CASSELL & THE PUBLISHERS ASSOCIATION

DIRECTORY OF PUBLISHING

UNITED KINGDOM, COMMONWEALTH AND OVERSEAS

1997

CASSELL

London and New York

Cassell
Wellington House
125 Strand
London WC2R 0BB

127 West 24th Street
New York, NY 10011

First Edition 1960
Second Edition 1962
Third Edition 1964
Fourth Edition 1966
Fifth Edition 1968
Sixth Edition 1970
Seventh Edition 1973
Eighth Edition 1976
Ninth Edition 1979
Tenth Edition 1982
Eleventh Edition 1984
Twelfth Edition 1986
Thirteenth Edition 1987
Fourteenth Edition 1988
Fifteenth Edition 1989
Sixteenth Edition 1990
Seventeenth Edition 1991
Eighteenth Edition 1992
Nineteenth Edition 1993
Twentieth Edition 1994
Twenty-first Edition 1995
Twenty-second Edition 1996

British Library Cataloguing in Publication Data

A record entry for this book is available from the British Library.

ISBN 0-304-33823-0

Research and editing by First Edition Translations, Cambridge
Data input by Argee Technical Services Ltd
Text processing and typesetting by John & Pamela Ainslie
Printed by Redwood Books, Trowbridge, Wiltshire

Contents

1   Introduction
    Foreword   v
    How to obtain British books   vi
    Comment obtenir des livres anglais   viii
    Bezug englischer Bücher   x
    Cómo adquirir libros británicos   xii
    The Publishers Association   xiv

2   Publishers
    2.1 United Kingdom   1
    2.2 Commonwealth & Overseas
         Australia   172
         Canada   187
         Ghana   211
         Hong Kong   212
         India   213
         Irish Republic   233
         Jamaica   237
         Kenya   238
         Malaysia   240
         Malta   241
         New Zealand   242
         Nigeria   247
         Pakistan   247
         Singapore   249
         South Africa   251
         Sri Lanka   255
         Swaziland   256
         Tanzania   256
         Zambia   257
         Zimbabwe   257

3   Packagers   259

4   Authors' Agents
     United Kingdom   267
     Australia   279
     Canada   279
     India   280
     Irish Republic   280
     New Zealand   280
     South Africa   281

5   Trade & Allied Associations
     5.1 International   282
     5.2 United Kingdom   284
     5.3 Commonwealth & Overseas   305

6   Trade & Allied Services
     6.1 Editorial Services   315
     6.2 Design & Production Services   318
     6.3 Electronic Publishing Services   320
     6.4 Translation Services   323
     6.5 Sales & Marketing Services   324
     6.6 Distributors   333
     6.7 Remainder Merchants   349
     6.8 Main Wholesalers   352
     6.9 Main Library Suppliers   357
     6.10 Book Clubs   359
     6.11 Literary & Trade Events   361
     6.12 Publishing Reference Books & Periodicals   364
     6.13 Training   374

7   Appendices
     7.1 UK Publishers classified by Fields of Activity   377
     7.2 Ownership of UK Publishers   399
     7.3 Publishers' Overseas Representatives   403
     7.4 Overseas Published represented in the UK   431
     7.5 Authors'Agents: Overseas Representation   435
     7.6 Index of ISBN Prefixes   440
     7.7 Index of Personal Names   446
     7.8 Index of Companies & Imprints   469
     7.9 UK Publishers by Postcode   504

1 Introductory

FOREWORD

The 22nd edition of the *Directory of Publishing* published by Cassell & The Publishers Association contains details of more than 1450 publishers from 21 countries, as well as over 110 authors' agents from 7 of them. It has been revised this year in order to accommodate the needs of new media publishers. Significant changes include a new section, Electronic Publishing Services, in the Trade and Allied Services listings, and other trade sections have been enhanced to include this area of publishing. This year, the directory lists over 650 organizations associated with publishing, including packagers, distributors, book clubs and translation services. Appendices include analyses of the UK publishers by fields of activity and indexes of companies and imprints, including a listing of UK publishers by postal code. The Ownership of UK Publishers index reflects recent changes in the industry.

The directory is updated annually. Previous entrants are sent last year's entry and new entrants a questionnaire. We are grateful to all those who have provided information for this edition. We have done all we can to ensure accuracy and completeness, but cannot accept responsibility for errors or omissions that escaped us. New entrants either approached the publisher or were discovered by monitoring various sources — the trade press, publishers' catalogues, exhibitions, book fairs, and the files of the Publishers Association itself.

As in the previous edition we have not excluded all organizations which have failed to reply to our mailings. Instead we have re-run their 1996 entries (in abbreviated form) and marked them with an asterisk. However, such organizations will be deleted from the next edition if they fail to update their entries for the second year running.

This new 1997 edition provides an indispensable guide to mainstream publishing and book trade activity throughout the UK, Commonwealth countries and other countries which are major English-language publishers (excluding only the USA). Cassell's reference list for the publishing trade also includes the third edition of *The Handbook of Copyright in British Publishing Practice* and the *Multilingual Dictionary of Publishing, Printing and Bookselling*.

We welcome all comments and suggestions from readers for improvements. We are also happy to receive details of possible new entries, but please note these must meet our criteria for inclusion. A UK publisher must either be a PA member or be of a certain size (publishing at least 5 new titles a year or employing at least 4 people). Overseas publishers must produce at least 8 new titles a year.

All organizations are entered free of charge.

Cassell

ABBREVIATIONS

* Asterisked entries indicate 1996 data.

International Direct Dialling

Where an area code is given following an IDD prefix, a dash above the first digit indicates that it should be retained when dialling from within that country, but excluded for international dialling.

UK Book Trade Association Membership

PA – Publishers Association
BA – Booksellers Association
BDC – Book Development Council
EPC – Educational Publishers Council
IGSMTP – International Group of Scientific, Medical & Technical Publishers
CAPP – Council of Academic & Professional Publishers
IPG – Independent Publishers Guild

HOW TO OBTAIN BRITISH BOOKS

This introduction is particularly intended for booksellers ordering from a British publisher for the first time.

HOW TO ORDER

1   If you have not previously ordered from a publisher, you should write for details on:

Trade discounts;
credit facilities;
catalogue mailing.

Please enclose in your letter information including:

name and address of your bank;

names and addresses of one or two publishers, preferably British, with whom you already do business. In certain circumstances you may be directed to a local stockist, agent or representative.

2   When the publisher agrees to supply you, your order should include:

your full name and address;
order date and order number;
insurance instructions (if any);
dispatch instructions: where you want the books to be sent—
where you want the invoice sent;
carriage instructions:
surface post
special carrier (e.g. shipper)
air freight
Accelerated Surface Post
invoicing instructions:
if you want a separate invoice by airmail
minimum number of copies your require
full details of the book:
number of copies you need
title
author/editor
cased/limp/paperback
international standard book number (ISBN)

3   Orders Clearing, Mardev Ltd, IBIS House, Riverside Estate, London Colney, St Albans, Hertfordshire AL2 1DX

(tel: 01727 825209, fax: 01727 826461) have an Orders Clearing system: by sending all your orders for different publishers to the one address, you can save yourself money. Similarly, Orders Clearing operates a service for the payment of publishers' accounts, the Overseas Booksellers' Clearing House (OBCH). Booksellers' may send one cheque for various accounts and OBCH will then distribute the payments to the different publishers.

4   An Orders Clearing Service is also offered by the Booksellers Order Distribution Ltd (BOD). Their address is 49 Victoria Road, Aldershot, Hampshire GU11 1SJ (tel: 01252 20697, fax: 01252 20697).

5   A teleordering service exists which is capable of extension to overseas territories. This is operated by TeleOrdering Ltd, 3 The Windmills, Turk Street, Alton, Hants (tel: 01420 544177, fax: 01420 543930). For further details, see section 6.15 of this Directory.

FOR REFERENCE

1   **Whitakers Books in Print:**
(Formerly *British Books in Print*) published annually in print form and updated monthly and bi-monthly as *Bookbank CD-ROM* by J. Whitaker & Sons Ltd, 12 Dyott Street, London WC1A 1DF (tel: 0171 836 8911, fax: 0171 836 2909). A weekly microfiche service gives details of new and forthcoming books added to the Whitaker database.

2   **The Bookseller:**
The British book trade journal, published weekly by Whitaker, containing correspondence, articles, trade news, together with a list of books published each week. (See section 6.13 for details of other periodicals and reference books of the trade.)

3   **British National Bibliography:**
A subject list of new British books arranged by Dewey classification. Published weekly with interim cumulations and an annual cumulation by the British Library, National

Bibliographic Service, Boston Spa, Wetherby, West Yorkshire LS23 7BQ (tel: 01937 546585, fax: 01937 546586).

4 Book Data:
Printed and computer-based information services primarily on CD-ROM, on current and forthcoming titles from UK and international publishers, selectable by subject and readership. From Book Data Ltd, Northumberland House, 2 King Street, Twickenham, Middlesex TW1 3RZ (tel: 0181 892 2272, fax: 0181 892 9109).

5 Individual publishers will normally provide catalogues of their own publications on request.

HOW TO PAY
You can pay by:
    cheque, bank draft or letter of credit
    bill of exchange drawn by the publisher on your giro or postal account
    international money order/postal order
    UNESCO coupons

IMPORTANT
Please make sure the publisher receives the *full amount* of the invoice value, free of all bank charges and transfer fees;
    pay *promptly*;
    if you have any problems, please also raise them *promptly*;
    if you have any difficulty in paying, consult your local bank manager, or the British Embassy, Consulate or High Commission.

WHEN YOU HAVE DIFFICULTY IN OBTAINING BRITISH BOOKS
1   If you have a problem of a *general* nature, please write to the Publishers Association, 19 Bedford Square, London WC1B 3HJ (tel: 0171 580 6321, fax: 0171 636 5375). The Association cannot intervene in problems which may arise between individual booksellers and publishers.

2 British Council
Your nearest branch may be able to help you with library facilities, reference works and advice. Their address is obtainable from: British Council, Information Department, 10 Spring Gardens, London SW1A 2BN (tel: 0171 930 8466, fax: 0171 839 6347).

PUBLISHERS' ABBREVIATED ANSWERS
Most publishers use one of the answers below when books are not available, and give an explanation of their answer codes at the bottom of the invoice.

NK   Not known, not ours, or so far in the future or so long out of print that it is unknown to the trade department
OO/TF   On order, to follow shortly
B8 or BDG8   Binding, will be available in August
B/ND   Binding (no date)
RP/June or **RP/6**   Reprint available in June
RP/2M   Reprint available in 2 months
NYP   Not yet published
NEP   New edition in preparation
RPUC   Reprint under consideration
OP   Out of print
OO/USA   On order, to be supplied by USA
TOP   Temporarily out of print
OS   Out of stock
RP/ND   Reprinting, no date

TECHNICAL TERMS
Firm
Books are normally supplied 'firm'. This means you will accept the books, pay for them, and will not be able to return them without first getting the publisher's permission.

See-safe or On approval
Some publishers are prepared to supply books on the basis that they are paid for at normal credit terms, but if the books remain unsold they may be returned to the publisher for crediting against future orders. You will be expected to return the books at your own expense. You should always obtain in writing details from publishers of any such agreements they are prepared to offer to their customers.

Standing Orders
Some publishers operate a scheme which allows a bookseller automatically to receive books in given subjects as they are published. These are normally supplied 'on approval'. You should write to individual publishers for details of their schemes.

Continuation Orders
Continuation Orders can be placed for books published in series and multi-volume works. This means that each new volume that appears will be sent to you automatically.

Pro-forma Invoice
Some publishers may prefer to supply initial orders by means of a pro-forma invoice which has to be paid before the books are sent.

COMMENT OBTENIR DES LIVRES ANGLAIS

Cette introduction est plus particulièrement destinée aux libraires qui passent une commande pour la première fois à un éditeur britannique.

COMMENT PASSER UNE COMMANDE

1   Si vous commandez des livres à un éditeur pour la première fois, vous devez écrire pour obtenir des détails concernant:
  les remises accordées aux libraires;
  les facilités de crédit;
  l'envoi de catalogues.
Prière de joindre à votre lettre les renseignements suivants:
  identité bancaire;
  nomme et adresse d'un ou de deux éditeurs, de préférence britanniques, avec lesquels vous êtes déjà en relations commerciales.
Dans certains cas vous pourrez être dirigé sur un dépositaire local, agent ou représentant.

2   Si l'éditeur accepte de vous fournir, votre commande devra comprendre:
  votre raison sociale et votre adresse complètes;
  la date et le numéro de votre commande;
  vos instructions concernant l'assurance requise (le cas échéant);
  vos instructions concernant l'envoi: la destination des livres et celle de la facture;
  vos instructions concernant le transport:
    par courrier postal
    par agence de transport
    par fret aérien
    par Accelerated Surface Post (courrier spécial pour les livres)
  vos instructions concernant la facturation:
    si vous souhaitez recevoir la facture par courrier aérien séparé
    le nombre de doubles désirés
  des renseignements complets concernant le livre:
    le nombre d'exemplaires
    le titre
    l'auteur – le rédacteur

relié/broché/livre de poche
ISBN

3   La société Orders Clearing, Mardev Ltd, IBIS House, Riverside Estate, London Colney, St Albans, Hertfordshire AL2 1DX (tel: 01727 825209, fax: 01727 826461), dispose d'un système de ventilation des commandes. En envoyant toutes vos commandes, même si elles sont destinées à différents éditeurs, à une seule adresse, vous économiserez de l'argent. Orders Clearing a aussi un service qui procède au règlement des comptes des éditeurs, le Overseas Booksellers' Clearing House (OBCH). Les libraires peuvent envoyer un seul chèque destiné à plusieurs comptes et c'est l'OBCH qui se charge ensuite d'effectuer les paiements à l'attention des différents éditeurs.

4   La Booksellers Order Distribution Ltd (BOD), 49 Victoria Road, Aldershot, Hampshire GU11 1SJ (tel: 01252 20697, fax: 01252 20697), offre également un service de ventilation des commandes.

5   Un service de commande à distance existant peut être étendu aux pays étrangers. Il est opéré par TeleOrdering Ltd, 3 The Windmills, Turk Street, Alton, Hants GU34 1EF (tel: 01420 544177, fax: 01420 543930). Pour plus de détails, reportez vous au paragraphe 6.15 de cet annuaire.

POUR CONSULTATION

1   **Whitakers Books in Print**
(Anciennement *British Books in Print*) impression annuelle. Mise à jour mensuelle et bi-mensuelle intitulée *Bookbank CD-ROM* par J. Whitaker & Sons Ltd, 12 Dyott Street, Londres WC1A 1DF (tel: 0171 836 8911, fax: 0171 836 2909). Un service hebdomadaire sur microfiches donne la liste des nouvelles publications et des ouvrages à paraître qui seront ajoutés à la base de données Whitaker.

2   **The Bookseller**
Revue hebdomadaire du livre anglais, publiée par Whitaker, contenant courrier, articles et nouvelles de la profession, ainsi

qu'une liste des livres publiés chaque semaine. (Voir le paragraphe 6.13; il contient des détails sur d'autres revues et livres de référence sur la profession.)

3   British National Bibliography
Une liste thématique des nouveaux livres britanniques établie par classification Dewey. C'est une publication hebdomadaire rééditée sous forme cumulée intérimaire et annuelle par la British Library, National Bibliographic Service, Boston Spa, Wetherby, West Yorkshire LS23 7BQ (tel: 01937 546585, fax: 01937 546586).

4   Book Data
Renseignements informatisés et publiés principalement sur CD-ROM, sur les titres courants et prochains des éditeurs du R.U. et d'autres pays pouvant être obtenus par thème et lectorat auprès de Book Data Ltd, Northumberland House, 2 King Street, Twickenham, Middlesex TW1 3RZ (tel: 0181 892 2272, fax: 0181 892 9109).

5   En général les éditeurs particuliers fournissent sur demande des catalogues de leurs propres éditions.

PAIEMENT
Vous pouvez payer par:
   chèque, virement bancaire ou lettre de crédit
   lettre de change tirée sur vous par l'éditeur
   compte courant postal
   mandat poste international
   coupons UNESCO

IMPORTANT
Veillez à ce que l'éditeur reçoive le *montant total* de sa facture franco de frais bancaires et de transfert;
   payez *rapidement*;
   si un problème se présente, informez-en également l'éditeur *rapidement*;
   si vous avez des difficultés de paiement, consultez le directeur de l'agence locale de votre banque, l'Ambassade britannique, le Consulat ou la Haute Commission.

SI VOUS AVEZ DES DIFFICULTES POUR OBTENIR DES LIVRES ANGLAIS
1   Si vous avez un problème d'ordre *général*, veuillez écrire à la Publishers Association, 19 Bedford Square, Londres WC1B 3HJ (tel: 0171 580 6321, fax: 0171 636 5375). Mais l'Association n'intervient pas dans les litiges survenant entre libraires et éditeurs particuliers.

2   British Council:
La représentation la plus proche pourrait éventuellement vous aider en mettant à votre disposition sa bibliothèque et tous ses ouvrages de référence, tout en vous dispensant ses conseils. Vous pouvez en obtenir l'adresse au British Council, Information Department, 10 Spring Gardens, Londres SW1A 2BN (tel: 0171 930 8466, fax: 0171 839 6347).

REPONSES DES EDITEURS EN ABREGE
La plupart des éditeurs utilisent l'une des réponses ci-dessous quand les ouvrages ne sont pas disponibles et donnent, au bas de leur facture, l'explication de leurs abréviations.

NK – Inconnu, n'est pas publié par nos soins, ou sera publié dans un avenir indéterminé ou est épuisé depuis si longtemps qu'il est inconnu de notre Service Commercial
OO/TF – En commande, suivra sous peu
B8 ou **BDG8** – Reliure, sera disponible en août
B/ND – Reliure (sans date)
RP/June ou **RP/6** – En réimpression – disponible en juin
RP/2M – En réimpression – disponible dans deux mois
NYP – Pas encore publié
NEP – Nouvelle édition en préparation
RPUC – Réimpression à l'étude
OP – Epuisé
OO/USA – En commande, sera livré depuis les Etats-Unis
TOP – Provisoirement épuisé
OS – Pas en stock
RP/ND – En réimpression, sans date

TERMES TECHNIQUES
Firm (Ferme)
En général, les livres sont fournis 'firm'. C'est-à-dire que vous devrez les accepter et les payer sans pouvoir les retourner avant d'en avoir obtenu l'autorisation de la part de l'éditeur.

See-safe ou **On approval** (à l'examen)
Certains éditeurs acceptent de livrer des livres sur la base de conditions de paiement habituelles mais si les livres ne sont pas vendus, ils pourront être retournés, à vos frais, à l'éditeur qui vous créditera du montant correspondant lors de commandes ulterieures. Demandez à recevoir par écrit des détails des procédures que les éditeurs sont disposés à offrir a leurs clients.

Standing Orders (Commandes permanentes)
Certains éditeurs utilisent un système qui permet aux libraires de recevoir automatiquement des ouvrages sur un sujet donné dès leur publication. Ces livres sont normalement fournis 'sur examen'. Adressez-vous directment aux éditeurs pour obtenir les détails de cette procédure.

Continuation Orders (Commandes de parutions successives)
Vous pouvez passer des commandes de livres publiés en série ou en plusieurs volumes. Cela signifie que chaque nouveau volume vous sera automatiquement envoyé dès sa parution.

Pro-forma Invoice (Facture pro forma)
Certains éditeurs préfèrent livrer leur première commande en envoyant auparavant une facture pro forma qui devra être payée avant l'envoi des livres.

BEZUG ENGLISCHER BÜCHER

Diese Einführung ist insbesondere für Buchhändler gedacht, die zum ersten Mal bei einem englischen Verlag bestellen.

BESTELLVERFAHREN

1 Wenn Sie bisher noch nichts von einem Verlag bezogen haben, sollten Sie schriftlich Angaben über:
  Handelsrabatte
  Zahlungsfristen
  Prospekt- und Katalogsversand
  Schreiben
anfordern. Ihr Schreiben sollte folgende Angaben enthalten:
  Name und Anschrift Ihrer Bank
  Name und Anschrift eines oder zweier – möglichst britischer – Verlage, mit denen Sie bereits Geschäftsbeziehungen unterhalten.
Mitunter wird man Sie an eine örtliche Lagerhaltung oder Vertretung verweisen.

2 Wenn der Verlag bereit ist, Sie zu beliefern, sollten Ihre Bestellungen folgende Angaben enthalten:
  Ihren vollen Namen und Anschrift
  Bestelldatum und -nummer
  ggf. Versicherungsanweisungen
  Versandanschriften für Bücher und Rechnungen (falls verschieden)
  Versandanweisung:
  –per Drucksache
  –über Spediteur
  –per Luftfracht/-post
  –per Accelerated Surface Post (Sonderpostzustellung für Bücher)
  Fakturierungsanweisung:
  –falls Sie die Rechnung separat per Luftpost wünschen
  –gewünschte Anzahl von Rechnungskopien
  genaue Angaben über das Buch:
  –Anzahl gewünschter Exemplare
  –Titel
  –Verfasser oder Herausgeber
  –Einband: gebunden, flexibel, broschiert (Paperback)
  –ISBN

3 Die Fa. Orders Clearing, Mardev Ltd, IBIS House, Riverside Estate, London Colney, St Albans, Hertfordshire AL2 1DX (tel: 01727 825209, fax: 01727 826461), betreibt ein Bestellverteilungssystem ('Zettelbörse'), d.h. Sie können Ihre Bestellungen für alle Verlage an die eine Anschrift zur Weiterleitung schicken und so Porto sparen. Dank dem Sammelzahlungsdienst der Orders Clearing, dem Overseas Booksellers' Clearing House (OBCH), können Sie auck verschiedene Zahlungen auf einen Scheck setzen; OBCH übernimmt die Zahlungsüberweisung auf die einzelnen Konten.

4 Auch The Booksellers Order Distribution Ltd (BOD), 49 Victoria Road, Aldershot, Hampshire GU11 1SJ (tel: 01252 20697, fax: 01252 20697), bietet einen Bestellverteilungsdienst.

5 Es gibt auch einen Fernbestelldienst, mit dem Überseegebiete erreicht werden können. Dieser wird von TeleOrdering Ltd, 3 The Windmills Turk Street, Alton, Hants GU34 1EF (tel: 01420 544177, fax: 01420 543930), betrieben. Weitere Einzelheiten finden Sie unter Punkt 6.15 dieses Nachschlagwerks.

FACHLITERATUR

1 Whitakers Books in Print
(Ursprünglich *British Books in Print*) erscheint jährlich bei J. Whitaker & Sons Ltd, 12 Dyott Street, London WC1A 1DF (tel: 0171 836 8911, fax: 0171 836 2909), und wird monatlich und bimonatlich als *Bookbank CD-ROM* veröffentlicht. Ein wöchentlicher Mikrofilmkartendienst gibt Einzelheiten neuer und in Kürze erscheinender Bücher, die der Whitaker-Datenbank hinzugefügt sind.

2 The Bookseller
Die Britische Buchhandler Fachzeitschrift erscheint wöchentlich bei J. Whitaker & Sons Ltd. Enthält Korrespondenz, Artikel, Handelsnachrichten und das wöchentliche Verzeichnis der erschienenen Bücher. In Punkt

6.13 finden Sie Einzelheiten über weitere Zeitschriften und Nachschlagwerke des Handels.

3 British National Bibliography
Eine Sachgebietsliste neuer, in Großbritannien erschienener Bücher, geordnet nach dem Dewey-Dezimalsystem. Erscheint wöchentlich, mit periodischen Kumulativbänden und einem Jahreskumulativband, veröffentlicht von der British Library, National Bibliographic Service, Boston Spa, Wetherby, West Yorkshire LS23 7BQ (tel: 01937 546585, fax: 01937 546586).

4 Bücherdaten
Computerisierter Informationsdienst, hauptsächlich auf CD-ROM, hinsichtlich im Druck erscheinender und demnächst zu erscheinender Büchertitel britischer und internationaler Herausgeber, wählbar nach Fachgebiet und Leserschaft, erhältlich von Book Data Ltd, Northumberland House, 2 King Street, Twickenham, Middlesex TW1 3RZ (tel: 0181 892 2272, fax: 0181 892 9109).

5 Die einzelnen Verlage versenden auf Wunsch normalerweise ihre eigenen Verlagsverzeichnisse und Prospekte.

ZAHLUNGSWEISE
Ihre Zahlung kann erfolgen:
  durch Scheck, Tratte oder Kreditbrief
  durch vom Verlag auf Sie gezogenen Wechsel
  durch Postscheck- oder Banküberweisung
  durch internationale Postanweisung
  durch UNESCO-Kupons

WICHTIG:
Achten Sie darauf, daß der Verlag den *vollen Rechnungsbetrag* frei von Bank- und Überweisungsspesen erhält;
  bitte *pünktlich* zahlen;
  falls Sie Schwierigkeiten haben, bitte *sofort* nachfragen;
  falls Sie Probleme mit der Zahlung haben, ziehen Sie bitte Ihre Bank oder die britische Botschaft bzw. das britische Konsulat zu Rate.

WENN SIE SCHWIERIGKEITEN BEI DEM BEZUG ENGLISCHER BÜCHER HABEN
1 Bei Problemen *allgemeiner Art* schreiben Sie bitte an The Publishers Association (International Division), 19 Bedford Square, London WC1B 3HJ (tel: 0171 580 6321, fax: 0171 636 5375). Die Publishers Association hat keine Eingriffsbefugnis bei Auseinandersetzungen zwischen einzelnen Buchhändlern und Verlagen.

2 British Council:
Die Ihnen nächstgelegene Niederlassung kann Ihnen oft mit Bibliotheksdiensten, Nachschlagewerken und Bibliographien beistehen. Die Anschrift ist vom British Council, 10 Spring Gardens, London SW1A 2BN (tel: 0171 930 8466, fax: 0171 839 6347), erhältlich.

HANDELSÜBLICHE KURZANTWORTEN
Die meisten Verlage benutzen die unten aufgeführten Kurzantworten, wenn ein Titel nicht lieferbar ist. Ein Schlüssel für diese Antworten erscheint normalerweise auch auf den Fakturen.

NK – Unbekannt, nicht von uns, oder so weit in der Zukunft oder so lange nicht mehr in Druck, daß es der Handelsabteilung unbekannt ist.
OO/TF – In Auftrag gegeben, folgt bald
B8 oder **BDG8** – Wird gebunden – im August lieferbar
B/ND – Wird gebunden – ohne Termin
RP/June oder **RP/6** – Nachdruck im Juni lieferbar
RP/2M – Nachdruck in zwei Monaten lieferbar
NYP – Noch nicht erschienen
NEP – Neuauflage in Vorbereitung
RPUC – Nachdruck in Erwägung gezogen
OP – Vergriffen
OO/USA – Für Lieferung aus den USA in Auftrag gegeben
TOP – z. Z. vergriffen
OS – Nicht am Lager
RP/ND – Nachdruck erfolgt – kein Termin

FACHAUSDRÜCKE
Firm (fest)
Bücher werden normalerweise 'fest' geliefert. Das bedeutet, daß Sie die Bücher annehmen, bezahlen und sie nicht ohne Genehmigung des Verlags zurücksenden.

See Safe oder **'on approval'** ('mit RR' bzw. 'zur Ansicht')
Einige Verleger sind bereit, Bücher unter normalen Kreditbedingungen zu senden und bei Nichtabnahme zurückzunehmen und für zukünftige Bestellungen gutzuschreiben und zu verrechnen. Die Remission muß portofrei erfolgen. Man sollte sich immer schriftlich bestätigen lassen, welche Dienstleistungen die Verlage ihren Kunden zu bieten bereit sind.

Standing Orders (Neuerscheinungszusendung)
Viele Verlage bieten den Service eines 'Standing Order System'. Hierbei erhält der Buchhändler die Neuerscheinungen in von ihm ausgewählten Gebieten automatisch mit Rückgaberecht zugesandt. Die einzelnen Verlage geben gerne Auskunft über ihre Systeme.

Continuation Orders (Fortsetzungen)
Fortsetzungen können für mehrbändige oder serienweise veröffentliche Werke bestellt werden. D.h., daß jeder neu erscheinende Band Ihnen automatisch zugesandt wird.

Pro-forma Invoice (Vorausrechnung)
Einige Verlage ziehen es vor, Erstaufträge gegen Vorausrechnung zu beliefern.

CÓMO ADQUIRIR LIBROS BRITÁNICOS

Esta introducción va especialmente dirigida a los libreros que encargan por primera vez a una editorial británica.

CÓMO SE HACEN LOS PEDIDOS

1   Si no ha efectuado anteriormente pedidos a una editorial, usted tiene que escribir a su oficina principal solicitando datos sobre:

descuentos comerciales;
facilidades de crédito;
envíos de catálogos.

Junto a su carta tiene usted que mandar información que incluya:

nombre y dirección de su banco;
nombre y direcciones de una o dos editoriales, de preferencia británicas, con las que ya realice transacciones. En ciertas circunstancias, posiblemente se le dirigirá a un almacén local o a un agente o representante.

2   Cuando una editorial acuerda suministrarle mercancía, tiene que hacer constar en su pedido:

su nombre y dirección completos;
fecha y número del pedido;
instrucciones para el seguro (si se requiere);
instrucciones para el envío: adónde hay que enviar los libros, y adónde hay que enviar la factura;
forma de transporte:
–vía terrestre/marítima
–transportista especial (p. ej. expedidor)
–flete aéreo
–vía terrestre/marítima acelerada
instrucciones para la facturación:
–si necesita una factura aparte por correo aéreo
–número mínimo de copias que necesita
datos completos sobre el libro:
–número de ejemplares
–título
–autor/editor
–con tapas/flexible/rústica
–ISBN

3   Orders Clearing, Mardev Ltd, IBIS House, Riverside Estate, London Colney, St Albans, Hertfordshire AL2 1DX (tel: 01727 825209, fax: 01727 826461), tiene un sistema de Canalización de Pedidos: enviando a una sola dirección todos los pedidos de distintas editoriales, se puede ahorrar dinero. La Orders Clearing ofrece además un servicio de pago a editoriales, el 'Overseas Booksellers' Clearing House' (OBCH). Los libreros pueden enviar un solo cheque para saldar varias cuentas, y el OBCH se encarga de distribuir los pagos a las editoriales correspondientes.

4   Un servicio similar (de distribución de pedidos) lo ofrece la organización Booksellers Order Distribution Ltd (BOD), 49 Victoria Road, Aldershot, Hampshire GU11 1SJ (tel: 01252 20697, fax: 01252 20697).

5   Existe un servicio por el que su pueden pasar los pedidos telefónicamente que se extiende al extranjero. Este servicio corre a cargo de TeleOrdering Ltd, 3 The Windmills, Turk Street, Alton, Hants GU34 1EF (tel: 01420 544177, fax: 01420 543930). Para más detalles ver sección 6.15 de esta guía.

PARA CONSULTA

1   **Whitakers Books in Print**
(Antes *British Books in Print*) publicado anualmente (impreso), puesto al día mensualmente y bimensualmente cómo *Bookbank CD-ROM* por J. Whitaker & Sons Ltd, 12 Dyott Street, Londres WC1A 1DF (tel: 0171 836 8911, fax: 0171 836 2909). Un servicio semanal de microfichas proporciona detalles de libros neuvos y de próxima publicación agregados a la base de datos Whitaker.

2   **The Bookseller**
La revista del ramo britanico, publicada semanalmente por Whitaker, con correspondencia, artículos, noticias del ramo, junto con una lista de los libros publicados cada semana. (Ver sección 6.13 para más detalles de otras publicaciones y libros de consulta.)

3 British National Bibliography

Una lista por temas de nuevos libros británicos clasificados de acuerdo con el sistema Dewey. Publicada semanalmente con acumulaciones interinas y una acumulación anual por la British Library, National Bibliographic Service, Boston Spa, Wetherby, West Yorkshire LS23 7BQ (tel: 01937 546585, fax: 01937 546586).

4 Book Data

Servicios de información, principalmente sobre CD-ROM, impresa y basada en ordenador sobre títulos actuales y a publicarse por editoriales del Reino Unido y de otra parte, clasificado por tema y lectores, de Book Data Ltd, Northumberland House, 2 King Street, Twickenham, Middlesex TW1 3RZ (tel: 0181 892 2272, fax: 0181 892 9109).

5   Las casas editoriales remiten normalmente catálogos de sus publicaciones si se les solicita.

FORMA DE PAGO

Puede pagar por:
  cheque, giro bancario o carta de crédito
  letra de cambio girada sobre la editorial
  'giro' o postal
  orden de pago internacional/postal
  cupones UNESCO

IMPORTANTE:

Sírvase comprobar que la editorial reciba el *valor total* de la factura, exento de todas las cargas bancarias y derechos de transferencia;
  pague *sin demora*;
  si se le presentan problemas, sírvase también comunicarlos *sin demora*;
  si tiene alguna dificultad en el pago, consulte al gerente de su banco, o a la Embajada Británica, al Consulado o a la High Commission.

CUANDO TENGA DIFICULTAD EN CONSEGUIR LIBROS BRITÁNICOS

1   Si se le presenta un problema de carácter *general*, sírvase escribir a la Publishers Association (International Division), 19 Bedford Square, London WC1B 3HJ (tel: 0171 580 6321, fax: 0171 636 5375). Este organismo no puede intervenir en problemas particulares que se puedan presentar entre libreros y editores.

2 British Council

La sucursal que usted tenga más próxima le podrá ayudar con su biblioteca, libros de consulta y asesoramiento. Puede obtener la dirección escribiendo a: British Council Information Department, 10 Spring Gardens, London SW1A 2BN (tel: 0171 930 8466, fax: 0171 839 6347).

CONTESTACIONES ABREVIADAS DE LAS EDITORIALES

La mayoría de las casas editoriales usan una de las contestaciones que a continuación se indican cuando los libros no están disponibles, explicando al pie de la factura el significado de estos códigos.

NK – Desconocido, no nuestro, o tan a largo plazo en el futuro o tanto tiempo agotado que le es desconocido al Departamento Comercial

OO/TF – En pedido, seguirá en breve

B8 o BDG8 – Encuadernación, disponible en agosto

B/ND – Encuadernación (sin fecha)

RP/June o RP/6 – Ambos significan que la reimpresión estará disponible en junio

RP2M – Reimpresión disponible en 2 meses

NYP – No publicado aún

NEP – Nueva edición en preparación

RPUC – Se estudia la reimpresión

OP – Agotado

OO/USA – En pedido, a suministrar por los EE.UU.

TOP – Momentáneamente agotado

OS – Fuera de existencias

RP/ND – Reimprimiendo, sin fecha

TÉRMINOS TÉCNICOS

Firm (en firme)
Los libros se suministran normalmente 'en firme'. Esto quiere decir que usted aceptará los libros, los pagará y no podrá devolverlos sin antes obtener el permiso de la editorial.

See-safe (a aceptación)
Algunas editoriales están dispuestas a suministrar libros en regimen de pago bajo condiciones de crédito normales, pero sí no se venden pueden ser devueltos a la editorial para ser abonados contra futuros pedidos. La devolución de estos libros correrá a su cargo. Siempre debe obtener detalles por escrito de las editoriales de tales términos que estén dispuestos a ofrecer a sus clientes.

Standing Orders (Pedidos permanentes)
Algunas editoriales tienen un sistema que le permite al librero recibir automáticamente libros sobre ciertos temas en cuanto se publican. Normalmente se suministran estos libros 'see-safe'. Diríjase a las editoriales individualmente solicitando detalles del sistema.

Continuation Orders (Pedidos de continuación)
Pueden pasarse pedidos de continuación para libros publicados en serie y obras en varios volúmenes. De esta manera cada nuevo volumen que salga se le remitirá automáticamente.

Pro-forma Invoice (Factura proforma)
Es posible que algunas editoriales prefieran suministrar los pedidos iniciales por medio de factura proforma que se tiene que pagar antes del envío de los libros.

THE PUBLISHERS ASSOCIATION

19 Bedford Square, London WC1B 3HJ
Telephone: +44 0171-580 6321
Fax: +44 0171-636 5375

Chief Executive: Clive Bradley
Director of Educational and Professional Publishing: John Davies
Director of International and Trade Service: Ian Taylor
Director of Management Services: Peter Kilborn

The Publishers Association represents the interests of United Kingdom book, journal and electronic publishers to the UK Government, the European Commission, foreign governments, other bodies in the book trade, and the public at large. It provides members with comprehensive information about developments affecting their operations through its monthly publications, its *Headlines* overnight fax bulletin service, educational newsletters, and circulars and notices, organises a wide range of seminars and forums, and offers advisory services in areas of professional interest including copyright, contracts, publishing finance, distribution, production, credit, employment, market trends, and technology and standards. It organises participation in overseas and educational trade fairs, sponsors the Book House Training Centre, and participates in the management of many specialist services for the book trade. It represents the British industry in publishing's international bodies. The PA provides specialist services to significant sectors of the industry through its specialist divisions described below, and arranges group meetings for children's, religious, medical, legal and journal publishers, and for other specialist interests. Details of membership supplied on request to the Membership Secretary.

INTERNATIONAL DIVISION
The International Division is the PA's Export Division, providing members with expert services to assist them in exporting their books to the UK's extensive export markets throughout the world. The International Division Board advises the Association and its members on export policy, with expert input from regional working parties, and the International Division works closely with the Department of Trade and Industry's export services, and with the British Council, to promote the sales of British books in other countries. It publishes *Export News* for members, and organises participation in a wide range of trade fairs.

GENERAL BOOK COUNCIL
GBC provides members with an invaluable forum for discussion of key trade issues; publishers benefit from the PA's wide experience in all areas of consumer publishing.

EDUCATIONAL PUBLISHERS COUNCIL (Schools Div)
EPC, the school publishing division of the PA, provides an extensive range of services for school publishers, and campaigns vigorously for proper financial provision for books in schools and school libraries. EPC represents the interests of its members to the Department of Education and Science, to educational bodies, and to the schools themselves, and provides expert guidance for members on school supply and the process of educational reform. It organises an extensive programme of book exhibitions for teachers in all parts of the UK.

COUNCIL OF ACADEMIC AND PROFESSIONAL PUBLISHERS
CAPP represents the interests of publishers of college, academic, professional and business books and journals, and campaigns to secure proper standards of textbook availability for students, and to encourage student book buying, high standards of book provision in libraries, and awareness of the value of books in the professions and in business. It represents the interests of academic and professional publishers to DES, the university and college authorities, and in further and continuing education. It provides regular information for members on market opportunities, and organises occasional exhibitions at subject conferences. CAPP has specialist groups for journal, medical and law publishers.

ELECTRONIC PUBLISHERS FORUM
Through EPF the PA provides full support for CD-ROM and online publishing and organises a popular programme of seminars and meetings enabling publishers of electronic material to share their problems and discuss market opportunities.

2 Publishers

2.1 United Kingdom

1001

AA PUBLISHING
The Automobile Association, Fanum House,
Basingstoke, Hants RG21 2EA
Telephone: 01256 20123
Fax: 01256 22575

Orders & Authorised Returns:
Exel Logistics Media Services, Invicta House,
Sir Thomas Longley Road,
Medway City Estate, Rochester, Kent
ME2 4DU
Telephone: 01634 297123
Fax: 01634 298000

Directors: J. V. Howard *(Managing)*
M. D. Buttler *(Editorial)*
S. J. Mesquita *(Marketing & International
    Sales)*
P. Hornby *(UK Sales)*
A. Symonds *(Production)*

*Atlases & Maps; Guide Books; Scientific &
Technical; Travel & Topography*

New Titles: 50 (1995), 45 (1996)
No of Employees: 130

ISBNs, Imprints & Series:
0 7495, 0 86145 Automobile Association

Parent Company:
Automobile Association

Distributor for:
British Tourist Authority; De Agostini
Editions; English Tourist Board; N. Ireland
Tourist Board; Pastime Publications; Duncan
Petersen; Regional Tourist Boards; Scottish
Tourist Board; Thomas Cook Publishing

Book Trade Association Membership: PA,
BA

1002

ABC – THE ALL CHILDREN'S CO LTD
33 Museum Street, London WC1A 1LD
Telephone: 0171 436 6300
Fax: 0171 240 6923

Warehouse:
D Services, 6 Euston Street,
Freemen's Common, Leicester LE2 7SS
Telephone: 0166 254 7671
Fax: 0166 254 4670

Directors: Susan Tarsky *(Managing)*
Timothy Chadwick *(Chairman)*
Michael Raine *(Financial)*

Children's Books

New Titles: 25 (1995), 25 (1996)
No of Employees: 15

ISBNs, Imprints & Series:
1 85406 All Books for Children
1 85704 SoftbABCks

Overseas Representation *(see §7.3)*:
Australia: CIS Publishers, Carlton, Vic
Japan: Yohan Co Ltd, London, UK
Singapore: Pansing Distribution Sdn Bhd

1003

ABC-CLIO LTD
[incorporating Clio Press Ltd]
Old Clarendon Ironworks,
35A Great Clarendon Street, Oxford OX2 6AT
Telephone: 01865 311350
Fax: 01865 311358

Orders:
Plymbridge Distributors Ltd, Estover Road,
Estover, Plymouth PL6 7PZ
Telephone: 01752 202301
Fax: 01752 202331

Directors: Tony Slogget *(Managing)*
Robert Neville *(UK Editorial & Production)*
Managers: Suzanne Wheatley *(Promotions)*
Sarah Pape *(Managing Editor, ABM)*
Guy Westwood *(Accountant)*

*Academic & Scholarly; Bibliography &
Library Science; Biography & Autobiography;
Electronic (Educational); Electronic
(Professional & Academic); Fine Art & Art
History; History & Antiquarian; Military &*

*War; Nautical; Photography; Reference Books,
Directories & Dictionaries*

New Titles: 20 (1995), 44 (1996)
No of Employees: 12

ISBNs, Imprints & Series:
0 87436 ABC–Clio (USA and UK)
0 903450, 1 85109 ABC-Clio (UK)

Parent Company:
ABC-Clio *(USA)*

Overseas Representation *(see §7.3)*:
Greece: K. C. Enterprises, Athens
Japan: Yushodo Fantas Corporation, Tokyo
USA: ABC-Clio, Santa Barbara, CA

1004

ABSOLUTE PRESS
Scarborough House, 29 James Street West,
Bath BA1 2BT
Telephone: 01225 316013
Fax: 01225 445836

**Accounts, Warehouse, Trade Enquiries &
Orders:**
Central Books Ltd, 99 Wallis Road, London
E9 5LN
Telephone: 0181 986 4854
Fax: 0181 533 5821

Publisher & Editorial: Jon Croft
Managers: Bronwen Douglas *(Marketing)*
Aidan Lunn *(Sales)*

*Cookery, Wines & Spirits; Guide Books;
Theatre, Drama & Dance; Travel &
Topography*

New Titles: 15 (1995), 20 (1996)
No of Employees: 4

ISBNs, Imprints & Series:
0 948230 Absolute Classics, Absolute Press

Distributor for:
USA: Smith & Kraus Inc; Streetwise Maps Inc

Overseas Representation (see §7.3):
Australia: Currency Press, Paddington
Canada: Theatre Books, Toronto
Europe: Nigel Thomas Associates, London, UK
New Zealand: Birch Tree Books, Auckland
USA (Absolute Classics only): Theatre Communications Group, New York, USA

Book Trade Association Membership: IPG

1005

ACADEMIC PRESS LTD
24–28 Oval Road, London NW1 7DX
Telephone: 0171 482 2893
Fax: 0171 267 0362
Web Site: http://www.apnet.com

Warehouse (Books), Customer Service & Journal Subscriptions:
High Street, Foots Cray, Kent DA14 5HP
Telephone: 0181 300 3322
Fax: 0181 309 0807
Web Site: http://www.harcourtbrace.com/apcs

Directors: J. J. M. Velterop (*Managing & Editorial*)
Pat Scott (*Personnel & Administrative*)
Michael Ewins (*Production*)
Jamie Shmer (*Finance & Distribution*)
Managers: Vincent Cassidy (*Marketing*)
Des Brennan (*Sales*)
Sheila O'Reilly (*Customer Service*)

Academic & Scholarly; Agriculture; Archaeology; Bibliography & Library Science; Biology & Zoology; Chemistry; Computer Science; Economics; Educational & Textbooks; Electronic (Professional & Academic); Engineering; Geography & Geology; Languages & Linguistics; Mathematics & Statistics; Medical (incl. Self Help & Alternative Medicine); Natural History; Physics; Psychology & Psychiatry; Reference Books, Directories & Dictionaries; Scientific & Technical; Sociology & Anthropology; Veterinary Science

New Titles: 90 (1995), 85 (1996)
No of Employees: 35
Annual Turnover: £22M

ISBNs, Imprints & Series:
0 12 Academic Press, APP (Academic Press Professional)
0 85661 T. & A. D. Poyser

Parent Company:
Academic Press Inc (*USA*)

Overseas Representation (see §7.3):
Australia & New Zealand: Harcourt Brace & Co (Australia) Pty Ltd, Marrickville, Australia
Brazil: Academic Press do Brasil Editora Ltda, São Paulo
Canada: Harcourt Brace & Co Canada Ltd, Toronto
India & Middle East: Harcourt Brace & Co International, Orlando, FL, USA
Israel: Carmel Libraries, Gan Yavne
Italy, Spain & Portugal: Marcello SNC, Padua, Italy
Japan & Korea: Academic Press Japan Inc, Tokyo, Japan
Philippines: Felta Book Sales Co, Quezon City

South East Asia: Harcourt Brace & Co International, Singapore
USA: Academic Press Inc, San Diego, CA

Book Trade Association Membership: PA, IGSMTP

1006

ACADEMY GROUP LTD
42 Leinster Gardens, London W2 3AN
Telephone: 0171 402 2141 (General Enquiries) & 402 3442 (Sales & Marketing)
Fax: 0171 723 9540

Warehouse, Trade Enquiries & Orders:
ITPS, Cheriton House, North Way, Andover, Hants SP10 5BE
Telephone: 01264 342832
Fax: 01264 342787

Managing Director: John Stoddart
Sales & Marketing: Robert Creffield
Production: Lorraine Mallon
Editorial: Maggie Toy
Design: Andrea Bottella

Antiques & Collecting; Architecture & Design; Fine Art & Art History; Philosophy

New Titles: 50 (1995), 55 (1996)
No of Employees: 22

ISBNs, Imprints & Series:
0 85670, 1 85490 Academy Editions, Architectural Design, Architectural Monographs, Art & Design

Parent Company:
VCH Verlagsgesellschaft mbH (*Germany*)

Associated & Subsidiary Companies:
VCH Publishers (UK) Ltd. *Germany:* VCH Verlagsgesellschaft mbH. *Switzerland:* VCH Verlags AG. *USA:* VCH Publishers Inc

Overseas Representation (see §7.3):
Germany: VCH Verlagsgesellschaft mbH, Weinheim
USA: National Book Network, Lanham, MD

Book Trade Association Membership: PA, Periodical Publishers Association

1007

ACC PUBLICATIONS
Association of County Councils, Eaton House, 66a Eaton Square, London SW1W 9BH
Telephone: 0171 235 1200
Fax: 0171 235 8458

Publisher: Michael R. Baker

Academic & Scholarly; Agriculture; Educational & Textbooks; Industry, Business & Management; Transport

ISBNs, Imprints & Series:
0 901783, 1 85862

Parent Company:
Association of County Councils

1008

ACCOUNTANCY BOOKS
40 Bernard Street, London WC1N 1LD
Telephone: 0171 833 8982
Fax: 0171 833 9034

Customer Services:
ICAEW, Gloucester House, 399 Silbury Boulevard, Milton Keynes MK9 2LO
Telephone: Milton Keynes 01908 248000
Fax: 01908 248001

Directors: Trevor D'Cruz (*Managing*)
Nick el Rio (*Publications*)
Managers: Diane Garnell (*Commissioning*)
Jo-ann Shore (*Customer Services*)
Judy Hubbard (*Marketing—Books*)

Accountancy & Taxation; Educational & Textbooks; Industry, Business & Management

ISBNs, Imprints & Series:
0 85291, 1 85355 Accountancy Books

Parent Company:
The Institute of Chartered Accountants in England & Wales (*Accountancy Business Group*)

Book Trade Association Membership: PA

1009

ACE BOOKS
1268 London Road, Norbury, London SW16 4ER
Telephone: 0181 679 8000
Fax: 0181 679 6069

Trade Distributor:
Biblios Publishers Distribution Service Ltd, Star Road, Partridge Green, West Sussex RH13 8LD
Telephone: 01403 710971
Fax: 01403 711143

Publishing Manager: Richard Holloway (*Rights & Permissions*)
Books Marketing Officer: Michael Addison (*Home & Export Sales*)

Academic & Scholarly; Accountancy & Taxation; Cookery, Wines & Spirits; Crafts & Hobbies; Gardening; Health & Beauty; Law; Medical (incl. Self Help & Alternative Medicine); Reference Books, Directories & Dictionaries; Transport

New Titles: 15 (1995), 12 (1996)
No of Employees: 3
Annual Turnover: £0.5M

ISBNs, Imprints & Series: 0 86242

Parent Company:
Age Concern

Book Trade Association Membership: PA

1010

ACOL-BIOTOL
Unit 42, Butterly Avenue, Dartford Trade Park, Dartford, Kent DA1 1JG
Telephone: 0181 331 9600

Fax: 0181 331 9672
Email: acol@gre.ac.uk

Manager: Dr J. D. Barnes
Director: Prof. Edwin Metcalfe
Editor: David Ando
Unit Administrator: Linda Johnson

*Academic & Scholarly; Biography &
Autobiography; Educational & Textbooks;
Electronic (Educational); Scientific &
Technical*

New Titles: 5 (1995), 5 (1996)
No of Employees: 4

ISBNs, Imprints & Series:
1 874529 Analytical Chemistry by Open
Learning/Biotechnology by Open Learning
(ACOL/BIOTOL), Greenwich University
Press

Parent Company:
UGMT Ltd

Overseas Representation *(see §7.3)*:
Australia: EMA Open Learning (Pty) Ltd,
South Melbourne
Canada (ACOL/BIOTOL): Open Learning
Agency, Burnaby, BC, Canada

1011

ADAM MATTHEW PUBLICATIONS
8 Oxford Street, Marlborough, Wiltshire
SN8 1AP
Telephone: 01672 511921
Fax: 01672 511663

Publishers: William Pidduck
David Tyler

*Academic & Scholarly; Economics; Gender
Studies; History & Antiquarian; Literature &
Criticism; Reference Books, Directories &
Dictionaries*

ISBNs, Imprints & Series: 1 85711

Overseas Representation *(see §7.3)*:
Japan: Maruzen Co Ltd, Tokyo
USA: Norman Ross Publishing Inc, New York

1012

ADAMANTINE PRESS LTD
3 Henrietta Street, London WC2E 8LU
Telephone: 0171 240 0856
Fax: 0171 379 0609

Warehouse, Trade Enquiries & Orders:
EDS, 3 Henrietta Street, London WC2E 8LU
Telephone: 0171 240 0856
Fax: 0171 379 0609

Editorial: Jeremy Geelan

*Academic & Scholarly; Politics & World
Affairs; Twenty-First Century Studies*

New Titles: 5 (1995), 7 (1996)

ISBNs, Imprints & Series: 0 7449

Parent Company:
Adamantine Press Ltd

Overseas Representation *(see §7.3)*:
Australia: DA Books, Melbourne
Europe & Middle East: Eurospan STM Group,
London, UK
India: Viva Marketing, New Delhi
Pakistan: Book Bird, Lahore
Philippines: Philippean Futuristic Society,
Manila

1013

ADDAX RETAIL PUBLISHING LTD
The Offices, The Square, Hadlow,
Nr Tonbridge, Kent TN11 0DD
Telephone: 01732 852030
Fax: 01732 852031

Managing Director: John Twiggs
Production Manager: Tracey Pennington

*Children's Books; History & Antiquarian;
Illustrated & Fine Editions; Military & War;
Natural History; Nautical*

New Titles: 9 (1995), 22 (1996)
No of Employees: 3

ISBNs, Imprints & Series: 1 86007

Book Trade Association Membership: PA

1014

ADDISON WESLEY LONGMAN LTD
Edinburgh Gate, Harlow, Essex CM20 2JE
Telephone: 01279 623623
Fax: 01279 431059

Distribution & Finance Centre:
Fourth Avenue, Pinnacles, Harlow, Essex
CM19 5SR
Telephone: 01279 623623
Fax: 01279 431067

Ordering Information:
PO Box 88, Fourth Avenue, Harlow, Essex
CM19 5SR
Telephone: 0800 579579 (Freephone)(School
Orders) & 0500 527528 (Trade Orders)
Fax: 01279 414130 (UK Orders) & 01279
623627 (International Orders)

Executive Directors: J. L. Jones *(Chairman &
Chief Executive Officer (US based))*
R. N. Woodward *(Chief Financial Officer (US
based))*
D. A. Smith *(Executive Vice-President (US
based))*
T. C. Davy *(Executive Vice-President
International ELT Group)*
J. E. Robinson *(Group Corporate Services
Director & Company Secretary)*
International ELT Group: R. A. J. Francis
(Managing Director)
R. Cauthery *(Sales & Marketing Director)*
M. Craig *(Managing Director, Consumer)*
G. Negus *(Publishing Director)*
T. Mann *(Production & Administration
Director)*
A. Mansell *(Human Resources Director)*
D. Summers *(Director, Dictionaries)*
G. S. Taylor *(Market Development Director)*
Higher Education Group: D. Hall *(Head,
Europe)*
M. S. Beyers *(Managing Director)*
F. Baker *(Human Resources Director, HE &
Schools division)*

C. Harrison *(Publishing Director, Social
Science & Study Guides)*
J. Jones *(Sales & Marketing Director)*
C. Lander *(Production Director)*
R. Lomax *(Publishing Director, Science &
Technology)*
A. Ware *(Director, AW Publishing)*
B. Willan *(Publishing Director, Academic)*
Longman Schools Group: J. Penrose *(Head of
Longman Schools)*
J. Andrew *(Managing Director)*
J. Pixton *(Managing Director, Logotron)*
A. Ransom *(Director, Interactive Learning)*
P. Uttley *(Sales & Marketing Director)*
L. Cocking *(Publishing Director, Secondary &
Vocational)*
J. Stanton *(Publishing Director, Primary)*
H. Davies *(Publishing Services Director)*
K. Roberts *(Director, International
Department)*
J. Pares *(Publishing Director, International
Department)*
Group Corporate Services: M. W. Todd
(Director UK Operations)
J. Mumford *(Head of Human Resources,
Operations)*
J. Ayre *(Head of Distribution)*
J. Heals *(Head of Customer Services)*
J. Mills *(Director Longman Finance)*
L. Owen *(Rights & Contracts Director)*
T. Tippler *(Head of Information Technology)*
T. Williams *(Head of Facilities Management)*
L. Meiller *(Corporate Communications)*

*Academic & Scholarly; Agriculture;
Archaeology; Architecture & Design; Atlases
& Maps; Audio Books; Biography &
Autobiography; Biology & Zoology;
Chemistry; Children's Books; Cinema, Video,
TV & Radio; Computer Science; Economics;
Educational & Textbooks; Electronic
(Educational); Electronic (Professional &
Academic); Engineering; English as a Foreign
Language; Environment & Development
Studies; Gender Studies; Geography &
Geology; History & Antiquarian; Industry,
Business & Management; Languages &
Linguistics; Law; Literature & Criticism;
Mathematics & Statistics; Military & War;
Natural History; Nautical; Philosophy;
Photography; Physics; Poetry; Politics &
World Affairs; Psychology & Psychiatry;
Reference Books, Directories & Dictionaries;
Religion & Theology; Scientific & Technical;
Sociology & Anthropology; Veterinary
Science; Vocational Training & Careers*

No of Employees: 1724
Annual Turnover: £114.6M

ISBNs, Imprints & Series:
Addison-Wesley, Addison-Wesley Interactive,
Benjamin/Cummings, Cuisenaire, Dale
Seymour/Logotron, Longman, Peachpit
Press, Planet Dexter, Scott Foresman/
Addison Wesley

Parent Company:
Pearson Plc

Associated & Subsidiary Companies:
Addison Wesley Longman Inc; Addison
Wesley Longman Ltd. *Australia:* Addison
Wesley Longman Australia Pty Ltd. *Botswana:*
Longman Botswana (Pty) Ltd. *P. R. of China:*
Shanghai AWL Education Software Ltd. *Egypt:*
The Egyptian International Publishing Co—

Longman. *France:* Editions Addison-Wesley France SA; Longman France SA. *Germany:* Addison Wesley Longman Verlag; Langenscheidt/Longman GmbH. *Greece:* Longman Hellas Publishing SA. *Hong Kong:* Longman Asia Ltd; Orient Longman Ltd. *Italy:* Addison-Wesley Italia Editoriale SpA; Direct English Srl; Longman Italia Srl. *Japan:* Longman Japan KK. *Lesotho:* Longman Lesotho (Pty) Ltd. *Malaysia:* Longman Malaysia Sdn Bhd. *Mexico:* Longman de Mexico SA de CV. *Namibia:* Longman Namibia (Pty) Ltd. *Netherlands:* Addison Wesley Longman Nederland BV; Addison Wesley Longman Publishers BV. *New Zealand:* Addison Wesley Longman New Zealand Ltd. *Nigeria:* Longman Nigeria Plc. *Singapore:* Longman Singapore Publishers Ltd. *South Africa:* Maskew Miller Longman (Pty) Ltd. *Spain:* Alhambra Longman SA. *Zambia:* Longman Zambia Ltd. *Zimbabwe:* Longman Zimbabwe (Pvt) Ltd

Overseas Representation *(see §7.3):*
Argentina: Longman Representative, Buenos Aires
Australia: Longman Australia Pty Ltd, Melbourne
Barbados: Louis A. Forde, St Michael
Botswana: Longman Botswana (Pty) Ltd, Gaborone
Brazil: Longman ELT, São Paulo
Egypt: Sphinx Bookshop, Cairo
France: Longman France, Paris
Ghana: Sedco Publishing Ltd, Accra
Hong Kong: Longman Hong Kong
India (medical books): BI Publications Pvt Ltd, New Delhi & Bombay, India
India (other titles): Orient Longman Ltd, Hyderabad, India
Italy: Longman Italia SRL, Milan
Jamaica: Carlong Publishers (Caribbean) Ltd, Kingston
Japan: Longman Japan KK, Tokyo
Jordan: Longman Arab World Centre, Amman
Kenya: Longhorn Kenya Ltd, Nairobi
Lebanon: Longman Arab World Centre, Beirut
Lesotho: Longman Lesotho (Pty) Ltd, Maseru
Malawi: Dzuka Publishing Ltd, Blantyre
Malaysia: Longman Malaysia Sdn Bhd, Petaling Jaya
Mexico: Longman de Mexico, Mexico DF
New Zealand: Longman Paul Ltd, Auckland
Nigeria: Longman Nigeria PK, Ikeja
Portugal: Longman Penguin Portugal, Lisbon
Singapore: Longman Singapore Publishers (Pte) Ltd
South Africa: Maskew Miller Longman Pty Ltd, Cape Town
Sudan: Longman Arab World Centre, Khartoum
Swaziland: Longman Swaziland (Pty) Ltd, Manzini
Syria: Librairie Sayegh, Damascus
Taiwan: Longman Taiwan, Taipei
Tanzania: Ben & Co Ltd, Dar es Salaam
Trinidad: Longman Trinidad Ltd, Trincity
Turkey: Longman Turkey, Istanbul
USA (medical titles): Churchill Radius Inc, Clifton, NJ, USA
USA (other titles): Longman Publishing Group, White Plains, NY, USA
Venezuela: Longman Representative, Caracas
Zimbabwe: Longman Zimbabwe (Pvt) Ltd, Harare

Book Trade Association Membership: PA, BDC, EPC, IGSMTP, CAPP, NBA (Signatory)

1015 ▬▬▬▬

ADLARD COLES NAUTICAL
35 Bedford Row, London WC1R 4JH
Telephone: 0171 242 0946
Fax: 0171 831 8478

Warehouse:
Howard Road, Eaton Socon, St Neots, Cambs PE19 3EZ
Telephone: 01480 212666
Fax: 01480 405014

Directors: Janet Murphy *(Editorial)*
Paul Langridge *(Rights)*
Manager: Susan Kodicek *(Home Sales)*
Chairman: Charles Black *(Export Sales)*

Nautical

New Titles: 20 (1995), 31 (1996)
No of Employees: 3

ISBNs, Imprints & Series:
0 229, 0 245, 0 333, 0 7136, 0 85177 Adlard Coles, Nautical Books, Stanford Maritime

Parent Company:
A. & C. Black (Publishers) Ltd

Distributor for:
USA: Sheridan House Inc

Overseas Representation *(see §7.3):*
See: A. & C. Black (Publishers) Ltd, London, UK

1016 ▬▬▬▬

ADVISORY UNIT: COMPUTERS IN EDUCATION
126 Great North Road, Hatfield, Herts AL9 5JZ
Telephone: 01707 266714
Fax: 01707 273684
Email: info@advunit.demon.co.uk
Web Site: http://www.rmplc.co.uk/eduweb/sites/advunit/index.html

Directors: M. Aston *(Export Sales)*
C. King *(Technical)*
A. Hinder *(Training)*
Ms D. Freeman *(Rights & Permissions)*
Sales Manager: M. Barnard

Academic & Scholarly; Atlases & Maps; Educational & Textbooks; Electronic (Educational); Electronic (Professional & Academic); English as a Foreign Language; Geography & Geology; Languages & Linguistics; Mathematics & Statistics

New Titles: 6 (1995), 7 (1996)
No of Employees: 8
Annual Turnover: £350,000

ISBNs, Imprints & Series: 1 874164

Distributor for:
Denmark: Orfeus Software Publishing.
Finland: Softmill Oy. *Germany:* CoMet Verlag. *Netherlands:* Visiria. *Norway:* Nasjonal Læremiddelscenter. *Russia:* The Almanac Software Publishing Co; St Petersberg Shipbuilding Institute. *South Africa:*

Afrisoft Grahamstown. *Spain:* Edicinco.
Sweden: Gävle. *USA:* Harvard Associates Inc

Overseas Representation *(see §7.3):*
Australia: Acorn (Australia) Ltd, Abbotsford; East West Computers Pty Ltd, Riddells Creek, Vic; Fingertip Concepts, Perth, WA
Canada: Olivetti/Acorn Canada, Markham
Denmark: Orfeus, Egå; Mikro Værkstedet, Odense
Egypt: Rehabco, Cairo
Finland: MFKA-Kustannus Oy, Helsinki
India: Interprint Publications, New Delhi
Netherlands: TES Nederland BV, The Hague; NIAM, The Hague
New Zealand: Acorn Computers (NZ) Ltd, Auckland; Special Education Service, Wellington
Pakistan: PACES, Karachi
South Africa: Oak Tree Technologies, Johannesburg; Educational Software, Bedfordview
USA: Roykore Inc, San Francisco; Harvard Associates Inc, Cambridge, MA

Book Trade Association Membership:
Educational Software Publishers Association, BESA

1017 ▬▬▬▬

AFRICANA PUBLISHING CO
244A London Road, Hadleigh, Essex SS7 2DE
Telephone: 01702 552912
Fax: 01702 556095

Directors: Miriam Holmes *(Managing)*
Doreen Mann *(Operations)*
Dan Levey *(Marketing)*
Sales Manager: Celia Stocks

Academic & Scholarly; Agriculture; Animal Care & Breeding; Atlases & Maps; Biology & Zoology; Environment & Development Studies; History & Antiquarian; Politics & World Affairs

ISBNs, Imprints & Series: 0 8419

Parent Company:
Holmes & Meier *(USA)*

1018 ▬▬▬▬

*AHMADIYYA MUSLIM PUBLICATIONS
Islamabad, Sheephatch Lane, Tilford, Surrey GU10 2AQ
Telephone: 01252 783155
Fax: 01252 783148

Orders:
The London Mosque, 16 Gressenhall Road, London SW18 5QL
Telephone: 0181 870 8517
Fax: 0181 870 1095

Managing Director: M. D. Shams *(Marketing)*
Sales Manager: Hashim M. Saeed

Children's Books; Religion & Theology

ISBNs, Imprints & Series:
1 85372 Islam International Publications Ltd, Al-Shirkatul Islamiyyah

Parent Company:
Al-Shirkatul Islamiyyah

Overseas Representation *(see §7.3)*:
Australia: Islam International Publications,
Riverstone
Bangladesh: Islam International Publications,
Dacca
Belgium: Islam International Publications,
Brussels
Canada: Baitul Islam, Maple
Denmark: Islam International Publications,
Copenhagen
Fiji: Islam International Publications, Suva
France: Islam International Publications, Saint
Prix
Gambia: Islam International Publications,
Banjul
Germany: Islam International Publications,
Frankfurt
Ghana: Islam International Publications, Accra
Guyana: Ahmadiyya Muslim Mission,
Georgetown
India: Islam International Publications, Qadian
Indonesia: Islam International Publications,
Jakarta
Ivory Coast: Ahmadiyya Muslim Mission,
Abidjan
Japan: Islam International Publications,
Nagoya
Kenya: Islam International Publications,
Nairobi
Liberia: Islam International Publications,
Monrovia
Mauritius: Islam International Publications,
Rose Hill
Myanmar (Burma): Islam International
Publications, Rangoon, Myanmar
Netherlands: Islam International Publications,
The Hague
Nigeria: Islam International Publications,
Lagos
Norway: Ahmadiyya Muslim Mission, Oslo
Philippines: Islam International Publications,
Zamboanga City
Sierra Leone: Islam International Publications,
Freetown
Singapore: Islam International Publications
South Africa: Islam International Publications,
Cape Town
Spain: Mission Ahmadiyya del Islam, Cordoba
Sri Lanka: Islam International Publications,
Colombo
Suriname: Ahmadiyya Muslim Mission,
Paramaribo
Sweden: Nasir Moské Islams Ahmadiyya
Församling, Göteborg
Switzerland: Islam International Publications,
Zurich
Tanzania: Islam International Publications, Dar
es Salaam
Trinidad & Tobago: Islam International
Publications, Tunapuna, Trinidad
Uganda: Islam International Publications,
Kampala
USA: Islam International Publications, Silver
Spring, MD
Zaire: Islam International Publications,
Kinshasa
Zambia: Islam International Publications,
Lusaka

1019

AIRDATA PUBLICATIONS
Southside, Manchester Airport, Wilmslow,
Cheshire SK9 4LL

Telephone: 0161 499 0024
Fax: 0161 499 0298
Email: books@airdata.u-net.com

Managing Director: Jeremy M. Pratt

Aviation; Military & War; Transport

New Titles: 9 (1995), 16 (1996)

ISBNs, Imprints & Series:
0 85979 Airdata Publications
0 907579 Goodall Publications
1 873454 Wingham Press
1 874783 Airplan Flight Equipment Ltd

Distributor for:
Germany: Flugzeug Publikations. *USA:*
Aviation Publications Inc

Overseas Representation *(see §7.3)*:
Worldwide: Books for Europe Ltd,
Bournemouth, UK

1020

AIRLIFE PUBLISHING LTD
101 Longden Road, Shrewsbury SY3 9EB
Telephone: 01743 235651
Fax: 01743 232944

Directors: A. D. R. Simpson *(Managing,*
Rights)
Andrew Johnston *(Export Sales)*
Peter Holmes *(Financial)*
Managers: Judith Sale *(Publicity)*
Peter Coles *(Managing Editor)*

Antiques & Collecting; Aviation; Biography &
Autobiography; Illustrated & Fine Editions;
Military & War; Natural History; Nautical;
Transport; Outdoor Pursuits

New Titles: 80 (1995), 90 (1996)
No of Employees: 25
Annual Turnover: £3.5M

ISBNs, Imprints & Series:
0 906393, 0 9504543, 1 85310 Airlife, Swan
Hill Press, Waterline

Distributor for:
Aerospace Publishing; International Marine;
Naval Institute Press; Robert Pooley Ltd;
Smithsonian (History of Aviation Series);
Stoeger Publishing Co; Tab/Aero Books Inc;
Voyageur Press

Overseas Representation *(see §7.3)*:
Australia: Peribo Pty Ltd, Mount Kuring-gai,
NSW
Canada: Vanwell Publishing Ltd, St
Catherines, Ont
New Zealand: South Pacific Books (Imports)
Ltd, Auckland
South Africa: Southern Book Publishers,
Halfway House

1021

ALBYN PRESS
2 Caversham Street, Chelsea, London
SW3 4AH
Telephone: 0171 351 4995
Fax: 0171 351 4995

Director: James Hughes *(Editorial)*

Fiction; Fine Art & Art History; Geography &
Geology; Guide Books; History & Antiquarian;
Illustrated & Fine Editions; Literature &
Criticism; Poetry; Reference Books,
Directories & Dictionaries; Scottish Books

New Titles: 10 (1995), 8 (1996)
No of Employees: 5

ISBNs, Imprints & Series: 0 284

Parent Company:
Charles Skilton Ltd

Associated & Subsidiary Companies:
Charles Skilton Publishing Group; Tallis Press

Book Trade Association Membership: IPG

1022

IAN ALLAN LTD
Coombelands House, Coombelands Lane,
Addlestone, Surrey KT15 1HY
Telephone: 01932 855909
Fax: 01932 854750

Distribution:
Littlehampton Book Services,
10–14 Eldon Way, Lineside Estate,
Littlehampton, West Sussex BN17 7HG
Telephone: 01903 721596
Fax: 01903 730914

Chairman: David Allan
Directors: Tony Saunders *(General Manager)*
Bill Lucas *(Sales)*
Nicholas Lerwill *(Production)*

Atlases & Maps; Aviation; Cookery, Wines &
Spirits; Gardening; Guide Books; History &
Antiquarian; Military & War; Sports & Games;
Transport; Travel & Topography

New Titles: 70 (1995), 80 (1996)
No of Employees: 100
Annual Turnover: £4M

ISBNs, Imprints & Series:
0 7110 Ian Allan, Dial House

Parent Company:
Ian Allan Group Ltd

Distributor for:
Atlantic Transport Publishing; Belgrove
Publishing; Millstream Books; Pendragon
Partnership; Runpast Publishing; Windrow &
Green; World of Transport. *USA:* Howell Press;
Stoddart

Overseas Representation *(see §7.3)*:
Australia & New Zealand: Peribo Pty Ltd,
Mount Kuring-gai, NSW, Australia
Canada: Vanwell Publishing Ltd, St
Catherines, Ont
France, Austria, Italy, Greece, Switzerland &
Yugoslavia: Juliusz Komarnicki, Massagno,
Switzerland
Germany, Netherlands, Luxembourg &
Belgium: PKB – Robbert J. Pleysier, Heerde,
Netherlands
India, Pakistan, Middle East, Singapore,
Malaysia, Thailand & Indonesia: PIM
(Publishers International Management),
Sheffield, MA, USA

Irish Republic & Northern Ireland: Brian Blennerhasset, Dublin, Irish Republic
Poland & Czech & Slovak Republics: Books International, Farnborough, Hants, UK
Scandinavia: D. Richard Bowen, Malmö, Sweden
South Africa: Ian Allan Publishing, Addlestone, Surrey, UK
Spain, Portugal & Gibraltar: Iberian Book Services SL, Madrid, Spain
USA: Specialist Marketing International, Herndon, VA

1023

J. A. ALLEN & CO LTD
1 Lower Grosvenor Place, London SW1W 0EL
Telephone: 0171 834 0090
Fax: 0171 976 5836

Warehouse & Shipping:
Trade Counter Ltd, The Airfield, Norwich Road, Mendlesham, Suffolk IP14 5NA
Telephone: 01449 766629
Fax: 01449 767122

Sales Ledger Accounts:
c/o Sheed & Ward Ltd, 14 Coopers Row, London EC3N 2BH
Telephone: 0171 702 9799
Fax: 0171 702 3583

Managing Director & Chairman: Joseph A. Allen
Company Secretary: Mrs A. Haistor
Publishing & Sales Director: Caroline Burt *(Rights & Permissions)*
Managing Editor: Jane Lake
Marketing Manager: Hugh Davie

Equine & Equestrian

New Titles: 17 (1995), 28 (1996)
No of Employees: 4

ISBNs, Imprints & Series:
0 85131 Caduceus Press

Distributor for:
BHS Bridleways Publications; The Pony Club

Book Trade Association Membership: IPG

1024

ALLIED MOUSE LTD
41a Spring Gardens, Buxton, Derbyshire SK17 6BJ
Telephone: 01298 72218

Directors: Sitakumari
Nick Sidle

Children's Books

New Titles: 1 (1996)
Annual Turnover: £120,000

ISBNs, Imprints & Series: 0 9513492

Book Trade Association Membership: PA

1025

ALLISON & BUSBY
179 King's Cross Road, London WC1X 9BZ

Telephone: 0171 833 1042
Fax: 0171 833 1044

Warehouse/Distribution & UK Sales:
Exel Logistics Media Services, Invicta House, Sir Thomas Longley Road, Medway City Estate, Rochester, Kent ME2 4BU
Telephone: 01634 297123
Fax: 01634 298000

Publisher: Peter Day
Assistant: Vanessa Unwin
Publicity: Jennifer Chapman
Finance & Administration: Geoffrey Chapman

Biography & Autobiography; Do-It-Yourself; Fiction; History & Antiquarian; Politics & World Affairs

New Titles: 36 (1995), 36 (1996)

ISBNs, Imprints & Series:
0 74900, 0 85031

Parent Company:
Wilson & Day Ltd

Overseas Representation *(see §7.3)*:
Africa: Len Ainsworth, Aldbourne, UK
Australia & New Zealand: Peribo Pty Ltd, Mount Kuring-gai, NSW, Australia
Canada: General Publishing Co Ltd, North York, Ont
Caribbean: Humphrys Roberts Associates, London, UK
Europe: Penguin Books Ltd, London, UK
France & Germany: Cantaluppi & Hug, Zurich, Switzerland
Hong Kong: Publishers' Associates Ltd
Japan: Macmillan Shuppan KK, Tokyo
Malaysia, Singapore, Indonesia & Brunei: Pansing Distribution Sdn Bhd, Singapore
Netherlands: Nilsson & Lamm BV, Weesp
Switzerland: Azed Bucher, Basle
Taiwan: Bookman Books Ltd, Taipei
Thailand & Philippines: Balatbat & Sons International, Quezon City, Philippines

Book Trade Association Membership: PA

1026

ALPINE FINE ART BOOKS LTD
43 Manchester Street, London W1M 5PE
Telephone: 0171 935 0797
Fax: 0171 935 0656

Warehouse & Fulfilment Centre:
Vine House Distribution, Waldenbury, North Common, Chailey, East Sussex BN8 4DR
Telephone: 01825 723398
Fax: 01825 724188

Managing Director: Gordon M. Saks
Home & Export Sales: Mary Ellen Upton

Fine Art & Art History; East European Art

New Titles: 5 (1995), 5 (1996)

ISBNs, Imprints & Series:
0 88168 Cromwell Editions
0 933516 Alpine Fine Arts Collection

Associated & Subsidiary Companies:
Cromwell Editions

Distributor for:
USA: Konecky & Konecky

Overseas Representation *(see §7.3)*:
Australia: Bookwise International, Findon, SA
Bulgaria: Any Bancheva, Sofia
Europe: Books for Europe, J. Komarnicki, Lugano, Switzerland
Italy, Spain & Portugal: Penny Padovani, London, UK
Middle East: Peter Ward Book Exports, London, UK
Scandinavia: D. Richard Bowen, Malmö, Sweden
Slovenia: East West Operations, Ljubljana

Book Trade Association Membership: PA

1027

THE AMAISING PUBLISHING HOUSE LTD
Unit 7, Greendykes Industrial Estate, Broxburn EH52 6PG
Telephone: 01506 857570
Fax: 01506 858100

Directors: Katrena Allan *(Managing)*
Gordon Allan *(Production)*

Children's Books

New Titles: 3 (1995), 3 (1996)
No of Employees: 15
Annual Turnover: £150,000

ISBNs, Imprints & Series: 1 871512

Book Trade Association Membership:
Scottish PA

1028

AMBER LANE PRESS LTD
Cheorl House, Church Street, Charlbury, Oxon OX7 3PR
Telephone: 01608 810024
Fax: 01608 810024

Managing Editor & Director: Judith Scott

Music; Theatre, Drama & Dance

New Titles: 3 (1995), 5 (1996)

ISBNs, Imprints & Series:
0 906399, 1 872868

Distributor for:
Three Rivers Books

Overseas Representation *(see §7.3)*:
Australia & New Zealand: Keith Ainsworth Pty Ltd, Penrith, NSW, Australia

1029

AMERICAN LIBRARY ASSOCIATION
3 Henrietta Street, Covent Garden, London WC2E 8LU
Telephone: 0171 240 0856
Fax: 0171 379 0609

Directors: Michael Geelan *(Managing)*
Danny Maher *(Sales)*
Product Manager: Clare Sutton

Bibliography & Library Science; Reference Books, Directories & Dictionaries

ISBNs, Imprints & Series:
0 8389, 0 910230

1030

AMERICAN PSYCHIATRIC PRESS
3 Henrietta Street, Covent Garden, London
WC2E 8LU
Telephone: 0171 240 0856
Fax: 0171 379 0609

Warehouse:
Plymbridge Distributors Ltd, Estover Road,
Plymouth PL6 7PZ
Telephone: 01752 735251 & 695745
(customer services)
Fax: 01752 695699

Contact: Michael Geelan

Psychology & Psychiatry

New Titles: 60 (1995), 60 (1996)

ISBNs, Imprints & Series:
0 88048, 0 89042, 1 88210, 1 882013

1031

AMERICAN PSYCHOLOGICAL ASSOCIATION
3 Henrietta Street, Covent Garden, London
WC2E 8LU
Telephone: 0171 240 0856
Fax: 0171 379 0609

Directors: Michael Geelan *(Managing)*
Danny Maher *(Sales)*
Product Manager: Clare Sutton

Psychology & Psychiatry

ISBNs, Imprints & Series:
0 912704, 1 555798

1032

AMNESTY INTERNATIONAL INTERNATIONAL SECRETARIAT
1 Easton Street, London WC1X 8DJ
Telephone: 0171 413 5500
Fax: 0171 956 1157
Email: amnestyis@amnesty.org

Secretary General: Pierre Sané
Director, Media Program: Anita Tiessen
Director, Publications Program: Sarah
Bennison

Human Rights

New Titles: 8 (1995), 10 (1996)
No of Employees: 300

ISBNs, Imprints & Series:
0 86210, 0308 6887

Overseas Representation *(see §7.3)*:
Algeria: Amnesty International, Alger

Argentina: Amnistía Internacional, Buenos Aires
Australia: Amnesty International, Broadway, NSW
Austria: Amnesty International, Vienna
Bangladesh: Amnesty International, Dhaka
Belgium: Amnesty International, Antwerp; Amnesty International, Brussels
Benin: Amnesty International, Cotonou
Bermuda: Amnesty International, Hamilton
Brazil: Anistia Internacional, São Paulo
Canada: Amnesty International, Vanier, Ont; Amnistie Internationale, Montreal
Chile: Amnistía Internacional, Santiago
Colombia: Señores, Bogota
Denmark: Amnesty International, Copenhagen
Ecuador: Amnistía Internacional, Quito
Faroe Islands: Amnesty International, Tórshavn, Faroe Islands
Finland: Amnesty International, Helsinki
France: Amnesty International, Paris
Germany: Amnesty International, Bonn
Ghana: Amnesty International, Koforidua
Greece: Amnesty International, Athens
Guyana: Amnesty International, Georgetown
Hong Kong: Amnesty International, Kowloon
Iceland: Amnesty International, Reykjavik
India: Amnesty International, Delhi
Irish Republic: Amnesty International, Dublin
Israel: Amnesty International, Tel Aviv
Italy: Amnesty International, Rome
Ivory Coast: Amnesty International, Abidjan
Japan: Amnesty International, Tokyo
Korea: Amnesty International, Daegu, Korea, South
Luxembourg: Amnesty International
Mauritius: Amnesty International, Rose-Hill
Mexico: Amnistía Internacional, Mexico DF
Nepal: Amnesty International, Kathmandu
Netherlands: Amnesty International, Amsterdam
New Zealand: Amnesty International, Wellington
Nigeria: Amnesty International, Lagos
Norway: Amnesty International, Oslo
Peru: Señores, Lima
Philippines: Amnesty International, Manila
Portugal: Amnistia Internacional, Lisbon
Puerto Rico: Amnistía Internacional, Rio Piedras
Senegal: Amnesty International, Dakar
Sierra Leone: Amnesty International, Freetown
Slovenia: Amnesty International, Ljubljana
Spain: Amnesty International, Madrid
Sweden: Amnesty International, Stockholm
Switzerland: Amnesty International, Berne
Tanzania: Amnesty International, Dar es Salaam
Tunisia: Amnesty International, Tunis
Uruguay: Amnistía Internacional, Montevideo
USA: Amnesty International of the USA (AIUSA), New York, NY
Venezuela: Amnistía Internacional, Caracas

1033

ANDERSEN PRESS LTD
20 Vauxhall Bridge Road, London SW1V 2SA
Telephone: 0171 973 9720
Fax: 0171 233 6263
Email: 101370.533@compuserve.com

Warehouse, Orders & Payments:
Tiptree Book Services Ltd, Tiptree, Colchester,
Essex CO5 0SR
Telephone: Tiptree 01621 816362
Fax: 01621 819011

Address for Returns Requests:
Sales Department, Random House,
(address as above)
Telephone: *(as above)*

Directors: Klaus Flugge *(Managing & Publisher)*
J. Flugge *(Company Secretary)*
P. W. Durrance
Denise Johnstone-Burt *(Editorial)*
Editor: Audrey Adams
Sales Managers: Mike Dougdale *(Home Sales)*
David Parrish *(Export Sales)*
Rights & Permissions: Sarah Pakenham
Marketing & Publicity: Lucy Chapman

Children's Books

New Titles: 42 (1995), 45 (1996)
No of Employees: 6
Annual Turnover: £4M

ISBNs, Imprints & Series:
0 86264, 0 905478 Andersen Artists (greetings cards), Andersen Press, Andersen Young Readers' Library, Children's Picture Books, Tigers — Read Alone Fiction

Associated & Subsidiary Companies:
Random House

Overseas Representation *(see §7.3)*:
Canada (Library Institutions): Nelson Canada, Scarborough, Canada
Canada (Trade): General Publishing Co Ltd, North York, Ont, Canada
Other overseas markets See: Random House UK Ltd, London, UK

1034

PETER ANDREW PUBLISHING CO LTD
4 Charlecot Road, Droitwich, Worcs WR9 7RP
Telephone: 01905 778543
Fax: 01905 795077

Directors: Philip Checkley
Joan Checkley *(Sales)*

Academic & Scholarly; Accountancy & Taxation; Economics; Engineering; Health & Beauty; Industry, Business & Management; Law; Sports & Games; Theatre, Drama & Dance

ISBNs, Imprints & Series: 0 946796

Book Trade Association Membership: Book Data

1035

ANDROMEDA INTERACTIVE LTD
9–15 The Vineyard, Abingdon, Oxon
OX14 3PX
Telephone: 01235 529595
Fax: 01235 559122
Email: medical@andromeda.co.uk
Web Site: http://www.andromeda.co.uk/medical.html

Chief Executive Officer: Jonathan Taylor
Directors: Therese Maitland *(Marketing)*
Michael Holyoak *(Production)*

Sales Managers: Louisa Perry
Emily Gillingham

Electronic (Educational); Medical (incl. Self Help & Alternative Medicine)

New Titles: 1 (1995), 5 (1996)

1036 ∎

ANGLO-GERMAN FOUNDATION FOR THE STUDY OF INDUSTRIAL SOCIETY
17 Bloomsbury Square, London WC1A 2LP
Telephone: 0171 404 3137
Fax: 0171 405 2071

Orders:
BEBC, 15 Albion Close, Parkstone, Poole, Dorset BH12 3YD
Telephone: 01800 262260
Fax: 01800 262266

Secretary-General: Dr Connie Martin

Academic & Scholarly; Economics; Industry, Business & Management; Politics & World Affairs

New Titles: 7 (1995), 16 (1996)
No of Employees: 5

ISBNs, Imprints & Series:
0 905492, 1 900834

Overseas Representation *(see §7.3)*:
Germany: Deutsch-Britische Stiftung für das Studium der Industriegesellschaft, Bonn

Book Trade Association Membership:
IGSMTP, ALPSP, SYP

1037 ∎

ANN ARBOR PUBLISHERS LTD
PO Box 1, Belford, Northumberland NE70 7JX
Telephone: 01668 214460
Fax: 01668 214484

Managing Director: Peter D. Laverack

Educational & Textbooks; High Interest Low Reading Level Novels; Tests for Learning Difficulty; Work Books for Dyslexic Pupils

New Titles: 10 (1995), 10 (1996)
No of Employees: 3

ISBNs, Imprints & Series:
0 87879, 0 931421, 1 900506

Distributor for:
Academic Therapy Publications; Ann Arbor Publishers; High Noon Books; Psychological & Educational Publications

Book Trade Association Membership: BEEA

1038 ∎

ANNESS PUBLISHING LTD
Hermes House, 88 Blackfriars Road, London SE1
Telephone: 0171 401 2077
Fax: 0171 633 9499

Trade (represents Lorenz Books):
Aurum Press, 25 Bedford Avenue, London WC1B 3AT
Telephone: 0171 637 3225
Fax: 0171 580 2469

Directors: Paul Anness *(Sales)*
Denise Lie *(Rights)*
Publisher: Joanna Lorenz

Animal Care & Breeding; Children's Books; Cookery, Wines & Spirits; Crafts & Hobbies; Do-It-Yourself; Gardening; Health & Beauty; Photography; Sports & Games

New Titles: 150 (1995), 200 (1996)
No of Employees: 60

ISBNs, Imprints & Series:
1 85967 Lorenz Books
1 86035 Ultimate Editions

Associated & Subsidiary Companies:
Australia: Anness Publishing Pty. *USA:* Anness Publishing

Overseas Representation *(see §7.3)*:
Australia: The Five Mile Press, Noble Park, Vic
Canada: Raincoast Distribution, Vancouver, BC
USA: Anness Publishing, London, UK

1039 ∎

ANTIQUE COLLECTORS' CLUB LTD
5 Church Street, Woodbridge, Suffolk IP12 1DS
Telephone: 01394 385501
Fax: 01394 384434 & 388994 (Sales)

Warehouse:
The Old Maltings, Crown Place, off Quay Street, Woodbridge, Suffolk IP12 1BU
Telephone: *(as above)*
Fax: *(as above)*

Directors: Diana Steel
Brian Cotton *(Sales)*
Manager: Sarah Smye *(Sales Office)*

Antiques & Collecting; Architecture & Design; Fine Art & Art History; Gardening; Humour; Reference Books, Directories & Dictionaries

New Titles: 22 (1995), 28 (1996)
No of Employees: 65

ISBNs, Imprints & Series:
0 902028, 0 907462, 1 85149, 1 870673

Associated & Subsidiary Companies:
Garden Art Press

Distributor for:
Arsenale Editrice; Bard Graduate Centre; George Braziller; Canal & Stamperia; Colonial Williamsburg; Jonathan Horne Publications; Museum of Fine Arts, Boston; Packard Publishing; Peabody Museum; Scala Books; Ursus Press; Winterthur

Overseas Representation *(see §7.3)*:
Australia: Peribo Pty Ltd, Mount Kuring-gai, NSW
Belgium: Jenny Gosling, Reading, UK

Far East: Asia Publisher Services Ltd, Hong Kong; Asia Publishers Services, Petaling Jaya, Malaysia; APD Singapore Pte Ltd, Singapore
France: David Pearson, Wheathampstead, UK
India: TBI Publishers' Distributors, New Delhi
Irish Republic & Northern Ireland: Robert Towers, Monkstown, Irish Republic
Italy, Spain & Portugal: Penny Padovani, London, UK
Near & Middle East: Michael Morris Associates, Saffron Walden, UK
Netherlands: Consul Books, Blaricum
New Zealand: Techbook Distributors, Auckland
Scandinavia & Iceland: Hanne Rotovnik, Klampenborg, Denmark
South Africa: Trinity Books CC, Randburg
USA: Antique Collectors' Club Ltd, Wappinger Falls

1040 ∎

ANVIL PRESS POETRY
69 King George Street, London SE10 8PX
Telephone: 0181 858 2946
Fax: 0181 858 2946

Distributors:
Clipper Distribution Service Ltd, Windmill Grove, Porchester, Hants PO16 9HT
Telephone: 01705 200080
Fax: 01705 200090

Representation:
Password (Books) Ltd, 23 New Mount Street, Manchester M4 4DE
Telephone: 0161 953 4009
Fax: 0161 953 4090

Editorial, Administration & Production:
Peter Jay *(Managing Director)*

Poetry

New Titles: 8 (1995), 15 (1996)
No of Employees: 2

ISBNs, Imprints & Series:
0 85646, 0 900977 Anvil Editions, Poetica

Overseas Representation *(see §7.3)*:
Australia: St Clair Press Pty Ltd, Rozelle, NSW

1041 ∎

AP INFORMATION SERVICES
Roman House, 296 Golders Green Road, London NW11 9PZ
Telephone: 0181 455 4550
Fax: 0181 455 6381

Partners: Alan Philipp *(Managing)*
Gail Philipp *(Financial)*
Associate Publishers: Alex Kaminsky *(Editorial)*
Tony Margolis *(Sales)*
Managers: Andy Bloom *(Computer)*
Sally Rodoham *(Sales Administration)*

Reference Books, Directories & Dictionaries; Directories

New Titles: 2 (1995)
No of Employees: 23
Annual Turnover: £1-2M

ISBNs, Imprints & Series:
0 906247, 0 906285

Overseas Representation *(see §7.3):*
USA: Money Market Directories,
  Charlottesville, VA; Kennedy Publications,
  Fitzwilliam, NH

Book Trade Association Membership: IPG,
Directory Publishers Association

1042 ▬▬▬▬▬▬

APPLETREE PRESS LTD
19–21 Alfred Street, Belfast BT2 8DL
Telephone: 01232 243074
Fax: 01232 246756
Email: 100407.1304@compuserve.com
Web Site: http://www.appletree.co.uk/

Distribution in UK:
Bookpoint Ltd, 39 Milton Park, Abingdon,
Oxon OX14 4TD
Telephone: 01235 835001
Fax: 01235 832066

London Office:
Appletree Press, 80-82 Chiswick High Road,
London W4 1SY
Telephone: 0181 987 9439
Fax: 0181 987 9443
Email: 100407.1304@compuserve.com

Directors: John Murphy *(Managing)*
David Ross *(Sales & Marketing—London
  office)*
Douglas Marshall *(Editorial)*
Jim White *(Financial)*
Paul McAvoy *(Production)*

*Academic & Scholarly; Archaeology; Atlases
& Maps; Cookery, Wines & Spirits;
Gardening; Guide Books; Humour; Illustrated
& Fine Editions; Languages & Linguistics;
Literature & Criticism; Music; Photography;
Politics & World Affairs; Reference Books,
Directories & Dictionaries; Sports & Games;
Transport; Irish Interest Non-Fiction*

New Titles: 35 (1995), 35 (1996)
No of Employees: 15

ISBNs, Imprints & Series:
0 86281, 0 904651

Overseas Representation *(see §7.3):*
Australia & New Zealand: Peribo Pty Ltd,
  Mount Kuring-gai, NSW, Australia
Canada: Vanwell Publishing Ltd, St
  Catherines, Ont
Europe: Janet Clark, London, UK
USA: Irish Books & Media, Minneapolis, MN

Book Trade Association Membership: CLÉ
(Irish PA)

1043 ▬▬▬▬▬▬

**ARCHITECTURAL ASSOCIATION
PUBLICATIONS**
34–36 Bedford Square, London WC1B 3ES
Telephone: 0171 636 0974
Fax: 0171 414 0782

Architecture Marketing Manager: Kirsten
  Morphet
Editorial: Pamela Johnston

Architecture & Design

New Titles: 5 (1995), 6 (1996)
No of Employees: 5

ISBNs, Imprints & Series:
0 904503, 1 870890

Distributor for:
USA: ANY

Overseas Representation *(see §7.3):*
Europe: Books for Europe Ltd, Bournemouth,
  UK

1044 ▬▬▬▬▬▬

ARCHIVAL FACSIMILES LTD
52 Crown Street, Banham, Norwich, Norfolk
NR16 2HW
Telephone: 01953 887277
Fax: 01953 888361

Director: Crispin de Boos
Consultant: Stephen Easton

*Academic & Scholarly; History & Antiquarian;
Illustrated & Fine Editions; Travel &
Topography*

New Titles: 7 (1995), 3 (1996)
No of Employees: 2

ISBNs, Imprints & Series:
0 948285, 1 85297 Archival Facsimiles,
  Erskine Press

Book Trade Association Membership: IPG

1045 ▬▬▬▬▬▬

ARGYLL PUBLISHING
Glendaruel, Argyll PA22 3AE
Telephone: 01369 820229
Fax: 01369 820229

Publisher: Derek Rodger

*Biography & Autobiography; Cookery, Wines
& Spirits; Fiction; Guide Books; Natural
History; Poetry; Sports & Games; Health &
Self-help*

New Titles: 15 (1995), 15 (1996)

ISBNs, Imprints & Series: 1 874640

Book Trade Association Membership:
Scottish PA

1046 ▬▬▬▬▬▬

ARIS & PHILLIPS LTD
Teddington House, Church Street, Warminster,
Wilts BA12 8PQ
Telephone: 01985 213409
Fax: 01985 212910

Warehouse:
La Haule Books Ltd, La Haule, Jersey,
Channel Islands
Telephone: Central 01534 44957
Fax: 01534 47414

Directors: A. A. Phillips *(Managing)*
L. M. Phillips *(Sales)*
Evelyn A. Aris *(Company Secretary)*

Elizabeth A. Aris
Sales & Promotion: Janet Davis *(Advertising
  Manager)*

*Academic & Scholarly; Archaeology;
Bibliography & Library Science; History &
Antiquarian; Languages & Linguistics;
Literature & Criticism; Reference Books,
Directories & Dictionaries; Sociology &
Anthropology; Oriental & Classical Studies*

New Titles: 15 (1995), 12 (1996)
No of Employees: 6

ISBNs, Imprints & Series:
0 85668 Central Asian Studies, Classical Texts,
  Hispanic Classics, Modern Egyptology

Associated & Subsidiary Companies:
La Haule Books Ltd

Distributor for:
The British School of Archaeology in Egypt;
The Gibb Memorial Trust; The Griffith Institute
of the University of Oxford. *Australia:* The
Australian Centre for Egyptology

Overseas Representation *(see §7.3):*
Australia: Hieroglyphics, Carlton South
India: UBS Publishers' Distributors Ltd, New
  Delhi
Spain & Portugal: Iberian Book Services SL,
  Madrid, Spain
USA: David Brown Book Co, Oakville, CT

1047 ▬▬▬▬▬▬

ARMS & ARMOUR PRESS
Wellington House, 125 Strand, London
WC2R 0BB
Telephone: 0171 420 5555
Fax: 0171 240 7261

Distribution:
Cassell Plc, 3 Fleets Lane, Poole, Dorset
BH15 3AJ
Telephone: 01202 665432
Fax: 01202 666219

Directors: Philip Sturrock *(Chairman)*
Roderick Dymott *(Editorial)*
Geoffrey Charters *(Production)*
Martyn Chapman *(Commercial & Distribution)*
Frank Roney *(Finance)*
Kevin Bristow *(Sales & Marketing)*
Michael Goff *(International Sales)*
Andrew Macmillan *(UK Trade Sales)*
Managers: Chris White *(Book Clubs)*
David Williams *(Special Sales)*
Joanna Lawrie *(Rights)*

*Atlases & Maps; Aviation; Biography &
Autobiography; Crafts & Hobbies; History &
Antiquarian; Military & War; Nautical;
Politics & World Affairs; Reference Books,
Directories & Dictionaries; Scientific &
Technical; Transport*

ISBNs, Imprints & Series:
0 85368, 1 85409

Parent Company:
Cassell Plc

Associated & Subsidiary Companies:
Blandford Press; Cassell; Victor Gollancz;
New Orchard Editions; Ward Lock

Distributor for:
USA: DBI Books Inc

Overseas Representation *(see §7.3):*
see: Cassell Plc, UK

1048 ▬▬▬▬▬▬▬

ARNOLD
338 Euston Road, London NW1 3BH
Telephone: 0171 873 6000
Fax: 0171 873 6325

Distribution Centre:
Bookpoint Ltd, 39 Milton Park, Abingdon,
Oxon OX14 4TD
Telephone: 01235 400400
Fax: 01235 400445

Managing Director: Richard Stileman
UK Sales: Philip Saunderson
International Sales: Barbara Moeller
Marketing: Jane Skinner
Production: Helen Whitehorn
Publishing: Georgina Bentliff
Humanities Publishing: Christopher Wheeler
Applied Science Publishing: Nicki Dennis

*Academic & Scholarly; Computer Science;
Engineering; Geography & Geology; History
& Antiquarian; Languages & Linguistics;
Literature & Criticism; Medical (incl. Self Help
& Alternative Medicine); Psychology &
Psychiatry; Reference Books, Directories &
Dictionaries; Scientific & Technical*

New Titles: 125 (1995), 140 (1996)
No of Employees: 42
Annual Turnover: £6.5M

ISBNs, Imprints & Series:
0 340 Hodder & Stoughton
0 7131 Arnold

Parent Company:
Hodder Headline Plc

Associated & Subsidiary Companies:
Headline Book Publishing Ltd

Overseas Representation *(see §7.3):*
Australia: Hodder Headline (Australia) Pty
Ltd, Rydalmere
Canada: Byford University Press, Don Mills,
Ont
Europe: Andrew B. Durnell, Tunbridge Wells,
UK
Ghana: EPP Book Services, Accra
Hong Kong, Taiwan & China: Asia Publisher
Services Ltd, Hong Kong
India: Affiliated East-West Press Pvt Ltd, New
Delhi; BI Publications Pvt Ltd, New Delhi;
Viva Marketing, New Delhi
Indonesia, Philippines, Singapore & Thailand:
Toppan Co (S) Pte Ltd, Singapore
Jamaica & Bahamas: Kingston Bookshop,
Kingston, Jamaica
Japan (for Medicine): Nankodo Co Ltd, Tokyo,
Japan
Kenya: Pan Africa Book Services, Mombasa;
Book Distributors Ltd, Nairobi
Leeward Islands, St Kitts & Dominica: R. J.
Laws & Son Agencies, Basseterre, St Kitts
Malaysia: Toppan Co (S) Pte Ltd, Selangor

Mauritius: Editions de l'Ocean Indien Ltd,
Rose Hill
Middle East: James & Lorin Watt, Oxford, UK
New Zealand: Hodder Moa Beckett Publishers
Ltd, Auckland
Nigeria: Mr Olu Anulopo, Ibadan
Southern Africa: Book Promotions Pty Ltd,
Plumstead, South Africa
St Lucia: Juliette Forde, St Michael, Barbados
Tanzania: Entrepreneur International (T) Ltd,
Dar es Salaam
Trinidad, Tobago & Guyana: RIK Services
Ltd, San Fernando, Trinidad
USA (for Humanities & Social Sciences): St
Martin's Press Inc, New York, NY, USA
USA (for Medicine): Oxford University Press,
New York, USA
Zimbabwe: Academic Press Pvt Ltd, Harare

Book Trade Association Membership:
IGSMTP, STM

1049 ▬▬▬▬▬▬▬

ARROW BOOKS LTD
Random House, 20 Vauxhall Bridge Road,
London SW1V 2SA
Telephone: 0171 973 9700
Fax: 0171 233 6127

Distribution Centre:
Tiptree Book Services Ltd, Tiptree, Colchester,
Essex CO5 0SR
Telephone: 01621 816362
Fax: 01621 819011

Managing Director: Simon King
Sales Director: Mike Broderick
Managers: Alison Wood *(Finance)*
Stephen Esson *(Production)*
Ronald Beard *(UK Sales)*
Andy McKillop *(Editorial – Arrow)*
Susan Sandon *(Publicity)*
John Jarrold *(Editorial – Legend)*
Kate Parkin *(Publisher)*
David Parrish *(Export Sales)*
Juliet Annan *(Rights)*

*Biography & Autobiography; Cinema, Video,
TV & Radio; Crime; Fiction; Health & Beauty;
History & Antiquarian; Humour; Industry,
Business & Management; Literature &
Criticism; Military & War; Politics & World
Affairs; Scientific & Technical; Travel &
Topography*

New Titles: 110 (1995), 105 (1996)
Annual Turnover: £15,500

ISBNs, Imprints & Series:
0 09 9 Arrow

Parent Company:
Random House UK Ltd

Overseas Representation *(see §7.3):*
Australia: Random Australia Pty Ltd, Sydney
Canada: Random House of Canada Ltd,
Mississauga
Caribbean: Random House Inc, New York,
USA; Random House UK Ltd, London, UK
Latin America: Random House Inc, New York,
USA
Middle East: Peter Ward Book Exports,
London, UK
New Zealand: Random House New Zealand
Ltd, Auckland

Singapore: Pansing Distribution Sdn Bhd
South Africa: Random House South Africa Pty
Ltd, Rosebank, Johannesburg

Book Trade Association Membership: PA,
Bookdata

1050 ▬▬▬▬▬▬▬

ART BOOKS INTERNATIONAL
1 Stewart's Court, 220 Stewart's Road, London
SW8 4UD
Telephone: 0171 720 1503
Fax: 0171 720 3158

Directors: Stanley Kekwick *(Managing)*
Fiona Smith *(Administrative)*
Head of Accounts Department: Stephen Coke

Fine Art & Art History

New Titles: 2 (1995), 2 (1996)
No of Employees: 7
Annual Turnover: £720,000

ISBNs, Imprints & Series: 1 874044

Distributor for:
Art Books International; Barbican Art Gallery
(single title); Cygnet Press; Dulwich Picture
Gallery *(single title)*; Festerman *(single title)*;
Flowers East; Francis Graham-Dixon Gallery;
Handsaw; Thomas Heneage *(selected titles)*;
Images *(single title)*; Bernard Jacobson
Gallery; Kala Press; Christopher Lennox-Boyd
(single title); Manchester City Art Galleries;
Museum of London; Peter Nahum *(single title)*;
Purdy Hicks Gallery *(single title)*; Raab
Gallery; Station Press; Temple Gallery *(single
title)*; Trojan Horse *(selected titles)*; The Water
Press; Zelda Cheatle Press. *Argentina:* La
Azotea. *Belgium:* Exhibitions International;
Mercator Fonds. *Brazil:* Editora Index.
Canada: Galerie Amrad African Art; Verulam
Publishing. *France:* ACR; Assouline;
Biblioteque De L'image; Bookking
International; Eiffel Editions *(single title)*;
Flohic; Maeght Editeur; Marval; Editions
Menges; MH Editions; Paris Musees; Editions
Plume; Editions Somogy. *Germany:* Die
Gestalten Verlag; Grabert Verlag; Hirmer
Verlag; Vitra Design Museum. *India:* Motilal.
Italy: Arcadia; Be-Ma Editrice; Centro Di;
Charta; Einaudi; Electa; Galleria Editrice
(single title); Hopeful Monster; Editrice
Militare *(single title)*; Motta; Nuova Alfa;
Sagep; Monica Smith *(single title)*. *Japan:*
Artis *(selected titles)*; Ikeda & Lokker *(single
title)*. *Netherlands:* Art Unlimited *(two titles
only)*; Kempen. *New Zealand:* David Bateman
(single title). *Portugal:* Edicoes Inapa. *Spain:*
Arco Editorial; Electa España; Lunwerg
Editores. *Switzerland:* ABC Verlag; Edition
Galerie Bruno Bischofberger; Edition
Stemmle. *USA:* Hudson Hills Press; L. A.
Louver Gallery; MJS Books *(single title)*;
Tasende Gallery

Overseas Representation *(see §7.3):*
Germany, Switzerland, Benelux & Austria:
Michael Geoghegan, London, UK
Scandinavia, Spain & Portugal: Katie
McNeish, London, UK

1051 ▬▬▬

ARTECH HOUSE
Portland House, Stag Place, London
SW1E 5XA
Telephone: 0171 973 8077
Fax: 0171 630 0166

Distribution:
Vale Packaging, 420 Vale Road, Tonbridge,
Kent TN9 1TD
Telephone: 01732 359387

Director, Sales & Marketing: Anne Fraser
Commissioning Editor: Julie Lancashire

Engineering; Scientific & Technical

New Titles: 55 (1995), 60 (1996)
No of Employees: 7
Annual Turnover: £1.2M

ISBNs, Imprints & Series: 0 89006

Parent Company:
Horizon House Inc *(USA)*

Associated & Subsidiary Companies:
USA: Artech House

1052 ▬▬▬

*ASHGATE PUBLISHING LTD
Gower House, Croft Road, Aldershot, Hants
GU11 3HR
Telephone: 01252 331551
Fax: 01252 344405

Warehouse & Mailing Shop, Orders:
Ashgate Distribution Services, Unit 3,
Lower Farnham Road, Aldershot, Hants
GU12 4DL
Telephone: 01252 317707
Fax: 01252 317446

Chairman: N. A. E. Farrow
Directors: Edward Elgar *(Managing – Edward
    Elgar Publishing)*
J. L. Irwin *(Managing – Dartmouth Publishing
    Co)*
Nigel Young *(Finance & Administration)*
Editorial: John Smedley *(Variorum)*
Josephine Gooderham *(Arena & Avebury)*
John Hindley *(Avebury Aviation)*
S. McNaughton
Alec McAulay *(Scolar Press)*
Sarah Markham *(Avebury)*

*Academic & Scholarly; Agriculture;
Archaeology; Aviation; Computer Science;
Economics; Educational & Textbooks;
Engineering; Fine Art & Art History; Gender
Studies; History & Antiquarian; Illustrated &
Fine Editions; Industry, Business &
Management; Law; Literature & Criticism;
Music; Philosophy; Politics & World Affairs;
Psychology & Psychiatry; Reference Books,
Directories & Dictionaries; Scientific &
Technical; Sociology & Anthropology;
Transport*

ISBNs, Imprints & Series:
0 291 Avebury Aviation
0 85967 Scolar Press
0 86078 Variorum
1 85278, 1 85898 Edward Elgar Publishing
1 85521 Dartmouth Publishing Co

1 85628, 1 85972 Avebury
1 85742 Arena

Parent Company:
Ashgate Publishing Group

Associated & Subsidiary Companies:
Dartmouth Publishing Co; Edward Elgar
Publishing Ltd; Gower Publishing Co Ltd;
Gregg Publishing Co Ltd. *Australia:* Gower
Asia Pacific. *Singapore:* Gower Asia Pacific.
USA: Ashgate Publishing Co

Overseas Representation *(see §7.3):*
Australia: Gower Asia Pacific Pte Ltd, Avalo,
    NSW
Japan: United Publishers Services Ltd, Tokyo;
    Publishers International Corporation, Tokyo
*South East Asia, Malaysia, Philippines, China,
    Hong Kong, Taiwan, Myanmar (Burma) &
    South Korea:* Gower Asia Pacific Pte Ltd,
    Singapore
USA: Ashgate Publishing Co, Brookfield, VT

Book Trade Association Membership: IPG

1053 ▬▬▬

*ASHGROVE PRESS LTD
7 Locksbrook Road Estate, Bath, Avon
BA1 3DZ

Director: Robin Campbell *(Editorial &
    Production, Rights)*
Managers: Charlotte Fyfe *(Marketing &
    Publicity)*
Norma Pitman *(Trade)*

*Health & Beauty; Magic & the Occult; Medical
(incl. Self Help & Alternative Medicine);
Philosophy; Psychology & Psychiatry;
Religion & Theology*

ISBNs, Imprints & Series:
0 906798, 1 85398

Associated & Subsidiary Companies:
Ashgrove Distribution

Distributor for:
Arcania Publications; Cornish Connection;
East-West Publications; Findhorn Press;
Golden Gates Press; Gothic Image
Publications; Solos Press. *Australia:* In-Tune
Books. *USA:* Anchor Press; Keats; Larson; Self
Realization Fellowship

Overseas Representation *(see §7.3):*
Australia & New Zealand: Peribo Pty Ltd,
    Mount Kuring-gai, NSW, Australia
Canada: Temeron Books Inc, Calgary
Europe: Bill Bailey Publishers
    Representatives, Newton Abbot, UK
Malaysia: Vintrade Sdn Bhd, Kuala Lumpur
South Africa: Faradawn CC, Saxonwold
USA: Book People, Oakland, CA; New Leaf
    Distribution, Lithia Springs, GA

Book Trade Association Membership: IPG

1054 ▬▬▬

**ASHMOLEAN MUSEUM
PUBLICATIONS**
Ashmolean Museum, Beaumont Street, Oxford
OX1 2PH

Telephone: 01865 278010
Fax: 01865 278018

Warehouse, Trade Enquiries & Orders:
Gazelle Book Services Ltd, Falcon House,
Queen Square, Lancaster LA1 1RN
Telephone: 01524 68765
Fax: 01524 63232

General Manager: R. I. H. Charlton
Home & Export Sales: D. McCarthy

*Academic & Scholarly; Archaeology; Fine Art
& Art History; History & Antiquarian;
Numismatics*

New Titles: 5 (1995), 6 (1996)
No of Employees: 5

ISBNs, Imprints & Series:
0 900090, 0 907849, 1 85444

Parent Company:
Ashmolean Museum, University of Oxford

Overseas Representation *(see §7.3):*
Australasia: S. G. Gray International
    Booksellers, Bondi Beach, NSW, Australia
Canada: Scholarly Book Services Inc, Toronto
Europe: Gazelle Book Services Ltd, Lancaster,
    UK
USA: Arthur Schwartz & Co, Woodstock, NY

Book Trade Association Membership: IPG,
Museums & Galleries Publishing Group

1055 ▬▬▬

**ASLIB (THE ASSOCIATION FOR
INFORMATION MANAGEMENT)**
Information House, 20–24 Old Street, London
EC1V 9AP
Telephone: 0171 253 4488 & 01252 317700
(Customer Services)
Fax: 0171 430 0514
Email: pub@aslib.co.uk
Web Site: http://www.aslib.co.uk/aslib/

Publishing Division: Brian Thackray
(Advertising/Marketing)
Moira Duncan *(Editorial)*

*Academic & Scholarly; Bibliography &
Library Science; Languages & Linguistics;
Reference Books, Directories & Dictionaries;
Information Management*

New Titles: 8 (1996)
No of Employees: 33

ISBNs, Imprints & Series:
0 85142 Aslib, Aslib Directories, Aslib Guide
to Copyright, Informatics, ITI Conference
Proceedings, Know How Series, Online
Guides, Translating and the Computer Series

Distributor for:
CEC Information Market Observatory (IMO)
reports

Overseas Representation *(see §7.3):*
Australia: DA Information Services, Mitcham,
    Vic
India: Allied Publishers Pte Ltd, New Delhi &
    Calcutta
Japan: Kinokuniya Co Ltd, Tokyo

South East Asia: Gower Asia Pacific Pte Ltd, Singapore

1056 ▬▬▬▬▬▬▬▬▬▬

ASSOCIATION OF COMMONWEALTH UNIVERSITIES (ACU)
John Foster House, 36 Gordon Square, London WC1H 0PF
Telephone: 0171 387 8572
Fax: 0171 387 2655
Email: pubinf@acu.ac.uk

Secretary General: Prof Michael Gibbons
Publications & Information: Gillian B. Woolven *(Director)*
Sue Kirkland *(Head—Market Development, Rights & Permissions)*

Academic & Scholarly; Educational & Textbooks; Reference Books, Directories & Dictionaries

New Titles: 8 (1995), 10 (1996)
No of Employees: 19
Annual Turnover: £302,000

ISBNs, Imprints & Series: 0 85143

Overseas Representation *(see §7.3):*
Canada, China (excluding Hong Kong) & Korea: University of British Columbia Press, Vancouver, BC, Canada
India: UBS Publishers' Distributors Ltd, New Delhi
USA, its dependencies & Japan: Stockton Press, New York, NY, USA

Book Trade Association Membership: Directory Publishers Association

1057 ▬▬▬▬▬▬▬▬▬▬

ATHEY EDUCATIONAL
Tibthorpe, East Yorkshire YO25 9LA
Telephone: 01377 229320
Fax: 01377 229320

Partners: Lionel Athey
Jill Athey

Children's Books; Educational & Textbooks

New Titles: 1 (1995), 2 (1996)
Annual Turnover: £164,000

ISBNs, Imprints & Series:
1 871993 Secondary Selection Portfolio Series

Book Trade Association Membership: PA, EPC

1058 ▬▬▬▬▬▬▬▬▬▬

THE ATHLONE PRESS LTD
1 Park Drive, London NW11 7SG
Telephone: 0181 458 0888
Fax: 0181 201 8115

Distributors:
The Athlone Press, c/o Book Systems Plus, 2B Priors Hall Farm, Widdington, Saffron Walden, Essex CB11 3SB
Telephone: 01799 542254
Fax: 01799 540229

Chairman: Brian Southam *(Editorial)*
Managing Director: Doris Southam *(Rights & Permissions)*
Production & Publicity Manager: Helen Drake

Academic & Scholarly; Archaeology; Architecture & Design; Bibliography & Library Science; Chemistry; Economics; Educational & Textbooks; Gender Studies; Geography & Geology; History & Antiquarian; Industry, Business & Management; Languages & Linguistics; Law; Literature & Criticism; Medical (incl. Self Help & Alternative Medicine); Philosophy; Psychology & Psychiatry; Reference Books, Directories & Dictionaries; Religion & Theology; Sociology & Anthropology

ISBNs, Imprints & Series: 0 485

Overseas Representation *(see §7.3):*
Australia & New Zealand: Ashgate-Gower Asia Pacific Pte Ltd, Avalon, NSW, Australia
Austria, Switzerland & France: Juliusz Komarnicki, Massagno, Switzerland
Benelux & Germany: PKB—Robbert J. Pleysier, Heerde, Netherlands
India: Maya Publishers Pvt Ltd, New Delhi
India (Beckett & Stenlake, Practical Pharmaceutical Chemistry Vols, only*):* United Books & Periodicals, Bombay, India
Italy, Spain, Portugal, Gibraltar & Greece: Patrick Bygate, Massagno, Switzerland
Japan: United Publishers Services Ltd, Tokyo; Kinokuniya Co Ltd, Tokyo; Maruzen Co Ltd, Tokyo
Scandinavia: Ove B. Poulsen, Glostrup, Denmark
South East Asia, Hong Kong, China & Taiwan: Ashgate Asia Pacific Pte Ltd, Singapore
USA: The Athlone Press, Atlantic Highlands, NJ

Book Trade Association Membership: IPG

1059 ▬▬▬▬▬▬▬▬▬▬

ATLANTIC EUROPE PUBLISHING CO LTD
Greys Court Farm, Greys Court, Henley on Thames, Oxon RG9 4PG
Telephone: 01491 628188
Fax: 01491 628189
Email: info@aepublish.com

Trade Orders:
Windrush Press Ltd, Windrush House, Little Window, High Street, Moreton in Marsh, Glos. GL56 0LL
Telephone: 01608 652012

Directors: Dr B. J. Knapp *(Education, Editorial)*
D. L. R. McCrae *(Rights, Sales & Permissions, Production)*

Children's Books; Educational & Textbooks; Geography & Geology; Reference Books, Directories & Dictionaries; Scientific & Technical

ISBNs, Imprints & Series: 1 869860

Associated & Subsidiary Companies:
Earthscape Editions

Book Trade Association Membership: IPG

1060 ▬▬▬▬▬▬▬▬▬▬

AURELIAN INFORMATION LTD
129 Leighton Gardens, London NW10 3PS
Telephone: 0181 960 7918

Distribution:
BECB Distribution, PO Box 1496, Poole, Dorset BH12 3YD
Telephone: 0800 262260
Fax: 0800 262266

Directors: Paul Petzold
Kim Worts *(Company Secretary)*

Industry, Business & Management; Reference Books, Directories & Dictionaries; Charities & Voluntary Organisations

New Titles: 13 (1995)
No of Employees: 2

ISBNs, Imprints & Series:
1 899247 Aurelian, Charities Address Book—UK, Charities on Disk, Who's Who in the Voluntary Sector

1061 ▬▬▬▬▬▬▬▬▬▬

AURUM PRESS
25 Bedford Avenue, London WC1B 3AT
Telephone: 0171 637 3225
Fax: 0171 580 2469

Distribution & Warehouse:
Exel Logistics, Invicta House, Sir Thomas Longley Road, Medway City Estate, Rochester, Kent
Telephone: 01634 297123
Fax: 01634 298000

Directors: W. J. McCreadie *(Managing)*
Piers Burnett *(Editorial)*
Sheila Murphy *(Marketing & Rights)*
Manager: Geoff Barlow *(Production)*

Cinema, Video, TV & Radio; Crafts & Hobbies; Guide Books; Sports & Games

New Titles: 44 (1995), 42 (1996)
No of Employees: 10
Annual Turnover: £1.75M

ISBNs, Imprints & Series:
0 906053, 0 948149, 1 85410

Distributor for:
Lorenz Books; Sheldrake Press

Overseas Representation *(see §7.3):*
Australia: Lothian Books, Port Melbourne
Austria, Belgium, France, Germany & Switzerland: Anselm Robinson, London, UK
Canada: General Publishing Co Ltd, North York, Ont
Far East (excluding Japan): Gunnar Lie & Associates, London, UK
Italy & Scandinavia: McNeish Publishing Services, London, UK
Netherlands: Consul Books, Blaricum
New Zealand: Forrester Books Ltd, Auckland
South Africa: Trinity Books CC, Randburg
Spain & Portugal: Iberian Book Services SL, Madrid, Spain

1062

AVON BOOKS
1 Dovedale Studios, 465 Battersea Park Road,
London SW11 4LR
Telephone: 0171 978 4825
Fax: 0171 924 2979

*Academic & Scholarly; Biography &
Autobiography; Children's Books; Cookery,
Wines & Spirits; Educational & Textbooks;
Environment & Development Studies; Fiction;
Fine Art & Art History; Gardening; Gender
Studies; Humour; Magic & the Occult; Military
& War; Music; Nautical; Poetry; Religion &
Theology; Science Fiction; Transport; Travel
& Topography*

New Titles: 150 (1995)

ISBNs, Imprints & Series:
1 86033 Avon Books London

Book Trade Association Membership: PA,
Christian Publishers Association

1063

AWARD PUBLICATIONS LTD
1st Floor, 27 Longford Street, London
NW1 3DZ
Telephone: 0171 388 7800
Fax: 0171 388 7887

Warehouse & Showroom:
The Old Riding School, The Welbeck Estate,
Worksop, Notts
Telephone: Worksop 01909 478170
Fax: 01909 484632

Managing Director: Ronald Wilkinson

Children's Books

New Titles: 40 (1995), 40 (1996)

ISBNs, Imprints & Series:
0 86163, 1 89976

1064

B & W PUBLISHING LTD
233 Cowgate, Edinburgh EH1 1NQ
Telephone: 0131 220 5551
Fax: 0131 220 5552

Directors: Campbell Brown
Steven Wiggins

*Biography & Autobiography; Fiction; Guide
Books; Law; Sports & Games*

New Titles: 15 (1995), 18 (1996)
No of Employees: 5

ISBNs, Imprints & Series:
0 9515151, 1 873631

Distributor for:
Novelsound; Rutland Press

Overseas Representation *(see §7.3):*
USA: Firebird Distributing, Eureka, CA

1065

BERNARD BABANI (PUBLISHING) LTD
The Grampians, Shepherds Bush Road, London
W6 7NF
Telephone: 0171 603 2581/7296
Fax: 0171 603 8203

Directors: Michael H. Babani *(Sales,
Production, Managing)*
Mrs S. Babani

*Computer Science; Crafts & Hobbies;
Educational & Textbooks; Electronic
(Educational); Electronic (Entertainment);
Electronic (Professional & Academic);
Engineering; Mathematics & Statistics;
Scientific & Technical; Radio & Electronics*

New Titles: 30 (1995), 35 (1996)

ISBNs, Imprints & Series:
0 85934, 0 900162 Babani Press

Associated & Subsidiary Companies:
Bernards (Publishers) Ltd

Book Trade Association Membership: IPG

1066

BAHÁ'Í PUBLISHING TRUST
6 Mount Pleasant, Oakham, Leics LE15 6HU
Telephone: 01572 722780
Fax: 01572 724280
Email: sales@bahaibooks

Warehouse & Shipping:
The Maltings, Station Road, Ketton, Leics
Telephone: 01780 720691

Directors: H. Adamson
Mrs Vivian Bartlett
Mrs Caroline Wade
Dr Wendi Momen
Trevor Finch
Dr J. Parris
P. Hulme
Dr I. Palin
Hon B. Leith
Manager: Gordon J. Kerr *(General, Chief
Editor)*

*Academic & Scholarly; Biography &
Autobiography; Children's Books;
Educational & Textbooks; Environment &
Development Studies; Fiction; Gender Studies;
Philosophy; Politics & World Affairs; Religion
& Theology; Sociology & Anthropology*

New Titles: 12 (1995), 15 (1996)
No of Employees: 7
Annual Turnover: £350,000

ISBNs, Imprints & Series:
0 900125, 1 870989 Nightingale Books

Parent Company:
National Spiritual Assembly of Bahá'ís of the
United Kingdom

Distributor for:
George Ronald, Publisher. *Australia:* Bahá'í
Publishing Trust. *Canada:* Association for
Bahá'í Studies; Bahá'í Publications Canada.
Germany: Bahá'í Verlag GmbH. *India:* Bahá'í
Publishing Trust. *Japan:* Bahá'í Publishing

Trust of Japan. *USA:* Bahá'í Publishing Trust;
Kalimát Press

Overseas Representation *(see §7.3):*
Australia: Bahá'í Publications Australia, Mona
Vale
Canada: Bahá'í Distribution Service, Thornhill
Germany: Bahá'í Verlag GmbH, Hofheim
India: Bahá'í Publishing Trust, New Delhi
Japan: Bahá'í Publishing Trust of Japan, Tokyo
New Zealand: New Zealand Library
Committee, Auckland
USA: Bahá'í Publishing Trust, Wilmette, IL

1067

BAILLIÈRE TINDALL
24–28 Oval Road, London NW1 7DX
Telephone: 0171 267 4466
Fax: 0171 482 2293

**Warehouse (Books), Customer Service &
Journal Subscriptions:**
High Street, Foots Cray, Kent DA15 5HP
Telephone: 0181 300 3322
Fax: 0181 309 0807

Directors: W. M. Barnett *(Managing)*
Jamie Sehmer *(Financial & Distribution)*
Michael Ewins *(Production)*
Peter McKay *(Sales & Marketing)*
Sean Duggan *(Editorial)*
Managers: Ian Banbery *(Marketing)*
Des Brennan *(Sales)*
Sheila O'Reilly *(Customer Service)*

*Agriculture; Animal Care & Breeding; Biology
& Zoology; Medical (incl. Self Help &
Alternative Medicine); Psychology &
Psychiatry; Reference Books, Directories &
Dictionaries; Scientific & Technical;
Veterinary Science; Nursing*

ISBNs, Imprints & Series: 0 7020

Parent Company:
Harcourt Brace & Co Ltd

Overseas Representation *(see §7.3):*
Australia: Harcourt Brace & Co (Australia) Pty
Ltd, Marrickville
Canada: W. B. Saunders Canada Ltd, Toronto
Italy & Portugal: Marcello SNC, Padua, Italy
Japan: Harcourt Brace Japan Inc, Tokyo
Spain: Interamerica SA, Madrid
USA: W. B. Saunders, Philadelphia

Book Trade Association Membership: PA,
BDC, EPC, IGSMTP, CAPP

1068

*BALNAIN BOOKS
Druim House, Lochloy Road, Nairn IV12 5LF
Telephone: 01667 452940
Fax: 01667 455099

Director: Sarah Fraser *(Rights, Editorial &
Publicity)*

*Animal Care & Breeding; Biography &
Autobiography; Fiction; Literature &
Criticism*

ISBNs, Imprints & Series:
0 9509792, 1 872557

Book Trade Association Membership:
Scottish PA

1069

THE BANNER OF TRUTH TRUST
3 Murrayfield Road, Edinburgh EH12 6EL
Telephone: 0131 337 7310
Fax: 0131 346 7484

Trustees: Iain H. Murray *(Editorial Director)*
Mervyn T. Barter *(General Manager, Home &*
Export Sales, Rights & Permissions)
Murdo MacLeod *(Production & Sales*
Manager)

Religion & Theology

New Titles: 14 (1995), 14 (1996)
No of Employees: 15

ISBNs, Imprints & Series: 0 85151

Associated & Subsidiary Companies:
USA: The Banner of Truth

Overseas Representation *(see §7.3):*
Australia: Greenwood Saunders & Co, West
Pennant Hills, NSW
New Zealand: Sovereign Grace Books,
Auckland
Nigeria: Amazing Grace Ltd, Kano
Philippines: Evangelical Outreach Inc, Quezon
City
South Africa: Farel Distributors (Pty) Ltd,
North Riding
USA: The Banner of Truth Trust, Carlisle, PA

1070

BAREFOOT BOOKS
18 Highbury Terrace, London N5 1UP
Telephone: 0171 704 6492
Fax: 0171 359 5798
Email: gopinder@barefoot-books.com

Educational Sales:
The Watts Publishing Group, c/o Jill Sharpe
Telephone: 0171 739 2929
Fax: 0171 739 2318

Warehouse:
Tiptree Book Services, Church Road, Tiptree,
Colchester, Essex CO5 0SR
Telephone: 01621 819600
Fax: 01621 819717

Publisher: Tessa Strickland
Director: Nancy Traversy *(Managing, Rights)*
Manager: Gopinder Panesar

Children's Books

New Titles: 15 (1995), 21 (1996)

ISBNs, Imprints & Series:
1 898000 Barefoot Beginners, Barefoot Books,
Barefoot Collections, Little Barefoot Books

Overseas Representation *(see §7.3):*
Australia & New Zealand: Educational
Concepts Sales (Pty) Ltd, Frenchs Forest,
NSW, Australia
Europe: Janet Clark, London, UK
Gibraltar, Italy, Portugal, Slovenia & Spain:
Penny Padovani, London, UK

Irish Republic & Northern Ireland: Gill &
Macmillan Ltd, Dublin, Irish Republic
Middle East, Cyprus, Pakistan & North Africa:
Anthony Rudkin Associates, Oxford, UK
South Africa & Swaziland: Leo Books,
Roggebaai & Cape Town, South Africa

1071

BARRIE & JENKINS LTD
Random House, 20 Vauxhall Bridge Road,
London SW1V 2SA
Telephone: 0171 973 9710
Fax: 0171 233 6057

Trade Orders:
Tiptree Book Services Ltd, Tiptree, Colchester,
Essex CO5 0SR
Telephone: 01621 816362
Fax: 01621 815706

Directors: Julian Shuckburgh *(Managing)*
Amelia Thorpe
Gail Rebuck

Antiques & Collecting; Architecture & Design;
Fine Art & Art History; Illustrated & Fine
Editions

ISBNs, Imprints & Series: 0 7126

Parent Company:
Random House UK Ltd

Overseas Representation *(see §7.3):*
Australia: Random Australia Pty Ltd, Sydney
Canada: Random House of Canada Ltd,
Mississauga
Far East & Caribbean: Ralph & Sheila
Summers, London, UK
India: Dass Media Pte Ltd, New Delhi
Irish Republic: Gill Hess Ltd, Skerries
Japan: YOHAN (Western Publications
Distribution Agency), Tokyo
Middle East: Peter Ward Book Exports,
London, UK
New Zealand: Random House New Zealand
Ltd, Auckland
South Africa: Random House South Africa Pty
Ltd, Rosebank, Johannesburg
USA: David & Charles Inc, North Pomfret, VT

1072

B. T. BATSFORD LTD
4 Fitzhardinge Street, London W1H 0AH
Telephone: 0171 486 8484
Fax: 0171 487 4296

**Warehouse, Trade Orders & Order
Enquiries:**
PO Box 4, Springwood Industrial Estate,
Rayne Road, Braintree, Essex CM7 7QY
Telephone: 01376 321276
Fax: 01376 552854

Directors: Jules Perel *(Chief Executive)*
Timothy Auger *(Editorial & Foreign Rights*
Sales)
Roger Huggins *(Production)*
James Gallacher *(Financial)*
Penny Daniels *(Sales & Marketing)*

Academic & Scholarly; Antiques & Collecting;
Archaeology; Architecture & Design; Cinema,
Video, TV & Radio; Crafts & Hobbies; Do-It-

Yourself; Educational & Textbooks; Fashion &
Costume; Gardening; Sports & Games

New Titles: 123 (1995), 108 (1996)
No of Employees: 60

ISBNs, Imprints & Series:
Christopher Helm (horticulture/botany/
gardening titles only), Seaby Books
0 7136, 0 900652, 1 85264

Parent Company:
Labyrinth Group Plc

Associated & Subsidiary Companies:
The Dryad Press Ltd

Distributor for:
BFP Books; Cadogan Chess; Chilton Book Co;
Meredith Books; Storey/Garden Way
Publishing; The Taunton Press

Overseas Representation *(see §7.3):*
Australia: Capricorn Link (Australia) Pty Ltd,
Baulkham Hills, NSW
Canada: Hushion House Ltd, Toronto, Ont
France & Switzerland: Juliusz Komarnicki,
Massagno, Switzerland
Germany, Netherlands, Belgium &
Luxembourg: PKB – Robbert J. Pleysier,
Heerde, Netherlands
Greece: Patrick Bygate, Massagno,
Switzerland
Hong Kong, Indonesia, Korea, Taiwan, West
Indies, Japan, Malaysia, Brunei States &
Singapore: Ralph & Sheila Summers,
London, UK
India, Bangladesh, Nepal & Sri Lanka: Maya
Publishers Pvt Ltd, New Delhi, India
Middle East, Israel, Turkey, Malta & Cyprus:
Ashton International Marketing Services,
Larkfield, UK
New Zealand: Random House New Zealand
Ltd, Auckland
Pakistan: S. I. Gillani, Lahore
Scandinavia: Sven Gade, Hørsholm,
Denmark
South Africa: Book Promotions, Claremont
Spain, Portugal & Italy: Penny Padovani,
London, UK
USA: Trafalgar Square Publications, North
Pomfret, VT

1073

COLIN BAXTER PHOTOGRAPHY LTD
Grantown-on-Spey PH26 3NA
Telephone: 01479 873999
Fax: 01479 873888

Representation (England only):
Derek Searle Associates, Burlington House,
14 High Street, Slough, Bucks SL1 1EE
Telephone: 01753 539295

Directors: Colin Baxter *(Managing)*
Colin Kirkwood *(Marketing & Rights)*

Architecture & Design; Biography &
Autobiography; Illustrated & Fine Editions;
Natural History; Photography; Travel &
Topography

New Titles: 12 (1995), 12 (1996)
No of Employees: 12

ISBNs, Imprints & Series:
0 948661, 1 900455 Worldlife Library

Overseas Representation *(see §7.3)*:
USA: Voyageur Press, Stillwater, MN

1074 ▬▬▬▬

BAY VIEW BOOKS LTD
The Red House, 25–26 Bridgeland Street,
Bideford, Devon EX39 2PZ
Telephone: 01237 479225 & 421285
Fax: 01237 421286

Trade Enquiries & Orders:
Chris Lloyd Sales & Marketing,
463 Ashley Road, Parkstone, Poole, Dorset
BH14 0AX
Telephone: 01202 715349
Fax: 01202 736191

Directors: L. C. Herridge
B. C. T. Herridge

Transport

ISBNs, Imprints & Series: 1 870979

1075 ▬▬▬▬

BBC BOOKS
BBC Worldwide Ltd, Woodlands,
80 Wood Lane, London W12 0TT
Telephone: 0181 576 2595
Fax: 0181 749 8766

Distribution & Management Services:
Exel-Logistics Media Services, Invicta House,
Sir Thomas Longley Road,
Medway City Estate, Rochester, Kent
ME2 4DU
Telephone: 01634 297123
Fax: 01634 298000

Directors: Chris Weller *(BBC Books)*
Stuart Biles *(Sales & Marketing)*
Sheila Ableman *(Editorial)*
Managers: Suzanna Zsohar *(Book Promotion*
& Publicity)
Richard Gay *(International Rights & Export)*
Brian Dickson *(Production)*

Audio Books; Children's Books; Cookery,
Wines & Spirits; Crafts & Hobbies;
Gardening; Humour; Languages &
Linguistics; Natural History; Sports & Games

New Titles: 150 (1995), 125 (1996)
No of Employees: 62

ISBNs, Imprints & Series: 0 563

Parent Company:
BBC Worldwide Ltd

Distributor for:
BBC Radio Collection

Overseas Representation *(see §7.3)*:
Africa: Len Ainsworth, Aldbourne, UK
Australia: Reed Books Australia, Melbourne,
Vic
Canada: McClelland & Stewart, Toronto &
Markham
Europe (excluding Scandinavia): Onslow
Books Ltd, London, UK
Hong Kong: Asia Publisher Services Ltd

India: Maya Publishers Pvt Ltd, New Delhi
Japan: Japan English Services Inc, Chiba-ken
Malaysia & Singapore: APD Singapore Pte
Ltd, Singapore
Middle East: Peter Ward Book Exports,
London, UK
Netherlands: Van Ditmar BV, Amsterdam
New Zealand: Reed Publishing Group,
Auckland
Pakistan: Mackwin & Co, Karachi
Scandinavia: Saga Books ApS, Copenhagen,
Denmark
South Africa: Jonathan Ball Publishers (Pty)
Ltd, Johannesburg
South America & West Indies: Humphrys
Roberts Associates, London, UK

Book Trade Association Membership: PA

1076 ▬▬▬▬

BBC EDUCATIONAL PUBLISHING
White City, 201 Wood Lane, London W12 7TS
Telephone: 0181 752 5263
Fax: 0181 752 5340
Email: richard@central.education.bbc.co.uk

Distribution:
PO Box 234, Wetherby, West Yorkshire
LS23 7EU
Telephone: 01937 541001
Fax: 01937 845381

Director: (to be appointed)
Managers: Sarah Dann *(Editorial)*
Juliet Waugh *(Sales & Marketing)*
Julia King *(Design)*
Susan Ross *(Production)*

Educational & Textbooks; Electronic
(Educational); Audio & Video Cassettes; CD-
ROMs

New Titles: 180 (1995), 180 (1996)
No of Employees: 23

ISBNs, Imprints & Series: 0 563

Parent Company:
BBC Enterprises Ltd

Book Trade Association Membership: EPC

1077 ▬▬▬▬

BBC ENGLISH
[part of BBC Worldwide Publishing]
Room A3148, Woodlands, 80 Wood Lane,
London W12 0TT
Telephone: 0181 576 3560
Fax: 0181 576 3570

Warehouse/Distribution:
BEBC Distribution, 15 Albion Close, Poole
BH12 3YD
Telephone: 01202 715555
Fax: 01202 715556

Head of Sales & Marketing: Charles Hyde
Head of Publishing: Martin Mulloy
Head of Partworks & IV: Douglas Cooksey
Sales Executives: Deborah Cook *(Far East)*
Jane Trinder *(Americas, UK & West Europe)*
Bee Greene *(East Europe & former Soviet*
Union)
Deborah Cook *(Middle East & Africa)*

English as a Foreign Language

ISBNs, Imprints & Series: 1 85497

Parent Company:
BBC

1078 ▬▬▬▬

BEACONSFIELD PUBLISHERS LTD
20 Chiltern Hills Road, Beaconsfield, Bucks
HP9 1PL
Telephone: 01494 672118
Fax: 01494 672118

Distribution:
Haigh & Hochland Ltd, Precinct Centre,
Oxford Road, Manchester M13 9QA
Telephone: 0161 273 7122
Fax: 0161 273 4340

Managing Director: John Churchill

Medical (incl. Self Help & Alternative
Medicine); Homoeopathy; Nursing; Patient
Care; Veterinary

New Titles: 3 (1995), 3 (1996)
No of Employees: 1
Annual Turnover: £196,000

ISBNs, Imprints & Series: 0 906584

Overseas Representation *(see §7.3)*:
Australia: Astam Books Pty Ltd, Leichhardt,
NSW
New Zealand: Viking Sevenseas Ltd,
Paraparaumu

Book Trade Association Membership: IPG

1079 ▬▬▬▬

BEAVER PUBLISHING LTD
9 Orchard Green, Alderley Edge, Cheshire
SK9 7DT
Telephone: 01625 586670
Fax: 01625 586782

Warehouse, Distribution & Orders:
Pegasus Distribution Ltd, Unit 350,
Glenfield Park Site 2, Blakewater Road,
Blackburn, Lancs BB1 5QH
Telephone: 01254 696768
Fax: 01254 697060

Directors: Tony Palmer *(Managing, Sales &*
Marketing)
Alison Palmer *(Editorial)*

Children's Books; Travel & Topography

New Titles: 8 (1995), 10 (1996)
No of Employees: 3
Annual Turnover: £600,000

ISBNs, Imprints & Series: 1 85962

1080 ▬▬▬▬

BELITHA PRESS LTD
London House, Great Eastern Wharf,
Parkgate Road, London SW11 4NQ
Telephone: 0171 978 6330
Fax: 0171 223 4936

Warehouse, Distribution & Trade Orders:
Bailey Distribution Ltd, Learoyd Road,
Mountfield Road Industrial Estate,
New Romney, Kent TN28 8XU
Telephone: 01797 366905
Fax: 01797 366638

Directors: Peter Osborn *(Managing)*
Cameron Brown *(Chairman)*
Mark Collins
Mary-Jane Wilkins *(Editorial)*
Kate MacPhee *(Production)*
Managers: Madeleine Ehm *(Foreign Rights)*
Helen James *(Design)*
to be appointed *(Sales & Marketing)*

*Atlases & Maps; Children's Books;
Educational & Textbooks; Electronic
(Educational); Fine Art & Art History; Natural
History; Reference Books, Directories &
Dictionaries*

New Titles: 50 (1995), 60 (1996)
No of Employees: 15
Annual Turnover: £2M

ISBNs, Imprints & Series:
0 947553, 1 85561

Parent Company:
Collins & Brown Ltd

Overseas Representation *(see §7.3)*:
Australia: Reed Books Australia, Melbourne,
    Vic
India: Rupa & Co, New Delhi
New Zealand: South Pacific Books (Imports)
    Ltd, Auckland
Singapore & Malaysia: Publishers Marketing
    Services Ltd, Singapore
South Africa: Struik Book Distributors Pty Ltd,
    Johannesburg, Cape Town & Maitland

Book Trade Association Membership: Book
Packagers Association, International Book
Development

1081 ▬▬▬▬

BELLEW PUBLISHING
Nightingale Centre, 8 Balham Hill, London
SW12 9EA
Telephone: 0181 673 5611
Fax: 0181 675 3542

Distribution:
Plymbridge Distributors, Estover Road,
Plymouth PL6 7PZ
Telephone: 01752 695745
Fax: 01752 695699

Managing Director: Ib Bellew

*Bibliography & Library Science; Biography &
Autobiography; Fiction; Fine Art & Art
History; Literature & Criticism; Poetry*

New Titles: 6 (1995), 6 (1996)
No of Employees: 2
Annual Turnover: £650,000

ISBNs, Imprints & Series: 1 85725

Overseas Representation *(see §7.3)*:
Australia: Bookwise International, Findon, SA
South Africa: Judith Wengrowe Agencies,
    Northcliff, Johannesburg

1082 ▬▬▬▬

THE BELMONT PRESS
29 Tenby Avenue, Harrow HA3 8RU
Telephone: 0181 907 4700
Fax: 0181 907 7354

Managing Director: John Lawes

Inland Waterways

New Titles: 6 (1995), 8 (1996)
No of Employees: 6

ISBNs, Imprints & Series:
0 905366 Belmont series of books, Navigator
    series of maps

Parent Company:
Belmont (1948) Ltd

1083 ▬▬▬▬

BERG PUBLISHERS LTD
150 Cowley Road, Oxford OX4 1JJ
Telephone: 01865 245104
Fax: 01865 791165
Email: kearle@berg.demon.co.uk
Web Site: http://www.bookshop.co.uk/berg/

Distribution & Returns:
Biblios Publishers Distribution Services,
Star Road, Partridge Green, West Sussex
RH13 8LD
Telephone: 01403 710971
Fax: 01403 711143

Managing Director: Peter Cowell
Sales & Marketing: Joanna Kaptein
Rights & Permissions: Kathryn Earle
Production: Sara Everett

*Academic & Scholarly; Educational &
Textbooks; Environment & Development
Studies; Fashion & Costume; Gay & Lesbian
Studies; Gender Studies; History &
Antiquarian; Literature & Criticism; Military
& War; Politics & World Affairs; Sociology &
Anthropology*

New Titles: 37 (1995), 40 (1996)
No of Employees: 4

ISBNs, Imprints & Series:
0 85496, 1 85973

Associated & Subsidiary Companies:
USA: Berg Publishers

Overseas Representation *(see §7.3)*:
Australia: Thomas Nelson (Australia) Pty Ltd,
    South Melbourne, Vic
India: Maya Publishers Pvt Ltd, New Delhi
Irish Republic: Mike Wilson, Anglesey,
    Gwynedd
Israel: Astra Agency, Jerusalem
Japan: United Publishers Services Ltd, Tokyo
Pakistan: Tahir Lodhi, Lahore
*South East Asia (including Philippines,
    Indonesia, Brunei, Thailand, Malaysia,
    Hong Kong, Papua New Guinea, Vietnam,
    Laos, Cambodia, Taiwan & Korea):*
    Combined Representatives Worldwide Inc,
    Manila, Philippines
USA: Berg Publishers, Dulles, VA

Western Europe & Scandinavia: Andrew B.
    Durnell, Tunbridge Wells, UK
Zimbabwe: Barbie Keene, Harare

1084 ▬▬▬▬

BERLITZ PUBLISHING CO LTD
Berlitz House, Peterley Road, Oxford
OX4 2TX
Telephone: 01865 747033
Fax: 01865 779700

Distribution:
Littlehampton Book Services Ltd,
10–14 Eldon Way, Lineside Industrial Estate,
Littlehampton, West Sussex BN17 7HE
Telephone: 01903 721596
Fax: 01903 730914

Directors: Roger Kirkpatrick *(Managing)*
Managers: Byron Russell *(International
    Sales)*
Sue Whittaker *(International Marketing)*

*Electronic (Educational); Languages &
Linguistics; Reference Books, Directories &
Dictionaries; Travel & Topography*

New Titles: 90 (1995), 100 (1996)

ISBNs, Imprints & Series:
2 8315 Berlitz, Discover, Travellers

Parent Company:
Berlitz International *(USA)*

Associated & Subsidiary Companies:
USA: Berlitz Inc

Distributor for:
USA: Berlitz Publishing Co Inc

Overseas Representation *(see §7.3)*:
Australia: Universal Press Pty Ltd, Sydney,
    NSW
Austria: Buchhandlung Othmar Edelmann,
    Vienna
Baltic States: Nordis, Riga, Latvia
Belgium: Diffusion Daphné, Ghent
China: China National Publications Import &
    Export Corporation (CNPIEC), Beijing, P.
    R. of China
Commonwealth of Independent States:
    Sovaminco, Moscow, Russia
Cyprus: K. P. Kyriakou (Books-stationery) Ltd,
    Limassol
Czech Republic: Mega Books International,
    Prague; Bohemian Ventures spol sro, Prague
Denmark: Centrum Publishing, Viby
Egypt: Al Ahram Distribution Agency, Cairo
Finland: Tammi Publishers, Helsinki
France: NQL International, Paris
France (self-teach materials): Berlitz-Fixot,
    Paris, France
Germany: Falk Verlag, Hamburg
Germany (self-teach materials): Transpress,
    Berlin, Germany
Greece: Hellenic Distribution Agency Ltd,
    Alimos
Hong Kong: Far East Media Ltd
Hungary: Welcome Publishing House,
    Budapest
Iceland: Ordabokautgafan, Reykjavik
India: India Book Distributors, Bombay
Indonesia: P. T. Isawandi Lestari, Jakarta
Israel: Steimatzky Ltd, Bnei Brak
Italy: Messaggerie Internazionali Srl, Rozzano

Japan: YOHAN (Western Publications
Distribution Agency), Tokyo
Jordan: Jordan Distribution Agency, Amman
Kenya: Textbook Centre Ltd, Nairobi
Korea: International Publications Service Inc,
Seoul, Korea, South
Kuwait: Kuwait Bookshops Co Ltd, Safat
Lebanon: Levant Distributors, Paris, France
Malta: Merlin Library, Blata-l-Bajda
Morocco: Sochepresse, Casablanca
Netherlands: Kosmos – Z & K, Utrecht
Netherlands (all non-Dutch titles): Nilsson &
Lamm BV, Weesp, Netherlands
New Zealand: Universal Press, Auckland
Norway: Gyldendal Norsk Forlag, Oslo
Poland: OXPOL/OUP Office, Lodz
Portugal: Distri Cultural, Sacvem
Saudi Arabia: Tihama Distribution Company,
Jeddah
Singapore: Berkeley Books Pvt Ltd
Slovenia: Cankarjeva Zalozba (Centre Oxford),
Ljubljana
South Africa: Macdonald Purnell (Pty) Ltd,
Cleveland
Spain: Comercial Atheneum SA, Barcelona
Sri Lanka: K. V. G. de Silva & Sons (Colombo)
Ltd, Colombo
Sweden: Wahlström & Widstrand, Stockholm
Switzerland: Hallwag AG, Berne
Taiwan: Caves Books Ltd, Taipei
Thailand: Asia Book Co, Bangkok
Tunisia: Ceres/Demeter, Tunis
Turkey: Globus, Istanbul
*USA, Argentina, Bahamas, Bermuda, Brazil,
Canada, Chile, Guyana, Jamaica, Peru,
Puerto Rico, Trinidad, US Virgin Islands,
Caribbean & Venezuela:* Berlitz Publishing
Co Inc, New York, USA

1085 ∎

BFI PUBLISHING
British Film Institute, 21 Stephen Street,
London W1P 2LN
Telephone: 0171 255 1444
Fax: 0171 436 7950

Distribution & Mail Order Sales:
Plymbridge Distributors Ltd, Estover,
Plymouth PL6 7PZ
Telephone: 01752 202301
Fax: 01752 202331

Head of Publishing: Edward Buscombe
Managers: John Smoker *(Production)*
Roma Gibson *(Editorial)*
Marketing: John Atkinson

*Academic & Scholarly; Cinema, Video, TV &
Radio; Educational & Textbooks*

New Titles: 30 (1995), 30 (1996)
No of Employees: 8
Annual Turnover: £500,000

ISBNs, Imprints & Series: 0 85170

Parent Company:
British Film Institute

Overseas Representation *(see §7.3):*
Asia: Roger Ward, London, UK
Australia & New Zealand: Peribo Pty Ltd,
Mount Kuring-gai, NSW, Australia
Europe: Onslow Books Ltd, London, UK
USA & Canada: Indiana University Press,
Bloomington, IN, USA

Book Trade Association Membership: PA,
CAPP

1086 ∎

BIBLE READING FELLOWSHIP
Peter's Way, Sandy Lane West, Oxford
OX4 5HG
Telephone: 01865 748227
Fax: 01865 771350

Chief Executive Officer: R. Fisher

Religion & Theology

ISBNs, Imprints & Series: 0 7459

Overseas Representation *(see §7.3):*
Australia: Albatross Books Pty Ltd, Sutherland
Malta: Fr D. Spiteri, Floriana
New Zealand: Scripture Union Wholesale,
Wellington
South Africa: Struik Book Distributors Pty Ltd,
Maitland
USA: H. Griffiths, Winter Park, FL

1087 ∎

BIBLIAGORA
PO Box 77, Feltham, Middx TW14 8JF
Telephone: 0181 898 1234
Fax: 0181 844 1777
Email: 100525.1225@compuserve.com

Directors: David Rex-Taylor *(Managing)*
Sev Hepton *(Sales)*
K. Gee *(Executive, Sales)*
Stuart Green *(Distribution, Export)*
Editorial: A. Cutting
Sales: E. Taylor
Accounts: S. Stonard
Out-of-Print: K. Gee *(Manager)*
Lineage: M. Gandy *(Research Director)*

*Crafts & Hobbies; Philosophy; Sports &
Games*

ISBNs, Imprints & Series:
0 906031 Bibliagora, Bridge Book Club,
Lineage Research Unit, St George & Dragon
Press

Associated & Subsidiary Companies:
Bridge Book Club; Lineage Research Unit

Distributor for:
USA: American Contract Bridge League;
Autobridge; Bridge World

Book Trade Association Membership: PA,
BA

1088 ∎

BIRLINN LTD
14 High Street, Edinburgh EH1 1TE
Telephone: 0131 556 6660
Fax: 0131 558 1500

Distribution:
Scottish Book Source, 137 Dundee Street,
Edinburgh EH11 1BG
Telephone: 0131 229 6800
Fax: 0131 229 9070

Managing Director: Hugh Andrew

*Archaeology; Guide Books; Humour; Local
Interest*

New Titles: 15 (1995), 18 (1996)
No of Employees: 1
Annual Turnover: £150,000

ISBNs, Imprints & Series:
0 951602, 1 874744

Distributor for:
Maclean Press

Book Trade Association Membership:
Scottish PA

1089 ∎

A. & C. BLACK (PUBLISHERS) LTD
35 Bedford Row, London WC1R 4JH
Telephone: 0171 242 0946
Fax: 0171 831 8478
Email: 160726.1035@compuserve.com

Sales & Distribution Centre:
Howard Road, Eaton Socon, Huntingdon,
Cambs PE19 3EZ
Telephone: 01480 212666
Fax: 01480 405014

Directors: Charles Black *(Chairman & Joint
Managing)*
Jill Coleman *(Joint Managing & Children's
Books)*
David Gadsby *(Deputy Chairman)*
Janet Murphy *(Adlard Coles Nautical)*
Paul Langridge *(Rights)*
Oscar Heini *(Production)*
Robert Kirk *(Christopher Helm Ornithology)*
Trade Department: Jenny Aspinall *(Company
Secretary)*
Terry Rouelett *(Distribution Director)*
Home & European Sales Manager: Susan
Kodicek
Publicity Manager: Rosanna Bortoli

*Aviation; Children's Books; Crafts & Hobbies;
Educational & Textbooks; Guide Books;
Literature & Criticism; Music; Nautical;
Reference Books, Directories & Dictionaries;
Religion & Theology; Sports & Games;
Theatre, Drama & Dance; Ornithology*

New Titles: 130 (1995), 130 (1996)
No of Employees: 95
Annual Turnover: £6.4M

ISBNs, Imprints & Series:
Blue Guides, Draw Books, Know the Game,
New Mermaids, New Testament
Commentaries
0 229 Adlard Coles
0 510 Ernest Benn
0 540 Stanford Maritime
0 7136 A. & C. Black
0 7158 EP Publishing
0 7470 Christopher Helm
0 85177 Nautical Books
1 871569 The Herbert Press

Parent Company:
A. & C. Black Plc

Associated & Subsidiary Companies:
Adlard Coles Nautical; Alphabooks;
Christopher Helm Ltd; The Herbert Press;
Nautical Publishing Co Ltd

Distributor for:
Applause Books; The Herbert Press; Magi
Publications; RSPB; Sunflower Books

Overseas Representation *(see §7.3)*:
Australia: Hodder Headline (Australia) Pty
Ltd, Rydalmere
Canada: Fitzhenry & Whiteside Ltd, Markham
Caribbean, East & West Africa: Kelvin van
Hasselt Publishing Services, Lymington, UK
Europe: Books for Europe, J. Komarnicki,
Lugano, Switzerland
Hong Kong: Publishers' Associates Ltd
India: T. R. Publications Pvt Ltd, Madras
Japan: Japan English Services Inc, Chiba-ken
Middle East: Eurab Ltd, Rottingdean, UK
New Zealand: Random House New Zealand
Ltd, Auckland
Singapore, Malaysia & Brunei: STP
Distributors Pte Ltd, Singapore
Southern Africa: Book Promotions Pty Ltd,
Plumstead, South Africa

Book Trade Association Membership: PA,
BDC, EPC, Music Publishers Association

1090

BLACK ACE BOOKS
Duns, Berwickshire TD11 3SG
Telephone: 01361 890370
Fax: 01361 890287

Publisher & Rights: Hunter Steele
Publicity & Sales: Boo Wood

*Academic & Scholarly; Fiction; History &
Antiquarian; Philosophy*

ISBNs, Imprints & Series: 1 872 988

Parent Company:
Black Ace Enterprises

Book Trade Association Membership:
Scottish PA

1091

BLACKSTAFF PRESS LTD
3 Galway Park, Dundonald, Belfast BT16 0AN
Telephone: 01232 487161
Fax: 01232 489552

Distribution:
Gill & Macmillan UK Distribution,
13–14 Goldenbridge Industrial Estate, Dublin 8
Telephone: 010 3531 4531005
Fax: 010 3531 4541688

Managing Director: Anne Tannahill
Editors: Hilary Bell
Carina Rourke
Sales & Marketing: Lawrence Greer
Publicity: Stephen Hawthorne
Design: Wendy Dunbar
Production: Elena Seymenliyska

*Academic & Scholarly; Biography &
Autobiography; Fiction; Humour; Illustrated
& Fine Editions; Literature & Criticism;
Natural History; Poetry; Politics & World
Affairs*

New Titles: 23 (1995), 25 (1996)
No of Employees: 9

ISBNs, Imprints & Series: 0 85640

Parent Company:
W. G. Baird *(Irish Republic)*

Overseas Representation *(see §7.3)*:
Australia: Keith Ainsworth Pty Ltd, Penrith,
NSW
Canada: Riverwood Publishers Ltd,
Newmarket, Ont
Southern Africa: Trade Winds Press (Pty) & Co
Ltd, Durban North, South Africa
USA: Dufour Editions Inc, Chester Springs, PA
Western Europe: Michael Geoghegan, London,
UK

Book Trade Association Membership: CLÉ
(Irish PA)

1092

BLACKSTONE PRESS LTD
9–15 Aldine Street, London W12 8AW
Telephone: 0181 740 1173
Fax: 0181 743 2292

Directors: Alistair MacQueen *(Managing)*
Jeremy Stein *(Sales & Marketing)*
Heather Saward *(Editorial)*

Law

New Titles: 18 (1995), 34 (1996)

ISBNs, Imprints & Series: 1 85431

Distributor for:
Australia: The Federation Press

Overseas Representation *(see §7.3)*:
Australia: The Federation Press, Annandale
Hong Kong: Asia Publisher Services Ltd
India: Book Marketing Services, Madras
Japan: Kay (Kaoru) Kato, Kanagawa
Malaysia: APD Malaysia, Petaling Jaya
North America: Wm. W. Gaunt & Sons Inc,
Holmes Beach FL, USA
Pakistan: Pakistan Law House, Karachi
Singapore: APD Singapore Pte Ltd

1093

BLACKWELL PUBLISHERS LTD
108 Cowley Road, Oxford OX4 1JF
Telephone: 01865 791100
Fax: 01865 791347
Email: general@blackwellpublishers.co.uk
Web Site: http://www.blackwellpublishers.co.
uk

Distribution:
Marston Book Services Ltd, PO Box 269,
Abingdon, Oxon OX14 4YN
Telephone: 01235 465500
Fax: 01235 465555

Trade & Customer Services (Direct Line):
Telephone: 01865 791100
Fax: 01865 791347
Email: general@blackwellpublishers.co.uk
Web Site: http://blackwellpublishers.co.uk

Directors: Rene Olivieri *(Managing)*
Julian Blackwell
Nigel Blackwell *(Chairman)*
John Davey *(Editorial)*
Philip Carpenter *(Editorial)*

Mark Houlton *(Financial)*
George Bain
Sue Corbett *(Journals)*
Carolyn Dougherty *(Sales & Marketing)*
Nigel Banister
Mike Fenton *(Systems)*
Manager: Stella Welford *(Rights)*

*Academic & Scholarly; Archaeology;
Computer Science; Economics; Electronic
(Educational); Electronic (Professional &
Academic); Gender Studies; Geography &
Geology; History & Antiquarian; Industry,
Business & Management; Literature &
Criticism; Philosophy; Politics & World
Affairs; Psychology & Psychiatry; Reference
Books, Directories & Dictionaries; Religion &
Theology; Sociology & Anthropology;
Vocational Training & Careers; Cultural
Theory; Finance; Information Technology*

New Titles: 200 (1995), 210 (1996)
No of Employees: 232
Annual Turnover: £22.3M

ISBNs, Imprints & Series:
0 631 Blackwell Journals, Blackwell Publishers
0 7456 Polity Press
0 85012, 1 85554 InfoSource International,
NCC Blackwell
1 55786 Blackwell Publishers Inc

Associated & Subsidiary Companies:
Blackwell Polity; Marston Book Services;
NCC Blackwell. *USA:* Blackwell Publishers;
InfoSource Inc

Overseas Representation *(see §7.3)*:
Australia (Academic books): Allen & Unwin
Pty Ltd, St Leonards, NSW, Australia
Benelux: Netwerk, Academic Book Agency,
Rotterdam, Netherlands
Eastern Europe: Michael Timperley
Marketing, Hong Kong
Hong Kong, Taiwan & Korea: Knowledge
Craft Ltd, Hong Kong
India: Maya Publishers Pvt Ltd, New Delhi
Japan: United Publishers Services Ltd, Tokyo
Middle East: James & Lorin Watt, Oxford, UK
New Zealand: Macmillan NZ, Auckland
Scandinavia: Colin Flint, Harlow, UK
Singapore & Malaysia: APD Singapore Pte
Ltd, Singapore
South Africa: Academic Marketing Services,
Auckland Park
Southern Europe: Turnkey Projects Ltd,
Buckingham, UK
USA: Basil Blackwell Inc, Cambridge, MA

Book Trade Association Membership: PA,
BDC, EPC, CAPP

1094

*BLACKWELL SCIENCE LTD
Osney Mead, Oxford OX2 0EL
Telephone: 01865 206206
Fax: 01865 721205

London Office:
25 John Street, London WC1N 2BL
Telephone: 0171 404 4101
Fax: 0171 831 6745

Edinburgh Office:
23 Ainslie Place, Edinburgh EH3 6AJ

Telephone: 0131 226 7232
Fax: 0131 226 3803

Distribution:
Marston Book Services Ltd, Osney Mead,
Oxford OX2 0DT
Telephone: 01865 791155
Fax: 01865 791927

Directors: Nigel Blackwell *(Chairman)*
Robert Campbell *(Managing)*
John Strange *(Production)*
Jon Conibear *(Sales & Marketing)*
Peter Saugman *(Editorial)*
Martin Wilkinson *(Finance)*
Non-Executive Directors: Clark Brundin
David Owen
Editors: Simon Rallison *(Science Editor-in-Chief)*
Richard Miles *(Professional)*
Lisa Field *(Nursing & Allied Health)*
Stuart Taylor *(Medicine)*
Andrew Robinson *(Medicine)*
Managers: Elizabeth Whelan *(London Office)*
Nigel Palmer *(Edinburgh Office)*
Edward Crutchley *(Sales)*
Ian Bannerman *(Journal Sales)*
Martine Cariou-Keen *(Advertising Sales)*
Wayne Ellis *(Distribution)*
Viv Harvey *(Product—Professional)*
Anna Rivers *(Product—Science)*
To be appointed *(Product—Medicine)*
Sarah Pollard *(Rights & Translations)*
Stephen Goodchild *(I.T.)*

*Agriculture; Animal Care & Breeding;
Architecture & Design; Aviation; Biology &
Zoology; Chemistry; Educational & Textbooks;
Electronic (Professional & Academic);
Engineering; Geography & Geology; Industry,
Business & Management; Law; Medical (incl.
Self Help & Alternative Medicine); Scientific &
Technical; Veterinary Science; Nursing/Allied
Health*

ISBNs, Imprints & Series:
0 632 Blackwell Science Ltd
0 85238 Fishing News Books
0 86542 Blackwell Science Inc
0 86793 Blackwell Science (Australia) Pty Ltd

Associated & Subsidiary Companies:
Australia: Blackwell Science Pty Ltd. *France:*
Arnette Blackwell. *Germany:* Blackwell
Wissenschafts-Verlag. *Japan:* Blackwell
Science Japan. *USA:* Blackwell Science Inc

Distributor for:
Futura Publishing; McGraw-Hill

Overseas Representation *(see §7.3):*
Australia: Blackwell Science (Australia) Pty
Ltd, Carlton, Vic
Benelux: Frans Janssen, Rotterdam,
Netherlands
Canada (medicine): Times Mirror Professional
Publishers, Markham, Ont, Canada
Canada (science & professional): Oxford
University Press, Don Mills, Canada
Caribbean: Kelvin van Hasselt Publishing
Services, Lymington, UK
Central Europe: The John Wilde Partnership,
London, UK
India: Oxford University Press Indian Branch,
New Delhi, Bombay, Calcutta & New Delhi,
Madras

Iran: McIntyre Information Services
Representatives Ltd, Tehran
Middle East: Anthony Rudkin Associates,
Oxford, UK
Scandinavia: Colin Flint, Harlow, UK
Spain: McGraw-Hill InterAmericana de
España SA, Madrid
USA: Blackwell Science Inc, Cambridge, MA

Book Trade Association Membership: PA,
BDC, IGSMTP, CAPP

1095

BLAKE PUBLISHING LTD
3 Bramber Court, 2 Bramber Road, London
W14 9PB
Telephone: 0171 381 0666
Fax: 0171 381 6868

Distributors:
Biblios Publishers Distribution Service Ltd,
Star Road, Partridge Green, West Sussex
RH13 8LD
Telephone: 01403 710971
Fax: 01403 711143

Managing Director: John Blake
Assistant Publisher: Rosie Ries
Rights Consultant: Lesley Toll

Biography & Autobiography; Crime; Fiction

New Titles: 20 (1995), 20 (1996)
No of Employees: 4

ISBNs, Imprints & Series: 1 85782

Overseas Representation *(see §7.3):*
Australia: Peribo Pty Ltd, Mount Kuring-gai,
NSW
Germany: Michael Mellor, Munich
New Zealand: David Bateman Ltd, Auckland
USA: Peter Miller, New York

1096

BLANDFORD PRESS
Wellington House, 125 Strand, London
WC2R 0BB
Telephone: 0171 420 5555
Fax: 0171 240 7261

Distribution:
Cassell Plc, 3 Fleets Lane, Poole, Dorset
BH15 3AJ
Telephone: 01202 665432
Fax: 01202 666219

Directors: Philip Sturrock *(Chairman)*
Rod Dymott *(Editorial)*
Geoffrey Charters *(Production)*
Martyn Chapman *(Commercial & Distribution)*
Frank Roney *(Financial)*
Kevin Bristow *(Sales & Marketing)*
Michael Goff *(International Sales)*
Adrienne Maguire *(Marketing)*
Andrew Macmillan *(UK Trade Sales)*
Managers: Christopher White *(Book Clubs)*
David Williams *(Special Sales)*
Dinah Parkinson *(Production)*
Joanna Lawrie *(Rights)*

*Animal Care & Breeding; Antiques &
Collecting; Biology & Zoology; Crime;
Environment & Development Studies; History*

*& Antiquarian; Music; Natural History;
Reference Books, Directories & Dictionaries;
Sports & Games; Transport; Travel &
Topography; New Age*

ISBNs, Imprints & Series: 0 7137

Parent Company:
Cassell Plc

Associated & Subsidiary Companies:
Arms & Armour Press Ltd; Cassell; New
Orchard Editions; Studio Vista; Ward Lock

Distributor for:
USA: Sterling Publishing Co

Overseas Representation *(see §7.3):*
see: Cassell Plc, UK

1097

BLOODAXE BOOKS LTD
PO Box 1SN, Newcastle upon Tyne NE99 1SN
Telephone: 0191 232 5988
Fax: 0191 222 0020

Chairman: Simon Thirsk
Managing Director: Neil Astley *(Editorial)*
Company Secretary: Nansi Thirsk
Publicity Officer: Andrew McAllister
Finance Manager: Karen Buchan
Distribution: Pat Manning
Rights & Permissions: Linda Healy
Marketing Officer: Alison Davis

*Biography & Autobiography; Fiction; Gender
Studies; Literature & Criticism; Photography;
Poetry; Politics & World Affairs; Theatre,
Drama & Dance*

New Titles: 32 (1995), 46 (1996)
No of Employees: 10
Annual Turnover: £0.5M

ISBNs, Imprints & Series:
0 906427, 1 85224 Bloodaxe Books
1 85557 Pandon Press

Associated & Subsidiary Companies:
Pandon Press Ltd

Distributor for:
Pandon Press

Overseas Representation *(see §7.3):*
Australia: Keith Ainsworth Pty Ltd, Penrith,
NSW
Caribbean: Hugh Dunphy, Kingston, Jamaica
Europe: Michael Geoghegan, London, UK
Irish Republic: Gregory Carr, Ashbourne
Italy: Penny Padovani, London, UK
North America: Dufour Editions Inc, Chester
Springs, PA, USA

1098

BLOOMSBURY PUBLISHING PLC
2 Soho Square, London W1V 6HB
Telephone: 0171 494 2111
Fax: 0171 434 0151
Email: bloomsbury.com

Distributor:
Invicta House, Sir Thomas Longley Road,
Medway City Industrial Estate, Rochester,
Kent ME2 4DU
Telephone: 01634 297123
Fax: 01634 298000
Email: nigel–newton@bloomsbury.com

Directors: Nigel Newton *(Managing)*
David Reynolds *(Deputy Managing, Editorial)*
Liz Calder *(Editorial, Fiction)*
Kathy Rooney *(Editorial, Reference)*
Alan Wherry *(Editorial, General)*
Sarah Beal *(Sales & Marketing)*
Colin Adams *(Finance)*
Ruth Logan *(Rights)*
Florence Whyte *(Publicity)*
Penny Edwards *(Production)*
Emma Kirby *(Export, Club)*
Matthew Hamilton *(Paperbacks)*
Barry Cunningham *(Children's)*

*Biography & Autobiography; Children's
Books; Cookery, Wines & Spirits; Fiction;
Health & Beauty; Military & War; Politics &
World Affairs; Reference Books, Directories &
Dictionaries*

New Titles: 220 (1995), 200 (1996)
No of Employees: 58
Annual Turnover: £11.4M

ISBNs, Imprints & Series: 0 7475

Distributor for:
Carlton Books; Granta

Overseas Representation *(see §7.3):*
Australia: Allen & Unwin Pty Ltd, St Leonards,
NSW
Canada: Little Brown & Co (Canada) Ltd,
Toronto
Europe: Michael Geoghegan, London, UK
*Hong Kong, Macau, China, Taiwan, Korea,
Philippines & Thailand:* Roger Ward,
London, UK
India: Maya Publishers Pvt Ltd, New Delhi
Irish Republic & Northern Ireland: Rep Force
Ireland, Monkstown, Irish Republic
Italy: Penguin Italia Srl, Milan
Japan: Roger Ward, London, UK
Middle East: Peter Ward Book Exports,
London, UK
Netherlands: Penguin Books Netherlands bv,
Amsterdam
New Zealand: Hodder Moa Beckett Ltd,
Auckland
Pakistan: Shams Quaraeshi, Karachi
Scandinavia: Hanne Rotovnik, Klampenborg,
Denmark
Singapore & Malaysia: Pansing Distribution
Sdn Bhd, Singapore
South Africa: Jonathan Ball Publishers (Pty)
Ltd, Johannesburg
USA: Trafalgar Square Publications, North
Pomfret, VT

1099 ■■■■■■

*BLUEPRINT
[an imprint of Chapman & Hall]
2–6 Boundary Row, London SE1 8HN
Telephone: 0171 865 0066
Fax: 0171 522 9623

Warehouse:
ITPS, Andover

Telephone: 01264 332424

Direct Sales Unit:
ITPS
Telephone: 0171 522 9966
Fax: 0171 522 9623

Publisher: Vivien James

*Desktop Publishing; Directories; Image/Film/
TV/Video; Printers & graphic arts industries;
Professional & reference for publishers;
Sound/Music/Multimedia*

ISBNs, Imprints & Series:
0 948905, 1 85713

Parent Company:
Chapman & Hall

Associated & Subsidiary Companies:
see: Chapman & Hall

Distributor for:
see: Chapman & Hall

Overseas Representation *(see §7.3):*
see: Chapman & Hall Ltd, London, UK

Book Trade Association Membership: PA

1100 ■■■■■■

BMJ PUBLISHING GROUP
BMA House, Tavistock Square, London
WC1H 9JR
Telephone: 0171 387 4499
Fax: 0171 383 6662

Executive Director: Stella Dutton
Manager Books Division: Neil Poppmacher
(Sales & Rights)
Group Product Manager (Books): Jane
Daniel *(Marketing & European Rights)*
Commissioning Editor: Mary Banks

*Biography & Autobiography; Medical (incl.
Self Help & Alternative Medicine)*

New Titles: 31 (1995), 35 (1996)
No of Employees: 150
Annual Turnover: £26M

ISBNs, Imprints & Series:
0 7279 BMJ Publishing Group, British Medical
Association, British Medical Journal

Parent Company:
British Medical Association

Associated & Subsidiary Companies:
Professional & Scientific Publications

Distributor for:
Professional & Scientific Publications.
Germany: Schaltauer. *USA:* American
Academy of Ophthalmology; American
College of Physicians

Overseas Representation *(see §7.3):*
Australia: AMA Services (WA) Pty Ltd,
Nedlands
Canada: Canadian Medical Association,
Ottawa
Far East (excluding Japan & Taiwan): APAC
Publishers Services, Singapore
Germany: F. K. Schattauer, Stuttgart

Hungary: Literatura Medica, Budapest
Japan: Ohi Shoten, Tokyo
North America: American College of
Physicians, Philadelphia, USA
South Africa: Medical Association of South
Africa, Pinelands
Taiwan: HWA Eng Trading Co, Taipei
USA & Mexico: American College of
Physicians, Philadelphia, USA

Book Trade Association Membership:
IGSMTP, ALPS

1101 ■■■■■■

*BMP
[Business & Medical Publications Ltd]
Saxeway, Chartridge, Bucks HP5 2SH
Telephone: 01494 792621
Fax: 01494 793098

Managing Director: Geoffrey Hall
Publisher: Jeffrey Archer
Production Manager: Caroline Duncan

*Aviation; Law; Medical (incl. Self Help &
Alternative Medicine)*

1102 ■■■■■■

BOOK DATA LTD
Northumberland House, 2 King Street,
Twickenham TW1 3RZ
Telephone: 0181 892 2272
Fax: 0181 892 9109
Email: info@bookdata.co.uk
Web Site: http://www.bookdata.co.uk/

Directors: Francis Bennett *(Managing)*
Ka Meechan *(Sales)*
Managers: Tracy Heron *(Financial)*
Vesna Nall *(Customer Services)*
Pam Roud *(Sales)*
Promotions & Publicity Executive: Rupinder
Sohal

Information Services

Book Trade Association Membership: PA,
BDC, CAPP, DPA

1103 ■■■■■■

THE BOOK GUILD LTD
Temple House, 25 High Street, Lewes,
East Sussex BN7 2LU
Telephone: 01273 472534
Fax: 01273 476472

Trade Enquiries & Orders:
Vine House Distribution, Waldenbury,
North Common, Chailey, East Sussex
BN8 4DR
Telephone: 01825 723398
Fax: 01825 724188

Directors: G. M. Nissen, CBE *(Chairman)*
C. Biss *(Managing, Editorial, Rights &
Permissions)*
Paul White *(Secretary)*
J. Nissen
D. Ross
Publicity: Max Crisfield
Editorial: Chantal Porter
Production: J. Wrench

Academic & Scholarly; Biography &
Autobiography; Children's Books; Crime;
Fiction; Fine Art & Art History; Literature &
Criticism; Military & War; Nautical; Poetry;
Religion & Theology; Theatre, Drama &
Dance; Transport; Travel & Topography

New Titles: 75 (1995), 94 (1996)
No of Employees: 13
Annual Turnover: £800,000

ISBNs, Imprints & Series:
0 86332, 1 85776 Book Guild, Seagull Books,
Temple House Books

Overseas Representation (see §7.3):
Africa: Dr Kunle Krown Banwo, Ibsdan,
Nigeria
Australia: Keith Ainsworth Pty Ltd, Penrith,
NSW
Canada: Cordillera Books, Vancouver, BC
Europe: Books for Europe, J. Komarnicki,
Lugano, Switzerland
Hong Kong: Asia 2000
India: Applied Media, New Delhi
Israel: Charles Rollings, Tel Aviv
New Zealand: South Pacific Books (Imports)
Ltd, Auckland
Philippines: Factfinder Collection Corporation,
Manila
Singapore & Malaysia: Globe Enterprise,
Selangor, Malaysia
South East Asia: GeoVistas, Lewes, UK
USA (distributors): State Mutual Book &
Periodical Service Ltd, New York, USA
USA (fiction rights): Lyle Steele & Co, New
York, USA

Book Trade Association Membership: PA,
IPG

1104 ▬▬▬▬

*BOOKMAN PROJECTS LTD
Mirror Group, 1 Canada Square, Canary Wharf,
London E14 5AP
Telephone: 0171 293 3468
Fax: 0171 293 3020

Publisher: Nick Kent

Guide Books; Humour; Sports & Games

ISBNs, Imprints & Series: 1 898718

Parent Company:
Mirror Group

Overseas Representation (see §7.3):
USA: Seven Hills Book Distributors,
Cincinnati, OH

1105 ▬▬▬▬

BOOKMARKS
265 Seven Sisters Road, Finsbury Park, London
N4 2DE
Telephone: 0181 802 6145
Fax: 0181 802 3835

Editor: Rob Hoverman (Rights & Export
Sales)
Home Sales: Lindi Gonzalez

Economics; History & Antiquarian; Politics &
World Affairs

New Titles: 11 (1995), 5 (1996)
No of Employees: 1

ISBNs, Imprints & Series:
0 905998 Socialist Workers Party
0 906224 Bookmarks

Distributor for:
Australia: Bookmarks Melbourne. USA:
Bookmarks Chicago

Overseas Representation (see §7.3):
USA: Bookmarks, Chicago, IL

1106 ▬▬▬▬

*BOOKS FROM INDIA (UK) LTD
45 Museum Street, London WC1A 1LR
Telephone: 0171 405 7226 & 3784
Fax: 0171 831 4517

Directors: S. Vidyarthi
Mrs S. Vidyarthi

Health & Beauty; Languages & Linguistics;
Medical (incl. Self Help & Alternative
Medicine); Military & War; Music; Reference
Books, Directories & Dictionaries; Scientific &
Technical

ISBNs, Imprints & Series:
0 86186, 0 948724, 0 948725, 1 85127

Associated & Subsidiary Companies:
Asia Publishing House; Asian Educational
Press; Asian Health Press; Homoeopathic Book
Service; Linguasia; Tricolour Books;
Worldsmith

Distributor for:
India: Abhinav Publications; Ajanta
Publications; Chetana (Bombay);
HarperCollins India; Orient Paperbacks;
Oxford & IBH; Rupa & Co

Overseas Representation (see §7.3):
India: Abhinav Publications, New Delhi
USA: Asia Publishing House Inc, Cincinnati,
OH

1107 ▬▬▬▬

BOOKS INTERNATIONAL
69B Lynchford Road, Farnborough, Hants
GU14 6EY
Telephone: 01252 376564
Fax: 01252 370181

Proprietor: Kris Machala

Aviation; Military & War; Nautical;
Modelling; Motoring

New Titles: 4 (1995)
No of Employees: 6
Annual Turnover: £320,000

ISBNs, Imprints & Series:
83 86208 A J-Press, Aircraft Monographs,
Armour in Detail, Camouflage and Markings

Parent Company:
Books International (Poland) (Poland)

Associated & Subsidiary Companies:
Poland: A J-Press

Distributor for:
Hikoki Publications. Poland: A J-Press

Overseas Representation (see §7.3):
France, Switzerland, Hungary, Czech & Slovak
Republics: Juliusz Komarnicki, Massagno,
Switzerland
Germany & Austria: PKB – Robbert J. Pleysier,
Heerde, Netherlands
Greece, Italy, Portugal, Spain (including
Gibraltar), Slovenia & Croatia: Patrick
Bygate & Juliusz Komarnicki, Massagno,
Switzerland
Netherlands, Belgium & Luxembourg: Reinier
A. Pleysier, Heerde, Netherlands
Poland: Books International, Warsaw
Scandinavia: Ove B. Poulsen, Glostrup,
Denmark
USA & Canada: Motorbooks International
Publishers & Wholesalers Inc, Osceola, WI,
USA

1108 ▬▬▬▬

BOOKS UK LTD
Research Station, Davy Bank, Wallsend,
Tyne & Wear NE28 6UZ
Telephone: 0191 295 0100
Fax: 0191 295 0432

Director: David F. Wilson

Children's Books; Cookery, Wines & Spirits;
Do-It-Yourself; Educational & Textbooks;
Gardening; Health & Beauty; Poetry; Sports &
Games; Travel & Topography

ISBNs, Imprints & Series: 1 871612

Book Trade Association Membership: PA,
EPC

1109 ▬▬▬▬

**BOOSEY & HAWKES MUSIC
PUBLISHERS LTD**
295 Regent Street, London W1R 8JH
Telephone: 0171 580 2060
Fax: 0171 436 5675

Warehouse, Trade Enquiries & Orders:
The Hyde, Edgware Road, London NW9 6JN
Telephone: 0181 205 3861
Fax: 0181 200 3737

Directors: R. A. Fell (Chairman & Managing)
T. Glover (Managing)
A. P. Pool (Legal)
S. G. Davidson (Commercial)
S. A. Richards (Printed Music)
R. Holland (Group Chief Executive)

Educational & Textbooks; Electronic
(Entertainment); Music

New Titles: 100 (1995), 100 (1996)
No of Employees: 88
Annual Turnover: £14.9M

ISBNs, Imprints & Series: 0 851

Parent Company:
Boosey & Hawkes Plc

Associated & Subsidiary Companies:
Germany: Boosey & Hawkes Musikverlag;
Bote & Bock. USA: Boosey & Hawkes Inc

Distributor for:
Cramer; Guildhall School of Music. *Hungary:*
EMB. *Italy:* Ricordi. *USA:* Carl Fischer

Book Trade Association Membership: PA

1110 ▬▬▬▬▬

BOOTH-CLIBBORN EDITIONS
12 Percy Street, London W1P 9FB
Telephone: 0171 736 0463

Warehouse & Orders:
Tiptree Book Services, Tiptree, Colchester,
Essex
Telephone: 0171 637 4255
Fax: 0171 637 4251

Sales Director: James Booth-Clibborn
Editor: Edward Booth-Clibborn

Architecture & Design; Fine Art & Art History

ISBNs, Imprints & Series: 1 873968

Parent Company:
Internos Books

Distributor for:
Switzerland: Graphis. *USA:* Hearst Books
International; Lars Muller Publishers; Rockport

Overseas Representation *(see §7.3):*
Worldwide: Hearst Books International, New
York, USA

Book Trade Association Membership: BA

1111 ▬▬▬▬▬

BOSSINEY BOOKS
Land's End, St Teath, Bodmin, Cornwall
PL30 3JH
Telephone: 01840 213401

Publishers: Michael Williams
Sonia Williams
Editorial: Angela Larcombe

*Guide Books; Magic & the Occult; Travel &
Topography; Local Interest Books*

New Titles: 3 (1996)
Annual Turnover: £56,000

ISBNs, Imprints & Series: 0 948158

1112 ▬▬▬▬▬

BOWKER-SAUR
Maypole House, Maypole Road,
East Grinstead, West Sussex RH19 1HU
Telephone: 01342 330100
Fax: 01342 330190

Distribution & Customer Services:
address as above
Telephone: 01342 330100
Fax: 01342 330191

Managing Director: Charles Halpin
Managers: Gerard Dummett
Phillipa Southern *(Finance)*
Publisher: Geraldine Turpie *(Library &
Information Science)*
Chairman: Ira Siegal

*Bibliography & Library Science; Biography &
Autobiography; Industry, Business &
Management; Politics & World Affairs;
Reference Books, Directories & Dictionaries*

ISBNs, Imprints & Series:
0 8352, 0 85935 Bowker
0 8379 Marquis Who's Who
0 86291 Bowker-Saur
0 87217 National Register Publishing
0 905450 Hans Zell
0 909532 D. W. Thorpe
1 85739 Bowker-Saur
1 873836 Hans Zell
3 598 Martindale-Hubbell, KG Saur

Parent Company:
Reed Reference Publishing

Associated & Subsidiary Companies:
Australia: D. W. Thorpe. *Germany:* K. G. Saur
Verlag. *New Zealand:* D. W. Thorpe.
Singapore: Malayan Law Journal Pte Ltd. *USA:*
R. R. Bowker; Marquis Who's Who;
Martindale-Hubbell; National Register
Publishing

Distributor for:
Australia: D. W. Thorpe. *Germany:* K. G. Saur.
New Zealand: D. W. Thorpe. *USA:* R. R.
Bowker; Marquis Who's Who; Martindale-
Hubbell; National Register Publishing

Overseas Representation *(see §7.3):*
Australia: D. W. Thorpe, Port Melbourne
*Germany, Austria, Switzerland &
Liechtenstein:* K. G. Saur Verlag, Munich,
Germany
Hong Kong: Info Access & Distribution
India, Sri Lanka & Bangladesh: Butterworths
India, New Delhi, India
Japan: Elsevier Science Japan, Tokyo
Korea: Shinwon Datanet Inc, Seoul, Korea,
South
Malaysia (books only): Malayan Law Journal
Sdn Bhd, Selangor, Malaysia
Middle East, Greece & Cyprus: Anthony
Rudkin Associates, Oxford, UK
New Zealand: D. W. Thorpe (New Zealand),
Wellington
Pakistan: Butterworth-Heinemann, Lahore
*Singapore, Taiwan, Thailand, Malaysia (CD-
ROM only), Philippines, Indonesia,
Myanmar, Vietnam, Laos, Cambodia &
China:* Information Access & Distribution
Pte Ltd, Singapore
South Africa: Butterworth Publishers (Pty) Ltd,
Durban
USA & Canada: Reed Reference Publishing,
New Providence, NJ, USA

Book Trade Association Membership: BA,
IGSMTP, CAPP, Directory Publishers'
Association

1113 ▬▬▬▬▬

*BOXTREE
2nd Floor, Broadwall House, 21 Broadwall,
London SE1 9PL
Telephone: 0171 928 9696
Fax: 0171 928 5632

Warehouse, Trade Enquiries & Orders:
Littlehampton Book Services, 14 Eldon Way,
Lineside Industrial Estate, Littlehampton,
West Sussex BN17 7HE

Telephone: Littlehampton 01903 726410

Chairman: Peter Roche
Directors: Sarah Mahaffy *(Managing)*
David Inman *(Sales & Marketing)*
Adrian Sington *(Publishing)*
Christine Brown *(Finance)*
Michael Alcock *(Publishing)*
Susanna Wadeson *(Editorial)*
Humphrey Price *(Editorial)*
Christine Corton *(Publishing)*
Rights Manager: Chantal Noel

*Children's Books; Cinema, Video, TV & Radio;
Fine Art & Art History; Gardening; Health &
Beauty; Humour; Military & War; Natural
History; Transport; Cookery; Mind, Body,
Spirit*

ISBNs, Imprints & Series:
New Leaf *(Mind, Body, Spirit)*, Sapling
(Children's Books)
0 7522, 1 85823

Distributor for:
Museum Quilts; Piccadilly Press; Rosendale;
Smith Gryphon

Overseas Representation *(see §7.3):*
Australia: Random House Australia Pty Ltd,
Sydney, NSW
New Zealand: Random House New Zealand
Ltd, Auckland

1114 ▬▬▬▬▬

MARION BOYARS PUBLISHERS LTD
24 Lacy Road, London SW15 1NL
Telephone: 0181 788 9522
Fax: 0181 789 8122

Managing Director: Marion Boyars
(Editorial, Publicity, Rights & Permissions)
Managers: S. M. Mawani *(Production)*
Michael Walmer *(Sales, Trade Enquiries)*

*Academic & Scholarly; Biography &
Autobiography; Cinema, Video, TV & Radio;
Environment & Development Studies; Fiction;
Gender Studies; Industry, Business &
Management; Literature & Criticism; Music;
Philosophy; Poetry; Politics & World Affairs;
Psychology & Psychiatry; Sociology &
Anthropology; Theatre, Drama & Dance;
Travel & Topography*

No of Employees: 5
Annual Turnover: ££0.5M

ISBNs, Imprints & Series:
0 7145 Marion Boyars, Briefings, Ideas in
Progress

Associated & Subsidiary Companies:
USA: Marion Boyars Publishers Inc

Overseas Representation *(see §7.3):*
Australia & New Zealand: Peribo Pty Ltd,
Mount Kuring-gai, NSW, Australia
*Netherlands, Belgium, France, Germany,
Austria & Switzerland:* Michael Geoghegan,
London, UK
Scandinavia: Croft & Croft, Leominster, UK
Spain, Portugal & Gibraltar: Iberian Book
Services SL, Madrid, Spain
USA: Marion Boyars Publishers Inc, New York

Book Trade Association Membership: PA

1115 ■

BOYDELL & BREWER LTD
PO Box 9, Woodbridge, Suffolk IP12 3DF
Telephone: 01394 411320
Fax: 01394 411477

Directors: R. W. Barber *(Managing)*
A. B. Cocks *(Sales)*
H. R. Barber *(Promotion)*
P. S. Harrison *(Production)*
D. S. Brewer
S. R. M. Wilson

*Academic & Scholarly; Archaeology; Guide
Books; History & Antiquarian; Languages &
Linguistics; Literature & Criticism; Military &
War; Music; Theatre, Drama & Dance*

ISBNs, Imprints & Series:
0 85115 Boydell Press
0 85991 D. S. Brewer

Associated & Subsidiary Companies:
USA: Boydell & Brewer Inc; University of
Rochester Press; Tamesis

Distributor for:
Camden House; Canterbury & York Society;
Colleagues Press; Early English Text Society;
Hakluyt Society; Henry Bradshaw Society;
Lincoln Records Society; Pallas Athene; Royal
Society of Literature; Suffolk Record Society.
USA: University of Rochester Press

1116 ■

BPP PUBLISHING LTD
Aldine House, Aldine Place, London
W12 8AW
Telephone: 0181 740 1111
Fax: 0181 740 1184

Warehouse:
Unit 6, Grand Union Industrial Estate, London
NW10 7UL
Telephone: 0181 965 8898

Directors: Justin West *(Managing)*
Clare Donnelly *(Production)*
Paul Roberts *(Sales & Marketing)*
Richard Baron *(Publishing)*

*Academic & Scholarly; Accountancy &
Taxation; Economics; Educational &
Textbooks; Industry, Business & Management;
Law*

ISBNs, Imprints & Series:
0 7517 BPP
1 871824 Password

Parent Company:
BPP Holdings Plc

Associated & Subsidiary Companies:
Blackstone Press Ltd; BPP (Letts Educational)
Ltd; DP Publications Ltd

Overseas Representation *(see §7.3):*
Botswana: Botswana Centre for Accounting
Studies, Gaborone
Cyprus: BPP (Cyprus), Nicosia

Hong Kong: Hon Wing Book Co Ltd;
Bloomsbury Books Ltd; The Commercial
Press Ltd; Swindon Book Co, Kowloon
India: M & J Services, Bombay
Irish Republic: A. Hanna, Dublin; Hodges
Figgis, Dublin; Liam Ruiseal Teo, Cork;
O'Mahony & Co Ltd, Limerick
Jamaica: Acorn Connections Ltd, Kingston
Kenya: Graffins College, Nairobi
Malaysia: Crescent News (KL) Sdn Bhd, Kuala
Lumpur
Mauritius: Editions Le Printemps, Vacoas
Singapore: ICPAS; MPH Distributors (S) Pte
Ltd
South Africa: Johannesburg Agencies,
Johannesburg
Sri Lanka: Pitraban, Colombo
West Indies: Herman Marcano & Associates
Ltd, Port of Spain, Trinidad

1117 ■

BRADT PUBLICATIONS
41 Nortoft Road, Chalfont St Peter, Bucks
SL9 0LA
Telephone: 01494 873478
Fax: 01494 873478

British Orders (Distributor):
Springfield Books Ltd, Norman Road,
Denby Dale, Huddersfield HD8 8TH
Telephone: Huddersfield 01484 864955
Fax: 01484 865443

Director: Mrs Hilary Bradt *(Rights &
Permissions, Editorial)*
Manager: Mrs Janet Mears *(Sales)*

*Guide Books; Travel & Topography; Rail
Guides*

New Titles: 17 (1995), 8 (1996)
No of Employees: 4

ISBNs, Imprints & Series:
0 946983 Backpacking Guide Series
1 898323 Guide to Series

Overseas Representation *(see §7.3):*
Australia: Peribo Pty Ltd, Mount Kuring-gai,
NSW
Belgium, France & Netherlands: Craenen
bvba, Winksele-Herent, Belgium
Canada: ITMB Publishing, Vancouver
Denmark: Scanvik Books APS, Copenhagen
Germany: Brettschneider Fernreisebedarf,
Munich
Italy: InterOrbis SpA, Corsico (Milan)
Kenya: Camerapix Publishers International,
Nairobi
South Africa: Media House Publications Pty
Ltd, Sandton
Spain: Libreria Altair SA, Barcelona
Sweden: Lantmateriet Kartbutiken, Stockholm
& Vällingby
Switzerland: Artou Diffusion, Geneva
USA: The Globe Pequot Press, Old Saybrook,
CT

Book Trade Association Membership: IPG

1118 ■

BRASSEY'S (UK) LTD
33 John Street, London WC1N 2AT
Telephone: 0171 753 7777
Fax: 0171 753 7795

Trade Enquiries & Orders:
Marston Book Services, PO Box 269,
Abingdon, Oxon OX14 4SD
Telephone: 01235 465500
Fax: 01235 465555

Directors: Jenny Shaw *(Publishing)*
Alan J. Steel

*Academic & Scholarly; Aviation; Biography &
Autobiography; History & Antiquarian;
Illustrated & Fine Editions; Military & War;
Nautical; Politics & World Affairs; Reference
Books, Directories & Dictionaries; Scientific &
Technical*

New Titles: 53 (1995), 115 (1996)
No of Employees: 20
Annual Turnover: £1M

ISBNs, Imprints & Series:
0 85 Conway Maritime Press, Putnam
Aeronautical Books
1 57488 Brassey's Inc (Washington)
1 85753 Brassey's

Parent Company:
R. S. Holdings Ltd

Associated & Subsidiary Companies:
USA: Brassey's Inc

Overseas Representation *(see §7.3):*
Australia: DLS Australia (Pty) Ltd, Dingley,
Vic
Canada (Conway & Putnam only): Vanwell
Publishing Ltd, St Catherines, Ont, Canada
*Far East (including Japan, Singapore &
Malaysia):* Ralph & Sheila Summers,
London, UK
Middle East, India, Pakistan & Bangladesh:
Ashton International Marketing Services,
Larkfield, UK
New Zealand: N.A.M. Books, Rotherham
Northern Europe: Angell Eurosales, Newton
Abbot, UK
Scandinavia: Saga Books ApS, Copenhagen,
Denmark
*Southern Europe (including Portugal, Spain,
Gibraltar, Malta, Italy, Yugoslav States &
Greece):* Bookport Associates, Bologna,
Italy
USA: Brassey's Inc, McLean, VA

1119 ■

**NICHOLAS BREALEY PUBLISHING
LTD**
21 Bloomsbury Way, London WC1A 2TH
Telephone: 0171 430 0224
Fax: 0171 404 8311

Orders & Warehouse:
Tiptree Book Services, Tiptree, Colchester,
Essex CO5 0SR
Telephone: 01621 816362
Fax: 01621 719717

Managing Director: Nicholas Brealey
(Editorial & Marketing)
Foreign Rights: Gilly Duff
UK Trade Sales: John Wilson *(Booksales Ltd)*
Export Marketing Manager: Angie Tainsh

*Accountancy & Taxation; Economics;
Industry, Business & Management; Politics &
World Affairs; Vocational Training & Careers*

ISBNs, Imprints & Series:
0 85290 Industrial Society (acquired titles)
1 85788 Nicholas Brealey

Overseas Representation *(see §7.3):*
Asia: Roger Ward, London, UK
Australia: Allen & Unwin Pty Ltd, St Leonards, NSW
Belgium: Angie Tainsh, London, UK
Europe (excluding Belgium): Janet Clark, London, UK
India: Ajay Parmar, Delhi
Irish Republic: Carr O'Connell, Ashbourne
Netherlands: Scriptum Books, Schiedan
Scandinavia: Hanne Rotovnik, Klampenborg, Denmark
South Arica: Book Services International, Sandton, South Africa
Switzerland: AZED AG, Muttenz

Book Trade Association Membership: PA, IPG

1120 ▬▬▬

BREEDON BOOKS PUBLISHING CO LTD
44 Friar Gate, Derby DE1 1DA
Telephone: 01332 384235
Fax: 01332 292755

Chairman & Managing Director: Anton Rippon *(Editorial)*
Director: Graham Hales *(Production)*

Biography & Autobiography; History & Antiquarian; Sports & Games

New Titles: 32 (1995), 35 (1996)
No of Employees: 8
Annual Turnover: £1M

ISBNs, Imprints & Series:
0 907969, 1 85983, 1 873626

1121 ▬▬▬

BREESE BOOKS LTD
164 Kensington Park Road, London W11 2ER
Telephone: 0171 727 9426
Fax: 0171 229 3395
Email: mbreese999@aol.com
Web Site: http://www.herefordshire.com/breese-books/

Distribution:
Clipper Distribution Ltd, Windmill Grove, Portchester, Hampshire PO16 9HT
Telephone: 01705 200080
Fax: 01705 200090

Directors: Martin R. Breese *(Managing)*
Andrea de Belleroche *(Editorial)*
Production Manager: George Levin

Antiques & Collecting; Bibliography & Library Science; Biography & Autobiography; Cookery, Wines & Spirits; Crime; Crafts & Hobbies; Fiction; Psychology & Psychiatry; Travel & Topography; Conjuring

New Titles: 10 (1995), 10 (1996)

ISBNs, Imprints & Series:
0 947533 Breese Books, Breese Books Collector's Series, Dreamer's Guide Series

Associated & Subsidiary Companies:
Retrograph Archive Ltd

Overseas Representation *(see §7.3):*
Australia: Alfred Hayes, Sydney
Japan: Ton Onosaka, Tokyo
USA: LPC Group (Losin), Milford, CT

Book Trade Association Membership: IPG

1122 ▬▬▬

BRIDGE BOOKS
61 Park Avenue, Wrexham, Clwyd LL12 7AW
Telephone: 01978 358661
Fax: 01978 262377

Trade Enquiries & Orders:
Wingett House, 25a Chester Street, Wrexham, Clwyd LL13 8BG
Telephone: 01978 358661
Fax: 01978 358661

Partners: W. Alister Williams
Susan A. Williams

History & Antiquarian; Military & War; Travel & Topography

New Titles: 6 (1995), 6 (1996)
No of Employees: 2

ISBNs, Imprints & Series:
0 9508285, 1 872424

Associated & Subsidiary Companies:
Maelor Interactive Publishing; Sand Sedge Publishers

1123 ▬▬▬

BRILLIANT PUBLICATIONS
PO Box 143, 8 Glebe Place, Leamington Spa CV31 1EB
Telephone: 01926 422178
Fax: 01926 422178

Publisher: Priscilla Hannaford

Educational & Textbooks

New Titles: 6 (1995), 8 (1996)
No of Employees: 2

ISBNs, Imprints & Series: 1 897675

1124 ▬▬▬

BRIMAX BOOKS
4–5 Studlands Park Industrial Estate, Newmarket, Suffolk CB8 7AU
Telephone: 01638 664611
Fax: 01638 665220

Directors: Patricia Gillette *(Managing)*
Ian Golding *(Publishing)*
Finance Controller: Adrian Swallow
Rights Manager: Carol Owen

Children's Books

No of Employees: 17
Annual Turnover: £5M

ISBNs, Imprints & Series: 0 86112

Parent Company:
Reed International Books Ltd

Overseas Representation *(see §7.3):*
Australia: Reed Books Australia, Melbourne, Vic
Canada: H. B. Fenn & Co Ltd, Mississauga
East Asia: Reed Consumer Books, Metro Manila, Philippines
New Zealand: Reed Publishing Group, Auckland
Singapore & Malaysia: Reed International (Singapore) Pte Ltd, Singapore
South Africa: Struik Book Distributors Pty Ltd, Johannesburg, Cape Town & Maitland
USA: Brimax Books, Bethlehem, PA

1125 ▬▬▬

BRITISH & FOREIGN BIBLE SOCIETY
[trading as Bible Society]
Stonehill Green, Westlea, Swindon SN5 7DG
Telephone: 01793 418100
Fax: 01793 418118

Director: Ashley Scott *(Commercial)*
Managers (within Publishing Division):
Derek Hill *(Production)*
Brian Lincoln *(Corporate PR)*
Donald Page *(Distribution)*
Peter Duke *(Home & Export Sales)*
Tim Carr *(Marketing, Editorial & Rights)*
Financial Services Manager: Paul Clark
Customer Services: Richard Dlucik

Religion & Theology

New Titles: 15 (1996)
Annual Turnover: £4M

ISBNs, Imprints & Series:
0 564 The Bible Societies, Bible Society, British & Foreign Bible Society

Associated & Subsidiary Companies:
Bible Society in Northern Ireland; National Bible Society of Scotland. *Irish Republic:* National Bible Society of Ireland

Distributor for:
Cambridge University Press; Harper Collins; Hodder & Stoughton; Oxford University Press. *USA:* American Bible Society; Thomas Nelson *(Bibles). Worldwide:* National Bible Societies

Book Trade Association Membership:
Christian Booksellers Association, Christian Booksellers Convention

1126 ▬▬▬

BRITISH AGENCIES FOR ADOPTION & FOSTERING
[BAAF]
200 Union Street, London SE1 0LX
Telephone: 0171 593 2000
Fax: 0171 593 2001

Trade Enquiries:
Turnaround Distribution, 27 Horsell Road, London N5 1XL
Telephone: 0171 609 7836
Fax: 0171 700 1205

Director: Felicity Collier
Publishing Manager: Shaila Shah
(Production, Sales & Rights)

Academic & Scholarly; Children's Books;
Educational & Textbooks; Law; Medical (incl.
Self Help & Alternative Medicine); Psychology
& Psychiatry; Sociology & Anthropology

New Titles: 10 (1995), 10 (1996)
No of Employees: 60

ISBNs, Imprints & Series:
0 903534, 1 873868

Book Trade Association Membership: IPG

1127 ▬▬▬▬

BRITISH LIBRARY, DOCUMENT
SUPPLY CENTRE
Boston Spa, Wetherby, West Yorkshire
LS23 7BQ
Telephone: 01937 546078
Fax: 01937 546333
Email: dsc-publish-section@bl.uk
Web Site: http://portico.bl.uk/dsc

Orders:
Turpin Distribution Services, Blackhorse Road,
Letchworth, Herts SG6 1HN
Telephone: 01462 672555
Fax: 01462 480947

Director: David Bradbury

Bibliography & Library Science

New Titles: 2 (1995), 2 (1996)

ISBNs, Imprints & Series: 0 7123

Parent Company:
British Library

Distributor for:
National Library of Medicine

Book Trade Association Membership: PA,
BDC, CAPP, ALPSP

1128 ▬▬▬▬

BRITISH LIBRARY, HUMANITIES &
SOCIAL SCIENCES
41 Russell Square, London WC1B 3DG
Telephone: 0171 323 7704
Fax: 0171 323 7768

Orders:
The British Library,
Turpin Distribution Services, Blackhorse Road,
Letchworth, Herts SG6 1HN
Telephone: 01462 672555
Fax: 01462 480947

Head of Publications: Jane Carr
Editorial & Rights: David Way
Non-book Publishing: Anne Young
Sales & Marketing: Jenny McKinley

Academic & Scholarly; Bibliography &
Library Science; Fine Art & Art History;
History & Antiquarian; Illustrated & Fine
Editions; Languages & Linguistics; Music

ISBNs, Imprints & Series:
0 7123 Bibliography of British Newspapers,
The British Library, British Library
Occasional Papers, The British Library
Studies in the History of the Book, Corpus of

British Medieval Library Catalogues,
National Sound Archive, Newsplan, The
Panizzi Lectures

Overseas Representation *(see §7.3)*:
Canada & USA: University of Toronto Press,
Downsview, Ont, Canada
Middle East: Ashton International Marketing
Services, Larkfield, UK
Netherlands: Consul Books, Blaricum
Portugal, Spain, Italy & France: Associated
Marketing Services, Woking, UK
Rest of Europe: Onslow Books Ltd, London,
UK

Book Trade Association Membership: PA,
BA, BDC, CAPP

1129 ▬▬▬▬

BRITISH LIBRARY, NATIONAL
BIBLIOGRAPHIC SERVICE
Boston Spa, Wetherby, West Yorkshire
LS23 7BQ
Telephone: 01937 546613
Fax: 01937 546586

Head of Publications: Arthur Cunningham

Bibliography & Library Science; Reference
Books, Directories & Dictionaries

ISBNs, Imprints & Series:
Books in English *(microfiche)*, British National
Bibliography, British National Film & Video
Guide, Name Authority List *(microfiche)*

Book Trade Association Membership: PA,
BDC

1130 ▬▬▬▬

THE BRITISH LIBRARY, PUBLIC
SERVICES PUBLISHING
Great Russell Street, London WC1B 3DG
Telephone: 0171 412 7704
Fax: 0171 412 7768
Email: david.way@bl.uk

Distribution:
Turpin Distribution Services Ltd,
Blackhorse Road, Letchworth, Herts SG6 1MN
Telephone: 01462 672555
Fax: 01462 480947

Director: Jane Carr
Publishing Manager: David Way

Bibliography & Library Science; Biography &
Autobiography; Electronic (Educational); Fine
Art & Art History; History & Antiquarian;
Illustrated & Fine Editions; Music; Natural
History; Reference Books, Directories &
Dictionaries

New Titles: 28 (1995), 30 (1996)
No of Employees: 6
Annual Turnover: £900,000

ISBNs, Imprints & Series: 0 7123

Overseas Representation *(see §7.3)*:
Australia & New Zealand: Bookwise
International, Findon, SA, Australia
Europe (excluding Italy, France, Spain &
Netherlands): Onslow Books Ltd, London,
UK

Irish Republic: Yale Representation Ltd,
London, UK
Italy, Spain & France: Associated Marketing
Services, Woking, UK
Middle East & Far East: AIMS, Larkfield, UK
Netherlands: Consul Books, Blaricum
North America & Canada (selected titles only):
University of Toronto Press, Downsview,
Ont, Canada

Book Trade Association Membership: PA,
BA, BDC, CAPP

1131 ▬▬▬▬

THE BRITISH LIBRARY, SCIENCE
REFERENCE & INFORMATION
SERVICE
25 Southampton Buildings, Chancery Lane,
London WC2A 1AW
Telephone: 0171 412 7469
Fax: 0171 412 7947
Email: maggie.taylor@bl.uk
Web Site: http://portico.bl.uk/sris/

Orders:
Turpin Distribution Services Ltd,
Blackhorse Road, Letchworth, Herts SG6 1HN
Telephone: 01462 672555
Fax: 01462 480947

Marketing & Public Relations: Paul Baxter

Bibliography & Library Science; Industry,
Business & Management; Medical (incl. Self
Help & Alternative Medicine); Reference
Books, Directories & Dictionaries; Scientific &
Technical

ISBNs, Imprints & Series: 0 7123

Overseas Representation *(see §7.3)*:
Japan: NGB Corporation, Tokyo
New Zealand: The Library Supply Co Ltd,
Auckland

1132 ▬▬▬▬

BRITISH MUSEUM PRESS
46 Bloomsbury Street, London WC1B 3QQ
Telephone: 0171 323 1234
Fax: 0171 436 7315

Trade Distributor:
Thames & Hudson Ltd, 44 Clockhouse Road,
Farnborough, Hants GU14 7QZ
Telephone: 01252 541602
Fax: 01252 377380

Managing Director: Patrick M. M. Wright
Company Secretary: Douglas Holford
Head of Publishing: Emma Way
Managers: Teresa Francis *(Editorial)*
Alasdair MacLeod *(Marketing & Rights)*
Julie Young *(Production)*

Academic & Scholarly; Antiques & Collecting;
Archaeology; Children's Books; Fine Art & Art
History; Sociology & Anthropology

ISBNs, Imprints & Series: 0 7141

Parent Company:
British Museum Publications Ltd

Book Trade Association Membership: PA

1133

BRITISH PSYCHOLOGICAL SOCIETY (BPS BOOKS)
St Andrews House, 48 Princess Road East,
Leicester LE1 7DR
Telephone: 0116 254 9568
Fax: 0116 247 0787

Distribution:
Plymbridge Distributors Ltd, Estover House,
Estover Road, Plymouth, Devon PL6 7PZ
Telephone: 01752 202300
Fax: 01752 202330

Publications Manager: Joyce Collins
Rights: Susan Pacitti

Academic & Scholarly; Educational & Textbooks; Health & Beauty; Psychology & Psychiatry; Vocational Training & Careers; Human Resources; Psychometrics

ISBNs, Imprints & Series: 1 85433

Overseas Representation *(see §7.3):*
Europe: Book Representation & Distribution
Ltd, Hadleigh, UK

Book Trade Association Membership: IPG,
ALPSP

1134

*BRITISH TOURIST AUTHORITY
Thames Tower, Black's Road, Hammersmith,
London W6 9EL
Telephone: 0181 846 9000
Fax: 0171 259 9187

Head of Sales & Distribution: Melvyn Colby

Travel & Topography; Cartography

ISBNs, Imprints & Series: 0 7095

Overseas Representation *(see §7.3):*
Australia: Bookwise International, Findon, SA
Canada: Fitzhenry & Whiteside Ltd, Markham
Japan: Toppan Co Ltd, Tokyo
New Zealand: British Travel Books, Auckland
Singapore: Changi International Distribution
Services Pte Ltd
USA: Seven Hills Book Distributors,
Cincinnati, OH

Book Trade Association Membership: PA

1135

BROWN WATSON LTD
The Old Mill, 76 Fleckney Road,
Kibworth Beauchamp, Leicester LE8 OHG
Telephone: 0116 279 6333
Fax: 0116 279 6303

Directors: Michael McDonald *(Managing)*
Dawn Mahon *(Production & Editorial)*

Children's Books

ISBNs, Imprints & Series: 0 7097

Parent Company:
McDonald Publishing

1136

BROWN, SON & FERGUSON, LTD
4–10 Darnley Street, Glasgow G41 2SD
Telephone: 0141 429 1234/5922
Fax: 0141 420 1694

Chairman & Production Director: T. Nigel
Brown
Company Secretary & Editorial Director: L.
Ingram-Brown
Sales Manager: D. H. Provan

Nautical; Theatre, Drama & Dance

New Titles: 4 (1995), 4 (1996)
No of Employees: 18
Annual Turnover: £800,000

ISBNs, Imprints & Series: 0 85174

Associated & Subsidiary Companies:
James Gowans (Trade Bookbinders) Ltd; James
Munro & Co

Book Trade Association Membership:
Scottish PA

1137

BRUCE SMITH BOOKS LTD
PO Box 382, St Albans, Herts AL2 3JD
Telephone: 01923 894355
Fax: 01923 894366
Email: bruce.smith-books@compuserve.com

Warehouse, Trade Enquiries & Orders:
Computer Bookshops Ltd, 205 Formans Road,
Birmingham B11 3AX
Telephone: 0121 778 3333

Directors: Mark Webb
Bruce Smith

Cinema, Video, TV & Radio; Computer Science; Crafts & Hobbies; Electronic (Educational); Electronic (Entertainment); Electronic (Professional & Academic); Reference Books, Directories & Dictionaries

ISBNs, Imprints & Series: 1 873308

Overseas Representation *(see §7.3):*
Denmark: Sall Data, Hammel
USA: JCV Computing International, Santa
Ana, CA

1138

BSA/CML BOOKSHOP
3 Savile Row, London W1X 1AF
Telephone: 0171 437 0655
Fax: 0171 287 0109

Director-General: Adrian Coles
Deputy Director-General: Ronald Armstrong
Senior Management: Christopher French
(Head of Financial Policy)
Michael Coogan *(Head of Legal Services)*
Peter Williams *(Head of Research & External
Affairs)*
Jane Jones *(Head of Personnel, Finance &
Administration)*
Katherine Besomi *(Publications Services
Officer)*
John Murray *(Under Secretary – Rights,
Marketing & Corporate Events)*

Economics; Housing

New Titles: 8 (1995), 6 (1996)

ISBNs, Imprints & Series: 1 869839

1139

BTL PUBLISHING
The B.I.C., Angel Way, Bradford BD7 1BX
Telephone: 01274 841320
Fax: 01274 841322
Email: matth@btlpub.demon.co.uk
Web Site: http://www.demon.co.uk/btlpub

Chairman: Dr I. R. Gomersall
Publishing: Matthew Hill
Business Development: John Winkley
Development Manager: Mark Rouse

Academic & Scholarly; Atlases & Maps; Biology & Zoology; Chemistry; Educational & Textbooks; Electronic (Educational); Guide Books; Physics; Vocational Training & Careers

New Titles: 3 (1995), 8 (1996)
No of Employees: 15

Parent Company:
Bradford Technology Ltd

Distributor for:
Automobile Association; Morgan Interactive

Overseas Representation *(see §7.3):*
Denmark: Industriens Forlag, Copenhagen
Norway: Tecknodidakt, Oslo
Sweden: Terco AB, Stockholm
USA: Modern School Supplies, Hartford, CT

1140

THE BUILDING SERVICES RESEARCH & INFORMATION ASSOCIATION
Old Bracknell Lane West, Bracknell, Berks
RG12 7AH
Telephone: 01344 426511
Fax: 01344 487575

Director: G. Baker
Sales Manager: Brian Brown

Bibliography & Library Science; Engineering; Scientific & Technical; Construction

New Titles: 24 (1995), 12 (1996)
No of Employees: 120
Annual Turnover: £4.3M

ISBNs, Imprints & Series: 0 86022

Overseas Representation *(see §7.3):*
Korea: Jeong Jie Lee, Seoul, Korea, South

1141

BURNS & OATES LTD
Wellwood, North Farm Road, Tunbridge Wells,
Kent TN2 3DR
Telephone: 01892 510850
Fax: 01892 515903

Directors: Countess de la Bedoyère
(Managing, Rights & Permissions)
Hans Küpfer
Paul Burns *(Editor)*

Julie Wood *(Designer)*
Mrs Inger Arthur *(Production Manager)*
Ruth B. Saunders *(Home & Export Sales)*

*Academic & Scholarly; Biography &
Autobiography; Literature & Criticism;
Philosophy; Psychology & Psychiatry;
Reference Books, Directories & Dictionaries;
Religion & Theology*

New Titles: 9 (1995), 10 (1996)
No of Employees: 13

ISBNs, Imprints & Series:
0 86012 Burns & Oates, Liberation &
Theology, Search Press, Springs of Wisdom

Overseas Representation *(see §7.3)*:
Canada: Meakin & Associates, Nepean
Commonwealth Africa & Ethiopia: Kelvin van
Hasselt Publishing Services, Lymington, UK
*Europe (including Germany, Netherlands,
Belgium, Luxembourg, Austria, France &
Switzerland):* Book Representation &
Distribution Ltd, Hadleigh, UK
*Far East, Pacific, West Indies, Japan &
Taiwan:* Ralph & Sheila Summers, London,
UK
India: Asian Trading Corporation, Bangalore
Malaysia, Singapore & Brunei: Vintrade Sdn
Bhd, Kuala Lumpur, Malaysia
Middle East: Eurab Ltd, Rottingdean, UK
New Zealand: Catholic Supplies (NZ) Ltd,
Wellington
Scandinavia: D. Richard Bowen, Malmö,
Sweden
South Africa: Challenge Distributors CC,
Johannesburg

Book Trade Association Membership: IPG

1142 ▬▬▬▬▬▬

BUSINESS EDUCATION PUBLISHERS
Leighton House, 10 Grange Crescent,
Stockton Road, Sunderland SR2 7BN
Telephone: 0191 567 4963
Fax: 0191 514 3277

Warehouse:
Unit 11, Hartlepool Workshops,
Usworth Road Industrial Estate, Usworth Road,
Hartlepool, Cleveland TS25 1PD

Managing Director: Paul Callaghan *(Rights &
Permissions)*
Production Editor: Gerard Callaghan

*Academic & Scholarly; Computer Science;
Educational & Textbooks; Health & Beauty;
Industry, Business & Management; Law*

New Titles: 6 (1995), 10 (1996)
No of Employees: 5
Annual Turnover: £450,000

ISBNs, Imprints & Series: 0 907679

Book Trade Association Membership: Book
Data

1143 ▬▬▬▬▬▬

**THE INTERNATIONAL BUSINESS
LIBRARY LTD**
94 Bromfelde Road, London SW4 6PS

Telephone: 0171 622 0229
Fax: 0171 498 5155

Directors: David Costello *(Administration &
Marketing)*
John T. Murphy *(Editorial)*

Industry, Business & Management; Law

New Titles: 1 (1995), 6 (1996)
No of Employees: 4
Annual Turnover: £250,000

ISBNs, Imprints & Series: 1 898769

Book Trade Association Membership: PA

1144 ▬▬▬▬▬▬

BUTTERFINGERS
Unit 10, Burnett Business Park, Gypsy Lane,
Burnett, Keynsham, Bristol BS18 2ED
Telephone: 0117 986 6680
Fax: 0117 986 6690
Email: mailbox@hub.co.uk
subject:Butterfingers
Web Site: http://www.hub.co.uk/intercafe/
market/butterfingers/index.html

Director: L. H. R. Collard *(Rights)*
Sales Manager: Ms C. G. Coleman

Sports & Games

New Titles: 1 (1995)
No of Employees: 5
Annual Turnover: £250,000

ISBNs, Imprints & Series:
0 9513240, 1 898591

Distributor for:
Circustuff. *Germany:* Die Jonglerie. *USA:*
Brian Dubé Inc; Finesse Press; Solipaz
Publishing Co

Book Trade Association Membership: PA

1145 ▬▬▬▬▬▬

*BUTTERWORTH-HEINEMANN
Linacre House, Jordan Hill, Oxford OX2 8DP
Telephone: 01865 310366
Fax: 01865 310898

Distribution:
Reed Book Services, Northampton Road,
Rushden, Northants NN10 6PU
Telephone: 01933 58521
Fax: 01933 50284

Managing Director: Philip Shaw

*Academic & Scholarly; Agriculture; Animal
Care & Breeding; Architecture & Design;
Chemistry; Cinema, Video, TV & Radio;
Computer Science; Economics; Educational &
Textbooks; Electronic (Professional &
Academic); Engineering; Industry, Business &
Management; Mathematics & Statistics;
Medical (incl. Self Help & Alternative
Medicine); Photography; Physics; Reference
Books, Directories & Dictionaries; Scientific &
Technical; Veterinary Science*

ISBNs, Imprints & Series:
0 240 Focal Press

0 250 Ann Arbor Science
0 407 Butterworth Medical
0 408 Butterworth Scientific
0 409 Butterworth Overseas Subsidiary
Companies
0 434 Heinemann Professional Publishing
0 592 Iliffe Books Ltd
0 7506 Butterworth-Heinemann

Parent Company:
Reed International Books Ltd

Associated & Subsidiary Companies:
USA: Butterworth-Heinemann

Overseas Representation *(see §7.3)*:
Australia & New Zealand: Butterworths
Australia, North Ryde, NSW, Australia
*Cayman Islands, Belize, Bahamas, Turks &
Caicos & Jamaica:* West Indies Publishing
Ltd, Kingston, Jamaica
Central America: Humphrys Roberts
Associates, London, UK
Hong Kong: Asia Publisher Services Ltd
India: Butterworths India, New Delhi
Korea & Taiwan: STM Publishing Services Pte
Ltd, Singapore
Leeward & Windward Islands: C. D. A.
Walker, Christchurch, Barbados
Malaysia: Butterworths Malaysia, Selangor
Malta (excluding Made Simple): Kekoo Modi,
San Pawl Tat-Targa, Malta
Malta (Made Simple only): Audio Visual
Centre Ltd, Sliema, Malta
Mexico: Leslie Croaker, Mexico DF
Middle East: Anthony Rudkin Associates,
Oxford, UK
Nigeria: Heinemann Educational Books
(Nigeria) Ltd, Ibadan
Pakistan: Tahir Lodhi, Lahore
*Singapore, Indonesia, Philippines &
Thailand:* Butterworths Asia, Singapore
South Africa: Butterworth Publishers (Pty) Ltd,
Durban; Butterworth Publishers (Pty) Ltd,
Durban
South America: Humphrys Roberts Associates,
Cotia, Brazil
Trinidad: KLP Agencies Ltd, Port of Spain
Uganda: Rorash Enterprises, Kampala
USA & Canada: Butterworth-Heinemann Inc,
Newton, MA, USA

Book Trade Association Membership: BA,
IGSMTP

1146 ▬▬▬▬▬▬

*BUTTERWORTHS LTD
Halsbury House, 35 Chancery Lane, London
WC2A 1EL
Telephone: 0171 400 2500
Fax: 0171 400 2842

Distribution:
Reed Book Services, Northampton Road,
Rushden, Northants NN10 6PU
Telephone: 01933 58521
Fax: 01933 50284

Chairman: Neville Cusworth

Accountancy & Taxation; Law

ISBNs, Imprints & Series: 0 406

Parent Company:
Reed Elsevier UK

Overseas Representation *(see §7.3):*
Australia: Butterworths Australia, North Ryde, NSW
Canada: Butterworths Canada, Markham, Ont
Caribbean: Butterworths Caribbean, San Juan, Puerto Rico
Irish Republic: Butterworths Ireland, Dublin
Malaysia: Butterworths Malaysia, Selangor
New Zealand: Butterworths of New Zealand, Wellington
Singapore: Butterworths Asia
South Africa: Butterworth Publishers (Pty) Ltd, Durban
USA: Butterworths, United States, Salem, NH

1147 ∎

CADOGAN BOOKS PLC
London House, Great Eastern Wharf, Parkgate Road, London SW11 4NQ
Telephone: 0171 738 1965
Fax: 0171 924 5491
Email: guides@cadogan.demon.co.uk & chess@cadogan.demon.co.uk

Trade Orders & Enquiries:
Grantham Book Services, Isaac Newton Way, Alma Park Industrial Estate, Grantham NG31 9SD
Telephone: 01476 67421
Fax: 01476 590223

Warehouse & Distribution:
B. T. Batsford, PO Box 4, Springwood Industrial Estate, Braintree, Essex CM7 7QY
Telephone: 01376 321276
Fax: 01376 552854

Directors: Bill Colegrave *(Chairman)*
Vicki Ingle *(Managing)*
Rachel Fielding *(Publisher)*
Managers: Robert Beard *(Sales & Distribution)*
Paul Shaw *(Financial)*
Rupert Wheeler *(Production)*

Guide Books; Sports & Games; Chess

No of Employees: 18

ISBNs, Imprints & Series:
0 08 Cadogan Pergamon Chess, Pergamon Chess
0 946313, 0 947754 Cadogan Books, Cadogan Guides
1 85744 Cadogan Bridge Books, Cadogan Chess Books

Associated & Subsidiary Companies:
David Campbell Publishers Ltd

Overseas Representation *(see §7.3):*
Australia (Cadogan Guides & Chess): Capricorn Link (Australia) Pty Ltd, Castle Hill, NSW, Australia
Belgium, Luxembourg & Germany (Cadogan Guides): Robbert Pleysier Books for Europe, Enschede, Netherlands
Far East & Caribbean (Cadogan Guides & Chess): Ralph & Sheila Summers, London, UK
Germany, Belgium, Netherlands & Luxembourg (Chess): PKB – Robbert J. Pleysier, Heerde, Netherlands
Italy, Spain, Greece, Portugal, Gibraltar, Slovenia & Croatia (Cadogan Guides &

Chess): Patrick Bygate, Massagno, Switzerland
Middle East & Cyprus (Cadogan Guides): Michael Morris Associates, Saffron Walden, UK
Middle East (Chess): Ashton International Marketing Services, Larkfield, UK
Netherlands (Cadogan Guides): Nilsson & Lamm BV, Weesp, Netherlands
Philippines (Cadogan Guides & Chess): R&S Summers, Metro Manila, Philippines
Scandinavia (Cadogan Guides & Chess): Ove B. Poulsen, Glostrup, Denmark
Singapore (Cadogan Guides & Chess): R&S Summers, Singapore
South Africa (Cadogan Guides & Chess): Verbatim Distributors, Steenberg, South Africa
Switzerland, France, Austria, Poland, Hungary, Czech & Slovak Republics (Cadogan Guides) & France, Austria, Switzerland, Czech Republic & Poland (Chess): Juliusz Komarnicki, Massagno, Switzerland
USA & Canada (Cadogan Guides): The Globe Pequot Press, Old Saybrook, CT, USA
USA & Canada (Chess): Simon & Schuster Paramount Publishing, New York, USA

1148 ∎

CALDER PUBLICATIONS LTD
179 King's Cross Road, London WC1X 9BZ
Telephone: 0171 833 1300

Trade Counter & Warehouse:
Combined Book Services Ltd, 406 Vale Road, Tonbridge, Kent TN9 1XR
Telephone: 01732 357755
Fax: 01732 770219

Director: John Calder *(Managing, Editorial & Publicity, & Rights)*
Production: Susan Herbert *(Rights & Permissions)*

Biography & Autobiography; Fiction; Literature & Criticism; Music; Photography; Poetry; Politics & World Affairs; Theatre, Drama & Dance; Opera

ISBNs, Imprints & Series:
0 7145 Calder Publications, Calderbooks Paperbacks, ENO Opera Guides, French Surrealism, German Expressionism, Historical Perspectives, Illustrated Musical Biographies, New Paris Editions, Opera Library, Platform Books, Playscripts, Scottish Library, Signature Series, World in Crisis Series

Parent Company:
The Calder Educational Trust

Associated & Subsidiary Companies:
USA: Riverrun Press Inc

Distributor for:
Vita Books. *Canada:* Mosaic Press *(a few selected titles)*

Overseas Representation *(see §7.3):*
Canada: Mosaic Press, Oakville, Ont
New Zealand: Brick Row Publishing Co Ltd, Auckland
USA: Riverrun Press Inc, New York

Book Trade Association Membership: PA

1149 ∎

CAMBRIDGE UNIVERSITY PRESS
The Edinburgh Building, Shaftesbury Road, Cambridge CB2 2RU
Telephone: 01223 312393
Fax: 01223 315052
Email: information@cup.cam.ac.uk
Web Site: http://www.cup.cam.ac.uk/

Orders:
Telephone: 01223 325964
Fax: 01223 325959
Email: trade@cup.cam.ac.uk

University Printer & Chief Executive of the Press: Tony Wilson
Deputy Chief Executive & Managing Director, Publishing Division: Jeremy Mynott
Publishing Division Directors: Nigel Atkinson *(UK Sales)*
James Berry *(Press Financial)*
Ian Bradie *(Distribution)*
Andrew Brown *(Humanities)*
Adrian Du Plessis *(Press Communications)*
Colin Hayes *(ELT)*
Michael Holdsworth *(Publishing Operations & Sales)*
Simon Mitton *(STM & Electronic Publishing)*
Nicholas Reckert *(International Sales)*
Christopher Scarles *(Administration)*
Publishing Division Associate Directors & Senior Managers: Alan Crowden *(Science, Technology & Medicine)*
Simon Capelin *(Physical Sciences)*
Bill Davies *(Press Syndicate Office)*
Peter Davison *(ELT & Educational Sales & Development)*
Peter Donovan *(ELT)*
Paul Driver *(Customer Services)*
Richard Fisher *(Social Sciences)*
Andrew Gilfillan *(Educational)*
Sonja Thein *(Rights)*
Conrad Guettler *(Journals)*
Lynn Hieatt *(Bibles)*
Peter Langworth *(Academic Sales & Development)*
Christine Lawless *(Personnel)*
Hamish McIlwrick *(Production)*
Chris Milne *(Computer Dept)*
Charly Nobbs *(Warehouse)*
David Tranah *(Mathematical Sciences)*

Academic & Scholarly; Agriculture; Archaeology; Architecture & Design; Bibliography & Library Science; Biography & Autobiography; Biology & Zoology; Chemistry; Children's Books; Computer Science; Economics; Educational & Textbooks; Electronic (Educational); Engineering; English as a Foreign Language; Environment & Development Studies; Fine Art & Art History; Gender Studies; Geography & Geology; History & Antiquarian; Industry, Business & Management; Languages & Linguistics; Law; Literature & Criticism; Mathematics & Statistics; Medical (incl. Self Help & Alternative Medicine); Music; Natural History; Philosophy; Physics; Politics & World Affairs; Psychology & Psychiatry; Reference Books, Directories & Dictionaries; Religion & Theology; Scientific & Technical; Sociology & Anthropology; Theatre, Drama & Dance; Animal Behaviour; Astronomy; Biotechnology;

Classics; Ecology; History & Philosophy of Science

New Titles: 1800 (1995), 1800 (1996)

ISBNs, Imprints & Series: 0 521

Associated & Subsidiary Companies:
Cambridge University Press (Printing Division). *Australia:* Cambridge University Press. *USA:* Cambridge University Press

Distributor for:
USA: Stanford University Press *(outside North America)*

Overseas Representation *(see §7.3):*
Contact: Karen White, UK

Book Trade Association Membership: PA, EPC, CAPP, BML, IBD

1150

*CAMPBELL BOOKS
12 Half Moon Court, London EC1A 7HE
Telephone: 0171 600 1693
Fax: 0171 600 2043

Warehouse & Distribution Centre:
Grantham Book Services Ltd,
Isaac Newton Way,
Alma Park Industrial Estate, Grantham, Lincs NG31 9SD
Telephone: 01476 67421
Fax: 01476 67314

Directors: Rod Campbell *(Managing)*
William McRobert
Managers: Penny Welton *(Rights)*
Debra Noakes *(Production)*
Caroline Bidwell *(Publishing)*

Children's Books

ISBNs, Imprints & Series: 1 85292

Parent Company:
Campbell Books Ltd

1151

*DAVID CAMPBELL PUBLISHERS
79 Berwick Street, London W1V 3PF
Telephone: 0171 287 0035
Fax: 0171 287 0038

Sales:
Random House UK, 20 Vauxhall Bridge Road, London SW1B 2SA
Telephone: 0171 973 9730

Publisher: David Campbell
Director: Mark Bicknell

Children's Books; Fiction; Poetry; Travel & Topography

ISBNs, Imprints & Series:
1 85715 Everyman Guides, Everyman's Library

Book Trade Association Membership: PA

1152

CAMRA BOOKS
230 Hatfield Road, St Albans, Herts AL1 4LW
Telephone: 01727 867201
Fax: 01727 848795
Email: camra@camra.org.uk

Managing Editor: Mark Webb

Cookery, Wines & Spirits; Guide Books; Travel & Topography

New Titles: 4 (1995), 5 (1996)
No of Employees: 2

ISBNs, Imprints & Series: 1 85249

Parent Company:
Campaign for Real Ale Ltd

Overseas Representation *(see §7.3):*
USA, Canada, Australasia & European Community: Verulam Publishing Ltd, St Albans, UK

1153

CANONGATE BOOKS
14 High Street, Edinburgh EH1 1TE
Telephone: 0131 557 5111
Fax: 0131 557 5211
Email: canon.gate@almac.co.uk
Web Site: http://www.scotweb.co.uk/whisky/maltfile

Warehouse:
Scottish Book Source, 32 Finlas Street, Springburn, Glasgow G22 5DU
Telephone: 0141 558 1355
Fax: 0141 557 0189

Orders:
Scottish Book Source, 137 Dundee Street, Edinburgh EH11 1BG
Telephone: 0131 229 6800
Fax: 0131 229 9070

Joint Managing Directors: Jamie Byng *(Rights)*
Hugh Andrew *(Sales)*

Audio Books; Biography & Autobiography; Children's Books; Cookery, Wines & Spirits; Crime; Crafts & Hobbies; Fiction; Fine Art & Art History; Guide Books; History & Antiquarian; Humour; Literature & Criticism; Military & War; Music; Natural History; Photography; Poetry; Reference Books, Directories & Dictionaries; Sports & Games; Afro-American & Jamaican Culture

New Titles: 50 (1995), 75 (1996)
No of Employees: 6
Annual Turnover: £1M

ISBNs, Imprints & Series:
0 86241 Canongate Classics, Canongate Kelpies, General list, Payback Press, Rebel Inc
1 85968 Canongate Audio

Associated & Subsidiary Companies:
USA: Interlink Books

Distributor for:
USA: Interlink

Overseas Representation *(see §7.3):*
Australia: Tower Books Wholesalers Pty Ltd, Frenchs Forest, NSW
France, Belgium, Netherlands, Luxembourg, Germany, Austria, Switzerland & Greece: Ted Dougherty, London, UK
New Zealand: Nationwide Book Distributors, Christchurch
Scandinavia: McNeish Publishing Services, London, UK
Southern Africa: Gondwana Books, Vorna Valley, South Africa
USA: Interlink Books, Northampton, MA

Book Trade Association Membership:
Scottish PA

1154

CAPALL BANN PUBLISHING
Freshfields, Chieveley, Berks RG20 8TF
Telephone: 01635 46455
Fax: 01635 46455

Editorial:
Telephone: 01635 248711
Fax: 01635 248711

Sales & Rights: Jon Day
Administration: Julia Day

Animal Care & Breeding; Archaeology; Computer Science; Cookery, Wines & Spirits; Crafts & Hobbies; Educational & Textbooks; Electronic (Educational); Electronic (Professional & Academic); Environment & Development Studies; Gender Studies; Guide Books; Health & Beauty; History & Antiquarian; Humour; Magic & the Occult; Medical (incl. Self Help & Alternative Medicine); Music; Natural History; Nautical; Religion & Theology; Theatre, Drama & Dance

New Titles: 30 (1995), 46 (1996)

ISBNs, Imprints & Series: 1 898307

Distributor for:
Broomtail Publications; Isle of Avalon Press

Overseas Representation *(see §7.3):*
Australia (Nautical): Boat Books, Australia
Australia (New Age): Mind Mint Distributors, Australia
Europe (excluding Netherlands): Books for Europe Ltd, Bournemouth, UK
Netherlands: Bernard Croft, Leominster, UK
New Zealand: Peaceful Living Publications, Tauranga
USA: New Leaf Distribution, Lithia Springs, GA

1155

CARCANET PRESS LTD
406 Corn Exchange Buildings, Manchester M4 3BY
Telephone: 0161 834 8730
Fax: 0161 832 0084

Distribution, Trade Enquiries & Orders:
Littlehampton Book Services Ltd,
Lineside Estate, Littlehampton, West Sussex
Telephone: 01903 721596
Fax: 01903 730914

Chairman: Kate Gavron
Director: Michael Schmidt *(Managing & Editorial)*

Academic & Scholarly; Biography & Autobiography; Educational & Textbooks; Literature & Criticism; Poetry; Religion & Theology

New Titles: 40 (1995), 40 (1996)
No of Employees: 5

ISBNs, Imprints & Series:
0 85635, 0 902145, 1 85754 Carcanet Press, Fyfield Books

Parent Company:
Folio Holdings

Overseas Representation *(see §7.3)*:
Canada: Scholarly Book Services Inc, Toronto
USA: Paul & Company, Concord, MA

1156

CARDIFF ACADEMIC PRESS
St. Fagans Road, Fairwater, Cardiff CF5 3AE
Telephone: 01222 560333
Fax: 01222 554909

Managing Director: R. G. Drake
Managers: Mrs J. Smith *(Accounts)*
Mrs M. de Lange *(Marketing)*

Academic & Scholarly; Architecture & Design; Bibliography & Library Science; Biography & Autobiography; Biology & Zoology; Children's Books; Cinema, Video, TV & Radio; Computer Science; Educational & Textbooks; English as a Foreign Language; Environment & Development Studies; Fiction; Fine Art & Art History; Gay & Lesbian Studies; Gender Studies; Geography & Geology; Guide Books; History & Antiquarian; Languages & Linguistics; Literature & Criticism; Medical (incl. Self Help & Alternative Medicine); Music; Natural History; Philosophy; Poetry; Politics & World Affairs; Psychology & Psychiatry; Religion & Theology; Sociology & Anthropology; Theatre, Drama & Dance

ISBNs, Imprints & Series: 1 899025

Book Trade Association Membership: PA, BA, BDC, EPC, CAPP, IPG

1157

CARLTON BOOKS LTD
20 St Anne's Court, London W1V 3AW
Telephone: 0171 734 7338
Fax: 0171 434 1196

Directors: J. Goodman *(Managing)*
J. Maynard *(Operations)*
P. Murray Hill *(Editorial)*
R. Porter *(Art)*
A. Whitton *(Financial)*
K. Allen Jones *(Sales)*

Cinema, Video, TV & Radio; Computer Science; Health & Beauty; Music; Natural History; Science Fiction; Sports & Games

New Titles: 40 (1995), 50 (1996)
No of Employees: 30
Annual Turnover: £10M

ISBNs, Imprints & Series: 1 85868

Parent Company:
Carlton Communications Plc

1158

CAROL PUBLISHING GROUP
Cedar House, 35 Chichele Road, Oxted, Surrey RH8 0AE
Telephone: 01883 730207
Fax: 01883 730188
Email: 101341.1235@compuserve.com

Warehouse, Trade Enquiries & Orders:
Biblios, Star Road, Partridge Green, West Sussex RH13 8LD
Telephone: 01403 710971
Fax: 01403 711143

UK Managing Director: Adrian Parker

Biography & Autobiography; Cinema, Video, TV & Radio; Cookery, Wines & Spirits; English as a Foreign Language; Fiction; Gay & Lesbian Studies; Health & Beauty; History & Antiquarian; Humour; Languages & Linguistics; Literature & Criticism; Magic & the Occult; Military & War; Music; Natural History; Philosophy; Poetry; Politics & World Affairs; Psychology & Psychiatry; Reference Books, Directories & Dictionaries; Religion & Theology; Science Fiction; Sociology & Anthropology; Sports & Games; Theatre, Drama & Dance

ISBNs, Imprints & Series:
0 8065 Citadel Press
0 8184 Lyle Stuart
0 8216 Carol Publishing
0 89746 Gambling Times
1 55972 Birch Lane Press

Parent Company:
Carol Publishing Group *(USA)*

1159

JON CARPENTER PUBLISHING
The Spendlove Centre, Charlbury OX7 3PQ
Telephone: 01608 811969
Fax: 01608 811969

Trade Orders:
Central Books, 99 Wallis Road, London E9 5LN
Telephone: 0181 986 4854
Fax: 0181 533 5821

Contact: Jon Carpenter

Academic & Scholarly; Economics; Environment & Development Studies; Magic & the Occult; Medical (incl. Self Help & Alternative Medicine); Philosophy; Politics & World Affairs; Sociology & Anthropology

New Titles: 6 (1995), 8 (1996)
No of Employees: 1

ISBNs, Imprints & Series: 1 897766

Distributor for:
New Consumer Publications. *Australia:* Envirobook Pty; Willow Park Press. *Canada:* Black Rose Books. *Netherlands:* International Books. *USA:* Apex Press; Bootstrap Press;

Common Knowledge Press; New Society Publishers

Overseas Representation *(see §7.3)*:
USA: In Book, Chicago, IL

1160

CARRICK MEDIA
2–7 Galt House, 31 Bank Street, Irvine KA12 0LL
Telephone: 01294 311322
Fax: 01294 311322

Editorial: Kenneth Roy
Production: Fiona MacDonald

Reference Books, Directories & Dictionaries; Periodicals; Scotland; The Media

ISBNs, Imprints & Series: 0 946724

1161

FRANK CASS & CO LTD
Newbury House, 890–900 Eastern Avenue, Newbury Park, Ilford, Essex IG2 7HH
Telephone: 0181 599 8866
Fax: 0181 599 0984

Trade Enquiries, Orders & Warehouse:
Biblios, Glenside Ind Est, Star Road, Partridge Green, Horsham, West Sussex RH13 8LD
Telephone: Horsham 01403 710971
Fax: 01403 711143

Directors: Frank Cass *(Managing)*
Stewart Cass *(Commercial)*
M. P. Zaidner, ACWA, ACIS *(Financial)*
Managers: Lydia Linford *(Editorial)*
Joan Dale-Lace *(Editorial)*
Randal Gray *(Editorial)*
Jonathan Manley *(Editorial)*
Robert Easton *(Editorial)*
Cathy Jennings *(Editorial)*
Daphne Weiss *(Production)*
Ray Green *(Production)*
Pat Wemyss *(Permissions)*
Lindy Burleigh *(Rights & Publicity)*
Patrick McLaughlin *(Marketing – Books, Sales)*
Anne Kidson *(Marketing – Academic Journals)*
Hayley Osen *(Marketing)*
Joanna Legg *(Trade)*
Jerry Quy *(Journal Subscriptions)*

Academic & Scholarly; Military & War; Politics & World Affairs

New Titles: 80 (1995), 80 (1996)
No of Employees: 25

ISBNs, Imprints & Series:
0 7130 Woburn Press
0 7146 Frank Cass
0 85303 Vallentine Mitchell
1 874774 The Littman Library of Jewish Civilization

Associated & Subsidiary Companies:
Irish Republic: Irish Academic Press

Overseas Representation *(see §7.3)*:
USA: International Specialized Book Services Inc, Portland, OR

Book Trade Association Membership: IPG

1162

CASSELL PLC
Wellington House, 125 Strand, London
WC2R 0BB
Telephone: 0171 420 5555
Fax: 0171 240 7261

Distribution:
Cassell Plc, Stanley House, 3 Fleets Lane,
Poole, Dorset BH15 3AJ
Telephone: 01202 665432
Fax: 01202 666219

Directors (Holding Co): Philip Sturrock
(Chairman & Chief Executive Officer)
Frank Roney *(Finance)*
Stewart Binne *(Non-Executive)*
Stephen Jaeger *(Non-Executive)*
Clifford Jakes *(Non-Executive)*
Directors (Operating Companies): Stephen
Butcher *(Managing—Academic & Religious
Division)*
Martyn Chapman *(Distribution & Commercial)*
Kevin Bristow *(Sales & Marketing,
General Division)*
Liz Knights *(Gollancz Editorial)*
Jane Blackstock *(Gollancz Rights)*
Alan Smith *(Publishing Services)*
Michael Goff *(International Trade Sales)*
Geoffrey Charters *(Production)*
George Sharp *(Art)*
Adrienne Maguire *(Group Trade Publicity &
Marketing)*
Roderick Dymott *(Editorial Arms & Armour &
Blandford)*
Alison Goff *(Editorial Cassell General & Ward
Lock)*
Andrew Macmillan *(UK Trade Sales)*

*Academic & Scholarly; Accountancy &
Taxation; Agriculture; Animal Care &
Breeding; Antiques & Collecting; Architecture
& Design; Aviation; Bibliography & Library
Science; Biography & Autobiography;
Computer Science; Cookery, Wines & Spirits;
Crafts & Hobbies; Do-It-Yourself; Economics;
Educational & Textbooks; English as a Foreign
Language; Fashion & Costume; Fine Art & Art
History; Gardening; Geography & Geology;
Guide Books; Health & Beauty; History &
Antiquarian; Humour; Illustrated & Fine
Editions; Industry, Business & Management;
Languages & Linguistics; Law; Magic & the
Occult; Military & War; Music; Natural
History; Nautical; Philosophy; Photography;
Poetry; Politics & World Affairs; Psychology &
Psychiatry; Reference Books, Directories &
Dictionaries; Religion & Theology; Sociology
& Anthropology; Sports & Games; Theatre,
Drama & Dance; Transport; Travel &
Topography; Vocational Training & Careers*

New Titles: 800 (1995), 900 (1996)
Annual Turnover: £23.1M

ISBNs, Imprints & Series:
0 304 Cassell

Associated & Subsidiary Companies:
Arms & Armour Press; Blandford Press;
Cassell Educational; Cassell Publishers;
Geoffrey Chapman; Victor Gollancz; Leicester
University Press; Mansell Publishing;
Mowbray; New Orchard Editions; Pinter;
Studio Vista; Ward Lock Ltd

Distributor for:
Wisley Handbooks (Royal Horticultural
Society). *Australia:* Sally Milner. *USA:* DBI
Books Inc; Heinemann Inc (Education list);
Lark Publishing; St Vladimir's Seminary Press;
Sterling Publishers Inc

Overseas Representation *(see §7.3)*:
Australia (Academic): Astam Books Pty Ltd,
Leichhardt, NSW, Australia
Australia (Cassell Trade & Reference):
Capricorn Link (Australia) Pty Ltd, Castle
Hill, NSW, Australia
Australia (Religion): Charles Paine Pty Ltd,
North Paramatta, NSW, Australia
*Austria, Belgium, France, Germany,
Luxembourg & Switzerland (Cassell
Trade):* European Marketing Services,
London, UK
Canada (Academic): Cassell Representative
Office, New York, USA
*Canada (Ward Lock Gardening & DIY &
Wisley Handbooks):* Cavendish Books Inc,
North Vancouver, Canada
Caribbean (Cassell Trade & Reference):
Humphrys Roberts Associates, London, UK
*Caribbean (excluding Jamaica & Trinidad)
(Academic only):* C. D. A. Walker,
Christchurch, Barbados
*Caribbean (excluding Trinidad) (Religious
only):* Harris Religious Supplies, St Philip,
Barbados
*Eastern & Central Africa (Cassell all
imprints):* PMC International, Durban
North, South Africa
*Europe & Scandinavia (Academic &
Religious):* Andrew B. Durnell, Tunbridge
Wells, UK
*Hong Kong, Taiwan, Korea, China (Cassell all
imprints):* Asia Publisher Services Ltd, Hong
Kong
*Hungary, Czech Republic, Slovakia, Slovenia
& Croatia (Cassell all imprints):* CLB
Marketing Services, Kecskemet, Hungary
*India (Cassell Trade & Reference, Academic
& Religious):* Maya Publishers Pvt Ltd,
New Delhi, India
Israel (Academic & Religious): Rouven Ziv,
Holon, Israel
Italy (Arms & Armour Press only): Tuttostoria,
Parma, Italy
Jamaica (Academic only): Times Store,
Kingston, Jamaica
Japan (Academic): United Publishers Services
Ltd, Tokyo, Japan
Japan (Cassell Trade & Reference): Japan
English Services Inc, Chiba-ken, Japan
Malaysia (Cassell all imprints): APD Kuala
Lumpur, Petaling Jaya, Malaysia
*Middle East & North Africa (Academic &
Religious):* International Publishers
Representatives (IPR), Nicosia, Cyprus
Middle East (Cassell Trade & Reference)):
Eurab Ltd, Rottingdean, UK
Netherlands (Cassell Trade & Reference):
Nilsson & Lamm BV, Weesp, Netherlands
New Zealand (Arms & Armour Press only):
Forrester Books Ltd, Auckland, New
Zealand
*New Zealand (Cassell Trade & Reference
excluding Arms & Armour Press):* David
Bateman Ltd, Auckland, New Zealand
Nigeria (Academic & Religious): Bounty Press
Ltd, Ibadan, Nigeria
Pakistan (Cassell all imprints): Mackwin &
Co, Karachi, Pakistan

Scandinavia (Cassell Trade & Reference): Ove
B. Poulsen, Glostrup, Denmark
*Singapore, Indonesia & Thailand (Cassell all
imprints):* APD Singapore Pte Ltd,
Singapore
South Africa (Cassell Religious & Academic):
David Philip Publishers Pty Ltd, Claremont,
South Africa
South Africa (Cassell Trade & Reference):
Kudu Books Pty Ltd, Cape Town, South
Africa
South America (Cassell all imprints):
Humphrys Roberts Associates, Cotia, Brazil
*Southern Europe (including Gibraltar, Italy,
Portugal & Spain; Cassell Trade &
Reference):* Penny Padovani, London, UK
Trinidad & Tobago (Academic & Religious):
RIK Services Ltd, San Fernando, Trinidad
USA & Canada (Academic): Cassell
Representative Office, Herndon, VA, USA
USA (Religious only): Morehouse, Ridgefield
CT, USA
USA (Trade & Reference): Sterling Publishing
Co Inc, New York, NY, USA

1163

CASTLEMAIN BOOKS
Unit 3, Fountain Way, Parkend, Glos GL15 6JD
Telephone: 01594 564508

Warehouse, Trade Enquiries & Orders:
West Country Books, Halsgrove House,
Lower Moor Way, Tiverton Business Park,
Tiverton, Devon EX16 6SS

Directors: John Pemberthy *(Sales & Editorial)*
Sam Wootten *(Company Secretary)*

*Archaeology; Biography & Autobiography;
Guide Books; History & Antiquarian; Hobbies;
Touring; Walking*

New Titles: 2 (1995), 1 (1996)
No of Employees: 1

ISBNs, Imprints & Series:
0 904110, 0 946328

Book Trade Association Membership: BA

1164

CASTLEMEAD PUBLICATIONS
12 Little Mundells, Welwyn Garden City, Herts
AL7 1EW
Telephone: 01707 320220
Fax: 01707 331012

Proprietor: Susan D. M. Lee

*Guide Books; Medical (incl. Self Help &
Alternative Medicine); Military & War;
Natural History; Transport*

New Titles: 2 (1995), 1 (1996)
No of Employees: 5
Annual Turnover: £41,370

ISBNs, Imprints & Series: 0 948555

Associated & Subsidiary Companies:
Ward's Publishing Services

Book Trade Association Membership: PA

1165 ▬▬▬▬

KYLE CATHIE LTD
20 Vauxhall Bridge Road, London SW1V 2SA
Telephone: 0171 973 9710
Fax: 0171 821 9258

Distributors:
Littlehampton Book Services Ltd,
14 Eldon Way, Lineside Estate, Littlehampton,
West Sussex BN17 7EH
Telephone: Littlehampton 01903 726410
Fax: 01903 730914

Director: Emma Bittleston *(Publicity &
Marketing)*
Rights: Sara-Jane Vere Nicoll

*Biography & Autobiography; Cookery, Wines
& Spirits; Gardening; Health & Beauty;
History & Antiquarian; Natural History;
Reference Books, Directories & Dictionaries*

New Titles: 24 (1995), 28 (1996)
No of Employees: 6

Overseas Representation *(see §7.3)*:
Australia & New Zealand: Lothian Books, Port
Melbourne, Australia
Canada: McClelland & Stewart, Toronto &
Markham
Singapore, Malaysia & Brunei: Pansing
Distribution Sdn Bhd, Singapore
South Africa: Kudu Books Pty Ltd, Cape Town
USA: Trafalgar Square Publications, North
Pomfret, VT

1166 ▬▬▬▬

THE CATHOLIC TRUTH SOCIETY
192 Vauxhall Bridge Road, London
SW1V 1PD
Telephone: 0171 834 4392
Fax: 0171 630 1124

Retail Bookshop & Mail order:
25 Ashley Place, London SW1P 1LT
Telephone: 0171 834 1363
Fax: 0171 630 1124

Directors: Rt Rev Peter Smith, DCL, Bishop of
East Anglia *(Chairman)*
Fergal Martin *(General Secretary, Editorial,
Rights & Permissions, Accounts)*
John Dilger *(Hon Treasurer)*
Production: Tom Cutler
Sales: William Carson
Systems: Laurence Benkhabeb

*Biography & Autobiography; Religion &
Theology*

New Titles: 35 (1995), 30 (1996)
No of Employees: 12
Annual Turnover: £0.5M

ISBNs, Imprints & Series:
0 85183 The Incorporated Catholic Truth
Society, CTS Publications

Distributor for:
Vatican City: Osservatore Romano

Book Trade Association Membership: BA

1167 ▬▬▬▬

CAUSEWAY PRESS LTD
129 New Court Way, PO Box 13, Ormskirk,
Lancs L39 5HP
Telephone: 01695 576048 & 573360
Fax: 01695 570714

Warehouse & Distribution:
The Trade Counter, The Airfield, Mendlesham,
Suffolk IP14 5NA
Telephone: Mendlesham 01449 766629
Fax: 01449 767122

Directors: Michael Haralambos
Pauline Haralambos
David Gray
David Alcorn
Accounts: Ingrid Hamer

*Academic & Scholarly; Economics;
Educational & Textbooks; Geography &
Geology; History & Antiquarian; Industry,
Business & Management; Mathematics &
Statistics; Politics & World Affairs; Sociology
& Anthropology*

New Titles: 19 (1995), 21 (1996)
No of Employees: 9
Annual Turnover: £1.7M

ISBNs, Imprints & Series:
0 946183, 1 873929

Overseas Representation *(see §7.3)*:
Australia: Mentone Educational Centre,
Ashburton
Pakistan: Danesh Publication (Pvt) Ltd,
Karachi
South East Asia: Academic Library Services,
Singapore
USA: Sheridan House Inc, Dobbs Ferry, NY

Book Trade Association Membership: IPG

1168 ▬▬▬▬

PAUL CAVE PUBLICATIONS LTD
74 Bedford Place, Southampton SO15 2DF
Telephone: 01703 333457
Fax: 01703 227190

Chairman: Paul Cave *(Editorial – Books &
Magazines)*
Directors: Joan Cave
Adrienne Burrows
Advertising: Mrs Debbie Venables

*Guide Books; History & Antiquarian; Sports &
Games*

ISBNs, Imprints & Series:
0 86146, 0 9501735

Book Trade Association Membership: PA,
Periodical Publishers Association

1169 ▬▬▬▬

CAVENDISH PUBLISHING LTD
The Glass House, Wharton Street, London
WC1X 9PX
Telephone: 0171 278 8000
Fax: 0171 278 8080
Email: enquiries@cavendishpublishing.co.uk

Warehouse:
Unit D, Trading Estate Road, London
NW10 7LU
Telephone: 0181 963 0322
Fax: 0181 965 9765

Directors: Sonny Leong *(Publishing, Sales &
Marketing)*
Jo Reddy *(Managing Editor)*

*Academic & Scholarly; Educational &
Textbooks; Law; Medical (incl. Self Help &
Alternative Medicine)*

New Titles: 100 (1995), 80 (1996)
No of Employees: 10

ISBNs, Imprints & Series:
1 85941, 1 874241

Associated & Subsidiary Companies:
Australia: Cavendish Publishing (Australia)
Pty Ltd

Distributor for:
Australia: Cavendish Publishing (Australia)
Pty Ltd. *Canada:* Emond Montgomery
Publications. *USA:* Little Brown & Co *(Law
titles)*; Nolo Press Inc

Overseas Representation *(see §7.3)*:
Australia: Cavendish Publishing (Australia)
Pty Ltd, Sydney
Canada: Emond Montgomery Publications
Ltd, Toronto, Ont
Hong Kong & Taiwan: Transglobal Publishers
Services Ltd, Tsuen Wan, Hong Kong
India: Aditya Books, New Delhi
Malaysia: Publishers Marketing Services,
Petaling Jaya
Singapore & Brunei: Publishers Marketing
Services Ltd, Singapore

Book Trade Association Membership: PA,
BDC, CAPP, IPG

1170 ▬▬▬▬

CBD RESEARCH LTD
Chancery House, 15 Wickham Road,
Beckenham, Kent BR3 2JS
Telephone: 0181 650 7745
Fax: 0181 650 0768
Email: 100702.32@compuserve.com

Director: Cris Henderson

*Crime; Reference Books, Directories &
Dictionaries*

New Titles: 1 (1995), 1 (1996)
No of Employees: 7
Annual Turnover: £300,000

ISBNs, Imprints & Series:
0 900 246 CBD Research, Chancery House
Press

Overseas Representation *(see §7.3)*:
USA: Gale Research Co, Detroit; Reference
Press, Austin, TX

Book Trade Association Membership: IPG,
Directory Publishers Association, European
Association of Directory Publishers

1171

CCBI PUBLICATIONS
Inter-Church House, 35–41 Lower Marsh,
London SE1 7RL
Telephone: 0171 620 4444
Fax: 0171 928 0010

Managers: David J. Rudiger *(Sales)*
Richard L. Bong *(Distribution)*

*Academic & Scholarly; Biography &
Autobiography; Gender Studies; History &
Antiquarian; Reference Books, Directories &
Dictionaries; Religion & Theology*

New Titles: 6 (1995), 4 (1996)
No of Employees: 50

ISBNs, Imprints & Series: 0 85169

Parent Company:
Council of Churches for Britain & Ireland

Distributor for:
New Zealand: Pace Communications.
Switzerland: Conference of European
Churches; World Council of Churches

Book Trade Association Membership: PA,
BA

1172

CCH EDITIONS LTD
Telford Road, Bicester, Oxon OX6 0XD
Telephone: 01869 253300
Fax: 01869 245814

Managing Director: Hans Staal
Company Secretary: Chris Plews
Managers: David Johnston *(Sales)*
Gary Palmer *(Marketing)*
John Flint *(Production)*
Adrian Magson *(Commercial Services)*

*Accountancy & Taxation; Industry, Business &
Management; Law*

ISBNs, Imprints & Series: 0 86325

Parent Company:
Wolters Kluwer NV *(Netherlands).* CCH Inc
(USA)

Overseas Representation *(see §7.3):*
Belgium, Netherlands & Luxembourg: Nicole
de Ruyck, Putte, Belgium
France, Monaco & Switzerland (French):
Patrick Kielty, Epernon, France
*Germany, Austria, Denmark & Switzerland
(German):* David Duffy, Wiesbaden,
Germany

1173

THE CENTRAL BUREAU
10 Spring Gardens, London SW1A 2BN
Telephone: 0171 389 4886
Fax: 0171 389 4426

Director: A. H. Male
Press & Publicity: Nicola Davis
Publishing: Thom Sewell

Guide Books; Travel & Topography

New Titles: 2 (1995), 2 (1996)

ISBNs, Imprints & Series:
0 900087, 1 898601

Book Trade Association Membership: PA

1174

**CENTRAL EUROPEAN UNIVERSITY
PRESS**
25 Belsize Park, London NW3 4DU
Telephone: 0171 794 4759
Fax: 0171 794 4759

Warehouse & Trade Enquiries:
Oxford University Press, Corby

Directors: Frances Pinter *(Executive)*
Pauline Wickham *(Editorial)*
Marketing & Rights Manager: Sue Wilson

*Academic & Scholarly; Economics; Fiction;
Law; Politics & World Affairs; Sociology &
Anthropology*

New Titles: 10 (1995), 12 (1996)
No of Employees: 4

ISBNs, Imprints & Series: 1 85866

Overseas Representation *(see §7.3):*
Worldwide: Oxford University Press, Oxford,
UK

Book Trade Association Membership: PA

1175

**CENTRE FOR ECONOMIC POLICY
RESEARCH**
25–28 Old Burlington Street, London
W1X 1LB
Telephone: 0171 878 2900
Fax: 0171 878 2999
Email: cepr@cepr.org

Director: Richard Portes
Publications Manager: Kate Millward

*Academic & Scholarly; Economics; Industry,
Business & Management; Politics & World
Affairs*

New Titles: 9 (1995), 8 (1996)
No of Employees: 23
Annual Turnover: £1.7M

ISBNs, Imprints & Series:
1 898128 Bulletin (quarterly), Conference
Reports (irregular), European Economic
Perspectives (bi-monthly), Monitoring
European Integration (annual)

Overseas Representation *(see §7.3):*
USA & Canada: The Brookings Institution,
Washington, DC, USA

1176

**CENTRE FOR INFORMATION ON
LANGUAGE TEACHING & RESEARCH**
20 Bedfordbury, London WC2N 4LB
Telephone: 0171 379 5101
Fax: 0171 379 5082
Email: publications@cilt.org.uk

Mail Order:
PO Box 8, Llandysul, Dyfed SA44 4ZB
Telephone: 01559 370422
Fax: 01559 370464

Head of Publications: Ute Hitchin

Languages & Linguistics

New Titles: 15 (1995), 16 (1996)
No of Employees: 20
Annual Turnover: £150,000

ISBNs, Imprints & Series:
0 903466, 0 948003, 0 9500528, 1 874016

Overseas Representation *(see §7.3):*
Australia & New Zealand: Intext Book Co Pty
Ltd, Melbourne & Fairfield, Australia
*Worldwide (excluding Australia & New
Zealand):* Delta Ltd, Addlestone, Surrey, UK

Book Trade Association Membership: PA,
EPC

1177

*CHADWYCK-HEALEY LTD
The Quorum, Barnwell Road, Cambridge
CB5 8SW
Telephone: 01223 215512
Fax: 01223 215514

Directors: Sir C. E. Chadwyck-Healey
(Chairman)
Lady A. M. Chadwyck-Healey
D. McCrae *(Finance)*
S. Hall *(Sales)*
Ms A. Moss *(Publishing)*
Managers: J. C. Russell *(Promotions)*
Ms I. Markan *(Production)*

*Academic & Scholarly; Architecture & Design;
Atlases & Maps; Bibliography & Library
Science; Biology & Zoology; Cinema, Video,
TV & Radio; Economics; Electronic
(Educational); Electronic (Professional &
Academic); Fine Art & Art History; Gender
Studies; Geography & Geology; History &
Antiquarian; Languages & Linguistics;
Literature & Criticism; Mathematics &
Statistics; Music; Poetry; Politics & World
Affairs; Reference Books, Directories &
Dictionaries; Theatre, Drama & Dance*

ISBNs, Imprints & Series: 0 85964

Overseas Representation *(see §7.3):*
France: Chadwyck-Healey France SARL,
Paris
Spain: Chadwyck-Healey SL, Madrid
USA: Chadwyck-Healey Inc, Alexandria, VA

1178

**THE CHALFORD PUBLISHING CO
LTD**
St Mary's Mill, Chalford, Glos GL6 8NX
Telephone: 01453 883300
Fax: 01453 883233

Directors: Nick Murphy *(Managing)*
Alan Sutton
Michael Walton *(Finance)*
Production Manager: Simon Thraves
Commissioning Editor: David Buxton

Aviation; History & Antiquarian;
Photography; Travel & Topography

New Titles: 90 (1995), 130 (1996)
No of Employees: 15
Annual Turnover: £1M

ISBNs, Imprints & Series:
0 7524 The Archive Photographs Series

Associated & Subsidiary Companies:
France: Editions Alan Sutton. *USA:* Chalford
Publishing Corporation

Overseas Representation *(see §7.3)*:
France: Stephane Mallegol, Joué-lès-Tours
USA: James Burkinshaw, Dover, NH

1179 ▬▬▬▬▬▬▬▬▬▬▬▬

CHALKSOFT LTD
PO Box 49, Spalding, Lincs PE11 1NZ
Telephone: 01775 769518
Fax: 01775 762618

Managing Director: David Baldwin
Office Manager: Mrs Gillian Baldwin *(Sales
& Rights)*

Academic & Scholarly; Animal Care &
Breeding; Children's Books; Educational &
Textbooks; Electronic (Educational);
Gardening; Geography & Geology;
Mathematics & Statistics; Music; Natural
History; Scientific & Technical

New Titles: 10 (1995), 15 (1996)
No of Employees: 12

ISBNs, Imprints & Series:
1 85116 Chalksoft, Nene Valley Publishing,
School Garden Co, SGC Books

Associated & Subsidiary Companies:
Nene Valley Publishing; School Garden Co

Book Trade Association Membership: IPG

1180 ▬▬▬▬▬▬▬▬▬▬▬▬

**CHANCEREL INTERNATIONAL
PUBLISHERS LTD**
120 Long Acre, London WC2E 9PA
Telephone: 0171 240 2811
Fax: 0171 836 4186

Editorial Manager: P. A. Cassidy
Director: W. D. B. Prowse

Educational & Textbooks; Languages &
Linguistics

ISBNs, Imprints & Series:
0 899888, 0 905703

1181 ▬▬▬▬▬▬▬▬▬▬▬▬

CHANNEL 4 LEARNING
Leah House, 10A Great Titchfield Street,
London W1P 7AA
Telephone: 0171 580 8181
Fax: 0171 580 9350
Email: etc@schools.channel4.co.uk
Web Site: http://www.schools.channel4.co.uk/
c4schools

Trade Enquiries & Orders:
PO Box 100, Warwick CV34 6TZ
Telephone: 01926 433333
Fax: 01926 450178

Publications Manager: Penny Vogler
Chief Executive: Davina Lloyd
Finance: Phillip Bond

Children's Books; Cinema, Video, TV & Radio;
Educational & Textbooks; Electronic
(Educational); Poetry

1182 ▬▬▬▬▬▬▬▬▬▬▬▬

GEOFFREY CHAPMAN
Wellington House, 125 Strand, London
WC2R 0BB
Telephone: 0171 420 5555
Fax: 0171 240 7261

Distribution:
Cassell Plc, Stanley House, 3 Fleets Lane,
Poole, Dorset BH15 3AJ
Telephone: 01202 665432
Fax: 01202 666219

Directors: Philip Sturrock *(Chairman)*
Stephen Butcher *(Managing)*
Frank Roney *(Finance)*
Ruth McCurry *(UK Sales)*
Martyn Chapman *(Distribution & Commercial)*
Managers: Rebecca Seymour *(Export Sales)*
Gill Paterson *(Publisher)*

Religion & Theology

New Titles: 40 (1995), 40 (1996)

ISBNs, Imprints & Series: 0 225

Parent Company:
Cassell Plc

Associated & Subsidiary Companies:
see: Cassell Plc

Overseas Representation *(see §7.3)*:
See: Cassell Plc, UK

1183 ▬▬▬▬▬▬▬▬▬▬▬▬

PAUL CHAPMAN PUBLISHING LTD
144 Liverpool Road, London N1 1LA
Telephone: 0171 609 5315/5316
Fax: 0171 700 1057

Distribution:
Plymbridge Distributors, Estover, Plymouth
PL6 7PZ
Telephone: 01752 202300
Fax: 01752 202330

Directors: Paul Chapman *(Managing)*
Marianne Lagrange *(Editorial)*

Academic & Scholarly; Accountancy &
Taxation; Economics; Educational &
Textbooks; Environment & Development
Studies; Geography & Geology; Industry,
Business & Management; Law

New Titles: 29 (1995), 34 (1996)

ISBNs, Imprints & Series: 1 85396

Associated & Subsidiary Companies:
USA: Markus Wiener *(accountancy list)*;
Stenhouse Publishers

Overseas Representation *(see §7.3)*:
Australia & New Zealand: Eleanor Brasch
Associates, Artarmon, NSW, Australia
Canada: Irwin Publishing Inc, West Concord
Caribbean & Africa: Kelvin van Hasselt
Publishing Services, Lymington, UK
Far East: Simon & Schuster (Asia) Pte Ltd,
Singapore
Germany, Austria & Switzerland: The John
Wilde Partnership, Oxford, UK
India: Disvan Enterprises, New Delhi
Italy, Greece & Malta: Turnkey Projects Ltd,
Buckingham, UK
Latin America: Publishing, Marketing &
Research Associates, New York, USA
Middle East & Cyprus: Berj Jamkojian,
Vienna, Austria
Netherlands, Belgium & France: Kemper
Conseil, Voorburg, Netherlands
Scandinavia: Colin Flint, Harlow, UK
South Africa: Academic Marketing Services,
London, UK
Spain & Portugal: Arie Ruitenbeek, Madrid,
Spain
USA: Taylor & Francis Inc, Bristol, PA
Zimbabwe, Malawi & Zambia: Barbie Keene,
Harare, Zimbabwe

Book Trade Association Membership: IPG

1184 ▬▬▬▬▬▬▬▬▬▬▬▬

CHAPMAN & HALL LTD
2–6 Boundary Row, London SE1 8HN
Telephone: 0171 865 0066
Fax: 0171 522 9623
Email: needtoknow@chall.co.uk
Web Site: http://www.chaphall.com/chaphall.
html

Warehouse:
Cheriton House, North Way, Andover, Hants
SP10 5BE
Telephone: 01264 332424
Fax: 01264 364418

Directors: Dana Dreibelbis *(USA)*
Michael Dixon *(Managing)*
Barend ter Haar *(Marketing)*
Alan Davis *(Financial)*
Gavin McDonald *(Production)*
Anna Bisztyga *(Rights)*
Publishing Directors: John Lavender
(Electronic)
Phillip Read *(Spon)*
Nick Dunton *(Biomedical)*
John Buckingham *(Scientific Data)*

Academic & Scholarly; Agriculture;
Architecture & Design; Biology & Zoology;
Chemistry; Computer Science; Engineering;
Geography & Geology; Industry, Business &
Management; Mathematics & Statistics;
Reference Books, Directories & Dictionaries;
Scientific & Technical

New Titles: 444 (1995), 472 (1996)
No of Employees: 140

ISBNs, Imprints & Series:
0 412 Chapman & Hall
0 419 Spon
0 7514 Blackie Academic & Professional

Parent Company:
The Thomson Corporation

Associated & Subsidiary Companies:
Blackie Academic & Professional; E. & F. N.
Spon

Distributor for:
USA: American Public Health Association;
Humana Press

Overseas Representation *(see §7.3)*:
Australia & New Zealand: Chapman & Hall
Australia, South Melbourne, Australia
*Australia (for professional and reference books
only) (non exclusive supplier)):* DA
Information Services, Mitcham, Vic,
Australia
Botswana & Zambia: The Educational Book
Service (Pty) Ltd, Gabarone, Botswana
China, Hong Kong & Macau: Asia Publisher
Services Ltd, Hong Kong
Eastern Europe: Chapman & Hall Ltd, London,
UK
Germany: Chapman & Hall GmbH, Weinheim
Ghana: J. A. Amoah, Accra
India: R. Seshadri, Madras
Iran: Vijeh Nashr International, Tehran
Irish Republic: Susanne Baines, Dublin
Italy: Marcello SNC, Padua
Japan, Korea & Taiwan: Chapman & Hall
Japan, Tokyo, Japan
Korea: International Thomson Publishing –
Asia, Seoul, Korea, South
Malaysia: International Thomson Publishing
Asia, Petaling Jaya
Middle East & North Africa: Z. Kaviani, Dubai,
UAE
Nigeria: Publisher Support Services Ltd, Ikeja
Singapore, Philippines, Indonesia & Brunei:
International Thomson Publishing Asia,
Singapore
South Africa: Fergus Hall, Halfway House
South America: Michael Bates, Rio de Janeiro,
Brazil
Taiwan: International Thomson Publishing –
Asia, Taipei
Thailand: International Thomson Publishing
Asia, Bangkok
Uganda: MK General School Supplies Ltd,
Kampala
USA & Canada: Chapman & Hall, New York,
USA
West Africa: J. A. Amoah, Accra, Ghana
Zimbabwe: Barbie Keene, Harare

Book Trade Association Membership: PA

1185

CHAPMANS
[Imprint of The Orion Publishing Group Ltd]
Orion House, 5 Upper St Martins Lane,
Covent Garden, London WC2H 9EA
Telephone: 0171 240 3444
Fax: 0171 240 4822

Distribution:
Littlehampton Book Services,
10–14 Eldon Way, Lineside Estate,
Littlehampton BN17 7HE
Telephone: 01903 726410
Fax: 01903 730914

*Biography & Autobiography; Cinema, Video,
TV & Radio; Economics; Fiction; Humour;*

*Illustrated & Fine Editions; Politics & World
Affairs; Sports & Games; Memoirs*

ISBNs, Imprints & Series: 1 85592

Parent Company:
The Orion Publishing Group Ltd

Associated & Subsidiary Companies:
Northcliffe Books

Overseas Representation *(see §7.3)*:
see: The Orion Publishing Group Ltd, London,
UK

1186

**THE CHARTERED INSTITUTE OF
PUBLIC FINANCE & ACCOUNTANCY**
3 Robert Street, London WC2N 6BH
Telephone: 0171 543 5600
Fax: 0171 543 5700

Publications Manager: Stephen Wilkins

Accountancy & Taxation; Economics

New Titles: 97 (1995), 90 (1996)
No of Employees: 250
Annual Turnover: £17M

ISBNs, Imprints & Series: 0 85299

Book Trade Association Membership:
ALPSP

1187

**CHARTWELL-BRATT (PUBLISHING &
TRAINING) LTD**
Old Orchard, Bickley Road, Bromley, Kent
BR1 2NE
Telephone: 0181 467 1956
Fax: 0181 467 1754
Email: philip@chartwel.demon.co.uk
Web Site: http://www.studli.se/chartwell.html

Warehouse:
The Trade Counter, The Airfield,
Norwich Road, Mendlesham, Suffolk
IP14 5NA

Manager, Software & Publishing: Philip
Yorke

*Academic & Scholarly; Computer Science;
Educational & Textbooks; Electronic
(Educational); Electronic (Professional &
Academic); Engineering; Industry, Business &
Management; Languages & Linguistics;
Mathematics & Statistics; Philosophy;
Physics; Reference Books, Directories &
Dictionaries; Religion & Theology; Scientific
& Technical; Sociology & Anthropology*

New Titles: 28 (1995), 28 (1996)

ISBNs, Imprints & Series:
0 86238, 91 44

Parent Company:
Studentlitteratur AB *(Sweden)*

Distributor for:
Sweden: Lund University Press

Overseas Representation *(see §7.3)*:
Germany: Bratt-Institut für Neues Lernen
GmbH, Goch
Irish Republic: Academic Book Marketing
(Ireland), Ashbourne
Japan: Toppan Co Ltd, Tokyo
Scandinavia: Studentlitteratur AB, Lund,
Sweden

1188

*CHATTO & WINDUS LTD
Random House, 20 Vauxhall Bridge Road,
London SW1V 2SA
Telephone: 0171 973 9000
Fax: 0171 233 6123

Warehouse & Orders:
Tiptree Book Services Ltd, St Lukes Chase,
Tiptree, Essex CO5 0SR
Telephone: 01621 816362
Fax: 01621 819011

Directors: Alison Samuel *(Editorial)*
Jonathan Burnham *(Editorial)*
Barry Featherstone *(Production)*
Anthony McConnell *(Finance)*
Company Secretary: Roger Smith

*Cookery, Wines & Spirits; Crime; Fiction;
Gardening; Poetry; Politics & World Affairs*

ISBNs, Imprints & Series:
0 7011 Chatto & Windus
0 7012 The Hogarth Press

Parent Company:
Random House UK Ltd

Associated & Subsidiary Companies:
Arrow Books Ltd; Barrie & Jenkins Ltd; The
Bodley Head Ltd; Jonathan Cape Ltd; Century
Publishing Co Ltd; Hutchinson Books Ltd;
Stanley Paul & Co Ltd

Overseas Representation *(see §7.3)*:
Australia: Random House Australia Pty Ltd,
Sydney, NSW
Canada: Random House of Canada Ltd,
Mississauga
Europe: Random House UK Ltd, London, UK
India: Rupa & Co Ltd, New Delhi
New Zealand: Random House New Zealand
Ltd, Auckland
South Africa: Random House South Africa Pty
Ltd, Rosebank, Johannesburg
West Indies: Emily Feffer, New York, USA

Book Trade Association Membership: PA,
BDC, CAPP

1189

**CHILD'S PLAY (INTERNATIONAL)
LTD**
Ashworth Road, Bridgemead, Swindon, Wilts
SN5 7YD
Telephone: 01793 616286
Fax: 01793 512795

Chairman: Michael Twinn
Sales Director: Jane Hickson
Managers: Peter Constable *(Distribution)*
Paul Gerrish *(Export)*
Alan Johnson *(Production)*

Children's Books

New Titles: 29 (1995), 17 (1996)
No of Employees: 20

ISBNs, Imprints & Series:
0 85953 Child's Play
0 85985 Questron

Distributor for:
Germany: F. X. Schmid

Overseas Representation *(see §7.3):*
Australia: Child's Play Australia, Terrey Hills, NSW
Canada: Child's Play, Mississauga
France: Child's Play France, St Meloir des Ondes
Greece: Child's Play Greece, Athens
Hong Kong, Taiwan, Korea, People's Republic of China & Micronesia: Knowledge Craft Ltd, Hong Kong
Malta: Child's Play Malta, Valletta
New Zealand: Educational Equipment Wholesale Ltd, Auckland
Poland: Wydawnictwo i Ksiegarnie, Elzbieta Jarmolkiewicz, Warsaw
Singapore: Kiwikraft
South Africa: Leo Books, Roggebaai & Cape Town
United Arab Emirates: Child's Play Dubai, Dubai, UAE
USA: Child's Play USA, Lewiston, ME

Book Trade Association Membership: BDC, EPC, IPG

1190 ▄▄▄▄▄▄▄▄▄▄▄

CHIVERS PRESS LTD
Windsor Bridge Road, Bath BA2 3AX
Telephone: 01225 335336
Fax: 01225 310771

Directors: Simon Gibbs *(Managing)*
Julian R. Batson *(Publishing)*
Nicole Kirkman *(Editorial, Rights & Permissions)*
Mike Bowen *(Financial)*

Biography & Autobiography; Children's Books; Crime; Fiction; Large Print Editions; Spoken Word Cassettes

New Titles: 996 (1995), 993 (1996)
No of Employees: 74
Annual Turnover: £9M

ISBNs, Imprints & Series:
0 7451 Cherrytree Books, Children's Large Print Galaxy, Large Print Chivers, Paragon Softcover Large Print, Softcover Large Print Camden
0 85046
0 85119
0 85997 Gunsmoke Westerns
0 86220 Black Dagger Crime, Cavalcade Story Cassettes, Windsor Large Print

Parent Company:
The Gieves Group Plc

Associated & Subsidiary Companies:
Cherrytree Press Ltd

Distributor for:
USA: G. K. Hall & Co (Large Print Books only)

Overseas Representation *(see §7.3):*
Australia: Southern Scene (Pty) Ltd, Kingsgrove, NSW
Canada (Books only): S & B Large Print & Special Lines Ltd, Toronto, Canada
New Zealand (Cherrytree only): Peribo Pty Ltd, Mount Kuring-gai, NSW, Australia
New Zealand (large print, audio and normal print books excluding Cherrytree): The Library Supply Co Ltd, Auckland, New Zealand
Singapore & Malaysia: Publishers Marketing Services Ltd, Singapore
South Africa (audio only): Listeners Library Pty Ltd, Parkhurst, South Africa
South Africa (Cherrytree only): Southern Book Publishers, Halfway House, South Africa
South Africa (large print only): Maureen Hargraves, Claremont, South Africa

1191 ▄▄▄▄▄▄▄▄▄▄▄

CHRISTIAN FOCUS PUBLICATIONS
Geanies House, Fearn, Tain, Ross-shire IV20 1TW
Telephone: 01862 871541
Fax: 01862 871699

Managing Director: William MacKenzie
General Manager: Ian Thompson
Managing Editor: Malcolm Maclean

Children's Books; Religion & Theology

New Titles: 60 (1995), 65 (1996)
No of Employees: 20
Annual Turnover: £600,000

ISBNs, Imprints & Series:
0 906731, 1 85792, 1 871676

Parent Company:
Balintore Holdings

Associated & Subsidiary Companies:
Focus on the Bible; Mentor

Distributor for:
Rutherford House

Overseas Representation *(see §7.3):*
Australia & New Zealand: Scripture Union Wholesale, Wellington, New Zealand
Canada: Beacon Distributing, Paris, Ont
South Africa: Dayspring, Durban
USA: Spring Arbor Distributors, Belleville

Book Trade Association Membership:
Evangelical Christian Publishers Association (USA), Christian Booksellers Association, Christian Booksellers Convention

1192 ▄▄▄▄▄▄▄▄▄▄▄

CHRISTIAN RESEARCH ASSOCIATION
Vision Building, 4 Footscray Road, Eltham, London SE9 2TZ
Telephone: 0181 294 1989
Fax: 0181 294 0014
Email: 100616.1657@compuserve.com

Publishing Director: Dr Peter Brierley *(Rights & Permissions)*
Marketing Manager: Miss Heather Wraight *(Home & Export Sales)*

Reference Books, Directories & Dictionaries; Religion & Theology

New Titles: 5 (1995), 3 (1996)
No of Employees: 5

ISBNs, Imprints & Series:
0 947697, 1 85321

Distributor for:
MARC International. *Australia:* Christian Research Association

Overseas Representation *(see §7.3):*
Australia: Christian Research Association, Kew
Finland: Soumen World Vision, Helsinki
Norway: China Institute, Oslo
South Africa: Christian Info, Welkom
USA: MARC International, Monrovia, CA

1193 ▄▄▄▄▄▄▄▄▄▄▄

*CHURCH HOUSE PUBLISHING
Church House, Great Smith Street, London SW1P 3NZ
Telephone: 0171 222 9011
Fax: 0171 340 0281

Trade Distribution:
Canterbury Press Norwich, St Mary's Works, St Mary's Plain, Norwich NR3 3BH
Telephone: Norwich 01603 616563
Fax: 01603 624483

Managers: Alan Mitchell *(Publishing, Rights & Permissions)*
Helena Smalman-Smith *(Promotions)*
Hamish Bruce *(Commissioning Editor)*
Katharine Allenby *(Editorial)*

Children's Books; Educational & Textbooks; Reference Books, Directories & Dictionaries; Religion & Theology

ISBNs, Imprints & Series:
0 7151 Church House Publishing, National Society / Church House Publishing
0 901819 The National Society

Parent Company:
General Synod of the Church of England

Overseas Representation *(see §7.3):*
Australia: Charles Paine Pty Ltd, North Paramatta, NSW

Book Trade Association Membership: PA

1194 ▄▄▄▄▄▄▄▄▄▄▄

CHURCHILL LIVINGSTONE
[a division of Pearson Professional Ltd]
Robert Stevenson House, 1–3 Baxter's Place, Leith Walk, Edinburgh EH1 3AF
Telephone: 0131 556 2424
Fax: 0131 558 1278

Warehouse:
see Pearson Professional Ltd

London Editorial:
Churchill Livingstone, 102-108 Clerkenwell Road, London EC1M 5SA
Telephone: 0171 282 8401
Fax: 0171 282 8355

Directors: Andrew Stevenson *(Managing)*
Timothy Wright *(Sales)*
Peter Shepherd *(Nursing & Allied Health)*
Peter Richardson *(Health Care Information & Management)*
John Richardson *(Publishing Services)*
Eileen Horne *(Personnel & Administration)*
Mary Law *(Editorial – Nursing)*
Managers: Timothy Horne *(Publishing)*
Gaye Turner *(Rights)*
Susan Jerdan-Taylor *(Marketing)*
Tony Histed *(UK Sales)*
Caroline McNamara *(European Sales)*

Academic & Scholarly; Electronic (Professional & Academic); Medical (incl. Self Help & Alternative Medicine)

New Titles: 120 (1995), 150 (1996)
No of Employees: 147
Annual Turnover: £32M

ISBNs, Imprints & Series: 0 443

Parent Company:
Pearson Professional Ltd

Associated & Subsidiary Companies:
USA: Churchill Livingstone Inc

Distributor for:
USA: Little, Brown Medical

Book Trade Association Membership: PA, IGSMTP, CAPP

1195 ▬▬

CICERONE PRESS
2 Police Square, Milnthorpe, Cumbria LA7 7PY
Telephone: 015395 62069
Fax: 015395 63417

Directors: D. Unsworth *(Sales)*
W. Unsworth *(Editorial, Rights & Permissions)*
R. B. Evans *(Production)*
A. Evans *(Production)*

Guide Books; History & Antiquarian; Natural History; Sports & Games; Travel & Topography

New Titles: 28 (1995), 24 (1996)
No of Employees: 7

ISBNs, Imprints & Series:
0 902363, 1 85284

Overseas Representation *(see §7.3)*:
Europe: Bill Bailey Publishers Representatives, Newton Abbot, UK

1196 ▬▬

*CLAIBORNE PUBLICATIONS
Kiln Farm, East End Green, Brightlingsea, Colchester, Essex CO7 0SX
Telephone: 01206 305554
Fax: 01206 304545

Crafts & Hobbies; Environment & Development Studies

1197 ▬▬

T. & T. CLARK
59 George Street, Edinburgh EH2 2LQ
Telephone: 0131 225 4703
Fax: 0131 220 4260

Director: Dr Geoffrey F. Green *(Managing & Publishing, Rights & Permissions)*
Production: J.L. Law
Publicity: Jane Grounsell *(Home & Export Sales)*

Academic & Scholarly; Educational & Textbooks; Law; Philosophy; Religion & Theology

New Titles: 50 (1995), 60 (1996)
No of Employees: 16

ISBNs, Imprints & Series: 0 567

Distributor for:
USA: Eerdmans *(selected titles only)*; HarperCollins San Francisco *(selected titles only)*; Scribners *(selected titles only)*; Westminster/John Knox Press *(selected titles only)*

Overseas Representation *(see §7.3)*:
Austria, Croatia, Czech & Slovak Republics, France, Gibraltar, Greece, Hungary, Italy, Poland, Portugal, Slovenia, Spain & Switzerland: Patrick Bygate & Juliusz Komarnicki, Massagno, Switzerland
Belgium, Luxembourg, Netherlands & Germany: PKB – Robbert J. Pleysier, Heerde, Netherlands
Denmark, Finland, Iceland, Norway & Sweden: Ove B. Poulsen, Glostrup, Denmark
USA: Books International Inc, Herndon, VA

1198 ▬▬

ANTHONY CLARKE BOOKS
16 Garden Court, Wheathampstead, Herts AL4 8RF
Telephone: 01582 832460

Directors: Anthony Clarke *(Managing, Sales)*
Elaine Clarke *(Secretary)*
Overseas Sales: Denis Clarke

Philosophy; Religion & Theology

ISBNs, Imprints & Series:
0 85650 Marian Series

Associated & Subsidiary Companies:
USA: Source Books

Distributor for:
USA: Abbey Press; Loyola University Press; Oakwood Publishers; Source Books California

Overseas Representation *(see §7.3)*:
Australia: Charles Paine Pty Ltd, North Paramatta, NSW
India: Examiner Bookshop, Bombay
New Zealand: Catholic Supplies (NZ) Ltd, Wellington
USA: Source Books, Trabuco, CA

1199 ▬▬

JAMES CLARKE & CO
PO Box 60, Cambridge CB1 2NT

Telephone: 01223 350865
Fax: 01223 66951
Email: lutterworth.pr@dial.pipex.com

Managing Director: Adrian Brink *(Rights)*
Managers: Colin Lester *(Sales)*
Ken Johnson *(Production)*
Terèsine Milner *(Permissions)*
Customer Service: Christine Hutchinson

Academic & Scholarly; History & Antiquarian; Philosophy; Reference Books, Directories & Dictionaries; Religion & Theology

New Titles: 1 (1995), 2 (1996)
No of Employees: 7

ISBNs, Imprints & Series:
0 227 James Clarke
0 906554 Acorn Editions

Associated & Subsidiary Companies:
The Lutterworth Press

Overseas Representation *(see §7.3)*:
Australia: Keith Ainsworth Pty Ltd, Penrith, NSW
New Zealand (religious books only): Catholic Supplies (NZ) Ltd, Wellington, New Zealand
Spain & Portugal: Iberian Book Services SL, Madrid, Spain

Book Trade Association Membership: PA, IPG

1200 ▬▬

NIGEL J. CLARKE PUBLICATIONS
Unit 2, Russell House, Lym Close, Lyme Regis, Dorset
Telephone: 01297 442513
Fax: 01297 442513

Manager: Penny Hall

Aviation; Educational & Textbooks; Guide Books; History & Antiquarian; Magic & the Occult; Natural History; Nautical

ISBNs, Imprints & Series: 0 907683

Book Trade Association Membership: IPG

1201 ▬▬

CLASS PUBLISHING
Barb House, Bard Mews, London W6 7PA
Telephone: 0171 371 2119
Fax: 0171 371 2878
Email: class@classpub.eunet.co.uk

Trade Enquiries & Orders & Distribution:
Plymbridge Distributors Ltd,
Plymbridge House, Estover Road, Plymouth, Devon PL6 7PZ
Telephone: 01752 695745
Fax: 01752 695668

Manager: Richard Warner
Law Editor: Melissa Chapman

Health & Beauty; History & Antiquarian; Law; Medical (incl. Self Help & Alternative Medicine); Scientific & Technical

ISBNs, Imprints & Series: 1 872362

Distributor for:
USA: Jones & Bartlett Inc

Book Trade Association Membership: IPG

1202 ▬▬▬▬▬▬

E. W. CLASSEY LTD
Oxford House, Marlborough Street, Faringdon,
Oxon SN7 7JP
Telephone: 01367 244700
Fax: 01367 244800

Mailing Address:
PO Box 93, Faringdon, Oxon SN7 7DR

Directors: Peter D. Classey *(Managing)*
Eric W. Classey

*Biography & Autobiography; Biology &
Zoology; Geography & Geology; Illustrated &
Fine Editions; Natural History*

New Titles: 7 (1995), 19 (1996)
No of Employees: 4

ISBNs, Imprints & Series:
Classey Books, Hedera Press

Distributor for:
France: Publications Sci. Nat.

Book Trade Association Membership: PA,
BA, IPG

1203 ▬▬▬▬▬▬

CLT PROFESSIONAL PUBLISHING
Wrens Court, 52–54 Victoria Road,
Sutton Coldfield, Birmingham B72 1SX
Telephone: 0121 355 0900
Fax: 0121 355 5517

Marketing Manager: Andrew Griffin
Publishers: Jane Belford
Andrew Prideaux

*Academic & Scholarly; Accountancy &
Taxation; Electronic (Professional &
Academic); Industry, Business & Management;
Law*

New Titles: 26 (1995), 27 (1996)

ISBNs, Imprints & Series: 1 85811

Overseas Representation *(see §7.3):*
Hong Kong: Bloomsbury Books Ltd

Book Trade Association Membership: IPG

1204 ▬▬▬▬▬▬

COACHWISE LTD
114 Cardigan Road, Headingley, Leeds
LS6 3BJ
Telephone: 0113 231 1310
Fax: 0113 231 9606

Deliveries only:
Units 2/3 Chelsea Close, off Amberley Road,
Armley, Leeds LS12 4HW
Telephone: 0113 231 1310
Fax: 0113 231 9606

Managing Director: Dr Tony Byrne
General Manager: Miss Kath Leonard
Head of Customer Care: Mrs Karen Wright

*Health & Beauty; Sports & Games; Leisure &
recreational management; Physical education;
Sports coaching; Sports equipment; Sports
science & sports medicine*

ISBNs, Imprints & Series: 0 947850

Parent Company:
The National Coaching Foundation

Book Trade Association Membership: PA,
Direct Marketing Association

1205 ▬▬▬▬▬▬

*LLOYD COLE
37 College Avenue, Maidenhead SL6 6AZ
Telephone: 01628 20809

*Children's Books; Gender Studies; Health &
Beauty; Industry, Business & Management;
Literature & Criticism; Philosophy; Poetry;
Reference Books, Directories & Dictionaries;
Crossword Puzzle Books; Driving*

ISBNs, Imprints & Series: 1 874052

Overseas Representation *(see §7.3):*
USA: Paul & Co Publishers Consortium Inc,
New York

Book Trade Association Membership: PA

1206 ▬▬▬▬▬▬

PETER COLLIN PUBLISHING LTD
1 Cambridge Road, Teddington, Middlesex
TW11 8DT
Telephone: 0181 943 3386
Fax: 0181 943 1673

Distributor:
Marston Book Services, PO Box 269,
Abingdon, Oxon OX14 4YN
Telephone: 01235 465500
Fax: 01235 465555

Directors: P. H. Collin *(Managing, Rights &
Permissions)*
S. M. H. Collin *(Technical, Sales)*

*Electronic (Educational); English as a Foreign
Language; Industry, Business & Management;
Reference Books, Directories & Dictionaries*

New Titles: 10 (1995), 10 (1996)

ISBNs, Imprints & Series: 0 948549

Overseas Representation *(see §7.3):*
Africa & Caribbean: Kelvin van Hasselt
Publishing Services, Lymington, UK
France: Editions Foucher, Paris
Greece, Cyprus & Middle East: Anthony
Rudkin Associates, Oxford, UK
Hong Kong: Transglobal Publishers Services
Ltd, Tsuen Wan
*Hungary, Czech Republic, Russia & Central
Europe:* Michael Timperley Marketing,
London, UK
Iran: Anthony Rudkin Iran, Tehran
Israel: London Publishers Agency, Ramat
HaSharon

Japan: Toppan Co Ltd, Tokyo
Mexico: Libreria Britanica SA, Mexico City
Netherlands: Intertaal, Amsterdam
Scandinavia: Croft & Croft, Leominster, UK
South East Asia: Reed International
(Singapore) Pte Ltd, Singapore
Spain & Portugal: Iberian Book Services SL,
Madrid, Spain
USA: ibd Ltd, Kinderhook, NY

Book Trade Association Membership: IPG

1207 ▬▬▬▬▬▬

COLLINS & BROWN
London House, Great Eastern Wharf,
Parkgate Road, London SW11 4NQ
Telephone: 0171 924 2575
Fax: 0171 924 7725

Distribution:
Biblios Distribution Services Ltd, Star Road,
Partridge Green, West Sussex RH13 8LD
Telephone: Partridge Green 01403 710971
Fax: 01403 711143

Rights & Co-editions: Cameron Brown
Publisher: Mark Collins
Directors: Kate MacPhee *(Production)*
Stuart Henderson *(Sales)*
Cindy Richards *(Editorial)*
Sarah Hoggett *(Editorial)*
Managers: Marian Silvester *(Sales)*
Sonia Pugh *(Marketing)*
Suzi Elsden *(Publicity)*

*Antiques & Collecting; Architecture & Design;
Biography & Autobiography; Cookery, Wines
& Spirits; Crafts & Hobbies; Do-It-Yourself;
Fine Art & Art History; Gardening; History &
Antiquarian; Illustrated & Fine Editions;
Literature & Criticism; Music; Natural
History; Photography; Travel & Topography*

New Titles: 27 (1995), 34 (1996)
No of Employees: 36

ISBNs, Imprints & Series:
1 85470, 1 85585

Associated & Subsidiary Companies:
Anaya Publishing Ltd; Belitha Press

Overseas Representation *(see §7.3):*
Australia: Peribo Pty Ltd, Mount Kuring-gai,
NSW
Canada: apply to London Office
Europe (excluding Netherlands): Onslow
Books Ltd, London, UK
Middle-East: Hugh C. Thomas, London, UK
Netherlands: Consul Books, Blaricum
New Zealand: Lothian Books NZ Ltd,
Auckland
South Africa: Struik Book Distributors,
Sandton
South East Asia (including Japan): Roger
Ward, London, UK

1208 ▬▬▬▬▬▬

**COMPUTATIONAL MECHANICS
PUBLICATIONS**
Ashurst Lodge, Ashurst, Southampton,
Hampshire SO40 7AA
Telephone: 01703 293223
Fax: 01703 292853

Email: cmp@cmp.co.uk
Web Site: http://www.cmp.co.uk/

Chairman: Prof. C. A. Brebbia
Managing Director: L. Sucharov *(Sales & Rights)*
Production Manager: (to be appointed)
Marketing: Ms Suzanne Drew
Sales & Ordering: Mrs Myra Mouland

Academic & Scholarly; Architecture & Design; Computer Science; Engineering; Mathematics & Statistics; Scientific & Technical; Environmental Modelling

New Titles: 50 (1995), 50 (1996)
No of Employees: 10
Annual Turnover: £0.5M

ISBNs, Imprints & Series:
0 905451, 1 85312 Advances in Fluid Mechanics, Computational Engineering Services, Engineering Software, Progress in Engineering, Topics in Engineering

Parent Company:
Computational Mechanics International Ltd

Overseas Representation *(see §7.3)*:
Australia & New Zealand: DA Information Services, Mitcham, Vic, Australia
Japan: Maruzen Co Ltd, Tokyo; Aims Corporation, Tokyo; Kaigai Publications Ltd, Tokyo
Korea: Kumi Trading Co Ltd, Seoul, Korea, South
USA: Computational Mechanics Inc, Billerica, MA

1209 ■

*CONRAN OCTOPUS
37 Shelton Street, London WC2H 9HN
Telephone: 0171 240 6961
Fax: 0171 836 9951

Distribution:
Reed Book Services, Northampton Road, Rushden, Northants NN10 6PU
Telephone: 01933 58521
Fax: 01933 50284

Publishing Director: John Wallace

Antiques & Collecting; Architecture & Design; Children's Books; Cookery, Wines & Spirits; Crafts & Hobbies; Do-It-Yourself; Gardening; Health & Beauty; Travel & Topography

ISBNs, Imprints & Series: 1 85029

Parent Company:
Reed International Books Ltd

Overseas Representation *(see §7.3)*:
Australia: Reed Books Australia, Melbourne, Vic
Canada: General Publishing Co Ltd, North York, Ont
East Asia: Reed Consumer Books, Metro Manila, Philippines
India: Reed Consumer Books, New Delhi
Japan: Reed Consumer Books, Tokyo
New Zealand: Reed Publishing Group, Auckland
Singapore: Reed International (Singapore) Pte Ltd

South Africa: Struik Book Distributors Pty Ltd, Johannesburg, Cape Town & Maitland

1210 ■

CONSERVATIVE POLITICAL CENTRE
32 Smith Square, Westminster, London SW1P 3HH
Telephone: 0171 222 9000
Fax: 0171 896 4163

Director: Alistair B. Cooke, OBE

Politics & World Affairs

New Titles: 12 (1995), 12 (1996)

ISBNs, Imprints & Series: 0 85070

Parent Company:
Conservative Central Office

1211 ■

CONSTABLE & CO LTD
3 The Lanchesters, 162 Fulham Palace Road, London W6 9ER
Telephone: 0181 741 3663
Fax: 0181 748 7562

Distributors:
Tiptree Book Services Ltd, Church Road, Tiptree, Colchester, Essex CO5 0SR
Telephone: 01621 816362
Fax: 01621 819011

Directors: Benjamin Glazebrook *(Chairman & Managing Director)*
Carol O'Brien *(Editorial)*
Richard Dodman *(Sales)*
Richard Tomkins *(Production)*
Yvette Evans-Foster *(Publicity)*
Financial: Adrian Andrews
Rights & Permissions: Benjamin Glazebrook

Archaeology; Biography & Autobiography; Crime; Fiction; Fine Art & Art History; Guide Books; History & Antiquarian; Military & War; Music; Photography; Psychology & Psychiatry; Reference Books, Directories & Dictionaries; Sociology & Anthropology; Travel & Topography; Celtic Studies

ISBNs, Imprints & Series:
0 09 Constable
0 486 Dover Publications Inc

Distributor for:
USA: Dover Publications Inc; Eland Books; Spellmount

Overseas Representation *(see §7.3)*:
Australia: Lothian Books, Port Melbourne
Canada: McClelland & Stewart, Toronto & Markham
Far East (excluding Japan): CKK Ltd Publishers' International Management, London, UK
India, Nepal, Bangladesh & Sri Lanka: Dass Media Pte Ltd, New Delhi, India
Italy & Greece: Penny Padovani, London, UK
Japan: Japan English Services Inc, Chiba-ken
Middle East & North Africa (excluding Ethiopia, Iran & Sudan), Western Europe (including Belgium, France, Germany, Austria & Switzerland): Richard Dodman, London, UK

Netherlands: Nilsson & Lamm BV, Weesp
New Zealand: Greene Phoenix Marketing, Helensville
Scandinavia: Saga Books Aps, Horsholm, Denmark
South Africa, Namibia & Zimbabwe: MacDonald Purnell (Pty) Ltd, Randburg, South Africa
Spain, Portugal & Gibraltar: Peter Prout, Madrid, Spain

Book Trade Association Membership: PA

1212 ■

COPPER BEECH PUBLISHING LTD
PO Box 159, East Grinstead, Sussex RH19 4FS
Telephone: 01342 314734
Fax: 01342 314734

Rights: Jan Barnes
Editorial: Julie Lessels

History & Antiquarian; Gift Books

New Titles: 7 (1995)

ISBNs, Imprints & Series:
0 9516295, 1 898617

Book Trade Association Membership: IPG

1213 ■

IVAN CORBETT PUBLISHING
Islington Wharf, Penryn, Cornwall TR10 8AT
Telephone: 01326 374339
Fax: 01326 378340

Partners: Ivan Corbett
Paul White

Guide Books; History & Antiquarian; Travel & Topography

ISBNs, Imprints & Series:
0 85025 Tor Mark Press
0 904836 Ivan Corbett Publishing

Associated & Subsidiary Companies:
Tor Mark Press

Distributor for:
Dyllansow Truran; Hillside Publications

1214 ■

COTTAGE PUBLICATIONS
15 Ballyhay Road, Donaghadee, Co Down BT21 0NG
Telephone: 01247 883876
Fax: 01247 883876

Partners: Timothy S. Johnston
Alison Johnston

Illustrated & Fine Editions

New Titles: 4 (1995), 4 (1996)
No of Employees: 3

ISBNs, Imprints & Series: 0 9516402

Book Trade Association Membership: PA

1215

COUNCIL FOR BRITISH ARCHAEOLOGY
Bowes Morrell House, 111 Walmgate, York
YO1 2UA
Telephone: 01904 671417
Fax: 01904 671384
Email: 100271.456@compuserve.com
Web Site: http://britac3.britac.ac.uk/cba/

Director: Richard Morris
Managing Editor: Christine Pietrowski
Officers: Carol Pyrah *(Conservation)*
Donald Henson *(Education)*
Michael Heyworth *(Information)*
Peter Olver *(Finance)*

Archaeology

New Titles: 10 (1995), 10 (1996)
No of Employees: 13
Annual Turnover: £0.5M

ISBNs, Imprints & Series:
0 900312, 0 906780, 1 872414 Archaeological
Yearbook, Archaeology of Lincoln,
Archaeology of York, CBA Research
Reports, Practical Handbooks in
Archaeology

Overseas Representation *(see §7.3):*
USA: Humanities Press International Inc,
Atlantic Highlands, NJ

Book Trade Association Membership:
ALPSP

1216

COUNTRYSIDE BOOKS
2 Highfield Avenue, Newbury, Berks
RG14 5DS
Telephone: 01635 43816
Fax: 01635 551004

Publisher: Nicholas Battle
Partner: Suzanne Battle

*Guide Books; Travel & Topography; Local
History*

New Titles: 60 (1995), 60 (1996)

ISBNs, Imprints & Series:
0 86368, 0 905392, 1 85306, 1 85455

Parent Company:
Countryside Book UK

Associated & Subsidiary Companies:
Local Heritage Books UK

Distributor for:
Bracken Publishing; Cube Publications Ltd;
John Donald Ltd *(Discovering Series only)*;
The Dovecote Press; Kent County Council;
Meridian Books; Power Publications

1217

COUNTYVISE LTD
1 and 3 Grove Road, Rock Ferry, Birkenhead
L42 3XS
Telephone: 0151 645 2311/2872
Fax: 0151 645 8999

Directors: John Emmerson *(Managing)*
Jean Emmerson
Sales: Melanie Holt

*Biography & Autobiography; History &
Antiquarian; Humour; Natural History;
Religion & Theology; Sports & Games;
Transport*

New Titles: 8 (1995), 16 (1996)

ISBNs, Imprints & Series:
0 907768
0 9516129 Merseyside Port Folios
1 871201 Liver Press
1 873245 Picton Press (Liverpool)

Book Trade Association Membership: PA,
IPG

1218

COVENANT PUBLISHING CO LTD
8 Blades Court, Deodar Road, Putney, London
SW15 2NU
Telephone: 0181 877 9010
Fax: 0181 871 4770

Accountant: A. Gibb

Religion & Theology

New Titles: 1 (1995), 1 (1996)
Annual Turnover: £26,000

ISBNs, Imprints & Series: 0 85205

Distributor for:
USA: Bonnie Gaunt; Covenant Media
Production; Destiny Publishers

Overseas Representation *(see §7.3):*
USA: Covenant Media Production, Thousand
Oaks, CA

Book Trade Association Membership: PA

1219

COVER TO COVER CASSETTES LTD
PO Box 112, Marlborough, Wilts SN8 3UG
Telephone: 01264 731227
Fax: 01264 731390

Representation:
Frances Lincoln Ltd, 4 Torriano Mews, London
NW5 2RZ

Managing Director: Helen Nicoll

Audio Books; Gardening

New Titles: 20 (1995), 20 (1996)
No of Employees: 7

ISBNs, Imprints & Series:
0 95270 Oxenwood Press (Gardening Books)
1 85549 Cover to Cover Cassettes (Audio
Cassettes)

Associated & Subsidiary Companies:
Oxenwood Press

1220

CRABTREE PUBLISHING CO
73 Lime Walk, Headington, Oxford OX3 7AD

Telephone: 01865 67575
Fax: 01865 750079

President: James Lavis *(Trade/Educational)*
Marketing Co-ordinator: Kathy Middleton
(Trade/Educational)
Warehouse Manager: Adrian Lavis *(Trade/
Educational)*
Customer Service: Fay Lavis *(Trade/
Educational)*

Children's Books; Educational & Textbooks

New Titles: 20 (1995), 30 (1996)

ISBNs, Imprints & Series:
0 86505 Animals & their Ecosystems Series,
Arctic World Series, Crabapples Series,
Crabtree Environment Series, Early Settler
Life Series, Endangered Animals Series,
Everyday Science Series, Great African
American Series, Historic Community
Series, Holidays & Festivals Series, In My
World Series, Lands Peoples & Cultures
Series, North American Wildlife Series,
Primary Ecology Series, Wonders of the
World Series

Parent Company:
Crabtree Publishing Co *(Canada)*

1221

CREATION BOOKS
83 Clerkenwell Road, London EC1R 5AR
Telephone: 0171 430 9878
Fax: 0171 242 5527

Directors: James Williamson *(Managing)*
Peter Colebrook
Editor: Laurence Raine

*Cinema, Video, TV & Radio; Crime; Fiction;
Gender Studies; Literature & Criticism; Magic
& the Occult; Music; Poetry; Science Fiction*

New Titles: 15 (1995), 15 (1996)

Parent Company:
Butcherbest Ltd

Overseas Representation *(see §7.3):*
Australia & New Zealand: Peribo Pty Ltd,
Mount Kuring-gai, NSW, Australia
Canada: Marginal Distribution, Peterborough
Europe: Turnaround Publishers Services Ltd,
London, UK
Japan: Charles E. Tuttle Co Inc, Kanagawa
USA: Subterranean Co, Monroe, OR

Book Trade Association Membership: PA

1222

CRÉCY BOOKS LTD
Unit 2A, Newbridge Trading Estate,
Newbridge Close, Bristol BS4 4AX
Telephone: 0117 972 4248
Fax: 0117 971 1056

Directors: Colin West
Clive Williams

Aviation; Military & War; Nautical

New Titles: 15 (1995), 10 (1996)

ISBNs, Imprints & Series: 0 947554

Overseas Representation *(see §7.3)*:
Australia: Peribo Pty Ltd, Mount Kuring-gai,
   NSW
Canada: Vanwell Publishing Ltd, St
   Catherines, Ont

1223

CRESCENT MOON PUBLISHING
18 Chaddesley Road, Kidderminster, Worcs
DY10 3AD
Telephone: 01622 209122

Director: Jeremy Robinson
Editors: C. Hughes
C. Hellawell
Design: Jean Kazan

*Academic & Scholarly; Biography &
Autobiography; Children's Books; Cinema,
Video, TV & Radio; Fiction; Fine Art & Art
History; Gardening; Gender Studies;
Literature & Criticism; Magic & the Occult;
Music; Philosophy; Photography; Poetry;
Reference Books, Directories & Dictionaries;
Religion & Theology; Sociology &
Anthropology; Theatre, Drama & Dance;
Travel & Topography*

New Titles: 11 (1995), 20 (1996)

ISBNs, Imprints & Series:
1 86171
1 871846 Crescent Moon
1 898283 Joe's Press

Overseas Representation *(see §7.3)*:
USA: State Mutual Book & Periodical Service
Ltd, New York

1224

CRESSRELLES PUBLISHING CO LTD
Unit 10, Station Road Industrial Estate,
Colwall, Malvern, Worcs WR13 6RN
Telephone: 01684 540154
Fax: 01684 540154

*History & Antiquarian; Theatre, Drama &
Dance; Travel & Topography*

New Titles: 4 (1995)

ISBNs, Imprints & Series: 0 85956

Associated & Subsidiary Companies:
Actinic Press; Kenyon-Deane; J. Garnet Miller
Ltd

Distributor for:
USA: Anchorage Press Inc *(through Kenyon-
Deane)*; I. E. Clarke Inc *(through J. Garnet
Miller)*

1225

PAUL H. CROMPTON LTD
102 Felsham Road, London SW15 1DQ
Telephone: 0181 780 1063
Fax: 0181 780 1063

Distribution:
Airlift Book Co, 26 Eden Grove, London
N7 8EF

Telephone: 0171 607 5792 & 5798
Fax: 0171 607 6714

Editorial, Production: Paul Crompton
   (Information Co-ordination)
Sales: Rosalie Brookhouse
Artistic, Design Director: Melissa Crompton
Book Rights: Henrietta Crompton

Martial Arts; Oriental Therapies; Survival

New Titles: 8 (1995), 12 (1996)
No of Employees: 6

ISBNs, Imprints & Series:
0 901764, 1 874250

Distributor for:
Canada: Masters. *France:* Budo-Store. *USA:*
Dragon Door Publications; High View
Publications; YMAA

Overseas Representation *(see §7.3)*:
Australia: Zen Imports Pty, Rozelle
South East Asia: APD Singapore Pte Ltd,
   Singapore
USA & Canada: The Talman Co, New York,
   NY, USA

1226

CRONER PUBLICATIONS LTD
Croner House, London Road,
Kingston upon Thames, Surrey KT2 6SR
Telephone: 0181 547 3333
Fax: 0181 547 2637

Directors: Hans Staal *(Managing)*
Chris Hilton-Childs *(Finance &
   Administration)*
Transport & Specialist: Michael Gilliat
Health & Safety, Insurance: Ruth Chapman
Employment/Business: David Johnston

*Accountancy & Taxation; Educational &
Textbooks; Industry, Business & Management;
Law; Reference Books, Directories &
Dictionaries; Transport*

ISBNs, Imprints & Series:
0 900319, 1 85452, 1 85524 Croner
   Publications
0 903393, 1 870080 Kluwer Publishing

Parent Company:
Wolters Kluwer NV *(Netherlands)*

1227

THE CROWOOD PRESS LTD
The Stable Block, Crowood Lane, Ramsbury,
Marlborough, Wiltshire SN8 2HR
Telephone: 01672 520320
Fax: 01672 520280

Distributors:
Bookpoint, 39 Milton Park, Abingdon, Oxon
OX14 4TD
Telephone: 01235 400400
Fax: 01235 832068

Chairman: John Dennis *(Publisher)*
Director: Ken Hathaway *(Managing)*
Rights & Permissions: Madeleine Hacking

*Animal Care & Breeding; Crafts & Hobbies;
Gardening; Natural History; Nautical; Sports
& Games; Transport*

New Titles: 52 (1995), 57 (1996)
No of Employees: 10

ISBNs, Imprints & Series:
0 946284, 1 85223, 1 86126

Overseas Representation *(see §7.3)*:
Australia: Peribo Pty Ltd, Mount Kuring-gai,
   NSW
Canada: Cavendish Books Inc, North
   Vancouver
Netherlands: Nilsson & Lamm BV, Weesp
New Zealand: David Bateman Ltd, Auckland
Scandinavia: D. Richard Bowen, Malmö,
   Sweden
Singapore, Malaysia & Brunei: Publishers
   Marketing Services Ltd, Singapore
South Africa: Verbatim Distributors,
   Constantia Hills
Southern Europe: Bookport Associates,
   Bologna, Italy
USA: Trafalgar Square Publications, North
   Pomfret, VT
Western Europe: Anselm Robinson, London,
   UK

1228

JAMES CURREY PUBLISHERS
54B Thornhill Square, Islington, London
N1 1BE
Telephone: 0171 609 9026
Fax: 0171 609 9605

Trade Enquiries & Orders:
Plymbridge Distribution Ltd, Estover,
Plymouth PL6 7PZ
Telephone: 01752 202301
Fax: 01752 202330

Chairman & Managing Director: James
   Currey
Editorial & Administration: Clare Currey
   (Director, Rights & Permissions)
Marketing & Sales: Keith Sambrook
   (Director)

*Academic & Scholarly; Agriculture;
Archaeology; Economics; Geography &
Geology; History & Antiquarian; Languages &
Linguistics; Law; Literature & Criticism;
Politics & World Affairs; Religion & Theology;
Sociology & Anthropology; Studies of Africa,
Caribbean; Studies of Third World*

New Titles: 26 (1995), 26 (1996)
No of Employees: 3

ISBNs, Imprints & Series: 0 85255

Overseas Representation *(see §7.3)*:
Caribbean: Ian Randle Publishers Ltd,
   Kingston, Jamaica
Kenya: East African Educational Publishers
   Ltd, Nairobi
South Africa: David Philip Publishers Pty Ltd,
   Claremont

1229

CURZON PRESS LTD
St John's Studios, Church Road, Richmond,
Surrey TW9 2QA

Telephone: 0181 948 5322/6
Fax: 0181 332 6735
Email: 100067.214@compuserve.com

Distribution:
Marston Book Services, PO Box 269,
Abingdon, Oxon OX14 4SD
Telephone: 01235 465500
Fax: 01235 465555

Chairman: Malcolm G. Campbell
Company Secretary: Martina B. Campbell

*Academic & Scholarly; Archaeology; History
& Antiquarian; Languages & Linguistics;
Literature & Criticism; Philosophy; Reference
Books, Directories & Dictionaries; Religion &
Theology; Sociology & Anthropology; Oriental
& African Studies*

New Titles: 50 (1995), 60 (1996)

ISBNs, Imprints & Series:
0 7007 Acta Kurdica, Collected Papers on
South Asia, Curzon Press, Durham
Indological Series, London Studies on South
Asia, Scandinavian Institute of Asian Studies
Monograph Series, Scandinavian Institute of
Asian Studies Occasional Papers, Studies on
Asian Topics
1 55729 IEAS
1 873410 China Library, Japan Library

Distributor for:
USA: IEAS *(selected titles)*

Overseas Representation *(see §7.3)*:
Australia: Eleanor Brasch Associates,
Artarmon, NSW
India: T. R. Publications Pvt Ltd, Madras
Japan: United Publishers Services Ltd, Tokyo
Korea: ICK, Seoul, Korea, South
Middle East: Berj Jamkojian, Vienna, Austria
Netherlands: Consul Books, Blaricum
Scandinavia: D. Richard Bowen, Malmö,
Sweden
Singapore: APD Singapore Pte Ltd
Spain & Portugal: Iberian Book Services SL,
Madrid, Spain
*USA & Canada (all titles except Middle East/
Islam, Judaism, Central Asia):* University of
Hawaii Press, USA
*USA & Canada (titles on Middle East/Islam,
Judaism, Central Asia:* Paul & Co Publishers
Consortium Inc, New York, USA

Book Trade Association Membership: IPG

1230 ▬▬▬▬▬▬▬▬▬▬▬▬▬

CYP LTD – CHILDREN'S AUDIO
The Fairway, Bush Fair, Harlow, Essex
CM18 6LY
Telephone: 01279 444707
Fax: 01279 445570

Directors: Paul Thorp *(Finance)*
Michael Kitson *(Managing)*
John Bassett *(Sales & Marketing)*

*Audio Books; Children's Books; Electronic
(Educational)*

New Titles: 23 (1995), 46 (1996)
No of Employees: 32

ISBNs, Imprints & Series:
1 85781 CYP (Children's Audio)
1 87144 PT (Playtime)

Distributor for:
Germany: Green Submarine

Overseas Representation *(see §7.3)*:
Australia: ABC Music, Artarmon, NSW
Far East: Richard Blady Booksales,
Macclesfield, UK
Germany: Verlag An der Ruhr, Mülheim
New Zealand: Golden Press Ltd, Auckland
*Saudi Arabia, United Arab Emirates, Quatar,
Oman, Bahrain & Kuwait:* Timbuktu
Records (UK) Ltd, London, UK
South Africa: Macdonald Purnell (Pty) Ltd,
Cleveland
South America: Humphrys Roberts Associates,
Cotia, Brazil; Humphrys Roberts Associates,
London, UK; Associacion De Distribuidores
y Editores, De Materiales De Ingles AC,
Mexico, DF, Mexico
Spain: Iberian Book Services SL, Madrid

Book Trade Association Membership: PA

1231 ▬▬▬▬▬▬▬▬▬▬▬▬▬

DALESMAN PUBLISHING CO LTD
Stable Courtyard, Broughton Hall, Skipton,
North Yorkshire BD23 3AE
Telephone: 01756 701381
Fax: 01756 701326

Warehouse, Trade Enquiries & Orders:
Clapham, via Lancaster LA2 8EB
Telephone: 015242 51225
Fax: 015242 51708

Chairman: Timothy Benn
Managing Director: C. G. Benn
General Manager: Robert Flanagan
Editor: Terry Fletcher
Marketing Manager: Barry Cox

*Crafts & Hobbies; Geography & Geology;
Guide Books; History & Antiquarian; Humour;
Travel & Topography*

ISBNs, Imprints & Series:
0 85206, 1 85568

1232 ▬▬▬▬▬▬▬▬▬▬▬▬▬

***DANCE BOOKS LTD**
15 Cecil Court, St Martins Lane, London
WC2N 4EZ
Telephone: 0171 836 2314
Fax: 0171 497 0473

Warehouse, Trade Enquiries & Orders:
Vine House Distribution, Waldenbury,
North Common, Chailey, East Sussex
BN8 4DR
Telephone: 01825 723398
Fax: 01825 724188

Editorial & Production: David Leonard
Sales: Richard Holland

*Academic & Scholarly; Music; Theatre, Drama
& Dance*

ISBNs, Imprints & Series:
0 903102, 1 85273

Distributor for:
USA: Dance Horizons; Princeton Book Co

Overseas Representation *(see §7.3)*:
Australia: Astam Books Pty Ltd, Leichhardt,
NSW
USA: Princeton Book Co, Princeton, NJ

Book Trade Association Membership: BA

1233 ▬▬▬▬▬▬▬▬▬▬▬▬▬

THE C. W. DANIEL COMPANY LTD
1 Church Path, Saffron Walden, Essex
CB10 1JP
Telephone: 01799 521909 & 526216
Fax: 01799 513462

Warehouse:
Unit 7, Saffron Business Centre,
Elizabeth Close, off Elizabeth Way,
Saffron Walden, Essex
Telephone: 01799 526633

Small Orders:
L. N. Fowler & Co Ltd, 1201 High Road,
Chadwell Heath, Romford, Essex RM6 4DH
Telephone: 0181 597 2491
Fax: 0181 598 2428

Directors: Ian Miller
Jane Miller *(Editor & Rights)*
Managers: Sharon Dare *(Accounts)*
Genevieve Miller *(Home & Export Sales)*
David Godfrey *(Warehouse)*

*Health & Beauty; Magic & the Occult; Medical
(incl. Self Help & Alternative Medicine);
Veterinary Science*

New Titles: 12 (1995), 14 (1996)
No of Employees: 5
Annual Turnover: £1M

ISBNs, Imprints & Series:
0 85032 Health Science Press
0 85207 The C. W. Daniel Company Ltd
0 85435, 0 85978 Neville Spearman Publishers

Distributor for:
Belgium: Editions Haug. *Germany:* Karl F.
Haug Verlag. *USA:* Brotherhood of Life

Overseas Representation *(see §7.3)*:
Australia: Gemcraft Books, Burwood, Vic
Canada: Biocosmic Books Inc, Barrie, Ont
Greece, Italy, Spain & Portugal: Bookport
Associates, Bologna, Italy
Irish Republic: Genny Kelliher Publishers
Representative, Monkstown
Israel: Astra Agency, Jerusalem
*Japan, Korea, Taiwan, Indonesia, Cambodia &
Vietnam:* Scott Brodie, Sydney, NSW,
Australia
Middle East: Michael Morris Associates,
Saffron Walden, UK
Netherlands & Scandinavia: Croft & Croft,
Leominster, UK
New Zealand: Forrester Books NZ Ltd,
Takapuna
Singapore: Asiapac Books Pte Ltd
South Africa: Alternative Books, Randburg
South East Asia: CKK Ltd Publishers'
International Management, London, UK
Sweden: Cedeseus AB, Halmstad
USA: New Leaf Distribution, Lithia Springs,
GA; National Book Network, Lanham, MD

1234

DANIELS MEDICA
38 Cambridge Place, Cambridge CB2 1NS
Telephone: 01223 467144
Fax: 01223 467145

Partner: Victor G. Daniels

*Academic & Scholarly; Biology & Zoology;
Chemistry; Educational & Textbooks; Health
& Beauty; Industry, Business & Management;
Mathematics & Statistics; Medical (incl. Self
Help & Alternative Medicine); Physics;
Scientific & Technical; Vocational Training &
Careers; Contract Publishing*

New Titles: 6 (1995), 6 (1996)
No of Employees: 3

Book Trade Association Membership: IPG

1235

DARTMOUTH PUBLISHING CO LTD
Gower House, Croft Road, Aldershot, Hants
GU11 3HR
Telephone: 01252 331551
Fax: 01252 344405

Distribution:
Ashgate Distribution Services, Unit 3,
Lower Farnham Road, Aldershot, Hants
Telephone: 01252 331551
Fax: 01252 344405

Chairman: Nigel Farrow
Managing Director: John Irwin
Company Secretary: Nigel Young

*Academic & Scholarly; Economics; Law;
Military & War; Philosophy; Politics & World
Affairs; Psychology & Psychiatry; Reference
Books, Directories & Dictionaries;
Management*

New Titles: 90 (1995), 110 (1996)
No of Employees: 9

ISBNs, Imprints & Series:
0 900178 Parliamentary Research Services
1 85521 Dartmouth Publishing Co

Overseas Representation *(see §7.3)*:
Australia: Ashgate-Gower Asia Pacific Pte Ltd,
Avalon, NSW
Japan: Maruzen Co Ltd, Tokyo; United
Publishers Services Ltd, Tokyo
South East Asia & Philippines: Ashgate Asia
Pacific Pte Ltd, Singapore
USA: Ashgate Publishing Co, Brookfield, VT

1236

*DARTON, LONGMAN & TODD LTD
1 Spencer Court,
140–142 Wandsworth High Street, London
SW18 4JJ
Telephone: 0181 875 0155
Fax: 0181 875 0133

Warehouse & Shipping:
Unit 9, Amor Way, Dunhams Lane,
Letchworth, Herts SG6 1UG
Telephone: 01462 673470
Fax: 01462 482742

Directors: Peter Green *(Accounts)*
Morag Reeve *(Editorial)*
Martin Sheppard *(Sales & Marketing)*
Mary Chapman *(Trade)*
Trevor Price *(Distribution)*
Helen Porter *(Freelance Editorial)*
Christine Amer *(Permissions)*
Fleure Dorrell *(Publicity)*

*Academic & Scholarly; Biography &
Autobiography; Philosophy; Psychology &
Psychiatry; Religion & Theology*

ISBNs, Imprints & Series:
0 232 Darton, Longman & Todd

Distributor for:
Clematis Press; Spa Books

Overseas Representation *(see §7.3)*:
*African, Caribbean Commonwealth & Far
East:* Kelvin van Hasselt Publishing
Services, Lymington, UK
Australia: Charles Paine Pty Ltd, North
Paramatta, NSW
Canada: Meakin & Associates, Nepean
Irish Republic: National Bible Society of
Ireland, Dublin
Malta: Preca Library, Societas Doctrinae
Christianae, M.U.S.E.U.M., Bajda
New Zealand: Catholic Supplies (NZ) Ltd,
Wellington
South Africa: Challenge Distributors CC,
Johannesburg

Book Trade Association Membership: PA

1237

DAVID & CHARLES PUBLISHERS
Brunel House, Newton Abbot, Devon
TQ12 4PU
Telephone: 01626 61121
Fax: 01626 64463
Email: dcpublishers.co.uk

Warehouse & Distribution:
Exel Logistics Media Services, Invicta House,
Sir Thomas Longley Road,
Medway City Estate, Rochester, Kent
ME2 4DU
Telephone: 01634 297123
Fax: 01634 298000

Directors: Piers Spence *(Publishing)*
John Allgrove *(Sales & Marketing)*
Neil Page *(Finance)*

*Antiques & Collecting; Architecture & Design;
Crafts & Hobbies; Do-It-Yourself; Fine Art &
Art History; Gardening; Natural History;
Photography; Transport*

New Titles: 55 (1995), 52 (1996)
No of Employees: 75
Annual Turnover: £20M

ISBNs, Imprints & Series:
0 7153
0 907115 Pevensey Press

Associated & Subsidiary Companies:
Readers' Union Group of Book Clubs

Distributor for:
Reader's Digest Books

Overseas Representation *(see §7.3)*:
Australia: Peribo Pty Ltd, Mount Kuring-gai,
NSW
*Austria, Belgium, Denmark, Finland, France,
Germany, Iceland, Luxembourg, Norway,
Sweden, Switzerland & Netherlands:* Angell
Eurosales, Newton Abbot, UK
*Caribbean, Mauritius, Kenya, Gambia,
Botswana & Zimbabwe:* Kelvin van Hasselt
Publishing Services, Lymington, UK
*Cyprus, Turkey, Israel, Arab & Arabian
Peninsula, North Africa & Iran:* Ashton
International Marketing Services, Larkfield,
UK
*Hong Kong, Macau, Taiwan, China, Korea &
Philippines:* Asia Publisher Services Ltd,
Hong Kong
India, Bangladesh, Nepal & Sri Lanka: Maya
Publishers Pvt Ltd, New Delhi, India
Japan: Japan English Services Inc, Chiba-ken
*Malaysia, Singapore, Thailand, Indonesia &
Brunei:* Prime Editions, Subang Jaya,
Malaysia
New Zealand: David Bateman Ltd, Auckland
*Portugal, Gibraltar, Spain, Italy, Malta &
Greece:* Bookport Associates, Bologna, Italy
South Africa: Trinity Books CC, Randburg
USA & Canada: Sterling Publishing Co Inc,
New York, NY, USA

Book Trade Association Membership: PA

1238

DAVID BENNETT BOOKS LTD
23B Albion Road, St Albans, Herts AL1 5EB
Telephone: 01727 855878
Fax: 01727 864085

Trade Enquiries:
Ragged Bears, Ragged Appleshaw, Andover,
Hants SP11 9HX
Telephone: 01264 772269
Fax: 01264 772391

Managing Director: David Bennett *(Artistic
Direction & US Sales, English Language
World Sales Manager)*
Managers: Phyllis Avery *(Production,
Foreign Sales)*
Sarah York *(Contracts & Business
Administration, Multimedia, UK Trade
Sales)*

Children's Books

New Titles: 30 (1995)
No of Employees: 6
Annual Turnover: £2.6M

ISBNs, Imprints & Series: 1 85602

1239

DE AGOSTINI EDITIONS
Interpark House, 7 Down Street, London
W1Y 7DS
Telephone: 0171 318 8000
Fax: 0171 629 6235
Email: irobertson@deagostini.co.uk

Warehouse & Distribution:
Exel Logistics, Invicta House,
Sir Thomas Longley Road,
Medway City Estate, Rochester, Kent
ME2 4DU

Telephone: 01634 297123
Fax: 01634 298000

Chairman & Publisher: Simon McMurtrie
Directors: Frances Gertler *(Publishing)*
Tim Foster *(Art)*
Lee Matthews *(Production)*
Joanna Everard *(Rights)*
Isobel Robertson *(Sales)*
Children's Publisher: Anna McQuinn

Antiques & Collecting; Children's Books; Fine Art & Art History; Health & Beauty; History & Antiquarian; Music

New Titles: 3 (1995), 27 (1996)
No of Employees: 23

ISBNs, Imprints & Series:
1 898883 De Agostini Children's Books, De Agostini Editions

Parent Company:
Instituto Geografico de Agostini *(Italy)*

Overseas Representation *(see §7.3):*
Europe (excluding Netherlands & Irish Republic): Books for Europe, Massagno, Switzerland
Irish Republic: Brookside Publishing Services, Dublin
Middle & Far East: Ashton International Marketing Services, Larkfield, UK
Netherlands: Nilsson & Lamm BV, Weesp
Scandinavia: Anglo-Nordic Books, Godalming, UK
South Africa: Struik Book Distributors Pty Ltd, Maitland
USA & Canada: Stewart, Taboori & Chang, New York, USA

Book Trade Association Membership: PA

1240 ▬▬▬

DEDALUS LTD
Langford Lodge, St Judith's Lane, Sawtry, Cambs PE17 5XE
Telephone: 01487 832382
Fax: 01487 832382

Distribution, Warehouse & Invoicing:
Central Books Ltd, 99 Wallis Road, London E9 5LN
Telephone: 0181 986 4854
Fax: 0181 533 5821

Chief Executive: George Barrington *(Sales)*
Directors: Robert Irwin *(Editorial)*
Juri Gabriel *(Chairman & Rights)*

Cookery, Wines & Spirits; Fiction; Literature & Criticism

New Titles: 16 (1995), 16 (1996)
Annual Turnover: £180,000

ISBNs, Imprints & Series:
0 946626, 1 873982 Dedalus European Classics, Empire of the Senses, Europe 1992–95, Modern English Fiction, Surrealism

Associated & Subsidiary Companies:
USA: Hippocrene Books Inc

Overseas Representation *(see §7.3):*
Australia & New Zealand: Peribo Pty Ltd, Mount Kuring-gai, NSW, Australia
Canada: Marginal Distribution, Peterborough
France, Belgium, Germany, Switzerland, Austria & Netherlands: Michael Geoghegan, London, UK
Irish Republic: Troika Ltd, London, UK
Italy: Penny Padovani, London, UK
Scandinavia: Bernard Croft, Leominster, UK
Spain & Portugal: Janet Clark, London, UK
USA: Hippocrene Books Inc, New York

1241 ▬▬▬

DEFIANT PUBLICATIONS
190 Yoxall Road, Shirley, Solihull, West Midlands B90 3RN
Telephone: 0121 745 8421

Proprietor: Peter Bernard Hands

Humour; Transport

New Titles: 5 (1995), 5 (1996)
Annual Turnover: £48,000

ISBNs, Imprints & Series:
0 946857 British Railways Series

Book Trade Association Membership: PA

1242 ▬▬▬

DELECTUS BOOKS
27 Old Gloucester Street, London WC1N 3XX
Telephone: 0181 963 0979
Fax: 0181 963 0502

Trade Orders:
Turnaround Distribution, 27 Horsell Road, London N5 1XL
Telephone: 0171 609 7836
Fax: 0171 700 1205

Fiction; Literature & Criticism; Erotic Literature; Horror

New Titles: 8 (1995), 6 (1996)
No of Employees: 5
Annual Turnover: £100,000

ISBNs, Imprints & Series:
1 897767 Delectus Classics of Erotic Literature, Delectus Vampire Classics

Overseas Representation *(see §7.3):*
Australia & New Zealand: Peribo Pty Ltd, Mount Kuring-gai, NSW, Australia
Canada: Marginal Distribution, Peterborough
USA: Xclusiv Distributors Inc, New York, NY; Koen Book Distributors Inc, Moorestown, NJ

1243 ▬▬▬

J M DENT
[Imprint of The Orion Publishing Group Ltd]
Orion House, 5 Upper St Martins Lane, London WC2H 9EA
Telephone: 0171 240 3444
Fax: 0171 240 4822

Trade Counter & Warehouse:
Littlehampton Book Services Ltd, 14 Eldon Way, Lineside Estate, Littlehampton, West Sussex BN17 7HE

Telephone: 01903 726410
Fax: 01903 730914

Director: Hilary Laurie *(Publishing— Everyman Paperbacks)*

Academic & Scholarly; Biography & Autobiography; Children's Books; Economics; Fiction; Gardening; History & Antiquarian; Law; Literature & Criticism; Music; Reference Books, Directories & Dictionaries; Scientific & Technical; Everyman classics

ISBNs, Imprints & Series:
0 460 J M Dent, Everyman Paperbacks

Parent Company:
The Orion Publishing Group Ltd

Overseas Representation *(see §7.3):*
see: The Orion Publishing Group Ltd, London, UK

1244 ▬▬▬

*ANDRÉ DEUTSCH LTD
106 Great Russell Street, London WC1B 3LJ
Telephone: 0171 580 2746
Fax: 0171 631 3253

Trade Orders:
Littlehampton Book Services Ltd, 14 Eldon Way, Lineside Estate, Littlehampton, W. Sussex BN17 7HE
Telephone: 01903 721596
Fax: 01903 730914

Chairman & Managing Director: T. G. Rosenthal *(Sales & Rights)*
Directors: Anthony Thwaite *(Editorial)*
Julian Tobin
David Wilson *(Editorial)*
John Cleary *(Production)*
Katherine Hockley *(Publicity)*

Architecture & Design; Biography & Autobiography; Crime; Fiction; Fine Art & Art History; Guide Books; Humour; Illustrated & Fine Editions; Literature & Criticism; Military & War; Music; Photography; Poetry; Politics & World Affairs; Psychology & Psychiatry; Reference Books, Directories & Dictionaries; Religion & Theology; Science Fiction; Sociology & Anthropology; Sports & Games; Theatre, Drama & Dance; Travel & Topography

ISBNs, Imprints & Series: 0 233

Overseas Representation *(see §7.3):*
Australia & New Zealand: Peribo Pty Ltd, Mount Kuring-gai, NSW, Australia
Canada: General Publishing Co Ltd, North York, Ont
Europe (excluding Netherlands): Gaffney-Dodds Associates, Hemel Hempstead, UK
Hong Kong: Asia Publisher Services Ltd
India: Rupa & Co, New Delhi
Japan: Japan English Services Inc, Chiba-ken
Netherlands: Nilsson & Lamm BV, Weesp
Scandinavia: Saga Books ApS, Copenhagen, Denmark
Singapore & Malaysia: Publishers Marketing Services Ltd, Singapore
South Africa: Verbatim Distributors, Steenberg
USA: Trafalgar Square Publications, North Pomfret, VT

Book Trade Association Membership: PA

1245 ▬▬▬▬▬▬▬▬▬

DIAL PUBLICATIONS
[a division of Reed Telepublishing Ltd]
Windsor Court, East Grinstead House,
East Grinstead, West Sussex RH19 1XA
Telephone: 01342 326972
Fax: 01342 326920

Publishing Director: Derek Barley
Editorial: Jan Brazier *(Managing Editor)*
Denise White *(Editor)*
Sales: Brian Gallagher *(National Sales Manager)*
Marketing: Julie Mason *(Product Manager)*

Electronic (Professional & Academic); Engineering; Industry, Business & Management; Reference Books, Directories & Dictionaries

ISBNs, Imprints & Series:
0 907850 Dial Electrical/Electronics 1996, Dial Engineering 1996

Parent Company:
Reed Information Services [a division of Reed Telepublishing Ltd] *(a member of the Reed Elsevier Plc Group)*

Associated & Subsidiary Companies:
Kelly's Directories; Kompass Publishers

Book Trade Association Membership:
Association of British Directory Publishers,
European Association of Directory Publishers

1246 ▬▬▬▬▬▬▬▬▬

JOHN DONALD PUBLISHERS LTD
138 St Stephen Street, Edinburgh EH3 5AA
Telephone: 0131 225 1146
Fax: 0131 220 0567

Warehouse:
2-12 Marionville Road, Edinburgh
Telephone: 0131 652 0823

Directors: Gordon Angus *(Distribution & Sales Promotion)*
Donald Morrison *(Publishing & Production)*
J. Elder *(Finance)*

Academic & Scholarly; Archaeology; Architecture & Design; Guide Books; History & Antiquarian; Military & War; Music; Sports & Games

New Titles: 18 (1995)
No of Employees: 7
Annual Turnover: £200,000

ISBNs, Imprints & Series:
0 85976 John Donald, Sportsprint

1247 ▬▬▬▬▬▬▬▬▬

DONHEAD PUBLISHING LTD
Lower Coombe, Donhead St Mary,
Shaftesbury, Dorset SP7 9LY
Telephone: 01747 828422
Fax: 01747 828522

Directors: Jill Pearce
Chris Hall

Architecture & Design; Scientific & Technical; Building Conservation; Heritage & Museum Studies

New Titles: 4 (1995), 7 (1996)
No of Employees: 2

ISBNs, Imprints & Series: 1 873394

Overseas Representation *(see §7.3)*:
USA: PRG, Rockport, MD

Book Trade Association Membership: IPG

1248 ▬▬▬▬▬▬▬▬▬

*DORLING KINDERSLEY LTD
9 Henrietta Street, London WC2E 8PS
Telephone: 0171 836 5411
Fax: 0171 836 7570

Distributors:
International Book Distributors Ltd,
Magna Park, Coventry Road, Lutterworth,
Leics LE17 4XH
Telephone: 01442 882212
Fax: 01442 882200

Directors: Peter Kindersley *(Chairman)*
Christopher Davis *(Deputy Chairman)*
Martyn Longley *(Operations – Adult Books, Production)*
Lyn Blackman *(Finance)*
Rod Hare *(Group Managing)*
Linda Davis *(Publisher – Children's Books)*
Sue Unstead *(Children's Editorial)*
David Holmes *(Managing – UK Publishing)*
Anne-Marie Bulat *(Art – Adult)*
Linda Cole *(Art – Children's)*
Roger Priddy *(Art – Children's)*
David Lamb *(Editorial – Adult)*
Stuart Jackman *(International Design)*
Alan Buckingham *(Multimedia)*
Jackie Douglas *(Editorial – Reference)*
John Adams *(DK Vision)*
Annie Frankland *(International Sales – Children's)*
Michael Devenish *(International Sales – Adult)*
Ruth Sandys *(Education)*
Netie Brooke *(Special Markets)*
Managers: Gillian Hawkins *(Sales)*
Ros Wesson *(Adult Marketing)*
Fenella Hunt *(Children's Marketing)*
Commonwealth Sales: Simonne Waud
Book Club Sales: Caroline Gibson

Animal Care & Breeding; Antiques & Collecting; Atlases & Maps; Children's Books; Cookery, Wines & Spirits; Crafts & Hobbies; Fashion & Costume; Gardening; Geography & Geology; Health & Beauty; Medical (incl. Self Help & Alternative Medicine); Music; Natural History; Reference Books, Directories & Dictionaries

ISBNs, Imprints & Series:
0 7513, 0 86318

Associated & Subsidiary Companies:
USA: Microsoft *(20% shareholder)*

Distributor for:
Germany: SDK Verlags GmbH. *USA:* Dorling Kindersley Inc

Overseas Representation *(see §7.3)*:
Australia: Random Australia Pty Ltd, Sydney

Austria, Italy, Switzerland, Belgium, Luxembourg, France, Greece, Yugoslav Republics, Germany, Spain, Portugal & Gibraltar: Walton Marketing Services, Chislehurst, UK
Central & South America: Humphrys Roberts Associates, London, UK
East, Central & West Africa: Len Ainsworth, Aldbourne, UK
Far East, Parkistan & Caribbean: Ralph & Sheila Summers, London, UK
India: Dass Media Pte Ltd, New Delhi
Middle East: Peter Ward Book Exports, London, UK
Netherlands: Consul Books, Blaricum
New Zealand: Random House New Zealand Ltd, Auckland
Scandinavia: Saga Books ApS, Copenhagen, Denmark
South Africa: Struik Book Distributors Pty Ltd, Johannesburg, Cape Town & Maitland

---

1249 ▬▬▬▬▬▬▬▬▬

DORSET PUBLISHING CO
Wincanton Press, National School,
North Street, Wincanton, Somerset BA9 9AT
Telephone: 01963 32583

Distributors:
Westcountry Books, Halsgrove House,
Lower Moor Way, Tiverton, Devon EX16 6SS
Telephone: 01884 243242
Fax: 01884 243325

Publisher: Rodney Legg
Sales Manager: Colin Cole

Archaeology; Guide Books; History & Antiquarian; Military & War

New Titles: 11 (1995), 9 (1996)
No of Employees: 2
Annual Turnover: £50,000

ISBNs, Imprints & Series:
0 902129 Dorset Publishing Co
0 948699 Dorset Publishing Co, Wincanton Press

Associated & Subsidiary Companies:
Wincanton Press

1250 ▬▬▬▬▬▬▬▬▬

DOWNLANDER PUBLISHING
88 Oxendean Gardens, Lower Willingdon,
Eastbourne BN22 0RS
Telephone: 01323 500437

Directing Editor: Derek Bourne-Jones
Deputy Editor: Hilary Clare *(Production)*

Poetry

New Titles: 5 (1996)
No of Employees: 4

ISBNs, Imprints & Series: 0 906369

1251 ▬▬▬▬▬▬▬▬▬

DP PUBLICATIONS & LETTS EDUCATIONAL
Aldine House, Aldine Place,
142–144 Uxbridge Road, London W12 8AW
Telephone: 0181 740 2266

Fax: 0181 743 8451
Email: 100767.272@compuserv.com

Warehouse:
The Trade Counter, The Airfield,
Norwich Road, Mendlesham, Suffolk
IP14 5NA
Telephone: 01449 766629
Fax: 01449 767122

Directors: Jonathan Harris (Managing)
Richard Carr (Publishing/Commissioning)
Catherine Tilley (Production & Editorial)
Edward Peppitt (Marketing)

Accountancy & Taxation; Computer Science;
Economics; Educational & Textbooks;
Electronic (Professional & Academic);
Mathematics & Statistics; Vocational Training
& Careers

New Titles: 50 (1995)
No of Employees: 22

ISBNs, Imprints & Series:
1 85758 A Level Questions & Answers, A
Level Study Guides, Assess Your Child's
Progress at Key Stage 2, Back to Basics,
Letts/Channel 4 Exam Kit, GCSE Passcards,
GCSE Questions & Answers, GCSE Study
Guides, GCSE Textbooks, Getting to Grips,
Key Stage 2 National Tests, Key Stage 3
National Tests, Key Stage 3 Study Guides,
Keyfacts GCSE Passbooks, Letts Explore
Literature Guides, Multimedia Revision
Guides for GCSE, Parent's Guides to the
National Curriculum, Study Skills

Parent Company:
BPP Holdings Plc

Associated & Subsidiary Companies:
Blackstone Press Ltd; BPP Publishing Ltd;
Letts Educational

Overseas Representation (see §7.3):
Ghana: EPP Book Services, Accra
Hong Kong: Pilot Publishers Services Ltd,
Kowloon; The Commercial Press Ltd
Jamaica: Ian Randle Publishers Ltd, Kingston
Kenya: Textbook Centre Ltd, Nairobi; Savani's
Book Centre, Nairobi
Malaysia: APD Kuala Lumpur, Petaling Jaya
Malta: Mireva Bookshop, Msida
Mauritius: Editions Le Printemps, Vacoas
Nigeria: Odusote Bookstores Ltd, Ibadan;
Abiola Bookshop Ltd, Lagos; Spectrum
Books Ltd, Ibadan; Mosuro Booksellers,
Ibadan
Pakistan: Book Bird, Lahore
Singapore: APD Singapore Pte Ltd
Sri Lanka: Pitraban, Colombo
Trinidad & Tobago: RIK Services Ltd, San
Fernando, Trinidad
Zimbabwe: Kingstons Ltd, Harare

1252 ∎

DRAGON'S WORLD LTD
High Street, Limpsfield, Surrey RH8 0DY
Telephone: 01883 715044
Fax: 01883 716032

**Editorial, Design, Production & Public
Relations:**
7 St Georges Square, London SW1V 2HX

Telephone: 0171 630 9955
Fax: 0171 630 9921

Distribution:
Exel Logistics Media Services, Invicta House,
Sir Thomas Langley Road,
Medway City Industrial Estate, Rochester,
Kent ME2 4DU
Telephone: 01634 297123
Fax: 01634 298000

Directors: Hubert Schaafsma (Managing)
Pippa Rubinstein (Editorial)
Leslie Cramphorn (Sales)
Production: Roger Matthews (Manager)
Public Relations: Amanda Marshall

Children's Books; Crafts & Hobbies; Do-It-
Yourself; Guide Books; Health & Beauty;
Illustrated & Fine Editions; Music; Natural
History; Photography; Science Fiction;
Astrology; Fantasy; Mythology

New Titles: 41 (1995), 40 (1996)
No of Employees: 18

ISBNs, Imprints & Series:
0 905895, 1 85028 Dragon's World Books,
Paper Tiger Books

Overseas Representation (see §7.3):
Japan: Aoki Hideo, Tokyo
USA & Canada: Allan Lang International Book
Marketing Ltd, Princeton, NJ, USA

1253 ∎

**DRAKE EDUCATIONAL ASSOCIATES
LTD**
St Fagans Road, Fairwater, Cardiff CF5 3AE
Telephone: 01222 560333
Fax: 01222 554909

Managing Director: R. Geoffrey Drake
(Home & Export Sales, Rights &
Permissions)
UK Exhibitions: R. Jonathan Drake

Children's Books; Educational & Textbooks;
English as a Foreign Language; Geography &
Geology; Languages & Linguistics

Parent Company:
Drake Group Ltd

Associated & Subsidiary Companies:
Educational Productions Ltd; Gwasg Addysgol
Drake Cyf

Distributor for:
American Guidance Services; Brookline
Books; Eleanor Curtain; Highsmith; Pembroke
Publishers

Book Trade Association Membership: PA,
EPC

1254 ∎

DRAMATIC LINES
7 Shaftesbury Way, Twickenham TW2 5RN
Telephone: 0181 898 3819
Fax: 0181 898 3819

Chief Executive: John Nicholas
Sales, Marketing & Production: Heather
Stephens
Development: Irene Palko

Theatre, Drama & Dance

New Titles: 1 (1995), 2 (1996)

ISBNs, Imprints & Series: 0 952222

Overseas Representation (see §7.3):
USA, Canada, Australia & Africa: Empire
Publishing Service, Studio City, CA, USA

Book Trade Association Membership: PA

1255 ∎

GERALD DUCKWORTH & CO LTD
48 Hoxton Square, London N1 6PB
Telephone: 0171 729 5986
Fax: 0171 729 0015

Directors: Robin Baird-Smith (Publisher &
Managing)
Ray Davies (Production)
Jonathan Earl (Sales & Marketing)
Deborah Blake (Editorial)
Company Secretary: Christine Halsey

Academic & Scholarly; Fiction; Nautical

New Titles: 80 (1995), 100 (1996)
No of Employees: 17
Annual Turnover: £1.1M

ISBNs, Imprints & Series:
0 7156
1 85399 Bristol Classical Press
1 86176 Chatham Publishing

Associated & Subsidiary Companies:
Bristol Classical Press; Chatham Publishing

Distributor for:
Classical Press of Wales

Overseas Representation (see §7.3):
Australia: Eleanor Brasch Associates,
Artarmon, NSW
Europe & Scandinavia: Bill Bailey Publishers
Representatives, Newton Abbot, UK
Middle East: Eurab Ltd, Rottingdean, UK
New Zealand: David Bateman Ltd, Auckland
South East Asia & Far East: Richard Blady
Booksales, Macclesfield, UK

1256 ∎

DUN & BRADSTREET LTD
Business Reference Services,
Holmers Farm Way, High Wycombe, Bucks
HP12 4UL
Telephone: 01494 423690
Fax: 01494 422260

Managers: Carol Hannawin (Telesales)
Nigel Dickinson (Sales & Development)
Sales Administration Supervisor: Iris
Willsher

Industry, Business & Management; Reference
Books, Directories & Dictionaries

ISBNs, Imprints & Series:
0 900625 Key British Enterprises, Who Owns
Whom Series

Parent Company:
The Dun & Bradstreet Corporation

Distributor for:
Dun & Bradstreet

Book Trade Association Membership: BA,
Directory Publishers' Association, European
Association of Directory Publishers

1257

MARTIN DUNITZ LTD
The Livery House, 7–9 Pratt Street, London
NW1 0AE
Telephone: 0171 482 2202
Fax: 0171 267 0159 & 1404
Email: martin–dunitz–ltd@compuserve.com

Trade Orders:
Marston Book Services, PO Box 87,
Osney Mead, Oxford OX2 0DT
Telephone: 01865 791155
Fax: 01865 791927

Sales, Rights & Permissions: Martin Dunitz
(*Managing Director*)
Directors: Rosemary Allen (*Production*)
John Slaytor (*Financial*)
Export Service Manager: Teresa Davey

*Medical (incl. Self Help & Alternative
Medicine); Scientific & Technical*

New Titles: 25 (1995), 36 (1996)
No of Employees: 23
Annual Turnover: £2.8M

ISBNs, Imprints & Series:
0 906348, 0 948269, 1 853170, 1 853171

Overseas Representation (*see §7.3*):
Argentina: Editorial Atlanta Argentina, Capital
Australia: Mosby-Williams & Wilkins Pty Ltd,
Artarmon
Brazil: Interlivros Edicoes Ltda, Rio de Janeiro
Egypt: Mass Publishing Co Sae, Kokki Gaza
Europe: Waverly Europe Ltd, London, UK
India: Jaypee Brothers Medical Publishers Ltd,
New Delhi
Israel: Franklins, Gane Yuan
Korea: Jin-Myong International Inc, Seoul,
Korea, South
Middle East: Median Books Ltd, Machynlleth,
UK
Pakistan: Pak Book Corporation, Lahore
Philippines: F & J de Jesus Inc, Metro Manila
Singapore & Hong Kong: Toppan Co (S) Pte
Ltd, Singapore
South Africa: Oxford University Press,
Capetown
Taiwan: HWA Eng Trading Co, Taipei
Turkey: Nobel Tip Kitabevlei, Istanbul

1258

DUNROD PRESS
8 Brown's Road, Antrim Road,
Newtownabbey, Co Antrim BT36 8RN
Telephone: 01232 832362
Fax: 01232 848780

Chief Executive: Ken Lindsay (*General
Manager*)
Sales: James Crawford
Publicity: John Graham

*History & Antiquarian; Politics & World
Affairs*

New Titles: 3 (1995), 3 (1996)
No of Employees: 7

ISBNs, Imprints & Series: 0 86202

Associated & Subsidiary Companies:
Irish Republic: Dunrod Press

1259

EAGLE
St Nicholas House, The Mount, Guildford,
Surrey GU2 5HN
Telephone: 01483 306309
Fax: 01483 579196

**Warehouse, Trade Enquiries & Orders (for
Religious Trade):**
c/o STL, PO Box 300, Kingstown Broadway,
Carlisle, Cumbria CA3 0QS
Telephone: 01228 512512
Fax: 01228 514949

**Warehouse, Trade Enquiries & Orders (for
General Trade):**
Combined Book Services

Managing Director: David Wavre

*Psychology & Psychiatry; Religion &
Theology; Colour gift book; Self-Help*

New Titles: 24 (1995), 24 (1996)
No of Employees: 4
Annual Turnover: £500,000

ISBNs, Imprints & Series:
0 86347 Eagle

Parent Company:
Inter Publishing Service (IPS) Ltd

Overseas Representation (*see §7.3*):
Australia: Openbook Publishers, Adelaide, SA
Irish Republic: Columba Book Service, Dublin
New Zealand: Scripture Union Wholesale,
Wellington
Singapore: Campus Crusade Asia Ltd
USA: Harold Shaw Publishers, Wheaton, IL

Book Trade Association Membership: PA

1260

EAGLEMOSS PUBLICATIONS LTD
7 Cromwell Road, London SW7 2HR
Telephone: 0171 581 1371
Fax: 0171 581 7977

Directors: Patrick Cavendish (*Chairman*)
Beverley Hilton (*Non-Executive*)
Mark Stanley (*Chief Executive*)
Judy Sibley (*Commercial*)
Matthew Lebus (*Marketing*)
Isabel Moore (*Editorial*)

*Aviation; Children's Books; Crime; Crafts &
Hobbies; Gardening; Photography; Sports &
Games*

New Titles: 2 (1995), 4 (1996)
No of Employees: 110
Annual Turnover: £45M

ISBNs, Imprints & Series: 1 85629

Associated & Subsidiary Companies:
Germany: Eaglemoss International GmbH.
Japan: Eaglemoss International Ltd

1261

EARTHSCAN PUBLICATIONS LTD
120 Pentonville Road, London N1 9JN
Telephone: 0171 278 0433
Fax: 0171 278 1142
Email: earthinfo@earthscan.co.uk
Web Site: http://www.earthscan.co.uk

Directors: Jonathan Sinclair-Wilson
(*Publishing*)
Jo O'Driscoll (*Managing Editor*)
Julie McNair (*Export Sales*)
Andrew Young (*Marketing*)
Mike Baggallay (*Home Sales*)

*Academic & Scholarly; Agriculture;
Economics; Educational & Textbooks;
Environment & Development Studies; Gender
Studies; Geography & Geology; Politics &
World Affairs; Reference Books, Directories &
Dictionaries; Transport*

New Titles: 42 (1995), 50 (1996)
No of Employees: 6

ISBNs, Imprints & Series: 1 85383

Parent Company:
Kogan Page Ltd

Distributor for:
Island Press; St Lucie Press; World Resources
Institute

Overseas Representation (*see §7.3*):
Australia: Boobook Publications Pty Ltd, Tea
Gardens, NSW
Canada: Gage Educational Publishing Co,
Agincourt, Ont
Caribbean: English House Services Publishers
International Management, Cinderford, UK
Hong Kong, South Korea & Taiwan: Asia
Publisher Services Ltd, Hong Kong
India: Viva Marketing, New Delhi
Japan: Kay Kato, Kamakura
Middle East: Peter Ward Book Exports,
London, UK
New Zealand: Tandem Press, Auckland
Pakistan: Book Bird, Lahore
Singapore, Malaysia & Brunei: Publishers
Marketing Services Ltd, Singapore;
Publishers Marketing Services, Petaling
Jaya, Malaysia
South Africa: Book Promotions Pty Ltd,
Plumstead
*Thailand, Burma, China, Philippines &
Vietnam:* STM Publishing Services Pte Ltd,
Singapore
USA: Island Press, Washington, DC
Western Europe & Scandinavia: Andrew B.
Durnell, Tunbridge Wells, UK

Book Trade Association Membership: PA,
BDC, CAPP, IPG

1262

EAST-WEST PUBLICATIONS (UK) LTD
8 Caledonia Street, London N1 9DZ
Telephone: 0171 837 5061
Fax: 0171 278 4429

Warehouse (for East-West):
Ashgrove Press, 4 Brassmill Centre,
Brassmill Lane, Bath BA1 3JN
Telephone: 01225 425539
Fax: 01225 319137

Warehouse (for Gallery):
The Trade Counter, The Airfield,
Norwich Road, Mendlesham, Suffolk
IP14 5NA
Telephone: 01449 766629
Fax: 01449 767122

Directors: L. W. Carp *(Chairman)*
B. G. Thompson *(Managing, Rights &
Permissions, Sales)*

*Biography & Autobiography; Children's
Books; Fiction; Guide Books; History &
Antiquarian; Music; Photography; Poetry;
Religion & Theology*

ISBNs, Imprints & Series:
0 85692 East-West, Gallery Children's Books
1 872571 Britannia Press

Associated & Subsidiary Companies:
The Britannia Press

Overseas Representation *(see §7.3)*:
Australia: The Five Mile Press, Noble Park,
Vic
USA (for Book Trade): Associated Publishers
Group (APG), Nashville, TN, USA
USA (for Gift Trade): The Evergreen Press,
Pleasant Hill, CA, USA

Book Trade Association Membership: PA,
BDC

1263

THE ECONOMIST BOOKS
[published in association with Profile Books
Ltd]
62 Queen Anne Street, London W1M 9LA
Telephone: 0171 486 6010
Fax: 0171 486 6012
Email: 101766.1201@compuserve.com

Orders:
Tiptree Book Services, Church Road, Tiptree,
Essex CO5 0SR
Telephone: 01621 819000
Fax: 01621 819717

Directors: Andrew Franklin *(Publishing)*
Stephen Brough *(Editorial)*
Editor: Nicky White

*Economics; Industry, Business &
Management; Politics & World Affairs;
Reference Books, Directories & Dictionaries*

ISBNs, Imprints & Series: 1 86197

Book Trade Association Membership: IPG

1264

EDINBURGH UNIVERSITY PRESS
22 George Square, Edinburgh EH8 9LF
Telephone: 0131 650 4218
Fax: 0131 662 0053

Trade Enquiries:
Marston Book Services, PO Box 269,
Abingdon, Oxon OX14
Telephone: 01235 465500
Fax: 01235 465555

Publisher: Vivian Bone *(Editorial, Rights &
Permissions)*
Business Manager: Allan Woods
Production: Ian Davidson
Marketing: Alison Munro

*Academic & Scholarly; Archaeology; Gender
Studies; History & Antiquarian; Languages &
Linguistics; Law; Literature & Criticism;
Philosophy; Reference Books, Directories &
Dictionaries; Sociology & Anthropology;
Botany & Environment; Cultural Studies;
Islamic Studies; Scottish Studies*

New Titles: 50 (1996)
No of Employees: 15

ISBNs, Imprints & Series:
0 7486, 0 85224

Associated & Subsidiary Companies:
Polygon

Overseas Representation *(see §7.3)*:
Australia: James Bennett Library Services,
Collaroy, NSW
Benelux: Frans Janssen, Rotterdam,
Netherlands
Caribbean, Central, East & West Africa:
Kelvin van Hasselt Publishing Services,
Lymington, UK
Central America: Humphrys Roberts
Associates, London, UK
Germany, Austria & Switzerland: The John
Wilde Partnership, Lauf, Germany
Hong Kong, Taiwan & Korea: Knowledge
Craft Ltd, Hong Kong
India: Maya Publishers Pvt Ltd, New Delhi
Iran: McIntyre Information Services
Representatives Ltd, Tehran
Japan: United Publishers Services Ltd, Tokyo
Malaysia: APD Kuala Lumpur, Petaling Jaya
Mexico: Humphrys Roberts Associates,
Colonia Doctores
Middle East: International Publishers
Representatives (IPR), Nicosia, Cyprus
New Zealand: Macmillan New Zealand,
Auckland
Pakistan: Afro-Asian Book Co, Karachi
Philippines: Combined Book Representatives,
Manila
Scandinavia: Colin Flint, Harlow, UK
Singapore: APD Singapore Pte Ltd
South Africa: Juta & Co Ltd, Isando
South America: Humphrys Roberts Associates,
Cotia, Brazil
USA & Canada (most titles, orders): Columbia
University Press, New York, USA
USA & Canada (most titles, enquiries):
Columbia University Press, New York, USA

Book Trade Association Membership:
Scottish PA

1265

**EDUCATIONAL LOW-PRICED BOOKS
SCHEME (ELBS)**
IBD Ltd, The Swan Centre, Fishers Lane,
Chiswick, London W4 1RX
Telephone: 0181 742 8232
Fax: 0181 747 8715

Head, ELBS Administration: Eileen Gillow
Assistant Editor: Joe De Souza.

*Academic & Scholarly; Accountancy &
Taxation; Agriculture; Animal Care &
Breeding; Biology & Zoology; Chemistry;
Computer Science; Economics; Educational &
Textbooks; Engineering; English as a Foreign
Language; Geography & Geology; Industry,
Business & Management; Law; Mathematics &
Statistics; Medical (incl. Self Help &
Alternative Medicine); Physics; Scientific &
Technical; Veterinary Science*

Overseas Representation *(see §7.3)*:
India: Viva Marketing, New Delhi
Nigeria: Mosuro Booksellers, Ibadan

Book Trade Association Membership:
International Book Development Ltd

1266

*EDUCATIONAL PLANNING BOOKS
PO Box 63, Hathersage, Sheffield S30 1DJ
Telephone: 01433 620220
Fax: 01433 620602

Managing Director: G. N. S. Garner

Educational & Textbooks

Book Trade Association Membership: PA,
EPC

1267

ELC INTERNATIONAL
109 Uxbridge Road, Ealing, London W5 5TL
Telephone: 0181 566 2288
Fax: 0181 566 4931

Managing Director: Don Wildey
Publications Manager: David King

*Industry, Business & Management; Reference
Books, Directories & Dictionaries;
Advertising; Directories; Marketing*

New Titles: 3 (1995), 3 (1996)
No of Employees: 10
Annual Turnover: £250,000

ISBNs, Imprints & Series:
0 948058 Largest Companies Series

Parent Company:
Clemis Group Ltd

Associated & Subsidiary Companies:
Goulden Reports Ltd; IAL Consultants Ltd

Distributor for:
Denmark: Okonomisk Litteratur. *Norway:*
Okonomisk Litteratur. *Sweden:* Okonomisk
Litteratur

Overseas Representation *(see §7.3):*
Asia: IRM Inc, Tokyo, Japan
Norway: A/S Okonomisk Literatur, Oslo
Sweden: Ekonomisk Litteratur AB, Vallingby
USA: Dun's Marketing Services, Parsipanny,
NJ

1268

ELECTRONIC PUBLISHING SERVICES
26 Rosebery Avenue, London EC1R 4SX
Telephone: 0171 837 3345
Fax: 0171 837 8901
Email: eps@epsltd.demon.co.uk

No of Employees: 8

Book Trade Association Membership: PA

1269

ELEMENT BOOKS LTD
Old School House, Bell Street, Shaftesbury,
Dorset SP7 8BP
Telephone: 01747 851448
Fax: 01747 855721

Directors: Michael Mann *(Chairman &*
Publisher)
David Alexander *(Managing)*
Annie Wilson *(Rights)*
Julia McCutcheon *(Editorial)*
Roger Lane *(Production)*
Ian Griffiths *(Finance)*
Theresa Franklin *(Sales & Marketing)*

Biography & Autobiography; Gender Studies;
Health & Beauty; Philosophy; Psychology &
Psychiatry; Reference Books, Directories &
Dictionaries; Religion & Theology;
Complementary Medicine; Esoteric Traditions;
Self Help

New Titles: 95 (1995), 111 (1996)
No of Employees: 33
Annual Turnover: £8M

ISBNs, Imprints & Series:
0 906540, 1 85230, 1 86204 Element Books,
Nadder Books
1 85404 Broadcast Books

Parent Company:
Element Communications Ltd

Associated & Subsidiary Companies:
Broadcast Books Ltd. *USA:* Element Inc

Distributor for:
Nadder Books; Oneworld Publications

Overseas Representation *(see §7.3):*
All other countries: Penguin Export Sales Dept,
London, UK
Australia: Jacaranda Wiley Ltd, North Ryde,
NSW
Australia (orders): Jacaranda Wiley Ltd,
Milton, Queensland, Australia
Canada: Penguin Books Canada Ltd,
Newmarket, Ont
Central & South America & Caribbean:
Humphrys Roberts Associates, London, UK
France: Penguin France SA, Toulouse
Germany & Austria: Penguin Books
Deutschland GmbH, Frankfurt, Germany
Greece, Cyprus & Israel: Penguin Hellas Ltd,
Athens, Greece

India, Sri Lanka, Pakistan & Bangladesh:
Penguin Books India Pvt Ltd, New Delhi,
India
Italy: Penguin Italia Srl, Milan
Japan: Penguin Books Japan, Tokyo
Netherlands: Penguin Books Netherlands bv,
Amsterdam
New Zealand: Forrester Books Ltd, Auckland
Scandinavia, Belgium & Luxembourg: Sophie
Piquemal, London, UK
South Africa: Longman Penguin South Africa,
Bertsham
South East Asia & Far East: Ms C. Cumming
Penguin Books Ltd, Hong Kong
Spain: Penguin Books SA, Madrid
USA: Viking Penguin Inc, New York

Book Trade Association Membership: IPG

1270

ELFANDE LTD
Unit 39, Bookham Industrial Park,
Church Road, Bookham, Surrey KT23 3EU
Telephone: 01372 459559
Fax: 01372 459699

Trade Enquiries:
Lavis Marketing, 73 Lime Walk, Headington,
Oxford OX3 7AD
Telephone: 01865 67575
Fax: 01865 750079

Director: Nicholas Gould *(Sales &*
Production)

Illustrated & Fine Editions; Photography;
Design; Illustration

ISBNs, Imprints & Series:
1 870458 Contact Illustrators, Contact
Illustration Agents, Contact Photographers,
European Contact

Overseas Representation *(see §7.3):*
USA: Books Nippan, Carson, CA

1271

EDWARD ELGAR PUBLISHING LTD
8 Lansdown Place, Cheltenham, Glos
GL50 2HU
Telephone: 01242 226934
Fax: 01242 262111
Email: edward@e-elgar.co.uk
Web Site: http://www.e-elgar.co.uk

Production Distribution Services:
Ashgate Distribution Services, Unit 3,
Lower Farnham Road, Aldershot, Hants
GU12 4DY
Telephone: 01252 331551
Fax: 01252 344405

Chairman: Nigel Farrow
Company Secretary: Nigel Young
Managing Director: Edward Elgar
Rights & Permissions: Sandy Elgar
Director: Mark Blaug
Marketing, Publicity & Sales: Hilary Quinn

Academic & Scholarly; Economics; Reference
Books, Directories & Dictionaries; Sociology
& Anthropology

New Titles: 154 (1995), 200 (1996)
No of Employees: 22

ISBNs, Imprints & Series:
1 85278, 1 85898

Overseas Representation *(see §7.3):*
Australia & New Zealand: Ashgate Asia
Pacific Pte Ltd, Surrey Hills, NSW, Australia
Japan: United Publishers Services Ltd, Tokyo
North & South America: Edward Elgar
Publishing Co, Brookfield, VT, USA
South East Asia, Philippines, Myanmar
(Burma), China, Hong Kong & South Korea:
Ashgate Asia Pacific Pte Ltd, Singapore

1272

ELLIOT RIGHT WAY BOOKS
Kingswood Buildings, Brighton Road,
Lower Kingswood, Tadworth, Surrey
KT20 6TD
Telephone: 01737 832202
Fax: 01737 830311

Directors: A. Clive Elliot *(Home & Export*
Sales)
Malcolm G. Elliot *(Production, Rights &*
Permissions)
Management: Chris Maynard *(Distribution &*
Accounts)

Animal Care & Breeding; Cookery, Wines &
Spirits; Crafts & Hobbies; Gardening;
Humour; Industry, Business & Management;
Law; Medical (incl. Self Help & Alternative
Medicine); Politics & World Affairs;
Psychology & Psychiatry; Reference Books,
Directories & Dictionaries; Sports & Games;
Transport

New Titles: 12 (1995), 16 (1996)

ISBNs, Imprints & Series:
Right Way
0 7160 Paperfronts
1 899606 Clarion

Parent Company:
Andrew Elliot & Sons Ltd

Overseas Representation *(see §7.3):*
Australia: Keith Ainsworth Pty Ltd, Penrith,
NSW
East & West Africa: Len Ainsworth,
Aldbourne, UK
Far East & West Indies: Ralph & Sheila
Summers, London, UK
Middle East & North Africa: Peter Ward Book
Exports, London, UK
South Africa: Alternative Books, Randburg

1273

AIDAN ELLIS PUBLISHING
Cobb House, Nuffield, Henley-on-Thames,
Oxon RG9 5RT
Telephone: 01491 641496
Fax: 01491 641678
Email: aidan@aepub.demon.co.uk
Web Site: http://www.demon.co.uk/aepub/

Invoicing & Credit, Books & Warehouse:
Cassell Plc, Stanley House, 3 Fleets Lane,
Poole, Dorset BH15 3AJ
Telephone: 01202 665432
Fax: 01202 666219

Partners: Aidan Ellis
Lucinda Ellis

Biography & Autobiography; Cookery, Wines & Spirits; Fiction; Fine Art & Art History; Gardening; History & Antiquarian; Illustrated & Fine Editions; Literature & Criticism; Natural History; Nautical; Travel & Topography

New Titles: 6 (1995), 13 (1996)
No of Employees: 2
Annual Turnover: £200,000

ISBNs, Imprints & Series: 0 85628

Overseas Representation (see §7.3):
Australia & New Zealand: Keith Ainsworth Pty Ltd, Penrith, NSW, Australia
Europe: Ted Dougherty, London, UK
Iberia: Peter Prout, Madrid, Spain
Scandinavia: Hanne Rotovnik, Klampenborg, Denmark

1274

ELM PUBLICATIONS
Seaton House, Kings Ripton, Huntingdon PE17 2NJ
Telephone: 01487 773238
Fax: 01487 773359

Managing Director: Sheila Ritchie (Home & Export Sales)

Bibliography & Library Science; Educational & Textbooks; Electronic (Educational); Industry, Business & Management; Training

ISBNs, Imprints & Series:
0 946139, 0 9505828, 1 85450

Parent Company:
Elm Training

1275

ELSEVIER ADVANCED TECHNOLOGY
PO Box 150, Kidlington, Oxford OX5 1AS
Telephone: 01865 843848
Fax: 01865 843971

Director: David Bousfield
Managers: Nick Baker (Publisher)
Andrew Fletcher (Associate Publisher)
Guy Kitteringham (Associate Publisher)
Nikki Spencer (Sales & Marketing)

Electronic (Professional & Academic); Engineering; Industry, Business & Management; Computer Security; Electronics; Materials Technology

New Titles: 34 (1995), 30 (1996)
No of Employees: 70
Annual Turnover: £1.6M

ISBNs, Imprints & Series:
0 904705, 0 946395, 0 948577, 1 85617

Parent Company:
Elsevier Science Ltd

Associated & Subsidiary Companies:
Trade & Technical Press

Overseas Representation (see §7.3):
Japan: Elsevier Science Japan, Tokyo
Netherlands: Elsevier Science BV, Amsterdam
USA: Elsevier Science Inc, New York

Book Trade Association Membership: PA, IGSMTP

1276

ELSEVIER SCIENCE LTD
The Boulevard, Langford Lane, Kidlington, Oxford OX5 1GB
Telephone: 01865 843000
Fax: 01865 843010

Warehouse:
Yeoman's Drive, Brickhill Street, Blakelands, Milton Keynes MK14 1LY

Directors: Michael Boswood (Managing)
F. Verhagen (Financial)
Ian Liddiard (Production)
A. F. Moon (Subsidiary Rights)
D. Sar (Marketing)

Academic & Scholarly; Chemistry; Educational & Textbooks; Medical (incl. Self Help & Alternative Medicine); Scientific & Technical

New Titles: 120 (1995), 100 (1996)
No of Employees: 600

ISBNs, Imprints & Series:
0 08 Elsevier Advanced Technology, Elsevier Applied Science, Elsevier Trends Journals, Pergamon

Parent Company:
Elsevier Science BV (Netherlands)

Associated & Subsidiary Companies:
USA: Elsevier Science Inc

Overseas Representation (see §7.3):
Australia: DA Information Services, Mitcham, Vic
Brazil: Editora Campus Ltda, Rio de Janeiro
India: Surinder Lijhara, New Delhi
Japan: Elsevier Science Japan, Tokyo
Korea: Elsevier Science, Seoul, Korea, South
Pakistan: Rae & Sons Publishers Representatives, Lahore

Book Trade Association Membership: STM

1277

EMMA BOOKS LTD
Little Orchard House, Mill Lane, Beckington, Somerset BA3 6SN
Telephone: 01373 831215
Fax: 01373 831216

Directors: David Bailey
Richard Powell
Andrew Mailey

Children's Books

New Titles: 24 (1995), 24 (1996)
No of Employees: 4
Annual Turnover: £1.6M

ISBNs, Imprints & Series: 1 874644

Associated & Subsidiary Companies:
Treehouse Children's Books

1278

ENCYCLOPAEDIA BRITANNICA INTERNATIONAL LTD
Carew House, Station Approach, Wallington, Surrey SM6 0DA
Telephone: 0181 669 4355
Fax: 0181 773 3631

Editorial:
Shropshire House, 179 Tottenham Court Road, London W1P 9LF
Telephone: 0171 580 8375
Fax: 0171 580 6653

Warehouse & Shipping:
c/o Hammond, Salbrook Road, Salfords, Redhill, Surrey RH1 5HB
Telephone: 01293 785555
Fax: 01293 820608

Directors: Guisseppie Annoscia (Managing)
William Bowe
Roger Pytel
Sales & Marketing: Jane Waterman
Trade Sales: Lesley Cowen
Mail Order: Lesley Craven
Editorial, Rights & Permissions: James Somerville
Administration: Peter Grala
Finance: Michael Rose

Reference Books, Directories & Dictionaries; CD-ROM

ISBNs, Imprints & Series:
0 85229 Britannica Book of the Year, Children's Britannica Yearbook, Children's Britannica, Compton's Interactive Encyclopaedia, Encyclopaedia Britannica, Great Books of the Western World, Medical & Health Annual, Yearbook of Science & the Future

Parent Company:
Encyclopaedia Britannica Inc (USA)

Distributor for:
France: Encyclopaedia Universalis

Book Trade Association Membership: EPC

1279

*ENGLISH HERITAGE
Keysign House, 429 Oxford Street, London W1R 2HD
Telephone: 0171 973 3000
Fax: 0171 973 3430

Distributor:
Bailey Distribution Ltd, Learoyd Road, Mountfield Industrial Estate, New Romney, Kent TN28 8XU
Telephone: 01797 366905
Fax: 01797 366638

Home Sales Agent: Chris Lloyd (Sales & Marketing Services)
Managers: Ken Glen (Educational Publications)
Val Horsler (General Publications)

Archaeology; Architecture & Design; Educational & Textbooks; History & Antiquarian; Travel & Topography; Conservation (UK)

ISBNs, Imprints & Series: 1 85074

1280

ENTERPRISE TRANSPORT BOOKS LTD
3 Barnsway, Kings Langley, Herts WD4 9PW
Telephone: 01923 268392
Fax: 01923 268418
Email: khumberstone@cix.compulink.co.uk

Warehouse & Orders:
3B Colwell Drive, Abingdon, Oxon OX14 1AU
Telephone: 01235 527544
Fax: 01235 530435

Directors: David Affleck *(Managing)*
Karl Humberstone *(Finance & Administration)*

Transport

New Titles: 22 (1995), 20 (1996)
No of Employees: 2
Annual Turnover: £250,000

1281

ENTRA PUBLICATIONS LTD
3 Finway Court, Whippendell Road, Watford
WD1 7EN
Telephone: 01923 243730
Fax: 01923 213144

Sales & Distribution:
PO Box 75, Stockport, Cheshire SK4 1PH
Telephone: 0161 480 5285
Fax: 0161 474 7502

Director: P. M. Farrer *(Watford)*
Managers: J. Atkinson *(Warehouse &*
Distribution—Stockport)
Mrs B. M. Bowsher *(Company Secretary,*
Rights & Permissions—Watford)
Miss S. Deane *(Editorial—Watford)*

Educational & Textbooks; Engineering;
Scientific & Technical; Vocational Training &
Careers

New Titles: 36 (1995), 30 (1996)
No of Employees: 20
Annual Turnover: £1.25M

ISBNs, Imprints & Series: 0 85083

Parent Company:
Engineering Training Authority

1282

EPWORTH PRESS
Methodist Publishing House, 20 Ivatt Way,
Peterborough PE3 7PG
Telephone: 01733 332202
Fax: 01733 331201

Promotion & Distribution:
SCM Press Ltd, 9–17 St Albans Place, London
N1 0NX
Telephone: 0171 359 8033
Fax: 0171 359 0049

Editorial: Revd Gerald Burt

Religion & Theology

New Titles: 10 (1995), 10 (1996)

ISBNs, Imprints & Series: 0 7162

Overseas Representation *(see §7.3):*
USA: Trinity Press International, Valley Forge,
PA
Worldwide (except USA): SCM Press, London,
UK

1283

ERA TECHNOLOGY LTD
Cleeve Road, Leatherhead, Surrey KT22 7SA
Telephone: 01372 367000
Fax: 01372 367099
Email: info@era.co.uk
Web Site: http://www.era.co.uk/

Manager: Mrs P. Church *(Publications)*

Electronic (Professional & Academic);
Engineering; Environment & Development
Studies; Industry, Business & Management;
Reference Books, Directories & Dictionaries;
Scientific & Technical

New Titles: 22 (1995), 30 (1996)
No of Employees: 465
Annual Turnover: £20M

ISBNs, Imprints & Series: 0 7008

Overseas Representation *(see §7.3):*
Singapore: ERA Technology (Asia) Pte Ltd
USA: ERA Technology Inc, Houston, TX

1284

*ESTATE PUBLICATIONS
Bridewell House, Tenterden, Kent TN30 6EP
Telephone: 01580 764225
Fax: 01580 763720

Sales: R. J. E. Taylor
Rights: C. M. G. Davies

Maps

ISBNs, Imprints & Series: 0 86084

Distributor for:
Ordnance Survey; Ordnance Survey of
Northern Ireland. *Canada:* International Travel
Maps & Books (ITMB). *Irish Republic:*
Ordnance Survey

Overseas Representation *(see §7.3):*
Australia: Rex Map Centre, Lane Cove, NSW
Germany: Gleumes & Co, Cologne
USA & Canada: International Travel Maps &
Books, Vancouver, Canada

1285

EUROBOOK LTD
PO Box 52, Wallingford, Oxon OX10 0XU
Telephone: 01865 749033
Fax: 01865 749044

Managing Director: P. S. Lowe

Gardening; Natural History; Reference Books,
Directories & Dictionaries

ISBNs, Imprints & Series:
0 85654 Peter Lowe

1286

EUROFI LTD
44 Melville Street, Edinburgh EH3 7HF
Telephone: 0131 225 8451
Fax: 0131 220 1972

Director: Tony Reid
Publications Co-ordinator: Verna Ingram

Industry, Business & Management

ISBNs, Imprints & Series:
0 907304, 1 900104 Eurofi Guide to European
Community Grants and Loans, Guide des
Prêts et Subventions de la Communauté
Européenne

1287

EUROMONITOR PLC
60–61 Britton Street, London EC1M 5NA
Telephone: 0171 251 8024
Fax: 0171 608 3149
Email: info@euromonitor.com
Web Site: http://www.euromonitor.com

Warehouse:
The Trade Counter, Unit D,
Trading Estate Road, North Acton, London
NW10 7LU
Telephone: 0181 963 0322
Fax: 0181 965 9765

Directors: Trevor Fenwick *(Managing)*
Robert Senior *(Chairman)*
Andrew Maslen *(Marketing)*
Manager: David Gudgin *(Marketing &*
Promotions)

Economics; Industry, Business &
Management; Reference Books, Directories &
Dictionaries

New Titles: 25 (1995), 40 (1996)
No of Employees: 85
Annual Turnover: £5M

ISBNs, Imprints & Series: 0 86338

Parent Company:
Euromonitor Plc

Associated & Subsidiary Companies:
USA: Euromonitor International Inc

Distributor for:
USA: Findex *(Cambridge Information Group)*

Overseas Representation *(see §7.3):*
India: Viva Marketing, New Delhi
Japan: Toppan Co Ltd, Tokyo
Scandinavia: Croft & Croft, Leominster, UK
Singapore, Malaysia & Brunei: Publishers
Marketing Services Ltd, Singapore
Spain & Portugal: Iberian Book Services SL,
Madrid, Spain
USA: Gale Research Co, Detroit; FIND/SVP,
New York, NY

Book Trade Association Membership:
Directory Publishers Association, European
Association of Directory Publishers

1288 ▄▄▄▄▄▄▄▄▄▄▄▄▄▄▄▄▄▄▄▄▄▄▄▄

EUROPA PUBLICATIONS LTD
18 Bedford Square, London WC1B 3JN
Telephone: 0171 580 8236 & 4139
Fax: 0171 636 1664

Chairman: C. H. Martin, OBE, TD
Directors: P. A. McGinley *(Managing)*
Peter Jackson *(Home & Export Sales, Rights &*
  Permissions)
A. G. Oliver *(Editorial)*
J. P. Desmond *(Accounts)*
R. M. Hughes *(Financial)*
J. Quinney
M. R. Milton *(Company Secretary)*
Marketing Manager: Mary Sweny

Industry, Business & Management; Politics &
World Affairs; Reference Books, Directories &
Dictionaries

New Titles: 9 (1995), 11 (1996)
No of Employees: 50

ISBNs, Imprints & Series:
0 905118, 0 946653, 1 85743

Parent Company:
Martins Printing Group UK Ltd

Overseas Representation *(see §7.3)*:
Australia: James Bennett Pty Ltd, Collaroy
  Beach, NSW
Bangladesh: World Agencies Ltd, Dhaka
India: Disvan Enterprises, New Delhi
Japan: Maruzen Co Ltd, Tokyo
Pakistan: Book Bird, Lahore
Scandinavia: Croft & Croft, Leominster, UK
Singapore: PMS Publishers Marketing
  Services Pte Ltd
Spain & Portugal: Iberian Book Services SL,
  Madrid, Spain

Book Trade Association Membership: IPG,
Directory Publishers Association

1289 ▄▄▄▄▄▄▄▄▄▄▄▄▄▄▄▄▄▄▄▄▄▄▄▄

**EVANGELICAL PRESS & SERVICES
LTD**
12 Wooler Street, Darlington, Co Durham
DL1 1RQ
Telephone: 01325 380232
Fax: 01325 466153
Email: 100113.3603@compuserve.com

Warehouse:
Blossomgate, Ripon, North Yorks HG4 2AJ
Telephone: 01765 602362
Fax: 01765 602362

Managers: J. H. Rubens *(General & Sales)*
P. Cooper *(Production)*

Religion & Theology

New Titles: 15 (1995), 15 (1996)
No of Employees: 15

ISBNs, Imprints & Series:
0 85234 Evangelical Press
0 946462 Grace Publications

Associated & Subsidiary Companies:
France: Europresse SARL

Distributor for:
Carey Publications; FIEC; Free Presbyterian
Publishing; Go Teach Publications; Gospel
Standard Publications; Knox Press; Sovereign
Publications. *USA:* Baker Book House;
Hendricksen Publishers; Pilgrim Publications;
Presbyterian & Reformed

Book Trade Association Membership:
Christian Booksellers Association

1290 ▄▄▄▄▄▄▄▄▄▄▄▄▄▄▄▄▄▄▄▄▄▄▄▄

EVANGELICAL PRESS OF WALES
Bryntirion, Bridgend, Mid Glamorgan
CF31 4DX
Telephone: 01656 655886
Fax: 01656 656095

Chief Executive: Gerallt Wyn Davies

Religion & Theology

New Titles: 5 (1995), 5 (1996)
No of Employees: 4
Annual Turnover: £85,000

ISBNs, Imprints & Series:
0 900898, 0 9502686, 1 85049 Evangelical
  Library of Wales
0 900898, 1 85049 Evangelical Movement of
  Wales, Evangelical Press of Wales

Parent Company:
Evangelical Movement of Wales

Distributor for:
Association of Christian Teachers of Wales;
Evangelical Library (London); Yr Undeb
Cristnogol

Overseas Representation *(see §7.3)*:
Australia: Reformers' Bookroom, Sydney
New Zealand: Sovereign Grace Books,
  Auckland
Philippines: Evangelical Outreach Inc, Quezon
  City
Singapore: Bethesda Book Centre
South Africa: Farel Distributors (Pty) Ltd,
  North Riding; Barnabas Book Room,
  Randburg
USA & Canada: Trinity Book Service,
  Montville, NJ, USA; Cumberland Valley
  Bible Book Service, Carlisle, PA, USA;
  Gospel Mission Inc, Choteau, MT, USA

Book Trade Association Membership:
Undeb Cyhoeddwyr a Llyfrwerthwyr Cymru,
(The Union of Welsh Publishers and
Booksellers)

1291 ▄▄▄▄▄▄▄▄▄▄▄▄▄▄▄▄▄▄▄▄▄▄▄▄

EVANS BROTHERS LTD
2a Portman Mansions, Chiltern Street, London
W1M 1LE
Telephone: 0171 935 7160
Fax: 0171 487 5034

Warehouse, Trade Enquiries & Orders:
Bookpoint Ltd, 39 Milton Park, Abingdon,
Oxon OX14 4TD
Telephone: 01235 400400 & 400407
Fax: 01235 861038 & 832068

Directors: Stephen Pawley *(Managing, Rights*
  & Permissions)

Brian Jones *(International Publishing)*
Managers: Jennifer Mulvanny *(Production)*
Jill Hole *(UK Sales)*
Jason McGovern *(Export Sales)*
Julia Posen *(Rights)*
Su Swallow

Children's Books; Educational & Textbooks

New Titles: 38 (1995), 46 (1996)
No of Employees: 10
Annual Turnover: £2M

ISBNs, Imprints & Series:
0 237 Cloverleaf, Evans Brothers

Associated & Subsidiary Companies:
Cameroon: Evans Brothers Ltd. *Ghana:* Evans
Brothers Ltd. *Kenya:* Evans Brothers (Kenya)
Ltd. *Nigeria:* Evans Brothers (Nigeria
Publishers) Ltd. *Sierra Leone:* Evans Brothers
Ltd

Overseas Representation *(see §7.3)*:
Australia: Macmillan Education Australia
  (Pty) Ltd, Melbourne, Vic & Drummoyne,
  NSW
Barbados, St Lucia & St Vincent: Ezra
  Crichlow, St Thomas, Barbados
Botswana, Mozambique & Zambia: The
  Educational Book Service (Pty) Ltd,
  Gabarone, Botswana
Cameroon: Evans Brothers Ltd, Bamenda
Canada: Fitzhenry & Whiteside Ltd, Markham
Ghana: MES Equipment Ltd, Accra North
Grenada: Thompson C. Crosby, St Mark's
Hong Kong: Federal Publications (HK) Ltd,
  Kowloon
Jamaica, Belize & Bahamas: Kingston
  Bookshop, Kingston, Jamaica; Sangster's
  Book Stores Ltd, Kingston, Jamaica
Kenya: Evans Brothers (Kenya) Ltd, Nairobi
Malawi: Dzuka Publishing Ltd, Blantyre
Middle East: Al-Dar al-Arabia Lil Nashr Wa
  Al-Tawzeia, Cairo, Egypt
New Zealand: South Pacific Books (Imports)
  Ltd, Auckland
Nigeria: Evans Brothers (Nigeria Publishers)
  Ltd, Ibadan
Sierra Leone, Liberia & Gambia: Evans
  Brothers Ltd, Freetown, Sierra Leone
Singapore, Malaysia & Brunei: Pansing
  Distribution Sdn Bhd, Singapore
South Africa, Swaziland, Lesotho & Namibia:
  Nolwazi Educational Publishers Pty Ltd,
  Braamfontein, South Africa
Spain: Iberian Book Services SL, Madrid
*St Kitts, British Virgin Isles, Netherlands
  Antilles, Montserrat, Anguilla, Antigua &
  Dominica:* R. J. Laws & Son Agencies,
  Basseterre, St Kitts
Tanzania: NGM Ltd, Dar-es-Salaam
Uganda: Fountain Publishers, Kampala
USA: Trafalgar Square Publications, North
  Pomfret, VT
Zimbabwe: Academic Press Pvt Ltd, Harare

Book Trade Association Membership: PA,
BA, BDC, EPC

1292 ▄▄▄▄▄▄▄▄▄▄▄▄▄▄▄▄▄▄▄▄▄▄▄▄

EX LIBRIS PRESS
1 The Shambles, Bradford on Avon, Wiltshire
BA15 1JS
Telephone: 01225 863595
Fax: 01225 863595

Stockists:
West Country Books, Tiverton, Devon
Telephone: 01884 243242
Fax: 01884 243325

Proprietor: Roger Jones

Biography & Autobiography; Geography & Geology; Guide Books; History & Antiquarian; Humour; Natural History; Transport; Travel & Topography

New Titles: 9 (1995), 9 (1996)
Annual Turnover: £65,000

ISBNs, Imprints & Series:
0 948578 Seaflower Books

Book Trade Association Membership: BA, IPG

1293 ▬▬▬▬▬▬▬▬▬

EXECUTIVE GRAPEVINE INTERNATIONAL LTD
New Barnes Mill, Cottonmill Lane, St Albans
AL5 2MA
Telephone: 01727 844335
Fax: 01727 844779

Managing Director: Helen Barrett
Managers: Sue Salisbury *(Research)*
Lyn Codrai *(Office, Sales)*

Industry, Business & Management; Reference Books, Directories & Dictionaries; Banking; Human Resources

New Titles: 9 (1995), 9 (1996)
No of Employees: 14

ISBNs, Imprints & Series: 1 870441

Book Trade Association Membership:
Directory Publishers Association

1294 ▬▬▬▬▬▬▬▬▬

UNIVERSITY OF EXETER PRESS
Reed Hall, Streatham Drive, Exeter EX4 4QR
Telephone: 01392 263066
Fax: 01392 263064
Email: uep@exeter.ac.uk
Web Site: http://www.ex.ac.uk/uep/

Distribution:
Plymbridge Distributors Ltd
Telephone: 01752 202301
Fax: 01752 202331

Publisher: Simon Baker
Sales: Genevieve Davey

Academic & Scholarly; Archaeology; Geography & Geology; History & Antiquarian; Languages & Linguistics; Literature & Criticism; Arabic & American Studies; Classical Studies; French/Spanish/ Italian Literature; Maritime History; Medieval English Texts & Studies

New Titles: 20 (1995), 30 (1996)
No of Employees: 5

ISBNs, Imprints & Series:
0 85989, 0 900771

Overseas Representation *(see §7.3)*:
Australia & New Zealand: Eleanor Brasch Associates, Artarmon, NSW, Australia
Far East: Roger Ward, London, UK
France, Greece, Germany, Spain, Portugal, Gibraltar, Scandinavia, Benelux, Italy, Switzerland & Austria: Books for Europe Ltd, Bournemouth, UK
Middle East: Hugh Thomas, Brighton, UK
USA & Canada: Northwestern University Press, Evanston, IL, USA

Book Trade Association Membership: PA

1295 ▬▬▬▬▬▬▬▬▬

EXLEY PUBLICATIONS LTD
16 Chalk Hill, Watford, Herts WD1 4BN
Telephone: 01923 250505
Fax: 01923 818733

Directors: Helen M. Exley *(Managing & Editorial)*
Richard A. Exley *(Finance & Chairman)*
Lincoln Exley *(Sales & Marketing)*
Managers: Peter Swift *(UK Sales)*
Frances Riley *(Foreign Rights)*
Mark Jeffrey *(Customer Services)*
Michael Illingworth *(Export Sales)*
Billy Adair *(National Accounts)*
Lynne Clark *(Business Development)*

Children's Books; Educational & Textbooks; Humour; Gift Books

New Titles: 50 (1995), 50 (1996)
No of Employees: 45

ISBNs, Imprints & Series: 1 85015

Associated & Subsidiary Companies:
France: Exley SA. *USA:* Exley Giftbooks

Overseas Representation *(see §7.3)*:
Australia: Lothian Books, Port Melbourne; Macmillan Education Australia (Pty) Ltd, Melbourne, Vic & Drummoyne, NSW
Canada: Tanager Press, Mississauga; Goods Trading Co, Richmond Hill, Ont
Europe: Roger Smith, Enfield, UK
India: Maya Publishers Pvt Ltd, New Delhi
Irish Republic: Island Publications Ltd, Dublin
Israel: Astra Agency, Jerusalem
Malta: Audio Visual Centre Ltd, Sliema
Middle East: Michael Morris Associates, Saffron Walden, UK
New Zealand: David Bateman Ltd, Auckland
Philippines: Balatbat & Sons International, Quezon City
Singapore: Pansing Distribution Sdn Bhd
Southern Africa: Southern Book Publishers, Halfway House, South Africa

Book Trade Association Membership: IPG

1296 ▬▬▬▬▬▬▬▬▬

EXPRESS NEWSPAPERS PLC
245 Blackfriars Road, London SE1 9UX
Telephone: 0171 928 8000
Fax: 0171 922 7966

Books Department Manager: Sue Bailey
Rupert Editor: Ian Robinson

Atlases & Maps; Children's Books; Gardening; Humour; Sports & Games; Transport

Parent Company:
United Newspapers Ltd

1297 ▬▬▬▬▬▬▬▬▬

FABER & FABER LTD
3 Queen Square, London WC1N 3AU
Telephone: 0171 465 0045
Fax: 0171 465 0034

Distribution & Accounts:
16 Burnt Mill, Elizabeth Way, Harlow, Essex
CM20 2HX
Telephone: 01279 417134
Fax: 01279 417366

Chairman & Managing Director: Matthew Evans
Directors: T. E. Faber
Joanna Mackle *(Publishing)*
Giles de la Mare
Tom Kelleher
John Bodley
Dennis Crutcher *(Production)*
Peter Simpson *(Finance)*
Robert McCrum *(Editorial)*
Patrick Curran *(Distribution)*
Valerie Eliot
Editorial: Chris Reid *(Poetry)*
Janice Thomson *(Children's)*
Peggy Butcher *(Plays)*
Walter Donohue *(Film)*
Michael Durnin *(Music)*
Belinda Matthews *(Wine & Food)*
Julian Loose *(Non-fiction)*
Jacket & Cover Design: Pentagram
Head of Rights: Ros Edwards
Sales: Tim Davies
Nick Kenney

Biography & Autobiography; Children's Books; Cinema, Video, TV & Radio; Cookery, Wines & Spirits; Fiction; Literature & Criticism; Music; Poetry; Politics & World Affairs; Theatre, Drama & Dance

New Titles: 250 (1995), 210 (1996)
No of Employees: 114
Annual Turnover: £11.4M

ISBNs, Imprints & Series: 0 571

Associated & Subsidiary Companies:
Geoffrey Faber Holdings Ltd; Faber Music Ltd.
USA: Faber & Faber Inc

Distributor for:
Faber Music Ltd; Walker Books Ltd. *USA:*
Faber & Faber Inc

Overseas Representation *(see §7.3)*:
Africa (excluding Southern Africa): Len Ainsworth, Aldbourne, UK
Australia: Penguin Books Australia Ltd, Ringwood, Vic
Canada: Penguin Books Canada Ltd, Newmarket, Ont
Caribbean & Latin America: Intermedia Americana, London, UK
France, Belgium & Luxembourg: Penguin France SA, Toulouse, France
Germany & Austria: Penguin Books Deutschland GmbH, Frankfurt, Germany

Greece, Israel & Cyprus: Penguin Hellas Ltd,
Athens, Greece
Hong Kong: Publishers' Associates Ltd
India: Rupa & Co, New Delhi
Irish Republic: Gill Hess Ltd, Skerries
Italy: Penguin Italia Srl, Milan
Japan: Macmillan Shuppan KK, Tokyo
Malta, Central Europe & Scandinavia:
Penguin Books Ltd, London, UK
Middle East: Sarah Fitzpatrick, London, UK
Netherlands: Nilsson & Lamm BV, Weesp
New Zealand: Penguin Books (New Zealand)
Ltd, Auckland
Pakistan: Oxford University Press, Karachi
*South East Asia (including Malaysia,
Singapore, Indonesia & Brunei):* Pansing
Distribution Sdn Bhd, Singapore
Southern Africa: Longman Penguin South
Africa, Bertsham, South Africa
Spain: Penguin Books SA, Madrid
Switzerland: AZED AG, Muttenz
Taiwan: Bookman Books Ltd, Taipei
Thailand & Philippines: Balatbat & Sons
International, Quezon City, Philippines
Turkey: Penguin Turkey, Istanbul
USA: Faber & Faber Inc, Winchester, MA

Book Trade Association Membership: PA

1298 ▬▬▬▬

FABIAN SOCIETY
11 Dartmouth Street, London SW1H 9BN
Telephone: 0171 222 8877
Fax: 0171 976 7153
Email: fabian-society@geo2.poptel.org.uk

General Secretary: Simon Crine
Sales: Giles Wright
Administrators: Clair Wilcox *(Conferences)*
Stephen Pollard *(Publications)*

*Academic & Scholarly; Economics; Politics &
World Affairs*

New Titles: 30 (1995), 30 (1996)

ISBNs, Imprints & Series:
0 7163 Fabian Pamphlet

Associated & Subsidiary Companies:
NCLC Publishers Ltd

Distributor for:
NCLC Publishers Ltd

Overseas Representation *(see §7.3):*
Australia: Australian Fabian Society

Book Trade Association Membership: PA,
BA

1299 ▬▬▬

THE FACTORY SHOP GUIDE
1 Rosebery Mews, Rosebery Road, London
SW2 4DQ
Telephone: 0181 678 0593
Fax: 0181 674 1594
Email: factshop@macline.co.uk

Partners: Gillian Cutress
Rolf Stricker

*Gardening; Guide Books; Industry, Business &
Management; Travel & Topography*

New Titles: 8 (1995), 8 (1996)

ISBNs, Imprints & Series:
0 948965 The Factory Shop Guides

Book Trade Association Membership: IPG

1300 ▬▬▬▬

FACTS ON FILE
c/o Roundhouse Publishing Ltd, PO Box 140,
Oxford OX2 7FF
Telephone: 01865 728399
Fax: 01865 59594
Email: 100637.3571@compuserve.com

Warehouse & Distribution:
Bookpoint Ltd, 39 Milton Park, Abingdon,
Oxon OX14 4TD
Telephone: Abingdon 01235 400400
Fax: 01235 832068

Directors: Alan Goodworth *(Home & Export
Sales)*
Christine Ramos *(Rights & Permissions)*

*Cinema, Video, TV & Radio; Fine Art & Art
History; Geography & Geology; History &
Antiquarian; Literature & Criticism; Medical
(incl. Self Help & Alternative Medicine);
Military & War; Music; Natural History;
Politics & World Affairs; Reference Books,
Directories & Dictionaries; Sports & Games;
Theatre, Drama & Dance*

New Titles: 125 (1995), 125 (1996)

ISBNs, Imprints & Series:
0 8160, 0 87196, 0 948894 Facts On File

Parent Company:
Facts On File Inc *(USA)*

Overseas Representation *(see §7.3):*
Africa: PMC International, Durban North,
South Africa
Australia: Capricorn Link (Australia) Pty Ltd,
Baulkham Hills, NSW
China: Cassidy & Associates Inc, New York,
USA
Europe (East): MTM, Hong Kong
Europe (West) (excluding Scandinavia): Ted
Dougherty, London, UK
Hong Kong & Taiwan: Edwin Chu, Hong Kong
India: Viva Marketing, New Delhi
Irish Republic (Reference/Academic): Carr
O'Connell, Ashbourne, Irish Republic
Japan: United Publishers Services Ltd, Tokyo
Middle East: International Publishers
Representatives (IPR), Nicosia, Cyprus
New Zealand: Forrester Books NZ Ltd,
Takapuna
Pakistan: Tahir Lodhi, Lahore
Philippines: F & J de Jesus Inc, Metro Manila
Scandinavia: Hanne Rotovnik, Klampenborg,
Denmark
Singapore & Malaysia: Publishers Marketing
Services Ltd, Singapore
South America: Terry Roberts, Cotia SP, Brazil
USA, Canada, Korea, Thailand & Indonesia:
Facts On File Inc, New York, USA

1301 ▬▬▬▬

FALMER PRESS LTD
1 Gunpowder Square, London EC4A 3DE

Telephone: 0171 583 0490
Fax: 0171 583 0581

Warehouse, Trade Enquiries & Orders:
Taylor & Francis, Rankine Road, Basingstoke,
Hants RG24 0PR
Telephone: 01256 813000
Fax: 01256 479438

Directors: Malcolm Clarkson *(Managing,
Editorial)*
Roger Horton *(Sales)*
Editor: Anna Clarkson
Managers: Alison Woodhead *(Promotion)*
Jo Gearing *(Marketing Assistant)*
Jackie Day *(Production)*
Peter Moran *(Sales)*
Foreign Rights & Permissions: Mary
Elverson
Secretary: Emma Jackson

*Academic & Scholarly; Educational &
Textbooks; Gender Studies; Psychology &
Psychiatry; Sociology & Anthropology;
Vocational Training & Careers*

New Titles: 55 (1995), 55 (1996)
No of Employees: 8
Annual Turnover: £1.2M

ISBNs, Imprints & Series:
0 75070, 1 85000

Parent Company:
Taylor & Francis Group

Associated & Subsidiary Companies:
USA: Taylor & Francis Inc

Overseas Representation *(see §7.3):*
Australia: Edward Arnold (Australia) Ltd,
Rydalmere, NSW
Canada: Gage Educational Publishing Co,
Agincourt, Ont
Hong Kong: Information Publications Pte Ltd,
Kowloon
India: UBS Publishers' Distributors Ltd, New
Delhi
Japan: Kinokuniya Co Ltd, Tokyo
New Zealand: Book Reps (New Zealand) Ltd,
Auckland
South East Asia: Information Publications Pte
Ltd, Singapore
USA: Taylor & Francis Inc, Bristol, PA

Book Trade Association Membership: PA,
EPC

1302 ▬▬▬

*FANTAIL BOOKS
27 Wrights Lane, London W8 5TZ
Telephone: 0171 416 3000
Fax: 0171 416 3099

Also at:
Bath Road, Harmondsworth, Middx
Telephone: 0181 899 4000
Fax: 0181 899 4099

*Children's Books; Cinema, Video, TV & Radio;
Fiction; Humour; Music; Television*

ISBNs, Imprints & Series: 0 14 09

Parent Company:
Penguin Books

Overseas Representation *(see §7.3):*
See: Penguin Books Ltd, London, UK

1303

FARMING PRESS
Wharfedale Road, Ipswich, Suffolk IP1 4LG
Telephone: 01473 241122
Fax: 01473 240501
Email: 101573.2030@compuserve.com

Manager: R. G. Smith *(Books)*
Sales: Catherine Britton
Editorial: Claire Newbery

Agriculture; Animal Care & Breeding; Humour; Veterinary Science; Countryside Interest

New Titles: 25 (1995), 39 (1996)
No of Employees: 12

ISBNs, Imprints & Series:
0 85236 Farming Press

Parent Company:
United Newspapers Ltd

Distributor for:
David Taylor

Overseas Representation *(see §7.3):*
Australia: Butterworth-Heinemann, Chatswood, NSW
India: UBS Publishers' Distributors Ltd, New Delhi
Irish Republic: Carr O'Connell, Ashbourne
New Zealand: David Bateman Ltd, Auckland
Southern Africa: Southern Book Publishers, Glenhills, Durban, South Africa
USA & Canada: Diamond Farm Book Publishers, Brighton, Canada

1304

FEDERAL TRUST
11 Tufton Street, London SW1P 3QB
Telephone: 0171 799 2818
Fax: 0171 799 2820
Email: gm@fedtrust.compulink.co.uk
Web Site: http://www.compulink.co.uk/~fedtrust/

Director: Andrew Duff
Publication Officer: Guillaume McLaughlin

Academic & Scholarly; Economics; Politics & World Affairs

New Titles: 8 (1995), 7 (1996)
No of Employees: 5

ISBNs, Imprints & Series: 0 90157

1305

FERNHURST BOOKS
Duke's Path, High Street, Arundel, West Sussex BN18 9AJ
Telephone: 01903 882277
Fax: 01903 882715

Managing Director: Tim Davison
Managers: Karen Rafferty *(Commercial)*
Annie Buckley *(Sales)*

Humour; Nautical; Sports & Games

New Titles: 10 (1995), 10 (1996)
No of Employees: 3

ISBNs, Imprints & Series:
0 906754, 1 898660

Distributor for:
Seloc *(Outboard manuals)*; Nat Young Surfing Books

Overseas Representation *(see §7.3):*
Australia: Boat Books, Crows Nest, NSW; Boat Books, St Kilda, Vic; Boat Books, Brisbane, Qld; Boat Books, Perth, WA
Canada (Canadian chandleries): Transat Marine, Barrie, Ont, Canada
Caribbean & Commonwealth Africa: Kelvin van Hasselt Publishing Services, Lymington, UK
Europe: Books for Europe, J. Komarnicki, Lugano, Switzerland
Middle & Near East: Eurab Ltd, Rottingdean, UK
New Zealand: David's Marine Books, Westhaven, Auckland
North America: Armchair Sailor Bookstore, Newport, RI, USA
North America, Canadian bookstores & South America: East Shore Sailing, Ithaca, NY, USA
South Africa: Media House Publications Pty Ltd, Sandton

Book Trade Association Membership: IPG, South Coast Publishers' Group (founder)

1306

FHG PUBLICATIONS LTD
Abbey Mill Business Centre, Seedhill, Paisley PA1 1TJ
Telephone: 0141 887 0428
Fax: 0141 889 7204

Book Trade Representative:
WLM, The Hollow, Littleover, Derby DE3 7BS

Publishing Director: P. M. Clark
Production Manager: G. Pratt

Guide Books; Sports & Games

New Titles: 15 (1995), 15 (1996)
No of Employees: 14

ISBNs, Imprints & Series: 1 85055

Parent Company:
Link House Media Ltd

Book Trade Association Membership: PPA

1307

FINDHORN PRESS
The Park, Findhorn, Forres, Moray IV36 0TZ
Telephone: 01309 690582
Fax: 01309 690036
Email: karin@findhorn.org
Web Site: http://www.gaia.org/findhornpress/

Publisher: Thierry Bogliolo
Sales Manager: Karin Bogliolo

Ecology; Healing & Self Help; Humour; Metaphysical; Mind, Body, Spirit; New Age

New Titles: 14 (1995), 16 (1996)
No of Employees: 3

ISBNs, Imprints & Series: 0 905249

Overseas Representation *(see §7.3):*
Australia: Gemcraft Books, Burwood, Vic
Irish Republic, Europe & South Africa: Ashgrove Press, Bath, UK
USA: New Leaf Distribution, Lithia Springs, GA; Book People, Oakland, CA

Book Trade Association Membership: IPG, Scottish PA

1308

FIREBIRD BOOKS LTD
463 Ashley Road, Parkstone, Poole, Dorset BH14 0AX
Telephone: 01202 715349
Fax: 01202 736191

Postal Address:
PO Box 327, Poole, Dorset BH15 2RG

Editorial/ Production Office:
41 Victoria Road, Blandford Forum, Dorset DT11 7JR
Telephone: 01258 454675
Fax: 01258 456023

Directors: Chris Lloyd *(Commercial)*
Stuart Booth *(Editorial)*
Kathryn S. A. Booth *(Design/Production)*

History & Antiquarian; Humour; Military & War; Music; Sports & Games

New Titles: 4 (1995), 4 (1996)
No of Employees: 3

ISBNs, Imprints & Series:
1 85314 Firebird Books, Heroes & Warriors Series, Wise Owl Quiz Promotions

Distributor for:
The Comic Book Price Guide (Price Guide Productions)

Overseas Representation *(see §7.3):*
Australia: Capricorn Link (Australia) Pty Ltd, Baulkham Hills, NSW
France, Benelux, Germany, Switzerland & Austria: European Marketing Services, London, UK
Italy, Malta, Greece, Spain & Portugal: Bookport Associates, Bologna, Italy
New Zealand: South Pacific Books (Imports) Ltd, Auckland
Scandinavia: Croft & Croft, Leominster, UK
Southern Africa: PMC International, Durban North, South Africa
USA (selected titles only): Sterling Publishing Co Inc, New York, NY, USA

1309

FIRST & BEST IN EDUCATION LTD
32 Nene Valley Business Park, Oundle, Peterborough PE8 4HJ
Telephone: 01832 275285
Fax: 01832 275281
Web Site: http://www.schools.co.uk

Finance Manager: Sue Quincey
Managing Director: Tony Attwood

Editors: Vivienne Hill
Kirsty Meadows

Educational & Textbooks; Electronic (Educational); Industry, Business & Management

New Titles: 200 (1995), 200 (1996)
No of Employees: 14
Annual Turnover: £0.5M

ISBNs, Imprints & Series:
1 860 First & Best Business Press, First & Best in Education Ltd, Multi-Sensory Learning

Book Trade Association Membership: PA, EPC

1310 ◼️

FLICKS BOOKS
29 Bradford Road, Trowbridge, Wilts
BA14 9AN
Telephone: 01225 767728
Fax: 01225 760418

Directors: Matthew Stevens
Aletta Stevens

Cinema, Video, TV & Radio

New Titles: 4 (1995), 12 (1996)

ISBNs, Imprints & Series: 0 948911

1311 ◼️

BURALL FLORAPRINT LTD
PO Box 29, Oldfield Lane, Wisbech,
Cambridgeshire PE13 2TH
Telephone: 01945 461165
Fax: 01945 474396

Distribution:
Biblios Publishers Distribution Services,
Star Road, Partridge Green, West Sussex
RH13 8LD
Telephone: 01403 710971
Fax: 01403 711143

Managing Director: B. Pinker

Gardening

New Titles: 1 (1995), 1 (1996)
No of Employees: 27
Annual Turnover: £5M

ISBNs, Imprints & Series:
0 903001 Floraprint

Parent Company:
Burall Ltd

Overseas Representation *(see §7.3):*
Australia: Macbird Floraprint Pty Ltd,
Scoresby, Vic
Austria: Floraprint GmbH, Vienna
Belgium: Floraprint NV, Antwerp
Canada: John Markham Associates, Sidney,
BC
France: Mauryflor SA, Malesherbes
Germany: Verlagsgesellschaft Grun ist Leben
mbH, Pinneberg
Liechtenstein: Floraprint International GmbH,
Vaduz
Netherlands: Floraprint BV, Lisse

New Zealand: Floraprint New Zealand,
Wellington
Norway: Floraprint Norge A/S, Stavanger
South Africa: Floraprint Southern Africa,
Florida
Spain: Floraprint España, Valencia
Sweden: Floraprint Sverige AB, Staffanstorp
Switzerland: Floraprint AG, Egg
Taiwan: Floraprint Taiwan Ltd, Taipei

1312 ◼️

FLORIS BOOKS
15 Harrison Gardens, Edinburgh EH11 1SH
Telephone: 0131 337 2372
Fax: 0131 346 7516

Editorial: Christopher Moore
Chief Executive: Christian Maclean

*Academic & Scholarly; Children's Books;
Crafts & Hobbies; Philosophy; Religion &
Theology*

New Titles: 16 (1995), 16 (1996)
No of Employees: 3
Annual Turnover: £350,000

ISBNs, Imprints & Series:
0 86315, 0 903540 Floris Books

Distributor for:
Lindisfarne Press

Overseas Representation *(see §7.3):*
Australia: Astam Books Pty Ltd, Leichhardt,
NSW
Canada: Mandragore, Richmond Hill, Ont
New Zealand: Steinerbooks NZ, Auckland
South Africa: Verbatim Distributors,
Constantia Hills
USA (34 Children's & Parents' titles):
Gryphon House Inc, Mt Rainier, MD, USA
USA (44 Religious & Children's titles): New
Leaf Distribution, Lithia Springs, GA, USA
USA (all titles): Anthroposophic Press Inc,
Hudson, NY, USA

Book Trade Association Membership: PA,
Scottish Publishers Association

1313 ◼️

FOLENS LTD
Albert House, Apex Business Centre,
Boscombe Road, Dunstable, Beds
Telephone: 01582 472788
Fax: 01582 472575

Chairman: Dirk Folens
Directors: Malcolm G. Watson *(Managing,
Export Sales)*
John O'Connor *(Sales & Marketing)*
Colm Holmes *(Finance)*
Patricia Harrison *(Publishing)*
Managers: Philip Haywood *(Distribution)*
Simon Kemp *(Production)*
Peter Haywood *(Finance)*

Educational & Textbooks

ISBNs, Imprints & Series:
1 85276 Scholarstown Educational Publishers

Distributor for:
Belair Publications. *USA:* Frank Shaffer
Publications; Teacher Created Materials

Overseas Representation *(see §7.3):*
Australia: Southern Cross Educational,
Caulfield; The Dominie Group, Brookvale,
NSW; Modern Teaching Aids, Brookvale,
NSW
Canada: Bacon & Hughes, Nepean
New Zealand: South Pacific Books (Imports)
Ltd, Auckland
Singapore, Malaysia & Brunei: EPB Publishers
Pte Ltd, Singapore; Integrated Learning
Resources, Singapore
USA: Evan Moor Corp, Monterey CA

Book Trade Association Membership: PA

1314 ◼️

FOOD TRADE PRESS LTD
Station House, Hortons Way, Westerham, Kent
TN16 1BZ
Telephone: 01959 563944
Fax: 01959 561285

Directors: Howard Binsted *(Publishing)*
Adrian Binsted *(Sales)*

*Agriculture; Chemistry; Reference Books,
Directories & Dictionaries; Food Science &
Technology*

New Titles: 11 (1995), 14 (1996)
No of Employees: 7

ISBNs, Imprints & Series: 0 900379

Associated & Subsidiary Companies:
Attwood & Binsted Ltd

Distributor for:
Campden Food Preservation Research
Association; Leatherhead Food Research
Association; Management Publications;
Society of Dairy Technologists. *Australia:*
Hospitality Publications Ltd. *Denmark:*
Mercantila Publishing AS. *France:* Regies
Actions Publicitaires. *Italy:* Chiriotti Editori
Srl. *Spain:* Montagud Editores SA.
Switzerland: Binsted Frères SA. *USA:*
American Association of Cereal Chemists;
American Institute of Baking; Chemical
Publishing Co Inc; CTI Publications Inc; Food
& Nutrition Press Inc; Food Processors
Institute; Edward E. Judge & Sons

1315 ◼️

FOOTPRINT HANDBOOKS
[formerly Trade & Travel Publications]
6 Riverside Court, Riverside Road,
Lower Bristol Road, Bath BA2 3DZ
Telephone: 01225 469141
Fax: 01225 469461
Email: handbooks@footprint.compulink.co.
uk

Directors: James Dawson *(Managing)*
Patrick Dawson *(Editorial)*
Ro Dawson *(Publicity & PR Manager)*

Travel & Topography

New Titles: 9 (1995), 13 (1996)
No of Employees: 10

ISBNs, Imprints & Series:
0 900751 Footprint/Trade & Travel Handbooks
1 900949 Footprint Handbooks

Distributor for:
Wexas International

Overseas Representation *(see §7.3)*:
Australia: Peribo Pty Ltd, Mount Kuring-gai,
   NSW
Europe: D. Richard Bowen, Malmö, Sweden
India: Roli Books, New Delhi
South Africa: Faradawn CC, Saxonwold
South America: Humphrys Roberts Associates,
   Cotia, Brazil
South East Asia: Höfer Communications,
   Singapore
USA: Passport Books a division of NTC
   Contemporary Publishing, Lincolnwood, IL

Book Trade Association Membership:
International Map Dealers Association

1316 ■

FOOTPRINT PRESS LTD
19 Moseley Street, Ripley, Derbys DE5 3DA
Telephone: 01773 512143
Fax: 01773 512143

Managing Director: John N. Merrill *(Sales,*
   Editorial & Production, Rights &
   Permissions)
Retail Mail Orders: Mrs J. Piggott *(Manager)*
Publicity: Nigel Wilson

Biography & Autobiography; Guide Books;
Sports & Games; Travel & Topography

New Titles: 47 (1995), 89 (1996)
No of Employees: 8
Annual Turnover: £250,000

ISBNs, Imprints & Series:
0 907496, 1 874754

Associated & Subsidiary Companies:
USA: Suncrest Ventures Ltd

Overseas Representation *(see §7.3)*:
Canada: International Book Distributors,
   Vancouver
USA: Alpenbooks, Mukilteo, WA

1317 ■

FORBES PUBLICATIONS LTD
Inigo House, 29 Bedford Street, London
WC2E 9ED
Telephone: 0171 379 1299
Fax: 0171 379 6740

Orders & Distribution:
Plymbridge Distributors, Estover, Plymouth
PL6 7PZ
Telephone: 01752 202300 & 202301
(Customer Service)
Fax: 01752 202330 & 202331 (Customer
Service)

Directors: Judith Bloor *(Managing)*
Mary Anne Fitzgerald *(Publishing)*

Academic & Scholarly; Children's Books;
Cookery, Wines & Spirits; Educational &
Textbooks; Health & Beauty; Medical (incl.
Self Help & Alternative Medicine)

New Titles: 6 (1995), 10 (1996)

ISBNs, Imprints & Series:
0 901762, 1 899527

Parent Company:
Rapport Learning Ltd

Overseas Representation *(see §7.3)*:
Australia: Mentone Educational Centre,
   Ashburton

1318 ■

FOREST BOOKS
20 Forest View, Chingford, London E4 7AY
Telephone: 0181 529 8470
Fax: 0181 524 7890
Email: brenda@fores.demon.co.uk
Web Site: http://www.kaapeli.fi/forest/

Distribution:
Grantham Book Services, Isaac Newton Way,
Alma Park Estate, Grantham, Lincs NG31 9SD

Director: Brenda Walker

Drama in Translation; Fiction in Translation;
Poetry in Translation; Prose in Translation

New Titles: 3 (1995), 3 (1996)
No of Employees: 2

ISBNs, Imprints & Series:
0 948259, 0 9509487, 1 85610

Overseas Representation *(see §7.3)*:
Australia & New Zealand: Biramo Books,
   Warners Bay, NSW, Australia
Central & Eastern Europe: Gutke Verlag,
   Cologne, Germany
Scandinavia, Benelux, France & Middle East:
   Jim Osgerby, Yateley, UK
USA & Canada: Dufour Editions Inc, Chester
   Springs, PA, USA

1319 ■

ADRIAN FORMAN BOOKS
PO Box 25, Minehead, Somerset TA24 8YX
Telephone: 01643 862511
Fax: 01643 862511

Contact: Adrian Forman

Military & War

New Titles: 1 (1995), 2 (1996)
Annual Turnover: £120,000

ISBNs, Imprints & Series:
0 912138 R. J. Bender Publishing
0 9523571 Adrian Forman Books

Associated & Subsidiary Companies:
USA: R. J. Bender Publishing

Distributor for:
USA: R. J. Bender Publishing

Overseas Representation *(see §7.3)*:
USA: R. J. Bender Publishing, San Jose, CA

Book Trade Association Membership: PA

1320 ■

G. T. FOULIS & CO
Sparkford, Yeovil, Somerset BA22 7JJ

Telephone: 01963 440635
Fax: 01963 440023

Mail Orders & Despatch:
(as above)
Telephone: 01963 440614
Fax: 01963 440001

Chairman: J. H. Haynes
Editorial: D. J. Reach
Sales: T. Kemp
Marketing: D. Keel
Export Sales: M. Adams
Rights: R. Jackson
Finance: C. Davies
Production: K. Perrett

Do-It-Yourself; Reference Books, Directories
& Dictionaries; Transport; Motorcycling;
Motoring

New Titles: 8 (1995), 9 (1996)

ISBNs, Imprints & Series:
0 72323, 0 75080, 0 85429, 0 85614, 0 908081,
0 946137

Parent Company:
Haynes Publishing Group Plc

Associated & Subsidiary Companies:
J. H. Haynes & Co Ltd; Oxford Illustrated
Press; Oxford Publishing Co (OPC); Patrick
Stephens Ltd

Overseas Representation *(see §7.3)*:
USA: Motorbooks International Publishers &
   Wholesalers Inc, Osceola, WI
USA, Canada & Mexico: Haynes Publications
   Inc, Newbury Park, CA, USA

1321 ■

W. FOULSHAM & CO LTD
The Publishing House, Bennetts Close,
Cippenham, Berks SL1 5AP
Telephone: 01753 526769
Fax: 01753 535003

Distribution:
Macmillan Distribution Ltd, Houndmills,
Basingstoke RG21 2XS
Telephone: 01256 29242
Fax: 01256 812558

Directors: Barry Belasco *(Managing)*
Graham Kitchen *(Financial)*

Accountancy & Taxation; Antiques &
Collecting; Cookery, Wines & Spirits; Crafts &
Hobbies; Educational & Textbooks;
Gardening; Guide Books; Health & Beauty;
Humour; Magic & the Occult; Medical (incl.
Self Help & Alternative Medicine); Reference
Books, Directories & Dictionaries; Travel &
Topography

ISBNs, Imprints & Series: 0 572

Distributor for:
Priory Publications; Ramblers Association

Overseas Representation *(see §7.3)*:
Australia: Capricorn Link (Australia) Pty Ltd,
   Castle Hill, NSW
Canada: Diffusion Prologue, Boisbriand

New Zealand: Forrester Books NZ Ltd,
Takapuna
South Africa: Alternative Books, Randburg
USA: Atrium, Santa Rosa, CA

Book Trade Association Membership: PA,
BA

1322 ▬

**THE FOUNDATIONAL BOOK
COMPANY**
[for The John W. Doorly Trust]
PO Box 659, London SW3 6SJ
Telephone: 0171 584 1053

Trustee for Publications: Mrs P. M. Brook

Religion & Theology

ISBNs, Imprints & Series: 0 85241

Overseas Representation *(see §7.3):*
USA: Rare Book Co, Freehold, NJ; The
Bookmark, Santa Clara, CA

1323 ▬

FOUNTAIN PRESS LTD
Fountain House, 2 Gladstone Road,
Kingston-upon-Thames, Surrey KT1 3HD
Telephone: 0181 541 4050
Fax: 0181 547 3022

Directors: H. M. Ricketts *(Publisher)*
Mrs A. K. Ricketts *(Rights)*
John Mole *(Sales)*

*Cinema, Video, TV & Radio; Cookery, Wines &
Spirits; Crafts & Hobbies; Music; Natural
History; Photography; Automotive*

New Titles: 11 (1995), 13 (1996)
No of Employees: 3
Annual Turnover: £600,000

ISBNs, Imprints & Series: 0 86343

Distributor for:
The Carbery Press; Classic Collection; Hove
Books; Hove Collectors Books; Hove Foto
Books; Mitchell-Filby; Outline Press Ltd
(Balafon); Pineloft Publications; Toccata Press.
Canada: Sound & Vision. *USA:* Fisher Books;
Kodak Publications; Marling Menu Masters;
The Saunders Group; Silver Pixel Press

Overseas Representation *(see §7.3):*
Africa: Southern Book Publishers, Glenhills,
Durban, South Africa
Australia: Brighton House Publishing Pty Ltd,
Brighton, Vic
*Austria, Benelux, France, Germany &
Switzerland:* Angell Eurosales, Newton
Abbot, UK
*Cyprus, Turkey, Middle East, Indian Continent
& Far East:* Ashton International Marketing
Services, Larkfield, UK
Italy, Spain, Portugal & Greece: Bookport
Associates, Bologna, Italy
Scandinavia: D. Richard Bowen, Malmö,
Sweden
USA & Canada (Book trade): Fisher Books,
Tucson, AZ, USA
USA & Canada (Photographic Trade): The
Saunders Group, Rochester, NY, USA

1324 ▬

FOURTH ESTATE LTD
6 Salem Road, London W2
Telephone: 0171 727 8993 & 0171 243 1382
Fax: 0171 792 3176
Email: 101514.3365@compuserve.com

Distribution:
Tiptree Book Services Ltd, Tiptree, Colchester,
Essex CO5 0SR
Telephone: 01621 816362

Directors: Victoria Barnsley *(Managing)*
Christopher Potter *(Editorial)*
Joanna Prior *(Publicity)*
Stephen Page *(Sales)*
Patric Duffy *(Finance)*

*Biography & Autobiography; Cinema, Video,
TV & Radio; Cookery, Wines & Spirits; Crime;
Fiction; Health & Beauty; Humour; Literature
& Criticism; Politics & World Affairs;
Reference Books, Directories & Dictionaries;
Sports & Games; Travel & Topography*

New Titles: 60 (1995), 75 (1996)
No of Employees: 22
Annual Turnover: £3M

ISBNs, Imprints & Series:
0 947795, 1 872180 Blueprint Monographs,
Guardian Books

Overseas Representation *(see §7.3):*
Australia: Allen & Unwin Pty Ltd, St Leonards,
NSW
Canada: McClelland & Stewart, Toronto &
Markham
Europe: Janet Clark, London, UK
New Zealand: Random House New Zealand
Ltd, Auckland
South Africa: Trans S.A. Book Distributors,
Sandton & Johannesburg
USA: Trafalgar Square Publications, North
Pomfret, VT

1325 ▬

L. N. FOWLER & CO LTD
1201–1203 High Road, Chadwell Heath,
Romford, Essex RM6 4DH
Telephone: 0181 597 2491
Fax: 0181 598 2428

Managing Director & Trade Manager: C. J.
Nagle

*Health & Beauty; Medical (incl. Self Help &
Alternative Medicine); Religion & Theology;
Astrology; Creative Thought*

No of Employees: 5
Annual Turnover: £250,000

ISBNs, Imprints & Series: 0 85243

Distributor for:
Anodyne Publishing Services; C. W. Daniel Co
Ltd; L. N. Fowler & Co Ltd; Honey Press;
Knights Templar of Aquarius; Pilgrim Book
Services; Roximillion Publications Co; White
Eagle Publishing Trust. *Australia:* The Holistic
Centre; Inwardpath Publishers;
Weirknightsbridge & Associates. *France:*
Amrita Editions; Aureus Editions (Editions
Saint Michel). *USA:* American Federation of

Astrologers; Blue Dolphin Publishing Inc;
CRCS; CSA Press; Data News Press; De Vorss
& Co; Expansion Publishing Co; Frank Amato
Publications Inc; The Golden Sufi Centre;
Moeller Foundation; New Millennium
Publishing; Penthe Publishing Co; Valor
Foundation; Wisdome Press; Yoga
Publications Society

Overseas Representation *(see §7.3):*
Australia: Specialist Publications, Mortlake,
NSW
USA: New Leaf Distribution, Lithia Springs,
GA

1326 ▬

**FRAMEWORK PRESS EDUCATIONAL
PUBLISHERS LTD**
Parkfield, Greaves Road, Lancaster LA1 4TZ
Telephone: 01524 39602
Fax: 01524 841520

Directors: David R. Green
Brenda V. Abercrombie *(Editorial)*
Nicholas Abercrombie
Managers: Pamela Dymock *(Sales)*
Christine Needham *(Marketing)*
Controllers: Pamela Ebdon *(Financial)*
Christine Needham *(Production)*

*Educational & Textbooks; Vocational Training
& Careers*

New Titles: 20 (1995), 22 (1996)
No of Employees: 8
Annual Turnover: £320,000

ISBNs, Imprints & Series: 1 85008

Book Trade Association Membership: PA,
IPG

1327 ▬

FREE ASSOCIATION BOOKS
57 Warren Street, London WIP 5PA
Telephone: 0171 388 3182/3
Fax: 0171 388 3187
Email: fab@melmoth.demon.co.uk

Trade Distribution:
Sheed & Ward, 14 Coopers Row, London
EC3N 2BH
Telephone: 0171 702 9799
Fax: 0171 702 3583

Distribution:
Book Representation & Distribution (BRAD)
Ltd, 244a London Road, Hadleigh, Essex
SS7 2DE
Telephone: 01702 552912
Fax: 01702 556095

Directors: Gill Davies *(Managing Editor)*
Trevor E. Brown
Home & Export Sales: Jeff Archer
Rights & Permissions: Cathy Miller

*Academic & Scholarly; Medical (incl. Self Help
& Alternative Medicine); Psychology &
Psychiatry; Psychoanalysis; Psychotherapy*

New Titles: 15 (1995), 20 (1996)
No of Employees: 5

ISBNs, Imprints & Series:
0 946960, 1 85343 ,

Overseas Representation *(see §7.3):*
Australia: Astam Books Pty Ltd, Leichhardt, NSW
Europe: Books for Europe Ltd, Bournemouth, UK
North America: New York University Press, New York, USA
Scandinavia: D. Richard Bowen, Malmö, Sweden

Book Trade Association Membership: IPG

1328 ▬▬▬

FREEDOM PRESS
84b Whitechapel High Street, London E1 7QX
Telephone: 0171 247 9249
Fax: 0171 377 9526
Web Site: http://www.lglobal.com/TAO/freedom

Philosophy; Politics & World Affairs; Sociology & Anthropology

New Titles: 5 (1995), 7 (1996)

ISBNs, Imprints & Series:
0 900384 Anarchist Classics Series, Centenary Series

Distributor for:
AK Press; ASP; Calabria Press; DS4 A; Elephant Editions; Phoenix Press; Pirate Press; Kate Sharpley Library. *USA:* Michael E. Coughlin; Left Bank Books; See Sharp Press

Overseas Representation *(see §7.3):*
Australia: Jura Books, Petersham, NSW
Europe: Bokhandeln Info, Stockholm, Sweden
USA: See Sharp Press, San Francisco, CA; Left Bank Distribution, Seattle, WA

1329 ▬▬▬

W. H. FREEMAN
at Macmillan Press, Houndmills, Basingstoke, Hants RG21 6XS
Telephone: 01256 332807
Fax: 01256 330688

Trade Orders & Warehouse:
Macmillan Distribution Ltd, Houndmills, Basingstoke, Hants RG21 6XS
Telephone: 01256 29242
Fax: 01256 64733
Email: christis@macmillan.co.uk
Web Site: http://www.macmillan-press.co.uk

Managing Director: Elizabeth Warner
Marketing Manager: Jana Bek

Academic & Scholarly; Biology & Zoology; Chemistry; Computer Science; Geography & Geology; Mathematics & Statistics; Politics & World Affairs; Psychology & Psychiatry

ISBNs, Imprints & Series:
0 7167 Computer Science Press, W. H. Freeman & Co Ltd, Spektrum UK
0 87893 Sinauer
0 87901 Worth
0 89454 Scientific American Medicine Books
0 935702 University Science Books

Parent Company:
W. H. Freeman & Co *(USA)*

Associated & Subsidiary Companies:
USA: Scientific American Inc

Distributor for:
Spektrum Academic Publishers UK; University Science Books; Worth Publishers. *USA:* W. H. Freeman & Co; Scientific American Books Inc; Sinauer Associates

Overseas Representation *(see §7.3):*
Australia & New Zealand: Macmillan Education Australia (Pty) Ltd, Melbourne, Vic & Drummoyne, NSW, Australia
Hong Kong & China: Macmillan Publishers (China) Ltd, Hong Kong
Japan: Macmillan Shuppan KK, Tokyo
Puerto Rico: Kelvin van Hasselt Publishing Services, Lymington, UK
Singapore, Korea, Taiwan, Malaysia, Philippines, Indonesia & Thailand: Toppan Co (S) Pte Ltd, Singapore
USA: W. H. Freeman & Co, New York

Book Trade Association Membership:
IGSMTP, CAPP

1330 ▬▬▬

SAMUEL FRENCH LTD
52 Fitzroy Street, London W1P 6JR
Telephone: 0171 387 9373
Fax: 0171 387 2161

Directors: Charles Van Nostrand *(Chairman)*
John Bedding *(Managing)*
Amanda Smith
Paul Taylor

Theatre, Drama & Dance

New Titles: 50 (1995), 35 (1996)
No of Employees: 50

ISBNs, Imprints & Series: 0 573

Parent Company:
Samuel French Inc

Distributor for:
USA: Samuel French Inc

Overseas Representation *(see §7.3):*
Australia: The Dominie Group, Brookvale, NSW
East Africa: Phoenix Players Ltd, Nairobi, Kenya
Irish Republic: Thomas J. Mooney, Dublin
Malta: Dingli Co International, Valletta
New Zealand: Play Bureau of New Zealand Ltd, New Plymouth
South Africa, Namibia, Swaziland, Botswana & Lesotho: Dalro (Pty) Ltd, Johannesburg, South Africa
Zimbabwe: National Theatre Organization, Harare

Book Trade Association Membership: PA

1331 ▬▬▬

*FRIENDS OF THE EARTH
26–28 Underwood Street, London N1 7JQ
Telephone: 0171 490 1555
Fax: 0171 490 0881

Distributor:
Worldly Goods, 10–12 Picton Street, Montpelier, Bristol BS6 5QA
Telephone: 01179 420165
Fax: 01179 420164

Managers: Sarah Finch *(Editorial)*
Nick Watts *(Marketing)*
Head of Publications & Information: Athena Lamnisos

Academic & Scholarly; Agriculture; Educational & Textbooks; Environment & Development Studies

ISBNs, Imprints & Series: 1 85750

1332 ▬▬▬

FT LAW & TAX
21–27 Lamb's Conduit Street, London WC1N 3NJ
Telephone: 0171 242 2548
Fax: 0171 831 8119
Web Site: http://www.ftlawandtax.com

Managing Director: Chris Stibbs
Business Analyst: Ian Folkes
Directors: Janson Woodall *(Production)*
Alan Wells *(Editorial)*
Marie Staunton *(Publishing)*

Law

New Titles: 79 (1995), 85 (1996)
No of Employees: 100

ISBNs, Imprints & Series:
0 75200, 0 85120, 0 85121

Parent Company:
Pearson Professional

Book Trade Association Membership: PA, Directory Publishers Association

1333 ▬▬▬

DAVID FULTON PUBLISHERS LTD
2 Barbon Close, Great Ormond Street, London WC1N 3JX
Telephone: 0171 405 5606
Fax: 0171 831 4840

Warehouse:
Marston Book Services Ltd, PO Box 269, Abingdon, Oxon OX14 4YN
Telephone: 01235 465500
Fax: 01235 465555

Directors: David Fulton *(Managing)*
Pamela Fulton *(Marketing)*
Alan Craig *(Production)*
John Owens *(Editorial)*

Academic & Scholarly; Educational & Textbooks; Geography & Geology; Psychology & Psychiatry

New Titles: 52 (1995), 52 (1996)
No of Employees: 4
Annual Turnover: £600,000

ISBNs, Imprints & Series: 1 85346

Overseas Representation (see §7.3):
Asia: STM Publishing Services Pte Ltd,
 Singapore
Australia: PRO-ED Australia, Nerang, Qd
Pakistan: Book Bird, Lahore
South Africa: Book Promotions Pty Ltd,
 Plumstead
USA: Taylor & Francis Inc, Bristol, PA

Book Trade Association Membership: IPG

1334 ▮▮▮▮▮▮▮

GAIA BOOKS LTD
66 Charlotte Street, London W1P 1LR
Telephone: 0171 323 4010
Fax: 0171 323 0435

Also at:
20 High Street, Stroud, Glos GL5 1AS
Telephone: 01453 752985
Fax: 01453 752987
Web Site: http://www.bookshop.co.uk/
GaiaBooks

Distribution:
D Services, 6 Euston Street,
Freemen's Common, Leicester LE2 7SS
Telephone: 01162 547671
Fax: 01162 544670

Directors: Joss Pearson *(Managing)*
Suzy Boston *(Sales)*
Patrick Nugent *(Art)*
Eleanor Lines *(UK Publishing — Sales, Rights &*
 Permissions)
David Pearson *(Company Secretary)*
Susan Walby *(Production)*
Managers: Francesca Ovington *(Sales)*
Frank Chambers *(Sales, Southern Europe)*
Pip Morgan *(Managing Editor)*

Atlases & Maps; Gender Studies; Health &
Beauty; Natural History; Ecology;
Environment; Mind; Natural Health

New Titles: 8 (1995), 11 (1996)
No of Employees: 22
Annual Turnover: £1.8M

ISBNs, Imprints & Series: 1 85675

Overseas Representation (see §7.3):
Australia: Banyan Tree Book Distributors,
 Stirling, SA
Caribbean, India & Middle East: D-Services,
 Leicester, UK
Europe & Scandinavia: Onslow Books Ltd,
 London, UK
Far East: CKK Ltd Publishers' International
 Management, London, UK
South Africa: Faradawn CC, Saxonwold

1335 ▮▮▮▮▮▮▮

GAIRM PUBLICATIONS
29 Waterloo Street, Glasgow G2 6BZ
Telephone: 0141 221 1971
Fax: 0141 221 1971

Editorial Director: Derick S. Thomson
 (Rights & Permissions)
Publicity: Margaret MacLeod *(Home & Export*
 Sales)

Academic & Scholarly; Biography &
Autobiography; Fiction; Languages &

Linguistics; Literature & Criticism; Poetry;
Reference Books, Directories & Dictionaries;
Gaelic Editions; Music (Gaelic)

New Titles: 10 (1995), 10 (1996)
No of Employees: 2

ISBNs, Imprints & Series:
0 901771, 1 871901

1336 ▮▮▮▮▮▮▮

***GALE RESEARCH INTERNATIONAL
LTD**
Routledge, 11 New Fetter Lane, London
EC4P 4EE
Telephone: 0171 842 2145
Fax: 0171 842 2306

Warehouse & Distribution:
PO Box 699, Cheriton House, North Way,
Andover SP10 5YE
Telephone: 01264 342962
Fax: 01264 342763

Directors: Clare Fletcher *(Marketing &*
 Promotions)
Judith Watts *(Marketing & Promotions)*

Bibliography & Library Science; Biography &
Autobiography; Cinema, Video, TV & Radio;
Environment & Development Studies; Gender
Studies; Industry, Business & Management;
Literature & Criticism; Reference Books,
Directories & Dictionaries; Theatre, Drama &
Dance

ISBNs, Imprints & Series:
St James Press, TAFT, Visible Ink Press

Parent Company:
International Thomson Publishing

Associated & Subsidiary Companies:
USA: Gale Research Inc

Overseas Representation (see §7.3):
Iran: Behruz Neirami, Tehran
Spain & Portugal: Peter Prout, Madrid, Spain
Switzerland, Belgium & France: David
 Charles, Maisons-Laffitte, France

Book Trade Association Membership:
Directory Publishers' Association

1337 ▮▮▮▮▮▮▮

GARLAND PUBLISHING INC
Middlesex House, 2nd Floor,
34–42 Cleveland Street, London W1P 5FB
Telephone: 0171 637 7332
Fax: 0171 637 7352

Orders:
Marston Book Services Ltd, PO Box 269,
Abingdon, Oxon OX14 4YN
Telephone: 01235 465500
Fax: 01235 465556

Editorial Director Scientific Books: Miranda
 Robertson

Biology & Zoology; Chemistry; Educational &
Textbooks; Physics; Reference Books,
Directories & Dictionaries; Scientific &
Technical

New Titles: 6 (1995), 10 (1996)
No of Employees: 5
Annual Turnover: £0.5M

ISBNs, Imprints & Series: 0 8153

Parent Company:
Garland Publishing Inc *(USA)*

Associated & Subsidiary Companies:
Current Biology

1338 ▮▮▮▮▮▮▮

GARNET PUBLISHING LTD
8 Southern Court, South Street, Reading
RG1 4QS
Telephone: 01734 597847
Fax: 01734 597356

Distribution:
Clipper Distribution Services, Windmill Grove,
Portchester, Hants PO16 9HT
Telephone: 01705 200080
Fax: 01705 200090

Managing Director: K. Banerji
Managers: Anna Watson *(Editorial)*
Ms Shirley Hibbert *(Administration)*
Sue Coll *(Permissions)*

Architecture & Design; Guide Books; History
& Antiquarian; Literature & Criticism;
Photography; Travel & Topography

ISBNs, Imprints & Series:
1 85964, 1 873938

Associated & Subsidiary Companies:
Ithaca Press

Overseas Representation (see §7.3):
Australia: Oriental Publications, Adelaide, SA
Europe: Books for Europe Ltd, Bournemouth,
 UK
Near & Middle East: Anthony Rudkin
 Associates, Oxford, UK
Southern Africa: Verbatim Distributors,
 Constantia Hills, South Africa
USA: Paul & Co Publishers Consortium Inc,
 Concord, MA

1339 ▮▮▮▮▮▮▮

GATEWAY BOOKS
The Hollies, Wellow, Bath, Somerset BA2 8QJ
Telephone: 01225 835127
Fax: 01225 840012

Warehouse & Trade Counter:
Airlift Book Co, 8 The Arena,
Mollinson Avenue, Enfield, Middx EN5 7NJ
Telephone: 0181 804 0400
Fax: 0181 804 0044

Editorial & Production: Alick Bartholomew
Publicity: Tina Currie
Marketing: Kevin Redpath
Rights & Permissions: Christine Nalder
Customer Services: Mari Bartholomew

Environment & Development Studies;
Psychology & Psychiatry; Sociology &
Anthropology; Alternative Medicine &
Science; Earth Mysteries; Metaphysics

New Titles: 8 (1995), 12 (1996)
No of Employees: 5

ISBNs, Imprints & Series:
0 944256, 0 946551, 1 85860

Associated & Subsidiary Companies:
Amethyst Books

Overseas Representation *(see §7.3):*
Australia: Banyan Tree Book Distributors,
   Stirling, SA
Canada: Temeron Books Inc, Calgary
New Zealand: Peaceful Living Publications,
   Tauranga
Singapore & Malaysia: Pansing Distribution
   Sdn Bhd, Singapore
South Africa: Wizard's Warehouse, Cape Town
USA: National Book Network, Lanham, MD

Book Trade Association Membership: IPG,
SPG

1340 ━━━━━━━━━━━

GEOGRAPHERS' A–Z MAP CO LTD
Fairfield Road, Borough Green, Sevenoaks,
Kent TN15 8PP
Telephone: 01732 781000
Fax: 01732 780677

Showrooms:
44 Gray's Inn Road, London WC1X 8LR
Telephone: 0171 242 9246
Fax: 0171 430 2081

Directors: Phyllis Pearsall *(Chairman & Joint
   Managing)*
J. N. Syrett *(Joint Managing)*
J. G. Archibald
D. W. Churchill
K. A. Palmer
P. J. Stevens
J. P. Frankel

Atlases & Maps

New Titles: 14 (1995), 12 (1996)
No of Employees: 108

ISBNs, Imprints & Series: 0 85039

1341 ━━━━━━━━━━━

**GEOLOGICAL SOCIETY PUBLISHING
HOUSE**
Unit 7, Brassmill Enterprise Centre,
Brassmill Lane, Bath BA1 3JN
Telephone: 01225 445046
Fax: 01225 442836

Manager: Mike Collins

Geography & Geology

New Titles: 25 (1995), 30 (1996)
No of Employees: 8
Annual Turnover: £1M

ISBNs, Imprints & Series:
0 903317, 1 897799 Geological Society

Distributor for:
USA: Association of American Petroleum
Geologists; Geological Society of America;
SEPM

Overseas Representation *(see §7.3):*
Australia: AMF, Glenside
India: EWP, New Delhi
Japan: Kanda Book Trading Co, Tokyo
USA: AAPG, Tulsa

Book Trade Association Membership:
ALPSP

1342 ━━━━━━━━━━━

GEORGE RONALD PUBLISHER LTD
46 High Street, Kidlington, Oxford OX5 2DN
Telephone: 01865 841515
Fax: 01865 841230
Email: sales@grpubl.demon.co.uk

Directors: Hassan Sabri
May Ballerio
Erica Leith *(General)*
Manager: Wendi Momen *(Sales, Rights &
   Permissions)*

*Academic & Scholarly; Biography &
Autobiography; Children's Books; Poetry;
Politics & World Affairs; Religion & Theology;
Bahá'í Faith; Islamic Studies*

New Titles: 11 (1995), 9 (1996)
No of Employees: 4
Annual Turnover: £188,000

ISBNs, Imprints & Series: 0 85398

Overseas Representation *(see §7.3):*
Australia: Bahá'í Publications Australia, Mona
   Vale
Canada: Nine Pines Publishing, Manotick, Ont
India: Bahá'í Publishing Trust, New Delhi
New Zealand: Bahá'í Distribution Service,
   Blenheim
USA: George Ronald Books, St Louis, MO

1343 ━━━━━━━━━━━

STANLEY GIBBONS PUBLICATIONS
5 Parkside, Christchurch Road, Ringwood,
Hants BH24 3SH
Telephone: 01425 472363
Fax: 01425 470247
Email: info@stangib.demon.co.uk
Web Site: http://www.stanleygibbons.co.uk

Operations Director: A. J. Pandit
Editorial: D. J. Aggersberg *(Catalogue Editor)*
H. Jefferies *(Magazine Editor)*
Managers: James New *(Commercial &
   Advertising)*
Mrs M. Leamon *(Sales)*

*Antiques & Collecting; Crafts & Hobbies;
Reference Books, Directories & Dictionaries*

New Titles: 12 (1995), 15 (1996)
No of Employees: 60
Annual Turnover: £3M

ISBNs, Imprints & Series: 0 85259

Parent Company:
Stanley Gibbons Holdings Plc

Distributor for:
Netherlands: Davo Publications

Overseas Representation *(see §7.3):*
Australia: Lighthouse Philatelics (Aust) Pty
   Ltd, Strawberry Hills, NSW
Belgium & Luxembourg: Davo, Brussels,
   Belgium
Canada: Lighthouse Publications (Canada)
   Ltd, Montreal
Denmark: Davo, Hammel
Finland: Davo, Helsinki
France: Davo France (Casteilla), St Quentin
   Yvelines
Germany & Austria: Leuchtturm Albenverlag,
   Geesthacht, Germany
Hong Kong: Po-on Stamp Service
Israel: Capital Stamps, Jerusalem
Italy: Secrian Srl, Milan
Japan: Japan Philatelic Co Ltd, Tokyo
Netherlands: Davo Publications, Deventer
New Zealand: Stanley Gibbons (New Zealand)
   Ltd, Wellington
Norway: Davo Norge A/S, Oslo
Singapore: Stanley Gibbons (Singapore) Pte
   Ltd
South Africa: Republic Coin & Stamps
   Accessories (Pty) Ltd, Johannesburg
Sweden: Chr Winther Soerensen AB, Knaered
Switzerland: Phila Services, Riehen
USA: Lighthouse Publications Inc,
   Hackensack, NJ
West Indies & Caribbean: Hugh Dunphy,
   Kingston, Jamaica

Book Trade Association Membership: PA

1344 ━━━━━━━━━━━

**ROBERT GIBSON & SONS
(GLASGOW) LTD**
17 Fitzroy Place, Glasgow G3 7SF
Telephone: 0141 248 5674
Fax: 0141 221 8219

Warehouse:
57 Fitzroy Lane, Glasgow G3
Telephone: 0141 248 5674
Fax: 0141 221 8219

Directors: R. G. C. Gibson *(Managing)*
Mrs M. M. Pinkerton *(Financial, Permissions)*
Mrs H. C. Crawford *(Editorial)*
N. J. Crawford *(Editorial, Export Sales)*

*Bibliography & Library Science; Educational
& Textbooks*

ISBNs, Imprints & Series:
0 7169 First Aid in English, Prepare to Pass,
   World Wide Adventures

Overseas Representation *(see §7.3):*
Singapore: Cannon International

Book Trade Association Membership: BA

1345 ━━━━━━━━━━━

*GINN & CO
Prebendal House, Parson's Fee, Aylesbury,
Bucks HP20 2QZ
Telephone: 01296 394442
Fax: 01296 393433

Warehouse:
Unit 1, Block H, Industrial Estate, Long Eaton,
Nottingham NG10 1GG
Telephone: 0115 972 0535

Managing Director: Nigel Hall

Educational & Textbooks

ISBNs, Imprints & Series: 0 602

Parent Company:
Reed International Books Ltd

Overseas Representation *(see §7.3):*
Argentina: Kel Ediciones SA, Buenos Aires;
  Mary Anne Warburton, Buenos Aires
Australia: Rigby-Heinemann (Australia) Ltd,
  Port Melbourne
Barbados & Eastern Caribbean: C. D. A.
  Walker, Christchurch, Barbados
Botswana, Lesotho & Swaziland: Heinemann
  Educational Botswana, Gaborone, Botswana
Brazil: Carlos Barbisan, São Paulo
Canada: Ginn & Co, Scarborough
Egypt: International Language Bookshop, Giza
Ghana: A. Ott-Attafua & Co Ltd, Accra
Hong Kong: Transglobal Publishers Services
  Ltd, Tsuen Wan
India: Oxford University Press Indian Branch,
  New Delhi, Bombay, Calcutta & New Delhi,
  Madras
Irish Republic: International Education
  Service, Leixlip; STA Ltd, Dublin
Jamaica: Schools Promotion Services,
  Kingston
Japan: YOHAN (Western Publications
  Distribution Agency), Tokyo
Kenya: Benjamin Kithyaka, Nairobi; Textbook
  Centre Ltd, Nairobi
Malta: Agius & Agius Ltd, Valletta
New Zealand: Reed Publishing Group,
  Auckland
Pakistan: Oxford University Press, Karachi
Singapore & South East Asia: Reed
  International (Singapore) Pte Ltd, Singapore
Southern Africa: Heinemann Publishers (Pty)
  Ltd, Houghton & Isando, South Africa
Trinidad: RIK Services Ltd, San Fernando
Uganda: Rorash Enterprises, Kampala
Uruguay: Bookshop SA, Montevideo
Zimbabwe: Textbook Sales (PVT) Ltd, Harare

1346 ▬▬▬▬

GLOBAL BOOKS LTD
PO Box 219, Folkestone CT20 3LZ
Telephone: 01303 226799
Fax: 01303 243087

Trade Counter & Warehouse:
Grantham Book Services, Isaac Newton Way,
Alma Park Industrial Estate, Grantham , Lincs
NG31 9SD
Telephone: 01476 67421
Fax: 01476 67314

Directors: Paul Norbury *(Publishing)*
David Burns *(Financial)*
Sales & Marketing Manager: Janet Johnston

*Biography & Autobiography; Languages &
Linguistics; Religion & Theology; Travel &
Topography; Oriental*

New Titles: 11 (1995), 20 (1996)
No of Employees: 3

ISBNs, Imprints & Series:
1 86034 Global Oriental, Simple Guides

Overseas Representation *(see §7.3):*
Australia: Bookwise International, Findon, SA
Middle East: Berj Jamkojian, Vienna, Austria
Pacific Rim: CKK Ltd Publishers' International
  Management, London, UK
Scandinavia: D. Richard Bowen, Malmö,
  Sweden
South Africa: Gondwana Books, Vorna Valley
USA: The Talman Co, New York, NY

1347 ▬▬▬▬

GMP PUBLISHERS LTD
PO Box 247, Swaffham, Norfolk PE37 8PA
Telephone: 01366 328101
Fax: 01366 328102
Email: aubreyordavid@gmppubs.demon.co.
uk

Warehouse, Trade Enquiries & Orders:
Central Books, 99 Wallis Road, London
E9 5LN
Telephone: 0181 986 4854
Fax: 0181 533 5821

Distribution:
Turnaround Distribution, 27 Horsell Road,
London N5 1XL
Telephone: 0171 609 7836
Fax: 0171 700 1205

Directors: David Fernbach *(Managing,
  (Publisher—Fiction, Non-fiction & Heretic))*
Aubrey Walter *(Publisher—Art &
  Photography)*

*Academic & Scholarly; Crime; Fiction; Fine
Art & Art History; Guide Books; History &
Antiquarian; Humour; Literature & Criticism;
Photography; Politics & World Affairs;
Science Fiction; Sociology & Anthropology;
Gay Studies*

New Titles: 11 (1995), 20 (1996)

ISBNs, Imprints & Series:
0 85449 Éditions Aubrey Walter, The Gay
  Men's Press, GMP
0 946097 Heretic Books Ltd

Distributor for:
Heretic Books Ltd

Overseas Representation *(see §7.3):*
Australia & New Zealand: Bulldog Books,
  New South Wales, Australia
Far East: Ashton International Marketing
  Services, Larkfield, UK
*France, Benelux, Germany, Austria &
  Switzerland:* Michael Geoghegan, London,
  UK
Italy: Leslie Durham, Bagnaria
North America: In Book, Chicago, IL, USA

Book Trade Association Membership: IPG

1348 ▬▬▬▬

**GOLDEN COCKEREL PRESS LTD,
ASSOCIATED UNIVERSITY PRESSES**
16 Barter Street, London WC1A 2AH
Telephone: 0171 405 7979
Fax: 0171 404 3598
Email: lindesay@ibm.net

Warehouse, Trade Enquiries & Orders :
Biblios Distribution Services, Star Road,
Partridge Green, West Sussex RH13 8LD
Telephone: Partridge Green 01403 710971
Fax: 01403 711143

Directors: Ms Tamar Lindesay
Andrew Lindesay

Academic & Scholarly

New Titles: 100 (1995), 100 (1996)

ISBNs, Imprints & Series:
0 8386 Fairleigh Dickinson University Press
0 8387 Bucknell University Press
0 8453 Cornwall Books
0 87413 University of Delaware Press
0 87982 Philadelphia Art Alliance
0 918016 Folger Shakespeare Library
0 934223 Lehigh University Press
0 940866 University of Scranton Press
0 941664, 0 945636 Susquehanna University
  Press
0 944190 Balch Institute Press
1 900541 Cygnus Arts

Parent Company:
Associated University Presses Inc *(USA)*

Overseas Representation *(see §7.3):*
Canada: Associated University Presses,
  Mississauga
Rest of World: Feffer & Simons Inc, New York,
  USA
USA: Associated University Presses, Cranbury,
  NJ

1349 ▬▬▬▬

VICTOR GOLLANCZ LTD
Wellington House, 125 Strand, London
WC2R 0BB
Telephone: 0171 420 5555
Fax: 0171 240 7261

Warehouse, Trade Enquiries & Orders:
See Cassell Plc

Directors: Philip Sturrock *(Chairman)*
Jane Blackstock *(Rights)*
Chris Kloet *(Children's)*
Elizabeth Dobson *(Production)*
Liz Knights *(Publisher)*
Kevin Bristow *(Sales & Marketing)*
Adrienne Maguire *(Marketing)*
Michael Goff *(Export Sales)*
Frank Roney *(Finance)*
Andrew Macmillan *(UK Sales)*

*Architecture & Design; Biography &
Autobiography; Children's Books; Crime;
Fiction; Gender Studies; Humour; Music;
Natural History; Politics & World Affairs;
Science Fiction; Sports & Games; Travel &
Topography*

ISBNs, Imprints & Series:
0 575 Master Bridge Series, Victor Gollancz
  Ltd, Gollancz Children's Paperbacks,
  Gollancz Paperbacks, Indigo, VG Crime, VG
  Horror, VGSF, Vista, H. F. & G. Witherby

Parent Company:
Cassell Plc

Overseas Representation *(see §7.3):*
see: Cassell Plc, UK

1350

GOMER PRESS
Llandysul, Dyfed SA44 4BQ
Telephone: 01559 362371
Fax: 01559 363758

Directors: J. H. Lewis *(Managing)*
Sue Davies *(Sales)*
Jonathan Lewis
Editors: D. Elis-Gruffydd
Mairwen Prys Jones
Accounts: Carol Bignell

Academic & Scholarly; Children's Books;
Educational & Textbooks; Guide Books;
Languages & Linguistics; Welsh Language
Publications

New Titles: 95 (1995), 100 (1996)
No of Employees: 35
Annual Turnover: £1.4M

ISBNs, Imprints & Series:
0 85088, 0 86383, 1 85902 Pont

Parent Company:
J. D. Lewis & Sons Ltd

Overseas Representation *(see §7.3):*
USA: Ford & Bailie, Belmont, MA

Book Trade Association Membership: BA,
Union of Welsh Publishers & Booksellers

1351

ADAM GORDON
Priory Cottage, Chetwode, Nr Buckingham,
Bucks MK18 4LB
Telephone: 01280 848650

Proprietor: Adam Gordon

Religion & Theology; Transport

New Titles: 5 (1995), 7 (1996)
Annual Turnover: £60,000

ISBNs, Imprints & Series: 1 874422

Book Trade Association Membership: PA

1352

THE ROBERT GORDON UNIVERSITY
School of Information & Media,
352 King Street, Aberdeen AB9 2TQ
Telephone: 01224 262951
Fax: 01224 262969
Email: slis@rgu.ac.uk
Web Site: http://www.rgu.ac.uk/~sim/sim.htm

Head, School of Information and Media: I.
M. Johnson
Publishing Studies: J. M. Royle *(Postgraduate*
Course Leader)
P.M. Evans *(Undergraduate Course Leader)*
L. Gunn *(Placement Co-ordinator)*

No of Employees: 55

Book Trade Association Membership: PA

1353

GOTHIC IMAGE PUBLICATIONS
7 High Street, Glastonbury, Somerset BA6 9DP
Telephone: 01458 831453
Fax: 01458 831666

Trade Orders:
Airlift Book Company, The Arena,
Mollison Avenue, Enfield EN3 7NJ
Telephone: 0181 804 0400
Fax: 0181 804 0044

Directors: Frances Howard-Gordon *(All titles*
— Editorial & Commissioning)
Jamie George *(Export Sales)*
Cat Gray *(Financial Controller)*

Biography & Autobiography; Guide Books;
Magic & the Occult; Philosophy; Politics &
World Affairs; Religion & Theology

New Titles: 3 (1995), 4 (1996)
Annual Turnover: £50,000

ISBNs, Imprints & Series: 0 906362

Overseas Representation *(see §7.3):*
Australia: Gemcraft Books, Burwood, Vic
Canada: Cherev Canada Ltd, Markdale, Ont
South Africa: Wizard's Warehouse, Cape Town
USA: New Leaf Distribution, Lithia Springs,
GA; Book People, Oakland, CA

Book Trade Association Membership: BA

1354

GOWER PUBLISHING LTD
Gower House, Croft Road, Aldershot, Hants
GU11 3HR
Telephone: 01252 331551
Fax: 01252 344405

Customer Service Department:
3 Lower Farnham Road, Aldershot, Hants
GU12 4DY
Telephone: 01252 317700
Fax: 01252 343151
Web Site: http://www.ashgate.com/gower/

Management: N. A. E. Farrow *(Chairman)*
C. J. Simpson *(Managing Director)*
N. R. Young *(Finance Director)*
C. Barber *(Production)*
M. Stern *(Editorial Director)*
Rachel Maund *(Marketing Director)*

Accountancy & Taxation; Bibliography &
Library Science; Chemistry; Engineering;
Industry, Business & Management; Reference
Books, Directories & Dictionaries; Scientific &
Technical; Vocational Training & Careers

ISBNs, Imprints & Series:
0 347, 0 566, 0 7161 Gower
0 7045 Wildwood House

Associated & Subsidiary Companies:
Australia: Gower Asia-Pacific Pte Ltd.
Singapore: Gower Asia-Pacific Pte Ltd. *USA:*
Gower Publishing Co Inc

Overseas Representation *(see §7.3):*
Australia & New Zealand: Gower Asia Pacific
Pte Ltd, Avalo, NSW, Australia
Benelux, Scandinavia & France: Academic
Book Promotions, Bovenkarspel,
Netherlands
India: Maya Publishers Pvt Ltd, New Delhi
Irish Republic: Carr O'Connell, Ashbourne
Italy: Marcello SNC, Padua
Pakistan: Book Bird, Lahore
South East Asia, Philippines, Myanmar
(Burma), China, Hong Kong & South Korea:
Gower Asia Pacific Pte Ltd, Singapore
Spain: Marcello Iberia SA, Madrid
USA: Gower Publishing Co, Brookfield, VT

Book Trade Association Membership: PA,
IPG

1355

GRACE PUBLICATIONS TRUST
The Christian Bookshop, Sevenoaks Road,
Pratts Bottom, Orpington, Kent BR6 7SQ
Telephone: 01689 854117

Trade Enquiries & Orders:
12 Wooler Street, Darlington, Co. Durham
DL1 1RQ
Telephone: 01325 380232
Fax: 01325 466153

Editorial: P. Arthur *(General Editor)*
H. John Appleby *(Associate Editor, Rights &*
Permissions)

Religion & Theology

ISBNs, Imprints & Series: 0 946462

Overseas Representation *(see §7.3):*
Canada: Purpose Products, Aurora; Sovereign
Grace Book Ministry, Oromocto
USA: Presbyterian & Reformed Publishing Co,
Philipsburg, NJ; Spring Arbor Distributors,
Belleville; East Coast Distributors,
Somerville, NJ; Evangelical Press,
Philipsburg, NJ

Book Trade Association Membership: PA

1356

GRACEWING/FOWLER WRIGHT BOOKS LTD
Gracewing House, 2 Southern Avenue,
Leominster, Herefordshire HR6 0QF
Telephone: 01568 616835
Fax: 01568 613289

Managing Director: Tom Longford *(Export*
Sales)
Managers: Jo Ratcliffe *(Publishing, Rights &*
Permissions)
Maire Mannion *(Home Sales)*
Adrian Hodnett *(Customer Service, USA*
Agencies)
Sybil Caslin *(Accounts)*
Monica Manwaring *(Publicity)*

Academic & Scholarly; Biography &
Autobiography; Cookery, Wines & Spirits;
Gender Studies; Guide Books; Philosophy;
Religion & Theology

New Titles: 45 (1995), 40 (1996)
No of Employees: 12

ISBNs, Imprints & Series:
0 85244 Fowler Wright Books, Gracewing

Distributor for:
Family Publications; Grail Publications.
Australia: Open Book. *Canada:* Novalis. *USA:*
Bell Tower; Marian Communications;
Montfort Publications; Morehouse Publishing;
Mount; New City; Our Sunday Visitor; Paulist
Press; Sheed & Ward; St Bede's Publications;
SVS Press (Icons); Templegate

Overseas Representation *(see §7.3):*
Australia: Charles Paine Pty Ltd, North
   Paramatta, NSW
Canada: Meakin & Associates, Nepean
USA: Morehouse, Ridgefield CT

1357

*GRAFFHAM PRESS LTD
6 York Place, Edinburgh EH1 3EP
Telephone: 0131 556 7887
Fax: 0131 556 1129

Directors: T. J. Clark
Mrs R. Davidson

*Medical (incl. Self Help & Alternative
Medicine)*

ISBNs, Imprints & Series:
1 85886 Annals of Experimental and Clinical
   Medicine, Current Topics in Drug Researh,
   Graffham Press

Book Trade Association Membership: PA

1358

GRAHAM & WHITESIDE LTD
Tuition House, 5–6 Francis Grove, London
SW19 5DT
Telephone: 0181 947 1011
Fax: 0181 947 1163

Warehouse:
Clipper Distribution Services Ltd,
Windmill Grove, Portchester, Hants PO16 9HP
Telephone: 01705 200080
Fax: 01705 200090

Directors: A. M. W. Graham *(Managing)*
H. C. H. Whiteside *(Electronic Publishing)*
Editorial: R. Eastwood
Marketing Managers: P. Murphy *(Lists
   rental)*
B. Joseph *(Sales & Orders)*

*Industry, Business & Management; Reference
Books, Directories & Dictionaries*

New Titles: 12 (1995), 19 (1996)
No of Employees: 10
Annual Turnover: £1.2M

ISBNs, Imprints & Series: 1 86099

Overseas Representation *(see §7.3):*
Australia & New Zealand: DA Information
   Services, Mitcham, Vic, Australia
Korea: Pan Korea Book Corporation, Seoul,
   Korea, South
Singapore, Malaysia & Brunei: Publishers
   Marketing Services Ltd, Singapore
USA & Canada: Gale Research Co, Detroit,
   USA

Book Trade Association Membership:
Directory Publishers Association

1359

**W. F. GRAHAM (NORTHAMPTON)
LTD**
2 Pondwood Close, Moulton Park,
Northampton NN3 6RT
Telephone: 01604 645537
Fax: 01604 648414

Directors: Ronnie Graham
Chris Graham
Tim Graham
Managers: Ian Wilson *(General)*
Mrs Rosemary Good *(Sales)*

Children's Books

New Titles: 15 (1995), 15 (1996)
No of Employees: 13
Annual Turnover: £1.8M

ISBNs, Imprints & Series: 1 85128

Overseas Representation *(see §7.3):*
Far East: CKK Ltd Publishers' International
   Management, London, UK
West Indies: Humphrys Roberts Associates,
   London, UK

1360

GRANDREAMS LTD
Jadwin House, 205-211 Kentish Town Road,
London NW5 2JU
Telephone: 0171 485 0648
Fax: 0171 482 4947

Foreign Rights Department:
6 Old King Street, Bath, Avon BA1 2JW
Telephone: 01225 429383
Fax: 01225 428161

Warehouse:
Unit 4/c Airfield Industrial Estate, Hixon,
Stafford
Telephone: 01889 270125
Fax: 01889 270917

Directors: Brian D. Babani *(Joint Managing)*
Peter L. Babani *(Joint Managing)*
Christine L. Swift *(Publishing)*
Andrew H. Rabin *(Sales)*
Neil Rodol *(Financial)*
Paul Scheinberg *(Grandreams USA)*
Nigel Money *(Production)*
Managers: Catherine Lyn-Jones *(Rights)*
David Taylor *(UK Sales)*

*Atlases & Maps; Children's Books;
Educational & Textbooks; Music; Sports &
Games*

New Titles: 200 (1995), 200 (1996)

ISBNs, Imprints & Series:
Bow Wow Books, Goodnight, Sleeptight
   Books

Overseas Representation *(see §7.3):*
USA: Grandreams USA, Howell, NJ

1361

GRANT & CUTLER LTD
55–57 Great Marlborough Street, London
W1V 2AY
Telephone: 0171 734 2012
Fax: 0171 734 9272
Email: martin@grant-c.demon.co.uk

*Academic & Scholarly; Bibliography &
Library Science; Languages & Linguistics;
Literature & Criticism*

New Titles: 10 (1995), 8 (1996)

ISBNs, Imprints & Series:
0 7293 Critical Guides to Spanish Texts,
   Critical Guides to French Texts, Critical
   Guides to German Texts, Research
   Bibliographies & Checklists

Book Trade Association Membership: BA

1362

GRANTA
2–3 Hanover Yard, Noel Road, London N1 8BE
Telephone: 0171 704 9776
Fax: 0171 704 0474(editorial) & 354 3469
(sales & administration)

Trade Orders:
Exel Logistics Media Services, Invicta House,
Sir Thomas Langley Road,
Medway City Estate, Rochester, Kent
ME2 4DU
Telephone: 01634 297123
Fax: 01634 298000

Sales Director: Kate Griffin
Publisher: Frances Coady
Managers: Claire Paterson *(Publicity)*
Isobel Rorison *(Production)*

*Biography & Autobiography; Fiction; History
& Antiquarian; Politics & World Affairs;
Travel & Topography*

New Titles: 40 (1996)
No of Employees: 6

ISBNs, Imprints & Series: 1 86207

Parent Company:
Granta Publications Ltd

Associated & Subsidiary Companies:
USA: Granta USA Ltd

1363

GRANTA EDITIONS
25–27 High Street, Chesterton, Cambridge
CB4 1ND
Telephone: 01223 352790
Fax: 01223 460718
Email: bpccam.demon.co.uk
Web Site: http://www.infragence.com

Warehouse:
William Guppy & Son Ltd, The Paper Centre,
Farringdon Avenue, Harold Hill, Romford,
Essex RN3 8SP
Telephone: 01708 346722
Fax: 01708 370279

London Office:
Book Production Consultants Plc,
c/o Bermuda Trust (UK) Ltd,
Austin Friars House, Austin Friars, London
EC2N 2HE
Telephone: 0171 256 4010
Fax: 0171 256 4010
Email: sz@bpclon.demon.co.uk

Joint Managing Directors: Tony Littlechild
Colin Walsh
Managers: Stephanie Zarach *(Business
Development)*
Roz Williams *(Editorial)*
Sue Gray *(Production)*
Franca Holden *(Sales)*

*Academic & Scholarly; Accountancy &
Taxation; Agriculture; Educational &
Textbooks; Environment & Development
Studies; Guide Books; Health & Beauty;
Reference Books, Directories & Dictionaries;
Scientific & Technical*

New Titles: 41 (1995), 48 (1996)
No of Employees: 22

ISBNs, Imprints & Series: 0 906782

Parent Company:
Book Production Consultants Plc

Associated & Subsidiary Companies:
Book Connections Ltd; NCT Publishing Ltd

Distributor for:
Book Connections; Chartered Insurance
Institute; NCT Publishing Ltd *(Membership
only)*; University of Cambridge – Dept of Land
Economy

Book Trade Association Membership: IPG

1364 ▬

**W. GREEN THE SCOTTISH LAW
PUBLISHER**
21 Alva Street, Edinburgh EH2 4PS
Telephone: 0131 225 4879
Fax: 0131 225 2104

Director: Anthony Kinahan *(Managing)*
Manager: Miss Gilly Michie *(Marketing)*
Commissioning Editor: Elanor Bower

Law

New Titles: 30 (1995), 35 (1996)
No of Employees: 19
Annual Turnover: £3.5M

ISBNs, Imprints & Series: 0 414

Parent Company:
International Thomson Corporation

Overseas Representation *(see §7.3)*:
Australia: The Law Book Co Ltd, North Ryde
Bangladesh: Karim International, Dhaka
Botswana: Kerrison Book Services, Gabarone
Canada: The Carswell Co Ltd, Agincourt
Ghana: J. A. Amoah, Accra
India: N. M. Tripathi Pte Ltd, Bombay
Israel: Steimatzky Ltd, Bnei Brak
Japan: Macmillan Shuppan KK, Tokyo

Kenya, Tanzania, Uganda & Mauritius: Kelvin
van Hasselt Publishing Services, Lymington,
UK
Malawi, Zambia & Zimbabwe: Barbie Keene,
Harare, Zimbabwe
Malaysia, Singapore & Brunei: Malayan Law
Journal Pte Ltd, Singapore
Pakistan: Pakistan Law House, Karachi

Book Trade Association Membership:
Scottish PA

1365 ▬

GREEN BOOKS
Foxhole, Dartington, Totnes, Devon TQ9 6EB
Telephone: 01803 863843 & 863260
Fax: 01803 863843

UK Trade Distributor:
Images Booksellers & Distribution,
The Wells House, Holy Well Road,
Malvern Wells WR14 4LH
Telephone: 01684 893990
Fax: 01684 893993
Email: 101233.2413@compuserve.com.uk

Managing Director: John Elford
Sales & Marketing Manager: Paul Rossiter

*Architecture & Design; Biography &
Autobiography; Do-It-Yourself; Economics;
Environment & Development Studies; Fine Art
& Art History; Gardening; Health & Beauty;
Literature & Criticism; Natural History;
Philosophy; Politics & World Affairs*

New Titles: 4 (1995), 9 (1996)
No of Employees: 2

ISBNs, Imprints & Series:
0 9527302 Themis Books
1 870098 Green Books & Resurgence Books
1 900322 Green Earth Books

Distributor for:
USA: Chelsea Green Publishing Co *(selected
titles)*; Council Oak Books *(selected titles)*

Overseas Representation *(see §7.3)*:
Australia: Astam Books Pty Ltd, Leichhardt,
NSW
South Africa: Titles, Durban
*USA (Green Books, Resurgence Books &
Themis Books):* Council Oak Books, Tulsa,
OK, USA
USA (Green Earth Books): Chelsea Green
Publishing Co, White River Junction, VT,
USA

Book Trade Association Membership: IPG

1366 ▬

**GREENHILL BOOKS / LIONEL
LEVENTHAL LTD**
Park House, 1 Russell Gardens, London
NW11 9NN
Telephone: 0181 458 6314
Fax: 0181 905 5245

Warehouse:
Bookpoint Ltd, 39 Milton Park, Abingdon,
Oxon OX14 4TD
Telephone: Abingdon 01235 835001
Fax: 01235 832068

Director: Lionel Leventhal
Manager: Mark Wray *(Sales)*

Aviation; Military & War

New Titles: 26 (1995), 30 (1996)

ISBNs, Imprints & Series:
0 947898 Napoleonic Library, Vintage
Aviation Library

Parent Company:
Lionel Leventhal Ltd

Distributor for:
Hong Kong: Concord Publications Co. *USA:*
Combined Books; Emperors Press; Presidio
Press; Savas Woodbury; Stackpole Books

Overseas Representation *(see §7.3)*:
Australia & New Zealand: Peribo Pty Ltd,
Mount Kuring-gai, NSW, Australia
*Austria, Switzerland, Italy, Spain (including
Gibraltar) & Portugal:* Patrick Bygate,
Massagno, Switzerland
Canada: Fortress Publications Inc, Stoney
Creek, Ont
France: Greenhill Books, London, UK
Germany: PKB – Robbert J. Pleysier, Heerde,
Netherlands
New Zealand: South Pacific Books (Imports)
Ltd, Auckland
Norway, Sweden, Finland & Denmark: Ove B.
Poulsen, Glostrup, Denmark
South Africa: Book Services International,
Sandton
USA: Stackpole Books, Harrisburg, PA

1367 ▬

GREENWICH UNIVERSITY PRESS
Unit 42, Butterfly Avenue,
Dartford Trade Park, Dartford, Kent DA1 1JG
Telephone: 0181 331 9600
Fax: 0181 331 9672

Director: Prof. John Parsonage
Manager: Iain Moir *(Editorial)*
Unit Administrator: Linda Johnson

*Academic & Scholarly; Biography &
Autobiography; Educational & Textbooks*

New Titles: 12 (1995), 12 (1996)
No of Employees: 7

ISBNs, Imprints & Series:
1 874529 Greenwich University Press

Parent Company:
UGMT Ltd

Overseas Representation *(see §7.3)*:
Germany, Austria & Switzerland: SHS
Publishers' Consultants and Representatives,
Berlin, Germany
Japan & South Korea: United Publishers
Services Ltd, Tokyo, Japan
USA & Canada: New York University Press,
New York, USA

1368 ▬

GREENWOOD PUBLISHING GROUP
3 Henrietta Street, London WC2E 8LU
Telephone: 0171 240 0856
Fax: 0171 379 0609

Marketing Director: Michael Geelan
Marketing Manager: Imogen Adams

*Academic & Scholarly; Bibliography &
Library Science; Biography & Autobiography;
Cinema, Video, TV & Radio; Economics;
Gender Studies; History & Antiquarian;
Industry, Business & Management; Law;
Literature & Criticism; Medical (incl. Self Help
& Alternative Medicine); Military & War;
Music; Philosophy; Politics & World Affairs;
Psychology & Psychiatry; Reference Books,
Directories & Dictionaries; Religion &
Theology; Science Fiction; Sociology &
Anthropology; Sports & Games; Theatre,
Drama & Dance*

New Titles: 600 (1995), 600 (1996)

ISBNs, Imprints & Series:
0 275 Praeger Publishers
0 313, 0 8371 Greenwood Press
0 86569 Auburn House
0 89789 Bergin & Garvey
0 89930 Quorum Books

1369 ▰▰▰▰▰▰

GREY SEAL BOOKS
28 Burgoyne Road, London N4 1AD
Telephone: 0181 340 6061
Fax: 0181 340 6061

Trade Enquiries & Orders:
Central Books, 99 Wallis Road, London
E9 5LN
Telephone: 0181 986 4854
Fax: 0181 533 5821

Proprietor: John E. Duncan

Academic & Scholarly; Religion & Theology

New Titles: 4 (1995), 4 (1996)

ISBNs, Imprints & Series: 1 85640

Parent Company:
Grey Seal (Publications) Ltd

Overseas Representation *(see §7.3):*
India: S. Janakiraman, Madras

Book Trade Association Membership: IPG

1370 ▰▰▰▰▰▰

PETER GROSE LTD
Lower House, Mitchel Troy, Monmouth,
Gwent NP5 4BL
Telephone: 01600 740230
Fax: 01600 740483

Warehouse & Trade Enquiries:
Bookpoint Ltd, 39 Milton Park, Abingdon,
Oxon OX14 4TD
Telephone: 01235 400400
Fax: 01235 861038

Directors: Peter Grose *(Managing)*
Roslyn Grose
Senior Editor: Tamara Grose

*Cookery, Wines & Spirits; Crafts & Hobbies;
Guide Books; Health & Beauty; Sports &
Games*

New Titles: 5 (1995), 5 (1996)
Annual Turnover: £200,000

ISBNs, Imprints & Series:
1 898885 Peter Grose Ltd
1 900018 Big Books
1 900019 Sunday Books

Overseas Representation *(see §7.3):*
Australia: Peribo Pty Ltd, Mount Kuring-gai,
NSW
New Zealand: David Bateman Ltd, Auckland

1371 ▰▰▰▰▰▰

GROSVENOR BOOKS
12 Palace Street, London SW1E 5JF
Telephone: 0171 828 6591
Fax: 0171 828 7609

Directors: D. W. Locke *(Sales, Rights &
Permissions)*
Elizabeth B. Locke *(Editorial)*
Company Secretary: C. Hutchinson
Manager: Blair Cummock *(Production)*

*Biography & Autobiography; Politics & World
Affairs; Religion & Theology*

New Titles: 4 (1995), 4 (1996)

ISBNs, Imprints & Series:
0 901269, 1 85239

Parent Company:
Grosvenor Productions Ltd

Distributor for:
Moral Re-Armament (The Oxford Group)

Overseas Representation *(see §7.3):*
Australia: Grosvenor Books, Toorak, Vic
Canada: Grosvenor Books, Ottawa
New Zealand: Grosvenor Books, Wellington
South Africa: Verbatim Distributors, Steenberg
USA: Grosvenor USA, Salem, OR

Book Trade Association Membership: PA

1372 ▰▰▰▰▰▰

GRUB STREET
The Basement, 10 Chivalry Road, London
SW11 1HT
Telephone: 0171 924 3966 & 0171 738 1008
Fax: 0171 738 1009

Distribution:
Bailey Distribution, Units 1a/1b Learoyd Road,
Mountfield Industrial Estate, New Romney,
Kent TN28 8XU
Telephone: 01679 66905
Fax: 01679 66638

Director: John Davies

*Aviation; Cookery, Wines & Spirits; Humour;
Military & War*

New Titles: 24 (1995), 22 (1996)
No of Employees: 3
Annual Turnover: £0.5M

ISBNs, Imprints & Series:
0 948817, 1 898697

Overseas Representation *(see §7.3):*
Australia: Capricorn Link (Australia) Pty Ltd,
Baulkham Hills, NSW
Canada: Fortress Publications Inc, Stoney
Creek, Ont
*Europe (including France, Belgium,
Netherlands, Germany, Austria &
Switzerland):* European Marketing Services,
London, UK
Middle East: McGuire Marketing Publishers'
International Management, Soham, Cambs,
UK
New Zealand: Forrester Books Ltd, Auckland
Pacific Rim: Electra Media Group Pty Ltd,
Sydney, NSW, Australia
Scandinavia: Angell Eurosales, Newton Abbot,
UK
South Africa: Verbatim Distributors, Steenberg
Southern Europe: Joe Portelli, Bologna, Italy
USA: Seven Hills Book Distributors,
Cincinnati, OH

1373 ▰▰▰▰▰▰

**GUILD OF MASTER CRAFTSMAN
PUBLICATIONS LTD**
166 High Street, Lewes, East Sussex BN7 1XU
Telephone: 01273 478449 & 477374
Fax: 01273 486300

Warehouse:
Mail International, Braybon Business Park,
Consort Way, Burgess Hill, West Sussex
RH15 9ND
Telephone: 01444 871111
Fax: 01444 248997

Trade Enquiries & Orders:
Chris Lloyd Sales & Marketing Services,
463 Ashley Road, Parkstone, Poole, Dorset
BH14 0AX
Telephone: 01202 715349
Fax: 01202 736191

Publisher: Alan Phillips

*Antiques & Collecting; Architecture & Design;
Crafts & Hobbies; Do-It-Yourself*

New Titles: 14 (1995), 21 (1996)
No of Employees: 10
Annual Turnover: £1M

ISBNs, Imprints & Series:
0 946819, 1 861080

Overseas Representation *(see §7.3):*
Australia: Capricorn Link (Australia) Pty Ltd,
Baulkham Hills, NSW
North America: Sterling Publishing Co Inc,
New York, NY, USA
UK & Europe: Chris Lloyd, Poole, UK

Book Trade Association Membership: IPG

1374 ▰▰▰▰▰▰

GUILDHALL PRESS
41 Great James Street, Derry BT48 7DF
Telephone: 01504 364413
Fax: 01504 372949

Project Manager: Paul Hippsley

*Academic & Scholarly; Educational &
Textbooks; Guide Books; History &
Antiquarian*

New Titles: 3 (1995), 4 (1996)
No of Employees: 17
Annual Turnover: £10,000

ISBNs, Imprints & Series:
0 946451 Derry's Walls, Seeing is Believing? –
　Murals in Derry

Overseas Representation *(see §7.3)*:
Australia: Irish Book Centre, Melbourne

Book Trade Association Membership: CLÉ
(Irish PA)

1375 ▬▬▬▬

GUILFORD PRESS
27 Church Road, Hove, East Sussex BN3 2FA
Telephone: 01273 207411
Fax: 01273 205612
Email: polly@psypress.co.uk or
info@guilford.com

Trade Enquiries & Orders:
Direct Distribution *(address as above)*
Telephone: 01273 748427
Fax: 01273 722180

Managing Director: Michael Forster
Managers: Polly Strauss *(Marketing)*
Linda Jarret *(Sales)*

*Gender Studies; Philosophy; Psychology &
Psychiatry; Sociology & Anthropology*

New Titles: 65 (1995), 80 (1996)

ISBNs, Imprints & Series:
0 89862, 1 57230

Parent Company:
Guilford Press Inc *(USA)*

Overseas Representation *(see §7.3)*:
Australia: Astam Books Pty Ltd, Leichhardt,
NSW

1376 ▬▬▬▬

GUINNESS PUBLISHING LTD
33 London Road, Enfield, Middx EN2 6DJ
Telephone: 0181 367 4567
Fax: 0181 367 5912

Distribution:
Macmillan Trade & Warehouse, Brunel Road,
Houndmills, Basingstoke, Hants RG21 2XS
Telephone: 01256 29242
Fax: 01256 812558

Chairman: Ian Chapman, CBE
Managing Director: Chris Irwin
Finance: Sarah Brown
Sales & Marketing: Fred Buxton
Production: Chris Lingard
Editorial: Ian Castello-Cortes
Michael Feldman

*Cinema, Video, TV & Radio; Cookery, Wines &
Spirits; Do-It-Yourself; Humour; Music;
Reference Books, Directories & Dictionaries;
Sports & Games; Theatre, Drama & Dance;
Transport*

New Titles: 40 (1995), 30 (1996)
No of Employees: 45
Annual Turnover: £7.5M

ISBNs, Imprints & Series: 0 85112

Parent Company:
Guinness Plc

Associated & Subsidiary Companies:
Guinness World of Records Inc

Overseas Representation *(see §7.3)*:
Australia: Pan Macmillan Books (Australia)
　Pty Ltd, Sydney, NSW
Canada: Canadian Manda Group, Toronto
Caribbean, Bahamas & Bermuda: Macmillan
　Caribbean, Basingstoke, UK
Hong Kong: Federal Publications (HK) Ltd,
　Kowloon
Hungary, Czech Republic & Slovak Republic:
　CLB Marketing Services, Kecskemet,
　Hungary
India: India Book Distributors, Bombay
Irish Republic: Donald O'Mahoney,
　Castleknock
Italy, Greece & Yugoslavia: Bookport
　Associates, Bologna, Italy
Kenya: Textbook Centre Ltd, Nairobi
Korea, Taiwan & Thailand: Allscript
　Establishment (S) Pte Ltd, Singapore
Middle East: Peter Ward Book Exports,
　London, UK
Netherlands: Consul Books, Blaricum
New Zealand: Pan Macmillan New Zealand
　Ltd, Auckland
Pakistan: Paramount Books (Pvt) Ltd, Karachi
*Scandinavia, Finland, France, Belgium,
　Luxembourg, Germany, Austria &
　Switzerland:* Hanne Rotovnik,
　Klampenborg, Denmark
South Africa: Pan Macmillan, Johannesburg
South America: Humphrys Roberts Associates,
　Cotia, Brazil
*South East Asia (including Singapore,
　Malaysia, Brunei & Indonesia):* STP
　Distributors Pte Ltd, Singapore
Spain, Portugal & Gibraltar: Iberian Book
　Services SL, Madrid, Spain

Book Trade Association Membership: PA,
BDC, Book Marketing Council

1377 ▬▬▬▬

GWASG Y DREF WEN
28 Church Road, Yr Eglwys Newydd, Cardiff
CF4 2EA
Telephone: 01222 617860
Fax: 01222 610507

Managing Director: Roger Boore *(Editorial &
　Production)*
Sales Manager: Gwilym Boore
Finance: Anne Boore

*Audio Books; Children's Books; Educational &
Textbooks; Fiction; Languages & Linguistics*

New Titles: 5 (1995), 85 (1996)
No of Employees: 2

ISBNs, Imprints & Series:
0 904910, 0 946962, 1 85596

Book Trade Association Membership: Union
of Welsh Publishers & Booksellers

1378 ▬▬▬▬

PETER HADDOCK LTD
Pinfold Lane, Bridlington, East Yorkshire
YO16 5BT
Telephone: 01262 678121
Fax: 01262 400043

Directors: David Haddock *(Sales)*
Pat Hornby *(Rights)*
Peter Haddock *(Chairman & Managing)*
Managers: John Hornby *(Shipping)*
Brian Pannhausen *(Warehouse)*

*Children's Books; Reference Books,
Directories & Dictionaries*

New Titles: 200 (1995), 200 (1996)
No of Employees: 35
Annual Turnover: £8M

ISBNs, Imprints & Series:
Big Time 0 7105

Parent Company:
D. C. Thomsen & Co Ltd

1379 ▬▬▬▬

ROBERT HALE LTD
Clerkenwell House, Clerkenwell Green,
London EC1R 0HT
Telephone: 0171 251 2661
Fax: 0171 490 4958

Warehouse & Returns:
4 Vestry Road, Vestry Industrial Estate,
Sevenoaks, Kent
Telephone: 01732 459852

Directors: John Hale *(Managing)*
Robert Kynaston *(General Manager)*
Martin Kendall *(Marketing)*
Betty Weston *(Rights)*
Managers: Yolanda Cerdá *(Publicity)*
April Jones *(Advertising)*
Iris Kynaston *(Credit Control)*
Lorraine Hall *(Trade Enquiries)*

*Animal Care & Breeding; Antiques &
Collecting; Archaeology; Aviation; Biography
& Autobiography; Cinema, Video, TV & Radio;
Cookery, Wines & Spirits; Crime; Crafts &
Hobbies; Do-It-Yourself; Fiction; Gardening;
Guide Books; Health & Beauty; History &
Antiquarian; Humour; Literature & Criticism;
Magic & the Occult; Military & War; Music;
Natural History; Nautical; Photography;
Poetry; Politics & World Affairs; Reference
Books, Directories & Dictionaries; Sociology
& Anthropology; Sports & Games; Theatre,
Drama & Dance; Transport; Travel &
Topography*

New Titles: 280 (1995), 290 (1996)
No of Employees: 20

ISBNs, Imprints & Series:
0 7090, 0 7091, 0 7198 NAG Press

Associated & Subsidiary Companies:
NAG Press Ltd

Distributor for:
Aperture Foundation

Overseas Representation *(see §7.3):*
Australia & New Zealand: Peribo Pty Ltd, Mount Kuring-gai, NSW, Australia
France, Germany, Netherlands, Austria & Switzerland: Ted Dougherty, London, UK
Italy, Spain, Portugal & Greece: Penny Padovani, London, UK
Scandinavia: Sven Gade, Hørsholm, Denmark
South Africa: Trinity Books CC, Randburg
USA & Canada: Atrium, Santa Rosa, CA, USA

1380

THE HAMBLEDON PRESS
102 Gloucester Avenue, London NW1 8HX
Telephone: 0171 586 0817
Fax: 0171 586 9970
Email: hambledon@cityscape.co.uk

Publisher: Martin Sheppard
Sales Manager: Eva Osborne

Academic & Scholarly; History & Antiquarian; Law; Literature & Criticism

New Titles: 20 (1995), 20 (1996)
No of Employees: 2

ISBNs, Imprints & Series:
0 907628, 0 9506882, 1 85285

Overseas Representation *(see §7.3):*
USA: The Hambledon Press, Rio Grande

Book Trade Association Membership: IPG

1381

HAMISH HAMILTON LTD
27 Wrights Lane, London W8 5TZ
Telephone: 0171 416 3100
Fax: 0171 416 3295

Orders:
Penguin Books Ltd, Bath Road, Harmondsworth, Middx
Telephone: 0181 899 4000
Fax: 0181 899 4099

Directors: Peter Carson *(Editor-in-Chief— Penguin Books)*
Clare Alexander *(Publishing)*

Biography & Autobiography; Children's Books; Fiction; History & Antiquarian; Illustrated & Fine Editions; Music; Natural History; Politics & World Affairs; Psychology & Psychiatry; Travel & Topography

ISBNs, Imprints & Series:
0 241 Hamish Hamilton Children's Books Ltd

Parent Company:
Penguin Books Ltd

Overseas Representation *(see §7.3):*
Australia: Penguin Books Australia Ltd, Ringwood, Vic
Canada: Penguin Books Canada Ltd, Newmarket, Ont
France: Penguin France SA, Toulouse
Germany & Austria: Penguin Books Deutschland GmbH, Frankfurt, Germany
Greece, Israel & Cyprus: Penguin Hellas Ltd, Athens, Greece

India, Bangladesh, Pakistan & Sri Lanka: Penguin Books India Pvt Ltd, New Delhi, India
Italy: Penguin Italia Srl, Milan
Japan: Penguin Books Japan, Tokyo
Korea: Addison-Wesley Korea, Seoul, Korea, South
Malaysia: STP Distributors (M) Sdn Bhd, Shah Alam
Netherlands: Penguin Books Netherlands bv, Amsterdam
New Zealand: Penguin Books (New Zealand) Ltd, Auckland
Portugal: Longman Penguin Portugal, Lisbon
Singapore: STP Distributors Pte Ltd
South Africa: Longman Penguin South Africa, Bertsham
South America: Humphrys Roberts Associates, Cotia, Brazil
Spain: Penguin Books SA, Madrid
Switzerland: OLF SA, Fribourg
Turkey: Sezai, Istanbul

1382

HAMLYN
Michelin House, 81 Fulham Road, London SW3 6RB
Telephone: 0171 581 9393
Fax: 0171 225 9458

Distribution:
Reed Book Services, Northampton Road, Rushden, Northants NN10 6PU
Telephone: 01933 58521
Fax: 01933 50284

International Sales Department:
(as principal address)
Telephone: 0171 581 9393
Fax: 0171 225 9371

Publishing Director: Laura Bamford

Cookery, Wines & Spirits; Crafts & Hobbies; Do-It-Yourself; Gardening; Health & Beauty; Magic & the Occult; Music; Reference Books, Directories & Dictionaries; Sports & Games

ISBNs, Imprints & Series:
0 600 Hamlyn
0 7064 Octopus
0 907486, 1 85152 Chancellor
1 85051 Treasure
1 85052 Peerage
1 85510 Pyramid

Parent Company:
Reed Elsevier Plc

Overseas Representation *(see §7.3):*
Australia: Reed Books Australia, Melbourne, Vic
Canada: Reed Publishing Canada, Markham, Ont
East Asia: Reed Consumer Books, Metro Manila, Philippines
India: Reed Consumer Books, New Delhi
Japan: Reed Consumer Books, Tokyo
New Zealand: Reed Publishing Group, Auckland
Singapore: Reed International (Singapore) Pte Ltd
South Africa: Struik Book Distributors Pty Ltd, Johannesburg, Cape Town & Maitland

1383

HAMLYN CHILDREN'S REFERENCE
Michelin House, 81 Fulham Road, London SW3 6RB
Telephone: 0171 581 9393
Fax: 0171 225 9406

Distribution:
Reed Book Services, Northampton Road, Rushden, Northants NN10 6PU
Telephone: 01933 58521
Fax: 01933 50284

International Sales Department:
(as principal address)
Telephone: 0171 581 9393
Fax: 0171 225 9371

Divisional Managing Director: Jane Winterbotham

Children's Books

ISBNs, Imprints & Series:
0 600 Hamlyn
0 603 Dean

Parent Company:
Reed Elsevier Plc

Overseas Representation *(see §7.3):*
Australia: Reed Books Australia, Melbourne, Vic
Canada: Reed Publishing Canada, Markham, Ont
East Asia: Reed Consumer Books, Metro Manila, Philippines
India: Reed Consumer Books, New Delhi
Japan: Reed Consumer Books, Tokyo
New Zealand: Reed Publishing Group, Auckland
Singapore: Reed International (Singapore) Pte Ltd
South Africa: Struik Book Distributors Pty Ltd, Johannesburg, Cape Town & Maitland

1384

HARCOURT BRACE & CO LTD
24–28 Oval Road, London NW1 7DX
Telephone: 0171 267 4466
Fax: 0171 482 2293 & 485 4752

Warehouse (Books):
High Street, Foots Cray, Sidcup, Kent DA15 5HP

Customer Service & Journal Subscriptions:
High Street, Footscray, Kent DA15 5HP
Telephone: 0181 300 3322
Fax: 0181 309 0807

Directors: W. M. Barnett *(Managing)*
Peter McKay *(Sales & Marketing)*
M. Ewins *(Production)*
S. Duggan *(Editorial)*
J. J. Velterop *(Academic Press)*
P. Scott *(Personnel)*
J. Sehmer *(Financial & Distribution)*
Managers: Sheila O'Reilly *(Customer Service)*
Des Brennan *(Sales)*

Academic & Scholarly; Accountancy & Taxation; Agriculture; Animal Care & Breeding; Archaeology; Bibliography &

*Library Science; Biology & Zoology;
Chemistry; Computer Science; Economics;
Electronic (Educational); Engineering;
Geography & Geology; History &
Antiquarian; Industry, Business &
Management; Languages & Linguistics;
Mathematics & Statistics; Medical (incl. Self
Help & Alternative Medicine); Natural
History; Nautical; Physics; Psychology &
Psychiatry; Reference Books, Directories &
Dictionaries; Religion & Theology; Scientific
& Technical; Sociology & Anthropology;
Veterinary Science*

ISBNs, Imprints & Series:
0 03 Holt, Rinehart & Winston
0 12 Academic Press
0 15 Harcourt Brace & Co
0 7020 Baillière Tindall
0 7216 W. B. Saunders
0 8089 Grune & Stratton
0 8566 T. & A. D. Poyser

Parent Company:
Harcourt Brace & Co Inc *(USA)*

Associated & Subsidiary Companies:
Academic Press Ltd; Baillière Tindall Ltd;
Grune & Stratton Ltd; Holt, Rinehart &
Winston; Johnson Reprint Co Ltd; The
Psychological Corporation; W. B. Saunders Co
Ltd; Scutari Press

Distributor for:
Australia: Harcourt Brace & Co (Australia) Pty
Ltd. *USA:* Academic Press Inc; Grune &
Stratton Inc; Harcourt Brace & Co; The
Psychological Corporation

Overseas Representation *(see §7.3):*
Australia: Harcourt Brace & Co (Australia) Pty
Ltd, Marrickville
Brazil: Academic Press do Brasil Editora Ltda,
São Paulo
Canada: Harcourt Brace & Co Canada Ltd,
Toronto
Italy: Marcello SNC, Padua
Japan: Harcourt Brace Japan Inc, Tokyo
Middle East: International Publishers
Representatives (IPR), Nicosia, Cyprus
South East Asia: Harcourt Brace & Co
International, Singapore
USA: Harcourt Brace & Co International,
Orlando, FL

Book Trade Association Membership: PA,
BDC, EPC, IGSMTP, CAPP

<hr>

1385

HARLEQUIN MILLS & BOON LTD
Eton House, 18–24 Paradise Road, Richmond,
Surrey TW9 1SR
Telephone: 0181 948 0444
Fax: 0181 288 2899

Warehouse, Orders, Returns & Payments:
Exel Logistics Media Services, Invicta House,
Sir Thomas Langley Road,
Medway City Estate, Rochester, Kent
ME2 4DU
Telephone: 01634 297123
Fax: 01634 298000

Chairman: John T. Boon
Editor Emeritus: A. W. Boon
Directors: R. Guzner *(Managing)*

S.L. Cummings *(Finance)*
D. Elliott *(Direct Marketing)*
A. Meredith *(Production)*
K. Stoecker *(Editorial)*
H. O'Neil *(Marketing, Sales & Export)*
G. Howe *(UK Sales)*
J. Oldham *(Human Resources)*
Managers: S. Critchlow *(Export Sales)*
C. J. Stevens *(Sales Operations)*
P. Bulos *(Rights & Permissions)*
J. Kirkup *(Marketing)*

Fiction

New Titles: 675 (1995), 692 (1996)
No of Employees: 130
Annual Turnover: £15M

ISBNs, Imprints & Series:
0 263 Mills & Boon
0 373 Silhouette
1 55166 Mira

Parent Company:
Harlequin Enterprises Ltd *(Canada)*

Associated & Subsidiary Companies:
Australia: Harlequin Mills & Boon Pty Ltd.
Brazil: Editora Abril. *Bulgaria:* Harlequin
Bulgaria EOOD. *Canada:* Harlequin
Enterprises Ltd. *Czech Republic:* Harlequin
Publishers SR, O. *Denmark:* Aller Leaser
Service. *Finland:* Harlequin Finland. *France:*
Harlequin SA. *Germany:* Cora Verlag GmbH &
Co. *Greece:* Harlenic Hellas SA. *Hungary:*
Harlequin KFT. *Italy:* Harlequin Mondadori
SPA. *Japan:* Harlequin KK. *Mexico:* Harmex.
Netherlands: Harlequin Enterprises BV. *New
Zealand:* C/- Network Distributors; Harlequin
Publishers (NZ) Ltd. *Philippines:* Philippine
Book Distributors Inc. *Poland:* Arlekin
Wydawnictwo. *Spain:* Harlequin Iberica SA.
Sweden: Forlaget Harlekin AB. *Switzerland:*
Harlequin Enterprises BV. *Taiwan:* Harlequin
Taiwan Ltd. *Turkey:* Harlequin Yayincilik Ltd
Sti

Distributor for:
Mira Books; Silhouette Books

Overseas Representation *(see §7.3):*
Middle East: Peter Ward Book Exports,
London, UK

Book Trade Association Membership: PA
(International Division)

<hr>

1386

HARPERCOLLINS CARTOGRAPHIC
[a division of HarperCollins Publishers]
HarperCollins Publishers,
77–85 Fulham Palace Road, London W6 8JB
Telephone: 0181 741 7070
Fax: 0181 307 4813

Branch:
Westerhill Road, Bishopbriggs, Glasgow
G64 2QT
Telephone: 0141 772 3200
Fax: 0141 306 3130 & 3144

Directors: Jeremy Westwood *(Managing)*
Chris Moore *(Cartographic Publishing)*
Alex Elder *(Cartographic)*
David Rye *(Production)*
Abigail Dawson *(Marketing)*

Financial Controller: Stephen Muncaster
Manager: Simon Fox *(Premium)*

*Atlases & Maps; Guide Books; Travel &
Topography*

New Titles: 76 (1995), 80 (1996)
No of Employees: 130
Annual Turnover: £13M

ISBNs, Imprints & Series:
0 00 360 Collins Longman
0 00 447 Collins Cartographic
0 7028 Bartholomew, Nicholson
0 7230 Times Books

Parent Company:
HarperCollins

Distributor for:
Switzerland: Hallwag

Overseas Representation *(see §7.3):*
Australia: HarperCollins Publishers, Pymble,
NSW & North Ryde, NSW
Belgium: Geocart, Sint Niklaas
Canada: HarperCollins Publishers, Toronto &
Scarborough
Denmark: Scanvik Books APS, Copenhagen
France: Editions Geographiques Generales,
Paris
Germany & Austria: Internationales
Landkartenhaus Geocenter, Stuttgart,
Germany
India: Dass Media Pte Ltd, New Delhi
Italy: InterOrbis SpA, Corsico (Milan)
Japan: Maruzen Co Ltd, Tokyo
Netherlands: Nilsson & Lamm BV, Weesp
New Zealand: HarperCollins Publishers,
Auckland
Singapore & Malaysia: Pansing Distribution
Sdn Bhd, Singapore
South Africa: HarperCollins Publishers,
Johannesburg
Sweden: Lantmateriet Kartbutiken, Stockholm
& Vällingby
Thailand: Asia Book Co, Bangkok
USA: Hammond Inc, Maplewood, NJ

Book Trade Association Membership: PA,
Scottish PA

<hr>

1387

HARPERCOLLINS PUBLISHERS LTD
77–85 Fulham Palace Road, London W6 8JB
Telephone: 0181 741 7070
Fax: 0181 307 4440

**Glasgow Office (Warehouse, Trade Orders
& Distribution):**
Westerhill Road, Bishopbriggs, Glasgow
G64 2QT
Telephone: 0141 772 3200
Fax: 0141 772 3200 x3119

Directors: Eddie Bell *(Executive Chairman,
Publisher)*
David Houston *(Group Finance)*
Adrian Bourne *(Managing, Group Sales)*
Tom Armstrong *(UK Business Systems &
Services)*
John McDougall *(Human Resources)*
Stephen Bray *(Managing, Publishing
Operations)*
Eileen Campbell *(Managing, Thorsons/
Religious)*

Ian Craig *(Children's Publisher)*
Helen Ellis *(Publicity)*
Margaret Halton *(Rights)*
Adrian Laing *(Legal Affairs)*
Cresta Norris *(Film & TV)*
Martin Palmer *(UK Sales)*
David Singer *(Marketing, Direct)*
John Stachiewicz *(International Sales)*
Kate Harris *(Managing, Education)*
Robin Wood *(Managing, General Reference &*
 Dictionaries)
Publishing Directors: Stuart Proffitt
 (Publisher, Trade Division)
Malcolm Edwards *(Trade Fiction)*
Nick Sayers *(Trade Fiction)*
Michael Fishwick *(Trade Non-Fiction)*
Julia Wisdom *(Crime Club)*
Gail Penston *(Children's)*
Philip Gwyn Jones *(Flamingo)*

Atlases & Maps; Biography & Autobiography;
Children's Books; Cookery, Wines & Spirits;
Crime; Crafts & Hobbies; Do-It-Yourself;
Educational & Textbooks; Electronic
(Educational); Electronic (Professional &
Academic); English as a Foreign Language;
Fiction; Gardening; Gender Studies;
Geography & Geology; Guide Books; Health &
Beauty; History & Antiquarian; Humour;
Literature & Criticism; Magic & the Occult;
Medical (incl. Self Help & Alternative
Medicine); Natural History; Poetry; Politics &
World Affairs; Psychology & Psychiatry;
Reference Books, Directories & Dictionaries;
Religion & Theology; Science Fiction; Sports
& Games; Travel & Topography

New Titles: 1500 (1995)
No of Employees: 1900
Annual Turnover: £152.2M

ISBNs, Imprints & Series:
0 00 Armada, Collins, Collins Bibles, Collins
 Classics, Collins COBUILD, Collins Crime,
 Collins English Dictionaries, Collins
 Liturgical, Collins New Naturalist Library,
 Collins-Longman, CollinsEducational,
 CollinsGems, CollinsWillow, Flamingo,
 Fontana Press, Fount, HarperCollins,
 HarperCollins Audiobooks, HarperCollins
 Audio, HarperCollinsPublishers,
 HarperCollinsReligious, Jets, Lions, Picture
 Lions, Tracks, Young Lions
0 002 HarperCollins Science Fiction & Fantasy
0 00219, 0 00220 Collins Natural History
0 0044 Collins Cartographic
0 006 HarperCollins Paperbacks
0 01 HarperCollins Audio,
 HarperCollinsPublishers, Jets
0 04 CollinsEducational, Pandora, Tolkien
0 06 HarperSanFrancisco, US
0 09
0 246
0 261 HarperCollins, HarperCollinsPublishers,
 Tolkien
0 310 Zondervan Publishing House, US
0 411 HarperCollins Audio
0 551 Marshall Pickering
0 583
0 586 Eclipse
0 7225 Thorsons
0 7230 Times Books
0 85030 Aquarian
0 851
0 85152 Bartholomew
0 85269 Thorsons
0 85543

0 85924 Collins Dove, Australia
0 86358 Pandora
0 900568
1 85538 Aquarian

Parent Company:
The News Corp Ltd

Overseas Representation *(see §7.3)*:
Australia: HarperCollins Publishers, Pymble,
 NSW & North Ryde, NSW
Canada: HarperCollins Publishers, Toronto &
 Scarborough
New Zealand: HarperCollins Publishers,
 Auckland
Worldwide (except countries listed):
 HarperCollins Publishers Ltd, Glasgow &
 London, UK

Book Trade Association Membership: PA

1388 ■■■■■

HARPERCOLLINS RELIGIOUS
77–85 Fulham Palace Road, Hammersmith,
London W6 8JB
Telephone: 0181 741 7070
Fax: 0181 307 4064

Customer Service Dept:
HarperCollins Publishers Ltd, Westerhill Road,
Bishopbriggs, Glasgow G64 2QT
Telephone: 0141 772 3200
Fax: 0141 306 3119

Directors: Eileen Campbell *(Managing)*
Jeremy Yates-Round *(Publishing-Marshall*
 Pickering Bibles, Music)
Editors: Murray White *(Fount)*
Kathy Dyke *(Music)*
Export: Ray Potts

Biography & Autobiography; Children's
Books; Music; Religion & Theology

ISBNs, Imprints & Series:
0 00 512 Bibles (including Good News Bible)
0 00 599 General Religious
0 00 627 Fount
0 551 Marshall Pickering, Music

Parent Company:
News International

Distributor for:
USA: HarperCollins Sanfrancisco; Zondervan

Overseas Representation *(see §7.3)*:
Australia & New Zealand: HarperCollins
 Publishers, Pymble, NSW & North Ryde,
 NSW, Australia
Canada: HarperCollins Publishers, Toronto &
 Scarborough
North America: HarperCollins US, New York,
 USA; The Zondervan Corporation, Grand
 Rapids, MI, USA; HarperSanFrancisco, San
 Francisco, CA, USA
South Africa: HarperCollins Publishers,
 Johannesburg

Book Trade Association Membership: PA

1389 ■■■■■

HARRAP
45 Annandale Street, Edinburgh EH7 4AZ

Telephone: 0131 557 4571
Fax: 0131 557 2936

Distribution:
Telephone: 01256 29242
Fax: 01256 812521 & 812558

Chairman: John Clement
International Sales: Robert Snuggs
Manager: Katharine Coates *(Publishing)*

English as a Foreign Language; Languages &
Linguistics; Reference Books, Directories &
Dictionaries

New Titles: 33 (1995), 7 (1996)
No of Employees: 11
Annual Turnover: £5M

ISBNs, Imprints & Series: 0 245

Parent Company:
Larousse Plc

1390 ■■■■■

HARVARD UNIVERSITY PRESS
Fitzroy House, Chenies Street, London
WC1E 7ET
Telephone: 0171 306 0603
Fax: 0171 306 0604
Email: 100315.1423@compuserve.com
Web Site: http://www.hup.harvard.edu

Orders & Warehouse:
c/o John Wiley & Sons,
Southern Cross Trading Estate,
1 Oldlands Way, Bognor Regis, West Sussex
PO22 9SA
Telephone: 01243 779777
Fax: 01243 829121
Email: customer@wiley.co.uk

Managing Director: Ann Sexsmith
Publicity & Promotion Manager: Jean
 Heffernan

Academic & Scholarly; Biology & Zoology;
Economics; Fine Art & Art History; Gender
Studies; History & Antiquarian; Literature &
Criticism; Music; Natural History;
Philosophy; Politics & World Affairs;
Psychology & Psychiatry; Sociology &
Anthropology

New Titles: 150 (1995), 150 (1996)
No of Employees: 3

ISBNs, Imprints & Series:
0 674 Loeb Classical Library

Parent Company:
Harvard University Press *(USA)*

Overseas Representation *(see §7.3)*:
China: Cassidy & Associates Inc, New York,
 USA
Germany, Austria, Switzerland & Italy: Uwe
 Luedemann, Berlin, Germany
India: Mediamatics, Calcutta
Israel: Rodney Franklin Agency, Tel Aviv
Japan, Taiwan, Hong Kong & South Korea:
 American University Press Group, Tokyo,
 Japan
Mexico, Central America, Caribbean & South
 America: Harvard University Press,
 Cambridge, MA, USA

Scandinavia, Netherlands, Luxembourg, Belgium, France & Liechtenstein: Fred Hermans, Bovenkarspel, Netherlands
South Africa: Cory Voigt Associates, Braamfontein
South East Asia: Toppan Co (S) Pte Ltd, Singapore
Spain & Portugal: Arie Ruitenbeek, Madrid, Spain

1391

HARVEYS BOOKS
Magna Road, Wigston, Leicester LE18 4ZH
Telephone: 0116 278 5154
Fax: 0116 278 2534

Chief Executive: Vance Harvey
Directors: Andrew Tindall *(Sales)*
K. E. Harvey
Managers: Robert Guy *(Export)*
Paul Bennett *(Operations)*
Barry May *(Business Development)*
Gilberto Fiocco *(Export)*

Animal Care & Breeding; Antiques & Collecting; Aviation; Children's Books; Cinema, Video, TV & Radio; Cookery, Wines & Spirits; Crafts & Hobbies; Gardening; Military & War; Music; Natural History; Nautical; Sports & Games; Transport; Art

New Titles: 150 (1995), 75 (1996)
No of Employees: 25

ISBNs, Imprints & Series:
0 948509, 1 85422 Magna Books

Parent Company:
Harveys Books Ltd

Associated & Subsidiary Companies:
USA: Magna Books Inc

Distributor for:
Magna Books

Book Trade Association Membership: PA, BA

1392

THE HARVILL PRESS
84 Thornhill Road, London N1 1RD
Telephone: 0171 609 1119
Fax: 0171 609 2019

UK Sales Representation:
4th Estate, 6 Salem Road, London W2 4BU
Telephone: 0171 727 8993
Fax: 0171 792 3176

Distribution:
Exel Logistics, Invicta House,
Sir Thomas Longley Road,
Medway City Estate, Rochester, Kent
ME2 4DU
Telephone: 01634 297123
Fax: 01634 298000

Chairman & Publisher: Christopher Maclehose
Directors: John Mitchinson *(Managing)*
Guido Waldman *(Editorial)*
Rachael Kerr *(Marketing)*
Editor: Sarah Westcott

Rights Manager and Sales Administration Assistant: Katharina Bielenberg

Biography & Autobiography; Fiction; Illustrated & Fine Editions; Literature & Criticism; Poetry; Travel & Topography

New Titles: 50 (1995), 60 (1996)
No of Employees: 12

ISBNs, Imprints & Series:
0 00 2 Collins Harvill
1 86046 The Harvill Press

Overseas Representation *(see §7.3)*:
Africa (excluding South Africa): Anita Zih, London, UK
Australia: HarperCollins Publishers, Pymble, NSW & North Ryde, NSW
Canada: General Publishing Co Ltd, North York, Ont
Central & Southern America & Caribbean: David Williams IMA, London, UK
Central Europe: Janet Clark, London, UK
Eastern Europe: Michael Timperley Marketing, London, UK
Far East: Ashton International Marketing Services, Larkfield, UK
New Zealand: Archetype, Wellington
South Africa: Trinity Books CC, Randburg
USA: HarperCollins US, New York

1393

HAWK BOOKS
Suite 309, Canalot Studios, 222 Kensal Road, London W10 5BN
Telephone: 0181 969 8091
Fax: 0181 968 9012

Distributor:
Bookpoint Ltd, 35 Milton Park, Abingdon, Oxon OX14 4TD
Telephone: 01235 400400
Fax: 01235 832068

Director: P. Hawkey

Children's Books; Electronic (Entertainment); Illustrated & Fine Editions; Science Fiction

New Titles: 9 (1995), 10 (1996)
No of Employees: 1
Annual Turnover: £300,000

ISBNs, Imprints & Series:
0 948248 American Nostalgia Library, Hawk Comics, Sparrowhawk

Parent Company:
Hostaction Ltd

1394

HAWKER PUBLICATIONS
13 Park House, 140 Battersea Park Road, London SW11 4NB
Telephone: 0171 720 2108
Fax: 0171 498 3023

Directors: Dr R. Hawkins *(Managing)*
P. Petker *(Sales)*

Health & Beauty; Medical (incl. Self Help & Alternative Medicine); Vocational Training & Careers

New Titles: 6 (1995), 8 (1996)
No of Employees: 14
Annual Turnover: £1.4M

ISBNs, Imprints & Series:
1 874790 Care Concern Handbook Series, Better Care Guides, Hawker Publications

Associated & Subsidiary Companies:
Hawker Consumer Publishing

Book Trade Association Membership: IPG

1395

HAWKSMERE GROUP LTD
12–18 Grosvenor Gardens, London
SW1W 0DH
Telephone: 0171 824 8257
Fax: 0171 730 4293

Trade Orders:
Bookpoint Ltd, 39 Milton Park, Abingdon, Oxon OX14 4TD
Telephone: 01235 835001
Fax: 01235 832068

Directors: Neil Thomas *(Managing)*
Neill Ross *(Marketing)*
Marketing Manager: Simone Davies
Publishing Executive: Angela Spall

Accountancy & Taxation; Engineering; Industry, Business & Management; Law; Music

New Titles: 20 (1996)
No of Employees: 40
Annual Turnover: £5M

ISBNs, Imprints & Series: 1 85418

Associated & Subsidiary Companies:
Acorn Publications Ltd; Hawksmere Plc; Thorogood Ltd

Overseas Representation *(see §7.3)*:
Hong Kong: Asia Publisher Services Ltd
South East Asia: APD Singapore Pte Ltd, Singapore

1396

HAWTHORN PRESS
Hawthorn House, 1 Lansdown Lane, Stroud, Glos GL5 1BJ
Telephone: 01453 757040
Fax: 01453 751138

Partners: Martin Large
Judy Large
Joyce Ballinger
Ann Mayer

Academic & Scholarly; Crafts & Hobbies; Educational & Textbooks; Gender Studies; Industry, Business & Management; Psychology & Psychiatry

New Titles: 10 (1995), 8 (1996)
No of Employees: 5
Annual Turnover: £35,000

ISBNs, Imprints & Series:
1 869890 Biography, Biography & Self Development, Conflict, Lifeways, Rudolf Steiner Education, Social Ecology

Overseas Representation *(see §7.3)*:
Australia: Astam Books Pty Ltd, Leichhardt, NSW
New Zealand: Steinerbooks NZ, Auckland
South Africa: Rudolf Steiner Publications, Randburg
USA: New Leaf Distribution, Lithia Springs, GA; Anthroposophic Press Inc, Hudson, NY

Book Trade Association Membership: IPG

1397

HAWTHORNS PUBLICATIONS LTD
Pond View House, 6a High Street, Otford, Sevenoaks, Kent TN14 5PQ
Telephone: 01959 522325
Fax: 01959 522368

Biography & Autobiography; Educational & Textbooks; Guide Books

ISBNs, Imprints & Series:
1 871044 Pond View

Overseas Representation *(see §7.3)*:
India: Applied Media, New Delhi
Philippines: Combined Book Representatives, Manila

Book Trade Association Membership: PA

1398

J. H. HAYNES & CO LTD
[trading as Haynes Publishing]
Sparkford, Yeovil, Somerset BA22 7JJ
Telephone: 01963 440635
Fax: 01963 440825

Mail Orders & Despatch:
Sparkford, Yeovil, Somerset BA22 7JJ
Telephone: 01963 440614
Fax: 01963 440001

Motor Trade Editorial:
Telephone: 01963 440635
Fax: 01963 440645

Special Interest Editorial:
Telephone: 01963 440635
Fax: 01963 440023

Home & Leisure Editorial:
Telephone: 01963 440635
Fax: 01963 440740

Chairman: J. H. Haynes
Directors: K. C. Fullman, A.C.A. *(Managing)*
A. Sperring *(Production)*
Editorial: Scott Mauck *(Motor Trade)*
Matthew Minter *(Motor Trade)*
D. J. Reach *(Special Interest)*
Nicholas Barnard *(Home & Leisure)*
Sales & Marketing: S. L. Reed *(UK & Europe)*
Rights: E. Oakley *(Motor Trade)*
R. Jackson *(Special Interest, Home & Leisure)*
Export Sales: G. Cook
Marketing: D. Keel
Permissions: J. Austin *(Motor Trade)*

Atlases & Maps; Crafts & Hobbies; Do-It-Yourself; Educational & Textbooks; Reference Books, Directories & Dictionaries; Sports & Games; Transport; Cycling; Motoring

New Titles: 108 (1995), 107 (1996)
No of Employees: 150
Annual Turnover: £10.8M

ISBNs, Imprints & Series:
0 85696, 0 900550, 1 85010, 1 85960

Parent Company:
Haynes Publishing Group Plc

Associated & Subsidiary Companies:
G. T. Foulis & Co; OPC; Oxford Illustrated Press; Oxford Publishing Co; Patrick Stephens Ltd. *France:* Editions Haynes SA. *USA:* Haynes North America Inc

Distributor for:
Motorbooks International Inc

Overseas Representation *(see §7.3)*:
Europe (excluding France) (Motor Trade): Joe Portelli, Bologna, Italy
Europe (Special Interest, Home & Leisure): Angell Eurosales, Newton Abbot, UK
France: Editions Haynes SA, Paris
Scandinavia: Haynes Publishing, Uppsala, Sweden
USA & Canada: Haynes Publications Inc, Newbury Park, CA, USA

1399

HAZAR PUBLISHING LTD
147 Chiswick High Road, London W4 2DT
Telephone: 0181 742 8578
Fax: 0181 994 1407

Distribution & Warehouse:
Macmillan Distribution Ltd, Brunel Road, Houndmills, Basingstoke RG21 6XS
Telephone: 01256 302775
Fax: 01256 51437

Managing Director: Greg Hill *(Company Secretary)*
Manager: Miss Marie Clayton *(Publishing)*

Architecture & Design; Children's Books; Illustrated & Fine Editions

New Titles: 7 (1995), 17 (1996)
No of Employees: 3
Annual Turnover: £400,000

ISBNs, Imprints & Series: 1 874371

Parent Company:
Areen Projects (Jersey)

Associated & Subsidiary Companies:
Lebanon: Hazar Graphics. *Saudi Arabia:* Dar Al Reisha

Overseas Representation *(see §7.3)*:
Australia & New Zealand: Bookwise International, Findon, SA, Australia
Hong Kong, Macau, Singapore, Taipei & Bangkok: Asia 2000, Hong Kong
Italy: Logos Impex srl, Modena
Netherlands: Van Buren Uitgeverij BV, Weert
South Africa: Verbatim Distributors, Constantia Hills

Book Trade Association Membership: IPG

1400

HAZLETON PUBLISHING LTD
3 Richmond Hill, Richmond, Surrey TW10 6RE
Telephone: 0181 948 5151
Fax: 0181 948 4111

Sales Representation:
Derek Searle Associates Ltd, Burlington House, 14 High Street, Slough, Berks SL1 1EE
Telephone: 01753 539295
Fax: 01753 551863

Distribution:
Biblios Ltd, Star Road, Partridge Green, West Sussex RH13 8LD
Telephone: 01403 710971
Fax: 01403 711143

Publisher & Managing Director: Richard Poulter
Managers: Simon Maurice *(Business Development)*
Steven Palmer *(Production)*
Editor: Peter Lovering

Sports & Games

New Titles: 1 (1995)

ISBNs, Imprints & Series:
0 905138, 1 874557

Overseas Representation *(see §7.3)*:
Australia: Technical Book & Magazine Co, Melbourne
New Zealand: David Bateman Ltd, Auckland
USA: Motorbooks International Publishers & Wholesalers Inc, Osceola, WI

1401

HEADLINE BOOK PUBLISHING LTD
338 Euston Road, London NW1 3BH
Telephone: 0171 873 6000
Fax: 0171 873 6124

Distribution Centre:
Bookpoint Ltd, 39 Milton Park, Abingdon, Oxon OX14 4TD
Telephone: 01235 400400
Fax: 01235 400445

Directors: Tim Hely-Hutchinson *(Chairman)*
Siân Thomas *(Managing)*
Alan Brooke *(Non-fiction Publishing)*
Richard Adam *(Financial)*
Liz Allen *(Production)*
Simon Littlewood *(Deputy Managing Director/ Sales & Marketing)*
Diane Rowley *(Publicity)*
Louise Weir *(Marketing)*
Jane Morpeth *(Fiction Publishing)*
Sarah Thomson *(Rights)*
Managers: Peter Newsom *(Export Sales)*
Jenny Gray *(Sales Administration)*
Catherine Newman *(UK Sales)*

Antiques & Collecting; Architecture & Design; Biography & Autobiography; Cinema, Video, TV & Radio; Cookery, Wines & Spirits; Crime; Crafts & Hobbies; Fiction; Gardening; Guide Books; Health & Beauty; Humour; Military & War; Natural History; Photography; Science Fiction; Sports & Games

New Titles: 641 (1995), 680 (1996)
No of Employees: 50
Annual Turnover: £17M

ISBNs, Imprints & Series:
0 7472 Headline, Headline Delta, Headline
Feature, Headline Liaison, Headline Review

Parent Company:
Hodder Headline Plc

Associated & Subsidiary Companies:
Arnold

Overseas Representation (see §7.3):
Africa (excluding South Africa): Headline
Book Publishing, London, UK
Australia & Papua New Guinea: Hodder
Headline (Australia) Pty Ltd, Rydalmere,
Australia
Canada: General Publishing Co Ltd, North
York, Ont
Caribbean, Central & South America:
Humphrys Roberts Associates, London, UK
Europe, India, Far East & Caribbean: Hodder
& Stoughton Ltd, London, UK
Middle East: Peter Ward Book Exports,
London, UK
New Zealand: Hodder Moa Beckett Publishers
Ltd, Auckland
South Africa: Jonathan Ball Publishers (Pty)
Ltd, Johannesburg

Book Trade Association Membership: IPG

1402

*HEADSTART HISTORY
PO Box 41, Bangor, Gwynedd LL57 1SB
Telephone: 01248 351816
Fax: 01248 362115

Distributor:
Headstart, PO Box 628, Oxford OX1 2NL
Telephone: 01374 412474

Proprietor: Judith Ann Loades

*Academic & Scholarly; Archaeology; Fiction;
History & Antiquarian; Literature & Criticism;
Natural History; Religion & Theology*

ISBNs, Imprints & Series:
1 873041 Babbage Press (Local History),
Catesby Press (Historical Novels), Headstart
(General Academic Titles), Headstart
History Papers, Headstart Lecture Series

Associated & Subsidiary Companies:
Phoenix Press (Oxford) *(formerly Swansea)*;
Umberleigh Press

1403

HEALTH EDUCATION AUTHORITY
Hamilton House, Mabledon Place, London
WC1H 9TX
Telephone: 0171 383 3833
Fax: 0171 413 0339

Distribution:
Marston Book Services,
MBA Customer Services, PO Box 269,
Abingdon, Oxon OX14 4YN
Telephone: 01235 465565
Fax: 01235 465556

Representation in the UK:
HMSO Books, Publications Centre,
51 Nine Elms Lane, London SW8 5DR
Fax: 0171 873 8203

Managing Director: Simon Boyd
Publishing Manager: Chris Owen
Commissioning Editors: Flair Milne
Delphine Verroest
Managers: Bill Cosans *(Production)*
Dolores Ashton *(Sales & Marketing)*
John Billingham *(Logistics)*

*Cinema, Video, TV & Radio; Educational &
Textbooks; Health & Beauty; Medical (incl.
Self Help & Alternative Medicine)*

New Titles: 113 (1995), 80 (1996)
No of Employees: 17
Annual Turnover: £600,000

ISBNs, Imprints & Series:
0 7521, 1 85448

Book Trade Association Membership: PA,
BDC, EPC, CAPP

1404

WILLIAM HEINEMANN
Michelin House, 81 Fulham Road, London
SW3 6RB
Telephone: 0171 581 9393
Fax: 0171 225 9095

Distribution:
Reed Book Services, Northampton Road,
Rushden, Northants NN10 6PU
Telephone: 01933 58521
Fax: 01933 50284

International Sales Department:
(as principal address)
Telephone: 0171 581 9393
Fax: 0171 225 9371

Publisher: Tom Weldon

*Biography & Autobiography; Fiction; History
& Antiquarian; Politics & World Affairs;
Travel & Topography*

ISBNs, Imprints & Series: 0 434

Parent Company:
Reed Elsevier Plc

Overseas Representation (see §7.3):
Australia: Reed Books Australia, Melbourne,
Vic
Canada: Reed Publishing Canada, Markham,
Ont
East Asia: Reed Consumer Books, Metro
Manila, Philippines
India: Reed Consumer Books, New Delhi
Japan: Reed Consumer Books, Tokyo
New Zealand: Reed Publishing Group,
Auckland
Singapore: Reed International (Singapore) Pte
Ltd
South Africa: Struik Book Distributors Pty Ltd,
Johannesburg, Cape Town & Maitland

1405

HEINEMANN EDUCATIONAL
Halley Court, Jordan Hill, Oxford OX2 8EJ

Telephone: 01865 311366
Fax: 01865 310043

**Warehouse (NB Orders to Oxford address
above):**
Reed Book Services Ltd, Northampton Road,
Rushden, Northants NN10 6PU
Telephone: 01933 58521
Fax: 01933 50284

Managing Director: Bob Osborne

*Atlases & Maps; Educational & Textbooks;
Electronic (Educational); African Writers
Series; Caribbean Writers Series; School
Library Books*

ISBNs, Imprints & Series:
0 431, 0 435 Heinemann Educational,
Heinemann International Education,
Heinemann Library

Parent Company:
Reed International Books Ltd

Overseas Representation (see §7.3):
Australia: Rigby-Heinemann (Australia) Ltd,
Port Melbourne
Barbados, Windwards & Leewards: C. D. A.
Walker, Christchurch, Barbados
Botswana: Heinemann Educational Botswana,
Gaborone
Canada: General Publishing Co Ltd, North
York, Ont
Egypt: Cairo Trade Centre, Cairo
Ghana: A. Ott-Attafua & Co Ltd, Accra
Hong Kong & East Asia: Transglobal
Publishers Services Ltd, Tsuen Wan, Hong
Kong
Jamaica: West Indies Publishing Ltd, Kingston
Malawi: Ann Jhala, Blantyre
Malaysia: Reed International (Singapore) Pte
Ltd, Singapore
Mauritius: Editions de l'Ocean Indien Ltd,
Rose Hill
Namibia: New Namibia Books, Windhoek
New Zealand: Reed Publishing Group,
Auckland
Nigeria: Heinemann Educational Books
(Nigeria) Ltd, Ibadan
Pakistan: Publishers Marketing Associates,
Karachi
Sierra Leone: New Horizons, Freetown
South Africa: Heinemann Publishers (Pty) Ltd,
Houghton & Isando
Sri Lanka: K. V. G. de Silva & Sons (Colombo)
Ltd, Colombo
Tanzania: Afriservices, Dar es Salaam
Trinidad: KLP Agencies Ltd, Port of Spain
Uganda: Rorash Educational Publishers,
Kampala
USA: Heinemann Educational Books Inc,
Portsmouth, NH
Zambia: Insaka Press, Lusaka

1406

**HEINEMANN ENGLISH LANGUAGE
TEACHING**
Halley Court, Jordan Hill, Oxford OX2 8EJ
Telephone: 01865 311366
Fax: 01865 314193

**Warehouse (NB Orders to Oxford address
above):**
Reed Book Services, Northampton Road,
Rushden, Northants NN10 6PU

Telephone: 01933 58521
Fax: 01933 50284

Managing Director: Mike Esplen

English as a Foreign Language

ISBNs, Imprints & Series: 0 435

Parent Company:
Reed International Books Ltd

Overseas Representation *(see §7.3)*:
Argentina: Mary Anne Warburton, Buenos
    Aires
Australia: Rigby-Heinemann (Australia) Ltd,
    Port Melbourne
Austria: Big Ben Bookshop, Vienna; The
    British Bookshop, Vienna
Belgium, Luxembourg & Netherlands: Benelux
    Studiecentrum NV, Roosendaal,
    Netherlands
Botswana: Heinemann Educational Botswana,
    Gaborone
Brazil: Guy Gerlach, São Paulo
Canada: Monarch Books of Canada Ltd,
    Downsview
Caribbean: Heinemann Publishers (Caribbean)
    Ltd, Kingston, Jamaica; KLP Agencies Ltd,
    Port of Spain, Trinidad; C. D. A. Walker,
    Christchurch, Barbados
Chile: Eurotex Limitada, Santiago; Kuatro
    Ltda, Santiago; South American Way,
    Santiago
Colombia: Harla SA Decv, Sante Fe de Bogota
Czech Republic: Reed International Books,
    Prague
Denmark: Dansk Centralagentur DCA,
    Copenhagen; English Center, Randers
Ecuador: English Book Centre, Guayaquil
Egypt: Cairo Trade Centre, Cairo
Finland: Kielipalvelu Ky Oy, Pukkila
France: Heinemann ELT, Oxford, UK;
    Editions Magnard, Paris
Germany: Hans Heinrich Petersen Buchimport
    GmbH, Hamburg; Buchhandlung Stäheli &
    Co ELT Dept, Spaichingen
Ghana: A. Ott-Attafua & Co Ltd, Accra
Greece: Heinemann ELT, Zografou;
    Heinemann ELT, Thessaloniki
Hong Kong: Hong Kong University Press
Hungary: Varga János, Budapest
Iceland: Bokabud Mals Og Meriningar,
    Reykjavik
India: Dass Media Pte Ltd, New Delhi
Irish Republic: International Books, Dublin;
    Modern Languages, Dublin
Italy: Felice Le Monnier SpA, Grassina
Japan: Heinemann International Japan Liaison
    Office, Tokyo
Korea: Moon Yae Dang, Seoul, Korea, South
Lebanon: Malik's Bookshop, Beirut
Malta: Audio Visual Centre Ltd, Sliema
Mauritius: Editions de l'Ocean Indien Ltd,
    Rose Hill
Mexico: Heinemann, Mexico DF
Myanmar (Burma): Innwa Book Store,
    Yongon, Myanmar
Namibia: New Namibia Books, Windhoek
New Zealand: OPG New Zealand Ltd,
    Auckland
Nigeria: Heinemann Educational Books
    (Nigeria) Ltd, Ibadan
Norway: Scandinavian University Press SA,
    Oslo
Pakistan: Publishers Marketing Associates,
    Karachi

Paraguay: Jose Luis Morales, Montevideo,
    Uruguay
Peru: Heinemann, Montevideo
Poland (North): ELT Books Ltd, Gdansk,
    Poland
Poland (South): ELT Books & Press, Wraclow,
    Poland
Russia: English for Youngsters, Zug,
    Switzerland
Slovakia: EFA Trading, Bratislava
Slovenia: DZS, Ljubljana
South Africa: Heinemann Publishers (Pty) Ltd,
    Houghton & Isando
South East Asia: Reed International
    (Singapore) Pte Ltd, Singapore
Spain: Heinemann Iberia, Madrid
Sri Lanka: K. V. G. de Silva & Sons (Colombo)
    Ltd, Colombo
Sweden: Corona AB, Malmo
Switzerland: Kurt Stäheli & Co, Zurich
Taiwan: Tung Hua Book Co Ltd, Taipei
Tanzania: Afriservices, Dar es Salaam
Thailand: Book Services & Promotion,
    Bangkok
Turkey: Heinemann International Türkiye,
    Istanbul
Uganda: Rorash Enterprises, Kampala
Uruguay: Jose Luis Morales, Montevideo
USA: Delta Systems Inc, McHenry, IL
Venezuela: Heinemann, Caracas

HEINEMANN YOUNG BOOKS
Michelin House, 81 Fulham Road, London
SW3 6RB
Telephone: 0171 581 9393
Fax: 0171 225 9406

Distribution:
Reed Book Services, Northampton Road,
Rushden, Northants NN10 6PU
Telephone: 01933 58521
Fax: 01933 50284

International Sales Department:
(as principal address)
Telephone: 0171 581 9393
Fax: 0171 225 9371

Divisional Managing Director: Jane
    Winterbotham

Children's Books

ISBNs, Imprints & Series:
0 434 Heinemann Young Books
1 85270 Parent & Child
1 85591 Buzz

Parent Company:
Reed Elsevier Plc

Overseas Representation *(see §7.3)*:
Australia: Reed Books Australia, Melbourne,
    Vic
Canada: Reed Publishing Canada, Markham,
    Ont
East Asia: Reed Consumer Books, Metro
    Manila, Philippines
India: Reed Consumer Books, New Delhi
Japan: Reed Consumer Books, Tokyo
New Zealand: Reed Publishing Group,
    Auckland
Singapore: Reed International (Singapore) Pte
    Ltd

South Africa: Struik Book Distributors Pty Ltd,
    Johannesburg, Cape Town & Maitland

HELICON
42 Hythe Bridge Street, Oxford OX1 2EP
Telephone: 01865 204204
Fax: 01865 204205
Email: 74777.3250@compuserve.com

Trade Enquiries & Orders:
Tiptree Book Services Ltd, Tiptree, Colchester,
Essex CO5 0SR
Telephone: 01621 819600
Fax: 01621 819717

Directors: David Attwooll *(Managing)*
Michael Upshall *(Publishing)*
Brigid Macleod *(Sales & Marketing)*
Anne-Lucie Norton *(Editorial)*
Hilary McGlynn *(Associate Editorial)*
Managers: Clare Painter *(Rights)*
Jenny Diment *(Market Development)*

*Electronic (Educational); Electronic
(Professional & Academic); Environment &
Development Studies; History & Antiquarian;
Medical (incl. Self Help & Alternative
Medicine); Military & War; Music; Politics &
World Affairs; Reference Books, Directories &
Dictionaries; Scientific & Technical*

New Titles: 33 (1995), 25 (1996)
No of Employees: 22

ISBNs, Imprints & Series: 1 85986

Overseas Representation *(see §7.3)*:
Canada: Oxford University Press, Don Mills
New Zealand: Reed Publishing Group,
    Auckland
Singapore: Reed International (Singapore) Pte
    Ltd
South Africa: Random House South Africa Pty
    Ltd, Rosebank, Johannesburg

Book Trade Association Membership: PA

HENDERSON PUBLISHING PLC
Tide Mill Way, Woodbridge, Suffolk IP12 1BY
Telephone: 01394 380622
Fax: 01394 380618

Warehouse & Distribution:
International Book Distributors,
Customer Service–DK, Magna Park,
Coventry Road, Lutterworth, Leics LE17 4XH
Telephone: 01442 882214
Fax: 01442 882200

Directors: Barrie Henderson *(Managing)*
Alan Cunningham *(Commercial)*
Managers: Steve Evans *(UK Sales)*
Lucy Bater *(Managing Editor)*
Mike Kudar *(Production)*
Simon Couchman *(Art & Design)*
Sarah Leask *(Publicity, Promotion &
    Advertising)*

Children's Books

New Titles: 108 (1995), 153 (1996)
No of Employees: 44
Annual Turnover: £6.4M

ISBNs, Imprints & Series:
0 85597, 1 85597 Clever Clogs, Fun Files,
Funfax, Junior Funfax, Henderson Study
System, Home Time, Know Alls, Loony
Balloonies, Mad Jack, Make-A-Model
Books, Master Class, My Little Funfax,
Scallywag, Sticky History Books

Parent Company:
Dorling Kindersley Ltd

Overseas Representation *(see §7.3):*
Australia: Ashton Scholastic Pty Ltd, Gosford
Malta: Miller Distributors Ltd, Luqa
Middle East: Peter Ward Book Exports,
London, UK
New Zealand: Ashton Scholastic Ltd, Auckland
Other Overseas Enquiries: Export Sales
Department Dorling Kindersley Ltd,
London, UK

1410 ▬▬▬

IAN HENRY PUBLICATIONS LTD
20 Park Drive, Romford, Essex RM1 4LH
Telephone: 01708 749119

Managing Director: Ian Wilkes

*Cookery, Wines & Spirits; Educational &
Textbooks; Fiction; History & Antiquarian;
Medical (incl. Self Help & Alternative
Medicine); Theatre, Drama & Dance;
Transport*

New Titles: 9 (1995), 12 (1996)

ISBNs, Imprints & Series: 0 86025

Distributor for:
USA: Players Press

Overseas Representation *(see §7.3):*
Scandinavia: D. Richard Bowen, Malmö,
Sweden
USA: Empire Publishing Service, Studio City,
CA

Book Trade Association Membership: IPG

1411 ▬▬▬

HENSTON LTD
[Veterinary Business Development Ltd]
Olympus House, Werrington Centre,
Peterborough PE4 6NA
Telephone: 01733 325522
Fax: 01733 325512
Email: 100303.1416@compuserve.com

Editor: Allan Henderson, BVMS MRCVS
Directors: Douglas Hutchison, BVMS
MRCVS *(Managing)*
Pippa Hutchison *(Operations)*

Animal Care & Breeding; Veterinary Science

New Titles: 1 (1996)
No of Employees: 11

ISBNs, Imprints & Series: 1 85054

Parent Company:
Veterinary Business Development Ltd

1412 ▬▬▬

THE HERBERT PRESS
35 Bedford Row, London WC1R 4JH
Telephone: 0171 4045621
Fax: 0171 4047706

Distributors:
A. & C. Black, Howard Road, Eaton Socon,
Huntingdon, Cambs PE19 3EZ
Telephone: 01480 212666
Fax: 01480 405014

Chairman: Charles Black
Directors: David Herbert *(Managing, Sales,
Rights & Permissions)*
Jill Coleman

*Archaeology; Architecture & Design; Crafts &
Hobbies; Fashion & Costume; Fine Art & Art
History; Illustrated & Fine Editions; Natural
History; Photography; Travel & Topography*

New Titles: 5 (1995), 5 (1996)
No of Employees: 3

ISBNs, Imprints & Series:
0 906969, 1 871569 Design Handbooks, The
Herbert History of Art & Architecture,
Illustrated Biographies

Parent Company:
A. C. Black Plc

Overseas Representation *(see §7.3):*
Australia: Hodder Headline (Australia) Pty
Ltd, Rydalmere
Benelux & Germany: Reinier A. Pleysier,
Heerde, Netherlands
Canada: Fitzhenry & Whiteside Ltd, Markham
France, Greece, Italy & Yugoslavia: PKB,
Massagno, Switzerland
Hong Kong: United Publishers Services (Hong
Kong) Ltd
India: Allied Publishers Pte Ltd, New Delhi &
Calcutta
Japan: YOHAN (Western Publications
Distribution Agency), Tokyo
Malaysia: STP Distributors (M) Sdn Bhd, Shah
Alam
Middle East: Eurab Ltd, Rottingdean, UK
New Zealand: Random House New Zealand
Ltd, Auckland
Scandinavia: Patrick Bygate, Massagno,
Switzerland
Singapore & Brunei: STP Distributors Pte Ltd,
Singapore
South Africa: Book Promotions Pty Ltd,
Plumstead
Spain, Portugal & Gibraltar: Patrick Bygate,
Massagno, Switzerland
Thailand: Far East Publications Ltd, Bangkok

Book Trade Association Membership: PA

1413 ▬▬▬

NICK HERN BOOKS
14 Larden Road, London W3 7ST
Telephone: 0181 740 9539
Fax: 0181 746 2006

Distributor:
Tiptree Book Services Ltd, Tiptree, Colchester,
Essex CO5 0SR
Telephone: 01621 819600
Fax: 01621 819698

Managing Director: Nick Hern
Senior Editor: Jackie Bodley

Theatre, Drama & Dance

New Titles: 44 (1995), 40 (1996)
No of Employees: 3
Annual Turnover: £250,000

ISBNs, Imprints & Series: 1 85459

Distributor for:
USA: Drama Book Publishers; Theatre
Communications Group

Overseas Representation *(see §7.3):*
Australia: Currency Press, Paddington
Canada: Theatre Books, Toronto
New Zealand: Birch Tree Books, Auckland
Singapore: Select Books Pte Ltd
South Africa: African Business Enterprises,
Benmore
USA: Theatre Communications Group, New
York

1414 ▬▬▬

**UNIVERSITY OF HERTFORDSHIRE
PRESS**
University of Hertfordshire, College Lane,
Hatfield AL10 9AD
Telephone: 01707 284681
Fax: 01707 284666
Email: UHPress@herts.ac.uk

Publisher: Bill Forster
Sales & Distribution: Sue Mariscal

*Academic & Scholarly; Bibliography &
Library Science; Educational & Textbooks;
History & Antiquarian; Psychology &
Psychiatry; Scientific & Technical*

New Titles: 13 (1995), 10 (1996)
No of Employees: 2

ISBNs, Imprints & Series:
0 900458 Document Management Yearbook
(for Cimtech) – Series, The Interface
Collection Series, Key Issues in the
Information Business Series

Parent Company:
University of Hertfordshire

Associated & Subsidiary Companies:
Cimtech

1415 ▬▬▬

HIGHLAND BOOKS
Two High Pines, Knoll Road, Godalming,
Surrey GU7 2EP
Telephone: 01483 424560
Fax: 01483 424388
Email: 100443.712@compuserve.colm

Distribution / Trade Orders:
STL, PO Box 300, Kingstown Broadway,
Carlisle, Cumbria CA3 0QS
Telephone: 01228 512512
Fax: 01228 514949

Director: Philip Ralli

Religion & Theology

New Titles: 8 (1995), 12 (1996)
No of Employees: 2
Annual Turnover: £120,000

ISBNs, Imprints & Series:
0 946616, 1 897913 Highland

Overseas Representation (see §7.3):
Australia: Openbook Publishers, Adelaide, SA
New Zealand: Scripture Union Wholesale,
Wellington
South Africa: Methodist Wholesale, Cape
Town

1416 ▬

HILMARTON MANOR PRESS
Calne, Wilts SN11 8SB
Telephone: 0124 976 0208
Fax: 0124 976 0379

Directors: C. Baile de Laperriere
S. Baile de Laperriere

*Antiques & Collecting; Architecture & Design;
Fine Art & Art History; Reference Books,
Directories & Dictionaries*

New Titles: 4 (1995), 6 (1996)

ISBNs, Imprints & Series:
0 904722, 0 9500508

Distributor for:
France: Henri Addor & Associates; ADEC;
Edition de l'Amateur; ARC Edition;
Bibliotheque des Arts; Guide Emer; GRUND;
Mayer Edition; Servedit-Acatos; Tardy;
Editions Van Wilder. *Germany:* Art Address
Verlag; Muller GmbH & Co KG. *Netherlands:*
Interbook International. *Switzerland:* Editions
Acatos; Bibliotheque des Arts. *USA:* ABAGE
Publications; Apollo Books; Sound View Press

1417 ▬

THE HISTORICAL ASSOCIATION
59a Kennington Park Road, London SE11 4JH
Telephone: 0171 735 3901
Fax: 0171 582 4989

Chief Executive: Mrs Madeline Stiles

History & Antiquarian

New Titles: 8 (1995), 8 (1996)
No of Employees: 8

ISBNs, Imprints & Series: 0 85278

1418 ▬

HLT PUBLICATIONS
The Gatehouse, Ruck Lane, Horsmonden,
Tonbridge, Kent TN12 8EA
Telephone: 01892 724371
Fax: 01892 724206

Warehouse:
Unit 5, 92–104 Carnwath Road, London
SW6 3HW
Telephone: 0171 371 7461
Fax: 0171 371 8627

Orders:
200 Greyhound Road, London W14 9RY

Telephone: 0171 385 3377
Fax: 0171 381 3377

Chairman: John Grenier
Manager: Steve Turner *(Sales & Marketing)*
Managing Editor: Jonathan Levy
Accounts Supervisor: Terence Griffiths
Publisher: Andrea Dowsett
Trade Enquiries: Jean Ravine

*Academic & Scholarly; Accountancy &
Taxation; Economics; Educational &
Textbooks; Industry, Business & Management;
Law; Mathematics & Statistics*

New Titles: 120 (1995), 152 (1996)
No of Employees: 12
Annual Turnover: £700,000

ISBNs, Imprints & Series:
1 85352, 0 7510 HLT Publications, Wise Owl
Books
1 85836 Old Bailey Press

Parent Company:
The HLT Group Ltd

Book Trade Association Membership: PA,
BDC, EPC, CAPP, IPG

1419 ▬

HMSO BOOKS
St Crispins, Duke Street, Norwich NR3 1PD
Telephone: 01603 622211
Fax: 01603 695317
Email: book.enquiries@hmso.gov.uk
Web Site: http://www.hmsoinfo.gov.uk

Sales & Distribution:
51 Nine Elms Lane, London SW8 5DR
Telephone: 0171 873 0011
Fax: 0171 873 8463
Web Site: http://www.hmsoinfo.gov.uk

Directors: Mike Lynn *(Controller & Chief
Executive)*
Brian Minett *(Distribution Director,
Publications Centre)*
John Hudson *(Sales)*
Publishing: Alan Cole *(Director, Client
Publishing)*
Eric Hendry *(Director, Parliamentary &
Statutory Publishing)*
John Saville *(Head of Electronic Publishing)*
Export, Sales, Rights & Permissions: Ian
Stevens
Managers: Michael Eaton *(General, Accounts)*
Chris Allen *(International Sales Agency)*
John Smith *(UK Sales)*
Andrew Cullua *(Head of Publicity)*
Mick Spencer *(Editorial Services)*
Phillip Brooks *(Head of Client Publishing)*

*Academic & Scholarly; Accountancy &
Taxation; Agriculture; Animal Care &
Breeding; Archaeology; Architecture &
Design; Aviation; Bibliography & Library
Science; Biography & Autobiography; Biology
& Zoology; Chemistry; Computer Science;
Crafts & Hobbies; Economics; Educational &
Textbooks; Electronic (Professional &
Academic); Engineering; Fine Art & Art
History; Gardening; Gender Studies;
Geography & Geology; Guide Books; Health &
Beauty; History & Antiquarian; Industry,
Business & Management; Law; Mathematics &*

*Statistics; Medical (incl. Self Help &
Alternative Medicine); Military & War; Music;
Natural History; Nautical; Photography;
Politics & World Affairs; Psychology &
Psychiatry; Reference Books, Directories &
Dictionaries; Scientific & Technical; Sociology
& Anthropology; Transport; Travel &
Topography; Veterinary Science; Vocational
Training & Careers*

New Titles: 11000 (1995), 10000 (1996)
No of Employees: 920
Annual Turnover: £74M

ISBNs, Imprints & Series:
0 10 Parliamentary Publications
0 11 Non-Parliamentary Publications
0 1149 Scottish Publications
0 337 Northern Ireland Publications
1 55 International Monetary Fund
92 International Organisations

Distributor for:
Austria: International Atomic Energy Agency
(IAEA). *Belgium:* World Customs
Organisation. *Denmark:* Nordic Council of
Ministers. *France:* Council of Europe;
Organisation of Economic Cooperation &
Development (OECD); UNESCO. *Irish
Republic:* Office of Public Works. *Italy:* Food
& Agriculture Organisation (FAO). *Japan:*
United Nations University (UNU).
Luxembourg: European Communities (EC).
Spain: World Tourism Organization (WTO).
Switzerland: United Nations (UN); World
Health Organisation (WHO); World Trade
Organisation. *USA:* Bernan Press; International
Monetary Fund (IMF). *Worldwide:* British
Consultants Bureau (BCB); National
Radiological Protection Board; UK Atomic
Energy Authority

Overseas Representation (see §7.3):
Australia: Hunter Publications, Collingwood;
DA Information Services, Mitcham, Vic
Bangladesh (stockist): Karim International,
Dhaka, Bangladesh
Belgium & Luxembourg: Jean de Lannoy,
Brussels, Belgium
Cyprus: Bridgehouse Bookshop, Nicosia
Denmark: Arnold Busck, Copenhagen
Europe (trade representation): Bill Bailey
Publishers Representatives, Newton Abbot,
UK
Far East: Toppan Co (S) Pte Ltd, Singapore
Finland: Akateeminen Kirjakauppa, Helsinki
France: World Data, Paris; WH Smith The
English Bookshop, Paris
Germany: Alexander Horn, Wiesbaden
Gibraltar: Gibraltar Bookshop
Greece: G. C. Eleftheroudakis SA, Athens
Hong Kong: Swindon Book Co, Kowloon
Iceland: Boksala Studenta, Reykjavik
India: Viva Marketing, New Delhi
Israel: R.O.Y. International, Tel Aviv
Japan: Maruzen Co Ltd, Tokyo
Jordan: Jordan Book Centre Co Ltd, Amman
Korea (Trade Representation): Information &
Culture Korea, Seoul, Korea, South
Kuwait: Kuwait Bookshops Co Ltd, Safat
Middle East (Trade Representation): Eurab
Ltd, Rottingdean, UK
Netherlands: Bookshop Kooyker, Leiden
Norway: Narvesens Information Centre, Oslo
Philippines: I. J. Sagun Enterprises Inc, Rizal
South Africa: Technical Books (Pty) Ltd, Cape
Town

Sweden: Fritzes Fackboksforetaget, Stockholm
Switzerland: Wepf & Co, Basel; Kurt Stäheli & Co, Zurich
United Arab Emirates: All Prints Publishers & Distributors, Abu Dhabi, UAE; Al Mutanabbi Bookshop, Dubai, UAE
USA & Canada: Seven Hills Book Distributors, Cincinnati, OH, USA
USA & Canada (Specialist Books & Documents): Unipub, Lanham, MD, USA

Book Trade Association Membership: PA, BA, Directory Publishers Association

1420 ▬▬▬▬▬

HOBSONS PUBLISHING PLC
Bateman Street, Cambridge CB2 1LZ
Telephone: 01223 354551
Fax: 01223 323154 & 301506
Web Site: http://www.hobsons.co.uk

Distributor:
Biblios Publishers' Distribution Services Ltd
Telephone: 01403 710971
Fax: 01403 711143

Orderline:
Telephone: 01403 710851
Fax: 01403 711143

Directors: M. Morgan *(Managing)*
Gillian Moore *(Publishing)*
Sales Manager: Julie Bushell

Educational & Textbooks; Electronic (Educational); Reference Books, Directories & Dictionaries; Scientific & Technical; Vocational Training & Careers; Education Choices

ISBNs, Imprints & Series:
0 86021 CRAC
1 85324 Hobsons

Parent Company:
Daily Mail & General Trust Group

Associated & Subsidiary Companies:
Harmsworth Publishing Ltd; Johansens Publications Ltd

Overseas Representation *(see §7.3)*:
Australia: New Hobsons Press Pty Ltd, Surry Hill, NSW
Caribbean, Honduras, Israel, Papua New Guinea & Zambia: Amday-B Import/Export Agents, Wolverhampton, UK
Middle East, United Arab Emirates, South Africa, India & Southern Europe: McGuire Marketing Publishers' International Management, Soham, Cambs, UK

Book Trade Association Membership:
Directory Publishers Association

1421 ▬▬▬▬▬

HOCHLAND & HOCHLAND LTD
174A Ashley Road, Hale, Cheshire WA15 9SF
Telephone: 0161 929 0190
Fax: 0161 929 1818

Warehouse, Trade Enquiries & Orders:
Butterworth Heinemann,
c/o Reed Book Services, Northampton Road, Rushden, Northants NN10 6PU

Telephone: 01933 58521
Fax: 01933 50284

Managing Director: Henry Hochland

Medical (incl. Self Help & Alternative Medicine)

ISBNs, Imprints & Series:
1 869888, 1 898507

Distributor for:
Department of Adult & Higher Education, University of Manchester; The Royal Marsden Hospital, Patient Information Group

Overseas Representation *(see §7.3)*:
Europe & North America: Butterworth-Heinemann Ltd, Oxford, UK

Book Trade Association Membership: PA

1422 ▬▬▬▬▬

HODDER & STOUGHTON EDUCATIONAL
338 Euston Road, London NW1 3BH
Telephone: 0171 873 6000
Fax: 0171 873 6299

Distribution Centre:
Bookpoint Ltd, 39 Milton Park, Abingdon, Oxon OX14 4TD
Telephone: 01235 400400
Fax: 01235 400445

Directors: Brian Steven *(Managing)*
Tim Gregson-Williams *(Educational Publishing)*
Philip Walters *(Sales & Marketing)*
Elisabeth Tribe *(Educational Publishing)*
Lucy Purkis *(Trade Educational Publishing)*

Academic & Scholarly; Chemistry; Crafts & Hobbies; Do-It-Yourself; Educational & Textbooks; Electronic (Educational); Engineering; Geography & Geology; Health & Beauty; Industry, Business & Management; Languages & Linguistics; Literature & Criticism; Mathematics & Statistics; Natural History; Physics; Politics & World Affairs; Psychology & Psychiatry; Reference Books, Directories & Dictionaries; Religion & Theology; Scientific & Technical; Sports & Games; Vocational Training & Careers

New Titles: 301 (1995), 400 (1996)
No of Employees: 68
Annual Turnover: £12M

ISBNs, Imprints & Series:
0 340 Hodder & Stoughton
0 7131 Arnold

Parent Company:
Hodder Headline Plc

Associated & Subsidiary Companies:
Arnold; Headline Book Publishing Ltd

Overseas Representation *(see §7.3)*:
Arab Middle East & Iran: International Publishers Representatives (IPR), Nicosia, Cyprus
Australia: Hodder Headline (Australia) Pty Ltd, Rydalmere
Canada: Pippin Publishing, Markham

Europe & USA: Hodder & Stoughton Educational, London, UK
Ghana: Oshiapem Publishing Services Ltd, Accra
Hong Kong: Federal Publications (HK) Ltd, Kowloon
India: Affiliated East-West Press Pvt Ltd, New Delhi; BI Publications Pvt Ltd, New Delhi & Bombay
Jamaica & Bahamas: Kingston Bookshop, Kingston, Jamaica
Japan: Nankodo Co Ltd, Tokyo; United Publishers Services Ltd, Tokyo
Kenya: Book Distributors Ltd, Nairobi; Pan Africa Book Services, Mombasa
Leeward Islands, St Kitts & Dominica: R. J. Laws & Son Agencies, Basseterre, St Kitts
Mauritius: Editions de l'Ocean Indien Ltd, Rose Hill
New Zealand: Hodder Moa Beckett Ltd, Auckland
Nigeria: Bounty Press Ltd, Ibadan
Pakistan: Publishers Marketing Associates, Karachi
Singapore, Malaysia, Indonesia, Philippines & Thailand: Toppan Co (S) Pte Ltd, Singapore
Southern Africa: Hodder & Stoughton Educational Southern Africa, Randburg, South Africa; Randhill, Randburg, South Africa
St Lucia: Juliette Forde, St Michael, Barbados
Tanzania: Entrepreneur International (T) Ltd, Dar es Salaam
Trinidad, Tobago, Barbados & Guyana: RIK Services Ltd, San Fernando, Trinidad
Uganda: Pan Africa Book Service (U), Kampala
Zimbabwe: Academic Press Pvt Ltd, Harare

1423 ▬▬▬▬▬

HODDER & STOUGHTON GENERAL
338 Euston Road, London NW1 3BH
Telephone: 0171 873 6000
Fax: 0171 873 6195

Distribution Centre:
Bookpoint Ltd, 39 Milton Park, Abingdon, Oxon OX14 4TD
Telephone: 01235 400400
Fax: 01235 400445

Directors: Martin Neild *(Managing)*
Sue Fletcher *(Deputy Managing)*
Amanda Ridout *(Sales)*
Karen Geary *(Publicity)*
Clare Armstrong *(Production)*
Publishers: Rupert Lancaster *(Audio)*
Roland Philipps *(Non-fiction)*
Carole Welch *(Editorial — Sceptre)*
Subsidiary Rights: Petra Sluka
Head of Marketing: Jamie Hodder-Williams
Managers: Richard Tucker *(UK Sales)*
Christopher Lewis *(Export Sales)*

Biography & Autobiography; Cinema, Video, TV & Radio; Cookery, Wines & Spirits; Crime; Crafts & Hobbies; Fiction; History & Antiquarian; Humour; Military & War; Politics & World Affairs; Reference Books, Directories & Dictionaries; Science Fiction; Sports & Games; Travel & Topography

New Titles: 529 (1995), 553 (1996)
No of Employees: 75
Annual Turnover: £21M

ISBNs, Imprints & Series:
Coronet, Sceptre
0 340 Hodder & Stoughton
0 450 New English Library

Parent Company:
Hodder Headline Plc

Associated & Subsidiary Companies:
Headline Book Publishing Ltd

Overseas Representation *(see §7.3)*:
Australia: Hodder Headline (Australia) Pty
   Ltd, Rydalmere
Brazil (paperbacks): Agencia Siciliano de
   Livros, São Paulo, Brazil
Canada (Christian trade): Lawson Falle Ltd,
   Cambridge, Canada
Canada (educational): Pippin Publishing,
   Markham, Canada
Canada (trade & paperbacks): General
   Publishing Co Ltd, North York, Ont, Canada
Ghana: Oshiapem Publishing Services Ltd,
   Accra
Hong Kong: Publishers' Associates Ltd
India (paperbacks): India Book House,
   Bombay, India
India (trade): BI Publications Pvt Ltd, New
   Delhi & Bombay, India
Israel (paperbacks): Steimatzky Ltd, Bnei
   Brak, Israel
Jamaica (paperbacks): Novelty Trading Co
   Ltd, Kingston, Jamaica
Malta (paperbacks): Progress Press Co Ltd,
   Valletta, Malta
Netherlands (paperbacks): Van Ditmar BV,
   Amsterdam, Netherlands
Netherlands (trade): Nilsson & Lamm BV,
   Weesp, Netherlands
New Zealand: Hodder Moa Beckett Publishers
   Ltd, Auckland
Pakistan (paperbacks): Liberty Books (Pvt)
   Ltd, Karachi, Pakistan
Pakistan (trade): Shams Quaraeshi, Karachi,
   Pakistan
Peru: Liberias ABC SA, San Isidro
Singapore: Pansing Distribution Sdn Bhd
Southern Africa (paperbacks): Struik Book
   Distributors Pty Ltd, Johannesburg, Cape
   Town & Maitland, South Africa
Southern Africa (trade & paperbacks): Struik
   Book Distributors Pty Ltd, Maitland, South
   Africa
Switzerland (paperbacks): OLF SA, Fribourg,
   Switzerland
Thailand (paperbacks): Asia Book Co,
   Bangkok, Thailand

1424 ■■■■■■■■■■■■■■■■■

HODDER & STOUGHTON RELIGIOUS
338 Euston Road, London NW1 3BH
Telephone: 0171 873 6000
Fax: 0171 873 6059

Distribution Centre:
Bookpoint Ltd, 39 Milton Park, Abingdon,
Oxon OX14 4TD
Telephone: 01235 400400
Fax: 01235 400445

Chairman: Mary Tapissier
Directors: Charles Nettleton *(Managing)*
Tim Moyler *(Sales)*
Judith Longman *(Editorial, Religious Trade)*
Emma Sealey *(Editorial, Bibles & Liturgical)*
Manager: Annabel Robson *(Publicity)*

Religion & Theology

New Titles: 86 (1995), 100 (1996)
No of Employees: 14
Annual Turnover: £4M

ISBNs, Imprints & Series:
0 340 Hodder & Stoughton

Parent Company:
Hodder Headline Plc

Associated & Subsidiary Companies:
Edward Arnold Ltd; Headline Book Publishing
Ltd

Overseas Representation *(see §7.3)*:
Australia: Hodder Headline (Australia) Pty
   Ltd, Rydalmere
Brazil (paperbacks): Agencia Siciliano de
   Livros, São Paulo, Brazil
Canada (Christian trade): R. G. Mitchell,
   Willowdale, Ont, Canada
Ghana: Oshiapem Publishing Services Ltd,
   Accra
Hong Kong: Publishers' Associates Ltd
India (paperbacks): India Book House,
   Bombay, India
India (trade): BI Publications Pvt Ltd, New
   Delhi & Bombay, India
Israel (paperbacks): Steimatzky Ltd, Bnei
   Brak, Israel
Jamaica (paperbacks): Novelty Trading Co
   Ltd, Kingston, Jamaica
Malta (paperbacks): Progress Press Co Ltd,
   Valletta, Malta
Netherlands (paperbacks): Van Ditmar BV,
   Amsterdam, Netherlands
Netherlands (trade): Nilsson & Lamm BV,
   Weesp, Netherlands
New Zealand: Hodder Moa Beckett Publishers
   Ltd, Auckland
Pakistan (paperbacks): Liberty Books (Pvt)
   Ltd, Karachi, Pakistan
Pakistan (trade): Shams Quaraeshi, Karachi,
   Pakistan
Peru: Liberias ABC SA, San Isidro
Singapore: Pansing Distribution Sdn Bhd
Southern Africa: Struik Christian Books, Cape
   Town, South Africa
Switzerland (paperbacks): OLF SA, Fribourg,
   Switzerland
Thailand (paperbacks): Asia Book Co,
   Bangkok, Thailand
USA: Spring Arbor Distributors, Belleville

1425 ■■■■■■■■■■■■■■■■■

HODDER CHILDREN'S BOOKS
338 Euston Road, London NW1 3BH
Telephone: 0171 873 6000
Fax: 0171 873 6229

Distribution Centre:
Bookpoint Ltd, 39 Milton Park, Abingdon,
Oxon OX14 4TD
Telephone: 01235 400400
Fax: 01235 400445

Chairman: Tim Hely-Hutchinson
Directors: Mary Tapissier *(Managing)*
Fiona Kenshole *(Publishing)*
Andrea Reece *(Marketing)*
Nancy Miles *(Rights)*
Clare Armstrong *(Production)*

Children's Books

New Titles: 300 (1995), 320 (1996)
No of Employees: 20
Annual Turnover: £4.8M

ISBNs, Imprints & Series: 0 340

Parent Company:
Hodder Headline Plc

Associated & Subsidiary Companies:
Arnold; Headline Book Publishing Ltd

Overseas Representation *(see §7.3)*:
Australia: Hodder Headline (Australia) Pty
   Ltd, Rydalmere
Brazil (paperbacks): Agencia Siciliano de
   Livros, São Paulo, Brazil
Canada (Christian trade): Lawson Falle Ltd,
   Cambridge, Canada
Canada (educational): Pippin Publishing,
   Markham, Canada
Canada (trade & paperbacks): General
   Publishing Co Ltd, North York, Ont, Canada
Ghana: Oshiapem Publishing Services Ltd,
   Accra
Hong Kong: Publishers' Associates Ltd
India (paperbacks): India Book House,
   Bombay, India
India (trade): BI Publications Pvt Ltd, New
   Delhi & Bombay, India
Israel (paperbacks): Steimatzky Ltd, Bnei
   Brak, Israel
Jamaica (paperbacks): Novelty Trading Co
   Ltd, Kingston, Jamaica
Malta (paperbacks): Progress Press Co Ltd,
   Valletta, Malta
Netherlands (paperbacks): Van Ditmar BV,
   Amsterdam, Netherlands
Netherlands (trade): Nilsson & Lamm BV,
   Weesp, Netherlands
New Zealand: Hodder Moa Beckett Publishers
   Ltd, Auckland
Pakistan (paperbacks): Liberty Books (Pvt)
   Ltd, Karachi, Pakistan
Pakistan (trade): Shams Quaraeshi, Karachi,
   Pakistan
Peru: Liberias ABC SA, San Isidro
Singapore: Pansing Distribution Sdn Bhd
Southern Africa (paperbacks): Struik Book
   Distributors Pty Ltd, Johannesburg, Cape
   Town & Maitland, South Africa
Southern Africa (trade & paperbacks): Struik
   Book Distributors Pty Ltd, Maitland, South
   Africa
Switzerland (paperbacks): OLF SA, Fribourg,
   Switzerland
Thailand: Asia Book Co, Bangkok

1426 ■■■■■■■■■■■■■■■■■

HOLLAND ENTERPRISES LTD
18 Bourne Court, Southend Road,
Woodford Green, Essex IG8 8HD
Telephone: 0181 551 7711
Fax: 0181 551 1266

Warehouse:
c/o Spacehire, M62 Trading Estate, Goole,
North Humberside DN14 8JW

Directors: W. C. Holland *(Managing,
   Children's Publications)*
J. W. Holland *(Commercial)*
T. C. Railton *(Sales)*

Children's Books

New Titles: 45 (1995), 68 (1996)
No of Employees: 15

ISBNs, Imprints & Series: 1 85038

1427 ▬▬▬

HOLLIS DIRECTORIES LTD
Harlequin House, 7 High Street, Teddington,
Middlesex TW11 8EY
Telephone: 0181 977 7711
Fax: 0181 977 1133
Email: 101320.3015@compuserve.com
Web Site: http://www.hollis-pr.com.uk/

Directors: Gary Zabel *(Managing)*
Rosemary Sarginson *(Publishing)*

*Industry, Business & Management; Reference
Books, Directories & Dictionaries*

New Titles: 2 (1995), 1 (1996)
No of Employees: 22
Annual Turnover: £1.3M

ISBNs, Imprints & Series:
0 900967 Hollis Arts Funding Handbook,
    Hollis Business Entertainment (the annual
    guide to corporate hospitality), Hollis
    Europe, Hollis Press & Public Relations
    Annual, Hollis Sponsorship & Donations
    Yearbook, Hollis Sponsorship Newsletter

Book Trade Association Membership:
Directory Publishers Association

1428 ▬▬▬

HOLMES & MEIER PUBLISHING
244A London Road, Hadleigh, Essex SS7 2DE
Telephone: 01702 552912
Fax: 01702 556095

Directors: Miriam Holmes *(Managing)*
Doreen Mann *(Operations)*
Dan Levey *(Marketing)*
Sales Manager: Celia Stocks

*Academic & Scholarly; Archaeology;
Architecture & Design; Cinema, Video, TV &
Radio; Economics; Environment &
Development Studies; Fashion & Costume;
Gender Studies; History & Antiquarian;
Politics & World Affairs; Psychology &
Psychiatry; Religion & Theology; Sociology &
Anthropology*

ISBNs, Imprints & Series: 0 8419

Parent Company:
Holmes & Meier *(USA)*

1429 ▬▬▬

HOLT, RINEHART & WINSTON
24–28 Oval Road, London NW1 7DX
Telephone: 0171 267 4466
Fax: 0171 482 2293

**Warehouse, Customer Service & Journal
Subscriptions:**
High Street, Foots Cray, Kent DA15 5HP
Telephone: 0181 300 3322
Fax: 0181 309 0807

Directors: W. M. Barnett *(Managing)*
Jamie Sehmer *(Financial & Distribution)*

Peter McKay *(Sales & Marketing)*
Managers: Des Brennan *(Sales)*
Sheila O'Reilly *(Customer Service)*

*Academic & Scholarly; Accountancy &
Taxation; Biology & Zoology; Chemistry;
Computer Science; Economics; Educational &
Textbooks; Electronic (Educational);
Electronic (Professional & Academic);
Engineering; Industry, Business &
Management; Languages & Linguistics;
Mathematics & Statistics; Physics; Reference
Books, Directories & Dictionaries; Scientific &
Technical; Sociology & Anthropology*

ISBNs, Imprints & Series: 0 03

Parent Company:
Harcourt Brace & Co

Overseas Representation *(see §7.3)*:
Australia: W. B. Saunders Co Ltd, Marrickville
Canada: W. B. Saunders Canada Ltd, Toronto
Italy: Marcello SNC, Padua
Japan: Harcourt Brace Japan Inc, Tokyo
Mexico: Nueva Editorial Interamericana SA de
    CV, Mexico
New Zealand: Holt, Rinehart & Winston
    Publishing New Zealand Ltd, Auckland

Book Trade Association Membership: PA,
EPC, CAPP

1430 ▬▬▬

***HOME HEALTH EDUCATION
SERVICE**
Alma Park, Grantham, Lincs NG31 9SL
Telephone: 01476 591800
Fax: 01476 77144

*Children's Books; Health & Beauty; Religion
& Theology*

ISBNs, Imprints & Series: 0 904748

Parent Company:
Stanborough Press Ltd

Book Trade Association Membership: PA

1431 ▬▬▬

**HOUGHTON MIFFLIN CO
INTERNATIONAL**
PO Box 269, Abingdon, Oxon OX14 4YN
Telephone: 01235 833827
Fax: 01235 833829

Warehouse, Trade Enquiries & Orders:
Marston Book Services, PO Box 269,
Abingdon, Oxon OX14 4YN
Telephone: 01235 465500
Fax: 01235 465555

Manager: Nicholas Edwards *(Home & Export
    Sales)*

*Academic & Scholarly; Accountancy &
Taxation; Biography & Autobiography;
Chemistry; Children's Books; Computer
Science; Crafts & Hobbies; Economics;
Educational & Textbooks; Electronic
(Educational); Fiction; Gardening; Gender
Studies; History & Antiquarian; Industry,
Business & Management; Languages &
Linguistics; Literature & Criticism;*

*Mathematics & Statistics; Medical (incl. Self
Help & Alternative Medicine); Natural
History; Poetry; Politics & World Affairs;
Psychology & Psychiatry; Reference Books,
Directories & Dictionaries; Scientific &
Technical*

New Titles: 250 (1995), 250 (1996)
No of Employees: 6

ISBNs, Imprints & Series: 0 395

Parent Company:
Houghton Mifflin Co *(USA)*

Associated & Subsidiary Companies:
Cassell Plc

Distributor for:
USA: Mayfield Publishing Co

Overseas Representation *(see §7.3)*:
All countries other than those listed: Houghton
    Mifflin, Boston, MA, USA
*Australia, New Zealand, Papua New Guinea &
    Fiji (academic):* Jacaranda Wiley Ltd,
    Milton, Queensland, Australia
Caribbean (trade & reference): Ian Randle
    Publishers Ltd, Kingston, Jamaica
India (academic & trade): Maya Publishers Pvt
    Ltd, New Delhi, India
Israel (academic & trade): Rodney Franklin
    Agency, Tel Aviv, Israel
Japan (academic & trade): MK International
    Ltd, Tokyo, Japan
Mexico (academic & trade): Robert G. Blake,
    Mexico DF, Mexico
*Middle East (excluding Israel) & North Africa
    (academic & trade):* Berj Jamkojian,
    Vienna, Austria
Pakistan (academic & trade): Tahir Lodhi,
    Lahore, Pakistan
South Africa (academic & trade): Oxford
    University Press, Capetown, South Africa
South America (academic & trade): Inter Book
    Marketing Services, Rio de Janeiro, Brazil
*South East Asia (including Singapore,
    Indonesia, Brunei, Malaysia, Thailand,
    Philippines, Hong Kong, China, Taiwan &
    Korea (academic & trade):* International
    Thomson Publishing Asia, Singapore

1432 ▬▬▬

HOW TO BOOKS LTD
Plymbridge House, Estover Road, Plymouth,
Devon PL6 7PZ
Telephone: 01752 202369 & 202300
Fax: 01752 202369 & 202331

Managing Director: Roger Ferneyhough

*Cinema, Video, TV & Radio; Educational &
Textbooks; Industry, Business & Management;
Law; Travel & Topography; Vocational
Training & Careers; Business Skills;
Expatriate Handbooks; Family Reference;
International Business Handbooks; Personal
Achievement; Writers Handbooks*

New Titles: 23 (1995), 50 (1996)

ISBNs, Imprints & Series:
1 85703 How To Books
1 85876 International Venture Handbooks

Overseas Representation *(see §7.3)*:
Asia: Electra Media Group Pty Ltd, Sydney, NSW, Australia
Australia & New Zealand: Astam Books Pty Ltd, Leichhardt, NSW, Australia
Europe: Books for Europe Ltd, London, UK
Hong Kong: Federal Publications (HK) Ltd, Kowloon
Poland & Russia: Duet Literary Agency, Warsaw, Poland
Scandinavia: D. Richard Bowen, Malmö, Sweden
West Indies: Hugh Dunphy, Kingston, Jamaica

1433 ▬▬▬▬▬▬

HUGO'S LANGUAGE BOOKS LTD
Old Station Yard, Marlesford, Woodbridge, Suffolk IP13 0AG
Telephone: 01728 746546
Fax: 01728 746236

Directors: Peter G. Lock *(Managing, Sales)*
Robin Batchelor-Smith *(Editorial)*

English as a Foreign Language; Languages & Linguistics; Reference Books, Directories & Dictionaries

New Titles: 18 (1995), 18 (1996)
No of Employees: 8
Annual Turnover: £1.1M

Distributor for:
John Catt Educational Ltd; Pisces Publications

Overseas Representation *(see §7.3)*:
Australia: Random House Australia Pty Ltd, Sydney, NSW
Canada: Riverwood Publishers Ltd, Newmarket, Ont
Europe (excluding Scandinavia, Iceland, Gibraltar, Portugal & Spain): Ted Dougherty, London, UK
Far East: Kelvin van Hasselt Publishing Services, Lymington, UK
Gibraltar, Portugal & Spain: Iberian Book Services SL, Madrid, Spain
Irish Republic: Gill Hess Ltd, Skerries
Japan: Toppan Co Ltd, Tokyo
Middle East: Peter Ward Book Exports, London, UK
New Zealand: Techbook Distributors, Auckland
Scandinavia & Iceland: Hanne Rotovnik, Klampenborg, Denmark
South Africa: Faradawn CC, Saxonwold

1434 ▬▬▬▬▬▬

HUMAN KINETICS (EUROPE) LTD
Units C2/C3, Wira Business Park, West Park Ring Road, West Park, Leeds LS16 6EB
Telephone: 0113 278 1708
Fax: 0113 278 1709

Sales Representation:
Datum Book Marketing (address as above)
Telephone: (as above)
Fax: (as above)

Managing Director: Karl Waddicor
Managers: Sara Cooper *(Sales & Marketing)*
Lloyd Barkham *(Finance)*
Karen Ingram *(Fulfilment)*

Sian Owens *(Sales & Marketing Assistant)*
Karen Robinson *(Administrative Assistant)*

Academic & Scholarly; Educational & Textbooks; Electronic (Educational); Sports & Games

New Titles: 90 (1995), 100 (1996)
No of Employees: 7

ISBNs, Imprints & Series:
0 87322, 0 88011, 0 918438, 0 931250

Parent Company:
Human Kinetics Inc *(USA)*

Associated & Subsidiary Companies:
Australia: Human Kinetics. *Canada:* Human Kinetics. *New Zealand:* Human Kinetics

Overseas Representation *(see §7.3)*:
Australia: Human Kinetics (Australia), Melrose Park, SA
Brazil: Centro de Estudos do Laboratorio de Aptidao Fisica de Sao Caetano do Sul (CELAFISCS), Sao Paulo
Canada: Human Kinetics (Canada), Windsor, Ont
Hong Kong, Taiwan, Philippines & Korea: I. J. Sagun Enterprises Inc, Rizal, Philippines
India: UBS Publishers' Distributors Ltd, New Delhi
Japan: Japan Publications Trading Co, Tokyo
Malaysia: Flo Enterprise Sdn Bhd, Selangor
New Zealand: Human Kinetics (New Zealand), Auckland
Singapore: Corporate Fitness
South Africa (academic & coaching titles): Vigor Book Agents, Clubview, South Africa
South Africa (bookstores order): Real Books CC, Randburg, South Africa
Taiwan: Unifacmanu Trading Co Ltd, Taipei
USA: Human Kinetics, Champaign, IL

1435 ▬▬▬▬▬▬

HUNT AND THORPE
Laurel House, Station Approach, New Alresford, Hants SO24 9JH
Telephone: 01962 735633
Fax: 01962 735320

Sales, Distribution, Enquiries & Orders:
STL, PO Box 300, Kingston Broadway, Carlisle CA3 0QS
Telephone: 01228 512512
Fax: 01800 282530

Sales, Distribution, Enquiries & Orders:
Bookpoint Ltd, 39 Milton Park, Abingdon, Oxon OX14 4TD
Telephone: 01235 400400
Fax: 01235 821511

Managers: Niamh Irving *(Home & Export Sales)*
John Hunt *(Rights)*

Children's Books; Religion & Theology

New Titles: 20 (1995), 20 (1996)
No of Employees: 3
Annual Turnover: £1.5M

ISBNs, Imprints & Series: 1 85608

Associated & Subsidiary Companies:
Godsfield Press Ltd

Overseas Representation *(see §7.3)*:
Australia: Hunt & Thorpe Australia Pty Ltd, Rydalmere
New Zealand: Omega Distributors Ltd, Auckland

1436 ▬▬▬▬▬▬

C. HURST & CO (PUBLISHERS) LTD
38 King Street, London WC2E 8JZ
Telephone: 0171 240 2666
Fax: 0171 240 2667
Email: hurst@atlas.co.uk

Distributor:
Marston Book Services, PO Box 269, Abingdon, Oxon OX14 4YN
Telephone: 01235 465500
Fax: 01235 465555

Directors: Christopher A. R. Hurst *(Managing)*
Michael Dwyer

Academic & Scholarly; Economics; Gender Studies; Politics & World Affairs; Religion & Theology; Sociology & Anthropology

New Titles: 18 (1995), 18 (1996)
No of Employees: 2

ISBNs, Imprints & Series:
0 903983, 0 905838, 1 85065

Overseas Representation *(see §7.3)*:
Australia: Bushbooks, Gosford South, NSW
Benelux, France & Suisse Romande: Kemper Conseil, Voorburg, Netherlands
Germany, Austria & German-speaking Switzerland: SHS Publishers' Consultants and Representatives, Berlin, Germany
Hong Kong, People's Republic of China: Hong Kong University Press, Hong Kong
Japan: United Publishers Services Ltd, Tokyo
Middle East: Berj Jamkojian, Vienna, Austria
Nordic countries: Colin Flint, Harlow, UK
South East Asia: Toppan Co (S) Pte Ltd, Singapore
Southern Europe: Charles Gibbes, Buckingham, UK

Book Trade Association Membership: PA

1437 ▬▬▬▬▬▬

HUTCHINSON
20 Vauxhall Bridge Road, London SW1V 2SA
Telephone: 0171 973 9000
Fax: 0171 233 7870

Warehouse, Trade Enquiries & Orders:
Tiptree Book Services, Tiptree, Essex CO5 0SR
Telephone: 01621 819600

Directors: Sue Freestone *(Publishing)*
Paul Sidey *(Editorial)*
Tony Whittome *(Editorial)*
Neil Bradford *(Production)*
Alex Hippsley Cox *(Publicity)*
Mark McCallum *(Marketing)*
Simon King *(Managing)*

Crime; Fiction; History & Antiquarian; Humour; Military & War; Politics & World Affairs

New Titles: 35 (1995), 32 (1996)

ISBNs, Imprints & Series: 0 09

Parent Company:
Random House UK Ltd

1438 ▬▬▬▬

HUTTON PRESS LTD
130 Canada Drive, Cherry Burton, Beverley, North Humberside HU17 7SB
Telephone: 01964 550573
Fax: 01964 550573

Directors: Charles F. Brook *(Managing)*
Christine R. Barker *(Company Secretary & Editorial)*
Davina C. Brook *(Publicity & Sales)*
Michael E. Ulyatt *(Marketing)*

Academic & Scholarly; Biography & Autobiography; Fiction; Guide Books; History & Antiquarian; Humour; Photography; Sports & Games; Travel & Topography

New Titles: 9 (1995), 12 (1996)
No of Employees: 3
Annual Turnover: £100,000

ISBNs, Imprints & Series:
0 907033, 1 872167

1439 ▬▬▬▬

HYMNS ANCIENT & MODERN LTD &
[Canterbury Press Norwich/Religious & Moral Educ. Press]
St Mary's Works, St Mary's Plain, Norwich, Norfolk NR3 3BH
Telephone: 01603 616563 & 615995
Fax: 01603 624483

Also at:
Chansitor Publications Ltd, 16 Blyburgate, Beccles, Suffolk
Telephone: 01502 711231
Fax: 01502 711585

UK Representation (in bookshops):
Christian Publishers Representatives, Holy Trinity Church, Marylebone Road, London
Telephone: 0171 387 5282
Fax: 0171 388 2352

Also at:
Canterbury Press, Norwich Bridge House, 181 Queen Victoria Street, London EC4V 6DD
Telephone: 0171 248 4759
Fax: 0171 329 0575

Chief Executive: G. A. Knights *(Home & Export Sales)*
Marketing: S. Ager
Publishers: Mrs C. Smith *(Canterbury Press)*
Mrs M. Mears *(RMEP)*
Sales: Miss J. Speed *(Hymns A & M Ltd/ Canterbury Press)*
Mrs J. Poole *(Chansitor Publications)*
Mrs S. Fletcher *(Religious & Moral Education Press)*

Rights & Permissions: Miss J. Wright
Editorial: K. Baker *(Canterbury Press)*

Educational & Textbooks; Music; Religion & Theology

New Titles: 50 (1995), 60 (1996)
No of Employees: 39
Annual Turnover: £2.8M

ISBNs, Imprints & Series:
0 900274, 1 85175 Chansitor Publications Ltd, Religious & Moral Education Press
0 907547 Hymns Ancient & Modern
1 85311 Canterbury Press Norwich

Associated & Subsidiary Companies:
Chansitor Publications Ltd; John Hart Publicity Ltd; G. D. Palmer & Sons Ltd *(Church Times)*

Distributor for:
Church House Publications; William Clowes (Publishers) Ltd. *Canada:* Anglican Book Centre

Overseas Representation *(see §7.3)*:
Australia: Charles Paine Pty Ltd, North Paramatta, NSW
Canada: Meakin & Associates, Nepean
New Zealand: Church Book Stores, Auckland
USA: Morehouse, Ridgefield CT
USA (copyrights only): Hope Publishing, Carol Stream, IL, USA
West Indies: Hugh Dunphy, Kingston, Jamaica

Book Trade Association Membership: IPG

1440 ▬▬▬▬

IBC BUSINESS PUBLISHING
37–41 Mortimer Street, London W1N 7RJ
Telephone: 0171 637 4383
Fax: 0171 636 6414

Subscriptions & Orders:
IBC House, Vickers Drive, Brooklands Industrial Park, Weybridge, Surrey KT13 0XS
Telephone: 01932 355244
Fax: 01932 354576
Email: 100340.647@compuserve.com
Web Site: http://www.intbuscom.com/

Directors: Tony Powell *(Managing)*
Heather Mckenzie *(Special Projects)*
Tim Molloy *(Publisher, MCI)*
Niàmh Bourke *(Marketing)*

Accountancy & Taxation; Industry, Business & Management; Law; Financial Technology

New Titles: 6 (1995), 8 (1996)
No of Employees: 28

ISBNs, Imprints & Series: 1 85271

Parent Company:
IBC Group Plc

Associated & Subsidiary Companies:
Banking Technology Ltd; Mobile Communications International Ltd

Overseas Representation *(see §7.3)*:
USA: IBC USA (Publications) Inc, Ashland, MA

Book Trade Association Membership: IPG

1441 ▬▬▬▬

ICA (INSTITUTE OF CONTEMPORARY ARTS)·
12 Carlton House Terrace, London SW1Y 5AH
Telephone: 0171 930 0493
Fax: 0171 873 0051

Publications Co-ordinator: Ian Farr *(Sales, Rights & Permissions, Print Buying, Publicity)*

Academic & Scholarly; Architecture & Design; Audio Books; Electronic (Professional & Academic); Fine Art & Art History; Philosophy; Photography; Sociology & Anthropology

New Titles: 6 (1995), 6 (1996)
Annual Turnover: £60,000

ISBNs, Imprints & Series:
0 905263, 1 900300

Associated & Subsidiary Companies:
ICA Video

Overseas Representation *(see §7.3)*:
Europe: Cornerhouse Publications, Manchester, UK
USA: Distributed Arts Publishers, New York

Book Trade Association Membership: BA

1442 ▬▬▬▬

*ICC INFORMATION GROUP LTD
Field House, 72 Oldfield Road, Hampton, Middx TW12 2HQ
Telephone: 0181 783 0922
Fax: 0181 783 1940

Information Services:
16–26 Banner Street, London EC1Y 8QE
Telephone: 0171 251 0941
Fax: 0171 251 4616

Business Publications General Manager:
Gina Blackham
Publications Sales Manager: Eoin Duane

Academic & Scholarly; Educational & Textbooks; Guide Books; Industry, Business & Management; Reference Books, Directories & Dictionaries

Parent Company:
Hoppenstedt Bonnier Information GmbH *(Germany)*

Distributor for:
Business Ratio Plus; Financial Surveys; Keynote Reports; Regional Sales Leads

Book Trade Association Membership:
Directory Publishers Association

1443 ▬▬▬▬

ICSA PUBLISHING LTD
Campus 400, Maylands Avenue, Hemel Hempstead, Herts HP2 7EZ
Telephone: 01442 881900
Fax: 01442 882099

Orders, Customer Service & Accounts:
International Book Distributors Ltd,
Campus 400, Maylands Avenue,
Hemel Hempstead, Herts HP2 7EZ
Telephone: 01442 881900
Fax: 01442 882099

Distribution Centre:
International Book Distributors Ltd,
Coventry Road, Magna Park, Lutterworth
LE17 4XH
Telephone: 01442 881900
Fax: 01442 882177

President, Prentice Hall Europe: Joseph J.
Marcelle
Editorial Director: Clare Grist
Rights & Permissions: Jean Spurr

Economics; Educational & Textbooks;
Industry, Business & Management; Reference
Books, Directories & Dictionaries

ISBNs, Imprints & Series: 0 902197

Associated & Subsidiary Companies:
Philip Allan; Harvester Wheatsheaf; Prentice
Hall; Woodhead-Faulkner

1444

**IMAGES PUBLISHING (MALVERN)
LTD**
The Wells House, Holywell Road,
Malvern Wells, Worcs WR14 4LH
Telephone: 01684 893990
Fax: 01684 893993
Email: 101233.2413@compuserve.com.uk

Distribution:
Biblios Publishers' Distribution Services Ltd,
Star Road, Partridge Green, West Sussex
RH13 8LD
Telephone: 01403 710971
Fax: 01403 711143

Directors: A. E. Harold *(Managing)*
C. L. Whiting
Publisher: A. Harthill
Production: C. Redman

Aviation; Biography & Autobiography;
Military & War; Transport

New Titles: 25 (1995), 30 (1996)
No of Employees: 15
Annual Turnover: £2M

ISBNs, Imprints & Series:
0 947993 The Malvern Publishing Co Ltd
1 897817 Images
1 898839 Rampant Horse Ltd

Distributor for:
The Amaising Publishing House Ltd; Argyll
Publishing; Berlinn Ltd; Broadcast Books;
Centre for Alternative Technology; Fast
Forward; Metropolis Promotions Ltd; New
Lifestyle Publishing; The Pall Mall Publishing
Co; Passport Publications; The Sporting Press.
USA: ABC Clio Ltd

Book Trade Association Membership: BA

1445

IMPACT BOOKS / OLIVE PRESS
70 Newcomen Street, London SE1 1YT
Telephone: 0171 403 3541
Fax: 0171 407 6437

Trade Orders:
Verulam Publishing Ltd,
152A Park Street Lane, Park Street, St Albans,
Herts AL2 2AU
Telephone: 01727 872770
Fax: 01727 873866

Publisher: Jean-Luc Barbanneau *(Rights)*
Directors: David Skinner
David Collins *(Home & Export Sales)*

Biography & Autobiography; Children's
Books; Illustrated & Fine Editions;
Photography; Reference Books, Directories &
Dictionaries; Travel & Topography

ISBNs, Imprints & Series:
0 245, 1 874687 Impact Books
0 946889 Olive Press

Overseas Representation *(see §7.3):*
Worldwide: Verulam Publishing Ltd, St
Albans, UK

Book Trade Association Membership: IPG

1446

IMPERIAL COLLEGE PRESS
516 Sherfield Building, Imperial College,
London SW7 2AZ
Telephone: 0171 594 9568
Fax: 0171 591 0876
Email: edit@icpress.demon.co.uk

Trade Enquiries & Orders:
World Scientific Publishing, 57 Shelton Street,
London WC2H 9HE
Telephone: 0171 836 0888
Fax: 0171 836 2020
Email: wspc@wspc.demon.co.uk
Web Site: http://www.wspc.co.uk

Editors: Richard Lim
Tony Moore

Academic & Scholarly; Biology & Zoology;
Chemistry; Computer Science; Economics;
Educational & Textbooks; Electronic
(Educational); Electronic (Professional &
Academic); Engineering; Environment &
Development Studies; Geography & Geology;
Mathematics & Statistics; Medical (incl. Self
Help & Alternative Medicine); Physics;
Scientific & Technical

New Titles: 2 (1995), 50 (1996)

ISBNs, Imprints & Series: 1 86094

Overseas Representation *(see §7.3):*
Hong Kong: World Scientific Publishing (HK)
Co Ltd
India: World Scientific Publishing Co Pte Ltd,
Bangalore
Singapore: World Scientific Publishing Co Pte
Ltd
Taiwan: World Scientific Publishing Co Pte
Ltd, Taipei

USA: World Scientific Publishing Co Inc, River
Edge, NJ

Book Trade Association Membership: PA

1447

**IMRAY LAURIE NORIE & WILSON
LTD**
Wych House, The Broadway, St Ives,
Huntingdon PE17 4BT
Telephone: 01480 462114
Fax: 01480 496109
Email: gen@imray.com
Web Site: http://www.imray.com

Directors: William Wilson
E. N. Wilson
Eric Rippington *(Finance)*
Accountant: David Clarke

Geography & Geology; Nautical; Transport;
Travel & Topography

New Titles: 8 (1995), 6 (1996)
No of Employees: 20

ISBNs, Imprints & Series: 0 85288

Distributor for:
HMSO; Hydrographic Department; J. M.
Pearson & Sons; Tetra Publications Ltd.
France: Grafocarte; Editions Vagnon. *Irish*
Republic: Irish Cruising Club. *Netherlands:*
ANWB; Hydrographic Office. *USA:* W. W.
Norton & Co; RCC Pilotage Foundation;
University of Hawaii Press

1448

IN PRINT PUBLISHING LTD
9 Beaufort Terrace, Brighton BN2 2SU
Telephone: 01273 682836
Fax: 01273 620958

Trade Orders:
Bailey Distribution Ltd, Learoyd Road,
Mountfield Industrial Estate, New Romney,
Kent TN28 8XU
Telephone: 01679 66905
Fax: 01679 66638

Directors: John Edmondson *(Home Sales,*
Rights & Permissions)
Alastair Dingwall *(Export Sales)*

Biography & Autobiography; English as a
Foreign Language; Guide Books; Literature &
Criticism; Travel & Topography

ISBNs, Imprints & Series:
1 873047 Traveller's Literary Companion
Series

Overseas Representation *(see §7.3):*
South East Asia: Publishers Marketing Services
Ltd, Singapore

Book Trade Association Membership: IPG

1449

THE INDUSTRIAL SOCIETY
48 Bryanston Square, London W1H 7LN
Telephone: 0171 262 2401
Fax: 0171 706 1096

Orders:
The Industrial Society, 49 Calthorpe Road,
Birmingham B15 1TH
Telephone: 0121 454 6769
Fax: 0121 456 3824

Head of Publishing: Sheridan Maguire
Multimedia Product Manager: Henrietta
  Walker *(A/V)*
Marketing Adviser: Dawn Marley
Editorial: Clemency Marlowe

*Educational & Textbooks; Industry, Business &
Management; Vocational Training & Careers*

New Titles: 10 (1995), 15 (1996)
No of Employees: 6
Annual Turnover: £1M

ISBNs, Imprints & Series:
0 85290, 1 85835

Parent Company:
The Industrial Society

Distributor for:
BBC for Business Videos; Nicholas Bredey
Publishing; Training Media Group (Videos)

Book Trade Association Membership: PA,
IPG

1450 ▬▬▬▬▬▬▬▬▬▬▬▬▬▬

**INSTITUTE FOR EMPLOYMENT
STUDIES**
Mantell Building, University of Sussex,
Brighton BN1 9RF
Telephone: 01273 686751
Fax: 01273 690430
Email: ies@fastnet.co.uk

Distributors:
BEBC Distribution Ltd, PO Box 1496,
Parkstone, Poole, Dorset BH12 3YD
Telephone: 01202 715555
Fax: 01202 715556

Publishing & Marketing Manager: Andy
  Davidson

*Gender Studies; Industry, Business &
Management; Vocational Training & Careers*

New Titles: 22 (1995), 25 (1996)
No of Employees: 60
Annual Turnover: £200,000

ISBNs, Imprints & Series:
1 85184 IES Report Series

Overseas Representation *(see §7.3)*:
Australia: DA Information Services, Mitcham,
  Vic
Worldwide (excluding Australia): Broadcast
  Book Services, London, UK

1451 ▬▬▬▬▬▬▬▬▬▬▬▬▬▬

INSTITUTE FOR FISCAL STUDIES
Third Floor, 7 Ridgmount Street, London
WC1E 7AE
Telephone: 0171 636 3784
Fax: 0171 323 4780
Email: mailbox@ifs.org.uk
Web Site: http://www1.ifs.org.uk/

Director: Andrew Dilnot

*Academic & Scholarly; Accountancy &
Taxation; Economics*

New Titles: 30 (1995), 25 (1996)
No of Employees: 30
Annual Turnover: £1.6M

ISBNs, Imprints & Series:
0 902992, 1 873357 Commentary, Report,
  Working Paper

1452 ▬▬▬▬▬▬▬▬▬▬▬▬▬▬

**INSTITUTE OF DEVELOPMENT
STUDIES**
University of Sussex, Brighton, East Sussex
BN1 9RE
Telephone: 01273 606261
Fax: 01273 621202

Administration: N. W. Posnett *(Head of
  Information Resource Unit)*
Editorial/Production: Katherine Henry
  (Editor, Rights & Permissions)
Sales & Mailing List: Andrew Proctor

*Academic & Scholarly; Agriculture;
Bibliography & Library Science; Economics;
Educational & Textbooks; Industry, Business &
Management; Politics & World Affairs;
Sociology & Anthropology*

New Titles: 41 (1995), 36 (1996)

ISBNs, Imprints & Series:
0 903354, 1 85864 Institute of Development
  Studies
0 903715 Bulletin, Development
  Bibliographies, Discussion Papers, IDS
  Commisioned Studies, Research Reports,
  Working Papers

1453 ▬▬▬▬▬▬▬▬▬▬▬▬▬▬

INSTITUTE OF EDUCATION
20 Bedford Way, London WC1H 0AL
Telephone: 0171 580 1122
Fax: 0171 612 6126
Email: d.spring@ioe.ac.uk

Trade Distributor:
(for Bedford Way Series,
London Ed'n Studies & London File)
Turnaround, 27 Horsell Road, London N5 1XL
Telephone: 0171 609 7836

Publications Officer: Deborah Spring

*Academic & Scholarly; Educational &
Textbooks*

ISBNs, Imprints & Series: 0 85473

Book Trade Association Membership: IPG,
ALPSP

1454 ▬▬▬▬▬▬▬▬▬▬▬▬▬▬

THE INSTITUTE OF MANAGEMENT
Management House, Cottingham Road, Corby,
Northants NN17 1TT
Telephone: 01536 204222
Fax: 01536 201651
Email: institute@easynet.co.uk

Warehouse & Distribution:
Burston Distribution Services, Unit 2A,
Newbridge Trading Estate, Bristol BS4 4AX
Telephone: 0117 9724248
Fax: 0117 9711056

Head of Publishing: Jeremy Kourdi

Industry, Business & Management

New Titles: 30 (1995), 40 (1996)
No of Employees: 120
Annual Turnover: £6M

ISBNs, Imprints & Series:
0 85946 Research Reports

Book Trade Association Membership: BA

1455 ▬▬▬▬▬▬▬▬▬▬▬▬▬▬

**THE INSTITUTE OF MARINE
ENGINEERS**
The Memorial Building, 76 Mark Lane,
London EC3R 7JN
Telephone: 0171 481 8493
Fax: 0171 488 1854
Email: books@imare.org.uk
Web Site: http://www.engc.org.uk/IMarE/

Head of Information Services: Tony Watts
  (Assistant Secretary)
Publications Editor/Manager: Nicola
  McGrath *(Sales)*

*Biography & Autobiography; Engineering;
Military & War; Nautical*

New Titles: 5 (1995), 5 (1996)
No of Employees: 4

ISBNs, Imprints & Series:
0 900976, 0 907206

Overseas Representation *(see §7.3)*:
North America & Mexico: Information Today
  Inc, Medford, NJ, USA

Book Trade Association Membership: The
Association of Learned and Professional
Society Publishers

1456 ▬▬▬▬▬▬▬▬▬▬▬▬▬▬

THE INSTITUTE OF MATERIALS
1 Carlton House Terrace, London SW1Y 5DB
Telephone: 0171 839 4071
Fax: 0171 839 2078

Regional Centre:
Shelton House, Stoke Road, Stelton, Stoke-on-
Trent ST4 2DR

Also at:
11 Hobart Place, London SW1W 0HL

Secretary: Dr J. A. Catterall
Deputy Secretary: R. Millbank
Publisher: M. Jackson

*Academic & Scholarly; Archaeology;
Chemistry; Electronic (Educational);
Engineering; Industry, Business &
Management; Mathematics & Statistics;
Physics; Reference Books, Directories &
Dictionaries; Scientific & Technical*

New Titles: 22 (1995), 37 (1996)
No of Employees: 90

ISBNs, Imprints & Series:
0 901462, 0 901716, 0 904357

Overseas Representation *(see §7.3):*
India: Current Technical Literature Co Pvt Ltd,
Bombay
Japan: Usaco Corp, Tokyo
USA & Canada: Ashgate Publishing Co,
Brookfield, VT, USA

Book Trade Association Membership: BA,
ALPSP

1457 ▬▬▬

**INSTITUTE OF PERSONNEL &
DEVELOPMENT**
35 Camp Road, Wimbledon, London
SW19 4UW
Telephone: 0181 971 9000
Fax: 0181 263 3333
Email: ipd@ipd.co.uk
Web Site: http://www.ipd.co.uk

Distribution Centre:
Plymbridge Distributors Ltd, Estover,
Plymouth PL6 7PZ
Telephone: Plymouth 01752 695745
Fax: 01752 695699

Managers: Judith Tabern *(Publishing)*
Brian Eagle *(Distribution, Plymbridge
Distributors)*
Commissioning Editors: Matthew Reisz
Anne Cordwent
Sales: Cathy Doyle
Rights & Permissions: Beryll Camplin

*Industry, Business & Management;
Management; Personnel Management*

New Titles: 28 (1995), 24 (1996)
No of Employees: 5
Annual Turnover: £800,000

ISBNs, Imprints & Series: 0 85292

Overseas Representation *(see §7.3):*
Australia, New Zealand & Papua New Guinea:
Astam Books Pty Ltd, Leichhardt, NSW,
Australia
*Austria, Italy, Switzerland, Benelux, France,
Greece, Germany, Gibraltar, Portugal,
Spain & Scandinavia:* Books for Europe Ltd,
Bournemouth, UK
*Hong Kong, Singapore, Taiwan, Vietnam,
Myanmar (Burma) & Malaysia:* STM
Publishing Services Pte Ltd, Singapore
Pakistan: S. I. Gillani, Lahore

Book Trade Association Membership: IPG

1458 ▬▬▬

**INSTITUTION OF CHEMICAL
ENGINEERS**
165–189 Railway Terrace, Rugby CV21 3HQ
Telephone: 01788 578214
Fax: 01788 547262
Email: pvarey@icheme.org.uk

Director of Publications: Peter Varey
Managing Editor, Books: Betty Brammer
Marketing Officer: Jacqueline Wilson

Engineering; Scientific & Technical

New Titles: 20 (1995), 20 (1996)
No of Employees: 6
Annual Turnover: £400,000

ISBNs, Imprints & Series: 0 85295

Distributor for:
USA: Aloray Inc; American Institute of
Chemical Engineers (AIChE)

Overseas Representation *(see §7.3):*
Australia & New Zealand: DA Books,
Mitcham, Vic, Australia
Europe: Momenta Publishing Ltd, London, UK
Far East: APAC Publishers Services,
Singapore
Germany, Austria & Switzerland: SHS
Publishers' Consultants and Representatives,
Berlin, Germany
South Africa: Russell Friedman Information
Services (Pty) Ltd, Cape Town

Book Trade Association Membership: PA

1459 ▬▬▬

**INSTITUTION OF ELECTRICAL
ENGINEERS**
Michael Faraday House, Six Hills Way,
Stevenage, Herts SG1 2AY
Telephone: 01438 313311
Fax: 01438 313465
Email: books@iee.org.uk
Web Site: http://www.iee.org.uk/publish/

Warehouse, Trade Enquiries & Orders:
PO Box 96, Stevenage, Herts SG1 2SD
Telephone: 01438 313311
Fax: 01438 742792

Director of Publishing: R. Mellors-Bourne
Director of Marketing: J. Ashling

*Academic & Scholarly; Computer Science;
Electronic (Professional & Academic);
Engineering; Scientific & Technical*

New Titles: 45 (1995), 45 (1996)

ISBNs, Imprints & Series:
0 85296, 0 86341, 0 901223, 0 906048

Associated & Subsidiary Companies:
Peter Peregrinus Ltd

Overseas Representation *(see §7.3):*
Belgium & Netherlands: Momenta Publishing
Ltd, London, UK
Far East: Clarke Associates Ltd, Bristol, UK
Middle East: Anthony Rudkin Associates,
Oxford, UK
USA & Canada: IEE/PPL, Piscataway, NJ,
USA

Book Trade Association Membership:
IGSMTP

1460 ▬▬▬

INTELLECT LTD
E.F.A.E., Earl Richards Road North, Exeter
EX2 6AS
Telephone: 01392 475110
Fax: 01392 475110

Distribution:
Lavis Marketing, 73 Lime Walk, Oxford
OX3 7AD
Telephone: 01865 67575
Fax: 01865 750079
Email: intellect@dial.pipex.com
Web Site: http://www.intellect-net.com/

Editor-in-Chief: M. Yazdani
Manager: Robin Beecroft

*Academic & Scholarly; Computer Science;
Educational & Textbooks; Electronic
(Educational); Electronic (Professional &
Academic); Gender Studies; History &
Antiquarian; Languages & Linguistics;
Scientific & Technical; Theatre, Drama &
Dance*

New Titles: 10 (1995), 11 (1996)
No of Employees: 2

ISBNs, Imprints & Series: 1 871516

Overseas Representation *(see §7.3):*
Europe: Andrew B. Durnell, Tunbridge Wells,
UK
India: Capital Books Pte Ltd, New Delhi
USA: Cromland Inc, Allentown, PA

1461 ▬▬▬

INTER-VARSITY PRESS
38 De Montfort Street, Leicester LE1 7GP
Telephone: 0116 255 1700 & 255 1754
Fax: 0116 254 2044
Email: UCCF@cix.compulink.co.uk

Warehouse, Sales, Sales Accounts:
Norton Street, Nottingham NG7 3HR
Telephone: 0115 978 1054
Fax: 0115 942 2694
Email: IVP@ivpnottm.compulink.co.uk

Directors: Frank R. Entwistle *(Chief
Executive)*
Brian Wilson *(Commercial)*
Managing Editor: Mrs Stephanie Heald

*Academic & Scholarly; Reference Books,
Directories & Dictionaries; Religion &
Theology*

New Titles: 49 (1995), 53 (1996)
No of Employees: 32

ISBNs, Imprints & Series:
0 85110, 0 85111 Apollos, Frameworks, Inter-
Varsity Press
0 85684 Crossway Books

Parent Company:
Universities & Colleges Christian Fellowship

Distributor for:
Christian Medical Fellowship; Crossway
Books

Overseas Representation *(see §7.3):*
Australia: Albatross Books Pty Ltd, Sutherland
Canada: Inter-Varsity Press, Markham
East Africa: Keswick Book Society, Nairobi,
Kenya
Netherlands: Inter-Media/Pelgrim,
Westervoort
New Zealand: Scripture Union Wholesale,
Wellington

Philippines: Evangelical Outreach Inc, Quezon City; Overseas Missionary Fellowship, Manila; Overseas Missionary Fellowship, Manila
Singapore: Bethesda Book Centre
South Africa: Protestant Book Centre, Cape Town
South Korea: Word of Life Press Bible Book House, Seoul, Korea, South
Sweden: DetStar Skrivet, Gothenburg
USA: Inter-Varsity Press, Downers Grove, IL

Book Trade Association Membership: PA

1462 ▬▬▬▬▬▬

INTERCEPT LTD
PO Box 716, Andover, Hants SP10 1YG
Telephone: 01264 334748 & 334749
Fax: 01264 334058

Distribution:
Unit 2B, Dukes Close, West Way, Walworth Industrial Estate, Andover, Hants SP10 5AR
Telephone: *as above*
Fax: *as above*

Directors: Pierre Fenouil
Patrick Fenouil
Gilberte Lafolie
Managers: Gill Parker *(Office)*
Andrew Cook

Academic & Scholarly; Agriculture; Biology & Zoology; Chemistry; Environment & Development Studies; Geography & Geology; Medical (incl. Self Help & Alternative Medicine); Natural History; Scientific & Technical

New Titles: 6 (1995), 8 (1996)
No of Employees: 5

ISBNs, Imprints & Series:
0 946707 Intercept
1 898298 Natural History Museum (Bulletins), RightAngle Books

Parent Company:
Lavoisier Tec et Doc *(France)*

Distributor for:
Natural History Museum Publications; The Ray Society. *France:* Degremont; Lavoisier Publishing

Overseas Representation *(see §7.3):*
France: Lavoisier Technique et Documentation, Cachan Cedex
India (non-exclusive): CBS Publishers & Distributors, Delhi, India; Asian Books Pvt Ltd, New Delhi, India
Japan: Toppan Co Ltd, Tokyo
Korea: Kumi Trading Co Ltd, Seoul, Korea, South
Malaysia, Singapore & Brunei: Parry's Book Centre Sdn Bhd, Kuala Lumpur, Malaysia
USA & Canada: Lavoisier Publishing Inc, Newark, NJ, USA

1463 ▬▬▬▬▬▬

INTERMEDIATE TECHNOLOGY PUBLICATIONS LTD
103–105 Southampton Row, London WC1B 4HH

Telephone: 0171 436 9761
Fax: 0171 436 2013
Email: itpubs@gn.api.org
Web Site: http://www.oneworld.org/itdg/

Trade Enquiries & Orders:
Plymbridge Distributors Ltd, Plymbridge House, Estover Road, Plymouth PL6 7PZ

Directors: N. E. Burton *(Managing)*
Edmund Marsden *(Chairman)*
N. D. Sinker
R. E. Holland
Sales & Marketing Manager: Guy Bentham

Agriculture; Economics; Educational & Textbooks; Engineering; Industry, Business & Management; Reference Books, Directories & Dictionaries; Scientific & Technical

New Titles: 40 (1995), 40 (1996)

ISBNs, Imprints & Series:
0 903031, 0 946688, 1 85339

Parent Company:
Intermediate Technology Development Group Ltd

Distributor for:
Canada: International Development Research Centre (IDRC). *Netherlands:* KIT Press *(Royal Tropical Institute)*

Overseas Representation *(see §7.3):*
Australia: Astam Books Pty Ltd, Leichhardt, NSW
Bangladesh: The University Press Ltd, Dhaka
Belgium: Atol vzw, Leuven
Botswana: Botswana Book Centre, Gaborone
India: Maya Publishers Pvt Ltd, New Delhi
Japan: United Nations Universlty Press, Tokyo
Kenya: Textbook Centre Ltd, Nairobi
Malaysia, Singapore, Indonesia & Brunei: Publishers Marketing Services Ltd, Singapore
Pakistan: Mirza Book Agency, Lahore
South Africa: David Philip Publishers Pty Ltd, Claremont
Spain: Ecoserveis, Barcelona
Sri Lanka: Lake House Bookshop, Colombo
Taiwan, Korea, Vietnam, Thailand & China: STM Publishing Services Pte Ltd, Singapore
USA: Women Ink, New York
Zimbabwe: Grassroots Books (Pvt) Ltd, Harare

Book Trade Association Membership: BA

1464 ▬▬▬▬▬▬

INTERNATIONAL BUSINESS IMAGES LTD
1 Taber Place, Witham, Essex CM8 3YP
Telephone: 01376 512412
Fax: 01376 515561
Email: ibi@business.english.co.uk
Web Site: http://.netforcenet/business-english

Managing Director: David G. Perry

Electronic (Educational); English as a Foreign Language

New Titles: 3 (1995), 3 (1996)

ISBNs, Imprints & Series:
1 899399 Business English Video Magazine, Business Terms (Pocket Books)

Book Trade Association Membership: PA

1465 ▬▬▬▬▬▬

INTERNATIONAL LABOUR OFFICE
Vincent House, Vincent Square, London SW1P 2NB
Telephone: 0171 828 6401
Fax: 0171 233 5925

Manager: Marion Motts

Academic & Scholarly; Economics; Gender Studies; Industry, Business & Management; Safety & Health; Statistics

1466 ▬▬▬▬▬▬

INTERNATIONAL MUSIC PUBLICATIONS LTD
Woodford Trading Estate, Southend Road, Woodford Green, Essex IG8 8HN
Telephone: 0181 551 6131
Fax: 0181 551 3919, 551 9121 (Sales) & 551 1595 (Permissions)
Email: imp@dial.pipex.com

Sales Department:
Fax: 0181 551 9121

Archives:
Telephone: 0181 550 0550
Fax: 0181 551 8188

Music Mail (mail order):
Telephone: 01474 813813
Fax: 0181 551 7104

Managing Director: Ron Fry
Managers: Trevor Callaghan *(Financial & Administration)*
Stephen Clark *(Copyright, Permissions & Publishing)*
David Taylor *(Warehouse)*
Mark Mumford *(Education)*
Roy Strode *(Sales)*
Roger Wood *(Distribution)*
Paul Smith *(Financial Controller)*

Music

No of Employees: 65

ISBNs, Imprints & Series:
0 86175 EMI
0 86359 IMP & Warner Chappell
0 88188 Hal Leonard
0 907188 Babylon

Parent Company:
Warner Music Group

Distributor for:
Academy Manuscript; Almo Music Inc; Anglo-Pic Music Co Ltd; Ardmore & Beechwood Ltd; Ascherberg, Hopwood & Crew Ltd; ATV Music; Axle Music Ltd; Belwin Mills Publishing Corporation; Irving Berlin (London); Big Pig Music Ltd; Bourne Music Ltd; Bowmar Publications; Bradbury Wood; Bright Music Ltd; British & Continental Music Agencies Ltd; Bill Buckley Music; Bucks Music; Burlington Music Co Ltd; Carlin Music

Corporation; Cary & Co; Chappell Music Ltd; Chappell Plays Ltd; Chappell-Aznavour Ltd; Chappell-Morris Ltd; Cherry Lane Music Inc; Cirone Publications; Clarabella Music Ltd; Colgems-EMI Music Ltd; Columbia Pictures Publications; Franco Columbo; Creole Music Ltd; Herman Darewski; Francis Day & Hunter Ltd; De Wolfe Ltd; Deshon Music Inc; Dick Leahy Music Ltd; Disney; Dix Ltd; Donna Music Ltd; Byron Douglas Publications; Elstree Music Ltd; EMI Film Music Ltd; EMI Music Publishing Ltd; EMI Songs Ltd; EMI-Virgin Music Ltd; Feldman & Co Ltd; Filmtrax Plc; J. Fisher & Bros; Charles Foley Inc; Sam Fox Publishing Co; Freeman & Co Ltd; Goodlife Publications; H. W. Gray Co Inc; Hotlicks; Intersong Music Ltd; Ipanema Music Ltd; Jewel Music Publishing Co Ltd; Jobete Music (UK) Ltd; Edwin F. Kalmus Music Publications; KPM Music Group; Hal Leonard; Leosong Copyright Services Ltd; Lionheart Music; Lowery-Chappell; Martin-Coulter Music Ltd; Peter Maurice Music Co Ltd; Mautoglade Music Ltd; MCA Music Inc; McAfee Music Corporation; Robert Mellin Ltd; Memory Lane Music Ltd; Mews Music Ltd; Mills Music Inc; Minder Music Ltd; Morrison Leahy Ltd; Musicord Publications; Noon Music Ltd; Paganiniana Books (THF Publications Ltd); Panopus Manuscript; Patricia Music Ltd; Plymouth Music Inc; PMP Guitar Publications; Post Music Ltd; Pro Art Publications; Keith Prowse Music Publishing Co Ltd; Queen Music Ltd; RAK Publishing Ltd; Redwood Music Ltd; REH Music; Reward Music Ltd; Reynolds Music; RJX Publications Inc; Robbins Music Corp Ltd; Rocket Publishing; Rondor Music; Schmitt Publications; Screen Gems EMI Music Ltd; Shadows Music Ltd; Sher Music; Skratch Music Publishing & Productions; Sky Writing (Publishing) Ltd; Spindrift Music Ltd; Springfield Music; Stonebridge Music; Stratford Music Ltd; Studio PR; Summit Publications; Summy Birchard; Tristan Music Ltd; Volkwein Bros; Warner Chappell Music Ltd; Warner Chappell Plays; Williamson Music Ltd; Willis Music Co; Dale Zdenek Publications. *Canada:* Warner Bros. Publications Inc. *USA:* Warner Bros. Publications Inc

Overseas Representation *(see §7.3):*
Australia: Warner Chappell Music Group, North Sydney
France: International Music Publications Ltd
Germany & Switzerland: International Music Publications GmbH, Munich, Germany
Italy & Spain: Nuova Carisch Spa, Italy
Scandinavia: Nodeservice A/S, Græsted, Denmark

Book Trade Association Membership: Music Publishers Association

1467 ■

IOP PUBLISHING
Techno House, Redcliffe Way, Bristol
BS1 6NX
Telephone: 0117 929 7481
Fax: 0117 929 4318

Warehouse:
Burston Distribution Services, Unit 2A, Newbridge Trading Estate, Newbridge Close, Bristol BS4 4AX

Telephone: 0117 972 4248
Fax: 0117 971 1056

Directors: J. Cowhig *(Managing)*
S. Prendiville *(Financial)*
Dr K. Paulus *(Operations)*
A. Singleton *(Editorial)*
M. Ware *(Publishing)*
Managers: A. Davenport *(International Sales)*
B. Trigg *(Rights)*
S. Toop *(Production)*
A. Pomroy *(Customer Services & Order Processing)*
D. Reaney *(Marketing)*

Academic & Scholarly; Biography & Autobiography; Computer Science; Educational & Textbooks; Electronic (Educational); Mathematics & Statistics; Physics; Reference Books, Directories & Dictionaries; Scientific & Technical

New Titles: 34 (1995), 48 (1996)
No of Employees: 160
Annual Turnover: £15.1M

ISBNs, Imprints & Series:
0 7503, 0 85274 Adam Hilger, IOP Publishing
0 85498 Institute of Physics

Overseas Representation *(see §7.3):*
Australia, New Zealand & Papua New Guinea: DA Information Services, Mitcham, Vic, Australia
Austria, Belgium, Denmark, Finland, Germany, Iceland, Italy, Netherlands, Norway, Sweden, Switzerland, Spain, Portugal & Greece: Andrew B. Durnell, Tunbridge Wells, UK
Europe: Suzanne Hardy, Paris, France
Far East: Richard Field, Bristol, UK
Japan: Eastern Book Service Inc, Tokyo
Korea: Kumi Trading Co Ltd, Seoul, Korea, South
Kuwait, Bahrain & Abu Dhabi: Kuwait Bookshops Co Ltd, Safat, Kuwait
Middle East & North Africa: Anthony Rudkin Associates, Oxford, UK
Pakistan: Pak Book Corporation, Lahore
USA & Canada: IOP Publishing, Williston, VT, USA

Book Trade Association Membership: PA, BA, BDC, CAPP, ALPSP, IASTMP

1468 ■

ISIS PUBLISHING LTD
Unit 7, Centremead, Osney Mead, Oxford
OX2 0ES
Telephone: 01865 250333
Fax: 01865 790358

Distribution (Northern Ireland):
Gavin Smyth Booksellers, Educational & Library Supplies, Unit 4, Windsor Business Park, Boucher Place, Belfast BT12 6HT
Telephone: 01232 668033

Director: John Durrant *(Managing)*
Executive Editor: Veronica Babington Smith *(General Books)*
Managers: Lesley Chaundy *(Distribution)*
Betty Smith *(Financial)*
Don Loader *(Production)*

Robert Poulton *(Promotions)*
David Meggs *(Sales & Marketing)*

Audio Books; Biography & Autobiography; Crime; Crafts & Hobbies; English as a Foreign Language; Fiction; Poetry; Large Print Publications

New Titles: 336 (1995), 400 (1996)
No of Employees: 20

ISBNs, Imprints & Series:
0 7531, 1 85089, 1 85695

Overseas Representation *(see §7.3):*
Australia (Large print & Audio books only): Australian Large Print Pty Ltd, Tullamarine, Australia
Canada: S & B Large Print & Special Lines Ltd, Toronto
Denmark: Bierman & Bierman A/S, Grindsted
Irish Republic: Michael O'Brien, Dublin
Japan: PIC, Tokyo
New Zealand: The Library Supply Co Ltd, Auckland
Norway: Lydlitteratur, Nesoya
South Africa (Audio): Booktalk, Parkhurst, South Africa
Sweden: Bibliotekstjanst AB, Lund
USA (Audio): Dual Dolphin Publishing Inc, Norfolk, MA, USA
USA (Large print): ISIS Transaction Publishers, New Brunswick, NJ, USA

1469 ■

*ISLAM INTERNATIONAL PUBLICATIONS LTD
Islamabad, Sheep Hatch Lane, Tilford, Surrey
GU10 2AQ
Telephone: 01252 783155
Fax: 01252 783148

Orders:
The London Mosque, 16 Gressenhall Road, London SW18 5QL
Telephone: 0181 870 8517
Fax: 0181 870 1095

Chairman: A. B. Arshad
Managing Director: M. D. Shams *(Marketing)*

Children's Books; Religion & Theology

ISBNs, Imprints & Series:
1 85372 Islam International Publications Ltd, Al-Shirkatul Islamiyyah

Parent Company:
Al Shirkatul Islamiyyah

Associated & Subsidiary Companies:
Elite International Publications Ltd; Al Shirkatul Islamiyyah; The London Mosque Publications; Muslim Publications Ltd; Raqeen Press

Overseas Representation *(see §7.3):*
Australia: Islam International Publications, Riverstone
Bangladesh: Islam International Publications, Dacca
Belgium: Islam International Publications, Brussels
Canada: Baitul Islam, Maple
Denmark: Islam International Publications, Copenhagen

Fiji: Islam International Publications, Suva
France: Islam International Publications, Saint Prix
Gambia: Islam International Publications, Banjul
Germany: Islam International Publications, Frankfurt
Ghana: Islam International Publications, Accra
Guyana: Ahmadiyya Muslim Mission, Georgetown
India: Islam International Publications, Qadian
Indonesia: Islam International Publications, Jakarta
Ivory Coast: Ahmadiyya Muslim Mission, Abidjan
Japan: Islam International Publications, Nagoya
Kenya: Islam International Publications, Nairobi
Liberia: Islam International Publications, Monrovia
Mauritius: Islam International Publications, Rose Hill
Myanmar (Burma): Islam International Publications, Rangoon, Myanmar
Netherlands: Islam International Publications, The Hague
Nigeria: Islam International Publications, Lagos
Norway: Ahmadiyya Muslim Mission, Oslo
Philippines: Islam International Publications, Zamboanga City
Sierra Leone: Islam International Publications, Freetown
Singapore: Islam International Publications
South Africa: Islam International Publications, Cape Town
Spain: Mission Ahmadiyya del Islam, Cordoba
Sri Lanka: Islam International Publications, Colombo
Suriname: Ahmadiyya Muslim Mission, Paramaribo
Sweden: Nasir Moské Islams Ahmadiyya Församling, Göteborg
Switzerland: Islam International Publications, Zurich
Tanzania: Islam International Publications, Dar es Salaam
Trinidad & Tobago: Islam International Publications, Tunapuna, Trinidad
Uganda: Islam International Publications, Kampala
USA: Islam International Publications, Silver Spring, MD
Zaire: Islam International Publications, Kinshasa
Zambia: Islam International Publications, Lusaka

1470 ▬▬▬▬▬▬▬

THE ISLAMIC FOUNDATION
Markfield Dawah Centre, Ratby Lane,
Markfield, Leicester LE67 9RN
Telephone: 01530 244944/5
Fax: 01530 244946

Publications Unit:
Unit 9, The Old Dunlop Factory,
62 Evington Valley Road, Leicester LE5 5LJ
Telephone: 0116 273 4860
Fax: 0116 273 4860

Director-General: M. M. Ahsan *(Editorial)*
Sales Manager: T. A. Dale

Children's Books; Economics; Islam

New Titles: 4 (1995), 5 (1996)
No of Employees: 20

ISBNs, Imprints & Series: 0 86037

Distributor for:
Kuwait: Islamic Book Publishers. *Pakistan:* Institute of Policy Studies. *USA:* Institute of Islamic Thought

Overseas Representation *(see §7.3):*
Kuwait: Karamat Sheikh, Safat

1471 ▬▬▬▬▬▬▬

THE ISLAMIC TEXTS SOCIETY
PO Box 842, Bartlow, Cambridge CB1 6PX
Telephone: 01223 314387
Fax: 01223 324342
Email: ITSoc@cityscape.co.uk
Web Site: http://www.cityscape.co.uk/users/ep77/

Trade Enquiries:
Central Books Ltd, 99 Wallis Road, London E9 5LN
Telephone: 0181 986 4854
Fax: 0181 533 5821

Trust Secretary: Fatima Azzam
Publishing Co-ordinator: Batul Salazar

Religion & Theology; Comparative Religion; Islam

ISBNs, Imprints & Series:
0 946621, 1 870196 Al-Ghazali Series, Golden Palm Series, Quinta Essentia

Associated & Subsidiary Companies:
Golden Palm Books; The Green Street Book Shop Mail Order; Quinta Essentia

Distributor for:
USA: Sunna Books *(selected titles)*

Overseas Representation *(see §7.3):*
Australia: Quest Book Agency, Sydney
USA: Atrium, Santa Rosa, CA

Book Trade Association Membership: PA, BA

1472 ▬▬▬▬▬▬▬

ITHACA PRESS
[Books on The Middle East]
8 Southern Court, South Street, Reading RG1 4QS
Telephone: 01734 597847
Fax: 01734 597356

Distribution:
Clipper Distribution Services, Windmill Grove, Portchester, Hants PO16 9HT
Telephone: 01705 200080
Fax: 01705 200090

Managing Director: K. Banerji
Managers: Anne Watson *(Editorial)*
Ms Shirley Hibbert *(Administration)*
Sue Coll *(Permissions)*

Academic & Scholarly; History & Antiquarian; Languages & Linguistics; Politics & World Affairs; Sociology & Anthropology

ISBNs, Imprints & Series:
0 86372, 0 903729 Middle East Cultures Series, St Antonys Middle East Series

Parent Company:
Garnet Publishing Ltd

Overseas Representation *(see §7.3):*
Australia: Oriental Publications, Adelaide, SA
Canada: Canadian Scholars Press, Toronto, Ont
Europe: Books for Europe Ltd, Bournemouth, UK
Near & Middle East: Anthony Rudkin Associates, Oxford, UK
Southern Africa: Verbatim Distributors, Constantia Hills, South Africa
USA: Paul & Co Publishers Consortium Inc, Concord, MA

1473 ▬▬▬▬▬▬▬

IW BOOKS
PO Box 71, Rotherham, South Yorkshire S60 1SU
Telephone: 0114 243 8058
Fax: 0114 261 8424

Executive: David Hyland
Editorial: Chris Marsden
Finance: Colleen Smith
Production: Mick England

Politics & World Affairs

New Titles: 2 (1995), 6 (1996)
No of Employees: 4

ISBNs, Imprints & Series:
0 929087 Labor Publications
1 873045 IW Books

Parent Company:
Labor Publications *(USA)*

Distributor for:
USA: Labor Publications

Overseas Representation *(see §7.3):*
Australia: Labour Press, Marrickville, NSW
Germany: Arbeiterpresse Verlag, Essen
USA: Labor Publications, Oak Park, MI

1474 ▬▬▬▬▬▬▬

*JADE PUBLISHERS
15 Stoatley Rise, Haslemere, Surrey GU27 1AF
Telephone: 01428 644846
Fax: 01428 645267

Distribution warehouse, Invoicing & Returns:
Bookpoint Ltd, 39 Milton Park, Abingdon, Oxon OX14 4TD
Telephone: 01235 835001
Fax: 01235 861038 & 832068

Partner: C. P. de Laszlo

Children's Books; Crafts & Hobbies

ISBNs, Imprints & Series:
0 903461 Jade Publishers
1 872610 Bonnington Books

1475 ▬▬▬▬▬▬▬▬▬▬▬▬▬

JAI PRESS LTD
38 Tavistock Street, London WC2E 7PB
Telephone: 0171 379 8834
Fax: 0171 379 8835
Email: jai@cix.compulink.co.uk

Trade Orders, Warehousing & Distribution:
JAI Press Ltd, c/o Marston Book Services Ltd,
PO Box 269, Abingdon, Oxon OX14 4YN
Telephone: 01235 465500
Fax: 01235 465555

Chairman: Herbert M. Johnson *(USA)*
Managing Director: Piers R. Allen *(Editorial, Publishing & Sales)*
Marketing Manager: Madeleine V. Johnston *(Marketing & Promotion)*

Academic & Scholarly; Accountancy & Taxation; Bibliography & Library Science; Biology & Zoology; Chemistry; Computer Science; Economics; Educational & Textbooks; Industry, Business & Management; Medical (incl. Self Help & Alternative Medicine); Philosophy; Politics & World Affairs; Reference Books, Directories & Dictionaries; Religion & Theology; Scientific & Technical; Sociology & Anthropology; Management

New Titles: 160 (1995), 170 (1996)
No of Employees: 4

ISBNs, Imprints & Series:
Armstrong Publishing Corp (children's books) *see* JAI Press, Johnson Associates *see* JAI Press
0 7623, 0 89232, 1 55938, 1 885108

Parent Company:
JAI Press Inc *(USA)*

Associated & Subsidiary Companies:
USA: Armstrong Publishing Corp

Distributor for:
USA: Armstrong Publishing Corp; JAI Press Inc; JAI Software Publishing; Johnson Associates Inc

Overseas Representation *(see §7.3):*
Far East, USA, Canada, South and Central America: Marty Smolar, Greenwich CT, USA
France: Pascal Brien, Versailles
Germany, Austria & Switzerland: Piers Allen, Hampton Hill, Middx, UK
India & Bangladesh: Capital Books Pte Ltd, New Delhi, India
Italy: Marcello SNC, Padua
Middle East, North Africa, Pakistan, Greece, Turkey & Cyprus: Anthony Rudkin Associates, Oxford, UK
Portugal & Spain: Marcello Iberia SA, Madrid, Spain
Scandinavia, Belgium & Netherlands: Jan Norbye, Ølstykke, Denmark
Worldwide (except countries listed): Piers Allen, Hampton Hill, Middx, UK

Book Trade Association Membership: IPG (Serials Group)

1476 ▬▬▬▬▬▬▬▬▬▬▬▬▬

JAMES & JAMES (PUBLISHERS) LTD
Gordon House Business Centre,
6 Lissenden Gardens, London NW5 1LX
Telephone: 0171 482 4596
Fax: 0171 284 0448

Managing Director: Hamish MacGibbon

Academic & Scholarly; History & Antiquarian

New Titles: 10 (1995), 8 (1996)
No of Employees: 4
Annual Turnover: £550,000

ISBNs, Imprints & Series: 0 907383

Book Trade Association Membership: PA

1477 ▬▬▬▬▬▬▬▬▬▬▬▬▬

JAMES & JAMES (SCIENCE PUBLISHERS) LTD
Waterside House, 47 Kentish Town Road,
London NW1 8NZ
Telephone: 0171 284 3833
Fax: 0171 284 3737
Email: jjspl@demon.co.uk
Web Site: http://www.jxj.com

Publisher: Edward Milford
Managers: Mark Chaloner *(Sales & Marketing)*
John Pacione *(Production)*
Philip Denby *(Advertising Sales)*

Academic & Scholarly; Archaeology; Architecture & Design; Engineering; Environment & Development Studies; Scientific & Technical

New Titles: 20 (1995), 22 (1996)
No of Employees: 18
Annual Turnover: £900,000

ISBNs, Imprints & Series:
0 907383, 1 873936

Distributor for:
Robertson Scientific Publications

Overseas Representation *(see §7.3):*
North America: International Publishers Marketing Inc, Herndon, VA, USA

Book Trade Association Membership: IPG

1478 ▬▬o▬▬▬▬▬▬▬▬▬▬

ARTHUR JAMES LTD
4 Broadway Road, Evesham, Worcs
WR11 6BH
Telephone: 01386 446566
Fax: 01386 446717

Directors: I. Carlile *(Managing)*
J. Hunt *(Editorial)*
Mrs B. Coles
Mrs M. Wiseman

Biography & Autobiography; Humour; Poetry; Psychology & Psychiatry; Religion & Theology; Sociology & Anthropology

New Titles: 24 (1996)
No of Employees: 4
Annual Turnover: £200,000

ISBNs, Imprints & Series: 0 85305

Overseas Representation *(see §7.3):*
Australia: W. A. Buchanan & Co, Brisbane
New Zealand: Omega Distributors Ltd, Auckland

1479 ▬▬▬▬▬▬▬▬▬▬▬▬▬

JANE'S INFORMATION GROUP LTD
163 Brighton Road, Coulsdon, Surrey
CR5 2NH
Telephone: 0181 700 3700
Fax: 0181 763 1006
Email: Rupert.Webb@Janes.co.uk
Web Site: http://www.janes.com/janes.html

Jane's Defence & Data, Sentinel:
(as above)
Telephone: *(as above)*

Directors: A. Rolington *(Managing)*
R. Hutchinson *(New Products)*
M. Staton *(Commercial)*
S. Kay *(Publishing, Defence Magazines)*

Aviation; Electronic (Professional & Academic); Military & War; Nautical; Reference Books, Directories & Dictionaries; Transport

New Titles: 52 (1995), 80 (1996)
No of Employees: 170

ISBNs, Imprints & Series: 0 7106

Parent Company:
International Thomson Corporation

Overseas Representation *(see §7.3):*
Australia: Hinton Information Services, Eastwood, NSW
China & Russia: Jane's Information Group, UK
Egypt: Middle East Agency, Cairo
Indonesia: International Thomson Publishing Asia, Singapore
Iran: Eideh Information Services Co Ltd, Tehran
Israel: NPK Technology Services Ltd, Tel Aviv
Korea: International Thomson Publishing Asia, Youngdeungpo-ku, Korea, South
Kuwait: National Consulting Bureau, Safat
Malaysia: International Thomson Publishing Asia, Petaling Jaya
New Zealand: Standards New Zealand, Wellington
North & South America: Jane's Information Group Inc, Alexandria, VA, USA
Saudi Arabia: Arabian Advanced Systems, Riyadh
Singapore: Pansing Distribution Sdn Bhd
South Africa: Avex Air Training Pty Ltd, Halfway House
Taiwan: International Thomson Publishing Asia, Bangkok, Thailand
USA: Jane's Information Group Inc, Alexandria, VA
Worldwide (excluding countries listed): Jane's Information Group, UK

1480

JANUS PUBLISHING CO LTD
Edinburgh House, 19 Nassau Street, London
W1N 7RE
Telephone: 0171 580 7664
Fax: 0171 636 5756

Warehouse & Orders:
Bailey Distribution Ltd, Units 1a/1b,
Learoyd Road,
Mountfield Road Industrial Estate,
New Romney, Kent TN28 8XU
Telephone: 01797 366905
Fax: 01797 366638

Directors: R. Ross Stanton *(Managing, Rights
& Permissions)*
Melissa Hill *(Publicity)*
Production Manager: John Crabb

*Biography & Autobiography; Crime; Fashion
& Costume; Fiction; Humour; Magic & the
Occult; Medical (incl. Self Help & Alternative
Medicine); Military & War; Nautical; Poetry;
Politics & World Affairs; Religion & Theology;
Science Fiction*

New Titles: 50 (1995), 54 (1996)
No of Employees: 5
Annual Turnover: £325,000

ISBNs, Imprints & Series:
1 85756 Janus Poetry Series

Overseas Representation *(see §7.3)*:
Australia: Biramo Book Distributors, New
Lambton, NSW
*Austria, Italy, Spain, Portugal, Gibraltar &
Greece:* Patrick Bygate & Juliusz
Komarnicki, Massagno, Switzerland
Benelux & Germany: PKB – Robbert J.
Pleysier, Heerde, Netherlands
France & Switzerland: Juliusz Komarnicki,
Massagno, Switzerland
Malaysia, Singapore & Brunei: Publishers
Marketing Services Ltd, Singapore
New Zealand: Biramo Book Distributors,
Auckland
Scandinavia: Ove B. Poulsen, Glostrup,
Denmark
South Africa: Phambili Agencies (Jean
Knopperson), Kensington
USA & Canada: Paul & Company, Concord,
MA, USA

Book Trade Association Membership: PA,
IPG

1481

JARROLD PUBLISHING
Whitefriars, Norwich NR3 1TR
Telephone: 01603 763300
Fax: 01603 662748

Managing Director: Antony Jarrold
Managers: Tony Thompson *(Sales)*
Caroline Jarrold *(Publishing)*

*Gardening; Guide Books; Poetry; Sports &
Games; Travel & Topography*

New Titles: 10 (1995), 22 (1996)
No of Employees: 40

ISBNs, Imprints & Series:
0 7117, 0 85306

Overseas Representation *(see §7.3)*:
Australia & New Zealand: Peribo Pty Ltd,
Mount Kuring-gai, NSW, Australia
Canada: Fitzhenry & Whiteside Ltd, Markham
Far East: Electra Media Group Pty Ltd,
Sydney, NSW, Australia
Irish Republic: Island Publications Ltd, Dublin
Netherlands & Belgium: Nilsson & Lamm BV,
Weesp, Netherlands
*Switzerland (E.T.B./W.T.B. & Healthy Breaks
only):* Wepf & Co, Basel, Switzerland
USA: Seven Hills Book Distributors,
Cincinnati, OH

1482

JOLLY LEARNING
Tailours House, High Road, Chigwell, Essex
IG7 8DL
Telephone: 0181 501 0405
Fax: 0181 500 1696

Managing Director: Christopher Jolly
Administrator: Mandy Roads

Educational & Textbooks

New Titles: 7 (1995), 2 (1996)
No of Employees: 3
Annual Turnover: £250,000

ISBNs, Imprints & Series: 1 870946

1483

**JONES & BARTLETT
INTERNATIONAL**
Barb House, Barb Mews, London W6 7PA
Telephone: 0171 371 2119
Fax: 0171 371 2878
Email: classpub@classpub.eunet.co.uk

Warehouse, Trade Enquiries & Orders:
Plymbridge Distributors Ltd,
Plymbridge House, Estover Road, Plymouth,
Devon PL6 7PZ
Telephone: 01752 695745
Fax: 01752 695668

Managers: Richard Warner
Melissa Chapman *(Marketing)*

*Biology & Zoology; Chemistry; Computer
Science; Geography & Geology; Mathematics
& Statistics; Medical (incl. Self Help &
Alternative Medicine); Scientific & Technical*

ISBNs, Imprints & Series: 0 86720

Parent Company:
Jones & Bartlett Inc *(USA)*

Associated & Subsidiary Companies:
Exeter Multimedia

Overseas Representation *(see §7.3)*:
Continental Europe: Andrew B. Durnell,
Tunbridge Wells, UK
Middle East: Anthony Rudkin Associates,
Oxford, UK

1484

JORDAN PUBLISHING LTD
21 St Thomas Street, Bristol BS1 6JS
Telephone: 0117 923 0600
Fax: 0117 925 0486

Directors: Richard Hudson *(Managing)*
Martin West *(Publishing)*
Managers: David Chaplin *(Marketing)*
Beverley Brown *(Customer Service &
Distribution)*
Mollie Dickenson *(Managing Editor)*

*Accountancy & Taxation; Electronic
(Professional & Academic); Industry, Business
& Management; Law*

ISBNs, Imprints & Series:
0 85308, 0 85938 Family Law, Jordan
Publishing Ltd

Parent Company:
West of England Trust

1485

**MICHAEL JOSEPH LTD & PELHAM
BOOKS**
27 Wrights Lane, London W8 5TZ
Telephone: 0171 416 3200
Fax: 0171 416 3293

Warehouse:
Penguin Books Ltd, Bath Road,
Harmondsworth, Middx UB7 0DA
Telephone: 0181 759 1984 & 5722
Fax: 0181 759 3570

Directors: Susan Watt *(Publishing)*
Max Adam *(Export Sales)*
Luigi Bonomi *(Editorial)*
Jenny Dereham *(Editorial)*
Roger Clarke *(Financial)*
Nellie Flexner *(Marketing & Publicity)*
Louise Haines *(Editorial)*
Joy Harrison *(Production)*
Tim Whitfield *(Rights)*
Deborah Wright *(Sales)*
Cecily Engle *(Company Secretary)*

*Biography & Autobiography; Cinema, Video,
TV & Radio; Cookery, Wines & Spirits;
Fiction; Gardening; Guide Books; Humour;
Military & War; Natural History;
Photography; Sports & Games; Travel &
Topography*

ISBNs, Imprints & Series:
0 7181 Michael Joseph
0 7207 Pelham

Parent Company:
Penguin Books Ltd

Overseas Representation *(see §7.3)*:
See: Penguin Books Ltd, London, UK

Book Trade Association Membership: PA,
BDC

1486

RICHARD JOSEPH PUBLISHERS LTD
Unit 2, Monks Walk, Farnham, Surrey
GU9 8HT

Telephone: 01252 734347
Fax: 01252 734307

Managing Director: Richard Joseph
Compiler: M. Goulding
Production Manager: Alison Lake

Reference Books, Directories & Dictionaries

New Titles: 10 (1995), 10 (1996)
No of Employees: 4
Annual Turnover: £160,000

ISBNs, Imprints & Series:
1 872699 Sheppard

Book Trade Association Membership: IPG

1487 ■■■■■■

H. KARNAC (BOOKS) LTD
58 Gloucester Road, London SW7 4QY
Telephone: 0171 584 3303
Fax: 0171 823 7743
Email: books@karnac.demon.co.uk

Retail Shop:
118 Finchley Road, London NW3 5HJ
Telephone: 0171 431 1075

Directors: Cesare D. S. Sacerdoti *(Managing, Publishing, Trade, Retail, Distribution)*
Mrs J. F. Sacerdoti *(Secretary)*
Managers: Malcolm Smith *(Retail, Publishing)*
Larry Fisher *(Mail Order)*
Graham Sleight *(Publishing & Distribution)*
Jaqui Clarke *(Trade)*

Medical (incl. Self Help & Alternative Medicine); Psychology & Psychiatry

New Titles: 28 (1995), 24 (1996)
No of Employees: 16
Annual Turnover: £1.5M

ISBNs, Imprints & Series:
0 946439, 1 85575 Institute of Psycho-Analysis, London, Karnac Books, Library of Analytical Psychology, Maresfield Library, Systemic Thinking Theory & Practice Series, Tavistock Institute of Marital Studies (TIMS), Winnicott Studies (Series)

Distributor for:
Clunie Press; Tavistock Institute of Marital Studies. *USA:* The Analytic Press; Chiron Publications

Overseas Representation *(see §7.3):*
North America: Brunner/Mazel Inc, New York, USA

Book Trade Association Membership: BA

1488 ■■■■■■

KEGAN PAUL INTERNATIONAL LTD
PO Box 256, 118 Bedford Court Mansions, Bedford Avenue, London WC1B 3SW
Telephone: 0171 580 5511
Fax: 0171 436 0899
Email: books@keganpau.demon.co.uk
Web Site: http://www.demon.co.uk/keganpaul/

Warehouse & Distribution:
John Wiley & Sons Ltd,
Southern Cross Trading Estate, Bognor Regis, West Sussex PO22 9SA
Telephone: 01243 829121
Fax: 01243 820250

Directors: Peter Hopkins *(Chairman & Managing)*
Kaori O'Connor *(Editorial)*

Academic & Scholarly; Antiques & Collecting; Archaeology; Architecture & Design; Biography & Autobiography; Cookery, Wines & Spirits; Economics; Environment & Development Studies; Fashion & Costume; Fiction; Fine Art & Art History; Geography & Geology; Guide Books; History & Antiquarian; Illustrated & Fine Editions; Languages & Linguistics; Natural History; Philosophy; Poetry; Politics & World Affairs; Reference Books, Directories & Dictionaries; Religion & Theology; Sociology & Anthropology; Travel & Topography

ISBNs, Imprints & Series:
0 7103 Publications of the Graduate Institute of International Studies, Geneva, Japanese Studies Series, KPI Paperbacks, Library of Arabic Linguistics, Pacific Basin Books, Studies in Egyptology

Overseas Representation *(see §7.3):*
Africa (sub-Saharan): Len Ainsworth, Aldbourne, UK
Australia & New Zealand: James Bennett Pty Ltd, Collaroy Beach, NSW, Australia
Bangladesh: Karim International, Dhaka
East Africa: Ben & Co Ltd, Dar es Salaam, Tanzania
Europe: Exlibris International Marketing Ltd, Stolberg, Germany
India (stockholding distributors): Selectbook Service Syndicate, New Delhi, India; Segment Book Distributors, New Delhi, India
India (stockholding representative): T. R. Publications Pvt Ltd, Madras, India
Middle East, North Africa, Cyprus, Malta & Turkey: Peter Ward Book Exports, London, UK
Pakistan: Afro-Asian Book Co, Karachi
South East Asia & Far East (including Japan, Hong Kong, Korea, Taiwan, Malaysia, Singapore, Indonesia & Thailand): Kegan Paul International, London, UK
Southern Africa: Verbatim Distributors, Constantia Hills, South Africa
USA & Canada: Columbia University Press, New York, USA
West Africa: Sedco Publishing Ltd, Accra, Ghana

1489 ■■■■■■

*KEMPS PUBLISHING LTD
11 The Swan Courtyard, Charles Edward Road, Yardley, Birmingham B26 1BU
Telephone: 0121 765 4144
Fax: 0121 706 3491

Sales Office:
4th Floor, Newgate House, Newgate Street, Newcastle-on-Tyne NE1 5UQ
Telephone: 0191 222 1223
Fax: 0191 230 0034

Directors: Frank Markham *(Managing)*
Stuart Walters *(Sales)*

Educational & Textbooks; Electronic (Professional & Academic); Fashion & Costume; Reference Books, Directories & Dictionaries

ISBNs, Imprints & Series: 0 86259

Book Trade Association Membership: DPA, EADP

1490 ■■■■■■

THE KENILWORTH PRESS LTD
Addington, Buckingham, Bucks MK18 2JR
Telephone: 01296 715101
Fax: 01296 715148

Warehouse:
Hoddle Doyle Meadows Ltd, Station Road, Linton, Cambs CB1 6UK
Telephone: 01223 893855
Fax: 01223 893852

Directors: David Blunt
Deirdre Blunt
Managing Editor: Lesley Gowers

Animal Care & Breeding; Natural History; Sports & Games; Veterinary Science

New Titles: 10 (1995), 10 (1996)
No of Employees: 6
Annual Turnover: £0.5M

ISBNs, Imprints & Series:
0 901366, 1 872082 Threshold Books/The Kenilworth Press Ltd
0 939481 Half Halt Press
1 872082 The Kenilworth Press

Distributor for:
Half Halt Press Inc

Overseas Representation *(see §7.3):*
Australia: Equine Educational, Lochinvar, NSW
South Africa: Trinity Books CC, Randburg
USA: Half Halt Press, Middletown, MD

Book Trade Association Membership: IPG

1491 ■■■■■■

KENNEDY'S PUBLICATIONS LTD
12 Blackstock Mews, London N4 2BT
Telephone: 0171 226 3423
Fax: 0171 354 5372

Chairwoman: Mrs C. Kennedy
Directors: A. Kennedy *(Managing, Rights)*
J. Kennedy *(Managing, Finance)*
Managers: Matthew Rowlands *(Editorial)*
Sarah Niel *(Editorial)*
Richard Robins *(Production)*
Graham Turner *(Production)*
Patricia Streotin *(Marketing)*
Andrea Jenn *(Sales)*
Suzanne Rollinson *(Sales)*

Cookery, Wines & Spirits; Engineering; Guide Books; Industry, Business & Management; Reference Books, Directories & Dictionaries; Scientific & Technical

No of Employees: 10

ISBNs, Imprints & Series: 0 904725

Distributor for:
Belgium: Chocolate World. *Malaysia:* Atlanto Publishing. *USA:* VNR

Overseas Representation *(see §7.3):*
Japan: Echo Agencies

1492

KENSINGTON WEST PRODUCTIONS
5 Cattle Market, Hexham, Northumberland NE46 1NJ
Telephone: 01434 609933
Fax: 01434 600066

Managing Director: Julian West
Managers: Janet West *(Finance)*
Martin Ellis *(Sales & Marketing)*
Diane Ridley *(Design)*

Photography; Sports & Games; Travel & Topography

ISBNs, Imprints & Series: 1 871349

Overseas Representation *(see §7.3):*
Canada: Temeron Books Inc, Calgary
USA: Bookworld Services Inc, Sarasota, FL

Book Trade Association Membership: IPG

1493

KENYON-DEANE LTD
10 Station Road Industrial Estate, Colwall, Malvern, Worcs WR13 6RN
Telephone: 01684 540154
Fax: 01684 540154

Theatre, Drama & Dance

New Titles: 6 (1995)

ISBNs, Imprints & Series: 0 7155

Parent Company:
Cressrelles Publishing Co Ltd

Distributor for:
USA: Anchorage Press

1494

KERSHAW PUBLISHING CO LTD
3 Henrietta Street, London WC2E 8LU
Telephone: 0171 240 0856
Fax: 0161 764 8213

Warehouse:
H. T. (Book Distribution) Ltd, Bolholt, Walshaw Road, Bury, Lancs BL8 1RP
Telephone: 0161 764 2296
Fax: 0161 764 8213

Directors: Peter Kershaw Taylor *(Managing)*
Elizabeth Taylor
Company Secretary: Susan K. V. Taylor
Sales: Christine Williams

Academic & Scholarly; Educational & Textbooks; Mathematics & Statistics

New Titles: 2 (1995), 2 (1996)

ISBNs, Imprints & Series:
0 901665 International Studies in Mathematics

Book Trade Association Membership: PA

1495

KIBWORTH BOOKS
Imperial Road, Kibworth Beauchamp, Leicester LE8 0HR
Telephone: 0116 279 6333
Fax: 0116 279 6303

Managing Director: Michael McDonald

Children's Books

ISBNs, Imprints & Series: 0 7239

Parent Company:
McDonald Publishing Ltd

1496

LAURENCE KING PUBLISHING
71 Great Russell Street, London WC1B 3BN
Telephone: 0171 831 6351
Fax: 0171 831 8356

Distribution:
Thames & Hudson Ltd, 44 Clockhouse Road, Farnborough, Hants GU14 7QZ
Telephone: 01252 541602
Fax: 01252 377380
Email: 101456.1525@compuserve.com

Chairman: Robin Hyman
Directors: Laurence King *(Managing)*
Judy Rasmussen *(Production)*
Lee Ripley Greenfield *(Editorial–College & Fine Art)*
Sales Manager: Christine Macgregor

Architecture & Design; Fine Art & Art History; Illustrated & Fine Editions; Photography

New Titles: 17 (1995), 14 (1996)
No of Employees: 19
Annual Turnover: £722,000

ISBNs, Imprints & Series: 1 85669

Parent Company:
Calmann & King Ltd

Book Trade Association Membership: PA

1497

KING'S FUND
11–13 Cavendish Square, London W1M 0AN
Telephone: 0171 307 2400
Fax: 0171 307 2801

Distribution:
Bournemouth English Book Centre, PO Box 1496, Poole BH12 3YD
Telephone: 0800 262260 (Freefone)
Fax: 0800 262266 (Freefax)

Head of Communications: Ian Wylie *(Rights & Permissions)*
Chief Executive: Robert J. Maxwell
Business Manager, Communications: Katie Stone
Editor: Giovanna Ceroni
Marketing Manager: Lyndsey Unwin

Academic & Scholarly; Educational & Textbooks; Medical (incl. Self Help & Alternative Medicine)

New Titles: 20 (1995), 20 (1996)
No of Employees: 250

ISBNs, Imprints & Series:
1 85717 King's Fund

1498

JESSICA KINGSLEY PUBLISHERS
116 Pentonville Road, London N1 9JB
Telephone: 0171 833 2307
Fax: 0171 837 2917

Trade Enquiries & Orders:
Kogan Page Ltd, 120 Pentonville Road, London N1
Telephone: 0171 278 0433
Fax: 0171 837 6348

Managing Director: Jessica Kingsley *(Editorial, Rights & Permissions)*
Home & Export Sales: Imogen Farrow
Production: Anna French

Academic & Scholarly; Economics; Educational & Textbooks; Geography & Geology; Law; Psychology & Psychiatry; Reference Books, Directories & Dictionaries; Sociology & Anthropology; Theatre, Drama & Dance

New Titles: 51 (1995), 75 (1996)
No of Employees: 9

ISBNs, Imprints & Series:
1 85302 Case Studies for Practice, Children in Charge, Disability and Rehabilitation Series, Educational Sciences Series co-published with UNESCO, Forensic Focus, Higher Education Policy Series, Jessica Kingsley Publishers, Penton Press, Regional Policy and Development Series, Research Highlights in Social Work

Distributor for:
Australia: MacLennan & Petty. *Netherlands:* Lemma. *Norway:* Sigma Forlag. *USA:* Paul H. Brookes; Health Professions Press; Love Publishing

Overseas Representation *(see §7.3):*
Australia & New Zealand: MacLennan & Petty Pty Ltd, Artarmon, NSW, Australia
Canada: Gage Educational Publishing Co, Agincourt, Ont
China, Hong Kong, Korea, Taiwan & Thailand: STM Publishing Services Pte Ltd, Singapore
Europe: Andrew B. Durnell, Tunbridge Wells, UK
Japan: United Publishers Services Ltd, Tokyo
Singapore, Malaysia, Brunei & Indonesia: Publishers Marketing Services Ltd, Singapore
Singapore, Malaysia, Brunei, Indonesia & Thailand: Publishers Marketing Services, Petaling Jaya, Malaysia
USA: Taylor & Francis Inc, Bristol, PA

Book Trade Association Membership: PA, IPG

1499

KINGSWAY PUBLICATIONS LTD
Lottbridge Drove, Eastbourne, East Sussex
BN23 6NT
Telephone: 01323 410930
Fax: 01323 411970

Distribution & Warehouse:
STL Wholesale, PO Box 300,
Kingstown Broadway, Carlisle, Cumbria
CA3 0QS
Telephone: 01228 512512
Fax: 01228 514949

Chief Executive Officers: John Paculabo
Brian Davies
Managers: Paul Mogford *(Sales)*
Phil Bacon *(Marketing)*
Richard Herkes *(Editorial, Rights &*
Permissions)
William Owen *(Finance & Administration)*
Richard Martin *(Overseas, Export Sales)*

Audio Books; Children's Books; Religion &
Theology

New Titles: 50 (1995), 40 (1996)

ISBNs, Imprints & Series:
0 85476, 0 85491, 0 86065, 0 86239, 0 902088
Kingsway

Parent Company:
Kingsway Communications Ltd

Associated & Subsidiary Companies:
Kingsway Music; The Rainbow Co (Retail);
Thankyou Music

Distributor for:
David C. Cook; Nova

Overseas Representation *(see §7.3):*
Australia: CMC Australia Pty Ltd, Belmont,
Vic
Canada: Beacon Distributing, Paris, Ont
Europe: Winfried Bluth, Remscheid, Germany
Hong Kong: Cross (HK) Co
Japan: Christian Literature Crusade, Tokyo
Malaysia: Salvation Book Centre, Petaling
Jaya
New Zealand: CMC Australasia Pty Ltd,
Havelock North
Singapore: Alby Commercial Enterprises Pte
Ltd
South Africa: Struik Christian Books, Cape
Town

Book Trade Association Membership: PA

1500

KINNELL PUBLICATIONS LTD
21 Brewster Road, Leyton, London E10 6RG
Telephone: 0181 556 2800

Distribution:
Vine House Distribution, Waldenbury,
North Common, Chailey, East Sussex
BN8 4DR
Telephone: 0182 572 3398
Fax: 0182 572 4188

Rights & Acquisitions, Sales & Promotion:
R. G. Lewis
Editorial: R. G. Lewis

Fiction; Science Fiction

ISBNs, Imprints & Series: 1 870532

1501

KLUWER LAW INTERNATIONAL
Sterling House, 66 Wilton Road, London
SW1V 1DE
Telephone: 0171 821 1123
Fax: 0171 630 5229
Web Site: http://www.kli.com

Warehouse & Orders:
Kluwer Academic Publishers Group,
Distribution Centre & Sales Department,
Kamerlingh Onnesweg 7–11, PO Box 322,
3300 AH Dordrecht, Netherlands
Telephone: +31 (70) 3081562

Directors: M. Nieuwenhuis *(General)*
S. Willcox *(Marketing)*
A. Visser *(Managing)*
Editorial: T. Hook *(Production)*
S. Hoedt *(Law)*
L. Claerhout *(Law)*
Marketing Managers: M. Nixon *(Law)*
G. Steddy *(Law)*
R. Uttley *(Sales)*
N. Gallehawk *(Law)*

Accountancy & Taxation; Law; International
Relations

New Titles: 200 (1995), 220 (1996)
No of Employees: 45

ISBNs, Imprints & Series:
0 7923, 1 85333, 90 411, 90 6544

Parent Company:
Wolters Kluwer NV *(Netherlands)*

Overseas Representation *(see §7.3):*
Australia & New Zealand: DA Information
Services, Mitcham, Vic, Australia
Bangladesh: Karim International, Dhaka
India: Allied Publishers Pte Ltd, New Delhi &
Calcutta
Japan: Maruzen Co Ltd, Tokyo; Kinokuniya
Co Ltd, Tokyo
Korea: Panmun Book Co Ltd, Seoul, Korea,
South
Malaysia: Parry's Book Centre Sdn Bhd, Kuala
Lumpur
Pakistan: Pakistan Law House, Karachi; Pak
American Commercial Inc, Karachi
USA & Canada: Kluwer Law International,
Cambridge, MA, USA

Book Trade Association Membership:
Directory Publishers Association, STM

1502

KOGAN PAGE LTD
120 Pentonville Road, London N1 9JN
Telephone: 0171 278 0433
Fax: 0171 837 6348
Email: kpinfo@kogan-page.cc.uk or
kpsales@kogan-page.co.uk

Warehouse:
Hoddle Doyle Meadows, Dalgety Building,
Station Road, Linton, Cambs CB1 6UX
Telephone: 01223 893855
Fax: 01223 893852

Directors: Philip Kogan *(Managing)*
Gordon Watts *(Financial)*
Pauline Goodwin *(Publishing—Professional &*
Reference)
Peter Chadwick *(Production)*
Philip Mudd *(Publishing—Education &*
Training)
Mike Baggallay *(Sales)*
Associate Directors: Linda Batham *(Foreign*
Rights & Marketing Services)
Julie McNair *(Head—Export Sales)*

Academic & Scholarly; Accountancy &
Taxation; Educational & Textbooks; Industry,
Business & Management; Reference Books,
Directories & Dictionaries; Transport;
Vocational Training & Careers

New Titles: 256 (1995), 260 (1996)
No of Employees: 60
Annual Turnover: £6.8M

ISBNs, Imprints & Series:
0 7494, 0 85038, 1 85091

Associated & Subsidiary Companies:
Earthscan Publications

Distributor for:
Earthscan Publications; Jessica Kingsley;
Penton Press; Telegraph Books. *Netherlands:*
Uitgeverij Lemman BV. *Norway:* MacLennan
& Petty. *USA:* Island Press; Paul H. Brookes; St
Lucie Press

Overseas Representation *(see §7.3):*
Australia: Astam Books Pty Ltd, Leichhardt,
NSW
Canada: Gage Educational Publishing Co,
Agincourt, Ont
Caribbean: English House Services Publishers
International Management, Cinderford, UK
Hong Kong, South Korea & Taiwan: Asia
Publisher Services Ltd, Hong Kong
India: Viva Marketing, New Delhi
Japan: Kay Kato, Kamakura
Middle East: Peter Ward Book Exports,
London, UK
Pakistan: Book Bird, Lahore
Singapore, Malaysia & Brunei: Publishers
Marketing Services Ltd, Singapore;
Publishers Marketing Services, Petaling
Jaya, Malaysia
South Africa: Book Promotions Pty Ltd,
Plumstead
Thailand, Myanmar (Burma), China,
Philippines & Vietnam: STM Publishing
Services Pte Ltd, Singapore
Western Europe: Andrew B. Durnell,
Tunbridge Wells, UK

Book Trade Association Membership: PA,
BDC, CAPP, IPG, Euro Business Publishing
Network, Directory Publishers Association

1503

*KUPERARD (LONDON) LTD
No 9, Hampstead West, 224 Iverson Road,
West Hampstead, London NW6 2HL
Telephone: 0171 372 4722
Fax: 0171 372 4599

Invoicing & Distribution (Orders to London
address above):
Bailey Distribution, Learoyd Road,
New Romney, Kent TN28 8XU

Telephone: 01797 366905
Fax: 01797 366638

Managing Director: Joshua Kuperard
Managers: Peter Roberts *(Sales & Marketing)*
Juliet Thorp *(Promotions, Publicity & Special Sales)*

Atlases & Maps; Guide Books; Languages & Linguistics; Literature & Criticism; Reference Books, Directories & Dictionaries; Religion & Theology; Travel & Topography; Vocational Training & Careers

ISBNs, Imprints & Series:
1 857330, 1 857331, 1 870668 At A Glance Maps, Culture Shock! Guides, Everyday Phrase Books, Michael's Guides, Les Routiers Guides

Distributor for:
Central Bureau; Les Routiers; Survival Books. *Australia:* Gadabout Guides. *Canada:* Maplehouse Press. *Germany:* Berndtson & Berndtson (Maps); Ravenstein (Maps). *Israel:* Inbal Travel Information Ltd *(Travel – The New Michael's Guides)*; Prolog. *Portugal:* Vista Iberica. *Singapore:* Times Editions *(Travel)*. *USA:* Jason Aronson *(Judaica)*; Basic Books *(Judaica)*; Gousha *(Road Atlases, North America)*; Jewish Publication Society *(Judaica)*; Kar-Ben Copies Inc *(Judaica)*; The Modern Library *(Classic Literature)*; Random House Inc *(Judaica)*; Schocken Books; Simon & Schuster *(Judaica)*; Summit Books *(Judaica)*

Overseas Representation *(see §7.3)*:
Australia: CIS Publishers, Carlton, Vic
Canada: Librairie Ulysse Inc, Montreal
Europe: Books for Europe Ltd, Bournemouth, UK
Netherlands: Penguin Books Netherlands bv, Amsterdam
Scandinavia & Finland (At A Glance): Sälta, Göteborg, Sweden
Scandinavia & Finland (Channel Tunnel At A Glance): Statenskartwerk, Honefoss, Norway
Scandinavia & Finland (Culture Shock): Platypus Förlag, Helsingborg, Sweden
South Africa: Trinity Books CC, Randburg
USA: Seven Hills Book Distributors, Cincinnati, OH

Book Trade Association Membership: PA, BA

1504 ■■■■■■

LADYBIRD BOOKS LTD
Beeches Road, Loughborough, Leics LE11 2NQ
Telephone: 01509 268021
Fax: 01509 234672

Directors: (to be appointed) *(Managing)*
Will Howarth *(Finance)*
Michael Gabb *(Publishing)*
David King *(International Sales)*
Charles Sanderson *(UK & Irish Republic Sales)*
Jeff Satterley *(Production)*
Managers: Dennis McGuirk *(National Accounts Sales)*
John Mackay *(Field Sales)*
Janet Riley *(Marketing)*
Mary Hagger *(Publicity)*
David Kidger *(Sales Development)*

Yvonne Francis *(International Sales – Australia, New Zealand, Caribbean & L. America)*
Nina Bueno Del Carpio *(International Sales – Europe, Middle East & Africa)*
Permissions: Pat Ross *(Editorial Administrator)*

Children's Books

New Titles: 148 (1995), 165 (1996)
No of Employees: 260
Annual Turnover: £20M

ISBNs, Imprints & Series:
0 7214 Ladybird

Parent Company:
Penguin Group

Overseas Representation *(see §7.3)*:
Asia (excluding Japan), India, Pakistan & Sri Lanka: Rhian Owen International Manager, Hong Kong
Australia (Ladybird only): Penguin Books Australia Ltd, Ringwood, Vic, Australia
Australia, New Zealand, Caribbean & Latin America: Yvonne Francis, Loughborough, UK
Brazil: Terry Roberts, Cotia SP
Canada: Penguin Books Canada Ltd, Newmarket, Ont
Caribbean Islands: Louis A. Forde, St Michael, Barbados
Europe, Middle East & Africa: Nina Bueno Del Carpio, Loughborough, UK
Greece: Educational Books & Records SA, Athens
India: Rupa & Co, New Delhi
Italy: Penguin Italia Srl, Milan
Jamaica: Carlong Publishers (Caribbean) Ltd, Kingston
Japan: Penguin Books Japan, Tokyo
Korea: Kwon Sung June, Seoul, Korea, South
Lebanon (Ladybird only): Librairie du Liban, Beirut, Lebanon
Malaysia, Brunei & Singapore: Longman Malaysia Sdn Bhd, Petaling Jaya, Malaysia
Malta: Merlin Library, Blata-l-Bajda
New Zealand: Penguin Books (New Zealand) Ltd, Auckland
Oman: Family Bookshop, Ruwi
Papua New Guinea, Kiribati, Soloman Islands, Vanuatu & Western Samoa: Pacific Press, Mount Waverley, Vic, Australia
Philippines: I. J. Sagun Enterprises Inc, Rizal
Qatar: Family Bookshop, Doha
South Africa: Maskew Miller Longman Pty Ltd, Cape Town
Syria: Librairie Sayegh, Damascus
Taiwan: Caves Books Ltd, Taipei
Uganda: Matovu Books & Stationery Ltd, Kampala
USA & Canada: Yvonne Francis, Loughborough, UK

Book Trade Association Membership: PA

1505 ■■■■■■

LANGUAGE TEACHING PUBLICATIONS
35 Church Road, Hove, East Sussex BN3 2BE
Telephone: 01273 736344
Fax: 01273 720898

Directors: Michael Lewis
Jimmie Hill
Home & Export Sales: Stuart Tipping

English as a Foreign Language

New Titles: 6 (1995), 6 (1996)
No of Employees: 4

ISBNs, Imprints & Series:
0 906717, 1 899396

Overseas Representation *(see §7.3)*:
Argentina: Acme Agency SA, Buenos Aires; Kel Ediciones SA, Buenos Aires; Libreria Blackpool, Cordoba
Australia & New Zealand: Melting Pot Press, Chippendale, Australia
Austria: The British Bookshop, Vienna
Belgium: W. H. Smith, Brussels; Papyrus Book Agency, Brussels
Brazil: Livraria Martins Fontes, Sao Paulo
Canada: Monarch Books of Canada Ltd, Downsview
Croatia: Algoritam Ltd, Zagreb
Cyprus: Bridgehouse Bookshop, Nicosia
Czech Republic: Mega Books International, Prague; Jiri Fraus, Plzen
Denmark: Eric Paludan, Copenhagen
Finland: Akateeminen Kirjakauppa, Helsinki
France: Attica-Diffusion, Paris; NQL International, Paris; Librairie Decitre, Lyon
Germany: Buchhandlung Stäheli & Co ELT Dept, Spaichingen
Germany & Austria (selected titles): Ernst Klett Verlag, Stuttgart, Germany
Greece: English School Book Co, Athens; Eurobook, Athens
Hong Kong: Transglobal Publishers Services Ltd, Tsuen Wan
Hungary: BELT, Budapest
Irish Republic: Modern Languages, Dublin; International Books, Dublin
Italy: Expolingua Italia, Turin
Japan: Meynard Publishing Ltd, Tokyo
Korea: Segroo Publishers Ltd, Seoul, Korea, South
Malaysia: S. Abdul Majeed & Co, Kuala Lumpur
Mexico: Libreria Britanica SA, Mexico City
Netherlands: Intertaal, Amsterdam
Norway: Juul Moller AS, Oslo
Poland: English Book Centre Bookshop, Krakow; Omnibus Bookshop, Poznan
Portugal: Livraria Escolar, Lisbon; Editóra Replicação, Lisbon
Slovenia: Cankarjeva Zalozba (Centre Oxford), Ljubljana
Spain: Heinemann Iberia, Madrid
Sweden: Akademibokhandeln, Stockholm; English Book Centre, Stockholm
Switzerland: Kurt Stäheli & Co, Zurich
Taiwan: New Schoolmate Business Group, Taipei; Hua Excellent Resources, Taipei
Turkey: Dunya Education, Istanbul
Ukraine, Russia, Estonia, Byelorussia, Lithuania, Bulgaria & Latvia: Parallel Publishing Services Ltd, Eastbourne, UK
USA: Delta Systems Inc, McHenry, IL; Alta Book Center, Burlingame, CA

1506 ■■■■■■

LAROUSSE PLC
Elsley House, 24–30 Great Titchfield Street, London W1P 7AD

Telephone: 0171 631 0878
Fax: 0171 323 4694

Also at:
45 Annandale Street, Edinburgh EH7 4AZ
Telephone: 0131 557 4571
Fax: 0131 557 2936

Distribution:
Macmillan Distribution Ltd, Brunel Road,
Houndmills, Basingstoke, Hants RG21 6XS
Telephone: 01256 29242
Fax: 01256 812521 & 812558

Chairman: John Clement
Directors: Marc Zagar *(Finance)*
Donald Smith *(UK Sales)*
Robert Snuggs *(International Sales &
    Marketing)*
Robert Allen *(Publishing—Larousse)*
Chester Fisher *(Publishing—Kingfisher—Non-
    fiction)*
Ann-Janine Murtagh *(Publishing—
    Kingfisher—Fiction)*
Christine De Poortere *(Rights—Kingfisher)*
Catherine Potter *(UK Rights)*
John Richards *(Production)*

*Children's Books; Educational & Textbooks;
Electronic (Educational); Electronic
(Entertainment); English as a Foreign
Language; Gardening; Guide Books;
Languages & Linguistics; Natural History;
Reference Books, Directories & Dictionaries*

New Titles: 196 (1995), 151 (1996)
No of Employees: 95
Annual Turnover: £17M

ISBNs, Imprints & Series:
0 550, 1 85296 Chambers
0 7523, 2 034 Larousse
0 86272, 1 85697 Kingfisher

Parent Company:
Groupe de la Cité

Associated & Subsidiary Companies:
Harrap

Overseas Representation *(see §7.3)*:
USA: Larousse, Kingfisher, Chambers Inc,
    New York

1507

ROGER LASCELLES
47 York Road, Brentford, Middx TW8 0QP
Telephone: 0181 847 0935
Fax: 0181 568 3886

Manager: Roger Lascelles

*Atlases & Maps; Guide Books; Travel &
Topography*

ISBNs, Imprints & Series:
0 903909, 1 85879, 1 872815

Distributor for:
Thomas Cook Rail Maps; Daily Telegraph
Maps; Heritage House; Iberia Press; Pictorial
Publications; Trailblazer Publications; UKHM;
Vacation Work. *Australia:* Cornelius Books.
Brazil: Streamline. *France:* Editions Blay;
Editions Edisud; Editions Charles Massin.
Germany: Ravenstein Verlag. *Hungary:* Park

Publications. *Italy:* Litografia Artistica
Cartografica Srl; Casa Editrice Tabacco. *Spain:*
Firestone Hispania SA. *Thailand:* T & R
United. *USA:* American Map Corporation; H.
M. Gousha Co; Kistler Graphics; World
Leisure Corporation

Overseas Representation *(see §7.3)*:
Australia: Rex Map Centre, Lane Cove, NSW
Canada: The Map Store of Canada, Ottawa
India: English Bookstore, New Delhi
Netherlands: Nilsson & Lamm BV, Weesp
Scandinavia: D. Richard Bowen, Malmö,
    Sweden
Switzerland: Travel Bookshop, Zurich

1508

LATIN AMERICA BUREAU
1 Amwell Street, London EC1R 1UL
Telephone: 0171 278 2829
Fax: 0171 278 0165
Email: labegn.apc.org

Trade Enquiries & Orders:
Central Books Ltd, 99 Wallis Road, London
E9 5LN
Telephone: 0181 986 4854
Fax: 0181 533 5821

Sales & Marketing: Chris Lee
Rights: James Ferguson
Production: Liz Morrell
Editorial: Duncan Green

*Environment & Development Studies; Politics
& World Affairs*

New Titles: 5 (1995), 10 (1996)
No of Employees: 5

ISBNs, Imprints & Series:
0 906156, 1 899365 In Focus Country guides
    series

Distributor for:
USA: Resource Center (Country Guide Series)

Overseas Representation *(see §7.3)*:
Australia: Bushbooks, Gosford South, NSW
Canada: Fernwood Books Ltd, Halifax, NS
Caribbean: Ian Randle Publishers Ltd,
    Kingston, Jamaica
Germany: Lateinamerika Nachrichten, Berlin
Netherlands: Ruurd Ruward, Ruward BV, The
    Hague
USA: Monthly Review Press, New York

1509

LAW PACK PUBLISHING LTD
10–16 Cole Street, London SE1 4YH
Telephone: 0171 357 0367
Fax: 0171 357 0347
Email: lawpack@lawpack.co.uk
Web Site: http://www/lawpack.co.uk

Managing Director: Thomas Coles
Marketing Manager: Jamie Ross

Computer Science; Law

New Titles: 1 (1995), 10 (1996)
No of Employees: 4

ISBNs, Imprints & Series: 1 898217

Parent Company:
E–Z Legal Forms Inc *(USA)*

Distributor for:
USA: Garrett Publishing Inc

1510

**LAW SOCIETY PUBLICATIONS &
MULTIMEDIA**
50 Chancery Lane, London WC2A 1SX
Telephone: 0171 242 1222
Fax: 0171 404 1124

Head of Publications & Multimedia: Ruth
    Lawrence
Publisher: Carl Upsall
Managers: Debra Salvoni *(Projects)*
Liz Dawson *(Marketing & Distribution)*
Projects Editor: Angela Atcheson

Law

New Titles: 31 (1995), 30 (1996)
No of Employees: 18

ISBNs, Imprints & Series:
1 85328 The Law Society

Parent Company:
The Law Society

Book Trade Association Membership:
Director Publishers Association

1511

LAWRENCE & WISHART LTD
99a Wallis Road, London E9 5LN
Telephone: 0181 533 2506
Fax: 0181 533 7369

Distributors:
Central Books Ltd, 99 Wallis Road, London
E9 5LN
Telephone: 0181 986 4854
Fax: 0181 533 5821

Director: S. Davison *(Managing)*
Department Chief: Avis Greenaway
    (Permissions, Finance & Rights)
S. Williams *(Sales, Marketing Publicity)*

*Academic & Scholarly; Biography &
Autobiography; Economics; Educational &
Textbooks; Gay & Lesbian Studies; Gender
Studies; History & Antiquarian; Politics &
World Affairs; Marxism; Sexual Politics*

New Titles: 15 (1995), 20 (1996)
No of Employees: 3
Annual Turnover: £150,000

ISBNs, Imprints & Series: 0 85315

Overseas Representation *(see §7.3)*:
Australia & New Zealand: Peribo Pty Ltd,
    Mount Kuring-gai, NSW, Australia
Belgium: De Groene Waterman, Bercham
Canada: University of British Columbia Press,
    Vancouver, BC
India: T. R. Publications Pvt Ltd, Madras
Japan: Far Eastern Booksellers, Tokyo
Netherlands: Ruurd Ruward, Ruward BV, The
    Hague
Scandinavia: D. Richard Bowen, Malmö,
    Sweden

South Africa: Phambili Agencies (Jean Knopperson), Kensington
USA: Humanities Press International Inc, Atlantic Highlands, NJ

Book Trade Association Membership: IPG

1512 ▬▬▬▬▬▬▬▬▬

*LEADING EDGE PRESS & PUBLISHING
The Old Chapel, Burtersett, Hawes, North Yorks DL8 3PB
Telephone: 01969 677566
Fax: 01969 667788

Sales:
World Leisure Marketing Ltd, Downing Road, West Meadows Industrial Estate, Derby DE21 6HA
Telephone: 01332 343332
Fax: 01332 340464

Distribution:
Grantham Book Services Ltd,
Isaac Newton Way,
Alma Park Industrial Estate, Grantham, Lincs NG31 9SD
Telephone: 01476 67421
Fax: 01476 590223

Director: Stan Abbott *(Chairman)*
Editorial Manager: Barbara Allen
Company Secretary: Bridget Swann *(Sales)*

Architecture & Design; Do-It-Yourself; Guide Books; Natural History; Transport; Travel & Topography

ISBNs, Imprints & Series:
0 948135 Leading Edge Press & Publishing, RailTrail

Distributor for:
Transport for Leisure

Book Trade Association Membership: IPG, SPG

1513 ▬▬▬▬▬▬▬▬▬

LEARNING DEVELOPMENT AIDS (LDA)
Duke Street, Wisbech, Cambs PE13 2AE
Telephone: 01945 363441
Fax: 01945 587361

Editorial & Marketing:
Abbeygate House, East Road, Cambridge CB1 1DB
Telephone: 01223 357744
Fax: 01223 460557

Trade Enquiries & Orders:
Chris Lloyd Sales & Marketing,
463 Ashley Road, Parkstone, Poole, Dorset BH14 0AX
Telephone: 01202 715349
Fax: 01202 736191

Managing Director: Simon Lyne *(Exports & Rights)*
Product Development Manager: Joanne Browning Wroe

Children's Books; Educational & Textbooks; Gender Studies

No of Employees: 51

ISBNs, Imprints & Series:
0 905114, 1 85503 LDA

Parent Company:
Living & Learning (Cambridge) Ltd

Associated & Subsidiary Companies:
Educational Software for Microcomputers (ESM); Living & Learning. *USA:* Living & Learning Inc

Distributor for:
France: Nathan. *Germany:* Sensor Verlag. *Switzerland:* Schubi. *USA:* Cuisenaire Co of America; Learning Resources

Overseas Representation *(see §7.3)*:
Australia: The Educational Experience Pty Ltd, Newcastle, NSW
Austria: Der Spielzeugmacher, St Georgen
Barbados: Quest, Christ Church
Belgium: Baert Sprl, Brussels
Canada: Quality International, Scarborough, Ont; Louise Kool & Galt Ltd, Scarborough, Ont
Denmark: Forlaget Gonge, Braband
Finland: Early Learning OY, Helsinki
France: Mot a Mot, Paris
Germany: Verlag An der Ruhr, Mülheim
Greece: Andreas Leon, Athens
Hong Kong: Artsberg Enterprises Ltd
Iceland: Err Namsgogn, Varma; Namsgagnastofnun, Reykjavik
Irish Republic: K. & M. Evans, Dublin; Surgisales Teaching Aids, Dublin; International Education Service, Leixlip
Israel: Applegames Educational Games & Learning Materials, Holon
Italy: La Favelliana, Milan; Edizioni Centro Studio Erickson, Trento
Malaysia: BMEC Rehab (M) Sdn Bhd, Petaling Jaya
Malta: Royal Trading Agency, Valletta
Netherlands: Dalcomtext, Paterswolde; Swets & Zeitlinger bv, Lisse
Norway: Okani Laermidler, Bergen
Portugal: PSICO, Lisbon; ABACO, Lisbon
Puerto Rico: Camera Mundi Inc, Caguas
Singapore: Didacta; Smart Kids Pte Ltd
South Africa: Play & Schoolroom Pty, Parklands; Educational Toy Centre, Johannesburg
Spain: Distesa, Madrid
Sweden: Playing & Learning, Danderyd; Beta Pedagog, Skällinge
Thailand: Productivity Corp Ltd, Bangkok
USA: Didax, Peabody, MA; Living & Learning Inc, Salem, OR

Book Trade Association Membership: IPG, BESA

1514 ▬▬▬▬▬▬▬▬▬

LEARNING TOGETHER
18 Shandon Park, Belfast BT5 6NW
Telephone: 01232 402086

Distributors:
Biblios Publisher's Distribution Services Ltd, Star Road, Partridge Green, West Sussex RH13 8LD
Telephone: 01403 710971
Fax: 01403 711143

Managing Director: Janet McConkey
Author/Publisher: Stephen McConkey

Educational & Textbooks

New Titles: 1 (1995)
No of Employees: 2
Annual Turnover: £46,000

ISBNs, Imprints & Series:
1 873385 Practice Tests In Series

Book Trade Association Membership: PA

1515 ▬▬▬▬▬▬▬▬▬

LEGAL ACTION GROUP
242 Pentonville Road, London N1 9UN
Telephone: 0171 833 2931
Fax: 0171 837 6094
Email: lag@online.rednet.co.uk

Director: Roger Smith
Managers: Jonathan Pearce *(Publisher)*
James Lamb *(Editorial)*
Stephen Davies *(Finance & Distribution)*
Fiona Razvi *(Marketing)*

Law

New Titles: 8 (1995), 10 (1996)
No of Employees: 12

ISBNs, Imprints & Series: 0 905099

Book Trade Association Membership: IPG

1516 ▬▬▬▬▬▬▬▬▬

LEICESTER UNIVERSITY PRESS
Wellington House, 125 Strand, London WC2R 0BB
Telephone: 0171 420 5555
Fax: 0171 240 7261

Distribution:
see Cassell Plc

Directors: Janet Joyce *(Publishing)*
Ruth McCurry *(UK Sales)*
Managers: Catherine Johnston *(Promotion)*
Rebecca Seymour *(Export Sales)*

Academic & Scholarly; Archaeology; History & Antiquarian; Politics & World Affairs; Art Theory; Communication Studies; Cultural Studies; Museum Studies

New Titles: 40 (1995), 40 (1996)

ISBNs, Imprints & Series: 0 7185

Parent Company:
Cassell Plc

Overseas Representation *(see §7.3)*:
see: Cassell Plc, UK

1517 ▬▬▬▬▬▬▬▬▬

LEMOS & CRANE
20 Pond Square, Highgate, London N6 6BA
Telephone: 0181 348 8263
Fax: 0181 347 5740
Email: admin@lemos.demon.co.uk

Warehouse:
Vale Packaging, 420 Vale Road, Tonbridge,
Kent TN9 1TD
Telephone: 01732 359387
Fax: 01732 770620

Partners: Gerard Lemos
Paul Crane

*Educational & Textbooks; Industry, Business &
Management; Law; Reference Books,
Directories & Dictionaries*

New Titles: 4 (1995), 12 (1996)
No of Employees: 3

ISBNs, Imprints & Series: 1 898001

Book Trade Association Membership: IPG

1518 ■■■■

LETTERLAND INTERNATIONAL LTD
Barton, Cambridge CB3 7AY
Telephone: 01223 262675
Fax: 01223 264126

Distribution:
HarperCollins Publishers Ltd, 77-
85 Fulham Palace Road, London W6 8JB
Telephone: 0181 741 7070
Fax: 0181 307 4440

Director: John Wendon

*Children's Books; Educational & Textbooks;
Electronic (Educational); Sports & Games*

ISBNs, Imprints & Series: 0 907345

Overseas Representation *(see §7.3):*
Australia: Ed Source, Bayswater, WA;
    Australian Special Book Service, Kew, Vic;
    Learning Logic, Canterbury, Vic; Readright
    Educational Services, Thornleigh, NSW
New Zealand: Wardell Educational Services,
    Manurewa; Oakdale Trading Ltd, Upper
    Hutt
South Africa: Educational Ideas, Johannesburg
USA: ABC Educators, Norfolk, VA

Book Trade Association Membership: PA,
EPC

1519 ■■■■

LETTERMEN PUBLISHING LTD
9 Tideway Yard, Mortlake High Street, London
SW14 8SN
Telephone: 0181 876 7622
Fax: 0181 392 2975

Sales:
Derek Searle Associates, The Coach House,
Cippenham Lodge, Cippenham Lane, Slough,
Berks SL1 5AN
Telephone: 01753 539295
Fax: 01753 551863

Directors: Simon Fearnehough *(Home &
    Export Sales, Rights)*
Roger Knights *(Author)*

Children's Books

New Titles: 6 (1995), 12 (1996)
No of Employees: 2
Annual Turnover: £150,000

ISBNs, Imprints & Series: 0 948535

1520 ■■■■

LEVINSON BOOKS LTD
Greenland Place, 115–123 Bayham Street,
London NW1 0AG
Telephone: 0171 424 0488
Fax: 0171 424 0499

Trade Sales & Distribution:
Ragged Bears Ltd, Ragged Appleshaw,
Andover, Hants SP11 9HX
Telephone: 01264 772269
Fax: 01264 772391

Directors: Joanna Levinson *(Managing)*
Louise Miller *(Art)*
Sales Managers: Neil Burden
Linda Watters
Senior Editor: Kate Burns

Children's Books

New Titles: 5 (1995), 30 (1996)
No of Employees: 12

ISBNs, Imprints & Series: 1 899607

1521 ■■■■

LEVINSON CHILDREN'S BOOKS LTD
Greenland Place, 115–123 Bayham Street,
London NW1 0AG
Telephone: 0171 424 0488
Fax: 0171 424 0499

Senior Editor: Kate Burns
International Sales: Alison Morris
Managers: Neil Burden *(Sales)*
Graham Cook *(Production)*

Children's Books

New Titles: 5 (1995), 34 (1996)
No of Employees: 12

ISBNs, Imprints & Series: 1 899607

Distributor for:
Levinson Books

Overseas Representation *(see §7.3):*
*South Africa, Irish Republic, Netherlands &
    Far East:* Ragged Bears Ltd, Andover, UK

1522 ■■■■

JOHN LIBBEY & COMPANY LTD
13 Smiths Yard, Summerley Street, London
SW18 4HR
Telephone: 0181 947 2777
Fax: 0181 947 2664
Email: libbey@earlsfield.win-uk.net

Distributor:
Faber & Faber Ltd, Burnt Mill, Elizabeth Way,
Harlow, Essex CM20 2HX
Telephone: 01279 417134
Fax: 01279 417366

Directors: John Libbey *(Managing)*
Gilles Cahn

Editorial & Rights: Dr Andy Colborne
Marketing & Sales: Angie Needs

*Cinema, Video, TV & Radio; Medical (incl. Self
Help & Alternative Medicine)*

New Titles: 12 (1995), 10 (1996)
No of Employees: 12

ISBNs, Imprints & Series: 0 86196

Associated & Subsidiary Companies:
Australia: John Libbey & Co Pty Ltd. *France:*
John Libbey Eurotext Ltd. *Italy:* John Libbey
CIC srl

Overseas Representation *(see §7.3):*
Australia, New Zealand & Papua New Guinea:
    DA Information Services, Mitcham, Vic,
    Australia
France: John Libbey Eurotext Ltd, Montrouge
Italy: John Libbey CIC Srl, Rome
USA: Books International Inc, Herndon, VA

1523 ■■■■

**LIBRARY & INFORMATION
STATISTICS UNIT (LISU)**
Loughborough University, Loughborough,
Leics LE11 3TU
Telephone: 01509 223071
Fax: 01509 223072
Email: lisu@lboro.ac.uk
Web Site: http://info.lboro.ac.uk/departments/
dils/lisu/lisuhp.html

Director: John W. Sumsion

Bibliography & Library Science

New Titles: 4 (1995), 5 (1996)
No of Employees: 5

ISBNs, Imprints & Series:
0 948848 LISU Reports

Parent Company:
Loughborough University

1524 ■■■■

LIBRARY ASSOCIATION PUBLISHING
7 Ridgmount Street, London WC1E 7AE
Telephone: 0171 636 7543
Fax: 0171 636 3627
Email: lapublishers@la-hq.org.uk

Warehouse:
Bookpoint Ltd, 39 Milton Park, Abingdon,
Oxon OX14 4TD
Telephone: 01235 400400
Fax: 01235 832068 & 861038

Managing Director: Janet Liebster
Managers: Kathryn Beecroft *(Production)*
Rohini Ramachandran *(Sales)*
Publisher: Helen Carley
Marketing Executive: Anna Tamar Thame

*Bibliography & Library Science; Reference
Books, Directories & Dictionaries*

New Titles: 19 (1995), 39 (1996)
No of Employees: 7

ISBNs, Imprints & Series:
0 85157, 1 85604 Clive Bingley Ltd

0 85365, 1 85604 Library Association
Publishing Ltd

Parent Company:
The Library Association

Associated & Subsidiary Companies:
Clive Bingley Ltd

Distributor for:
Canada: Canadian Library Association

Overseas Representation *(see §7.3):*
Australia & New Zealand: James Bennett Pty
Ltd, Collaroy Beach, NSW, Australia
Canada & USA: Unipub, Lanham, MD, USA
Europe: Andrew B. Durnell, Tunbridge Wells,
UK
Japan: United Publishers Services Ltd, Tokyo
Scandinavia: D. Richard Bowen, Malmö,
Sweden
Singapore, Malaysia, Indonesia & Indochina:
Gower Asia Pacific Pte Ltd, Singapore
South Africa: Libriger Book Distributors,
Bloemfontein
Spain & Portugal: Iberian Book Services SL,
Madrid, Spain
Taiwan, Hong Kong, Korea & Philippines:
Toppan Co (S) Pte Ltd, Singapore

Book Trade Association Membership: PA,
CAPP

1525 ▬▬▬

FRANCES LINCOLN LTD
4 Torriano Mews, Torriano Avenue, London
NW5 2RZ
Telephone: 0171 284 4009
Fax: 0171 485 0490

Warehouse, Trade Enquiries & Orders:
Bookpoint Ltd, 39 Milton Park, Abingdon,
Oxon OX14 4TD
Telephone: 01235 400400
Fax: 01235 861038

Directors: Frances Lincoln *(Managing)*
Nicky Bowden *(Production & Deputy
Managing)*
Erica Hunnigher *(Editorial – Adult Books)*
Janetta Otter-Barry *(Editorial – Children's
Books)*
Caroline Hillier *(Art – Adult Books)*
Judith Escreet *(Art – Children's Books)*
Paula Saunders *(Sales – UK, Australia, N
Zealand, S Africa, Canada, Far East &
Export)*
Katherine Judge *(US Rights)*
Managers: Sara Borthwick *(Business)*
Sarah Roberts *(Finance)*
Claire Nozières *(Foreign Rights)*
Elspeth Greig *(UK Sales)*
Avril Litchmore *(Production)*
Andrea Shallcross *(Contracts & Permissions)*

*Children's Books; Crafts & Hobbies;
Gardening; Health & Beauty; History &
Antiquarian*

New Titles: 50 (1995), 60 (1996)
No of Employees: 40

ISBNs, Imprints & Series: 0 7112

Distributor for:
Cover to Cover Cassettes Ltd

Overseas Representation *(see §7.3):*
All countries other than those listed: Frances
Lincoln, London, UK
Australia: Peribo Pty Ltd, Mount Kuring-gai,
NSW
New Zealand: Forrester Books Ltd, Auckland
South Africa: Struik Book Distributors Pty Ltd,
Johannesburg, Cape Town & Maitland

1526 ▬▬▬

LINGUAPHONE INSTITUTE LTD
St Giles House, 50 Poland Street, London
W1V 4AX
Telephone: 0171 287 4050
Fax: 0171 734 0469

Warehouse:
Bartholomews Distribution Services,
Woodside Road,
Boyatt Wood Industrial Estate, Eastleigh, Hants
SO5 5XZ
Telephone: Eastleigh 01703 629369
Fax: 01703 650117

Directors: Timothy Sherwen *(Executive
Chairman)*
Peter Peacock *(Managing)*

*Educational & Textbooks; English as a Foreign
Language; Industry, Business & Management;
Languages & Linguistics*

New Titles: 52 (1995), 15 (1996)
No of Employees: 50
Annual Turnover: £14M

ISBNs, Imprints & Series: 0 85320

Parent Company:
Centaur Communications Ltd

Associated & Subsidiary Companies:
Hong Kong: Linguaphone Institute (Hong
Kong) Ltd. *Japan:* Linguaphone Japan KK.
Malaysia: Linguapac Distributors Pte Ltd.
Singapore: Linguapac Distributors Pte Ltd

1527 ▬▬▬

LION PUBLISHING PLC
Peter's Way, Sandy Lane West, Oxford
OX4 5HG
Telephone: 01865 747550
Fax: 01865 747568

Directors: David Alexander
Mark Beedell *(Managing)*
Pat Alexander
Rebecca Winter *(Publishing)*
Tony Wales *(International)*
Denis Cole
Sales Managers: Colin Nutt *(UK Sales)*
Robert Wendover *(Export Sales)*
Accountant: Dy Leyland
International Rights: Paul Whitton
Subsidiary Rights: Philip Henderson
Production: Charles Wallis

*Children's Books; Educational & Textbooks;
Electronic (Educational); Religion & Theology*

New Titles: 105 (1995), 95 (1996)
No of Employees: 102
Annual Turnover: £6.7M

ISBNs, Imprints & Series:
0 7459, 0 85648 Aslan, Lion, Lion Library,
Lion Manuals, Little Lions, Young Lions

Associated & Subsidiary Companies:
USA: Lion Publishing Corp

Distributor for:
Australia: Albatross Books

Overseas Representation *(see §7.3):*
Australia: Albatross Books Pty Ltd, Sutherland
South Africa: Struik Book Distributors Pty Ltd,
Johannesburg, Cape Town & Maitland

Book Trade Association Membership: PA,
BDC, EPC

1528 ▬▬▬

*LITTLE, BROWN & CO (UK)
Brettenham House, Lancaster Place, London
WC2E 7EN
Telephone: 0171 911 8000
Fax: 0171 911 8100

Distribution Centre:
Tiptree Book Services Ltd, Church Road,
Tiptree, Colchester, Essex CO5 0SR
Telephone: 01621 816362 & 819600 (Orders)
Fax: 01621 819011 & 819717 (Orders)

Directors: Philippa Harrison *(Managing)*
Nigel Batt *(Finance)*
Alan Samson *(Publishing)*
Barbara Boote *(Publishing)*
David Kent *(Home Sales)*
Nann du Sautoy *(Rights)*
Terry Jackson *(Group Marketing)*
Charles Viney *(Export Sales)*
Jane Warren *(Marketing)*
Peter Cotton *(Art)*
Rosalie MacFarlane *(Publicity)*
Pat James *(Permissions)*
Managers: Christina Macphail *(Export Sales)*
Hilary Hale *(Little, Brown/Warner)*
Vivien Bowler *(Illustrated)*
Richard Beswick *(Abacus)*
Kathy Law *(Sales Administration)*
Imogen Taylor *(Little, Brown/Warner)*
Liz Mammat *(Bibliographic)*

*Biography & Autobiography; Children's
Books; Cookery, Wines & Spirits; Crime;
Crafts & Hobbies; Fiction; Gardening; Health
& Beauty; Humour; Illustrated & Fine
Editions; Photography; Science Fiction*

ISBNs, Imprints & Series:
0 316 Little, Brown
0 349 Abacus
0 7515 Warner
0 8212 Bulfinch
0 8487 Sunset
1 85723 Orbit
1 85823 Warner-Futura

Parent Company:
Little, Brown & Co Inc *(USA)*

Overseas Representation *(see §7.3):*
Australia: Penguin Books Australia Ltd,
Ringwood, Vic
*Belgium, Luxembourg, Scandinavia, Eastern
Europe, Gibraltar, Malta & Portugal:*
Penguin Books Ltd, London, UK

Canada: Little Brown & Co (Canada) Ltd,
Toronto
*Central America, Caribbean, East Africa,
Korea, Philippines, Sri Lanka & South
America:* Little Brown & Co, London, UK
France: Penguin Books Ltd, Toulouse
Germany & Austria: Penguin Books
Deutschland GmbH, Frankfurt, Germany
Greece, Israel, Turkey & Cyprus: Penguin
Hellas Ltd, Athens, Greece
Hong Kong: Far East Media Ltd
India: India Book Distributors, Bombay
Israel: Steimatzky Ltd, Bnei Brak
Italy: Penguin Italia Srl, Milan
Japan: Charles E. Tuttle Co Inc, Kanagawa
Malta: Audio Visual Centre Ltd, Sliema
Middle East: Ashton International Marketing
Services, Larkfield, UK
Netherlands: Penguin Books Netherlands bv,
Amsterdam
New Zealand: Penguin Books (New Zealand)
Ltd, Auckland
Pakistan: Liberty Books (Pvt) Ltd, Karachi
Singapore & Malaysia: MPH Distributors (S)
Pte Ltd, Singapore
South Africa: Macdonald Purnell (Pty) Ltd,
Cleveland
Spain: Penguin Books SA, Madrid
Switzerland: OLF SA, Fribourg
Thailand: Asia Book Co, Bangkok

Book Trade Association Membership: PA,
Book Marketing Ltd

1529

**THE LITTMAN LIBRARY OF JEWISH
CIVILIZATION**
PO Box 645, Oxford OX2 6AS
Telephone: 01235 868104
Fax: 01235 868104

Distribution:
Biblios Publishers' Distribution Services,
Star Road, Partridge Green, West Sussex
RH13 8LD
Telephone: 01403 710971
Fax: 01403 711143

UK Representation:
Frank Cass, Newbury House,
899–900 Eastern Avenue, Newbury Park,
Ilford, Essex IG2 7HH
Telephone: 0181 599 8866
Fax: 0181 599 0984
Email: littman@frankcass.com
Web Site: http://www.frankcass.com

Managing Editor: Connie Wilsack *(Editorial
& Rights)*
Directors: Ludo Craddock
Colette Littman
Robert Littman

*Academic & Scholarly; Biography &
Autobiography; Educational & Textbooks;
History & Antiquarian; Literature & Criticism;
Music; Philosophy; Politics & World Affairs;
Religion & Theology; Sociology &
Anthropology*

New Titles: 7 (1996)

ISBNs, Imprints & Series:
0 19, 1 874774 Littman Library of Jewish
Civilization
0 631 Polin Series

Overseas Representation *(see §7.3):*
Australia & New Zealand: Judaica Direct,
North Sydney, NSW, Australia
Israel: Sefer Ve Sefel, Jerusalem
USA & Canada: ISBS, Portland, OR, USA

1530

LIVERPOOL UNIVERSITY PRESS
PO Box 147, Liverpool L69 3BX
Telephone: 0151 794 2233
Fax: 0151 794 2235

Sales & Distribution:
Burston Distribution Services, Unit 2A,
Newbridge Trading Estate, Newbridge Close,
off Whitby Road, Bristol BS4 4AX
Telephone: 0117 972 4248
Fax: 0117 971 1056

Publisher: Robin Bloxsidge
Production Editor: Julie Rainford
Promotion Co-ordinator: Sandra Robinson

*Academic & Scholarly; Archaeology;
Architecture & Design; Educational &
Textbooks; Fine Art & Art History; Geography
& Geology; History & Antiquarian; Literature
& Criticism; Religion & Theology; Science
Fiction; Sociology & Anthropology; Veterinary
Science*

New Titles: 30 (1995), 40 (1996)
No of Employees: 4

ISBNs, Imprints & Series: 0 85323

Distributor for:
Australia: Fremantle Arts Centre Press;
Macquarrie University Ancient History
Documentary Research Centre. *Canada:*
Dovehouse Editions Inc

Overseas Representation *(see §7.3):*
Far East (excluding Japan): STM Publishing
Services Pte Ltd, Singapore
Scandinavia & Iceland: D. Richard Bowen,
Malmö, Sweden

Book Trade Association Membership: PA,
CAPP

1531

LLANERCH PUBLISHERS
Llanerch, Felinfach, Lampeter, Dyfed
SA48 8PJ
Telephone: 01570 470567
Fax: 01570 470567

Proprietor: D. Bryce

*Academic & Scholarly; Archaeology; History
& Antiquarian; Philosophy; Poetry; Religion
& Theology; Oriental (Chinese Philosophy/
Mysticism)*

ISBNs, Imprints & Series:
0 947992, 1 897853

1532

LLOYD'S REGISTER OF SHIPPING
71 Fenchurch Street, London EC3M 4BS
Telephone: 0171 709 9166
Fax: 0171 488 4796

Managers: R. M. Lewell
G. N. White *(Deputy)*
C. J. Dean *(Assistant)*

*Archaeology; Engineering; History &
Antiquarian; Mathematics & Statistics;
Nautical; Scientific & Technical; Transport*

ISBNs, Imprints & Series:
0 076, 0 141, 0 260, 0 261, 0 264, 0 268
0 900, 0 963

Overseas Representation *(see §7.3):*
USA: Lloyd's Register of Shipping, New York,
NY

Book Trade Association Membership: PA

1533

LLP LTD
Sheepen Place, Colchester, Essex CO3 3LP
Telephone: 01206 772277
Fax: 01206 772880

London Office:
One Singer Street, London EC2A 4LQ
Telephone: 0171 250 1500
Fax: 0171 250 0660

Group Chief Executive: I. Lindsay-Smith
Directors: P. Miller *(Finance)*
D. Lodge *(Central Resources)*
D. Winter *(Systems & Communications)*
K. Brownlie *(Personnel)*
D. Gilbertson *(Deputy Managing)*
J. Cramp *(Legal Publishing)*
J. Quilter *(Chief Executive, Lloyd's List
Publishing)*
B. Waller *(International Sales)*

*Atlases & Maps; Aviation; Economics;
Educational & Textbooks; Electronic
(Professional & Academic); Industry, Business
& Management; Law; Reference Books,
Directories & Dictionaries; Transport*

New Titles: 37 (1995), 43 (1996)
No of Employees: 420

ISBNs, Imprints & Series: 1 85044

Associated & Subsidiary Companies:
Hong Kong: LLP (Asia) Ltd. *USA:* LLP Inc

Overseas Representation *(see §7.3):*
Hong Kong: LLP (Asia) Ltd
USA: LLP Inc, New York

Book Trade Association Membership: PA,
British Directory Publishers Association,
European Directory Publishers Association,
Periodical Publishers Association

1534

HOUSE OF LOCHAR
Isle of Colonsay, Argyll PA61 7YR
Telephone: 01951 200232
Fax: 01951 200232
Email: 100676.623@compuserve.com

Scottish Trade Representation:
SEOL Ltd, 14 High Street, Edinburgh EH1 1TE
Telephone: 0131 558 1500
Fax: 0131 558 1500

Principal: Kevin Byrne
Manager: Georgina Hobhouse *(Manager)*
Sales: Hugh Andrew

History & Antiquarian; Transport; Travel & Topography; Scottish Non-fiction

New Titles: 6 (1995), 8 (1996)
No of Employees: 3
Annual Turnover: £90,000

ISBNs, Imprints & Series: 1 899863

Book Trade Association Membership:
Scottish PA

1535

BARRY LONG BOOKS
42 North Street, Wiveliscombe, Somerset
TA4 2UJ
Telephone: 01984 623426
Fax: 01984 624446

Trade Enquiries & Orders:
Ashgrove Press, 7 Locksbrook Road Estate,
Bath BA1 3DZ
Telephone: 01225 425539
Fax: 01225 319137

Managing Editor: Clive Tempest
Managers: Lina Lotto *(Marketing)*
Neal Bowhay *(Production)*
Finance: Simon Campbell

Audio Books; Philosophy

New Titles: 6 (1995), 8 (1996)
No of Employees: 6

ISBNs, Imprints & Series:
0 9508050, 1 899324

Parent Company:
The Barry Long Foundation

Overseas Representation *(see §7.3):*
USA: Warwick Associates, Sonoma, CA

Book Trade Association Membership: IPG

1536

LUATH PRESS LTD
Barr, Ayrshire KA26 9TN
Telephone: 01465 861636
Fax: 01465 861625

Directors: Mrs R. Atkinson *(Sales)*
T. W. Atkinson *(Managing, Editorial)*

Biography & Autobiography; Fiction; Guide Books; Poetry; Travel & Topography

New Titles: 4 (1995), 4 (1996)
No of Employees: 4
Annual Turnover: £150,000

ISBNs, Imprints & Series:
0 946487 The Blew Blanket Library, Guides to
the West of Scotland

Book Trade Association Membership: PA,
Scottish PA

1537

LUND HUMPHRIES PUBLISHERS LTD
Park House, 1 Russell Gardens, London
NW11 9NN
Telephone: 0181 458 6314
Fax: 0181 905 5245

Trade Distribution:
Bookpoint Ltd, 39 Milton Park, Abingdon,
Oxon OX14 4TD
Telephone: 01235 835001
Fax: 01235 832068

Director: Lionel Leventhal
Editorial Consultant: John Taylor
Editorial Director: Lucy Myers
Manager: Mark Wray *(Sales)*

*Academic & Scholarly; Antiques & Collecting;
Architecture & Design; Fine Art & Art History;
Languages & Linguistics*

New Titles: 24 (1995), 29 (1996)

ISBNs, Imprints & Series: 0 85331

Distributor for:
Canada: Hartley & Marks

Overseas Representation *(see §7.3):*
Australia: Peribo Pty Ltd, Mount Kuring-gai,
NSW
Belgium: Exhibitions International, Leuven
*Finland, Sweden, Norway, Denmark &
Iceland:* Hanne Rotovnik, Klampenborg,
Denmark
France: Lund Humphries Publ., London, UK
Germany, Austria, Switzerland & Belgium: Ted
Dougherty, London, UK
Greece, Italy & Yugoslavia: Juliusz
Komarnicki, Massagno, Switzerland
Japan: United Publishers Services Ltd, Tokyo
Netherlands: Consul Books, Blaricum
New Zealand: South Pacific Books (Imports)
Ltd, Auckland
South Africa: Book Services International,
Sandton
Spain, Portugal & Gibraltar: Patrick Bygate,
Massagno, Switzerland

1538

THE LUTTERWORTH PRESS
PO Box 60, Cambridge CB1 2NT
Telephone: 01223 350865
Fax: 01223 366951
Email: lutterworth.pr@dial.pipex.com

Managing Director: Adrian Brink *(Rights)*
Managers: Colin Lester *(Sales)*
Chris Bates *(Accounts)*
Teresine Milnes
Customer Service: Christine Hutchinson
Production: Ken Johnson

*Academic & Scholarly; Animal Care &
Breeding; Antiques & Collecting; Architecture
& Design; Bibliography & Library Science;
Biography & Autobiography; Biology &
Zoology; Children's Books; Crafts & Hobbies;
Educational & Textbooks; Fine Art & Art
History; Illustrated & Fine Editions; Military
& War; Natural History; Religion & Theology;
Sports & Games*

New Titles: 14 (1995), 15 (1996)
No of Employees: 7

ISBNs, Imprints & Series:
0 7188 The Lutterworth Press
0 7444 Patrick Hardy

Parent Company:
James Clarke & Co Ltd

Overseas Representation *(see §7.3):*
Australia: Keith Ainsworth Pty Ltd, Penrith,
NSW
New Zealand (religious books only): Catholic
Supplies (NZ) Ltd, Wellington, New Zealand
Spain & Portugal: Iberian Book Services SL,
Madrid, Spain

Book Trade Association Membership: PA,
BDC, EPC, CAPP

1539

*LYLE PUBLICATIONS LTD
Glenmayne, Galashiels TD1 3NR
Telephone: 01896 752005
Fax: 01896 754696

Managing Director: Tony Curtis

Antiques & Collecting

ISBNs, Imprints & Series: 0 86248

Book Trade Association Membership: PA

1540

LYRIC BOOKS LTD
Central House, 7–8 Ritz Parade, London
W5 3RA
Telephone: 0181 810 6111
Fax: 0181 566 9666

Distribution:
Biblios Publishers Distribution Services Ltd,
Star Road, Partridge Green, West Sussex
RH13 8LD
Telephone: 01403 710971
Fax: 01403 711143

Director: David Moeller *(Managing)*

Crafts & Hobbies

New Titles: 12 (1995)

ISBNs, Imprints & Series:
0 7111 Harmony Guides

1541

MACDONALD YOUNG BOOKS
61 Western Road, Hove, East Sussex BN3 1JD
Telephone: 01273 722561
Fax: 01273 723526

Warehouse:
Bailey Bros Distribution Ltd, Unit 1A/
1B Learoyd Road, Mountfield Industrial Estate,
New Romney, Kent TN28 8XU
Telephone: 01797 366905
Fax: 01797 366638

General Manager: Roberta Bailey
Directors: Nigel Padbury *(Finance)*
Michael McWhinne *(Sales Development)*

Phil Hughes *(Production)*
Steve White-Thomson *(Editorial)*
Export Sales Executive: Oonagh Gretton
Marketing Executive: Naomi Cooper
Foreign Rights Manager: Jane Ward

Children's Books

New Titles: 352 (1995), 270 (1996)
No of Employees: 79
Annual Turnover: £9.5M

ISBNs, Imprints & Series:
0 7500 Macdonald Young Books
0 7502 Wayland Publishers

Parent Company:
Wolters Kluwer NV *(Netherlands)*

Overseas Representation *(see §7.3):*
Australia: Lothian Books, Port Melbourne
Canada: Nelson Canada, Scarborough
Caribbean: Humphrys Roberts Associates,
London, UK
Egypt: International Language Bookshop, Giza
Hong Kong: Federal Publications (HK) Ltd,
Kowloon
Irish Republic: Gill & Macmillan Ltd, Dublin
Kuwait: Al Lugain Co, Salmiya
Lebanon: Universal Book House for Print &
Distribution, Saida
Malaysia: Publishers Marketing Services,
Petaling Jaya
New Zealand: Forrester Books Ltd, Auckland
*Papua New Guinea, Solomon Islands, Vanuatu,
Fiji & Tonga:* La Galamo Office & School
Supplies Pty Ltd, Lae, Papua New Guinea
Philippines, Taiwan, South Korea & Japan:
Combined Representatives Worldwide Inc,
Rizal, Philippines
Singapore, Brunei & Indonesia: Publishers
Marketing Services Ltd, Singapore
South Africa: Southern Book Publishers,
Halfway House
*Western Europe (excluding Scandinavia &
Greece):* Michael Geoghegan, London, UK

Book Trade Association Membership: PA,
EPC

1542 ▬▬▬▬▬▬

McGRAW-HILL PUBLISHING CO
Shoppenhangers Road, Maidenhead, Berks
SL6 2QL
Telephone: 01628 23432
Fax: 01628 35895 & 770224

Directors: Fred Perkins *(Managing & Group
Vice President Europe)*
Steven Gardiner *(Production)*
Peter Kitley *(Financial & Administrative)*
Carolyn Hird *(Trade & Professional
Publishing)*
Andrew Phillips *(Educational Publishing)*
Brian Newson *(Operations)*
Managers: (to be appointed) *(University &
College Marketing)*
Lawrence Mitchell *(Professional & Reference
Marketing)*

*Academic & Scholarly; Accountancy &
Taxation; Architecture & Design; Biology &
Zoology; Chemistry; Computer Science;
Economics; Educational & Textbooks;
Electronic (Educational); Electronic
(Professional & Academic); Engineering;*

*Geography & Geology; Industry, Business &
Management; Mathematics & Statistics;
Medical (incl. Self Help & Alternative
Medicine); Physics; Politics & World Affairs;
Psychology & Psychiatry; Reference Books,
Directories & Dictionaries; Scientific &
Technical; Sociology & Anthropology;
Transport; Vocational Training & Careers*

ISBNs, Imprints & Series: 0 07

Parent Company:
McGraw-Hill Inc *(USA)*

Associated & Subsidiary Companies:
Australia: McGraw-Hill Book Co Australia Pty
Ltd. *Canada:* McGraw-Hill Ryerson Ltd.
Colombia: McGraw-Hill/InterAmericana
(Colombia) SA. *India:* Tata-McGraw-Hill
Publishing Co Ltd. *Italy:* McGraw-Hill Libri
Italia srl. *Japan:* McGraw-Hill Book Co.
Mexico: Libros McGraw-Hill de Mexico SA de
CV. *Portugal:* McGraw-Hill/Interamericana de
Portugal Ltda. *Singapore:* McGraw-Hill
International Book Co. *Spain:* McGraw-Hill/
Interamericana de España SA. *USA:* Osborne
TAB. *Venezuela:* McGraw-Hill/
InterAmericana (Venezuela) SA

Distributor for:
USA: Amacom; Berrett-Koehler; Harvard
Business School Press; World Trade Press

Book Trade Association Membership: PA,
BA

1543 ▬▬▬▬▬▬

MACMILLAN CHILDREN'S BOOKS
Brunel Road, Houndmills, Basingstoke, Hants
RG21 6XS
Telephone: 0171 881 8000
Fax: 0171 881 8001

Trade Enquiries:
Houndmills, Basingstoke, Hants RG21 2YT
Telephone: 01256 464481
Fax: 01256 460675

Directors: A. Soar *(Chairman)*
Kate Wilson *(Executive)*
David North *(Sales)*
Susie Gibbs *(Editorial–Non-Fiction)*

Children's Books

New Titles: 200 (1995), 200 (1996)

ISBNs, Imprints & Series:
0 330, 0 333 Campbell Books, Macmillan
Children's Books, Pan Books

Parent Company:
Macmillan Ltd

Book Trade Association Membership:
Children's Book Circle, PA Children's Book
Group

1544 ▬▬▬▬▬▬

MACMILLAN EDUCATION LTD
Houndmills, Basingstoke, Hants RG21 6XS
Telephone: 01256 29242
Fax: 01256 814642

Chairman: A. Soar
Directors: Christopher Harrison *(Managing)*
Alison Hubert *(Publishing)*
Richard Hartgill *(Finance)*
Christopher West *(Latin America)*
John Peacock *(Production)*
John Watson *(Marketing)*
Christopher Paterson
Company Secretary: M. E. Powter

*Academic & Scholarly; Animal Care &
Breeding; Atlases & Maps; Bibliography &
Library Science; Biography & Autobiography;
Biology & Zoology; Chemistry; Children's
Books; Cinema, Video, TV & Radio; Computer
Science; Economics; Educational &
Textbooks; English as a Foreign Language;
Environment & Development Studies; Fiction;
Geography & Geology; Guide Books; History
& Antiquarian; Languages & Linguistics;
Literature & Criticism; Mathematics &
Statistics; Medical (incl. Self Help &
Alternative Medicine); Physics; Poetry;
Reference Books, Directories & Dictionaries;
Religion & Theology; Veterinary Science*

New Titles: 200 (1995), 200 (1996)

ISBNs, Imprints & Series: 0 333

Parent Company:
Holtzbrinck Publishers Holdings Ltd

Associated & Subsidiary Companies:
Macmillan General Books Ltd; Macmillan
Press Ltd; Macmillan Publishers Ltd. *USA:*
Stockton Press Inc

Overseas Representation *(see §7.3):*
See: Macmillan Publishers Ltd, Basingstoke,
UK

Book Trade Association Membership: PA

1545 ▬▬▬▬▬▬

MACMILLAN GENERAL BOOKS LTD
25 Eccleston Place, London SW1W 9NF
Telephone: 0171 881 8000
Fax: 0171 881 8001
Email: books@macmillan.co.uk

Warehouse, Trade Enquiries & Orders:
Macmillan Distribution Ltd, Houndmills,
Basingstoke, Hants RG21 6XS
Telephone: 01256 24292
Fax: 01256 842084
Email: mdl@macmillan.co.uk

Directors: A. Soar *(Chairman)*
I. S. Chapman *(Managing)*
D. North *(Sales)*
R. Gibb *(Australia)*
I. J. Metcalfe *(Financial)*
C. Gibson *(Production)*
P. Straus *(Editor-in-chief)*
S. Baboneau *(Executive Publisher)*
Ms F. Carpenter *(Art)*
Ms M. Rejt *(Macmillan Publishing)*
J. Riley *(Literary Publishing)*
Ms M. Fry *(Marketing)*
Jeremy Trevathan *(Rights)*
Associate Directors: Ms G. Morley *(Non-
fiction)*
P. Lavery *(Fiction)*

Cinema, Video, TV & Radio; Fiction;
Gardening; Guide Books; Health & Beauty;
History & Antiquarian; Literature & Criticism;
Science Fiction; Sports & Games; Travel &
Topography

New Titles: 600 (1995), 600 (1996)

ISBNs, Imprints & Series:
0 283 S & J
0 330 Pan, Picador
0 333 Macmillan, Papermac

Parent Company:
Holtzbrinck Publishers Holdings Ltd

Associated & Subsidiary Companies:
Macmillan Children's Books Ltd; Macmillan
London Ltd; Macmillan Press Ltd; Macmillan
Publishers Ltd; Pan Books Ltd; Sidgwick &
Jackson Ltd

Distributor for:
Michael O'Mara; St Martins Press

Overseas Representation (see §7.3):
All other areas – send orders to: Export
  Department Macmillan Distribution Ltd,
  Basingstoke, UK
Australia: Pan Macmillan Books (Australia)
  Pty Ltd, Sydney, NSW
Canada: McClelland & Stewart, Toronto &
  Markham
East Africa, Zimbabwe, Ghana & Nigeria:
  Macmillan Education, Basingstoke, UK
Europe: Macmillan Publishers Ltd,
  Basingstoke, UK
Hong Kong: Macmillan Publishers (China) Ltd
India: Rupa & Co, New Delhi
Irish Republic: Fiona Killeen, Dublin
Japan: Macmillan Shuppan KK, Tokyo
Mexico & Central America: Editorial
  Macmillan de Mexico SA de CV, Mexico
  DF, Mexico
Netherlands: Nilsson & Lamm BV, Weesp;
  Van Ditmar BV, Amsterdam
New Zealand: Pan Macmillan New Zealand
  Ltd, Auckland
South Africa: Pan Macmillan, Johannesburg
South East Asia: Pansing Distribution Sdn Bhd,
  Singapore
West Indies & Caribbean: Macmillan
  Caribbean, Basingstoke, UK

Book Trade Association Membership: PA

1546 ▬▬▬

MACMILLAN PRESS LTD
Houndmills, Basingstoke, Hants RG21 6XS
Telephone: 01256 29242
Fax: 01256 479476

Chairman: A. Soar
Managing Director: D. J. G. Knight
Finance: R. H. Hartgill
Academic Marketing: M. Hewinson
Production: J. W. Peacock
Sales: G. Warner *(W. H. Freeman)*
College Publishing: S. Kennedy
Further Education: J. R. Winckler
Academic: T. M. Farmiloe
Journals: J. Marks
Reference: S. O'Neill
Macmillan Business: S. Rutt
Publishing Services: T. Fox
Electronic Publishing Services: J. Vernay

*Academic & Scholarly; Accountancy &
Taxation; Biology & Zoology; Chemistry;
Computer Science; Economics; Educational &
Textbooks; Engineering; Gender Studies;
Geography & Geology; History &
Antiquarian; Industry, Business &
Management; Languages & Linguistics; Law;
Literature & Criticism; Mathematics &
Statistics; Medical (incl. Self Help &
Alternative Medicine); Music; Philosophy;
Physics; Politics & World Affairs; Psychology
& Psychiatry; Reference Books, Directories &
Dictionaries; Religion & Theology; Scientific
& Technical; Sociology & Anthropology;
Theatre, Drama & Dance; Vocational Training
& Careers*

New Titles: 393 (1995), 567 (1996)

ISBNs, Imprints & Series: 0 333

Parent Company:
Macmillan Ltd

Associated & Subsidiary Companies:
Macmillan General Books Ltd; Macmillan
Publishers Ltd. *USA:* Stockton Press Inc

Distributor for:
W. H. Freeman; Jinaver Associates; Spectrum;
University Science Books; Worth Publishers

Overseas Representation (see §7.3):
See: Macmillan Publishers Ltd, Basingstoke,
UK

Book Trade Association Membership: IPG,
BDPA, STM

1547 ▬▬▬

MACMILLAN PUBLISHERS LTD
25 Eccleston Place, London SW1W 9NF
Telephone: 0171 881 8000
Fax: 0171 881 8001

**Trade Enquiries, Orders & Registered
Office:**
Brunel Road, Houndmills, Basingstoke, Hants
RG21 6XS
Telephone: 01256 29242
Fax: 01256 479476

Directors: N. G. Byam Shaw *(Chairman)*
M. J. Barnard
A. Soar
R. Barker
The Hon. D. M. B. Macmillan
G. R. U. Todd
C. J. Paterson
A. J. Sutherland
Company Secretary: P. S. Trotman

Parent Company:
Macmillan Ltd

Associated & Subsidiary Companies:
Austen Cornish Publishers Ltd; Campbell
Books Ltd; Globe Publishing Ltd; Grove's
Dictionaries of Music Ltd; Hospital & Social
Service Publications Ltd; Macmillan Accounts
and Administration Ltd; Macmillan Children's
Books Ltd; The Macmillan Dictionary of Art
Ltd; Macmillan Direct Ltd; Macmillan
Distribution Ltd; Macmillan Education Ltd;
Macmillan General Books Ltd; Macmillan
Information Systems Ltd; Macmillan Journals

Ltd; Macmillan Journals Subscriptions Ltd;
Macmillan London Ltd; Macmillan Magazines
Ltd; Macmillan Multimedia Ltd; Macmillan
Press Ltd; Macmillan Press UK Ltd; Macmillan
Production Ltd; Macmillan Reference
Publications Ltd; Macmillan Subscriptions Ltd;
Macmillan US Subscriptions Ltd; New Media
Investments Ltd; Pan Books (Holdings) Ltd;
Pan Books Ltd; Pan Bookshops Ltd; Sidgwick
& Jackson Ltd; Stockton Press Ltd; TFPL
Multimedia Ltd. *Australia:* Macmillan
Publishers Australia Pty Ltd; Pan Macmillan
Australia Pty Ltd; Sun Books Pty Ltd.
Botswana: Macmillan Botswana Publishing Co
(Pty) Ltd. *Brazil:* Macmillan do Brasil. *Hong
Kong:* Macmillan Publishers (China) Ltd;
Macmillan Publishers (Hong Kong) Ltd;
Peninsula Production & Distribution Ltd.
India: Macmillan India Ltd. *Irish Republic:*
Gill & Macmillan Ltd. *Japan:* Macmillan
Language House Ltd; Macmillan Shuppan KK;
Nature Japan KK. *Kenya:* Macmillan Kenya
(Publishers) Ltd. *Mexico:* Editorial Macmillan
de Mexico SA de CV. *New Zealand:* Macmillan
Publishers New Zealand Ltd. *Nigeria:*
Macmillan Nigeria Publishers Ltd; Northern
Nigerian Publishing Co Ltd. *Swaziland:*
Macmillan Boleswa Publishers Pty Ltd;
Macmillan Swaziland National Publishing Co
(Pty) Ltd. *Uganda:* Macmillan Uganda Ltd.
USA: Grove's Dictionaries Inc; Nature
America Inc; St Martin's Enterprises Inc; St
Martin's Press Inc; Stockton Press Inc. *Zambia:*
Macmillan Publishers (Zambia) Ltd.
Zimbabwe: College Press Publishers (Pvt) Ltd

Distributor for:
see: Macmillan Children's Books Ltd;
Macmillan General Books Ltd; Macmillan
Press Ltd; Macmillan Reference Books

Overseas Representation (see §7.3):
Australia: Macmillan Publishers, South
  Melbourne
Canada: McClelland & Stewart, Toronto &
  Markham
East & Central Africa: Macmillan Kenya
  (Publishers) Ltd, Nairobi, Kenya
Ghana: Unimax Publishers (Sic) Ltd, Accra
Hong Kong: Macmillan Publishers (China) Ltd
India: Macmillan India Ltd, Bangalore
Irish Republic: Gill & Macmillan Ltd, Dublin
Japan: Macmillan Shuppan KK, Tokyo;
  Macmillan Language House, Tokyo
Mexico & Central America: Editorial
  Macmillan de Mexico SA de CV, Mexico
  DF, Mexico
Netherlands: Nilsson & Lamm BV, Weesp;
  Van Ditmar BV, Amsterdam
New Zealand: Macmillan Publishers New
  Zealand Ltd, Albany
Nigeria: Macmillan Nigeria Publishers Ltd,
  Lagos
Singapore: Pansing Distribution Sdn Bhd
South Africa (Macmillan Press only): Cory
  Voigt Associates, Braamfontein, South
  Africa
Zimbabwe: College Press Publishers (Pvt) Ltd,
  Harare

Book Trade Association Membership: PA

1548 ▬▬▬

MACMILLAN REFERENCE BOOKS
25 Eccleston Place, London SW1W 9NF

Telephone: 0171 881 8000
Fax: 0171 881 8001

Also at:
Houndmills, Basingstoke, Hants RG21 6XS
Telephone: 01256 29242
Fax: 01256 479476

Directors: Adrian Soar *(Chairman)*
David North *(Sales)*
Chris Paterson *(Marketing)*
Georgina Morley *(Editorial)*
Cookery Editor: Judith Hannam
Company Secretary: M. E. Powter

Cookery, Wines & Spirits; Music; Reference Books, Directories & Dictionaries; Travel & Topography

New Titles: 12 (1995), 16 (1996)
No of Employees: 28

ISBNs, Imprints & Series: 0 333

Parent Company:
Holtzbrinck Publishers Holdings Ltd

Associated & Subsidiary Companies:
Macmillan General Books Ltd; Macmillan Press Ltd; Macmillan Publishers Ltd. *USA:* Stockton Press Inc

Overseas Representation *(see §7.3):*
See: Macmillan Publishers Ltd, Basingstoke, UK

Book Trade Association Membership: PA

1549

MAGNA LARGE PRINT BOOKS
Magna House, Long Preston, Skipton, North Yorks BD23 4ND
Telephone: 01729 840225 & 840526
Fax: 01729 840683

Directors: David Thorpe *(Chairman)*
John Cressey *(Managing)*
Diane Allen
David Mellin

Large Print Books; Story Sound Audio Cassettes

New Titles: 240 (1995), 280 (1996)
No of Employees: 20
Annual Turnover: £1.8M

ISBNs, Imprints & Series:
0 86009, 1 85057, 1 85389, 1 86110 Large Print
1 85903, 1 87267 Audio

Parent Company:
The Ulverscroft Group

Distributor for:
Mills & Boon Large Print

Overseas Representation *(see §7.3):*
Worldwide: Ulverscroft Large Print Books, UK

1550

MAINSTREAM PUBLISHING CO (EDINBURGH) LTD
7 Albany Street, Edinburgh EH1 3UG

Telephone: 0131 557 2959
Fax: 0131 556 8720

Distribution, Trade Enquiries & Orders:
Tiptree Book Services, Tiptree, Colchester, Essex CO5 0SR
Telephone: 01621 816362
Fax: 01621 819011

Directors: Bill Campbell *(Production)*
Peter MacKenzie *(Sales & Marketing)*
John Beaton *(Editorial)*
Manager: Raymond Cowie *(Sales – UK)*

Biography & Autobiography; Cookery, Wines & Spirits; Fiction; Fine Art & Art History; Guide Books; Health & Beauty; Illustrated & Fine Editions; Literature & Criticism; Music; Photography; Politics & World Affairs; Sports & Games

New Titles: 100 (1995), 100 (1996)
No of Employees: 20
Annual Turnover: £2.5M

ISBNs, Imprints & Series:
0 906391, 1 85158

Overseas Representation *(see §7.3):*
Australia: Capricorn Link (Australia) Pty Ltd, Baulkham Hills, NSW
Canada: Hushion House Ltd, Toronto, Ont
Europe: Bill Bailey Publishers Representatives, Newton Abbot, UK
USA: David & Charles Inc, North Pomfret, VT

Book Trade Association Membership:
Scottish PA

1551

MAMMOTH
Michelin House, 81 Fulham Road, London SW3 6RB
Telephone: 0171 581 9393
Fax: 0171 225 9406

Distribution:
Reed Book Services, Northampton Road, Rushden, Northants NN10 6PU
Telephone: 01933 58521
Fax: 01933 50284

International Sales Department:
Michelin House, 81 Fulham Road, London SW3 6RB
Telephone: 0171 581 9393
Fax: 0171 225 9371

Divisional Managing Director: Jane Winterbotham

Children's Books

ISBNs, Imprints & Series:
0 7497 Mammoth, Little Mammoth, Teens

Parent Company:
Reed Elsevier Plc

Overseas Representation *(see §7.3):*
Australia: Reed Books Australia, Melbourne, Vic
Canada: Reed Publishing Canada, Markham, Ont
East Asia: Reed Consumer Books, Metro Manila, Philippines

India: Reed Consumer Books, New Delhi
Japan: Reed Consumer Books, Tokyo
New Zealand: Reed Publishing Group, Auckland
Singapore: Reed International (Singapore) Pte Ltd
South Africa: Struik Book Distributors Pty Ltd, Johannesburg, Cape Town & Maitland

1552

MANAGEMENT BOOKS 2000 LTD
Cowcombe House, Cowcombe Hill, Chalford, Glos GL6 8HP
Telephone: 01285 760722
Fax: 01285 760708

Managing Director: Nicholas Dale-Harris

Accountancy & Taxation; Economics; Electronic (Professional & Academic); Industry, Business & Management; Law; Reference Books, Directories & Dictionaries

ISBNs, Imprints & Series:
1 85251, 1 85252

Distributor for:
Mercury Business Books. *USA:* Motivation Cassettes

Overseas Representation *(see §7.3):*
Australia & New Zealand: Woodslane Pty Ltd, Mona Vale, NSW, Australia
Austria, Switzerland & Italy: Patrick Bygate, Massagno, Switzerland
Belgium, Luxembourg & Netherlands: Reinier A. Pleysier, Heerde, Netherlands
Denmark, Norway, Sweden, Finland & Iceland: D. Richard Bowen, Malmö, Sweden
Far East, Japan, Singapore, West Indies, Central & South America: c/o Management Books 2000 Ltd, Didcot, UK
France, Greece & Yugoslavia: Graham Powell, Bournemouth, UK
Germany: PKB – Robbert J. Pleysier, Heerde, Netherlands
Portugal, Spain & Gibraltar: Patrick Bygate, Massagno, Switzerland
South Africa: Kelvin van Hasselt Publishing Services, Lymington, UK

Book Trade Association Membership: IPG

1553

MANCHESTER UNIVERSITY PRESS
Oxford Road, Manchester M13 9NR
Telephone: 0161 273 5539
Fax: 0161 274 3346
Email: mup@man.ac.uk

Directors: Glen Innes *(Sales & Marketing)*
Vanessa Graham *(Editorial History)*
David Rodgers *(Production)*
Editorial: Matthew Frost *(Humanities & Art)*
Nikki Viinikka *(Politics & Economics)*
Manager: Norma Ashton *(Accounts)*
Rights & Permissions: Clare Blick

Academic & Scholarly; Accountancy & Taxation; Architecture & Design; Cinema, Video, TV & Radio; Economics; Educational & Textbooks; Fashion & Costume; Fine Art & Art History; Gender Studies; History & Antiquarian; Industry, Business & Management; Languages & Linguistics; Law;

Literature & Criticism; Military & War; Philosophy; Photography; Politics & World Affairs; Sociology & Anthropology; Theatre, Drama & Dance; Transport

New Titles: 120 (1995), 140 (1996)
No of Employees: 27
Annual Turnover: £2M

ISBNs, Imprints & Series: 0 7190

Overseas Representation *(see §7.3)*:
Canada: University of British Columbia Press, Vancouver, BC
East & South East Asia & Australasia: Roger Ward, London, UK
Europe: Andrew B. Durnell, Tunbridge Wells, UK
India: T. R. Publications Pvt Ltd, Madras
Japan: United Publishers Services Ltd, Tokyo
Middle East, Cyprus & North Africa: Hugh C. Thomas, London, UK
North America: St Martin's Press Inc, New York, NY, USA
Pakistan: S. I. Gillani, Lahore
Southern Africa: Russell Friedman Information Services (Pty) Ltd, Cape Town, South Africa

Book Trade Association Membership: PA, BDC, IPG, CAPP

1554

MANDARIN
Michelin House, 81 Fulham Road, London SW3 6RB
Telephone: 0171 581 9393
Fax: 0171 225 9095

Distribution:
Reed Book Services, Northampton Road, Rushden, Northants NN10 6PU
Telephone: 01933 58521
Fax: 01933 50284

International Sales Department:
(as above)
Telephone: 0171 581 9393
Fax: 0171 225 9371

Publisher: Tom Weldon

Biography & Autobiography; Crime; Fiction; History & Antiquarian; Humour; Politics & World Affairs; Travel & Topography

ISBNs, Imprints & Series: 0 7493

Parent Company:
Reed Elsevier Plc

Overseas Representation *(see §7.3)*:
Australia: Reed Books Australia, Melbourne, Vic
Canada: Reed Publishing Canada, Markham, Ont
East Asia: Reed Consumer Books, Metro Manila, Philippines
India: Reed Consumer Books, New Delhi
Japan: Reed Consumer Books, Tokyo
New Zealand: Reed Publishing Group, Auckland
Singapore: Reed International (Singapore) Pte Ltd
South Africa: Struik Book Distributors Pty Ltd, Johannesburg, Cape Town & Maitland

1555

MANDRAKE OF OXFORD
PO Box 250, Oxford OX1 1AP
Telephone: 01865 243671
Fax: 01865 243671
Email: krm@mandrake.compulink.co.uk
Web Site: http://www.compulink.co.uk/
~mandrake/welcome.htm

Directors: Kris Morgan
Ruth Mandrake

Crime; Fine Art & Art History; Literature & Criticism; Magic & the Occult; New Science

New Titles: 6 (1995), 10 (1996)

ISBNs, Imprints & Series:
1 869928 Golden Dawn, Mandrake of Oxford

Overseas Representation *(see §7.3)*:
Australia: Peribo Pty Ltd, Mount Kuring-gai, NSW
Benelux: Henco Associates, Utrecht, Netherlands
Northern Europe: Henco Associates, Utrecht, Netherlands
USA: New Leaf Distribution, Lithia Springs, GA; Abyss, Chester, MA; Samuel Weiser Inc, York, ME

Book Trade Association Membership: IPG, SPG

1556

MANSELL PUBLISHING
Wellington House, 125 Strand, London WC2R 0BB
Telephone: 0171 420 5555
Fax: 0171 240 7261

Distribution:
Cassell Plc, Stanley House, 3 Fleets Lane, Poole, Dorset BH15 3AJ
Telephone: 01202 665432
Fax: 01202 666219

Chairman: Philip Sturrock
Directors: Stephen Butcher *(Managing)*
Frank Roney *(Finance)*
Janet Joyce *(Publishing)*
Martyn Chapman *(Commercial & Distribution)*
Ruth McCurry *(UK Sales)*
Senior Managers: Catherine Johnston *(Promotion)*
Rebecca Seymour *(Export Sales)*
Veronica Higgs *(Editorial)*

Academic & Scholarly; Architecture & Design; Bibliography & Library Science; Educational & Textbooks; Gender Studies; Geography & Geology; History & Antiquarian; Industry, Business & Management; Law; Literature & Criticism; Philosophy; Politics & World Affairs; Reference Books, Directories & Dictionaries; Religion & Theology; Sociology & Anthropology; CD-Rom Reference

New Titles: 40 (1995), 40 (1996)

ISBNs, Imprints & Series: 0 7201

Parent Company:
Cassell Plc

Associated & Subsidiary Companies:
see: Cassell Plc

Overseas Representation *(see §7.3)*:
see: Cassell Plc, UK

Book Trade Association Membership:
Library Association

1557

MANSON PUBLISHING LTD
73 Corringham Road, London NW11 7DL
Telephone: 0181 905 5150
Fax: 0181 201 9233
Email: manson-publishing@compuserv.com

Managing Director: Michael Manson

Agriculture; Animal Care & Breeding; Biology & Zoology; Geography & Geology; Medical (incl. Self Help & Alternative Medicine); Scientific & Technical; Veterinary Science

New Titles: 8 (1995), 15 (1996)
No of Employees: 3

ISBNs, Imprints & Series: 1 874545

Associated & Subsidiary Companies:
The Veterinary Press Ltd

Distributor for:
British Small Animal Veterinary Association (BSAVA)

Overseas Representation *(see §7.3)*:
Australia & New Zealand (stockholding distributor): McGraw-Hill Book Co Australia Pty Ltd, Roseville, NSW, Australia
Canada (stockholding distributor): W. B. Saunders Canada Ltd, Toronto, Canada
Greece, Turkey & Middle East: James & Lorin Watt, Oxford, UK
India (stockholding distributors): Jaypee Brothers Medical Publishers Ltd, New Delhi, India; Oxford University Press Indian Branch Head Office, New Delhi, India; K. M. Varghese Co, Bombay, India
Irish Republic, Continental Europe, Africa, Asia & Latin America (Representation and availability through OUP branches): Oxford University Press, Oxford, UK
Japan (stockholding distributor): Oxford University Press KK, Tokyo, Japan
Pakistan (stockholding distributor): Oxford University Press, Karachi, Pakistan
Singapore, Malaysia, Thailand, Indonesia & Hong Kong (stockholding distributor): Toppan Co (S) Pte Ltd, Singapore

Book Trade Association Membership: PA, IPG

1558

MANTICORE EUROPE LTD
Silver Birches, Heronsgate, Rickmansworth, Herts WD3 5DN
Telephone: 01923 282772
Fax: 01923 282772

Managing Director: R. D. Warman
Sales: Mrs L. Fernandez

Medical (incl. Self Help & Alternative Medicine)

ISBNs, Imprints & Series: 1 900887

Associated & Subsidiary Companies:
Canada: Manticore Publishers Inc

Distributor for:
Canada: Manticore Publishers Inc

Book Trade Association Membership: PA

1559

KENNETH MASON PUBLICATIONS LTD
Dudley House, 12 North Street, Emsworth,
Hants PO10 7DQ
Telephone: 01243 377977
Fax: 01243 379136

Distribution:
Biblios PDS Ltd, Star Road, Partridge Green,
West Sussex RH13 8LD
Telephone: 01403 710971
Fax: 01403 711143

Directors: K. Mason *(Chairman)*
M. Mason
P. Mason *(Managing)*
A. Mason

*Cookery, Wines & Spirits; Crafts & Hobbies;
Guide Books; Health & Beauty; Law; Medical
(incl. Self Help & Alternative Medicine);
Nautical; Sports & Games*

ISBNs, Imprints & Series:
0 85937 Kenneth Mason, Seafile
1 873432 Boatswain Press, Essential Series,
 Handbag Books

Associated & Subsidiary Companies:
Boatswain Press Ltd; Jumpahead Ltd; A. E.
Norris Ltd

Book Trade Association Membership: PA

1560

MECHANICAL ENGINEERING PUBLICATIONS
Northgate Avenue, Bury St Edmunds, Suffolk
IP32 6BW
Telephone: 01284 763277
Fax: 01284 704006
Email: sales@IMechE.org.uk
Web Site: http://www.imeche.org.uk

Director: J. D. Cameron *(Publications)*
Managers: P. A. Williams *(Sales)*
J. Entwiste-Baker *(Rights & Permissions)*
D. Fidler *(Finance)*
B. Eliot *(Production)*

*Academic & Scholarly; Aviation; Computer
Science; Engineering; Medical (incl. Self Help
& Alternative Medicine); Nautical; Scientific &
Technical; Transport*

New Titles: 28 (1995), 50 (1996)
No of Employees: 30
Annual Turnover: £3M

ISBNs, Imprints & Series:
0 85298, 1 86058

Parent Company:
Institution of Mechanical Engineers

Distributor for:
USA: American Society of Mechanical
Engineers

Overseas Representation *(see §7.3):*
Australia: DA Information Services, Mitcham,
Vic
India: Allied Publishers Ltd, Madras
Japan: Kinokuniya Co Ltd, Tokyo; Maruzen
Co Ltd, Tokyo
Malaysia, Singapore & Brunei: Parry's Book
Centre Sdn Bhd, Kuala Lumpur, Malaysia
Middle East (not stockholding): Berj
Jamkojian, Vienna, Austria
South Korea: Kumi Trading Co Ltd, Seoul,
Korea, South
USA & Canada: American Society of
Mechanical Engineers, Fairfield, NJ, USA

Book Trade Association Membership:
IGSMTP, ALPSP, UK Serials Group (UKSG),
STM, National Acquisitions Group (NAG)

1561

MECKLERMEDIA LTD
4th Floor, Artillery House, Artillery Row,
London SW1P 1RT
Telephone: 0171 976 0405
Fax: 0171 976 0506

Trade Orders:
McGraw-Hill Europe, Shoppenhangers Road,
Maidenhead, Berks SL6 2QL

Managing Director: Matthew Finlay

*Computer Science; Industry, Business &
Management; Scientific & Technical; Library
Science*

New Titles: 10 (1995)
No of Employees: 5

ISBNs, Imprints & Series: 0 88736

Parent Company:
Mecklermedia Publishing Corporation *(USA)*

Overseas Representation *(see §7.3):*
Australia & New Zealand: Kirby Book Co,
Sydney, NSW, Australia
Europe: McGraw-Hill Book Co (Europe) Ltd,
Maidenhead, UK
North & South America: Meckler Media,
Westport, CT, USA

Book Trade Association Membership: IPG

1562

MEDIA RESEARCH PUBLISHING LTD
Lister House, 117 Milton Road,
Weston-super-Mare, North Somerset
BS23 2UX
Telephone: 01934 644309
Fax: 01934 644402

Chairman: Cliff Dane
Director: Margaret Dane
Administration Manager: Alison Press

*Academic & Scholarly; Accountancy &
Taxation; Cinema, Video, TV & Radio; Music*

New Titles: 2 (1995), 3 (1996)
No of Employees: 2

ISBNs, Imprints & Series:
0 9521414 UK Record Industry Annual Survey
1995, Rock Accounts 1995

Book Trade Association Membership: PA

1563

THE MEDICI SOCIETY LTD
34–42 Pentonville Road, London N1 9HG
Telephone: 0171 837 7099
Fax: 0171 837 9152

Managers: John Marsh *(Sales)*
Catriona Mitchell *(Export)*

*Children's Books; Fine Art & Art History;
Natural History*

New Titles: 1 (1995), 5 (1996)
No of Employees: 150

ISBNs, Imprints & Series: 0 85503

Overseas Representation *(see §7.3):*
Australia: Roy McMillan Agencies, Church
Point, NSW
Canada: Casablanca, Streetsville, Ont
Irish Republic: George R. Allen & Co Ltd,
Dublin
New Zealand: Oxted Resources Ltd, Auckland
South Africa: H. R. & L. Shapiro, Cape Town
USA: Rose Cottage, Yardley, PA

1564

MELROSE PRESS LTD
3 Regal Lane, Soham, Ely, Cambs CB7 5BA
Telephone: 01353 721091
Fax: 01353 721839

Chairman: R. A. Kay
Managing Director: N. S. Law
Chief Executive: J. E. Pearson
Company Secretary: C. Emmett
Production: J. Timothy
Senior Manager: D. Abraham

Reference Books, Directories & Dictionaries

New Titles: 7 (1995)
No of Employees: 32

ISBNs, Imprints & Series:
0 900332 Melrose Press
0 948875 International Biographical Centre,
 Melrose Press

Distributor for:
Eddison Press Ltd; Pentland Press Ltd

Overseas Representation *(see §7.3):*
Australia: James Bennett Pty Ltd, Collaroy
Beach, NSW
India: Viva Marketing, New Delhi
People's Republic of China: China Book
Import Centre, Beijing, P. R. of China
USA & Canada: Taylor & Francis Inc, Bristol,
PA, USA

1565

MERCAT PRESS
c/o James Thin, 53–59 South Bridge,
Edinburgh EH1 1YS
Telephone: 0131 556 6743

Fax: 0131 557 8149
Email: james.thin.ltd@almac.co.uk

Editorial & Sales, Publicity: Tom Johnstone
Seán Costello

*History & Antiquarian; Literature & Criticism;
Reference Books, Directories & Dictionaries;
Travel & Topography; Scottish*

ISBNs, Imprints & Series:
0 901824, 1 873644 Mercat Press

Parent Company:
James Thin Ltd

Book Trade Association Membership: BA,
Scottish PA

1566 ▬▬▬▬▬▬▬▬▬▬▬▬▬▬▬▬▬▬▬

MEREHURST FAIRFAX
Ferry House, 51–57 Lacy Road, Putney,
London SW15 1PR
Telephone: 0181 780 1177
Fax: 0181 780 1714

Distribution & Invoicing:
Bookpoint Ltd, 39 Milton Park, Abingdon,
Oxon OX14 4TD
Telephone: 01235 400400
Fax: 01235 832068

Directors: Shirley Patton *(Editorial)*
Debbie Kent *(Sales)*
Kirsten Schlesinger *(Marketing & Foreign
Rights)*
Company Secretary: Roger Potter

*Children's Books; Cookery, Wines & Spirits;
Crafts & Hobbies; Gardening*

ISBNs, Imprints & Series:
0 948075, 1 85391 Merehurst Books
1 86343, 1 874567 J. B. Fairfax

Parent Company:
J. B. Fairfax International *(Australia)*

Associated & Subsidiary Companies:
J. B. Fairfax Press Ltd. *Australia:* J. B. Fairfax
Pty Ltd. *USA:* Michael Friedman Publishing
Group

Distributor for:
Future Publishing

Overseas Representation *(see §7.3):*
Australia: Herron Book Distributors Pty Ltd,
Fortitude Valley, Qld
Europe: Roger Smith, Enfield, UK
*Hong Kong, Singapore, Malaysia, Thailand,
Taiwan, Indonesia & South Korea:* Richard
Blady Booksales, Macclesfield, UK
Japan: YOHAN (Western Publications
Distribution Agency), Tokyo
Middle East: Peter Ward Book Exports,
London, UK
New Zealand: Beckett Sterling Ltd, Auckland
New Zealand (craft titles): David Bateman Ltd,
Auckland, New Zealand
Scandinavia: Books for Europe, Glostrup,
Denmark
South Africa: Struik Book Distributors, Cape
Town
South America & Caribbean: Humphrys
Roberts Associates, London, UK

USA & Canada: Foxwood International Ltd,
Milton, Ont, Canada

1567 ▬▬▬▬▬▬▬▬▬▬▬▬▬▬▬▬▬▬▬

MERIDIAN BOOKS
40 Hadzor Road, Oldbury, Warley,
West Midlands B68 9LA
Telephone: 0121 429 4397

Publisher: Peter Groves

*Guide Books; History & Antiquarian; Travel &
Topography*

New Titles: 3 (1995), 5 (1996)
No of Employees: 1
Annual Turnover: £20,000

ISBNs, Imprints & Series:
0 906070 Tetradon Publications
1 869922 Meridian Books

Overseas Representation *(see §7.3):*
North America: The Denali Press, Juneau, AK,
USA

Book Trade Association Membership: IPG

1568 ▬▬▬▬▬▬▬▬▬▬▬▬▬▬▬▬▬▬▬

MERLIN BOOKS LTD
Stonycroft, East Hill, Braunton, Devon
EX33 2LD
Telephone: 01271 812117
Fax: 01271 812117

Warehouse, Trade Enquiries & Orders:
40 East Street, Braunton, Devon EX33 2EA
Telephone: 01271 816430
Fax: 01271 812117

Managing Director: Derek Stockwell
Company Secretary: Barbara M. Stockwell
General Office Manager: Pam Stevens
Editor: E. A. Edwards
Trade Counter Returns: Keith Chapman

*Academic & Scholarly; Aviation; Biography &
Autobiography; Military & War; Poetry*

New Titles: 38 (1995), 40 (1996)
No of Employees: 8
Annual Turnover: £200,000

ISBNs, Imprints & Series: 0 86303

Book Trade Association Membership: BA

1569 ▬▬▬▬▬▬▬▬▬▬▬▬▬▬▬▬▬▬▬

*MERLIN PRESS LTD
10 Malden Road, London NW5 3HR
Telephone: 0171 267 3399
Fax: 0171 284 3092

Trade Orders:
Central Books Ltd, 99 Wallis Road, London
E9 5NL
Telephone: 0181 986 4854
Fax: 0181 533 5821

Joint Managing Directors: Martin Eve
*(Merlin Press & Seafarer Books – Editorial
& Rights)*
Julie Millard *(Green Print – Editorial & Rights)*

*Academic & Scholarly; Nautical; Philosophy;
Politics & World Affairs*

ISBNs, Imprints & Series:
0 85036 Seafarer
1 85425 Green Print

Overseas Representation *(see §7.3):*
Australia: Boobook Publications Pty Ltd, Tea
Gardens, NSW
Canada: Diffusion Prologue, Boisbriand
Europe: Books for Europe Ltd, Bournemouth,
UK
India: Rupa & Co, New Delhi
South Africa: Judith Wengrowe Agencies,
Northcliff, Johannesburg

1570 ▬▬▬▬▬▬▬▬▬▬▬▬▬▬▬▬▬▬▬

**MERRELL HOLBERTON PUBLISHERS
LTD**
Axe and Bottle Court, 70 Newcomen Street,
London SE1 1YT
Telephone: 0171 403 2047
Fax: 0171 407 6437
Email: merrholb@dircon.co.uk

Warehouse, Distributor:
Biblios, Star Road, Partridge Green,
West Sussex RH13 8LD
Telephone: 01403 710851
Fax: 01403 711143

Directors: Hugh Merrell *(Marketing,
Production)*
Paul Holberton *(Editorial)*

*Academic & Scholarly; Architecture & Design;
Fine Art & Art History; Illustrated & Fine
Editions; Photography*

ISBNs, Imprints & Series: 1 85894

Overseas Representation *(see §7.3):*
Austria: Seth Meyer-Bruhns, Vienna
*Denmark, Norway, Sweden, Finland &
Iceland:* D. Richard Bowen, Malmö, Sweden
France: Fischbacher International, Paris
Germany: Eckhard Becksmann, Frankfurt;
Andreas Böttcher, Berlin; Michael Franke &
Till Meyer-Bruhns, Hamburg; Henner Voss,
Bergheim-Zieverich; Mälte Würzner,
Dusseldorf
Italy: Penny Padovani, Montanare di Cortona
Netherlands, Belgium & Luxembourg:
Continent Books, Amsterdam, Netherlands
Spain & Portugal: Arie Ruitenbeek, Madrid,
Spain
Switzerland: Buch und Information AG, Zurich
USA (all other Art titles): University of
Washington Press, Seattle, WA, USA
USA (contemporary Art titles): D.A.P., New
York, USA

1571 ▬▬▬▬▬▬▬▬▬▬▬▬▬▬▬▬▬▬▬

METHODIST PUBLISHING HOUSE
20 Ivatt Way, Peterborough PE3 7PG
Telephone: 01733 332202
Fax: 01733 331201

Chairman: Dudley Coates
Chief Executive: Brian Thornton *(General
Manager)*
Marketing Manager: Christopher Pursehouse
Editorial: Gerald Burt

Electronic (Professional & Academic); Music; Religion & Theology

New Titles: 22 (1995), 20 (1996)
No of Employees: 23
Annual Turnover: £1M

ISBNs, Imprints & Series:
0 716204 Epworth
0 946550, 1 85852 The Foundery Press,
  Methodist Publishing House

Parent Company:
The Methodist Church

Distributor for:
USA: The Upper Room Nashville

Book Trade Association Membership: PA,
BA

1572 ▬▬▬▬▬

METHUEN
Michelin House, 81 Fulham Road, London
SW3 6RB
Telephone: 0171 581 9393
Fax: 0171 225 9095

Distribution:
Reed Book Services, Northampton Road,
Rushden, Northants NN10 6PU
Telephone: 01933 58521
Fax: 01933 50284

International Sales Department:
(as principal address)
Telephone: 0171 581 9393
Fax: 0171 225 9371

Publisher: Michael Earley

Biography & Autobiography; Fiction; History & Antiquarian; Humour; Politics & World Affairs; Theatre, Drama & Dance

ISBNs, Imprints & Series: 0 413

Parent Company:
Reed Elsevier Plc

Overseas Representation *(see §7.3)*:
Australia: Reed Books Australia, Melbourne,
  Vic
Canada: Reed Publishing Canada, Markham,
  Ont
East Asia: Reed Consumer Books, Metro
  Manila, Philippines
India: Reed Consumer Books, New Delhi
Japan: Reed Consumer Books, Tokyo
New Zealand: Reed Publishing Group,
  Auckland
Singapore: Reed International (Singapore) Pte
  Ltd
South Africa: Struik Book Distributors Pty Ltd,
  Johannesburg, Cape Town & Maitland

1573 ▬▬▬▬▬

METHUEN CHILDREN'S BOOKS
Michelin House, 81 Fulham Road, London
SW3 6RB
Telephone: 0171 581 9393
Fax: 0171 225 9731

Distribution:
Reed Book Services, Northampton Road,
Rushden, Northants NN10 6PU
Telephone: 01933 58521
Fax: 01933 50284

International Sales Department:
Michelin House, 81 Fulham Road, London
SW3 6RB
Telephone: 0171 581 9393
Fax: 0171 225 8456

Divisional Managing Director: Jane
  Winterbotham

Children's Books

ISBNs, Imprints & Series: 0 416

Parent Company:
Reed Elsevier Plc

Overseas Representation *(see §7.3)*:
Australia: Reed Books Australia, Melbourne,
  Vic
Canada: Reed Publishing Canada, Markham,
  Ont
East Asia: Reed Consumer Books, Metro
  Manila, Philippines
India: Reed Consumer Books, New Delhi
Japan: Octopus Publishing Group, Tokyo
New Zealand: Reed Publishing Group,
  Auckland
Singapore: Reed International (Singapore) Pte
  Ltd
South Africa: Struik Book Distributors Pty Ltd,
  Johannesburg, Cape Town & Maitland

1574 ▬▬▬▬▬

METRO BOOKS
19 Gerrard Street, London W1V 7LA
Telephone: 0171 734 1411
Fax: 0171 734 1811

Distribution (Warehouse):
Exel Logistics, Invicta House,
Sir Thomas Longley Road,
Medway City Estate, Rochester, Kent
ME2 4DU
Telephone: 01634 298000
Fax: 01634 297123

Directors: Susanne McDadd *(Managing)*
David Furse-Roberts *(Finance)*
Beth McDougall *(Publicity)*
David Bann *(Production)*
Rights Manager: Lesley Toll

Cookery, Wines & Spirits; Gardening; Guide Books; Health & Beauty; Humour; Medical (incl. Self Help & Alternative Medicine); Psychology & Psychiatry; Reference Books, Directories & Dictionaries; Sports & Games; Travel & Topography

New Titles: 8 (1996)
No of Employees: 5

ISBNs, Imprints & Series: 1 900512

Overseas Representation *(see §7.3)*:
Asia, Eastern Europe & South America: Tony
  Moggach IMA, London, UK
Australia: Peribo Pty Ltd, Mount Kuring-gai,
  NSW

Europe: Derek Searle Associates Ltd, Slough,
  UK
South Africa: Trinity Books CC, Randburg

Book Trade Association Membership: IPG

1575 ▬▬▬▬▬

MICHELIN TYRE PLC
The Edward Hyde Building,
38 Clarendon Road, Watford WD1 1SX
Telephone: 01923 415000
Fax: 01923 415052

Warehouse/Returns:
Michelin Tyre Plc, Maps & Guides,
Building 71 Campbell Road, Stoke on Trent,
Staffs ST4 4EY

Head of Tourism: D. C. Brown *(Editorial/*
  Production/Sales)
Sales Manager: J. Lewis *(UK)*

Atlases & Maps; Children's Books; Travel & Topography

ISBNs, Imprints & Series:
2 06, 3 92107 Michelin Tourist Guides (Red &
  Green)

Parent Company:
Manufacture Française des Pneumatiques
Michelin *(France)*

Overseas Representation *(see §7.3)*:
Austria: Michelin Reifenverkaufs GmbH,
  Vienna
Belgium & Luxembourg: S.A. Belge du
  Pneumatique Michelin, Brussels, Belgium
Canada: Ste Canadienne des Pneus Michelin
  Ltée, Dorval
Germany: Michelin Reifenwerke KGaA,
  Karlsruhe
Greece: Elastika Michelin AE, Athens
Italy: Michelin Italiana SPA, Milan
Japan: Nihon Michelin Tire KK, Tokyo
Spain: SAFE de Neumaticos Michelin, Madrid
Switzerland: S.A. des Pneumatiques Michelin,
  Givisiez
USA: Michelin Travel Publications, Greenville,
  SC

1576 ▬▬▬▬▬

**MICROFORM ACADEMIC
PUBLISHERS**
Main Street, East Ardsley, Wakefield,
West Yorkshire WF3 2AT
Telephone: 01924 825700
Fax: 01924 871005
Email: micro.image@cix.compulink.co.uk

Directors: Nigel Le Page *(Managing)*
Angela Jarman *(Publishing)*

Academic & Scholarly; Archaeology; Economics; Geography & Geology; History & Antiquarian; Law; Literature & Criticism; Medical (incl. Self Help & Alternative Medicine); Music; Natural History; Nautical; Philosophy; Physics; Psychology & Psychiatry; Religion & Theology; Sociology & Anthropology

Overseas Representation *(see §7.3)*:
Japan: Far Eastern Booksellers, Tokyo

USA & Canada: Norman Ross Publishing Inc, New York, USA

1577

MIDDLETON PRESS
Easebourne Lane, Midhurst, Sussex GU29 9AZ
Telephone: 01730 813169
Fax: 01730 812601

Author & Proprietor: J. C. V. Mitchell

Aviation; Military & War; Transport

New Titles: 24 (1995), 20 (1996)

ISBNs, Imprints & Series:
0 906520, 1 873793

1578

MIDLAND COUNTIES PUBLICATIONS (AEROPHILE) LTD
24 The Hollow, Earl Shilton, Leicester LE9 7NA
Telephone: 01455 847256
Fax: 01455 841805

Warehouse & Trade Counter:
Unit 3, Maizefield, Hinckley Fields Estate, Hinckley, Leics LE10 1YF
Telephone: 01455 233747
Fax: 01455 233737

Directors: N. P. Lewis
C. J. Salter

Aviation; Military & War

New Titles: 3 (1995), 3 (1996)

ISBNs, Imprints & Series: 0 904597

Associated & Subsidiary Companies:
Midland Publishing Ltd

Overseas Representation *(see §7.3):*
USA: Specialty Press, North Branch, MN

1579

MIDLAND PUBLISHING LTD
24 The Hollow, Earl Shilton, Leicester LE9 7NA
Telephone: 01455 847256
Fax: 01455 841805

Warehouse & Trade Counter:
c/o Midland Counties Publications, Unit 3, Maizefield, Hinckley Fields Estate, Hinckley, Leics LE10 1YF
Telephone: 01455 233747
Fax: 01455 233737

Directors: N. P. Lewis
C. J. Salter
T. G. Ferris

Aviation; Military & War; Transport

New Titles: 15 (1995), 18 (1996)

ISBNs, Imprints & Series:
1 85780 Aerofax

Associated & Subsidiary Companies:
Midland Counties Publications (Aerophile) Ltd

Overseas Representation *(see §7.3):*
USA: Specialty Press, North Branch, MN

1580

*HARVEY MILLER PUBLISHERS
[an imprint of G&B Arts International Ltd]
197 Knightsbridge, London SW7 1RB
Telephone: 0171 584 7676
Fax: 0171 823 7696

Trade Distribution Orders:
Biblios, Glenside Industrial Estate, Partridge Green, West Sussex RH13 8LD
Telephone: 01403 710971
Fax: 01403 711143

Directors: Harvey Miller
Elly Miller
Marketing Manager: Peter Churcher

Fine Art & Art History

ISBNs, Imprints & Series:
0 905203, 1 872501 Corpus of Spanish Drawings, Corpus Rubenianum Ludwig Burchard, Survey of Manuscripts Illuminated in the British Isles

Overseas Representation *(see §7.3):*
Asia: IPD (Pte) Ltd, Singapore
Continental Europe: Gordon & Breach Arts, Basle, Switzerland
USA: International Publishers Distributor, Langhorne, PA

Book Trade Association Membership: PA

1581

MILLER FREEMAN INFORMATION SERVICES
Riverbank House, Angel Lane, Tonbridge, Kent TN9 1SE
Telephone: 01732 362666
Fax: 01732 367301

Directors: Roger Michael *(Managing)*
Les Kelly *(Publishing)*
Elaine Soni *(Sales)*
Sara Creech *(Publishing)*
Gwen Young *(Data Services)*

Aviation; Chemistry; Cinema, Video, TV & Radio; Do-It-Yourself; Electronic (Professional & Academic); Engineering; Industry, Business & Management; Medical (incl. Self Help & Alternative Medicine); Nautical; Reference Books, Directories & Dictionaries; Travel & Topography

New Titles: 3 (1995), 2 (1996)
No of Employees: 130

ISBNs, Imprints & Series: 0 86382

Parent Company:
United News & Media Plc

Associated & Subsidiary Companies:
Miller Freeman Plc

Book Trade Association Membership: DPA, EADP

1582

MINERVA
Michelin House, 81 Fulham Road, London SW3 6RB
Telephone: 0171 581 9393
Fax: 0171 225 9095

Distribution:
Reed Book Services, Northampton Road, Rushden, Northants NN10 6PU
Telephone: 01933 58521
Fax: 01933 40284

International Sales Department:
(as above)
Telephone: 0171 581 9393
Fax: 0171 225 9371

Editorial Director: Geoff Mulligan

Biography & Autobiography; Fiction; History & Antiquarian; Literature & Criticism

ISBNs, Imprints & Series: 0 7493

Parent Company:
Reed Elsevier Plc

Overseas Representation *(see §7.3):*
Australia: Reed Books Australia, Melbourne, Vic
Canada: Reed Publishing Canada, Markham, Ont
East Asia: Reed Consumer Books, Metro Manila, Philippines
India: Reed Consumer Books, New Delhi
Japan: Reed Consumer Books, Tokyo
New Zealand: Reed Publishing Group, Auckland
Singapore: Reed International (Singapore) Pte Ltd
South Africa: Struik Book Distributors Pty Ltd, Johannesburg, Cape Town & Maitland

1583

MINIMAX BOOKS LTD
Broadgate House, Church Street, Deeping St James, Peterborough PE6 8HD
Telephone: 01778 347609
Fax: 01778 341198

Directors: Lynn Green
Robert Lavender

Children's Books; Educational & Textbooks; Local Interest Books

ISBNs, Imprints & Series: 0 906791

Distributor for:
Anglia Young Books

1584

THE MIT PRESS LTD
Fitzroy House, 11 Chenies Street, London WC1E 7ET
Telephone: 0171 306 0603
Fax: 0171 306 0604
Email: 100315.1423@compuserve.com
Web Site: http://www-mitpress.mit.edu

Trade & Warehouse:
John Wiley & Sons Ltd, Distribution Centre,
Southern Cross Trading Estate,
1 Oldlands Way, Bognor Regis, West Sussex
PO22 9SA
Telephone: 01243 779777
Fax: 01243 820250
Email: customer@wiley.co.uk

Managers: Ann Sexsmith *(General)*
Ann Twiselton *(Publicity)*
Mary Starkey *(Texts/Exhibitions)*

*Academic & Scholarly; Architecture & Design;
Bibliography & Library Science; Biography &
Autobiography; Biology & Zoology;
Chemistry; Computer Science; Economics;
Educational & Textbooks; Engineering; Fine
Art & Art History; Industry, Business &
Management; Languages & Linguistics; Law;
Mathematics & Statistics; Medical (incl. Self
Help & Alternative Medicine); Music; Natural
History; Philosophy; Photography; Physics;
Politics & World Affairs; Psychology &
Psychiatry; Reference Books, Directories &
Dictionaries; Scientific & Technical; Sociology
& Anthropology*

New Titles: 180 (1995), 180 (1996)
No of Employees: 5

ISBNs, Imprints & Series:
0 262 American Association for Artificial
Intelligence Press, Bradford Books, MIT
Press

Parent Company:
MIT Press *(USA)*

Distributor for:
Zone Books (Urzone Publishing Ltd)

Overseas Representation *(see §7.3):*
Australia: Astam Books Pty Ltd, Leichhardt,
NSW
*Belgium, France, Netherlands, Norway,
Sweden, Finland & Denmark:* Fred
Hermans, Bovenkarspel, Netherlands
Germany, Austria, Switzerland & Italy: Uwe
Luedemann, Berlin, Germany
Japan: United Publishers Services Ltd, Tokyo
Morocco: Librarie Internationale, Ramat
Pakistan: Pak Book Corporation, Lahore
South Africa: Cory Voigt Associates,
Braamfontein
South East Asia: Toppan Co (S) Pte Ltd,
Singapore
Spain & Portugal: Arie Ruitenbeek, Madrid,
Spain

1585 ▬▬▬

MITCHELL BEAZLEY
Michelin House, 81 Fulham Road, London
SW3 6RB
Telephone: 0171 581 9393
Fax: 0171 225 9458

Distribution:
Reed Book Services, Northampton Road,
Rushden, Northants NN10 6PU
Telephone: 01933 58521
Fax: 01933 50284

Publishing Director: Jane Aspden

*Antiques & Collecting; Architecture & Design;
Cookery, Wines & Spirits; Gardening; Magic
& the Occult; Natural History; Photography;
Reference Books, Directories & Dictionaries*

ISBNs, Imprints & Series:
0 85533, 1 85732

Parent Company:
Reed Elsevier Plc

Overseas Representation *(see §7.3):*
Australia: Reed Books Australia, Melbourne,
Vic
Canada: Reed Publishing Canada, Markham,
Ont
East Asia: Reed Consumer Books, Metro
Manila, Philippines
India: Reed Consumer Books, New Delhi
Japan: Reed Consumer Books, Tokyo
New Zealand: Reed Publishing Group,
Auckland
Singapore: Reed International (Singapore) Pte
Ltd
South Africa: Struik Book Distributors Pty Ltd,
Johannesburg, Cape Town & Maitland

1586 ▬▬▬

MOONLIGHT PUBLISHING LTD
36 Stratford Road, London W8 6QA
Telephone: 0171 376 0299
Fax: 0171 937 8921

Trade Enquiries & Orders:
Ragged Bears Ltd, Ragged Appleshaw,
Andover, Hants SP11 9HX
Telephone: 01264 772269
Fax: 01264 772391

Director: Christine Baker *(Editor)*

Children's Books

ISBNs, Imprints & Series:
1 85103 Discoverers, First Discovery,
Moonlight First Encyclopaedia, Pocket
Bears, Pocket Worlds, Tales of Heaven &
Earth

Distributor for:
Ragged Bears Ltd

Overseas Representation *(see §7.3):*
Australia: Era Publications, Brooklyn Park
Canada: Douglas & McIntyre, Toronto
New Zealand & South Africa: Ragged Bears
Ltd, Andover, UK

1587 ▬▬▬

MOORLAND PUBLISHING CO LTD
Moor Farm Road, Ashbourne, Derbys
DE6 1HD
Telephone: 01335 344486
Fax: 01335 346397

Distributors:
Grantham Book Services,
Alma Park Industrial Estate, Grantham, Lincs
Telephone: 01476 67421
Fax: 01476 590223

Managing Director: C. L. M. Porter

Gardening; Guide Books

New Titles: 38 (1995), 60 (1996)
No of Employees: 10
Annual Turnover: £1.1M

ISBNs, Imprints & Series: 0 86190

Distributor for:
Little Hills Press *(travel titles only)*; The RHS
Plant Finder

Overseas Representation *(see §7.3):*
Australia: Little Hills Press Pty Ltd, Crows
Nest (Sydney), NSW
Central & Eastern Europe: Michael Timperley
Marketing, Karmelave, Lithuania; Michael
Timperley Marketing, Budapest, Hungary
Middle East: Eurab Ltd, Rottingdean, UK
Northern Europe: Angell Eurosales, Newton
Abbot, UK
Russian Federation & CIS: Michael Timperley
Marketing, Hong Kong
South Africa: Faradawn CC, Saxonwold
South East Asia: Keith Hardy, Bangkok,
Thailand
Southern Europe: Bookport Associates,
Bologna, Italy

1588 ▬▬▬

MOORLEY'S PRINT & PUBLISHING
23 Park Road, Ilkeston, Derbyshire DE7 5DA
Telephone: 0115 932 0643
Fax: 0115 932 0643

Managing Director: John R. Moorley

*Music; Poetry; Religion & Theology; Theatre,
Drama & Dance*

New Titles: 14 (1995), 16 (1996)
No of Employees: 9

ISBNs, Imprints & Series:
0 86071, 0 901495

Parent Company:
Moorley's Bible & Bookshop Ltd

Associated & Subsidiary Companies:
Truedata Computer Services

Distributor for:
Cliff College Publishing; Darby Publications;
Freedom Ministries; Mainstream Baptists for
Life & Growth; Nimbus Press; T. Young

1589 ▬▬▬

MOTOR RACING PUBLICATIONS LTD
Unit 6, The Pilton Estate, 46 Pitlake, Croydon,
Surrey CR0 3RY
Telephone: 0181 681 3363
Fax: 0181 760 5117

UK representatives:
Book Rep Services, 2 Hamble Road, Didcot,
Oxon OX11 7QT
Telephone: 01235 812834
Fax: 01235 813535

Orders:
Biblios Publishers' Distribution Services Ltd,
Star Road, Partridge Green, West Sussex
RH13 8LD
Telephone: 01403 710971 & 710851
Fax: 01403 711143

Managing Director: John Blunsden *(Rights & Permissions)*
Editor: Anne Jackson
Manager: Jim Starr *(Production & Sales)*

Sports & Games; Transport

New Titles: 8 (1995), 10 (1996)
No of Employees: 3
Annual Turnover: £470,000

ISBNs, Imprints & Series:
0 900549, 0 947981, 1 899870 Motor Racing
Publications
0 948358 The Fitzjames Press

Associated & Subsidiary Companies:
The Fitzjames Press

Overseas Representation *(see §7.3):*
Austria, France, Greece, Switzerland,
Slovenia, Croatia, Poland, Hungary, Czech
& Slovak Republics: Patrick Bygate &
Juliusz Komarnicki, Massagno, Switzerland
Benelux & Germany: PKB – Robbert J.
Pleysier, Heerde, Netherlands
Italy, Malta, Spain, Gibraltar & Portugal:
Bookport Associates, Bologna, Italy
Scandinavia: D. Richard Bowen, Malmö,
Sweden
USA: Motorbooks International Publishers &
Wholesalers Inc, Osceola, WI

1590

MOWBRAY
Wellington House, 125 Strand, London
WC2R 0BB
Telephone: 0171 420 5555
Fax: 0171 240 7261

Distribution:
Cassell Plc, 3 Fleets Lane, Poole, Dorset
BH15 3AJ
Telephone: 01202 665432
Fax: 01202 666219

Directors: Philip Sturrock *(Chairman)*
Stephen Butcher *(Managing)*
Frank Roney *(Finance)*
Martyn Chapman *(Commercial & Distribution)*
Ruth McCurry *(UK Sales)*
Senior Managers: Rebecca Seymour *(Export Sales)*
Gill Paterson *(Publisher)*

Religion & Theology

New Titles: 40 (1995)

ISBNs, Imprints & Series:
0 264 Mowbray

Parent Company:
Cassell Plc

Associated & Subsidiary Companies:
see: Cassell Plc

Distributor for:
USA: St Vladimir's Seminary Press

Overseas Representation *(see §7.3):*
see: Cassell Plc, UK

1591

MULTILINGUAL MATTERS LTD
Frankfurt Lodge, Clevedon Hall,
Victoria Road, Clevedon, North Somerset
BS21 7SJ
Telephone: 01275 876519
Fax: 01275 343096
Email: multi@mulm.demon.co.uk

Distribution:
Plymbridge Distributors, Plymbridge House,
Estover Road, Plymouth PL6 7PZ
Telephone: 01752 202301
Fax: 01752 202331

Directors: Mike Grover *(Managing, Home & Export Sales)*
Marjukka Grover *(Rights & Permissions)*
Ken Hall *(Production)*
Kathryn King *(Marketing)*

Academic & Scholarly; Educational &
Textbooks; Languages & Linguistics;
Psychology & Psychiatry; Sociology &
Anthropology; Transport

New Titles: 30 (1995), 30 (1996)
No of Employees: 7
Annual Turnover: £600,000

ISBNs, Imprints & Series:
0 905028, 1 85359 Bera Dialogues, Bilingual
Education & Bilingualism, French
Sociolinguistics, Intercommunication,
Language & Education Library, Mispol,
Modern Languages in Practice, Multilingual
Matters, Topics in Translation
1 873150 Channel View Publication

Overseas Representation *(see §7.3):*
Australia & New Zealand: Helios Bookshop,
Adelaide, Australia
Benelux: Kemper Conseil, Voorburg,
Netherlands
Canada: Guidance Centre OISE, Toronto, Ont
Far East: Roger Ward, London, UK
Germany: The John Wilde Partnership, Lauf
Irish Republic: Carr O'Connell, Ashbourne
Japan: Kinokuniya Book Import Dept, Tokyo;
Maruzen Co Ltd, Tokyo
Malaysia: PMS Marketing Services, Selangor
Singapore: Publishers Marketing Services Ltd
South Africa: Judith Wengrowe Agencies,
Northcliff, Johannesburg
Spain: Iberian Book Services SL, Madrid
USA: Taylor & Francis Inc, Bristol, PA

Book Trade Association Membership: IPG

1592

MULTIMEDIA LIBRARY LTD
Four Seasons House, 102B Woodstock Road,
Witney, Oxon OX8 6DY
Telephone: 01993 778077
Fax: 01993 778246

Managing Director: Les Burnham
Marketing Executive: Charlotte J. Holt

Educational & Textbooks; Electronic
(Educational); History & Antiquarian;
Literature & Criticism; Natural History;
Reference Books, Directories & Dictionaries

New Titles: 20 (1995), 20 (1996)

ISBNs, Imprints & Series:
1 56779 World Library Ltd
1 85993 Zigzag Publishing
1 885582, 1 882807 Cambrix Publishing

Associated & Subsidiary Companies:
Zigzag Publishing. *USA:* Cambrix Publishing
Ltd; Remedia; World Library Ltd

Distributor for:
Zigzag Publishing. *USA:* Cambrix Publishing
Ltd; Remedia; World Library Ltd

1593

MURCHISON'S PANTHEON LTD
11–12 West Smithfield, London EC1A 9JR
Telephone: 0171 329 1515
Fax: 0171 329 0150
Email: 100450.1105@compuserve.com

Directors: Andrew Hayes *(Managing)*
Charles Blount *(Finance)*
Peter Stevenson
Sales Manager: Emmanuelle Kreh

Audio Books; Guide Books; Travel &
Topography

New Titles: 6 (1996)
No of Employees: 4
Annual Turnover: £100,000

ISBNs, Imprints & Series: 1 900652

Book Trade Association Membership: PA

1594

JOHN MURRAY PUBLISHERS LTD
50 Albemarle Street, London W1X 4BD
Telephone: 0171 493 4361
Fax: 0171 499 1792

**UK Orders & Invoicing, Payments & Credit
Control & Warehouse:**
Grantham Book Services, Isaac Newton Way,
Alma Park Industrial Estate, Grantham, Lincs
NG31 9SD
Telephone: 01476 67421
Fax: 01476 590223

Directors: John R. Murray *(Chairman,
General Books Marketing)*
Nicholas Perren *(Managing)*
Grant McIntyre *(General Books Editorial)*
Judith Reinhold *(Educational Marketing)*
Company Secretary & Chief Accountant:
Philip Carter
Managers: Barbara Smith *(Production)*
Bridget Moon *(Rights)*
Stephanie Allen *(Publicity)*

Accountancy & Taxation; Biography &
Autobiography; Biology & Zoology;
Chemistry; Economics; Educational &
Textbooks; Fine Art & Art History; Geography
& Geology; Guide Books; History &
Antiquarian; Industry, Business &
Management; Languages & Linguistics;
Mathematics & Statistics; Military & War;
Physics; Scientific & Technical; Travel &
Topography

New Titles: 80 (1995), 85 (1996)
No of Employees: 46

ISBNs, Imprints & Series:
0 7195 John Murray Publishers, Success Study
Books

Distributor for:
Irish Republic: Abbeville Press Inc

Overseas Representation *(see §7.3)*:
Australia: Octopus Publishing Group Australia
Pty Ltd, Port Melbourne
Bangladesh: The University Press Ltd, Dhaka
Cameroon: Evans Brothers Ltd, Bamenda
Canada: General Publishing Co Ltd, North
York, Ont
Caribbean (East): RIK Services Ltd, San
Fernando, Trinidad
East Africa: EAEP Ltd, Nairobi, Kenya
Egypt, Greece, Malta & Middle East:
International Publishers Representatives
(IPR), Nicosia, Cyprus
Ghana: A. Ott-Attafua & Co Ltd, Accra
Hong Kong (Educational): Pilot Publishers
Services Ltd, Kowloon, Hong Kong
Hong Kong (General Books): Asia Publisher
Services Ltd, Hong Kong
India: Maya Publishers Pvt Ltd, New Delhi
Italy, France, Spain & Portugal: Patrick
Bygate, Massagno, Switzerland
Japan: United Publishers Services Ltd, Tokyo
Malaysia: APD KL Ltd, Selangor Darul
Mauritius: Editions Le Printemps, Vacaos
Netherlands: Nilsson & Lamm BV, Weesp
New Zealand: OPG New Zealand Ltd,
Auckland
Nigeria: African Universities Press, Ibadan
Pakistan & Afghanistan: Oxford University
Press, Karachi, Pakistan
Scandinavia & Finland: Saga Books ApS,
Copenhagen, Denmark
Sierra Leone: African Universities Press,
Freetown
Singapore, East Malaysia & Brunei: APD
Singapore Pte Ltd, Singapore
Southern Africa (educational books): Book
Promotions Pty Ltd, Plumstead, South Africa
Southern Africa (general books): Random
House South Africa Pty Ltd, Rosebank,
Johannesburg, South Africa
Switzerland: Dr H. R. Conrad, Meilen
Tanzania: Gilbert Mwakalukwa, Dar-es-
Salaam
Uganda: John Budds, Nairobi, Kenya
Zimbabwe: Academic Press Pvt Ltd, Harare

Book Trade Association Membership: PA,
BDC, EPC, CAPP, IPG

1595 ▬▬▬▬▬▬▬

**NATE (NATIONAL ASSOCIATION FOR
THE TEACHING OF ENGLISH)**
50 Broadfield Road,
Broadfield Business Centre, Sheffield S8 0XJ
Telephone: 0114 2 555419
Fax: 0114 2 555296

General Secretary: Anne Barnes
Publications Officer: Rhonda Jenkins

*Educational & Textbooks; Theatre, Drama &
Dance*

New Titles: 2 (1995), 4 (1996)
No of Employees: 8

ISBNs, Imprints & Series: 0 901291

Book Trade Association Membership: PA,
EPC

1596 ▬▬▬▬▬▬▬

NATIONAL ACADEMY PRESS
12 Hid's Copse Road, Cumnor Hill, Oxford
OX2 9JJ
Telephone: 01865 865466
Fax: 01865 862763
Email: nap@oxfpubp.demon.co.uk

Warehouse & Distribution:
Plymbridge Distributors, Estover, Plymouth
PL6 7PZ
Telephone: 01752 202300
Fax: 01752 202330

Marketing Managers: Sue Miller
Alice Meadows

*Academic & Scholarly; Agriculture; Animal
Care & Breeding; Biology & Zoology;
Chemistry; Engineering; Environment &
Development Studies; Geography & Geology;
Industry, Business & Management; Medical
(incl. Self Help & Alternative Medicine);
Natural History; Nautical; Psychology &
Psychiatry; Scientific & Technical*

ISBNs, Imprints & Series: 0 309

Parent Company:
National Academy Press *(USA)*

1597 ▬▬▬▬▬▬▬

**NATIONAL CHRISTIAN EDUCATION
COUNCIL**
1020 Bristol Road, Selly Oak, Birmingham
B29 6LB
Telephone: 0121 472 4242
Fax: 0121 472 7575

Head of Publishing: David Trenaman
Marketing & Sales: Bernard Morgan

*Biography & Autobiography; Children's
Books; Educational & Textbooks; Music;
Religion & Theology; Theatre, Drama &
Dance*

New Titles: 12 (1995), 15 (1996)

ISBNs, Imprints & Series:
0 7197, 0 85213

Associated & Subsidiary Companies:
Hillside Publishing; International Bible
Reading Association

Distributor for:
Australia: Joint Board of Christian Education

Book Trade Association Membership: PA,
BA, EPC

1598 ▬▬▬▬▬▬▬

**NATIONAL EXTENSION COLLEGE
TRUST LTD**
18 Brooklands Avenue, Cambridge CB2 2HN
Telephone: 01223 316644
Fax: 01223 313586
Email: nec@dial.pipex.com

Warehouse:
Unit 23, Clifton Road, Cambridge CB1 4ZB
Telephone: 01223 316644
Fax: 01223 313586

Director: Ros Morpeth
Heads of Department: Robert Leach
(Education)
Roger Merritt *(Sales, Rights & Permissions)*
Anna Russell *(Learner Support)*
John Elrtul *(Finance)*
Senior Editor: Trevor Weston
Customer Services: Pat Gouldstone

*Educational & Textbooks; Electronic
(Educational); Vocational Training & Careers*

New Titles: 30 (1995), 40 (1996)
No of Employees: 75
Annual Turnover: £4M

ISBNs, Imprints & Series:
0 86082, 1 85356

Book Trade Association Membership: IPG

1599 ▬▬▬▬▬▬▬

**NATIONAL FOSTER CARE
ASSOCIATION (NFCA)**
Leonard House, 5–7 Marshalsea Road, London
SE1 1EP
Telephone: 0171 828 6266
Fax: 0171 357 6668

Director: Gerri McAndrew
Communications Manager: Katrina Phillips

*Children's Books; Educational & Textbooks;
Child Care*

New Titles: 5 (1995), 5 (1996)

ISBNs, Imprints & Series: 0 946015

Book Trade Association Membership: IPG

1600 ▬▬▬▬▬▬▬

**NATIONAL GALLERY PUBLICATIONS
LTD**
5–6 Pall Mall East, London SW1Y 5BA
Telephone: 0171 839 8544
Fax: 0171 930 0108

Director of Book Publishing: Patricia
Williams
Publisher: F. Luard
Managing Editor: J. Green
Editorial Assistant: K. Eyston
Production: S. Curnow
Retail: C. Parrish
Mail Order: C. Sobro
Financial Controller: H. R. Armstrong

*Academic & Scholarly; Children's Books;
Cinema, Video, TV & Radio; Fine Art & Art
History*

New Titles: 18 (1995), 19 (1996)
No of Employees: 91
Annual Turnover: £5.5M

ISBNs, Imprints & Series:
0 901791, 0 947645

Parent Company:
The National Gallery Trust

Distributor for:
USA: Yale University Press

Overseas Representation *(see §7.3):*
USA: Yale University Press, New Haven, CT
Worldwide (excluding USA): Yale
  Representation Ltd, London, UK

1601

NATIONAL INSTITUTE OF ADULT CONTINUING EDUCATION
21 De Montfort Street, Leicester LE1 7GE
Telephone: 0116 255 1451
Fax: 0116 285 4514

Trade Distributors:
Central Books Ltd, Wallis Road, London
E9 5LN

Senior Publication Officer: Virman Man

Educational & Textbooks

New Titles: 12 (1995), 12 (1996)

ISBNs, Imprints & Series:
0 900559, 1 872941

1602

NATIONAL MUSEUMS OF SCOTLAND
Publications Office, NMS, Chambers Street,
Edinburgh EH1 1JF
Telephone: 0131 225 7534
Fax: 0131 247 4012
Email: fhk@nms.ac.uk

Distribution (Scotland):
Scottish Book Source, 137 Dundee Street,
Edinburgh EH11 1BG
Telephone: 0131 229 6800
Fax: 0131 229 9070

Distribution (Rest of UK):
Gazelle Book Services Ltd, Falcon House,
Queen Square, Lancaster LA1 1RN
Telephone: 01524 68765
Fax: 01524 63232

Head of Publications: Jenni Calder *(Sales,
  Rights & Permissions)*
Editor: Helen Kemp *(Sales, Rights &
  Permissions)*
Designer: Liz Robertson

*Academic & Scholarly; Archaeology;
Architecture & Design; Biology & Zoology;
Children's Books; Educational & Textbooks;
Fine Art & Art History; Geography & Geology;
History & Antiquarian; Military & War;
Natural History; Scientific & Technical;
Sociology & Anthropology; Transport*

New Titles: 12 (1995), 11 (1996)
No of Employees: 2
Annual Turnover: £100,000

ISBNs, Imprints & Series: 0 948636

Overseas Representation *(see §7.3):*
Australia: Reg Tigwell Art Agency, Bowral,
  NSW

Europe: Gazelle Book Services Ltd, Lancaster,
  UK
USA: Arthur Schwartz & Co, Woodstock, NY

Book Trade Association Membership:
Scottish PA

1603

NATIONAL PORTRAIT GALLERY PUBLICATIONS
National Portrait Gallery, 2 St Martin's Place,
London WC2H 0HE
Telephone: 0171 306 0055
Fax: 0171 306 0056

Warehouse & Trade Enquiries:
Biblios Publishers' Distribution Services Ltd,
Star Road, Partridge Green, West Sussex
Telephone: 01403 710971

Head of Publications & Retailing: Robert
  Carr-Archer *(Publisher)*
Manager: Louisa Hearnden
Rights & Permissions: Shruti Patel

*Biography & Autobiography; Fine Art & Art
History; Photography*

New Titles: 2 (1995), 8 (1996)

ISBNs, Imprints & Series:
0 904017, 1 85514

Overseas Representation *(see §7.3):*
Canada: Fitzhenry & Whiteside Ltd, Markham
France: Interart sarl, Paris
Spain: Edimport, Madrid
USA: Antique Collectors' Club Ltd, Wappinger
  Falls

Book Trade Association Membership: BA

1604

THE NATIONAL TRUST
36 Queen Anne's Gate, London SW1H 9AS
Telephone: 0171 222 9251
Fax: 0171 222 5097

Trade Enquiries:
Derek Searle Associates Ltd,
The Coach House, Cippenham Lodge,
Cippenham Lane, Slough, Berks SL1 5AN
Telephone: 01753 539295
Fax: 01753 551863

Warehouse:
Bookpoint Ltd, 39 Milton Park, Abingdon,
Oxon OX14 4TD
Telephone: 01235 400400
Fax: 01235 861038

Publisher: Margaret Willes
Publishing Administrator: Morwenna Wallis

*Architecture & Design; Children's Books;
Cookery, Wines & Spirits; Fashion & Costume;
Fine Art & Art History; Gardening; Guide
Books; History & Antiquarian*

New Titles: 15 (1995), 15 (1996)
No of Employees: 11

ISBNs, Imprints & Series: 0 7078

Book Trade Association Membership: BA

1605

NATIONAL YOUTH AGENCY
17–23 Albion Street, Leicester LE1 6GD
Telephone: 0116 247 1200
Fax: 0116 247 1043

Head of Communications: Mary Durkin
Publishing Co-ordinator: Andy Hopkinson

*Academic & Scholarly; Educational &
Textbooks; Gender Studies; Sociology &
Anthropology; Vocational Training & Careers*

ISBNs, Imprints & Series:
0 86155 Youth Work Press

1606

THE NATURAL HISTORY MUSEUM – PUBLICATIONS SECTION
Cromwell Road, London SW7 5BD
Telephone: 0171 938 8761
Fax: 0171 938 8709
Email: t.brannan@nhm.ac.uk
Web Site: http://www.nhm.ac/publications/

Production & Foreign Rights: Lynn
  Millhouse
Editor & Permissions: Trudy Brannan
Head of Publications: Chris Mills

*Academic & Scholarly; Biology & Zoology;
Fine Art & Art History; Geography & Geology;
Natural History; Scientific & Technical*

No of Employees: 3

ISBNs, Imprints & Series:
0 565 The Natural History Museum –
  Publications Section

Book Trade Association Membership: IPG

1607

NAXOS AUDIOBOOKS
HR House, 447 High Road, Finchley, London
N12 0AF
Telephone: 0181 346 6816
Fax: 0181 346 6496

Distribution:
Select Music & Video,
34A Holmethorpe Avenue, Redhill, Surrey
RH1 2NN
Telephone: 01737 760020
Fax: 01737 766316

Director: Nicolas Soames
Production Executive: Anna Britten

Audio Books

ISBNs, Imprints & Series: 0 962634

Parent Company:
HNH International *(Hong Kong)*

Overseas Representation *(see §7.3):*
Australia: Sonart, Balgowlah, NSW
Austria: Gramola Co, Vienna, Australia
Brazil: RKR Musical, Sao Paulo
Canada: McClelland & Stewart, Toronto &
  Markham; Naxos of Canada Ltd,
  Scarborough, Ont

Czech Republic: Classic Music Distribution, Prague
Denmark: Olga Musik, Ry
Finland: FG Distribution, Helsinki
France: Naxos of France, Paris; Naxos & Marco Polo, Paris
Germany: Fono Schallplatten GmbH, Laer; MVD , Munich
Greece: Greek Record Club, Athens
Hungary: Phoenix Studio, Budapest
Iceland: JAPIS, Reykjavik
Irish Republic: Cosmic Sounds Ltd, Dublin
Israel: MCI Records, Tel Aviv
Japan: Naxos Japan, Nagoya & Tokyo
Korea: Hae Dong Co Ltd, Seoul, Korea, South
Malaysia: AV Masters Sdn Bhd, Kuala Lumpar
Netherlands: Vanguard Classics, Nieuwegein
New Zealand: Triton Music Ltd, Auckland
Norway: Musikkdistribusjon AS, Oslo
Philippines: Universal Records, Kalookan City
Singapore: Naxos Pte Ltd
Slovak Republic: Slovart Music, Bratislava, Slovakia
South Africa: RPM Record Co, Johannesburg
Spain: FERYSA, Madrid
Sri Lanka: Titus Stores, Columbo
Sweden: Naxos Sweden, Orebro
Switzerland: FAME, Meggen (Lucerne)
Taiwan: Rock Records & Tapes, Taipei
Thailand: Media Plus & Broadcasting Network Ltd, Bangkok
Turkey: Haci Emin Elendi Sokak, Istanbul
USA: Naxos of America Inc, Cherry Hill, NJ

Book Trade Association Membership:
Spoken Word Publishers' Association

1608

NCT PUBLISHING LTD
25–27 High Street, Chesterton, Cambridge CB4 1ND
Telephone: 01223 352790
Fax: 01223 460718
Email: bpccam@demon.co.uk

Editorial:
1 Beetley Grange, Beetley, Dereham, Norfolk NR20 4TD
Telephone: 01362 860082
Fax: 01362 861175

Distribution:
HMSO Books, HMSO Publications Centre, PO Box 276, London SW8 5DT
Telephone: 0171 873 9090
Fax: 0171 873 8200

Directors: Colin Walsh
Daphne Metland *(Editorial)*
Production Manager: Deborah Wayment
Sales Co-ordinator: Franca Holden

Gender Studies; Health & Beauty; Medical (incl. Self Help & Alternative Medicine); Reference Books, Directories & Dictionaries; Sociology & Anthropology; Vocational Training & Careers; Childbirth; Maternity; Pregnancy

New Titles: 10 (1996)

ISBNs, Imprints & Series:
011 701 HMSO

Parent Company:
Book Production Consultants Plc; National Childbirth Trust

Associated & Subsidiary Companies:
Book Production Consultants Plc

Overseas Representation *(see §7.3):*
Worldwide: HMSO Books, London, UK

1609

NCVO PUBLICATIONS
[incorporating Bedford Square Press]
National Council for Voluntary Organisations, Regent's Wharf, 8 All Saints Street, London N1 9RL
Telephone: 0171 713 6161
Fax: 0171 713 6300

Head of Marketing & Members' Services:
Angela Galvin

Reference Books, Directories & Dictionaries; Sociology & Anthropology; Voluntary Sector Management

New Titles: 10 (1995), 15 (1996)
No of Employees: 60

ISBNs, Imprints & Series:
0 7199 NCVO Management Guides, NCVO Publications

Parent Company:
National Council for Voluntary Organisations

Distributor for:
USA: National Center for Non-Profit Boards

1610

NEIL WILSON PUBLISHING LTD
303A Pentagon Centre, 36 Washington Street, Glasgow G3 8AZ
Telephone: 0141 221 1117
Fax: 0141 221 5363
Email: nwp@cqm.co.uk
Web Site: http://www.nwp.co.uk

Distributor, Sales Ledger & Trade Orders:
Exel Logistics Media Services, Invicta House, Sir Thomas Longley Road, Medway City Industrial Estate, Rochester, Kent ME2 4DU
Telephone: 01634 297123
Fax: 01634 298000

Managing Director: Neil Wilson *(Sales, Rights & Permissions)*

Biography & Autobiography; Cookery, Wines & Spirits; Crime; History & Antiquarian; Humour; Sports & Games; Irish Interest; Scottish Interest

New Titles: 10 (1995), 11 (1996)
No of Employees: 4
Annual Turnover: £240,000

ISBNs, Imprints & Series: 1 897784

Overseas Representation *(see §7.3):*
France, Belgium, Germany, Austria & Switzerland: European Marketing Services, London, UK

Netherlands: Novelty Books International bv, Weesp
USA: Interlink International Inc, Northampton, MA

Book Trade Association Membership:
Scottish PA

1611

THOMAS NELSON & SONS LTD
Nelson House, Mayfield Road, Walton-on-Thames, Surrey KT12 5PL
Telephone: 01932 252211
Fax: 01932 246109

Warehouse, Orders, Customer Service & Credit Control:
International Thomson Publishing Services Ltd, Cheriton House, North Way, Andover, Hants SP10 1YN
Telephone: 01264 342992
Fax: 01264 364418

Directors: R. E. Gauvin *(Managing)*
John Tuttle *(Sales & Marketing)*
Nick White *(Finance)*
David Fothergill *(Publishing)*
Managers: N. Jones *(International Sales Development)*
Tim Dare *(UK Sales)*

Educational & Textbooks; Electronic (Educational); Languages & Linguistics

ISBNs, Imprints & Series:
0 17 Thomas Nelson & Sons Ltd
0 216 Blackie
0 333 Macmillan Schoolbooks

Parent Company:
The Thomson Corporation

Distributor for:
Australia: Nelson. *USA:* South Western Publishing Co (School Division)

Overseas Representation *(see §7.3):*
Argentina: Kel Ediciones SA, Buenos Aires
Australia: Thomas Nelson (Australia) Pty Ltd, South Melbourne, Vic
Bahamas: Nassau Stationers, Nassau
Barbados, Antigua, Dominica, St Lucia & St Vincent: Ezra Crichlow, St Thomas, Barbados
Belize: The Book Center, Belize City
Brunei: Pustaha Remaja
Canada: Nelson Canada, Scarborough
Chile: South American Way, Santiago, P. R. of China
Gambia: Jim Heffernan, Banjul
Ghana: A. Ott-Attafua & Co Ltd, Accra
Grenada: Grenada Teacher's School Supplies, St George's, Guyana
Indonesia: Book Covers of Indonesia, Jakarta
Irish Republic (Modern Languages only): Modern Languages, Dublin, Irish Republic
Jamaica: Kingston Bookshop, Kingston
Kenya: Book Distributors Ltd, Nairobi; Textbook Centre Ltd, Nairobi
Malawi: Dzuka Publishing Ltd, Blantyre
Malaysia, Brunei & Thailand: Delta Editions Sdn Bhd, Selangor Darul Ehsan, Malaysia
Malta contact: Thomas Nelson International Sales Department, Malta
Middle East: I.P.R. (International Publishers' Representatives), Nicosia, Cyprus

Pakistan: Danesh, Karachi
Singapore: Nelson Publishers (SEA) Pte Ltd
South Africa, Namibia, Swaziland, Lesotho &
  Botswana (secondary & ELT): Macdonald
  Purnell (Pty) Ltd, Cleveland, South Africa
South Africa, Namibia, Swaziland, Lesotho &
  Botswana (New Way & Gay Way series):
  Macmillan Boleswa, Braamfontein, South
  Africa
St Kitts, Aguilla, Br Virgin Islands, Montzerrat
  & St Maarten: R. J. Laws, Basseterre, St
  Kitts, St Kitts
Tanzania: M & K Publishers & Agencies, Dar
  es Salaam
Trinidad, Guyana, Barbados & Tobago: RIK
  Services Ltd, San Fernando, Trinidad
Uganda: MK Publishers Ltd, Kampala
Uruguay: Noelie Bermudez, Montevideo
USA (Primary Language Arts only): Around
  the World Books, Monroville, PA, USA
USA (Secondary Science & Maths only): South
  Western Publishing Co, Cincinnati, OH,
  USA
Zambia: Insaka Press, Lusaka
Zimbabwe: College Press Publishers (Pvt) Ltd,
  Harare

Book Trade Association Membership: BDC,
EPC

1612

NEW CAVENDISH BOOKS
3 Denbigh Road, London W11 2SJ
Telephone: 0171 229 6765, 792 9984
Fax: 0171 792 0027

Director: Narisa Chakra
Manager: Chris Shelley

Antiques & Collecting

New Titles: 5 (1995), 4 (1996)
No of Employees: 4
Annual Turnover: £0.5M

ISBNs, Imprints & Series:
0 904568, 1 872727

Associated & Subsidiary Companies:
Thailand: River Books

Overseas Representation *(see §7.3):*
Australia & New Zealand: Frank Barker &
  Sons Pty Ltd, Mona Vale, NSW, Australia
Thailand: River Books, Bangkok
USA: Pincushion Enterprises Inc, Tampa, FL

Book Trade Association Membership: PA,
BA

1613

NEW ERA PUBLICATIONS UK LTD
Saint Hill Manor, Saint Hill, East Grinstead,
West Sussex RH19 4JY
Telephone: 01342 314846
Fax: 01342 314857

Managing Director: Margaret Blunden
Managers: Nic Webb *(Sales)*
Eugene Bustamante *(Sales)*
Robert Springall *(Public Relations)*

Academic & Scholarly; Audio Books;
Educational & Textbooks; Fiction; Health &
Beauty; Medical (incl. Self Help & Alternative

Medicine); Philosophy; Religion & Theology;
Science Fiction; Horror

New Titles: 5 (1995), 7 (1996)
No of Employees: 7
Annual Turnover: £1M

ISBNs, Imprints & Series:
1 870451 Mission Earth

Parent Company:
New Era Publication International *(Denmark)*

Associated & Subsidiary Companies:
Australia: N E Publications. *South Africa:*
Continental Publications. *USA:* Bridge
Publications

Overseas Representation *(see §7.3):*
Europe: Walton Marketing Services,
Chislehurst, UK

1614

NEW HOLLAND (PUBLISHERS) LTD
24 Nutford Place, London W1H 6DQ
Telephone: 0171 724 7773
Fax: 0171 724 6184
Email: newhollandpublishing.co.uk
Web Site: vobis@newhollandpublishing.co.uk

Warehouse:
Littlehampton Book Services,
10–14 Eldon Way, Lineside Estate,
Littlehampton, West Sussex BN17 7HE
Telephone: 01903 721596
Fax: 01903 730914

Directors: John Beaufoy *(Managing)*
Charlotte Parry-Crooke *(Publishing)*
Yvonne McFarlane *(Publishing—Lifestyle*
  Books)
Managers: Elena Mannion *(Sales & Foreign*
  Rights)
Martin Oestreicher *(UK Sales & Marketing)*
Tim Jollands *(Publishing—Globetrotter*
  Division)
Jo Hemmings *(Publishing—Natural History &*
  Travel)
Heather White *(Publicity)*
Keith Ireland *(Production)*
Sandy Caven *(Accounts)*
Amanda Spiers *(Trade)*

Antiques & Collecting; Atlases & Maps;
Cookery, Wines & Spirits; Crafts & Hobbies;
Do-It-Yourself; Gardening; Guide Books;
History & Antiquarian; Natural History;
Photography; Travel & Topography

New Titles: 70 (1995), 80 (1996)
No of Employees: 27
Annual Turnover: £4.2M

ISBNs, Imprints & Series:
0 900470, 0 946323 Holland Press
1 85238 Letts
1 85368 New Holland

Associated & Subsidiary Companies:
Australia: National Book Distributors

Distributor for:
Japan: Weatherhill Inc. *South Africa:* Berlitz;
Struik Publishers

Overseas Representation *(see §7.3):*
Australia: National Book Distributors, Frenchs
  Forest, NSW
India: India Book Distributors, Bombay
Japan: YOHAN (Western Publications
  Distribution Agency), Tokyo
Korea, Taiwan & Philippines: Combined
  Representatives Worldwide Inc, Rizal,
  Philippines
Middle East: Peter Ward Book Exports,
  London, UK
New Zealand: South Pacific Books (Imports)
  Ltd, Auckland
Scandinavia: Katie McNeish, London, UK
Singapore & Malaysia: STP Distributors Pte
  Ltd, Singapore
South America & Caribbean: Humphrys
  Roberts Associates, London, UK
Southern Africa: Struik Book Distributors Pty
  Ltd, Johannesburg, Cape Town & Maitland,
  South Africa
Spain & Portugal: Iberian Book Services SL,
  Madrid, Spain
Western Europe: Ted Dougherty, London, UK

Book Trade Association Membership: PA

1615

NEW ORCHARD EDITIONS
Wellington House, 125 Strand, London
WC2R 0BB
Telephone: 0171 420 5555
Fax: 0171 240 7261

Distribution:
Cassell Plc, 3 Fleets Lane, Poole, Dorset
BH15 3AJ
Telephone: 01202 665432
Fax: 01202 666219

Directors: Philip Sturrock *(Chairman &*
  Managing)
Kevin Bristow *(Sales & Marketing)*
Martyn Chapman *(Commercial)*
Geoffrey Charters *(Production)*
Managers: Alison Nicholls *(Sales, Editorial &*
  Marketing)
John Mills *(Export Sales)*
David Williams *(Special Sales)*

Antiques & Collecting; Children's Books;
Cookery, Wines & Spirits; Fine Art & Art
History; Gardening; History & Antiquarian;
Illustrated & Fine Editions; Military & War;
Natural History; Reference Books, Directories
& Dictionaries; Transport; Travel &
Topography

New Titles: 15 (1995), 15 (1996)

ISBNs, Imprints & Series: 1 85079

Parent Company:
Cassell Plc

Associated & Subsidiary Companies:
Arms & Armour Press; Blandford Press;
Cassell; Victor Gollancz; Studio Vista; Ward
Lock

Overseas Representation *(see §7.3):*
see: Cassell Plc, UK

1616

NEW PLAYWRIGHTS' NETWORK
17 Heyes Lane, Timperley, Altrincham,
Cheshire WA15 6EF
Telephone: 0161 969 8755

Also at:
4 Brocklehurst Manor,
25 Brocklehurst Avenue, Macclesfield
SK10 2RX
Telephone: 01625 425312
Fax: 01625 425312

Managing Proprietor: J. C. F. Gray
Production: Ian Hornby
Rights: Denis Cartwright

Theatre, Drama & Dance

New Titles: 50 (1995), 75 (1996)
No of Employees: 4
Annual Turnover: £60,000

ISBNs, Imprints & Series: 0 86319

Overseas Representation *(see §7.3)*:
New Zealand: Play Bureau of New Zealand
Ltd, New Plymouth
South Africa: Dalro (Pty) Ltd, Johannesburg

1617

**THE NEW YORK ACADEMY OF
SCIENCES**
3 Henrietta Street, Covent Garden, London
WC2E 8LU
Telephone: 0171 240 0856
Fax: 0171 379 0609

Director: Danny Maher

*Biology & Zoology; Chemistry; Scientific &
Technical*

New Titles: 35 (1995), 35 (1996)

ISBNs, Imprints & Series: 0 89766

1618

NEXUS SPECIAL INTERESTS
Nexus House, Boundary Way,
Hemel Hempstead, Herts HP2 7ST
Telephone: 01442 66551
Fax: 01442 66998

Distribution:
Bailey Distribution Ltd, Units 1a/
1b Learoyd Road,
Mountfield Road Industrial Estate,
New Romney, Kent TN28 8XU
Telephone: 01797 366905
Fax: 01797 366638

Trade Enquiries:
C. Lloyd Sales & Marketing, 463 Ashley Road,
Parkstone, Poole, Dorset
Telephone: 01202 715349
Fax: 01202 736191

Publisher: Beverly Laughlin

*Aviation; Cookery, Wines & Spirits; Crafts &
Hobbies; Engineering; Health & Beauty;
Military & War; Nautical; Scientific &
Technical; Sports & Games; Transport*

ISBNs, Imprints & Series:
0 85242, 0 90084, 1 85486

Overseas Representation *(see §7.3)*:
Australia: Capricorn Link (Australia) Pty Ltd,
Baulkham Hills, NSW
Canada: Riverwood Publishers Ltd,
Newmarket, Ont
New Zealand: Technical Books, Auckland
South Africa: Media House Publications Pty
Ltd, Sandton
USA: Motorbooks International Publishers &
Wholesalers Inc, Osceola, WI

Book Trade Association Membership: IPG

1619

NFER-NELSON PUBLISHING CO LTD
Darville House, 2 Oxford Road East, Windsor,
Berks SL4 1DF
Telephone: 01753 858961
Fax: 01753 856830

Warehouse:
1–2 Wyndham Road, Hawksworth Estate,
Swindon, Wilts SN2 1EJ
Telephone: 01793 526698
Fax: 01793 432603

Directors: M. Jackson *(Managing)*
I. Florance *(Business Development)*
Fiona Penn *(Commercial)*
Dr Robert Fellham *(Research)*

Tests & Assessments

ISBNs, Imprints & Series:
0 7005, 0 85633

Parent Company:
NFER (National Foundation for Educational
Research) & The Thomson Corporation

Distributor for:
Australia: Australian Council for Educational
Research (ACER). *New Zealand:* New Zealand
Council for Educational Research (NZCER).
USA: AGS; CESA 5; DLM Teaching
Resources; IPAT; PAR; Pro-Ed; WPS

Overseas Representation *(see §7.3)*:
Australia: ACER Ltd, Camberwell, Vic;
Professional Resources Services,
Coldstream, Vic
Canada: Nelson Canada, Scarborough
Cyprus: HAD Centre Ltd, Nicosia
Denmark: Dansk Psykologisk Forlag,
Copenhagen
Finland: Psykologien Kustannus Oy, Helsinki
France: Editions du Centre de Psychologie
Appliquée, Paris
Germany, Austria & Switzerland: Testzentrale,
Göttingen, Germany
Hong Kong: Transglobal Publishers Services
Ltd, Tsuen Wan
India: Manasayan, Shakarpur, Delhi
Irish Republic: ETCC, Dublin
Italy: Organizzazioni Speciali, Florence
Malta: Malta Union of Professional
Psychologists, Valletta
Netherlands & Belgium: Swets & Zeitlinger bv,
Lisse, Netherlands
New Zealand: NZCER, Wellington
Norway: Norsk Psykologforening, Oslo
Norway (selected lists only): Universitets
Forlaget, Oslo, Norway

Portugal: PSICO, Lisbon
Singapore, Malaysia, Indonesia & Thailand:
Nelson Publishers (SEA) Pte Ltd, Singapore
South Africa (selected tests only): Occupational
& Medical Suppliers, Johannesburg, South
Africa
Sweden: Psykologiförlaget AB, Stockholm
Taiwan: Unifacmanu Trading Co Ltd, Taipei
USA: Western Psychological Services, Los
Angeles, CA
USA (selected tests only): Stoelting, Wood
Dale, IL, USA; PAR Inc, Odessa, FL, USA

Book Trade Association Membership: PA,
EPC

1620

NILE & MACKENZIE LTD
13 John Prince's Street, London W1M 9HB
Telephone: 0171 493 0351
Fax: 0171 495 0128

Warehouse:
Rapat Freight Ltd, Rapat House,
Amberley Way, off Green Lane, Hounslow,
Middlesex TW4 6BH
Telephone: 0181 570 7777

Managing Director: Daljit Sehbai

*Children's Books; Educational & Textbooks;
Reference Books, Directories & Dictionaries*

ISBNs, Imprints & Series: 0 86031

Distributor for:
India: Living Media India Ltd

Overseas Representation *(see §7.3)*:
Ghana: FEP International Ghana, Accra
India: Thomson Press (India) Ltd, New Delhi
Jamaica: Kingston Publishers Ltd, Kingston
Philippines: Jade Book Distributors Inc,
Quezon City
Singapore: Daystar Publishers Pte Ltd
Trinidad: Caribbean Book Distributors, Port of
Spain

1621

JAMES NISBET & CO LTD
78 Tilehouse Street, Hitchin, Herts SG5 2DY
Telephone: 01462 438331
Fax: 01462 431528

Directors: E. M. Mackenzie-Wood
(Chairman)
A. A. C. Bierrum *(Company Secretary)*

*Educational & Textbooks; Electronic
(Educational); Industry, Business &
Management*

ISBNs, Imprints & Series: 0 7202

Overseas Representation *(see §7.3)*:
New Zealand: David Bateman Ltd, Auckland
Southern Africa: Book Promotions Pty Ltd,
Plumstead, South Africa

1622

**NORTHCOTE HOUSE PUBLISHERS
LTD**
Plymbridge House, Estover Road, Plymouth,
Devon PL6 7PY

Telephone: 01752 202368
Fax: 01752 202330

Distributors:
Plymbridge Distributors Ltd, Estover,
Plymouth PL6 7PY
Telephone: 01752 202301
Fax: 01752 202331

Managing Director: Brian Hulme
Accounts: Michael Beevers, FCA *(Company
Secretary)*

*Educational & Textbooks; Literature &
Criticism; Theatre, Drama & Dance;
Vocational Training & Careers*

New Titles: 10 (1995), 35 (1996)
No of Employees: 2

ISBNs, Imprints & Series:
0 7463, 1 85461 Northcote House, Resources in
Education, Starting Out...., Writers and Their
Work

Overseas Representation *(see §7.3)*:
Arab Middle East, Cyprus & Malta: Eurab Ltd,
Rottingdean, UK
Australia: Astam Books Pty Ltd, Leichhardt,
NSW
Austria & Switzerland: Patrick Bygate,
Massagno, Switzerland
Canada: Scholarly Book Services Inc, Toronto
Caribbean: Hugh Dunphy, Kingston, Jamaica
France, Greece, Italy & Yugoslavia: Juliusz
Komarnicki, Massagno, Switzerland
Germany: PKB – Robbert J. Pleysier, Heerde,
Netherlands
Hong Kong & Philippines: Electra Media
Group Pty Ltd, Sydney, NSW, Australia
India: Maya Publishers Pvt Ltd, New Delhi
Netherlands, Belgium & Luxembourg: Reinier
A. Pleysier, Heerde, Netherlands
Pakistan: Book Bird, Lahore
Portugal, Spain & Gibraltar: Patrick Bygate,
Massagno, Switzerland
Scandinavia: D. Richard Bowen, Malmö,
Sweden
Singapore & Malaysia: Publishers Marketing
Services Ltd, Singapore
South Africa: Judith Wengrowe Agencies,
Northcliff, Johannesburg
USA: University Press of Mississippi, Jackson,
MS
Zimbabwe, Zambia & Malawi: Barbie Keene,
Harare, Zimbabwe

Book Trade Association Membership: IPG

1623 ▬▬▬▬▬▬▬

W. W. NORTON & CO LTD
10 Coptic Street, London WC1A 1PU
Telephone: 0171 323 1579
Fax: 0171 436 4553

Distribution:
John Wiley & Sons Ltd, 1 Oldlands Way,
Shripney, Bognor Regis, Sussex PO22 9SA
Telephone: 01243 779777
Fax: 01243 820250

Directors: R. A. Cameron *(Managing)*
D. S. Lamm *(USA)*
V. Schmalzer *(USA)*
Lord Bullock, FBA
R. A. Denniston

E. Barber *(USA)*
W. D. McFeely *(USA)*
S. R. Lawrence *(USA)*
G. Luciano *(USA)*
Managers: Ariadne van de Ven *(Publicity)*
Judith Pamplin *(Sales)*
Victoria Keown-Boyd *(Marketing)*

*Architecture & Design; Biology & Zoology;
Cinema, Video, TV & Radio; Computer
Science; Economics; Fine Art & Art History;
Gender Studies; History & Antiquarian;
Literature & Criticism; Mathematics &
Statistics; Music; Natural History; Nautical;
Philosophy; Physics; Poetry; Politics & World
Affairs; Psychology & Psychiatry; Sports &
Games; Theatre, Drama & Dance*

ISBNs, Imprints & Series:
0 393 Norton
0 87140 Liveright

Parent Company:
W. W. Norton & Co *(USA)*

Distributor for:
USA: Ecco Press; New Directions Publishing
Corporation

Overseas Representation *(see §7.3)*:
Africa: Kelvin van Hasselt Publishing Services,
Lymington, UK
India: Viva Marketing, New Delhi
Irish Republic: Sheila Lavery, Ashbourne, Co
Meath
Middle East, North Africa & Pakistan:
International Publishers Representatives
(IPR), Nicosia, Cyprus

1624 ▬▬▬▬▬▬▬

NORWOOD PUBLISHERS
3 Chapel Street, Norwood Green, Halifax,
West Yorkshire HR3 8QU
Telephone: 01274 602454
Fax: 01274 676665

Partners: M. H. Wolfenden
Mrs A. M. Wolfenden

Educational & Textbooks

ISBNs, Imprints & Series: 1 873784

1625 ▬▬▬▬▬▬▬

NTC PUBLICATIONS LTD
Farm Road, Henley-on-Thames, Oxfordshire
RG9 1EJ
Telephone: 01491 411000
Fax: 01491 571188

Directors: David Roberts *(Managing)*
Andrew Denham *(Production)*
Leo Zeglovskis *(Finance)*
Managers: Bob Hulks *(Publisher –
Advertising & Media)*
Lynn Marshall *(Office)*
Suzanne Timbers *(Accounts)*

*Economics; Industry, Business &
Management; Reference Books, Directories &
Dictionaries*

New Titles: 42 (1995), 44 (1996)
No of Employees: 28
Annual Turnover: £2.8M

ISBNs, Imprints & Series: 1 870562

Parent Company:
Allied Information Technologies Ltd

Associated & Subsidiary Companies:
Advertising Press Ltd; Industry Forecasts Ltd;
NTC Publications Ltd; NTC Research Ltd

Book Trade Association Membership: PA,
DPA

1626 ▬▬▬▬▬▬▬

OBERON BOOKS LTD
521 Caledonian Road, London N7 9RH
Telephone: 0171 607 3637
Fax: 0171 607 3629

Sales Representation:
Troika, 179 King's Cross Road, London
WC1X 9BZ
Telephone: 0171 833 8441
Fax: 0171 833 8442

Publishing Director: James Hogan
Orders: W. Sutcliffe

Theatre, Drama & Dance

New Titles: 10 (1995), 24 (1996)
No of Employees: 3

ISBNs, Imprints & Series:
1 870259 Oberon Classics, Oberon Modern
Playwrights, Oberon/Lamda (London
Academy of Music & Dramatic Art)

Overseas Representation *(see §7.3)*:
New Zealand: Birch Tree Books, Auckland

1627 ▬▬▬▬▬▬▬

OLDCASTLE BOOKS LTD
18 Coleswood Road, Harpenden, Herts
AL5 1EQ
Telephone: 01582 761264
Fax: 01582 712244
Email: noxitpress@aol.com

**Distributor (excluding Cardoza
Publications):**
Turnaround Distribution

Orders (Cardoza Publications):
Oldcastle Books Ltd *(address as above)*
Telephone: *as above*
Fax: *as above*

Director: Ion Mills *(Home & Export Sales)*

*Crime; Fiction; Sports & Games; Gambling
Books*

ISBNs, Imprints & Series:
0 948353, 1 874061 No Exit Press (Fiction),
Oldcastle Books Gambling Books

Distributor for:
USA: Cardoza Publications

Overseas Representation *(see §7.3)*:
Australia: Capricorn Link (Australia) Pty Ltd,
Baulkham Hills, NSW
Eastern Europe: MTM, London, UK
Far East: AIMS, Larkfield, UK

Irish Republic: Brookside Publishing Services, Dublin
Middle East: Eurab Ltd, Rottingdean, UK
Rest of Europe: Janet Clark, London, UK
Scandinavia: Katie McNeish, London, UK
South Africa: MacDonald Purnell (Pty) Ltd, Randburg

Book Trade Association Membership: IPG

1628

*OM PUBLISHING
PO Box 300, Carlisle CA3 0QS
Telephone: 01228 512512
Fax: 01228 514949

Director of Publishing Services: Pieter Kwant
Publishing Manager: Jeremy Mudditt

Biography & Autobiography; Children's Books; Religion & Theology

ISBNs, Imprints & Series:
0 903843, 1 85078

Parent Company:
Send The Light Ltd

1629

MICHAEL O'MARA BOOKS LTD
9 Lion Yard, Tremadoc Road, London SW4 7NQ
Telephone: 0171 720 8643
Fax: 0171 627 8953 (editorial) & 627 3041 (sales & marketing)
Email: lesleyo'mara.100773. 1774@compuserve.com
Web Site: http://www.bookshop.co.uk/ omarabooks/

Warehouse/Trade Enquiries & Orders:
Macmillan Distribution, Brunel Road, Houndmills, Basingstoke, Hants RG21 2XS
Telephone: 01256 29242
Fax: 01256 479476

Chairman: Michael O'Mara
Directors: Lesley O'Mara *(Managing, Rights & Sales)*
David Roberts *(Editorial)*

Biography & Autobiography; Children's Books; Crafts & Hobbies; Fiction; Health & Beauty; History & Antiquarian; Humour; Illustrated & Fine Editions; Military & War

New Titles: 50 (1995), 40 (1996)
No of Employees: 18

ISBNs, Imprints & Series:
0 948397, 1 85479

Overseas Representation *(see §7.3):*
Australia: National Book Distributors, Frenchs Forest, NSW
Canada: Fitzhenry & Whiteside Ltd, Markham
New Zealand: HarperCollins Publishers, Auckland
South Africa: Struik Book Distributors Pty Ltd, Maitland
USA (Children's and Gift Books only): Associated Publishers Group (APG), Nashville, TN, USA

1630

OMNIBUS PRESS
8–9 Frith Street, London W1V 5TZ
Telephone: 0171 434 0066
Fax: 0171 734 2246

Warehouse:
Music Sales Ltd, Newmarket Road, Bury St Edmunds, Suffolk IP33 3YB
Telephone: 01284 702600
Fax: 01284 768301

Directors: Robert Wise *(Managing)*
Malcolm Grabham *(Financial)*
Managers: Andrew King *(Rights)*
Hilary Donlon *(Marketing)*
Editor: Chris Charlesworth

Biography & Autobiography; Music

New Titles: 40 (1995), 40 (1996)

ISBNs, Imprints & Series:
0 7119 Bobcat Books, Omnibus Press

Parent Company:
Music Sales Ltd

Associated & Subsidiary Companies:
Australia: Music Sales (Pty) Ltd. *USA:* Music Sales Corp

Distributor for:
BBC Music Guides; Gramophone; Independent Music Press; Music Master

Overseas Representation *(see §7.3):*
Asia & Far East: Ashton International Marketing Services, Larkfield, UK
Australia: Music Sales Pty Ltd, Findon, SA
Central America, Mexico & Caribbean: Humphrys Roberts Associates, London, UK
Cyprus & Middle East: Peter Ward Book Exports, London, UK
Eastern European States (including Hungary, Czech Republic & Slovakia): Michael Timperley Marketing, Hong Kong
Germany, Switzerland, Austria, Belgium, France & Netherlands: Michael Geoghegan, London, UK
India: Book Channel, Bombay
New Zealand: c/o Bookwise International, Auckland
Scandinavia: Katie McNeish, London, UK
South Africa: Trinity Books CC, Randburg
South America: Humphrys Roberts Associates, Cotia, Brazil
Spain, Portugal, Gibraltar & Italy: Janet Clark, London, UK
USA: Music Sales Corporation, New York

Book Trade Association Membership: PA

1631

ONEWORLD PUBLICATIONS
185 Banbury Road, Oxford OX2 7AR
Telephone: 01865 310597
Fax: 01865 310598
Email: oneworld@cix.compulink.co.uk

Trade Enquiries & Orders:
Penguin Books, Harmondsworth, Middx UB7 0DA

Directors: Novin Doostdar *(Sales & Marketing)*
Juliet Mabey *(Editorial)*
Senior Editor: Helen Coward
Rights: Linda Lloyd

Gender Studies; Philosophy; Politics & World Affairs; Psychology & Psychiatry; Religion & Theology; Sociology & Anthropology; Social Concerns

ISBNs, Imprints & Series: 1 85168

Overseas Representation *(see §7.3):*
Canada: Penguin Books Canada Ltd, Newmarket, Ont
USA: Penguin Books, New York

1632

OPC (OXFORD PUBLISHING COMPANY)
Sparkford, Yeovil, Somerset BA22 7JJ
Telephone: 01963 440635
Fax: 01963 440023

Mail Orders & Despatch:
(as above)
Telephone: 01963 440614
Fax: 01963 440001

Director: J. H. Haynes *(Chairman)*
Editorial: D. J. Reach
Sales: T. Kemp
Export Sales: M. Adams
Editor: P. Nicholson
Rights: R. Jackson
Marketing: D. Keel
Finance: C. Davies
Production: K. Perrett

Transport

New Titles: 5 (1995), 5 (1996)

ISBNs, Imprints & Series: 0 86093

Parent Company:
Haynes Publishing Group Plc

Associated & Subsidiary Companies:
G. T. Foulis & Co; J. H. Haynes & Co Ltd; Oxford Illustrated Press; Patrick Stephens Ltd

Overseas Representation *(see §7.3):*
USA, Canada & Mexico: Haynes Publications Inc, Newbury Park, CA, USA

1633

OPEN GATE PRESS
51 Achilles Road, London NW6 1DZ
Telephone: 0171 431 4391
Fax: 0171 431 5088

Trade Enquiries & Orders:
Book Representation & Distribution Ltd, 244A London Road, Hadleigh, Essex SS7 2DE
Telephone: 01702 552912
Fax: 01702 556095

Editorial: Jeannie Cohen
Production: Elisabeth Petersdorff

Academic & Scholarly; Philosophy; Politics & World Affairs; Psychology & Psychiatry

New Titles: 4 (1995), 4 (1996)
No of Employees: 4

ISBNs, Imprints & Series: 1 871871

Distributor for:
Cambridge International Publishers

Overseas Representation *(see §7.3)*:
Mainland Europe: Books for Europe Ltd,
Bournemouth, UK
Southern Africa: Judith Wengrowe Agencies,
Northcliff, Johannesburg, South Africa
USA & Canada: Paul & Co Publishers
Consortium Inc, Concord, MA, USA

Book Trade Association Membership: PA,
IPG

1634 ■■■■■■■■■■■■■■■■■■■■■■

THE OPEN UNIVERSITY
Walton Hall, Milton Keynes MK7 6AA
Telephone: 01908 653515
Fax: 01908 652436

Also at:
OUEE Ltd, 12 Cofferidge Close,
Stony Stratford, Milton Keynes MK11 1BY
Telephone: 01908 261662
Fax: 01908 261001

Managing Editor, Book Trade: John Taylor

*Academic & Scholarly; Architecture & Design;
Biology & Zoology; Chemistry; Economics;
Educational & Textbooks; Electronic
(Educational); Engineering; Gender Studies;
Geography & Geology; History &
Antiquarian; Industry, Business &
Management; Mathematics & Statistics;
Medical (incl. Self Help & Alternative
Medicine); Music; Natural History;
Philosophy; Physics; Politics & World Affairs;
Psychology & Psychiatry; Religion &
Theology; Scientific & Technical; Sociology &
Anthropology*

ISBNs, Imprints & Series: 0 7492

Associated & Subsidiary Companies:
Open University Educational Enterprises Ltd

Overseas Representation *(see §7.3)*:
Australia & New Zealand (all products): EMA
Open Learning (Pty) Ltd, South Melbourne,
Australia
*Botswana, Kenya, Lesotho, Mauritius,
Mozambique, South Africa, Seychelles,
Swaziland, South West Africa/Namibia &
Transkei (all products):* Advtech Video
Training, Johannesburg, South Africa
Greece & Cyprus (all products): Open
University Educational Enterprises Ltd,
Milton Keynes, UK
*Hong Kong, Macau & People's Republic of
China (all products):* Educational Film
Services Ltd, Hong Kong
Irish Republic (all products): National
Distance Education Centre, Dublin, Irish
Republic
Italy (video): Cinehollywood Srl, Milan, Italy
Japan (all products): General Educational
Media Corp, Tokyo, Japan
Malaysia (all products): Educational Film
Services Sdn Bhd, Kuala Lumpur, Malaysia

*Middle East, North Africa & Turkey (all
products, video/English & Arabic
languages):* Audio Visual Source,
Crowborough, UK
*Middle East, North Africa & Turkey (video/film
— Broadcast Sales in Arabic version):* Media
Consultants, Amman, Jordan
*Nigeria, Ivory Coast, Ghana, Gambia, Senegal
& The Cameroons (all products):* Open
University Educational Enterprises Ltd,
Milton Keynes, UK
Pakistan (video/film): Didactic Films Ltd,
Oxford, UK
*Singapore, Brunei, Indonesia & Thailand (all
products):* Educational Film Services Pte
Ltd, Singapore
Spain (video/film): Technea Iberica SL,
Barcelona, Spain
Taiwan (all products): Educational Film
Services (Taiwan) Ltd, Taipei, Taiwan
*Uganda, Zaire, Zambia & Zimbabwe (all
products):* Advtech Video Training,
Johannesburg, South Africa
USA (video/film): Open University Educational
Enterprises Ltd, Milton Keynes, UK

Book Trade Association Membership: PA,
IPG

1635 ■■■■■■■■■■■■■■■■■■■■■■

**OPEN UNIVERSITY EDUCATIONAL
ENTERPRISES LTD**
12 Cofferidge Close, Stony Stratford,
Milton Keynes MK11 1BY
Telephone: 01908 261662
Fax: 01908 261001

Chairman: Dr J. S. Daniel
Directors: P. D. Bowen *(Managing)*
J. N. Chapple
J. A. Clarke *(Deputy Managing & Company
Secretary)*
Prof S. Hall
P. Marsh
N. H. Smith
Prof A. W. J. Thomson
Managers: Sue Hitchen *(Business — Print)*
Diana Ruault *(Media—A/V)*
Philip Rathkey *(General)*
Edmund Dixon *(Marketing Development)*
John Beer *(Business—Professional Training
Materials)*

*Academic & Scholarly; Architecture & Design;
Biology & Zoology; Chemistry; Economics;
Educational & Textbooks; Electronic
(Educational); Engineering; Geography &
Geology; History & Antiquarian; Industry,
Business & Management; Mathematics &
Statistics; Philosophy; Physics; Politics &
World Affairs; Psychology & Psychiatry;
Scientific & Technical; Sociology &
Anthropology*

ISBNs, Imprints & Series: 0 7492

Distributor for:
The Open University

Overseas Representation *(see §7.3)*:
*Algeria, Bahrain, Egypt, Ethiopia, Iran, Iraq,
Jordan, Kuwait, Lebanon, Libya, Morocco,
North Yemen (video/film — broadcast sales in
Arabic version):* Media Consultants,
Amman, Jordan

Australia & New Zealand: EMA Open
Learning (Pty) Ltd, South Melbourne,
Australia
*Botswana, South Africa, Namibia &
Zimbabwe:* Viewcom (Pty) Ltd, Randburg,
South Africa
Greece & Cyprus: Educational Materials
Enterprises Ltd, Athens, Greece
*Hong Kong, Macau & People's Republic of
China:* Educational Film Services Ltd, Hong
Kong
Irish Republic: National Distance Education
Centre, Dublin
Italy (Video): Cinehollywood Srl, Milan, Italy
Japan: General Educational Media Corp,
Tokyo
Malaysia: Educational Film Services Sdn Bhd,
Kuala Lumpur
*Middle East, North Africa & Turkey (video/
English & Arabic languages):* Audio Visual
Source, Crowborough, UK
*Middle East, North Africa & Turkey (video/film
— Broadcast Sales in Arabic version):* Media
Consultants, Amman, Jordan
*Nigeria, Ivory Coast, Ghana, Gambia, Senegal
& The Cameroons (all products):* Open
University Educational Enterprises Ltd,
Milton Keynes, UK
*Oman, Qatar, Saudi Arabia, Somalia, South
Yemen, Sudan, Syria, Tunisia, Turkey &
United Arab Emirates (video/film —
Broadcast sales in Arabic version):* Media
Consultants, Amman, Jordan
Pakistan (video/film): Didactic Films Ltd,
Oxford, UK
Singapore, Brunei, Indonesia, & Thailand:
Educational Film Services Pte Ltd,
Singapore
Spain (video/film): Ancora Audiovisual SA,
Barcelona, Spain
Taiwan: Educational Film Services (Taiwan)
Ltd, Taipei
USA: Open University Educational Enterprises
Ltd, Milton Keynes, UK

Book Trade Association Membership: PA

1636 ■■■■■■■■■■■■■■■■■■■■■■

OPEN UNIVERSITY PRESS
Celtic Court, 22 Ballmoor, Buckingham
MK18 1XW
Telephone: 01280 823388
Fax: 01280 823233
Email: enquiries@openup.co.uk
Web Site: http://www.bookshop.co.uk/openup

Trade Counter:
Telephone: 01280 822211
Fax: 01280 823681
Email: enquiries@openup.co.uk
Web Site: http://www.bookshop.co.uk/openup

Directors: John Skelton *(Managing)*
Barry Clarke *(Financial)*
Sue Hadden *(Production)*
Jacinta Evans *(Publishing)*
Managers: Barbara Martin *(Sales & Rights)*
Gary Hall *(Home & Export Marketing)*

*Academic & Scholarly; Educational &
Textbooks; Gay & Lesbian Studies; Gender
Studies; Medical (incl. Self Help & Alternative
Medicine); Politics & World Affairs;
Psychology & Psychiatry; Sociology &
Anthropology*

New Titles: 91 (1995), 90 (1996)
No of Employees: 30
Annual Turnover: £3M

ISBNs, Imprints & Series:
0 335 Open University Press, Society for Research into Higher Education Series

Distributor for:
USA: Indiana University Press

Overseas Representation *(see §7.3)*:
Australia & New Zealand: Allen & Unwin Pty Ltd, St Leonards, NSW, Australia
Canada: Scholarly Book Services Inc, Toronto
Hong Kong, China, Korea, Taiwan & Philippines: Asia Publisher Services Ltd, Hong Kong
India: Viva Marketing, New Delhi
Japan: Kinokuniya Book Import Dept, Tokyo
Malaysia: APD Kuala Lumpur, Petaling Jaya
Pakistan: Book Bird, Lahore
Singapore, Brunei, Indonesia & Thailand: APD Singapore Pte Ltd, Singapore
South Africa, Botswana, Lesotho, Mauritius, Namibia & Swaziland: Book Promotions Pty Ltd, Plumstead, South Africa
USA: Taylor & Francis Inc, Bristol, PA

Book Trade Association Membership: PA, IPG

1637

*ORCHARD BOOKS
[a division of The Watts Publishing Group]
96 Leonard Street, London EC2A 4RH
Telephone: 0171 739 2929
Fax: 0171 739 2318

Warehouse & Distribution:
see The Watts Publishing Group

Directors: Marlene Johnson *(Managing – Watts Publishing Group)*
Francesca Dow *(Publishing)*
Rita Ireland *(Production)*
George Spicer *(Trade Sales)*
Sarah Odedina *(Group Rights)*
Managers: Linda Banner *(Promotions)*
Catharine Snow *(Rights)*
Paul Moreton *(Marketing)*

Children's Books

ISBNs, Imprints & Series:
1 85213, 1 86039

Parent Company:
The Watts Publishing Group *(a division of Grolier Ltd)*

Associated & Subsidiary Companies:
Australia: Franklin Watts Australia. *USA:* Orchard Books [a division of Franklin Watts Inc]

Overseas Representation *(see §7.3)*:
Australia & New Zealand: Franklin Watts Australia, Lane Cove, Australia
Europe: Roger Smith, Enfield, UK
Hong Kong, Indonesia & India: Balatbat & Sons International, Quezon City, Philippines
Irish Republic: Rep Force Ireland, Monkstown
Japan: Japan English Services Inc, Chiba-ken
Middle East, Cyprus & Pakistan: Anthony Rudkin Associates, Oxford, UK

Scandinavia: D. Richard Bowen, Malmö, Sweden
South Africa & Swaziland: Leo Books, Roggebaai & Cape Town, South Africa

Book Trade Association Membership: PA, LBA

1638

ORDNANCE SURVEY
Romsey Road, Maybush, Southampton SO9 4DH
Telephone: 01703 792000 ext. 2768
Fax: 01703 792494

Director of Consumer & Education Markets: Don Davies
Managers: John Miell *(Joint Commercial Publications)*
Karen McGrath *(Joint Commercial Publications)*
Paul Franklin *(Publishing – Small Scale Mapping)*
Mike Cranidge *(Branch – Trade Sales)*
Robin Knights *(Copyright)*

Atlases & Maps; Educational & Textbooks; Electronic (Educational); Geography & Geology; Guide Books

ISBNs, Imprints & Series: 0 319

Book Trade Association Membership: PA, BA, CAPP

1639

ORION BOOKS LTD
Orion House, 5 Upper St Martins Lane, London WC2H 9EA
Telephone: 0171 240 3444
Fax: 0171 240 4822

Trade Counter & Warehouse:
Littlehampton Book Services Ltd,
14 Eldon Way, Lineside Estate, Littlehampton, West Sussex BN17 7HE
Telephone: 01903 726410
Fax: 01903 730914

Publisher: Rosie Cheetham *(Orion Books)*
Managing Directors: Susan Lamb *(Orion Paperbacks)*
Judith Elliott *(Orion Children's)*
Publishing Director: Jane Wood *(Orion Books)*

Biography & Autobiography; Children's Books; Fiction; Science Fiction; Fantasy

ISBNs, Imprints & Series:
1 85592 Chapmans
1 85797 Orion
1 85798 Millennium
1 85799 Phoenix
1 85881 Orion Children's
1 89758 Orion Paperbacks, Phoenix House

Parent Company:
The Orion Publishing Group Ltd

Overseas Representation *(see §7.3)*:
see: The Orion Publishing Group Ltd, London, UK

1640

THE ORION PUBLISHING GROUP LTD
Orion House, 5 Upper St Martins Lane, London WC2H 9EA
Telephone: 0171 240 3444
Fax: 0171 240 4822

Trade Counter & Warehouse:
Littlehampton Book Services Ltd,
14 Eldon Way, Lineside Estate, Littlehampton, West Sussex BN17 7HE
Telephone: 01903 726410
Fax: 01903 730914

Chairman: Lord Cuckney
Chief Executive: Anthony Cheetham
Directors: Peter Roche *(Managing)*
Dallas Manderson *(Group Sales)*
Jonathan King *(Home Sales)*
Mark Streatfeild *(Export Sales)*
Richard Hussey *(Production)*
Matthew O'Sullivan *(Deputy Finance)*
Clare Hegarty *(Art)*
Group Financial Controller: Carl Stott

New Titles: 300 (1995), 300 (1996)
No of Employees: 180
Annual Turnover: £27M

ISBNs, Imprints & Series:
0 297 Weidenfeld & Nicolson
0 460 Artus Books, J M Dent, Everyman Paperbacks, Northcliffe House Books, Orion Paperbacks
1 85592 Chapmans
1 85797 Orion
1 85798 Millennium
1 85799 Phoenix
1 85881 Orion Children's
1 89758 Phoenix House

Associated & Subsidiary Companies:
J M Dent Ltd; Littlehampton Book Services Ltd; Orion Books Ltd; George Weidenfeld and Nicolson Ltd

Distributor for:
Peter Halban Publishers

Overseas Representation *(see §7.3)*:
Australia: Allen & Unwin Pty Ltd, St Leonards, NSW
Canada: Douglas & McIntyre, Toronto
East Africa: Len Ainsworth, Aldbourne, UK
Europe (excluding Scandinavia & Netherlands)): Onslow Books Ltd, London, UK
India, Sri Lanka & Bangladesh: Maya Publishers Pvt Ltd, New Delhi, India
Israel: Rodney Franklin Agency, Tel Aviv
Middle East & North Africa: Ashton International Marketing Services, Larkfield, UK
Netherlands: Consul Books, Blaricum
New Zealand: Hodder Moa Beckett Publishers Ltd, Auckland
Scandinavia: Sven Gade, Hørsholm, Denmark
South Africa: Jonathan Ball Publishers (Pty) Ltd, Johannesburg
South America: Humphrys Roberts Associates, São Paulo, Brazil
South East Asia, Caribbean, Pakistan & Japan: Ralph & Sheila Summers, London, UK
USA & Other Territories: The Orion Publishing Group Ltd, London, UK

1641 ▬▬▬▬▬▬▬▬▬▬▬▬▬

OSMOSIS PUBLICATIONS
55 Kellner Road, London SE28 0AX
Telephone: 0181 855 5497
Fax: 0181 316 5840

Proprietor: Brian C. J. Warnes

Accountancy & Taxation; Industry, Business & Management

ISBNs, Imprints & Series: 0 9509432

Book Trade Association Membership: PA

1642 ▬▬▬▬▬▬▬▬▬▬▬▬▬

OSPREY
Michelin House, 81 Fulham Road, London
SW3 6RB
Telephone: 0171 581 9393
Fax: 0171 225 9458

Distribution:
Reed Book Services, Northampton Road,
Rushden, Northants NN10 6PU
Telephone: 01933 58521
Fax: 01933 50284

International Sales Department:
(as above)
Telephone: 0171 581 9393
Fax: 0171 225 9371

Managing Director: Jonathan Parker

Aviation; Military & War; Transport

ISBNs, Imprints & Series:
0 85045, 1 85532

Parent Company:
Reed Elsevier Plc

Overseas Representation *(see §7.3):*
Australia: Reed Books Australia, Melbourne,
  Vic
Canada: Reed Publishing Canada, Markham,
  Ont
East Asia: Reed Consumer Books, Metro
  Manila, Philippines
India: Reed Consumer Books, New Delhi
Japan: Reed Consumer Books, Tokyo
New Zealand: Reed Publishing Group,
  Auckland
Singapore: Reed International (Singapore) Pte
  Ltd
South Africa: Struik Book Distributors Pty Ltd,
  Johannesburg, Cape Town & Maitland

1643 ▬▬▬▬▬▬▬▬▬▬▬▬▬

**OVERSEAS DEVELOPMENT
INSTITUTE**
Regent's College, Inner Circle, Regent's Park,
London NW1 4NS
Telephone: 0171 487 7413
Fax: 0171 487 7590
Email: publications@odi.org.uk
Web Site: http://www.oneworld.org/odi/

Publications & IT Officer: Peter Gee
Assistant Publications Officer: Pippa Leask

*Agriculture; Economics; Politics & World
Affairs; Sociology & Anthropology*

New Titles: 30 (1995), 35 (1996)

ISBNs, Imprints & Series: 0 85003

Book Trade Association Membership:
ALPSP

1644 ▬▬▬▬▬▬▬▬▬▬▬▬▬

PETER OWEN LTD
73 Kenway Road, London SW5 0RE
Telephone: 0171 373 5628 & 0171 370 6093
Fax: 0171 373 6760

Trade Counter & Warehouse:
Littlehampton Book Services, Lineside Estate,
Littlehampton, West Sussex BN17 7HE
Telephone: 01903 721596
Fax: 01903 730914

Managing Director: Peter Owen *(Rights &
  Permissions)*
Editorial: Stephen Stuart-Smith
Production: Juliet Standing
Sales: Lorna Casimir
Publicity: Gary Pulsifer

*Biography & Autobiography; Fashion &
Costume; Fiction; Gay & Lesbian Studies;
Literature & Criticism; Theatre, Drama &
Dance*

New Titles: 35 (1995), 35 (1996)
No of Employees: 6

ISBNs, Imprints & Series: 0 7206

Overseas Representation *(see §7.3):*
Australia: Peribo Pty Ltd, Mount Kuring-gai,
  NSW
Canada: Scholarly Book Services Inc, Toronto
Europe (excluding Scandinavia): Onslow
  Books Ltd, London, UK
New Zealand: Brick Row Publishing Co Ltd,
  Auckland
Scandinavia & Iceland: D. Richard Bowen,
  Malmö, Sweden
South East Asia: Balabat & Sons Int, Metro
  Manila, Philippines
USA: Dufour Editions Inc, Chester Springs, PA

1645 ▬▬▬▬▬▬▬▬▬▬▬▬▬

OXBOW BOOKS
Park End Place, Oxford OX1 1HN
Telephone: 01865 241249
Fax: 01865 794449
Email: oxbow@patrol.i-way.co.uk

Managing Director: David Brown
Sales & Marketing: Liz Jones
Finance: Jane Lovell
US Manager: Michael Hagen

*Archaeology; History & Antiquarian;
Classical Studies; Egyptology*

New Titles: 12 (1995), 15 (1996)

ISBNs, Imprints & Series:
0 946897 Oxbow Monographs in Archaeology
  1 900188

Distributor for:
The British Institute of Archaeology at Ankara;
The British School at Rome; British School of
Archaeology in Iraq; Edinburgh University,

Dept of Archaeology; Oxford University
Committee for Archaeology; Society of
Antiquaries of Scotland; York University, Dept
of Archaeology. *USA:* American Early
Medieval Studies; International Monographs in
Prehistory; Prehistory Press

Overseas Representation *(see §7.3):*
USA & Canada: David Brown Book Co,
  Oakville, CT, USA

Book Trade Association Membership: BA,
American Booksellers Association

1646 ▬▬▬▬▬▬▬▬▬▬▬▬▬

OXFAM PUBLISHING
274 Banbury Road, Oxford OX2 7DZ
Telephone: 01865 313921
Fax: 01865 313925
Email: publish@oxfam.org.uk

Warehouse:
BEBC, PO Box 1496, Parkstone, Dorset
BH12 3YD
Telephone: 01202 715555
Fax: 01202 715556

Trade Distribution & Trade Enquiries:
Central Books, 99 Wallis Road, London
E9 5LN
Telephone: 0181 986 4854
Fax: 0181 533 5821

**Oxfam Publications, Oxfam Education,
  Oxfam Audio-Visual:** Robert Cornford

*Agriculture; Atlases & Maps; Economics;
Educational & Textbooks; Environment &
Development Studies; Gender Studies; Medical
(incl. Self Help & Alternative Medicine);
Politics & World Affairs*

New Titles: 40 (1995), 40 (1996)

ISBNs, Imprints & Series:
0 85598 Oxfam Publications
0 870727 Oxfam Education, Oxfam
  Information
1 870727 Oxfam Audio-Visual

Overseas Representation *(see §7.3):*
Australia: Bushbooks, Gosford South, NSW
India: K. Krishnamurthy (Books), Madras
Netherlands: Ruurd Ruward, Ruward BV, The
  Hague
North America: Humanities Press International
  Inc, Atlantic Highlands, NJ, USA
*South Africa, Botswana, Swaziland, Lesotho,
  Zimbabwe & Namibia:* David Philip
  Publishers Pty Ltd, Claremont, South Africa

1647 ▬▬▬▬▬▬▬▬▬▬▬▬▬

**OXFORD INSTITUTE FOR ENERGY
STUDIES**
57 Woodstock Road, Oxford OX2 6FA
Telephone: 01865 311377
Fax: 01865 310527
Email: energy.studies@mail.wolfson.ox.ac.uk
Web Site: http://www.wolfson.ox.ac.uk/
energy/

Director: Robert Mabro
Marketing: Richard Hepworth
Order Fulfilment: Margaret Ko

*Academic & Scholarly; Economics;
Environment & Development Studies*

New Titles: 8 (1995), 10 (1996)
No of Employees: 15

ISBNs, Imprints & Series: 0 948061

Overseas Representation *(see §7.3):*
USA: PennWell Books, Tulsa, OK

1648 ■■■■■■■

OXFORD UNIVERSITY PRESS
Walton Street, Oxford OX2 6DP
Telephone: 01865 56767
Fax: 01865 56646

Corby Office:
Oxford University Press Dist. Services,
Saxon Way West, Corby, Northants NN18 9ES
Telephone: Corby 01536 741519
Fax: 01536 746337

**Chief Executive & Secretary to the
  Delegates:** James Arnold-Baker
Finance Director: R. Boning
Director of International Division: P.
  Mothersole
Director of Distribution: N. R. Killip
President of OUP USA: E. W. Barry
Arts & Reference Division: Ivon Asquith
  (Managing Director)
Simon Wratten *(Director Sales & Marketing)*
George Taylor *(UK Sales Director)*
David Wynn *(Head of Rights)*
Education Division: Fiona Clarke *(Managing
  Director)*
Martin Cuss *(Sales Director)*
English Language Teaching Division: W. R.
  Andrewes *(Managing Director)*
David Stewart *(Sales Director)*
**Science, Medical & Journals Division
  (including IRL Press):** John Manger
  (Managing Director)
Christoph Chesher *(Sales & Marketing
  Director)*

*Academic & Scholarly; Accountancy &
Taxation; Antiques & Collecting; Archaeology;
Architecture & Design; Atlases & Maps;
Bibliography & Library Science; Biography &
Autobiography; Biology & Zoology;
Chemistry; Children's Books; Cinema, Video,
TV & Radio; Computer Science; Economics;
Educational & Textbooks; Electronic
(Educational); Engineering; English as a
Foreign Language; Fine Art & Art History;
Gender Studies; Geography & Geology;
History & Antiquarian; Illustrated & Fine
Editions; Industry, Business & Management;
Languages & Linguistics; Law; Literature &
Criticism; Mathematics & Statistics; Medical
(incl. Self Help & Alternative Medicine);
Military & War; Music; Natural History;
Philosophy; Photography; Physics; Poetry;
Politics & World Affairs; Psychology &
Psychiatry; Reference Books, Directories &
Dictionaries; Religion & Theology; Scientific
& Technical; Sociology & Anthropology;
Theatre, Drama & Dance; Veterinary Science*

ISBNs, Imprints & Series:
0 19 Clarendon Press, IRL Press, Oxford
  University Press

Associated & Subsidiary Companies:
Nigeria: University Press Ltd. *Thailand:*
LIBRIS (Thailand) Co Ltd

Distributor for:
American Institute of Physics; American
Mathematical Society; Bibliographical
Society; British Academy; Classical
Association; Early English Text Society;
German Historical Institute, London; Institute
of Historical Research, University of London;
International African Institute; International
Agency for Research on Cancer; Malone
Society; The Naur Foundation; Nuffield
Provincial Hospitals Trust; Oriental Institute,
Oxford; Oxford Institute for Energy Studies;
Pasold Research Fund; Scandinavian
University Press; School of Oriental & African
Studies. *New Zealand:* Auckland University
Press. *Norway:* Norwegian University Press.
Sweden: Stockholm International Peace
Research Institute. *USA:* The Bruschettini
Foundation; Islamic Art Foundation, New
York; World Bank Publications

Overseas Representation *(see §7.3):*
  *NOTE: For English Language Teaching offices
  overseas apply to:* Oxford University Press,
  Oxford, UK
Australia: Oxford University Press, South
  Melbourne
Bangladesh: Mohiuddin Ahmed, Dacca
Barbados & Bermuda: C. D. A. Walker,
  Christchurch, Barbados
Botswana: David Barrett-Jolly, Gaborone
Canada: Oxford University Press, Don Mills
Ghana: Emmanuel Publishing Services, Accra
  North
Guyana: Lloyd Austin, Demarara
Hong Kong & East Asia: Oxford University
  Press, Hong Kong
India: Oxford University Press Indian Branch,
  New Delhi, Bombay, Calcutta & New Delhi,
  Madras
Iran: Hooshang Momeni, Tehran
Jamaica: Kingston Bookshop, Kingston
Japan: Oxford University Press KK, Tokyo
Kenya: Oxford University Press, Nairobi
Malaysia: Penerbit Fajar Bakti Sdn Bhd, Kuala
  Lumpur
New Zealand: Oxford University Press,
  Auckland
Nigeria: University Press Ltd, Ibadan
Pakistan: Oxford University Press, Karachi
Philippines: Edwin Makabenta Jr, Quezon City
Singapore: Oxford University Press Pte Ltd
South Africa: Oxford University Press
  Southern African Branch, Cape Town,
  Pietersburg, Umtata, Pinetown & Melrose
  North
Spain: Oxford University Press Espana, Madrid
Taiwan: Oxford University Press, Taipei
Tanzania: Oxford University Press East &
  Central Africa Branch, Dar es Salaam
Thailand: Libris (Thailand) Co Ltd, Bangkok
Trinidad & Tobago: Mrs Edna Dawson, Diego
  Martin, Trinidad
Uganda: Betty Lumu, Kampala
USA: Oxford University Press, New York
Zimbabwe: College Press Publishers (Pvt) Ltd,
  Harare

Book Trade Association Membership: BDC,
EPC, IGSMTP, CAPP, Book Marketing Ltd,
The Music Publishers Association Ltd

1649 ■■■■■■■

PACKARD PUBLISHING LTD
Forum House, Stirling Road, Chichester,
West Sussex PO19 2EN
Telephone: 01243 537977
Fax: 01243 537977

Warehouse:
c/o Clipper Distribution Services,
Windmill Grove, Portchester, Hants PO16 9HT

Director: Michael Packard *(Managing, Sales,
  Rights & Permissions)*

*Academic & Scholarly; Agriculture;
Architecture & Design; Biology & Zoology;
Educational & Textbooks; Environment &
Development Studies; Gardening; Geography
& Geology; Languages & Linguistics; Music;
Natural History; Reference Books, Directories
& Dictionaries; Scientific & Technical; Sports
& Games*

New Titles: 1 (1995), 6 (1996)

ISBNs, Imprints & Series:
0 906527, 1 85341 Packard
0 948690 Packard (Arabic titles)

Distributor for:
Australia: Surrey Beatty. *Lebanon:* Librairie du
Liban. *USA:* Carolina Biological Supply Co Inc
(Biology Readers only); Stipes Publishing Co

Overseas Representation *(see §7.3):*
Australasia (biology, ecology & landscape):
  Surrey Beatty Pty Ltd, Chipping Norton,
  NSW, Australia
*North America (landscape architecture &
  planning):* Antique Collectors' Club Ltd,
  Wappinger Falls, USA
North America (science books): University
  Science Books, Mill Valley, CA, USA

Book Trade Association Membership: IPG

1650 ■■■■■■■

PALLAS ATHENE
59 Linden Gardens, London W2 4HJ
Telephone: 0171 229 2798
Fax: 0171 792 1067

Trade Enquiries & Orders:
Boydell & Brewer, PO Box 9, Woodbridge,
Suffolk IP12 3DF
Telephone: 01394 411320
Fax: 01394 411477

President & Publisher: Alexander Fyjis-
Walker

*Architecture & Design; Fine Art & Art History;
Guide Books; Travel & Topography*

New Titles: 2 (1995), 7 (1996)

ISBNs, Imprints & Series:
1 873429 Pallas Guides

Overseas Representation *(see §7.3):*
Iberia: Peter Prout, Madrid, Spain
Scandinavia: Hanne Rotovnik, Klampenborg,
  Denmark

1651

PARTHENON PUBLISHING GROUP LTD
Casterton Hall, Carnforth, Lancs LA6 2LA
Telephone: 015242 72084
Fax: 015242 71587
Email: mail@parthpub.com
Web Site: http://www.parthpub.com

Directors: David G. T. Bloomer *(Managing)*
Paula F. Bloomer *(Secretary)*
Foreign Rights: Yvonne Baillie
Production: Margaret Clarke
Editorial: Jean Wright

Environment & Development Studies; Medical (incl. Self Help & Alternative Medicine); Scientific & Technical

New Titles: 70 (1995), 70 (1996)

ISBNs, Imprints & Series: 1 85070

Associated & Subsidiary Companies:
USA: Parthenon Publishing Group Inc

Distributor for:
USA: The Parthenon Publishing Group Inc

Overseas Representation *(see §7.3):*
Australia: DA Information Services, Mitcham, Vic
Far East (excluding Japan): Toppan Co (S) Pte Ltd, Singapore
India: Jaypee Brothers Medical Publishers Ltd, New Delhi
Japan (non-exclusive): Igaku Shoin Ltd, Tokyo, Japan
Japan (non-medical books)(exclusive): Eastern Book Service Inc, Tokyo, Japan
Near & Middle East & North Africa: Ajamiam Brothers International Publishers Representatives Ltd, Nicosia, Cyprus

1652

PASTEST
Egerton Court, Parkgate Estate, Knutsford, Cheshire WA16 8DX
Telephone: 01565 755226
Fax: 01565 650264
Email: pastest@dial.pipex.com

Director: Mrs F. G. Campbell
Publishing Manager: Ms J. Bowler

Industry, Business & Management; Medical (incl. Self Help & Alternative Medicine)

New Titles: 9 (1995), 9 (1996)
No of Employees: 15

ISBNs, Imprints & Series: 0 906896

Distributor for:
ETS/Warner Publications (GMAT & MBA)

Overseas Representation *(see §7.3):*
Europe: Andrew B. Durnell, Tunbridge Wells, UK

Book Trade Association Membership: IPG

1653

PATERNOSTER PUBLISHING
PO Box 300, Carlisle, Cumbria CA3 0QS
Telephone: 01228 512512
Fax: 01228 514949
Email: 100526.3434@compuserve.com

Managing Director: Pieter Kwant
Managers: Ian Blakemore *(Commercial)*
John Lewis *(International Sales)*
(to be appointed) *(Editorial)*

Academic & Scholarly; Biography & Autobiography; Children's Books; Illustrated & Fine Editions; Religion & Theology

New Titles: 140 (1995), 110 (1996)
No of Employees: 9
Annual Turnover: £1.25M

ISBNs, Imprints & Series:
Paternoster Periodicals, Regnum, Rutherford House, Solway, WEF
0 85364 The Paternoster Press
0 903843, 1 85078 OM Publishing

Parent Company:
Send the Light Ltd

Distributor for:
Alliance Music; Candle Books; Eagle; Highland; Hunt and Thorpe; Kingsway Music; Kingsway Publications; Tear Fund. *USA:* Baker Bookhouse; Harper Collins Religious; IVP; Harold Shaw

Overseas Representation *(see §7.3):*
Australia: Crossroad Distributors Pty Ltd, Rydalmere, NSW
Korea: Korea Christian Book Service, Seoul, Korea, South
New Zealand: Scripture Union Wholesale, Wellington

1654

PATHFINDER PRESS
47 The Cut, London SE1 8LL
Telephone: 0171 261 1354
Fax: 0171 928 7970

Distribution:
Plymbridge Distributors Ltd, Estover, Plymouth PL6 7PZ
Telephone: 01752 202300
Fax: 01752 202330

Manager: M. FitzGerald

Academic & Scholarly; Economics; Gender Studies; History & Antiquarian; Military & War; Philosophy; Politics & World Affairs; Sociology & Anthropology

ISBNs, Imprints & Series:
0 87348, 0 913460, 0 937091 Pathfinder

Distributor for:
USA: Pathfinder Press

Overseas Representation *(see §7.3):*
Australia, Asia & Pacific: Pathfinder Press, Haymarket, NSW, Australia
Canada: Pathfinder, Montreal; Pathfinder, Montreal
Iceland: Pathfinder, Reykjavik

New Zealand: Pathfinder, Auckland
Sweden: Pathfinder, Stockholm
USA, Caribbean & Latin America: Pathfinder Press, New York, USA

1655

PAVIC PUBLICATIONS
Sheffield Hallam University,
36 Collegiate Crescent, Sheffield S10 2BP
Telephone: 0114 253 2380
Fax: 0114 253 2471

Administrator: Monica Moseley

Computer Science; Educational & Textbooks; Electronic (Professional & Academic); Engineering; English as a Foreign Language; Gender Studies; Military & War; Poetry; Politics & World Affairs; Scientific & Technical; Sports & Games

New Titles: 21 (1995), 25 (1996)
No of Employees: 4
Annual Turnover: £100,000

ISBNs, Imprints & Series: 0 86339

1656

PAVILION BOOKS LTD
26 Upper Ground, London SE1 9PD
Telephone: 0171 620 1666
Fax: 0171 620 1314

Distribution:
Bookpoint Ltd, 39 Milton Park, Abingdon, Oxon OX14 4TD
Telephone: 01235 400400
Fax: 01235 861038 & 832068

Directors: Colin Webb *(Publisher)*
Vivien James *(Publishing – Adult)*
Pamela Webb *(Publishing – Children's)*
Sarah Wherry *(Publicity)*
Terry Shaughnessy *(Sales)*
Andrea Russo *(Special Sales)*
International Sales Manager: Toby Ashmore
Financial Controller: Mark McKell

Biography & Autobiography; Children's Books; Cookery, Wines & Spirits; Crafts & Hobbies; Fine Art & Art History; Gardening; Guide Books; Health & Beauty; Humour; Illustrated & Fine Editions; Music; Sports & Games; Theatre, Drama & Dance; Travel & Topography; Gift; TV Tie-Ins

New Titles: 150 (1996)
No of Employees: 37

ISBNs, Imprints & Series:
1 85145, 1 85793, 1 86205

Overseas Representation *(see §7.3):*
Africa, Middle East, Eastern Europe & CIS States: Intermedia Americana, London, UK
Canada: Raincoast Distribution, Vancouver, BC

1657

PAVILION PUBLISHING (BRIGHTON) LTD
8 St George's Place, Brighton, East Sussex BN1 4GB
Telephone: 01273 623222

Fax: 01273 625526
Email: pavpub@pavilion.co.uk

Warehouse:
45 Gloucester Street, Brighton, East Sussex
Telephone: 01273 609585

Directors: Jan Alcoe
Chris Parker

*Academic & Scholarly; Medical (incl. Self Help
& Alternative Medicine); Psychology &
Psychiatry; Sociology & Anthropology;
Vocational Training & Careers*

New Titles: 20 (1995), 35 (1996)
No of Employees: 25

ISBNs, Imprints & Series:
1 86165 Pennant Professional Books
1 871080, 1 900600 Pavilion Publishing

Distributor for:
Cumbria Social Services; University of
Dundee; Educational Broadcasting Trust;
EHSSB; EMFEC; FPA; Gower Publishing;
NSPCC; University of St Andrews; University
of Sussex; Trust Study for Adolescence;
Winslow Press. *USA:* Attainment Inc

Overseas Representation *(see §7.3):*
USA & Canada: TRACIL, Calgary, Canada

*PC PUBLISHING
4 Brook Street, Tonbridge, Kent TN9 2PJ
Telephone: 01732 770893
Fax: 01732 770268

Proprietor: Philip Chapman

*Engineering; Music; Scientific & Technical;
Computers*

ISBNs, Imprints & Series: 1 870775

Distributor for:
Orpheus Publications. *Belgium:* Appa.
Netherlands: De Muiderkring. *USA:* Old
Colony

Overseas Representation *(see §7.3):*
Australia: Astam Books Pty Ltd, Leichhardt,
NSW
Middle East: Eurab Ltd, Rottingdean, UK
USA: Cimino Publishing Group, Carle Place,
NY
West Europe: Andrew B. Durnell, Tunbridge
Wells, UK

Book Trade Association Membership: IPG

PEARSON PROFESSIONAL LTD
Maple House, 149 Tottenham Court Road,
London W1P 9LL
Telephone: 0171 896 2000
Fax: 0171 896 2099

Orders:
Pearson Professional Distribution Centre,
Slaidburn Crescent, Fylde Road, Southport,
Merseyside PR9 9YF
Telephone: 01704 26881
Fax: 01704 231970

Directors: Peter Warwick *(Chief Executive)*
Steve Barlow *(Operations)*
John Stroud *(IT)*
Mark Silver *(Finance)*
Graham Elton
Henry Reece
Alison MacDougall *(Legal)*
Christine Watson *(Human Resource)*

*Accountancy & Taxation; Electronic
(Professional & Academic); Industry, Business
& Management; Law; Medical (incl. Self Help
& Alternative Medicine)*

ISBNs, Imprints & Series:
0 186067 Cartermill
0 273 Pitman Publishing
0 443 Churchill Livingstone
0 75200 FT Law and Tax

Parent Company:
Pearson Plc

Distributor for:
USA: Adam Software; Little, Brown Medical;
Springer Publishing; Sybex; Waite Group

Overseas Representation *(see §7.3):*
Australia: Pearson Professional (Australia) Pty
Ltd, Melbourne, Vic
Hong Kong: Pearson Professional (Hong
Kong) Ltd
Singapore: Pearson Professional (Singapore)
Pte Ltd

Book Trade Association Membership: PA,
IGSMTP, CAPP

PEN & SWORD BOOKS LTD
47 Church Street, Barnsley, South Yorkshire
S70 2AS
Telephone: 01226 734555
Fax: 01226 734438

Chairman: Sir Nicholas Hewitt, Bt
Director: T. G. Hewitt *(Company Secretary)*

History & Antiquarian; Military & War

ISBNs, Imprints & Series:
0 436
0 85052 Leo Cooper
0 9507892 Wharncliffe 1 871647

Parent Company:
Barnsley Chronicle Holdings Ltd

Associated & Subsidiary Companies:
Wharncliffe Publishing Ltd

Overseas Representation *(see §7.3):*
Australia: Peribo Pty Ltd, Mount Kuring-gai,
NSW
Canada: Vanwell Publishing Ltd, St
Catherines, Ont
New Zealand: South Pacific Books (Imports)
Ltd, Auckland
USA: Combined Books Inc, Conshohocken, PA

Book Trade Association Membership: PA,
BA

PENGUIN BOOKS LTD
Bath Road, Harmondsworth, Middx UB7 0DA
Telephone: 0181 899 4000
Fax: 0181 899 4099
Email: penguin.com

Publishing Office:
27 Wrights Lane, London W8 5TZ
Telephone: 0171 416 3000
Fax: 0171 416 3099

Directors: Peter Mayer *(Chairman & Chief
Executive)*
Anthony Forbes Watson *(Managing,
Publishing — Ladybird)*
Pat McCarthy *(Computer Services)*
Fran Supple *(Personnel)*
Peter Carson *(Editor-in-Chief)*
John Rolfe *(Publishing Operations)*
Jonathan Yglesias *(Production)*
Tony Lacey *(Publishing — Penguin)*
Philippa Milnes-Smith *(Publishing —
Children's)*
Clare Alexander *(Publishing — Viking)*
Stephen Hall *(Group Development)*
Roger Clarke *(Chief Financial Officer)*
Sally Floyer *(Publishing — Frederick Warne)*
Susan Watt *(Publishing — Michael Joseph)*
Andrew Welham *(Marketing & Sales)*
Cecily Engle *(Legal)*
Max Adam *(International Sales)*

*Academic & Scholarly; Archaeology;
Architecture & Design; Atlases & Maps;
Biography & Autobiography; Biology &
Zoology; Chemistry; Children's Books;
Cinema, Video, TV & Radio; Computer
Science; Cookery, Wines & Spirits; Crime;
Crafts & Hobbies; Economics; Educational &
Textbooks; Electronic (Educational);
Electronic (Entertainment); English as a
Foreign Language; Fashion & Costume;
Fiction; Fine Art & Art History; Gardening;
Gender Studies; Guide Books; Health &
Beauty; History & Antiquarian; Humour;
Illustrated & Fine Editions; Industry, Business
& Management; Languages & Linguistics;
Law; Literature & Criticism; Mathematics &
Statistics; Medical (incl. Self Help &
Alternative Medicine); Music; Natural History;
Philosophy; Photography; Physics; Poetry;
Politics & World Affairs; Psychology &
Psychiatry; Reference Books, Directories &
Dictionaries; Religion & Theology; Science
Fiction; Scientific & Technical; Sociology &
Anthropology; Sports & Games; Theatre,
Drama & Dance; Transport; Travel &
Topography; Vocational Training & Careers*

ISBNs, Imprints & Series:
Joint ventures with BBC Paperbacks, Granta
0 14 Arkana, Buildings of England, Ireland,
Scotland and Wales, Creed, Dutton,
Ladybird, Mermaid, Pelham, Pelican,
Penguin, Penguin Audiobooks, Penguin
Electronic, Puffin, Roc, Signet, Syrens
0 216 Blackie
0 241 Hamish Hamilton, Hamish Hamilton
Children's Books
0 670 Viking, Viking Children's Books
0 7181 Michael Joseph
0 7232 Claremont, Frederick Warne

Parent Company:
The Penguin Publishing Company Ltd

Associated & Subsidiary Companies:
Godfrey Cave Holdings Ltd; Hamish Hamilton
Ltd; Michael Joseph Ltd; Ventura Publishing
Ltd; Frederick Warne (& Co) Ltd. *Australia:*
Penguin Books Australia Ltd. *Canada:* Penguin
Books Canada Ltd. *New Zealand:* Penguin
Books (NZ) Ltd. *USA:* Eden Toys Inc; Penguin
USA Inc

Distributor for:
Castle Communications; Consumers
Association; Element Books; Icon Books;
Monacelli; Rough Guides; Wisden

Overseas Representation *(see §7.3):*
Australia: Penguin Books Australia Ltd,
    Ringwood, Vic
Canada: Penguin Books Canada Ltd,
    Newmarket, Ont
France: Penguin France SA, Toulouse
Germany & Austria: Penguin Books
    Deutschland GmbH, Frankfurt, Germany
Greece, Israel & Cyprus: Penguin Hellas Ltd,
    Athens, Greece
India, Bangladesh, Pakistan & Sri Lanka:
    Penguin Books India Pvt Ltd, New Delhi,
    India
Italy: Penguin Italia Srl, Milan
Japan: Penguin Books Japan, Tokyo
Korea: Addison-Wesley Korea, Seoul, Korea,
    South
Malaysia: STP Distributors (M) Sdn Bhd, Shah
    Alam
Netherlands: Penguin Books Netherlands bv,
    Amsterdam
New Zealand: Penguin Books (New Zealand)
    Ltd, Auckland
Portugal: Longman Penguin Portugal, Lisbon
Singapore: STP Distributors Pte Ltd
South Africa: Longman Penguin South Africa,
    Bertsham
South America: Humphrys Roberts Associates,
    Cotia, Brazil
Spain: Penguin Books SA, Madrid
Switzerland: OLF SA, Fribourg
Turkey: Sezai, Istanbul

Book Trade Association Membership: PA

1662 ▬▬▬▬▬▬▬▬▬▬▬▬▬▬▬▬

**THE PENSIONS MANAGEMENT
INSTITUTE**
PMI House, 4–10 Artillery Lane, London
E1 7LS
Telephone: 0171 247 1452
Fax: 0171 375 0603

Secretary: Mrs S. M. Howlett
Deputy Secretary: P. J. B. Whiteing

Economics

No of Employees: 18
Annual Turnover: £1M

ISBNs, Imprints & Series:
0 946242, 1 898785 The PMI Tuition Service

1663 ▬▬▬▬▬▬▬▬▬▬▬▬▬▬▬▬

PENTATHOL PUBLISHING
PO Box 92, 40 Gibson Street, Wrexham,
Wrexham County LL13 7NS

Owner/Chief Executive: Athol E. Cowen

Poetry

Annual Turnover: £1,000

ISBNs, Imprints & Series: 1 8730

Book Trade Association Membership: PA

1664 ▬▬▬▬▬▬▬▬▬▬▬▬▬▬▬▬

PENTAXION LTD
180 New Bridge Street, Newcastle upon Tyne
NE1 2TE
Telephone: 0191 232 6189
Fax: 0191 232 6190

Directors: M. Baker *(Managing)*
B. Gillham *(Product Development)*
Company Secretary: A. Spooner

*Academic & Scholarly; Chemistry;
Engineering; Industry, Business &
Management; Law; Medical (incl. Self Help &
Alternative Medicine); Physics; Scientific &
Technical*

New Titles: 10 (1996)
No of Employees: 8

ISBNs, Imprints & Series: 1 874430

1665 ▬▬▬▬▬▬▬▬▬▬▬▬▬▬▬▬

THE PENTLAND PRESS LTD
Hutton Close, South Church, Bishop Auckland,
Co Durham DL14 6XB
Telephone: 01388 776555
Fax: 01388 776766

Warehouse, Trade Enquiries & Orders:
3 Regal Lane, Soham, Ely, Cambridgeshire
CB7 5BA
Telephone: 01353 723359
Fax: 01353 721839

Chairman: N. S. Law
Editorial Director: J. A. Phillips
Company Secretary: C. Emmett
Sales: Mark Leonard
Production: Mary Denton

*Biography & Autobiography; Fiction; History
& Antiquarian; Military & War; Poetry;
Religion & Theology*

New Titles: 100 (1995), 110 (1996)
No of Employees: 10
Annual Turnover: £1M

ISBNs, Imprints & Series:
0 946270, 1 85821

Parent Company:
Pentland Press Inc *(USA)*

Overseas Representation *(see §7.3):*
Australia: Biramo Books Ltd, New Lambton,
    NSW
Canada: Christie & Christie Associates,
    Cookstown, Ont
India: Applied Media, New Delhi
Malawi: Central Africana Ltd, Blantyre
New Zealand: Biramo Holdings Ltd, Auckland
Singapore & Malaysia: Publishers Marketing
    Services Ltd, Singapore
USA: Pentland Press Inc, Raleigh, NC

Book Trade Association Membership: IPG,
Scottish PA

1666 ▬▬▬▬▬▬▬▬▬▬▬▬▬▬▬▬

PERFECT WORDS AND MUSIC LTD
Purbeck, Mill Lane, Felbridge, Surrey
RH19 2PE
Telephone: 01342 322833
Fax: 01342 322833
Email: 101376.154@compuserve.com
Web Site: http://www.ipi.co.uk/docs/perfect-
words

General Manager: Allison Longstaff
Marketing: Allison Murray
Directors: Phil Murray *(Managing)*
Bill Marshall *(Rights)*

*Educational & Textbooks; Health & Beauty;
Magic & the Occult; Medical (incl. Self Help &
Alternative Medicine); Philosophy;
Psychology & Psychiatry; Religion & Theology*

New Titles: 7 (1995), 10 (1996)
No of Employees: 8
Annual Turnover: £350,000

ISBNs, Imprints & Series:
1 898716 The Esoteric Story Trilogy, The
    Health Series, The Phil Murray Success
    Programme

1667 ▬▬▬▬▬▬▬▬▬▬▬▬▬▬▬▬

PETERLOO POETS
2 Kelly Gardens, Calstock, Cornwall PL18 9SA
Telephone: 01822 833473

Editorial Production: Harry Chambers
    (Director)
Sales & Administration: Lynn Chambers
    (Rights & Permissions)

Poetry

New Titles: 12 (1995), 9 (1996)

ISBNs, Imprints & Series:
0 905291, 1 871471

Overseas Representation *(see §7.3):*
Australia: St Clair Press Pty Ltd, Rozelle, NSW

Book Trade Association Membership: IPG

1668 ▬▬▬▬▬▬▬▬▬▬▬▬▬▬▬▬

PHAIDON PRESS LTD
18 Regent's Wharf, All Saints Street, London
N1 9PA
Telephone: 0171 843 1000
Fax: 0171 843 1010

Trade Counter & Warehouse:
Unit 4, Lodge Causeway Trading Estate,
Fishponds, Bristol, Avon BS16 3JB
Telephone: 0117 958 4588
Fax: 0117 958 4599

Directors: Richard Schlagman *(Chairman)*
Paula Kahn *(Managing)*
Frances Johnson *(Production & Purchasing)*
Andrew Price *(Financial)*
Manager: Amanda Renshaw *(Rights)*

Academic & Scholarly; Antiques & Collecting; Architecture & Design; Children's Books; Crafts & Hobbies; Fine Art & Art History; Photography; Theatre, Drama & Dance

ISBNs, Imprints & Series: 0 7148

Associated & Subsidiary Companies:
Architecture Design & Technology Press (ADT)

Distributor for:
Germany: Belser

Overseas Representation *(see §7.3):*
Australia: Bookwise International, Findon, SA
Canada: Penguin Books Canada Ltd, Newmarket, Ont
Eastern Europe, Greece, Spain, Portugal, Belgium, Switzerland, Italy & Scandinavia: Macmillan Publishers Services Ltd, Basingstoke, UK
Far East & Japan: Ralph & Sheila Summers, London, UK
France: Michael Abbott, Peyrilhac
Germany & Austria: Heiner Meyer auf der Heyde, Dortmund, Germany
Irish Republic: Robert Towers, Monkstown
Middle East & Israel: Peter Ward Book Exports, London, UK
Netherlands: Nilsson & Lamm BV, Weesp
USA: Chronicle Books, San Francisco, CA

Book Trade Association Membership: PA

1669 ▬▬▬▬▬▬

THE PHARMACEUTICAL PRESS
1 Lambeth High Street, London SE1 7JN
Telephone: 0171 735 9141
Fax: 0171 735 7629

Orders:
The Pharmaceutical Press, PO Box 151, Wallingford, Oxon OX10 8QU
Telephone: 01491 824486
Fax: 01491 826090
Email: rpsgb@cabi.org

Director of Publications: C. Fry
Commissioning Editor: P. J. Weller
Marketing Manager: Ms J. Weir
Production Co-ordinator: J. Wilson

Medical (incl. Self Help & Alternative Medicine)

ISBNs, Imprints & Series: 0 85369

Parent Company:
The Royal Pharmaceutical Society of Great Britain

Overseas Representation *(see §7.3):*
Australia: Australian Pharmaceutical Publishing Co Ltd, Hawthorn; Pharmaceutical Society of Australia, Curtin
Germany, Austria & Switzerland: Deutscher Apotheker Verlag, Stuttgart, Germany
India: Arnold Publishers (India) Pvt Ltd, New Delhi
Japan: Maruzen Co Ltd, Tokyo
New Zealand: Pharmaceutical Society of New Zealand, Wellington
USA: Rittenhouse Book Distributors Inc, King of Prussia

Book Trade Association Membership:
ALPSP

1670 ▬▬▬▬▬▬

GEORGE PHILIP
Michelin House, 81 Fulham Road, London SW3 6RB
Telephone: 0171 581 9393
Fax: 0171 225 9406

Distribution:
Reed Book Services, Northampton Road, Rushden, Northants NN10 6PU
Telephone: 01933 58521
Fax: 01933 50284

International Sales Department:
(as principal address)
Telephone: 0171 581 9393
Fax: 0171 225 9371

Publishing Director: John Gaisford

Atlases & Maps; Guide Books; Travel & Topography

ISBNs, Imprints & Series: 0 540

Parent Company:
Reed Elsevier Plc

Overseas Representation *(see §7.3):*
Australia: Reed Books Australia, Melbourne, Vic
Canada: Reed Publishing Canada, Markham, Ont
East Asia: Reed Consumer Books, Metro Manila, Philippines
India: Reed Consumer Books, New Delhi
Japan: Reed Consumer Books, Tokyo
New Zealand: Reed Publishing Group, Auckland
Singapore: Reed International (Singapore) Pte Ltd
South Africa: Struik Book Distributors Pty Ltd, Johannesburg, Cape Town & Maitland

1671 ▬▬▬▬▬▬

PHILLIMORE & CO LTD
Shopwyke Manor Barn, Chichester, West Sussex PO20 6BG
Telephone: 01243 787636
Fax: 01243 787639

Directors: Philip Harris, JP *(Chairman)*
Noel H. Osborne *(Managing)*
Hilary Clifford Brown *(Marketing)*
Managers: Carol Cockaday *(Trade Counter)*
Jane Gunton *(Publicity, Rights & Permissions)*
Nicola Willmot *(Production)*

Academic & Scholarly; Archaeology; Architecture & Design; Atlases & Maps; History & Antiquarian; Military & War; Travel & Topography; Family History; Local History

New Titles: 55 (1995), 45 (1996)
No of Employees: 15
Annual Turnover: £1.26M

ISBNs, Imprints & Series:
0 7199 British Association for Local History
0 85033, 0 900592 Darwen County History, History from the Sources, Phillimore

Associated & Subsidiary Companies:
Darwen Finlayson Ltd

Distributor for:
British Association for Local History; Historical Publications Ltd

Overseas Representation *(see §7.3):*
Europe: D. Richard Bowen, Malmö, Sweden

Book Trade Association Membership: BA, IPG

1672 ▬▬▬▬▬▬

PHILOGRAPH PUBLICATIONS LTD
North Way, Andover, Hants SP10 5BA
Telephone: 01264 332171
Fax: 01264 332226

Warehouse:
Riverside Road, Barnstaple, Devon
Telephone: 01271 45061
Fax: 01271 23076

Directors: Jon Tacey *(Managing)*
E. A. Jarvis *(Finance & Company Secretary)*
Managers: H. L. Timpe *(Sales, UK)*
S. Williams *(Marketing & Export Sales)*

Children's Books; Crafts & Hobbies; Educational & Textbooks

ISBNs, Imprints & Series: 0 85370

Distributor for:
Philip & Tacey Ltd

Book Trade Association Membership: PA

1673 ▬▬▬▬▬▬

PHOENIX ELT
[a division of Simon & Schuster International]
Campus 400, Maylands Avenue, Hemel Hempstead, Herts HP2 7EZ
Telephone: 01442 881900
Fax: 01442 882151

Orders, Customer Services & Accounts:
International Book Distrbutors Ltd, Campus 400, Maylands Avenue, Hemel Hempstead, Herts HP2 7EZ
Telephone: 01442 881900
Fax: 01442 882099

Distribution Centre:
International Book Distributors Ltd, Coventry Road, Magna Park, Lutterworth LE17 4XH
Telephone: 01442 881900
Fax: 01442 882177

Sales & Marketing Director: Mike Thompson

ELT Material – Main Course; ELT – Reference & Grammar

ISBNs, Imprints & Series:
0 13 Cassell, Phoenix, Prentice Hall

Parent Company:
Viacom Inc *(USA)*

Associated & Subsidiary Companies:
see: Prentice Hall Europe (Academic Division)

Distributor for:
Prentice Hall Regents

Book Trade Association Membership: PA

1674 ▬▬▬▬▬▬▬▬▬▬

*PHOENIX PRESS (OXFORD)
PO Box 41, Bangor, Gwynedd LL57 1SB
Telephone: 01248 351816
Fax: 01248 362115

Warehouse, Trade Enquiries & Orders:
PO Box 628, Oxford OX1 2NL

Executive: Judith Loades

*Academic & Scholarly; Children's Books;
Cookery, Wines & Spirits; Educational &
Textbooks; History & Antiquarian; Military &
War; Poetry; Religion & Theology*

Parent Company:
Headstart History

Book Trade Association Membership: PA

1675 ▬▬▬▬▬▬▬▬▬▬

*PHOENIX PUBLICATIONS
PO Box 255, London SW16 6DA
Telephone: 0181 677 1813

Book Trade Association Membership: BA

1676 ▬▬▬▬▬▬▬▬▬▬

PIATKUS BOOKS
5 Windmill Street, London W1P 1HF
Telephone: 0171 631 0710
Fax: 0171 436 7137
Email: piatkus.books@dial.pipex.com

Distribution:
Grantham Book Services, Isaac Newton Way,
Alma Industrial Estate, Grantham, Lincs
NG31 9SD
Telephone: 01476 67421
Fax: 01476 590223

Directors: Judy Piatkus *(Managing)*
Philip Cotterell *(Marketing & Sales)*
Gill Cormode *(Non-Fiction Editorial)*
Home Sales Manager: Diane Hill
Rights & Permissions: Kate Callaghan

*Biography & Autobiography; Cookery, Wines
& Spirits; Crime; Fashion & Costume; Fiction;
Gender Studies; Health & Beauty; Humour;
Industry, Business & Management; Magic &
the Occult; Psychology & Psychiatry*

New Titles: 100 (1995), 100 (1996)
No of Employees: 19
Annual Turnover: £4.5M

ISBNs, Imprints & Series:
0 7499, 0 86188 Piatkus Books
1 81058 Inner Circle

Parent Company:
Judy Piatkus (Publishers) Ltd

Overseas Representation *(see §7.3)*:
Australia: Hodder Headline (Australia) Pty
Ltd, Rydalmere

Canada: General Publishing Co Ltd, North
York, Ont
New Zealand: David Bateman Ltd, Auckland
Singapore & Malaysia: Pansing Distribution
Sdn Bhd, Singapore
South Africa: Macdonald Purnell (Pty) Ltd,
Cleveland

Book Trade Association Membership: IPG

1677 ▬▬▬▬▬▬▬▬▬▬

*PICADOR
25 Eccleston Place, London SW1W 9NF

Chairman: Nicholas Byam Shaw
Directors: Ian S. Chapman *(Managing)*
David North *(Sales)*
David Macmillan *(Deputy Managing)*
Jilly Easterby *(Rights)*
Chris Gibson *(Production)*
Mark Jefferson *(Marketing)*
Peter Straus *(Publishing)*
Fiona Carpenter *(Art)*

*Biography & Autobiography; Fiction;
Humour; Philosophy; Politics & World Affairs;
Travel & Topography*

ISBNs, Imprints & Series: 0 330

Parent Company:
Macmillan Ltd

Distributor for:
Pan Books Ltd

Overseas Representation *(see §7.3)*:
see: Macmillan Ltd, UK

Book Trade Association Membership: PA,
BA, EPC, CAPP

1678 ▬▬▬▬▬▬▬▬▬▬

PICCADILLY PRESS
5 Castle Road, London NW1 8PR
Telephone: 0171 267 4492
Fax: 0171 267 4493

Warehouse & Distribution:
Tiptree Book Services, St Luke's Chase,
Church Road, Tiptree, Essex CO5 0SR
Telephone: 01621 816362
Fax: 01621 819011

Managing Director: Brenda Gardner
Production & Rights: Caroline Bidwell
Editorial: Ruth Williams
Rights: Margot Edwards
Financial Controller: Geoffrey Lill
Publicity: Emma O'Bryen

Children's Books; Books for Parents

New Titles: 30 (1995), 34 (1996)
No of Employees: 6
Annual Turnover: £0.5M

ISBNs, Imprints & Series:
0 946826, 1 85340

Overseas Representation *(see §7.3)*:
Australia: CIS Publishers, Carlton, Vic
Japan: Japan English Agency, Tokyo
Malaysia: Publishers Marketing Services,
Petaling Jaya

New Zealand: Forrester Books NZ Ltd,
Takapuna
Singapore: Publishers Marketing Services Ltd
Southern Africa: Trinity Books CC, Randburg,
South Africa

1679 ▬▬▬▬▬▬▬▬▬▬

**PICKERING & CHATTO
(PUBLISHERS) LTD**
21 Bloomsbury Way, London WC1A 2TH
Telephone: 0171 405 1005
Fax: 0171 405 6216

Distribution & Orders:
Turpin Distribution Ltd, Blackhorse Road,
Letchworth, Herts SG6 1HN
Telephone: 01462 672555
Fax: 01462 480947

Directors: Jane Mahony *(Managing)*
Lord Rees-Mogg *(Chairman)*
Editorial & Rights: Bridget Frost
Florence Hamilton
Sales & Marketing Manager: James Powell

*Academic & Scholarly; Economics; Gender
Studies; Literature & Criticism; Scientific &
Technical*

New Titles: 50 (1995), 70 (1996)
No of Employees: 10

ISBNs, Imprints & Series: 1 85196

Overseas Representation *(see §7.3)*:
Japan: Kinokuniya Co Ltd, Tokyo; Maruzen
Co Ltd, Tokyo
Spain & Portugal: Iberian Book Services SL,
Madrid, Spain
USA: Ashgate Publishing Co, Brookfield, VT

Book Trade Association Membership: IPG

1680 ▬▬▬▬▬▬▬▬▬▬

**PICTON PUBLISHING (CHIPPENHAM)
LTD**
Queensbridge Cottages, Patterdown,
Chippenham, Wilts SN15 2NS
Telephone: 01249 443430
Fax: 01249 443430 (Manual)

Managing Director: D. B. Picton-Phillips,
BSc, FISM, MIOP
Company Secretary: Mrs A. V. Picton-
Phillips, SRN

*Gardening; Military & War; Local History;
Railway*

New Titles: 6 (1995), 6 (1996)
No of Employees: 3
Annual Turnover: £75,000

ISBNs, Imprints & Series: 0 948251

Associated & Subsidiary Companies:
Barebones Books; Nutshell Press

Distributor for:
Canada: Kenlyn Publishing

Overseas Representation *(see §7.3)*:
Scandinavia & Western Europe: D. Richard
Bowen, Malmö, Sweden

1681 ▬▬▬▬

PINTER PUBLISHERS LTD
Wellington House, 125 Strand, London
WC2R 0BB
Telephone: 0171 420 5555
Fax: 0171 240 7261

Distribution:
Cassell Plc, Stanley House, 3 Fleets Lane,
Poole, Dorset BH15 3AJ
Telephone: 01202 665432
Fax: 01202 666219

Directors: Janet Joyce *(Publishing)*
Ruth McCurry *(UK Sales)*
Managers: Catherine Johnston *(Promotion)*
Rebecca Seymour *(International Sales)*
Petra Recter *(Editorial)*

*Academic & Scholarly; Archaeology;
Economics; History & Antiquarian; Industry,
Business & Management; Languages &
Linguistics; Law; Literature & Criticism;
Politics & World Affairs; Reference Books,
Directories & Dictionaries; Religion &
Theology*

New Titles: 90 (1995), 90 (1996)

ISBNs, Imprints & Series:
0 71851 Leicester University Press
0 86187, 0 903804, 1 85567 Pinter Publishers

Parent Company:
Cassell Plc

Overseas Representation *(see §7.3)*:
see: Cassell Plc, UK

1682 ▬▬▬▬

PION LTD
207 Brondesbury Park, London NW2 5JN
Telephone: 0181 459 0066 & 0067
Fax: 0181 451 6454
Email: sales@pion.demon.co.uk
Web Site: http://www.pion.co.uk

Distributor:
Turpin Distribution Services, Blackhorse Road,
Letchworth, Herts SG6 1HN
Telephone: 01462 672555
Fax: 01462 480947

Directors: Adam Gelbtuch *(Managing)*
John Ashby *(Editorial)*
UK & International Sales Manager: Diana
Mallett *(Rights & Permissions)*

*Academic & Scholarly; Architecture & Design;
Geography & Geology; Physics*

New Titles: 2 (1995), 1 (1996)

ISBNs, Imprints & Series:
London Papers (now European Research in
Regional Science) (Series), Studies in
Society & Space (Series) 0 85086

Associated & Subsidiary Companies:
Turpion *(joint venture with Royal Society of
Chemistry & Infosearch Ltd)*

Overseas Representation *(see §7.3)*:
Japan: Kinokuniya Book Import Dept, Tokyo

Book Trade Association Membership: IPG,
ALPSP, UK Serials Group

1683 ▬▬▬▬

PIRA INTERNATIONAL
Randalls Road, Leatherhead, Surrey
KT22 7RU
Telephone: 01372 802080
Fax: 01372 802079
Email: publications@pira.co.uk
Web Site: http://www.pira.co.uk/

Marketing Manager: Milan Taylor
Senior Editor: Gail Murray
Publisher: Marie Rushton
Principal Information Scientist: Diana Devin
Production Controller: Lewis Marshall
Commercial Director: Mike Hancock

*Academic & Scholarly; Electronic
(Professional & Academic); Industry, Business
& Management; Reference Books, Directories
& Dictionaries; Scientific & Technical;
Vocational Training & Careers*

New Titles: 34 (1995), 40 (1996)
No of Employees: 23
Annual Turnover: £850,000

ISBNs, Imprints & Series: 1 85802

Book Trade Association Membership: PA,
BA

1684 ▬▬▬▬

PITKIN GUIDES
Healey House, Dene Road, Andover, Hants
SP10 2AA
Telephone: 01264 334303
Fax: 01264 334110
Email: guides@pitkin.u-net.com

Managing Director: Ian Corsie

Guide Books

ISBNs, Imprints & Series:
0 85372 Pitkin Guides

Parent Company:
Reed International Books Ltd

1685 ▬▬▬▬

PITMAN PUBLISHING
[a division of Pearson Professional Ltd]
128 Long Acre, London WC2E 9AN
Telephone: 0171 447 2000
Fax: 0171 240 5771

Warehouse:
Southport Book Distributors,
12–14 Slaidburn Crescent, Southport,
Merseyside PR9 9YF
Telephone: 01704 26881 & 24331
Fax: 01704 231970

Directors: Rod Bristow *(Managing)*
John Knight *(Operations)*
Simon Lake *(Product Development)*
Mark Allin *(Publishing)*
Barry Finch *(Production & Administration)*
Peter Marshall *(Sales & Marketing)*
David Evans *(Distribution)*
Managers: Suzie Bloom *(Personnel)*

Simon Beale *(Export Sales)*
Valerie Roberts *(Rights & Contracts)*
Adrian Mellor *(Sales & Marketing)*
Ed Suthon *(Trade Marketing)*
Stephen Rangecroft *(Direct, Sales &
Marketing)*

*Accountancy & Taxation; Computer Science;
Economics; Educational & Textbooks;
Electronic (Educational); Electronic
(Professional & Academic); Industry, Business
& Management; Law; Reference Books,
Directories & Dictionaries; Vocational
Training & Careers; Banking; Finance;
Management*

ISBNs, Imprints & Series:
0 273 Allied Dunbar Board, Chartered Institute
of Bankers, Financial Times, IM Guides,
Investor's Chronicle, Nat West, Pitman
0 7121 BTEC, M & E

Parent Company:
Pearson Professional Ltd

Distributor for:
USA: MIS Press (M & T Books); Sybex

Overseas Representation *(see §7.3)*:
See: Pearson Professional Ltd, London, UK

Book Trade Association Membership: PA,
BDC, CAPP, IBD

1686 ▬▬▬▬

PLATEWAY PRESS
PO Box 973, Brighton BN2 2TG
Fax: 01273 693488

Directors: Keith Taylorson
Andrew Neale

Transport

New Titles: 4 (1995), 4 (1996)
No of Employees: 2
Annual Turnover: £66,000

ISBNs, Imprints & Series: 1 871980

Overseas Representation *(see §7.3)*:
Austria: Josef Otto Slezak, Vienna
Canada: North Kildonan Publications,
Winnepeg
Germany: Lok Report, Münster
Spain: Librimport, Barcelona
USA: Whistles in the Woods, Chicamauga, GA

1687 ▬▬▬▬

PLATFORM 5 PUBLISHING LTD
Wyvern House, Sark Road, Sheffield S2 4HG
Telephone: 0114 255 2625
Fax: 0114 255 2471

Director: P. Fox *(Editorial & General)*
Sales Assistant: A. Dyson

Transport; Travel & Topography

New Titles: 12 (1995), 12 (1996)
No of Employees: 7
Annual Turnover: £350,000

ISBNs, Imprints & Series:
0 906579, 1 872524

Distributor for:
British Bus Publishing; Bus Enthusiast
Publishing Co; Capital Transport Publishing;
Fearless Publications; Headstock Publications;
Milepost Publications; Quail Map Co; Rail
Photoprints; South Coast Transport Publishing

1688

PLAYERS PRESS (UK)
20 Park Drive, Romford, Essex RM1 4LH
Telephone: 01708 749119

British Manager: Ian Wilkes
President: William-Alan Landes

Theatre, Drama & Dance

New Titles: 17 (1995), 27 (1996)

ISBNs, Imprints & Series: 0 88734

Parent Company:
Players Press Inc *(USA)*

1689

PLENUM PUBLISHING CO LTD
101 Back Church Lane, London E1 1LU
Telephone: 0171 377 0686
Fax: 0171 247 0555

Managing Director: Ken Derham
Editor: Joanna Lawrence
European Sales: Theo van de Bilt
Marja-Liisa Puolakka
Customer Service Manager: Sean Ayres
Rights & Permissions: Georgia Prince
*(Plenum Publishing Corporation—New
York)*
Exhibitions/Advertising: Vikki Cookson

*Academic & Scholarly; Bibliography &
Library Science; Biology & Zoology;
Chemistry; Computer Science; Educational &
Textbooks; Industry, Business & Management;
Mathematics & Statistics; Medical (incl. Self
Help & Alternative Medicine); Physics;
Psychology & Psychiatry; Scientific &
Technical*

ISBNs, Imprints & Series:
0 306 Consultants Bureau, IFI/Plenum Data Co,
Plenum Insight, Plenum Medical Book Co,
Plenum Press, Plenum Publishing Co

Parent Company:
Plenum Publishing Corporation *(USA)*

Associated & Subsidiary Companies:
Russia: Plenum Publishing Corporation,
Moscow. *USA:* J. S. Canner; Human Sciences
Press; IFI Plenum Data Corporation

Distributor for:
USA: Plenum Publishing Corporation

Overseas Representation *(see §7.3):*
Australia, New Zealand & Papua New Guinea:
DA Information Services, Mitcham, Vic,
Australia
Near & Middle East, North Africa:
International Publishers Representatives
(IPR), Nicosia, Cyprus
*Singapore, Malaysia, Indonesia, Brunei, Hong
Kong, Taiwan, China, Thailand, South*

Korea & Philippines: APAC Publishers
Services, Singapore
South America: Michael Bates, Rio de Janeiro,
Brazil

Book Trade Association Membership: PA,
CAPP

1690

PLEXUS PUBLISHING LTD
55a Clapham Common Southside, London
SW4 9BX
Telephone: 0171 622 2440
Fax: 0171 622 2441
Email: plexus@plexusuk.demon.co.uk

Warehouse & Distribution:
Book Point, 39 Milton Park Trading Estate,
Abingdon, Oxford OX14 4TD
Telephone: 01235 400400
Fax: 01235 861038 & 832068

Directors: Sandra Wake *(Editorial, Rights &
Permissions)*
Terence Porter *(Production, Sales &
Marketing)*

*Cinema, Video, TV & Radio; Humour; Music;
Photography; Popular Culture*

New Titles: 12 (1995), 15 (1996)

ISBNs, Imprints & Series:
0 85965 Plexus
0 906008 Eel Pie

Overseas Representation *(see §7.3):*
*Belgium, Germany, Netherlands, Austria &
Switzerland:* Michael Geoghegan, London,
UK
Central & Eastern Europe: MTM, London, UK
*Denmark, Finland, Iceland, Norway &
Sweden:* Saga Books Aps, Horsholm,
Denmark
France: Pierre-Yves Cosmo, Paris
Italy, Spain, Portugal, Greece & Gibraltar:
Penny Padovani, London, UK; Penny
Padovani, Montanare di Cortona, Italy
Mexico, Central America & Caribbean:
Humphrys Roberts Associates, London, UK
South Africa: Trinity Books CC, Randburg
South America: Humphrys Roberts Associates,
Cotia, Brazil
USA: Publishers' Group West, Emeryville, CA

1691

PLUTO PUBLISHING LTD
345 Archway Road, London N6 5AA
Telephone: 0181 348 2724
Fax: 0181 348 9133
Email: pluto@plutobks.demon.co.uk

Trade Enquiries & Orders:
Marston Book Services, PO Box 269,
Abingdon, Oxon OX14 4YN
Telephone: 01235 465500
Fax: 01235 465555

Directors: Roger Van Zwanenberg
(Managing, Publisher)
Anne Beech *(Editorial)*
Gilly Duff *(Rights & Permissions)*
Head of Sales & Marketing: Jane Penrose

*Academic & Scholarly; Economics;
Environment & Development Studies;
Gardening; Gender Studies; Law; Literature &
Criticism; Philosophy; Politics & World
Affairs; Sociology & Anthropology*

New Titles: 50 (1995), 50 (1996)
No of Employees: 9
Annual Turnover: £850,000

ISBNs, Imprints & Series:
0 7453, 0 86104 Pluto Press
1 85172 Journeyman Press

Overseas Representation *(see §7.3):*
Australia: Eleanor Brasch Associates,
Artarmon, NSW
Germany (stock-holding distributor): Missing
Link Versandbuchhandlung, Bremen,
Germany
*Germany, Austria, Switzerland, Scandinavia,
Netherlands, Belgium, Luxembourg, France,
Italy, Greece & Malta:* Andrew B. Durnell,
Tunbridge Wells, UK
India: New Age International Ltd, New Delhi
Japan: United Publishers Services Ltd, Tokyo
North America: In Book, Chicago, IL, USA
Pakistan: Vanguard Books Pvt Ltd, Lahore
South Africa: Phambili Agencies (Jean
Knopperson), Kensington
South East Asia: Roger Ward, London, UK
Spain & Portugal: Iberian Book Services SL,
Madrid, Spain

Book Trade Association Membership: Small
Press Group

1692

POETRY WALES PRESS LTD
[publishing under the Seren imprint]
2 Wyndham Street, Bridgend, Mid Glamorgan
CF31 1FT
Telephone: 01656 767834
Fax: 01656 767834

Distributor:
Central Books, 99 Wallis Road, London
E9 5LN
Telephone: 0181 986 4854
Fax: 0181 533 5821

Managing Director: Mick Felton
Managers: Simon Hicks *(Marketing)*
Amy Wack *(Editorial)*

*Biography & Autobiography; Children's
Books; Educational & Textbooks; Fiction; Fine
Art & Art History; History & Antiquarian;
Literature & Criticism; Poetry; Theatre,
Drama & Dance*

New Titles: 19 (1995), 25 (1996)
No of Employees: 3
Annual Turnover: £100,000

ISBNs, Imprints & Series:
0 907476, 1 85411

Overseas Representation *(see §7.3):*
Irish Republic & all overseas enquiries: Troika
Ltd, London, UK
USA: Dufour Editions Inc, Chester Springs, PA

1693 ▬▬▬▬▬▬▬▬▬

POLITY PRESS
65 Bridge Street, Cambridge CB2 1UR
Telephone: 01223 324315
Fax: 01223 461385

Distribution Warehouse:
Marston Book Services, PO Box 269,
Abingdon, Oxon OX14 4YN
Telephone: 01235 465500
Fax: 01235 465555

Publicity & Production:
Blackwell Publishers Ltd, 108 Cowley Road,
Oxford OX4 1JF
Telephone: Oxford 01865 791100
Fax: 01865 791347

Directors: Anthony Giddens *(Editorial)*
David Held *(Editorial)*
John Thompson *(Editorial)*

*Academic & Scholarly; Archaeology; Cinema,
Video, TV & Radio; Economics; Educational &
Textbooks; Fine Art & Art History; Gender
Studies; Geography & Geology; History &
Antiquarian; Humour; Literature & Criticism;
Military & War; Philosophy; Politics & World
Affairs; Psychology & Psychiatry; Reference
Books, Directories & Dictionaries; Religion &
Theology; Sociology & Anthropology*

ISBNs, Imprints & Series: 0 7456

Overseas Representation *(see §7.3)*:
All other areas: Blackwell Publishers, Oxford,
UK
Australia: Allen & Unwin Pty Ltd, St Leonards,
NSW
Benelux: Netwerk, Academic Book Agency,
Rotterdam, Netherlands
Canary Islands: Turnkey Projects Ltd, Santa
Cruz de Tenerife, Spain
*Czech & Slovak Republics, Hungary, Romania,
Bulgaria, Slovenia, Macedonia & former
Yugoslavia:* Ms Sue Wilson, Budapest,
Hungary
Germany, Austria & Switzerland: The John
Wilde Partnership, Lauf, Germany
Hong Kong, China, Taiwan & Korea:
Knowledge Craft Ltd, Hong Kong
India: Maya Publishers Pvt Ltd, New Delhi;
Segment Book Distributors, New Delhi
Iran: Jahan Adib Co Ltd, Tehran
Irish Republic & Northern Ireland: Carr
O'Connell, Ashbourne, Irish Republic
Israel: Allied Scientific Presses, Jerusalem
Japan (academic): United Publishers Services
Ltd, Tokyo, Japan
Malaysia: APD Kuala Lumpur, Petaling Jaya
Middle East (Arabic countries): International
Publishers Representatives (IPR), Nicosia,
Cyprus
New Zealand: Macmillan NZ, Auckland
Pakistan: Afro-Asian Book Co, Karachi
*Poland, Lithuania, Latvia, Estonia, Belarus &
Ukraine:* Ms Andrea Hedgecock,
Karmelava, Lithuania
Russian Federation (CIS): Michael Timperley
Marketing, Oxford, UK
Scandinavia: Colin Flint, Harlow, UK
Singapore, Brunei & Thailand: APD Singapore
Pte Ltd, Singapore
South Africa: Academic Marketing Services,
Auckland Park

Southern Europe: Charles Gibbes,
Buckingham, UK

1694 ▬▬▬▬▬▬▬▬▬

POLYGON
22 George Square, Edinburgh EH8 9LF
Telephone: 0131 650 4689
Fax: 0131 662 0053

Trade:
Marston Book Services, PO Box 269,
Abingdon, Oxon OX14 4YN
Telephone: 01235 465500
Fax: 01235 465555

Warehouse:
Marston Book Services,
Book Distribution Centre, Unit 113,
Milton Park, Abingdon, Oxon OX14 4NR
Telephone: 01235 820123
Fax: 01235 821436

Publisher & Editor: Marion Sinclair *(Rights)*
Publicity: Jeanie Scott *(Permissions)*
Production: Pamela O'Connor

*Fiction; Poetry; Politics & World Affairs;
Sports & Games; Travel & Topography*

New Titles: 25 (1995), 27 (1996)
No of Employees: 3

ISBNs, Imprints & Series:
0 7486, 0 904919, 0 948275

Parent Company:
Edinburgh University Press

Overseas Representation *(see §7.3)*:
Australia: James Bennett Pty Ltd, Collaroy
Beach, NSW
Canada & Western Europe: c/o Edinburgh
University Press, Edinburgh, UK
Netherlands: Novelty Books International bv,
Weesp
North America: Small Press Distribution Inc,
Berkeley, CA, USA
Northern Europe: Troika Ltd, London, UK

Book Trade Association Membership: PA,
Scottish PA

1695 ▬▬▬▬▬▬▬▬▬

POOKIE PRODUCTIONS LTD
12 Craighouse Avenue, Edinburgh EH10 5LN
Telephone: 0131 447 6750
Fax: 0131 447 7372

Home Representation:
Images

Directors: Heather Bonning
Cherry Hope *(Company Secretary)*

Children's Books

ISBNs, Imprints & Series: 1 872885

Overseas Representation *(see §7.3)*:
South Africa: Verbatim Distributors,
Constantia Hills

Book Trade Association Membership:
Scottish PA

1696 ▬▬▬▬▬▬▬▬▬

DAVID PORTEOUS EDITIONS
PO Box 5, Chudleigh, Newton Abbot, Devon
TQ13 0YZ
Telephone: 01626 853310
Fax: 01626 853663

Warehouse, Trade Enquiries & Orders:
Bookpoint Ltd, 39 Milton Park, Abingdon,
Oxon OX14 4TD
Telephone: 01235 400400
Fax: 01235 861038/832068

Home Sales:
Derek Searle Associates, The Coach House,
Cippenham Lodge, Cippenham Lane, Slough,
Berks SL1 5AN
Telephone: 01753 539295
Fax: 01753 551863

Publisher: David Porteous *(Editorial, Rights)*

Crafts & Hobbies; Fine Art & Art History

New Titles: 2 (1995), 2 (1996)
No of Employees: 2

ISBNs, Imprints & Series: 1 870586

Overseas Representation *(see §7.3)*:
Australia: Little Hills Press Pty Ltd, Crows
Nest (Sydney), NSW
Canada: Vanwell Publishing Ltd, St
Catherines, Ont
Europe: Bill Bailey Publishers
Representatives, Newton Abbot, UK
Irish Republic: Derek Searle Associates Ltd,
Slough, UK
South Africa: Southern Book Publishers,
Halfway House
South East Asia: CKK Ltd Publishers'
International Management, London, UK
USA: Parkwest Publications Inc, Jersey City,
NJ

Book Trade Association Membership: IPG

1697 ▬▬▬▬▬▬▬▬▬

PORTLAND PRESS LTD
59 Portland Place, London W1N 3AJ
Telephone: 0171 580 5530
Fax: 0171 323 1136
Email: edit@portlandpress.co.uk
Web Site: http://www.portlandpress.co.uk

Distribution Centre:
Portland Press, Commerce Way, Colchester,
Essex CO2 8HP
Telephone: 01206 796351
Fax: 01206 799331
Email: sales@portlandpress.co.uk

Directors: Glyn Jones *(Managing)*
Rhonda Oliver *(Publishing)*
Chris Finch *(Financial)*
Managers: Adam Marshall *(Marketing)*
Shirley Day *(Sales)*

*Academic & Scholarly; Biology & Zoology;
Children's Books; Educational & Textbooks;
Medical (incl. Self Help & Alternative
Medicine); Scientific & Technical*

New Titles: 14 (1995), 19 (1996)
No of Employees: 50
Annual Turnover: £2.5M

ISBNs, Imprints & Series:
0 904498 Biochemical Society
1 85578 Portland Press

Parent Company:
The Biochemical Society

Distributor for:
Farrand Press; Journal of Reproduction &
Fertility Ltd; Society for Experimental Biology.
Australia: La Trobe University Press

Overseas Representation *(see §7.3):*
Brunei, Indonesia, Malaysia, Singapore &
Thailand: Prime Editions, Petaling Jaya,
Malaysia
China, Hong Kong, Korea, Philippines &
Taiwan: STM Publishers Services Pte Ltd,
Singapore
Europe: Jim Osgerby, Yateley, UK
Japan: Obi-Wan Kenobi Inc, Tokyo
USA & Canada: Ashgate Publishing Co,
Brookfield, VT, USA

Book Trade Association Membership:
IGSMTP, IPG, Association of Learned and
Professional Society Publishers

1698 ▬▬▬▬▬▬▬

PRENTICE HALL EUROPE
Campus 400, Maylands Avenue,
Hemel Hempstead, Herts HP2 7EZ
Telephone: 01442 881900
Fax: 01442 882099

Orders, Customer Services & Accounts:
International Book Distributors Ltd,
Campus 400, Maylands Avenue,
Hemel Hempstead, Herts HP2 7EZ
Telephone: 01442 881900
Fax: 01442 882099

Distribution Centre:
International Book Distributors Ltd,
Coventry Road, Magna Park, Lutterworth
LE17 4XH
Telephone: 01442 881900
Fax: 01442 882177

President, Prentice Hall Europe: Joseph J.
Marcelle
Editorial Director: Clare Grist
Rights & Permissions: Jean Spurr

Academic & Scholarly; Accountancy &
Taxation; Animal Care & Breeding; Biology &
Zoology; Chemistry; Computer Science;
Economics; Educational & Textbooks;
Electronic (Educational); Engineering;
English as a Foreign Language; Fine Art & Art
History; Geography & Geology; Industry,
Business & Management; Languages &
Linguistics; Mathematics & Statistics; Medical
(incl. Self Help & Alternative Medicine);
Music; Philosophy; Physics; Politics & World
Affairs; Psychology & Psychiatry; Scientific &
Technical; Sociology & Anthropology;
Theatre, Drama & Dance; Vocational Training
& Careers; Computer Books (Trade)

ISBNs, Imprints & Series:
0 13 Arco, Brady, Ellis Horwood, Prentice Hall
Regents, Prentice-Hall
0 205 Allyn & Bacon
0 7450 Harvester Wheatsheaf
0 8385 Appleton & Lange
0 85941 Woodhead Faulkner
0 88173 Fairmont Press
0 917072 Hayden, Macmillan Computer
Publishing, NRP, Prentice Hall Macmillan,
Que, Sams, Sams.Net, Yourdon Press

Parent Company:
Viacom Inc *(USA)*

Associated & Subsidiary Companies:
Australia: Simon & Schuster (Australia) Pty
Ltd. *Canada:* Prentice-Hall of Canada Ltd.
Germany: Markt & Technik. *India:* Prentice-
Hall of India Pte Ltd. *Japan:* Prentice-Hall of
Japan Inc. *Mexico:* Prentice-Hall
Hispanoamericana. *Singapore:* Simon &
Schuster (Asia) Pte Ltd. *USA:* Appleton-
Century-Crofts; Bureau of Business Practice;
Centre for Applied Research in Education;
National Foreman's Institute

Distributor for:
USA: Silicon Press

Book Trade Association Membership: PA

1699 ▬▬▬▬▬▬▬

PRENTICE HALL/ELLIS HORWOOD
[a division of Simon & Schuster International]
Campus 400, Maylands Avenue,
Hemel Hempstead, Herts HP2 7EZ
Telephone: 01442 881900
Fax: 01442 882099

Orders, Customer Services & Accounts:
International Book Distributors Ltd,
Campus 400, Maylands Avenue,
Hemel Hempstead, Herts HP2 7EZ
Telephone: 01442 881900
Fax: 01442 882099

Distribution Centre & Returns:
International Book Distributors Ltd,
Coventry Road, Magna Park, Lutterworth
LE17 4XH
Telephone: 01442 881900
Fax: 01442 882177

President, Prentice Hall Europe: Joseph J.
Marcelle
Editorial Director: Clare Grist
Rights & Permissions: Jean Spurr

Academic & Scholarly; Biology & Zoology;
Chemistry; Computer Science; Educational &
Textbooks; Engineering; Mathematics &
Statistics; Medical (incl. Self Help &
Alternative Medicine); Physics; Reference
Books, Directories & Dictionaries

ISBNs, Imprints & Series: 0 13

Parent Company:
Viacom Inc *(USA)*

Book Trade Association Membership:
IGSMTP

1700 ▬▬▬▬▬▬▬

**PRENTICE HALL/HARVESTER
WHEATSHEAF**
[a division of Simon & Schuster International]
Campus 400, Maylands Avenue,
Hemel Hempstead, Herts HP2 7EZ
Telephone: 01442 881900
Fax: 01442 252544

Orders, Customer Services & Accounts:
International Book Distributors Ltd,
Campus 400, Maylands Avenue,
Hemel Hempstead, Herts HP2 7EZ
Telephone: 01442 881900
Fax: 01442 882099

Distribution Centre:
International Book Distributors Ltd,
Coventry Road, Magna Park, Lutterworth
LE17 4XH
Telephone: 01442 881900
Fax: 01442 882177

President, Prentice Hall Europe: Joseph J.
Marcelle
Editorial Director: Clare Grist
Rights & Permissions: Jean Spurr

Academic & Scholarly; Economics; Gender
Studies; History & Antiquarian; Languages &
Linguistics; Literature & Criticism;
Philosophy; Politics & World Affairs;
Psychology & Psychiatry; Sociology &
Anthropology

ISBNs, Imprints & Series:
0 7108, 0 7450, 0 85527, 0 901759

Parent Company:
Viacom Inc *(USA)*

1701 ▬▬▬▬▬▬▬

**PRENTICE HALL/WOODHEAD
FAULKNER**
[a division of Simon & Schuster International]
Campus 400, Maylands Avenue,
Hemel Hempstead, Herts HP2 7EZ
Telephone: 01442 881900
Fax: 01442 882099

Orders, Customer Services, Accounts:
International Book Distributors Ltd,
Campus 400, Maylands Avenue,
Hemel Hempstead, Herts HP2 7EZ
Telephone: 01442 881900
Fax: 01442 882099

Distribution Centre:
International Book Distributors Ltd,
Coventry Road, Magna Park, Lutterworth
LE17 4XH
Telephone: 01442 881900
Fax: 01442 882177

President, Prentice Hall Europe: Joseph J.
Marcelle
Editorial Director: Clare Grist
Rights & Permissions: Jean Spurr

Accountancy & Taxation; Economics;
Educational & Textbooks; Industry, Business &
Management; Reference Books, Directories &
Dictionaries; Travel & Topography

ISBNs, Imprints & Series:
0 13 Prentice Hall
0 85941 Woodhead Faulkner (Publishers) Ltd
0 870555 Director Books

Parent Company:
Viacom Inc *(USA)*

Associated & Subsidiary Companies:
ICSA Publishing Ltd

Distributor for:
Euromoney Books; Institute of Fiscal Studies

Book Trade Association Membership:
Directory Publishers Association

1702 ■■■■

PRIM-ED PUBLISHING
Centenary Business Centre, Hammond Close,
Attleborough Industrial Estate, Nuneaton,
Warks CV11 6RY
Telephone: 01203 352002
Fax: 01203 326243
Email: 10455.724@compuserve.com

Managers: S. McGuinness *(General)*
D. Garner *(Sales)*

*Children's Books; Educational & Textbooks;
Environment & Development Studies;
Languages & Linguistics; Mathematics &
Statistics; Sports & Games; Theatre, Drama &
Dance*

New Titles: 50 (1995), 60 (1996)
No of Employees: 9
Annual Turnover: £0.5M

ISBNs, Imprints & Series: 1 86400

Parent Company:
R.I.C. (Australia) *(Australia)*

Distributor for:
Australia: R.I.C.

Book Trade Association Membership: PA

1703 ■■■■

PRIMARY SOURCE MEDIA
PO Box 45, Reading RG1 8HF
Telephone: 01189 577213
Fax: 01189 394334

Directors: Marga Beuth *(Sales & Marketing)*
Mark Holland *(Publisher)*

*Academic & Scholarly; Gender Studies;
History & Antiquarian; Languages &
Linguistics; Literature & Criticism*

ISBNs, Imprints & Series:
Research Publications International

Distributor for:
USA: Primary Source Media

Overseas Representation *(see §7.3)*:
France: Josiane Stern, Courbevoie
Spain: Peter Prout, Madrid

Book Trade Association Membership: PA,
Library Association, National Acquisitions
Group

1704 ■■■■

**PRISM PRESS BOOK PUBLISHERS
LTD**
The Thatched Cottage, Partway Lane,
Hazelbury Bryan, Sturminster Newton, Dorset
DT10 2DP
Telephone: 01258 817164
Fax: 01258 817635

**Trade Counter, Warehouse, Payments &
Returns:**
Bailey Distribution Ltd, Units 1A/
1B Learoyd Road, Mountfield Industrial Estate,
New Romney, Kent TN28 8XU
Telephone: 01797 366905
Fax: 01797 366638

Home Trade Representation:
Chris Lloyd Sales & Marketing Services Ltd,
463 Ashley Road, Parkstone, Poole, Dorset
BH14 0AX
Telephone: 01202 715349
Fax: 01202 736191

Foreign Rights:
Cathy Miller, 10 Filmer Road Studios,
75 Filmer Road, London SW6 7JF

Directors: Julian King *(Managing)*
Diana King *(Editorial)*

*Academic & Scholarly; Agriculture; Animal
Care & Breeding; Architecture & Design;
Biology & Zoology; Cookery, Wines & Spirits;
Do-It-Yourself; Geography & Geology; Health
& Beauty; Magic & the Occult; Medical (incl.
Self Help & Alternative Medicine); Music;
Natural History; Philosophy; Politics & World
Affairs; Psychology & Psychiatry; Religion &
Theology; Scientific & Technical; Sociology &
Anthropology*

New Titles: 6 (1995), 6 (1996)
No of Employees: 2

ISBNs, Imprints & Series:
0 904727, 0 907061, 1 85327

Overseas Representation *(see §7.3)*:
Australia (selected titles): Max Harrell,
Malvern, Vic, Australia
*Austria, Germany, Switzerland, Benelux,
France & Netherlands:* Anselm Robinson,
London, UK
Canada: Temeron Books Inc, Calgary
Greece, Italy, Portugal & Spain: Joe Portelli,
Bologna, Italy
New Zealand: Peaceful Living Publications,
Tauranga
Scandinavia: Croft & Croft, Leominster, UK
South Africa: Trinity Books CC, Randburg
USA: Atrium, Santa Rosa, CA

1705 ■■■■

PROFESSIONAL PUBLISHING LTD
100 Avenue Road, London NW3 3PG
Telephone: 0171 538 5386
Fax: 0171 538 8623

Warehouse:
21 The Business Centre, Molly Millars Lane,
Wokingham, Berkshire RG11 2PY
Telephone: 01734 771997

Directors: R. Sutton *(Publishing)*
K. Allen *(Marketing)*
R. Cressey *(Financial)*
S. Short *(Production)*
P. Lake *(Managing)*
E. Bramwell *(Police Review)*
S. Fathers *(Electronic)*
I. Dyson *(Customer Service)*

*Accountancy & Taxation; Industry, Business &
Management; Law*

No of Employees: 130

ISBNs, Imprints & Series:
0 85258 Gee & Co
0 900382 Franey & Co
0 946559 Professional Publishing

Parent Company:
The Thomson Corporation

Associated & Subsidiary Companies:
Franey & Co; Gee & Co; Police Review
Publishing Co Ltd

Distributor for:
USA: American Management Association
(Self-Study Manuals)

1706 ■■■■

PROFILE BOOKS LTD
62 Queen Anne Street, London W1M 9LA
Telephone: 0171 486 6010
Fax: 0171 486 6012
Email: 101766.1201@compuserve.com

Orders:
Tiptree Book Services, Church Road, Tiptree,
Essex CO5 0SR
Telephone: 01621 819000
Fax: 01621 819717

Directors: Andrew Franklin *(Publisher &
Managing)*
Stephen Brough *(Editorial)*
Editor: Nicky White

*Economics; History & Antiquarian;
Philosophy; Politics & World Affairs;
Psychology & Psychiatry; Sociology &
Anthropology*

New Titles: 10 (1996)

ISBNs, Imprints & Series: 1 86197

Book Trade Association Membership: IPG

1707 ■■■■

PROMETHEUS BOOKS UK
10 Crescent View, Loughton, Essex IG10 4PZ
Telephone: 0181 508 2989
Email: 100023.2355@compuserve.com
Web Site: http://www.cs.man.ac.uk/aig/staff/
toby/prometheus/index.html

Distributor:
Lavis Marketing, 73 Lime Walk, Headington,
Oxford OX3 7AD
Telephone: 01865 67575
Fax: 01865 750079

Proprietor: Mike Hutchinson

Academic & Scholarly; Magic & the Occult;
Philosophy; Politics & World Affairs; Religion
& Theology

New Titles: 45 (1995), 50 (1996)
No of Employees: 1

ISBNs, Imprints & Series:
0 87975, 1 57392

Distributor for:
USA: Prometheus Books

1708

PROMOTIONAL REPRINT CO LTD
Kiln House, 210 New Kings Road, London
SW6 4NZ
Telephone: 0171 736 5666
Fax: 0171 736 5777

Directors: Suneel Jaitly *(Managing)*
Jo Messham *(Deputy Managing)*
Managers: Kevin Phillips *(Commercial)*
Alison Percival *(Production)*

*Animal Care & Breeding; Antiques &
Collecting; Atlases & Maps; Aviation;
Cookery, Wines & Spirits; Crafts & Hobbies;
Do-It-Yourself; Fine Art & Art History;
Gardening; Guide Books; Health & Beauty;
History & Antiquarian; Magic & the Occult;
Medical (incl. Self Help & Alternative
Medicine); Military & War; Natural History;
Nautical; Reference Books, Directories &
Dictionaries; Sports & Games; Transport*

New Titles: 120 (1995), 150 (1996)
No of Employees: 12
Annual Turnover: £5M

ISBNs, Imprints & Series:
1 85648 PRC (Promotional Reprint Co)
1 85778 Sunburst Books
1 85820 Kids

1709

**PSYCHOLOGY PRESS OF ERLBAUM
(UK) TAYLOR & FRANCIS**
27 Church Road, Hove, East Sussex BN3 2FA
Telephone: 01273 207411
Fax: 01273 205612

Warehouse:
Vale Packaging, 420 Vale Road, Tonbridge,
Kent TN9 1TD
Telephone: 01732 359387
Fax: 01732 770620

Trade Enquiries & Orders:
Direct Distribution, 27 Church Road, Hove
BN3 2FA
Telephone: 01273 748427
Fax: 01273 722180

Directors: Michael Forster *(Managing)*
Anthony R. Selvey
Stephen B. Neal
Managing Editor: Rohays Perry
Company Secretary: Anthony M. Foye

*Computer Science; Educational & Textbooks;
Psychology & Psychiatry*

New Titles: 18 (1995), 40 (1996)
No of Employees: 25

ISBNs, Imprints & Series:
0 86377 Psychology Press of Erlbaum (UK)
   Taylor & Francis
1 898931 Immediate Publishing

Parent Company:
Taylor & Francis

Overseas Representation *(see §7.3)*:
Australia: Astam Books Pty Ltd, Leichhardt,
   NSW
Japan: United Publishers Services Ltd, Tokyo;
   Maruzen Co Ltd, Tokyo; Kinokuniya Co Ltd,
   Tokyo; My Book Service, Tokyo; Kaigai
   Publications Ltd, Tokyo
South Africa: Michael Brightmore, London,
   UK
Southern Europe & France: Turnkey Projects
   Ltd, Buckingham, UK
Taiwan: Unifacmanu Trading Co Ltd, Taipei

1710

QUAKER HOME SERVICE
Friends House, Euston Road, London
NW1 2BJ
Telephone: 0171 387 3601
Fax: 0171 388 1977

Trade Enquiries & Orders:
Friends Book Centre *(address as above)*

Sales & Distribution: Graham Garner
   (Manager, Friends Book Centre)
Rights & Permissions: David Goddard

Religion & Theology

New Titles: 4 (1995)
No of Employees: 2

ISBNs, Imprints & Series: 0 85245

Parent Company:
Religious Society of Friends (Quakers)

Distributor for:
USA: Friends General Conference; Friends
United Press; Pendle Hill Publications

Book Trade Association Membership: BA

1711

QUARTET BOOKS
27 Goodge Street, London W1P 2LD
Telephone: 0171 636 3992
Fax: 0171 637 1866
Email: quartetbooks@easynet.co.uk

Warehouse:
Plymbridge Distributors Ltd, Estover Road,
Plymouth PL6 7PZ
Telephone: 01752 695745
Fax: 01752 695699

Directors: Jeremy Beale *(Managing)*
Stella Kane *(Publishing)*
Managers: Susie Craigie-Halkett *(Publicity)*

*Biography & Autobiography; Fiction; History
& Antiquarian; Music; Theatre, Drama &
Dance*

New Titles: 45 (1995), 50 (1996)
No of Employees: 8

ISBNs, Imprints & Series:
0 7043 Quartet Encounters
0 86072 Robin Clark

Parent Company:
Namara Group

Associated & Subsidiary Companies:
Robin Clark; The Literary Review; Pipeline
Books; The Wire; The Women's Press

Overseas Representation *(see §7.3)*:
Australia: Allen & Unwin Pty Ltd, St Leonards,
   NSW
Denmark, Finland, Norway & Sweden: Hanne
   Rotovnik, Klampenborg, Denmark
*France, Belgium, Germany, Austria,
   Switzerland, Portugal, Spain, Italy &
   Greece:* Ted Dougherty, London, UK
India: Maya Publishers Pvt Ltd, New Delhi
Japan: Japan English Services Inc, Chiba-ken
Netherlands: Nilsson & Lamm BV, Weesp

1712

QUEEN ANNE PRESS
Windmill Cottage, Mackerye End, Harpenden,
Herts AL5 5DR
Telephone: 01582 715866
Fax: 01582 715121
Email: lennard@nettec.co.uk
Web Site: http://www.nettec.co.uk/cricketer/

Trade Orders:
B. T. Batsford, 1 Bradbury Drive,
Springwood Industrial Estate, Braintree, Essex
CM7 2QY
Telephone: 01376 321276
Fax: 01376 552854

Director: Adrian Stephenson *(Managing)*
Editor: Chris Hawkes

Sports & Games; Yearbooks

New Titles: 8 (1995), 10 (1996)
No of Employees: 3
Annual Turnover: £0.5M

ISBNs, Imprints & Series: 1 85291

Parent Company:
Lennard Associates Ltd

Overseas Representation *(see §7.3)*:
Australia: Davis & Yvonne Inwood, Castle
   Hill, NSW
Canada: Hushion House Ltd, Toronto, Ont
*Denmark, Iceland, Sweden, Finland &
   Norway:* Saga Books ApS, Copenhagen,
   Denmark
*Far East, Caribbean, Japan, China, Hong
   Kong, Taiwan, Singapore & Thailand:* Ralph
   & Sheila Summers, London, UK
*France, Czech & Slovak Republics, Austria,
   Switzerland & Poland:* Juliusz Komarnicki,
   Massagno, Switzerland
*Germany, Belgium, Netherlands &
   Luxembourg:* PKB – Robbert J. Pleysier,
   Heerde, Netherlands
Greece, Croatia & Slovenia: Patrick Bygate,
   Massagno, Switzerland
India, Sri Lanka, Bangladesh & Nepal: Surit
   Mitra & Bikram Grewal, New Delhi, India
*Middle East, Israel, Cyprus, Turkey & United
   Arab Emirates:* Ashton International
   Marketing Services, Larkfield, UK

New Zealand: Random House New Zealand Ltd, Auckland
Pakistan: S. I. Gillani, Lahore
South Africa: Book Promotions Pty Ltd, Claremont
Spain, Portugal, Italy & Gibraltar: Penny Padovani, London, UK
USA: Trafalgar Square Publications, North Pomfret, VT

1713

QUILLER PRESS LTD
46 Lillie Road, London SW6 1TN
Telephone: 0171 499 6529 & 0171 381 8941
Fax: 0171 381 8941

Distribution:
CBS, 406 Vale Road, Tonbridge, Kent
Telephone: 01732 357755
Fax: 01732 770219

Directors: J. J. Greenwood *(Managing)*
A. E. Carlile

Antiques & Collecting; Architecture & Design; Biography & Autobiography; Cookery, Wines & Spirits; Gardening; Guide Books; Humour; Industry, Business & Management; Travel & Topography

New Titles: 12 (1995), 15 (1996)
No of Employees: 2
Annual Turnover: £400,000

ISBNs, Imprints & Series:
0 907621, 1 870948, 1 899163

Overseas Representation *(see §7.3):*
Africa: PMC International, Durban North, South Africa
Australia: Tower Books Wholesalers Pty Ltd, Frenchs Forest, NSW
Europe (excluding Spain, Italy & Portugal): Ted Dougherty, London, UK
New Zealand: Nationwide Book Distributors, Christchurch
Scandinavia: Hanne Rotovnik, Klampenborg, Denmark
Spain, Italy & Portugal: Penny Padovani, London, UK
USA: Cimino Publishing Group, Carle Place, NY

1714

QUINTESSENCE PUBLISHING CO LTD
2 Blagdon Road, New Malden, Surrey KT3 4AD
Telephone: 0181 949 6087
Fax: 0181 336 1484

Director: Mrs Joyce Ronald *(Marketing, Sales Distribution, Advertising & Promotion)*
Sales Consultant: Jim Osgerby

Medical (incl. Self Help & Alternative Medicine)

New Titles: 17 (1995), 24 (1996)
No of Employees: 7

ISBNs, Imprints & Series:
0 86715, 1 85097, 4 87417

Parent Company:
Quintessenz Verlag *(Germany)*

Associated & Subsidiary Companies:
Japan: Quintessence Publishing Co Ltd. *USA:* Quintessence Publishing Co Inc

Distributor for:
Germany: Quintessenz Verlags GmbH. *Japan:* Quintessence Publishing Co Ltd. *USA:* Quintessence Publishing Co Inc

Overseas Representation *(see §7.3):*
Africa: Libriger Book Distributors, Bloemfontein, UK
Australia: Martin Halas Dental Co Pty Ltd, Sydney
Brazil: Quintessence Editora Ltda, São Paulo
Middle East: International Publishers Representatives (IPR), Nicosia, Cyprus

Book Trade Association Membership: PA, BDC

1715

QUOTES LTD
The Book Barn, Church Way, Whittlebury, Northants NN12 8XS
Telephone: 01327 858301
Fax: 01327 858302

Director: Clive Birch

History & Antiquarian; Military & War; Natural History; Sports & Games; Transport

New Titles: 12 (1995), 20 (1996)
No of Employees: 6

ISBNs, Imprints & Series:
0 86023 Baron, In Camera, Quotes, Saga, Sporting & Leisure Press

Book Trade Association Membership: IPG

1716

RAC PUBLISHING
RAC House, PO Box 100, South Croydon, Surrey CR2 6XW
Telephone: 0181 681 8512
Fax: 0181 688 2882

Distribution:
Bookpoint Ltd, 39 Milton Park, Abingdon, Oxon OX14 4TD
Telephone: 01235 400400
Fax: 01235 861038

Publisher: Jacqui Bruff
Sales Fulfilment Manager: Joanne Gillam

Atlases & Maps; Guide Books; Travel & Topography

New Titles: 9 (1995), 9 (1996)
No of Employees: 3
Annual Turnover: £2.2M

ISBNs, Imprints & Series: 0 86211

Parent Company:
RAC Motoring Services

Overseas Representation *(see §7.3):*
Australia: Bookwise International, Findon, SA

1717

RADCLIFFE MEDICAL PRESS LTD
18 Marcham Road, Abingdon, Oxon OX14 1AA
Telephone: 01235 528820
Fax: 01235 528830
Email: medical@radpress.win-uk.net

Directors: Andrew Bax *(Managing)*
Gillian Nineham *(Editorial)*
Margaret McKeown *(Financial)*
Managers: Allison Collins *(Rights & Permissions)*
Jamie Etherington *(Editorial)*
Lorraine Beele *(Production)*
Gregory Moxon *(Marketing)*

Electronic (Educational); Electronic (Professional & Academic); Industry, Business & Management; Medical (incl. Self Help & Alternative Medicine); Reference Books, Directories & Dictionaries

New Titles: 31 (1995), 55 (1996)
No of Employees: 14

ISBNs, Imprints & Series:
1 85775, 1 870905

Overseas Representation *(see §7.3):*
Australia & New Zealand: MacLennan & Petty Pty Ltd, Artarmon, NSW, Australia
Scandinavia: Jim Osgerby, Yateley, UK
South East Asia: McGraw-Hill Book Co, Singapore
USA & Canada: Radcliffe Medical Press Inc, New York, USA

1718

THE RADCLIFFE PRESS
Victoria House, Bloomsbury Square, London WC1B 4DZ
Telephone: 0171 916 1069
Fax: 0171 916 1068

Distributor:
Biblios Publishers' Distribution Services, Star Road, Partridge Green, West Sussex RH13 8LD
Telephone: 01403 710971
Fax: 01403 711143

Publisher: Lester Crook

Biography & Autobiography; History & Antiquarian; Military & War; Politics & World Affairs; Travel & Topography

New Titles: 14 (1995), 21 (1996)

ISBNs, Imprints & Series:
1 85043, 1 86064

Overseas Representation *(see §7.3):*
USA: St Martin's Press Inc, New York, NY

1719

RAGGED BEARS LTD
Ragged Appleshaw, Andover, Hants SP11 9HX
Telephone: 01264 772269
Fax: 01264 772391
Email: books@ragged-bears.co.uk
Web Site: http://www.ragged-bears.co.uk

Returns:
Ragged Bears Ltd, c/o The Trade Counter,
The Airfield, Norwich Road, Mendlesham,
Suffolk IP14 5NA

Directors: Mrs Charles Shirley
Henrietta Stickland
Marketing Manager: Angela Espley

Children's Books

New Titles: 5 (1995), 9 (1996)
No of Employees: 9

ISBNs, Imprints & Series:
1 85714, 1 870817

Distributor for:
A Vos Marques Cassettes; Annick Press; Peter
Bedrick Books; David Bennett Books; Douglas
& McIntyre; Electric Paper; Era Publications
(trade titles); Gallery Children's Books; Happy
Cat Books; Levinson Children's Books; Little
Ark Books (Allen & Unwin Pty); Moonlight
Publishing; Mr Humpty Cassettes; Neugebauer
Press; North-South Books; Owl Man; R&S
Books; Spindlewood; Star Bright Books;
Templar Publishing; Tundra Books;
Watchword Videos & Cassettes

Overseas Representation *(see §7.3)*:
Australia: Lothian Books, Port Melbourne
France: Mrs C. Shirley, Andover, UK
Netherlands, Belgium & Germany: Marietta
   Snell, Maarssenbroek, Netherlands
New Zealand: Forrester Books Ltd, Auckland
South East Asia: CKK Ltd Publishers'
   International Management, London, UK

1720 ▬▬▬▬▬▬▬

RAMPANT HORSE LTD
The Wells House, Holywell Road,
Malvern Wells, Worcs WR14 4LH
Telephone: 01684 893990
Fax: 01684 893993
Email: 101233.2413@compuserve.com.uk

Orders & Warehouse:
Images Booksellers & Distributors Ltd,
The Wells House, Holywell Road,
Malvern Wells, Worcs WR14 4LH
Telephone: 01684 893990
Fax: 01684 893993
Email: 101233.2413@compuserve.com.uk

Directors: Tony Harold *(Managing)*
Catherine Whiting *(Publishing)*
Rights: Andre Harthill
Editorial: Alan Martin

Fiction

New Titles: 15 (1995), 10 (1996)
No of Employees: 4
Annual Turnover: £250,000

ISBNs, Imprints & Series: 1 898839

Overseas Representation *(see §7.3)*:
Europe: Troika Ltd, London, UK

Book Trade Association Membership: IPG

1721 ▬▬▬▬▬▬▬▬▬▬▬▬▬▬▬▬▬▬

**RANDOM HOUSE CHILDREN'S
BOOKS**
20 Vauxhall Bridge Road, London SW1V 2SA
Telephone: 0171 973 9000
Fax: 0171 233 6129

Distribution & Accounts:
Tiptree Book Services, St Luke's Chase,
Colchester, Essex
Telephone: 01621 816362
Fax: 01621 819717

Chairman: Piet Snyman
Directors: Martina Challis *(Managing)*
Ian Hudson *(Deputing Managing)*
Sally-Ann Campbell *(Sales)*
Ruth Jones *(Marketing)*
Alan Lee *(Production)*
Linda Summers
Publisher: Caroline Roberts *(Trade)*

Children's Books

New Titles: 275 (1995), 230 (1996)

ISBNs, Imprints & Series:
0 09 Hutchinson
0 099 Red Fox
0 224 Jonathan Cape
0 370 Bodley Head
1 85656 Random House New Media, Tellastory

Parent Company:
Random House UK Ltd

1722 ▬▬▬▬▬▬▬

RANDOM HOUSE UK LTD
Random House, 20 Vauxhall Bridge Road,
London SW1V 2SA
Telephone: 0171 973 9000
Fax: 0171 233 6129

Warehouse & Orders:
Tiptree Book Services Ltd, St Lukes Chase,
Tiptree, Essex CO5 0SR
Telephone: 01621 816362
Fax: 01621 819011

Directors: Simon Master
Simon King
Amelia Thorpe
Gail Rebuck
Piet Snyman
Anthony McConnell
Alberto Vitale
Company Secretary: Anthony McConnell
Sales: Mike Broderick
Production: Stephen Esson
Rights: Juliet Annan
Marketing: Susan Sandon

*Animal Care & Breeding; Antiques &
Collecting; Audio Books; Biography &
Autobiography; Children's Books; Cookery,
Wines & Spirits; Crime; Crafts & Hobbies;
Electronic (Entertainment); Fiction; Fine Art
& Art History; Gardening; Guide Books;
Health & Beauty; Humour; Illustrated & Fine
Editions; Industry, Business & Management;
Literature & Criticism; Medical (incl. Self Help
& Alternative Medicine); Military & War;
Music; Natural History; Photography; Poetry;
Politics & World Affairs; Reference Books,
Directories & Dictionaries; Science Fiction;*

*Sports & Games; Theatre, Drama & Dance;
Travel & Topography*

ISBNs, Imprints & Series:
0 091 Hutchinson
0 091, 0 7126, 0 8522 Barrie & Jenkins, Ebury
   Press, Helicon, Stanley Paul, Vermilion
0 099 Arrow Books, Legend, Vintage
0 224 Jonathan Cape
0 3562 Optima, Studio Editions
0 370 Bodley Head
0 6790 Fodor
0 7011 Chatto & Windus
0 7012 The Hogarth Press
0 712 Pimlico
0 7126 Century
1 8568 Random House Audio Books
1 85681 Julia MacRae

Parent Company:
Advance Publications Inc *(USA)*

Associated & Subsidiary Companies:
Arrow Books Ltd; Barrie & Jenkins Ltd; The
Bodley Head Ltd; Jonathan Cape Ltd; Century
Publishing Co Ltd; Chatto & Windus Ltd; The
Hogarth Press Ltd; Hutchinson Books Ltd;
Stanley Paul & Co Ltd; Studio Editions Ltd.
Australia: Random House Australia Pty Ltd.
New Zealand: Random House (New Zealand)
Ltd. *South Africa:* Random House South Africa
(Pty) Ltd

Distributor for:
USA: Random House Inc

Overseas Representation *(see §7.3)*:
Australia: Random Australia Pty Ltd, Sydney
Canada: Random House of Canada Ltd,
   Mississauga
Europe: Random House UK Ltd, London, UK
Hong Kong, China, Taiwan & South Korea:
   Stanson Yeung, Hong Kong
India: Rupa & Co, New Delhi
Japan: Yuki Tagaya, Tokyo
Middle East: Peter Ward Book Exports,
   London, UK
New Zealand: Random House New Zealand
   Ltd, Auckland
Philippines & Guam: Balatbat & Sons
   International, Quezon City, Philippines
South Africa: Random House South Africa Pty
   Ltd, Rosebank, Johannesburg
*West Indies, Central & South America &
   Caribbean:* Emily Feffer, New York, USA

Book Trade Association Membership: PA,
BDC, EPC, CAPP

1723 ▬▬▬▬▬

RANSOM PUBLISHING
Ransom House, 2 High Street, Watlington,
Oxon OX9 5PS
Telephone: 01491 613711
Fax: 01491 613733
Email: ransom@dial.pipex.com
Web Site: http://www.ransom.co.uk

Distribution:
Marston Book Services, PO Box 269,
Abingdon, Oxon OX14 4YN
Telephone: 01235 465500
Fax: 01235 465555

Managing Director: Jenny Ertle
Managers: Shaun Lancaster *(Sales & Marketing)*
Robert Ertle *(IT & Project)*
Editor: Lizzy Whittingham

Biology & Zoology; Educational & Textbooks; Electronic (Educational); Electronic (Entertainment); Environment & Development Studies; Geography & Geology; Natural History

New Titles: 1 (1995), 8 (1996)
No of Employees: 4

ISBNs, Imprints & Series:
1 900127 Biodiversity 2000

Distributor for:
Coral Cay Conservation. *Australia:* Webster Publishing

Overseas Representation *(see §7.3):*
Denmark: Compact Data, Frederiksberg
Europe: Intertape Ltd, Mollis, Switzerland
Greece: Pliroforiki Technognosia, Athens
India: ABI Info Access, New Delhi
Netherlands: ROM Soft, Ridderkerk; New Media, The Hague
Poland: Axall Media, Paris, France
Singapore & Malaysia: Graphic Multimedia, Singapore
South Africa: African Business Enterprises, Benmore

1724

RAPID SCIENCE PUBLISHERS
2–6 Boundary Row, London SE1 8HN
Telephone: 0171 865 0198
Fax: 0171 410 6600

American Office:
Rapid Science Publishers, Suite 750, 400 Market Street, Philadelphia, PA 19106, USA
Telephone: +1 (215) 574 2266
Fax: +1 (215) 574 2292

Order Fulfilment:
ITPS, Cheriton House, North Way, Andover SP10 5BE
Telephone: 01264 342773
Fax: 01264 342807

Directors: Dr Michael Dixon *(Managing)*
Anthony Gresford *(Sales)*
Peter McKay *(Marketing)*
Anthony Watkinson *(Publishing)*
Caroline Black *(Publishing)*

Academic & Scholarly; Medical (incl. Self Help & Alternative Medicine); Scientific & Technical

New Titles: 5 (1995), 5 (1996)
No of Employees: 50

ISBNs, Imprints & Series:
1 85922 Rapid Science Publishers
1 869868 CNS Publications

Parent Company:
International Thomson Publishing *(USA)*

Associated & Subsidiary Companies:
Chapman & Hall; Routledge

Book Trade Association Membership: PA, IGSMTP, CAPP

1725

RAVETTE PUBLISHING LTD
Unit 3, Tristar Centre, Star Road, Partridge Green, West Sussex RH13 8RA
Telephone: 01403 711443
Fax: 01403 711554

Warehouse, Invoicing & Accounts:
Telephone: 01254 696768
Fax: 01254 697060

Director: Mrs M. Lamb *(Home & Export Sales)*
UK Sales Manager: B. Camichel

Children's Books; Crafts & Hobbies; Educational & Textbooks; Guide Books; Humour; Industry, Business & Management

No of Employees: 3

ISBNs, Imprints & Series:
0 906710 Garfield
0 948456, 1 85304 Albums, Bluffers Guides, C.O.N.DOMS Series, Disney Studio Albums, Everyone's Guide To (Art) Series, Garfield, Golfer's Dictionary, Golfermania, Management Guides, Shakespeare Series, Traveller's Phrase Book & Dictionary Series, World's Toughest Tongue Twisters, Xenophobe's Guides

Overseas Representation *(see §7.3):*
Australia: Transworld Publishers (Australia) Pty Ltd, Sydney
Europe, Israel & Scandinavia: Walton Marketing Services, Chislehurst, UK
Middle East: Eurab Ltd, Rottingdean, UK
Philippines, Korea, Taiwan, Thailand & Indonesia: I. J. Sagun Enterprises Inc, Rizal, Philippines
Singapore & Malaysia: Pansing Distribution Sdn Bhd, Singapore
South Africa: Macdonald Purnell (Pty) Ltd, Cleveland
USA: Associated Publishers Group (APG), Nashville, TN

1726

REAKTION BOOKS LTD
11 Rathbone Place, London W1P 1DE
Telephone: 0171 580 9928
Fax: 0171 580 9935
Email: 101274.2232@compuserve.com

Distributor (Trade):
Littlehampton Book Services Ltd, 14 Eldon Way, Lineside Estate, Littlehampton, W Sussex BN17 7HE
Telephone: 01903 726410
Fax: 01903 730914

Managers: Jane Franks *(Sales)*
Truda Spruyt *(Publicity)*
Harry Gilonis *(Permissions)*
General Editor: Michael R. Leaman

Architecture & Design; Fine Art & Art History; History & Antiquarian

New Titles: 10 (1995), 12 (1996)
No of Employees: 4

ISBNs, Imprints & Series: 0 948462

Overseas Representation *(see §7.3):*
Australia & Far East: Reaktion Books Ltd, London, UK
Austria, Belgium, France, Germany, Switzerland, Slovenia & Turkey: Onslow Books Ltd, London, UK
Greece, Italy, Portugal & Spain: Bookport Associates, Bologna, Italy
Irish Republic & Northern Ireland: Robert Towers, Monkstown, Irish Republic
Netherlands: Nilsson & Lamm BV, Weesp
New Zealand: Harry Howell, Lane Cove, Australia
Scandinavia & Iceland: Hanne Rotovnik, Klampenborg, Denmark

1727

REDCLIFFE PRESS LTD
22 Canynge Square, Clifton, Bristol BS8 3LA
Telephone: 0117 973 7207
Fax: 0117 921 5431

Trade Orders:
Westcountry Books, Halsgrove House, Lower Moor Way, Tiverton Business Park, Tiverton, Devon

Director: John Sansom *(Rights & Permissions)*
Editorial & Production: John Sansom
Home & Export Sales: Angela Sansom

Fine Art & Art History; Guide Books; Industry, Business & Management; Literature & Criticism; West Country History

New Titles: 11 (1995), 20 (1996)
No of Employees: 3
Annual Turnover: £150,000

ISBNs, Imprints & Series:
0 905459, 0 948265, 1 872971 Sansom & Co, Whitetree Books

1728

REDEMPTORIST PUBLICATIONS
Alphonsus House, Chawton, Alton, Hants GU34 3HQ
Telephone: 01420 88222
Fax: 01420 88805
Email: rp@redempt.demon.co.uk
Web Site: http://www.redempt.org

Executive Director: J. D. McKell
Managers: J. A. James *(Sales Office)*
M. P. Roberts *(Distribution)*

Religion & Theology

New Titles: 9 (1995), 10 (1996)
No of Employees: 20

ISBNs, Imprints & Series: 0 85231

Distributor for:
USA: Ave Maria Press; Dimension Books; Doubleday *(Religious)*; ICS Publications; Liguori; Regina Press; Servant Publications; St Anthony Messenger Press; Tabor Publishing

Book Trade Association Membership: PA, BA

1729

REDSTONE PRESS
7a St Lawrence Terrace, London W10 5SU
Telephone: 0171 352 1594
Fax: 0171 352 8749

Distributor (outside London):
Central Books Ltd, 99 Wallis Road, London
E9 5LN
Telephone: 0181 986 4854
Fax: 0181 533 5821

Proprietor: Julian Rothenstein

Fine Art & Art History; Literature & Criticism

New Titles: 4 (1995), 3 (1996)
No of Employees: 1
Annual Turnover: £100,000

ISBNs, Imprints & Series: 1 870003

Associated & Subsidiary Companies:
USA: Shambhala/Redstone

Overseas Representation *(see §7.3)*:
Europe: Idea Books, Amsterdam, Netherlands

1730

REED BOOKS
Michelin House, 81 Fulham Road, London
SW3 6RB
Telephone: 0171 581 9393
Fax: 0171 225 9424

Distribution:
Reed Book Services, Northampton Road,
Rushden, Northants NN10 6PU
Telephone: 01933 58521
Fax: 01933 50284

Chief Executive: Sandy Grant

*Antiques & Collecting; Architecture & Design;
Atlases & Maps; Audio Books; Aviation;
Biography & Autobiography; Children's
Books; Cookery, Wines & Spirits; Crime;
Crafts & Hobbies; Do-It-Yourself; Fiction;
Fine Art & Art History; Gardening; Geography
& Geology; Guide Books; Health & Beauty;
History & Antiquarian; Humour; Illustrated &
Fine Editions; Literature & Criticism; Magic &
the Occult; Military & War; Music; Natural
History; Philosophy; Photography; Poetry;
Politics & World Affairs; Reference Books,
Directories & Dictionaries; Religion &
Theology; Science Fiction; Sports & Games;
Theatre, Drama & Dance; Transport; Travel &
Topography*

ISBNs, Imprints & Series:
Bounty Books, Brimax, Buzz Books, Cedar,
Conran Octopus, Dean, Hamlyn, Hamlyn
Children's Reference, William Heinemann,
Heinemann Young Books, Mammoth,
Mandarin, Methuen, Methuen Children's
Books, Millers, Minerva, Mitchell Beazley,
Osprey, Parent & Child, George Philip's,
Pitkin Guides, Martin Secker & Warburg,
Sinclair-Stevenson

Parent Company:
Reed Elsevier Plc

Overseas Representation *(see §7.3)*:
see: individual imprints, UK

1731

*REED EDUCATIONAL PUBLISHING
Halley Court, Jordan Hill, Oxford OX2 8EJ
Telephone: 01865 311366
Fax: 01865 310043

Managing Director: William Shepherd

*Educational & Textbooks; English as a Foreign
Language*

ISBNs, Imprints & Series:
Ginn, Heinemann, Heinemann Educational,
Heinemann English Language Teaching,
Heinemann Library, Rigby

Parent Company:
Reed International Books Ltd

Associated & Subsidiary Companies:
Australia: Rigby Heinemann. *Botswana:*
Heinemann Educational Botswana Pty Ltd.
Brazil: Heinemann (Latin America). *Italy:*
Heinemann Le Monnier (50%). *South Africa:*
Heinemann Publishers (50%). *Spain:*
Heinemann Iberia SA. *USA:* Heinemann USA;
Mimosa Publications (50%); Reed Educational
Publishing USA; Rigby Education USA

Overseas Representation *(see §7.3)*:
see: individual imprints, UK

1732

REGENCY HOUSE PUBLISHING LTD
The Grange, Grange Yard, London SE1 3AG
Telephone: 0171 232 0565
Fax: 0171 232 0113

Warehouse & Distribution:
Regency House Publishing Ltd
(address as above)

Managing Director: Miss N. Trodd
Managers: B. H. Trodd
Annabel Trodd

*Architecture & Design; Aviation; Children's
Books; Crafts & Hobbies; Magic & the Occult;
Military & War*

New Titles: 30 (1995), 30 (1996)
No of Employees: 3

ISBNs, Imprints & Series:
1 85361 Troddy Books

1733

**RESEARCH INSTITUTE FOR THE
STUDY OF CONFLICT & TERRORISM
(RISCT)**
136 Baker Street, London W1M 1FH
Telephone: 0171 224 2659
Fax: 0171 486 3064

Distribution:
J. Allen, 133 Downhall Road, Rayleigh, Essex
SS6 9PB
Telephone: 01268 784725

Director: Prof William Gutteridge
Public Relations & Editorial Officer: Joan
Bates *(Rights & Permissions)*
Distributor: Jenny Allen
Administrator: Joan Donald

*Economics; Military & War; Politics & World
Affairs*

New Titles: 10 (1995), 10 (1996)

ISBNs, Imprints & Series:
Conflict Studies

1734

RESEARCH STUDIES PRESS LTD
24 Belvedere Road, Taunton, Somerset
TA1 1HD
Telephone: 01823 336197
Fax: 01823 253252
Email: vaw@rspltd.demon.co.uk

Orders:
John Wiley & Sons Ltd,
Southern Cross Trading Est, Shripney Road,
Bognor Regis PO22 9SA
Telephone: 01243 829121
Fax: 01243 820250

Publisher: William G. Askew
Managing Director: Veronica Wallace
(Permissions)

*Academic & Scholarly; Biology & Zoology;
Chemistry; Computer Science; Engineering;
Scientific & Technical*

New Titles: 11 (1995), 14 (1996)

ISBNs, Imprints & Series: 0 86380

Overseas Representation *(see §7.3)*:
Worldwide: John Wiley & Sons Ltd,
Chichester, UK

Book Trade Association Membership: IPG

1735

*RHINEGOLD PUBLISHING LTD
241 Shaftesbury Avenue, London WC2H 8EH
Telephone: 0171 333 1721
Fax: 0171 333 1769

Directors: Anthony C. Gamble *(Managing)*
Keith Diggle *(Marketing)*
Managers: Richard Thomas *(Marketing)*
Thérèse Claffey *(Advertising)*

*Music; Reference Books, Directories &
Dictionaries; Theatre, Drama & Dance;
Vocational Training & Careers; Arts
Management; Opera*

ISBNs, Imprints & Series: 0 946890

1736

RIAD EL-RAYYES BOOKS LTD
56 Knightsbridge, London SW1X 7NJ
Telephone: 0171 235 4240
Fax: 0171 235 9305

Manager: Z. El-Rayyes *(Sales, Export &
Marketing)*

Biography & Autobiography; Cookery, Wines & Spirits; Fiction; Gender Studies; History & Antiquarian; Literature & Criticism; Photography; Poetry; Politics & World Affairs; Religion & Theology; Travel & Topography

ISBNs, Imprints & Series:
1 85513, 1 869844

Overseas Representation *(see §7.3)*:
Germany: Tabbara, Osnabruck
Jordan: Jordan Distribution Agency, Amman
Lebanon: Allied Printers & Publishers, Beirut
Morocco: Sochepresse, Casablanca
Saudi Arabia: Dar Al Rifai, Riyadh
Switzerland: Librairie Arabe l'Olivier, Geneva
United Arab Emirates: Emirates Bookshop, Al-Ain, UAE

Book Trade Association Membership: PA, BA

1737 ▬▬▬▬

RIBA PUBLICATIONS
Finsbury Mission, 39 Moreland Street, London EC1V 8BB
Telephone: 0171 251 0791 (Sales), 0171 250 0060 (Admin.)
Fax: 0171 608 2375

Retail Counter & Bookshop:
66 Portland Place, London W1N 4AD
Telephone: 0171 251 0791
Fax: 0171 608 2375

Directors: Geoffrey Denner *(Managing)*
Mike Stribbling *(Production)*
Alaine Hamilton *(Editorial)*
Bob Hawkins *(Bookshops)*
Liza Kershaw *(Mail Order)*

Architecture & Design

No of Employees: 25

ISBNs, Imprints & Series:
0 900630, 0 947877, 1 85946

Parent Company:
RIBA Companies Ltd *(wholly owned division of the Royal Institute of British Architects)*

Associated & Subsidiary Companies:
National Building Specification (NBS); RIBA Information Services

Distributor for:
Chartered Society of Designers; Landscape Institute; National Joint Consultative Committee for Building

Overseas Representation *(see §7.3)*:
USA: International Specialized Book Services Inc, Portland, OR

1738 ▬▬▬▬

THE RICHMOND PUBLISHING CO LTD
PO Box 963, Slough SL2 3RS
Telephone: 01753 643104
Fax: 01753 646553

Managing Director: Mrs S. J. Davie

Academic & Scholarly; Biology & Zoology; Educational & Textbooks; Natural History; Scientific & Technical

ISBNs, Imprints & Series:
0 85546 Richmond Publishing
0 916422 Mad River Press
1 85153 Field Studies Council
3 85604 Mykologia Lucerne

Distributor for:
Field Studies Council; WWF United Kingdom.
Switzerland: Mykologia Lucerne. *USA:* Mad River Press (all titles)

Overseas Representation *(see §7.3)*:
USA: Mad River Press, Eureka, CA

1739 ▬▬▬▬

LYNNE RIENNER PUBLISHERS
3 Henrietta Street, Covent Garden, London WC2E 8LU
Telephone: 0171 240 0856
Fax: 0171 379 0609

Contact: Imogen Adam

Academic & Scholarly; Agriculture; Economics; Politics & World Affairs; Sociology & Anthropology

New Titles: 30 (1995), 30 (1996)

ISBNs, Imprints & Series:
0 931477, 0 946510, 1 55587, 1 55598

1740 ▬▬▬▬

RINGPRESS BOOKS LTD
PO Box 8, Lydney, Glos GU5 6YD
Telephone: 01594 563800
Fax: 01594 563808

Trade Enquiries:
Biblios Publishers' Distribution Services, Star Road, Partridge Green, West Sussex RH13 8LD
Telephone: 01403 710971

Director: John Sellers
Editorial: Julia Barnes
Marketing: Nick Kent

Animal Care & Breeding

New Titles: 20 (1995), 22 (1996)
No of Employees: 5
Annual Turnover: £400,000

ISBNs, Imprints & Series:
0 948955 Book of the Breed, Pet Owners' Guide, Ringpress Books Ltd

Distributor for:
USA: Howell Book House

Overseas Representation *(see §7.3)*:
Australia & New Zealand: Kirby Book Co, Sydney, NSW, Australia
South Africa: Southern Book Publishers, Halfway House
Sweden: Akvaristen, Gothenburg
USA & Canada: Seven Hills Book Distributors, Cincinnati, OH, USA

1741 ▬▬▬▬

RIVERS ORAM
144 Hemingford Road, London N1 1DE
Telephone: 0171 607 0823
Fax: 0171 609 2776

Warehouse:
Clipper Distribution, Windmill Grove, Porchester, Hants PO16 0HT
Telephone: 01705 200080
Fax: 01705 200900

Directors: Elizabeth Fidlon *(Managing, Sales, Editorial)*
Anthony Harris *(Financial)*
Managers: Shirley Dow *(Marketing)*
Katherine Bright-Holmes *(Rights, Editorial)*

Academic & Scholarly; Biography & Autobiography; Gay & Lesbian Studies; Gender Studies; History & Antiquarian; Photography; Politics & World Affairs; Sociology & Anthropology

New Titles: 10 (1995), 15 (1996)
No of Employees: 6

ISBNs, Imprints & Series:
1 85489 Institute of Public Policy Research titles – Series

Overseas Representation *(see §7.3)*:
Australia: Manic Ex-Poseur Pty Ltd, Carlton North, Vic
Germany: Missing Link Versandbuchhandlung, Bremen
India: T. R. Publications Pvt Ltd, Madras
Irish Republic: Brookside Publishing Services, Dublin
Japan: United Publishers Services Ltd, Tokyo
Malaysia, Brunei, Singapore, Thailand & Indonesia: Charles Kang, Petalinga Jaya, Malaysia
Philippines: Combined Representatives Worldwide Inc, Manila
Scandinavia: Saga Books ApS, Copenhagen, Denmark
South America: Emir Sader, Rio de Janeiro, Brazil
USA & Canada: Paul & Co Publishers Consortium Inc, Concord, MA, USA

Book Trade Association Membership: IPG

1742 ▬▬▬▬

ROADMASTER PUBLISHING
PO Box 176, Chatham, Kent ME5 9AQ
Telephone: 01634 862843
Fax: 01634 201555

Sales Manager: Malcolm Wright

Geography & Geology; Guide Books; Nautical; Transport; Travel & Topography

ISBNs, Imprints & Series: 1 871814

1743 ▬▬▬▬

ROBSON BOOKS LTD
Bolsover House, 5–6 Clipstone Street, London W1P 8LE
Telephone: 0171 323 1223 & 0171 637 5937/8
Fax: 0171 636 0798

Warehouse:
Units 3 & 4, The Peacock Estate,
20 White Hart Lane, Tottenham, London N17

Directors: Jeremy Robson (Managing)
Carole Robson (Home & Export Sales)
Managers: Robert Crocker (Production)
Editorial Head: Louise Dixon
Accounts: David Pickin

Biography & Autobiography; Cinema, Video,
TV & Radio; Cookery, Wines & Spirits;
Gardening; Guide Books; Health & Beauty;
Humour; Sports & Games; Theatre, Drama &
Dance; Travel & Topography

New Titles: 70 (1995), 80 (1996)
No of Employees: 13
Annual Turnover: £1.4M

ISBNs, Imprints & Series:
0 86051, 0 903895, 1 86105

Overseas Representation (see §7.3):
Australia: Peribo Pty Ltd, Terrey Hills, NSW
Canada: Hushion House Ltd, Toronto, Ont
Europe (excluding Spain & Portugal): Ted
    Dougherty, London, UK
New Zealand: David Bateman Ltd, Auckland
Scandinavia: Croft & Croft, Leominster, UK
South Africa: Trinity Books CC, Randburg
South East Asia: CKK Ltd Publishers'
    International Management, London, UK
Spain & Portugal: Peter Prout, Madrid, Spain

Book Trade Association Membership: PA

1744 ▬▬▬

ROMER PUBLICATIONS
Smith Yard, Unit 5, 29A Spelman Street,
London E1 6LQ
Telephone: 0171 247 3581
Fax: 0171 247 3581

Director: Dr H. de Brouwer (Chairman)
Marketing Manager: H. Melkman (Sales)
Administration: Mike Holland
Editorial: Anthony Wall

Children's Books; Educational & Textbooks;
History & Antiquarian; Law; Religion &
Theology; Scientific & Technical

New Titles: 1 (1995), 2 (1996)
No of Employees: 3
Annual Turnover: £10,000

ISBNs, Imprints & Series:
0 9511508 History of Christian Doctrine Series,
    Nebula Encounters Series

Parent Company:
de Brouwer & Melkman Publishing
(Netherlands)

Associated & Subsidiary Companies:
Excalibur Press; Hebreware

Distributor for:
Excalibur Press; Hebreware. Netherlands: de
Brouwer & Melkman Publishing

Overseas Representation (see §7.3):
Belgium: W. Melkman, Amsterdam,
    Netherlands
Netherlands: H. De Brouwer, Amsterdam

Book Trade Association Membership: EPC,
IPG, Small Press Group, Association of Little
Presses

1745 ▬▬▬

ROSENDALE PRESS LTD
Premier House, 10 Greycoat Place, London
SW1P 1SB
Telephone: 0171 222 8866
Fax: 0171 799 1416
Email: maureen@rosendal.demon.co.uk

Warehouse & Distribution:
Littlehampton Book Services Ltd,
10–14 Eldon Way, Lineside Estate,
Littlehampton, West Sussex BN17 7HE
Telephone: 01903 721596
Fax: 01903 730914

Chairman: T. S. Green
Editorial Director: Maureen Green

Cookery, Wines & Spirits; Guide Books; Health
& Beauty; Industry, Business & Management;
Psychology & Psychiatry; Travel &
Topography

New Titles: 4 (1995), 6 (1996)
No of Employees: 3

ISBNs, Imprints & Series:
0 9509182, 1 872803

Book Trade Association Membership: IPG

1746 ▬▬▬

ROUNDHOUSE PUBLISHING LTD
PO Box 140, Oxford OX2 7FF
Telephone: 01865 512682
Fax: 01865 59594
Email: 100637.3571@compuserve.com

Warehouse & Distribution:
BookPoint Ltd, 39 Milton Park, Abingdon,
Oxon OX14 4TD
Telephone: 01235 400400
Fax: 01235 832068

Managing Director: Alan Goodworth
    (Publisher)

Atlases & Maps; Cinema, Video, TV & Radio;
Guide Books; Literature & Criticism; Medical
(incl. Self Help & Alternative Medicine);
Music; Philosophy; Psychology & Psychiatry;
Reference Books, Directories & Dictionaries;
Theatre, Drama & Dance

New Titles: 10 (1995), 12 (1996)

ISBNs, Imprints & Series: 1 85710

Associated & Subsidiary Companies:
Roundhouse Reference Books

Distributor for:
Facts on File; Headstart History; Health Press.
Canada: Canadian Museum of Civilization;
Douglas & McIntyre Ltd; Fitzhenry &
Whiteside; Greystone Books; Natural Heritage
Books; Self-Counsel Press. Italy: Gremese
International. USA: American Map
Corporation; Barricade Books; Chatham House
Publishers; Continuum Publishing Group;
Facts on File, US; Mapeasy; Marshall

Cavendish, US; North Star Publications;
Paragon House; University Press of
Mississippi; World Music Press; Writings of
Mary Baker Eddy

Overseas Representation (see §7.3):
Africa: PMC International, Durban North,
    South Africa
Europe (East): MTM, Hong Kong
Europe (Spain & Portugal only): Iberian Book
    Services SL, Madrid, Spain
Europe (West) (excluding Scandinavia): Ted
    Dougherty, London, UK
India: Viva Marketing, New Delhi
Irish Republic: Carr O'Connell, Ashbourne
Middle East: International Publishers
    Representatives (IPR), Nicosia, Cyprus
Pakistan: Tahir Lodhi, Lahore
Scandinavia: Hanne Rotovnik, Klampenborg,
    Denmark

1747 ▬▬▬

ROUTLEDGE
11 New Fetter Lane, London EC4P 4EE
Telephone: 0171 583 9855
Fax: 0171 842 2298

Warehouse, Trade Enquiries & Orders:
ITPS, Cheriton House, North Way, Andover,
Hants SP10 5BE
Telephone: 01264 332424
Fax: 01264 364418

Directors: Robert Kiernan (Chairman)
David Tebbutt (Finance)
Andy Roper (Financial Controller)
Tim Westbrook (Marketing)
Tony Short (Production, Publishing Services &
    IT)
Peter Sowden (Publishing)

Academic & Scholarly; Archaeology;
Economics; Educational & Textbooks; Gender
Studies; Geography & Geology; History &
Antiquarian; Industry, Business &
Management; Languages & Linguistics;
Literature & Criticism; Philosophy; Politics &
World Affairs; Psychology & Psychiatry;
Reference Books, Directories & Dictionaries;
Sociology & Anthropology; Theatre, Drama &
Dance; Classics; Media; Social Welfare

ISBNs, Imprints & Series:
0 415 Routledge

Parent Company:
The Thomson Corporation

Associated & Subsidiary Companies:
Australia: Law Book Co. Canada: Routledge,
Chapman & Hall Inc. USA: Routledge,
Chapman & Hall Inc

Overseas Representation (see §7.3):
Australia: The Law Book Co Ltd, North Ryde
Botswana & Zambia: The Educational Book
    Service (Pty) Ltd, Gabarone, Botswana
Caribbean: Choice Publishing & Marketing Co
    Ltd, St Michael, Barbados
Central America: Humphrys Roberts
    Associates, London, UK
Ghana: J. A. Amoah, Accra
Hong Kong: Asia Publisher Services Ltd
India: R. Seshadri, Madras
Israel: Franklins, Gane Yuan
Japan: United Publishers Services Ltd, Tokyo

Malaysia: Asia Publishers Services, Petaling Jaya
Middle East: Chapman & Hall Ltd, London, UK
New Zealand: Hodder Moa Beckett Publishers Ltd, Auckland
Nigeria: Publisher Support Services Ltd, Ikeja
Pakistan: Afro-Asian Book Co, Karachi
Philippines: I. J. Sagun Enterprises Inc, Rizal
Rest of World: Routledge, London, UK
Singapore, Indonesia, Thailand & Brunei: APD Singapore Pte Ltd, Singapore
South Africa: Book Promotions Pty Ltd, Plumstead
South America: Humphrys Roberts Associates, São Paulo, Brazil
Trinidad & East Caribbean: Longman Trinidad Ltd, Trincity, Trinidad
USA & Canada: Routledge Inc, New York, NY, USA
Zimbabwe: Barbie Keene, Harare

Book Trade Association Membership: PA, BDC, CAPP

1748

ROYAL COLLEGE OF GENERAL PRACTITIONERS
14 Princes Gate, Hyde Park, London SW7 1PU
Telephone: 0171 581 3232
Fax: 0171 225 3047

Publications Office:
9 Marlborough Road, Exeter EX2 4TJ
Telephone: 01392 57938
Fax: 01392 413449

Honorary Editor: Prof D. J. Pereira Gray
Assistant Editor: Mrs Jill Pereira Gray
Head of Services: Mrs Jane Austin
Sales Administrator: Mrs Maria Phantis

Medical (incl. Self Help & Alternative Medicine); Psychology & Psychiatry

New Titles: 8 (1995), 12 (1996)
No of Employees: 120
Annual Turnover: £3.5M

ISBNs, Imprints & Series: 0 85084

Book Trade Association Membership: ALPSP

1749

THE ROYAL SOCIETY
6 Carlton House Terrace, London SW1Y 5AG
Telephone: 0171 839 5561
Fax: 0171 930 2170 & 976 1837

Warehouse:
Two-Ten Communications, PO Box 210, Wetherby, Yorkshire LS23 7EL

Director of Publishing: John Taylor

Academic & Scholarly; Biography & Autobiography; Biology & Zoology; Chemistry; Physics; Scientific & Technical

Annual Turnover: £1.3M

ISBNs, Imprints & Series: 0 85403

Book Trade Association Membership: ALPSP

1750

THE ROYAL SOCIETY OF CHEMISTRY
Sales & Promotion Dept,
Thomas Graham House, Science Park,
Milton Road, Cambridge CB4 4WF
Telephone: 01223 420066
Fax: 01223 423429
Email: sales@rsc.org
Web Site: http://chemistry.rsc.org/rsc/

Warehouse:
Turpin Distribution Services Ltd,
Blackhorse Road, Letchworth, Herts SG6 1HN
Telephone: 01462 672555
Fax: 01462 480947
Email: turpin@rsc.org
Web Site: http://www.worldserver.pipex.com/ turpin/turpinxp.htm

Director: Robert Welham *(Information Services)*
Managers: Barry Anderson *(Home & Export Sales & Promotion)*
Robert Andrews *(Editorial, Rights & Permissions)*
Alan Cubitt *(Book Production)*

Academic & Scholarly; Chemistry; Educational & Textbooks; Electronic (Educational); Electronic (Professional & Academic); Reference Books, Directories & Dictionaries; Scientific & Technical

New Titles: 45 (1995), 45 (1996)
No of Employees: 350
Annual Turnover: £13.5M

ISBNs, Imprints & Series: 0 85186, 0 85404

Distributor for:
USA: American Chemical Society

Overseas Representation *(see §7.3):*
Asia, Australia & New Zealand: Clarke Associates Ltd, Bristol, UK
Australia, New Zealand & Papua New Guinea: DA Information Services, Mitcham, Vic, Australia
India: UBS Publishers' Distributors Ltd, New Delhi; S. Janakiraman, Madras
Irish Republic: George Sainsbury, Bleasby, UK
Israel: Franklins, Gane Yuan
Japan: OBK, Obi-Wan Kenobi Inc, Tokyo
Middle East, Pakistan, Algeria, Malta, Afghanistan, Greece, Turkey, Tunisia & Morocco: Anthony Rudkin Associates, Oxford, UK
Middle East, Pakistan, Algeria, Malta, Afghanistan, Greece, Turkey, Tunisia & Morocco: Farhad Maftoon, Tehran, Iran
Nigeria: Mr Olu Anulopo, Ibadan
Scandinavia & Iceland: Colin Flint, Harlow, UK
Singapore, Brunei, Malaysia, Indonesia, Philippines, Thailand, Hong Kong & Korea: APAC Publishers Services, Singapore
South America: Terry Roberts, Cotia SP, Brazil
Spain & Portugal: Arie Ruitenbeek, Madrid, Spain

Book Trade Association Membership: ALPSP

Book Trade Association Membership: PA, Association of Learned Society Publishers

1751

ROYAL SOCIETY OF MEDICINE PRESS LTD
1 Wimpole Street, London W1M 8AE
Telephone: 0171 290 2922
Fax: 0171 290 2929

Warehousing & Distribution:
Hoddle Doyle Meadows Ltd, Station Road, Linton, Cambs CB1 6UX
Telephone: 01223 893855
Fax: 01223 893852

Managing Director: Howard Croft
Production Executive: Brian Weight
Marketing: Dominic Bentham
Editorial & Sales: Yvonne Rue
Finance: Michael Hellyar

Medical (incl. Self Help & Alternative Medicine)

New Titles: 17 (1995), 19 (1996)
No of Employees: 11
Annual Turnover: £951,000

ISBNs, Imprints & Series:
1 85315 Controversies and Dilemmas Series, Eponymists in Medicine Series, International Congress and Symposium Series, Key Paper Conferences Series, Round Table Series

Parent Company:
Royal Society of Medicine

Overseas Representation *(see §7.3):*
USA: Royal Society of Medicine Foundation Inc, New York

Book Trade Association Membership: PA, ALPSP

1752

RUNNING PRESS BOOK PUBLISHERS
Cedar House, 35 Chichele Road, Oxted, Surrey RH8 0AE
Telephone: 01883 730207
Fax: 01883 730188
Email: 101341.1235@compuserve.com

Warehouse, Trade Enquiries & Orders:
Biblios Publishers' Distribution Services, Star Road, Partridge Green, West Sussex RH13 8LD
Telephone: 01403 710971
Fax: 01403 711143

Director of Sales UK: Adrian Parker

Antiques & Collecting; Archaeology; Atlases & Maps; Children's Books; Cookery, Wines & Spirits; Crafts & Hobbies; Fiction; Fine Art & Art History; Gardening; Gender Studies; Geography & Geology; Humour; Literature & Criticism; Natural History; Photography; Poetry; Psychology & Psychiatry; Sports & Games; Travel & Topography; Miniature Books; Postcard Books

ISBNs, Imprints & Series:
0 89471 Running Press Miniature Editions™

0 91 4294 Start Exploring™
1 56138 Courage Books

Parent Company:
Running Press *(USA)*

1753 ▬▬▬▬▬▬▬▬▬▬▬▬▬

*THE RUTLAND PRESS
[formerly Rias Publishing]
15 Rutland Square, Edinburgh EH1 2BE
Telephone: 0131 229 7545
Fax: 0131 228 2188

Distribution:
Albany Publishers' Distribution Ltd,
32 Finlas Street, Glasgow G22 5DU
Telephone: 0141 558 5012
Fax: 0141 557 0189

Representation:
Seol, 13 Roseneath Street, Edinburgh EH9 1JH
Telephone: 0131 228 6189

Managers: Helen Leng *(Publishing)*
John Pelan *(Sales & Marketing)*

Architecture & Design

ISBNs, Imprints & Series:
0 7073, 0 950, 1 8515, 1 873190

Parent Company:
Royal Incorporation of Architects in Scotland

Book Trade Association Membership: BA,
Scottish PA

1754 ▬▬▬▬▬▬▬▬▬▬▬▬▬

SAGE PUBLICATIONS LTD
6 Bonhill Street, London EC2A 4PU
Telephone: 0171 374 0645
Fax: 0171 374 8741
Email: info@sagepub.co.uk
Web Site: http://www.sagepub.co.uk

Directors: David Hill *(Managing)*
Lynn Adams *(Administration)*
Ian Eastment *(Marketing)*
Stephen Barr *(Editorial)*
Mike Birch *(Systems)*
Sara Miller McCune
David McCune
Matt Jackson
Sales Manager: John Gavin
Rights & Permissions: Vivienne Dunlop

*Academic & Scholarly; Economics; Electronic
(Educational); Gender Studies; Industry,
Business & Management; Mathematics &
Statistics; Politics & World Affairs; Psychology
& Psychiatry; Reference Books, Directories &
Dictionaries; Sociology & Anthropology*

New Titles: 350 (1995), 375 (1996)
No of Employees: 81

ISBNs, Imprints & Series: 0 8039

Parent Company:
Sage Publications Inc *(USA)*

Associated & Subsidiary Companies:
India: Sage Publications Pvt Ltd. *USA:*
Altamira Press Inc; Corwin Press Inc; Pine

Forge Press Inc; Sage Publications Inc; Sage
Publications Software; Scolari

Overseas Representation *(see §7.3)*:
Australia & New Zealand: Astam Books Pty
Ltd, Leichhardt, NSW, Australia
Europe: Andrew B. Durnell, Tunbridge Wells,
UK
Japan: United Publishers Services Ltd, Tokyo
South Africa: Academic Marketing Services,
Auckland Park

Book Trade Association Membership: PA,
IPG

1755 ▬▬▬▬▬▬▬▬▬▬▬▬▬

*SAINSBURY PUBLISHING LTD
Auldearn, Main Street, Bleasby, Notts
NG14 7GH
Telephone: 01636 830499
Fax: 01636 830175

Directors: George Sainsbury
Angela Sainsbury

Humour; Natural History

ISBNs, Imprints & Series: 1 870655

Distributor for:
A. K. Peters

1756 ▬▬▬▬▬▬▬▬▬▬▬▬▬

SAINT ANDREW PRESS
121 George Street, Edinburgh EH2 4YN
Telephone: 0131 225 5722
Fax: 0131 220 3113

Managers: Lesley A. Taylor *(Editorial, Rights
& Permissions)*
Derek Auld *(Sales & Production)*
Ian Dunnet *(Warehouse)*

History & Antiquarian; Religion & Theology

New Titles: 11 (1995), 10 (1996)
No of Employees: 6
Annual Turnover: £232,286

ISBNs, Imprints & Series:
0 7152, 0 86153

Parent Company:
Church of Scotland's Board of Communication

Distributor for:
Church of Scotland Stationery; Pathway
Productions; Wild Goose Publications

Overseas Representation *(see §7.3)*:
Australia: Openbook Publishers, Adelaide, SA
New Zealand: Omega Distributors Ltd,
Auckland
USA & Canada: Westminster/John Knox Press,
Louisville, KY, USA

Book Trade Association Membership:
Scottish PA

1757 ▬▬▬▬▬▬▬▬▬▬▬▬▬

ST PAULS
Morpeth Terrace, Victoria, London SW1P 1EP
Telephone: 0171 828 5582
Fax: 0171 828 3329

Managing Director: Sebastian Karamuelil
(Permissions)

*Children's Books; Philosophy; Religion &
Theology*

New Titles: 25 (1995), 10 (1996)

ISBNs, Imprints & Series: 0 85439

Associated & Subsidiary Companies:
Argentina: Ediciones San Pablo. *Australia:* St
Pauls. *Brazil:* Edições San Pablo. *Canada:*
Medias Paul. *Colombia:* Ediciones San Pablo.
France: Editions Mediaspaul. *India:* Better
Yourself Books; St Pauls. *Irish Republic:* St
Pauls. *Italy:* Edizioni San Palo. *Japan:*
Chuoshuppan-Sha. *Kenya:* St Pauls
Publications. *Korea, South:* St Pauls. *Mexico:*
Ediciones San Pablo. *Philippines:* St Pauls.
Portugal: Edições San Pablo. *Spain:* Ediciones
San Pablo. *USA:* Alba House. *Venezuela:*
Ediciones San Pablo

Distributor for:
St Pauls

Overseas Representation *(see §7.3)*:
Australia: St Pauls, Homebush
Kenya: St Paul Book Centre, Nairobi
Nigeria: St Paul Book Centre, Oke-Padi
Tanzania: St Paul Book Centre, Dar-es-Salaam
Uganda: St Paul Book Centre, Kampala

Book Trade Association Membership: BA

1758 ▬▬▬▬▬▬▬▬▬▬▬▬▬

SALAMANDER BOOKS
129–137 York Way, London N7 9LG
Telephone: 0171 267 4447
Fax: 0171 267 5112

Distributor:
Bookpoint Limited, 39 Milton Park, Abingdon,
Oxon OX14 4TD
Telephone: 01235 835861
Fax: 01235 861038

Directors: David Spence *(Managing)*
Richard Collins *(Editorial)*
Managers: Janet Cooper *(US Sales)*
Colin Gower *(Sales – Home & Export)*
Peter Thompson *(Production)*
Christine Chick *(Foreign Rights)*

*Animal Care & Breeding; Aviation; Children's
Books; Cookery, Wines & Spirits; Crafts &
Hobbies; Gardening; Military & War; Music;
Natural History; Sports & Games; Transport*

New Titles: 42 (1995), 54 (1996)
No of Employees: 31
Annual Turnover: £10.1M

ISBNs, Imprints & Series:
0 86101, 1 85600

Parent Company:
Salamander Holdings NV *(Belgium)*

Overseas Representation *(see §7.3)*:
*Greece, Africa (excluding South Africa),
Eastern Europe & Russia (English
Language):* IMA, London, UK
*India, Far East (excluding Singapore) &
Middle East (English Language):* Ashton

International Marketing Services, Larkfield, UK
Ireland (English Language): Gill & Macmillan Ltd, Dublin, Irish Republic
Philippines (English Language): Combined Book Representatives, Manila, Philippines

1759

SALVATIONIST PUBLISHING & SUPPLIES LTD
117–121 Judd Street, Kings Cross, London WC1H 9NN
Telephone: 0171 387 1656
Fax: 0171 383 3420

Mail Order:
Campfield Road, St Albans, Herts AL1 5HY
Telephone: 01727 852371
Fax: 01727 832006

Directors: Michael Williams *(Managing, Rights & Permissions)*
David Napier
Gordon Camsey *(Company Secretary)*
Gordon Becker
Ramsey Caffull
John Rowlanes
Buyer: John Driscoll

Biography & Autobiography; Children's Books; Educational & Textbooks; Music; Poetry; Religion & Theology; Theatre, Drama & Dance

New Titles: 2 (1995), 2 (1996)
No of Employees: 50
Annual Turnover: £3M

ISBNs, Imprints & Series: 0 85412

Book Trade Association Membership: BA, Christian Booksellers Association

1760

SANGAM BOOKS LTD
57 London Fruit Exchange, Brushfield Street, London E1 6EP
Telephone: 0171 377 6399
Fax: 0171 375 1230

Manager: A. A. DeSouza

Academic & Scholarly; Agriculture; Bibliography & Library Science; Biography & Autobiography; Biology & Zoology; Chemistry; Children's Books; Cinema, Video, TV & Radio; Cookery, Wines & Spirits; Crafts & Hobbies; Economics; Educational & Textbooks; Engineering; English as a Foreign Language; Fine Art & Art History; Gender Studies; Geography & Geology; Guide Books; Humour; Illustrated & Fine Editions; Industry, Business & Management; Languages & Linguistics; Law; Literature & Criticism; Mathematics & Statistics; Medical (incl. Self Help & Alternative Medicine); Music; Natural History; Philosophy; Physics; Poetry; Politics & World Affairs; Psychology & Psychiatry; Reference Books, Directories & Dictionaries; Religion & Theology; Scientific & Technical; Sociology & Anthropology; Sports & Games

Annual Turnover: £100,000

ISBNs, Imprints & Series:
0 86125, 0 86131, 0 86132, 0 86311

Associated & Subsidiary Companies:
India: Orient Longman Ltd

Distributor for:
India: Academic Publishers; Indus Publishing House; Konark Publishers; Popular Prakashan Pvt Ltd; Radiant Publishers; Sangam Books (India) Pvt Ltd; Universities Press (India) Pvt Ltd; Vikas Publishing House Pvt Ltd

Book Trade Association Membership: PA

1761

SAQI BOOKS
26 Westbourne Grove, London W2 5RH
Telephone: 0171 221 9347
Fax: 0171 229 7492

Distribution:
Bailey Distribution Ltd, Units 1A/1B, Learoyd Road,
Mountfield Road Industrial Estate,
New Romney, Kent TN28 8XU
Telephone: 01797 366905
Fax: 01797 366638

Editor: Mai Ghoussoub
Sales Director: André Gaspard

Architecture & Design; Fiction; Arab World; Art; Islam; Middle East; World Affairs

New Titles: 10 (1995), 12 (1996)
No of Employees: 3
Annual Turnover: £120,000

ISBNs, Imprints & Series:
0 86356 Saqi Books
187 339 Echoes

Parent Company:
Dar Al Jaqi Sarl *(Lebanon)*

Overseas Representation *(see §7.3):*
Other overseas markets: Drake International Services, Oxford, UK
USA: Interlink International Inc, Northampton, MA

Book Trade Association Membership: PA, BA, BDC, CAPP

1762

SAREMA PRESS (PUBLISHERS) LTD
15 Beeches Walk, Carshalton, Surrey SM5 4JS
Telephone: 0181 770 1953
Fax: 0181 770 1957

Directors: Gordon Rookledge *(Managing & Sales)*
Jennie Rookledge *(Accounts & Distribution)*
Editorial: Sarah Rookledge
Rights & Sales: Emma Rookledge

Architecture & Design; Atlases & Maps; Fine Art & Art History

No of Employees: 4
Annual Turnover: £7,000

ISBNs, Imprints & Series:
1 870758 Rookledge International Publications, Sarema Press Publishers

Overseas Representation *(see §7.3):*
Europe (excluding Sweden): Sven Uffe Reumert ApS, Copenhagen, Denmark
Sweden: C52 – Graphic Design, Goteborg
USA & Canada: Moyer Bell, Rhode Island, USA

1763

W. B. SAUNDERS CO LTD
24–28 Oval Road, London NW1 7DX
Telephone: 0171 267 4466
Fax: 0171 482 2293
Web Site: http://www.hbuk.co.uk/wbs/

Warehouse, Customer Service & Journal Subscription:
High Street, Footscray, Kent DA15 5HP
Telephone: 0181 300 3322
Fax: 0181 309 0807

Directors: W. M. Barnett
Jamie Sehmer *(Financial)*
Sean Duggan *(Publishing/Medical)*
Michael Ewins *(Production)*
Peter McKay *(Sales & Marketing)*
Managers: Ian Banbery *(Marketing)*
Des Brennan *(Sales)*
Sheila O'Reilly *(Customer Service)*

Academic & Scholarly; Animal Care & Breeding; Medical (incl. Self Help & Alternative Medicine); Veterinary Science; Nursing

ISBNs, Imprints & Series:
0 7020, 0 7216

Parent Company:
Harcourt Brace & Co

Distributor for:
USA: W. B. Saunders Inc

Overseas Representation *(see §7.3):*
Africa, Middle East, India & Pakistan: contact London Office, UK
Australia: W. B. Saunders Co Ltd, Marrickville
Brazil: Editoria Guanabara, Rio de Janeiro
Canada: W. B. Saunders Canada Ltd, Toronto
Colombia: Editorial Interamericana SA, Bogota
Ecuador: Libros Tecnicos Liteja Cia Ltda, Quito
Greece: G. Zevelekakis & Co EE, Athens
Italy & Portugal: Marcello SNC, Padua, Italy
Japan & Korea: Harcourt Brace Japan Inc, Tokyo, Japan
Mexico: Nueva Editorial Interamericana SA de CV, Mexico
New Zealand: Holt, Rinehart & Winston Publishing New Zealand Ltd, Auckland
Nigeria: University Press Ltd, Ibadan
Spain: Interamerica SA, Madrid
Uruguay: Editorial Tecnica Interamericana, Montevideo
USA: W. B. Saunders, Philadelphia

Book Trade Association Membership: PA, BDC, IGSMTP, CAPP

1764

SAVE THE CHILDREN
17 Grove Lane, London SE5 8RD
Telephone: 0171 703 5400
Fax: 0171 703 2278
Web Site: http://www.oneworld.org/scf/

Head of Publications: Bo Priestley
Publications Marketing: Madeleine Parkyn

*Academic & Scholarly; Educational &
Textbooks; Medical (incl. Self Help &
Alternative Medicine); Politics & World
Affairs; Sociology & Anthropology*

ISBNs, Imprints & Series:
1 870322, 1 899120

Book Trade Association Membership: PA

1765

SAWD BOOKS
Plackett's Hole, Bicknor, Sittingbourne, Kent
ME9 8BA
Telephone: 01795 472262
Fax: 01795 422633

Distribution:
Sawd Publications, Unit 1, Centre 2000,
St Michael's Road, Sittingbourne, Kent
ME10 3DZ
Telephone: 01795 472262
Fax: 01795 422633

Partners: Susannah Wainman
Allison Wainman

*Cookery, Wines & Spirits; Gardening; Guide
Books; Humour*

New Titles: 1 (1995)
No of Employees: 3
Annual Turnover: £100,000

ISBNs, Imprints & Series: 1 872489

Parent Company:
Sawd Publications

Book Trade Association Membership: IPG

1766

S. B. PUBLICATIONS
c/o 19 Grove Road, Seaford, East Sussex
BN25 1TP
Telephone: 01323 893498

Distribution:
Biblios Publishers' Distribution Services,
Partridge Green, West Sussex RH13 8LD
Telephone: 01403 710971
Fax: 01403 711143

Owner/Manager: Stephen Benz

*Guide Books; History & Antiquarian;
Nautical; Sports & Games; Transport; Local
History; Walking*

New Titles: 18 (1995), 20 (1996)
No of Employees: 3

ISBNs, Imprints & Series:
1 85770, 1 870708 A Portrait in Old Picture
Postcards (series)

Associated & Subsidiary Companies:
Brampton Publications

Distributor for:
Brampton Publications; Pomegranate Press

1767

SCARLET PRESS
5 Montague Road, London E8 2HN
Telephone: 0171 241 3702
Fax: 0171 275 0031

Orders:
Plymbridge Distributors Ltd,
Plymbridge House, Estover Road, Plymouth
PL6 7PZ
Telephone: 01752 202301
Fax: 01752 202331

Director: Avis Lewallen *(Editorial, Rights &
Sales)*

*Academic & Scholarly; Gay & Lesbian Studies;
Gender Studies; Health & Beauty*

New Titles: 5 (1995), 9 (1996)
No of Employees: 3

ISBNs, Imprints & Series: 1 85727

Overseas Representation *(see §7.3):*
Australia: Peribo Pty Ltd, Mount Kuring-gai,
NSW
Germany: Missing Link
Versandbuchhandlung, Bremen
South Africa: Judith Wengrowe Agencies,
Northcliff, Johannesburg
USA & Canada: In Book, Chicago, IL, USA

1768

SCARTHIN BOOKS
The Promenade, Scarthin, Cromford,
Derbyshire DE4 3QF
Telephone: 01629 823272
Fax: 01629 825094

Marketing: David Mitchell
Customer Services: Wendy Cooper

*Academic & Scholarly; Guide Books; History
& Antiquarian*

New Titles: 7 (1995), 7 (1996)
No of Employees: 2

ISBNs, Imprints & Series:
0 907758 Family Walks Series, Scarthin Books

Book Trade Association Membership: BA,
IPG

1769

SCHOFIELD & SIMS LTD
Dogley Mill, Fenay Bridge, Huddersfield
HD8 0NQ
Telephone: 01484 607080
Fax: 01484 606815

Chairman: J. S. Nesbitt
Directors: J. S. Platts *(Managing)*

J. Brierley *(Company Secretary, Sales, Rights
& Permissions)*

*Atlases & Maps; Biology & Zoology;
Chemistry; Children's Books; Cinema, Video,
TV & Radio; Educational & Textbooks;
Electronic (Educational); Geography &
Geology; Languages & Linguistics;
Mathematics & Statistics; Music; Physics;
Poetry; Reference Books, Directories &
Dictionaries; Religion & Theology*

New Titles: 40 (1995), 45 (1996)
No of Employees: 28
Annual Turnover: £1.8M

ISBNs, Imprints & Series: 0 7217

Overseas Representation *(see §7.3):*
Australia: INT Press, Pascoe Vale South, Vic
Canada: Bacon & Hughes, Nepean
*Caribbean (Barbados, Windward & Leeward
Islands):* C. D. A. Walker, Christchurch,
Barbados
Hong Kong: Transglobal Publishers Services
Ltd, Tsuen Wan
New Zealand: Educational Distributors Ltd, Te
Atatu North
Philippines: I. J. Sagun Enterprises Inc, Rizal
Singapore & Malaysia: Falcon Press Sdn Bhd,
Petaling Jaya, Malaysia
Southern Africa: Faradawn CC, Saxonwold,
South Africa

Book Trade Association Membership: IPG

1770

SCHOLASTIC LTD
Villiers House, Clarendon Avenue,
Leamington Spa, Warwickshire CV32 5PR
Telephone: 01926 887799
Fax: 01926 883331

**Accounts, Warehouse, Trade Enq., Orders
& Scholastic Bookfairs:**
Westfield Road, Southam, Leamington Spa,
Warks CV33 0JH
Telephone: 01926 813910
Fax: 01926 817727

Children's Division:
Commonwealth House,
1—19 New Oxford Street, London WC1A 1NU
Telephone: 0171 421 9000
Fax: 0171 421 9001

Directors: David M. R. Kewley *(Managing)*
Anne Peel *(Publishing—Educational)*
David Fickling *(Editorial—Children's)*
Gavin Lang *(Sales)*
David Bleasdale *(Production, Operations &
Distribution)*
Ian Bloodworth *(Financial, IT)*
Victoria Birkett *(Buying—Direct Marketing)*
Rights Manager: Anne Murray

*Children's Books; Crafts & Hobbies;
Educational & Textbooks*

New Titles: 280 (1995), 300 (1996)
No of Employees: 400
Annual Turnover: £27M

ISBNs, Imprints & Series:
0 590 Adlib, André Deutsch Children's Books,
Educational Publishing, Hippo, Point,
Scholastic

Parent Company:
Scholastic Inc *(USA)*

Associated & Subsidiary Companies:
Usborne Publishing Ltd. *Australia:* Scholastic
Australia Pty Ltd. *Canada:* Scholastic Canada
Ltd. *New Zealand:* Scholastic New Zealand Ltd

Overseas Representation *(see §7.3):*
Australia: Scholastic Australia Ltd, Gosford,
NSW
Canada: Scholastic Canada Ltd, Richmond
Hill
*Far East (excluding Singapore, Malaysia &
Indonesia):* Knowledge Craft Ltd, Hong
Kong
New Zealand: Ashton Scholastic Ltd, Auckland
Singapore, Malaysia & Indonesia: Pansing
Distribution Sdn Bhd, Singapore
South Africa: Struik Book Distributors,
Sandton

Book Trade Association Membership: PA,
EPC, Periodical Publishers Association

1771 ▬▬▬

**SCHOOL OF ORIENTAL AND
AFRICAN STUDIES (UNIVERSITY OF
LONDON)**
Thornhaugh Street, Russell Square, London
WC1H 0XG
Telephone: 0171 637 2388
Fax: 0171 436 3844
Email: md2@soas.ac.uk

Manager: M. J. Daly *(Publications Officer)*

*Academic & Scholarly; Bibliography &
Library Science; Languages & Linguistics;
Religion & Theology*

New Titles: 11 (1995), 10 (1996)
No of Employees: 4

ISBNs, Imprints & Series:
0 7286, 0 901877

Overseas Representation *(see §7.3):*
South Asia: Heritage Publishers, New Delhi,
India

1772 ▬▬▬

SCIENCE MUSEUM PUBLICATIONS
Science Museum, Exhibition Road, London
SW7 2DD
Telephone: 0171 938 8136
Fax: 0171 938 8213
Email: a.hodson@nmsi.ac.uk
Web Site: http://www.nmsi.ac.uk/researchers/
books.html

Sales (including mail order):
Dillons, Science Museum, Exhibition Road,
London SW7 2DD
Telephone: 0171 938 8255
Fax: 0171 938 8118

Manager: Anna Hodson

*Academic & Scholarly; Guide Books; History
& Antiquarian; Scientific & Technical*

ISBNs, Imprints & Series: 0 901805

1773 ▬▬▬

SCM PRESS LTD
9–17 St Albans Place, London N1 0NX
Telephone: 0171 359 8033
Fax: 0171 359 0049

Warehouse & Distribution:
The Trade Counter,
Mendlesham Industrial Estate, Norwich Road,
Mendlesham, Suffolk IP14 5NA

Directors: Ven. Derek Hayward *(Chairman)*
Rev Dr John Bowden *(Editor & Managing)*
Miss Margaret Lydamore *(Company Secretary
& Rights, Associate Editor)*
Roger Pygram *(Finance)*
Managers: Jennifer Ellis *(Sales)*
Susan Molyneux *(Publicity)*
Stephen Rogers *(Production)*

*Academic & Scholarly; Philosophy; Religion &
Theology; Judaica*

New Titles: 50 (1995), 55 (1996)
No of Employees: 10
Annual Turnover: £1M

ISBNs, Imprints & Series:
0 334
1 85931 Xpress Reprints

Parent Company:
SCM Press Trust

Distributor for:
Epworth Press. *USA:* Continuum Publishing
Co; Polebridge Press; Trinity Press
International; Westminster John Knox Press

Overseas Representation *(see §7.3):*
Australia & New Zealand: Openbook
Publishers, Adelaide, SA, Australia
Canada: Meakin & Associates, Nepean
USA: Trinity Press International, Valley Forge,
PA

Book Trade Association Membership: PA

1774 ▬▬▬

*SCOLAR PRESS
Gower House, Croft Road, Aldershot
GU11 3HR
Telephone: 01252 331551
Fax: 01252 344405

Director: Nigel Farrow *(Chairman)*
Managers: Anne Burbage *(Sales)*
Alex McAulay *(Publisher – History)*
Rachel Lynch *(Editor – Music)*

*Academic & Scholarly; Architecture & Design;
Bibliography & Library Science; Fine Art &
Art History; History & Antiquarian; Illustrated
& Fine Editions; Literature & Criticism; Music*

ISBNs, Imprints & Series: 0 85967

Parent Company:
Ashgate Publishing Ltd

Overseas Representation *(see §7.3):*
Australia: Gower Asia Pacific Pte Ltd, Avalo,
NSW
Singapore: Gower Asia Pacific Pte Ltd
USA: Ashgate Publishing Co, Brookfield, VT

1775 ▬▬▬

SCOPE INTERNATIONAL LTD
Forestside House, Forestside, Rowlands Castle,
Hants PO9 6EE
Telephone: 01705 631468 & 631751 (Sales)
Fax: 01705 631777 & 631322 (Sales)

Directors: Nicholas J. Pine *(Managing)*
William Smith

*Economics; Industry, Business &
Management; Philosophy; Politics & World
Affairs*

New Titles: 4 (1995), 6 (1996)
No of Employees: 22
Annual Turnover: £1.7M

ISBNs, Imprints & Series:
0 906619 Scope Special Reports

Associated & Subsidiary Companies:
Milestone Publications

Book Trade Association Membership: IPG

1776 ▬▬▬

SCOTTISH ACADEMIC PRESS
56 Hanover Street, Edinburgh EH2 2DX
Telephone: 0131 225 7483
Fax: 0131 225 7662

Consultant Editor: Dr Douglas Grant

*Academic & Scholarly; Architecture & Design;
Educational & Textbooks; Geography &
Geology; History & Antiquarian; Literature &
Criticism; Religion & Theology*

New Titles: 9 (1995), 14 (1996)
No of Employees: 4

ISBNs, Imprints & Series:
0 7073 Scottish Academic Press, Scottish
Gaelic Texts Society

1777 ▬▬▬

**SCOTTISH COUNCIL FOR RESEARCH
IN EDUCATION**
15 St John Street, Edinburgh EH8 8JR
Telephone: 0131 557 2944
Fax: 0131 556 9454
Email: SCRE@ed.ac.uk
Web Site: http://www.ed.ac.uk/~webscre

Director: Prof. W. Harlen
Deputy Director: B. Somekh
Head of Administrative Services: D. Gilhooly
Head of Information Services: Mrs R. Wake

Educational & Textbooks

New Titles: 17 (1995), 17 (1996)
No of Employees: 40
Annual Turnover: £1.2M

ISBNs, Imprints & Series:
0 901116, 1 86003

Distributor for:
Australia: Australian Council for Educational Research Ltd. *Canada:* Ontario Institute for Studies in Education. *New Zealand:* New Zealand Council for Educational Research

Overseas Representation *(see §7.3):*
Australia: Australian Council for Educational Research Ltd, Hawthorn
Canada: Ontario Institute for Studies in Education, Toronto
New Zealand: New Zealand Council for Educational Research, Wellington

Book Trade Association Membership:
Scottish PA

1778

SCOTTISH CULTURAL PRESS
PO Box 106, Aberdeen AB11 7ZE
Telephone: 01224 583777
Fax: 01224 575337

Trade Counter, Returns:
13 Millburn Street, Aberdeen AB1 2SS
Telephone: 01224 583777
Fax: 01224 575337

Director: Jill Dick

Archaeology; Biography & Autobiography; Children's Books; Environment & Development Studies; Geography & Geology; History & Antiquarian; Languages & Linguistics; Literature & Criticism; Military & War; Natural History; Nautical; Poetry; Sociology & Anthropology; Theatre, Drama & Dance; Scottish Culture

New Titles: 38 (1995), 50 (1996)
No of Employees: 2
Annual Turnover: £150,000

ISBNs, Imprints & Series:
1 898218 Scottish Cultural Press
1 899827 Scottish Children's Press

Distributor for:
Scottish Text Society

Book Trade Association Membership:
Scottish PA

1779

ASSOCIATION FOR SCOTTISH LITERARY STUDIES
c/o Dept of Scottish History,
University of Glasgow, 9 University Gardens,
Glasgow G12 8QH
Telephone: 0141 330 5309
Email: cmc@arts.gla.ac.uk

General Manager: Catherine McInerney

Academic & Scholarly; Educational & Textbooks; Languages & Linguistics; Literature & Criticism

New Titles: 3 (1995), 6 (1996)
No of Employees: 2
Annual Turnover: £40,000

ISBNs, Imprints & Series: 0 948877

Book Trade Association Membership: PA

1780

THE SCOUT ASSOCIATION
Baden-Powell House, Queen's Gate, London
SW7 5JS
Telephone: 0171 584 7030
Fax: 0171 581 9953

Trade Enquiries, Warehouse & Orders:
Scout Shops Ltd, Churchill Industrial Estate,
Lancing, West Sussex BN15 8UG
Telephone: 01903 755352
Fax: 01903 750993

General Editor: David Easton

Children's Books

ISBNs, Imprints & Series: 0 85165

1781

SCRIPTURE UNION PUBLISHING
Scripture Union, 207–209 Queensway,
Bletchley, Milton Keynes, Bucks MK2 2EB
Telephone: 01908 856000
Fax: 01908 856111

Warehouse, Trade Enquiries & Mail Order & Accounts Department:
Lion Distribution

Publishing Director: John Grayston
Director International Publishing & Development: David Rosser
Managers: Tony Hobbs *(Co-ordinator)*
Penny Boshoff *(Co-ordinator)*
Accounts: Andrew Turnbull
Rights: Rosemary North
Promotions: Bret Pitchfork

Children's Books; Educational & Textbooks; Music; Religion & Theology

ISBNs, Imprints & Series:
0 85421, 0 86201 Scripture Union
1 873824 Tamarind

Overseas Representation *(see §7.3):*
Australasia, East Asia & Pacific: Scripture Union, Lidcombe, NSW, Australia
Canada: Scripture Union, Pickering
New Zealand: Scripture Union Wholesale, Wellington
South Africa: Scripture Union Publishing Agency, Rondebosch
USA: Scripture Union Publishing, Upper Darby, PA

Book Trade Association Membership: PA, BDC, EPC

1782

SCUTARI PRESS
24–28 Oval Road, London NW1 7DX
Telephone: 0171 267 4466
Fax: 0171 482 2293
Web Site: http://www.hbuk.co.uk/wbs

Distributor:
Harcourt Brace, High Street, Foots Cray, Kent
DA15 5HP
Telephone: 0181 300 3322
Fax: 0181 309 0807

Directors: Bill Barnett *(Managing)*
Sean Duggan *(Editorial)*

Health Science; Midwifery; Nursing

New Titles: 16 (1995), 7 (1996)

ISBNs, Imprints & Series: 0 871364

Parent Company:
Royal College of Nursing, Baillière Tindall, Harcourt Brace

Book Trade Association Membership: PA

1783

SEARCH PRESS LTD
Wellwood, North Farm Road, Tunbridge Wells,
Kent TN2 3DR
Telephone: 01892 510850
Fax: 01892 515903

Directors: Countess de la Bedoyère
(Managing)
Ruth B. Saunders
Editors: Clare Turner
John Dalton
Designer: Julie Wood
Production Manager: Mrs Inger Arthur

Cookery, Wines & Spirits; Crafts & Hobbies; Do-It-Yourself; Educational & Textbooks; Fine Art & Art History; Gardening; Philosophy

New Titles: 18 (1995), 20 (1996)
No of Employees: 13

ISBNs, Imprints & Series:
0 85532 Art of Painting on Silk, Burns & Oates, The Craft Library Series, Key to Art Series, Leisure Art Series, Organic Handbooks Series, Search Press, Springs of Wisdom, Understand How to Draw Series

Associated & Subsidiary Companies:
Burns & Oates

Overseas Representation *(see §7.3):*
Australia: Keith Ainsworth Pty Ltd, Penrith, NSW
Canada: Fitzhenry & Whiteside Ltd, Markham
Commonwealth Africa & Ethiopa: Kelvin van Hasselt Publishing Services, Lymington, UK
Europe (Germany, Netherlands, Belgium, Luxembourg, Austria, France & Switzerland): Book Representation & Distribution Ltd, Hadleigh, UK
Far East, West Indies, Japan & Taiwan: Ralph & Sheila Summers, London, UK
India: Maya Publishers Pvt Ltd, New Delhi
Italy, Spain & Portugal: Penny Padovani, London, UK
Middle East: Eurab Ltd, Rottingdean, UK
New Zealand: David Bateman Ltd, Auckland
Scandinavia: D. Richard Bowen, Malmö, Sweden
Southern Africa: Trinity Books CC, Randburg, South Africa
Southern Africa (Leisure Arts & Understand How to Draw Series): Ashley & Radmore (Pty) Ltd, Springfield, South Africa
USA: Arthur Schwartz & Co, Woodstock, NY

Book Trade Association Membership: IPG

1784 ∎

MARTIN SECKER & WARBURG
Michelin House, 81 Fulham Road, London
SW3 6RB
Telephone: 0171 581 9393
Fax: 0171 225 9095

Distribution:
Reed Book Services, Northampton Road,
Rushden, Northants NN10 6PU
Telephone: 01933 58521
Fax: 01933 50284

International Sales Department:
(as principal address)
Telephone: 0171 581 9393
Fax: 0171 225 9371

Publisher: Max Eilenberg

*Biography & Autobiography; Fiction; History
& Antiquarian; Literature & Criticism; Poetry;
Politics & World Affairs; Travel & Topography*

ISBNs, Imprints & Series: 0 436

Parent Company:
Reed Elsevier Plc

Overseas Representation *(see §7.3)*:
Australia: Reed Books Australia, Melbourne,
Vic
Canada: Reed Publishing Canada, Markham,
Ont
East Asia: Reed Consumer Books, Metro
Manila, Philippines
India: Reed Consumer Books, New Delhi
Japan: Reed Consumer Books, Tokyo
New Zealand: Reed Publishing Group,
Auckland
Singapore: Reed International (Singapore) Pte
Ltd
South Africa: Struik Book Distributors Pty Ltd,
Johannesburg, Cape Town & Maitland

1785 ∎

SERIF
47 Strahan Road, London E3 5DA
Telephone: 0181 981 3990
Fax: 0181 981 3990

Warehouse, Trade Enquiries & Orders:
Central Books Ltd, 99 Wallis Road, London
E9 5LN
Telephone: 0181 986 4854
Fax: 0181 553 5821

Publisher: Stephen Hayward
Chair: Paul Westlake
Publicity/Marketing: Nana Yaa Mensah

*Architecture & Design; Biography &
Autobiography; Cookery, Wines & Spirits;
Fiction; History & Antiquarian; Literature &
Criticism; Politics & World Affairs*

ISBNs, Imprints & Series: 1 897959

Parent Company:
Threshold Publishing Ltd

Overseas Representation *(see §7.3)*:
Australia & New Zealand: Peribo Pty Ltd,
Mount Kuring-gai, NSW, Australia

*Austria, Belgium, Luxembourg, France,
Germany, Greece, Italy & Switzerland:* Ted
Dougherty, London, UK
Netherlands: Novelty Books International bv,
Weesp
*South Africa, Namibia, Botswana, Lesotho &
Swaziland:* Judith Wengrowe Agencies,
Northcliff, Johannesburg, South Africa
Spain & Portugal: Peter Prout, Madrid, Spain
*Sweden, Norway, Denmark, Finland &
Iceland:* D. Richard Bowen, Malmö, Sweden
USA & Canada: Login Publishers Consortium,
Chicago, IL, USA

1786 ∎

SERINDIA PUBLICATIONS
10 Parkfields, Putney, London SW15 6NH
Telephone: 0181 788 1966
Fax: 0181 785 4789

Distribution:
Wisdom Publications Ltd, 402 Hoe Street,
London E17 9AA
Telephone: 0181 520 5588
Fax: 0181 520 0932

Proprietor & Managing Director: Anthony
Aris

*Fine Art & Art History; Illustrated & Fine
Editions; Travel & Topography*

Overseas Representation *(see §7.3)*:
Europe: Bill Bailey Publishers
Representatives, Newton Abbot, UK

1787 ∎

SERPENT'S TAIL LTD
4 Blackstock Mews, London N4 2BT
Telephone: 0171 354 1949
Fax: 0171 704 6467
Email: serpent@dial.pipex.com
Web Site: http://www.serpentstail.com

Distribution:
Plymbridge Distributors Ltd, Estover Road,
Plymouth PL6 7PZ
Telephone: 01752 202301 (customer service)
202300 (reception)
Fax: 01752 202330

Representation:
Troika, 179 King's Cross Road, London
WC1X 9BZ
Telephone: 0171 833 8441
Fax: 0171 833 8442

Publisher: Pete Ayrton
Managers: Frances Hollingdale *(Sales)*
Deirdre Clark *(Production)*
Lisa Clarke *(Publicity)*

*Biography & Autobiography; Cinema, Video,
TV & Radio; Crime; Fiction; Gay & Lesbian
Studies; Gender Studies; Literature &
Criticism; Music; Politics & World Affairs*

New Titles: 40 (1995)
No of Employees: 3

ISBNs, Imprints & Series:
1 85242 Extraordinary Classics, High Risk
Books, Mask Noir, Midnight Classics

Associated & Subsidiary Companies:
USA: Serpent's Tail

Overseas Representation *(see §7.3)*:
Australia & New Zealand: Allen & Unwin Pty
Ltd, St Leonards, NSW, Australia
Canada: Stewart House a division of
McClelland & Stewart, Markham, Ont
Europe: Macmillan Publishers Ltd,
Basingstoke, UK
*France, Belgium, Switzerland & Southern
Europe:* Michael Abbott, Peyrilhac, France
Germany & Austria: Heiner Meyer auf der
Heyde, Dortmund, Germany
Irish Republic: Dudley Smith, Dunboyne
Netherlands & Scandinavia: Stephen Jackson,
UK
*Singapore, Malaysia, Indonesia, Thailand,
Indochina & Brunei:* Pansing Distribution
Sdn Bhd, Singapore
South Africa: David Philip Publishers Pty Ltd,
Claremont
USA (editorial & publicity): Ira Silverberg,
New York, USA
USA (selected Serpent's Tail titles):
Consortium Inc, St Paul, MN, USA

1788 ∎

SESSIONS OF YORK
The Ebor Press, Huntington Road, York
YO3 9HS
Telephone: 01904 659224
Fax: 01904 637068
Email: hk81@dial.pipex.com

Chairman: W. K. Sessions
Managing Director: W. Mark Sessions
Manager: R. J. Sissons *(Ebor Press Division)*
Publishing Manager: Richard York

*Archaeology; Biography & Autobiography;
History & Antiquarian; Industry, Business &
Management; Natural History; Poetry;
Religion & Theology*

New Titles: 22 (1995), 20 (1996)
No of Employees: 180
Annual Turnover: £9.5M

ISBNs, Imprints & Series:
1 85072 Sessions of York

Parent Company:
William Sessions Holdings Ltd

Book Trade Association Membership:
Quakers Uniting in Publishing

1789 ∎

SETTLE PRESS
10 Boyne Terrace Mews, London W11 3LR
Telephone: 0171 243 0695

Warehouse & Invoicing:
Biblios PDS Ltd, Star Road, Partridge Green,
West Sussex RH13 8LD
Telephone: 01403 710971

Directors: David Settle *(Managing, Editorial,
Rights & Permissions, Home & Export
Sales)*
Margaret Carter *(Education & Administration)*

Guide Books; Travel & Topography

New Titles: 12 (1995), 12 (1996)

ISBNs, Imprints & Series:
0 907070, 1 872876

Overseas Representation *(see §7.3)*:
Northern Europe: D. Richard Bowen, Malmö,
Sweden

Book Trade Association Membership: IPG

1790

SEVERN HOUSE PUBLISHERS LTD
9–15 High Street, Sutton, Surrey SM1 1DF
Telephone: 0181 770 3930
Fax: 0181 770 3850

Distribution:
Tiptree Book Services, Tiptree, Colchester,
Essex CO5 0SR
Telephone: 01621 816362
Fax: 01621 819011

Chairman: Edwin Buckhalter *(Sales)*
Publisher: Humphrey Price
Acquisitions Editor: Deborah Smith

Crime; Fiction; Science Fiction

New Titles: 140 (1995), 140 (1996)

ISBNs, Imprints & Series: 0 7278

Parent Company:
Severn House Books (Holdings) Ltd

Associated & Subsidiary Companies:
USA: Severn House Publishers Inc

Overseas Representation *(see §7.3)*:
Australia: DLS Australia (Pty) Ltd, Dingley,
Vic
Hong Kong: Book Marketing Ltd
*Singapore, Malaysia, Indonesia, Brunei &
Thailand:* Publishers Marketing Services
Ltd, Singapore
South Africa: Hargraves Library Service,
Claremont & Cape Town
USA: Severn House Publishers Inc, New York

Book Trade Association Membership: Crime
Writers Association, Romantic Novelists
Association

1791

SGC BOOKS
PO Box 49, Spalding, Lincs PE11 1NZ
Telephone: 01775 712424
Fax: 01775 762618

Directors: David Baldwin *(Managing)*
Gillian Baldwin *(Home Sales, Rights)*

*Children's Books; Gardening; Health &
Beauty; Natural History*

New Titles: 3 (1995), 4 (1996)
No of Employees: 5

ISBNs, Imprints & Series: 1 85116

Parent Company:
Chalksoft Ltd

Associated & Subsidiary Companies:
Nene Valley Publishing

Book Trade Association Membership: IPG

1792

SHAW & SONS LTD
21 Bourne Park, Bourne Road, Crayford, Kent
DA1 4BZ
Telephone: 01322 550676
Fax: 01322 550553
Email: 100666.2201@compuserve.com

Directors: M. B. Johnson *(Managing)*
David C. Hubber *(Publishing)*
R. H. Smith *(Finance)*
Managing Editor: Crispin Williams

*Academic & Scholarly; Educational &
Textbooks; Law; Reference Books, Directories
& Dictionaries; Transport*

New Titles: 8 (1995), 8 (1996)
No of Employees: 23
Annual Turnover: £408,000

ISBNs, Imprints & Series:
0 7219 Shaw & Sons, Shaway

Parent Company:
The Gordon Press Ltd

Book Trade Association Membership: PA,
CAPP, Law Services Association

1793

*SHEED & WARD LTD
14 Coopers Row, London EC3N
Telephone: 0171 702 9799
Fax: 0171 702 3583

Directors: Martin Redfern *(Managing)*
K. G. Darke *(Non-Executive)*
A. Moira Redfern *(Non-Executive)*
Manager: Leslie Nunn *(Accountant)*

*Academic & Scholarly; Biography &
Autobiography; Educational & Textbooks;
History & Antiquarian; Philosophy; Reference
Books, Directories & Dictionaries; Religion &
Theology*

ISBNs, Imprints & Series:
0 7220 Heythrop Monographs, Prayer &
Practice, Sheed & Ward, Spiritual Masters,
Stagbooks

Distributor for:
J. A. Allen & Co Ltd; Chancellor Publications
Ltd; Christian Classics Inc; Free Association
Books; Interfisc Publishing; The Pony Club;
Quintessence Publishing Co Ltd; University
Central Admissions System (University &
College Entrance); Wuerz Publishing Co Ltd

Overseas Representation *(see §7.3)*:
Australia: Charles Paine Pty Ltd, North
Paramatta, NSW
Hong Kong: Catholic Truth Society
India: Asian Trading Corporation, Bangalore
Italy: Libreria Ancora, Rome
New Zealand: Catholic Supplies (NZ) Ltd,
Wellington

1794

SHEFFIELD ACADEMIC PRESS
Mansion House, 19 Kingfield Road, Sheffield
S11 9AS
Telephone: 0114 255 4433
Fax: 0114 255 4626
Email: admin@sheffac.demon.co.uk
Web Site: http://www.shef.ac.uk/uni/
companies/shap

Warehouse:
100 Prospect Road, Sheffield S3
Telephone: 0114 250 8562

Directors: Prof. David J. A. Clines
Dr Philip R. Davies
Michael J. Mallett
Jean Allen *(Managing)*
Sales Office Supervisor: Sylvia Sanderson

*Academic & Scholarly; Archaeology;
Languages & Linguistics; Literature &
Criticism; Religion & Theology; Scientific &
Technical*

New Titles: 102 (1995), 102 (1996)
No of Employees: 32
Annual Turnover: £1.3M

ISBNs, Imprints & Series:
1 85075 JSOT Press, Sheffield Academic Press

Distributor for:
Anglo-Catalan Society

Overseas Representation *(see §7.3)*:
USA: Cornell University Press, Ithaca, NY

1795

SHELDON PRESS
SPCK, Holy Trinity Church, Marylebone Road,
London NW1 4DU
Telephone: 0171 387 5282
Fax: 0171 388 2352 & 388 1921
Email: publishing@spck.co.uk

Accounts & Orders:
Trade Department (Sheldon Press),
7 Castle Street, Reading, Berks RG1 7SB
Telephone: 0118 959 9011
Fax: 0118 959 9240

Warehouse & Distribution:
SPCK (Sheldon Press), 13 Markham Centre,
Station Road, Theale, Berks RG7 4PE
Telephone: 0118 932 3667
Fax: 0118 930 2474

Director of Publishing: Simon Kingston
Financial Secretary: Timothy Leates
Publisher: Joanna Moriarty
Managers: Brian Keen *(Sales)*
Michael Salinger *(Production)*
Rights Administrator: Sheena Daley

*Gender Studies; Health & Beauty; Industry,
Business & Management; Medical (incl. Self
Help & Alternative Medicine); Psychology &
Psychiatry*

New Titles: 20 (1995), 25 (1996)

ISBNs, Imprints & Series: 0 85969

Parent Company:
The Society for Promoting Christian
Knowledge (SPCK)

Overseas Representation *(see §7.3)*:
Australia: Charles Paine Pty Ltd, North
 Paramatta, NSW
Canada: Milestone Publications, Vancouver
India: ISPCK, Delhi
Japan: Atlantic Book Service, Tokyo
Middle East: Family Bookshop Group Co Ltd,
 Limassol, Cyprus
New Zealand: Forrester Books Ltd, Auckland
South Africa: Alternative Books, Randburg

Book Trade Association Membership: PA

1796 ▬▬▬▬▬▬▬▬▬▬

**SHEPHEARD-WALWYN (PUBLISHERS)
LTD**
Suite 34, 26 Charing Cross Road, London
WC2H 0DH
Telephone: 0171 240 5992
Fax: 0171 379 5770

Orders:
Bailey Distribution Ltd, 1A/1B Learoyd Road,
Mountfield Road Industrial Estate,
New Romney, Kent TN28 8XU
Telephone: 01797 366905
Fax: 01797 366638

Directors: Anthony R. A. Werner *(Managing)*
Mrs M. M. Werner

*Economics; History & Antiquarian; Illustrated
& Fine Editions; Philosophy; Politics & World
Affairs; Religion & Theology; Scottish Interest*

New Titles: 4 (1995), 4 (1996)
Annual Turnover: £150,000

ISBNs, Imprints & Series:
Who's Who in British History series 0 85683

Distributor for:
Sherwood Press

Overseas Representation *(see §7.3)*:
Australia: Keith Ainsworth Pty Ltd, Penrith,
 NSW
USA & Canada: Paul & Co Publishers
 Consortium Inc, New York, USA

Book Trade Association Membership: IPG

1797 ▬▬▬▬▬▬▬▬▬▬

SHERWOOD PUBLISHING
Sherwood House, 7 Oxhey Road, Watford
WD1 4QF
Telephone: 01923 224737
Fax: 01923 210648
Email: 100526.3633@compuserve.com

Chief Executive: Mrs Julie Hay

*Industry, Business & Management; Psychology
& Psychiatry*

New Titles: 1 (1995), 1 (1996)
No of Employees: 1
Annual Turnover: £10,000

ISBNs, Imprints & Series: 0 9521964

Overseas Representation *(see §7.3)*:
India: Creative Communication and
 Management Center, Bombay

Book Trade Association Membership: PA

1798 ▬▬▬▬▬▬▬▬▬▬

SHIRE PUBLICATIONS LTD
Cromwell House, Church Street,
Princes Risborough, Aylesbury, Bucks
HP17 9AA
Telephone: 01844 344301
Fax: 01844 347080

Directors: John W. Rotheroe *(Managing)*
Jacqueline P. Rotheroe *(Editorial)*
Managers: Sue Ross *(Home & Export Sales)*
Patience Dizon *(Rights & Permissions)*

*Antiques & Collecting; Archaeology;
Architecture & Design; Gardening; Guide
Books; History & Antiquarian; Military &
War; Natural History; Sociology &
Anthropology; Transport; Travel &
Topography*

New Titles: 17 (1995), 16 (1996)
No of Employees: 10

ISBNs, Imprints & Series:
0 7478, 0 85263

Overseas Representation *(see §7.3)*:
Denmark, Finland, Norway & Sweden: D.
 Richard Bowen, Malmö, Sweden

1799 ▬▬▬▬▬▬▬▬▬▬

SIDGWICK & JACKSON LTD
25 Eccleston Place, London SW1W 9NF
Telephone: 0171 881 8000
Fax: 0171 881 8001

Warehouse, Trade Enquiries & Orders:
Macmillan Distribution Centre, Brunel Road,
Basingstoke, Hants
Telephone: 01256 29242
Fax: 01256 479476

Directors: William Armstrong *(Managing)*
Antonia Bailey *(Publicity)*
Ian Chapman *(Chairman)*
Paul Davies *(Rights)*
Minna Fry *(Marketing)*
David North *(Sales)*

*Biography & Autobiography; Cinema, Video,
TV & Radio; Cookery, Wines & Spirits; History
& Antiquarian; Industry, Business &
Management; Magic & the Occult; Military &
War; Politics & World Affairs; Sports &
Games; Travel & Topography*

ISBNs, Imprints & Series: 0 283

Parent Company:
Pan Macmillan Ltd *(A member of Group –
ultimate holding to Macmillan Ltd)*

Associated & Subsidiary Companies:
Pan Ltd

Overseas Representation *(see §7.3)*:
Asia: Pansing Distribution Sdn Bhd, Singapore
Australia: Pan Macmillan Australia Ltd,
 Sydney

Canada: McClelland & Stewart, Toronto &
 Markham
India: Rupa & Co, New Delhi
New Zealand: Pan Books (New Zealand) Ltd,
 Auckland

Book Trade Association Membership: BA

1800 ▬▬▬▬▬▬▬▬▬▬

SIGMA PRESS
1 South Oak Lane, Wilmslow, Cheshire
SK9 6AR
Telephone: 01625 531035
Fax: 01625 536800
Email: sigma.press@zetnet.co.uk
Web Site: http://www.zetnet.cok.uk/coms/
sigma-press/

Warehouse:
Thomas Lyster Ltd, Unit 9,
Ormskirk Industrial Park, Old Boundary Way,
Burscough Road, Ormskirk, Lancs L39 2YW

Senior Editor: Graham Beech *(Computing/
 Scientific)*
Assistant Editor: Diana Beech
Marketing Assistant: Annie Eastwood

*Computer Science; Cookery, Wines & Spirits;
Electronic (Educational); Electronic
(Entertainment); Electronic (Professional &
Academic); Guide Books; Magic & the Occult;
Scientific & Technical; Sports & Games*

New Titles: 50 (1995), 60 (1996)
No of Employees: 6

ISBNs, Imprints & Series:
0 905104, 1 85058 Sigma Leisure, Sigma
Science

Overseas Representation *(see §7.3)*:
USA: Coronet Books Inc, Philadelphia, PA

Book Trade Association Membership: IPG

1801 ▬▬▬▬▬▬▬▬▬▬

SILENT BOOKS LTD
10 Market Street, Swavesey, Cambridge
CB4 5QG
Telephone: 01954 232199 & 231000
Fax: 01954 232199

Warehouse:
P & H Thermal Control, 37 Hilton Street, Over,
Cambs CB4 5PU

Managing Director: Carole A. Green
Publishing Consultant: Geoff Green
Publishing Assistant: Sylvia Sharp
Marketing Executive: Sue Smith

*Antiques & Collecting; Cookery, Wines &
Spirits; Crafts & Hobbies; Gardening; Art
(general)*

New Titles: 9 (1995), 11 (1996)
No of Employees: 4

ISBNs, Imprints & Series:
1 85183 Midsummer Books, West Meadow
 Books

Distributor for:
USA: Timber Press

Overseas Representation *(see §7.3)*:
Australia & New Zealand: Gilbert Teague, Balmain, NSW, Australia
Denmark, Finland, Sweden & Iceland: D. Richard Bowen, Malmö, Sweden
France, Germany, Austria, Switzerland, Italy, Netherlands, Belgium & Greece: Ted Dougherty, London, UK
Irish Republic: Hibernian Book Services, Dublin
Japan: ALIS, Tokyo
South Africa: Judith Wengrowe Agencies, Northcliff, Johannesburg
Spain, Portugal & Gibraltar: Peter Prout, Madrid, Spain

Book Trade Association Membership: PA

1802

SILVER LINK PUBLISHING LTD
Unit 5, Home Farm Close, Church Street, Wadenhoe, Peterborough PE8 5TE
Telephone: 01832 720440
Fax: 01832 720531
Email: pete@slinkp-p.demon.co.uk

Distribution:
Bookpoint Ltd, Milton Park, Abingdon, Oxon
Telephone: 01235 400400
Fax: 01235 861038

Sales:
Amalgamated Book Services, Suite 1, Royal Star Arcade, High Street, Maidstone, Kent ME14 1JL
Telephone: 01622 764555
Fax: 01622 763197

Managing Director: Peter Townsend *(Publisher)*
Production Manager: Michael Sanders
Managing Editor: Will Adams
Director/Company Secretary: Frances Townsend

Crime; History & Antiquarian; Humour; Military & War; Nautical; Transport; Nostalgia

ISBNs, Imprints & Series:
0 947971, 1 85794 Silver Link Publishing Ltd
1 85895 Past & Present Publishing Ltd

Associated & Subsidiary Companies:
Past & Present Publishing Ltd

Distributor for:
Past & Present Publishing Ltd

1803

SIMON & SCHUSTER
West Garden Place, Kendal Street, London W2 2AQ
Telephone: 0171 316 1900
Fax: 0171 402 0639
Email: @prenhall.co.uk

Orders, Customer Services, Accounts:
International Book Distributors Ltd, Campus 400, Maylands Avenue, Hemel Hempstead, Herts HP2 7EZ
Telephone: 01442 881900
Fax: 01442 882099
Email: @prenhall.co.uk

Distribution Centre:
International Book Distributors Ltd, Coventry Road, Magna Park, Lutterworth, Leics LE17 4XH
Telephone: 01442 881900
Fax: 01442 882177
Email: @prenhall.co.uk

Trade Publisher: Nick Webb
Sales: Bob Kelly
Editorial: Joanna Frank *(Fiction)*
Martin Fletcher *(Pocket)*
Helen Gummer *(Non-Fiction)*
Publicity: Cathy Schofield
Production: Caroline Burns
Rights: Mary Pachnos
Finance: Tom Bulgarelli

Audio Books; Biography & Autobiography; Crime; Fiction; Guide Books; Health & Beauty; Humour; Medical (incl. Self Help & Alternative Medicine); Music; Politics & World Affairs; Reference Books, Directories & Dictionaries; Science Fiction; Scientific & Technical; Sports & Games; Travel & Topography

New Titles: 268 (1995), 260 (1996)
No of Employees: 53
Annual Turnover: £16M

ISBNs, Imprints & Series:
0 671 Pocket
0 671, 0 684 Simon & Schuster
0 859 Marlin Books

Parent Company:
Simon & Schuster Inc *(USA)*

Associated & Subsidiary Companies:
see: Simon & Schuster International Group (Academic Division)

Distributor for:
USA: Baen; Betty Crocker; Fireside; Free Press; Frommer; Macmillan; Pocket; Prentice-Hall Press; Scribner; Simon & Schuster Audio; Simon & Schuster Inc; Summit; Touchstone; Webster's New World Dictionaries

Overseas Representation *(see §7.3)*:
Australia & New Zealand: Simon & Schuster Australia, East Roseville, NSW, Australia
Canada: Distican, Richmond Hill, Ont
India: India Book Distributors, Bombay
Japan: Prentice Hall Regents of Japan, Tokyo
South Africa: Media House Publications Pty Ltd, Sandton
South America: Humphrys Roberts Associates, Cotia, Brazil
South East Asia: Simon & Schuster (Asia) Pte Ltd, Singapore

Book Trade Association Membership: PA

1804

SINCLAIR-STEVENSON
Michelin House, 81 Fulham Road, London SW3 6RB
Telephone: 0171 581 9393
Fax: 0171 225 9095

Distribution:
Reed Book Services, Northampton Road, Rushden, Northants NN10 6PU

Telephone: 01933 58521
Fax: 01933 50284

International Sales Department:
(as principal address)
Telephone: 0171 581 9393
Fax: 0171 225 9371

Senior Editorial Director: Penny Hoare

Biography & Autobiography; Crime; Fiction; History & Antiquarian; Literature & Criticism; Music; Natural History; Photography; Politics & World Affairs; Theatre, Drama & Dance; Travel & Topography

ISBNs, Imprints & Series: 1 85619

Parent Company:
Reed Elsevier Plc

Overseas Representation *(see §7.3)*:
Australia: Reed Books Australia, Melbourne, Vic
Canada: Reed Publishing Canada, Markham, Ont
East Asia: Reed Consumer Books, Metro Manila, Philippines
India: Reed Consumer Books, New Delhi
Japan: Reed Consumer Books, Tokyo
New Zealand: Reed Publishing Group, Auckland
Singapore: Reed International (Singapore) Pte Ltd
South Africa: Struik Book Distributors Pty Ltd, Johannesburg, Cape Town & Maitland

1805

SINGULAR PUBLISHING GROUP INC
19 Compton Terrace, London N1
Telephone: 0171 359 9030
Fax: 0171 359 7150

Distribution:
Plymbridge Distributors, Estover Road, Plymouth PL6 7PZ

General Manager: Noel McPherson

Medical (incl. Self Help & Alternative Medicine)

New Titles: 60 (1995), 70 (1996)
No of Employees: 14

ISBNs, Imprints & Series:
1 56593, 1 879105

Parent Company:
Singular Publishing Group Inc *(USA)*

Overseas Representation *(see §7.3)*:
Australia & New Zealand: Thomas Nelson (Australia) Pty Ltd, South Melbourne, Vic, Australia

1806

SKOOB BOOKS LTD
11A-17 Sicilian Avenue, off Southampton Row, Holborn, London WC1A 2QH
Telephone: 0171 404 3063
Fax: 0171 404 4398
Email: books@skoob.demon.co.uk

Web Site: http://www.bozell.com.mylbozell/
skoob/skoob.html

President: I. K. Ong
Directors: M. Lovell *(Editorial)*
Editor: Ms C. Y. Loh
Publicity: Adam Wilson

*Literature & Criticism; Magic & the Occult;
Poetry; Reference Books, Directories &
Dictionaries; Theatre, Drama & Dance*

New Titles: 10 (1995), 5 (1996)
No of Employees: 8
Annual Turnover: £0.5M

ISBNs, Imprints & Series:
1 871438 Skoob Esoterica, Skoob Pacifica,
Skoob Seriph

Distributor for:
Skoob Books Publishing Ltd

1807

SLS LEGAL PUBLICATIONS (NI)
School of Law, Queen's University, Belfast
BT7 1NN
Telephone: 01232 245133 & 335224
Fax: 01232 325590

Director: Mrs E. Harkness
Manager: Mrs S. Gamble

Academic & Scholarly; Law

New Titles: 3 (1995), 5 (1996)
No of Employees: 5

ISBNs, Imprints & Series: 0 85389

Book Trade Association Membership: PA,
CAPP

1808

ADAM SMITH INSTITUTE
23 Great Smith Street, London SW1P 3BL
Telephone: 0171 222 4995
Fax: 0171 222 7544

Director: Dr Eamonn Butler
President: Dr Madsen Pirie

Economics; Politics & World Affairs

New Titles: 15 (1995)
No of Employees: 5

ISBNs, Imprints & Series:
0 906517, 1 870109

Parent Company:
ASI (Research) Ltd

1809

SMITH GRYPHON PUBLISHERS
Swallow House, 11–21 Northdown Street,
London N1 9BN
Telephone: 0171 278 2444
Fax: 0171 833 5680

Representation:
Boxtree Ltd, 2nd Floor, Broadwall House,
21 Broadwall, London SE1 9PL

Telephone: 0171 928 9696
Fax: 0171 928 5632

Warehouse:
Tiptree Book Services Ltd, Tiptree, Colchester,
Essex CO5 0SR
Telephone: 01621 816362
Fax: 01621 819011

Directors: Robert Smith *(Chairman &
Managing)*
Lesley Toll *(Rights)*

*Animal Care & Breeding; Antiques &
Collecting; Biography & Autobiography;
Cinema, Video, TV & Radio; Cookery, Wines &
Spirits; Crime; Health & Beauty; Industry,
Business & Management; Music; Politics &
World Affairs; Theatre, Drama & Dance;
Travel & Topography*

New Titles: 18 (1995), 20 (1996)
No of Employees: 3

ISBNs, Imprints & Series: 1 85685

Parent Company:
Smith Gryphon Ltd

Overseas Representation *(see §7.3)*:
Australia & New Zealand: Allen & Unwin Pty
Ltd, St Leonards, NSW, Australia
Far East: International Book Marketing,
London, UK
Singapore & Malaysia: Pansing Distribution
Sdn Bhd, Singapore
South Africa: Jonathan Ball Publishers (Pty)
Ltd, Jeppestown

1810

SMITH SETTLE LTD
Ilkley Road, Otley, West Yorkshire LS21 3JP
Telephone: 01943 467958
Fax: 01943 850057

Director: Kenneth Smith

*Biography & Autobiography; Fine Art & Art
History; History & Antiquarian; Illustrated &
Fine Editions; Travel & Topography*

New Titles: 7 (1995), 10 (1996)
No of Employees: 1
Annual Turnover: £250,000

ISBNs, Imprints & Series:
1 85825, 1 870071

Distributor for:
Fig Tree Press; MTD Rigg; Spredden Press

Book Trade Association Membership: IPG

1811

COLIN SMYTHE LTD
PO Box 6, Gerrards Cross, Bucks SL9 8XA
Telephone: 01753 886000
Fax: 01753 886469

Warehouse & Despatch only:
Clipper Distribution Services Ltd,
Windmill Grove, Portchester, Hants PO16 9HT
Telephone: 01705 200080
Fax: 01705 200090

Managing Director: Colin Smythe *(Sales,
Editorial & Production)*

*Academic & Scholarly; Bibliography &
Library Science; Biography & Autobiography;
Literature & Criticism; Theatre, Drama &
Dance; Heraldry; Orders of Knighthood*

New Titles: 12 (1995), 10 (1996)
No of Employees: 2
Annual Turnover: £1.45M

ISBNs, Imprints & Series:
Van Duren
0 85105 Dolmen Press
0 86140, 0 900675, 0 901072, 0 905715

Distributor for:
Canada: P. D. Meany Co Inc. *Irish Republic:*
Skellig Press Ltd; Tir Eolas. *USA:* ELT Press

Overseas Representation *(see §7.3)*:
Ireland: Hibernian Book Services, Dublin,
Irish Republic
USA & Canada: Dufour Editions Inc, Chester
Springs, PA, USA

Book Trade Association Membership: PA,
IPG

1812

**THE SOCIETY FOR PROMOTING
CHRISTIAN KNOWLEDGE**
Holy Trinity Church, Marylebone Road,
London NW1 4DU
Telephone: 0171 387 5282
Fax: 0171 388 2352 & 388 1921
Email: publishing@SPCK.co.uk

Accounts & Orders:
Trade Department, SPCK, 7 Castle Street,
Reading, Berks RG1 7SB
Telephone: 0118 959 9011
Fax: 0118 959 9240

Warehouse & Distribution:
SPCK, 13 Markham Centre, Station Road,
Theale, Berks RG7 4PE
Telephone: 0118 932 3667
Fax: 0118 930 2474

Director of Publishing: Simon Kingston
Publisher: Joanna Moriarty
Editors: Rachel Boulding
Lucy Gasson
Robin Keeley *(Lynx)*
Naomi Starkey *(Triangle)*
Alex Wright
Managers: Brian Keen *(Sales)*
Michael Salinger *(Production)*
Rights Administrator: Sheena Daley
Financial Secretary: Timothy Leates

Religion & Theology

New Titles: 50 (1995), 45 (1996)
No of Employees: 45
Annual Turnover: £2.4M

ISBNs, Imprints & Series:
0 281 SPCK, Triangle Books
0 7459 Lynx Communication
0 85969 Sheldon Press

Distributor for:
USA: Cowley Publications

Overseas Representation *(see §7.3)*:
Australia: Charles Paine Pty Ltd, North Paramatta, NSW
Canada: Meakin & Associates, Nepean
India (North): ISPCK, Delhi, India
India (South), Pakistan & Bangladesh: Asian Trading Corporation, Bangalore, India
Japan: Atlantic Book Service, Tokyo
Middle East: Family Bookshop Group Co Ltd, Limassol, Cyprus
New Zealand: Omega Distributors Ltd, Auckland
South Africa: Struik Book Distributors Pty Ltd, Johannesburg, Cape Town & Maitland
South East Asia: Alby Commercial Enterprises Pte Ltd, Singapore
USA: Abingdon Press, Nashville, TN
Western Europe: Books for Europe Ltd, Bournemouth, UK

Book Trade Association Membership: PA

1813 ▬▬▬▬

THE SOCIETY OF METAPHYSICIANS LTD
Archers' Court, Stonestile Lane, The Ridge, Hastings, East Sussex TN35 4PG
Telephone: 01424 751577
Fax: 01424 722387

Managing Director: Dr J. J. Williamson
Business Secretary: Mrs P. Owens
General Secretary: Ms E. Swift
Scientific & Literary Research: A. J. Mayne
Philosophical Research: Mrs J. Rawson

Academic & Scholarly; Environment & Development Studies; Magic & the Occult; Philosophy; Scientific & Technical; Esoteric; Neometaphysics; Paraphysics; Parapsychology

New Titles: 100 (1995), 300 (1996)
No of Employees: 8

ISBNs, Imprints & Series:
0 900680, 1 85228, 1 85810

Associated & Subsidiary Companies:
Metaphysical Research Group. *Belgium:* Society of Metaphysicians . *France:* Society of Metaphysicians. *Nigeria:* Society of Metaphysicians (Nigeria) Ltd

Distributor for:
USA: Ars Obscura *(Archival Reproductions)*; J. Green Books; Sun Books

Overseas Representation *(see §7.3)*:
Australia: Magic Circle Bookshop, Perth
Belgium: L'Univers Particulier, Brussels; Ignoramus, As
Germany: Verlag Hermann Bauer, Freiburg im Breisgau
Netherlands: Boekhandel Synthese, 's Gravenhage
New Zealand: Bennet's Bookshop, Palmerston North
Spain: Eyras Editorial, Madrid
Tenerife: Soluciones, Tenerife, Canary Islands, Spain
USA: Llewellyns Inc, St Paul, MN

1814 ▬▬▬▬▬▬▬▬▬▬▬▬▬▬▬▬▬▬

SOUTHGATE PUBLISHERS
15 Barnfield Avenue, Exmouth, Devon EX8 2QE
Telephone: 01395 223801
Fax: 01395 223818

Distribution:
Biblios Publishers' Distribution Services, Star Road, Partridge Green, West Sussex RH13 8LD

Managing Director: Drummond Johnstone
Production Manager: Marlene Buckland

Educational & Textbooks; Environment & Development Studies

New Titles: 9 (1995), 10 (1996)
No of Employees: 3

ISBNs, Imprints & Series: 1 85741

Associated & Subsidiary Companies:
Mosaic Educational Publications

Distributor for:
Learning Through Landscapes Trust.
Australia: Ready-Ed

Overseas Representation *(see §7.3)*:
Canada: Bacon & Hughes, Nepean

1815 ▬▬▬▬

SOUVENIR PRESS LTD
43 Great Russell Street, London WC1B 3PA
Telephone: 0171 580 9307/8 & 0171 637 5711/ 2/3
Fax: 0171 580 5064

Distributors & Warehouse:
Bookpoint Ltd, 39 Milton Trading Estate, Abingdon, Oxon OX14 4TD
Telephone: 01235 835001
Fax: 01235 832068

Managing Director & Chairman: Ernest Hecht
Director: Jeanne Manchee *(Executive, Accounts)*
Editor: Tessa Harrow

Academic & Scholarly; Animal Care & Breeding; Antiques & Collecting; Archaeology; Biography & Autobiography; Crime; Crafts & Hobbies; Fiction; Gardening; Gender Studies; Health & Beauty; Humour; Industry, Business & Management; Literature & Criticism; Magic & the Occult; Medical (incl. Self Help & Alternative Medicine); Military & War; Natural History; Philosophy; Psychology & Psychiatry; Religion & Theology; Sociology & Anthropology; Sports & Games; Theatre, Drama & Dance; Veterinary Science

New Titles: 55 (1995), 55 (1996)

ISBNs, Imprints & Series:
0 285 Condor Books, Human Horizons, Souvenir Press Ltd

Associated & Subsidiary Companies:
Pictorial Presentations Ltd; Pop Universal Ltd; Souvenir Press (Educational & Academic) Ltd

Overseas Representation *(see §7.3)*:
Australia: Lothian Books, Port Melbourne
India: Rupa & Co, New Delhi
New Zealand: Forrester Books NZ Ltd, Takapuna
Scandinavia: Saga Books ApS, Copenhagen, Denmark
South Africa: Calico Books International, Sandton

1816 ▬▬▬▬

SPA BOOKS LTD
PO Box 47, Stevenage, Herts SG2 8UH
Telephone: 01438 816896
Fax: 01438 310104

Managing Director: Steven Apps
Sales Director: Aileen Apps

Antiques & Collecting; Biography & Autobiography; Fine Art & Art History; History & Antiquarian; Military & War; List of Books on Scotland (History, Art)

ISBNs, Imprints & Series:
0 907590, 1 871048

Associated & Subsidiary Companies:
Strong Oak Press

Distributor for:
Pollock's Toy Theatres; The Strong Oak Press Ltd; John Taylor Book Ventures *(Desktop Publishing Series)*; Tom Donovan Publishing Ltd. *Canada:* Collector Grade Publications. *South Africa:* William Waterman Publications *(including Ashanti Publishing & Justified Press)*

Overseas Representation *(see §7.3)*:
Australia & New Zealand: Peribo Pty Ltd, Mount Kuring-gai, NSW, Australia
South Africa: Media House Publications Pty Ltd, Sandton
USA: Seven Hills Book Distributors, Cincinnati, OH

1817 ▬▬▬▬

SPELLMOUNT LTD
The Old Rectory, Staplehurst, Kent TN12 0AZ
Telephone: 01580 893730
Fax: 01580 893731

Warehouse & Trade Enquiries:
CBS Ltd, 406 Vale Road, Tonbridge, Kent TN9 1XR
Telephone: 01732 357755
Fax: 01732 770219

Managing Director: Jamie Wilson

History & Antiquarian; Military & War

New Titles: 20 (1995), 20 (1996)
No of Employees: 1
Annual Turnover: £250,000

ISBNs, Imprints & Series:
0 946771, 1 871876, 1 873376

Distributor for:
USA: Sarpedon Publishers

Overseas Representation *(see §7.3)*:
Australia & New Zealand: Peribo Pty Ltd,
Mount Kuring-gai, NSW, Australia
Austria, Belgium, France, Germany &
Switzerland: European Marketing Services,
London, UK
Scandinavia: D. Richard Bowen, Malmö,
Sweden

Book Trade Association Membership: PA

1818 ▬

SPINDLEWOOD
70 Lynhurst Avenue, Barnstaple, Devon
EX31 2HY
Telephone: 01271 71612
Fax: 01271 25906

Orders:
Ragged Bears Ltd, Ragged Appleshaw,
Andover, Hants SP11 9HX

Director: Michael Holloway

Children's Books

New Titles: 5 (1995), 5 (1996)
No of Employees: 3

ISBNs, Imprints & Series: 0 907349

Book Trade Association Membership: PA,
EPC, IPG

1819 ▬

SPLASH! PUBLISHING LTD
55 Austhorpe Road, Cross Gates, Leeds
LS15 8EQ
Telephone: 01132 939433/4
Fax: 01132 939435

Sales & Distribution:
Macmillan S & D, Houndmills, Basingstoke,
Hants RG21 6XS
Telephone: 01256 29242
Fax: 01256 842084

Chairman: Ian Harding
Company Secretary: F. Milton
Sales & Production Director: R. Dever

Children's Books

New Titles: 9 (1995), 18 (1996)
No of Employees: 5
Annual Turnover: £750,000

ISBNs, Imprints & Series:
1 900207 Little Wizard

Parent Company:
SPLASH! Holdings Ltd

Associated & Subsidiary Companies:
SPLASH! Animation Ltd

1820 ▬

SPOKESMAN
Bertrand Russell House, Gamble Street,
Nottingham NG7 4ET
Telephone: 0115 978 4504 & 970 8318
Fax: 0115 942 0433

Home Representation:
Troika Ltd, 179 Kings Cross Road, London
WC1X 9BZ

Managers: Ken Fleet *(General)*
Tony Simpson *(Publications)*
Editor: Ken Coates

Economics; History & Antiquarian; Military &
War; Politics & World Affairs; Psychology &
Psychiatry; Europe; Works of Bertrand Russell

New Titles: 9 (1995), 10 (1996)

ISBNs, Imprints & Series:
0 85124 European Labor Forum (Elf Books)

Associated & Subsidiary Companies:
Bertrand Russell Peace Foundation Ltd

Overseas Representation *(see §7.3)*:
Germany, Austria & Switzerland: PS
Publishers' Services, Frankfurt, Germany
Irish Republic: Troika Ltd, London, UK

1821 ▬

E. & F. N. SPON
2–6 Boundary Row, London SE1 8HN
Telephone: 0171 865 0066
Fax: 0171 522 9623
Email: needtoknow@chall.co.uk
Web Site: http://www.chaphall.com/chaphall.
html

Other Details:
see Chapman & Hall Ltd

Directors: Phillip Read *(Publishing)*
Barend ter Haar *(Marketing)*
Gavin McDonald *(Production)*
Ian Johnston *(Sales)*
Alan Davis *(Finance)*
Rights & Permissions: Anna Bisztyga

Architecture & Design; Engineering; Scientific
& Technical; Sports & Games

New Titles: 82 (1995), 80 (1996)

ISBNs, Imprints & Series: 0419

Parent Company:
Chapman & Hall

Overseas Representation *(see §7.3)*:
See: Chapman & Hall Ltd, London, UK

Book Trade Association Membership: See:
Chapman & Hall Ltd

1822 ▬

THE SPORTSMAN'S PRESS
25 King Charles Walk, London SW19 6JA
Telephone: 0181 789 0229
Fax: 0181 891 5567

Warehouse & Invoicing:
Biblios Publishers Distribution Services Ltd,
Star Road, Partridge Green, West Sussex
RH13 8LD
Telephone: 01403 710971
Fax: 01403 711143

Publisher: Kenneth Kemp

Animal Care & Breeding; Antiques &
Collecting; Biography & Autobiography;
Fiction; Fine Art & Art History; Humour;
Natural History; Sports & Games

New Titles: 4 (1995), 3 (1996)

ISBNs, Imprints & Series: 0 948253

Overseas Representation *(see §7.3)*:
Australia: Max Harrell, Malvern, Vic
Europe (excluding Scandinavia): Books for
Europe Ltd, Bournemouth, UK
Irish Republic: Hibernian Book Services,
Dublin
New Zealand: Halcyon Publications, Auckland
Scandinavia: Saga Books ApS, Copenhagen,
Denmark
USA: Trafalgar Square Publications, North
Pomfret, VT

Book Trade Association Membership: IPG

1823 ▬

*SPRINGER-VERLAG LONDON LTD
Sweetapple House, Catteshall Road,
Godalming, Surrey GU7 3DJ
Telephone: 01483 418800
Fax: 01483 415144

Directors: J. R. Watson *(Managing)*
Prof. Dr D. Götze
C. Michaletz
Editors: N. Pinfield *(Engineering)*
Dr A. J. Colborne *(Medical)*
B. Ford *(Computing)*
Managers: D. Anderson *(Sales & Marketing*
Director)
R. Dobbing *(Book Production)*
C. Notarmarco *(Journals Production)*
P. Roberts *(Sales)*

Computer Science; Engineering; Medical (incl.
Self Help & Alternative Medicine)

ISBNs, Imprints & Series: 3 540

Parent Company:
Springer Verlag GmbH & Co KG *(Germany)*

Book Trade Association Membership: PA,
IGSMTP, CAPP

1824 ▬

SPRINGFIELD BOOKS LTD
Norman Road, Denby Dale, Huddersfield
HD8 8TH
Telephone: 01484 864955
Fax: 01484 865443

Directors: Brian Lewis *(Managing & Sales)*
Walter Puszczynski *(Finance)*
Sales Manager: Paula Brennan

Atlases & Maps; Guide Books; Sports &
Games; Travel & Topography

New Titles: 2 (1995)
No of Employees: 9

ISBNs, Imprints & Series:
0 947655, 1 85688

Distributor for:
Bradt Publications; Hostelling International;

Logis of Great Britain; Marwain Publishing;
Northern Bee Books; Swallow Press; Trafton.
Australia: Gregory's. *Austria:* Freytag &
Berndt. *Belgium:* Geocart. *France:* Fivedit.
Germany: Falk; Karto & Graphic. *USA:* Karen
Brown Guides; Globe Pequot; Hunter
Publishing; Lyons & Burford; Rand McNally

Overseas Representation *(see §7.3)*:
Australia: Tower Books Wholesalers Pty Ltd,
   Brookvale
South Africa: Media House Publications Pty
   Ltd, Sandton

1825 ▬▬▬▬

SQUARE ONE BOOKS LTD
Iron Bridge House, Chalk Farm, London
NW1 8BD
Telephone: 0171 734 3251
Fax: 0171 439 2391

Orders:
Guinness Publishing Ltd
Telephone: 0181 367 4567
Fax: 0181 367 5912

Warehouse:
Macmillan Distribution, Unit 8,
Lye Industrial Estate, Pontardulais, Swansea
SA4 1QD
Telephone: 01702 885598

Directors: Colin Larkin *(Managing, Publisher
   & Art Director)*
David Japp
Freddy Bienstock
John Reiss *(Financial)*
Company Secretary: Colin Larkin

*Fiction; Fine Art & Art History; Music;
Reference Books, Directories & Dictionaries;
Theatre, Drama & Dance*

New Titles: 3 (1995), 2 (1996)
No of Employees: 2

ISBNs, Imprints & Series:
1 872747 Encyclopedia of Popular Music, Leah
   Manning Trust, Square One Books

Associated & Subsidiary Companies:
USA: Carlin Music Corp

Overseas Representation *(see §7.3)*:
Italy, Portugal, Spain, Greece & France:
   Bookport Associates, Bologna, Italy

1826 ▬▬▬▬

STAINER & BELL LTD
PO Box 110, 23 Gruneisen Road, London
N3 1DZ
Telephone: 0181 343 3303
Fax: 0181 343 3024

Directors: Keith Wakefield *(Joint Managing,
   Marketing, Permissions, Accounts &
   Distribution)*
Carol Wakefield *(Joint Managing, Editorial &
   Production)*
Antony Kearns *(Sales)*

*Academic & Scholarly; Biography &
Autobiography; History & Antiquarian; Music;
Reference Books, Directories & Dictionaries;*

*Religion & Theology; Theatre, Drama &
Dance*

New Titles: 14 (1995), 20 (1996)
No of Employees: 11
Annual Turnover: £550,000

ISBNs, Imprints & Series:
0 85249 Augener, Early English Church Music,
   Galliard, Music for London Entertainment,
   Musica Britannica, Stainer & Bell, Weekes,
   Joseph Williams

Associated & Subsidiary Companies:
Galliard Ltd

Distributor for:
USA: ECS Publishing Co *(Rental Library)*;
Hope Publishing Co *(selected titles)*

Overseas Representation *(see §7.3)*:
USA (hymn copyrights & selected titles): Hope
   Publishing, Carol Stream, IL, USA
USA (Rental Library): ECS Publishing Co,
   Boston, MA, USA

Book Trade Association Membership: The
Music Publishers Association Ltd

1827 ▬▬▬▬

HAROLD STARKE PUBLISHERS LTD
Pixey Green, Stradbroke, Eye, Suffolk
IP21 5NG
Telephone: 0137 938 8334
Fax: 0137 938 8335

Also (not for trade enquiries or orders) at:
203 Bunyan Court, Barbican, London
EC2Y 8DH
Telephone: 0171 588 5195

Directors: Harold K. Starke *(Home & Export
   Sales)*
Naomi Galinski *(Rights & Permissions)*

*Medical (incl. Self Help & Alternative
Medicine); Natural History; Reference Books,
Directories & Dictionaries; Scientific &
Technical*

ISBNs, Imprints & Series:
0 287 Harold Starke Publishers Ltd
1 872457 Harold Starke Medical

Book Trade Association Membership: PA,
BDC

1828 ▬▬▬▬

RUDOLF STEINER PRESS
51 Queen Caroline Street, London W6 9QL
Telephone: 0181 563 2759
Fax: 0181 748 5451

Trade Enquiries & Orders:
Biblios Publishers' Distribution Services,
Star Road, Partridge Green, Horsham,
West Sussex RH13 8LD
Telephone: 01403 710971
Fax: 01403 711143

Manager: Sevak Gulbekian

*Agriculture; Architecture & Design;
Biography & Autobiography; Educational &
Textbooks; Fine Art & Art History; Magic & the*

*Occult; Medical (incl. Self Help & Alternative
Medicine); Music; Natural History;
Philosophy; Religion & Theology; Sociology &
Anthropology; Theatre, Drama & Dance*

New Titles: 10 (1995), 10 (1996)
No of Employees: 2
Annual Turnover: £132,283

ISBNs, Imprints & Series:
0 85440, 1 85584 Mercury Arts Publications,
   New Knowledge Books, Sophia Books,
   Rudolf Steiner Press
0 88010, 0 91014 Anthroposophic Press

Associated & Subsidiary Companies:
USA: Anthroposophic Press

Distributor for:
Mercury Arts Publications; New Knowledge
Books. *Switzerland:* Verlag am Goetheanum.
USA: Anthroposophic Press

Overseas Representation *(see §7.3)*:
USA: Anthroposophic Press Inc, Hudson, NY

Book Trade Association Membership: IPG

1829 ▬▬▬▬

PATRICK STEPHENS LTD
Sparkford, Nr Yeovil, Somerset BA22 7JJ
Telephone: 01963 440635
Fax: 01963 440023

Mail Orders & Despatch:
(as above)
Telephone: 01963 440614
Fax: 01963 440001

Chairman: J. H. Haynes
Sales: T. Kemp
Export Sales: M. Adams
Editorial: D. Reach
Rights: R. Jackson
Marketing: D. Keel
Finance: C. Davies
Production: K. Perrett

*Aviation; Biography & Autobiography;
Military & War; Nautical; Transport; Maritime
& Naval; Motoring; Motor Racing; Motor
Cycling; Railways; Railway Modelling*

New Titles: 35 (1995), 32 (1996)

ISBNs, Imprints & Series:
0 85059, 1 85260

Parent Company:
Haynes Publishing Group Plc

Associated & Subsidiary Companies:
G. T. Foulis & Co; J. H. Haynes & Co Ltd;
Oxford Illustrated Press; Oxford Publishing Co
(OPC)

Overseas Representation *(see §7.3)*:
USA: Motorbooks International Publishers &
   Wholesalers Inc, Osceola, WI
USA, Canada & Mexico: Haynes Publications
   Inc, Newbury Park, CA, USA

1830

STOBART DAVIES LTD
2 Priory House, Priory Street, Hertford, Herts
SG14 1RN
Telephone: 01992 501518
Fax: 01992 501519

Director: Brian Davies *(Publishing)*

*Crafts & Hobbies; Natural History; Scientific
& Technical*

New Titles: 3 (1995), 3 (1996)
No of Employees: 5
Annual Turnover: £280,000

ISBNs, Imprints & Series: 0 85442

Parent Company:
Stobart Publishing Ltd

Distributor for:
India: International Book Distributors

Overseas Representation *(see §7.3):*
*Africa (including South Africa), Caribbean &
 Far East:* Kelvin van Hasselt Publishing
 Services, Lymington, UK
Australia & New Zealand: Astam Books Pty
 Ltd, Leichhardt, NSW, Australia
*France, Switzerland, Poland, Hungary, Czech
 & Slovak Republics:* Juliusz Komarnicki,
 Massagno, Switzerland
Germany & Austria: PKB—Robbert J. Pleysier,
 Heerde, Netherlands
*Greece, Italy, Portugal, Spain (including
 Gibraltar), Slovenia & Croatia:* Patrick
 Bygate & Juliusz Komarnicki, Massagno,
 Switzerland
India: International Book Distributors, Dehra
 Dun
Netherlands, Belgium & Luxembourg: Reinier
 A. Pleysier, Heerde, Netherlands
Scandinavia: Ove B. Poulsen, Glostrup,
 Denmark

Book Trade Association Membership: BA

1831

ARTHUR H. STOCKWELL LTD
Elms Court, Torrs Park, Ilfracombe,
North Devon EX34 8BA
Telephone: 01271 862557
Fax: 01271 862557

Directors: R. J. G. Stockwell *(Trade Manager)*
P. J. Nicholas *(Sales Manager)*
S. F. McGowan *(Production Manager)*

*Antiques & Collecting; Biography &
Autobiography; Children's Books; Crafts &
Hobbies; Fiction; Literature & Criticism;
Military & War; Poetry; Religion & Theology;
Sports & Games; Travel & Topography*

No of Employees: 13

ISBNs, Imprints & Series: 0 7223

1832

STOKESBY HOUSE PUBLICATIONS
Stokesby, Norfolk NR29 3ET
Telephone: 01493 750645
Fax: 01493 750146

Publisher & Marketing: Pamela Minett

*Educational & Textbooks; Environment &
Development Studies*

New Titles: 2 (1995), 1 (1996)

ISBNs, Imprints & Series:
0 9514490, 1 873600

Book Trade Association Membership: PA,
EPC

1833

STRAIGHTFORWARD PRESS LTD
39A Welbeck Street, London W1M 7HF
Telephone: 0181 905 5050

Contact: Richard Astor

New Titles: 2 (1996)

ISBNs, Imprints & Series: 1 8739994

Book Trade Association Membership: PA

1834

**INTERNATIONAL INSTITUTE FOR
STRATEGIC STUDIES**
23 Tavistock Street, London WC2E 7NQ
Telephone: 0171 379 7676 & 872 0770
Fax: 0171 836 3108
Email: iiss@iiss.org.uk
Web Site: http://www.fsk.ethz.ch/iiss/

Editorial (Production): Rachel Neaman
 (Publications Manager)
Marketing: Jane Martin
Andrea Nicholls *(OUP)*
Managers: Nina Curtis *(OUP)*
Julie Atkins *(OUP)*

*Academic & Scholarly; Military & War;
Politics & World Affairs*

New Titles: 9 (1995), 12 (1996)
No of Employees: 35
Annual Turnover: £1.9M

ISBNs, Imprints & Series:
1 85753 Adelphi Papers (Monograph Series),
 The Military Balance (Annual), Strategic
 Survey (Annual)

Overseas Representation *(see §7.3):*
USA & Canada: Oxford University Press,
 Cary, NC, USA
Worldwide (excluding USA & Canada): Oxford
 University Press, Oxford, UK

1835

STRIDE PUBLICATIONS
11 Sylvan Road, Exeter, Devon EX4 6EW
Email: rml@madbear.demon.co.uk
Web Site: http://www.poptel.org.uk/password/
home.html

Trade:
Password (Books) Ltd, 23 New Mount Street,
Manchester M4
Telephone: 0161 953 4009
Fax: 0161 953 4001

Managing Editor: R. M. Loydell

*Fiction; Fine Art & Art History; Literature &
Criticism; Music; Poetry*

New Titles: 11 (1995), 12 (1996)
No of Employees: 1
Annual Turnover: £35,000

ISBNs, Imprints & Series:
0 946699, 1 873012, 1 900152

Associated & Subsidiary Companies:
Apparitions Press; Taxus Press; Trombone
Press

Distributor for:
Magwood Press. *USA:* Cornerstone Press
(selected titles); New Earth Press *(selected
titles)*

Overseas Representation *(see §7.3):*
Canada (selected titles): Marginal Distribution,
 Peterborough, Canada
USA (selected titles): Small Press Distribution
 Inc, Berkeley, CA, USA

1836

THE STROKE ASSOCIATION
CHSA House, Whitecross Street, London
EC1Y 8JJ
Telephone: 0171 490 7999
Fax: 0171 490 2686

Chief Editor, Director General: Sylvia
 McLauchlan, MB, ChB, MSc, FFPHM

*Medical (incl. Self Help & Alternative
Medicine)*

New Titles: 3 (1995), 2 (1996)

Book Trade Association Membership: PA

1837

*STUDIO EDITIONS LTD
Princess House, 50 Eastcastle Street, London
W1N 7AP
Telephone: 0171 636 5070
Fax: 0171 580 3001

Warehouse:
Grantham Book Services, Isaac Newton Way,
Alma Park Industrial Estate, Grantham, Lincs
NG31 9SD
Telephone: 01476 67421
Fax: 01476 590223

Directors: Sonia Land *(Chairman)*
Kenneth R. L. Webb *(Managing)*
Tony Curtis *(Financial & Company Secretary)*
David Nash *(Managing—Studio Designs)*
Ruth Binney *(Publishing)*
Lionel Foot *(Sales—Books)*
K. T. Forster *(Rights)*
Gary Grant *(Production)*
Managers: Ken Fox *(Sales—BPL)*
Linda Sheridan *(Publicity)*

*Antiques & Collecting; Architecture & Design;
Atlases & Maps; Aviation; Children's Books;
Fashion & Costume; Fine Art & Art History;
Guide Books; Health & Beauty; History &
Antiquarian; Illustrated & Fine Editions;
Military & War; Natural History; Reference
Books, Directories & Dictionaries; Religion &*

Theology; Transport; Travel & Topography; Paperbacks

ISBNs, Imprints & Series:
0 946495 Bracken Books
1 85170 Senate Paperbacks, Studio Designs, Studio Editions

Overseas Representation *(see §7.3)*:
Australia: Karlov Marketing Services Pty Ltd, Castle Hill, NSW
Europe (excluding Netherlands, Spain, Portugal & Scandinavia): Janet Clark, London, UK
France (studio designs only): Royal Garden, Arcueil, France
Hong Kong, Taiwan, Korea, Philippines & China: Allscript Establishment (S) Pte Ltd, Singapore
India & Pakistan: Nadeem Ansari, New Delhi, India
Italy (studio designs only): Giorgio Bernadini Editore srl, Milan, Italy
Middle East, Turkey, Cyprus & North Africa: Peter Ward Book Exports, London, UK
Netherlands: Nilsson & Lamm BV, Weesp
Netherlands (studio designs only): Ter Maat BV, Hertogenbosch, Netherlands
Scandinavia: Anglo-Nordic Books, Godalming, UK
Singapore, Malaysia, Thailand, Indonesia & Brunei: APD Singapore Pte Ltd, Singapore
South Africa: Macdonald Purnell (Pty) Ltd, Cleveland
Spain & Portugal: Isabel Leao, London, UK
USA & South America: Colt Associates, Wheathampstead, UK
USA (studio designs only): Renaissance Greeting Cards Inc, Sandford, ME, USA

1838 ▪▪▪▪▪

SUMMERSDALE PUBLISHERS
46 West Street, Chichester, West Sussex
PO19 1RP
Telephone: 01243 771107
Fax: 01243 786300
Email: 100102.776@compuserve.com

Warehouse, Trade Enquiries & Orders:
Littlehampton Book Services,
Lineside Industrial Estate, Littlehampton,
West Sussex BN17 7HE
Telephone: 01903 721596
Fax: 01903 730914

Editorial Directors: Alastair Williams
Stewart Ferris

Biography & Autobiography; Cookery, Wines & Spirits; English as a Foreign Language; Guide Books; Humour; Industry, Business & Management; Military & War; Poetry; Psychology & Psychiatry; Reference Books, Directories & Dictionaries; Sports & Games; Travel & Topography; Vocational Training & Careers

New Titles: 27 (1995), 45 (1996)
No of Employees: 3
Annual Turnover: £150,000

ISBNs, Imprints & Series:
0 943231 Howell Press
0 964664 Alexandria Press
1 873475 Summersdale Publishers, Tip-Top Guides Series

Distributor for:
Alexandria Press; Europa Pages; Protection Publications. *USA:* Howell Press

Overseas Representation *(see §7.3)*:
South Africa: Judith Wengrowe Agencies, Northcliff, Johannesburg
USA (Cookery books only): Howell Press, Charlottesville, VA, USA

1839 ▪▪▪▪▪

SUNBURST BOOKS
Kiln House, 210 New Kings Road, London
SW6 4NZ
Telephone: 0171 736 5666
Fax: 0171 736 5777
Email: prc–co@compuserve.com

Distributor:
Macmillan Distribution Ltd, Brunel Road, Houndmills, Basingstoke, Hants RG21 2XS
Telephone: 01256 29242
Fax: 01256 812521

Directors: Suneel Jaitly *(Managing)*
Keith Baxter *(Trade Sales)*
Joanne Messham *(Deputy Managing)*
Trade/Sales Administrator: Michelle Baring
Managers: Kevin Phillips *(Commercial)*
Alison Percival *(Production)*

Animal Care & Breeding; Antiques & Collecting; Architecture & Design; Atlases & Maps; Aviation; Cookery, Wines & Spirits; Crime; Crafts & Hobbies; Do-It-Yourself; Fine Art & Art History; Gardening; Health & Beauty; History & Antiquarian; Illustrated & Fine Editions; Magic & the Occult; Medical (incl. Self Help & Alternative Medicine); Military & War; Music; Natural History; Nautical; Photography; Reference Books, Directories & Dictionaries; Sports & Games; Transport; Travel & Topography

New Titles: 109 (1995), 70 (1996)
No of Employees: 12
Annual Turnover: £5M

ISBNs, Imprints & Series: 1 85778

Parent Company:
Promotional Reprint Co Ltd

1840 ▪▪▪▪▪

SUNFLOWER BOOKS
12 Kendrick Mews, London SW7 3HG
Telephone: 0171 589 1862
Fax: 0171 589 1862

Distributors:
A & C Black, Howard Road, Eaton Socon
PE19 3EZ
Telephone: 01480 212666
Fax: 01480 405014

Joint Managing Directors: Pat Underwood
John Seccombe

Travel & Topography

New Titles: 6 (1995), 6 (1996)

ISBNs, Imprints & Series:
0 948513, 1 85691 Landscapes Series

Parent Company:
P. A. Underwood Ltd

Distributor for:
Portugal: Francisco Ribeiro

1841 ▪▪▪▪▪

SUPERNET
Supernet House, 12–14 David Place, St Helier, Jersey, Channel Islands JE2 4TD
Telephone: 01534 880044
Fax: 01534 509555

Director, Electronic Publishing: Nick Ogden

Academic & Scholarly; Educational & Textbooks; Electronic (Educational); Electronic (Entertainment); Electronic (Professional & Academic); Industry, Business & Management; Reference Books, Directories & Dictionaries

Parent Company:
Multi Media Investments Ltd

Book Trade Association Membership: PA, International Electronic Book Publishers Association, UK Electronic Book Publishers Association, USA Electronic Book Publishers Association

1842 ▪▪▪▪▪

SUPPORTIVE LEARNING PUBLICATIONS (SLP)
23 West View, Chirk, Wrexham LL14 5HL
Telephone: 01691 774778
Fax: 01691 774849

Partner: Phil Roberts

Educational & Textbooks; Geography & Geology; History & Antiquarian; Humour; Mathematics & Statistics; Sports & Games; Theatre, Drama & Dance

New Titles: 97 (1995), 85 (1996)
No of Employees: 9
Annual Turnover: £400,000

ISBNs, Imprints & Series: 1 871585

Distributor for:
USA: Ellison Educational

Book Trade Association Membership: PA, EPC

1843 ▪▪▪▪▪

*ALAN SUTTON PUBLISHING LTD
Phoenix Mill, Far Thrupp, Stroud, Glos
GL5 2BU
Telephone: 01453 731114
Fax: 01453 731117

Distribution:
Littlehampton Book Services,
10–14 Eldon Way, Lineside Estate,
Littlehampton, West Sussex BN17 7HE
Telephone: 01903 721596
Fax: 01903 730914

Directors: David Hogg *(Managing)*
Peter Clifford *(Publishing, Foreign Rights & Permissions)*

Richard Bryant *(Academic)*
Nicholas Mills
Christopher Sackett
Alan Plank *(Book Production)*
Managers: James Kinnear *(Sales Development)*
F. Henderson *(Publicity)*
David Hodge *(Management Accountant)*
Nicola Wood *(Sales)*

Academic & Scholarly; Archaeology; Architecture & Design; Aviation; Biography & Autobiography; Fine Art & Art History; Gardening; Guide Books; History & Antiquarian; Illustrated & Fine Editions; Literature & Criticism; Military & War; Natural History; Nautical; Photography; Transport; Travel & Topography

ISBNs, Imprints & Series:
0 7509, 0 86299, 0 904387 Pocket Classics Series

Parent Company:
The Guernsey Press Co

Distributor for:
Brigantia Monographs; Cambridgeshire Records Society; University of Exeter Press; Ian Faulkner Publishing; Glasgow University, Department of Archaeology; Gloucester Reprints; Guernsey Museums and Galleries; Hampshire Field Club; Hertfordshire Archaeological Trust; Kent Archaeological Society; National Museum of Wales; Newnham College, Cambridge; Oxfordshire Record Society; Railway and Canal Historical Society; The Richard III and Yorkist History Trust; The Richard III Society; Royal Commission on Ancient & Historical Monuments in Wales; Societe Jersaise; South Wales Record Society; Southampton City Museums; Western Archaeological Trust

Overseas Representation *(see §7.3)*:
Australia, New Zealand & Papua New Guinea: Peribo Pty Ltd, Mount Kuring-gai, NSW, Australia
Europe (except Netherlands, Italy & Scandinavia): Michael Geoghegan, Cookham Dean, Berks, UK
Italy: Penny Padovani, London, UK
Middle East, Greece, Cyprus & Turkey: Eurab Ltd, Rottingdean, UK
Netherlands: Consul Books, Blaricum
Scandinavia: D. Richard Bowen, Malmö, Sweden

1844

*SWEET & MAXWELL LTD
South Quay Plaza, 183 Marsh Wall, London
E14 9FT
Telephone: 0171 538 8686
Fax: 0171 538 8625

Accounts & Distribution:
Cheriton House, North Way, Andover, Hants
SP10 5BE
Telephone: 01264 332424
Fax: 01264 364418

Directors: S. White *(Managing)*
C. Blake *(Deputy Managing)*
A. Lourie *(Marketing)*
P. W. Riddle *(Production)*
I. Drane *(Finance)*

B. Grandage *(Editorial)*
C. Tullo *(Publishing)*

Law; Reference Books, Directories & Dictionaries

ISBNs, Imprints & Series:
0 414 W. Green & Son
0 420 Stevens & Sons
0 421 Sweet & Maxwell
0 906214 ESC Publishing

Parent Company:
The Thomson Corporation

Associated & Subsidiary Companies:
ESC Publishing; L.I.R. (Legal Information Resources)

Overseas Representation *(see §7.3)*:
Australia: The Law Book Co Ltd, North Ryde
Bangladesh: Karim International, Dhaka
Canada & USA: Thomson Professional Publishing, Scarborough, Ont, Canada
India: N. M. Tripathi Pte Ltd, Bombay

Book Trade Association Membership: PA

1845

TABB HOUSE
7 Church Street, Padstow, Cornwall PL28 8BG
Telephone: 01841 532316
Fax: 01841 532316

Distributors:
West Country Books, Lower Moor Way, Tiverton Business Park, Devon EX16 6SS
Telephone: 01884 243242
Fax: 01884 243325

Director: Caroline White *(Editorial)*
Promotion & Marketing Manager: K. Bickmore
Finance: Sandra Daniels

Biography & Autobiography; Fiction; Literature & Criticism; Poetry; Local History & Factual

New Titles: 6 (1995), 11 (1996)
No of Employees: 4

ISBNs, Imprints & Series:
0 907018 Encore Series, Humphrey Series (for Children)

Overseas Representation *(see §7.3)*:
USA (selected titles): Seven Hills Book Distributors, Cincinnati, OH, USA

Book Trade Association Membership: IPG

1846

TAKE THAT LTD
PO Box 200, Harrogate HG1 4XB
Telephone: 01423 507545
Fax: 01423 526035
Email: sales@takethat.co.uk
Web Site: http://www.bookshop.co.uk/takethat/

Sales:
Verulam Publishing, 152a Park Street Lane, Park Street, St Albans, Herts AL2 2AU
Telephone: 01727 872770

Fax: 01727 873866
Email: 100124.2375@compuserve.com

Partner: Chris Brown *(Sales, Rights & Permissions)*

Computer Science; Humour; Industry, Business & Management; Sports & Games

New Titles: 10 (1995), 15 (1996)

ISBNs, Imprints & Series:
0 9519489, 1 873668 Take That Books
1 873668 Net.works

Distributor for:
Australia: Beercan Books; Maxi Books; Pacific View Press

Overseas Representation *(see §7.3)*:
Australia & New Zealand: Maximedia Pty Ltd, Springwood, Australia

1847

TANGO BOOKS
3D West Point, 36–37 Warple Way, London
W3 0RG
Telephone: 0181 746 1171
Fax: 0181 746 1170

Distribution:
Bookpoint Ltd, 39 Milton Park, Abingdon, Oxon OX14 4TD
Telephone: 01235 835001
Fax: 01235 861038

Directors: David Fielder
Sheri Safran

Children's Books

ISBNs, Imprints & Series: 1 85707

Parent Company:
Sadie Fields Productions Ltd

1848

TARQUIN PUBLICATIONS
Stradbroke, Diss, Norfolk IP21 5JP
Telephone: 01379 384218
Fax: 01379 384289

Editorial: Gerald Jenkins *(Rights & Permissions)*
Sales & Promotion: Barry Graystone
Financial: Jean Howlett

Atlases & Maps; Children's Books; Crafts & Hobbies; Educational & Textbooks; Mathematics & Statistics; Do-it-Yourself Pop-up Books

New Titles: 5 (1995), 10 (1996)
No of Employees: 10

ISBNs, Imprints & Series:
0 906212, 1 899618

Overseas Representation *(see §7.3)*:
Australia: Latitude Media & Marketing, Glen Waverley, Vic; Beyond Toys, Lane Cove, NSW; H. E. Wootton & Sons, Toorak, Vic
New Zealand: Eton Press (Auckland) Ltd, Auckland
Portugal: Editóra Replicação, Lisbon

USA: Parkwest Publications Inc, Jersey City, NJ

Book Trade Association Membership: IPG

1849 ▬▬▬▬▬▬▬▬▬▬

TATE GALLERY PUBLISHING LTD
Millbank, London SW1P 4RG
Telephone: 0171 887 8869/70/71
Fax: 0171 887 8878

Warehouse, Trade Enquiries & Orders:
Telephone: 0171 887 8867

Managers: Celia Clear *(Managing Director)*
Mark Eastment *(Marketing)*
Brian McGahon *(Senior & Company Secretary)*
Tim Holton *(Production)*
Rosemary Bennett *(Retail)*

Fine Art & Art History

New Titles: 18 (1995), 18 (1996)
No of Employees: 43
Annual Turnover: £4.5M

ISBNs, Imprints & Series:
0 905005, 0 946590, 1 85437

Distributor for:
USA: Guggenheim Museum

Overseas Representation *(see §7.3)*:
Australia: Thames & Hudson (Australia) Pty Ltd, Port Melbourne, Vic
Canada: University of British Columbia Press, Vancouver, BC
Far East: Ralph & Sheila Summers, London, UK
France: Interart sarl, Paris
Japan: Maruzen Co Ltd, Tokyo
Middle East: Peter Ward Book Exports, London, UK
Netherlands: Idea Books, Amsterdam
Scandinavia: Saga Books Aps, Horsholm, Denmark
USA: University of Washington Press, Seattle, WA
Western Europe: Onslow Books Ltd, London, UK

1850 ▬▬▬▬▬▬▬▬▬▬

I. B. TAURIS & CO LTD
Victoria House, Bloomsbury Square, London WC1B 4DZ
Telephone: 0171 916 1069
Fax: 0171 916 1068

Distribution:
Biblios Publishers' Distribution Services Ltd, Star Road, Partridge Green, Horsham, West Sussex RH13 8LD
Telephone: 01403 710971
Fax: 01403 711143

Directors: Iradj Bagherzade *(Managing)*
Jonathan McDonnell *(Sales & Marketing)*

Academic & Scholarly; Archaeology; Architecture & Design; Biography & Autobiography; Cinema, Video, TV & Radio; Fine Art & Art History; Gender Studies; Guide Books; History & Antiquarian; Military & War; Politics & World Affairs; Reference

Books, Directories & Dictionaries; Sociology & Anthropology

New Titles: 73 (1995), 84 (1996)

ISBNs, Imprints & Series:
1 85043, 1 86064 International Library of African Studies, International Library of Historical Studies, Isma'ili Heritage Series, Library of International Relations, Library of Modern Middle East Studies, Society and Culture in the Modern Middle East

Associated & Subsidiary Companies:
British Academic Press; Tauris Academic Studies; Tauris Parke Books

Distributor for:
USA: Institute for Palestine Studies; The New Press

Overseas Representation *(see §7.3)*:
Bangladesh: Karim International, Dhaka
Central & South America: Humphrys Roberts Associates, London, UK
Europe: Andrew B. Durnell, Tunbridge Wells, UK
Europe (Tauris Parke only): Books for Europe Ltd, Bournemouth, UK
India: Viva Marketing, New Delhi
Iran: Behruz Neirami, Tehran
Japan: United Publishers Services Ltd, Tokyo
Middle East & North Africa: Eurab Ltd, Rottingdean, UK
Pakistan: Afro-Asian Book Co, Karachi
South Africa: Judith Wengrowe Agencies, Northcliff, Johannesburg
South-East Asia, Hong Kong, Taiwan & Korea: STM Publishing Services Pte Ltd, Singapore
USA & Canada: St Martin's Press Inc, New York, NY, USA

Book Trade Association Membership: IPG

1851 ▬▬▬▬▬▬▬▬▬▬

TAYLOR & FRANCIS LTD
Rankine Road, Basingstoke, Hants RG24 8PR
Telephone: 01256 813000
Fax: 01256 479438

President: Sir Nevill Mott, FRS
Directors: B. R. Coles *(Chairman)*
K. W. Keohane *(Vice-Chairman)*
A. R. Selvey *(Managing)*
H. Baum
S. B. Neal *(Editorial)*
E. Ferguson
D. J. Banister
K. R. Courtney
A. M. Foye *(Financial)*
R. Horton *(Sales & Marketing)*

Academic & Scholarly; Biology & Zoology; Chemistry; Educational & Textbooks; Engineering; Geography & Geology; Languages & Linguistics; Mathematics & Statistics; Medical (incl. Self Help & Alternative Medicine); Natural History; Philosophy; Photography; Physics; Politics & World Affairs; Psychology & Psychiatry; Scientific & Technical; Transport

ISBNs, Imprints & Series:
0 85066 Taylor & Francis
0 905273, 1 85000 Falmer Press Ltd

Associated & Subsidiary Companies:
Falmer Press Ltd. *USA:* Taylor & Francis Inc

Overseas Representation *(see §7.3)*:
Australia: Edward Arnold (Australia) Ltd, Rydalmere, NSW
India: UBS Publishers' Distributors Ltd, New Delhi
Japan: Kinokuniya Co Ltd, Tokyo
Singapore: Information Publications Pte Ltd
South Africa: Book Promotions Pty Ltd, Plumstead

1852 ▬▬▬▬▬▬▬▬▬▬

TAYLOR GRAHAM PUBLISHING
500 Chesham House, 150 Regent Street, London W1R 5FA

Director: Peter J. Taylor

Academic & Scholarly; Bibliography & Library Science; Computer Science; Scientific & Technical

ISBNs, Imprints & Series: 0 947568

Overseas Representation *(see §7.3)*:
USA & Canada: Taylor Graham Publishing, Los Angeles, CA, USA

Book Trade Association Membership: UK Serials Group

1853 ▬▬▬▬▬▬▬▬▬▬

THOMAS TELFORD SERVICES LTD
Thomas Telford House, 1 Heron Quay, London E14 4JD
Telephone: 0171 987 6999
Fax: 0171 538 4101

Warehouse:
21–23 Westferry Road, London E14 8JH
Telephone: 0171 538 5441

Retail Bookshop:
1–7 Great George Street, London SW1P 3AA
Telephone: 0171 222 7722
Fax: 0171 222 7500

Head of Publications Division: Graham James
Managers: Steven Cross *(Books Publisher)*
Peter Scarlett *(Sales Administration)*
Glen Wilders *(Directories Publisher)*
Leon Heward-Mills *(Journals & Electronic Products Publisher)*

Engineering

New Titles: 37 (1995), 50 (1996)

ISBNs, Imprints & Series:
0 7277 British Nuclear Energy Society, Institution of Civil Engineers, Thomas Telford

Parent Company:
Institution of Civil Engineers

Distributor for:
British Geotechnical Society; British Nuclear Energy Society; Fédération Internationale de la Précontrainte (Slough, UK); H. R. Wallingford

Overseas Representation *(see §7.3)*:
Australia: DA Information Services, Mitcham, Vic
Far East: APAC Publishers Services, Singapore
Germany: Bernd Feldmann, Berlin
India: Book Marketing Services, Madras
Japan: Maruzen Co Ltd, Tokyo
Malaysia & Singapore: Publishers Marketing Services Ltd, Singapore
Middle East: Berj Jamkojian, Vienna, Austria
Netherlands, Belgium, Italy, France, Spain, Portugal & Greece: Momenta Publishing Ltd, London, UK
Scandinavia: Jan Norbye, Ølstykke, Denmark
USA: American Society of Civil Engineers, New York

Book Trade Association Membership: IPG, APLSP, Directory Publishers Association

1854 ▬▬▬▬

TFPL PUBLISHING
17–18 Britton Street, London EC1M 5NQ
Telephone: 0171 251 5522
Fax: 0171 251 8318
Email: central@tfpl.demon.co.uk
Web Site: http://www.tfpl.com

Publishing Manager: Peter Kibby

Bibliography & Library Science; Industry, Business & Management; Reference Books, Directories & Dictionaries

New Titles: 6 (1995), 7 (1996)
No of Employees: 7
Annual Turnover: £750,000

ISBNs, Imprints & Series: 1 870889

Parent Company:
TFPL Ltd

Associated & Subsidiary Companies:
USA: TFPL Inc

Distributor for:
USA: Online Inc; Simba Information Inc

Book Trade Association Membership:
Directory Publishers Association

1855 ▬▬▬▬

THAMES & HUDSON LTD
30–34 Bloomsbury Street, London WC1B 3QP
Telephone: 0171 636 5488
Fax: 0171 636 4799

Warehouse, Accounts & Returns:
Thames & Hudson (Distributors) Ltd,
44 Clockhouse Road, Farnborough, Hants
GU14 7QZ
Telephone: 01252 541602
Fax: 01252 377380

Directors: Thomas Neurath *(Managing)*
Timothy Evans *(Sales & Marketing)*
Jamie Camplin *(Editorial)*
Ian Middleton *(Rights & Permissions)*
Eric Bates
Timothy Flood *(Financial)*
Christopher Ferguson *(Production)*
Constance Kaine *(Design)*

Simon Huntley *(General)*
UK Sales Manager: Trevor Naylor
Export Area Managers: Diana Jones
Ian Bartley
Andrew Freeman

Academic & Scholarly; Antiques & Collecting; Archaeology; Architecture & Design; Biography & Autobiography; Children's Books; Crafts & Hobbies; Environment & Development Studies; Fashion & Costume; Fine Art & Art History; History & Antiquarian; Illustrated & Fine Editions; Literature & Criticism; Music; Philosophy; Photography; Psychology & Psychiatry; Reference Books, Directories & Dictionaries; Religion & Theology; Sociology & Anthropology; Theatre, Drama & Dance; Travel & Topography

New Titles: 181 (1995), 180 (1996)

ISBNs, Imprints & Series:
0 500 Thames & Hudson
0 642 National Gallery of Australia
0 7141 British Museum Press
0 87070 Museum of Modern Art, New York
1 85669 Laurence King
1 881616 Scalo, Zurich
208 Flammarion SA, France
3 7913 Prestel Verlag, Munich

Parent Company:
T & H Holdings Ltd

Associated & Subsidiary Companies:
Thames & Hudson (Distributors) Ltd.
Australia: Thames & Hudson (Australia) Pty Ltd. *France:* Interart sarl; Editions Thames & Hudson sarl. *Singapore:* Thames & Hudson (S) Pte Ltd. *USA:* Thames & Hudson Inc

Distributor for:
British Museum Press; Laurence King.
Australia: National Gallery of Australia.
France: Flammarion SA. *Germany:* Prestel Verlag, Munich. *Switzerland:* Scalo, Zurich.
USA: Museum of Modern Art, New York

Overseas Representation *(see §7.3)*:
Australia: Thames & Hudson (Australia) Pty Ltd, Port Melbourne, Vic
Brazil & South America: Humphrys Roberts Associates, Cotia, Brazil
Canada: Douglas & McIntyre, Toronto
France: Interart sarl, Paris
Germany (Central): Claus Schmögner, Heidelberg, Germany
Germany (North): Ingo Meyer, Eckernförde, Germany
Germany (South): Wolfgang Willmann & Susanne Sieger, Munich, Germany
Hong Kong, Korea, Taiwan, China & Philippines: Asia Publisher Services Ltd, Hong Kong
Hungary, Czech Republic & Slovakia: Csaba Lengyel de Bagota, Kécskemét, Hungary
India: contact our Export Sales Department
Irish Republic: Genny Kelliher Publishers Representative, Monkstown
Israel: Lonnie Kahn & Co Ltd, Tel Aviv
Japan: YOHAN (Western Publications Distribution Agency), Tokyo
Malaysia: Thames & Hudson (S) Pte Ltd, Petaling Jaya
Mexico & Central America: Humphrys Roberts Associates, London, UK
Netherlands: Nilsson & Lamm BV, Weesp

New Zealand: David Bateman Ltd, Auckland
Singapore, Brunei & Indonesia: Thames & Hudson (S) Lte Ltd, Singapore
South Africa: Oxford University Press Southern African Branch, Cape Town, Pietersburg, Umtata, Pinetown & Melrose North
Thailand: Asia Book Co, Bangkok
West Indies: Hugh Dunphy, Kingston, Jamaica
Western Europe (excluding Netherlands, France, Italy & Germany): Onslow Books Ltd, London, UK

Book Trade Association Membership: PA

1856 ▬▬▬▬

THARPA PUBLICATIONS
15 Bendemeer Road, London SW15 1JX
Telephone: 0181 788 7792
Fax: 0171 589 9611

Distribution & Accounts Office:
Kilnwick Percy Hall, Pocklington, York
YO4 2UF
Telephone: 01759 306446
Fax: 01759 306397
Email: tharpa@rmplc.co.uk
Web Site: http://www.luna.co.uk/tharpa

Director: Hugh W. P. Clift
General Manager: Jeremy Sloan

Religion & Theology

New Titles: 1 (1995), 1 (1996)
No of Employees: 5
Annual Turnover: £250,000

ISBNs, Imprints & Series: 0 948006

Overseas Representation *(see §7.3)*:
Australia: Quest Book Agency, Sydney
Hong Kong: The Buddhist Merit & Wisdom Service
New Zealand: Peaceful Living Publications, Tauranga
Singapore: Allscript Establishment (S) Pte Ltd
USA: Atrium, Santa Rosa, CA
USA (Sales office): Tharpa Publications, Seattle, WA, USA

Book Trade Association Membership: IPG

1857 ▬▬▬▬

THE POLICY PRESS
University of Bristol, Rodney Lodge,
Grange Road, Bristol BS8 4EA
Telephone: 0117 973 8797
Fax: 0117 973 7308
Email: tpp@bris.ac.uk

Publishing Manager: Alison Shaw
Sales & Marketing: Julia Mortimer
Editorial: Dawn Louise Pudney
Journal Manager: Liz McCarty

Academic & Scholarly; Economics; Educational & Textbooks; Gender Studies; Geography & Geology; Industry, Business & Management; Politics & World Affairs; Sociology & Anthropology

New Titles: 40 (1996)
No of Employees: 3
Annual Turnover: £173,000

ISBNs, Imprints & Series:
0 86292 University of Bristol Press
1 86134 The Policy Press
1 873575 SAUS Publications

1858

THEOSOPHICAL BOOKS LTD
50 Gloucester Place, London W1H 3HJ
Telephone: 0171 935 9201
Fax: 0171 935 9543

Chairman: Miss L. Storey
Manager: N. Hedges

Magic & the Occult; Philosophy; Psychology & Psychiatry; Religion & Theology

ISBNs, Imprints & Series:
0 7229, 0 8356

Parent Company:
English Theosophical Trust

Distributor for:
India: Theosophical Publishing House. *USA:*
Theosophical Publishing House

Overseas Representation *(see §7.3):*
Australia: Quest Book Agency, Sydney
Denmark: Miss A. Bildsoe, Copenhagen
Finland: Miss S. Kivilinna, Helsinki
France: Editions Adyar, Paris
India: Theosophical Publishing House, Madras
Netherlands: Uitgeverij Theosofische,
   Amsterdam
New Zealand: Auckland Book Depot,
   Auckland
Sweden: Bokhandeln Studio, Stockholm
USA: The Theosophical Publishing House,
   Wheaton, IL

Book Trade Association Membership: BA

1859

THOEMMES PRESS
11 Great George Street, Bristol BS1 5RR
Telephone: 0117 929 1377
Fax: 0117 922 1918
Email: 100633.1133@compuserve.com

Distribution:
Biblios Publishers Distribution Services Ltd,
Star Road, Partridge Green, West Sussex
RH13 8LD
Telephone: 01403 710971
Fax: 01403 711143

Director: Rudi Thoemmes *(Managing & Editorial)*
Managers: Deborah Mann *(Marketing & Sales)*
Daniel Broughton *(Production)*
Linda Keeble *(Finance)*
Jane Williamson

Academic & Scholarly; Philosophy

New Titles: 76 (1995), 57 (1996)
No of Employees: 11

ISBNs, Imprints & Series:
1 85506 , Nico Editions

Parent Company:
Thoemmes Antiquarian Books Ltd

Overseas Representation *(see §7.3):*
Canada: Scholarly Book Services Inc, Toronto
India: T. R. Publications Pvt Ltd, Madras
Irish Republic: Brookside Publishing Services,
   Dublin
Japan (main stockist): Kinokuniya Co Ltd,
   Tokyo, Japan
Korea: Information & Culture Korea, Seoul,
   Korea, South
Philippines: I. J. Sagun Enterprises Inc, Rizal
Scandinavia: D. Richard Bowen, Malmö,
   Sweden
Singapore, Malaysia, Thailand & Indonesia:
   APD Singapore Pte Ltd, Singapore
Taiwan: Unifacmanu Trading Co Ltd, Taipei
USA: International Publishers Marketing Inc,
   Dulles, VA

Book Trade Association Membership: IPG

1860

THOMAS COOK PUBLISHING
PO Box 227, Peterborough PE3 8BQ
Telephone: 01733 269300
Fax: 01733 267052
Email: publishing@thomascook.tmailuk.
sprint.com
Web Site: http://www.thomascook.com

Warehouse, Trade Enquiries & Orders:
AA Publishing, Exel Logistics MS,
Invicta House, Sir Thomas Longley Road,
Medway City Estate, Rochester, Kent
ME2 4DU
Telephone: 01634 297123
Fax: 01634 298000

Head of Publishing: Jennifer Rigby
Product Development Manager: Stephen
   York

Transport; Travel & Topography

New Titles: 13 (1995), 12 (1996)
No of Employees: 18
Annual Turnover: £2M

ISBNs, Imprints & Series: 0 906273

Parent Company:
Thomas Cook Group Ltd

Overseas Representation *(see §7.3):*
Australia: Bookwise International, Findon, SA
Germany: Brettschneider Fernreisebedarf,
   Munich
Italy (book trade): Bookport Associates,
   Bologna, Italy
Italy (travel trade): L.E.D., Turin, Italy
Netherlands: Schuyt & Co bv, Haarlem
Scandinavia: D. Richard Bowen, Malmö,
   Sweden
Singapore, Thailand, Malaysia, Hong Kong &
   Philippines: Höfer Communications,
   Singapore
South Africa (book trade): Faradawn CC,
   Saxonwold, South Africa
South Africa (travel trade): Houston Travel
   Marketing Services, Gardenview, South
   Africa
USA: Forsyth Travel Library Inc, Shawnee
   Mission, KS; Passport Books a division of
   NTC Contemporary Publishing,
   Lincolnwood, IL

Book Trade Association Membership: IPG

1861

STANLEY THORNES (PUBLISHERS) LTD
[incorporating Mary Glasgow Publications]
Ellenborough House, Wellington Street,
Cheltenham, Glos GL50 1YW
Telephone: 01242 228888
Fax: 01242 221914

Warehouse:
Old Station Drive, Leckhampton, Cheltenham,
Glos GL53 0DN
Telephone: 01242 228888
Fax: 01242 221914

Directors: D. J. Smith *(Managing)*
P. Vinson *(Production)*
B. D. Carvell *(Market Development)*
O. Gadsby *(Market Development)*
K. Waterman *(Finance)*
Managers: E. Heasman *(Export)*
M. van de Weijer *(Distribution)*

*Accountancy & Taxation; Biology & Zoology;
Chemistry; Children's Books; Computer
Science; Cookery, Wines & Spirits; Economics;
Educational & Textbooks; Electronic
(Educational); Engineering; Environment &
Development Studies; Fashion & Costume;
Geography & Geology; Health & Beauty;
History & Antiquarian; Industry, Business &
Management; Languages & Linguistics;
Mathematics & Statistics; Physics; Politics &
World Affairs; Religion & Theology; Scientific
& Technical; Sociology & Anthropology;
Vocational Training & Careers*

New Titles: 213 (1995), 290 (1996)
No of Employees: 196
Annual Turnover: £21M

ISBNs, Imprints & Series:
0 7175 Hulton Educational Publications Ltd
0 7487
0 85950 Stanley Thornes (Publishers) Ltd
0 85973 Stam Press Ltd
0 86158, 1 85234 Mary Glasgow Publications 1
871402

Parent Company:
Wolters Kluwer (UK) (plc) *(Netherlands)*

Distributor for:
The Financial Training Co

Overseas Representation *(see §7.3):*
Australia: Jacaranda Wiley Ltd, Milton,
   Queensland
Botswana: The Educational Book Service (Pty)
   Ltd, Gabarone
Canada: The Resource Centre, Waterloo;
   Bacon & Hughes, Nepean
Caribbean (excluding Trinidad & Guyana): Ian
   Randle Publishers Ltd, Kingston, Jamaica
Guyana & Trinidad: RIK Services Ltd, San
   Fernando, Trinidad
Hong Kong: Pilot Publishers Services Ltd,
   Kowloon
India: Maya Publishers Pvt Ltd, New Delhi
Middle East: Eurab Ltd, Rottingdean, UK
New Zealand: Educational Distributors Ltd,
   Auckland
Pakistan: Publishers Marketing Associates,
   Karachi
Singapore & Malaysia: APD Singapore Pte
   Ltd, Singapore

South Africa: Shuter & Shooter Pty Ltd, Pietermaritzburg
Zimbabwe: College Press Publishers (Pvt) Ltd, Harare

Book Trade Association Membership: PA, BDC, EPC, CAPP

1862 ■

F. A. THORPE (PUBLISHING) LTD
The Green, Bradgate Road, Anstey, Leicester LE7 7FU
Telephone: 0116 236 4325
Fax: 0116 234 0205
Email: ulverscroft@dial.pipex.com
Web Site: http://dspace.dial.pipex.com/town/plaza/hf33/

Chairman & Managing Director: D. F. Thorpe
President: F. A. Thorpe, OBE, JP

Large Print Leisure

New Titles: 450 (1995), 450 (1996)

ISBNs, Imprints & Series:
0 7089 Charnwood Hardback Series, Linford Soft Cover Series, Ulverscroft Hard Cover Series

Associated & Subsidiary Companies:
Ulverscroft Large Print Books Ltd

Distributor for:
Soundings Audio Books

Overseas Representation *(see §7.3):*
Australia: Sandra Lavender, Crows Nest
Canada: Mrs Irene Hanson, Burlington, Ont
New Zealand: Frank & Lois Dew, Feilding
USA: Ulverscroft Large Print (USA) Inc, West Seneca, NY

1863 ■

TIMBER PRESS
10 Market Street, Swavesey, Cambridge CB4 5QG
Telephone: 01954 232959
Fax: 01954 206040

Publisher: Robert B. Conklin
Marketing Director: Michael Alan Fox
Managers: Deborah D. Garman *(Publicity)*
Darcel Warren *(Production)*
Managing Editors: Dale E. Johnson
Karen Kirtley *(Amadeus Press)*

Agriculture; Gardening; Music; Scientific & Technical

New Titles: 20 (1995), 25 (1996)
Annual Turnover: £100,000

ISBNs, Imprints & Series:
0 88192 Timber Press
0 917304 Timber Press (old)
0 931146 Dioscorides Press
0 931340 Amadeus Press

Parent Company:
Timber Press Inc *(USA)*

Overseas Representation *(see §7.3):*
Belgium, France, Netherlands, Germany, Italy, Switzerland & Greece: Ted Dougherty, London, UK
Irish Republic: Hibernian Book Services, Dublin
Scandinavia & Iceland: D. Richard Bowen, Malmö, Sweden
Spain: Peter Prout, Madrid

1864 ■

TIME-LIFE BOOKS
Time Life UK, 4 Furzeground Way, Stockley Park, Uxbridge, Middx UB11 1DP
Telephone: 0181 606 3097
Fax: 0181 606 3108

Distributor:
Bookpoint Ltd, 39 Milton Park, Abingdon, Oxon OX14 4JD
Telephone: 01235 400400
Fax: 01235 861038

Academic & Scholarly; Children's Books; Cookery, Wines & Spirits; Crime; Crafts & Hobbies; Do-It-Yourself; Military & War; Natural History; Poetry; Reference Books, Directories & Dictionaries

ISBNs, Imprints & Series:
0 7054, 0 8094

Distributor for:
USA: Cy Decosse

1865 ■

TITAN BOOKS LTD
42–44 Dolben Street, London SE1 0UP
Telephone: 0171 620 0200
Fax: 0171 620 0032
Email: 101447.2455@compuserve.com

Comics & Specialist Shop Distribution:
Diamond Comic Distributors, Unit 1, Empson Street, London E3 3LT
Telephone: 0171 538 8300
Fax: 0171 987 6744

General Book Trade Distribution:
Exel Logistics Media Services, Invicta House, Sir Thomas Longley Road, Medway City Estate, Rochester, Kent ME2 4DU
Telephone: 01634 297123
Fax: 01634 298000

Directors: Nick Landau *(Managing)*
Katy Wild *(Editorial, Rights & Permissions)*
Siobhan Flynn *(Marketing, Home & Export Sales)*
Marketing Officer: Robin King
Trade Representation: John Masters *(Amalgamated Book Services)*
Production Controller: Bob Kelly

Biography & Autobiography; Children's Books; Cinema, Video, TV & Radio; Crime; Fiction; Humour; Music; Science Fiction; Erotic Fiction; Graphic Novels; Paperbacks; True Crime; TV

New Titles: 65 (1995), 70 (1996)
No of Employees: 21

ISBNs, Imprints & Series:
0 907610, 1 85286 Eros Plus

Associated & Subsidiary Companies:
Forbidden Planet Ltd, UK

Overseas Representation *(see §7.3):*
Australia: HarperCollins Publishers, Pymble, NSW & North Ryde, NSW
Benelux, Germany, France, Austria & Switzerland: Janet Clark, London, UK
Far East & Japan: EM International, Seattle, WA, USA
New Zealand: Propaganda Distributors, Auckland
Scandinavia & Italy: Katie McNeish, London, UK
South Africa: Walton Marketing Services, Chislehurst, UK
Spain & Portugal: Iberian Book Services SL, Madrid, Spain

1866 ■

*TIXERANT DEAN PUBLICATIONS/STEPPING STONES
PO Box 679, Amersham, Bucks HP7 0NB
Telephone: 01494 726374

Marketing Manager: Chris Tixerant
Secretary, Sales: Cathryn Weekes

Children's Books; Fun Work Books; Nursery School

ISBNs, Imprints & Series:
1 899524 Stepping Stones

1867 ■

UNIVERSITY OF TORONTO PRESS
Trevor Brown Associates,
114–115 Tottenham Court Road,
Midford Place, London W1P 0BY
Telephone: 0171 388 8500
Fax: 0171 388 5950

General Book Trade Distribution:
Marston Book Services Ltd, PO Box 269, Abingdon, Oxon OX14 4YN
Telephone: 01235 465500
Fax: 01235 465555

Director: J. Trevor Brown
Manager: A. Simpson-Muellner *(European Sales)*

Academic & Scholarly; Bibliography & Library Science; Educational & Textbooks; Environment & Development Studies; History & Antiquarian; Languages & Linguistics; Literature & Criticism; Military & War; Music; Natural History; Philosophy; Politics & World Affairs; Reference Books, Directories & Dictionaries; Scientific & Technical; Sociology & Anthropology

ISBNs, Imprints & Series:
0 8020
0 88854 Royal Ontario Museum

Parent Company:
University of Toronto Press *(Canada)*

Distributor for:
Canada: Royal Ontario Museum Publications

1868

TOUCAN PRESS
rue des Monts, Delancy Park, St Sampson,
Guernsey
Telephone: 01481 57017

Executive: G. Stevens-Cox

*Academic & Scholarly; Antiques & Collecting;
Archaeology; Bibliography & Library Science;
Children's Books; Fashion & Costume;
History & Antiquarian; Poetry; Reference
Books, Directories & Dictionaries; Travel &
Topography*

ISBNs, Imprints & Series: 0 85694

1869

TRANSWORLD PUBLISHERS LTD
61–63 Uxbridge Road, London W5 5SA
Telephone: 0181 579 2652
Fax: 0181 579 5479

Warehouse & Distribution:
PO Box 17, Wellingborough, Northants
NN8 4BU
Telephone: 01933 225761
Fax: 01933 271235

Directors: Stephen Rubin *(Chairman)*
Mark Barty-King *(Managing)*
John Blake *(International)*
Alun Davies *(USA)*
George Greenfield *(Production)*
William Hayhurst *(Company Secretary &
    Personnel)*
Barry Hempstead *(Financial & Deputy
    Managing)*
Patrick Janson-Smith *(Publisher: Adult Trade
    Books)*
Anthony Mott *(Publisher: Paperbacks)*
Terry Pink *(Distribution)*
Geoff Rumpf *(Australia)*
Philippa Dickinson *(Publisher: Children's &
    Young Adult Books)*
Larry Finlay *(Marketing)*
Sally Gaminara *(Publishing: Bantam Press)*
Liz Laczynska *(Art)*
Francesca Liversidge *(Publishing: Bantam
    Paperbacks)*
Ursula Mackenzie *(Publisher: Hardbacks)*
Ian Manhire *(Sales Administration)*
Diane Pearson *(Editorial: Corgi)*
Garry Prior *(Home Sales)*
Judy Turner *(Publicity)*
Marianne Velmans *(Publishing: Doubleday)*
John Saddler *(Editorial)*
Bill Scott-Kerr *(Editorial: Corgi, Black Swan)*
Mike Webster *(Distribution)*
Rebecca Winfield *(Rights)*
Editorial: Debbie Beckerman *(Partridge
    Press)*
Broo Doherty *(Bantam Press)*
Annie Eaton *(Children's Fiction)*
Penny Walker *(Children's Novelty & Picture
    Books)*

*Audio Books; Biography & Autobiography;
Children's Books; Cinema, Video, TV & Radio;
Cookery, Wines & Spirits; Crime; Electronic
(Educational); Electronic (Entertainment);
Electronic (Professional & Academic);
Fiction; Gardening; Health & Beauty;
Humour; Politics & World Affairs; Science
Fiction; Sports & Games; Psychic*

ISBNs, Imprints & Series:
0 385 Delacorte, Doubleday
0 440 Dell Yearling
0 552 Black Swan, Corgi, Freeway, Pathway,
    Picture Corgi, Young Corgi
0 553 Bantam, Choose Your Own Adventure,
    Sweet Dreams, Sweet Valley High, Sweet
    Valley Kids, Sweet Valley Twins
0 593 Bantam Press
0 903 Expert Gardening Books
1 85225 Partridge Press

Parent Company:
Bantam Doubleday Dell Inc *(USA)*

Associated & Subsidiary Companies:
Australia: Transworld Publishers (Australia)
Pty Ltd. *Canada:* Bantam Books (Canada) Inc /
Doubleday Canada Ltd. *New Zealand:*
Transworld Publishers (NZ) Ltd. *South Africa:*
Trans-SABD (Pty) Ltd

Distributor for:
IDG Computer Books; Private Eye Books

Overseas Representation *(see §7.3)*:
Australia: Transworld Publishers (Australia)
    Pty Ltd, Sydney
Canada: Bantam Books (Canada) Inc /
    Doubleday Canada Ltd, Toronto
New Zealand: Transworld Publishers (NZ) Ltd,
    Auckland
South Africa: Trans-SABD (Pty) Ltd,
    Braamfontein

Book Trade Association Membership: PA,
BDC

1870

**TREEHOUSE CHILDREN'S BOOKS
LTD**
Melbourne House, 36 Chamberlain Street,
Wells, Somerset BA5 2PJ
Telephone: 01749 679651
Fax: 01749 679725

Distribution:
Macmillan Distribution Ltd, Brunel Road,
Houndmills, Basingstoke, Hants RG21 6XS

Directors: Richard Powell
David Bailey *(Home & Export Sales)*
Andrew Bailey *(Foreign Rights)*
Dawn Powell

Children's Books

New Titles: 16 (1995), 12 (1996)
No of Employees: 3
Annual Turnover: £1M

ISBNs, Imprints & Series: 1 85576

Associated & Subsidiary Companies:
Emma Books Ltd

1871

TRENTHAM BOOKS
Westview House, 734 London Road, Oakhill,
Stoke on Trent ST4 5NP
Telephone: 01782 745567
Fax: 01782 745553
Email: tb@trentham-books.co.uk
Web Site: http://www.ftech.net/~trentham

Directors: John Eggleston *(Chairman, Rights
    & Permissions)*
Gillian Klein *(Editor)*
Barbara Wiggins *(Sales Manager)*

*Academic & Scholarly; Educational &
Textbooks; Politics & World Affairs*

New Titles: 25 (1995), 30 (1996)
No of Employees: 7
Annual Turnover: £280,000

ISBNs, Imprints & Series:
0 948080, 0 9507735, 1 85856

Associated & Subsidiary Companies:
Trentham Print Design Ltd

Distributor for:
Arts Council *(selected titles)*; Central TV
(selected educational videos); Design and
Technology Association *(all priced
publications)*. *France:* European Institute of
Education & Social Policy; UNESCO Institute
for Educational Planning *(selected titles)*

Overseas Representation *(see §7.3)*:
Australia & New Zealand: Terry Carr, West
    Lakes, Australia
Canada: Bacon & Hughes, Nepean
Spain & Portugal: Iberian Book Services SL,
    Madrid, Spain

Book Trade Association Membership: PA

1872

TROTMAN & CO LTD
12 Hill Rise, Richmond, Surrey TW10 6UA
Telephone: 0181 940 5668
Fax: 0181 948 9267
Email: ar@trotman.demon.co.uk
Web Site: http://www.trotman.co.uk

Warehouse:
Vale Packaging, 420 Vale Road, Tonbridge
Telephone: 01732 359387
Fax: 01732 770620

Directors: Andy Fiennes Trotman *(Managing)*
Morfydd Jones *(Publishing)*
Alastair George *(Finance)*

*Educational & Textbooks; Reference Books,
Directories & Dictionaries; Vocational
Training & Careers*

New Titles: 50 (1995), 70 (1996)
No of Employees: 20

ISBNs, Imprints & Series: 0 85660

Associated & Subsidiary Companies:
Australia: Trotman Australia Pty Ltd. *South
Africa:* Trotman Africa Pte Ltd

Overseas Representation *(see §7.3)*:
Singapore, Malaysia & Brunei: Publishers
    Marketing Services Ltd, Singapore

Book Trade Association Membership: IPG,
Directory Publishers Association, The Galley
Club

1873

DYLLANSOW TRURAN
Croft Prince, Mount Hawke, Truro TR4 8EE
Telephone: 01209 891134
Fax: 01209 891134

Trade Enquiries:
Tor Mark Press, Islington Wharf, Penryn,
Cornwall TR10 8AT

Contact: Ivan Corbett

*Geography & Geology; Guide Books; History
& Antiquarian; Languages & Linguistics;
Natural History; Reference Books, Directories
& Dictionaries*

New Titles: 4 (1996)
Annual Turnover: £35,000

ISBNs, Imprints & Series:
0 9506431, 0 907566, 1 85022

1874

TURTON & CHAMBERS
Unit 5, Station Road Industrial Estate,
Woodchester, Stroud, Glos GL5 5EQ
Telephone: 01453 878598
Fax: 01453 878599

Directors: Aidan Chambers
David Turton

Children's Books; Fiction; Poetry

ISBNs, Imprints & Series: 1 872148

1875

TWELVEHEADS PRESS
Chy Mengleth, Twelveheads, Truro, Cornwall
TR4 8SN
Telephone: 01209 820978
Fax: 01719 196417
Email: 12heads@celtic.co.uk

Partners: Alan Kittridge
Michael Messenger
John Stengelhofen

*Archaeology; Guide Books; History &
Antiquarian; Nautical; Transport*

New Titles: 2 (1995), 4 (1996)

ISBNs, Imprints & Series: 0 906294

1876

UCL PRESS LTD
University College London, Gower Street,
London WC1E 6BT
Telephone: 0171 380 7707
Fax: 0171 413 8392
Email: n.staff@ucl.ac.uk
Web Site: http://www.bookshop.co.uk/ucl/

Distributor:
Marston Book Services, PO Box 269,
Abingdon, Oxon OX14 4YN
Telephone: 01235 465500
Fax: 01235 465555

Publisher & Chief Executive: Roger Jones
Marketing Director: Nicholas Esson

*Academic & Scholarly; Archaeology;
Computer Science; Engineering; Environment
& Development Studies; Fine Art & Art
History; Geography & Geology; History &
Antiquarian; Military & War; Philosophy;
Physics; Politics & World Affairs; Psychology
& Psychiatry; Sociology & Anthropology*

New Titles: 73 (1995), 69 (1996)
No of Employees: 14

ISBNs, Imprints & Series: 1 85728

Distributor for:
Australia: Allen & Unwin. *Canada:* McGill-
Queen's University Press. *USA:* University of
Minnesota Press; Northwestern University
Press

Overseas Representation *(see §7.3):*
Australia & New Zealand: Allen & Unwin Pty
Ltd, St Leonards, NSW, Australia
Benelux: Frans Janssen, Rotterdam,
Netherlands
Canada: University of British Columbia Press,
Vancouver, BC
Caribbean: Ian Randle Publishers Ltd,
Kingston, Jamaica
Eastern & Central Europe: Michael Timperley
Marketing, Hong Kong
India: Research Press, New Delhi
Irish Republic: Brookside Publishing Services,
Dublin
Japan: United Publishers Services Ltd, Tokyo
Mexico & Central America: Chris Humphrys,
London, UK
Middle East: Anthony Rudkin Associates,
Oxford, UK
Nigeria: Mosuro Booksellers, Ibadan
Pakistan: Afro-Asian Book Co, Karachi
Scandinavia: Colin Flint, Harlow, UK
South America: Terry Roberts, Cotia SP, Brazil
Southeast & East Asia: STM Publishers
Services Pte Ltd, Singapore; STM Publishers
Pte Ltd, Taipei, Taiwan
Southern Africa: Book Promotions Pty Ltd,
Plumstead, South Africa
Southern Europe: Charles Gibbes,
Buckingham, UK
USA: Taylor & Francis Inc, Bristol, PA

Book Trade Association Membership: IPG

1877

UFO MUSIC LTD
18 Hanway Street, London W1P 9DD
Telephone: 0171 636 1281
Fax: 0171 636 0738
Email: ufomusic@dircon.co.uk

Executives: Zi Siddique *(Rights & Publishing)*
Acrelda Farrell *(Sales & Marketing)*
Managing Director: Mark Hayward

Music

New Titles: 15 (1995), 20 (1996)
No of Employees: 8

ISBNs, Imprints & Series: 1 873884

Book Trade Association Membership: PA

1878

ULSTER HISTORICAL FOUNDATION
Balmoral Buildings, 12 College Square East,
Belfast BT1 6DD
Telephone: 01232 332288
Fax: 01232 239885
Email: enquiry@uhf.dnet.co.uk
Web Site: http://www.unite.net/customers/uhf

Retail Outlet/Mail Order:
Familia, 64 Wellington Place, Belfast BT1 6GG
Telephone: 01232 235392
Fax: 01232 239885

Chairperson of Board of Trustees: Prof.
Richard Clarke
Administrator: Shane McAteer
Sales & Marketing: Richard Tobin

*Academic & Scholarly; Biography &
Autobiography; Educational & Textbooks;
History & Antiquarian; Reference Books,
Directories & Dictionaries*

New Titles: 8 (1995), 11 (1996)
No of Employees: 32

ISBNs, Imprints & Series:
Directory of Irish Family History Research
0 901905 Educational Series, Familia,
Gravestone Inscription Series, Historical
Series

Distributor for:
Australia: New South Wales University Press.
Canada: Toronto University Press

Book Trade Association Membership: PA,
BA

1879

**UNITED KINGDOM COUNCIL FOR
HUMAN RIGHTS (UKCHR)**
17 Ravenscroft, Harpenden, Herts AL5 1ST
Telephone: 01582 715070

Co-ordinator: Dr Mark Ponnampalam, FRCS

*History & Antiquarian; Politics & World
Affairs; Sociology & Anthropology*

New Titles: 1 (1995), 2 (1996)

ISBNs, Imprints & Series: 0 9513759

1880

**UNITED WRITERS PUBLICATIONS
LTD**
Ailsa, Castle Gate, Penzance, Cornwall
TR20 8BG
Telephone: 01736 65954
Fax: 01736 65954

Editorial & Sales: M. Sheppard
Production: T. Sully

*Biography & Autobiography; Cinema, Video,
TV & Radio; Educational & Textbooks;
Fiction; Humour; Industry, Business &
Management; Science Fiction; Travel &
Topography*

New Titles: 6 (1995), 6 (1996)

ISBNs, Imprints & Series:
0 901976, 1 85200

1881 ▬▬▬▬▬▬

USBORNE PUBLISHING LTD
Usborne House, 83–85 Saffron Hill, London
EC1N 8RT
Telephone: 0171 430 2800
Fax: 0171 242 0974 & 430 1562

Warehouse:
D Services, Euston Street, Freemen's Common,
Aylestone Road, Leics LE2 7SS
Telephone: 01162 547671
Fax: 01162 544670

Director: T. P. Usborne *(Managing)*
Associate Directors: D. M. Lowe *(General
   Manager)*
Robert Jones *(Production)*
J. Tyler *(Editorial)*
D. Harte
L. Hunt
K. M. Ball *(Company Secretary)*
Rights Controller: E. Wright

*Children's Books; Computer Science; Crafts &
Hobbies; Fiction; Natural History; Reference
Books, Directories & Dictionaries; Scientific &
Technical; Sports & Games*

New Titles: 105 (1995), 120 (1996)
No of Employees: 110
Annual Turnover: £18M

ISBNs, Imprints & Series:
0 7460, 0 86020

Book Trade Association Membership: PA

1882 ▬▬▬▬▬▬

VACATION WORK
9 Park End Street, Oxford OX1 1HJ
Telephone: 01865 241978
Fax: 01865 790885

Director: Charles James
Accounts: Anne Hunt *(Book Sales)*
Editorial: David Woodworth

*English as a Foreign Language; Guide Books;
Travel & Topography; Vocational Training &
Careers*

New Titles: 12 (1995), 13 (1996)
No of Employees: 6

ISBNs, Imprints & Series:
0 907638, 0 911285, 1 85458, 4 385

Distributor for:
France: Vac Job. *USA:* Peterson's Guides

Overseas Representation *(see §7.3)*:
Australia: Bookwise International, Findon, SA
Benelux: Nilsson & Lamm BV, Weesp,
   Netherlands
USA: Peterson's Guides, Princeton, NJ

1883 ▬▬▬▬▬▬

VCH PUBLISHERS (UK) LTD
8 Wellington Court, Wellington Street,
Cambridge CB1 1HZ

Telephone: 01223 321111
Fax: 01223 313321

Managing Director: Christine White

*Biology & Zoology; Chemistry; Law;
Philosophy; Physics; Reference Books,
Directories & Dictionaries; Scientific &
Technical*

Parent Company:
VCH Verlagsgesellschaft *(Germany)*

Associated & Subsidiary Companies:
Academy Group Ltd. *Germany:* Akademie
Verlag; Ernst & Sohn Verlag. *Switzerland:*
VCH Verlag AG. *USA:* VCH Publishers Inc

Distributor for:
Germany: Carl Hanser Verlag; Siemens; VCH
Verlagsgesellschaft. *USA:* VCH Publishers Inc

Book Trade Association Membership: PA

1884 ▬▬▬▬▬▬

VELOCE PUBLISHING PLC
Godmanstone, Dorset DT2 7AE
Telephone: 01300 341602
Fax: 01300 341065

Directors: Rod Grainger
Judith Brooks

*Biography & Autobiography; Illustrated &
Fine Editions; Sports & Games; Transport*

New Titles: 10 (1995), 11 (1996)
No of Employees: 2
Annual Turnover: £250,000

ISBNs, Imprints & Series: 1 874105

Overseas Representation *(see §7.3)*:
Australia & New Zealand: Capricorn Link
   (Australia) Pty Ltd, Baulkham Hills, NSW,
   Australia
France: Trame Selection, Boulogne
Germany: Heel-Verlag, Konigswinter; Mehne
   Automobil Access, Bad Rappenau
Germany, Austria & Benelux: Anselm
   Robinson, London, UK
Japan: Shinada & Co Inc, Tokyo; Bookstore
   Co Ltd, Aichi-ken; Hokuto Corporation,
   Tokyo
Scandinavia: D. Richard Bowen, Malmö,
   Sweden
South Africa: Motor Books, Bryanston
Spain & Italy: Bookport Associates, Bologna,
   Italy
USA: Motorbooks International Publishers &
   Wholesalers Inc, Osceola, WI

1885 ▬▬▬▬▬▬

VERSO
6 Meard Street, London W1V 3HR
Telephone: 0171 437 3546 / 0171 434 1704
Fax: 0171 734 0059
Email: 100434.1414@compuserve.com

Distribution:
Marston Book Services

Directors: Lucy Heller *(Executive Chairman)*
Colin Robinson *(Managing)*
Tony Stevenson *(Finance)*

Managers: Malcolm Imrie *(Editorial)*
Amelia la Fuente Sanchez *(Marketing & Sales)*
Sophie Arditti *(Production)*
Gil McNeil *(Rights)*

*Academic & Scholarly; Economics;
Educational & Textbooks; Gender Studies;
History & Antiquarian; Literature & Criticism;
Philosophy; Politics & World Affairs;
Psychology & Psychiatry; Sociology &
Anthropology*

New Titles: 40 (1995), 48 (1996)
Annual Turnover: £2M

ISBNs, Imprints & Series:
0 86091, 1 85984

Overseas Representation *(see §7.3)*:
Australia & New Zealand: Allen & Unwin Pty
   Ltd, St Leonards, NSW, Australia
Belgium, Luxembourg & Netherlands:
   Netwerk, Academic Book Agency,
   Rotterdam, Netherlands
Canada: Routledge Inc, New York, NY, USA
Eastern Europe: Ms Sue Wilson, Budapest,
   Hungary
France, Spain, Italy, Portugal & Greece:
   Charles Gibbes, Buckingham, UK
Germany, Switzerland & Austria: The John
   Wilde Partnership, Lauf, Germany
Greece: Mark Tremlow, Vaula
Hong Kong, Taiwan & Korea: Knowledge
   Craft Ltd, Hong Kong
India: Maya Publishers Pvt Ltd, New Delhi
Japan: United Publishers Services Ltd, Tokyo
Malaysia: APD KL Ltd, Selangor Darul
Middle East & North Africa: International
   Publishers Representatives, Nicosia, Cyprus
Pakistan: Afro-Asian Book Co, Karachi
Philippines: Combined Book Representatives,
   Manila
Scandinavia: Ben Greig, Cambridge, UK
Singapore, Thailand & Brunei: APD Singapore
   Pte Ltd, Singapore
South Africa & Zimbabwe: David Philip
   Publishers Pty Ltd, Claremont, South Africa
Spain: Robery Pryor, Madrid
Turkey: Metis'Yayinlari, Istanbul
USA: Verso, New York, NY

1886 ▬▬▬▬▬▬

VERULAM PUBLISHING LTD
152a Park Street Lane, Park Street, St Albans,
Herts AL2 2AU
Telephone: 01727 872770
Fax: 01727 873866
Email: 100124.2375@compuserve.com

Distribution:
International Book Distributors Ltd,
Campus 400, Maylands Avenue,
Hemel Hempstead, Herts HP2 7EZ
Telephone: 01442 881900
Fax: 01442 882288

Directors: David Collins *(Managing)*
Penny Collins

*Humour; Languages & Linguistics; Transport;
Vocational Training & Careers*

ISBNs, Imprints & Series:
0 8442 NTC Publishing Group
0 88029 Dorset Press
0 902726 Thornton Cox Publishers

0 907938 Century 22
0 951553 Diamond Publishing
1 55013 Key Porter Books
1 55853 Rutledge Hill Press
1 85249 CAMRA
1 85882 Eric Dobby Publishing
1 873668 Take That Ltd
1 874504 Verulam
1 874687 Impact Books
1 874735 b small publishing

Distributor for:
b small publishing; CAMRA (Campaign for
Real Ale); Century 22; Diamond Publishing;
Eric Dobby Publishing; Impact Books; Take
That Ltd; Thornton Cox Publishers; Verbaid
Ltd; Working Books Ltd. *Canada:* Key Porter
Books. *USA:* Dorset Press/Barnes & Noble
Books; NTC Publishing Group; Rutledge Hill
Press

Overseas Representation *(see §7.3):*
Africa & Middle East: Len Ainsworth,
Aldbourne, UK
Canada: General Publishing Co Ltd, North
York, Ont
Europe: Bill Bailey Publishers
Representatives, Newton Abbot, UK
Irish Republic: Gill & Macmillan Ltd, Dublin
New Zealand: Greene Phoenix Marketing,
Helensville
South Africa: Alternative Books, Randburg

1887

**VICTORIA & ALBERT MUSEUM
PUBLICATIONS**
160 Brompton Road, London SW3 1HW
Telephone: 0171 938 9663
Fax: 0171 938 8370
Web Site: http://www.vam.ac.uk

Distribution:
Littlehampton Book Services Ltd,
14 Eldon Way, Littlehampton, West Sussex
BN17 7HE
Telephone: 01903 721596
Fax: 01903 730914
Email: 100067.1631@compuserve.com

Head of Publishing: Mary Butler
Editor: Miranda Harrison
Production: Lesley Burton

*Academic & Scholarly; Antiques & Collecting;
Architecture & Design; Fashion & Costume;
Fine Art & Art History; Theatre, Drama &
Dance*

New Titles: 2 (1995), 11 (1996)
No of Employees: 4

ISBNs, Imprints & Series:
0 905209, 0 948107, 1 85177

Parent Company:
Victoria & Albert Museum

Overseas Representation *(see §7.3):*
*Austria, Belgium, Germany, Luxembourg,
Switzerland & Yugoslav Republics:* Michael
Geoghegan, London, UK
Canada: Antique Collectors' Club Ltd,
Wappinger Falls, USA
Caribbean: Humphrys Roberts Associates,
London, UK
France: Critiques Livres, Bagnolet

Greece, Italy, Portugal & Spain: Janet Clark,
London, UK
Hong Kong, China, Taiwan & Korea: Asia
Publisher Services Ltd, Hong Kong
Japan: Japan English Services Inc, Chiba-ken
Middle East & Cyprus: Peter Ward Book
Exports, London, UK
Netherlands: Nilsson & Lamm BV, Weesp
New Zealand: Random House New Zealand
Ltd, Auckland
Pakistan: Shams Quaraeshi, Karachi
Scandinavia: Saga Books ApS, Copenhagen,
Denmark
Singapore, Malaysia, Indonesia & Thailand:
APD Singapore Pte Ltd, Singapore
*South & Central America, East, Central & West
Africa & India:* Cassell Plc (Sales Dept),
London, UK
South Africa: Random House South Africa Pty
Ltd, Rosebank, Johannesburg
USA: Trafalgar Square Publications, North
Pomfret, VT

Book Trade Association Membership:
International Association of Museum
Publishers

1888

VINYL EXPERIENCE LTD
18 Hanway Street, London W1P 9DD
Telephone: 0171 636 1281
Fax: 0171 636 0738

Director: Mark Hayward *(Foreign Sales)*
Publishing Executive: Zi Siddique
Design: Mike Edgar
Accounts: Hillen Shah

*Audio Books; Cinema, Video, TV & Radio;
Music*

New Titles: 30 (1996)
No of Employees: 10
Annual Turnover: £1.2M

ISBNs, Imprints & Series: 1 873884

1889

VIRAGO PRESS
[Imprint of Little, Brown & Co (UK)]
Brettenham House, Lancaster Place, London
WC2E 7EN
Telephone: 0171 911 8000
Fax: 0171 911 8100

Sales & Distribution:
Random Century House,
20 Vauxhall Bridge Road, London SW1V 2SA
Telephone: 0171 973 9740
Fax: 0171 233 6123

Publisher & Editor: Lennie Goodings
Editor: Sally Abbey
Editorial: Sarah White

*Biography & Autobiography; Crime; Fiction;
Gender Studies; History & Antiquarian;
Literature & Criticism; Politics & World
Affairs; Psychology & Psychiatry; Sociology &
Anthropology; Drama, Creative & Criticism*

New Titles: 55 (1995), 55 (1996)
No of Employees: 3

ISBNs, Imprints & Series:
0 86068, 1 85381, 1 86049

Parent Company:
Little, Brown & Co (UK)

Overseas Representation *(see §7.3):*
See: Little, Brown & Co (UK), UK

1890

VIRGIN PUBLISHING
332 Ladbroke Grove, London W10 5AH
Telephone: 0181 968 7554
Fax: 0181 968 0929

Directors: Rob Shreeve *(Managing)*
John Bond *(Marketing)*
Ray Mudie *(Home Sales)*
Nicky Stonehill *(Publicity)*
Michael Cohen *(Finance)*
Managers: Graham Eames *(Export Sales)*
Gill Woolcott *(Production)*
Editors: Rod Green *(General Editorial)*
Philip Dodd *(Illustrated)*
Peter Darvill-Evans *(Fiction)*

*Biography & Autobiography; Children's
Books; Cinema, Video, TV & Radio; Crime;
Fiction; Guide Books; Humour; Magic & the
Occult; Music; Reference Books, Directories &
Dictionaries; Sports & Games; Theatre,
Drama & Dance; Travel & Topography;
Leisure; Television*

ISBNs, Imprints & Series:
0 352 Blacklace, Nexus
0 426 Doctor Who
0 86369 Virgin (paperback)
1 85227 Virgin (hardback)

Parent Company:
Virgin Group Ltd

Overseas Representation *(see §7.3):*
Africa (excluding South Africa): Len
Ainsworth, Aldbourne, UK
Australia: Hodder Headline (Australia) Pty
Ltd, Rydalmere
Canada: General Publishing Co Ltd, North
York, Ont
Europe: Onslow Books Ltd, London, UK
Middle East: AIMS, Larkfield, UK
New Zealand: Hodder Moa Beckett Publishers
Ltd, Auckland
South Africa: Trinity Books CC, Randburg
West Indies, Central & South America:
Humphrys Roberts Associates, London, UK

1891

VIRTUE BOOKS LTD
Edward House, Tenter Street, Rotherham
S60 1LB
Telephone: 01709 365005
Fax: 01709 829982

Directors: Michael Virtue *(Sales)*
Peter Russum *(Managing)*

Cookery, Wines & Spirits

New Titles: 3 (1996)

ISBNs, Imprints & Series: 0 900778

Parent Company:
E. Russum & Sons Ltd

Overseas Representation *(see §7.3)*:
Australia: The Cookery Book, Crows Nest,
NSW
Caribbean: Kelvin van Hasselt Publishing
Services, Lymington, UK
Cyprus: Pergamon Bookhouse, Nicosia
Hong Kong: I.I.H.T.
Malta: Kekoo Modi, San Pawl Tat-Targa
New Zealand: Virtue Books (NZ), Auckland
South Africa: PMC International, Durban North

1892

STUDIO VISTA
Wellington House, 125 Strand, London
WC2R 0BB
Telephone: 0171 420 5555
Fax: 0171 240 7261

Distribution:
Cassell Plc, Stanley House, 3 Fleets Lane,
Poole, Dorset BH15 3AJ
Telephone: 01202 665432
Fax: 01202 666219

Directors: Philip Sturrock *(Chairman)*
Geoffrey Charters *(Production)*
Frank Roney *(Finance)*
Alison Goff *(Editorial)*
Martyn Chapman *(Distribution & Commercial)*
Kevin Bristow *(Sales & Marketing)*
Andrew Macmillan *(UK Sales)*
Michael Goff *(Export Sales)*
Adrienne Maguire *(Marketing)*
Commissioning Editor: Barry Holmes
Managers: John Mills *(Export Sales)*
Chris White *(Book Clubs)*
David Williams *(Special Sales)*
Joanna Lawrie *(Rights)*

*Antiques & Collecting; Architecture & Design;
Cinema, Video, TV & Radio; Fine Art & Art
History; Illustrated & Fine Editions;
Photography*

ISBNs, Imprints & Series: 0 289

Parent Company:
Cassell Plc

Associated & Subsidiary Companies:
Blandford Press; Cassell; Ward Lock

Overseas Representation *(see §7.3)*:
See: Cassell Plc, UK

1893

VOLCANO PRESS LTD
PO Box 139, Leicester LE2 2YH
Telephone: 0116 270 6714
Fax: 0116 270 6714

Warehouse:
121 Devana Road, Leicester LE2 1PL

Sales, Rights & Permissions: A. Hussain
Editorial: F. Hussain

*Academic & Scholarly; Educational &
Textbooks; Gender Studies; Guide Books;
Politics & World Affairs; Reference Books,
Directories & Dictionaries; Religion &
Theology; Sociology & Anthropology*

New Titles: 3 (1996)

ISBNs, Imprints & Series: 1 870127

Book Trade Association Membership: IPG

1894

VOLTAIRE FOUNDATION LTD
99 Banbury Road, Oxford OX2 6JX
Telephone: 01865 284600
Fax: 01865 284610
Email: email@voltaire.ox.ac.uk
Web Site: http://www.voltaire.ox.ac.uk

Executive Director: Andrew Brown *(Sales,
Rights & Permissions)*

*Academic & Scholarly; Bibliography &
Library Science; History & Antiquarian;
Languages & Linguistics; Literature &
Criticism*

ISBNs, Imprints & Series: 0 7294

Parent Company:
University of Oxford

Overseas Representation *(see §7.3)*:
France: Universitas, Paris

1895

UNIVERSITY OF WALES PRESS
6 Gwennyth Street, Cathays, Cardiff CF2 4YD
Telephone: 01222 231919
Fax: 01222 230908
Email: press@wales.ac.uk
Web Site: http://www.swan.ac.uk/uwp/home.
htm

Director: Ned Thomas
Sales: Richard Houdmont *(Commercial
Manager)*
Permissions: Ms Liz Powell *(Editor)*
Editorial: Susan Jenkins *(Senior Editor)*

*Academic & Scholarly; Archaeology;
Biography & Autobiography; Educational &
Textbooks; Gender Studies; History &
Antiquarian; Languages & Linguistics;
Literature & Criticism; Reference Books,
Directories & Dictionaries; Religion &
Theology*

New Titles: 55 (1995), 60 (1996)
No of Employees: 15
Annual Turnover: £350,000

ISBNs, Imprints & Series:
0 7083, 0 900768 GPC Books, Gwasg Prifysgol
Cymru, University of Wales Press

Parent Company:
University of Wales

Distributor for:
The Glamorgan County History Trust; National
Museum of Wales; Temple University Press
(one title); Zena Publications *(one title)*

Overseas Representation *(see §7.3)*:
Australia: St Clair Press Pty Ltd, Rozelle, NSW

Europe: Book Representation & Distribution
(BRAD), Hadleigh, UK
USA & Canada: Paul & Co Publishers
Consortium Inc, Concord, MA, USA

Book Trade Association Membership: Union
of Welsh Publishers

1896

WALKER BOOKS LTD
87 Vauxhall Walk, London SE11 5HJ
Telephone: 0171 793 0909
Fax: 0171 587 1123

**Trade Orders & Customer Service
Enquiries:**
Faber Book Services, Burnt Mill,
Elizabeth Way, Harlow, Essex CM20 2HX
Telephone: 01279 417134
Fax: 01279 417366

Chairman & Editorial: David Lloyd
Directors: David Heatherwick *(Financial,
Managing)*
Judy Burdsall *(Merchandise)*
Wendy Boase *(Editorial)*
Henryk Wesolowski *(Sales & Marketing)*
Export: Fiona MacDonald
Foreign Rights: Caroline Muir

Children's Books

New Titles: 300 (1995), 300 (1996)
No of Employees: 115

ISBNs, Imprints & Series:
0 7445 Read & Wonder, Sprinters, Walker
Books

Associated & Subsidiary Companies:
Australia: Walker Books. *USA:* Candlewick
Press Inc

Overseas Representation *(see §7.3)*:
Australia: Walker Books Australia, Sydney
Canada: Candlewick Press Inc, Toronto
*Caribbean (excluding Jamaica & Trinidad) &
Netherlands Antilles:* C. D. A. Walker,
Christchurch, Barbados
Europe: Books for Europe Ltd, Bournemouth,
UK
Gulf Area: Media & Marketing Network,
Dubai, UAE
Hong Kong, Taiwan & Korea: Richard Blady
Booksales, Macclesfield, UK
India, Pakistan & Philippines: Balatbat & Sons
International, Quezon City, Philippines
Jamaica, Trinidad & Latin America:
Humphrys Roberts Associates, London, UK
Japan: Macmillan Shuppan KK, Tokyo
Middle East & North Africa: Eastern Company
for Publications, Beirut, Lebanon
New Zealand: Random House New Zealand
Ltd, Auckland
Scandinavia: Saga Books ApS, Copenhagen,
Denmark
Singapore, Thailand, Malaysia & Brunei:
Pansing Distribution Sdn Bhd, Singapore
South Africa: Random House South Africa Pty
Ltd, Rosebank, Johannesburg
USA: Candlewick Press, Cambridge, MA

1897 ▬▬▬▬▬▬▬▬

WARD LOCK LTD
Wellington House, 125 Strand, London
WC2R 0BB
Telephone: 0171 420 5555
Fax: 0171 240 7261

Trade Counter & Warehouse:
Cassell Plc, Stanley House, 3 Fleets Lane,
Poole, Dorset BH15 3AJ
Telephone: 01202 665432
Fax: 01202 666219

Directors: Philip Sturrock (Chairman)
Alison Goff (Editorial)
Geoffrey Charters (Production)
Frank Roney (Finance)
Martyn Chapman (Commercial & Distribution)
Kevin Bristow (Sales & Marketing)
Andrew Macmillan (UK Trade Sales)
Michael Goff (International Sales)
Joanna Lawrie (Rights)
Managers: Chris White (Book Clubs)
David Williams (Central Accounts)
John Mills (Export Sales)
Dinah Parkinson (Production)

Cookery, Wines & Spirits; Crafts & Hobbies;
Do-It-Yourself; Gardening; Guide Books;
Health & Beauty; Reference Books, Directories
& Dictionaries; Sports & Games

ISBNs, Imprints & Series: 0 7063

Parent Company:
Cassell Plc

Overseas Representation (see §7.3):
See: Blandford Press, UK

1898 ▬▬▬▬▬▬▬▬

WARD LOCK EDUCATIONAL CO LTD
1 Christopher Road, East Grinstead,
West Sussex RH19 3BT
Telephone: 01342 318980
Fax: 01342 410980

**Warehouse (Orders, Returns to West Sussex
address above):**
Bookpoint Ltd, 39 Milton Park, Abingdon,
Oxon OX14 4TD
Telephone: 01235 400400
Fax: 01235 832068

Director: Au Bak Ling (Chairman—Hong
Kong)
Editorial: Rose Hill
Managers: Penny Kitchenham (General)
John Gamble (Finance & Administration)

Biology & Zoology; Chemistry; Educational &
Textbooks; Geography & Geology;
Mathematics & Statistics; Music; Physics;
Religion & Theology; English

New Titles: 30 (1995), 30 (1996)
No of Employees: 7

ISBNs, Imprints & Series: 0 7062

Parent Company:
Ling Kee (UK) Ltd

Associated & Subsidiary Companies:
BLA Publishing Ltd

Overseas Representation (see §7.3):
see: Cassell Plc, UK

1899 ▬▬▬▬▬▬▬▬

FREDERICK WARNE & CO LTD
27 Wrights Lane, London W8 5TZ
Telephone: 0171 416 3000
Fax: 0171 416 3199

Warehouse, Trade Enquiries & Orders:
Penguin Books Ltd, Bath Road,
Harmondsworth, Middx
Telephone: 0181 899 4000
Fax: 0181 899 4099

Directors: Sally Floyer (Publisher)
Stephen Hall (Group Development)
John Rolfe (Publishing Operations)

Children's Books; Illustrated & Fine Editions

ISBNs, Imprints & Series: 0 7232

Parent Company:
Penguin Books Ltd

Overseas Representation (see §7.3):
Australia: Penguin Books Australia Ltd,
Ringwood, Vic
Canada: Penguin Books Canada Ltd,
Newmarket, Ont
France: Penguin France SA, Toulouse
Germany & Austria: Penguin Books
Deutschland GmbH, Frankfurt, Germany
Greece, Israel & Cyprus: Penguin Hellas Ltd,
Athens, Greece
India, Bangladesh, Pakistan & Sri Lanka:
Penguin Books India Pvt Ltd, New Delhi,
India
Italy: Penguin Italia Srl, Milan
Japan: Penguin Books Japan, Tokyo
Korea: Addison-Wesley Korea, Seoul, Korea,
South
Malaysia: STP Distributors (M) Sdn Bhd, Shah
Alam
Netherlands: Penguin Books Netherlands bv,
Amsterdam
New Zealand: Penguin Books (New Zealand)
Ltd, Auckland
Portugal: Longman Penguin Portugal, Lisbon
Singapore: STP Distributors Pte Ltd
South Africa: Longman Penguin South Africa,
Bertsham
South America: Humphrys Roberts Associates,
Cotia, Brazil
Spain: Penguin Books SA, Madrid
Switzerland: OLF SA, Fribourg
Turkey: Sezai, Istanbul

1900 ▬▬▬▬▬▬▬▬

THE WATTS PUBLISHING GROUP
[a division of Grolier Ltd]
96 Leonard Street, London EC2A 4RH
Telephone: 0171 739 2929
Fax: 0171 739 6487

Warehouse & Distribution:
Tiptree Book Services Ltd, Tiptree, Colchester,
Essex CO5 0SR
Telephone: 01621 816362
Fax: 01621 819011

Directors: Marlene Johnson (Managing/
Finance & Operations)
Francesca Dow (Publisher: Orchard)

Philippa Stewart (Editorial: Franklin Watts)
Rita Ireland (Production)
George Spicer (Trade Sales)
Sarah Odedina (Group Rights)
Jill Sharpe (Educational Sales)
Managers: Linda Banner (Promotion)
Anne Marimuthu (Finance)
Directors: Jill Thorpe (International Sales)

Audio Books; Children's Books; Educational &
Textbooks; Fiction; Poetry; Reference Books,
Directories & Dictionaries; Books for Babies;
Novelty Books

New Titles: 300 (1995), 300 (1996)
No of Employees: 49
Annual Turnover: £9M

ISBNs, Imprints & Series:
Aladdin/Watts, Franklin Watts, Orchard Books,
Two-can/Watts, Watts Books

Parent Company:
Grolier Inc (USA)

Distributor for:
Aladdin; Two-can

Overseas Representation (see §7.3):
Australia & New Zealand: Franklin Watts
Australia, Lane Cove, Australia
Europe: Roger Smith, Enfield, UK
Irish Republic & Northern Ireland: Gill Hess
Ltd, Skerries, Irish Republic
Japan: Japan English Services Inc, Chiba-ken
Middle East, Cyprus & Pakistan: Anthony
Rudkin Associates, Oxford, UK
Pacific Islands (excluding Australia & New
Zealand): La Galamo Office & School
Supplies Pty Ltd, Lae, Papua New Guinea
Scandinavia: D. Richard Bowen, Malmö,
Sweden
South Africa, Swaziland, Kwazulu &
Bophutatswana: Leo Books, Roggebaai &
Cape Town, South Africa

Book Trade Association Membership: PA,
BDC, EPC

1901 ▬▬▬▬▬▬▬▬

WAYLAND PUBLISHERS LTD
61 Western Road, Hove, East Sussex BN3 1JD
Telephone: 01273 722561
Fax: 01273 329314/723526

Warehouse:
Bailey Bros Distribution, Unit 1, Learoyd Rd,
Mountfield Est, New Romney, Kent
TN28 8XU
Telephone: 01679 66905
Fax: 01679 66638

Directors: J. P. Dubois (Chairman)
John Lewis (Managing)
Stephen White-Thomson (Editorial)
Bernard Nevin (UK Sales)
Keith Lilley (International Sales & Foreign
Rights)
Martin Jane (Finance)
Operations Manager: Oonagh Gretton

Children's Books; Educational & Textbooks

ISBNs, Imprints & Series:
0 7502, 0 85078, 0 85340, 0 904724, 1 85210, 1
85485

Parent Company:
Wolters Kluwer UK Plc

Associated & Subsidiary Companies:
Priory Press Ltd; Sovereign Books Ltd

Overseas Representation *(see §7.3):*
Australia: Lothian Books, Port Melbourne
Brunei, Indonesia, Singapore & Thailand:
  Publishers Marketing Services Ltd,
  Singapore
Canada: Nelson Canada, Scarborough
Caribbean: Humphrys Roberts Associates,
  London, UK
Finland: Interbook Interkirja Oy, Helsinki
Irish Republic: Gill & Macmillan Ltd, Dublin
Kuwait: Al Lugain Co, Salmiya
Lebanon: Universal Book House for Print &
  Distribution, Saida
Malaysia: Publishers Marketing Services,
  Petaling Jaya
New Zealand: Forrester Books Ltd, Auckland
Papua New Guinea, Solomon Islands &
  Vanuatu: La Galamo Office & School
  Supplies Pty Ltd, Lae, Papua New Guinea
Philippines, Taiwan, South Korea & Japan:
  Combined Book Representatives, Manila,
  Philippines
South Africa: Southern Book Publishers,
  Hurlyvale

Book Trade Association Membership: PA,
EPC, BEEA

1902 ▬▬▬▬▬▬

**WEBSTERS INTERNATIONAL
PUBLISHERS LTD**
Axe and Bottle Court, 70 Newcomen Street,
London SE1 1YT
Telephone: 0171 407 2846/5956
Fax: 0171 407 6437

Directors: Susannah Webster *(Publishing)*
Adrian Webster *(Chairman & Managing, Sales
  & Rights)*
Claire Harcup *(Editorial)*
Jean-Luc Barbanneau *(Managing)*

*Cookery, Wines & Spirits; Guide Books; Health
& Beauty; Travel & Topography*

New Titles: 6 (1995), 6 (1996)
No of Employees: 60
Annual Turnover: £3M

Associated & Subsidiary Companies:
Adrian Webster Ltd; Websters Multimedia Ltd

1903 ▬▬▬▬▬▬

WEIDENFELD & NICOLSON
[Imprint of The Orion Publishing Group Ltd]
Orion House, 5 Upper St Martin's Lane,
London WC2H 9EA
Telephone: 0171 240 3444
Fax: 0171 240 4822

Trade Counter & Warehouse:
Littlehampton Book Services Ltd,
14 Eldon Way, Lineside Estate, Littlehampton,
West Sussex BN17 7HE
Telephone: 01903 726410
Fax: 01903 730914

Publishing Directors: Ion Trewin *(General)*
Michael Dover *(Illustrated)*

*Academic & Scholarly; Architecture & Design;
Biography & Autobiography; Cookery, Wines
& Spirits; Crafts & Hobbies; Economics;
Educational & Textbooks; Fiction; Fine Art &
Art History; Gardening; Guide Books;
Humour; Illustrated & Fine Editions; Industry,
Business & Management; Law; Literature &
Criticism; Philosophy; Photography; Politics
& World Affairs; Sports & Games; Travel &
Topography*

ISBNs, Imprints & Series: 0 297

Parent Company:
The Orion Publishing Group Ltd

Overseas Representation *(see §7.3):*
see: The Orion Publishing Group Ltd, London,
UK

1904 ▬▬▬▬▬▬

WESTERN PUBLISHING CO INC
25–31 Tavistock Place, London WC1H 9SU
Telephone: 0171 323 1212
Fax: 0171 255 2051

Warehouse & Trade Enquiries:
Nedlloyd Districenters, Unit 185B,
Milton Park, Milton, Nr Abingdon, Oxon
OX14 4PR
Telephone: 01235 821100
Fax: 01235 821101

Directors: David Guild *(Managing)*
Vytas Karpavicius *(Sales)*
Financial Controller: Paul Price
Managers: Ian Wallace *(Rights)*
John Wilson *(Export)*

Children's Books; Electronic (Entertainment)

New Titles: 45 (1995), 35 (1996)
No of Employees: 15
Annual Turnover: £5M

Parent Company:
Western Publishing Co Inc *(USA)*

1905 ▬▬▬▬▬▬

WESTVIEW PRESS
12 Hid's Copse Road, Cumnor Hill, Oxford
OX2 9JJ
Telephone: 01865 865466
Fax: 01865 862763
Email: westview@oxfpubp.demon.co.uk

Warehouse:
Plymbridge Distributors Ltd, Estover,
Plymouth PL6 7PZ
Telephone: 01752 202300
Fax: 01752 202330

Managers: Sue Miller *(Rights & Permissions,
  General Enquiries, Editorial, Marketing)*
Alice Meadows *(Rights & Permissions,
  General Enquiries, Marketing)*

*Academic & Scholarly; Agriculture;
Economics; Environment & Development
Studies; Gay & Lesbian Studies; Gender
Studies; Geography & Geology; Law; Military
& War; Philosophy; Politics & World Affairs;
Psychology & Psychiatry; Sociology &
Anthropology*

ISBNs, Imprints & Series:
0 8133, 0 86531, 0 89158

Parent Company:
Westview Press *(USA)*

Book Trade Association Membership: IPG

1906 ▬▬▬▬▬▬

WHARNCLIFFE PUBLISHING LTD
47 Church Street, Barnsley, South Yorkshire
S70 2AS
Telephone: 01226 734241
Fax: 01226 734438
Email: p&sword@barnsley-chronicle.co.uk
Web Site: http://www.yorkshire-web.co.uk/ps/
pshome.html

Chairman & Managing Director: Sir
  Nicholas Hewitt, Bt
**Deputy Managing Director & Company
  Secretary:** T. G. Hewitt
Managers: Barbara Bramall *(Book Publishing)*
Alan Twiddle *(Business Development)*
Consultant: J. B. Bayne

*Atlases & Maps; Aviation; Cookery, Wines &
Spirits; Guide Books; History & Antiquarian;
Military & War; Sports & Games; Transport*

New Titles: 5 (1995), 5 (1996)
No of Employees: 6

ISBNs, Imprints & Series: 0 871647

Parent Company:
The Barnsley Chronicle Ltd

Associated & Subsidiary Companies:
Pen & Sword Books Ltd

Overseas Representation *(see §7.3):*
Australia: Peribo Pty Ltd, Mount Kuring-gai,
  NSW
Canada: Vanwell Publishing Ltd, St
  Catherines, Ont
New Zealand: South Pacific Books (Imports) ,
  Ltd, Auckland
USA: Trans-Atlantic Publications Inc,
  Philadelphia, PA

Book Trade Association Membership: PA

1907 ▬▬▬▬▬▬

WHELDON & WESLEY LTD
Lytton Lodge, Codicote, Hitchin, Herts
SG4 8TE
Telephone: 01438 820370
Fax: 01438 821478
Email: wheldwes@dircon.co.uk

Chairman: A. H. Swann
Managing Director: Christopher K. Swann

*Biology & Zoology; Gardening; Natural
History*

ISBNs, Imprints & Series: 0 85486

Book Trade Association Membership: BA,
ABA

1908

WHICH? BOOKS
2 Marylebone Road, London NW1 4DF
Telephone: 0171 830 6000
Fax: 0171 830 7660
Email: editor@which.co.uk

Trade Enquiries:
Penguin Books Ltd, 27 Wrights Lane, London
W8
Telephone: 0171 416 3166
Fax: 0171 416 3198

Assistant Director: Kim Lavely
Head of Publishing: Gill Rowley
Production Manager: Brenda Follett

*Crafts & Hobbies; Do-It-Yourself; Gardening;
Guide Books; Travel & Topography; Legal and
Practical Advice for Consumers; Personal
Finance*

New Titles: 26 (1995), 23 (1996)

ISBNs, Imprints & Series:
0 85202 Which? Consumer Guides, Which?
Travel Guides

Parent Company:
Which? Ltd *(part of Consumers' Association)*

Book Trade Association Membership: PA

1909

J. WHITAKER & SONS LTD
12 Dyott Street, London WC1A 1DF
Telephone: 0171 420 6000
Fax: 0171 836 2909

Directors: David Whitaker, OBE *(Chairman)*
Sally Whitaker *(Managing)*
Martin Whitaker
Peter Allsop, CBE, FBIM, FRSA
Paul Pounsford
R. F. Baum
Jonathan Nowell
Tom Sweetman, FCA
John Lycett
Chris Ostrom
Sales Manager: Simon Skinner

*Bibliography & Library Science; Reference
Books, Directories & Dictionaries*

ISBNs, Imprints & Series: 0 85021

Associated & Subsidiary Companies:
BookTrack Ltd; Standard Book Numbering
Agency Ltd; TeleOrdering Ltd; UK Standard
Address Numbering Agency Ltd; UK Standard
Book Numbering Agency Ltd

Overseas Representation *(see §7.3)*:
Australia: D. W. Thorpe, Port Melbourne
India: Aditya Books, New Delhi
Japan: United Publishers Services Ltd, Tokyo
New Zealand: D. W. Thorpe (New Zealand),
Wellington
Singapore: Information Access & Distribution
Pte Ltd
South Africa: Oxford University Press,
Capetown
Spain: Iberian Book Services SL, Madrid
USA & Canada: R. R. Bowker, New
Providence, NJ, USA

USA (Whitaker's Almanack only): Gale
Research Co, Detroit, USA

Book Trade Association Membership: PA,
IPG, DPA

1910

WHITE EAGLE PUBLISHING TRUST
New Lands, Brewells Lane, Liss, Hants
GU33 7HY
Telephone: 01730 893300
Fax: 01730 892235

Editorial: Mrs Y. G. Hayward
J. C. Hayward *(Production/Sales Promotion)*
Treasurer: G. R. H. Dent *(Sales, Rights &
Permissions)*

Religion & Theology

New Titles: 2 (1995), 1 (1996)
No of Employees: 12
Annual Turnover: £181,000

ISBNs, Imprints & Series: 0 85487

Overseas Representation *(see §7.3)*:
Australia: The White Eagle Lodge of
Australasia Ltd, Maleny; Quest Book
Agency, Sydney
Irish Republic: Cosmic Sounds Ltd, Dublin
South Africa: Richford Enterprises Pty,
Durban; Chris and Candy Legg, Cape Town
USA: De Vorss & Co Inc, Marina del Rey, CA

Book Trade Association Membership: IPG

1911

WHITTET BOOKS LTD
18 Anley Road, London W14 0BY
Telephone: 0171 603 1139
Fax: 0171 603 8154

Warehouse:
Biblios Publishers Distribution Services,
Star Industrial Estate, Partridge Green,
Horsham, West Sussex RH13 8LD
Telephone: 01403 710971
Fax: 01403 711143

Managing Director: Annabel Whittet

*Animal Care & Breeding; Biology & Zoology;
Illustrated & Fine Editions; Natural History;
Transport; Travel & Topography*

New Titles: 6 (1995), 7 (1996)

ISBNs, Imprints & Series:
0 905483, 1 873580

Parent Company:
A. Whittet & Co Ltd

Overseas Representation *(see §7.3)*:
USA & Canada: Diamond Farm Book
Publishers, Brighton, Canada

1912

WHITTLES PUBLISHING
Roseleigh House, Harbour Road,
Latheronwheel, Caithness KW5 6DW
Telephone: 01593 741240
Fax: 01593 741360

Warehouse/Distributor:
Scottish Book Source, 137 Dundee Street,
Edinburgh EH11 1BG
Telephone: 0131 229 6800
Fax: 0131 229 9070

Proprietor: Dr Keith Whittles *(Publisher)*

*Academic & Scholarly; Engineering;
Geography & Geology; Scientific & Technical;
General*

New Titles: 3 (1995), 9 (1996)
No of Employees: 4

ISBNs, Imprints & Series: 1 870325

Overseas Representation *(see §7.3)*:
Australia: DA Books, Mitcham, Vic
Germany: Sven von Loga, Köln-Raderberg
South East & North East Asia: STM Publishers
Services Pte Ltd, Singapore
Southern Africa: Russell Friedman Information
Services (Pty) Ltd, Cape Town, South Africa

Book Trade Association Membership:
Scottish PA

1913

WHURR PUBLISHERS LTD
19b Compton Terrace, London N1 2UN
Telephone: 0171 359 5979
Fax: 0171 226 5290

Warehouse, Trade Enquiries & Orders:
Turpin Distribution Services Ltd,
Blackhorse Road, Letchworth, Herts SG6 1HN
Telephone: 01462 672555
Fax: 01462 480947

Managing Director: Colin Whurr
Marketing Executive: Sarah Vicary
Editorial: Margaret Gallagher

*Industry, Business & Management; Medical
(incl. Self Help & Alternative Medicine);
Psychology & Psychiatry; Scientific &
Technical*

ISBNs, Imprints & Series:
1 870332 Whurr Publishers
1 871381 Cole & Whurr

Distributor for:
Cole & Whurr Ltd

Overseas Representation *(see §7.3)*:
USA & Canada: Singular Publishing Group
Inc, San Diego, USA

Book Trade Association Membership: PA,
BDC, CAPP, IPG

1914

WILD GOOSE PUBLICATIONS
Unit 15, Six Harmony Row, Glasgow G51 3UU
Telephone: 0141 440 0985
Fax: 0141 440 2338
Email: ionacomm@mainland.demon.co.uk

Production Controller:
Morning Mist, Horsecombe Vale,
Combe Down, Bath BA2 5QR
Telephone: 01225 837313
Fax: 01225 837313

Trade Orders:
St Andrew Press, 121 George Street, Edinburgh
EH2 4YN
Telephone: 0131 225 5722
Fax: 0131 220 3113

Managing Editor: Sarelle Reid

*Music; Religion & Theology; Theatre, Drama
& Dance*

New Titles: 5 (1995), 5 (1996)
No of Employees: 3
Annual Turnover: £174,000

ISBNs, Imprints & Series:
0 947988, 0 9501351 Songs of the World
   Church, Wild Goose Prints (Drama), Wild
   Goose Song Books

Parent Company:
The Iona Community

Distributor for:
Sweden: Utryck

Overseas Representation *(see §7.3):*
Australia & New Zealand: Willow Connection
   Pty Ltd, Manly Vale, NSW, Australia
North America: GIA Publications, Chicago, IL,
   USA

Book Trade Association Membership:
Scottish PA

1915 ▬▬▬

JOHN WILEY & SONS LTD
Baffins Lane, Chichester, West Sussex
PO19 1UD
Telephone: 01243 779777
Fax: 01243 775878
Email: europe@wiley.co.uk
Web Site: http://www.wiley.co.uk

Packaging & Distribution Centre:
Shripney Road, Bognor Regis, West Sussex
PO22 9SA
Telephone: 01243 779777
Fax: 01243 820250

Directors: P. W. Ferris *(I.T. & Production)*
C. J. Dicks *(Financial)*
Dr M. Dixon *(Publishing STM)*
C. R. Ellis *(USA)*
Dr J. Jarvis *(Managing)*
R. Long *(Sales & Marketing)*
R. S. Mair *(Publishing Professional)*
UK Sales Manager: T. Armstrong
Rights & Permissions: Mrs S. Morris
   (Director of Copyright & Licensing)
Mrs D. Southern *(Permissions)*
Mrs F. Naylor *(Rights)*
Promotion & Export Sales: P. Kisray
   (General Sales Manager)
P. Holmes *(Marketing)*

*Academic & Scholarly; Accountancy &
Taxation; Agriculture; Architecture & Design;
Biography & Autobiography; Biology &
Zoology; Chemistry; Computer Science;
Economics; Electronic (Educational);
Electronic (Professional & Academic);
Engineering; Environment & Development
Studies; Geography & Geology; Health &
Beauty; History & Antiquarian; Industry,
Business & Management; Languages &*

*Linguistics; Law; Mathematics & Statistics;
Medical (incl. Self Help & Alternative
Medicine); Natural History; Physics; Politics
& World Affairs; Psychology & Psychiatry;
Reference Books, Directories & Dictionaries;
Scientific & Technical; Travel & Topography;
Veterinary Science; Vocational Training &
Careers*

New Titles: 390 (1995), 400 (1996)
No of Employees: 355
Annual Turnover: £41.5M

ISBNs, Imprints & Series:
0 470, 0 471

Parent Company:
Wiley Europe Ltd

Associated & Subsidiary Companies:
Chancery Law Publishing Ltd; Wiley Heyden
Ltd

Distributor for:
Institute of Petroleum; Kegan Paul
International; Pentech Press; Research Studies
Press. *USA:* California University Press;
Columbia University Press; Dorset House
Publishing Co Inc; Harvard University Press;
Indiana University Press; Loeb; The MIT Press;
W. W. Norton & Co Ltd; Princeton University
Press; The University of Chicago Press; Yale
University Press

Overseas Representation *(see §7.3):*
Australia: Jacaranda Wiley Ltd, Milton,
   Queensland
Canada: John Wiley & Sons Canada Ltd,
   Rexdale
Japan: John Wiley & Sons Ltd, Tokyo
*Mexico & Latin America, Pakistan & North
   Africa:* John Wiley & Sons Inc, New York,
   USA
Singapore & Asia: John Wiley & Sons (Asia)
   Pte Ltd, Singapore

Book Trade Association Membership: PA,
BDC, IEPRC, CAPP

1916 ▬▬▬

TONY WILLIAMS PUBLICATIONS
Helland, North Curry, Taunton, Somerset
TA3 6DU
Telephone: 01823 490694
Fax: 01823 490281

Sales: George Brown
Tony Williams

Sports & Games

ISBNs, Imprints & Series: 1 869833

1917 ▬▬▬

PHILIP WILSON PUBLISHERS LTD
143–149 Great Portland Street, London
W1N 5FB
Telephone: 0171 436 4485
Fax: 0171 436 4403

Directors: Philip Wilson *(Chairman)*
Antony White *(Managing)*
Peter Jawardena *(Finance)*
Anne Jackson *(Publishing, Editorial)*
Mary Osborne *(Production)*

Managers: Elisabeth Wilson *(Rights)*
Elaine Lewis *(Sales)*
Dan Giles *(Publishing)*

*Antiques & Collecting; Architecture & Design;
Fine Art & Art History*

New Titles: 21 (1995), 17 (1996)
No of Employees: 17
Annual Turnover: £646,000

ISBNs, Imprints & Series:
0 302 Zwemmer
0 85667 Sotheby's Publications, Philip Wilson
1 85759, 1 870248 Scala Publications
1 871489 Flint River Press

Associated & Subsidiary Companies:
Flint River Press Ltd; Scala Publications Ltd

Overseas Representation *(see §7.3):*
Australia: Thames & Hudson (Australia) Pty
   Ltd, Port Melbourne, Vic
Benelux: Exhibitions International, Leuven,
   Belgium
Brazil: Livraria Gaudi Ltda, São Paulo
France: Interart sarl, Paris
*Hong Kong, Japan, Korea, Macau, Taiwan &
   China:* Asia Publisher Services Ltd, Hong
   Kong
India (New Delhi only): TBI Publishers'
   Distributors, New Delhi, India
Israel: David Wine, Jerusalem
Italy: Penny Padovani, London, UK
Middle East: Michael Morris Associates,
   Saffron Walden, UK
Scandinavia: Hanne Rotovnik, Klampenborg,
   Denmark
Singapore, Indonesia & Thailand: APD
   Singapore Pte Ltd, Singapore
South Africa: Verbatim Distributors,
   Constantia Hills
Spain, Portugal & Switzerland: Janet Clark,
   London, UK
USA & Canada: Antique Collectors' Club Ltd,
   Wappinger Falls, USA

Book Trade Association Membership: PA

1918 ▬▬▬

WINDHORSE PUBLICATIONS
Unit 1/316, The Custard Factory, Gibb Street,
Digbeth, Birmingham B9 4AA
Telephone: 0121 604 1640
Fax: 0121 604 1640
Email: 100331.3327@compuserve.com

Editorial:
Telephone: 0121 604 9977
Fax: 0121 604 1640
Email: 100545.2201@compuserve.com

Chairman, Editor in Chief: Terence Pilchick
   (Rights & Permissions)
Operations: Alan Sabatini

*Biography & Autobiography; Philosophy;
Poetry; Religion & Theology*

New Titles: 8 (1995), 10 (1996)
No of Employees: 10
Annual Turnover: £250,000

ISBNs, Imprints & Series:
0 904766, 1 899579

Distributor for:
Dharmachakra Tapes; Weatherlight Press;
Western Buddhist Review. *USA:* Dharma
Publishing

Overseas Representation *(see §7.3):*
Australia & New Zealand: Windhorse Books,
Newtown, NSW, Australia
India: Windhorse India, Poona
USA: Windhorse Publications Inc, Newmarket,
NH

Book Trade Association Membership: IPG

1919 ▬▬▬

WINDROW & GREENE
5 Gerrard Street, London W1V 7LS
Telephone: 0171 240 4570
Fax: 0171 494 0583

Warehouse:
Littlehampton Book Services Ltd,
10–14 Eldon Way, Lineside Estate,
Littlehampton BN17 7HE
Telephone: 01903 721596
Fax: 01903 730914

Directors: Alan Greene *(Managing)*
Martin Windrow *(Editorial)*

*Aviation; Crafts & Hobbies; Military & War;
Transport*

New Titles: 24 (1995), 27 (1996)
No of Employees: 3
Annual Turnover: £700,000

ISBNs, Imprints & Series:
1 872004 Europa Militaria Series, Wag Books

Overseas Representation *(see §7.3):*
Australia & New Zealand: Peribo Pty Ltd,
Mount Kuring-gai, NSW, Australia
Austria, Switzerland & Italy: Juliusz
Komarnicki, Massagno, Switzerland
Far East: Richard Blady Booksales,
Macclesfield, UK
France, Greece & Yugoslavia: Books for
Europe Ltd, Bournemouth, UK
*Germany, Belgium, Luxembourg &
Netherlands:* PKB – Robbert J. Pleysier,
Heerde, Netherlands
Portugal, Spain, Gibraltar & Greece: Patrick
Bygate, Massagno, Switzerland
Scandinavia: Ove B. Poulsen, Glostrup,
Denmark
South Africa (Transport only): Motor Books,
Bryanston, South Africa
USA: Motorbooks International Publishers &
Wholesalers Inc, Osceola, WI; Combined
Books Inc, Conshohocken, PA
USA (Hobby titles): Specialty Book Marketing,
New York, NY, USA

Book Trade Association Membership: IPG

1920 ▬▬▬

WINDRUSH PRESS LTD
Little Window, High Street, Moreton in Marsh,
Glos GL56 0LL
Telephone: 01608 652012 & 652025
Fax: 01608 652125

**Returns (after authorisation from Windrush
Press):**
Hoddle, Doyle, Meadows, Station Road,
Linton, Cambs CB1 6UX
Telephone: 01223 893855
Fax: 01223 893852

Directors: Geoffrey Smith *(Managing, Home
& Export Sales)*
Victoria Huxley *(Editorial, Rights &
Permissions)*

*Biography & Autobiography; Guide Books;
History & Antiquarian; Humour; Military &
War; Books local to Cotswolds/Gloucestershire*

New Titles: 10 (1995), 10 (1996)
No of Employees: 2
Annual Turnover: £400,000

ISBNs, Imprints & Series:
0 88088 Peter Pauper Press
0 900075 Traveller's Histories, Windrush
Island Guides
0 934977 Italica Press
1 869860 Atlantic Europe

Distributor for:
Atlantic Europe Children's Books; Signpost
Books. *Australia:* Watermark Press. *USA:*
Aslan Publishing; Atrium Publishers Group;
Avo Books; Culinary Arts; Delphi Press;
Dharma Cloud; Earth Heart; Elliott & Clark;
Freestone Collective; Hermetician Press; Italica
Press; Light Technology; Mamre Press;
Maypop Books; Peter Pauper Press; Royal
Priest Publishing; Sierra Press; Swan Raven &
Co; Tree of Life Publications; Valley of the
Sun; Wild Flower Press; Yes International

Overseas Representation *(see §7.3):*
Europe: Angell Eurosales, Newton Abbot, UK
Italy: Penny Padovani, London, UK
Scandinavia & Northern Europe: D. Richard
Bowen, Malmö, Sweden
Spain & Portugal: Peter Prout, Madrid, Spain

1921 ▬▬▬

WINSLOW PRESS LTD
Telford Road, Bicester, Oxon OX6 0TS
Telephone: 01869 244644
Fax: 01869 320040

Customer Service:
Telephone: 01869 244733
Fax: 01869 320040

Directors: Ian Franklin *(Managing)*
Catherine McAllister *(Editorial & Rights)*
Managers: Alyson Carr *(Customer Service)*
Sarah Wilson *(Sales Development)*
Sue Halliday *(Publishing)*

*Educational & Textbooks; English as a Foreign
Language; Health & Beauty; Languages &
Linguistics; Medical (incl. Self Help &
Alternative Medicine); Psychology &
Psychiatry; Care of the Elderly; Occupational
Therapy; Physiotherapy; Speech Therapy*

New Titles: 8 (1995), 11 (1996)
No of Employees: 22
Annual Turnover: £2.3M

ISBNs, Imprints & Series: 0 86388

Distributor for:
Canada: Hanen Programme

1922 ▬▬▬

WISDOM BOOKS
402 Hoe Street, London E17 9AA
Telephone: 0181 520 5588
Fax: 0181 520 0932
Email: 100660.2464@compuserve.com

Managing Director: Dennis Heslop
Managers: Jonathan Steyn *(Order Processing)*
Philip Bradley *(Office)*
Mike Gilmore *(Customer Services)*

Religion & Theology

No of Employees: 6
Annual Turnover: £300,000

ISBNs, Imprints & Series: 1 872921

Distributor for:
Aukana; Buddhist Publishing Group; The
Buddhist Society; Insight Books; Kodansha;
Pali Text Society; Rider; RIGPA Publications;
Serindia Publications; Tharpa Publications
(Artwork); Triple Gem Press; Tuttle; Zen
Centre (London). *France:* Anako Editions.
India: Library of Tibetan Works and Archives;
Lotsawa; Mahayana Publications; Motilal
Banarsidass. *Japan:* Kosei; Kyoto Zen Centre;
Rinsen; Windbell. *Malaysia:* Dharmafarer.
Singapore: Rinchen Editions. *Sri Lanka:*
Buddhist Publication Society. *Thailand:*
Buddhadhamma Foundation. *USA:* Asian
Humanities Press; Clear Point Press; Dharma
Communications; Dharma Drum; Jain
Publishing; Jewel Publishing House; Lame
Turtle Press; Mahayana Sutra & Tantra Press;
Nine Gates Press; Padma Publishing; Ranjung
Yeshe; Rato Publicatins; Shambhala; Snow
Lion Graphics; Snow Lion Publications USA;
Thubten Dhargye Ling; Vippassana Dhura;
Wisdom Publications (Boston)

Overseas Representation *(see §7.3):*
Southern Europe: Bookport Associates,
Bologna, Italy

1923 ▬▬▬

WITHERBY & CO LTD
32–36 Aylesbury Street, London EC1R 0ET
Telephone: 0171 251 5341
Fax: 0171 251 1296

Managing Director: Alan Witherby
Trade Sales Manager: Brian Dawes

*Educational & Textbooks; Industry, Business &
Management; Law; Nautical; Reference Books,
Directories & Dictionaries; Scientific &
Technical*

New Titles: 15 (1995), 20 (1996)
No of Employees: 6
Annual Turnover: £1.5M

ISBNs, Imprints & Series:
0 900886 Witherby
0 900886, 0 948691 Witherby Monument

Distributor for:
Institute of Risk Management; International
Chamber of Shipping; International Tanker

Owners' Pollution Federation; Oil Companies International Marine Forum; The Society of Consulting Marine Engineers and Ship Surveyors; Society of International Gas Tanker & Terminal Operators; Tanker Structure Co-operative Forum

Overseas Representation *(see §7.3)*:
Australia: Boat Books, St Kilda, Vic
Hong Kong: Bloomsbury Books Ltd
Japan: Cornes & Co, Tokyo
Singapore: Motion Smith
USA: New York Nautical, New York

Book Trade Association Membership: PA, BA

1924 ■■■■

THE WOMEN'S PRESS
34 Great Sutton Street, London EC1V 0DX
Telephone: 0171 251 3007
Fax: 0171 608 1938

Warehouse:
Plymbridge Distributors Ltd, Estover Road, Plymouth PL6 7PZ
Telephone: 01752 735251
Fax: 01752 695699

Directors: Mary Hemming *(Sales)*
Kathy Gale *(Publishing)*
Stephanie Dowrick
Rights: Helen Windrath

Biography & Autobiography; Crime; Fiction; Gender Studies; Humour; Literature & Criticism; Poetry; Politics & World Affairs; Science Fiction; Teenage

New Titles: 60 (1995), 60 (1996)
No of Employees: 9

ISBNs, Imprints & Series: 0 7043

Associated & Subsidiary Companies:
The Women's Press Book Club

Overseas Representation *(see §7.3)*:
Australia & New Zealand: Allen & Unwin Pty Ltd, St Leonards, NSW, Australia
Europe: Hanne Rotovnik, Klampenborg, Denmark; Ted Dougherty, London, UK
Irish Republic: Fergus Corcoran, Dun Laoghaire
Middle & Far East: Ashton International Marketing Services, Larkfield, UK
Southern Africa: David Philip Publishers Pty Ltd, Claremont, South Africa

1925 ■■■■

WOODHEAD PUBLISHING LTD
Abington Hall, Abington, Cambridge CB1 6AH
Telephone: 01223 891358
Fax: 01223 893694
Email: woodhead@dial.pipex.com
Web Site: http://dspace.dial.pipex.com/town/square/ca97/

Warehouse & Distribution:
Combined Book Services, 406 Vale Road, Tonbridge, Kent TN9 1XR
Telephone: 01732 357755
Fax: 01732 770219

Directors: Martin Woodhead *(Managing)*
Duncan Leeper
Marketing Manager: Rosemary Parravani
Editors: Amanda Thomas *(Production)*
Patricia Morrison *(Commissioning)*

Engineering; Industry, Business & Management; Scientific & Technical

New Titles: 20 (1995), 30 (1996)
No of Employees: 10
Annual Turnover: £900,000

ISBNs, Imprints & Series:
1 85573 Abington Publishing, Gresham Books, Woodhead Publishing

Distributor for:
Germany: Beuth (The German Standards Institute); Stahleisen (The German Iron & Steel Institute); VDI (The Association of German Engineers). *USA:* The American Welding Society

Overseas Representation *(see §7.3)*:
Australia: DA Information Services, Mitcham, Vic
Greece, Middle East & Pakistan: Anthony Rudkin Associates, Oxford, UK
India: Viva Marketing, New Delhi
Italy: Marcello SNC, Padua
Japan: OBK, Obi-Wan Kenobi Inc, Tokyo
Netherlands, Belgium & Luxembourg: Netwerk, Academic Book Agency, Rotterdam, Netherlands
Scandinavia: Colin Flint, Harlow, UK
South East Asia: APAC Publishers Services, Singapore

Book Trade Association Membership: IPG

1926 ■■■■

WORD PUBLISHING
[Word (UK) Ltd]
9 Holdom Avenue, Bletchley, Bucks MK1 1QU
Telephone: 01908 648440
Fax: 01908 648592

Managing Director: Graham Williams

Children's Books; Religion & Theology

New Titles: 40 (1995), 30 (1996)
No of Employees: 55
Annual Turnover: £5.5M

ISBNs, Imprints & Series:
0 85009, 1 86024

Parent Company:
Thomas Nelson Inc; Word Inc *(USA)*

Distributor for:
USA: Thomas Nelson Inc; Word Inc; Yuam Focus on the Family

Overseas Representation *(see §7.3)*:
Australia: Word Australia, Kilsyth
Hong Kong: Jensco
Malaysia: Salvation Book Centre, Petaling Jaya
New Zealand: Christian Marketing New Zealand, Havelock North
Singapore: Alby Commercial Enterprises Pte Ltd; Campus Crusade Asia Ltd

South Africa: Struik Book Distributors Pty Ltd, Johannesburg, Cape Town & Maitland

1927 ■■■■

WORDS ON SPORT LTD
PO Box 382, St Albans, Herts AL2 3JD
Telephone: 01923 894355
Fax: 01923 894366
Email: bruce–smith–books@compuserve.com

Sales:
Derek Searle Associates, Burlington House, 14 High Street, Slough, Berks SL1 1EE
Telephone: 01753 539295
Fax: 01753 551863

Distribution:
Bookpoint Ltd, Abingdon, Oxon OX14 4JD
Telephone: 01235 400400
Fax: 01235 861038

Managing Director: Bruce Smith *(Rights & Export)*
Sales Manager: Bob Cripps *(Home Sales – Derek Searle Associates)*

Sports & Games

New Titles: 9 (1995), 4 (1996)

ISBNs, Imprints & Series: 1 898351

1928 ■■■■

WORDSWORTH EDITIONS LTD
Cumberland House, Crib Street, Ware, Herts SG12 9ET
Telephone: 01920 465167
Fax: 01920 462267
Email: 101512.3577@compuserve.com (Head Office & Accounts)
Web Site: http://www.BookWeb.co.uk/wordsworth/home

Orders & Accounts:
Email: 101512.3577@compuserve.com

Editorial:
Email: 100434.276@compuserve.com

Distribution (Scotland):
Lomond Books, 36 West Shore Road, Granton, Edinburgh EH5 1QD

Managing Director: Michael C. W. Trayler
Company Secretary: Clive Reynard
Sales Manager: Dennis R. Hart *(Home & Export)*
Editorial Director: Marcus Clapham

Children's Books; Literature & Criticism; Poetry; Reference Books, Directories & Dictionaries

New Titles: 110 (1995), 118 (1996)
No of Employees: 13
Annual Turnover: £5M

ISBNs, Imprints & Series: 1 85326

Overseas Representation *(see §7.3)*:
Australia & Papua New Guinea: Peribo Pty Ltd, Mount Kuring-gai, NSW, Australia
Cyprus: Huckleberry Trading, Tala Paphos
Czech Republic: Bohemian Ventures spol sro, Prague

France: Copernicus Diffusion, Paris
Germany: GLBmbH (Bargain, Promotional &
Remainder Shops), Cologne; Tradis Verlag
und Vertrieb GmbH (Bookshops), Cologne
India: OM Book Service, Delhi
Irish Republic: Wordsworth Editions Ltd,
Ware, UK
Israel: Timmy Marketing Ltd, Jerusalem
Italy: Magis Books srl, Reggio Emilia
New Zealand & Fiji: Allphy Book Distributors
Ltd, Auckland, New Zealand
North America: Universal Sales & Marketing,
New York, USA
Philippines: I. J. Sagun Enterprises Inc, Rizal
Portugal: International Publishing Services
Ltd, Lisbon
Singapore, Malaysia & Brunei: Paul &
Elizabeth Book Services Pte Ltd, Singapore
Slovak Republic: Slovak Ventures spol sro,
Nitra, Slovakia
Southern, Central & East Africa: P.M.C.
International Importers & Exporters CC,
Durban North, South Africa
Spain: Ribera Libros, SL, Arrigorriaga

1929

WORLD INTERNATIONAL PUBLISHING LTD
Deanway Technology Centre, Wilmslow Road,
Handforth, Cheshire SK9 3FB
Telephone: 01625 650011
Fax: 01625 650040

Directors: Ian Findlay *(Managing)*
Mike Herridge *(Creative)*
David Smith *(Financial)*
David Sheldrake *(Production & Rights
Manager)*
Peter Hey *(Marketing)*

Children's Books

New Titles: 96 (1996)
No of Employees: 30

ISBNs, Imprints & Series:
0 7235, 0 7498 Character Colour/Activity, Fun
to Learn, I Can Learn, Learning Rewards, Mr
Men Library

Parent Company:
Egmont *(Denmark)*

1930

WRITERS & READERS LTD
6–9 Cynthia Street, London N1 9JF
Telephone: 0171 713 0386
Fax: 0171 833 4804

Distribution:
Airlift Book Co, 8 The Arena,
Mollison Avenue, Enfield, Middlesex EN3 7NJ
Telephone: 0181 804 0400
Fax: 0181 804 0044

Publisher, Director: Glenn Thompson
Accountant: Sandi

*Audio Books; Biography & Autobiography;
Children's Books; Educational & Textbooks;
Gender Studies; Music; Philosophy;
Photography; Poetry; Politics & World Affairs;
Psychology & Psychiatry; Religion &
Theology; Theatre, Drama & Dance*

New Titles: 15 (1995), 15 (1996)

ISBNs, Imprints & Series:
0 86316 For Beginners, Black Butterfly
Children's Books, Harlem River Press

Parent Company:
Writers & Readers Publishing Inc *(USA)*

Overseas Representation *(see §7.3):*
Australia: Tower Books Wholesalers Pty Ltd,
Brookvale
Czech Republic: Foreign Rights Ltd, Vienna,
Austria
Greece: Omiros Avramides Literary Agency,
Markopoulo
Italy: The Living Literary Agency, Milan
Japan: The English Agency (Japan) Ltd, Tokyo
Spain: Ute Körner, Barcelona

Book Trade Association Membership: PA

1931

THE X PRESS
55 Broadway Market, London E8 4PH
Telephone: 0171 729 1199
Fax: 0171 729 1771
Email: xpress@maxis.co.uk
Web Site: http://www.maxis.co.uk/xpress

Distribution:
Turnaround Distribution, 27 Horsell Road,
London N7
Telephone: 0171 609 7836
Fax: 0171 700 1205

Managing Directors: Steve Pope
Dotun Adebayo

Fiction

New Titles: 17 (1995), 20 (1996)
No of Employees: 4
Annual Turnover: £250,000

1932

Y LOLFA CYF
Hen Swyddfa'r Heddlu, Talybont, Ceredigion
SY24 5HE
Telephone: 01970 832304
Fax: 01970 832782
Email: ylolfa@netwales.co.uk
Web Site: http://www.ylolfa.wales.comm/

Director: Robat Gruffudd
Administrator: Heddwen Pugh-Evans
Editor: Elena Morus
Marketing: Garmon Gruffudd
Projects Editor: Eiry Jones

*Children's Books; Cookery, Wines & Spirits;
Humour; Languages & Linguistics; Music;
Politics & World Affairs; Welsh Language
Books*

New Titles: 28 (1995), 30 (1996)
No of Employees: 15

ISBNs, Imprints & Series:
0 86243, 0 904864 Y Lolfa

Overseas Representation *(see §7.3):*
Worldwide: Drake International Services,
Oxford, UK

Book Trade Association Membership: Union
of Welsh Publishers & Booksellers

1933

YALE UNIVERSITY PRESS LONDON
23 Pond Street, London NW3 2PN
Telephone: 0171 431 4422
Fax: 0171 431 3755

Warehouse & Fulfilment:
John Wiley & Sons Ltd, Distribution Centre,
Shripney Road, Bognor Regis, W Sx PO22 9SA
Telephone: 01243 829121
Fax: 01243 82050

Directors: John Nicoll *(Editorial/Production
& Managing)*
Robert Baldock *(Editorial)*
Gillian Malpass *(Editorial)*
Kate Pocock *(Marketing)*
Publicity: Hazel Hutchison
Promotion: Linda Keene
Rights & Permissions: Linden Lawson
Sales: Chris Oliver
Accountant: Donal Burke
Production: Patricia Rennie

*Academic & Scholarly; Archaeology;
Architecture & Design; Bibliography &
Library Science; Biography & Autobiography;
Biology & Zoology; Economics; Fine Art & Art
History; Gender Studies; Geography &
Geology; History & Antiquarian; Illustrated &
Fine Editions; Languages & Linguistics; Law;
Literature & Criticism; Mathematics &
Statistics; Medical (incl. Self Help &
Alternative Medicine); Military & War; Music;
Natural History; Philosophy; Photography;
Poetry; Politics & World Affairs; Psychology &
Psychiatry; Reference Books, Directories &
Dictionaries; Religion & Theology; Sociology
& Anthropology; Theatre, Drama & Dance*

ISBNs, Imprints & Series: 0 300

Parent Company:
Yale University Press *(USA)*

Associated & Subsidiary Companies:
Yale Representation Ltd

Overseas Representation *(see §7.3):*
Austria, Germany, Italy & Switzerland: Uwe
Luedemann, Berlin, Germany
*Benelux, Denmark, Finland, France, Iceland,
Norway & Sweden:* Fred Hermans,
Bovenkarspel, Netherlands
Hong Kong & Philippines: Asia Publisher
Services Ltd, Hong Kong
India: S. Janakiraman, Madras
Middle East: International Publishers
Representatives (IPR), Nicosia, Cyprus
New Zealand: The University Press Group,
Toronto, Ont, Canada
Nigeria: Bounty Press Ltd, Ibadan
Singapore, Malaysia, Brunei & Indonesia:
Pansing Distribution Sdn Bhd, Singapore
South Africa: Cory Voigt Associates,
Braamfontein
Spain & Portugal: Arie Ruitenbeek, Madrid,
Spain
*USA, Central & South America, Mexico,
Canada, Australia, Japan, Korea & Taiwan:*
Yale University Press, New Haven, CT, USA

Book Trade Association Membership: PA,
BDC, CAPP

1934 ■■■■■■■■■■■■■■■■■■■■■■■■■■■■■■

ROY YATES BOOKS
Smallfields Cottage, Cox Green, Rudgwick,
Horsham, West Sussex RH12 3DE
Telephone: 01403 822299
Fax: 01403 823012

Directors: Roy Yates *(Marketing, Distribution
& Accounts)*
Constance Yates

*Children's Books; English as a Foreign
Language*

New Titles: 6 (1996)
No of Employees: 2
Annual Turnover: £120,000

ISBNs, Imprints & Series:
0 907264 Roy Yates
1 870045 Ingham Yates

Distributor for:
Jennie Ingham Associates Ltd; Luzac
Storytellers

Overseas Representation *(see §7.3)*:
Australia: Global Language Books,
Greystanes, NSW
USA & Canada: Multicultural Books & Video
Inc, Tecumseh, Ont, Canada

1935 ■■■■■■■■■■■■■■■■■■■■■■■■■■■■■■

*YOUNG LIBRARY LTD
3 The Old Brushworks, 56 Pickwick Road,
Corsham, Wilts SN13 9BX
Telephone: 01249 712025
Fax: 01249 715558

**Warehouse, Distribution & Customer
Accounts:**
Young Library Ltd,
c/o Clipper Distribution Services,
Windmill Grove, Portchester, Hants PO16 9HT
Telephone: 01705 200080
Fax: 01705 200090

Director: Roger Bonnett *(Managing,
Editorial, Production, Rights &
Permissions)*
Manager: Gina Rotherford *(Sales,
Administration)*

Children's Books; Educational & Textbooks

ISBNs, Imprints & Series:
0 946003, 1 85429

Overseas Representation *(see §7.3)*:
Canada: Saunders Book Co, Collingwood
New Zealand: South Pacific Books (Imports)
Ltd, Auckland
Singapore: Educational Publishers Bureau Pte
Ltd

1936 ■■■■■■■■■■■■■■■■■■■■■■■■■■■■■■

ZED BOOKS LTD
7 Cynthia Street, London N1 9JF
Telephone: 0171 837 4014 & 0384
Fax: 0171 833 3960

Distribution:
Plymbridge Distributors Ltd, Estover,
Plymouth PL6 7PZ
Telephone: 01752 202301
Fax: 01752 202331

Trade Representation – UK & Ireland:
Troika

Commissioning Editors: Louise Murray
Robert Molteno
Mohammed Umar *(Rights)*

Michael Pallis *(Computer Information)*
Production: Anne Rodford
Sales & Distribution: Farouk Sohawon
Marketing: Kathryn Perry
Margaret Ling
Helen Salmon *(Promotion)*
Accounts: Diane Blackbourn *(Company
Secretary)*
Alison Roberts

*Academic & Scholarly; Economics; Gender
Studies; Politics & World Affairs; Sociology &
Anthropology; Cultural Studies*

New Titles: 42 (1995), 40 (1996)
No of Employees: 12
Annual Turnover: £900,000

ISBNs, Imprints & Series:
0 86232, 0 905762, 1 85649 Zed Books
0 901787 Panaf Books

Overseas Representation *(see §7.3)*:
Australia: Peribo Pty Ltd, Mount Kuring-gai,
NSW
Bangladesh: The University Press Ltd, Dhaka
Belgium: De Groene Waterman, Bercham
Canada: Fernwood Books Ltd, Halifax, NS
Germany: Missing Link
Versandbuchhandlung, Bremen
Hong Kong: Hong Kong University Press
Japan: Yushodo Fantas Corporation, Tokyo
Netherlands: Ruurd Ruward, Ruward BV, The
Hague
New Zealand: One World Books, Auckland
Pakistan: Vanguard Books Pvt Ltd, Lahore
Singapore: Academic Marketing Services
South Africa: David Philip Publishers Pty Ltd,
Claremont
USA: Humanities Press International Inc,
Atlantic Highlands, NJ
Zimbabwe: Grassroots Books (Pvt) Ltd, Harare

Book Trade Association Membership: PA,
BDC, CAPP

2 Publishers

2.2 Commonwealth & Overseas

AUSTRALIA

2001

*ABORIGINAL STUDIES PRESS
GPO Box 553, Canberra, ACT 2601
Telephone: +61 (Õ6) 246 1111
Fax: +61 (Õ6) 249 7310

Trade Enquiries & Orders:
Cambridge University Press, GPO Box 85,
Oakleigh, Vic 3166
Telephone: +61 (Õ3) 568 0322
Fax: +61 (Õ3) 563 1517

Director of Publications: Dr David Horton
(Rights & Permissions)
Senior Editor: Stephanie Haygarth
Marketing Manager: Margaret Ruhfus

*Academic & Scholarly; Archaeology;
Biography & Autobiography; Children's
Books; Educational & Textbooks; Electronic
(Educational); Geography & Geology; History
& Antiquarian; Languages & Linguistics;
Music; Natural History; Politics & World
Affairs; Reference Books, Directories &
Dictionaries; Sociology & Anthropology*

ISBNs, Imprints & Series: 0 85575

Parent Company:
Australian Institute of Aboriginal and Torres
Strait Islanders Studies *(Australia)*

Book Trade Association Membership:
Australian Book PA

2002

ACCESS PRESS
PO Box 132, Northbridge, Perth, WA 6865
Telephone: +61 (Õ9) 328 9188
Fax: +61 (Õ9) 328 4605

Location:
35 Stuart Street, Perth, WA 6003
Telephone: *(as above)*
Fax: *(as above)*

Directors: Helen Weller *(Managing)*
John Harper-Nelson *(Rights & Permissions)*

Biography & Autobiography

New Titles: 10 (1995), 11 (1996)
No of Employees: 2

ISBNs, Imprints & Series:
0 86445 Reeve Books
0 908112 The Nine Club
0 949795 Access Press

Parent Company:
Reeve Pty Ltd *(Australia)*

Associated & Subsidiary Companies:
Australia: Reeve Books

2003

ALBATROSS BOOKS PTY LTD
55 East Parade, (PO Box 320), Sutherland,
NSW 2232
Telephone: +61 (Õ2) 9521 4455
Fax: +61 (Õ2) 9521 1515
Email: albatross@albatross.com.au

Director: John Waterhouse
Editor: Ken Goodlet
Sales Manager: Richard Dwyer
Customer Enquiries: Laura Pentecost

*Biography & Autobiography; Children's
Books; Fiction; Religion & Theology*

New Titles: 60 (1995), 55 (1996)
No of Employees: 9

ISBNs, Imprints & Series:
0 7324, 0 86760

Overseas Representation *(see §7.3)*:
UK: Lion Publishing, Oxford

2004

*ALLEN & UNWIN PTY LTD
9 Atchison Street, St Leonards, NSW 2065
Telephone: +61 (Õ2) 901 4088
Fax: +61 (Õ2) 906 2218

Warehouse:
Unit A/2, 1–3 Rodborough Road,
Frenchs Forest, NSW 2086
Telephone: +61 (Õ2) 451 9225
Fax: +61 (Õ2) 975 3581

Managing Director: Patrick Gallagher
Directors: Paul Donovan *(Sales & Marketing)*
Peter Eichhorn *(Business & Administration,
Company Secretary)*
Rights: Angela Namoi

*Academic & Scholarly; Biography &
Autobiography; Children's Books; Crime;
Crafts & Hobbies; Economics; Fiction; Gender
Studies; History & Antiquarian; Industry,
Business & Management; Military & War;
Politics & World Affairs; Sociology &
Anthropology; Vocational Training & Careers*

ISBNs, Imprints & Series:
Little Ark Books, Rathdowne Publishing

Overseas Representation *(see §7.3)*:
Canada (trade titles): McClelland & Stewart,
Toronto & Markham, Canada
Hong Kong: Asia Publisher Services Ltd
Japan: United Publishers Services Ltd, Tokyo
Singapore: Reed International (Singapore) Pte
Ltd
UK (academic titles): University College
London Press, London, UK
UK (children's titles): Ragged Bears Ltd,
Andover, UK
UK (trade titles): Cassell Plc (Sales Dept),
London, UK
USA (academic titles): Paul & Co Publishers
Consortium Inc, New York, USA
USA (trade titles): IPG, Chicago, IL, USA

Book Trade Association Membership:
Australian Book PA

2005

ARTEMIS PUBLISHING
PO Box 151, Market Street PO, Melbourne,
Vic 8007
Telephone: +61 (Õ3) 9614 3920
Fax: +61 (Õ3) 9670 1252 & 9417 3588

Editor, Manager: J. Terry *(Rights & Permissions)*
Sales & Marketing: Erica Travers
Finance: Helen Cunningham

Biography & Autobiography; Crime; Educational & Textbooks; Gender Studies; Law; Politics & World Affairs; Sociology & Anthropology

New Titles: 5 (1995), 7 (1996)

ISBNs, Imprints & Series:
1 875656 Artemis, Artemis Crime Series, Women's Studies Series, Women's Voices, Women's Lives Series

Overseas Representation *(see §7.3)*:
Germany: Kiel & Kiel Literatur Agentur, Hamburg

Book Trade Association Membership:
Australian PA, Publish Australia

2006

AUSLIB PRESS
PO Box 622, Blackwood, SA 5051
Telephone: +61 (08) 278 4303
Fax: +61 (08) 278 4000
Email: auslib@mail.camtech.net.au

Manager: Judith Bundy
Editorial Director: Dr Alan Bundy

Academic & Scholarly; Bibliography & Library Science

New Titles: 8 (1995), 9 (1996)
Annual Turnover: $150,000

ISBNs, Imprints & Series:
1 875145 Library Challenges Series

2007

*AUSTED PUBLISHING CO
4 Panton Road, Manourah, WA 6210
Telephone: +61 (09) 581 8299
Fax: +61 (09) 581 8288

Also at:
PO Box 1104, Booragoon, WA 6154

Managing Directors: W. B. R. Banks
K. A. Chesson

Academic & Scholarly; Animal Care & Breeding; Educational & Textbooks; Health & Beauty; History & Antiquarian; Humour; Mathematics & Statistics; Natural History; Psychology & Psychiatry; Sports & Games

ISBNs, Imprints & Series:
0 9592597, 1 86307

Parent Company:
Aesthetic Holdings Pty Ltd *(Australia)*

2008

AUSTRALIAN ACADEMY OF SCIENCE
Ian Potter House, Gordon Street, Acton, ACT 2601
Telephone: +61 (06) 247 5385
Fax: +61 (06) 257 4620
Email: aas@asap.unimelb.edu.au

Web Site: http://www.asap.unimelb.edu.au/aas/aashome.htm

Managing Editor: Maureen Swanage
Finance & Business Officer: Ros Greenwood
Executive Secretary: Peter Vallee

Educational & Textbooks

New Titles: 3 (1995)
No of Employees: 5
Annual Turnover: $1.4M

ISBNs, Imprints & Series: 0 85847

Book Trade Association Membership:
Australian PA

2009

AUSTRALIAN COUNCIL FOR EDUCATIONAL RESEARCH (ACER)
19 Prospect Hill Road, Camberwell, Vic
Telephone: +61 (03) 277 5555
Fax: +61 (03) 277 5500
Email: fraser@acer.edu.au

Postal Address:
Private Bag 55, Camberwell, Vic 3124

Managers: Ian C. Fraser *(Publishing, Rights & Permissions)*
Tricia Genat *(Marketing)*

Academic & Scholarly; Educational & Textbooks; Psychology & Psychiatry; Computer Software; Parenting; Personnel

ISBNs, Imprints & Series: 0 86431

Overseas Representation *(see §7.3)*:
New Zealand: New Zealand Council for Educational Research, Wellington
UK: NFER-Nelson, Windsor

Book Trade Association Membership:
Australian PA, Australian Booksellers' Association

2010

AUSTRALIAN GOVERNMENT PUBLISHING SERVICE
GPO Box 84, Canberra, ACT 2601
Telephone: +61 (06) 295 4411
Fax: +61 (06) 295 4455

General Manager: Alan Law

Biology & Zoology; Economics; Gender Studies; Industry, Business & Management; Government Publications

New Titles: 3822 (1995), 3465 (1996)

ISBNs, Imprints & Series:
0 642, 0 644

Parent Company:
Department of Administrative Services (DAS) *(Australia)*

Book Trade Association Membership:
Australian PA, Australian Booksellers Association

2011

AUSTRALIAN INSTITUTE OF CRIMINOLOGY
GPO Box 2944, Canberra 2601
Telephone: +61 (06) 260 9200
Fax: +61 (06) 260 9260
Email: aicpress@aic.gov.au

Publishing Manager: Merril Thompson *(Sales, Rights & Permissions)*

Academic & Scholarly; Educational & Textbooks; Law; Sociology & Anthropology; Criminology

New Titles: 5 (1995), 5 (1996)
No of Employees: 3

ISBNs, Imprints & Series:
CA, Trends & Issues in Crime & Criminal Justice

Overseas Representation *(see §7.3)*:
USA: Criminal Justice Press, Monsey, NY

Book Trade Association Membership:
Australian Book PA

2012

AUSTRALIAN LARGE PRINT AUDIO & VIDEO PTY LTD
17 Mohr Street, Tullamarine, Vic 3043
Telephone: +61 (03) 9338 0666
Fax: +61 (03) 9335 1903
Email: alpav@c031.aone.net.au

Marketing Manager: Rebecca Walshe
Sales Consultant: Felicity Nottingham
Promotions Co-ordinator: Jeanette Laffan

Audio Books; Large Print Books

New Titles: 28 (1995), 50 (1996)
No of Employees: 15
Annual Turnover: $3.5M

ISBNs, Imprints & Series:
1 86340 Bolinda Audio, Bolinda Press, Compass Press, Ghost Gum Press, Goanna Crime, Sagebrush

Overseas Representation *(see §7.3)*:
UK: Isis Publishing Ltd, Oxford
USA: Thomas T. Beeter, Hampton Falls

2013

AUSTRALIAN SCHOLARLY PUBLISHING
Suite 208, 222 Collins Street, Melbourne, Vic 3000
Telephone: +61 (03) 9817 5208
Fax: +61 (03) 9817 6431
Email: nwalker@aurora.cc.monash.edu.au

Also at:
Ken Pryse & Associates, 156 Collins Street, Melbourne, Vic 3000

Director: Nicholas S. Walker *(Sales & Marketing)*
Senior Editor: Dr Diane Carlyle

Academic & Scholarly; Biography & Autobiography; Fiction; History &

Antiquarian; Poetry; Politics & World Affairs;
Scientific & Technical; Sociology &
Anthropology

New Titles: 12 (1995), 15 (1996)
No of Employees: 4

ISBNs, Imprints & Series: 1 875606

Book Trade Association Membership:
Australian PA

2014

BLACKWELL SCIENCE PTY LTD
54 University Street, Carlton, Vic 3053
Telephone: +61 (03) 9347 0300
Fax: +61 (03) 9347 5001
Email: 100036.2662@compuserve.com
Web Site: http://www.blacksci.co.uk

Warehouse:
26 Albert Street, Brunswick, Vic 3056
Telephone: +61 (03) 9387 2427
Fax: +61 (03) 9387 7498

Directors: Mark Ian Robertson *(Managing)*
Jon Conibear *(Chairman)*
Audrey Chin *(Finance)*
Neil Walsh *(Operations)*

Academic & Scholarly; Agriculture; Biology &
Zoology; Geography & Geology; Medical
(incl. Self Help & Alternative Medicine);
Scientific & Technical; Veterinary Science

New Titles: 2 (1995), 3 (1996)
No of Employees: 39
Annual Turnover: £4.2M

ISBNs, Imprints & Series: 0 86793

Parent Company:
Blackwell Science Ltd *(UK)*

Overseas Representation *(see §7.3)*:
UK: Blackwell Science Ltd, Oxford &
  Edinburgh
USA & Canada: Blackwell Science Inc,
  Cambridge, MA, USA

2015

BOOLARONG PRESS
35 Hamilton Road, Moorooka, Qld 4105
Telephone: +61 (07) 3848 8200
Fax: +61 (07) 3848 8007

General Manager: Russell Keirnan

Biography & Autobiography; Crafts &
Hobbies; Fine Art & Art History; Industry,
Business & Management; Military & War

New Titles: 23 (1995), 25 (1996)
No of Employees: 3

ISBNs, Imprints & Series: 0 86439

Parent Company:
Artists Associated Pty Ltd *(Australia)*

Overseas Representation *(see §7.3)*:
Singapore: APD Singapore Pte Ltd

2016

BUTTERWORTHS
[a division of Reed International Books
Australia Pty Ltd]
271–273 Lane Cove Road, PO Box 345,
North Ryde, NSW 2113
Telephone: +61 (02) 335 4444
Fax: +61 (02) 335 4655
Web Site: http://www.butterworths.com.au

Directors: D. Day *(Managing)*
J. Broadfoot *(Editorial, Marketing & Deputy*
  Managing, Rights & Permissions)
D. Bishop *(Deputy Editorial)*
J. Seward *(Commercial)*
Associate Directors: E. Dickinson *(Human*
  Resources)
M. Piper *(Marketing & Sales)*
P. Cauwood *(Finance)*

Academic & Scholarly; Accountancy &
Taxation; Educational & Textbooks; Law;
Commercial

ISBNs, Imprints & Series: 0 409

Parent Company:
Reed Elsevier Australia Pty Ltd *(a part of Reed*
Elsevier Plc) (Australia)

Overseas Representation *(see §7.3)*:
Canada: Butterworths Canada, Markham, Ont
France: Editions du Juris-Classeur, Paris
Italy: Dott. A. Giuffrè Editore, Milan
Malaysia: Malayan Law Journal Sdn Bhd,
  Selangor
New Zealand: Butterworths of New Zealand,
  Wellington
Singapore: Butterworths Asia
South Africa: Butterworth Publishers (Pty) Ltd,
  Durban
UK: Butterworth & Co (Publishers) Ltd,
  London
USA: Michie, Charlottesville, VA

Book Trade Association Membership:
Australian PA, Australian National Book
Council

2017

**CAMBRIDGE UNIVERSITY PRESS
AUSTRALIAN BRANCH**
10 Stamford Road, Oakleigh, Vic 3166
Telephone: +61 (03) 568 0322
Fax: +61 (03) 563 1517
Email: kwh@cup.edu.au

Directors: Kim W. Harris
A. L. Davies *(Deputy)*

Academic & Scholarly; Educational &
Textbooks; English as a Foreign Language;
Reference Books, Directories & Dictionaries

Parent Company:
Cambridge University Press *(UK)*

Overseas Representation *(see §7.3)*:
New Zealand: Archetype Book Agency,
  Newtown

Book Trade Association Membership:
Australian PA

2018

*R. J. CLEARY
86/77 Riley Street, East Sydney, NSW 2010
Telephone: +61 (02) 360 6777
Fax: +61 (02) 360 6777

Principal: R. J. Dick Cleary

Accountancy & Taxation; Children's Books;
Computer Science; Cookery, Wines & Spirits;
Crafts & Hobbies; Do-It-Yourself; Educational
& Textbooks; Electronic (Educational);
Electronic (Professional & Academic); English
as a Foreign Language; Gardening; Humour;
Industry, Business & Management; Law;
Mathematics & Statistics; Photography;
Psychology & Psychiatry; Vocational Training
& Careers

ISBNs, Imprints & Series: 0 85567

2019

CRAFTSMAN HOUSE
PO Box 480, Roseville, NSW 2069
Telephone: +61 (02) 417 1670 & 417 1033
Fax: +61 (02) 417 1501 & 417 1045

Location:
20 Barcoo Street, Roseville East, NSW 2069
Fax: as above

Distributor (nationally):
Thames & Hudson (Australia) Pty Ltd,
11 Central Boulevard, Portside Business Park,
Port Melbourne, Vic 3207
Telephone: +61 (03) 9646 7788
Fax: +61 (03) 9646 8790

Chairman: Martin Gordon
Managers: Nevill Drury *(Publishing)*
Nichola Dyson Walker *(Sales & Marketing)*
Caroline de Fries *(Assistant Publisher)*

Architecture & Design; Crafts & Hobbies;
Fashion & Costume; Fine Art & Art History

New Titles: 31 (1995), 40 (1996)
No of Employees: 8

ISBNs, Imprints & Series:
90 5703, 976 6410, 976 8097

Parent Company:
Gordon & Breach Arts International
(Netherlands)

Associated & Subsidiary Companies:
Australia: Fine Arts Press Pty Ltd

Overseas Representation *(see §7.3)*:
Asia: IPD (Pte) Ltd, Singapore
Europe: G + B Arts International, Basle,
  Switzerland
USA (direct sales): IPD, Newark, NJ, USA
USA (trade sales): Independent Publishers
  Group, Chicago, IL, USA

2020

CSIRO PUBLISHING
150 Oxford Street, PO Box 1139, Collingwood,
Vic 3066
Telephone: +61 (03) 9662 7500
Fax: +61 (03) 9662 7555

Email: info@publish.csiro.au
Web Site: http://www.publish.csiro.au/

General Manager: Paul W. Reekie
Publishers: Kevin Jeans *(Academic & Reference)*
Nick Alexander *(Education & General)*
Laurie Martinelli *(Academic & Reference)*
Sales Manager: Ted Hamilton *(Sales & Distribution)*

Academic & Scholarly; Agriculture; Bibliography & Library Science; Biology & Zoology; Chemistry; Electronic (Educational); Electronic (Professional & Academic); Environment & Development Studies; Gardening; Natural History; Physics; Scientific & Technical

ISBNs, Imprints & Series: 0 643

Parent Company:
CSIRO Australia *(Australia)*

Overseas Representation *(see §7.3)*:
USA & Canada: International Specialized Book Services Inc, Portland, OR, USA

Book Trade Association Membership:
Australian PA

2021

CURRENCY PRESS
330 Oxford Street, Paddington, NSW 2021
Telephone: +61 (02) 332 1300
Fax: +61 (02) 332 3848
Email: currency@magna.com.au
Web Site: http://www.currency.com.au

Distribution:
Cambridge University Press
Telephone: +61 (03) 9568 0322
Fax: +61 (03) 9569 9292

Chairman: Nicholas Parsons
Publisher: Katharine Brisbane *(Editorial)*

Biography & Autobiography; Children's Books; Cinema, Video, TV & Radio; Music; Theatre, Drama & Dance; Australian Life

New Titles: 34 (1995), 45 (1996)
No of Employees: 5
Annual Turnover: £750,000

ISBNs, Imprints & Series: 0 86819

Overseas Representation *(see §7.3)*:
New Zealand: Playmarket, Wellington
UK: Gazelle Book Services Ltd, Lancaster

Book Trade Association Membership:
Australian PA

2022

CURRICULUM CORPORATION
141 Rathdowne Street, Carlton, Vic 3053
Telephone: +61 (03) 639 0699
Fax: +61 (03) 639 1616

Chief Executive Officer: Bruce Wilson
Marketing: Lyn Thane

Educational & Textbooks

New Titles: 50 (1995), 50 (1996)
No of Employees: 40
Annual Turnover: $12M

ISBNs, Imprints & Series: 1 86366

Book Trade Association Membership:
Australian PA

2023

*ELEANOR CURTAIN PUBLISHING
906 Malvern Road, Armadale, Melbourne, Vic 3143
Telephone: +61 (03) 822 0344
Fax: +61 (03) 824 8851

Managing Director: Eleanor Curtain

Educational & Textbooks

ISBNs, Imprints & Series: 1 875327

Overseas Representation *(see §7.3)*:
New Zealand: Ashton Scholastic Ltd, Auckland
North America: Peguis Publishers, Winnipeg, Canada
Singapore: Publishers Marketing Services Ltd

Book Trade Association Membership:
Australian Book PA, Publish Australia Group Enterprises

2024

DELLASTA
3a Evans Street, Burwood, Vic 3125
Telephone: +61 (03) 9888 9188
Fax: +61 (03) 9888 7806
Email: chrisdella@peg.apc.org

Trade Enquiries & Orders:
PO Box 777, Mount Waverley, Vic 3149

Directors: Christopher Roering *(Managing & Publisher)*
Dawn Roering *(Administration)*
Production Manager: Irene Beattie
Accountant: Irene Horwood

Accountancy & Taxation; Biography & Autobiography; Economics; Educational & Textbooks; Environment & Development Studies; Medical (incl. Self Help & Alternative Medicine); Music; Reference Books, Directories & Dictionaries; Travel & Topography

New Titles: 20 (1995), 26 (1996)
No of Employees: 5

ISBNs, Imprints & Series:
0 947138, 1 875627

Associated & Subsidiary Companies:
Australia: Ashwood Medical

Overseas Representation *(see §7.3)*:
New Zealand: EDL, Auckland
USA: Mondo, Washington, NY

Book Trade Association Membership:
Publish Australia

2025

E. J. DWYER (AUSTRALIA) PTY LTD
Unit 13, Perry Park, 33 Maddox Street, Alexandria, Sydney, NSW 2015
Telephone: +61 (02) 550 2355
Fax: +61 (02) 519 3218

Publishers: Catherine Hammond *(E. J. Dwyer)*
Carol Floyd *(Millenium Books)*
Sales: Anthony Dwyer

Academic & Scholarly; Biography & Autobiography; Children's Books; Crafts & Hobbies; Guide Books; Health & Beauty; Industry, Business & Management; Philosophy; Religion & Theology; Travel & Topography

New Titles: 20 (1995), 24 (1996)
No of Employees: 20

ISBNs, Imprints & Series:
0 85574 E. J. Dwyer
1 86429 Millennium Books

Parent Company:
E. J. Dwyer (Holdings) Pty Ltd *(Australia)*

Overseas Representation *(see §7.3)*:
Canada (E. J. Dwyer): Novalis, Toronto, Ont, Canada
India (E. J. Dwyer): Examiner Bookshop, Bombay, India
New Zealand (E. J. Dwyer): Catholic Supplies (NZ) Ltd, Wellington, New Zealand
New Zealand (Millennium Books): Tandem Press, Auckland, New Zealand
UK & Irish Republic (E. J. Dwyer): Columba Book Service, Dublin, Irish Republic
UK & Irish Republic (Millennium Books): Deep Books Ltd, London, UK
USA (E. J. Dwyer & Millennium): Morehouse, Ridgefield CT, USA

Book Trade Association Membership:
Christian Booksellers Association of Australia, Australian PA

2026

EA BOOKS (ENGINEERS AUSTRALIA PTY LTD)
PO Box 588, Crows Nest, NSW 2065
Telephone: +61 (02) 438 5355
Fax: +61 (02) 438 5343
Email: eabooks@eol.ieaust.org.au

General Manager: Bruce Roff
Sales: Robert Barber

Agriculture; Computer Science; Electronic (Professional & Academic); Engineering; Scientific & Technical; Transport

New Titles: 8 (1995), 17 (1996)
No of Employees: 7

ISBNs, Imprints & Series: 0 85825

Parent Company:
Institution of Engineers *(Australia)*

Overseas Representation *(see §7.3)*:
Canada & USA: Accents Publications Service Inc, Silver Spring, MD, USA

Japan (non-exclusive): Technicon Document Services, Tokyo, Japan; Aims Corporation, Tokyo, Japan

2027 ▬

DEPARTMENT FOR EDUCATION AND CHILDREN'S SERVICES, SOUTH AUSTRALIA
Publishing Unit, Banksia Avenue, Seacombe Gardens, SA 5047
Telephone: +61 (08) 377 0399
Fax: +61 (08) 377 0341

Orders:
Curriculum Resources,
Customer Service Centre, PO Box 33, Campbelltown, SA 5074
Telephone: +61 (08) 373 6077
Fax: +61 (08) 234 5086

Managing Editor: Pamela Ball *(Rights & Permissions)*
Marketing Manager: Robert Muir *(Home & Export Sales)*

Educational & Textbooks

ISBNs, Imprints & Series:
0 7243, 0 7308 Government of South Australia

Book Trade Association Membership:
Australian PA

2028 ▬

EDUCATIONAL SUPPLIES LTY LTD
[Publishing Division of the Dominie Group]
8 Cross Street, Brookvale, NSW 2100
Telephone: +61 (02) 9905 0201
Fax: +61 (02) 9905 5209

Directors: Ross Martin *(Managing)*
Toy Martin
Sales: Pauline Ralston
Financial Controller: Ronnie Trenter
Accountant: Tracey Trenter

Educational & Textbooks; Music

New Titles: 10 (1995), 10 (1996)
No of Employees: 10

ISBNs, Imprints & Series:
0 86251, 0 86799, 0 908540, 0 909268

Parent Company:
The Dominie Group *(Australia)*

2029 ▬

FINE ARTS PRESS
20 Barcoo Street, PO Box 480, Roseville, NSW 2069
Telephone: +61 (02) 417 1033
Fax: +61 (02) 417 1045
Email: info@gbpub.com.au

Directors: Dr Robin Derricourt *(Managing)*
Dinah Dysart *(Deputy)*
Nevill Drury *(Publishing)*
Hari Ho *(Production)*

Fine Art & Art History; Scientific & Technical

No of Employees: 25

ISBNs, Imprints & Series:
0 86917 Fine Arts Press
90 5703 Craftsman House

2030 ▬

THE FIVE MILE PRESS PTY LTD
22 Summit Road, Noble Park, Vic 3174
Telephone: +61 (03) 9790 5000
Fax: +61 (03) 9790 6888

Management Division: David Horgan *(Managing Director)*
Alan Reynolds *(Administration Manager, Accountant)*
Sales Division: Mary Mumford *(Manager)*
Production Department: Emma Borghesi *(Publishing Manager, Rights & Permissions)*
Editorial Department: Maggie Pinkney *(Senior Editor)*

Children's Books; Cookery, Wines & Spirits; Crafts & Hobbies; Gardening; Guide Books; Natural History; Sports & Games; Travel & Topography

No of Employees: 33

ISBNs, Imprints & Series: 0 86788

Overseas Representation *(see §7.3):*
UK: Chris Lloyd, Poole

Book Trade Association Membership:
Australian PA

2031 ▬

FREMANTLE ARTS CENTRE PRESS
193 South Terrace, South Fremantle, (PO Box 320), WA 6162
Telephone: +61 (09) 430 6331
Fax: +61 (09) 430 5242
Email: facp@anythink.iinet.net.au
Web Site: http://www.iinet.net.au/~bryce/facp.html

General Manager: Clive Newman
Publisher: Ray Coffey

Biography & Autobiography; Children's Books; Fiction; Fine Art & Art History; Literature & Criticism; Poetry; Sociology & Anthropology

New Titles: 28 (1995), 35 (1996)
No of Employees: 10
Annual Turnover: $1M

ISBNs, Imprints & Series:
Sandcastle Books
0 909144, 0 949206, 1 86368

Book Trade Association Membership:
Australian PA

2032 ▬

HALE & IREMONGER
19–21 Eve Street, Erskineville, NSW 2043
Telephone: +61 (02) 565 1955
Fax: +61 (02) 550 2012

Distribution:
E. J. Dwyer, Locked Bag 71, Alexandria, NSW 2015

Telephone: +61 (02) 550 2355
Fax: +61 (02) 519 3218

Director: Sylvia Hale
Managers: Kerrie McLeod *(Business)*
Sheila Drummond *(Marketing)*
Permissions: Heather Cam
Publisher: Rhonda Black

Academic & Scholarly; Do-It-Yourself; Educational & Textbooks; Fine Art & Art History; Health & Beauty; History & Antiquarian; Poetry; Sociology & Anthropology

New Titles: 37 (1995), 22 (1996)
No of Employees: 6
Annual Turnover: $600,000

ISBNs, Imprints & Series:
0 86806, 0 908094

Overseas Representation *(see §7.3):*
Canada: Marginal Distribution, Peterborough
Malaysia: Pelanduk Publications (M) Sdn Bhd, Petaling Jaya
New Zealand: Biramo Book Distributors, Auckland
UK: Turnaround Publishers Services Ltd, London

Book Trade Association Membership:
Australian PA, National Book Council, Galley Club, Women in Publishing

2033 ▬

HARCOURT BRACE & CO, AUSTRALIA PTY LTD
30–52 Smidmore Street, Marrickville, NSW 2204
Telephone: +61 (02) 517 8999
Fax: +61 (02) 517 2249 (Customer Service) & 550 6007 (Admin.)

Victoria Branch Office:
Level 3, 71 Queens Road, Melbourne, Vic 3004
Telephone: +61 (03) 9529 1533
Fax: +61 (03) 9510 5157

Auckland Branch Office:
Level 1, 236–238 Dominion Road, Mt Eden, Auckland 3, New Zealand
Telephone: +64 (09) 630 1675
Fax: +64 (09) 630 1674

Managing Director: Brian M. Brennan
Financial Controller/Operations Manager: Jim Robinson

Academic & Scholarly; Accountancy & Taxation; Biology & Zoology; Chemistry; Computer Science; Economics; Educational & Textbooks; Industry, Business & Management; Languages & Linguistics; Mathematics & Statistics; Medical (incl. Self Help & Alternative Medicine); Physics; Psychology & Psychiatry; Reference Books, Directories & Dictionaries; Scientific & Technical; Sociology & Anthropology; Veterinary Science

New Titles: 19 (1995)
No of Employees: 60

ISBNs, Imprints & Series:
0 7295 Baillière Tindall, Harcourt Brace, Holt,
Rinehart & Winston, The Psychological
Corporation, W. B. Saunders

Parent Company:
Harcourt General Inc *(USA)*

Associated & Subsidiary Companies:
Australia: Academic Press; The Dryden Press;
Grune & Stratton; Holt, Rinehart & Winston;
The Psychological Corporation; W. B.
Saunders Co

Book Trade Association Membership:
Australian PA

2034

***HARPER EDUCATIONAL
(AUSTRALIA)**
[a division of HarperCollins Publishers]
PO Box 321, Pymble, NSW 2073
Telephone: +61 (Õ2) 952 5000
Fax: +61 (Õ2) 952 5600

Location:
25 Ryde Road, Pymble, NSW 2073
Telephone: as above
Fax: as above

Managing Director: Barrie Hitchon
Managers: Mark Tredinnick *(General)*
David Evans *(Sales & Marketing)*
Jim Davidson *(Publisher)*
Ms Julie Ganner *(Production)*
Beryl Skellern *(Promotions)*

*Accountancy & Taxation; Biology & Zoology;
Chemistry; Computer Science; Economics;
Educational & Textbooks; Engineering;
Industry, Business & Management;
Mathematics & Statistics; Medical (incl. Self
Help & Alternative Medicine); Physics;
Psychology & Psychiatry; Scientific &
Technical; Sociology & Anthropology;
Veterinary Science*

ISBNs, Imprints & Series:
0 0650, 006 04, 0 673 HarperCollins
0 314 West
0 397 J. B. Lippincott
0 7817, 0 87630, 0 88167 Raven
0 8153, 0 8240 Garland
0 834, 0 8718 Apsen
0 87901 Worth
1 87373 Campion Press

Parent Company:
HarperCollins Publishers Pty Ltd *(Australia)*

Associated & Subsidiary Companies:
UK: HarperCollins Publishers. *USA:*
HarperCollins Publishers Inc

Book Trade Association Membership:
Australian Book PA, United States Book PA

2035

***HARPERCOLLINS PUBLISHERS
(MELBOURNE)**
[member of HarperCollins Publishers (Aus) Pty
Ltd Group]
22–24 Joseph Street, North Blackburn,
Vic 3130 (PO Box 316, Blackburn, Vic 3130)

Telephone: +61 (Õ3) 895 8105
Fax: +61 (Õ3) 895 8181

Managers: Paul Pels *(Business)*
Bert Eadon *(Operations)*
Peter Cribb *(Publishing)*
Frank Priatel *(Sales & Marketing)*
Lesley Thwaites *(Production)*
Publishers: Kevin Mark *(Religious)*
Robin Freeman *(Health & Personal
Development)*

*Educational & Textbooks; Health & Beauty;
Religion & Theology*

ISBNs, Imprints & Series:
0 85924, 1 86371

Book Trade Association Membership:
Australian Book PA

2036

HARPERCOLLINSRELIGIOUS
[formerly Collins Dove]
19 Terracotta Drive, Blackburn, Vic 3130
Fax: +61 (Õ2) 9952 5588

Managing Director: Barrie Hitchon
Managers: Frank Priatel *(Sales & Marketing)*
Gerard Mullen *(Trade Sales)*
Publisher: Cathy Jenkins

Educational & Textbooks; Religion & Theology

New Titles: 101 (1996)

ISBNs, Imprints & Series:
0 85924, 1 86371

Parent Company:
HarperCollinsPublishers (Australia) Pty Ltd
Group *(Australia)*

Overseas Representation *(see §7.3):*
Canada: HarperCollins Publishers, Toronto &
Scarborough
New Zealand: HarperCollins Publishers,
Auckland
South Africa: HarperCollins Publishers,
Johannesburg
UK & Irish Republic: Gill & Macmillan Ltd,
Dublin, Irish Republic
USA: HarperCollins Publishers, San Francisco,
CA

Book Trade Association Membership:
Australian PA

2037

ROLAND HARVEY STUDIOS
62 Beach Street, Port Melbourne, Vic 3207
Telephone: +61 (Õ3) 9646 8711
Fax: +61 (Õ3) 9646 2245

Warehouse:
Rear 420 South Road, Moorabbin, Vic
Telephone: +61 (Õ3) 9532 1880
Fax: +61 (Õ3) 9532 0059

Director: Roland Harvey
Marketing Manager: Dinah Lewis *(Trade
Books, Rights & Export Sales)*

Children's Books

New Titles: 2 (1995), 5 (1996)
No of Employees: 6
Annual Turnover: $1.5M

ISBNs, Imprints & Series:
0 949714 Roland Harvey Books

Parent Company:
Green Croc Pty Ltd *(Australia)*

Overseas Representation *(see §7.3):*
New Zealand: Ashton Scholastic Ltd, Auckland

Book Trade Association Membership:
Australian PA, Friends of Dromkeen

2038

**HILL OF CONTENT PUBLISHING CO
PTY LTD**
86 Bourke Street, Melbourne, Vic 3000
Telephone: +61 (Õ3) 662 2282
Fax: +61 (Õ3) 662 2527

Warehouse:
180 Wellington Street, Collingwood, Vic 3066
Telephone: +61 (Õ3) 417 7611
Fax: +61 (Õ3) 416 2401

Directors: M. Zifcak *(Managing)*
M. Anderson *(Publishing & Export Sales)*

*Health & Beauty; Psychology & Psychiatry;
General; Leisure*

ISBNs, Imprints & Series: 0 85572

Overseas Representation *(see §7.3):*
South Africa: Southern Books, Halfway House
UK: Deep Books Ltd, London
USA: Seven Hills Book Distributors,
Cincinnati, OH

Book Trade Association Membership:
Australian PA, National Book Council

2039

HODDER EDUCATION
10–16 South Street, Rydalmere, NSW 2116
Telephone: +61 (Õ2) 638 5299
Fax: +61 (Õ2) 684 4942

Directors: Malcolm Edwards *(Managing)*
Richard Bartlett

Educational & Textbooks

New Titles: 17 (1995), 27 (1996)
No of Employees: 10
Annual Turnover: £1.5M

ISBNs, Imprints & Series:
0 340, 0 7131, 0 733

Parent Company:
Hodder Headline Australia Pty Ltd *(Australia)*

Overseas Representation *(see §7.3):*
New Zealand: Hodder Moa Beckett Publishers
Ltd, Auckland
Southern Africa: Hodder & Stoughton
Educational Southern Africa, Randburg,
South Africa

Book Trade Association Membership:
Australian PA

2040 ▬

HODDER HEADLINE (AUSTRALIA) PTY LTD
Rydalmere Business Park, 10–16 South Street,
Rydalmere, NSW 2116
Telephone: +61 (Õ2) 638 5299
Fax: +61 (Õ2) 684 4942

Directors: Malcolm Edwards *(Managing)*
Lisa Highton *(Publishing)*
Mary Howell *(Sales)*
Richard Bartlett *(Education Publishing &
Sales)*
David Cocking *(Finance)*

*Academic & Scholarly; Biography &
Autobiography; Children's Books; Cookery,
Wines & Spirits; Educational & Textbooks;
Fiction; History & Antiquarian; Natural
History*

New Titles: 162 (1995), 185 (1996)
No of Employees: 101
Annual Turnover: $15M

ISBNs, Imprints & Series:
0 340 Hodder & Stoughton
0 450 NEL
0 7131 Edward Arnold

Parent Company:
Hodder Headline Plc *(UK)*

Overseas Representation *(see §7.3)*:
Canada: Raincoast Distribution, Vancouver,
BC
New Zealand: Hodder Moa Beckett Publishers
Ltd, Auckland
South Africa: Southern Book Publishers,
Halfway House; Southern Books, Halfway
House
UK: Hodder Headline Plc, London

Book Trade Association Membership:
Australian PA, Christian Booksellers
Association of Australia

2041 ▬

HORWITZ PUBLICATIONS PTY LTD
55 Chandos Street, St Leonards, NSW 2065
Telephone: +61 (Õ2) 9901 6100
Fax: +61 (Õ2) 9901 6166

Educational & Textbooks

ISBNs, Imprints & Series:
0 7253 Martin Education
0 7255 Horwitz Publications

Overseas Representation *(see §7.3)*:
USA: Crouch International Ltd, New York, NY

2042 ▬

HOSPITALITY PRESS PTY LTD
38 Riddell Parade, (PO Box 426), Elsternwick,
Vic 3185
Telephone: +61 (Õ3) 9528 5021
Fax: +61 (Õ3) 9528 2645
Email: hosppress@publishaust.net.au

Directors: David Cunningham *(Managing,
Sales & Permissions)*
Jean Cunningham *(Publicity, Accounts)*

*Cookery, Wines & Spirits; Educational &
Textbooks; Industry, Business & Management;
Languages & Linguistics; Vocational Training
& Careers*

New Titles: 5 (1995), 7 (1996)
No of Employees: 4
Annual Turnover: £250,000

ISBNs, Imprints & Series: 0 86250

Overseas Representation *(see §7.3)*:
New Zealand: Virtue Books (NZ), Auckland
UK & Europe: Eddington Hook Ltd, Tunbridge
Wells, UK

Book Trade Association Membership:
Publish Australia

2043 ▬

**HYLAND HOUSE PUBLISHING PTY
LTD**
Hyland House, 387–389 Clarendon Street,
South Melbourne, Vic 3205
Telephone: +61 (Õ3) 9696 9064
Fax: +61 (Õ3) 9696 9065
Email: hylandhouse@peg.apc.org

Distribution:
Australian Book Distribution Group,
Calway Street (PO Box 130), Drouin, Vic 3818
Telephone: +61 (Õ56) 25 4290
Fax: +61 (Õ56) 25 4272

Publisher: Al Knight
Editorial: Anne Godden
Rose Kitching
Marketing: Andrew Wilkins *(Sales)*
Production: Susie Godden *(Rights &
Permissions)*
Promotions: Najiye Nihat

*Biography & Autobiography; Children's
Books; Cookery, Wines & Spirits; Crafts &
Hobbies; Do-It-Yourself; Fiction; Gardening;
Gender Studies; Health & Beauty; History &
Antiquarian; Poetry; Asian Studies*

New Titles: 18 (1995)
No of Employees: 6
Annual Turnover: $0.75M

ISBNs, Imprints & Series:
The Hyland House/Monash Asia Institute
Series, Young Hylanders (children's
paperback reprint)
0 908090, 0 947062, 1 875657

Overseas Representation *(see §7.3)*:
France: Agence Litteraire, Paris
Netherlands: Translit Literary Agents,
Amsterdam
New Zealand: Greene Phoenix Marketing,
Helensville
Spain: Kerrigan/Miro/Calonje Literary
Agency, Barcelona
UK: Gazelle Book Services Ltd, Lancaster
USA: Seven Hills Book Distributors,
Cincinnati, OH; The Australian Book
Source, Davis, CA

Book Trade Association Membership:
Australian PA, Publish Australia

2044 ▬

**THE IMAGES PUBLISHING GROUP
PTY LTD**
6 Bastow Place, Mulgrave, Vic 3170
Telephone: +61 (Õ3) 9561 5544
Fax: +61 (Õ3) 9561 4860
Email: books@images.com.au

Joint Managing Directors: Paul A. Latham
Alessina R. Brooks

*Architecture & Design; Fashion & Costume;
Fine Art & Art History; Reference Books,
Directories & Dictionaries*

New Titles: 12 (1995), 15 (1996)
No of Employees: 10
Annual Turnover: $3.5M

ISBNs, Imprints & Series: 1 875498

Associated & Subsidiary Companies:
Australia: Images Australia P/c

Overseas Representation *(see §7.3)*:
Asia & Japan: Nippon Nippon, Japan; Shuppan
Hanbai, Japan; Nippon IPS, Japan
USA: McGraw-Hill Inc, International Group,
Hightstown, NJ & New York; AIA Press

2045 ▬

**INSTITUTE FOR ABORIGINAL
DEVELOPMENT (IAD) PRESS**
3 South Terrace, (PO Box 2531), Alice Springs,
NT 0871
Telephone: +61 (Õ89) 51 1311
Fax: +61 (Õ89) 52 2527

Distributor:
Tower Books, 2 Sydenham Road, Brookvale,
NSW 2100
Telephone: +61 (Õ2) 9975 5566
Fax: +61 (Õ2) 9975 5599

Publications Officer: Mark Maclean
Editor: Marg Bowman
Designer: Louise Wellington
Production Manager: Brenda Thornley
Sales & Marketing: Josie Douglas

*Academic & Scholarly; Educational &
Textbooks; Languages & Linguistics*

New Titles: 9 (1995), 12 (1996)
No of Employees: 5
Annual Turnover: £75,000

ISBNs, Imprints & Series: 0 949659

Overseas Representation *(see §7.3)*:
UK & Europe: Gazelle Book Services Ltd,
Lancaster, UK

Book Trade Association Membership:
Australian PA

2046 ▬

JACARANDA WILEY LTD
PO Box 1226, Milton, Qld 4064
Telephone: +61 (Õ7) 3859 9755
Fax: +61 (Õ7) 3859 9715
Email: headoffice@jacwiley.com.au

Location:
33 Park Road, Milton, Qld 4064

Warehouse & Shipping:
56 Edmonstone Road, Bowen Hills, Qld 4006
Telephone: +61 (07) 3252 1149
Fax: +61 (07) 3257 1106

Victoria Office:
184–186 Glenferrie Road, Malvern, Vic 3144
Telephone: +61 (03) 957 61011
Fax: +61 (03) 957 61132

NSW Office:
Suite 4A, 113 Wicks Road, North Ryde,
NSW 2113
Telephone: +61 (02) 9805 1100
Fax: +61 (02) 9805 1597
Email: sydney@jacwiley.com.au

Managing Director: Peter Donoughue *(Export Sales)*
Director: Quentin Smith *(Finance & Administration)*
Managers: Peter van Noorden *(School Division)*
Lucy Russell *(Tertiary Division)*
Shawn Casey *(Professional, Reference & Trade Division)*
David Wilson *(Editorial/Production)*
Chris Prebble *(Technology & Services)*
Rights & Permissions: Ann Braben

Academic & Scholarly; Accountancy & Taxation; Agriculture; Architecture & Design; Atlases & Maps; Chemistry; Children's Books; Computer Science; Cookery, Wines & Spirits; Economics; Educational & Textbooks; Electronic (Educational); Electronic (Professional & Academic); Engineering; Geography & Geology; Industry, Business & Management; Languages & Linguistics; Law; Literature & Criticism; Mathematics & Statistics; Medical (incl. Self Help & Alternative Medicine); Physics; Psychology & Psychiatry; Reference Books, Directories & Dictionaries; Scientific & Technical; Theatre, Drama & Dance; Vocational Training & Careers

New Titles: 69 (1995), 55 (1996)
No of Employees: 120
Annual Turnover: $18M

ISBNs, Imprints & Series:
0 471 John Wiley & Sons
0 7016 The Jacaranda Press
0 86440 Brooks Waterloo

Parent Company:
John Wiley & Sons Inc *(USA)*

Associated & Subsidiary Companies:
Canada: John Wiley & Sons Canada Ltd.
India: Wiley Eastern Ltd. *Singapore:* John Wiley & Sons (SEA) Pte Ltd. *UK:* John Wiley & Sons Ltd

Book Trade Association Membership:
Australian PA

2047 ▬▬▬▬▬▬▬▬▬▬▬▬▬▬▬

THE JOINT BOARD OF CHRISTIAN EDUCATION
PO Box 1245, Collingwood, Vic 3006
Telephone: +61 (03) 9416 4262

Fax: +61 (03) 9416 4264
Email: jbce@jbce.com.au

Executive Director: John A. Emmett
Books Manager: Hugh McGinlay
Editorial: Rev Colville Crowe *(Associate Director)*
Rights & Permissions: Mrs Jan Scutt

Religion & Theology; Christian Education

New Titles: 66 (1995), 64 (1996)
No of Employees: 15

ISBNs, Imprints & Series:
0 85819, 1 86407

Associated & Subsidiary Companies:
Australia: Uniting Church Press

Overseas Representation *(see §7.3):*
Canada: United Church Publishing House, Etobicoke, Ont
New Zealand: Epworth Bookshop, Wellington
UK: National Christian Education Council, Birmingham
USA: Morehouse, Ridgefield CT

Book Trade Association Membership:
Christian Bookselling Association of Australia

2048 ▬▬▬▬▬▬▬▬▬▬▬▬▬▬▬

KANGAROO PRESS PTY LTD
3 Whitehall Road, Kenthurst, NSW 2156
Telephone: +61 (02) 654 1502
Fax: +61 (02) 654 1338
Email: 100231.2308@compuserve.com

Postal Address:
PO Box 6125, Dural Delivery Centre,
NSW 2158

Managing Director: David Rosenberg *(Editorial & Production, Export Sales, Rights & Permissions)*
Publicity Director: Scilla Rosenberg *(Distribution)*
Sales Manager: Van McCune

Agriculture; Animal Care & Breeding; Antiques & Collecting; Biography & Autobiography; Children's Books; Crafts & Hobbies; Do-It-Yourself; Gardening; Guide Books; History & Antiquarian; Military & War; Natural History; Sports & Games; Transport; Travel & Topography

New Titles: 75 (1995), 75 (1996)
No of Employees: 9
Annual Turnover: £1.4M

ISBNs, Imprints & Series:
0 949924, 0 86417 Growing Series, Kangaroo Press, Picture Roo Books

Overseas Representation *(see §7.3):*
New Zealand: Penguin Books (New Zealand) Ltd, Auckland
South Africa: Leo Books, Roggebai
UK: Hi Marketing, London
USA: Seven Hills Book Distributors, Cincinnati, OH
USA (craft books): Unicorn Books and Crafts Inc, Petaluma, CA, USA

Book Trade Association Membership:
Australian PA

2049 ▬▬▬▬▬▬▬▬▬▬▬▬▬▬▬

LANSDOWNE PUBLISHING
Level 5, 70 George Street, Sydney, NSW 2000
Telephone: +61 (02) 240 9222
Fax: +61 (02) 241 4818
Email: lansdowne@magna.com.au

Directors: Jane Curry *(Chief Executive Officer, Publisher)*
Steven Morris *(Sales)*
Managers: Sally Stokes *(Production)*
Debbie Zampieri *(Marketing)*
Edwina Ferris *(Finance & IT)*
Deborah Nixon *(Publishing)*

Animal Care & Breeding; Cookery, Wines & Spirits; Gardening; Health & Beauty; Australiana; Gift Books; New Age/History/Mythology

New Titles: 20 (1995), 30 (1996)
No of Employees: 18

ISBNs, Imprints & Series:
0 7018 Lansdowne Press
0 7254 Ure Smith Press
0 7270 Rigby Publishers
1 86302 Harbour, Lansdowne Publishing (formerly Weldon Publishing)

Parent Company:
Kirin Publishing Pty Ltd *(Australia)*

Book Trade Association Membership:
Australian PA

2050 ▬▬▬▬▬▬▬▬▬▬▬▬▬▬▬

LBC INFORMATION SERVICES
[formerly The Law Book Co Ltd]
44–50 Waterloo Road, North Ryde, NSW 2113
Telephone: +61 (02) 9936 6444
Fax: +61 (02) 888 9706

Director: E. Costigan *(Managing)*
Managers: B. Crane *(Sales)*
A. M. O'Neill *(Publisher)*
C. Simmons *(Marketing & Sales)*
P. Finneran *(Production)*

Accountancy & Taxation; Educational & Textbooks; Law

New Titles: 48 (1995), 50 (1996)
No of Employees: 350

ISBNs, Imprints & Series: 0 455

Parent Company:
Thomson Corporation Ltd *(Canada)*

Associated & Subsidiary Companies:
Australia: Centre for Professional Development (Australia) Pty Ltd; Newsletter Information Services Pty Ltd. *New Zealand:* Brookers

Overseas Representation *(see §7.3):*
Singapore: Thomson Information Services
UK & Europe: Sweet & Maxwell Ltd, London, UK

USA & Canada: Carswell Legal Publications, Scarborough, Canada; Wm. W. Gaunt & Sons Inc, Holmes Beach FL, USA

Book Trade Association Membership:
Australian Booksellers Association, Australian PA

2051

*LEARNING SOLUTIONS
(Rear) 444 Cambridge Street, Floreat, WA 6014
Telephone: +61 (Õ9) 383 7966
Fax: +61 (Õ9) 383 7967

Postal Address (For all literature):
PO Box 325, Jolimont, WA 6014

Directors: Ian Ritchie *(Managing)*
Denyse Ritchie *(Head of Production)*

Educational & Textbooks

ISBNs, Imprints & Series: 1 86399

Parent Company:
Ebony Holdings Pty Ltd *(Australia)*

Overseas Representation *(see §7.3):*
South Africa: The Caxton Bookshop, Cape Town

Book Trade Association Membership:
Australian Book PA

2052

LITTLE HILLS PRESS PTY LTD
Suite 11, Regent House,
37–43 Alexander Street, Crows Nest,
NSW 2065
Telephone: +61 (Õ2) 437 6995
Fax: +61 (Õ2) 438 5762
Email: littlehills@peg.apc.org
Web Site: http://www.peg.apc.org/~littlehills

Director: Charles Burfitt

Biography & Autobiography; Crafts & Hobbies; Gardening; Religion & Theology; Travel & Topography

New Titles: 10 (1995), 11 (1996)
No of Employees: 6

ISBNs, Imprints & Series:
0 949773, 1 86315 At Cost Travel Guides, Mount Series

Overseas Representation *(see §7.3):*
Canada: Ulysses Books & Maps, Montreal
Europe: D. Richard Bowen, Malmö, Sweden
Singapore: Graham Brash Pte Ltd
Southern Africa: P.M.C. International Importers & Exporters CC, Durban North, South Africa
UK & Europe (travel titles only): Moorland Publishing Co, Ashbourne, UK
USA (certain travel titles only): Pelican Publishing Co, Gretna, LA, USA

2053

*LONELY PLANET PUBLICATIONS PTY LTD
192 Burwood Road, PO Box 617, Hawthorn, Vic 3122
Telephone: +61 (Õ3) 819 1877
Fax: +61 (Õ3) 819 6459

Directors: Tony Wheeler
Maureen Wheeler
Jim Hart
General Managers: Richard Evenst
Steve Hibbard
Andy Neilson *(Rights & Permissions)*
Tom Danby *(Regional Sales)*
Graham Imeson *(Art & Production)*
Anna Bolger *(Promotions)*
Publishers: Sue Galley *(Guidebooks)*
Rob van Driesum *(Guidebooks)*
Rob Flynn *(Multimedia)*
Sally Steward *(Phrase Books)*
Paul Smitz *(Travel Atlases)*
Michelle de Kretzer *(Travel Literature)*

Atlases & Maps; Guide Books; Languages & Linguistics; Travel & Topography

ISBNs, Imprints & Series:
0 86442, 0 908086

Associated & Subsidiary Companies:
France: Lonely Planet. *UK:* Lonely Planet Publications. *USA:* Lonely Planet Publications Inc

Overseas Representation *(see §7.3):*
France: Lonely Planet, Paris
UK: Lonely Planet Publications, London
USA: Lonely Planet Publications Inc, Oakland, CA

Book Trade Association Membership:
Australian Book PA

2054

LONGMAN AUSTRALIA PTY LTD
95 Coventry Street, South Melbourne, Vic 3205
Telephone: +61 (Õ3) 9697 0666
Fax: +61 (Õ3) 9699 2041
Email: @awl.com.au

NSW Branch:
Level 1, 2 Lincoln Street, Lane Cove,
NSW 2066
Telephone: +61 (Õ2) 428 8000
Fax: +61 (Õ2) 427 9922

Queensland Branch:
Paddington Market, Unit 17,
261–267 Given Terrace, Paddington, Qld 4064
Telephone: +61 (Õ7) 3369 2114
Fax: +61 (Õ7) 3369 2137

Western Australia Branch:
1174 Hay Street, West Perth, WA 6005
Telephone: +61 (Õ9) 322 6054
Fax: +61 (Õ9) 321 0054

Directors: R. W. Fisher *(Managing)*
B. Ashcroft-Hawley *(Finance Director & Company Secretary)*
R. D. Harper *(Business Development)*
P. J. Field
R. Stagg
Rights & Permissions: A. Peterson

Sales: E. Anders *(Primary)*
M. Spears *(Secondary)*
D. Barnett *(Tertiary)*
S. Judd *(Trade)*
J. Holt *(Export)*

Academic & Scholarly; Accountancy & Taxation; Economics; Educational & Textbooks; English as a Foreign Language; Geography & Geology; History & Antiquarian; Industry, Business & Management; Languages & Linguistics; Mathematics & Statistics; Politics & World Affairs; Sociology & Anthropology

New Titles: 288 (1995), 325 (1996)
No of Employees: 150

ISBNs, Imprints & Series:
0 201 Addison-Wesley
0 582 Longman Australia
0 7015 Cheshire Publishing
0 8053 Benjamin/Cummings
1 5600 Peachpit Press

Parent Company:
Pearson Plc *(UK)*

Overseas Representation *(see §7.3):*
Hong Kong: Longman Asia Ltd
Malaysia: Longman Malaysia Sdn Bhd, Petaling Jaya
New Zealand: Addison Wesley Longman New Zealand Pty Ltd, Auckland
Singapore: Longman Singapore Publishers (Pte) Ltd; Addison-Wesley (Singapore) Pte Ltd
UK: Addison Wesley Longman UK, Harlow

Book Trade Association Membership:
Australian PA, National Book Council

2055

LOTHIAN BOOKS
11 Munro Street, Port Melbourne, Vic 3207
Telephone: +61 (Õ3) 9645 1544
Fax: +61 (Õ3) 9646 4882
Email: books@lothian.com.au and custserv@iaccess.com.au

NSW Branch:
Suite 192, 392 Jones Street, Ultimo, NSW 2007
Telephone: +61 (Õ2) 692 9099 & 9267
Fax: +61 (Õ2) 552 2310

Queensland Branch:
47 Marsh Street, Cannon Hill, Qld 4170
Telephone: +61 (Õ7) 3395 6905
Fax: +61 (Õ7) 3395 6905

South Australia Branch:
1 John Street, Kingswood, SA 5062
Telephone: +61 (Õ8) 272 4182
Fax: +61 (Õ8) 271 4854

Western Australia Branch:
PO Box 130, Darlington, WA 6070
Telephone: +61 (Õ9) 299 7348
Fax: +61 (Õ9) 299 7348

Directors: Peter Lothian *(Managing & Chairman, Export Sales)*
Ms E. McDonald *(Publishing, Rights & Commissions)*

Gary J. Matthews *(Company Secretary,*
  Finance & Distribution)
Bruce Hilliard *(Sales)*

Children's Books; Cookery, Wines & Spirits;
Crafts & Hobbies; Do-It-Yourself; Gardening;
Health & Beauty; Gift; New Age; Self Help

New Titles: 55 (1995), 60 (1996)
No of Employees: 38

ISBNs, Imprints & Series: 0 85091

Parent Company:
Thomas C. Lothian Pty Ltd *(Australia)*

Associated & Subsidiary Companies:
Australia: Lothian Books; Taltrade Sales Pty
Ltd

Overseas Representation *(see §7.3):*
Canada: Vanwell Publishing Ltd, St
  Catherines, Ont
Hong Kong: Mediaplus Books Ltd
Malaysia & Singapore: PMS Books Pte Ltd,
  Singapore
New Zealand: Forrester Books Ltd, Auckland
South Africa: Southern Book Publishers,
  Halfway House
UK: Gazelle Book Services Ltd, Lancaster
USA: Seven Hills Book Distributors,
  Cincinnati, OH

Book Trade Association Membership:
Australian PA

2056

**McGRAW-HILL BOOK CO
AUSTRALIA PTY LTD**
4 Barcoo Street, Roseville, NSW 2069
Telephone: +61 (Õ2) 417 4288
Fax: +61 (Õ2) 417 8872

Directors: Firgal Adams *(Managing)*
Graham Foxcroft *(Finance)*
Managers: Jeremy Fisher *(Tertiary Division)*
Tony Wong *(School Division)*
Penny Martin *(Production)*
John Rowe *(Professional & Reference
  Division)*

Academic & Scholarly; Architecture & Design;
Educational & Textbooks; Electronic
(Educational); Engineering; Industry, Business
& Management; Medical (incl. Self Help &
Alternative Medicine); Veterinary Science

New Titles: 86 (1995), 92 (1996)
No of Employees: 106
Annual Turnover: $154M

ISBNs, Imprints & Series:
0 07 Osborne
0 8168, 0 8306, 0 89433 Tab Books

Parent Company:
McGraw-Hill Inc *(USA)*

Associated & Subsidiary Companies:
New Zealand: McGraw-Hill Book Co New
Zealand Ltd

Overseas Representation *(see §7.3):*
Canada: McGraw Hill Ryerson, Scarborough
Mexico: McGraw-Hill Interamericana de
  Mexico, SA de C.V., Naucalpan

Portugal: McGraw-Hill Interamericana de
  Portugal Ltda, Lisbon
Singapore: McGraw-Hill Book Co
Spain: McGraw-Hill InterAmericana de
  España SA, Madrid
UK: McGraw-Hill Book Co (Europe) Ltd,
  Maidenhead
USA: McGraw-Hill Inc, International Group,
  Hightstown, NJ & New York

Book Trade Association Membership:
Australian PA, US Book PA

2057

MACLENNAN & PETTY PTY LTD
4/809 Botany Road, (PO Box 145), Rosebery,
NSW 2018
Telephone: +61 (Õ2) 9669 5755
Fax: +61 (Õ2) 9669 5997

Directors: Pamela Petty *(Managing)*
Friedel Gehring *(Finance & Operations)*
Jenny Curtis *(Publishing)*
Rod Mead *(Special Projects)*
Co-ordinators: Laura Yuen *(Marketing
  Services)*
Deidre Cox *(Foreign Rights)*

*Educational & Textbooks; Medical (incl. Self
Help & Alternative Medicine); Psychology &
Psychiatry*

New Titles: 6 (1995), 9 (1996)
No of Employees: 14

ISBNs, Imprints & Series: 0 86433

Overseas Representation *(see §7.3):*
Europe & UK: Jessica Kingsley Publishers,
  London, UK
South East Asia: APAC Publishers Services,
  Singapore
USA: F. A. Davis Co, Philadelphia, PA

2058

MELBOURNE UNIVERSITY PRESS
268 Drummond Street, Carlton, Vic 3103
Telephone: +61 (Õ3) 9347 3455
Fax: +61 (Õ3) 9349 2527

Warehouse & Australian Trade Enquiries:
Penguin Books Australia Pty Ltd,
487 Maroondah Highway, Ringwood, Vic 134
Telephone: +61 (Õ3) 9871 2400
Fax: +61 (Õ3) 9870 6086

Retail Sales:
Melbourne University Bookroom,
University Grounds, Parkville, Vic 3052
Telephone: +61 (Õ3) 9344 6217
Fax: +61 (Õ3) 9344 5621
Email: publish@mup.unimelb.edu.au

Managers: Brian Wilder *(Director)*
Andrew Watson *(Assistant Director –
  Editorial, Production, Electronic
  Publishing)*
John Meckan *(Assistant Director – Finance,
  Operations)*
Bruce Allardice *(Assistant Director – Retail)*
Teresa Pitt *(Commissioning Editor)*
Allison Jones *(Marketing)*

Academic & Scholarly; Agriculture;
Archaeology; Biography & Autobiography;

*Chemistry; Economics; Educational &
Textbooks; Environment & Development
Studies; Fine Art & Art History; Gender
Studies; Geography & Geology; History &
Antiquarian; Law; Literature & Criticism;
Medical (incl. Self Help & Alternative
Medicine); Military & War; Natural History;
Politics & World Affairs; Psychology &
Psychiatry; Reference Books, Directories &
Dictionaries; Sociology & Anthropology;
Theatre, Drama & Dance*

New Titles: 55 (1995), 58 (1996)

ISBNs, Imprints & Series:
0 522 Melbourne University Press, Miegunyah
  Press

Overseas Representation *(see §7.3):*
Japan: United Publishers Services Ltd, Tokyo
New Zealand: Penguin Books (New Zealand)
  Ltd, Auckland
UK & Europe: Gazelle Book Services Ltd,
  Lancaster, UK
USA & Canada: Paul & Co Publishers
  Consortium Inc, New York, USA

Book Trade Association Membership:
Australian PA

2059

***MIMOSA PUBLISHING LTD**
PO Box 779, Hawthorn, Vic 3122
Telephone: +61 (Õ3) 9819 0511
Fax: +61 (Õ3) 9819 0524

Location:
8 Yarra Street, Hawthorn, Vic
Telephone: +61 (Õ3) 9819 0511
Fax: +61 (Õ3) 9819 0524

Directors: Sue Donovan
John Gilder
Managing Editor: Janet Hillman

Children's Books; Educational & Textbooks

ISBNs, Imprints & Series:
0 7327 Creciendo con matemáticas, Literacy
  Links/2000, Moving into Math, Science
  Alive

Parent Company:
Weldon International *(Australia)*

Associated & Subsidiary Companies:
UK: Kingscourt Publishing. *USA:* Mimosa
Publications

Book Trade Association Membership:
Australian Book PA

2060

MURDOCH BOOKS
213 Miller Street, North Sydney, NSW 2060
Telephone: +61 (Õ2) 9956 1000
Fax: +61 (Õ2) 9956 1922

Publisher: Anne Wilson
Managers: Mark Newman *(International)*
Mark Smith *(Marketing)*
Catie Ziller *(Publishing)*
Dianne Bedford *(International)*

Children's Books; Cookery, Wines & Spirits; Crafts & Hobbies; Do-It-Yourself; Gardening; Natural History; Sports & Games

New Titles: 90 (1995), 105 (1996)
No of Employees: 45
Annual Turnover: $20M

ISBNs, Imprints & Series:
0 86411 Better Homes & Gardens, Family Circle, Murdoch Books
1 86378 Bay Books

Parent Company:
Murdoch Magazines Pty Ltd *(Australia)*

Overseas Representation *(see §7.3)*:
Canada: Whitecap Books, Vancouver, BC
New Zealand: Golden Press Ltd, Auckland
South Africa: Struik Book Distributors, Sandton, Johannesburg
UK: ACP (UK) Ltd, Northampton

Book Trade Association Membership:
Australian PA

2061 ■■■■■

NATIONAL GALLERY OF AUSTRALIA
PO Box 1150, Canberra, ACT 2601
Telephone: +61 (06) 2406 411
Fax: +61 (06) 2406 427

Home Representation:
Thames & Hudson (Australia) Pty Ltd,
11 Central Boulevard, Portside Business Park,
Port Melbourne, Vic 3207

Marketing & Publications Manager: Suzie Campbell
Rights & Permissions Officer: Jane Hyden

Fine Art & Art History; Photography

ISBNs, Imprints & Series:
0 642130 Australian National Gallery, National Gallery of Australia

Overseas Representation *(see §7.3)*:
UK: Thames & Hudson Ltd, London
USA: Thames & Hudson Inc, New York

Book Trade Association Membership:
Australian PA

2062 ■■■■■

NATIONAL GALLERY OF VICTORIA
180 St Kilda Road, Melbourne, Vic 3004
Telephone: +61 (03) 920 8222
Fax: +61 (03) 9208 0241

Merchandise Manager: Philip Jago

Academic & Scholarly; Fashion & Costume; Fine Art & Art History

New Titles: 8 (1995), 6 (1996)

ISBNs, Imprints & Series: 0 7241

Overseas Representation *(see §7.3)*:
UK: Arts Bibliographic, London

2063 ■■■■■

NATIONAL LIBRARY OF AUSTRALIA
Parkes Place, Canberra, ACT 2600
Telephone: +61 (06) 262 1474
Fax: +61 (06) 273 4493

Director, Publications & Marketing: Paul Hetherington
Manager, Sales & Marketing: Greg Turner

Bibliography & Library Science; History & Antiquarian; Illustrated & Fine Editions

New Titles: 12 (1995), 14 (1996)
No of Employees: 20

ISBNs, Imprints & Series: 0 642106

Book Trade Association Membership:
Australian PA

2064 ■■■■■

THOMAS NELSON AUSTRALIA
102 Dodds Street, South Melbourne, Vic 3205
Telephone: +61 (03) 968 54111
Fax: +61 (03) 968 54199

NSW Office:
Suite 7, 50 Great North Road, Five Dock, NSW 2046
Telephone: +61 (02) 712 2666
Fax: +61 (02) 712 2555

Queensland Office:
Suite 4, 727 Stanley Street, Woolloongabba, Qld 4102
Telephone: +61 (07) 3891 2144
Fax: +61 (07) 3891 2188

Directors: Edward Gannan *(Managing)*
John Mehan *(Finance & Operations)*
Greg Browne *(School Division)*
Rights & Permissions: Michelle Atkins

Educational & Textbooks; Electronic (Educational); Scientific & Technical; Vocational Training & Careers

ISBNs, Imprints & Series: 0 17

Parent Company:
The Thomson Corporation *(Canada)*

Associated & Subsidiary Companies:
New Zealand: Nelson Price Milburn

Overseas Representation *(see §7.3)*:
Canada: Nelson Canada, Scarborough
New Zealand: Nelson Price Milburn Ltd, Wellington
UK: Thomas Nelson & Sons Ltd, Walton-on-Thames

Book Trade Association Membership:
Australian PA

2065 ■■■■■

UNIVERSITY OF NEW SOUTH WALES PRESS
Sydney, NSW 2052
Telephone: +61 (02) 398 8900
Fax: +61 (02) 398 3408

Warehouse:
Govett Street, Randwick, NSW 2031

Directors: Oliver Freeman *(Chairman)*
Peter Sharpe *(Managing)*
Jeremy Davis
Barry Garner
Graham Bradley
Group Accountant: John Szabo *(Company Secretary)*
Production & Design: Diane Quick
Sales & Marketing: Maria Foster

Academic & Scholarly; Accountancy & Taxation; Agriculture; Biology & Zoology; Educational & Textbooks; Gardening; Natural History; Politics & World Affairs; Reference Books, Directories & Dictionaries; Scientific & Technical

New Titles: 35 (1995), 35 (1996)
No of Employees: 15
Annual Turnover: £1M

ISBNs, Imprints & Series:
0 86840 University of New South Wales Press
0 908237 Tafe Educational Books

Overseas Representation *(see §7.3)*:
Canada & USA: International Specialized Book Services Inc, Portland, OR, USA

Book Trade Association Membership:
Australian PA

2066 ■■■■■

OPENBOOK PUBLISHERS
PO Box 1368, GPO, Adelaide, SA 5001
Telephone: +61 (08) 223 5468
Fax: +61 (08) 223 4552
Email: openbook.@enet.com.au

Location:
205 Halifax Street, Adelaide, SA 5000
Telephone: *(as above)*
Email: *(as above)*

Managers: Warren Schirmer *(General)*
Chris Pfeiffer *(Marketing, Trade Sales & Exports)*
John Altus *(Administrative Services, Rights & Permissions)*

Children's Books; Religion & Theology

New Titles: 15 (1995), 28 (1996)
No of Employees: 72
Annual Turnover: $7.9M

ISBNs, Imprints & Series: 0 85910

Overseas Representation *(see §7.3)*:
New Zealand: Omega Distributors Ltd, Auckland
UK: Fowler Wright Books Ltd, Leominster
USA: Concordia Publishing House, Saint Louis

Book Trade Association Membership:
Australian PA, Christian Bookselling Association of Australia

2067 ■■■■■

PASCOE PUBLISHING PTY LTD
PO Box 42, Apollo Bay, Vic 3233

Telephone: +61 (Ō52) 379 227 & 376 311
Fax: +61 (Ō52) 376 559

Directors: Bruce Pascoe *(Senior Editor)*
Lyn Harwood *(Assistant Editor)*

Fiction; Literature & Criticism

New Titles: 5 (1995), 4 (1996)

ISBNs, Imprints & Series: 0 947087

Associated & Subsidiary Companies:
Australia: Cape Distribution

Book Trade Association Membership:
Australian PA, Australian BA, Society of
Editors, Australian Society of Authors,
Fellowship of Australian Writers, Amnesty
International (Writers)

2068

PENGUIN BOOKS AUSTRALIA LTD
487–493 Maroondah Highway, Ringwood,
Vic 3134
Telephone: +61 (Ō3) 9871 2400
Fax: +61 (Ō3) 9870 9618

Directors: P. J. Field *(Managing)*
P. W. Dart *(Information Services)*
R. W. Fisher
R. E. Ford *(Trade Services)*
P. M. Mayer
R. P. Sessions *(Publishing)*
J. C. Strike *(Finance & Administration)*
Chief Accountant: J. Elkin
Warehouse Operations Manager: R.
  Caithness
Editorial: Julie Gibbs *(Publisher – Viking)*
Bryony Cosgrove *(Publisher – Penguin/
  McPhee Gribble)*
Julie Watts *(Publisher – Children's)*
Peg McColl *(Rights & Permissions)*
Marketing Managers: Patricia Adam
  (Children's Books)
Gabrielle Coyne *(Adult Books)*
Sales Managers: Margaret Thompson
  (Paperback)
Lyn Amy *(Hardback)*
Paula Hurley *(Education)*

*Architecture & Design; Atlases & Maps;
Biography & Autobiography; Children's
Books; Cookery, Wines & Spirits; Crime;
Crafts & Hobbies; Economics; Educational &
Textbooks; Electronic (Professional &
Academic); Fiction; Fine Art & Art History;
Gardening; Guide Books; Health & Beauty;
History & Antiquarian; Humour; Literature &
Criticism; Natural History; Poetry; Politics &
World Affairs; Reference Books, Directories &
Dictionaries; Science Fiction; Sociology &
Anthropology; Sports & Games; Travel &
Topography*

No of Employees: 315

ISBNs, Imprints & Series:
0 14 Fantail, Pelican, Penguin, Puffin
0 241 Hamish Hamilton
0 451 Mentor, Onyx, ROC, Signet, Topaz
0 452 Meridian, Meridian Classic, Plume
0 453 NAL
0 525 Dutton
0 670 Viking
0 7181 Michael Joseph

0 7207 Pelham Books
0 7214 Ladybird
0 7232 Frederick Warne
0 8037 Dial
0 86914 McPhee Gribble
0 88677 DAW

Parent Company:
Penguin Publishing Co Ltd *(UK)*

Associated & Subsidiary Companies:
Australia: Addison Wesley Longman; Pearson
Professional Pty Ltd. *Canada:* Penguin Books
Canada Ltd. *New Zealand:* Penguin Books
(New Zealand) Ltd. *UK:* Addison-Wesley;
Churchill Livingstone; Hamish Hamilton Ltd;
Michael Joseph Ltd; Ladybird Books Ltd;
Longman Group Ltd; Oliver & Boyd; Penguin
Books Ltd; Frederick Warne. *USA:* Penguin
Books USA Inc

Book Trade Association Membership:
Australian PA

2069

*PHOENIX EDUCATION PTY LTD
PO Box 197, Albert Park, Vic 3206
Telephone: +61 (Ō3) 699 8377
Fax: +61 (Ō3) 699 9242

Interstate Office:
102 Charles Street, Putney, NSW 2112
Telephone: +61 (Ō2) 809 3579
Fax: +61 (Ō2) 808 1430

Chairman: Barney Rivers
General Manager: David Stewart
Editorial & Production Director: Ruth Siems

Educational & Textbooks

ISBNs, Imprints & Series: 1 875695

Book Trade Association Membership:
Australian Book PA

2070

PLUTO PRESS AUSTRALIA
PO Box 199, Leichhardt, NSW 2040
Telephone: +61 (Ō2) 519 3299
Fax: +61 (Ō2) 519 8940
Email: pluto@socialchange.net.au
Web Site: http://www.pluto.socialchange.net.
au

**Warehouse, Trade Representation &
Distribution:**
University of New South Wales Press,
22 King Street, Randwick 2031
Telephone: +61 (Ō2) 398 8900
Fax: +61 (Ō2) 398 3408

Directors: Ric Sissons *(Managing)*
Sean Kidney

*Gender Studies; Law; Politics & World Affairs;
Industrial Relations*

New Titles: 15 (1995), 15 (1996)
Annual Turnover: £125,000

ISBNs, Imprints & Series:
0 949138, 1 86403

Associated & Subsidiary Companies:
Australia: Social Change Media

2071

DEPARTMENT OF PRIMARY
INDUSTRIES
GPO Box 46, Brisbane, Qld 4001
Telephone: +61 (Ō7) 3239 3100
Fax: +61 (Ō7) 3239 0860
Email: books@dpi.qld.gov.au

*Agriculture; Animal Care & Breeding;
Electronic (Educational); Electronic
(Professional & Academic); Gardening;
Veterinary Science*

ISBNs, Imprints & Series: 0 7242

Overseas Representation *(see §7.3)*:
Europe & UK: Books Express, Saffron
  Walden, UK
India, Bhutan, Pakistan & Nepal: United
  Publishers, Assam, India
New Zealand: Techbook Distributors,
  Auckland
Singapore, Malaysia & Brunei: Publishers
  Marketing Services Ltd, Singapore
USA: agAccess, Davis, CA

Book Trade Association Membership:
Australian PA

2072

PROSPECT MEDIA PTY LTD
Level 11, Carlton Centre,
55–63 Elizabeth Street, Sydney, NSW 2000
Telephone: +61 (Ō2) 221 6199
Fax: +61 (Ō2) 221 5923
Email: oliver@well.com
Web Site: http://www.prospectmedia.com.au

Bookshop:
Legal Books, 60–70 Elizabeth Street, Sydney,
NSW 2000
Telephone: +61 (Ō2) 231 6547
Fax: +61 (Ō2) 233 1602
Email: legalb@slmflim.flnfw.gov.au and
legalbooks.com.au

Managing Director: Oliver Freeman
Managers: Sue Howard *(Sales)*
Matthew Langman *(Marketing)*
Managing Editor: Jenny Berich
Financial Accountant: Vicky Mahadeva

*Accountancy & Taxation; Educational &
Textbooks; Industry, Business & Management;
Law*

New Titles: 12 (1995), 12 (1996)
No of Employees: 20
Annual Turnover: £1.5M

ISBNs, Imprints & Series:
0 186316 Australian Business Network, Legal
  Books, Prospect Media, Prospect Publishing

Parent Company:
Oliver Freeman Pty Ltd *(Australia)*

Book Trade Association Membership:
Australian PA, Publish Australia Group
Enterprises

2073 ▬▬▬▬▬▬▬▬▬▬▬▬▬

*THE UNIVERSITY OF QUEENSLAND PRESS
PO Box 42, St Lucia, Qld 4067
Telephone: +61 (07) 365 2127
Fax: +61 (07) 365 1988

Warehouse & Orders:
Penguin Books, Australia Ltd, PO Box 257,
Ringwood, Vic 3134
Telephone: (03) 871 2555
Fax: (03) 870 6086

Director & General Manager: Laurie Muller
Managers: Keith McDonald *(Finance & Administration)*
Dr Craig Munro *(Editorial & Publishing, Rights & Permissions)*
Robert Brown *(Marketing & Sales)*
Terry Farley *(Production)*

Academic & Scholarly; Accountancy & Taxation; Agriculture; Biography & Autobiography; Children's Books; Crafts & Hobbies; Economics; Educational & Textbooks; Fiction; Geography & Geology; Guide Books; History & Antiquarian; Industry, Business & Management; Law; Literature & Criticism; Military & War; Natural History; Philosophy; Poetry; Politics & World Affairs; Psychology & Psychiatry; Religion & Theology; Science Fiction; Sociology & Anthropology; Sports & Games

ISBNs, Imprints & Series: 0 7022

Overseas Representation *(see §7.3):*
New Zealand: Tandem Press, Auckland
USA: International Specialized Book Services Inc, Portland, OR

Book Trade Association Membership:
Australian Association of University Presses

2074 ▬▬▬▬▬▬▬▬▬▬▬▬▬

READER'S DIGEST (AUSTRALIA) PTY LTD
26–32 Waterloo Street, Surry Hills, NSW 2010
Telephone: +61 (02) 690 6111
Fax: +61 (02) 699 8165

Distributor:
Hodder Headline Australia Pty Ltd,
10–16 South Street, Rydalmere, NSW 2116
Telephone: +61 (02) 638 5299
Fax: +61 (02) 684 4942

Retail Publishing Division: Robert Sarsfield *(Publisher – Catalogue & Trade Books)*
Tony Philip *(National Sales Manager – Trade Books)*
General Books Editorial Division: Carol Natsis *(Editor-in-Chief)*
Directors: William B. Toohey *(Managing)*
Claire Cavanaugh *(Finance)*

Atlases & Maps; Children's Books; Cookery, Wines & Spirits; Crafts & Hobbies; Do-It-Yourself; Gardening; Natural History; Reference Books, Directories & Dictionaries; Sports & Games

New Titles: 135 (1995), 355 (1996)

ISBNs, Imprints & Series:
0 86438 Reader's Digest Books
0 86450 RD Press

Parent Company:
The Reader's Digest Association Inc *(USA)*

Book Trade Association Membership:
Australian PA, New Zealand Book PA,
Australian National Book Council

2075 ▬▬▬▬▬▬▬▬▬▬▬▬▬

*REED BOOKS
[part of Reed Books Australia (Reed International)]
PO Box 5335, West Chatswood, NSW 2057
Telephone: +61 (02) 372 5252
Fax: +61 (02) 419 6159

Postal Address:
PO Box 460, Port Melbourne, Vic 3207
Telephone: +61 (03) 245 7183

Publisher: Bill Templeman
Managing Editor: Mary Halbmeyer

Agriculture; Biology & Zoology; Gardening; Natural History; Nautical; Botanical/Horticultural

ISBNs, Imprints & Series: 0 7301

Parent Company:
Reed Books Australia [a division of Reed International Books Australia Pty Ltd] *(Australia)*

Overseas Representation *(see §7.3):*
Worldwide: Reed/Elsevier, UK

Book Trade Association Membership:
Australian Book PA

2076 ▬▬▬▬▬▬▬▬▬▬▬▬▬

RIGBY HEINEMANN
[a part of Reed Books Australia]
22 Salmon Street, Port Melbourne, Vic 3207
Telephone: +61 (03) 9245 7111
Fax: +61 (03) 9245 7333
Email: heinemann@reedbooks.com.au
Web Site: http://www.reedbooks.com.au

New South Wales Office:
Level 9, North Tower, 1–5 Railway Street,
Chatswood, NSW 2067
Telephone: +61 (02) 372 5299
Fax: +61 (02) 419 7149

Queensland Office:
Ground Floor, Oxley House, 25 Donkin Street,
West End, Qld 4101
Telephone: +61 (07) 3844 0775
Fax: +61 (07) 3844 0900

South Australia Office:
18 Dequetteville Terrace, Kent Town, SA 5067
Telephone: +61 (08) 363 2055
Fax: +61 (08) 363 2557

Western Australia Office:
69 Guthrie Street, Osborne Park, WA 6017
Telephone: +61 (09) 244 1700
Fax: +61 (09) 446 1661

Directors: Louise Rice *(Managing)*
Col Gillespie *(Rigby Publishing)*
Christine Vale *(Rigby Marketing)*
Elio Guarnuccio *(Export/Languages)*
Managers: Kathy Hatzi *(Heinemann Marketing)*
David Kellock *(Heinemann Publishing)*
Fiona McDonald *(Heinemann Managing Editor)*
Jane Pennells *(Design/Production)*
State Managers Heinemann: Rachel Slattery *(Vic & Tas)*
Doreen Vostinar *(NSW)*
Bev Clasohm *(SA)*
State Managers Rigby: Joan Stewart *(Vic & Tas)*
Glenice Bland *(NSW)*
Bill McConnell *(Qld)*
Mary Witts *(SA)*
Bernadette McKinlay *(WA)*

Atlases & Maps; Educational & Textbooks; Electronic (Educational); Reference Books, Directories & Dictionaries

New Titles: 157 (1995), 402 (1996)
No of Employees: 120
Annual Turnover: £12M

ISBNs, Imprints & Series:
0 7312 Rigby
0 86462 Heinemann

Parent Company:
Reed Books Australia [a division of Reed International Books Australia Pty Ltd] *(a member of the Reed Elsevier Group) (Australia)*

2077 ▬▬▬▬▬▬▬▬▬▬▬▬▬

RMIT PUBLISHING
33–37 Hotham Street, Collingwood, Vic 3066
Telephone: +61 (03) 419 6611
Fax: +61 (03) 416 0463

Postal Address:
PO Box 388, Abbotsford, Vic 3067
Telephone: +61 (03) 419 6611
Fax: +61 (03) 416 0463

Publisher: Judy Benson

Academic & Scholarly; Accountancy & Taxation; Agriculture; Architecture & Design; Audio Books; Computer Science; Cookery, Wines & Spirits; Economics; Educational & Textbooks; Electronic (Educational); Engineering; Fashion & Costume; Industry, Business & Management; Reference Books, Directories & Dictionaries; Scientific & Technical; Vocational Training & Careers

New Titles: 20 (1995), 20 (1996)
No of Employees: 7
Annual Turnover: £500

ISBNs, Imprints & Series:
RMIT Press, TAFE Publications
7241, 7306, 86459

Overseas Representation *(see §7.3):*
Asia: McGraw-Hill Book Co, Singapore
USA, UK & Europe: PIM (Publishers International Management), Sheffield, MA, USA

Book Trade Association Membership:
Australian PA, Australian National Book
Council

2078 ▬▬▬▬▬▬▬▬▬▬

***SALLY MILNER PUBLISHING PTY
LTD**
558 Darling Street, Rozelle, Sydney,
NSW 2039
Telephone: +61 (02) 555 7899
Fax: +61 (02) 555 1403

Managers: Liz Kaydos *(Home Sales)*
Lisa Hanrahan *(Production)*
Director: Sally Milner *(Export Sales)*
Editor, Rights & Permissions: Jenny Cattell

*Crafts & Hobbies; Do-It-Yourself; Health &
Beauty; Sports & Games*

ISBNs, Imprints & Series:
1 86351 Milner, Milner Craft Series

Overseas Representation *(see §7.3):*
UK (craft list): Cassell Plc (Sales Dept),
London, UK
UK (health list): Gazelle Book Services Ltd,
Lancaster, UK
USA (craft list): Sterling Publishing Co Inc,
New York, NY, USA
USA (health list): Seven Hills Book
Distributors, Cincinnati, OH, USA

Book Trade Association Membership:
Australian Book PA

2079 ▬▬▬▬▬▬▬▬▬▬

*SCHOLASTIC PTY LTD
Lot 14 Railway Crescent, Lisarow,
NSW 2250 (PO Box 579, Gosford, NSW 2250)
Telephone: +61 (043) 283555
Fax: +61 (043) 233827

Publishing Dept:
345 Pacific Highway, Lindfield, 2070
Telephone: +61 (02) 416 4000
Fax: +61 (02) 416 9877

Directors: Ken Jolly *(Managing,
Administration)*
Bob Bateman *(Finance)*
David Harris *(Publishing)*
Myra Lee *(Book Club)*
Managers: Leonie Sweeney *(Marketing)*
Peter Cleal *(Operations)*
Maureen Hadden *(Warehouse & Distribution
Services)*
Gavin Shepherd *(Sales)*

*Academic & Scholarly; Children's Books;
Educational & Textbooks; Electronic
(Educational); Electronic (Professional &
Academic)*

ISBNs, Imprints & Series:
0 86896 AS
1 86291 Omnibus

Associated & Subsidiary Companies:
Canada: Scholastic Canada. *New Zealand:*
Ashton Scholastic. *UK:* Scholastic UK. *USA:*
Scholastic Inc

Overseas Representation *(see §7.3):*
Canada: Scholastic Canada Ltd, Richmond
Hill
New Zealand: Ashton Scholastic Ltd, Auckland
UK: Scholastic UK
USA: Scholastic Inc

Book Trade Association Membership:
Australian National Book Council, Australian
Book PA, CBC

2080 ▬▬▬▬▬▬▬▬▬▬

STATE LIBRARY OF NSW PRESS
Macquarie Street, Sydney, NSW 2000
Telephone: +61 (02) 230 1514
Fax: +61 (02) 223 8807
Email: jkelly@planet.slnsw.gov.au
Web Site: http://www.slnsw.gov.au/home.htp

General Publishing, Manager: Judith Kelly

*Biography & Autobiography; Cookery, Wines
& Spirits; Fine Art & Art History; History &
Antiquarian; Illustrated & Fine Editions;
Industry, Business & Management; Natural
History; Sociology & Anthropology;
Australian History; Cultural History
(Australia)*

New Titles: 7 (1995), 6 (1996)
No of Employees: 3
Annual Turnover: $300,000

ISBNs, Imprints & Series:
0 7305, 0 7310

Parent Company:
Library Council of NSW *(Australia)*

Overseas Representation *(see §7.3):*
UK & USA: Drake International Services,
Oxford, UK

Book Trade Association Membership:
Australian PA

2081 ▬▬▬▬▬▬▬▬▬▬

**SUMMER INSTITUTE OF
LINGUISTICS (AUSTRALIAN
ABORIGINES & ISLANDERS BRANCH)**
Post Office, Berrimah, NT 0828
Telephone: +61 (089) 844 488
Fax: +61 (089) 844 0321
Email: sildarwin@taunet.net.au

Academic Editor: Susanne Hargrave
Production: Alan Rogers
Sales: Lorraine Prosser

*Academic & Scholarly; Languages &
Linguistics*

New Titles: 10 (1995), 12 (1996)
No of Employees: 4
Annual Turnover: $10,000

Parent Company:
Summer Institute of Linguistics International
(USA)

Associated & Subsidiary Companies:
Australia: Pitjantjatjava Bible Translation
Project; St Matthew's Ngukurr – Kriol; Yapaka
– Warlpiri

Overseas Representation *(see §7.3):*
USA: SIL (Academic Publications Dept),
Dallas, TX

2082 ▬▬▬▬▬▬▬▬▬▬

THE TEXT PUBLISHING CO PTY LTD
171 LaTrobe Street, Melbourne, Vic 3000
Telephone: +61 (03) 9272 4700
Fax: +61 (03) 9272 4799

Distribution & Sales:
Penguin Books, 487 Maroondah Highway,
Ringwood, Vic 3134
Telephone: +61 (03) 9871 2400
Fax: +61 (03) 9879 6187
Email: (surname)@penguin.com.au

Managing Director: Diana Gribble
Publisher: Michael Heyward
Marketing & Publicity Manager: Patty
Brown *(Sales)*

*Biography & Autobiography; Crime; Fiction;
Literature & Criticism; Politics & World
Affairs*

New Titles: 8 (1995), 12 (1996)
No of Employees: 4

ISBNs, Imprints & Series: 1 87584

Overseas Representation *(see §7.3):*
Italy: Grandi and Vitali, Milan
Japan: The English Agency (Japan) Ltd, Tokyo
Switzerland (for German language rights):
Mohrbooks Literary Agency, Zurich,
Switzerland

Book Trade Association Membership:
Australian PA

2083 ▬▬▬▬▬▬▬▬▬▬

**THAMES & HUDSON (AUSTRALIA)
PTY LTD**
11 Central Boulevard, Portside Business Park,
Port Melbourne, Vic 3207
Telephone: +61 (03) 9646 7788
Fax: +61 (03) 9646 8790

Managing Director: R. M. Gilmour

*Archaeology; Architecture & Design; Fashion
& Costume; Fine Art & Art History; History &
Antiquarian; Literature & Criticism;
Photography; Travel & Topography*

Parent Company:
Thames & Hudson Ltd *(UK)*

Book Trade Association Membership:
Australian PA

2084 ▬▬▬▬▬▬▬▬▬▬

D. W. THORPE
18 Salmon Street, Port Melbourne, Vic 3207
Telephone: +61 (03) 9245 7370
Fax: +61 (03) 9245 7395

Managers: Michael Webster *(Managing
Director)*
Deirdre Morris *(Publishing)*
Paulene Morey *(Administration)*
Oriana Ruffini *(Advertising)*

Bibliography & Library Science; Reference Books, Directories & Dictionaries

ISBNs, Imprints & Series:
0 909532, 1 875589 Thorpe

Parent Company:
Reed/Elsevier Plc *(UK)*

Overseas Representation *(see §7.3)*:
New Zealand: Heinemann Reference, Auckland
Singapore & Far East: Butterworths Asia, Singapore
UK & EEC Countries: Bowker-Saur Ltd, East Grinstead, UK
USA: R. R. Bowker, New Providence, NJ

Book Trade Association Membership:
Australian PA, ABA

2085

TRANSWORLD PUBLISHERS (AUST) PTY LTD
15–25 Helles Avenue, Moorebank, NSW 2170
Telephone: +61 (02) 601 7122
Fax: +61 (02) 821 1334

Publishing & Marketing:
40 Yeo Street, Neutral Bay, NSW 2089
Telephone: +61 (02) 908 4366
Fax: +61 (02) 953 8563

Directors: Geoffrey Rumpf *(Managing)*
Greg Little *(Executive, Operations)*
Jacki Heppard *(Marketing & Sales)*
Editors: Julie Stanton *(Executive)*
Laura Paterson *(Acquisitions)*
Howard Gelman *(Senior)*
Fiona Henderson *(Senior)*
Managers: Chris Raine *(Sales)*
Therese Haussener *(Inventory & Publishing Operations)*
Maggie Hamilton *(Head of Publicity)*
Trevor Anderson *(Information Technology)*
Warwick Teale *(Financial Controller)*

Biography & Autobiography; Children's Books; Fiction; Gardening; Gender Studies; Health & Beauty; Humour; Philosophy; Politics & World Affairs; Psychology & Psychiatry; Religion & Theology; Sports & Games; Diaries & Calendars; General non-fiction; Parenting/Childcare

New Titles: 815 (1995), 640 (1996)
No of Employees: 81
Annual Turnover: £14M

ISBNs, Imprints & Series:
0 863, 0 947 Bantam Australia
0 868 Doubleday Australia

Parent Company:
Transworld Publishers Ltd *(UK)*

Associated & Subsidiary Companies:
New Zealand: Transworld Publishers (NZ) Ltd.
UK: Transworld Publishers Ltd. *USA:* Bantam Doubleday Dell Publishing Group Inc

Overseas Representation *(see §7.3)*:
See: Transworld Publishers Ltd, London, UK

Book Trade Association Membership:
Australian Book Publishers Association

2086

TURTON & ARMSTRONG PTY LTD
21 Lister Street, Wahroonga, NSW 2076
Telephone: +61 (02) 489 6719
Fax: +61 (02) 489 6719

Publisher: Paul Armstrong
Editor: Jill Caldwell
Sales: James Throssell

Aviation; Biography & Autobiography; Cinema, Video, TV & Radio; Cookery, Wines & Spirits; Crafts & Hobbies; Economics; Educational & Textbooks; Electronic (Educational); Electronic (Professional & Academic); Engineering; History & Antiquarian; Illustrated & Fine Editions; Industry, Business & Management; Medical (incl. Self Help & Alternative Medicine); Military & War; Music; Nautical; Reference Books, Directories & Dictionaries; Sociology & Anthropology; Transport

New Titles: 6 (1995), 8 (1996)
No of Employees: 4

ISBNs, Imprints & Series: 0 908031

Overseas Representation *(see §7.3)*:
UK (Motoring Titles only): Menoshire Ltd, Perivale, UK
USA (Motoring Titles only): Motorbooks International Publishers & Wholesalers Inc, Osceola, WI, USA

2087

USQ PRESS
PO Box 58, Darling Heights, Toowoomba, Qld 4350
Telephone: +61 (076) 312630
Fax: +61 (076) 311758

Orders:
Herron Book Distributors,
39 Commercial Road, Fortitude Valley, Qld 4006
Telephone: +61 (07) 3257 1711
Fax: +61 (07) 3257 1686

Manager: Brenda Tait *(USQ Press, Production, Rights & Permissions)*
Editor: Jennifer Wright *(Australasian Science – Editorial & Permissions)*
Customer Service: *(to be appointed) (Sales, Subscription Management, Accounts)*

Educational & Textbooks; History & Antiquarian

New Titles: 2 (1995), 10 (1996)
No of Employees: 4
Annual Turnover: $450,000

ISBNs, Imprints & Series: 0 949414

Parent Company:
University of Southern Queensland *(Australia)*

Book Trade Association Membership:
National Book Council, Australian PA, Galley Club, Queensland Writers Centre, Society of Editors, Queensland, CAL (Copyright Agency Ltd)

2088

*THE WATERMARK PRESS
308 Darling Street, Balmain, 2041
Telephone: +61 (02) 818 5677
Fax: +61 (02) 818 5581

Postal Address:
PO Box 603, Balmain, 2041

Publisher: Simon Blackall *(General Books, Export Sales)*
Rights Manager: Diane Hall *(Rights & Permissions)*
Senior Commissioning Editor: Diane Wallis

Animal Care & Breeding; Architecture & Design; Cookery, Wines & Spirits; Crafts & Hobbies; Do-It-Yourself; Fashion & Costume; Gardening; Guide Books; Health & Beauty; Humour; Reference Books, Directories & Dictionaries; Veterinary Science

ISBNs, Imprints & Series: 0 949284

Overseas Representation *(see §7.3)*:
Hong Kong: The Guide Book Co
UK: The River Press, Twickenham; Windrush

Book Trade Association Membership:
Australian Book PA

2089

WIZARD BOOKS PTY LTD
214 Sturt Street, Ballarat, Vic 3350
Telephone: +61 (053) 323 435
Fax: +61 (053) 311 488
Email: wizard@peg.apc.org

Directors: Valerie McRoberts
Richard McRoberts

Academic & Scholarly; Audio Books; Children's Books; Educational & Textbooks; Fiction; Literature & Criticism

New Titles: 18 (1995), 20 (1996)
No of Employees: 4
Annual Turnover: $195,000

ISBNs, Imprints & Series:
1 875739 Wizard Classroom Kits, Wizard English Teaching Modules, Wizard Fiction, Wizard Study Guides

Book Trade Association Membership:
Australian PA, Publish Australia

2090

WRIGHTBOOKS PTY LTD
PO Box 270, Elsternwick, 3185
Telephone: +61 (03) 9532 7082
Fax: +61 (03) 9532 7084

Also at:
5 Horne Street, Elsternwick, 3185

Directors: Geoff Wright *(Managing, Sales & Rights)*
Ms Lesley Beaumont *(Publishing)*

Finance; Investment; Management; Personal Development

New Titles: 16 (1995), 19 (1996)
No of Employees: 4
Annual Turnover: $500,000

ISBNs, Imprints & Series:
0 947351, 1 875857

Overseas Representation *(see §7.3)*:
New Zealand: Forrester Books Ltd, Auckland
Singapore & Hong Kong: Reed International
  (Singapore) Pte Ltd, Singapore

Book Trade Association Membership:
Australian PA

CANADA

2091 ▬▬▬▬

*LES ÉDITIONS D'ACADIE
CP 885, Moncton, NB E1C 8N8
Telephone: +1 (506) 857 8490
Fax: +1 (506) 855 3130

General Director: Marcel Ouellette

Children's Books; Cookery, Wines & Spirits;
Educational & Textbooks; Electronic
(Educational); Fiction; Gender Studies; Guide
Books; History & Antiquarian; Languages &
Linguistics; Literature & Criticism; Poetry

ISBNs, Imprints & Series: 2 7600

Overseas Representation *(see §7.3)*:
France: Geste Editions, Mougon
Rest of World: Export Livres, Saint-Lambert,
  PQ, Canada

Book Trade Association Membership:
Association nationale des éditeurs de livres,
Atlantic Publishers Association, Regroupement
de editeurs canadiens de langue française

2092 ▬▬▬▬

UNIVERSITY OF ALBERTA PRESS
141 Athabasca Hall, The University of Alberta,
Edmonton, Alberta T6G 2E8
Telephone: +1 (403) 492 3662
Fax: +1 (403) 492 0719
Email: uap@gpu.srv.ualberta.ca

Warehouse, Trade Enquiries & Orders:
UBC Press, University of British Columbia,
6344 Memorial Road, Vancouver, BC V6T 1Z2
Telephone: +1 (604) 822 5959

Director: Glenn Rollans
Editor: Mary Mahoney-Robson

Academic & Scholarly; Archaeology;
Educational & Textbooks; Natural History;
Politics & World Affairs

New Titles: 10 (1995), 15 (1996)
No of Employees: 3

ISBNs, Imprints & Series:
0 88864 Pica Pica Press

Overseas Representation *(see §7.3)*:
UK & Western Europe: Lavis Marketing,
  Oxford, UK

Book Trade Association Membership:
Association of Canadian Publishers, Book
Publishers Association of Alberta, Association
of Canadian University Presses, Association of
American University Presses

2093 ▬▬▬▬

AMPERSAND COMMUNICATIONS INC
5606 Scobie Crescent, Manotick,
Ont K4M 1B7
Telephone: +1 (613) 692 2080
Fax: +1 (613) 692 1419
Email: editors@magi.com

President: Edward C. Matheson
Vice-President: Eunice A. Thorne

Reference Books, Directories & Dictionaries

New Titles: 1 (1995), 1 (1996)
No of Employees: 2
Annual Turnover: $175,000

ISBNs, Imprints & Series: 0 929262

2094 ▬▬▬▬

ANNICK PRESS LTD
15 Patricia Avenue, Willowdale,
Ont M2M 1H9
Telephone: +1 (416) 221 4802
Fax: +1 (416) 221 8400

Co-Directors Trade Publishing: Rick Wilks
Anne W. Millyard
Marketing: Jennifer Kroezen
Rights & Permissions: Maral Bablanian
Production: Heather Davies

Children's Books; Educational & Textbooks

New Titles: 29 (1995), 27 (1996)
No of Employees: 8
Annual Turnover: $3.5M

ISBNs, Imprints & Series:
0 920236, 0 920303, 1 55037

Overseas Representation *(see §7.3)*:
UK: Ragged Bears Ltd, Andover

Book Trade Association Membership:
Association of Canadian Publishers

2095 ▬▬▬▬

ARNOLD PUBLISHING LTD
Suite 101, 10301-104 Street NW, Edmonton,
Alberta T5J 1B9
Telephone: +1 (403) 426 2998/(800) 563 2665
(Toll Free)
Fax: +1 (403) 426 4607
Email: info@arnold.ca
Web Site: http://www.arnold.ca

Mailing address for United States:
PO Box 5686, Springfield, MO 65801
Telephone: +1 (800) 563 2665
Fax: +1 (403) 426 4607

President: Phyllis Arnold
Editor-in-Chief: Karen Iversen

Educational & Textbooks; Electronic
(Educational); Geography & Geology; History
& Antiquarian

New Titles: 5 (1995), 5 (1996)
No of Employees: 18

ISBNs, Imprints & Series:
0 919913, 1 896081

Book Trade Association Membership: Book
Publishers Association of Alberta

2096 ▬▬▬▬

ARSENAL PULP PRESS
103, 1014 Homer Street, Vancouver,
BC V6B 2W9
Telephone: +1 (604) 687 4233
Fax: +1 (604) 669 8250

Managing Editor: Brian Lam
Marketing: Blaine Kyllo

Fiction; Gay & Lesbian Studies; Gender
Studies; Humour; Sociology & Anthropology

New Titles: 9 (1996)
No of Employees: 2

ISBNs, Imprints & Series:
0 88978, 1 55152

Book Trade Association Membership:
Association of Canadian Publishers

2097 ▬▬▬▬

BEACH HOLME PUBLISHERS
4252 Commerce Circle, Victoria, BC V8Z 4M2
Telephone: +1 (604) 727 6514
Fax: +1 (604) 727 6418
Email: bhp@pine.com
Web Site: http://www.beachholme.bc.ca

Warehouse:
1800 Steeles Avenue, Concord, Ont L4K 2P3

Literary Press Group:
301–2 Gloucester Street, Toronto,
Ont M4Y 1L5

Trade Enquiries & Orders:
General Publishing Ltd, 30 Lesmill Road,
Don Mills, Ont M3B 2T6

Managing Editor: Joy Gugeler
Sales Director: Melissa Pitts
Senior Editor: Antonia Banyard

Fiction; Literature & Criticism; Magic & the
Occult; Poetry; Young adult fiction

New Titles: 8 (1995), 7 (1996)
No of Employees: 2

ISBNs, Imprints & Series:
0 88878 Beach Holme, Porcepic

Overseas Representation *(see §7.3)*:
USA: Inland Books, NJ

Book Trade Association Membership:
Association of Canadian Publishers, Literary
Press Group, Association of Book Publishers of
British Columbia

2098

BETWEEN THE LINES
720 Bathurst Street, Suite 404, Toronto,
Ont M5S 2R4
Telephone: +1 (416) 535 9914
Fax: +1 (416) 535 1484

Distribution:
University of Toronto Press,
5201 Dufferin Street, Downsview,
Ont M3H 5T8
Telephone: +1 (416) 667 7791
Fax: +1 (416) 667 7832

Managers: Marg Anne Morrison *(Production, Finance)*
Paul Eprile *(Promotion, Publicity, Marketing)*

Biography & Autobiography; Cinema, Video, TV & Radio; Economics; Gender Studies; History & Antiquarian; Industry, Business & Management; Politics & World Affairs; Sociology & Anthropology

New Titles: 5 (1995), 4 (1996)
No of Employees: 2
Annual Turnover: $140,000

ISBNs, Imprints & Series:
0 919946, 0 921284, 1 896357

Overseas Representation *(see §7.3):*
USA: Left Bank Distribution, Seattle, WA

Book Trade Association Membership:
Association of Canadian Publishers

2099

BLACK ROSE BOOKS LTD
CP 1258, Succ. Place du Parc, Montreal,
PQ H2W 2R3
Telephone: +1 (514) 844 4076
Fax: +1 (514) 849 1956
Email: blakrose@web.apc.org
Web Site: http://www.blackrosebooks.com

Distribution:
University of Toronto Press,
5201 Dufferin Street, Downsview,
Ont M3H 5T8
Telephone: +1 (716) 683 4547 & +1 (800) 565 9523
Fax: +1 (416) 667 7832

Editorial: J. Nataf
Managers: J. Roux *(Production)*
G. Briffin *(Sales)*
Rebecca Laurier
Alexander Negri *(Rights & Permissions)*

Academic & Scholarly; Cinema, Video, TV & Radio; Economics; Environment & Development Studies; Gender Studies; History & Antiquarian; Law; Philosophy; Politics & World Affairs; Psychology & Psychiatry; Sociology & Anthropology; Canadian Studies; Ecology

New Titles: 55 (1995), 35 (1996)

ISBNs, Imprints & Series:
0 919618, 0 919619, 0 920057, 0 921689, 1 55164, 1 551640 1 895431

Associated & Subsidiary Companies:
Canada: Editions Ecosociété; Our Generation

Overseas Representation *(see §7.3):*
Australia: Astam Books Pty Ltd, Leichhardt, NSW
Europe: Central Books Ltd, London, UK
Japan & Korea: United Publishers Services Ltd, Tokyo, Japan
USA: Black Rose Books

Book Trade Association Membership:
Association of Canadian Publishers, Canadian Booksellers Association, Canadian Book Marketing Centre, COSMEP (USA), Publishers Marketing Association (USA)

2100

BLIZZARD PUBLISHING
73 Furby Street, Winnipeg, MB R3C 2A2
Telephone: +1 (204) 775 2923
Fax: +1 (204) 775 2947
Email: atwood@blizzard.mb.ca
Web Site: http://www.blizzard.mb.ca/catalog/

Distributor:
General Distribution Services,
34 Lesmill Road, Don Mills, Ont M3B 2T6
Telephone: +1 (800) 387 0172
Fax: +1 (416) 445 5967

Managing Editor: Anna Synenko
Editorial Assistant: Todd Scarth

Academic & Scholarly; Gay & Lesbian Studies; Theatre, Drama & Dance

New Titles: 14 (1995), 12 (1996)
No of Employees: 3

ISBNs, Imprints & Series:
Bain & Cox, Publishers

Overseas Representation *(see §7.3):*
European Union: Gazelle Book Services Ltd, Lancaster, UK

2101

EDITIONS DU BORÉAL
4447 rue Saint-Denis, Montreal, PQ H2J 2L2
Telephone: +1 (514) 287 7401
Fax: +1 (514) 287 7664
Email: editions–boreal@infopuq.uquebec.ca

Trade Enquiries & Orders:
Diffusion Dimedia, 539 boulevard Lebeau,
Ville Saint-Laurent, Montreal, PQ H4N 1S2
Telephone: +1 (514) 336 3941
Fax: +1 (514) 331 3916

General Manager: Pascal Assathiany
Director Publisher: Jean Bernier

Biography & Autobiography; Children's Books; Fiction; History & Antiquarian; Politics & World Affairs; Sociology & Anthropology; Theatre, Drama & Dance

New Titles: 63 (1995), 65 (1996)
No of Employees: 10

ISBNs, Imprints & Series:
2 89052 Boréal, Boréal Compact, Boréal Express, Boréal Inter, Boréal Junior,

Dominique, Kami-Case, Madeleine, Papiers collés, Pour en finir

Overseas Representation *(see §7.3):*
Europe: Editions du Seuil, Paris, France
USA: Export Livres, Saint-Lambert, PQ, Canada

2102

BOREALIS PRESS LTD
9 Ashburn Drive, Ottawa, Ont K2E 6N4
Telephone: +1 (613) 224 6837
Fax: +1 (613) 829 7783

President: Frank Tierney
Vice-President: Glenn Clever

Academic & Scholarly; Fiction; Literature & Criticism; Poetry; Reference Books, Directories & Dictionaries; Theatre, Drama & Dance

New Titles: 10 (1996)
No of Employees: 5
Annual Turnover: $100,000

ISBNs, Imprints & Series:
0 88887, 1 896133

Associated & Subsidiary Companies:
Canada: The Tecumseh Press Ltd

Overseas Representation *(see §7.3):*
Europe: EBSCO Europe, Aalsmeer, Netherlands
USA: Baker & Taylor, Momence, IL; Blackwell North America, Blackwood, NJ; EBSCO Subscription Service, Birmingham, AL

Book Trade Association Membership:
Canadian Booksellers Association

2103

THE BOSTON MILLS PRESS
132 Main Street, Erin, Ontario N0B 1T0
Telephone: +1 (519) 833 2407
Fax: +1 (519) 833 2195

Warehouse, Trade Enquiries & Orders:
Stoddart Publishing, Toronto

President: John Denison

Antiques & Collecting; Guide Books; History & Antiquarian; Illustrated & Fine Editions

New Titles: 19 (1995), 20 (1996)
No of Employees: 4

ISBNs, Imprints & Series:
0 919783, 0 919822, 1 55046

Parent Company:
Stoddart Publishing *(Canada)*

Book Trade Association Membership:
Ontario Publishers Association

2104

BREAKWATER BOOKS LTD
100 Water Street, PO Box 2188, St John's,
Nfld A1C 6E6
Telephone: +1 (709) 722 6680
Fax: +1 (709) 753 0708

President: Clyde Rose
Managing Director: Laura Woodford

*Academic & Scholarly; Atlases & Maps;
Biography & Autobiography; Children's
Books; Cookery, Wines & Spirits; Educational
& Textbooks; Electronic (Educational);
Electronic (Professional & Academic);
Environment & Development Studies; Fiction;
Guide Books; History & Antiquarian; Humour;
Literature & Criticism; Natural History;
Photography; Poetry; Reference Books,
Directories & Dictionaries; Theatre, Drama &
Dance; Travel & Topography*

New Titles: 12 (1995), 10 (1996)
No of Employees: 10

ISBNs, Imprints & Series:
0 88760, 0 906397, 0 919519, 0 919948, 0
920911, 1 55081

Associated & Subsidiary Companies:
Canada: Breakwater Books Ltd; Softwaves
Educational Software Inc

Overseas Representation *(see §7.3):*
UK: Roundhouse Publishing Ltd, Oxford
USA: Paul & Co Publishers Consortium Inc,
Concord, MA

Book Trade Association Membership:
Association of Canadian Publishers, Canadian
Booksellers Association, Association for the
Export of Canadian Books, Canadian Book
Information Centre, Literary Press Group

2105 ▬▬▬▬▬▬▬

*BRICK BOOKS
431 Boler Road, Box 20081, London,
Ont N6K 4G6
Telephone: +1 (519) 657 8579
Fax: +1 (519) 657 8579

Distributors:
General Distribution Services,
30 Lesmill Road, Don Mills, Ont M3B 2T6
Telephone: +1 (416) 445 3333
Fax: +1 (416) 445 5967

Managers: Kitty Lewis *(General)*
Sue Schenk *(Production)*
Editors: Don McKay
Jan Zwicky
John Donlan

Poetry

ISBNs, Imprints & Series: 0 919626

Overseas Representation *(see §7.3):*
USA: Inland Book Co Inc, East Haven, CT

Book Trade Association Membership:
Association of Canadian Publishers, Literary
Press Group, Canadian Book Marketing
Council

2106 ▬▬▬▬▬▬▬

BROADVIEW PRESS LTD
PO Box 1243, Peterborough K9J 7H5
Telephone: +1 (705) 743 8990
Fax: +1 (705) 743 8353

Returns:
71 Princess Street, Peterborough, Ont K9J 2A8

Western Office:
627-604 1st Street SW, Calgary, AB T2P 1M7
Telephone: +1 (403) 232 6863

President: Don LePan
Vice-President: Michael Harrison
Accounts/Customer Service: Carol
Richardson
Paula Huhtala
Rights & Permissions, Production: Barbara
Conolly
Production: George Kirkpatrick
Warehouse: Ken Hone

*Academic & Scholarly; Architecture & Design;
Educational & Textbooks; English as a Foreign
Language; Fine Art & Art History; History &
Antiquarian; Languages & Linguistics;
Literature & Criticism; Philosophy; Politics &
World Affairs; Sociology & Anthropology*

New Titles: 16 (1995), 24 (1996)
No of Employees: 11
Annual Turnover: $750,000

ISBNs, Imprints & Series:
0 921149, 1 55111

Associated & Subsidiary Companies:
USA: Broadview Press

Overseas Representation *(see §7.3):*
UK: Book Representation & Distribution
(BRAD), Hadleigh
USA: Broadview Press, Orchard Park, NY

Book Trade Association Membership:
Association of Canadian Publishers

2107 ▬▬▬▬▬▬▬

**BROKEN JAW PRESS/M. A.
PRODUCTIONS**
Box 596, Stn A, Fredericton, NB E3B 5A6
Telephone: +1 (506) 454 5127
Fax: +1 (506) 454 5127
Email: jblades@nbnet.nb.ca

Trade Distribution:
General Distribution Services,
30 Lesmills Road, Don Mills, Ont M3B 2T6
Telephone: +1 (416) 445 3333
Fax: +1 (416) 445 5967

Owner/Publisher: Joe Blades

*Audio Books; History & Antiquarian;
Literature & Criticism; Poetry*

New Titles: 8 (1995), 10 (1996)
No of Employees: 1
Annual Turnover: $15,000

ISBNs, Imprints & Series:
0 921411 Book Rat, Dead Sea Physh Products
1 896647 Cowgirlsinkilts, New Muse Award
(annual)

Associated & Subsidiary Companies:
Canada: Spare Time Editions

Overseas Representation *(see §7.3):*
USA: General Distribution Services, Buffalo,
NY

Book Trade Association Membership:
Association of Canadian Publishers, Atlantic
Publishers Marketing Association

2108 ▬▬▬▬▬▬▬

UNIVERSITY OF CALGARY PRESS
2500 University Drive NW, Calgary,
Alberta T2N 1N4
Telephone: +1 (403) 220 7578
Fax: +1 (403) 282 0085
Email: sonn@ucdasuml.admin.ucalgary.ca
Web Site: http://www.ucalgary.ca/uofc/
departments/up

Courier Address:
Room 816 MacKimmie Library Tower,
404 University Court NW, Calgary, Alberta
Telephone: +1 (403) 220 7578
Fax: +1 (403) 282 0085

Orders:
UBC Press, 6344 Memorial Road, Vancouver,
BC V6T 1Z2
Telephone: +1 (604) 822 5959
Fax: +1 (604) 822 6083 & +1 (800) 668 0821
(Toll Free)

Director: Shirley A. Onn *(Management,
Operations, Acquisitions, Fund
Development & Marketing)*
Accounts: Barb Semple *(Financial Records)*
Production Editor: John King
Journals Assistant: Judy Powell
Publicity Editor: Sharon Boyle *(Rights &
Permissions)*
Editorial Secretary: Joan Barton
Fulfilment Supervisor: Leslie Moore

*Academic & Scholarly; Agriculture;
Archaeology; Bibliography & Library Science;
Biography & Autobiography; Biology &
Zoology; Chemistry; Economics; Educational
& Textbooks; Engineering; Fine Art & Art
History; Gender Studies; Geography &
Geology; Guide Books; History & Antiquarian;
Illustrated & Fine Editions; Industry, Business
& Management; Languages & Linguistics;
Law; Literature & Criticism; Medical (incl.
Self Help & Alternative Medicine); Music;
Natural History; Philosophy; Politics & World
Affairs; Psychology & Psychiatry; Religion &
Theology; Scientific & Technical; Sociology &
Anthropology; Travel & Topography; Political
Science*

New Titles: 15 (1995), 12 (1996)
No of Employees: 8

ISBNs, Imprints & Series:
African Occasional Papers, Canadian Archival
Inventory Series, Canadian Energy Research
Institute, Canadian Institute of Resources
Law Series
0 895176, 0 919813 The Banff Centre for
Management, The University of Calgary
Press

Parent Company:
The University of Calgary *(Canada)*

Overseas Representation *(see §7.3):*
Continental Europe: Trevor Brown Associates,
London, UK
UK: Mike Wilson, Anglesey; David Grant,
Tunbridge Wells; Tony Lawrence,

Altrincham; Donald Macdonald, Glasgow; Adele Rogers, London

Book Trade Association Membership:
Association of Canadian Publishers, Association of Canadian University Presses, Book Publishers Association of Alberta, Canadian Book Marketing Centre

2109

CANADA COMMUNICATION GROUP-PUBLISHING
45 Sacre-Coeur Boulevard, Room A-2403, Hull, Quebec K1A 0S9
Telephone: +1 (819) 956 1612
Fax: +1 (819) 994 1498

Enquiries & Order Processing:
Room D-2202, 45 Sacre-Coeur Boulevard, Hull, Quebec K1A 0S9
Telephone: +1 (819) 956 4800
Fax: +1 (819) 994 1498

Warehouse & Distribution:
1770 Pink Road, Aylmer, PQ K1A 1L3
Telephone: +1 (819) 956 4800

Director: Leslie-Ann Scott *(Publishing)*
Manager: Pauline Hawkes *(Commercial Network & Promotion Marketing)*

Academic & Scholarly; Agriculture; Archaeology; Aviation; Bibliography & Library Science; Economics; Educational & Textbooks; English as a Foreign Language; Fine Art & Art History; Gender Studies; Geography & Geology; History & Antiquarian; Languages & Linguistics; Law; Medical (incl. Self Help & Alternative Medicine); Military & War; Natural History; Nautical; Politics & World Affairs; Reference Books, Directories & Dictionaries; Scientific & Technical; Sociology & Anthropology; Transport; Vocational Training & Careers

New Titles: 4674 (1995), 4000 (1996)
No of Employees: 62

ISBNs, Imprints & Series:
0 660, 0 662 Government of Canada

Overseas Representation *(see §7.3)*:
Australia: Jean-Louis Boglio, Currumbin, Qld
Austria: International Network for Terminology (TERMNET), Vienna
Bangladesh: Asia Book House, Dhaka
Finland: Academic Book Store, Helsinki
France: Canadian Books Express, Paris
Japan: Naigai Trading Co Ltd, Tokyo; Harcourt Brace Japan Inc, Tokyo
UK: E. W. Classey Ltd, Faringdon, Oxon; Books Express, Saffron Walden; GBS Distribution & Marketing Ltd, Rainham, Essex; Natural History Book Service Ltd, Totnes; MicroInfo Ltd
USA: International Specialized Book Services Inc, Portland, OR; Accents Publications Service Inc, Silver Spring, MD; Interpharm Press Inc, Buffalo Grove, IL; Bioquip Products, Gardena, CA; Franciscan University of Steubenville, Steubenville, OH; J. J. Keller & Associates, Neenah, WI; Robert Hale & Co, Bellevue, WA

Book Trade Association Membership:
Canadian Booksellers Association; Canadian

Book Publishers Council, Association of Canadian Publishers, Licensing Executive Society, Canadian Library Association, Assn pour l'avancement des sciences et des techniques de la documentation, Assn Nationale des Editeurs de livres

2110

CANADIAN INSTITUTE OF UKRAINIAN STUDIES PRESS
Department of Slavic Languages and Literatures, University of Toronto, 21 Sussex Avenue, Toronto, Ont M5S 1A1
Telephone: +1 (416) 978 8240
Fax: +1 (416) 978 2672
Email: tarn@epas.utoronto.ca

Trade Enquiries & Orders:
352 Athabasca Hall, University of Alberta, Edmonton, Alberta T6G 2E8
Telephone: +1 (403) 492 2972
Fax: +1 (403) 492 4967

Director: Maxim Tarnawsky *(Toronto)*
Marketing, Distribution: Khrystyna Kohut *(Edmonton)*

Academic & Scholarly

New Titles: 4 (1995), 6 (1996)
No of Employees: 4
Annual Turnover: $30,000

ISBNs, Imprints & Series:
0 920862, 1 895571

Book Trade Association Membership:
Association of Canadian Publishers

2111

THE CANADIAN INSTITUTE OF STRATEGIC STUDIES (CISS)
76 St Clair Avenue West, Suite 502, Toronto, Ont M4V 1N2
Telephone: +1 (416) 964 6632
Fax: +1 (416) 964 5833
Email: ciss@inforamp.net
Web Site: http:/www.ciss.ca

Directors: Alex Morrison *(Executive)*
James Hanson *(Associate Executive)*
Mark Larsen *(Finance & Administration)*
Susan McNish *(Publications)*

Academic & Scholarly; Aviation; History & Antiquarian; Military & War; Politics & World Affairs

New Titles: 9 (1995), 7 (1996)

ISBNs, Imprints & Series: 0 919769

Associated & Subsidiary Companies:
Canada: Pearson Peacekeeping Centre – The Peacekeeping Press

Book Trade Association Membership:
Canadian Booksellers Association

2112

CANADIAN MUSEUM OF CIVILIZATION
100 Laurier Street, PO Box 3100, Station B, Hull, PQ J8X 4H2

Telephone: +1 (819) 776 8395
Fax: +1 (819) 776 8300

Senior Production Officer: Deborah Brownrigg
Senior Development Officer: Cathrine Wanezycki
Programmes Administrator: Pam Coulas
Publisher: Jean-François Blanchette

Academic & Scholarly; Antiques & Collecting; Archaeology; Educational & Textbooks; Fine Art & Art History; Illustrated & Fine Editions; Languages & Linguistics; Reference Books, Directories & Dictionaries; Sociology & Anthropology

New Titles: 14 (1995), 8 (1996)
No of Employees: 7
Annual Turnover: $100,000

ISBNs, Imprints & Series: 0 660

Overseas Representation *(see §7.3)*:
France: Editions Maisonneuve et Laiose, Paris
UK: Roundhouse Publishing Ltd, Oxford
USA: University of Washington Press, Seattle, WA

Book Trade Association Membership:
Association of Canadian Publishers, Association for the Export of Canadian Books

2113

*CANADIAN SCHOLARS' PRESS
180 Bloor Street West, Suite 402, Toronto, Ont M5S 2V6
Telephone: +1 (416) 929 2774
Fax: +1 (416) 929 1926

Warehouse:
TTS Distributing Inc, 45 Tyler Street, PO Box 425, Aurora, Ont L4G 3L5

Publisher: Jack Wayne
Managers: Brad J. Lambertus *(Managing Editor)*
Rodney Fishbien *(Customer Service)*
Brad Horning *(Production)*
Helen Jager *(Administration)*
Ian Wayne *(Marketing Associate)*
Marketing Associates: Julie Sternberg
Catherine Trarelle

Academic & Scholarly; Educational & Textbooks; Languages & Linguistics; Sociology & Anthropology

ISBNs, Imprints & Series:
0 921627, 1 55130

Overseas Representation *(see §7.3)*:
UK: Book Representation & Distribution (BRAD), Hadleigh

Book Trade Association Membership:
Ontario Publishers Group, Society for Scholarly Publishing, Association of Canadian Publishers

2114

CARLETON UNIVERSITY PRESS
1400 CTTC, 1125 Colonel By Drive, Ottawa, Ont K1S 5B6
Telephone: +1 (613) 520 3740

Fax: +1 (613) 520 2893
Email: cu.press@ccs.carleton.ca

President & Chief Executive Officer: John
  Flood
Associate Director: Naomi Griffiths
Administrative Assistant: Suzanne Stott
Orders & Accounts Manager: Jeff Sloan
Production Editors: Jennie Strickland
Diane Dupuis *(Marketing & Promotion)*
Pauline McKillop
Typesetter: Barbara Cumming
Permissions Editor: Christine LaBlanc
  (Course Packs)
Graduate Studies Intern: Nahlah Ayed
Packing/Shipping: Denise Strong

*Academic & Scholarly; Biography &
Autobiography; Economics; Fine Art & Art
History; Gender Studies; Geography &
Geology; History & Antiquarian; Law;
Literature & Criticism; Military & War;
Photography; Poetry; Politics & World Affairs;
Sociology & Anthropology*

New Titles: 20 (1995), 35 (1996)
No of Employees: 7

ISBNs, Imprints & Series:
0 88629 Carleton Contemporary Series,
  Carleton Library Series, Carleton University
  Press , Public Policy Series, Women's
  Experience Series

Overseas Representation *(see §7.3)*:
UK: Cardiff Academic Press, Cardiff

Book Trade Association Membership:
Association of Canadian University Presses,
Association of Canadian Publishers, Canadian
Book Marketing Centre, Canadian Booksellers
Association, Literary Press Group,
Organization of Book Publishers of Ontario

2115 ▬▬▬▬▬▬▬▬▬▬▬▬▬▬▬▬▬

CCH CANADIAN LTD
6 Garamond Court, North York, Ont M3C 1Z5
Telephone: +1 (416) 441 0086 & (800) 268
4522
Fax: +1 (416) 444 9011 & (800) 461 4131
Web Site: http://www.ca.cch.com

President: J. Pineo
Managers: T. Hemmingway *(Vice-President
  Content Management)*
Greg Nordal *(Vice-President Sales &
  Marketing)*
Janet Murray *(Vice-President Administration
  & Finance)*
R. Savolainen *(Plant & Operations)*
Michael Sloly *(Company Secretary)*

*Accountancy & Taxation; Educational &
Textbooks; Electronic (Professional &
Academic); Industry, Business & Management;
Law; Human Resources*

New Titles: 20 (1995), 20 (1996)
No of Employees: 200

ISBNs, Imprints & Series:
0 88796, 1 55141

Parent Company:
Commerce Clearing House Inc *(part of the
Wolters Kluwer group of companies) (USA)*

Associated & Subsidiary Companies:
Canada: CCH/FM Ltée

Overseas Representation *(see §7.3)*:
*Asia (excluding Japan, Hong Kong & South
  Korea):* CCH Asia Ltd, Singapore
Australia: CCH Australia Ltd, North Ryde,
  NSW
Europe: CCH Editions Ltd, Wiesbaden,
  Germany
Hong Kong: CCH Hong Kong Ltd
Japan: CCH Japan Ltd, Tokyo
Korea (South): International Professional
  Associates, Seoul, Korea, South
New Zealand: Commerce Clearing House New
  Zealand Ltd, Auckland
UK: CCH Editions Ltd, Bicester
USA: CCH Inc, Chicago, IL

Book Trade Association Membership: Book
Publishers Professional Association, Canadian
Booksellers Association

2116 ▬▬▬▬▬▬▬▬▬▬▬▬▬▬▬▬▬

CHA PRESS
17 York Street, Suite 100, Ottawa, Ont K1N 9J6
Telephone: +1 (613) 241 8005
Fax: +1 (613) 241 5055

President: Tim Julien *(Acting)*
Editor-in-Chief: Eleanor Sawyer *(Editorial,
  Administration, Rights & Permissions)*
Manager: Lyne Sauvé *(Sales)*

Educational & Textbooks; Guide Books

New Titles: 8 (1995), 8 (1996)

ISBNs, Imprints & Series:
0 919100, 1 896151

Parent Company:
Canadian Healthcare Association *(Canada)*

2117 ▬▬▬▬▬▬▬▬▬▬▬▬▬▬▬▬▬

THE CHARLTON PRESS
2010 Yonge Street, Toronto, Ont M4S 1Z9
Telephone: +1 (416) 488 4653
Fax: +1 (416) 488 4656

Publisher: William K. Cross
Managing Director: Nicola Leedham
Office Manager: Jean Dale
Editor: Sandra Tooze

*Antiques & Collecting; Crafts & Hobbies;
Reference Books, Directories & Dictionaries*

New Titles: 25 (1995), 25 (1996)
No of Employees: 8

ISBNs, Imprints & Series: 0 88968

Book Trade Association Membership:
Independent Publishers Group

2118 ▬▬▬▬▬▬▬▬▬▬▬▬▬▬▬▬▬

*CHEMTEC PUBLISHING
38 Earswick Drive, Toronto-Scarborough,
Ont M1E 1C6
Telephone: +1 (416) 265 2603
Fax: +1 (416) 265 1399

Manager: Anna Wypych
Publisher: George Wypych

*Academic & Scholarly; Chemistry; Electronic
(Educational); Engineering; Scientific &
Technical*

ISBNs, Imprints & Series: 1 895198

2119 ▬▬▬▬▬▬▬▬▬▬▬▬▬▬▬▬▬

LES EDITIONS DE LA CHENELIÈRE
215 Jean Talon Est, Montreal, PQ H2R 1S9
Telephone: +1 (514) 273 1066
Fax: +1 (514) 276 0324

Educational President: Michel de la
  Chenelière

*History & Antiquarian; Industry, Business &
Management; Medical (incl. Self Help &
Alternative Medicine); Reference Books,
Directories & Dictionaries; Religion &
Theology; Sociology & Anthropology*

New Titles: 50 (1995), 60 (1996)
No of Employees: 38

ISBNs, Imprints & Series:
2 89310 Chenelière
2 89461 Chenelière/McGraw-Hill

Overseas Representation *(see §7.3)*:
France: Ediscience International, Paris

Book Trade Association Membership:
Canadian Book Publishers Council

2120 ▬▬▬▬▬▬▬▬▬▬▬▬▬▬▬▬▬

*COACH HOUSE PRESS INC
50 Prince Arthur Avenue, Suite 107, Toronto,
Ont M5R 1B5
Telephone: +1 (416) 921 3910
Fax: +1 (416) 921 4403

Trade Enquiries & Orders:
Stewart House, c/o Canbook Distribution,
1220 Nicholson Road, Newmarket,
Ont L3Y 7V1
Telephone: +1 (905) 713 1852
Fax: +1 (905) 836 6728

Publisher: Margaret McClintock
Sales & Marketing: Pamela Robinson

*Fiction; Literature & Criticism; Poetry;
Theatre, Drama & Dance*

ISBNs, Imprints & Series: 0 88910

Book Trade Association Membership:
Organization of Book Publishers of Ontario

2121 ▬▬▬▬▬▬▬▬▬▬▬▬▬▬▬▬▬

**COMMONWEALTH PUBLICATIONS
INC**
9764 45 Avenue, Edmonton, AB T6E 5C5
Telephone: +1 (403) 432 1100
Fax: +1 (403) 432 9409
Email: lions@worldgate.com
Web Site: http://www.commonwealthpub.com

President: Don Phelan
Vice-Presidents: Ken Molloy *(Operations)*
Michael Bryan *(Marketing)*

Directors: Chris Brilz *(Advertising)*
Amber Toullelan *(Acquisitions)*
Corrine Millroy *(Production)*
Managing Editor: Kirsten Osland
Head Pressman: Robert Mead

*Children's Books; Crime; Fiction; Humour;
Medical (incl. Self Help & Alternative
Medicine); Poetry*

New Titles: 90 (1995), 300 (1996)
No of Employees: 60

ISBNs, Imprints & Series:
1 55197, 1 896329

Book Trade Association Membership:
Canadian Booksellers Association, American
Booksellers Association, Periodical Marketers
Council of Canada (Associate Member)

2122 ▬

*COPP CLARK LTD
2775 Matheson Boulevard East, Mississauga,
Ont L4W 4P7
Telephone: +1 (905) 238 6074
Fax: +1 (905) 238 6075

Directors: Peter Warwick
S. J. Mills *(President & CEO)*
R. F. Gurnham *(Vice-President, Finance &
Operations)*
Marion Elliott *(Publications, Managing Editor
– School Division)*
Dawn Morrison *(Vice-President – School
Division)*
L. Petriw *(Vice-President College,
Professional & Trade)*
Vice-President Production & Promotion:
Susan Cline
Order Services: Lynn Burden
Executive Editor: Jeff Miller *(College
Division)*
Rights & Permissions: Dana Bailey

*Academic & Scholarly; Computer Science;
Educational & Textbooks; Electronic
(Educational); Electronic (Professional &
Academic); Geography & Geology; Industry,
Business & Management; Languages &
Linguistics; Mathematics & Statistics; Medical
(incl. Self Help & Alternative Medicine);
Scientific & Technical*

ISBNs, Imprints & Series: 0 7730

Parent Company:
Pearson Professional Ltd *(UK)*

Book Trade Association Membership:
Canadian Book Publishers Council

2123 ▬

CORMORANT BOOKS INC
RR1, Dunvegan, Ont K0C 1J0
Telephone: +1 (613) 527 3348
Fax: +1 (613) 527 2262

Orders:
General Distribution Services,
30 Lesmill Road, Don Mills, Ont M3B 2T6
Telephone: +1 (416) 445 3333
Fax: +1 (416) 445 5967, 5991 & 6967

Publisher: Jan Geddes
Marketing Director: Jeannine Rosenberg
(Stoddard Publishing Co Ltd)

Fiction

New Titles: 7 (1995), 6 (1996)
No of Employees: 2
Annual Turnover: $300,000

ISBNs, Imprints & Series: 0 920953

Book Trade Association Membership:
Association of Canadian Publishers,
Association for the Export of Canadian Books,
Literary Press Group, Organization of Book
Publishers of Ontario, Canadian Booksellers
Association

2124 ▬

COTEAU BOOKS
[Thunder Creek Publishing Co-op]
401–2206 Dewdney Avenue, Regina,
Sask S4R 1H3
Telephone: +1 (306) 777 0170
Fax: +1 (306) 522 5152

Orders:
General Distribution Services,
30 Lesmill Road, Don Mills, Ont M3B 2T6
Telephone: +1 (416) 445 3333
Fax: +1 (416) 445 5913

Publisher: Geoffrey Ursell
Acquisitions Editor: Barbara Sapergia
Managers: Ruth Linka *(Production)*
Erica Smishek *(Marketing)*
Accounts & Fulfilment: Karen Thomas

*Children's Books; Fiction; Literature &
Criticism; Poetry; Theatre, Drama & Dance*

New Titles: 12 (1995), 13 (1996)
No of Employees: 5

ISBNs, Imprints & Series:
0 919926, 1 55050

Book Trade Association Membership:
Literary Press Group, Canadian Booksellers
Association (associate member), Association of
Canadian Publishers, Canadian Telebook
Agency

2125 ▬

LA COURTE ECHELLE
5243 Boulevard St Laurent, Montreal,
PQ H2T 1S4
Telephone: +1 (514) 274 2004
Fax: +1 (514) 270 4160

Distribution:
Diffusion Prologue, 1650 boulevard Lionel-
Bertrand, Boisbriand, PQ J7H 1N7
Telephone: +1 (514) 434 0306
Fax: +1 (514) 434 2627

President: Bertrand Gauthier
Foreign Rights Director: Barbara Creary
Managers: Helene Derome *(Production)*
Martine Benard *(Administration)*

Children's Books; Literature & Criticism

New Titles: 24 (1995), 33 (1996)
No of Employees: 11

ISBNs, Imprints & Series: 2 89021

Overseas Representation *(see §7.3):*
Belgium: Au Gai Savoir, Ransart
France: Le Colporteur Diffusion, La Roche
Blanche
Switzerland: Redim Diffusion, St Sulpice
USA: Firefly Books Ltd, Willowdale, Ont,
Canada
Western Europe: Export Livres, Saint-Lambert,
PQ, Canada

Book Trade Association Membership:
Association of Canadian Publishers,
L'Association Nationale des Editeurs de Livres

2126 ▬

ROBERT DAVIES PUBLISHING
4999 St Catherine Street West, Suite 311,
Westmount, Quebec H3Z 1T3
Telephone: +1 (514) 481 2440
Fax: +1 (514) 481 9973

Trade Manager: Robert Davies

*Children's Books; Cookery, Wines & Spirits;
Crafts & Hobbies; Do-It-Yourself; Economics;
Fiction; Gender Studies; Health & Beauty;
History & Antiquarian; Humour; Illustrated &
Fine Editions; Literature & Criticism;
Philosophy; Politics & World Affairs; Religion
& Theology; Sociology & Anthropology;
Sports & Games; Theatre, Drama & Dance;
Travel & Topography*

New Titles: 32 (1995), 26 (1996)
No of Employees: 2
Annual Turnover: $700,000

ISBNs, Imprints & Series:
1 895854 Robert Davies Publishing
2 89019 L'Etincelle
2 89462 Editions RD

Parent Company:
L'Etincelle Editeur *(Canada)*

Overseas Representation *(see §7.3):*
France & Belgium: Quorum/Magnard, Ivry sur
Seine, France
Switzerland: Diffulivre, St Sulpice
UK & Irish Republic: Drake International
Services, Oxford, UK
USA: Associated Publishers Group, Nashville,
TN

Book Trade Association Membership:
Association of Canadian Publishers, ANEL,
AEAQ, Canadian Booksellers Association,
Canadian Book Publishers Council

2127 ▬

DETSELIG ENTERPRISES LTD
210, 1220 Kensington Road NW, Calgary,
Alta T2N 3P5
Telephone: +1 (403) 283 0900
Fax: +1 (403) 283 6947

President: T. E. Giles
Editor: Linda Berry
Fulfilment: May Misfeldt
Sales Manager: Karen McMullin

Academic & Scholarly; Biography &
Autobiography; Do-It-Yourself; Economics;
Educational & Textbooks; English as a Foreign
Language; Gender Studies; History &
Antiquarian; Politics & World Affairs;
Psychology & Psychiatry; Reference Books,
Directories & Dictionaries; Sociology &
Anthropology

New Titles: 22 (1995), 18 (1996)
No of Employees: 6

ISBNs, Imprints & Series:
0 920490, 1 55059

Overseas Representation (see §7.3):
Malaysia: International Book Service, Petaling
  Jaya
UK: Canadabooks International, Saffron
  Walden

Book Trade Association Membership: Book
PA of Alberta

2128 ■■■■■■■■■■■■■■■■■■■■■■■■■■■■■

DISTICAN INC
[formerly PaperJacks Ltd]
35 Fulton Way, Richmond Hill, Ont L4B 2N4
Telephone: +1 (905) 764 0073
Fax: +1 (905) 764 0086
Email: mail@distican.com

President: Susan Stoddart
Vice-Presidents: Andrew Nopper (Executive)
John Rosenberg (Sales & Marketing, Mass
  Market Division)
Trudy Ledsham (Sales & Marketing, Trade
  Division)
Jim Palmieri (Controller)

Biography & Autobiography; Children's
Books; Crime; Fiction; Reference Books,
Directories & Dictionaries; Science Fiction

No of Employees: 96

ISBNs, Imprints & Series:
0 7701 PaperJacks

Book Trade Association Membership:
Canadian Book Publishers Council

2129 ■■■■■■■■■■■■■■■■■■■■■■■■■■■■■

DOUGLAS & McINTYRE LTD
1615 Venables Street, Vancouver,
BC V5L 2H1
Telephone: +1 (604) 254 7191 & +1 (800) 667
6902
Fax: +1 (604) 254 9099
Email: dm@douglas-mcintyre.com

Customer Service:
Kym Lyons at above address
Telephone: +1 (604) 254 8218 & +1 (800) 667
6902
Fax: +1 (604) 254 9099 & +1 (800) 263 9099

Toronto Address:
585 Bloor Street W, 2nd Floor, Toronto,
Ont M6G 1K5
Telephone: +1 (416) 537 2501
Fax: +1 (416) 537 4647

Vice-Presidents/Publishers: Rob Sanders
  (Greystone Books)

Patsy Aldana (Children's)
Managers: Susan McIntosh (Vice-President,
  Sales & Marketing)
Janice Bearg (General)
Polly Manguel (Export Sales)

Architecture & Design; Biography &
Autobiography; Children's Books; Cookery,
Wines & Spirits; Fiction; Fine Art & Art
History; Guide Books; History & Antiquarian;
Natural History; Politics & World Affairs;
Sociology & Anthropology; Sports & Games;
Travel & Topography

New Titles: 43 (1995), 50 (1996)
No of Employees: 28

ISBNs, Imprints & Series:
0 88833, 0 88894 Greystone
0 88894, 1 55054 Douglas & McIntyre
0 88899, 1 85103 Groundwood

Overseas Representation (see §7.3):
Australia (children's books): Ashton
  Scholastic Pty Ltd, Gosford, Australia
UK & Europe (adult books): Roundhouse
  Publishing Ltd, Oxford, UK
UK & Europe (children's books): Ragged
  Bears Ltd, Andover, UK

Book Trade Association Membership:
Association of Canadian Publishers,
Association of Book Publishers of British
Columbia

2130 ■■■■■■■■■■■■■■■■■■■■■■■■■■■■■

DOVEHOUSE EDITIONS CANADA
1890 Fairmeadow Crescent, Ottawa,
Ont K1H 7B9
Telephone: +1 (613) 731 7601

Executive: Donald Beecher
Sales & Marketing: Sophie Beecher
Production: Christina Theile
Editorial: Massimo Ciavolella

Academic & Scholarly; Fiction; Literature &
Criticism; Theatre, Drama & Dance

New Titles: 8 (1995), 8 (1996)
No of Employees: 2
Annual Turnover: $28,000

ISBNs, Imprints & Series:
Barnabe Riche Society in Early English Prose
  Fiction, University of Toronto Italian Studies
0 919473 Carleton Renaissance Plays — in
  Translation Series
1 985537 Ottawa Hispanic Studies

2131 ■■■■■■■■■■■■■■■■■■■■■■■■■■■■■

THE DUNDURN GROUP
2181 Queen Street East, Suite 301, Toronto,
Ontario M4E 1E5
Telephone: +1 (416) 698 0454
Fax: +1 (416) 698 1102
Email: orders@dundurn.com

President & Publisher: J. Kirk Howard
Comptroller: Ian A. B. Low (Export Sales)
Rights & Permissions: Carl Brand

Academic & Scholarly; Bibliography &
Library Science; Biography & Autobiography;
Children's Books; Crime; Fiction; Fine Art &

Art History; History & Antiquarian; Literature
& Criticism; Military & War; Natural History;
Poetry; Politics & World Affairs; Reference
Books, Directories & Dictionaries; Theatre,
Drama & Dance

New Titles: 45 (1995), 50 (1996)
No of Employees: 17

ISBNs, Imprints & Series:
0 8882, 0 88924, 0 919670, 1 55002

Associated & Subsidiary Companies:
Canada: Hounslow Press; Simon & Pierre
Publishing Ltd

Overseas Representation (see §7.3):
UK & Europe: Dundurn Distribution, Oxford,
  UK
USA: Dundurn Press, Niagara Falls, NY

Book Trade Association Membership:
Association of Canadian Publishers, Canadian
Book Information Centre, Canadian
Booksellers Association

2132 ■■■■■■■■■■■■■■■■■■■■■■■■■■■■■

DURKIN HAYES PUBLISHING LTD
3375 North Service Road, Burlington,
Ont L7N 3G2
Telephone: +1 (905) 335 0393
Fax: +1 (905) 332 3008

Chief Executive Officer: Patrick J. Hayes
Chief Financial Officer: Donald L. Matheson
Managing Editor: Willem VanZon

Audio Books; Children's Books

New Titles: 72 (1995), 75 (1996)
No of Employees: 25

ISBNs, Imprints & Series:
0 88625 DHP Books
0 88646 Durkin Hayes Audio/Paperback Audio

Associated & Subsidiary Companies:
USA: Durkin Hayes Publishing Ltd

Book Trade Association Membership:
Canadian Book Publishers' Council, Canadian
Booksellers Association, Canadian Library
Association, Ontario Library Association,
American Booksellers Association, American
Library Association

2133 ■■■■■■■■■■■■■■■■■■■■■■■■■■■■■

ECW PRESS
2120 Queen Street East, Suite 200, Toronto,
Ont M4E 1E2
Telephone: +1 (416) 694 3348
Fax: +1 (416) 698 9906
Email: ecw@sympatico.ca

President: Jack David
Vice-President: Robert Lecker
Production Manager: Paul Davies

Academic & Scholarly; Bibliography &
Library Science; Biography & Autobiography;
Educational & Textbooks; Gender Studies;
Literature & Criticism; Poetry; Reference
Books, Directories & Dictionaries; Sports &
Games

New Titles: 32 (1995), 30 (1996)
No of Employees: 8
Annual Turnover: $800,000

ISBNs, Imprints & Series:
0 920763, 0 920802, 1 55022

Overseas Representation *(see §7.3)*:
Canada & USA (selected titles): General
 Publishing Co Ltd, North York, Ont, Canada
USA (selected titles): In Book, Chicago, IL,
 USA
Worldwide (excluding Canada & USA): Cardiff
 Academic Press, Cardiff, UK

Book Trade Association Membership:
Association of Canadian Publishers, Literary
Press Group

2134

*EKSTASIS EDITIONS
Box 8474, Main Road, Victoria, BC V8W 3S1
Telephone: +1 (604) 385 3378
Fax: +1 (604) 385 3378

Publisher/Editor: Richard Olafson
Editor: Carol Ann Solcoloff

*Academic & Scholarly; Children's Books;
Fiction; Literature & Criticism; Music;
Philosophy; Poetry; Religion & Theology;
Science Fiction; Theatre, Drama & Dance*

ISBNs, Imprints & Series: 0 921215

Book Trade Association Membership:
Association of Canadian Publishers,
Association of Book Publishers of British
Columbia

2135

**EMOND MONTGOMERY
PUBLICATIONS LTD**
58 Shaftesbury Avenue, Toronto,
Ont M4T 1A3
Telephone: +1 (416) 975 3925
Fax: +1 (416) 975 3924
Email: emplaw@io.org
Web Site: http://www.io.org/~emplaw

Warehouse:
240 Edward Street, Aurora, Ont L4G 3S9
Telephone: +1 (905) 841 6472

Directors: Desmond Harty *(Marketing &
 Sales)*
Nora Rock *(Acquisitions & New Product
 Development)*
Office Manager/Production Co-ordinator:
 Teresa van den Heuvel

*Academic & Scholarly; Educational &
Textbooks; Environment & Development
Studies; Gay & Lesbian Studies; Law; Medical
(incl. Self Help & Alternative Medicine);
Reference Books, Directories & Dictionaries*

New Titles: 8 (1995), 8 (1996)
No of Employees: 4

ISBNs, Imprints & Series: 0 920722

Parent Company:
Cartwright Omni Corporation *(Canada)*

Associated & Subsidiary Companies:
Canada: Canada Law Book; Dye & Durham

Overseas Representation *(see §7.3)*:
UK: Cavendish Publishing Ltd, London

2136

FIFTH HOUSE PUBLISHERS
201-165 3rd Avenue South, Saskatoon,
SK S7K 1L8
Telephone: +1 (306) 242 4936
Fax: +1 (306) 242 7667

Distributor:
University of Toronto Press,
5201 Dufferin Street, Downsview,
Ont M3H 5T8
Telephone: +1 (416) 667 7791
Fax: +1 (416) 667 7832

Publisher: Fraser Seely
Editors: Charlene Dobmeier *(Managing)*
Nora Russell *(Production)*
Promotion Manager: Caroline Walker *(Rights
 & Permissions)*

*Biography & Autobiography; Children's
Books; Gardening; History & Antiquarian;
Natural History; Photography*

New Titles: 14 (1995), 11 (1996)
No of Employees: 4

ISBNs, Imprints & Series:
0 920079, 1 895618

Book Trade Association Membership:
Saskatchewan Publishers Group

2137

THE FRASER INSTITUTE
626 Bute Street, 2nd Floor, Vancouver,
BC V6E 3M1
Telephone: +1 (604) 688 0221
Fax: +1 (604) 688 8539
Web Site: http://www.fraserinstitute.ca

Toronto Office:
Ste 2550 – 55 King Street West, Toronto,
Ont M5K 1E7
Telephone: +1 (416) 363 6575
Fax: +1 (416) 601 7322

Orders:
Telephone: +1 (800) 665 3558 (Toll free)

Directors: Dr M. A. Walker *(Editorial)*
Victor Waese *(Finance & Administration)*
David Hanley *(Communication)*
Kristin McCahon *(Production)*
Brian April *(Development)*

*Economics; Industry, Business &
Management; Politics & World Affairs;
Sociology & Anthropology*

New Titles: 5 (1995), 5 (1996)
No of Employees: 22

ISBNs, Imprints & Series: 0 88975

Overseas Representation *(see §7.3)*:
Australia: Libertarian Review, Mona Vale
New Zealand: Chaunter Editorial Associates
 Ltd, Wellington

Norway: Ideer om Frihet, Bergen
Sweden: AB Timbro, Stockholm
UK: Blackwell Publishers, Oxford
USA: Baker & Taylor Companies, Somerville,
 NJ & Momence, IL

Book Trade Association Membership:
Association of Book Publishers of British
Columbia, Canadian Booksellers Association,
Canadian Book Information Centre

2138

GAËTAN MORIN PUBLISHER
171 de Mortagne, Boucherville, PQ J4B 6G4
Telephone: +1 (514) 449 2369
Fax: +1 (514) 449 7808

President: Gaëtan Morin
Publishing: Céline Laprise
Sales & Promotion Director: Jacqueline
 Mallet
Rights & Permissions: Catherine Vallet

*Academic & Scholarly; Educational &
Textbooks*

New Titles: 26 (1995), 22 (1996)
No of Employees: 70

ISBNs, Imprints & Series: 2 89105

Associated & Subsidiary Companies:
Canada: Graficor; Presses de l'Université de
Montréal (University of Montreal Press);
Presses de l'Université d'Ottawa (University of
Ottawa Press)

Overseas Representation *(see §7.3)*:
Europe: Initiatives Santé, Vélizy, France

2139

**GAGE EDUCATIONAL PUBLISHING
CO**
164 Commander Boulevard, Scarborough,
Ont M1S 3C7
Telephone: +1 (416) 293 8141
Fax: +1 (416) 293 9009

Promotion: Helen Richardson
President: Ronald Besse
Vice-President: Chris Besse
Publisher: Joe Banel
College/Prof. Manager: Caroline
 Hebblethwaite
Business: Tim McDonald
Rights: Elizabeth Long
Production: Anna Kress

*Atlases & Maps; Aviation; Chemistry;
Children's Books; Cookery, Wines & Spirits;
Educational & Textbooks; Electronic
(Educational); Electronic (Professional &
Academic); Environment & Development
Studies; Geography & Geology; Health &
Beauty; History & Antiquarian; Mathematics
& Statistics; Reference Books, Directories &
Dictionaries; Vocational Training & Careers*

New Titles: 26 (1995), 20 (1996)
No of Employees: 30

ISBNs, Imprints & Series:
0 7705, 0 7715

Parent Company:
Canada Publishing Corporation *(Canada)*

Associated & Subsidiary Companies:
Canada: Diffulivre Inc; Gage Distribution;
Global Press; Macmillan Canada

Overseas Representation *(see §7.3):*
USA: Dominie Press Inc, San Diego

Book Trade Association Membership:
Canadian Book Publishers Council

2140 ■

GARAMOND PRESS
77 Mowat Avenue, Suite 403, Toronto,
Ont M6K 3E3
Telephone: +1 (416) 516 2709
Fax: +1 (416) 516 0571
Email: garamond@web.apc.org
Web Site: http://www.garamond.ca/garamond/

Warehouse:
TTS Distributing, 45 Tyler Street, Aurora,
Ont M6K 3E3

Directors: Peter Saunders
Bob Mawhinney *(Marketing)*

*Academic & Scholarly; Environment &
Development Studies; Gender Studies; History
& Antiquarian; Politics & World Affairs;
Reference Books, Directories & Dictionaries;
Sociology & Anthropology*

New Titles: 8 (1995), 10 (1996)
No of Employees: 3

ISBNs, Imprints & Series:
0 920059, 1 55193

Overseas Representation *(see §7.3):*
Australia: St Clair Press Pty Ltd, Rozelle, NSW
UK: Book Representation & Distribution
(BRAD), Hadleigh
USA: Garamond Press, Niagara Falls, NY

Book Trade Association Membership:
Ontario Book PA

2141 ■

GENERAL PUBLISHING CO LTD
30 Lesmill Road, North York, Ont M3B 2T6
Telephone: +1 (416) 445 3333
Fax: +1 (416) 445 5991

President: Nelson Doucet
Vice-President: Kevin Chapman

*Atlases & Maps; Cookery, Wines & Spirits; Do-
It-Yourself; Gardening; Guide Books; Music;
Photography; Reference Books, Directories &
Dictionaries; Travel & Topography*

New Titles: 43 (1995), 50 (1996)
No of Employees: 150
Annual Turnover: $30M

ISBNs, Imprints & Series:
1 55144 élan press

Parent Company:
General *(Canada)*

Book Trade Association Membership:
Association for the Export of Canadian Books

2142 ■

GOOSE LANE EDITIONS
469 King Street, Fredericton, NB E3B 1E5
Telephone: +1 (506) 450 4251
Fax: +1 (506) 459 4991

Canadian Distributor:
General Distribution Services,
30 Lesmill Road, Don Mills, Ont M3B 2T6
Telephone: +1 (416) 445 3333
Fax: +1 (416) 445 5967

Foreign Rights:
Bill Hanna, Stoddart Publishing,
30 Lesmill Road, Don Mills, Ont M3B 2T6
Telephone: +1 (416) 445 3333
Fax: +1 (416) 445 5967

Publisher: Susanne Alexander
Senior Editor: Laurel Boone
Art Director: Julie Scriver

*Academic & Scholarly; Architecture & Design;
Biography & Autobiography; Cookery, Wines
& Spirits; Crime; Fiction; Fine Art & Art
History; Gender Studies; Guide Books; History
& Antiquarian; Humour; Literature &
Criticism; Music; Photography; Poetry*

New Titles: 14 (1995), 15 (1996)
No of Employees: 7
Annual Turnover: $750,000

ISBNs, Imprints & Series:
0 86492 Goose Lane Editions
0 920110 Fiddlehead Poetry Books

Associated & Subsidiary Companies:
Canada: Acadiensis Press; Art Gallery of Nova
Scotia; Beaverbrook Art Gallery; Breton
Books; Lower Saint John River Association;
New Brunswick Geographic Information
Corporation; University College of Cape
Breton Press

Book Trade Association Membership:
Association of Canadian Publishers, Canadian
Booksellers Association, Atlantic Publishers
Association, Canadian Copyright Agency,
Literary Press Group of Canada

2143 ■

*GROUNDWOOD BOOKS
585 Bloor Street West, 2nd Floor, Toronto,
Ont M6G 1K5
Telephone: +1 (416) 537 2501
Fax: +1 (416) 537 4647

Warehouse:
University of Toronto Press,
5201 Dufferin Street, Toronto, Ont M3H 5T8
Telephone: +1 (416) 667 7791
Fax: +1 (416) 667 7832

President & Publisher: Patricia Aldana
Vice-President, Sales & Marketing: Susan
McIntosh
Senior Editor: Shelley Tanaka

Children's Books

ISBNs, Imprints & Series: 0 88899

Overseas Representation *(see §7.3):*
Australia: Ashton Scholastic Pty Ltd, Gosford
USA: Firefly Books Ltd, Willowdale, Ont,
Canada

2144 ■

GUERNICA EDITIONS
PO Box 117, Station P, Toronto, Ont M5S 2S6
Telephone: +1 (416) 658 9888
Fax: +1 (416) 657 8885
Email: 120260.1333@compuserve.com
Web Site: http://ourworld.compuserve.com/
homepages/guernica

Editorial Director: Antonio D'Alfonso
(Fiction/Poetry)
Marketing: Emilia Chiocca
Editorial: Pasquale Verdicchio

*Academic & Scholarly; Biography &
Autobiography; Cinema, Video, TV & Radio;
Fiction; Gender Studies; Poetry; Theatre,
Drama & Dance*

New Titles: 14 (1995), 20 (1996)
No of Employees: 2

ISBNs, Imprints & Series:
0 919349, 0 920717, 1 55071 Drama Series,
Essay Series, Essential Poets Series, Picas
Series, Prose Series
2 89135 Voix (Collection)

Overseas Representation *(see §7.3):*
UK: Gazelle Book Services Ltd, Lancaster
USA (East): LPC/Inbook, Chicago, IL, USA
USA (West): Small Press Distribution Inc,
Berkeley, CA, USA

2145 ■

RAGWEED PRESS/ GYNERGY BOOKS
PO Box 2023, Charlottetown, PEI C1A 7N7
Telephone: +1 (902) 566 5750
Fax: +1 (902) 566 4473
Email: gb@gynergy.com & rp@ragweed.com

Distribution:
General Distribution Services,
30 Lesmill Road, Don Mills, Ont M3B 2T6
Telephone: +1 (416) 445 3333
Fax: +1 (416) 445 5967

Publisher: Louise Fleming *(Rights)*
Managers: Sibyl Frei *(Production, Rights)*
Inga Petri *(Marketing, Sales)*

*Biography & Autobiography; Children's
Books; Cookery, Wines & Spirits; Crime;
Fiction; Gay & Lesbian Studies*

New Titles: 12 (1995), 11 (1996)
No of Employees: 5

ISBNs, Imprints & Series:
0 920304, 0 921556 Ragweed Press
0 921881 gynergy books

Overseas Representation *(see §7.3):*
UK: Turnaround Publishers Services Ltd,
London
USA: LPC/Inbook, Chicago, IL

Book Trade Association Membership:
Association of Canadian Publishers

2146 ∎

HANCOCK HOUSE PUBLISHERS LTD
19313 Zero Avenue, Surrey, BC V4P 1M7
Telephone: +1 (604) 538 1114
Fax: +1 (604) 538 2262
Email: hancock@uniserve.com

President: David Hancock
Comptroller: David Baker
Managers: Georg Wilson *(Sales)*
Nancy Miller *(Promotions)*
Myron Shutty *(Production)*

Animal Care & Breeding; Aviation; Biology & Zoology; Guide Books; History & Antiquarian; Natural History

New Titles: 24 (1995), 13 (1996)
No of Employees: 8
Annual Turnover: $700,000

ISBNs, Imprints & Series:
0 88839, 0 919654

Overseas Representation *(see §7.3):*
Africa: PMC International, Durban North, South Africa
Europe & UK: Gazelle Book Services Ltd, Lancaster, UK

2147 ∎

HARBOUR PUBLISHING CO LTD
Box 219, Madeira Park, BC V0N 2H0
Telephone: +1 (604) 883 2730
Fax: +1 (604) 883 9451

Editorial: Howard White *(Publisher)*
Director: Mary White
Managers: Peter Robson
Marisa Alps
Dani Lacusta *(Office)*

Audio Books; Aviation; Biography & Autobiography; Children's Books; Cookery, Wines & Spirits; Crafts & Hobbies; Gay & Lesbian Studies; Guide Books; History & Antiquarian; Industry, Business & Management; Literature & Criticism; Nautical; Poetry

New Titles: 17 (1995), 19 (1996)
No of Employees: 7

ISBNs, Imprints & Series:
0 88971, 0 920080, 1 55017

Book Trade Association Membership:
Association of Canadian Publishers,
Association of Book Publishers of BC

2148 ∎

HARLEQUIN ENTERPRISES LTD
225 Duncan Mill Road, Don Mills,
Ont M3B 3K9
Telephone: +1 (416) 445 5860
Fax: +1 (416) 445 8655
Web Site: http://www.romance.net

Chairman: D. A. Galloway
President: B. E. Hickey *(Chief Executive Officer)*
Executive Vice-President: S. J. Campbell *(Direct Marketing)*
Vice-Presidents: Candy Lee *(Publisher)*

W. M. Catto *(Corporate Finance)*
B. A. Stevenson *(Administration & Legal Affairs)*
A. Flynn

Fiction

ISBNs, Imprints & Series:
0 373 Gold Eagle, Harlequin, Silhouette, Worldwide
1 55166 Mira

Parent Company:
Torstar Corporation *(Canada)*

Associated & Subsidiary Companies:
Australia: Harlequin Enterprises (Australia) Pty Ltd. *France:* Harlequin SA. *Germany:* Cora Verlag AG. *Greece:* Harlenic Hellas AE. *Hungary:* Harlequin Kft. *Italy:* Harlequin-Mondadori SpA. *Poland:* Harlequin Poland. *Spain:* Harlequin Iberica SA. *Switzerland:* Harlequin Books SA. *UK:* Harlequin; Mills & Boon Ltd. *USA:* Harlequin Retail Inc

Overseas Representation *(see §7.3):*
Japan: Harlequin K. K., Tokyo
Netherlands: Harlequin Holland, Amsterdam
Sweden: Forlaget Harlequin AB, Stockholm
USA: Harlequin Distribution Center, Depew, NY

Book Trade Association Membership:
Association of Canadian Publishers

2149 ∎

***D. C. HEATH CANADA LTD**
200 Adelaide Street West, 3rd Floor, Toronto, Ont M5H 1W7
Telephone: +1 (416) 977 1345
Fax: +1 (416) 977 3135

Warehouse:
2775 Matheson Boulevard East, Mississauga, Ont L4W 4P7
Telephone: +1 (905) 238 6108
Fax: +1 (905) 625 8008

President: Robbie Ross
Vice-President & Director of School Operations: Ron Cornelius
Vice-President Finance: David Kirkwood
Managers: Tim McCleary *(College Division)*
Trevor Hills *(Sales & Marketing—School Division)*
Gaynor Fitzpatrick *(Editorial & Production)*

Academic & Scholarly; Children's Books; Educational & Textbooks; Electronic (Educational); Geography & Geology; History & Antiquarian; Languages & Linguistics; Literature & Criticism; Mathematics & Statistics; Physics; Politics & World Affairs; Vocational Training & Careers

ISBNs, Imprints & Series: 0 669

Parent Company:
Raytheon International Inc *(USA)*

Overseas Representation *(see §7.3):*
USA: D. C. Heath & Co, Lexington, MA

Book Trade Association Membership:
Canadian Book Publishers' Council

2150 ∎

HERALD PRESS
490 Dutton Drive, Waterloo, Ont N2L 6H7
Telephone: +1 (519) 747 5722
Fax: +1 (519) 747 5721
Email: hpcan%mph@mcimail.com
Web Site: http://www.mph.lm.com/hp.html

New Titles: 29 (1995), 28 (1996)
No of Employees: 8
Annual Turnover: $97,389

Overseas Representation *(see §7.3):*
Australia: W. A. Buchanan & Co, Brisbane
Colombia: CLARA, Bogota
Korea: Bible Book House, Seoul, Korea, South; Korea Christian Book Service, Seoul, Korea, South
Netherlands: Pelgrim International Boeken, Westervoort
New Zealand: Omega Distributors, Auckland
South Africa: Rainbow Distributors, Kenilworth
Sweden: DetStar Skrivet, Gothenburg
UK: Metanoia Book Service, London

Book Trade Association Membership:
Christian Booksellers Association International, Christian Booksellers Association Canadian Chapter, Protestant Church Owned Publishers Association

2151 ∎

EDITIONS HERITAGE INC
300 rue Arran, Saint-Lambert, PQ J4R 1K5
Telephone: +1 (514) 875 0327
Fax: +1 (514) 672 1481

President: Jacques Payette *(Editorial)*
Vice-President: Luc Payette *(Marketing)*
Assistants: Ginette Guetat *(to the Editor)*
Pierre Simard *(to the President)*
Public Relations: Francesco Ferri

Children's Books; Cookery, Wines & Spirits

New Titles: 212 (1995), 198 (1996)
No of Employees: 47

ISBNs, Imprints & Series: 2 7625

Overseas Representation *(see §7.3):*
Belgium: Les Presses de Belgique, Wavre
France: Le Colporteur Diffusion, La Roche Blanche
Switzerland: Redim Diffusion, St Sulpice

Book Trade Association Membership:
CTMA, Canadian BA

2152 ∎

HIGHWAY BOOK SHOP
Highway 11 South, Cobalt, Ont P0J 1C0
Telephone: +1 (705) 679 8375
Fax: +1 (705) 679 8511
Email: bookshop@onlink.net
Web Site: http://www.onlink.net/cybermall/bookshop/index.htm

Owner-Manager: Dr Douglas C. Pollard
Managers: Lois Pollard *(Assistant)*
Paul Bogart *(Production)*

History & Antiquarian

New Titles: 5 (1995), 5 (1996)
No of Employees: 10

ISBNs, Imprints & Series: 0 88954

Book Trade Association Membership:
Association of Canadian Publishers, Canadian
Book Information Centre

2153 ▬▬▬

HMS PRESS:BOOKS ON DISK
Box 340, Stn B, London, Ont N6A 4W1
Telephone: +1 (519) 433 8994
Email: resource.center@onlinesys.com
Web Site: http://www.bb.com

President: Wayne Ray
Editor ADP titles: Regena Bennett

Academic & Scholarly; Audio Books;
Bibliography & Library Science; Biography &
Autobiography; Children's Books; Crime; Do-
It-Yourself; Educational & Textbooks;
Electronic (Educational); Electronic
(Entertainment); Electronic (Professional &
Academic); English as a Foreign Language;
Fiction; Gardening; Gay & Lesbian Studies;
History & Antiquarian; Humour; Literature &
Criticism; Military & War; Music; Natural
History; Philosophy; Poetry; Reference Books,
Directories & Dictionaries; Religion &
Theology; Science Fiction; Sociology &
Anthropology; Theatre, Drama & Dance;
PACKAGER ONLY

New Titles: 100 (1995), 100 (1996)

ISBNs, Imprints & Series:
0 919957 HMS Press Publishing
1 571060 HMS Press: Atlantic Disk Publishers
1 895700 HMS Press: Books on Disk, Canadian
Poetry Association: Bookclub

Parent Company:
HMS Press *(Canada)*

Associated & Subsidiary Companies:
USA: HMS Press: Atlantic Disk Publishers

2154 ▬▬▬

**HORSDAL & SCHUBART PUBLISHERS
LTD**
Suites 618 & 623, 425 Simcoe Street, Victoria,
BC V8V 4T3
Telephone: +1 (604) 360 2031
Fax: +1 (604) 360 0829

President: Marlyn Horsdal
Secretary: Michael Schubart

Biography & Autobiography; History &
Antiquarian; Natural History; Nautical; Travel
& Topography

New Titles: 10 (1995), 7 (1996)
Annual Turnover: $150,000

ISBNs, Imprints & Series: 0 920663

Book Trade Association Membership:
Association of Canadian Publishers,
Association of Book Publishers of British
Columbia

2155 ▬▬▬

HOUNSLOW PRESS
2181 Queen Street East, Suite 301, Toronto,
Ont M4E 1E5
Telephone: +1 (416) 698 0454
Fax: +1 (416) 698 1102

President: Kirk Howard
General Manager: Tony Hawke

Aviation; Children's Books; Cookery, Wines &
Spirits; Crime; Do-It-Yourself; Fiction; Health
& Beauty; Humour; Illustrated & Fine
Editions; Literature & Criticism; Magic & the
Occult; Poetry

New Titles: 10 (1995), 12 (1996)
No of Employees: 2

ISBNs, Imprints & Series: 0 88882

Parent Company:
Dundurn Press *(Canada)*

Overseas Representation *(see §7.3)*:
UK & Europe: Dundurn Distribution, Oxford,
UK

Book Trade Association Membership:
Association of Canadian Publishers

2156 ▬▬▬

HOUSE OF ANANSI PRESS LTD
1800 Steeles Avenue W, Concord,
Ont L4K 2P3
Telephone: +1 (905) 660 0611
Fax: +1 (905) 660 0676

Orders, Customer Service & Accounting:
34 Lesmill Road, Don Mills, Ont M3B 2T6
Telephone: +1 (416) 445 3333
Fax: +1 (416) 445 5967
Email: anasi@irwin-pub.com
Web Site: http://www.irwin-pub.com/irwin/
anansi

Publisher: Michael Byron Davis
Export Sales, Rights & Permissions: William
B. Hanna
Editor: Martha Sharpe

Fiction; Literature & Criticism; Poetry;
Politics & World Affairs

New Titles: 14 (1995), 10 (1996)
No of Employees: 3

ISBNs, Imprints & Series: 0 88784

Parent Company:
Stoddart Publishing *(Canada)*

Overseas Representation *(see §7.3)*:
UK, Irish Republic & Europe: Lavis
Marketing, Oxford, UK

Book Trade Association Membership:
Association of Canadian Publishers, Literary
Press Group

2157 ▬▬▬

HYPERION PRESS LTD
300 Wales Avenue, Winnipeg, Man R2M 2S9

Telephone: +1 (204) 256 9204
Fax: +1 (204) 255 7845

President: Dr Marvis Tutiah
Vice-President: Arlene O. Osen

Children's Books; Crafts & Hobbies; Do-It-
Yourself; Natural History; Art

New Titles: 8 (1995), 11 (1996)
No of Employees: 5

ISBNs, Imprints & Series:
0 920534, 1 895340

Overseas Representation *(see §7.3)*:
USA: Sterling Publishing Co Inc, New York,
NY; The Walt Disney Co Inc, New York

2158 ▬▬▬

**INSTITUTE OF PSYCHOLOGICAL
RESEARCH INC**
34 Fleury Street West, Montreal, PQ H3L 1S9
Telephone: +1 (514) 382 3000
Fax: +1 (514) 382 3007

President & Executive Director: Jean-Marc
Chevrier *(Rights & Permissions)*
Sales Manager: Michel Ratthé
Chief Accountant: Line Pellerin
Associate Publisher: Malko von Osten

Academic & Scholarly; Educational &
Textbooks; Psychology & Psychiatry

New Titles: 5 (1995), 5 (1996)
No of Employees: 12

ISBNs, Imprints & Series:
0 88509, 2 89109

Parent Company:
JMC Press Ltd *(Canada)*

Overseas Representation *(see §7.3)*:
Belgium: Editions Editest, Brussels
France: Librairie Vuibert, Paris

2159 ▬▬▬

**INTERNATIONAL SELF-COUNSEL
PRESS LTD**
1481 Charlotte Road, North Vancouver,
BC V7J 1H1
Telephone: +1 (604) 986 3366
Fax: +1 (604) 986 3947
Email: selfcoun@pmc.com
Web Site: http://www.swiftg.com/scp/

Eastern Office & Warehouse:
4 Bram Court, Brampton, Ont L6W 3R6
Telephone: +1 (905) 450 0336
Fax: +1 (905) 450 7626

President: Diana Douglas *(Rights &*
Permissions)
Directors: Colleen Davies *(Export Sales)*
Pat Touchie *(Marketing, Home Sales)*

Do-It-Yourself; Industry, Business &
Management; Law; Psychology & Psychiatry;
Reference Books, Directories & Dictionaries

New Titles: 12 (1995), 14 (1996)
No of Employees: 24

ISBNs, Imprints & Series:
1 55180, 1 88908 Self-Counsel Series

Associated & Subsidiary Companies:
USA: Self-Counsel Press Inc

Overseas Representation *(see §7.3):*
Australia: Astam Books Pty Ltd, Leichhardt,
NSW
India: Dipak Kumar Guha, New Delhi
Malaysia, Singapore, Brunei & Indonesia:
Delta Editions Sdn Bhd, Selangor Darul
Ehsan, Malaysia
New Zealand: South Pacific Books (Imports)
Ltd, Auckland
South Africa: Alternative Books, Randburg
UK & Europe: Roundhouse Publishing Ltd,
Oxford, UK
West Indies & Venezuela: Universal Multitrade
& Associates, Trinidad

Book Trade Association Membership:
Association of Canadian Publishers,
Association of American Publishers

2160 ━━━━━

IRWIN PUBLISHING
[Educational Division of General Publishing]
1800 Steeles Avenue West, Concord,
Ont L4K 2P3
Telephone: +1 (905) 660 0611
Fax: +1 (905) 660 0676
Email: irwin@irwin.pub.com
Web Site: http://www.irwin-pub.com/irwin/

Trade Enquiries & Orders:
34 Lesmill Road, Don Mills, Ont M3B 2T6
Telephone: +1 (416) 445 3333
Fax: +1 (416) 445 5967

President: Brian O'Donnell
Vice-President: Michael Byron Davis
Managers: Steve Walker *(Community
College)*
Terry Nikkel *(Professional Training)*
Jennifer MacDougall *(Business Education)*
Sharon Port *(Sales & Marketing)*

*Academic & Scholarly; Biography &
Autobiography; Chemistry; Educational &
Textbooks; Geography & Geology; Languages
& Linguistics; Physics; Politics & World
Affairs; Religion & Theology; Theatre, Drama
& Dance*

New Titles: 19 (1995), 22 (1996)
No of Employees: 20

ISBNs, Imprints & Series:
0 7720, 0 7725

Parent Company:
General Publishing Co Ltd *(Canada)*

Book Trade Association Membership:
Canadian Book Publishers Council

2161 ━━━━━

ITP NELSON CANADA
[a division of Thomson Canada Ltd]
1120 Birchmount Road, Scarborough,
Ont M1K 5G4
Telephone: +1 (416) 752 9100
Fax: +1 (416) 752 9646

Email: ldarroch@nelson.com
Web Site: http://www.nelson.com/nelson.html

President & Chief Executive Officer: Herb
Hilderley
Executive Vice-Presidents: Dic Parkinson
(Finance & Chief Financial Officer)
Dave Dimmell *(Market & Product
Development)*
David Morrow *(Business Development &
Emerging Markets)*
Ken Proctor *(Sales & Customer Satisfaction)*
Directors: Loren Darroch *(Communications)*
Jim Black *(Human Resources)*

*Cinema, Video, TV & Radio; Environment &
Development Studies; Industry, Business &
Management; Psychology & Psychiatry;
Reference Books, Directories & Dictionaries*

New Titles: 106 (1995), 110 (1996)
No of Employees: 265

ISBNs, Imprints & Series: 0 17

Parent Company:
The Thomson Corporation *(Canada)*

Overseas Representation *(see §7.3):*
Australia: Thomas Nelson (Australia) Pty Ltd,
South Melbourne, Vic
UK: Thomas Nelson & Sons Ltd, Walton-on-
Thames

Book Trade Association Membership:
Canadian Book Publishers' Council

2162 ━━━━━

JESPERSON PRESS LTD
39 Jame Lane, St John's, NF A1E 3H3
Telephone: +1 (709) 753 0633
Fax: +1 (709) 753 5507
Email: jp@public.compusult.nf.ca

President: John Symonds *(Home & Export
Sales)*
Vice-President Production: Russ Thomas
Accounts: Dulcie Coombs
Supervisor: Donna Snelgrove

Educational & Textbooks

New Titles: 8 (1995), 8 (1996)
No of Employees: 9

ISBNs, Imprints & Series:
0 920502, 0 921692

2163 ━━━━━

KEY PORTER BOOKS LTD
70 The Esplanade, Toronto, Ont M5E 1R2
Telephone: +1 (416) 862 7777
Fax: +1 (416) 862 2304

Orders & Distribution:
General Publishing, 1800 Steeles Avenue West,
Concord, Ont L4K 2P3
Telephone: +1 (905) 660 0470
Fax: +1 (905) 660 1753

Publisher & Chief Executive Officer: Anna
Porter
President & Editor-in-Chief: Susan Renouf
Vice-Presidents: Allan Ibarra *(Finance,
Treasurer)*

Clare McKeon *(Production)*
Managers: Bonnie Harris *(Promotion)*
Jean Peters *(Creative Director)*
Arden Boehm *(International Rights)*

*Children's Books; Gardening; Health &
Beauty; Illustrated & Fine Editions; Natural
History; Photography*

New Titles: 47 (1995), 50 (1996)
No of Employees: 21

ISBNs, Imprints & Series:
0 919493, 1 55013

Associated & Subsidiary Companies:
Canada: Lester & Orpen Dennys; Lester
Publishing Ltd

Overseas Representation *(see §7.3):*
UK: Verulam Publishing Ltd, St Albans
USA: Firefly Books Ltd, Willowdale, Ont,
Canada

Book Trade Association Membership:
Association of Canadian Publishers

2164 ━━━━━

KIDS CAN PRESS
29 Birch Avenue, Toronto, Ont M4V 1E2
Telephone: +1 (416) 925 5437
Fax: +1 (416) 960 5437

Warehouse & Fulfilment:
5201 Dufferin Street, Downsview,
Ont M3H 5T8
Telephone: +1 (416) 667 7791
Fax: +1 (416) 667 7856

President: Valerie Hussey *(Publisher &
Contracts)*
Vice President: Ricky Englander *(Promotion
& Sales)*
Rights Manager: Barbara Howson

Children's Books

New Titles: 37 (1995), 56 (1996)
No of Employees: 19

ISBNs, Imprints & Series:
0 919964, 0 921103, 1 55074 Kids Can Press

Book Trade Association Membership:
Association of Canadian Publishers, Canadian
Booksellers Association, Canadian Library
Association, Book Promoters Association of
Canada, Ontario Publishers Association

2165 ━━━━━

KINDRED PRODUCTIONS
4-169 Riverton Avenue, Winnipeg,
MB R2L 2E5
Telephone: +1 (204) 669 6575
Fax: +1 (204) 654 1865
Email: kindred@cdnmbconf.ca

Warehouse & Shipping:
315 South Lincoln Street, Hillsboro, KS 67063,
USA
Telephone: +1 (316) 947 3151
Fax: +1 (316) 947 3266

Managers: Marilyn Hudson *(Director—
   Canadian Office)*
Arlene Schale *(Fulfilment—US Office)*

*Biography & Autobiography; Children's
Books; Fiction; Music; Religion & Theology*

New Titles: 4 (1995), 6 (1996)
No of Employees: 1
Annual Turnover: $145,000

ISBNs, Imprints & Series:
0 921788, 0 919797

Parent Company:
Mennonite Brethren Church of North America
(USA)

Overseas Representation *(see §7.3)*:
USA: Winfried Bluth

Book Trade Association Membership:
Canadian Christian Booksellers Association

2166 ▰▰▰▰▰▰▰▰▰▰

**LES PRESSES DE L'UNIVERSITÉ
LAVAL**
2336 chemin Ste-Foy, Ste-Foy,
Quebec G1K 7P4
Telephone: +1 (418) 656 3001
Fax: +1 (418) 656 3305

Warehouse:
Distribution Univers, 845 rue Marie-Victorin,
St-Nicolas, Quebec G0S 3L0
Telephone: +1 (418) 831 7474
Fax: +1 (418) 831 4021

Senior Editor: Denis Dion
Editor-in-Chief: Denis Vaugeois

Academic & Scholarly

New Titles: 48 (1995), 56 (1996)
No of Employees: 8

ISBNs, Imprints & Series: 2 7637

Overseas Representation *(see §7.3)*:
France: La librairie du Quebec, Paris

Book Trade Association Membership:
Association Nationale des Éditeurs de Livres,
Association québécoise des Presses
Universitaires, Association of Canadian
University Presses

2167 ▰▰▰▰▰▰▰▰▰▰

LE LOUP DE GOUTTIÈRE INC
347 rue Saint-Paul, PQ G1K 3X1
Telephone: +1 (418) 694 2224
Fax: +1 (418) 694 2225

President/Director General: Francine Vernac
Editorial: Jeannine Dumont
Production: Geneviève Dumas

*Fiction; Fine Art & Art History; Philosophy;
Poetry; Psychology & Psychiatry*

New Titles: 14 (1995), 20 (1996)
No of Employees: 3

ISBNs, Imprints & Series:
2 921310 Imprimerie Richard Vézma Inc

Overseas Representation *(see §7.3)*:
France: Editions Anne Sigier—France, Marq-
   en-Baroeul

Book Trade Association Membership:
Association nationale des éditeurs de livres du
Québec (ANEL)

2168 ▰▰▰▰▰▰▰▰▰▰

*LESTER PUBLISHING LTD
56 The Esplanade, Suite 507A, Toronto,
Ont M5E 1A7
Telephone: +1 (416) 362 1032
Fax: +1 (416) 362 1647

Warehouse, Orders & Distribution:
2775 Matheson Boulevard E, Mississauga,
Ont L4W 4P7
Telephone: +1 (905) 238 0707
Fax: +1 (905) 625 8008

President & Publisher: Malcolm Lester
Editors: Kathy Lowinger *(Executive)*
Janice Weaver

*Biography & Autobiography; Children's
Books; Economics; Fiction; Illustrated & Fine
Editions; Industry, Business & Management;
Literature & Criticism; Military & War;
Politics & World Affairs*

ISBNs, Imprints & Series: 1 895555

Associated & Subsidiary Companies:
Canada: Key Porter Books Ltd

Overseas Representation *(see §7.3)*:
France: F. Porretta Agency, Paris
Spain: Ute Körner, Barcelona

Book Trade Association Membership:
Organization of Book Publishers of Ontario,
Association of Canadian Publishers

2169 ▰▰▰▰▰▰▰▰▰▰

*McCLELLAND & STEWART INC
481 University Avenue, Suite 900, Toronto,
Ont M5G 2E9
Telephone: +1 (416) 598 1114
Fax: +1 (416) 598 7764

**Warehouse, Distribution, Trade Enquiries
& Orders:**
Canbook Distribution Services,
1220 Nicholson Road, Newmarket,
Ont L3Y 7V1
Telephone: +1 (905) 713 3852
Fax: +1 (905) 940 8864

**Chairman, President & Chief Executive
   Officer:** Avie Bennett
Vice-Presidents: William Hushion *(Senior,
   Rights & Permissions)*
Chris Keen *(Purchasing)*
Ken Thomson *(Sales)*
George Goodwin *(Corporate Development)*
Publisher: Douglas Gibson

*Academic & Scholarly; Architecture & Design;
Atlases & Maps; Aviation; Biography &
Autobiography; Children's Books; Cinema,
Video, TV & Radio; Cookery, Wines & Spirits;
Crime; Crafts & Hobbies; Do-It-Yourself;
Educational & Textbooks; Fiction; Gardening;
Gender Studies; Guide Books; Health &*

*Beauty; Humour; Illustrated & Fine Editions;
Industry, Business & Management; Medical
(incl. Self Help & Alternative Medicine);
Military & War; Natural History;
Photography; Poetry; Politics & World Affairs;
Reference Books, Directories & Dictionaries;
Religion & Theology; Science Fiction; Sports
& Games; Travel & Topography*

ISBNs, Imprints & Series:
0 7710 Canadian Social History, Douglas
   Gibson Books, M & S Paperback, New
   Canadian Library, Signature
1 895246 Stewart House

Overseas Representation *(see §7.3)*:
Germany: Literatur-Agentur Koln, Lohmar
Italy & Spain: Studio Nabu, Florence, Italy
Japan: Japan Uni Agency Inc, Tokyo
Netherlands: Translit Literary Agents,
   Amsterdam
Scandinavia: Bookman Literary Agency,
   Copenhagen, Denmark
Singapore & Malaysia: The Golden Mountain
   Agency, Singapore
USA: International Book Marketing, New York

Book Trade Association Membership:
Canadian Book Publishers Council, Ontario
Library Association, Organization of Book
Publishers of Ontario, Association of Canadian
Publishers

2170 ▰▰▰▰▰▰▰▰▰▰

MACFARLANE WALTER & ROSS
37A Hazelton Avenue, Toronto, Ont M5R 2E3
Telephone: +1 (416) 924 7595
Fax: +1 (416) 924 4254
Email: mwandr@interlog.com

Sales, Warehouse, Orders & Enquiries:
Stoddart Sales Group, General Publishing,
30 Lesmill Road, Don Mills, Ont M3B 2T6
Telephone: +1 (416) 445 3333
Fax: +1 (416) 445 5967

President: Jan Walter

*Architecture & Design; Biography &
Autobiography; Economics; Fiction; Guide
Books; Humour; Industry, Business &
Management; Literature & Criticism; Music;
Natural History; Photography; Politics &
World Affairs; Psychology & Psychiatry;
Scientific & Technical; Sports & Games;
Financial Self Help; Future Trends/Social
Issues; Urban Affairs*

New Titles: 10 (1995), 11 (1996)
No of Employees: 4

ISBNs, Imprints & Series:
0 921912, 1 55199

Associated & Subsidiary Companies:
Canada: General Publishing

Book Trade Association Membership:
Association of Canadian Publishers

2171 ▰▰▰▰▰▰▰▰▰▰

**McGILL-QUEEN'S UNIVERSITY
PRESS**
3430 McTavish Street, Montreal, PQ H3A 1X9
Telephone: +1 (514) 398 3750

Fax: +1 (514) 398 4333
Email: mqup@printing.lan.mcgill.ca
Web Site: http://www.mcgill.ca/mqupress

Warehousing & Invoicing (Order Fulfilment):
University of Toronto Press,
5201 Dufferin Street, Downsview,
Ont M3H 5T8
Telephone: +1 (416) 667 7791
Fax: +1 (416) 667 7832

Editorial Office:
Queen's University, Kingston, Ont K7L 3N2
Telephone: +1 (613) 545 2155
Fax: +1 (613) 545 6822
Email: mqup@qucdn.queensu.ca

Executive Director: Philip Cercone *(Editor, Sales, Rights & Permissions)*
Editors: Donald H. Akenson *(Queen's University)*
Joan Harcourt *(Queen's University)*
Arden Ford *(Business Manager, McGill University)*
Peter B. Blaney *(Acquisitions, McGill University)*
Joan McGilvray *(Manuscript, McGill University)*
Managers: Susanne McAdam *(Production)*
Roy Ward *(Marketing & Sales)*

Academic & Scholarly; Architecture & Design; Biography & Autobiography; Economics; Educational & Textbooks; Gender Studies; Geography & Geology; History & Antiquarian; Illustrated & Fine Editions; Literature & Criticism; Military & War; Natural History; Philosophy; Photography; Politics & World Affairs; Religion & Theology; Sociology & Anthropology; Sports & Games

New Titles: 75 (1995), 70 (1996)
No of Employees: 17

ISBNs, Imprints & Series: 0 7735

Overseas Representation *(see §7.3)*:
Japan: United Publishers Services Ltd, Tokyo; United Publishers Services Ltd, Tokyo; Kinokuniya Co Ltd, Tokyo
South East & East Asia (excluding Japan): STM Publishing Services Pte Ltd, Singapore; STM Publishers Pte Ltd, Taipei, Taiwan
UK, Irish Republic, Europe, Africa, Middle East, Asia (excluding Japan, China & Hong Kong, Latin America & Caribbean: UCL Press Ltd, London, UK
UK, Irish Republic, Europe, Africa, Middle East, Asia (excluding Japan, China & Hong Kong), Latin America & Caribbean (orders): Marston Book Services Ltd, Oxford, UK

Book Trade Association Membership:
Association of American University Presses, Association of Canadian University Presses, Association of Canadian Publishers

2172 ▬▬▬

McGRAW-HILL RYERSON LTD
300 Water Street, Whitby, Ontario L1N 9B6
Telephone: +1 (905) 430 5006
Fax: +1 (905) 430 5191
Email: johnd@mcgrawhill.ca
Web Site: http://www.mghr.com

President & Chief Executive Officer: John Dill
Vice-Presidents: Marshall Morris *(Customer Satisfaction)*
Murray Lamb *(School Division)*
Ron Munro *(College Division)*
Gary Krikler *(Finance, Chief Financial Officer, IS+T)*
Carl Posluns *(Human Resources)*
Julia Woods *(Trade, Professional & Medical)*
Clive Powell *(Director of Production)*

Accountancy & Taxation; Aviation; Biography & Autobiography; Computer Science; Cookery, Wines & Spirits; Do-It-Yourself; Economics; Educational & Textbooks; Geography & Geology; Industry, Business & Management; Mathematics & Statistics; Philosophy; Politics & World Affairs; Psychology & Psychiatry; Sociology & Anthropology; Vocational Training & Careers

New Titles: 100 (1995), 80 (1996)
No of Employees: 272
Annual Turnover: $27.6M

ISBNs, Imprints & Series:
0 07 McGraw-Hill, McGraw-Hill Ryerson

Parent Company:
McGraw-Hill Inc *(USA)*

Overseas Representation *(see §7.3)*:
All international markets (other than those detailed below): McGraw-Hill Inc, International Group, Hightstown, NJ & New York, USA
Australia: McGraw-Hill Book Co Australia Pty Ltd, Roseville, NSW
Caribbean: McGraw-Hill Interamericana Del Caribe Inc, Rio Piedras, Puerto Rico
Colombia: McGraw-Hill Interamericana Colombia SA, Bogotá
France: Ediscience International, Paris
India: Tata McGraw-Hill Publishing Co Ltd, New Delhi
Italy: McGraw-Hill Libri Italia srl, Milan
Japan: McGraw-Hill Book Co Japan Ltd, Tokyo
Mexico: McGraw-Hill Interamericana de Mexico, SA de C.V., Naucalpan
New Zealand: McGraw-Hill Book Co New Zealand Ltd, Manukan
Portugal: McGraw-Hill Interamericana de Portugal Ltda, Lisbon
South East Asia: McGraw-Hill Book Co, Singapore
Spain: McGraw-Hill InterAmericana de España SA, Madrid
UK & Germany: McGraw-Hill Book Co (Europe) Ltd, Maidenhead, UK
Venezuela: McGraw-Hill Interamericana Venezuela CA, Caracas

Book Trade Association Membership:
Canadian Book Publishers Council

2173 ▬▬▬

MACMILLAN CANADA
[a division of Canada Publishing Corporation]
29 Birch Avenue, Toronto, Ont M4V 1E2
Telephone: +1 (416) 963 8830
Fax: +1 (416) 923 4821

Orders & Warehouse:
164 Commander Boulevard, Agincourt,
Ont M1S 3C7
Telephone: +1 (416) 293 8141
Fax: +1 (416) 293 0846

President: Mike Richardson
Publisher: Karen O'Reilly
National Sales Manager: Cari Burrows
Managing Editor: Susan Girvan
Managers: Ann Nelles *(Contracts, Rights & Permissions)*
Sheron Metcalf *(Promotion & Advertising)*

Biography & Autobiography; Cookery, Wines & Spirits; Crime; Health & Beauty; Humour; Industry, Business & Management; Reference Books, Directories & Dictionaries; Sports & Games

New Titles: 22 (1995), 31 (1996)
No of Employees: 29

ISBNs, Imprints & Series:
0 7705, 0 7715

Parent Company:
Canada Publishing Corporation *(Canada)*

Associated & Subsidiary Companies:
Canada: Diffulivre Inc; Gage Educational Publishing; Global Press

Book Trade Association Membership:
Association of Canadian Publishers, Canadian Book Publishers Council

2174 ▬▬▬

UNIVERSITY OF MANITOBA PRESS
Suite 244, 15 Gillson Street,
University of Manitoba, Winnipeg,
Man R3T 5V6
Telephone: +1 (204) 474 9495
Fax: +1 (204) 275 2270

Distribution:
University of Toronto Press,
5201 Dufferin Street, Downsview,
Ont M3H 5T8
Telephone: +1 (416) 667 7846
Fax: +1 (416) 667 7832

Director & Editor: D. Carr
Promotions Co-ordinator: A. Campbell
Managing Editor: C. Dahlstrom

Academic & Scholarly; Gender Studies; History & Antiquarian; Sociology & Anthropology; Native Studies

New Titles: 3 (1995), 5 (1996)
No of Employees: 3

ISBNs, Imprints & Series: 0 88755

Overseas Representation *(see §7.3)*:
UK: Lavis Marketing, Oxford

Book Trade Association Membership:
Association of Canadian University Presses, International Association of Scholarly Publishers, Association of Canadian Publishers, Association of Manitoba Book Publishers

2175

*THE MERCURY PRESS
137 Birmingham Street, Stratford,
Ont N5A 2T1
Telephone: +1 (519) 273 7083
Fax: +1 (519) 273 7932

Distribution:
General Distribution Services,
30 Lesmill Road, Don Mills, Ont M3B 2T6
Telephone: +1 (416) 445 3333
Fax: +1 (416) 445 5967

Co-Publishers: Donald Daurio *(Managing
Editor)*
Beverley Daurio *(Editor-in-Chief)*

*Biography & Autobiography; Fiction;
Literature & Criticism; Poetry; Politics &
World Affairs; Sociology & Anthropology*

ISBNs, Imprints & Series:
0 920544, 1 555128

Overseas Representation *(see §7.3):*
USA: In Book, East Haven, CT

Book Trade Association Membership:
Association of Canadian Publishers, Literary
Press Group (Canada), Ontario Book
Publishers Organization

2176

**LES PRESSES DE L'UNIVERSITÉ DE
MONTRÉAL**
CP 6128, Succursale Centre-ville, Montreal,
PQ H3C 3J7
Telephone: +1 (514) 343 6929
Fax: +1 (514) 343 2232
Email: pumedit@are.umontreal.ca

Also at:
171 boulevard de Mortagne, Boucherville,
PQ J4B 6G4
Telephone: +1 (514) 449 2369
Fax: +1 (514) 449 7808
Email: presses@gmorin.qc.ca

Managers: Marie-Claire Borgo *(General)*
Marise Labresque *(Publishing)*
Jean-Francois Brisson *(Promotion & Sales)*
Roger LeGarrec *(Production)*

*Academic & Scholarly; Reference Books,
Directories & Dictionaries*

New Titles: 20 (1995), 20 (1996)
No of Employees: 7

ISBNs, Imprints & Series: 2 7606

Overseas Representation *(see §7.3):*
France: Initiatives Santé, Vélizy

2177

*MOSAIC PRESS
Units 1 & 2, 1252 Speers Road, PO Box 1032,
Oakville, Ont L6L 5N9
Telephone: +1 (905) 825 2130
Fax: +1 (905) 825 2130

*Fiction; Literature & Criticism; Politics &
World Affairs; Theatre, Drama & Dance*

ISBNs, Imprints & Series: 0 88962

Associated & Subsidiary Companies:
USA: Mosaic Press

Overseas Representation *(see §7.3):*
UK: Drake International Services, Oxford

2178

MOVING PUBLICATIONS LTD
44 Upjohn Road, Suite 100, Don Mills,
Ont M3B 2W1
Telephone: +1 (416) 441 1168
Fax: +1 (416) 441 1641
Email: movingto@idirect.com
Web Site: http://www.movingto.com

President/Publisher: Anita Wood

New Titles: 8 (1995), 8 (1996)
No of Employees: 4

2179

NATIONAL GALLERY OF CANADA
Publications Division, 380 Sussex Drive,
PO Box 427, Ottawa, Ont K1N 9N4
Telephone: +1 (613) 990 0539
Fax: +1 (613) 990 7460

Warehouse, Trade Enquiries & Orders:
The Bookstore Mail Order Service
Telephone: +1 (613) 990 0962
Fax: +1 (613) 990 1972

Publications: Serge Thériault *(Chief)*
Head of Retail & Marketing: Anne Hurley
(The Bookstore)

*Academic & Scholarly; Fine Art & Art History;
Photography*

New Titles: 3 (1995), 2 (1996)

ISBNs, Imprints & Series: 0 88884

Overseas Representation *(see §7.3):*
Africa & Europe (French titles): National
Gallery of Canada, Ottawa, Ont, Canada
*Europe (English titles), France, Belgium &
Switzerland (French title books only):*
National Gallery of Canada, Canada
*USA, Central & South America, Australia,
Europe, Middle East, Africa:* University of
Chicago Press, Chicago, IL, USA

Book Trade Association Membership: The
Book Trade in Canada, Canadian Booksellers
Association, American Booksellers
Association, Museum Store Association

2180

**NATIONAL MUSEUM OF SCIENCE &
TECHNOLOGY CORPORATION**
PO Box 9724, Station T, Ottawa, Ont K1G 5A3
Telephone: +1 (613) 991 2986
Fax: +1 (613) 990 3635

Distributor (English titles):
University of Toronto Press (UTP),
5201 Dufferin Street, Downsview,
Ont M3H 5T8
Telephone: +1 (416) 667 7791, (800) 363 2864
(toll free)

Fax: +1 (416) 667 7832, (800) 361 8088 (toll
free)

Distributor (French titles):
Diffusion Prologue,
1650 boulevard Lionel Bertrand, Boisbriand,
PQ J7E 4H4
Telephone: +1 (514) 434 0306
Fax: +1 (514) 434 2627

Director, Publishing & Product Marketing:
Wendy McPeake

*Academic & Scholarly; Aviation; Children's
Books; Engineering; History & Antiquarian;
Military & War; Scientific & Technical*

New Titles: 4 (1995), 4 (1996)

ISBNs, Imprints & Series:
0 660 Material History Review, Profiles in
Aeronautical History, Transformation Series

Parent Company:
National Museum of Science and Technology
Corp *(Canada)*

Associated & Subsidiary Companies:
Canada: National Aviation Museum

Overseas Representation *(see §7.3):*
Worldwide: University of Chicago Press,
Chicago, USA

Book Trade Association Membership:
Canadian Booksellers Association, Association
of Canadian Publishers, Canadian Book
Information Centre, Canadian Magazine
Publishers Association

2181

**NATURAL HERITAGE/NATURAL
HISTORY INC**
PO Box 95, Station 'O', Toronto, Ont M4C 4X3
Telephone: +1 (416) 694 7907
Fax: +1 (416) 690 0819

Warehouse:
TTS Distributing, 45 Tyler Street, Toronto, Ont
Telephone: +1 (905) 841 3898
Fax: +1 (905) 841 3026

President: Barry Penhale *(Rights, Sales)*
Editor-in-Chief: Jane Gibson

*Biography & Autobiography; Geography &
Geology; History & Antiquarian; Military &
War; Natural History; Poetry*

New Titles: 10 (1995), 10 (1996)
No of Employees: 10

ISBNs, Imprints & Series:
0 920474 Natural Heritage

Overseas Representation *(see §7.3):*
*UK, Irish Republic, Europe, Middle East,
Africa & Indian Sub-continent:* Roundhouse
Publishing Ltd, Oxford, UK

2182

NEW SOCIETY PUBLISHERS
PO Box 189, Gabriola Island, BC V0R 1X0
Telephone: +1 (604) 247 9737
Fax: +1 (604) 247 7471

Email: nsp@island.net
Web Site: http://www.swiftly.com/nsp/

Distributor:
General Distribution Services,
30 Lesmill Road, Don Mills, Ont M3B 2T6
Telephone: +1 (800) 387 0172

Editorial: Christopher Plant
Marketing: Judith Plant

*Architecture & Design; Economics;
Educational & Textbooks; Environment &
Development Studies; Gender Studies; Law;
Politics & World Affairs; Psychology &
Psychiatry; Sociology & Anthropology*

New Titles: 10 (1995), 7 (1996)
No of Employees: 5
Annual Turnover: $600,000

ISBNs, Imprints & Series:
0 86571, 1 55092

Parent Company:
New Society Publishers Ltd *(Canada)*

Associated & Subsidiary Companies:
USA: New Society Publishers

Overseas Representation *(see §7.3)*:
USA: LPC/Inbook, Chicago, IL

Book Trade Association Membership:
Association of Canadian Publishers, Literary
Press Group, Association of Book Publishers of
British Columbia

2183 ▬

NEW STAR BOOKS LTD
2504 York Avenue, Vancouver, BC V6K 1E3
Telephone: +1 (604) 738 9429
Fax: +1 (604) 738 9332

Trade Enquiries & Orders:
General Distribution Services,
30 Lesmill Road, Don Mills, Ont M3B 2T6
Telephone: +1 (416) 445 3333
Fax: +1 (416) 445 5967

Publisher: Rolf Maurer
Marketing Director: Carolyn Stewart

*Academic & Scholarly; Fiction; Gender
Studies; History & Antiquarian; Natural
History; Poetry; Politics & World Affairs*

New Titles: 10 (1995), 10 (1996)
No of Employees: 2

ISBNs, Imprints & Series:
0 919573, 0 919888, 0 921586

Overseas Representation *(see §7.3)*:
USA: LPC/Inbook, Chicago, IL; General
Distribution Services, Niagara Falls, NY

Book Trade Association Membership:
Association of Canadian Publishers,
Association of Book Publishers of British
Columbia

2184 ▬

NEWEST PUBLISHERS LTD
Suite 310, 10359 82 Avenue, Edmonton,
Alberta T6E 1Z9
Telephone: +1 (403) 432 9427
Fax: +1 (403) 432 9429
Email: newest@planet.eon.net

Orders:
General Distribution Services,
30 Lesmill Road, Don Mills, Ont M3B 2T6
Telephone: +1 (416) 445 3333
Fax: +1 (416) 445 5967

Managers: Liz Grieve *(General)*
Eva Radford *(Editorial)*
Kathleen McLean *(Administrative)*

*Fiction; Literature & Criticism; Theatre,
Drama & Dance*

New Titles: 8 (1995), 7 (1996)
No of Employees: 4

ISBNs, Imprints & Series:
0 920897, 0 920316, 1 896300

Overseas Representation *(see §7.3)*:
Worldwide: Dundurn Distribution, Oxford, UK

Book Trade Association Membership:
Association of Canadian Publishers, Canadian
Booksellers Association

2185 ▬

*NIMBUS PUBLISHING LTD
3731 Mackintosh Street, PO Box 9301,
Station A, Halifax, NS B3K 5N5
Telephone: +1 (902) 455 4286
Fax: +1 (902) 455 3652

President: John Marshall
Managing Editor: Dorothy Blythe
Sales Manager: Dan Soucoup *(Rights &
Permissions)*

*Academic & Scholarly; Architecture & Design;
Biography & Autobiography; Children's
Books; Cookery, Wines & Spirits; Crafts &
Hobbies; Educational & Textbooks; Fiction;
Fine Art & Art History; Gardening; Geography
& Geology; Guide Books; History &
Antiquarian; Industry, Business &
Management; Military & War; Natural
History; Nautical; Photography*

ISBNs, Imprints & Series:
0 919380 Petheric Press
0 920852, 0 921054, 0 921128, 1 55109 Nimbus
Publishing

Parent Company:
H. H. Marshall Ltd *(Canada)*

Overseas Representation *(see §7.3)*:
UK & Europe: Gazelle Book Services Ltd,
Lancaster, UK
UK & Europe (nautical titles): Seafarer Books,
London, UK
USA: Chelsea Green Publishing Co, White
River Junction, VT

2186 ▬

NORBRY PUBLISHING LTD
15838 Shaws Creek Road, Terra Cotta,
Ont L0P 1N0
Telephone: +1 (905) 838 2800
Fax: +1 (905) 838 0214
Email: norbry@norbry.com
Web Site: http://www.norbry.com/norbry

President: Mike Pembry *(Export Sales)*
Sales Representative: Michelle Goossen
Editorial: Rebecca Pembry
Production: Deron Douglas
Finance: Ivy Flett

*Educational & Textbooks; Electronic
(Educational); Electronic (Professional &
Academic); Multimedia Tutorials-Educational
& Trade*

New Titles: 10 (1995), 12 (1996)
Annual Turnover: $500,000

ISBNs, Imprints & Series:
0 921282 Comprehensive, Computerized
Interactive Tutorials (CITs), Step-by-Step

Book Trade Association Membership:
Canadian Booksellers Association, Publishers'
Marketing Association

2187 ▬

NORTHSTONE PUBLISHING INC
330–1980 Cooper Road, Kelowna,
BC V1Y 9G8
Telephone: +1 (250) 766 2926 & +1 (800) 299
2926 (orders)
Fax: +1 (250) 766 1201
Email: info@northstone.com

Warehouse:
3396 Sexsmith Road, Kelowna, BC V1V 1L6
Telephone: +1 (250) 765 6152

Editor: Mike Schwartzentruber
Publisher: David Cleary
Sales & Marketing: Ann Wallin
Rights & Permissions: Lindy Jones
Production: Gene Longson

Children's Books; Religion & Theology

New Titles: 14 (1996)
No of Employees: 5
Annual Turnover: $200,000

ISBNs, Imprints & Series: 1 55145

Book Trade Association Membership:
Association of Book Publishers of British
Columbia

2188 ▬

OBERON PRESS
400-350 Sparks Street, Ottawa,
Ontario K1R 7S8
Telephone: +1 (613) 238 3275
Fax: +1 (613) 238 3275

President: Michael Macklem *(Home & Export
Sales)*
Vice-Presidents: Nicholas Macklem *(Home &
Export Sales)*
Anne Hardy

Secretary-Treasurer: Dilshad Engineer
(*Rights & Permissions*)

Biography & Autobiography; Fiction;
Literature & Criticism; Poetry

New Titles: 17 (1995), 15 (1996)
No of Employees: 4
Annual Turnover: £150,000

ISBNs, Imprints & Series:
0 7780, 0 88750

Book Trade Association Membership:
Association of Canadian Publishers

2189 ▬

*OISE PRESS
252 Bloor Street West, Toronto, Ont M5S 1Y6
Telephone: +1 (413) 923 6641
Fax: +1 (413) 926 4725

Distributor:
Scholarly Book Services Inc,
77 Mowat Avenue, Suite 403, Toronto,
Ont M6K 3E3
Telephone: +1 (416) 533 5490
Fax: +1 (416) 533 5652

Managing Editor: Ann Nicholson
Senior Editor: John McConnell

Academic & Scholarly; Educational &
Textbooks; Gender Studies

ISBNs, Imprints & Series: 0 7744

Parent Company:
Ontario Institute for Studies in Education
(Canada)

Book Trade Association Membership:
Association of Canadian University Presses,
Ontario Book Publishers Organization,
Canadian Book Marketing Centre

2190 ▬

OOLICHAN BOOKS
PO Box 10, Lantzville, BC V0R 2H0
Telephone: +1 (604) 390 4839
Fax: +1 (604) 390 4839
Email: oolichan@island.net

Distributor:
General Distribution Services,
30 Lesmill Road, Don Mills, Ont M3B 2T6
Telephone: +1 (416) 445 3333
Fax: +1 (416) 445 5967

Managing Editor: Rhonda Bailey *(Sales &*
Publicity & Co-Publisher)
Production Manager & Fiction Editor: Jay
Connolly
Co-Publisher & Poetry Editor: Ron Smith

Biography & Autobiography; Children's
Books; Fiction; History & Antiquarian;
Humour; Literature & Criticism; Medical (incl.
Self Help & Alternative Medicine); Nautical;
Poetry; Politics & World Affairs; Religion &
Theology

New Titles: 8 (1995), 10 (1996)
No of Employees: 3

ISBNs, Imprints & Series: 0 88982

Overseas Representation *(see §7.3)*:
USA: LPC/Inbook, Chicago, IL

Book Trade Association Membership:
Association of Canadian Publishers,
Association of Book Publishers of British
Columbia, Literary Press Group, Canadian
Booksellers Association

2191 ▬

UNIVERSITY OF OTTAWA PRESS
542 King Edward, Ottawa, Ont K1N 6N5
Telephone: +1 (613) 562 5246
Fax: +1 (613) 562 5247
Email: press@uottawa.ca

Director: Marie-Claire Borgo
Editor: Suzanne Bossé *(English & French)*
Marketing: Jean-Francois Brisson
Production: Roger Legarrel

Academic & Scholarly; Bibliography &
Library Science; Biography & Autobiography;
Economics; Educational & Textbooks; English
as a Foreign Language; Gender Studies;
Health & Beauty; History & Antiquarian;
Industry, Business & Management; Languages
& Linguistics; Literature & Criticism; Medical
(incl. Self Help & Alternative Medicine);
Philosophy; Politics & World Affairs;
Psychology & Psychiatry; Reference Books,
Directories & Dictionaries; Religion &
Theology; Sociology & Anthropology

New Titles: 20 (1995)
No of Employees: 5

ISBNs, Imprints & Series:
0 7766 English titles
2 7603 French titles

Overseas Representation *(see §7.3)*:
Benelux (French titles): Diffusion Nord-Sud,
Brussels, Belgium
Europe (excluding Belgium) (French titles):
Initiatives Santé, Vélizy, France
Rest of World: Export Livres, Saint-Lambert,
PQ, Canada
Senegal: Librairie Clairafrique, Dakar
USA (English titles): Paul & Co Publishers
Consortium Inc, New York, USA

Book Trade Association Membership:
Association for the Export of Canadian Books

2192 ▬

OXFORD UNIVERSITY PRESS
(CANADA)
70 Wynford Drive, Don Mills, Ont M3C 1J9
Telephone: +1 (416) 441 2941
Fax: +1 (416) 441 0345

Orders, Customer Service & Accounts:
(as above)
Telephone: (as above)
Fax: +1 (416) 444 0427

Managing Director: Susan Froud
Directors: Joanna Gertler *(Production/Design)*
Greg Chiykowski *(Finance)*
Anne Erickson *(Trade & Medical Divisions)*
Ric Kitowski *(College Division)*

Phyllis Wilson *(Managing Editor, Trade &*
College)
Foreign Rights & Permissions: Ann Checchia

Academic & Scholarly; Atlases & Maps;
Educational & Textbooks; English as a Foreign
Language; Literature & Criticism; Poetry;
Reference Books, Directories & Dictionaries

New Titles: 50 (1995), 60 (1996)
No of Employees: 89

ISBNs, Imprints & Series: 0 19 54

Parent Company:
Oxford University Press *(UK)*

Overseas Representation *(see §7.3)*:
Worldwide: Oxford University Press, Oxford,
UK

Book Trade Association Membership:
Canadian Book Publishers Council

2193 ▬

*PEGUIS PUBLISHERS LTD
100–318 McDermot Avenue, Winnipeg,
Manitoba R3A 0A2
Telephone: +1 (204) 987 3500
Fax: +1 (204) 947 0080

President: Mary Dixon *(Managing Editor,*
Export Sales, Rights & Permissions)
Director of Sales & Marketing: Ryan Dixon

Architecture & Design; Educational &
Textbooks

ISBNs, Imprints & Series:
0 919566, 0 920541, 1 895411

Associated & Subsidiary Companies:
Canada: Portage & Main Press

Book Trade Association Membership:
Association of Manitoba Book Publishers,
Association of Canadian Publishers

2194 ▬

PEMBROKE PUBLISHERS LTD
538 Hood Road, Markham, Ont L3R 3K9
Telephone: +1 (905) 477 0650
Fax: +1 (905) 477 3691

Publisher & Foreign Rights: Mary Macchiusi
Managing Director & Finance: Claudia
Connolly

Children's Books; Educational & Textbooks

New Titles: 13 (1995), 15 (1996)
No of Employees: 3

ISBNs, Imprints & Series:
0 921217, 1 55138

Overseas Representation *(see §7.3)*:
Australia & New Zealand: Thomas Nelson
(Australia) Pty Ltd, South Melbourne, Vic,
Australia
UK & Europe: Drake Marketing Services,
Cardiff, UK
USA: Heinemann Educational Books Inc,
Portsmouth, NH; The Wright Group,
Bothell, WA

Book Trade Association Membership:
Canadian Book Publishers Council, The
Canadian Children's Book Centre

2195

PEMMICAN PUBLICATIONS
Unit 2, 1635 Burrows Avenue, Winnipeg,
Manitoba R2X 0T1
Telephone: +1 (204) 589 6346
Fax: +1 (204) 589 2063
Email: pemmican@fox.nstn.ca
Web Site: http://fox.nstn.ca/~pemmican

Manager: Sue MacLean *(Rights &
Permissions)*
Sales: Suzanne Flett

*Children's Books; Fiction; History &
Antiquarian; Poetry*

New Titles: 5 (1995), 4 (1996)
No of Employees: 2

ISBNs, Imprints & Series:
0 921827, 0 919143

Book Trade Association Membership:
Association of Canadian Publishers

2196

*PIPPIN PUBLISHING LTD
[formerly Dominie Press Ltd]
380 Esna Park Drive, Markham, Ont L3R 1H5
Telephone: +1 (905) 513 3759
Fax: +1 (905) 513 6977

President: Jonathan Lovat Dickson
Vice-President: Paul Lockwood *(Sales &
Marketing)*
Administrative Co-ordinator: Jocelyn Ong
Controller: Barry Kadoch

*Academic & Scholarly; Educational &
Textbooks; English as a Foreign Language*

ISBNs, Imprints & Series: 0 88751

Book Trade Association Membership:
Organization of Book Publishers of Ontario

2197

PLAYWRIGHTS CANADA PRESS
[imprint of Playwrights Union of Canada]
54 Wolseley Street, 2nd Floor, Toronto,
Ontario M5T 1A5
Telephone: +1 (416) 703 0201
Fax: +1 (416) 703 0059
Email: cdplays@interlog.com
Web Site: http://www.puc.ca

Publisher: Angela Rebeiro *(Promotion/
Publicity, Rights & Permissions — Books)*
Managing Editor: Tony Hamill *(Publication,
Rights & Permissions — Books)*
Customer Service Manager: Robert Alton
Rights & Permissions: Jodi Armstrong
(Amateur Performance)

Theatre, Drama & Dance

New Titles: 8 (1995), 7 (1996)
No of Employees: 4

ISBNs, Imprints & Series:
0 88754, 0 919834

Parent Company:
Playwrights Union of Canada *(Canada)*

Book Trade Association Membership:
Association of Canadian Publishers, Canadian
Booksellers Association, Literary Presses
Group, Organization of Ontario Book
Publishers

2198

POLESTAR BOOK PUBLISHERS
1011 Commercial Drive, 2nd Floor,
Vancouver, BC V5L 3X1
Telephone: +1 (604) 251 9718
Fax: +1 (604) 251 9738

Publisher: Michelle Benjamin
Marketing & Promotions: Emiko Morita

*Environment & Development Studies; Fiction;
Gardening; Gay & Lesbian Studies;
Geography & Geology; Humour; Music;
Natural History; Photography; Poetry; Sports
& Games; Veterinary Science*

New Titles: 10 (1995), 10 (1996)
No of Employees: 3

ISBNs, Imprints & Series:
0 919591, 1 896095

Overseas Representation *(see §7.3):*
European Union: Canadabooks International,
Saffron Walden, UK

2199

PONTIFICAL INSTITUTE OF
MEDIAEVAL STUDIES
59 Queen's Park Crescent East, Toronto,
Ont M5S 2C4
Telephone: +1 (416) 926 7144
Fax: +1 (416) 926 7258

Director of Publications: Ron B. Thomson
Editors: Jean Hoff
Fred Unwalla

Academic & Scholarly

New Titles: 8 (1995), 8 (1996)
No of Employees: 4
Annual Turnover: $200,000

ISBNs, Imprints & Series:
0 88844 Etienne Gilson Series, Greek Index
Project Series, Mediaeval Sources in
Translation, Papers in Mediaeval Studies,
Pontifical Institute of Mediaeval Studies,
Publications de l'Institut d'Études
Médiévales, Publications of the Dictionary
of Old English, Studies & Texts, Subsidia
Mediaevalia, Toronto Medieval Latin Texts

Overseas Representation *(see §7.3):*
Europe: Brepols Publishers, Turnhout,
Belgium

Book Trade Association Membership:
Association of Canadian Publishers,
Association of Canadian University Presses

2200

THE PORCUPINE'S QUILL
68 Main Street, Erin, Ont N0B 1T0
Telephone: +1 (519) 833 9158
Fax: +1 (519) 833 9158

President, Acquisitions: Tim Inkster
General Manager: Elke Inkster
Acquisitions: John Metcalf

*Academic & Scholarly; Fiction; Literature &
Criticism; Poetry*

New Titles: 8 (1995), 9 (1996)
No of Employees: 5
Annual Turnover: $250,000

ISBNs, Imprints & Series: 0 88984

Overseas Representation *(see §7.3):*
USA: LPC/Inbook, Chicago, IL

Book Trade Association Membership:
Literary Press Group, Association of Canadian
Publishers

2201

ÉDITIONS PRISE DE PAROLE
CP 550, Succursale B, Sudbury, Ont P3E 4R2
Telephone: +1 (705) 675 6491
Fax: +1 (705) 673 1817
Email: pdp@vianet.on.ca

Warehouse & Orders:
111 Elm Street, Sudbury, Ont P3C 1T3
Telephone: +1 (705) 675 6491
Fax: +1 (705) 673 1817
Email: pdp@vianet.on.ca

Executive Director: Denise Truax
General Manager: Alain Mayotte

*Academic & Scholarly; Educational &
Textbooks; Fiction; Literature & Criticism;
Poetry; Theatre, Drama & Dance*

New Titles: 11 (1995), 10 (1996)
No of Employees: 2

ISBNs, Imprints & Series:
0 920814, 0 921573, 2 89423

Book Trade Association Membership:
Association of Canadian Publishers,
Association Nationale des Éditeurs de Livres,
Regroupement des Éditeurs Canadiens de
Langue Française

2202

PRODUCTIVE PUBLICATIONS
PO Box 7200, Station A, Toronto,
Ont M5W 1X8
Telephone: +1 (416) 483 0634
Fax: +1 (416) 322 7434

Owner: Iain Williamson
General Manager: Vicki Demmsico

*Accountancy & Taxation; Computer Science;
Do-It-Yourself; Economics; Industry, Business
& Management; Vocational Training &
Careers; Small Business & Entrepreneurship*

New Titles: 22 (1995), 20 (1996)
No of Employees: 2

ISBNs, Imprints & Series:
0 920847, 1 896210

2203

*QUARRY PRESS INC
PO Box 1061, Kingston, Ont K7L 4Y5
Telephone: +1 (613) 548 8429
Fax: +1 (613) 548 1556

Distribution:
Stoddart Publishing, 34 Lesmill Road,
Don Mills, Ont M3B 2T6
Telephone: +1 (416) 445 3333

Trade Publishing: Bob Hilderley *(Editor, Publisher)*

Academic & Scholarly; Bibliography & Library Science; Biography & Autobiography; Children's Books; Fiction; Fine Art & Art History; Guide Books; History & Antiquarian; Literature & Criticism; Poetry

ISBNs, Imprints & Series:
0 919627, 1 55082 Quarry B.M.S. (Body. Mind. Spirit), Canadian Children's Classics, Silhouette Folktales for Children, International Authors Series, New Canadian Novelists Series, New Canadian Poets Series, Canadian Radio Drama Series, Quarry Rocks!

Associated & Subsidiary Companies:
Canada: Poetry Canada Review; Quarry Magazine

Overseas Representation *(see §7.3):*
UK: Cardiff Academic Press, Cardiff

Book Trade Association Membership:
Association of Canadian Publishers, Literary Press Group (Canada), American Booksellers Association

2204

PRESSES DE L'UNIVERSITÉ DU QUÉBEC
2875 boulevard Laurier, Ste-Foy,
Quebec G1V 2M3
Telephone: +1 (418) 657 4399
Fax: +1 (418) 657 2096

Warehouse:
845 rue Marie-Victorin, Saint-Nicolas,
Quebec G0S 3L0
Telephone: +1 (418) 831 7474
Fax: +1 (418) 831 4021

Marketing Director: Gilles Lachance *(Home & Export Sales)*
Director General: Angèle Tremblay *(Rights & Permissions)*

Economics; History & Antiquarian; Languages & Linguistics; Mathematics & Statistics; Philosophy; Politics & World Affairs; Psychology & Psychiatry; Sociology & Anthropology

New Titles: 51 (1995), 52 (1996)
No of Employees: 8
Annual Turnover: $1.5M

ISBNs, Imprints & Series:
0 7770, 2 7605 Presses de l'Université du Québec
2 920073 Québec Science Editeur

Overseas Representation *(see §7.3):*
Europe: Éditions ESKA, Paris, France

Book Trade Association Membership:
Association of Canadian University Presses, Association of University Presses of Quebec, Association Québecoises presses universitaires (AQPU), Assocation nationale des éditeurs de livres (ANEL)

2205

LES EDITIONS QUÉBEC/AMÉRIQUE INC
425 rue Saint-Jean-Baptiste, Montreal,
PQ H2Y 2Z7
Telephone: +1 (514) 393 1450
Fax: +1 (514) 866 2430
Email: montreal@editionsqa.qc.ca

Warehouse:
1380A rue De Couloumb, Boucherville,
PQ J4B 7J4
Telephone: +1 (514) 655 6084
Fax: +1 (514) 655 5166

Chief Executive Officer: Jacques Fortin
Directors: Jean-Pierre Servant *(International Marketing)*
Francois Fortin *(International Division)*
General Manager: Luc Roberge

Electronic (Professional & Academic); Literature & Criticism; Reference Books, Directories & Dictionaries

New Titles: 50 (1995), 50 (1996)
No of Employees: 50

2206

RAINCOAST BOOK DISTRIBUTION LTD
8680 Cambie Street, Vancouver, BC V6P 6M9
Telephone: +1 (604) 323 7100
Fax: +1 (604) 323 2600
Email: info@raincoast.com

President & Publisher: Mark Stanton
Vice-Presidents: Allan MacDougall *(Marketing & Sales)*
Kevin Williams *(Operations & Export Sales)*
Managing Editor: Michael Carroll
Production Manager: Ruth Linka
Controller: Elona Ewing

Biography & Autobiography; Children's Books; Cookery, Wines & Spirits; Gardening; Guide Books; History & Antiquarian; Humour; Natural History; Photography; Politics & World Affairs; Sports & Games; Travel & Topography

New Titles: 35 (1995), 41 (1996)
No of Employees: 66

ISBNs, Imprints & Series:
0 920417, 1 55192, 1 895714

Associated & Subsidiary Companies:
Canada: Book Express

Book Trade Association Membership:
Association of Canadian Publishers, American Booksellers Association, Canadian Booksellers Association, Association of Book Publishers of British Columbia

2207

THE READER'S DIGEST ASSOCIATION (CANADA) LTD
215 Redfern Avenue, Westmount, Montreal,
PQ H3Z 2V9
Telephone: +1 (514) 934 0751
Fax: +1 (514) 932 3637

Director: Joe H. Beauduin *(President & Chief Executive Officer)*
Company Secretary: Barbara Robins
Sales & Marketing: Bernard Poirier
Production: Marisol Santos
Art: Jean Brouillet
Rights & Permissions: Enid Ferdinand *(Magazines)*
Wadad Bashour *(Books)*

Atlases & Maps; Children's Books; Cookery, Wines & Spirits; Do-It-Yourself; Gardening; Medical (incl. Self Help & Alternative Medicine); Reference Books, Directories & Dictionaries; Religion & Theology; Travel & Topography

ISBNs, Imprints & Series: 0 88850

Parent Company:
Reader's Digest Association Inc *(USA)*

2208

*REED BOOKS CANADA
204 Richmond Street West, Suite 300, Toronto,
Ont M5V 1V6
Telephone: +1 (416) 598 0045
Fax: +1 (416) 598 0358

Warehouse:
75 Clegg Road, Markham, Ont L6G 1A1
Telephone: +1 (905) 479 1992

Managing Director: Susan Jasper
Publisher: Oliver Salzmann
Managers: Joe March *(Marketing)*
Jennifer Smith *(National Sales)*

Antiques & Collecting; Architecture & Design; Atlases & Maps; Audio Books; Biography & Autobiography; Children's Books; Computer Science; Cookery, Wines & Spirits; Crafts & Hobbies; Do-It-Yourself; Educational & Textbooks; Electronic (Educational); Fiction; Fine Art & Art History; Gardening; Guide Books; Health & Beauty; Humour; Illustrated & Fine Editions; Military & War; Music; Philosophy; Photography; Poetry; Sports & Games; Theatre, Drama & Dance; Travel & Topography

ISBNs, Imprints & Series:
0 204 Focal Press
0 408, 0 409, 0 433 Reed Books Canada
0 413 Methuen Children's, Methuen Drama, Methuen London
0 434 William Heinemann, Heinemann Young Books
0 435 Heinemann Drama US
0 436 Secker & Warburg
0 540 George Philips

0 600 Hamlyn
0 603 Dean
0 7493 Mandarin
0 74939 Minerva
0 7497 Mammoth
0 7506 Butterworth-Heinemann Business
0 7900 Pacific Writers Series, Reed New
Zealand
0 85533, 1 85732 Mitchell Beazley [use
Hamlyn imprint]
0 90748, 1 85051, 1 85052, 1 85152 Bounty
1 85029 Conran Octopus
1 85561, 1 86330 Reed Australia
1 85591 Buzz Books
1 85619 Sinclair-Stevenson

Parent Company:
Reed Elsevier *(UK)*

Associated & Subsidiary Companies:
Canada: Butterworths. *USA:* Butterworth-
Heinemann

Overseas Representation *(see §7.3):*
ASEAN Region: Reed Publishing Services Asia
Pte Ltd, Singapore
Australia: Reed Books Australia, Melbourne,
Vic; Rigby-Heinemann (Australia) Ltd, Port
Melbourne
Barbados, Leeward & Windward Isles: C. D.
A. Walker, Christchurch, Barbados
Botswana: Heinemann Educational Botswana,
Gaborone
Egypt: Cairo Trade Centre, Cairo
Europe: Reed International Books Ltd,
London, UK
Ghana: A. Ott-Attafua & Co Ltd, Accra
Hong Kong: Far East Media Ltd; Transglobal
Publishers Services Ltd, Tsuen Wan
India: Reed Consumer Books, New Delhi;
Maya Publishers Pvt Ltd, New Delhi
Jamaica: West Indies Publishing Ltd, Kingston
Japan: Reed Consumer Books, Tokyo
Kenya: East African Educational Publishers
Ltd, Nairobi
Mauritius: Editions de l'Ocean Indien Ltd,
Rose Hill
Middle East: Anthony Rudkin Associates,
Oxford, UK
Namibia: New Namibia Books, Windhoek
Netherlands: Nilsson & Lamm BV, Weesp
New Zealand: Reed Publishing Group,
Auckland
Nigeria: Heinemann Educational Books
(Nigeria) Ltd, Ibadan
*Philippines, Hong Kong, Korea, China &
Taiwan:* Reed Consumer Books, Metro
Manila, Philippines
Sierra Leone: New Horizons, Freetown
Singapore, Malaysia & Indonesia: Reed
International (Singapore) Pte Ltd, Singapore
South Africa: Struik Book Distributors Pty Ltd,
Maitland
South Africa (Lesotho): Heinemann Publishers
(Pty) Ltd, Houghton & Isando, South Africa
Tanzania: Afriservices, Dar es Salaam
Trinidad & Tobago: KLP Agencies Ltd, Port of
Spain, Trinidad
Uganda: Rorash Educational Publishers,
Kampala
USA: Trafalgar Square Publications, North
Pomfret, VT
USA (Methuen Drama only): Heinemann
Educational Books Inc, Portsmouth, NH,
USA

Book Trade Association Membership:
Canadian Book Publishers Council, Canadian
Library Association

2209 ▬▬▬▬▬▬▬

REIDMORE BOOKS INC
1200 Energy Square, 10109-106 Street,
Edmonton, Alberta T5J 3L7
Telephone: +1 (403) 424 4420
Fax: +1 (403) 441 9919
Email: reidmore@compusmart.ab.ca
Web Site: http://www.reidmore.com

Warehouse:
14339 – 112 Avenue, Edmonton, Alta T5M 2V3
Telephone: +1 (403) 452 7905

President: Patrick Reid
Director: Cathie Crooks *(Marketing)*
Editor-in-Chief: Leah-Ann Lymer
Designer: James Manis

*Academic & Scholarly; Children's Books;
Educational & Textbooks; Electronic
(Educational)*

New Titles: 16 (1995), 16 (1996)
No of Employees: 8

ISBNs, Imprints & Series:
0 919091, 1 895073

Overseas Representation *(see §7.3):*
UK & Europe: Canadabooks International,
Saffron Walden, UK

2210 ▬▬▬▬▬▬▬

**EDITIONS DU RENOUVEAU
PÉDAGOGIQUE INC**
5757 rue Cypihot, Saint-Laurent, PQ H4S 1X4
Telephone: +1 (514) 334 2690
Fax: +1 (514) 334 4720
Email: erpidlm@odyssee.net

President: Normand Cléroux
Vice-Presidents: Luc Garneau *(Finance)*
Pierre Prud'Homme *(School Division)*
Jean Tardif *(Diffusion du Livre Mirabel)*
Ino Algranti *(Second Languages Division)*
Production Manager: Mireille de Palma
Director: Jean-Pierre Albert *(College
Division)*

*Academic & Scholarly; Atlases & Maps;
Biology & Zoology; Educational & Textbooks;
English as a Foreign Language; Geography &
Geology; History & Antiquarian; Mathematics
& Statistics; Physics; Psychology &
Psychiatry; Scientific & Technical*

New Titles: 40 (1995), 40 (1996)
No of Employees: 100

ISBNs, Imprints & Series: 2 7613

Parent Company:
Diffusion du Livre Mirabel *(Canada)*

Book Trade Association Membership:
Association Nationale des editeurs

2211 ▬▬▬▬▬▬▬

ROCKY MOUNTAIN BOOKS
4 Spruce Centre SW, Calgary, AB T3C 3B3

Telephone: +1 (403) 249 9490
Fax: +1 (403) 249 2968
Email: tonyd@cadvision.com
Web Site: http://www.culturenet.ca/rmb/

Publisher: Tony Daffern
President: Gillean Daffern
Sales Manager: Joanne Godziuk
Editor: Janice Redlin

*Cookery, Wines & Spirits; Guide Books; Sports
& Games; Travel & Topography*

New Titles: 5 (1995), 8 (1996)
No of Employees: 3
Annual Turnover: $300,000

ISBNs, Imprints & Series: 0 921102

Overseas Representation *(see §7.3):*
UK: Cordee, Leicester
USA: Alpenbooks, Mukilteo, WA

Book Trade Association Membership: Book
Publishers Association of Alberta

2212 ▬▬▬▬▬▬▬

THE ROEHER INSTITUTE
Kinsmen Building, York University,
4700 Keele Street, North York, Ont M3J 1P3
Telephone: +1 (416) 661 9611
Fax: +1 (416) 661 5701

Directors: Marcia H. Rioux *(Executive)*
Cameron Crawford *(Assistant)*
Senior Researcher: Michael Bach
Managing Editor: Laura Lee
Desktop Publishing: Dean McCallum
Translation (French): Dana Carciumaru
Danielle Raitzes
Book Distribution Clerk: Nadia Dyman

*Academic & Scholarly; Educational &
Textbooks; Social Policy & Human Rights*

New Titles: 14 (1995), 10 (1996)
No of Employees: 15

ISBNs, Imprints & Series:
0 920121, 0 9690438, 1 895070

Overseas Representation *(see §7.3):*
Australia: McLennan & Petty, Rosebery, NSW

2213 ▬▬▬▬▬▬▬

**ROYAL BRITISH COLUMBIA
MUSEUM**
675 Belleville Street, Victoria, BC V8V 1X4
Telephone: +1 (604) 387 6357
Fax: +1 (604) 387 5360
Email: gtruscott@rbml01.rbcm.gov.bc.ca
Web Site: http://www.rbcm1.rbcm.gov.bc.ca

Distributor:
UBC Press, 6344 Memorial Road, Vancouver,
BC V6T 1W5

Publishing Services: Gerry Truscott

*Academic & Scholarly; Archaeology; Biology
& Zoology; Electronic (Educational);
Electronic (Professional & Academic); History
& Antiquarian; Natural History; Scientific &
Technical; Sociology & Anthropology*

New Titles: 5 (1995), 4 (1996)
No of Employees: 1

ISBNs, Imprints & Series:
0 7718, 0 7726, 0 7748

Overseas Representation *(see §7.3)*:
See: UBC Press, Canada

Book Trade Association Membership:
Association of Canadian Publishers,
Association of Book Publishers of British
Columbia, Association for the Export of
Canadian Books

2214 ■■■■■

ROYAL ONTARIO MUSEUM
Publications Dept, 100 Queen's Park, Toronto,
Ont M5S 2C6
Telephone: +1 (416) 586 5581
Fax: +1 (416) 586 5827
Email: sandras@rom.on.ca

Warehouse, Trade Enquiries & Orders:
University of Toronto Press,
Order Fulfilment Division,
5201 Dufferin Street, Downsview,
Ont M3H 5T8
Telephone: +1 (416) 667 7791
Fax: +1 (416) 667 7832
Email: utpbooks@gpu.utcc.utoronto.ca

Head of Publication Services: Sandra Shaul
(Rights & Sales)
Managing Editor: Glen Ellis *(Editorial,*
Permissions)

Academic & Scholarly; Archaeology; Biology
& Zoology; Children's Books; History &
Antiquarian; Natural History; Sociology &
Anthropology

New Titles: 6 (1995), 5 (1996)
No of Employees: 5

ISBNs, Imprints & Series: 0 88854

Overseas Representation *(see §7.3)*:
UK: University of Toronto Press, Abingdon

Book Trade Association Membership:
Canadian Book Publishers Council, Society for
Scholarly Publishing

2215 ■■■■■

SECOND STORY PRESS
720 Bathurst Street #301, Toronto,
Ont M5S 2R4
Telephone: +1 (416) 537 7850
Fax: +1 (416) 537 0588
Email: secstory@fox.nstn.ca

Distribution & Fulfilment:
University of Toronto Press,
5201 Dufferin Street, Downsview,
Ont M3H 5T8
Telephone: +1 (416) 667 7791
Fax: +1 (416) 667 7832

Editors & Rights: Margie Wolfe *(Children's,*
Adult Non-fiction, Marketing & Promotion)
Lois Pike *(Adult Fiction/Non-fiction, Finance,*
Distribution & Permissions)

Children's Books; Fiction; Gender Studies;
Health & Beauty; Politics & World Affairs;
Sociology & Anthropology

New Titles: 11 (1995), 9 (1996)
No of Employees: 4
Annual Turnover: $275,000

ISBNs, Imprints & Series:
0 921299 Second Story Press (Amanita)
0 929005 Second Story Press

Overseas Representation *(see §7.3)*:
UK & Europe: Airlift Book Co, London, UK
USA: LPC/Inbook, Chicago, IL

Book Trade Association Membership:
Association of Canadian Publishers,
Organization of Book Publishers of Ontario,
Canadian Booksellers Association (associate
membership)

2216 ■■■■■

SIMON & PIERRE PUBLISHING CO
LTD
2181 Queen Street East, Suite 301, Toronto,
Ont M4E 1E5
Telephone: +1 (416) 698 0454
Fax: +1 (416) 698 1102

President: J. Kirk Howard
Publisher: Jean Paton

Biography & Autobiography; Crime;
Educational & Textbooks; Fiction; Literature
& Criticism; Theatre, Drama & Dance

New Titles: 8 (1995), 8 (1996)
No of Employees: 2

ISBNs, Imprints & Series:
0 88924, 0 9690454 Bastet Books, Canplay

Parent Company:
Dundurn Press *(Canada)*

Overseas Representation *(see §7.3)*:
UK & Europe: Dundurn Distribution, Oxford,
UK

Book Trade Association Membership:
Association of Canadian Publishers

2217 ■■■■■

*SISTER VISION PRESS
PO Box 217, Station E, Toronto, Ont M6H 4E2
Telephone: +1 (416) 533 2184
Fax: +1 (416) 533 2397

Distribution:
General Publishing Co Ltd, 30 Lesmill Road,
Don Mills, Ont M3B 2T6
Telephone: +1 (416) 445 3333
Fax: +1 (416) 445 5967

Literary Press: Kelly Watt *(Ontario)*
Group Representatives: Melissa Pitts
(Toronto & area)
Jana Williams *(BC)*
Tim Brandt *(Prairies)*
Debra Surette *(Atlantic/Quebec)*
Managers: Stephanie Martin *(Sales)*
Makeda Silvera *(Rights & Permissions)*

Children's Books; Fiction; Gender Studies;
Poetry

ISBNs, Imprints & Series: 0 920813

Overseas Representation *(see §7.3)*:
Caribbean: deBrosse, Redman & Black,
Kingston, Jamaica
UK: Turnaround Publishers Services Ltd,
London
USA: Book People, Oakland, CA; Inland Book
Co Inc, East Haven, CT

Book Trade Association Membership:
Association of Canadian Publishers

2218 ■■■■■

SOGIDES LTÉE
955 rue Amherst, Montreal, PQ H2L 3K4
Telephone: +1 (514) 523 1182
Fax: +1 (514) 597 0370

Warehouse, Trade Enquiries & Orders:
1751 Richardson, Point St Charles, Montreal,
PQ H3K 1G6

President: Pierre Lespérance
Executive Vice-President: André Massicotte
Vice-President & Publisher: James de Gaspé
Bonar
Directors of Sales: Jacques Leclerc
(Consignment)
Pierre Burdon *(Retail)*
Marc-André Dandurand *(Bookstores)*
Huguette Laurent *(Associate Publisher—*
Europe)
Director of Production: Francis Vincent
Director of Finances: Sylvain Lamoureux

Academic & Scholarly; Antiques & Collecting;
Architecture & Design; Aviation; Biography &
Autobiography; Biology & Zoology;
Children's Books; Cookery, Wines & Spirits;
Crime; Crafts & Hobbies; Do-It-Yourself;
Educational & Textbooks; Fiction; Fine Art &
Art History; Gardening; Guide Books; Health
& Beauty; History & Antiquarian; Humour;
Industry, Business & Management; Politics &
World Affairs; Psychology & Psychiatry;
Sports & Games

New Titles: 200 (1995), 155 (1996)
No of Employees: 500
Annual Turnover: $58M

ISBNs, Imprints & Series:
Utilis
2 7619 Les Editions de l'Homme
2 89029 Les Editions Domino
2 89043 Les Editions la Presse
2 89044 Le Jour Editeur
2 89117 Les Presses Libre

Associated & Subsidiary Companies:
Canada: Les Editions françaises; La Librairie
Garneau; Le Groupe Ville-Marie Littérature

Overseas Representation *(see §7.3)*:
Belgium & Luxembourg: Les Presses de
Belgique, Wavre, Belgium
Canada & USA: Les Messageries ADP,
Montreal, Canada
France & Africa: Inter Forum, Paris, France
Switzerland: Transat SA, Geneva

Book Trade Association Membership:
Association nationale des éditeurs de livres,
Association for the Export of Canadian Books

2219 ▬▬▬▬

SOMERVILLE HOUSE BOOKS LTD
3080 Yonge Street, Suite 5000, Toronto,
Ont M4N 3N1
Telephone: +1 (416) 488 5938
Fax: +1 (416) 488 5506
Email: sombooks@goodmedia.com
Web Site: http://www.goodmedia.com/
somervillehouse

Distribution & Orders:
Thomas Allen & Son Ltd,
390 Steelcase Road E, Markham, Ont L3R 1G2
Telephone: +1 (416) 475 9126
Fax: +1 (416) 475 6747

President: Jane Somerville
Directors: Patrick Crean *(Editorial)*
Nick Harris *(Marketing)*
Managers: Michelle Bennett *(Assistant
Production)*
Paula Fisher *(Production)*
Comptroller: David Maxwell

*Children's Books; Crafts & Hobbies;
Environment & Development Studies; Fiction;
Medical (incl. Self Help & Alternative
Medicine); Philosophy; Sports & Games*

New Titles: 15 (1995), 26 (1996)
No of Employees: 17

ISBNs, Imprints & Series:
Patrick Crean Books (for adult titles only)
0 921051 Somerville House Publishing 1
895897

Overseas Representation *(see §7.3):*
Australia: Lothian Books, Port Melbourne
Japan: Tuttle-Mori Agency Ltd, Tokyo
New Zealand: David Bateman Ltd, Auckland
Spain: Julio F. Yañez, Barcelona
UK: D-Services, Leicester

2220 ▬▬▬▬

SONO NIS PRESS
1725 Blanshard Street, Victoria, BC V8W 2J8
Telephone: +1 (604) 382 1024
Fax: +1 (604) 382 0775

President: Darryl E. Morriss
Publisher: Ann J. West
Editorial Assistant: A. Kemball
Designer: J. Bennett

*Aviation; Biography & Autobiography; Fine
Art & Art History; History & Antiquarian;
Literature & Criticism; Nautical; Poetry*

New Titles: 8 (1995), 7 (1996)
No of Employees: 2

ISBNs, Imprints & Series:
0 919203, 0 919462, 1 55039

Parent Company:
Morriss Publishing *(Canada)*

Book Trade Association Membership:
Association of Canadian Publishers,

Association of Book Publishers of British
Columbia

2221 ▬▬▬▬

***SOUTHAM MAGAZINE &
INFORMATION GROUP**
[a division of Southam Inc]
1450 Don Mills Road, Don Mills,
Ont M3B 2X7
Telephone: +1 (416) 445 6641
Fax: +1 (416) 442 2200

General Manager: Ian Rhind

*Industry, Business & Management; Law;
Politics & World Affairs; Reference Books,
Directories & Dictionaries; Environment*

Parent Company:
Southam Inc *(Canada)*

Associated & Subsidiary Companies:
Canada: Corpus Information Services

2222 ▬▬▬▬

TALON BOOKS LTD
104-3100 Production Way, Burnaby,
BC V5A 4R4
Telephone: +1 (604) 444 4889
Fax: +1 (604) 444 4119
Email: talon@pinc.com
Web Site: http://www.swiftycom/talon

Warehouse & Fulfillment:
General Distribution Services,
30 Lesmill Road, Don Mills, Ont M3B 2T6
Telephone: +1 (416) 445 3333
Fax: +1 (416) 445 5967

President & Managing Editor: Karl H.
Siegler

*Academic & Scholarly; Architecture & Design;
Atlases & Maps; Bibliography & Library
Science; Biography & Autobiography;
Cookery, Wines & Spirits; Fiction; Fine Art &
Art History; Gender Studies; Geography &
Geology; Literature & Criticism; Philosophy;
Poetry; Politics & World Affairs; Sociology &
Anthropology; Theatre, Drama & Dance*

New Titles: 6 (1995), 12 (1996)
No of Employees: 2

ISBNs, Imprints & Series: 0 88922

Overseas Representation *(see §7.3):*
Europe: Book Representation & Distribution
(BRAD), Hadleigh, UK
USA (complete list): General Distribution
Services, Buffalo, NY, USA
USA (selected titles only): In Book/LPC Group,
Milford, CT, USA

Book Trade Association Membership:
Association of Canadian Publishers,
Association of Book Publishers of British
Columbia, Canadian Booksellers Association

2223 ▬▬▬▬

TAMOS BOOKS INC
300 Wales Avenue, Winnipeg,
Manitoba R2M 2S9

Telephone: +1 (204) 256 9204
Fax: +1 (204) 255 7845

President & Editor-in-Chief: Dr Marvis
Tutiah

Crafts & Hobbies; Do-It-Yourself

New Titles: 5 (1995), 5 (1996)
No of Employees: 5

ISBNs, Imprints & Series: 1 895569

Overseas Representation *(see §7.3):*
USA, UK, Australia & New Zealand: Sterling
Publishing Co Inc, New York, NY, USA

2224 ▬▬▬▬

*THEYTUS BOOKS LTD
PO Box 20040, Penticton, BC V2A 8K3
Telephone: +1 (604) 493 7181
Fax: +1 (604) 493 5302

Manager: Greg Young-Ing

*Academic & Scholarly; Children's Books;
Educational & Textbooks; Fiction; Languages
& Linguistics; Literature & Criticism; Natural
History; Photography; Poetry; Science
Fiction; Native American Authors*

ISBNs, Imprints & Series: 0 919441

Book Trade Association Membership:
Association of Canadian Publishers, Canadian
Booksellers Association

2225 ▬▬▬▬

THISTLEDOWN PRESS LTD
633 Main Street, Saskatoon, Sask S7H 0J8
Telephone: +1 (306) 244 1722
Fax: +1 (306) 244 1762

President: Glen Sorestad
Vice-President: Patrick O'Rourke *(Editor-in-
Chief)*
Directors: Sonia Sorestad *(Financial,
Treasurer)*
Allan Forrie *(Production, Secretary)*

*Fiction; Literature & Criticism; Poetry; Young
Adult*

New Titles: 19 (1995), 8 (1996)
No of Employees: 2

ISBNs, Imprints & Series:
0 920066, 0 920633, 1 895449

Overseas Representation *(see §7.3):*
Australia & New Zealand: St Clair Press Pty
Ltd, Rozelle, NSW, Australia
USA: General Distribution Services, Niagara
Falls, NY

Book Trade Association Membership:
Association of Canadian Publishers, Literary
Press Group (Canada), Saskatchewan
Publishers Group

2226 ▬▬▬▬▬▬▬

**THOMPSON EDUCATIONAL
PUBLISHING INC**
14 Ripley Avenue, Suite 105, Toronto,
Ont M6S 3N9
Telephone: +1 (416) 766 2763
Fax: +1 (416) 766 0398
Email: thompson@canadabooks.ingenia.com
Web Site: http://www.canadabooks.ingenia.
com

Orders:
General Distribution Services,
30 Lesmill Road, Don Mills, Ont M3B 2T6
Telephone: +1 (800) 387 0141 (Toll Free) &
387 0172
Fax: +1 (416) 445 5967

President: Keith Thompson

*Economics; Educational & Textbooks; Gender
Studies; Politics & World Affairs; Sociology &
Anthropology*

New Titles: 9 (1995), 5 (1996)
No of Employees: 2
Annual Turnover: $260,000

ISBNs, Imprints & Series:
0 921332, 1 55077

Book Trade Association Membership:
Association of Canadian Publishers

2227 ▬▬▬▬▬▬▬

***TRIFOLIUM BOOKS INC**
238 Davenport Road, Suite 28, Toronto,
Ont M5R 1J6
Telephone: +1 (416) 925 0765
Fax: +1 (416) 485 5563 & 925 2360

**Educational, College, P&R (excluding The
Technological Classroom):**
Guidance Centre, 712 Gordon Baker Road,
Toronto, Ont M2H 3R7
Telephone: +1 (416) 502 1262
Fax: +1 (416) 502 1101 & (800) 668 6247 (Toll
Free)

**Educational, College, P&R (The
Technological Classroom):**
Irwin Publishing, 1800 Steeles Avenue West,
Concord, Ont L4K 2B3
Telephone: +1 (905) 736 4561 & 660 0611
Fax: +1 (905) 660 0676

Trade:
Stoddart Publishing Co Ltd, 34 Lesmill Road,
Don Mills, Ont M3B 2T6
Telephone: +1 (416) 445 3333
Fax: +1 (416) 445 5967

Career Connections Series:
Weigl Educational Publishers Ltd,
1902 11th Street SE, Calgary, Alberta T2G 3G2
Telephone: +1 (403) 233 7747
Fax: +1 (403) 233 7769 & (800) 668 0766 (Toll
Free)

President: Trudy L. Rising *(Rights &
Permissions, Acquisitions—El-hl, College,
P&R)*
Vice-Presidents: Mary Kay Winter *(Finance,
Publisher—Science & Technology)*

Grace Deutsch *(Marketing,
Acquisitions—Trade)*

*Academic & Scholarly; Educational &
Textbooks; Industry, Business & Management;
Scientific & Technical; Vocational Training &
Careers*

ISBNs, Imprints & Series: 1 895579

Overseas Representation *(see §7.3):*
*USA (Educational, P&R excluding The Career
Connections Series & The Technological
Classroom):* Eric/Cass, USA
USA (Trade—Select titles): DBM Publishing,
USA
Worldwide (Trade only/Foreign Rights):
Stoddart Publishing, Don Mills, Ont, Canada

Book Trade Association Membership:
Association of Canadian Publishers, Canadian
Book Publishers' Council, Canadian
Booksellers' Association, Canadian Telebook
Agency, Cancopy: The Canadian Reprography
Collective

2228 ▬▬▬▬▬▬▬

TUNDRA BOOKS INC
481 University Avenue, Suite 802, Toronto,
Ont M5G 2E9
Telephone: +1 (416) 598 4786
Fax: +1 (416) 598 0247

Editor-in-Chief: Kathy Lorringer *(Editor,
Foreign Rights)*
Marketing: Catherine Mitchell *(Home Sales,
Rights & Permissions)*

*Children's Books; Illustrated & Fine Editions;
Art*

New Titles: 11 (1995), 12 (1996)
No of Employees: 3

ISBNs, Imprints & Series: 0 88776

Parent Company:
McClelland & Stewart *(Canada)*

Associated & Subsidiary Companies:
USA: Tundra Books of Northern New York

Overseas Representation *(see §7.3):*
Australia & New Zealand: Stafford Books, St
Leonards, NSW, Australia
France: Le Colporteur Diffusion, La Roche
Blanche
UK: Ragged Bears Ltd, Andover
USA: Ron Doussard & Associates, Lake in the
Hills, IL; Errett Stuart Associates, Camarillo,
CA; Ryen, Re Associates, Oradell, NJ; Gary
White ,Chuck Gregg, Cumberland, ME;
Horace McQueen Associates, Houston, TX;
Morris & Associates, Clearwater, FL

Book Trade Association Membership:
Canadian Booksellers Association, American
Booksellers Association, Association nationale
des éditeurs de livre, Canadian Library
Association, American Library Association

2229 ▬▬▬▬▬▬▬

TURNSTONE PRESS LTD
607-100 Arthur Street, Winnipeg,
Manitoba R3B 1H3

Telephone: +1 (204) 947 1556
Fax: +1 (204) 942 1555
Email: marketing@turnstonepress.mb.ca

Orders:
General Distribution Services,
30 Lesmill Road, Don Mills, Ont M3B 2T6
Telephone: +1 (416) 445 3333
Fax: +1 (416) 445 5967

Managing Editor: James V. Hutchison *(Rights
& Permissions)*
Managers: Christine Dulat *(Promotion &
Marketing)*
Manuela Dias *(Production)*

*Fiction; Literature & Criticism; Poetry; Non-
fiction: travel/adventure*

New Titles: 10 (1995), 11 (1996)
No of Employees: 3

ISBNs, Imprints & Series: 0 88801

Overseas Representation *(see §7.3):*
USA (Midwest, New York & Mid-Atlantic):
LPC/Inbook, Chicago, IL, USA

Book Trade Association Membership:
Association of Canadian Publishers, Literary
Press Group, Canadian Booksellers
Association (Associate)

2230 ▬▬▬▬▬▬▬

UBC PRESS
University of British Columbia,
6344 Memorial Road, Vancouver, BC V6T 1Z2
Telephone: +1 (604) 822 3259
Fax: +1 (604) 822 6083
Email: orders@ubcpress.ubc.ca
Web Site: http://www.ubcpress.ubc.ca

Warehouse:
8591 Fraser Street, Vancouver, BC V5X 3Y1
Telephone: +1 (604) 327 6591
Fax: +1 (604) 327 1009

Director: R. Peter Milroy *(Rights &
Permissions)*
Senior Editor: Jean Wilson
Managers: George Maddison *(Production)*
Evie Mandel *(Business)*
Berit Kraus *(Advertising & Promotion)*
Julia Sedger *(Sales)*

*Academic & Scholarly; Archaeology; Atlases
& Maps; Economics; Educational &
Textbooks; Geography & Geology; History &
Antiquarian; Law; Natural History; Politics &
World Affairs; Reference Books, Directories &
Dictionaries; Sociology & Anthropology*

New Titles: 23 (1995), 30 (1996)
No of Employees: 16
Annual Turnover: $1M

ISBNs, Imprints & Series:
0 7748 Canada & International Relations, First
Nations Languages Series, The Pioneers of
British Columbia Series, Sustainability &
The Environment, Urbanization in Asia

Overseas Representation *(see §7.3):*
*Australia, New Zealand, East & South East
Asia & Pacific:* East-West Export Books,
Honolulu, Hawaii, USA

Germany, Scandinavia, Italy, Switzerland, Austria, Netherlands, Spain, France & Belgium: Trevor Brown Associates, London, UK
South America: Terry Roberts, Cotia SP, Brazil
UK: Mike Wilson, Anglesey; David Grant, Tunbridge Wells; Tony Lawrence, Altrincham; Donald Macdonald, Glasgow; Adele Rogers, London
USA: University of Washington Press, Seattle, WA

Book Trade Association Membership:
Association of Canadian Publishers, Association of American University Presses, Association of Canadian University Presses, Canadian BA, Canadian Book Information Centre, Association of Book Publishers of British Columbia

2231 ▬▬▬▬▬

VANWELL PUBLISHING LTD
1 Northrup Cr, PO Box 2131, St Catharines, Ont L2M 6P5
Telephone: +1 (416) 937 3700
Fax: +1 (416) 937 1760

Vancouver Office:
202-1224 Hamilton Street, Vancouver, BC V6B 2S8
Telephone: +1 (604) 688 6918
Fax: +1 (604) 687 4624

Edmonton Office:
15003-76th Avenue, Edmonton, AB T5R 2Z7
Telephone: +1 (403) 487 6170
Fax: +1 (403) 487 6321

Calgary Office:
2312-16A Street SW, Calgary, AB T2T 4K4
Telephone: +1 (403) 245 8393
Fax: +1 (403) 245 8393

Ontario & Quebec:
6 Donlands Avenue, PO Box 70, Sharon, Ont L0G 1V0
Telephone: +1 (905) 478 8396
Fax: +1 (905) 478 8380

Eastern Canada:
70 Old Windsor Highway, Mount Uniacke, NS B0N 1Z0
Telephone: +1 (902) 866 0832
Fax: +1 (902) 866 4258

President: Ben Kooter *(Sales)*
Editor: Angela Dobler *(Rights)*

Aviation; Children's Books; Military & War; Nautical

New Titles: 10 (1995), 14 (1996)

ISBNs, Imprints & Series:
0 920277, 1 55068, 1 55125

Associated & Subsidiary Companies:
Canada: Troll Bookclubs

Overseas Representation *(see §7.3)*:
UK: Airlife Publishing, Shrewsbury
USA: Publishers' Distribution Service, Grawn, MI

Book Trade Association Membership:
Canadian Booksellers Association

2232 ▬▬▬▬▬

VÉHICULE PRESS
PO Box 125, Place du Parc, Station, Montreal, PQ H2W 2M4
Telephone: +1 (514) 844 6073
Fax: +1 (514) 844 7543
Email: upress@com.org

Distribution:
General Publishing, 30 Lesmill Road, Don Mills, Ont M3B 2T6

Publisher: Simon Dardick
Promotion Manager: Vicki Marcok
Editor: Michael Harris *(Poetry)*

Academic & Scholarly; Fiction; Gender Studies; Literature & Criticism; Poetry

New Titles: 13 (1995), 13 (1996)
No of Employees: 2

ISBNs, Imprints & Series:
0 919890, 1 55065

Overseas Representation *(see §7.3)*:
USA: LPC/Inbook, Chicago, IL

Book Trade Association Membership:
Association of Canadian Publishers, Literary Press Group, English Language Publishers Association of Quebec (AEAQ)

2233 ▬▬▬▬▬

*VOYAGEUR PUBLISHING
Maple Avenue, RR2, Prescott, Ont K0E 1T0
Telephone: +1 (613) 925 2111
Fax: +1 (613) 925 0029

Academic & Scholarly; Literature & Criticism; Politics & World Affairs; Canadian Issues

ISBNs, Imprints & Series: 0 921842

2234 ▬▬▬▬▬

WARWICK PUBLISHING INC
24 Mercer Street, Toronto, Ont M5V 1H3
Telephone: +1 (416) 596 1555
Fax: +1 (416) 596 1520

Distributor:
Firefly Books Ltd, 3680 Victoria Park Avenue, Willow Dale, Ont M2H 3K1
Telephone: +1 (416) 499 8412
Fax: +1 (416) 499 8313

President: James Williamson
Publisher: Nicholas Pitt
Controller: Paul Hillcrup
Art Director: Kimberly Davison
Editor: Harry Endrulat
Designer: Diane Farewick

New Titles: 18 (1995), 20 (1996)
No of Employees: 8
Annual Turnover: $1.5M

ISBNs, Imprints & Series: 1 895629

Parent Company:
Warwick Publishing Group Inc *(Canada)*

Associated & Subsidiary Companies:
Canada: Canadian Golf Press Inc; Warwick Interactive Inc

Overseas Representation *(see §7.3)*:
USA: Firefly Books Ltd, Willowdale, Ont, Canada

2235 ▬▬▬▬▬

WEIGL EDUCATIONAL PUBLISHERS
1902 – 11th Street SE, Calgary, AB T2G 3G2
Telephone: +1 (403) 233 7747
Fax: +1 (403) 233 7769
Email: weigl@agt.net
Web Site: http://www.weigl.com

Publisher: Linda A. Weigl
Secretary – Treasurer: David Rylands
Project Co-ordinator: Amanda Woodrow
Marketing Co-ordinator: Lauri Seidlitz

Educational & Textbooks

New Titles: 14 (1995), 10 (1996)
No of Employees: 8

2236 ▬▬▬▬▬

JOHN WILEY & SONS CANADA LTD
22 Worcester Road, Rexdale, Ontario M9W 1L1
Telephone: +1 (416) 675 3580
Fax: +1 (416) 675 6599
Email: dwood@jwiley.com
Web Site: http://www.wiley.com

Courier Address:
5353 Dundas Street West, 4th Floor, Etobicoke, Ont M9B 6H8
Telephone: +1 (416) 236 4433
Fax: +1 (416) 236 4446(College Production)/ (416) 236 4447(Executive/Acnts)

President: Diane Wood *(College Division)*
Vice-Presidents: Beth Bruder *(Professional, Reference & Trade)*
Paul Anonen *(Finance & Administration)*
Human Resources Manager: Berni Galway

Academic & Scholarly; Chemistry; Computer Science; Economics; Educational & Textbooks; Electronic (Educational); Electronic (Professional & Academic); Engineering; Geography & Geology; Industry, Business & Management; Mathematics & Statistics; Medical (incl. Self Help & Alternative Medicine); Physics; Psychology & Psychiatry; Reference Books, Directories & Dictionaries; Scientific & Technical

New Titles: 10 (1995), 20 (1996)
No of Employees: 71

ISBNs, Imprints & Series:
0 470, 0 471

Parent Company:
John Wiley & Sons Inc *(USA)*

Associated & Subsidiary Companies:
Australia: Jacaranda Wiley Ltd. *Singapore:* John Wiley & Sons (SEA) Pte Ltd. *UK:* John Wiley & Sons Ltd. *USA:* John Wiley & Sons Inc

Book Trade Association Membership:
Canadian Book Publishers Council

2237 ▬▬▬▬▬▬▬

WILFRID LAURIER UNIVERSITY PRESS
75 University Avenue West, Waterloo,
Ont N2L 3C5
Telephone: +1 (519) 884 0710 ext 6124
Fax: +1 (519) 725 1399
Email: press@mach1.wlu.ca
Web Site: http://www.info.wlu.co/
~wwwpress/

Director: Sandra Woolfrey
Marketing Manager: *(to be appointed)*
Production Co-ordinator: Doreen
  Armbruster
Financial Supervisor: *(to be appointed)*

*Academic & Scholarly; Cinema, Video, TV &
Radio; Environment & Development Studies;
Gender Studies; History & Antiquarian;
Literature & Criticism; Religion & Theology*

New Titles: 12 (1995), 16 (1996)
No of Employees: 12

ISBNs, Imprints & Series: 0 88920

Overseas Representation *(see §7.3):*
Australia: Michael Romano, Groton, NY, USA
UK & Continental Europe: Trevor Brown
  Associates, Horsham, Sussex, UK
USA: Wilfrid Laurier University Press, Groton,
  NY

Book Trade Association Membership:
Association of Canadian Publishers, Canadian
Booksellers Association, American
Association of University Presses, Association
of Canadian University Presses

2238 ▬▬▬▬▬▬▬

WOOD LAKE BOOKS INC
10162 Newene Road, Winfield, BC, V4V 1R2
Telephone: +1 (250) 766 2778
Fax: +1 (250) 766 2736
Email: info@woodlake.com

Warehouse:
3396 Sexsmith Road, Kelowna, BC V1V 1L6
Telephone: +1 (250) 765 6152

Editor: Mike Schwartzentruber
Publisher: David Cleary
Sales & Marketing: Ann Wallin
Rights & Permissions: Lindy Jones
Production: Gene Longson

Children's Books; Religion & Theology

New Titles: 10 (1995), 5 (1996)
No of Employees: 23
Annual Turnover: $1.5M

ISBNs, Imprints & Series:
0 919599, 0 929032, 1 55145, 1 895562

Overseas Representation *(see §7.3):*
Australia: MediaCom Associates, Unlay

Book Trade Association Membership:
Association of Book Publishers of British
Columbia

2239 ▬▬▬▬▬▬▬

WUERZ PUBLISHING LTD
895 McMillan Avenue, Winnipeg,
Manitoba R3M 0T2
Telephone: +1 (204) 453 7429
Fax: +1 (204) 453 6598

Editorial: Steve Wuerz
Sales & Marketing: Kate Wood
Production: Lance Rosolowich

*Academic & Scholarly; Chemistry;
Educational & Textbooks; Electronic
(Educational); Electronic (Professional &
Academic); Languages & Linguistics;
Mathematics & Statistics; Medical (incl. Self
Help & Alternative Medicine); Physics;
Scientific & Technical*

New Titles: 14 (1995), 18 (1996)
No of Employees: 4

ISBNs, Imprints & Series: 0 920063

Overseas Representation *(see §7.3):*
UK, Irish Republic, Greece & Israel: UPM –
  University Presses Marketing, Wantage, UK

Book Trade Association Membership:
Association of Canadian Publishers, Canadian
Book Publishers' Council, Publishers
Marketing Association (USA), Society for
Scholarly Publishing (USA), National
Association of College Stores (USA)
(application pending)

GHANA

2240 ▬▬▬▬▬▬▬

AFRAM PUBLICATIONS (GH) LTD
PO Box M.18, Accra
Telephone: +233 (Ō21) 774248
Fax: +233 (Ō21) 778715

Managing Director: Eric Ofei *(Editorial,
  Rights & Permissions)*
Managers: George Braye *(Production, Sales)*
  Emmanuel Manful *(Marketing)*
  David Dackson M. Patawah *(Accountant)*

Children's Books; Educational & Textbooks

New Titles: 10 (1995), 30 (1996)
No of Employees: 17
Annual Turnover: $1M

ISBNs, Imprints & Series: 9964 70

Book Trade Association Membership: Ghana
Book PA, Afro-Asian Book Council, African
Books Collective Ltd

2241 ▬▬▬▬▬▬▬

AFRICA CHRISTIAN PRESS
PO Box 30, Achimota
Telephone: +233 (Ō21) 220271
Fax: +233 (Ō21) 220271

General Manager: Richard A. B. Crabbe
Assistant Editor: Mrs Margaret Saah
Marketing Managers: A. Dei-Awuku
  (Export)
  Esther Dordoe *(Home Sales)*

*Children's Books; Fiction; Religion &
Theology*

New Titles: 2 (1995), 6 (1996)
No of Employees: 7

ISBNs, Imprints & Series: 9964 87

Overseas Representation *(see §7.3):*
Kenya: Keswick Book Society, Nairobi
Nigeria: Scripture Union, Ibadan
South Africa: Scripture Union Publishing
  Agency, Rondebosch
UK: ACP, Worthing
USA: ACP, Bloomingdale, IL
Zambia: Scripture Union, Kitwe
Zimbabwe: Scripture Union, Harare

Book Trade Association Membership: Ghana
Book PA

2242 ▬▬▬▬▬▬▬

**ASEMPA PUBLISHERS CHRISTIAN
COUNCIL OF GHANA**
PO Box 919, Accra
Telephone: +233 (Ō21) 221706 & 233084
Fax: +233 (Ō21) 776725 & 233130

Manager: Rev Emmanuel Borlabi Bortey
  (General)
Editors: Samuel Loring Asiedu *(Home &
  Export Sales)*
  Mrs Sarah Apronti *(Production)*

*Biography & Autobiography; Children's
Books; Educational & Textbooks; Fiction;
Music; Poetry; Religion & Theology*

New Titles: 5 (1995), 6 (1996)
No of Employees: 14

ISBNs, Imprints & Series: 9964 78

Book Trade Association Membership: Ghana
PA

2243 ▬▬▬▬▬▬▬

FRANK PUBLISHING LTD
PO Box M.414, Ministry Branch Post Office,
Accra

Managing Director: Francis K. Dzokoto
Sales Manager: Moses K. Dzokoto

Children's Books; Educational & Textbooks

New Titles: 6 (1996)
No of Employees: 4
Annual Turnover: $50,000

ISBNs, Imprints & Series: 9964 959

Book Trade Association Membership: Ghana
Book PA

2244 ▬▬▬▬▬▬▬

SAM-WOODE LTD
273/4, Dr Nanka Bruce Road, Laterbiokoshie,
PO Box 12719 Accra-North
Telephone: +233 (Ō21) 220257
Fax: +233 (Ō21) 662210

Showroom:
First Floor, Kaneshie Market Complex, Accra

Telephone: +233 (Õ21) 220257
Fax: +233 (Õ21) 662210

Executive Chairman: Kwesi Sam-Woode
  (Rights & Permissions)
Managers: Vincent Owusu-Ansah *(Marketing,
  Home & Export Sales)*
Kweku E. Sam-Woode *(Production)*
Ms Pamela Woode *(Editorial)*

Children's Books; Educational & Textbooks

New Titles: 6 (1995), 10 (1996)
No of Employees: 10
Annual Turnover: $150,000

ISBNs, Imprints & Series: 9964 979

Book Trade Association Membership: Ghana
Book PA

2245

SEDCO PUBLISHING LTD
Sedco House, Tabon Street, North Ridge,
PO Box 2051, Accra
Telephone: +233 (Õ21) 221332
Fax: +233 (Õ21) 220107

Directors: C. K. Segbawu *(Managing)*
Mrs F. G. Segbawu *(Sales & Executive)*
Marketing Manager: F. K. Segbawu
Editor: E. K. Sallah

*Accountancy & Taxation; Biology & Zoology;
Chemistry; Children's Books; Educational &
Textbooks; Fiction; Guide Books; History &
Antiquarian; Law; Mathematics & Statistics;
Theatre, Drama & Dance*

New Titles: 3 (1995), 15 (1996)
No of Employees: 18

ISBNs, Imprints & Series: 9964 72

Book Trade Association Membership: Ghana
Book PA

2246

GHANA UNIVERSITIES PRESS
PO Box 4219, Accra

Director: K. M. Ganu
Business Manager: J. K. Bosomtwe
Assistant Editors: Linda Tsevi
Victor K. Boadu

*Academic & Scholarly; Agriculture; Biology &
Zoology; Educational & Textbooks;
Environment & Development Studies; History
& Antiquarian; Languages & Linguistics; Law;
Music; Sociology & Anthropology*

New Titles: 4 (1995), 15 (1996)
No of Employees: 15
Annual Turnover: $17,000

ISBNs, Imprints & Series: 9964 3

Overseas Representation *(see §7.3):*
UK: African Books Collective Ltd, Oxford

Book Trade Association Membership: Ghana
Book Publishers Association (Foundation
member), International Association of
Scholarly Publishers (Foundation member)

2247

WOELI PUBLISHING SERVICES
PO Box K601, Accra New Town
Telephone: +233 (Õ21) 229294 & 227182
Fax: +233 (Õ21) 226206 & 777098

Managing Director: W. A. Dekutsey
Editor/Manageress: Mrs Agatha Akonor-
  Mills

*Academic & Scholarly; Agriculture;
Children's Books; Fiction; Fine Art & Art
History; Health & Beauty; Literature &
Criticism; Medical (incl. Self Help &
Alternative Medicine); Military & War;
Poetry; Politics & World Affairs; Theatre,
Drama & Dance; Travel & Topography*

New Titles: 6 (1995), 15 (1996)
No of Employees: 5
Annual Turnover: $5,000

ISBNs, Imprints & Series: 9964 978

Overseas Representation *(see §7.3):*
Europe & North America: African Books
  Collective Ltd, Oxford, UK

Book Trade Association Membership: Ghana
Book Publishers Association, African
Publishing Network

HONG KONG

2248

ASIA 2000 LTD
1101 Seabird House, 22–38 Wyndham Street,
Central
Telephone: +852 2530 1409
Fax: +852 2526 1107
Email: info@asia2000.com.hk
Web Site: http://www.asia2000.com.hk

Managing Director: Michael Morrow
Managers: Edowan Bersma *(Sales &
  Distribution)*
John Fowler *(Office)*
Chief Editor: Alan Sargent *(Rights)*

*Atlases & Maps; Biography & Autobiography;
Fiction; Humour; Industry, Business &
Management; Law; Photography; Politics &
World Affairs; Travel & Topography*

New Titles: 4 (1995), 6 (1996)
No of Employees: 6

ISBNs, Imprints & Series: 962 7160

Book Trade Association Membership:
American Booksellers Association, Hong Kong
TDC

2249

THE CHINESE UNIVERSITY PRESS
The Chinese University of Hong Kong, Shatin,
New Territories
Telephone: +852 2609 6508
Fax: +852 2603 6692
Email: cup@cuhk.edu.hk
Web Site: http://www.cuhk.edu.hk/cupress/wl.
htm

Director: Paul S. L. Wong
Managers: Angelina L. F. Wong *(Business,
  Rights & Permissions)*
Kingsley K. H. Ma *(Production)*
Y. K. Fung *(Editorial)*
Yvonne Tam *(Finance & Administration)*

*Academic & Scholarly; Accountancy &
Taxation; Educational & Textbooks; Industry,
Business & Management; Languages &
Linguistics; Chinese Studies*

New Titles: 36 (1995), 40 (1996)
No of Employees: 37
Annual Turnover: $800,000

ISBNs, Imprints & Series: 962 201

Book Trade Association Membership:
Association of American University Presses
Inc

2250

**THE COMMERCIAL PRESS (HONG
KONG) LTD**
Kiu Ying Building, 2D Finnie Street,
Quarry Bay
Telephone: +852 256 51371
Fax: +852 256 45277 & 256 51113

Warehouse & Sales Department:
2nd Floor, Heng Ngai Jewelry Centre,
4 Hok Yuen Street East, Hunghom, Kowloon
Telephone: +852 326 26207
Fax: +852 276 42418 & 236 54129

Editor: Dr Chan Man Hung *(Managing
  Director & Chief)*
Deputy General Manager: Dr Steven K. Luk
Deputy Chief Editor: Wong To
Assistant General Managers: Ms Lui Siu
  Ping *(Branch Operations)*
Ms Chan Yun King *(Financial Controller)*

*Children's Books; Educational & Textbooks;
English as a Foreign Language; Illustrated &
Fine Editions; Languages & Linguistics; Law;
Medical (incl. Self Help & Alternative
Medicine); Philosophy; Reference Books,
Directories & Dictionaries*

ISBNs, Imprints & Series:
962 07 The Commercial Press (Hong Kong)
  Ltd
962 255 Genius Publishing Co
962 290 Hong Kong Educational Publishing Co
962 329 Hong Kong Tai Ping Book Co

Parent Company:
Sino United Publishing (Holdings) Ltd

Associated & Subsidiary Companies:
P. R. of China: The Commercial Press
International Co Ltd. *Hong Kong:* Genius
Publishing Co; Hong Kong Educational
Publishing Co; Hong Kong Tai Ping Book Co.
Malaysia: K. L. Commercial Book Co (M) Sdn
Bhd. *Singapore:* The Commercial Press
(Singapore) Ltd

Book Trade Association Membership: Hong
Kong Book & Magazine Trade Association
Ltd, The Chinese General Chamber of
Commerce, Hong Kong, The Hong Kong
Chinese Enterprises Association, The Hong
Kong Chinese Importers & Exporters Association

2251

*FEDERAL PUBLICATIONS LTD
Units 903–905, Hunghom Commercial Centre,
Tower B, 37 Ma Tau Wai Road, Hunghom,
Kowloon
Telephone: +852 2334 2421
Fax: +852 2764 5095

Director & General Manager: Tom Ng
Publishing Manager: Tsze Sun Li
Marketing Managers: Stewart Lee *(Trade &*
Magazines)
Vincent Wong *(Educational)*
Managers: Douglas Cheng *(Direct Selling)*
Edmond Leung *(Retail)*
Angel Fong *(Library Supplier)*

Children's Books; Educational & Textbooks

ISBNs, Imprints & Series: 962 302

Parent Company:
Times Publishing Ltd *(Singapore)*

Associated & Subsidiary Companies:
Singapore: Federal Publications (S) Pte Ltd.
UK: Marshall Cavendish Ltd

Book Trade Association Membership:
Educational Booksellers Association, Hong
Kong Educational PA, Hong Kong Publishing
Federation

2252

**THE HONG KONG UNIVERSITY
PRESS**
The University of Hong Kong,
139 Pokfulam Road, Hong Kong
Telephone: +852 2550 2703
Fax: +852 2875 0734
Email: hkupress@hkucc.hku.hk

Publisher: Barbara Clarke
Managing Editor: Dennis W. C. Cheung
Sales Manager: Robin Chew Hee Leong
Sales Executive: Winnie Y. W. Chau
Editors: Ms P. T. So
Ms Clara Ho

*Academic & Scholarly; Archaeology;
Architecture & Design; Bibliography &
Library Science; Biology & Zoology;
Economics; Educational & Textbooks; English
as a Foreign Language; Environment &
Development Studies; Fine Art & Art History;
Gender Studies; Geography & Geology;
History & Antiquarian; Industry, Business &
Management; Languages & Linguistics; Law;
Literature & Criticism; Mathematics &
Statistics; Medical (incl. Self Help &
Alternative Medicine); Natural History;
Philosophy; Politics & World Affairs;
Reference Books, Directories & Dictionaries;
Sociology & Anthropology; Theatre, Drama &
Dance; Transport*

New Titles: 25 (1995), 40 (1996)
No of Employees: 13

ISBNs, Imprints & Series: 962 209

Parent Company:
The University of Hong Kong *(Hong Kong)*

Overseas Representation *(see §7.3)*:
Australia & New Zealand: Harry Howell, Lane
Cove, Australia
Philippines: I. J. Sagun Enterprises Inc, Rizal
*UK, Europe, Africa & Middle East (marine
biology & zoology):* Universal Book
Services, Oegstgeest, Netherlands
*UK, Europe, Indian sub-continent & Southern
Africa:* Drake International Services,
Oxford, UK

Book Trade Association Membership:
Anglo-Chinese Textbook Publishers
Organization, International Association of
Scholarly Publishers, Hong Kong
Reprographic Rights Licensing Society

2253

**OXFORD UNIVERSITY PRESS (CHINA)
LTD**
18F Warwick House, 979 King's Road,
Taikoo Place, Quarry Bay
Telephone: +852 2516 3222
Fax: +852 2565 8491
Email: leehelen@oupchina.com.hk

Warehouse:
25/F Dynamic Cargo Centre,
188 Yeung Uta Road, Tsuen Wan,
New Territories
Telephone: +852 2615 5839
Fax: +852 2408 8070
Email: yeungpeg@oupchina.com.hk

Taiwan Office:
9F-8, 79 Roosevelt Road, Section 2,
Taipei, Taiwan
Telephone: +886 2362 2984
Fax: +886 2362 0924

Regional Director: A. F. D. Scott
Editorial Directors: Wong Wai-Man
Mrs Fiona Lauder
Ms Rebecca Ng
Educational Marketing: S. Li
Academic & General Marketing: F. Tse
Design: Mrs W. Sin
Production: P. Ling
Finance/Systems: J. Lau

*Academic & Scholarly; Educational &
Textbooks; English as a Foreign Language;
History & Antiquarian; Literature & Criticism;
Politics & World Affairs; Reference Books,
Directories & Dictionaries*

New Titles: 387 (1995), 300 (1996)
No of Employees: 145

ISBNs, Imprints & Series:
0 19 584, 0 19 585

Parent Company:
Oxford University Press *(UK)*

Associated & Subsidiary Companies:
Hong Kong: Oxford Jardine Electronic
Publications Ltd; Sino Group Enterprises Ltd

Overseas Representation *(see §7.3)*:
Worldwide: Oxford University Press, Oxford,
UK

Book Trade Association Membership:
Anglo-Chinese Textbook Publishers
Organization, Hong Kong Educational
Publishers Association

2254

SUN YA PUBLICATIONS (HK) LTD
Room 1306, Eastern Centre, 1065 King's Road,
Quarry Bay
Telephone: +852 2562 0161
Fax: +852 2565 9951

**Managing Director, Editor-in-Chief &
Managing Editor:** Mrs Yim Ng Seen Ha
Sales Manager: C. C. Chan

Children's Books; Educational & Textbooks

New Titles: 114 (1995), 102 (1996)
No of Employees: 44
Annual Turnover: $4.18M

ISBNs, Imprints & Series:
962 08 Jumping Bean, Parent's Monthly, Sun
Ya Publications (HK) Ltd

Book Trade Association Membership: Hong
Kong Booksellers & Stationers Association Co
Ltd, Anglo-Chinese Textbook Publishers
Organization

INDIA

2255

**A.I.T.B.S. PUBLISHERS &
DISTRIBUTORS**
J-5/6 Krishan Nagar, Delhi 110 051
Telephone: +91 (Õ11) 246 0494
Fax: +91 (Õ11) 221 8401

Warehouse & Trade Enquiries:
F-8/23 Krishan Nagar, Delhi 110 051
Telephone: +91 (Õ11) 224 9313 & 224 3416
Fax: +91 (Õ11) 221 8401

Managing Partner: Virender Kumar Arya
Managers: Shri S. S. Mehta *(Accounts)*
B. C. Paul *(Sales)*

*Accountancy & Taxation; Computer Science;
Economics; Educational & Textbooks; English
as a Foreign Language; Industry, Business &
Management; Mathematics & Statistics;
Medical (incl. Self Help & Alternative
Medicine)*

New Titles: 20 (1995), 40 (1996)
No of Employees: 10

ISBNs, Imprints & Series:
81 7473, 81 85386

Parent Company:
All India Traveller Book Seller *(India)*

Book Trade Association Membership: Indian
PA, Indian Booksellers Association

2256

*ABHINAV PUBLICATIONS
E-37 Hauz Khas, New Delhi 110 016
Telephone: +91 (Õ11) 666 387

Managing Director: Shakti Kumar Malik
Managers: Ateev Malik
Abhinav Malik *(Deputy, Production)*

Academic & Scholarly; Agriculture;
Archaeology; Architecture & Design;
Economics; Environment & Development
Studies; Fashion & Costume; Fiction; Fine Art
& Art History; Gardening; Gender Studies;
History & Antiquarian; Illustrated & Fine
Editions; Literature & Criticism; Music;
Philosophy; Poetry; Psychology & Psychiatry;
Religion & Theology; Sociology &
Anthropology; Theatre, Drama & Dance

ISBNs, Imprints & Series: 81 7017

Overseas Representation *(see §7.3)*:
UK: Books from India Ltd, London
USA: South Asia Books, Columbia, MO

Book Trade Association Membership: Indian
PA, Federation of Indian Publishers

2257

ADVAITA ASHRAMA
5 Dehi Entally Road, Calcutta 700 014
Telephone: +91 (Õ33) 245 2383 & 244 0898
Fax: +91 (Õ33) 245 0050

Manager: Swami Bodhasarananda

Biography & Autobiography; Children's
Books; Philosophy; Religion & Theology

New Titles: 76 (1995), 100 (1996)
No of Employees: 35
Annual Turnover: £172,000

ISBNs, Imprints & Series:
81 7505, 81 85301

Overseas Representation *(see §7.3)*:
Argentina: Ramakrishna Ashrama, Buenos
   Aires
Canada: Vedanta Society of Toronto, Toronto,
   Ont
Fiji: Ramakrishna Mission, Nadi
France: Centre Vedantique Ramakrichna,
   Gretz
Mauritius: Ramakrishna Mission, Vacoas
Singapore: Ramakrishna Mission
Sri Lanka: Ramakrishna Mission, Colombo
Switzerland: Ramakrishna Vedanta Centre,
   Corsier/Geneva
UK: Ramakrishna Vedanta Centre, Bourne End
USA: Ramakrishna Vedanta Society, Boston,
   MA; Vedanta Society of Berkeley, Berkeley,
   CA; Vedanta Society of (S) California,
   Hollywood, CA; Ramakrishna Vivekananda
   Center, New York; Vedanta Society,
   Portland, OR; Vedanta Society, Providence,
   RI; Vedanta Society of St Louis, St Louis,
   MI; Vedanta Society of Northern California,
   San Francisco, CA; Vedanta Society of
   Sacramento, Carmichael, CA; Vedanta
   Society of Western Washington, Seattle,
   WA; Vivekananda Vedanta Society,
   Chicago, IL

2258

*AJANTA BOOKS INTERNATIONAL
1 UB Jawahar Nagar, Bunglow Road,
Delhi 110 007

Telephone: +91 (Õ11) 292 6182 & 725 8630
Fax: +91 (Õ11) 713 2908 & 721 2361

Also at:
2687 Outram Lane (Basement), SGTB Nagar,
Delhi 110 009

Educational Director: S. Balwant *(Exports,*
   Rights & Permissions)
Sales: Amit Atwal
Sneh Atwal

Academic & Scholarly; Accountancy &
Taxation; Agriculture; Archaeology;
Bibliography & Library Science; Biography &
Autobiography; Children's Books; Cinema,
Video, TV & Radio; Computer Science; Do-It-
Yourself; Economics; Educational &
Textbooks; English as a Foreign Language;
Fiction; Fine Art & Art History; Gender
Studies; Geography & Geology; Guide Books;
History & Antiquarian; Industry, Business &
Management; Languages & Linguistics;
Literature & Criticism; Mathematics &
Statistics; Medical (incl. Self Help &
Alternative Medicine); Military & War;
Philosophy; Poetry; Politics & World Affairs;
Reference Books, Directories & Dictionaries;
Religion & Theology; Sociology &
Anthropology; Sports & Games; Theatre,
Drama & Dance; Vocational Training &
Careers

ISBNs, Imprints & Series: 81 202

Associated & Subsidiary Companies:
India: Ajanta Publications; Ambe Books;
Takshica Hardbounds

Overseas Representation *(see §7.3)*:
UK: Books from India Ltd, London;
   Independent Publishing Co Ltd, London;
   Heffers Booksellers, Cambridge
USA: South Asia Books, Columbia, MO

Book Trade Association Membership:
Federation of Indian Publishers, Federation of
Educational Publishers, Delhi State
Booksellers & Publishers Association,
Federation of Publishers & Booksellers
Associations of India, Asian Association of
Scholarly Publishers

2259

AKSHAT PUBLICATIONS
Maitri Chaaya Apartments,
T-4 Usha Chambers, Ashok Vihar,
Central Market, Delhi 52
Telephone: +91 (Õ11) 711 4425, 724 0483 &
724 7234
Fax: +91 (Õ11) 725 4734

Branch Office:
B-250 Ashok Vihar-I, Delhi 110 052
Telephone: +91 (Õ11) 723 1293 & 713 2411
Fax: +91 (Õ11) 721 8836

Directors: Dr Roopa Vohra
Seema Bharti
President: K. L. Jain

Gender Studies; History & Antiquarian;
Psychology & Psychiatry; Religion & Theology

New Titles: 19 (1996)
No of Employees: 7

ISBNs, Imprints & Series: 81 85069

Overseas Representation *(see §7.3)*:
UK, USA & Canada: UBS Publishers'
   Distributors Ltd, New Delhi, India

Book Trade Association Membership:
Federation of Indian Publishers

2260

AMBAR PARKASHAN
888 East Park Road, Karol Bagh,
New Delhi 110 005
Telephone: +91 (Õ11) 752 5528
Fax: +91 (Õ11) 777 6058

Partners: Ved Bhushan *(Home & Export*
   Sales, Rights & Permissions, Executive &
   Finance)
Jaideep Aggarwal *(Production)*
Marketing Manager: Manish Aggarwal
Editor: Manish Aggarwal

Children's Books; Educational & Textbooks;
Reference Books, Directories & Dictionaries

ISBNs, Imprints & Series: 81 7289

Parent Company:
Pitambar Publishing Co Pvt Ltd *(India)*

Associated & Subsidiary Companies:
India: Bharat Publishing House; Piyush
Printers Publishers Pvt Ltd

Overseas Representation *(see §7.3)*:
Australia: Anita International, Surrey Hills
Sri Lanka: Jeya Agency (Pvt) Ltd, Colombo
UK & Western Europe: Books from India Ltd,
   London, UK
United Arab Emirates: Arora Book Centre,
   Sharjah, UAE

Book Trade Association Membership: The
Federation of Publishers & Booksellers
Associations, Federation of Indian Publishers,
The Federation of Educational Publishers of
India

2261

AMERIND PUBLISHING CO PVT LTD
Oxford Building, N-56 Connaught Circus,
New Delhi 110 001
Telephone: +91 (Õ11) 331 3584 & 331 4957
Fax: +91 (Õ11) 332 2639 & 371 3275
Email: oxford.publ@axcess.net.in

Warehouse:
Plot No. 6, Sector 27A, Industrial Area,
Faridabad
Telephone: +91 (Õ11) 825 5814
Fax: +91 (Õ11) 332 2639

Director: Gulab Primlani
Manager: Veeraraghavan

Academic & Scholarly; Agriculture; Biology &
Zoology; Scientific & Technical

New Titles: 8 (1995), 10 (1996)
No of Employees: 8
Annual Turnover: $100,000

Associated & Subsidiary Companies:
USA: Science Publishers Inc

Overseas Representation *(see §7.3):*
USA: Science Publishers Inc, Lebanon, NH

Book Trade Association Membership:
Federation of Indian Publishers

2262 ▬

ANANDA PUBLISHERS PVT LTD
45 Beniatola Lane, Calcutta 700 009
Telephone: +91 (Õ33) 241 4352 & 241 3417
Fax: +91 (Õ33) 225 3240 & 225 3241

Manager: D. N. Basu

*Academic & Scholarly; Biography &
Autobiography; Children's Books; Computer
Science; Cookery, Wines & Spirits; Economics;
Fiction; Gardening; History & Antiquarian;
Humour; Languages & Linguistics; Literature
& Criticism; Philosophy; Poetry; Reference
Books, Directories & Dictionaries; Sports &
Games; Theatre, Drama & Dance; Travel &
Topography*

New Titles: 93 (1995), 100 (1996)

ISBNs, Imprints & Series:
81 7066, 81 7215

Book Trade Association Membership: The
Federation of Indian Publishers New Delhi,
Publishers & Booksellers Association of
Bengal Calcutta, Publishers & Booksellers
Guild Calcutta

2263 ▬

ARUN PUBLISHING HOUSE PVT LTD
SCO 49–51, Sector 17C, Post Box 52,
Chandigarh 160 017
Telephone: +91 (Õ172) 702 189 & 702 318
Fax: +91 (Õ172) 702 189

Directors: S. R. Sharma *(General
Administration)*
Nalin Sharma *(Sales, Accounts)*
Anil Sharma *(Managing, Production, Export,
Rights & Permissions)*

*Academic & Scholarly; Bibliography &
Library Science; Computer Science;
Educational & Textbooks; Environment &
Development Studies; Fiction; Gender Studies;
Health & Beauty; Industry, Business &
Management; Literature & Criticism; Magic &
the Occult; Medical (incl. Self Help &
Alternative Medicine); Reference Books,
Directories & Dictionaries; Religion &
Theology; Scientific & Technical*

New Titles: 16 (1995), 24 (1996)
No of Employees: 6
Annual Turnover: $25,000

ISBNs, Imprints & Series: 81 85212

Parent Company:
New Era Book Agency *(India)*

Book Trade Association Membership: The
Federation of Publishers & Booksellers of
India, New Delhi, All India Hindi Publishers'
Association, Delhi

2264 ▬

ASHISH PUBLISHING HOUSE
8/81 Punjabi Bagh, New Delhi 110 026
Telephone: +91 (Õ11) 510 0581, 541 0924, 328
5807 & 327 4050 (Showroom)
Fax: +91 (Õ11) 328 5585

Trade Enquiries & Orders:
5 Ansari Road, Darya Ganj, New Delhi 110 002
Telephone: +91 (Õ11) 327 4050 & 328 5807
Fax: +91 (Õ11) 328 5585

Editorial: Shashi Bhushan Nangia *(Rights &
Permissions, Export Sales)*
Manager: Gopal Sharma *(Home Sales, Trade)*

*Academic & Scholarly; Accountancy &
Taxation; Agriculture; Aviation; Bibliography
& Library Science; Biography &
Autobiography; Biology & Zoology;
Chemistry; Computer Science; Crime;
Economics; Educational & Textbooks;
Environment & Development Studies; Fiction;
Gender Studies; Geography & Geology;
Health & Beauty; History & Antiquarian;
Industry, Business & Management; Languages
& Linguistics; Law; Literature & Criticism;
Music; Natural History; Philosophy; Politics &
World Affairs; Psychology & Psychiatry;
Religion & Theology; Scientific & Technical;
Sociology & Anthropology; Veterinary Science*

New Titles: 120 (1995), 150 (1996)
No of Employees: 20

ISBNs, Imprints & Series: 81 7024

Book Trade Association Membership:
Federation of Indian Publishers, Delhi State
Booksellers & Publishers Association,
Chemicals & Allied Products Export
Promotion Council (Books Division)

2265 ▬

ASIAN EDUCATIONAL SERVICES
C-2/15, SDA, New Delhi 110 016
Telephone: +91 (Õ11) 685 1586, 660 187 &
668 594
Fax: +91 (Õ11) 685 2805

Branch Office:
5 Sripuram First Street, Madras 600 014
Telephone: +91 (Õ44) 826 5040 & 613 980
Fax: +91 (Õ44) 826 5040

Warehouse:
17 Shahpur Jat, New Delhi 110 016

Trade Enquiries & Orders:
31 Hauz Khas Village, New Delhi 16

Managing Director: Jagdish Jetley
Branch Managers: W. J. Suresh *(Madras)*
Gautam Jetley *(Bombay)*
Publicity: Mrs Saroj Jetley
Rights & Permissions: Gaurav Jetley
Home Sales: S. N. Ghosal

*Archaeology; Biography & Autobiography;
History & Antiquarian; Languages &
Linguistics; Military & War; Music; Natural
History; Philosophy; Reference Books,
Directories & Dictionaries; Religion &
Theology; Sociology & Anthropology; Travel
& Topography*

New Titles: 100 (1995), 120 (1996)
No of Employees: 20
Annual Turnover: £220,000

ISBNs, Imprints & Series: 81 206

Associated & Subsidiary Companies:
India: Antiquarian Publication & Reprographic
Services Pvt Ltd

Overseas Representation *(see §7.3):*
Canada: Laurier Books Ltd, Ottawa, Ont
France: Editions Kailash, Paris
Sri Lanka: Lake House Bookshop, Colombo
UK: Jeremy Tenniswood, Aldershot; Bay
Foreign Language Books, Romney Marsh;
Books from India Ltd, London
USA: South Asia Books, Columbia, MO;
French & European Publications, New York;
Hippocrene Books Inc, New York

Book Trade Association Membership:
Federation of Indian Publishers, Federation of
Publishers' & Booksellers' Associations in
India

2266 ▬

ASIAN PUBLISHERS
3911 Roshanpura, Nai Sarak, Delhi 110 006
Telephone: +91 (Õ11) 291 5650 & 294 1531
Fax: +91 (Õ11) 291 5650

Managers: Anil Mehta *(Business)*
Salil Mehta *(Office)*

*Architecture & Design; Biology & Zoology;
Chemistry; Computer Science; Educational &
Textbooks; Electronic (Educational);
Engineering; Guide Books; Industry, Business
& Management; Mathematics & Statistics;
Physics; Reference Books, Directories &
Dictionaries; Scientific & Technical; Travel &
Topography; Vocational Training & Careers*

New Titles: 30 (1995), 45 (1996)
No of Employees: 8

ISBNs, Imprints & Series:
81 7317, 81 7318

Parent Company:
New Asian Publishers *(India)*

Associated & Subsidiary Companies:
India: New Asian Publishers (Export Division)

2267 ▬

ASSOCIATED PUBLISHING HOUSE
E-22 Preet Vihar, Vikas Marg,
New Delhi 110 092
Telephone: +91 (Õ11) 242 9392

Sales:
C-113 Preet Vihar, Vikas Marg,
New Delhi 110 092
Telephone: +91 (Õ11) 242 9392

Publisher: R. K. Paul
Directors: Mrs Sharda Paul *(Sales & Publicity)*
Ashok Paul *(Editorial)*

*Academic & Scholarly; Agriculture; Biography
& Autobiography; Economics; History &
Antiquarian; Literature & Criticism;
Philosophy; Politics & World Affairs; Religion*

& Theology; Sociology & Anthropology; Travel & Topography

New Titles: 8 (1995), 10 (1996)

ISBNs, Imprints & Series: 81 7045

Overseas Representation *(see §7.3)*:
UK: UBS Publishers Distributors Ltd, Harrow & London

2268 ▬

ASSOCIATION OF INDIAN UNIVERSITIES
AIU House, 16 Kotla Marg, New Delhi 110 002
Telephone: +91 (0̃11) 323 0159
Fax: +91 (0̃11) 323 6105

Sales & Publication: B. M. Dureja *(Deputy Secretary)*

Academic & Scholarly

New Titles: 20 (1995), 20 (1996)

2269 ▬

ATLANTIC PUBLISHERS & DISTRIBUTORS
4346/4C, Ansari Road, Darya Ganj,
New Delhi 110 002
Telephone: +91 (0̃11) 328 5873 & 327 3880
Fax: +91 (0̃11) 328 5873

Warehouse:
B-2, Vishal Enclave, New Delhi 110 027
Telephone: +91 (0̃11) 541 3460 & 542 9987

Directors: Manish Kumar *(Production & Sales)*
K. R. Gupta *(Managing)*

Academic & Scholarly; Accountancy & Taxation; Agriculture; Bibliography & Library Science; Biology & Zoology; Economics; Educational & Textbooks; English as a Foreign Language; Fiction; History & Antiquarian; Industry, Business & Management; Languages & Linguistics; Law; Literature & Criticism; Mathematics & Statistics; Military & War; Natural History; Philosophy; Politics & World Affairs; Psychology & Psychiatry; Reference Books, Directories & Dictionaries; Religion & Theology; Sociology & Anthropology

New Titles: 60 (1995), 85 (1996)
No of Employees: 95

Book Trade Association Membership: Delhi Publishers & Booksellers Association

---

2270 ▬

SRI AUROBINDO ASHRAM PUBLICATION DEPARTMENT
Sri Aurobindo Ashram, Pondicherry 605 002
Telephone: +91 (0̃413) 34445
Fax: +91 (0̃413) 38132 (Attn SABDA)

Trade Enquiries & Orders:
SABDA, as above
Telephone: +91 (0̃413) 34980 & 34072
Fax: +91 (0̃413) 38132

Trustees: Harikant Patel *(Publication Department)*

Manoj Das Gupta *(Rights & Permissions)*
Managers: Ranganath *(Production)*
Mira Gupta *(Sales)*

Literature & Criticism; Philosophy; Poetry; Politics & World Affairs; Psychology & Psychiatry; Religion & Theology

New Titles: 50 (1995), 50 (1996)
No of Employees: 15
Annual Turnover: $2M

ISBNs, Imprints & Series: 81 7058

Overseas Representation *(see §7.3)*:
Canada: Centre Sri Aurobindo, Montreal
France: Adi Shakti, Paris
Germany: Hinder & Deelmann, Gladenbach
UK: Batstone Books, Malmesbury
USA: Sri Aurobindo Association, Berkeley, CA

Book Trade Association Membership: Indian PA, Indian Booksellers Association

---

2271 ▬

K. P. BAGCHI & CO
286 B B Ganguli Street, Calcutta 700 012
Telephone: +91 (0̃33) 26 7474 & 26 9496
Fax: +91 (0̃33) 248 2973

Warehouse & Despatch:
Kusum Book Agency, Kalyan Nagar,
PO Pansila, Dist North 24-Parganas, W Bengal
Telephone: +91 (0̃33) 553 2225

Partners: P. K. Bagchi *(Educational Publisher)*
K. K. Bagchi

Academic & Scholarly

New Titles: 15 (1995), 20 (1996)
No of Employees: 12
Annual Turnover: $90,000

ISBNs, Imprints & Series: 81 7074

Overseas Representation *(see §7.3)*:
Germany: Broner & Daentler, Eichstatt
UK: Heffers Booksellers, Cambridge
USA: South Asia Books, Columbia, MO

Book Trade Association Membership:
Federation of Indian Publishers, Federation of Publishers & Booksellers Associations of India

---

2272 ▬

BAHRI PUBLICATIONS
997a Street No 9, PO Box 4453, Gobindpuri,
Kalkaji, New Delhi 110 019
Telephone: +91 (0̃11) 644 8606 & 644 5710
Fax: +91 (0̃11) 641 6116

Managing Director: Ujjal Singh Bahri

Academic & Scholarly; English as a Foreign Language; Fiction; History & Antiquarian; Languages & Linguistics; Literature & Criticism; Poetry; Politics & World Affairs; Reference Books, Directories & Dictionaries; Religion & Theology; Sociology & Anthropology

New Titles: 6 (1995), 12 (1996)
No of Employees: 2
Annual Turnover: $0.4M

ISBNs, Imprints & Series:
81 7034 Language Forum Monograph Series (LSMF), Series in Indian Languages and Linguistics (SILL), Series in Indian Studies in Theoretical and Applied Linguistics (SISTAL), Series in Semiotics and Linguistics, Series in Semiotics and Literature

Associated & Subsidiary Companies:
India: Bahri Books & Periodicals

Overseas Representation *(see §7.3)*:
Europe & USA: Lincom Europe, Munich, Germany

Book Trade Association Membership:
Federation of Publishers & Booksellers Associations in India

2273 ▬

BHARAT LAW HOUSE PVT LTD
4779/23 Ansari Road, Darya Ganj,
New Delhi 110 002
Telephone: +91 (0̃11) 327 8282
Fax: +91 (0̃11) 327 5884

Also at:
222 Tarun Enclave, Pitampura, Delhi 110 034
Telephone: +91 (0̃11) 701 6884 & 702 5884
Fax: +91 (0̃11) 701 2323

Directors: D. C. Puliani
Ashok Puliani
Ravi Puliani
Mahesh Puliani

Law; Reference Books, Directories & Dictionaries

New Titles: 36 (1995), 40 (1996)

Associated & Subsidiary Companies:
India: Bharat Law House; Bharat Publishing House; BLH Publishers' Distributors Pvt Ltd

Book Trade Association Membership: Delhi State Booksellers' & Publishers' Association

---

2274 ▬

BHARAT PUBLISHING HOUSE
123 Durga Chambers,
1333 Desh Bandhu Gupta Road, Karol Bagh,
New Delhi 110 005
Telephone: +91 (0̃11) 575 7081
Fax: +91 (0̃11) 777 6058

Partner: Manish Aggarwal

Children's Books; Educational & Textbooks; Reference Books, Directories & Dictionaries

New Titles: 10 (1995), 10 (1996)
No of Employees: 5
Annual Turnover: $60,000

ISBNs, Imprints & Series: 81 86378

Parent Company:
Pitambar Publishing Co P. Ltd *(India)*

Associated & Subsidiary Companies:
India: Ambar Parkashan

Book Trade Association Membership:
Federation of Indian Publishers, New Delhi

2275 ▬▬▬▬▬▬▬▬▬▬▬▬▬▬▬▬

BISHEN SINGH MAHENDRA PAL SINGH
23a Connaught Place, PO Box 137, Dehra Dun, 248 001
Telephone: +91 (Õ135) 655748
Fax: +91 (Õ135) 680107
Email: bsmpsisnet@axcessnet.in

Storage:
14 Old Connaught Place,
Dehra Dun 248 001 (UP)

Managing Partner: Gajendra Singh Gahlot

Academic & Scholarly; Agriculture; Biology & Zoology; Environment & Development Studies; Gardening; Natural History; Scientific & Technical

New Titles: 26 (1995), 40 (1996)
No of Employees: 10

ISBNs, Imprints & Series: 81 211

Overseas Representation *(see §7.3):*
Germany: Sven Koltz, Koenigstein

Book Trade Association Membership:
Federation of Indian Publishers, Federation of Publishers & Booksellers Associations of India, CAPEXIL, Indian Booksellers Association

2276 ▬▬▬▬▬▬▬▬▬▬▬▬▬▬▬▬

BRIGHT CAREERS INSTITUTE
1525 Nai Sarak, Delhi 110 006
Telephone: +91 (Õ11) 328 2227
Fax: +91 (Õ11) 326 9227

Corporate Office:
Bright House, 2767 Darya Ganj,
New Delhi 110 002
Telephone: +91 (Õ11) 327 6554 & 3282226
Fax: +91 (Õ11) 326 9227

Managing Partner: Pritam Singh *(Printer & Publisher)*
Managing Editor: D. S. Phull
Director: Ms Davinder Kaur

Academic & Scholarly; Accountancy & Taxation; Biology & Zoology; Chemistry; Guide Books; Reference Books, Directories & Dictionaries

New Titles: 52 (1995), 75 (1996)
No of Employees: 50
Annual Turnover: £600,000

ISBNs, Imprints & Series: 81 7122

Associated & Subsidiary Companies:
India: Bright Careers Ltd; Bright Distributing Co; Bright Media Impex (P) Ltd; C. R. Competition Refresher (P) Ltd; J. S. R. Junior Science Refresher (P) Ltd

Book Trade Association Membership:
Federation of Indian Publishers, Federation of

Publishers & Booksellers Associations of India, Indian Newspaper Society, Audit Bureau of Circulation

2277 ▬▬▬▬▬▬▬▬▬▬▬▬▬▬▬▬

CHILDREN'S BOOK TRUST
Nehru House, 4 Bahadur Shah Zafar Marg,
New Delhi 110 002
Telephone: +91 (Õ11) 331 6970/4
Fax: +91 (Õ11) 372 1090

Managers: Ravi Shankar *(General)*
H. R. Khurana *(Sales)*
Editor: G. C. Kurup

Children's Books

New Titles: 25 (1995), 35 (1996)

ISBNs, Imprints & Series: 81 7011

Book Trade Association Membership: Indian PA, Indian Booksellers Association

2278 ▬▬▬▬▬▬▬▬▬▬▬▬▬▬▬▬

CHOWKHAMBA SANSKRIT SERIES OFFICE
K 37/99 Gopal Mandir Lane, PO Box 1008,
Varanasi 221 001
Telephone: +91 (Õ542) 333458

Partner: Brajmohan Das Gupta

Archaeology; Biology & Zoology; Economics; Fine Art & Art History; History & Antiquarian; Medical (incl. Self Help & Alternative Medicine); Music; Philosophy; Physics; Poetry; Politics & World Affairs; Psychology & Psychiatry; Reference Books, Directories & Dictionaries; Religion & Theology; Veterinary Science

New Titles: 15 (1995), 20 (1996)
No of Employees: 5

Book Trade Association Membership:
Federation of Publishers & Booksellers Association in India

2279 ▬▬▬▬▬▬▬▬▬▬▬▬▬▬▬▬

CHRONICLE PUBLICATIONS (P) LTD
208 Shivlok House-I,
Karampura Commercial Complex,
New Delhi 110 015
Telephone: +91 (Õ11) 541 9131
Fax: +91 (Õ11) 545 1177

Editor & Managing Director: N. N. Ojha
Managers: Shiv Dutt *(General)*
K. L. Joseph *(General)*
Amrendra Kumar *(Production)*
S. Rehman *(Finance)*

Academic & Scholarly; Biology & Zoology; Educational & Textbooks; Geography & Geology; Guide Books; Industry, Business & Management; Mathematics & Statistics; Physics; Scientific & Technical; Sociology & Anthropology; Vocational Training & Careers

New Titles: 25 (1995), 30 (1996)
No of Employees: 60
Annual Turnover: $430,000

ISBNs, Imprints & Series:
81 7368 Chronicle Books, Chronicle Group of Publications

Book Trade Association Membership: Indian Newspaper Society

2280 ▬▬▬▬▬▬▬▬▬▬▬▬▬▬▬▬

CHUGH PUBLICATIONS
2 Strachey Road, Civil Lines,
Allahabad 211 001
Telephone: +91 (Õ532) 623561

Also at:
20 Mahatma Gandhi Marg, Civil Lines,
Allahabad
Telephone: +91 (Õ532) 623561

Director: Ramesh Chugh
Marketing: Ritu Chugh
Sales: Rajiv Chugh

Accountancy & Taxation; Agriculture; Bibliography & Library Science; Biography & Autobiography; Biology & Zoology; Economics; Educational & Textbooks; Environment & Development Studies; Geography & Geology; History & Antiquarian; Industry, Business & Management; Law; Military & War; Religion & Theology; Sociology & Anthropology; Transport; Vocational Training & Careers

New Titles: 17 (1995), 15 (1996)
No of Employees: 7

ISBNs, Imprints & Series:
81 85076, 81 85613

Book Trade Association Membership: Indian PA

2281 ▬▬▬▬▬▬▬▬▬▬▬▬▬▬▬▬

CLARION BOOKS
18–19 Dilshad Garden, G.T. Road,
Delhi 110 095
Telephone: +91 (Õ11) 229 7792 & 229 7793
Fax: +91 (Õ11) 228 2332

Directors: D. N. Malhotra *(Managing)*
Shekhar Malhotra

Archaeology; Computer Science; Environment & Development Studies; History & Antiquarian; Illustrated & Fine Editions; Philosophy; Poetry; Religion & Theology; Theatre, Drama & Dance

New Titles: 8 (1995), 12 (1996)
No of Employees: 20

ISBNs, Imprints & Series: 81 85120

Parent Company:
Hind Pocket Books (P) Ltd *(India)*

Book Trade Association Membership:
Federation of Indian Publishers, Indian PA

2282 ▬▬▬▬▬▬▬▬▬▬▬▬▬▬▬▬

*CONCEPT PUBLISHING CO
A/15–16 Commercial Block, Mohan Garden,
New Delhi 110 059

Telephone: +91 (Õ11) 555 4042 & 550 4042
Fax: +91 (Õ11) 559 8898

Showroom:
4788/23 Ansari Road, Daryaganj,
New Delhi 110 002
Telephone: +91 (Õ11) 327 2187
Fax: +91 (Õ11) 559 8898

Chief Executive: Ashok Kumar Mittal
Head of Sales: Arvind Kumar Mittal

*Academic & Scholarly; Agriculture;
Bibliography & Library Science; Economics;
Gender Studies; Geography & Geology;
Medical (incl. Self Help & Alternative
Medicine); Politics & World Affairs;
Psychology & Psychiatry; Reference Books,
Directories & Dictionaries; Sociology &
Anthropology*

ISBNs, Imprints & Series: 81 7022

Associated & Subsidiary Companies:
USA: South Asia Books

Overseas Representation *(see §7.3):*
North America: South Asia Books, Columbia,
MO, USA

Book Trade Association Membership:
Federation of Indian Publishers, International
Association of Scholarly Publishers, Delhi
State Booksellers & Publishers Association

2283

COSMO PUBLICATIONS
24-B Ansari Road, Daryaganj,
New Delhi 110 002
Telephone: +91 (Õ11) 327 8779 & 328 0455
Fax: +91 (Õ11) 327 4597

Editorial, Exports & Imports:
4 W/16, Patel Nagar, New Delhi 110 008
Telephone: +91 (Õ11) 572 4395 & 578 6269
Fax: +91 (Õ11) 327 4597

Directors: Mrs Rani Kapoor *(Managing)*
Sunil Kapoor *(Home Sales, Rights &
Permissions)*
Manager: Subodh Kapoor *(Editorial, New
Projects, Export Sales)*

*Academic & Scholarly; Agriculture; Animal
Care & Breeding; Archaeology; Architecture
& Design; Bibliography & Library Science;
Biology & Zoology; Crime; Economics;
Educational & Textbooks; English as a Foreign
Language; Fine Art & Art History; Gender
Studies; Geography & Geology; History &
Antiquarian; Illustrated & Fine Editions;
Languages & Linguistics; Literature &
Criticism; Music; Natural History;
Philosophy; Poetry; Politics & World Affairs;
Psychology & Psychiatry; Reference Books,
Directories & Dictionaries; Religion &
Theology; Scientific & Technical; Sociology &
Anthropology; Veterinary Science*

New Titles: 76 (1995), 125 (1996)
No of Employees: 24

ISBNs, Imprints & Series:
81 7020 Cosmo Dictionaries, Cosmo Key
Facts, Falcon Books, Siddhi Books

Parent Company:
Genesis Publishing Pvt Ltd *(India)*

Associated & Subsidiary Companies:
India: Cosmopolitan Book House

Overseas Representation *(see §7.3):*
UK: UBS Publishers Distributors Ltd, Harrow
& London

Book Trade Association Membership:
Federation of Indian Publishers, Federation of
Booksellers & Publishers Associations of India,
Delhi State Booksellers & Publishers
Association

2284

*D. C. BOOKS AND CURRENT BOOKS
Kottayam, Kerala 686 001
Telephone: +91 (Õ481) 563 114
Fax: +91 (Õ481) 564 758

Co-Publishing:
Kairali Childrens Book Trust & Kairali
Mudralayam, Kottayam, Kerala 686 001
Telephone: +91 (Õ481) 560 018 & 563 226
Fax: +91 (Õ481) 564 758

Managers: V. R. Radhakrishnan Nair *(Home
& Export Sales)*
G. Sreekumar *(Rights & Permissions)*

*Fine Art & Art History; Gardening; Humour;
Illustrated & Fine Editions; Politics & World
Affairs; Religion & Theology; Sports & Games;
Travel & Topography*

ISBNs, Imprints & Series: 81 7130

Book Trade Association Membership:
Kerala Publishers & Booksellers Association,
Federation of Indian Publishers

2285

D. K. PRINTWORLD (P) LTD
Sri Kunj, F-52 Bali Nagar, New Delhi 110 015
Telephone: +91 (Õ11) 545 3975
Fax: +91 (Õ11) 546 5926

Directors: Susheel Kumar Mittal
Lata Mittal

*Academic & Scholarly; Archaeology; Fine Art
& Art History; History & Antiquarian;
Philosophy; Reference Books, Directories &
Dictionaries; Theatre, Drama & Dance*

New Titles: 15 (1995), 20 (1996)
No of Employees: 10
Annual Turnover: $1M

ISBNs, Imprints & Series: 81 246

Parent Company:
D. K. Agencies (P) Ltd *(India)*

Associated & Subsidiary Companies:
India: Decent Books

Overseas Representation *(see §7.3):*
Australia: Navigator Books Pty Ltd, Nerang,
Qld
USA: South Asia Books, Columbia, MO

Book Trade Association Membership:
Federation of Indian Publishers, New Delhi,
Delhi State Booksellers' & Publishers'
Association, New Delhi

2286

DAYA PUBLISHING HOUSE
1123/74 Deva Ram Park, Tri Nagar,
Delhi 110 035
Telephone: +91 (Õ11) 722 0593 & 723 1826
Fax: +91 (Õ11) 719 8902

Director: Anil Mittal

*Agriculture; Biology & Zoology; Environment
& Development Studies*

New Titles: 12 (1995), 20 (1996)
No of Employees: 3
Annual Turnover: £30,000

ISBNs, Imprints & Series: 81 7035

Book Trade Association Membership: Delhi
State Booksellers & Publishers Association,
Federation of Indian Publishers

2287

*DEEP & DEEP PUBLICATIONS
F-159 Sawhney Apartments, Rajouri Garden,
New Delhi 110 027
Telephone: +91 (Õ11) 543 5369 & 544 0916
Fax: +91 (Õ11) 544 0916

Partners: G. S. Bhatia
K. D. S. Bhatia
H. S. Bhatia

*Academic & Scholarly; Agriculture; Biography
& Autobiography; Economics; Educational &
Textbooks; English as a Foreign Language;
Gender Studies; History & Antiquarian;
Industry, Business & Management; Law;
Mathematics & Statistics; Military & War;
Politics & World Affairs*

ISBNs, Imprints & Series: 81 7100

Book Trade Association Membership: Delhi
State Book Sellers & Publishers Association,
Federation of Publishers & Booksellers
Associations in India

2288

**DK PUBLISHERS DISTRIBUTORS
(PVT) LTD**
A-6, Nimri Community Centre, Ashok Vihar,
Phase-IV, Delhi 110 052
Telephone: +91 (Õ11) 743 0113
Fax: +91 (Õ11) 326 4368

Sales:
1 Ansari Road, Darya Ganj, New Delhi 2
Telephone: +91 (Õ11) 327 8368
Fax: +91 (Õ11) 713 8265

Directors: Parmil Mittal *(Home Sales)*
Pradeep Mittal *(Home Sales)*
Praveen Mittal *(Editorial, Publicity, Accounts,
Export Orders & Printing)*

*Academic & Scholarly; Agriculture;
Archaeology; Architecture & Design;
Bibliography & Library Science; Biography &*

Autobiography; Crime; Economics; Fashion & Costume; Fiction; Fine Art & Art History; Gender Studies; Geography & Geology; Health & Beauty; History & Antiquarian; Languages & Linguistics; Law; Literature & Criticism; Medical (incl. Self Help & Alternative Medicine); Military & War; Music; Natural History; Philosophy; Poetry; Politics & World Affairs; Psychology & Psychiatry; Reference Books, Directories & Dictionaries; Religion & Theology; Sociology & Anthropology; Theatre, Drama & Dance

New Titles: 125 (1995), 150 (1996)
No of Employees: 25
Annual Turnover: £0.5M

ISBNs, Imprints & Series:
81 7018 B R Publishing Corporation

Associated & Subsidiary Companies:
India: B R Publishing Corporation; Books for All; Low Price Publications

Overseas Representation *(see §7.3):*
USA: South Asia Books, Columbia, MO

2289

DOABA HOUSE
1688 Nai Sarak, Delhi 110 006
Telephone: +91 (011) 327 4669
Fax: +91 (011) 696 8735

Educational & Textbooks; English as a Foreign Language; Languages & Linguistics; Literature & Criticism

New Titles: 20 (1995), 20 (1996)
No of Employees: 6

ISBNs, Imprints & Series: 81 85173

Associated & Subsidiary Companies:
India: Creative Career Publishers

Book Trade Association Membership: The Federation of Publishers & Booksellers Associations of India

---

2290

EASTERN BOOK COMPANY
34 Lalbagh, Lucknow, Uttar Pradesh 226 001
Telephone: +91 (0522) 224 328 & 226 517
Fax: +91 (0522) 224 328

Directors: P. L. Malik *(Sales – Inland & Rights)*
Vijay Malik *(Export Division)*
C. L. Malik *(Distribution)*
Kamal Malik *(Production)*
Chief Editor: Surendra Malik
Senior Manager: Sumain Malik
   (Phototypesetting & Computer Division)

Law; Reference Books, Directories & Dictionaries

New Titles: 45 (1995), 50 (1996)
No of Employees: 30

ISBNs, Imprints & Series: 81 7012

Associated & Subsidiary Companies:
India: Current Legal Publications; Eastern Book Co (Sales); Eastern Book Co Pvt Ltd;

Eastern Book Publishing Co; EBC Publishing Pvt Ltd; Law Times Press; Manav Law House

Overseas Representation *(see §7.3):*
Bangladesh: Anupam Gyan Bhandar, Dhaka
Japan: Kokusai Shobo, Japan
Malaysia: Malayan Law Journal Sdn Bhd, Selangor
Nepal: Nepal Law Book Co, Kathmandu
Nigeria: The Law Book Vendors, Lagos
Pakistan: Pakistan Law House, Karachi
Singapore: Reed International (Singapore) Pte Ltd
Sri Lanka: M. D. Gunasena & Co Ltd, Colombo
Thailand: Bookseller Co Ltd, Bangkok
Trinidad & Tobago: Gurley & Associates Ltd, Port of Spain, Trinidad
UK: Legal Library Services Ltd, Yeovil; Wildy & Sons Ltd, London; Cavendish Publishing Ltd, London
USA: State Mutual Book & Periodical Service Ltd, New York

Book Trade Association Membership: Indian PA, Indian Booksellers Association

---

2291

EASTERN LAW HOUSE PVT LTD
54 Ganesh Chunder Avenue, Calcutta 700 013
Telephone: +91 (033) 274 989 & 272 301
Fax: +91 (033) 260 491

Delhi Sales Branch:
36 Netaji Subhash Marg, Daryaganj, New Delhi 110 002
Telephone: +91 (011) 327 9982
Fax: +91 (011) 941 111

Managers: Asok De
S. Chakraborti

Accountancy & Taxation; Law; Politics & World Affairs; Reference Books, Directories & Dictionaries

New Titles: 26 (1995), 31 (1996)
No of Employees: 26

Overseas Representation *(see §7.3):*
Singapore: Malayan Law Journal Pte Ltd

Book Trade Association Membership: The Federation of Publishers' & Booksellers' Associations of India, The Federation of Indian Publishers

---

2292

FERTILISER DEVELOPMENT AND CONSULTATION ORGANISATION
204 Bhanot Corner, 1–2 Pamposh Enclave, New Delhi 110 048
Telephone: +91 (011) 641 7801
Fax: +91 (011) 643 5850

Director: Dr H. L. S. Tandon

Agriculture; Gardening; Guide Books; Reference Books, Directories & Dictionaries; Scientific & Technical

New Titles: 5 (1995), 5 (1996)
No of Employees: 2

ISBNs, Imprints & Series: 81 85116

Book Trade Association Membership: The Federation of Publishers & Booksellers Associations of India

---

2293

GALGOTIA BOOKSOURCE PVT LTD
PO Box 141, 3B-12, Uttri Marg, Rajinder Nagar, New Delhi 110 060
Telephone: +91 (011) 575 2506
Fax: +91 (011) 575 2506

Managing Director: Neeraj Galgotia

Chemistry; Computer Science; Educational & Textbooks; Electronic (Educational); Electronic (Professional & Academic); Engineering; Reference Books, Directories & Dictionaries; Scientific & Technical; Vocational Training & Careers

Book Trade Association Membership: Delhi State Booksellers & Publishers Association

---

2294

GALGOTIA PUBLICATIONS (PVT) LTD
5 Ansari Road, Darya Ganj, New Delhi 110 002
Telephone: +91 (011) 326 3334 & 328 8134
Fax: +91 (011) 328 1909

Also at:
G-64, Mansarover Business Complex, Noida (UP)

Managing Director: Suneel Galgotia

Computer Science; Engineering; Guide Books; Scientific & Technical

Parent Company:
E. D. Galgotia & Sons *(India)*

Book Trade Association Membership:
Federation of Publishers & Booksellers Association in India

2295

GENERAL BOOK DEPOT
1691 Nai Sarak, PO Box 1220, Delhi 110 006
Telephone: +91 (011) 326 3695
Fax: +91 (011) 371 2710 & 294 0861

Publishing Division:
Goyl SaaB Publishers & Distributors, 86 University Block, Jawahar Nagar, Delhi 110 007
Telephone: +91 (011) 291 2186
Fax: +91 (011) 371 2710 & 294 0861

Directors: Kaushal Goyal
Ashwani Goyal
Head Foreign Language Dept: Mrs Anita Kolb-Goyal
Managers: Nikunj Gupta *(Sales)*
Rajesh Sood *(Accounts)*
Vijay Bansal *(Production)*

Children's Books; Educational & Textbooks; English as a Foreign Language; Guide Books; Languages & Linguistics; Reference Books, Directories & Dictionaries

New Titles: 25 (1995), 20 (1996)
No of Employees: 26
Annual Turnover: $250,000

ISBNs, Imprints & Series:
81 85288 Goyl SaaB

Book Trade Association Membership: The
Federation of Indian Publishers, The Federation
of Educational Publishers in India, Delhi State
Booksellers & Publishers Association,
Federation of Career & Competition Book
Publishers, Nai Sarak Booksellers & Publishers
Association

2296 ▬▬▬▬▬▬▬

**GOYL SAAB PUBLISHERS &
DISTRIBUTORS**
86 University Block, Jawahar Nagar,
Delhi 110 007
Telephone: +91 (Ō11) 291 2186 & 291 8362
Fax: +91 (Ō11) 371 2710 & 294 0861

Distributors:
General Book Depot, 1691 Nai Sarak,
PO Box 1220, Delhi 110 006
Telephone: +91 (Ō11) 326 3695
Fax: +91 (Ō11) 371 2710 & 294 0861

Directors: Ashwani Goyal
Kaushal Goyal
Head Foreign Language Dept: Mrs Anita
Kolb-Goyal
Managers: Nikunj Gupta *(Sales)*
Rajesh Sood *(Accounts)*
Vijay Bansal *(Production)*

*Children's Books; Educational & Textbooks;
English as a Foreign Language; Guide Books;
Languages & Linguistics; Reference Books,
Directories & Dictionaries*

New Titles: 25 (1995), 20 (1996)
No of Employees: 26
Annual Turnover: $200,000

ISBNs, Imprints & Series: 81 85288

Parent Company:
General Book Depot *(India)*

2297 ▬▬▬▬▬▬▬

GYAN BOOKS (P) LTD
5 Ansari Road, New Delhi 110 002
Telephone: +91 (Ō11) 326 1060 & 328 2060
Fax: +91 (Ō11) 328 5914

Warehouse:
C-30 Satyawati Colony,
Near Laxmi Bai College, Phase III, Delhi

Managing Director: B. P. Garg
Sales Manager: R. P. Yadav
Editors: S. K. Sharma
Amit Garg

*Academic & Scholarly; Agriculture;
Archaeology; Bibliography & Library Science;
Biography & Autobiography; Cinema, Video,
TV & Radio; Economics; Environment &
Development Studies; Gender Studies;
Geography & Geology; History &
Antiquarian; Industry, Business &
Management; Languages & Linguistics; Law;
Music; Natural History; Philosophy; Politics &*

*World Affairs; Religion & Theology; Sociology
& Anthropology; Sports & Games; Theatre,
Drama & Dance*

New Titles: 46 (1995), 53 (1996)
No of Employees: 23
Annual Turnover: $200,000

ISBNs, Imprints & Series:
81 212 Gyan Publishing House

Book Trade Association Membership:
Federation of Indian Publishers & Booksellers
Associations in India

2298 ▬▬▬▬▬▬▬

HEMKUNT PRESS PUBLISHERS
A-78 Naraina Industrial Area I,
New Delhi 110 028
Telephone: +91 (Ō11) 579 5079, 579 2083, 579
0032 & 579 3317
Fax: +91 (Ō11) 301 3705

Chief Executive: G. P. Singh
Managers: Deepinder Singh *(Sales)*
Arvinder Singh *(Rights & Permissions)*

*Children's Books; Educational & Textbooks;
Reference Books, Directories & Dictionaries;
Religion & Theology; Folklore; Mythology*

New Titles: 25 (1995), 20 (1996)

ISBNs, Imprints & Series: 81 7010

Associated & Subsidiary Companies:
India: Coco Creations; Hemkunt Publishers (P)
Ltd

Overseas Representation *(see §7.3):*
USA: Lotus Enterprises, Walnut Creek, CA

Book Trade Association Membership:
Federation of Indian Publishers

2299 ▬▬▬▬▬▬▬

HERITAGE PUBLISHERS
32 Prakash Apartments, Ansari Road,
New Delhi 110 001
Telephone: +91 (Ō11) 326 6258
Fax: +91 (Ō11) 326 3050

Proprietor: B. R. Chawla
Business Manager: Himanshu Chawla *(Sales)*

*Academic & Scholarly; Economics;
Environment & Development Studies; Gender
Studies; Geography & Geology; History &
Antiquarian; Languages & Linguistics;
Literature & Criticism; Philosophy; Religion &
Theology; Sports & Games*

New Titles: 6 (1995), 10 (1996)
No of Employees: 10
Annual Turnover: £320,000

ISBNs, Imprints & Series: 81 7026

Associated & Subsidiary Companies:
India: Disha Publications; Heritage Impex
Worldwide

Book Trade Association Membership: Delhi
State Booksellers & Publishers Association,

Federation of Publishers & Booksellers
Association of India

2300 ▬▬▬▬▬▬▬

HIND POCKET BOOKS PVT LTD
GT Road, Shahadara, Delhi 110 032
Telephone: +91 (Ō11) 228 2467, 229 7792/93/
94
Fax: +91 (Ō11) 228 2332

Directors: D. N. Malhotra *(Chairman)*
Miss Madhvi Malhotra *(Managing)*
C. Shekhar Malhotra
Ms Poonam Malhotra
S. L. Shaily

*Archaeology; Computer Science; Educational
& Textbooks; Electronic (Professional &
Academic); Humour; Illustrated & Fine
Editions; Industry, Business & Management;
Poetry; Religion & Theology; Theatre, Drama
& Dance*

New Titles: 250 (1995), 280 (1996)

ISBNs, Imprints & Series: 81 216

Associated & Subsidiary Companies:
India: Clarion Books; Global Business Press

Book Trade Association Membership:
Federation of Indian Publishers, Delhi State
Publishers & Booksellers Association

2301 ▬▬▬▬▬▬▬

***HINDI PRACHARAK SANSTHAN**
C21/30 Pishachmochan, PO No 1106,
Varanasi 221 001
Telephone: +91 (Ō542) 358 470, 350 425, 350
670, 355 168, 356 850 & 361 452

Directors: Krishna Chand Beri
Vijay Prakash Beri
Rajendra Prasad Beri
Anil Beri
Manager: Vivek Beri

*Academic & Scholarly; Educational &
Textbooks; Fiction*

Associated & Subsidiary Companies:
India: Hindi Pracharak Publications Pvt Ltd;
HPS Publications Pvt Ltd; Sahitya Bharati
Publications Pvt Ltd

Book Trade Association Membership: The
Federation of Publishers' & Booksellers'
Associations in India, The Federation of Indian
Publishers, Akhil Bhartiya Hindi Prakashak
Sangh, All India Federation of Master Printers

2302 ▬▬▬▬▬▬▬

HIRALAL PRINTING WORKS LTD
Plot No. D-41/1, MIDC, TTC Industrial Area,
Opp Turbhe Telephone Exchange, Turbhe,
New Bombay 400 613
Telephone: +91 (Ō22) 767 2726 & 768 3013
Fax: +91 (Ō22) 763 1191

Registered Office:
Apt No 5, 3rd Floor, Readmoney Terrace, AR.
AB Road, Worli, Bombay 400 018
Telephone: +91 (Ō22) 493 6216 & 493 3671
Fax: +91 (Ō22) 492 9904

Export Manager: Hemant Mehta *(Children's Books)*

Children's Books; Fashion & Costume

New Titles: 80 (1995), 100 (1996)
Annual Turnover: £25M

ISBNs, Imprints & Series:
81 85559 Keep Busy Series of Books

Parent Company:
Conway Printers Pvt Ltd *(India)*

Book Trade Association Membership: The Federation of Indian Publishers, The Federation of Publishers & Booksellers Associations in India

2303 ▬▬▬▬▬▬▬▬

INDIA BOOK HOUSE PVT LTD
Mahalaxmi Chambers, 5th Floor,
22 Bhulabhai Desai Road, Bombay 400 026
Telephone: +91 (Õ22) 492 3409 & 495 3827
Fax: +91 (Õ22) 493 8406

Distribution:
412–415 Tulsiani Chambers,
212 Backbay Reclamation, Nariman Point,
Bombay 400 021
Telephone: +91 (Õ22) 284 0626, 284 0165 & 284 0678
Fax: +91 (Õ22) 204 8163

Directors: Deepak Mirchandani *(Managing)*
Padmini G. Mirchandani *(Publishing, Rights & Permissions)*
Lata Vasvani *(Marketing)*
Managers: Mohan Shahani *(Export)*
Anand Kanekar *(Sales)*
Editors: Dinesh Raheja *(Movie Magazine)*
Chandralekha Maitra *(Books)*

Children's Books; Cinema, Video, TV & Radio; Cookery, Wines & Spirits; Illustrated & Fine Editions; Medical (incl. Self Help & Alternative Medicine); Religion & Theology; Travel & Topography

ISBNs, Imprints & Series: 81 85028

Parent Company:
Mirchandani & Co Ltd *(India)*

Overseas Representation *(see §7.3)*:
USA & Canada: ACK Agency, Los Altos, CA, USA

Book Trade Association Membership:
Federation of Indian Publishers, Bombay Booksellers' Association, Federation of Publishers & Booksellers Associations of India, Distripress

2304 ▬▬▬▬▬▬▬▬

INDIAN BOOKS CENTRE
40/5 Shakti Nagar, Delhi 110 007
Telephone: +91 (Õ11) 712 6497 & 743 4930
Fax: +91 (Õ11) 722 7336

Managing Director: Naresh Gupta *(Exports & Sales)*
Directors: Anil Gupta *(Sales & Publicity)*
Virender Gupta *(Production & Rights)*
Sunil Gupta *(Exports & Purchase)*

Academic & Scholarly; Archaeology; Fine Art & Art History; Gender Studies; Languages & Linguistics; Music; Philosophy; Reference Books, Directories & Dictionaries; Religion & Theology; Theatre, Drama & Dance

New Titles: 65 (1995), 60 (1996)
No of Employees: 10
Annual Turnover: $350,000

ISBNs, Imprints & Series: 81 7030

Associated & Subsidiary Companies:
India: Bibliotheca Indo-Buddhica Series Office; Sri Garib Dass Oriental Series Office; Monumenta Indica Series; Sri Satguru Publications; Studies on Sri Lanka Series Office

Overseas Representation *(see §7.3)*:
UK: Books from India Ltd, London
USA: South Asia Books, Columbia, MO

Book Trade Association Membership:
CAPEXIL Calcutta, The Federation of Educational Publishers of India

2305 ▬▬▬▬▬▬▬▬

INDIAN COUNCIL OF AGRICULTURAL RESEARCH
Krishi Bhavan, Dr Rajendra Prasad Road,
New Delhi 110 001
Telephone: +91 (Õ11) 338 8991
Fax: +91 (Õ11) 387 293
Email: dare@400-nicgw.nic.in & dare@icar-ven.nic.in

Publications & Information Division Office:
Krishi Anusandhan Bhavan, Pusa,
New Delhi 110 012
Telephone: +91 (Õ11) 573 1350, 571 3657 & 571 8649
Fax: +91 (Õ11) 578 1327

Editors: Shri Kuldip Sharma *(Chief, Hindi Publications)*
Shri R. R. Lokeshwar *(English Publications)*
Shri R. S. Gupta *(English Publications)*
Managers: Shri V. K. Bharti *(Chief Production Officer)*
Shri A. K. Chakravarty *(Chief Artist–Design)*
Shri Sunil K. Jashi *(Business, Sales & Advertising)*
Mrs Shashi Razdan *(Administration, Under Secretary (P&I))*
Compiler ARIC Unit: Shri Hans Raj *(Information Systems Officer)*

Agriculture; Animal Care & Breeding; Gardening

2306 ▬▬▬▬▬▬▬▬

THE INDIAN SOCIETY FOR PROMOTING CHRISTIAN KNOWLEDGE
[ISPCK]
1654 Madarsa Road, Kashmere Gate,
PO Box 1585, Delhi 110 006
Telephone: +91 (Õ11) 296 6323
Fax: +91 (Õ11) 296 5490

Calcutta Bookshop:
51 Chowringhee Road, Calcutta 700 071
Telephone: +91 (Õ33) 242 1804

Nagpur Bookshop:
Opp Liberty Cinema, Residency Road, Sadar,
Nagpur 440 001
Telephone: +91 (Õ712) 543 425

Associate General Secretary: Ashish Amos *(Marketing & Distribution)*

Philosophy; Religion & Theology; Sociology & Anthropology

New Titles: 96 (1995), 115 (1996)
No of Employees: 22
Annual Turnover: $2M

ISBNs, Imprints & Series: 81 7214

Parent Company:
Society for Promoting Christian Knowledge *(UK)*

Associated & Subsidiary Companies:
India: Nav Din Prakashan Kendra

Overseas Representation *(see §7.3)*:
Canada: Meditatio, Montreal; Christian Meditation Media Meditation Chretienne, Verdun, PQ
UK: Christian Meditation Media, London

Book Trade Association Membership: Delhi State Booksellers & Publishers Association, Federation of Publishers & Booksellers Association of India, Association of Christian Publishers and Booksellers in India

2307 ▬▬▬▬▬▬▬▬

INDUS PUBLISHING CO
FS-5, Tagore Garden, New Delhi 110 027
Telephone: +91 (Õ11) 535 289

Archaeology; Economics; Fine Art & Art History; Philosophy; Sociology & Anthropology; Environment; Forestry; Himalayas

New Titles: 25 (1995), 25 (1996)

ISBNs, Imprints & Series: 81 7387

Book Trade Association Membership: Delhi State Booksellers' & Publishers' Association

2308 ▬▬▬▬▬▬▬▬

INTERNATIONAL BOOK DISTRIBUTING CO
Chaman Studio Building, 2nd Floor,
Charbagh Lucknow 226 004
Telephone: +91 (Õ522) 450 004, 381 622, 450 007 & 342 433
Fax: +91 (Õ522) 219 605

Branch Office:
23/4787 (Ground Floor) G-5 Ansari Road,
Daryaganj, New Delhi 2
Telephone: +91 (Õ11) 328 7461

Managing Partners: Suneel Gomber *(Distribution Division)*
Sushil Arora *(Distribution Division)*
Partners: Ms Sweety Gomber *(Publishing Division)*
Ms Jyoti Arora *(Publishing Division)*

Agriculture; Animal Care & Breeding; Gardening; Veterinary Science

New Titles: 10 (1995), 20 (1996)
No of Employees: 20

ISBNs, Imprints & Series: 81 85860

Associated & Subsidiary Companies:
India: M/S Apex Book Distributors

Book Trade Association Membership: The Federation of Publishers' & Booksellers' Associations in India

2309

INTERPRINT
Mehta House, 16-A, Naraina II,
New Delhi 110 028
Telephone: +91 (Ō11) 570 4234 & 570 4450, 1, 2
Fax: +91 (Ō11) 570 2138 & 570 0644

Publisher: S. N. Mehta *(Rights & Permissions)*
Marketing Manager: G. P. S. Bawa *(Home & Export Sales)*

Medical (incl. Self Help & Alternative Medicine)

New Titles: 6 (1995), 6 (1996)
No of Employees: 12
Annual Turnover: $250,000

ISBNs, Imprints & Series: 81 85017

Parent Company:
Calendar Makers Corp *(India)*

Book Trade Association Membership:
Federation of Indian Publishers, New Delhi,
Federation of Publishers & Booksellers
Associations in India, Afro-Asian Book
Council

2310

B. JAIN PUBLISHERS (P) LTD
1921 Chuna Mandi, Street 10th, PB 5775,
Paharganj, New Delhi 110 055
Telephone: +91 (Ō11) 777 0430, 777 0572 & 753 4618
Fax: +91 (Ō11) 751 0471 & 753 6420
Email: kjain@giasdlo1.vsnl.net

Warehouse:
7 Wazirpur Printing Complex, Ring Road,
Delhi
Telephone: +91 (Ō11) 710 4100

Chairman: Dr P. N. Jain *(Publishing & Printing)*
Directors: Ashok Jain *(Rights & Permissions)*
Kuldeep Jain *(Sales, Promotion & Publicity)*

Health & Beauty; Medical (incl. Self Help & Alternative Medicine); Homoeopathy

New Titles: 55 (1995), 68 (1996)
No of Employees: 38
Annual Turnover: $5M

ISBNs, Imprints & Series: 81 7021

Book Trade Association Membership:
Federation of Indian Publishers

2311

JAIN BROTHERS
16/873 East Park Road, Karol Bagh,
New Delhi 110 005
Telephone: +91 (Ō11) 751 8426

Also at:
Vidhy Vihar, Pilani (Raj), BITS Campus

*Academic & Scholarly; Agriculture;
Chemistry; Cinema, Video, TV & Radio;
Computer Science; Educational & Textbooks;
Engineering; Environment & Development
Studies; Mathematics & Statistics; Physics;
Scientific & Technical*

New Titles: 8 (1995), 10 (1996)
No of Employees: 6

Book Trade Association Membership: Delhi
State Publishers & Booksellers Association,
New Delhi

2312

*KHANNA PUBLISHERS
2-B Nath Market, Nai Sarak, Delhi 110 006
Telephone: +91 (Ō11) 291 2380, 722 4179

Despatch Office:
11-Community Centre, Ashok Vihar, Phase-II,
Delhi 110 052
Telephone: +91 (Ō11) 722 4179

Head of Organization: R. C. Khanna
Senior Personnel: Vineet Khanna

*Chemistry; Computer Science; Electronic
(Educational); Engineering; Mathematics &
Statistics; Scientific & Technical*

Book Trade Association Membership:
Federation of Indian Publishers

2313

*LANCER PUBLISHERS & DISTRIBUTORS
56 Gautam Nagar, New Delhi 110 049
Telephone: +91 (Ō11) 686 7339
Fax: +91 (Ō11) 686 2077

Sales: Sunil Madan
Rights & Permissions: Jagdish Nair

*Academic & Scholarly; Children's Books;
Fiction; Humour; Military & War*

ISBNs, Imprints & Series:
Indian Defence Review, Lancer International,
Lancer Paperbacks, Lancer Publishers &
Distributors

Associated & Subsidiary Companies:
UK: Spantech & Lancer. *USA:* Indian Defence
Review; Spantech & Lancer

Overseas Representation *(see §7.3)*:
Europe: Spantech & Lancer, South Godstone,
UK
North America: Spantech & Lancer, Hartford,
WI, USA; NAFTA, Indian Defence Review,
Fort Salonga, NY, USA

Book Trade Association Membership:
Federation of Indian Publishers

2314

LAW PUBLISHERS
Sardar Patel Marg, PO Box 1077,
Allahabad 211 001
Telephone: +91 (Ō532) 622 758
Fax: +91 (Ō532) 622 781

Chief Executive: S. Sagar
Director: V. Sagar *(General Management)*
Manager: K. P. Tiwari *(Export)*

Law

New Titles: 5 (1995), 12 (1996)
No of Employees: 60
Annual Turnover: $30,000

ISBNs, Imprints & Series: 81 7111

Overseas Representation *(see §7.3)*:
USA: Media One Inc, Chicago, IL

Book Trade Association Membership:
Federation of Publishers & Booksellers
Association of India

2315

LAXMI PUBLICATIONS
7/21 Ansari Road, Daryaganj,
New Delhi 110 002
Telephone: +91 (Ō11) 327 6799, 325 2574 & 327 9646
Fax: +91 (Ō11) 325 2572

Also at:
37 Motilal Street, T. Nagar, Madras 600 017

Managing Director: R. K. Gupta

*Academic & Scholarly; Educational &
Textbooks; Engineering; Guide Books;
Mathematics & Statistics*

New Titles: 100 (1995), 125 (1996)
No of Employees: 70
Annual Turnover: $1.5M

ISBNs, Imprints & Series: 81 7008

Associated & Subsidiary Companies:
India: A. Saurabh & Co Pvt Ltd

Book Trade Association Membership: The
Federation of Educational Publishers in India,
The Federation of Publishers' & Booksellers'
Associations in India

2316

LEARNERS PRESS
L-11, Green Park Extension,
New Delhi 110 016
Telephone: +91 (Ō11) 685 1028 & 669 560
Fax: +91 (Ō11) 685 1028 & 688 6646

Managing Partners: Vikas Ghai
Gaurav Ghai
Chief Editor: Ms Mary Joseph

*Children's Books; Computer Science; Do-It-
Yourself; Educational & Textbooks; Science
Fiction*

New Titles: 30 (1995), 50 (1996)
No of Employees: 8
Annual Turnover: £1M

ISBNs, Imprints & Series: 81 7181

Parent Company:
Sterling Publishers Pvt Ltd *(India)*

2317

M D PUBLICATIONS PVT LTD
B/231-E, Greater Kailash I, New Delhi 110 048
Telephone: +91 (Ō11) 641 4048
Fax: +91 (Ō11) 647 5450

New Titles: 30 (1995), 50 (1996)

ISBNs, Imprints & Series:
81 7533, 81 85880

Parent Company:
M/S Prints India *(India)*

2318

MAHAJAN PUBLISHERS PVT LTD
Super Market Basement, Near Natraj Cinema,
Ashram Road, Ahmedabad 380 009
Telephone: +91 (Ō79) 408 537
Fax: +91 (Ō79) 469101

Directors: Dinker Mahajan *(Managing)*
Pratibha Mahajan
Managers: Rramukhbhai Patel *(Marketing)*
W. M. Parmar *(Sales)*

Academic & Scholarly; Scientific & Technical

New Titles: 5 (1995), 20 (1996)
No of Employees: 5
Annual Turnover: $70,000

ISBNs, Imprints & Series: 81 85401

Book Trade Association Membership: The
Federation of Publishers' & Booksellers'
Associations in India

2319

**MINERVA ASSOCIATES
(PUBLICATIONS) PVT LTD**
7-B Lake Place, Calcutta 700 029
Telephone: +91 (Ō33) 466 3783

Directors: Sushil Mukherjea *(Managing,
Publications)*
T. K. Mukherjee *(Sales)*

*Academic & Scholarly; Economics; History &
Antiquarian; Literature & Criticism; Natural
History; Philosophy; Politics & World Affairs;
Psychology & Psychiatry; Sociology &
Anthropology*

New Titles: 10 (1995), 10 (1996)
No of Employees: 4
Annual Turnover: $10,000

ISBNs, Imprints & Series: 81 85195

Book Trade Association Membership:
Publishers & Booksellers Guild, Calcutta

2320

***MITRA & GHOSH PUBLISHERS PVT
LTD**
10 Shyama Charan De Street, Calcutta 700 073
Telephone: +91 (Ō33) 314 431
Fax: +91 (Ō33) 316 420

Warehouse:
65 Keshab Chandra Sen Street,
Calcutta 700 009

Home Sales: Manish Chakravorty
Export Sales: Tapan Chakravorty

*Academic & Scholarly; Chemistry;
Educational & Textbooks; Environment &
Development Studies; Fiction; Fine Art & Art
History; Geography & Geology; Health &
Beauty; History & Antiquarian; Humour;
Literature & Criticism; Medical (incl. Self Help
& Alternative Medicine); Natural History;
Philosophy; Religion & Theology; Science
Fiction*

Book Trade Association Membership:
Publishers' & Booksellers' Guild, Calcutta,
Publishers' & Booksellers' Association, West
Bengal, West Bengal Literary Publishers'
Association

2321

**MOTILAL BANARSIDASS
PUBLISHERS**
41 UA Bungalow Road, Jawahar Nagar,
Delhi 110 007
Telephone: +91 (Ō11) 291 1985 & 291 8335
Fax: +91 (Ō11) 293 0689

**Warehouse, Trade Enquiries, Orders &
Printing:**
A45, Naraina Industrial Area, Phase 1,
New Delhi 110 028
Telephone: +91 (Ō11) 579 3423 & 579 5180
Fax: +91 (Ō11) 579 7221

Partners: N. P. Jain *(Editing, Rights &
Permissions)*
J. P. Jain *(Home Sales)*
R. P. Jain *(Export Sales)*
Ravi P. Jain *(Finance)*
Rajiv P. Jain *(Home Sales)*
Anurag Jain *(Publishing)*

*Academic & Scholarly; Archaeology;
Architecture & Design; Atlases & Maps; Fine
Art & Art History; History & Antiquarian;
Languages & Linguistics; Literature &
Criticism; Magic & the Occult; Mathematics &
Statistics; Medical (incl. Self Help &
Alternative Medicine); Music; Philosophy;
Psychology & Psychiatry; Reference Books,
Directories & Dictionaries; Religion &
Theology; Theatre, Drama & Dance; Indology;
Sanskrit Literature*

New Titles: 36 (1995), 40 (1996)
No of Employees: 200
Annual Turnover: $1.4M

ISBNs, Imprints & Series:
81 208 Ancient Indian Tradition & Mythology,
Buddhist Tradition Series, Encyclopedia of
Indian Philosophies, Kala Mula Shastra,
Kala Tattva Kosha, Lala Sunderlal Jain
Series, MLBD Series in Linguistics,

Performing Art Series, Sacred Books of the
East

Associated & Subsidiary Companies:
India: Excel Books; MLBD Books
International; Motilal Banarsidass Publishers
Pvt Ltd; Shri Jaintendra Press

Overseas Representation *(see §7.3)*:
UK: Motilal Books (UK) Ltd, Oxford
USA: South Asia Books, Columbia, MO

Book Trade Association Membership:
Chemicals & Allied Products Export
Promotion Council, Calcutta, Delhi State
Booksellers Association, Federation of Indian
Publishers, Association of Hindi Publishers,
Federation of Publishers & Booksellers
Associations of India

2322

**MUNSHIRAM MANOHARLAL
PUBLISHERS PVT LTD**
PO Box 5715, 54 Rani Jhansi Road,
New Delhi 110 055
Telephone: +91 (Ō11) 777 1668 & 777 3650
Fax: +91 (Ō11) 751 2745
Email: mrmlpub.mrml@axcess.net.in

Directors: Devendera Jain *(Managing,
Editorial)*
Ashok Jain *(Sales)*
Manager: Pankaj Jain *(Sales, Rights &
Permissions)*

*Archaeology; Fine Art & Art History; Gender
Studies; History & Antiquarian; Languages &
Linguistics; Music; Philosophy; Reference
Books, Directories & Dictionaries; Religion &
Theology; Theatre, Drama & Dance; Travel &
Topography*

New Titles: 56 (1995), 70 (1996)
No of Employees: 32
Annual Turnover: $0.5M

ISBNs, Imprints & Series:
81 215 Munshiram Manoharlal Publishers Pvt
Ltd
81 7069 Oriental Books Reprint Corporation

Overseas Representation *(see §7.3)*:
Japan: Nagara Books Ltd, Tokyo
Switzerland: Inforel Book Service, Basle

Book Trade Association Membership: Delhi
State Booksellers & Publishers Association,
Federation of Publishers & Booksellers
Associations of India, Federation of Indian
Publishers

2323

NARESH PUBLISHERS
111 Shankar Road Market,
New Rajinder Nagar, New Delhi 110 060
Telephone: +91 (Ō11) 572 3235 & 575 4442
Fax: +91 (Ō11) 574 6485

Directors: N. K. Chowdhry
M. K. Chowdhry

Educational & Textbooks

New Titles: 18 (1996)
No of Employees: 8
Annual Turnover: $110,000

ISBNs, Imprints & Series: 81 7005

Associated & Subsidiary Companies:
India: Paramount Sales (India) Pvt Ltd

Book Trade Association Membership:
Federation of Indian Publishers, Federation of
Educational Publishers, Federation of
Publishers & Booksellers Associations of India

2324

NAROSA PUBLISHING HOUSE
6 Community Centre, Panchsheel Park,
New Delhi 110 017
Telephone: +91 (011) 643 3992
Fax: +91 (011) 646 8717

Managing Director: N. K. Mehra
Managers: M. S. Sejwal *(Production)*
S. Mehra *(Marketing)*

*Agriculture; Biology & Zoology; Chemistry;
Computer Science; Engineering; Mathematics
& Statistics; Medical (incl. Self Help &
Alternative Medicine); Philosophy; Physics;
Scientific & Technical; Veterinary Science*

New Titles: 12 (1995), 30 (1996)
No of Employees: 40

ISBNs, Imprints & Series:
81 7319, 81 85015, 81 85198 Narosa
Publishing House
81 85015 Springer International Student
Edition

Associated & Subsidiary Companies:
India: Narosa Book Distributors Pvt Ltd;
Springer Books (India) Pvt Ltd

Overseas Representation *(see §7.3):*
Australia: DA Information Services, Mitcham,
Vic
Japan: Eastern Book Service Inc, Tokyo
UK: Eurospan STM Group, London

Book Trade Association Membership:
Federation of Indian Publishers, Federation of
Booksellers & Publishers Associations of India,
Delhi State Booksellers & Publishers
Association

2325

*NATIONAL BOOK ORGANISATION
H-39 Green Park Extension,
New Delhi 110 016
Telephone: +91 (011) 696 0389 & 685 4179

Also at:
Municipal Flat 18, Bangalow Road,
opposite Jawahar Nagar, Delhi 110 007
Telephone: +91 (011) 292 9583

Director: Mrs A. H. Marwah

*Agriculture; Architecture & Design;
Economics; Fiction; Geography & Geology;
History & Antiquarian; Law; Literature &
Criticism; Military & War; Philosophy;
Poetry; Politics & World Affairs; Psychology &*

*Psychiatry; Religion & Theology; Theatre,
Drama & Dance; Child Care & Development*

ISBNs, Imprints & Series: 81 85135

Overseas Representation *(see §7.3):*
UK: J. Whitaker & Sons Ltd, London
USA: R. R. Bowker, New Providence, NJ;
South Asia Books, Columbia, MO

Book Trade Association Membership:
Federation of Indian Publishers

2326

NATIONAL BOOK SHOP
32-B Pleasure Garden Market,
Chandni Chowk, Delhi 110 006
Telephone: +91 (011) 327 8392

Manager: Paramjit Singh *(Punjabi Books —
Fiction & Non-Fiction)*

History & Antiquarian; Religion & Theology

New Titles: 9 (1995), 15 (1996)
No of Employees: 5
Annual Turnover: $35,000

ISBNs, Imprints & Series: 81 7116

Associated & Subsidiary Companies:
India: Satwant Book Agency

Overseas Representation *(see §7.3):*
UK: Star Books International, Hayes

Book Trade Association Membership:
Federation of Indian Publishers

2327

NAVRANG, BOOKSELLERS &
PUBLISHERS
RB-7 Inderpuri, New Delhi 110 012
Telephone: +91 (011) 578 9914 & 572 2197
Fax: +91 (011) 572 2197 & 576 2467

Proprietor: Mrs Nirmal Singal
Sales, Editing & Publishing: Sushil Singal
Listing: Mrs Nisha Singal

*Academic & Scholarly; Archaeology; Fine Art
& Art History; Religion & Theology*

New Titles: 25 (1995), 25 (1996)
No of Employees: 7
Annual Turnover: $200,000

ISBNs, Imprints & Series: 81 7013

Overseas Representation *(see §7.3):*
USA: Navrang Inc, Blacksburg, VA

Book Trade Association Membership:
Export Promotion Council, Federation of
Indian Publishers, Federation of Publishers &
Booksellers Association of India

2328

NEW ASIAN PUBLISHERS
3911 Roshanpura, Nai Sarak, Delhi 110 006
Telephone: +91 (011) 291 5650 & 294 1531
Fax: +91 (011) 291 5650

Warehouse:
295 Jagriti Enclave, Vikas Marg, Delhi 110 092

Managers: Anil Mehta *(Business)*
Salil Mehta *(Office)*
Proprietor: Ravinder Kumar Mehta

*Architecture & Design; Biology & Zoology;
Chemistry; Computer Science; Educational &
Textbooks; Electronic (Educational);
Engineering; Guide Books; Industry, Business
& Management; Mathematics & Statistics;
Physics; Reference Books, Directories &
Dictionaries; Scientific & Technical; Travel &
Topography; Vocational Training & Careers*

New Titles: 30 (1995), 45 (1996)
No of Employees: 8
Annual Turnover: $14,000

ISBNs, Imprints & Series:
81 7317, 81 7318

Associated & Subsidiary Companies:
India: Asian Publishers; New Asian Publishers
(Export Division)

Book Trade Association Membership: The
Federation of Publishers' & Booksellers'
Associations in India

2329

OMSONS PUBLICATIONS
T-7 Rajouri Garden, New Delhi 110 027
Telephone: +91 (011) 541 2452

Also at:
Prakash House, 4379/4B Ansari Road,
New Delhi 2
Telephone: +91 (011) 328 9353

Manager: Satish Kumar

*Agriculture; Animal Care & Breeding;
Bibliography & Library Science; Biography &
Autobiography; Children's Books; Economics;
Educational & Textbooks; Environment &
Development Studies; Fiction; Gender Studies;
Geography & Geology; History &
Antiquarian; Industry, Business &
Management; Literature & Criticism;
Philosophy; Psychology & Psychiatry;
Sociology & Anthropology; Theatre, Drama &
Dance; Travel & Topography; Veterinary
Science*

New Titles: 11 (1995), 17 (1996)
No of Employees: 4
Annual Turnover: $24,000

ISBNs, Imprints & Series: 81 7117

Parent Company:
Western Book Depot *(India)*

2330

ORIENT LONGMAN LTD
3-6-272 Himayatnagar, Hyderabad 500 029
Telephone: +91 (040) 240305
Fax: +91 (040) 240393
Email: info@orienth.uunet.in

Bombay Office:
Kamani Marg, Ballard Estate, Bombay 400 038

Telephone: +91 (022) 261 6918 & 261 6919
Fax: +91 (022) 262 1278

Calcutta Office:
17 Chittaran jan Avenue, Calcutta 700 072
Telephone: +91 (033) 279 884 & 279 885
Fax: +91 (033) 271 292

Madras Office:
160 Anna Salai, Madras 600 002
Telephone: +91 (044) 852 3346 & 852 3358
Fax: +91 (044) 852 2231

New Delhi Office:
1/24 Asaf Ali Road, New Delhi 110 002
Telephone: +91 (011) 323 5901
Fax: +91 (011) 323 9172

Bangalore Office:
80/1 Mahatma Gandhi Road,
Bangalore 560 001
Telephone: +91 (080) 559 9761 & 559 9760

Guwahati Office:
S. C. Goswami Road, Panbazar,
Guwahati 781 001
Telephone: +91 (0361) 31889

Lucknow Office:
Patiala House, 28/31 Ashok Marg,
Lucknow 226 001
Telephone: +91 (0522) 283 850 & 283 854

Patna Office:
City Centre Ashok, Govind Mitra Road,
Patna 800 004
Telephone: +91 (0612) 650 838 & 663 334

Bhubaneshwar Office:
Plot 365, Saheed Nagar,
Bhubaneshwar 751 007
Telephone: +91 (0674) 417 175

Cochin Office:
41/316 Gour Mohan, Ambady Lane,
Chittoor Road, Cochin 682 011
Telephone: +91 (0484) 374 577

Chairman: J. Rameshwar Rao
Managers: E. Raghavan *(General, Export)*
Jagan Mohan Reddy *(Finance)*
J. Krishnadev Rao *(Sales & Marketing)*
Girish S. Mondkar *(Production)*
Secretary: R. Sunandan Reddy
Publishers: Priya B. Adarkar
Madhu Reddy

*Academic & Scholarly; Atlases & Maps;
Biography & Autobiography; Biology &
Zoology; Chemistry; Children's Books;
Cinema, Video, TV & Radio; Computer
Science; Cookery, Wines & Spirits; Economics;
Educational & Textbooks; Engineering;
English as a Foreign Language; Fiction;
Gender Studies; Guide Books; History &
Antiquarian; Illustrated & Fine Editions;
Industry, Business & Management; Literature
& Criticism; Mathematics & Statistics;
Medical (incl. Self Help & Alternative
Medicine); Physics; Poetry; Politics & World
Affairs; Reference Books, Directories &
Dictionaries; Scientific & Technical; Sociology
& Anthropology; Sports & Games*

New Titles: 143 (1995), 175 (1996)
No of Employees: 282

ISBNs, Imprints & Series:
81 250 Disha Books, Orient Longman

Associated & Subsidiary Companies:
India: OSDATA (Orient Software
Development & Training Co Ltd); Sangam
Books (I) Ltd; Universities Press (I) Ltd.
Malaysia: Pustaka Baiduri Sdn Bhd *(South
East Asia). UK:* Sangam Books Ltd

Overseas Representation *(see §7.3):*
South East Asia: Pustaka Baiduri Sdn Bhd,
Kuala Lumpur, Malaysia
UK: Sangam Books Ltd, London

Book Trade Association Membership: The
Federation of Publishers & Booksellers
Associations in India, The Federation of Indian
Publishers, The International Association of
Scholarly Publishers

2331 ▬▬▬▬▬▬▬▬

ORIENT PAPERBACKS
Madarsa Road, Kashmere Gate, Delhi 110 006
Telephone: +91 (011) 251 2267 & 7001
Fax: +91 (011) 291 6315

Branch:
24 Feroze Gandhi Road, Lajpat Nagar III,
New Delhi 110 024
Telephone: +91 (011) 683 6470 & 683 6480
Fax: +91 (011) 683 6490

Branch:
Vasant, Ground Floor, 3-B Peddar Road,
Bombay
Telephone: +91 (022) 492 9343 & 496 0229

Branch:
3-6-280/A/5 Himayat Nagar,
Hyderabad 500 029
Telephone: +91 (040) 24 3252

Directors: Sudhir Malhotra *(Managing &
Marketing)*
Kapil Malhotra *(Editorial)*
Editors: Veena Baswani
O. P. Jaggi

*Biography & Autobiography; Children's
Books; Cookery, Wines & Spirits; Crafts &
Hobbies; Do-It-Yourself; Fiction; Gardening;
Guide Books; Health & Beauty; Humour;
Magic & the Occult; Philosophy; Reference
Books, Directories & Dictionaries; Religion &
Theology; Sports & Games; Fitness; IQ/
Puzzle/Brain Teasers; Lifestyle; Yoga*

New Titles: 45 (1995), 50 (1996)
No of Employees: 40
Annual Turnover: $1M

ISBNs, Imprints & Series:
81 222 Anand Paperbacks

Parent Company:
Vision Books Pvt Ltd *(India)*

Associated & Subsidiary Companies:
India: Big Database Publishing Pvt Ltd; Orient
Book Club; Rajpal & Sons; Ravindra Printing
Press; Shiksha Bharati

Overseas Representation *(see §7.3):*
Mauritius: Nalanda & Co, Port Louis
Singapore: P & M Studyaids Centre

UK & Europe: Books from India Ltd, London,
UK; Independent Publishing Co Ltd,
London, UK

Book Trade Association Membership: Indian
PA, Indian Booksellers Association, Delhi
State Booksellers & Publishers Association

2332 ▬▬▬▬▬▬▬▬

**OXFORD & IBH PUBLISHING CO PVT
LTD**
66 Janpath, (2nd Floor), New Delhi 110 001
Telephone: +91 (011) 332 4578
Fax: +91 (011) 332 2639

Directors: Mohan Primlani *(Home & Export
Sales)*
Gulab Primlani
Raju Primlani *(Home & Export Sales)*
Manager: Vijay Primlani *(Marketing, Home &
Export Sales)*

*Agriculture; Biology & Zoology; Engineering;
Geography & Geology; Industry, Business &
Management; Natural History; Reference
Books, Directories & Dictionaries; Scientific &
Technical; Veterinary Science*

New Titles: 106 (1995), 115 (1996)
No of Employees: 45

ISBNs, Imprints & Series:
81 204, 81 205, 81 7087, 1 886106

Associated & Subsidiary Companies:
USA: Science Publishers Inc

Overseas Representation *(see §7.3):*
USA: Science Publishers Inc, Lebanon, NH

Book Trade Association Membership:
Federation of Indian Publishers

2333 ▬▬▬▬▬▬▬▬

**OXFORD UNIVERSITY PRESS (INDIAN
BRANCH)**
YMCA Library Building, Jai Singh Road,
New Delhi 110 001
Telephone: +91 (011) 373 2990, 373 4769 &
374 7124/5
Fax: +91 (011) 373 2312

Delhi Branch:
2/11 Ansari Road, Daryaganj,
New Delhi 110 002
Telephone: +91 (011) 327 3841/2 & 325 3647
Fax: +91 (011) 327 7812

Calcutta Branch:
5 Lala Lajpat Rai Sarani (3rd Floor),
Elgin Road, Calcutta 700 020
Telephone: +91 (033) 247 8983, 406 745 &
406 915
Fax: +91 (033) 247 9116

Bombay Branch:
Oxford House, Apollo Bunder,
Bombay 400 039
Telephone: +91 (022) 202 1029 & 202 1198
Fax: +91 (022) 204 1268

Madras Branch:
Oxford House, Anna Salai (Mount Road),
Madras 600 006

Telephone: +91 (044) 827 2267/8 & 827 2299
Fax: +91 (044) 826 0962

Bangalore Showroom:
94 Industrial Area, 4th B Cross, 5th Block,
Koramangala, Bangalore 560 095
Telephone: +91 (080) 553 4286

Pune Showroom:
Gayatri Sadan (1st Floor), 2060 Sadashiv Peth,
Vijaynagar Colony, Pune 411 030
Telephone: +91 (0212) 434 537

Patna Showroom:
Bharati Bhawan, Rishi Bazar,
Thakurbari Road, Kadam Kuan, Patna 800 003
Telephone: +91 (0612) 650 325 & 651 356

Lucknow Showroom:
B-49 Mandir Marg, Mahanagar Extn,
Lucknow 226 006
Telephone: +91 (0522) 77702 & 79049

Hyderabad Showroom:
3-5-1107 Narayanaguda, Hyderabad 500 029,
AP
Telephone: +91 (040) 510 155

Guwahati Showroom:
Danish Road, Panbazar, Guwahati 781 001
Telephone: +91 (0361) 524 050

Directors: Manzar Khan *(Managing)*
A. Roy Chowdhury *(Educational)*
A. K. Rai Chowdhury *(Finance)*
Prabir Bhambal *(IT)*
Sanjeev Goswami *(Academic Marketing)*
Regional Directors: J. K. Sen *(East)*
R. B. Patel *(West)*
Neil Todd *(North)*
N. V. Iyer *(South)*
Managers: Rukun Advani *(Academic
Publishing Division)*
S. Seshadari *(Educational Division)*
Arvind Srivastava *(Chief Accountant)*
Sharmila Bose *(Editorial, Educational
Division)*
T. Bhaumik *(Production)*

*Academic & Scholarly; Atlases & Maps;
Biography & Autobiography; Biology &
Zoology; Children's Books; Economics;
Educational & Textbooks; Environment &
Development Studies; Fine Art & Art History;
Gender Studies; Geography & Geology;
History & Antiquarian; Industry, Business &
Management; Law; Literature & Criticism;
Medical (incl. Self Help & Alternative
Medicine); Natural History; Philosophy;
Poetry; Politics & World Affairs; Psychology &
Psychiatry; Reference Books, Directories &
Dictionaries; Scientific & Technical; Sociology
& Anthropology; Theatre, Drama & Dance*

New Titles: 172 (1995), 200 (1996)
No of Employees: 296
Annual Turnover: £6M

ISBNs, Imprints & Series:
0 19 560, 0 19 561, 0 19 562, 0 19 563

Parent Company:
Oxford University Press *(UK)*

Overseas Representation *(see §7.3)*:
Worldwide: Oxford University Press, Oxford,
UK

Book Trade Association Membership:
Federation of Publishers & Booksellers
Associations of India, Federation of Indian
Publishers

2334 ▬

OXONIAN PRESS PVT LTD
N-56 Connaught Circus, New Delhi 110 001
Telephone: +91 (011) 331 4957 & 3584
Fax: +91 (011) 332 2639 & 371 3275
Email: oxford.publ@axcess.net.in

Warehouse:
Plot No 6, Sector 27A, Industrial Area,
Faridabad
Telephone: +91 (011) 827 5814
Fax: +91 (011) 332 2639

Directors: Gulab Primlani
Dr A. M. Primlani

*Agriculture; Biology & Zoology; Scientific &
Technical*

New Titles: 10 (1995), 12 (1996)
No of Employees: 6
Annual Turnover: $75,000

ISBNs, Imprints & Series: 81 7087

Associated & Subsidiary Companies:
India: Amerind Publishing Co Pvt Ltd; Oxford
& IBH Publishing Co Pvt Ltd; Oxford Book &
Stationery Co

Overseas Representation *(see §7.3)*:
USA: Science Publishers Inc, Lebanon, NH
Worldwide (excluding USA): A. A. Balkema
Publishers, Rotterdam, Netherlands; E. J.
Brill & Co, Leiden, Netherlands

Book Trade Association Membership:
Federation of Indian Publishers

2335 ▬

PALANI PARAMOUNT PUBLICATIONS
69D Anna Nagar, Palani, Tamil Nadu 624 602
Telephone: +91 (04545) 43212 & 42332
Fax: +91 (04545) 42119

Also at:
Paramount Laser Service,
1047 Gandhipuram 5th Street,
Combatore 641 012

Managing Director: Mrs P. Sarojini
Editor-in-Chief: Dr S. Palanichamy

Biology & Zoology; Environmental Science

New Titles: 11 (1995), 15 (1996)

ISBNs, Imprints & Series: 81 85517

Book Trade Association Membership: Indian
PA, Indian Booksellers Association

2336 ▬

*PANTHER PUBLISHERS PVT LTD
29 3rd Cross, 16th Main,
Koramangala IV Block, Bangalore 560 034
Telephone: +91 (080) 553 3819 & 223 4562
Fax: +91 (080) 553 7145

Also at:
39 6th Cross, Wilson Gardens,
Bangalore 560 034
Telephone: +91 (080) 223 4562
Fax: +91 (080) 553 7145

Director: P. T. Rajasekharan *(Publishing &
Rights)*

*Academic & Scholarly; Biography &
Autobiography; Reference Books, Directories
& Dictionaries*

ISBNs, Imprints & Series: 81 85457

Book Trade Association Membership: Indian
PA, Bangalore Publishers & Booksellers
Association

2337 ▬

PARAMOUNT SALES (INDIA) PVT LTD
PO Box 2860, 484 Double Storey,
New Rajinder Nagar, New Delhi 110 060
Telephone: +91 (011) 572 3235 & 575 4442
Fax: +91 (011) 574 6485

Directors: Naresh Kumar Chowdhry
Mohinder Kumar Chowdhry

Educational & Textbooks

New Titles: 10 (1996)
No of Employees: 2
Annual Turnover: $24,000

ISBNs, Imprints & Series: 81 7103

Associated & Subsidiary Companies:
India: Naresh Publishers

2338 ▬

PATRA BHARATI
1/1 Brindaban Mallick Lane, Calcutta 700 009
Telephone: +91 (033) 350 1944
Fax: +91 (033) 239 3510

Trade Enquiries & Orders:
3/1 College Row, Calcutta 700 009
Telephone: +91 (033) 241 1175
Fax: +91 (033) 239 3510

Editorial: Ms Chumki Chatterjee
Hasir Mallick
Production: Nazrul Islam
Marketing: Debashis Chakraborty
Sales: Goutam Chakraborty
Finance & Accounts: Tarapada Ray

*Children's Books; Crafts & Hobbies; Do-It-
Yourself; Electronic (Entertainment)*

New Titles: 30 (1995), 75 (1996)
No of Employees: 20
Annual Turnover: $50,000

Associated & Subsidiary Companies:
India: Amrita Prakashan; Shishuswapna
Prakashan

Book Trade Association Membership:
Publishers & Booksellers Guild, Publishers &
Booksellers Association of Bengal

2339 ■■■■■■■■■

PENGUIN BOOKS INDIA PVT LTD
210 Chiranjiv Tower, 43 Nehru Place,
New Delhi 110 019
Telephone: +91 (Õ11) 644 6122
Fax: +91 (Õ11) 642 0866
Email: sales.penguin@axcess.net.in

Chief Executive: Vinod Jethra
Financial Controller: Sudha Mahapatra
Managers: Zamir Ansari *(General – Sales &*
  Marketing)
Sajal Srivastava *(Assistant – Marketing)*
Production Administrator: Nirmalya Roy
  Chaudhuri
Editor/Publisher: David Davidar
Contracts & Rights Assistant: Geeta Bhatia

Biography & Autobiography; Children's
Books; Cookery, Wines & Spirits; Environment
& Development Studies; Fiction; History &
Antiquarian; Humour; Illustrated & Fine
Editions; Industry, Business & Management;
Medical (incl. Self Help & Alternative
Medicine); Philosophy; Photography; Poetry;
Politics & World Affairs; Psychology &
Psychiatry; Reference Books, Directories &
Dictionaries; Religion & Theology; Sociology
& Anthropology; Sports & Games; Travel &
Topography; Vocational Training & Careers

New Titles: 86 (1995), 120 (1996)
No of Employees: 40
Annual Turnover: £2M

ISBNs, Imprints & Series:
014 Penguin

Parent Company:
Penguin Books Ltd *(UK)*

Overseas Representation *(see §7.3)*:
Australia: Penguin Books Australia Ltd,
  Ringwood, Vic
Canada: Penguin Books Canada Ltd, Toronto,
  Ont
New Zealand: Penguin Books (New Zealand)
  Ltd, Auckland
South Africa: Longman Penguin South Africa,
  Bertsham
USA: Penguin Books, New York

Book Trade Association Membership:
Federation of Publishers & Booksellers
Associations in India, Federation of Indian
Publishers

2340 ■■■■■■■■■

PITAMBAR PUBLISHING CO PVT LTD
888 East Park Road, Karol Bagh,
New Delhi 110 005
Telephone: +91 (Õ11) 752 5528, 777 0067 &
777 6058
Fax: +91 (Õ11) 777 6058

Packing & Stocking:
415/1/3, Mundlea Village, New Delhi 110 041
Telephone: +91 (Õ11) 547 2629
Fax: +91 (Õ11) 777 6058

Directors: Ved Bhushan *(Managing, Home*
  Sales)
Anand Bhushan *(Export Sales)*
Sushil Bhushan *(Chairman, Rights &*
  Permissions)

Jaideep Aggarwal *(Production)*
Manish Aggarwal *(Editorial)*
Dr V. B. Aggarwal *(Computerization &*
  Accounts)
General Manager: Prem Chand

Academic & Scholarly; Accountancy &
Taxation; Chemistry; Children's Books;
Computer Science; Educational & Textbooks;
Electronic (Educational); Electronic
(Professional & Academic); Industry, Business
& Management; Mathematics & Statistics;
Physics; Poetry; Religion & Theology

New Titles: 120 (1995), 150 (1996)
No of Employees: 125
Annual Turnover: $2.5M

ISBNs, Imprints & Series: 81 209

Associated & Subsidiary Companies:
India: Ambar Prakashan; Bharat Publishing
House; Pitambar Coated Papers Ltd

Overseas Representation *(see §7.3)*:
UK & Western Europe: Books from India Ltd,
  London, UK
United Arab Emirates: Arora Book Centre,
  Sharjah, UAE

Book Trade Association Membership:
Federation of Indian Publishers, Federation of
Educational Publishers in India, All India Hindi
Publishers Association, Delhi State Booksellers
& Publishers Association

2341 ■■■■■■■■■

POINTER PUBLISHERS
Vyas Building, S. M. S. Highway, Jaipur,
Rajasthan 302 003
Telephone: +91 (Õ141) 568159 & 518286
Fax: +91 (Õ141) 562000

Proprietor: Shashi Jain *(Educational,*
  Reference, Rights & Permissions)
Manager: Vipin Jain *(Home & Export Sales)*

Academic & Scholarly; Accountancy &
Taxation; Agriculture; Biology & Zoology;
Economics; Environment & Development
Studies; Geography & Geology; History &
Antiquarian; Industry, Business &
Management; Literature & Criticism; Politics
& World Affairs; Psychology & Psychiatry

New Titles: 24 (1995), 50 (1996)

ISBNs, Imprints & Series:
81 7132 Contemporary Issues in Accounting
Series

Parent Company:
Aavishkar Publishers' Distributors *(India)*

Book Trade Association Membership:
Rajasthan Pustak Vyavsaya Sangh, Jaipur, The
Federation of Publishers' & Booksellers'
Associations in India

2342 ■■■■■■■■■

POPULAR PRAKASHAN (PTE) LTD
35-C Pandit Madan Mohan Malaviya Road,
Tardeo, Bombay 400 034
Telephone: +91 (Õ22) 494 1656
Fax: +91 (Õ22) 494 5790 & 495 2627

Email: info.vans@axcess.net.in
Web Site: http://www.accessindia.com

New Delhi Sales Office:
4648/1 Ansari Road, New Delhi 110 002
Telephone: +91 (Õ11) 326 5245
Fax: +91 (Õ11) 327 9203
Email: popular.vans@axcess.net.in
Web Site: http://www.accessindia.com

Calcutta Sales Office:
16 Southern Avenue, Calcutta 700 026
Telephone: +91 (Õ33) 760 812
Fax: +91 (Õ33) 466 4514
Email: mandira.vans@axcess.net.in
Web Site: http://www.accessindia.com

Directors: Ramdas Bhatkal *(Managing)*
R. N. Gokarn
Harsha Bhatkal *(Exports, Rights &*
  Permissions)

Medical (incl. Self Help & Alternative
Medicine); Sociology & Anthropology

New Titles: 18 (1995), 20 (1996)
No of Employees: 41
Annual Turnover: $222,982

ISBNs, Imprints & Series:
81 7154 Focus Books
81 85604 Sanya, Stree

Parent Company:
Popular Book Depot *(India)*

Associated & Subsidiary Companies:
India: Bhatkal & Sen; Bhatkal Books
International; Vans Information & Investor
Services Ltd

Overseas Representation *(see §7.3)*:
UK: Sangam Books Ltd, London
USA: South Asia Books, Columbia, MO

Book Trade Association Membership:
Bombay Booksellers Association, Federation
of Indian Publishers, International Association
of Scholarly Publishers

2343 ■■■■■■■■■

PRABHAT PRAKASHAN
4/19 Asaf Ali Road, New Delhi 110 002
Telephone: +91 (Õ11) 328 9555, 328 9666 &
326 4676
Fax: +91 (Õ11) 325 3233

Branch Office:
205 Chawri Bazar, Delhi 110 006
Telephone: +91 (Õ11) 326 4676 & 327 6316

Chief Executive: Pawan Agrawal
Business Executive: Piyush Agrawal
Managers: Raghuvir Agrawal *(Sales)*
Dharamvir Agrawal *(Finance)*
Parasnath Agrawal *(Marketing)*
Rajendra Singh *(Production)*
Chief Editor: Nabab Singh Chauhan

Bibliography & Library Science; Biography &
Autobiography; Children's Books;
Environment & Development Studies; Fiction;
Humour; Languages & Linguistics; Literature
& Criticism; Mathematics & Statistics;
Medical (incl. Self Help & Alternative
Medicine); Poetry; Psychology & Psychiatry;

Reference Books, Directories & Dictionaries;
Religion & Theology; Science Fiction; Sports
& Games; Theatre, Drama & Dance; Travel &
Topography

New Titles: 60 (1995), 75 (1996)
No of Employees: 15

ISBNs, Imprints & Series: 81 7315

Associated & Subsidiary Companies:
India: Granth Akademi; Gyan Ganga; Pratibha
Pratishthan; Satsahitya Prakashan; Vidya Vihar

Book Trade Association Membership:
Federation of Indian Publishers, Akhil
Bharatiya Hindi Prakashak Sangh

2344 ▬▬▬

*PRAGATI PUBLICATIONS
9926 Library Road, Azad Market,
Delhi 110 006
Telephone: +91 (011) 751 4747
Fax: +91 (011) 545 5952

Warehouse:
3/56 West Punjabi Bagh, New Delhi 110 026
Telephone: +91 (011) 502 109
Fax: +91 (011) 777 7476

Director: Vinod Kapoor
Editorial & Production: Pramod Kapoor
Sales: Ms Vandana Kapoor

*Academic & Scholarly; Archaeology;
Bibliography & Library Science; Economics;
Educational & Textbooks; Gender Studies;
History & Antiquarian; Literature & Criticism;
Philosophy; Politics & World Affairs;
Psychology & Psychiatry; Sociology &
Anthropology*

ISBNs, Imprints & Series: 81 7307

Overseas Representation *(see §7.3):*
USA: Rajdeep Books, York, PA

Book Trade Association Membership: The
Federation of Indian Publishers' &
Booksellers' Associations

2345 ▬▬▬

PRESTIGE BOOKS
3/28 East Patel Nagar, New Delhi 110 008
Telephone: +91 (011) 573 7849 & 550 7139
Fax: +91 (011) 575 4111 & 573 6111

Educational Director: Ms D. Renu *(Sales,
Rights & Permissions)*
Executive: Sumesh Dhawan
Sales: Suresh
Editorial: Dr R. K. Dhawan

*Fiction; Gender Studies; Literature &
Criticism; Poetry*

New Titles: 25 (1995), 30 (1996)
No of Employees: 5
Annual Turnover: $15,000

ISBNs, Imprints & Series:
81 7551, 81 85218

Associated & Subsidiary Companies:
India: Indian Society for Commonwealth
Studies

Overseas Representation *(see §7.3):*
UK: Blackwell Publishers, Oxford

2346 ▬▬▬

*PUSTAK MAHAL
F-2/16 Ansari Road, Daryaganj,
New Delhi 110 002
Telephone: +91 (011) 327 2783/4, 327 6539 &
326 0518
Fax: +91 (011) 292 4673 & 326 0518

Showroom & Sales:
10-B Netaji Subhash Marg, Daryaganj,
New Delhi 110 002
Telephone: +91 (011) 326 8292/3 & 327 9900
Fax: +91 (011) 292 4673 & 326 0518

Bombay Branch:
23/25 Zaoba Wadi, Thakurdwar,
Bombay 400 002
Telephone: +91 (022) 201 0941

Bangalore Branch:
22/2 Mission Road (Shama Rao's Compound),
Bangalore 560 027
Telephone: +91 (080) 223 4025

Patna Branch:
Khemka House, Opp. Women's Hospital,
Ashok Rajpath, Patna
Telephone: +91 (0612) 653 644

Directors: Dr Ashok Kumar Gupta *(Executive)*
Ramesh Kumar Gupta *(Home Sales)*
Amit Gupta *(Marketing, Export Sales)*
Vikas Gupta *(Technical, Editorial, Rights &
Permissions)*
Vinod Gupta *(Executive & Production)*

*Children's Books; Computer Science; Cookery,
Wines & Spirits; Crafts & Hobbies; Do-It-
Yourself; Educational & Textbooks; Electronic
(Professional & Academic); Fiction; Guide
Books; Health & Beauty; Humour; Languages
& Linguistics; Magic & the Occult; Medical
(incl. Self Help & Alternative Medicine);
Music; Reference Books, Directories &
Dictionaries; Scientific & Technical; Sports &
Games; Travel & Topography; Vocational
Training & Careers*

Associated & Subsidiary Companies:
India: Family Books Pvt Ltd; Hind Pustak
Bhandar; Book Makers; SBP Consultants &
Engineers Pvt Ltd

Book Trade Association Membership:
Federation of Indian Publishers, Federation of
Booksellers & Publishers Associations in India,
Federation of Educational Publishers,
Chemical & Allied Export Promotion Council,
All India Hindi Publishers' Association

2347 ▬▬▬

RAMESH PUBLISHING HOUSE
12-H New Darya Ganj Road,
New Delhi 110 002
Telephone: +91 (011) 327 5124
Fax: +91 (011) 327 5124

Showroom/Trade Enquiries:
4457 Nai Sarak, Delhi 110 006
Telephone: +91 (011) 291 8938
Fax: +91 (011) 327 5124

Partners: Om Parkash Gupta
Alok Gupta
Manager: Anurag Gupta
Writer: Anjani Gupta

*Educational & Textbooks; English as a Foreign
Language; Guide Books; Reference Books,
Directories & Dictionaries; Vocational
Training & Careers*

New Titles: 35 (1995), 40 (1996)
No of Employees: 17
Annual Turnover: $235,000

ISBNs, Imprints & Series: 81 86224

Book Trade Association Membership: Delhi
State Booksellers' & Publishers' Association

2348 ▬▬▬

RASTOGI PUBLICATIONS
Shivaji Road, Meerut 250 002
Telephone: +91 (0121) 510 688, 516 080 &
521 546
Fax: +91 (0121) 521 545

Exports & Rights: H. K. Rastogi
Production: R. K. Rastogi

*Academic & Scholarly; Agriculture; Biology &
Zoology; Educational & Textbooks;
Environment & Development Studies*

New Titles: 125 (1995), 150 (1996)
No of Employees: 25
Annual Turnover: $625,000

ISBNs, Imprints & Series:
81 7133, 81 85711

Associated & Subsidiary Companies:
India: Rastogi & Co

Book Trade Association Membership:
Federation of Indian Publishers

2349 ▬▬▬

RAWAT PUBLICATIONS
3-Na-20 Jawahar Nagar, Jaipur 302 004
Telephone: +91 (0141) 567 022
Fax: +91 (0141) 567 748

Directors: Kailash Rawat *(Managing,
Publishing)*
Pranit Rawat *(Export Sales)*
Sachin Rawat *(Home Sales)*

*Agriculture; Crime; Economics; Educational
& Textbooks; Environment & Development
Studies; Gender Studies; Geography &
Geology; Sociology & Anthropology*

New Titles: 60 (1995), 75 (1996)
No of Employees: 10
Annual Turnover: $25,000

ISBNs, Imprints & Series: 81 7033

Overseas Representation *(see §7.3):*
UK: K. G. Khandelwal, London

USA: South Asia Books, Columbia, MO; Dr S. Gupta, Chicago, IL

2350

RELIANCE PUBLISHING HOUSE
3026/7H Ranjit Nagar, New Delhi 110 008
Telephone: +91 (Õ11) 572 2605, 578 6889 & 573 7377
Fax: +91 (Õ11) 574 4633

Warehouse:
J-436 Baljeet Nagar (Prem Nagar Road), New Delhi 110 008
Telephone: +91 (Õ11) 573 7377
Fax: +91 (Õ11) 574 4633

Proprietor: Dr S. K. Bhatia *(Rights & Permissions)*
Managers: Manish K. Bhatia *(General)*
Mrs Durgesh Bhatia *(Sales)*
Miss Geeta Bhatia *(Publicity, Editorial)*
Miss Anita Mehta *(Enquiry)*
Mrs Anju Sehgal *(Office)*
Miss Meenu Sharma *(Office)*

Academic & Scholarly; Accountancy & Taxation; Agriculture; Archaeology; Architecture & Design; Atlases & Maps; Bibliography & Library Science; Biography & Autobiography; Biology & Zoology; Children's Books; Cinema, Video, TV & Radio; Computer Science; Cookery, Wines & Spirits; Crime; Crafts & Hobbies; Do-It-Yourself; Economics; Educational & Textbooks; Electronic (Educational); Electronic (Entertainment); Electronic (Professional & Academic); English as a Foreign Language; Environment & Development Studies; Fashion & Costume; Fiction; Fine Art & Art History; Gardening; Gender Studies; Geography & Geology; Guide Books; Health & Beauty; History & Antiquarian; Humour; Illustrated & Fine Editions; Industry, Business & Management; Languages & Linguistics; Law; Literature & Criticism; Magic & the Occult; Mathematics & Statistics; Medical (incl. Self Help & Alternative Medicine); Military & War; Music; Natural History; Philosophy; Photography; Poetry; Politics & World Affairs; Psychology & Psychiatry; Reference Books, Directories & Dictionaries; Religion & Theology; Science Fiction; Scientific & Technical; Sociology & Anthropology; Sports & Games; Theatre, Drama & Dance; Transport; Travel & Topography; Vocational Training & Careers

New Titles: 50 (1995), 50 (1996)
No of Employees: 12

ISBNs, Imprints & Series:
81 7510, 81 85047, 81 85972

Associated & Subsidiary Companies:
India: Geeta Graphics; Gita Enterprises

Book Trade Association Membership:
Federation of Indian Publishers, Delhi State Booksellers & Publishers Association, Federation of Booksellers & Publishers Associations of India, Federation of Career & Competition Publishers, Federation of Educational Publishers, Indian Society of Authors, Indian Library Association

2351

RESEARCH PRESS
PO Box 7208, Flat 212A Vardaan House, 7/28 Ansari Road, Darya Ganj, New Delhi 110 002
Telephone: +91 (Õ11) 328 1819
Fax: +91 (Õ11) 688 3369

Environment & Development Studies; Geography & Geology; Industry, Business & Management; Sociology & Anthropology

New Titles: 10 (1995), 12 (1996)
No of Employees: 5
Annual Turnover: £40,000

ISBNs, Imprints & Series: 81 7314

Overseas Representation *(see §7.3):*
Worldwide: UCL Press, London, UK

2352

RITANA BOOKS
81 Defence Colony Flyover Market, New Delhi 110 024
Telephone: +91 (Õ11) 464 3764 & 461 7278
Fax: +91 (Õ11) 463 6063

Directors: Rock Furtado *(Managing)*
Blossom Furtado *(Executive)*

Aviation; Fiction; Industry, Business & Management; Military & War; Travel & Topography; Vocational Training & Careers

New Titles: 16 (1995), 20 (1996)
No of Employees: 20

ISBNs, Imprints & Series: 81 85250

Book Trade Association Membership: The Federation of Publishers' & Booksellers' Associations in India, Delhi State Booksellers & Publishers Association

2353

RUPA & CO
15 Bankim Chatterjee Street, (PO Box 12333), Calcutta 700 073
Telephone: +91 (Õ33) 241 0691, 241 7401 & 241 6597
Fax: +91 (Õ33) 241 0691

Warehouse:
1 Thakurdas Chakraborty Lane, Calcutta 700 006
Telephone: +91 (Õ33) 241 2611

Bombay Branch:
Ghaswala Tower, P. G. Solanki Path, off Lamington Road, Bombay 400 007
Telephone: +91 (Õ22) 3082 631 & 3088 212
Fax: +91 (Õ22) 3088 212

Delhi Branch:
7/16 Makhanlal Street, Ansari Road, Daryaganj, New Delhi 110 002
Telephone: +91 (Õ11) 327 2161 & 327 8586
Fax: +91 (Õ11) 327 7294

Allahabad Branch:
135 South Malaka, Allahabad, Uttar Pradesh 211 001

Telephone: +91 (Õ532) 606 833
Fax: +91 (Õ532) 611 020

Partners: D. Mehra *(Chief Executive)*
R. N. Barman *(Sales)*
R. K. Mehra *(Production)*
C. K. Mehra *(Publicity & Promotion)*
S. K. Mehra *(Accounts)*

Biography & Autobiography; Children's Books; Cinema, Video, TV & Radio; Cookery, Wines & Spirits; Crime; English as a Foreign Language; Fashion & Costume; Fiction; Industry, Business & Management; Literature & Criticism; Philosophy; Poetry; Psychology & Psychiatry; Reference Books, Directories & Dictionaries; Religion & Theology; Sports & Games; Theatre, Drama & Dance; Travel & Topography

No of Employees: 84

ISBNs, Imprints & Series: 81 7167

2354

SAGE PUBLICATIONS INDIA PVT LTD
32 M-Block Market, Greater Kailash-I, PO Box 4215, New Delhi 110 048
Telephone: +91 (Õ11) 648 5884 & 644 4958
Fax: +91 (Õ11) 647 2426

Managing Director: Tejeshwar Singh
Finance: Anjul Kalra
Marketing: Sunanda Ghosh
Editorial: Harsh Sethi

Academic & Scholarly; Economics; Environment & Development Studies; Gender Studies; Industry, Business & Management; Politics & World Affairs; Psychology & Psychiatry; Sociology & Anthropology

New Titles: 50 (1995), 60 (1996)
No of Employees: 63
Annual Turnover: $800,000

ISBNs, Imprints & Series: 81 7036

Parent Company:
Sage Publications Inc *(USA)*

Associated & Subsidiary Companies:
UK: Sage Publications Ltd

Overseas Representation *(see §7.3):*
UK: Sage Publications Ltd, London
USA: Sage Publications Inc, Thousand Oaks, CA

Book Trade Association Membership:
Federation of Booksellers & Publishers Associations of India

2355

*SANGAM BOOKS (I) LTD
3-5-820 Hyderguda, Hyderabad 500 029
Telephone: +91 (Õ40) 232 543
Fax: +91 (Õ40) 240 393

Accountant: D. Yoga Reddy

Biography & Autobiography; Educational & Textbooks; Fiction; Gender Studies; Sociology & Anthropology

Overseas Representation *(see §7.3)*:
South East Asia: Pustaka Baiduri Sdn Bhd,
Kuala Lumpur, Malaysia
UK: Sangam Books Ltd, London

Book Trade Association Membership: The
Federation of Indian Publishers

2356 ▬▬▬▬▬▬▬

SRI SATGURU PUBLICATIONS
40/5 Shakti Nagar, Delhi 110 007
Telephone: +91 (Ō11) 712 6497 & 743 4930
Fax: +91 (Ō11) 722 7336

Directors: Anil Gupta *(Publicity &*
Production)
Naresh Gupta *(Sales)*
Virender Gupta *(Rights & Sales)*
Sunil Gupta *(Exports)*

Academic & Scholarly; History & Antiquarian;
Music; Philosophy; Reference Books,
Directories & Dictionaries; Religion &
Theology; Theatre, Drama & Dance

New Titles: 65 (1995), 60 (1996)
No of Employees: 10
Annual Turnover: $305,000

ISBNs, Imprints & Series: 81 7030

Parent Company:
Indian Books Centre *(India)*

Associated & Subsidiary Companies:
India: Asian Arts & Archaeology Series Office;
Bibliotheca Indo-Buddhica Series Office; Sri
Garib Dass Oriental Series Office; Monumenta
Indica Series; Studies on Sri Lanka Series
Office

Overseas Representation *(see §7.3)*:
UK: Books from India Ltd, London
USA: South Asia Books, Columbia, MO

2357 ▬▬▬▬▬▬▬

SATPRAKASHAN SANCHAR KENDRA
PB 507, Bhanwarkua, Madhya Pradesh,
Indore 452 001
Telephone: +91 (Ō731) 475 744 & 63733
Fax: +91 (Ō731) 475 731

Children's Books; Cinema, Video, TV & Radio;
Gender Studies; Religion & Theology;
Sociology & Anthropology

New Titles: 8 (1995), 10 (1996)
No of Employees: 15
Annual Turnover: $50,000

ISBNs, Imprints & Series:
81 85357, 81 85428

Book Trade Association Membership: SVD
International

2358 ▬▬▬▬▬▬▬

SCHOLAR PUBLISHING HOUSE (P)
LTD
85 Model Basti, New Delhi 110 005
Telephone: +91 (Ō11) 752 8303 & 354 1299
Fax: +91 (Ō11) 777 6565

Bangalore Office:
10 Sheshadri Road, Bangalore 560 009
Telephone: +91 (Ō80) 287 5296 & 287 4925

Calcutta Office:
23-G/4 Baederaipur Road, Jadavpur,
Calcutta 700 032

Gauhati Office:
M. C. Road, Opp. Gauhati Club,
Gauhati 793 001
Telephone: +91 (Ō361) 547 146

Haderabad Office:
7-1-65/16 Vidhaya Apartments,
Flat No 203 Dharam Karam Road, Ameerpet,
Hyderabad 500 016
Telephone: +91 (Ō40) 374 8759

Imphal Office:
Paona Bazar, Near Victory Cinema,
Imphal 795 001
Telephone: +91 (Ō385) 225 839 & 223 880

Madras Office:
A. P. 642, 49th Street, 9 Sector, K.K. Nagar,
Madras 600 078
Telephone: +91 (Ō44) 483 7232

Directors: Y. P. Ranade *(Managing, Finance*
& Rights)
I. J. Sharma *(Production & Editorial)*
S. K. Ranade *(Sales)*
Ramesh Ranade *(Marketing)*

Atlases & Maps; Children's Books;
Educational & Textbooks; Languages &
Linguistics; Reference Books, Directories &
Dictionaries

New Titles: 200 (1995), 250 (1996)
No of Employees: 15
Annual Turnover: $1.7M

ISBNs, Imprints & Series: 81 7172

Associated & Subsidiary Companies:
India: Alvina Publishing House; Schemeco
Enterprises; Seminery Publishers

Overseas Representation *(see §7.3)*:
Kenya: Textbook Centre Ltd, Nairobi
Mauritius: Robert Lee, Port Louis
South Africa: Mrs Dense Padayachee,
Dormerton
Tanzania: Rasiad-Said Khamis, Dar Es Salaam
Zimbabwe: The Book Centre, Harare

Book Trade Association Membership: Afro-
Asian Book Council, Chemicals & Allied
Products Export Promotion Council – Book
Division, Federation of Educational Publishers
in India, National Book Development Council,
All India Map Charts Publishers Association,
Educational Publishers Association (Delhi)

2359 ▬▬▬▬▬▬▬

SCIENTIFIC BOOK AGENCY
56-D Mirza Ghalib Street, Post Bag 9003,
Calcutta 700 016
Telephone: +91 (Ō33) 292 915
Fax: +91 (Ō33) 464 4650

Trade Enquiries, Orders & Warehouse:
79/2 Mahatma Gandhi Road, Calcutta 700 009
Telephone: +91 (Ō33) 315 278

Also at:
PO Box 239, Calcutta 700 001

Also at:
49/13 Hindusthan Park, Calcutta 700 029

Partners: J. Sinha *(Managing)*
S. Sinha *(Production)*
Satin Sinha *(Trade Sales)*
Editors: Atish Sinha *(Engineering &*
Technology)
Mrs Prakriti Sinha *(Chief)*
Snehamay Sinha *(Copy, Sales Promotion &*
Publicity, & Science)
Swapan Mitra *(Supervisor)*
Mrs Rajashi Sinha *(Export Sales, Rights &*
Permissions)

Academic & Scholarly; Accountancy &
Taxation; Agriculture; Animal Care &
Breeding; Archaeology; Architecture &
Design; Biology & Zoology; Chemistry;
Computer Science; Do-It-Yourself; Economics;
Educational & Textbooks; Electronic
(Educational); Electronic (Professional &
Academic); Engineering; Geography &
Geology; Guide Books; History & Antiquarian;
Industry, Business & Management; Law;
Literature & Criticism; Mathematics &
Statistics; Medical (incl. Self Help &
Alternative Medicine); Natural History;
Philosophy; Physics; Politics & World Affairs;
Psychology & Psychiatry; Reference Books,
Directories & Dictionaries; Scientific &
Technical; Travel & Topography; Veterinary
Science

New Titles: 11 (1995), 15 (1996)
No of Employees: 12

Book Trade Association Membership: New
Delhi: Federation of Indian Publishers &
Booksellers Association, Calcutta: Publishers
& Booksellers Association of West Bengal

2360 ▬▬▬▬▬▬▬

SCIENTIFIC PUBLISHERS
New Pali Road, PO Box 91, Jodhpur 342 001
Telephone: +91 (Ō291) 33323
Fax: +91 (Ō291) 613 480

Warehouse:
Opposite Police Line, Jodhpur
Telephone: +91 (Ō291) 624 154

Director: Pawan Kumar

Academic & Scholarly; Agriculture; Biology &
Zoology; Engineering; Geography & Geology;
Scientific & Technical

New Titles: 26 (1995), 32 (1996)
No of Employees: 10

ISBNs, Imprints & Series:
81 07233, 81 85046

Parent Company:
United Book Traders *(India)*

Associated & Subsidiary Companies:
India: Divya Jyoti

Book Trade Association Membership:
Federation of Publishers & Booksellers of
India, Federation of India Publishers

2361

SHIPRA PUBLICATIONS
115-A, 3rd Floor, Vikas Marg, Shakarpur,
Delhi 110 092
Telephone: +91 (Õ11) 220 0954 & 245 8662
Fax: +91 (Õ11) 242 3078

Director of Publications: M. K. Jain
Administration Officer: Ms Jyoti Nijhawan

*Academic & Scholarly; Agriculture;
Bibliography & Library Science; Biography &
Autobiography; Children's Books; Crime;
Economics; Educational & Textbooks;
Environment & Development Studies; Fiction;
Humour; Industry, Business & Management;
Law; Literature & Criticism; Military & War;
Politics & World Affairs; Reference Books,
Directories & Dictionaries; Sociology &
Anthropology*

New Titles: 26 (1995), 30 (1996)
No of Employees: 10

ISBNs, Imprints & Series: 81 85402

Book Trade Association Membership: Delhi
State Booksellers & Publishers Association

2362

SOUTH ASIAN PUBLISHERS PVT LTD
50 Sidharth Enclave, PO Jangpura,
New Delhi 110 014
Telephone: +91 (Õ11) 692 5315 & 683 5713

Warehouse:
H 65 Sector IX, Noida, UP

Editorial & Rights: Vinod Kumar
Sales & Promotion: Y. P. Pandey

*Agriculture; Chemistry; Mathematics &
Statistics; Philosophy; Politics & World Affairs*

New Titles: 21 (1995), 24 (1996)
No of Employees: 6
Annual Turnover: $20,000

ISBNs, Imprints & Series: 81 7003

2363

*SPECTRUM PUBLICATIONS
PO Box 45, Panbazar Main Road,
Guwahati 781 001
Telephone: +91 (Õ361) 32059
Fax: +91 (Õ361) 544 791

Distributors:
United Publishers, Pan Bazar, PO Box 82,
Guwahati 781 001
Telephone: +91 (Õ361) 546 244
Fax: +91 (Õ361) 544 791

Publisher: Krishan Kumar
Editorial: Ms Aarti Kumar
Export Sales & Rights: Ms Anita Kumar
Publicity: Sanchit Kumar

*Atlases & Maps; Children's Books; Guide
Books; Law; Reference Books, Directories &
Dictionaries; Sociology & Anthropology;
Travel & Topography*

ISBNs, Imprints & Series:
81 85319 Aarti Books, Neha Mini Katha,
Sunny Classics

Parent Company:
The Modern Book Depot *(India)*

Book Trade Association Membership:
Federation of Indian Publishers

2364

STAR PUBLICATIONS (P) LTD
4/5 B Asaf Ali Road, New Delhi 110 002
Telephone: +91 (Õ11) 327 4874 & 326 8651
Fax: +91 (Õ11) 327 3335
Email: del.starpub@axcess.net.in

Exports:
N-33 Greater Kailash-I, New Delhi 110 048
Telephone: +91 (Õ11) 648 1565
Fax: +91 (Õ11) 648 1565
Email: del.starpub@axcess.net.in

Directors: Amarnath Varma *(Managing)*
Anil Varma *(Sales)*
Sunil Varma *(Exports)*
Sanjay Varma *(Finance)*

Languages & Linguistics

New Titles: 50 (1995), 30 (1996)
No of Employees: 48

ISBNs, Imprints & Series:
Hindi Book Centre, Star Publications (P) Ltd

Overseas Representation *(see §7.3)*:
UK: Asian Bookshop, London

Book Trade Association Membership:
Federation of Indian Publishers

2365

STERLING INFORMATION TECHNOLOGIES
L-11, Green Park Extension,
New Delhi 110 016
Telephone: +91 (Õ11) 685 1023 & 669 560
Fax: +91 (Õ11) 685 1028 & 688 6646

Partners: Vikas Ghai
Gaurav Ghai
Administration Executive: Sam Chacko

*Computer Science; Languages & Linguistics;
Management*

New Titles: 25 (1995), 25 (1996)
No of Employees: 3
Annual Turnover: $50,000

ISBNs, Imprints & Series:
81 7359 Sterling, Sterling Languages, Sterling
Management

Parent Company:
Sterling Publishers Pvt Ltd *(India)*

Associated & Subsidiary Companies:
India: Learners Press

2366

STERLING PUBLISHERS PVT LTD
L-10 Green Park Extension, New Delhi 110 016

Telephone: +91 (Õ11) 669 560, 660 904 & 685
1023
Fax: +91 (Õ11) 685 1028 & 688 6646

Chairman & Managing Director: S. K. Ghai
Directors: Vikas Ghai
Gaurav Ghai
General Manager: H. J. Seghal
Editor: Vijaya Kumar

*Academic & Scholarly; Biography &
Autobiography; Cookery, Wines & Spirits;
Economics; Educational & Textbooks; English
as a Foreign Language; Fiction; Gender
Studies; Poetry; Politics & World Affairs*

New Titles: 50 (1995), 60 (1996)
No of Employees: 35
Annual Turnover: £500,000

ISBNs, Imprints & Series: 81 207

Overseas Representation *(see §7.3)*:
Bangladesh: The University Press Ltd, Dhaka
Pakistan: Vanguard Books Pvt Ltd, Lahore
Sri Lanka: Charles Subasinghe & Sons (P) Ltd,
Colombo
UK: Soma Books, London
USA: South Asia Books, Columbia, MO

Book Trade Association Membership:
Federation of Indian Publishers, Delhi State
Booksellers & Publishers Association,
International Association of Scholarly
Publishers

2367

SULTAN CHAND & SONS
23 Daryaganj, New Delhi 110 002
Telephone: +91 (Õ11) 327 8659, 327 7843 &
327 9080
Fax: +91 (Õ11) 325 4295

Production & Editorial: Shri Prakash Chand
Marketing: Shri Manohar Pant

*Accountancy & Taxation; Chemistry;
Computer Science; Do-It-Yourself; Economics;
Educational & Textbooks; Electronic
(Educational); Industry, Business &
Management; Law; Mathematics & Statistics;
Physics; Politics & World Affairs; Scientific &
Technical; Vocational Training & Careers*

New Titles: 45 (1995), 50 (1996)
No of Employees: 48
Annual Turnover: $2M

ISBNs, Imprints & Series: 81 7014

Associated & Subsidiary Companies:
India: Premier Book Co

Book Trade Association Membership:
Federation of Booksellers & Publishers
Associations of India

2368

SURYA INTERNATIONAL PUBLICATIONS
4-B Nashville Road, Dehra Dun 248 001 (UP)
Telephone: +91 (Õ135) 650172

*Academic & Scholarly; Agriculture; Biology &
Zoology; Chemistry; Economics; Educational*

& Textbooks; Environment & Development
Studies; Geography & Geology; Natural
History; Physics; Psychology & Psychiatry;
Sociology & Anthropology

New Titles: 6 (1995), 10 (1996)
No of Employees: 5

ISBNs, Imprints & Series: 81 85276

2369

TBS PUBLISHERS' DISTRIBUTORS
TBS Building, G H Road, Calicut 673 001
Telephone: +91 (Ō495) 64025, 60085 & 60086
Fax: +91 (Ō495) 64314

Partner: N. E. Manohar
Managing Partner: Balakrishnan

Academic & Scholarly; Biography &
Autobiography; Biology & Zoology;
Chemistry; Children's Books; Cookery, Wines
& Spirits; Economics; Educational &
Textbooks; Electronic (Educational);
Engineering; Fiction; Gardening; Guide
Books; Humour; Literature & Criticism;
Mathematics & Statistics; Philosophy;
Physics; Poetry; Reference Books, Directories
& Dictionaries

New Titles: 45 (1995), 70 (1996)
No of Employees: 60
Annual Turnover: £1.5M

ISBNs, Imprints & Series:
81 7180 Poorna Publications

Book Trade Association Membership:
Federation of Indian Publishers, International
Publishers Association

2370

THE THEOSOPHICAL PUBLISHING HOUSE
Adyar, Madras 600 020
Telephone: +91 (Ō44) 491 1338
Fax: +91 (Ō44) 491 5552

Manager: D. K. Govindaraj
Publications Officer: K. N. Anantharaman

Magic & the Occult; Philosophy; Religion &
Theology; Metaphysics; Oriental; Theosophy

New Titles: 4 (1995), 20 (1996)
No of Employees: 28
Annual Turnover: $40,000

ISBNs, Imprints & Series: 81 7059

Associated & Subsidiary Companies:
Philippines: The Theosophical Publishing
House. UK: Theosophical Books Ltd. USA:
The Theosophical Publishing House

Overseas Representation (see §7.3):
Philippines: The Theosophical Publishing
House, Quezon City
UK: Theosophical Books Ltd, London
USA: The Theosophical Publishing House,
Wheaton, IL

2371

TODAY & TOMORROW'S PRINTERS & PUBLISHERS
24B/5 Desh Bandhu Gupta Road, Karol Bagh,
New Delhi 110 005
Telephone: +91 (Ō11) 572 1928 & 572 7770
Fax: +91 (Ō11) 572 1928

Managing Director: Shri R. K. Jain
Manager: Shri S. K. Jain

Academic & Scholarly; Agriculture;
Bibliography & Library Science; Biology &
Zoology; Geography & Geology; Natural
History; Reference Books, Directories &
Dictionaries; Religion & Theology; Sociology
& Anthropology

New Titles: 15 (1995), 15 (1996)
No of Employees: 12

ISBNs, Imprints & Series: 81 7019

Overseas Representation (see §7.3):
USA: Scholarly Publications, Houston, TX

Book Trade Association Membership:
Federation of Indian Publishers, Chemical &
Allied Export Promotion Council

2372

UNIVERSAL BOOK TRADERS
80 Gokhale Market,
Opposite Tishazari New Courts, Delhi 110 054
Telephone: +91 (Ō11) 291 1966, 251 1288 &
291 4487
Fax: +91 (Ō11) 292 4152 & 745 9023

Branch (Retail Sales):
C-27/1, Connaught Place, New Delhi 110 001
Telephone: +91 (Ō11) 332 3277 & 371 3671
Fax: +91 (Ō11) 292 4152

Directors: M. G. Arora (Managing)
Pradeep Arora (Imports & Exports, Rights &
Permissions)
Sanjeev Arora (Home Sales)
Manish Arora (Editing & Production)
Managers: Labhaya Ram (Sales Promotion)
J. N. Magan (Sales)

Accountancy & Taxation; Industry, Business &
Management; Law

New Titles: 52 (1995), 50 (1996)

ISBNs, Imprints & Series:
81 7494, 81 85200

Overseas Representation (see §7.3):
Australia: The Law Book Co Ltd, North Ryde;
The Point of Law, Sydney
Canada: Carswell Legal Publications,
Scarborough
Hong Kong: Bloomsbury Books Ltd; Swindon
Book Co, Kowloon
Malaysia: Malayan Law Journal Sdn Bhd,
Selangor; Crescent News (KL) Sdn Bhd,
Kuala Lumpur
Pakistan: Pakistan Law House, Karachi
Singapore: Minican Law Books Pte Ltd
South Africa: Butterworth Publishers (Pty) Ltd,
Durban; Juta & Company Ltd, Cape Town &
Johannesburg

UK: Hammicks Law Bookshop, London;
LAMBS (Legal & Medical Bookshop Ltd),
London; Wildy & Sons Ltd, London
USA: Fred B. Rothman & Co, Littleton

Book Trade Association Membership: Delhi
State Booksellers & Publishers Association,
The Federation of Publishers' & Booksellers'
Associations in India

2373

UNIVERSITIES PRESS (I) LTD
3-5-820 Hyderguda, Hyderabad 500 029
Telephone: +91 (Ō40) 232 543
Fax: +91 (Ō40) 240 393
Email: info@orienth.uunet.in

Editor: Madhu Reddy

Architecture & Design; Chemistry; Computer
Science; Engineering; Industry, Business &
Management; Mathematics & Statistics;
Physics; Scientific & Technical

New Titles: 8 (1995), 15 (1996)
No of Employees: 2
Annual Turnover: £30,000

ISBNs, Imprints & Series: 81 7371

Parent Company:
The Agricultural Development, Commercial
Credit & Industrial Investment Co Ltd; Orient
Longman Ltd; Sangam Books (India) Ltd
(India)

Overseas Representation (see §7.3):
South East Asia: Pustaka Baiduri Sdn Bhd,
Kuala Lumpur, Malaysia
UK: Sangam Books Ltd, London

Book Trade Association Membership: The
Federation of Indian Publishers

2374

VIDYARTHI PRAKASHAN (PVT) LTD
Bhagat Singh Marg, Post Box 161,
Saharanpur 247 001
Telephone: +91 (Ō132) 726 724
Fax: +91 (Ō132) 727 104

Also at:
Trisea Publications, Post Box 161,
Saharanpur 247 001
Telephone: +91 (Ō132) 726 724
Fax: +91 (Ō132) 727 104

Children's Books; Crafts & Hobbies; Do-It-
Yourself; Educational & Textbooks; English as
a Foreign Language; Environment &
Development Studies

New Titles: 35 (1995), 30 (1996)
No of Employees: 60

ISBNs, Imprints & Series:
81 86765 Trisea Publications
81 86766 Vidyarthi Prakashan (P) Ltd

Associated & Subsidiary Companies:
India: Trisea Publications. Nepal: Nepal
Sahitya Kendra

Overseas Representation (see §7.3):
Nepal: Nepal Sahitya Kendra, Kathmandu

Book Trade Association Membership: Indian PA, The Federation of Educational Publishers in India

2375

VISION BOOKS PVT LTD
Madarsa Road, Kashmere Gate, Delhi 110 006
Telephone: +91 (Õ11) 251 2267 & 251 7001
Fax: +91 (Õ11) 291 6315

Branch:
24 Feroze Gandhi Road, Lajpat Nagar III,
New Delhi 110 024
Telephone: +91 (Õ11) 683 6480 & 683 6470
Fax: +91 (Õ11) 683 6490

Branch:
3-B Pedder Road, 'Vasant', Ground Floor,
Bombay 400 026
Telephone: +91 (Õ22) 492 9343 & 496 0029

Branch:
3-6-280/A/5 Himayat Nagar,
Hyderabad 500 029
Telephone: +91 (Õ40) 243252

Directors: Sudhir Malhotra *(Marketing)*
Kapil Malhotra *(Publishing)*

*Accountancy & Taxation; Agriculture;
Biography & Autobiography; Cookery, Wines
& Spirits; Economics; Fiction; Health &
Beauty; Industry, Business & Management;
Literature & Criticism; Magic & the Occult;
Medical (incl. Self Help & Alternative
Medicine); Military & War; Philosophy;
Politics & World Affairs; Sports & Games;
Travel & Topography; Vocational Training &
Careers; Astrology; Finance & Investment*

New Titles: 50 (1995), 60 (1996)
No of Employees: 45
Annual Turnover: $1M

ISBNs, Imprints & Series:
81 7094 Anand Paperbacks, Orient Paperbacks

Associated & Subsidiary Companies:
India: Big Database Publishing Pvt Ltd; Rajpal
& Son; Ravindra Printing Press; Shiksha
Bharati

Overseas Representation *(see §7.3)*:
UK & Europe: Books from India Ltd, London,
UK

Book Trade Association Membership: Indian
PA, Indian Booksellers Association, Delhi
State Booksellers & Publishers Association

2376

A. H. WHEELER & CO LTD
23 L. B. Shastri Marg, Allahabad 211 001
Telephone: +91 (Õ532) 623346, 624661 &
624662
Fax: +91 (Õ532) 623345

Warehouse:
54 National Park, Lajpat Nagar IV,
New Delhi 110 024

Director: Arunjeet Banerjee
Managers: S. Chatterjee *(General—Finance)*
R. Taneja *(Branch)*

K. Joyson *(Assistant)*
Assistant Editor: K. Anand

*Academic & Scholarly; Accountancy &
Taxation; Chemistry; Computer Science; Do-
It-Yourself; Educational & Textbooks;
Engineering; English as a Foreign Language;
Guide Books; Health & Beauty; Philosophy;
Physics; Politics & World Affairs; Reference
Books, Directories & Dictionaries; Scientific &
Technical; Sociology & Anthropology*

New Titles: 25 (1995), 30 (1996)
No of Employees: 500
Annual Turnover: $80M

Book Trade Association Membership:
Federation of Indian Publishers, New Delhi,
Federation of Publishers & Booksellers
Associations of India, New Delhi

IRISH REPUBLIC

2377

AN GÚM
44 Upper O'Connell Street, Dublin 1
Telephone: +353 (Õ1) 873 4700
Fax: +353 (Õ1) 873 1140

Trade Enquiries:
The Stationery Office, 4–5 Harcourt Road,
Dublin 2
Telephone: +353 (Õ1) 613111
Fax: +353 (Õ1) 878 0645

Senior Editor: Caoimhín Ó Marcaigh
  (General, Rights & Permissions)
Production: John Dixon *(Production)*
Finance: Barra Mac Aoilha Bhuí

*Children's Books; Educational & Textbooks;
Music; Reference Books, Directories &
Dictionaries*

New Titles: 42 (1995), 50 (1996)
No of Employees: 17
Annual Turnover: £370,000

ISBNs, Imprints & Series: 1 85791

Parent Company:
Department of Education *(Irish Republic)*

Book Trade Association Membership: CLÉ
(Irish PA), Irish Educational PA

2378

ANVIL BOOKS/CHILDREN'S PRESS
45 Palmerston Road, Dublin 6
Telephone: +353 (Õ1) 497 3628

Director: Margaret Dardis *(Rights)*
Manager: Rena Dardis *(Sales, Editorial &
  Production)*

*Biography & Autobiography; Children's
Books; Cookery, Wines & Spirits; History &
Antiquarian; Humour*

New Titles: 7 (1995), 5 (1996)

ISBNs, Imprints & Series:
0 900068, 0 947962

Overseas Representation *(see §7.3)*:
UK: Turnaround Publishers Services Ltd,
London
USA: Irish Books & Media, Minneapolis, MN

2379

ATTIC PRESS LTD
29 Upper Mount Street, Dublin 2
Telephone: +353 (Õ1) 661 6128
Fax: +353 (Õ1) 661 6176
Email: atticirl@iol.ie
Web Site: http://www.iol.ie/~atticirl/

Publisher: Róisín Conroy

*Fiction; Gender Studies; Politics & World
Affairs*

New Titles: 21 (1995), 23 (1996)

ISBNs, Imprints & Series:
0 946211, 1 85594

Overseas Representation *(see §7.3)*:
Netherlands & Germany: Brigitte Axster,
Frankfurt, Germany
UK (excluding Northern Ireland): Central
Books Ltd, London, UK
USA: Koen Book Distributors Inc,
Moorestown, NJ; Irish Books & Media,
Minneapolis, MN

Book Trade Association Membership: CLÉ
(Irish PA)

2380

BLACKWATER PRESS
Juliette House, Broomhill Business Park,
Broomhill Road, Tallaght, Dublin 24
Telephone: +353 (Õ1) 451 5311
Fax: +353 (Õ1) 451 5308 & 451 5306 (Orders)

Directors: John O'Connor *(Managing)*
Colm Holmes *(Production)*
Editorial Managers: Anna O'Donovan
  (General—Rights & Permissions)
Deirdre Whelan *(Children's—Rights &
  Permissions)*

*Biography & Autobiography; Fiction; Politics
& World Affairs; Sports & Games*

ISBNs, Imprints & Series: 0 86121

Parent Company:
Folens Publishing Co *(Irish Republic)*

Overseas Representation *(see §7.3)*:
UK: Folens Ltd, Dunstable

2381

BRANDON BOOK PUBLISHERS LTD
Cooleen, Dingle, Co Kerry
Telephone: +353 (Õ66) 51463
Fax: +353 (Õ66) 51234

Warehouse, Trade Orders:
Gill & Macmillan, Goldenbridge, Inchicore,
Dublin 8
Telephone: +353 (Õ1) 531005
Fax: +353 (Õ1) 541688

Directors: Steve MacDonogh *(Editorial, Sales, Rights & Permissions)*
Bernard Goggin *(Financial)*

Biography & Autobiography; Fiction; Literature & Criticism; Politics & World Affairs; Travel & Topography

New Titles: 14 (1995), 14 (1996)
No of Employees: 5
Annual Turnover: £400,000

ISBNs, Imprints & Series: 0 86322

Overseas Representation *(see §7.3)*:
UK (excluding Northern Ireland): Turnaround Publishers Services Ltd, London, UK
USA: Irish Books & Media, Minneapolis, MN

Book Trade Association Membership: CLÉ (Irish PA)

2382

*CITIS LTD
2 Rosemount Terrace, Blackrock, Co Dublin
Telephone: +353 (01) 288 6227
Fax: +353 (01) 288 5971

Directors: Donal P. Murphy *(Managing)*
K. D. Murphy *(Marketing)*
Marketing Manager: Kenneth Kelly

Electronic (Professional & Academic); Engineering; Reference Books, Directories & Dictionaries; Scientific & Technical; CD-ROM databases

ISBNs, Imprints & Series: 0 948564

Overseas Representation *(see §7.3)*:
USA & Canada: CITIS, New York, USA

Book Trade Association Membership:
ALPSP (UK), CLÉ (Irish PA)

2383

CLÓ IAR-CHONNACHTA
Indreabhán, Conamara, Co Galway
Telephone: +353 (091) 593307
Fax: +353 (091) 593362
Email: cic@iol.ie
Web Site: http://www.wombat.ie/cic

Managing Director: Micheal Ó Conghaile *(Rights)*
Sales, Marketing & Exports: Déirdre Ní Thuathail
Editor: Nóirín Ní Ghrádaigh

Audio Books; Biography & Autobiography; Children's Books; Educational & Textbooks; Fiction; History & Antiquarian; Languages & Linguistics; Literature & Criticism; Music; Poetry; Theatre, Drama & Dance

New Titles: 15 (1995), 15 (1996)
No of Employees: 4
Annual Turnover: £200,000

ISBNs, Imprints & Series:
1 874700, 1 900693

Overseas Representation *(see §7.3)*:
Australia: Roibeard Mac Eoin, Sydney; Grub Street Bookshop, Fitzroy, Vic

UK: Connolly Publications, London
USA: The Irish Book Shop, New York; Steve Griffin, Medford, MA; Irish Books & Media, Minneapolis, MN

Book Trade Association Membership: CLÉ (Irish PA)

2384

COLUMBA
55A Spruce Avenue, Stillorgan Industrial Park, Blackrock, Co Dublin
Telephone: +353 (01) 294 2556
Fax: +353 (01) 294 2564
Email: columba@indigo.ie
Web Site: http://www.bookshop.co.uk/columba

Managing Director & Publisher: Séan O Boyle
Sales Director: Cecilia West *(Rights & Permissions)*

History & Antiquarian; Medical (incl. Self Help & Alternative Medicine); Psychology & Psychiatry; Religion & Theology

New Titles: 25 (1995), 25 (1996)
No of Employees: 2

ISBNs, Imprints & Series:
0 948183, 1 85607 The Columba Press

Associated & Subsidiary Companies:
USA: Twenty-Third Publications

Overseas Representation *(see §7.3)*:
Australia: E. J. Dwyer (Australia) Pty Ltd, Alexandria, NSW
USA: Twenty-Third Publications, Mystic, CT

Book Trade Association Membership: CLÉ (Irish PA), Booksellers Association

---

2385

CORK UNIVERSITY PRESS
University College, Cork
Telephone: +353 (021) 902980
Fax: +353 (021) 273553

Orders & Distribution (Irish Republic, Northern Ireland & Europe):
Gill & Macmillan Distribution, Golden Bridge, Inchicore, Dublin 8
Telephone: +353 (01) 453 1005
Fax: +353 (01) 454 1688

Representation (Irish Republic & Northern Ireland):
Robert Towers, 2 The Crescent, Monkstown, Co Dublin
Telephone: +353 (01) 280 6532
Fax: +353 (01) 280 6020

Publisher: Sara Wilbourne
Production Editor: Eileen O'Carroll
Publicity & Promotion: Anne Lee
Secretary/PA: Patricia Carroll
Marketing: Seamus O'Reilly

Academic & Scholarly; Archaeology; Economics; Gender Studies; History & Antiquarian; Literature & Criticism

ISBNs, Imprints & Series:
0 902561, 1 85918 Undercurrents

Overseas Representation *(see §7.3)*:
Germany, Austria & Switzerland (Rights only): Brigitte Axster, Frankfurt, Germany
Japan: United Publishers Services Ltd, Tokyo
North America: International Specialized Book Services Inc, Portland, OR, USA
UK: Troika, London
UK & Europe: Central Books Ltd, London, UK

Book Trade Association Membership: CLÉ (Irish PA)

2386

*THE DEDALUS PRESS
24 The Heath, Cypress Downs, Dublin 6W
Telephone: +353 (01) 4902582

Director: John F. Deane

Fiction; Poetry

ISBNs, Imprints & Series:
0 948268, 1 873790 Peppercanister Series

Overseas Representation *(see §7.3)*:
Worldwide: Password, Manchester, UK

Book Trade Association Membership: CLÉ (Irish PA)

2387

DOMINICAN PUBLICATIONS
42 Parnell Square, Dublin 1
Telephone: +353 (01) 872 1611
Fax: +353 (01) 873 1760
Email: dompubs@iol.ie

Religion & Theology

New Titles: 4 (1995), 5 (1996)
No of Employees: 4

ISBNs, Imprints & Series:
0 907271, 0 9504797, 1 871552

Book Trade Association Membership: CLÉ (Irish PA)

2388

ECONOMIC & SOCIAL RESEARCH INSTITUTE
4 Burlington Road, Dublin 4
Telephone: +353 (01) 667 1525
Fax: +353 (01) 668 6231

Director: Prof K. A. Kennedy
Secretary: John Roughan
Research Professors: J. J. Sexton *(Economics)*
J. D. Fitz Gerald *(Economics)*
D. Conniffe *(Economics/Statistics)*
P. Honohan *(Economics)*
J. Bradley *(Economics)*
E. W. Henry *(Economics)*
B. Nolan *(Economics)*
B. J. Whelan *(Economics/Head of Survey Unit)*
D. Hannan *(Sociology & Social Policy)*
C. T. Whelan *(Sociology & Social Policy)*

Academic & Scholarly; Agriculture; Economics; Psychology & Psychiatry; Sociology & Anthropology

New Titles: 11 (1995), 10 (1996)
No of Employees: 80
Annual Turnover: £3.8M

ISBNs, Imprints & Series:
0 7070 Research Series

Book Trade Association Membership:
Association of Irish Learned Journals

2389 ▬▬▬▬▬▬▬▬▬▬

**EUROPEAN FOUNDATION FOR THE
IMPROVEMENT OF LIVING AND
WORKING CONDITIONS**
Loughlinstown House, Shankill, Co Dublin
Telephone: +353 (Õ1) 282 6888
Fax: +353 (Õ1) 282 6456

Head of Information: Norman Wood
Publications Officer: Susan Ryan-Sheridan
Editor EF News : Brid Nolan

*Academic & Scholarly; Gender Studies;
Reference Books, Directories & Dictionaries;
Scientific & Technical; Sociology &
Anthropology; Transport; Environment;
Health & Safety; Industrial Relations*

New Titles: 100 (1995), 120 (1996)
No of Employees: 80

ISBNs, Imprints & Series: 92 826

Parent Company:
Commission of the European Communities
(Belgium)

Associated & Subsidiary Companies:
Luxembourg: Office for Official Publications

Overseas Representation *(see §7.3):*
Australia: Hunter Publications, Collingwood
Austria: Manz'sche Verlags- und
    Universitätsbuchhandlung, Vienna
Belgium: Moniteur belge, Brussels
Canada: Renouf Publishing Co Ltd, Ottawa
Denmark: Schultz EF-publikationer,
    Copenhagen
France: European Community Information
    Service, Paris
Germany: Bundesanzeiger Verlag, Cologne
Greece: G. C. Eleftheroudakis SA, Athens
Hungary: Agroinform, Budapest
Italy: LICOSA–Libreria Comm. Sansoni SpA,
    Florence
Japan: Kinokuniya Co Ltd, Tokyo
Luxembourg: Messageries Paul Kraus,
    Luxembourg
Netherlands: Staatsdrukkerij- en
    uitgeverijbedrijf, 's-Gravenhage
Poland: Business Foundation, Warsaw
Portugal: Imprensa Nacional Casa da Moeda
    EP, Lisbon
Rest of World: Office for Official Publications
    of the European Community, Luxembourg
Spain: Boletín Oficial del Estado, Madrid
Sweden: BTJ, Lund
Switzerland: OSEC, Zurich
Turkey: Pres Dagitim Ticaret ve sanayi AS,
    Istanbul
UK: HM Stationery Office, London
USA: Unipub, Lanham, MD
Yugoslavia: Privredni Vjesnik, Belgrade

Book Trade Association Membership: CLÉ
(Irish PA)

2390 ▬▬▬▬▬▬▬▬▬▬

A. & A. FARMAR
78 Ranelagh Village, Dublin 6
Telephone: +353 (Õ1) 496 3625
Fax: +353 (Õ1) 497 0107
Email: 102021.150@compuserve.com

Trade Orders (Irish):
Brookside, Dundrum, Co Dublin

Trade Orders (UK):
Central Books, 99 Wallis Road,
London E9 5LN
Telephone: 0181 986 4854

Editorial: Anna Farmar
Production: Tony Farmar

*Cookery, Wines & Spirits; Fiction; Business
history*

New Titles: 5 (1995), 10 (1996)
No of Employees: 2

ISBNs, Imprints & Series: 1 899047

Overseas Representation *(see §7.3):*
UK: Oldcastle Books Ltd, Harpenden

Book Trade Association Membership: CLÉ
(Irish PA)

2391 ▬▬▬▬▬▬▬▬▬▬

FOLENS PUBLISHING CO
Juliette House, Broomhill Business Park,
Broomhill Road, Tallaght, Dublin 24
Telephone: +353 (Õ1) 4515311
Fax: +353 (Õ1) 4515308

Directors: John O'Connor *(Managing)*
Colm Holmes
Clare Manning *(Finance)*

*Biography & Autobiography; Educational &
Textbooks*

ISBNs, Imprints & Series: 0 86121

Parent Company:
Folens Investment Co *(Irish Republic)*

Associated & Subsidiary Companies:
UK: Folens Ltd

Overseas Representation *(see §7.3):*
UK: Folens Ltd, Dunstable

Book Trade Association Membership:
European Educational Publishers Group

2392 ▬▬▬▬▬▬▬▬▬▬

FOUR COURTS PRESS
Kill Lane, Blackrock, Co Dublin
Telephone: +353 (Õ1) 289 2922
Fax: +353 (Õ1) 289 3072
Email: fcp@indigo.ie

Distributor:
Gill & Macmillan, Goldenbridge, Inchicore,
Dublin 8
Telephone: +353 (Õ1) 453 1005
Fax: +353 (Õ1) 454 1688

Managing Director: Michael Adams
Marketing: Ronan Gallagher
Production: Martin Healy
Editorial: Martin Fanning

*Academic & Scholarly; Fine Art & Art History;
History & Antiquarian; Philosophy; Religion
& Theology*

New Titles: 17 (1995), 30 (1996)
No of Employees: 4

ISBNs, Imprints & Series:
0 906127, 1 85182

Overseas Representation *(see §7.3):*
USA: International Specialized Book Services
    Inc, Portland, OR

Book Trade Association Membership: CLÉ
(Irish PA)

2393 ▬▬▬▬▬▬▬▬▬▬

THE GALLERY PRESS
Loughcrew, Oldcastle, Co Meath
Telephone: +353 (Õ49) 41779
Fax: +353 (Õ49) 41779

Director: Peter Fallon *(Editorial, Production)*
Administration: Jean Barry
Sales & Accounts: Patricia Nicol

Fiction; Poetry; Theatre, Drama & Dance

New Titles: 13 (1995), 12 (1996)
No of Employees: 3

ISBNs, Imprints & Series:
0 902996, 0 904011, 1 85235

Associated & Subsidiary Companies:
USA: Deerfield Publications Inc

2394 ▬▬▬▬▬▬▬▬▬▬

GILL & MACMILLAN LTD
Goldenbridge, Inchicore, Dublin 8
Telephone: +353 (Õ1) 453 1005
Fax: +353 (Õ1) 454 1688

Directors: M. H. Gill *(Managing)*
H. J. Mahony *(Publishing)*
P. A. Thew *(Marketing & Sales)*
M. D. O'Dwyer *(Financial)*
M. O'Keeffe *(Production)*
M. D. O'Brien *(Distribution)*

*Academic & Scholarly; Biography &
Autobiography; Children's Books; Cookery,
Wines & Spirits; Economics; Educational &
Textbooks; Guide Books; History &
Antiquarian; Industry, Business &
Management; Law; Literature & Criticism;
Medical (incl. Self Help & Alternative
Medicine); Politics & World Affairs;
Psychology & Psychiatry; Reference Books,
Directories & Dictionaries; Religion &
Theology; Travel & Topography*

New Titles: 85 (1995), 85 (1996)
No of Employees: 50

ISBNs, Imprints & Series: 0 7171

Overseas Representation *(see §7.3)*:
Australia (Education titles): Macmillan Education Australia, South Melbourne, Vic, Australia
Australia (Religious titles): E. J. Dwyer (Australia) Pty Ltd, Alexandria, NSW, Australia
Europe: Michael Geoghegan, Cookham Dean, Berks, UK
Hong Kong, China, Thailand, Taiwan & Philippines: Macmillan Publishers (China) Ltd, Hong Kong
Japan: Macmillan Shuppan KK, Tokyo
New Zealand: Macmillan NZ, Auckland
Singapore, Indonesia, Brunei & Malaysia: Pansing Distribution Sdn Bhd, Singapore
South Africa (Education titles): Macmillan Boleswa, Braamfontein, South Africa
South Africa (Religious titles): Struik Christian Books, Cape Town, South Africa
UK (Irish interest, academic & general titles): Oldcastle Books Ltd, Harpenden, UK
UK (Religious titles): A. Guy Taylor, Ripon, UK
West Indies: Macmillan Caribbean, Basingstoke, UK

Book Trade Association Membership: CLÉ (Irish PA)

2395 ▬▬▬

INSTITUTE OF PUBLIC ADMINISTRATION
57–61 Lansdowne Road, Dublin 4
Telephone: +353 (Õ1) 668 6233
Fax: +353 (Õ1) 668 9135

Publications Division:
Institute of Public Administration, Vergemount Hall, Clonskeagh, Dublin 6
Telephone: +353 (Õ1) 2697011
Fax: +353 (Õ1) 2698644

Head of Publishing: Jim O'Donnell *(Rights & Permissions)*
Editorial: Tony McNamara
Production: Kathleen Harte
Sales: Eileen Kelly *(Home & Export)*

Academic & Scholarly; Economics; Law; Politics & World Affairs; Reference Books, Directories & Dictionaries; Sociology & Anthropology

New Titles: 8 (1995), 8 (1996)
No of Employees: 8

ISBNs, Imprints & Series:
0 906980, 1 872002

Overseas Representation *(see §7.3)*:
World (excluding North America): Euromonitor, London, UK

Book Trade Association Membership: CLÉ (Irish PA)

2396 ▬▬▬

IRISH ACADEMIC PRESS
Kill Lane, Blackrock, Co Dublin
Telephone: +353 (Õ1) 2892922
Fax: +353 (Õ1) 2893072
Email: fcp@indigo.ie

Distribution:
Gill & Macmillan, Goldenbridge, Inchicore, Dublin 8
Telephone: +353 (Õ1) 453 1005
Fax: +353 (Õ1) 454 1688

Academic & Scholarly; History & Antiquarian; Military & War

New Titles: 15 (1995), 22 (1996)

ISBNs, Imprints & Series:
0 7165 Irish Academic Press, Irish University Press

Overseas Representation *(see §7.3)*:
USA: International Specialized Book Services Inc, Portland, OR

Book Trade Association Membership: CLÉ (Irish PA)

2397 ▬▬▬

THE LILLIPUT PRESS LTD
4 Rosemount Terrace, Arbour Hill, Dublin 7
Telephone: +353 (Õ1) 671 1647
Fax: +353 (Õ1) 671 1647

Distributors (Trade Orders):
Gill & Macmillan, Goldenbridge, Inchicore, Dublin 8
Telephone: +353 (Õ1) 531005
Fax: +353 (Õ1) 541688

Director: Antony Farrell
Co-Directors: David Dickson
W. J. McCormack
Vincent Hurley
Terence Brown
Vivienne Guinness

Academic & Scholarly; Biography & Autobiography; Fiction; History & Antiquarian; Literature & Criticism; Reference Books, Directories & Dictionaries

New Titles: 18 (1995), 18 (1996)
No of Employees: 3
Annual Turnover: £200,000

ISBNs, Imprints & Series:
0 946640, 1 874675 ETCH (Essays & Texts in Cultural History), The Lilliput Press

Overseas Representation *(see §7.3)*:
France: Lora Fountain Agency, Paris
UK: Central Books Ltd, London

Book Trade Association Membership: CLÉ (Irish PA)

2398 ▬▬▬

MENTOR PUBLICATIONS
43 Furze Road, Sandyford Industrial Estate, Dublin 18
Telephone: +353 (Õ1) 295 2112/3
Fax: +353 (Õ1) 295 2114

General Manager: Daniel C. McCarthy

Economics; Educational & Textbooks; Geography & Geology; Guide Books; History & Antiquarian; Industry, Business & Management; Mathematics & Statistics; Poetry; Scientific & Technical

New Titles: 40 (1995), 12 (1996)
No of Employees: 15

2399 ▬▬▬

MERCIER PRESS LTD
5 French Church Street, Cork
Telephone: +353 (Õ21) 275040
Fax: +353 (Õ21) 274969

Managing Director: John F. Spillane *(Rights & Permissions)*
Sales Manager: Liam Clooney

Children's Books; History & Antiquarian; Humour; Law; Music; Religion & Theology

New Titles: 40 (1995), 50 (1996)
No of Employees: 21
Annual Turnover: £1,500

ISBNs, Imprints & Series:
0 85342, 1 85635

Overseas Representation *(see §7.3)*:
Australia: Keith Ainsworth Pty Ltd, Penrith, NSW
Europe: Hans Heinrich Petersen Buchimport GmbH, Hamburg, Germany
UK: Oldcastle Books Ltd, Harpenden
USA: Irish Books & Media, Minneapolis, MN; Dufour Editions Inc, Chester Springs, PA

2400 ▬▬▬

*THE O'BRIEN PRESS
20 Victoria Road, Rathgar, Dublin 6
Telephone: +353 (Õ1) 492 3333
Fax: +353 (Õ1) 492 2777

Trade Orders:
Gill & Macmillan, Goldenbridge Industrial Estate, Inchicore, Dublin 8
Telephone: +353 (Õ03) 453 1005
Fax: +353 (Õ1) 454 1688

Directors: Michael O'Brien *(Rights)*
Ivan O'Brien
Íde Ní Laoghaire
Sales & Marketing: Chenile Keogh
Mary Webb

Archaeology; Biography & Autobiography; Children's Books; Cookery, Wines & Spirits; Economics; Educational & Textbooks; Fiction; History & Antiquarian; Natural History; Politics & World Affairs; Reference Books, Directories & Dictionaries; Sociology & Anthropology

ISBNs, Imprints & Series:
0 86278 O'Brien Educational, O'Brien Press
0 905140 O'Brien Press

Associated & Subsidiary Companies:
Irish Republic: O'Brien Educational

Overseas Representation *(see §7.3)*:
Australia: Keith Ainsworth Pty Ltd, Penrith, NSW
Germany (Trade Orders): HHP Buchimport GmbH, Hamburg, Germany
UK & Ireland: Gill & Macmillan Ltd, Dublin, Irish Republic
USA: Irish Books & Media, Minneapolis, MN

USA & Canada (Trade & Library Orders):
Dufour Editions Inc, Chester Springs, PA, USA

2401

ROBERTS RINEHART PUBLISHERS
Trinity House, Charleston Road, Ranelagh, Dublin 6
Telephone: +353 (Ö1) 497 6860
Fax: +353 (Ö1) 497 6861
Email: rinehart@iol.ie

President: Rick Rinehart
Vice-President: Jack Van Zandt
Marketing & Publicity: Shelley Daigh
Rights: Mary Hegarty

Architecture & Design; Audio Books; Biography & Autobiography; Children's Books; Cookery, Wines & Spirits; Fiction; Fine Art & Art History; Geography & Geology; Guide Books; History & Antiquarian; Music; Natural History; Photography; Poetry; Travel & Topography

ISBNs, Imprints & Series:
0 911797, 0 939643, 1 879373 Roberts Rinehart (including Mizen Books, Rhino Books, Little Rhino Books)
0 911797, 1 57098, 1 879373, 1 882092, 1 916567
0 939643 Audio Press

Parent Company:
Roberts Rinehart *(USA)*

Associated & Subsidiary Companies:
USA: Roberts Rinehart Publishers

Overseas Representation *(see §7.3)*:
Canada: Publishers Group West, Emeryville, CA, USA
CIS: PIC Publishers, Moscow, Russia
Czech Republic: Foreign Rights Ltd, Vienna, Austria
France: Lora Fountain Agency, Paris
Germany: Thomas Schlück, Garbsen
Japan: Nicholas Smith, New York, USA
New Zealand: David Bateman Ltd, Auckland
Scandinavia: ICBS, Copenhagen, Denmark
Spain: Julio F. Yañez, Barcelona
UK: Airlift Book Co, London

Book Trade Association Membership: CLÉ (Irish PA), ABA (USA), Publishers Association (USA)

2402

*THE ROUND HALL PRESS
Kill Lane, Blackrock, Co Dublin
Telephone: +353 (Ö1) 289 2922
Fax: +353 (Ö1) 289 3072

Distribution:
Gill & Macmillan, Goldenbridge, Inchicore, Dublin 8
Telephone: +353 (Ö1) 453 1005
Fax: +353 (Ö1) 454 1688

Managing Director: Michael Adams
Promotions Manager: Terri McDonnell
Editor: Eilish McGuire

Law

ISBNs, Imprints & Series:
, 0 9508725, 1 85800

Parent Company:
Irish Academic Press *(Irish Republic)*

2403

ROYAL IRISH ACADEMY
Academy House, 19 Dawson Street, Dublin 2
Telephone: +353 (Ö1) 676 2570 & 676 4222
Fax: +353 (Ö1) 676 2346

Executive Secretary: Patrick Buckley *(Rights & Permissions)*
Sales Executive: Hugh Shiels *(Home & Export Sales)*
Editor: Barbara Young

Academic & Scholarly; Atlases & Maps; Biology & Zoology; History & Antiquarian; Languages & Linguistics; Reference Books, Directories & Dictionaries

New Titles: 6 (1995), 5 (1996)
No of Employees: 5

ISBNs, Imprints & Series:
0 901714, 1 874045

Book Trade Association Membership: CLÉ (Irish PA)

2404

VERITAS PUBLICATIONS
Veritas House, 7–8 Lower Abbey Street, Dublin 1
Telephone: +353 (Ö1) 788177
Fax: +353 (Ö1) 786507

Warehouse, Trade Enquiries & Orders:
8 Hanover Quay, Dublin 2

Managing Editor: Fiona Biggs
Commercial Manager: Tom Griffin
Publicity & Marketing: Brian Lynch
Rights & Permissions: Rita Singleton

Religion & Theology

New Titles: 35 (1995), 28 (1996)
No of Employees: 9

ISBNs, Imprints & Series:
0 85390, 0 86217, 1 85390

Parent Company:
Catholic Communications Institute of Ireland *(Irish Republic)*

Associated & Subsidiary Companies:
UK: Veritas Book & Video Distribution Ltd

Overseas Representation *(see §7.3)*:
Australia: Charles Paine Pty Ltd, North Paramatta, NSW
Canada: Emmets Religious Supply Ltd, Toronto
Malta: Libreria Taghlim Nisrani, Sliema
New Zealand: Christian Distribution Centre, Auckland
USA: Ignatius Press, San Francisco, CA

Book Trade Association Membership: CLÉ (Irish PA)

2405

WOLFHOUND PRESS
68 Mountjoy Square, Dublin 1
Telephone: +353 (Ö1) 874 0354
Fax: +353 (Ö1) 872 0207

Managing Director: Seamus Cashman *(Publisher)*
Editorial: Susan Houlden

Academic & Scholarly; Biography & Autobiography; Children's Books; Fiction; Gender Studies; Literature & Criticism; Sports & Games

New Titles: 31 (1995), 36 (1996)
No of Employees: 8

ISBNs, Imprints & Series: 0 86327

Overseas Representation *(see §7.3)*:
Australia: Keith Ainsworth Pty Ltd, Penrith, NSW
UK: Ion Mills, Harpenden; Turnaround Publishers Services Ltd, London
USA: Dufour Editions Inc, Chester Springs, PA

Book Trade Association Membership: CLÉ (Irish PA)

JAMAICA

2406

CARLONG PUBLISHERS (CARIBBEAN) LTD
[formerly Longman Jamaica Ltd]
2 East Avenue, Kingston 5
Telephone: +1 (809) 960 9364–6
Fax: +1 (809) 968 1353

Also at:
33 Second Street, Newport West, PO Box 489, Kingston 10
Telephone: +1 (809) 923 7019 & 7008
Fax: +1 (809) 923 7003

Marketing Manager: Steve Ashman
Rights & Permissions: Dorothy Noel

Academic & Scholarly; Children's Books; Educational & Textbooks; Geography & Geology

New Titles: 4 (1995), 10 (1996)
No of Employees: 31

ISBNs, Imprints & Series:
976 8010 Carlong Assessment Tests Series, Carlong Practice Papers for Common Entrance Series, Carlong Primary Social Studies Series, First Steps in Science Series, Fun with Phonics Series, Let's Learn to Write Series, Reading Readiness Series

Book Trade Association Membership: Book Industry Association of Jamaica, Jamaican Booksellers Association

2407

KINGSTON PUBLISHERS LTD
LOJ Complex, Building 10, 7 Norman Road, Kingston

Telephone: +1 (809) 928 8898
Fax: +1 (809) 928 5719

Warehouse:
7 Norman Road, Kingston
Telephone: +1 (809) 928 5719
Fax: +1 (809) 928 5719

Chairman: L. Michael Henry
Managers: Daphne Taylor *(Educational Sales)*
Dawn Chambers *(Overseas Marketing)*
Editorial Director: Kim Robinson

*Academic & Scholarly; Atlases & Maps;
Biography & Autobiography; Children's
Books; Cookery, Wines & Spirits; Educational
& Textbooks; Fiction; Guide Books; History &
Antiquarian; Music; Politics & World Affairs;
Religion & Theology; Travel & Topography*

New Titles: 9 (1995), 24 (1996)
No of Employees: 10
Annual Turnover: $1M

Overseas Representation *(see §7.3):*
Bahamas: Bahamian News Ltd, Nassau
Barbados: Choice Publishing & Marketing Co
Ltd, St Michael
Far East: Fep International Pvt Ltd, Singapore
Trinidad: Caribbean Book Distributors, Port of
Spain
UK: Gazelle Book Services Ltd, Lancaster
USA: African World Press, Lawrenceville, NJ;
A & B Books, Brooklyn, NY; D & J Books,
Laurelton, NY

Book Trade Association Membership: Book
Industry Association of Jamaica, Jamaican PA,
Jamaican Booksellers Association

2408

**THE PRESS UNIVERSITY OF THE
WEST INDIES**
1A Aqueduct Flats, Mona, Kingston 7
Telephone: +1 (809) 977 2659
Fax: +1 (809) 977 2660
Email: lcameron@uwimona.edu.jm

Director: Linda D. Cameron
Managers: Nadine Buckland *(Business)*
Glynis Salmon *(Marketing)*
Managing Editor: Pansy Benn

*Academic & Scholarly; Archaeology; Atlases
& Maps; Bibliography & Library Science;
Biography & Autobiography; Environment &
Development Studies; Geography & Geology;
Languages & Linguistics; Reference Books,
Directories & Dictionaries; Religion &
Theology; Sociology & Anthropology*

New Titles: 19 (1995), 25 (1996)
No of Employees: 12
Annual Turnover: $200,000

ISBNs, Imprints & Series: 976

Parent Company:
The University of the West Indies *(Jamaica)*

Associated & Subsidiary Companies:
Jamaica: Canoe Press UWI

Overseas Representation *(see §7.3):*
Barbados: UWI Bookshop, Cave Hill
Canada: Sandberry Press, Toronto

Trinidad & Tobago: UWI Bookshop, St
Augustine, Trinidad
UK & Europe: Central Books Ltd, London, UK
USA: Kelani Caribbean, Orlando FL

Book Trade Association Membership: Book
Industry Association of Jamaica

2409

IAN RANDLE PUBLISHERS LTD
206 Old Hope Road, Box 686, Kingston 6
Telephone: +1 (809) 927 2085
Fax: +1 (809) 977 0243

Managing Director & Publisher: Ian Randle
Business Manager: Carlene Randle

*Academic & Scholarly; Biography &
Autobiography; Cookery, Wines & Spirits;
Educational & Textbooks; Electronic
(Professional & Academic); Gender Studies;
Law; Sports & Games*

New Titles: 16 (1995), 30 (1996)
No of Employees: 10
Annual Turnover: $675,000

ISBNs, Imprints & Series: 976 8100

Associated & Subsidiary Companies:
Jamaica: The Caribbean Law Publishing Co
Ltd

Overseas Representation *(see §7.3):*
UK: Africa Books Centre Ltd, London

Book Trade Association Membership: Book
Industry Association of Jamaica

2410

WEST INDIES PUBLISHING LTD
7 Norman Road, Kingston CSO
Telephone: +1 (809) 928 9081
Fax: +1 (809) 928 5269

Directors: D. Andrew Rousseau *(Managing)*
Managers: Julia Newbluard *(Finance)*
Diane Browne *(Publishing)*
Sales & Marketing: Emma Lewis

*Academic & Scholarly; Children's Books;
Cookery, Wines & Spirits; Educational &
Textbooks*

New Titles: 1 (1995), 5 (1996)

ISBNs, Imprints & Series: 976 605

Associated & Subsidiary Companies:
Jamaica: The Book Shop Ltd (Retailers); Book
Traders (Caribbean) Ltd (Distributors)

Overseas Representation *(see §7.3):*
Barbados: Cloister Book Store Ltd,
Bridgetown
Canada: Barrington Huie, Agincourt, Ont
Dominica: Jays Bookstore, Roseau
Guyana: National Stationery & Book Centre,
Georgetown
St Lucia: Nato's Educational Supplies, Castrie
Trinidad: KLP Agencies Ltd, Port of Spain

Book Trade Association Membership: Book
Industry Association of Jamaica, American
Booksellers Association

KENYA

2411

AFRICA BOOK SERVICES (EA) LTD
PO Box 45245, Quran House, Mfangano Street,
Nairobi
Telephone: +254 (Õ2) 223641
Fax: +254 (Õ2) 330272

Directors: M. B. Dar *(Managing)*
Noreen Dar *(Finance)*
S. M. Dar *(Sales)*
Talat Lone *(Marketing)*

*Accountancy & Taxation; Children's Books;
Computer Science; Educational & Textbooks;
Fiction; Reference Books, Directories &
Dictionaries*

New Titles: 3 (1995), 5 (1996)
No of Employees: 20
Annual Turnover: £450,000

Book Trade Association Membership: Kenya
PA, Kenya Booksellers & Stationers
Association, Kenya Library Association,
Booksellers Association of Great Britain &
Ireland

2412

AMECEA GABA PUBLICATIONS
PO Box 4002, Elboret
Telephone: +254 (Õ321) 61218
Fax: +254 (Õ321) 62570

Editor: Agatha Raboli
Dispatch Co-ordinator: Hesbon Nyongesa
Accountant: John Mwika Githae

Religion & Theology

New Titles: 7 (1995), 8 (1996)
No of Employees: 5

ISBNs, Imprints & Series:
9966 836 Spearhead Monograph Series

2413

CAMERAPIX
PO Box 45048, Nairobi
Telephone: +254 (Õ2) 223511 & 334398
Fax: +254 (Õ2) 217244

London Office:
8 Ruston Mews, London W11 1RB
Telephone: 071-221 0077
Fax: 071-792 8105

Chief Executive: Mohamed Amin
Editor: Brian Tetley
Sales Executive: Rukhsana Haq
Photo Editor: Duncan Willetts
General Manager: Steve Gill

*Guide Books; Illustrated & Fine Editions;
Natural History; Travel & Topography*

ISBNs, Imprints & Series: 1 874041

Associated & Subsidiary Companies:
Pakistan: Camerapix. *Seychelles:* Camerapix
Publishers Ltd. *Tanzania:* Camerapix. *UK:*
Camerapix

Overseas Representation *(see §7.3)*:
UK: Camerapix, London

Book Trade Association Membership: IPG

2414 ▬▬▬▬▬▬▬

**EAST AFRICAN EDUCATIONAL
PUBLISHERS LTD**
Brick Court, Mpaka Road / Woodvale Grove,
PO Box 45314, Nairobi
Telephone: +254 (Õ2) 444700 & 445260/1
Fax: +254 (Õ2) 448753

**Warehouse, Finance, Sales & Marketing
Departments:**
PO Box 45314, Nairobi
Telephone: +254 (Õ2) 503132 & 502881
Fax: +254 (Õ2) 501616

Warehouse:
East African Books Distribution Ltd,
Mombasa Road, PO Box 10324, Nairobi
Telephone: +254 (Õ2) 220520 (Direct line)
Fax: +254 (Õ2) 501616

City Centre Forwarding Office:
East African Book Distributors Ltd,
Kijabe Street, PO Box 10324, Nairobi
Fax: +254 (Õ2) 228949

Chairman: Richard Kemoli
Directors: Henry Chakava *(Managing & Chief
    Executive, Rights)*
Joseph Arap Leting
Prof. Shem Wandiga
Dr Ben Kipkoir
Fabian Murugu *(Financial)*
Jimmi Makotsi *(Publishing)*
C. Oduor Munjal *(Warehouse)*
R. Mutua Nzioki *(Sales & Marketing)*
Managers: Onyango Ogutu *(Office,
    Administration)*
Barrack O. Muluka *(Publishing & ELT Editor)*
Mark Abonyo *(Accountant)*
James Ogola *(Publicity)*
Editors: Anne Mithamo *(Secondary)*
Jeremy Nganga *(Tertiary & Further Education)*
Lilian Dhahabu *(Kiswahili)*
Secretaries: Jane Mbaya *(to Managing
    Director & Chief Executive)*
Greta Ooro *(to Publishing Director)*

*Academic & Scholarly; Accountancy &
Taxation; Agriculture; Atlases & Maps;
Biography & Autobiography; Biology &
Zoology; Chemistry; Children's Books;
Cookery, Wines & Spirits; Crime; Crafts &
Hobbies; Economics; Educational &
Textbooks; English as a Foreign Language;
Fiction; Fine Art & Art History; Geography &
Geology; Guide Books; Health & Beauty;
History & Antiquarian; Industry, Business &
Management; Languages & Linguistics; Law;
Literature & Criticism; Mathematics &
Statistics; Medical (incl. Self Help &
Alternative Medicine); Music; Natural History;
Philosophy; Physics; Poetry; Politics & World
Affairs; Reference Books, Directories &
Dictionaries; Religion & Theology; Scientific
& Technical; Sociology & Anthropology;
Sports & Games; Theatre, Drama & Dance;
Travel & Topography*

New Titles: 25 (1995), 60 (1996)

ISBNs, Imprints & Series:
9966 46 East African Educational Publishers,
    Elementary, Readers, Junior Readers,
    Secondary Readers Series, Modern African
    Writers Library, Spear Books, Wandishi wa
    Kiafrika (African Writers in Kiswahili)
9966 848 Kenway Publications

Associated & Subsidiary Companies:
Kenya: East African Educational Publishers
Distribution; Kenway Publications

Overseas Representation *(see §7.3)*:
Uganda: East African Educational Publishers
    (Uganda) Ltd, Kampala
UK: Heinemann Educational Books Ltd,
    Oxford; James Currey Publishers, London
USA: Heinemann Educational Books Inc,
    Portsmouth, NH
Zimbabwe: Zimbabwe Publishing House (Pvt)
    Ltd, Harare

Book Trade Association Membership: Kenya
PA, Africa Books Collective, African
Publishing Network, Pan African Children's
Book Fair (Nairobi)

2415 ▬▬▬▬▬▬▬

*JACARANDA DESIGNS LTD
PO Box 76691, Nairobi
Telephone: +254 (Õ2) 569736
Fax: +254 (Õ2) 568353

Managing Director: Susan Scull-Carvalho
    (Rights & Permissions)
Manager: Brown Onduso *(Marketing, Sales &
    Distribution)*

Children's Books; Literature & Criticism

ISBNs, Imprints & Series: 9966 884

Overseas Representation *(see §7.3)*:
USA: Jacaranda Designs Ltd, Boulder, CO

Book Trade Association Membership: Kenya
PA, Multi-Cultural Publishers Exchange
Association

2416 ▬▬▬▬▬▬▬

**LAKE PUBLISHERS & ENTERPRISES
LTD**
Jomo Kenyatta Highway, PO Box 1743,
Kisumu
Telephone: +254 (Õ35) 21715 & 22707
Fax: +254 (Õ35) 22291 & 22707

Warehouse & Printing:
address as above
Telephone: +254 (Õ35) 21715, 22291 & 22707
Fax: +254 (Õ35) 22291 & 22707

Directors: Mrs Asenath Bole Odaga
    (Managing)
James C. Odaga *(Sales, Rights & Permissions)*
Managers: Peter N. Odhiambo *(Marketing)*
Moses Okech *(Sales)*
Editor: Habel Andati
Marketing: Michael Juma

*Academic & Scholarly; Accountancy &
Taxation; Agriculture; Biology & Zoology;
Chemistry; Children's Books; Cookery, Wines
& Spirits; Economics; Educational &
Textbooks; Electronic (Educational); Fiction;*

*Gender Studies; Geography & Geology;
Industry, Business & Management; Languages
& Linguistics; Law; Literature & Criticism;
Mathematics & Statistics; Music; Natural
History; Philosophy; Poetry; Politics & World
Affairs; Reference Books, Directories &
Dictionaries; Religion & Theology; Theatre,
Drama & Dance*

New Titles: 6 (1995), 12 (1996)
No of Employees: 8

ISBNs, Imprints & Series: 9966 847

Overseas Representation *(see §7.3)*:
UK: Hogarth Representation Books from
    Africa, London

Book Trade Association Membership: Kenya
PA, Kenya BA, African Publishers' Network
(APNET)

2417 ▬▬▬▬▬▬▬

LONGHORN KENYA LTD
PO Box 18033, Funzi Road, Nairobi
Telephone: +254 (Õ2) 532579
Fax: +254 (Õ2) 540037

General Manager: Janet Njoroge
Finance: N. Mthenge
Marketing: David Omuruli
Editorial: Simon Sossion

*Children's Books; Educational & Textbooks;
Fiction; Guide Books*

New Titles: 5 (1995), 10 (1996)
No of Employees: 45
Annual Turnover: £1.2M

ISBNs, Imprints & Series: 9966 49

Associated & Subsidiary Companies:
Uganda: Longhorn Publishers (Uganda) Ltd

Overseas Representation *(see §7.3)*:
Tanzania: Ben & Co Ltd, Dar es Salaam

Book Trade Association Membership: Kenya
PA

2418 ▬▬▬▬▬▬▬

MACMILLAN KENYA PUBLISHERS
PO Box 30797, Kijabe Street, Nairobi
Telephone: +254 (Õ2) 224488
Fax: +254 (Õ2) 212179

Directors: David N. Muita *(Managing)*
Mrs Shahida Shah *(Finance)*
Managers: Gad N. Munyaka *(Field Sales)*
Miss Mary Mbuthia *(Marketing)*
David Nganga *(Editor)*

*Academic & Scholarly; Agriculture; Atlases &
Maps; Biology & Zoology; Chemistry;
Children's Books; Computer Science;
Educational & Textbooks; Engineering;
Fiction; Gender Studies; Geography &
Geology; Guide Books; History & Antiquarian;
Illustrated & Fine Editions; Industry, Business
& Management; Languages & Linguistics;
Literature & Criticism; Mathematics &
Statistics; Medical (incl. Self Help &
Alternative Medicine); Music; Natural History;
Philosophy; Physics; Poetry; Politics & World*

Affairs; Psychology & Psychiatry; Reference Books, Directories & Dictionaries; Religion & Theology; Scientific & Technical; Sports & Games; Theatre, Drama & Dance; Travel & Topography; Veterinary Science; Vocational Training & Careers

New Titles: 23 (1995), 10 (1996)
No of Employees: 18
Annual Turnover: £500,000

ISBNs, Imprints & Series:
0 333, 9966 885

Parent Company:
Macmillan Education *(UK)*

Book Trade Association Membership: Kenya PA

2419

NEWSPREAD INTERNATIONAL
PO Box 46854, Nairobi
Telephone: +254 (02) 331402
Fax: +254 (02) 607252

Executive Editor: Kul Bhushan
Publishing Manager: Benedict Nzomo

Guide Books; Reference Books, Directories & Dictionaries

New Titles: 2 (1995), 1 (1996)

ISBNs, Imprints & Series:
0 378 Kenya Factbook

Associated & Subsidiary Companies:
India: Newstech Publishing Inc

2420

OXFORD UNIVERSITY PRESS EASTERN AFRICA
PO Box 72532, ABC Place, Waiyaki Way, Westlands, Nairobi
Telephone: +254 (02) 440555-8
Fax: +254 (02) 443972

Warehouse:
PO Box 72532, Kijabe Street, Nairobi
Telephone: +254 (02) 226184 & 339169
Fax: +254 (02) 335193

Managing Director: K. Abdulla Ismaily
Managers: H. A. Mohamed *(Trade)*
A. M. Fondo *(Publishing, Rights & Permissions)*
Philip O. Omondi *(Financial Controller)*
John Kiarie *(Regional Marketing)*

Children's Books; Educational & Textbooks; Law; Reference Books, Directories & Dictionaries; Religion & Theology; Theatre, Drama & Dance

New Titles: 13 (1995), 21 (1996)
No of Employees: 60
Annual Turnover: £1.6M

ISBNs, Imprints & Series: 0 19 572

Parent Company:
Oxford University Press *(UK)*

Associated & Subsidiary Companies:
Tanzania: Oxford University Press. *Uganda:* Oxford University Press

Overseas Representation *(see §7.3):*
Worldwide: Oxford University Press, Oxford, UK

Book Trade Association Membership: Kenya PA

2421

PAULINES PUBLICATIONS
PO Box 49026, Nairobi
Telephone: +254 (02) 442097
Fax: +254 (02) 442144

Warehouse:
Paulines Publications-Africa, PO Box 49026, Nairobi
Telephone: +254 (02) 442097
Fax: +254 (02) 442144

Director: Sister Teresa Marcazzan
Sales Representative: Sister Rosemary Ballini
Accountant: Sister Maria Pezzini

Biography & Autobiography; Children's Books; Educational & Textbooks; History & Antiquarian; Religion & Theology; African Studies

New Titles: 49 (1995), 40 (1996)
No of Employees: 3

ISBNs, Imprints & Series: 9966 21

Overseas Representation *(see §7.3):*
Italy: San Paolo Multimedia, Rome
Mozambique: F. S. P., Maputo
Nigeria: St Paul Book Centre, Oke-Padi; F.S.P., Lagos
South Africa: Daughters of St Paul, Johannesburg
Tanzania: Cathedral Bookshop, Dar es Salaam
Uganda: St Paul Book Centre, Kampala
Zambia: Catholic Bookshop, Lusaka

2422

PHOENIX PUBLISHERS LTD
3rd Floor, Coffee Plaza, Haile Selassie Avenue, PO Box 18650, Nairobi
Telephone: +254 (02) 222309 & 223262
Fax: +254 (02) 339875

Directors: Waruingi Gacheche *(Managing & Chief Editor)*
J. W. Kabugi *(Sales)*
Manager: Muthoni Karega *(Senior Editor, Rights & Permissions)*

Children's Books

New Titles: 7 (1995), 10 (1996)
No of Employees: 8

ISBNs, Imprints & Series:
9966 47 Modern African Library, Phoenix Young Readers Library

Book Trade Association Membership: Kenya PA

2423

TEXT BOOK CENTRE LTD
PO Box 47540, Nairobi
Telephone: +254 (02) 300340
Fax: +254 (02) 225779

Managing Director: S. V. Shah
Managers: C. D. Shah *(General)*
Arvimd A. Shah *(Sales)*
Ashok A. Shah *(Marketing)*

PACKAGER ONLY

No of Employees: 90
Annual Turnover: $8.9M

Book Trade Association Membership: Kenya Booksellers & Stationers Association

MALAYSIA

2424

ALPHA SIGMA PTE LTD
14 A/B Jalan SS 26/6, Taman Mayang Jaya, 47301 Petaling Jaya
Telephone: +60 (03) 704 1672
Fax: +60 (03) 704 1673

Managing Director: Jeremy Thor *(Executive, Finance & Marketing)*

Children's Books; Educational & Textbooks; English as a Foreign Language; Fiction; Industry, Business & Management; Mathematics & Statistics; Reference Books, Directories & Dictionaries

New Titles: 40 (1995), 80 (1996)
No of Employees: 12
Annual Turnover: $0.5M

ISBNs, Imprints & Series: 967 966

Parent Company:
Johor State Economic Development Corp *(Malaysia)*

Book Trade Association Membership:
Malaysian Book PA

2425

DELTA PUBLISHING SDN BHD
18 Jalan 51A/223, 46100 Petaling Jaya
Telephone: +60 (03) 757 0000
Fax: +60 (03) 757 6688

Manager: Wong Chin Teng *(Export Sales & Rights)*
Managing Director: Lim Kim Wah

Academic & Scholarly; Children's Books; Cookery, Wines & Spirits; Educational & Textbooks; Philosophy; Sports & Games; Travel & Topography

New Titles: 300 (1995), 350 (1996)
No of Employees: 300
Annual Turnover: $10M

ISBNs, Imprints & Series: 983 9808

Parent Company:
Delta Publishing Group of Companies
(Malaysia) *(Malaysia)*

Associated & Subsidiary Companies:
Malaysia: Delta Editions Sdn Bhd; Gedung
Ilmu Sdn Bhd; Jayatinta Sdn Bhd; Pustaka
Delta Pelajaran Sdn Bhd; Tempo Publishing
Sdn Bhd

Overseas Representation *(see §7.3):*
Australia: Oriental Publications, Adelaide, SA
Europe & Irish Republic: Gazelle Book
   Services Ltd, Lancaster, UK
North America: Weatherhill Inc, New York,
   NY, USA
Singapore: Select Books Pte Ltd

Book Trade Association Membership:
Malaysian Book PA

2426

FEDERAL PUBLICATIONS SDN BHD
Times Subang 46,
Jalan Persiaran Teknologi Subang,
Subang Hi-Tech Industrial Park, Batu 3,
40000 Shah Alam
Telephone: +60 (Õ75) 735 1511
Fax: +60 (Õ75) 736 4620

General Manager: Stephen Lim Kee Soon

*Children's Books; Computer Science; Crafts &
Hobbies; Do-It-Yourself; Educational &
Textbooks; Gardening; Industry, Business &
Management; Reference Books, Directories &
Dictionaries; Sports & Games; Trade
Directories*

New Titles: 150 (1995), 180 (1996)
No of Employees: 90
Annual Turnover: £2.5M

ISBNs, Imprints & Series: 967 91

Parent Company:
Times Publishing Ltd *(Singapore)*

Associated & Subsidiary Companies:
Hong Kong: Federal Publications Ptd Ltd.
Singapore: Federal Publications Ptd Ltd

Book Trade Association Membership:
Malaysian Book PA

2427

*S. ABDUL MAJEED & CO
7 Jalan 3/82B, Bangsar Utama,
59000 Kuala Lumpur
Telephone: +60 (Õ3) 283 2230
Fax: +60 (Õ3) 282 5670

Warehouse:
107-C Jalan Raja Laut, 50746 Kuala Lumpur
Telephone: +60 (Õ3) 4424486

Penang Office:
35 Jalan Sekerat, (Off Transfer Road),
PO Box 507, 10760 Penang
Telephone: +60 (Õ4) 368929 & 373360
Fax: +60 (Õ4) 372054

Managers: Mohamed Rafique *(Sales)*
Akbar Ali *(Marketing)*

Ams Alawdeen *(General)*
Partner: Peer Mohamed

ISBNs, Imprints & Series:
983 9629 Business Information Books, Eastern
   Dragon Series, Health Resource Series, Sam
   Language Series, Synergy Books
   International

Book Trade Association Membership:
Malaysian Book PA, Malaysia Book Importers
Association, Malaysian Book Sellers
Association

2428

PRESTON CORPORATION SDN BHD
No 18 Jalan 19/3, 46300 Petaling Jaya
Telephone: +60 (Õ3) 756 3734/5
Fax: +60 (Õ3) 757 3607

Warehouse & Printing:
Preston-Times Printing & Publishing Sdn Bhd,
Lots 2, 4 & 6 Kawasan Miel, Phase 3,
Shah Alam Industrial Estate
Telephone: +60 (Õ3) 559 1067
Fax: +60 (Õ3) 559 1067

Corporate Treasurer: Lorinne Kon
Accountant: Mrs Lam Yuk Lean
Marketing: Han Moh Neoh
Area Managers: Raymond Chan *(Sales)*
Johnny Loke *(Sales)*
Managing Editors: Felicia Hen
Wan Mun Ching
Managers: Ranjit Kuar *(Production)*
Chang Chee Kong *(Printing)*

*Chemistry; Children's Books; Cookery, Wines
& Spirits; Educational & Textbooks; English as
a Foreign Language; Languages &
Linguistics; Mathematics & Statistics; Physics;
Reference Books, Directories & Dictionaries*

New Titles: 105 (1995), 110 (1996)
No of Employees: 95
Annual Turnover: $3M

ISBNs, Imprints & Series: 967 917

Parent Company:
Preston Corporation (Pte) Ltd *(Singapore)*

Associated & Subsidiary Companies:
Hong Kong: Vista Productions Ltd. *Malaysia:*
Preston-Times Printing & Publishing Co Sdn
Bhd; Times Educational Co Sdn Bhd

Book Trade Association Membership:
Malaysian Book PA, Singapore Book PA

2429

TIMES EDUCATIONAL CO SDN BHD
No 22 Jalan 19/3, 46300 Petaling Jaya
Telephone: +60 (Õ3) 757 1766
Fax: +60 (Õ3) 757 3607

Warehouse & Printing:
Preston-
Times Printing & Publishing Co Sdn Bhd,
Lots 2, 4 & 6 Kawasan Miel, Phase 3,
Shah Alam Industrial Estate
Telephone: +60 (Õ3) 559 1067
Fax: +60 (Õ3) 559 1067

General Manager: Foong Chui Lin
Accountant: Pat Than Sow Hoon
Area Managers: Phang Yow Kow
Kuek Tang Ling
Managing Editors: Felicia Hen
Wan Mun Ching
Managers: Ranjit Kuar *(Production)*
Chang Chee Kong *(Printing)*
Lai Nam Koong

*Children's Books; Cookery, Wines & Spirits;
Educational & Textbooks; English as a Foreign
Language; Languages & Linguistics;
Mathematics & Statistics; Reference Books,
Directories & Dictionaries*

New Titles: 85 (1995), 95 (1996)
No of Employees: 72
Annual Turnover: $2.5M

ISBNs, Imprints & Series: 967 919

Parent Company:
Times Educational Co Ltd *(Hong Kong)*

Associated & Subsidiary Companies:
Hong Kong: Times Educational Co Ltd; Vista
Productions Ltd. *Malaysia:* Preston
Corporation Sdn Bhd; Preston-Times Printing
& Publishing Co Sdn Bhd. *Singapore:* Preston
Corporation (Pte) Ltd

Book Trade Association Membership:
Malaysian Book PA, The Anglo-Chinese
Textbook Publishers Organization

MALTA

2430

GOZO PRESS
Mgarr Road, Gh'sielem
Telephone: +356 551534
Fax: +356 560857

Director: Achilles F. Cauchi
Manager: Carmel Mizzi
Production: Tony Bezzina

*Academic & Scholarly; Archaeology;
Bibliography & Library Science; Biography &
Autobiography; Children's Books; Crafts &
Hobbies; Educational & Textbooks; Guide
Books; History & Antiquarian; Poetry;
Religion & Theology*

New Titles: 6 (1995), 12 (1996)
No of Employees: 6
Annual Turnover: £100,000

2431

PROGRESS PRESS CO LTD
Strickland House, 341 St Paul's Street,
Valletta VLT 07
Telephone: +356 241464/9 & 241411/2
Fax: +356 237150

Publications Department:
4 Castille Place, Valletta VLT 07
Telephone: as above exts: 220 & 272
Fax: +356 237150

Chairman: Ronald Agius
Managing Director: Wilfrid Asciak
Publications Manager: Joseph Tortell

Antiques & Collecting; Archaeology;
Architecture & Design; Aviation; Cookery,
Wines & Spirits; Fiction; Fine Art & Art
History; Gardening; Geography & Geology;
Guide Books; History & Antiquarian;
Languages & Linguistics; Military & War;
Natural History; Reference Books, Directories
& Dictionaries

New Titles: 18 (1995), 10 (1996)

ISBNs, Imprints & Series:
999093 Progress Press Publications

Parent Company:
Allied Newspapers Ltd *(Malta)*

Overseas Representation *(see §7.3):*
UK: Bay Foreign Language Books, Romney
Marsh

NEW ZEALAND

2432 ━━━━━━━━━━━━━━━

AUCKLAND UNIVERSITY PRESS
University of Auckland, Private Bag 92019,
Auckland
Telephone: +64 (09) 373 7528
Fax: +64 (09) 373 7465
Email: e.caffin@auckland.ac.nz

Trade Enquiries & Orders:
HarperCollins NZ, PO Box 1, Auckland
Telephone: +64 (09) 443 9400
Fax: +64 (09) 443 9403

Wellington Office:
PO Box 3058, Wellington
Telephone: +64 (04) 495 2540
Fax: +64 (04) 495 2541

Chairman: Prof. Ian Carter
Director: Elizabeth Caffin *(all enquiries)*
Publisher: Bridget Williams

Academic & Scholarly; Archaeology;
Biography & Autobiography; Fine Art & Art
History; Gender Studies; Geography &
Geology; History & Antiquarian; Literature &
Criticism; Poetry; Politics & World Affairs;
Reference Books, Directories & Dictionaries;
Sociology & Anthropology

New Titles: 21 (1995), 26 (1996)
No of Employees: 8
Annual Turnover: £350,000

ISBNs, Imprints & Series:
1 86940 Auckland University Press, Auckland
University Press/Bridget Williams Books

Overseas Representation *(see §7.3):*
Australia: James Bennett Library Services,
Collaroy, NSW
UK: Academic & University Publishers Group,
London
USA: Paul & Co Publishers Consortium Inc,
Concord, MA

Book Trade Association Membership: Book
Publishers Association of New Zealand,
Booksellers New Zealand Ltd, International
Association of Scholarly Publishers

2433 ━━━━━━━━━━━━━━━

DAVID BATEMAN LTD
30 Tarndale Grove, off Bush Road, Albany,
North Shore, (PO Box 100-242) Auckland
Telephone: +64 (09) 415 7664
Fax: +64 (09) 415 8892

Publisher: David Bateman *(Chairman)*
Managing Directors: Paul Bateman
(Publishing, Rights & Permissions)
Paul C. Parkinson *(General/Marketing)*
Managing Editor: Tracey Borgfeldt

Agriculture; Antiques & Collecting;
Architecture & Design; Aviation; Biography &
Autobiography; Biology & Zoology;
Children's Books; Cookery, Wines & Spirits;
Crafts & Hobbies; Do-It-Yourself; Educational
& Textbooks; Fine Art & Art History;
Gardening; Geography & Geology; Guide
Books; Health & Beauty; History &
Antiquarian; Humour; Illustrated & Fine
Editions; Industry, Business & Management;
Law; Medical (incl. Self Help & Alternative
Medicine); Military & War; Natural History;
Nautical; Politics & World Affairs; Reference
Books, Directories & Dictionaries; Scientific &
Technical; Sports & Games; Travel &
Topography

New Titles: 50 (1995), 59 (1996)
No of Employees: 14

ISBNs, Imprints & Series:
0 908610, 1 86953

Book Trade Association Membership: Book
Publishers Association of New Zealand,
Booksellers New Zealand Ltd

2434 ━━━━━━━━━━━━━━━

THE BUSH PRESS
PO Box 33-029, Takapuna, Auckland 9
Telephone: +64 (09) 486 2667
Fax: +64 (09) 486 2667

Warehouse & Billing:
Forrester Books (NZ) Ltd

Governing Director: Gordon Ell

Archaeology; Architecture & Design; Biology
& Zoology; Children's Books; Crafts &
Hobbies; Gardening; Geography & Geology;
Guide Books; History & Antiquarian; Natural
History; Photography; Transport; Travel &
Topography; Fishing (Trout)

New Titles: 10 (1995), 8 (1996)
No of Employees: 2

ISBNs, Imprints & Series:
0 908608 Beginners' Nature Guides, Best of
New Zealand, Bush Pictorials, The Bush
Press, The Children's Guides to New
Zealand Nature, Discover New Zealand,
Nature Detectives, New Zealand Past and
Present, Pictures from the Past

Parent Company:
Bush Press Communications Ltd *(New
Zealand)*

Associated & Subsidiary Companies:
New Zealand: Bush Films; Bush Press
Production

Book Trade Association Membership:
Booksellers New Zealand

2435 ━━━━━━━━━━━━━━━

**BUTTERWORTHS OF NEW ZEALAND
LTD**
203–207 Victoria Street, Wellington 1
Telephone: +64 (04) 3851 479
Fax: +64 (04) 3851 598
Email: kirkp@bwthsnz.attmail.com
Web Site: http://www.butterworths.co.nz

Butterworths Bookshop:
Plaza Level, NML Complex, Shortland Street,
Auckland 1
Telephone: +64 (09) 309 9171
Fax: +64 (09) 377 9861
Email: kellewayj@bwthsnz.attmail.com
Web Site: http://www.butterworths.co.nz

Directors: Philip Kirk *(Managing, Marketing)*
Jeffery Bull *(Finance)*
Executives: Karen Balasaglou *(Human
Resources)*
James Clarke *(Editorial)*
John Hoffman *(Publishing Systems)*

Accountancy & Taxation; Electronic
(Professional & Academic); Law

ISBNs, Imprints & Series: 0 408

Parent Company:
Reed-Elsevier *(UK)*

Overseas Representation *(see §7.3):*
Asia: Butterworths Asia, Singapore
Australia: Butterworths Australia, North Ryde,
NSW
South Africa: Butterworths South Africa,
Durban
UK: Butterworth & Co (Publishers) Ltd,
London
USA: Michie, Charlottesville, VA

Book Trade Association Membership: Book
Publishers Association of New Zealand

2436 ━━━━━━━━━━━━━━━

CANTERBURY UNIVERSITY PRESS
University of Canterbury, Private Bag 4800,
Christchurch
Telephone: +64 (03) 364 2046
Fax: +64 (03) 364 2044
Email: m.bradstock@cup.canterbury.ac.nz

Distribution:
HarperCollins Publishers (NZ) Ltd, PO Box 1,
Auckland
Telephone: +64 (09) 443 9401
Fax: +64 (09) 443 9402

Managing Editor: Michael Bradstock
Production Manager: Richard King

Academic & Scholarly; Biography &
Autobiography; Biology & Zoology; Fiction;
History & Antiquarian; Natural History;
Politics & World Affairs; Scientific &
Technical

New Titles: 8 (1995), 10 (1996)
No of Employees: 3

ISBNs, Imprints & Series: 0 908812

Overseas Representation *(see §7.3):*
UK & Europe: Book Representation &
Distribution Ltd, Hadleigh, UK

Book Trade Association Membership: Book
Publishers Association of New Zealand,
Booksellers New Zealand

CRAIG POTTON PUBLISHING LTD
PO Box 555, Nelson
Telephone: +64 (Õ3) 548 9009
Fax: +64 (Õ3) 546 9192
Email: burton@cpp.co.nz

Director: Craig Potton
Managing Editor: Robbie Burton *(Sales,
Rights & Permissions)*

*Architecture & Design; Guide Books; Natural
History; Photography*

New Titles: 4 (1995), 5 (1996)
No of Employees: 11
Annual Turnover: £680,000

ISBNs, Imprints & Series: 0 9416458

Book Trade Association Membership: Book
Publishers Association of New Zealand,
Booksellers Association of New Zealand Inc

CRAIG PRINTING CO LTD
PO Box 99, 67 Tay Street, Invercargill 9501
Telephone: +64 (Õ3) 218 7029
Fax: +64 (Õ3) 218 4811

General Manager: Colin W. Smith

*Aviation; Children's Books; Cookery, Wines &
Spirits; Crafts & Hobbies; Fine Art & Art
History; Guide Books; History & Antiquarian;
Sports & Games*

New Titles: 10 (1995), 10 (1996)
No of Employees: 62

ISBNs, Imprints & Series: 0 908629

Book Trade Association Membership: Book
Publishers Association of New Zealand

DAVID LING PUBLISHING LTD
67 Hinemoa Street, PO Box 34-601,
Birkenhead, Auckland 10
Telephone: +64 (Õ9) 418 2785
Fax: +64 (Õ9) 418 2785

Sales & Distribution:
Transworld Publishers,
3 William Pickering Drive, North Harbour,
Auckland
Telephone: +64 (Õ9) 415 6210
Fax: +64 (Õ9) 415 6221

Managing Director: David Ling

*Biography & Autobiography; Crafts &
Hobbies; Fiction; History & Antiquarian;
Illustrated & Fine Editions; Natural History;
Travel & Topography*

New Titles: 11 (1995), 12 (1996)
No of Employees: 2

ISBNs, Imprints & Series: 0 908990

Book Trade Association Membership: Book
Publishers Association of New Zealand,
Booksellers New Zealand

DUNMORE PRESS LTD
109 Napier Road, (PO Box 5115),
Palmerston North
Telephone: +64 (Õ6) 358 7169
Fax: +64 (Õ6) 357 9242

Managing Director: Murray Gatenby

*Academic & Scholarly; Accountancy &
Taxation; Biography & Autobiography;
Educational & Textbooks; Industry, Business &
Management; Sociology & Anthropology*

New Titles: 20 (1995), 22 (1996)
No of Employees: 7
Annual Turnover: $0.5M

ISBNs, Imprints & Series: 0 86469

Overseas Representation *(see §7.3):*
Australia: The Federation Press, Annandale

Book Trade Association Membership: Book
Publishers Association of New Zealand

ESA PUBLICATIONS (NZ) LTD
Box 9453, Newmarket, Auckland
Telephone: +64 (Õ9) 520 2886
Fax: +64 (Õ9) 524 0089
Email: info@esa.co.nz
Web Site: http://www.esa.co.nz/

Warehouse:
Level 3, Hayes Building, 8 Teed Street,
Newmarket
Telephone: +64 (Õ9) 522 2537
Fax: *(as above)*
Email: *(as above)*
Web Site: *(as above)*

Managing Director: Mark Sayes

Educational & Textbooks

New Titles: 2 (1995), 4 (1996)
No of Employees: 11

ISBNs, Imprints & Series:
0 908756 ESA Books
0 908906 Ibis Books

Parent Company:
Sayes Corporation Ltd *(New Zealand)*

Associated & Subsidiary Companies:
New Zealand: Ibis Books Ltd

Book Trade Association Membership: Book
Publishers Association of New Zealand,
Educational & Professional Dvn

G P PUBLICATIONS LTD
PO Box 12-052, Wellington
Telephone: +64 (Õ4) 473 8211
Fax: +64 (Õ4) 472 9915

Location:
10 Mulgrave Street, Wellington
Telephone: as above
Fax: as above

General Manager: Ann Clifford
Customer Services: Jackie Hutchings
Publisher: Ann Clifford
Marketing: Sarah Maxwell

*Economics; Educational & Textbooks;
Languages & Linguistics; Nautical; Reference
Books, Directories & Dictionaries*

New Titles: 8 (1995), 8 (1996)
No of Employees: 6

ISBNs, Imprints & Series: 1 86956

Parent Company:
Whitcoulls Group *(New Zealand)*

Book Trade Association Membership: Book
Publishers Association of New Zealand

GODWIT PUBLISHING LTD
PO Box 34-683, Birkenhead, Auckland
Telephone: +64 (Õ9) 480 5410
Fax: +64 (Õ9) 480 5930

Warehouse, Trade Enquiries & Orders:
c/o Reed Publishing, Private Bag, Birkenhead,
Auckland
Fax: +64 (Õ9) 480 4970

Directors: Jane Connor *(Rights &
Permissions)*
Brian Phillips *(Sales)*

*Biography & Autobiography; Cookery, Wines
& Spirits; Fiction; Fine Art & Art History;
Gardening; Natural History; Poetry*

New Titles: 20 (1995), 20 (1996)

ISBNs, Imprints & Series:
0 908877, 1 86962

Book Trade Association Membership: Book
Publishers Association of New Zealand,
Booksellers Association of New Zealand Inc

GRANTHAM HOUSE PUBLISHING
24 Messines Road, PO Box 17-256, Karori,
Wellington 5
Telephone: +64 (Õ4) 476 4625
Fax: +64 (Õ4) 476 3048

Marketing, Sales & Warehouse:
Hodder Moa Beckett Ltd, PO Box 3858,
Auckland

Telephone: +64 (09) 444 8036
Fax: +64 (09) 444 1967

Publisher, Chief Executive: Graham C.
Stewart
Manager: Julie Green *(Home Sales)*
Export Director: Anne Stewart

*Antiques & Collecting; Architecture & Design;
Aviation; History & Antiquarian; Illustrated &
Fine Editions; Military & War; Nautical;
Transport*

New Titles: 6 (1995), 6 (1996)
No of Employees: 4
Annual Turnover: £250,000

ISBNs, Imprints & Series: 1 86934

Parent Company:
Bookprint Consultants Ltd *(New Zealand)*

Overseas Representation *(see §7.3)*:
Australia: Biramo Books Pty Ltd, New
Lambton, NSW

Book Trade Association Membership:
Booksellers Association of New Zealand Inc

2445

HALCYON PUBLISHING LTD
[The Halcyon Press]
PO Box 360, Auckland 1
Telephone: +64 (09) 489 5337
Fax: +64 (09) 444 2399

Warehouse:
64E Ellice Road, Glenfield, Auckland
Telephone: +64 (09) 489 5337
Fax: +64 (09) 444 2399

Directors: Graham Gurr *(Managing, Sales &
Export)*
Tony Entwistle *(Editorial)*
Dave Shaw *(Research)*

*Sports & Games; Diving; Fishing; Hunting;
Outdoors; Sailing; Shooting*

New Titles: 9 (1995), 6 (1996)

ISBNs, Imprints & Series: 0 90865

Overseas Representation *(see §7.3)*:
Australia: ADRF, Croydon, Vic

Book Trade Association Membership: Book
Publishers Association of New Zealand,
Booksellers New Zealand

2446

**HARPERCOLLINS PUBLISHERS (NEW
ZEALAND) LTD**
31 View Road, Glenfield, Auckland 10
Telephone: +64 (09) 443 9400
Fax: +64 (09) 443 9403

Postal Address:
PO Box 1, Auckland

Managers: Ian Watt *(Publishing, Rights &
Export Sales)*
Tony Fisk *(Marketing, Home Sales)*
Karen Avery *(Finance)*

*Biography & Autobiography; Cookery, Wines
& Spirits; Crafts & Hobbies; Do-It-Yourself;
Gardening; Geography & Geology; Natural
History; Reference Books, Directories &
Dictionaries; Sports & Games; Transport;
Young adult fiction*

New Titles: 36 (1995), 30 (1996)
No of Employees: 72

ISBNs, Imprints & Series:
Tui, Tui Junior and Tui Turbo young fiction 1
86950

Parent Company:
HarperCollins Publishers Inc *(USA)*

Overseas Representation *(see §7.3)*:
Australia: HarperCollins Publishers, Pymble,
NSW & North Ryde, NSW
UK: HarperCollins Publishers Ltd, Glasgow &
London
USA: HarperCollins US, New York

Book Trade Association Membership: Book
Publishers Association of New Zealand,
Booksellers Association of New Zealand Inc

2447

HAZARD PRESS LTD
62 Gloucester Street, Christchurch 1
Telephone: +64 (03) 370370
Fax: +64 (03) 370390
Email: quentinw@hazard.co.nz
Web Site: http://www.hazard.co.nz

Postal Address:
PO Box 2151, Christchurch

Managing Editor: Quentin Wilson
Accounts: Jill Hammond
Editorial: Sarah Bowden

*Children's Books; Cookery, Wines & Spirits;
Fiction; Fine Art & Art History; Gender
Studies; History & Antiquarian; Humour;
Illustrated & Fine Editions; Literature &
Criticism; Photography; Poetry; Theatre,
Drama & Dance; General non-fiction*

New Titles: 15 (1995), 18 (1996)
No of Employees: 3

ISBNs, Imprints & Series:
0 908790 Hazard Poets Series, Hazard Short
Fiction Series 1 877161

Associated & Subsidiary Companies:
New Zealand: Orca Publishing Services Ltd

Overseas Representation *(see §7.3)*:
Australia: Biramo Books Ltd, New Lambton,
NSW
USA: Aubrey Books International Ltd, Silver
Spring, MD

Book Trade Association Membership: Book
Publishers Association of New Zealand,
Booksellers New Zealand

2448

*IPL BOOKS
28 Grey Street, Wellington
Telephone: +64 (04) 499 3032
Fax: +64 (04) 499 6599

Publisher: G. B. Churchman
Secretary: L. Born

*Architecture & Design; Aviation; Cinema,
Video, TV & Radio; Cookery, Wines & Spirits;
Crafts & Hobbies; Guide Books; History &
Antiquarian; Illustrated & Fine Editions;
Transport*

ISBNs, Imprints & Series: 0 908876

Parent Company:
IPL Publishing Group Ltd *(New Zealand)*

Associated & Subsidiary Companies:
Australia: IPL Books. *New Zealand:* IPL
Books; IPL Video; IPL Wordprint

Overseas Representation *(see §7.3)*:
Australia: Gary Allen Pty Ltd, Smithfield,
NSW
UK: Ian Allan Publishing, Addlestone, Surrey

Book Trade Association Membership: Book
Publishers Association of New Zealand,
Australian Book PA

2449

LEARNING MEDIA LTD
PO Box 3293, Wellington
Telephone: +64 (04) 472 5522
Fax: +64 (04) 472 6444
Email: info@learningmedia.co.nz

Warehouse & Orders:
Learning Media Distribution Centre,
PO Box 39-055, Petone
Telephone: +64 (04) 568 7547
Fax: +64 (04) 568 3584

Sales: Pat Starkey
Rights & Permissions: Lois Thompson

Children's Books; Educational & Textbooks

New Titles: 250 (1995), 250 (1996)
No of Employees: 54

ISBNs, Imprints & Series:
0 477 Applications, Choices, He Purapura,
Reading Science, Ready to Read, School
Journal, Story Library, Tupu

Overseas Representation *(see §7.3)*:
Australia: Troll Books of Australia, Roseville,
NSW
Canada: Irwin Publishing Inc, West Concord
Pacific: Read Pacific, Auckland, New Zealand
USA: Richard C. Owen Publishers Inc,
Katonah, NY

Book Trade Association Membership: Book
Publishers' Association of New Zealand

2450

LONGMAN PAUL LTD
46 Hillside Road, Glenfield, Auckland 10
Telephone: +64 (09) 444 4968
Fax: +64 (09) 444 4957
Email: rosemary.stagg@awl.co.nz

Postal Address:
Private Bag 102908, North Shore Mail Centre,
Glenfield, Auckland 10

Telephone: +64 (09) 444 4968
Fax: +64 (09) 444 4957

Directors: Rosemary Stagg *(Managing)*
Elizabeth Nelson *(Sales)*
Robert Fisher
B. V. Ashcroft-Hawley

Academic & Scholarly; Educational &
Textbooks; Industry, Business & Management

New Titles: 70 (1995), 55 (1996)
No of Employees: 25
Annual Turnover: £2M

ISBNs, Imprints & Series: 0 582

Parent Company:
Addison Wesley Longman Ltd *(UK)*

Book Trade Association Membership: Book
Publishers Association of New Zealand

2451

MACMILLAN PUBLISHERS
Private Bag, North Shore Mail Centre,
Auckland
Telephone: +64 (09) 415 6677
Fax: +64 (09) 415 6659
Email: name@macmillan.co.nz

Director: Joan Mackenzie *(Managing)*
Manager: Jill Rawnsley *(Promotions)*
Stock Controller: Michelle Newton

Biography & Autobiography; Children's
Books; Crafts & Hobbies; Fiction; Gardening;
Health & Beauty; Humour; Reference Books,
Directories & Dictionaries; Science Fiction

ISBNs, Imprints & Series:
0 283 Sidgwick & Jackson
0 312 St Martins Press
0 330 Pan, Picador, Piccolo, Piper
0 333 Macmillan
0 671, 0 731 Simon & Schuster
0 908 Shoal Bay Press

Parent Company:
Pan Books Ltd *(UK)*

Associated & Subsidiary Companies:
Australia: Pan Macmillan Australia Ltd

Overseas Representation *(see §7.3)*:
Australia: Pan Macmillan Australia Ltd
Rest of World: Macmillan Ltd, UK

Book Trade Association Membership:
Booksellers New Zealand

2452

*MACMILLAN PUBLISHERS NEW ZEALAND LTD
6 Ride Way, Albany, Auckland
Telephone: +64 (09) 415 6672
Fax: +64 (09) 415 6676

Managing Director & Publisher: David Joel
School Publisher: Chris Chittenden
Editor: Elizabeth Rawlings

Academic & Scholarly; Atlases & Maps;
Educational & Textbooks; Electronic

(Educational); Industry, Business &
Management

Parent Company:
Verlagsgruppe Georg von Holtzbrink GmbH
(Germany). Macmillan Publishers Ltd *(UK)*

Book Trade Association Membership:
Booksellers New Zealand

2453

MALLINSON RENDEL PUBLISHERS LTD
7 Grass Street, PO Box 9409, Wellington
Telephone: +64 (04) 385 7340
Fax: +64 (04) 385 4235

Managing Director: Ann Mallinson
Chairman: David Rendel
Sales Manager: Judy Harper

Children's Books

New Titles: 8 (1995), 8 (1996)
No of Employees: 4
Annual Turnover: £300,000

ISBNs, Imprints & Series: 0 908783

Book Trade Association Membership:
Booksellers New Zealand

2454

NELSON PRICE MILBURN LTD
PO Box 38-945, Wellington Mail Centre
Telephone: +64 (04) 568 7179
Fax: +64 (04) 568 2115

Director: Ted Gannon
General Manager: Greg Browne *(Home &*
Export Sales)

Children's Books; Educational & Textbooks

New Titles: 126 (1995), 65 (1996)
No of Employees: 11
Annual Turnover: $4M

ISBNs, Imprints & Series:
0 7055 Highgate/Price Milburn Ltd
1 86955 Nelson Price Milburn Ltd

Parent Company:
Thomson Australia Holdings Ltd *(Australia)*

Overseas Representation *(see §7.3)*:
Australia: Thomas Nelson (Australia) Pty Ltd,
South Melbourne, Vic
Canada: Nelson Canada, Scarborough
USA: The Wright Group, Bothell, WA; Rigby,
Crystal Lane, IL

Book Trade Association Membership: Book
Publishers Association of New Zealand

2455

NEW HOUSE PUBLISHERS LTD
PO Box 33376, Takapuna, Auckland 1309
Telephone: +64 (09) 410 6517
Fax: +64 (09) 410 6329
Email: david:newhouse.co.nz

Publisher: David Heap

Educational & Textbooks; Reference Books,
Directories & Dictionaries

New Titles: 20 (1995), 20 (1996)
No of Employees: 3
Annual Turnover: £650,000

ISBNs, Imprints & Series: 1 86946

2456

*NEW WOMEN'S PRESS LTD
PO Box 6401, Dunedin North
Telephone: +64 (03) 482 1399
Fax: +64 (03) 482 1399

Publisher & Managing Director: Wendy
Harrex

Fiction; Gender Studies; Health & Beauty

ISBNs, Imprints & Series: 0 908652

Overseas Representation *(see §7.3)*:
USA & Canada: Inland Book Co Inc, East
Haven, CT, USA

Book Trade Association Membership: Book
Publishers Association of New Zealand

2457

NEW ZEALAND COUNCIL FOR EDUCATIONAL RESEARCH
178 Willis Street (PO Box 3237), Wellington
Telephone: +64 (04) 3847 939
Fax: +64 (04) 3847 933
Email: sales@nzcer.org.nz

Director: Anne Meade
Export Sales: Joan Kirby
Publications Officer: Peter J. Ridder *(Rights*
& Permissions)

Academic & Scholarly; Educational &
Textbooks; Reference Books, Directories &
Dictionaries

New Titles: 16 (1995), 17 (1996)
No of Employees: 5
Annual Turnover: $380,000

ISBNs, Imprints & Series:
0 908567, 0 908916

Overseas Representation *(see §7.3)*:
Australia: ACER Ltd, Camberwell, Vic
UK: National Foundation for Educational
Research, Slough; NFER-Nelson, Windsor

2458

UNIVERSITY OF OTAGO PRESS
PO Box 56, Dunedin
Telephone: +64 (03) 479 8807
Fax: +64 (03) 479 8385

Distributor:
HarperCollins, PO Box 1, Auckland
Telephone: +64 (09) 443 9400
Fax: +64 (09) 443 9403

Managing Editor: Wendy Harrex
Administrative Assistant: Martine O'Shea
Publicist: Philippa Jamieson
Production Editor: Jenny Cooper

Academic & Scholarly; Educational & Textbooks; Fiction; Gender Studies; Literature & Criticism; Medical (incl. Self Help & Alternative Medicine); Natural History

New Titles: 12 (1995), 15 (1996)
No of Employees: 4

ISBNs, Imprints & Series:
0 908569, 1 877133

Overseas Representation *(see §7.3)*:
Australia: Biramo Books, Warners Bay, NSW
North America: International Specialized Book Services Inc, Portland, OR, USA

Book Trade Association Membership: Book Publishers Association of New Zealand

2459 ━━━━━━━━━━━━━━

OXFORD UNIVERSITY PRESS (NEW ZEALAND BRANCH)
PO Box 11-149, Ellerslie, Auckland 5
Telephone: +64 (Ō9) 525 8020
Fax: +64 (Ō9) 525 1072

Location:
540 Great South Road, Greenlane, Auckland 5
Telephone: +64 (Ō9) 525 8020
Fax: +64 (Ō9) 525 1072

Publisher: Linda Cassells

Academic & Scholarly; Educational & Textbooks; Reference Books, Directories & Dictionaries

ISBNs, Imprints & Series: 0 19 558

Parent Company:
Oxford University Press *(UK)*

Overseas Representation *(see §7.3)*:
Worldwide: Oxford University Press, Oxford, UK

Book Trade Association Membership: Book Publishers Association of New Zealand

2460 ━━━━━━━━━━━━━━

*PENGUIN BOOKS (NZ) LTD
182–190 Wairau Road, Glenfield, Auckland 10
Telephone: +64 (Ō9) 444 4965
Fax: +64 (Ō9) 444 8582

Postal Address:
Private Bag 102-902, North Shore Mail Centre, Auckland 10
Telephone: (as above)
Fax: +64 (Ō9) 444 1470

Directors: Tony Harkins *(Managing)*
Colin Cox *(Sales)*
Geoff Walker *(Publishing)*
Karen Ferns *(Marketing)*
Operations Manager: Gerard Burns

Children's Books; Cookery, Wines & Spirits; Fiction; Gardening; Natural History

ISBNs, Imprints & Series:
0 14 Pelican, Penguin, Puffin
0 17 Nelson
0 241 Hamish Hamilton
0 349 Abacus

0 451, 0 452 NAL
0 571 Faber
0 670 Viking
0 7181 Michael Joseph, Mermaid
0 7226 Viking Kestrel
0 7232 Frederick Warne
0 8289 Stephen Greene

Parent Company:
Penguin Books Ltd *(UK)*

Associated & Subsidiary Companies:
New Zealand: Longman Paul Ltd

Overseas Representation *(see §7.3)*:
Australia: Penguin Books Australia Ltd, Ringwood, Vic
Canada: Penguin Books Canada Ltd, Newmarket, Ont
UK: Penguin Books Ltd, London
USA: Viking Penguin Inc, New York

Book Trade Association Membership: Book Publishers Association of New Zealand, Booksellers New Zealand Inc

2461 ━━━━━━━━━━━━━━

RANDOM HOUSE NEW ZEALAND LTD
Private Bag 102-950, North Shore Mail Centre, Glenfield, Auckland 10
Telephone: +64 (Ō9) 444 7197
Fax: +64 (Ō9) 444 7524

Directors: J. Rogers *(Managing)*
R. Jacobson *(Finance & Administration)*
M. Moynahan *(Sales & Marketing)*
Manager: H. Allan *(Publishing & Rights)*

Biography & Autobiography; Cookery, Wines & Spirits; Fiction; Gardening; Health & Beauty; Illustrated & Fine Editions

New Titles: 30 (1995), 25 (1996)
No of Employees: 30

ISBNs, Imprints & Series: 1 86941

Parent Company:
Random House Group Ltd *(UK)*

Associated & Subsidiary Companies:
Australia: Random House Australia Pty Ltd.
South Africa: Random House South Africa Ltd.
UK: Random House Group Ltd. *USA:* Random House Inc

Overseas Representation *(see §7.3)*:
Australia: Random Australia Pty Ltd, Sydney
South Africa: Random House South Africa Pty Ltd, Rosebank, Johannesburg
UK: Random House UK Ltd, London
USA: Random House Inc, New York

Book Trade Association Membership: Book Publishers Association of New Zealand, New Zealand Book Marketing Council, Booksellers New Zealand

2462 ━━━━━━━━━━━━━━

RUGBY PUBLISHING LTD
PO Box 100243, North Shore Mail Centre, Auckland 10
Telephone: +64 (Ō9) 443 0147
Fax: +64 (Ō9) 443 7448

Warehouse:
67–73 View Road, Glenfield, Auckland
Telephone: *(as above)*
Fax: *(as above)*

Editor: R. J. Howitt
Publisher: W. D. Honeybone *(Home Sales, Export Sales & Rights)*
Managing Director: D. D. Sutherland

Biography & Autobiography; Sports & Games

New Titles: 6 (1995), 8 (1996)
No of Employees: 2

ISBNs, Imprints & Series:
0 908630 Rugby Press
0 908757 Harlen Books
0 9597884 The Sporting Press

Parent Company:
Medialine Holdings Ltd *(New Zealand)*

Overseas Representation *(see §7.3)*:
Australia: Herron Book Distributors Pty Ltd, Fortitude Valley, Qld

Book Trade Association Membership:
Booksellers New Zealand, Book Publishers Association of New Zealand

2463 ━━━━━━━━━━━━━━

SAINT PUBLISHING LTD
PO Box 8157, Auckland 1
Telephone: +64 (Ō9) 623 2510
Fax: +64 (Ō9) 623 2890

Warehouse & Distributors:
Saint Publishing Ltd, 56 Mount Eden Road, Auckland
Telephone: +64 (Ō9) 623 2510
Fax: +64 (Ō9) 623 2890

Director: Selwyn Jacobson *(Managing)*

Cookery, Wines & Spirits; Fine Art & Art History; Humour; Photography; Sports & Games

New Titles: 2 (1995), 5 (1996)
No of Employees: 7
Annual Turnover: $1M

Overseas Representation *(see §7.3)*:
Australia: The Five Mile Press, Noble Park, Vic; Bissett Marketing Services Plc, Melbourne

Book Trade Association Membership:
Booksellers Association of New Zealand Inc

2464 ━━━━━━━━━━━━━━

SCHOLASTIC NEW ZEALAND LTD
Private Bag 94407, Greenmount, Auckland
Telephone: +64 (Ō9) 274 8112
Fax: +64 (Ō9) 274 8114

Managing Director: Joan Baker *(Rights & Permissions)*
Managers: Sharron Barber *(Book Fairs)*
Rob Southam *(Sales)*
Anne de Lautour *(Trade)*
Company Secretary: David Peagram *(Finance)*

Children's Books; Educational & Textbooks

New Titles: 40 (1995), 40 (1996)

ISBNs, Imprints & Series: 1 86943

Parent Company:
Scholastic Inc *(USA)*

Associated & Subsidiary Companies:
Australia: Scholastic Australia. *Canada:*
Scholastic Canada. *UK:* Scholastic
Publications

Overseas Representation *(see §7.3)*:
Australia: Scholastic Australia Ltd, Gosford,
  NSW
Canada: Scholastic Canada Ltd, Richmond
  Hill
UK: Scholastic Publications, Leamington Spa
USA: Scholastic Inc, New York, NY

Book Trade Association Membership: New
Zealand Book PA, Book Publishers
Association of New Zealand

2465

*SHEARWATER ASSOCIATES LTD
PO Box 54-224, Mana, Wellington
Telephone: +64 (Õ4) 233 8548
Fax: +64 (Õ4) 233 8548

Director: Michael Keith

Children's Books; Educational & Textbooks

ISBNs, Imprints & Series:
0 908864 Shearwater Books, Nga Rerenga o te
Titi Tuhiwai

Book Trade Association Membership: Book
Publishers Association of New Zealand

2466

SHOAL BAY PRESS LTD
PO Box 1251, Christchurch 1
Telephone: +64 (Õ3) 377 0370
Fax: +64 (Õ3) 377 0390
Email: shoalbay@shoalbay.co.nz
Web Site: http://www.shoalbay.co.nz

Directors: David Elworthy *(Publishing)*
Ros Henry *(Production)*
Luke Elworthy *(Sales & Marketing)*

*Aviation; Crafts & Hobbies; Gardening;
Industry, Business & Management; Natural
History; Reference Books, Directories &
Dictionaries; Sports & Games*

New Titles: 16 (1995), 21 (1996)
No of Employees: 5
Annual Turnover: £400,000

ISBNs, Imprints & Series: 0 908704

Book Trade Association Membership: Book
Publishers Association of New Zealand,
Booksellers Association of New Zealand Inc

2467

TANDEM PRESS
PO Box 34-272, Birkenhead, Auckland

Telephone: +64 (Õ9) 480 1452
Fax: +64 (Õ9) 480 1455

Also at:
c/o Forrester Books, Private Bag 93514,
Takapuna, Auckland 9

Directors: Bob Ross *(Publishing)*
Helen Benton *(Marketing)*

*Cookery, Wines & Spirits; Fiction; Gender
Studies; Health & Beauty; Humour; Illustrated
& Fine Editions; Industry, Business &
Management; Photography; Psychology &
Psychiatry*

New Titles: 13 (1995), 19 (1996)
No of Employees: 5
Annual Turnover: $1.2M

ISBNs, Imprints & Series: 0 908884

Book Trade Association Membership: Book
Publishers Association of New Zealand

2468

VICTORIA UNIVERSITY PRESS
PO Box 600, Wellington
Telephone: +64 (Õ4) 496 6580
Fax: +64 (Õ4) 496 6581

Trade Orders:
Harper Collins Ltd, PO Box 1, Auckland
Telephone: +64 (Õ9) 443 9401
Fax: +64 (Õ9) 443 9402

Editor: Fergus Barrowman
Chairperson, Board of VUP: Prof A. H.
Angelo

*Academic & Scholarly; Fiction; Poetry;
Theatre, Drama & Dance*

New Titles: 15 (1995), 20 (1996)
No of Employees: 2

ISBNs, Imprints & Series: 0 86473

Book Trade Association Membership: Book
Publishers Association of New Zealand,
Booksellers Association of New Zealand Inc

2469

*BRIDGET WILLIAMS BOOKS LTD
PO Box 11-294, Wellington
Telephone: +64 (Õ4) 495 2540
Fax: +64 (Õ4) 495 2541

Distribution:
HarperCollins, PO Box 1, Auckland
Telephone: +64 (Õ9) 443 9400
Fax: +64 (Õ9) 443 9403

Managing Director: Bridget Williams

*Academic & Scholarly; Biography &
Autobiography; Gardening; Gender Studies;
History & Antiquarian; Politics & World
Affairs; Sociology & Anthropology*

ISBNs, Imprints & Series: 0 908912

Book Trade Association Membership: Book
Publishers Association of New Zealand,
Booksellers New Zealand Ltd

NIGERIA

2470

JOHN WEST PUBLICATIONS LTD
Plot 2, Block A, Acme Road,
Ogba Industrial Estate, PMB 21401, Ikeja
Telephone: +234 (Õ1) 4925459 & 921010
Fax: +234 (Õ1) 921010

Directors: Dr Alhaji L. K. Jakande *(Chairman
  & Chief Executive Officer)*
Chief Bayo Fadoju *(Group Managing)*
Dr Lai Olurode *(Executive)*
Alhaji S. A. S. Ajala *(Non-Executive)*
Chief (Mrs) C. O. Ademuyiwa *(Executive)*
Rev N. O. Sholesi *(Executive)*
Lukeman K. Jakande *(Non-Executive)*
Managers: Hakeem Gaffar *(Chief Accountant)*
Victor Nmakwe *(Production)*
Anthony Aridegbe *(Editorial)*

*Academic & Scholarly; Biography &
Autobiography; Children's Books; Economics;
Educational & Textbooks; Politics & World
Affairs; Reference Books, Directories &
Dictionaries; Sociology & Anthropology*

New Titles: 12 (1996)
No of Employees: 39
Annual Turnover: $100,000

ISBNs, Imprints & Series: 978 163

Book Trade Association Membership:
Nigerian PA

PAKISTAN

2471

**ECONOMIC & INDUSTRIAL
PUBLICATIONS**
Al-Masiha Building, 3rd Floor,
47 Abdullah Haroon Road, Karachi 74400
Telephone: +92 (Õ21) 7728957, 7728434 &
7728963
Fax: +92 (Õ21) 7727582

Business: Saleem Haidari
Editorial: Iqbal Haidari
Corporate Affairs: Shireen Mohammad Ali
  (Secretary)

*Agriculture; Economics; Industry, Business &
Management; Politics & World Affairs*

New Titles: 2 (1995), 4 (1996)
No of Employees: 50
Annual Turnover: $1M

Associated & Subsidiary Companies:
Pakistan: Economic Forecasting Service;
Economic Review; EIP Investors' Service;
Industrial Research Service; IR – Multiclient
Studies

Overseas Representation *(see §7.3)*:
UK: Sultan-ul-Hassan Farooqui, London

2472

FAZLEESONS (PVT) LTD
507/3 Temple Road, Urdu Bazar,
Karachi 74200

Telephone: +92 (021) 2633853 & 2633851
Fax: +92 (021) 2633887
Email: fazlee@biruni.erum.com.pk

Chief Executive: Tarique Rehman
Managers: Chand Mian *(General)*
Muhammad Aslam *(Sales)*
Noor Ahmed *(Marketing)*
Jameel Ahmed *(Production)*
Qaseemuddin Sheikh *(Editorial)*

Biography & Autobiography; Children's Books; Fiction; History & Antiquarian; Literature & Criticism; Poetry; Politics & World Affairs; Religion & Theology; Travel & Topography

New Titles: 9 (1995), 15 (1996)
No of Employees: 120
Annual Turnover: $0.65M

ISBNs, Imprints & Series: 969 441

Book Trade Association Membership:
Pakistan Publishers & Booksellers Association, Pakistan Association of Printers & Graphic Art Industry

2473 ━━━━

*HAMDARD FOUNDATION PRESS
Hamdard Centre, Nazimabad No 3, Karachi 74600
Telephone: +92 (021) 6616001 (4 lines)
Fax: +92 (021) 6641766

Sales Officer: Mohammad Abid Taimuri *(Sales)*
Director General: Furqan Ahmad Shamsi *(Rights & Permissions)*

Academic & Scholarly; Bibliography & Library Science; Biography & Autobiography; Chemistry; Children's Books; Religion & Theology; Science Fiction; Travel & Topography

ISBNs, Imprints & Series: 969 412

Book Trade Association Membership:
Pakistan Publishers & Booksellers Association

2474 ━━━━

ISLAMIC BOOK CENTRE
Head Office, 25b Masson Road, Lahore 54000
Telephone: +92 (042) 636 1803
Fax: +92 (042) 636 0955

Counter Sales & Showroom:
6-7 Malik Jalal Trust Building, Chowk Urdu Bazar, PO Box 1625, Lahore 54000
Telephone: +92 (042) 636 1803
Fax: +92 (042) 636 0955

Managing Director: Mrs Muhammad Sajid Saeed *(Home & Export Sales)*
Sales Executive: Mrs Suberleena Sajid

Academic & Scholarly; Educational & Textbooks; Languages & Linguistics; Philosophy; Religion & Theology

New Titles: 9 (1995), 11 (1996)
No of Employees: 5
Annual Turnover: $150,000

ISBNs, Imprints & Series: 969 436

Overseas Representation *(see §7.3)*:
Australia: Muslim Book Club, Lakemba, NSW
Bangladesh: Book Centre, Dhaka
Fiji: Fiji Muslim Youth Organisation, Suva
Kenya: Haji Muhammad & Sons, Mombasa
Kuwait: Kuwait Bookshops Co Ltd, Safat
Malaysia: A. S. Noordeen, Kuala Lumpur
South Africa: Taj Co, Durban
Sri Lanka: Cargills (Ceylon) Ltd, Colombo
Trinidad: Islamic Missionary Guild, Port of Spain
UK: Heffers Booksellers, Cambridge
USA: Halal Books, Detroit, MI; Bodhi Tree Book Store, West Hollywood, CA

Book Trade Association Membership:
Pakistan Publishers & Booksellers Association

2475 ━━━━

*ISLAMIC PUBLICATIONS (PTE) LTD
13-E Shahalam Market, Lahore 54000
Telephone: +92 (042) 325243 & 7664504
Fax: +92 (042) 7658674

Sales Depot:
Al-Karim Market, Urdu Bazar, Lahore 54000
Telephone: +92 (042) 7237467

Managing Director: Rana Allah Dad Khan
General Manager: Abdul Waheed Khan
Assistant Managers: Syed Hasan Zaidi *(Sales)*
Shabbir Ahmad *(Production)*
Chief Accountant: Naved Islam Siddiqui

Children's Books; Economics; Educational & Textbooks; History & Antiquarian; Law; Politics & World Affairs; Religion & Theology

Overseas Representation *(see §7.3)*:
UK: Islamic Foundation, Leicester
USA: ICNA, Jamaica, NY

Book Trade Association Membership:
Pakistan Publishers & Booksellers Association

2476 ━━━━

MACKWIN & CO
6 Krishna Mansions, Inverarity Road, Saddar, Karachi 74400
Telephone: +92 (021) 568 1461 & 512 368
Fax: +92 (021) 722 8253 & 568 1461

Manager: Masood Husain Khan
Marketing: Precy Alfonso

No of Employees: 6

ISBNs, Imprints & Series: 969 466

Book Trade Association Membership:
Pakistan Publishers & Booksellers Association, Afro-Asian Book Council

2477 ━━━━

PAKISTAN INSTITUTE OF DEVELOPMENT ECONOMICS
PO Box 1091, Islamabad 44000
Telephone: +92 (051) 824070 & 826991
Fax: +92 (051) 210886
Email: arshad%pide@sdnpk.undp.org

Director: Prof. Sarfraz K. Qureshi
Chief Literary Editor: Prof. A. Alamghir Hashmi
Senior Publication Officer: Afraz Abbasi

Agriculture; Bibliography & Library Science; Economics; Environment & Development Studies; PACKAGER ONLY

New Titles: 4 (1995), 3 (1996)
No of Employees: 196
Annual Turnover: £12,000

ISBNs, Imprints & Series: 969 461

Overseas Representation *(see §7.3)*:
France: Dawson France, Palaisea
Japan: Maruzen Co Ltd, Tokyo
Netherlands: Martinus Nijhoff International, The Hague; Faxon Europe, Amsterdam; Swets & Zeitlinger bv, Lisse
Switzerland: Karger Libri AG, Basle
UK: Dawson Bumps, Olney
USA: EBSCO Subscription Service, Birmingham, AL

2478 ━━━━

*SANG-E-MEEL PUBLICATIONS
25 Lower Mall, PO Box 997, Lahore 54000
Telephone: +92 (042) 722 100, 722 8143 & 354 429
Fax: +92 (042) 724 5101

Director: Ahmad Niaz *(Publishing, Rights & Permissions)*
Managers: Ahmad Ijaz *(Home Sales)*
Ahmad Afzaal *(Exports & Imports)*

Academic & Scholarly; Agriculture; Archaeology; Bibliography & Library Science; Biography & Autobiography; Children's Books; Cookery, Wines & Spirits; Fiction; History & Antiquarian; Humour; Languages & Linguistics; Literature & Criticism; Philosophy; Poetry; Politics & World Affairs; Psychology & Psychiatry; Reference Books, Directories & Dictionaries; Religion & Theology; Sociology & Anthropology; Theatre, Drama & Dance

ISBNs, Imprints & Series: 939 35

Book Trade Association Membership:
Pakistan Publishers & Booksellers Association

2479 ━━━━

MALIK SIRAJUDDIN & SONS
Kashmiri Bazar, Lahore 8
Telephone: +92 (042) 765 7527
Fax: +92 (042) 765 7490

Also at:
18–19 Jh, Chowk Urdu Bazar, Lahore
Telephone: +92 (042) 766 6226 & 722 4713
Fax: +92 (042) 765 7490

General Manager: Malik Abdul Rouf

Educational & Textbooks; Law; Religion & Theology

ISBNs, Imprints & Series: 969 29

Associated & Subsidiary Companies:
Pakistan: M/S Ayaz Bookbinding Works; M/S Siraj Mohammadi Press

2480

*VANGUARD BOOKS PVT LTD
45 The Mall, Lahore
Telephone: +92 (042) 724 3779
Fax: +92 (042) 724 5097

Branch Office:
Mashriq Shopping Centre,
Sir Shah Suleman Road, Gulshan Iqbal,
Karachi
Telephone: +92 (021) 494 9175 & 494 4178

Branch Office:
Jinnah Super Market, Islamabad
Telephone: +92 (051) 215 215 & 210 099

Director: Ms Maimanat Mohsin *(Publisher)*
Chief Accountant: Aleem Ansari

*Academic & Scholarly; Economics;
Educational & Textbooks; Reference Books,
Directories & Dictionaries*

ISBNs, Imprints & Series: 969 402

Book Trade Association Membership:
Pakistan Publishers & Booksellers Association

SINGAPORE

2481

APAC PUBLISHERS SERVICES
35 Tannery Road, Tannery Block No 10-06,
Ruby Industrial Complex, Singapore 1334
Telephone: +65 747 8662
Fax: +65 747 8916
Email: sgohapac@singnet.com.sg

Managing Director: Steven Goh

*Medical (incl. Self Help & Alternative
Medicine); Scientific & Technical*

New Titles: 2 (1995), 5 (1996)
No of Employees: 3

ISBNs, Imprints & Series: 981 3045

Book Trade Association Membership:
Singapore Book PA

2482

**ASHGATE PUBLISHING ASIA PACIFIC
PTE LTD**
41 Kallang Pudding Road, #04-03,
Golden Wheel Building, Singapore 349316
Telephone: +65 741 5166
Fax: +65 742 9356
Email: ashgate@asianconnect.com

Managing Director: Barry Clarke
Managers: Bessie Tay *(General)*
Jeffrey Lim *(Sales)*

*Academic & Scholarly; Aviation; Economics;
Environment & Development Studies; Fine Art
& Art History; Industry, Business &
Management; Law; Music; Philosophy;*

*Politics & World Affairs; Vocational Training
& Careers*

No of Employees: 13

Parent Company:
Ashgate Publishing Group *(UK)*

Associated & Subsidiary Companies:
Australia: Ashgate-Gower Asia Pacific Pte Ltd

Book Trade Association Membership:
Singapore PA, Publishers Association of
Singapore

2483

ASIAPAC BOOKS PTE LTD
629 Aljunied Road, #04-06,
Cititech Industrial Building, Singapore 389838
Telephone: +65 745 3868
Fax: +65 745 3822
Email: apacbks@singnet.com.sg
Web Site: http://www.span.com.au/asiapac.
htm

Publisher: Lim Li Kok
Business Director: Anthony Chung
Managing Editor: Lydia Lum

*Children's Books; Humour; Philosophy;
Comics on Chinese culture*

New Titles: 35 (1995), 30 (1996)
No of Employees: 23
Annual Turnover: $1.6M

ISBNs, Imprints & Series:
981 3029, 981 3068, 9971 985

Overseas Representation *(see §7.3):*
Australia: Oriental Publications, Adelaide, SA;
China Books, Melbourne, Vic
China: China National Publications Import &
Export Corporation (CNPIEC), Beijing, P.
R. of China; China Book Import Centre,
Beijing, P. R. of China
Hong Kong: Peace Book Co Ltd
Indonesia: Times The Bookshop, Jakarta
Malaysia: Cahaya Vista Bakti Sdn Bhd,
Petaling Jaya
Taiwan: Caves Books Ltd, Taipei; Kinokuniya
Bookstores of Taiwan Co Ltd, Taipei
Thailand: DK Book House Co Ltd, Bangkok
UK: Millbank Books Ltd, Bishop's Stortford
USA: China Books & Periodicals Inc, San
Francisco

Book Trade Association Membership:
Singapore PA

2484

*GRAHAM BRASH PTE LTD
32 Gul Drive, Singapore 2262
Telephone: +65 861 1336
Fax: +65 861 4815

Directors: D. G. Campbell *(Research)*
K. C. Campbell *(Publishing)*
C. I. Campbell *(Managing)*
Managers: Ms Evelyn Lee *(General)*
Mr Garesan Kasee *(Home Sales)*
James Scullion *(Export Sales)*
Editor: Ms Gael Lee

*Children's Books; Educational & Textbooks;
Fiction; Guide Books; Sports & Games*

ISBNs, Imprints & Series: 981 218

Associated & Subsidiary Companies:
UK: Tynron Press Ltd

Overseas Representation *(see §7.3):*
Asia: Graham Brash Pte Ltd, Singapore
Australia: Stafford Books, St Leonards, NSW
Canada: McClelland & Stewart, Toronto &
Markham
New Zealand: South Pacific Books (Imports)
Ltd, Auckland
UK & Europe: Gazelle Book Services Ltd,
Lancaster, UK; Tynron Press Ltd,
Lutterworth, UK
USA (excluding Hawaii): Heian International
Inc, Torrance, CA, USA

Book Trade Association Membership:
Singapore Book PA, Malaysian Book
Importers Association, Malaysian PA

2485

*CANNON INTERNATIONAL
Block 86, Marine Parade Central, 03-213,
Singapore 1544
Telephone: +65 344 7801 & 440 7409
Fax: +65 447 0897

Publisher: Wu Cheng Tan

*Children's Books; Educational & Textbooks;
English as a Foreign Language*

ISBNs, Imprints & Series:
981 00, 9971 83, 9971 84 Kingsway Publishers

Associated & Subsidiary Companies:
Hong Kong: Publisher Marketing Ltd.
Mauritius: University Bookshop

Book Trade Association Membership:
Singapore Book PA

2486

EPB PUBLISHERS PTE LTD
Block 162, Bukit Merah Central #04-3545,
Singapore 150162
Telephone: +65 278 0881
Fax: +65 278 2456 & 276 6970
Email: epbpublr@singnet.com.sg
Web Site: http://www.infront.com.sg/epb/

Warehouse:
Block 3, Alexandra Distripark, #09-01/
08 Pasir Panjang Road, Singapore 118483
Telephone: +65 271 1310
Fax: +65 270 9845
Web Site: http://www.infront.com.sg/epb/

Managers: Roger Phua *(General)*
Tan Poay Lim *(Rights & Permissions)*

*Children's Books; Educational & Textbooks;
Electronic (Educational); Health & Beauty;
Industry, Business & Management; Literature
& Criticism; Reference Books, Directories &
Dictionaries*

New Titles: 200 (1995), 200 (1996)
No of Employees: 140
Annual Turnover: $17M

ISBNs, Imprints & Series:
9971 0 EPB, Young Generation Series

Parent Company:
SNP Corporation Ltd *(Singapore)*

Associated & Subsidiary Companies:
Singapore: EPB Retail Pte Ltd; SNP Publishers Pte Ltd

Overseas Representation *(see §7.3):*
Malaysia: Pan Asia Publications Sdn Bhd, Petaling Jaya
UK: Gazelle Book Services Ltd, Lancaster

Book Trade Association Membership:
Publishers Association of Singapore

2488 ▬▬▬▬▬▬▬

INSTITUTE OF SOUTHEAST ASIAN STUDIES
Heng Mui Keng Terrace, Pasir Panjang,
Singapore 119596
Telephone: +65 778 0955
Fax: +65 775 6259
Email: triena@merlion.iseas.ac.sg
Web Site: http://www.merlion.iseas.ac.sg/pub/html

Managing Editor: Triena Ong *(Publishing, Rights & Sales)*
Director: Prof Chan Heng Chee

Academic & Scholarly; Economics; Politics & World Affairs; Sociology & Anthropology

New Titles: 38 (1995), 42 (1996)

ISBNs, Imprints & Series:
981 ISEAS

Overseas Representation *(see §7.3):*
Australia & New Zealand: James Bennett Pty Ltd, Collaroy Beach, NSW, Australia
Germany: Asia Books, Neckargemund
Japan: United Publishers Services Ltd, Tokyo
South East Asia: Ashgate Publishing Asia Pacific Pte Ltd, Singapore

Book Trade Association Membership:
Publishers Association of Singapore,
International Association of Scholarly Publishers

2488 ▬▬▬▬▬▬▬

MANHATTAN PRESS (S) PTE LTD
16 Fan Yoong Road, Singapore 629793
Telephone: +65 261 6288
Fax: +65 261 6088

Managers: Chua Hong Koon *(Acting General)*
Jerry Goh *(Marketing)*
Brenda Goh *(Production)*
Managing Editor: Margaret Tan
Accounts Executive: Steven Teo

*Academic & Scholarly; Atlases & Maps;
Biology & Zoology; Chemistry; Children's
Books; Economics; Educational & Textbooks;
English as a Foreign Language; Geography &
Geology; Humour; Literature & Criticism;
Mathematics & Statistics; Physics; Poetry;
Reference Books, Directories & Dictionaries*

New Titles: 80 (1995), 120 (1996)
No of Employees: 39
Annual Turnover: $4.7M

ISBNs, Imprints & Series: 981 215

Parent Company:
Pan Pacific Public Co Ltd *(Singapore)*

Associated & Subsidiary Companies:
Hong Kong: Manhattan Press (HK) Ltd.
Malaysia: Eastview Publications Sdn Bhd.
Singapore: Pan Pacific Publications (S) Pte Ltd

Overseas Representation *(see §7.3):*
Brunei: Booker International, Bandar Seri
Begawan; Q-Pac Publishing Sdn Bhd,
Bandar Seri Beganan
Hong Kong: Manhattan Press (HK) Ltd
Malaysia: Eastview Publications Sdn Bhd,
Petaling Jaya
Mauritius: Editions de l'Ocean Indien Ltd,
Rose Hill; University Bookshop, Port Louis;
Editions Le Printemps, Vacoas
Pakistan: Paramount Books (Pvt) Ltd, Karachi
Taiwan: Shin Ya Ltd, Taipei

Book Trade Association Membership:
Singapore PA

2489 ▬▬▬▬▬▬▬

EDITIONS DIDIER MILLET
593 Havelock Road #02-01/02,
Isetan Office Building, Singapore 169641
Telephone: +65 735 7990
Fax: +65 735 8981
Email: edm@pacific.net.sg

Publisher: Didier Millet
General Manager: Charles Orwin
Editorial Director: Timothy Auger

*Architecture & Design; Cookery, Wines &
Spirits; Crafts & Hobbies; Environment &
Development Studies; Fine Art & Art History;
Guide Books; Illustrated & Fine Editions;
Natural History; Photography; Reference
Books, Directories & Dictionaries; Travel &
Topography*

New Titles: 20 (1995), 20 (1996)
No of Employees: 35
Annual Turnover: $7.5M

ISBNs, Imprints & Series:
981 3018 Archipelago Press, Les Editions du Pacifique

2490 ▬▬▬▬▬▬▬

OXFORD UNIVERSITY PRESS PTE LTD
37 Jalan Pemimpin,
03-03 Union Industrial Building,
Singapore 2057
Telephone: +65 259 7122
Fax: +65 259 8622

Managing Director: Clarence Lim
Manager: Elaine Yap *(Finance)*
Editors: Asha Kumaran *(Educational)*
Claire Goh *(Educational)*
Grace Kan *(Educational)*
Assistant Marketing Manager: Gan Bee Lian
Marketing Executives: Richard Seet
Kelvyn Chong

Rosalind Yeow
Constance Tan
Assistant Warehouse Manager: Roger Phay

Educational & Textbooks

New Titles: 120 (1995), 100 (1996)
No of Employees: 26
Annual Turnover: £2.3M

ISBNs, Imprints & Series:
0 19 584 OUP Singapore
0 19 587, 0 19 588 The Asia Collection, Images
of Asia, Oxford in Asia Hardback Reprints,
Oxford in Asia Studies in Ceramics, Oxford
in Asia Students Editions, Oxford
Paperbacks, South East Asian Social Science
Monographs

Parent Company:
Oxford University Press *(UK)*

Overseas Representation *(see §7.3):*
Worldwide: Oxford University Press, Oxford, UK

Book Trade Association Membership:
Publishers Association of Singapore

2491 ▬▬▬▬▬▬▬

PAN PACIFIC PUBLICATIONS (S) PTE LTD
16 Fan Yoong Road, Singapore 629793
Telephone: +65 261 6288
Fax: +65 261 6088

Managing Director: Chong Huai Seng
Managers: Chua Hong Koon *(Acting General)*
Jerry Goh *(Marketing & Media Development)*

*Academic & Scholarly; Atlases & Maps;
Biology & Zoology; Chemistry; Children's
Books; Economics; Educational & Textbooks;
English as a Foreign Language; Geography &
Geology; Humour; Literature & Criticism;
Mathematics & Statistics; Physics; Poetry;
Reference Books, Directories & Dictionaries*

New Titles: 80 (1995), 100 (1996)
No of Employees: 39
Annual Turnover: $4.7M

ISBNs, Imprints & Series:
981 208, 981 215

Associated & Subsidiary Companies:
Hong Kong: Manhattan Press (HK) Ltd.
Malaysia: Eastview Publications Sdn Bhd;
Jacaranda Buku Sdn Bhd. *Singapore:* Mandarin
Educational Publishers Pte Ltd; Manhattan
Press (S) Pte Ltd

Overseas Representation *(see §7.3):*
Brunei: Booker International, Bandar Seri
Begawan; Bandar Seri Begawan; Q-Pac
Publishing Sdn Bhd, Bandar Seri Beganan
Hong Kong: Manhattan Press (HK) Ltd
Malaysia: Eastview Publications Sdn Bhd,
Petaling Jaya
Mauritius: Editions de l'Ocean Indien Ltd,
Rose Hill; University Bookshop, Port Louis;
Editions Le Printemps, Vacoas
Pakistan: Paramount Books (Pvt) Ltd, Karachi
Taiwan: Shin Ya Ltd, Taipei

Book Trade Association Membership:
Singapore Book PA

2492 ▬▬▬▬▬▬▬▬▬▬

SINGAPORE UNIVERSITY PRESS PTE LTD
Yusof Ishak House, Kent Ridge,
Singapore 119260
Telephone: +65 776 1148 & 772 2382
Fax: +65 774 0652
Email: supbooks@nus.sg
Web Site: http://www.nus.sg

Managing Editor: Patricia Tay

Academic & Scholarly

New Titles: 15 (1995), 15 (1996)
No of Employees: 4

ISBNs, Imprints & Series:
9971 69 Ridge Books, Singapore University Press

Overseas Representation *(see §7.3)*:
Australia: James Bennett Library Services, Collaroy, NSW
Japan: United Publishers Services Ltd, Tokyo
Malaysia, Thailand, Indonesia, Brunei, Hong Kong, Korea & Taiwan: Ashgate Publishing Asia Pacific Pte Ltd, Singapore
UK & Europe: Drake International Services, Oxford, UK
USA: Coronet Books Inc, Philadelphia, PA

Book Trade Association Membership:
Singapore PA, International Association of Scholarly Publishers

2493 ▬▬▬▬▬▬▬▬▬▬

TIMES PUBLISHING LTD
Times Centre, 1 New Industrial Road,
Singapore 1953
Telephone: +65 284 8844
Fax: +65 288 9254
Email: tplchh@corp.tpl.com.sg
Web Site: http://www.tpl.com.sg

President & Chief Executive Officer: Kua Hong Pak
Senior Vice-President: Chiam Heng Him
Executive Vice-President: Colin Yam

Academic & Scholarly; Accountancy & Taxation; Agriculture; Antiques & Collecting; Architecture & Design; Biography & Autobiography; Biology & Zoology; Chemistry; Children's Books; Cookery, Wines & Spirits; Crime; Crafts & Hobbies; Economics; Educational & Textbooks; English as a Foreign Language; Fashion & Costume; Fiction; Gardening; Gender Studies; Guide Books; Health & Beauty; History & Antiquarian; Humour; Illustrated & Fine Editions; Industry, Business & Management; Languages & Linguistics; Literature & Criticism; Magic & the Occult; Mathematics & Statistics; Natural History; Physics; Poetry; Politics & World Affairs; Reference Books, Directories & Dictionaries; Theatre, Drama & Dance; Travel & Topography

New Titles: 350 (1995), 380 (1996)
No of Employees: 2000
Annual Turnover: £218M

ISBNs, Imprints & Series:
Asia Pacific Press, Earlybird Books, Eastern University Press, Federal Publications, Les Editions du Pacifique, Times Academic Press, Times Books International, Times Editions

Associated & Subsidiary Companies:
Australia: Marshall Cavendish (Australia) Pty Ltd; Reed Books Pty Ltd. *France:* ALP Snc. *Germany:* Sammelwerk Redaktions Service GmbH. *Hong Kong:* Far East Publications Ltd; Far East Trade Press Business Publications Ltd; Far East Trade Press Ltd; Federal Publications Ltd; United Publishers Services (HK) Ltd; United Publishers Services Ltd. *Japan:* Kabushiki Kaisha Union Enterprises. *Malaysia:* Federal Publications Sdn Bhd. *Singapore:* Federal Publications (S) Pte Ltd; FETP Business Publications Pte Ltd; Times Editions Pte Ltd; Times Trade Directories Pte Ltd; United Publishers Services Pte Ltd. *UK:* Marshall Cavendish Books Ltd; Marshall Cavendish International Ltd; Marshall Cavendish Partworks Ltd. *USA:* Marshall Cavendish Corporation; H. S. Stuttman Inc; Webster's Unified Inc

Overseas Representation *(see §7.3)*:
Africa: Trade Winds Press Pty Ltd, Randburg, South Africa
Australia: Bookland Pty Ltd, East Perth; Bookwise International, Findon, SA; CIS Publishers, Carlton, Vic
Hong Kong: Asia Publisher Services Ltd; APS Singapore Pte Ltd, Singapore; Federal Publications (HK) Ltd, Kowloon
India: Times Books International, New Delhi; Teksons Bookshop, New Delhi
Indonesia: P. T. Isawandi Lestari, Jakarta; PT Transito Tatemedia, Jakarta; PT Gramedia, Jakarta
Malaysia: STP Distributors (M) Sdn Bhd, Shah Alam
Netherlands: Nilsson & Lamm BV, Weesp
Sri Lanka: Sansoni Warehouse Ltd, Colombo
Taiwan: Lai Lai Book Co, Taipei
Thailand: Far East Publications Ltd, Bangkok; Shin Ya Ltd, Taipei, Taiwan; ISBN Co Ltd, Bangkok; Asia Book Co, Bangkok
UK: Millbank Books Ltd, Bishop's Stortford
USA: China Books & Periodicals Inc, San Francisco; Eastwind Books & Arts Inc, San Francisco, CA; Graphic Arts, Portland, OR

Book Trade Association Membership:
Singapore PA

2494 ▬▬▬▬▬▬▬▬▬▬

*WORLD SCIENTIFIC PUBLISHING CO PTE LTD
1022 Hougang Avenue 1 05-3520,
Tai Seng Industrial Estate, Singapore 1953
Telephone: +65 382 5663
Fax: +65 382 5919

Editor: Gillian Chee
Sales Manager: Siew Lan Tan

Academic & Scholarly; Biology & Zoology; Chemistry; Computer Science; Economics; Educational & Textbooks; Engineering; Environment & Development Studies; Mathematics & Statistics; Medical (incl. Self Help & Alternative Medicine); Physics; Psychology & Psychiatry; Reference Books,

Directories & Dictionaries; Scientific & Technical

Associated & Subsidiary Companies:
Hong Kong: World Scientific Publishing (HK) Co Ltd. *India:* World Scientific Publishing Co Pte Ltd. *Taiwan:* World Scientific Publishing Co Pte Ltd. *UK:* World Scientific Publishing Co. *USA:* World Scientific Publishing Co Inc

Overseas Representation *(see §7.3)*:
Australia: DA Information Services, Mitcham, Vic
India: Allied Publishers Ltd, New Delhi
Japan: Kaigai Publications Ltd, Tokyo; Neutrino Inc, Tokyo; Kinokuniya Book Import Dept, Tokyo; Maruzen Co Ltd, Tokyo

Book Trade Association Membership:
IGSMTP

SOUTH AFRICA

2495 ▬▬▬▬▬▬▬▬▬▬

JONATHAN BALL PUBLISHERS
PO Box 33977, Jeppestown, 2043
Telephone: +27 (011) 622 2900
Fax: +27 (011) 622 7610

Director: Jonathan Ball *(General Manager)*

Biography & Autobiography; History & Antiquarian; Natural History; Politics & World Affairs; Reference Books, Directories & Dictionaries

ISBNs, Imprints & Series:
0 86852, 0 949937 Ad. Donker
0 908387 Delta
0 947464, 1 86842 Jonathan Ball Publishers

Parent Company:
National Press *(South Africa)*

Associated & Subsidiary Companies:
South Africa: Delta Books (Pty) Ltd; Ad. Donker (Pty) Ltd

Book Trade Association Membership:
Publishers Association of South Africa

2496 ▬▬▬▬▬▬▬▬▬▬

BRABY'S BUSINESS DIRECTORIES
PO Box 1426, Pinetown, 3600
Telephone: +27 (031) 701 7021
Fax: +27 (031) 701 7036

Directors: G. Rechner *(Finance)*
T. Stagg *(Production)*
Mrs N. Baye *(Sales)*
Marketing Manager: Mrs P. Dahn
Company Secretary: G. Cleveland

Atlases & Maps; Electronic (Professional & Academic); Reference Books, Directories & Dictionaries; PACKAGER ONLY

No of Employees: 800

Parent Company:
Kohler *(South Africa)*

Associated & Subsidiary Companies:
South Africa: A. C. Braby; Caversham Printing
& Publishing; Intratex; Swan Publishing

2497 ■■■■■■

AD DONKER (PTY) LTD
PO Box 33977, Jeppestown, 2043
Telephone: +27 (Õ11) 622 2900
Fax: +27 (Õ11) 622 7610

Sales: J. A. B. Ball

*Literature & Criticism; Poetry; Reference
Books, Directories & Dictionaries*

ISBNs, Imprints & Series:
0 86852, 0 949937

Parent Company:
National Press *(South Africa)*

Associated & Subsidiary Companies:
South Africa: Jonathan Ball Publishers (Pty)
Ltd; Delta Books (Pty) Ltd

2498 ■■■■■■

**HARPERCOLLINS PUBLISHERS (SA)
(PTY) LTD**
PO Box 33977, Jeppestown, 2043
Telephone: +27 (Õ11) 622 2900
Fax: +27 (Õ11) 622 3553

General Manager: J. Ball
Sales & Marketing: Alastair Steyn
Finance: Dirk van der Toorn

Parent Company:
National Press *(South Africa)*

2499 ■■■■■■

HEINEMANN PUBLISHERS (PTY) LTD
PO Box 371, Isando, 1600
Telephone: +27 (Õ11) 974 1181
Fax: +27 (Õ11) 974 4311 (Admin/Marketing)
& 974 2142 (Publishing)

Directors: K. Kroeger *(Managing)*
Robert Sulley *(Textbook Publishing Division)*
Sabelo Zulu *(Language Publishing Division)*
Laura Czerniewicz *(Strategy & Staff
Development)*
Mike Smuts *(Financial)*
Jannie Wilken *(Sales & Marketing)*
Margarethe Mostert *(Higher & Further
Education)*
General Manager, Sales & Marketing:
Bunny Castle

Academic & Scholarly

New Titles: 100 (1995), 150 (1996)
No of Employees: 117
Annual Turnover: £10M

ISBNs, Imprints & Series:
1 86813 Butterworth–Heinemann, Centaur,
Ginn, Heinemann, Heinemann-Centaur,
Isando Books, Lexicon

Parent Company:
CNA Gallo *(South Africa)*. Reed-Elsevier *(UK)*

Associated & Subsidiary Companies:
South Africa: Heinemann Higher & Further
Education

Book Trade Association Membership:
Publishers Association of South Africa

2500 ■■■■■■

HUMAN & ROUSSEAU PTY LTD
PO Box 5050, Cape Town, 8000
Telephone: +27 (Õ21) 25 1280
Fax: +27 (Õ21) 419 2619

Location:
State House, 3–9 Rose Street, Cape Town, 8001
Telephone: +27 (Õ21) 25 1280
Fax: +27 (Õ21) 419 2619

Managers: C. T. Breytenbach *(General)*
R. Hauman *(Operations)*
M. Coetzee *(Transvaal Office)*
C. Stoffberg *(Accounting)*
E. Wolfaard *(Sales)*
Editors: A. Kühn *(Cookery & Leisure Books)*
E. Naudé *(Trade Co-productions & Mass
Market Books)*
A. Potgieter *(Fiction)*
M. Fryer *(Crafts & Gardening)*
L. Viljoen *(Non-fiction)*
A. Lategan *(Children's Books)*

*Academic & Scholarly; Architecture & Design;
Biography & Autobiography; Children's
Books; Cookery, Wines & Spirits; Crafts &
Hobbies; Do-It-Yourself; Fiction; Fine Art &
Art History; Gardening; Guide Books; Health
& Beauty; History & Antiquarian; Industry,
Business & Management; Literature &
Criticism; Music; Natural History; Poetry;
Politics & World Affairs; Reference Books,
Directories & Dictionaries; Theatre, Drama &
Dance; Travel & Topography*

New Titles: 140 (1995), 150 (1996)
No of Employees: 34
Annual Turnover: £4.1M

ISBNs, Imprints & Series:
0 7981 Human & Rousseau

Parent Company:
Nasionale Boekhandel Beperk *(South Africa)*

Book Trade Association Membership:
Publishers Association of South Africa

2501 ■■■■■■

JUTA & CO LTD
PO Box 30, Cape Town, 8000
Telephone: +27 (Õ21) 797 5101
Fax: +27 (Õ21) 762 7424
Email: jutabooks%jin@juta.co.za
Web Site: http://www.juta.com

Directors: R. J. Cooke *(Managing)*
J. C. Potgieter *(Educational Publishing)*
S. P. Sephton *(Law & Professional Publishing,
Rights & Permissions)*
E. Horwitz *(Academic Publishing, Rights &
Permissions)*

*Academic & Scholarly; Accountancy &
Taxation; Educational & Textbooks; Electronic
(Professional & Academic); Industry, Business*

*& Management; Law; Medical (incl. Self Help
& Alternative Medicine)*

New Titles: 330 (1995), 605 (1996)
No of Employees: 360

ISBNs, Imprints & Series: 0 7021

Parent Company:
Juta Holdings (Pty) Ltd *(South Africa)*

Associated & Subsidiary Companies:
South Africa: Jutastat (Pty) Ltd. *Zambia:*
School & College Press (Zambia) Ltd.
Zimbabwe: Juta Zimbabwe (Pvt) Ltd

Overseas Representation *(see §7.3):*
Australia: The Law Book Co Ltd, North Ryde
Australia (Law titles): Blackstone Press Pty
Ltd, Sydney, NSW, Australia
*Europe (including UK: Academic & Medical
titles):* Book Representation & Distribution
(BRAD), Hadleigh, UK
Europe (including UK: Law titles): Hammicks
Law Bookshop, London, UK
Malaysia (Law & Medical titles): Legal Circle,
Klang, Malaysia
USA & Canada (Academic & Medical titles):
International Specialized Book Services Inc,
Portland, OR, USA
USA & Canada (Law titles): Wm Gaunt & Sons
Inc, Holmes Drive, FL, Canada

Book Trade Association Membership:
Publishers Association of South Africa,
Associated Booksellers of Southern Africa

2502 ■■■■■■

*KAGISO PUBLISHERS
PO Box 629, Pretoria, 0001
Telephone: +27 (Õ12) 328 4620
Fax: +27 (Õ12) 328 4706

Directors: P. S. Scholtz *(Publishing)*
S. F. du Toit *(Marketing)*
L. Mabandla *(Research & Development)*

*Academic & Scholarly; Accountancy &
Taxation; Agriculture; Atlases & Maps;
Biology & Zoology; Chemistry; Children's
Books; Computer Science; Economics;
Educational & Textbooks; Electronic
(Educational); Engineering; English as a
Foreign Language; Fiction; Gardening;
Geography & Geology; History &
Antiquarian; Industry, Business &
Management; Languages & Linguistics;
Literature & Criticism; Mathematics &
Statistics; Medical (incl. Self Help &
Alternative Medicine); Natural History;
Physics; Poetry; Reference Books, Directories
& Dictionaries; Religion & Theology;
Scientific & Technical; Theatre, Drama &
Dance; Vocational Training & Careers*

ISBNs, Imprints & Series: 0 7986

Book Trade Association Membership:
Publishers' Association of South Africa

2503 ■■■■■■

N. G. KERK-UITGEWERS
33 Waterkant Street, PO Box 4539, Cape Town,
8001

Telephone: +27 (021) 21 5540
Fax: +27 (021) 419 1865

**Warehouse, Trade Enquiries, Orders &
Wholesale:**
3 Skietlood Street, Isando Ext. 3, 1610
Telephone: +27 (011) 392 3005
Fax: +27 (011) 392 3738

Chief Executive Officer: Stephan Spies
Managers: F. du Plessis *(Administration)*
Mrs E. M. Volschenk *(Marketing)*
Editor-in-Chief: Mrs H. Venter *(Rights &
Permissions)*
Production Manager: P. van Schuik

Religion & Theology

New Titles: 35 (1995), 30 (1996)
No of Employees: 45

ISBNs, Imprints & Series: 0 86991

Associated & Subsidiary Companies:
South Africa: Lux Verbi; Waterkant Publishers

Book Trade Association Membership:
Christian Booksellers of South Africa

2504

KNOWLEDGE UNLIMITED (PTY) LTD
Private Bag 16, Centurion, 0046
Telephone: +27 (011) 652 1800
Fax: +27 (011) 314 2984

Managing Director: M. A. C. Jacklin
Managers: C. Gregory *(Financial)*
A. Fouché *(Sales)*
B. H. Mason *(Production)*
Marketing: H. Hodgkins
Head, Editorial: H. J. M. Retief

*Children's Books; Educational & Textbooks;
Fiction; African languages*

New Titles: 300 (1995), 300 (1996)

ISBNs, Imprints & Series: 1 86839

Parent Company:
Time Warner Publishing BV *(South Africa)*

2505

LUX VERBI LTD
33 Waterkant Street, PO Box 1822, Cape Town
Telephone: +27 (021) 21 5540
Fax: +27 (021) 419 1865

Chief Executive Officer: Stephan Spies
Managers: F. du Plessis *(Administration)*
Mrs E. M. Volschenk *(Marketing)*
Editor-in-Chief: Mrs H. Venter *(Rights &
Permissions)*

*Academic & Scholarly; Children's Books;
Educational & Textbooks; Poetry; Religion &
Theology*

New Titles: 47 (1995), 45 (1996)
No of Employees: 37

ISBNs, Imprints & Series: 0 86997

Associated & Subsidiary Companies:
South Africa: N. G. Kerk-Uitgewers; Waterkant
Publishers

Book Trade Association Membership: South
African Book PA, South African Booksellers
Association

2506

MACDONALD PURNELL (PTY) LTD
PO Box 40533, Cleveland, 2022
Telephone: +27 (011) 616 8248
Fax: +27 (011) 616 7943

Directors: Peter Matthews *(Managing)*
John Keppler *(Operations)*
Muoneen Lang *(Financial)*
Janine O'Connor *(Sales & Marketing)*

*Academic & Scholarly; Antiques & Collecting;
Children's Books; Cinema, Video, TV & Radio;
Cookery, Wines & Spirits; Crafts & Hobbies;
Do-It-Yourself; Educational & Textbooks;
Fiction; Fine Art & Art History; Gardening;
Health & Beauty; Military & War; Natural
History; Photography; Religion & Theology;
Science Fiction; Sports & Games; Travel &
Topography*

No of Employees: 26

ISBNs, Imprints & Series:
Abacus, Belair, Berlitz, Bulfinch, C.Y.P.
Audio, Constable, Duckworth, Duns Tew,
Early Childhood Learning, Holloway House,
Hyperion, Little, Brown UK, Little, Brown
USA, No Exit Press, Oldcastle Press, Orbit,
Piatkus Books, Ravette, Southern Printing,
Studio Editions, Thomas Nelson UK, Tiger
Books, Virago, Warner UK, World
International

Book Trade Association Membership:
Publishers Association of South Africa

2507

**MASKEW MILLER LONGMAN (PTY)
LTD**
PO Box 396, Cape Town, 8000
Telephone: +27 (021) 531 7750
Fax: +27 (021) 531 4049

Chief Executive: M. Peacock
Directors: F. Dada *(Managing, Education
Division)*
S. Connolly *(Managing, Development
Division)*
C. Gillitt *(Sales & Marketing, Education
Division)*
C. Vamvadelis *(Group Corporate Services)*

*Children's Books; Educational & Textbooks;
Adult Non-fiction*

ISBNs, Imprints & Series: 0 636

Parent Company:
Khula Educational Investments (50%) *(South
Africa)*. Longman Group Ltd (50%) *(UK)*

Associated & Subsidiary Companies:
Namibia: Longman (Namibia) (Pty) Ltd;
Sached Books (Pty) Ltd

Overseas Representation *(see §7.3)*:
Botswana: Longman Botswana (Pty) Ltd,
Gaborone
Lesotho: Longman Lesotho (Pty) Ltd, Maseru
Namibia: Longman (Namibia) (Pty) Ltd,
Windhoek
UK: Longman Group (UK) Ltd, Harlow
Zimbabwe: Longman Zimbabwe (Pvt) Ltd,
Harare

Book Trade Association Membership:
Publishers Association of South Africa

2508

METHODIST PUBLISHING HOUSE
3rd Floor, Creative House,
31 Parliament Street, (PO Box 708),
Cape Town, 8000
Telephone: +27 (021) 461 8214
Fax: +27 (021) 461 8249

Wholesale Division:
(as above)
Telephone: +27 (021) 461 8275
Fax: +27 (021) 461 8249

Religion & Theology

New Titles: 5 (1995), 7 (1996)
No of Employees: 7
Annual Turnover: $120,000

ISBNs, Imprints & Series: 1 947450

2509

UNIVERSITY OF NATAL PRESS
PO Box 01 Scottsville, 3209
Telephone: +27 (0331) 260 5226
Fax: +27 (0331) 260 5599
Email: books@press.unp.ac.za

Director: Ms M. P. Moberly
Editor: Dr J. J. Edley
Administration Officer: Ms H. Khoosal

*Academic & Scholarly; Gender Studies;
History & Antiquarian; Literature & Criticism;
Medical (incl. Self Help & Alternative
Medicine); Military & War; Natural History*

New Titles: 6 (1995), 14 (1996)
No of Employees: 5
Annual Turnover: £32,000

ISBNs, Imprints & Series:
0 8690 Hadeda Books, Killie Campbell
Africana Library, University of Natal Press

Overseas Representation *(see §7.3)*:
North America: International Specialized Book
Services Inc, Portland, OR, USA
UK: Africa Book Centre, London

Book Trade Association Membership:
Publishers Association of South Africa

2510

**OXFORD UNIVERSITY PRESS
(SOUTHERN AFRICA)**
PO Box 1141, Cape Town, 8000
Telephone: +27 (021) 45 7266
Fax: +27 (021) 45 7265
Email: oxford@oup.co.za

Johannesburg Branch Office:
PO Box 41390, Craighall, 2024
Telephone: +27 (0̄11) 442 8862, 788 3617 &
880 1523
Fax: +27 (0̄11) 880 5481
Email: rose@oup.co.za

Durban Branch Office:
311 Perm Building, 13–17 Crompton Street,
Pinetown, 3600
Telephone: +27 (0̄31) 72 8125 (Education) &
709 1577 (Academic)
Fax: +27 (0̄31) 72 8522

Umtata Branch Office:
PO Box 327, Umtata, Transkei
Telephone: +27 (0̄471) 31 0111
Fax: +27 (0̄471) 31 0111

Pietersburg Branch Office:
PO Box 5799, Pietersburg North, 0750
Telephone: +27 (0̄1521) 291 3116
Fax: +27 (0̄1521) 291 4303

Directors: Kate McCallum *(Managing)*
Robert Marsh *(Financial)*
Colleen McCallum *(Sales & Marketing)*
Hanri Pieterse *(Publishing)*

*Academic & Scholarly; Agriculture;
Economics; Educational & Textbooks;
Geography & Geology; History &
Antiquarian; Industry, Business &
Management; Languages & Linguistics;
Literature & Criticism; Mathematics &
Statistics; Medical (incl. Self Help &
Alternative Medicine); Politics & World
Affairs; Psychology & Psychiatry; Reference
Books, Directories & Dictionaries; Scientific &
Technical; Sociology & Anthropology; Sports
& Games; Veterinary Science*

New Titles: 50 (1995), 70 (1996)
No of Employees: 75
Annual Turnover: £4M

ISBNs, Imprints & Series:
0 19 570, 0 19 571

Parent Company:
Oxford University Press *(UK)*

Overseas Representation *(see §7.3)*:
Australia: Oxford University Press, South
Melbourne
Bangladesh: Mohiuddin Ahmed, Dacca
Barbados & Bermuda: C. D. A. Walker,
Christchurch, Barbados
Botswana: David Barrett-Jolly, Gaborone
Canada: Oxford University Press, Don Mills
Caribbean: Austin's Book Services,
Georgetown, Guyana
China & Hong Kong: Oxford University Press,
Hong Kong
Germany: OUP GmbH, Cologne
Ghana: Emmanuel Publishing Services, Accra
North
India: Oxford University Press Indian Branch,
New Delhi, Bombay, Calcutta & New Delhi,
Madras
Iran: Hooshang Momeni, Tehran
Jamaica: Steadman A. R. Fuller, Kingston
Japan: Oxford University Press KK, Tokyo
Kenya: Oxford University Press, Nairobi
Malaysia: Penerbit Fajar Bakti Sdn Bhd, Kuala
Lumpur

New Zealand: Oxford University Press,
Auckland
Nigeria: Mosuro Booksellers, Ibadan
Pakistan: Oxford University Press, Karachi;
Oxford University Press, Karachi; Oxford
University Press, Islamabad
Philippines: Edwin Makabenta Jr, Quezon City
Singapore: Oxford University Press Pte Ltd
Spain: Oxford University Press Espana, Madrid
Taiwan: Oxford University Press, Taipei
Tanzania: Oxford University Press East &
Central Africa Branch, Dar es Salaam
Thailand: Libris (Thailand) Co Ltd, Bangkok
Trinidad & Tobago: Mrs Edna Dawson, Diego
Martin, Trinidad
Uganda: Betty Lumu, Kampala
UK: Oxford University Press, Academic
Division, Oxford; Zwemmer OUP Music &
Books, London; Oxford University Press
Distribution Services, Corby
USA: Oxford University Press, New York
Zimbabwe: College Press Publishers (Pvt) Ltd,
Harare

Book Trade Association Membership:
Publishers Association of South Africa

2511 ▄▄▄▄▄▄▄▄

***RANDOM HOUSE SOUTH AFRICA
(PTY) LTD**
PO Box 337, Bergvlei, 2012
Telephone: +27 (0̄11) 786 2983
Fax: +27 (0̄11) 887 5077

Trade Enquiries:
Telephone: +27 2241 2667
Fax: +27 2241 2667

Sales Manager: Colin McGee
Directors: Stephen Johnson *(Managing)*
Peter Hains *(Finance & Administration)*
Ronald Napier *(Chairman)*
Dawn Mokhobo

ISBNs, Imprints & Series: 0 947

Parent Company:
Random House Group *(UK)*

Book Trade Association Membership:
Publishers Association of South Africa

2512 ▄▄▄▄▄▄▄▄

RAVAN PRESS (PTY) LTD
PO Box 145, Randburg, 2125
Telephone: +27 (0̄11) 789 7636
Fax: +27 (0̄11) 789 7653

Managing Director: Gerald de Villiers
General Manager: Monica Seeber *(Rights &
Permissions, Export Sales)*
Production: Matthew Seal
Home Sales: Ipuseng Kotsokoane

*Academic & Scholarly; Gender Studies;
History & Antiquarian; Literature & Criticism;
Politics & World Affairs*

New Titles: 15 (1995), 20 (1996)
No of Employees: 5
Annual Turnover: £270,000

ISBNs, Imprints & Series: 0 86975

Parent Company:
Hodder & Stoughton Educational *(South
Africa)*

Overseas Representation *(see §7.3)*:
North America: Ohio University Press, Athens,
OH, USA

Book Trade Association Membership:
Publishers Association of South Africa

2513 ▄▄▄▄▄▄▄▄

**SOUTHERN BOOK PUBLISHERS (PTY)
LTD**
PO Box 3103, Halfway House, Transvaal, 1685
Telephone: +27 (0̄11) 315 3633
Fax: +27 (0̄11) 315 3810

Orders:
PSD Warehouse
Telephone: +27 (0̄11) 397 5054
Fax: +27 (0̄11) 823 3941

Directors: Basil Van Rooyen *(Managing)*
Erroll Marx *(Production)*
Barrie Wood *(Financial)*
Louise Grantham *(Publishing)*
Debby de Groot *(Sales—SA product)*
Paul Steedman *(Sales—Agencies)*

*Atlases & Maps; Cookery, Wines & Spirits;
Crafts & Hobbies; Environment &
Development Studies; Fine Art & Art History;
Gardening; Guide Books; History &
Antiquarian; Illustrated & Fine Editions;
Industry, Business & Management; Natural
History; Politics & World Affairs; Reference
Books, Directories & Dictionaries; Sports &
Games; Travel & Topography; Vocational
Training & Careers*

New Titles: 42 (1995), 48 (1996)
No of Employees: 27
Annual Turnover: £3M

ISBNs, Imprints & Series: 1 86812

Associated & Subsidiary Companies:
South Africa: Southern Directories

Overseas Representation *(see §7.3)*:
UK: Millbank Books Ltd, Bishop's Stortford

Book Trade Association Membership:
Publishers Association of South Africa

2514 ▄▄▄▄▄▄▄▄

TAFELBERG PUBLISHERS
PO Box 879, Cape Town, 8000
Telephone: +27 (0̄21) 24 1320
Fax: +27 (0̄21) 24 2510

Sales Representation:
PO Box 879, Cape Town 8000
Telephone: +27 (0̄21) 24 1320
Fax: +27 (0̄21) 24 2510

Warehouse & Orders:
PO Box 487, Bellville, 7535
Telephone: +27 (0̄21) 951 6611
Fax: +27 (0̄21) 951 4903

Managers: J. J. Labuschagne *(General)*
R. V. Taylor *(Production)*
A. Swanepoel *(Marketing, Home Sales)*

Promotions: Ms R. Scheepers
Chief Editors: Ms L. Steyn *(Children's Books)*
C. Fryer *(Fiction)*
J. Steyn *(Non-Fiction)*

*Children's Books; Cookery, Wines & Spirits;
Crafts & Hobbies; Fiction; Literature &
Criticism; Poetry; Theatre, Drama & Dance*

New Titles: 91 (1995), 94 (1996)
No of Employees: 43

ISBNs, Imprints & Series:
0 624 Tafelberg
1 86826 Delos/Tafelberg

Parent Company:
Nasionale Pers *(South Africa)*

Associated & Subsidiary Companies:
South Africa: Jonathan Ball Publishers; Human
& Rousseau; Kwela Books; Leo Books; Nasou;
J. L. van Schaik Publishers; Via Afrika

Book Trade Association Membership:
Publishers Association of South Africa, South
African Booksellers Association

2515

UNISA PRESS
PO Box 392, Pretoria, 0001
Telephone: +27 (0̄12) 429 3051
Fax: +27 (0̄12) 429 3221
Email: moolmsj@alpha.unisa.ac.za
Web Site: http://www.unisa.ac.za/

Director: Phoebe van der Walt
Head, Publishing Section: Saric Moolman
Business Section: Nellie Swart
Production Manager: Dirk van Corter

*Academic & Scholarly; Accountancy &
Taxation; Bibliography & Library Science;
Computer Science; Educational & Textbooks;
Electronic (Educational); Environment &
Development Studies; History & Antiquarian;
Languages & Linguistics; Law; Literature &
Criticism; Mathematics & Statistics;
Philosophy; Psychology & Psychiatry;
Reference Books, Directories & Dictionaries;
Religion & Theology*

New Titles: 29 (1995), 30 (1996)
No of Employees: 40

ISBNs, Imprints & Series: 0 86981

Book Trade Association Membership:
Publishers Association of South Africa

2516

J. L. VAN SCHAIK PUBLISHERS
PO Box 12681, Hatfield, Pretoria, 0028
Telephone: +27 (0̄12) 342 2765
Fax: +27 (0̄12) 43 3563
Email: mbotha@nbh.naspers.co.za

Warehouse & Orders:
Nasionale Boekhandel Wholesale Services,
PO Box 4886, Randburg, 2125
Telephone: +27 (0̄11) 792 2213
Fax: +27 (0̄11) 792 3308

Directors: T. Vosloo *(Chairman)*
J. F. Malherbe

H. G. Raubenheimer *(Executive)*
L. M. Taunyane
F. J. Wiese
Prof E. Botha

*Academic & Scholarly; Accountancy &
Taxation; Agriculture; Biography &
Autobiography; Biology & Zoology;
Chemistry; Economics; Educational &
Textbooks; Fiction; Fine Art & Art History;
Guide Books; Industry, Business &
Management; Languages & Linguistics; Law;
Literature & Criticism; Mathematics &
Statistics; Medical (incl. Self Help &
Alternative Medicine); Music; Natural History;
Physics; Politics & World Affairs; Psychology
& Psychiatry; Reference Books, Directories &
Dictionaries; Religion & Theology; Sociology
& Anthropology; Theatre, Drama & Dance*

No of Employees: 24

ISBNs, Imprints & Series: 0 627

Parent Company:
Nasionale Boekhandel Bpk *(South Africa)*

Book Trade Association Membership:
Publishers Association of South Africa

2517

VIA AFRIKA
PO Box 151, Pretoria, 0001
Telephone: +27 (0̄12) 342 1964
Fax: +27 (0̄12) 342 1846

Warehouse:
PO Box 4886, Randburg, 2125
Telephone: +27 (0̄11) 792 2213/4/5
Fax: +27 (0̄11) 792 3308

Managers: D. Schroeder *(General)*
E. R. Arnold *(Publications, Rights &
    Permissions)*
A. Gouws *(Marketing & Sales)*
C. van Jaarsveld *(Administration)*
Publishers: P. Mtinshilana *(African
    Languages)*
C. Hougaard *(African Languages)*
L. Cohen *(African Languages)*
B. Schouwstra *(Technological, Technical &
    Religious)*
J. Pym *(Social Sciences, Commercial)*
D. Fratsanos *(General Science, Biology,
    Physical Science)*
H. Kotze *(Adult Education & Special Projects)*

*Academic & Scholarly; Agriculture;
Educational & Textbooks; Electronic
(Educational); English as a Foreign Language;
Gardening; Geography & Geology; Languages
& Linguistics; Literature & Criticism;
Scientific & Technical*

New Titles: 34 (1995), 40 (1996)
No of Employees: 280

ISBNs, Imprints & Series:
0 18749 Afritech
0 7994 Via Afrika
0 86817 Acacia

Parent Company:
National Educational Group *(South Africa)*

Associated & Subsidiary Companies:
South Africa: Afro Publishers (Eastern Cape);
Atlas Publishers (North West Province);
Bateleur Books (Northern Province)

Book Trade Association Membership:
Publishers Association of South Africa, South
African BA

2518

**WITWATERSRAND UNIVERSITY
PRESS**
PO Wits, 2050
Telephone: +27 (0̄11) 484 5907
Fax: +27 (0̄11) 484 5971
Email: wup@iafrica.com

Distributors:
Book Promotions, PO Box 5, Plumstead, 7800
Telephone: +27 (0̄21) 720 332
Fax: +27 (0̄21) 720 383
Email: bookpro@aztec.co.za

Acting Director: Franscois McHardy
Publishing Manager: Pat Tucker
Commissioning Editor: Cheryl Brant
Administration Assistant: Winnie Sibeko

*Academic & Scholarly; Accountancy &
Taxation; Archaeology; Biography &
Autobiography; Biology & Zoology;
Economics; Educational & Textbooks;
Environment & Development Studies; Fiction;
Fine Art & Art History; Gender Studies;
History & Antiquarian; Industry, Business &
Management; Languages & Linguistics;
Literature & Criticism; Medical (incl. Self Help
& Alternative Medicine); Music; Natural
History; Philosophy; Politics & World Affairs;
Reference Books, Directories & Dictionaries;
Religion & Theology; Sociology &
Anthropology; Theatre, Drama & Dance*

New Titles: 25 (1995), 25 (1996)
No of Employees: 6

ISBNs, Imprints & Series: 1 86814

Parent Company:
University of the Witwatersrand *(South Africa)*

Overseas Representation *(see §7.3)*:
Europe: Africa Book Centre, London, UK

Book Trade Association Membership:
Publishers Association of South Africa

SRI LANKA

2519

**BUDDHIST PUBLICATION SOCIETY
INC**
PO Box 61, 54 Sangharaja Mawatha, Kandy
Telephone: +94 (0̄8) 223679
Fax: +94 (0̄8) 223679

President/Editor-in-Chief: Bhikkhu Bodhi
Executive Director: T. B. Talwatte
Administration Secretary: A. Bokalamulla

Philosophy; Religion & Theology

New Titles: 6 (1995), 6 (1996)
No of Employees: 21
Annual Turnover: $110,837

ISBNs, Imprints & Series: 955 24

Overseas Representation *(see §7.3):*
Malaysia: Sukhi Hotu, Penang
Singapore: Evergreen Buddhist Cultural
Service
UK & Irish Republic: Lavis Marketing, Oxford,
UK
USA: Wisdom Publications, Boston, MA

2520 ━━━━━

KARUNARATNE & SONS LTD
647 Kularatne Mawata, Colombo 10
Telephone: +94 (01) 692295
Fax: +94 (01) 850256

Factory:
Lot 67, Industrial Complex, Katuwana Road,
Homagama
Telephone: +94 (01) 855520
Fax: +94 (01) 855520

Directors: M. W. Karunaratne *(Managing)*
R. W. Karunaratne *(Production)*

Children's Books; Gender Studies; History &
Antiquarian; Philosophy; Reference Books,
Directories & Dictionaries; Religion &
Theology; Sociology & Anthropology

New Titles: 13 (1995), 12 (1996)
No of Employees: 28
Annual Turnover: £30,000

ISBNs, Imprints & Series: 955 9098

Associated & Subsidiary Companies:
Sri Lanka: Buddhist Publication Society;
CENWOR (Centre for Women's Research);
Post Graduate Institute of Pali & Buddhist
Studies; Social Scientists Association

Overseas Representation *(see §7.3):*
UK: Wisdom Books, London

Book Trade Association Membership:
Publishers Association of Sri Lanka

2521 ━━━━━

LAKE HOUSE INVESTMENTS LTD
41 W. A. D. Ramanayake Mawatha, Colombo 2
Telephone: +94 (01) 435175, 433272/3 &
439331
Fax: +94 (01) 447848

Directors: R. S. Wijewardene *(Chairman)*
L. C. Gooneratne
Mrs N. M. Wickremesinghe
V. L. C. Walatara
A. David
A. B. T. Wijeratne
D. N. Wijewardene
Editorial & Production: Henry
Samaranayake *(Managerial Consultant)*
Miss Mangalika Bandupala *(Sales, Rights &*
Permissions)
Gamini Jayawickrema

Academic & Scholarly; Accountancy &
Taxation; Agriculture; Animal Care &
Breeding; Archaeology; Architecture &

Design; Biography & Autobiography; Biology
& Zoology; Chemistry; Children's Books;
Cinema, Video, TV & Radio; Cookery, Wines &
Spirits; Crime; Economics; Educational &
Textbooks; English as a Foreign Language;
Fiction; Fine Art & Art History; Gardening;
Geography & Geology; Guide Books; Health &
Beauty; History & Antiquarian; Languages &
Linguistics; Law; Literature & Criticism;
Mathematics & Statistics; Medical (incl. Self
Help & Alternative Medicine); Music; Natural
History; Philosophy; Physics; Poetry; Politics
& World Affairs; Psychology & Psychiatry;
Reference Books, Directories & Dictionaries;
Religion & Theology; Scientific & Technical;
Sociology & Anthropology; Sports & Games;
Theatre, Drama & Dance

New Titles: 15 (1995), 12 (1996)
No of Employees: 9
Annual Turnover: $117,445

ISBNs, Imprints & Series: 955 552

Book Trade Association Membership: Book
Publishers Association of Sri Lanka

SWAZILAND

2522 ━━━━━

MACMILLAN BOLESWA PUBLISHERS
PTY LTD
PO Box 1235, Manzini
Telephone: +268 (09268) 84533
Fax: +268 (09268) 85247

Trade Enquiries:
Boleswa Services Office, PO Box 32484,
Braamfontein, 2017
Telephone: +27 (011) 339 2935
Fax: +27 (011) 403 1627

Chairman: C. J. Pateson
Directors: L. A. Balarin *(Managing)*
T. Ball *(Marketing)*
J. Webb *(Finance)*
P. Murby *(Publishing)*
E. Ndwandwe *(Managing—Swaziland)*
P. Davis *(Production)*
D. Moloantoa *(Sales)*
K. Rakhudu *(Sales—BLS)*
Senior Managers: D. Diamond *(African*
Languages Publishing)
N. Cooles *(ELT Publishing)*
W. Uiterwijk *(General—Botswana)*

Educational & Textbooks

New Titles: 140 (1995), 160 (1996)
No of Employees: 200

ISBNs, Imprints & Series:
Aids Readers, Babhali Besiswati, Chambers-
Macmillan Dictionaries, Crime Prevention
Readers, Dipalo, Impilo Enhle, Ipalele,
Junior Secondary Social Studies, Kagiso
Readers, Macmillan Atlases, Macmillan
Library Series, Macmillan Primary English
Project (MAPEP), Macmillan Primary
English Readers, Macmillan Primary Maths,
MELTS Readers, Middle School Maths,
Mmaletsatsi, Monate Wa Setswana,
Mosupatsela, New Dimensions in Maths,
New Horizons, New Ventures in History,
Ngwao Boswa, Pepet letso, Primary Maths

(Botswana), Primary Science, Primary
Social Studies, Project in Secondary
Mathematics (PRISM), Science for All,
Tshedimoso, Wise (University of the
Witwatersrand Initiative in Science
Education)

Parent Company:
Macmillan Publishers *(UK)*

Associated & Subsidiary Companies:
Botswana: Macmillan Botswana Publishing
Co. *Lesotho:* Macmillan Boleswa (Lesotho)
Publishing Co. *Namibia:* Gamsberg Macmillan
Publishers. *South Africa:* Macmillan South
Africa (Pty) Ltd; Nolwazi Educational
Publishers Pty Ltd. *Swaziland:* Macmillan
Swaziland National Publishing Co

Overseas Representation *(see §7.3):*
UK: Macmillan Publishers Ltd, Basingstoke
Zimbabwe: College Press Publishers (Pvt) Ltd,
Harare

Book Trade Association Membership:
International Book Distributors Association

TANZANIA

2523 ━━━━━

BILAL MUSLIM MISSION OF
TANZANIA
PO Box 20033, Dar Es Salaam
Telephone: +255 (051) 20111
Fax: +255 (051) 46333

Hon. Treasurer: M. G. Lalji
Editor: F. H. Abdullah
Hon. Secretary: P. M. Shnji
Production Manager: J. J. Kiambu

Religion & Theology

New Titles: 19 (1995), 25 (1996)
No of Employees: 15

ISBNs, Imprints & Series: 9976 956

Parent Company:
Federation of K.S.I. Jarnaats of Africa
(Tanzania)

2524 ━━━━━

CENTRAL TANGANYIKA PRESS
PO Box 1129, Dodoma
Telephone: +255 (061) 24180
Fax: +255 (061) 24565

Acting Publishing Manager: Canon James
Lifa
Marketing Officer: David J. Tuppa

Children's Books; Religion & Theology

ISBNs, Imprints & Series: 9976 66

Overseas Representation *(see §7.3):*
Kenya: Uzima Press, Nairobi
Nigeria: Daystar Press, Ibadan
Uganda: Centenary Publishing House,
Kampala

Book Trade Association Membership: World
Association for Christian Communication,

Tanzanian Evangelical Literature Ministry,
Publishers Association of Tanzania

2525

NDANDA MISSION PRESS
PO Box 1004, Ndanda, via Mtwara

Production: Markus Forster
Marketing & Editorial: Fr S. Hofbeck

*Children's Books; Educational & Textbooks;
Fiction; Medical (incl. Self Help & Alternative
Medicine); Religion & Theology*

New Titles: 30 (1995), 24 (1996)
No of Employees: 35
Annual Turnover: $165,000

ISBNs, Imprints & Series:
9976 63 Benedictine Publications

ZAMBIA

2526

POINTER BOOKS LTD
Private Bag 274X, Ridgeway, Lusaka
Telephone: +260 (Õ1) 263270

Managing Director: Isidore Gerd Ntoshya
Managers: Ms Meva Daka *(Finance)*
Ms Unity Mwanza
Sammy Kamota *(Production)*
Caroline Ntoshya *(Marketing)*

Children's Books; Educational & Textbooks

New Titles: 3 (1995), 15 (1996)
No of Employees: 10

Book Trade Association Membership:
Booksellers and Publishers Association of
Zambia, Editors Forum (Zambia)

2527

**ZAMBIA EDUCATIONAL PUBLISHING
HOUSE**
PO Box 32708, Lusaka
Telephone: +260 (Õ1) 222324
Fax: +260 (Õ1) 225073

Managing Director: Henry Chipewo
Company Secretary: Fine Chilomo
Managers: Alfred Sikajanga *(Publishing)*
Enoch Mwale *(Finance)*
Ray Munamwimbu *(Marketing)*
Benito Mulota *(Commercial)*
Michael Funga *(Works)*

Educational & Textbooks

New Titles: 5 (1995), 7 (1996)
No of Employees: 300
Annual Turnover: $1.5M

ISBNs, Imprints & Series:
9982 00 Educational Titles
9982 01 General Titles

Book Trade Association Membership:
Booksellers & Publishers Association of
Zambia

ZIMBABWE

2528

BAOBAB BOOKS (PVT) LTD
PO Box 567, Harare
Telephone: +263 (Õ4) 755035-9
Fax: +263 (Õ4) 759052

Executive: A. Wallace
Finance: Mrs J. Chant
Sales: A. Muchaziwepi
Marketing: G. McCullough
Production: N. Hattle
Editorial: Mrs I. Staunton
Rights: Mrs P. Brine

*Academic & Scholarly; Children's Books;
Educational & Textbooks; Fiction*

New Titles: 4 (1995), 10 (1996)
No of Employees: 14

ISBNs, Imprints & Series: 0 908311

Parent Company:
Academic Books *(Zimbabwe)*

Overseas Representation *(see §7.3)*:
South Africa: David Philip Publishers Pty Ltd,
Claremont
UK, Europe & USA: African Books Collective
Ltd, Oxford, UK

Book Trade Association Membership:
Zimbabwe Book Development Council,
Zimbabwe PA

2529

**COLLEGE PRESS PUBLISHERS (PVT)
LTD**
15 Douglas Road, PO Box 3041, Workington,
Harare
Telephone: +263 (Õ4) 754145
Fax: +263 (Õ4) 754256

Directors: Ben Mugabe *(Managing, Rights &
Permissions)*
E. Busangabanye *(Financial)*
Engelbert Luphahla *(Production, Export &
Import Sales)*
Cletus Ngwaru *(Home & Export Sales)*
Mazvita Partricia Madondo *(Managing Editor)*

*Agriculture; Chemistry; Children's Books;
Economics; Educational & Textbooks; Fashion
& Costume; Fiction; Geography & Geology;
Mathematics & Statistics; Music; Poetry;
Religion & Theology*

New Titles: 27 (1995), 24 (1996)
No of Employees: 65

ISBNs, Imprints & Series:
0 86925, 1 77990

Overseas Representation *(see §7.3)*:
UK: Macmillan Publishers Ltd, Basingstoke

Book Trade Association Membership:
Zimbabwe Book PA, Zimbabwe Booksellers
Association

2530

LONGMAN ZIMBABWE (PVT) LTD
Tourle Road, Harare Drive, Arbennie, Harare
Telephone: +263 (Õ4) 621661-7
Fax: +263 (Õ4) 621670

Managing Director: N. Dlodlo
Directors: G. Varghese *(Finance)*
D. R. Mackenzie *(Operations)*

Educational & Textbooks

New Titles: 25 (1995), 52 (1996)
No of Employees: 56

ISBNs, Imprints & Series:
0 582, 0 908308, 0 908310, 1 77903

Parent Company:
Addison Wesley Longman Ltd *(UK)*

Overseas Representation *(see §7.3)*:
Worldwide: Addison Wesley Longman UK,
Harlow, UK

Book Trade Association Membership:
Zimbabwe Book PA

2531

MAMBO PRESS
PO Box 779, Gweru
Telephone: +263 (Õ54) 4016/7
Fax: +263 (Õ54) 51991

Wholesale Department:
Telephone: *as above*
Fax: *as above*

Managers: Leonz Fischer *(General)*
Patrick Rukodzi *(Deputy)*
Vonai B. Paradza *(Publishing)*
Obrien Mutero *(Marketing)*
Nicasio M. Takawira *(Retail, Bookshops)*

*Academic & Scholarly; Children's Books;
Fiction; Guide Books; Languages &
Linguistics; Literature & Criticism; Poetry;
Reference Books, Directories & Dictionaries;
Religion & Theology; Theatre, Drama &
Dance*

New Titles: 30 (1995), 20 (1996)
No of Employees: 100
Annual Turnover: $1.8M

ISBNs, Imprints & Series: 0 86922

Associated & Subsidiary Companies:
Zimbabwe: Moto Magazine (Pvt) Ltd

Overseas Representation *(see §7.3)*:
Switzerland: NZM Verlag, Immensee
UK: Leishman & Taussig African & Caribbean
Book Services, Southwell

Book Trade Association Membership:
Zimbabwe Book PA, Zimbabwe Booksellers
Association

2532

MERCURY PRESS (PVT) LTD
22 Kaguvi Street, PO Box 23ı́ 3, Harare
Telephone: +263 (Õ14) 751515/6
Fax: +263 (Õ14) 737640

Managing Director: D. F. Sutherland
Administrator: D. A. Byrom
Sales Manager: E. Siyangapi
Chief Editor: P. C. Clifford

*Academic & Scholarly; Educational &
Textbooks; Vernacular Languages – Language
Study; Vernacular Languages – Fiction &
Poetry*

New Titles: 12 (1995), 12 (1996)
No of Employees: 10
Annual Turnover: £50,000

ISBNs, Imprints & Series: 0 7974

Parent Company:
Central African Correspondence College (Pvt)
Ltd *(Zimbabwe)*

Book Trade Association Membership:
Zimbabwe PA, Zimbabwe Booksellers
Association

2533 ▬▬▬▬▬▬▬▬

**UNIVERSITY OF ZIMBABWE
PUBLICATIONS**
Publications Office, University of Zimbabwe,
PO Box MP 203, Mt Pleasant, Harare

Telephone: +263 (0̃4) 303211 Ext 1236
Fax: +263 (0̃4) 333407

Publications Officer: Samuel Matsangaise

*Academic & Scholarly; Educational &
Textbooks*

New Titles: 8 (1995), 12 (1996)
No of Employees: 8

ISBNs, Imprints & Series:
0 908307 Supplements to Zambezia Series

Overseas Representation *(see §7.3)*:
UK, Europe, USA, Canada & Commonwealth
countries (excluding Africa): African Books
Collective Ltd, Oxford, UK

Book Trade Association Membership:
Zimbabwe Book PA, Zimbabwe Book
Development Council

2534 ▬▬▬▬▬▬▬▬▬▬▬▬▬▬▬

ZIMBABWE PUBLISHING HOUSE
PO Box 350, Harare
Telephone: +263 (0̃14) 497555
Fax: +263 (0̃14) 882340 & 497554

Warehouse:
97 Coventry Road, Workington, Harare
Telephone: +263 (0̃14) 67170
Fax: +263 (0̃14) 882340 & 497554

Chairman: David M. Martin *(Marketing)*

*Academic & Scholarly; Children's Books;
Cookery, Wines & Spirits; Educational &
Textbooks; English as a Foreign Language;
Fiction; Gender Studies; Geography &
Geology; History & Antiquarian; Literature &
Criticism; Poetry; Politics & World Affairs;
Sports & Games; Theatre, Drama & Dance;
Vocational Training & Careers*

New Titles: 15 (1995), 10 (1996)
No of Employees: 40

ISBNs, Imprints & Series:
0 908300 Secondary Shona
0 949225 Primary Shona 1 77901

Overseas Representation *(see §7.3)*:
UK: African Books Collective Ltd, Oxford

Book Trade Association Membership:
Zimbabwe Book PA, Zimbabwe Book
Development Council

3 Packagers

3001 ▬▬▬▬▬▬▬▬▬▬

*ALADDIN BOOKS LTD
28 Percy Street, London W1P 9FF
Telephone: 0171 323 3319
Fax: 0171 323 4829

Directors: Charles Nicholas *(Managing)*
Lynn Lockett

Children's Books

3002 ▬▬▬▬▬▬▬▬▬▬

ALBION PRESS LTD
Spring Hill, Idbury, Oxon OX7 6RU
Telephone: 01993 831094
Fax: 01993 831982

Directors: Emma Bradford *(Managing)*
Neil Philip *(Editorial)*

Children's Books

New Titles: 7 (1995), 9 (1996)
No of Employees: 2

3003 ▬▬▬▬▬▬▬▬▬▬

ALPHABET & IMAGE LTD
Marston House, Marston Magna, Yeovil,
Somerset BA22 8DH
Telephone: 01935 851331
Fax: 01935 851331

Warehouse, Trade Enquiries & Orders:
c/o Bailey Bros, Unit 1a/1b Learoyd Road,
Mountfield Road Industrial Estate,
New Romney, Kent TN28 8XU
Telephone: 01797 366905
Fax: 01797 366638

Directors: Anthony Birks-Hay *(Managing,
Sales, Finance, Production)*
Leslie Birks-Hay *(Editorial, Commissioning)*

*Academic & Scholarly; Architecture & Design;
Crafts & Hobbies; Fine Art & Art History;
Gardening; Illustrated & Fine Editions*

ISBNs, Imprints & Series:
0 9517700 Marston House 1 899296

Overseas Representation *(see §7.3):*
Worldwide: Chris Lloyd, Poole, UK

Book Trade Association Membership: IPG,
Book Packagers Association

3004 ▬▬▬▬▬▬▬▬▬▬

ANDROMEDA OXFORD LTD
9–15 The Vineyard, Abingdon, Oxon
OX14 3PX
Telephone: 01235 550296
Fax: 01235 550330
Email: books@andromeda.co.uk
Web Site: http://www.andromeda.co.uk

Directors: Mark Ritchie *(Managing)*
Michele Smith *(Finance)*
Derek Hall *(Children's Publishing)*
Clive Sparling *(Production)*
Graham Bateman *(Adult Publishing)*

*Atlases & Maps; Children's Books; Geography
& Geology; History & Antiquarian; Natural
History; Reference Books, Directories &
Dictionaries*

New Titles: 15 (1995), 17 (1996)
No of Employees: 32

ISBNs, Imprints & Series:
1 861990, 1 871869 Andromeda Oxford,
Vineyard Books

Parent Company:
M.33 Ltd

Associated & Subsidiary Companies:
Andromeda Interactive Ltd; Publishing
Copyrights Ltd

Overseas Representation *(see §7.3):*
Australia: Electra Media Group Pty Ltd,
Sydney, NSW
Europe: Ted Dougherty, London, UK
Italy: Bookport Associates, Bologna
Japan: Tuttle-Mori Agency Ltd, Tokyo
Korea: Eric Yang Agency, Seoul, Korea, South

Middle East: Ashton International Marketing
Services, Larkfield, UK
South Africa: Verbatim Distributors,
Constantia Hills
Spain: Iberian Book Services SL, Madrid
Taiwan: Big Apple Tuttle-Mori Agency Inc,
Taipei
Thailand: Big Apple Tuttle-Mori Agency Inc,
Bangkok

3005 ▬▬▬▬▬▬▬▬▬▬

AS PUBLISHING
73 Montpelier Rise, London NW11 9DU
Telephone: 0181 458 3552
Fax: 0181 458 0618

Managing Director: Angela Sheehan

*Atlases & Maps; Children's Books;
Educational & Textbooks*

3006 ▬▬▬▬▬▬▬▬▬▬

B SMALL PUBLISHING
Pinewood, 3A Coombe Ridings,
Kingston upon Thames, Surrey KT2 7JT
Telephone: 0181 974 6851
Fax: 0181 974 6845

Sales Representation:
Verulam Publishing, 152A Park Street Lane,
Park Street, St Alban's, Herts AL2 2AU
Telephone: 01727 872770
Fax: 01727 873866

Warehouse:
International Book Distributors
Telephone: 01442 882016
Fax: 01442 882288

Foreign Rights:
Penny Pumphrey
Telephone: 0181 672 3192
Fax: 0181 682 2648

Editorial: Catherine Bruzzone
UK Sales: David Collins *(Verulam Publishing)*

Children's Books; Languages & Linguistics

ISBNs, Imprints & Series: 1 874735

Overseas Representation *(see §7.3):*
Australia (selected activity books): Herron
Book Distributors Pty Ltd, Fortitude Valley,
Qld, Australia

Book Trade Association Membership: IPG,
Book Packagers Association

3007

*PAUL BARNETT EDITORIAL
17 Polsloe Road, Exeter, Devon EX1 2HL
Telephone: 01392 74524 & 73780
Fax: 01392 74524

Proprietors: Paul Barnett *(Editorial)*
Catherine Stewart *(Art & Design)*

*Cinema, Video, TV & Radio; Fiction; Humour;
Physics; Reference Books, Directories &
Dictionaries; Science Fiction; Editorial
Packaging & Commissioning; Freelance
Editing; Rewriting; Writing to Order*

Book Trade Association Membership: West
Country Writers' Association

3008

*BCS PUBLISHING LTD
1 Bignell Park Barns, Kirtlington Road,
Chesterton, Bicester, Oxon OX6 8TD
Telephone: 01869 324423
Fax: 01869 324385

Directors: Steve McCurdy *(Managing)*
Candida Hunt *(Publishing)*
Deena Daher

*Archaeology; Cinema, Video, TV & Radio;
English as a Foreign Language; History &
Antiquarian; Natural History; Transport*

3009

BENDER RICHARDSON WHITE
PO Box 266, Uxbridge UB9 5NX
Telephone: 01895 832444
Fax: 01895 835213

Directors: Lionel Bender *(Editorial)*
Kim Richardson *(Sales & Production)*
Ben White *(Art & Design)*

*Biology & Zoology; Children's Books; Natural
History*

3010

*BERKSWELL PUBLISHING CO LTD
PO Box 420, Warminster, Wilts BA12 9XB
Telephone: 01985 840189
Fax: 01985 840189

Directors: J. Stidolph *(Managing)*
S. A. Abbott *(Sales & Mail Order)*
Editor: A. McGregor

*Biography & Autobiography; Heritage; Local
interest*

ISBNs, Imprints & Series:
0 904631 Berkswell Illustrated Guides

Overseas Representation *(see §7.3):*
USA: Worldwide Media Service Inc, Jersey
City, NJ

Book Trade Association Membership: IPG

3011

BLA PUBLISHING LTD
1 Christopher Road, East Grinstead,
West Sussex RH19 3BT
Telephone: 01342 318980
Fax: 01342 410980

Chairman: Au Bak Ling
Manager: Penny Kitchenham *(Sales, Rights &
Permissions)*
Finance: John Gamble

*Antiques & Collecting; Aviation; Biology &
Zoology; Chemistry; Children's Books;
Computer Science; Medical (incl. Self Help &
Alternative Medicine); Military & War; Music;
Natural History; Nautical; Physics; Reference
Books, Directories & Dictionaries; Religion &
Theology*

ISBNs, Imprints & Series:
Thames Head

Parent Company:
Ling Kee (UK) Ltd

Associated & Subsidiary Companies:
Ward Lock Educational Co Ltd

3012

BOOK PACKAGING AND MARKETING
3 Murswell Lane, Silverstone, Towcester,
Northants NN12 8UT
Telephone: 01327 858380
Fax: 01327 858380

Director: Martin F. Marix Evans

*Guide Books; Health & Beauty; Illustrated &
Fine Editions; Photography; Reference Books,
Directories & Dictionaries; Sports & Games;
Travel & Topography; Day Books & Diaries;
Gift Books*

Book Trade Association Membership: IPG,
Book Packagers Association

3013

DELIAN BOWER PUBLISHING
18 Devonshire Place, Exeter EX4 6JA
Telephone: 01392 436329
Fax: 01392 436329

Partners: Delian Bower
Susie Bower

*Children's Books; Cinema, Video, TV & Radio;
Fine Art & Art History; Humour; Music;
Philosophy; Psychology & Psychiatry;
Religion & Theology; Theatre, Drama &
Dance*

New Titles: 3 (1995), 5 (1996)
No of Employees: 2

3014

BRESLICH & FOSS LTD
20 Wells Mews, London W1P 3FJ
Telephone: 0171 580 8774
Fax: 0171 580 8784

Director: Paula Breslich

*Children's Books; Crafts & Hobbies; Fine Art
& Art History; Gardening; Health & Beauty*

New Titles: 9 (1995), 8 (1996)
No of Employees: 5
Annual Turnover: £1M

Book Trade Association Membership: Book
Packagers Association

3015

BROWN PACKAGING (BOOKS) LTD
255–257 Liverpool Road, London N1 1LX
Telephone: 0171 607 9039
Fax: 0171 609 5823

Directors: Stasz Gnych *(Managing)*
Sara Ballard *(Rights)*
Alastair Gourlay *(Production)*

*Aviation; Crafts & Hobbies; Gardening;
Military & War; Music; Sports & Games*

New Titles: 20 (1995), 30 (1996)
No of Employees: 6
Annual Turnover: £1.5M

ISBNs, Imprints & Series:
1 897884 Brown Books

Book Trade Association Membership: Book
Packagers Association

3016

BROWN WELLS & JACOBS LTD
Foresters Hall, 25–27 Westow Street, London
SE19 3RY
Telephone: 0181 771 5115
Fax: 0181 771 9994

Director: Graham Brown *(Managing, Design,
Sales & Production)*
Publisher: Ailsa Brown

Children's Books; Natural History

New Titles: 16 (1995), 8 (1996)
No of Employees: 2
Annual Turnover: £3.25M

ISBNs, Imprints & Series: 1 873829

Distributor for:
Brown Wells & Jacobs Ltd (Publishing)

3017

CALMANN & KING LTD
71 Great Russell Street, London WC1B 3BN
Telephone: 0171 831 6351
Fax: 0171 831 8356
Email: 101456.1525@compuserve.com

Chairman: Robin Hyman
Directors: Laurence King *(Managing)*
Judy Rasmussen *(Production)*

Lee Ripley Greenfield *(Editorial – College &
Fine Art)*
Manager: Christine Macgregor *(Rights &
Permissions)*

*Architecture & Design; Fine Art & Art History;
History & Antiquarian; Illustrated & Fine
Editions; Music; Natural History;
Photography*

New Titles: 12 (1995), 15 (1996)
No of Employees: 19
Annual Turnover: £2.9M

ISBNs, Imprints & Series:
Laurence King Publishing

Associated & Subsidiary Companies:
Laurence King Publishing

Overseas Representation *(see §7.3)*:
Italy: Natoli Stefan & Oliva, Milan

3018

CAMERON BOOKS
PO Box 1, Moffat, Dumfriesshire DG10 9SU
Telephone: 01683 220808
Fax: 01683 220012

Directors: Ian A. Cameron
Jill Hollis

*Antiques & Collecting; Architecture & Design;
Cinema, Video, TV & Radio; Cookery, Wines &
Spirits; Environment & Development Studies;
Fine Art & Art History; Natural History;
Poetry; Reference Books, Directories &
Dictionaries*

New Titles: 4 (1995), 5 (1996)

ISBNs, Imprints & Series:
0 906506 Cameron & Hollis

3019

PHILIP CLARK LTD
53 Calton Avenue, Dulwich Village, London
SE21 7DF
Telephone: 0181 693 5605
Fax: 0181 299 4647

Managing Director: Philip Clark

*Cookery, Wines & Spirits; Gardening; Guide
Books; Travel & Topography*

ISBNs, Imprints & Series:
The Traveller's Wine Guides

Book Trade Association Membership: Book
Packagers Association

3020

*CLB PUBLISHING LTD
Godalming Business Centre, Woolsack Way,
Godalming, Surrey
Telephone: 01483 426277
Fax: 01483 426947

Sales Directors: Bill Dancer *(International,
English Language Rights)*
Keith Allen-Jones *(English Language)*
Marketing Manager: Moira McCann
(Foreign Language Rights & Co-editions)

*Atlases & Maps; Children's Books; Cookery,
Wines & Spirits; Crafts & Hobbies; Do-It-
Yourself; Gardening; Health & Beauty;
Military & War; Natural History; Sports &
Games; Transport; Travel & Topography*

Parent Company:
Colour Library Books Ltd

Associated & Subsidiary Companies:
Waverley 1770; Zigzag Publishing Ltd

Book Trade Association Membership: Book
Packagers Association

3021

**DIAGRAM VISUAL INFORMATION
LTD**
195 Kentish Town Road, London NW5 8SY
Telephone: 0171 482 3633
Fax: 0171 482 4932

Managing Director: Bruce Robertson

*Educational & Textbooks; Fine Art & Art
History; Geography & Geology; Health &
Beauty; Natural History; Reference Books,
Directories & Dictionaries; Sports & Games*

New Titles: 17 (1995), 16 (1996)
No of Employees: 5
Annual Turnover: £750,000

Overseas Representation *(see §7.3)*:
China: Big Apple Tuttle-Mori Agency Inc,
Taipei, Taiwan
Eastern Europe: DS Druck- und Verlags
service, Stuttgart, Germany
Germany: Rose Meerwein, Berlin
Italy: Tipress Deutschland GmbH, Turin
Japan: Tuttle-Mori Agency Ltd, Tokyo
Korea: DRT International, Seoul, Korea, South
Netherlands & Scandinavia: Jan Michael,
Amsterdam, Netherlands
Thailand: Big Apple Tuttle-Mori Agency Inc,
Bangkok

3022

**DUNCAN PETERSEN PUBLISHING
LTD**
31 Ceylon Road, London W14 0YP
Telephone: 0171 371 2356
Fax: 0171 371 2507

Warehouse Trade Enquiries & Orders:
World Leisure Marketing, 9 Downing Road,
West Meadows Industrial Estate, Derby
DE21 6HA
Telephone: 01332 343332
Fax: 01332 340464
Email: office@wlmsales.demon.co.uk

Directors: Andrew Duncan *(Editorial & Sales)*
Mel Petersen *(Design & Production)*
Rights Manager: Penny Pumphrey

*Atlases & Maps; Cookery, Wines & Spirits;
Crafts & Hobbies; Do-It-Yourself; Gardening;
Guide Books; Health & Beauty; Natural
History*

New Titles: 3 (1995), 5 (1996)
No of Employees: 6

ISBNs, Imprints & Series:
3-D City Guides, Back Roads (One Word)
Guides, Charming Small Hotel Guides,
Versatile Guides 1 872576

Overseas Representation *(see §7.3)*:
Australia & New Zealand: Bookwise
International, Findon, SA, Australia
South East Asia: Electra Media Group Pty Ltd,
Sydney, NSW, Australia

3023

SARA DUNN
1a Summerhouse Road, London N16 0NA
Telephone: 0171 241 4448
Fax: 0171 254 4485

*Crafts & Hobbies; Do-It-Yourself;
Environment & Development Studies; Fashion
& Costume; Gay & Lesbian Studies;
Geography & Geology; Health & Beauty;
Natural History; Poetry; Sports & Games*

Book Trade Association Membership: Book
Packagers Association

3024

EARTHSCAPE EDITIONS
Greys Court Farm, Greys Court,
Henley on Thames, Oxon RG9 4PG
Telephone: 01491 628188
Fax: 01491 628189
Email: info@aepublish.com

Educational: Dr B. J. Knapp *(Technical
Director)*
Library & Reference: D. L. R. McCrae
(Rights Director)

*Academic & Scholarly; Children's Books;
Educational & Textbooks; Geography &
Geology; Reference Books, Directories &
Dictionaries; Scientific & Technical*

Associated & Subsidiary Companies:
Atlantic Europe Publishing

Book Trade Association Membership: IPG

3025

EDDISON SADD EDITIONS LTD
St Chad's House, 148 King's Cross Road,
London WC1X 9DH
Telephone: 0171 837 1968
Fax: 0171 837 2025
Email: postmaster@edd-sadd.demon.co.uk

Directors: Nick Eddison *(Managing)*
Ian Jackson *(Editorial)*
Maria White *(Rights)*
David Owen *(Financial)*
Elaine Partington *(Art)*
Charles James *(Production)*

*Animal Care & Breeding; Crafts & Hobbies;
Gardening; Health & Beauty; Humour;
Medical (incl. Self Help & Alternative
Medicine); Natural History; Reference Books,
Directories & Dictionaries*

New Titles: 13 (1995), 10 (1996)
No of Employees: 20
Annual Turnover: £3.5M

Overseas Representation *(see §7.3)*:
Japan: Tuttle-Mori Agency Ltd, Tokyo

Book Trade Association Membership: Book Packagers Association

3026 ▬▬▬

ENDEAVOUR GROUP UK
85 Larkhall Rise, London SW4 6HR
Telephone: 0171 652 5737
Fax: 0171 652 5738

Rights: Charles Merullo
Editorial: Annabel Merullo
Production: Robert Gray

History & Antiquarian; Travel & Topography

New Titles: 1 (1995), 2 (1996)
No of Employees: 3
Annual Turnover: £600,000

3027 ▬▬▬

THE FOUNDRY CREATIVE MEDIA CO LTD
The Long House, Antrobus Road, Chiswick, London W4 5HY
Telephone: 0181 987 9530
Fax: 0181 987 9540
Email: info@foundry.co.uk
Web Site: http://www.foundry.co.uk

Directors: Nick Wells *(Managing)*
Patrick McCreeth *(Art)*
Frances Banfield *(Development)*

Architecture & Design; Biography & Autobiography; Children's Books; Cinema, Video, TV & Radio; Crafts & Hobbies; Fine Art & Art History; Illustrated & Fine Editions; Music; Poetry

ISBNs, Imprints & Series: 1 874634

Associated & Subsidiary Companies:
Firebox Audiovisual Productions; Flame Tree Publishing; The Ideas Factory

3028 ▬▬▬

FREELANCE PRESS SERVICES
Cumberland House, Lissadel Street, Salford, Manchester M6 6GG
Telephone: 0161 702 8225
Fax: 0161 745 8865

Editorial: Mrs S. E. Williams
Circulation: Miss Samantha Williams

Educational & Textbooks; Literature & Criticism; Photography; Freelance Writing & Photography

No of Employees: 3

Distributor for:
USA: Writer Inc; Writer's Digest

3029 ▬▬▬

GRAHAM-CAMERON PUBLISHING & ILLUSTRATION
The Studio, 23 Holt Road, Sheringham, Norfolk NR26 8NB

Telephone: 01263 821333
Fax: 01263 821334

Directors: Mike Graham-Cameron
(Managing, Sales & Editorial)
Helen Graham-Cameron *(Art & Editorial)*

Biography & Autobiography; Children's Books; Educational & Textbooks

No of Employees: 43

ISBNs, Imprints & Series: 0 947672

Associated & Subsidiary Companies:
Graham-Cameron Illustration

Book Trade Association Membership: IPG, Cambridge Book Association, Pica Club

3030 ▬▬▬

HALDANE MASON LTD
59 Chepstow Road, London W2 5BP
Telephone: 0171 792 2123
Fax: 0171 221 3965

Directors: Ron Samuels
Miss Sydney Francis

Animal Care & Breeding; Cookery, Wines & Spirits; Crafts & Hobbies; Do-It-Yourself; Fashion & Costume; Gardening; Guide Books; Health & Beauty; Magic & the Occult; Medical (incl. Self Help & Alternative Medicine); Natural History; Photography; Sports & Games; Transport; Travel & Topography

Book Trade Association Membership: Book Packagers Association

3031 ▬▬▬

INK INC LTD
1 Anglesea Road, Kingston on Thames, Surrey KT1 2EW
Telephone: 0181 549 3174
Fax: 0181 546 2415

Managing Director: Richard Parkes
Editor: Barbara Leedham

Accountancy & Taxation; Agriculture; Architecture & Design; Environment & Development Studies; Guide Books; Illustrated & Fine Editions; Industry, Business & Management; Military & War; Music; Politics & World Affairs; Reference Books, Directories & Dictionaries; Sports & Games; Transport; Travel & Topography; Vocational Training & Careers

3032 ▬▬▬

JOHN TAYLOR BOOK VENTURES
7 Cranborne Road, Hatfield, Herts AL10 8AW
Telephone: 01707 265908
Fax: 01707 270536

Distributors (Desktop publishing titles):
Spa Books Ltd, PO Box 47, Stevenage, Herts SG2 8UH
Telephone: 01438 816896
Fax: 01438 310104

Distributors (Art books):
Lund Humphries Publishers, Park House, 1 Russell Gardens, London NW11 9NN
Telephone: 0181 458 6314
Fax: 0181 905 5245

Partners: John Taylor
Ann Taylor

Academic & Scholarly; Antiques & Collecting; Architecture & Design; Computer Science; Fine Art & Art History

Annual Turnover: £100,000

ISBNs, Imprints & Series: 0 871224

3033 ▬▬▬

JOSHUA MORRIS
4 North Parade, Bath BA1 1LF
Telephone: 01225 312200
Fax: 01225 460942

Distributors:
Littlehampton Book Services Ltd
Telephone: 01903 721596
Fax: 01903 730914

Chairman: Michael J. Morris
Directors: Andrew Hewetson *(Managing)*
Garry Manning *(International Sales)*
Roger Hibbert *(UK & Export Sales)*
Sales Administration: Penny Davis

Children's Books; Novelty Books

New Titles: 65 (1995), 77 (1996)

ISBNs, Imprints & Series:
Wishing Well

Parent Company:
The Reader's Digest Association Inc *(USA)*

Associated & Subsidiary Companies:
USA: Joshua Morris Publishing Inc; Readers Digest Young Families

Overseas Representation *(see §7.3)*:
USA: Readers Digest Young Families, Westport, CT

3034 ▬▬▬

*KINGFISHER DESIGN SERVICES
59 Twyford Avenue, London N2 9NR
Telephone: 0181 444 4666
Fax: 0181 444 5637

Partners: Pedro Pra-Lopez
Frances Pra-Lopez

Children's Books; Cookery, Wines & Spirits; Crafts & Hobbies; Do-It-Yourself; Gardening; Guide Books; Health & Beauty; History & Antiquarian; Military & War; Natural History; Theatre, Drama & Dance

Book Trade Association Membership: Book Packagers Association

3035 ▬▬▬

LABYRINTH PUBLISHING (UK) LTD
32 Leighton Road, Kentish Town, London NW5 2QE

Telephone: 0171 284 4783
Fax: 0171 284 3038

Directors: Robert Gwyn Palmer *(Managing)*
Geoffrey Chesler *(Editorial)*
Rights Manager: Francesca Fisher

*Magic & the Occult; Philosophy; Religion &
Theology; Sociology & Anthropology*

New Titles: 8 (1995), 12 (1996)
No of Employees: 4
Annual Turnover: £2.3M

Parent Company:
Labyrinth Group Plc

Associated & Subsidiary Companies:
B. T. Batsford

3036

LENNARD ASSOCIATES LTD
[Imprint of Lennard Publishing]
Windmill Cottage, Mackerye End, Harpenden,
Herts AL5 5DR
Telephone: 01582 715866
Fax: 01582 715121
Email: lennard@nettec.co.uk
Web Site: http://www.nettec.co.uk/cricketer/

Sales & Marketing:
B. T. Batsford Ltd, 1 Bradbury Drive,
Springwood Industrial Estate, Braintree, Essex
CM7 2QY
Telephone: 01376 321276
Fax: 01376 552854

Managing Director: Adrian Stephenson
Rights & Permissions: Rosemary Stephenson
Editorial: Chris Hawkes

Sponsored Books; Television Tie-ins

New Titles: 6 (1995), 2 (1996)
No of Employees: 3
Annual Turnover: £100,000

ISBNs, Imprints & Series:
1 85291 Lennard Publishing

Overseas Representation *(see §7.3)*:
Australasia: Capricorn Link (Australia) Pty
Ltd, Baulkham Hills, NSW, Australia; Davis
& Yvonne Inwood, Castle Hill, NSW,
Australia
Canada: Hushion House Ltd, Toronto, Ont
*Denmark, Iceland, Sweden, Finland &
Norway:* Saga Books ApS, Copenhagen,
Denmark
*Far East, Caribbean, Japan, China, Hong
Kong, Taiwan, Singapore & Thailand:* Ralph
& Sheila Summers, London, UK
France, Czech & Slovak Republics: Juliusz
Komarnicki, Massagno, Switzerland
*Germany, Belgium, Netherlands &
Luxembourg:* PKB – Robbert J. Pleysier,
Heerde, Netherlands
Greece, Croatia & Slovenia: Patrick Bygate,
Massagno, Switzerland
India, Sri Lanka, Bangladesh & Nepal: Surit
Mitra & Bikram Grewal, New Delhi, India
*Middle East, Israel, Cyprus, Turkey & United
Arab Emirates:* Ashton International
Marketing Services, Larkfield, UK
New Zealand: Random House New Zealand
Ltd, Auckland

Pakistan: S. I. Gillani, Lahore
South Africa: Book Promotions Pty Ltd,
Claremont
Spain, Portugal, Italy & Gibraltar: Penny
Padovani, London, UK
USA: Trafalgar Square Publications, North
Pomfret, VT

3037

LEXUS LTD
205 Bath Street, Glasgow G2 4HZ
Telephone: 0141 221 5266
Fax: 0141 226 3139
Email: pt@lexus.win-uk.net

Director: Peter Terrell

Reference Books, Directories & Dictionaries

New Titles: 8 (1995), 11 (1996)
No of Employees: 6
Annual Turnover: £180,000

3038

LITTLE PEOPLE BOOKS
No 6 4th Avenue, Selly Park, Birmingham
B29 7EU
Telephone: 0121 471 2363
Fax: 0121 472 7372

Directors: Grant Jessé *(Production, Managing
Editor)*
Helen Wallis *(Rights, Finance)*
Publicity Manager: Gareth Willis *(Marketing)*

*Architecture & Design; Audio Books;
Children's Books; Multimedia; Water
Environment*

ISBNs, Imprints & Series: 1 899573

Parent Company:
Grant Jessé Associates

Associated & Subsidiary Companies:
Virtuosity : Animations; Grant Jessé;
Karavadra : Multimedia; TVRT Studios
(Sound)

Book Trade Association Membership: IPG,
Book Packagers Association

3039

LOW PRICED BRITISH BOOKS (LPBB)
IBD Ltd, The Swan Centre, Fishers Lane,
Chiswick, London W4 1RX
Telephone: 0181 742 8232
Fax: 0181 747 8715

Head, Administration: Eileen Gillow
Promotion Manager: Joe De Souza

*Accountancy & Taxation; Economics; English
as a Foreign Language; Industry, Business &
Management*

Parent Company:
International Book Development Ltd

Book Trade Association Membership:
International Book Development Ltd

3040

MARKET HOUSE BOOKS LTD
Market House, Market Square, Aylesbury,
Bucks HP20 1TN
Telephone: 01296 84911
Fax: 01296 437073

Directors: Dr Alan Isaacs
Dr John Daintith
Peter Sapsed
Chief Editor: Miss Elizabeth Martin

*Computer Science; Industry, Business &
Management; Medical (incl. Self Help &
Alternative Medicine); Reference Books,
Directories & Dictionaries; Scientific &
Technical*

New Titles: 12 (1995), 12 (1996)
No of Employees: 20

Book Trade Association Membership: Book
Packagers Association

3041

MARSHALL CAVENDISH BOOKS
[a division of Marshall Cavendish Partworks
Ltd]
119 Wardour Street, London W1V 3TD
Telephone: 0171 734 6710
Fax: 0171 439 1423
Email: ellend@mcmedia.com
Web Site: http://www.mcmedia.com

Managers: Ellen Dupont *(Head of Books)*
Lisa Simpson *(Sales)*
Foreign Rights: Richard Elman
Olivine Henry *(Eastern Europe)*

*Antiques & Collecting; Aviation; Cookery,
Wines & Spirits; Crafts & Hobbies; Do-It-
Yourself; Educational & Textbooks;
Gardening; Illustrated & Fine Editions; Magic
& the Occult; Military & War; Natural History;
Photography; Sports & Games; Transport*

ISBNs, Imprints & Series: 1 85435

Parent Company:
Times Publishing Ltd *(Singapore)*

3042

MARSHALL INFORMATION LTD
170 Piccadilly, London W1V 9DD
Telephone: 0171 629 0079
Fax: 0171 834 0785

Directors: Richard Harman *(Chief Executive)*
Bruce Marshall *(Publisher)*
Barbara Anderson *(Sales, Rights &
Permissions)*
Ed Day *(Creative)*
Barry Baker *(Commercial)*

*Architecture & Design; Atlases & Maps;
Aviation; Children's Books; Cinema, Video, TV
& Radio; Computer Science; Cookery, Wines &
Spirits; Crafts & Hobbies; Do-It-Yourself;
Fashion & Costume; Gardening; Health &
Beauty; Industry, Business & Management;
Medical (incl. Self Help & Alternative
Medicine); Military & War; Natural History;
Nautical; Photography; Scientific & Technical;
Sports & Games; Travel & Topography*

Parent Company:
Mediakey Plc

Associated & Subsidiary Companies:
Marshall Editions Developments Ltd; Marshall
Media Ltd

Overseas Representation *(see §7.3)*:
Eastern Europe: DS Druck- und Verlags
service, Stuttgart, Germany
France: Mary Kling, Paris
Germany: Rose Meerwein, Berlin
Spain: Angela Reynolds, Barcelona

Book Trade Association Membership: Book
Packagers Association

3043 ▬

MEDALLION PUBLISHING LTD
42 South Molton Street, London W1Y 1HB
Telephone: 0171 629 1018
Fax: 0171 629 1019

Managing Director: Tamar Karet

*Cookery, Wines & Spirits; Crafts & Hobbies;
Health & Beauty; Illustrated & Fine Editions*

Book Trade Association Membership: Book
Packagers Association

3044 ▬

OPUS PUBLISHING LTD
36 Camden Square, London NW1 9XA
Telephone: 0171 267 1034
Fax: 0171 267 6026

Chairman & Managing Director: Martin
Heller

*Archaeology; Architecture & Design; Fine Art
& Art History*

3045 ▬

OYSTER BOOKS LTD
Unit 4b, Kirklea Farm, Badgworth, Somerset
BS26 2QH
Telephone: 01934 732251
Fax: 01934 732514

Directors: Jenny Wood *(Managing)*
Ali Brooks *(Production)*
Tim Wood *(Financial)*

Children's Books

New Titles: 22 (1995), 34 (1996)
No of Employees: 11
Annual Turnover: £1.5M

ISBNs, Imprints & Series: 0 948240

3046 ▬

PINWHEEL PUBLISHING LTD
c/o Felgates, 11 Heathmans Road,
Parsons Green, London SW6 4TJ
Telephone: 0171 610 6010
Fax: 0171 610 6868

Managing Directors: Sarah Hewetson
Patricia Jennings

Children's Books

3047 ▬

PLAYNE BOOKS LTD
Chapel House, Trefin, Haverfordwest,
Pembrokeshire SA62 5AU
Telephone: 01348 837073
Fax: 01348 837063

Editorial Director: Gill Davies
Production: David Playne

*Children's Books; Crafts & Hobbies; Health &
Beauty; Theatre, Drama & Dance; Travel &
Topography*

New Titles: 4 (1995), 9 (1996)
No of Employees: 2
Annual Turnover: £110,000

Associated & Subsidiary Companies:
Playne Plays

3048 ▬

PORTHILL PUBLISHERS
PO Box 311, Edgware, Middx HA9 9EA
Telephone: 0181 958 6783
Fax: 0181 905 4516

Director: Radomir Putnikovich
Secretary: Penelope Putnikovich

*Children's Books; Fine Art & Art History;
Humour*

New Titles: 6 (1995), 9 (1996)
No of Employees: 5

ISBNs, Imprints & Series: 1 870732

Book Trade Association Membership: Book
Packagers Association

3049 ▬

MATHEW PRICE LTD
The Old Glove Factory, Bristol Road,
Sherborne, Dorset DT9 4HP
Telephone: 01935 816010
Fax: 01935 816310
Email: 100413.2100@compuserve.com

Chairman: Mathew Price *(Sales & Rights)*
Production Co-ordinator: Karen Pearce
Financial Manager: James Williams

Children's Books

New Titles: 3 (1995), 5 (1996)
No of Employees: 6
Annual Turnover: £100,000

ISBNs, Imprints & Series:
0 948867 Meher Baba Books
0 9516844 Mathew Price Ltd

Distributor for:
USA: Sheriar Press Ltd

Overseas Representation *(see §7.3)*:
Japan: Mari Koga, Tokyo
Spain: Nueva Agencia Literaria Int, Madrid

Book Trade Association Membership: PA,
Children's Book Council, Book Packagers
Association

3050 ▬

PRION BOOKS LTD
Unit L, 32–34 Gordon House Road, London
NW5 1LP
Telephone: 0171 482 4248
Fax: 0171 482 4203
Email: Books@prion.co.uk

Distribution:
Exel Logistics, 3 Sheldon Way, Larkfield,
Aylesford, Kent ME20 6SF
Telephone: 01634 297123
Fax: 01634 298000

Managing Director: Barry Winkleman
Production Manager: Jim Pope
Export Sales, Rights & Permissions:
Christine Regan
Editorial: Andrew Goodfellow

*Cinema, Video, TV & Radio; Cookery, Wines &
Spirits; Guide Books; Health & Beauty;
Natural History; Psychology & Psychiatry;
Theatre, Drama & Dance; Transport; Travel &
Topography*

New Titles: 15 (1995), 25 (1996)
No of Employees: 7

ISBNs, Imprints & Series:
1 85375 Prion

Overseas Representation *(see §7.3)*:
Australia: Peribo Pty Ltd, Mount Kuring-gai,
NSW
Hungary, Germanay, Spain & Italy: Books for
Europe, Massagno, Switzerland
Japan & Far East: Roger Ward, London, UK
Middle East: Peter Ward Book Exports,
London, UK
Netherlands: Nilsson & Lamm BV, Weesp
New Zealand: South Pacific Books (Imports)
Ltd, Auckland
Scandinavia: D. Richard Bowen, Malmö,
Sweden
South Africa: Verbatim Distributors,
Constantia Hills

3051 ▬

QUARTO PUBLISHING PLC
The Old Brewery, 6 Blundell Street, London
N7
Telephone: 0171 700 6700
Fax: 0171 700 4191 & 0077

Chairman & Chief Executive: L. F. Orbach
Directors: M. J. Mousley *(Finance)*
C. H. Bhote *(Finance)*
M. E. Nelson *(Sales & Marketing)*
R. J. Morley
Charlotte Gascoigne *(Publisher)*

*Animal Care & Breeding; Antiques &
Collecting; Architecture & Design; Children's
Books; Cookery, Wines & Spirits; Crafts &
Hobbies; Fine Art & Art History; Gardening;
Health & Beauty; Military & War; Natural
History; Photography; Transport*

Parent Company:
The Quarto Group Inc *(USA)*

Associated & Subsidiary Companies:
Apple Press; QED Publishing Ltd; Quarto

Children's Books Ltd; Quill Publishing Ltd;
Quintet Publishing Ltd

3052 ▰▰▰▰▰▰▰▰▰▰▰▰▰▰▰▰▰▰

RAVELIN LTD
Braceborough, Stamford, Lincs PE9 4NT
Telephone: 01778 560 637
Fax: 01778 560 604

Directors: Diane Moore
John Moore

*Aviation; Educational & Textbooks; Military &
War; Transport*

ISBNs, Imprints & Series:
1 898994 Order of Battle Series, Ravelin,
   Warplanes (Interactive CD-ROM Series)

Associated & Subsidiary Companies:
Talos Books

3053 ▰▰▰▰▰▰▰▰▰▰▰▰▰▰▰▰▰▰

WILLIAM REED DIRECTORIES
Broadfield Park, Crawley, West Sussex
RH11 9RT
Telephone: 01293 613400
Fax: 01293 610322
Email: online@foodanddrink.co.uk
Web Site: http://www.foodanddrink.co.uk

Orders:
William Reed Publishing Ltd, Broadfield Park,
Crawley, West Sussex RH11 9RT
Telephone: 01293 613400
Fax: 01293 610322

Managing Director: Maria Atkin
Managers: Belinda Marston *(Sales)*
Helen Turner *(Editorial)*
Billie Moore *(Marketing)*

*Cookery, Wines & Spirits; Industry, Business &
Management; Reference Books, Directories &
Dictionaries*

New Titles: 7 (1995), 10 (1996)
No of Employees: 22

ISBNs, Imprints & Series: 0 901595

Parent Company:
William Reed Publishing Ltd

Book Trade Association Membership:
Directory Publishers Association

3054 ▰▰▰▰▰▰▰▰▰▰▰▰▰▰▰▰▰▰

ROUGH GUIDES LTD
1 Mercer Street, London WC2H 9QL
Telephone: 0171 379 3329
Fax: 0171 379 3055

Sales & Distribution:
Penguin Books, 27 Wrights Lane, London
W8 5TZ
Telephone: 0171 416 3000

Directors: Mark Ellingham
Martin Dunford
John Fisher
Susanne Hillen
Manager: Richard Trillo *(Rights & Marketing)*

*Computer Science; Guide Books; Music;
Travel & Topography*

New Titles: 40 (1995), 43 (1996)
No of Employees: 30

ISBNs, Imprints & Series:
0 85828 The Rough Guides

Overseas Representation *(see §7.3)*:
Australia: Penguin Books Australia Ltd,
   Ringwood, Vic
New Zealand: Penguin Books (New Zealand)
   Ltd, Auckland
USA & Canada: Penguin Books, New York,
   USA

3055 ▰▰▰▰▰▰▰▰▰▰▰▰▰▰▰▰▰▰

SADIE FIELDS PRODUCTIONS LTD
3d West Point, 36–37 Warple Way, London
W3 0RG
Telephone: 0181 746 1171
Fax: 0181 746 1170

Directors: Sheri Safran
David Fielder

Children's Books

ISBNs, Imprints & Series:
1 85707 Tango Books

Associated & Subsidiary Companies:
USA: Sadie Fields Management Inc

Book Trade Association Membership:
Children's Book Circle

3056 ▰▰▰▰▰▰▰▰▰▰▰▰▰▰▰▰▰▰

SIGNPOST BOOKS LTD
25 Eden Drive, Headington, Oxford OX3 0AB
Telephone: 01865 60444
Fax: 01865 751399

Distribution (Adult titles):
Biblios Ltd, Star Road, Partridge Green,
West Sussex RH13 3LD
Telephone: 01403 710971
Fax: 01403 711143

Directors: D. Wood *(Managing, Rights &
   Permissions)*
S. L. Wood *(Finance)*

Children's Books; History & Antiquarian

New Titles: 4 (1995), 4 (1996)
No of Employees: 2
Annual Turnover: £200,000

ISBNs, Imprints & Series: 1 874785

3057 ▰▰▰▰▰▰▰▰▰▰▰▰▰▰▰▰▰▰

TEENEY BOOKS LTD
Arlington House, 72 Fore Street, Trowbridge,
Wilts BA14 8HD
Telephone: 01225 775657
Fax: 01225 775676

Directors: Tiny de Vries *(Managing)*
Martyn Lewis *(Production)*
Debbie Backhouse *(Sales)*

Children's Books

ISBNs, Imprints & Series: 0 85952

3058 ▰▰▰▰▰▰▰▰▰▰▰▰▰▰▰▰▰▰

THE TEMPLAR CO PLC
Pippbrook Mill, London Road, Dorking, Surrey
RH4 1JE
Telephone: 01306 876361
Fax: 01306 889097

Distribution:
Ragged Bears Ltd, Ragged Appleshaw,
Andover, Hants SP11 9HX
Telephone: 01264 772269
Fax: 01264 772391

Directors: Richard Carlisle *(Creative)*
Amanda Wood *(Managing)*
Graeme East *(Financial)*
Ruth Huddleston *(Sales)*

*Children's Books; Educational & Textbooks;
Natural History*

New Titles: 204 (1995), 250 (1996)
No of Employees: 28
Annual Turnover: £6M

ISBNs, Imprints & Series:
1 870956 Templar Publishsing

Overseas Representation *(see §7.3)*:
Australia: Karlov Marketing Services Pty Ltd,
   Castle Hill, NSW

3059 ▰▰▰▰▰▰▰▰▰▰▰▰▰▰▰▰▰▰

TOUCAN BOOKS LTD
Fourth Floor, 32–38 Saffron Hill, London
EC1N 8BS
Telephone: 0171 404 8181
Fax: 0171 404 8282

Directors: Robert Sackville-West *(Managing)*
Jane Macandrew

*Architecture & Design; Atlases & Maps;
Cookery, Wines & Spirits; Crime; Crafts &
Hobbies; Do-It-Yourself; Fine Art & Art
History; Geography & Geology; History &
Antiquarian; Illustrated & Fine Editions;
Natural History; Reference Books, Directories
& Dictionaries; Sports & Games; Travel &
Topography*

New Titles: 9 (1995), 14 (1996)
No of Employees: 4
Annual Turnover: £1.5M

Book Trade Association Membership: Book
Packagers Association

3060 ▰▰▰▰▰▰▰▰▰▰▰▰▰▰▰▰▰▰

TUCKER SLINGSBY
3G London House,
66–68 Upper Richmond Road, Putney, London
SW15 2RP
Telephone: 0181 874 3400
Fax: 0181 874 3004

Partners: Del Tucker
Janet Slingsby

*Children's Books; Cookery, Wines & Spirits;
Crafts & Hobbies; Gardening*

New Titles: 10 (1995), 20 (1996)
No of Employees: 4

3061

LAURENCE URDANG INC
PO Box 199, Aylesbury, Bucks HP20 2HY
Telephone: 01296 395880

President: Laurence Urdang *(Editorial)*
Administration: Mrs Hazel Hall *(Assistant to the President)*

Languages & Linguistics; Reference Books, Directories & Dictionaries

ISBNs, Imprints & Series:
Verbatim 0 930454

Parent Company:
Laurence Urdang Inc *(USA)*

Associated & Subsidiary Companies:
Verbatim Books

Overseas Representation *(see §7.3):*
USA: Laurence Urdang Inc, Old Lyme, CT

3062

VENTURA PUBLISHING LTD
27 Wrights Lane, London W8 5TZ
Telephone: 0171 416 3000
Fax: 0171 416 3070

Publishing Director: Sally Floyer
Directors: Deborah Hooper *(Marketing)*
Susan Winton *(Rights)*

Children's Books

ISBNs, Imprints & Series:
Mr Little, Spot Books

Parent Company:
Penguin Group

Overseas Representation *(see §7.3):*
See: Penguin, UK

3063

VICTORIA HOUSE PUBLISHING LTD
4 North Parade, Bath BA1 1LF
Telephone: 01225 463401
Fax: 01225 460942

Chairman: Michael J. Morris
Directors: Andrew Hewetson *(Managing)*
Jennifer Fifield *(Sales — Southern Europe)*
Cristina Externest *(Sales — Northern Europe)*
Garry Manning *(International Sales)*
Roger Hibbert *(UK Sales)*
Stewart Cowley *(Publishing)*
Robert Kendrew *(Production)*
Managers: Trish Fernandez *(Sales — Scandinavia & Iceland)*
Agnes Vogt *(Sales — Netherlands, Belgium, Italy)*

Children's Books; Novelty Books

New Titles: 65 (1995), 77 (1996)
No of Employees: 30

ISBNs, Imprints & Series:
Joshua Morris

Parent Company:
The Reader's Digest Association Inc *(USA)*

Associated & Subsidiary Companies:
USA: Joshua Morris Publishing Inc; Readers Digest Young Families

Overseas Representation *(see §7.3):*
USA: Readers Digest Young Families, Westport, CT

3064

WEBB & BOWER (PUBLISHERS) LTD
9 Duke Street, Dartmouth, Devon TQ6 9PY
Telephone: 01803 835525
Fax: 01803 835552

Director: Richard Webb *(Managing)*

Parent Company:
Richard Webb Ltd

Associated & Subsidiary Companies:
Country Diary of an Edwardian Lady Ltd

3065

WHITE LINE PUBLISHING SERVICES
4 Prospect Street, Rawdon, Leeds LS19 6DP
Telephone: 0113 250 2043
Fax: 0113 250 2043
Email: 100660.3664@compuserve.com
Web Site: http://ourworld.compuserve.com/homepages/whiteline/

Also at:
1A Headingley Mount, Leeds LS6 3EL

Partners: Philip Gardner *(Editorial/Production)*
Noel Whittall *(Sales/Administration)*

Guide Books; Sports & Games; Travel & Topography

No of Employees: 2

ISBNs, Imprints & Series:
0 948205 What's That Over There? (Series)

3066

ROSEMARY WILKINSON PUBLISHING
4 Lonsdale Square, London N1 1EN
Telephone: 0171 607 8819
Fax: 0171 607 9842

Principal: Rosemary Wilkinson

Cookery, Wines & Spirits; Crafts & Hobbies

Book Trade Association Membership: Book Packagers Association

3067

WORDWRIGHT
25 Oakford Road, London NW5 1AJ
Telephone: 0171 284 0056
Fax: 0171 284 0041

Directors: Charles Perkins *(Publisher)*
Veronica Davis *(Rights & Permissions)*

Aviation; Children's Books; Cookery, Wines & Spirits; Fine Art & Art History; Gardening; Geography & Geology; Military & War; Natural History; Sports & Games; Social History & Comment

New Titles: 2 (1995), 3 (1996)

Parent Company: Wordwright

Book Trade Association Membership: Book Packagers' Association

3068

ZIGZAG PUBLISHING
The Barn, Randolph's Farm, Brighton Road, Hurstpierpoint, West Sussex BN6 9EL
Telephone: 01273 832777
Fax: 01273 835511
Email: zigzag-publishing@dial.pipex.com

Directors: Dr Tony Potter *(Managing)*
Operations Manager: Sheila Mortimer

Children's Books

ISBNs, Imprints & Series:
1 85993 Zigzag Books

Parent Company: Quadrillion Publishing Ltd

Book Trade Association Membership: PA, Packagers Association

3069

ZOË BOOKS LTD
15 Worthy Lane, Winchester, Hants SO23 7AB
Telephone: 01962 851318
Fax: 01962 843015

Warehouse & Orders:
Bailey Distribution Ltd, Learoyd Road, Mountfield Industrial Estate, New Romney, Kent TN28 8XU
Telephone: 01797 366905
Fax: 01797 366638

Directors: Imogen Z. Dawson *(Managing, Publishing)*
Bob Davidson *(Financial, Rights)*

Children's Books; Educational & Textbooks

New Titles: 20 (1995), 30 (1996)

ISBNs, Imprints & Series:
1 874488
All about food series, Clothes and Crafts series, Discovering Series, A First Guide to..... Series, First sports science series, Geography Detective Series, Great 20th Century Expeditions, Great Battles & Sieges, Hidden Worlds, History Detectives, History Starters Series, Pictures from the past series, Postcards from.....Series, A Zoë Book

Overseas Representation *(see §7.3):*
Australia & New Zealand: Reed Books Australia, Melbourne, Vic, Australia
Canada: Vanwell Publishing Ltd, St Catherines, Ont
South Africa, Namibia, Botswana, Zimbabwe, Swaziland, Lesotho, Malawi, Mozambique & Kenya: Southern Books, Halfway House, South Africa

4 Authors' Agents

4001 ▬▬▬▬

A & B PERSONAL MANAGEMENT LTD
5th Floor, Plaza Suite, 114 Jermyn Street, London SW1Y 6HJ
Telephone: 0171 839 4433
Fax: 0171 930 5738

Director: R. W. Ellis

Specialization: plays & screenplays for theatre, film & TV, & any novel/MS that lends itself to the above.

4002 ▬▬▬▬

THE AGENCY (LONDON) LTD
24 Pottery Lane, Holland Park, London W11 4LZ
Telephone: 0171 727 1346
Fax: 0171 727 9037

Executives: Stephen Durbridge
Sheila Lemon
Leah Schmidt
Sebastian Born
Julia Kreitman
Girsha Reid
Wendy Gresser
Bethan Evans
Hilary Delamere

Specialization: theatre, film, TV & radio. Children's authors and illustrators in all media. Novels represented for existing clients. No reading fee but preliminary letter and return postage essential.

Associated & Subsidiary Companies:
Harvey Unna & Stephen Durbridge Ltd. *UK:* Lemon Unna & Durbridge Ltd

4003 ▬▬▬▬

AITKEN & STONE LTD
29 Fernshaw Road, London SW10 0TG
Telephone: 0171 351 7561
Fax: 0171 376 3594

Directors: Gillon Aitken *(Managing)*
Brian Stone
Sally Riley
Antony Harwood
J. H. Linsky *(Company Secretary)*
Foreign Rights: Sally Riley

All MSS except plays, film & TV scripts, short stories & articles if not by existing clients.

Specialization: quality full-length fiction & non-fiction.

4004 ▬▬▬▬

JACINTHA ALEXANDER ASSOCIATES
47 Emperor's Gate, London SW7 4HJ
Telephone: 0171 373 9258
Fax: 0171 373 4374
Email: 101641.154@compuserve.com

Contacts: Julian Alexander
Kirstan Romano

All MSS except scripts for theatre and children's books.

Specialization: fiction, commercial & literary; all kinds of non-fiction.

Rights Representative in UK for:
Spain: Ute Korner Literary Agency, Barcelona
USA: Ivan R. Dee Inc, Chicago, IL; Sarah Lazin Books, New York, NY; Wendy Lipkind Literary Agency, New York, NY; Mcpherson & Co, Kingston, NY

Overseas Representation *(see §7.5):*
France: Frédérique Porretta, Paris
Germany: Michael Meller Agency, Munich
Italy: Roberta Oliva
Japan: Tuttle-Mori Agency, Tokyo
Netherlands: Jan Michael, Amsterdam
Russia: Alexander Korzhenevski, Moscow
Scandinavia: Licht & Licht Literary Agency, Charlottenlund, Denmark
USA: Wendy Lipkind Literary Agency, New York, NY

4005 ▬▬▬▬

DARLEY ANDERSON LITERARY, TV & FILM AGENCY
Estelle House, 11 Eustace Road, London SW6 1JB
Telephone: 0171 385 6652
Fax: 0171 386 5571

Sole Proprietor: Darley Anderson

All MSS except academic and children's.

Specialization: fiction: all types of thrillers & all types of women's fiction including contemporary, 20th century romantic sagas, erotica, women in jeopardy; also crime (cosy/hard-boiled/historical), horror, fantasy, comedy & Irish novels; non-fiction: celebrity autobiographies, biographies, 'true life' woman in jeopardy, popular psychology, self-improvement, diet, health, beauty & fashion, gardening, cookery, inspirational & religious.

Overseas Representation *(see §7.5):*
Argentina: International Editors Co, Buenos Aires
Brazil: Mrs Karin Schindler, São Paulo
Bulgaria: Anthea Literary Agency, Varna
China: Wu Herong, Nanning, P. R. of China
Czech & Slovak Republics: Andrew Nurnberg Associates, Prague, Czech Republic
France: Frédérique Porretta, Paris
Germany: Thomas Schlück, Garbsen
Greece: O A Literary Agency, Markopoulo
Hungary: Balla & Co, Budapest
Israel: The Book Publishers Association of Israel, Tel Aviv
Italy: Natoli Stefan & Oliva Agenzia Letteraria, Milan
Japan: The English Agency Japan Ltd, Tokyo; Tuttle- Mori Agency Inc, Tokyo
Korea: Eric Yang Agency, Seoul, Korea, South
Netherlands: Jan Michael, Amsterdam
Poland: Graal Ltd, Warsaw
Russia: Prava I Prevodi, Moscow
Scandinavia: Jan Michael, Amsterdam, Netherlands
Slovak Republic: Gerd Plessl Agentur, Bratislava, Slovakia

Spain & Portugal: International Editors Co,
Barcelona, Spain
Taiwan: Tuttle Mori Agency, Taipei
Thailand: Sharon Ng, Bangkok
USA (for fiction): Darley Anderson Books,
London, UK
USA (for film): Renaissance-Swan Film
Agency Inc, Los Angeles, CA, USA
USA (for non-fiction): Mitchell Rose, New
York, USA

4006

**AQUARIUS LITERARY AGENCY &
PICTURE LIBRARY**
[a division of SPM London Ltd]
PO Box 5, 136 Emmanuel Road, Hastings
TN34 3ZY
Telephone: 01424 721196
Fax: 01424 717704

Postal Address:
PO Box 5, Hastings, East Sussex TN34 1HR
Telephone: 01424 721196
Fax: 01424 717704

Directors: Gilbert Gibson *(Managing)*
David Corkill *(Picture Library)*

*All MSS except fiction. No unsolicited MSS.
(Prior letter with SAE required from
unpublished authors.)*

*Specialization: showbusiness features (films &
TV), profiles, interviews, gossip columns,
Hollywood candid photography, film stills (old
& new, colour & b/w), showbusiness
personalities, biographies & autobiographies,
books on films and all other aspects of
international showbusiness and mass
entertainment.*

Parent Company:
Sun-Pacific Music (London) Ltd

Overseas Representation *(see §7.5):*
Japan & Hong Kong: Cosmos, Tokyo, Japan

4007

**BLAKE FRIEDMANN LITERARY
AGENCY LTD**
37–41 Gower Street, London WC1E 6HH
Telephone: 0171 631 4331
Fax: 0171 323 1274

Directors: Carole Blake *(Book Sales)*
Julian Friedmann *(Film, TV & Radio Sales)*
Barbara Jones *(Finance)*
Conrad Williams *(Film, TV & Radio Sales)*
Manager: Isobel Dixon *(Serial & Audio
Rights)*

*All MSS except science fiction, plays, poetry &
juvenile.*

*Specialization: placing book rights
internationally; film, television & radio rights;
placing journalism & short stories for existing
clients.*

Rights Representative in UK for:
Canada: Bella Pomer Inc, Toronto
South Africa: Human & Rousseau, Cape Town;
Queillerie, Cape Town; Tafelberg, Cape
Town

USA: Stuart Krichevsky Literary Agency Inc,
Irvington, NY; Putnam Berkley Inc, New
York, NY; Nancy Stauffer Associates, New
York, NY; Writers House Inc, New York,
NY

Overseas Representation *(see §7.5):*
Asia (excluding Japan, Taiwan & China):
Electra Media Group Pty Ltd, Sydney, NSW,
Australia
Bulgaria: Anthea Literary Agency, Varna
Canada: Bella Pomer Inc, Toronto
China: Bardon Chinese Media Agency, New
York, USA
Czech Republic: Dilia (Czechoslovak
Theatrical & Literary Agency), Prague
France: La Nouvelle Agence, Paris
Germany: Liepman AG, Zurich, Switzerland
Greece: JLM Agency, Halandri
Hungary: Katai & Bolza, Budapest
Israel: Ilana Pikarski Literary Agency, Tel
Aviv
Italy: Natoli Stefan & Oliva Agenzia Letteraria,
Milan
Japan: The English Agency Japan Ltd, Tokyo;
Tuttle-Mori Agency, Tokyo
Korea: DRT International Ltd, Seoul, Korea,
South
Poland: Graal Ltd, Warsaw
Romania: Simona Kessler Literary Agency,
Bucharest
Russia: Elizabeth van Lear Agency, Moscow
Scandinavia: Leonhardt Literary Agency,
Copenhagen, Denmark
Spain, Brazil & Portugal: Mercedes Casanovas
Agency, Barcelona, Spain
Taiwan: Bardon Agency, Taipei
Turkey: Ackali & Tuna, Istanbul
USA: Writers House Inc, New York, NY

4008

DAVID BOLT ASSOCIATES
12 Heath Drive, Send, Surrey GU23 7EP
Telephone: 01483 721118
Fax: 01483 721118

*All MSS except short stories, articles, verse,
original play & film scripts, stories for very
young children. Preliminary letter with SAE
appreciated. Consideration fee on application.*

*Specialization: fiction, African writers,
biography, history, military, theology.*

Associated & Subsidiary Companies:
USA: Maxwell Aley Associates; Writers House

Rights Representative in UK for:
USA: Maxwell Aley Associates, New York,
NY

Overseas Representation *(see §7.5):*
Denmark & Finland: A/S Bookman Literary
Agency, Copenhagen, Denmark
France: La Nouvelle Agence, Paris
Germany: Mohrbooks Literary Agency,
Zurich, Switzerland
Italy: Agenzia Letteraria Internazionale Srl,
Milan
Japan: Tuttle-Mori Agency, Tokyo
Netherlands & Belgium: T&L Literary Agents,
Amsterdam, Netherlands
Norway, Iceland & Sweden: Suzanne Palme
Literary Agency, Oslo, Norway
South America: Carmen Balcells Agencia
Literaria, Rio de Janeiro, Brazil

Spain & Portugal: Carmen Balcells Agencia
Literaria, Barcelona, Spain

4009

FELICITY BRYAN
2a North Parade, Banbury Road, Oxford
OX2 6PE
Telephone: 01865 513816
Fax: 01865 310055

Director: Felicity Bryan

*All MSS except science fiction, fantasy,
children's, romance.*

*Specialization: adult fiction & general non-
fiction, history & popular science.*

Overseas Representation *(see §7.5):*
Europe & Russia: Andrew Nurnberg
Associates Ltd, London, UK
Scandinavia: Sane Töregard Agency,
Karlsham, Sweden

4010

ROSEMARIE BUCKMAN
Ryman's Cottage, Little Tew, Oxford OX7 4JJ
Telephone: 01608 683677
Fax: 01608 683449

*Specialization: handling of translation rights in
all foreign rights markets for fiction and non-
fiction.*

4011

*DIANE BURSTON
46 Cromwell Avenue, London N6 5HL
Telephone: 0181 340 6130

Proprietor: Diane Burston

All MSS except children's & poetry.

*Specialization: general non-fiction & fiction,
good general fiction, women's fiction &
detective/crime novels preferred. Short stories
suitable for women's magazines. Reading
service available on request. Initial telephone
call or letter describing work (with SAE)
necessary.*

4012

**CAMPBELL THOMSON &
McLAUGHLIN LTD**
1 King's Mews, London WC1N 2JA
Telephone: 0171 242 0958
Fax: 0171 242 2408

Directors: John McLaughlin *(Managing)*
Charlotte Bruton
Hal Cheetham

*All MSS except children's, poetry, SF; book
length MSS only.*

Associated & Subsidiary Companies:
Peter Janson-Smith Ltd

Rights Representative in UK for:
USA: The Fox Chase Agency Inc, Philadelphia,
PA; Raines & Raines Agency, New York,
NY

4013 ▬

CASAROTTO CO LTD
National House, 60–66 Wardour Street,
London W1V 3HP
Telephone: 0171 287 4450
Fax: 0171 287 9128

Directors: Jenne Casarotto
Giorgio R. Casarotto
Agents: Greg Hunt
Tracey Smith
Tom Erhardt
Mel Kenyon
Rachel Swann
Sara Pritchard
Catherine O'Shea

*All MSS except scientific, technical, poetry,
educational.*

Specialization: film & TV, theatre.

Associated & Subsidiary Companies:
UK: Casarotto Marsh Ltd; Casarotto Ramsay
Ltd

4014 ▬

CASAROTTO RAMSAY LTD
60 Wardour Street, London W1V 3HP
Telephone: 0171 287 4450
Fax: 0171 287 9128

Directors: Jenne Casarotto
Tom Erhardt

*All MSS except novels, short stories, prose &
poetry, etc.*

*Specialization: play agents – stage plays, TV,
radio & film.*

4015 ▬

SERAFINA CLARKE
98 Tunis Road, London W12 7EY
Telephone: 0181 749 6979
Fax: 0181 740 6862

Proprietor: Serafina Clarke
Associate: Amanda White

*All MSS except science-fiction, poetry and short
stories.*

Rights Representative in UK for:
USA: Permanent Press, Sag Harbor, NY

Overseas Representation *(see §7.5):*
France: Lora Fountain, Paris
*German, Scandinavian & Japanese
translations:* Jennifer Luithlen, Leicester,
UK
Italy: Grandi & Vitali, Milan
Spain & Portugal: Acer, Madrid, Spain

4016 ▬

MARY CLEMMEY LITERARY AGENT
6 Dunollie Road, London NW5 2XP
Telephone: 0171 267 1290
Fax: 0171 267 1290

Literary Agent: Mary Clemmey

*All MSS except science fiction, horror, fantasy
or children's books. No unsolicited MSS.*

*Specialization: fiction and non-fiction, high
quality work with an international market. TV,
film, radio and theatre scripts from existing
clients only. Please approach by preliminary
letter and synopsis (SAE essential).*

Rights Representative in UK for:
Canada: The Bukowski Agency, Toronto, Ont
USA: Lynn C. Franklin Associates Ltd, New
York, NY; Frederick Hill Associates Literary
Agency, San Francisco, CA; The Miller
Agency, New York; Roslyn Targ Literary
Agency Inc, New York; The Weingel Fidel
Agency, New York

Overseas Representation *(see §7.5):*
USA: Elaine Markson Literary, New York

4017 ▬

JONATHAN CLOWES LTD
10 Iron Bridge House, Bridge Approach,
London NW1 8BD
Telephone: 0171 722 7674
Fax: 0171 722 7677

Directors: Jonathan Clowes
Ann Evans
Brie Burkeman

All MSS except stories & articles.

Specialization: films, TV, books.

Overseas Representation *(see §7.5):*
France, Netherlands, Italy, Spain & Germany:
Andrew Nurnberg Associates Ltd, London,
UK
Scandinavia: Sane Töregard Agency,
Karlsham, Sweden

4018 ▬

*ELSPETH COCHRANE AGENCY
11–13 Orlando Road, London SW4 0LE
Telephone: 0171 622 0314
Fax: 0171 622 5815

Proprietor: Elspeth Cochrane

4019 ▬

ROSICA COLIN LTD
1 Clareville Grove Mews, London SW7 5AH
Telephone: 0171 370 1080
Fax: 0171 244 6441

All MSS except poetry.

*Specialization: theatre, film, television, radio &
foreign rights.*

4020 ▬

JANE CONWAY-GORDON
1 Old Compton Street, London W1V 5PH
Telephone: 0171 494 0148
Fax: 0171 287 9264

Sole Proprietor: Jane Conway-Gordon

*All MSS except science fiction, poetry, short
pieces; return postage essential.*

Rights Representative in UK for:
USA: Helen McGrath Associates, Concord, CA

Overseas Representation *(see §7.5):*
Germany: Liepman AG, Zurich, Switzerland
Israel: I. Pikarski Literary Agency, Tel Aviv
Japan: The English Agency Japan Ltd, Tokyo
Netherlands: Lijnkamp Literary Agents,
Amsterdam
Scandinavia: Lijnkamp Literary Agents,
Amsterdam, Denmark
Spain: International Editors Co, Barcelona
USA: McIntosh & Otis Inc, New York, NY

4021 ▬

THE COPYRIGHTS CO (UK) LTD
Manor Barn, Milton, Banbury, Oxon
Telephone: 01295 721188
Fax: 01295 720145

Also at:
7 Square Rigger Row, Plantation Wharf,
York Road, Battersea, London SW11 3TZ
Telephone: 0171 924 3292
Fax: 0171 924 3208

Directors: Nicholas Durbridge *(Managing)*
Linda Pooley
Julie Nellthorp
Karen Addison

*Specialization: merchandise agency licensing
the work of writers & artists.*

Associated & Subsidiary Companies:
Australia: Copyrights Australasia (Pty) Ltd.
Japan: Copyrights Japan Ltd. *UK:* The
Copyrights Co (Europe) Ltd *(for Europe)*; The
Copyrights Group Ltd. *USA:* Copyrights
America Inc

Overseas Representation *(see §7.5):*
Australia & New Zealand: Copyrights
Australasia Pty Ltd, Brunswick, Australia
Continental Europe: Copyrights Europe,
Hamburg, Germany
USA: Copyrights America Inc, Morristown, NJ

4022 ▬

RUPERT CREW LTD
[International Literary Representation]
1a King's Mews, London WC1N 2JA
Telephone: 0171 242 8586
Fax: 0171 831 7914

Founder: F. Rupert Crew
Chairman: Kathleen Crew
Directors: Doreen Montgomery *(Deputy
Chairman & Managing)*
Caroline Montgomery *(Company Secretary)*

*All MSS except science fiction, short stories,
poetry, film & TV scripts.*

*Specialization: international business
management for authors, desiring world
representation. Preliminary letter required.
Also act as publishers' consultants.*

Overseas Representation *(see §7.5):*
France: Frédérique Porretta, Paris
Germany: Paul & Peter Fritz AG Literary
Agency, Zurich, Switzerland
Japan: Tuttle-Mori Agency, Tokyo

Russia: Andrew Nurnberg Literary Agency,
Moscow
Scandinavia & Spain: Sane Töregard Agency,
Karlsham, Sweden
USA: Allan Lang International Book Marketing
Ltd, Princeton, NJ
Worldwide (Film/TV): The Sharland
Organisation, London, UK

4023

CRUICKSHANK CAZENOVE LTD
97 Old South Lambeth Road, London
SW8 1XU
Telephone: 0171 735 2933
Fax: 0171 820 1081

Director: Harriet Cruickshank

All MSS except fiction.

*Specialization: plays, TV & film scripts only.
Preliminary letter & stamped addressed
envelope required.*

4024

CURTIS BROWN
4th Floor, Haymarket House,
28–29 Haymarket, London SW1Y 4SP
Telephone: 0171 396 6600
Fax: 0171 396 0110

Directors & Agents: Peter Murphy
(Managing)
Tim Curnow *(Curtis Brown (Australia) Pty
Ltd)*
Sue Freathy
Jonathan Lloyd
Diana Mackay
Anthea Morton-Saner
Peter Robinson
Vivienne Schuster
Michael Shaw
Elizabeth Stevens
Giles Gordon
Mark Collingbourne

All MSS except short stories & poetry.

*Specialization: negotiation in all publishing
markets; and television, film & dramatic
writing, directing and presenting.*

Associated & Subsidiary Companies:
Australia: Curtis Brown (Australia) Pty Ltd

Rights Representative in UK for:
USA: Gelfman Schneider Literary Agents Inc,
New York

Overseas Representation *(see §7.5):*
Australia: Curtis Brown (Australia) Pty Ltd,
Paddington, NSW
USA: Scovil Chichak Galen Literary Agents
Inc, New York, NY

4025

FELIX DE WOLFE
Manfield House, 1 Southampton Street,
London WC2R 0LR
Telephone: 0171 379 5767
Fax: 0171 836 0337

Proprietor: Felix de Wolfe

All MSS except non-fiction, children's.

Overseas Representation *(see §7.5):*
France: Michelle Lapautre, Paris
Italy: Liepman AG, Zurich, Switzerland

4026

DORIAN LITERARY AGENCY
Upper Thornehill, 27 Church Road,
St Marychurch, Torquay, Devon TQ1 4QY
Telephone: 01803 312095
Fax: 01803 312095

Proprietor: Dorothy Lumley

All MSS except poetry, plays or technical.

*Specialization: all types of fiction for adults,
plus a little non-fiction.*

Overseas Representation *(see §7.5):*
Czech Republic: Interlit Services, Prague
France: Agence Litteraire Lenclud
Germany: Thomas Schlück, Garbsen
Italy: Agenzia Letteraria Internazionale Srl,
Milan
Japan: The English Agency Japan Ltd, Tokyo
Scandinavia: A/S Bookman Literary Agency,
Copenhagen, Denmark
South Africa: International Press Agency Pty
Ltd, Howard Place, Cape Town
Spain: NALI

4027

TOBY EADY ASSOCIATES LTD
9 Orme Court, London W2 4RL
Telephone: 0171 792 0092
Fax: 0171 792 0879
Email: 100571.2263@compuserve.com

Directors: Toby Eady
Alexandra Pringle

*All MSS except pornographic & vicariously
violent.*

*Specialization: fiction & non-fiction; travel
writing. Africa, China, India and the Middle
East are of great interest; politics of a Swiftean
nature.*

Overseas Representation *(see §7.5):*
France: La Nouvelle Agence, Paris
Germany: Mohrbooks Literary Agency,
Zurich, Switzerland
Japan: The English Agency Japan Ltd, Tokyo
Netherlands: Jan Michael, Amsterdam
Scandinavia & Spain: Rosemarie Buckman,
Oxford, UK

4028

**PETER ELEK ASSOCIATES/ELEK
INTERNATIONAL RIGHTS AGENT
USA**
14a Bedford Road, Chiswick, London W4 1JH
Telephone: 0181 747 9150
Fax: 0181 749 7377

Rights: Gaye Facer
Executive: Peter Elek

All MSS except poetry.

*Specialization: representing US and Canadian
agents and publishers in the UK.*

Parent Company:
Peter Elek Associates *(USA)*

Associated & Subsidiary Companies:
USA: The Content Co Inc

Rights Representative in UK for:
Canada: Madison Press, Toronto
USA: Knox Burger Associates, New York, NY;
The Content Co Inc, New York; Peter Elek
Associates, New York, NY; Lynn C.
Franklin Associates Ltd, New York, NY;
Goodman Associates, New York, NY; Sarah
Lazin Books, New York, NY; The Sagalyn
Agency, Washington, DC; Rhoda Weyr
Agency, New York, NY

Overseas Representation *(see §7.5):*
France: Michelle Lapautre, Paris
Germany: Corry Theegarten-Schlotterer
Verlags- und Autoren-Agentur, Munich
Italy: TiPress Deutschland, Turin
Japan: Motovun Co Ltd, Tokyo
Netherlands: Lijnkamp Literary Agents,
Amsterdam
Spain: Ute Korner Literary Agency, Barcelona

4029

*FAITH EVANS ASSOCIATES
Clerkenwell House, 45 Clerkenwell Green,
London EC1R 0EB
Telephone: 0171 490 2535
Fax: 0171 490 4958

*Specialization: Small, select agency. No phone
calls or unsolicited MSS.*

4030

FRENCH'S
9 Elgin Mews South, London W9 1VZ
Telephone: 0171 266 3321
Fax: 0171 286 6716

Director: John French

*Specialization: reading service on all
manuscripts. Details on request.*

4031

VERNON FUTERMAN ASSOCIATES
159 Goldhurst Terrace, London NW6 3EU
Telephone: 0171 625 9601
Fax: 0171 625 9601 (Direct)

Submissions Dept:
17 Deanhill Road, London SW14 7DQ
Telephone: 0181 878 9766
Fax: 0181 878 9766

Directors: Vernon E. Futerman *(Managing)*
Alexandra Groom *(Associate)*
Guy Rose *(Associate)*

*All MSS except poetry; no short stories unless
by established authors.*

*Specialization: quality fiction including crime,
academic, art, politics, current affairs,
biographies and autobiographies, history,
literary criticism, film and TV scripts.*

Overseas Representation (see §7.5):
Germany: Brigitte Axster, Frankfurt am Main

4032 ▬▬▬▬▬▬▬▬▬▬

PETER GALLINER ASSOCIATES
PO Box 312, London NW8 6DE
Telephone: 0171 722 5217
Fax: 0171 722 5217

Director: Peter Galliner
Manager: Mrs Hildegard Abraham

Specialization: representing foreign publishers as scouts & representatives; foreign rights; international coproductions.

4033 ▬▬▬▬▬▬▬▬▬▬

ERIC GLASS LTD
28 Berkeley Square, London W1X 6HD
Telephone: 0171 629 7162
Fax: 0171 499 6780

Director: Janet Glass

All MSS except children's books, articles, short stories & poetry.

Specialization: plays (stage & TV), screenplays, books (fiction & non-fiction).

Rights Representative in UK for:
France: Société des Auteurs et Compositeurs Dramatiques, Paris; Société Civil des Auteurs Multimedia (Société des Gens de Lettres), Paris

Overseas Representation (see §7.5):
Agents in the following countries: USA, Australasia, France, Germany, Netherlands, Scandinavia, Italy, Spain, Poland, Czechoslovakia, Greece, Japan, South America

4034 ▬▬▬▬▬▬▬▬▬▬

CHRISTINE GREEN AUTHORS' AGENT
40 Doughty Street, London WC1N 2LF
Telephone: 0171 831 4956
Fax: 0171 405 3935

Director: Christine Green

All MSS except poetry, plays, children's.

Specialization: fiction.

Overseas Representation (see §7.5):
Eastern Europe, CIS, Netherlands, Italy & Spain: Andrew Nurnberg Associates Ltd, London, UK
France: Frédérique Porretta, Paris
Germany: Paul & Peter Fritz AG Literary Agency, Zurich, Switzerland
Greece: JLM Literary Agency, Athens
Israel: Ilana Pikarski Literary Agency, Tel Aviv
Japan: Tuttle-Mori Agency, Tokyo
Korea: DRT International Ltd, Seoul, Korea, South
Scandinavia: Sane Töregard Agency, Karlsham, Sweden
Taiwan: Big Apple Tuttle Mori, London, UK

4035 ▬▬▬▬▬▬▬▬▬▬

GREENE & HEATON LTD
37 Goldhawk Road, London W12 8QQ
Telephone: 0181 749 0315
Fax: 0181 749 0318

Directors: Carol Heaton
Timothy Webb *(Company Secretary)*
Associate Agent: Judith Murray

All MSS except plays, TV & film-scripts, articles & poetry, stories (other than from existing clients), science fiction or fantasy and children's. Preliminary letter and return postage required.

Rights Representative in UK for:
USA: Knox Burger Associates, New York, NY; Jed Mattes Inc, New York, NY; Jean V. Naggar Literary Agency, New York, NY; The Sagalyn Literary Agency, Bethesda, MD

Overseas Representation (see §7.5):
France: La Nouvelle Agence, Paris
German-speaking countries: Paul & Peter Fritz AG Literary Agency, Zurich, Switzerland
German-speaking countries (for Carol Heaton's authors): Liepman AG, Zurich, Switzerland
Italy: Agenzia Antonella Antonelli, Milan
Japan: Tuttle-Mori Agency, Tokyo
Netherlands, Eastern Europe & USSR: Andrew Nurnberg Associates Ltd, London, UK
Spain: Carmen Balcells Agencia Literaria, Barcelona
USA: Jed Mattes Inc, New York, NY
USA (for Carol Heaton's authors): Jean V. Naggar Literary Agency, New York, NY, USA

4036 ▬▬▬▬▬▬▬▬▬▬

THE JANE GREGORY AGENCY
3 Barb Mews, London W6 7PA
Telephone: 0171 610 4676
Fax: 0171 610 4686

Proprietor: Jane Gregory *(Literary Agent)*

Specialization: See: Gregory & Radice Authors' Agents

Associated & Subsidiary Companies:
UK: Gregory & Radice Authors' Agents

Rights Representative in UK for:
USA: March 10th Inc, Haworth, NJ

Overseas Representation (see §7.5):
See: Gregory & Radice Authors' Agents, UK

4037 ▬▬▬▬▬▬▬▬▬▬

GREGORY & RADICE AUTHORS' AGENTS
3 Barb Mews, London W6 7PA
Telephone: 0171 610 4676
Fax: 0171 610 4686

Partners & Literary Agents: Jane Gregory
Dr Lisanne Radice *(Editorial)*
Pippa Dyson *(Film & TV Rights)*

All MSS except children's, juvenile, academic & technical books, poetry & plays, TV & film scripts, short stories. Preliminary letter with

synopsis, first three chapters and SAE essential.

Specialization: crime, suspense fiction & thrillers, commercial & literary fiction. Also represent politicians & political journalists. Editorial advice given to own authors. Film & TV rights for own published authors only, no original scripts.

Associated & Subsidiary Companies:
The Jane Gregory Agency

Overseas Representation (see §7.5):
Bulgaria: Interrights Literary & Translation Agency, Sofia
Czech Republic: Interlit Services, Prague
France: La Nouvelle Agence, Paris
Hungary: Lex Copyright, Budapest
Italy: Living Literary Agency, Milan
Japan: Tuttle-Mori Agency, Tokyo
Korea: Imprima Korea, Seoul, Korea, South
Russia: Andrew Nurnberg Associates Ltd, London, UK
Scandinavia: Leonhardt Literary Agency, Copenhagen, Denmark
Spain: Carmen Balcells Agencia Literaria, Barcelona

4038 ▬▬▬▬▬▬▬▬▬▬

MARGARET HANBURY
27 Walcot Square, London SE11 4UB
Telephone: 0171 735 7680
Fax: 0171 793 0316

Proprietor/Literary Agent: Margaret Hanbury

All MSS except science fiction, horror, fantasy, books for children, plays, scripts, poetry. Preliminary letter plus s.a.e. essential. Represented in all other countries. Commission: home 15%, overseas 20%.

Specialization: quality fiction and non-fiction.

Rights Representative in UK for:
USA: Robin Straus Literary Agency, New York, NY

Overseas Representation (see §7.5):
Germany: Mohrbooks Literary Agency, Zurich, Switzerland
Italy: Luigi Bernabó Associates Srl, Milan
Netherlands: Jan Michael, Amsterdam
Scandinavia (including Finland): Licht & Licht Literary Agency, Charlottenlund, Denmark
USA: Robin Straus Literary Agency, New York, NY

4039 ▬▬▬▬▬▬▬▬▬▬

RICHARD HATTON LTD
29 Roehampton Gate, London SW15 5JR
Telephone: 0181 876 6699
Fax: 0181 876 8278

Director: Richard Hatton

Specialization: Theatre, TV, broadcasting and film production, and publication associated. Corresponding agents overseas.

4040 ▬

A. M. HEATH & CO LTD
79 St Martins Lane, London WC2N 4AA
Telephone: 0171 836 4271
Fax: 0171 497 2561

Chairman: Mark Hamilton
Directors: Michael Thomas *(Joint Managing & Company Secretary)*
William Hamilton *(Joint Managing)*
Sara Fisher
Sarah Molloy

All MSS except scientific, technical for the layman only.

Rights Representative in UK for:
USA: Miriam Altshuler Literary Agency, Red Hook, NY; Brandt & Brandt Inc, New York, NY; Jane Jordan Browne, Chicago, IL; Jane Chelius Literary Agency, Brooklyn, NY; Anita Diamant Inc, New York, NY; Hyperion-Disney Publishing Co, New York; Kidde, Hoyt & Picard, New York, NY; Lescher & Lescher Ltd, New York, NY; Ellen Levine Literary Agency Inc, New York, NY; Gina Maccoby Literary Agency, New York, NY; McIntosh & Otis Inc, New York, NY; Lori Perkins, Riverdale, NY; Russell & Volkening Inc, New York, NY; Scott Meredith Literary Agency Inc, New York, NY; Wallace Literary Agency, New York, NY; Harriet Wasserman Literary Agency Inc, New York, NY

4041 ▬

DAVID HIGHAM ASSOCIATES LTD
5–8 Lower John Street, Golden Square, London W1R 4HA
Telephone: 0171 437 7888
Fax: 0171 437 1072

Directors: Bruce Hunter
Jacqueline Korn
Anthony Crouch
Elizabeth Cree
Anthony Goff
Ania Corless

All MSS except highly specialist & academic works.

Specialization: fiction & non-fiction, plays & short stories, film, radio & TV scripts. Preliminary letter and return postage essential.

Rights Representative in UK for:
USA: Harold Ober Associates Inc, New York, NY; The Wendy Weil Agency Inc, New York, NY

Overseas Representation *(see §7.5):*
Afrikaans: International Press Agency Pty Ltd, Howard Place, Cape Town, South Africa
Bulgarian: Nika Literary Agency, Sofia, Bulgaria
Chinese: Bardon Chinese Media Agency, New York, USA; Big Apple Tuttle-Mori Agency Inc, Taipei, Taiwan
Danish & Finnish: Licht & Licht Literary Agency, Charlottenlund, Denmark
Dutch: Lijnkamp Literary Agents, Amsterdam, Netherlands
French: Agence Hoffman, Paris, France

German: Mohrbooks Literary Agency, Zurich, Switzerland
Greek: JLM Literary Agency, Athens, Greece
Hebrew: Orly Pecker Literary Agency, Tel Aviv, Israel
Hungarian: Katai & Bolza, Budapest, Hungary
Italian: Luigi Bernabó Associates Srl, Milan, Italy
Japanese: The English Agency Japan Ltd, Tokyo, Japan; Japan Uni Agency Inc, Tokyo, Japan; Tuttle-Mori Agency, Tokyo, Japan
Norwegian & Swedish: Suzanne Palme Literary Agency, Oslo, Norway
Portuguese in Brazil: Agencia Literaria Balcells, Mello e Souza, Riff, Rio de Janeiro, Brazil
Spanish & Portuguese: Carmen Balcells Agencia Literaria, Barcelona, Spain
Turkish: Nurcihan Kesim Literary Agency, Istanbul, Turkey
USA: Harold Ober Associates Inc, New York, NY

4042 ▬

VANESSA HOLT LTD
59 Crescent Road, Leigh-on-Sea, Essex SS9 2PF
Telephone: 01702 73787
Fax: 01702 471890

Director: Vanessa Holt
Assistant: Brenda White

All MSS except specialized non-fiction & children's books.

Specialization: commercial fiction & crime. Preliminary letter essential but very limited capacity to represent new authors.

Rights Representative in UK for:
USA: JCA Literary Agency Inc, New York, NY

Overseas Representation *(see §7.5):*
France: La Nouvelle Agence, Paris
German-speaking: Liepman AG, Zurich, Switzerland
Japan: The English Agency Japan Ltd, Tokyo
Netherlands: Andrew Nurnberg Associates Ltd, London, UK
Portugal: Ilidio da Fonseca Matos, Lisbon
Scandinavia: Sane Töregard Agency, Karlsham, Sweden
Spanish-speaking: International Editors Co, Barcelona, Spain
USA (for US rights): Gelfman Schneider Literary Agents Inc, New York, USA

4043 ▬

TANJA HOWARTH LITERARY AGENCY
19 New Row, London WC2N 4LA
Telephone: 0171 240 5553 & 836 4342
Fax: 0171 379 0969

All MSS except children's, plays and science fiction.

Specialization: full-length MSS. General fiction and non-fiction, thrillers, contemporary and historical women's novels and sagas and general non-fiction (home 15%, USA & translation 20%). Please submit preliminary letter, synopsis and three sample chapters with return postage. No reading fee.

Rights Representative in UK for:
Germany: DTV, Munich; Kiepenheuer & Witsch, Cologne
Norway: H. Aschehoug & Co, Oslo

4044 ▬

MICHAEL IMISON PLAYWRIGHTS LTD
28 Almeida Street, Islington, London N1 1TD
Telephone: 0171 354 3174
Fax: 0171 359 6273
Email: 100130.2516@compuserve.com

Directors: Michael Imison
Tamsyn Imison

All MSS except unsolicited MSS & most writers other than our existing clients. No novels, short stories, etc.

Specialization: plays & dramatic works.

4045 ▬

INFORMATION AGENTS LTD
26 Rosebery Avenue, London EC1R 4SX
Telephone: 0171 837 3345
Fax: 0171 837 8901
Email: ial@epsltd.demon.co.uk
Web Site: http://www.epsltd.com

Chairman: David R. Worlock
Senior Consultant: Tony Feldman

Specialization: representing publishers of printed information and authors in the negotiation and sale of electronic publishing rights. Will handle rights for resale to database vendors, for online or CD-ROM use. Negotiation of contracts with audiotex service providers for the re-use of book-based information in voice information services.

Parent Company:
Electronic Publishing Services Ltd *(51%) (UK)*

Associated & Subsidiary Companies:
UK: Electronic Publishing Services (Publications) Ltd; Interactive Media Publications Ltd

4046 ▬

INTERCONTINENTAL LITERARY AGENCY
The Chambers, Chelsea Harbour, London SW10 0XF
Telephone: 0171 351 4763
Fax: 0171 351 4809

Specialization: translation rights exclusively.

Associated & Subsidiary Companies:
UK: Peters Fraser & Dunlop Group *(including the June Hall Agency).* USA: Harold Matson Co Inc

4047 ▬

THE INTERNATIONAL PRESS AGENCY
19 Avenue South, Surbiton, Surrey KT5 8PJ
Telephone: 0181 390 4414
Fax: 0181 390 4414

Managing Editor: U. A. Barnett

Specialization: children's books only.

Associated & Subsidiary Companies:
South Africa: The International Press Agency
(Pty) Ltd

Rights Representative in UK for:
South Africa: Human & Rousseau, Cape Town;
   Maskew Miller Longman, Cape Town;
   Tafelberg, Cape Town

Overseas Representation *(see §7.5):*
Japan: Japan Foreign Rights Centre, Tokyo
South Africa: The International Press Agency,
   Ndabeni

4048 ▬▬▬▬▬▬▬▬

INTERNATIONAL SCRIPTS LTD
1 Norland Square, Holland Park, London
W11 4PX
Telephone: 0171 229 0736
Fax: 0171 792 3287

Accounts:
38 Lakeside, Brook Lane, Snodland, Kent
ME6 5LD
Telephone: 01634 241203

Managing Director: Bob Tanner
Company Secretary: Jill Lawson
Associate: Pat Hornsey

All MSS except poetry and short stories.
Preliminary letter required. Return postage
required for MSS plus a £25 reading fee (for
which a report will be provided).

Specialization: contemporary & women's
fiction, general non-fiction, self-improvement,
horror & thrillers, business books.

Rights Representative in UK for:
USA: Barricade Books Inc, New York;
   Barron's Publishers of General and
   Educational Books, Hauppauge;
   Masquerade Books, New York; Singer
   Media Corporation, San Clemente, CA;
   Spectrum Literary Agency, New York, NY

Overseas Representation *(see §7.5):*
Bulgaria: Interrights Literary & Translation
   Agency, Sofia
Eastern Europe: Prava & Prevodi, Belgrade,
   Yugoslavia
France: Eliane Benisti, Paris
Germany: Thomas Schlück, Garbsen
Japan: Japan Uni Agency Inc, Tokyo; Tuttle-
   Mori Agency, Tokyo
South America: Agencia Siciliano, São Paulo,
   Brazil
Spain: Julio F. Yañez Agencia Literaria,
   Barcelona
USA (selected titles): Singer Media
   Corporation, San Clemente, CA, USA;
   Ralph M. Vicinanza Ltd *(selected titles),*
   New York, USA

4049 ▬▬▬▬▬▬▬▬

JOHN JOHNSON LTD
45–47 Clerkenwell Green, London EC1R 0HT
Telephone: 0171 251 0125
Fax: 0171 251 2172

Directors: Andrew Hewson
Margaret Hewson

All MSS except short stories, TV, radio and
playscripts.

Specialization: full length MSS only. No
reading fee but preliminary letter & return
postage essential.

Rights Representative in UK for:
USA: Holiday House Inc, New York; Soho
   Press, New York, NY

Overseas Representation *(see §7.5):*
France: Agence Hoffman, Paris
German-speaking: Paul & Peter Fritz AG
   Literary Agency, Zurich, Switzerland
Greece: Educational Materials Enterprises Ltd,
   Athens
Israel: I. Pikarski Literary Agency, Tel Aviv
Italy: Agenzia Antonella Antonelli, Milan
Japan: Tuttle-Mori Agency, Tokyo
*Netherlands, Spain & Portugal (Russian-
   speaking):* Andrew Nurnberg Associates
   Ltd, London, UK
Scandinavia: Sane Töregard Agency,
   Karlsham, Sweden
Turkey: Nurcihan Kesim Literary Agency,
   Istanbul

4050 ▬▬▬▬▬▬▬▬

JANE JUDD LITERARY AGENCY
18 Belitha Villas, London N1 1PD
Telephone: 0171 607 0273
Fax: 0171 607 0623

Proprietor: Jane C. Judd

All MSS except plays, poetry and short stories.

Specialization: general non-fiction & fiction.

Rights Representative in UK for:
Canada: Penguin Canada, Toronto, Ont
USA: Avon Books, New York; Mercury House,
   San Francisco, CA; Marian Young, New
   York, NY

Overseas Representation *(see §7.5):*
France: La Nouvelle Agence, Paris
Germany: Thomas Schlück, Garbsen
Italy: Living Literary Agency, Milan
Netherlands & Scandinavia: Jan Michael,
   Amsterdam, Netherlands
Spain & Portugal: Julio F. Yañez Agencia
   Literaria, Barcelona, Spain
USA: Christine Tomasino RLR Associates,
   New York

4051 ▬▬▬▬▬▬▬▬

THE FRANCES KELLY AGENCY
111 Clifton Road, Kingston-upon-Thames,
Surrey KT2 6PL
Telephone: 0181 549 7830
Fax: 0181 547 0051

Proprietor: Frances Kelly

Specialization: general non-fiction, all
academic & professional disciplines; return
postage & preliminary letter requested.

4052 ▬▬▬▬▬▬▬▬

KNIGHT FEATURES
20 Crescent Grove, London SW4 7AH

Telephone: 0171 622 1467
Fax: 0171 622 1522

Proprietor: Peter Knight
Associates: Ann King-Hall
Gaby Martin
Giovanna Farrell-Vinay
Andrew Knight

All MSS except short stories, poetry &
unsolicited MSS (reading fee).

Specialization: worldwide selling of strip
cartoons, major features and serializations.
Exclusive syndication agent in UK & Irish
Republic for United Feature Syndicate
(Peanuts, etc.) & Newspaper Enterprise
Association (Frank & Ernest, Born Loser, King
Baloo, etc.), also Paws Inc (Garfield).

Rights Representative in UK for:
Canada: Fitzhenry & Whiteside, Markham,
   Ont
USA: Meadowbrook Press, Deephaven, MN;
   United Media, New York

4053 ▬▬▬▬▬▬▬▬

CAT LEDGER LITERARY AGENCY
33 Percy Street, London W1P 9FG
Telephone: 0171 436 5030
Fax: 0171 631 4273

Director: Catherine Ledger

All MSS except children's books, poetry or
plays. No reading fee, but preliminary letter
with SAE essential.

Specialization: general fiction and non-fiction;
full-length MSS.

4054 ▬▬▬▬▬▬▬▬

BARBARA LEVY LITERARY AGENCY
64 Greenhill, Hampstead High Street, London
NW3 5TZ
Telephone: 0171 435 9046
Fax: 0171 431 2063

Associate: John F. Selby

Specialization: general fiction & non-fiction,
including illustrated books; TV & radio.

Rights Representative in UK for:
USA: Arcadia, Danbury, CT; Richard Parks,
   New York

Overseas Representation *(see §7.5):*
Foreign Language Markets: The Marsh
   Agency, London, UK
USA: Arcadia, Danbury, CT

4055 ▬▬▬▬▬▬▬▬

**CHRISTOPHER LITTLE LITERARY
AGENCY**
48 Walham Grove, London SW6 1QR
Telephone: 0171 386 1800
Fax: 0171 381 2248
Email: 100555.3137@compuserve.com

Proprietor: Christopher John Little
Managers: Patrick Walsh
Bryony Evens

All MSS except short stories.

Specialization: women's fiction, crime, thrillers, horror, romance, children's, narrative & investigative non-fiction, sport, biography. Also handles commercial and literary full-length fiction, non-fiction, and film/TV/play scripts. No reading fee. Send detailed letter plus synopsis and three sample chapters, and SAE in first instance.

Rights Representative in UK for:
USA: IMG Literary, New York; The Evan Marshall Agency, Pinebrook, NJ

4056

LONDON INDEPENDENT BOOKS
26 Chalcot Crescent, London NW1 8YD
Telephone: 0171 706 0486
Fax: 0171 724 3122

Literary Agent: Carolyn Whitaker

All MSS except computers & young children's.

Specialization: fiction & non-fiction, particularly travel & fantasy.

4057

ANDREW LOWNIE LITERARY AGENCY
122 Bedford Court Mansions, Bedford Square, London WC1B 3AH
Telephone: 0171 636 4917
Fax: 0171 436 1898

Proprietor: Andrew Lownie

All MSS except poetry, children's books, horror, science fiction, romantic fiction, drama or educational. Return postage essential. No reading fee. Commission 15% worldwide.

Specialization: non-fiction and in particular history, biography and popular reference. Titles agented include the Oxford Classical Dictionary, Cambridge Guide to Literature in English, *the memoirs of Gloria Huniford, John Grigg's magisterial six-volume life of Lloyd George, Norma Major's books on Joan Sutherland and Chequers, Juliet Barker, numerous books about the SAS and a series of male thrillers.*

Overseas Representation *(see §7.5):*
Worldwide: The Marsh Agency, London, UK

4058

JENNIFER LUITHLEN AGENCY
88 Holmfield Road, Leicester LE2 1SB
Telephone: 0116 273 8863
Fax: 0116 273 5697

Agent: Jennifer Luithlen

Specialization: children's books fiction and non-fiction, pony books of particular interest. Adult fiction—sagas, historical, crime. Specialist market for translation; the Nordic countries, Germany and Netherlands. Not accepting new clients.

4059

LUTYENS & RUBINSTEIN
231 Westbourne Park Road, London W11 1EB
Telephone: 0171 792 4855
Fax: 0171 792 4833
Email: name@luru.demon.co.uk

Partners: Felicity Rubinstein
Sarah Lutyens

All MSS except childrens' books, science fiction, fantasy, poetry, screenplays, scripts for theatre and/or TV and radio.

Specialization: general adult non-fiction and fiction.

4060

ANDREW MANN LTD
1 Old Compton Street, London W1V 5PH
Telephone: 0171 734 4751
Fax: 0171 287 9264

Directors: Anne Dewe
Tina Betts

Specialization: fiction, general non-fiction & film/TV/radio scripts. No unsolicited MSS. Preliminary letter, synopis and SAE essential. No reading fee.

Rights Representative in UK for:
USA: Richard McDonough, Cambridge, MA

Overseas Representation *(see §7.5):*
Czech Republic: Andrew Nurnberg Associates, Prague
Germany: Thomas Schlück, Garbsen
Hungary: Katai & Bolza, Budapest
Italy: Living Literary Agency, Milan
Korea: Shin Won Agency Co, Seoul, Korea, South
Poland: Maria Strarz-Kánska Literary Agency Ltd, Krakow
Russia: Prava I Prevodi, Moscow
Spain, Scandinavia, Portugal & Brazil: Sane Töregard Agency, Karlsham, Sweden
Taiwan: Big Apple Tuttle-Mori Agency Inc, Taipei
USA: McIntosh & Otis Inc, New York, NY

4061

THE MARSH AGENCY
138 Buckingham Palace Road, London SW1W 9SA
Telephone: 0171 730 1124
Fax: 0171 730 0037
Email: 100614.1702@compuserve.com

Agents: Paul Marsh
Susanna Nicklin
Junior Agent: Juliet Matthews

Specialization: selling of translation rights in the work of English-language writers throughout the world, representing a number of British and American agencies and publishers. No unsolicited submissions.

4062

BLANCHE MARVIN
21a St Johns Wood High Street, London NW8 7NG

Telephone: 0171 722 2313
Fax: 0171 722 2313

Director: Blanche Marvin

Specialization: theatre, film, TV, radio & publishing for UK & USA. MSS from published authors only.

4063

MBA LITERARY AGENTS
45 Fitzroy Street, London W1P 5HR
Telephone: 0171 387 2076 & 4785
Fax: 0171 387 2042
Email: 101572.353@compuserve.com

Directors: Diana Tyler *(Managing)*
John Richard Parker
Meg Davis
Ruth Needham
Timothy Webb *(Financial)*

All MSS except poetry, short stories and children's fiction.

Specialization: fiction and non-fiction. Also scripts for film, TV, radio & theatre.

Rights Representative in UK for:
USA: Bill Fawcett & Associates, Wanconde, IL; Jabberwocky (Joshua Bilmes), Sunnyside, NY; Donald Maass Agency, New York, NY; Susan Schulman, New York, NY

Overseas Representation *(see §7.5):*
Asia: Electra Media Group Pty Ltd, Sydney, NSW, Australia
Czech & Slovak Republics: Interlit Services, Prague, Czech Republic
Eastern Europe: Prava & Prevodi, Belgrade, Yugoslavia
France: Lora Fountain, Paris
Germany: Thomas Schlück, Garbsen
Greece: JLM Literary Agency, Athens
Hungary: Inter Codex/Inter Licence, Budapest; Lex Copyright Office, Budapest
Israel: I. Pikarski Literary Agency, Tel Aviv
Italy: Living Literary Agency, Milan
Japan: The English Agency Japan Ltd, Tokyo; Tuttle-Mori Agency, Tokyo
Korea: Eric Yang Agency, Seoul, Korea, South
Russia: Alexander Korzhenevski, Moscow
Scandinavia: Rosemarie Buckman, Oxford, UK
South America: International Editors Co, Buenos Aires, Argentina
Spain: Carmen Balcells Agencia Literaria, Barcelona; International Editors Co, Barcelona
Taiwan: Big Apple Tuttle-Mori Agency Inc, Taipei
Thailand: Tuttle-Mori Big Apple Agency (Thailand) Co Ltd, Bangkok
Turkey: Nurcihan Kesim Literary Agency, Istanbul
USA: Donald Maass Agency, New York, NY

4064

THE CATHY MILLER FOREIGN RIGHTS AGENCY
10 Filmer Road Studios, 75 Filmer Road, London SW6 7JF
Telephone: 0171 384 1198
Fax: 0171 384 1135

Also at:
9 Broadway Mansions, Effie Road, London
SW16 1EL
Telephone: 0171 731 2540

Principal: Cathy Miller

All MSS except poetry & educational.

*Specialization: foreign rights; acting as
consultants to publishers on sales of foreign
rights of non-fiction titles (psychoanalysis,
medical, business & management, esoteric,
philosophy, health & general trade books);
handling market research for lists or one-off
projects; helping to set up rights departments;
advising on all matters concerning translation
rights and negotiations with foreign publishers.*

Rights Representative in UK for:
Canada: Golden Globe Publishing, Montreal,
PQ
Switzerland: Edi Inter SA, Geneva; Editions
Godefroy, Chesières
USA: Alliance Books, New York; Humanities
Press, Atlantic Highlands, NJ

Overseas Representation *(see §7.5)*:
Australia: Electra Media Group Pty Ltd,
Sydney, NSW

4065 ▬▬▬

RICHARD MILNE LTD
15 Summerlee Gardens, London N2 9QN
Telephone: 0181 883 3987
Fax: 0181 883 3987

Directors: R. M. Sharples
K. N. Sharples

*Specialization: scripts for films and TV. Unable
to represent any additional authors at present.*

4066 ▬▬▬

WILLIAM MORRIS AGENCY (UK) LTD
31–32 Soho Square, London W1V 5DG
Telephone: 0171 434 2191
Fax: 0171 437 0238

Managing Director: Steve Kenis
Literary Agent: Stephanie Cabot

*All MSS except poetry, technical, educational
or academic material.*

*Specialization: general fiction & non-fiction;
no reading fee; preliminary letter essential.*

Parent Company:
William Morris Agency Inc *(USA)*

Overseas Representation *(see §7.5)*:
USA & foreign: William Morris Agency Inc,
New York, USA

4067 ▬▬▬

*MICHAEL MOTLEY LTD
Flat 4, 42 Craven Hill Gardens, London
W2 3EA
Telephone: 0171 723 2973
Fax: 0171 262 4566

Director: Michael Motley

*All MSS except freelance journalism (ie short
MSS), poetry & original dramatic material.*

Associated & Subsidiary Companies:
UK: The Casarotto Co Ltd *(dramatic rights)*

Rights Representative in UK for:
USA: J de S Associates Inc, South Norwalk, CT

Overseas Representation *(see §7.5)*:
Brazil: Carmen Balcells Agencia Literaria, Rio
de Janeiro
France: Michelle Lapautre, Paris
Greece: Educational Materials Enterprises Ltd,
Athens
Israel: I. Pikarski Literary Agency, Tel Aviv
Italy: Cooperation, Munich, Germany
Japan: Japan Uni Agency Inc, Tokyo
Netherlands: Andrew Nurnberg Associates
Ltd, London, UK
Scandinavia: Licht & Licht Literary Agency,
Charlottenlund, Denmark
Spain: Carmen Balcells Agencia Literaria,
Barcelona
Switzerland: Mohrbooks Literary Agency,
Zurich
Turkey: Nurcihan Kesim Literary Agency,
Istanbul
USA: JCA Literary Agency Inc, New York, NY

4068 ▬▬▬

**THE MAGGIE NOACH LITERARY
AGENCY**
21 Redan Street, London W14 0AB
Telephone: 0171 602 2451
Fax: 0171 603 4712

Proprietor: Maggie Noach

*All MSS except scientific, academic or
specialist non-fiction, romantic fiction, poetry,
plays, short stories or books for the very young.
Unsolicited MSS not welcome.*

*Specialization: general fiction & non-fiction.
Approach by letter (not by telephone), giving a
brief description of the book and enclosing a
few sample pages. Return postage essential. No
reading fee. Commission: Home 15%, USA &
translation 20%.*

4069 ▬▬▬

**ANDREW NURNBERG ASSOCIATES
LTD**
45-47 Clerkenwell Green, London EC1R 0HT
Telephone: 0171 417 8800
Fax: 0171 417 8812
Email: 100663.727@compuserve.com

Directors: Andrew Nurnberg *(Managing)*
Klaasje Mul
Sarah Nundy

*Specialization: sale of translation rights
throughout the world, representing leading
British & American agents & authors.*

Associated & Subsidiary Companies:
Bulgaria: Andrew Nurnberg Associates, Sofia.
Czech Republic: Andrew Nurnberg Associates,
Prague. *Hungary:* Andrew Nurnberg
Associates, Budapest. *Poland:* Andrew
Nurnberg Associates, Warsaw. *Romania:*
Andrew Nurnberg Associates, Bucharest.

Russia: Andrew Nurnberg Literary Agency
(Moscow)

4070 ▬▬▬

DAVID O'LEARY LITERARY AGENTS
10 Lansdowne Court, Lansdowne Rise, London
W11 2NR
Telephone: 0171 229 1623
Fax: 0171 727 9624

Director: David O'Leary

*All MSS except plays, film & TV scripts, poetry
& children's books.*

*Specialization: fiction: commercial & literary;
non-fiction, particularly historical & scientific.*

Overseas Representation *(see §7.5)*:
Japan: Tuttle-Mori Agency, Tokyo
Scandinavia, Spain, Portugal & Latin America:
Sane Töregard Agency, Karlsham, Sweden
USA: JCA Literary Agency Inc, New York, NY

4071 ▬▬▬

DEBORAH OWEN LTD
78 Narrow Street, Limehouse, London
E14 8BP
Telephone: 0171 987 5119 & 5441
Fax: 0171 538 4004

Literary Agents: Deborah Owen
Gemma Hirst

*All MSS except poetry, children's books, all
scripts for TV, film & theatre, short stories.
Preliminary letter & return postage essential.
No new authors at present.*

*Specialization: works of fiction & non-fiction
with international sales potential.*

4072 ▬▬▬

MARK PATERSON & ASSOCIATES
10 Brook Street, Wivenhoe, Colchester
CO7 9DS
Telephone: 01206 825433
Fax: 01206 822990

Proprietor: Mark Paterson
Associate: Mary Swinney

*All MSS except short stories, articles, song and
play scripts, poetry. Preliminary letter and
return postage required.*

*Specialization: professional psychology,
psychoanalysis, psychotherapy, history,
education.*

Associated & Subsidiary Companies:
Sigmund Freud Copyrights. *UK:* Quentin
Books Ltd

Rights Representative in UK for:
USA: Jason Aronson Inc [translation only],
Northvale, NJ; Brunner Mazel Inc, New
York, NY; Gardner Press, Lakeworth, FL;
The Guilford Press, New York, NY;
International Universities Press, Madison,
CT; Albert Whitman & Co, Morton Grove,
IL

4073

JOHN PAWSEY
60 High Street, Tarring, Worthing, West Sussex
BN14 7NR
Telephone: 01903 205167
Fax: 01903 205167

Sole Proprietor: John Pawsey

*All MSS except poetry, short stories,
journalism, original film & stage scripts.*

*Specialization: sport, leisure, business, current
affairs, popular fiction.*

Rights Representative in UK for:
USA: Marcia Amsterdam, New York; Bonus
Books Inc, Chicago, IL; Columbia Literary
Associates, Elliott City, MD; Marilyn
Connor, New York, NY; Ethan Ellenberg
Literary Agency, New York, NY; IMG
Literary, New York; Lyons & Burford, New
York; Lynn Seligman, Upper Montclair, NJ;
Bobbe Siegel, New York

Overseas Representation *(see §7.5):*
China: Bardon Agency, Taipei, Taiwan
France: Lora Fountain, Paris
Germany: Thomas Schlück, Garbsen
Hungary: Lex Copyright, Budapest
Italy: Living Literary Agency, Milan
Japan: The English Agency Japan Ltd, Tokyo
Netherlands & Scandinavia: Jennifer Luithlen,
Leicester, UK
Russia: Prava I Prevodi, Moscow
Spain & South America: International Editors
Co, Barcelona, Spain
Turkey: Nurcihan Kesim Literary Agency,
Istanbul
USA: IMG Literary, New York
Yugoslav States: Prava & Prevodi, Belgrade,
Yugoslavia

4074

**MAGGIE PEARLSTINE ASSOCIATES
LTD**
31 Ashley Gardens, Ambrosden Avenue,
Westminster, London SW1P 1QE
Telephone: 0171 828 4212
Fax: 0171 834 5546
Email: mp@authsagt.demon.co.uk

Translation Rights:
Aitken & Stone Ltd, London

Director: Maggie Pearlstine

*All MSS except poetry, plays, film scripts,
children's and short stories (other than from
existing clients). Preliminary letter required
with SAE.*

*Specialization: full length fiction & general
non-fiction. Member of Association of Authors'
Agents.*

4075

**THE PENMAN LITERARY SERVICE
(AGENCY DEPARTMENT)**
185 Daws Heath Road, Benfleet, Essex
SS7 2TF
Telephone: 01702 557431

Director: Mark Sorrell

All MSS except plays.

*Specialization: most types of fiction and non-
fiction.*

4076

**THE PETERS FRASER & DUNLOP
GROUP LTD**
503–504, The Chambers, Chelsea Harbour,
Lots Road, London SW10 0XF
Telephone: 0171 344 1000
Fax: 0171 352 7356 & 351 1756
Email: rscoular@pfd.co.uk

Joint Chairmen: Anthony Jones
Michael Sissons
Directors: Anthony Baring *(Managing)*
Kenneth Ewing
Pat Kavanagh
Tim Corrie
Maureen Vincent
Norman North
Mark Lucas
Caroline Dawnay
Ginette Chalmers

*All MSS except foreign. No unsolicited MSS.
Please write with full synopsis.*

*Specialization: fiction, film & TV scripts, plays,
general non-fiction, children's books,
electronic and multimedia.*

Rights Representative in UK for:
USA: SLL Inc, New York, NY

Overseas Representation *(see §7.5):*
USA: Chelsea West Inc, New York; SLL Inc,
New York, NY

4077

PHOEBE PHILLIPS
57 Melrose Avenue, Wimbledon Park, London
SW19 8BU
Telephone: 0181 897 7130
Fax: 0181 897 7130

*Specialization: non-fiction illustrated and
children's books, history and the Arts.*

4078

LAURENCE POLLINGER LTD
18 Maddox Street, Mayfair, London W1R 0EU
Telephone: 0171 629 9761
Fax: 0171 629 9765

Managing Director: Gerald J. Pollinger
Directors: Miss Heather Chalcroft
(Translation & Anthology Rights)
Miss Juliet Burton *(Fiction and Non-Fiction)*
Mrs Lesley Hadcroft *(Children's Books)*
Company Secretary: Denzil de Silva

*All MSS except poetry & plays, film scripts &
articles.*

Rights Representative in UK for:
USA: James Allen, Milford, PA; Max
Gartenberg, New York, NY; Ben F. Kamsler
Ltd, Van Nuys, CA; Virginia Kidd Literary
Agency, Milford, PA; Mystery Writers of
America, New York, NY; New Directions
Publishing Corporation, New York, NY;
John K. Payne Literary Agency Inc, New

York, NY; Evelyn Singer Agency Inc, White
Plains, NY

Overseas Representation *(see §7.5):*
Asia Pacific Region: Electra Media Group Pty
Ltd, Sydney, NSW, Australia
Denmark & Finland: Licht & Licht Literary
Agency, Charlottenlund, Denmark
France: Michelle Lapautre, Paris
Hungary: Lex Copyright, Budapest
Italy: Luigi Bernabó Associates Srl, Milan
Japan: Tuttle-Mori Agency, Tokyo
Netherlands: Lijnkamp Literary Agents,
Amsterdam
Norway: Suzanne Palme Literary Agency, Oslo
Portugal & Brazil: Ilidio da Fonseca Matos,
Lisbon, Portugal
Russia: Prava I Prevodi, Moscow
Spain & South America: Carmen Balcells
Agencia Literaria, Barcelona, Spain
Sweden: Gösta Dahl & Son, Bromma
Switzerland: Mohrbooks Literary Agency,
Zurich
*Yugoslav States, Bulgaria, Poland, Czech/
Slovak Rep. & Romania:* Prava & Prevodi,
Belgrade, Yugoslavia

4079

*MURRAY POLLINGER
222 Old Brompton Road, London SW5 0BZ
Telephone: 0171 373 4711
Fax: 0171 373 3775

Adult Books: Murray Pollinger *(Proprietor)*
Sara Menguc *(Associate Agent)*
Children's Books: Gina Pollinger
Translation Rights: Kiran Kataria

*All MSS except poetry, plays & articles. No
unsolicited MSS will be considered without
prior letter.*

*Specialization: fiction MSS, general non-
fiction, children's books.*

Rights Representative in UK for:
USA: The Helen Brann Agency, Bridgewater,
CT; John Hawkins & Associates, New York,
NY; Lila Karpf, New York, NY; The Martell
Agency, New York, NY; Philip G. Spitzer
Literary Agency, New York, NY

Overseas Representation *(see §7.5):*
Brazil: Agencia Literaria CB Ltda, Rio de
Janeiro
Eastern Europe: Lex Copyright, Budapest,
Hungary
France: Michelle Lapautre, Paris
German-speaking: Mohrbooks Literary
Agency, Zurich, Switzerland
Italy: Agenzia Letteraria Internazionale Srl,
Milan
Japan: Tuttle-Mori Agency, Tokyo
Netherlands: Kooy & van Gelderen,
Amsterdam
Portugal & Spanish-speaking: Carmen
Balcells Agencia Literaria, Barcelona, Spain
Scandinavia: Leonhardt Literary Agency,
Copenhagen, Denmark

4080

**SHELLEY POWER LITERARY
AGENCY LTD**
Le Montaud, 24220 Berbiguières, France
Telephone: +33 53 29 62 52

Fax: +33 53 29 62 54
Email: puissant@easynet.fr

Agent: Shelley Power

*All MSS except short stories & features, plays &
poetry, children's books. Please send SAE with
submissions but preliminary letter essential.*

*Specialization: general fiction and non-fiction;
business, true crime & exposés; film &
entertainment; self-help.*

Rights Representative in UK for:
USA: The Connor Agency, Edina, MN;
   Marlowe & Co, New York; Martha Millard
   Agency, Madison; Thunder's Mouth Press,
   New York, NY

Overseas Representation *(see §7.5)*:
France: Agence Littéraire Hoffman, Paris,
   Netherlands
Germany: Liepman AG, Zurich, Switzerland
Greece: JLM Literary Agency, Athens
Israel: Ilana Pikarski Literary Agency, Tel
   Aviv
Italy: Eulama Srl, Rome
Scandinavia: Ulla Løhren Literary Agency,
   Bagsvaerd, Denmark
South Africa: International Press Agency Pty
   Ltd, Howard Place, Cape Town
Spain: Julio F. Yañez Agencia Literaria,
   Barcelona
USA: Martha Millard Agency, Madison

4081

PVA MANAGEMENT LIMITED
Hallow Park, Worcester WR2 6PG
Telephone: 01905 640663
Fax: 01905 641842

Managing Director: Paul Vaughan
Assistant to Managing Director: Lisa Ventura

All MSS except short MSS.

*Specialization: non-fiction with some fiction,
together with established film, television and
radio scriptwriters. (Home and overseas 15%).*

4082

*RADALA & ASSOCIATES
17 Avenue Mansions, Finchley Road, London
NW3 7AX
Telephone: 0171 794 4495
Fax: 0171 431 7636

Director: Richard Gollner
Associates: Neil Hornick
Anna Swan
Andy Marino

All MSS except badly written ones.

*Specialization: fiction, biography, writing from
Eastern Europe, psychotherapy. Also handle:
theatre, TV & radio scripts, audio tapes,
computer software.*

Associated & Subsidiary Companies:
USA: Waterside Productions Inc; Writer's
House Inc

Overseas Representation *(see §7.5)*:
USA: Waterside Productions Inc, Cardiff-by-
   the-Sea, CA; Writers House Inc, New York,
   NY

4083

ROGERS, COLERIDGE & WHITE LTD
20 Powis Mews, London W11 1JN
Telephone: 0171 221 3717
Fax: 0171 229 9084

Directors: Deborah Rogers
Gill Coleridge
Pat White *(USA)*
Consultant: Ann Warnford-Davies
Foreign Rights: Clare Loeffler
Carol Jackson

*All MSS except poetry, plays & technical books.
No unsolicited MSS please, and no submission
via Fax.*

Rights Representative in UK for:
USA: Donadio & Ashworth, New York, NY;
   Maxine Groffsky Inc, New York, NY; ICM,
   New York, NY; Melanie Jackson, New York,
   NY

Overseas Representation *(see §7.5)*:
Germany: Paul & Peter Fritz AG Literary
   Agency, Zurich, Switzerland
Italy: Roberto Santachiara Literary Agency,
   Pavia

4084

HILARY RUBINSTEIN BOOKS
61 Clarendon Road, London W11 4JE
Telephone: 0171 792 4282
Fax: 0171 221 5291

Managing Director: Hilary Rubinstein

*All MSS except plays, scripts, poetry or
children's books. No reading fee but no
unsolicited MSS without preliminary letter or
call.*

*Specialization: full-length MSS. Fiction and
non-fiction (home 10%, overseas 20%). Will
suggest revision where appropriate.*

Overseas Representation *(see §7.5)*:
Canada: Lucinda Vardey Agency, Toronto
European Community: Andrew Nurnberg
   Associates Ltd, London, UK
USA: Ellen Levine Literary Agency Inc, New
   York, NY

4085

TESSA SAYLE AGENCY
11 Jubilee Place, London SW3 3TE
Telephone: 0171 823 3883
Fax: 0171 823 3363

Partners: Rachel Calder *(Books)*
Jane Villiers *(TV & Film)*

All MSS except children's, poetry.

Specialization: books, TV & film scripts.

Rights Representative in UK for:
USA: Darhansoff & Verrill Literary Agency,
   New York, NY

Overseas Representation *(see §7.5)*:
Brazil: Mrs Karin Schindler, São Paulo
China & Taiwan: Big Apple Tuttle-Mori
   Agency Inc, Taipei, Taiwan
France: Michelle Lapautre, Paris
Germany: Liepman AG, Zurich, Switzerland
Hungary: Lex Copyright, Budapest
Israel: I. Pikarski Literary Agency, Tel Aviv
Italy: Agenzia Letteraria Internazionale Srl,
   Milan
Japan: Tuttle-Mori Agency, Tokyo
Netherlands & Russia: Andrew Nurnberg
   Associates Ltd, London, UK
Scandinavia: The Marsh Agency, London, UK
Spain: International Editors Co, Barcelona
Turkey: Nurcihan Kesim Literary Agency,
   Istanbul
USA: Darhansoff & Verrill Literary Agency,
   New York, NY
*Yugoslav States, Poland, Czech & Slovak Rep,
   Greece & Bulgaria:* Prava & Prevodi,
   Belgrade, Yugoslavia

4086

SHEIL LAND ASSOCIATES LTD
43 Doughty Street, London WC1N 2LF
Telephone: 0171 405 9351
Fax: 0171 831 2127

Foreign Rights Department:
19 John Street, London WC1N 2DL
Telephone: 0171 405 7473
Fax: 0171 405 5239

Chief Executive: Sonia Land
Chairman: Anthony Sheil
Literary Agents: Vivien Green
Robert Kirby
Simon Trewin
Film/TV Agent: John Rush
Foreign Rights Agent: Benita Edzard

*Specialization: handles full-length general and
literary fiction, biography, travel, cookery and
humour. Also theatre, film and TV scripts.
Foreign rights. Sheil Land represents over 270
established clients and welcomes approaches
from new clients looking to start or to develop
their careers. Preliminary letter with SAE
essential. No reading fee. Clients include Peter
Ackroyd, Melvyn Bragg, Catherine Cookson,
John Fowles, Susan Hill, HRH The Prince of
Wales, Michael Ignatieff, John Keegan,
Richard Mabey, Eddy Shah, Tom Sharpe, Rick
Smolan, Rose Tremain. Commission: home
10%, US & translation 20%.*

Rights Representative in UK for:
USA: Farrar, Straus & Giroux (Richard Scott
   Simon)

Overseas Representation *(see §7.5)*:
USA: Georges Borchardt Inc (Richard Scott
   Simon); Ed Breslin Agency Ltd (Sheil Land
   Associates Ltd)

4087

**CAROLINE SHELDON LITERARY
AGENCY**
71 Hillgate Place, London W8
Telephone: 0171 727 9102

Literary Agent: Caroline Sheldon

All MSS except short stories.

Specialization: fiction, women's fiction & children's books.

Overseas Representation *(see §7.5):*
Europe & Japan: Jennifer Luithlen, Leicester, UK

4088

JEFFREY SIMMONS
10 Lowndes Square, London SW1X 9HA
Telephone: 0171 235 8852
Fax: 0171 235 9733

All MSS except children's books, cookery, science-fiction, romances & some specialist subjects.

Specialization: biography & memoirs; cinema, drama & the arts; general fiction; history; law & crime; literature; politics & world affairs; travel.

Overseas Representation *(see §7.5):*
France: Jean-Pierre Boscq, Paris
Germany: Michael Meller Agency, Munich
Greece: JLM Literary Agency, Athens
Japan: The English Agency Japan Ltd, Tokyo; Japan Uni Agency, Tokyo
Spain: Julio F. Yañez Agencia Literaria, Barcelona

4089

*CAROL SMITH LITERARY AGENCY
25 Hornton Court, Kensington High Street, London W8 7RT
Telephone: 0171 937 4874/5
Fax: 0171 938 5323

Proprietor: Carol Smith

All MSS except technical & children's.

Specialization: new fiction.

Overseas Representation *(see §7.5):*
Denmark, Finland, Norway & Sweden: Licht & Licht Literary Agency, Charlottenlund, Denmark
France: La Nouvelle Agence, Paris
Germany: Liepman AG, Zurich, Switzerland
Greece: Educational Materials Enterprises Ltd, Athens
Israel: I. Pikarski Literary Agency, Tel Aviv
Italy: Susanna Zevi, Milan
Japan: The English Agency Japan Ltd, Tokyo
Netherlands: Andrew Nurnberg Associates Ltd, London, UK
Spain: International Editors Co, Barcelona
USA: Jonathan Dolger, New York, NY

4090

SOLO LITERARY AGENCY LTD
49–53 Kensington High Street, London W8 5ED
Telephone: 0171 376 2166
Fax: 0171 938 3165

Chairman & Managing Director: Don Short
Company Secretary: Wendy Short

Specialization: autobiographies, biographies: celebrities, statesmen & international figures; worldwide newspaper syndication chain. All

non-fiction MSS. Fiction from professional writers only.

Parent Company:
Solo Syndication Ltd *(UK)*

Associated & Subsidiary Companies:
Solo Books Ltd; Solo Vision Ltd

4091

ABNER STEIN
10 Roland Gardens, London SW7 3PH
Telephone: 0171 373 0456
Fax: 0171 370 6316

Director: Abner Stein

All MSS except unsolicited MSS unless they are preceded by a preliminary letter describing the work.

Specialization: full-length fiction & non-fiction.

Overseas Representation *(see §7.5):*
Worldwide (translation only): Rosemarie Buckman, Oxford, UK

4092

PETER TAUBER PRESS AGENCY
94 East End Road, London N3 2SX
Telephone: 0181 346 4165

Directors: Peter Tauber
Robert Tauber

All MSS except poetry, short stories, children's, scripts, technical & foreign language. Non-returnable submission fee of £50 plus SAE must be sent with all submissions.

Specialization: women's fiction, horror, thrillers, fantasy, crime and autobiographies of the famous only.

Rights Representative in UK for:
USA: Acropolis Books Ltd, Reston, VA; Avery Publishing Group Inc, Garden City Park, NY; New Century Publishers, Piscataway, NJ

4093

J. M. THURLEY MANAGEMENT
213 Linen Hall, 162–168 Regent Street, London W1R 5TA
Telephone: 0171 437 9545
Fax: 0171 287 9208

Executive: Jon Thurley
Editorial: Patricia Preece

All MSS except short stories & poetry.

Specialization: will give editorial help by arrangement on all types of projects.

4094

LAVINIA TREVOR
6 The Glasshouse, 49A Goldhawk Road, London W12 8QP
Telephone: 0181 749 8481
Fax: 0181 749 7377

Agent: Lavinia Trevor

All MSS except poetry, academic or technical work, film scripts and plays.

Specialization: general non-fiction and fiction. Material must be accompanied by an sae.

4095

ED VICTOR LTD
6 Bayley Street, Bedford Square, London WC1B 3HB
Telephone: 0171 304 4100
Fax: 0171 304 4111

Directors: Ed Victor *(Managing)*
Leon Morgan
Carol Ryan
Margaret Phillips
Graham Greene, CBE
Sophie Hicks *(Foreign Rights & Children's Books)*

All MSS except short stories; poetry; technical.

Specialization: fiction; biography; children's books.

Overseas Representation *(see §7.5):*
Worldwide: Andrew Nurnberg Associates Ltd, London, UK

4096

*S. WALKER LITERARY AGENCY
96 Church Lane, Goldington, Bedford MK41 0AS
Telephone: 01234 216229

Partners: Alan Oldfield
Cora-Louise Oldfield
Consultant: E. K. Walker

All MSS except short topical articles, poetry & children's stories. No unsolicited synopses or MSS.

4097

WARNER CHAPPELL PLAYS LTD
[formerly English Theatre Guild]
129 Park Street, London W1Y 3FA
Telephone: 0171 514 5236
Fax: 0171 514 5201
Email: warner.chappell@dial.pipex.com

Manager: Michael Callahan

Specialization: dramatic works, publishing plays, acquisition of stage rights & promotion of plays.

Parent Company:
Warner Chappell Music Ltd

Rights Representative in UK for:
USA: Dramatists Play Service Inc, New York, NY

Overseas Representation *(see §7.5):*
Australia: Warner Chappell & Co (Australia) Pty Ltd, North Sydney, NSW
Canada & USA: Dramatists Play Service Inc, New York, NY, USA
New Zealand: Play Bureau (NZ) Ltd, New Plymouth

South Africa: Dalro (Pty) Ltd, Johannesburg
Zimbabwe: National Theatre Organization,
  Harare

4098

WATSON, LITTLE LTD
12 Egbert Street, London NW1 8LJ
Telephone: 0171 722 9514
Fax: 0171 586 7649

Directors: Sheila Watson
Amanda Little
Foreign & Electronic Rights: Sugra Zaman

*All MSS except short stories, plays, poetry,
works for very small children & articles (except
by established columnists).*

*Specialization: fiction, non-fiction &
multimedia; popular science, psychology, self
help; history; business books; gardening.*

Associated & Subsidiary Companies:
UK: The Sharland Organisation *(Dramatic
Associate)*

Rights Representative in UK for:
USA: Barrie Van Dyck Agency Inc,
  Philadelphia, PA
USA (Juvenile list): McIntosh & Otis Inc, New
  York, NY, USA

Overseas Representation *(see §7.5):*
Bulgaria: Interrights Literary & Translation
  Agency, Sofia
Czech & Slovak Republics: Interlit Services,
  Prague, Czech Republic
France: La Nouvelle Agence, Paris
Germany, Austria & Switzerland: Mohrbooks
  Literary Agency, Zurich, Switzerland
Greece: JLM Literary Agency, Athens
Hungary: Lex Copyright, Budapest
Israel: Ilana Pikarski Literary Agency, Tel
  Aviv
Italy: Agenzia Letteraria Internazionale Srl,
  Milan
Japan: Tuttle-Mori Agency, Tokyo
Korea: DRT International Ltd, Seoul, Korea,
  South
Netherlands: Lijnkamp Literary Agents,
  Amsterdam
Poland: Helfa Ltd Literary Agency, Warsaw;
  Maria Strarz-Kánska Literary Agency Ltd,
  Krakow
Romania: Simona Kessler Literary Agency,
  Bucharest
Scandinavia & Iceland: Suzanne Palme
  Literary Agency, Oslo, Norway
South Africa: The International Press Agency,
  Ndabeni
South America: Carmen Balcells Agencia
  Literaria, Rio de Janeiro, Brazil
Spain & Portugal: Carmen Balcells Agencia
  Literaria, Barcelona, Spain
Taiwan: Big Apple Tuttle-Mori Agency Inc,
  Taipei
Thailand: Tuttle-Mori Big Apple Agency
  (Thailand) Co Ltd, Bangkok
USA: McIntosh & Otis Inc, New York, NY

4099

A. P. WATT LTD
20 John Street, London WC1N 2DR
Telephone: 0171 405 6774
Fax: 0171 831 2154

Directors: Caradoc King
Linda Shaughnessy
Rod Hall
Lisa Eveleigh
Nick Marston
Derek Johns

All MSS except poetry.

Rights Representative in UK for:
USA: The Axelrod Agency, Lenox, MA; The
  Robbins Office Inc, New York, NY; Scovil
  Chichak Galen Literary Agents Inc, New
  York, NY

Overseas Representation *(see §7.5):*
Brazil: Mrs Karin Schindler, São Paulo
Bulgaria: Planeta Literary Agency, Sofia
Czech Republic: Petra Tobiskova, Prague
France: La Nouvelle Agence, Paris
Germany: Mohrbooks Literary Agency,
  Zurich, Switzerland
Greece: Nelly Moucacou, Halandri
Hungary: Artisjus Agency for Literature &
  Theatre, Budapest
Israel: Ilana Pikarski Literary Agency, Tel
  Aviv
Netherlands: Andrew Nurnberg Associates
  Ltd, London, UK
Poland: Maria Strarz-Kánska Literary Agency
  Ltd, Krakow
Romania: International Copyright Agency Ltd,
  Bucharest
Russia: Andrew Nurnberg Literary Agency,
  Moscow
Spain & Portugal: Carmen Balcells Agencia
  Literaria, Barcelona, Spain
Turkey: Nurcihan Kesim Literary Agency,
  Istanbul
USA: Scovil Chichak Galen Literary Agents
  Inc, New York, NY

4100

*JOHN WELCH
Milton House, 28 Fen Road, Milton,
Cambridge CB4 6AD
Telephone: 01223 860641
Fax: 01223 440575

Proprietor: John Welch

All MSS except poetry, plays, film & TV scripts.

*Specialization: military history, art, biography,
history, some sports, children's books &
theology. Preliminary letter required.*

4101

DINAH WIENER LTD
27 Arlington Road, London NW1 7ER
Telephone: 0171 388 2577
Fax: 0171 388 7559

Directors: Dinah Wiener
D. P. Wiener
B. M. Wiener

*All MSS except juvenile, plays, film scripts,
poetry & short stories.*

Specialization: general fiction and non-fiction.

AUSTRALIA

4102

CURTIS BROWN (AUSTRALIA) PTY LTD
27 Union Street, Paddington, Sydney,
NSW 2021
Telephone: +61 (02) 331 5301 & 361 6161
Fax: +61 (02) 360 3935

Chairman: Jonathan Lloyd
Directors: Tim Curnow *(Managing)*
Fiona Inglis
Anthea Morton Saner *(UK)*
Diana Mackay *(UK)*
Agents (in Australia): Tim Curnow
Fiona Inglis

*Specialization: fiction & non-fiction,
children's, stage, film, TV scripts.*

Parent Company:
Curtis Brown Group Ltd *(UK)*

Associated & Subsidiary Companies:
Canada: Curtis Brown Ltd. *UK:* Curtis Brown
Ltd

CANADA

4103

AUTHORS' MARKETING SERVICES LTD
200 Simpson Avenue, Suite 200, Toronto,
Ont M4K 1A6
Telephone: +1 (416) 463 7200
Fax: +1 (416) 469 4494
Email: 102047.1111@compuserve.com

President: Larry Hoffman
Vice-President: Antonia Hoffman

*All MSS except screenplays, poetry & short
stories.*

*Specialization: fiction (action/adventure,
romance & woman's interest), business, self-
help & parenting.*

4104

BELLA POMER AGENCY INC
22 Shallmar Blvd PH2, Toronto, Ont M5N 2Z8
Telephone: +1 (416) 781 8597
Fax: +1 (416) 782 4196

President: Bella Pomer

*All MSS except how-to books, cook books,
religious, popular psychology, fantasy or
science-fiction, horror, thrillers.*

*Specialization: a wide range of fiction from
commercial to literary; general interest non-
fiction. No unsolicited manuscripts. List is
closed at present to additional authors.*

Overseas Representation *(see §7.5):*
Australia: Australian Literary Management
Brazil: International Editors Co
*Czech & Slovak Republics, Poland, Russia &
  Yugoslavia:* Prava I Prevodi, Moscow,
  Russia
France: Michelle Lapautre, Paris

Germany: Liepman AG, Zurich, Switzerland
Greece: JLM Literary Agency, Athens
Hungary: Katai & Bolza, Budapest
Israel: I. Pikarski Literary Agency, Tel Aviv
Italy: Grandi & Vitali, Milan
Japan: The English Agency Japan Ltd, Tokyo
Korea: Imprima Korea, Seoul, Korea, South
Netherlands: Andrew Nurnberg Associates
Romania: Simona Kessler Literary Agency, Bucharest
Scandinavia: Suzanne Palme Literary Agency, Oslo, Norway
Spain & Portugal: International Editors Co, Barcelona, Spain
Taiwan: Big Apple Tuttle-Mori Agency Inc, Taipei
Turkey: Akcali & Tuna, Istanbul
UK: Blake Friedmann Literary Agency, London

4105

BEVERLEY SLOPEN LITERARY AGENCY
131 Bloor Street West, Suite 711, Toronto, Ont M5S 1S3
Telephone: +1 (416) 964 9598
Fax: +1 (416) 921 7726
Email: slopen@inforamp.net

All MSS except children's, drama, technical, screenplays, poetry, short stories, cook books & how-to books.

Specialization: general list of trade titles; mainly Canadian authors. We do not accept unsolicited MSS.

Overseas Representation *(see §7.5):*
France: Michelle Lapautre, Paris
Germany: Paul & Peter Fritz AG Literary Agency, Zurich, Switzerland
Italy: Agenzia Letteraria Internazionale Srl, Milan
Japan: Tuttle-Mori Agency, Tokyo
Scandinavia: Ulla Løhren Literary Agency, Oslo, Norway
Spain: Julio F. Yañez Agencia Literaria, Barcelona
UK: Lavinia Trevor Literary Agency, London

4106

WESTWOOD CREATIVE ARTISTS LTD
[formerly Lucinda Vardey Agency]
10 St Mary Street, Suite 510, Toronto, Ont M4Y 1P9
Telephone: +1 (416) 922 0250
Fax: +1 (416) 925 4943

Chairman: Michael Levine
President/Agent: Bruce Westwood
Associate Agents: Janice Whitford
Linda McKnight

All MSS except children's books, textbooks, academic titles, science-fiction, romance, poetry & plays.

Specialization: general trade, fiction & non-fiction; titles with emphasis on the international marketplace. Authors must be Canadian residents.

Overseas Representation *(see §7.5):*
Bulgaria: Nika Literary Agency, Sofia

China, Korea & Japan: Tuttle-Mori Agency, Tokyo, Japan
Croatia: Maja Mihic
France: Michelle Lapautre, Paris
Germany: Liepman AG, Zurich, Switzerland
Greece: Educational Materials Enterprises Ltd, Athens
Israel: I. Pikarski Literary Agency, Tel Aviv
Italy: Agenzia Antonella Antonelli, Milan
Netherlands & CIS: Andrew Nurnberg Associates Ltd, London, UK
Poland: Maria Strarz-Kánska Literary Agency Ltd, Krakow
Scandinavia: Licht & Licht Literary Agency, Charlottenlund, Denmark
Slovakia: GP Agentur, Bratislava
Spain, Portugal & South America: Mercedes Casanovas Agency, Barcelona, Spain
Turkey: Akcali & Tuna, Istanbul
UK: Felicity Bryan

INDIA

4107

JAFFE PUBLISHING MANAGEMENT SERVICE
Kunnuparambil Buildings, Kurichy, Kottayam 686 549
Telephone: +91 (0481) 430 470
Fax: +91 (0481) 561 190

President: K. P. Punnoose
Chief Executive: Shaji Jacob
Managing Editor: Jaffe K. Punnoose

Specialization: promoting the exchange of publishing rights between publishers in India and other countries, free information, feedback and guidance to authors interested in selling rights to India and to overseas publishers who want to buy rights from India.

Parent Company:
Jaffe Punnoose & Co *(India)*

Associated & Subsidiary Companies:
India: Jaffe International Education Service

IRISH REPUBLIC

4108

JONATHAN WILLIAMS LITERARY AGENCY
2 Mews, 10 Sandycove Avenue West, Sandycove, Co Dublin
Telephone: +353 (01) 280 3482
Fax: +353 (01) 280 3482

Director: Jonathan Williams

All MSS except plays or film scripts. Return postage and packing is appreciated.

Specialization: typescripts of Irish interest.

NEW ZEALAND

4109

GLENYS BEAN LITERARY AGENCY
PO Box 47098, Auckland

Telephone: +64 (09) 378 6287
Fax: +64 (09) 378 6287

Director: Fay Weldon

Specialization: full length MSS, fiction, non-fiction, juvenile, educational; film, TV & radio.

Overseas Representation *(see §7.5):*
Europe (translation): Benita Edzard Sheil Land, London, UK
USA: Dan Mandel, New York

4110

MICHAEL GIFKINS & ASSOCIATES
Box 6496, Auckland 1
Telephone: +64 (09) 630 3562
Fax: +64 (09) 630 3562

Location:
7 Carrick Place, Mt Eden, Auckland 3
Telephone: *(as above)*
Fax: *(as above)*

Executive: Michael Gifkins

Specialization: literary fiction; general trade books; children's fiction, film & TV; co-publications; literary event management; editorial and consultancy services. International representation.

4111

PLAYMARKET
PO Box 9767, Te Aro, Wellington
Telephone: +64 (04) 382 8462
Fax: +64 (04) 382 8461

Location:
Level 2, 16 Cambridge Terrace, Wellington
Telephone: *(as above)*

Executive Officer: John McDavitt
Script Advisor: Susan Wilson
Administrative Assistant: Stephanie Creed

Specialization: agency for New Zealand's playwrights and script development & marketing service.

Associated & Subsidiary Companies:
Australia: Currency Press

4112

RICHARDS LITERARY AGENCY
PO Box 31240, Milford, Auckland
Telephone: +64 (09) 410 5681
Fax: +64 (09) 410 6389

Street Address:
49c Aberdeen Road, Castor Bay, Auckland
Telephone: (as above)
Fax: (as above)

Partners: Ray Richards
Barbara Richards

All MSS except articles, short stories, verse.

Specialization: adult fiction & non-fiction; juvenile & young adult; educational; academic, scientific & technical; drama for films, TV and radio; photography & illustrations.

4113

TFS TOTAL FICTION SERVICES
PO Box 29-023, Ngaio, Wellington
Telephone: +64 (04) 479 6746
Fax: +64 (04) 479 6746
Email: else@ihug.co.nz

Partners: Chris Else
Barbara Else

All MSS except journalism, single short stories, film, TV or stage scripts, specialist non-fiction or poetry.

Specialization: literary agency & manuscript assessment, working with writers through its assessment service to develop projects to publication standard and beyond. Fiction, children's, general non-fiction. English language only. Preliminary letter essential.

Associated & Subsidiary Companies:
UK: TFS Literary Agency

Overseas Representation *(see §7.5)*:
UK: TFS Literary Agency

SOUTH AFRICA

4114

FRANCES BOND LITERARY SERVICES
32b Stanley Teale Road, Westville North, Kwazulu, 3630
Telephone: +27 (031) 82 4532
Fax: +27 (031) 82 2620

Postal Address:
PO Box 223, Westville, Kwazulu, 3630
Fax: +27 (031) 82 2620

Managing Editor: Frances Bond
Chief Editor: Eileen Molver

All MSS except poetry & short stories.

Specialization: fiction, non-fiction & children's fiction.

Overseas Representation *(see §7.5)*:
Worldwide: Forest Publishers, South Africa

4115

CHEROKEE LITERACY AGENCY
3 Blythwood Road, Rondebosch, Cape, 7700
Telephone: +27 (021) 61 4508

Executive: Donna Kay Lee

Specialization: negotiation of contracts with overseas publishers for children's picture books in translation—mainly into Afrikaans, Xhosa, Zulu, South Sotho and Tswana.

4116

INTERNATIONAL PRESS AGENCY LTD
PO Box 67, Howard Place, 7450
Telephone: +27 (021) 531 1926
Fax: +27 (021) 531 8789

Manager: Terry Temple

Specialization: agents for South African publishers and authors for the sale of translation and other rights, children's and young readers' books only: sub-agents for British, American and other publishers and agents for the sale of translation rights in South Africa, children's books only. Also handle serial rights in South Africa in adult books, English and Afrikaans.

Overseas Representation *(see §7.5)*:
UK: Dr Ursula A. Barnett, Surbiton

4117

*LITERARY DYNAMICS
Suite 222, PO Box 51037, Musgrave 4062
Telephone: +27 (031) 3092913
Fax: +27 (031) 3092913

Also at:
2 Beirnfels, 170 Cowey Road, Berea, Durban, 4001

Director: Isabel Cooke

All MSS except poetry, short stories, articles, children's literature.

Specialization: adult fiction, women's issues, non-fiction & TV scripts. Will provide fiction writing tuition. Public speaking consultant, corporate consultant.

4118

SANDTON LITERARY AGENCY
PO Box 785799, Sandton 2146
Telephone: +27 (011) 442 8624
Fax: +27 (011) 442 8624

Directors: V. Canning
M. Sutherland

All MSS except poetry or books for children under 12 years old.

Specialization: MSS for commercial gain. Reading fee, mainly for fiction, for which editing and a report, will be provided. Services for accepted MSS include US & Commonwealth rights, film, TV & radio rights.

Rights Representative in UK for:
USA: Renaissance-Swan Film Agency Inc, Los Angeles, CA

Overseas Representation *(see §7.5)*:
Zimbabwe: Rosemary Kimberley, Harare

5 Trade & Allied Associations

5.1 INTERNATIONAL

5001

**AGENCE FRANCOPHONE POUR LA NUMÉROTATION
INTERNATIONALE DU LIVRE (AFNIL)**
30 rue Dauphine, 75006 Paris, France
Telephone: +33 1 44 41 28 00
Fax: +33 1 44 07 20 33

Director: Mrs Martine Gueguen

Founded in 1972 for the allocation and operation of International Book
Numbering for books published in France or by French language
publishers in Belgium, Switzerland and Francophone African countries.

5002

ASSOCIATION INTERNATIONALE DE BIBLIOPHILIE
58 rue Richelieu, 75084 Paris Cédex 02, France
Telephone: +33 1 47 03 77 57
Fax: +33 1 47 03 75 70

Also at:
1 rue Sully, 77004 Paris, France

President: Anthony R. A. Hobson
Treasurer: Bernard Skalli

Organizes congresses and colloquium. The XX Congrès international de
Bibliophilie will be held in Netherlands, September 1997.

5003

CAB INTERNATIONAL
Wallingford, Oxon OX10 8DE
Telephone: 01491 832111
Fax: 01491 833508

Director of Publishing: Tony Llewellyn
Deputy Director General, Information: Dr Colin Ogbourne

CAB INTERNATIONAL (CABI) is dedicated to improving human
welfare worldwide through the dissemination, application and generation
of scientific knowledge in support of sustainable development, with
emphasis on agriculture, forestry, human health and the management of
natural resources, and with particular attention to the needs of developing
countries.
    CABI is a treaty level, international, intergovernmental organization
with 39 member countries. Originally established to assist agricultural

development in Commonwealth countries the organization was granted
international status in 1985 and member countries now include the
following non-Commonwealth countries: China, Colombia, Hungary,
Vietnam, Pakistan, Myanmar and the Philippines.
    The CAB INTERNATIONAL Information Institute (CABI-II) is an
international centre for the collection, organization and dissemination of
information on agriculture, forestry, the management of natural
resources, and related sciences including human nutrition and health. It
gives particular attention to the needs of developing countries. CABI-II's
central function is the compilation of bibliographic databases from the
world's technical literature. CABI-II is also an international institute for
information science, with a programme of innovation, project
development and research. It pays special regard to opportunities to
exploit the advance of technology.
    CABI has four scientific institutes: three provide identification and
taxonomic services in the specialities of entomology, mycology and
parasitology. In addition they undertake funded projects in plant
protection, field surveys of pests and beneficial organisms, specialist
research into hygiene and communicable diseases and training for these
topics in many parts of the world as well as in the UK. The fourth institute
has for more than 65 years provided a global service in research, training
and information on integrated pest management (IPM) with emphasis on
biological control.
    A new, corporate information for development programme (IFD),
distinct from CABI's publishing programme, and based on partnership
and collaboration, covers three main areas: capacity-building; sponsored
supply of information products and service; development of new products
and services. The programme's Steering Group comprises: Dr Colin
Ogbourne, Deputy DG (Information), Dr Stephen Rudgard, Head,
Development Projects Unit, and Margot Bellamy, Head of Training and
Development, with assistance from other parts of CABI, including
regional offices in Africa, Asia and the Caribbean.

5004

ENGLISH-SPEAKING UNION OF THE COMMONWEALTH
37 Charles Street, London W1X 8AB
Telephone: 0171 493 3328
Fax: 0171 495 6108

President: HRH The Duke of Edinburgh, KG, KT, OM
Chairman: The Baroness Brigstocke
Director General: Valerie Mitchell

The English-Speaking Union is an international organization with
headquarters in London and in New York. It is a voluntary body and
registered charity existing to promote international friendship and
understanding through a variety of educational and cultural programmes.
    The Books-Across-the-Sea programme is a scheme established during
the Second World War to exchange between Britain and the US books that
were well-written, well-produced and not readily available in each other's

country. A high proportion of the books chosen have not had their publishing rights sold outside their country of origin. The scheme has also occasionally operated between Britain and the countries of the Commonwealth and Eastern Europe. Books selected are exhibited and advertised through the 'Ambassador' booklists.

5005

EUROPEAN CHRISTIAN BOOKSELLERS ASSOCIATION
Grampian House, 144 Deansgate, Manchester M3 3ED
Telephone: 0161 833 3003
Fax: 0161 835 3000

Editor & General Manager: Paul Mitchell
Managers: Steve Mimmack *(Advertising)*
Barry Holmes *(Production)*
Executive Vice-Chairman: John Macdonald

Trade association looking after the interests of member Christian bookshops, publishers, etc throughout the UK, Europe and nearly 50 countries worldwide. Publishes the *European Christian Bookstore Journal*, reflecting all news, activities, companies, personnel, personalities, events, new books, music, video and CD-ROM material produced in the UK for the religious bookstores worldwide. Monitors developments in the publishing industry and media, with special emphasis on Christianity. Produces annual *Buyers Directory of Suppliers & Services* and monthly *Preview Directory* of all new Christian titles.

5006

FÉDÉRATION DES ÉDITEURS EUROPÉENS (FEE)
[Federation of European Publishers (FEP)]
Avenue de Tervuren 92, 1040 Brussels, Belgium
Telephone: +32 (02) 736 36 16
Fax: +32 (02) 736 19 87

President: Volker Schwarz *(Germany)*
Director: Mechthild von Alemann *(Germany)*

Founded in 1967, the Federation of European Publishers (FEP) represents jointly the interests of the European Communities for all matters arising from the treaties. FEP also offers opportunities for exchanging experience and information on issues which are of common concern to the member States of the European Community.
    Activities include lobbying officials of the European Commission and members of the European Parliament about matters relating to books (VAT, price of books, postal rates, etc).

5007

THE FOLKLORE SOCIETY
University College London, Gower Street, London WC1E 6BT
Telephone: 0171 387 5894 *(answerphone)*

President: Jacqueline Simpson
Publicity Officer: Doc Rowe
Hon Secretary & Katharine Briggs Folklore Award Convenor: Dr
    Juliette Wood
Events Officer: George Monger
Publications Officer: Jennifer Chandler

Founded in 1878, the Folklore Society attracts members from all over the world, acting as a point of contact for those interested in folk traditions. Based in London, the Society's library, archive and information service constitute a unique resource for the study of folklore, both old and new, and its role in people's lives. It also embraces a number of specialist groups and encourages the formation of such specific sections based on the particular interests of members.
    Folklore Society events include lectures, conferences and exhibitions held both in London and around the UK.
    Publications: *Folklore*, a journal published annually; a monograph series; *FLS News*, a newsletter; occasional booklets; *New Books in Folklore* and *Current Contents in Folklore*, current awareness publications.
    The Children's Folklore Group, which is a specialist section within the Society devoted to the study of children's traditional culture, organizes its own events and publishes a newsletter for those with an interest in childlore.
    Members receive free copies of *Folklore* and *FLS News*; reduced rates for *New Books in Folklore*, *Current Contents in Folklore* and other selected publications; reduced rates for Society events; access to the Society's library and archives; reduced subscriptions to the Children's Folklore Group.

5008

IBBY – INTERNATIONAL BOARD ON BOOKS FOR YOUNG PEOPLE
Nonnenweg 12, Postfach, 4003 Basle, Switzerland
Telephone: +41 (061) 272 29 17
Fax: +41 (061) 272 27 57

Secretariat (Switzerland): Leena Maissen

Promotion of children's books and reading worldwide.

5009

INTERNATIONAL ASSOCIATION OF SCHOLARLY PUBLISHERS
Aarhus University Press, 8000 Aarhus C, Denmark
Telephone: +45 86 19 70 33
Fax: +45 86 19 84 33

Membership Enquiries:
IASP, J. Paul Getty Museum, Box 2112, Santa Monica, CA 90407-2112, USA
Telephone: +1 (310) 459 7611
Fax: +1 (310) 454 8156

President: Tønnes Bekker-Nielsen
Secretary-General: Christopher Hudson

Founded in 1972, affiliated to IPA. Eligible for membership are the scholarly publishing divisions of regularly constituted colleges, universities and other institutions of higher education, and other publishers not directly related to such institutions who publish a substantial amount of scholarly research. Members must publish two or more scholarly books, or an equivalent amount of material in journal or electronic form, each year.
    Publications: *IASP Newsletter* (6 issues a year; free to members), proceedings from meetings.
    Membership fees: US$120 per year. Subscription to *IASP Newsletter*: US$60. Membership enquiries to: Christopher Hudson, at address above. *Newsletter* subscriptions may be ordered direct from Aarhus University Press or through any major subscription agency.

5010

INTERNATIONAL BOOKSELLERS FEDERATION (IBF)
Bd Lambermont 140/1, 1030 Brussels, Belgium
Telephone: +32 (02) 242 0957
Fax: +32 (02) 242 0957

President: John K. Hedgecock
General Secretary: Christiane Vuidar

The International Booksellers Federation was founded in 1956 to promote closer cooperation, the exchange of information and the discussion of common trade problems. There are 22 national booksellers' associations and over 150 individual members from 20 countries. Matters dealt with regularly include retail price maintenance for books, market research, cooperative advertising, commercial practices, taxes and duties, comparative management, young booksellers in all countries, public relations for booksellers and cooperation between booksellers' trade journals. International congresses are held every four years, and the IBF International Congress of Young Booksellers is held each year in a different country. IBF publishes a number of reports and documents, and also the *Bulletin*, the *Booksellers International* and the trade journal *Fellow* (for young booksellers).

5011

INTERNATIONAL ISBN AGENCY
Staatsbibliothek zu Berlin, 10772 Berlin, Germany
Telephone: +49 (Õ30) 266 2338, 2481 & 2498
Fax: +49 (Õ30) 266 2378 & 2800

Also at:
Potsdamer Straße 33, 10785 Berlin, Germany

Director: Dr Hartmut Walravens
Managers: Sabine Behle
Gerd Weidemann

Functions:
    to supervise the use of the ISBN system;
    to approve the definition and structure of groups;
    to allocate identifiers to groups;
    to advise groups on the setting up and functioning of group agencies;
    to advise group agencies on the allocation of publisher identifiers;
    to promote the worldwide use of the system;
    to publish the *ISBN Review*, the *ISBN Newsletter*, the *Publishers' International ISBN Directory*.

5012

INTERNATIONAL LEAGUE OF ANTIQUARIAN BOOKSELLERS (ILAB)
PO Box 323, Victoria Stn, Montreal, PQ H3Z 2V8
Telephone: +1 (514) 844 5344
Fax: +1 (514) 499 9274

President: Anton Gerits
Treasurer: Poul Jan Poulsen
General Secretary: Helen R. Kahn

The International League of Antiquarian Booksellers was founded in 1948. Their concept of an affiliation of antiquarian booksellers throughout the world gained ready acceptance and the various national associations joined in creating the ILAB. It exists to promote the interests of its members everywhere. Currently its membership includes antiquarian booksellers in 18 countries. Its activities include the promotion of international congresses, international antiquarian book fairs, the publication of the *International Directory of Antiquarian Booksellers*, the periodic circulation of a newsletter, the issue of a dictionary for the antiquarian book trade in nine languages, and the award of a prize for bibliography. The last edition of the *International Directory* was published in autumn 1994 at the price of US$35.

5013

INTERNATIONAL PUBLISHERS ASSOCIATION (IPA)
avenue de Miremont 3, 1206 Geneva, Switzerland
Telephone: +41 (Õ22) 346 30 18
Fax: +41 (Õ22) 347 57 17

President 1996–2000: Alain Gründ
Secretary-General: J. Alexis Koutchoumow

Founded in 1896, IPA aims to ensure the publisher's right to publish and distribute the products of the human mind, campaign to end illiteracy, encourage the circulation of books and other published works, and ensure copyright protection. It is a non-governmental organization of 60 national publishers' associations, and in addition a number of specialist groups.
    A world congress is held every four years, the next in Barcelona, Spain, 22–26 April 1996. A symposium is held every four years, the last in Torino, Italy, 23–25 May 1994.

5014

INTERNATIONAL TRANSLATIONS CENTRE
Schuttersveld 2, 2611 WE Delft, Netherlands
Telephone: +31 (Õ15) 2142242
Fax: +31 (Õ15) 2158535
Email: itc@library.tudelft.nl

Director: Mrs M. Risseeuw

The Centre, a foundation under Dutch law, is directed by an international board of management from eight countries. The object of the Centre is to encourage, improve and facilitate the use of literature published in less accessible languages and of interest to science and industry and also to promote international cooperation in this field. The Centre compiles, processes and disseminates information on existing scientific and technical translations from any language source into Western languages.
    Publications: *World Translations Index* (*WTI*, formerly *World Transindex*, vol 1-9, 1978-86, and *Translations Register-Index*), published 10 times a year with an annual source and author index; *WTI Database*, available on ESA/IRS as file 33 containing 420,000 references of translations, also available on Dialog as file 295.
    WTI lists approximately 35,000 records per year in 11 updates; *Five-Year Cumulations* of the former publication *World Index of Scientific Translations* 1967-71 and 1972-6; *WTI Nine-Year Cumulation* 1977-85; *Journals in Translation*, listing cover-to-cover or selectively translated journals, published irregularly (5th edition April 1991). From 1995 onwards updated twice yearly on diskette and in paper edition.

5015

THE INTERNATIONAL YOUTH LIBRARY
Schloss Blutenburg, 81247 Munich, Germany
Telephone: +49 (Õ89) 891 21 10
Fax: +49 (Õ89) 811 75 53

Director: Dr Barbara Scharioth
Head of Research and Reference: Dr Andreas Bode

The International Youth Library is the largest institution in the world devoted to the collection of international children's literature and the documentation and exchange of information about it. Not only does the IYL maintain an examination collection of almost half a million children's books in 120 languages, it also organizes up to five exhibitions a year in Germany and abroad to promote exchange, both in a commercial and non-commercial sense, of children's books. The staff maintains contact with publishers throughout the world, serves as international intermediaries for rights and information exchange, and compiles bibliographies and catalogues. The library is represented at the Children's Book Fair in Bologna each spring. Publication list is available upon request. Scholarships are available to subject specialists including publishers or editors for research and study of up to three months at the library.

5016

PRIVATE LIBRARIES ASSOCIATION
Ravelston, South View Road, Pinner, Middx HA5 3YD

President: Robin De Beaumont
Hon Secretary: Frank Broomhead
Hon Editor: David Chambers
Hon Treasurer: Derek White

An international society of book collectors, run on a voluntary basis.
    Publications include a quarterly journal and *The Exchange List*, which circulate among member collectors throughout the world, *Private Press Books*, an annual bibliography, and other books concerned with book collecting.

5.2   UNITED KINGDOM

5017

YR ACADEMI GYMREIG
3rd Floor, Mount Stuart House, Mount Stuart Square, Cardiff CF1 6DQ
Telephone: 01222 492064 (Welsh), 492025 (English)
Fax: 01222 492930

Welsh Section: Dafydd Rogers *(Director)*
Caerwyn Williams *(President)*
Nesta Wyn Jones *(Chairman)*
English Language Section: Kevin Thomas *(Director)*
Dannie Abse *(President)*
Sally Roberts Jones *(Chairman)*

The Welsh Section was founded in 1959 to promote Welsh literature. Existing members elect new members on the basis of their contribution to Welsh literature or literary criticism. It publishes a journal, *Taliesin*, books of Welsh literature and translations of modern European classics into Welsh, and awards biennially the Griffith John Williams Memorial Prize. It also organizes readings and conferences and has published an up-to-date English/Welsh dictionary.

The English Language Section was formed in 1968 and aims to promote Anglo-Welsh literature through readings, conferences, creative writing weekends and work in schools. It has published reprints by Anglo-Welsh authors, writers' leaflets on Anglo-Welsh writers and a resource pack for schools, *Writing in Wales*. In 1986 University of Wales Press and Oxford University Press published *The Companion to the Literature of Wales / Cydymaith I Lenyddiaeth Cymru* on the Academy's behalf.

All enquiries should be addressed to the Administrator of the appropriate Section at the above address.

5018

ALLIANCE OF LITERARY SOCIETIES
71 Stepping Stones Road, Coventry CV5 8JT
Telephone: 01203 592231

Chairman: J. Hunt
Hon Secretary: Bill Adams
Editor of Newsletter 'Chapter One': K. Oultram

Member societies may send delegates to the annual convention and use the ALS logo on letterheads/publicity material, and will receive an allocation of the official publication, *Chapter One*.

The Alliance is your referral and support organization and maintains your society's printed material for distribution in response to general enquiries. The ALS also compiles a regularly updated register of member societies (available free upon receipt of an A5 stamped addressed envelope).

Annual Subscription: £5 (for societies with less than 100 members), £10 (less than 500), £15 (less than 1000), £20 (over 1000).

Secretariat/Hon Treasurer: address as above. For single copies of *Chapter One* send 4 × 18 pence stamps to the Editor, Clatterwick House, Little Leigh, Northwich CW8 4RJ.

5019

ARTS COUNCIL OF ENGLAND
14 Great Peter Street, London SW1P 3NQ
Telephone: 0171 333 0100
Fax: 0171 973 6590

Chairman: Lord Gowrie
Secretary-General: Mary Allen

Incorporated under Royal Charter in 1946, and granted a new Charter of Incorporation in 1994, for the purpose of developing and improving the knowledge, understanding and practice of the arts, and to increase their accessibility to the public.

5020

ARTS COUNCIL OF WALES
Museum Place, Cardiff CF1 3NX
Telephone: 01222 394711
Fax: 01222 221447

Director: Emyr Jenkins
Literature Director: Tony Bianchi
Literature Officers: Gwen Davies
Emyr Williams

The object of the Arts Council of Wales, with respect to literature, is to establish an environment in which writers enjoy suitable financial rewards, publishers are encouraged to improve and extend their activities, better services are provided for the book-buying public of Wales, and access to writing opportunities is actively promoted. These ends are currently pursued through the following and other schemes:

1) writers' prizes and bursaries;
2) revenue and production grants to literary book publishers and periodicals;

3) revenue grants to national organizations such as the Welsh Books Council, the Welsh Academy and Tŷ Newydd writers' centre;
4) community and educational initiatives, including Writers on Tour and writers' residencies;
5) funding of the HMSO Oriel Bookshop in Cardiff and a national retail outreach scheme;
6) funding of various projects, particularly translations.

5021

ASLIB (THE ASSOCIATION FOR INFORMATION MANAGEMENT)
Information House, 20–24 Old Street, London EC1V 9AP
Telephone: 0171 253 4488
Fax: 0171 430 0514
Email: pubs@aslib.co.uk
Web Site: http://www.aslib.co.uk/aslib/

Also at:
122–124 Rue Joseph II, 1040 Brussels, Belgium
Telephone: +32 2 230 7737
Fax: +32 2 230 8337

Chief Executive: Roger Bowes
Managers: Sarah Blair *(Publications)*
S. Marshall *(Finance & Administration)*
Brian Thackray *(Marketing)*

With over 2000 members worldwide, Aslib promotes the better management of information as a key strategic resource. Aslib organizes short practical training courses and seminars, and publishes 15 professional journals and a comprehensive range of books and directories, including the *Aslib Directory of Information Sources*.

Other services include Aslib Professional Recruitment, a specialist recruitment agency, and The One Stop Information Shop, a complete information service providing information solutions from immediate query response to full scale consultancy.

5022

ASSOCIATION OF ART HISTORIANS
Dog & Partridge House, Byley, Cheshire CW10 9NJ
Telephone: 01606 835517
Fax: 01606 834799

Chair: Dr Anthea Callen
Hon Secretary: Dr Fintan Cullen
Administrator: Kate Woodhead

The Association of Art Historians, formed in 1974, welcomes the individual membership of all those who are directly concerned with the advancement of the study of the history of art, which is conceived as a broad and developing field involving the study of all aspects of the visual arts, architecture, design and the history of photography and film.

Members are students and graduates in academic and curatorial positions but other professions including journalists, publishers, artists and designers are represented. There are sections within the Association catering specifically for students, museums and galleries, schools, universities and freelance art historians.

The Association publishes a quarterly journal, *Art History*, and mails a newsletter, *Bulletin*, to members four times a year. An annual weekend conference / book fair is arranged and attended by 500+ delegates.

The 1997 conference / book fair will take place at the Courtauld Institute of Art, London, from 4 to 6 April.

5023

ASSOCIATION OF AUTHORS' AGENTS
c/o Greene & Heaton Ltd, 37 Goldhawk Road, London W12 8QQ
Telephone: 0181 749 0315
Fax: 0181 749 0318

President: Caroline Dawnay
Vice-President: Andrew Nurnberg
Treasurer: Brian Stone
Secretary: Carol Heaton

Founded in 1974 to institute and maintain a code of professional behaviour, to discuss matters of common professional interest and to provide a vehicle for representing the view of authors' agents in discussions on matters of common interest with other professional bodies.

5024

ASSOCIATION OF BRITISH SCIENCE WRITERS
23 Savile Row, London W1X 2NB
Telephone: 0171 439 1205
Fax: 0171 973 3051

Chair: Richard Stevenson
Secretary: Dr Peter Briggs *(Executive Secretary – British Assoc for the Advancement of Science)*

Visits, lunches, seminars and briefings on all aspects of science. Monthly newsletter.

5025

ASSOCIATION OF LEARNED & PROFESSIONAL SOCIETY PUBLISHERS
c/o Secretary-General ALPSP, 48 Kelsey Lane, Beckenham, Kent BR3 3NE
Telephone: 0181 658 0459
Fax: 0181 663 3583
Email: donovan@alpsp.demon.co.uk
Web Site: http://www.alpsp.org.uk

Administrator:
Eileen Storrie, 17 Orchard Close, Shillingford, Oxon OX10 7HQ

Editor: Mrs Hazel Bell
Secretary-General: Prof B. T. Donovan

Founded in 1972 to protect and advance the publishing interests of learned and professional societies and institutions. Members should be either publishers of learned journals, transactions, monographs and so forth, or publish on behalf of learned organizations or allied organizations whose membership would contribute to the objectives of the Association.

5026

ASSOCIATION OF LITTLE PRESSES
86 Lytton Road, Oxford OX4 3NZ
Telephone: 01865 718266

Membership:
89a Petherton Road, London N5 2QT

Co-ordinator: Chris Jones
Chairman: Ian Robinson
Membership Secretary: Bob Cobbing
Treasurer: Peter Finch
Editors: Stan Trevor *(Palpi)*
Paul Green *(Newsletter)*

The ALP was formed in 1966. It acts as an information exchange, advice centre and general promoter of the benefits of small publishing. ALP currently represents over 300 publishers and associates throughout Britain. Membership costs £12.50 a year and is open to presses and magazines as well as interested individuals and institutions.

The Association produces a *Catalogue of Small Press Books in Print*; a thrice yearly magazine *Poetry and Little Press Information* (PALPI); a regular ALP newsletter; *Getting your Poetry Published*, a pamphlet of basic advice, and *Publishing Yourself – Not Too Difficult After All*, which advises those who are thinking of self-publishing. In addition, ALP has co-operated with Oriel Bookshop to produce the regularly updated *Small Presses and Little Magazines* in the UK and Ireland – an address list, which contains information on over a thousand publishers. The ALP also organizes a book fair.

ALP members produce everything from comics and cookery hints to novels and naval history.

5027

AUTHORS' CLUB
40 Dover Street, London W1X 3RB
Telephone: 0171 499 8581
Fax: 0171 409 0913

Secretary: Ann Carter

Founded in 1891. A social club for writers. Literary prizes awarded.

5028

AUTHORS' FOUNDATION
84 Drayton Gardens, London SW10 9SB
Telephone: 0171 373 6642

Trustees: Lady Antonia Fraser
Michael Holroyd
Secretary: Mark Le Fanu

Founded in 1984 to mark the centenary of the Society of Authors, the Foundation offers grants to published writers who need additional funding for research, travel, etc. Open to fiction, poetry and non-fiction.

The Foundation incorporates the Phoenix Trust. Annual closing date for applications: 30 April.

5029

AUTHORS' LICENSING & COLLECTING SOCIETY (ALCS)
74 New Oxford Street, London WC1A 1EF
Telephone: 0171 255 2034
Fax: 0171 323 0486
Email: alcs@alcs.co.uk
Web Site: http://www.alcs.co.uk

Secretary-General: Christopher Zielinski

Formed in 1977, ALCS is a collecting society for writers. It is non-profit-making. Its purpose is to enable writers to receive payment for the use of those rights from which they cannot benefit except through an organization of this kind in the fields of overseas lending right, cable and satellite TV, reprography, off-air and private recording. It has agreements with several overseas collecting societies. Together with the Publishers Licensing Society it formed the Copyright Licensing Agency to offer licences for reprographic or duplicated reproduction of copyright material. ALCS is also a member of the Educational Recording Agency, which licenses off-air recording in educational institutions. ALCS distributes payments from these schemes to writers.

5030

E. F. BENSON SOCIETY
88 Tollington Park, London N4 3RA
Telephone: 0171 272 3375
Fax: 0171 580 0763

Chair: Keith Cavers
Secretary: Allan Downend
Treasurer: Chris Roby

Aims to promote interest in E. F. Benson and the Benson family. The Society promotes knowledge of E. F. Benson through its annual journal, *The Dodo*. It purchases Benson books for its library at Lamb House and for resale to its members. It publishes Benson material which has been out of print for some time, both in its journal and as individual titles. Booksellers/Publishers advertise in *The Dodo*; rates can be obtained from the Society. The Society gives talks on E. F. Benson and promotes his books at these. It also holds exhibitions.

5031

BOOK AID INTERNATIONAL (RANFURLY LIBRARY SERVICE)
39–41 Coldharbour Lane, Camberwell, London SE5 9NR
Telephone: 0171 733 3577

Fax: 0171 978 8006
Email: ris@gn.apc.org

Patron: HRH The Duke of Edinburgh, KG, KT, OM
President: The Countess of Ranfurly, OBE
Chairman: Tim Rix
Director: Mrs Sara Harrity, MBE
Deputy Director: David Membrey

Book Aid International is Britain's largest book-aid charity, sending books to schools, libraries and other institutions in the less-developed world which are experiencing severe book shortages. Last year over 670,000 books were selected, packed and despatched to about 65 countries; since it was founded, over 16 million books have been sent overseas.

Book Aid International is dependent on donations of used and new books from a number of different sources within the UK, including schools, libraries, publishers, professional organizations and individuals. It is particularly keen to strengthen links and obtain support from the publishing and book trades. These sectors currently pulp vast quantities of books which are surplus to requirements; the books are however a potentially valuable resource to readers in the less-developed world.

For further information about how you can help education and literacy programmes, please write to or phone the Book Acquisitions Officer.

5032

BOOK INDUSTRY COMMUNICATION
39–41 North Road, London N7 9DP
Telephone: 0171 607 0021
Fax: 0171 607 0415
Email: brian@bic.org.uk
Web Site: http://www.bic.org.uk/bic

Chairman: Tony Hall
Deputy Chairman: Malcolm Peters
Treasurer: Christopher Sweeten
Managing Agent: Brian Green

Book Industry Communication (BIC) was set up in 1991 to facilitate the provision and communication of information throughout the book industry and to be responsible for the development and promotion of standards for the format and transmission of bibliographic information, commercial messages and other information designed to increase efficiency and effectiveness in trading and supply within the industry.

BIC is funded and sponsored by the Publishers Association, the Booksellers Association, the British Library and the Library Association who formed BIC to continue and expand the work on electronic communication done by BEDIS (the Book Trade Electronic Data Interchange Standards Committee), BTECC (the Book Trade Electronic Communications Committee) and many other committees and working parties. Book industry systems suppliers are also closely involved with the work of BIC.

BIC produces a regular newsletter and publishes standard formats and user guides for electronic messages, machine readable codes etc. and organizes seminars and forums. BIC has links with counterpart associations internationally with a view to developing international standards to facilitate interchange of electronic information.

5033

BOOK PACKAGERS ASSOCIATION
93a Blenheim Crescent, London W11 2EQ
Telephone: 0171 221 9089

Secretary: Rosemary Pettit

The BPA was founded in 1985 to provide book packagers with a forum for the exchange of ideas and information and to represent the interests of its members in dealing with other bodies in the book trade. Membership is open to companies which conceive, edit, design and produce books for sale to publishers and others; associate membership is available for sole traders.

The Association holds meetings and seminars, takes a joint stand at the London Book Fair and provides standard contracts applicable to packaging and publishing.

5034

BOOK TRADE BENEVOLENT SOCIETY
Dillon Lodge, The Retreat, Kings Langley, Herts WD4 8LT
Telephone: 01923 263128
Fax: 01923 270732

President: Paul Sherer
Warden: Ann Rosina Brown
The Secretariat: Mrs A. R. Brown, AMBIM, FIPD
Chief Executive: David Hicks

Formed 1 January 1968 as a single benevolent society replacing the old-established trade friendly societies to administer funds subscribed for the relief in adversity of workers or their dependants in all branches of the book trade in the United Kingdom and for the maintenance of dwellings at the Retreat for such persons.

5035

BOOK TRUST
Book House, 45 East Hill, London SW18 2QZ
Telephone: 0181 870 9055
Fax: 0181 874 4790

Book Trust (Scotland):
The Scottish Book Centre, 137 Dundee Street, Edinburgh EH11 1BG
Telephone: 031-229 3663
Fax: 031-228 4293

Executive Director: Brian Perman
Head of Young Book Trust: Lindsey Fraser *(Scotland)*

Book Trust is an educational charity which exists to promote the role of books and literature as a means of enrichment and enjoyment; to represent and further the interests of readers and to campaign for the basic freedom of access to books and reading for people of all ages, races and cultures.

The various ways in which these aims are met include the administration of many prestigious book prizes; the Book Trust Information Service which deals with all telephone queries about books; publications ranging from profiles of contemporary writers to an annual selection of the best paperbacks for children; book campaigns and research when necessary; BookFax – the service offering instant information on authors, books, and book prizes via fax; the advisory and promotion work of Young Book Trust; the children's book libraries in both London and Scotland housing all publications of the past two years.

Enquiries about membership of Book Trust or subscriptions to Young Book Trust are encouraged and welcomed.

5036

BOOKSELLERS ASSOCIATION OF GREAT BRITAIN AND IRELAND
Minster House, 272 Vauxhall Bridge Road, London SW1V 1BA
Telephone: 0171 834 5477
Fax: 0171 834 8812
Email: 100437.2261@compuserve.com

President: Willie Anderson
Chief Executive: Tim Godfray

Founded in 1895. Over 3300 members. Promotes and looks after the interests of booksellers, helps booksellers become more efficient, fights for better distribution in the trade, helps booksellers increase sales and reduce costs and gives advice on opening and running a bookshop. Among other services, the Association produces catalogues for distribution throughout the retail trade at Christmas.

The Association awards a Diploma in Professional Bookselling and organizes a programme of training courses and seminars.

5037

BRITISH ASSOCIATION OF COMMUNICATORS IN BUSINESS
3 Locks Yard, High Street, Sevenoaks, Kent TN13 1LT
Telephone: 01732 459331
Fax: 01732 461757

Director: Allen Brobyn
Projects Administrator: Richard Kingsley

The Association aims to be the market leader for those involved in corporate media management and practice by providing professional, authoritative, dynamic, supportive and innovative services.

Membership is open to all individuals engaged in internal corporate communication. Major activities include the annual Editing for Industry award scheme, an annual study conference and a regular programme of educational and training events. Publications include the *BACB Membership and Services Directory* (annual), the *Editor's Handbook*, a loose-leaf manual and reference book, and *Crucible and Communicators in Business* magazine.

5038

THE BRITISH ASSOCIATION OF PICTURE LIBRARIES AND AGENCIES (BAPLA)
18 Vine Hill, London EC1R 5DX
Telephone: 0171 713 1780
Fax: 0171 713 1211
Email: bapla@dial.pipex.com
Web Site: http://www.dspace.dial.pipex.com/town/plaza/raa00/index. htm

Administrator: Sarah Saunders

BAPLA was founded in 1975, became a company limited by guarantee in 1993, and now has a membership of 300 picture collections, which gives its clients, picture users of all kinds, access to over 300 million images. Its aim is to promote fair and honest trading and high standards of professional conduct amongst members. It also has an educational role to establish the commercial value of pictures. Any photograph, print etc that has the impact to sell or illustrate a book or promote a product has a market value for that use.

BAPLA maintains contact with foreign organizations with allied aims. Further information is available from the Administrator.

Publications: *Annual Directory of Members* with subject index of their collections; biannual BAPLA *Journal*, available on subscription. Terms and conditions of submission and reproduction of pictures.

5039

BRITISH COPYRIGHT COUNCIL
29–33 Berners Street, London W1P 4AA
Telephone: 0171 359 1895
Fax: 0171 359 1895

President of Honour: Denis de Freitas, OBE
Chairman: Maureen Duffy, FRSL
Secretary: Geoffrey Adams

The British Copyright Council is an association of bodies representing those who create, or hold interests or rights in literary, dramatic, musical and artistic works in which rights of copyright subsist under the UK Copyright, Designs and Patents Act 1988, and those who perform such works.

The Council operates as a liaison committee, providing its members with a forum for the discussion of copyright matters, and as a pressure group for changes in the law, where necessary.

It does not provide any advisory services, nor have any individual members.

5040

BRITISH COUNCIL
10 Spring Gardens, London SW1A 2BN
Telephone: 0171 930 8466
Fax: 0171 839 6347

Libraries, Books and Information Division:
UK Headquarters, Medlock Street, Manchester M15 4AA
Telephone: 0161 957 7000
Fax: 0161 957 7111

Chairman: Sir Martin Jacomb
Director-General: Sir John Hanson
Chairman, Publishing Advisory Committee: Philip Attenborough

The British Council promotes Britain abroad. It is an independent, non-political organization. It provides access to British ideas, talents and experience in education and training, books and periodicals, the English language, the arts, sciences and technology.

The Council works in 229 cities in 108 countries. Around the world it runs 180 offices, 143 libraries, 75 English language schools and 29 resource centres; it employs 1600 staff in its London and Manchester headquarters and in university towns in the United Kingdom. Its annual turnover is £416 million, including government grants and overseas aid programmes: its revenue exceeds £70 million.

The Council's lending and reference libraries throughout the world help to cater for the needs of the serious reader and act as show-cases for the latest British publications. They vary in size from small reference collections to comprehensive libraries of up to 74,000 volumes, stocked with up-to-date books for loan and reference works, a selection of British periodicals reviewing new books and, increasingly, stocks of audio-visual materials and computer software. Bibliographies of British books on special subjects are prepared on request.

Working in close collaboration with book trade associations, the British Council organizes book and electronic publishing exhibitions for showing overseas. These exhibitions range from small specialist displays of fewer than 100 titles to bigger trade fair exhibits of over 1000 titles mounted annually at Frankfurt and at other locations.

The Council's publications include *Writers and Their Work,* a series of booklets on classic and contemporary authors, of which over 200 have appeared, and a series of literary bibliographies. A catalogue of publications is available on request. Well-known British authors lecture overseas under Council auspices and booksellers are invited to Britain for visits or training.

The Council acts as the agent of the Overseas Development Administration for book aid projects in developing countries.

The Council is an authority on teaching English as a second or foreign language and gives advice and information on curriculum, methodology, materials and testing through its English Language and Literature Division.

Further information about the British Council is available from the Press and Public Relations Department, The British Council, 10 Spring Gardens, London SW1A 2BN.

The Council's overseas offices and representatives are listed below.

Albania
Liaison Officer: Elsona Agolli
Office of the British Chargé d'Affaires, Rruga Vaso Pasha 7/1, Tirana
Telephone: +355 429508 **Fax:** +355 429508

Algeria
Office Manager: Hafida Gabouze
British Council, c/o British Embassy, 7 Chemin des Glycines, BP 43, Alger-Gare 1600, Algiers
Telephone: +213 (Õ2) 692601, 692831, 692411 & 692038 **Fax:** +213 (Õ2) 69 24 10

Argentina
Director: Mike P. Potter
Marcelo T. de Alvear 590, 1058 Buenos Aires
Telephone: +54 (Õ1) 311 9814 & 311 7519 **Fax:** +54 (Õ1) 311 7747

Australia
Director: James Potts
Edgecliff Centre, 401/203 New South Head Road, (PO Box 88), Edgecliff, Sydney, NSW 2027
Telephone: +61 (Õ2) 326 2022 **Fax:** +61 (Õ2) 327 4868
Email: bc.sydney@bc-sydney.sprint.com

Austria
Director: David Handforth
Schenkenstrasse 4, A-1010 Vienna
Telephone: +43 (Õ1) 533 26 18 **Fax:** +43 (Õ1) 533 26 1685
Email: bc.vienna@british-council.sprint.com

Azerbaijan
DTO Manager: James Shipton

Baku Institute of Social Management and Politology, 74 Lermentov
Street, Baku
Telephone: +99 412 989236 **Fax:** +99 412 989236

Bahrain
Director: John Shorter
AMA Centre, 146 Shaikh Salman Highway, Manama 356 (PO Box 452,
Manama)
Telephone: +973 261555 **Fax:** +973 241272

Baltic States
Director: Arthur Sanderson, MBE
Lazaretes Iela 3, LV-1010 Riga, Latvia
Telephone: +371 7320468 & 7321165 **Fax:** +371 7830031
Email: bc.riga@british-council.sprint.com

and offices in Lithuania and Estonia

Bangladesh
Director: Keith Burd, OBE
5 Fuller Road, Dhaka 1000 (PO Box 161, Ramna, Dhaka 2)
Telephone: +880 (Õ2) 868905-7 & 868867-8 **Fax:** +880 (Õ2) 863375
Email: bcdhaka.barlow@pradeshta.net

and an office in Chittagong

Belarus
Resource Centre Co-ordinator: Andrew Houghton
English Teachers' Resource Centre, Institute of Foreign Languages, Ul.
Zakharova 21, 220662 Minsk
Telephone: +7 (0172) 367 953 **Fax:** +7 (0172) 364 047
Email: bc.minsk@british-council.sprint.com

Belgium & Luxembourg
Director: Dr Ken Churchill, OBE
Liefdadigheidstraat, rue de la Charité 15, 1040 Brussels
Telephone: +32 (Õ2) 227 0840 **Fax:** +32 (Õ2) 227 0849
Email: bc.brussels@bc-brussels.sprint.com

Bosnia-Herzegovina
Director: Sue Barnes
The British Embassy, 8 Tina Ujevica, Sarajevo
Telephone: +387 (71) 444429 & 663922 **Fax:** +387 (71) 444429

Botswana
Director: Anne Hewling
British High Commission Building, Queen's Road, The Mall, Gaborone
(PO Box 439, Gaborone)
Telephone: +267 353602 **Fax:** +267 356643
Email: bc.gaborone@british-council.sprint.com

Brazil
Director: Patrick Early, OBE
SCRN 708-9 BLF Nos. 1-3 (Caixa Postal 6104), 70.740-780 Brasilia, DF
Telephone: +55 (Õ61) 272 3060 **Fax:** +55 (Õ61) 272 3455
Email: 0007465808@mcimail.com

and offices in Recife, Rio de Janeiro and São Paulo

Brunei
Manager: Susan Matthews
Hong Kong Bank Chambers, Jalan Pemancha, (PO Box 3049), Bandar
Seri Begawan 2085, Negara Brunei Darussalam
Telephone: +673 (Õ2) 227480 & 227531 **Fax:** +673 (Õ2) 241769
Email: bc.brunei@pso.brunet.bn

Bulgaria
Director: David Stokes
7 Tulovo Street, 1504 Sofia
Telephone: +359 (Õ2) 467133 & 9460099 **Fax:** +359 (Õ2) 9460102
Email: bc.sofia@british-council.sprint.com

Burma (Myanmar)
Director/Cultural Attaché: Chris Harrison
British Embassy, 80 Strand Road, PO Box 638, Rangoon
Telephone: +95 (Õ1) 281700, 281702/3, 295300 & 295309 **Fax:** +95 (Õ1)
283895, 550292 & 289566

Cameroon
Director: Terry Humphreys
avenue Charles de Gaulle, BP 818, Yaoundé
Telephone: +237 21 16 96 & 20 31 72 **Fax:** +237 21 56 91

Canada
Director: John Harniman, OBE
c/o British High Commission, 80 Elgin Street, Ottawa, Ont K1P 5K7
Telephone: +1 (613) 237 1530 **Fax:** +1 (613) 569 1478
Email: af572@freenet,carleton.ca

and an office in Montreal

Caribbean
Acting Director: David Tarr
PCMB Building, 64 Knutsford Boulevard, PO Box 575, Kingston 5,
Jamaica
Telephone: +1 (809) 92 96915 & 92 97049 **Fax:** +1 (809) 92 97090
Email: bc.kingston@toj.com

and an office in Trinidad

Chile
Director: Robin Evans
Eliodoro Yañex 832, Casilla 115 Correo 55, Santiago
Telephone: +56 (Õ2) 236 0193, 236 1199 & 235 6660 **Fax:** +56 (Õ2) 235
7375
Email: bc.chile@mailnet.rdc.cl

China
Counsellor (Cultural): Martin Davidson
British Embassy, Cultural & Education Section, Landmark Building, 8
North Dongsanhuan Road, Chaoyang District, Beijing 100006
Telephone: +86 (Õ1) 6501 1903 **Fax:** +86 (Õ1) 6501 1977
Email: bc.beijing@bc-beijing.sprint.com

and offices in Shanghai and Hong Kong

Colombia
Director: Kate Board
Calle 87 No 12-79, (Apartado Aéreo 089231), Santa Fe de Bogotá
Telephone: +57 (Õ1) 618 0175, 218 7518 & 257 6188 **Fax:** +57 (Õ1) 218
7754

Croatia
Director: Ian Stewart
PO Box 55, Ilica 12/1, Zagreb 41001
Telephone: +385 (Õ41) 273491/2 & 424888 **Fax:** +385 (Õ41) 421725

Cyprus
Director: Robert Frost
3 Museum Street, 1097 Nicosia (PO Box 5654, 1387 Nicosia)
Telephone: +357 (Õ2) 442152 **Fax:** +357 (Õ2) 477257

Czech Republic
Director/Cultural Counsellor: Mary O'Neill
Narodni 10, 12501 Prague 1
Telephone: +42 (Õ2) 2491 2179/83 **Fax:** +42 (Õ2) 2491 3839
Email: bcprague@britcoun.anet.cz

Denmark
see Nordic countries

East Jerusalem & Gaza
Director: Peter Skelton
Al-Nuzha Building, 2 Abu Obeida Street, PO Box 19136, East Jerusalem
Telephone: +972 (Õ2) 282545 **Fax:** +972 (Õ2) 283021
Email: 100726.332@compuserve.com

and offices in Gaza, Hebron and Nablus

Ecuador
Director: Anthony Deyes
Av. da Amazonas 1646, Orellana, (Casilla 17-07-8829), Quito
Telephone: +593 (Õ2) 540 225, 225 421 & 508 282 **Fax:** +593 (Õ2) 508
283 & 223 396
Email: erey@britcoun.org.ec

Egypt
Director: Howard Thompson, OBE
192 Sharia el Nil, Agouza, Cairo
Telephone: +20 (Õ2) 303 1514 **Fax:** +20 (Õ2) 344 3076
Email: bc.cairo@bc-cairo.sprint.com

and an office in Alexandria

Eritrea
Director: Dr Negusse Araya
Lorenzo Ta'zaz Street 23, PO Box 997, Asmara
Telephone: +2911 123415 **Fax:** +2911 127230

Estonia
see Baltic States

Ethiopia
Director: Michael Sargent
Artistic Building, Adwa Avenue, Addis Ababa (PO Box 1043, Addis
Ababa)
Telephone: +251 (Õ1) 55 00 22 **Fax:** +251 (Õ1) 55 25 44
Email: britcoun@padis.gn.apc.org

European Community
Director: Michele Saward
European Commission Relations Office, Liefdadigheidstraat, rue de la
Charité 15, 1040 Brussels
Telephone: +32 (Õ2) 227 0852 **Fax:** +32 (Õ2) 227 0853
and
Head: Fiona Clouder Richards
United Kingdom Research and Higher Education European Office. rue de
la Loi 83, BP10, 1040 Brussels
Telephone: +32 (Õ2) 230 5275 **Fax:** +32 (Õ2) 230 4803

Finland
see Nordic countries

France
Director/Cultural Counsellor: Dr Christine Gamble
9–11 rue de Constantine, 75007 Paris
Telephone: +33 1 49 55 73 00 **Fax:** +33 1 47 05 77 02
Email: bc.paris@bc-paris.sprint.com

Georgia
Director Russia is responsible for work in Georgia
Tskhvedadze 36, Tbilisi *(mail via The British Council, Moscow)*
Telephone: +788 (32) 952361 **Fax:** +788 (32) 220253

Germany
Director: Keith Dobson, OBE
Hahnenstrasse 6, 50667 Cologne
Telephone: +49 (Õ221) 20 64 40 **Fax:** +49 (Õ221) 20 64 455
Email: bc.cologne@british-council.sprint.com

and offices in Berlin, Leipzig, Hamburg and Munich

Ghana
Director: Tom Cowin
Liberia Road, PO Box 771, Accra
Telephone: +233 (Õ21) 663414 & 663979 **Fax:** +233 (Õ21) 663337
Email: bcaccra@britcoun.aau.org

and an office in Kumasi

Greece
Director: Dr John Munby, OBE
17 Plateia Philikis, Etairias, Kolonaki Square, (PO Box 3488), 102 10
Athens
Telephone: +30 (Õ1) 3633211/15 **Fax:** +30 (Õ1) 3634769
Email: british.council@bc-athens.sprint.com

and an office in Thessaloniki

Hong Kong
Director: Tom Buchanan
Easey Commercial Building, 255 Hennessy Road, Wanchai, Hong Kong

Telephone: +852 2879 5138 & 2859 5115 *(English Language Centre)*
Fax: +852 2507 5731 & 2877 7540 *(English Language Centre)*
Email: bc.hongkong@bc-hongkong.sprint.com

Hungary
Director: Dr Paul Dick, OBE
Benczur utca 26, 1068 Budapest VI
Telephone: +36 (Õ1) 322 8246 & 351 2032/4 **Fax:** +36 (Õ1) 342 5728
Email: hungary@britcoun.hu

India
Minister (Cultural Affairs): Colin Perchard, OBE
British High Commission, British Council Division, 17 Kasturba Gandhi
Marg, New Delhi
Telephone: +91 (Õ11) 371 1401, 371 0111 & 371 0555 **Fax:** +91 (Õ11)
371 0717
Email: delhi@bcdd.ernet.in

and offices in Bombay, Calcutta and Madras

Indonesia
Director: Dr Neil Kemp
S Widjojo Centre, Jalan Jenderal Sudirman 71, Jakarta 12190
Telephone: +62 (Õ21) 2524126, 2524115 & 2524122 **Fax:** +61 (Õ21)
2524129
Email: bc.jakarta@bc-jakarta.sprint.com

Irish Republic
Director: Harold Fish, OBE
Newmount House, 22–24 Lower Mount Street, Dublin 2
Telephone: +353 (Õ1) 6764088 **Fax:** +353 (Õ1) 6766945

Israel
Director: Harley Brookes
140 Hayarkon Street, PO Box 3302, Tel Aviv 61032
Telephone: +972 (Õ3) 5222 194, 5242 558 & 5241 350/1 **Fax:** +972 (Õ3)
5221 229

and offices in West Jerusalem and Nazareth

Italy
Director: Richard Alford, OBE
Via Quattro Fontane 20, 00184 Rome
Telephone: +39 (Õ6) 478141 **Fax:** +39 (Õ6) 4740483
Email: bc.rome@british-council.sprint.com

and offices in Bologna, Milan and Naples

Jamaica
see Caribbean

Japan
Director: Michael Barrett, OBE
2 Kagurazaka 1-chome, Shinjuku-ku, Tokyo 162
Telephone: +81 (Õ3) 3235 8031 **Fax:** +81 (Õ3) 3235 8040
Email: bc.tokyo@bc-tokyo.sprint.com

and an office in Kyoto

Jordan
Director: Dr David Burton
Rainbow Street (off First Circle), Jabal Amman, PO Box 634, Amman
11118
Telephone: +962 (Õ6) 636147/8 **Fax:** +962 (Õ6) 656413

Kazakhstan
Director: Elizabeth White
Ul. Panifilova 158/17, 480064 Almaty
c/o The British Council, Mailing Section (Almaty), 10 Spring Gardens,
London SW1A 2BN
Telephone: +7 3272 633339 **Fax:** +7 3272 633443
Email: bc@britcoun.almaty.kz

Kenya
Director: Bill Harvey
ICEA Building, Kenyatta Avenue, PO Box 40751, Nairobi

Telephone: +254 (Õ2) 334811, 334855/6/7, 334881 & 334885 **Fax:** +254 (Õ2) 339854, 333801 & 334875
Email: bc.nairobi@british-council.sprint.com

and offices in Kisumu and Mombasa

Korea
Director: Terry Toney
Anglican Church Building, 1st Floor, 3-7 Chung-dong, Choong-ku, Seoul 100-120
Telephone: +82 2 737 7157 **Fax:** +82 2 737 9911
Email: bc.seoul@bc-seoul.sprint.com

and an office in Pusan

Kuwait
Director: Aidan Broderick
2 Al Arabi Street, Block 2, PO Box 345, 13004 Safat, Mansouriya
Telephone: +965 252 0067/8, 253 3204, 251 5512 & 253 3227 **Fax:** +965 252 0069 & 255 1376
Email: dirkuw@kuwait,net

Kyrgyzstan
see Kazakhstan

Latvia
see Baltic States

Lebanon
Director: Ann Malamah-Thomas, MBE
Sidani Street, Azar Building, Beirut
Telephone: +961 (1) 803979/80 **Fax:** +961 (1) 864534

Lesotho
Manager: Sella Cweba
Hobson's Square, PO Box 429, Maseru 100
Telephone: +266 312609 **Fax:** +266 310363
Email: bc.lesotho@british-council.sprint.com

Lithuania
see Baltic States

Macedonia
see Yugoslavia (Eastern Adriatic)

Madagascar
see Mauritius

Malawi
Director: James Kennedy
Plot No 13/20, City Centre, PO Box 30222, Lilongwe 3
Telephone: +265 783244 & 783419 **Fax:** +265 782945
Email: bc.lilongwe@unima.wn.apc.org

and an office in Blantyre

Malaysia
Director: Ted Edmundsen
Jalan Bukit Aman, PO Box 10539, 50480 Kuala Lumpur
Telephone: +60 (Õ3) 2987555 & 2926076 *(Director)* **Fax:** +60 (Õ3) 2937214 & 2930807
Email: brcokl@britkl.po.my

and offices in Sarawak, Sabah and Penang

Maldive Islands
see Sri Lanka

Malta
Information Centre Manager: Anne Bradley
British High Commission, 7 St Anne Street, Floriana VLT 15
Telephone: +356 226227 **Fax:** +356 226207
Email: 100077.41@compuserve.com

Mauritius
Director: Michael Bootle

Royal Road, PO Box 111, Rose Hill
Telephone: +230 454 9550/1/2 **Fax:** +230 454 9553

Mexico
Director: Dr Frank Edwards
Maestro Antonio Caso 127, Col San Rafael, Apdo Postal 30-588, Mexico City 06470 DF
Telephone: +52 (Õ5) 566 6144, 566 6191, 566 6743, 566 6595, 566 6384 & 566 6187 **Fax:** +52 (Õ5) 535 59 84

Morocco
Director: Tony O'Brien
36 rue de Tanger, BP 427, Rabat
Telephone: +212 (Õ7) 76 08 36 **Fax:** +212 (Õ7) 76 08 50

Mozambique
Director: Paul Woods
Rua John Issa 226, PO Box 4178, Maputo
Telephone: +258 1 421571/2/3/4 **Fax:** +258 1 421577
Email: root@bcmaputo.uem.mz

Namibia
Director: Deborah Crowe
74 Bülow Strasse, PO Box 24224, Windhoek 9000
Telephone: +264 (Õ61) 226 878 & 226 776 **Fax:** +264 (Õ61) 227 530
Email: bc.namibia@british-council.sprint.com

Nepal
Director: Sarah Ewans
Kantipath, PO Box 640, Kathmandu
Telephone: +977 (Õ1) 221305, 223796 & 222698 **Fax:** +977 (Õ1) 224076
Email: bcnepal@britcoun.mos.com.np

Netherlands
Director: Tim Butchard
Keizersgracht 343, 1016 EH Amsterdam
Telephone: +31 (Õ20) 622 36 44 **Fax:** +31 (Õ20) 620 73 89
Email: bc.amsterdam@british-council.sprint.com

New Zealand
Director: Paul Smith
c/o British High Commission, 44 Hill Street, PO Box 1812, Wellington
Telephone: +64 (Õ4) 4726 049 **Fax:** +64 (Õ4) 4736 261

Nigeria
Director: Dr John Hawkins
11 Kingsway Road, Ikoyi, PO Box 3702, Lagos
Telephone: +234 (Õ1) 269 2188–2192 **Fax:** +234 (Õ1) 269 2193 & 0646
Email: bc.lagos@bc-lagos.sprint.com

and offices in Enugu, Kaduna, Kano, Ibadan and Port Harcourt

Nordic countries
Director Nordic Area: Len Tyler
Gammel Mont 12/3, 1117 Copenhagen K, Denmark
Telephone: +45 33 11 20 44 **Fax:** +45 33 32 15 01

and offices in Helsinki, Oslo and Stockholm

Oman
Director: Clive Bruton
Road One, Medinat Qaboos West, PO Box 73, Postal Code 115, Muscat
Telephone: +968 600548 **Fax:** +968 699163
Email: bc.muscat@bc-muscat.sprint.com

and offices in Salalah and Sohar

Pakistan
Director: Peter Elborn, OBE
Block 14, Civic Centre G6 (PO Box 1135), Islamabad
Telephone: +92 (Õ51) 829041-4 **Fax:** +92 (Õ51) 276683
Email: firstname.lastname@bc.islamabad.sprint.com

and offices in Karachi, Lahore and Peshawar

Peru
Director: Chris Brown

Calle Alberto Lynch 110, San Isidro, Lima 27 (Apartado 14-0114, Santa
  Beatriz, Lima 14)
Telephone: +51 (Õ1) 221 7552 & 221 7600 **Fax:** +51 (Õ1) 21 52 15
Email: bc.lima@bc-lima.sprint.com

Philippines
Director: Dr Kate Bailey
10F Taipan Place, Emerald Avenue, Ortigas Complex, Pasig City, Manila
Telephone: +63 (Õ2) 9141011-14 **Fax:** +63 (Õ2) 9141020
Email: bc@kilaw.admu.edu.ph

Poland
Director: Ed Pugh
Al Jerozolimskie 59, 00-697 Warsaw
Telephone: +48 (Õ2) 6287401-3 & 6287188 **Fax:** +48 (Õ2) 6219955

Portugal
Director: Bill Jefferson, OBE
Rua de São Marçal 174, 1294 Lisbon Codex
Telephone: +351 (Õ1) 347 61 41–7 **Fax:** +351 (Õ1) 347 61 52
Email: bc.lisbon@bc-lisbon.sprint.com

and offices in Parede, Coimbra and Oporto

Qatar
Director: Brian Austin
93 Al Sadd Street, PO Box 2992, Doha
Telephone: +974 426193/4, 426185 & 426159 **Fax:** +974 320065

Romania
Director/Cultural Attaché: Claus Henning
Calea Dorobantilor 14, Bucharest 71132
Telephone: +40 (Õ1) 2105347 & 2100314 **Fax:** +40 (Õ1) 2100310
Email: bc.romania@bc-bucharest.sprint.com

Russia
Director: Tony Andrews
Biblioteka Inostrannoi Literaturi, Ulitsa Nikoloyamskaya 1, Moscow
  109189
Telephone: +7 (0095) 915 3511 **Fax:** +7 (0095) 975 2561
Email: bc.moscow@bc-moscow.sprint.com

and offices in St Petersburg, Ekaterinburg and Nizhni Novgorod

Saudi Arabia
Director: Anthony Lewis
Al Mousa Centre, Tower B, Olaya Main Road, PO Box 58012, Riyadh
  11594
Telephone: +966 (Õ1) 462 1818 & 465 4993 *(Director)* **Fax:** +966 (Õ1)
  462 0663
Email: enquiries@bc-riyadh.sprint.com

and offices in Jeddah, Dammam and Jubail

Senegal
Director: Roger Budd
34–36 Boulevard de la République, Immeuble Sonatel, BP 6232, Dakar
Telephone: +221 22 20 15, 22 20 48 **Fax:** +221 21 81 36
Email: bc.dakar@endadak.gn.apc.org

Seychelles
see Mauritius

Sierra Leone
Director: Joe Docherty
Tower Hill, PO Box 124, Freetown
Telephone: +232 (Õ22) 222223, 222227, 224683 & 224684 **Fax:** +232
  (Õ22) 224123
Email: bcouncil@sl.baobab.com

Singapore
Director: John Grote
30 Napier Road, Singapore 1025
Telephone: +65 437 1111 & 479 7481 *(ECS)* **Fax:** +65 472 1010
Email: britcoun@britcoun.org.sg

Slovakia
Director: Susan Wallace-Shaddad
PO Box 68, Panska 17, 81499 Bratislava, Slovakia
Telephone: +42 (Õ7) 5331793, 5331185, 5331074 & 5331261 **Fax:** +42
  (Õ7) 334705
Email: bc.slovakia@british-council.sprint.com

Slovenia
Director: Francis King, OBE
Stefanova l/III, 61000 Ljubljana
Telephone: +38 (Õ61) 125 9032 & 125 9292 **Fax:** +38 (Õ61) 125 9139

South Africa
Director: Les Phillips, OBE, FSA
76 Juta Street, PO Box 30637, Braamfontein, 2017 Johannesburg
Telephone: +27 (Õ11) 403 3316 **Fax:** +27 (Õ11) 339 7806 & 339 3715
Email: bc.johannesburg@british-council.sprint.com

and offices in Cape Town and Durban

Spain
Director: Peter Taylor, OBE
Paseo del General Martinez Campos 31, 28010 Madrid
Telephone: +34 (Õ1) 337 3500 & 337 3600 *(DTO Manager)* **Fax:** +34
  (Õ1) 337 3573
Email: bc.madrid@british-council.sprint.com

and offices in Barcelona, Bilbao, Oviedo, Segovia, Sevilla, Valencia,
  Palma de Mallorca and Las Palmas de Gran Canaria

Sri Lanka
Director: Peter Ellwood
49 Alfred House Gardens, PO Box 753, Colombo 3
Telephone: +94 (Õ1) 581171/2, 587078, 580301, 502487, 582449 &
  595348 **Fax:** +94 (Õ1) 587079
Email: enquiry@britcoun.lanka.net

and an office in Kandy

Sudan
Director: Don Sloan
14 Abu Sin Street, PO Box 1253, Khartoum
Telephone: +249 (Õ11) 780817 **Fax:** +249 (Õ11) 774935

Swaziland
Director: Felciity Townsend
British High Commission Building, Alister Miller Street, Mbabane
  (Private Bag, Mbabane)
Telephone: +268 43101/3 & 42918 **Fax:** +268 42641
Email: bc.swaziland@british-council.sprint.com

Sweden
see Nordic countries

Switzerland
Director: Caroline Morrissey
c/o British Embassy, Thunstrasse 50, PO Box 265, 30004 Berne 15
Telephone: +41 (Õ31) 352 7025 **Fax:** +41 (Õ31) 352 7029

Syria
Director: Dr Peter Clark, OBE
Abu Rumaneh Rowda, Masr Street, Hasibi/Azem Building, PO Box
  33105, Damascus
Telephone: +963 (Õ11) 333 3109 & 331 0631/2 **Fax:** + 963 (Õ11) 331
  0630

Taiwan
Director Operations: Dr Patrick Hart
7th floor, Fu Key Building, 99 Jen Al Road, Section 2, Taipei 10625
Telephone: +886 (Õ2) 3962238 **Fax:** +886 (Õ2) 3415749
Email: atecmark@aol.com

Tanzania
Director: Robert Sykes
Samora Avenue/Ohio Street, PO Box 9100, Dar es Salaam
Telephone: +255 (Õ51) 46486-90 **Fax:** +255 (Õ51) 112669
Email: bc.tanzania@british-council.sprint.com

Thailand
Director: Dr John Richards
254 Chulalongkorn Soi 64, Siam Square, Phyathai Road, Pathumwan,
    Bangkok 10330
Telephone: +66 (Õ2) 252 6136/7/8 **Fax:** +66 (Õ2) 253 5312
Email: bc.bangkok@british-council.sprint.com

and an office in Chiang Mai

Trinidad
see Caribbean

Tunisia
Director: Colin Stevenson
c/o British Embassy, BP 229, 5 place de la Victoire, Tunis 1015 RP
Telephone: +216 (Õ1) 259053 & 351754 **Fax:** +216 (Õ1) 353411

Turkey
Director: David Marler, OBE
c/o British Embassy, Kirklangic Sokak 9, Gazi Osman Pasa, Ankara
    06700
Telephone: +90 (312) 468 6192 & 468 6199 **Fax:** +90 (312) 427 6182
Email: bc.ankara@bc-ankara.sprint.com

and offices in Istanbul and Izmir

Uganda
Director: Roger Wilkins
IPS Building, PO Box 7070, Parliament Avenue, Kampala
Telephone: +256 (Õ41) 257301, 257303 & 257054-9 **Fax:** +256 (Õ41)
    254853

Ukraine
Director: John Day
9/1 Bessarabska Ploshcha, Flat 9, Kiev 252004
Telephone: +7 (044) 294 5518, 294 5528 & 294 5578 **Fax:** +7 (044) 294
    5507
& 294 5588

and offices in Kharkiv, Lviv and Odessa

United Arab Emirates
Director: David Latta
Villa no.7, Al Nasr Street, Khalidiya, Abu Dhabi
Telephone: +971 (Õ2) 659300 **Fax:** +971 (Õ2) 664340
Email: firstname.lastname@bc-abudhabi.sprint.com

and an office in Dubai

USA
Cultural Attaché: David Evans
British Embassy, 3100 Massachusetts Avenue NW, Washington, DC
    20008
Telephone: +1 (202) 898 4275, 462 1340 & 898 4407 **Fax:** +1 (202) 898
    4612
Email: bc.washington@bc-washington.sprint.com

Uzbekistan
see Turkey

Venezuela
Director: Paul de Quincey
Torre la Noria, Piso 6, Paseo Enrique Eraso, Las Mercedes, Sector San
    Román, Apartado 65131, Caracas 1065
Telephone: +58 (Õ2) 91 52 22, 91 55 43, 91 53 43 & 91 54 43 **Fax:** +58
    (Õ2) 91 59 43
Email: firstname.lastname@bc-caracas.sprint.com

and an office in Valencia

Vietnam
Director: Ian Simm
18b Cao Ba Quat, Ba Dinh District, Hanoi
Telephone: +844 8434941 & 8434943/4 **Fax:** +844 8434962
Email: bc.hanoi@british-council.sprint.com

Yemen
Director: Brendan McSharry, MBE
As-Sabain St 7, PO Box 2157, Sana'a
Telephone: +967 (Õ1) 244121/2 & 244153/4 **Fax:** +967 (Õ1) 244120

Yugoslavia/Eastern Adriatic
Director: Jim McGrath
Generala Zdanova 34-Mazanin, PO Box 248, 11001 Belgrade
Telephone: +38 (Õ11 1) 332 441/2, 327 910 **Fax:** +38 (Õ11 1) 324 9013

and an office in Montenegro

Zambia
Director: Mark Fryars
Heroes Place, Cairo Road, PO Box 34571, Lusaka
Telephone: +260 (Õ1) 223602 & 228332/3/4 **Fax:** +260 (Õ1) 214122
Email: cchatham@zamnet.zm *(Assistant Director)*

and an office in Ndola

Zimbabwe
Director: Dr Jerry Eyres
23 Jason Moyo Avenue, PO Box 664, Harare
Telephone: +263 (Õ4) 790 627/8/9 & 793 792/3 **Fax:** +263 (Õ4) 737 877
Email: britcoun@harare.iafrica.com

and an office in Bulawayo

5041

BRITISH FANTASY SOCIETY
2 Harwood Street, Heaton Norris, Stockport SK4 1JJ
Telephone: 0161 476 5368
Email: bfs@pavilion.co.uk

President: Ramsey Campbell
Vice-President: Jan Edwards
Secretary: Robert Parkinson
Editors: Peter Coleborn *(Winter Chills)*
David Howe *(Newsletter)*
Mike Chinn *(Mystique)*
Phil Williams *(Dark Horizons)*

Formed for devotees of fantasy, horror and related fields in literature, art
and the cinema. Publications include the *British Fantasy Newsletter* (bi-
monthly), featuring news and reviews, and various accompanying
booklets listing fiction and non-fiction of interest, including *Masters of
Fantasy*, a series of booklets on individual authors, and *Winter Chills*, an
annual fiction booklet. There is a small press library and an annual
convention. The British Fantasy Awards are sponsored by the Society.
    Membership fees: UK £17; Europe £20; USA $35; Rest of World £25.

5042

BRITISH FILM INSTITUTE
21 Stephen Street, London W1P 2LN
Telephone: 0171 255 1444
Fax: 0171 436 7950

Director: Wilf Stevenson
Head of Research: Colin MacCabe
Head of Publishing: Ed Buscombe
Deputy Head of Publishing: John Smoker

The British Film Institute exists to encourage the development of film,
TV and video in the UK, and to promote knowledge, understanding and
enjoyment of the culture of the moving image. Its activities include the
National Film and Television Archive; the National Film Theatre; the
Museum of the Moving Image; the London Film Festival; the production
and distribution of film and video; funding and support for regional
activities; library and information services; stills, posters and designs;
research; publishing and education; and the monthly *Sight and Sound*
magazine.

5043

THE BRITISH GUILD OF TRAVEL WRITERS
90 Corringway, London W5 3HA
Telephone: 0181 998 2223

Chairman: John Bell
Hon Secretary: John Harrison

The Guild has a membership of around 150, all professional journalists, broadcasters and photographers who derive the majority of their earnings from travel writing or broadcasting. Monthly meetings are devoted to discussion of travel topics, usually with outside speakers, and take place at a variety of venues. There is a monthly *Newsletter*.
    A list of members can be purchased with details of who they write for, interests, etc.

5044

BRITISH PRINTING INDUSTRIES FEDERATION (BPIF)
11 Bedford Row, London WC1R 4DX
Telephone: 0171 242 6904
Fax: 0171 405 7784

Director General: Tom Machin
Deputy Director General: David Padbury
Directors: John Arnold *(Corporate and Policy Affairs)*
Andrew Brown *(Employment Affairs)*
Leigh Martins *(Sections)*

The BPIF is the trade association and employers' organization representing some 3000 employers in the general commercial sector of the UK printing industry.
    Publications include a monthly management journal and specialist books on costing and cost accountancy, book production, recruitment, print buying, industrial relations, law, careers, health and safety and technical subjects.

5045

BRITISH STANDARDS INSTITUTION
389 Chiswick High Road, London W4 4AL
Telephone: 0181 996 9000
Fax: 0181 996 7400

Sales Department:
Linford Wood, Milton Keynes MK14 6LE

Chief Executive: Sir Neville Purvis, KCB

BSI is the national, independent Royal Charter body responsible for compiling and publishing British Standards. There are some 12,000 British Standards covering products and processes for all industries and technologies. These are listed in the BSI *Catalogue* (issued annually) and are available by mail order from the Sales Department, BSI.

5046

THE BRONTË SOCIETY
Brontë Parsonage Museum, Haworth, Keighley, West Yorkshire
BD22 8DR
Telephone: 01535 642323
Fax: 01535 647131

President: Lord Briggs of Lewes, MA, FBA

The principal activities of the Society are the preservation of the literary works of the Brontë family and of manuscripts and other objects related to or connected with the family; the maintenance and development of the Brontë Parsonage Museum and Library at Haworth; the holding of meetings, lectures and exhibitions, and the publication of information relating to the Brontë family; and the acquisition of new material as it becomes available.

5047

THE BROWNING SOCIETY
100 Townshend Court, Mackennal Street, London NW8 6LD
Telephone: 0171 722 4170

Also at:
The Director, Armstrong Browning Library, Baylor University,
PO Box 97152, Waco, TX 76798-7152, USA

President: Dr Peter Kelley
Hon Secretary: Dr M. Calcraft-Rennie

The aims of the Society are to widen the appreciation and understanding of the poetry of Robert Browning and Elizabeth Barrett Browning and other Victorian writers and poets; and also to collect and exchange relevant items of special literary and biographical interest. The Society arranges an annual programme of lectures, visits etc, in London and elsewhere.
    Members from Britain and overseas are kept in touch through the regular interchange of news and information. The subscription is £15 per year. Membership enquiries should be made to the Secretary.

5048

THE BYRON SOCIETY
Byron House, 6 Gertrude Street, London SW10 0JN
Telephone: 0171 352 5112
Fax: 0171 352 8226

Chairman: Derek Wise
Deputy Chairman: Rt Hon Michael Foot, PC
Hon Director: Mrs Elma Dangerfield, OBE
Secretary: Mrs Rosemary Smith
Hon Treasurer: Justin Glass

To promote interest and research into the work and life of the poet, Lord Byron.

5049

RANDOLPH CALDECOTT SOCIETY
Clatterwick Hall, Little Leigh, Northwich, Cheshire CW8 4RJ
Telephone: 01606 891303 *(office hours)*

Hon Secretary: Kenn Oultram

The Society (founded in 1983) exists to honour and promote the life and works of Randolph Caldecott, the Chester-born illustrator, artist and sculptor, who died in St Augustine, Florida, USA in 1886. Meetings are held twice-yearly in Chester (and occasionally in London) and a Newsletter is produced.

5050

DARESBURY LEWIS CARROLL SOCIETY
Clatterwick Hall, Little Leigh, Northwich, Cheshire CW8 4RJ
Telephone: 01606 891303 *(office hours)*

Hon Secretary: Kenn Oultram

The Daresbury Lewis Carroll Society (founded in 1970) exists to study the life, times and works of Lewis Carroll. Within the next two years it is hoped to open a study centre/library in Daresbury which would be made available for students, researchers etc. Meetings are held twice annually in Daresbury, Cheshire (Carroll's village of birth). Newsletters are issued which refer to new Carrollian books and publications.

5051

CHILDREN'S BOOK CIRCLE
c/o Anne Marley, County Library HQ, 81 North Walls, Winchester
SO23 8BY
Telephone: 01962 846086
Fax: 01962 856615
Email: libjam@hants.gov.uk

Chair: Anne Marley *(Hampshire County Library)*

Founded in 1962. An informal association of people involved in the publishing of children's books which aims to promote friendship and to encourage the spread of information and ideas among those concerned with children's books. Approximately once a month discussion meetings are held, at which talks are given by people inside and outside the publishing trade such as authors, reviewers, booksellers, librarians and parents. In 1965 the Circle instituted the annual Eleanor Farjeon Award. Membership: 350.

5052

CHILDREN'S BOOKS HISTORY SOCIETY
c/o Secretary, 25 Field Way, Hoddesdon, Herts EN11 0QN
Telephone: 01992 464885
Fax: 01992 464885

Chairman: Brian Alderson *(temp. Joint Editor)*
Secretary: Pat Garrett *(temp. Joint Editor)*
Treasurer: Sarah Jardine-Willoughby
Newsletter Editor: John Coles
Committee: Dennis Butts
Mary Cadogan
Margaret Clark
Margaret Heaton
Margaret Payne
Dr Michael Taylor

The Children's Books History Society aims to promote an appreciation of children's books, and to study their history, bibliography and literary content. By means of its meetings, Newsletters and Occasional Papers which are issued to members containing articles, book reviews, news of exhibitions and collections, auctions and other items, it encourages the distribution and exchange of information on the history of children's literature. The Society welcomes new members whether their interest is amateur or professional.

In 1990 the Society established its biennial 'Harvey Darton Award' for a book published in English, which extends our knowledge of some aspect of British children's literature of the past.

Meetings and talks are held in London about six times a year with occasional provincial meetings.

The Society constitutes the British branch of the Friends of Osborne in Toronto, Canada. The Society is also in liaison with the Library Association. Members are welcome at each other's meetings, and British members may purchase the Toronto annual giftbook.

The annual subscription is £7.50, and should be sent to the Secretary at the above address. A copy of the current newsletter and programme will be sent with your receipt.

5053

CHILDREN'S WRITERS & ILLUSTRATORS GROUP
The Society of Authors, 84 Drayton Gardens, London SW10 9SB
Telephone: 0171 373 6642
Fax: 0171 373 5768

Secretary: Gareth Shannon

The Children's Writers and Illustrators Group is an organization, founded in 1963, for writers and illustrators of children's books, who are members of the Society of Authors. Meetings are held regularly, with opportunities for members to meet each other, as well as to hear talks or discussions on various aspects of their work.

5054

CIRCLE OF WINE WRITERS
44 Oaklands Avenue, Droitwich, Worcs WR9 7BT
Telephone: 01905 773707
Fax: 01905 773707

President: Julian Jeffs
Chairman: Steven Spurrier
Vice-Chairman: Philippe Boucheron

Aims to improve the standard of writing, lecturing and broadcasting about wine and to contribute in those ways to the growth of knowledge and interest in wine.

5055

COMHAIRLE NAN LEABHRAICHEAN / THE GAELIC BOOKS COUNCIL
Department of Celtic, University of Glasgow, Glasgow G12 8QQ
Telephone: 0141 330 5190

Chairman: Prof Donald MacAulay
Chief Executive: Ian MacDonald

Set up in 1968 to administer the Gaelic Books Grant awarded to the University by the Scottish Education Department, the Council's purpose is to stimulate Gaelic publishing. It normally has ten members, and a paid staff of two. In April 1983 the Scottish Arts Council became its main funding body.

The Council provides financial assistance in the form of publication grants (paid to the publisher) for individual Gaelic books, and also commission grants for authors. Editorial advice is available, and a typing and proof-reading service.

As a retailer, the Council runs a bookselling service and stocks all Gaelic and Gaelic-related works in print, regular lists of these being published in its catalogue, *Leabhraichean Gàidhlig*.

5056

THE CONFEDERATION OF INFORMATION COMMUNICATION INDUSTRIES
19 Bedford Square, London WC1B 3HJ
Telephone: 0171 580 6321
Fax: 0171 636 5375

Director: Clive Bradley
Manager: Brian Green

The Confederation of Information Communication Industries (CICI) is a confederation of trade and professional associations and public organizations in the information products and services industries.

CICI provides representative and support services to strengthen the role of the UK's information industries and expand their international and domestic markets.

5057

THE JOSEPH CONRAD SOCIETY (UK)
c/o POSK, 238–46 King Street, London W6 0RF

President: Philip Conrad
Chairman: Keith Carabine
Secretary: Hugh Epstein
Treasurer: Allan Simmons
Editor: Andrew Roberts *(The Conradian)*

The Joseph Conrad Society (UK) has been in existence for 20 years. It aims to promote interest in and bring together scholars and readers of Conrad's works. The Society holds an annual international Conrad conference (usually in London) early in July, which is attended by leading Conrad scholars. It also publishes a journal, *The Conradian*, which appears twice a year and contains articles on Conrad and reviews of recent publications relating to Conrad and his work.

5058

THE COPYRIGHT LICENSING AGENCY LTD
90 Tottenham Court Road, London W1P 0LP
Telephone: 0171 436 5931
Fax: 0171 436 3896
Email: cla@cla.co.uk
Web Site: http://www.cla.co.uk

Directors: Maureen Duffy *(Chair)*
Nicolas Thompson *(Vice-Chair)*
Secretary: Colin P. Hadley *(Chief Executive)*

Formed by the Authors' Licensing and Collecting Society (ALCS) and the Publishers Licensing Society (PLS) and incorporated in 1983 as a single source for authorization of copying and to establish and implement licensing schemes for institutions and professions where extensive photocopying of books, periodicals and journals occurs. The fees collected, after the deduction of administration costs, are distributed to authors and publishers via their respective societies. Since 1987 CLA has distributed nearly £23M.

5059

COUNCIL OF ACADEMIC AND PROFESSIONAL PUBLISHERS

[Academic & Professional Div. of The Publishers Assoc.]
19 Bedford Square, London WC1B 3HJ
Telephone: 0171 580 6321
Fax: 0171 636 5375

Chair (1996–99): John Jarvis
Director: John R. M. Davies

Formed in 1977 as a division of the Publishers Association, the Council of Academic and Professional Publishers represents the interests of publishers serving higher education and the professional and commercial market. Collective activities are organized on their behalf. Membership is open to any publisher in membership of the Publishers Association who produces books or similar published material for these markets.

5060

CRIME WRITERS' ASSOCIATION
PO Box 172, Tring, Herts HP23 5LP

Chairman: Peter Walker
Vice-Chairman: Kate Charles
Treasurer: Vanessa Daubney
Secretary: Anthea Fraser
Membership Secretary: Barry Musto

Founded in 1953 with the object of improving standards of crime writing and providing a forum for crime writers. The Association holds monthly meetings in London, usually with a speaker, and annual weekend conferences. It issues a monthly news bulletin, *Red Herrings*, for members only, and presents annual awards for the best crime fiction of the year chosen by reviewers. A separate panel judges non-fiction. Since 1986, Cartier have sponsored a Diamond Dagger for outstanding contributions to the genre. The recipients have been Eric Ambler, P. D. James, John le Carré, Dick Francis, Julian Symons, Ruth Rendell, Leslie Charteris, Ellis Peters and Michael Gilbert.

5061

CRITICS' CIRCLE
47 Bermondsey Street, London SE1 3XT
Telephone: 0171 403 1818
Fax: 0171 403 1418

President: Stephen Pettitt
Honorary General Secretary: Peter Hepple

Founded in 1913 by J. T. Grein, S. R. Littlewood and John Parker. Aims to promote the art of criticism and to uphold its integrity in practice; to foster and safeguard the professional interests of its members and to provide opportunities for social intercourse among them and to support the advancement of the arts. Membership is only by invitation of the Council and is confined to persons engaged professionally, regularly and substantially in the writing or broadcasting of criticism of drama, music, cinema and ballet. There is no literary section *per se.*

5062

CROMPTON BEQUEST FUND
84 Drayton Gardens, London SW10 9SB
Telephone: 0171 373 6642
Fax: 0171 373 5768

Trustees: The Society of Authors

Founded by the late R. H. Crompton, to aid financially from time to time the publication of a limited number of works of real merit and some permanent importance which might otherwise remain unpublished owing to the improbability of their proving financially successful.

5063

DESIGN AND ARTISTS COPYRIGHT SOCIETY LTD
Parchment House, 13 Northburgh House, London EC1V 0AH
Telephone: 0171 336 8811
Fax: 0171 336 8822
Email: 101741.2676@compuserve.com

Chief Executive: Rachel Duffield
Deputy Chief Executive: Janet Ibbotson
Rights Administrators: Magnus Nelson
Janet Tod

Founded in 1983 by artists for artists. DACS is a non-making profit organization established to administer and protect the rights of artists in the UK.

Membership is open to any artist of any discipline and to the estate of an artist still in copyright.

DACS represents over 40,000 artists, including Picasso, Dali, Matisse, Wadsworth, Hamilton, Spencer and Lichtenstein.

Any publisher wishing to reproduce works of art in copyright should contact DACS in the first instance to obtain clearance prior to publication.

5064

DICKENS FELLOWSHIP
48 Doughty Street, London WC1N 2LF
Telephone: 0171 405 2127
Fax: 0171 831 5175

Hon General Secretary: Edward G. Preston
Editor: Dr Malcolm Andrews

An international organization for persons interested in the life and works of Charles Dickens. The Fellowship publishes a scholarly journal, *The Dickensian*, three times a year. Regular meetings. Annual conference. Branches throughout the world.

5065

DIRECT MARKETING ASSOCIATION (UK) LTD
Haymarket House, 1 Oxendon Street, London SW1Y 4EE
Telephone: 0171 321 2525
Fax: 0171 321 0191

Chief Executive: Colin Lloyd
Directors: Colin Fricker *(Legal Affairs)*
David Robottom *(Development)*

The Direct Marketing Association (UK) Ltd (DMA) is a leading authoritative voice of the direct marketing industry in the UK. Its aim is to promote the understanding and use of direct marketing. The membership includes companies who supply services to the direct marketing industry and companies who use direct marketing as part of the marketing mix. There are a number of publishers enjoying the benefits of membership: benefits such as being kept in touch with latest developments in the industry; playing an active role in the DMA and influencing negotiations with the government, the Post Office and other official bodies on matters which affect the way the industry operates; and attending conferences, courses, seminars and lunches at special discount rates.

5066

DIRECTORY PUBLISHERS ASSOCIATION
93a Blenheim Crescent, London W11 2EQ
Telephone: 0171 221 9089

Chairman: Trevor Fenwick
Secretary: Rosemary Pettit

Founded in 1970 to provide for the exchange of information between members in directory publishing; to devise and maintain a code of professional practice for the protection of the public; and in general to protect and promote the interests of directory publishers. The Association has 85 companies in membership and is affiliated to the European Association of Directory Publishers, Brussels; the Periodical Publishers Association and the Advertising Association.

5067

EDINBURGH BIBLIOGRAPHICAL SOCIETY
Dept of Special Collections, Edinburgh University Library, George Square, Edinburgh EH8 9LJ
Telephone: 0131 650 3412
Fax: 0131 650 6863
Email: exkb33@srv1.lib.ed.ac.uk

Secretary: M. C. T. Simpson

The Society's *Transactions* are issued approximately once every two years. At present they are issued to members, individual and institutional (annual subscription £7), who may also purchase such back numbers as are available. Other publications are issued occasionally and can be purchased by non-members.

5068

EDUCATIONAL PUBLISHERS COUNCIL
[Schools Division of The Publishers Association]
19 Bedford Square, London WC1B 3HJ
Telephone: 0171 580 6321
Fax: 0171 636 5375

Chairman (1995–97): Jeff Andrew
Director: John R. M. Davies

Formed in 1969 as a division of The Publishers Association, the Educational Publishers Council is particularly concerned with making known, both to the educational system and to the general public, the nature and importance of educational publishers' work. It is charged with assessing and putting forward the co-ordinated views of educational publishers.
   Membership is open to any firm which is in membership of the Publishers Association and gives proof of a *bona fide* interest in publishing or producing books or other permanent forms of instruction intended for classroom use.

5069

EDUCATIONAL WRITERS GROUP
The Society of Authors, 84 Drayton Gardens, London SW10 9SB
Telephone: 0171 373 6642
Fax: 0171 373 5768

Secretary: Kate Pool

The Educational Writers Group is a subsidiary group of the Society of Authors. Its purpose is to advise members on their publishing and broadcasting problems etc, to study the conditions peculiar to the market at home and overseas, to watch developments in teaching as they affect the educational writer, and to hold meetings at which experience can be pooled, surveys presented and matters of mutual interest discussed.

5070

THE EIGHTEEN NINETIES SOCIETY
97d Brixton Road, London SW9 6EE
Telephone: 0171 582 4690

Patron: HRH Princess Michael of Kent
President: The Countess of Longford, CBE
Chairman: Martyn Goff, OBE
Treasurer: Martin Paisner
Hon Secretary: G. Krishnamurti

Founded in 1963 as The Francis Thompson Society, the Eighteen Nineties Society widened its scope in 1972 to embrace the entire artistic and literary scene of the 1890 decade. Its activities include exhibitions, lectures and poetry readings. It publishes biographies of neglected authors

and artists of the period, also checklists, bibliographies etc. Its *Journal* appears periodically, and includes biographical, bibliographical and critical articles and book reviews. The *Journal* is free to members, and is not for public sale. There is also a quarterly newsletter, *Keynotes*.

5071

THE GEORGE ELIOT FELLOWSHIP
71 Stepping Stones Road, Coventry CV5 8JT
Telephone: 01203 592231

Secretary: Mrs Kathleen Adams

The George Eliot Fellowship is a registered charity and exists to honour George Eliot and to promote interest in her life and works. Its objects are to gather together admirers of the novelist and to encourage the collection of books, manuscripts, letters, portraits and other articles associated with her for public display as well as to observe her birthday each year.
   The Fellowship's annual programme includes a programme of readings from George Eliot's novels, essays and letters, wreath-laying ceremonies in the George Eliot Memorial Gardens, Nuneaton, and in Poets' Corner, Westminster Abbey, a George Eliot Memorial Lecture and a Birthday Luncheon in November on the Sunday nearest to her birthday. Other events which vary from year to year are also held.
   A free quarterly newsletter and an annual magazine are published. The annual subscription is £8.

5072

THOMAS ELLIS MEMORIAL FUND
University Registry, University of Wales, Cathays Park, Cardiff CF1 3NS
Telephone: 01222 382656
Fax: 01222 396040

Secretary General: J. D. Pritchard

Fund raised in memory of the late Thomas Edward Ellis, MP for Merioneth 1886–99. Grants from the fund are made to assist research into the language, literature, history and antiquities of Wales and Monmouthshire and the publication of such research.

5073

GAY AUTHORS WORKSHOP
BM Box 5700, London WC1N 3XX
Telephone: 0181 520 5223

Secretary: Kathryn Byrd

Gay Authors Workshop is an association of lesbians, gay men and bisexuals who are creative writers—poets, dramatists, fiction writers. Its aim is to raise the standard of gay literature by providing opportunities for gay writers to meet, read, discuss and criticize their work in a constructive way. Monthly meetings are held at different places in the London area for that purpose, and to share information about publishing outlets and competitions. Although London-based, it is a national organization. The quarterly newsletter (print and tape) keeps members in touch with activities.
   Membership is open to all gay writers, beginners as well as published authors. The subscription is £5 a year, £2 unwaged.

5074

GIBB MEMORIAL TRUST
c/o Deloitte & Touche, Leda House, Station Road, Cambridge CB1 2RN
Telephone: 01223 460222
Fax: 01223 350839

Clerk to the Trustees: P. R. Bligh

The Trust is a registered charity whose aim is to support the publication of works of scholarly research within the areas of the history, literature, philosophy and religion of the Persians, Turks and Arabs. Its activities are in financing and organizing the production of books, and in the distribution and marketing of the published works.

5075

GRAPHICAL, PAPER & MEDIA UNION
Keys House, 63–67 Bromham Road, Bedford MK4O 2AG
Telephone: 01234 351521
Fax: 01234 270580

General Secretary: A. D. Dubbins
Deputy General Secretary: T. Burke
General President: D. Douglas

Trade union.

5076

THE HAKLUYT SOCIETY
c/o Map Library, The British Library, Great Russell Street, London
WC1B 3DG
Telephone: 01986 788359
Fax: 01986 788181

President: Prof P. E. H. Hair
Series Editors: Dr W. F. Ryan
Mrs Sarah Tyacke
Hon Secretary: Anthony Payne
Administrative Officer: Mrs Fiona Easton

The objects of the Society, founded in 1846, are to advance education by the publication of scholarly editions of records of voyages, travels and other geographical material of the past and to promote public knowledge of these matters. Membership is open to all who are interested in its work. Members receive all volumes (except extra series) issued by the Society during the period of their membership; may purchase earlier volumes (if still in print) and additional copies of current volumes at special prices; may purchase volumes issued in the extra series at special prices; may purchase at a discount reprints of certain out-of-print volumes; and receive the annual report, the list of publications in print and the news bulletin.

5077

THE THOMAS HARDY SOCIETY
PO Box 1438, Dorchester, Dorset DT1 1YH
Telephone: 01305 251501

Chairman: Geoffrey Tapper
Hon Secretary: Miss E. M. Johnson
Editor of Journal: Dr Simon Curtis

The Thomas Hardy Society was founded in 1967 when it was set up to organize a festival marking the fortieth anniversary of Hardy's death. It continues as an organization dedicated to advancing education in the works of Thomas Hardy by promoting appreciation and study of these works.
   The Society is for anyone interested in Hardy's writings, his life and his times. Every other year it organizes a summer conference which attracts lecturers and students from all over the world. It also arranges Hardy events in Wessex, in London and in Sheffield. *The Thomas Hardy Journal* is published three times a year and is sent free to members.

5078

INDEPENDENT PUBLISHERS GUILD
25 Cambridge Road, Hampton, Middx TW12 2JL
Telephone: 0181 979 0250
Fax: 0181 979 6393

Secretary: Yvonne Messenger

The Independent Publishers Guild was founded in 1962 to offer a forum for the exchange of ideas and information and to represent the interests of its members. Membership is open to publishing companies which publish and produce books under their own imprint, to packagers and to publishing suppliers, and it is usually restricted to those who are independent of any owning group or consortium. New and established publishers are welcome to apply for membership. The Guild's *Bulletin* is regularly sent to all members.

Regular meetings are held to discuss issues of interest to members and to the book trade in general. Each year the Guild holds a spring weekend conference, which affords an opportunity for concentrated discussion within the Guild. The Guild mounts joint exhibitions at international trade fairs.

5079

INSTITUTE OF PRINTING
8 Lonsdale Gardens, Tunbridge Wells, Kent TN1 1NU
Telephone: 01892 538118 & 518028
Fax: 01892 518028

Chairman: C. H. Williams

Founded in 1961 as an independent professional body for those who practise or are directly engaged in the development of printing, bookbinding and associated technologies. Aims to promote the advancement of the science and art of printing and bookbinding, to lay down standards for admission to its various grades of membership and to establish scholarships, grants, awards and prizes.

5080

INSTITUTE OF SCIENTIFIC AND TECHNICAL COMMUNICATORS (ISTC)
Kings Court, 2–16 Goodge Street, London W1P 1FF
Telephone: 0171 436 4425
Fax: 0171 580 0747

President: Dave Griffiths
Executive Director: Allen Brobyn, FRSA
Editor: Rick Webster *(Communicator – ISTC Journal)*

Formed in 1972 as a result of the amalgamation of the Presentation of Technical Information Group (1948), the Institution of Technical Authors and Illustrators (originally the Technical Publications Association), formed in 1953, and the Institute of Technical Publicity and Publications (1963).
   The Institute aims to establish and maintain professional codes of practice for those employed in all branches of scientific and technical communication. It provides a forum for the exchange of views between its members, and aims to further their expectations and interests. The membership embodies a wide range of specialist knowledge of the principles and modern practices of effective communication of scientific and technical information. Through its publications and meetings, the Institute disseminates this experience to a growing profession and to those who employ the services of its members.
   The Institute represents Great Britain on the International Council for Technical Communication (INTECOM).
   Publications: *The Communicator* (UK subscription: £25 per year).

5081

INSTITUTE OF TRANSLATION & INTERPRETING
377 City Road, London EC1V 1NA
Telephone: 0171 713 7600
Fax: 0171 713 7650
Email: 101376.1430@compuserve.com

The Institute was founded in 1986 with the aim of serving all those concerned with translation and interpreting in industry, commerce, literature, science, research, law and administration, and of promoting high professional standards and a better status for translation and interpreting services. Its members must meet the requirements of the Institute's Council with regard to experience and competence in particular fields of technical, scientific, commercial and literary translation work, or in a variety of fields of interpretation. There is a register of members and the Institute office can also provide enquirers with the names of suitable members for any particular assignment. The office can advise on translating and interpreting fees, and also on staff translators' salaries.

5082

ISSN UK CENTRE
The British Library, Boston Spa, Wetherby, West Yorkshire LS23 7BQ

Telephone: 01937 546958
Fax: 01937 546979
Email: issn-uk@bl.uk

Assigns ISSN (International Standard Serial Numbers) to serial titles published in the UK.

5083

JANE AUSTEN MEMORIAL TRUST
Jane Austen's House, Chawton, Alton, Hants GU34 1SD
Telephone: 01420 83262
Fax: 01420 83262

Chairman: Thomas F. Carpenter, TD
Curator: Miss Jean K. Bowden

Founded in 1949, inaugurated under the auspices of Thomas Edward Carpenter, to advance the study of English literature, and in particular the works of Jane Austen, and in so doing to commemorate her. The Trust is also a memorial to his son, Lt Philip John Carpenter, 1st Battalion East Surrey Regiment, killed in action in Italy on 30 June 1944. The house is open daily from March to December (excluding Christmas Day and Boxing Day), in January and February open weekends only plus February half-term. Books by and about Jane Austen are on sale.

5084

CHARTERED INSTITUTE OF JOURNALISTS
2 Dock Offices, Surrey Quays Road, London SE16 2XU
Telephone: 0171 252 1187
Fax: 0171 232 2302
Email: cioj@dircon.co.uk

General Secretary: Christopher Underwood

The senior professional society of journalists. Incorporated by Royal Charter in 1890, it had its origin in the National Association of Journalists, which was founded in 1884 and converted into the Institute in 1889. Its primary object is 'the promotion by all reasonable means of the interests of journalists and journalism'. Representing the profession as a whole, it is a completely independent body free of political partiality. It gives equal rights of membership to all members of the profession, including radio and television journalists, press photographers and public relations officers with journalistic qualifications. Trade union representation is provided by the IOJ (TU), an independent certificated trade union.

5085

KEATS-SHELLEY MEMORIAL ASSOCIATION
Hon Treasurer, 10 Lansdowne Road, Tunbridge Wells, Kent TN1 2NJ
Telephone: 01892 533452
Fax: 01892 519142

Italy:
Keats-Shelley Memorial House, 26 Piazza di Spagna, 00187 Rome, Italy
Telephone: +39 (06) 678 4235
Fax: +39 (06) 678 4167

Chairman: Kenneth Prichard-Jones
Company Secretary: David Leigh-Hunt
Curator, Rome: Miss Bathsheba Abse

The Association exists to educate the public generally in the appreciation of the works of John Keats and Percy Bysshe Shelley and to preserve and maintain the house at 26 Piazza di Spagna, Rome, as a public memorial to these two poets. The Association produces the *Keats-Shelley Review* annually, edited by Angus Graham-Campbell, at Eton College.

5086

THE KIPLING SOCIETY
PO Box 68, Haslemere, Surrey GU27 2YR
Telephone: *(Secretary)* 01428 652709

Secretary: N. Entract
President: Dr M. Brock, CBE

Editor: G. H. Webb, OBE, CMG
US Secretary: Professor Enamul Karim
Secretary, Melbourne Branch, Australia: Mrs Rosalind Kennedy

A registered charity, whose aims are: the advancement of public education by the promotion of the study and appreciation of the life and works of Rudyard Kipling. The Society publishes a quarterly journal, holds meetings and discussions and maintains a library.

5087

LIBRARY ASSOCIATION
7 Ridgmount Street, London WC1E 7AE
Telephone: 0171 636 7543
Fax: 0171 436 7218
Email: info@la-hq.org.uk
Web Site: http://www.fdgroup.co.uk/la.htm

Chief Executive: R. Shimmon, FLA
Managing Director, LA Enterprises: Mrs J. Liebster
Publisher, LA Publishing: Mrs H. Carley
Directors: Ray Templeton *(Information Services)*
Ms S. Jespersen *(Professional Services)*
M. Wright *(Management Services)*

Founded in 1877. Primarily concerned with the promotion of a better, more widespread library service, it seeks to improve the status and qualifications of librarians by monitoring courses in schools of librarianship and maintaining a professional register of 25,000 members. It holds national and local conferences and meetings, provides information services and issues periodicals, books and reports on bibliographical and library matters.

5088

MECHANICAL-COPYRIGHT PROTECTION SOCIETY LTD
Elgar House, 41 Streatham High Road, London SW16 1ER
Telephone: 0181 664 4400
Fax: 0181 769 8792
Web Site: http://www.mcps.co.uk

Irish Republic:
MCPS (Ireland) Ltd, Pembroke Row, Lower Baggot Street, Dublin 2, Irish Republic
Telephone: +353 (01) 676 6940
Fax: +353 (01) 661 1316

Chief Executive: Frans de Wit
Commercial Operations Controller: G. J. Churchill
General Licensing Controller: Mark Isherwood

Founded in 1910, the MCPS represents more than 10,000 composer and music publisher members, issuing licences and collecting royalties on their behalf. The Society's primary function is to protect the interests of its members whenever their works are recorded either in the UK or abroad and to provide an efficient central clearing house for the music user.
Its main office is in London (there is a separate office in Dublin for the assistance of users in Eire), but its regional managers operate nationally and are available by contacting the Field Operations Department on 0181 664 4400.

5089

MEDICAL WRITERS GROUP
The Society of Authors, 84 Drayton Gardens, London SW10 9SB
Telephone: 0171 373 6642
Fax: 0171 373 5768

The Medical Writers Group, established in 1979, is a subsidiary organization of the Society of Authors. Its principal objects are to represent its members in all matters affecting their interests as medical writers; to hold meetings from time to time for the discussion of matters of common interest; and to provide, through the Society, advice to members on the special problems of medical authorship. Authors who have had a book accepted for publication, but not yet published, can join the Society as associate members and obtain advice.

5090 ▬▬▬▬▬▬▬▬▬▬▬▬▬▬▬▬▬▬▬▬▬▬▬▬▬▬▬

THE MERVYN PEAKE SOCIETY
2 Mount Park Road, Ealing, London W5 2RP
Telephone: 0181 567 9307
Fax: 0181 991 0559

Newsletter Office:
37 Byron Avenue East, Sutton, Surrey SM1 3RB

Honorary President: Sebastian Peake
Secretary: Frank Surry

The Society exists to promote a wider understanding of Peake's work. It publishes a yearly review and a quarterly newsletter, as well as other publications of Peake's work.

5091 ▬▬▬▬▬▬▬▬▬▬▬▬▬▬▬▬▬▬▬▬▬▬▬▬▬▬▬

NATIONAL ACQUISITIONS GROUP
Westfield House, North Road, Horsforth, Leeds, West Yorkshire LS18 5HG
Telephone: 0113 259 1447
Fax: 0113 259 1447
Email: swolfe@nag.eunet.co.uk

Chair: Jenny Glayzer
Hon. Secretary: Mary Morley
Hon. Treasurer: Richard Wake
Administrator: Sally Wolfe
Publications Officer: Ray Attwood

Established in 1986, NAG is a broadly based organization which stimulates, co-ordinates and publicizes developments in library acquisitions and the book trade. The membership includes individuals and organizations within publishing, bookselling and systems supply, as well as librarians responsible for choosing and buying books for academic, public, national, government and special institutions.

NAG has two main aims:
— to bring together all those in any way concerned with library acquisitions, to assist them in exchanging information and comment and to promote understanding and good practice between them;
— to seek to influence other organizations and individuals to adopt its opinions and standards.

NAG's objectives are to:
— provide a forum for discussion and the exchange of information;
— extend knowledge and understanding of technological developments;
— promote the dissemination of information about library acquisitions;
— develop the awareness of producers, suppliers and librarians;
— act as a channel of communication with Government and other bodies.

5092 ▬▬▬▬▬▬▬▬▬▬▬▬▬▬▬▬▬▬▬▬▬▬▬▬▬▬▬

NATIONAL UNION OF JOURNALISTS
Acorn House, 314 Grays Inn Road, London WC1X 8DP
Telephone: 0171 278 7916
Fax: 0171 837 8143

Irish Republic:
Liberty Hall, Eden Quay, Dublin 1
Telephone: +353 (01) 748694
Fax: +353 (01) 749250

Scotland:
63 Carlton Place, Glasgow G5 9TW
Telephone: 041-429 7239
Fax: 041-429 4039

The North:
Adamson House, Shambles Square, Manchester M3 1RE
Telephone: 061-834 0240
Fax: 061-832 8196

General Secretary: John Foster
Deputy General Secretary: Jacob Ecclestone

Senior Assistant Secretary: Robert Norris
Assistant Secretary (Ireland): Eoin Ronayne

The Union consists of journalists, including photographers and creative artists, working editorially in newspapers, magazines, books, broadcasting, public relations, teletext and viewdata, advertising and fashion photographers, and full-time officials of the Union.

The objects of the Union are to defend and promote the professional and financial interests and the welfare of its members; the principles and practice of journalism; the freedom of the Press, broadcasting, speech and information; trade union principles and organization; equality of opportunity for all its members and staff and the elimination of discrimination; peace, social justice and civil liberty; to establish out-of-work, benevolent and death benefits; and to determine all questions affecting the professional conduct of members.

5093 ▬▬▬▬▬▬▬▬▬▬▬▬▬▬▬▬▬▬▬▬▬▬▬▬▬▬▬

NUFFIELD FOUNDATION
28 Bedford Square, London WC1B 3EG
Telephone: 0171 631 0566
Fax: 0171 323 4877

Director: Anthony Tomei

Founded 1943. While not a literary foundation, being rather concerned with the advancement of health, education and social well-being through scientific research, the Foundation from time to time supports projects of interest to publishers, particularly in the field of the social sciences. The Foundation rarely acts as publisher itself and most of the work resulting from its grants is published through commercial channels. In the case of the large-scale school curriculum development programmes sponsored by the Foundation in recent years (in such subjects as science, mathematics and modern languages), the resulting materials are published by appropriate firms of educational publishers.

5094 ▬▬▬▬▬▬▬▬▬▬▬▬▬▬▬▬▬▬▬▬▬▬▬▬▬▬▬

THE PENMAN CLUB
185 Daws Heath Road, Benfleet, Essex SS7 2TF
Telephone: 01702 557431

General Secretary: Mark Sorrell

Literary society for writers, published and unpublished, throughout the world; members in many countries. Benefits of membership include criticism of all MSS without additional charge; marketing and general literary advice. Prospectus available from the General Secretary, send SAE.

5095 ▬▬▬▬▬▬▬▬▬▬▬▬▬▬▬▬▬▬▬▬▬▬▬▬▬▬▬

PERFORMING RIGHT SOCIETY LTD
29–33 Berners Street, London W1P 4AA
Telephone: 0171 580 5544
Fax: 0171 306 4050

South-West England & Wales:
1st floor, ICL House, 143 Redcliff Street, Bristol BS1 6PS
Telephone: 0117 930 0036
Fax: 0117 927 5200

Scotland:
3 Rothesay Place, Edinburgh EH3 7SL
Telephone: 0131 226 5320
Fax: 0131 220 4541

North-West:
Empire Court, 51 Winmarleigh Street, Warrington, Cheshire WA1 1LE
Telephone: 01925 234456
Fax: 01925 234996

East:
Elwes House, 19 Church Walk, Peterborough, Cambs PE1 2UZ
Telephone: 01733 312712
Fax: 01733 312912

Chairman: Andrew Potter
General Manager: John Axon

Founded in 1914. An association of composers, authors and publishers of music, formed to administer the public performance and broadcasting rights in its members' copyright musical works, and those of its affiliated societies overseas.
  Publications: *PRS News*; *PRS Yearbook*; *PRS Handbook*.
  Composers and authors with at least 3 published or commercially recorded musical works and music publishers with a catalogue of at least 15 works are eligible for membership.

5096

THE POETRY SOCIETY
22 Betterton Street, London WC2H 9BU
Telephone: 0171 240 4810
Fax: 0171 240 4818
Email: poetrysoc@dial.pipex.com
Web Site: http://www.bbcnc.org.uk/online/poetry

Director: Chris Meade
Editor: Peter Forbes

The Society's principal activities include: the quarterly publication of *Poetry Review*; the promotion of national tours and London events; an Advice and Information Service (including a quarterly newsletter); the National Poetry Competition which awards over £4000 in prizes each year and has brought many poets to national attention; administering the prestigious European Poetry Translation Prize; the administration of the WH Smith Poets in Schools Scheme, the BP Teachers' Resources File, and *Schools Poetry Review*.

5097

THE BEATRIX POTTER SOCIETY
32 Etchingham Park Road, Finchley, London N3 2DT
Telephone: 0181 346 8031

Chairman: Judy Taylor
Membership Secretary: Margaret Heaton
Secretary: Marian Werner
Sales Manager: Jenny Akester

The Society was founded in 1980 by a group of people professionally involved in the curatorship of Beatrix Potter material. It exists to promote the study and appreciation of the life and works of Beatrix Potter (1866–1943).
  The Society holds regular talks and meetings in London, and arranges visits to other places connected with Beatrix Potter. An annual Linder Memorial Lecture is given each spring to commemorate the contribution to Beatrix Potter studies made by Leslie and Enid Linder. Biennial study conferences are held in the Lake District and are attended by many of our overseas members.
  The Society issues a quarterly newsletter, sent free to members, which contains information about forthcoming meetings and visits; reviews of books and exhibitions; members' letters, and a variety of articles on aspects of Beatrix Potter's life and work. News is also given on the collections of Beatrix Potter material both in the UK and elsewhere. The Society also publishes the proceedings of its study conferences.
  The Society is a registered charity and its membership is worldwide. In view of our many American members special liaison officers have been appointed in the US to look after their interests.

5098

PUBLIC LENDING RIGHT
Bayheath House, Prince Regent Street, Stockton-on-Tees TS18 1DF
Telephone: 01642 604699
Fax: 01642 615641
Email: registrar@plr.octacon.co.uk

Registrar: Jim Parker

Public Lending Right (PLR) exists to make payments to authors for the borrowing of their books from public libraries. PLR is funded by the Department of National Heritage and is headed by a registrar. To qualify,

authors must register their books with the PLR office. Payment calculations are based on book loans from a representative sample of public libraries. Payments are made annually. No author may receive more than £6000.

5099

THE PUBLISHERS ASSOCIATION
19 Bedford Square, London WC1B 3HJ
Telephone: 0171 580 6321
Fax: 0171 636 5375

President: Simon Master
Vice-President: Trevor Glover
Chief Executive & Secretary: Clive Bradley

Including the International Division (Book Development Council), the Educational Publishers Council (School Books Division), and the Council of Academic and Professional Publishers.
  The Association represents the interests of UK publishers of books, book-related materials and journals, to governments, other bodies in the trade and the public at large. It seeks to promote the sales of British books by all suitable means, and provides members with a wide range of services and help on publishing problems and opportunities.

5100

PUBLISHERS LICENSING SOCIETY LTD
90 Tottenham Court Road, London W1P 9HE
Telephone: 0171 436 5931
Fax: 0171 436 3986
Email: c.elmslie@pls.org.uk

Chairman: Nicolas Thompson
Secretary & Manager: Caroline Elmslie
Consultant: Richard Balkwill

The Publishers Licensing Society obtains mandates from publishers which grant PLS the authority to license photocopying of pages from published works.
  PLS aims to maximize revenue from licences for mandating publishers and to expand the range and repertoire of mandated publishers available to licence holders. It supports the Copyright Licensing Agency (CLA) in its efforts to increase the number of legitimate users through the issuing of licences and vigorously pursues any infringements of copyright works belonging to rights' holders.

5101

PUBLISHERS PUBLICITY CIRCLE
48 Crabtree Lane, London SW6 6LW
Telephone: 0171 385 3708
Fax: 0171 385 3708

Secretary/Treasurer: Christina Thomas

For over 50 years, the Publishers Publicity Circle has enabled book publicists – both from publishing houses and freelance PR agencies – to meet and share information regularly. Representatives of the media are invited to speak about the ways in which they can feature authors and their books, and how book publicists can provide most effectively the information and material needed.
  Annual prizes are awarded for the best publicity campaigns of the year. In 1991 two new prizes were given: the Young Telegraph/PPC awards for children's fiction and non-fiction.
  A directory of the PPC membership is published each year and distributed to over 2000 media contacts, providing the names of publicity staff, their fax and telephone numbers.

5102

ROMANTIC NOVELISTS ASSOCIATION
35 Ruddlesway, Windsor, Berks SL4 5SF
Telephone: 01753 867100

Public Relations / Publicity:
Southfield Farm, Bridgehampton, Yeovil, Somerset BA22 8HQ

Chairman: Elizabeth Buchan
Hon Secretary: Joyce Bell
Hon Treasurer: Alannah Hubbart
Membership Secretary & New Writers Scheme Organizer: Hilary Johnson

The Association aims to raise the prestige of good quality romantic fiction and makes annual awards for the best romantic (including historical) novel, and for the best first novel by a hitherto unpublished writer accepted for publication.

5103

ROYAL LITERARY FUND
144 Temple Chambers, Temple Avenue, London EC4Y 0DA
Telephone: 0171 353 7150

President: His Honour Judge Stephen Tumim *(Chairman of Management Committee)*
Secretary: Mrs Fiona Clark *(Administrator)*

Founded 1790. Grants are made to authors of published works of approved literary merit who are in want or distress; single non-repeatable grants are made to the dependants of deceased eligible authors. Applicants should write to the Secretary for a form.

5104

ROYAL SOCIETY OF LITERATURE
1 Hyde Park Gardens, London W2 2LT
Telephone: 0171 723 5104
Fax: 0171 402 0199

President: Rt Hon Lord Jenkins of Hillhead, OM, FRSL
Chairman: John Mortimer, QC, CBE, FRSL
Secretary: Maggie Parham

The Society's purpose is to sustain all that is best, whether traditional or experimental, in English Letters, and to encourage a catholic appreciation of literature.
   Lectures and poetry readings take place monthly in the Society's rooms and a selection of the lectures is published from time to time in volume form. The Society administers a number of trusts for the advancement of Letters. The Royal Society of Literature Award under the Heinemann bequest is presented annually to one or more writers on the strength of a published work of high literary merit. The Winfred Holtby Memorial Award is a yearly prize for a regional novel.

5105

RSA (THE ROYAL SOCIETY FOR THE ENCOURAGEMENT OF ARTS, MANUFACTURES AND COMMERCE)
8 John Adam Street, London WC2N 6EZ
Telephone: 0171 930 5115
Fax: 0171 839 5805
Email: rsa@rsa.ftech.co.uk

Chairman: Prue Leith, OBE
Director: Peter Cowling

Publishes monthly *RSA Journal* and reports, conference papers and occasional books.

5106

THE RUSKIN SOCIETY OF LONDON
c/o Ivy Books, 351 Woodstock Road, Oxford OX2 7NX
Telephone: 01865 310987 & 515962

Hon Secretary: Miss O. E. Madden

A literary society, founded to further the life and works of John Ruskin and his contemporaries. All meetings and functions are held in London.

5107

THE DOROTHY L. SAYERS SOCIETY
Rose Cottage, Malthouse Lane, Hurstpierpoint, West Sussex BN6 9JY
Telephone: 01273 833444
Fax: 01273 835988
Email: jasmine@bredon.demon.co.uk

Chairman: Christopher Dean
Hon Secretaries: Lenelle Davis
Jasmine Simeone
Hon Treasurer: John Brading
Archivist: Bunty Parkinson

The Dorothy L. Sayers Society was founded in 1976 to promote the study of the life, works and thoughts of the writer, to encourage the performance of her plays and the publication of books by and about her, to preserve original material and to provide assistance for researchers. It acts as a forum and information centre, putting members in touch with one another and providing for study purposes material not otherwise available. It holds regular meetings and annual seminars whose proceedings are published. The archives contain over 1200 items, including articles and pamphlets by members. Six bulletins are issued each year. Membership is currently £9 or $18 a year, with reduction under 25 years of age.

5108

SCHOOL LIBRARY ASSOCIATION
Liden Library, Barrington Close, Liden, Swindon, Wilts SN3 6HF
Telephone: 01793 617838

Executive Secretary: *to be appointed*

The School Library Association is an independent organization working to promote the development of school libraries, primary and secondary. Services to members include advice and information from office base, publications at reduced prices, quarterly journal of articles and reviews, training courses and a network of area groups. Membership includes schools, colleges, local education authorities, public libraries, publishers and individuals in the United Kingdom and overseas.

5109

SCOTTISH PUBLISHERS ASSOCIATION
Scottish Book Centre, 137 Dundee Street, Edinburgh EH11 1BG
Telephone: 0131 228 6866
Fax: 0131 228 3220

Chairman: Mike Miller
Vice-Chairman: Lesley Taylor
Treasurer: Christian Maclean
Director: Lorraine Fannin
Publicist: Susanne Dickson

The Scottish Publishers Association (SPA) was formed in 1974 by a group of small trade publishers to serve the interests of Scottish-based houses. The SPA has now grown to include virtually every Scottish publishing house.
   The SPA represents its members' interests in a number of capacities, primarily in the cooperative promotion and marketing of their books. This takes the form of attendance at international book fairs, publication of a variety of catalogues, joint catalogue mailings, export services and the administration of the Scottish Book Marketing Group.

5110

THE SHAW SOCIETY
51 Farmfield Road, Downham, Bromley, Kent BR1 4NF
Telephone: 0181 697 3619
Fax: 0181 697 3619

Treasurer:
155a North View Road, London N8 7ND
Telephone: 0181 348 7411

Hon General Secretary: Ms B. Smoker
Hon Treasurer: D. Sutherland

The Shaw Society is a literary society, founded in 1941, to promote a wider interest in and deeper understanding of the word of Bernard Shaw.

Meetings (mostly comprising a lecture followed by discussion) are held in Conway Hall, 25 Red Lion Square, London WC1 (near Holborn station) usually on the last Friday of January, March, April, May, June, September, October and November, at 7 pm; the AGM takes place on the last Friday of February, followed by a mini-social and book auction.

The Society sponsors an open-air Shavian performance on the lawn of Shaw's Corner, Ayot St Lawrence, Hertfordshire, on the Saturday and Sunday closest to Shaw's birthday (July 26), at 6.30 pm.

Publications: *The Shavian*, edited by T. F. Evans, annual, and an informative newsletter four times a year, edited by Anthony Ellis, both being sent free to members.

Subscriptions: UK individual and library members £9; family membership (single mailing) £12; USA and Canada $15.

5111

SOCIETY OF ARCHIVISTS
Information House, 20–24 Old Street, London EC1V 9AP
Telephone: 0171 253 5087/4488 ext 65
Fax: 0171 253 3942

Executive Secretary: Patrick Cleary

Publication of texts/periodicals on archives and records management. Conferences and training courses.

5112

SOCIETY OF AUTHORS
84 Drayton Gardens, London SW10 9SB
Telephone: 0171 373 6642
Fax: 0171 373 5768

President: Sir Victor Pritchett, CH, CBE
General Secretary: Mark Le Fanu

An independent trade union for authors. Its purpose is to further the interests of its 6000 members through individual advice and general campaigning. It is controlled by an elected Committee of Management and administered by a staff with long experience in the business and legal aspects of authorship. Members have access to a comprehensive advisory service and may seek advice on all forms of contracts. The Society also serves the corporate interests of specialist writers through a number of subsidiary groups – viz the Broadcasting Group, the Translators Association, Children's Writers and Illustrators, Educational Writers and Medical Writers Groups. It makes representations to government departments and promotes campaigns on behalf of the profession as a whole (eg public lending right, tax concessions for authors, etc). It also administers literary estates, publishes a quarterly journal, *The Author*, issues numerous *Quick Guides* to its members and manages a variety of awards and trust funds for authors.

5113

SOCIETY OF AUTHORS PENSION FUND
84 Drayton Gardens, London SW10 9SB

Secretary: Mark Le Fanu

A small number of pensions is granted by the Pension Fund Committee to authors over the age of 60 who have been members of the Society for 10 years. Pensions normally range from £500 to £600 per annum.

5114

SOCIETY OF FREELANCE EDITORS & PROOFREADERS
38 Rochester Road, London NW1 9JJ
Telephone: 0171 813 3113

Chairwoman: Michèle Clarke
Secretary: Valerie Elliston
Press Officer: Lionel Browne

Founded in 1988 with the twin aims of promoting high editorial standards and achieving recognition of its members' professional status, the Society works to disseminate information and training, foster good relations between members and their clients, and combat the isolation often experienced by freelances. It supports recognized standards of training and accreditation for editors and proofreaders, and is working towards establishing recognized standards for its own members. Membership in April 1996 was over 1200.

Benefits of membership include: annual directory of members seeking work; free regular newsletter; local groups throughout the country; annual conference; meetings and training sessions in several centres, covering aspects of current professional practice and business matters; reference books available at a discount.

5115

SOCIETY OF INDEXERS
38 Rochester Road, London NW1 9JJ
Telephone: 0171 916 7809

Registrar:
25 Leyborne Park, Kew Gardens, Surrey TW9 3HB
Telephone: 0181 940 4771

Secretary: Mrs H. C. Troughton
Registrar: Mrs E. Wallis

Founded 1957 to raise the standards of indexing of books, periodicals and documents by holding meetings, courses and conferences and to issue a journal, *The Indexer*, and regular newsletters. Publishes and runs an open-learning course 'Training in Indexing'. The Society maintains a Register of members competent to do indexing in a wide range of both simple and specialized subject fields. Publishers and authors may be supplied with suitable names on application to the Registrar. Minimum scales of payment are recommended by the Society for use by members as a basis for negotiation with publishers. The Society wishes to impress on both publishers and authors the need for adequate and competent indexes in non-fiction works.

5116

SOCIETY OF PICTURE RESEARCHERS AND EDITORS (SPRED)
455 Finchley Road, London NW3 6HN
Telephone: 0171 431 9886
Fax: 0171 431 9887

SPREd exists to further the interests of picture researchers and picture editors. It provides members with information and advice, and operates a register for experienced freelancers. Its code of practice ensures a high standard of professionalism amongst members. It holds regular meetings and publishes a quarterly magazine, which is free to members and available on subscription to others.

5117

THE SOCIETY OF WOMEN WRITERS AND JOURNALISTS
110 Whitehall Road, Chingford, London E4 6DW
Telephone: 0181 529 0886

Hon Secretary: Jean Hawkes

The society holds lunch-time meetings in London each month and a monthly informal workshop meeting. The AGM and Country Members' Day takes place in London; there are also occasional get-togethers in various parts of the country.

Manuscripts, including poetry, can be brought to the monthly workshop meetings for reading and criticism. Out-of-town members may send their work by post. *The Woman Journalist*, the Society's publication, appears three times a year, and includes articles, reviews of members' work and information about events and activities.

Competitions, with awards, are held regularly for members working in all areas of writing. There is also a scholarship to the weekend school.

5118

SOCIETY OF YOUNG PUBLISHERS
12 Dyott Street, London WC1A 1DF

Chair: Suzanne Collier
Careers Adviser: Victoria Smith
Press Officer: Daniel Hume
Inprint Editor: Nick Baxter

Founded 1949. Provides a lively forum for discussion on subjects relevant to its members in every publishing department. Typical monthly meetings have recently included such subjects as bookclubs, audio and multimedia, film and TV tie-ins, copyright, the future of publishing, design, music publishing and remaindering. Other activities include an annual conference, study tours within the UK and regular social events. A newsletter, *Inprint*, is issued monthly.

Applications for membership are invited from anyone under 35 employed in publishing, printing, bookselling or allied trades, with associate membership available for anyone over 35. Meetings are held at the Publishers Association, 19 Bedford Square, London WC1 on the last Wednesday in the month at 6.30 pm (free to members, £2 to non-members). Current annual subscription is £20.

5119

STANDARD BOOK NUMBERING AGENCY LTD
c/o J. Whitaker & Sons Ltd, 12 Dyott Street, London WC1A 1DF
Telephone: 0171 836 8911
Fax: 0171 836 4342

Chairman: D. Whitaker, OBE
Directors: L. Baum
R. F. Baum
A. Mollison
Sally Whitaker
M. Whitaker
Manager: L. K. Andreasen

Formed in 1966 by collaboration between J. Whitaker & Sons Ltd, the British National Bibliography and the Publishers Association, with the aim of facilitating the ordering of books by publishers and booksellers in Great Britain.

The Standard Book Numbering Agency is responsible for allocating International Standard Book Numbers (ISBNs) and for the maintenance of the ISBN system in Great Britain. An ISBN is a number which identifies a book, its publisher and the country or group of countries of its publication. The number is unique to one title or edition of that title, and can never be used again, even if the original book has been out of print for many years.

In 1969 total numbering was achieved in Great Britain.

5120

THE TOLKIEN SOCIETY
Flat 6, 8 Staverton Road, Oxford OX2 6XJ
Telephone: 01865 58646
Fax: 01865 278855

Chairman: Chris Crawshaw
Secretary: Anne Haward
Treasurer: Mike Percival

The Society is dedicated to promoting research into and educating the public in the life and works of Professor J. R. R. Tolkien. It publishes a bi-monthly bulletin, *Amon Hen*, and an annual journal, *Mallorn*; and holds regular meetings in Oxford, London and elsewhere in the UK.

5121

TRANSLATORS ASSOCIATION
84 Drayton Gardens, London SW10 9SB
Telephone: 0171 373 6642
Fax: 0171 373 5768

Secretary: Gordon Fielden

The Translators Association is a subsidiary of the Society of Authors and advises literary translators on such matters as contracts and fees. Publishers seeking book translators can contact the Association for advice.

5122

TRAVELLING SCHOLARSHIP FUND
84 Drayton Gardens, London SW10 9SB
Telephone: 0171 373 6642
Fax: 0171 373 5768

Secretary: Mark Le Fanu

Founded in 1944 by an anonymous donor, to enable British creative writers to travel and to keep in touch with their colleagues abroad. A special committee annually reviews the field of contemporary literature before making its awards, which are not for open candidature, and are normally made to established writers of over 30 years of age.

The Fund is administered by the Society of Authors.

5123

EDGAR WALLACE SOCIETY
Kohlbergsgracht 40, 6462 CD Kerkrade, Netherlands

President: Penelope Wallace
Organizer: Kai Jörg Hinz

The Edgar Wallace Society was founded in 1969 to provide members with information on matters of interest about Edgar Wallace, including details of books to be published and those in current print, news of films, plays, television and radio broadcasts etc. New members receive a biography of Edgar Wallace and a cross-referenced list of all published book titles. The Society has members in 20 countries. Members receive the quarterly *Crimson Circle* magazine, which contains articles and other contributions of interest from members. Annual subscription is £15; concessions available.

5124

WELSH BOOKS COUNCIL / CYNGOR LLYFRAU CYMRU
Castell Brychan, Aberystwyth, Ceredigion, Wales SY23 2JB
Telephone: 01970 624151
Fax: 01970 625385

Director: Gwerfyl Pierce Jones
Deputy Director: Pedr ap Llwyd
Head of Department: Elgan Davies *(Design)*
Dewi Morris Jones *(Editorial)*
D. Philip Davies *(Marketing)*
Menna Lloyd Williams *(Children's Books)*
Dafydd Charles Jones *(Distribution)*
Arwyn Roderick *(Finance)*

Established in 1961 to promote an awareness of books from Wales, to act as a central agency co-ordinating the interests of authors, publishers and booksellers, and to develop the Welsh book trade in all possible ways. Editorial, design, marketing, children's books and wholesale distribution departments provide services to publishers.

Also responsible, since 1979, for distributing the Welsh Office grant towards Welsh-language publications.

5125

WOMEN IN PUBLISHING
c/o 12 Dyott Street, London WC1A 1DF

Committee Members: Jane Middleton *(Membership)*
Sheila Davies *(Information)*
Rajni Boswell *(WiPlash Editor)*

Women in Publishing works to promote the status of women working in publishing and related trades. It provides them and all women interested in publishing with the opportunity to meet and network. Activities include a monthly evening meeting, regular training courses, special events and publications, and a monthly newsletter. Membership is £20 per annum (£15 unwaged or students, and £25 for those paid for by their companies), which includes entrance to meetings and the newsletter.

Further information, and information about Women in Publishing branches outside London, is available from the Information Officer.

5126 ▬▬▬

WORSHIPFUL COMPANY OF STATIONERS AND NEWSPAPER MAKERS
Stationers' Hall, Ave Maria Lane, London EC4M 7DD
Telephone: 0171 248 2934
Fax: 0171 489 1975

Master: R. K. Haselden
Clerk: Captain P. Hames, RN

The Worshipful Company of Stationers had its beginnings in a Guild dating back at least to 1403; the original Charter was granted in 1557. The Company was expanded in modern times (1933) to include the Newspaper Makers. For nearly four centuries it was essential for the protection of copyright to register books at Stationers' Hall; since 1924 an extensively used system of voluntary registration has been in force.
   The Company's object has always been to promote the interests of the printing and allied trades, among them publishing and bookbinding. Its activities at the present day include the binding of apprentices and the award of scholarships to young men and women in these trades and the provision of pensions and financial help for tradesmen and their widows. The Company also plays a full part in the life of the City of London.
   The Stationers' Hall may be hired for functions.

5127 ▬▬▬

WRITERS' GUILD OF GREAT BRITAIN
430 Edgware Road, London W2 1EH
Telephone: 0171 723 8074
Fax: 0171 706 2413

President: Rosemary Anne Sisson
Co-Chair: Julia Jones
John Scotney
General Secretary: Alison Gray

Formed in May 1959. The Guild is a TUC Affiliated Union which now represents film, television, radio, book and theatre writers in Great Britain. Its basic function is to advise and assist any of its members and generally to act on their behalf, either individually or as a body, in solving the numerous problems which confront them. The Guild is affiliated to the TUC, Writers' Guild of America East and West, The Writers' Guild of Canada, Australian Writers Guild, New Zealand Writers Guild, Société des Auteurs, Recherchistes, Documentalistes et Compositeurs, The Confederation of Entertainment Unions, Performers Alliance, British Copyright Council, Congress of European Writers Organisation and International Confederation of Societies of Authors and Composers.

5128 ▬▬▬

YOUNG BOOK TRUST
Book Trust, Book House, 45 East Hill, Wandsworth, London SW18 2QZ
Telephone: 0181 870 9055
Fax: 0181 874 4790

Scottish Book Centre:
137 Dundee Street, Edinburgh EH11 1BG
Telephone: 0131 229 3663
Fax: 0131 228 4293

Patron: HRH the Prince Philip, Duke of Edinburgh
Chief Executive: Brian Perman
Chairman: Richard Hoggart

Young Book Trust, originally the Children's Book Foundation, is the children's division of Book Trust, the national educational charity for books and the reader. It was established in 1987 to act as a national focal point for everything to do with children's books and reading. It is in continuous discussion with publishers, booksellers, librarians, teachers and parents.
   Young Book Trust houses a unique collection of every children's book published in the UK in the last two years. It offers an information service on all aspects of children's books and reading, together with a wide range of promotional material and publications. Young Book Trust provides information on children's writers and illustrators. A subscription service is available for organizations such as schools and libraries.

5.3   COMMONWEALTH & OVERSEAS

AUSTRALIA

5129 ▬▬▬

AUSTRALIAN BOOKSELLERS ASSOCIATION
PO Box 1088, Carlton, Vic 3053
Telephone: +61 (03) 9663 7888
Fax: +61 (03) 9663 7557
Email: ausbook@ozemail.com.au

Location:
Suite 4/21 Drummond Place, Carlton, Vic 3053

Executive Director: Celia Pollock

The Australian Booksellers Association Inc protects and promotes the interests of booksellers throughout Australia. The Association has its origins in State Associations formed early this century and later amalgamated into a Federal Association.
   The objectives of the Association are to: establish bonds between booksellers all over Australia; enhance the unique role of books in our society; foster and encourage the selling of books; provide a national forum for member booksellers; provide technical advice and information to booksellers; represent booksellers' interests in contacts with organizations within the book trade, the government and the commercial world.
   The Australian Booksellers Association provides a range of services to its members including seminars and training courses, an annual conference, a monthly news bulletin, an annual economic survey, advice on legal and trade matters and Australian book vouchers.

5130 ▬▬▬

AUSTRALIAN COPYRIGHT COUNCIL
Suite 3, 245 Chalmers Street, Redfern, NSW 2016
Telephone: +61 (02) 318 1788
Fax: +61 (02) 698 3536

Chairman: Peter Banki
Executive Officer: Libby Baulch

Founded in 1968. The Council comprises 22 organizations or associations of owners and creators of copyright material. These include the Australian Society of Authors, the Australian Writers Guild and the Australian Book Publishers Association. The Council aims to represent the interests of copyright owners and to undertake research and give advice on all questions of copyright.
   Publications: *Australian Copyright Council Bulletin* and *Copyright Reporter*.

5131 ▬▬▬

AUSTRALIAN GOVERNMENT PUBLISHING SERVICE
GPO Box 84, Canberra, ACT 2601
Telephone: +61 (06) 295 4411
Fax: +61 (06) 295 4455

General Manager: Alan Law

The Australian Government Publishing Service (AGPS) is a business unit of the Department of Administrative Services.
   The AGPS's role is to provide printing, publishing and distribution services to the Australian Parliament, government departments and some statutory authorities.
   The AGPS General Manager is the AGPS head. He is supported by three assistant general managers and a number of managers each responsible for a discrete section. These sections cover the functional areas of information solutions, publishing, printing, publication sales, communications services, technical and electronic publishing services, finance, human resource and information technology management. Total AGPS staff numbers are approximately 570.

5132 ▬▬▬▬▬▬▬▬▬▬▬

AUSTRALIAN LIBRARY & INFORMATION ASSOCIATION
PO Box E441, Queen Victoria Terrace, ACT 2600
Telephone: +61 (06) 285 1877
Fax: +61 (06) 282 2249
Email: enquiry@alia.org.au
Web Site: http://www.alia.org.au

Executive Director: Virginia Walsh

The professional association for the library and information services industry. It aims to: promote and improve the services of libraries and other information agencies; improve the standard of library and information personnel and foster their professional interests and aspirations; represent the interests of members to governments, other organizations and the community; encourage people to contribute to the improvement of library and information services by supporting the association.

The association has over 7000 members throughout Australia and overseas. Any interested person or organization is most welcome to join.

5133 ▬▬▬▬▬▬▬▬▬▬▬

AUSTRALIAN PUBLISHERS ASSOCIATION LTD
Suite 60, Level 3, 89 Jones Street, Ultimo, NSW 2007
Telephone: +61 (02) 281 9788
Fax: +61 (02) 281 1073

President: Peter Donoughue
Executive Director: Susan Blackwell

Founded in 1949. Represents the interests of all firms actively engaged in publishing in Australia. Membership: 150, about 70% Australian-owned firms; the rest are Australian subsidiaries of overseas firms, mainly British and American.

5134 ▬▬▬▬▬▬▬▬▬▬▬

AUSTRALIAN SOCIETY OF AUTHORS LTD
98 Pitt Street, Redfern, NSW 2016
Telephone: +61 (02) 318 0877
Fax: +61 (02) 318 0530
Email: asauthors@peg.pegasus.oz.au

Postal Address:
PO Box 1566, Strawberry Hills, NSW 2012

Chair: Anne Deveson
Executive Director: Lynne Spender

The Australian Society of Authors Ltd was established in 1963 to promote and protect the general professional interests of all who create literary, musical or dramatic material.

Services include contract advice, intervention in disputes between authors and publishers and a comprehensive advisory service on all aspects of the profession of writing, including electronic and multimedia authorship. The Society publishes a quarterly journal, *Australian Author*, and a 6-weekly newsletter. The Society operates an electronic membership through Artsnet.

5135 ▬▬▬▬▬▬▬▬▬▬▬

AUSTRALIAN SOCIETY OF INDEXERS
GPO Box 1251, Melbourne, Vic 3001
Telephone: +61 (03) 9571 6341
Fax: +61 (03) 9571 6341
Email: mindexer@interconnect.com.au
Web Site: http://www.zeta.org.au/~aussi

Webmaster:
2/1 Nelson Street, Randwick, 2031
Telephone: +61 (02) 398 6726
Fax: +61 (02) 438 3729
Email: aussi@zeta.org.au

President: John Simkin
Treasurer: Joyce Gillespie
Secretary: Ian Odgers
Editor/Webmaster: Dwight Walker
Vice-President: Max McMaster

Objectives:
— to improve the quality of indexing in Australia — book, CD-ROM, Web, periodicals, database, picture
— to promote the training, continuing professional development, status and interest of indexers in Australia
— to act as an advisory board for indexing for authors, editors and publishers
— to provide opportunities for those interested in indexing to meet and exchange information, ideas and experience
— to establish and maintain relationships with bodies with related interests
— to publish information in accord with the above.

Services:
— to publishers and authors:
  — *Register of Indexers* — listing members whose work has been accepted by the Society's Panel of Assessors as being of high competence
  — *Indexers Available* — twice yearly — lists all members, registered and unregistered; all expect to take a commission
  — *The Medal* — annual award for excellence for an index published in Australia or New Zealand in the last two years
  — Web Indexing Prize (aussi@zeta.org.au) — to foster electronic indexing
— to indexers:
  — *Register of Indexers* — competence is recognized
  — current awareness of new methods, media and technology through newsletter, courses, meetings, workshops and Web site.

Membership: $AU40: Melbourne, Sydney, ACT; $AU30: rest of Australia; $AU35: rest of world; students half-price; electronic Newsletter available.

5136 ▬▬▬▬▬▬▬▬▬▬▬

LITERATURE FUND OF THE AUSTRALIA COUNCIL
PO Box 788, Strawberry Hills, NSW 2012
Telephone: +61 (02) 9950 9000
Fax: +61 (02) 9950 9111
Web Site: http://www.ozco.govt.au

Also at:
181 Lawson Street, Redfern, NSW 2016

Chairperson: Edmund Campion
Fund Manager: Irene Stevens
Programme Manager: Jose Borghino

The Literature Fund is a specialist fund of the Australia Council, replacing the Commonwealth Literary Fund (est 1908). The Australia Council, established in January 1973 and made a statutory body in March 1975, is responsible to the Australian government for the provision of financial support to the arts, and for advising on and assisting in the advancement of the status of the arts in Australia.

The Literature Fund plays a key role in ensuring that Australian writing is an increasingly vital part of Australia's life and culture. The Fund supports the writing and publication of all forms of creative literature through fellowships and project grants (for short-term projects) to Australian writers. By offering publishing subsidies to Australian book and magazine publishers, the Fund aims to encourage the publication of a wide range of work by Australian creative writers.

The Fund actively encourages the publication of Australian writing overseas and offers translation subsidies to international publishers who plan to publish Australian creative writing in a language other than English (closing date: 15 August annually). International publishing subsidies also assist international literary magazines which feature special editions devoted to Australian creative writing (closing date: 15 August annually).

International Promotions subsidies are also available to overseas organizations to promote Australian writers and the sale of their work overseas. Applications may be made for assistance with the attendance of Australian writers at overseas readings, conferences, seminars etc, and for promotional tours by Australian writers, organized by the overseas publishers of their books (closing date: 15 August annually; there is also a provision for approving some applications under $5000 through a Quick Response Scheme).

5137

NATIONAL LIBRARY OF AUSTRALIA
Parkes Place, Canberra, ACT 2600
Telephone: +61 (06) 262 1111
Fax: +61 (06) 273 4493

Director, Publishing & Marketing Branch: Paul Hetherington
Marketing Manager: Greg Turner

The National Library produces regular publications for the library community and the book trade as part of its collecting and resource sharing activities. The Library also publishes a wide range of books, prints and cards from the special collections to promote awareness of this material and its use by scholars and the general public.

CANADA

5138

ASSOCIATION FOR THE EXPORT OF CANADIAN BOOKS
504-1 Nicholas, Ottawa, Ont K1N 7B7
Telephone: +1 (613) 562 2324
Fax: +1 (613) 562 2329
Email: aecb@magi.com
Web Site: http://infoweb.magi.com/~aecb

Director: Luc Jutras *(Executive)*
International Program Officer: Carmen Tremblay
Information Officer: Veronica Schami

Established in 1972, the AECB is a non-profit organization composed of the various national publishers associations of Canada for the purpose of promoting exports of Canadian books. The organization is under the direction of a Board of Directors consisting of delegates from the various member associations: l'Association nationale des éditeurs de livres, Association of Canadian Publishers, Canadian Book Publishers Council and the Association of Canadian University Presses. Representatives from the Federal Departments of Canadian Heritage and Foreign Affairs are also members of AECB's Board.
The AECB's mandate is to help Canadian publishers develop foreign markets for Canadian books and increase the profitability of Canadian publishing houses by promoting export sales.

5139

ASSOCIATION OF CANADIAN PUBLISHERS
2 Gloucester Street, Suite 301, Toronto, Ont M4Y 1L5
Telephone: +1 (416) 413 4929
Fax: +1 (416) 413 4920

Executive Director: Paul Davidson
Communications & Research: Albert Tan
Financial Officer: Linda Liu
Executive Secretary: Boaden Burns

The Association of Canadian Publishers (ACP) is a national trade association representing Canadian-owned book publishers. Founded in 1971, it now represents over 140 publishers.
The ACP represents its members' interests by lobbying federal and provincial governments, maintaining close contact with federal departments and the Canada Council, and working to improve copyright protection for Canadian books. It represents its membership at international book fairs and on trade missions, and serves the professional educational needs of its members through an active programme of professional development seminars.
The ACP works closely with other groups within the publishing industry — writers, booksellers, periodical publishers and librarians — to deal with common problems. It is actively involved with the work of the Canadian Telebook Agency whose recently implemented Telebook is the network set up to allow booksellers to transmit their book orders by

microcomputer to publishers. Regional organizations of publishers affiliated with the ACP operate in a number of provinces.

5140

ASSOCIATION OF CANADIAN UNIVERSITY PRESSES / ASSOCIATION DES PRESSES UNIVERSITAIRES CANADIENNES
35 Spadina Road, Toronto, Ont M5R 2S9
Telephone: +1 (416) 975 9366
Fax: +1 (416) 975 1839

The Association addresses problems common to university presses and scholarly publishing in Canada, such as financial support, innovative technology and joint marketing.

5141

ASTED INC
3414 avenue du Parc, Bureau 202, Montreal, PQ H2X 2H5
Telephone: +1 (514) 281 5012
Fax: +1 (514) 281 8219
Email: info@asted.org

Director: Louis Cabral
Chairman: Joanne Cournoyer
Outgoing President: Pierre Meunier
Secretary: Julie Gauthier
Treasurer: Louise Lallier

ASTED (the association for the advancement of information sciences and techniques) is a national, professional association which groups together French speakers involved in documentation procedures both in Quebec and in French Canada. Its aims are to promote the high quality of services and personnel provided by libraries, to influence the legislation applicable to the latter and to take an important part in library economics as well as in information and documentation sciences. ASTED has an annual publication list of five news bulletins, announcing the association's proposed activities and programme, and four issues of the professional review *Documentation et bibliothèques* (information and libraries). Other publications include a translation of *Anglo-American Cataloguing Rules*. ASTED handles the distribution of several other publications dealing with a variety of subjects.

5142

BIBLIOGRAPHICAL SOCIETY OF CANADA
PO Box 575, Postal Station P, Toronto, Ont M5S 2T1
Web Site: http://www.utowuto.ca/~bsc

President: Tom Vincent
Secretary: Anne Dondertman

Founded in 1946. The principal aims of the Society are to promote bibliographical publications; to encourage the preservation and to extend the knowledge of printed works and manuscripts, particularly those relating to Canada; to facilitate the exchange of information concerning rare Canadiana; to co-ordinate bibliographical activity and to set standards.

5143

BOOK AND PERIODICAL COUNCIL
35 Spadina Road, Toronto, Ont M5R 2S9
Telephone: +1 (416) 975 9366
Fax: +1 (416) 975 1839

Executive Director: Nancy B. Fleming
Administration Co-ordinator: Nicola Lutte

An umbrella organization representing associations of authors, editors, publishers, book manufacturers, distributors, booksellers & librarians in the book and periodical industries in Canada. Thirteen full members represent approximately 6000 individuals and 5500 firms and institutions; 12 associate members represent an additional several thousand individuals, firms and institutions.

The Book and Periodical Council was formed in 1975 to provide a forum for discussion for associations and to serve as a venue in which mutual concerns are addressed, and projects undertaken for the benefit of Canadian writing and publishing.

5144

THE CANADA COUNCIL
350 Albert Street, PO Box 1047, Ottawa, Ont K1P 5V8
Telephone: +1 (613) 566 4365/6
Fax: +1 (613) 566 4390
Web Site: http://www.culturenet.ca/cc

Chair: Donna M. Scott
Director: Roch Carrier

The Canada Council (Le Conseil des Arts du Canada) is an independent agency created by the Parliament of Canada in 1957 to foster and promote the arts. The Council is headed by 11 members, including a Chairman and a Vice-Chairman appointed by the Government of Canada and drawn from every province. Its decisions on policies, programmes, grants and other matters are implemented by a staff headed by a Director appointed by the Governor in Council.

The Canada Council offers various grants to Canadian authors to research and write works of fiction, poetry, drama, children's literature, biographies, studies, essays and criticism, and provides financial help to Canadian publishers for the publication of Canadian literary works. It also operates several programmes in support of literary and arts periodicals, promotion and distribution of Canadian books and periodicals, and translation of Canadian works. The Council also awards literary prizes to Canadian authors and administers some international literary prizes.

5145

CANADIAN AUTHORS ASSOCIATION
275 Slater Street, Suite 500, Ottawa, Ont K1P 5H9
Telephone: +1 (613) 233 2846
Fax: +1 (613) 235 8237

President: Cora Taylor

The Canadian Authors Association (CAA) was founded in 1921 to foster and develop a climate favourable to Canadian writers and their works. Its main objectives are: to work for the protection of Canadian writers and other artists producing copyrightable material; to act as a spokesman before government and other community inquiries; to sponsor a system of awards and otherwise encourage work of literary and artistic merit; to publish periodicals and other publications.

There are currently 730 members of the CAA and 16 branches. Members and branches co-ordinate the publication of *Canadian Author* magazine, *The Canadian Writer's Guide*, *National Newsline* and numerous anthologies and newsletters. Contests include the CAA Literary Awards, the Air Canada Award, and Vicky Metcalf Awards for children's writing. The Association holds a conference each June in conjunction with its Annual Meeting. The conference draws writers, editors and publishers together for seminars, workshops, panel discussions, readings by award-winning authors and many social events.

5146

CANADIAN BOOK PUBLISHERS COUNCIL
250 Merton Street, Suite 203, Toronto, Ont M4S 1B1
Telephone: +1 (416) 322 7011
Fax: +1 (416) 322 6999

Executive Director: Jacqueline Hushion
President: Gordon Bain
Vice-Presidents: Brian O'Donnell *(1st)*
John Neale *(2nd)*
Secretary-Treasurer: Andrew Nopper

The Canadian Book Publishers' Council (CBPC), a national trade association of book publishers founded in 1910, is the major voice in the book publishing industry in Canada. The 44 members account for over 80% of the sales of English-language books in Canada and more than 70% of the sales of English-language Canadian books. They employ more than 3000 Canadians and contribute more than $25 million annually to the Canadian book manufacturing sector.

CBPC members publish and distribute elementary, high school and post-secondary textbooks and ancillary materials, general trade books, mass market paperbacks, audio-visual materials, business and educational software, and legal and other professional and reference books.

The Council represents the Canadian publishing community on the international level as the official English-language member of the International Publishers Association and is a member of the International Federation of Reprographic Rights Organizations. The CBPC also maintains liaison with other Canadian professional publishers' associations, the Association of American Publishers and the British Publishers Association, as well as Canadian colleagues in all areas of the literary arts, and the educational, library and retail communities.

5147

CANADIAN BOOKSELLERS ASSOCIATION
301 Donlands Avenue, Toronto, Ont M4J 3R8
Telephone: +1 (416) 467 7883
Fax: +1 (416) 467 7886

Executive Director: John J. Finlay

The CBA is a national trade association representing retail trade and campus booksellers. It is committed to ensuring the continued importance of books in the culture of Canada.

It publishes the *CBA Booksellers' Manual*, which is updated yearly. All CBA active, provisional and mail order members receive one free copy of the manual. This publication lists over 250 publishers with addresses, phone numbers, contact names, discount structures and returns policies.

CBA provides all members with a copy of *Canadian Bookseller* magazine which is published 10 times a year. The association also owns and operates the only annual national Convention and Trade Show in June of each year. The 1997 show will be in Toronto from 25 to 30 June.

The CBA publishes an annual directory of its members and can provide mailing lists in a variety of formats. The Association also offers a variety of courses and educational programmes for booksellers, including the only national Bookselling School for prospective booksellers. A new programme, Professional Book Retailing: Training Innovations for the Future, was introduced in 1996.

5148

THE CANADIAN CHILDREN'S BOOK CENTRE
35 Spadina Road, Toronto, Ont M5R 2S9
Telephone: +1 (416) 975 0010
Fax: +1 (416) 975 1839
Email: ccbc@lglobal.com
Web Site: http://www.lglobal.com/~ccbc

Executive Director: Charlotte Teeple
Programmes Co-ordinator: Jeffrey Canton

The Canadian Children's Book Centre is a national, non-profit organization founded in 1976 to support the Canadian children's publishing industry. It promotes and encourages the reading, writing and illustrating of Canadian children's books.

It is dedicated to the goal of introducing Canadian children to books and the pleasures of reading.

It offers the services of a comprehensive reference library of contemporary Canadian children's books and extensive information on authors, illustrators, book production and publishing to all members of the Centre. It is a resource for authors and illustrators. Professional staff can provide full reference services by phone, fax or mail.

Publications include:
Our Choice—$5.95—annual buying guide to the best in Canadian children's books; these fully annotated listings are organized by subject with assigned reading and interest levels.

Get Published: The Writing for Children Kit—$14.95—includes an author/illustrator guide offering practical advice on how to submit manuscripts and portfolios; also includes a list of Canadian publishers who accept unsolicited manuscripts.

All publications of the Canadian Children's Book Centre can be ordered directly through the Centre.

5149

CANADIAN ISBN AGENCY
National Library of Canada, 395 Wellington Street, Ottawa,
Ont K1A 0N4
Telephone: +1 (819) 994 6872
Fax: +1 (819) 997 7517
Email: isbn@nlc-bnc.ca

Executive: David Balatti

In January 1975, the National Library of Canada was asked to assume
responsibility for the assignment of International Standard Book
Numbers in Canada. The assignment of numbers for French-language
publishers in the Province of Quebec has been undertaken by the
Bibliothèque Nationale du Québec. The Canadian ISBN Agency
maintains records of assignments of blocks of numbers to Canadian
publishers and notifies the International ISBN Agency in Berlin of
assignments. The agency provides information and advice to new
publishers, provides logbooks for their use and promotes the use of ISBNs
among the Canadian book trade. It also publishes the *ISBN Users' Manual*
and the *Canadian ISBN Publishers' Directory*, the latest edition of which
listed some 10,000 publishers, their addresses and ISBN publisher
prefixes.

5150

CANADIAN LIBRARY ASSOCIATION
200 Elgin Street, Room 602, Ottawa, Ont K2P 1L5
Telephone: +1 (613) 232 9625
Fax: +1 (613) 563 9895

Directors: Karen Adams *(Executive)*
Leacy O'Brien *(Member Services)*
Ed Reed *(Financial & Administrative Services)*

National library association, dedicated to the development and promotion
of excellence in library and information services. Founded in 1946. More
than 5000 personal and institutional members. Non-profit, charitable
organization concerned with issues from intellectual freedom to inter-
library loan systems; activities and professional development
opportunities tailored to specific needs of those who work in college and
university libraries; public, special and school libraries; and those who
serve on library boards. Maintains international liaison with library
associations of other nations. Publishes range of titles relevant to library/
information services area.

5151

**SOCIAL SCIENCES AND HUMANITIES RESEARCH
COUNCIL**
350 Albert Street, Box 1610, Ottawa, Ont K1P 6G4
Telephone: +1 (613) 992 0691
Fax: +1 (613) 992 1787
Email: pwi@sshrc.ca

President: Lynn Penrod
Secretary General: Dr Louise Dandurand
Director of Communications: Pamela Wiggin

The Social Sciences and Humanities Research Council (SSHRC) was
created in 1978 by Act of Parliament. The SSHRC is the federal granting
agency which promotes research and advanced training in the social
sciences and humanities. Through a vigorous peer review process it offers
grants for a full range of subject matters within the social sciences and
humanities; grants for strategic research in specific areas of national
concern; doctoral and postdoctoral fellowships; scholarly exchanges,
journals, scholarly publishing and conferences.

GHANA

5152

**GEORGE PADMORE RESEARCH LIBRARY ON AFRICAN
AFFAIRS**
PO Box 2970, Accra

Telephone: +233 (021) 228402

Librarian: Mrs Sarah Dorothy Kanda

Established in 1961 as a monument to the ideals of Pan-Africanism and a
memorial to George Padmore, the aim of the library is to collect materials
on Africa. Subject areas covered are anthropology, economics,
geography, history and literature. A greater emphasis is placed on
collecting materials on Ghana to build a comprehensive national
collection.
 The Library is the National Bibliographic Agency for Ghana and
publishes the *Ghana National Bibliography*. This lists books and
pamphlets deposited with the Library in consonance with the Book and
Newspaper Registration Act, 1961, and is used by libraries and other
agencies to acquire an awareness of the country's literature. Other
materials listed are:
 (a) acquisitions of the Library covered publications in whatever forms
or language originating from Ghana, by Ghanaians and non-Ghanaians;
 (b) publications about Ghana published abroad;
 (c) new serial titles;
 (d) articles from books, pamphlets, periodicals and newspapers which
have Ghana as the subject.
 The Library is also the Legal Deposit Library, ISBN Centre for Ghana,
ISSN Centre for Ghana, Centre for International Loans and Exchange.

5153

GHANA BOOK PUBLISHERS ASSOCIATION
PO Box M430, Accra
Telephone: +233 (021) 229178
Fax: +233 (021) 220271

President: Richard Crabbe
Executive Secretary: Peter Kokoi
Treasurer: Mary Asirifi

Aims to bring together all book publishers in Ghana with a view to
establishing a vigorous and viable publishing industry.
 Disseminates information about publishing in Ghana; solves problems
related to the publishing industry; organizes courses, fairs, seminars, etc;
enters into cooperative ventures with interested parties, etc.

HONG KONG

5154

**THE ANGLO-CHINESE TEXTBOOK PUBLISHERS
ORGANIZATION LTD**
6/F Block B, Hong Kong Industrial Centre, 489–491 Castle Peak Road,
Kowloon
Telephone: +852 2745 1133
Fax: +852 2745 1998

Chairman: Sing Wong

Objectives:
 to maintain the status and professional standing of educational
publishers in Hong Kong;
 to promote and develop the products of educational publishers in Hong
Kong;
 to negotiate with all government, educational and other competent
authorities concerned with educational products;
 to promote and enable members to achieve a better understanding of
the policies formulated by the Hong Kong Government.
 The organization now has 40 members. All of them are textbook
publishers.

5155

HONG KONG LIBRARY ASSOCIATION
PO Box 10095, General Post Office, Hong Kong

President: Grace Cheng
Vice-President: Terry Lee
Hon Secretary: Louisa Lam
Hon Treasurer: Monica Pang

The Hong Kong Library Association (founded 1958) has the following objectives: to unite those engaged in library work or interested in libraries in Hong Kong; to encourage the establishment and development of libraries in Hong Kong; to encourage professional education and training for librarianship; and to organize activities appropriate to the attainment of the above objectives.

Activities include talks by visiting librarians, visits to libraries and other institutions, seminars on topics of professional interest, exhibitions and workshops. A major concern is the sponsorship of local training courses in librarianship.

Publications: *Newsletter* (5 times a year); *Journal* (annual); membership directory (annual), Year Book (annual).

There are seven categories of membership: honorary fellows, fellows, full, associate (for those without a professional qualification in librarianship), student, retired and institutional. Enquiries regarding membership subscription rates, and requests for application forms, should be addressed to the Hon Secretary.

INDIA

5156

DELHI STATE BOOKSELLERS' & PUBLISHERS' ASSOCIATION
3026/7H Ranjit Nagar, New Delhi 110 008
Telephone: +91 (011) 5737377, 5722605 & 5786889

President: K. L. Sabharwal
Secretary: Kailash Balani
Vice-President: Dr S. K. Bhatia
Joint Secretary: M. S. Bhalla
Treasurer: S. K. Jain

Delhi State Booksellers' & Publishers' Association has more than 400 members in Delhi alone. The Association looks after the welfare of members with regard to publishing and bookselling and also offers other services to members. In addition to protecting the interests of members, it guides other allied associations. The Association has introduced the Children Bookmindedness Scheme. Future plans are to introduce schemes for the benefit of publishing and bookselling etc.

5157

THE FEDERATION OF EDUCATIONAL PUBLISHERS IN INDIA
19 Rani Jhansi Road, New Delhi 110 055
Telephone: +91 (011) 522 697 & 753 6103

President: Y. P. Ranade
Secretary General: O. P. Shastri

The Federation co-ordinates the activities of the major Indian publishers and the Indian government to:
—improve the standard of educational books and to promote their export to Africa, Asia and the Middle East;
—combat illiteracy with cheaper books and to promote reading in the general population;
—organize Book Exhibitions/Fairs and conduct seminars and workshops on behalf of the educational publishing industry;
—provide a forum for complaints within and against the publishing industry, and for improving its relations with outside agencies.

IRISH REPUBLIC

5158

IRISH BOOK PUBLISHERS ASSOCIATION (CLÉ)
The Writers' Centre, 19 Parnell Square, Dublin 1
Telephone: +353 (01) 872 9090
Fax: +353 (01) 872 2035

President: Jo O'Donoghue
Administrator: Hilary Kennedy

The Irish Book Publishers Association (Clé) promotes the publication, distribution, sale and publicity of books at home and abroad. There are 46 members of the association. Clé is a member of the Federation of European Publishers and of the International Publishers Association.

5159

IRISH EDUCATIONAL PUBLISHERS ASSOCIATION
c/o Gill & Macmillan Ltd, Goldenbridge Industrial Estate, Inchicore, Dublin 8
Telephone: +353 (01) 453 1005
Fax: +353 (01) 454 9813

Secretary: Hubert Mahony

Contact the Association for information about activities and membership.

JAMAICA

5160

JAMAICA LIBRARY ASSOCIATION
PO Box 58, Kingston 5

President: Miss Gloria Clarke
Secretary: Mrs Patricia Duff
Treasurer: Mrs Valerie Reid

The Association was founded in 1949 to:
—unite all persons engaged in or interested in library work in Jamaica and provide opportunities for their meeting together to discuss matters relating to libraries;
—encourage co-operation between libraries and promote the active development and maintenance of libraries throughout Jamaica;
—promote a high standard of education and training of library staff and work towards improving the status of librarians;
—promote a wider knowledge of library work and to form an educated public opinion on libraries.

KENYA

5161

KENYA LITERATURE BUREAU
Belle Vue, off Mombasa Road, PO Box 30022, Nairobi
Telephone: +254 (02) 506142 & 506143

Managing Director: S. C. Lang'at
Marketing & Sales Manager: J. K. Muraya
Publishing Manager: Gitau Githenji

Kenya Literature Bureau is a state owned corporation. It was established in 1980 to:
    publish, print and distribute educational books;
    promote and encourage local writers;
    promote and distribute low priced textbooks and other materials throughout the country.

NEW ZEALAND

5162

BOOK PUBLISHERS' ASSOCIATION OF NEW ZEALAND INC
PO Box 36477, Auckland 1309
Telephone: +64 (09) 480 2711
Fax: +64 (09) 480 1130

Also at:
Corner College Road and Kilmam Avenue, Northcote, Auckland 1309
Telephone: *(as above)*
Fax: *(as above)*

President: Wendy Harrex
Vice-President: Daphne Brasell

Founded in 1977 as an amalgamation of the Publishers Representatives
Association (1944) and the New Zealand Book Publishers Association
(1962).
   Publication: *The Publisher* (12 issues a year).

5163

BOOKSELLERS NEW ZEALAND
PO Box 11-377, Wellington
Telephone: +64 (õ4) 472 8678
Fax: +64 (õ4) 472 8628

Chief Executive: Josephine Breese
Office Manager: Ann Kerr
Marketing & Promotions Manager: John Barr
Co-ordinator: Alaina Beattie *(Administrative)*
Booksellers Tokens: Jo Duncan

Booksellers New Zealand was established to foster, promote and
encourage the development of retail bookselling. It operates generally to
promote, protect and safeguard the interests of the members in industry
matters. Its principal focus is on the marketing and promotion of books.
   Booksellers New Zealand organizes major book promotions such as
the children's festival book awards, Listener Women's Book Festival and
Christmas catalogue; operates the booksellers tokens scheme through the
subsidiary, Book Tokens (NZ) Ltd; organizes an annual conference,
providing opportunities for interaction and exchange of information;
lobbies government; liaises with related organizations in New Zealand
and overseas; provides training seminars/workshops for bookseller staff;
and facilitates research.
   The organization also offers a comprehensive membership service.

5164

CHRISTIAN BOOKSELLERS' ASSOCIATION (NZ CHAPTER)
PO Box 4017, New Plymouth 4615
Telephone: +64 (õ6) 758 4912
Fax: +64 (õ6) 758 4912

Secretary/Treasurer: Peter G. Stark

CBANZ offers the following services:
   newletters, monthly;
   yearly national convention in August;
   national promotions of products;
   training materials;
   collective orders for directories, microfiche, bags and CBA – USA
resources;
   yearly awards;
   book token exchange;
   group member of Booksellers NZ (BNZ) and its services;
   group member of CBA – USA – International and its services,
bookstore journal and resources;
   news from CBA – Australia and European CBA;
   exchange of ideas, expertise, problem solving and fellowship
nationally and regionally.

5165

GP PUBLICATIONS
PO Box 12-052, Wellington
Telephone: +64 (õ4) 473 7211
Fax: +64 (õ4) 472 7715

Publisher: Ann Clifford

GP Publications publishes a small range of non-fiction titles and is a
distributor for a number of government reports, such as *NZ Year Book*,
Directory of Official Information, *NZ Statutes*.

5166

INTERNATIONAL STANDARD BOOK NUMBERING AGENCY
National Library of New Zealand, PO Box 1467, Wellington 1
Telephone: +64 (õ4) 474 3000 x 8653
Fax: +64 (õ4) 474 3161

ISBN Librarian: Linda Bevan Smith
Sarah Pearce *(Assistant)*

To maintain the number of International Standard Book Numbers
allocated to monographs published in New Zealand. To increase
awareness of International Standard Book Numbers to publishers and
printers throughout New Zealand.

5167

NEW ZEALAND BOOK COUNCIL
PO Box 11-377, Wellington
Telephone: +64 (õ4) 499 1569
Fax: +64 (õ4) 499 1424

Executive Director: Philippa Christmas

The New Zealand Book Council was established in 1972, during
International Book Year, to foster a love of books and reading.
   Its aims are:
   – to increase interest in books for information, education, and
recreation;
   – to encourage easy access to books;
   – to bring together organizations and individuals who have an interest
in and concern for books;
   – to publish and circulate information about books and to encourage
ownership and use of books;
   – to persuade the government to give every support to books.
   It is associated with Booksellers NZ, NZ Children's Book Foundation,
NZ Library and Information Association, PEN (NZ Centre) and *New
Zealand Books*.

5168

NEW ZEALAND COUNCIL FOR EDUCATIONAL RESEARCH
Education House, 178–182 Willis Street (PO Box 3237), Wellington 1
Telephone: +64 (õ4) 3847 939
Fax: +64 (õ4) 3847 933
Email: sales@nzcer.org.nz

Director: Anne Meade
Publications Officer: Peter Ridder
Periodicals Editor: Judith Wright

Founded in 1934, the Council covers four broad categories of publishing
activities; research monographs, research reports, large-scale tests and
periodical publications.

5169

NEW ZEALAND LIBRARY AND INFORMATION ASSOCIATION – TE RAU HERENGA O AOTEAROA
PO Box 12-212, Wellington
Telephone: +64 (õ4) 473 5834
Fax: +64 (õ4) 499 1480
Email: nzlia@netlink.co.nz
Web Site: http://www.netlink.co.nz/~nzlia

Location:
Level 8, 86 Lambton Quay, Wellington
Telephone: +64 (õ4) 473 5834
Fax: +64 (õ4) 499 1480

Executive Director: Lydia Klimovitch

A professional association, publishing a monthly newsletter (*Library
Life*) and a quarterly journal (*New Zealand Libraries*), as well as periodic
publication of directories, reports, etc.

5170 ▬▬▬▬▬▬▬▬▬▬▬▬▬▬▬▬▬▬▬▬▬

PRINTING INDUSTRIES NEW ZEALAND (INC)
Huddart Parker Building, Post Office Square, (PO Box 1422),
Wellington 1
Telephone: +64 (04) 472 3497
Fax: +64 (04) 472 3534

Chief Executive Officer: W. R. Johnson

Founded in 1907. Aims to advance the prestige of the printing industry in
New Zealand, to present the viewpoint of printers of New Zealand to the
government and elsewhere.

NIGERIA

5171 ▬▬▬▬▬▬▬▬▬▬▬▬▬▬▬▬▬▬▬▬▬

NIGERIAN PUBLISHERS ASSOCIATION
14 Awosika Avenue, off Oshuntokun Avenue, Old Bodija, PO Box 2541,
Ibadan
Telephone: +234 (02) 8102684

President: A. O. Echebiri
Vice-President: J. A. Fawibe
Executive Members: Wale Olaniawo
Bodunde Bankole
O. M. Lawal-Solarin
Akin Fasemore

SIERRA LEONE

5172 ▬▬▬▬▬▬▬▬▬▬▬▬▬▬▬▬▬▬▬▬▬

SIERRA LEONE LIBRARY BOARD
PO Box 326, Rokel Street, Freetown
Telephone: +232 (022) 23848

Chief Librarian: Mrs Irene O'Brien-Coker
Chairman: Mrs Talabi A. Lucan
Deputy Chief Librarian: Mrs Marian Lisk

The Sierra Leone Library Board, founded in 1959, establishes, equips,
manages and maintains libraries in Sierra Leone.
The Central Library in Freetown, opened in 1964, provides a public
library service, functions as the headquarters of the National Library
Service, and serves as a legal deposit library (three copies of every
document published in Sierra Leone must be deposited at the library).
Administratively the Board operates three regional libraries each
located in the regional headquarter towns of Bo (Southern Province),
Kenema (Eastern Province) and Makeni (Northern Province), nine branch
libraries each located in the district headquarter towns of Bonthe,
Bumbuna, Kabala, Kailahun, Kambia, Koidu, Magburaka, Mattru and
Pujehun and one in Freetown. Branch libraries in Kailahun, Koidu,
Mattru and Pujehun have been temporarily closed owing to the rebel
incursion.
Publications: *Sierra Leone Library Board Report* (annual); *Sierra
Leone Publications* (annual, subscription $6).

SINGAPORE

5173 ▬▬▬▬▬▬▬▬▬▬▬▬▬▬▬▬▬▬▬▬▬

**NATIONAL BOOK DEVELOPMENT COUNCIL OF
SINGAPORE**
c/o Bukit Merah Branch Library, Bukit Merah Central, Singapore 0315
Telephone: +65 273 2730
Fax: +65 270 6139

Executive Director: Mrs Vasantha Kumaree Siva

The National Book Development Council of Singapore was registered
as a non-profit society on 19 December 1968 and was formally
inaugurated on 13 February 1969. Beginning with 21 official members

representing educational, cultural, publishing, printing, library, and
bookselling associations and institutions, the Board of the Council now
consists of 35 official members and 9 individual members. An Executive
Committee is elected from members of the Board.
The Council's objectives are twofold:
1. to promote and encourage the reading of books amongst all sections
of the population in Singapore for the purposes of education, information
and culture;
2. to cooperate and liaise with all members of the national and
international book world.
In striving to achieve these objectives, the Council has organized a
variety of programmes to promote reading, improve book production and
distribution standards, and encourage local writing. It has also developed
close contacts with many national and international organizations
devoted to the same objectives.

5174 ▬▬▬▬▬▬▬▬▬▬▬▬▬▬▬▬▬▬▬▬▬

SEAMEO REGIONAL LANGUAGE CENTRE
30 Orange Grove Road, Singapore 1025
Telephone: +65 737 9044
Fax: +65 734 2753

Director: Edwin Goh
Registrar: Thomas Khng
Publications Manager: William Wang
Bursar: Lau Chor Yau
Librarian: Miss Yolanda Beh

The Regional Language Centre (RELC), established in 1968 and located
in Singapore, is an educational project of the Southeast Asian Ministers of
Education Organization (SEAMEO).
The general objective of RELC is to assist SEAMEO member countries
in the development of language education in relation to social and
economic development in the multi-lingual context of Southeast Asia.
This is carried out through training and advanced studies programmes
leading to postgraduate degrees and through seminars, research,
publications and information dissemination.

5175 ▬▬▬▬▬▬▬▬▬▬▬▬▬▬▬▬▬▬▬▬▬

SINGAPORE BOOK PUBLISHERS ASSOCIATION
Blk 86, Marine Parade Central, #03-213, Singapore 1544
Telephone: +65 344 7801 & 440 7409
Fax: +65 447 0897

President: K. P. Sivam *(Europhone Language Institute Pte Ltd)*
Hon Secretary: Tan Wu Cheng *(Cannon International)*
Treasurer: N. T. Nair *(Print World Services Pte Ltd)*

The Association jointly organizes the Festival of Books and Book Fair
with the National Book Development Council of Singapore.
The members of the Association are engaged in the following areas of
business:
— Publishing and distribution of educational books, general and
scholarly works, audio-visual materials and electronic publications.
— Publishing and distribution of consumer and trade magazines and
periodicals, and the importation and distribution of a wide range of
magazines and periodicals from overseas.
— Importation and distribution of textbooks, mass market publications,
reference books and educational toys.
— Co-publishing, translations and joint venture arrangements with
international publishers for regional and export markets.
— Sales and purchase of rights for both Singapore and foreign published
books.
— Arrangements for printing in Singapore on behalf of overseas
publishers.

SOUTH AFRICA

5176 ▬▬▬▬▬▬▬▬▬▬▬▬▬▬▬▬▬▬▬▬▬

ASSOCIATED BOOKSELLERS OF SOUTHERN AFRICA
PO Box 870, Bellville, 7530
Telephone: +27 (021) 951 6611
Fax: +27 (021) 951 4903

President: Mrs M. Hargraves
General Secretary: R. Stoltenkamp

5177

PUBLISHERS' ASSOCIATION OF SOUTH AFRICA (PASA)
PO Box 1001, Kalk Bay, 7990
Telephone: +27 (0̃21) 788 6470
Fax: +27 (0̃21) 788 6469

Chair: Basil van Rooyen
Secretary: Mary Monteith
Chairs: Kate McCallum *(Educational Publishers Group)*
Richard Cooke *(Academic & Tertiary)*
Eve Horwitz *(Copyright Committee)*
Nicholas Combrinck *(General)*
Laura Czerniewicz *(Development & Training)*

An association for promoting the interests of book publishers, importers and distributors in the Republic of South Africa. Member of the International Publishers Association and of the Book Development Council of South Africa (BDCSA).

SRI LANKA

5178

EDUCATIONAL PUBLICATIONS DEPARTMENT
Isurupaya, Battaramulla
Telephone: +94 (0̃1) 564815
Fax: +94 (0̃1) 564815

Commissioner: M. K. J. A. Alwis
Accountant: M. J. B. Fernando

The Educational Publications Department is a Government Institution started in 1966. It produces and publishes school text books distributed free of charge to pupils in classes 1 to 11 in all the schools on the island. These books are printed in Sinhala and Tamil, the two local languages. Relevant reading materials are published in English too.
   It also produces books for tertiary education, which are sold at reasonable prices. In this process the Department is engaged in original writing, purchase of translation rights and translation into the two local languages of higher education books.
   It also produces extra reading books, reference books, glossaries and dictionaries for local use.

5179

SRI LANKA NATIONAL LIBRARY SERVICES BOARD
14 Independence Avenue, Colombo 07
Telephone: +94 (0̃1) 685201 & 685203
Fax: +94 (0̃1) 685201

Director: Upali Amarasiri

The Sri Lanka National Library Services Board (SLNLSB) is a statutory body which was established in 1970 to plan library services nationally. It is funded by the government and is placed under the Ministry of Education and Higher Education. The Board of Directors consists of nine members including a full-time chairman.
   Responsibilities of the SLNLSB include the establishment and maintenance of the National Library of Sri Lanka, advising on the organization of library services of schools, public libraries and departments, organizing training courses for librarians, assisting authors and publishers, introducing new technology to library services and maintaining relationships with international organizations.
   Publications include: *Sri Lanka ISBN Publishers Directory*, *Directory of Libraries, Information Centres and Databases in Sri Lanka*, *Library News* (quarterly) and *Sri Lanka National Bibliography* (monthly).

ZAMBIA

5180

BOOKSELLERS AND PUBLISHERS ASSOCIATION OF ZAMBIA (BPAZ)
PO Box 31838, Lusaka, Zambia
Telephone: +260 (0̃1) 222647
Fax: +260 (0̃1) 222647

Also at:
Lotti House (Old Wing), 1st floor, Room 6, Cairo Road, Lusaka, Zambia
Telephone: +260 (0̃1) 222647
Fax: +260 (0̃1) 222647

Executive Director & Secretary: Basil Mbewe
Chairman: Ray Munamwimbu
Treasurer: Bharat Nayee

The Booksellers and Publishers Association of Zambia (BPAZ) is a voluntary non-governmental and non-profit-making organization for publishers, booksellers, institutions in related fields and individuals with a direct or indirect interest in the book industry in Zambia.
   The objectives of the association, among others, are to:
   a) encourage the development of the book industry in Zambia;
   b) promote the consumption of books by the general public through book fairs, exhibitions, etc;
   c) provide a forum for the exchange of information and ideas to its members;
   d) co-operate with government departments, local institutions and authorities, etc in securing the furtherance of its objectives.
   The association organizes seminars, workshops, conferences, etc for its members, and hosts the annual Zambis National Book Fair. It further organizes training sessions for its members; allocates and manages the ISBN in the country; and most importantly, it provides an enabling environment conducive for the cross-fertilisation of ideas on book publishing and selling.

5181

DIRECTORY PUBLISHERS OF ZAMBIA LTD
PO Box 30963, Plot 10826 Close, Olympia Park, Lusaka
Telephone: +260 (0̃1) 292845
Fax: +260 (0̃1) 292845

General Manager: Warwick Wratten
National Sales Manager: Claire Suckling

Parent Company: Intratex Printing & Publishing Ltd *(South Africa)*

ZIMBABWE

5182

THE LITERATURE BUREAU
Ministry of Education, PO Box CY 749, Causeway, Harare
Telephone: +263 (0̃4) 726929

Chief Publications Officer: B. C. Chitsike

The Literature Bureau aims to provide reading material to all, especially to schools, university and teachers' colleges. Its functions are:
   to assess manuscripts;
   to advise authors;
   to publish books and booklets;
   to sponsor books for publication;
   to distribute published books to schools, bookshops and booksellers;
   to translate books and other material into local languages and English;
   to organize and sponsor writers' workshops;
   to encourage authorship in Zimbabwe;
   to research into readership requirements;
   to participate in cultural exchange programmes on an international level.

5183 ▃▃▃▃▃▃▃▃▃▃▃▃▃▃▃▃▃▃▃▃▃▃▃▃▃▃▃▃▃▃▃▃

ZIMBABWE LIBRARY ASSOCIATION
PO Box 3133, Harare

Chairman: Aaron Ngwenya
Vice-Chairperson: Mrs Josephine Gurira
Secretary: Driden Kunaka

Editor: Sabelo Mapasure
Treasurer: Langton Mavhudzi

The Zimbabwe Library Association is the professional body representing the library and information science profession. It publishes, twice a year, an in-house journal called the *Zimbabwe Librarian*.

The Zimbabwe Library Association is affiliated to the Commonwealth Library Association (COMLA) and to the International Federation of Library Associations (IFLA).

6 Trade & Allied Services

6.1 EDITORIAL SERVICES

6001

AAB EDITORIAL RESEARCH CENTRE – OXFORD
PO Box 342, PSBC Unit 8, Oxford OX1 1NN
Telephone: 01865 792610 & 790686
Fax: 01865 792611
Email: info@booksbbs.demon.co.uk
Web Site: http://www.booksbbs.co.uk/books-rare

Directors: Louis de Sybaris
Luigi Gigliotti

The book trade, academics and members of the public are allowed to use this centre for tracking down their publications provided they cover the costs of the search fee, the publication when found, the handling costs, packing, postage and insurance. Using worldwide contacts the service will trace documents and publications listed in the *AAB Register of Wanted Publications*, updated daily.

6002

ASGARD PUBLISHING SERVICES
1a Headingley Mount, Leeds LS6 3EL
Telephone: 0113 274 1037
Fax: 0113 274 1037

Personnel: Philip Gardner
Michael Scott Rohan
Allan Scott
Andrew Shackleton

Established in 1984. Full editorial service, including writing and re-writing, translating, copy-editing, proof-reading, indexing, design and layout, including DTP, and multimedia projects. Illustrated reference books are a speciality. Projects can be taken from manuscript to camera-ready artwork. A range of audio-visual services is offered.

6003

AUTHORS' ADVISORY SERVICE
21 Campden Grove, Kensington, London W8 4JG
Telephone: 0171 937 5583

Editor: Jan Siegler

Established in 1972, this advisory service offers constructive criticism, based on the founder's long professional experience as a publisher's editor, both in-house and freelance. All general typescripts, including fiction and children's books, in English and French, evaluated and edited. Talks given to writers' circles and other groups.

6004

BROOKE PUBLICATIONS LTD
16 Scott Park Road, Burnley BB11 4JR

Also at:
21 Barnfield, Urmston, Manchester M41 9DW

Chairman: William R. Mills
Managing Director: Alan E. Mitton
Director: Michael Z. Brooke

Brooke Publications (founded in 1979, incorporated in 1987, reformed in 1991) undertakes contract writing, editing and designing for numerous clients in the public and private sectors; publications range from a brief newsletter to a 500-page directory. It specializes in research and writing on international trade and investment.

6005

COPYTRAIN
Pitts, Great Milton, Oxford OX44 7NF
Telephone: 01844 279345
Fax: 01844 279345

Proprietor: Richard Balkwill

Copytrain provides a consultancy and advisory service to publishers in the training and copyright fields.
   Training: Book House lecturer in editorial management, financial planning, time and people managing. Seminars in contracts, copyright and rights. Courses in all aspects of publishing and management.
   Copyright: Advice to publishers on rights and copyright matters. Review of authors' and suppliers' contracts and agreements.
   Clients include Scholastic and the British Council.
   Copytrain provides 'work-for-hire' writing commissions, especially in the children's reference area (non-fiction, history, railways).

6006

DD EDITORIAL SERVICES
Withens, 3 The Greenway, Beccles, Suffolk NR34 9UJ
Telephone: 01502 717735

Contact: J. Nicholls

DD Editorial Services offers the following services: proof-reading, English and foreign – all stages – with or without copy; copy-editing; compilation of diaries, English & foreign.

6007

DEESON EDITORIAL SERVICES
Ewell House, Faversham, Kent ME13 8UP
Telephone: 01795 535468
Fax: 01795 535469

Also at:
100 Grove Vale, London SE22 8DR
Telephone: 0181 693 3383
Fax: 0181 299 0862

Chairman: Dr Tony Deeson *(Editor-in-Chief)*
Managing Director: Dominic Deeson
Research: Jane Deeson
Finance: Susan Hamilton

Deeson Editorial Services was founded in 1959. It provides a research/writing/editing and publishing service to book and magazine publishers, central government, local authorities and a wide spectrum of industrial concerns. An area of particular expertise is historical works. Technically, it is particularly at home in presenting medical research to the layman, and in the construction, papermaking, electronic and engineering industries.

6008

EDITION
PO Box 1, Moffat, Dumfriesshire DG10 9SU
Telephone: 01683 220808
Fax: 01683 220012

Directors: Jill Hollis
Ian Cameron

In association with Cameron Books, Edition offers a complete range of services up to delivery of finished books. Services include: editing, proof-reading, indexing, in-house typesetting, photography, picture research, design, production. Edition is able to offer an editing, design and production package including whatever ancillary services a particular title demands, and is an experienced producer of museum and exhibition catalogues and educational books as well as titles for general trade distribution.

6009

FIRST EDITION TRANSLATIONS LTD
6 Wellington Court, Wellington Street, Cambridge CB1 1HZ
Telephone: 01223 356733
Fax: 01223 321488

Contacts: Judy Boothroyd
Sarah Walsh

First Edition offers complete and specialized editorial and translation services, including all necessary liaison: copy origination, editing, proofreading, indexing, desktop publishing, film or bromide output.

6010

FLAG COMMUNICATIONS
Middlewhite Barn, St George's Way, Impington, Cambridge CB4 4AF
Telephone: 01223 233882
Fax: 01223 237121
Email: info@flagcomms.co.uk
Web Site: http://www.flagcomms.co.uk

Managing Director: Liz Toms
Chairman: Robin Cameron

Flag provides a complete service – writing and editing; design, typesetting and artwork production; print buying. The company has undertaken a variety of corporate publishing projects including histories, biographies and guides to the application of high technology to business.

The founder, Rodney Dale, is a practising author whose name has appeared on 16 titles in as many years.
Clients include Railtrack, The Post Office, Brown & Root, Logica, Total Oil and BP.

6011

GUILDFORD READING SERVICES
17 Burrwood Gardens, Ash Vale, Aldershot, Hants GU12 5HN
Telephone: 01483 504325 or 01252 317950

Managing Director: B. V. Varney
Manager: T. Hoskins *(Head Reader)*

Guildford Reading Services provide an efficient and rapid proof-reading and copy preparation service to publishers, printers, studios and typesetters.

6012

LIBRARY RESEARCH AGENCY
Burberry, Devon Road, Salcombe, South Devon TQ8 8HJ
Telephone: 0154 884 2769
Fax: *(by arrangement)*

Director: D. J. Langford

Research and information service for writers, MPs, journalists and businessmen from libraries, archives, museums, public records, newspapers etc in the UK, USA and Europe.
Research may be short or long term, on commercial or academic subjects. Maps, prints, books acquired and translations made in Russian, Serbo-Croat and Bulgarian, in addition to French and German.

6013

MEDIA RESOURCE SERVICE
41 Portland Place, London W1N 4BN
Telephone: 0171 631 1634, 0171 580 0100, 0171 323 0938/9
Fax: 0171 637 2127

Head of Information: Dr Chris Langley
Information Officers: Tim Conyers
Jan Pieter Emans
Janice Leeming

The Media Resource Service is a free referral service available to all journalists, media researchers and authors who are seeking reliable sources of information in all science, technology and medicine areas. Contact is usually by telephone to the Media Resource Service although for authors seeking substantial information letters are advisable. The Service operates through a register of (currently) over 6000 experts in the UK and other Western European countries who have agreed to provide, in the first instance, background comment on a non-attributable basis. Experts are often willing to provide more information or to be interviewed, but these arrangements are left to the journalist and expert to sort out between themselves. It is staffed during the working week by people with a training in science in widely different disciplines and is open from 9 am to 6 pm (UK time). Outside these hours an answerphone operates.

6014

MEDITEXT
45 Woodland Grove, Weybridge, Surrey KT13 9EQ
Telephone: 01932 847629
Fax: 01932 821610
Email: bjhc@bcs.org.uk

Studio:
Unit 4, Haland House, 66 York Road, Weybridge, Surrey KT13 9DR
Telephone: Weybridge 01932 857036
Fax: 01932 858035

Owner/Chief Editor: Dr H. de Glanville
Graphic Designer: R. Jackman
Manager/Typesetting: Mrs Karen Flower

Meditext offers editing services, typesetting, journal/magazine/book production to camera-ready copy and arranges printing. Database services, publishers' list management, etc.

6015

ROGER PALMER LTD MEDIA CONTRACTS & COPYRIGHT
18 Maddox Street, Mayfair, London W1R 9PL
Telephone: 0171 499 8875
Fax: 0171 499 9580

Managing Director: Roger Palmer
Company Secretary: Judith E. Palmer
Senior Consultant: Stephen Aucutt

Roger Palmer Ltd drafts, advises on and negotiates all media contracts (on a regular or ad hoc basis) for publishers, agents, packagers, charities and others. The company also manages and operates clients' complete contracts, literary and merchandizing functions, undertakes contractual audits, devises contracts systems, advises on copyright and related issues and provides training and seminars. Growing private client list, with special rates for members of the Society of Authors.

6016

READING & RIGHTING (ROBERT LAMBOLLE SERVICES)
618b Finchley Road, London NW11 7RR
Telephone: 0181 455 4564
Fax: 0181 455 4564

Director: Robert Lambolle

Established in 1987, Reading & Righting is an independent script consultancy offering evaluation and editing services, based on wide-ranging agency and publishing experience. Detailed assessment, analysis of prospects and next-step guidelines for fiction, non-fiction, screenplays, plays and poetry. Full follow-up editing service by separate negotiation, one-to-one tutorials, lectures, creative writing courses, and research. Write or phone for leaflet outlining procedures and terms.

'Are You Reading Me?', an associated creative venture, under the auspices of The Phantom Captain company, provides book-themed entertainment especially tailored for enhancement of literary festivals, conferences, award ceremonies, promotions, launches, luncheons, dinners, writing courses and related functions.

6017

ROBERT ROLLASON ASSOCIATES
Chepping House, Church Road, Penn, High Wycombe, Bucks HP10 8EL
Telephone: 01494 813299
Fax: 01494 670227

Partners: Robert Rollason *(Creative Consultant)*
Jean Rollason *(Creative Consultant)*

Consultant and writer for advertisements, catalogues, brochures and trade newspapers/magazines.

6018

SMALL PRINT
The Old School House, 74 High Street, Swavesey, Cambridge CB4 5QU
Telephone: 01954 231713
Fax: 01954 232777
Email: info@smallprt.demon.co.uk

Proprietor: Naomi Laredo

Publishing and translation service, specializing in the following areas: educational and academic books; ELT and foreign language courses; business and professional packages; audio production; music and arts publishing.

Comprehensive publishing service covers: research and specification; commissioning authors and illustrators; copy-editing and on-screen editing in English and a range of foreign languages; design and picture research (own colour library); DTP and typesetting, specializing in

foreign languages; proofreading; complete studio production service for audio material.

Translation by native speakers to and from most European and Asian languages.

Clients to date include: Berlitz, Cambridge University Press, Heinemann Educational, Hugo's Language Books, Linguaphone Institute, Longman, Macmillan Press, Stanley Thornes.

6019

STRAND EDITORIAL SERVICES
16 Mitchley View, South Croydon, Surrey CR2 9HQ
Telephone: 0181 657 1247
Fax: 0181 657 1247

Principal: Derek Bradley, FCIS, MBACB
Partner: Irene Bradley

Provides a comprehensive service to publishers, editorial departments and public relations and advertising agencies at any stage of the production process. Proofreading a speciality. Will also take over entire magazine production cycle from start to finish. Contracts accepted on both an on-going and short-term basis. Emergencies handled if required. Current full-time contracts include consultant editorship of *Business Executive* (Association of Business Executives), and proofreading for five organizations.

6020

SUMMIT PUBLISHING PROMOTION SERVICES
58 Rocky Lane, Great Barr, Birmingham B42 1PA
Telephone: 0121 356 8533

Managing Director: Roger Arthur

The provision of, or consultancy for, mail order promotion copywriting for general non-fiction books. Catalogues, newsletters, reviews, jacket blurbs, off-the-page advertisement copy, etc. Prompt, expert service by former Chief Copywriter of the Readers Union Group of Book Clubs. Especially for such subjects as art, crafts, biography, entertainment, theatre, drama, fashion, education, music, TV, radio and film, history, science fiction and sport.

6021

WORDWISE
37 Elmthorpe Road, Wolvercote, Oxford OX2 8PA
Telephone: 01865 510098
Fax: 01865 310556

Director: Valerie Mendes

Wordwise is a comprehensive publishing and editorial consultancy. Founded in Oxford in 1990 by author, editor and publisher, Valerie Mendes, Wordwise provides a range of support services, from creative writing, editing, promotion and publicity to report analysis and full project management.

Specialisms and skills include: creative writing, especially for the younger market; editing children's fiction and non-fiction; all aspects of educational publishing from primary to postgraduate level; arts and humanities publishing; English Language Teaching publishing; and writing and presenting training projects for the professional publishing market.

Wordwise can brief and commission illustrators, picture researchers, photographers, designers and typesetters.

Project-management services include budget and schedule maintenance, team co-ordination, trouble-shooting and liaison, and providing regular progress reports for the in-house publishing team.

6022

HANS ZELL PUBLISHING CONSULTANTS
11 Richmond Road, PO Box 56, Oxford OX1 2SJ
Telephone: 01865 511428
Fax: 01865 311534

Director: Hans M. Zell
Associate: Cécile Lomer

Specialization in services to publishers and the book community in Third World countries, providing specific expertise in these areas. Undertakes a broad range of general publishing consultancies (both for books and journals publishing), including research and project evaluation, feasibility studies, list development, management, administration and sub-editorial work. Also organizes joint exhibits at African/Third World studies associations' meetings and conventions, etc and provides specialist mailing list services in the African studies and development field.

6.2 DESIGN & PRODUCTION SERVICES

6023

BOOK CREATION SERVICES LTD
21 Carnaby Street, London W1V 1PH
Telephone: 0171 287 0214
Fax: 0171 287 8547

Directors: Hal Robinson *(Sales)*
Gill Paul *(Managing)*

Book Creation Services provides editorial, translation, design and packaging/repackaging services, using Apple Macintosh and IBM technology, to text and layouts or final film, primarily in illustrated non-fiction, partworks, dictionaries and general reference, often involving re-use of existing illustrative or text resources.
Book Creation Services is structured with high creative input and low overheads so that both services and costs can be tailored precisely to clients' needs, working as independently or closely as required within a defined budget and schedule.

6024

BOOK PRODUCTION CONSULTANTS PLC
25–27 High Street, Chesterton, Cambridge CB4 1ND
Telephone: 01223 352790
Fax: 01223 460718
Email: bpc@bpccam.demon.co.uk
Web Site: http://www.infragence.com/bpc/home.htm

Also at:
c/o Bermuda Trust (UK) Ltd, Austin Friars House, 2–6 Austin Friars, London EC2N 2HE
Telephone: 0171 256 5377
Fax: 0171 638 9335
Email: sz@bpclon.demon.co.uk

Directors: Tony Littlechild
Colin Walsh
Production Consultants: Sue Gray
Debbie Wayment
Tricia Rowland
Jannie Brightman
Charlotte Cartwright
Manager: Roz Williams *(Editorial)*

A totally comprehensive publishing service including editing, sub-editing, designing, technical mark-up, illustrating, technical drawing, estimating, paper buying, typesetting and film origination. BPC arranges the printing and binding of black-and-white or colour publications in the UK or overseas and supervises quality control and delivery schedules; also computer software packs including design of packaging and manufacture of boxes, tapes and discs. Other specialities include the design and production of illustrated books, music and foreign language setting projects, academic journals and institutional publications, producing company sponsored books and company histories. Electronic publishing and CD-ROM origination, particularly as joint ventures, form part of current expansion.

6025

CHASE PRODUCTION SERVICES
Chase House, Chalford Oaks, Chipping Norton, Oxon OX7 5QR
Telephone: 01608 644162
Fax: 01608 644162

Director: Ray Addicott

Chase provide a complete book production service – editing, design and artwork, typesetting (keying or from disk), materials purchasing, printing and binding. Professional help at affordable cost. Single projects or a complete production management service.

6026

COOPER DALE
1a Dalling Road, London W6 0RA
Telephone: 0181 748 6824
Fax: 0181 748 5689

Partners: Roger Pring *(Design Director)*
Roger Hearn *(Editorial Director)*

Cooper-Dale is a design–editorial partnership which will produce entire books and CD-ROMs or assist with any part of the process. Though most commissions are to fulfil both design and editorial aspects, either can be undertaken on its own. The partners have extensive experience in their fields and over the last ten years have produced work for publishers and other clients in the USA and Europe as well as the UK. Cooper Dale also has proven strengths in publicity/advertising design and copywriting, exhibition design and modelmaking.

6027

DESIGN SYSTEMS
Holbrook House, 105 Rose Hill, Oxford OX4 4HT
Telephone: 01865 770490

Partner: Peter Tucker *(Consultant)*

Design Systems is a consultancy providing both technical and design expertise in the implementation and use of both Macs and PCs in graphics and publishing industries. Agents include Adobe, Aldus, Corel Systems, Micrografx, Lotus, SPC, Quark, Ventura Software, Monotype, Linotype. Affiliated to Holbrook Design Oxford Ltd, for many years designers in publishing and print.

6028

ELECTRONIC PUBLISHING SERVICES LTD
26 Rosebery Avenue, London EC1R 4SX
Telephone: 0171 837 3345
Fax: 0171 837 8901
Email: eps@epsltd.demon.co.uk
Web Site: epsltd.com

Chairman: David R. Worlock
Director: David J. Powell

EPS offers strategic and market-based advice on the use of 'new tchnology' for the communication of publishers' content. EPS concerns itself primarily with what the technology (e.g. CD-ROM, audiotex, online, magnetic media, etc) can do rather than how it does it.
EPS publishes *EP.Journal* (ISSN 0954-3244), the international electronic publishing newsletter, as well as various multi-client studies, such as 'Network Publishing'. An associate company publishes *Interactive Media International*.

6029

EPUBLISHING
9 Lakesmere Close, Kidlington Business Centre, Oxford OX5 1LG
Telephone: 01865 372111
Fax: 01865 372112

Divisional Head: Steve Johnston
Technical Manager: Steve Allam

ePublishing provides electronic media solutions for publishers. ePublishing will develop innovative electronic concepts for the 'repurposing' of content, and will propose effective strategies for the creation of new content; whether it is for CD-ROM, floppy disc or the Internet. It delivers working prototypes of titles promptly and within budget, and will decide on, plan and manage the most appropriate full development route. This may involve third party companies, freelance specialists or ePublishing's own creative team.

Parent Company: The Data Business Ltd *(UK)*

6030

GRAHAM-CAMERON ILLUSTRATION
The Studio, 23 Holt Road, Sheringham, Norfolk NR26 8NB
Telephone: 01263 821333
Fax: 01263 821334

Partners: Mike Graham-Cameron
Helen Graham-Cameron

This illustration agency has some 43 professional artists who use a wide range of techniques, media and skills. They specialize in educational, children's, architectural and costume pictures.

6031

HOLBROOK DESIGN OXFORD LTD
Holbrook House, 105 Rose Hill, Oxford OX4 4HT
Telephone: 01865 770490

Directors: Peter Tucker *(Design)*
Alex Tucker *(Production)*

Holbrook Design Oxford Ltd was founded as PGT Design in 1974. It offers the following services: typography, editorial design and art direction, photography; from concept through dummies, mark-up and typesetting, page layouts to artwork, in consultation with photographers, illustrators and printers. Clients include many national and international publishers. Holbrook Design has particular experience in educational and general publishing; subject areas covered range from science to religion, cookery to history and first readers to A-level.

6032

D. & J. HUNTER
100 Ravenscroft Road, Beckenham, Kent BR3 4TW
Telephone: 0181 659 3579
Fax: 0181 659 3579
Email: djhunter@su.span.com

Art Director: Jenny Hunter
Manager: David Oliver Hunter *(Production)*

Design company specializing in book and magazine production. The company is involved in many fields of educational publishing. It has recently been specializing in the design and development of ELT, modern languages, resource packs. D. & J. Hunter work with QuarkXpress, Photoshop and Freehand on Macintosh as page layout programs and system. The company will commission illustrators and photographers (it holds a substantial portfolio of illustrators).

6033

IMAGO PUBLISHING LTD
Station Yard, Thame, Oxon OX9 3UH
Telephone: 01844 261555
Fax: 01844 261666
Email: reception@imago.co.uk

Directors: Richard Hayes
Erik Pordes
Cherry Jaquet

Colin Risk
Jim Allpass

Offers production consultancy and print broking to the publishing industry. With offices in the UK, Hong Kong, Singapore, New York and California, the group is able to locate and control sources of manufacture on a world-wide basis.
   The group works with a wide range of customers, and can offer its extensive expertise in a range of ways, from running all the production needs for small publishers/packagers, to sourcing and arranging for the manufacture of individual projects on a competitive brokerage basis. All types of work are handled, including colour separation, children's books, novelty products, short- and long-run general books and magazines.

6034

INTERNATIONAL IMAGING
10 North End, Bassingbourn, Royston, Herts SG8 5NX
Telephone: 01763 245811
Fax: 01763 243692

Manager: D. A. Chapman

Specialized services for publishers, libraries, academic institutions and general business for high security image capture, including scanning and digitizing; also comprehensive range of archive and preservation microfilming services.

6035

LEADING EDGE PRESS & PUBLISHING
The Old Chapel, Burtersett, Hawes, North Yorks DL8 3PB
Telephone: 01969 667566
Fax: 01969 667788

Chairman: Stan Abbott *(Editorial Director)*
Company Secretary: Bridget Swann *(Trade Sales)*
Manager: Barbara Allen *(Managing Editor)*
Advertising Sales: Maggie Campbell

Leading Edge Press & Publishing provides a range of publishing and public relations services from writing and research to design and make-up. We are also print buyers and offer a packaging service to the publishing trade. We operate the latest Apple Macintosh desktop technology, with in-house laser printing, or full typeset quality through trade contacts. We can convert text-only disks to customers' specifications and produce type in galleys from any disk. We also offer a disk-based French–English translation service.

6036

LEGASTAT COPYING & SCANNING
57 Carey Street, London WC2A 2JB
Telephone: 0171 405 9178
Fax: 0171 405 3877
Email: postmaster@legastat.demon.co.uk

Proprietor: John Eddowes *(Customer Relations)*
Manager: David Thompson
Accountant: Jacquie Ward

Legastat is a copying and scanning service in central London, specializing in the rapid xeroxing of manuscripts, advance information sheets, publicity information, etc for publishers and literary agents. The reproduction of galleys, camera-ready art work, and large charts, roughs and posters, is also undertaken, by xerographic machinery. Collection and delivery to ensure rapid turnround times are provided. Clients include many of the major publishers. Legastat is open from 9 am to 9 pm.

6037

JOHN MARTIN & ARTISTS LTD
26 Danbury Street, Islington, London N1 8JU
Telephone: 0171 734 9000
Fax: 0171 226 6069

Directors: W. Bowen-Davies *(Managing)*
C. M. Bowen-Davies
B. L. Bowen-Davies

Originated as an illustrators' agency in 1956 and has since that date done work in all branches of publishing where illustrating is required. Currently they have on their books 40 freelance illustrators who work in individual specialized fields.

6038

THE PINPOINT DESIGN CO
The Mill, 1 Old Road, Linslade, Leighton Buzzard, Beds LU7 7RB
Telephone: 01525 383550
Fax: 01525 850279

Partner/Manager: Martin Kerr

A complete design service to the publishing industry. From board books to encyclopedias — fact & fiction: concept development, visualizing, mockups, covers, spreads, book design & production, publicity & promotion.

6039

PRIMARY SOURCE MEDIA
PO Box 45, Reading RG1 8HF
Telephone: 0118 956 8844
Fax: 0118 939 4334
Email: sales@psmedia.co.uk
Web Site: http://www.psmedia.com/psmedia.html

Also at:
12 Lunar Drive / Drawer AB, Woodbridge, CT 06525, USA

Directors: David Lucas *(Chief Executive Officer)*
John Cook *(Finance)*
Reg Readings *(Indexing & IT)*
Marga Beuth *(Sales & Marketing)*
Mark Holland *(Publisher)*
Managers: Helen Agutter *(Customer Services)*
Bethan Simpson *(Marketing)*

Academic and scholarly, in microform, CD-ROM and print formats. Compilers and publishers of *The Times Index* and *Chaucer: Life & Times* (CD-ROM). Publishers of rare printed materials, unpublished manuscript collections and newspapers.

6040

Q-MULTIMEDIA (UK) LTD
Orwell House, 2 Orwell Road, Cowley Road, Cambridge CB4 4WY
Telephone: 01223 576616
Fax: 01223 576617
Email: 100754.2723@compuserve.com

Directors: P. F. Poulter *(Managing)*
M. Lebi
Chief Designer: R. Stock

Employed by leading publishers in the design and development of multimedia CDs for education, commerce and the home market. Specialists in user interface design combined with advanced production and programming skills. Experts in the integration of existing content into creative multimedia formats, especially for magazine publishing and interactive catalogues.

6041

TRAIT DESIGN
Logan House, Church Road, Tiptree, Essex CO5 0AB
Telephone: 01621 817905
Fax: 01621 816373

Director: Bruce MacWillson

A graphic design company, founded in 1976. A wide range of experience in the publishing industry. Providing research, editing, concepts, visuals, finished artwork, mono and full colour illustration, generated on our Mac system. Outputting bromide and film. Disc translation facilities.
    Clients include educational, financial and children's book publishers.
    Other activities include print management, corporate design, brochure and exhibition design.

6042

VILLIERS PUBLICATIONS LTD
19 Sylvan Avenue, London N3 2LE
Telephone: 0181 343 3704
Fax: 0181 343 3704

Managing Director: John V. Sankey *(Editorial Production)*

Villiers Publications Ltd undertakes production for other publishing companies.

6.3 ELECTRONIC PUBLISHING SERVICES

6043

VIRGINIA BARDER
8 Trevelyan Road, London SW17 9LN
Telephone: 0181 682 0601
Fax: 0181 682 0965
Email: vbarder@cix.compulink.co.uk

Multimedia production and consultancy services.

6044

CAMBRIDGE MULTIMEDIA SYSTEMS PLC
St Andrews, North Street, Burwell, Cambridge CB5 0BB
Telephone: 01638 743121
Fax: 01638 743572
Email: cmsisl.dungeon.com
Web Site: http://www.tela.co.uk/cms

Directors: Robin Sewell *(Marketing)*
Tony Blake *(Sales)*
Sales Manager: Peter Skipper
Administrator: Ruth Cresswell

Cambridge Multimedia Systems Plc (CMS) is a specialist multimedia systems house of 12 years' standing. It provides consultancy, hardware, software and bureau services to intending publishers of CD-based programmes. All formats of CD are covered.
    Specialist areas are large image databases and software for rapid access to images stored on optical media.
    CMS is a distributor of CD writers and peripherals for Philips, Sony and most makes of related hardware and software.

6045

CASTELL COMPUTER & SYSTEMS TELECOMMUNICATIONS LTD
20 Grange Road, Wickham Bishops, Witham, Essex CM8 3LT
Telephone: 01621 891776
Fax: 01621 892553
Email: cstll01@ibm.net

Chairman: Dr Stephen Castell

Independent, professional consultancy services in software and systems, telecommunications, broadcasting, marketing, publishing and the media.
    Expert witnesses experienced in all aspects of computer disputes and litigation, well-known and respected by legal professionals internationally.
    Entrepreneurial new business development specialists.

6046

CD PUBCO INC
1500, 715 –5th Avenue SW, Calgary, Alberta T2P 2X6, Canada
Telephone: +1 (403) 294 0080
Fax: +1 (403) 294 0082
Email: jbreslawski@cdpubco.com

President: Joe Breslawski

Founded in 1987, CD PubCo Inc, one of Canada's oldest CD-ROM publishers, researches and develops large database technology for applications primarily within the energy industry.
    The first energy database was published on CD-ROM is October 1988. This was quickly followed by the release of production data on CD-ROM in the sopring of 1989. CD PubCo Inc has developed an advanced Windows NT-based indexing and retrieval system, GEOVISTA, to access the energy databases published. Targeting small to junior-sized exploration companies, CD Pubco Inc provides information to a wide range of clients, including exploration companies, financial institutions, consultant firms, government departments and educational centres.
    Present databases are Western Canada Drilling Data, Western Canada Production Data, Western Canada Survey Data (actual and theoretical), Western Canada Oil & Gas Reserves Data, Alberta AOF Pressure Data and Hydrology & Culture. The Western Canada Environmental Data Base is under development.

6047

ELECTRONIC PUBLISHING SERVICES LTD
26 Rosebery Avenue, London EC1R 4SX
Telephone: 0171 837 3345
Fax: 0171 837 8901
Email: eps@epsltd.demon.co.uk
Web Site: http://www.epsltd.com

Chairman: David R. Worlock
Director: David J. Powell
Research Manager: Bridgid C. Nzekwu

Consultancy concerning the use of electronic media for the delivery of information products and services.
    Publishing – industry newsletters (*EPJournal* and *Interactive Media International*), reports and multi-client studies.

6048

EXOTERICA CORPORATION, PUBLISHING SOFTWARE
1545 Carling Avenue, Suite 404, Ottawa, Ont K1Z 8P9, Canada
Telephone: +1 (613) 722 1700
Fax: +1 (613) 722 5706

Sales Manager: Eric Skinner

Exoterica develops, markets and supports OmniMark, the established hypertext programming language based on SGML and open standards technology. OmniMark is used by a wide range of industry-leading companies, including over 600 customers in 34 countries, for development of on-line, Web, CD-ROM and print-on-demand applications.

6049

MIKE GILBERT PRODUCTIONS
45 Burntwood Lane, Earlsfield, London SW17 0JY
Telephone: 0181 947 7706
Fax: 0181 947 7706
Email: mikegilbe@atlas.co.uk

Sole Proprietor: Mike Gilbert

Mike Gilbert Productions is a freelance multimedia design, production and consultancy service provider to electronic publishing, WWW, CD-ROM and presentation publishers and producers.
    Services include: multimedia software prototyping; concept demonstrator production for fund-raising purposes; CD-ROM and WWW interactive authoring in MM Director 5 / Shockwave with Lingo

programming; image processing and graphics; cross-platform and Web file translation/compression; animation; presentations and slide shows; still photograph and Hi8 video content production; international software localization; interactive and user-interface design.
    Previous customers: Apple Training Europe Inc; Apple UK Business Marketing; EC COMETT and ESPRIT offices (R&D); Adplates (New Media); First Information Group (FlagTower); Benefits Agency Video Unit. Most recent major project: 'War in the Pacific' – documentary CD-ROM. Post-production services to First Information Group (FlagTower).

6050

GRASHOFF CONSULTING GROUP
35 Whellock Road, London W4 1DY
Telephone: 0181 994 6528
Fax: 0181 742 0196
Email: tudor@handbook.co.uk
Web Site: http://www.handbook.co.uk

Director: Tudor Grashoff

The company's aim is to help publishers succeed in new media publishing: CD-ROM, multimedia, the Internet. The involvement often starts with a review for CD-ROM / multimedia publishing opportunities and setting strategies to exploit those opportunities. Advice is also given on implementation issues such as joint ventures, distribution and software selection. Other services include project management, and setting up and managing in-house electronic publishing departments.
    Advice given is business-led rather than technology-driven, and is based on practical experience. Publication types advised on include: directories, scientific journals, business journals, abstracts, reports, consumer fiction.

6051

IEPRC – INTERNATIONAL ELECTRONIC PUBLISHING RESEARCH CENTRE
Pira House, Randalls Road, Leatherhead, Surrey KT22 7RU
Telephone: 01372 802003
Fax: 01372 802244
Email: admin.ieprc@pira.co.uk
Web Site: http://www.pira.co.uk

Administrator (after UK office hours):
Telephone: 01372 278335

Chief Executive: Brian W. Blunden
Company Secretary & Administrator: Dr Margot H. Blunden-Willms
Research Manager: Roberto Minio

IEPRC serves its members by providing information on electronic publishing developments (databank: *World Publishing Monitor*, monthly abstracts journal, *Pre-press Commentary*, *Publishing Technology Review*), conferences, study tours and workshops. It undertakes general research related to multimedia publishing and multi-client R&D projects. IEPRC acts as a centre of influence for the development of the electronic publishing business.

6052

INFORMATION AGENTS LTD
26 Rosebery Avenue, London EC1R 4SX
Telephone: 0171 837 3345
Fax: 0171 837 8901
Email: eps@epsltd.demon.co.uk
Web Site: http://www.epsltd.com

Chairman: David R. Worlock
Senior Consultant: A. S. Feldman
Director: David J. Powell

Negotiation of rights for exploitation of content in electronic products and services.

6053

INNOTECH MULTIMEDIA CORPORATION
2005 Sheppard Avenue East, North York, Ont M2J 5B4, Canada
Telephone: +1 (416) 492 3838
Fax: +1 (416) 492 3843
Email: marketg.innoteched.com
Web Site: http://www.innoteched.com

President & Chief Executive Officer: Norman Vokey
Vice-President, Development & Client Services: Simon Arnison

Innotech is a leading developer of database management software, specializing in CD-ROM applications, Innotech's proprietary database management technology consists of database creation tools, one of the world's fastest and most efficient search and retrieval engines, and multimedia authoring tools. These tools are excellent for archiving and providing quick access to large amounts of information. The tools are also used in multimedia titles development. Innotech provides services to satisfy the information management needs of large corporations and is a publisher of CD-ROM titles.

6054

INSOFT LTD
15/16 Lower Park Row, Bristol BS1 5BN
Telephone: 0117 925 3373
Fax: 0117 925 3374
Email: 100751.1327@compuserve.com
Web Site: http://www.insoft.co.uk

Managing Director: S. C. Robinson

Insoft provides a wide range of electronic publishing services, enabling publishers to distribute information on CD-ROM and across the Internet. The company also develops full text retrieval software.

6055

MILEX DATA CORPORATION
Euston House, 81–103 Euston Street, London NW1 2ET
Telephone: 0171 383 5210
Fax: 0171 383 4145
Web Site: http://www.d-net.com

Also at:
PO Box 20, Norwich, Norfolk NR6 6TL
Telephone: 01603 419645
Fax: 01603 414716

Directors: David Armstrong *(Managing)*
Lysa Schwartz *(Operations)*
David Longfoot *(Technical)*

Services include system building, electronic product development, data compilation, processing and manipulation.
Publishers of the European edition of *Directory Publishing: A Practical Guide.*

6056

MPW LASEC SOFTWARE LTD
London House, 100 New Kings Road, London SW6 4LX
Telephone: 0171 731 8199
Fax: 0171 731 8312
Email: 76111.301@compuserve.com

Managing Director: Frank Bevis

MPW Lasec Software specialize in the development of electronic publications on CD-ROM and the Internet for commercial publishing and in-company applications.
The company's state-of-the-art development and retrieval system Lasec OptiSearch® 2 allows users fast and extremely easy access to critical information, and offers features important to directory publishers: on-screen advertising and logos, on-screen enquiry/order forms, security-

controlled mailing lists, 'try before you buy' demonstration directories, incorporation of multimedia elements, etc.
Publishers can either take advantage of the company's 'full service' concept, or alternatively use its tool kit to develop CD-ROM and multimedia CD titles themselves in-house.

6057

OPTONICA LTD
1 The Terrace, High Street, Lutterworth, Leics LE17 4BA
Telephone: 01455 558282
Fax: 01455 559386
Email: post@optonica.com

Directors: Lee Gibson *(Managing)*
Kevin Stevens *(Technical)*
Sales & Marketing Manager: Carl Gamble

Optonica publishes CD-ROM based reference/information/training products as well as providing full in-house facilities for publishing on all types of electronic media including the Internet and CD-ROM.
In-house services include 2D/3D graphic design, software engineering, video production and editing, photography, audio production, photo scanning and production.

6058

ROBERT PRINCE – PUBLISHING SOLUTIONS
2(B) Langstone High Street, Havant, Hants PO9 1RY
Telephone: 01705 492655
Fax: 01705 492655

Contact: Robert Prince

Robert Prince – Publishing Solutions supplies the following services to publishers who wish to convert hard copy publications to electronic media based publications:
— initial data capture,
— OCR/ICR scanning,
— image scanning,
— SGML/HTML tagging.
In addition, convential typesetting or laser printing can also be supplied.

6059

REED TECHNOLOGY & INFORMATION SERVICES
39a Bowling Green Lane, London EC1R 0BJ
Telephone: 0171 837 9846
Fax: 0171 837 9856
Email: peterc@ocs.com

European Sales Manager: Peter Camilleri

RTIS provides electronic publishing services to publishers, database producers, libraries and corporations. These services include data conversion, data capture, database creation, online delivery systems, Internet publishing and CD-ROM development.

6060

SAZTEC EUROPE LTD
Maritime House, North Crescent Road, Ardrossan, Ayrshire KA22 8LR
Telephone: 01294 461081
Fax: 01294 461019
Email: pub@saztec.com

Vice-President & General Manager: Mike Dale
Financial Controller & Treasurer: John Kerr
General Manager & Secretary: Anne Barlow

Data conversion, i.e. library cards to tape/CD-ROM.

6061

SOUTRON LTD
Jerome House, Hallam Fields, Fields Road, Ilkeston DE7 4BH

Telephone: 0115 944 1664
Fax: 0115 944 1626

Contact: Louise Storry

6062

WISE & LOVEYS LTD
4 Meadway Court, Rutherford Close, Stevenage, Herts SG1 2EF
Telephone: 01438 759210
Fax: 01438 759833
Email: 100710.3071@compuserve.com
Web Site: http://www.wiseloveys.com

Directors: Tim Wise
Chris Loveys

Formed in 1991, Wise & Loveys Ltd is a specialist software developer to the publishing industry offering the following services to directory and information publishers:
—development of database, text-retrieval and multimedia titles on CD-ROM and diskette;
—development of interactive Internet applications including real-time database-to-HTML;
—development of hybrid CD-ROM/Internet solutions;
—technical support help-line and password fulfilment services;
—development of internal databases for data collection and data management purposes;
—development of output routines enabling publication direct from database to print via DTP.
    Clients include: Cassell, Chapman & Hall, EMAP, Euromonitor, Reed Elsevier, John Wiley & Sons and a number of smaller specialist publishers.

6.4   TRANSLATION SERVICES

6063

FIRST EDITION TRANSLATIONS LTD
6 Wellington Court, Wellington Street, Cambridge CB1 1HZ
Telephone: 01223 356733
Fax: 01223 321488

Contacts: Judy Boothroyd
Sarah Walsh

Translations—commercial, technical, academic and of any length—undertaken in any language according to publisher's requirements. Editing, proofreading, indexing, typesetting / desktop publishing by linguists. Film or bromide output. Quotations given without obligation.

6064

INTERCULTURAL NETWORKING LTD (ICN)
133 John Trundle Court, London EC2Y 8DJ
Telephone: 0171 628 5876
Fax: 0171 628 9147
Email: icn@dircon.co.uk

Directors: Atsuko Takenaka *(Managing)*
Bob Brown

Principally, ICN provides non-fiction book translation services Japanese—English and English—Japanese, including editorial and illustration services in both languages if required. The company specializes in business, economics, financial, social issues, current affairs and some technical fields.
    In addition, ICN directly represents several Japanese non-fiction authors in placing their work in English translation with English-language publishers. It would be pleased to hear from further Japanese authors. It has no facilities to receive MSS from others.
    ICN from time to time informally represents Japanese publishers in Europe.

6065

SATRAP PUBLISHING & TRANSLATION
Suite 21, London House, 271 King Street, Hammersmith, London W6 9LZ
Telephone: 0181 748 9397
Fax: 0181 748 9394

Managing Director: Ahmad Vahdat
Manager: Mrs Homa Lohrasb *(Technical)*

Satrap Publishing is a UK-based international company, specializing in the fields of translation, typesetting and print services in Oriental and East European languages.
    The company produces promotional literature, exhibition catalogues, information pamphlets, books, reports, manuals, business stationery, product labels, diaries etc for Western European companies, trade centres and various organizations.
    The human resources and advanced technical facilities available are ideal for those clients who wish to target ethnic minorities for their social, cultural and educational programmes. Satrap Publishing offers a complete package of expert translation, state-of-the-art laser typesetting, professional graphic design as well as printing. Production of exclusive greeting cards and wedding stationery in non-European languages are among other services from Satrap Publishing.

6066

SERVICES FOR EXPORT AND LANGUAGE (SEL)
Crescent House, University of Salford, Manchester M5 4WT
Telephone: 0161 745 7480
Fax: 0161 745 5110
Email: sel@mod-lang.salford.ac.uk
Web Site: http://www.salford.ac.uk/modlang/sel/selhome.html

Translations Manager: Patrick Murphy

SEL provides translations, simultaneous and consecutive interpreters and can arrange voice-overs in most sectors, in over 30 languages.
    SEL also provides language training and country briefing.
    Clients include a number of advertising agencies, Kogan Page and Gordon and Breach.

6067

UPS TRANSLATIONS
111 Baker Street, London W1M 1FE
Telephone: 0171 837 8300
Fax: 0171 486 3272

Managing Director: Bernard Silver
Head of Translation: Judith Alsop
Marketing Manager: Nicola Birch

UPS Translations offers a specialist packaging service, based on translations into and from English:
—translation to highest literary standards;
—adaptation of published material;
—heavy adaptation (eg cookery books);
—editing and proof-checking;
—design and typography;
—mechanical production and film stages.
    It can match a book's design exactly or take work on DTP diskette from the original publishers. The parent company, United Publicity Services Plc, has been in book publishing for 49 years and some of the largest publishers in the world use its services.
    The company also translate:
—national newspapers;
—periodicals and magazines;
—promotional material;
—house journals;
—advertising copy;
—audio-visual presentations.

6.5 SALES & MARKETING SERVICES

6068

3 & 5 PROMOTION
Crag House, Witherslack, Grange-over-Sands, Cumbria LA11 6RW
Telephone: 015395 52286
Fax: 015395 52013
Email: musicbks@rdooley.demon.co.uk

Manager: Rosemary Dooley

3 & 5 Promotion provides publicity services for publishers: collaborative publishers' exhibitions at academic conferences, catalogues, mailings, launches. Specialization in music, film, health care.

6069

AFRICAN BOOKS COLLECTIVE
The Jam Factory, 27 Park End Street, Oxford OX1 1HU
Telephone: 01865 726686
Fax: 01865 793298 & 01993 709265
Email: abc@dial.pipex.com
Web Site: http://www.sas.upenn.edu/African-Studies/Publications/ABC-Menu.html

Warehouse:
Unit 3, off Pytts Lane, Burford, Oxon OX18 4SJ
Telephone: 01993 823650

Consultant: Mary Jay

Founding member publishers:
East Africa: East African Educational Publishers Ltd
Ghana: Ghana Publishing Corporation
Ghana Universities Press
Woeli Publishing Services
Nigeria: Fourth Dimension Publishing Co Ltd
Ibadan University Press
New Horn Press Ltd
Nigerian Institute of International Affairs
Obafemi Awolowo University Press

University of Lagos Press
University of Nigeria Press
University of Port Harcourt Press
Senegal: Council for the Development of Science and Technology (CODESRIA)
South Africa: Skotaville Publishers
Tanzania: Dar es Salaam University Press
Mkuki na Nyota Publishers
Tanzania Publishing House
Zimbabwe: Zimbabwe Publishing House Ltd

Other members:
Botswana: Foundation for Education with Production
Ghana: Afram Publications
Freedom Publishers
Sankofa Educational Publishers
Kenya: Academy Science Publishers
Nairobi University Press
Lesotho: Institute of Southern African Studies
Malawi: Centre for Social Research
Mauritius: Editions de l'Ocean Indien
Namibia: New Namibia Books (Pty) Ltd
Nigeria: Bookcraft Ltd
Heinemann Educational Books (Nigeria)
Malthouse Press Ltd
Sankore Publishers
Saros International Publishers
Spectrum Books Ltd
University Press Plc

Senegal: Environmental Development Action in the Third World (ENDA)
South Africa: Buchu Books
Tanzania: Tanzania Commission for Science and Technology
Uganda: Fountain Publishers
Zambia: Multimedia Zambia
Zimbabwe: Africa Community Publishing & Development Trust
Baobab Books
Southern African Printing and Publishing House / SAPES Trust
Southern African Research and Documentation Centre (SARDC)
University of Zimbabwe Publications
Zimbabwe Book Publishers Association
Zimbabwe Women Writers

African Books Collective is a major initiative to promote African-published books in Europe, North America, and in Commonwealth countries outside Africa. It is owned by the founding member publishers, is donor-organization supported and non-profit making on its own behalf. It therefore offers preferential terms to its participating member publishers. Centralized billing and shipping is provided from Oxford; a wide range of joint catalogues and other promotional material is mailed to libraries and other book buyers. English-language material only is stocked initially, but orders for back-list titles not stocked are forwarded to publishers for processing. In addition to titles being available for individual purchase, standing order / blanket order plans are available and can be geared to meet libraries' specific requirements or acquisitions 'profiles'. Trading started in May 1990.

6070

AMALGAMATED BOOK SERVICES LTD
Suite 1, Royal Star Arcade, High Street, Maidstone, Kent ME14 1JL
Telephone: 01622 764555
Fax: 01622 763197

Director: John Masters *(Sales)*

Amalgamated Book Services provides a comprehensive sales and marketing service for publishers. ABS offers nationwide representation through our fully trained and experienced sales team. Regular presentations, at head office level, to the retail and wholesale multiples in the book trade. Selling is done on an eight-weekly cycle, which allows for a comprehensive coverage of the UK.
   Regular meetings are held with clients to discuss and decide upon future publishing programmes. ABS sees active participation with clients as a vital part of its services, and frequently advises on format, jacket treatment, publicity and promotions.

6071

BILL BAILEY PUBLISHERS' REPRESENTATIVES
16 Devon Square, Newton Abbot, Devon TQ12 2HR
Telephone: 01626 331079 **Fax:** 01626 331080

Proprietor: Bill Bailey
Partner: Matt Parsons

Publishers represented include:
Airlift Book Co
Arkitektens Forlag *(Iceland, Norway, Sweden & Finland)*
Boxtree (Littlehampton Distribution)
Cornerhouse (Trade Counter)
Deep Books
Duckworth
Geocenter (Insight Guides, Langenscheidt Dictionaries) (Grantham Book Services)
Gustavo Gili *(Iceland, Scandinavia & Finland)*
Harvest (Harcourt Brace – San Diego)
Hi Marketing (Tiptree) *(Chronicle in Iceland, Scandinavia, Belgium, Netherlands & Cyprus)*

Kodansha/Tuttle (Biblios) *(not France, Germany, Austria, Switzerland & Greece)*
Mainstream (Bookpoint)
University Press of Mississippi
University of Nebraska Press
University of New Mexico Press
David Porteous Editions (Bookpoint)
Rizzoli/Biblios Marketing *(Iceland, Sweden, Norway & Finland)*
Rutgers University Press
Scanvik Books *(Iceland, Norway, Sweden & Finland)*
Serindia/Kiscadale (Wisdom)
Terrail *(Iceland, Scandinavia & Finland)*
Verulam (IBD)
World Leisure Marketing (Grantham Book Services)

Orders for the following should be sent c/o Bill Bailey:
Carol Publishing Group (New Jersey & Biblios)
HMSO *(not Cyprus & Greece)*
National Textbook Co

Worldwide Media / Adrian Parker Associates / Running Press (Biblios)

Sales representatives, freelance, to UK and USA publishers, visiting 750 bookshops in Continental Europe twice per year.

6072

BEST MAILING SERVICES LTD
Merlin Way, North Weald, Epping, Essex CM16 6HR
Telephone: 01992 524343
Fax: 01992 524552

Managing Director: Mrs Lyn Reed

BMS offers a complete direct mail production facility.
   Comprehensive services include database management, data capture, laser printing, mail order fulfilment, subscription management, machine and hand enclosing, bulk despatch, overseas and UK postal discounts.

6073

BIBLIOS MARKETING SERVICES
Star Road, Partridge Green, West Sussex RH13 8LD
Telephone: 01403 710971 (orderline: 710851)
Fax: 01403 711143
Email: biblios@compuserve.com

Also at:
Biblios 2, Old London Road, Washington, West Sussex RH20 3BN
Telephone: 01903 892346
Fax: 01903 893383

Managing Director: Anthony Wagstaff
Managers: Louise Mallard *(Sales)*
David Mansfield *(Client Services)*
Ian Dumbleton *(Financial Controller)*
David Brown *(Accounts)*
David Hamill *(Warehouse)*
Philip Cranfield *(IT)*
Helen Negus *(Administration)*

Sales and Distribution provided for:

Arlington Books	Johansens
Berghaus Oberauer Offset	Lannoo
Cedco Calendars	Learning Together
CRS Records	Kenneth Mason
CSA Telltapes	Montignac Publishing
Dalebank Books	Pendulum Gallery Press
Evening Standard	Rizzoli International Publications
Floraprint Books	Inc
Robert Frederick	Universe Publishing
Hobsons / CRAC	John Van Weenen
Norman Hudson	Veloce Publishing

With a Sales Manager and a team of representatives covering the United Kingdom, the Republic of Ireland and Europe, Biblios Marketing Services handle sales and marketing requirements for a wide variety of publishers. Marketing, sales and physical distribution are all under one control and one roof, ensuring a flexible approach and services which can be tailored exactly to a client/publisher's requirements.

6074

THE BOOK DEPOT
111 Woodcote Avenue, London NW7 2PD
Telephone: 0181 906 3708
Fax: 0181 906 3708

Proprietors: Conrad Wiberg
George Depotex

Sales, marketing, promotion campaigns, special sales service, out of print and antiquarian bookfinding service.

6075

BOOK MARKETING LTD
7a Bedford Square, London WC1B 3RA
Telephone: 0171 580 7282
Fax: 0171 580 7236

Chairman: Tim Rix
Managing Director: Clare Harrison

Book Marketing Ltd offers a complete marketing research service to all those involved in the book business. Services include market research, information provision and market sector reports/publications.
   BML also administers the ongoing research study, Books and the Consumer.
   Syndicated/collective activities and one-off private commissions are undertaken.

6076

BOOK REPRESENTATION AND DISTRIBUTION LTD (BRAD)
244a London Road, Hadleigh, Essex SS7 2DE
Telephone: 01702 552912
Fax: 01702 556095

Managing Director: Dan Levey
Company Secretary: Doreen Mann
Company Accountant: John Fielder
Sales Manager: Celia Stocks

Sales Territories: UK and Irish Republic, Austria, Belgium, Denmark, Egypt, Finland, France, Germany, Greece, Iceland, Iran, Iraq, Israel, Italy, Jordan, Lebanon, Libya, Luxembourg, Netherlands, Norway, Portugal, Saudi, Spain, Sweden, Switzerland, Syria, Turkey.
   Specialization: Acedemic books, quality general titles.
   Services: Distribution – worldwide. Marketing – consultancy for Europe and USA. Origination and design of marketing material, printing and mailing.

6077

BOOKLINK
43 Maycock Grove, Northwood, Middx HA6 3PU
Telephone: 01923 828612
Fax: 01923 828455

Managing Director: Evelyne Duval

An international connection for foreign rights sales. Representing French, English and American publishers/packagers.

6078

BOOKS CONTINENTAL LTD
4–12 Old Christchurch Road, Bournemouth BH1 1LG
Telephone: 01202 528263
Fax: 01202 537595

Director: Graham Powell

Provides sales, mailing and marketing services specializing in:
   – export of finished books to Europe,
   – advice and organization of sales of foreign-based publishers' books in UK market and rest of world.

6079

BOOKWATCH LTD
15-Up East Street, Lewin's Yard, Chesham, Bucks HP5 1HQ
Telephone: 01494 792269
Fax: 01494 784850
Email: 100615.1643@compuserve.com

Directors: Peter Harland *(Managing)*
Jennifer Harland *(Company Secretary)*
Editorial Assistant, 'Books in the Media': Sue Harris *(Advertising)*
Senior Researcher: Steve Butler
Subscriptions: Marjorie Davenport

Bookwatch compiles weekly bestseller lists for *The Sunday Times*, *The Bookseller*, *The Sunday Telegraph*, *The Daily Telegraph*, *The Mail on Sunday*, *The Irish Times*, etc; and offers sales research and statistics for publishers based on a weekly national sample of more than 650 bookshops. It also offers syndicated book reviews for newspapers etc, and publishes the weekly, *Books in the Media*, which lists titles reviewed in the Press, serialized or linked to TV, radio, films, etc.

6080

CEDAR TREE HOUSE
7–9 Church Hill, Loughton, Essex IG10 1QP
Telephone: 0181 508 8856
Fax: 0181 508 8856

Directors: Roger Barnett
Marie L. Barnett

Distributors and agents for overseas publishers of high quality professional and reference information on Europe for business, industry, libraries, academic and official institutions.

6081

THE CENTRE FOR INTERFIRM COMPARISON
Capital House, Andover Road, Winchester, Hants SO23 7BH
Telephone: 01962 844144
Fax: 01962 843180

Director: Hon H. W. Palmer

An independent organization established in 1959 by the British Institute of Management and the British Productivity Council specifically to meet the demand for a neutral specialist body to conduct interfirm comparisons (IFCs) and benchmarking projects on a confidential basis as a service to management.
    In 1965, in conjunction with the Publishers Association, the Centre began a series of IFCs specifically designed for book publishers. These comparisons provide objective yardsticks for assessing how overall performance compares; where and why it differs; and lines of action for improvement. The comparisons are based on information supplied confidentially, in depth, and using carefully defined definitions, by participating firms.
    The Centre is also a leading organization in the conduct of benchmarking projects for firms and organizations of all kinds and has carried out projects for journal publishers.

6082

*CLARKE ASSOCIATES – EUROPE LTD
The Rackhay, Queen Charlotte Street, Bristol BS1 4HJ
Telephone: 0117 926 8864 or 922 5864
Fax: 0117 922 6437

Directors: Malcolm Clarke *(Managing)*
Sue Phillips *(Finance)*

Importers and distributors of scientific and technical books, primarily from US societies, providing integrated marketing and distribution throughout UK, Europe, Middle East and Africa. The company has extensive mailing lists of individuals, libraries and booksellers. Books are supplied from the large stock of current and new titles held in the UK.

6083

COLMAN GETTY LTD
Carrington House, 126–130 Regent Street, London W1R 5FE
Telephone: 0171 439 1783
Fax: 0171 439 1784
Email: dotti@colqetpr.demon.co.uk

Chief Executive: Dotti Irving
Director, Publishing Division: Liz Sich

Colman Getty PR is a London-based consumer PR consultancy, founded in 1987 and headed by Dotti Irving, formerly Publicity Director of Penguin Books. The agency specializes in book publishing and issues-related PR and has an established reputation for handling complex, high-profile campaigns, individual promotions, literary awards and longer term consultancies. As well as offering a wide-based expertise in marketing, PR and publicity, Colman Getty can also handle every aspect of marketing projects – from copywriting and print production to sales promotion and advertising. Client list includes The Booker Prize, The NLR Award for Non Fiction, The Red House Children's Book Club, Waterstone's, The Everyman's Library, Richard Cohen Books and a number of high-profile individual authors such as Sir Roy Strong and Robert Harris. Other clients include The Employers Forum on Age and sculptor David Wynne.

6084

MERRIC DAVIDSON, MARKETING CONSULTANCY
Oakwood, Ashley Park, Tunbridge Wells, Kent TN4 8UA
Telephone: 01892 514282
Fax: 01892 514282

Proprietor: Merric Davidson

Marketing, sales and editorial skills in publishing combine to offer a special long-term arrangement for publicity and promotion needs. All aspects of the marketing campaign are covered through trade, media and public relations.

6085

DRAKE INTERNATIONAL SERVICES
Market House, Market Place, Deddington, Oxford OX15 0SF
Telephone: 01869 338240
Fax: 01869 338310

Directors: Norman Drake *(Managing)*
Ashley Drake *(Sales)*
Joy Drake *(Promotions & Export)*
Accounts Manager: Julie Jones

Clients:

Australia: State Library of New South Wales Press
Austria: University of Salzburg Studied in English Literature
Bangladesh: The University Press Bangladesh
Canada: Bayeux Publishers
Robert Davies Publishing
The Golden Dog
Mosaic Press
Peguis Publishers
Pippin Publishing
Trifolium Books
TSAR Publications
Hong Kong: Hong Kong University Press
India: New Age Publications *(academic)*
TR Publications
Netherlands: VU University Press
Russia: Panorama Information Group
Singapore: Singapore University Press
UK: Alpha Press

Bath University Press
Bramcote Press
Continuing Education Press
Educational Heretics Press
Adam Hart Publishers
Hearthstone Publications
Hisarlik Press
John Jones Publishing
Libris Ltd
Margaret Lowenfeld Trust
Modern Welsh Publications
Mustaqim
New Cherwell Press
Reed Information Services
Saqi Books
Shepheard-Walwyn *(academic)*
Staple First Editions
Sussex Academic Press
Tallents Press
Welsh Academic Press
Wishwa Prakashan
Y Lolfa
USA: Ballena Press
Caddo Gap Press
Duquesne University Press

Drake International Services offers an international marketing, sales and distribution service to academic and scholarly publishers in association with Bailey Distribution.

6086

ANDREW DURNELL – PUBLISHERS EUROPEAN MARKETING AGENCY
2 Linden Close, Tunbridge Wells TN4 8HH
Telephone: 01892 544272
Fax: 01892 511152
Email: 100442.1665@compuserve.com

Proprietors: Andrew B. Durnell
Julia Lippiatt

Sales and marketing organization specializing in the sale and promotion of English-language academic and professional publications to Western Europe & Scandinavia. Coverage includes extensive and regular academic institute and book-trade calling. Team of representatives visit individual teaching staff to promote potential textbooks, visit European booksellers to sell and promote clients' new and existing lists and arrange exhibitions and other promotional events.

All academic and professional subjects covered.

6087

DURRANT'S PRESS CUTTINGS LTD
103 Whitecross Street, London EC1Y 8QT
Telephone: 0171 588 3671
Fax: 0171 374 8171

Directors: J. M. Finn *(Chairman)*
A. J. Law *(Managing)*
A. M. Law
B. Swidecki

Rates begin at £150 per hundred cuttings. Coverage: British and overseas press.

6088

EAST WEST NIGEL CARR PUBLISHERS CONSULTANTS
6 Lintott Gardens, Horsham, West Sussex RH13 5TY
Telephone: 01306 627428
Fax: 01306 627026

Managing Director: Nigel Carr

East West specializes in publishing services to South East Asia, Hong Kong, China, Korea and Taiwan. It covers all aspects of the business including sales and marketing, co-publishing, foreign rights, special editions and market surveys on a country-by-country or regional basis.

East West maintains close links with the Book Trade in each region through regular visits each year.

Foreign Rights has become an important part of its business, as has the setting up of effective agency arrangements. East West will also run them for you if you would like them to do so.

6089

ENGLISH HOUSE PUBLISHING SERVICES
Higgs Farm, New Road, Flaxley, Gloucester GL14 1JS
Telephone: 01452 760250
Fax: 01452 760214

Partners: Neil Morley
Sally Morley

International field-based sales and marketing services are available to publishers.

English House specializes in overseas markets, and has been a principal agency in the *Business Books Project* involving over 40 publishers (Eastern Europe, Southern Africa), and in the CD-ROM focused *Electronic Information Services* demonstration projects (Middle East).

Other commissions cover the management of marketing networks in the Caribbean, and the selling of children's, academic, business and general trade titles to various English-speaking countries. Market research programmes are also undertaken.

6090

FLETEL BUSINESS SERVICES
Henbury House, Gables Road, Fleet, Hants GU13 0QZ
Telephone: 01252 622415
Fax: 01252 620729
Email: fletel@zetnet.co.uk
Web Site: http://www.fletel.co.uk

Proprietor: Stan Googe

Fletel Business Services offers American mailing lists and competitively priced shared and solus mailings to the USA. Mailing lists include over 720,000 American professors, selectable by subject, the American Medical Association and the American Libraries Association lists, as well as lists of all American scientists and engineers. Most of our American lists can be delivered within seven working days.

6091

GBS DISTRIBUTION & MARKETING LTD
Units A1/2 Star Business Centre, Fairview Industrial Estate, Marsh Way, Rainham, Essex RM13 8UH
Telephone: 01708 525544
Fax: 01708 524615

Directors: Miss Karen Fox
Mrs Lesley Down

UK distributor/representative for:
Singapore: Mighty Minds   Hohm Press
   Corporation Ltd   Home Planners Inc
USA: C & T Publishing   School Zone Publishing Co

Supplier of distribution services, primarily for the small to medium sized publisher based either in the UK or abroad.

These services cover all aspects of distribution; marketing, stocking in a purpose built warehouse, a pick-pack operation, delivery and invoicing with full computerized documentation. The publisher can choose all or any combination of our services.

6092

GIVEN & PARTNERS
Nahanni Gate, Dipley, Hartley Wintney, Hants RG27 8JP
Telephone: 01252 843265
Fax: 01252 844092

Partner: Morwenna Given

Given & Partners is a trans-Atlantic consultancy specializing in providing soft marketing services for exporters of all kinds of books and materials except computer and software publishers: North American publishers in Europe, British publishers in North America.

Services include: arranging sales and distribution facilities, marketing strategy, market research, merchandizing and sales presentations, publicity, promotion, and public relations activities either on a corporate or author/title basis (author tours, reviews, features, events etc).

6093

DIPAK KUMAR GUHA
PO Box 3205, New Delhi 110 013, India
Telephone: +91 (011) 550 0998
Fax: +91 (011) 646 9018
Email: guha.dk@sma.sprintrpg.sprint.com

Also at:
2 Haly Close, Bradwell Village, Milton Keynes MK13 9BY
Telephone: 01908 225206
Fax: 01908 670587

Rights: D. K. Guha
Executive: Ashok Kumar
Marketing: Ms Sandhya

Founded in 1986 the company specializes in negotiating reprint and syndication licenses, co-editions, special sales on behalf of overseas partners, both in English and Indian languages.

Services include CD-ROM rights (entertainment and reference) and OEM sales in particular on behalf of book publishers who have started with a CD-ROM program.

Activities are also directed at publishers in the USA, Canada and Australia who want a separate licensing agreement in India for their titles instead of blanket agreements with UK firms.

The company specializes in health, self help/improvement, productivity, business and management, reference pocket book fiction and general interest areas plus syndication from wire services into magazines and newspapers.

The company does not handle culturally incompatible subjects.

6094 ▬▬▬▬▬▬

HI MARKETING LTD
38 Carver Road, London SE24 9LT
Telephone: 0171 738 7751
Fax: 0171 274 9160

Joint Managing Directors: Medwyn Hughes
Catherine Parson
Manager: Claire Lavedan

Sales and marketing for publishers in the UK and Europe. Services offered include representation, warehousing, invoicing, collection, stock control, and marketing advice.

6095 ▬▬▬▬▬▬

HPR
22 Mount View Road, London N4 4HX
Telephone: 0181 348 1234
Fax: 0181 341 0748
Email: hpr@heritage.co.uk
Web Site: http://www.heritage.co.uk/heritage/bmol.html

Directors: Gwyn Headley
Yvonne Seeley

Organizations who have used HPR's services include:
Czech Republic: Czech Publishers & Booksellers Association
UK: Apex Publishing
BBC Publications
Boydell & Brewer
Chelsea Football Club
Exley
Faber & Faber
Folly Fellowship
Foulsham
Hamish Hamilton
Heinemann
Infobase
Michael Joseph
Lawson-Price
Macmillan
Oxford University Press
Pavilions of Splendour
Pilkington Brothers
Tarmac
Trinity Estates
University of Wales Press
Webb & Bower
Welsh Rugby Union
John Wiley & Sons
World One Day Novel Cup

HPR provides consultant and/or executive functions in most aspects of book publishing excluding book design and production. Particular strengths: publicity; copywriting; Quark Xpress DTP; slide presentations; 35mm photography; corporate image presentations; cybermarketing, HTML, VRML, World Wide Web site design, creation and maintenance; costings; creative ideas; design and artwork; direct mail; exhibitions; extract and rights sales; lectures; market analysis; merchandizing; parties and receptions; premium deals; press relations; promotional tours; public affairs consulting; sales briefings; sales promotions; strategic planning, etc.

6096 ▬▬▬▬▬▬

HUMBERSIDE INDUSTRIAL PUBLICATIONS
Friary Chambers, Whitefriargate, Hull, North Humberside HU1 2HA
Telephone: 01482 23427
Fax: 01482 214024
Email: 101325.355@compuserve.com

Principal: John Davis

Public relations consultant, house journal publishers, desk-top publishers.

6097 ▬▬▬▬▬▬

HUMPHRYS ROBERTS ASSOCIATES
24 High Street, London E11 2AQ
Telephone: 0181 530 5028
Fax: 0181 530 7870

Also at:
Terry Roberts, Caixa Postal 801-0, Ag Jardim da Gloria, 06700-970 Cotia SP, Brazil
Telephone: +55 (11) 492 4496 & 492 6697
Fax: +55 (11) 492 6896

Directors: Christopher Humphrys
Terry Roberts

Publishers' agents and representatives representing UK and US publishers in Latin America and the West Indies.

6098 ▬▬▬▬▬▬

INFORMATION AGENTS LTD
26 Rosebery Avenue, London EC1R 4SX
Telephone: 0171 837 3345
Fax: 0171 837 8901
Email: ial@epsltd.demon.co.uk
Web Site: epsltd.com

Director (Chairman): David R. Worlock
Senior Consultant: Tony Feldman

Information Agents Ltd (IAL) was established to provide an electronic rights broking service—that is, to assist publishers and other rights holders to find suitable partners to exploit their information assets in electronic form, and to negotiate contracts appropriate to such exploitation. All electronic media are covered, especially all CD-based platforms, audiotex, online, etc.

6099 ▬▬▬▬▬▬

THE INTERNET BOOKSHOP
6 Isis Business Centre, Pony Road, Oxford OX4 3DR
Email: stuart.rivett@bookshop.co.uk
Web Site: http://www.bookshop.co.uk

Chief Executive: Darryl Mattocks
Managers: Stuart Rivett *(Book Sales)*
Adrian Pritchard *(Publisher Sales)*
Design Consultant: Gary Newbrook

The Internet Bookshop is one of Europe's largest on-line bookshops. It is a facility for marketing and selling books and journals on the Internet.

6100 ▬▬▬▬▬▬

IRISH BOOK SALES
18 Coleswood Road, Harpenden, Herts AL5 1EQ
Telephone: 01582 761264
Fax: 01582 712244
Email: ionmills@aol.com

Manager: Ion Mills

Irish companies represented:
Irish Republic: Gill & Macmillan *(general list)*
Lilliput Press
Mercier Press
New Island Books
O'Brien Press
Wolfhound Press

6101 ▬▬▬▬▬▬

THE JOHNSTON EDUCATIONAL SERVICE
25 Middleton Road, Horsham, Sussex RH12 1JS
Telephone: 01403 253382

Proprietor: T. V. W. Johnston

Promotion agent specializing in mobile exhibition of publishers' material in the technical college and college of education fields.

6102 ▬▬▬▬▬▬

KEY PERSPECTIVES
The Leys, Gaddesby, Leicestershire LE7 8XF
Telephone: 01664 840160
Fax: 01664 840160

Also at:
2 Ivy Cottages, Ponsanooth, Truro, Cornwall TR3 7ET

Telephone: 01872 862173
Fax: 01872 862173

Partners: Dr Alma Swan
Sheridan Brown

Key Perspectives provides high quality strategic research and
consultancy services to the publishing industry. The range of activities
offered include:
— business strategy reviews and planning
— new market development strategy
— new product development strategy and portfolio planning
— information systems strategy
— electronic publishing and project management
— marketing and promotion strategy
— market research

Key Perspectives publish a number of *Strategic Briefings* on key
aspects of the publishing industry, focusing on business opportunities.
Topics include: the potential of the intranet; targeting end users; targeting
the corporate market; and effective organizational design for publishers.

6103

KSB PUBLISHERS' SERVICES
Eagle House, Landgate, Rye, East Sussex TN31 7LH
Telephone: 01797 225650
Fax: 01797 225652

Partners: J. F. Burnett
Marion Koenig

Specialist academic book and journal publicists. Concentrating on one
discipline at a time, KSB organize small exhibitions in series of between
15 and 20 universities, teaching hospitals, polytechnics or other
institutions, one day in each. Subjects include natural, social and
environmental sciences, technology, medicine, humanities, education,
business studies and economics. Exhibition tours take place in UK, West
Germany, Belgium and the Netherlands, Denmark, Norway and Sweden,
Italy, Switzerland and Iberia.

6104

LAVIS MARKETING
73 Lime Walk, Headington, Oxford OX3 7AD
Telephone: 01865 67575
Fax: 01865 750079

Directors: James H. Lavis *(Managing)*
Fay W. Lavis

Clients include:
Canada: Alberta University Press	IOS Press
Boardwalk	*Norway:* Solum Forlag AS
Crabtree Publishing Co	*Sri Lanka:* Buddhist Publication
Dundurn Press	Society
Formac	*Thailand:* Silkworm Books
Hounslow	White Orchid Press
ISER	*UK:* Elfande Art Publishing
James Lorimer & Co	Intellect
University of Manitoba Press	Kiscadale
NC Press	Malthouse Publishing
Newest	Motilal Books
Simon & Pierre	Pali Text Society
Stoddart (Anansi)	Royal Asiatic Society
France: ASA Editions	Tarragon Press
Italy: Bibliopolis	*USA:* Edgemore Enterprises
Netherlands: Amsterdam	Prometheus Books
University Press	*Yugoslav Republics:* International
Ercomer	Centre for Public Enterprises

Lavis Marketing provides a full range of services for academic, scholarly
and specialist publishers worldwide. The services include trade
representation, marketing and promotion, major book fair displays,
warehousing and distribution, direct mail fulfilment and distribution.

6105

CHRIS LLOYD SALES & MARKETING SERVICES
463 Ashley Road, Parkstone, Poole, Dorset BH14 0AX
Telephone: 01202 715349 **Fax:** 01202 736191

Proprietor: Christopher Lloyd

Publishers & Imprints represented & distributed:
Australia: The Five Mile Press	Learning Development Aids
Off The Shelf Publishing	M&J Publications
France: Histoires & Collections	Marston House Books
Switzerland: Translegal	Nexus Special Interests
UK: Alpha Press	Premier Books
Amateur Winemaker Publications	Prism Press
Bay View Books	RAF Benevolent Fund
Creel Publishing	Stilwell Publishing
DC Publishing	Two Heads Publishing
English Heritage	Winslow
Firebird Books	*USA:* Bicycle Books Inc
GMC Publications	Meadowbrook Press
Guild of Master Craftsman	
Publications	

An independent sales and marketing agency for small and medium sized
publishers. Formed in collaboration with book distributor, Bailey Book
Distribution Ltd.

6106

MARDEV LTD
[incorporating IBIS]
151–153 Wardour Street, London W1V 3TB
Telephone: 0171 411 2666
Fax: 0171 287 1098

Managing Director: Rosemary Smith
Directors: John Beale
Lisa Long
Nick Martin
Shane Redding
Robert Howells *(New York)*

IBIS is now part of Mardev Ltd, a Reed-Elsevier company.
The IBIS Worldwide Academic and Library File continues to provide
carefully researched names and addresses of academics and librarians
around the world, selectable by subject and area. Medical, business and
professional names are also available.
Through Mardev, access is available to a wide range of brokered and
managed lists as well as to the listholdings from the Reed Database.
Individual customer mailings are undertaken at competitive prices. Co-
operative, shared cost mailings are also regularly organized.

6107

MEDIAN BOOKS LTD
Ty Derw, Dinas Mawddwy, Machynlleth, Powys SY20 9LR
Telephone: 01650 531444
Fax: 01650 531337
Email: 100124.1201@compuserve.com

Directors: Ian G. McIntyre
Mrs K. A. McIntyre

Median Books Ltd operates in the following areas: export bookselling to
the Middle East; representation of publishers in the Middle East.

6108

MELIA PUBLISHING SERVICES
Broadway House, 21 Broadway, Maidenhead, Berks SL6 1JK
Telephone: 01628 410537
Fax: 01628 789758

Directors: Terry Melia *(Managing)*
David Owen *(Financial)*

Represents:
Canada: McClelland & Stewart   Geoscience
UK: Connections   Oxmoor House
Deirdre McDonald Books   Putnam Publishing Group
Usha Publications   Time Warner Publisher Services
USA: Berkley Publishing Group   International
Creative Editions   Workman Publishing

MPS offers a sales and marketing and distribution service to English language publishers throughout the UK and overseas markets.

6109

MIDAS PUBLIC RELATIONS LTD
7–8 Kendrick Mews, London SW7 3HG
Telephone: 0171 584 7474
Fax: 0171 584 7123
Email: midaspr@dial.pipex.com

Proprietors: Steven Williams
Tony Mulliken

Complete trade promotions of individual books or series, or authors. Campaign planning – and implementation – of publicity and promotion for authors and books at publication including press releases, launch parties, feature coverage, review lists, radio and TV interviews and bookshop promotion. Compilation, design and production of leaflets, advertisements, catalogues, display and POS material. Promotion and marketing of academic, technical, specialist and reference books.

6110

MOMENTA PUBLISHING LTD
Broadway House, The Broadway, London SW19 1RH
Telephone: 0181 542 2465
Fax: 0181 542 2465

Director: Robert Leech
Company Secretary: Mahara Collier

Founded 1972. Momenta represents various publishing houses, mainly specializing in academic, scholastic, technical, scientific and medical books, located in continental Europe and the USA as well as the UK.
  Momenta offers the following services:
  full sales representation in the UK and Western Europe;
  visits to bookshops, sci-tech, academic and medical centres, universities, polytechnics, libraries;
  medical and sci-tech lecturers and personnel;
  participation in book fairs, congresses and exhibitions;
  detailed visit reports containing comments, impressions and recommendations;
  market research;
  contact with overdue debtors;
  book distribution if required.
  Momenta is a dynamic company with a wide experience in book sale and promotion.

6111

OXFORD PUBLICITY PARTNERSHIP
12 Hid's Copse Road, Oxford OX2 9JJ
Telephone: 01865 865466
Fax: 01865 862763
Email: opp@oxfpubp.demon.co.uk

Partners: Sue Miller
Alice Meadows

The Oxford Publicity Partnership offers academic, educational and professional publishers and other institutions with publishing interests a comprehensive range of publicity services. These services are available on a regular or one-off basis and are geared to the budgets of both small and large publishers.
  Our range of work includes consultancy, preparing, designing and (if required) printing catalogues, leaflets and other mailshots, mailing list research and implementation, compiling press packs and press releases, copywriting, proof-reading, review list compilation, organizing press and media launches, author tours, etc.
  OPP also runs a number of training courses on various aspects of publishing – further details are available on request.

6112

PAGEANT PUBLISHING
1 Weir Gardens, Pershore, Worcs WR10 1DX
Telephone: 01386 561125
Fax: 01386 561119

Director: Gillian Page

A consultancy service on all aspects of academic publishing for learned societies, scholarly publishers and anyone who sells services to them. Questions that Pageant Publishing can help with include: business policy and finance; subcontracting the whole publishing process or some elements of it; editorial policy, marketing, promotion and distribution. It can help organize training; negotiate the purchase or sale of journals; or conduct surveys on a confidential basis. Pageant also publishes journals.
  Clients include commercial publishers, learned societies and university presses in Britain, the USA, and Western Europe.

6113

PETER WARD BOOK EXPORTS
231 Royal College Street, London NW1 9LT
Telephone: 0171 267 4374
Fax: 0171 267 5014

Warehouse:
Unit 20, Grays Farm Production Village, St Pauls Cray, Orpington, Kent BR5 3BD
Telephone: 0181 300 1733
Fax: 0181 309 7437

Senior Partner: Peter Ward
Partner: Richard Ward
Export Sales Co-ordinator: Sean Sweeney
Financial Controller: Ranga Nathan

Publishers' sales representatives and wholesalers in Middle East, North Africa, Cyprus, Turkey, Far East, South America and South Africa.

6114

PHIPPS PUBLIC RELATIONS LTD
Woburn Buildings, 1–7 Woburn Walk, London WC1H 0JJ
Telephone: 0171 388 2525
Fax: 0171 387 6411
Email: 101527.1257@compuserve.com

Directors: Penny Phipps
Miranda Page Wood
Dr Miriam Stoppard

Marketing and PR strategy from a team with over 20 years' experience in event management, sponsorship, media relations and retail. All programmes are handled by specialist staff who bring expertise from the world of entertainment, leisure and f.m.c.g. to the challenge of promoting and marketing books, publishers, retailers and writers.

6115

PLATO PUBLISHING
20 Highgate West Hill, London N6 6NP
Telephone: 0181 340 8845
Fax: 0181 340 8845

Director: Priscilla Oakeshott

Plato Publishing is a consultancy offering management analysis, advice and market research on publishing, copyright and contracts, especially in the academic and educational areas, both UK and overseas.
  Clients range from individual publishers and learned societies to large international organizations. Assignments may be one-off or provide

continuing help and back-up: recurring problems handled range from general publishing management to author and publisher contracts, export sales (including the sale of rights), pricing and distribution.

6116

POWERHOUSE (PR) LTD
26 Westbourne Grove, London W2 5RH
Telephone: 0171 221 3754
Fax: 0171 221 0723
Email: phouse@easynet.co.uk

Chairman: Vikki Stace
Directors: Harriet Hastings
Adrian Weston

Powerhouse is a public relations consultancy specializing in all aspects of the book trade – publishing, retailing, exhibitions and trade associations.
Services include media relations, author promotion, serial rights sales, copywriting, advertising, point of sale material, competitions, launch events, sponsorship, exhibitions, seminars, conferences and research.

6117

PIPPA RANN BOOKS
Pineview House, 58 Ridgway Road, Farnham, Surrey GU9 8NS
Telephone: 01252 713643
Fax: 01252 718282

Proprietor: Pippa Rann
Executive Consultant: Prabhu Guptara

Pippa Rann Books publishes, distributes and markets books, and acts as a publishing consultant, especially for books first published overseas – which gives rise to its interest in translation. It has particular interests in South Asia, literature, films, religion, communication, business and management.

6118

RESOLUTIONS LTD
Forde House, 51 Cloth Fair, London EC1A 7JQ
Telephone: 0171 606 0900
Fax: 0171 606 0226

Directors: Caroline Thomas
Liz Walsh

In addition to the organizing of fairs and conferences, Resolutions provides services to trade associations including the publishing of newsletters and trade directories.

6119

ANTHONY RUDKIN ASSOCIATES
PO Box 15, 51 Cornmarket Street, Oxford OX1 3EB
Telephone: 01865 724627
Fax: 01865 792309

Partners: Anthony Rudkin
Ann Rudkin
Associate: Adam Dent

Representatives of academic, scientific, medical, technical, educational and trade publishers in Greece, Cyprus, Malta, the Middle East and Pakistan.
Regular visits to educational institutions, relevant ministries, libraries, commercial and industrial companies and bookshops throughout the territories. Extensive promotional activities and publisher and customer liaison carried out from offices in Oxford and Tehran.

6120

JOHN RULE SALES & MARKETING
40 Voltaire Road, London SW4 6DH
Telephone: 0171 498 0115
Fax: 0171 498 2245

Sales and distribution services offered to small publishers to the UK market.

6121

DEREK SEARLE ASSOCIATES LTD
Burlington House, 14 High Street, Slough, Berks SL1 1EE
Telephone: 01753 539295
Fax: 01753 551863

Directors: Derek Searle
June Searle
Bob Cripps

DSA is a professional, productive and cost-effective sales and marketing agency for publishers. It employs an experienced team of sales people providing full representation throughout the UK and Irish book market and maintains close contacts with all major trade outlets as well as key specialist and non-trade outlets. The company also provides export and premium/promotional sales support, full administration and support services, and is expert in all aspects of marketing, publicity and promotion for small, medium or large publishers. Close communication with clients is ensured through regular field/contact reports and meetings.

6122

WILLIAM SNYDER PUBLISHING ASSOCIATES
5 Five Mile Drive, Oxford OX2 8HT
Telephone: 01865 513186
Fax: 01865 513186
Email: 100072.2511@compuserve.com

Managing Director: W. A. Snyder

Publishers represented include:
Canada: Canadian Almanac & Directory Publishing Co	Grey House Publishing Omnigraphics
France: French Company Handbook	Peachtree Publishers The Reference Press
Germany: Germany's Top 500	Science Press NY
Spain: SPA	Transnational Juris Publications
USA: Art Direction Book Co	Universal Reference Publishing
Association Management Press	Worldwide Government
Columbia Books Inc	Directories Inc

A specialist provider of business information on companies, people and regions. The company has formed links with several US and Canadian producers of information in reference book form, journals and in electronic formats.
In addition, a consultancy service for organizations interested in international publishing and marketing is provided.

6123

SOVEREIGN SYSTEMS
The Old Workshop, 4a East Avenue, Oxford OX4 1XW
Telephone: 01865 202570
Fax: 01865 202790

Proprietor & Managing Director: John Davis
Managers: Andrew Moore *(Client)*
Kevin Naylor *(Technical)*

Sovereign Systems is a computer bureau specializing in processing names and addresses. Of particular interest to publishers is CLIENT, a software solution specifically developed to hold their marketing data on our computers.
CLIENT can:
– hold any numbers of names and addresses
– process data from and to any media
– postcode to Royal Mail standards
– prevent, detect and remove duplicates
– hold up to 16 subjects on each entry
– combine geographical and subject selection
– merge and purge your data with other lists
– process gone-aways quickly and efficiently

Sovereign offer selection quotes on the same day with despatch of output within 24 hours. Alternatively we offer a complete posting and fulfilment service. Telephone Andrew Moore for details.

6124

SPA BOOKS LTD
PO Box 47, Stevenage, Herts SG2 8UH
Telephone: 01438 816896
Fax: 01438 310104

Directors: Steven Apps *(Managing)*
Aileen Apps

Spa Books Ltd is a publishing company offering a range of services to other publishers. It most commonly undertakes basic distribution and marketing for other small companies.

It is also developing a range of services whereby titles created by companies and institutions which are not themselves publishers can be taken into the company's own list and presented to the book trade at large. Any of these services is available to UK companies and enquiries from other countries are welcomed.

6125

PETER STOCKHAM ASSOCIATES
4 & 6 Dam Street, Lichfield, Staffs WS13 6AA
Telephone: 01543 264093

Managing Director: Peter Stockham

Consultancy specializing in services to the book trade, particularly publishing, but also new and second-hand, antiquarian bookselling, libraries, museums etc.

Services have included stocktaking, design problems and ideas, editorial and picture research, product development, future growth planning, retail problems, series planning, publishing ideas, marketing, board participation, publicity, products for museums and art galleries, detecting where profit lies, acquisition and disposals and crystal ball gazing.

The consultancy also has consultancy rooms in the centre of London, near Trafalgar Square, London WC2.

6126

TELEDYNAMICS
[a division of Taylor Nelson – AGB Plc]
Brenchley House, Week Street, Maidstone, Kent ME14 1RF
Telephone: 01622 778899
Fax: 01622 778880

Directors: P. Dray *(Managing)*
B. F. Stott *(Sales)*
Sales Manager: Ms S. Randall

Specialists in providing telemarketing and telesales for the publishing industry. Projects undertaken utilizing highly skilled staff and specially designed software systems include subscription sales, appointment making, prospect list building and cleaning, reader registration and research. ABC members.

6127

TROIKA
179 King's Cross Road, London WC1X 9BZ
Telephone: 0171 833 8441
Fax: 0171 833 8442

Managing Director: Aidan Lunn

Troika provides a full range of representation and marketing services for the independent publisher in the UK and Ireland. The majority of its clients publish in the literary, cultural or academic domain, and a significant proportion of titles are generally paper (or dual) editions.

6128

VERULAM PUBLISHING LTD
152a Park Street Lane, Park Street, St Albans AL2 2AU
Telephone: 01727 872770
Fax: 01727 873866
Email: 100124.2375@compuserve.com

Directors: David Collins
Penny Collins

Clients include:

Canada: Key Porter Books Ltd	Thornton Cox Travel Guides
UK: b small publishing	Working Books
CAMRA Ltd	*USA:* Barnes & Noble Inc
Century 22 Ltd	NTC Publishing Group
Diamond Publishing Group	Rutledge Hill Press
Eric Dobby Publishing	Stoddart Publishing Ltd
Impact Books	

Sales, marketing and distribution of third-party publishers to the book trade.

6129

DEREK WALKER PARTNERSHIP
97 Gunnergate Lane, Marton-in-Cleveland, Middlesbrough, Cleveland TS7 8JA
Telephone: 01642 315938
Fax: 01642 316503

Partners: Derek Walker
David Gregor

Publishers' sales representation on a free-lance basis, including some distribution. Territory covered: North of England and Scotland (including Isle of Man, Orkney and Shetland).

6130

JOHN WILSON BOOKSALES
1 High Street, Princes Risborough, Bucks HP27 0AG
Telephone: 01844 275927
Fax: 01844 274402

Directors: John S. Wilson *(Managing)*
Pat Wilson *(Administration)*

An exclusive sales and marketing organization providing comprehensive sales coverage to all types of bookselling outlets, with 12 representatives in the UK and Ireland, and overseas agents retained where required. Strong working contacts with most major distributors and publicity houses.

6131

WINDSOR BOOKS INTERNATIONAL
The Boundary, Wheatley Road, Garsington, Oxford OX44 9DT
Telephone: 01865 361122
Fax: 01865 361133

Managing Director: Geoff Cowen

UK Distributor/Representative for:

Billboard Books	*Switzerland:* Rotovision SA
C & T Publishing	*UK:* Bonfini Art Books
Getty Trust Publications	Garnet Publishing
RAC Callbooks	TimeLife Books
Universe Publishing	*USA:* Allworth Press

Windsor Books International provides distribution combined with sales representation and marketing in the UK and European markets. Full distribution is organized using Windsor's own facilities or those of independent fulfilment houses such as Bookpoint. The Windsor sales team consists of seven representatives in the UK and Irish Republic and four covering West and Eastern Europe.

6132

WING FORWARD – PUBLISHERS REGIONAL SERVICE
10 Aylesby Close, Knutsford, Cheshire WA16 8AE
Telephone: 01565 651116
Fax: 01565 651116

Managing Director: Barrie B. Hodgson
Secretary: Josanne Hodgson

Wing Forward – Publishers Regional Service has been providing selling and promotional services for publishers in the area of the North of England and the Midlands for over 19 years.
A comprehensive coverage is provided in our selling and promotional service to academic and general bookshops, library suppliers, and specialist outlets when required.

6133

WORLD LEISURE MARKETING
9 Downing Road, West Meadows Industrial Estate, Derby DE21 6HA
Telephone: 01332 343332
Fax: 01332 340464

Directors: John Whitby *(Managing)*
Judy Whitby *(Promotions)*
Jan Cundy *(Finance)*
Gavin Miller *(Chairman)*
Phil Richards *(Sales)*

The company is an independent sales and marketing organization specializing in leisure related books and electronic publishing. The company represents 40 publishers throughout the UK and Europe. It works on behalf of several major guidebook and cartographic publishers.
World Leisure Marketing offers a full marketing consultancy and sales operation.

6134

YVONNE COURTNEY PR
6 Rabbit Row, London W8 4DX
Telephone: 0171 229 2292
Fax: 0171 229 9891

Director: Yvonne Courtney
Account Executive: Rebecca Davies
Office Manager: David Chadwick

Independent arts PR consultancy – over 60% of our clientele are visual art/non-fiction publishers.
A full PR/marketing service is provided – either handling entire lists or individual titles.
The consultancy generates publicity campaigns within the media, launch events, author signings, direct mail opportunities within specialist mailings, etc.

6.6 DISTRIBUTORS

6135

AIRLIFT BOOK COMPANY
8 The Arena, Mollison Avenue, Enfield, Middlesex EN3 7NJ
Telephone: 0181 804 0400
Fax: 0181 804 0044

Directors: Beth Grossman *(Managing)*
Don Skirving *(Financial)*
John Bailey *(Sales)*
Pat Graves *(Distribution)*

Publishers represented:
Canada: Second Story Press
UK: Angel Books
Atlas Press
Barton House
Black Spring Press

Paul H. Crompton
Eden Grove Editions
Gale Centre Publications
Llewellyn
Onlywomen Press

Quest Books
SAF Publishing
Silver Moon Books
Touchstone Publications
Wellspring Publications
USA: ACS Publications
Aurora Press
Barrytown Ltd
Beacon Press
Bear & Co
Black Sparrow Press
Book Publishing Co
Cassandra Press
Celestial Arts
Chiron Publications
City Lights
Conari Press
CRCS Publications
Crossing Press
Firebrand Books
David R. Godine
Hay House
Hazelden
Healing Tao Books
Health Communications
Humanics New Age
Impact
Inner City Books
H. J. Kramer

Love Line Books
Naiad Press
Nataraj Publishing
New Falcon Publications
New Harbinger
New World Library
Newcastle Publishing
North Atlantic Books
Phanes Press
Real People Press
ReSearch
Roberts Rinehart Publishers
Seal Press
Shambhala Publications
Sigo Press
Gibbs M. Smith
Spinsters Ink
Spring Publications
Station Hill Press
Stillpoint Publishing
Ten Speed Press
Thunders Mouth
Vivation Publishing
Samuel Weiser Inc
White Dove International
Whitford Press
Writers & Readers Publishing Inc
Zephyr Press

6136

THE ANGLO-AMERICAN BOOK CO LTD
Underwood, St Clears, Carmarthen, Dyfed SA33 4NE
Telephone: 01994 230400
Fax: 01994 230064

Chairperson: Mrs G. Roberts
Directors: Dr M. Roberts *(Managing)*
D. S. Bowman *(Marketing)*
Mrs K. J. Bowman *(Rights)*

UK Distributor/Representative for:
USA: Ages Publications
Bramble Books US
Center Press
Facticity Trainings
Futurepace Inc
Gestalt Journal Press
Great Ocean Publishing
Grinder Delozier and Associates
Hudson Centre
International Society for General
  Semantics
Kendall/Hunt
Learning Strategies Corporation
Lifestar
Magination Press
Meta Publications

Metasystems
Mind Matters
Morgen Publishing
NLP Comprehensive
Outcomes Incorporated
Positive Changes
Project Renaissance
Purelight Publishing
Science and Behavior Books
Success Strategies
Syntony Publishing
Turning Point
Westwood Publishing
Yurisha Press
Zephyr Press

The Anglo-American Book Co is a stockholding distributor of American books with particular expertise in the NLP, personal growth, hypnotherapy, accelerated learning and psychotherapy fields. Stock book orders received by 2.30 pm are dispatched the same day.
Order Department opening times: 9–5 Monday to Friday. Basic trade terms 20–35%, no p&p in UK; credit/debit cards accepted.

6137

APEX BOOKS CONCERN
Darus Salaam, 13 Trimley Close, Luton LU4 9HJ
Telephone: 01582 572216
Fax: 01582 572216

Managing Director: S. Dean
Publicity & Sales: A. Dean
Acquisition: Mrs M. Hughes

UK Distributor for:

Bangladesh: Dhaka University
   Press
Joy Books
Research Publications
Egypt: Elias Publishing
France: R. Laffont
Germany: O. Harrassowitz
India: Habib & Co
Hussami Book Depot
Kitab Bhavan
Dairat al Marif
Seven Seas
Taj Co
Lebanon: Dar el Ilm
Netherlands: E. J. Brill

Pakistan: Sh Muhammad Ashraf
Ferozsons Ltd
Hamdard Foundation
Institute of Islamic Culture
Iqbal Academy
Islamic Research Institute
Kazi Publications
National Book Foundation
Vanguard Publications
USA: American Trust Publications
Fellowship Press
Kazi Publications, Chicago
University of Texas Press
University of Utah Press
Vantage Press

Distributors to overseas publishers; book publication; specialist in
Islamic and other religious studies; supplies books in English, French,
German, Arabic, Farsi and Urdu.

6138 ▬

ART BOOKS INTERNATIONAL LTD
1 Stewart's Court, 220 Stewart's Road, London SW8 4UD
Telephone: 0171 720 1503
Fax: 0171 720 3158

Managing Director: Stanley Kekwick
Managers: Stephen Coke *(Head of Accounts)*
Fiona Smith *(Sales)*

Publishers represented:

Argentina: La Azotea
Belgium: Exhibitions
   International
Mercator Fonds
Brazil: Editora Index
Canada: Galerie Amrad African
   Art
Verulam Publishing
France: ACR
Editions Assouline
Bibliothèque de l'Image
Bookking International
Eiffel Editions *(single title)*
Flohic
Maeght Editeur
Marval
Editions Menges
MH Editions
Paris Musées
Editions Plume
Editions Somogy
Germany: Die Gestalten Verlag
Grabert Verlag
Hirmer-Verlag
Vitra Design Museum
India: Motilal
Italy: Arcadia
Be-Ma Editrice
Centro Di
Charta
Einaudi
Electa *(including Mondadori Arte*
   & Nuova Alfa)
Galleria Editrice *(single title)*
Hopeful Monster
Editrice Militare *(single title)*
Motta
Sagep
Monica Smith *(single title)*
Japan: Artis *(selected titles)*
Ikeda & Lokker *(single title)*

Netherlands: Art Unlimited *(two*
   titles only)
Kempen Pers BV
New Zealand: David Bateman
   (single title)
Portugal: Edições Inapa
Spain: Arco Editorial
Electa España
Lunwerg Editores
Switzerland: ABC Verlag
Edition Galerie Bruno
   Bischofberger
Edition Stemmle
UK: Art Books International Ltd
Barbican Art Gallery *(single title)*
Zelda Cheatle Press
Cygnet Press *(single title)*
Dulwich Picture Gallery *(single*
   title)
Festerman *(single title)*
Flowers East Gallery
Francis Graham-Dixon Gallery
Handsaw Press *(single title)*
Thomas Heneage *(selected titles)*
Images *(single title)*
Bernard Jacobson Gallery
Kala Press
Christopher Lennox-Boyd *(single*
   title)
Manchester City Art Galleries
Museum of London
Peter Nahum *(single title)*
Purdy Hicks Gallery *(single title)*
Raab Gallery
Station Press
Temple Gallery *(single title)*
Trojan Horse *(selected titles)*
The Water Press
USA: Hudson Hills Press
L. A. Louver Gallery
MJS Books *(single title)*
Tasende Gallery

Specialist distributor and publisher of books on fine art, architecture,
design and photography.

6139 ▬

ART DATA
12 Bell Industrial Estate, Cunnington Street, London W4 5HB
Telephone: 0181 747 1061
Fax: 0181 742 2319

Director: T. G. Borton

Distributor for:

Uitgeverij 010
Aedes Gallery
Albright-Knox Gallery
Arcadia
Arnolfini Gallery
Art Data
Art Gallery of New South Wales
Art Institute of Chicago
Art Metropole
Art Random
Artists Bookwork
Baltimore Museum of Art
Bauhaus Archive
Benteli Verlag
Braus
Brooklyn Museum of Art
Edition Cantz
Center for Creative Photography
Centre d'Arts Plastiques
   Contemporains
Centre Georges Pompidou
Charta
CPC Publishing
Anthony d'Offay Gallery
Delft University Press
Elefanten Press
Focus
Fragment
Barry Friedman
Fundacion Caja de Pensiones
Galerie Claude Bernard
Galerie Isy Brachot
Galerie Lelong
Galerie Thaddeus Ropac
Gustavo Gili
Good Books
Grassfield Press
Groninger Museum
Guggenheim Museum
Haags Gemeentemuseum
Hanover Gallery
Edition Hansjorg Mayer
Hatje
Hazan Editions
Heibonsha
Houston Fine Art Press
Idea Books Edizioni
Institute of Contemporary Art
Fred Jahn Galerie
La Jolla Museum of
   Contemporary Art
JPL Fine Art

Kettle's Yard
Walther Konig
Kunsthaus Zürich
Kyoto Shoin
Lapis Press
Libro Port
Locker Verlag
Marlborough Fine Art
Edition Marzona
Mazzota Editore
McPherson & Co
Robert Miller Gallery
Ministero de Cultura (Spain)
Minneapolis Institute of Art
Mississippi Museum of Art
Museum of Modern Art (Oxford)
Museum of New Mexico Press
Musée de la Mode et du Costume
Musée de Marseille
Nieswand Verlag
Pace Gallery
Parco View
Paris Audiovisuel
Philadelphia Museum of Art
Photographers Gallery
Photovision
Portikus
Reflex Publishers
Rhode Island School of Design
Gerrit Rietveld Academie
Ritter Verlag
San Francisco Museum of Art
Schellman Edition
Schirmer-Mosel
Schirn Kunsthalle (Frankfurt)
SDU Publishers
Seibu Museum
Serpentine Gallerie
Shikosha
Stills Gallery
Tanam Press
Textile Museum
Thoth Uitgeverij
Treville
Twelve Trees Press
Twin Palms Publishing
University Art Museum (Santa
   Barbara)
Van Abbe Museum
Wellesley College Museum
Whitechapel

Publisher of the Master of Art series of monographs on contemporary
artists and art movements and also other books on the visual arts.
Represents many British and foreign museums, galleries and publishers
specializing in all aspects of the arts.

6140 ▬

ASHGROVE PRESS
7 Locksbrook Road Estate, Bath, Avon BA1 3DZ
Telephone: 01225 425539
Fax: 01225 319137

Director: Robin Campbell
Managers: Charlotte Fyfe *(Publicity)*
Jeanette Woods *(Credit Controller)*
Norma Pitman *(Trade)*

Sales, invoicing, distribution and cash collection service for:

Arcania Press	Solos Press
Ashgrove Press	*Australia:* In-Tune Books
Cornish Connection	*USA:* Anchor Press *(selected titles*
East-West Publications	*only)*
Findhorn Press	Keats
Golden Gates Press	Larson
Gothic Image Publications	Self-Realization Fellowship

6141 ▬▬▬▬▬▬▬▬▬▬

AURA BOOKS PLC
14–15 Fairway Drive, Greenford, Middlesex UB6 8PW
Telephone: 0181 575 6193
Fax: 0181 578 5857

Directors: Andrew Bailey
Allan Beesley
Diane White
Alan Shields
Divisional Sales Managers: Dorothy Robins *(Leisure & Garden Centre)*
Danny Carey *(Children's, Gift & Creative)*
Tony Cullis *(Multiples & Own Brand)*

Aura Books offers book distribution and merchandising service. A full time sales force covers the entire UK and Northern Ireland, supported by three senior managers.

Operating from its computerized distribution centre at Greenford, Aura offers over 8000 titles from stock totally geared to the specialist markets it services, delivered fast. Aura's range extends to gardening, DIY and the home, cookery, natural history, travel and leisure, illustrated stationery, gift books, needlecraft, practical art, health, pet books and children's books. Aura supplies books mainly to garden centres, home and DIY outlets, the natural history / heritage markets and more recently the gift sector.

Aura Books has established a separate division, First Lines Children's Books, which has been allowed to develop a specialist service to non-traditional children's book outlets.

Aura's stock base has been selected without bias to any publisher. Being totally independent, Aura carries titles on merit only. Selections can be tailored to meet individual requirements.

6142 ▬▬▬▬▬▬▬▬▬▬

BAILEY DISTRIBUTION LTD
Learoyd Road, Mountfield Road Industrial Estate, New Romney, Kent TN28 8XU
Telephone: 01797 366905
Fax: 01797 366638

Managing Director: Robin Mortimore
Managers: Alan Crabb *(Distribution)*
David Addison *(DP)*
Tony Lamberton *(Warehouse)*
Darran Quinn *(Accounts)*

Distribution for:

Alpha Press	Good Company for Children Co
Bay View Books	Grub Street
Belitha Press Ltd	Histoires & Collections
Bicycle Books	In Print Publishing
Marion Boyars Publishers	Janus Publishing Co
Centre for Policy on Ageing	Kahn & Averill
Continuing Education Press	Kapco Library Products
DC Publishing	Kuperard (London)
Drake International Services	Learning Development Aids
Dulwich Press	Chris Lloyd Sales & Marketing
Educational Heretic Press	Services
English Heritage	M & J Publications
Firebird Books	Macdonald Young Books
Five Mile Press	Marston House
GMC Publications	Meadowbrook Press

Nexus Specialist Interests	Thames Publishing
Norden Publishing House	Translegal
Premier Books	Two Heads Publishing
Prism Press	Wayland Publishers
RAF Benevolent Fund	Winslow Press
Stilwell Publishing	Zoe Books

Bailey Distribution Ltd is owned by Bailey Bros & Swinfen Ltd, and continues the company's involvement in the book trade dating back to 1870. A complete sales, marketing and distribution service is offered to trade publishers. Educational and specialist publishers also use the service which operates out of modern warehousing located on the south coast of Kent.

6143 ▬▬▬▬▬▬▬▬▬▬

BBL DISTRIBUTION SERVICES LTD
PO Box 324, Borehamwood, Herts WD6 1NB
Telephone: 0181 905 1244
Fax: 0181 905 1108
Email: bbl@com.bbt.se

Managing Director: R. J. McLennan

Distributor for:

USA: Govardhan Hill	*Worldwide:* Bhaktivedanta Book
Torchlight Publishing	Trust

Distributor of books and other materials dealing with the philosophy, religion and culture of India.

BBL Distribution Services Ltd supply Hare Krishna temples with approximately 1 million books a year and provide a mail order service to individuals, the book trade and wholesale outlets in India.

6144 ▬▬▬▬▬▬▬▬▬▬

BEBC DISTRIBUTION
PO Box 1496, Parkstone, Poole, Dorset BH12 3YD
Telephone: 01202 715555
Fax: 01202 715556

Also at:
15 Albion Close, Parkstone, Poole, Dorset BH12 3YD
Telephone: *as above*
Fax: *as above*

Managing Director: John Walsh
Managers: Philippa Monks *(General Distribution)*
Karen Ball *(ELT Distribution)*

UK Distributor/Representative for:

UK: BBC English	King's Fund Centre
Business Books Direct	Oxfam Trading *(non-trade only)*
Clarity English Software	Policy Studies Institute
Institute Manpower Studies	Richmond Publishing

Distribution of publishers involved with social policy, local government, cultural trends, medical policy, health reports, business books and English language teaching.

6145 ▬▬▬▬▬▬▬▬▬▬

BIBLIOS PUBLISHERS DISTRIBUTION SERVICES LTD
Star Road, Partridge Green, West Sussex RH13 8LD
Telephone: 01403 710971; *(orderline:* 710851)
Fax: 01403 711143
Email: biblios@compuserve.com

Also at:
Biblios 2, Old London Road, Washington, West Sussex RH20 3BN
Telephone: 01903 892346
Fax: 01903 893383

Director: Anthony Wagstaff *(Managing)*
Managers: Louise Mallard *(Sales)*
Helen Negus *(Administration)*
Ian Dumbleton *(Financial Controller)*

David Brown *(Accounts)*
David Mansfield *(Client Services)*
Philip Cranfield *(IT)*
David Hamill *(Warehouse)*

Distribution facilities provided for:

Academic & University
  Publishers Group (AUPG)
Age Concern
Anaya Publishers
Arlington Books Publishers
Ashley Courtenay
Balloon Books
Berg Publishers
Biscuit Music
Blake Publishing
Bookman Projects
Boosey & Hawkes Music
  Publishers
Broadcast Book Services
Brown Books
Carol Publishing
Frank Cass
Cedco Publishing
Chambers & Partners
Collins & Brown
CSA Telltapes
Dalebank Books
Direction Book Sales
Dorling Kindersley Marketing
  Services
Edition Belvedere
Educational Bookshelf
Elms Hunt International
European Library Publishers
Fast Forward
Floraprint Books
Robert Frederick
Golden Cockerel Press
Peter Grose
Harbinger International
Hardens Guides
Hazleton Publishing
Hobsons Publishing
Hollanden Publishing
Honeyglen Publishing
Norman Hudson
Images Publishing
Immel Publishing
Independent Magazines
The Institute for Palestine Studies
Japan Publication Trading Co
  (JPT)
Johansens/CRAC
Kodansha Europe
Lannoo Publications

Learning Together
Leisure Books
Lettermen Publishing
Limetree Calendars
Lyric Books
Management Books 2000
Kenneth Mason Publications
Merrell Holberton Publishers
Montignac Publishing
Motor Racing Publications
Museum Quilts Publications
National Portrait Gallery
The New Press
Nippan Educational Books
Nippan Visual Art Books
OPA Overseas Publishing
Parker Associates
Pendulum Gallery Press
Premier Book Marketing
Princeton Architectural Press
Radcliffe Press
Ringpress Books
Rizzoli International Publications
  Inc
Robson Books *(export)*
John Rule Sales & Marketing
Running Press
Michael Russell
SB Publications
Settle Press
Southgate Publishing
The Sportsman's Press
St Anne's Music Society
Stable
Stacey International
Rudolf Steiner Press
Sussex Videos
I. B. Tauris
Tauris Parke
Pierre Terrail Editions
Thoemmes Antiquarian Press
Thoth Publishing
Universe Publishing
University Book Marketing
John van Weenan
Veloce Publishing
J. Whitaker & Sons
White Wolf
Whittet Books
Worldwide Media

Based in a fully-equipped warehouse, 60 minutes from London, Biblios' services cover all aspects of sales, distribution and accounting to the publishing industry throughout the world.

6146 ▬▬▬▬▬▬▬▬

BOOKPOINT LTD
39 Milton Park, Abingdon, Oxon OX14 4TD
Telephone: 01235 400400
Fax: 01235 400450

Chairman: Mark Opzoomer
Directors: Peter Oldham *(Managing)*
John Hunt *(Financial)*
Tony Bryars *(Operations)*
Alec Price *(IT)*
Frank Garofalo *(Customer & Client Services)*

Distributor for:
UK: Active Press

Amalgamated Book Services

Annuals Publishing
Appletree Press
Edward Arnold
Berol Ltd
Bespoke Audio Ltd
Britannia Crest
Burke's Peerage
Concorde
Cover to Cover Cassettes
Crowood Press
CYP Ltd
Daltons Weekly
Debrett's Peerage
Deneway Guides
Evans Brothers
Facts on File
W. G. Foyle Ltd
Godsfield Press
Greenhill Books
Gremese
Peter Grose Books
Hawksmere
Hayit Publishing GB Ltd
Headline Book Publishing
Hi Marketing
Hodder & Stoughton
Hostaction Ltd
Hunt & Thorpe
IMP
Industrial Society
Ion Press
Jade Publishers
Library Association

Frances Lincoln
Lund Humphries Publishers
Media Masters Pty Ltd
Memorabilia Pack Co
Merehurst
Music Collection International
National Trust
Oldcastle Books
Pavilion Books
Pedigree Books
Plexus Publishing
David Porteous Associates
Prima Publishing
RAC Motoring Services
Roundhouse Publishing
Rushmere Wynne Ltd
Salamander Books
Derek Searle Associates
Shaw & Sons Ltd
Sidan Press
Silverlink Publishing
Skyblue Publishing
Souvenir Press
Tango Books
Time Life Books
Usborne Books at Home
Vinyl Experience
Ward Lock Educational
Watershed Productions Ltd
John Wilson (Booksales) Ltd
Words on Sport
USA: Bob Adams
Prima Publishing

Over 100 publishers use distribution services by Bookpoint. Services encompass order processing, accounting, royalty maintenance, management reporting, warehousing, despatch and ancillary functions, through use of our VISTA New Books system.

6147 ▬▬▬▬▬▬▬▬

BRADT PUBLICATIONS
41 Nortoft Road, Chalfont St Peter, Bucks SL9 0LA
Telephone: 01494 873478
Fax: 01494 873478

Editorial:
Grey House Flat, Beeches Drive, Farnham Common, Bucks SL2 3JU
Telephone: 01753 646850
Fax: 01753 646850

Proprietor: Ms Hilary Bradt
Manager: Mrs Janet Mears

Publisher and distributor of maps, guides and books emphasizing travel off the beaten path.

6148 ▬▬▬▬▬▬▬▬

TREVOR BROWN ASSOCIATES
114–115 Tottenham Court Road, Midford Place, London W1P 0BY
Telephone: 0171 388 8500
Fax: 0171 388 5950

Director: J. Trevor Brown
Administrator: Carole Crampton
UK Sales: Adrian Greenwood

Foreign university presses represented in UK include:
Canada: Wilfrid Laurier
  University Press
University of Toronto Press
Norway: Scandinavian University
  Press (Universitetsforlaget)
USA: University of Hawaii Press
University of Illinois Press

University Press of Kentucky
University of Michigan Press
University of North Carolina Press
University of Texas Press
Texas A & M University Press
Vanderbilt University Press
University of Washington Press

6149

BURSTON DISTRIBUTION SERVICES
Unit 2a, Newbridge Trading Estate, Newbridge Close, off Whitby Road,
Bristol BS4 4AX
Telephone: 0117 972 4248
Fax: 0117 971 1056

Proprietor: Leighton Burston

Burston Distribution Services offers a complete order processing,
distribution and warehousing facility. Fast efficient distribution with the
latest CIS.PUB order processing system.

6150

BUSHWOOD BOOKS
84 Bushwood Road, Kew Gardens, Surrey TW9 3BQ
Telephone: 0181 948 8119 & 332 2667
Fax: 0181 948 3232

Director: Richard Hansen
PA: Victoria Hansen

Exclusive distributor for:
Canada: J. J. Fedorowicz
USA: Schiffer Publishing Ltd *(Military Aviation)*

Distributor for:
USA: Schiffer Collectibles Arts & Crafts

The company also carries in stock hundreds of titles on antiques and
collectibles, predominantly horology, jewellery, ceramics and glass. It
specializes in providing a service for UK customers to purchase from
North American and Canadian publishers.
  Bushwood Books is one of the leading UK distributors of German
World War II titles in English.

6151

CAMBRIDGE CD-ROM LTD
Combs Tannery, Stowmarket, Suffolk IP14 2EN
Telephone: 01449 774658
Fax: 01449 677600

Directors: G. A. Butler *(Financial)*
R. D. Smith *(Managing)*
Managers: Ms S. Henbrey *(Office)*
R. Kendrick *(Technical)*

Distributors include:

Book Data	Knight Ridder
Bowker Saur	Macmillan
The British Library	McGraw Hill
Cambridge University Press	Microsoft
Cartermill	News Multimedia
Chadwyck Healey	Oxford University Press
Collins	Penguin Books
Context	Random House
Dorling Kindersley	Reed Information
EBSCO	Times Mirror International
Encyclopaedia Britannica	J. Whitaker & Sons
Heinemann	Yorkshire International Thomson
HMSO	Multimedia
Hodder Headline	

Sole distributor of:
Philips School 2000 CD-i educational software

Cambridge CD-ROM Ltd, part of the Cambridge Multimedia Group
founded in 1983, is a specialist supplier of CD-ROM and CD-i software
for libraries, schools and colleges. The company offers customers 'Try
Before Buy' approval facilities, library CD-ROM subscription
management, free technical support and friendly advice. The company
also specializes in the supply and support of CD writing hardware and
software.

Cambridge CR catalogues describing over 900 titles from more than
175 publishers are available free on request.

6152

CENTRAL BOOKS
99 Wallis Road, London E9 5LN
Telephone: 0181 986 4854
Fax: 0181 533 5821

Directors: William Norris *(Managing)*
David Cope *(Company Secretary)*
Mark Chilver *(Sales)*
David Crystal *(Warehouse)*
Managers: Bob Moheebob *(Accountant)*
Kirstie Kemp *(Marketing)*

Distribution for:

Australia: Ocean Press	Comedia Publications *(selected*
Rastar Pty Ltd	*titles)*
St Louis Press	Comerford, Miller & Associates
Sybylla Co-operative Press	Community Health Foundation
Wakefield Press	The Consortium
Canada: Black Rose Books	Cruelty-Free London
France: Mediterraneans	Dedalus
Médecins sans Frontières	Democratic Left
The Noble Rider	Demos
Germany: European Photography	Disability Alliance
Hans-Nietsch-Verlag	Dog Publishing Inc
Intrac	ECRA Publishing Ltd
Minus	Escreet Publications
Michael Schwinn	Estamp
Greece: Adam Editions	Ethical Consumer
Kedros Publishing	European Business Books Ltd
Irish Republic: Aran Book	Everywoman
Publishers	Five Leaves Publications
Black Cat Press Ltd	Floodlight
Cork University Press	Frontline
Lilliput Press Ltd	Fuse Press
New Island Books	GMP Publishers Ltd
Oak Tree Press	Golgonooza
Oishin Publishing	Green Book
Picture Press	Greenprint
Road Books	Greenwich Exchange
Italy: Giancarlo Politi Editore	Grey Seal
Malaysia: Consumers Association	The Guardian
Penang	Harbord Publishing
Netherlands: De Geus	Hyphen Press
Uitgeverij Uniepers bv	Icon Press
Switzerland: Parkett Verlag	Institute for African Alternatives
UK: Absolute Press	Institute for Public Policy
AKME Publications	Research
Aktok	Islamic Texts Society
Allegretto Publications	Kala Press
Amanda Publications	Labour Research Department
Amnesty Publications	Lancaster House Pub.
Art Review	Latin American Bureau
Article 19	Lawrence & Wishart
Aurora Metro Publications	Libertarian Education
Benefactum Publishing Ltd	London Review of Books
Black Pudding Press	Malice Aforethought Press
Blackberry Books	Menard Press
Blueprint	Merlin
Bogle-L'Ouverture Press Ltd	Middlesex University Press
Boulevard	Minority Rights Group
Bowerdean Publishing	Moscovitch & Co
Jon Carpenter Publishing	Mushroom Bookshop
Catholic Institute for International	Mute Records
Relations	National Council for Civil
Chalcott Marketing	Liberties
Cheerman Ltd	New Clarion Press
Chelsea Green	New Internationalist Books
Child Poverty Action Group	NIACE (National Institute for
Children's Society	Adult Continuing Education)
Civil Liberties Trust	Oxfam
Colporteur	Oxford Literary Review
Comedia	Panos Institute

Panurge	Ten 8
Peridot Press	Unemployment Unit
Pi34 Publishing	Verrocchio Arts
Poetry Review	Watershed Arts Trust Ltd
Porcupine Press	Wordsearch
Presswork	Working Press
Prince's Trust Events Ltd	WorldView Publications
Proper Pictures	Youthaid
Pulp Faction	Zoilus Press
Quilliam	*USA:* Alyson Publications
Quinta Essentia	Ariadne Press
Redstone Press	Autonomedia
Roof Publications	Bootstrap & Apex Press
Angela Royal Publishing	Heinemann Drama
Satrap	Humanities Press
Seafarer	International Publishers NY
Searchlight	Knowledge Systems (GB)
Sempringham Publishing	Monthly Review Foundation
Seren	New Horizons Press
Serif	New Society Publishers
Shola	Pamphleteer's Press
Socialist Health Association	Penrose Press
Spare Tyre Publications	Diana E. H. Russell
Stonewall Press	Semiotext
Sunk Island Publishing	Smith & Krauss
Cath Tate	Woodpond Press

The main activity and purpose of Central Books is to assist small and independent publishers to reach the widest possible audience for their books. Central Books offer warehousing, distribution, representation and some help with marketing and promotion. It supplies booksellers and library suppliers throughout the world.

The company also acts as subscription agent and handles subscription lists for about ten magazines, and distributes magazines and journals to bookshops.

6153

COMBINED BOOK SERVICES
406 Vale Road, Tonbridge, Kent TN9 1XR
Telephone: 01732 357755
Fax: 01732 770219

Directors: David Turner *(Managing)*
Charles Turner

Distributors for:

Alma House	Grail Publishing
Applause Theatre Books	Millbank Books
APS	Morpheus International
Benedikt Taschen	New Cavendish
John Calder Ltd	Octopus Distribution
Character Publishing	Parapress Ltd
Chatham House Publishers	PTB
Debut Books	Quiller Press
Diamond Books	Spellmount Ltd
Eagle Publishing	Straw Hat
Eddington Hook	Te Neues Publishing
Factwell Ltd	Woodhead Publishing
Good Books	

Combined Book Services provides full sales and distribution services for publishers worldwide. The service includes invoicing and cash collection together with a comprehensive range of management reports. Direct mail response handling, cash sales and list building are available as an integral part of our computer systems.

6154

D SERVICES
6 Euston Street, Freemen's Common, Leicester LE2 7SS
Telephone: 0116 254 7671
Fax: 0116 254 4670

Managers: Trevor Martin *(General)*
Richard Curry *(Marketing)*
John Timmis *(Sales)*

Publishers represented:

ABC Books	Modello
Barrons	John Muir
BBC *(remainders)*	Parragon
Gaza Books	RAC *(remainders)*
M & M Publishing	Usborne

D Services is a trading division of W. H. Smith. Publishers are provided with a combination of services, from marketing support and sales representation, through all aspects of physical stock management, to accounting and debtor management.

D Services operates in two markets: the Booktrade and the Newstrade:

Books: D Services employs an experienced sales team of professional territory managers in the UK and a network of fully managed agents overseas to ensure that publishers' books are sold into all potential buying outlets including multiple chain and independent bookshops, wholesalers, library suppliers, educational and institutional suppliers, schools and colleges, mail order catalogue suppliers, premiums and incentives suppliers, newstrade wholesalers, cash and carry outlets, book clubs and overseas territories.

News: D Services operates alongside W. H. Smith News, and has powerful trading relationships with all multiple and independent wholesalers providing access to 40,000 retail newsagents in the UK.

6155

DEEP BOOKS LTD
Unit 33, Cannon Wharf Business Centre, 35 Evelyn Street, London SE8 4RT
Telephone: 0171 232 2747
Fax: 0171 237 0067

Managing Director: Chris Custance

Client publishers:

Australia: Millenium Books	Inner Traditions International
Milne Books Pty Ltd	Jewish Lights Publishing
New Humanity Books	Oral Traditions
UK: Khaniqahi Nimatullahi	Philosophical Research Society
Publications (KNP)	(PRS)
USA: ARE Press	Phoenix Publishing Inc
Beyond Words Publishing Inc	Sevenstar Communications
Blue Poppy Press	Sparrow Hawk Press
Crystal Clarity Publishers	Threshold Books
Dawn Publications	Timeless Books
Earthspirit Inc	Tough Dove Books

Specialist mind body spirit distributors. Deep Books handles publishers lists from the UK, the USA and Australia. It provides sales and distribution for these publishers throughout the UK, Irish Republic, mainland Europe and Scandinavia and acts as their exclusive agents in that territory.

6156

DIFFULIVRE INC
817 rue McCaffrey, Saint-Laurent, PQ H4T 1N3, Canada
Telephone: +1 (514) 738 2911
Fax: +1 (514) 738 8512
Email: mlaberge@interlink.net

President: Marc Laberge
Controller: Serge Poulin
Directors: Christian Bélair *(Sales & Marketing)*
Colette Laberge *(Trade & Publishing)*
Public Relations: Marie Marsolais

Distributors of coffee-table, nature and practical books, dictionaries and reference books, general trade, children's, computer-software, school, university/college and cookery books.

6157

DIRECT DISTRIBUTION
27 Palmeira Mansions, Church Road, Hove, East Sussex BN3 2FA
Telephone: 01273 748427
Fax: 01273 205612

Warehouse (returns only):
Vale Packaging Ltd, 420 Vale Road, Tonbridge, Kent TN9 1TD
Telephone: 01732 359387
Fax: 01732 770620

Managing Director: Michael Forster
Managers: David Pettifor *(Distribution)*
Bill Heaney *(Sales)*

Distributor for:
Ablex Publishing Corporation
Brunner/Mazel Publishers
Lawrence Erlbaum Associates
Guilford Press
Immediate Publishing
Morgan Kaufmann Publishers

6158

DOUBLEDAY
[division of Bantam Doubleday Dell Inc]
100 Wigmore Street, London W1H 9DR
Telephone: 0171 935 1269
Fax: 0171 935 4840

London Office Rights Director: Sarah Birdsey

6159

ELECTRONICA BOOKS LTD
Unit E4, Sunbury International Business Centre, Brooklands Close,
Sunbury-on-Thames, Middx TW16 7DX
Telephone: 01932 765119 **Fax:** 01932 765429

Directors: Howard Barkway
Anthony Head
Jan Kimber *(Administrator)*

Worldwide service and supply centre for:
IEEE
IEEE Computer Society

Also stocked and supplied:
Computer Technology Research Corp
The Minerals Metals and Materials Society (TMS)
Society for Industrial and Applied Mathematics (SIAM)

6160

EUROPEAN SCHOOLBOOKS LTD
Ashville Trading Estate, The Runnings, Cheltenham GL51 9PQ
Telephone: 01242 245252
Fax: 01242 224137
Email: esb.co.uk

Managing Director: Frank Preiss
Sales & Marketing Director: David Young

Distributor for:
Canada: Editions Rényi
Denmark: Grafisk Forlag
France: 10/18
Assimil
Pierre Bordas & fils
Bordas
Casterman
CLE International
Armand Colin
Didier
Documentation Française
Dunod
Ecole des loisirs
Editions du Fallois
Editions 'des femmes'
Flammarion
Folio
Foucher
Gallimard
Garnier
Garnier Flammarion

Gault Millau
Gautier-Langereau
Gautier-Villars
Gründ
Hachette
Hatier
J'ai lu
Jeux Nathan
Larousse
Livres de poche
Livres de poche classique
Minuit
Nathan
Presses de la cité
Presses Pocket
Presses Universitaires de France
Presses Universitaires de
  Grenoble
Editions du Seuil
Germany: Bibliographisches
  Institut Mannheim

Brockhaus
Carlsen
Cornelsen-Velhagen & Klasing
Deutscher Taschenbuch Verlag
Verlag Moritz Diesterweg
dtv
Duden
Verlag Dürr & Kessler
Eilers & Schunemann
Verlag Enzyklopädie
Fischer
Gilde Buchhandlung
Goldmann
Harenberg Kommunikation
Heyne
Max Hueber Verlag
Insel
Kiepenheuer & Witsch
Knaur
Langenscheidt
Luchterhand
Reclam
Rowohlt
Suhrkamp
Tessloff
Ullstein
Verlag für Deutsch
Westermann
Italy: Bonacci Editore
European Language Institute
Fabbri-Bompiani
Feltrinelli
Garzanti
Guerra
Hoepli
Mondadori
Ugo Mursia
Oscar
Rizzoli
Rux

Zanichelli
Portugal: Lidel Edições Técnicas
Porto Editora
Spain: Alfaguara
Alianza
Anaya
Austral
Bruguera
Castalia
Catedra
Colegio de España
Destino
Difusión
EDELSA (Ediseis)
Ediciones SM
Espasa-Calpe
Everest
Grijalbo
Juventud
Molino
Mondadori España
Paraninfo
Planeta
Plaza & Janes
Santillana
Seix Barral
SGEL
Sopena
Javier Vergara
Switzerland: Diogenes
UK: Accent Educational
  Publishers Ltd
European Schoolbooks Publishing
  Ltd
European Schoolbooks Hatier Ltd
Links Publications
Understanding Global Issues
USA: EMC Publishing
National Textbook Co
The Olivia & Hill Press

Distributors of some 10,000 titles in the main European languages on
behalf of around 75 publishers. Large-scale promotion in all sectors of the
foreign languages educational market. Suppliers of foreign-published
stock to academic and general bookshops. General wholesale service for
non-stock titles.

6161

THE EUROSPAN GROUP
3 Henrietta Street, Covent Garden, London WC2E 8LU
Telephone: 0171 240 1003
Fax: 0171 379 0609
Email: eurospan.co.uk

Directors: Danny Maher *(Chief Executive)*
Michael Geelan *(Managing)*

Exclusive Sales & Distribution Agents for UK & Europe for:
University of Alabama Press
University Press of America
American Academy of
  Orthopaedic Surgeons
American Enterprise Institute
American Library Association
American Psychiatric Press
American Psychological
  Association
AMS *(not reprints)*
Jason Aronson Publishers
Auburn House Publishing Co
Austin & Winfield
Bergin & Garvey
Catholic University of America
  Press
Curator *(journal)*
Da Capo Press

Ethics & Public Policy Centre
University Press of Florida
Fordham University Press
Freedom House
Gardner Press
University of Georgia Press
Greenwood Press
Hampton Press
Human Sciences Press *(books and
  journals)*
Idea Group Publishing
International Scholars
  Publications
Iowa State University Press
University Press of Kansas
Kent State University Press
Krieger Publishing Co
Libraries Unlimited

University of Massachusetts Press
University of Missouri Press
Narosa Publishing House (India)
Neal-Schuman Publishers
University of Nevada Press
The New York Academy of
 Sciences
University of Notre Dame Press
Ohio State University Press
University of Oklahoma Press
Open Court Publishing Co
The Oryx Press
Penn State Press
University of Pittsburgh Press
PMA Publishing
Popular Culture, Inc
Praeger Publishers

Quorum Books
Lynne Rienner, Publishers
Rowman & Littlefield Publishers
Scholarly Resources Inc
M. E. Sharpe Publishing
Statistics Canada
Syracuse University Press
Teacher Ideas Press
Teachers' College Press
Temple University Press
Thomas International Publishing
 Co
Urban Institute Press
The University Press of Virginia
Wayne State University Press
Who's Who in Italy
University of Wisconsin Press

6162

EXEL LOGISTICS MEDIA SERVICES
Christchurch House, Beaufort Court, Sir Thomas Longley Road,
Medway City Estate, Rochester, Kent ME2 4FX
Telephone: 01634 297123
Fax: 01634 298000

Distribution:
Shaw Close, Park Farm Industrial Estate, Wellingborough, Northants
NN8 2BN

Distribution also at:
Unit 4, Sheldon Way, Larkfield, Kent ME20 6SF

International Head Office:
The Merton Centre, 45 St Peters Street, Bedford MK40 2UB

Directors: Paul Goodland *(Managing)*
Tony Hartley *(Key Accounts)*
John Sexton *(Development)*
Neil MacGowan *(Commercial)*
Client Services Executive: Bridget Radnedge
Head of IT: John Davidson

Distribution of books for the following publishers:

AA Publishing
Advanced Marketing (UK) Ltd
Allison & Busby
Aurum Press
BBC Books
Bloomsbury Publishing Ltd
Chart Books
Richard Cohen
David & Charles
De Agostini Editions
Do Not Press
Dragon's World
Mary Ford
Golden Memories
Harlequin Mills & Boon

Harrods Publishing
Harvill Press
Metro Publishing
John Napir
Notting Hill Publishers
Poolbeg Group Services
Prion
Readers Digest
Solo Books
Times Mirror International
 Publishing
Titan Books
Virgin Publishing
Neil Wilson Publishing
World International

6163

FACE DISTRIBUTION
Centre Studios, Englands Lane, London NW3 4YD
Telephone: 0171 483 3732
Fax: 0171 916 3170

Director: Chris Parish
Managers: Malcolm Hedley
Paula Hollings *(Marketing)*

FACE Distribution is a small book, audio, video and magazine
distribution company. It distributes four books by Andrew Cohan,
American author and lecturer, published by Moksha Foundation.

6164

FOLENS DISTRIBUTION
Albert House, Apex Business Centre, Boscombe Road, Dunstable,
Bedfordshire LU5 4RL
Telephone: 01582 472788
Fax: 01582 472575

Distribution:
Folens Distribution Centre, DE Block, Boscombe Road, Dunstable,
Bedfordshire LU5 4SE
Telephone: 01582 662353
Fax: 01582 666883

General Manager: Philip Hayward

Established in 1995, Folens Distribution serves the needs of UK business
and also includes an increasing portfolio of imported product, especially
from North America, Hong Kong and Singapore.
 Utilizing its personnel, systems and facilities, Folens Distribution
distributes a wide range of educational products, including posters, music
cassettes and discs, stationery items and more recently computer
software, in addition to the core distribution of books.
 Core business is the provision of a complete fulfilment service for
Folens publishers to UK primary educational establishments, book shops
and an increasing home delivery address service. Small, one parcel orders
are efficiently handled.
 In addition to complete order fulfilment, Folens Distribution also
provides a number of product assembly and packaging services,
assembling point-of-sale display packages, collating and placing sets of
books in these packages, packaging books with other products such as
music cassettes, shrink wrapping and stickering with promotional or price
information.

6165

FREELANCE PRESS SERVICES
Cumberland House, Lissadel Street, Salford, Manchester M6 6GG
Telephone: 0161 702 8225
Fax: 0161 745 8865

Managing Editor: Mrs Saundrea Williams

Sole Distributor for:
USA: Writer Inc *(books on writing)*

Distributor for:
USA: Writer's Digest Books *(books on writing)*

6166

GAZELLE BOOK SERVICES LTD
Falcon House, Queen Square, Lancaster LA1 1RN
Telephone: 01524 68765
Fax: 01524 63232
Email: gazelle4go@aol.com

Directors: Chris Timms *(Managing)*
Trevor Witcher *(Sales)*
Brian Haywood *(Company Secretary)*
Managers: Mark Trotter *(Customer Services)*
Graham Chamberlain *(Warehouse)*
Julie Patten *(Promotions)*
Pat Fawley *(Publicity)*
Bookkeeper: Margaret Shaw

Sales & Distribution facilities provided for:

Australia: Aird Books Pty Ltd
Angus & Robertson Publishers
 (selected titles)
Australian Doll Digest
Business & Professional
 Publishers Pty Ltd
Currency Press Pty Ltd
Hyland House Publishers Pty
Institute for Aboriginal
 Development

Lothian Books
Melbourne University Press
Sally Milner Publishing
University of New England Press
Triad Publishers Pty Ltd
Austria: Ennsthaler GmbH & Co
 KG
Belgium: Kluwer Algemene
 Uitgeverijen *(UK & Irish
 Republic only)*

Presses Interuniv. Européennes
(UK, Irish Republic &
Scandinavia only)
VUB University Press
Canada: Blizzard Publishing
(including Africa)
Creative Bound Inc
Digirule Inc
Guernica Editions Inc
Hancock House Ltd
Learned Enterprises International
Nimbus Publishing
Rosetree Publishing Inc
Shoestring Publications
Denmark: Museum Tusculanum
Press
France: Parasol (including Hong
Kong, Singapore & South
Africa)
Parkstone Press (UK, Irish
Republic & Scandinavia only)
Sapphire Publishing Corporation
Whitter Nohedes
Germany: Nierwand Verlag
GmbH (UK & Southern Europe
only)
Trescher Verlag GmbH
Vista Point Verlag GmbH (UK &
Irish Republic only)
Weingarten GmbH, Kunstverlag
Greece: Efstathiadis Group
Hong Kong: Chopsticks
Publications Ltd
India: Mapin Publishing Pvt Ltd
(excluding Italy & France)
Irish Republic: Sean Glyn
(excluding Irish Republic &
Northern Ireland)
Italy: I Libri del Bargello
(excluding France, Germany &
Italy)
Piccin Editore (UK, Scandinavia
& Netherlands only)
S1 Editrice Srl
Jamaica: Kingston Publishers Ltd
Malaysia: Delta Editions Sdn Bhd
Wilmette Publications Sdn Bhd
Netherlands: Bekking & Blitz
Uitgevers bv (UK only)
The Greyhound Press
International Chess Enterprises
Inc
International Theatre Bookshop
(excluding Benelux)
New Zealand: Leonard Ring
Associates Ltd
Norway: Grondahl Dreyers Forlag
AS (excluding Scandinavia but
including Iceland)
Russia: Interbook Business Co
Madoc Books
Singapore: Graham Brash Pte Ltd
East West Express
EPB Publishers Pte Ltd
World Scientific (warehousing &
shipping only)
Switzerland: Bergli Books AG
Taiwan: Hilit Publishing Co Ltd
UK: Ashmolean Museum
Aspen Gold Books
Audrey Babington's Workbox
Bellevue Books
Belvedere Fine Publishing Co
British Deaf Association
Castle Kent Associates
Clinical Press
Fleetfoot Books

Elektor Electronics (excluding
Finland)
Grant Books
Gursharan Sahota
Helix Editions Ltd
Impala Books
Insect Publications
Interworld Publications
Evelyn Kent Associates
National Museums of Scotland
Neptune Press
Oxford School of Learning Ltd
Parallax Press
Parkstone Press (UK, Irish
Republic & Scandinavia only)
Polo Publishing
Rollo Publishing Co
Royal College of Nursing
Publications
Royal College of Physicians
Skoob Books
Soho Book Co Ltd
Taffeta Publications
Thunder Bay Publishing Co
Training Publications
(distribution only)
Tynron Press
University Publishing Inc
Valhalla Publishing
Cynthia Venn
Veterinary Business Development
Ltd
White Line Press (EC countries
only)
Winning International (UK & Irish
Republic only)
World Scientific Publishing Co
Pte Ltd
The World's Best Loved Hotels
Zardos Books
USA: 3-D Revelations
Abdo & Daughters Publishing
Academy Chicago Publishers Ltd
Acrobat Books Publishers
Acropolis South LC
Adventures Unlimited
Amalgam Publishing Co
America West Distributors
American Technical Publishers
Inc
Anatomical Chart Co
Angel City Press
Annual Reviews Inc
Architectural Book Publishers Co
Inc
Babelcom
Banmar Inc
Frederic Beil Publisher Inc
Bergh Publishing Inc
Berkshire House Publishers
Blake Publishing (excluding Italy
& Italian-speaking
Switzerland)
Bonus Books Inc
Books Americana Inc
Bookworld Services Inc
Branden Publishing Co
Bristol Publishing Enterprises Inc
Britain Books
Bull Publishing
CD Specialties
Cimino Publishing Group Inc
Cin-Dav Inc
Clear Light Publishers
Cliffs Notes Inc (excluding
Germany)
CMC Publishing

Cobble & Mickle Books
Colorado University Press
Companion Press
Contemporary Books Inc
Cortina Learning International Inc
Costa Rica Books
Country Roads Press
Countryman Press Inc
Creatures at Large Press
Crown Outlet (selected titles only)
Current Clinical Strategies
Publishing
Davis Publications Inc
Ivan R. Dee Inc
Demos Vermande
DermaPet Inc
Devyn Press Inc
Doral Publishing Inc
Dramaline Publications
Dynotech Ltd (UK only)
Earth Magic Productions Inc
El-Sayed Publications
Carlos H. Elmer Publishing
Elysium Growth Press
Enterprises Publishers
Ermor Enterprises
Excalibur Publishing
Fairview Press
Feedback Theatrebooks
The Feminist Press
Samuel French Trade
Galde Press Inc
Gallaudet University Press
Gateway Books & Tapes
Gateways Books
Golden Aura Publishing
Good Books
Gorham House Publishing
Warren H. Green Inc
Griffin Publishing (including the
whole of Africa)
Hackett Publishing Co Inc
Harlan Davidson Inc
Harvard Common Press
Hastings House
Heathcoat Publishing
HighText Publications Inc
Hippocrene Books Inc
Ron Hirshberg Publishing
Hobby House Press
Horizon Publishers & Distributors
Inc
Howells House
HRD Human Resource
Development Press
Hunter House Inc
ICS Books Inc
Impact Publications
Industrial Press Inc (distribution
only)
Inner Light Publications
International Broadcasting
Services Ltd
International Chess Enterprises
Inc
International Jewelry Publications
Irvington Publishers Inc
Ishiyaku EuroAmerica Inc
J&S Publishing Co Inc
Michael Kesend Publishing Ltd
Krause Publications
Laurel House Publishing Co Inc
Hugh Lauter Levin Associates
Lifetime Books Inc
Limelight Editions
Lion's Den Publications Inc
Lip Smackers Inc

Little, Brown & Co
Living Quest
Login Publishers Consortium
Lone Eagle Publishing Co
Love Child Publishing
Louis E. Madison
Magic Image Filmbooks
Manderino Books
Market Street Press
Marlowe & Co
Masters Press
Mercury House
Meriwether Publishing Ltd
The Michigan State University
Press
Miller Freeman Inc
Mind and Miracles
Morgan & Morgan Inc
Moyer Bell Ltd
Multicom Publishing Inc
Mike Murach & Associates Inc
Mustang Publishing
National Book Network
National League for Nursing
National Press Books
Naturist Society
Nelson-Hall Inc
New Amsterdam Books
New Chapter Press
New York Zoetrope Inc
Noble Porter Press
Nova Science Publishers Inc
Open Horizons Publishing Co
Open Road Publishing
Packard Publishing Co
Paris Publishing
F. E. Peacock Publishers Inc
Pendulum Plus Inc
Penton Overseas Inc
Point Loma Publications Inc
Precept Press Inc
Pruett Publishing Co
Publishers Distribution Services
Punches Productions
Random House Group (selected
titles only)
Renaissance House Publishers
Sagamore Publishing Inc
Searchlight Inc
Shade Tree Press
The Shoe String Press Inc
Silman James Press
Sky Books
Sports Support Syndicate Inc
Stabur Corp
Stemmer House Publishers Inc
Summit Beacon International
Sunset Books
Surrey Books
Taylor Publishing Co
TeakWood Press Inc
Teitan Press Inc
Todd Publications
Travelus Publishing
Trimarket Co (excluding
Scandinavia)
Vagabond Publishing Inc
Vestal Press Ltd
Wei-Chuan Publishing Inc
Westgate Press
Westport Publishers Inc
Whereabouts Press
Wide World Publishing/Tetra
Michael Wiese Production
Williamson Publishing Co
Woodbine House
Woodbridge Press Publishing Co

Wordware Publishing Inc
Wright Publishing

Write Stuff Syndicate Inc
Wyrick & Co

Gazelle Book Services handles both trade and academic lists and covers the whole of the UK and Europe. It provides:
    fast order turn-round;
    comprehensive stock and regular stock replenishment;
    efficient reporting and information service to customers;
    regular sales calling and regular liaison with booksellers in connection with promotion, exhibitions, special events, etc;
    following through;
    friendly, helpful service;
    regular and adaptable reporting to publishers;
    flexibility and co-operation.

6167

GRANTHAM BOOK SERVICES LTD
Isaac Newton Way, Alma Park Industrial Estate, Grantham, Lincs NG31 9SD
Telephone: 01476 67421
Fax: 01476 590223 *(orders:* 67314)

Directors: David Pemberton *(Chairman)*
Bob Anderson *(Managing)*
Graham Miller *(Finance)*
Managers: Jeff Chambers *(Warehouse)*
Paul Drury *(Warehouse)*
Dave Paxton *(Warehouse)*
David Goodere *(Sales Ledger)*
Julie Nix *(Trade & Cash Sales)*
Stephen Spick *(General Services)*
Michael Sedgwick *(Project)*

Distribution services for:

Abbeville Press	Moorland Publishing
Apple Press	John Murray
BPL	Pepin Press
Bracken Books	Piatkus Books
Cadogan Books	Senate
Camerapix	Sport in Word
Geocentre International UK Ltd	Stewart Tabori & Chang
Peter Haddock	Taschen UK
Leopard Books	Workman Publishing
Lonely Planet	World Leisure Marketing
Melia Publishing Services	

Grantham Book Services provides a very fast and efficient distribution service for publishers. Service includes order receipt by post, fax, telephone and teleordering; invoicing and despatch. A next day delivery service, from receipt of order to delivery of books, is provided to the UK trade.
    Also sales ledger and cash collection service. Comprehensive range of computer reports; plus all the usual ancillary work such as shrinkwrapping, repricing, dumpbin and counterpack make up etc.

6168

HT (BOOK DISTRIBUTION) LTD
Bolholt, Walshaw Road, Bury, Lancs BL8 1RP
Telephone: 0161 764 2296
Fax: 0161 764 8213

Managing Director: Peter Kershaw Taylor
Company Secretary: Susan K. V. Taylor

HT (Book Distribution) Ltd is an associate company of Harry Taylor (Bury) Ltd which has been involved in general warehousing and distribution since 1922. Started to handle out-of-the-ordinary book and journal material, HTBD now warehouses and distributes books and journals for some 16 British and American imprints whose product line ranges from scholarly reprints and textbooks to multi-volume reference works, journals, annuals and general trade books. Approximately 9500 titles are stocked in a single-storey 14,500 sq ft warehouse.

6169

HUNKYDORY DESIGNS LTD
Crown House, Millboard Road, Bourne End, Bucks SL8 5XD
Telephone: 01628 529621
Fax: 01628 529488

Directors: John Harper *(Managing)*
Brian Johnston *(Finance)*
Peter Prado *(Distribution)*
Murray Mahon *(Marketing)*
Ronald Lee *(Operations)*
Jemima Haddock *(Sales)*

Stationery and gift designers and distributors. Distributors of gift stationery, children's books, cookery books and gift books to the gift trade.

6170

INFO TECHNOLOGY SUPPLY LTD (ITS)
Talbot House, 204–226 Imperial Drive, Harrow HR2 7HH
Telephone: 0181 429 3970
Fax: 0181 429 3642
Email: lts@ltsltd.demon.co.uk

Marketing Manager: Radomir Dabanovic
Accounts Administrator: Ms Manisha Patel
Sales Executives: Ms Diane Keen
Ms Deborah Bartley
Bob Kalyan
Senior Product Manager: Pedja Pavlicic
Technical Support Managers: Rudy Harding
James Wright

Distributor for:

BSI	Knight Ridder
Cartermill	Micromedex
Chadwyck Healey	Micropatent
CIS	OCLC
CITIS	Pergamon Press
Computer Library	Reed Information Services
Context	SilverPlatter
Engineering Index	TFPL
HMSO	UMI
ILI	J. Whitaker & Sons
ISI	H. W. Wilson Co.
Jane's Information	

Distributors of CD-ROM.

6171

INFORMATION PUBLICATIONS INTERNATIONAL
White Swan House, Godstone, Surrey RH9 8LW
Telephone: 01883 744123
Fax: 01883 744024
Email: umi@ipi.demon.co.uk

Chairman: Nigel Farrow
Managing Director: Tim Smartt
Sales Director: Susan Orchard *(Area Manager—Australasia)*
Managers: Richard Hollingsworth *(Area—Middle East & Africa)*
Karen Christopherson *(Area—Spain, Italy, Portugal & Greece)*
Suzanne O'Hare *(Promotions)*
Liz Hunt *(Area—Germanic, Norway & Denmark)*
Jonathan Wynne *(Area—France, Benelux & UK)*
Birgit Bartels *(Area—Eastern Europe, Sweden & Finland)*

IPI is the agent in Europe, Africa, the Middle East and Australasia for UMI, publishers of CD-ROM databases, doctoral dissertations, serials in microform, research collections and out-of-print books. Both microform and paper publications are available.
    In conjunction with the British Library, IPI makes available in paper and micro formats British theses in all subject areas accepted by British universities.

6172 ▬▬▬▬▬▬▬▬▬▬▬▬▬▬▬▬▬▬▬▬▬▬▬▬▬

INTERACTIVE IDEAS LTD
276 Chase Road. London N14 6HA
Telephone: 0181 447 9288
Fax: 0181 447 8944

Directors: Michael Trup *(Managing)*
Grahame Fernback *(Operations)*

Distributor for:
Belgium: AIM Productions   *USA:* Transparent Language

Distributors of CD-ROM in the UK. Interactive Ideas stocks over 1500 different titles, mainly aimed at the lifestyle and education markets. A next-day-service is provided to many bookstores both in the UK and in Europe.

6173 ▬▬▬▬▬▬▬▬▬▬▬▬▬▬▬▬▬▬▬▬▬▬▬▬▬

INTERNATIONAL BOOK DISTRIBUTORS LTD
Campus 400, Maylands Avenue, Hemel Hempstead, Herts HP2 7EZ
Telephone: 01442 881900
Fax: 01442 882099

Orders, Customer Services, Accounts:
as principal address above

Distribution & Returns:
Coventry Road, Magna Park, Lutterworth, Leics LE17 4XH
Telephone: 01442 881900
Fax: 01442 882177

Directors: Keith Pratt *(Operations)*
Roger Antrobus *(Distribution)*
Other Executives: Alan Myles *(Finance)*
Liz Shearn *(Customer Services)*

Distribution service for:
Dorling Kindersley   Pocket Books
Harvester Wheatsheaf   Prentice Hall International
Ellis Horwood   Simon & Schuster Trade
ICSA Publishing Ltd   West Publishing Co
Martin Books   Woodhead-Faulkner

6174 ▬▬▬▬▬▬▬▬▬▬▬▬▬▬▬▬▬▬▬▬▬▬▬▬▬

INTERNATIONAL THOMSON PUBLISHING SERVICES LTD
[a division of The Thomson Corporation]
Cheriton House, North Way, Andover, Hants SP10 5BE
Telephone: 01264 332424
Fax: 01264 364418

Directors: Barry Glynn *(Managing)*
David McGregor *(Finance)*
Rodney Peake *(Customer Service)*
David Silk *(Operations)*
Customer Service Managers: Wendy Edge *(Home)*
Ted Pashley *(Home)*
John Perrett *(International)*
Jacqui Edge *(International)*

Distributors for:
Australia: Law Book Co of   Chapman & Hall *(incorporating*
    Australia *(3)*   *all companies marked (1) in this*
Thomas Nelson Australia *(4)*   *list & ex- VCH)*
Canada: Carswell Co of Canada   Clark Boardman Callaghan *(3)*
    (3)   Clinical Neuroscience
UK: Academy Group   Croom Helm *(academic; 2)*
Altman Publications *(1)*   Elsevier *(applied science; 1)*
E. J. Arnold *(5)*   ESC Books *(3)*
Blackie Educational *(5)*   European Law Centre *(3)*
Blackie Scientific *(1)*   W. Green & Sons *(3)*
Blueprint Publishing *(1)*   HarperCollins ELT *(5)*
BMMR *(1)*   HarperCollins Medical *(1)*
Building & Construction Books   Harrap Educational *(5)*
    (1)

International Thomson   Thomson Professional Publishing
    Publications *(incorporating all*   *(3)*
    companies marked (4) in this   Unwin Hyman *(academic; 2)*
    list)   Unwin Hyman *(science; 1)*
Janes Information Group   *USA:* American Public Health
Lawyers Co-operative *(3)*   Association *(1)*
H. K. Lewis *(1)*   boyd & fraser *(4)*
Macmillan Educational *(5)*   Brooks Cole *(4)*
Thomas Nelson *(incorporating all* Course Technology Inc *(4)*
    companies marked (5) in this   Delmar *(4)*
    list)   Gale Research International
NFER Routledge *(2)*   Heinle & Heinle *(5)*
O'Reilly Associates *(4)*   Humana Press *(distribution*
Rapid Communications of Oxford   *agreement; 1)*
Routledge *(incorporating all*   Milady Publications *(4)*
    companies marked (2) in this   PWS *(4)*
    list)   Singular Publications *(distribution*
Routledge Kegan Paul *(2)*   *agreement; 1)*
Scientific Press *(4)*   South Western *(4)*
E. & F. N. Spon *(1)*   St James Press
Stevens & Sons *(3)*   Taft
Sweet & Maxwell *(incorporating*   Van Nostrand Reinhold *(4)*
    all companies marked (3) in this Van Nostrand Reinhold *(part list*
    list)   *only; 1)*
Tavistock Publications *(2)*   Wadsworth Publishing *(4)*
Thomson Directories   Wadsworth Publishing *(part list*
                                        only; 1)

6175 ▬▬▬▬▬▬▬▬▬▬▬▬▬▬▬▬▬▬▬▬▬▬▬▬▬

KUPERARD (LONDON) LTD
7 Spectrum House, 32–34 Gordon House Road, London NW5 1LP
Telephone: 0171 424 0554
Fax: 0171 424 0556

Distributors:
Bailey Distribution, Learoyd Road, New Romney, Kent TN28 8XU
Telephone: 01797 369966
Fax: 01797 366638
Email: kuperard@dircon.co.uk
Web Site: http://www.bestware.co.uk/kuperard

Managing Director: Joshua Kuperard
Managers: Peter Roberts *(Sales & Marketing, Promotions, Publicity &*
    Special Sales)
Martin Kaye *(Judaica Sales)*

Publishers of:
At A Glance Self-folding Maps   Michael's Guides
Channel Tunnel at a Glance   Touring Australia Road Atlases
Culture Shock! Guides   Working Holidays Abroad
Everyday Phrase Books

Distributor for travel books:
France: Les Routiers Guides   *UK:* The Parents' Guide to
Germany: Ravenstein Verlag   *Children's Holidays*
    (maps)   Tea Rooms of Britain
Israel: Inbal Travel Information   *USA:* Gousha Road Atlases

Distributor for survival books:
Buying a Home in... Guides   Living & Working in... Guides

Distributor for Jewish interest books:
USA: Jason Aronson   Schocken Books / Random House
Basic Books   Simon & Schuster
Jewish Publication Society   Summit Books
Kar-Ben

Distributor for classic hardback literature:
USA: The Modern Library (Random House)

Kuperard acts as publishers, co-publishers and distributors, handling marketing and representation. Kuperard handle over 70 UK and overseas publishers. Stocklists, catalogues and brochures are available upon request.
   Travel subjects include leisure guides, maps, city plans, cross-cultural guides for business people and travellers. Kuperard publishes 'At a

Glance' self-folding city maps, and Channel Tunnel At A Glance. Judaica subjects covered include art, cookery, Israel, history, language, children, religion, literature, archaeology, holocaust and reference.

Kuperard specializes in the above subject lists, and makes particular efforts to guide books directly to their target markets.

6176 ━━━━━━━━━━━━━━━━━━━━━━━

LISTER ART BOOKS (OF SOUTHPORT)
PO Box 31, Southport, Lancs PR9 8BF
Telephone: 01704 232033
Fax: 01704 505926
Email: sales@laboox.demon.co.uk

Proprietor: Graham Lister
Manager: Joanne Proctor *(Sales & Marketing)*

USA companies represented:
USA: American Quilters Society   Merry Walk Antiques
Antique Publications   New Leaf Publishers
Sandra Bondhus   Reflected Images Publishing
Collector Books   Tomart Publications
Heart of America   Western World Publishers
LW Book Sales   Windmill Publishing

Lister Art Books are specialist distributors and wholesalers of books relating to antiques, collecting and quilting, from US and European publishing houses.

The company also offers a comprehensive service of distribution to the UK book and antiques trades. Books available on most collectable subjects from one source of supply.

Complete list of titles stocked available upon request.

6177 ━━━━━━━━━━━━━━━━━━━━━━━

LITTLEHAMPTON BOOK SERVICES LTD
10–14 Eldon Way, Littlehampton, West Sussex BN17 7HE
Telephone: 01903 721596
Fax: 01903 730914
Email: 100067.1631@compuserve.com

Directors: Peter Roche *(Chairman)*
Terence H. E. Giles *(Managing)*
Mark A. Stacey *(Finance)*
Nigel Montgomery *(IT)*

Clients include:
Ian Allan Publishing   Orion Children's *(1)*
Berlitz   Orion Group *(incorporating all*
Boxtree   *companies marked (1) in this*
Carcanet   *list)*
Kyle Cathie   Peter Owen
Chapmans *(1)*   Phoenix *(1)*
J. M. Dent *(1)*   Phoenix House *(1)*
André Deutsch   Reaktion
Dolphin *(1)*   Rosendale Press
Ellipsis London Ltd   Summersdale Publishers
Everyman *(1)*   Sutton Publishing Ltd
Farrar, Straus & Giroux   Victoria & Albert Museum
Peter Halban *(1)*   Victoria House Publishing
Millennium *(1)*   *(trading as Joshua Morris)*
New Holland *(including Charles*   Weidenfeld & Nicolson *(1)*
Letts Publishing Division)   Windrow & Greene Publishing
Orion *(1)*

Littlehampton Book Services provides publishers with full warehouse management and distribution services that include credit control and trust accounting, sophisticated management reporting, telesales and royalty accounting.

6178 ━━━━━━━━━━━━━━━━━━━━━━━

LONELY PLANET PUBLICATIONS
The Barley Mow Centre, 10 Barley Mow Passage, Chiswick, London W4 4PH
Telephone: 0181 742 3161
Fax: 0181 742 2772

Email: 100413.3551@compuserve.com
Web Site: http://www.lonelyplanet.com/

General Manager UK: C. Hindle

Handles Lonely Planet books sales, marketing, distribution, publicity and promotion for the UK, Europe and Africa.

6179 ━━━━━━━━━━━━━━━━━━━━━━━

B. MCCALL BARBOUR
28 George IV Bridge, Edinburgh EH1 1ES
Telephone: 0131 225 4816
Fax: 0131 225 4816

Managing Partner: Rev Dr T. C. Danson-Smith
Despatch Manager: Miss G. A. Danson-Smith

USA companies represented:
USA: AMG Publishers   John Peterson Music
Chick Publications   Riverside Bibles
Dake Bible Sales   Schoettle Publishing House
Discovery House   Singspiration Inc
Bob Jones University Press   Stamps Baxter Music
Living Stories Inc   Sword of the Lord Publishers
Loizeaux Brothers Inc   Zondervan Corporation
Thomas Nelson & Sons

6180 ━━━━━━━━━━━━━━━━━━━━━━━

MACMILLAN DISTRIBUTION LTD
Houndmills, Basingstoke, Hants RG21 6XS
Telephone: 01256 29242   **Fax:** 01256 841426
Email: lawrencj@macmillan.co.uk

Directors: Lawrence Jennings *(Managing)*
Roger Woodham *(Client & Customer Services)*
David Smith *(Distribution)*

Client Publishers:
Andromeda Interactive Ltd   Magazine Design & Publishing
Andromeda Oxford Ltd   Ltd
Duncan Baird Publishers   Michael O'Mara Books Ltd
W. Foulsham & Co Ltd   Poddington Publishing
W. H. Freeman & Co Ltd   Quadrille Publishing Ltd
Guinness Publishing Ltd   Ripping Publishing
Hazar Publishing Ltd   Ryland Peters & Small
Henry Holt   The Short Publishing Co Ltd
Ice Publishing   Splash Publishing
JPM Publications SA   Sunburst Books
Larousse Group   Tasman Studio
Little Wizard Ltd   Treehouse Children's Books
Macmillan Book Publishing
Group

6181 ━━━━━━━━━━━━━━━━━━━━━━━

MARSTON BOOK SERVICES LTD
PO Box 269, Abingdon, Oxon OX14 4YN
Telephone: 01235 465500
Fax: 01235 465555

Distribution & Returns:
Unit 113, Milton Park, Abingdon, Oxon OX14 4NR
Telephone: 01235 820123
Fax: 01235 821436

Directors: Charles Ashford *(Managing)*
Mark Oliver *(Finance)*
Wayne Ellis *(Operations)*
Micheline Jebb *(Customer Services)*

Distributors for:
Abingdon Press   American Society of
Alban Books   Microbiology
Allen & Unwin   American Society of Neurological
University of Arizona Press   Surgeons

Augsburg
Blackwell Business
Blackwell Publishers
Blackwell Science
Brassey (UK & US) Ltd
Peter Collin Publishing Ltd
Conway Maritime Press
Crossroads
Curzon Press
Martin Dunitz Ltd
Edinburgh University Press
Wm B. Eerdmans
Fishing News Books
Fitzroy Dearborn Publishers
Fortress Press
David Fulton Publishers
Futura
Garland Publishing Inc
Gordon & Breach
Harwood Academic Publishers
Health Education Authority
D. C. Heath
Houghton Mifflin Co Inc *(college list, trade & reference)*
C. Hurst & Co (Publishers) Ltd
Infosource International

International Publishers Distributor
JAI Press Ltd
Japan Library
Journeyman
Keyboard
Mayfield Publishing Co
McGill Queen's University Press
McGraw Hill Healthcare & Medical
Medical Economics
University of Minnesota Press
NCC Blackwell
Northwestern University Press
Orbis Books
Pluto Press Ltd
Polity Press
Polygon
Putnam Aeronautical
Ransom Publishing Ltd
University of Toronto Press
UBC Press
UCL Press Ltd
Verso
Waverly Europe Ltd *(physical distribution only)*

6182

MICROINFO LTD
PO Box 3, Omega Park, Alton, Hants GU34 2PG
Telephone: 01420 86848
Fax: 01420 89889
Email: cdrom@ukminfo.demon.co.uk

Directors: Roy Selwyn *(Joint Managing)*
Cyril Fish *(Joint Managing)*
Associate Directors: Mrs Nicola S. Temple *(Sales & Marketing)*
Mrs Maureen Main *(Operations)*
Aidan Selwyn *(Systems & Technology)*

Distributor of CD-ROM titles for:
ABC-Clio International
Academic Press
ADAM Software
American Conference of Governmental Industrial Hygienists
Andromeda Interactive
Aslib
Association for Computing Machinery
BioCommerce Data
BNA International
Book Data
Bowker-Saur
Britannica Software Inc
British Library
BSI Standards
Building Services Research & Information Association
Bureau Development Inc
Bureau van Dijk
Butterworth-Heinemann
Canada Communication Group
Canadian Centre for Occupational Health & Safety
Capscan
Cartermill Publishing
Cerved International
Chadwyck-Healey Ltd
Chapman & Hall
Chemical Abstracts Service
Churchill Livingstone
CMC ReSearch Inc
Computer Library
Context Ltd

Congressional Information Service
Corel Systems Corp.
Data Service & Information
DataMedia
Derwent Scientific & Patent Information
Digital Media Resources
Dun & Bradstreet
EBSCO Publishing
ECCTIS 2000 Ltd
ELLIS Publications
Encyclopaedia Britannica International
Enerdata
Euromonitor
European Patent Office
Faulkner Information Services
FT Law & Tax
Gale Research
Government Printing Office
Gower Publishing
Grolier Electronic Publishing
HarperCollins
Harrap
Helsinki School of Economics & Business
HM Stationery Office
Hulton Deutsch
ICL
IMSWorld Publications Ltd
Informania
Information Access Co
Innotech Inc
Interactive Media Publications

International Academy at Santa Barbara
International Computer Programs
International Labour Organization
Jaeger & Waldmann
Jane's Information Group
Japan Information Center of Science & Technology
Jones & Barlett
Knight-Ridder Information OnDisc
Kompass (Reed Information Services)
Leatherhead Food RA
Library of Congress
J. B. Lippincott
Little, Brown & Co
McGraw-Hill
Medical Economics Data
Micromedex Inc
Microsoft
National Information Services Corp
National Oceanographic & Atmospheric Administration
National Technical Information Service, US Dept of Commerce
NATO – Publications Office
News Multimedia
Orda-B
Organisation for Economic Cooperation & Development (OECD)
OVP – Editions du Vidal
Oxford University Press
Penguin
PJB Publications
Political Risk Services
Prentice Hall
Preston Publications
Primary Source Media
Prous Science Publishers
R&R Enterprises
RAPRA
Reed Information Services
Research Information Systems

Retail Entertainment Data
Roth Publishing
Royal Melbourne Institute of Technology
Russian Federation Chamber of Commerce & Industry
Scientific American Medicine
SilverPlatter
Software Toolworks
Solutions Software
SPC Software Publishing
Springer-Verlag
Statistical Office of the European Communities
Statistics Canada
Taylor Nelson
TDS Inform
Technical Indexes
TELDAN Information Systems
Thomas Marketing & Distribution
Times Mirror International
Tri Star Publishing
TWI (The Welding Institute)
UN Food & Agriculture Organization
UNESCO
United Nations
University Microfilms Inc
US Patent & Trademark Office
VNU Business Publications
Vocational Technologies
Walters Lexikon
Water Research Centre
Waverly Europe
Wayzata Technology
WeatherDisc Associates Inc
Wer liefert was?
J. Whitaker & Sons
John Wiley & Sons
World Bank
World Book – Childcraft International
World Intellectual Property Organisation
World Library Inc
World Trade Organization

Microinfo is a private company established in 1970 as a publisher and library supplier, specializing in the preparation and distribution of information products and services for industrial, government, academic, research, business and other professional sectors.

Products offered include paper and microfiche copies of technical and scientific reports; subscription services; computer software on magnetic tape and diskette; computerized databases; online computer services and database services on CD-ROM. Many CD-ROMs are exclusive to Microinfo in the UK.

Microinfo also undertakes special information acquisition, preparation, publishing and distribution programmes on behalf of official agencies in the UK and elsewhere.

6183

MILLBANK BOOKS LTD
The Court Yard, The Old Monastery, Windhill, Bishop's Stortford, Herts CM23 2PE
Telephone: 01279 655233
Fax: 01279 655244
Email: millbank.demon.co.uk
Web Site: http://www.millbank.co.uk

Directors: Diana Walsh
Christine Walsh

Titles held:
Canada: Lesome Press
Malaysia: Konsep Lagendia
Pelanduk Publications

Singapore: Asiapac Publications
Didier-Millet
Times Editions

South Africa: Fernwood Press   *USA:* Schiffer Publishing
Southern Book Publishers   Zon International

Millbank Books is a book distributor, importing specialist titles from overseas. All our books are warehoused and physically distributed by Combined Book Services, Kent. Millbank Books has a team of 11 representatives who sell our list throughout the UK, Europe and the Middle East.

All marketing and promotion is handled in-house and attention is paid to the specialist categories.

The list comprises books from North America, Australia, South Africa, Singapore and Malaysia, and all are high quality, illustrated non-fiction with an emphasis on antiques and collecting, travel/photographic, natural history and international cookery.

6184

MONDADORI UK LTD
43–45 Charlotte Street, London W1P 1HA
Telephone: 0171 637 0348
Fax: 0171 637 0352

Managing Director: Leslie Viney

UK sales representative of Arnoldo Mondadori Editore Printing Division.

6185

MOTILAL BOOKS (UK)
73 Lime Walk, Headington, Oxford OX3 7AD
Telephone: 01865 67575
Fax: 01865 750079

Managers: R. Hilsdon
P. Hilsdon
A. Lavis *(Trade)*

Trade distributor and stockist of Motilal Banarsidass publications. Importer of Indian publications in English to special order, including single copies, conferences, standing orders and non-trade items. Where needed, bibliographical research on these items will be included. Aims to enable British and European booksellers to obtain Indian publications in the English language with the minimum of inconvenience and costs.

6186

MUSIC BOOK DISTRIBUTORS LTD
44 Station Way, Buckhurst Hill, Essex IG9 6LN
Telephone: 0181 559 1522
Fax: 0181 559 1522

Director: Neil Taylor

MBD specializes in distributing the publications of music publishers to the book trade. Titles included in our stock list cover the full spectrum of classical, jazz and popular music plus the bestselling tutorial books. Any titles not stocked are supplied on a special order basis. Also carried is a range of books about music and musicians.

6187

PANDEMIC LTD
112 Sydney Road, London N10 2RN
Telephone: 0181 442 1783
Fax: 0181 442 1783
Email: 101454.301@compuserve.com

Managing Director: Jack Stacey

Publishers' sales agents.

6188

PASSWORD (BOOKS) LTD
23 New Mount Street, Manchester M4 4DE
Telephone: 0161 953 4009
Fax: 0161 953 4090

Email: password-books@mcr1.poptel.org.uk
Web Site: http://www.poptel.org.uk/password/home.html

Managing Director: David Parrish
Publicity Officer: Pauline Clarke
Sales Representatives: Rob Richardson *(South & London)*
Leandra Holder *(North & Scotland)*
Distribution & Accounts Manager: Arlene Graham

Sales representation agency and distributor for publishers of literature based in the UK and abroad.

Password provides training courses for small publishers.

6189

PEBBLESHORE LTD
Lewes Enterprise Centre, 112 Malling Street, Lewes, Sussex BN7 2RJ
Telephone: 01273 483890
Fax: 01273 479645

Contact: John Hume

Pebbleshore publishes and distributes CD-ROM packs, mainly for education and training, in the field of social geography.

The CD-ROM packs include support print material and maps. They are available for sale through bookshops, library suppliers and other outlets, and enquiries are welcome.

Pebbleshore would be pleased to consider material, already published or not, in text or database form relating to geography and society in any part of the EU.

6190

PEGASUS DISTRIBUTION LTD
Unit 350, Glenfield Park Site 2, Blakewater Road, Blackburn, Lancashire BB1 5QH
Telephone: 01254 696768
Fax: 01254 697060

Managing Director: Tony Paulaskas

Distributor for:
Australia: Nightingale Press   Ravette Publishing Ltd
UK: Beaver Publishing Ltd   *USA:* Turner Publishing Inc

Pegasus Distribution Ltd, which operates out of new purpose-built premises, offers a sales, marketing and distribution service to the book trade. A professional trade sales team of freelance agents operates in the UK and in the Irish Republic.

Services can also incorporate sales invoicing, credit control and bad debt risk. Clients' stock is totally insured from the moment it arrives in the company's warehouse.

6191

PLYMBRIDGE DISTRIBUTORS LTD
Plymbridge House, Estover Road, Plymouth PL6 7PZ
Telephone: 01752 202300 *(customer services:* 202301*)*
Fax: 01752 202300 *(orders:* 202333*)*
Email: plym@plym.ennet.co.uk

Directors: Michael W. Beevers *(Managing)*
Brian G. Eagle *(Computer Systems)*
Ken R. Wasley *(Warehouse)*
Managers: Ian Wordsworth *(Data Processing)*
Ann Peters *(Customer Services)*

UK Agents for:
Belgium: Archibel SA	British Film Institute
UK: ABC-Clio Ltd	British Psychological Society
Albion Publishing	Paul Chapman Publishing
American Psychiatric Press	Robin Clark
Angell Editions	Class Publishing
Bellew Publishing Co	Clio Press
Berghahn Books	Current Science Group
Bild Publications	James Currey Publishers
Biography Press	Euromoney Publications

University of Exeter Press
Export Success
Forbes Publications
Hawker Publications
How to Books Ltd
Institute of Personnel
    Development
Intermediate Technology
Librapharm
Multilingual Matters
National Geographic *(books only)*
Northcote House Publishers
Pathfinder Distribution Ltd
Quartet Books Ltd
Readers International
Royal Institute of International
    Affairs
Scarlet Press
Serpent's Tail Publishing
Singular Publishing
Technical & Educational Services
UPM Agencies
Windrush Books
The Women's Press Ltd
Zed Books
USA: All Books for Children

American Association of
    Orthopedic Surgery
Aspen Publishers
Cornell University Press
Georgetown University Press
Gulf Publishing Co
Johns Hopkins University Press
Jones & Bartlett Publishers
Krieger
Lippincott-Raven Publishers
University of Michigan Press
National Academy Press
University Press of New England
State University of New York
    Press
New York University Press
A. K. Peters Ltd
Research & Education
    Association
Russell Sage Foundation
Smithsonian Institution Press
Stenhouse
United States Institute of Peace
Wesleyan University Press
Westview Press

6192

POCKETBOND LTD
PO Box 80, Welwyn, Herts AL6 0ND
Telephone: 01438 798593
Fax: 01438 798616

Director: Phillip Brook

Pocketbond Ltd is the UK importer of Squadron Signal Publications, USA. These lists are sold and distributed in the UK and the Irish Republic to bookshops, book wholesalers, etc.

Pocketbond is also the European representative for Squadron Signal Publications and identifies importers for the list in European countries.

6193

POMEGRANATE EUROPE LTD
Fullbridge House, Fullbridge, Maldon, Essex CM9 7LE
Telephone: 01621 851646
Fax: 01621 852426

Directors: Thomas Burke *(Managing)*
David Harris *(Sales)*

UK Distributor for:
USA: Pomegranate

Pomegranate (Europe) Ltd represent, distribute and publish a high-quality range of fine art and photographic calendars, posters, cards, diaries, books of days, postcards, books and much more.

6194

RAGGED BEARS LTD
The Orchards, Ragged Appleshaw, Andover, Hants SP11 9HX
Telephone: 01264 772269
Fax: 01264 772391
Email: books@ragged-bears.co.uk
Web Site: http://www.ragged-bears.co.uk

Returns:
c/o The Trade Counter, The Airfield, Norwich Road, Mendlesham, Suffolk IP14 5NA

Directors: Mrs Charles Shirley
Henrietta Stickland
Customer Service Clerk: Mrs M. Portsmouth
Marketing Manager: Angela Espley

UK agents for:
A Vos Marques Cassettes
Allen & Unwin *(Little Ark Books)*
Annick Press Ltd
Ars Edition
Peter Bedrick Books
David Bennett Books
Era Publications
Gallery Children's Books
Happy Cat Books
Levinson Children's Books

Moonlight Publishing Ltd
North-South Books *(including
    Neugebauer Press)*
Owl Man
Raben & Sjogren Bokforlag
Spindlewood
Star Bright Books
Templar Publishing
Tundra Books Inc
Watchword Videos & Cassettes

Marketing and distribution of children's books, stationery and advent calendars to the book and gift trades in the UK and export markets.

6195

THE RICHMOND PUBLISHING CO LTD
PO Box 963, Slough SL2 3RS
Telephone: 01753 643104
Fax: 01753 646553

Managing Director: Mrs S. J. Davie

Distributors for:
Field Studies Council *(all titles)*
Mad River Press *(all titles)*

WWF United Kingdom *(all titles)*
Switzerland: Mycologia Lucerne

Publishers of natural history books and sole distributors for a number of academic publishers. Co-publishers of several titles with WWF United Kingdom. Publishers of school texts and educational material.

One of the largest botanical retail booksellers in Britain specializing in imported titles and serving libraries, professionals and institutions around the world.

6196

JOHN RULE, PUBLISHERS SALES AGENT
40 Voltaire Road, London SW4 6DH
Telephone: 0171 498 0115
Fax: 0171 498 2245

Manager: John Rule

6197

SHELWING LTD
127 Sandgate Road, Folkestone, Kent CT20 2BL
Telephone: 01303 850501
Fax: 01303 850162

Warehouse:
4 Pleydell Gardens, Folkestone, Kent CT20 2DN
Telephone: 01303 850501
Fax: 01303 850162

Managing Director: J. R. Bailey
General Manager: John D. Poole
Publicity Manager: Eileen Marshall

UK Distributor for:
UK: Cambax Publishing *(one title
    only)*
Clark, Lawrence Publishers
Hart & Sole (Publishers) Ltd

Vineyard Press (London)
Wat Tyler Books
USA: McFarland & Co Inc
Scarecrow Press Inc

Also offers single copy and small publisher distribution service.

6198

SPRINGFIELD BOOKS LTD
Norman Road, Denby Dale, Huddersfield, West Yorkshire HD8 8TH
Telephone: 01484 864955
Fax: 01484 865443

Directors: Brian Lewis *(Managing)*
Walter Puszczynski *(Financial)*
Sales Manager: Paula Brennan *(Sales & Promotion)*

Springfield Books are publishers of high quality sports and travel books, that also offer a complete distribution service to many UK and overseas publishers.

6199

TIPTREE BOOK SERVICES LTD
St Luke's Chase, Church Road, Tiptree, Colchester, Essex CO5 0SR
Telephone: 01621 816362 (orders: 819600)
Fax: 01621 819011

Chairman: D. Pemberton
Directors: M. McCreanor *(Customer Services)*
I. Farnell *(Distribution)*
G. Miller *(Financial)*
M. A. Johnson *(IT)*
P. K. Martin *(Logistics)*
R. Anderson

Distribution services offered to:

Andersen Press Ltd	Hi-Marketing
Arrow	Internos Books
Nicholas Brealey	Little, Brown
John Brown Publishing	Piccadilly Press
Constable & Co	Random House
Dover Books	Severn House
Everyman	Smith Gryphon
Fodor	TSR
Fourth Estate	Virago Press
Helicon	The Watts Group
Nick Hern	

Distribution covers order receipt, by telephone, post and teleordering, telesales, cyclical invoicing, despatch via Omega Express, Ireland Freight, post and own vehicles. Also included is a full sales ledger and cash collection service. Sales and stock information and royalties are offered. Ancillary work such as mailing, shrink-wrapping, repricing, dump-bin and counterpack make up is also available.

6200

THE TRADE COUNTER LTD
Unit D, Trading Estate Road, London NW10 7LU
Telephone: 0181 963 0322
Fax: 0181 965 9765

Also at:
Mendlesham Industrial Estate, Norwich Road, Mendlesham, Suffolk IP14 5NA
Telephone: 01449 766629
Fax: 01449 767122

Managing Director: B. A. Barron

Storage, packing and distribution of publications for publishers.

6201

TURNAROUND PUBLISHER SERVICES LTD
27 Horsell Road, London N5 1XL
Telephone: 0171 609 7836/7
Fax: 0171 700 1205

Directors: Bill Godber *(Managing & Sales)*
Claire Thompson *(Marketing)*
Kiel Shaw *(Financial & Company Secretary)*

Clients include:

Irish Republic: Brandon Books	*USA:* Four Walls Eight Windows
UK: GMP	Red Sea Press
X-Press	

Turnaround provides a sales, marketing and distribution service for independent publishers, both from the UK and overseas. Sales reps cover the whole of the UK, Irish Republic and Europe and can offer a repping-only service if required.

6202

TURPIN DISTRIBUTION SERVICES LTD
Blackhorse Road, Letchworth, Herts SG6 1HN
Telephone: 01462 672555
Fax: 01462 480947
Email: turpin@rsc.org

Managing Director: Robert Welham
Director & General Manager: Lorna Summers
Marketing Services & Development Manager: Gervase Muller

Clients include:

Abington Publishing	Liverpool University Press
ALPSP	Pickering & Chatto
American Chemical Society	Pion
Arnold	Royal Anthropological Institute
Beech Tree	Royal Society of Chemistry
Brasseys	Society for Endocrinology
The British Library	Society of Chemical Industry
British Psychological Society	Turpion
Current Science	Whurr
In Print	Woodhead Publishing
Kogan Page	Wrightson Biomedical
Liberty Fund	

Turpin Distribution Services specialize in worldwide distribution of learned and academic publications offering either a bureau or a full service option. Membership society requirements can also be cared for.

Turpin invoice in the publisher's name and use their trading terms. ABC circulation figures can be provided on publications carrying advertising.

Turpin provides EDI facilities for both journals and books and can also interface with information provided to bill for electronic products. Turpin reports can analyse both electronic and paper purchases.

6203

UBS PUBLISHERS' DISTRIBUTORS LTD
475 North Circular Road, Neasden, London NW2 7QG
Telephone: 0181 450 8667
Fax: 0181 452 6612 attn UBS
Email: delhi.ubspd@axcess.netin.axcess.delhi.ubspd

Marketing Manager: M. K. Kalsi

Represents over 400 Indian and foreign publishers; maintains selection of nearly 40,000 titles and holds inventory of over 2 million books in India (most operations fully computerized). Participates in all major international book fairs and organizes frequent exhibitions at overseas centres in association with local booksellers and institutions. Network of UBSPD branches in India (New Delhi, Bombay, Bangalore, Madras, Calcutta, Patna and Kanpur) enables speedy provision of any Indian book or journal published commercially and also government, academic, research and scholarly publications including back volumes of journals.

6204

THE UNIVERSITY PRESSES OF CALIFORNIA, COLUMBIA & PRINCETON LTD
John Wiley & Sons Ltd, Distribution Centre, 1 Oldlands Way, Bognor Regis, West Sussex PO22 9SA
Telephone: 01243 842165
Fax: 01243 842167
Email: lois@upccp.demon.co.uk

6205

VINE HOUSE DISTRIBUTION
Waldenbury, North Chailey, East Sussex BN8 4DR
Telephone: 01825 723398
Fax: 01825 724188

Warehouse:
Mullany Business Park, Golden Cross, East Sussex BN27 3RP

Partners: Richard Squibb
Sarah Squibb

Clients include:

Alderney Books	Masquerade Publications
Alpine Fine Art Books	Melstamps
Atlantis	Messidor Books
George Beldam Collection	Michaelmas Books
The Book Guild	Nott Organisation
Boundary Books	ONT
Bracken Publishing	Oval Publishing
British Institute of Radiology	Pica Press
Creative Monochrome	Quest Books
Crossroads of Prague	Scriptmate Editions
Dance Books	Simply Classics
DCM Publications	Sportsbooks
Deerhurst Publications	Take One Publications
Dido Press	Temple House Books
Electronic Meeting Services	Voluntary Sector Press
Good Food Retailing Publications	*Australia:* Florilegium
Granta Editions	*Italy:* Free Lance Press
Haymarket Specialist Motoring	Vallardi e Associati
Publications	*Netherlands:* Van + Van
Helm Information	Publiciteit
Martin Holmes Rallying	*Spain:* Editorial Moll
International Business Library	*Switzerland:* Chronosports
Keytone Publications	Editions JR
Kinnell Publications	*USA:* Dance Horizons
Kozmik Press	Graphic Arts Center
Land Rover	Konecky & Konecky
Madison Publishing	Princeton Book Co

Vine House Distribution provides a comprehensive range of services for small and medium sized book publishers, including representation, distribution, marketing, publicity and promotion, and mail order fulfilment.

6206

MRS MARIELLA WOLF
17 Chiltern Court, Baker Street, London NW1 5TD
Telephone: 0171 487 5956
Fax: 0171 487 5956

Overseas companies represented:
USA: K. S. Giniger Co Inc

6207

WORLDWIDE MEDIA SERVICE INC
c/o Biblios, Star Road, Partridge Green, West Sussex RH13 8LD
Telephone: 01403 710971
Fax: 01403 711143

UK Manager: Adrian Parker

Publishers currently stocked and represented in the UK are:

Avery Publishing Group	Leisure Books
Blue Moon Books	Masquerade Books
Carol	Newmarket Press
Carroll & Graf	

Worldwide Media Service Inc is an American firm representing American publishers throughout the world outside the North American continent. The UK branch stocks and sells most available titles from these publishers through the distribution services of Biblios. Representation of these titles to the book trade is by means of a team of freelance representatives under the control of the UK manager. Eight representatives cover the UK and Irish Republic and a team of four representatives covers continental Europe.

6.7 REMAINDER MERCHANTS

6208

AB BOOKS
21 Chalice Court, Hedge End, Southampton SO30 4TA
Telephone: 01489 799082
Fax: 01489 799082

Proprietor: A. C. Butler

Remainder and bargain book sales.

6209

AURORA ENTERPRISES LTD
Unit 9, Bradley Fold Trading Estate, Radcliffe Moor Road, Bradley Fold, Bolton BL2 6RT
Telephone: 01204 370752/3
Fax: 01204 370751

Directors: Andrew Walsh *(Managing)*
Dawn Robinson *(Editorial)*
Sales Managers: Peter Scott *(Wholesale/Retail)*
Alan Gurney *(Direct)*

Publishing: mainly local interest but also general books. We also have our own publications (ISBN: 1 85926). Wholesaling: our own full-price titles. Remainders.

6210

BARGAIN BOOK SALES
2-B Moore Park Road, London SW6 2JT
Telephone: 0171 385 7007
Fax: 0171 385 9727

Director: Graham Snell
Secretary: Diana Snell

Wholesale booksellers of remainders and bargain reprints, specializing in: the fine and applied arts, graphics, music, architecture, film.

6211

BIBLIOPHILE BOOKS
5 Thomas Road, London E14 7BN
Telephone: 0171 515 9222
Fax: 0171 538 4115

Editor & Buyer: Anne Quigley

Bibliophile purchases publishers' remainders and sells them by mail to private buyers. Ten catalogues are published each year.

6212

BLAKETON HALL LTD
Unit One, 26 Marsh Green Road, Exeter, Devon EX2 8QD
Telephone: 01392 210602
Fax: 01392 421165

Directors: John Shillingford
Patricia Anne Shillingford
Managers: Martin Shillingford *(Office)*
Mike Smith *(Warehouse)*

Buyers and sellers of remainder books. Suppliers to the trade of remainder books. Library suppliers of remainder books and new but out-of-print titles. Wholesale distributors worldwide specializing in bargain books and remainders. Exporters of remainders worldwide. Publishers of reprints. Importers of publishers' overstocks and remainders.

6213

ROY BLOOM LTD
4–5 Academy Buildings, Fanshaw Street, London N1 6LQ

Telephone: 0171 729 5373
Fax: 0171 729 2375

Directors: Roy Bloom *(Managing)*
A. L. Bloom
Paul White *(Sales)*
M. E. Pritchard *(Financial)*
Secretary: M. I. Bloom

Leading remainder dealers, offering books on most subjects at greatly reduced prices.

6214

BOOKMARK INTERNATIONAL
Alpha House, Scarne Industrial Estate, Launceston, Cornwall PL15 9HT
Telephone: 01566 772709
Fax: 01566 776061

Administrator: Mrs Doreen Cowling

Founded in 1982, Bookmark International operates exclusively as a remainder merchant. Its list is a very comprehensive one, with particular emphasis on the serious book. No attempt is made to cater for the glossy manufactured remainder. All books are genuine surpluses from reputable publishers. Particular attention is devoted to specialist book-dealers (military, maritime, transport) for whom a well-tailored telephone ordering service has been developed. 24-hour delivery is achieved from a total in-house operation. Offers from publishers are invited.

6215

BOOKMART LTD
Desford Road, Enderby, Leicester LE9 5AD
Telephone: 0116 275 1800
Fax: 0116 275 0507

Directors: P. E. Parkin *(Managing)*
P. Wareing *(Sales)*

Remainder and promotional books.

6216

BOOKS EXPORTS
137 Hale Lane, Edgware, Middlesex HA8 9QP
Telephone: 0181 959 4099
Fax: 0181 959 2137

Partner: B. P. Lakhani *(Export Manager)*

Books Exports supply remainders, specialize in paperbacks and export all publishers' publications to booksellers, universities, libraries and individuals. Suppliers of ELBS and LPBB editions.

6217

BPL REMAINDERS LTD
Princess House, 50–60 Eastcastle Street, London W1N 7AP
Telephone: 0171 636 5070
Fax: 0171 580 3001

Managing Director: Ken Webb
General Manager: Ken Fox

BPL Remainders purchase general remainders which it sells into the bargain book trade throughout the world. It also publishes promotional reprints and the Senate range of paperbacks.

6218

THE BRIDGE BOOK CO LTD
Unit 4, Goldsworth Park Trading Estate, Woking, Surrey GU21 3BA
Telephone: 01483 720505
Fax: 01483 756143

Directors: M. J. Pemberton *(Managing)*
E. B. Pemberton
J. Steward

The Bridge Book Co is an independent company and has been trading for over 30 years in publishers' overstocks and remainders to the home and export market.
The Bridge Book Co specializes in sagas, historical romances, science fiction, trade paperbacks, hardbacks and children's books. The range covers over 2500 titles in an overall stock of five million.
The company exhibits at all the major trade fairs including Frankfurt, ABA, the London International Book Fair, CIROBE and the Remainder and Promotional Fair in London.

6219

BROCKHAMPTON PRESS LTD
20 Bloomsbury Street, London WC1B 3QJ
Telephone: 0171 636 7171
Fax: 0171 636 1922

Directors: John Maxwell *(Managing)*
Jack Cooper *(Sales)*
Terry Price *(Trade)*
Paul Gregory *(Special Sales)*
Office Manager: Jean Lyne *(Bought & Sales Ledgers)*

One of the leading promotional and remainder book companies, both in the UK and overseas. An increasing range of titles covering art, cookery, reference, and many other general interest subjects.

Parent Company: Hodder Headline Plc *(UK)*

6220

GODFREY CAVE ASSOCIATES
[a division of Penguin Books]
42 Bloomsbury Street, London WC1B 3QJ
Telephone: 0171 636 9177
Fax: 0171 636 9091

Warehouse:
D Services, 6 Euston Street, Freemans Common, Leicester LE2 7SS
Telephone: 01533 547671
Fax: 01533 544670

Directors: Kevin Bristow *(Managing)*
Deborah Wright *(Sales)*
Manager: Roz Scott *(Editorial)*

First established in 1974, Godfrey Cave is a major international dealer in publishers overstocks and promotional reprints, supplying world-wide markets with a range of high quality publications in all categories, from classic art volumes to promotional lines, fiction, childrens and mass market subjects.
Subsidiaries: Godfrey Book Sales Ltd; Bloomsbury Books — publishing imprint for new, reprint and facsimile editions.
Parent Company: Penguin Books Ltd.

6221

MIKE DAVIES BOOKS
PO Box 3, Ware, Herts SG12 0QZ
Telephone: 01920 486333
Fax: 01920 486777

Director: Mike Davies

Remainder book wholesaler specializing in illustrated non-fiction titles.

6222

FRASER STEWART BOOK WHOLESALE LTD
Unit 3B, Colwell Drive, Abingdon, Oxon OX14 1AU
Telephone: 01235 527544
Fax: 01235 530435
Email: khumberstone@cix.compulink.co.uk

Managing Director: David Affleck
Company Secretary: Karl Humberstone

Remainder dealer.

6223

WALTER H. GARDNER LTD
16 Chalton Drive, London N2 0QW
Telephone: 0181 458 3202
Fax: 0181 458 8499

Managing Director: W. H. Gardner
Director: D. Gardner

The company purchases and sells remainders and overstocks in all fields in the home and export markets with particular emphasis on specialist and expensive titles.

6224

GRANGE BOOKS PLC
The Grange, Grange Yard, London SE1 3AG
Telephone: 0171 232 0565
Fax: 0171 232 0113

Directors: Michael Ash *(Managing)*
Heather Staples *(Company Secretary)*
Stephen Ash *(Sales)*
Kevin Matthews *(Financial)*
Managers: John Norman *(International Sales)*
Bob Siwecki *(Sales & Marketing)*

Grange Books Plc has been in the book selling business for 24 years, and has built its reputation on being able to supply a continual and changing selection of quality promotional titles and reprints as well as overstocks.
It is particularly strong on children's titles and adult non-fiction. Its large customer base extends throughout the world, and export is a major part of the business. To satisfy demand, Grange Books is always looking for the following:
—new promotional titles
—promotional reprints
—remainders with the potential to become promotional reprints
—remainders
Subjects include: art, architecture, transport, natural history, transport, cookery, crafts, travel, sport, militaria, general hobbies and interests.
Overstocks can be disposed of discreetly, so as not to interfere with existing trade stocks and we honour territorial restrictions.
If you have any titles you would like to discuss, or any ideas you think we may be able to work together on, please contact: Michael Ash.

6225

GREENWICH EDITIONS
Bibliophile House, 10 Blenheim Court, Brewery Road, London N7 9NT
Telephone: 0171 700 7444
Fax: 0171 704 6442
Email: 101600.604@compuserve.com

Chief Executive: J. E. Needleman
Managing Editor: A. Brown
Editor: L. Burnand

Value publishing and promotional book publisher.

6226

HARVEYS BOOKS (MAGNA BOOKS)
Magna Road, Wigston, Leicester LE18 4ZH
Telephone: 0116 278 5154
Fax: 0116 278 2534

Directors: Vance Harvey *(Managing)*
Andrew Tindall *(Sales)*

Harveys Books is a publisher and wholesaler of promotional and remainder books, distributing worldwide. It has a comprehensive range of mass market and illustrated books and can offer a wide coverage in the fields of large format art, postcard books and general interest titles. Many of these are published under the Magna Books imprint. Remainders are available in most subjects.

6227

HOLLAND ENTERPRISES LTD
18 Bourne Court, Southend Road, Woodford Green, Essex IG8 8HD
Telephone: 0181 551 7711
Fax: 0181 551 1266

Directors: William C. Holland *(Managing)*
Sheila M. Holland *(Company Secretary)*
Thomas C. Railton *(Sales)*
Jonathan W. Holland *(Commercial)*

Holland Enterprises Ltd are publishers of children's colouring, activity and story books (approximately 240 titles). A range of gift boxes and bags of books is always available. These publications are sold into the wholesale and multiple retail trades, and overseas markets, particularly Australia, New Zealand, South Africa, India, France and the Far East.

6228

MURRAY REMAINDERS
Bibliophile House, 10 Blenheim Court, Brewery Road, London N7 9NT
Telephone: 0171 700 7444
Fax: 0171 704 6442
Email: 101600.604@compuserve.com

Warehouse:
The Trade Counter, The Airfield, Norwich Road, Mendlesham, Suffolk
Telephone: 01449 766402
Fax: 01449 766309

Chief Executive: J. E. Needleman

Offering books in the following subject areas: children's, crime, fiction, health and beauty.

6229

OCTAGON BOOKS (WHOLESALE) LTD
Hill View, Hare Lane, Little Kingshill, Great Missenden, Bucks HP16 0EF
Telephone: 01494 863184
Fax: 01494 890595

Director: Ron Ive

All types of remainders and promotional reprints.

6230

JIM OLDROYD BOOKS
14–18 London Road, Sevenoaks, Kent TN13 1AJ
Telephone: 01732 763232
Fax: 01732 763766

Director: Jim Oldroyd
Managers: Paula Ireland
David Lines *(Sales)*

Remainders, bargain books and overstocks of adult and children's books. All ages and all interests.

6231

H. PORDES LTD
383 Cockfosters Road, Cockfosters, Herts EN4 0JS
Telephone: 0181 449 2524
Fax: 0181 441 9595

Directors: Henry Pordes
Rita Pordes

Dealers in remainders, reprints of learned and scientific books as well as popular classics, modern Judaica reprints, antiquarian learned periodicals in all languages and subjects.

Supply dealers (at discount prices according to quantity) and internal university libraries.

6232 ▬▬▬▬▬▬▬▬

HENRY PORDES BOOKS LTD
58–60 Charing Cross Road, London WC2H 0BB
Telephone: 0171 836 9031
Fax: 0181 886 2201

Manager: Gino Della-Ragione

Retail and wholesale sales of antiquarian and remainder books. The company carries a constantly changing, very large stock of books on every subject.

6233 ▬▬▬▬▬▬▬▬

RAMBORO BOOKS
Bibliophile House, 10 Blenheim Court, Brewery Road, London N7 9NT
Telephone: 0171 700 7444
Fax: 0171 704 6442
Email: 101600.604@compuserve.com

Chief Executive: J. E. Needleman
Marketing: T. Finch
UK Sales: R. Cortie

Europe's foremost remainder wholesaler.

6234 ▬▬▬▬▬▬▬▬

SANDERSON BOOKS LTD
Front Street, Klondyke, Cramlington, Northumberland NE23 6RF
Telephone: 01670 735855
Fax: 01670 730974

Director: John Sanderson
Manager: Anne Pearson

6235 ▬▬▬▬▬▬▬▬

SANDPIPER BOOKS LTD
24 Langroyd Road, London SW17 7PL
Telephone: 0181 767 7421
Fax: 0181 682 0280
Email: sandpiper@sandpiper.co.uk
Web Site: http://www.sandpiper.co.uk/postscript

Managing Director: Robert Collie

Sandpiper Books Ltd is a company specializing in scholarly, literary and art remainders. Titles stocked include those on anthropology, religion, economics, politics, history, literature, art and design. The company buys extensively from university presses and the scholarly divisions of major publishers as well as from smaller companies, and supplies an extensive network of trade and non-trade outlets both in the UK and overseas.

6236 ▬▬▬▬▬▬▬▬

SELLQUICK CO LTD
Unit 3B, Colwell Drive, Abingdon, Oxon OX14 1AU
Telephone: 01235 527544
Fax: 01235 530435
Email: khumberstone@cix.compulink.co.uk

Directors: David Affleck (Managing)
Theo de Boer (Purchasing)
Karl Humberstone (Finance)

Remainder dealer.

6237 ▬▬▬▬▬▬▬▬

TIGER BOOKS INTERNATIONAL PLC
26a York Street, Twickenham, Middx TW1 3LJ
Telephone: 0181 892 5577
Fax: 0181 891 6550

Directors: Grahame Parish (Managing)
Sue Parish (Production & Editorial)
Norman Lott (Financial)

Suppliers of books for the remainder, reprint and promotional book market worldwide. Specialization in two areas: hardcover, colour-illustrated books on cookery, gardening, art, military, reference, travel, entertainment, natural history, sport, history, transport, photography, children's books; and paperback fiction and non-fiction.

Remainders bought from major publishers; titles reprinted in liaison with publishers and packagers and distributed as bargain books. Products distributed in UK by sales representatives who carry Tiger books exclusively; export sales handled by direct contact with wholesalers, retailers or distributors in all major English language export markets.

Exhibits at London Book Fair, Frankfurt and ABA.

6238 ▬▬▬▬▬▬▬▬

W. E. ASSOCIATES (SWINDON) LTD
Unit 1, Marshgate, Stratton Road, Swindon, Wilts SN1 2PA
Telephone: 01793 490400
Fax: 01793 511408

Chairman: Malcolm Wetherill
Manager: Chris Holmes (Sales & Retail)

W. E. Associates stock an extensive range of paperback and hardback remainders and are well established in both the UK and export markets. They also now publish a complete range of print and blank books.

6239 ▬▬▬▬▬▬▬▬

GEOFF WEEDON BOOKS LTD
110 Alkham Road, Maidstone, Kent ME14 5PD
Telephone: 01622 761399
Fax: 01622 754556

Showroom:
4–5 Academy Buildings, Fanshaw Street, London N1 6LQ
Telephone: 0171 613 4446
Fax: 0171 613 4513

Managing Director: Geoff Weedon
Manager: George Pentney (Showroom)

Geoff Weedon Books carries a large and varied selection of remainder books.

6240 ▬▬▬▬▬▬▬▬

W. J. WILLIAMS & SON (BOOKS) LTD
Ashcroft, Barton-under-Needwood, Staffs DE13 8BA
Telephone: 01283 712948
Fax: 01283 716807

Managing Director: Anthony Williams
Warehouse & Sales Manager: Michael Taylor

Remainder wholesaler.

6.8 MAIN WHOLESALERS

6241 ▬▬▬▬▬▬▬▬

APB
[Petbridge Ltd trading as APB]
423/425 Caledonian Road, London N7 9BQ
Telephone: 0171 607 4335
Fax: 0171 700 6539

Also at:
848b Melton Road, Thurmaston, Leicester LE4 8BJ
Telephone: 0116 269 3861
Fax: 0116 264 0042

Directors: John Gibbins *(Managing)*
Ron Cheetham *(Sales)*
Managers: Bob Nichols *(Sales)*
Stephen Lowe *(General)*
Book Buyer: Diane Tennant

Part of APB Group. Wholesalers supplying paperbacks, magazines, maps
and guides, children's books, reference and selected hardbacks through
van-sales service (currently 28 representatives in London). Area covered:
Greater London, Home Counties, Sussex and Hampshire, Berkshire,
Suffolk, Bedfordshire, East Anglia.

6242

J. BARNICOAT LTD
Parkengue, Kernick Industrial Estate, Penryn, Cornwall TR10 9EP
Telephone: 01326 372628
Fax: 01326 377240

Chairman: Paul Barnicoat
Directors: Jonathan Barnicoat *(Managing)*
Glyn Barnicoat *(Distribution)*
Raymond Dyer *(Sales & Marketing)*
Sue Toseland *(Financial)*
Managers: Rowland Abram *(Operations)*
Stephen Averiss *(Logistics)*
Sue Bartlett *(Customer Services)*
Tim Briggs *(Library & Information)*
John Evans *(Sales)*
Bruce Izard *(Warehouse)*
Liz Pearce *(Marketing)*
New Title Buyer: Rachael Bastian
Stock Controllers: Matthew Hoben
Stephen Richards
Representatives: David Gilbert *(North)*
John Howkins *(South West)*
John Rose *(East Anglia)*
Darryl Tucker *(Western Area)*

A trade book wholesaler supplying to bookshops and libraries throughout
the UK, Europe and the rest of the world.

6243

BERTRAM BOOKS LTD
The Nest, Rosary Road, Norwich, Norfolk NR1 1TF
Telephone: 01603 766266 (Orders) & 216666 (Admin)
Fax: 01603 617999 (Orders) & 611201 (Admin)
Email: books@bertrams.co.uk

Directors: Kip Bertram *(Chairman)*
Mrs Elsie Bertram *(Company Secretary)*
Alison Bertram
Nigel Bertram
Julian Rivers *(Chief Executive)*
Managers: Barry Robinson *(Distribution)*
Kevin Allard *(IT)*
John Kingsmill *(Company Accountant)*
Kim Arthurton *(Sales)*
Mike Butler *(Buying)*

Publishers represented:

21st Century	Airlift Book Co
AA Publishing	Ian Allan Ltd
Abbeville	Allen Lane
Harry N. Abrams Inc	Allison & Busby
Absolute Press	Amalgamated Books
Acid Jazz	Anaya Publishers Ltd
Addax Retail Publishing	Andersen Press
Adlard Coles	Andromeda Interactive
Age Concern	Anglia Multimedia
Airlife Publishing	Annuals Publishing Ltd

APA Insight Guides
The Apple Press
Appletree Press Ltd
Aquafitness
Aquarian
Archway
Argus Books
Argyll Publishing
Arlington Books
Arms & Armour Press
Edward Arnold
Arrow
Artulen
Ashgrove Press Ltd
Attica Cybernetics
Aurum Press
Baillière Tindall
Bantam Press
Barefoot Books
Barrie & Jenkins
Barrons
Bartholomew & Son Ltd
Barton House
Batsford Ltd
Colin Baxter Photography
Bay View Books Ltd
BBC Books
Berlitz Publishing Co Ltd
Bespoke Audio Ltd
Bible Society
Bicycle Books
A. & C. Black Ltd
Blackie & Son Ltd
Blackwell Publishers
Blackwell Science
Blake Publishing
Blandford Press
Bloodaxe Books
Bloomsbury Publishing Ltd
Bloomsbury/Warne
Bodley Head
Bookmart Ltd
Bounty Books
Boxtree
Boydell Press
BPP Publishing
Bradt Books
Brassey Sports
Nicholas Brealey Publishing
Brimax Books
Britannia Press
British Mountaineering Council
British Museum Press
Brockhampton Press
Andrew Brodie Publications
Brooks/Cole
John Brown
BTL Publishing
Butterfingers
Butterworth Heinemann Ltd
Buzz Books
Cadogan Guides
Cambridge Academic
Cambridge Publishing Group
Cambridge University Press
Campbell Books Ltd
CAMRA
Canongate Publishing
Jonathan Cape
Carcanet Press Ltd
Carlton Books
Cassell
Castle Communications
Godfrey Cave Associates
Central Books Ltd (Distributors)
Central Bureau
Century

Chambers
Paul Chapman Publishing
Chapmans
Chatto & Windus
Child's Play
Chivers Press Ltd
Chronicle
Chronicle Books
Churchill Livingstone
Richard Cohen
Cole Group
Collins & Brown
Colt Books
Compass Star Publications
Conran-Octopus
Constable & Co
Conway Maritime Press
Leo Cooper
Cordee
Coronet
Cover to Cover Cassettes Ltd
The Crowood Press
C. W. Daniel Ltd
David & Charles
de Agostini
Debretts Peerage Ltd
J. M. Dent
André Deutsch
André Deutsch Children's Books
Diadem Books
Direct Distribution
Dorling Kindersley
Doubleday
Dover Thrift Editions
DP Publications Ltd
Dragon's World
G. Duckworth & Co Ltd
Dutton
Ebury Press
Eden Grove Editions
Element Books Ltd
Elliot Right Way Books
Aidan Ellis Publishing
EMAP Business Publications
EMI Distribution Centre
Erlbaum UK
Estate Publications
Evans Brothers Ltd
Evening Standard
Everyman Paperbacks
Everyman's Library
Excellent Press
Exley Publications
Expert
Faber & Faber
Falmer Press
Farming Press Books
Fernhurst
FHG 1996 Publications Ltd
Firebird Books Ltd
Five Mile Press
Floris Books
Fodor Guides
Mary Ford Publications
Foulsham
Fountain Press
Fourth Estate
W. H. Freeman & Co Ltd
Frontier Publishing
Gaia Publishers
Gallery Children's Books
Garland Publishers
Gateway Books
Geocentre International
Geographer
Gill & Macmillan
Glasgow Royal Concert Hall

Godsfield Press
Gollancz
Gracewing
Grange Books Plc
Granta Books
Peter Grose
Grub Street
Guild of Master Craftsmen
  Publishers
Guinness Publishing
Robert Hale
Hamish Hamilton
Hamlyn Publishing
Harlequin Mills & Boon
Harmsworth Publishing Co
Harp Publications
HarperCollins Electronic
HarperCollins Paperbacks
HarperCollins Publishers
Harrap
Harrods Publishing
Harvard University Press
Harvill Press
Hawk Books
Hay House
Haynes Publishing Group
Hazleton
Headline
Health Education Authority
William Heinemann
Heinemann Library
Heinemann Publishing Oxford
Helicon
Christopher Helm
Henderson Publishing Ltd
The Herbert Press
Nick Hern Books
Hippo
HMSO
Hobsons Publishing Plc
Hodder & Stoughton
Hodder Education
Hollanden Publishing
How to Books
Norman Hudson & Co
Hugo's Language Books Ltd
Hunt & Thorpe
Hutchinson
Icon Books
IDG Computer Books
Independent UK Sports
  Publications
Indigo
Infinity Press
Infobase
ISIS
Jarrold Publishing
Johansens
Jolly Learning Ltd
Michael Joseph
Kaye & Ward
Kenilworth Press Ltd
Kensington West Productions
KGP Publishing
Laurence King Publishers
Kingfisher Books
Klutz
Kogan Page Ltd
Kramer H. J.
Kuperard (London) Ltd
Kyle Cathie
Ladybird Books
Langenscheidt Dictionaries
Langsyne Publishers
Larousse Plc
Laughing Stock Productions
Learning Development Aids

Lennard Publishing
Letterland Direct Ltd
Lettermen Publishing
Letts (General Publishing
  Division)
Letts Educational
Levinson
Frances Lincoln
Link House
Lion Publishing Plc
Listen for Pleasure
Little Brown
Living Books
Chris Lloyd Sales & Marketing
Lonely Planet Publications
Longman Group
Lorenz Books
Peter Lowe
Lyle Publications
Lyric Books
M & M Publishing
Macdonald Young Books
Macmillan
Macmillan Education
Macmillan Interactive
Julia Macrae Books
Mainstream Publishing Co
Mandarin
Marco Polo Guides
Kenneth Mason
McGraw Hill Book Co
MCI (Music College
  International)
Media Masters
Melia Publishing Services
Merehurst
Merlin Unwin
Methuen Books
Metro Publishing
Michelin Tyre Plc
Microsoft
Midland Publishing Ltd
Millennium
Milner
Mindscape
Mirror Books
Mitchell Beazley
Moon Travel Handbooks
Moorland Publishing Co Ltd
Joshua Morris
Mowbray & Co Ltd
Frederick Muller
Multilingual Matters
Multimedia Solutions
John Murray Publishers
Museum Quilts Publications
National Gardens Scheme
National Trust
New Cavendish
New Holland Publishers Ltd
New World Library
Nexus
No Exit Press
Nottinghill
NTC
O'Brien Press
Michael O'Mara Books Ltd
Oberon Books
Oddball Publishing
Odyssey Illustrated Guides
Omnibus Press
Open University
Orchard Books
Ordnance Survey
Orion
Orion Paperbacks
Osborne Books

Osprey
Peter Owen Ltd
Oxford Childrens
Oxford Electronic
Oxford Publishing Co
Oxford University Press
Paddleless Press
Pallas Athene Publishers
Pan Books
Parragon
Partridge Press
Pastime Publications
Stanley Paul
Pavilion
Pedigree Books Ltd
Pelham
Pen & Sword Books Ltd
Penguin
Penguin Electronic
Penguin Popular Classics
Duncan Peterson
Phaidon Press
George Philip
Phoenix
Phoenix House
Phoenix Paperbacks
Piatkus Books
PIC
Pica Press
Piccadilly Press
Pimlico
Pitman Publishing
Erin Pizzy
Plexus Publishing
Pluto Press
Pocket Books
Polygram
Pony Club
Poolbeg
David Porteous Editions
Prentice-Hall International
Pride of Place Publishing
Prion
Prism Press
Psygnosis
The Publishing Corporation
Quadrille Publishing
Quartet Books
Queen Anne Press
Quiller Press
RAC Publishing
Ragged Bears Ltd
Rand McNally & Co
Random House Audio
Random New Media
Ravette Books
Reader's Digest
Red Fox Books
Redback (Audio)
Reed Audio
Reed Information Services
Reed Interactive
Max Reinhardt
Rider
Ringpress Books
Ringpull Press
Riverswift
Robinson Publishing
Robson Books
Alan Rogers Good
Rosendale Press
Rough Guides
Routledge Ltd
Running Press Mini Editions
Sage
Saint Andrews Press
Salamander Books

J. Salmon Ltd
Alastair Sawday Publishing
Scottish Cultural Press
Search Press Ltd
Secker & Warburg
Send the Light
Serpent's Tail
Sheldon Press
Shepheard-Walwyn
Shire
Sidgwick & Jackson
Signet
Simon & Schuster
Simon & Schuster Young Books
Sinclair Stevenson Ltd
Sleeping Bear
Smith Gryphon Ltd
Soccer Book Publishing
Sony Music
Souvenir Press
Spellmount Ltd
Spinal Publications (NZ) Ltd
Sportsman's Press
Springfield Books
Standard Catalogue Publishers
Stanley Thornes
Patrick Stephens
Sterling
Stevenson Publications
Stilwell Publishing
Studio Editions Ltd
Studio Vista
Summersdale
Sunburst Books
Alan Sutton Publishing
Swapmeet Ltd
Sweet & Maxwell
Taschen (Benedikt) UK Ltd
Tenspeed Press
TFH Publications
Thames & Hudson
Thorsons
Times Books
Times Mirror International
Times Warner International
Titan Books
Tolley Publishing
Touchstone
Trade & Travel
Tradewind Books
Transworld
Treehouse Children's Books
TSR
Turnaround Distribution
Two Heads Publishing
UCL Press
University of Chicago
University Press Princeton
University Western Australia
Usborne
Vacation Work
Verso
Verulam Publishing Ltd
Viking
Vine House Distribution
Vintage
Vinyl Experience
Virago
Virgin Books
Vista
Walker Books Ltd
Ward Lock
Frederick Warne
Warner Books
Watershed Productions
Watts Books
Wayland Paperbacks

Weatherhill
Weidenfeld & Nicolson
Western Publishing
Which? Books
J. Whitaker & Sons
Whittet Books Ltd
Paul Whittome
John Wiley
Neil Wilson Publishers Ltd
Windrow & Greene
Windrush
Wisden
Wisley Handbooks
H. F. & G. Witherby

Women's Press
Words on Sport
Wordsmith Publishing Co
Wordsworth Editions Ltd
World International
World Leisure Marketing
Writers & Readers
Xpress Publishers
Yorkshire Art Circus Ltd
Yorkshire TV Enterprises
Youth Hostel Association
Zebra Books
Zigzag Publishing Ltd

6244

BOOKWORLD WHOLESALE

7 Welch Gate, Bewdley, Worcs DY12 2AT
Telephone: 01299 404140
Fax: 01299 404140

Co-Owners: Janet Gainham *(Warehouse)*
Leslie Gainham *(Marketing Manager)*
Managers: Justin Gainham *(Sales)*
Lian Gainham *(Office & Home Sales)*

Transport and military book specialist distributor, now selling craft and doll books, mainly to the UK; some export sales to Europe and the USA.
Minimum order one book, full trade terms given but postage added to orders under £25 in value. Teleordering mnemonic BK WORLD.
Range of distribution whole of UK. Number of publishers for whom we distribute is in excess of 70.

6245

T. COX & SON (CASH & CARRY) LTD

1 Alder Close, Eastbourne, East Sussex BN21 6QF
Telephone: 01323 647444
Fax: 01323 721357

Book Buyer: Mrs P. Locke

Wholesale and retail newsagents with small book wholesaling operation.

6246

DEE BOOKS

Unit 3G, Brymau Three Industrial Estate, River Lane, Chester CH4 8RQ
Telephone: 01244 671177
Fax: 01244 680037

Partners: R. J. Mason *(General Manager)*
E. A. Wakley

General wholesalers specializing in hardbacked books from most general publishers, with complete stocks held for some; also good stocks of local publications and remainder books. Popular mass-market paperbacks now stocked.
Representation and van deliveries in North Wales and the North West.

6247

DELTA LTD

39 Alexandra Road, Addlestone, Surrey KT15 2PQ
Telephone: 01932 854776
Fax: 01932 849528

Managing Director: Nicholas Boisseau
Financial Director: Kevin Castle
Sales & Marketing Director: Eileen Fryer

Delta is one of the UK's leading export wholesalers, offering booksellers overseas a single source for all their British book requirements.
Delta North America offers a similar service to bookshops worldwide for American books.

Delta ELT. Delta holds a wide range of ELT materials in stock and offers bookshops both in the UK and overseas a fast and reliable wholesale service for ELT materials.

6248

ELSTEAD MAPS

Badgery, Hookley Lane, Elstead, Godalming, Surrey GU8 6JE
Telephone: 01252 703472
Fax: 01252 703971
Email: 100430.2720@compuserve.com
Web Site: http://www.elstead.co.uk

Proprietor: Stephen Colebrooke

Elstead Maps is a specialist map and guide wholesaler, offering a range of travel publications from most major publishers to all retailers. Deliveries are by Securicor next-day service to any address in mainland UK.
Elstead Maps provides a first-class service to all its customers. It can provide the company catalogue which is arranged by geographical area, stock check lists, and if customers request stock cards these can also be provided.

6249

R. T. & A. FAWCETT

White Quarry, Tadcaster, North Yorkshire LS24 9NQ
Telephone: 01937 833153
Fax: 01937 530327

Contact: R. T. Fawcett

General book wholesaling mainly paperback. Yorkshire, North Humberside and Cleveland only.

6250

GARDNERS BOOKS LTD

1 Whittle Drive, Willingdon Drove, Eastbourne, East Sussex BN23 6QH
Telephone: 01323 521555
Fax: 01323 521666
Email: mail@gardners-books.co.uk

Chairman: Alan Little
Directors: Jonathan Little *(Managing)*
Jean Little
Andrew Little *(Technical)*
Carol Little *(Finance)*
Bob Jackson *(Sales)*
Managers: Phil Edwards *(Buying)*
John Talbot *(Customer Service)*
Nicky Godfrey *(Credit Controller)*
Warwick Bailey *(Export Sales)*

Gardners are wholesalers who offer a comprehensive service to booksellers worldwide, from their stockholding of 80,000 hardback and paperback titles.
They are complete stockists of all the major paperback publishers and carry selective stock from nearly 300 other publishers. A comprehensive catalogue is issued twice a year and is indexed alphabetically by both title and author. All catalogues are available on CD-ROM with jackets illustrated in full colour.
All orders taken by 5.30 pm will be despatched the same day on a next day delivery service. Orders can be placed by telephone, answerphone, fax, teleordering, post (prepaid envelopes available), EDI and via Gardlink. Gardlink can also run a bookshops' special ordering service.
Additional services include new title monthly book guide for paperbacks and hardbacks. Title listings sorted by category are available along with many other computer listings arranged by both category and sales. Re-order slips are available giving basic bibliographical information; these slips, which are an effective form of stock control, will be inserted in each book. Promotional bulletins are usually topical and some offer additional discount.
Terms—35% discount.
Settlement—30 days.
Returns—a 5% return privilege is allowed.

6251

HEATHCOTE BOOKS
Hawkes Drive, Heathcote Estate, Warwick CV34 6LX
Telephone: 01926 821555
Fax: 01926 821607

General Manager: Graham Nelson
Managers: Ian Richards *(Finance)*
Andrew Whittaker *(Logistics)*

Trade wholesalers offering same-day despatch on orders received before 4.00 pm, UK and overseas. Services: 60,000 title range, comprising hardbacks, paperbacks, maps and tapes. Titles flagged on Bookbank and Bookfind CDs. Free stock directory and stock cards. The most comprehensive subscription service available. Electronic ordering and order confirmation via BUY*line*, Subs-on-Screen, CD-ROM.

6252

MERESBOROUGH BOOKS LTD
1 Saracen Close, Gillingham Business Park, Gillingham, Kent ME8 0QN
Telephone: 01634 388812
Fax: 01634 378501

Also at:
17 Station Road, Rainham, Gillingham, Kent ME8 7RS

Directors: Hamish Mackay Miller
Barbara Mackay Miller
Trade Manager: Judith Allen

Meresborough Books offers a comprehensive wholesale service to medium size and smaller bookshops. A wide range of titles from all the major hardback and paperback publishers and from many of the smaller ones is stocked. In addition, Meresborough Books offers a single copy ordering service for any title from these publishers. A list is available on request.
    Our stock of maps is particularly large, including all OS Pathfinders and many foreign maps.

6253

PATEMANS WHOLESALE BOOK SERVICE
2a Newington Road, Kingsthorpe, Northampton NN2 7TF
Telephone: 01604 721233
Fax: 01604 720677

Proprietor: Michael A. Pateman

Patemans offers a wholesale service with books from publishers covering a large range of topics. In addition to an order service, a cash-and-carry service is available, based on the warehouse and showroom containing a large selection of books. There is a van service to retail outlets in the Northampton, Leicester, Bedfordshire, Coventry, Nottingham and Derby areas. A full range of the latest paperbacks and hardbacks is stocked, and also a large selection of activity books for children.

6254

SCIENCE & TECHNOLOGY BOOK STORE
124 Caddy Road, Randalstown, Co Antrim BT41 3DW
Telephone: 01849 473580
Fax: 01849 479480
Email: mmann@scitec.dnet.co.uk
Web Site: http://www.dnet.co.uk

Sales Manager: Morris Mann
Customer Services: Moyra Mann
Accounts Supervisor: Harry Hamill

Wholesale booksellers, export only. Main areas served: Canada, USA and Scandinavia.

6255

SHOGUN INTERNATIONAL LTD
87 Gayford Road, London W12 9BY
Telephone: 0181 749 2022
Fax: 0181 740 1086

Manager: G. Blanc

Sole UK agent for:
Japan: Shufonotomo   *USA:* Dragon Books Publishing
Sweden: Japanska   Corp

Shogun International deals exclusively with wholesaling of martial arts goods and related sports books.

6256

TOTAL BOOK DISTRIBUTION (TBD)
Unit One, Rosevale Business Park, Newcastle-under-Lyme, Staffs ST5 7QT
Telephone: 01782 561000
Fax: 01782 564484

Customer Service:
Telephone: 01782 564455
Fax: 01800 626625 *(FreeFax UK only)*; 01782 564494

Directors: Alan Taylor *(Managing)*
R. W. Shingleton *(Sales)*
Graham Rand *(Buying)*

Major book wholesale distributor supplying the UK and overseas trade, including John Menzies Retail and independent booksellers. TBD has a range of 50,000 titles, including a wide range of travel, education and children's titles. TBD stocks over 1000 books on tape. Two issues of a *New Titles Guide* are produced every month, one for hardbacks and one for paperbacks. A range of subject catalogues and seasonal promotions are produced for customers. A national and key accounts manager and three representatives visit bookshops regularly and TBD also provides an export service for bookshops worldwide.

6257

VALLEY BOOKS TRUST LTD
Hadnock Road, Monmouth, Gwent NP5 3NQ
Telephone: 01600 712402
Fax: 01600 716075

Chief Executive: Christopher Ward
Managers: Luis Merola *(General)*
Michael Bounds *(Sales)*
Lawrence Williams *(Accounts)*

A registered charity and company limited by guarantee. Wholesale distributor of religious books.

6258

WELSH BOOKS COUNCIL: DISTRIBUTION CENTRE / CYNGOR LLYFRAU CYMRU: CANOLFAN DDOSBARTHU
Stad Glanyrafon, Llanbadarn Fawr, Aberystwyth, Ceredigion SY23 3AQ
Telephone: 01970 624455
Fax: 01970 625506

Marketing Department:
Welsh Books Council, Castell Brychan, Aberystwyth, Ceredigion SY23 2JB
Telephone: 01970 624151
Fax: 01970 625385

Director: Gwerfyl Pierce Jones
Head of Marketing Department: D. Philip Davies
Head of Administration: Pedr ap Llwyd
Distribution Centre Manager: Dafydd Charles Jones

Publishers represented include:

UK: Abercastle Publications
Yr Academi Gymreig / The Welsh
   Academy
Alaw
Alun Books
Amgueddfa Genedlaethol Cymru /
   National Museum of Wales
Annwn
Brefi Press
Bridge Books
D. Brown & Sons
Cadw
Canolfan Adnoddau CPC
   Aberystwyth / UCW
   Aberystwyth Resources Centre
Canolfan Astudiaethau Iaith /
   Language Studies Centre
Canolfan Genedlaethol Addysg
   Grefyddol / Welsh National
   Centre for Religious Education
Castle Publications
Child's Play
Ivan Corbett Publishing
Cwmni Cyhoeddi Gwynn
Cyd-Bwyllgor Addysg Cymru /
   Welsh Joint Education
   Committee
Cyhoeddiadau Barddas
Cyhoeddiadau Curiad
Cyhoeddiadau Modern Cymreig /
   Modern Welsh Publications
Cyhoeddiadau'r Gair
Cymdeithas Lyfrau Ceredigion
Christopher Davies
Y Ddraig Fach
Domino Books
The Ernest Press
Ferry Publications
Gwasg Addysgol Drake

Gwasg Cambria
Gwasg Carreg Gwalch
Gwasg Dwyfor
Gwasg Efengylaidd Cymru /
   Evangelical Press of Wales
Gwasg Ffrancon
Gwasg Gee
Gwasg Gomer / Gomer Press
Gwasg Gwalia
Gwasg Gwynedd
Gwasg Pantycelyn
Gwasg Prifysgol Cymru /
   University of Wales Press
Gwasg Taf
Gwasg y Dref Wen
Headstart History
Honno
HTV
Hughes a'i Fab
John Jones
Lily Publications
Llanerch Enterprises
Llyfrau'r Faner
Llyfrgell Genedlaethol Cymru /
   National Library of Wales
Ordnance Survey
Paladour Books
Parthian Books
Planet
Pont Books
Qualitex
Sain
Seren Books
Tafol
Tre Graig Press
Tŷ John Penry
Urdd Gobaith Cymru
Y Lolfa

Wholesale distributors of 6000 titles, including Welsh and Anglo-Welsh
books and English-language titles of relevance to Wales.

6.9   MAIN LIBRARY SUPPLIERS

6259 ▰▰▰▰▰▰▰▰▰▰▰▰▰▰▰▰▰▰

ALBANY BOOK CO LTD
30 Clydeholm Road, Glasgow G14 0BJ
Telephone: 0141 954 2271
Fax: 0141 958 1198

Directors: Andrew T. Haigh *(Managing)*
Jonathan Ridge *(Sales & Marketing)*
Joseph Halpin *(Financial)*
Managers: Peter Hughes *(Computer)*
Jane Churchill *(Children's Buyer)*
Ruth Simmons *(Adult Buyer)*

Supplies books, periodicals and journals to public, schools, academic and
special libraries in Scotland, the rest of the UK and overseas. Services
include worldwide ordering, library servicing, promotional lists,
catalogues and events and supply from a substantial stockholding.
Specializations include teenage, Scottish and education books.

6260 ▰▰▰▰▰▰▰▰▰▰▰▰▰▰▰▰▰▰

BURCHELL & MARTIN LTD
34 Granville Street, Birmingham B1 2LJ
Telephone: 0121 643 1888
Fax: 0121 631 3492

Directors: Mrs S. I. Martin *(Managing)*
H. K. I. Burchell

W. M. Kennedy
Company Accountant: M. Brookes
Managers: D. Gray *(General: Sales)*
M. Sutton *(Home Sales)*
Miss D. Smith *(Export Sales)*
Miss S. Little *(Export Projects)*
D. Hamill *(Quotations)*
Bibliographical Services: Miss C. Pillath

UK-based international library and institutional bookseller. Books of all
categories including non-book materials are supplied to all types of
libraries, business and professional organizations; in particular the supply
of educational text or research level books to governments and local
authorities is undertaken. Continuations and standing orders are serviced.
A wide range of book selection aids are available. Full book servicing,
binding and library support materials.

6261 ▰▰▰▰▰▰▰▰▰▰▰▰▰▰▰▰▰▰

DAWSON UK LTD
Cannon House, Folkestone, Kent CT19 5EE
Telephone: 01303 850101
Fax: 01303 850440

Also at:
Crane Close, Denington Road, Wellingborough, Northants NN8 2QG
Telephone: 01933 274444
Fax: 01933 225993

Directors: B. C. Ingleby *(Managing)*
G. Connolly *(Finance)*
Chairman: P. Brown

Three divisions provide a complete service for libraries in the UK and
worldwide.
   Subscriptions: The Subscription Division provides a comprehensive
serials management service in all media: subscription management,
consolidated airfreight services, standing orders, subscriptions on-line,
Key-Facts subscription analysis software, CD-ROM, back issue, single
issues.
   Books: Dawson Book Division offers a proven first-rate service for all
purchasers of British or overseas publications, with expertise in science,
technology, medicine, economics and business. Services include:
Dawson book service, Advance, books on-line, direct on-line link to
HMSO, standing orders, *Presto!* prompt service, antiquarian service.
   Technology: The Technology Division acts as European agent for
OCLC FirstSearch.
   Dawson also publishes *The Dawson Top 3000 Directories and
Annuals*, *Book Auction Records* and *Library & Information News*.

6262 ▰▰▰▰▰▰▰▰▰▰▰▰▰▰▰▰▰▰

T. C. FARRIES & CO LTD
Irongray Road, Lochside, Dumfries DG2 0LH
Telephone: 01387 720755
Fax: 01387 721105
Email: 100023.101@compuserve.com

Directors: D. W. N. Landale *(Chairman)*
T. C. Farries *(Life President)*
P. D. R. Landale *(Managing)*
Mrs L. Bennett *(Sales & Purchasing)*
J. McGrillis *(Financial & Systems)*

Extensive stocks of books, audio-visual products and computer software
held. Full range of services for libraries including processing, servicing,
approvals (UK customers only), bibliographic services, classified
stockroom, regular deliveries, mobile selection service (UK customers
only), subject and level specific lists and collections, publishers specific
promotions to libraries. Services to publishers include stockholding,
promotion special collections, mailing and approvals, mobile selections
service promotions, in-store promotions.
   Types of library customers include academic, public school, medical,
industrial government and institutional, both in the UK and overseas.
Showrooms and stockroom open to the public.

6263

HEFFERS BOOKSELLERS & LIBRARY SUPPLIERS
20 Trinity Street, Cambridge CB2 3NG
Telephone: 01223 568568
Fax: 01223 568591
Email: heffers@heffers.co.uk

Servicing:
Hollin Bridge Street, Bolton Road, Blackburn, Lancs BB2 4BB
Telephone: Blackburn 01254 52092
Fax: 01254 674292

Directors: M. K. Wait *(Managing)*
C. W. Cornell
M. A. Fuller
R. A. Dickinson *(Servicing)*

Established in 1876, Heffers offer access to one of the world's largest stockholding bookshops. A warm welcome awaits visiting librarians. A range of processing and servicing is provided to meet the needs of most libraries.

6264

HELLENIC BOOKSERVICE (THE GREEK BOOKSHOP)
91 Fortess Road, Kentish Town, London NW5 1AG
Telephone: 0171 267 9499
Fax: 0171 267 9498

Partner: Monica Constantinou Williams
Manager: Andrew Stoddart

Established 1966. Specialists in books on all aspects of Greece, Turkey, Latin classics, art, history (ancient and modern), classics, politics, travel, Teach-Yourself books (including cassettes), cookery, mythology, anthropology, Orthodoxy (Byzantium), Greek literature (ancient and modern) in Greek and English. Translations into Greek from many languages and Greek into English; books for children; poetry; maps and newspapers. Also supply the British Library and libraries generally, schools, universities worldwide and individual customers either in the shop or by post.

6265

THE HOLT JACKSON BOOK CO LTD
Preston Road, Lytham, Lancs FY8 5AX
Telephone: 01253 737464
Fax: 01253 733361
Email: info@holtjack.eunet.co.uk

Chairman: J. K. Holden
Directors: J. M. Pewtress
P. A. Jones
K. M. Spencer

6266

INTERNATIONAL PRESS PUBLICATIONS INC
90 Nolan Court, Suite 21, Markham, Ont L3R 4L9, Canada
Telephone: +1 (905) 946 9588
Fax: +1 (905) 946 9590

President: Bali Sethi
Vice-President, Operations: Mrs Rupa
Office Manager: Cissy Wang
Shipping: Savitrie Sookdeo
Accounts: Mr Robert
Finance: Joe Arcuri

Library suppliers of reference books, dictionaries, in all foreign languages, business, trade, medical, government and telephone directories from over 200 countries.
    Subscription agents for the supply of publications on all subjects from different countries.

Publishers and distributors of: *Canadian Research Directory, World Information Directory, Book Trade in Canada, Europa World Year Book, World of Learning, Who's Who in Canada.*

6267

JMLS LTD
PO Box 17, 24 Gamble Street, Nottingham NG7 4FJ
Telephone: 0115 970 8021
Fax: 0115 978 7718

Directors: Suzy Brain England *(Managing)*
O. C. Finnie *(Finance)*
P. A. O'Neill *(Technical Services)*
J. Aspinall *(Sales Strategist)*

Provides comprehensive acquisition service for monographs, continuations and complete bibliographic services to public libraries worldwide. Supported by the latest technology, including the LIBTEL on-line ordering system.

6268

MODERN BOOK SERVICE
33 Beehive Lane, Ilford, Essex IG1 3RG
Telephone: 0181 554 2871

Owner: J. W. S. Cairns

Book suppliers to main libraries, schools, hospitals and universities. Subscription agents for journals and periodicals.

6269

MORLEY BOOKS
Elmfield Road, Morley, Leeds LS27 0NN
Telephone: 0113 253 8811
Fax: 0113 252 7925

London Showroom:
Pegasus House, 116–120 Golden Lane, London EC1Y 0UD
Telephone: 0171 251 2551
Fax: 0171 490 2338

Directors: C. P. Watkins *(Managing)*
L. J. Wolfe
N. Lancaster
F. P. M. Johnston
M. L. A. Chiappelli
N. Ivel
Tim Bowdler

6270

STARKMANN LTD
6 Broadley Street, London NW8 8AE
Telephone: 0171 724 5335
Fax: 0171 724 9863

Delivery Address:
6 Plympton Place, London NW8 8AD

Managing Director: Bernhard Starkmann
Managers: Kishor Chandarana *(Accountant)*
Joachim Bartz *(Sales)*
John Airlie *(Operations)*
Rodney Latham *(I.T.)*

Suppliers of academic and scientific books to university, faculty, industrial and research libraries in Europe. Customers and potential customers receive frequent and accurate new book information. Distribution of the main line publishers from UK, USA, Netherlands, Germany and Switzerland. Supplies made at publisher's list price. Fast airfreight service of US books.

6271 ▬▬▬▬▬▬▬▬▬▬▬▬

WOODFIELD & STANLEY LTD
Broad Lane, Moldgreen, Huddersfield HD5 8DD
Telephone: 01484 421467 & 532401
Fax: 01484 510237

Chairman: J. A. Chadwick
Joint Managing Directors: P. G. Chadwick
R. G. Myers
Company Secretary: J. M. S. Turner
Directors: D. J. Morrell
A. J. Chadwick

Library supply booksellers.

6272 ▬▬▬▬▬▬▬▬▬▬▬▬

ROY YATES BOOKS
Smallfields Cottage, Cox Green, Rudgwick, Horsham, West Sussex
RH12 3DE
Telephone: 01403 822299
Fax: 01403 823012

Managing Director: Roy Yates

Specialist supplier of children's books to schools and libraries; distributes
multilingual books; distributes foreign-language books.

6.10 BOOK CLUBS

6273 ▬▬▬▬▬▬▬▬▬▬▬▬

ARTISTS' CHOICE LTD
The Old Post Office, Bythorn, Huntingdon, Cambs PE18 0QN
Telephone: 01832 710201
Fax: 01832 710488

Managing Director: Henry Malt

Book club aimed at the amateur artist.

6274 ▬▬▬▬▬▬▬▬▬▬▬▬

BCA
87 Newman Street, London W1P 4EN
Telephone: 0171 637 0341
Fax: 0171 323 5665

Chief Executive: Dr M. Herriger
General Manager: J. Roberts *(Editorial & Publishing)*

A partnership of Reed Books International Ltd and Bertelsmann Books
and Magazines Ltd.

Ancient History & Medieval Book Club
Simultaneous book club. Monthly. Founded 1972. Popular archaeology
and history.

Arts Guild
Simultaneous club, founded 1976. Quarterly. Wide range of arts-related
books.

Book Club of Ireland
Books in Ireland. Founded 1990.

Book of the Month Club
Simultaneous book club. Monthly. Founded 1974. General non-fiction
and fiction.

Books Direct
Founded 1988.

Children's Book of the Month Club
Founded 1987.

Classical Music Direct
A tape and compact disc club. Classical music. Bi-monthly. Founded
1981.

English Book Clubs
Founded 1974. English language books in Netherlands, Germany, France,
Sweden and Norway.

Executive World
Founded 1985. Business and management books.

Fantasy & SF Book Club
Simultaneous book club, founded 1978. Bi-monthly. Science fiction,
magic, occult, the unexplained, paranormal phenomena.

History Guild
Simultaneous book club, founded 1973. General history.

Home Computer Club
Founded 1984. Home computer software and related books.

The Literary Guild
Simultaneous book club. Monthly. Founded 1968. General non-fiction
and some fiction.

Military & Aviation Book Society
Simultaneous book club. Monthly. Warfare, ancient and modern, land,
sea and air. Founded 1977.

Music Direct
A tape and compact disc club. Popular music. Bi-monthly. Founded 1988.

Mystery & Thriller Guild
Simultaneous book club. Monthly. Founded 1972. Crime fiction.

New Home & Garden Guild
Relaunch of a simultaneous quarterly book club launched in 1977.

On the Road
Simultaneous club, founded 1981. Quarterly. Wide range of motor/
transport-related books.

QPD (Quality Paperbacks Direct)
Paperback books. Bi-monthly. Founded 1990.

Railway Book Club
Simultaneous club, founded 1979. Quarterly. Wide range of railway-
related books.

Readers Choice
Simultaneous book club. Quarterly. Founded 1976. Popular fiction and
non-fiction.

Video Direct
Founded 1989. Pre-recorded video tapes.

World Books
Previously The Reprint Society. Founded 1939. Monthly reprint book
club. Popular fiction and non-fiction.

6275 ▬▬▬▬▬▬▬▬▬▬▬▬

BIBLIOPHILE BOOKS
5 Thomas Road, London E14 7BN
Telephone: 0171 515 9222
Fax: 0171 538 4115

General Manager: Anne Quigley
Distribution Manager: Keith Higgins

Produces 10 catalogues a year, offering books at bargain prices to private
buyers. Range: general, eg biography, history, travel, handicrafts,
humour, literature.

6276 ▬▬▬▬▬▬▬▬▬▬▬▬▬▬▬▬▬▬

BOOKMARKS CLUB
265 Seven Sisters Road, London N4 2DE
Telephone: 0181 802 6145
Fax: 0181 802 3835

A book club for socialists offering the best of political paperbacks and hardbacks at a discount to members. Organized by Bookmarks Bookshop (membership requires taking a minimum quantity of books each year).

6277 ▬▬▬▬▬▬▬▬▬▬▬▬▬▬▬▬▬▬

BOOKS FOR CHILDREN
4 Furzeground Way, Stockley Park, Middx UB11 1DP
Telephone: 0181 606 3090
Fax: 0181 606 3099

Membership Services & Warehouse:
McIntyre & King, Harrington Dock, Liverpool L70 1AX
Telephone: 051-708 8141
Fax: 051-708 8125

Directors: Shelagh Casebourne *(Editorial)*
Brian Angle *(Finance)*
Paul Busby *(Marketing)*

Simultaneous book club. Fifteen previews per annum. Five divisions by age: 0–2, 2–4, 4–6, 6–9, 9–12.
Sponsors of The Mother Goose Award for the most exciting newcomer to British children's book illustrations, and the Eleanor Farjeon Award presented annually by the Children's Book Circle for distinguished services to children's books.

Parent Company: Time Life Entertainments Ltd.

6278 ▬▬▬▬▬▬▬▬▬▬▬▬▬▬▬▬▬▬

BOOKWORM BOOK CLUB
Heffers Booksellers, Rustat House, 60 Clifton Road, Cambridge CB1 4FY
Telephone: 01223 568650
Fax: 01223 568591
Email: clubs@heffers.co.uk

Manager: Philippa Reece

The Bookworm Club, now including the Early Worm Club, is a paperback bookclub run in schools and groups for children up to the age of 13. There are six fresh selections a year and each offers a wide range of books from all the major British publishers. Each child receives a copy of the *Club News* to take home and the *Teacher's Notes* give extra information and advice. There are free giveaways and posters throughout the year.

6279 ▬▬▬▬▬▬▬▬▬▬▬▬▬▬▬▬▬▬

LETTERBOX LIBRARY
2nd Floor, Leroy House, 436 Essex Road, London N1 3QP
Telephone: 0171 226 1633
Fax: 0171 226 1768

Co-operative Members: Gillian Harris
Alison Blake
Mai Kim Stern
Sally Hill
Angela Bovell
Susanna McKnight
Sue Slater

Letterbox Library is a children's book club specializing in non-sexist and multi-cultural books for all ages. Quarterly catalogues are produced with up to 50 new titles, offered at discounts to members. The books selected avoid stereotyped images of male and female roles showing, for example, adventurous girls and caring, sensitive boys, working mothers or men involved in child care. As far as possible books are chosen which will reflect the UK's multi-ethnic society. A small one-off membership fee of £5 entitles members to quarterly catalogues and newsletters.

Letterbox Library is run co-operatively. Apart from operating the book club they will do book displays for schools and libraries, attend exhibitions and give talks on sexism in children's literature.

6280 ▬▬▬▬▬▬▬▬▬▬▬▬▬▬▬▬▬▬

READERS UNION
Brunel House, Newton Abbot, Devon TQ12 2DW
Telephone: 01626 336424
Fax: 01626 331374

Directors: Colin Sage *(Operational)*
Neil Page *(Finance)*

Country Sports Book Society
Quarterly book club. Covers all field sports – technique and equipment, including game fishing.

Craftsman Book Society
Quarterly. Woodcrafts of all types.

Creative Books Plus
Quarterly book club. Covers all home/garden interests, craft and female interest.

Creative Living
Quarterly book club. Books on all aspects of the home (craft, decorating, entertaining, furnishing, etc) and garden.

Equestrian Book Society
Quarterly book club. Covers all aspects of equestrian sports.

Gardeners Book Society
Quarterly book club. Gardening, especially practical books.

Needlecrafts with Cross Stitch Book Society
Quarterly book club. Books on knitting, sewing, toymaking, embroidery, etc.

Photographic Book Society
Quarterly book club. Covers all aspects of photography to an advanced level.

Ramblers & Climbers Book Society
Quarterly book club. Covers all aspects of walking and climbing.

6281 ▬▬▬▬▬▬▬▬▬▬▬▬▬▬▬▬▬▬

RED HOUSE CHILDREN'S BOOK CLUB
Windrush Park, Witney, Oxon OX8 5YF
Telephone: 01993 774171 & 771144
Fax: 01993 776813

Director: David Teale

A book club selling books and cassettes for children of all ages and their parents. Members are mailed 13 times a year. School book clubs for ages 3 to 16 years.

6282 ▬▬▬▬▬▬▬▬▬▬▬▬▬▬▬▬▬▬

SCHOLASTIC LTD
Villiers House, Clarendon Avenue, Leamington Spa, Warks CV32 5PR
Telephone: 01926 887799
Fax: 01926 431590
Email: scholastic@tcns.co.uk
Web Site: http://www.scholastic.co.uk

Also at:
Westfield Road, Southam, Warks CV33 0JH
Telephone: 01926 887799
Fax: 01926 817727

and:
Scholastic Children's Books, 7–9 Pratt Street, London NW1 0AE

Managing Director: D. M. R. Kewley
Directors: Annie Peel
Gavin Lang
David Fickling
Ian Bloodworth
David Bleasdale
Marketing Managers: Gareth Evans *(Book Fairs & Educational Books)*
Colin Cole *(Book Clubs & Magazines)*

Scholastic Ltd operates five children's and teachers' book clubs; and
publishes teacher magazines, including *Child Education* and *Junior
Education*. Bright Ideas, Inspirations, Bright Ideas for Early Years
resource books and Hippo children's paperbacks, educational and
children's publishing division.

The four children's book clubs, *See-Saw* (0–6 years), *Lucky* (7–9
years), *Chip* (9–12 years) and *Scene* (12–16 years), are run in over 12,000
schools and playgroups throughout the UK. Each club offers a wide range
of books at special club prices, with a colourful copy of club news for each
child and a class poster with every monthly offer during term time.

As a special service to teachers who organize the children's clubs,
Criterion, the teachers' book club, offers the best of new material from
educational publishers.

Scholastic book fairs: four mobile book cases are delivered to the
school for six days. Children, parents and teachers can choose books. The
school gets commission on all purchases.

6283 ▬

THE SOFTBACK REVIEW
Time-Life UK, 4 Furzeground Way, Stockley Park, Middlesex
UB11 1DP
Telephone: 0181 606 3073
Fax: 0181 606 3099

Directors: Chris Holifield *(Publishing)*
Paul Burby *(Marketing)*
Brian Angle *(Financial)*

The Softback Review (TSP) is a general book club, specializing
particularly in serious non-fiction titles, such as history, science,
reference, psychology and philosophy, but also offering literary fiction
and some genre fiction. Founded in 1990, it has grown steadily and aims
to offer its members a wide range of stimulating and well-written books
which would appeal to the intelligent general reader. All titles are sourced
from publishers and most of them are printed by the publishers in the
softback format used by TSP.

TSP is a no-commitment club, meaning that the members are not
obliged to buy a set number of books from the club, but membership must
be for at least six Previews.

6.11 LITERARY & TRADE EVENTS

6284 ▬

**AMERICAN BOOKSELLERS ASSOCIATION CONVENTION
& TRADE EXHIBIT**
383 Main Avenue, Norwalk, CT 06851, USA
Telephone: +1 (203) 840 5614
Fax: +1 (203) 840 9614

Vice-President: Jon Leibowitz *(Organizer of Meetings & Conventions)*

The annual convention and trade exhibit has grown from a meeting of 35
booksellers to a convention of over 40,000 industry professionals:
booksellers, publishers, agents, libraries, and others active in the book
community. The ABA convention and trade exhibit is one of the leading
events for the business of books in all formats.

6285 ▬

APA AUSTRALIAN BOOK FAIR
c/o Australian Publishers Association Ltd, 60/89 Jones Street, Ultimo,
NSW, Australia 2007
Telephone: +61 (02) 281 9788
Fax: +61 (02) 281 1073

Executive Director: Susan Blackwell

The APA Australian Book Fair is held annually in July in Sydney. The fair
runs for four days. On the first two days the fair is open only to the book
trade. The fair is attracting many visitors from the Asia Pacific region and
it is becoming a focus for rights and co-edition negotiations in the region.
On the last two days, the weekend, the fair is open to the public of whom
over 80,000 attend. Books are sold on the public days and an extensive
programme of activities involving authors is organized. The fair has been
running since 1992.

6286 ▬

BOK & BIBLIOTEK
Box 5222, 40 227 Göteborg, Sweden
Telephone: +46 (31) 819655
Fax: +46 (31) 209103

Director: Bertil Falck
Sales Manager: Suzanne Ohlson
Conference Managers: Gunilla Sandin
Bo A. Karlsson
Administration: Siv Johansson-Falk

The Book and Library Fair in Göteborg is an annual event open to authors,
publishers, editors, agents, booksellers, journalists, teachers, librarians,
politicians and the public.

In conjunction with the Fair, there is a conference programme which
includes presentations, debates, readings, talks and discussions.

6287 ▬

BOOK PRINT (LONDON)
c/o PAMS Promotions Ltd, St Ives House, Faringdon Avenue,
Harold Hill, Romford, Essex RM3 8XL
Telephone: 01708 340059
Fax: 01708 342818

Exhibition Contact: Tracy Johnson

1997 Fair: 16–18 March at Olympia Grand Hall.

6288 ▬

**BOOK TRADE SERVICES REMAINDER & PROMOTIONAL
BOOKS (FRANKFURT)**
c/o PAMS Promotions Ltd, St Ives House, Faringdon Avenue,
Harold Hill, Romford, Essex RM3 8XL
Telephone: 01708 340059
Fax: 01708 342818

Exhibition Contact: Tracy Johnson

1995 Fair: 11–16 October.
1996 Fair: 2–7 October.
Venue: Frankfurt Book Fair, Hall 7.
Visitor attendance: 250,000; number of exhibitors: 8500; size of
exhibition: 80,000 sq m.
Times: 9 am to 6 pm Wednesday to Sunday; 9 am to 2 pm Monday.

6289 ▬

BOOKSELLERS ASSOCIATION ANNUAL CONFERENCE
Minster House, 272 Vauxhall Bridge Road, London SW1V 1BA
Telephone: 0171 834 5477
Fax: 0171 834 8812

Director: Tim Godfray
Conference Organizer: Meryl Halls

Major UK book trade event. The Conference provides opportunity for
those supplying or serving the retail book trade to meet trade customers
and for both to learn from business programme. **Details from:** above
address.

6290

CAIRO INTERNATIONAL BOOK FAIR
General Egyptian Book Organization, Cournich El-Nil, Boulac, Cairo, Egypt
Telephone: 775371
Fax: 5754213

Deputy Minister: Samir Saad Khalil

Annual. Ever since its establishment as a city more than 1000 years ago, Cairo has been a centre of cultural and trade activities and has attracted millions of visitors. The international reputation of the Cairo Fair derives from a dynamic orientation toward the future. This event is a major attraction both for the public at large and for the business professionals.
Details from: Samir Saad Khalil, General Director.

6291

CHELTENHAM FESTIVAL OF LITERATURE
Town Hall, Imperial Square, Cheltenham, Glos GL50 1QA
Telephone: 01242 521621
Fax: 01242 573902

Festival Administrator: Jeremy Tyndall
Festival Organizer: Sarah Smyth

Annual in October. Promoted by Cheltenham Arts Festivals Ltd. Performances, poetry readings, talks and discussions by literary personalities. Includes Book It! Festival for Children, Youth Drama Festival.
Details from: The Festival Organizer.

6292

CHILDREN'S BOOK WEEK
Book House, 45 East Hill, Wandsworth, London SW18 2QZ
Telephone: 0181 870 9055
Fax: 0181 874 4790
Email: booktrust@dial.pipex.com

Patron: HRH The Prince Philip, Duke of Edinburgh
Chief Executive: Brian Perman
Chairman: Martyn Goff, OBE

Children's Book Week is an annual event which takes place every October. It is administered by Young Book Trust. Book Week is a national event promoting the idea that reading and books are fun!
   Promotional material is available as is advice and support for those organizing book events for children. Schools, libraries, bookshops and book groups throughout the country are encouraged to participate. Young Book Trust works with all forms of the media to focus attention and raise awareness of children's books and reading, in their many guises, throughout the week. Subscribers to Young Book Trust automatically receive a free pack of Book Week material.

6293

CHRISTIAN BOOKSELLERS CONVENTION
Unit C, 41 Dace Road, London E3 2NG
Telephone: 0181 986 0178
Fax: 0181 986 1531

Held annually since 1976. Also includes a residential conference consisting of training seminars for bookshop managers and staff. **Details from:** Miss Jean S. Wilson.

6294

CIANA LTD
4/5 Academy Buildings, Fanshaw Street, London N1 6LQ
Telephone: 0171 613 4446
Fax: 0171 613 4513

Directors: Robert Collie
Sarah Isaac
Adam Bloom

Organizers of the annual London Remainder and Promotional Book Fair in September, and the Northern Remainder and Promotional Book Fair in January.

6295

EDINBURGH BOOK FESTIVAL
Scottish Book Centre, 137 Dundee Street, Edinburgh EH11 1BG
Telephone: 0131 228 5444
Fax: 0131 228 4333

Director: Jan Fairley

The Edinburgh Book Festival began in 1983. EBF is a biennial festival and the seven staged so far have seen over 1000 different author appearances. It exists to promote books and reading to all ages and is primarily for the public.
   Publishers are invited to take stands or submit titles for the general exhibition. All books are for sale and restocking and sales are all handled by EBF staff on behalf of the publishers.
   The next Edinburgh Book Festival will be held 9–25 August 1997.
Details from: above address.

6296

ELECTRONIC BOOKS
Mecklermedia Ltd, Artillery House, Artillery Row, London SW1P 1RT
Telephone: 0171 976 0405
Fax: 0171 976 0506

6297

ELECTRONIC PUBLISHING 96
Learned Information Europe Ltd, Woodside, Hinksey Hill, Oxford OX1 5BE
Telephone: 01865 730275
Fax: 01865 736354

Next: RSA Centre, London, 9–10 October 1996.
   Contact: Catherine Graham.

6298

EUSIDIC
PO Box 1416, 1014 Luxembourg
Fax: +352 250 750 222
Web Site: http://www.vito.be/eusidic

Eusidic, the association for the electronic information sector, is holding its 1996 annual conference from 14 to 16 October in Bologna. The conference will re-examine the developments that affect how information is created, distributed and consumed.

6299

FRANKFURT BOOK FAIR
PO Box 100116, 60001 Frankfurt am Main, Germany
Telephone: +49 69 2102 0
Fax: +49 69 2102 227 & 277
Email: weber@book-fair.com
Web Site: http://www.frankfurt-book-fair.com

Delivery Address:
Reineckstraße 3, 60313 Frankfurt am Main, Germany

Director: Peter Weidhaas
Deputy Executive Director: Joachim Kehl
   Contacts: Franz Fenke *(Technical Director (for exhibitors))*
Ronald Weber *(Promotion Manager (for trade visitors))*

The Frankfurt Book Fair is the largest event of its kind in the world. Annual participation stands at 8800 exhibitors from 97 countries and 320,000 visitors. The Multimedia Hall at the Frankfurt Book Fair is a showcase for the latest electronic media innovations.
   Open exclusively to the trade for four days and to the public for two days it attracts publishers, booksellers, authors, distributors and the whole range of multimedia companies.

1997 Fair: 15–20 October.
1998 Fair: 7–12 October.

6300

JERUSALEM INTERNATIONAL BOOK FAIR
8 Shlomzion Hamalka Street, PO Box 775, Jerusalem 91007, Israel
Telephone: +972 (02) 624 0663 & 624 5142
Fax: +972 (02) 624 3144

Managing Director: Zev Birger
Deputy Director: Yoel Makov
Events Co-ordinators: Ms Annette Aaronson
Assistant to Director: Ms Hila Nir

Biennial since 1963 under the sponsorship of the Municipality of
Jerusalem. Recent Book Fairs have seen tremendous growth, attendance
increasing to over 60,000, with 1200 publishing imprints from over 50
countries displaying their publications to publishers, editors, writers,
translators and agents.
   Events taking place during the Fair: the Jerusalem Prize, Aspen
Institute Jerusalem International Book Fair Forum, the Jerusalem
International Symposium on Encouraging Reading and Editorial
Fellowship Programme.
   The 18th Jerusalem International Book Fair will take place 6–11 April
1997.

6301

LEIPZIG BOOK FAIR
CZ Scientific Instruments, PO Box 43, 1 Elstree Way, Borehamwood,
Herts WD6 1NH
Telephone: 0181 953 1688
Fax: 0181 953 9456

Agency Director: Nicholas Bloxam

The Leipzig Book Fair is an independent, general book fair concentrating
on the German-speaking countries of Europe (Germany, Austria and
Switzerland). However, it also features international book art and is
additionally characterized by a general theme which changes from year to
year and which is highlighted by special events relating to this theme. The
commercial aspect of the Leipzig Book Fair is accompanied by a wide
range of fringe events, including a section for antique books and prints.
   Visitors to the Leipzig Book Fair are mainly made up of representatives
from publishers, the book trade, libraries, the newer media, the printing
industry, and all other areas connected with the production of books,
including book illustrators and graphic designers.
   1997 Fair: 20–23 March.

6302

LIBTECH – INTERNATIONAL LIBRARY TECHNOLOGY FAIR
University of Hertfordshire, College Lane, Hatfield, Herts AL10 9AD
Telephone: 01707 284665
Fax: 01707 248666

Next: 4–5 September 1996; University of Hertfordshire, UK.

6303

LONDON INTERNATIONAL BOOK FAIR
Oriel House, 26 The Quadrant, Richmond, Surrey TW9 1DL
Telephone: 0181 910 7933
Fax: 0181 910 7930

Director: Mike Allsopp
Manager: Helen McLachlan *(Marketing)*
Sales Executive: Kari Olsen

Established in 1971. An international trade marketplace held in the spring
at which several hundred UK and international publishers exhibit, as well
as other suppliers and service companies in the book trade. The Fair takes
place within the Grand Hall, Olympia, Kensington, London W14. Trade
visitors welcome, including literary agents, booksellers, librarians,
teachers, authors etc. The public will be allowed in at certain times.
   1997 Fair: 16–18 March.

6304

MILIA – INTERNATIONAL ILLUSTRATED BOOK & NEW MEDIA PUBLISHING FAIR
Reed Midem, 9–11 rue du Colonel Pierre Avia, BP 572,
75726 Paris Cedex, France
Telephone: +33 1 41 90 44 00
Fax: +33 1 41 90 44 50

Next: 9–12 February 1997; Palais des Festivals et des Congrès, Cannes,
France.

6305

ONLINE – EUROPEAN CONGRESS & FAIR FOR TECHNICAL COMMUNICATIONS
Online GmbH, Postfach 10 08 66, Nevigeser Strasse 131, 42553 Velbert,
Germany
Telephone: +49 2051 28520
Fax: +49 2051 28519

Next: 4–7 February 1997; Hamburg, Germany.
   Contact: Dipl. Ing. Albin Ockl.

6306

OVERSEAS BOOK SERVICE
Via Paradurone 16, 40053 Bazzano (BO), Italy
Telephone: +39 (051) 830588
Fax: +39 (051) 830588
Email: rod2410@iperbole.bologna.it

Partners: Thomas Sims
Kelly Galusha

Overseas Book Service is an independent collective book exhibitor
specializing in international book fairs.
   As well as exhibiting publishers' products, taking orders and
distributing publicity material, our staff will initiate the negotiation of
rights sales upon instruction. A special fair catalogue listing all titles and
publishers exhibiting on our stand is prepared for each show.
   Our stands are staffed at all times by people with experience in
publishing. Publicity mailings are made to a wide selection of
distributors, publishers and publishers' agents in advance of exhibitions.
After the fair a general report of the fair as well as detailed information on
the contacts made for each publisher exhibiting on our stand is produced.
   Some of the shows we will be attending in 1997 are:
   – London International Book Fair
   – Children's International Book Fair
   – Warsaw International Book Fair
   – Frankfurt International Book Fair.

6307

*PAMS PROMOTIONS
St Ives House, Faringdon Avenue, Harold Hill, Romford, Essex
RM3 8XL
Telephone: 01708 340059
Fax: 01708 342818

Exhibition Contact: Tracy Johnson

6308

SALON DU LIVRE
OIP, 62 rue de Miromesnil, 75008 Paris, France
Telephone: +33 (1) 49 53 27 00
Fax: +33 (1) 49 53 27 88

General Commissioner: Jean-Marc de Chauvigny
Fair Manager: Xavier Delmas
Communication: Henri Jobbé-Duval
Exhibitors Relations: Marie-Hélène Pasdeloup
Christophe Conte
Taya de Reyniès
Press Relations: Nadine Brianceau
Marie-Victoire Boudillet *(Assistant)*

Animations: Taya de Reyniès
Laurence Nérée

Annual public book fair, organized by the 'Syndicat National de
l'Edition'.
   Visitors attendance: 200,000; number of exhibitors: 1400 publishers
put together on 500 stands plus 120 multi-media exhibitors; size of
exhibition: 35,000 sq m; stands surface: 18,000 sq m; exhibitors profile:
publishers, CDI, CD-ROM makers.
   1997 Fair: 12–17 March at the Parc des Expositions, Porte de
Versailles, Hall 1, Paris. Theme: French, French speaking and foreign
edition. Times: daily from 10 am to 7 pm; late evening Thursday until 11
pm.

6309

SALON DU LIVRE DE JEUNESSE
OIP, 62 rue de Miromesnil, 75008 Paris, France
Telephone: +33 (1) 49 53 27 00
Fax: +33 (1) 49 53 27 88

Organization: Henriette Zoughebi
Communication & Press: Nathalie Donikian
Relations with Exhibitors: Xavier Delmas
Jean-Pascal Jullien

Annual, public book fair.
   The 1995 Fair, with an area covering 12,000 sq m, welcomed 55,000
visitors and 150 exhibitors.

6310

SALON DU LIVRE DE MONTREAL
480 St-Laurent, Ste 202, Montreal, PQ, Canada H2Y 3Y7
Telephone: +1 (514) 845 2365
Fax: +1 (514) 845 7119

General Manager: Francine Bois
Exhibitors Service: Noreen Belanger

The Salon du Livre de Montréal is a public book fair which aims to
promote reading.

6311

**SANTIAGO INTERNATIONAL BOOK FAIR (CÁMARA
CHILENA DEL LIBRO)**
Av. Libertador Bernardo O'Higgins 1370, Oficina 501, (Casilla Postal 13.
526), Santiago, Chile
Telephone: +56 (02) 6989519 & 6724088
Fax: +56 (02) 6989226

President: Eduardo Castillo
Manager: Carlos Franz

6312

SAUDI EDUCATION '97
Overseas Exhibition Services Ltd, 11 Manchester Square, London
W1M 5AB
Telephone: 0171 486 1951
Fax: 0171 935 8625

Project Manager: Philip Walsh
Project Director: Gerry Dobson

Saudi Education '97 is the ninth in a biennial series of education and
training events. It will take place at the Riyadh Exhibition Centre from 2
to 6 March 1997. An important aspect of the exhibit profile is relevant
literature, ie textbooks; English as a foreign language (EFL) material;
science, medical and technical (SMT) material; reference books;
children's books, etc.
   Saudi Education '97 runs alongside Saudi Computer '97, 14th
Computer and Computer Graphics Show.

6313

SCHOOL BOOK FAIRS LTD
5 Airspeed Road, Priory Industrial Park, Christchurch, Dorset BH23 4HD
Telephone: 01425 279171
Fax: 01425 275062

Directors: Philip J. Hodson *(Managing)*
Robert Merrell *(Operations)*
Manager: Laurence Pine *(Distribution)*

School Book Fairs offer a wide range of leisure reading books suitable for
children in the age range 5–13 years. Book Fairs are held in schools. All
leading publishers of children's books are represented.

6314

ZIMBABWE INTERNATIONAL BOOK FAIR
PO Box CY 1179, Causeway, 78 Kaguvi Street, Harare, Zimbabwe
Telephone: +263 (4) 750282
Fax: +263 (4) 751202
Email: zibf@mango.zw

Chairperson: Elliot Mugamu
Executive Director: Trish Mbanga

Independent Trust, representing publishers, booksellers, writers and
relevant ministry officials, formed to run the annual Zimbabwe
International Book Fair in Harare. Previous fairs, with participation from
countries throughout the region, and internationally, have established
Harare as the major event for publishing in Africa. Concurrent theme-
related events, including writers' workshop, ensure wide participation of
professionals and public.
   1997 Fair: 4–9 August. Main theme: Libraries.

6.12 PUBLISHING REFERENCE
BOOKS & PERIODICALS

6315

100 BEST BOOKS
Young Book Trust, Book House, 45 East Hill, Wandsworth, London
SW18 2QZ
Telephone: 0181 870 9055
Fax: 0181 874 4790

Patron: HRH The Prince Philip, Duke of Edinburgh
Executive Director: Brian Perman
Chairman: Martyn Goff, OBE
Head of Young Book Trust: Lindsey Fraser
Children's Co-ordinator: Marsha Cawthorne

ISBN: 0 85353 455 1

Published 10 April 1995, 32 pp, £1.

A guide to the best of new paperbacks for children. *100 Best Books: The
Big Stories for Children*, published by Young Book Trust, is an
independent guide to the best of new paperback fiction and picture books
for children from 0 to 12+ years.
   In an accessible 32-page A5 format, each book gets a snappy
introduction, an invaluable age range and interest level coding, plus all the
bibliographic details necessary for easy selection in bookshops and
libraries.

6316

THE AFRICAN BOOK PUBLISHING RECORD
Hans Zell Publishers, PO Box 56, Oxford OX1 2SJ
Telephone: 01865 511428
Fax: 01865 311534

Also at:
Hans Zell Publishers, Bowker-Saur, Maypole House, Maypole Road,
East Grinstead, West Sussex RH19 1HU

Telephone: 01342 330100
Fax: 01342 330191

Editor: Hans M. Zell
Assistant Editor: Cécile Lomer

ISSN: 0306-0322

Quarterly in March, June, September, December. £115 annually.

Comprehensive bibliographic coverage of new and forthcoming African publications in English and French, and significant new titles in African languages. Supplements and updates *African Books in Print*, and provides a buying and acquisitions tool for librarians and booksellers. Serves as a medium of communication between the African book professions, and features news, reports, interviews and articles about African book trade activities and developments. Also includes an extensive book review section, plus reviews of new African serials.
    Information about advertising rates available on request.

6317

THE AFRICAN BOOK WORLD & PRESS: A DIRECTORY / RÉPERTOIRE DU LIVRE ET DE LA PRESSE EN AFRIQUE
Hans Zell Publishers, Maypole House, Maypole Road, East Grinstead, West Sussex RH19 1HU
Telephone: 01342 330100
Fax: 01342 330191
Email: custserv@bowker-saur.co.uk
Web Site: http://www.bowker-saur.co.uk/service/

Editorial Office:
11 Richmond Road, PO Box 56, Oxford OX1 2SJ
Telephone: 01865 511428
Fax: 01865 311534 & 793298

Editor: Hans M. Zell

4th revised edition (1989), £79. 5th edition due 1995.

Provides comprehensive information in English and French on libraries, publishers, the retail book trade, research institutions with publishing programmes, magazines, periodicals, major newspapers and major printers throughout Africa. Total of over 4600 entries, arranged in country-by-country sections. There are subject indexes to special libraries and periodicals; a series of appendices provide information about book clubs, literary prizes, book fairs, news agencies in Africa; and there is an annotated directory of principal dealers in African books outside Africa.

6318

AFRICAN BOOKS IN PRINT
Customer Services Department, Bowker-Saur, Maypole House, Maypole Road, East Grinstead, West Sussex RH19 1HU
Telephone: 01342 330100
Fax: 01342 330191

Directors: Charles Halpin *(Managing)*
Gerard Dummett *(Marketing)*
John Sands *(Technical Services)*

ISBN: 1 873836 11 2

1993 edition, 2 vols, 1520 pp, £259.

6319

AFRICAN PUBLISHERS' NETWORK
78 Kaguvi Street, Harare, Zimbabwe
Telephone: +263 (04) 751202
Fax: +263 (04) 751202

Postal Address:
PO Box 3773, Harare, Zimbabwe

Editor: Humphrey Lesley

Networking of African publishers through their Publishers Associations.
    Newsletter *African Publishing Review* is published six times a year and distributed free to all African publishers. It is available to other organizations on subscription: US$25 (airmail US$30) inside Africa, US$40 (airmail US$50) outside Africa. Also available in French.

6320

AMERICAN BOOK TRADE DIRECTORY
Customer Services Department, Bowker-Saur, Maypole House, Maypole Road, East Grinstead, West Sussex RH19 1HU
Telephone: 01342 330100
Fax: 01342 330191

ISBN: 0 8352 3582 3

41st edition published June 1995; 1800 pp; £200.

Provides access to over 27,500 bookstores, wholesalers and distributors throughout the US and Canada, arranged alphabetically by state and city.

6321

AMERICAN LIBRARY DIRECTORY
Customer Services Department, Bowker-Saur, Maypole House, Maypole Road, East Grinstead, West Sussex RH19 1HU
Telephone: 01342 330100
Fax: 01342 330191

ISBN: 0 8352 3583 1

1995–96 edition, 2 vols July 1995; 2200 pp; £215.

Find the most complete up-to-date information available on more than 38,000 public, academic, special and governmental libraries.

6322

AUSTRALIAN BOOKS IN PRINT
D. W. Thorpe, 18 Salmon Street, Port Melbourne, Vic, Australia 3207
Telephone: +61 (03) 9245 7370
Fax: +61 (03) 9245 7395

Managing Director: Michael Webster
Manager: Victoria Matthews *(Bibliographic Services)*

6323

AUSTRALIAN BOOKSELLER & PUBLISHER
D. W. Thorpe, 18 Salmon Street, Port Melbourne, Vic, Australia 3207
Telephone: +61 (03) 9245 7370
Fax: +61 (03) 9245 7395

Managing Director: Michael Webster
Editor: Kim Hutchins
Advertising Manager: Oriana Ruffini

6324

THE AUTHOR
84 Drayton Gardens, London SW10 9SB
Telephone: 0171 373 6642

Editor: Derek Parker
Manager: Kate Pool

Free to members. £7, post free, per copy for others. Annual subscription: £24, post free.

The quarterly journal of the Society of Authors. Articles on the legal, commercial and technical side of authorship.

6325

BENN'S MEDIA
Miller Freeman Information Services, Riverbank House, Angel Lane, Tonbridge, Kent TN9 1SE

Telephone: 01732 362880
Fax: 01732 367301

Senior Marketing Executive: Craig Curtis
Publishing Manager: Sara Creech

ISBN: 0 86382 254 1 (UK volume); 0 86382 255 X (European volume); 0 86382 256 8 (World volume); 0 86382 233 9 (UK & European volumes); 0 86382 257 6 (UK & World volumes); 0 86382 258 4 (European & World volumes); 0 86382 259 2 (UK); 0 86382 260 6 (European & World volumes).

An annual publication in 3 volumes; the 1996 edition was published January 1996. Prices: £110 (individual volumes; UK, Europe, World); £210 (any two volumes); £265 (three-volume set). Freight prices: £4.50 post and packing if ordering within the UK; £15, 1 volume; £20, 2 volumes; £30, 3 volumes (to be added when ordering from outside the UK).

Benn's Media provides easy-to-use, essential information on newspapers, periodicals and broadcasting media throughout the world; plus in the UK volume, publishing houses, media organizations and services. International and Inflight Media are included in the Europe and World volumes.

'UK' gives complete coverage of the UK market. 'Europe' covers 48 European countries (excluding UK), and 'World' covers Asia (with the Middle East), Africa, the Americas and Australasia.

6326

BEST BOOKS FOR PUBLIC LIBRARIES
Customer Services Department, Bowker-Saur, Maypole House, Maypole Road, East Grinstead, West Sussex RH19 1HU
Telephone: 01342 330100
Fax: 01342 330191

ISBN: 0 8352 3073 2

Published December 1992. Imprint: R. R. Bowker, 840 pp, hbk, £65.

This brand new title provides a development guide for librarians, with over 10,000 descriptions and reviews. It targets the most acclaimed works in all categories, and presents positive reviews from a wealth of respected sources including: *Library Journal, Booklist, Choice, The New Yorker, The New York Times Book Review, Time* and many others.

6327

BIBLIOLOG
Trade Service Information Ltd, Cherryholt Road, Stamford, Lincolnshire PE9 2HT
Telephone: 01780 64331
Fax: 01780 482067

Managing Director: Michael Bullard
Managers: Glyn Reed *(Strategic Business Development)*
Derek Free *(Sales)*

Subscription: £9.50 per month.

Bibliolog is a directory of spoken word recordings that are currently available for rent or retail.

Thousands of spoken word recordings are indexed by author, performer/reader, title and genre, which makes finding titles easier than ever.

Bibliolog is used by public libraries and booksellers throughout the UK to keep track of new titles and all currently available recordings. Monthly updates make sure Bibliolog and its users are always up to date with spoken word recordings. ISBN and catalogue numbers, distributor and label information are all provided to aid the ordering process.

6328

BOOK NEWS INC
5600 NE Hassalo Street, Portland, OR 97213, USA
Telephone: +1 (503) 281 9230
Fax: +1 (503) 287 4485

Email: booknews@booknews.com
Web Site: http://www.books.com/booknews

Publisher: Fred Gullette
Editor: Jane Erskine

Books News Inc publishes two bibliographic periodicals that inform librarians and other book-buyers of newly published books from English-language publishers worldwide. The two periodicals give full bibliographic data with concise annotations for some 700–1000 new books in each issue.

SciTech Book News (1976–) is published eight times per year, concentrating on high-level books in technology, engineering, computers, medicine, and the physical and biological sciences.

Reference & Research Book News (1986–) is published eight times a year and focuses on reference and scholarly works. It now incorporates *University Press Book News*, and cites books from the world's university presses.

In addition to publishing the two periodicals, Book News makes use of its extensive database to enhance a number of online and CD-ROM book information sources and to produce store catalogues and direct mail promotions for bookstores and wholesalers.

Book News annotations and reviews are displayed full text on Bowker's CD-ROM, *Books in Print with Reviews PLUS*. Indexing is in *Book Review Index*.

6329

BOOKS FOR KEEPS
6 Brightfield Road, Lee, London SE12 8QF
Telephone: 0181 852 4953

Directors: Chris Powling *(Editor)*
Richard Hill *(Managing)*

ISSN: 0143-909X

6 issues pa. Annual subscription: £16.20 (UK).

Children's books review journal aimed at anyone who is involved with children and books. It contains reviews of fiction and non-fiction, articles, author features, practical information and news.

6330

BOOKS IN PRINT
Customer Services Department, Bowker-Saur, Maypole House, Maypole Road, East Grinstead, West Sussex RH19 1HU
Telephone: 01342 330100
Fax: 01342 330191

ISBN: 0 8352 3644 7

1995–96 edition, published October 1995, 10 volumes, 14750 pp, £395.

Full bibliographic and ordering information for over one million titles published or distributed in the USA. There are 174,000 titles new to this edition.

6331

BOOKS IN THE MEDIA
Bookwatch Ltd, 15-Up, East Street, Lewin's Yard, Chesham, Bucks HP5 1HQ
Telephone: 01494 792269
Fax: 01494 784850

Publisher: Peter Harland *(Advertising)*
Editor: Sophie Walker
Helpline: Jennifer Harland
Subscriptions: Marjorie Davenport

A comprehensive weekly listing of titles with British TV, radio, press or film tie-ins. Circulates widely to booksellers and libraries, who also use Bookwatch's Helpline service for tracking difficult customer queries. Bookwatch compiles bestseller lists.

6332

BOOKS IN WALES / LLAIS LLYFRAU
Welsh Books Council, Castell Brychan, Aberystwyth, Ceredigion
SY23 2JB
Telephone: 01970 624151
Fax: 01970 625385

Editorial Board: R. Gerallt Jones *(Chairman)*
Katie Gramich
Lorna Herbert

ISSN: 0024-5437

Quarterly. Annual subscription: £5 (UK), £6.50 (overseas).

The journal of the Welsh book trade. Published quarterly in both Welsh
and English, *Books in Wales* lists and reviews Welsh-language books and
books in English of Welsh interest and includes articles on the book trade,
the Welsh literary scene and Welsh writers. Includes special section on
children's books.

6333

BOOKS IRELAND
11 Newgrove Avenue, Dublin 4, Irish Republic
Telephone: +353 (01) 269 2185
Fax: +353 (01) 269 2185

Editors: Jeremy Addis *(Director)*
Shirley Kelly *(Features)*
Alan Titley *(Gaelic)*
Advertisement Manager: Anne O'Donnell

ISSN: 0376-6039

Monthly, except January, July and August. Annual subscription: £15,
IR£15, $22.

Summary (classified) and full reviews of titles of Irish interest and Irish
authorship; seasonal classified lists of forthcoming titles; Irish trade and
library news and articles. Annual index of books reviewed. An
independent magazine published since 1976, supported by the two Irish
Arts Councils and sold in bookshops throughout Ireland. Expatriate and
overseas library circulation in 29 countries.

6334

THE BOOKSELLER
J. Whitaker & Sons Ltd, 12 Dyott Street, London WC1A 1DF
Telephone: 0171 420 6000
Fax: 0171 420 6103

Editor: Louis Baum
Managing Director: Jonathan Nowell

ISSN: 0006-7539

Weekly £2. Annual subscription: £115 (inland), £138 (overseas, standard
rate, airmail extra).

The weekly newspaper of the book trade, offering in the course of a year
over 7000 pages of news, analysis, features, letters, advertising and lists
of books published in the UK. Major national and international events
reported, regular authoritative articles on matters of trade, special
features, book features and rights, stock market, legal and financial pages.
Twice a year a six-month special issue of nearly 900 pages provides the
best reference source for British publishers' publishing plans.

6335

BOOKSELLERS ASSOCIATION DIRECTORY OF MEMBERS
The Booksellers Association of GB & Ireland,
272 Vauxhall Bridge Road, London SW1V 1BA
Telephone: 0171 834 5477
Fax: 0171 834 8812
Email: 100437.2261@compuserve.com

Chief Executive: Tim Godfray
Editor: Kevin Ramage

Annual. 1996–97 edition, £25 (£29 overseas).

Gives information on over 3300 booksellers in membership of the
Booksellers Association. Main index arranged alphabetically by town
with additional index by shop name. Includes addresses, telephone
numbers and names of bookshop managers, subject specializations, BA
group membership, teleordering participation, other goods stocked and
services provided.

6336

THE BOWKER ANNUAL LIBRARY AND BOOK TRADE ALMANAC
Customer Services Department, Bowker-Saur, Maypole House,
Maypole Road, East Grinstead, West Sussex RH19 1HU
Telephone: 01342 330100
Fax: 01342 330191

ISBN: 0 8352 3613 7

40th edition, published May 1995, £140 (approx.).

Brings together in one volume a single source of information for the
library and book trade, news and statistics.

6337

CANADIAN BOOK REVIEW ANNUAL
Manu-Life Centre, 44 Charles Street West, Suite 3205, Toronto, Ont,
Canada M4Y 1R8
Telephone: +1 (416) 961 8537
Fax: +1 (416) 961 1855
Email: cbra@interlog.com
Web Site: http://www.interlog.com/~cbra

Publisher & Editor: Joyce M. Wilson

The Canadian Book Review Annual features original reviews by
specialists of more than 1500 Canadian trade, scholarly, reference and
children's books published each year, with bibliographic information,
description and critical commentary, and a comprehensive subject-
author-title index.

6338

CANADIAN BOOKS IN PRINT
University of Toronto Press, Suite 700, 10 St Mary Street, Toronto,
Ont M4Y 2W8
Telephone: +1 (416) 978 8651
Fax: +1 (416) 978 4738

Editors: Elizabeth Lumley *(Head of Bibliographic Publications)*
Marian Butler *(Canadian Books in Print)*

Canadian Books in Print is a bibliographic listing of all English-language
titles available in Canada.

6339

CAROUSEL – THE GUIDE TO CHILDREN'S BOOKS
7 Carrs Lane, Birmingham B4 7TG
Telephone: 0121 643 6411
Fax: 0121 643 3152

Editor: Jenny Blanch
Executive: David Blanch

Annual subscription: UK £8; overseas £10 (surface mail), £12 (airmail).

Published three times a year by Carousel.

Articles by authors, parents and reviewers on children's book publishing
and extensive reviews of children's books, and multi-media products.

6340

CD-ROM DIRECTORY 95
TFPL Publishing, 17–18 Britton Street, London EC1M 5NQ
Telephone: 0171 251 5522
Fax: 0171 251 8318
Email: 100067.1560@compuserve.com

ISBN: 1 870889 46 0

13th edition 1995.

6341

CHILDREN'S BOOKS IN PRINT
Customer Services Department, Bowker-Saur, Maypole House,
Maypole Road, East Grinstead, West Sussex RH19 1HU
Telephone: 01342 330100
Fax: 01342 330191

Directors: Charles Halpin *(Managing)*
Gerard Dummett *(Marketing)*

ISBN: 0 8352 3687 0

Published March 1996, 2 vols, 2500 pp; £135.

Most complete list of currently available children's books published in
the USA.

6342

THE COMPLETE DIRECTORY OF LARGE PRINT BOOKS AND SERIALS
Customer Services Department, Bowker-Saur, Maypole House,
Maypole Road, East Grinstead, West Sussex RH19 1HU
Telephone: 01342 330100
Fax: 01342 330191

ISBN: 0 8352 3750 8

15th edition, published March 1996. Imprint: R. R. Bowker, 1 volume
343 pp, pbk, £140.

Bigger than ever, this invaluable guide covers the large print field like no
other resource. Inside you'll discover current, accurate bookfinding and
ordering information on some 6500 titles.

6343

CURRENT TECHNOLOGY INDEX
Bowker-Saur Abstracts & Indexes, Maypole House, Maypole Road,
East Grinstead, West Sussex RH19 1HU
Telephone: 01342 330165
Fax: 01342 330191
Email: custserv@bowker-saur.co.uk

Editor: Peter Ellway

Hard copy: six bi-monthly issues and annual volume: £680 (EC), £735
(rest of world excluding USA).
Catni: three issues including annual cumulation: £180 (EC), £190 (rest
of world excluding USA). Catni is an alphabetical name index.
CD-ROM (includes CTI and Catni): CTI Plus (now includes Supertech
Plus) is issued quarterly, £875 per annum (plus VAT in UK only).
CTI is from 1993 an abstracting/indexing service covering over 300
mainly British technical periodicals. Free specimen copies are available.

6344

DIRECTORY OF BOOK PUBLISHERS, DISTRIBUTORS AND WHOLESALERS
The Booksellers Association of GB & I, 272 Vauxhall Bridge Road,
London SW1V 1BA
Telephone: 0171 834 5477
Fax: 0171 834 8812
Email: 100437.2261@compuserve.com

Director: Tim Godfray
Editor: Sydney Davies

Annual. Not available for sale to general public. 1996 edition, £43 (£48
overseas).

Contains addresses and comprehensive information about trade terms
offered by the major British and Irish publishers, distributors and book
wholesalers, including distribution arrangements in the UK for overseas
publications. Also includes details of remainder dealers and suppliers of
audio books, and a publishers subject specialization index.

6345

DIRECTORY OF PUBLISHERS 1996
J. Whitaker & Sons Ltd, 12 Dyott Street, London WC1A 1DF
Telephone: 0171 420 6000
Fax: 0171 836 2909

Sales Manager: Simon Skinner

ISBN: 0 85021 259 6

Annually. £15 post paid, £18 export (airmail postage included).

A list of names and addresses of over 2500 publishers of books in the
United Kingdom.

6346

DIRECTORY OF WRITERS' CIRCLES
Oldacre, Horderns Park Road, Chapel-en-le-Frith, Derbys SK12 6SY
Telephone: 01298 812305
Email: jillie@cix.compulink.co.uk

Editor: Jill Dick *(Compiler)*

The Directory of Writers' Circles contains addresses of several hundred
writers' circles, guilds, workshops and literary clubs throughout the UK,
with some overseas entries, and is published regularly by Laurence
Pollinger Ltd.
It is of use to a wide variety of people including: advertisers, publishers,
specialists and researchers. As membership of Writers' Circles varies
greatly, writers in search of fellow-scribes at professional, amateur and
general interest level also find this publication invaluable.
The current (7th edition) costs £4 post free from the above address.

6347

ELECTRONIC BIBLIOGRAPHY OF OUT-OF-PRINT BOOKS
AAB British Book Service, PO Box 342, PSBC Unit 8, Oxford OX1 1NN
Telephone: 01865 792610
Fax: 01865 792611
Email: info@booksbbs.demon.co.uk

Director: Luigi Gigliotti

Available on-line and in print format. Set of four parts: Part One – authors;
Part Two – titles; Part Three – categories; Part Four – subjects.

6348

ELECTRONIC REGISTER OF WANTED PUBLICATIONS
AAB British Book Service, PO Box 342, PSBC Unit 8, Oxford OX1 1NN
Telephone: 01865 792610
Fax: 01865 792611
Email: info@booksbbs.demon.co.uk

Director: Luigi Gigliotti

List of titles reported wanted by our members, clients in the UK and
worldwide. The Register is updated daily. It is available on-line or in print
format.
Set of four parts: Part One by authors; Part Two by titles; Part Three by
subjects; Part Four by categories.

6349

EPJOURNAL
Electronic Publishing Services Ltd, 26 Rosebery Avenue, London
EC1R 4SX
Telephone: 0171 837 3345
Fax: 0171 837 8901
Email: eps@epsltd.demon.co.uk
Web Site: http://www.epsltd.com

Editor:
48 Lawmill Gardens, St Andrews, Fife KY16 8QS
Telephone: 01334 478459
Fax: 01334 479833
Email: 100073.2215@compuserve.com

Editor: Hugh E. Look
Director: David J. Powell
Chairman: David R. Worlock

EPJournal is a newsletter covering market and strategic developments in
the field of electronic publishing. Coverage extends to all electronic
delivery media whether using telecommunications or some physical
carrier (e.g. floppy disks, CD-ROM).

6350

THE EUROPEAN BOOK WORLD
Anderson Rand Ltd, The Scotts Bindery, Russell Court, Cambridge
CB2 1HL

Authoritative book trade directory, providing trade professionals with
precise, up-to-date business contact details from listings of over 25,000
publishing organizations, 55,000 libraries and 40,000 booksellers.
    Over 150 indexes include: 4000 subject specialities, named staff,
library and bookseller types, telephone/fax, market types, non-book stock
and organization size.
    Superb sales and promotion mailing facility available with CD-ROM
version.

6351

EUROPEAN BOOKSELLER MAGAZINE
15 Micawber Street, London N1 7TB
Telephone: 0171 336 6650
Fax: 0171 336 6640
Email: beishon@ibm.net

Directors: Eva Skelley
Jessica Beishon *(Managing Editor)*
Marc Beishon *(Editor)*
John Beishon *(Publisher)*
Gwenda Beishon

Book trade magazine aimed at pan-European publishing and book trade
management. Circulation/readership: 6,000/20,000 booksellers,
publishers, literary agents and libraries.

6352

BOWKER/WHITAKER GLOBAL BOOKS IN PRINT PLUS
Customer Services Department, Bowker-Saur, Maypole House,
Maypole Road, East Grinstead, West Sussex RH19 1HU
Telephone: 01342 330100
Fax: 01342 330191

Annual subscription: £1695.

Monthly CD-ROM of over two million records of books from 90,000
publishers in over 60 countries where English-language titles are
published. Single most complete listing of English language titles.

6353

THE GOOD BOOK GUIDE
24 Seward Street, London EC1V 3PB
Telephone: 0171 490 9900 *(general)*; 0171 490 9902 *(editorial)*

Fax: 0171 490 9909
Email: enquiries@good-book-guide.co.uk

Directors: Peter F. Braithwaite *(Chairman)*
Pamela Costain *(Managing)*
Rosalie Wood *(Supplements)*
Nick Frost *(Financial)*
Bonnie Falconer *(Editorial)*

Annual subscription rates: £24 (UK); £28 (Europe); £33 (outside
Europe). The Guide is available on subscription only.

The Good Book Guide, twice winner of the Queen's Award for Export
Achievement, combines two elements: an independent monthly book
review magazine and an international book ordering service. Each issue
of the Guide reviews approximately 400 books, hardback and paperback,
available from British publishers, on a wide variety of subjects, plus
videos, audios and CD-ROMs. All titles recommended are then stocked
by the Guide's ordering service for immediate despatch to any country in
the world. The Guide is completely independent, with no connection with
any other publisher, and does not accept advertising or financial
contributions. Books are selected for inclusion solely on merit, on the
advice of the Guide's editorial advisers and reviewers.
    The Good Book Guide is *not* a book club: books are available by mail
order, but there is no commitment to buy books, and no books are sent
unless ordered.

6354

GUIDE TO MICROFORMS IN PRINT (GMIP)
Customer Services Department, Bowker-Saur, Maypole House,
Maypole Road, East Grinstead, West Sussex RH19 1HU
Telephone: 01342 330100
Fax: 01342 330191

Directors: Charles Halpin *(Managing)*
Gerard Dummett *(Marketing)*

ISBN: 3 598 11233 5

Published January 1996, 100 pp, pbk, £140.

Provides both author/title and subject listings of new titles.

6355

GUIDE TO NEW AUSTRALIAN BOOKS
Customer Services Department, Bowker-Saur, Maypole House,
Maypole Road, East Grinstead, West Sussex RH19 1HU
Telephone: 01342 330100
Fax: 01342 330191

ISSN: 1035 5391

Bi-monthly journal. Imprint: D. W. Thorpe (order directly from publisher
– Thorpe).

D. W. Thorpe and Monash University's National Centre for Australian
Studies have combined to produce the *Guide to New Australian Books*, a
comprehensive listing and description of all newly published Australian
books.

6356

INDEX TRANSLATIONUM
c/o HMSO Books, 51 Nine Elms Lane, London SW8 5DR
Telephone: 0171 873 0011 *(orders)*
Fax: 0171 873 8203

Managers: John Hudson *(Sales)*
Ian Stevens *(Export & Rights)*
Robin Henry *(Agency Publications, International Organizations)*

Provides an annual listing of translated books throughout the world.
    Enables the user to follow, from year to year, the flow of translations
from one country or cultural region to another and assists in tracing works
of a specific author as they appear in translation.

6357

INTERNATIONAL BOOKS IN PRINT 1994
Customer Services Department, Bowker-Saur, Maypole House,
Maypole Road, East Grinstead, West Sussex RH19 1HU
Telephone: 01342 330100
Fax: 01342 330191

Directors: Charles Halpin *(Managing)*
Gerard Dummett *(Marketing)*

14th edition, newly revised.

Part One: ISBN: 3 598 22130 4. Published August 1995. 2 vols, 3198 pp,
£340.
    Part Two: ISBN: 3 598 22132 1. Published September 1995. 2 vols,
2540 pp, £340.

Listings of English-language titles published in Africa, Asia, Australia,
Canada, Continental Europe, Latin America, New Zealand, Oceania and
Irish Republic. Over 250,000 titles from 6000 publishers.

6358

INTERNATIONAL LITERARY MARKET PLACE
Customer Services Department, Bowker-Saur, Maypole House,
Maypole Road, East Grinstead, West Sussex RH19 1HU
Telephone: 01342 330100
Fax: 01342 330191

Managing Director: Charles Halpin
Marketing Manager: Clive Hawkins

ISBN: 0 8352 9919 8

1996 edition, published October 1995, £139.

Instant access to over 15,500 organizations connected with books in 170
countries outside the USA and Canada.

6359

IRISH PUBLISHING RECORD
National Library of Ireland, Kildare Street, Dublin 2, Irish Republic
Telephone: +353 (0̃1) 661 8811
Fax: +353 (0̃1) 676 6690

Director: Patricia Donlon
Sales: Mary Hurley

ISSN: 0579 4056

Annual subscription: £IR15.

Annual listing of current reprints of the Irish Republic and Northern
Ireland. Entries arranged by Dewey Decimal Classification; includes
author and title indexes, with list of publishers and addresses. Order from:
National Library of Ireland.

6360

ISBN LISTING – ON MICROFICHE 1996
J. Whitaker & Sons Ltd, 12 Dyott Street, London WC1A 1DF
Telephone: 0171 420 6000
Fax: 0171 836 2909

Sales Manager: Simon Skinner
Marketing Director: Marie Lester

Published twice yearly in January and July. £195 + VAT UK, £195 plus
airmail postage export.

A listing on microfiche of over 1,500,000 titles on the Whitaker master
file including 800,000 OPs, in ISBN sequence.

6361

LITERARY MARKET PLACE 1994 – THE DIRECTORY OF AMERICAN BOOK PUBLISHING INDUSTRY
Customer Services Department, Bowker-Saur, Maypole House,
Maypole Road, East Grinstead, West Sussex RH19 1HU
Telephone: 01342 330100
Fax: 01342 330191

ISBN: 0 8352 3475 4

1996 edition, published September 1995, 2000 pp, pbk, £135.

Instant access to over 30,000 companies and professionals – publishers,
distributors, book clubs, literary agents, book producers, editorial, art
services, etc.

6362

LOGOS
Whurr Publishers Ltd, 19b Compton Terrace, London N1 2UN
Telephone: 0171 359 5979
Fax: 0171 226 5290

Editor: Gordon Graham
Associate Editor: Betty Graham
Publisher: Colin Whurr

Published quarterly from April 1990.

Logos is a journal for publishers, booksellers, librarians and all other
members of the international book community. *Logos* aims to provide an
independent and impartial medium for the in-depth examination of issues
which unite, divide, excite and concern the world of books.

6363

NEW ZEALAND BOOKS IN PRINT
D. W. Thorpe, Thorpe New Zealand, 203 Victoria Street, Wellington,
New Zealand
Telephone: +64 (0̃4) 802 7191
Fax: +64 (0̃4) 385 1598

Managing Director: Michael Webster
Managers: Deirdre Morris *(Publishing)*
Oriana Ruffini *(Advertising)*

6364

OP TITLE LISTING – ON MICROFICHE
J. Whitaker & Sons Ltd, 12 Dyott Street, London WC1A 1DF
Telephone: 0171 420 6000
Fax: 0171 836 2909

Sales Manager: Simon Skinner

£115 + VAT UK, £115 plus airmail postage export.

OP titles listing on microfiche. Over 400,000 titles, published 1976–95. In
addition to recording details of books published in UK, lists English
language titles published in Western Europe together with English
language titles published elsewhere in the world which were available in
the UK through a sole stockholding agent.
    Binder, instruction sheets, fiche panels and benchmark supplied with
each set.

6365

PAPER EUROPEAN DATA BOOK
M-G Information Services Ltd, Riverbank House, Angel Lane,
Tonbridge, Kent TN9 1SE
Telephone: 01732 362666
Fax: 01732 367301

Publishing Manager : Sara Creech

ISBN: 0 86382 199 5. **ISSN:** 0950-4478

1994 edition, published September 1993. £190 (UK); £209 (overseas).

Vital statistical analysis of the economies, raw material resources and pulp and paper industries of Western Europe in one easily accessible source. Global, regional and national data on pulp, paper and related industries. Trends in demand, capacity developments, corporate performance and price movements.

Financial results, product range and capacity of the market leaders. Analytical charts and tables to review markets at a glance.

6366

PAPERBOUND BOOKS IN PRINT
Customer Services Department, Bowker-Saur, Maypole House, Maypole Road, East Grinstead, West Sussex RH19 1HU
Telephone: 01342 330100
Fax: 01342 330191

Fall edition published November 1995. Imprint: R. R. Bowker, 6 volumes, 9850 pp, hbk, £190.

The spring edition is the seasonal guide to more than 413,000 titles. Virtually every paperback book in print is represented in these volumes.

6367

PHILLIPS INTERNATIONAL PAPER DIRECTORY
Miller Freeman Information Services Ltd, Miller Freeman Technical Ltd, Riverbank House, Angel Lane, Tonbridge, Kent TN9 1SE
Telephone: 01732 362666
Fax: 01732 367301, 770483 *(Customer Service)*

Publishing Director: Les Kelly
Associate Publisher: Elaine Soni
Managers: Sara Creech *(Publishing)*
Gwen Young *(Group Data)*
Paul Nash *(Production)*

1996 edition. £115 + postage.

Over 3000 pulp, paper and board mills; 1300 paper, board and paper products merchants; 1800 pulp and paper agents; 7000 machinery, equipment and materials manufacturers and/or suppliers in one cross-referenced book giving comprehensive coverage of the world paper industry. The 'Mills' section includes details of machinery, number of employees, executives, breakdown of tons/annum output. The directory also lists waste paper merchants and processors, Paper Trade Associations and a special UK Converters section as well as an index of world brand names and watermarks.

6368

PR PLANNER UK
Media Information Ltd, Hale House, 290–296 Green Lanes, London N13 5TP
Telephone: 0181 882 0155
Fax: 0181 886 0703

Annual subscription: £335 (1997). Now available on disk.

A monthly updated guide to the British Press. Monthly update, bulletin and cumulative index.

6369

PRINTING TRADES DIRECTORY
Miller Freeman Information Services Ltd, Miller Freeman Technical Ltd, Riverbank House, Angel Lane, Tonbridge, Kent TN9 1SE
Telephone: 01732 362666
Fax: 01732 367301

Publishing Manager: Sara Creech

ISBN: 0 86382 192 8. ISSN: 0079-5372

1995 edition, published May 1995. £97 (UK); £114 (export).

Covers all aspects of the printing industry. Printers and allied trade services are listed alphabetically, geographically (by town) and by the type of work undertaken. Manufacturers and suppliers of printers' machinery and equipment are listed alphabetically and by product/service. Information provided includes company name, address, telecommunication details, machinery and equipment, products and services, contact names.

Also included are brands and trade names, trade organizations, colleges and schools of printing and graphic arts, publishing houses.

6370

PUBLISHERS' INTERNATIONAL ISBN DIRECTORY
Customer Services Department, Bowker-Saur, Maypole House, Maypole Road, East Grinstead, West Sussex RH19 1HU
Telephone: 01342 330100
Fax: 01342 330191

22nd edition, published August 1995, 3800 pp, 3 vols, £310.

The most complete directory, derived from International ISBN Agency files, listing prefixes for over 200,000 publishers in 189 countries.

6371

PUBLISHING AND BOOK DEVELOPMENT IN SUB-SAHARAN AFRICA
Hans Zell Publishers, 11 Richmond Road, PO Box 56, Oxford OX1 2SJ
Telephone: 01865 511428
Fax: 01865 311534 & 793298

Orders:
Customer Services Dept, Bowker-Saur, Maypole House, Maypole Road, East Grinstead, West Sussex RH19 1HU
Telephone: 01342 330100
Fax: 01342 330198
Email: custserv@bowker-saur.co.uk

Editors: Hans Zell
Cécile Lomer

ISBN: 1 873836 46 5

Published March 1996, 424 pp, hbk, c. £60.

Charting the growth of publishing in Sub-Saharan Africa, this comprehensive annotated bibliography covers all segments of the continent's book industry, including book marketing and distribution, and the retail book trade.

A substantial number of citations relate to more specialist areas of publishing, such as children's book publishing, journals and magazine publishing, scholarly publishing and publishing in African languages. The bibliography also contains sections on complementary aspects of book development, among them authors and publishing, copyright, the reading habit, national book policies, and training for book industry personnel.

Other literature on relevant topics features book assistance and donation programmes, the book famine in Africa, the acquisition of African-published material, and publishing (in Africa and elsewhere) of African writers and African literature.

6372

PUBLISHING AND DEVELOPMENT IN THE THIRD WORLD
Customer Services Department, Bowker-Saur, Maypole House, Maypole Road, East Grinstead, West Sussex RH19 1HU
Telephone: 01342 330100
Fax: 01342 330191

ISBN: 1 873836 40 6

Published January 1992. Imprint: Hans Zell, 442 pp, hbk, £54.

Publishing and Development brings together fresh insights and analysis on a timely and important topic, to provide a full understanding of the complexity of book development in the Third World.

6373

PUBLISHING NEWS
43 Museum Street, London WC1A 1LY
Telephone: 0171 404 0304
Fax: 0171 242 0762

Editor: Fred Newman
Associate Editor: Rodney Burbeck
Advertisement Manager: Konrad Kochanski

Weekly. £75 a year (UK only), £85 (Europe), £99 (elsewhere).

Weekly newspaper of the book trade. Hardback and paperback reviews and extensive listings of new paperbacks. Interviews with leading personalities in the trade, authors, agents and features on specialist book areas. Full international coverage.

6374

RELIGIOUS BOOKS IN PRINT 1996
J. Whitaker & Sons Ltd, 12 Dyott Street, London WC1A 1DF
Telephone: 0171 420 6000
Fax: 0171 836 2909

Sales Manager: Simon Skinner

ISBN: 0 85021 258 8

Annually in March. £45 inland, £50 export (post paid).

A reference catalogue of 29,000 titles in print. Authors, titles and keywords in one alphabetical sequence: classified index using 18 principal classifications with 127 subsidiaries. Directory of over 2400 publishers and distributors listed.

6375

THE SCHOOL LIBRARIAN
Liden Library, Barrington Close, Liden, Swindon, Wilts SN3 6HF
Telephone: 01793 617838

Advertising:
Publications Secretary, 83 Warwick Street, Oxford OX4 1SZ
Telephone: 01865 722746

Editor: Ray Astbury
Review Editor: Keith Barker

Quarterly. Annual subscription: £45.

The School Librarian: the official journal of the School Library Association. Published in February, May, August and November. Free to members. Contents include professional news items and articles on school library practice and children's literature, with book reviews forming about half of each issue.

6376

SHEPPARD'S BOOK DEALERS
Richard Joseph Publishers Ltd, Unit 2, Monks Walk, Farnham, Surrey GU9 8HT
Telephone: 01252 734347
Fax: 01252 734307

Managing Director: Richard Joseph

All Sheppard directories contain lists of all known dealers in antiquarian and secondhand books throughout the relevant country. The entries are arranged geographically and are served by alphabetical, town and speciality indexes.
  Volumes include; British Isles, Europe, North America, Australia and New Zealand, India and the Orient, Japan, International Print Map Sellers, International Ephemera Dealers and dealers in collectables.

6377

SUBJECT GUIDE TO AUSTRALIAN CHILDREN'S BOOKS IN PRINT
Customer Services Department, Bowker-Saur, Maypole House, Maypole Road, East Grinstead, West Sussex RH19 1HU
Telephone: 01342 330100
Fax: 01342 330191

Managing Director: Charles Halpin

6378

THE TIMES LITERARY SUPPLEMENT
Admiral House, 66–68 East Smithfield, London E1 9XY
Telephone: 0171 782 3000
Fax: 0171 782 3100

Editor: Ferdinand Mount

The *TLS* is a weekly literary review, which carries notices by leading authorities on up to 3000 books a year on literature and language, history, politics, philosophy, the arts and music, social studies, economics, natural history and many other subjects. It also reviews exhibitions and performing arts, carries articles of general interest, publishes poetry and has a letters page which is the principal forum for literary debate. It is essential reading for librarians, booksellers and academics, and also for its broad, worldwide general readership.

6379

ULRICH'S INTERNATIONAL PERIODICALS DIRECTORY
Customer Services Department, Bowker-Saur, Maypole House, Maypole Road, East Grinstead, West Sussex RH19 1HU
Telephone: 01342 330100
Fax: 01342 330191

Managing Director: Charles Halpin
Marketing Manager: Clive Hawkins

ISBN: 0 8352 3676 5

34th edition, published November 1995, 5 volumes, £370.

Instant access to over 65,000 publishers. There are some 7000 new entries including 360 serials available on CD-ROM.

6380

UNESCO STATISTICAL YEARBOOK 1995
The UNESCO Press, Paris. UK Distributor: HMSO, 51 Nine Elms Lane, London SW8 5DR
Telephone: 0171 873 8372
Fax: 0171 873 8463

Managers: John Hudson *(Sales)*
Ian Stevens *(Exports & Rights)*
Robin Henry *(Agency Publications, International Organizations)*

ISBN: 923 002 887 8

Annual. Trilingual: English/French/Spanish. 1993 edition, £50.

Contains statistics from some 200 countries and territories on population, education, science and technology, libraries, museums, theatres, book production, newspapers and other periodicals, paper consumption, film and cinema, radio broadcasting and television.

6381

VERBATIM, THE LANGUAGE QUARTERLY
PO Box 199, Aylesbury, Bucks HP20 2HY
Telephone: 01296 395880

Also at:
4 Laurel Heights, Old Lyme, CT 06371, USA
Telephone: +1 (203) 434 2104

Editor: Laurence Urdang

Verbatim Books is an adjunct of *Verbatim, The Language Quarterly*. Founded in 1974, *Verbatim* reaches about 25,000 readers worldwide, in 80 countries. The main readership of *Verbatim* is among lay people, not academicians or specialists in linguistics.

6382

WALFORD'S GUIDE TO REFERENCE MATERIAL
Library Association Publishing, 7 Ridgmount Street, London WC1E 7AE
Telephone: 0171 636 7543
Fax: 0171 636 3627
Email: lapublishing@la-hq.org.uk

Marketing Executive: Anna Tamar Thame
Sales Manager: Rohier Ramachandran
Publisher: Helen Carley
Managing Director: Janet Leibster
Production: Kathryn Beecroft

In three volumes. Vol. 1 (7th edition, 1996, c. 1168 pp): Marilyn Mullay & Priscilla Schlicke (eds), 'Science and Technology' **(ISBN:** 1 85604 165 4, c. £135). Vol. 2 (6th edition, 1994, 1168 pp): Joan Harvey & Alan Day (compilers) 'Social & Historical Sciences, Philosophy & Religion' **(ISBN:** 1 85604 044 5, £130). Vol. 3 (5th edition, 1991, 1035 pp): Anthony Chalcraft, Ray Prytherch & Stephen Willis (eds) 'Generalia, Language & Literature, The Arts' **(ISBN:** 1 85604 137 9, £135).

6383

WEEKLY BOOK NEWSLETTER
D. W. Thorpe, 18 Salmon Street, Port Melbourne, Vic, Australia 3207
Telephone: +61 (03) 9245 7370
Fax: +61 (03) 9245 7395

Editor: Caroline Birrell
Managers: Oriana Ruffini *(Advertising)*
Deirdre Morris *(Publishing)*

6384

WHITAKER'S BOOKS IN PRINT 1996
J. Whitaker & Sons Ltd, 12 Dyott Street, London WC1A 1DF
Telephone: 0171 420 6000
Fax: 0171 836 2909

Sales Manager: Simon Skinner

ISBN: 0 85021 257 X

Annually in January. £295 inland; £325 export (post paid).

UK and European English language titles in print, recently out-of-print and forthcoming.

A microfiche edition is available. Completely updated every month on approx 110 fiche (48× reduction).
Annual subscription: £670 + VAT.

A CD-ROM edition is available. Completely updated each month, it includes forthcoming and recently out-of-print books.
Annual subscription: £1285 (monthly service), £905 (bi-monthly service). DOS and Windows versions.

6385

WHO'S WHO OF AUSTRALIAN WRITERS
Customer Services Department, Bowker-Saur, Maypole House, Maypole Road, East Grinstead, West Sussex RH19 1HU
Telephone: 01342 330100
Fax: 01342 330191

Managing Director: Charles Halpin

ISBN: 1 875589 20 1

Published June 1995. Imprint: D. W. Thorpe, 700 pp, hbk, £45.

This 2nd edition includes approximately 5000 entries on living writers of fiction, poetry, plays, radio and TV scripts.

6386

WORDS ON CASSETTE 1994
Customer Services Department, Bowker-Saur, Maypole House, Maypole Road, East Grinstead, West Sussex RH19 1HU
Telephone: 01342 330100
Fax: 01342 330191

Directors: Charles Halpin *(Managing)*
Gerard Dummett *(Marketing)*

ISBN: 0 8352 3765 6

Published February 1996, 1880 pp, £130.

6387

WORLD BOOK INDUSTRY
Jaffe Publishing Management Service, Kunnuparambil Buildings, Kurichy, Kottayam 686 549, India
Telephone: +91 (0481) 430470
Fax: +91 (0481) 561190

Editor & Publisher: K. P. Punnoose
Managing Editor: Jaffe K. Punnoose

Annual subscription: US$10 (including air mail charges).

Published since 1975, *World Book Industry* is a trade magazine promoting internationalism in the book business.

6388

WORLD GUIDE TO LIBRARIES
Customer Services Department, Bowker-Saur, Maypole House, Maypole Road, East Grinstead, West Sussex RH19 1HU
Telephone: 01342 330100
Fax: 01342 330191

Managing Director: Charles Halpin

ISBN: 3 598 20720 4

12th edition, published September 1995. Imprint: K. G. Saur, 1300 pp, hbk, £340.

World Guide to Libraries continues to be the most authoritative guide to library development. The 12th edition provides: updated information on nearly 47,000 libraries from 181 countries, details of national, state, regional and central university libraries, and library name, address and contact details.

6389

THE WORLD OF LEARNING
Europa Publications Ltd, 18 Bedford Square, London WC1B 3JN
Telephone: 0171 580 8236
Fax: 0171 636 1664

Editor: Michael Salzman

Annual. 46th edition, published January 1996, 2072 pp, £210.

Commences with detailed articles on UNESCO and summarized information on a large number of other international organizations; alphabetically arranged under countries. The rest of the book gives details of national academies, learned societies, research institutes, libraries, museums and art galleries, including the names of their chief officials; it also lists universities, with names of full professors with their subjects, higher colleges and schools of art and music. Covers every country in the world.

6390

WRITERS' & ARTISTS' YEARBOOK

A. & C. Black (Publishers) Ltd, 35 Bedford Row, London WC1R 4JH
Telephone: 0171 242 0946
Fax: 0171 831 8478

ISBN: 0 7136 4233 5

Annual. 1997 edition, to be published September 1996, £10.99.

A guide for free-lance writers and artists. Details of English-language periodicals; of British, American and Commonwealth publishers; of British, American and Continental literary agents; and of press, art and photographic agencies. Practical information on such topics as copyright, libel and income tax; and on word processing and desktop publishing. Articles on writing for newspapers and the periodical press, on films, television, radio, artists, music publishing, and markets for verse and drama.

6.13 TRAINING

6391

BOOK HOUSE TRAINING CENTRE

45 East Hill, Wandsworth, London SW18 2QZ
Telephone: 0181 874 2718
Fax: 0181 870 8985
Email: training@bhtc.eunet.co.uk

Chief Executive: Dag Smith
Managers: Jean Hindmarch *(Course Development)*
Orna O'Brien *(Course)*
Sheila Christie *(Marketing)*

Book House Training Centre is the Industry Training Organization (ITO) for the book and journal publishing industry. It was set up in 1979 as an educational charity.

BHTC offers over 60 different courses, most of which are run several times a year. Courses are between one and five days long and cover a wide range of publishing and management skills.

Most courses are held at BHTC's London premises, though some are residential, and are based mainly in the Oxford area.

In addition, BHTC offers:
— in-company courses in the UK and overseas;
— consultancy service;
— training needs analysis;
— books and videos;
— a free quarterly newsletter on training issues.

BHTC is responsible for the development and updating of the industry-agreed standards for each job function specific to publishing. It is an independent NVQ Assessment Centre for publishing NVQs. Through its network of trained freelance assessors, it can offer NVQ assessment of candidates wishing to take units or a full NVQ. The Centre Co-ordinator can advise candidates on their eligibility for schemes to fund NVQ assessment.

6392

CANADIAN CENTRE FOR STUDIES IN PUBLISHING

515 West Hastings Street, Vancouver, BC V6B 5K3, Canada
Telephone: +1 604 291 5242
Fax: +1 604 291 5239
Email: jray@sfu.ca
Web Site: http://www.harbour.sfu.ca/ccsp/ccsp.html

Director: Rowland Lorimer
Associate Director: Ann Cowan
Professional Fellow: Ralph Hancox
Projects Director: Ron Woodward
Instructor: Jane Cowan
Assistant to the Director: Jo Anne Ray

The Canadian Centre for Studies in Publishing (CCSP) is a teaching, research, innovation and information centre based at Simon Fraser University, Harbour Centre. The CCSP was founded in 1987. It is a university/industry initiative dedicated to the development of publishing in Canada and internationally. Its special focus is on books, magazines, multimedia and information systems. The CCSP is advised by an industry-based board drawn widely from the Canadian publishing industry.

6393

THE CENTRE FOR PUBLISHING STUDIES

University of Stirling, Stirling FK9 4LA
Telephone: 01786 467511/467496
Fax: 01786 466210
Email: engl1@stir.ac.uk
Web Site: http://www.stir.ac.uk/departments/publishing.html

Director: Dr Ian McGowan
Reader: Dr Douglas Mack
Lecturers: Andrew Wheatcroft
Mrs Fianach Lawry
James McCall
Dr A. Turnbull

The Centre specializes in the study of and teaching about the publishing industry internationally. Centre staff have experience in North America, Africa, East Asia and other areas, are engaged in editorial and marketing consultancy, and are active in publishing, training, and cultural organizations.

The Centre runs a well-established one year full-time MPhil course in Publishing Studies, with three main taught elements: contemporary publishing — publishing business, industry structure, authors, bookselling, marketing, financial, legal (copyright, contracts, defamation), group projects; editorial function — varieties of editing, practical skills in copy editing, proofreading; production — overview of manufacturing, computer typesetting, design, desktop publishing, Internet Web pages, practical projects; handprinting, papermaking facilities; students research 20,000-word dissertations on individual topics; there are visiting trade speakers. Most students go into editorial or marketing jobs. There are also PhD research students.

6394

GERMAN TUITION — BARBARA CLASSEN

2 Blackall Street, London EC2A 4AD
Telephone: 0171 613 3177
Fax: 0171 739 6242

Director/Tutor: Barbara Classen
Co-Tutor: Daniela Zimmermann

The company offers lively German tuition at all levels and specializes in German for the book trade. Students can choose between one-to-one tuition or small groups of 4–6.

Tutors are professional, experienced native speakers and offer free consultations with trial lesson. Students may work towards one of many recognized exams.

Clients include publishers, booksellers, journalists and other professionals.

Classes are held in the central London German Tuition office or in client's office/home 7 days a week.

6395

THE ROBERT GORDON UNIVERSITY

School of Information and Media, Robert Gordon University, 352 King Street, Aberdeen AB9 2TQ
Telephone: 01224 262952
Fax: 01224 262969
Email: p.evans@rgu.ac.uk

Course Leader: P. Evans
Lecturers: Ms J. M. Royle
Ms L. Gunn

Training in publishing:
1. BA/BA (Hons) Publishing Studies via full-time study.
2. Postgraduate certificate, diploma and master's degree (MA/MSc) via part-time, distance learning (commences January each year).

3. Research.
4. Consultancy.

6396

LONDON COLLEGE OF PRINTING AND DISTRIBUTIVE TRADES
Elephant & Castle, London SE1 6SB
Telephone: 0171 735 0810 & 793 0077

BTEC ND Graphic and Typographic Design: 2 years full-time.

The LCPDT offers a range of more general short courses which run throughout the year, including How to Publish Yourself; Publishing as a Small Business Venture; Publishing as a Career Option; An Introduction to Publishing; Editorial Management; Publishing Management; and several desk-top publishing courses. These vary from one-day intensive courses to ten-week evening classes, and are organised by the Professional Development Unit of the London Institute.

6397

THE LONDON INSTITUTE
65 Davies Street, London W1Y 2DA
Telephone: 0171 514 6000

College Diploma in Publishing Production and Diploma in Printing and Publishing Studies. Also BA (Hons) in Publishing.
  CAT Contact: Judith Chaney.

6398

LONDON SCHOOL OF PUBLISHING
47 Red Lion Street, London WC1R 4PF
Telephone: 0171 405 9801

Publishing courses available include Editorial, Editorial Workshop, Contracts and Rights, Picture Research and Desk Top Publishing.
  Apply to the Director of Publishing Studies.

6399

LOUGHBOROUGH UNIVERSITY
Loughborough, Leics LE11 3TU
Telephone: 01509 223052
Fax: 01509 223053
Email: dils@lboro.ac.uk
Web Site: http://info.lut.ac.uk/home.html

BA (Hons) in Information and Publishing.
  Contact: Derek Stevens or Heather Rees.

6400

MIDDLESEX UNIVERSITY
All Saints, White Hart Lane, London N17 8HR
Telephone: 0181 368 1299

MA/PgDip/PgCert in Computer-integrated Publishing.
  CAT Contact: Mr J. Garnett.

6401

NAPIER UNIVERSITY
East Craigs, Craighouse, Edinburgh
Telephone: 0131 444 2266

BA in Publishing.
  CAT Contact: Mr M. McDonagh, Educational Development Unit.

6402

OXFORD CENTRE FOR PUBLISHING STUDIES
Oxford Brookes University, Gipsy Lane, Headington, Oxford OX3 0BP
Telephone: 01865 484951
Fax: 01865 484952
Email: prichardson@brookes.ac.uk

Director: Paul Richardson

The Centre for Publishing Studies offers a B.A. in Publishing, a post-graduate Diploma in Advanced Studies in Publishing and an M.A. in Electronic Media. In addition, it provides evening and daytime short courses and bespoke training and consultancy for publishing companies and other organizations involved in publishing.

6403

PASSWORD TRAINING
23 Mount Street, Manchester M4 4BE
Telephone: 0161 953 4009

One- or two-day courses in London: Foundation Course in Publishing; Marketing for Publishers; Beginner's Guide to Desk-top Publishing. In-house and tailor-made courses are also available. Grants are provided for small publishers by the Paul Hamlyn Foundation.

6404

UNIVERSITY OF PLYMOUTH
Drake Circus, Plymouth, Devon PL4 8AA
Telephone: 01752 232370

MA/PgDip in Publishing and Book Production.
  Contact Dr Roger Adams, the CATS Coordinator.

6405

SWANSEA INSTITUTE OF HIGHER EDUCATION
Townhill Campus, Swansea SA2 0UT
Telephone: 01792 481263

BA (Hons) Art and Media Studied (Publishing and Print): 3 years full-time, part-time available.

6406

THAMES VALLEY UNIVERSITY
St Mary's Road, Ealing, London W5 5RF
Telephone: 0181 231 2902

BA (Hons) Information Management (Publishing and Information Studies): 3 years full-time. Postgraduate Diploma Information Management (Publishing): 1 year full-time or 2 years part-time. MA Information Management (Publishing): 1 year full-time or 2 years part-time.

6407

TRAINING MATTERS
15 Pitts Road, Headington Quarry, Oxford OX3 8BA
Telephone: 01865 66964

An independent training and consultancy organization, geared specifically for the publishing industry. Off-the-shelf or tailored in-house courses are available in the following areas: managing projects; team building; negotiating skills; appraisal training; influencing skills; introduction to publishing; time and self management; finance for non-financial staff; personal effectiveness/assertiveness; recruitment practice; telesales training
  They also offer consultancy and careers guidance services.

6408

WEST HERTS COLLEGE
Hempstead Road, Watford, Herts WD1 3EZ
Telephone: 01923 257654
Fax: 01923 257667
Email: watvcom@dircon.co.uk

HND in Printing, Publishing and Packaging.
  CAT Contact: Dr B. Pepper, Vice Principal (Academic).

UNIVERSITY OF WESTMINSTER
15–18 Metford House, Clipstone Street, London W1M 8JS
Telephone: 0171 911 5000

The Short Course Unit provides several evening and one-day, weekend or five-day courses in desk-top publishing, sub-editing and writing, aimed primarily at journalists.

7 Appendices

7.1 UK PUBLISHERS CLASSIFIED BY FIELDS OF ACTIVITY

The categories shown below are those in which the publishers listed have declared their interest. The list is intended to be neither exclusive nor comprehensive.

Packagers are shown in *italic* print.

ACADEMIC & SCHOLARLY

ABC-Clio Ltd
Academic Press Ltd
ACC Publications
Ace Books
Acol-Biotol
Adam Matthew Publications
Adamantine Press Ltd
Addison Wesley Longman Ltd
Advisory Unit: Computers in Education
Africana Publishing Co
Peter Andrew Publishing Co Ltd
Anglo-German Foundation for the Study of Industrial Society
Appletree Press Ltd
Archival Facsimiles Ltd
Aris & Phillips Ltd
Arnold
Ashgate Publishing Ltd
Ashmolean Museum Publications
ASLIB (The Association for Information Management)
Association of Commonwealth Universities (ACU)
The Athlone Press Ltd
Avon Books
Bahá'í Publishing Trust
B. T. Batsford Ltd
Berg Publishers Ltd
BFI Publishing
Black Ace Books
Blackstaff Press Ltd
Blackwell Publishers Ltd
The Book Guild Ltd
Marion Boyars Publishers Ltd
Boydell & Brewer Ltd
BPP Publishing Ltd
Brassey's (UK) Ltd

British Agencies for Adoption & Fostering
British Library, Humanities & Social Sciences
British Museum Press
British Psychological Society (BPS Books)
BTL Publishing
Burns & Oates Ltd
Business Education Publishers
Butterworth-Heinemann
Cambridge University Press
Carcanet Press Ltd
Cardiff Academic Press
Jon Carpenter Publishing
Frank Cass & Co Ltd
Cassell Plc
Causeway Press Ltd
Cavendish Publishing Ltd
CCBI Publications
Central European University Press
Centre for Economic Policy Research
Chadwyck-Healey Ltd
Chalksoft Ltd
Paul Chapman Publishing Ltd
Chapman & Hall Ltd
Chartwell-Bratt (Publishing & Training) Ltd
Churchill Livingstone
T. & T. Clark
James Clarke & Co
CLT Professional Publishing
Computational Mechanics Publications
Crescent Moon Publishing
James Currey Publishers
Curzon Press Ltd
Dance Books Ltd
Daniels Medica
Dartmouth Publishing Co Ltd
Darton, Longman & Todd Ltd
J M Dent
John Donald Publishers Ltd
Gerald Duckworth & Co Ltd
Earthscan Publications Ltd
Edinburgh University Press
Educational Low-Priced Books Scheme (ELBS)
Edward Elgar Publishing Ltd
Elsevier Science Ltd

University of Exeter Press
Fabian Society
Falmer Press Ltd
Federal Trust
Floris Books
Forbes Publications Ltd
Free Association Books
W. H. Freeman
Friends of the Earth
David Fulton Publishers Ltd
Gairm Publications
George Ronald Publisher Ltd
GMP Publishers Ltd
Golden Cockerel Press Ltd, Associated University Presses
Gomer Press
Gracewing/Fowler Wright Books Ltd
Grant & Cutler Ltd
Granta Editions
Greenwich University Press
Greenwood Publishing Group
Grey Seal Books
Guildhall Press
The Hambledon Press
Harcourt Brace & Co Ltd
Harvard University Press
Hawthorn Press
Headstart History
University of Hertfordshire Press
HLT Publications
HMSO Books
Hodder & Stoughton Educational
Holmes & Meier Publishing
Holt, Rinehart & Winston
Houghton Mifflin Co International
Human Kinetics (Europe) Ltd
C. Hurst & Co (Publishers) Ltd
Hutton Press Ltd
ICA (Institute of Contemporary Arts)
ICC Information Group Ltd
Imperial College Press
Institute for Fiscal Studies
Institute of Development Studies
Institute of Education
The Institute of Materials
Institution of Electrical Engineers
Intellect Ltd
Inter-Varsity Press
Intercept Ltd

International Labour Office
IOP Publishing
Ithaca Press
JAI Press Ltd
James & James (Publishers) Ltd
James & James (Science Publishers) Ltd
Kegan Paul International Ltd
Kershaw Publishing Co Ltd
King's Fund
Jessica Kingsley Publishers
Kogan Page Ltd
Lawrence & Wishart Ltd
Leicester University Press
The Littman Library of Jewish Civilization
Liverpool University Press
Llanerch Publishers
Lund Humphries Publishers Ltd
The Lutterworth Press
McGraw-Hill Publishing Co
Macmillan Education Ltd
Macmillan Press Ltd
Manchester University Press
Mansell Publishing
Mechanical Engineering Publications
Media Research Publishing Ltd
Merlin Books Ltd
Merlin Press Ltd
Merrell Holberton Publishers Ltd
Microform Academic Publishers
The MIT Press Ltd
Multilingual Matters Ltd
National Academy Press
National Gallery Publications Ltd
National Museums of Scotland
National Youth Agency
The Natural History Museum – Publications Section
New Era Publications UK Ltd
Open Gate Press
The Open University
Open University Educational Enterprises Ltd
Open University Press
Oxford Institute for Energy Studies
Oxford University Press
Packard Publishing Ltd
Paternoster Publishing

Pathfinder Press
Pavilion Publishing (Brighton) Ltd
Penguin Books Ltd
Pentaxion Ltd
Phaidon Press Ltd
Phillimore & Co Ltd
Phoenix Press (Oxford)
Pickering & Chatto (Publishers) Ltd
Pinter Publishers Ltd
Pion Ltd
Pira International
Plenum Publishing Co Ltd
Pluto Publishing Ltd
Polity Press
Portland Press Ltd
Prentice Hall Europe
Prentice Hall/Ellis Horwood
Prentice Hall/Harvester Wheatsheaf
Primary Source Media
Prism Press Book Publishers Ltd
Prometheus Books UK
Rapid Science Publishers
Research Studies Press Ltd
The Richmond Publishing Co Ltd
Lynne Rienner Publishers
Rivers Oram
Routledge
The Royal Society
The Royal Society of Chemistry
Sage Publications Ltd
Sangam Books Ltd
W. B. Saunders Co Ltd
Save the Children
Scarlet Press
Scarthin Books
School of Oriental and African Studies (University of London)
Science Museum Publications
SCM Press Ltd
Scolar Press
Scottish Academic Press
Association for Scottish Literary Studies
Shaw & Sons Ltd
Sheed & Ward Ltd
Sheffield Academic Press
SLS Legal Publications (NI)
Colin Smythe Ltd
The Society of Metaphysicians Ltd
Souvenir Press Ltd
Stainer & Bell Ltd
International Institute for Strategic Studies
Supernet
Alan Sutton Publishing Ltd
I. B. Tauris & Co Ltd
Taylor & Francis Ltd
Taylor Graham Publishing
Thames & Hudson Ltd
The Policy Press
Thoemmes Press
Time-Life Books
University of Toronto Press
Toucan Press
Trentham Books
UCL Press Ltd
Ulster Historical Foundation
Verso
Victoria & Albert Museum Publications
Volcano Press Ltd
Voltaire Foundation Ltd
University of Wales Press

Weidenfeld & Nicolson
Westview Press
Whittles Publishing
John Wiley & Sons Ltd
Yale University Press London
Zed Books Ltd
Alphabet & Image Ltd
Earthscape Editions
John Taylor Book Ventures

ACCOUNTANCY & TAXATION

Accountancy Books
Ace Books
Peter Andrew Publishing Co Ltd
BPP Publishing Ltd
Nicholas Brealey Publishing Ltd
Butterworths Ltd
Cassell Plc
CCH Editions Ltd
Paul Chapman Publishing Ltd
The Chartered Institute of Public Finance & Accountancy
CLT Professional Publishing
Croner Publications Ltd
DP Publications & Letts Educational
Educational Low-Priced Books Scheme (ELBS)
W. Foulsham & Co Ltd
Gower Publishing Ltd
Granta Editions
Harcourt Brace & Co Ltd
Hawksmere Group Ltd
HLT Publications
HMSO Books
Holt, Rinehart & Winston
Houghton Mifflin Co International
IBC Business Publishing
Institute for Fiscal Studies
JAI Press Ltd
Jordan Publishing Ltd
Kluwer Law International
Kogan Page Ltd
McGraw-Hill Publishing Co
Macmillan Press Ltd
Management Books 2000 Ltd
Manchester University Press
Media Research Publishing Ltd
John Murray Publishers Ltd
Osmosis Publications
Oxford University Press
Pearson Professional Ltd
Pitman Publishing
Prentice Hall Europe
Prentice Hall/Woodhead Faulkner
Professional Publishing Ltd
Stanley Thornes (Publishers) Ltd
John Wiley & Sons Ltd
Ink Inc Ltd
Low Priced British Books (LPBB)

AGRICULTURE

Academic Press Ltd
ACC Publications
Addison Wesley Longman Ltd
Africana Publishing Co
Ashgate Publishing Ltd
Baillière Tindall
Blackwell Science Ltd
Butterworth-Heinemann
Cambridge University Press
Cassell Plc
Chapman & Hall Ltd
James Currey Publishers

Earthscan Publications Ltd
Educational Low-Priced Books Scheme (ELBS)
Farming Press
Food Trade Press Ltd
Friends of the Earth
Granta Editions
Harcourt Brace & Co Ltd
HMSO Books
Institute of Development Studies
Intercept Ltd
Intermediate Technology Publications Ltd
Manson Publishing Ltd
National Academy Press
Overseas Development Institute
Oxfam Publishing
Packard Publishing Ltd
Prism Press Book Publishers Ltd
Lynne Rienner Publishers
Sangam Books Ltd
Rudolf Steiner Press
Timber Press
Westview Press
John Wiley & Sons Ltd
Ink Inc Ltd

ANIMAL CARE & BREEDING

Africana Publishing Co
Anness Publishing Ltd
Baillière Tindall
Balnain Books
Blackwell Science Ltd
Blandford Press
Butterworth-Heinemann
Capall Bann Publishing
Cassell Plc
Chalksoft Ltd
The Crowood Press Ltd
Dorling Kindersley Ltd
Educational Low-Priced Books Scheme (ELBS)
Elliot Right Way Books
Farming Press
Robert Hale Ltd
Harcourt Brace & Co Ltd
Harveys Books
Henston Ltd
HMSO Books
The Kenilworth Press Ltd
The Lutterworth Press
Macmillan Education Ltd
Manson Publishing Ltd
National Academy Press
Prentice Hall Europe
Prism Press Book Publishers Ltd
Promotional Reprint Co Ltd
Random House UK Ltd
Ringpress Books Ltd
Salamander Books
W. B. Saunders Co Ltd
Smith Gryphon Publishers
Souvenir Press Ltd
The Sportsman's Press
Sunburst Books
Whittet Books Ltd
Eddison Sadd Editions Ltd
Haldane Mason Ltd
Quarto Publishing Plc

ANTIQUES & COLLECTING

Academy Group Ltd
Airlife Publishing Ltd
Antique Collectors' Club Ltd

Barrie & Jenkins Ltd
B. T. Batsford Ltd
Blandford Press
Breese Books Ltd
British Museum Press
Cassell Plc
Collins & Brown
Conran Octopus
David & Charles Publishers
De Agostini Editions
Dorling Kindersley Ltd
W. Foulsham & Co Ltd
Stanley Gibbons Publications
Guild of Master Craftsman Publications Ltd
Robert Hale Ltd
Harveys Books
Headline Book Publishing Ltd
Hilmarton Manor Press
Kegan Paul International Ltd
Lund Humphries Publishers Ltd
The Lutterworth Press
Lyle Publications Ltd
Mitchell Beazley
New Cavendish Books
New Holland (Publishers) Ltd
New Orchard Editions
Oxford University Press
Phaidon Press Ltd
Promotional Reprint Co Ltd
Quiller Press Ltd
Random House UK Ltd
Reed Books
Running Press Book Publishers
Shire Publications Ltd
Silent Books Ltd
Smith Gryphon Publishers
Souvenir Press Ltd
Spa Books Ltd
The Sportsman's Press
Arthur H. Stockwell Ltd
Studio Editions Ltd
Sunburst Books
Thames & Hudson Ltd
Toucan Press
Victoria & Albert Museum Publications
Studio Vista
Philip Wilson Publishers Ltd
BLA Publishing Ltd
Cameron Books
John Taylor Book Ventures
Marshall Cavendish Books
Quarto Publishing Plc

ARCHAEOLOGY

Academic Press Ltd
Addison Wesley Longman Ltd
Appletree Press Ltd
Aris & Phillips Ltd
Ashgate Publishing Ltd
Ashmolean Museum Publications
The Athlone Press Ltd
B. T. Batsford Ltd
Birlinn Ltd
Blackwell Publishers Ltd
Boydell & Brewer Ltd
British Museum Press
Cambridge University Press
Capall Bann Publishing
Castlemain Books
Constable & Co Ltd
Council for British Archaeology
James Currey Publishers
Curzon Press Ltd
John Donald Publishers Ltd

Dorset Publishing Co
Edinburgh University Press
English Heritage
University of Exeter Press
Robert Hale Ltd
Harcourt Brace & Co Ltd
Headstart History
The Herbert Press
HMSO Books
Holmes & Meier Publishing
The Institute of Materials
James & James (Science
   Publishers) Ltd
Kegan Paul International Ltd
Leicester University Press
Liverpool University Press
Llanerch Publishers
Lloyd's Register of Shipping
Microform Academic Publishers
National Museums of Scotland
Oxbow Books
Oxford University Press
Penguin Books Ltd
Phillimore & Co Ltd
Pinter Publishers Ltd
Polity Press
Routledge
Running Press Book Publishers
Scottish Cultural Press
Sessions of York
Sheffield Academic Press
Shire Publications Ltd
Souvenir Press Ltd
Alan Sutton Publishing Ltd
I. B. Tauris & Co Ltd
Thames & Hudson Ltd
Toucan Press
Twelveheads Press
UCL Press Ltd
University of Wales Press
Yale University Press London
BCS Publishing Ltd
Opus Publishing Ltd

ARCHITECTURE & DESIGN

Academy Group Ltd
Addison Wesley Longman Ltd
Antique Collectors' Club Ltd
Architectural Association
   Publications
The Athlone Press Ltd
Barrie & Jenkins Ltd
B. T. Batsford Ltd
Colin Baxter Photography Ltd
Blackwell Science Ltd
Booth-Clibborn Editions
Butterworth-Heinemann
Cambridge University Press
Cardiff Academic Press
Cassell Plc
Chadwyck-Healey Ltd
Chapman & Hall Ltd
Collins & Brown
Computational Mechanics
   Publications
Conran Octopus
David & Charles Publishers
André Deutsch Ltd
John Donald Publishers Ltd
Donhead Publishing Ltd
English Heritage
Garnet Publishing Ltd
Victor Gollancz Ltd
Green Books
Guild of Master Craftsman
   Publications Ltd

Hazar Publishing Ltd
Headline Book Publishing Ltd
The Herbert Press
Hilmarton Manor Press
HMSO Books
Holmes & Meier Publishing
ICA (Institute of Contemporary
   Arts)
James & James (Science
   Publishers) Ltd
Kegan Paul International Ltd
Laurence King Publishing
Leading Edge Press & Publishing
Liverpool University Press
Lund Humphries Publishers Ltd
The Lutterworth Press
McGraw-Hill Publishing Co
Manchester University Press
Mansell Publishing
Merrell Holberton Publishers Ltd
The MIT Press Ltd
Mitchell Beazley
National Museums of Scotland
The National Trust
W. W. Norton & Co Ltd
The Open University
Open University Educational
   Enterprises Ltd
Oxford University Press
Packard Publishing Ltd
Pallas Athene
Penguin Books Ltd
Phaidon Press Ltd
Phillimore & Co Ltd
Pion Ltd
Prism Press Book Publishers Ltd
Quiller Press Ltd
Reaktion Books Ltd
Reed Books
Regency House Publishing Ltd
RIBA Publications
The Rutland Press
Saqi Books
Sarema Press (Publishers) Ltd
Scolar Press
Scottish Academic Press
Serif
Shire Publications Ltd
E. & F. N. Spon
Rudolf Steiner Press
Studio Editions Ltd
Sunburst Books
Alan Sutton Publishing Ltd
I. B. Tauris & Co Ltd
Thames & Hudson Ltd
Victoria & Albert Museum
   Publications
Studio Vista
Weidenfeld & Nicolson
John Wiley & Sons Ltd
Philip Wilson Publishers Ltd
Yale University Press London
Alphabet & Image Ltd
Calmann & King Ltd
Cameron Books
*The Foundry Creative Media Co
   Ltd*
Ink Inc Ltd
John Taylor Book Ventures
Little People Books
Marshall Information Ltd
Opus Publishing Ltd
Quarto Publishing Plc
Toucan Books Ltd

ATLASES & MAPS

AA Publishing
Addison Wesley Longman Ltd
Advisory Unit: Computers in
   Education
Africana Publishing Co
Ian Allan Ltd
Appletree Press Ltd
Arms & Armour Press
Belitha Press Ltd
BTL Publishing
Chadwyck-Healey Ltd
Dorling Kindersley Ltd
Express Newspapers Plc
Gaia Books Ltd
Geographers' A–Z Map Co Ltd
Grandreams Ltd
HarperCollins Cartographic
HarperCollins Publishers Ltd
J. H. Haynes & Co Ltd
Heinemann Educational
Kuperard (London) Ltd
Roger Lascelles
LLP Ltd
Macmillan Education Ltd
Michelin Tyre Plc
New Holland (Publishers) Ltd
Ordnance Survey
Oxfam Publishing
Oxford University Press
Penguin Books Ltd
George Philip
Phillimore & Co Ltd
Promotional Reprint Co Ltd
RAC Publishing
Reed Books
Roundhouse Publishing Ltd
Running Press Book Publishers
Sarema Press (Publishers) Ltd
Schofield & Sims Ltd
Springfield Books Ltd
Studio Editions Ltd
Sunburst Books
Tarquin Publications
Wharncliffe Publishing Ltd
Andromeda Oxford Ltd
AS Publishing
CLB Publishing Ltd
Duncan Petersen Publishing Ltd
Marshall Information Ltd
Toucan Books Ltd

AUDIO BOOKS

Addison Wesley Longman Ltd
BBC Books
Canongate Books
Cover to Cover Cassettes Ltd
CYP Ltd – Children's Audio
Gwasg y Dref Wen
ICA (Institute of Contemporary
   Arts)
ISIS Publishing Ltd
Kingsway Publications Ltd
Barry Long Books
Murchison's Pantheon Ltd
Naxos Audiobooks
New Era Publications UK Ltd
Random House UK Ltd
Reed Books
Simon & Schuster
Transworld Publishers Ltd
Vinyl Experience Ltd
The Watts Publishing Group
Writers & Readers Ltd
Little People Books

AVIATION

Airdata Publications
Airlife Publishing Ltd
Ian Allan Ltd
Arms & Armour Press
Ashgate Publishing Ltd
A. & C. Black (Publishers) Ltd
Blackwell Science Ltd
BMP
Books International
Brassey's (UK) Ltd
Cassell Plc
The Chalford Publishing Co Ltd
Nigel J. Clarke Publications
Crécy Books Ltd
Eaglemoss Publications Ltd
Greenhill Books / Lionel
   Leventhal Ltd
Grub Street
Robert Hale Ltd
Harveys Books
HMSO Books
Images Publishing (Malvern) Ltd
Jane's Information Group Ltd
LLP Ltd
Mechanical Engineering
   Publications
Merlin Books Ltd
Middleton Press
Midland Counties Publications
   (Aerophile) Ltd
Midland Publishing Ltd
Miller Freeman Information
   Services
Nexus Special Interests
Osprey
Promotional Reprint Co Ltd
Reed Books
Regency House Publishing Ltd
Salamander Books
Patrick Stephens Ltd
Studio Editions Ltd
Sunburst Books
Alan Sutton Publishing Ltd
Wharncliffe Publishing Ltd
Windrow & Greene
BLA Publishing Ltd
Brown Packaging (Books) Ltd
Marshall Cavendish Books
Marshall Information Ltd
Ravelin Ltd
Wordwright

BIBLIOGRAPHY &
LIBRARY SCIENCE

ABC-Clio Ltd
Academic Press Ltd
American Library Association
Aris & Phillips Ltd
ASLIB (The Association for
   Information Management)
The Athlone Press Ltd
Bellew Publishing
Bowker-Saur
Breese Books Ltd
British Library, Document Supply
   Centre
British Library, Humanities &
   Social Sciences
British Library, National
   Bibliographic Service
The British Library, Public
   Services Publishing

The British Library, Science Reference & Information Service
The Building Services Research & Information Association
Cambridge University Press
Cardiff Academic Press
Cassell Plc
Chadwyck-Healey Ltd
Elm Publications
Gale Research International Ltd
Robert Gibson & Sons (Glasgow) Ltd
Gower Publishing Ltd
Grant & Cutler Ltd
Greenwood Publishing Group
Harcourt Brace & Co Ltd
University of Hertfordshire Press
HMSO Books
Institute of Development Studies
JAI Press Ltd
Library & Information Statistics Unit (LISU)
Library Association Publishing
The Lutterworth Press
Macmillan Education Ltd
Mansell Publishing
The MIT Press Ltd
Oxford University Press
Plenum Publishing Co Ltd
Sangam Books Ltd
School of Oriental and African Studies (University of London)
Scolar Press
Colin Smythe Ltd
Taylor Graham Publishing
TFPL Publishing
University of Toronto Press
Toucan Press
Voltaire Foundation Ltd
J. Whitaker & Sons Ltd
Yale University Press London

BIOGRAPHY & AUTOBIOGRAPHY

ABC-Clio Ltd
Acol-Biotol
Addison Wesley Longman Ltd
Airlife Publishing Ltd
Allison & Busby
Argyll Publishing
Arms & Armour Press
Arrow Books Ltd
Avon Books
B & W Publishing Ltd
Bahá'í Publishing Trust
Balnain Books
Colin Baxter Photography Ltd
Bellew Publishing
Blackstaff Press Ltd
Blake Publishing Ltd
Bloodaxe Books Ltd
Bloomsbury Publishing Plc
BMJ Publishing Group
The Book Guild Ltd
Bowker-Saur
Marion Boyars Publishers Ltd
Brassey's (UK) Ltd
Breedon Books Publishing Co Ltd
Breese Books Ltd
The British Library, Public Services Publishing
Burns & Oates Ltd
Calder Publications Ltd
Cambridge University Press
Canongate Books

Carcanet Press Ltd
Cardiff Academic Press
Carol Publishing Group
Cassell Plc
Castlemain Books
Kyle Cathie Ltd
The Catholic Truth Society
CCBI Publications
Chapmans
Chivers Press Ltd
E. W. Classey Ltd
Collins & Brown
Constable & Co Ltd
Countyvise Ltd
Crescent Moon Publishing
Darton, Longman & Todd Ltd
J M Dent
André Deutsch Ltd
East-West Publications (UK) Ltd
Element Books Ltd
Aidan Ellis Publishing
Ex Libris Press
Faber & Faber Ltd
Footprint Press Ltd
Fourth Estate Ltd
Gairm Publications
Gale Research International Ltd
George Ronald Publisher Ltd
Global Books Ltd
Victor Gollancz Ltd
Gothic Image Publications
Gracewing/Fowler Wright Books Ltd
Granta
Green Books
Greenwich University Press
Greenwood Publishing Group
Grosvenor Books
Robert Hale Ltd
Hamish Hamilton Ltd
HarperCollins Publishers Ltd
HarperCollins Religious
The Harvill Press
Hawthorns Publications Ltd
Headline Book Publishing Ltd
William Heinemann
HMSO Books
Hodder & Stoughton General
Houghton Mifflin Co International
Hutton Press Ltd
Images Publishing (Malvern) Ltd
Impact Books / Olive Press
In Print Publishing Ltd
The Institute of Marine Engineers
IOP Publishing
ISIS Publishing Ltd
Arthur James Ltd
Janus Publishing Co Ltd
Michael Joseph Ltd & Pelham Books
Kegan Paul International Ltd
Lawrence & Wishart Ltd
Little, Brown & Co (UK)
The Littman Library of Jewish Civilization
Luath Press Ltd
The Lutterworth Press
Macmillan Education Ltd
Mainstream Publishing Co (Edinburgh) Ltd
Mandarin
Merlin Books Ltd
Methuen
Minerva
The MIT Press Ltd
John Murray Publishers Ltd

National Christian Education Council
National Portrait Gallery Publications
Neil Wilson Publishing Ltd
OM Publishing
Michael O'Mara Books Ltd
Omnibus Press
Orion Books Ltd
Peter Owen Ltd
Oxford University Press
Paternoster Publishing
Pavilion Books Ltd
Penguin Books Ltd
The Pentland Press Ltd
Piatkus Books
Picador
Poetry Wales Press Ltd
Quartet Books
Quiller Press Ltd
The Radcliffe Press
Random House UK Ltd
Reed Books
Riad El-Rayyes Books Ltd
Rivers Oram
Robson Books Ltd
The Royal Society
Salvationist Publishing & Supplies Ltd
Sangam Books Ltd
Scottish Cultural Press
Martin Secker & Warburg
Serif
Serpent's Tail Ltd
Sessions of York
Sheed & Ward Ltd
Sidgwick & Jackson Ltd
Simon & Schuster
Sinclair-Stevenson
Smith Gryphon Publishers
Smith Settle Ltd
Colin Smythe Ltd
Souvenir Press Ltd
Spa Books Ltd
The Sportsman's Press
Stainer & Bell Ltd
Rudolf Steiner Press
Patrick Stephens Ltd
Arthur H. Stockwell Ltd
Summersdale Publishers
Alan Sutton Publishing Ltd
Tabb House
I. B. Tauris & Co Ltd
Thames & Hudson Ltd
Titan Books Ltd
Transworld Publishers Ltd
Ulster Historical Foundation
United Writers Publications Ltd
Veloce Publishing Plc
Virago Press
Virgin Publishing
University of Wales Press
Weidenfeld & Nicolson
John Wiley & Sons Ltd
Windhorse Publications
Windrush Press Ltd
The Women's Press
Writers & Readers Ltd
Yale University Press London
Berkswell Publishing Co Ltd
The Foundry Creative Media Co Ltd
Graham-Cameron Publishing & Illustration

BIOLOGY & ZOOLOGY

Academic Press Ltd
Addison Wesley Longman Ltd
Africana Publishing Co
Baillière Tindall
Blackwell Science Ltd
Blandford Press
BTL Publishing
Cambridge University Press
Cardiff Academic Press
Chadwyck-Healey Ltd
Chapman & Hall Ltd
E. W. Classey Ltd
Daniels Medica
Educational Low-Priced Books Scheme (ELBS)
W. H. Freeman
Garland Publishing Inc
Harcourt Brace & Co Ltd
Harvard University Press
HMSO Books
Holt, Rinehart & Winston
Imperial College Press
Intercept Ltd
JAI Press Ltd
Jones & Bartlett International
The Lutterworth Press
McGraw-Hill Publishing Co
Macmillan Education Ltd
Macmillan Press Ltd
Manson Publishing Ltd
The MIT Press Ltd
John Murray Publishers Ltd
National Academy Press
National Museums of Scotland
The Natural History Museum— Publications Section
The New York Academy of Sciences
W. W. Norton & Co Ltd
The Open University
Open University Educational Enterprises Ltd
Oxford University Press
Packard Publishing Ltd
Penguin Books Ltd
Plenum Publishing Co Ltd
Portland Press Ltd
Prentice Hall Europe
Prentice Hall/Ellis Horwood
Prism Press Book Publishers Ltd
Ransom Publishing
Research Studies Press Ltd
The Richmond Publishing Co Ltd
The Royal Society
Sangam Books Ltd
Schofield & Sims Ltd
Taylor & Francis Ltd
Stanley Thornes (Publishers) Ltd
VCH Publishers (UK) Ltd
Ward Lock Educational Co Ltd
Wheldon & Wesley Ltd
Whittet Books Ltd
John Wiley & Sons Ltd
Yale University Press London
Bender Richardson White
BLA Publishing Ltd

CHEMISTRY

Academic Press Ltd
Addison Wesley Longman Ltd
The Athlone Press Ltd
Blackwell Science Ltd
BTL Publishing
Butterworth-Heinemann

Cambridge University Press
Chapman & Hall Ltd
Daniels Medica
Educational Low-Priced Books
 Scheme (ELBS)
Elsevier Science Ltd
Food Trade Press Ltd
W. H. Freeman
Garland Publishing Inc
Gower Publishing Ltd
Harcourt Brace & Co Ltd
HMSO Books
Hodder & Stoughton Educational
Holt, Rinehart & Winston
Houghton Mifflin Co International
Imperial College Press
The Institute of Materials
Intercept Ltd
JAI Press Ltd
Jones & Bartlett International
McGraw-Hill Publishing Co
Macmillan Education Ltd
Macmillan Press Ltd
Miller Freeman Information
 Services
The MIT Press Ltd
John Murray Publishers Ltd
National Academy Press
The New York Academy of
 Sciences
The Open University
Open University Educational
 Enterprises Ltd
Oxford University Press
Penguin Books Ltd
Pentaxion Ltd
Plenum Publishing Co Ltd
Prentice Hall Europe
Prentice Hall/Ellis Horwood
Research Studies Press Ltd
The Royal Society
The Royal Society of Chemistry
Sangam Books Ltd
Schofield & Sims Ltd
Taylor & Francis Ltd
Stanley Thornes (Publishers) Ltd
VCH Publishers (UK) Ltd
Ward Lock Educational Co Ltd
John Wiley & Sons Ltd
BLA Publishing Ltd

CHILDREN'S BOOKS

ABC—The All Children's Co Ltd
Addax Retail Publishing Ltd
Addison Wesley Longman Ltd
Ahmadiyya Muslim Publications
Allied Mouse Ltd
The Amaising Publishing House
 Ltd
Andersen Press Ltd
Anness Publishing Ltd
Athey Educational
Atlantic Europe Publishing Co Ltd
Avon Books
Award Publications Ltd
Bahá'í Publishing Trust
Barefoot Books
BBC Books
Beaver Publishing Ltd
Belitha Press Ltd
A. & C. Black (Publishers) Ltd
Bloomsbury Publishing Plc
The Book Guild Ltd
Books UK Ltd
Boxtree
Brimax Books

British Agencies for Adoption &
 Fostering
British Museum Press
Brown Watson Ltd
Cambridge University Press
Campbell Books
David Campbell Publishers
Canongate Books
Cardiff Academic Press
Chalksoft Ltd
Channel 4 Learning
Child's Play (International) Ltd
Chivers Press Ltd
Christian Focus Publications
Church House Publishing
Lloyd Cole
Conran Octopus
Crabtree Publishing Co
Crescent Moon Publishing
CYP Ltd—Children's Audio
David Bennett Books Ltd
De Agostini Editions
J M Dent
Dorling Kindersley Ltd
Dragon's World Ltd
Drake Educational Associates Ltd
Eaglemoss Publications Ltd
East-West Publications (UK) Ltd
Emma Books Ltd
Evans Brothers Ltd
Exley Publications Ltd
Express Newspapers Plc
Faber & Faber Ltd
Fantail Books
Floris Books
Forbes Publications Ltd
George Ronald Publisher Ltd
Victor Gollancz Ltd
Gomer Press
W. F. Graham (Northampton) Ltd
Grandreams Ltd
Gwasg y Dref Wen
Peter Haddock Ltd
Hamish Hamilton Ltd
Hamlyn Children's Reference
HarperCollins Publishers Ltd
HarperCollins Religious
Harveys Books
Hawk Books
Hazar Publishing Ltd
Heinemann Young Books
Henderson Publishing Plc
Hodder Children's Books
Holland Enterprises Ltd
Home Health Education Service
Houghton Mifflin Co International
Hunt and Thorpe
Impact Books / Olive Press
Islam International Publications
 Ltd
The Islamic Foundation
Jade Publishers
Kibworth Books
Kingsway Publications Ltd
Ladybird Books Ltd
Larousse Plc
Learning Development Aids
 (LDA)
Letterland International Ltd
Lettermen Publishing Ltd
Levinson Books Ltd
Levinson Children's Books Ltd
Frances Lincoln Ltd
Lion Publishing Plc
Little, Brown & Co (UK)
The Lutterworth Press
Macdonald Young Books

Macmillan Children's Books
Macmillan Education Ltd
Mammoth
The Medici Society Ltd
Merehurst Fairfax
Methuen Children's Books
Michelin Tyre Plc
Minimax Books Ltd
Moonlight Publishing Ltd
National Christian Education
 Council
National Foster Care Association
 (NFCA)
National Gallery Publications Ltd
National Museums of Scotland
The National Trust
New Orchard Editions
Nile & Mackenzie Ltd
OM Publishing
Michael O'Mara Books Ltd
Orchard Books
Orion Books Ltd
Oxford University Press
Paternoster Publishing
Pavilion Books Ltd
Penguin Books Ltd
Phaidon Press Ltd
Philograph Publications Ltd
Phoenix Press (Oxford)
Piccadilly Press
Poetry Wales Press Ltd
Pookie Productions Ltd
Portland Press Ltd
Prim-Ed Publishing
Ragged Bears Ltd
Random House Children's Books
Random House UK Ltd
Ravette Publishing Ltd
Reed Books
Regency House Publishing Ltd
Romer Publications
Running Press Book Publishers
St Pauls
Salamander Books
Salvationist Publishing &
 Supplies Ltd
Sangam Books Ltd
Schofield & Sims Ltd
Scholastic Ltd
Scottish Cultural Press
The Scout Association
Scripture Union Publishing
SGC Books
Spindlewood
SPLASH! Publishing Ltd
Arthur H. Stockwell Ltd
Studio Editions Ltd
Tango Books
Tarquin Publications
Thames & Hudson Ltd
Stanley Thornes (Publishers) Ltd
Time-Life Books
Titan Books Ltd
Tixerant Dean Publications/
 Stepping Stones
Toucan Press
Transworld Publishers Ltd
Treehouse Children's Books Ltd
Turton & Chambers
Usborne Publishing Ltd
Virgin Publishing
Walker Books Ltd
Frederick Warne & Co Ltd
The Watts Publishing Group
Wayland Publishers Ltd
Western Publishing Co Inc
Word Publishing

Wordsworth Editions Ltd
World International Publishing
 Ltd
Writers & Readers Ltd
Y Lolfa Cyf
Roy Yates Books
Young Library Ltd
Aladdin Books Ltd
Albion Press Ltd
Andromeda Oxford Ltd
AS Publishing
b small publishing
Bender Richardson White
BLA Publishing Ltd
Delian Bower Publishing
Breslich & Foss Ltd
Brown Wells & Jacobs Ltd
CLB Publishing Ltd
Earthscape Editions
*The Foundry Creative Media Co
 Ltd*
*Graham-Cameron Publishing &
 Illustration*
Joshua Morris
Kingfisher Design Services
Little People Books
Marshall Information Ltd
Oyster Books Ltd
Pinwheel Publishing Ltd
Playne Books Ltd
Porthill Publishers
Mathew Price Ltd
Quarto Publishing Plc
Sadie Fields Productions Ltd
Signpost Books Ltd
Teeney Books Ltd
The Templar Co Plc
Tucker Slingsby
Ventura Publishing Ltd
Victoria House Publishing Ltd
Wordwright
Zigzag Publishing
Zoë Books Ltd

CINEMA, VIDEO, TV &
 RADIO

Addison Wesley Longman Ltd
Arrow Books Ltd
Aurum Press
B. T. Batsford Ltd
BFI Publishing
Boxtree
Marion Boyars Publishers Ltd
Bruce Smith Books Ltd
Butterworth-Heinemann
Cardiff Academic Press
Carlton Books Ltd
Carol Publishing Group
Chadwyck-Healey Ltd
Channel 4 Learning
Chapmans
Creation Books
Crescent Moon Publishing
Faber & Faber Ltd
Facts on File
Fantail Books
Flicks Books
Fountain Press Ltd
Fourth Estate Ltd
Gale Research International Ltd
Greenwood Publishing Group
Guinness Publishing Ltd
Robert Hale Ltd
Harveys Books
Headline Book Publishing Ltd
Health Education Authority

Hodder & Stoughton General
Holmes & Meier Publishing
How To Books Ltd
Michael Joseph Ltd & Pelham
  Books
John Libbey & Company Ltd
Macmillan Education Ltd
Macmillan General Books Ltd
Manchester University Press
Media Research Publishing Ltd
Miller Freeman Information
  Services
National Gallery Publications Ltd
W. W. Norton & Co Ltd
Oxford University Press
Penguin Books Ltd
Plexus Publishing Ltd
Polity Press
Robson Books Ltd
Roundhouse Publishing Ltd
Sangam Books Ltd
Schofield & Sims Ltd
Serpent's Tail Ltd
Sidgwick & Jackson Ltd
Smith Gryphon Publishers
I. B. Tauris & Co Ltd
Titan Books Ltd
Transworld Publishers Ltd
United Writers Publications Ltd
Vinyl Experience Ltd
Virgin Publishing
Studio Vista
Paul Barnett Editorial
BCS Publishing Ltd
Delian Bower Publishing
Cameron Books
The Foundry Creative Media Co
  Ltd
Marshall Information Ltd
Prion Books Ltd

COMPUTER SCIENCE

Academic Press Ltd
Addison Wesley Longman Ltd
Arnold
Ashgate Publishing Ltd
Bernard Babani (Publishing) Ltd
Blackwell Publishers Ltd
Bruce Smith Books Ltd
Business Education Publishers
Butterworth-Heinemann
Cambridge University Press
Capall Bann Publishing
Cardiff Academic Press
Carlton Books Ltd
Cassell Plc
Chapman & Hall Ltd
Chartwell-Bratt (Publishing &
  Training) Ltd
Computational Mechanics
  Publications
DP Publications & Letts
  Educational
Educational Low-Priced Books
  Scheme (ELBS)
W. H. Freeman
Harcourt Brace & Co Ltd
HMSO Books
Holt, Rinehart & Winston
Houghton Mifflin Co International
Imperial College Press
Institution of Electrical Engineers
Intellect Ltd
IOP Publishing
JAI Press Ltd
Jones & Bartlett International

Law Pack Publishing Ltd
McGraw-Hill Publishing Co
Macmillan Education Ltd
Macmillan Press Ltd
Mechanical Engineering
  Publications
Mecklermedia Ltd
The MIT Press Ltd
W. W. Norton & Co Ltd
Oxford University Press
PAVIC Publications
Penguin Books Ltd
Pitman Publishing
Plenum Publishing Co Ltd
Prentice Hall Europe
Prentice Hall/Ellis Horwood
Psychology Press of Erlbaum
  (UK) Taylor & Francis
Research Studies Press Ltd
Sigma Press
Springer-Verlag London Ltd
Take That Ltd
Taylor Graham Publishing
Stanley Thornes (Publishers) Ltd
UCL Press Ltd
Usborne Publishing Ltd
John Wiley & Sons Ltd
BLA Publishing Ltd
John Taylor Book Ventures
Market House Books Ltd
Marshall Information Ltd
Rough Guides Ltd

COOKERY, WINES & SPIRITS

Absolute Press
Ace Books
Ian Allan Ltd
Anness Publishing Ltd
Appletree Press Ltd
Argyll Publishing
Avon Books
BBC Books
Bloomsbury Publishing Plc
Books UK Ltd
Breese Books Ltd
Camra Books
Canongate Books
Capall Bann Publishing
Carol Publishing Group
Cassell Plc
Kyle Cathie Ltd
Chatto & Windus Ltd
Collins & Brown
Conran Octopus
Dedalus Ltd
Dorling Kindersley Ltd
Elliot Right Way Books
Aidan Ellis Publishing
Faber & Faber Ltd
Forbes Publications Ltd
W. Foulsham & Co Ltd
Fountain Press Ltd
Fourth Estate Ltd
Gracewing/Fowler Wright Books
  Ltd
Peter Grose Ltd
Grub Street
Guinness Publishing Ltd
Robert Hale Ltd
Hamlyn
HarperCollins Publishers Ltd
Harveys Books
Headline Book Publishing Ltd
Ian Henry Publications Ltd
Hodder & Stoughton General

Michael Joseph Ltd & Pelham
  Books
Kegan Paul International Ltd
Kennedy's Publications Ltd
Little, Brown & Co (UK)
Macmillan Reference Books
Mainstream Publishing Co
  (Edinburgh) Ltd
Kenneth Mason Publications Ltd
Merehurst Fairfax
Metro Books
Mitchell Beazley
The National Trust
Neil Wilson Publishing Ltd
New Holland (Publishers) Ltd
New Orchard Editions
Nexus Special Interests
Pavilion Books Ltd
Penguin Books Ltd
Phoenix Press (Oxford)
Piatkus Books
Prism Press Book Publishers Ltd
Promotional Reprint Co Ltd
Quiller Press Ltd
Random House UK Ltd
Reed Books
Riad El-Rayyes Books Ltd
Robson Books Ltd
Rosendale Press Ltd
Running Press Book Publishers
Salamander Books
Sangam Books Ltd
Sawd Books
Search Press Ltd
Serif
Sidgwick & Jackson Ltd
Sigma Press
Silent Books Ltd
Smith Gryphon Publishers
Summersdale Publishers
Sunburst Books
Stanley Thornes (Publishers) Ltd
Time-Life Books
Transworld Publishers Ltd
Virtue Books Ltd
Ward Lock Ltd
Websters International Publishers
  Ltd
Weidenfeld & Nicolson
Wharncliffe Publishing Ltd
Y Lolfa Cyf
Cameron Books
Philip Clark Ltd
CLB Publishing Ltd
Duncan Petersen Publishing Ltd
Haldane Mason Ltd
Kingfisher Design Services
Marshall Cavendish Books
Marshall Information Ltd
Medallion Publishing Ltd
Prion Books Ltd
Quarto Publishing Plc
William Reed Directories
Toucan Books Ltd
Tucker Slingsby
Rosemary Wilkinson Publishing
Wordwright

CRIME

Arrow Books Ltd
Blake Publishing Ltd
Blandford Press
The Book Guild Ltd
Breese Books Ltd
Canongate Books
CBD Research Ltd

Chatto & Windus Ltd
Chivers Press Ltd
Constable & Co Ltd
Creation Books
André Deutsch Ltd
Eaglemoss Publications Ltd
Fourth Estate Ltd
GMP Publishers Ltd
Victor Gollancz Ltd
Robert Hale Ltd
HarperCollins Publishers Ltd
Headline Book Publishing Ltd
Hodder & Stoughton General
Hutchinson
ISIS Publishing Ltd
Janus Publishing Co Ltd
Little, Brown & Co (UK)
Mandarin
Mandrake of Oxford
Neil Wilson Publishing Ltd
Oldcastle Books Ltd
Penguin Books Ltd
Piatkus Books
Random House UK Ltd
Reed Books
Serpent's Tail Ltd
Severn House Publishers Ltd
Silver Link Publishing Ltd
Simon & Schuster
Sinclair-Stevenson
Smith Gryphon Publishers
Souvenir Press Ltd
Sunburst Books
Time-Life Books
Titan Books Ltd
Transworld Publishers Ltd
Virago Press
Virgin Publishing
The Women's Press
Toucan Books Ltd

CRAFTS & HOBBIES

Ace Books
Anness Publishing Ltd
Arms & Armour Press
Aurum Press
Bernard Babani (Publishing) Ltd
B. T. Batsford Ltd
BBC Books
Bibliagora
A. & C. Black (Publishers) Ltd
Breese Books Ltd
Bruce Smith Books Ltd
Canongate Books
Capall Bann Publishing
Cassell Plc
Claiborne Publications
Collins & Brown
Conran Octopus
The Crowood Press Ltd
Dalesman Publishing Co Ltd
David & Charles Publishers
Dorling Kindersley Ltd
Dragon's World Ltd
Eaglemoss Publications Ltd
Elliot Right Way Books
Floris Books
W. Foulsham & Co Ltd
Fountain Press Ltd
Stanley Gibbons Publications
Peter Grose Ltd
Guild of Master Craftsman
  Publications Ltd
Robert Hale Ltd
Hamlyn
HarperCollins Publishers Ltd

Harveys Books
Hawthorn Press
J. H. Haynes & Co Ltd
Headline Book Publishing Ltd
The Herbert Press
HMSO Books
Hodder & Stoughton Educational
Hodder & Stoughton General
Houghton Mifflin Co International
ISIS Publishing Ltd
Jade Publishers
Frances Lincoln Ltd
Little, Brown & Co (UK)
The Lutterworth Press
Lyric Books Ltd
Kenneth Mason Publications Ltd
Merehurst Fairfax
New Holland (Publishers) Ltd
Nexus Special Interests
Michael O'Mara Books Ltd
Pavilion Books Ltd
Penguin Books Ltd
Phaidon Press Ltd
Philograph Publications Ltd
David Porteous Editions
Promotional Reprint Co Ltd
Random House UK Ltd
Ravette Publishing Ltd
Reed Books
Regency House Publishing Ltd
Running Press Book Publishers
Salamander Books
Sangam Books Ltd
Scholastic Ltd
Search Press Ltd
Silent Books Ltd
Souvenir Press Ltd
Stobart Davies Ltd
Arthur H. Stockwell Ltd
Sunburst Books
Tarquin Publications
Thames & Hudson Ltd
Time-Life Books
Usborne Publishing Ltd
Ward Lock Ltd
Weidenfeld & Nicolson
Which? Books
Windrow & Greene
Alphabet & Image Ltd
Breslich & Foss Ltd
Brown Packaging (Books) Ltd
CLB Publishing Ltd
Duncan Petersen Publishing Ltd
Sara Dunn
Eddison Sadd Editions Ltd
The Foundry Creative Media Co Ltd
Haldane Mason Ltd
Kingfisher Design Services
Marshall Cavendish Books
Marshall Information Ltd
Medallion Publishing Ltd
Playne Books Ltd
Quarto Publishing Plc
Toucan Books Ltd
Tucker Slingsby
Rosemary Wilkinson Publishing

DO-IT-YOURSELF

Allison & Busby
Anness Publishing Ltd
B. T. Batsford Ltd
Books UK Ltd
Cassell Plc
Collins & Brown
Conran Octopus

David & Charles Publishers
Dragon's World Ltd
G. T. Foulis & Co
Green Books
Guild of Master Craftsman Publications Ltd
Guinness Publishing Ltd
Robert Hale Ltd
Hamlyn
HarperCollins Publishers Ltd
J. H. Haynes & Co Ltd
Hodder & Stoughton Educational
Leading Edge Press & Publishing
Miller Freeman Information Services
New Holland (Publishers) Ltd
Prism Press Book Publishers Ltd
Promotional Reprint Co Ltd
Reed Books
Search Press Ltd
Sunburst Books
Time-Life Books
Ward Lock Ltd
Which? Books
CLB Publishing Ltd
Duncan Petersen Publishing Ltd
Sara Dunn
Haldane Mason Ltd
Kingfisher Design Services
Marshall Cavendish Books
Marshall Information Ltd
Toucan Books Ltd

ECONOMICS

Academic Press Ltd
Adam Matthew Publications
Addison Wesley Longman Ltd
Peter Andrew Publishing Co Ltd
Anglo-German Foundation for the Study of Industrial Society
Ashgate Publishing Ltd
The Athlone Press Ltd
Blackwell Publishers Ltd
Bookmarks
BPP Publishing Ltd
Nicholas Brealey Publishing Ltd
BSA/CML Bookshop
Butterworth-Heinemann
Cambridge University Press
Jon Carpenter Publishing
Cassell Plc
Causeway Press Ltd
Central European University Press
Centre for Economic Policy Research
Chadwyck-Healey Ltd
Paul Chapman Publishing Ltd
Chapmans
The Chartered Institute of Public Finance & Accountancy
James Currey Publishers
Dartmouth Publishing Co Ltd
J M Dent
DP Publications & Letts Educational
Earthscan Publications Ltd
The Economist Books
Educational Low-Priced Books Scheme (ELBS)
Edward Elgar Publishing Ltd
Euromonitor Plc
Fabian Society
Federal Trust
Green Books
Greenwood Publishing Group
Harcourt Brace & Co Ltd

Harvard University Press
HLT Publications
HMSO Books
Holmes & Meier Publishing
Holt, Rinehart & Winston
Houghton Mifflin Co International
C. Hurst & Co (Publishers) Ltd
ICSA Publishing Ltd
Imperial College Press
Institute for Fiscal Studies
Institute of Development Studies
Intermediate Technology Publications Ltd
International Labour Office
The Islamic Foundation
JAI Press Ltd
Kegan Paul International Ltd
Jessica Kingsley Publishers
Lawrence & Wishart Ltd
LLP Ltd
McGraw-Hill Publishing Co
Macmillan Education Ltd
Macmillan Press Ltd
Management Books 2000 Ltd
Manchester University Press
Microform Academic Publishers
The MIT Press Ltd
John Murray Publishers Ltd
W. W. Norton & Co Ltd
NTC Publications Ltd
The Open University
Open University Educational Enterprises Ltd
Overseas Development Institute
Oxfam Publishing
Oxford Institute for Energy Studies
Oxford University Press
Pathfinder Press
Penguin Books Ltd
The Pensions Management Institute
Pickering & Chatto (Publishers) Ltd
Pinter Publishers Ltd
Pitman Publishing
Pluto Publishing Ltd
Polity Press
Prentice Hall Europe
Prentice Hall/Harvester Wheatsheaf
Prentice Hall/Woodhead Faulkner
Profile Books Ltd
Research Institute for the Study of Conflict & Terrorism (RISCT)
Lynne Rienner Publishers
Routledge
Sage Publications Ltd
Sangam Books Ltd
Scope International Ltd
Shepheard-Walwyn (Publishers) Ltd
Adam Smith Institute
Spokesman
The Policy Press
Stanley Thornes (Publishers) Ltd
Verso
Weidenfeld & Nicolson
Westview Press
John Wiley & Sons Ltd
Yale University Press London
Zed Books Ltd
Low Priced British Books (LPBB)

EDUCATIONAL & TEXTBOOKS

Academic Press Ltd
ACC Publications
Accountancy Books
Acol-Biotol
Addison Wesley Longman Ltd
Advisory Unit: Computers in Education
Ann Arbor Publishers Ltd
Ashgate Publishing Ltd
Association of Commonwealth Universities (ACU)
Athey Educational
The Athlone Press Ltd
Atlantic Europe Publishing Co Ltd
Avon Books
Bernard Babani (Publishing) Ltd
Bahá'í Publishing Trust
B. T. Batsford Ltd
BBC Educational Publishing
Belitha Press Ltd
Berg Publishers Ltd
BFI Publishing
A. & C. Black (Publishers) Ltd
Blackwell Science Ltd
Books UK Ltd
Boosey & Hawkes Music Publishers Ltd
BPP Publishing Ltd
Brilliant Publications
British Agencies for Adoption & Fostering
British Psychological Society (BPS Books)
BTL Publishing
Business Education Publishers
Butterworth-Heinemann
Cambridge University Press
Capall Bann Publishing
Carcanet Press Ltd
Cardiff Academic Press
Cassell Plc
Causeway Press Ltd
Cavendish Publishing Ltd
Chalksoft Ltd
Chancerel International Publishers Ltd
Channel 4 Learning
Paul Chapman Publishing Ltd
Chartwell-Bratt (Publishing & Training) Ltd
Church House Publishing
T. & T. Clark
Nigel J. Clarke Publications
Crabtree Publishing Co
Croner Publications Ltd
Daniels Medica
DP Publications & Letts Educational
Drake Educational Associates Ltd
Earthscan Publications Ltd
Educational Low-Priced Books Scheme (ELBS)
Educational Planning Books
Elm Publications
Elsevier Science Ltd
English Heritage
EnTra Publications Ltd
Evans Brothers Ltd
Exley Publications Ltd
Falmer Press Ltd
First & Best in Education Ltd
Folens Ltd
Forbes Publications Ltd
W. Foulsham & Co Ltd

Framework Press Educational
  Publishers Ltd
Friends of the Earth
David Fulton Publishers Ltd
Garland Publishing Inc
Robert Gibson & Sons (Glasgow)
  Ltd
Ginn & Co
Gomer Press
Grandreams Ltd
Granta Editions
Greenwich University Press
Guildhall Press
Gwasg y Dref Wen
HarperCollins Publishers Ltd
Hawthorn Press
Hawthorns Publications Ltd
J. H. Haynes & Co Ltd
Health Education Authority
Heinemann Educational
Ian Henry Publications Ltd
University of Hertfordshire Press
HLT Publications
HMSO Books
Hobsons Publishing Plc
Hodder & Stoughton Educational
Holt, Rinehart & Winston
Houghton Mifflin Co International
How To Books Ltd
Human Kinetics (Europe) Ltd
Hymns Ancient & Modern Ltd &
ICC Information Group Ltd
ICSA Publishing Ltd
Imperial College Press
The Industrial Society
Institute of Development Studies
Institute of Education
Intellect Ltd
Intermediate Technology
  Publications Ltd
IOP Publishing
JAI Press Ltd
Jolly Learning
Kemps Publishing Ltd
Kershaw Publishing Co Ltd
King's Fund
Jessica Kingsley Publishers
Kogan Page Ltd
Larousse Plc
Lawrence & Wishart Ltd
Learning Development Aids
  (LDA)
Learning Together
Lemos & Crane
Letterland International Ltd
Linguaphone Institute Ltd
Lion Publishing Plc
The Littman Library of Jewish
  Civilization
Liverpool University Press
LLP Ltd
The Lutterworth Press
McGraw-Hill Publishing Co
Macmillan Education Ltd
Macmillan Press Ltd
Manchester University Press
Mansell Publishing
Minimax Books Ltd
The MIT Press Ltd
Multilingual Matters Ltd
Multimedia Library Ltd
John Murray Publishers Ltd
NATE (National Association for
  the Teaching of English)
National Christian Education
  Council

National Extension College Trust
  Ltd
National Foster Care Association
  (NFCA)
National Institute of Adult
  Continuing Education
National Museums of Scotland
National Youth Agency
Thomas Nelson & Sons Ltd
New Era Publications UK Ltd
Nile & Mackenzie Ltd
James Nisbet & Co Ltd
Northcote House Publishers Ltd
Norwood Publishers
The Open University
Open University Educational
  Enterprises Ltd
Open University Press
Ordnance Survey
Oxfam Publishing
Oxford University Press
Packard Publishing Ltd
PAVIC Publications
Penguin Books Ltd
Perfect Words and Music Ltd
Philograph Publications Ltd
Phoenix Press (Oxford)
Pitman Publishing
Plenum Publishing Co Ltd
Poetry Wales Press Ltd
Polity Press
Portland Press Ltd
Prentice Hall Europe
Prentice Hall/Ellis Horwood
Prentice Hall/Woodhead Faulkner
Prim-Ed Publishing
Psychology Press of Erlbaum
  (UK) Taylor & Francis
Ransom Publishing
Ravette Publishing Ltd
Reed Educational Publishing
The Richmond Publishing Co Ltd
Romer Publications
Routledge
The Royal Society of Chemistry
Salvationist Publishing &
  Supplies Ltd
Sangam Books Ltd
Save the Children
Schofield & Sims Ltd
Scholastic Ltd
Scottish Academic Press
Scottish Council for Research in
  Education
Association for Scottish Literary
  Studies
Scripture Union Publishing
Search Press Ltd
Shaw & Sons Ltd
Sheed & Ward Ltd
Southgate Publishers
Rudolf Steiner Press
Stokesby House Publications
Supernet
Supportive Learning Publications
  (SLP)
Tarquin Publications
Taylor & Francis Ltd
The Policy Press
Stanley Thornes (Publishers) Ltd
University of Toronto Press
Trentham Books
Trotman & Co Ltd
Ulster Historical Foundation
United Writers Publications Ltd
Verso
Volcano Press Ltd

University of Wales Press
Ward Lock Educational Co Ltd
The Watts Publishing Group
Wayland Publishers Ltd
Weidenfeld & Nicolson
Winslow Press Ltd
Witherby & Co Ltd
Writers & Readers Ltd
Young Library Ltd
AS Publishing
Diagram Visual Information Ltd
Earthscape Editions
Freelance Press Services
Graham-Cameron Publishing &
  Illustration
Marshall Cavendish Books
Ravelin Ltd
The Templar Co Plc
Zoë Books Ltd

**ELECTRONIC
(EDUCATIONAL)**

ABC-Clio Ltd
Acol-Biotol
Addison Wesley Longman Ltd
Advisory Unit: Computers in
  Education
Andromeda Interactive Ltd
Bernard Babani (Publishing) Ltd
BBC Educational Publishing
Belitha Press Ltd
Berlitz Publishing Co Ltd
Blackwell Publishers Ltd
The British Library, Public
  Services Publishing
Bruce Smith Books Ltd
BTL Publishing
Cambridge University Press
Capall Bann Publishing
Chadwyck-Healey Ltd
Chalksoft Ltd
Channel 4 Learning
Chartwell-Bratt (Publishing &
  Training) Ltd
Peter Collin Publishing Ltd
CYP Ltd – Children's Audio
Elm Publications
First & Best in Education Ltd
Harcourt Brace & Co Ltd
HarperCollins Publishers Ltd
Heinemann Educational
Helicon
Hobsons Publishing Plc
Hodder & Stoughton Educational
Holt, Rinehart & Winston
Houghton Mifflin Co International
Human Kinetics (Europe) Ltd
Imperial College Press
The Institute of Materials
Intellect Ltd
International Business Images Ltd
IOP Publishing
Larousse Plc
Letterland International Ltd
Lion Publishing Plc
McGraw-Hill Publishing Co
Multimedia Library Ltd
National Extension College Trust
  Ltd
Thomas Nelson & Sons Ltd
James Nisbet & Co Ltd
The Open University
Open University Educational
  Enterprises Ltd
Ordnance Survey
Oxford University Press

Penguin Books Ltd
Pitman Publishing
Prentice Hall Europe
Radcliffe Medical Press Ltd
Ransom Publishing
The Royal Society of Chemistry
Sage Publications Ltd
Schofield & Sims Ltd
Sigma Press
Supernet
Stanley Thornes (Publishers) Ltd
Transworld Publishers Ltd
John Wiley & Sons Ltd

**ELECTRONIC
(ENTERTAINMENT)**

Bernard Babani (Publishing) Ltd
Boosey & Hawkes Music
  Publishers Ltd
Bruce Smith Books Ltd
Hawk Books
Larousse Plc
Penguin Books Ltd
Random House UK Ltd
Ransom Publishing
Sigma Press
Supernet
Transworld Publishers Ltd
Western Publishing Co Inc

**ELECTRONIC
(PROFESSIONAL &
ACADEMIC)**

ABC-Clio Ltd
Academic Press Ltd
Addison Wesley Longman Ltd
Advisory Unit: Computers in
  Education
Bernard Babani (Publishing) Ltd
Blackwell Publishers Ltd
Blackwell Science Ltd
Bruce Smith Books Ltd
Butterworth-Heinemann
Capall Bann Publishing
Chadwyck-Healey Ltd
Chartwell-Bratt (Publishing &
  Training) Ltd
Churchill Livingstone
CLT Professional Publishing
Dial Publications
DP Publications & Letts
  Educational
Elsevier Advanced Technology
ERA Technology Ltd
HarperCollins Publishers Ltd
Helicon
HMSO Books
Holt, Rinehart & Winston
ICA (Institute of Contemporary
  Arts)
Imperial College Press
Institution of Electrical Engineers
Intellect Ltd
Jane's Information Group Ltd
Jordan Publishing Ltd
Kemps Publishing Ltd
LLP Ltd
McGraw-Hill Publishing Co
Management Books 2000 Ltd
Methodist Publishing House
Miller Freeman Information
  Services
PAVIC Publications
Pearson Professional Ltd
Pira International

Pitman Publishing
Radcliffe Medical Press Ltd
The Royal Society of Chemistry
Sigma Press
Supernet
Transworld Publishers Ltd
John Wiley & Sons Ltd

ENGINEERING

Academic Press Ltd
Addison Wesley Longman Ltd
Peter Andrew Publishing Co Ltd
Arnold
Artech House
Ashgate Publishing Ltd
Bernard Babani (Publishing) Ltd
Blackwell Science Ltd
The Building Services Research &
    Information Association
Butterworth-Heinemann
Cambridge University Press
Chapman & Hall Ltd
Chartwell-Bratt (Publishing &
    Training) Ltd
Computational Mechanics
    Publications
Dial Publications
Educational Low-Priced Books
    Scheme (ELBS)
Elsevier Advanced Technology
EnTra Publications Ltd
ERA Technology Ltd
Gower Publishing Ltd
Harcourt Brace & Co Ltd
Hawksmere Group Ltd
HMSO Books
Hodder & Stoughton Educational
Holt, Rinehart & Winston
Imperial College Press
The Institute of Marine Engineers
The Institute of Materials
Institution of Chemical Engineers
Institution of Electrical Engineers
Intermediate Technology
    Publications Ltd
James & James (Science
    Publishers) Ltd
Kennedy's Publications Ltd
Lloyd's Register of Shipping
McGraw-Hill Publishing Co
Macmillan Press Ltd
Mechanical Engineering
    Publications
Miller Freeman Information
    Services
The MIT Press Ltd
National Academy Press
Nexus Special Interests
The Open University
Open University Educational
    Enterprises Ltd
Oxford University Press
PAVIC Publications
PC Publishing
Pentaxion Ltd
Prentice Hall Europe
Prentice Hall/Ellis Horwood
Research Studies Press Ltd
Sangam Books Ltd
E. & F. N. Spon
Springer-Verlag London Ltd
Taylor & Francis Ltd
Thomas Telford Services Ltd
Stanley Thornes (Publishers) Ltd
UCL Press Ltd
Whittles Publishing

John Wiley & Sons Ltd
Woodhead Publishing Ltd

ENGLISH AS A FOREIGN LANGUAGE

Addison Wesley Longman Ltd
Advisory Unit: Computers in
    Education
BBC English
Cambridge University Press
Cardiff Academic Press
Carol Publishing Group
Cassell Plc
Peter Collin Publishing Ltd
Drake Educational Associates Ltd
Educational Low-Priced Books
    Scheme (ELBS)
HarperCollins Publishers Ltd
Harrap
Heinemann English Language
    Teaching
Hugo's Language Books Ltd
In Print Publishing Ltd
International Business Images Ltd
ISIS Publishing Ltd
Language Teaching Publications
Larousse Plc
Linguaphone Institute Ltd
Macmillan Education Ltd
Oxford University Press
PAVIC Publications
Penguin Books Ltd
Prentice Hall Europe
Reed Educational Publishing
Sangam Books Ltd
Summersdale Publishers
Vacation Work
Winslow Press Ltd
Roy Yates Books
BCS Publishing Ltd
Low Priced British Books (LPBB)

ENVIRONMENT & DEVELOPMENT STUDIES

Addison Wesley Longman Ltd
Africana Publishing Co
Avon Books
Bahá'í Publishing Trust
Berg Publishers Ltd
Blandford Press
Marion Boyars Publishers Ltd
Cambridge University Press
Capall Bann Publishing
Cardiff Academic Press
Jon Carpenter Publishing
Paul Chapman Publishing Ltd
Claiborne Publications
Earthscan Publications Ltd
ERA Technology Ltd
Friends of the Earth
Gale Research International Ltd
Gateway Books
Granta Editions
Green Books
Helicon
Holmes & Meier Publishing
Imperial College Press
Intercept Ltd
James & James (Science
    Publishers) Ltd
Kegan Paul International Ltd
Latin America Bureau
Macmillan Education Ltd
National Academy Press
Oxfam Publishing

Oxford Institute for Energy
    Studies
Packard Publishing Ltd
Parthenon Publishing Group Ltd
Pluto Publishing Ltd
Prim-Ed Publishing
Ransom Publishing
Scottish Cultural Press
The Society of Metaphysicians
    Ltd
Southgate Publishers
Stokesby House Publications
Thames & Hudson Ltd
Stanley Thornes (Publishers) Ltd
University of Toronto Press
UCL Press Ltd
Westview Press
John Wiley & Sons Ltd
Cameron Books
Sara Dunn
Ink Inc Ltd

FASHION & COSTUME

B. T. Batsford Ltd
Berg Publishers Ltd
Cassell Plc
Dorling Kindersley Ltd
The Herbert Press
Holmes & Meier Publishing
Janus Publishing Co Ltd
Kegan Paul International Ltd
Kemps Publishing Ltd
Manchester University Press
The National Trust
Peter Owen Ltd
Penguin Books Ltd
Piatkus Books
Studio Editions Ltd
Thames & Hudson Ltd
Stanley Thornes (Publishers) Ltd
Toucan Press
Victoria & Albert Museum
    Publications
Sara Dunn
Haldane Mason Ltd
Marshall Information Ltd

FICTION

Albyn Press
Allison & Busby
Argyll Publishing
Arrow Books Ltd
Avon Books
B & W Publishing Ltd
Bahá'í Publishing Trust
Balnain Books
Bellew Publishing
Black Ace Books
Blackstaff Press Ltd
Blake Publishing Ltd
Bloodaxe Books Ltd
Bloomsbury Publishing Plc
The Book Guild Ltd
Marion Boyars Publishers Ltd
Breese Books Ltd
Calder Publications Ltd
David Campbell Publishers
Canongate Books
Cardiff Academic Press
Carol Publishing Group
Central European University Press
Chapmans
Chatto & Windus Ltd
Chivers Press Ltd
Constable & Co Ltd

Creation Books
Crescent Moon Publishing
Dedalus Ltd
Delectus Books
J M Dent
André Deutsch Ltd
Gerald Duckworth & Co Ltd
East-West Publications (UK) Ltd
Aidan Ellis Publishing
Faber & Faber Ltd
Fantail Books
Fourth Estate Ltd
Gairm Publications
GMP Publishers Ltd
Victor Gollancz Ltd
Granta
Gwasg y Dref Wen
Robert Hale Ltd
Hamish Hamilton Ltd
Harlequin Mills & Boon Ltd
HarperCollins Publishers Ltd
The Harvill Press
Headline Book Publishing Ltd
Headstart History
William Heinemann
Ian Henry Publications Ltd
Hodder & Stoughton General
Houghton Mifflin Co International
Hutchinson
Hutton Press Ltd
ISIS Publishing Ltd
Janus Publishing Co Ltd
Michael Joseph Ltd & Pelham
    Books
Kegan Paul International Ltd
Kinnell Publications Ltd
Little, Brown & Co (UK)
Luath Press Ltd
Macmillan Education Ltd
Macmillan General Books Ltd
Mainstream Publishing Co
    (Edinburgh) Ltd
Mandarin
Methuen
Minerva
New Era Publications UK Ltd
Oldcastle Books Ltd
Michael O'Mara Books Ltd
Orion Books Ltd
Peter Owen Ltd
Penguin Books Ltd
The Pentland Press Ltd
Piatkus Books
Picador
Poetry Wales Press Ltd
Polygon
Quartet Books
Rampant Horse Ltd
Random House UK Ltd
Reed Books
Riad El-Rayyes Books Ltd
Running Press Book Publishers
Saqi Books
Martin Secker & Warburg
Serif
Serpent's Tail Ltd
Severn House Publishers Ltd
Simon & Schuster
Sinclair-Stevenson
Souvenir Press Ltd
The Sportsman's Press
Square One Books Ltd
Arthur H. Stockwell Ltd
Stride Publications
Tabb House
Titan Books Ltd
Transworld Publishers Ltd

Turton & Chambers
United Writers Publications Ltd
Usborne Publishing Ltd
Virago Press
Virgin Publishing
The Watts Publishing Group
Weidenfeld & Nicolson
The Women's Press
The X Press
Paul Barnett Editorial

FINE ART & ART HISTORY

ABC-Clio Ltd
Academy Group Ltd
Albyn Press
Alpine Fine Art Books Ltd
Antique Collectors' Club Ltd
Art Books International
Ashgate Publishing Ltd
Ashmolean Museum Publications
Avon Books
Barrie & Jenkins Ltd
Belitha Press Ltd
Bellew Publishing
The Book Guild Ltd
Booth-Clibborn Editions
Boxtree
British Library, Humanities &
    Social Sciences
The British Library, Public
    Services Publishing
British Museum Press
Cambridge University Press
Canongate Books
Cardiff Academic Press
Cassell Plc
Chadwyck-Healey Ltd
Collins & Brown
Constable & Co Ltd
Crescent Moon Publishing
David & Charles Publishers
De Agostini Editions
André Deutsch Ltd
Aidan Ellis Publishing
Facts on File
GMP Publishers Ltd
Green Books
Harvard University Press
The Herbert Press
Hilmarton Manor Press
HMSO Books
ICA (Institute of Contemporary
    Arts)
Kegan Paul International Ltd
Laurence King Publishing
Liverpool University Press
Lund Humphries Publishers Ltd
The Lutterworth Press
Mainstream Publishing Co
    (Edinburgh) Ltd
Manchester University Press
Mandrake of Oxford
The Medici Society Ltd
Merrell Holberton Publishers Ltd
Harvey Miller Publishers
The MIT Press Ltd
John Murray Publishers Ltd
National Gallery Publications Ltd
National Museums of Scotland
National Portrait Gallery
    Publications
The National Trust
The Natural History Museum –
    Publications Section
New Orchard Editions
W. W. Norton & Co Ltd

Oxford University Press
Pallas Athene
Pavilion Books Ltd
Penguin Books Ltd
Phaidon Press Ltd
Poetry Wales Press Ltd
Polity Press
David Porteous Editions
Prentice Hall Europe
Promotional Reprint Co Ltd
Random House UK Ltd
Reaktion Books Ltd
Redcliffe Press Ltd
Redstone Press
Reed Books
Running Press Book Publishers
Sangam Books Ltd
Sarema Press (Publishers) Ltd
Scolar Press
Search Press Ltd
Serindia Publications
Smith Settle Ltd
Spa Books Ltd
The Sportsman's Press
Square One Books Ltd
Rudolf Steiner Press
Stride Publications
Studio Editions Ltd
Sunburst Books
Alan Sutton Publishing Ltd
Tate Gallery Publishing Ltd
I. B. Tauris & Co Ltd
Thames & Hudson Ltd
UCL Press Ltd
Victoria & Albert Museum
    Publications
Studio Vista
Weidenfeld & Nicolson
Philip Wilson Publishers Ltd
Yale University Press London
Alphabet & Image Ltd
Delian Bower Publishing
Breslich & Foss Ltd
Calmann & King Ltd
Cameron Books
Diagram Visual Information Ltd
*The Foundry Creative Media Co
    Ltd*
John Taylor Book Ventures
Opus Publishing Ltd
Porthill Publishers
Quarto Publishing Plc
Toucan Books Ltd
Wordwright

GARDENING

Ace Books
Ian Allan Ltd
Anness Publishing Ltd
Antique Collectors' Club Ltd
Appletree Press Ltd
Avon Books
B. T. Batsford Ltd
BBC Books
Books UK Ltd
Boxtree
Cassell Plc
Kyle Cathie Ltd
Chalksoft Ltd
Chatto & Windus Ltd
Collins & Brown
Conran Octopus
Cover to Cover Cassettes Ltd
Crescent Moon Publishing
The Crowood Press Ltd
David & Charles Publishers

J M Dent
Dorling Kindersley Ltd
Eaglemoss Publications Ltd
Elliot Right Way Books
Aidan Ellis Publishing
Eurobook Ltd
Express Newspapers Plc
The Factory Shop Guide
Burall Floraprint Ltd
W. Foulsham & Co Ltd
Green Books
Robert Hale Ltd
Hamlyn
HarperCollins Publishers Ltd
Harveys Books
Headline Book Publishing Ltd
HMSO Books
Houghton Mifflin Co International
Jarrold Publishing
Michael Joseph Ltd & Pelham
    Books
Larousse Plc
Frances Lincoln Ltd
Little, Brown & Co (UK)
Macmillan General Books Ltd
Merehurst Fairfax
Metro Books
Mitchell Beazley
Moorland Publishing Co Ltd
The National Trust
New Holland (Publishers) Ltd
New Orchard Editions
Packard Publishing Ltd
Pavilion Books Ltd
Penguin Books Ltd
Picton Publishing (Chippenham)
    Ltd
Pluto Publishing Ltd
Promotional Reprint Co Ltd
Quiller Press Ltd
Random House UK Ltd
Reed Books
Robson Books Ltd
Running Press Book Publishers
Salamander Books
Sawd Books
Search Press Ltd
SGC Books
Shire Publications Ltd
Silent Books Ltd
Souvenir Press Ltd
Sunburst Books
Alan Sutton Publishing Ltd
Timber Press
Transworld Publishers Ltd
Ward Lock Ltd
Weidenfeld & Nicolson
Wheldon & Wesley Ltd
Which? Books
Alphabet & Image Ltd
Breslich & Foss Ltd
Brown Packaging (Books) Ltd
Philip Clark Ltd
CLB Publishing Ltd
Duncan Petersen Publishing Ltd
Eddison Sadd Editions Ltd
Haldane Mason Ltd
Kingfisher Design Services
Marshall Cavendish Books
Marshall Information Ltd
Quarto Publishing Plc
Tucker Slingsby
Wordwright

GAY & LESBIAN STUDIES

Berg Publishers Ltd
Cardiff Academic Press
Carol Publishing Group
Lawrence & Wishart Ltd
Open University Press
Peter Owen Ltd
Rivers Oram
Scarlet Press
Serpent's Tail Ltd
Westview Press
Sara Dunn

GENDER STUDIES

Adam Matthew Publications
Addison Wesley Longman Ltd
Ashgate Publishing Ltd
The Athlone Press Ltd
Avon Books
Bahá'í Publishing Trust
Berg Publishers Ltd
Blackwell Publishers Ltd
Bloodaxe Books Ltd
Marion Boyars Publishers Ltd
Cambridge University Press
Capall Bann Publishing
Cardiff Academic Press
CCBI Publications
Chadwyck-Healey Ltd
Lloyd Cole
Creation Books
Crescent Moon Publishing
Earthscan Publications Ltd
Edinburgh University Press
Element Books Ltd
Falmer Press Ltd
Gaia Books Ltd
Gale Research International Ltd
Victor Gollancz Ltd
Gracewing/Fowler Wright Books
    Ltd
Greenwood Publishing Group
Guilford Press
HarperCollins Publishers Ltd
Harvard University Press
Hawthorn Press
HMSO Books
Holmes & Meier Publishing
Houghton Mifflin Co International
C. Hurst & Co (Publishers) Ltd
Institute for Employment Studies
Intellect Ltd
International Labour Office
Lawrence & Wishart Ltd
Learning Development Aids
    (LDA)
Macmillan Press Ltd
Manchester University Press
Mansell Publishing
National Youth Agency
NCT Publishing Ltd
W. W. Norton & Co Ltd
Oneworld Publications
The Open University
Open University Press
Oxfam Publishing
Oxford University Press
Pathfinder Press
PAVIC Publications
Penguin Books Ltd
Piatkus Books
Pickering & Chatto (Publishers)
    Ltd
Pluto Publishing Ltd
Polity Press

Prentice Hall/Harvester
Wheatsheaf
Primary Source Media
Riad El-Rayyes Books Ltd
Rivers Oram
Routledge
Running Press Book Publishers
Sage Publications Ltd
Sangam Books Ltd
Scarlet Press
Serpent's Tail Ltd
Sheldon Press
Souvenir Press Ltd
I. B. Tauris & Co Ltd
The Policy Press
Verso
Virago Press
Volcano Press Ltd
University of Wales Press
Westview Press
The Women's Press
Writers & Readers Ltd
Yale University Press London
Zed Books Ltd

GEOGRAPHY & GEOLOGY

Academic Press Ltd
Addison Wesley Longman Ltd
Advisory Unit: Computers in
Education
Albyn Press
Arnold
The Athlone Press Ltd
Atlantic Europe Publishing Co Ltd
Blackwell Publishers Ltd
Blackwell Science Ltd
Cambridge University Press
Cardiff Academic Press
Cassell Plc
Causeway Press Ltd
Chadwyck-Healey Ltd
Chalksoft Ltd
Paul Chapman Publishing Ltd
Chapman & Hall Ltd
E. W. Classey Ltd
James Currey Publishers
Dalesman Publishing Co Ltd
Dorling Kindersley Ltd
Drake Educational Associates Ltd
Earthscan Publications Ltd
Educational Low-Priced Books
Scheme (ELBS)
Ex Libris Press
University of Exeter Press
Facts on File
W. H. Freeman
David Fulton Publishers Ltd
Geological Society Publishing
House
Harcourt Brace & Co Ltd
HarperCollins Publishers Ltd
HMSO Books
Hodder & Stoughton Educational
Imperial College Press
Imray Laurie Norie & Wilson Ltd
Intercept Ltd
Jones & Bartlett International
Kegan Paul International Ltd
Jessica Kingsley Publishers
Liverpool University Press
McGraw-Hill Publishing Co
Macmillan Education Ltd
Macmillan Press Ltd
Mansell Publishing
Manson Publishing Ltd
Microform Academic Publishers

John Murray Publishers Ltd
National Academy Press
National Museums of Scotland
The Natural History Museum—
Publications Section
The Open University
Open University Educational
Enterprises Ltd
Ordnance Survey
Oxford University Press
Packard Publishing Ltd
Pion Ltd
Polity Press
Prentice Hall Europe
Prism Press Book Publishers Ltd
Ransom Publishing
Reed Books
Roadmaster Publishing
Routledge
Running Press Book Publishers
Sangam Books Ltd
Schofield & Sims Ltd
Scottish Academic Press
Scottish Cultural Press
Supportive Learning Publications
(SLP)
Taylor & Francis Ltd
The Policy Press
Stanley Thornes (Publishers) Ltd
Dyllansow Truran
UCL Press Ltd
Ward Lock Educational Co Ltd
Westview Press
Whittles Publishing
John Wiley & Sons Ltd
Yale University Press London
Andromeda Oxford Ltd
Diagram Visual Information Ltd
Sara Dunn
Earthscape Editions
Toucan Books Ltd
Wordwright

GUIDE BOOKS

AA Publishing
Absolute Press
Albyn Press
Ian Allan Ltd
Appletree Press Ltd
Argyll Publishing
Aurum Press
B & W Publishing Ltd
Birlinn Ltd
A. & C. Black (Publishers) Ltd
Bookman Projects Ltd
Bossiney Books
Boydell & Brewer Ltd
Bradt Publications
BTL Publishing
Cadogan Books Plc
Camra Books
Canongate Books
Capall Bann Publishing
Cardiff Academic Press
Cassell Plc
Castlemain Books
Castlemead Publications
Paul Cave Publications Ltd
The Central Bureau
Cicerone Press
Nigel J. Clarke Publications
Constable & Co Ltd
Ivan Corbett Publishing
Countryside Books
Dalesman Publishing Co Ltd
André Deutsch Ltd

John Donald Publishers Ltd
Dorset Publishing Co
Dragon's World Ltd
East-West Publications (UK) Ltd
Ex Libris Press
The Factory Shop Guide
FHG Publications Ltd
Footprint Press Ltd
W. Foulsham & Co Ltd
Garnet Publishing Ltd
GMP Publishers Ltd
Gomer Press
Gothic Image Publications
Gracewing/Fowler Wright Books
Ltd
Granta Editions
Peter Grose Ltd
Guildhall Press
Robert Hale Ltd
HarperCollins Cartographic
HarperCollins Publishers Ltd
Hawthorns Publications Ltd
Headline Book Publishing Ltd
HMSO Books
Hutton Press Ltd
ICC Information Group Ltd
In Print Publishing Ltd
Jarrold Publishing
Michael Joseph Ltd & Pelham
Books
Kegan Paul International Ltd
Kennedy's Publications Ltd
Kuperard (London) Ltd
Larousse Plc
Roger Lascelles
Leading Edge Press & Publishing
Luath Press Ltd
Macmillan Education Ltd
Macmillan General Books Ltd
Mainstream Publishing Co
(Edinburgh) Ltd
Kenneth Mason Publications Ltd
Meridian Books
Metro Books
Moorland Publishing Co Ltd
Murchison's Pantheon Ltd
John Murray Publishers Ltd
The National Trust
New Holland (Publishers) Ltd
Ordnance Survey
Pallas Athene
Pavilion Books Ltd
Penguin Books Ltd
George Philip
Pitkin Guides
Promotional Reprint Co Ltd
Quiller Press Ltd
RAC Publishing
Random House UK Ltd
Ravette Publishing Ltd
Redcliffe Press Ltd
Reed Books
Roadmaster Publishing
Robson Books Ltd
Rosendale Press Ltd
Roundhouse Publishing Ltd
Sangam Books Ltd
Sawd Books
S. B. Publications
Scarthin Books
Science Museum Publications
Settle Press
Shire Publications Ltd
Sigma Press
Simon & Schuster
Springfield Books Ltd
Studio Editions Ltd

Summersdale Publishers
Alan Sutton Publishing Ltd
I. B. Tauris & Co Ltd
Dyllansow Truran
Twelveheads Press
Vacation Work
Virgin Publishing
Volcano Press Ltd
Ward Lock Ltd
Websters International Publishers
Ltd
Weidenfeld & Nicolson
Wharncliffe Publishing Ltd
Which? Books
Windrush Press Ltd
Book Packaging and Marketing
Philip Clark Ltd
Duncan Petersen Publishing Ltd
Haldane Mason Ltd
Ink Inc Ltd
Kingfisher Design Services
Prion Books Ltd
Rough Guides Ltd
White Line Publishing Services

HEALTH & BEAUTY

Ace Books
Peter Andrew Publishing Co Ltd
Anness Publishing Ltd
Arrow Books Ltd
Ashgrove Press Ltd
Bloomsbury Publishing Plc
Books from India (UK) Ltd
Books UK Ltd
Boxtree
British Psychological Society
(BPS Books)
Business Education Publishers
Capall Bann Publishing
Carlton Books Ltd
Carol Publishing Group
Cassell Plc
Kyle Cathie Ltd
Class Publishing
Coachwise Ltd
Lloyd Cole
Conran Octopus
The C. W. Daniel Company Ltd
Daniels Medica
De Agostini Editions
Dorling Kindersley Ltd
Dragon's World Ltd
Element Books Ltd
Forbes Publications Ltd
W. Foulsham & Co Ltd
Fourth Estate Ltd
L. N. Fowler & Co Ltd
Gaia Books Ltd
Granta Editions
Green Books
Peter Grose Ltd
Robert Hale Ltd
Hamlyn
HarperCollins Publishers Ltd
Hawker Publications
Headline Book Publishing Ltd
Health Education Authority
HMSO Books
Hodder & Stoughton Educational
Home Health Education Service
Frances Lincoln Ltd
Little, Brown & Co (UK)
Macmillan General Books Ltd
Mainstream Publishing Co
(Edinburgh) Ltd
Kenneth Mason Publications Ltd

Metro Books
NCT Publishing Ltd
New Era Publications UK Ltd
Nexus Special Interests
Michael O'Mara Books Ltd
Pavilion Books Ltd
Penguin Books Ltd
Perfect Words and Music Ltd
Piatkus Books
Prism Press Book Publishers Ltd
Promotional Reprint Co Ltd
Random House UK Ltd
Reed Books
Robson Books Ltd
Rosendale Press Ltd
Scarlet Press
SGC Books
Sheldon Press
Simon & Schuster
Smith Gryphon Publishers
Souvenir Press Ltd
Studio Editions Ltd
Sunburst Books
Stanley Thornes (Publishers) Ltd
Transworld Publishers Ltd
Ward Lock Ltd
Websters International Publishers
  Ltd
John Wiley & Sons Ltd
Winslow Press Ltd
Book Packaging and Marketing
Breslich & Foss Ltd
CLB Publishing Ltd
Diagram Visual Information Ltd
Duncan Petersen Publishing Ltd
Sara Dunn
Eddison Sadd Editions Ltd
Haldane Mason Ltd
Kingfisher Design Services
Marshall Information Ltd
Medallion Publishing Ltd
Playne Books Ltd
Prion Books Ltd
Quarto Publishing Plc

HISTORY & ANTIQUARIAN

ABC-Clio Ltd
Adam Matthew Publications
Addax Retail Publishing Ltd
Addison Wesley Longman Ltd
Africana Publishing Co
Albyn Press
Ian Allan Ltd
Allison & Busby
Archival Facsimiles Ltd
Aris & Phillips Ltd
Arms & Armour Press
Arnold
Arrow Books Ltd
Ashgate Publishing Ltd
Ashmolean Museum Publications
The Athlone Press Ltd
Berg Publishers Ltd
Black Ace Books
Blackwell Publishers Ltd
Blandford Press
Bookmarks
Boydell & Brewer Ltd
Brassey's (UK) Ltd
Breedon Books Publishing Co Ltd
Bridge Books
British Library, Humanities &
  Social Sciences
The British Library, Public
  Services Publishing
Cambridge University Press

Canongate Books
Capall Bann Publishing
Cardiff Academic Press
Carol Publishing Group
Cassell Plc
Castlemain Books
Kyle Cathie Ltd
Causeway Press Ltd
Paul Cave Publications Ltd
CCBI Publications
Chadwyck-Healey Ltd
The Chalford Publishing Co Ltd
Cicerone Press
James Clarke & Co
Nigel J. Clarke Publications
Class Publishing
Collins & Brown
Constable & Co Ltd
Copper Beech Publishing Ltd
Ivan Corbett Publishing
Countyvise Ltd
Cressrelles Publishing Co Ltd
James Currey Publishers
Curzon Press Ltd
Dalesman Publishing Co Ltd
De Agostini Editions
J M Dent
John Donald Publishers Ltd
Dorset Publishing Co
Dunrod Press
East-West Publications (UK) Ltd
Edinburgh University Press
Aidan Ellis Publishing
English Heritage
Ex Libris Press
University of Exeter Press
Facts on File
Firebird Books Ltd
Garnet Publishing Ltd
GMP Publishers Ltd
Granta
Greenwood Publishing Group
Guildhall Press
Robert Hale Ltd
The Hambledon Press
Hamish Hamilton Ltd
Harcourt Brace & Co Ltd
HarperCollins Publishers Ltd
Harvard University Press
Headstart History
William Heinemann
Helicon
Ian Henry Publications Ltd
University of Hertfordshire Press
The Historical Association
HMSO Books
Hodder & Stoughton General
Holmes & Meier Publishing
Houghton Mifflin Co International
Hutchinson
Hutton Press Ltd
Intellect Ltd
Ithaca Press
James & James (Publishers) Ltd
Kegan Paul International Ltd
Lawrence & Wishart Ltd
Leicester University Press
Frances Lincoln Ltd
The Littman Library of Jewish
  Civilization
Liverpool University Press
Llanerch Publishers
Lloyd's Register of Shipping
House of Lochar
Macmillan Education Ltd
Macmillan General Books Ltd
Macmillan Press Ltd

Manchester University Press
Mandarin
Mansell Publishing
Mercat Press
Meridian Books
Methuen
Microform Academic Publishers
Minerva
Multimedia Library Ltd
John Murray Publishers Ltd
National Museums of Scotland
The National Trust
Neil Wilson Publishing Ltd
New Holland (Publishers) Ltd
New Orchard Editions
W. W. Norton & Co Ltd
Michael O'Mara Books Ltd
The Open University
Open University Educational
  Enterprises Ltd
Oxbow Books
Oxford University Press
Pathfinder Press
Pen & Sword Books Ltd
Penguin Books Ltd
The Pentland Press Ltd
Phillimore & Co Ltd
Phoenix Press (Oxford)
Pinter Publishers Ltd
Poetry Wales Press Ltd
Polity Press
Prentice Hall/Harvester
  Wheatsheaf
Primary Source Media
Profile Books Ltd
Promotional Reprint Co Ltd
Quartet Books
Quotes Ltd
The Radcliffe Press
Reaktion Books Ltd
Reed Books
Riad El-Rayyes Books Ltd
Rivers Oram
Romer Publications
Routledge
Saint Andrew Press
S. B. Publications
Scarthin Books
Science Museum Publications
Scolar Press
Scottish Academic Press
Scottish Cultural Press
Martin Secker & Warburg
Serif
Sessions of York
Sheed & Ward Ltd
Shepheard-Walwyn (Publishers)
  Ltd
Shire Publications Ltd
Sidgwick & Jackson Ltd
Silver Link Publishing Ltd
Sinclair-Stevenson
Smith Settle Ltd
Spa Books Ltd
Spellmount Ltd
Spokesman
Stainer & Bell Ltd
Studio Editions Ltd
Sunburst Books
Supportive Learning Publications
  (SLP)
Alan Sutton Publishing Ltd
I. B. Tauris & Co Ltd
Thames & Hudson Ltd
Stanley Thornes (Publishers) Ltd
University of Toronto Press
Toucan Press

Dyllansow Truran
Twelveheads Press
UCL Press Ltd
Ulster Historical Foundation
United Kingdom Council for
  Human Rights (UKCHR)
Verso
Virago Press
Voltaire Foundation Ltd
University of Wales Press
Wharncliffe Publishing Ltd
John Wiley & Sons Ltd
Windrush Press Ltd
Yale University Press London
Andromeda Oxford Ltd
BCS Publishing Ltd
Calmann & King Ltd
Endeavour Group UK
Kingfisher Design Services
Signpost Books Ltd
Toucan Books Ltd

HUMOUR

Antique Collectors' Club Ltd
Appletree Press Ltd
Arrow Books Ltd
Avon Books
BBC Books
Birlinn Ltd
Blackstaff Press Ltd
Bookman Projects Ltd
Boxtree
Canongate Books
Capall Bann Publishing
Carol Publishing Group
Cassell Plc
Chapmans
Countyvise Ltd
Dalesman Publishing Co Ltd
Defiant Publications
André Deutsch Ltd
Elliot Right Way Books
Ex Libris Press
Exley Publications Ltd
Express Newspapers Plc
Fantail Books
Farming Press
Fernhurst Books
Firebird Books Ltd
W. Foulsham & Co Ltd
Fourth Estate Ltd
GMP Publishers Ltd
Victor Gollancz Ltd
Grub Street
Guinness Publishing Ltd
Robert Hale Ltd
HarperCollins Publishers Ltd
Headline Book Publishing Ltd
Hodder & Stoughton General
Hutchinson
Hutton Press Ltd
Arthur James Ltd
Janus Publishing Co Ltd
Michael Joseph Ltd & Pelham
  Books
Little, Brown & Co (UK)
Mandarin
Methuen
Metro Books
Neil Wilson Publishing Ltd
Michael O'Mara Books Ltd
Pavilion Books Ltd
Penguin Books Ltd
Piatkus Books
Picador
Plexus Publishing Ltd

Polity Press
Quiller Press Ltd
Random House UK Ltd
Ravette Publishing Ltd
Reed Books
Robson Books Ltd
Running Press Book Publishers
Sainsbury Publishing Ltd
Sangam Books Ltd
Sawd Books
Silver Link Publishing Ltd
Simon & Schuster
Souvenir Press Ltd
The Sportsman's Press
Summersdale Publishers
Supportive Learning Publications
  (SLP)
Take That Ltd
Titan Books Ltd
Transworld Publishers Ltd
United Writers Publications Ltd
Verulam Publishing Ltd
Virgin Publishing
Weidenfeld & Nicolson
Windrush Press Ltd
The Women's Press
Y Lolfa Cyf
Paul Barnett Editorial
Delian Bower Publishing
Eddison Sadd Editions Ltd
Porthill Publishers

ILLUSTRATED & FINE
EDITIONS

Addax Retail Publishing Ltd
Airlife Publishing Ltd
Albyn Press
Appletree Press Ltd
Archival Facsimiles Ltd
Ashgate Publishing Ltd
Barrie & Jenkins Ltd
Colin Baxter Photography Ltd
Blackstaff Press Ltd
Brassey's (UK) Ltd
British Library, Humanities &
  Social Sciences
The British Library, Public
  Services Publishing
Cassell Plc
Chapmans
E. W. Classey Ltd
Collins & Brown
Cottage Publications
André Deutsch Ltd
Dragon's World Ltd
Elfande Ltd
Aidan Ellis Publishing
Hamish Hamilton Ltd
The Harvill Press
Hawk Books
Hazar Publishing Ltd
The Herbert Press
Impact Books / Olive Press
Kegan Paul International Ltd
Laurence King Publishing
Little, Brown & Co (UK)
The Lutterworth Press
Mainstream Publishing Co
  (Edinburgh) Ltd
Merrell Holberton Publishers Ltd
New Orchard Editions
Michael O'Mara Books Ltd
Oxford University Press
Paternoster Publishing
Pavilion Books Ltd
Penguin Books Ltd

Random House UK Ltd
Reed Books
Sangam Books Ltd
Scolar Press
Serindia Publications
Shepheard-Walwyn (Publishers)
  Ltd
Smith Settle Ltd
Studio Editions Ltd
Sunburst Books
Alan Sutton Publishing Ltd
Thames & Hudson Ltd
Veloce Publishing Plc
Studio Vista
Frederick Warne & Co Ltd
Weidenfeld & Nicolson
Whittet Books Ltd
Yale University Press London
Alphabet & Image Ltd
Book Packaging and Marketing
Calmann & King Ltd
The Foundry Creative Media Co
  Ltd
Ink Inc Ltd
Marshall Cavendish Books
Medallion Publishing Ltd
Toucan Books Ltd

INDUSTRY, BUSINESS &
MANAGEMENT

ACC Publications
Accountancy Books
Addison Wesley Longman Ltd
Peter Andrew Publishing Co Ltd
Anglo-German Foundation for the
  Study of Industrial Society
Arrow Books Ltd
Ashgate Publishing Ltd
The Athlone Press Ltd
Aurelian Information Ltd
Blackwell Publishers Ltd
Blackwell Science Ltd
Bowker-Saur
Marion Boyars Publishers Ltd
BPP Publishing Ltd
Nicholas Brealey Publishing Ltd
The British Library, Science
  Reference & Information
  Service
Business Education Publishers
The International Business
  Library Ltd
Butterworth-Heinemann
Cambridge University Press
Cassell Plc
Causeway Press Ltd
CCH Editions Ltd
Centre for Economic Policy
  Research
Paul Chapman Publishing Ltd
Chapman & Hall Ltd
Chartwell-Bratt (Publishing &
  Training) Ltd
CLT Professional Publishing
Lloyd Cole
Peter Collin Publishing Ltd
Croner Publications Ltd
Daniels Medica
Dial Publications
Dun & Bradstreet Ltd
The Economist Books
Educational Low-Priced Books
  Scheme (ELBS)
ELC International
Elliot Right Way Books
Elm Publications

Elsevier Advanced Technology
ERA Technology Ltd
Eurofi Ltd
Euromonitor Plc
Europa Publications Ltd
Executive Grapevine International
  Ltd
The Factory Shop Guide
First & Best in Education Ltd
Gale Research International Ltd
Gower Publishing Ltd
Graham & Whiteside Ltd
Greenwood Publishing Group
Harcourt Brace & Co Ltd
Hawksmere Group Ltd
Hawthorn Press
HLT Publications
HMSO Books
Hodder & Stoughton Educational
Hollis Directories Ltd
Holt, Rinehart & Winston
Houghton Mifflin Co International
How To Books Ltd
IBC Business Publishing
ICC Information Group Ltd
ICSA Publishing Ltd
The Industrial Society
Institute for Employment Studies
Institute of Development Studies
The Institute of Management
The Institute of Materials
Institute of Personnel &
  Development
Intermediate Technology
  Publications Ltd
International Labour Office
JAI Press Ltd
Jordan Publishing Ltd
Kennedy's Publications Ltd
Kogan Page Ltd
Lemos & Crane
Linguaphone Institute Ltd
LLP Ltd
McGraw-Hill Publishing Co
Macmillan Press Ltd
Management Books 2000 Ltd
Manchester University Press
Mansell Publishing
Mecklermedia Ltd
Miller Freeman Information
  Services
The MIT Press Ltd
John Murray Publishers Ltd
National Academy Press
James Nisbet & Co Ltd
NTC Publications Ltd
The Open University
Open University Educational
  Enterprises Ltd
Osmosis Publications
Oxford University Press
PasTest
Pearson Professional Ltd
Penguin Books Ltd
Pentaxion Ltd
Piatkus Books
Pinter Publishers Ltd
Pira International
Pitman Publishing
Plenum Publishing Co Ltd
Prentice Hall Europe
Prentice Hall/Woodhead Faulkner
Professional Publishing Ltd
Quiller Press Ltd
Radcliffe Medical Press Ltd
Random House UK Ltd
Ravette Publishing Ltd

Redcliffe Press Ltd
Rosendale Press Ltd
Routledge
Sage Publications Ltd
Sangam Books Ltd
Scope International Ltd
Sessions of York
Sheldon Press
Sherwood Publishing
Sidgwick & Jackson Ltd
Smith Gryphon Publishers
Souvenir Press Ltd
Summersdale Publishers
Supernet
Take That Ltd
TFPL Publishing
The Policy Press
Stanley Thornes (Publishers) Ltd
United Writers Publications Ltd
Weidenfeld & Nicolson
Whurr Publishers Ltd
John Wiley & Sons Ltd
Witherby & Co Ltd
Woodhead Publishing Ltd
Ink Inc Ltd
Low Priced British Books (LPBB)
Market House Books Ltd
Marshall Information Ltd
William Reed Directories

LANGUAGES &
LINGUISTICS

Academic Press Ltd
Addison Wesley Longman Ltd
Advisory Unit: Computers in
  Education
Appletree Press Ltd
Aris & Phillips Ltd
Arnold
ASLIB (The Association for
  Information Management)
The Athlone Press Ltd
BBC Books
Berlitz Publishing Co Ltd
Books from India (UK) Ltd
Boydell & Brewer Ltd
British Library, Humanities &
  Social Sciences
Cambridge University Press
Cardiff Academic Press
Carol Publishing Group
Cassell Plc
Centre for Information on
  Language Teaching & Research
Chadwyck-Healey Ltd
Chancerel International Publishers
  Ltd
Chartwell-Bratt (Publishing &
  Training) Ltd
James Currey Publishers
Curzon Press Ltd
Drake Educational Associates Ltd
Edinburgh University Press
University of Exeter Press
Gairm Publications
Global Books Ltd
Gomer Press
Grant & Cutler Ltd
Gwasg y Dref Wen
Harcourt Brace & Co Ltd
Harrap
Hodder & Stoughton Educational
Holt, Rinehart & Winston
Houghton Mifflin Co International
Hugo's Language Books Ltd
Intellect Ltd

Ithaca Press
Kegan Paul International Ltd
Kuperard (London) Ltd
Larousse Plc
Linguaphone Institute Ltd
Lund Humphries Publishers Ltd
Macmillan Education Ltd
Macmillan Press Ltd
Manchester University Press
The MIT Press Ltd
Multilingual Matters Ltd
John Murray Publishers Ltd
Thomas Nelson & Sons Ltd
Oxford University Press
Packard Publishing Ltd
Penguin Books Ltd
Pinter Publishers Ltd
Prentice Hall Europe
Prentice Hall/Harvester
  Wheatsheaf
Prim-Ed Publishing
Primary Source Media
Routledge
Sangam Books Ltd
Schofield & Sims Ltd
School of Oriental and African
  Studies (University of London)
Scottish Cultural Press
Association for Scottish Literary
  Studies
Sheffield Academic Press
Taylor & Francis Ltd
Stanley Thornes (Publishers) Ltd
University of Toronto Press
Dyllansow Truran
Verulam Publishing Ltd
Voltaire Foundation Ltd
University of Wales Press
John Wiley & Sons Ltd
Winslow Press Ltd
Y Lolfa Cyf
Yale University Press London
b small publishing
Laurence Urdang Inc

LAW

Ace Books
Addison Wesley Longman Ltd
Peter Andrew Publishing Co Ltd
Ashgate Publishing Ltd
The Athlone Press Ltd
B & W Publishing Ltd
Blackstone Press Ltd
Blackwell Science Ltd
BMP
BPP Publishing Ltd
British Agencies for Adoption &
  Fostering
Business Education Publishers
The International Business
  Library Ltd
Butterworths Ltd
Cambridge University Press
Cassell Plc
Cavendish Publishing Ltd
CCH Editions Ltd
Central European University Press
Paul Chapman Publishing Ltd
T. & T. Clark
Class Publishing
CLT Professional Publishing
Croner Publications Ltd
James Currey Publishers
Dartmouth Publishing Co Ltd
J M Dent
Edinburgh University Press

Educational Low-Priced Books
  Scheme (ELBS)
Elliot Right Way Books
FT Law & Tax
W. Green The Scottish Law
  Publisher
Greenwood Publishing Group
The Hambledon Press
Hawksmere Group Ltd
HLT Publications
HMSO Books
How To Books Ltd
IBC Business Publishing
Jordan Publishing Ltd
Jessica Kingsley Publishers
Kluwer Law International
Law Pack Publishing Ltd
Law Society Publications &
  Multimedia
Legal Action Group
Lemos & Crane
LLP Ltd
Macmillan Press Ltd
Management Books 2000 Ltd
Manchester University Press
Mansell Publishing
Kenneth Mason Publications Ltd
Microform Academic Publishers
The MIT Press Ltd
Oxford University Press
Pearson Professional Ltd
Penguin Books Ltd
Pentaxion Ltd
Pinter Publishers Ltd
Pitman Publishing
Pluto Publishing Ltd
Professional Publishing Ltd
Romer Publications
Sangam Books Ltd
Shaw & Sons Ltd
SLS Legal Publications (NI)
Sweet & Maxwell Ltd
VCH Publishers (UK) Ltd
Weidenfeld & Nicolson
Westview Press
John Wiley & Sons Ltd
Witherby & Co Ltd
Yale University Press London

LITERATURE & CRITICISM

Adam Matthew Publications
Addison Wesley Longman Ltd
Albyn Press
Appletree Press Ltd
Aris & Phillips Ltd
Arnold
Arrow Books Ltd
Ashgate Publishing Ltd
The Athlone Press Ltd
Balnain Books
Bellew Publishing
Berg Publishers Ltd
A. & C. Black (Publishers) Ltd
Blackstaff Press Ltd
Blackwell Publishers Ltd
Bloodaxe Books Ltd
The Book Guild Ltd
Marion Boyars Publishers Ltd
Boydell & Brewer Ltd
Burns & Oates Ltd
Calder Publications Ltd
Cambridge University Press
Canongate Books
Carcanet Press Ltd
Cardiff Academic Press
Carol Publishing Group

Chadwyck-Healey Ltd
Lloyd Cole
Collins & Brown
Creation Books
Crescent Moon Publishing
James Currey Publishers
Curzon Press Ltd
Dedalus Ltd
Delectus Books
J M Dent
André Deutsch Ltd
Edinburgh University Press
Aidan Ellis Publishing
University of Exeter Press
Faber & Faber Ltd
Facts on File
Fourth Estate Ltd
Gairm Publications
Gale Research International Ltd
Garnet Publishing Ltd
GMP Publishers Ltd
Grant & Cutler Ltd
Green Books
Greenwood Publishing Group
Robert Hale Ltd
The Hambledon Press
HarperCollins Publishers Ltd
Harvard University Press
The Harvill Press
Headstart History
Hodder & Stoughton Educational
Houghton Mifflin Co International
In Print Publishing Ltd
Kuperard (London) Ltd
The Littman Library of Jewish
  Civilization
Liverpool University Press
Macmillan Education Ltd
Macmillan General Books Ltd
Macmillan Press Ltd
Mainstream Publishing Co
  (Edinburgh) Ltd
Manchester University Press
Mandrake of Oxford
Mansell Publishing
Mercat Press
Microform Academic Publishers
Minerva
Multimedia Library Ltd
Northcote House Publishers Ltd
W. W. Norton & Co Ltd
Peter Owen Ltd
Oxford University Press
Penguin Books Ltd
Pickering & Chatto (Publishers)
  Ltd
Pinter Publishers Ltd
Pluto Publishing Ltd
Poetry Wales Press Ltd
Polity Press
Prentice Hall/Harvester
  Wheatsheaf
Primary Source Media
Random House UK Ltd
Redcliffe Press Ltd
Redstone Press
Reed Books
Riad El-Rayyes Books Ltd
Roundhouse Publishing Ltd
Routledge
Running Press Book Publishers
Sangam Books Ltd
Scolar Press
Scottish Academic Press
Scottish Cultural Press
Association for Scottish Literary
  Studies

Martin Secker & Warburg
Serif
Serpent's Tail Ltd
Sheffield Academic Press
Sinclair-Stevenson
Skoob Books Ltd
Colin Smythe Ltd
Souvenir Press Ltd
Arthur H. Stockwell Ltd
Stride Publications
Alan Sutton Publishing Ltd
Tabb House
Thames & Hudson Ltd
University of Toronto Press
Verso
Virago Press
Voltaire Foundation Ltd
University of Wales Press
Weidenfeld & Nicolson
The Women's Press
Wordsworth Editions Ltd
Yale University Press London
Freelance Press Services

MAGIC & THE OCCULT

Ashgrove Press Ltd
Avon Books
Bossiney Books
Capall Bann Publishing
Carol Publishing Group
Jon Carpenter Publishing
Cassell Plc
Nigel J. Clarke Publications
Creation Books
Crescent Moon Publishing
The C. W. Daniel Company Ltd
W. Foulsham & Co Ltd
Gothic Image Publications
Robert Hale Ltd
Hamlyn
HarperCollins Publishers Ltd
Janus Publishing Co Ltd
Mandrake of Oxford
Mitchell Beazley
Perfect Words and Music Ltd
Piatkus Books
Prism Press Book Publishers Ltd
Prometheus Books UK
Promotional Reprint Co Ltd
Reed Books
Regency House Publishing Ltd
Sidgwick & Jackson Ltd
Sigma Press
Skoob Books Ltd
The Society of Metaphysicians
  Ltd
Souvenir Press Ltd
Rudolf Steiner Press
Sunburst Books
Theosophical Books Ltd
Virgin Publishing
Haldane Mason Ltd
Labyrinth Publishing (UK) Ltd
Marshall Cavendish Books

**MATHEMATICS &
STATISTICS**

Academic Press Ltd
Addison Wesley Longman Ltd
Advisory Unit: Computers in
  Education
Bernard Babani (Publishing) Ltd
Butterworth-Heinemann
Cambridge University Press
Causeway Press Ltd

Chadwyck-Healey Ltd
Chalksoft Ltd
Chapman & Hall Ltd
Chartwell-Bratt (Publishing & Training) Ltd
Computational Mechanics Publications
Daniels Medica
DP Publications & Letts Educational
Educational Low-Priced Books Scheme (ELBS)
W. H. Freeman
Harcourt Brace & Co Ltd
HLT Publications
HMSO Books
Hodder & Stoughton Educational
Holt, Rinehart & Winston
Houghton Mifflin Co International
Imperial College Press
The Institute of Materials
IOP Publishing
Jones & Bartlett International
Kershaw Publishing Co Ltd
Lloyd's Register of Shipping
McGraw-Hill Publishing Co
Macmillan Education Ltd
Macmillan Press Ltd
The MIT Press Ltd
John Murray Publishers Ltd
W. W. Norton & Co Ltd
The Open University
Open University Educational Enterprises Ltd
Oxford University Press
Penguin Books Ltd
Plenum Publishing Co Ltd
Prentice Hall Europe
Prentice Hall/Ellis Horwood
Prim-Ed Publishing
Sage Publications Ltd
Sangam Books Ltd
Schofield & Sims Ltd
Supportive Learning Publications (SLP)
Tarquin Publications
Taylor & Francis Ltd
Stanley Thornes (Publishers) Ltd
Ward Lock Educational Co Ltd
John Wiley & Sons Ltd
Yale University Press London

MEDICAL (INCL. SELF HELP & ALTERNATIVE MEDICINE)

Academic Press Ltd
Ace Books
Andromeda Interactive Ltd
Arnold
Ashgrove Press Ltd
The Athlone Press Ltd
Baillière Tindall
Beaconsfield Publishers Ltd
Blackwell Science Ltd
BMJ Publishing Group
BMP
Books from India (UK) Ltd
British Agencies for Adoption & Fostering
The British Library, Science Reference & Information Service
Butterworth-Heinemann
Cambridge University Press
Capall Bann Publishing
Cardiff Academic Press

Jon Carpenter Publishing
Castlemead Publications
Cavendish Publishing Ltd
Churchill Livingstone
Class Publishing
The C. W. Daniel Company Ltd
Daniels Medica
Dorling Kindersley Ltd
Martin Dunitz Ltd
Educational Low-Priced Books Scheme (ELBS)
Elliot Right Way Books
Elsevier Science Ltd
Facts on File
Forbes Publications Ltd
W. Foulsham & Co Ltd
L. N. Fowler & Co Ltd
Free Association Books
Graffham Press Ltd
Greenwood Publishing Group
Harcourt Brace & Co Ltd
HarperCollins Publishers Ltd
Hawker Publications
Health Education Authority
Helicon
Ian Henry Publications Ltd
HMSO Books
Hochland & Hochland Ltd
Houghton Mifflin Co International
Imperial College Press
Intercept Ltd
JAI Press Ltd
Janus Publishing Co Ltd
Jones & Bartlett International
H. Karnac (Books) Ltd
King's Fund
John Libbey & Company Ltd
McGraw-Hill Publishing Co
Macmillan Education Ltd
Macmillan Press Ltd
Manson Publishing Ltd
Manticore Europe Ltd
Kenneth Mason Publications Ltd
Mechanical Engineering Publications
Metro Books
Microform Academic Publishers
Miller Freeman Information Services
The MIT Press Ltd
National Academy Press
NCT Publishing Ltd
New Era Publications UK Ltd
The Open University
Open University Press
Oxfam Publishing
Oxford University Press
Parthenon Publishing Group Ltd
PasTest
Pavilion Publishing (Brighton) Ltd
Pearson Professional Ltd
Penguin Books Ltd
Pentaxion Ltd
Perfect Words and Music Ltd
The Pharmaceutical Press
Plenum Publishing Co Ltd
Portland Press Ltd
Prentice Hall Europe
Prentice Hall/Ellis Horwood
Prism Press Book Publishers Ltd
Promotional Reprint Co Ltd
Quintessence Publishing Co Ltd
Radcliffe Medical Press Ltd
Random House UK Ltd
Rapid Science Publishers
Roundhouse Publishing Ltd

Royal College of General Practitioners
Royal Society of Medicine Press Ltd
Sangam Books Ltd
W. B. Saunders Co Ltd
Save the Children
Sheldon Press
Simon & Schuster
Singular Publishing Group Inc
Souvenir Press Ltd
Springer-Verlag London Ltd
Harold Starke Publishers Ltd
Rudolf Steiner Press
The Stroke Association
Sunburst Books
Taylor & Francis Ltd
Whurr Publishers Ltd
John Wiley & Sons Ltd
Winslow Press Ltd
Yale University Press London
BLA Publishing Ltd
Eddison Sadd Editions Ltd
Haldane Mason Ltd
Market House Books Ltd
Marshall Information Ltd

MILITARY & WAR

ABC-Clio Ltd
Addax Retail Publishing Ltd
Addison Wesley Longman Ltd
Airdata Publications
Airlife Publishing Ltd
Ian Allan Ltd
Arms & Armour Press
Arrow Books Ltd
Avon Books
Berg Publishers Ltd
Bloomsbury Publishing Plc
The Book Guild Ltd
Books from India (UK) Ltd
Books International
Boxtree
Boydell & Brewer Ltd
Brassey's (UK) Ltd
Bridge Books
Canongate Books
Carol Publishing Group
Frank Cass & Co Ltd
Cassell Plc
Castlemead Publications
Constable & Co Ltd
Crécy Books Ltd
Dartmouth Publishing Co Ltd
André Deutsch Ltd
John Donald Publishers Ltd
Dorset Publishing Co
Facts on File
Firebird Books Ltd
Adrian Forman Books
Greenhill Books / Lionel Leventhal Ltd
Greenwood Publishing Group
Grub Street
Robert Hale Ltd
Harveys Books
Headline Book Publishing Ltd
Helicon
HMSO Books
Hodder & Stoughton General
Hutchinson
Images Publishing (Malvern) Ltd
The Institute of Marine Engineers
Jane's Information Group Ltd
Janus Publishing Co Ltd

Michael Joseph Ltd & Pelham Books
The Lutterworth Press
Manchester University Press
Merlin Books Ltd
Middleton Press
Midland Counties Publications (Aerophile) Ltd
Midland Publishing Ltd
John Murray Publishers Ltd
National Museums of Scotland
New Orchard Editions
Nexus Special Interests
Michael O'Mara Books Ltd
Osprey
Oxford University Press
Pathfinder Press
PAVIC Publications
Pen & Sword Books Ltd
The Pentland Press Ltd
Phillimore & Co Ltd
Phoenix Press (Oxford)
Picton Publishing (Chippenham) Ltd
Polity Press
Promotional Reprint Co Ltd
Quotes Ltd
The Radcliffe Press
Random House UK Ltd
Reed Books
Regency House Publishing Ltd
Research Institute for the Study of Conflict & Terrorism (RISCT)
Salamander Books
Scottish Cultural Press
Shire Publications Ltd
Sidgwick & Jackson Ltd
Silver Link Publishing Ltd
Souvenir Press Ltd
Spa Books Ltd
Spellmount Ltd
Spokesman
Patrick Stephens Ltd
Arthur H. Stockwell Ltd
International Institute for Strategic Studies
Studio Editions Ltd
Summersdale Publishers
Sunburst Books
Alan Sutton Publishing Ltd
I. B. Tauris & Co Ltd
Time-Life Books
University of Toronto Press
UCL Press Ltd
Westview Press
Wharncliffe Publishing Ltd
Windrow & Greene
Windrush Press Ltd
Yale University Press London
BLA Publishing Ltd
Brown Packaging (Books) Ltd
CLB Publishing Ltd
Ink Inc Ltd
Kingfisher Design Services
Marshall Cavendish Books
Marshall Information Ltd
Quarto Publishing Plc
Ravelin Ltd
Wordwright

MUSIC

Amber Lane Press Ltd
Appletree Press Ltd
Ashgate Publishing Ltd
Avon Books
A. & C. Black (Publishers) Ltd

Blandford Press
Books from India (UK) Ltd
Boosey & Hawkes Music
 Publishers Ltd
Marion Boyars Publishers Ltd
Boydell & Brewer Ltd
British Library, Humanities &
 Social Sciences
The British Library, Public
 Services Publishing
Calder Publications Ltd
Cambridge University Press
Canongate Books
Capall Bann Publishing
Cardiff Academic Press
Carlton Books Ltd
Carol Publishing Group
Cassell Plc
Chadwyck-Healey Ltd
Chalksoft Ltd
Collins & Brown
Constable & Co Ltd
Creation Books
Crescent Moon Publishing
Dance Books Ltd
De Agostini Editions
J M Dent
André Deutsch Ltd
John Donald Publishers Ltd
Dorling Kindersley Ltd
Dragon's World Ltd
East-West Publications (UK) Ltd
Faber & Faber Ltd
Facts on File
Fantail Books
Firebird Books Ltd
Fountain Press Ltd
Victor Gollancz Ltd
Grandreams Ltd
Greenwood Publishing Group
Guinness Publishing Ltd
Robert Hale Ltd
Hamish Hamilton Ltd
Hamlyn
HarperCollins Religious
Harvard University Press
Harveys Books
Hawksmere Group Ltd
Helicon
HMSO Books
Hymns Ancient & Modern Ltd &
International Music Publications
 Ltd
The Littman Library of Jewish
 Civilization
Macmillan Press Ltd
Macmillan Reference Books
Mainstream Publishing Co
 (Edinburgh) Ltd
Media Research Publishing Ltd
Methodist Publishing House
Microform Academic Publishers
The MIT Press Ltd
Moorley's Print & Publishing
National Christian Education
 Council
W. W. Norton & Co Ltd
Omnibus Press
The Open University
Oxford University Press
Packard Publishing Ltd
Pavilion Books Ltd
PC Publishing
Penguin Books Ltd
Plexus Publishing Ltd
Prentice Hall Europe
Prism Press Book Publishers Ltd

Quartet Books
Random House UK Ltd
Reed Books
Rhinegold Publishing Ltd
Roundhouse Publishing Ltd
Salamander Books
Salvationist Publishing &
 Supplies Ltd
Sangam Books Ltd
Schofield & Sims Ltd
Scolar Press
Scripture Union Publishing
Serpent's Tail Ltd
Simon & Schuster
Sinclair-Stevenson
Smith Gryphon Publishers
Square One Books Ltd
Stainer & Bell Ltd
Rudolf Steiner Press
Stride Publications
Sunburst Books
Thames & Hudson Ltd
Timber Press
Titan Books Ltd
University of Toronto Press
UFO Music Ltd
Vinyl Experience Ltd
Virgin Publishing
Ward Lock Educational Co Ltd
Wild Goose Publications
Writers & Readers Ltd
Y Lolfa Cyf
Yale University Press London
BLA Publishing Ltd
Delian Bower Publishing
Brown Packaging (Books) Ltd
Calmann & King Ltd
*The Foundry Creative Media Co
 Ltd*
Ink Inc Ltd
Rough Guides Ltd

NATURAL HISTORY

Academic Press Ltd
Addax Retail Publishing Ltd
Addison Wesley Longman Ltd
Airlife Publishing Ltd
Argyll Publishing
Colin Baxter Photography Ltd
BBC Books
Belitha Press Ltd
Blackstaff Press Ltd
Blandford Press
Boxtree
The British Library, Public
 Services Publishing
Cambridge University Press
Canongate Books
Capall Bann Publishing
Cardiff Academic Press
Carlton Books Ltd
Carol Publishing Group
Cassell Plc
Castlemead Publications
Kyle Cathie Ltd
Chalksoft Ltd
Cicerone Press
Nigel J. Clarke Publications
E. W. Classey Ltd
Collins & Brown
Countyvise Ltd
The Crowood Press Ltd
David & Charles Publishers
Dorling Kindersley Ltd
Dragon's World Ltd
Aidan Ellis Publishing

Eurobook Ltd
Ex Libris Press
Facts on File
Fountain Press Ltd
Gaia Books Ltd
Victor Gollancz Ltd
Green Books
Robert Hale Ltd
Hamish Hamilton Ltd
Harcourt Brace & Co Ltd
HarperCollins Publishers Ltd
Harvard University Press
Harveys Books
Headline Book Publishing Ltd
Headstart History
The Herbert Press
HMSO Books
Hodder & Stoughton Educational
Houghton Mifflin Co International
Intercept Ltd
Michael Joseph Ltd & Pelham
 Books
Kegan Paul International Ltd
The Kenilworth Press Ltd
Larousse Plc
Leading Edge Press & Publishing
The Lutterworth Press
The Medici Society Ltd
Microform Academic Publishers
The MIT Press Ltd
Mitchell Beazley
Multimedia Library Ltd
National Academy Press
National Museums of Scotland
The Natural History Museum –
 Publications Section
New Holland (Publishers) Ltd
New Orchard Editions
W. W. Norton & Co Ltd
The Open University
Oxford University Press
Packard Publishing Ltd
Penguin Books Ltd
Prism Press Book Publishers Ltd
Promotional Reprint Co Ltd
Quotes Ltd
Random House UK Ltd
Ransom Publishing
Reed Books
The Richmond Publishing Co Ltd
Running Press Book Publishers
Sainsbury Publishing Ltd
Salamander Books
Sangam Books Ltd
Scottish Cultural Press
Sessions of York
SGC Books
Shire Publications Ltd
Sinclair-Stevenson
Souvenir Press Ltd
The Sportsman's Press
Harold Starke Publishers Ltd
Rudolf Steiner Press
Stobart Davies Ltd
Studio Editions Ltd
Sunburst Books
Alan Sutton Publishing Ltd
Taylor & Francis Ltd
Time-Life Books
University of Toronto Press
Dyllansow Truran
Usborne Publishing Ltd
Wheldon & Wesley Ltd
Whittet Books Ltd
John Wiley & Sons Ltd
Yale University Press London
Andromeda Oxford Ltd

BCS Publishing Ltd
Bender Richardson White
BLA Publishing Ltd
Brown Wells & Jacobs Ltd
Calmann & King Ltd
Cameron Books
CLB Publishing Ltd
Diagram Visual Information Ltd
Duncan Petersen Publishing Ltd
Sara Dunn
Eddison Sadd Editions Ltd
Haldane Mason Ltd
Kingfisher Design Services
Marshall Cavendish Books
Marshall Information Ltd
Prion Books Ltd
Quarto Publishing Plc
The Templar Co Plc
Toucan Books Ltd
Wordwright

NAUTICAL

ABC-Clio Ltd
Addax Retail Publishing Ltd
Addison Wesley Longman Ltd
Adlard Coles Nautical
Airlife Publishing Ltd
Arms & Armour Press
Avon Books
A. & C. Black (Publishers) Ltd
The Book Guild Ltd
Books International
Brassey's (UK) Ltd
Brown, Son & Ferguson, Ltd
Capall Bann Publishing
Cassell Plc
Nigel J. Clarke Publications
Crécy Books Ltd
The Crowood Press Ltd
Gerald Duckworth & Co Ltd
Aidan Ellis Publishing
Fernhurst Books
Robert Hale Ltd
Harcourt Brace & Co Ltd
Harveys Books
HMSO Books
Imray Laurie Norie & Wilson Ltd
The Institute of Marine Engineers
Jane's Information Group Ltd
Janus Publishing Co Ltd
Lloyd's Register of Shipping
Kenneth Mason Publications Ltd
Mechanical Engineering
 Publications
Merlin Press Ltd
Microform Academic Publishers
Miller Freeman Information
 Services
National Academy Press
Nexus Special Interests
W. W. Norton & Co Ltd
Promotional Reprint Co Ltd
Roadmaster Publishing
S. B. Publications
Scottish Cultural Press
Silver Link Publishing Ltd
Patrick Stephens Ltd
Sunburst Books
Alan Sutton Publishing Ltd
Twelveheads Press
Witherby & Co Ltd
BLA Publishing Ltd
Marshall Information Ltd

PHILOSOPHY

Academy Group Ltd
Addison Wesley Longman Ltd
Ashgate Publishing Ltd
Ashgrove Press Ltd
The Athlone Press Ltd
Bahá'í Publishing Trust
Bibliagora
Black Ace Books
Blackwell Publishers Ltd
Marion Boyars Publishers Ltd
Burns & Oates Ltd
Cambridge University Press
Cardiff Academic Press
Carol Publishing Group
Jon Carpenter Publishing
Cassell Plc
Chartwell-Bratt (Publishing & Training) Ltd
T. & T. Clark
Anthony Clarke Books
James Clarke & Co
Lloyd Cole
Crescent Moon Publishing
Curzon Press Ltd
Dartmouth Publishing Co Ltd
Darton, Longman & Todd Ltd
Edinburgh University Press
Element Books Ltd
Floris Books
Freedom Press
Gothic Image Publications
Gracewing/Fowler Wright Books Ltd
Green Books
Greenwood Publishing Group
Guilford Press
Harvard University Press
ICA (Institute of Contemporary Arts)
JAI Press Ltd
Kegan Paul International Ltd
The Littman Library of Jewish Civilization
Llanerch Publishers
Barry Long Books
Macmillan Press Ltd
Manchester University Press
Mansell Publishing
Merlin Press Ltd
Microform Academic Publishers
The MIT Press Ltd
New Era Publications UK Ltd
W. W. Norton & Co Ltd
Oneworld Publications
Open Gate Press
The Open University
Open University Educational Enterprises Ltd
Oxford University Press
Pathfinder Press
Penguin Books Ltd
Perfect Words and Music Ltd
Picador
Pluto Publishing Ltd
Polity Press
Prentice Hall Europe
Prentice Hall/Harvester Wheatsheaf
Prism Press Book Publishers Ltd
Profile Books Ltd
Prometheus Books UK
Reed Books
Roundhouse Publishing Ltd
Routledge
St Pauls

Sangam Books Ltd
SCM Press Ltd
Scope International Ltd
Search Press Ltd
Sheed & Ward Ltd
Shepheard-Walwyn (Publishers) Ltd
The Society of Metaphysicians Ltd
Souvenir Press Ltd
Rudolf Steiner Press
Taylor & Francis Ltd
Thames & Hudson Ltd
Theosophical Books Ltd
Thoemmes Press
University of Toronto Press
UCL Press Ltd
VCH Publishers (UK) Ltd
Verso
Weidenfeld & Nicolson
Westview Press
Windhorse Publications
Writers & Readers Ltd
Yale University Press London
Delian Bower Publishing
Labyrinth Publishing (UK) Ltd

PHOTOGRAPHY

ABC-Clio Ltd
Addison Wesley Longman Ltd
Anness Publishing Ltd
Appletree Press Ltd
Colin Baxter Photography Ltd
Bloodaxe Books Ltd
Butterworth-Heinemann
Calder Publications Ltd
Canongate Books
Cassell Plc
The Chalford Publishing Co Ltd
Collins & Brown
Constable & Co Ltd
Crescent Moon Publishing
David & Charles Publishers
André Deutsch Ltd
Dragon's World Ltd
Eaglemoss Publications Ltd
East-West Publications (UK) Ltd
Elfande Ltd
Fountain Press Ltd
Garnet Publishing Ltd
GMP Publishers Ltd
Robert Hale Ltd
Headline Book Publishing Ltd
The Herbert Press
HMSO Books
Hutton Press Ltd
ICA (Institute of Contemporary Arts)
Impact Books / Olive Press
Michael Joseph Ltd & Pelham Books
Kensington West Productions
Laurence King Publishing
Little, Brown & Co (UK)
Mainstream Publishing Co (Edinburgh) Ltd
Manchester University Press
Merrell Holberton Publishers Ltd
The MIT Press Ltd
Mitchell Beazley
National Portrait Gallery Publications
New Holland (Publishers) Ltd
Oxford University Press
Penguin Books Ltd
Phaidon Press Ltd

Plexus Publishing Ltd
Random House UK Ltd
Reed Books
Riad El-Rayyes Books Ltd
Rivers Oram
Running Press Book Publishers
Sinclair-Stevenson
Sunburst Books
Alan Sutton Publishing Ltd
Taylor & Francis Ltd
Thames & Hudson Ltd
Studio Vista
Weidenfeld & Nicolson
Writers & Readers Ltd
Yale University Press London
Book Packaging and Marketing
Calmann & King Ltd
Freelance Press Services
Haldane Mason Ltd
Marshall Cavendish Books
Marshall Information Ltd
Quarto Publishing Plc

PHYSICS

Academic Press Ltd
Addison Wesley Longman Ltd
BTL Publishing
Butterworth-Heinemann
Cambridge University Press
Chartwell-Bratt (Publishing & Training) Ltd
Daniels Medica
Educational Low-Priced Books Scheme (ELBS)
Garland Publishing Inc
Harcourt Brace & Co Ltd
Hodder & Stoughton Educational
Holt, Rinehart & Winston
Imperial College Press
The Institute of Materials
IOP Publishing
McGraw-Hill Publishing Co
Macmillan Education Ltd
Macmillan Press Ltd
Microform Academic Publishers
The MIT Press Ltd
John Murray Publishers Ltd
W. W. Norton & Co Ltd
The Open University
Open University Educational Enterprises Ltd
Oxford University Press
Penguin Books Ltd
Pentaxion Ltd
Pion Ltd
Plenum Publishing Co Ltd
Prentice Hall Europe
Prentice Hall/Ellis Horwood
The Royal Society
Sangam Books Ltd
Schofield & Sims Ltd
Taylor & Francis Ltd
Stanley Thornes (Publishers) Ltd
UCL Press Ltd
VCH Publishers (UK) Ltd
Ward Lock Educational Co Ltd
John Wiley & Sons Ltd
Paul Barnett Editorial
BLA Publishing Ltd

POETRY

Addison Wesley Longman Ltd
Albyn Press
Anvil Press Poetry
Argyll Publishing

Avon Books
Bellew Publishing
Blackstaff Press Ltd
Bloodaxe Books Ltd
The Book Guild Ltd
Books UK Ltd
Marion Boyars Publishers Ltd
Calder Publications Ltd
David Campbell Publishers
Canongate Books
Carcanet Press Ltd
Cardiff Academic Press
Carol Publishing Group
Cassell Plc
Chadwyck-Healey Ltd
Channel 4 Learning
Chatto & Windus Ltd
Lloyd Cole
Creation Books
Crescent Moon Publishing
André Deutsch Ltd
Downlander Publishing
East-West Publications (UK) Ltd
Faber & Faber Ltd
Gairm Publications
George Ronald Publisher Ltd
Robert Hale Ltd
HarperCollins Publishers Ltd
The Harvill Press
Houghton Mifflin Co International
ISIS Publishing Ltd
Arthur James Ltd
Janus Publishing Co Ltd
Jarrold Publishing
Kegan Paul International Ltd
Llanerch Publishers
Luath Press Ltd
Macmillan Education Ltd
Merlin Books Ltd
Moorley's Print & Publishing
W. W. Norton & Co Ltd
Oxford University Press
PAVIC Publications
Penguin Books Ltd
Pentathol Publishing
The Pentland Press Ltd
Peterloo Poets
Phoenix Press (Oxford)
Poetry Wales Press Ltd
Polygon
Random House UK Ltd
Reed Books
Riad El-Rayyes Books Ltd
Running Press Book Publishers
Salvationist Publishing & Supplies Ltd
Sangam Books Ltd
Schofield & Sims Ltd
Scottish Cultural Press
Martin Secker & Warburg
Sessions of York
Skoob Books Ltd
Arthur H. Stockwell Ltd
Stride Publications
Summersdale Publishers
Tabb House
Time-Life Books
Toucan Press
Turton & Chambers
The Watts Publishing Group
Windhorse Publications
The Women's Press
Wordsworth Editions Ltd
Writers & Readers Ltd
Yale University Press London
Cameron Books
Sara Dunn

The Foundry Creative Media Co Ltd

POLITICS & WORLD AFFAIRS

Adamantine Press Ltd
Addison Wesley Longman Ltd
Africana Publishing Co
Allison & Busby
Anglo-German Foundation for the Study of Industrial Society
Appletree Press Ltd
Arms & Armour Press
Arrow Books Ltd
Ashgate Publishing Ltd
Bahá'í Publishing Trust
Berg Publishers Ltd
Blackstaff Press Ltd
Blackwell Publishers Ltd
Bloodaxe Books Ltd
Bloomsbury Publishing Plc
Bookmarks
Bowker-Saur
Marion Boyars Publishers Ltd
Brassey's (UK) Ltd
Nicholas Brealey Publishing Ltd
Calder Publications Ltd
Cambridge University Press
Cardiff Academic Press
Carol Publishing Group
Jon Carpenter Publishing
Frank Cass & Co Ltd
Cassell Plc
Causeway Press Ltd
Central European University Press
Centre for Economic Policy Research
Chadwyck-Healey Ltd
Chapmans
Chatto & Windus Ltd
Conservative Political Centre
James Currey Publishers
Dartmouth Publishing Co Ltd
André Deutsch Ltd
Dunrod Press
Earthscan Publications Ltd
The Economist Books
Elliot Right Way Books
Europa Publications Ltd
Faber & Faber Ltd
Fabian Society
Facts on File
Federal Trust
Fourth Estate Ltd
Freedom Press
W. H. Freeman
George Ronald Publisher Ltd
GMP Publishers Ltd
Victor Gollancz Ltd
Gothic Image Publications
Granta
Green Books
Greenwood Publishing Group
Grosvenor Books
Robert Hale Ltd
Hamish Hamilton Ltd
HarperCollins Publishers Ltd
Harvard University Press
William Heinemann
Helicon
HMSO Books
Hodder & Stoughton Educational
Hodder & Stoughton General
Holmes & Meier Publishing
Houghton Mifflin Co International
C. Hurst & Co (Publishers) Ltd

Hutchinson
Institute of Development Studies
Ithaca Press
IW Books
JAI Press Ltd
Janus Publishing Co Ltd
Kegan Paul International Ltd
Latin America Bureau
Lawrence & Wishart Ltd
Leicester University Press
The Littman Library of Jewish Civilization
McGraw-Hill Publishing Co
Macmillan Press Ltd
Mainstream Publishing Co (Edinburgh) Ltd
Manchester University Press
Mandarin
Mansell Publishing
Merlin Press Ltd
Methuen
The MIT Press Ltd
W. W. Norton & Co Ltd
Oneworld Publications
Open Gate Press
The Open University
Open University Educational Enterprises Ltd
Open University Press
Overseas Development Institute
Oxfam Publishing
Oxford University Press
Pathfinder Press
PAVIC Publications
Penguin Books Ltd
Picador
Pinter Publishers Ltd
Pluto Publishing Ltd
Polity Press
Polygon
Prentice Hall Europe
Prentice Hall/Harvester Wheatsheaf
Prism Press Book Publishers Ltd
Profile Books Ltd
Prometheus Books UK
The Radcliffe Press
Random House UK Ltd
Reed Books
Research Institute for the Study of Conflict & Terrorism (RISCT)
Riad El-Rayyes Books Ltd
Lynne Rienner Publishers
Rivers Oram
Routledge
Sage Publications Ltd
Sangam Books Ltd
Save the Children
Scope International Ltd
Martin Secker & Warburg
Serif
Serpent's Tail Ltd
Shepheard-Walwyn (Publishers) Ltd
Sidgwick & Jackson Ltd
Simon & Schuster
Sinclair-Stevenson
Adam Smith Institute
Smith Gryphon Publishers
Spokesman
International Institute for Strategic Studies
I. B. Tauris & Co Ltd
Taylor & Francis Ltd
The Policy Press
Stanley Thornes (Publishers) Ltd
University of Toronto Press

Transworld Publishers Ltd
Trentham Books
UCL Press Ltd
United Kingdom Council for Human Rights (UKCHR)
Verso
Virago Press
Volcano Press Ltd
Weidenfeld & Nicolson
Westview Press
John Wiley & Sons Ltd
The Women's Press
Writers & Readers Ltd
Y Lolfa Cyf
Yale University Press London
Zed Books Ltd
Ink Inc Ltd

PSYCHOLOGY & PSYCHIATRY

Academic Press Ltd
Addison Wesley Longman Ltd
American Psychiatric Press
American Psychological Association
Arnold
Ashgate Publishing Ltd
Ashgrove Press Ltd
The Athlone Press Ltd
Baillière Tindall
Blackwell Publishers Ltd
Marion Boyars Publishers Ltd
Breese Books Ltd
British Agencies for Adoption & Fostering
British Psychological Society (BPS Books)
Burns & Oates Ltd
Cambridge University Press
Cardiff Academic Press
Carol Publishing Group
Cassell Plc
Constable & Co Ltd
Dartmouth Publishing Co Ltd
Darton, Longman & Todd Ltd
André Deutsch Ltd
Eagle
Element Books Ltd
Elliot Right Way Books
Falmer Press Ltd
Free Association Books
W. H. Freeman
David Fulton Publishers Ltd
Gateway Books
Greenwood Publishing Group
Guilford Press
Hamish Hamilton Ltd
Harcourt Brace & Co Ltd
HarperCollins Publishers Ltd
Harvard University Press
Hawthorn Press
University of Hertfordshire Press
HMSO Books
Hodder & Stoughton Educational
Holmes & Meier Publishing
Houghton Mifflin Co International
Arthur James Ltd
H. Karnac (Books) Ltd
Jessica Kingsley Publishers
McGraw-Hill Publishing Co
Macmillan Press Ltd
Metro Books
Microform Academic Publishers
The MIT Press Ltd
Multilingual Matters Ltd
National Academy Press

W. W. Norton & Co Ltd
Oneworld Publications
Open Gate Press
The Open University
Open University Educational Enterprises Ltd
Open University Press
Oxford University Press
Pavilion Publishing (Brighton) Ltd
Penguin Books Ltd
Perfect Words and Music Ltd
Piatkus Books
Plenum Publishing Co Ltd
Polity Press
Prentice Hall Europe
Prentice Hall/Harvester Wheatsheaf
Prism Press Book Publishers Ltd
Profile Books Ltd
Psychology Press of Erlbaum (UK) Taylor & Francis
Rosendale Press Ltd
Roundhouse Publishing Ltd
Routledge
Royal College of General Practitioners
Running Press Book Publishers
Sage Publications Ltd
Sangam Books Ltd
Sheldon Press
Sherwood Publishing
Souvenir Press Ltd
Spokesman
Summersdale Publishers
Taylor & Francis Ltd
Thames & Hudson Ltd
Theosophical Books Ltd
UCL Press Ltd
Verso
Virago Press
Westview Press
Whurr Publishers Ltd
John Wiley & Sons Ltd
Winslow Press Ltd
Writers & Readers Ltd
Yale University Press London
Delian Bower Publishing
Prion Books Ltd

REFERENCE BOOKS, DIRECTORIES & DICTIONARIES

ABC-Clio Ltd
Academic Press Ltd
Ace Books
Adam Matthew Publications
Addison Wesley Longman Ltd
Albyn Press
American Library Association
Antique Collectors' Club Ltd
AP Information Services
Appletree Press Ltd
Aris & Phillips Ltd
Arms & Armour Press
Arnold
Ashgate Publishing Ltd
ASLIB (The Association for Information Management)
Association of Commonwealth Universities (ACU)
The Athlone Press Ltd
Atlantic Europe Publishing Co Ltd
Aurelian Information Ltd
Baillière Tindall
Belitha Press Ltd

Berlitz Publishing Co Ltd
A. & C. Black (Publishers) Ltd
Blackwell Publishers Ltd
Blandford Press
Bloomsbury Publishing Plc
Books from India (UK) Ltd
Bowker-Saur
Brassey's (UK) Ltd
British Library, National
  Bibliographic Service
The British Library, Public
  Services Publishing
The British Library, Science
  Reference & Information
  Service
Bruce Smith Books Ltd
Burns & Oates Ltd
Butterworth-Heinemann
Cambridge University Press
Canongate Books
Carol Publishing Group
Carrick Media
Cassell Plc
Kyle Cathie Ltd
CBD Research Ltd
CCBI Publications
Chadwyck-Healey Ltd
Chapman & Hall Ltd
Chartwell-Bratt (Publishing &
  Training) Ltd
Christian Research Association
Church House Publishing
James Clarke & Co
Lloyd Cole
Peter Collin Publishing Ltd
Constable & Co Ltd
Crescent Moon Publishing
Croner Publications Ltd
Curzon Press Ltd
Dartmouth Publishing Co Ltd
J M Dent
André Deutsch Ltd
Dial Publications
Dorling Kindersley Ltd
Dun & Bradstreet Ltd
Earthscan Publications Ltd
The Economist Books
Edinburgh University Press
ELC International
Element Books Ltd
Edward Elgar Publishing Ltd
Elliot Right Way Books
Encyclopaedia Britannica
  International Ltd
ERA Technology Ltd
Eurobook Ltd
Euromonitor Plc
Europa Publications Ltd
Executive Grapevine International
  Ltd
Facts on File
Food Trade Press Ltd
G. T. Foulis & Co
W. Foulsham & Co Ltd
Fourth Estate Ltd
Gairm Publications
Gale Research International Ltd
Garland Publishing Inc
Stanley Gibbons Publications
Gower Publishing Ltd
Graham & Whiteside Ltd
Granta Editions
Greenwood Publishing Group
Guinness Publishing Ltd
Peter Haddock Ltd
Robert Hale Ltd
Hamlyn

Harcourt Brace & Co Ltd
HarperCollins Publishers Ltd
Harrap
J. H. Haynes & Co Ltd
Helicon
Hilmarton Manor Press
HMSO Books
Hobsons Publishing Plc
Hodder & Stoughton Educational
Hodder & Stoughton General
Hollis Directories Ltd
Holt, Rinehart & Winston
Houghton Mifflin Co International
Hugo's Language Books Ltd
ICC Information Group Ltd
ICSA Publishing Ltd
Impact Books / Olive Press
The Institute of Materials
Inter-Varsity Press
Intermediate Technology
  Publications Ltd
IOP Publishing
JAI Press Ltd
Jane's Information Group Ltd
Richard Joseph Publishers Ltd
Kegan Paul International Ltd
Kemps Publishing Ltd
Kennedy's Publications Ltd
Jessica Kingsley Publishers
Kogan Page Ltd
Kuperard (London) Ltd
Larousse Plc
Lemos & Crane
Library Association Publishing
LLP Ltd
McGraw-Hill Publishing Co
Macmillan Education Ltd
Macmillan Press Ltd
Macmillan Reference Books
Management Books 2000 Ltd
Mansell Publishing
Melrose Press Ltd
Mercat Press
Metro Books
Miller Freeman Information
  Services
The MIT Press Ltd
Mitchell Beazley
Multimedia Library Ltd
NCT Publishing Ltd
NCVO Publications
New Orchard Editions
Nile & Mackenzie Ltd
NTC Publications Ltd
Oxford University Press
Packard Publishing Ltd
Penguin Books Ltd
Pinter Publishers Ltd
Pira International
Pitman Publishing
Polity Press
Prentice Hall/Ellis Horwood
Prentice Hall/Woodhead Faulkner
Promotional Reprint Co Ltd
Radcliffe Medical Press Ltd
Random House UK Ltd
Reed Books
Rhinegold Publishing Ltd
Roundhouse Publishing Ltd
Routledge
The Royal Society of Chemistry
Sage Publications Ltd
Sangam Books Ltd
Schofield & Sims Ltd
Shaw & Sons Ltd
Sheed & Ward Ltd
Simon & Schuster

Skoob Books Ltd
Square One Books Ltd
Stainer & Bell Ltd
Harold Starke Publishers Ltd
Studio Editions Ltd
Summersdale Publishers
Sunburst Books
Supernet
Sweet & Maxwell Ltd
I. B. Tauris & Co Ltd
TFPL Publishing
Thames & Hudson Ltd
Time-Life Books
University of Toronto Press
Toucan Press
Trotman & Co Ltd
Dyllansow Truran
Ulster Historical Foundation
Usborne Publishing Ltd
VCH Publishers (UK) Ltd
Virgin Publishing
Volcano Press Ltd
University of Wales Press
Ward Lock Ltd
The Watts Publishing Group
J. Whitaker & Sons Ltd
John Wiley & Sons Ltd
Witherby & Co Ltd
Wordsworth Editions Ltd
Yale University Press London
Andromeda Oxford Ltd
Paul Barnett Editorial
BLA Publishing Ltd
Book Packaging and Marketing
Cameron Books
Diagram Visual Information Ltd
Earthscape Editions
Eddison Sadd Editions Ltd
Ink Inc Ltd
Lexus Ltd
Market House Books Ltd
William Reed Directories
Toucan Books Ltd
Laurence Urdang Inc

RELIGION & THEOLOGY

Addison Wesley Longman Ltd
Ahmadiyya Muslim Publications
Ashgrove Press Ltd
The Athlone Press Ltd
Avon Books
Bahá'í Publishing Trust
The Banner of Truth Trust
Bible Reading Fellowship
A. & C. Black (Publishers) Ltd
Blackwell Publishers Ltd
The Book Guild Ltd
British & Foreign Bible Society
Burns & Oates Ltd
Cambridge University Press
Capall Bann Publishing
Carcanet Press Ltd
Cardiff Academic Press
Carol Publishing Group
Cassell Plc
The Catholic Truth Society
CCBI Publications
Geoffrey Chapman
Chartwell-Bratt (Publishing &
  Training) Ltd
Christian Focus Publications
Christian Research Association
Church House Publishing
T. & T. Clark
Anthony Clarke Books
James Clarke & Co

Countyvise Ltd
Covenant Publishing Co Ltd
Crescent Moon Publishing
James Currey Publishers
Curzon Press Ltd
Darton, Longman & Todd Ltd
André Deutsch Ltd
Eagle
East-West Publications (UK) Ltd
Element Books Ltd
Epworth Press
Evangelical Press & Services Ltd
Evangelical Press of Wales
Floris Books
The Foundational Book Company
L. N. Fowler & Co Ltd
George Ronald Publisher Ltd
Global Books Ltd
Adam Gordon
Gothic Image Publications
Grace Publications Trust
Gracewing/Fowler Wright Books
  Ltd
Greenwood Publishing Group
Grey Seal Books
Grosvenor Books
Harcourt Brace & Co Ltd
HarperCollins Publishers Ltd
HarperCollins Religious
Headstart History
Highland Books
Hodder & Stoughton Educational
Hodder & Stoughton Religious
Holmes & Meier Publishing
Home Health Education Service
Hunt and Thorpe
C. Hurst & Co (Publishers) Ltd
Hymns Ancient & Modern Ltd &
Inter-Varsity Press
Islam International Publications
  Ltd
The Islamic Texts Society
JAI Press Ltd
Arthur James Ltd
Janus Publishing Co Ltd
Kegan Paul International Ltd
Kingsway Publications Ltd
Kuperard (London) Ltd
Lion Publishing Plc
The Littman Library of Jewish
  Civilization
Liverpool University Press
Llanerch Publishers
The Lutterworth Press
Macmillan Education Ltd
Macmillan Press Ltd
Mansell Publishing
Methodist Publishing House
Microform Academic Publishers
Moorley's Print & Publishing
Mowbray
National Christian Education
  Council
New Era Publications UK Ltd
OM Publishing
Oneworld Publications
The Open University
Oxford University Press
Paternoster Publishing
Penguin Books Ltd
The Pentland Press Ltd
Perfect Words and Music Ltd
Phoenix Press (Oxford)
Pinter Publishers Ltd
Polity Press
Prism Press Book Publishers Ltd
Prometheus Books UK

Quaker Home Service
Redemptorist Publications
Reed Books
Riad El-Rayyes Books Ltd
Romer Publications
Saint Andrew Press
St Pauls
Salvationist Publishing &
 Supplies Ltd
Sangam Books Ltd
Schofield & Sims Ltd
School of Oriental and African
 Studies (University of London)
SCM Press Ltd
Scottish Academic Press
Scripture Union Publishing
Sessions of York
Sheed & Ward Ltd
Sheffield Academic Press
Shepheard-Walwyn (Publishers)
 Ltd
The Society for Promoting
 Christian Knowledge
Souvenir Press Ltd
Stainer & Bell Ltd
Rudolf Steiner Press
Arthur H. Stockwell Ltd
Studio Editions Ltd
Thames & Hudson Ltd
Tharpa Publications
Theosophical Books Ltd
Stanley Thornes (Publishers) Ltd
Volcano Press Ltd
University of Wales Press
Ward Lock Educational Co Ltd
White Eagle Publishing Trust
Wild Goose Publications
Windhorse Publications
Wisdom Books
Word Publishing
Writers & Readers Ltd
Yale University Press London
BLA Publishing Ltd
Delian Bower Publishing
Labyrinth Publishing (UK) Ltd

SCIENCE FICTION

Avon Books
Carlton Books Ltd
Carol Publishing Group
Creation Books
André Deutsch Ltd
Dragon's World Ltd
GMP Publishers Ltd
Victor Gollancz Ltd
Greenwood Publishing Group
HarperCollins Publishers Ltd
Hawk Books
Headline Book Publishing Ltd
Hodder & Stoughton General
Janus Publishing Co Ltd
Kinnell Publications Ltd
Little, Brown & Co (UK)
Liverpool University Press
Macmillan General Books Ltd
New Era Publications UK Ltd
Orion Books Ltd
Penguin Books Ltd
Random House UK Ltd
Reed Books
Severn House Publishers Ltd
Simon & Schuster
Titan Books Ltd
Transworld Publishers Ltd
United Writers Publications Ltd

The Women's Press
Paul Barnett Editorial

SCIENTIFIC & TECHNICAL

AA Publishing
Academic Press Ltd
Acol-Biotol
Addison Wesley Longman Ltd
Arms & Armour Press
Arnold
Arrow Books Ltd
Artech House
Ashgate Publishing Ltd
Atlantic Europe Publishing Co Ltd
Bernard Babani (Publishing) Ltd
Baillière Tindall
Blackwell Science Ltd
Books from India (UK) Ltd
Brassey's (UK) Ltd
The British Library, Science
 Reference & Information
 Service
The Building Services Research &
 Information Association
Butterworth-Heinemann
Cambridge University Press
Chalksoft Ltd
Chapman & Hall Ltd
Chartwell-Bratt (Publishing &
 Training) Ltd
Class Publishing
Computational Mechanics
 Publications
Daniels Medica
J M Dent
Donhead Publishing Ltd
Martin Dunitz Ltd
Educational Low-Priced Books
 Scheme (ELBS)
Elsevier Science Ltd
EnTra Publications Ltd
ERA Technology Ltd
Garland Publishing Inc
Gower Publishing Ltd
Granta Editions
Harcourt Brace & Co Ltd
Helicon
University of Hertfordshire Press
HMSO Books
Hobsons Publishing Plc
Hodder & Stoughton Educational
Holt, Rinehart & Winston
Houghton Mifflin Co International
Imperial College Press
The Institute of Materials
Institution of Chemical Engineers
Institution of Electrical Engineers
Intellect Ltd
Intercept Ltd
Intermediate Technology
 Publications Ltd
IOP Publishing
JAI Press Ltd
James & James (Science
 Publishers) Ltd
Jones & Bartlett International
Kennedy's Publications Ltd
Lloyd's Register of Shipping
McGraw-Hill Publishing Co
Macmillan Press Ltd
Manson Publishing Ltd
Mechanical Engineering
 Publications
Mecklermedia Ltd
The MIT Press Ltd
John Murray Publishers Ltd

National Academy Press
National Museums of Scotland
The Natural History Museum –
 Publications Section
The New York Academy of
 Sciences
Nexus Special Interests
The Open University
Open University Educational
 Enterprises Ltd
Oxford University Press
Packard Publishing Ltd
Parthenon Publishing Group Ltd
PAVIC Publications
PC Publishing
Penguin Books Ltd
Pentaxion Ltd
Pickering & Chatto (Publishers)
 Ltd
Pira International
Plenum Publishing Co Ltd
Portland Press Ltd
Prentice Hall Europe
Prism Press Book Publishers Ltd
Rapid Science Publishers
Research Studies Press Ltd
The Richmond Publishing Co Ltd
Romer Publications
The Royal Society
The Royal Society of Chemistry
Sangam Books Ltd
Science Museum Publications
Sheffield Academic Press
Sigma Press
Simon & Schuster
The Society of Metaphysicians
 Ltd
E. & F. N. Spon
Harold Starke Publishers Ltd
Stobart Davies Ltd
Taylor & Francis Ltd
Taylor Graham Publishing
Stanley Thornes (Publishers) Ltd
Timber Press
University of Toronto Press
Usborne Publishing Ltd
VCH Publishers (UK) Ltd
Whittles Publishing
Whurr Publishers Ltd
John Wiley & Sons Ltd
Witherby & Co Ltd
Woodhead Publishing Ltd
Earthscape Editions
Market House Books Ltd
Marshall Information Ltd

SOCIOLOGY & ANTHROPOLOGY

Academic Press Ltd
Addison Wesley Longman Ltd
Aris & Phillips Ltd
Ashgate Publishing Ltd
The Athlone Press Ltd
Bahá'í Publishing Trust
Berg Publishers Ltd
Blackwell Publishers Ltd
Marion Boyars Publishers Ltd
British Agencies for Adoption &
 Fostering
British Museum Press
Cambridge University Press
Cardiff Academic Press
Carol Publishing Group
Jon Carpenter Publishing
Cassell Plc
Causeway Press Ltd

Central European University Press
Chartwell-Bratt (Publishing &
 Training) Ltd
Constable & Co Ltd
Crescent Moon Publishing
James Currey Publishers
Curzon Press Ltd
André Deutsch Ltd
Edinburgh University Press
Edward Elgar Publishing Ltd
Falmer Press Ltd
Freedom Press
Gateway Books
GMP Publishers Ltd
Greenwood Publishing Group
Guilford Press
Robert Hale Ltd
Harcourt Brace & Co Ltd
Harvard University Press
HMSO Books
Holmes & Meier Publishing
Holt, Rinehart & Winston
C. Hurst & Co (Publishers) Ltd
ICA (Institute of Contemporary
 Arts)
Institute of Development Studies
Ithaca Press
JAI Press Ltd
Arthur James Ltd
Kegan Paul International Ltd
Jessica Kingsley Publishers
The Littman Library of Jewish
 Civilization
Liverpool University Press
McGraw-Hill Publishing Co
Macmillan Press Ltd
Manchester University Press
Mansell Publishing
Microform Academic Publishers
The MIT Press Ltd
Multilingual Matters Ltd
National Museums of Scotland
National Youth Agency
NCT Publishing Ltd
NCVO Publications
Oneworld Publications
The Open University
Open University Educational
 Enterprises Ltd
Open University Press
Overseas Development Institute
Oxford University Press
Pathfinder Press
Pavilion Publishing (Brighton)
 Ltd
Penguin Books Ltd
Pluto Publishing Ltd
Polity Press
Prentice Hall Europe
Prentice Hall/Harvester
 Wheatsheaf
Prism Press Book Publishers Ltd
Profile Books Ltd
Lynne Rienner Publishers
Rivers Oram
Routledge
Sage Publications Ltd
Sangam Books Ltd
Save the Children
Scottish Cultural Press
Shire Publications Ltd
Souvenir Press Ltd
Rudolf Steiner Press
I. B. Tauris & Co Ltd
Thames & Hudson Ltd
The Policy Press
Stanley Thornes (Publishers) Ltd

University of Toronto Press
UCL Press Ltd
United Kingdom Council for
  Human Rights (UKCHR)
Verso
Virago Press
Volcano Press Ltd
Westview Press
Yale University Press London
Zed Books Ltd
Labyrinth Publishing (UK) Ltd

SPORTS & GAMES

Ian Allan Ltd
Peter Andrew Publishing Co Ltd
Anness Publishing Ltd
Appletree Press Ltd
Argyll Publishing
Aurum Press
B & W Publishing Ltd
B. T. Batsford Ltd
BBC Books
Bibliagora
A. & C. Black (Publishers) Ltd
Blandford Press
Bookman Projects Ltd
Books UK Ltd
Breedon Books Publishing Co Ltd
Butterfingers
Cadogan Books Plc
Canongate Books
Carlton Books Ltd
Carol Publishing Group
Cassell Plc
Paul Cave Publications Ltd
Chapmans
Cicerone Press
Coachwise Ltd
Countyvise Ltd
The Crowood Press Ltd
André Deutsch Ltd
John Donald Publishers Ltd
Eaglemoss Publications Ltd
Elliot Right Way Books
Express Newspapers Plc
Facts on File
Fernhurst Books
FHG Publications Ltd
Firebird Books Ltd
Footprint Press Ltd
Fourth Estate Ltd
Victor Gollancz Ltd
Grandreams Ltd
Greenwood Publishing Group
Peter Grose Ltd
Guinness Publishing Ltd
Robert Hale Ltd
Hamlyn
HarperCollins Publishers Ltd
Harveys Books
J. H. Haynes & Co Ltd
Hazleton Publishing Ltd
Headline Book Publishing Ltd
Hodder & Stoughton Educational
Hodder & Stoughton General
Human Kinetics (Europe) Ltd
Hutton Press Ltd
Jarrold Publishing
Michael Joseph Ltd & Pelham
  Books
The Kenilworth Press Ltd
Kensington West Productions
Letterland International Ltd
The Lutterworth Press
Macmillan General Books Ltd

Mainstream Publishing Co
  (Edinburgh) Ltd
Kenneth Mason Publications Ltd
Metro Books
Motor Racing Publications Ltd
Neil Wilson Publishing Ltd
Nexus Special Interests
W. W. Norton & Co Ltd
Oldcastle Books Ltd
Packard Publishing Ltd
PAVIC Publications
Pavilion Books Ltd
Penguin Books Ltd
Polygon
Prim-Ed Publishing
Promotional Reprint Co Ltd
Queen Anne Press
Quotes Ltd
Random House UK Ltd
Reed Books
Robson Books Ltd
Running Press Book Publishers
Salamander Books
Sangam Books Ltd
S. B. Publications
Sidgwick & Jackson Ltd
Sigma Press
Simon & Schuster
Souvenir Press Ltd
E. & F. N. Spon
The Sportsman's Press
Springfield Books Ltd
Arthur H. Stockwell Ltd
Summersdale Publishers
Sunburst Books
Supportive Learning Publications
  (SLP)
Take That Ltd
Transworld Publishers Ltd
Usborne Publishing Ltd
Veloce Publishing Plc
Virgin Publishing
Ward Lock Ltd
Weidenfeld & Nicolson
Wharncliffe Publishing Ltd
Tony Williams Publications
Words on Sport Ltd
Book Packaging and Marketing
Brown Packaging (Books) Ltd
CLB Publishing Ltd
Diagram Visual Information Ltd
Sara Dunn
Haldane Mason Ltd
Ink Inc Ltd
Marshall Cavendish Books
Marshall Information Ltd
Toucan Books Ltd
White Line Publishing Services
Wordwright

THEATRE, DRAMA & DANCE

Absolute Press
Amber Lane Press Ltd
Peter Andrew Publishing Co Ltd
A. & C. Black (Publishers) Ltd
Bloodaxe Books Ltd
The Book Guild Ltd
Marion Boyars Publishers Ltd
Boydell & Brewer Ltd
Brown, Son & Ferguson, Ltd
Calder Publications Ltd
Cambridge University Press
Capall Bann Publishing
Cardiff Academic Press
Carol Publishing Group

Cassell Plc
Chadwyck-Healey Ltd
Crescent Moon Publishing
Cressrelles Publishing Co Ltd
Dance Books Ltd
André Deutsch Ltd
Dramatic Lines
Faber & Faber Ltd
Facts on File
Samuel French Ltd
Gale Research International Ltd
Greenwood Publishing Group
Guinness Publishing Ltd
Robert Hale Ltd
Ian Henry Publications Ltd
Nick Hern Books
Intellect Ltd
Kenyon-Deane Ltd
Jessica Kingsley Publishers
Macmillan Press Ltd
Manchester University Press
Methuen
Moorley's Print & Publishing
NATE (National Association for
  the Teaching of English)
National Christian Education
  Council
New Playwrights' Network
Northcote House Publishers Ltd
W. W. Norton & Co Ltd
Oberon Books Ltd
Peter Owen Ltd
Oxford University Press
Pavilion Books Ltd
Penguin Books Ltd
Phaidon Press Ltd
Players Press (UK)
Poetry Wales Press Ltd
Prentice Hall Europe
Prim-Ed Publishing
Quartet Books
Random House UK Ltd
Reed Books
Rhinegold Publishing Ltd
Robson Books Ltd
Roundhouse Publishing Ltd
Routledge
Salvationist Publishing &
  Supplies Ltd
Scottish Cultural Press
Sinclair-Stevenson
Skoob Books Ltd
Smith Gryphon Publishers
Colin Smythe Ltd
Souvenir Press Ltd
Square One Books Ltd
Stainer & Bell Ltd
Rudolf Steiner Press
Supportive Learning Publications
  (SLP)
Thames & Hudson Ltd
Victoria & Albert Museum
  Publications
Virgin Publishing
Wild Goose Publications
Writers & Readers Ltd
Yale University Press London
Delian Bower Publishing
Kingfisher Design Services
Playne Books Ltd
Prion Books Ltd

TRANSPORT

ACC Publications
Ace Books
Airdata Publications

Airlife Publishing Ltd
Ian Allan Ltd
Appletree Press Ltd
Arms & Armour Press
Ashgate Publishing Ltd
Avon Books
Bay View Books Ltd
Blandford Press
The Book Guild Ltd
Boxtree
Cassell Plc
Castlemead Publications
Countyvise Ltd
Croner Publications Ltd
The Crowood Press Ltd
David & Charles Publishers
Defiant Publications
Earthscan Publications Ltd
Elliot Right Way Books
Enterprise Transport Books Ltd
Ex Libris Press
Express Newspapers Plc
G. T. Foulis & Co
Adam Gordon
Guinness Publishing Ltd
Robert Hale Ltd
Harveys Books
J. H. Haynes & Co Ltd
Ian Henry Publications Ltd
HMSO Books
Images Publishing (Malvern) Ltd
Imray Laurie Norie & Wilson Ltd
Jane's Information Group Ltd
Kogan Page Ltd
Leading Edge Press & Publishing
Lloyd's Register of Shipping
LLP Ltd
House of Lochar
McGraw-Hill Publishing Co
Manchester University Press
Mechanical Engineering
  Publications
Middleton Press
Midland Publishing Ltd
Motor Racing Publications Ltd
Multilingual Matters Ltd
National Museums of Scotland
New Orchard Editions
Nexus Special Interests
OPC (Oxford Publishing
  Company)
Osprey
Penguin Books Ltd
Plateway Press
Platform 5 Publishing Ltd
Promotional Reprint Co Ltd
Quotes Ltd
Reed Books
Roadmaster Publishing
Salamander Books
S. B. Publications
Shaw & Sons Ltd
Shire Publications Ltd
Silver Link Publishing Ltd
Patrick Stephens Ltd
Studio Editions Ltd
Sunburst Books
Alan Sutton Publishing Ltd
Taylor & Francis Ltd
Thomas Cook Publishing
Twelveheads Press
Veloce Publishing Plc
Verulam Publishing Ltd
Wharncliffe Publishing Ltd
Whittet Books Ltd
Windrow & Greene
BCS Publishing Ltd

CLB Publishing Ltd
Haldane Mason Ltd
Ink Inc Ltd
Marshall Cavendish Books
Prion Books Ltd
Quarto Publishing Plc
Ravelin Ltd

TRAVEL & TOPOGRAPHY

AA Publishing
Absolute Press
Ian Allan Ltd
Archival Facsimiles Ltd
Arrow Books Ltd
Avon Books
Colin Baxter Photography Ltd
Beaver Publishing Ltd
Berlitz Publishing Co Ltd
Blandford Press
The Book Guild Ltd
Books UK Ltd
Bossiney Books
Marion Boyars Publishers Ltd
Bradt Publications
Breese Books Ltd
Bridge Books
British Tourist Authority
David Campbell Publishers
Camra Books
Cassell Plc
The Central Bureau
The Chalford Publishing Co Ltd
Cicerone Press
Collins & Brown
Conran Octopus
Constable & Co Ltd
Ivan Corbett Publishing
Countryside Books
Crescent Moon Publishing
Cressrelles Publishing Co Ltd
Dalesman Publishing Co Ltd
André Deutsch Ltd
Aidan Ellis Publishing
English Heritage
Ex Libris Press
The Factory Shop Guide
Footprint Handbooks
Footprint Press Ltd
W. Foulsham & Co Ltd
Fourth Estate Ltd
Garnet Publishing Ltd
Global Books Ltd
Victor Gollancz Ltd
Granta
Robert Hale Ltd

Hamish Hamilton Ltd
HarperCollins Cartographic
HarperCollins Publishers Ltd
The Harvill Press
William Heinemann
The Herbert Press
HMSO Books
Hodder & Stoughton General
How To Books Ltd
Hutton Press Ltd
Impact Books / Olive Press
Imray Laurie Norie & Wilson Ltd
In Print Publishing Ltd
Jarrold Publishing
Michael Joseph Ltd & Pelham
  Books
Kegan Paul International Ltd
Kensington West Productions
Kuperard (London) Ltd
Roger Lascelles
Leading Edge Press & Publishing
House of Lochar
Luath Press Ltd
Macmillan General Books Ltd
Macmillan Reference Books
Mandarin
Mercat Press
Meridian Books
Metro Books
Michelin Tyre Plc
Miller Freeman Information
  Services
Murchison's Pantheon Ltd
John Murray Publishers Ltd
New Holland (Publishers) Ltd
New Orchard Editions
Pallas Athene
Pavilion Books Ltd
Penguin Books Ltd
George Philip
Phillimore & Co Ltd
Picador
Platform 5 Publishing Ltd
Polygon
Prentice Hall/Woodhead Faulkner
Quiller Press Ltd
RAC Publishing
The Radcliffe Press
Random House UK Ltd
Reed Books
Riad El-Rayyes Books Ltd
Roadmaster Publishing
Robson Books Ltd
Rosendale Press Ltd
Running Press Book Publishers
Martin Secker & Warburg

Serindia Publications
Settle Press
Shire Publications Ltd
Sidgwick & Jackson Ltd
Simon & Schuster
Sinclair-Stevenson
Smith Gryphon Publishers
Smith Settle Ltd
Springfield Books Ltd
Arthur H. Stockwell Ltd
Studio Editions Ltd
Summersdale Publishers
Sunburst Books
Sunflower Books
Alan Sutton Publishing Ltd
Thames & Hudson Ltd
Thomas Cook Publishing
Toucan Press
United Writers Publications Ltd
Vacation Work
Virgin Publishing
Websters International Publishers
  Ltd
Weidenfeld & Nicolson
Which? Books
Whittet Books Ltd
John Wiley & Sons Ltd
Book Packaging and Marketing
Philip Clark Ltd
CLB Publishing Ltd
Endeavour Group UK
Haldane Mason Ltd
Ink Inc Ltd
Marshall Information Ltd
Playne Books Ltd
Prion Books Ltd
Rough Guides Ltd
Toucan Books Ltd
White Line Publishing Services

VETERINARY SCIENCE

Academic Press Ltd
Addison Wesley Longman Ltd
Baillière Tindall
Blackwell Science Ltd
Butterworth-Heinemann
The C. W. Daniel Company Ltd
Educational Low-Priced Books
  Scheme (ELBS)
Farming Press
Harcourt Brace & Co Ltd
Henston Ltd
HMSO Books
The Kenilworth Press Ltd
Liverpool University Press

Macmillan Education Ltd
Manson Publishing Ltd
Oxford University Press
W. B. Saunders Co Ltd
Souvenir Press Ltd
John Wiley & Sons Ltd

VOCATIONAL TRAINING & CAREERS

Addison Wesley Longman Ltd
Blackwell Publishers Ltd
Nicholas Brealey Publishing Ltd
British Psychological Society
  (BPS Books)
BTL Publishing
Cassell Plc
Daniels Medica
DP Publications & Letts
  Educational
EnTra Publications Ltd
Falmer Press Ltd
Framework Press Educational
  Publishers Ltd
Gower Publishing Ltd
Hawker Publications
HMSO Books
Hobsons Publishing Plc
Hodder & Stoughton Educational
How To Books Ltd
The Industrial Society
Institute for Employment Studies
Kogan Page Ltd
Kuperard (London) Ltd
McGraw-Hill Publishing Co
Macmillan Press Ltd
National Extension College Trust
  Ltd
National Youth Agency
NCT Publishing Ltd
Northcote House Publishers Ltd
Pavilion Publishing (Brighton)
  Ltd
Penguin Books Ltd
Pira International
Pitman Publishing
Prentice Hall Europe
Rhinegold Publishing Ltd
Summersdale Publishers
Stanley Thornes (Publishers) Ltd
Trotman & Co Ltd
Vacation Work
Verulam Publishing Ltd
John Wiley & Sons Ltd
Ink Inc Ltd

7.2 OWNERSHIP OF UK PUBLISHERS

This section is an alphabetical index to holding and other companies which own the UK publishers listed in section 2 of the *Directory*.

The list was compiled using the Parent Company information section on the questionnaires completed by publishers. If a publisher did not supply this information it will not appear in this index.

It should be noted that the ownership structure of the larger groups can be quite complex — an 'owner' may be owned by another company or group.

We welcome users' information on any omissions, which will be added to the index in future editions.

ABC-Clio *(USA)*
   ABC-Clio Ltd
Advance Publications Inc *(USA)*
   Random House UK Ltd
Age Concern
   Ace Books
Ian Allan Group Ltd
   Ian Allan Ltd
Allied Information Technologies Ltd
   NTC Publications Ltd
Areen Projects (Jersey)
   Hazar Publishing Ltd
Ashgate Publishing Group
   Ashgate Publishing Ltd
   Scolar Press
ASI (Research) Ltd
   Adam Smith Institute
Associated University Presses Inc *(USA)*
   Golden Cockerel Press Ltd, Associated University Presses
Association of County Councils
   ACC Publications
Automobile Association
   AA Publishing
W. G. Baird *(Irish Republic)*
   Blackstaff Press Ltd
Balintore Holdings
   Christian Focus Publications
Bantam Doubleday Dell Inc *(USA)*
   Transworld Publishers Ltd
Barnsley Chronicle Holdings Ltd
   Pen & Sword Books Ltd
The Barnsley Chronicle Ltd
   Wharncliffe Publishing Ltd

The Barry Long Foundation
   Barry Long Books
BBC
   BBC English
BBC Enterprises Ltd
   BBC Educational Publishing
BBC Worldwide Ltd
   BBC Books
Belmont (1948) Ltd
   The Belmont Press
Berlitz International *(USA)*
   Berlitz Publishing Co Ltd
The Biochemical Society
   Portland Press Ltd
A. & C. Black (Publishers) Ltd
   Adlard Coles Nautical
   The Herbert Press
Black Ace Enterprises
   Black Ace Books
Book Production Consultants Plc
   Granta Editions
   NCT Publishing Ltd
Books International (Poland) *(Poland)*
   Books International
Boosey & Hawkes Plc
   Boosey & Hawkes Music Publishers Ltd
BPP Holdings Plc
   BPP Publishing Ltd
   DP Publications & Letts Educational
Bradford Technology Ltd
   BTL Publishing
British Film Institute
   BFI Publishing
British Library
   British Library, Document Supply Centre
British Medical Association
   BMJ Publishing Group
British Museum Publications Ltd
   British Museum Press
de Brouwer & Melkman Publishing *(Netherlands)*
   Romer Publications
Burall Ltd
   Burall Floraprint Ltd
Butcherbest Ltd
   Creation Books
The Calder Educational Trust
   Calder Publications Ltd
Calmann & King Ltd
   Laurence King Publishing

Campaign for Real Ale Ltd
   Camra Books
Carlton Communications Plc
   Carlton Books Ltd
Carol Publishing Group *(USA)*
   Carol Publishing Group
Cassell Plc
   Arms & Armour Press
   Blandford Press
   Geoffrey Chapman
   Victor Gollancz Ltd
   Leicester University Press
   Mansell Publishing
   Mowbray
   New Orchard Editions
   Pinter Publishers Ltd
   Studio Vista
   Ward Lock Ltd
CCH Inc *(USA)*
   CCH Editions Ltd
Centaur Communications Ltd
   Linguaphone Institute Ltd
Chalksoft Ltd
   SGC Books
Chapman & Hall
   Blueprint
   E. & F. N. Spon
Church of Scotland's Board of Communication
   Saint Andrew Press
James Clarke & Co Ltd
   The Lutterworth Press
Clemis Group Ltd
   ELC International
Collins & Brown Ltd
   Belitha Press Ltd
Colour Library Books Ltd
   CLB Publishing Ltd
Computational Mechanics International Ltd
   Computational Mechanics Publications
Conservative Central Office
   Conservative Political Centre
Council of Churches for Britain & Ireland
   CCBI Publications
Countryside Book UK
   Countryside Books
Crabtree Publishing Co *(Canada)*
   Crabtree Publishing Co
Cressrelles Publishing Co Ltd
   Kenyon-Deane Ltd

Daily Mail & General Trust Group
Hobsons Publishing Plc
Dar Al Jaqi Sarl *(Lebanon)*
Saqi Books
Dorling Kindersley Ltd
Henderson Publishing Plc
Drake Group Ltd
Drake Educational Associates Ltd
The Dun & Bradstreet Corporation
Dun & Bradstreet Ltd
Edinburgh University Press
Polygon
Egmont *(Denmark)*
World International Publishing Ltd
Element Communications Ltd
Element Books Ltd
Andrew Elliot & Sons Ltd
Elliot Right Way Books
Elm Training
Elm Publications
Elsevier Science Ltd
Elsevier Advanced Technology
Encyclopaedia Britannica Inc *(USA)*
Encyclopaedia Britannica International Ltd
Engineering Training Authority
EnTra Publications Ltd
English Theosophical Trust
Theosophical Books Ltd
Evangelical Movement of Wales
Evangelical Press of Wales
E–Z Legal Forms Inc *(USA)*
Law Pack Publishing Ltd
Facts On File Inc *(USA)*
Facts on File
J. B. Fairfax International *(Australia)*
Merehurst Fairfax
Folio Holdings
Carcanet Press Ltd
W. H. Freeman & Co *(USA)*
W. H. Freeman
Samuel French Inc
Samuel French Ltd
Garland Publishing Inc *(USA)*
Garland Publishing Inc
Garnet Publishing Ltd
Ithaca Press
General Synod of the Church of England
Church House Publishing
Stanley Gibbons Holdings Plc
Stanley Gibbons Publications
The Gleves Group Plc
Chivers Press Ltd
The Gordon Press Ltd
Shaw & Sons Ltd
Grant Jessé Associates
Little People Books
Granta Publications Ltd
Granta
Grey Seal (Publications) Ltd
Grey Seal Books
Grolier Inc *(USA)*
The Watts Publishing Group
Grosvenor Productions Ltd
Grosvenor Books
Groupe de la Cité
Larousse Plc
The Guernsey Press Co
Alan Sutton Publishing Ltd
Guilford Press Inc *(USA)*
Guilford Press
Guinness Plc
Guinness Publishing Ltd
Harcourt General Inc
Academic Press Ltd
Baillière Tindall
The Dryden Press
Harcourt Brace & Co Ltd

Holt, Rinehart & Winston
W. B. Saunders Co Ltd
Harlequin Enterprises Ltd *(Canada)*
Harlequin Mills & Boon Ltd
Haynes Publishing Group Plc
G. T. Foulis & Co
J. H. Haynes & Co Ltd
OPC (Oxford Publishing Company)
Patrick Stephens Ltd
Headstart History
Phoenix Press (Oxford)
The HLT Group Ltd
HLT Publications
HNH International *(Hong Kong)*
Naxos Audiobooks
Hodder Headline Plc
Arnold
Headline Book Publishing Ltd
Hodder & Stoughton Educational
Hodder & Stoughton General
Hodder & Stoughton Religious
Hodder Children's Books
Holmes & Meier *(USA)*
Africana Publishing Co
Holmes & Meier Publishing
Holtzbrinck Publishers Holdings Ltd
Macmillan Education Ltd
Macmillan General Books Ltd
Macmillan Reference Books
Hoppenstedt Bonnier Information GmbH
(Germany)
ICC Information Group Ltd
Horizon House Inc *(USA)*
Artech House
Hostaction Ltd
Hawk Books
Houghton Mifflin Co *(USA)*
Houghton Mifflin Co International
Human Kinetics Inc *(USA)*
Human Kinetics (Europe) Ltd
IBC Group Plc
IBC Business Publishing
The Institute of Chartered Accountants in England & Wales
Accountancy Books
Institution of Civil Engineers
Thomas Telford Services Ltd
Instituto Geografico de Agostini *(Italy)*
De Agostini Editions
Inter Publishing Service (IPS) Ltd
Eagle
Intermediate Technology Development Group Ltd
Intermediate Technology Publications Ltd
International Book Development Ltd
Low Priced British Books (LPBB)
Internos Books
Booth-Clibborn Editions
The Iona Community
Wild Goose Publications
Al-Shirkatul Islamiyyah
Ahmadiyya Muslim Publications
Islam International Publications Ltd
JAI Press Inc *(USA)*
JAI Press Ltd
Jones & Bartlett Inc *(USA)*
Jones & Bartlett International
Kingsway Communications Ltd
Kingsway Publications Ltd
Kogan Page Ltd
Earthscan Publications Ltd
Labor Publications *(USA)*
IW Books
Labyrinth Group Plc
B. T. Batsford Ltd
Labyrinth Publishing (UK) Ltd

Larousse Plc
Harrap
Lavoisier Tec et Doc *(France)*
Intercept Ltd
The Law Society
Law Society Publications & Multimedia
Lennard Associates Ltd
Queen Anne Press
Lionel Leventhal Ltd
Greenhill Books / Lionel Leventhal Ltd
J. D. Lewis & Sons Ltd
Gomer Press
The Library Association
Library Association Publishing
Ling Kee (UK) Ltd
Ward Lock Educational Co Ltd
BLA Publishing Ltd
Link House Media Ltd
FHG Publications Ltd
Little, Brown & Co (UK)
Virago Press
Little, Brown & Co Inc *(USA)*
Little, Brown & Co (UK)
Living & Learning (Cambridge) Ltd
Learning Development Aids (LDA)
Loughborough University
Library & Information Statistics Unit (LISU)
M.33 Ltd
Andromeda Oxford Ltd
McDonald Publishing Ltd
Brown Watson Ltd
Kibworth Books
McGraw-Hill Inc *(USA)*
McGraw-Hill Publishing Co
Macmillan Ltd
Macmillan Children's Books
Macmillan Press Ltd
Macmillan Publishers Ltd
Picador
Manufacture Française des Pneumatiques Michelin *(France)*
Michelin Tyre Plc
Martins Printing Group UK Ltd
Europa Publications Ltd
Institution of Mechanical Engineers
Mechanical Engineering Publications
Mecklermedia Publishing Corporation *(USA)*
Mecklermedia Ltd
Mediakey Plc
Marshall Information Ltd
The Methodist Church
Methodist Publishing House
Mirror Group
Bookman Projects Ltd
MIT Press *(USA)*
The MIT Press Ltd
Moorley's Bible & Bookshop Ltd
Moorley's Print & Publishing
Multi Media Investments Ltd
Supernet
Music Sales Ltd
Omnibus Press
Namara Group
Quartet Books
National Academy Press *(USA)*
National Academy Press
National Childbirth Trust
NCT Publishing Ltd
The National Coaching Foundation
Coachwise Ltd
The National Gallery Trust
National Gallery Publications Ltd
National Spiritual Assembly of Bahá'ís of the United Kingdom
Bahá'í Publishing Trust

Thomas Nelson Inc *(USA)*
　Word Publishing
New Era Publication International
　(Denmark)
　New Era Publications UK Ltd
The News Corp Ltd
　HarperCollins Publishers Ltd
News International
　HarperCollins Religious
NFER (National Foundation for
　Educational Research) & The Thomson
　Corporation
　NFER-Nelson Publishing Co Ltd
W. W. Norton & Co *(USA)*
　W. W. Norton & Co Ltd
The Orion Publishing Group Ltd
　Chapmans
　J M Dent
　Orion Books Ltd
　Weidenfeld & Nicolson
University of Oxford
　Voltaire Foundation Ltd
Pan Macmillan Ltd
　Sidgwick & Jackson Ltd
Pearson Plc
　Addison Wesley Longman Ltd
　Churchill Livingstone
　FT Law & Tax
　Pearson Professional Ltd
　Pitman Publishing
Penguin Books Ltd
　Fantail Books
　Hamish Hamilton Ltd
　Michael Joseph Ltd & Pelham Books
　Ladybird Books Ltd
　Ventura Publishing Ltd
　Frederick Warne & Co Ltd
The Penguin Publishing Company Ltd
　Penguin Books Ltd
Pentland Press Inc *(USA)*
　The Pentland Press Ltd
The Royal Pharmaceutical Society of Great
　Britain
　The Pharmaceutical Press
Judy Piatkus (Publishers) Ltd
　Piatkus Books
Players Press Inc *(USA)*
　Players Press (UK)
Plenum Publishing Corporation *(USA)*
　Plenum Publishing Co Ltd
Promotional Reprint Co Ltd
　Sunburst Books
Quadrillion Publishing Ltd
　Zigzag Publishing
The Quarto Group Inc *(USA)*
　Quarto Publishing Plc
Quintessenz Verlag *(Germany)*
　Quintessence Publishing Co Ltd
R. S. Holdings Ltd
　Brassey's (UK) Ltd
R.I.C. (Australia) *(Australia)*
　Prim-Ed Publishing
RAC Motoring Services
　RAC Publishing
Random House UK Ltd
　Arrow Books
　Business Books
　Jonathan Cape
　Century
　Chatto & Windus
　Cressit Books
　Ebury Press
　Hutchinson
　Legend
　Leopard
　Pimlico
　Random House Audio

Random House Children's Books
Random House New Media
Studio Designs
Studio Editions
Vermilion
Vintage
Rapport Learning Ltd
　Forbes Publications Ltd
The Reader's Digest Association Inc *(USA)*
　Joshua Morris
　Victoria House Publishing Ltd
Reed Books
　Bounty Books
　Brimax Books
　Conran Octopus
　Hamlyn Children's Reference
　Hamyln/Octopus
　William Heinemann
　Heinemann Young Books
　Mammoth
　Mandarin
　Methuen
　Methuen Children's Books
　Millers
　Minerva
　Mitchell Beazley
　Osprey
　George Philip
　Pitkin Guides
　Martin Secker & Warburg
　Sinclair-Stevenson
Reed Educational & Professional Publishing
　Butterworth-Heinemann
　Ginn & Co
　Heinemann Educational
　Heinemann English Language Teaching
　Heinemann International
　Heinemann Publishers Oxford
　Pergamon Open Learning
　Reed Educational Electronic Publishing
Reed Elsevier Plc
　Butterworths
　Elsevier Science UK
　IPC Magazines
　Reed Business Publishing
　Reed Consumer Books
　Reed Educational & Professional Publishing
　Reed Elsevier Legal Division
　Reed Exhibition Companies
　Reed Information Services
　Reed Travel Publishing
　Utell International
Reed Information Services
　Dial Publications
Reed International Plc
　see Reed Elsevier Plc
William Reed Publishing Ltd
　William Reed Directories
Reed Reference Publishing
　Bowker-Saur
Religious Society of Friends (Quakers)
　Quaker Home Service
RIBA Companies Ltd
　RIBA Publications
Royal College of Nursing, Baillière Tindall,
　Harcourt Brace
　Scutari Press
Royal Incorporation of Architects in
　Scotland
　The Rutland Press
Royal Society of Medicine
　Royal Society of Medicine Press Ltd
Running Press *(USA)*
　Running Press Book Publishers
E. Russum & Sons Ltd
　Virtue Books Ltd

Sadie Fields Productions Ltd
　Tango Books
Sage Publications Inc *(USA)*
　Sage Publications Ltd
Salamander Holdings NV *(Belgium)*
　Salamander Books
Sawd Publications
　Sawd Books
Scholastic Inc *(USA)*
　Scholastic Ltd
SCM Press Trust
　SCM Press Ltd
Send The Light Ltd
　OM Publishing
　Paternoster Publishing
William Sessions Holdings Ltd
　Sessions of York
Severn House Books (Holdings) Ltd
　Severn House Publishers Ltd
Simon & Schuster Inc *(USA)*
　Simon & Schuster
Singular Publishing Group Inc *(USA)*
　Singular Publishing Group Inc
Charles Skilton Ltd
　Albyn Press
Smith Gryphon Ltd
　Smith Gryphon Publishers
The Society for Promoting Christian
　Knowledge (SPCK)
　Sheldon Press
SPLASH! Holdings Ltd
　SPLASH! Publishing Ltd
Springer Verlag GmbH & Co KG *(Germany)*
　Springer-Verlag London Ltd
Stanborough Press Ltd
　Home Health Education Service
Stobart Publishing Ltd
　Stobart Davies Ltd
Studentlitteratur AB *(Sweden)*
　Chartwell-Bratt (Publishing & Training) Ltd
T & H Holdings Ltd
　Thames & Hudson Ltd
Taylor & Francis Group
　Falmer Press Ltd
　Psychology Press of Erlbaum (UK)
James Thin Ltd
　Mercat Press
Thoemmes Antiquarian Books Ltd
　Thoemmes Press
Thomas Cook Group Ltd
　Thomas Cook Publishing
D. C. Thomsen & Co Ltd
　Peter Haddock Ltd
The Thomson Corporation
　Chapman & Hall
　Derwent Information
　W. Green The Scottish Law Publisher
　IFR Publishing
　Information Access Co
　Institute for Scientific Information
　International Thomson Business Press
　International Thomson Computer Press
　International Thomson Multimedia
　Jane's Information Group
　Legal Information Resources
　Thomas Nelson & Sons
　NFER-Nelson
　Police Review Publishing Co
　Primary Source Media
　Professional Publishing
　Rapid Science Publishers
　Sweet & Maxwell
Threshold Publishing Ltd
　Serif
Timber Press Inc *(USA)*
　Timber Press

Times Publishing Ltd *(Singapore)*
Marshall Cavendish Books
UGMT Ltd
Acol-Biotol
Greenwich University Press
The Ulverscroft Group
Magna Large Print Books
P. A. Underwood Ltd
Sunflower Books
United News & Media Plc
Miller Freeman Information Services
United Newspapers Ltd
Express Newspapers Plc
Farming Press
**Universities & Colleges Christian
Fellowship**
Inter-Varsity Press
VCH Verlagsgesellschaft mbH *(Germany)*
Academy Group Ltd
VCH Publishers (UK) Ltd

Veterinary Business Development Ltd
Henston Ltd
Viacom Inc *(USA)*
Phoenix ELT
Prentice Hall Europe
Prentice Hall/Ellis Horwood
Prentice Hall/Harvester Wheatsheaf
Prentice Hall/Woodhead Faulkner
Virgin Group Ltd
Virgin Publishing
**National Council for Voluntary
Organisations**
NCVO Publications
Warner Music Group
International Music Publications Ltd
The Watts Publishing Group
Orchard Books
Richard Webb Ltd
Webb & Bower (Publishers) Ltd
West of England Trust
Jordan Publishing Ltd

Which? Ltd
Which? Books
A. Whittet & Co Ltd
Whittet Books Ltd
Wiley Europe Ltd
John Wiley & Sons Ltd
Wilson & Day Ltd
Allison & Busby
Wolters Kluwer NV *(Netherlands)*
CCH Editions Ltd
Croner Publications Ltd
Kluwer Law International
Macdonald Young Books
Stanley Thornes (Publishers) Ltd
Wolters Kluwer UK Plc
Wayland Publishers Ltd
Word Inc *(USA)*
Word Publishing
Writers & Readers Publishing Inc *(USA)*
Writers & Readers Ltd

7.3 PUBLISHERS' OVERSEAS REPRESENTATIVES

AAPG, PO Box 979, 1444 South Boulder, Tulsa, OK 74101-0979, USA
A & B Books, 149 Lawrence Street, Brooklyn, NY 11201, USA
ABACO, Trav. Légua de Póvoa, 30-A 1200 Lisbon, Portugal
Michael Abbott, Macmillan Publishers Ltd, Conore, 87510 Peyrilhac, France
ABC-Clio, 130 Cremona, Santa Barbara, CA 93116, USA
ABC Educators, 6111 Wythe Place, Norfolk, VA 23508, USA
ABC Music, 10A Campbell Street, Artarmon, NSW, Australia 2065
Abhinav Publications, E-37 Hauz Khas, New Delhi, India 110 016
ABI Info Access, B-6 & 7 Skipper Corner, 88 Nehru Place, New Delhi, India 110 019
Abingdon Press, 201 Eighth Avenue South, (PO Box 801), Nashville, TN 37202, USA
Abiola Bookshop Ltd, PO Box 7700, Zelikha Wuraola House, 362 Herbert Macauley Street, Yaba, Lagos, Nigeria
Abyss, RRI, Box 213, Chester Road, Chester, MA 01011-9735, USA
Academic Book Marketing (Ireland), 83 Tudor Grove, Ashbourne, Co Meath, Irish Republic
Academic Book Promotions, Hoofdstraat 261, 1611 AG Bovenkarspel, Netherlands
Academic Book Store, PO Box 128, 00100 Helsinki, Finland
Academic Library Services, 8 Pereira Road 02-02, Singapore 1336 & 30 East Coast Road, Suite 03-21, 22 Paramount Shopping Centre, Singapore 1542
Academic Marketing Services, 8 Pereira Road No 02-02, Singapore 1336
Academic Marketing Services, PO Box 519, Auckland Park, 2006 South Africa
Academic Marketing Services, 104 Sherbrooke Road, London SW6 7QN, UK
Academic Press do Brasil Editora Ltda, Rua des Armando Fairbanks 314, Butanta, 05501 São Paulo SP, Brazil
Academic Press Inc, 1250 Sixth Avenue, San Diego, CA 92101, USA
Academic Press Japan Inc, Ichibancho Central Building, 22-1 Ichibancho, Chiyoda-ku, Tokyo 102, Japan
Academic Press Pvt Ltd, PO Box 567, Harare, Zimbabwe
Academic & University Publishers Group, 1 Gower Street, London WC1E 6HA, UK
Accents Publications Service Inc, 721 Ellsworth Drive 203, Silver Spring, MD 20910, USA
ACER Ltd, 19 Prospect Hill Road, Camberwell, Vic, Australia 3124
ACK Agency, PO Box 1414, Los Altos, CA 94023-1616, USA
Acme Agency SA, Suipacha 245, Piso 1, 1008 Buenos Aires, Argentina
Acorn (Australia) Ltd, 335 Johnston Street, Abbotsford, Vic, Australia 3067
Acorn Computers (NZ) Ltd, 1 Ngaire Avenue, Epson, Auckland, New Zealand
Acorn Connections Ltd, 5 Oxford Road, Kingston 5, Jamaica
ACP, 50 Loxwood Avenue, Worthing, West Sussex BN14 7RA, UK
ACP, 130 North Bloomingdale Road, Suite 101, Bloomingdale, IL 60108, USA

ACP (UK) Ltd, 20 Galowhill Road, Brackmills, Northampton NN4 7EE, UK
Addison-Wesley Korea, 3rd Floor, 403-16 Seo Kyo Dong, Ma Po Ku, Seoul 121-210, Korea
Addison Wesley Longman New Zealand Pty Ltd, 46 Hillside, Glenfield, Auckland 10, New Zealand
Addison Wesley Longman UK, Edinburgh Gate, Harlow, Essex CM20 2JE, UK
Addison-Wesley (Singapore) Pte Ltd, 11 Cantonment Road, Singapore 089736
Adi Shakti, 9 rue Gutenberg, 75015 Paris, France
Jahan Adib Co Ltd, 70 Matahari Avenue, PO Box 15655-444, Tehran 15667, Iran
Aditya Books, H-2/16 Ansari Road, Daryaganj, New Delhi, India 110 002
ADRF, PO Box 454, Croydon, Vic, Australia 3136
Advtech Video Training, 364 Kent Avenue, Randburg, Johannesburg, 2914 South Africa
Editions Adyar, 4 Square Rapp, Paris, France
Affiliated East-West Press Pvt Ltd, G-1/16 Ansari Road, Darya Ganj, New Delhi, India 110 002
Africa Book Centre, 38 King Street, Covent Garden, London WC2E 8JT, UK
African Books Collective Ltd, The Jam Factory, 27 Park End Street, Oxford OX1 1HU (PO Box 56, OX1 3EL), UK
African Business Enterprises, PO Box 651793, Benmore, 2010 South Africa
African Universities Press, New Oluyole Ind Est, Phase 2, PO Box 5617, Ibadan-Lagos Expressway, Ibadan, Nigeria
African Universities Press, c/o Aureol Publishers, PO Box 395, 5 Laminah Sankoh St, Freetown, Sierra Leone
African World Press, 11d Princess Road, Lawrenceville, NJ 08648, USA
Afriservices, PO Box 3206, Dar es Salaam, Tanzania
Afro-Asian Book Co, 212-A Hashimi Centre, 2nd Floor, Preedy Street, Saddar, GPO Box 962, Karachi74200, Pakistan
Afro-Asian Book Co, GPO Box 962, Karachi 74200, Pakistan
agAccess, PO Box 2008, Davis, CA 95617, USA
Agence Litteraire, 70 rue d'Assas, 75006 Paris, France
Agencia Siciliano de Livros, Alameda Dino Bueno 492, 01217 São Paulo, Brazil
Agius & Agius Ltd, PO Box 352, 42a South Street, Valletta, Malta
Agroinform, Központ, Attila út 93, 1012 Budapest 1, Hungary
Ahmadiyya Muslim Mission, PO Box 10094, Georgetown, Guyana
Ahmadiyya Muslim Mission, 03 BP 416, Adjame, Abidjan 03, Ivory Coast
Ahmadiyya Muslim Mission, Forgnerveine 53, Oslo 2, Norway
Ahmadiyya Muslim Mission, Ephraimszegenweg 67, PO Box 2106, Paramaribo, Suriname
Mohiuddin Ahmed, 1st Floor, Post Box 88, Red Cross Building, 114 Motijheel, Dacca 2, Bangladesh

AIMS, 101 Marlowe Road, Lunsford Park, Larkfield, Kent ME20 6TU, UK

Aims Corporation, Asakawa Building, 1-16-10 Shinbashu, Minato-ku, Tokyo 105, Japan

Keith Ainsworth Pty Ltd, Unit 6, 88 Batt Street, Penrith, NSW, Australia 2750

Len Ainsworth, PO Box 992, Aldbourne, Marlborough, Wilts SN8 1ZA, UK

Airlife Publishing, 101 Longden Road, Shrewsbury, Shropshire SY3 9EB, UK

Airlift Book Co, 26–28 Eden Grove, London N7 8EF, UK

Ajamiam Brothers International Publishers Representatives Ltd, 4 Michalakis Karaolis Street, Engomi, Nicosia, Cyprus

Akademibokhandeln, Master Samuelsgatan 32, 103 94 Stockholm, Sweden

Akateeminen Kirjakauppa, Keskuskatu 1, PO Box 218, 00381 Helsinki, Finland

Akvaristen, PO Box 22105, 400 72 Gothenburg, Sweden

Al Ahram Distribution Agency, Galaa Street, Cairo, Egypt

Al-Dar al-Arabia Lil Nashr Wa Al-Tawzeia, 32 Abbas Al Akkad St, Nasser City, Apt 9, Cairo, Egypt

Albatross Books Pty Ltd, PO Box 320, Sutherland, NSW, Australia 2232

Alby Commercial Enterprises Pte Ltd, 60 Martin Road, 06-04-A/B, Singapore & 8 Kaki Bukit Road 2, Ruby Warehouse Complex, No 04-38, Singapore 1441

Algoritam Ltd, Gajeva 12, PO Box 23, 41000 Zagreb, Croatia

ALIS, 7-14-6 Todoroki, Setagaya-ku, Tokyo, 158 Japan

All Prints Publishers & Distributors, PO Box 857, Abu Dhabi, UAE

Ian Allan Publishing, Coombelands House, Coombelands Lane, Addlestone, Surrey KT15 1HY, UK

Gary Allen Pty Ltd, 9 Cooper Street, Smithfield, NSW, Australia 2164

George R. Allen & Co Ltd, 12 Ailesbury Grove, Dundrum, Dublin 16, Irish Republic

Piers Allen, c/o JAI Press Ltd, The Courtyard, 28 High Street, Hampton Hill, Middx TW12 1PD, UK

Allen & Unwin Pty Ltd, 9 Atchison Street, PO Box 8500, St Leonards, NSW, Australia 2065

Allied Printers & Publishers, Union Building, Beirut, Lebanon

Allied Publishers Ltd, 751 Mount Road, Madras, India 600 002; PO Box 155, 13/14 Asaf Ali Road, New Delhi, 110 002, India & 17 Chittaranjan Avenue, Calcutta, India 700 072

Allied Scientific Presses, PO Box 411, 8 Hahavatzelet Street, Jerusalem 91003, Israel

Allphy Book Distributors Ltd, 4–6 Charles Street, Eden Terrace, Auckland, New Zealand

Allscript Establishment (S) Pte Ltd, 605A Macpherson Road, 05–03 Citimac Industrial Complex, Singapore 368240

Alpenbooks, 3616 South Road, Mukilteo, WA 98275, USA

Alta Book Center, 14 Adrian Court, Burlingame, CA 94010, USA

Libreria Altair SA, Balmes 69, 08007 Barcelona, Spain

Alternative Books, PO Box 2428, Randburg, 2125 South Africa

AMA Services (WA) Pty Ltd, PO Box 133, Nedlands, WA,, Australia 6009

Amazing Grace Ltd, 31a Gold Coast Road, PO Box 173, Kano, Nigeria

Amday-B Import/Export Agents, 49 Leverton Rise, Oxley, Wolverhampton WV10 6HY, UK

American College of Physicians, PO Box 777 R-0270, Philadelphia, PA 19175, USA

American Society of Civil Engineers, 345 East 47th Street, New York, NY 10017, USA

American Society of Mechanical Engineers, ASME Order Department, 22 Law Drive, Box 2300, Fairfield, NJ 07007-2300, USA

American University Press Group, 3-21-18-206 Higashi-Shinagawa, Shinagawa-ku, Tokyo, 140 Japan

AMF, 63 Conyngham Street, Glenside,, Australia 5065

Amnesty International, Section Algérienne, BP 377, Alger RP 16004, Algeria

Amnesty International, Australian Section, Private Bag 23, Broadway, NSW, Australia 2007

Amnesty International, Austrian Section, Apostelgasse 25–27, 1030 Vienna, Austria

Amnesty International, Bangladesh Section, 100 Kalabagan, 1st Floor, 2nd Lane, Dhaka 1205, Bangladesh

Amnesty International, Belgium Section (*Flemish branch*), Kerkstraat 156, 2060 Antwerp, Belgium

Amnesty International, Section belge francophone, Rue Berckmans 9, 1060 Brussels, Belgium

Amnesty International, BP 01 3536, Cotonou, Benin

Amnesty International, Bermuda Section, PO Box HM 2136, Hamilton HM JX, Bermuda

Amnesty International, Canadian Section (*English-speaking branch*), 214 Montreal Road, 4th Floor, Vanier, Ont, Canada K1L 8L8

Amnesty International, Danish Section, Dyrkoeb 3, 1166 Copenhagen K, Denmark

Amnesty International, Faroe Islands Section, PO Box 1075, 110 Tórshavn, Faeroe Islands

Amnesty International, Finnish Section, Ruoholahdenkatu 24 D, 00180 Helsinki, Finland

Amnesty International, Section française, 4 rue de la Pierre Levée, 75553 Paris Cedex 11, France

Amnesty International, German Section, Heerstrasse 178, 53108 Bonn, Germany

Amnesty International, Ghanaian Section, PO Box 1173, Koforidua, ER, Ghana

Amnesty International, Greek Section, 30 Sina Street, 106 72 Athens, Greece

Amnesty International, Guyana Section, c/o PO Box 10720, Palm Court Building, 35 Main Street, Georgetown, Guyana

Amnesty International, Hong Kong Section, Unit C 3/F, Best-o-Best Building, 32–36 Ferry Street, Kowloon, Hong Kong

Amnesty International, Icelandic Section, PO Box 618, 121 Reykjavik, Iceland

Amnesty International, Indian Section, 13 Indra Prastha Building, E-109 Pandav Nagar, New Delhi-92, India

Amnesty International, Irish Section, 48 Fleet Street, Dublin 2, Irish Republic

Amnesty International, Israel Section, 98 Allenby Street, PO Box 14179, Tel Aviv 61141, Israel

Amnesty International, Italian Section, Viale Mazzini 146, 00195 Rome, Italy

Amnesty International, Section Ivoirienne, 04 BP 895, Abidjan 04, Ivory Coast

Amnesty International, Treichville Arras 2 (face ex-AITACI), Escalier 7, 2ème Etage, Porte 553, Abidjan, Ivory Coast

Amnesty International, Japanese Section, Sky Esta 2fl, 2-18-23 Nishi-Waseda, Shinjuku-ku, Tokyo, 165 Japan

Amnesty International, 706-600 Kyeong Buk RCO Box 36, Daegu, Korea

Amnesty International, Luxembourg Section, BP 1914, 1019 Luxembourg, Luxembourg

Amnesty International, Mauritius Section, BP 69, Rose-Hill, Mauritius

Amnesty International, Nepalese Section, PO Box 135, Bagbazar, Kathmandu, Nepal

Amnesty International, Dutch Section, Keizersgracht 620, 1017 ER Amsterdam, Netherlands

Amnesty International, New Zealand Section, PO Box 793, Wellington 1, New Zealand

Amnesty International, Nigerian Section, PMB 3061, Suru-Lere, Lagos, Nigeria

Amnesty International, Norwegian Section, PO Box 702 Sentrum, 0106 Oslo, Norway

Amnesty International, Philippines Section, PO Box 286, Sta Mesa Post Office, 1008 Sta Mesa, Manila, Philippines

Amnesty International, Senegalese Section, c/o Isma Daddis Sagna, Cabinet M'baye Jacques DIOP, 13 ruede Thiong, Dakar, Senegal

Amnesty International, Sierra Leone Section, PMB 1021, Freetown, Sierra Leone

Amnesty International, Komenskega 7, 61000 Ljubljana, Slovenia

Amnesty International, Sección Española, Calle Barquillo 17 6°B, 29004 Madrid, Spain

Amnesty International, Swedish Section, PO Box 23400, 104 35 Stockholm, Sweden

Amnesty International, Swiss Section, PO Box, 3001 Berne, Switzerland

Amnesty International, Tanzanian Section, PO Box 4331, Dar es Salaam, Tanzania

Amnesty International, Section Tunisienne, 48 Avenue Farhat Hached, 3ème Etage, 1001 Tunis, Tunisia

Amnesty International of the USA (AIUSA), 322 Eighth Avenue, New York, NY 10001, USA

Amnistía Internacional, Sección Argentina, 25 de Mayo 67, 4° Piso, 1002 Capital Federal, BuenosAires, Argentina

Amnistia Internacional, Rua dos Andredas 1560, Sala 2525, 90020-010, Porto Alegre, RS, CEP 04619-032,São Paulo, SP, Brazil

Amnistía Internacional, Sección Chilena, Casilla 4062, Santiago, Chile

Amnistía Internacional, Sección Ecuatoriana, Casilla 17-15-240-C, Quito, Ecuador

Amnistía Internacional, Calle Aniceto Ortega 624, (paralela a Gabriel Mancera, esq. Angel Urraza-eje 6Sur), Col. de Valle, Mexico DF, Mexico

Amnistia Internacional, Secção Portuguesa, Rua Fialho de Almeida, Nº 13, 1º, 1070 Lisbon, Portugal

Amnistía Internacional, Sección de Puerto Rico, Calle Robles No 54-Altos, Oficina 11, Rio Piedras00925, Puerto Rico

Amnistía Internacional, Sección Uruguaya, Trist Narvaja 1642, Apto 2, CP 11200 Montevideo, Uruguay

Amnistía Internacional, Sección Venezolana, Apartado Postal 5110, Carmelitas 1010-A, Caracas, Venezuela

Amnistie Internationale, Section canadienne francophone, 6250 boulevard Monk, Montreal, PQ, Canada H4E 3H7

J. A. Amoah, PO Box 2726, Accra, Ghana

Libreria Ancora, Via della Conciliazione, Rome, Italy

Ancora Audiovisual SA, Grana Via Corts Catalanes 645, 2º 0 8010 Barcelona, Spain

Angell Eurosales, PO Box 7, Newton Abbot, Devon TQ12 1QU, UK

Anglo-Nordic Books, 15 Marshall Road, Godalming, Surrey GU7 3AS, UK

Anita International, 510 Elizabeth Street, Surrey Hills, Sydney, Australia

Anness Publishing, Hermes House, 88 Blackfriars Road, London SE1, UK

Nadeem Ansari, 147 Zakir Bagh, New Delhi, India 110 025

Anthroposophic Press Inc, RR4, Box 94A1, Hudson, NY 12534, USA

Antique Collectors' Club Ltd, Market Street Industrial Park, Wappinger Falls, NY 12590, USA

Mr Olu Anulopo, Bounty Press Ltd, 57/1184 Odutala Runsewe Close, Orita Challenge, Ibadan, Nigeria

APAC Publishers Services, 35 Tannery Road, 10-06 Tannery Block, Ruby Industrial Complex, Singapore 1334

APD KL Ltd, 40B Jalan SS21/39, Damansara Utama, 47400 Petaling Jaya, Selangor Durul, Ehsan, Malaysia

APD Kuala Lumpur, No 18, Jalan SS3/41, 47300 Petaling Jaya, Selangor, Malaysia

APD Malaysia, 18 Jalan SS3/41, 47300 Petaling Jaya, Selangor Dural Ehsan, Malaysia

APD Singapore Pte Ltd, 5 Kallang Pudding Road, 06-07 Mactech Industrial Building, Singapore 349307

Applegames Educational Games & Learning Materials, 30 Efal Street, Holon 58510, Israel

Applied Media, 88 Bangla Sahib Marg, New Delhi, India 110 001

APS Singapore Pte Ltd, 60D Kallang Pudding Road, 02-07, Singapore 1334

Arabian Advanced Systems, PO Box 20129, Riyadh 11455, Saudi Arabia

Arbeiterpresse Verlag, Postfach 100105, 45001 Essen, Germany

Archetype, 7a Papawai Terrace, Mt Cook, Wellington, New Zealand

Archetype Book Agency, PO Box 68 085, Newtown, Auckland, New Zealand

Armchair Sailor Bookstore, 543 Thames Street, Newport, RI 02840-6709, USA

Edward Arnold (Australia) Ltd, Hodder Headline, Rydalmere Business Park, 10–16 South Street, Rydalmere, NSW, Australia

Arnold Publishers (India) Pvt Ltd, AB/9 1st Floor, Safdarjung Enclave, New Delhi, India 110 029

Arora Book Centre, PO Box 3284, Sharjah, UAE

Around the World Books, 4332 Old William Penn Highway, Monroeville, PA 15146-1438, USA

Artou Diffusion, 8 rue de Rive, 1204 Geneva, Switzerland

Arts Bibliographic, 37 Cumberland Business Park, Cumberland Avenue, London NW10 7SL, UK

Artsberg Enterprises Ltd, Unit 9, 13th Floor, Shing Yip Building, 19–21 Shing Yip Street, Kwun Tong,Kowloon, Hong Kong

Ashgate Asia Pacific Pte Ltd, Suite 12, Level 7, 8 Kippax Street, Surrey Hills, NSW, Australia 2010

Ashgate-Gower Asia Pacific Pte Ltd, 43 Albert Road, Avalon, NSW, Australia 2107

Ashgate Publishing Asia Pacific Pte Ltd, Golden Wheel Building, 41 Kallang Pudding, 04-03, Singapore 349316

Ashgate Publishing Co, Old Post Road, Brookfield, VT 05036, USA

Ashgrove Press, 4 Brassmill Centre, Brassmill Lane, Bath, Avon BA1 3JN, UK

Ashley & Radmore (Pty) Ltd, PO Box 57324, Springfield, 2137 South Africa

Ashton International Marketing Services, 101 Marlowe Road, Lunsford Park, Larkfield, Kent ME20 6TU, UK

Ashton Scholastic Ltd, 21 Lady Ruby Drive, East Tamaki, Auckland, New Zealand

Ashton Scholastic Pty Ltd, PO Box 579, Gosford, NSW, Australia 2250

Asia 2000, Winning Centre 7F, 46–48 Wyndham Street Central, Hong Kong

Asia Book Co, 5 Sukhumvit Road Soi 61, Prakhanong, PO Box 40, Bangkok 10110, Thailand

Asia Book House, 16/17 Bangaa Bazar, Dhaka 1100, Bangladesh

Asia Books, Bahnhofstrasse 132, 69151 Neckargemund, Germany

Asia Publisher Services Ltd, 16th Floor, Wing Fat Commercial Building, 218 Aberdeen Main Road, Aberdeen, Hong Kong

Asia Publishers Services, 40B Jalan SS21/39, Damansara Utama, 47400 Petaling Jaya, Selangor Darul, Ehsan, Malaysia

Asia Publishing House Inc, 10901 Reed Hartmann Highway, Suite 317, Cincinnati, OH 45242, USA

Asian Books Pvt Ltd, 7/28 Mahavir Gali, 1st Floor Ansari Road, Daryaganj, New Delhi, India 110 002

Asian Bookshop, 45 Graftons Way, London W1P 5LA, UK

Asian Trading Corporation, St Thomas Building, 150 Brigade Road, Bangalore, India 560 025

Asiapac Books Pte Ltd, 629 Aljunied Road, Cititech Industrial Building, 04-06 Singapore 1438

Associacion De Distribuidores y Editores, De Materiales De Ingles AC, Chihuahua 175-402, Col. Roma, Deleq. Cuauhtemoc, 06700 Mexico, DF, Mexico

Associated Marketing Services, 22 Mabel Street, Woking, Surrey GU21 1NN, UK

Associated Publishers Group (APG), 1501 County Hospital Road, Nashville, TN 37218, USA

Associated University Presses, PO Box 488, Port Credit, Mississauga, Ont, Canada

Associated University Presses, 440 Forsgate Drive, Cranbury, NJ 08512, USA

Astam Books Pty Ltd, 57–61 John Street, Leichhardt, NSW, Australia 2040

Astra Agency, PO Box 1567, Jerusalem, Israel

The Athlone Press, 165 First Avenue, Atlantic Highlands, NJ 07716, USA

Editorial Atlanta Argentina, Junin 827, 1113 Capital, Argentina

Atlantic Book Service, PO Box 78, Toshima, Tokyo, 170-91 Japan

Atol vzw, Blijde Inkomststraat 9, 3000 Leuven, Belgium

Atrium, 3356 Coffey Lane, Santa Rosa, CA 95403, USA

Attica-Diffusion, 63 rue de la folie Méricourt, 75011 Paris, France

Aubrey Books International Ltd, Silver Spring, MD, USA

Auckland Book Depot, 18 Belvedere Street, Epsom, Auckland 3, New Zealand

Audio Visual Centre Ltd, Mayflower Mansions, Bisazza Street, PO Box 58, Sliema SLM 01, Malta

Audio Visual Source, Item House, Beacon Road, Crowborough, East Sussex TN6 1AS, UK

Lloyd Austin, 144 Lindley Avenue, Nandy Park, East Bank, Demarara, Guyana

Austin's Book Services, 228 Camp Street, North Cummingsburg, Georgetown, Guyana

The Australian Book Source, 1309 Redwood Lane, Davis, CA 95616, USA

Australian Council for Educational Research Ltd, PO Box 210, Hawthorn, Vic, Australia 3122

Australian Large Print Pty Ltd, Unit 4, 8–10 Cataline Drive, Tullamarine, Vic, Australia 3058

Australian Pharmaceutical Publishing Co Ltd, 40 Burwood Road, Hawthorn, Victoria,, Australia 3122

Australian Special Book Service, Methodist Ladies College, 207 Barkers Road, Kew, Vic, Australia 3101

AV Masters Sdn Bhd, 18 Jalan Kemuja, off Jalan Bangsar, 59000 Kuala Lumpar, Malaysia

Avex Air Training Pty Ltd, PO Box 2259, Halfway House 1685 South Africa

Axall Media, 93 Rue Pascal, 75013 Paris, France

Brigitte Axster, Literarische Agentur, Postfach 7006 25, 60556 Frankfurt am Main, Germany
AZED AG, Hofackerstrasse 40, 4132 Muttenz, Switzerland
Azed Bucher, Dornacharstrasse 60/62, Postfach, 4002 Basle, Switzerland

Bacon & Hughes, 13 Deer Lane Avenue, Nepean, Ont, Canada K2E 6W7
Baert Sprl, avenue Firmin le Charlier, Jette, 1090 Brussels, Belgium
Bahamian News Ltd, Thompson Blvd. Leco Building, PO Box 8196, Nassau, Bahamas
Bahá'í Distribution Service, 7200 Leslie Street, Thornhill, Ont, Canada L3T 2A1
Bahá'í Distribution Service, PO Box 147, Blenheim, New Zealand
Bahá'í Publications Australia, PO Box 285, Mona Vale, NSW, Australia 2103
Bahá'í Publishing Trust, PO Box 19, New Delhi, India
Bahá'í Publishing Trust, 415 Linden Avenue, Wilmette, IL 60091, USA
Bahá'í Publishing Trust of Japan, Shinjuku 7-2-3, Shinjuku-ku, Tokyo, Japan
Bahá'í Verlag GmbH, Eppsteinerstrasse 89, W-6238 Hofheim, Germany
Bill Bailey Publishers Representatives, 16 Devon Square, Newton Abbot, Devon TQ12 2HR, UK
Susanne Baines, 2 Brookside, Dundrum Road, Dublin 14, Irish Republic
Baitul Islam, 10610 Jane Street, Maple, Ont, Canada L0J 1E0
Baker & Taylor, 501 Gladiola Street, Momence, IL 60954-1799, USA
Baker & Taylor Companies, PO Box 4500, 6 Kirby Avenue, Somerville, NJ 08876, USA & 501 S Gladiola Avenue, Momence, IL 60954, USA
Balatbat & Sons International, 22 Mount Stanford Street, Fitlinvest Home 1, Quezon City, Metro Manila, Philippines
A. A. Balkema Publishers, Lisplein 11, PO Box 1675, 3000 BR Rotterdam, Netherlands
Jonathan Ball Publishers (Pty) Ltd, 10-14 Watkins Street, Denver Extension 4, Johannesburg, PO Box 33977,Jeppestown, 2043 South Africa
Any Bancheva, Mladost 1, Block 32, Entrance 7 Apt 123, 1784 Sofia, Bulgaria
The Banner of Truth Trust, PO Box 621, Carlisle, PA 17013, USA
Bantam Books (Canada) Inc / Doubleday Canada Ltd, 105 Bond Street, Toronto, Ont, Canada M5B 1Y3
Dr Kunle Krown Banwo, GPO Box 1498, Ibsdan, Oyo State, Nigeria
Banyan Tree Book Distributors, PO Box 269, Stirling, SA, Australia 5152
Carlos Barbisan, Av Brig Luis Antonio 2367, CJ1104, São Paulo 01401-000, Brazil
Frank Barker & Sons Pty Ltd, PO Box 138, Mona Vale, NSW, Australia 2103
Barnabas Book Room, Suite 308, Postnet X10039, Randburg, 2125 South Africa
David Barrett-Jolly, Educational Book Services, Private Bag BR42, Gaborone, Botswana
David Bateman Ltd, PO Box 100-242, North Shore Mail Centre, Auckland 1330, New Zealand & Tarndale Grove, Albany Business Park, Bush Road, Albany, Auckland, New Zealand
Michael Bates, Inter-Book Marketing Services, Rua des Palmeiras 32-apto, 701 22270 Rio deJaneiro, Brazil
Batstone Books, 12 Gloucester Street, Malmesbury, Wilts SN16 0AA, UK
Verlag Hermann Bauer, Postfach 167, Kronenstraße 2, W-7800 Freiburg im Breisgau, Germany
Bay Foreign Language Books, 19 Dymchurch Road, St Mary's Bay, Romney Marsh, Kent TN29 0ET, UK
Beacon Distributing, PO Box 98, 55 Woodslee Avenue, Paris, Ont, Canada N3L 3E5
Beckett Sterling Ltd, 28 Poland Road, Auckland 10, New Zealand
Eckhard Becksmann, Rödelheimer Landstrasse 170, W-60489 Frankfurt, Germany
Thomas T. Beeter, Hampton Falls, USA
BELT, Bajvivo u. 8, 1027 Budapest II, Hungary
Ben & Co Ltd, PO Box 3164, Plot 3, Samora Machel Avenue, Dar es Salaam, Tanzania
R. J. Bender Publishing, PO Box 23456, San Jose, CA 95153, USA
Benelux Studiecentrum NV, Reditzaad 2, 4703 RC Roosendaal, Netherlands
Bennet's Bookshop, 38–42 Broadway, PO Box 138, Palmerston North, New Zealand

James Bennett Library Services & Pty Ltd, 4 Collaroy Street, Collaroy, NSW, Australia 2097
Berg Publishers, 22883 Quicksilver Drive, Dulles, VA 20166, USA
Berkeley Books Pvt Ltd, 2A Paterson Hill, Singapore 0923
Berlitz-Fixot, 24 avenue Marceau, 75008 Paris, France
Berlitz Publishing Co Inc, 257 Park Avenue South, 17th Floor, New York, NY 10010, USA
Noelie Bermudez, Alejandro Schroeder 6472, Galeria Azul Local 8, 11, 5000 Montevideo, Uruguay
Giorgio Bernadini Editore srl, Viale Bianca Maria 19, 20122 Milan, Italy
Beta Pedagog, Box 58, 430 17 Skällinge, Sweden
Bethesda Book Centre, Block 126, No. 551, Lorong 1, Toa Payoh, Singapore·12
Beyond Toys, Shop 2, 24 Birdwood Lane, Lane Cove, NSW, Australia 2066
Anupam Gyan Bhandar, 156 Dhaka Stadium, 1st Floor, Gate 14, Stair 28, Dhaka 2, Bangladesh
BI Publications Pvt Ltd, 43 Janpath, New Delhi, India 110 001 & 61-63 Lakshmi Building, 4th Fl, Sir Phirozshah Mehta Rd, Bombay, India 400 001
Bible Book House, PO Box 680, Kwang Hwa Moon, Seoul 110, Korea
Bibliotekstjanst AB, Box 200, Lund 221, Sweden
Bierman & Bierman A/S, Vestergade 126, 7200 Grindsted, Denmark
Big Apple Tuttle-Mori Agency Inc, 2nd Floor No. 8 Alley, 19 I-Tung Street, Taipei 10431, Taiwan
Big Apple Tuttle-Mori Agency Inc, 420/15 Soi Chomchoey, Sukhumuit 49, Bangkok 10110, Thailand
Big Ben Bookshop, Porzellangasse 24, 1090 Vienna, Austria
Miss A. Bildsoe, 27 Sct Knudsvej, 1903 Copenhagen V, Denmark
Biocosmic Books Inc, Unit 30, 110 Saunders Road, Barrie, Ont, Canada L4M 6E7
Bioquip Products, 17803 Lasalle Avenue, Gardena, CA 90248, USA
Biramo Book Distributors, PO Box 93, New Lambton, NSW, Australia 2305
Biramo Book Distributors, PO Box 14-640, Panmure, Auckland, New Zealand
Biramo Books Pty Ltd, PO Box 93, New Lambton, NSW, Australia 2305 & 7 King Street, Warners Bay, NSW, Australia 2282
Biramo Holdings Ltd, PO Box 14-640, Panmure, Auckland 6, New Zealand
Birch Tree Books, 3/103 Owens Road, Epsom, Auckland 3, New Zealand
Bissett Marketing Services Plc, Melbourne, Australia
A. & C. Black (Publishers) Ltd, 35 Bedford Row, London WC1R 4JH, UK
Libreria Blackpool, Dean Funes 395, 5000 Cordoba, Argentina
Blackstone Press Pty Ltd, PO Box 978, Bondi Junction, Sydney, NSW, Australia 2022
Basil Blackwell Inc, 238 Main Street, Suite 501, Cambridge, MA 02142, USA
Blackwell North America, 1001 Fries Mill Road, Blackwood, NJ 09012, USA
Blackwell Publishers, 108 Cowley Road, Oxford OX4 1JF, UK
Blackwell Science (Australia) Pty Ltd, 54 University Street, Carlton, Vic, Australia 3053
Blackwell Science Inc, Suite 500, 5th Floor, 238 Main Street, Cambridge, MA 02142, USA
Blackwell Science Ltd, Osney Mead, Oxford OX2 0EL, UK & 23 Ainslie Place, Edinburgh EH3 6AJ, UK
Richard Blady Booksales, Atlas House, Old Hall Street, Macclesfield SK10 2DT, UK
Robert G. Blake, Apartado Postal 41-533, Mexico DF 11000, Mexico
Brian Blennerhasset, Butler Sims, 78 Ranelagh Village, Dublin 6, Irish Republic
Bloomsbury Books Ltd, 702-4 Seabird House, 22–28 Wyndham Street, Central, Hong Kong
Winfried Bluth, Augustinusstrasse 43, W-42810 Remscheid, Germany
BMEC Rehab (M) Sdn Bhd, 31 Jalan PJS 9/12, Taman Bandar Sunway, 46150 Petaling Jaya, Malaysia
Boat Books, 214 St Kilda Road, St Kilda, Vic 3182, Melbourne, Australia; 31 Albany Street, Crows Nest, NSW 2065, Sydney, Australia; 109 Albert Street, Brisbane, Qld, Australia 4000 & 9 Axon Street, Subiaco, WA 6008, Perth, Australia
Bodhi Tree Book Store, 8585 Melrose Avenue, West Hollywood, CA 90069-5199, USA

Jean-Louis Boglio, Bookdealer, 26/31 Teemangum Street, PO Box 72, Currumbin, Qld, Australia 4223

Bohemian Ventures spol sro, Delnicka 13, 170 00 Prague 7, Czech Republic

Bokabud Mals Og Meriningar, Laugavegi 18, 101 Reykjavik, Iceland

Bokhandeln Info, Hornsgatan 151, 117 34 Stockholm, Sweden

Boksala Studenta, The University Bookshop, Haskola Islands, 101 Reykjavik, Iceland

Boletín Oficial del Estado, Trafalgar 27, 28010 Madrid, Spain

Boobook Publications Pty Ltd, PO Box 163, Tea Gardens, 2334 NSW, Australia

Book Bird, GPO Box 518, Mian Chambers, 3 Temple Road, Lahore, Pakistan

The Book Center, 144 North Front Street, PO Box 426, Belize City, Belize

Book Centre, DIT Annexe, Dilkhusha CA, Dhaka, Bangladesh

The Book Centre, PO Box 3799, 16 George Silundika Avenue, Harare, Zimbabwe

Book Channel, 21 Rajgir Chambers, 12–14 Shahid Bhagat, Singh Road, Opp Old Customs House,Bombay, India 400 023

Book Covers of Indonesia, J. I. Madrasah 14, Cilandak Timur, Jakarta 12560, Indonesia

Book Distributors Ltd, Weruga Lane (offf Haile Sellasie Avenue), Opposite Venus Metal, PO Box 47610,Nairobi, Kenya

Book Marketing Ltd, North Point Ind Building, 17/F Flat A, 499 King's Road, North Point, Hong Kong

Book Marketing Services, P-5 Rohini Gardens, Madras, India 600 028

Book People, 7900 Edgewater Drive, Oakland, CA 94621, USA

Book Promotions, 220 Werdmuller Centre, Newry Street, Claremont, 7700 South Africa

Book Promotions Pty Ltd, PO Box 23320, Claremont, 7735 South Africa & PO Box 5, Plumstead, 7800 South Africa

Book Representation & Distribution (BRAD), 244a London Road, Hadleigh, Essex SS7 2DE, UK

Book Reps (New Zealand) Ltd, 48 Lake Road, Northcote, (PO Box 36-105, Northcote Cen), Auckland 9, New Zealand

Book Services International, PO Box 782395, Sandton, Transvaal 2146 South Africa

Book Services & Promotion, 2220/31 Soi Ramkanhaeng 36/1, Ramkamhaeng Road, Huamaru, Bangkok, Thailand

Booker International, PO Box 2007, Bandar Seri Begawan, Negara, Brunei

Bookland Pty Ltd, Bookland House, 287–295 Lord Street, East Perth, WA, Australia 6000

Bookman Books Ltd, 2F-S, 88 Hsin Sheng South Road, Section 3, Taipei 106, Taiwan

Bookman Literary Agency, 12 Fiolstræde, 1171 Copenhagen, Denmark

The Bookmark, Box 801143, Santa Clara, CA 91380-1143, USA

Bookmarks, PO Box 16085, Chicago, IL 60616, USA

Bookport Associates, Casella Postale, 40040 Vado, Bologna, Italy

Books Express, PO Box 10, Saffron Walden, Essex CB11 4EW, UK

Books for Europe, PKB CPH Office, Hegnet 13, 2600 Glostrup, Denmark

Books for Europe, Casella Postale 196, 6900 Massagno, Switzerland

Books for Europe Ltd, 3 Sutton Court, 92 Grange Road, London W5 3PG, UK & PO Box 531, Bournemouth, Dorset BH1 1YA, UK

Books for Europe, J. Komarnicki, Lugano, Switzerland

Books for Europe (Robbert Pleysier), Walkottelanden 72, 7542 MT Enschede, Netherlands

Books from India Ltd, 45 Museum Street, London WC1A 1LR, UK

Books International, Ul. Lubelska 30/32, 03-308 Warsaw, Poland

Books International, 69B Lynchford Road, Farnborough, Hants GU14 6EJ, UK

Books International Inc, PO Box 605, Herndon, VA 20172, USA

Books Nippan, 1123 Dominguez Street, Unit K, Carson, CA 90746, USA

Bookseller Co Ltd, 81 Patpong Road, Bangkok, Thailand

Bookshop SA, J. M. Blanes 1170, Montevideo 11200, Uruguay

Bookstore Co Ltd, 1-2710 Akaike, Nisshin-shi, Aichi-ken, 470-01 Japan

Booktalk, PO Box 81340, Parkhurst, 2120 South Africa

Bookwise International, A.C.N. 005 526 045, 54 Crittenden Road, Findon, SA, Australia 5023

Bookwise International, PO Box 68.085, Auckland, New Zealand

Bookworld Services Inc, 1933 Whitfield Park Loop, Sarasota, FL 34243, USA

Botswana Book Centre, PO Box 91, Gabarone, Botswana

Botswana Centre for Accounting Studies, Private Bag 00319, Gabarone, Botswana

Andreas Böttcher, Pappelallee 6, W-10437 Berlin, Germany

Bounty Press Ltd, PO Box 23856, Mapo PO, Ibadan, Nigeria

D. Richard Bowen, PO Box 30037, 200 61 Malmö 30, Sweden

R. R. Bowker, 121 Chanlon Road, New Providence, NJ 07974, USA

Bowker-Saur Ltd, Maypole Road, East Grinstead, West Sussex RH19 1HH, UK

Marion Boyars Publishers Inc, 237 East 39th Street, New York, NY 10016, USA

BPP (Cyprus), PO Box 5215, Nicosia, Cyprus

Eleanor Brasch Associates, PO Box 586, 7 Pyrl Road, Artarmon, NSW, Australia 2064

Graham Brash Pte Ltd, 32 Gul Drive, Singapore 2262

Brassey's Inc, 1313 Dolley Madison Boulevard, Suite 401, McLean, VA 22101, USA

Bratt-Institut für Neues Lernen GmbH, Aspermuhle, Triftstraße 264, W-4180 Goch 5, Germany

Brepols Publishers, Steenweg op Tielen 68, 2300 Turnhout, Belgium

Brettschneider Fernreisebedarf, Hauptstrasse 5, 85586 Poing, Bei Munich, Germany

Brick Row Publishing Co Ltd, PO Box 100-057, Auckland 10, New Zealand

Bridgehouse Bookshop, Bridgehouse Building, Byron & Grivas Digenis Avenue, PO Box 4527, Nicosia, Cyprus

Pascal Brien, 2 rue Vauban, 78000 Versailles, France

Michael Brightmore, 104 Sherbrooke Road, London SW6 7QN, UK

Brighton House Publishing Pty Ltd, PO Box 98, Brighton, Vic, Australia 3186

E. J. Brill & Co, PO Box 9000, 2300 PA Leiden, Netherlands

Brimax Books, RD 3, Box 104, Black River Road, Bethlehem, PA 18015, USA

Libreria Britanica SA, Serapio Rendon 125, Col San Rafael, 06470 Mexico DF, Mexico

The British Bookshop, English Language Centre, Singerstraße 30, 1010 Vienna, Austria

University of British Columbia Press, 6344 Memorial Road, Vancouver, BC, Canada V6T 1Z2

British Travel Books, 3rd Floor, Dilworth Building, Auckland, New Zealand

Broadcast Book Services, 24 De Montfort Road, London SW16 1LZ, UK

Broadview Press, 3576 California Road, Orchard Park, NY 14127, USA

Scott Brodie, Electra Media Group Pty Ltd, GPO Box 1546, Sydney, NSW, Australia 2011

Broner & Daentler, Marktplatz 5, 8078 Eichstatt, Germany

The Brookings Institution, Dept 029, Washington, DC 20042-0029, USA

Brookside Publishing Services, 2 Brookside, Dundrum Road, Dundrum, Dublin 14, Irish Republic

David Brown Book Co, PO Box 511, 20 Main Street, Oakville, CT 06779, USA

Trevor Brown Associates, Biblios Publishers Distribution Services Ltd, Star Road, Partridge Green,Horsham, West Sussex RH13 8LD, UK & 114–115 Tottenham Court Road, Midford Place, London W1P 0BY, UK

Brunner/Mazel Inc, 9 Union Square West, New York, NY 10003, USA

BTJ, Box 200, 22100 Lund, Sweden

Buch und Information AG, Hofackerstrasse 13, 8032 Zurich, Switzerland

W. A. Buchanan & Co, 20 Morrisby Street, Geebung, Brisbane, Qld, Australia 4034

The Buddhist Merit & Wisdom Service, Shop A, Ground Floor, Jenny's Court, 241-3 Sai Yee Street, Mongkok, Kowloon, Hong Kong

John Budds, Evans Brothers (Kenya) Ltd, PO Box 44536, Nairobi, Kenya

Nina Bueno Del Carpio, c/o Ladybird Head Office, Beeches Road, Loughborough, Leics LE11 2NQ, UK

Bulldog Books, PO Box 155, Broadway, NSW,, Australia 2007

Bundesanzeiger Verlag, Breite Strasse, Postfach 10 80 06, 5000 Cologne 1, Germany

Van Buren Uitgeverij BV, Postbus 10356, 6000, GJ Weert, Netherlands

James Burkinshaw, Arcadia Publishing, Chalford Publishing Corporation, One Washington Centre,Dover, NH 03820, USA

Arnold Busck, Købmagergade 49, Copenhagen, Denmark

Bushbooks, PO Box 1370, Gosford South, NSW, Australia 2250

Business Foundation, ul Wspólna 1/3, 00 529 Warsaw, Poland
Butterworth & Co (Publishers) Ltd, Halsbury House, 35 Chancery Lane, London WC2A 1EL, UK
Butterworth-Heinemann, Level 9, North Tower, Chatswood Plaza, 1–5 Railway Street, Chatswood, NSW, Australia 2067
Butterworth-Heinemann, 7 Jahangir Street, Islamia Park, Poonch Road, Lahore, Pakistan
Butterworth-Heinemann Inc, 313 Washington Street, Newton, MA 02158, USA
Butterworth-Heinemann Ltd, Linacre House, Jordan Hill, Oxford OX2 8DP, UK
Butterworth Publishers (Pty) Ltd, 8 Walter Place, Waterval Park, Mayville, Durban, 4091 South Africa
Butterworths Asia, No 1, Temasek Avenue, #17-01 Millenia Tower, Singapore 039192
Butterworths Australia, 271–273 Lane Cove Road, PO Box 345, North Ryde, NSW, Australia 2113
Butterworths Canada, 75 Clegg Road, Markham, Ont, Canada L6G 1A1
Butterworths Caribbean, Butterworth of Puerto Rico Inc, Equity and Escreetinio, Legislativo Divisions, Paseo No 52, San Juan, 00906, Puerto Rico
Butterworths India, G-2 Vardaan House, 7/28 Mahavir Street, Ansari Road, Daryaganj, New Delhi 110 002, India
Butterworths Ireland, 26 Upper Ormand Quay, Dublin 7, Irish Republic
Butterworths Malaysia, No 3, Jalan PJS 11/20, Bandar Sunway, 46150 Petaling Jaya, Selangor, DarulEhsan, Malaysia
Butterworths of New Zealand, 205–207 Victoria Street, CPO Box 472, Wellington 1, New Zealand
Butterworths South Africa, 8 Walter Place, Mayville 4091, Durban, 4000, Natal, South Africa
Butterworths, United States, 8 Industrial Way, Building C, Salem, NH 03071, USA
Byford University Press, 70 Wynford Drive, Don Mills, Ont, Canada
Patrick Bygate & Juliusz Komarnicki, Casella Postale 196, 6900 Massagno, Switzerland

C52 – Graphic Design, Chalmersgatan 15, 411 35 Goteborg, Sweden
Cahaya Vista Bakti Sdn Bhd, J4-00-04 KNMK 3, Subang Jaya 47600, Petaling Jaya, Malaysia
Cairo Trade Centre, 35 Gamiat al-Doual al-Arabia, Mohandesien, Giza, Cairo, Egypt
Calico Books International, PO Box 782395, Sandton, Transvaal, 2146 South Africa
Camera Mundi Inc, Amatista Num 8, Villa Blanca, GPO Box 6840, Caguas, Puerto Rico
Camerapix, 8 Ruston Mews, London W11 1RB, UK
Camerapix Publishers International, PO Box 45048, Nairobi, Kenya
Campus Crusade Asia Ltd, 315 Outram Road, 06-08 Tan Boon, Liat Building, Singapore 0316
Editora Campus Ltda, Rua Barao de Itapagipe 55, Rio de Janeiro, Brazil
Canadabooks International, 2B Priors Hall Farm, Widdington, Saffron Walden, Essex CB11 3SB, UK
Canadian Books Express, The Abbey Bookshop, 29 rue de la Parcheminerie, 75005 Paris, France
Canadian Manda Group, One Atlantic Avenue, Suite 105, Toronto, Ont, Canada M6K 3E7
Canadian Medical Association, 1867 Alta Vista Drive, Ottawa, Ont, Canada K19 3Y6
Canadian Scholars Press, 180 Bloor Street West, Suite 402, Toronto, Ont, Canada M5S 2V6
Ste Canadienne des Pneus Michelin Ltée, 175 boulevard Bouchard, Dorval, PQ, Canada H9S 5T1
Candlewick Press, 2067 Massachusetts Avenue, Cambridge, MA 02140, USA
Candlewick Press Inc, via Douglas & McIntyre, 2nd Floor, 585 Bloor Street West, Toronto, Ont, Canada M6G 1K5
Cankarjeva Zalozba (Centre Oxford), 61000 Ljubljana, Kopitarjeva 2, Slovenia
Cannon International, Block 86, Marine Parade Central – 03–213, Singapore 1544
Cantaluppi & Hug, Freudenbergstrasse 142, 8044 Zurich, Switzerland
Capital Books Pte Ltd, PO Box No 7135, 7/28 (Part II) Manaveer St, Ansari Road, Daryagganj, New Delhi, India 110 002
Capital Stamps, PO Box 3769, 91036 Jerusalem, Israel

Capricorn Link (Australia) Pty Ltd, 2–13 Carrington Road, Castle Hill, NSW, Australia 2154 & PO Box 6651, Baulkham Hills BC, NSW, Australia 2153
Cardiff Academic Press, St Fagan's Road, Fairwater, Cardiff CF5 3AE, UK
Cargills (Ceylon) Ltd, York Street, Colombo, Sri Lanka
Caribbean Book Distributors, PO Box 462, Port of Spain, Trinidad
Carlong Publishers (Caribbean) Ltd, PO Box 489, 33 Second Street, Newport West, Kingston 13, Jamaica
Carmel Libraries, PO Box 54, Gan Yavne 70800, Israel
Gregory Carr, Carr O'Connell, 83 Tudor Grove, Ashbourne, Co Meath, Irish Republic
Terry Carr, 17 St Andrews Way, West Lakes, Australia 5021
Carr O'Connell, Book Marketing Services (Ireland), 83 Tudor Grove, Ashbourne, Co Meath, Irish Republic
The Carswell Co Ltd, 2330 Midland Avenue, Agincourt, Ont, Canada M1S 1P7
Carswell Legal Publications, Corporate Plaza, 2075 Kennedy Road, Scarborough, Ont, Canada M1T 3V4
Casablanca, PO Box 824, Streetsville, Ont, Canada L5M 2C4
Cassell Plc (Sales Dept), Wellington House, 125 Strand, London WC2R 0BB, UK
Cassell Representative Office, PO Box 605, Herndon, VA 20172, USA
Cassidy & Associates Inc, 470 West 24th Street, New York, NY 10011, USA
Cathedral Bookshop, PO Box 2381, Dar es Salaam, Tanzania
Catholic Bookshop, PO Box 36291, Lusaka, Zambia
Catholic Supplies (NZ) Ltd, 80 Adelaide Road, Wellington 1, New Zealand
Catholic Truth Society, Catholic Centre, PO Box 2984, Hong Kong
Cavendish Books Inc, Unit 5, 801 West 1st Street, North Vancouver, BC, Canada V7P 1A4
Cavendish Publishing (Australia) Pty Ltd, Sydney **AUS, Australia
Cavendish Publishing Ltd, The Glass House, Wharton Street, London WC1X 9PX, UK & 23A Countess Road, London NW5 2XH, UK
Caves Books Ltd, 103 Chung Shan North Road, Section 2, Taipei, Taiwan
The Caxton Bookshop, 278 Main Road, Kenilworth, Cape Town, 7700 South Africa
CBS Publishers & Distributors, 485 Jain Bhawan, Bhola Nath Nagar, Delhi, India 110 032
CCH Asia Ltd, 11-01, 11 Keppel Road, Singapore 089057
CCH Australia Ltd, Cnr Talavera & Khartoum Roads, North Ryde, NSW, Australia 2113
CCH Editions Ltd, Aarstrasse 67, 65195 Wiesbaden, Germany
CCH Editions Ltd, Telford Road, Bicester, Oxon OX6 0XD, UK
CCH Hong Kong Ltd, 701 Seabird House, 22–28 Wyndham Street, Central, Hong Kong
CCH Inc, 4025 West Peterson Avenue, Chicago, IL 60646, USA
CCH Japan Ltd, Ginza TK Building 3F, 1-1-7 Shintomi, Chuo-ku, Tokyo, 104 Japan
Cedeseus AB, Kungsgatan 15, 302 45 Halmstad, Sweden
Centenary Publishing House, PO Box 2776, Kampala, Uganda
Central Africana Ltd, PO Box 631, Blantyre, Malawi
Central Books Ltd, 99 Wallis Road, London E9 5LN, UK
Centro de Estudos do Laboratorio de Aptidao Fisica de Sao Caetano do Sul (CELAFISCS), Caixa Postal 268, CEP 09501, Sao Caetano Do Sul, Sao Paulo, Brazil
Edizioni Centro Studio Erickson, Piazzetta Anfiteatro 8, Trento, Italy
Editions du Centre de Psychologie Appliquée, 25 rue de la Plaine, 75980 Paris, Cedex 20, France
Centrum Publishing, Gunnar Clausenvej 66, 8260 Viby J, Denmark
Ceres/Demeter, Av Montplaisir 6, Tunis, Tunisia
Chadwyck-Healey France SARL, 50 rue de Paradis, 75010 Paris, France
Chadwyck-Healey Inc, 1101 King Street, Alexandria, VA 22314, USA
Chadwyck-Healey SL, Juan Bravo 18, 2°C, 28006 Madrid, Spain
Challenge Distributors CC, PO Box 7109, Primrose Hill, Johannesburg 1417 South Africa
Changi International Distribution Services Pte Ltd, Unit 15/17, Kaki Bukit Road 2, KB Warehouse Complex, Singapore 1441
Chapman & Hall, 115 5th Avenue, New York, NY 10003, USA
Chapman & Hall Australia, 102 Dodds Street, South Melbourne, Vic, Australia 3205
Chapman & Hall GmbH, Pappelallee 3, 69469 Weinheim, Germany

Chapman & Hall Japan, ITP Japan, Kywoa Building, 3F, 2-2-1 Hiakawacho, Chiyoda-ku, Tokyo 102, Japan

Chapman & Hall Ltd, 2–6 Boundary Row, London SE1 8HN, UK

David Charles, 21 les Graviers de Vieux Maisons, 26 rue de Paris, 78600 Maisons-Laffitte, France

Chaunter Editorial Associates Ltd, PO Box 17-159, Wellington 5, New Zealand

Chelsea Green Publishing Co, 205 Gates-Briggs Building, White River Junction, VT 05001, USA

Cherev Canada Ltd, PO Box 698, 25 Main Street East, Markdale, Ont, Canada N0C 1H0

University of Chicago Press, 5801 South Ellis Avenue, Chicago, IL 60637, USA

Child's Play, 120 Watline Avenue, Unit 5, Mississauga, Ont, Canada L4Z 2C1

Child's Play Australia, 5/53 Myoora Road, Terrey Hills, NSW, Australia 2084

Child's Play Dubai, PO Box 290, Dubai, UAE

Child's Play France, Le Vieux Vaulerault, 35350 St Meloir des Ondes, France

Child's Play Greece, Ithakis 38, Athens 11251, Greece

Child's Play Malta, Gasper Trading Agency, 2/5 Melita Street, Valletta, Malta

Child's Play USA, PO Box 821, Lewiston, ME 04240, USA

China Book Import Centre, 35 Chegongzhuang Xilu, PO Box 2825, Beijing, P. R. of China

China Books, 2nd Floor, 4 Tattersalls Lane, Melbourne, Vic, Australia 3000

China Books & Periodicals Inc, 2929 24th Street, San Francisco, CA 94110, USA

China Institute, Sinsenveien 15, 0572 Oslo 5, Norway

China National Publications Import & Export Corporation (CNPIEC), 16 Gongti East Road, 100020 Beijing, P. R. of China

Choice Publishing & Marketing Co Ltd, 15 Tenth Avenue Belleville, St. Michael, Barbados

Christian Distribution Centre, 2/193 Marua Road, Auckland 5, New Zealand

Christian Info, PO Box 2540, Welkom, 9460 South Africa

Christian Literature Crusade, 2-1-3 Surugadai Kanda, Chiyoda-ku, Tokyo, 101 Japan

Christian Marketing New Zealand, Private Bag, Havelock North, New Zealand

Christian Meditation Media Meditation Chretienne, 1283 Moffat Avenue, Verdun, PQ, Canada H4H 1Z1

Christian Meditation Media, 23 Kensington Square, London W8 7D, UK

Christian Research Association, Locked Bag 23, Kew,, Australia 3101

Christie & Christie Associates, PO Box 392, Cookstown, Ont, Canada L0L 1L0

Chronicle Books, 275 Fifth Street, San Francisco, CA 94013, USA

Edwin Chu, 2F, 5 Austin Avenue, Tsimshatsui, Kowloon, Hong Kong

Church Book Stores, 69 Great South Road, Remuera, Auckland 1005, New Zealand

Churchill Radius Inc, 1425 Broad Street, Clifton, NJ 07013, USA

Cimino Publishing Group, PO Box 174, Carle Place, NY 11514, USA

Cinehollywood Srl, Via Reguzzoni 15, 20125 Milan, Italy

CIS Publishers, 245–249 Cardigan Street, Carlton, Vic, Australia 3053

CITIS, 80 Eighth Avenue, Suite 303, New York, NY 10011, USA

CKK Ltd Publishers' International Management, Standard House, 16–22 Epworth Street, London EC2A 4JL, UK

Librairie Clairafrique, Place de l'Indépendance, BP 2005, Dakar, Senegal

CLARA, Carrera 15 # 32-78, Apartado Aereo 57-527, Bogota 2, Colombia

Janet Clark, 3 Beauchamp Close, Chiswick, London W4 5BT, UK & PF Box 445, London W3 0TN, UK

Clarke Associates Ltd, The Rackhay, Queen Charlotte Street, Bristol BS1 4HU, UK

E. W. Classey Ltd, PO Box 93, Faringdon, Oxon SN7 7DR, UK

Classic Music Distribution, Biskupcova 26, 130 00 Prague 3, Czech Republic

CLB Marketing Services, Szarvashaz Batthany Utca 4, Kecskemet 6000, Hungary

Cloister Book Store Ltd, Kinks Street, Bridgetown, Barbados

CMC Australasia Pty Ltd, Cooper Street, Havelock North, New Zealand

CMC Australia Pty Ltd, PO Box 519, Belmont, Vic, Australia 3216

College Press Publishers (Pvt) Ltd, 15 Douglas Road, Workington, Harare, Zimbabwe

Le Colporteur Diffusion, rue du Champ du Loup, BP 1, 63670 La Roche Blanche, France

Colt Associates, 4 Bury Green Cottages, Wheathampstead, Herts AL4 8AK, UK

Columba Book Service, The Rise, Mount Merrion, Blackrock, Co Dublin, Irish Republic

Columbia University Press, Marketing Department, 562 West 113th Street, New York, NY 10025, USA

Combined Book Representatives, PO Box 4571, CPO Manila 1099, Philippines

Combined Books Inc, 151 East 10th Avenue, Conshohocken, PA 19428, USA

Combined Representatives Worldwide Inc, 4 Topaz Road, Green Heights, Taytay, Rizal, Philippines & PO Box 4571, CPO Manila, Philippines

Comercial Atheneum SA, Joventnt 19, 08830 Sant Boi De Llobregat, Barcelona, Spain

Commerce Clearing House New Zealand Ltd, 17 Kahika Road, Beach Haven, Auckland 10, New Zealand

The Commercial Press Ltd, 2nd Floor, Heng Ngai Jewelry Centre, 4 Hok Yuen Street East, Hunghom, Kowloon, Hong Kong

Compact Data, Forchhammersvej 19, 1920 Frederiksberg C, Denmark

Computational Mechanics Inc, 25 Bridge Street, Billerica, MA 01821, USA

Concordia Publishing House, 3558 South Jefferson Avenue, Saint Louis, MO 63118, USA

Connolly Publications, Four Provinces Bookshop, 244–246 Grays Inn Road, London WC1X 8JR, UK

Dr H. R. Conrad, Rehmatt, 8706 Meilen, Switzerland

Consortium Inc, 1045 Westgate Drive, St Paul, MN 55114-0165, USA

Consul Books, Dr Catzlaan 21, 1261 CE Blaricum, Netherlands

Continent Books, Paulus Potterstraat 20, 1071 DA Amsterdam, Netherlands

The Cookery Book, 31 Albany Street, Crows Nest, NSW, Australia 2065

Copernicus Diffusion, 23 rue Saint Dominique, Paris 75007, France

Fergus Corcoran, 21 Cross Avenue, Dun Laoghaire, Co Dublin, Irish Republic

Cordee, 3A De Montfort Street, Leicester LE1 7HD, UK

Cordillera Books, 8415 Granville Street, Box 46, Vancouver, BC, Canada V6P 4Z9

Cornell University Press, 740 Cascadilla Street, PO Box 250, Ithaca, NY 14851, USA

Cornerhouse Publications, 70 Oxford Street, Manchester M1 5NH, UK

Cornes & Co, CPO Box 158, Tokyo, Japan

Corona AB, PO Box 5, 20120 Malmo, Sweden

Coronet Books Inc, 311 Bainbridge Street, Philadelphia, PA 19147, USA

Corporate Fitness, 509 Balasteir Road, Singapore 1232

Cosmic Sounds Ltd, 1 Vergemount, Clonskeagh, Dublin 6, Irish Republic

Pierre-Yves Cosmo, 17 Square des Cardours, Box 51, 75020 Paris, France

Council Oak Books, 1350 East 15th Street, Tulsa, OK 74120, USA

Covenant Media Production, PO Box 1497, Thousand Oaks, CA 91358, USA

Craenen bvba, Ijzerenberglaan 24, 3009 Winksele-Herent, Belgium

Creative Communication and Management Center, 2nd Floor, Raja Bahadur Building, 8 Ambalal Doshi Road, Bombay, India 400 023

Crescent News (KL) Sdn Bhd, 2104/5 Malayan Mansion, Jalan Masjid India, 50100 Kuala Lumpur, Malaysia

Ezra Crichlow, 15 Warren's Crescent, St Thomas, Barbados

Criminal Justice Press, PO Box 249, Monsey, NY 10952, USA

Critiques Livres, 56 rue Malmaison, BP 93, 93172 Bagnolet Cedex, France

Leslie Croaker, Dr Carmona Y Valle B-12-2, Edifico Sagitario Depto 904, Col Doctores, MexicoDF 06720, Mexico

Bernard Croft (Croft & Croft), The Highwood, Birches, Leominster, Herefordshire HR6 0GN, UK

Cromland Inc, 2200 Irving Street, Allentown, PA 18103, USA

Thompson C. Crosby, Victoria, St Mark's, Grenada

Cross (HK) Co, PO Box 4559, GPO, Hong Kong

Crossroad Distributors Pty Ltd, 9 Euston Street, Rydalmere, NSW, Australia 2116

Crouch International Ltd, Room 710, 1156 Avenue of the Americas, New York, USA

Csaba Lengyel de Bagota, Szarvasház Batthyany utca 4, 6000 Kécskemét, Hungary

Cumberland Valley Bible Book Service, PO Box 613, Carlisle, PA 17013, USA

Currency Press, 330 Oxford Street, PO Box 452, Paddington, NSW, Australia 2021

Current Technical Literature Co Pvt Ltd, India House, opp GPO, PO Box 1473, Bombay, India 400 001

James Currey Publishers, 54b Thornhill Square, Islington, London N1 1BE, UK

DA Books & Information Services, 648 Whitehorse Road, Mitcham, Victoria, Australia 3132

Dalcomtext, Postbus 76, 9765 ZH Paterswolde, Netherlands

Dalro (Pty) Ltd, Samro House, 73 Juta Street, Braamfontein, Johannesburg, 2001 South Africa

Danesh Publication (Pvt) Ltd, A-7 Amir Khusro Road, KDA 1, Karachi, Pakistan

Dansk Centralagentur DCA, Sluseholmen 6-8, 2450 Copenhagen, Denmark

Dansk Psykologisk Forlag, Hans Knudsens Plads 1a, 2100 Copenhagen, Denmark

D.A.P., 636 Broadway, EM 1208, New York, NY 10012, USA

Diffusion Daphné, Poortakkerstraat 29, 9051 Ghent, Belgium

Dar Al Rifai, PO Box 1590, Riyadh, Saudi Arabia

Dass Media Pte Ltd, 207 Bhandri House, 91 Nehru Place, New Delhi, India 110 019

Daughters of St Paul, Catholic Shop, PO Box 5141, Johannesburg, 2001 South Africa

David & Charles Inc, Trafalgar Square, Howe Hill Road, North Pomfret, VT 05053, USA

David's Marine Books, Corner of Gaunt & Beaumont Streets, Westhaven, Auckland, New Zealand

F. A. Davis Co, 1915 Arch Street, Philadelphia, PA 19103, USA

Davo, c/o Philac, Rue du Midi 48, Brussels 1000, Belgium

Davo, c/o Lindner Falzlos, Gl Randers vej 28, 8450 Hammel, Denmark

Davo, c/o Suomen Postimerkkeily, Ludvingkatu 5, 00130 Helsinki, Finland

Davo France (Casteilla), 10 Rue Leon Foucault, 78184 St Quentin Yvelines, Cedex, France

Davo Norge A/S, PO Box 738, Sentrum, 0105 Oslo, Norway

Davo Publications, PO Box 411, 7400 AK Deventer, Netherlands

Mrs Edna Dawson, Lot B, Hillock Terrace, Blue Range, Diego Martin, Trinidad

Dawson Bumps, Cowper Works, Olney, Bucks MK46 4BN, UK

Dawson France, 91871 Palaisea Cedex, France

Dayspring, PO Box 581, Westville, Durban, 3630 South Africa

Daystar Press, PO Box 2161, Ibadan, Nigeria

Daystar Publishers Pte Ltd, 45 Jalan Pemimpin 10-00, Foowah Industrial Building, Singapore 2057

H. De Brouwer, PO Box 10120, 1001 EC Amsterdam, Netherlands

Nicole de Ruyck, Brede Straat 131, 2580 Putte, Belgium

K. V. G. de Silva & Sons (Colombo) Ltd, 415 Galle Road, Colombo 4, Sri Lanka

De Vorss & Co Inc, PO Box 550, Marina del Rey, CA 90291, USA

deBrosse, Redman & Black, PO Box 507, Kingston 10, Jamaica

Librairie Decitre, 29 Place Bellecour, 69002 Lyon, France

Deep Books Ltd, Unit 13, Cannon Wharf Business Centre, 35 Evelyn Street, London SE8 5RT, UK

Delta Editions Sdn Bhd, Lot 18, Jalan 51A/223, PO Box 621, 46100 Petaling Jaya, Selangor Darul Ehsan, Malaysia

Delta Ltd, 39 Alexandra Road, Addlestone, Surrey KT15 2PQ, UK

Delta Systems Inc, 1400 Miller Parkway, McHenry, IL 60050-7030, USA

The Denali Press, PO Box 1535, Juneau, AK 99802, USA

DetStar Skrivet, Box 47069, 40258 Gothenburg, Sweden

Deutsch-Britische Stiftung für das Studium der Industriegesellschaft, Bonn, Germany

Deutscher Apotheker Verlag, Postfach 10 10 61, Birkenwaldstrasse 44, W-7000 Stuttgart 10, Germany

Frank & Lois Dew, PO Box 456, Feilding, New Zealand

Diamond Farm Book Publishers, RR3, Brighton, Ont, Canada K0K 1H0

Didacta, 1 Genting Link, 07-03 Perfect Industrial Building, Singapore 1334

Didactic Films Ltd, Oxford Educational Resources Ltd, PO Box 106, Kidlington, Oxford OX5 1HY, UK

Didax, 5 Fourth Street, Centennial Industrial Park, Peabody, MA 01960, USA

Diffulivre, 41 rue des Jordils, 1025 St Sulpice, Switzerland

Dingli Co International, 43–44 Zachary Street, Valletta, Malta

The Walt Disney Co Inc, 114 Fifth Avenue, New York, NY 10011, USA

Distesa, Puerto Rico 6, Madrid 16, Spain

Distican, 35 Fulton Way, Richmond Hill, Ont, Canada L4B 2NY

Distri Cultural, Rua Vasco da Gama 4-4A, 2686 Sacvem Codex, Portugal

Distributed Arts Publishers, 636 Broadway, 12th Floor, New York, NY 10012, USA

Disvan Enterprises, 25 Mayfair Apartments, Mayfair Gardens, New Delhi, India 110 016

D & J Books, 229-21B Merrick Boulevard, Laurelton, NY 11413, USA

DK Book House Co Ltd, 3rd Floor, Seacon Square, 904 Moo 6, Sri Nakarin Road, Nongbon, Praves, Bangkok 10260, Thailand

DLS Australia (Pty) Ltd, 6 Holly Drive, Dingley, Vic, Australia 3172

Richard Dodman, c/o Constable & Co Ltd, 3 The Lanchesters, 162 Fulham Palace Road, London W6 9ER, UK

The Dominie Group, 8 Cross Street, PO Box 33, Brookvale, NSW, Australia 2100

Dominie Press Inc, 11568 Sorrento Valley Road, Suite 12, San Diego, CA 92121, USA

Dorling Kindersley Ltd, 9 Henrietta Street, Covent Garden, London WC2E 8PS, UK

Ted Dougherty, 72 Hadley Street, London NW1 8TA, UK

Douglas & McIntyre, 2nd Floor, 585 Bloor Street West, Toronto, Ont, Canada M6G 1K5

Ron Doussard & Associates, 6 Castle Pines Court, Lake in the Hills, IL 60102, USA

Drake International Services, Market House, Market Place, Deddington, Oxford OX15 0SF, UK

Drake Marketing Services, St Fagan's Road, Fairwater, Cardiff CF5 3AE, UK

DRT International, 6th Floor, Garden Tower Building, 98-78 Unni-dong Chong, Seoul 110-350, Korea

DS Druck- und Verlags service, Burghaldenweg 53, 70469 Stuttgart, Germany

D-Services, 6 Euston Street, Freemen's Common, Leicester LE2 7SS, UK

Dual Dolphin Publishing Inc, 224 Dedham Street, Norfolk, MA 02056, USA

Duet Literary Agency, Gagarina 27m.19, 00-753 Warsaw, Poland

David Duffy, Parkstraße 71-73, W-6200 Wiesbaden, Germany

Dufour Editions Inc, PO Box 7, Byers Road, Chester Springs, PA 19425-0007, USA

Dun's Marketing Services, Three Century Drive, Parsipanny, NJ 07054, USA

Dundurn Distribution, c/o Lavis Marketing, 73 Lime Walk, Headington, Oxford OX3 7AD, UK

Dundurn Press, 1823 Maryland Avenue, Niagara Falls, NY 14302-1000, USA

Hugh Dunphy, PO Box 413, Kingston 10, Jamaica

Dunya Education, 34440 Bagcilar, Istanbul, Turkey

Leslie Durham, Cascina Antonietta 1, 27050 Bagnaria PV, Italy

Andrew B. Durnell, 2 Linden Close, Tunbridge Wells, Kent TN4 8HH, UK

E. J. Dwyer (Australia) Pty Ltd, Unit 13, Perry Park Industrial Estate, 33 Maddox Street, Alexandria, NSW, Australia 2015

DZS, Mestni trg 26, 61000 Ljubljana, Slovenia

Dzuka Publishing Ltd, PMB 39, Stadium Road, Ginnery Corner, Blantyre, Malawi

EAEP Ltd, Mpaka Road/Woodvale Grove, PO Box 45314, Nairobi, Kenya

Early Learning OY, Tynnyrintekijänkatu 2, 00580 Helsinki, Finland

East African Educational Publishers Ltd, Mpaka Road, Woodvale Grove, PO Box 45314, Nairobi, Kenya

East African Educational Publishers (Uganda) Ltd, Jinja Road, Pioneer House, 1st Floor Room 9, Plot 28, Kampala, Uganda

East Coast Distributors, PO Box 4200, Somerville, NJ 08876, USA

East Shore Sailing, 1000 East Shore Drive, Ithaca, NY 14850, USA

East West Computers Pty Ltd, PO Box 250, 172 Main Road, Riddells Creek, Vic, Australia 3431

East-West Export Books, c/o University of Hawaii Press, 2840 Kolowalu Street, Honolulu, HI 96822, USA
East West Operations, Copova 38, 61000 Ljubljana, Slovenia
Eastern Book Service Inc, 3-13 Hongo 3-chome, Bunkyo-ku, Tokyo, 113 Japan
Eastern Company for Publications, PO Box 6220, Beirut, Lebanon
Eastview Publications Sdn Bhd, 11 Lorong 51a/227c, 46100 Petaling Jaya, Selangor Darul Ehsan, Malaysia
Eastwind Books & Arts Inc, 1435 Stockton Street, Suite B3, San Francisco, CA 94133, USA
EBSCO Europe, PO Box 204, AE Aalsmeer, Netherlands
EBSCO Subscription Service, PO Box 1943, Birmingham, AL 35201-1943, USA
Ecoserveis, Ceramica 38, 08035, Spain
ECS Publishing Co, 138 Ipswich Street, Boston, MA 02215, USA
Ed Source, 47 Milne Street, Bayswater, WA, Australia 6053
Eddington Hook Ltd, PO Box 239, Tunbridge Wells, Kent TN4 0YQ, UK
Buchhandlung Othmar Edelmann, Rennweg 40, 1030 Vienna 1, Austria
Edimport, Burgos 24, 28039 Madrid, Spain
Edinburgh University Press, 22 George Square, Edinburgh EH8 9LF, UK
Ediscience International, 28 rue Beaunier, 75014 Paris, France
Editions Editest, Place Van Meyel 25, 1040 Brussels, Belgium
EDL, PO Box 45 089, Auckland, New Zealand
Educational Books & Records SA, Niriidon 14, Athens 116 34, Greece
The Educational Book Service (Pty) Ltd, PB BR42, Plot 10041, Noko Road, Broadhurst, Gabarone, Botswana
Educational Concepts Sales (Pty) Ltd, 4/1 Skyline Place, Frenchs Forest, NSW, Australia 2086
Educational Distributors Ltd, PO Box 45 089, Te Atatu North 1208, New Zealand
Educational Equipment Wholesale Ltd, PO Box 35586, Brown's Bay, Auckland 10, New Zealand
The Educational Experience Pty Ltd, PO Box 860, Newcastle, NSW, Australia 2300
Educational Film Services Ltd, 5/F Chinachem Johnston Plaza, 178 Johnston Road, Wanchai, Hong Kong
Educational Film Services Pte Ltd, 307C New Bridge Road, Singapore 0208
Educational Film Services Sdn Bhd, Suite 18-03A, 18th Floor Wisma MCA, 163 Jalan Ampang, 50450 Kuala Lumpur, Malaysia
Educational Film Services (Taiwan) Ltd, 5F-3, 26 Chung Shan Road Section 3, Taipei, Taiwan
Educational Ideas, PO Box 70354, Bryanston, Johannesburg 2021 South Africa
Educational Materials Enterprises Ltd, PO Box 3580, 102 10 Athens, Greece
Educational Publishers Bureau Pte Ltd, 3545C Block 162, Bukit Merah Central, Singapore 0315
Educational Software, 64 Talisman Avenue, Bedfordview, 2008, Transvaal, South Africa
Educational Toy Centre, PO Box 64082, 2037 Highlands North, Johannesburg, South Africa
EFA Trading, Drienova 3, 826 19 Bratislava, Slovakia
Eideh Information Services Co Ltd, 243 Ostad Motahari Avenue, PO Box 1871, Tehran 15875, Iran
Ekonomisk Litteratur AB, Box 2019, 16202 Vallingby, Sweden
Elastika Michelin AE, 89 Avenue d'Athenes, Athens 301, Greece
Electra Media Group Pty Ltd, 6/6 Challis Avenue, Potts Point, Sydney, NSW, Australia 2011 & GPO Box 1546, Sydney, NSW, Australia 2001
G. C. Eleftheroudakis SA, International Bookstore, 4 Nikis Street, 105 63 Athens, Greece
Edward Elgar Publishing Co, (Distributed by Ashgate Publishing Co), Old Post Road, Brookfield, VT 05036, USA
Elsevier Science, Tsunashima Building Annex, 3-20-12 Yushima, Bunkyo-ku, Tokyo, Japan
Elsevier Science, Room 711-1, Hanaro Bldg, 194-4 Insa-Dong, Chongno-ku, Seoul 110-290, Korea
Elsevier Science BV, Amsterdam, Netherlands
Elsevier Science Inc, Orders Dept, PO Box 1663, Grand Central Station, New York, NY 10163, USA
Elsevier Science Japan, 9–15 Higashi-Azabu 1-chome, Minato-ku, Tokyo, 106 Japan
ELT Books Ltd, ul Polanki 110, 80-308 Gdansk, Poland

ELT Books & Press, ul Mlodej Gwardii 1C P417, 51-608 Wraclow, Poland
EM International, 2102 31st Avenue South, Seattle, WA 98144, USA
EMA Open Learning (Pty) Ltd, 7 Martin Street, South Melbourne, Vic, Australia 3205
Emirates Bookshop, PO Box 15688, Al-Ain, Abu Dhabi, UAE
Emmanuel Publishing Services, PO Box 5282, Accra North, Ghana
Emmets Religious Supply Ltd, 4204b Dundas Street West, Toronto, Ont, Canada M8X 1C7
Emond Montgomery Publications Ltd, 58 Shaftesbury Avenue, Toronto, Ont, Canada M4T 1A3
Empire Publishing Service, PO Box 1344, Studio City, CA 91614-0344, USA
The English Agency (Japan) Ltd, Sakuragi Building 4F, 6-7-3 Minami-Aogama, Minato-ku, Tokyo, 107 Japan & 305 Azabu Empire Mansion, 4-11-28 Nishi Azabu, Minato-ku, Tokyo 106, Japan
English Book Centre, Acacias 613, PO Box 5164, Guayaquil, Ecuador
English Book Centre, Surbrunnsgatan 51, Box 6207, 102 34 Stockholm, Sweden
English Book Centre Bookshop, Krakow, Poland
English Bookstore, 17L Connaught Circus, New Delhi, India 110 001
English Center, Borup Byvej 162, 8900 Randers, Denmark
English for Youngsters, Rogns AG, Balinhofstrasse 27, 6304 Zug, Switzerland
English House Services Publishers International Management, Higgs Farm, New Road, Flaxley, Cinderford, Gloucester GL14 1JS, UK
English School Book Co, Themistocleous 23, 106 77 Athens, Greece
Entrepreneur International (T) Ltd, PO Box 1727, Dar es Salaam, Tanzania
EPB Publishers Pte Ltd, 162, Bukit Merah Central 04-3545, Singapore 0315
EPP Book Services, TUC Post Office, Accra, Ghana
Epworth Bookshop, PO Box 6133, Te Aro, Wellington 1, New Zealand
Equine Educational, Maroon, Lochinvar, NSW, Australia 2321
Era Publications, PO Box 231, Brooklyn Park, SA, Australia 5032
ERA Technology (Asia) Pte Ltd, 83 Science Park Drive Nº 03-02A, The Curie, Singapore Science Park, Singapore 0511
ERA Technology Inc, 16203 Park Row, Suite 175, Houston, TX 77084, USA
Errett Stuart Associates, 3118 Old Coach Drive, Camarillo, CA 93010, USA
Livraria Escolar, R. Do Vale Formoso 37, 1900 Lisbon, Portugal
Éditions ESKA, 27 rue Dunois, 75013 Paris, France
ETCC, 17 Leeson Park, Dublin 6, Irish Republic
Eton Press (Auckland) Ltd, 18 Portsea Place, Birkenhead, Auckland, New Zealand
Eurab Ltd, 47 Meadow Close, Rottingdean, East Sussex BN2 7FB, UK
Eurobook, 6 Alikarnassou St, 104 44 Athens, Greece
Euromonitor, 60–61 Britton Street, London EC1M 5NH, UK
European Community Information Service, 26 rue Desaix, 75727 Paris Cedex 15, France
European Marketing Services, 55 Mendora Road, London SW6 7ND, UK
Eurospan STM Group, 3 Henrietta Street, Covent Garden, London WC2E 8LU, UK
Eurotex Limitada, Casilla 174, Correo 12, Santiago, Chile
Evangelical Outreach Inc, 55 Miami Street, Cubao, 1102 Quezon City, Philippines
Evangelical Press, PO Box 29, Philipsburg, NJ 08865, USA
K. & M. Evans, 5 Mary's Alley, Dublin 7, Irish Republic
Evans Brothers (Kenya) Ltd, PO Box 44536, Nairobi, Kenya
Evans Brothers Ltd, PO Box 165, Bamenda, Cameroon
Evans Brothers Ltd, PMB 646, Spiritus House, 8 Howe Street, Freetown, Sierra Leone
Evans Brothers (Nigeria Publishers) Ltd, Jericho Road, PMB 5164, Ibadan, Nigeria
Evergreen Buddhist Cultural Service, 100 Eu Tong Sen Street, 03-17 Pearls Centre, Singapore 0105
The Evergreen Press, 3380 Vincent Road, Pleasant Hill, CA 94523, USA
EWP, Marketing Division, G-1/16 Ansari Road, Darya Ganji, New Delhi, 110 002, India
Examiner Bookshop, 35 Dalal Street, Bombay, India 400 023
Exhibitions International, Kol. Begaultaan 17, 3012 Leuven, Belgium

Exlibris International Marketing Ltd, Rennsbend 10, W-52224 Stolberg, Germany

Expolingua Italia, Via P. Micca 22, 101 22 Turin, Italy

Export Livres, CP 307, 128 rue d'Alsace, Saint-Lambert, PQ, Canada J4S 1M7

Eyras Editorial, Andres Mellado 42–46, 28015 Madrid, Spain

Faber & Faber Inc, 50 Cross Street, Winchester, MA 01890, USA

Factfinder Collection Corporation, PO Box 2282, CPO Manila, Philippines

Facts On File Inc, 11 Penn Plaza, New York, NY 10001-2006, USA

Falcon Press Sdn Bhd, PO Box 228, Jalan Sultan Post Office, 46720 Petaling Jaya, Selangor Darul Ehsan, Malaysia

Falk Verlag, Im Gleisdreieck 5, Postfach 80 02 60, 21002 Hamburg, Germany

FAME, Schloesslistrasse 34, 6045 Meggen (Lucerne), Switzerland

Family Bookshop, PO Box 376, Ruwi, Oman

Family Bookshop, PO Box 5769, Doha, Qatar

Family Bookshop Group Co Ltd, PO Box 1020, Limassol, Cyprus

Far East Media Ltd, 3rd Floor, Remex Centre, 42 Wong Chuk Hang Road, Aberdeen, Hong Kong

Far East Publications Ltd, Mahatun Plaza, 888 Ploenchit Road, 8th Floor, Unit Nos 84–85, Bangkok 10500, Thailand

Far Eastern Booksellers, Kanda, PO Box 72, Tokyo 101-91, Japan

Faradawn CC, PO Box 1903, Saxonwold, 2132 South Africa

Farel Distributors (Pty) Ltd, PO Box 272, North Riding, 2162 South Africa

Sultan-ul-Hassan Farooqui, 12 Burlington Road, London N10 1NJ, UK

La Favelliana, Via Val di Fiemme 21, 20128 Milan, Italy

Faxon Europe, PO Box 197, 1000 AD Amsterdam, Netherlands

Federal Publications (HK) Ltd, Units 903–905, Tower B, 9/F Hung Hom Commercial Centre, 37 Ma Tau Wai Road, Hung Hom, Kowloon, Hong Kong

The Federation Press, PO Box 45, Annandale, NSW, Australia 2038

Emily Feffer, c/o Random House US, 201 East 50th Street, New York, NY 10022, USA

Feffer & Simons Inc, 1114 Avenue of the Americas, New York, NY 10036, USA

Bernd Feldmann, SHS, Heinrich Roller Strasse 21, 10405 Berlin, Germany

Felice Le Monnier SpA, Via Meucci 2, PO Box 202, 50015 Grassina (Florence), Italy

Felta Book Sales Co, 58f Manalo Street, Cubao, Quezon City, Philippines

H. B. Fenn & Co Ltd, 1090 Lorimar Drive, Mississauga, Ont, Canada L5S 1R7

FEP International Ghana, PO Box 3166, Accra, Ghana

Fep International Pvt Ltd, Unit 05-01A, 108 Pasir Panjang Road, Singapore 0511

Fernwood Books Ltd, PO Box 4909, Station A, Halifax, NS, B3K 5S3, Canada

FERYSA, Isabel Colbrand, 10 (Venecia II) Nave 87, 28050 Madrid, Spain

FG Distribution, Fredrikinkaru 34, 00100 Helsinki, Finland

Richard Field, Sales Manager Asia, IOP Publishing, Techno House, Redcliffe Way, Bristol BS1 6NX, UK

Fiji Muslim Youth Organisation, PO Box 455, Suva, Fiji

FIND/SVP, 625 Avenue of the Americas, New York, NY 10011, USA

Fingertip Concepts, PO Box 8266, Stirling Street 6849, 102 Beaufort Street, Perth, WA, Australia

Firebird Distributing, 1945 P Street, Eureka, CA 95501, USA

Firefly Books Ltd, 3680 Victoria Park Avenue, Willowdale, Ont, Canada M2H 3K1

Fischbacher International, 33 rue de Seine, 75006 Paris, France

Fisher Books, PO Box 38040, Tucson, AZ 85740-8040, USA

Fitzhenry & Whiteside Ltd, 195 Allstate Parkway, Markham, Ont, Canada L3R 4T8

Sarah Fitzpatrick, Faber & Faber Ltd, 3 Queen Square, London WC1N 3AU, UK

The Five Mile Press, 22 Summit Road, Noble Park, Vic, Australia 3174

Colin Flint, Northgate, School Lane, Harlow, Essex CM20 2QB, UK

Flo Enterprise Sdn Bhd, 24 Lorong PJS 1/2A, Batu 6 Jalan Kelang Lama, Petaling Jaya 4600, Selangor Darul Ehsan, Malaysia

Floraprint AG, Gewerbestrasse 18, 8132 Egg/ZH, Switzerland

Floraprint BV, PO Box 276, Meer en Duin, 2160 AG Lisse, Netherlands

Floraprint España, Gremis 12, 46014 Valencia, Spain

Floraprint GmbH, Missindorfstrasse 21, 1140 Vienna, Austria

Floraprint International GmbH, Meierhofstrasse 2, Postfach 1245, 9490 Vaduz, Liechtenstein

Floraprint New Zealand, 127 Park Road, PO Box 1173, Miramar, Wellington, New Zealand

Floraprint Norge A/S, c/o Litografen AS, Postboks 117, 4001 Stavanger, Norway

Floraprint NV, Van den Hautelei 193, 2100 Deurne, Antwerp, Belgium

Macbird Floraprint Pty Ltd, 19 Koornang Road, Scoresby, Vic, Australia 3179

Floraprint Southern Africa, PO Box 825, Florida, 1710 South Africa

Floraprint Sverige AB, Hemmerstorp 3/9, 24592 Staffanstorp, Sweden

Floraprint Taiwan Ltd, PO Box 6-84, Peitou, Taipei 11203, Taiwan

Folens Ltd, Albert House, Apex Business Centre, Boscombe Road, Dunstable, Beds LU5 4RL, UK

Fono Schallplatten GmbH, Zum Hagenbach 4, Postfach 1 06, 48366 Laer, Germany

Ford & Bailie, PO Box 138, Belmont, MA 02178, USA

Juliette Forde, Mall 34, Broad Street, St Michael, Barbados

Louis A. Forde, Mall 34, Broad Street, St Michael, Barbados

Foreign Rights Ltd, Schlossgasse 15/4, 1050 Vienna, Austria

Forrester Books Ltd, 3/3 Marken Place, Glenfield, Private Bag 93514, Takapuna, Auckland, New Zealand

Forrester Books NZ Ltd, Private Bag 93514, Takapuna, Auckland, New Zealand

Forsyth Travel Library Inc, 9154 West 57th Street, PO Box 2975, Shawnee Mission, KS 66201-1375, USA

Fortress Publications Inc, 221 Barton Street East, PO Box 9241, Stoney Creek, Ont, Canada L8G 3X9

Editions Foucher, 31 rue de Fleurus, Paris 75006, France

Lora Fountain Agency, 7 rue de Belfort, 75011 Paris, France

Fountain Publishers, PO Box 488, Kampala, Uganda

Fowler Wright Books Ltd, Burgess Street, Leominster, Herefordshire HR6 8DE, UK

Foxwood International Ltd, PO Box 523, Milton, Ont, L9T 4Z1, Canada

Yvonne Francis, International Sales Manager, c/o Ladybird Head Office, Beeches Road, Loughborough, Leics LE11 2NQ, UK

Franciscan University of Steubenville, Franciscan Way, Steubenville, OH 43952, USA

Michael Franke & Till Meyer-Bruhns, Postfach 130971, W-20146 Hamburg, Germany

Rodney Franklin Agency, PO Box 37727, 5 Karl Netter Street, Tel Aviv 61376, Israel

Franklins, PO Box 111, Gane Yuan 70800, Israel

Jiri Fraus, Klatovskatr. 24, 301 27 Plzen, Czech Republic

W. H. Freeman & Co, 41 Madison Avenue, New York, NY 10010, USA

French & European Publications, 610 5th Avenue, New York, NY 10020-2497, USA

Fritzes Fackboksforetaget, PO Box 16356, 103 27 Stockholm, Sweden

F. S. P., Av. Agostinho Neto 1065, CP 3659, Maputo, Mozambique

F. S. P., PO Box 2748, Lagos, Nigeria

Steadman A. R. Fuller, Kingston Bookshop, 70B King Street, Kingston, Jamaica

Sven Gade, Saga Books ApS, 17 Mellemvang, 2970 Hørsholm, Denmark

Gaffney-Dodds Associates, 5 Badgers Croft, Leverstock Green, Hemel Hempstead, Herts HP2 4NE, UK

Gage Educational Publishing Co, 164 Commander Boulevard, Agincourt, Ont, Canada M1S 3C7

Au Gai Savoir, 60 rue de la Station, 6043 Ransart, Belgium

La Galamo Office & School Supplies Pty Ltd, PO Box 1405, Lae, Morabe Province, Papua New Guinea

Gale Research Co, 835 Penobscot Building, Detroit, MI 48202, USA

Garamond Press, 1823 Maryland Avenue, PO Box 1000, Niagara Falls, NY 14302-1000, USA

Livraria Gaudi Ltda, Rua Augusta 2872, CEP 01412, São Paulo, Brazil

Wm. W. Gaunt & Sons Inc, Gaunt Building, 3011 Gulf Drive, Holmes Beach, FL 34217-2199, USA

Gazelle Book Services Ltd, Falcon House, Queen Square, Lancaster LA1 1RN, UK

G + B Arts International, St Johanns-Vorstadt 19, Postfach, 4004 Basle, Switzerland

GBS Distribution & Marketing Ltd, Unit 1A/2A, Star Business Centre, Fairview Industrial Estate, March Way, Rainham, Essex RM13 8UH, UK

Gemcraft Books, 14 Duffy Street, Burwood, Vic, Australia 3125

General Distribution Services, 4600 Whitmer Industrial Estates 4, Niagara Falls, NY 14306, USA & 85 River Rock Drive, Suite 202, Buffalo, NY 14207-2170, USA

General Educational Media Corp, 7th Floor, Minamizuka Building, 2-17-3 Shibuya, Shibuya-ku, Tokyo, 150 Japan

General Publishing Co Ltd, 30 Lesmill Road, North York, Ont, Canada M3B 2T6

Geocart, Breedstraat 94, 9100 Sint Niklaas, Belgium

Michael Geoghegan, c/o Bloomsbury Publishing Plc, 2 Soho Square, London W1V 6HB, UK; Forest Lodge, Gibraltar Lane, Cookham Dean, Berks SL6 9TR, UK; 140 Bramley Close, Higham Hill, London E17 6EG, UK & 14 Frognal Gardens, London NW3 6UX, UK

Editions Geographiques Generales, 45 rue Broca, 75005 Paris, France

GeoVistas, 30 Cranedown, Lewes, East Sussex BN7 3NA, UK

Guy Gerlach, Av. Brig. Luis Antonio 2367, CJ 1104, 01401 São Paulo, Brazil

Geste Editions, BP 05, 79370 Mougon, France

GIA Publications, 7404 South Mason Avenue, Chicago, IL 60638, USA

Charles Gibbes, Cross Tree Cottage, Church Lane, Finmere, Bucks MK18 4AT, UK

Stanley Gibbons (New Zealand) Ltd, PO Box 80, Wellington, New Zealand

Stanley Gibbons (Singapore) Pte Ltd, Raffles City, PO Box 1689, Singapore 9117

Gibraltar Bookshop, 300 Main Street, Gibraltar

Gill & Macmillan Ltd, Goldenbridge Industrial Estate, Inchicore, Dublin 8, Irish Republic

S. I. Gillani, Surriaya Mansions, 65 The Mall, PO Box 1463, Lahore 54000, Pakistan

Ginn & Co, 3771 Victoria Park Avenue, Scarborough, Ont, Canada M1W 2P9

Dott. A. Giuffrè Editore, Via Busto Arsizio 40, 20151 Milan, Italy

GLBmbH (Bargain, Promotional & Remainder Shops), Schönhauser Strasse 25, 50968 Cologne, Germany

Gleumes & Co, Hohenstaufenring 47–51, W-5000 Cologne 1, Germany

Global Language Books, 88 Orange Street, Greystanes, NSW, Australia 2145

Globe Enterprise, PO Box 7322, 40710 Shah Alam, Selangor, Malaysia

The Globe Pequot Press, 6 Business Park Road, PO Box 833, Old Saybrook, CT 06475, USA

Globus, Dünya Basineri, 100 Yil Mahallesi, 34440 Bagcilar, Istanbul, Turkey

The Golden Mountain Agency, 5 Westbourne Road, 02-04, Singapore 0513

Golden Press Ltd, 31 View Road, Glenfield, Auckland 1, New Zealand

Gondwana Books, PO Box 11 684, Vorna Valley, 1686 South Africa

Forlaget Gonge, Engdalsvej 96b, 8220 Braband, Denmark

Goods Trading Co, 35 East Beaver Creek Road, Richmond Hill, Ont, Canada

Gordon & Breach Arts, Basle, Switzerland

Jenny Gosling, 1 Bucklebury Place, Upper Woolhampton, Reading, Berks RG7 5UD, UK

Gospel Mission Inc, Box M, Choteau, MT 59422, USA

Gower Asia Pacific Pte Ltd, 43 Albert Road, Avalo, NSW, Australia 2107

Gower Asia Pacific Pte Ltd, Golden Wheel Building, 41 Kallang Pudding, 04-03, Singapore 349316

Gower Publishing Co, Old Post Road, Brookfield, VT 05036-9704, USA

Graffins College, Peponi House, Moi Avenue, PO Box 45966, Nairobi, Kenya

PT Gramedia, Asri Media, Jln Gajah Mada 109, Jakarta 11140, Indonesia

Gramola Co, Graben 16, Vienna 1, Australia

Grandi and Vitali, Via Caradosa 12, 20123 Milan, Italy

Grandreams USA, 8 Arbour Road, Howell, NJ, USA

David Grant, Datum Book Marketing, 80 Ridgeway, Pembury, Tunbridge Wells, Kent TN2 4EZ, UK

Graphic Arts, PO Box 10306, 3019 NW Yeon, Portland, OR 97210, USA

Graphic Multimedia, 3 Shenton Way, #08-03 Shenton House, Singapore 068805

Grassroots Books (Pvt) Ltd, Box A267, 100 Jason Moyo Avenue, Avondale, Harare, Zimbabwe

S. G. Gray International Booksellers, PO Box 85, Bondi Beach, NSW, Australia 2826

Greek Record Club, Leski Publications Ltd, 57 Akadimias Street, 106 79 Athens, Greece

Greene Phoenix Marketing, 1 Captain Street, Helensville, North Island, New Zealand

Greenhill Books, Park House, 1 Russell Gardens, London NW11 9NN, UK

Greenwood Saunders & Co, PO Box W27, West Pennant Hills, NSW, Australia 2125

Ben Greig, Academic Representative, 6 York Street, Cambridge CB1 2PY, UK

Grenada Teacher's School Supplies, No 1 Grenville Street, St George's, Guyana

Steve Griffin, 9 Irvington Road, Medford, MA 02155, USA

H. Griffiths, PO Box M, Winter Park, FL 32790, USA

De Groene Waterman, Lange Pastoorstraat 25, 2600 Bercham, Belgium

Grosvenor Books, 226 Kooyong Road, Toorak, Vic, Australia 3142

Grosvenor Books, Suite 500, 251 Bank Street, Ottawa, Ont, Canada K2P 1X3

Grosvenor Books, Box 1834, Wellington 1, New Zealand

Grosvenor USA, 3735 Cherry Avenue NE, Salem, OR 97303, USA

Grub Street Bookshop, 317 Brunswick Street, Fitzroy, Vic, Australia 3065

Verlagsgesellschaft Grun ist Leben mbH, Bismarkstrasse 49, Postfach 1229, 25421 Pinneberg (PO Box 25402), Germany

Gryphon House Inc, Box 275, Mt Rainier, MD 20712, USA

Editoria Guanabara, Travessa de Ouvidor 11, Centro, 20042 Rio de Janeiro, Brazil

Dipak Kumar Guha, 33 Nizamuddin East, PO Box 3205, New Delhi, India 110 013

The Guide Book Co, 3rd Floor, 20 Hollywood Road, Central, Hong Kong, Hong Kong

M. D. Gunasena & Co Ltd, 217 Olcott Mawatha, Colombo II, Sri Lanka

Gunnar Lie & Associates, Thornton House, Thornton Road, London SW19 4NG, UK

Dr S. Gupta, 6720 North Lakewood Avenue apt 1, Chicago, IL 60626-4372, USA

Gurley & Associates Ltd, The Book Specialists, Unit No 4, Ground Floor, Temple Court Building, 31–33 Abercromby Street, Port of Spain, Trinidad

Gutke Verlag, Cologne, Germany

Gyldendal Norsk Forlag, Postboks 6860, St Olavs Plass, 0130 Oslo 1, Norway

Haci Emin Elendi Sokak, Tanis Ap., 4/5 Daire 4, Nisantasi, Istanbul, Turkey

HAD Centre Ltd, Flat 501, Capital Centre, 2–4 Makarios Avenue, PO Box 5366, Nicosia, Cyprus

Hae Dong Co Ltd, Grace Building, 5-13 Changjeon-Dong, Mapo-Gu, Seoul 121-190, Korea

Halal Books, PO Box 32457, Detroit, MI 48232-2457, USA

Martin Halas Dental Co Pty Ltd, 209–211 Bourke Street, Sydney, NSW, Australia 2010

Halcyon Publications, PO Box 360, Auckland 1, New Zealand

Robert Hale & Co, 1803-132 ND. Avenue NE, Ste 4, Bellevue, WA 98005, USA

Half Halt Press, 6416 Burkittsville Road, Middletown, MD 21769, USA

Fergus Hall, ITP South Africa, PO Box 2459, Halfway House, 1685 South Africa

Hallwag AG, Nordring 4, 3001 Berne, Switzerland

The Hambledon Press, PO Box 162, Rio Grande, OH 45672, USA

Hammicks Law Bookshop, 191–192 Fleet Street, London EC4A 2AH, UK

Hammond Inc, 515 Valley Street, Maplewood, NJ 07040-1396, USA

A. Hanna, Dublin, Irish Republic

Mrs Irene Hanson, PO Box 80038, Burlington, Ont, Canada L7L 6B1

Harcourt Brace & Co (Australia) Pty Ltd, 30–52 Smidmore Street, Marrickville, NSW, Australia 2204

Harcourt Brace & Co Canada Ltd, 55 Horner Avenue, Toronto, Ont, Canada M8Z 4X6

Harcourt Brace & Co International, 5611 North Bridge Road, 02-09 Eng Cheong Tower, Singapore 0719

Harcourt Brace & Co International, Orlando, FL 32887, USA

Harcourt Brace Japan Inc, Ichibancho Central Building, 22-1 Ichibancho, Chiyoda-ku, Tokyo, 102 Japan

Keith Hardy, SEA books, PO Box 53, Bangna, Bangkok 10260, Thailand

Suzanne Hardy, European Sales Manager, 9 Boulevard Voltaire, 75011 Paris, France

Maureen Hargraves, (Atrium Bookshop), PO Box 23832, Claremont, 7735 South Africa

Hargraves Library Service, PO Box 23495, Claremont, 7735 South Africa & 80 Jordaan Street (corner Carisbrook), Cape Town, 8001 South Africa

Harla SA Decv, Int. Bookshop de Columbia, Calle 79 N° 14-30, Sante Fe de Bogota, Colombia

Forlaget Harlequin AB, Nybrogatan 36, PO Box 5327, 102 46 Stockholm, Sweden

Harlequin Distribution Center, 3010 Walden Avenue, Depew, NY 14043, USA

Harlequin Holland, World Trade Centre B13, Strawinskylaan 1333, 1077 XX Amsterdam, Netherlands

Harlequin K. K., Aoyama Building, 9th Floor, 1-2-3 Kita Aoyama, Minato-ku, Tokyo, 107 Japan

HarperCollins Publishers, 25 Ryde Road, PO Box 321, Pymble, NSW, Australia 2073 & 7/31 Waterloo Road, North Ryde, NSW, Australia 2113

HarperCollins Publishers, Suite 2900, Hazelton Lanes, 55 Avenue Road, Toronto, Ont, Canada M5R 3L0 & 1995 Markham Road, Scarborough, Ont, Canada M1B 5M8

HarperCollins Publishers, 31 View Road, Glenfield, PO Box 1, Auckland 10, New Zealand

HarperCollins Publishers, 10–14 Watkins Street, Denver, Ext 4, Johannesburg, South Africa

HarperCollins Publishers, 1160 Battery Street, San Francisco, CA 94111-1213, USA

HarperCollins Publishers Ltd, Westerhill Road, Bishopbriggs, Glasgow G64 2QT, UK & 77–85 Fulham Palace Road, Hammersmith, London W6 8JB, UK

HarperCollins US, 10 East 53rd Street, New York, NY 10022-5299, USA

HarperSanFrancisco, Icehouse One 401, 151 Union Street, San Francisco, CA 94111-1299, USA

Max Harrell, 1351 Malvern Road, Malvern, Vic, Australia 3144

Harris Religious Supplies, Las Palmas, Marchfield, St Philip, Barbados

Harvard Associates Inc, 10 Holworthy Street, Cambridge, MA 02138, USA

Harvard University Press, Sales Department, 79 Garden Street, Cambridge, MA 02138, USA

University of Hawaii Press, Hawaii, USA

Alfred Hayes, 6 Wesley Arcade, 210 Pitt Street, Sydney, NSW, Australia 2000

Haynes Publications Inc, 861 Lawrence Drive, Newbury Park, CA 91320, USA

Haynes Publishing, Fyrisborgsgatan 5, 754 50 Uppsala, Sweden

Editions Haynes SA, 147/149 rue Saint Honore, 75001 Paris, France

Headline Book Publishing, Export Department, 338 Euston Road, London NW1 3BH, UK

Hearst Books International, 1350 Avenue of the Americas, New York, NY 10019, USA

D. C. Heath & Co, 125 Spring Street, Lexington, MA 02173, USA

Ms Andrea Hedgecock, Tulpiu 2, 4301 Karmelava, Kaunas Region, Lithuania

Heel-Verlag, Postfach 1220, 53622 Konigswinter, Germany

Jim Heffernan, PO Box 203, 6 Buckle Street, Banjul, Gambia

Heffers Booksellers, Rustat House, 60 Clifton Road, Cambridge CB1 4FY, UK

Heian International Inc, 1815 West 205th Street, Suite 301, Torrance, CA 90501, USA

Heinemann, Insurgentes Centro 51 Desp.204, Col. San Rafael, Mexico DF, Mexico

Heinemann, Av. Constituyente 1943, Apto 102, 11200 Montevideo, Peru

Heinemann, Distribuciones English Lab, Av. Urdaneta, Ed Centro Candoral Mezzanina,La Candelaria, Caracas, Venezuela

Heinemann Educational Botswana, PO Box 10103, Village Post Office, Gaborone, Botswana

Heinemann Educational Books Inc, 361 Hanover Street, Portsmouth, NH 03801-3509, USA

Heinemann Educational Books Ltd, Halley Court, Jordan Hill, Oxford OX2 8EJ, UK

Heinemann Educational Books (Nigeria) Ltd, Private Mail Bag, 5205 Ighodoro Road, Jericho, Ibadan, Nigeria

Heinemann ELT, 26 Vas Olgas (1st Floor), 54641 Thessaloniki, Greece & 80 Kousidi Street, 157 72 Zografou, Greece

Heinemann ELT, Halley Court, Jordan Hill, Oxford OX2 8EJ, UK

Heinemann Iberia, Almagro 2, Madrid 28010, Spain

Heinemann International Japan Liaison Office, San Nichibo Bldg 2-1, Sarugaku-cho 1 chome, Chiyoda-ku, Tokyo, 101 Japan

Heinemann International Türkiye, Inkilap Han, Ankara Caddesi No 99/2, Sirkeci 34410, Istanbul, Turkey

Heinemann Publishers (Caribbean) Ltd, 175–179 Mountain View Avenue, Kingston 6, Jamaica

Heinemann Publishers (Pty) Ltd, PO Box 2017, Houghton, 2041 South Africa & PO Box 371, Isando, 1600 South Africa

Heinemann Reference, 39 Rawene Road, Birkenhead, Auckland 10, New Zealand

Helios Bookshop, 95 Gilles Street, Adelaide, SA, Australia 5000

Hellenic Distribution Agency Ltd, 1 Digeni Street, 17456 Alimos, Greece

Henco Associates, Tannhauserdreef 22, 3561 HE Utrecht, Netherlands

Heritage Publishers, 32 Prakash Apartments, 5 Ansari Road, Daryaganj, New Delhi, India 110 002

Fred Hermans, Academic Book Promotions, Hoofdstraat 261, 1611 AG Bovenkarspel, Netherlands

Herron Book Distributors Pty Ltd, 39 Commercial Road, Fortitude Valley, Qld, Australia 4006

Gill Hess Ltd, 15 Church Street, Skerries, Co Dublin, Irish Republic

Heiner Meyer auf der Heyde, Macmillan Publishing Services, Rabenstraße 9, 44143 Dortmund 1, Germany

HHP Buchimport GmbH, Lederstraße 21, W-2000 Hamburg 54, Germany

Hi Marketing, 38 Carver Road, London SE24 9LT, UK

Hibernian Book Services, 18 Lorcan O'Toole Park, Kimmage Road West, Dublin 12, Irish Republic

Aoki Hideo, Motovun Co Ltd, Coop Nomura Ichibancho 103, 15-6 Ichibancho Chiyoda-ku, Tokyo,102, Japan

Hieroglyphics, PO Box 610, Carlton South, Victoria, Australia

Hinder & Deelmann, Postfach 1206, 3554 Gladenbach/Hessen, Germany

Hinton Information Services, Locked Bag 7, Eastwood, NSW, Australia 2122

Hippocrene Books Inc, 171 Madison Avenue, New York, NY 10016, USA

HM Stationery Office, HMSO Publications Centre, Agency Section, 51 Nine Elms Lane, London SW8 5DR, UK

HMSO Books, HMSO Publications Centre, PO Box 276, London SW8 5DT, UK

Hodder & Stoughton Educational, The Export Sales Department, 338 Euston Road, London NW1 3BH, UK

Hodder & Stoughton Educational Southern Africa, PO Box 3948, Randburg, 2125 South Africa

Hodder & Stoughton Ltd, 338 Euston Road, London NW1 3BH, UK

Hodder Headline (Australia) Pty Ltd, Rydalmere Business Park, 10–16 South Street, Rydalmere, NSW, Australia 2116 & PO Box 386, Rydalmere, NSW, Australia 2116

Hodder Headline Plc, 338 Euston Road, London NW1 3BH, UK

Hodder Moa Beckett Ltd, 4 Wheen Place, Mairingi Bay, Auckland 10, New Zealand

Hodder Moa Beckett Publishers Ltd, 4 Whetu Place, Mairangi Bay, Auckland 10, New Zealand

Hodges Figgis, Dawson Street, Dublin, Irish Republic

Höfer Communications, 38 Joo Koon Road, Singapore 2262

Hogarth Representation Books from Africa, 1 Birchington Court, Birchington Road, London N8 8HS, UK

Hokuto Corporation, 34-8 Yayaoicho 3-chome, Nakano-ku, Tokyo 164, Japan

Holt, Rinehart & Winston Publishing New Zealand Ltd, 10 Moa Street, Otahuhu, Auckland 6, New Zealand

Hon Wing Book Co Ltd, 63A Tung Choi Street, Ground Floor–2nd Floor Mongkok, Kowloon, Hong Kong

Hong Kong University Press, 139 Pokfulam Road, Hong Kong, Hong Kong

Hope Publishing, 380 South Main Place, Carol Stream, IL 60188, USA

Alexander Horn, Spiegelgasse 9, W-6200 Wiesbaden 1, Germany

Houghton Mifflin, 222 Berkley Street, Boston, MA 02116-3764, USA

Houston Travel Marketing Services, PO Box 75262, Gardenview, Transvaal, 2047 South Africa

Harry Howell, 54 Gordon Crescent, Lane Cove, NSW, Australia 2066
Howell Press, 1147 River Road, Suite 2, Charlottesville, VA 22901, USA
Hua Excellent Resources, Taipei, Taiwan
Huckleberry Trading, 3 Othos Avvey, Tala Paphos, Cyprus
Barrington Huie, 77 Ashridge Drive, Agincourt, Ont, Canada M1V 1P1
Human Kinetics, PO Box 5076, Champaign, IL 61825-5076, USA
Human Kinetics (Australia), PO Box 689, Melrose Park, SA, Australia
Human Kinetics (Canada), Box 2503, Windsor, Ont, Canada N8Y 4S2
Human Kinetics (New Zealand), PO Box 105-231, Auckland 1, New Zealand
Humanities Press International Inc, 165 First Avenue, Atlantic Highlands, NJ 07715-1289, USA
Chris Humphrys, 24 High Street, Wanstead, London E11 2AQ, UK
Humphrys Roberts Associates, Caixa Postal 801-0, Jardim da Gloria, 06700-970 Cotia SP, 131 São Paulo, Brazil & CP 22183, 01499 São Paulo SP, Brazil
Humphrys Roberts Associates, Dr Carmona Y Valle, B-12-2, Edisicio Sagitario, Depto 904,Colonia Doctores 06720, Mexico
Humphrys Roberts Associates, 32 Addison Road, London E11 2RG, UK & 24 High Street, Wanstead, London E11 2AQ, UK
Hunt & Thorpe Australia Pty Ltd, 9 Euston Street, Rydalmere, NSW, Australia 2116
Hunter Publications, 58a Gipps Street, Collingwood, Victoria,, Australia 3066
Hushion House Ltd, 36 Northline Road, Toronto, Ont, Canada M4B 3E2
HWA Eng Trading Co, PO Box 748, No 91 Po Ei Road, Taipei, Taiwan

IBC USA (Publications) Inc, 290 Eliot Street, PO Box 9104, Ashland, MA 01721–9104, USA
ibd Ltd, 24 Hudson Street, Kinderhook, NY 12106, USA
Iberian Book Services SL, Sector Islas, Bloque 112-1°B, 28760 Tres Cantos, Madrid, Spain
ICBS, Skindergade 3B, 1159 Copenhagen K, Denmark
ICK, Suite 1214, Life Combi Building, 61-4 Yoldo-dong, Yungdeungpo-ku, Seoul, 150-010, Korea
ICNA, 166-26 89th Avenue, Jamaica, NY 11432, USA
ICPAS, 16 Middle Road, 1CB Enterprise House, Singapore 0718
Idea Books, Nieuwe Herengracht 11, 1011 RK Amsterdam, Netherlands
Ideer om Frihet, Box 1134, 5001 Bergen, Norway
IEE/PPL, IEEE Service Center, 445 Hoes Lane, Piscataway, NJ 08854, USA
Igaku Shoin Ltd, Tokyo International, PO Box 5063, 1-28-36 Hongo, Bunkyo-ku, Tokyo, 113 Japan
Ignatius Press, 2515 McAllister Street, San Francisco, CA 94118, USA
Ignoramus, Stationsstraat 121, 3665 As, Belgium
I.I.H.T., 704 Tai Yau Bldg, 181 Johnston Road, Wanchai, Hong Kong, Hong Kong
IMA, PO Box 8734, London SE21 7ZF, UK
Imprensa Nacional Casa da Moeda EP, rua D. Francisco Manuel de Melo 5, 1092 Lisbon Codex, Portugal
In Book, PO Box 120261, East Haven, CT 06512, USA & 1436 West Randolph Street, Chicago, IL 60607, USA
In Book/LPC Group, 30 Commerce Park Road, Milford, CT 06460, USA
Independent Publishers Group, 814 North Franklin Street, Chicago, IL 60610, USA
Independent Publishing Co Ltd, 38 Kennington Lane, London SE11 4LS, UK
India Book Distributors, 107/108 Arcadia, 10th Floor, 195 Narman Point, Bombay, India 400 021
India Book House, 412–5 Tulsiani Chambers, 212 Backbay Recl, Nariman Point, Bombay, India 400 021
Indiana University Press, 10th & Morton Streets, Bloomington, IN 47405, USA
Industriens Forlag, Vesterbrogade 149, 1620 Copenhagen V, Denmark
Info Access & Distribution, Room 105, 1/F Federal Building, 369 Lockhart Road, Wanchai, Hong Kong
Inforel Book Service, Sulzerstrasse 16, Basle 4054, Switzerland
Information Access & Distribution Pte Ltd, 113 Eunos Avenue 3 N° 07-03, Gordon Industrial Building, Singapore 1440
Information & Culture Korea, Suite 1214, Life Combi Building, 61-4 Yoido-Dong, Yung Deungpo-ku, Seoul151-010, Korea
Information Publications Pte Ltd, Tung Shun Hing Centre, 20–22a Granville Road, Tsim Sha Tsui, Kowloon, Hong Kong
Information Publications Pte Ltd, 02-06 1st Floor, Pei-fu Industrial Bldg, 24 New Industrial Road, Singapore 1953

Information Today Inc, 143 Old Marlton Pike, Medford, NJ 08055, USA
Initiatives Santé, BP 60, 26 avenue de l'Europe, 78141 Vélizy Cedex, France
Inland Book Co Inc, 140 Commerce Street, PO Box 120261, East Haven, CT 06512, USA
Innwa Book Store, 232 Sule Padoga Road, Kyauktada Township, Yongon, Myanmar
Insaka Press, PO Box 50708, Lusaka, Zambia
INT Press, 65–69 Melville Road (PO Box 3), Pascoe Vale South, Vic, Australia 3044
Integrated Learning Resources, 809 Holland Road, Singapore 1027
Inter Book Marketing Services, Rua das Palmeiros 32, Apt 701, Rio de Janeiro 22270, Brazil
Inter Forum, 1 rue de l'Est, 75020 Paris, France
Inter-Media/Pelgrim, Mollevite 24, 6931 KG Westervoort, Netherlands
Inter-Varsity Press, 860 Denison Street, Unit 3, Markham, Ont, Canada L3R 4H1
Inter-Varsity Press, PO Box 1400, Downers Grove, IL 60515, USA
Interamerica SA, Manuel Ferrero 13, 28036 Madrid, Spain
Editorial Interamericana SA, Carrera 17 33-71, Apartado Aero 6131, Bogota, Colombia
Interart sarl, 1 rue de l'Est, 75020 Paris, France
Interbook Interkirja Oy, Työmiehenkatu 4, 00180 Helsinki 18, Finland
Interlink Books, 46 Crosby Street, Northampton, MA 01060, USA
Interlink International Inc, 46 Crosby Street, Northampton, MA 01060-1804, USA
Interlivros Edições Ltda, Rua Comandante Coelno 1085, CEP 21250 Cordouil, Rio de Janeiro/RJ, Brazil
Intermedia Americana, PO Box 8734, London SE21 7ZF, UK
International Book Distributors, PO Box 2290, Vancouver, BC, Canada V6B 3W5
International Book Distributors, 9/3 Rajpur Road, Dehra Dun, India 248 001
International Book Marketing, 2 Haythorn House, Vicarage Crescent, Battersea Village, London SW11 3LQ, UK
International Book Marketing, 27 West 20th Street, Suite 1001, New York, NY 10011, USA
International Book Service, 33 Jalan 20/16, 46300 Petaling Jaya, Selangor, Malaysia
International Books, 18 South Frederick Street, Dublin 2, Irish Republic
International Education Service, Weston Industrial Estate, Salmon Leap, Leixlip, Co Kildare, Irish Republic
International Language Bookshop, PO Box 53, Embaba, Giza, Cairo, Egypt
International Music Publications GmbH, Marstallstrasse 8, 80539 Munich, Germany
International Network for Terminology (TERMNET), Grungasse 9/17, 1050 Vienna, Austria
International Professional Associates, Tacho Building, 6th Floor, 99-15 Seogye-dong Yongsan-ku, Seoul, 140-140, Korea
International Publications Service Inc, Gongpyong Building 1104, 5-1 Gongpyong-dong, Chongro-ku, Seoul 110-604, Korea
International Publishers Distributor, Langhorne, PA, USA
International Publishers Marketing Inc, 22883 Quicksilver Drive, Dulles, VA 20166, USA & 13950 Park Center Road, Herndon, VA 22071, USA
International Publishers Representatives (IPR), 4 Michaelakis Karaclis Street, Engorra, Nicosia, Cyprus & PO Box 5731, 1386 Nicosia, Cyprus
International Publishing Services Ltd, Rua da Cruz da Carreira, 4B, 1100 Lisbon, Portugal
International Specialized Book Services Inc, 5804 NE Hassalo Street, Portland, OR 97213-3644, USA
International Thomson Publishing Asia, Suite 505, Life Combi Building, 61-4 Yoido-Wong, Youngdeungpo-ku, Korea & Suite 707, Hanshin Building, 136-1, Mapo-dong, Mapo-ku, Seoul, 121-050, Korea
International Thomson Publishing Asia, 22A Jalan 19/36, 46300 Petaling Jaya, Selangor Darul Ehsan, Malaysia
International Thomson Publishing Asia, Blk 211 Henderson Road, 08-03 Henderson Industrial Park, Singapore 159552
International Thomson Publishing Asia, Room 701, 121 Chung King S Road, Section 1, Taipei, Taiwan
International Thomson Publishing Asia, 342 Sriwara Road, Wang Thenglang, Bankapi, Bangkok 10310, Thailand
International Travel Maps & Books, PO Box 2290, Vancouver, Canada

Internationales Landkartenhaus Geocenter, Schockenried Straße 44, 7000 Stuttgart 80, Germany

InterOrbis SpA, Via Benedetto Croce 4, 20094 Corsico (Milan), Italy

Interpharm Press Inc, 1356 Busch Parkway, Buffalo Grove, IL 60089, USA

Interprint Publications, Mehta House, 16a Naraina II, New Delhi, India 110 028

Intertaal, Van Baerlestraat 76, Postbus 75410, 1070 AK Amsterdam, Netherlands

Intertape Ltd, Spinnereistrasse 21, 8753 Mollis, Switzerland

Intext Book Co Pty Ltd, 600 Smith Street, Clifton Hill, Melbourne, Victoria, Australia 3068 & 412 Heidelberg Road, Fairfield, Victoria, Australia 3078

Davis & Yvonne Inwood, Unit 2/13, Carrington Road, Castle Hill, NSW, Australia 2154

IOP Publishing, c/o AIDC, 2 Wintersport Lane, PO Box 20, Williston, VT 05495-0020, USA

IPD, PO Box 200029, Riverfront Plaza Station, Newark, NJ 07102-0301, USA

IPD (Pte) Ltd, 25 Tannery Road, Singapore 1334

IPG, 814 North Franklin Street, Chicago, IL 60610, USA

I.P.R. (International Publishers' Representatives), PO Box 5731, 1386 Nicosia, Cyprus

Irish Book Centre, GPO Box 1074J, Melbourne, Vic, Australia 3001

The Irish Book Shop, 580 Broadway, Room 1103, New York, NY 10012, USA

Irish Books & Media, Franklin Business Center, 1433 Franklin Avenue East, Minneapolis, MN 55404-2135, USA

IRM Inc, Rosei Building, 4 Higashi Azabu 1-chome, Minato Ku, Tokyo, 106 Japan

Irwin Publishing Inc, 1800 Steels Avenue, West Concord, Ont, Canada L4K 2P3

ISBN Co Ltd, 958 Moo 3, Moobaan Sinthorn Soi 10, Happyland Road, Khlongchan, Bangkapi, Bangkok 10240, Thailand

ISBS, 5804 NE Hassalo Street, Portland, OR 97213-3644, USA

Isis Publishing Ltd, 7 Centremead, Osneymead, Oxford OX2 0ES, UK

ISIS Transaction Publishers, Rutgers—The State University of New Jersey, New Brunswick, NJ, USA

Islam International Publications, PO Box 89, Riverstone, NSW, Australia 2765

Islam International Publications, 4 Baxi Bazar Road, Dacca 1, Bangladesh

Islam International Publications, Brussel Straat 3, 1744 Sint Ulriks-Kapelle (Dilbeek), Brussels, Belgium

Islam International Publications, Eriksminde Alle 2, Hvidovre, Copenhagen, Denmark

Islam International Publications, PO Box 3758, 82 Kings Road, Samabula, Suva, Fiji

Islam International Publications, 54 Lt Colonel Donzelle, 95390 Saint Prix, France

Islam International Publications, PO Box 383, Banjul, Gambia

Islam International Publications, Die Moschee Babenhauser, Landstraße 25, Frankfurt, Germany

Islam International Publications, PO Box 2327, Accra (OSU New Estates), Ghana

Islam International Publications, Darul Masih, Qadian, India 143 516

Islam International Publications, Jalan Balik Papan 1/10, Jakarta Pusat 10130, Indonesia

Islam International Publications, 2-1062 Kifu Ne, Me Ito Ku, Nagoya, 465 Japan

Islam International Publications, PO Box 40554, Fort Hall Road, Nairobi, Kenya

Islam International Publications, PO Box 618, 9 Lynch Street, Monrovia, Liberia

Islam International Publications, PO Box 6, Rose Hill, Mauritius

Islam International Publications, 191 28th Street, Rangoon, Myanmar

Islam International Publications, De Moschee, Oostduirlaan 79, The Hague, Netherlands

Islam International Publications, PO Box 418, 45 Idumagbo Avenue, Lagos, Nigeria

Islam International Publications, PO Box 385, Zamboanga City, Philippines

Islam International Publications, PO Box 353, Freetown, Sierra Leone

Islam International Publications, 111 Onan Road, Singapore 1542

Islam International Publications, PO Box 212, Gatesville, Cape Town, South Africa

Islam International Publications, 38 Kumaran Ratnam Road, Colombo 2, Sri Lanka

Islam International Publications, Mahmud Moschee, 323 Forschstraße, 8008 Zurich, Switzerland

Islam International Publications, PO Box 376, Libya Street, Dar es Salaam, Tanzania

Islam International Publications, 126 Eastern Main Road, Tunapuna, Trinidad

Islam International Publications, PO Box 98, Kampala, Uganda

Islam International Publications, 15000 Good Hope Road, Silver Spring, MD 20905, USA

Islam International Publications, PO Box 13856, Kinshasa, Zaire

Islam International Publications, PO Box 32345, Lusaka, Zambia

Islamic Foundation, Markfield Dawah Centre, Ratby Lane, Markfield, Leicester, UK

Islamic Missionary Guild, PO Box 800, Port of Spain, Trinidad

Island Press, 1718 Connecticut Avenue NW, Suite 300, Washington, DC 20009, USA

Island Publications Ltd, Unit 3 Cookstown Enterprise Park, Tallaght, Dublin 24, Irish Republic

ISPCK, Post Box 1815, Kashmere Gate, Delhi, India 110 006

ITMB Publishing, 736a Granville Street, Vancouver, BC, Canada V6Z 1G3

Jacaranda Designs Ltd, PO Box 7936, Boulder, CO 80306, USA

Jacaranda Wiley Ltd, PO Box 1226, Milton, Queensland, Australia 4064 & 4a, 113 Wicks Road, North Ryde, NSW, Australia 2113

Stephen Jackson, c/o Macmillan, UK

Jade Book Distributors Inc, Suite 412, Puzon Building, E Rodriguez Sr Ave, Quezon City, Philippines

Berj Jamkojian, Gruengasse 12/2, 1050 Vienna, Austria

S. Janakiraman, Book Marketing Services, P-5 Rohini Gardens, Madras, India 600 028

Jane's Information Group Inc, 1340 Braddock Place, Suite 300, Alexandria, VA 22313-2036, USA

Varga János, Torok Floris u. 128/A, Budapest 1204, Hungary

Frans Janssen, Netwerk Book Agency, Box 33228, 3005 EE Rotterdam, Netherlands

Japan English Agency, Sakuragi Building, 4F, 6-7-3 Minami Aoyama, Minato-ku, Tokyo, 107 Japan

Japan English Services Inc, 48-2 Minamidama, Oami Shirasato-machi, Sambu-gun, Chiba-ken, 299-32 Japan

Japan Philatelic Co Ltd, PO Box 2, Suginami-Minami, Tokyo, Japan

Japan Publications Trading Co, Box 5030, Tokyo International, Tokyo 100-31, Japan

Japan Uni Agency Inc, Naigai Building, 1-1 Kanda Jinbocho, Chiyoda-ku, Tokyo, 101 Japan

JAPIS, Brautarhold 2, Box 396, 121 Reykjavik, Iceland

Jaypee Brothers Medical Publishers Ltd, PO Box 7193, B-3 Emca House, 23/23B Ansari Road, Darya Ganj, New Delhi, India 110 002

Jays Bookstore, Corner Queens Mary Street & Kennedy Avenue, PO Box 254, Roseau, Dominica

JCV Computing International, 3619 West Warner Avenue, Santa Ana, CA 92704, USA

Jensco, PO Box 1987, Hong Kong, Hong Kong

Jeong Jie Lee, Seoul, Korea

F & J de Jesus Inc, PO Box 2063, Mokati, Metro Manila, Philippines

Jeya Agency (Pvt) Ltd, 99 Upper Ground Floor, People's Park Complex, Colombo 11, Sri Lanka

Ann Jhala, PO Box 1259, Blantyre, Malawi

Jin-Myong International Inc, GPA Box 7640, Seoul 100-676, Korea

Johannesburg Agencies, Johannesburg 2000 South Africa

Jordan Book Centre Co Ltd, University Street, PO Box 301, Al-Jubeiha, Amman, Jordan

Jordan Distribution Agency, PO Box 375, Amman, Jordan

Judaica Direct, PO Box 2187, Rose Bay, North Sydney, NSW, Australia 2030

Jura Books, 110 Crystal Street, Petersham, NSW, Australia 2049

Editions du Juris-Classeur, 141 rue de Javal, Paris, France

Juta & Co Ltd, PO Box 163, Isando, 1600 South Africa

Lonnie Kahn & Co Ltd, 5 Tel Givoram Street, PO Box 37613, Tel Aviv 68105, Israel

Kaigai Publications Ltd, PO Box 5020, Tokyo International, Tokyo, 100-31 Japan

Editions Kailash, 69 rue Saint Jacques, 75005 Paris, France

Kanda Book Trading Co, Tanikawa Building, 3-2 Kanda Surugadai, Chiyoda-ku, Tokyo, 101 Japan

Charles Kang, 24C Jalan SS 15/8, 47500 Suband Jaya, PO Box 316 Jalan Sultan, 46730 PetalingJaya, Selangor D.E., Malaysia

Karger Libri AG, Petersgraben 31, 4009 Basle, Switzerland

Karim International, GPR Box 2141, 64/1 Monipuri Para, Tejgaon, Dhaka 1215, Bangladesh

Karlov Marketing Services Pty Ltd, 9 Hughes Avenue, Castle Hill, NSW, Australia 2154

Kay Kato, 5-14 Gokurakuji, 1-chome, Kamakura, Kanagawa 248, Japan

Z. Kaviani, International Thomson Publishing, White Crown Building, Abu Dhabi Highway, PO Box 7184, Dubai, UAE

Kay (Kaoru) Kato, 5-14 Gokurakuji, 1-chome, Kamakura, Kanagawa, 248 Japan

Barbie Keene, PO Box MR67, Marlborough, Harare, Zimbabwe

K. C. Enterprises, PO Box 70, Glyfada, 166 10 Athens, Greece

Kegan Paul International, PO Box 256, London WC1B 3SW, UK

Kekoo Modi, Shanti Nivas, F. W. Ryan Street, San Pawl Tat-Targa, Naxxar NXR 06, Malta

Kel Ediciones SA, M. T. Alvear 1369, 1058 Buenos Aires, Argentina

Kelani Caribbean, 6225 Westgate Drive 705, Orlando, FL 32835, USA

J. J. Keller & Associates, R. & D., 7273 US Highway 45, Neenah, WI 54957, USA

Genny Kelliher Publishers Representative, 24 Longford Terrace, Monkstown, Co Dublin, Irish Republic

Kemper Conseil, Dr Beguinlaan 72, 2272 AL Voorburg, Netherlands

Kennedy Publications, Templeton Road, Fitzwilliam, NH 03447, USA

Kerrigan/Miro/Calonje Literary Agency, Traversera de Gracia 12 5923, 08021 Barcelona, Spain

Kerrison Book Services, 5635 Nakedi Road, Broadhurst, PO Box 40551, Gaborone, Botswana

Keswick Book Society, PO Box 10242, Nairobi, Kenya

Rasiad-Said Khamis, Box 33918, Uroja Wa Vijana Building, Morochoro Road, Dar Es Salaam, Tanzania

K. G. Khandelwal, 85 Briar Avenue, Norbury, London SW16 3AG, UK

Kiel & Kiel Literatur Agentur, Brauerknechtgraben 55, 20459 Hamburg, Germany

Kielipalvelu Ky Oy, Marjamaentie 7, 07560 Pukkila, Finland

Patrick Kielty, 7 rue du Marche a l'Avoine, 28230 Epernon, France

Fiona Killeen, 109 Upper Kilmacia Road, Stilcorgan, Dublin, Irish Republic

Jessica Kingsley Publishers, 118 Pentonville Road, London N1 9JB, UK

Kingston Bookshop, 70B King Street, Kingston, Jamaica

Kingston Publishers Ltd, 1a Norwood Avenue, Kingston 5, Jamaica

Kingstons Ltd, 4th Floor, Lenberu House, Union Avenue, PO Box 2374, Harare, Zimbabwe

Kinokuniya Book Import Dept, 38-1 Sakuragaoka 5-chome, Setagaya-ku, Tokyo, 156 Japan

Kinokuniya Bookstores of Taiwan Co Ltd, Rm 802, I. T. Building, No 205, Sec 1, Tun Hua South Road, Taipei, Taiwan

Kinokuniya Co Ltd, 38-1 Sakuragaoka 5-chome, Setagaya-ku, Tokyo, 156 Japan

Kirby Book Co, Unit 7, 19 Bowden Street, Alexandria, Sydney, NSW, Australia 2015

Benjamin Kithyaka, Nzomo Educational Supplies Ltd, PO Box 72796, Nairobi, Kenya

Miss S. Kivilinna, Vironkatu 7C2, 00170 Helsinki 17, Finland

Kiwikraft, 02-05 Coronation Shopping Plaza, 587 Bukit Timah Road, Singapore 1026

Ernst Klett Verlag, Stuttgart, Germany

Mary Kling, 7 rue Corneille, 75006 Paris, France

KLP Agencies Ltd, 1a Lazare Street, St James, PO Box 270, Port of Spain, Trinidad

Kluwer Law International, 675 Massachusetts Avenue, Cambridge, MA 02139, USA

Knowledge Craft Ltd, Room 601-2, Tung Shun Hing Centre, 20–22a Granville Rd, TST, Kowloon, Hong Kong

Koen Book Distributors Inc, 10 Twosome Drive, PO Box 600, Moorestown, NJ 08057, USA

Mari Koga, Motovun, Coop N. Ichibancho 153, 15-6 Ichibancho, Chiyoda-ku, Tokyo, 102 Japan

Kokusai Shobo, 5 Ogawanachi 3-chome, Kanda, Chiyoda-ku, Tokyo, 101 Japan

Sven Koltz, Koeltz Scientific Books, PO Box 1360, 61453 Koenigstein, Germany

Juliusz Komarnicki, Books for Europe, CP 196, 6900 Massagno, Switzerland

Louise Kool & Galt Ltd, 1149 Bellamy Road, Scarborough, Ont, Canada M1H 1H7

Bookshop Kooyker, Postbus 24, 2300 AA Leiden, Netherlands

Korea Christian Book Service, Gangnam PO Box 672, Seoul 135-606, Korea

Ute Körner, Rondo Guinardó 32-5º 5, Barcelona 08025, Spain

Kosmos – Z & K, Postbus 14095, St Jacobstraat 125, 3511 BP Utrecht, Netherlands

Messageries Paul Kraus, 5 rue Raiffeisen, 2411 Luxembourg, Luxembourg

K. Krishnamurthy (Books), 23 Thanikachalan Road, Madras, India 600 017

Wydawnictwo i Ksiegarnie, Elzbieta Jarmolkiewicz, ul Szara 10A apt. no. 210, 00-420 Warsaw, Poland

Kuatro Ltda, Pedro de Valdivia Nº 47, Casilla 171 Correo 10, Santiago, Chile

Kudu Books Pty Ltd, PO Box 193, Maitland, 7405, Cape Town, South Africa

Kumi Trading Co Ltd, 983-41, Bangbae-3 Dong, Seocho-ku, Seoul 137-063, Korea

Kuwait Bookshops Co Ltd, PO Box Safat 2942, 13030 Safat, Kuwait

K. P. Kyriakou (Books-Stationery) Ltd, Panagides Building, 3 Grivas Digenis Avenue, PO Box 159, Limassol, Cyprus

Labor Publications, 25900 Greenfield Road, Suite 258, Oak Park, MI 48237, USA

Labour Press, PO Box 7, Marrickville, NSW, Australia 2204

Okani Laermidler, PO Box 1764, 5011 Bergen-Nordnes, Norway

Lai Lai Book Co, 4F-1, 271, Sec 3, Roosevelt Road, Taipei, Taiwan

Lake House Bookshop, PO Box 244, 100 Sir Chittampalam Gardiner Mawata, Colombo 2, Sri Lanka

LAMBS (Legal & Medical Bookshop Ltd), London, UK

Allan Lang International Book Marketing Ltd, 234 Nassau Street, Princeton, NJ 08542, USA

Jean de Lannoy, Av du Roi 202, 1060 Brussels, Belgium

Lantmateriet Kartbutiken, Kungsgatan 74, 111 22 Stockholm, Sweden & 162 15 Vällingby, Sweden

Larousse, Kingfisher, Chambers Inc, 95 Madison Avenue, New York, NY 10016, USA

Lateinamerika Nachrichten, Gneisenaustraße 2, 10961 Berlin, Germany

Latitude Media & Marketing, 41 Martins Place, PO Box 120, Glen Waverley, Victoria, Australia 3150

Laurier Books Ltd, 1975 Fairbanks Avenue, Ottawa, Ont, Canada K1H 5Y5

Sandra Lavender, PO Box 953, Crows Nest, NSW, Australia 2065

Sheila Lavery, Kilbrew, Ashbourne, Co Meath, Irish Republic

Lavis Marketing, 73 Lime Walk, Headington, Oxford OX3 7AD, UK

Lavoisier Publishing Inc, Springer-Verlag Service Center, PO Box 19386, Newark, NJ 07195-9386, USA

Lavoisier Technique et Documentation, rue de Provigny 14, 94236 Cachan Cedex, France

The Law Book Co Ltd, 44–50 Waterloo Road, North Ryde, NSW, Australia 2113

The Law Book Vendors, Mabrochi International Co, PO Box 1509, Surulere, Lagos, Nigeria

Tony Lawrence, Datum Book Marketing, 10 Westmorland Close, Bowdon, Altrincham, Cheshire WA143QR, UK

R. J. Laws & Son Agencies, PO Box 63, Cayon Street, Basseterre, St Kitts

Lawson Falle Ltd, Box 1144, 341 Sheldon Drive, Cambridge, Ont, Canada N1R 6C9

Isabel Leao, 25 Elmhurst Avenue, Finchley, London N2 0LT, UK

Learning Logic, 17 Allenby Road, Canterbury, Vic, Australia 3126

L.E.D., Via Cassini 41, 10129 Turin, Italy

Robert Lee, University Bookshop, 16 S. S. Ramgoolam Street, Port Louis, Mauritius

Left Bank Distribution, 4142 Brooklyn NE, Seattle, WA 98105, USA

Legal Circle, 47B Jalan Satu Kan, 16 Berkeley Town Centre, 41300 Klang, Selangor Darul Eshan, Malaysia

Legal Library Services Ltd, Thorne House, Eastville, Yeovil, Somerset BA21 4JD, UK

Chris & Candy Legg, Box 3340, Cape Town, 8000 South Africa

Leishman & Taussig African & Caribbean Book Services,
2b Westgate, Southwell, Notts NG25 0JH, UK
Leo Books, PO Box 6836, Roggebaai 8012 South Africa &
Nasionale Pers Sentrum, Heerengracht 40, Cape Town 8001 South
Africa
Andreas Leon, 12B Androutsou Street, 15233 Athens, Greece
P. T. Isawandi Lestari, Artholoka Building, Ground Floor,
2 Jl Jenderal Sudirman, Jakarta 10220, Indonesia
Leuchtturm Albenverlag, Paul Koch KG AM Spakenberg 45,
Postfach 1340, 2054 Geesthacht, Germany
Levant Distributors, 88 avenue Victor Hugo, 75116 Paris, France
Librairie du Liban, BP 945, Beirut, Lebanon
John Libbey CIC Srl, Via L. Spallanzani 11, 00161 Rome, Italy
John Libbey Eurotext Ltd, 6 rue Blanche, 92120 Montrouge, France
Libertarian Review, PO Box 236, Mona Vale, NSW, Australia 2103
Liberty Books (Pvt) Ltd, 3 Rafiq Plaza, Karachi 3, Pakistan
Librairie Arabe l'Olivier, 5 rue de Fribourg, Geneva, Switzerland
La librairie du Quebec, 30 rue Gay Lussac, 75005 Paris, France
Librarie Internationale, 70 Rue Tssoule, MA 10001 Ramat, Morocco
The Library Supply Co Ltd, PO Box 8137, Symonds Street, Auckland,
New Zealand
Librerias ABC SA, Avenida Central 671 of 604, San Isidro, Peru
Libriger Book Distributors, 3 George Lubbe Street, Hamilton,
Bloemfontein, 9300 South Africa
Librimport, Provenza 277, 08037 Barcelona, Spain
Libris (Thailand) Co Ltd, PO Box 794, Prakanong, Bangkok 10110,
Thailand
Libros Tecnicos Liteja Cia Ltda, Avenida America 542, Apartado 455a,
Quito, Ecuador
LICOSA—Libreria Comm. Sansoni SpA, Via Benedetto Fortini 10,
50125 Florence, Italy
Lighthouse Philatelics (Aust) Pty Ltd, PO Box 763, Strawberry Hills,
NSW, Australia 2012
Lighthouse Publications (Canada) Ltd, 255 Duke Street, Montreal,
Quebec, H3C 2M2, Canada
Lighthouse Publications Inc, PO Box 705, 274 Washington Avenue,
Hackensack, NJ 07602-0705, USA
Surinder Lijhara, 20b/46 Tilak Nagar, New Delhi, India 110018
Frances Lincoln, 4 Torriano Mews, Torriano Avenue,
London NW5 2RZ, UK
Lincom Europe, Linguistic Sales & Distribution Market, PO Box 1316,
8044 Unterschleissheim/Munich, Germany
Lion Publishing, Sandy Lane West, Oxford, UK
Listeners Library Pty Ltd, PO Box 81340, Parkhurst, 2120 South
Africa
Literatur-Agentur Koln, Grunenborn 49m, 5204 Lohmar 21, Germany
Literatura Medica, 1027 Budapest, Frankel Leo U11. 11/8, 1539 Bp,
PO Box 603, Budapest, Hungary
Little Brown & Co, Brettenham House, Lancaster Place,
London WC2E 7EN, UK
Little Brown & Co (Canada) Ltd, 148 Yorkville Avenue, Toronto, Ont,
Canada M5R 1C2
Little Hills Press Pty Ltd, Regent House, 37–43 Alexander Street,
Crows Nest (Sydney), NSW, Australia 2065
Living & Learning Inc, 2195 Turnage Street, Salem, OR 97304, USA
The Living Literary Agency, Via Poliziano, 8, 20154 Milan, Italy
Llewellyns Inc, PO Box 43383, St Paul, MN 55114, USA
Chris Lloyd, 463 Ashley Road, (PO Box 327), Parkstone, Poole,
Dorset BH14 0AX, UK
Lloyd's Register of Shipping, 17 Battery Place, New York,
NY 10004-1195, USA
LLP (Asia) Ltd, Room 1101 Hollywood Centre, 233 Hollywood Road,
Hong Kong
LLP Inc, Suite 308, 611 Broadway, New York, NY 10012, USA
Tahir Lodhi, Al-Rehman Building, 2nd Floor, PO Box 2458,
65 The Mall, Lahore, Pakistan
Sven von Loga, Gerhard-vom-Rath-Strasse 55, 50968 Köln-Raderberg,
Germany
Login Publishers Consortium, 4029 West George Street, Chicago,
IL 60641, USA
Logos Impex srl, Strada Curtatona 5/F, 41100 Modena, Italy
Lok Report, Post Box 1280, 48002 Münster, Germany
London Publishers Agency, PO Box 1791, Ramat HaSharon, 47117,
Israel
Lonely Planet, 71 bis, rue du Cardinal Lemoine, 75005 Paris, France
Lonely Planet Publications, Devonshire House,
10 Barley Mow Passage, Chiswick, London W4 4PH, UK

Lonely Planet Publications Inc, 155 Filbert Street, Oakland, CA 94607,
USA
Longhorn Kenya Ltd, PO Box 18033, Funzi Road, Nairobi, Kenya
Longman Arab World Centre, PO Box 6587,
Al-Hujairi Building 4th Floor, Amir Mohammed Street,
Amman 11118, Jordan
Longman Arab World Centre, Butros Bustani Street, Zokak el Blat,
BP 11945, Beirut, Lebanon
Longman Arab World Centre, 15th Street, PO Box 10437, Khartoum,
Sudan
Longman Asia Ltd, Cornwall House, 18th Floor, Taikoo Trading Estate,
Tong Chong Street, Quarry Bay, Hong Kong
Longman Australia Pty Ltd, Kings Gardens, 95 Coventry Street,
Melbourne, Vic, Australia 3205
Longman Botswana (Pty) Ltd, PO Box 1083, Lobatse Road, Gaborone,
Botswana
Longman de Mexico, Amores No 2027, Colonia del Valle,
03100 Mexico DF, Mexico
Longman ELT, Av. Paulista, 807-cj 1502, 01311, São Paulo, Brazil
Longman France, 95 boulevard St Michel, 75005 Paris, France
Longman Group (UK) Ltd, Longman House, Burnt Mill, Harlow,
Essex CM20 2JE, UK
Longman Hong Kong, Taikoo Place, 979 King's Road, Hong Kong
Longman Italia SRL, Via F. Casati 20, 20124 Milan, Italy
Longman Japan KK, Gyokuroen Building, 1-13-19 Sekiguchi,
Bunkyo-ku, 112 Tokyo Japan
Longman Lesotho (Pty) Ltd, PO Box 1174, Christie House,
Orpen Road, Maseru, Lesotho
Longman Malaysia Sdn Bhd, 3 Jalan Kilang A, off Jalan Penchala,
Petaling Jaya 46050, Selangor, Malaysia
Longman (Namibia) (Pty) Ltd, PO Box 9251, Eros, Windhoek,
Namibia
Longman Nigeria PK, 52 Oba Akran Avenue, PMB 21036, Ikeja,
Nigeria
Longman Paul Ltd, 46 Hillside Road, Glenfield, Auckland 10, New
Zealand
Longman Penguin Portugal, Rua D. Pedro V, 60-1-D, 1200 Lisbon,
Portugal
Longman Penguin South Africa, Amethyst Street, Theta Ext 1,
Private Bag X08, Bertsham, Johannesburg, 2013 South Africa
Longman Publishing Group, Addison Wesley, 10 Bunk Street,
White Plains, NY 10606-1951, USA
Longman Representative, Marcelo T de Alvear 976 30K,
1058 Buenos Aires, Argentina
Longman Representative, Apartado 60543, Chaco, Caracas 1060-A,
Venezuela
Longman Singapore Publishers (Pte) Ltd, 25 First Lokang Road,
Jurong Town, Singapore 2262
Longman Swaziland (Pty) Ltd, PO Box 2207, Eyakho Building,
Nkoseluhlaza Street, Manzini, Swaziland
Longman Taiwan, 11F No 87-1 Ho-Ping East Road, Section 1, Taipei,
Taiwan
Longman Trinidad Ltd, PO Box 179,
Corner Macoya Road & Churchill Roosevelt Highway, Trincity,
Trinidad
Longman Turkey, Kozo Is Merkezi, B Block K4, Murbasan Sok, 80700,
Balmumca, Istanbul, Turkey
Longman Zimbabwe (Pvt) Ltd, PO Box ST125, Stand 1515,
Tourle Road, Southerton, Harare, Zimbabwe
Lothian Books, 11 Munro Street, Port Melbourne, Vic, Australia 3207
Lothian Books NZ Ltd, 3/3 Marken Place, Glenfield, Auckland 10, New
Zealand
Lotus Enterprises, 1890 Apollo Court, Walnut Creek, CA 94598, USA
LPC Group (Losin), 30 Commerce Park Road, Milford, CT 06460, USA
LPC/Inbook, 1436 West Randolf Street, Chicago, IL 60607, USA
Uwe Luedemann, Boddinstrasse 21, 12053 Berlin, Germany
Al Lugain Co, PO Box 2124, Salmiya, 22022, Kuwait
Betty Lumu, c/o Gustro Ltd, PO Box 1980, Kampala, Uganda
Lund Humphries Publ., Park House, 1 Russell Gardens,
London NW11 9NN, UK
Lydlitteratur, Postboks 69, Nesoya, Norway
Lyle Steele & Co, 511 East 73rd Street, New York, NY 10021, USA

McClelland & Stewart, 481 University Avenue, Suite 900, Toronto,
Ont, Canada M5G 2E9 & 380 Esna Park Drive, Markham, Ont,
Canada L3R 1H5

Donald Macdonald, Datum Book Marketing, 57 Essex Drive, Jordanhill, Glasgow G14 9LZ, UK

Macdonald Purnell (Pty) Ltd, PO Box 40533, Cleveland, 2022 South Africa; 5 Watkins Street, Denver Ext 4, Cleveland, TVL, 2022 South Africa & PO Box 1401, Randburg, 2125 South Africa

Roibeard Mac Eoin, 191 Brougham Street, Woolloomooloo, Sydney, NSW, Australia 2011

McGraw-Hill Book Co, 60 Tuas Basin Link, Singapore 638775

McGraw-Hill Book Co (Europe) Ltd, Shoppenhangers Road, Maidenhead, Berks SL6 2QL, UK

McGraw-Hill Book Co Australia Pty Ltd, 4 Barcoo Street, PO Box 239, Roseville, NSW, Australia 2069

McGraw-Hill Book Co Japan Ltd, 77 Building, 7th Floor, 4-14-11 Ginza, Chuo-ku, Tokyo, 104 Japan

McGraw-Hill Book Co New Zealand Ltd, 5 Joval Place, Wiri, Manukan, New Zealand

McGraw-Hill Inc, International Group, Princeton-Hightstown Road, Hightstown, NJ 08520, USA & 1221 Avenue of the Americas, New York, NY 10020, USA

McGraw-Hill Interamericana Colombia SA, Transversal 42b, No 19-77, Apartado Aereo 81078, Bogotá, Colombia

McGraw-Hill Interamericana de Mexico, SA de C.V., Atlacomulco 499–501, Fracionamiento, San Andres Atoto, 53500 Naucalpan, Mexico

McGraw-Hill Interamericana Del Caribe Inc, Avenida Munoz Rivera 1121, Rio Piedras, Puerto Rico

McGraw-Hill InterAmericana de España SA, Edifico Oasis A, c/ Basauri s/n, 1ª Planta, Ctra de la Coruna Km 12,28023 Aravaca Madrid, Spain

McGraw-Hill Interamericana Venezuela CA, 2da Calle de Bello Monte, Apartado Aereo 50785, Caracas 1050, Venezuela

McGraw-Hill Interamericana de Portugal Ltda, rua Rosa Damasceno 11A-B, 1900 Lisbon, Portugal

McGraw-Hill Libri Italia srl, Piazza Emilia 5, 20129 Milan, Italy

McGraw Hill Ryerson, 330 Progress Avenue, Scarborough, Ont, Canada M1P 2Z5

McGuire Marketing Publishers' International Management, 97 Guntons Close, Soham, Cambs CB7 5DL, UK

McIntyre Information Services Representatives Ltd, PO Box 15875/1733, Tehran, Iran

Mackwin & Co, 6 Krishna Mansions, Inverarity Road, Karachi 3, Pakistan

McLennan & Petty, Unit 4, 809 Botany Road, Rosebery, NSW 2018 (PO Box 145, Rosebery), Australia

MacLennan & Petty Pty Ltd, PO Box 425, Artarmon, NSW, Australia 2064

Macmillan Boleswa, PO Box 32484, Braamfontein, 2017 South Africa

Macmillan Caribbean, Houndmills, Basingstoke, Hants RG21 6XS, UK

Editorial Macmillan de Mexico SA de CV, Texas 118, Col Napoles, 03810 Mexico DF, Mexico

Macmillan Distribution Ltd, Houndmills, Basingstoke, Hants RG21 6XS, UK

Macmillan Education, Houndmills, Basingstoke, Hants RG21 6XS, UK

Macmillan Education Australia, 107 Moray Street,South Melbourne, Vic, Australia 3205

Macmillan India Ltd, 315–316 Raheja Chambers, 12 Museum Street, Bangalore, India 560 001

Macmillan Kenya (Publishers) Ltd, PO Box 30797, Kijabe Street, Nairobi, Kenya

Macmillan Language House, Hayakawa Bldg 1F, 5-14-7 Hakusan, Bunkyo-ku, Tokyo 112, Japan

Macmillan New Zealand, Private Bag, Northshore Mail Centre, Auckland 1306, New Zealand

Macmillan Nigeria Publishers Ltd, 4 Industrial Avenue, Ilupedu Estate, PO Box 264, Yaba, Lagos, Nigeria

Macmillan Publishers, 107 Moray Street, South Melbourne, Vic, Australia 3205

Macmillan Publishers (China) Ltd, Warwick House East, 19th Floor, Taikoo Place, 979 King's Road, Quarry Bay, Hong Kong

Macmillan Publishers Ltd, Houndmills, Basingstoke, Hants RG21 6XS, UK

Macmillan Publishers New Zealand Ltd, 6 Ride Way, North Harbour Industrial Estate, Albany, New Zealand

Macmillan Publishers Services Ltd, European Sales Department, Houndmills, Basingstoke, Hampshire RG21 6XS, UK

Macmillan Shuppan KK, Eikow Building, 10-9 Hongo, 1-chome, Bunkyo-ku, Tokyo, 113 Japan

Roy McMillan Agencies, 39 McCarrs Creek Road, Church Point, NSW, Australia 2105

Katie McNeish, McNeish Publishing Services, Bagley's Studio, York Way, London N1 0UZ, UK

McNeish Publishing Services, Bagley Studios, Kings Cross Freight Dept, York Way, London N1 0UZ, UK

Horace McQueen Associates, PO Box 35061, Houston, TX 77035, USA

Mad River Press, Route 2, Box 151-B, Eureka, CA 95501, USA

Farhad Maftoon, Anthony Rudkin Associates, PO Box 15115/133, Tehran, Iran

Magic Circle Bookshop, 409 Wellington Street, Perth, WA, Australia 6000

Magis Books srl, Via Raffaello 31/C, Zona Ind Mancasale, 42100 Reggio Emilia, Italy

Editions Magnard, 6 rue Lacépède, 75005 Paris, France

Editions Maisonneure et Laiose, 14 rue Victor Cousin, Paris 75005, France

S. Abdul Majeed & Co, 7 Jalan 3/82b, Bangsar Utama, off Jalan Bangsar, 59000 Kuala Lumpur, Malaysia

Edwin Makabenta Jr, 81 Talayan Street, Talayan Village, Quezon City, 1104, Philippines

Malayan Law Journal Pte Ltd, 3 Shenton Way, 14-03 Shenton House, Singapore 0106

Malayan Law Journal Sdn Bhd, No 3, Jalan PJS 11/20, Bandar Sunway, 46150 Petaling Jaya, Selangor Darul Ehsan, Malaysia

Malik's Bookshop, Bliss Street, Nr Aub Main Gate, PO Box 113-5149, Hanra, Beirut, Lebanon

Stephane Mallegol, Editions Alan Sutton, 21 Avenue de la République, 37300 Joué-lès-Tours, France

Malta Union of Professional Psychologists, PO Box 341, Valletta, Malta

Management Books 2000 Ltd, 125 The Broadway, Didcot, Oxon OX11 8AW, UK

Manasayan, Agarwal Complex, S-524, School Block, Shakarpur, Delhi, India 110 092

Mandragore, 127a Castlerock, Richmond Hill, Ont, Canada L4C 6A1

Manhattan Press (HK) Ltd, Units 1–6, Block B, Wah Tat Industrial Centre, 8–10 Wah Sing Street,Kwai Chung, New Territories, Hong Kong

Manic Ex-Poseur Pty Ltd, PO Box 8, Carlton North, Vic, Australia 3054

Manz'sche Verlags- und Universitätsbuchhandlung, Kohlmarkt 16, 1014 Vienna, Austria

The Map Store of Canada, 113 O'Connor Street, Ottawa, Canada K1P 5M8

MARC International, 121 East Huntingdon Drive, Monrovia, CA 91016-3400, USA

Herman Marcano & Associates Ltd, 12 Flament Street, Port of Spain, Trinidad

Marcello Iberia SA, C/. Bocangel 28, 28028 Madrid, Spain

Marcello SNC, Via P. Canal 12/1, 35137 Padua, Italy

Marginal Distribution, Unit 103, 277 George Street North, Peterborough, Ont, Canada K9J 3G9

John Markham Associates, 11210 Elderberry Way, RR3, Sidney, BC, V8L 5J6, Canada

Marston Book Services Ltd, PO Box 87, Osney Mead, Oxford OX2 0DT, UK

Livraria Martins Fontes, Rua Conselheiro Ramalho, 330, 01325. 000 Sao Paulo, Brazil

Maruzen Co Ltd, Book Division, PO Box 5050, Tokyo International, 100-31 Japan

Maskew Miller Longman Pty Ltd, PO Box 396, Howard Drive, Cape Town 8000 South Africa

Mass Publishing Co Sae, 9 Al Tahin Street, Kokki Gaza, Egypt

Matovu Books & Stationery Ltd, PO Box 4511, Kampala, Uganda

Mauryflor SA, Route d'Etampes, BP 12, 45331 Malesherbes Cedex, France

Maximedia Pty Ltd, PO Box 268, Springwood, NSW, Australia 2777

Maya Publishers Pvt Ltd, 1113-B Shahpur Jat, New Delhi, India 110 049

MCI Records, 21 Habarzel Street, Tel Aviv 69710, Israel

Meakin & Associates, Unit 17, 81 Auriga Drive, Nepean, Ottawa, Ont, Canada K2E 7Y5

Meckler Media, 20 Ketchum Street, Westport, CT 06880, USA

Media Consultants, Jabal Amman 3rd Circle, Jordanian Insurance Co, Building (C), PO Box 811738,Amman, Jordan

Media House Publications Pty Ltd, PO Box 782395, Sandton, Transvaal, 2146 South Africa

Media & Marketing Network, PO Box 16384, Dubai, UAE

Media One Inc, 3434 N. Elaine Place Road, Chicago, IL 60657, USA

Media Plus & Broadcasting Network Ltd, 192 Sukhumvit 49/12, Bangkok 10110, Thailand

MediaCom Associates, PO Box 610, Unlay, SA, Australia 5061

Mediamatics, 280 NSC Bose Road, PO Regent Park, Calcutta, India 700 040

Median Books Ltd, Ty Derw, Dinas Mawddwy, Machynlleth, Powys SY20 9LR, UK

Mediaplus Books Ltd, 203, 2/F Waysun Commercial Building, 28 Connaught Road West, Hong Kong

Medical Association of South Africa, MASA House, Central Square, Pinelands, 7405 South Africa

Meditatio, PO Box 552, Station NDG, Montreal, PQ, Canada H4A 3P0

Rose Meerwein, Reuterpfad 6–8, W-1000 Berlin/Grunewald 33, Germany

Mega Books International, Rostovska 4, 10100 Prague 10 Vrsovice, Czech Republic

Mehne Automobil Access, Wagnerstraße 66, 74906 Bad Rappenau, Germany

W. Melkman, c/o Michelangelostraat 26, 1077 CC Amsterdam, Netherlands

Michael Mellor, c/o Network, PO Box 400323, Munich 40, Germany

Melting Pot Press, 10 Grafton Street, Chippendale, NSW, Australia 2008

Menoshire Ltd, Unit 13, 21 Wadsworth Road, Perivale, Greenford, Middlesex UB6 7LQ, UK

Mentone Educational Centre, 40e Victory Boulevard, Ashburton, Vic, Australia 3147

Merlin Library, Mountbatten Street, Blata-l-Bajda, HMR 08, Malta

MES Equipment Ltd, PO Box 5786, Accra North, Ghana

Les Messageries ADP, 955 rue Amherst, Montreal, PQ, Canada H2L 3K4

Messaggerie Internazionali Srl, Via Alessandro Manzoni No 8, Rozzano, Italy

Metanoia Book Service, 14 Shepherds Hill, London N6 5AQ, UK

Methodist Wholesale, PO Box 708, Cape Town, 8000 South Africa

Ingo Meyer, Hasenheide 18, 24340 Eckernförde, Germany

Seth Meyer-Bruhns, Schottefeldgasse 82/16, 1070 Vienna, Austria

Meynard Publishing Ltd, 2-13-10 Shimo Meguro, Meguro ku, Tokyo, 153 Japan

MFKA-Kustannus Oy, Rautatielalsenkatu 6, 00520 Helsinki, Finland

Jan Michael, PO Box 15137, 1001 MC Amsterdam, Netherlands

S.A. Belge du Pneumatique Michelin, Quai de Willebrock 33, 1210 Brussels, Belgium

S.A. des Pneumatiques Michelin, Route Jo Siffert 36, 1762 Givisiez, Switzerland

Michelin Italiana SPA, Corso Sempione 66, 20154 Milan, Italy

Michelin Reifenverkaufs GmbH, Weigelestrasse 10, Postfach, 1230 Vienna, Austria

Michelin Reifenwerke KGaA, Bannwaldallee 60, W-7500 Karlsruhe 21, Germany

SAFE de Neumaticos Michelin, Calle de Doctor Esquerdo 157, 28007 Madrid, Spain

Michelin Travel Publications, PO Box 19001, Greenville, SC 29602-9001, USA

Michie, 701 E Water Street, Charlottesville, VA 22906-7587, USA

MicroInfo Ltd, Box 3, Omega Park, Hants, UK

Middle East Agency, 16B Maamal El Sukar Street, Apartment 18, Garden City, Cairo, Egypt

Milestone Publications, 3284 Heather Street, Vancouver, BC, V5Z 3K5, Canada

Millbank Books Ltd, The Courtyard, The Old Monastery, Windhill, Bishop's Stortford, Hertfordshire CM23 2PE, UK

Peter Miller, New York, USA

Miller Distributors Ltd, Miller House, Tarxien Road, Airport Way, Luqa, Malta

Ion Mills, 18 Coleswood Road, Harpenden, Herts AL5 1EQ, UK

Mireva Bookshop, Tarer Street, Msida, Malta

Mirza Book Agency, 65 Shahrah-e-Quaid-e-Azam, PO Box 729, Lahore 3, Pakistan

Missing Link Versandbuchhandlung, Westerstraße 118, 28199 Bremen, Germany

Mission Ahmadiyya del Islam, Mezquita Basharat, Pedro Abad, Cordoba, Spain

University Press of Mississippi, 3825 Ridgewood Road, Jackson, MS 39211-6492, USA

R. G. Mitchell, 565 Gordon Baker Road, Willowdale, Ont, Canada M2H 2W2

Surit Mitra & Bikram Grewal, 1113B Shapur Jat, New Delhi, India 110 049

M & J Services, Dadar, Bombay, India

MK General School Supplies Ltd, Ground Floor, Plot 1, Jinja Road, PO Box 12385, Kampala, Uganda

MK International Ltd, 203-1-50-7 Itabashi, Itabashi-ku, Tokyo 173, Japan

MK Publishers Ltd, Eagen Mansions, Plot 1, Ginje Road, O Box 12385, Kampala, Uganda

M & K Publishers & Agencies, PO Box 71025, Dar es Salaam, Tanzania

Modern Languages, 39 Westland Row, Dublin 2, Irish Republic

Modern School Supplies, PO Box 958, Hartford, CT 06143, USA

Modern Teaching Aids, PO Box 608, Brookvale, NSW, Australia 2100

Mohrbooks Literary Agency, Klasbachstrasse 110, 8032 Zurich, Switzerland

Juul Moller AS, Oslo, Norway

Hooshang Momeni, PO Box 14155-4315, Tehran, Iran

Momenta Publishing Ltd, Broadway House, The Broadway, Wimbledon, London SW19 1RH, UK

Monarch Books of Canada Ltd, U5000 Dufferin Street, Unit K, Downsview, Ont, Canada M3H 5T5

Mondo, 3 Sands Court Point, Washington, NY 11050, USA

Money Market Directories, 320 East Main Street, PO Box 1608, Charlottesville, VA 22901, USA

Moniteur belge, rue de Louvain 40–42, 1000 Brussels, Belgium

Monthly Review Press, 122 West 27th Street, New York, NY 10001, USA

Moon Yae Dang, 7th Floor Keunyoung Building, Yeoido-dong, Youngdeoungpo-ku, Seoul, Korea

Thomas J. Mooney, 282 Swords Road, Dublin 9, Irish Republic

Evan Moor Corp, 18 Lower Ragsdale, Monterey, CA 93940, USA

Moorland Publishing Co, Moor Farm Road West, Ashbourne, Derbyshire DE6 1HD, UK

Jose Luis Morales, Av. Constituyente 1943, Apto 102, 11200 Montevideo, Uruguay, Uruguay

Morehouse, 871 Ethan Allen Highway, Suite 204, Ridgefield, CT 06877, USA

Michael Morris Associates, Walden Road, Littlebury, Saffron Walden, Essex CB11 4TA, UK

Morris & Associates, 2300 Hazelwood Lane, Clearwater, FL 34623, USA

Mosaic Press, PO Box 1032, Oakville, Ont, Canada L6J 5N9

Mosby-Williams & Wilkins Pty Ltd, PO Box 431, Unit 19, 39 Herbert Street, Artarmon, NSW, Australia 2064

Mosuro Booksellers, PO Box 30201, Ibadan, Nigeria

Mot a Mot, 5 rue Dugommier, 75012 Paris, France

Motilal Books (UK) Ltd, 73 Lime Walk, Hedington, Oxford OX3 7AD, UK

Motion Smith, 78 Shenton Way, Singapore

Motor Books, Box 68801, Bryanston, 2021 South Africa

Motorbooks International Publishers & Wholesalers Inc, PO Box 1, Osceola, WI 54020-0001, USA

Moyer Bell, Rhode Island, USA

MPH Distributors (S) Pte Ltd, MPH House, 12 Tagore Drive, Singapore 2678

MTM, 10b Garden Terrace III, 8A Old Peak Road, Hong Kong

MTM, 118 Culford Road, London N1 4HU, UK

Haji Muhammad & Sons, PO Box 80849, Mombasa, Kenya

Multicultural Books & Video Inc, 12033 St Thomas Court, Tecumseh, Ont, Canada N8N 3V6

Music Sales Corporation, 257 Park Avenue South, New York, NY 10010, USA

Music Sales Pty Ltd, c/o Bookwise International, 54 Crittenden Road, Findon, SA, Australia 5923

Musikkdistribusjon AS, Sandakerveien 76, Postboks 4379/Torshov, 0402 Oslo 4, Norway

Muslim Book Club, PO Box 19, Lakemba NSW, Australia 2195

Al Mutanabbi Bookshop, Tariq bin Zaid Street, near Rashid Hospital, Dubai, UAE

MVD, Oberweg 21c – Halle V, 82008 Unterhaching, Munich, Germany

Gilbert Mwakalukwa, PO Box 3535, Olympio Street, Dar-es-Salaam, Tanzania

My Book Service, PO Box 12, Koganei, Tokyo, 184 Japan

NAFTA, Indian Defence Review, 12 Paddock Drive, Fort Salonga, NY 11768, USA

Nagara Books Ltd, Urushibara Building 705, 4-37-13, Hongo Bunkyo-ku, Tokyo, 113 Japan

Naigai Trading Co Ltd, 7-3-107 Hiroo 1-Chome, Shibuya-Ku, Tokyo 150, Japan

Nalanda & Co, 30 Bourbon Street, Port Louis, Mauritius

N.A.M. Books, Rotherham, North Canterbury, New Zealand

Namsgagnastofnun, Laugavegur 166, 105 Reykjavik, Iceland

Err Namsgogn, Box 172, 270 Varma, Iceland

Nankodo Co Ltd, PO Box 5272, Tokyo International, Tokyo 10031, Japan & 42-6 Hongo 3-Chome, Bunkyo-ku, Tokyo, 113 Japan

Narvesens Information Centre, PO Box 6125, Etterstad, 0602 Oslo 6, Norway

Vijeh Nashr International, PO Box 15815-1779, Tehran 16139, Iran

Nasir Moské Islams Ahmadiyya Församling, Tolvskillingsgatan 1, 414 82 Göteborg, Sweden

Nassau Stationers, PO Box N31378, Nassau, Bahamas

National Bible Society of Ireland, 41 Dawson Street, Dublin 2, Irish Republic

National Book Distributors, 3/2 Aquatic Drive, Frenchs Forest, NSW, Australia 2086

National Book Network, 4720A Boston Way, Lanham, MD 20706, USA

National Christian Education Council, 1020 Bristol Road, Selly Oak, Birmingham B20 6LB, UK

National Consulting Bureau, PO Box 5092, Safat 13051, Kuwait

National Distance Education Centre, Dublin City University, Collins Avenue Extension, Glassnevin, Dublin 9, Irish Republic

National Foundation for Educational Research, The Mere, Upton Park, Slough, Berks SL1 2DQ, UK

National Gallery of Canada, 380 Sussex Drive, Ottawa, Ont, Canada K1N 9N4

National Stationery & Book Centre, 78 Church Street, PO Box 101047, Georgetown, Guyana

National Theatre Organization, PO Box 2701, Harare, Zimbabwe

Nationwide Book Distributors, PO Box 4176, 30 Stewart Street, Christchurch, New Zealand

Nato's Educational Supplies, Brazil Street, PO Box 150, Castrie, St Lucia

Natoli Stefan & Oliva, Via Omboni 5, 20129 Milan, Italy

Natural History Book Service Ltd, 2 Wills Road, Totnes, Devon TQ9 5XN, UK

Navigator Books Pty Ltd, 7027 Nerang, Southport Road, Nerang, Qld, Australia 4211

Navrang Inc, PO Box 10056, 507 Seminole Drive, Blacksburg, VA 24062-0056, USA

Naxos Japan, Itohpia—Hisaya 603, 14-23 Izumi 1-chome, Higashiku, Nagoya, 461 Japan & Meitsu Fuyoku Nakameguro 313, 3-10-3 Kameguro, Meguro-Ku, Tokyo, 153 Japan

Naxos & Marco Polo, 34 rue de Richelieu, 75001 Paris, France

Naxos of America Inc, 1165 Markress Road, Suites E & F, Cherry Hill, NJ 08003, USA

Naxos of Canada Ltd, 3510 Pharmacy Avenue, Unit 5, Scarborough, Ont, Canada M1W 2T7

Naxos of France, 13 rue Molière, 75001 Paris, France

Naxos Pte Ltd, Toa Payoh North, Block 970, 04-18/20 Toa Payoh Industrial Estate

Naxos Sweden, Kryptongatan 6, 703 74 Orebro, Sweden

Behruz Neirami, PO Box 15875/1733, Tehran, Iran

Nelson Canada, 1120 Birchmount Road, Scarborough, Ont, Canada M1K 5G4

Thomas Nelson (Australia) Pty Ltd, 102 Dodds Street, South Melbourne, Vic, Australia 3205

Thomas Nelson & Sons Ltd, Nelson House, Mayfield Road, Walton-on-Thames, Surrey KT12 5PL, UK

Nelson Price Milburn Ltd, 1 Te Puni Street, Petone, Wellington, New Zealand

Nelson Publishers (SEA) Pte Ltd, 105 Sims Avenue 02-06, Chancerlodge Complex, Singapore 1438

Nepal Law Book Co, PB 2964, Ram Shah, Kathmandu, Nepal

Nepal Sahitya Kendra, Kamalpokhri, PO Box 4183, Kathmandu, Nepal

Netwerk, Academic Book Agency, PO Box 33228, 3005 EE Rotterdam, Netherlands

Neutrino Inc, Takahashi Building, 44-3 Fuda, 1-chome, Chofu-Shi, Tokyo 182, Japan

New Age International Ltd, 4835/24 Ansari Road, Darya Ganj, New Delhi, India 110 002

New Hobsons Press Pty Ltd, 22553 Elizabeth Street, Surry Hill, NSW, Australia 2010

New Horizons, 13 Howe Street, Freetown, Sierra Leone

New Leaf Distribution, 401 Thornton Road, Lithia Springs, GA 30057-1557, USA

New Media, Meteoorstraat 68—72, 2516 BP The Hague, Netherlands

New Namibia Books, PO Box 21601, Windhoek 9000, Namibia

New Schoolmate Business Group, B2, 465 Chung Shiao E. Road, Sec1, Taipei, Taiwan

New York Nautical, 140 West Broadway, New York, NY 10013, USA

New York University Press, Elmer Holmes Bobst Library, 70 Washington Square, New York, NY 10012-1091, USA

New Zealand Council for Educational Research, PO Box 3237, 178—182 Willis Street, Wellington, New Zealand

New Zealand Library Committee, PO Box 37-248, Parnell, Auckland, New Zealand

NFER-Nelson, Darville House, 2 Oxford Road East, Windsor, Berks SL4 1DF, UK

NGB Corporation, PO Box 521, Ark Mori Building 28F, 12-32 Akasaka 1-chome, Minato-ku, Tokyo, 107 Japan

NGM Ltd, PO Box 3535, 935 Olympio Street, Dar-es-Salaam, Tanzania

NIAM, Sweelinckplein 33, 2517 Den Haag, Netherlands

Nihon Michelin Tire KK, Shinjuku Center Bldg 46F, 25-1-1 Nishi Shinjuku, Shinjuku-ku, Tokyo, 160 Japan

Martinus Nijhoff International, PB 269, 2501 AX The Hague, Netherlands

Nilsson & Lamm BV, Pampuslaan 212–214, Postbus 195, 1380 AD Weesp, Netherlands

Nine Pines Publishing, 5536 Ann Street, PO Box 545, Manotick, Ontario, Canada K4M 1A5

Libreria Taghlim Nisrani, Centru Kateketiku Salesjan, 19 Triq Alexandra, Sliema, Malta

Nobel Tip Kitabevlei, Millet Cad No. 119, Capa, Istanbul, Turkey

Nodeservice A/S, Parupvej 44, 3230 Græsted, Denmark

Nolwazi Educational Publishers Pty Ltd, 7th Floor, Goldenhuys Building, 33 Jorissen Street, Braamfontein, 2017 South Africa

A. S. Noordeen, PO Box 10066, 50704 Kuala Lumpur, Malaysia

Jan Norbye, Jomsborgvej 22, 3650 Ølstykke, Denmark

Diffusion Nord-Sud, 150 rue Berthelot, 1190 Brussels, Belgium

Nordis, Stabu Str, IV-1001 Riga, Latvia

Norsk Psykologforening, Storgaten 10A, 0155 Oslo, Norway

North Kildonan Publications, Box 28006, 1453 Henderson Highway, Winnipeg, Manitoba, Canada R2G 4E9

Northwestern University Press, 625 Colfax Street, Evanston, IL 60208-4210, USA

Novalis, 49 Front Street East, 2nd Floor, Toronto, Ont, Canada M5E 2B3

Novelty Books International bv, PO Box 157, 1380 AD Weesp, Netherlands

Novelty Trading Co Ltd, PO Box 80, 53 Hanover Street, Kingston, Jamaica

NPK Technology Services Ltd, PO Box 10117, Tel Aviv 81100, Israel

NQL International, 78 Boulevard St Michel, 75280 Paris Cedex 06, France

Nueva Agencia Literaria Int, Maldonadas 9, 2º Dcha, 28005 Madrid, Spain

Nueva Editorial Interamericana SA de CV, Cedro 512, Apartado 26370, Mexico 06450 DF, Mexico

NZCER, Education House, 178 Willis Street, Wellington C1, New Zealand

NZM Verlag, Bethlehemweg, 6405 Immensee, Switzerland

Oak Tree Technologies, PO Box 5895, Rivonia, 2128, Johannesburg, South Africa

Oakdale Trading Ltd, Deep Creek, Paton Road, Mangaroa, Upper Hutt, New Zealand

Obi-Wan Kenobi Inc (OBK), T's Building, 3rd Floor, 1-38-11 Matsubara, Setagaya-ku, Tokyo, 156 Japan

Michael O'Brien, Library Supplier, 14 Beechlawn, Dundrum, Dublin 16, Irish Republic

Occupational & Medical Suppliers, PO Box 3393, Halfway House, Johannesburg, 1685 South Africa

Editions de l'Ocean Indien Ltd, Stanley, Rose Hill, Mauritius

Octopus Publishing Group, Shin Nichibo Building, Sarugaku-Cho 1-2-1, Chiyoda-ku, Tokyo, 101 Japan

Octopus Publishing Group Australia Pty Ltd, 22 Salmon Street, Port Melbourne, Vic, Australia 3207

Odusote Bookstores Ltd, 68 Lagos By-Pass, PO Box 244, Ibadan, Nigeria

Office for Official Publications of the European Community, 2 rue Mercier, Luxembourg

Ohi Shoten, Sun Square 403, 1-34-1 Miya-machi, Fuchu-shi, Tokyo, 183 Japan

Ohio University Press, Scott Quadrangle, Athens, OH 45701, USA

Guidance Centre OISE, 712 Gordon Baker Road, Toronto, Ont, Canada M2H 3R7

A/S Okonomisk Literatur, Sogsveien 70, 0855 Oslo 8, Norway

Oldcastle Books Ltd, 18 Coleswood Road, Harpenden, Herts AL5 1EQ, UK

OLF SA, Z.1.3 Corminboeuf, C.P. 1061, 1701 Fribourg, Switzerland

Olga Musik, Boeletvej 4, 8680 Ry, Denmark

Olivetti/Acorn Canada, 3190 Steeles Avenue East, Markham, Ont, Canada L3R 2G9

OM Book Service, 1690 First Floor, Nai Sarak, Delhi, India 110 006

Donald O'Mahoney, 22 Castleknock Pines, Castleknock, Co Dublin, Irish Republic

O'Mahony & Co Ltd, 120 O'Connell Street, Limerick, Irish Republic

Omega Distributors Ltd, 69 Great South Road, Remuera, Auckland, New Zealand & PO Box 2 6-222, Epsom, Auckland 3, New Zealand & PO Box 26-222, Epsom, Auckland, New Zealand

Omiros Avramides Literary Agency, 1 Kritis Street, 190 03 Markopoulo, Greece

Omnibus Bookshop, Poznan, Poland

One World Books, PO Box 68-419, Auckland 1, New Zealand

Ton Onosaka, Yamatoya Building, 3-5-2 Kayaba-cho, Nihonbashi, Chuo-ku, Tokyo, 103 Japan

Onslow Books Ltd, Tyler's Court, 111A Wardour Street, London W1V 3TD, UK

Ontario Institute for Studies in Education, 252 Bloor Street West, Toronto, Ont, Canada M5S 1V6

Open Learning Agency, 4355 Mathissi Place, Burnaby, BC, Canada V5G 4S8

Open University Educational Enterprises Ltd, 12 Cofferidge Close, Stony Stratford, Milton Keynes MK11 1BY, UK

Openbook Publishers, 205 Halifax Street, Adelaide, SA, Australia 5000 & GPO Box 1368, Adelaide, SA, Australia 5001

OPG New Zealand Ltd, 39 Rawene Road, (Private Bag), Birkenhead, Auckland 10, New Zealand

Ordabokautgafan, Bergstadstraeti 7, PO Box 124, 121 Reykjavik, Iceland

Orfeus, Skæring Skolevej 202, 8250 Egå, Denmark

Organizzazioni Speciali, Via Scipioni Ammirato 37, 50136 Florence, Italy

Orient Longman Ltd, 3-6-272 Himayatnagar, Hyderabad, India 500 029

Oriental Publications, 16 Market Street, Adelaide, SA, Australia 5000

The Orion Publishing Group Ltd, Orion House, 5 Upper St Martin's Lane, London WC2H 9EA, UK

OSEC, Stampfenbachstrasse 85, 8035 Zurich, Switzerland

Jim Osgerby, The Studio, Pondcroft, Reading Road, Yateley, Camberley, Surrey GU17 7UR, UK

Oshiapem Publishing Services Ltd, PO Box 5891, Accra, Ghana

A. Ott-Attafua & Co Ltd, Mission Ext Extension (off Cantonments Road), House/F686612, OSURE, PO Box2692, Accra, Ghana

OUP GmbH, Max-Planck-Strasse 35, W-50858 Cologne, Germany

Overseas Missionary Fellowship, PO Box 2217, Manila, Philippines

Rhian Owen International Manager, 2/F Cornwall House, Taikoo Place, 979 King's Road, Quarry Bay, Hong Kong, Hong Kong

Richard C. Owen Publishers Inc, Box 585, Katonah, NY 10536, USA

Oxford University Press, 253 Normanby Road, South Melbourne, Vic, Australia 3205

Oxford University Press, 70 Wynford Drive, Don Mills, Ont, Canada M3C 1J9

Oxford University Press, 18th Floor, Warwick House East, Taikoo Place, 979 King's Road, Hong Kong, Hong Kong

Oxford University Press, ABC Place, Waiyaki Way, Westlands, Nairobi, Kenya

Oxford University Press, PO Box 11-149, Ellerslie, Auckland 5, New Zealand

Oxford University Press, No. 7, 99 West, Shalimar Plaza, F-7 Blue Area, Islamabad, Pakistan

Oxford University Press, 5 Bangalore Town, Block 7 & 8, Sharae Faisal, PO Box 13033, Karachi, 75350, Pakistan

Oxford University Press, (Head Office) PO Box 1141, Capetown, 8000 South Africa

Oxford University Press, 9F-8, No 79 Roosevelt Road, Section 2, Taipei, Taiwan

Oxford University Press, Walton Street, Oxford OX2 6DP, UK

Oxford University Press, 2001 Evans Road, Cary, NC 27513, USA

Oxford University Press, 198 Madison Avenue, New York, NY 10016, USA

Oxford University Press, Academic Division, Walton Street, Oxford OX2 6DP, UK

Oxford University Press Distribution Services, Saxon Way West, Corby, Northants NN18 9ES, UK

Oxford University Press East & Central Africa Branch, Maktaba Street, PO Box 5299, Dar es Salaam, Tanzania

Oxford University Press España, Parque Empresarial San Fernando, Edificio E, Esc B Planta 2º,San Fernando de Henares, 28831 Madrid, Spain

Oxford University Press Indian Branch, (Head Office) YMCA Library Building, 1st Floor, Jai Singh Road, PO Box 43,New Delhi, India 110 001; Oxford House, Apollo Bunder, PO Box 31, Bombay 400 039;5 Lala Laipat Rai Sarani (3rd Floor), Calcutta, India 700 020 & 2/11 Ansari Road, Daryaganj, PO Box 7035, New Delhi 110 002;Oxford House, Anna Salai, PO Box 1079, Madras, India 600 006

Oxford University Press KK, 2-4-8 Kanamecho, Toshima-ku, Tokyo, 171 Japan

Oxford University Press Pte Ltd, 37 Jalan Pemimpin, 03-03 Union Industrial Building, Singapore 2057

Oxford University Press Southern African Branch, (Head Office) PO Box 1141, Cape Town, 8000;PO Box 5799, Pietersburg, North Transvaal 0750 South Africa; PO Box 327, Umtata, Transkei;310 Perm Building, 13–17 Crompton Street, Pinetown, 3600 South Africa & Suite 206, Willowbrook, Willowbrook Close, off Atholl Oaklands Road, MelroseNorth, 2196 South Africa

OXPOL/OUP Office, ul. Traugutta 21/23, Room 1012, 90-950 Lodz, Poland

Oxted Resources Ltd, PO Box 38907, Wellington Mail Centre, New Zealand

PACES, 1/4 Rimpa Skyline, Shahrah-e-Faisal, Karachi, Pakistan

Pacific Press, PO Box 777, Mount Waverley, Vic, Australia 3149

Mrs Dense Padayachee, PO Box 19043, Dormerton, 4015 South Africa

Penny Padovani, N. A. La Chiesa 9, 52040 Montanare di Cortona (AR), Italy

Penny Padovani, 56 Rosebank, Holyport Road, Fulham, London SW6 6LH, UK

Charles Paine Pty Ltd, 8 Ferris Street, North Paramatta, NSW, Australia 2151

Pak American Commercial Inc, PO Box 7359, Karachi 0301, Pakistan

Pak Book Corporation, Aziz Chambers, 21 Queen's Road, Lahore 54000, Pakistan

Pakistan Law House, Pakistan Chowk, GPO Box 90, Karachi 1, Pakistan

Eric Paludan, Fiolstraede 10, 11721 Copenhagen K, Denmark

Pan Africa Book Service (U), PO Box 14197, Kampala, Uganda

Pan Africa Book Services, PO Box 96131, Likoni, via Mombasa, Kenya

Pan Asia Publications Sdn Bhd, 25 Jalan SS26/6, Taman Mayang Jaya, 47301 Petaling Jaya, Selangor, Darul Ehsan, Malaysia

Pan Books (New Zealand) Ltd, PO Box 36-343, Northcote, Auckland, New Zealand

Pan Korea Book Corporation, 1-222, 2-Ga, Shinman-Ro, Chongno-ku, Seoul, Korea

Pan Macmillan, 2nd Floor North Block, Hyde Park Corner, Cnr Jan Smuts Avenue 1st Road,2196 Hyde Park, Johannesburg, South Africa

Pan Macmillan Australia Ltd, 63–71 Balfour Street, Chippendale, PO Box 124, Sydney, NSW, Australia 2008

Pan Macmillan Books (Australia) Pty Ltd, Level 18, St Martins Tower, 31 Market Street, Sydney, NSW, Australia 2000

Pan Macmillan New Zealand Ltd, 6 Ride Way, North Harbour Industrial Estate, Albany, Auckland, New Zealand

Panmun Book Co Ltd, PO Box 1016, Seoul, Korea

Pansing Distribution Sdn Bhd, 8 New Industrial Road, Singapore 536200

Papyrus Book Agency, Rue de l'Aqueduc 102, 1050 Brussels, Belgium

PAR Inc, PO Box 998, Odessa, FL 33556, USA

Parallel Publishing Services Ltd, Lanston House, 13 Commercial Road, Eastbourne, East Sussex BN21 3XE, UK

Paramount Books (Pvt) Ltd, 152/0 Block 2, Pechs 75400, Karachi 29, Pakistan

Parkwest Publications Inc, 451 Communipaw Avenue, Jersey City, NJ 07304, USA

Ajay Parmar, Research Press, Post Box 7208, 212A Vardaan House, 7/28 Ansari Road, New Delhi 110 002, India

Parry's Book Centre Sdn Bhd, PO Box 10960, 60 Jalan Negara, Taman Helawati, 53100 Kuala Lumpur, Malaysia

Passport Books a division of NTC Contemporary Publishing, 4255 West Touhy Avenue, Lincolnwood, IL 60646-1975, USA

Password, 23 New Mount Street, Manchester M4 4DE, UK

Pathfinder, 4581 rue St-Denis, Montreal, Quebec, H2J 2L4, Canada

Pathfinder, PO Box 233, 121 Reykjavik, Iceland

Pathfinder, PO Box 8730, Auckland, New Zealand

Pathfinder, Vikingagatan 10, 113 42 Stockholm, Sweden

Pathfinder Press, PO Box K879, Haymarket, NSW, Australia 2000

Pathfinder Press, 410 West Street, New York, NY 10014, USA

Paul & Co Publishers Consortium Inc, c/o PCS Data Processing Inc., 360 West 31st Street, New York, NY 10001, USA & PO Box 442, Concord, MA 01742, USA

Paul & Elizabeth Book Services Pte Ltd, 163 Tanglin Road No. 03-15/16, Tanglin Mall, Singapore 1024

Peace Book Co Ltd, Rm 1502 Wing On House, 71 Des Voeux Road, Central, Hong Kong

Peaceful Living Publications, PO Box 300, Tauranga, New Zealand

David Pearson, 1 Brownfield Way, Wheathampstead, Herts AL4 8LL, UK

Pearson Professional (Australia) Pty Ltd, 95 Coventry Street, GPO Box 1337, Melbourne, Vic, Australia 3205

Pearson Professional (Hong Kong) Ltd, Suite 1808, Asian House, 1 Hennessy Road, Wan Chai, Hong Kong

Pearson Professional Ltd, Maple House, 149 Tottenham Court Road, London W1P 9LL, UK

Pearson Professional (Singapore) Pte Ltd, 133 Cecil Street, 12-01 Keck Seng Tower, Singapore 0106

Peguis Publishers, 100-318 McDermot Avenue, Winnipeg, Manitoba, Canada R3A 0A2

Pelanduk Publications (M) Sdn Bhd, 24 Jalan 20/16A, 46300 Petaling Jaya, Malaysia

Pelgrim International Boeken, Mollevite 24, 6931 KG Westervoort, Netherlands

Pelican Publishing Co, PO Box 3110, Gretna, LA 70054-3110, USA

Penerbit Fajar Bakti Sdn Bhd, PO Box 160, Jalan Kelang Lama, 58700 Kuala Lumpur, Malaysia

Penguin Books, 375 Hudson Street, New York, NY 10014, USA

Penguin Books Australia Ltd, PO Box 257, 487 Maroondah Highway, Ringwood, Vic, Australia 3134

Penguin Books Canada Ltd, 10 Alcorn Avenue, Suite 300, Toronto, Ont, Canada M4V 3B2 & c/o Canbook Distribution Services, 1220 Nicholson Road, Newmarket, L3V 7V1, Canada

Penguin Books Deutschland GmbH, Metzlerstrasse 26, 60595 Frankfurt am Main, Germany

Penguin Books India Pvt Ltd, 706 Eros Apartments, 56 Nehru Place, New Delhi, India 110019

Penguin Books Japan, Ishikiribashi Building, 2-5-4 Suido, Bunkyo-ku, Tokyo, 112 Japan

Penguin Books Ltd, 17 rue Lejeune, 31000 Toulouse, France

Penguin Books Ltd, c/o Longman Asia, 2nd Floor, Cornwall House, Taikoo Place, 979 King's Road, Quarry Bay, Hong Kong

Penguin Books Ltd, 27 Wrights Lane, London W8 5TZ, UK

Penguin Books Netherlands bv, Keizergracht 231, 1016 DV Amsterdam, Netherlands

Penguin Books (New Zealand) Ltd, Private Bag 102902, North Shore Mail Centre, Auckland 10, New Zealand

Penguin Books SA, Bravo Murillo, 19-1B, 28015 Madrid, Spain

Penguin Export Sales Dept, 27 Wrights Lane, London W8 5TZ, UK

Penguin France SA, 17 rue Lejeune, 3100 Toulouse, France

Penguin Hellas Ltd, Dimocritou 3, 106 71 Athens, Greece

Penguin Italia Srl, Via Felice Casati 20, 20124 Milan, Italy

Penguin Turkey, Sezai Selek Sokak 10/2, Nisantas, Istanbul, Turkey

PennWell Books, 1421 South Sheridan, PO Box 1260, Tulsa, OK 74101, USA

Pentland Press Inc, 5124 Bur Oak Circle, Raleigh, NC 27612, USA

Pergamon Bookhouse, 16 King Paul Street, PO Box 5062, Nicosia, Cyprus

Peribo Pty Ltd, 26 Tepko Road, Terrey Hills, NSW, Australia 2084 & 58 Beaumont Road, Mount Kuring-gai, NSW, Australia 2080

Hans Heinrich Petersen Buchimport GmbH, Rugenbarg 256, 22549 Hamburg, Germany

Peterson's Guides, 202 Carnegie Center, Princeton, NJ 08543, USA

Phambili Agencies (Jean Knopperson), PO Box 28680, Kensington, 2101 South Africa

Pharmaceutical Society of Australia, Pharmaceutical House, PO Box 21, Curtin, ACT,, Australia 2605

Pharmaceutical Society of New Zealand, Pharmacy House, 124 Dixon Street, PO Box 11640, Wellington 1, New Zealand

Phila Services, Burgstrasse 160, 4125 Riehen, Switzerland

David Philip Publishers Pty Ltd, PO Box 23408, Claremont, CP 7735 South Africa

Philippean Futuristic Society, Manila, Philippines

Phoenix Players Ltd, PO Box 52383, Nairobi, Kenya

Phoenix Studio, Derkovics u. 26, 1183 Budapest, Hungary

PIC, Second Newfield Building, 42-43 Ohtsuka 3-chome, Bunkyo-ku, Tokyo, 112 Japan

PIC Publishers, 25 Tverskoy Bulvar, 103104 Moscow, Russia

Pilot Publishers Services Ltd, Ground Floor, 86 To Kwa Wan Road, Kowloon, Hong Kong

PIM (Publishers International Management), 16 Salisbury Road, PO Box 356, Sheffield, MA 01257, USA

Pincushion Enterprises Inc, 5245 Baywater Drive, Tampa, FL, USA

Pippin Publishing, 380 Esna Park Drive, Markham, Ont, Canada L3R 1H5

Sophie Piquemal, c/o Penguin Books Ltd, 27 Wrights Lane, London W8 5TZ, UK

Pitraban, 2nd Floor, Supermarket Complex, Reclamation Road, Colombo 11, Sri Lanka

PKB, Casella Postale 196, 6900 Massagno, Switzerland

Platypus Förlag, Inspektörsgatan 4, 25227 Helsingborg, Sweden

Play Bureau of New Zealand Ltd, PO Box 420, New Plymouth, New Zealand

Play & Schoolroom Pty, PO Box 47288, Parklands, 2121 South Africa

Playing & Learning, Branta Backen 7, 182 355 Danderyd, Sweden

Playmarket, PO Box 9767, Courtenay Place, Wellington, New Zealand

PKB – Robbert J. Pleysier, Looierspad 8, 8181 KH Heerde, Netherlands

Reinier A. Pleysier, Kerkdijk 21, PO Box 166, 8180 AD Heerde GLD, Netherlands

Pliroforiki Technognosia, 11B Konitsis Str, 15125 Maroussi, Athens, Greece

P & M Studyaids Centre, PO Box 80, Thompson Road PO, 9157 Singapore

PMC International Importers & Exporters CC, PO Box 201520, Durban North, Kwa-Zulu Natal, 4016 South Africa

PMS Books Pte Ltd, 10-C Jalan Ampas 07-01, Ho Seng Lee Flatted Warehouse, Singapore 1232

PMS Marketing Services, 28A Jalan 5521/58, Damensana Utama, 47400 Petaling Jaya, Selangor, Malaysia

PMS Publishers Marketing Services Pte Ltd, 10-C Jalan Ampas, 07-01 Ho Seng Lee Flatted Warehouse, Singapore 329513

Po-on Stamp Service, PO Box 2498, Hong Kong

The Point of Law, Sydney, Australia

F. Porretta Agency, Paris, France

Joe Portelli, Bookport Associates, Casella Postale, 40040 Vado, BO Bologna, Italy

Ove B. Poulsen, Books for Europe, Hegnet 13, 2600 Glostrup, Denmark

Graham Powell, Books for Europe, PO Box 531, Bournemouth, Dorset BH1 1YA, UK

Preca Library, Societas Doctrinae Christianae, M.U.S.E.U.M., Blata L-Bajda, Malta

Prentice Hall Regents of Japan, Nishi-Shinjuku KF Building 602, 8-14-24, Nishi-Shinjuku, Shinjuku-ku, Tokyo, 160 Japan

Pres Dagitim Ticaret ve sanayi AS, Narlibahçe Sokak No 15, Cağaloğlu, Istanbul, Turkey

Presbyterian & Reformed Publishing Co, PO Box 817, Philipsburg, NJ 08865, USA

Les Presses de Belgique, Boulevard de l'Europe 117, 1301 Wavre, Belgium

PRG, Rockport, MD, USA

Prime Editions, 215 Jalan USJ 12/1, 47630 Subang Jaya, Malaysia & PO Box 316, Jalan Sultan, 46730 Petaling Jaya, Selangor D.E., Malaysia

Princeton Book Co, PO Box 57, Princeton, NJ 08540, USA

Editions Le Printemps, 4 Club Road, Vacaos, Ile Maurice, Mauritius

Privredni Vjesnik, Bulevar Lenjina 171/XIV, 11070 Belgrade, Yugoslavia

PRO-ED Australia, PO Box 3161, Nerang, Qd, Australia 4211

Productivity Corp Ltd, 33/7 Sol Prompong, Sukhumvit Road, Klongton Klongtoey, Bangkok 10110, Thailand

Professional Resources Services, PO Box 71, Coldstream, Vic, Australia 3770

Progress Press Co Ltd, Strickland House, 341 St Paul Street, Valletta, Malta

Diffusion Prologue, 1650 Boulevard Lionel-Bertrand, Boisbriand, Quebec, Canada J1E 4H4

Propaganda Distributors, PO Box 582, Auckland, New Zealand

Protestant Book Centre, 61–65 Main Road, Mowbray, 7700, Cape Town, South Africa

Peter Prout, Iberian Book Services, Sector Islas, Bloque 12 1° B, 28760 Tres Cantos, Madrid, Spain

PS Publishers' Services, Ziegenhainer Strasse 169, 60433 Frankfurt, Germany

PSICO, Rua Luis Pastor de Macedo, Lote 29, 1700 Lisbon, Portugal

Psykologien Kustannus Oy, Kolmas Linja 12, 00530 Helsinki 53, Finland

Psykologiförlaget AB, Box 47054, 10074 Stockholm, Sweden

PT Transito Tatemedia, Gedung Pertintis, J1 Kebahaciaan 4 11, Jakarta 11140, Indonesia

Publisher Support Services Ltd, PO Box 9270, Ikeja, Lagos State, Nigeria

Publishers Group West, PO Box 8843, Emeryville, CA 94662, USA

Publishers International Corporation, 2nd Newfield Building, 42-3 Ohtsuka 3-chome, Bunkyo-ku, Tokyo, 112 Japan

Publishers Marketing Associates, PO Box 12602, Pechs, Karachi 75400, Pakistan

Publishers Marketing Services, 28A Jalan SS21/58, Damansara Utama, 47400 Petaling Jaya, Selangor, Malaysia

Publishers Marketing Services Ltd, 10-C Jalan Ampas, 07-01 Ho Seng Lee Flatted Warehouse, Singapore 329513

Publishers' Associates Ltd, 11th Floor, Warwick House East, 28 Tong Chong Street, Quarry Bay, Hong Kong

Publishers' Distribution Service, 6893 Sullivan Road, Grawn, MI 49637, USA

Publishers' Group West, PO Box 8843, Emeryville, CA 94698, USA

Publishing, Marketing & Research Associates, 79-01 35th Avenue, #5, Jackson Heights, Queens, New York, NY 11372, USA

Purpose Products, 81 Temperance Street, Aurora, Ont, Canada L4G 2R1

Pustaha Remaja, PO Box 1827, Bandar Seri Begawan 1918, Brunei Darussalam, Brunei

Pustaka Baiduri Sdn Bhd, 85 Jalan Perhentian Sentul, 51100 Kuala Lumpur, Malaysia

Q-Pac Publishing Sdn Bhd, 205 Plaza QAF, Gadong/Tutong Link Road, Bandar Seri Beganan 3188, Brunei

Quality International, 3401 McNicoll Avenue, Unit 12, Scarborough, Ont, Canada MV1 4B7

Shams Quaraeshi, 6 Krishna Mansions, Inverarity Road, Karachi 74400, Pakistan

Quest, PO Box 57W, Worthing, Christ Church, Barbados

Quest Book Agency, 1st Floor, Theosophy House, 484 Kent Street, Sydney, NSW, Australia 2000

Quintessence Editora Ltda, PO Box 801, São Paulo, Brazil

Quorum/Magnard, 129 rue Marcel Hartmann, 94400 Ivry sur Seine, France

Radcliffe Medical Press Inc, 141 Fifth Avenue, Suite N, New York, NY 10010, USA

Rae & Sons Publishers Representatives, E-187 Street 6, Cavalry Ground, Cantonment 13, Lahore, Pakistan

Ragged Bears Ltd, Ragged Appleshaw, Andover, Hants SP11 9HX, UK

Rainbow Distributors, PO Box 48, Kenilworth, 7745 South Africa

Raincoast Distribution, 8680 Cambie Street, Vancouver, BC, V6P 6M9, Canada

Rajdeep Books, 367 Hill-N-Dale Drive (North), York, PA 17403, USA

Ramakrishna Ashrama, Av. Gaspar Campos 1149, 1661 Bella Vista, Buenos Aires, Argentina

Ramakrishna Mission, Ashram Road, Post Box 716, Nadi, South Pacific, Fiji

Ramakrishna Mission, Quinze Cantons, Vacoas, Mauritius

Ramakrishna Mission, 179 Bartley Road, Singapore 1953

Ramakrishna Mission, 40 Ramakrishna Road, Colombo 6, Sri Lanka

Ramakrishna Vedanta Centre, 9 chemin des Gravannes, 1246, Corsier/ Geneva, Switzerland

Ramakrishna Vedanta Centre, Unity House, Blind Lane, Bourne End, Bucks SL8 5LG, UK

Ramakrishna Vedanta Society, 58 Deerfield Street, Boston, MA 02215, USA

Ramakrishna Vivekananda Center, 17 East 94th Street, New York, NY 10128, USA

Randhill, 4th Floor, 104 Bordeaux Drive, Bordeaux, Randburg, 2194 South Africa

Ian Randle Publishers Ltd, 206 Old Hope Road, Kingston 6, Jamaica

Random House Australia Pty Ltd, 1st Floor, 20 Alfred Street, Milsons Point, Sydney, NSW, Australia 2061

Random House Inc, 201 East 50th Street, New York, NY 10022, USA

Random House New Zealand Ltd, 18 Poland Street, Glenfield, Auckland 10, New Zealand & Private Bag, North Shore Mail Centre, Glenfield, Auckland 10, New Zealand

Random House of Canada Ltd, 1265 Aerowood Drive, Mississauga, Ont, Canada L4W 1B9

Random House South Africa Pty Ltd, PO Box 2263, Rosebank, Johannesburg, 2121 South Africa

Random House UK Ltd, Random House, 20 Vauxhall Bridge Road, London SW1V 2SA, UK

Rare Book Co, PO Box 6957, Freehold, NJ 07728, USA

Read Pacific, PO Box 21-637, Henderson, Auckland, New Zealand

Readers Digest Young Families, 355 Riverside Avenue, Westport, CT 06880, USA

Readright Educational Services, 4 Chilvers Road, Thornleigh, NSW, Australia 2120

Reaktion Books Ltd, Sales Department, 11 Rathbone Place, London W1P 1DE, UK

Redim Diffusion, Route Cantonale 116, 1025 St Sulpice, Switzerland

Reed Books Australia, 22 Salmon Street, PO Box 460, Melbourne, Vic, Australia 3207

Reed Consumer Books, PO Box 7208, 212A Vardaan House, 7/ 28 Ansari Road, New Delhi, India 110 002

Reed Consumer Books, Shin Nichibo Building, Sarugaku-Cho-1-2-1, Chiyoda-ku, Tokyo, 101 Japan

Reed Consumer Books, 57 Sta Teresita, Kapitolyo Pasig, Metro Manila, Philippines

Reed International Books, Obecni Dum PKS, Namesti Republiky 5, 11121 Prague 1, Czech Republic

Reed International Books Ltd, International Sales Department, Michelin House, 81 Fulham Road, London SW3 6RB, UK

Reed International (Singapore) Pte Ltd, 37 Jalan Pemimpin, 07-04, Block B, Union Industrial Building, Singapore 2057

Reed Publishing Canada, 75 Clegg Road, Markham, Ont, Canada L6G 1A1

Reed Publishing Group, 39 Rawene Road, Private Bag, Birkenhead, Auckland 10, New Zealand

Reed Publishing Services Asia Pte Ltd, 37 Jalan Pemimpin 07-04, Block B, Union Industrial Building, Singapore 2057

Reed Reference Publishing, 121 Chanlon Road, New Providence, NJ 07974, USA

Reference Press, Austin, TX, USA

Reformers' Bookroom, 140 Albany Road, Petersham, Sydney, NSW, Australia 2049

Rehabco, 10 Abi Emama, Dokki, Cairo Branch PO Box 1969, Egypt

Renaissance Greeting Cards Inc, 505 Main Street, Sandford, Maine 04073, USA

Renouf Publishing Co Ltd, 1294 Algoma Road, Ottawa, Ontario, Canada K1B 3W8

Rep Force Ireland, 12 Longford Terrace, Monkstown, Co Dublin, Irish Republic

Editóra Replicação, Avenida Infante Santo, 343/r/c, 1350 Lisbon, Portugal

Republic Coin & Stamps Accessories (Pty) Ltd, PO Box 11199, Johannesburg 2000 South Africa

Research Press, Post Box 7208, 212A Vardaan House, 7/ 28 Ansari Road, New Delhi, India 110 002

The Resource Centre, PO Box 190, Waterloo, Ont, Canada N2J 3Z9

Sven Uffe Reumert ApS, PO Box 1135, 1010 Copenhagen K, Denmark

Rex Map Centre, 388 Pacific Highway, Lane Cove, NSW, Australia 2066

Angela Reynolds, Pobla de Lillet 4,6, 08028 Barcelona, Spain

Ribera Libros, SL, Poligono Martiartu, Calle 1 – no 6, 48480 Arrigorriaga, Vizcaya, Spain

Richford Enterprises Pty, PO Box 4922, Durban, 4000 South Africa

Rigby, 450 Congress Parkway, Crystal Lake, IL 60014, USA

Rigby-Heinemann (Australia) Ltd, 22 Salmon Street, Port Melbourne, Vic, Australia 3207

RIK Services Ltd, 104 High Street, San Fernando, Trinidad

Rittenhouse Book Distributors Inc, 511 Feheley Drive, King of Prussia, PA 19406, USA

River Books, 396 Maharaj Road, Ta, Tien, Bangkok 10200, Thailand

The River Press, 17 St Peters Road, St Margarets, Twickenham, Middx TW1 1QY, UK

Riverrun Press Inc, 1170 Broadway, New York, NY 10001, USA

Riverwood Publishers Ltd, 471 Eagle Street, Newmarket, Ont, Canada L3Y 1K4

RKR Musical, Rua Apamas 44, 04084 Sao Paulo, Brazil

Terry Roberts, Caixa Postal 801-0, Ag. Jardim da Gloria, 06700-470 Cotia SP, Brazil

Robery Pryor, Rondo Da Segovia 45, 30, 28005 Madrid, Spain

Anselm Robinson, European Marketing Services, 55 Mendora Road, Fulham, London SW6 7ND, UK

Rock Records & Tapes, Kwang Fu S. Road, Lane 290 5/Floor (No. 3), Taipei ROC, Taiwan

Adele Rogers, Datum Book Marketing, 27 Chessington Mansions, Colworth Road, Leytonstone,London E11 1HZ, UK

Roli Books, M75 GKII Market, New Delhi, India 110 048

Charles Rollings, 6 Kikar Malchei Israel, Entrance B, Tel Aviv 64951, Israel

ROM Soft, Nikkelstraat 7, 2984 AM Ridderkerk, Netherlands

Michael Romano, Red Barn Booksellers, 481 Peruville Road, Groton, NY 13073, USA

George Ronald Books, PO Box 447, St Louis,MO 63166, USA

Rorash Educational Publishers, Office Suite 6, Jinja Road, Plot 28, PO Box 7642, Kampala, Uganda

Rorash Enterprises, PO Box 4329, 45 Junja Road, Kampala, Uganda

Rose Cottage, 1470 Greenmeadows Road, Yardley, PA 19067, USA

Norman Ross Publishing Inc, 330 West 58th Street, New York, NY 10019, USA

Fred B. Rothman & Co, 10368 West Centennial Road, Littleton, CO 80123, USA

Hanne Rotovnik, PO Box 5, Strandvejen 685 B, 2930 Klampenborg, Denmark

Roundhouse Publishing Ltd, PO Box 140, Oxford OX2 7FF, UK

Routledge, 11 New Fetter Lane, London EC4P 4EE, UK

Routledge Inc, 29 West 35th Street, New York, NY 10001-2291, USA

Rouven Ziv, 16 Pinsker Street, Holon 58411, Israel

R.O.Y. International, POB 13056, 17 Shimon Hatarassi Street, Tel Aviv 61130, Israel

Royal Garden, 79 avenue Aristolde Briand, 94118 Arcueil Cedex, France

Royal Society of Medicine Foundation Inc, 150 East 58th Street, New York, NY 10155, USA

Royal Trading Agency, PO Box 313, Valletta, Malta

Roykore Inc, 2215 Filbert Street, San Francisco, CA 94123-3414, USA

RPM Record Co, 1 Hood Avenue, Rosebank, PO Box 2807, Johannesburg, South Africa

Anthony Rudkin Associates, PO Box 15, 51 Cornmarket Street, Oxford OX1 3EB, UK

Anthony Rudkin Iran, PO Box 15115-133, Tehran, Iran

Verlag An der Ruhr, Postfach 10 22 51, 45422 Mulheim An der Ruhr, Germany

Liam Ruiseal Teo, The Fountain Bookshop, 49–50 Oliver Plunkett Street,Cork, Irish Republic

Arie Ruitenbeek, Calle Moreira 6, 28005 Madrid, Spain

Rupa & Co Ltd, 7/16 Makhanlal Street, Ansari Road, Daryaganj, New Delhi, India 110 002

Russell Friedman Information Services (Pty) Ltd, PO Box 73, Halfway House, Cape Town, 1685 South Africa

Ruurd Ruward, Ruward BV, Spui 231, 2511 BP The Hague, Netherlands

Ryen, Re Associates, 585 Seminole Street, Oradell, NJ 07649, USA

Emir Sader, Estrade da Bavea 827, Apt 1001–22610, Sao Contrado, Rio de Janeiro, Brazil

Saga Books ApS, 6 Siljangade, 4th Floor, 2300 Copenhagen S, Denmark & Mellemvang 17, Box 166, 2970 Hørsholm, Denmark

Sage Publications Inc, 2455 Teller Road, Thousand Oaks, CA 91320, USA

Sage Publications Ltd, 6 Bonhill Street, London EC2A 4PU, UK

I. J. Sagun Enterprises Inc, PO Box 4322, C.P.O. Manila 1099, 2 Topaz Road, Green Heights Village, Tatay,Rizal 1901, Philippines

George Sainsbury, Auldearn, Main Street, Bleasby, Notts NG14 7GH, UK

Sall Data, Borgergade 44, 8450 Hammel, Denmark

Sälta, Humlegardsgatan 8, 41224 Göteborg, Sweden

Salvation Book Centre, 23 Jalan SS2/64, 47300 Petaling Jaya, Selangor, Malaysia

San Paolo Multimedia, Via del Mascherino 94, 00193 Rome, Italy

Sandberry Press, 391 Bartlett Avenue, Toronto, Ont, Canada M6H 3G8

Sangam Books Ltd, 57 London Fruit Exchange, Brushfield Street, London E1 6EP, UK

Sangster's Book Stores Ltd, 101 Water Lane, Kingston, Jamaica

Sansoni Warehouse Ltd, 14 Anderson Road, Colombo 5, Sri Lanka

W. B. Saunders, The Curtis Center, Independence Square West, Philadelphia, PA 19106, USA

W. B. Saunders Co Ltd, 30–52 Smidmore Street, Marrickville, NSW, Australia 2204

Saunders Book Co, 199 Campbell Street, Box 308, Collingwood, Ont, Canada L9Y 3Z7

W. B. Saunders Canada Ltd, 55 Horner Avenue, Toronto, Ont, Canada N8Z 4XG

The Saunders Group, 21 Jetview Drive, Rochester, NY 14624-4996, USA

K. G. Saur Verlag, Ortlerstrasse 8, W-81373 Munich 70, Germany

Savani's Book Centre, PO Box 42157, Nairobi, Kenya

Librairie Sayegh, Salhie Street, PO Box 704, Damascus, Syria

S & B Large Print & Special Lines Ltd, 4132 Dundas Street West, Toronto, Ont, Canada M8X 1X3

Scandinavian University Press SA, PO Box 2959, Toyen, Oslo, Norway

Scanvik Books APS, Esplanaden 8B, 1263 Copenhagen K, Denmark

F. K. Schattauer, Lenzhalde 3, W-70192 Stuttgart, Germany

Thomas Schlück, Literarische Agentur, Hinter der Worth 12, 30827 Garbsen, Germany

Claus Schmögner, Albert-Mays-Straße 2, 6900 Heidelberg 1, Germany

Scholarly Book Services Inc, Suite 403, 77 Mowat Avenue, Toronto, Ont, Canada M6K 3E3

Scholarly Publications, 2825 Wilcrest Drive, Suite 255, Houston, TX 77042, USA

Scholastic Australia Ltd, PO Box 579, Gosford, NSW, Australia 2250

Scholastic Canada Ltd, 123 Newkirk Road, Richmond Hill, Ont, Canada L4C 3G5

Scholastic Inc, 730 Broadway, New York, NY 10003, USA

Scholastic Publications, Villiers House,Clarendon Avenue, Leamington Spa, Warwickshire CV32 5PR, UK

Schools Promotion Services, 34 Old Hope Road, Kingston 5, Jamaica

Schultz EF-publikationer, Møntergade 19, 1116 Copenhagen K, Denmark

Schuyt & Co bv, Gedempte oude Gracht 35, 2003 RN Haarlem, Netherlands

Arthur Schwartz & Co, 234 Meads Mountain Road, Woodstock, NY 12498, USA

Science Publishers Inc, 10 Water Street, Suite 310, Lebanon, NH 03766, USA

SCM Press, 9–17 St Albans Place, London N1 0NX, UK

Scriptum Books, Postbus 293, 3100 AG Schiedan, Netherlands

Scripture Union, PO Box 77, Lidcombe, NSW, Australia 2141

Scripture Union, 1885 Clements Road, Unit 226, Pickering, Ont, Canada L1W 3V4

Scripture Union, Box 4011, U. I. Ibadan, Oyo State, Nigeria

Scripture Union, PO Box 21689, Kitwe, Zambia

Scripture Union, PO Box 8467, Causeway, Harare, Zimbabwe

Scripture Union Publishing, 7000 Ludlow Street, Upper Darby, PA 19082, USA

Scripture Union Publishing Agency, 83 Camp Ground Road, Rondebosch, 7700 South Africa

Scripture Union Wholesale, PO Box 760, 9A Oxford Terrace, New Town, Wellington, New Zealand

Seafarer Books, Merlin Press, 10 Maldon Road, London NW5 3HR, UK

Derek Searle Associates Ltd, The Coach House, Cippenham Lodge, Cippenham Lane, Slough, Berks SL1 5AN, UK

Secrian Srl, Via Pantelleria 2, 20156, Milan, Italy

Sedco Publishing Ltd, PO Box 2051, Accra, Ghana

See Sharp Press, PO Box 6118, San Francisco, CA 94101, USA

Sefer Ve Sefel, 2 Yavetz Street, Jerusalem 94232, Israel
Segment Book Distributors, B-23/25, Kailash Colony, New Delhi, India 110 019
Segroo Publishers Ltd, 324-16, Sadang 3 – dong, Dongjak-ku, Seoul, Korea
Select Books Pte Ltd, 19 Tanglin Road 03-15 Tanglin Shopping Centre, Singapore 1024
Selectbook Service Syndicate, Shiel Sadan, E-10 Kailash Colony, New Delhi, India 110 048
Señores, Apartado Aéreo 76350, Bogota, Colombia
Señores, Casilla 659, Lima 18, Peru
R. Seshadri, 32 II Main Road, CIT East, Madras, India 600 035
Editions du Seuil, 27 rue Jacob, 75261 Paris Cedex 06, France
Seven Hills Book Distributors, 49 Central Avenue, Suite 300, Cincinnati, OH 45202, USA
Severn House Publishers Inc, 595 Madison Avenue, 15th Floor, New York, NY 10022, USA
Sezai, Selek Sokak 10/2, Nisantas, Istanbul, Turkey
H. R. & L. Shapiro, PO Box 2103, Cape Town, 8000 South Africa
Harold Shaw Publishers, Box 567, Wheaton, IL 60189, USA
Karamat Sheikh, Al-Baldani Trading Est, PO Box 1094, Safat, Kuwait
Sheridan House Inc, 145 Palisade Street, Dobbs Ferry, NY 10522, USA
Shin Ya Ltd, 3rd Floor 103 Section 2, Chung Shan North Road, Taipei, Taiwan
Shinada & Co Inc, 5-9-15 (Kyodo Building), Minani-Aoyana, Minato-ku, Tokyo, 107 Japan
Shinwon Datanet Inc, 2F Shinwon Building, 571-4 Yeonnam-Dong Maypo-Gu, Seoul, 121-240, Korea
Mrs C. Shirley, c/o Ragged Bears Ltd, Ragged Appleshaw, Andover, Hants SP11 9HX, UK
SHS Publishers' Consultants and Representatives, Heinrich-Roller-Strasse 21, 10405 Berlin, Germany
Shuter & Shooter Pty Ltd, 230 Church Street, PO Box 109, Pietermaritzburg, 3200 South Africa
Editions Anne Sigier – France, 28 rue de la Malterie, BP 3007, 59703 Marq-en-Baroeul, France
SIL (Academic Publications Dept), 7500 West Camp Wisdom Road, Dallas, TX 75236-5628, USA
Ira Silverberg, 180 Varick Street, 10th Floor, New York, NY 10014, USA
Simon & Schuster (Asia) Pte Ltd, 24 Pasir Panjang Road, 04-31 Psa Multi-Storey Complex, Singapore 0511
Simon & Schuster Australia, 20 Barcoo Street, PO Box 507, East Roseville, NSW, Australia 2069
Simon & Schuster Paramount Publishing, 1230 Avenue of the Americas, New York, NY 10020, USA
Singular Publishing Group Inc, 4284 41st Street, San Diego, CA 92105, USA
Josef Otto Slezak, Wiedner Hauptstrasse 42, 1040 Vienna, Austria
Slovak Ventures spol sro, Stefanikova 128, 94901 Nitra, Slovakia
Slovart Music, Jakubovo Nam 12, 81531 Bratislava, Slovakia
Small Press Distribution Inc, 1814 San Pablo Avenue, Berkeley, CA 94702, USA
Smart Kids Pte Ltd, 03-29 Centrepoint, 176 Orchard Road, Singapore 0923
Dudley Smith, The Gables, Dunboyne, Co Meath, Irish Republic
Nicholas Smith, 141 5th Avenue, 8N, New York, NY 10010, USA
Roger Smith, 38 Chase Green, Enfield EN2 8EB, UK
W. H. Smith, 71 boulevard Adolphe Max, Brussels, Belgium
WH Smith The English Bookshop, 248 rue de Rivoli, 75001 Paris, France
Marty Smolar, c/o JAI Press Inc, 55 Old Post Road No 2, PO Box 1678, Greenwich, CT 06836-1678, USA
Marietta Snell, Reigerskamp 228, 3607 HM Maarssenbroek, Netherlands
Sochepresse, Angles Rues Rahal Ben Ahmed & St Saens, 21700 Casablanca, Morocco
Chr Winther Soerensen AB, Box 43, 310 Knaered, Sweden
Soluciones, c/ Iriarte 43, Puerto de la Cruz, 38400 Tenerife, Canary Islands, Spain
Soma Books, 38 Kennington Lane, London SE11 4LS, UK
Sonart, Unit 6/14 Roseberry Street, Balgowlah, NSW, Australia 2095
Soumen World Vision, Kalevankatu 14 C13, 001 00 Helsinki, Finland
Source Books, PO Box 794, Trabuco Canyon, CA 92678, USA
South American Way, Avda Apoquinda 6856, Las Condes, Santiago, Chile
South Asia Books, PO Box 502, Columbia, MO 65205, USA

South Pacific Books (Imports) Ltd, 6 King Street, Grey Lynn, Auckland 2, New Zealand & PO Box 68097, Newton, Auckland, New Zealand
South Western Publishing Co, 5701 Madison Road, Cincinnati, OH 45227, USA
Southern Book Publishers, PO Box 3103, Halfway House, 1685 South Africa; 136 Rinaldo Road, Glenhills, 4051 Durban, South Africa & Africa Book Centre Wholesalers (Pty) Ltd, PO Box 15302, Hurlyvale, 1611 South Africa
Southern Books, 240 Old Pretoria Road, Midrand, South Africa
Southern Cross Educational, 348 Orrong Road, PO Box 161, Caulfield, Victoria, Australia 3162
Southern Scene (Pty) Ltd, 47–49 Kingsway, Kingsgrove, NSW, Australia 2208
Sovaminco, 11/4 Gertsen Str. Building 2, Moscow 103009, Russia
Sovereign Grace Book Ministry, RR No 3, Oromocto, NB, Canada E2V 2G3
Sovereign Grace Books, PO Box 62-159, Sylvia Park, Auckland 6, New Zealand
Spantech & Lancer, Spantech House, Lagham Road, South Godstone, Surrey RH9 8MB, UK
Spantech & Lancer, 3986 Ernst Road, Hartford, WI 53027, USA
Special Education Service, National Office, Vogel House, Wellington, New Zealand
Specialist Marketing International, PO Box 960, Herndon, VA 22070, USA
Specialist Publications, 1–5 Edwin Street, Mortlake, NSW, Australia 2137
Specialty Book Marketing, 443 Park Avenue South, Suite 801, New York, NY 10016, USA
Specialty Press, 11481 Kost Dam Road, North Branch, MN 55056, USA
Spectrum Books Ltd, Sunshine House, 1 Emmanuel Alayande Street, Oluyole Industrial Estate, PMB 5612, Ibadan, Nigeria
Sphinx Bookshop, 3 Shawarby Street, Kasr el Nil, Cairo, Egypt
Der Spielzeugmacher, Alkdersdorf 21, 4880 St Georgen, Austria
Fr D. Spiteri, The Malta Bible Society, c/o Catholic Institute, Floriana, Malta
Spring Arbor Distributors, 10885 Textile Road, MI 48111, USA
Centre Sri Aurobindo, 4125 rue Saint-Denis, Montreal, PQ, Canada H2W 2M7
Sri Aurobindo Association, 2288 Fulton Street, Suite 310, Berkeley, CA 94704, USA
St Clair Press Pty Ltd, PO Box 287, Rozelle, NSW, Australia 2039
St Martin's Press Inc, 257 Park Avenue South, 18th Floor, New York, NY 10010, USA
St Paul Book Centre, Kaunda Street, PO Box 30249, Nairobi, Kenya
St Paul Book Centre, GPO Box 19220, Dugbe, Oke-Padi, Nigeria
St Paul Book Centre, PO Box 2381, Dar-es-Salaam, Tanzania
St Paul Book Centre, PO Box 4392, Kampala, Uganda
St Pauls, 60–70 Broughton Road, Homebush, NSW, Australia 2140
STA Ltd, 132 Harolds Cross Road, Dublin 6W, Irish Republic
Staatsdrukkerij- en uitgeverijbedrijf, Christoffel Plantijnstraat, Postbus 20014, 2500 EA 's-Gravenhage, Netherlands
Stackpole Books, PO Box 1831, Harrisburg, PA 17105, USA
Stafford Books, Suite 25, 71 Chandos Street, PO Box 60, St Leonards, NSW, Australia 2065
Kurt Stäheli & Co, Bahnhofstrasse 70, 8021 Zurich, Switzerland
Buchhandlung Stäheli & Co ELT Dept, Am Marktplatz 20, 78549 Spaichingen, Germany
Standards New Zealand, 155 The Terrace, Private Bag 2439, Wellington 6020, New Zealand
Star Books International, 55 Crowland Avenue, Hayes, Middx, UK
State Mutual Book & Periodical Service Ltd, 17th Floor, 521 Fifth Avenue, New York, NY 10175-0105, USA
Statenskartwerk, 3500 Honefoss, Norway
Steimatzky Ltd, 11 Hakishon Street, PO Box 1444, Bnei Brak 51114, Israel
Rudolf Steiner Publications, PO Box 4891, Randburg, 2125 South Africa
Steinerbooks NZ, PO Box 11-336, Ellerslie, Auckland 5, New Zealand
Sterling Publishing Co Inc, 387 Park Avenue South, New York, NY 10016-8810, USA
Josiane Stern, 5 avenue Pasteur, 92400 Courbevoie, France
Stewart House (a division of McClelland & Stewart), 380 Esna Park Drive, Markham, Ont, Canada L3R 1H5
Stewart, Taboori & Chang, 575 Broadway, New York, NY 10012, USA

STM Publishers Pte Ltd, c/o 2/F, 2, Alley 9, Lane 316, Roosevelt Road, Section 3, Taipei, Taiwan

STM Publishers Services Pte Ltd, Block 113 Eunos Avenue 3, 07-03 Gordon Industrial Building, Singapore 1440 & 352 Lorong Chuan, 01-05 Laurel Park, Singapore 1955

Stockton Press, 345 Park Avenue South, 10th Floor, New York, NY 10010-1707, USA

Stoddart Publishing, 34 Lesmill Road, Don Mills, Ont, Canada M3B 2T6

Stoelting, Oakwood Centre, 620 Wheat Lane, Wood Dale, IL 60191, USA

STP Distributors (M) Sdn Bhd, 1st Floor, Bangunan, Times Publishing, Lot 46, Subang Hi Tech Ind Park, Batu Tiga, 40000 Shah Alam, Selangor Darul Ehsan, Malaysia

STP Distributors Pte Ltd, Books Division, Pasir Panjang Districentre, Block 1, 03-01 Pasir Panjang Road, Singapore 0511

Struik Book Distributors, Trade Division (Pty) Ltd, PO Box 624, Bergvlei, Wynberg, Sandton, 2012 South Africa; 32 Thora Crescent, Wynberg, Sandton, Johannesburg, South Africa; Graph Avenue, Montague Gardens, Cape Town, 7441 South Africa & PO Box 11204, Johannesburg, 2000 South Africa; PO Box 1144, Cape Town, 8000 South Africa & PO Box 193, Upper Camp Road, Maitland, 7405 South Africa

Struik Christian Books, Struik House, 80 McKenzie Street, Cape Town, 8001 South Africa

Studentlitteratur AB, Box 141, 221 00 Lund, Sweden

Bokhandeln Studio, Karlavagen 44, 114 49 Stockholm, Sweden

Studio Nabu, 50135 Settignano, Florence, Italy

Charles Subasinghe & Sons (P) Ltd, 720 Galle Road, Colombo 3, Sri Lanka

Subterranean Co, Box 160, 265 South 5th Street, Monroe, OR 97456, USA

Sukhi Hotu, 42-V Jln. Matang Kucing, 11500 Air Itam, Penang, Malaysia

R&S Summers, PO Box 1741, Ortigas Center, Pasig, Metro Manila 1657, Philippines

R&S Summers, 11–144 Holland Court, 144 Holland Road, Singapore 278576

Ralph & Sheila Summers, c/o Formtone, Dame Alice House, 10–12 Emerald Street, London WC1N 3QA, UK

Kwon Sung June, Addison-Wesley Publishing Co, 3rd Floor, 403-16h Seo Kyo dong, Ma Po Ku, Seoul 121-210, Korea

Surgisales Teaching Aids, 132 Harrolds Cross Road, Dublin 5, Irish Republic

Surrey Beatty Pty Ltd, 43–45 Rickard Road, Chipping Norton, NSW,, Australia 2170

Sweet & Maxwell Ltd, South Quay Plaza, 183 Marsh Walk, London E14 9FT, UK

Swets & Zeitlinger bv, Heereweg 347b, PO Box 820, 2160 SZ Lisse, Netherlands

Swindon Book Co, 13–15 Lock Road, Kowloon, Hong Kong

Boekhandel Synthese, Lange Voorhout 96, 2514 EJ 's Gravenhage, Netherlands

Tabbara, PO Box 4067, Osnabruck, Germany

Yuki Tagaya, Ikebukuro White House Building, Room 311, 120-2 Higashi-Ikebukuro, Toshima-ku, Tokyo 170, Japan

Angie Tainsh, Nicholas Brealey Publishing Ltd, 21 Bloomsbury Way, London WC1A 2TH, UK

Taj Co, 127 Prince Edward Street, Durban, Natal, 4001 South Africa

The Talman Co, Suite 201E–N, 131 Spring Street, New York, NY 10012, USA

Tammi Publishers, Eerikinkatu 28, 00180 Helsinki, Finland

Tanager Press, 145 Troy Street, Mississauga, Ont L5G I5, Canada

Tandem Press, PO Box 34272, Takapuna, Auckland 9, New Zealand

Tata McGraw-Hill Publishing Co Ltd, 4/12 Asaf Ali Road, 3rd Floor, New Delhi, India 110 002

A. Guy Taylor, 11 Thorpe Chase, Ripon, North Yorkshire HG4 1UA, UK

Taylor & Francis Inc, 1900 Frost Road, Suite 101, Bristol, PA 19007-1598, USA

Taylor Graham Publishing, 12021 Wilshire Boulevard, Suite 187, Los Angeles, CA 90025, USA

TBI Publishers' Distributors, 33-M Connaught Place, New Delhi, India 110 001

Gilbert Teague, Florilegium Press, 30 Cameron Street, Balmain, NSW, Australia 2041

Techbook Distributors, 378–380 Broadway, Private Bag 99939, Newmarket, Auckland, New Zealand

Technea Iberica SL, Grana Via de les Corts Catalanes 690–E°2ª 0 8010 Barcelona, Spain

Technical Book & Magazine Co, 289–299 Swanston Street, Melbourne, Vic, Australia 3000

Technical Books, 6 Morrow Street, Private Bag 39, Newmarket, Auckland, New Zealand

Technical Books (Pty) Ltd, 10th Floor, Aureith Centre, Hans Strijdom Avenue, Cape Town, 8001 South Africa

Technicon Document Services, Iidabaashi High Town Building, 15 Shimomiyabicho, Shinyuku-ku, Tokyo, Japan

Tecknodidakt, Postboks 36, Kalbakken, 0901 Oslo, Norway

Editorial Tecnica Interamericana, Av de Manuel Albo 2656/108, Montevideo, Uruguay

Teksons Bookshop, South Extension Market, Part 1, New Delhi, India 110 049

Temeron Books Inc, 210, 1220 Kensington Road NW, Calgary, Alberta, T2N 3P5, Canada

Jeremy Tenniswood, 28 Gordon Road, Aldershot, Hants GU11 1ND, UK

Ter Maat BV, Zilverenberg 3, 5202 CG's Hertogenbosch, Netherlands

Terco AB, 141 OS Huddings, Stockholm, Sweden

TES Nederland BV, Mercuriusweg 26–28, 2516 AW 's-Gravenhage, Netherlands

Testzentrale, Robert-Bosch-Breite 25, 37027 Göttingen, Germany

Textbook Centre Ltd, Kijabi Street, PO Box 47540, Nairobi, Kenya

Textbook Sales (PVT) Ltd, PO Box 3799, Harare, Zimbabwe

Thames & Hudson (Australia) Pty Ltd, 11 Central Boulevard, Portside Business Park, Port Melbourne, Vic, Australia 3207

Thames & Hudson Inc, 500 Fifth Avenue, New York, NY 10110, USA

Thames & Hudson Ltd, 30–34 Bloomsbury Street, London WC1B 3QP, UK

Thames & Hudson (S) Pte Ltd, c/o APD Kuala Lumpur, No. 18, Jalan SS3/41, 47300 Petaling Jaya, Selangor, Darul Ehsan, Malaysia

Thames & Hudson (S) Pte Ltd, 2 Kallang Pudding Road, 06-07, Mactech Industrial Building, Singapore 1334

Tharpa Publications, PO Box 85772, Seattle, WA 98145-1772, USA

Theatre Books, 11 St Thomas Street, Toronto, Ont, Canada M5S 2B7

Theatre Communications Group, 355 Lexington Avenue, New York, NY 10017, USA

Uitgeverij Theosofische, Tolstraat 154, 1074 VM Amsterdam, Netherlands

Theosophical Books Ltd, 50 Gloucester Place, London W1H 4EA, UK

Theosophical Publishing House, Adyar, Madras, India 600 020

The Theosophical Publishing House, 1 Iba Street, Quezon City, Philippines

The Theosophical Publishing House, 306 West Geneva Road, PO Box 270, Wheaton, IL 60189-0270, USA

Hugh Thomas, 47 Meadow Close, Rottingdean, Brighton BN2 7FB, UK

Hugh C. Thomas, Eurab Ltd, c/o Collins & Brown, London House, Great Eastern Wharf, Parkgate Road, London SW11 4NQ, UK

Nigel Thomas Associates, 26 Melrose Avenue, Wimbledon, London SW19 8BY, UK

Thomson Information Services, Lippo Centre, 1 Phillip Street, 03-01, Singapore 0104

Thomson Press (India) Ltd, 9K Block, Connaught Circus, New Delhi, India 110 001

Thomson Professional Publishing, Corporate Plaza, 2075 Kennedy Road, Scarborough, Ont, Canada M1T 3V4

D. W. Thorpe, PO Box 146, 18 Salmon Street, Port Melbourne, Vic, Australia 3207

D. W. Thorpe (New Zealand), CPO Box 472, Wellington, New Zealand

Reg Tigwell Art Agency, 5/78 Bendooley Street, Bowral, NSW, Australia 2576

Tihama Distribution Company, PO Box 9409, Jeddah 21413, Saudi Arabia

AB Timbro, R Näringslivets Presstjänst, B Jarlsgatan 6b, 114 34 Stockholm, Sweden

Timbuktu Records (UK) Ltd, 41/42 Bernes Street, London W1P 3AA, UK

Times Books International, 25a Khan Market, New Delhi, 110 003, India

Times Mirror Professional Publishers, 130 Flaska Drive, Markham, Ont, Canada

Times Store, 8–12 King Street, PO Box 152, Kingston, Jamaica

Times The Bookshop, Basement 1 Unit 84–85, Plaza Indonesia, Jln M. H. Thamrin Kav. 28–30, Jakarta 10350, Indonesia

Timmy Marketing Ltd, Israel Ben Zeev 12, Ramont Gimmel, Jerusalem, Israel

Michael Timperley Marketing, 10B Garden Terrace III, 8A Old Peak Road, Hong Kong, Hong Kong & c/o Activair (Hong Kong) Ltd, Unit 2, G/F Kenning Industrial Building, 19 WangHoi Road, Kowloon Bay, Hong Kong

Michael Timperley Marketing, c/o Ms Sue Wilson, Bartók Béla ut 41 (IV/4), 1114 Budapest, Hungary

Michael Timperley Marketing, c/o Ms A. Hedgecock, Tulpin 2, 4301 Karmelave, Kaunas Region, Lithuania

Michael Timperley Marketing, c/o Blackwell Publishers Ltd, 108 Cowley Road, Oxford OX4 1JF, UK & 118 Culford Road, London N1 4HU, UK

Tipress Deutschland GmbH, Via Cernaia 34, 10122 Turin, Italy

Titles, 45 Umhlanga Rocks Drive, Durban North 4051 South Africa

Titus Stores, PO Box 264, 98 Main Street, Columbo 11, Sri Lanka

Toppan Co Ltd, 2nd Floor, Shufunotomo Building, 1-6 Kanda Surugadai, Chiyoda-ku, Tokyo, 101 Japan

Toppan Co (S) Pte Ltd, Selangor, Malaysia

Toppan Co (S) Pte Ltd, 38 Liu Fang Road, Box 22, Jurong Town PO, Jurong, Singapore 2262

University of Toronto Press, 5201 Dufferin Street, Downsview, Ont, Canada M3H 5T8

University of Toronto Press, c/o Marston Book Services, PO Box 269, Abingdon, Oxon OX14 4SD, UK

Tower Books Wholesalers Pty Ltd, PO Box 231, Brookvale,, Australia 2100 & 9/19 Rodborough Road, Frenchs Forest, NSW, Australia 2086

Robert Towers, 2 The Crescent, Monkstown, Co Dublin, Irish Republic

T. R. Publications Pvt Ltd, PMG Complex, 11 Floor, 57 South Usman Road, Madras, Tamil Nagar, India 600 017

TRACIL, 3935 Point McKay Road NW, Calgary, Alberta, T3B 4V7, Canada

Trade Winds Press Pty & Co Ltd, PO Box 20194, Durban North, 4016 South Africa & EBA House, Corner Fabriek/Sterling Streets, Strydom Park, Randburg, 2125 South Africa

Tradis Verlag und Vertrieb GmbH (Bookshops), Postfach 90 03 69, 51113 Cologne, Germany

Trafalgar Square Publications, Howe Hill Road, North Pomfret, VT 05053, USA

Trame Selection, 62 boulevard Jean Jaures, 92100 Boulogne, France

Trans-Atlantic Publications Inc, 311 Bainbridge Street, Philadelphia, PA 19147, USA

Trans S.A. Book Distributors, Block A, Wierda Court, 107 Johan Avenue, Wierda Valley, Sandton, 2196 South Africa & PO Box 7724, Johannesburg, 2000 South Africa

Transat Marine, 240 Bayview Drive, Unit 6, Barrie, Ont, Canada L4N 4Y8

Transat SA, Route des Jeunes, 4 Ter, CP 125, 1211 Geneva 26, Switzerland

Transglobal Publishers Services Ltd, 27/F, Unit E, Shield Industrial Centre, 84–92 Chai Wan Kok Street, Tsuen Wan, New Territories, Hong Kong

Translit Literary Agents, Singel 450, 1017 AV Amsterdam, Netherlands

Transpress, Borkumstraße 2, PLZ 13161 Berlin, Germany

Transworld Publishers (Australia) Pty Ltd, 40 Yeo Street, Neutral Bay, Sydney, NSW, Australia 2089

Transworld Publishers Ltd, 61–63 Uxbridge Road, Ealing, London W5 5SA, UK

Transworld Publishers (NZ) Ltd, 3 William Pickering Drive, Albany, Auckland, New Zealand

Travel Bookshop, Rindermarkt 20, 8001 Zurich, Switzerland

Mark Tremlow, Sotociecus 33, 16673 Vaula, Attiki, Greece

Trinity Book Service, PO Box 569, Montville, NJ 07045, USA

Trinity Books CC, PO Box 242, Randburg, 2125 South Africa

Trinity Press International, PO Box 851, Valley Forge, PA 19482-0851, USA

N. M. Tripathi Pte Ltd, 164 Shamaldas Gandhi Marg, Bombay, India 400 002

Triton Music Ltd, 9 Marmion Street, Auckland, New Zealand

Troika Ltd, 179 Kings Cross Road, London WC1X 9BZ, UK & 99 Wallis Road, London E9 5LN, UK

Troll Books of Australia, PO Box 522, Roseville, NSW, Australia 2069

Tung Hua Book Co Ltd, 105 Omei Street, Taipei, Taiwan

Turnaround Publishers Services Ltd, 27 Horsell Road, London N5 1XL, UK

Turnkey Projects Ltd, General Mola 23, Santa Cruz de Tenerife, 38006, Canary Islands, Spain

Turnkey Projects Ltd, Cross Tree Cottage, Church Lane, Finmere, Buckingham MK18 4AT, UK

Charles E. Tuttle Co Inc, 21-13 Seki 1-chome, Tama-ku, Kawasaki, Kanagawa 214, Japan

Tuttle-Mori Agency Ltd, Fuji Building 8F, 2-15 Kanda Jimbocho, Chiyoda-ku, Tokyo, 101 Japan

Tuttostoria, Via S. Sonnino 34, 43100 Parma, Italy

Twenty-Third Publications, PO Box 180, Mystic, CT 06355, USA

Tynron Press Ltd, Unit 3, Turnpike Close, Lutterworth, Leics LE17 4JA, UK

UBS Publishers' Distributors Ltd, 5 Ansari Road, PB No 7015, New Delhi, India 110 002

UBS Publishers' Distributors Ltd, 222 Charlton Road, Kenton, Harrow, Middx HA3 9HJ, UK & 475 North Circular Road, Neasden, London NW2 7QG, UK

UCL Press, University College London, Gower Street, London WC1E 6BT, UK

UCL Press Ltd, University College London, Gower Street, London WC1E 6BTGrantham, Lincs NG31 9SD, UK

Ulverscroft Large Print (USA) Inc, 1881 Ridge Road, PO Box 1230, West Seneca, NY 14224-1230, USA

Librairie Ulysse Inc, 4176 St-Denis, CDN-Montreal, Quebec, Canada

Ulysses Books & Maps, 4176 St Denis, Montreal, PQ, Canada H2W 2M5

Unicorn Books and Crafts Inc, 1338 Ross Street, Petaluma, CA 94954-6502, USA

Unifacmanu Trading Co Ltd, 4F, 91 Ho-Ping East Road, Sec. 1, Taipei 10609, Taiwan

Unimax Publishers (Sic) Ltd, 42 Ring Road, West Industrial Area, Accra, Ghana

Unipub, 46 11-F Assembly Drive, Lanham, MD 20706-4391, USA

United Books & Periodicals, 7 Vishwadham, Prabhat Colony Road, Santa Cruz (E), Bombay, India 400 055

United Church Publishing House, 50 Bloor Street West, Etobicoke, Ont, Canada M8X 2Y4

United Nations University Press, 5-53-70 Jingumae, Shibuya-ku, Tokyo, 150 Japan

United Publishers, PO Box 82, Guwahati 781001, Assam, India

United Publishers Services (Hong Kong) Ltd, Stanhope House, 13th Floor, 734 King's Road, North Point, Hong Kong

United Publishers Services Ltd, Kenkyu-sha Building, 9 Kanda Surugadai 2-chome, Chiyoda-ku, Tokyo, Japan

L'Univers Particulier, 194 chaussée Dr Charleroi, 1060 Brussels, Belgium

Universal Book House for Print & Distribution, PO Box 11, Saida-Lebanon, Lebanon

Universal Book Services, Warmonderweg 80, 2341 K2 Oegstgeest, Netherlands

Universal Multitrade & Associates, 68 Norflock Street, Trinidad

Universal Press, 42 Olive Road, PO Box 12680 Penrose, Auckland 1135, New Zealand

Universal Press Pty Ltd, 1 Waterloo Road, Macquarie Centre, Sydney, NSW, Australia 2113

Universal Records, 135P Sevilla Street, Grace Park, Kalookan City, Metro Manila, Philippines

Universal Sales & Marketing, 230 Fifth Avenue, Suite 1212, New York, NY 10001, USA

Universitas, 62 avenue de Suffren, 75015 Paris, France

Universitets Forlaget, Postboks 2959, Toyen, Oslo 6, Norway

University Bookshop, 16 Desforges Street, Port Louis, Mauritius

University College London Press, Gower Street, London WC1E 6BT, UK

The University Press Group, 164 Hillside Avenue East, Toronto, Ont, Canada M45 1T5

The University Press Ltd, Red Crescent Building, 114 Motijheel Commercial Area, PO Box 2611, Dhaka 1000, Bangladesh

University Press Ltd, Three Crowns Building, Eleyiele Road, Jericho, PMB 5095, Ibadan, Nigeria

University Science Books, 20 Edgehill Road, Mill Valley, CA 94941, USA

UPM – University Presses Marketing, The Old Mill, Mill Street, Wantage, Oxfordshire OX12 9AB, UK

Laurence Urdang Inc, 4 Laurel Heights, Old Lyme, CT 06371, USA

Usaco Corp, Tsutsumi Building, 13-12 Shimbashi 1-chome, Minato Ku, Tokyo, 105 Japan

UWI Bookshop, University of the West Indies, Cave Hill, Barbados

UWI Bookshop, University of the West Indies, St Augustine, Trinidad

Uzima Press, PO Box 48127, Nairobi, Kenya

Mikro Værkstedet, Dockerslundsvej 33, 5000 Odense C, Denmark

Van Ditmar BV, Joan Muyskenweg 6–6a, 1096 CJ Amsterdam, Netherlands

Kelvin van Hasselt Publishing Services, Corner Cottage, Mayflower Close, Lymington, Hants SO41 3SN, UK

Vanguard Books Pvt Ltd, 45 The Mall, Lahore, Pakistan

Vanguard Classics, Groningenhaven 18, PO Box 1308, 3430 BH Nieuwegein, Netherlands

Vanwell Publishing Ltd, 1 Northrup Crescent, PO Box 2131, Stn B, St Catherines, Ont, Canada L2M 6P5

K. M. Varghese Co, 104–105 Hind Rajasthan Building, Dadasaheb Phalke Road, Dadar, Bombay, India 400 014

VCH Verlagsgesellschaft mbH, Pappelallee 3, Postfach 101161, 6940 Weinheim, Germany

Vedanta Society, 1157 SE 55th Avenue, Portland, OR 97215, USA & 224 Angell Street, Providence, RI 02906, USA

Vedanta Society of Berkeley, 2455 Bowditch Street, Berkeley, CA 94704, USA

Vedanta Society of Northern California, 2323 Vallejo Street, San Francisco, CA 94123, USA

Vedanta Society of Sacramento, 1337 Mission Avenue, Carmichael, CA 95608, USA

Vedanta Society of (S) California, 1946 Vedanta Place, Hollywood, CA 90068, USA

Vedanta Society of St Louis, 205 South Skinker Boulevard, St Louis, MI 63105, USA

Vedanta Society of Toronto, 120 Emmatt Avenue, Toronto, Ont, Canada M6M 2E6

Vedanta Society of Western Washington, 2716 Broadway East, Seattle, WA 98102, USA

Centre Vedantique Ramakrichna, 1 boulevard Romain Rolland, 77220 Gretz, France

Verbatim Distributors, PO Box 190, Steenberg, 7947 South Africa & 23 Bergandal Road, Constantia Hills, 7800 South Africa

Verso, 180 Varick Street, New York, NY 10014, USA

Verulam Publishing Ltd, 152A Park Street Lane, Park Street, St Albans, Herts AL2 2AU, UK

Viewcom (Pty) Ltd, 364 Kent Avenue, Randburg, 2914 South Africa

Vigor Book Agents, PO Box 13206, Clubview 0014 South Africa

Viking Penguin Inc, 375 Hudson Street, New York, NY 10014, USA

Viking Sevenseas Ltd, PO Box 152, Paraparaumu, New Zealand

Vintrade Sdn Bhd, 5 & 7 Lorong Datuk Sulaiman, Tujuh, Taman Tun Dr Ismail, 60000 Kuala Lumpur, Malaysia

Virtue Books (NZ), PO Box 36-357, Northcote, Auckland 9, New Zealand

Viva Marketing, 4327/3 Ansari Road, Daryaganj, New Delhi, India 110 002

Vivekananda Vedanta Society, 5423 South Hyde Park Boulevard, Chicago, IL 60615, USA

Cory Voigt Associates, PO Box 31487, Braamfontein, 2017 South Africa

Henner Voss, Zievericher Mühle 1, W-50126 Bergheim-Zieverich, Germany

Voyageur Press, 123 North Second Street, Stillwater, MN 55082, USA

Librairie Vuibert, 63 boulevard Saint-Germain, 75005 Paris, France

Wahlström & Widstrand, Tysta Gatan 10, 11524 Stockholm, Sweden

C. D. A. Walker, Golf View, Rockley New Road, Christchurch, Barbados

Walker Books Australia, 1st Floor, 335–341 Glebe Point Road, Glebe, Sydney, NSW, Australia 2037

Walton Marketing Services, 14 Woodclyffe Drive, Chislehurst, Kent BR7 5NT, UK

Mary Anne Warburton, Aronales 1514, (1602) Florida, Buenos Aires, Argentina

Peter Ward Book Exports, 231 Royal College Street, London NW1 9LT, UK

Roger Ward, International Book Marketing, 2 Haythorne House, Vicarage Crescent, Battersea Village, London SW11 3LQ, UK

Wardell Educational Services, Box 423, Manurewa, New Zealand

Warner Chappell Music Group, 1 Cassins Avenue, North Sydney, NSW, Australia 2060

Warwick Associates, 18900 Olive Avenue, Sonoma, CA 95476, USA

University of Washington Press, PO Box 50096, Suite 555, 1326 Fifth Avenue, Seattle, WA 98145-5096, USA

James & Lorin Watt, 1A Newtec Place, 66-72 Magdalen Road, Oxford OX4 1RE, UK

Franklin Watts Australia, 14 Mars Road, Lane Cove, NSW, Australia 2066

Waverly Europe Ltd, The Broadway Centre, 2–6 Fulham Broadway, London SW6 1AA, UK

Weatherhill Inc, 568 Broadway, Suite 705, New York, NY 10012-3225, USA

Samuel Weiser Inc, 97 Raydon Road, York, ME 03909, USA

Welcome Publishing House, Szerb u. 17–19 VI.em, 1056 Budapest, Hungary

Judith Wengrowe Agencies, PO Box 1080, Northcliff, Johannesbury, 2115 South Africa

Wepf & Co, Eisengasse 56, 4001 Basel, Switzerland

West Indies Publishing Ltd, Unit 33, 7–9 Norman Road, Kingston, Jamaica

Western Psychological Services, 12031 Wilshire Boulevard, Los Angeles, CA 90025, USA

Westminster/John Knox Press, 100 Witherspoon Street, Louisville, KY 40202-1396, USA

Whistles in the Woods, PO Box 309, Chicamauga, GA 30707, USA

J. Whitaker & Sons Ltd, 12 Dyott Street, London WC1A 5DF, UK

Gary White ,Chuck Gregg, 17 Edes Road, Cumberland, ME 04021, USA

The White Eagle Lodge of Australasia Ltd, Willomee MS 16, Tesch Road, Maleny, Qld, Australia 4552

Whitecap Books, 351 Lynn Avenue, North Vancouver, BC, Canada V7J 2C4

The John Wilde Partnership, Bei Schröder, Schützenstrasse 20, 77886 Lauf, Germany

The John Wilde Partnership, 31 Hodges Court, Whitehouse Road, Oxford OX1 4NX, UK & 65 Pymers Mead, Croxted Road, West Dulwich, London SE21 8NJ, UK

Wildy & Sons Ltd, Lincolns' Inn Archway, Carey Street, London WC2A 2JD, UK

John Wiley & Sons (Asia) Pte Ltd, 2 Clementi Loop, Jin Xing Distripark, Singapore 0512

John Wiley & Sons Canada Ltd, 22 Worcester Road, Rexdale, Ont, Canada M9W 1L1

John Wiley & Sons Inc, 605 Third Avenue, New York, NY 10158-0012, USA

John Wiley & Sons Ltd, Meguro Nishiguchi Mansion 2-403, 2-24-11 Kamiosaki, Shinagawa-ku, Tokyo, 141 Japan

John Wiley & Sons Ltd, Baffins Lane, Chichester, West Sussex PO19 1UD, UK

Wilfrid Laurier University Press, 481 Peruville Road, Groton, NY 13073, USA

Wolfgang Willmann & Susanne Sieger, c/o Glockenbachbuchhandlung, Hans-Sachs-Straße 11, 8000 Munich 5, Germany

Willow Connection Pty Ltd, Unit 7a, 3–9 Kenneth Road, Manly Vale, NSW, Australia 2093

Mike Wilson, Datum Book Marketing, Plas Berw, Pentre Berw, Anglesey, Gwynedd LL60 6LL, UK

Ms Sue Wilson, Bartok Bela Ut 41 (IV/4), 111 Budapest, Hungary

Windhorse Books, PO Box 574, Newtown, NSW, Australia 2042

Windhorse India, Dharmachakra Pravartana Mahavihara, Raja Harischandra Road, Dapadi, Poona, India 411 012

Windhorse Publications Inc, Aryaloka, Heartwood Circle, Newmarket, NH 03857, USA

David Wine, Astra Agency, Ramat Motza, PO Box 1567, Jerusalem, Israel

Wisdom Books, 402 Hoe Street, London E17 9AA, UK

Wisdom Publications, 361 Newbury Street, Boston, MA 02115, USA

Wizard's Warehouse, PO Box 3340, Cape Town, 3000 South Africa

Women Ink, 777 UN Plaza, New York, NY 10017, USA

Woodslane Pty Ltd, Unit 8, 101 Darley Street, PO Box 935, Mona Vale, NSW, Australia 2103

H. E. Wootton & Sons, 523 Malvern Road, Toorak, Vic, Australia 3142

Word Australia, 140 Canterbury Road, Kilsyth, Vic, Australia 3137

Word of Life Press Bible Book House, PO Box 680, Kuang Hwa Moon, Seoul 110-061, Korea

Wordsworth Editions Ltd, Cumberland House, Crib Street, Ware, Hertfordshire SG12 9ET, UK

World Agencies Ltd, 64/5 Lake Circus, Kalabagan, PO Box 2739, Dhaka 1205, Bangladesh

World Data, PO Box 4243, 75162 Paris, Cedex 04, France

World Scientific Publishing Co Pte Ltd, 4911, 9th Floor, High Point IV, 45 Palace Road, Bangalore, India 560 001

World Scientific Publishing Co Pte Ltd, Farrer Road, PO Box 128, Singapore 912805

World Scientific Publishing Co Pte Ltd, 5F-6, No. 88, Hsin-Sheng S Road, Taipei, Taiwan

World Scientific Publishing Co Inc, 1060 Main Street, River Edge, NJ 07661, USA

World Scientific Publishing (HK) Co Ltd, PO Box 72482, Kowloon Central Post Office, Hong Kong, Hong Kong

Worldwide Media Service Inc, 30 Montgomery Street, Jersey City, NJ 07302, USA

The Wright Group, 19201 120th Avenue NE, Bothell, WA 98011-9512, USA

Mälte Würzner, Binterimstrasse 12, W-40233 Dusseldorf, Germany

Xclusiv Distributors Inc, 451 50th Street, New York, NY 11220, USA

Yale Representation Ltd, 23 Pond Street, London NW3 2PN, UK

Yale University Press, 92A Yale Station, New Haven, CT 06520, USA

Julio F. Yañez, Via Augusta, 139, 6º, 2º, 08021 Barcelona, Spain

Eric Yang Agency, Pungsung Building, 8F51—12 Banpo-Dong, Secho-ku, Seoul, Korea

Metis' Yayinlari, Basmusahip Sok 3/2, Cagalaglu, Istanbul, Turkey

Stanson Yeung, 7th Floor, Sup Tower, 75/83 Kings Road, North Point, Hong Kong

Yohan Co Ltd, London House, 53–54 Haymarket, London SW1Y 4RP, UK

YOHAN (Western Publications Distribution Agency), 14-9 Okuba 3-chome, Shinjuku-ku, Tokyo, 169 Japan

Yushodo Fantas Corporation, Second Newfield Building, 42-43 Ohtsuka 3-chome, Bunkyo-ku, Tokyo, 112 Japan & Distribution Centre, 3-38-14 Doshida, Nerima-ku, Tokyo 179, Japan

Zen Imports Pty, PO Box 201, Rozelle, Sydney, NSW, Australia 2039

G. Zevelekakis & Co EE, Fidipidou 53 (Goudi), Athens 609, Greece

Anita Zih, 29 Thanet Court, Queens Drive, London W3 0HW, UK

Zimbabwe Publishing House (Pvt) Ltd, PO Box BW-350, Harare, Zimbabwe

The Zondervan Corporation, 1415 Lake Drive, Se, Grand Rapids, MI 49506, USA

Zwemmer OUP Music & Books, 26 Litchfield Street, London WC2H 9JNJ, UK

7.4 OVERSEAS PUBLISHERS REPRESENTED IN THE UK

ARGENTINA

La Azotea **1050**

AUSTRALIA

Albatross Books **1527**
Allen & Unwin **1876**
The Australian Centre for Egyptology **1046**
Australian Council for Educational Research (ACER) **1619**
Australian Council for Educational Research Ltd **1777**
Bahá'í Publishing Trust **1066**
Beercan Books **1846**
Bookmarks Melbourne **1105**
Cavendish Publishing (Australia) Pty Ltd **1169**
Christian Research Association **1192**
Cornelius Books **1507**
Envirobook Pty **1159**
The Federation Press **1092**
Fremantle Arts Centre Press **1530**
Gadabout Guides **1503**
Gregory's **1824**
Harcourt Brace & Co (Australia) Pty Ltd **1384**
The Holistic Centre **1325**
Hospitality Publications Ltd **1314**
In-Tune Books **1053**
Inwardpath Publishers **1325**
Joint Board of Christian Education **1597**
MacLennan & Petty **1498**
Macquarrie University Ancient History Documentary Research Centre **1530**
Maxi Books **1846**
Sally Milner **1162**
National Gallery of Australia **1855**
Nelson **1611**
New South Wales University Press **1878**
Open Book **1356**
Pacific View Press **1846**
R.I.C. **1702**
Ready-Ed **1814**
Surrey Beatty **1649**
D. W. Thorpe **1112**
La Trobe University Press **1697**
Watermark Press **1920**
Webster Publishing **1723**
Weirknightsbridge & Associates **1325**
Willow Park Press **1159**

AUSTRIA

Freytag & Berndt **1824**
International Atomic Energy Agency (IAEA) **1419**

BELGIUM

Appa **1658**
Chocolate World **1491**
Exhibitions International **1050**
Geocart **1824**
Editions Haug **1233**
Mercator Fonds **1050**
World Customs Organisation **1419**

BRAZIL

Editora Index **1050**
Streamline **1507**

CANADA

Galerie Amrad African Art **1050**
Anglican Book Centre **1439**
Association for Bahá'í Studies **1066**
Bahá'í Publications Canada **1066**
Black Rose Books **1159**
Canadian Library Association **1524**
Canadian Museum of Civilization **1746**
Collector Grade Publications **1816**
Douglas & McIntyre Ltd **1746**
Dovehouse Editions Inc **1530**
Emond Montgomery Publications **1169**
Fitzhenry & Whiteside **1746**
Greystone Books **1746**
Hanen Programme **1921**
Hartley & Marks **1537**
International Development Research Centre (IDRC) **1463**
International Travel Maps & Books (ITMB) **1284**
Kenlyn Publishing **1680**
Key Porter Books **1886**
Manticore Publishers Inc **1558**
Maplehouse Press **1503**
Masters **1225**
McGill-Queen's University Press **1876**
P. D. Meany Co Inc **1811**
Mosaic Press **1148**
Natural Heritage Books **1746**

Novalis **1356**
Ontario Institute for Studies in Education **1777**
Royal Ontario Museum Publications **1867**
Self-Counsel Press **1746**
Sound & Vision **1323**
Toronto University Press **1878**
Verulam Publishing **1050**
Warner Bros. Publications Inc **1466**

DENMARK

Mercantila Publishing AS **1314**
Nordic Council of Ministers **1419**
Okonomisk Litteratur **1267**
Orfeus Software Publishing **1016**

FINLAND

Softmill Oy **1016**

FRANCE

ACR **1050**
Henri Addor & Associates **1416**
ADEC **1416**
Edition de l' Amateur **1416**
Amrita Editions **1325**
Anako Editions **1922**
ARC Edition **1416**
Assouline **1050**
Aureus Editions (Editions Saint Michel) **1325**
Biblioteque De L'image **1050**
Bibliotheque des Arts **1416**
Editions Blay **1507**
Bookking International **1050**
Budo-Store **1225**
Council of Europe **1419**
Degremont **1462**
Editions Edisud **1507**
Eiffel Editions **1050**
Guide Emer **1416**
Encyclopaedia Universalis **1278**
European Institute of Education & Social Policy **1871**
Fivedit **1824**
Flammarion SA **1855**
Flohic **1050**
Grafocarte **1447**
GRUND **1416**
Lavoisier Publishing **1462**
Maeght Editeur **1050**

Marval **1050**
Editions Charles Massin **1507**
Mayer Edition **1416**
Editions Menges **1050**
MH Editions **1050**
Nathan **1513**
Organisation of Economic Cooperation &
    Development (OECD) **1419**
Paris Musees **1050**
Editions Plume **1050**
Publications Sci. Nat. **1202**
Regies Actions Publicitaires **1314**
Servedit-Acatos **1416**
Editions Somogy **1050**
Tardy **1416**
UNESCO **1419**
UNESCO Institute for Educational Planning
    1871
Vac Job **1882**
Editions Vagnon **1447**
Editions Van Wilder **1416**

GERMANY

Art Address Verlag **1416**
Bahá'í Verlag GmbH **1066**
Belser **1668**
Berndtson & Berndtson (Maps) **1503**
Beuth (The German Standards Institute) **1925**
CoMet Verlag **1016**
Falk **1824**
Flugzeug Publikations **1019**
Die Gestalten Verlag **1050**
Grabert Verlag **1050**
Green Submarine **1230**
Carl Hanser Verlag **1883**
Karl F. Haug Verlag **1233**
Hirmer Verlag **1050**
Die Jonglerie **1144**
Karto & Graphic **1824**
Muller GmbH & Co KG **1416**
Prestel Verlag, Munich **1855**
Quintessenz Verlags GmbH **1714**
Ravenstein (Maps) **1503**
Ravenstein Verlag **1507**
K. G. Saur **1112**
Schaltauer **1100**
F. X. Schmid **1189**
SDK Verlags GmbH **1248**
Sensor Verlag **1513**
Siemens **1883**
Stahleisen (The German Iron & Steel Institute)
    1925
VCH Verlagsgesellschaft **1883**
VDI (The Association of German Engineers)
    1925
Vitra Design Museum **1050**

HONG KONG

Concord Publications Co **1366**

HUNGARY

EMB **1109**
Park Publications **1507**

INDIA

Abhinav Publications **1106**
Academic Publishers **1760**
Ajanta Publications **1106**
Bahá'í Publishing Trust **1066**
Chetana (Bombay) **1106**
HarperCollins India **1106**
Indus Publishing House **1760**
International Book Distributors **1830**

Konark Publishers **1760**
Library of Tibetan Works and Archives **1922**
Living Media India Ltd **1620**
Lotsawa **1922**
Mahayana Publications **1922**
Motilal **1050**
Motilal Banarsidass **1922**
Orient Paperbacks **1106**
Oxford & IBH **1106**
Popular Prakashan Pvt Ltd **1760**
Radiant Publishers **1760**
Rupa & Co **1106**
Sangam Books (India) Pvt Ltd **1760**
Theosophical Publishing House **1858**
Universities Press (India) Pvt Ltd **1760**
Vikas Publishing House Pvt Ltd **1760**

IRISH REPUBLIC

Abbeville Press Inc **1594**
Irish Cruising Club **1447**
Office of Public Works **1419**
Ordnance Survey **1284**
Skellig Press Ltd **1811**
Tir Eolas **1811**

ISRAEL

Inbal Travel Information Ltd **1503**
Prolog **1503**

ITALY

Arcadia **1050**
Be-Ma Editrice **1050**
Centro Di **1050**
Charta **1050**
Chiriotti Editori Srl **1314**
Einaudi **1050**
Electa **1050**
Food & Agriculture Organisation (FAO) **1419**
Galleria Editrice **1050**
Gremese International **1746**
Hopeful Monster **1050**
Litografia Artistica Cartografica Srl **1507**
Editrice Militare **1050**
Motta **1050**
Nuova Alfa **1050**
Ricordi **1109**
Sagep **1050**
Monica Smith **1050**
Casa Editrice Tabacco **1507**

JAPAN

Artis **1050**
Bahá'í Publishing Trust of Japan **1066**
Ikeda & Lokker **1050**
Kosei **1922**
Kyoto Zen Centre **1922**
Quintessence Publishing Co Ltd **1714**
Rinsen **1922**
United Nations University (UNU) **1419**
Weatherhill Inc **1614**
Windbell **1922**

KUWAIT

Islamic Book Publishers **1470**

LEBANON

Librairie du Liban **1649**

LUXEMBOURG

European Communities (EC) **1419**

MALAYSIA

Atlanto Publishing **1491**
Dharmafarer **1922**

NETHERLANDS

ANWB **1447**
Art Unlimited **1050**
de Brouwer & Melkman Publishing **1744**
Davo Publications **1343**
Hydrographic Office **1447**
Interbook International **1416**
International Books **1159**
Kempen **1050**
KIT Press **1463**
Lemma **1498**
Uitgeverij Lemman BV **1502**
De Muiderkring **1658**
Visiria **1016**

NEW ZEALAND

Auckland University Press **1648**
David Bateman **1050**
New Zealand Council for Educational Research
    (NZCER) **1619**
New Zealand Council for Educational Research
    1777
Pace Communications **1171**
D. W. Thorpe **1112**

NORWAY

MacLennan & Petty **1502**
Nasjonal Læremiddelscenter **1016**
Norwegian University Press **1648**
Okonomisk Litteratur **1267**
Sigma Forlag **1498**

PAKISTAN

Institute of Policy Studies **1470**

POLAND

AJ-Press **1107**

PORTUGAL

Edições Inapa **1050**
Francisco Ribeiro **1840**
Vista Iberica **1503**

RUSSIA

The Almanac Software Publishing Co **1016**
St Petersberg Shipbuilding Institute **1016**

SEE

Chapman & Hall **1099**
Macmillan Children's Books Ltd **1547**
Macmillan General Books Ltd **1547**
Macmillan Press Ltd **1547**
Macmillan Reference Books **1547**

SINGAPORE

Rinchen Editions **1922**
Times Editions **1503**

SOUTH AFRICA

Afrisoft Grahamstown **1016**
Berlitz **1614**

Struik Publishers 1614
William Waterman Publications 1816

SPAIN

Arco Editorial 1050
Edicinco 1016
Electa España 1050
Firestone Hispania SA 1507
Lunwerg Editores 1050
Montagud Editores SA 1314
World Tourism Organization (WTO) 1419

SRI LANKA

Buddhist Publication Society 1922

SWEDEN

Gävle 1016
Lund University Press 1187
Okonomisk Litteratur 1267
Stockholm International Peace Research
    Institute 1648
Utryck 1914

SWITZERLAND

ABC Verlag 1050
Editions Acatos 1416
Bibliotheque des Arts 1416
Binsted Frères SA 1314
Edition Galerie Bruno Bischofberger 1050
Conference of European Churches 1171
Graphis 1110
Hallwag 1386
Mykologia Lucerne 1738
Scalo, Zurich 1855
Schubi 1513
Edition Stemmle 1050
United Nations (UN) 1419
Verlag am Goetheanum 1828
World Council of Churches 1171
World Health Organisation (WHO) 1419
World Trade Organisation 1419

THAILAND

Buddhadhamma Foundation 1922
T & R United 1507

USA

ABAGE Publications 1416
Abbey Press 1198
ABC Clio Ltd 1444
Academic Press Inc 1384
Adam Software 1659
AGS 1619
Aloray Inc 1458
Amacom 1542
American Academy of Ophthalmology 1100
American Association of Cereal Chemists
    1314
American Bible Society 1125
American Chemical Society 1750
American College of Physicians 1100
American Contract Bridge League 1087
American Early Medieval Studies 1645
American Federation of Astrologers 1325
American Institute of Baking 1314
American Institute of Chemical Engineers
    (AIChE) 1458
American Management Association 1705
American Map Corporation 1507, 1746
American Public Health Association 1184

American Society of Mechanical Engineers
    1560
The American Welding Society 1925
The Analytic Press 1487
Anchor Press 1053
Anchorage Press 1493
Anchorage Press Inc 1224
Anthroposophic Press 1828
ANY 1043
Apex Press 1159
Apollo Books 1416
Armstrong Publishing Corp 1475
Jason Aronson 1503
Ars Obscura 1813
Asian Humanities Press 1922
Aslan Publishing 1920
Association of American Petroleum Geologists
    1341
Atrium Publishers Group 1920
Attainment Inc 1657
Autobridge 1087
Ave Maria Press 1728
Aviation Publications Inc 1019
Avo Books 1920
Baen 1803
Bahá'í Publishing Trust 1066
Baker Book House 1289
Baker Bookhouse 1653
Barricade Books 1746
Basic Books 1503
Bell Tower 1356
R. J. Bender Publishing 1319
Berlitz Publishing Co Inc 1084
Bernan Press 1419
Berrett-Koehler 1542
Betty Crocker 1803
Blue Dolphin Publishing Inc 1325
Bonnie Gaunt 1218
Bookmarks Chicago 1105
Bootstrap Press 1159
R. R. Bowker 1112
Bridge World 1087
Paul H. Brookes 1498
Brotherhood of Life 1233
Karen Brown Guides 1824
The Bruschettini Foundation 1648
California University Press 1915
Cambrix Publishing Ltd 1592
Cardoza Publications 1627
Carolina Biological Supply Co Inc (Biology
    Readers only) 1649
CESA 5 1619
Chatham House Publishers 1746
Chelsea Green Publishing Co 1365
Chemical Publishing Co Inc 1314
Chiron Publications 1487
I. E. Clarke Inc 1224
Clear Point Press 1922
Columbia University Press 1915
Combined Books 1366
Common Knowledge Press 1159
Continuum Publishing Co 1773
Continuum Publishing Group 1746
Cornerstone Press 1835
Michael E. Coughlin 1328
Council Oak Books 1365
Covenant Media Production 1218
Cowley Publications 1812
CRCS 1325
CSA Press 1325
CTI Publications Inc 1314
Cuisenaire Co of America 1513
Culinary Arts 1920
Cy Decosse 1864
Dance Horizons 1232
Data News Press 1325
DBI Books Inc 1047, 1162

De Vorss & Co 1325
Delphi Press 1920
Destiny Publishers 1218
Dharma Cloud 1920
Dharma Communications 1922
Dharma Drum 1922
Dharma Publishing 1918
Dimension Books 1728
DLM Teaching Resources 1619
Dorling Kindersley Inc 1248
Dorset House Publishing Co Inc 1915
Dorset Press/Barnes & Noble Books 1886
Doubleday 1728
Dover Publications Inc 1211
Dragon Door Publications 1225
Drama Book Publishers 1413
Brian Dubé Inc 1144
Earth Heart 1920
Ecco Press 1623
ECS Publishing Co 1826
Eerdmans 1197
Eland Books 1211
Elliott & Clark 1920
Ellison Educational 1842
ELT Press 1811
Emperors Press 1366
Expansion Publishing Co 1325
Faber & Faber Inc 1297
Facts on File, US 1746
Findex 1287
Finesse Press 1144
Fireside 1803
Carl Fischer 1109
Fisher Books 1323
Food & Nutrition Press Inc 1314
Food Processors Institute 1314
Frank Amato Publications Inc 1325
Free Press 1803
W. H. Freeman & Co 1329
Freestone Collective 1920
Samuel French Inc 1330
Friends General Conference 1710
Friends United Press 1710
Frommer 1803
Garrett Publishing Inc 1509
Geological Society of America 1341
Globe Pequot 1824
The Golden Sufi Centre 1325
Gousha 1503
H. M. Gousha Co 1507
J. Green Books 1813
Grune & Stratton Inc 1384
Guggenheim Museum 1849
G. K. Hall & Co (Large Print Books only) 1190
Harcourt Brace & Co 1384
Harper Collins Religious 1653
HarperCollins San Francisco 1197
HarperCollins Sanfrancisco 1388
Harvard Associates Inc 1016
Harvard Business School Press 1542
Harvard University Press 1915
Health Professions Press 1498
Hearst Books International 1110
Heinemann Inc (Education list) 1162
Hendricksen Publishers 1289
Hermetician Press 1920
High View Publications 1225
Hope Publishing Co 1826
Howell Book House 1740
Howell Press 1022, 1838
Hudson Hills Press 1050
Humana Press 1184
Hunter Publishing 1824
ICS Publications 1728
IEAS 1229
Indiana University Press 1636, 1915
Institute for Palestine Studies 1850

Institute of Islamic Thought **1470**
Interlink **1153**
International Monetary Fund (IMF) **1419**
International Monographs in Prehistory **1645**
IPAT **1619**
Islamic Art Foundation, New York **1648**
Island Press **1502**
Italica Press **1920**
IVP **1653**
JAI Press Inc **1475**
JAI Software Publishing **1475**
Jain Publishing **1922**
Jewel Publishing House **1922**
Jewish Publication Society **1503**
Johnson Associates Inc **1475**
Jones & Bartlett Inc **1201**
Edward E. Judge & Sons **1314**
Kalimát Press **1066**
Kar-Ben Copies Inc **1503**
Keats **1053**
Kistler Graphics **1507**
Kodak Publications **1323**
Konecky & Konecky **1026**
L. A. Louver Gallery **1050**
Labor Publications **1473**
Lame Turtle Press **1922**
Lark Publishing **1162**
Lars Muller Publishers **1110**
Larson **1053**
Learning Resources **1513**
Left Bank Books **1328**
Light Technology **1920**
Liguori **1728**
Little Brown & Co **1169**
Little, Brown Medical **1194, 1659**
Loeb **1915**
Love Publishing **1498**
Loyola University Press **1198**
Lyons & Burford **1824**
Macmillan **1803**
Mad River Press (all titles) **1738**
Mahayana Sutra & Tantra Press **1922**
Mamre Press **1920**
Mapeasy **1746**
Marian Communications **1356**
Marling Menu Masters **1323**
Marquis Who's Who **1112**
Marshall Cavendish, US **1746**
Martindale-Hubbell **1112**
Mayfield Publishing Co **1431**
Maypop Books **1920**
University of Minnesota Press **1876**
MIS Press (M & T Books) **1685**
The MIT Press **1915**
MJS Books **1920**
The Modern Library **1503**
Moeller Foundation **1325**
Montfort Publications **1356**
Morehouse Publishing **1356**
Motivation Cassettes **1552**
Mount **1356**
Museum of Modern Art, New York **1855**
National Center for Non-Profit Boards **1609**
National Register Publishing **1112**
Thomas Nelson **1125**
Thomas Nelson Inc **1926**
New City **1356**
New Directions Publishing Corporation **1623**
New Earth Press **1835**
New Millennium Publishing **1325**
The New Press **1850**
New Society Publishers **1159**
Nine Gates Press **1922**
Nolo Press Inc **1169**
North Star Publications **1746**
Northwestern University Press **1876**
W. W. Norton & Co **1447**

W. W. Norton & Co Ltd **1915**
NTC Publishing Group **1886**
Oakwood Publishers **1198**
Old Colony **1658**
Online Inc **1854**
Our Sunday Visitor **1356**
Padma Publishing **1922**
PAR **1619**
Paragon House **1746**
The Parthenon Publishing Group Inc **1651**
Pathfinder Press **1654**
Paul H. Brookes **1502**
Paulist Press **1356**
Pendle Hill Publications **1710**
Penthe Publishing Co **1325**
Peter Pauper Press **1920**
Peterson's Guides **1882**
Pilgrim Publications **1289**
Players Press **1410**
Plenum Publishing Corporation **1689**
Pocket **1803**
Polebridge Press **1773**
Prehistory Press **1645**
Prentice-Hall Press **1803**
Presbyterian & Reformed **1289**
Presidio Press **1366**
Primary Source Media **1703**
Princeton Book Co **1232**
Princeton University Press **1915**
Pro-Ed **1619**
Prometheus Books **1707**
The Psychological Corporation **1384**
Quintessence Publishing Co Inc **1714**
Rand McNally **1824**
Random House Inc **1503, 1722**
Ranjung Yeshe **1922**
Rato Publicatins **1922**
RCC Pilotage Foundation **1447**
Regina Press **1728**
Remedia **1592**
University of Rochester Press **1115**
Rockport **1110**
Royal Priest Publishing **1920**
Rutledge Hill Press **1886**
Sarpedon Publishers **1817**
The Saunders Group **1323**
W. B. Saunders Inc **1763**
Savas Woodbury **1366**
Schocken Books **1503**
Scientific American Books Inc **1329**
Scribner **1803**
Scribners **1197**
Self Realization Fellowship **1053**
SEPM **1341**
Servant Publications **1728**
Frank Shaffer Publications **1313**
Shambhala **1922**
See Sharp Press **1328**
Harold Shaw **1653**
Sheed & Ward **1356**
Sheriar Press Ltd **3049**
Sheridan House Inc **1015**
Sierra Press **1920**
Silicon Press **1698**
Silver Pixel Press **1323**
Simba Information Inc **1854**
Simon & Schuster **1503**
Simon & Schuster Audio **1803**
Simon & Schuster Inc **1803**
Sinauer Associates **1329**
Smith & Kraus Inc **1004**
Snow Lion Graphics **1922**
Snow Lion Publications USA **1922**
Solipaz Publishing Co **1144**
Sound View Press **1416**
Source Books California **1198**

South Western Publishing Co (School Division) **1611**
Spellmount **1211**
Springer Publishing **1659**
St Anthony Messenger Press **1728**
St Bede's Publications **1356**
St Lucie Press **1502**
St Vladimir's Seminary Press **1162, 1590**
Stackpole Books **1366**
Stanford University Press **1149**
Sterling Publishers Inc **1162**
Sterling Publishing Co **1096**
Stipes Publishing Co **1649**
Stoddart **1022**
Streetwise Maps Inc **1004**
Summit **1803**
Summit Books **1503**
Sun Books **1813**
Sunna Books **1471**
SVS Press (Icons) **1356**
Swan Raven & Co **1920**
Sybex **1685, 1659**
Tabor Publishing **1728**
Tasende Gallery **1050**
Teacher Created Materials **1313**
Templegate **1356**
Theatre Communications Group **1413**
Theosophical Publishing House **1858**
Thubten Dhargye Ling **1922**
Timber Press **1801**
Touchstone **1803**
Tree of Life Publications **1920**
Trinity Press International **1773**
The University of Chicago Press **1915**
University of Hawaii Press **1447**
University Press of Mississippi **1746**
The Upper Room Nashville **1571**
Valley of the Sun **1920**
Valor Foundation **1325**
VCH Publishers Inc **1883**
Vippassana Dhura **1922**
VNR **1491**
Waite Group **1659**
Warner Bros. Publications Inc **1466**
Webster's New World Dictionaries **1803**
Westminster John Knox Press **1773**
Westminster/John Knox Press **1197**
Wild Flower Press **1920**
Wisdom Publications (Boston) **1922**
Wisdome Press **1325**
Word Inc **1926**
World Bank Publications **1648**
World Leisure Corporation **1507**
World Library Ltd **1592**
World Music Press **1746**
World Trade Press **1542**
WPS **1619**
Writer Inc **3028**
Writer's Digest **3028**
Writings of Mary Baker Eddy **1746**
Yale University Press **1600, 1915**
Yes International **1920**
YMAA **1225**
Yoga Publications Society **1325**
Yuam Focus on the Family **1926**
Zondervan **1388**

VATICAN CITY

Osservatore Romano **1166**

WORLDWIDE

British Consultants Bureau (BCB) **1419**
National Bible Societies **1125**
National Radiological Protection Board **1419**
UK Atomic Energy Authority **1419**

7.5 AUTHORS' AGENTS: OVERSEAS REPRESENTATION

Bold figures indicate an agent's UK rights representative; roman figures indicate foreign representation of a UK agent.

ARGENTINA

International Editors Co, Avenida Cabildo 1156, 1426 Buenos Aires: 4005, 4063

AUSTRALIA

Australian Literary Management: 4104
Copyrights Australasia Pty Ltd, 24 Merri Street, Brunswick 3056, Victoria: 4021
Curtis Brown (Australia) Pty Ltd, 27 Union Street, Paddington, NSW 2021: 4024
Electra Media Group Pty Ltd, PO Box 1546, Sydney, NSW 2001: 4007, 4063, 4064, 4078
Hickson, Vardey & Brunton, 128 Queen Street, Woollahra, NSW 2025:
Warner Chappell & Co (Australia) Pty Ltd, PO Box 618, North Sydney, NSW 2059: 4097

BRAZIL

Carmen Balcells Agencia Literaria, Rua João Lira 97/202, CP 33-113 Leblon, 20000 Rio de Janeiro: 4008, 4067, 4098
Agencia Literaria Balcells, Mello e Souza, Riff, Rua Visconde de Piraja 414, Sala 1.108, 22410 Rio de Janeiro: 4041
Dr J. E. Bloch Literary Agency, CP 19051, 04599 São Paulo:
Agencia Literaria CB Ltda, Caixa Postal 14.718, 22. 410 Rio de Janeiro R.J.: 4079
International Editors Co: 4104
Mrs Karin Schindler, CP 19051, 04599-970 São Paulo SP: 4005, 4085, 4099
Agencia Siciliano, Av. Raimundo Pereira de Magalhães 3305, CEP 05145, São Paulo SP: 4048
World View & Focus, Rua Major Diogo 784, Bela Vista, 01324 São Paulo:

BULGARIA

Anthea Literary Agency, 14 Strahill Street, Varna 9004: 4005, 4007
Interrights Literary & Translation Agency, 9 Graf Igatiev Street, Sofia 1000: 4037, 4048, 4098
Nika Literary Agency, 19 Anguel Kantchev Str., 1000 Sofia: 4041, 4106
Planeta Literary Agency, PO Box 1336, 1000 Sofia: 4099

CANADA

The Bukowski Agency, 125B Dupont Street, Toronto, Ont M5R 1V4: **4016**

Fitzhenry & Whiteside, 195 Allstate Parkway, Markham, Ont L3R 4T8: **4052**
Golden Globe Publishing, 4329 Oxford, Montreal, PQ H4A 2Y7: **4064**
Madison Press, 40 Madison Avenue, Toronto, Ont M5R 2S1: **4028**
Penguin Canada, 10 Alcorn Avenue, Suite 300, Toronto, Ont M4V 3B2: **4050**
Bella Pomer Inc, 22 Shallmar Boulevard PH2, Toronto M5N 2Z8: **4007**, 4007
Lucinda Vardey Agency, 297 Seaton Street, Toronto, Ont M5A 2T6: 4084

P. R. OF CHINA

Wu Herong, Vantage Agency, 68 Minzu Dadao, Nanning, Guangxi: 4005

CROATIA

Maja Mihic: 4106

CZECH REPUBLIC

Dilia (Czechoslovak Theatrical & Literary Agency), Polska 1, 12 000 Prague 2: 4007
Interlit Services, PO Box 125, 13000 Prague 3: 4026, 4037, 4063, 4098
Andrew Nurnberg Associates, Siefertova 81, Prague 3: 4005, 4060
Petra Tobiskova, Piseckd 18, 130 00 Prague 3: 4099

DENMARK

A/S Bookman Literary Agency, 45 Nørregade, 1165 Copenhagen K: 4008, 4026
Leonhardt Literary Agency, Studiestraede 35, 1455 Copenhagen: 4007, 4037, 4079
Licht & Licht Literary Agency, Maglemosevej 46, 2920 Charlottenlund: 4004, 4038, 4041, 4067, 4078, 4089, 4106
Lijnkamp Literary Agents, Brouwersgracht 288, 1013 HC Amsterdam: 4020
Ulla Løhren Literary Agency, 89 Vaerebrovej, 2880 Bagsvaerd: 4080

FRANCE

Agence Hoffman, 77 boulevard St-Michel, 75005 Paris: 4041, 4049
Eliane Benisti, 80 rue des Saints-Pères, 75007 Paris: 4048
Jean-Pierre Boscq, 20 rue Saint Nicolas, 75012 Paris: 4088
Lora Fountain, 7 rue de Belfort, 75011 Paris: 4015, 4063, 4073
Michelle Lapautre, 6 rue Jean Carriès, 75007 Paris: 4025, 4028, 4067, 4078, 4079, 4085, 4104, 4105, 4106
Agence Litteraire Lenclud: 4026
La Nouvelle Agence, 7 rue Corneille, 75006 Paris: 4007, 4008, 4027, 4035, 4037, 4042, 4050, 4089, 4098, 4099

Frédérique Porretta, Agence Litteraire, 70 rue d'Assas, 75006 Paris: 4004, 4005, 4022, 4034
Société Civil des Auteurs Multimedia (Société des Gens de Lettres), Hotel de Massa, 38 rue du Faubourg Saint Jacques, 75014 Paris: **4033**
Société des Auteurs et Compositeurs Dramatiques, 11bis rue Ballu, 75442 Paris Cedex 09: **4033**

GERMANY

Brigitte Axster, Drei Eich Strasse 43, 60594 Frankfurt am Main: 4031
Cooperation, PO Box 400 323, 80703 Munich: 4067
Copyrights Europe, Heilwigstraße 95, 20249 Hamburg 20: 4021
DTV, Postfach 40 04 22, 8000 Munich 40: **4043**
Kiepenheuer & Witsch, Rondorferstrasse 5, 50968 Cologne: **4043**
Michael Meller Agency, Osterwaldstrasse 9–10, 8000 Munich 40: 4004, 4088
Thomas Schlück, Hinter der Worth 12, 30827 Garbsen: 4005, 4026, 4048, 4050, 4060, 4063, 4073
Corry Theegarten-Schlotterer Verlags- und Autoren-Agentur, Kulmerstrasse 3, 81927 Munich 81: 4028

GREECE

Educational Materials Enterprises Ltd, PO Box 580, Athens 136: 4049, 4067, 4089, 4106
JLM Agency, PO Box 62080, 15210 Halandri: 4007
JLM Literary Agency, 54 Zoodohou Pigis Street, 106 81 Athens: 4034, 4041, 4063, 4080, 4088, 4098, 4104
Nelly Moucacou, PO Box 62080, 15210 Halandri: 4099
O A Literary Agency, 1 Kritis Street, 190 03 Markopoulo: 4005

HUNGARY

Artisjus Agency for Literature & Theatre, PO Box 593, Meszaros u. 15–17, 1538 Budapest: 4099
Balla & Co, Ulloi Ut 14:II:8:, 1085 Budapest: 4005
Inter Codex/Inter Licence, Csalogány u. 6–10, II/66, 1015 Budapest: 4063
Katai & Bolza, PO Box 1666, 1465 Budapest: 4007, 4104
Katai & Bolza, Kopia Office, Ulloi ut 14.11.8, 1085 Budapest: 4041, 4060
Lex Copyright, Szemere u.21, 1054 Budapest: 4037, 4063, 4073, 4078, 4079, 4085, 4098

ISRAEL

The Book Publishers Association of Israel, PO Box 20123, 29 Carlebach Street, Tel Aviv 67-132: 4005
Ilana Pikarski Literary Agency, PO Box 4006, 200 Hayarkon Street, Tel Aviv 61040: 4007, 4020, 4034, 4049, 4063, 4067, 4080, 4085, 4089, 4098, 4099, 4104, 4106
Orly Pecker Literary Agency, PO Box 33444, Tel Aviv 61333: 4041

ITALY

Agenzia Letteraria Internazionale Srl, Via Fratelli Gabba 3, 20121 Milan: 4008, 4026, 4079, 4085, 4098, 4105
Agenzia Antonella Antonelli, Via Brisa 15, 20123 Milan: 4035, 4049, 4106
Luigi Bernabó Associates Srl, Via Bianca di Savoia 4, 20122 Milan, Italy: 4038, 4041, 4078
Eulama Srl, Via Guido di Ruggiero 28, 00142 Rome: 4080
Grandi & Vitali, Via Caradosso 12, 20123 Milan: 4015, 4104
Living Literary Agency, Via Poliziano 8, 20154 Milan: 4037, 4050, 4060, 4063, 4073
Natoli Stefan & Oliva Agenzia Letteraria, Via Omboni 5, 20129 Milan: 4005, 4007
Roberta Oliva: 4004
Roberto Santachiara Literary Agency, Via Folperti 44, 27100 Pavia: 4083
TiPress Deutschland, Via Cernaia 34, 10122 Turin: 4028
Susanna Zevi, Via G. Marcora 6, 20121 Milan: 4089

JAPAN

Cosmos, CPO Box 571, Tokyo, 100: 4006

The English Agency Japan Ltd, 305 Azalon Empire Mansion, 4-11-28 Nishi Azalon, Minato-ku, Tokyo, 106: 4005, 4007, 4020, 4026, 4027, 4041, 4042, 4063, 4073, 4088, 4089, 4104
Japan Foreign Rights Centre, 27-18-804 Nakaochiai 2-chome, Shinjuku 161, Tokyo: 4047
Japan Uni Agency, Naigai Building, 1-1 Kanda Jinbocho, Chiyoda-ku, Tokyo 101: 4088
Japan Uni Agency Inc, Tokyodo Jinbocho No 2 Building, 1-27 Kanda Jinbocho, Chiyoda-ku, Tokyo, 101: 4041, 4048, 4067
Motovun Co Ltd, Coop Nomura Ichibancho, 15-6 Ichibancho Chiyoda-ku, Tokyo, 102: 4028
Tuttle-Mori Agency, Fuji Building, 2-15 Kanda Timbocho, Chiyoda-ku, Tokyo, 101: 4004, 4005, 4007, 4008, 4022, 4034, 4035, 4037, 4041, 4048, 4049, 4063, 4070, 4078, 4079, 4085, 4098, 4105, 4106

KOREA

DRT International Ltd, 6th Floor, Garden Tower Building, 98-78 Unni-dong, Chongo, Seoul 110-350: 4007, 4034, 4098
Imprima Korea, Suite 807, Samchang Plaza Building, 173 Dohwa-Dong, Mapo-ku, Seoul 121-04L: 4037, 4104
Shin Won Agency Co, 419-16 Hapjung-dong Mapo-ku, Seoul: 4060
Eric Yang Agency, Pungsung Building 8F, 51-12 Banpo-Dong, Secho-Ku, Seoul: 4005, 4063

NETHERLANDS

Agence Littéraire Hoffman, 77 boulevard Saint-Michel, 75005 Paris: 4080
Kooy & van Gelderen, Kerkstraat 301, 1017 GZ Amsterdam: 4079
Lijnkamp Literary Agents, Brouwersgracht 288, 1013 HG Amsterdam: 4020, 4028, 4041, 4078, 4098
Jan Michael, PO Box 15137, 1001 MC Amsterdam: 4004, 4005, 4005, 4027, 4038, 4050
Andrew Nurnberg Associates: 4104
T&L Literary Agents, Brouwersgracht 288, 1013 HG Amsterdam: 4008

NEW ZEALAND

Play Bureau (NZ) Ltd, PO Box 420, New Plymouth: 4097

NORWAY

H. Aschehoug & Co, Sehesteds Gate 3, Postboks 363 Sentrum, Oslo 1: 4043
Ulla Løhren Literary Agency, PO Box 150, 0801 Tåsen, Oslo 8: 4105
Suzanne Palme Literary Agency, Box 7112, Homansbyen, 0307 Oslo: 4008, 4041, 4078, 4098, 4104

POLAND

Graal Ltd, Ul Radna 12/15, 00-341 Warsaw: 4005, 4007
Helfa Ltd Literary Agency, Stepinska 6/8 appt 66a, 00-957 Warsaw 36: 4098
Maria Strarz-Kánska Literary Agency Ltd, Ul Filsacka 3a, 30-114 Krakow: 4060, 4098, 4099, 4106

PORTUGAL

Ilidio da Fonseca Matos, Avenida Gomes Pereira 105-30-B, 1500 Lisbon: 4042, 4078

ROMANIA

International Copyright Agency Ltd, Ion Campineanu 31, Bloc 4, Scara 4, Apt 94, Bucharest 1: 4099
Simona Kessler Literary Agency, Ion Campineanu 31, Bloc 4, Scara 4, Apt 94, Bucharest: 4007, 4098, 4104

RUSSIA

Alexander Korzhenevski, 7th, Parkovaya, 28-100, Moscow 105264: 4004, 4063

Elizabeth van Lear Agency, Ploshcad Kurchatova 1, Moscow 123182: 4007
Andrew Nurnberg Literary Agency, Floor 10, Bolshoy Gnezdikovsy 10, 103009 Moscow: 4022, 4099
Prava I Prevodi, Sadovaya- Trimphalnaya St 14-12, 103006 Moscow: 4005, 4060, 4073, 4078, 4104

SLOVAKIA

GP Agentur, Kukucinova 34, 83103 Bratislava: 4106
Gerd Plessl Agentur, PO Box 80, 830 08 Bratislava 38: 4005

SOUTH AFRICA

Dalro (Pty) Ltd, PO Box 9292, Johannesburg: 4097
Forest Publishers: 4114
Human & Rousseau, PO Box 5050, Cape Town, 8000 (children's & teen books only): 4007, 4047
International Press Agency Pty Ltd, PO Box 67, Howard Place 7405, Cape Town: 4026, 4041, 4047, 4080, 4098
Maskew Miller Longman, PO Box 396, Cape Town, 8000: 4047
Queillerie, 25 Robins Road, 7925 Observatory, Cape Town: 4007
Tafelberg, PO Box 879, Cape Town, 8000 (children's & teen books only): 4007, 4047

SPAIN

Acer, Amor de Dios 1, 28014 Madrid: 4015
Carmen Balcells Agencia Literaria, Diagonal 580, 08021 Barcelona: 4008, 4035, 4037, 4041, 4063, 4067, 4078, 4098, 4099
Mercedes Casanovas Agency, Teodora Lamadrid 29, 08022 Barcelona: 4007, 4106
International Editors Co, Rambla de Cataluna 63 3° 1ª, 08007 Barcelona: 4005, 4020, 4042, 4063, 4073, 4085, 4089, 4104
Ute Korner Literary Agency, Ronda Guinado 32 5° 5ª, 08025 Barcelona: 4004, 4028
NALI: 4026
Julio F. Yañez Agencia Literaria, Via Augusta 139 6° 2ª, 08021 Barcelona: 4048, 4050, 4080, 4088, 4105

SWEDEN

Gösta Dahl & Son, Aladdinsvägen 14, 161 38 Bromma: 4078
Sane Töregard Agency, Holländareplan 9, 374 34 Karlsham: 4009, 4017, 4022, 4034, 4042, 4049, 4060, 4070

SWITZERLAND

Edi Inter SA, route de Chancy 28, 1213 Petit Lancy 2, Geneva: 4064
Paul & Peter Fritz AG Literary Agency, Jupiterstrasse 1, 8032 Zurich: 4022, 4034, 4035, 4049, 4083, 4105
Editions Godefroy, Chalet Imniac, 1885 Chesières: 4064
Liepman AG, Maienburgweg 23, 8044 Zurich: 4007, 4020, 4025, 4035, 4042, 4080, 4085, 4089, 4104, 4106
Mohrbooks Literary Agency, Klosbachstrasse 110, 8032 Zurich: 4008, 4027, 4038, 4041, 4067, 4078, 4079, 4098, 4099

TAIWAN

Bardon Agency, 2F No 1-1, Hsin-Hai Road, Section 1, Taipei: 4007, 4073
Big Apple Tuttle-Mori Agency Inc, 2nd Floor, No 8, Alley 19, I-tung Street, Taipei 10431: 4041, 4060, 4063, 4085, 4098, 4104
Tuttle Mori Agency, 1-Tung Street, Alley 19, No 8 2nd Floor, Taipei 10431: 4005

THAILAND

Sharon Ng, PO Box 4-158, Sam Sen Nai, Bangkok 10400: 4005
Tuttle-Mori Big Apple Agency (Thailand) Co Ltd, 420/ 15 S01 Chomchoey, Sukhumvit 49, Bangkok 10110: 4063, 4098

TURKEY

Akcali & Tuna, Bahariye Caddesi 8/6, 81300 Kadiköy, Istanbul: 4007, 4104, 4106

Nurcihan Kesim Literary Agency, PO Box 868, Sirkeci, Istanbul: 4041, 4049, 4063, 4067, 4073, 4085, 4099

UK

Darley Anderson Books, Estelle House, 11 Eustace Road, London SW6 1JB: 4005
Dr Ursula A. Barnett, 19 Avenue South, Surbiton, Surrey KT5 8PJ: 4116
Big Apple Tuttle Mori, 58d Clifton Gardens, London W9 1AU: 4034
Blake Friedmann Literary Agency, 37–41 Gower Street, London WC1E 6HH: 4104
Felicity Bryan : 4106
Rosemarie Buckman, Ryman's Cottage, Little Tew, Oxford OX7 4JJ, UK: 4027, 4063, 4091
Gregory & Radice Authors' Agents: 4036
Jennifer Luithlen, 88 Holmfield Road, Leicester LE2 1SB: 4015, 4073, 4087
The Marsh Agency, 138 Buckingham Palace Road, London SW1W 9SA: 4054, 4057, 4085
Andrew Nurnberg Associates Ltd, Clerkenwell House, 45–47 Clerkenwell Green, London EC1R 0HT: 4009, 4017, 4034, 4035, 4037, 4042, 4049, 4067, 4084, 4085, 4089, 4095, 4099, 4106
The Sharland Organisation, 9 Marlborough Crescent, Bedford Park, London W4 1HE: 4022
Benita Edzard Sheil Land, 43 Doughty Street, London WC1N 2LF: 4109
TFS Literary Agency: 4113
Lavinia Trevor Literary Agency, 6 The Glasshouse, 49A Goldhawk Road, London W12 8QP: 4105

USA

Acropolis Books Ltd, Reston, VA 22090: 4092
James Allen, PO Box 278, 538 East Harford Street, Milford, PA 18337: 4078
Alliance Books, 133 West 72nd Street, Suite 304, New York, NY 10023: 4064
Miriam Altshuler Literary Agency, RR 1, Box 5, 5 Old Post Road, Red Hook, NY 12571: 4040
Marcia Amsterdam, 41 West 82nd Street, New York, NY 10024: 4073
Arcadia, 20A Old Neversink Road, Danbury, CT 06811: 4054, 4054
Jason Aronson Inc [translation only], 230 Livingston Street, Northvale, NJ 07647: 4072
Avery Publishing Group Inc, Garden City Park, NY 11040: 4092
Avon Books, 105 Madison Avenue, New York, NY 10016: 4050
The Axelrod Agency, 66 Church Street, Lenox, MA 01240: 4099
Bardon Chinese Media Agency, 55 Pineapple Street 2D, Brooklyn Heights, New York, NY 11201: 4007, 4041
Barricade Books Inc, 150 Fifth Avenue, New York, NY 10011: 4048
Barron's Publishers of General and Educational Books, 250 Wireless Blvd, Hauppauge, NY 11788: 4048
Bonus Books Inc, 160 East Illinois Street, Chicago, IL 60611: 4073
Georges Borchardt Inc (Richard Scott Simon): 4086
Brandt & Brandt Inc, 1501 Broadway, New York, NY 10036: 4040
The Helen Brann Agency, Curtis Road, Bridgewater, CT 06752: 4079
Ed Breslin Agency Ltd (Sheil Land Associates Ltd): 4086
Jane Jordan Browne, 410 South Michigan Avenue, Room 828, Chicago, IL 60605: 4040
Brunner Mazel Inc, 19 Union Square, New York, NY 10003: 4072
Knox Burger Associates, 39½ Washington Square South, New York, NY 10012: 4028, 4035
Jane Chelius Literary Agency, 548 2nd Street, Brooklyn, NY 11215: 4040
Chelsea West Inc, 156 Fifth Avenue, Suite 608, New York, NY 10010: 4076
Columbia Literary Associates, 7902 Nottingham Way, Elliott City, MD: 4073
Marilyn Connor, 640 West 153rd Street, New York, NY 10031: 4073
The Connor Agency, 7333 Gallagher Drive, Edina, MN 55435: 4080
The Content Co Inc, 457 Broome Street, New York, NY 10013: 4028
Copyrights America Inc, High Street Court, Suite 206, Morristown, NY 07960: 4021
Darhansoff & Verrill Literary Agency, 179 Franklin Street, New York, NY 10013: 4085, 4085
J de S Associates Inc, Shagbark Road, South Norwalk, CT 06840: 4067
Ivan R. Dee Inc, 1332 North Halsted Street, Chicago, IL: 4004

Anita Diamant Inc, Apartment 1508, 310 Madison Avenue, New York, NY 10017: **4040**

Jonathan Dolger, 49 East 96th Street, Apt 9B, New York, NY 10028: 4089

Donadio & Ashworth, 231 West 22nd Street, New York, NY 10011: **4083**

Dramatists Play Service Inc, 440 Park Avenue South, New York, NY 10016: **4097**, 4097

Peter Elek Associates, 457 Broome Street, New York, NY 10013: **4028**

Ethan Ellenberg Literary Agency, Suite 5E, 548 Broadway, New York, NY 10012: **4073**

Farrar, Straus & Giroux (Richard Scott Simon): **4086**

Bill Fawcett & Associates, 27861 Forest Garden Road, Wanconde, IL 60084-2838: **4063**

The Fox Chase Agency Inc, The Public Ledger Building, Independence Square, Philadelphia, PA 19106: **4012**

Lynn C. Franklin Associates Ltd, 386 Park Avenue South, NY 10016: **4016**, **4028**

Gardner Press, Suite 104, 6801 Lakeworth Road, Lakeworth, FL 33467: **4072**

Max Gartenberg, 521 Fifth Avenue, Suite 1700, New York, NY 10175: **4078**

Gelfman Schneider Literary Agents Inc, 250 West 57th Street, Suite 2515, New York, NY 10107: **4024**, 4042

Goodman Associates, 500 West End Avenue, New York, NY 10024: **4028**

Maxine Groffsky Inc, 2 Fifth Avenue, New York, NY 10004: **4083**

The Guilford Press, 72 Spring Street, New York, NY 10012: **4072**

John Hawkins & Associates, 71 West 23rd Street, Suite 1600, New York, NY 10010: **4079**

Frederick Hill Associates Literary Agency, 1842 Union Street, San Francisco, CA 94123: **4016**

Holiday House Inc, 425 Madison Avenue, New York, NY 10017: **4049**

Humanities Press, 105 First Avenue, Atlantic Highlands, NJ 07710-1023: **4064**

Hyperion-Disney Publishing Co, 114 Fifth Avenue, New York, NY 10011: **4040**

ICM, 40 West 57th Street, New York, NY 10019: **4083**

IMG Literary, 22 East 71st Street, New York, NY 10021-4911: **4055**, 4073, **4073**

International Universities Press, 59 Boston Post Road, Madison, CT 06443-1524: **4072**

Jabberwocky (Joshua Bilmes), 41-16 47th Avenue, 2D, Sunnyside, NY 11104-3040: **4063**

Melanie Jackson, 250 West 57th Street, New York, NY 10107: **4083**

JCA Literary Agency Inc, 27 West 20th Street, Suite 1103, New York, NY 10011: **4042**, 4067, 4070

Ben F. Kamsler Ltd, 5501 Noble Avenue, Van Nuys, CA 91411: **4078**

Lila Karpf, 225 East 63rd Street, New York, NY 10021: **4079**

Virginia Kidd Literary Agency, PO Box 278, 538 East Harford Street, Milford, PA 18337: **4078**

Kidde, Hoyt & Picard, 335 East 51st Street, New York, NY 10022: **4040**

Stuart Krichevsky Literary Agency Inc, One Bridge Street, Suite 26, Irvington, NY 10533: **4007**

Allan Lang International Book Marketing Ltd, 234 Nassau Street, Princeton, NJ 08542: 4022

Sarah Lazin Books, 126 Fifth Avenue, New York, NY 10011: **4004**, **4028**

Lescher & Lescher Ltd, 155 East 71st Street, New York, NY 10021: **4040**

Ellen Levine Literary Agency Inc, Suite 1801, 15 East 26th Street, New York, NY 10010: **4040**, 4084

Wendy Lipkind Literary Agency, 165 East 66th Street, New York, NY 10021: **4004**, 4004

Lyons & Burford, 31 West 21st Street, New York, NY 10010: **4073**

Donald Maass Agency, 157 West 57th Street, New York, NY 10019: **4063**, 4063

Gina Maccoby Literary Agency, 1123 Broadway, Suite 1010, New York, NY 10010: **4040**

Richard McDonough, 551 Franklin Street, Cambridge, MA 02139: **4060**

Helen McGrath Associates, 1406 Idaho Court, Concord, CA 94521: **4020**

McIntosh & Otis Inc, 310 Madison Avenue, New York, NY 10017: 4020, **4040**, 4060, **4098**, 4098

Mcpherson & Co, PO Box 1126, Kingston, NY 12401: **4004**

Dan Mandel, 55 Fifth Avenue, New York, NY 10003: 4109

March 10th Inc, 4 Myrtle Street, Haworth, NJ 07641: **4036**

Elaine Markson Literary, 44 Greenwich Avenue, New York, NY 10011: 4016

Marlowe & Co, 632 Broadway, 7th Floor, New York, NY 10012: **4080**

The Evan Marshall Agency, 6 Tristam Place, Pinebrook, NJ 07058: **4055**

The Martell Agency, 555 Fifth Avenue, Suite 1900, New York, NY 10017: **4079**

Masquerade Books, 801 Second Avenue, New York, NY 10017: **4048**

Jed Mattes Inc, 200 West 72nd Street #50, New York, NY 10023: **4035**, 4035

Maxwell Aley Associates, 145 East 35th Street, New York, NY 10016: **4008**

Meadowbrook Press, 18318 Minnetonka Boulevard, Deephaven, MN 55391: **4052**

Mercury House, 201 Filbert Street, Suite 400, San Francisco, CA 94133: **4050**

Martha Millard Agency, 204 Park Avenue, Madison, NJ 07940: **4080**, 4080

The Miller Agency, 801 West End Avenue, New York, NY 10025: **4016**

William Morris Agency Inc, 1325 Avenue of the Americas, New York, NY 10019: 4066

Mystery Writers of America, 17 East 47th Street, Sixth Floor, New York, NY 10017: **4078**

Jean V. Naggar Literary Agency, 216 East 75th Street, New York, NY 10021: **4035**, 4035

New Century Publishers, Piscataway, NJ: **4092**

New Directions Publishing Corporation, 80 Eighth Avenue, New York, NY 10011: **4078**

Harold Ober Associates Inc, 425 Madison Avenue, New York, NY 10017: **4041**, 4041

Richard Parks, 138 E16 Street, 5B, New York, NY 10003: **4054**

John K. Payne Literary Agency Inc, Box No. 1003, New York, NY 10276: **4078**

Lori Perkins, 5800 Arlington Avenue, Riverdale, NY 10471: **4040**

Permanent Press, Noyac Road, Sag Harbor, NY: **4015**

Putnam Berkley Inc, 200 Madison Avenue, New York, NY 10016: **4007**

Raines & Raines Agency, 71 Park Avenue, New York, NY 10016: **4012**

Renaissance-Swan Film Agency Inc, 8523 Sunset Boulevard, Los Angeles, CA 90069: 4005, **4118**

Christine Tomasino RLR Associates, 7 West 51st Street, New York, NY 10019: 4050

The Robbins Office Inc, 405 Park Avenue, New York, NY 10022: **4099**

Mitchell Rose, 688 Avenue of the Americas, Suite 303, New York, NY 10003: 4005

Russell & Volkening Inc, 50 West 29th Street, New York, NY 10001: **4040**

The Sagalyn Agency, 1520 New Hampshire Avenue NW, Washington, DC 20036: **4028**

The Sagalyn Literary Agency, 4635 Bethesda Avenue, Suite 302, Bethesda, MD 20814: **4035**

Susan Schulman, 454 West 44th Street, New York, NY 10036: **4063**

Scott Meredith Literary Agency Inc, 845 Third Avenue, New York, NY 10022: **4040**

Scovil Chichak Galen Literary Agents Inc, Suite 1020, 381 Park Avenue South, New York, NY 10016: 4024, **4099**, 4099

Lynn Seligman, 400 Highland Avenue, Upper Montclair, NJ 07043: **4073**

Bobbe Siegel, 41 West 83rd Street, New York, NY 10024: **4073**

Evelyn Singer Agency Inc, Box 594, White Plains, NY 10602: **4078**

Singer Media Corporation, Seaview Business Park, 1030 Calle Cordillera, Unit 106, San Clemente, CA 92673: **4048**, 4048

SLL Inc, 1 Madison Avenue, New York, NY 10010: **4076**, 4076

Soho Press, 853 Broadway, New York, NY 10003: **4049**

Spectrum Literary Agency, Room 1205, 432 Park Avenue South, New York, NY 10016: **4048**

Philip G. Spitzer Literary Agency, 50 Talmage Farm Lane, East Hampton, New York, NY 11937: **4079**

Nancy Stauffer Associates, 137 Fifth Avenue, New York, NY 10010: **4007**

Robin Straus Literary Agency, 229 East 79th Street, New York, NY 10021: **4038**, 4038

Roslyn Targ Literary Agency Inc, 105 West 13th Street, New York, NY 10011: **4016**

Thunder's Mouth Press, 632 Broadway, 7th Floor, New York, NY 10012: **4080**

United Media, 200 Park Avenue, New York, NY 10166: **4052**

Barrie Van Dyck Agency Inc, 217 Spruce Street, Philadelphia, PA 19106: **4098**

Ralph M. Vicinanza Ltd *(selected titles)*, 111 Eighth Avenue, Suite 1501, New York, NY 10011: 4048

Wallace Literary Agency, 177 East 70th Street, New York, NY 10021: **4040**

Harriet Wasserman Literary Agency Inc, 137 East 36th Street, New York, NY 10016: **4040**

Waterside Productions Inc, The Waterside Building, 2191 San Elijo Avenue, Cardiff-by-the-Sea, CA 92014: 4082

The Wendy Weil Agency Inc, Suite 1300, 232 Madison Avenue, New York, NY 10016: **4041**

The Weingel Fidel Agency, 310 East 46th Street, New York, NY 10017: **4016**

Rhoda Weyr Agency, 151 Bergen Street, Brooklyn, New York, NY 11217: **4028**

Albert Whitman & Co, 6340 Oakton Street, Morton Grove, IL 60053-2723: **4072**

Writers House Inc, 21 West 26th Street, New York, NY 10010: **4007**, 4007, 4082

Marian Young, 156 Fifth Avenue, Suite 608, New York, NY 10010: **4050**

YUGOSLAVIA

Prava & Prevodi, Koste Jovanovíca 18, 11000 Belgrade: 4048, 4063, 4073, 4078, 4085

ZIMBABWE

Rosemary Kimberley, 15 Cheshire Avenue, Avondale, Harare: 4118

National Theatre Organization, PO Box 2701, Harare: 4097

7.6 INDEX OF ISBN PREFIXES

0 00: **1387**
0 00 2: **1387, 1392**
0 00 219: **1387**
0 00 220: **1387**
0 00 360: **1386**
0 00 44: **1387**
0 00 447: **1386**
0 00 512: **1388**
0 00 599: **1388**
0 00 6: **1387**
0 00 627: **1388**
0 01: **1387**
0 03: **1384, 1429**
0 04: **1387**
0 06: **1387**
0 06 04: **2034**
0 06 50: **2034**
0 07: **1542, 2056, 2172**
0 07 6: **1532**
0 08: **1147, 1276**
0 09: **1211, 1387, 1437, 1721**
0 09 1: **1722**
0 09 9: **1049, 1721, 1722**
0 10: **1419**
0 11: **1419**
0 11 49: **1419**
0 11 701: **1608**
0 12: **1005, 1384**
0 13: **1673, 1698, 1699, 1701**
0 14: **1661, 2068, 2339, 2460**
0 14 09: **1302**
0 14 1: **1532**
0 15: **1384**
0 17: **1611, 2064, 2161, 2460**
0 19: **1529, 1648**
0 19 54: **2192**
0 19 558: **2459**
0 19 560: **2333**
0 19 561: **2333**
0 19 562: **2333**
0 19 563: **2333**
0 19 570: **2510**
0 19 571: **2510**
0 19 572: **2420**
0 19 584: **2253, 2490**

0 19 585: **2253**
0 19 587: **2490**
0 19 588: **2490**
0 201: **2054**
0 204: **2208**
0 205: **1698**
0 208: **1855**
0 216: **1611, 1661**
0 224: **1721, 1722**
0 225: **1182**
0 227: **1199**
0 229: **1015, 1089**
0 232: **1236**
0 233: **1244**
0 237: **1291**
0 240: **1145**
0 241: **1381, 1661, 2068, 2460**
0 245: **1015, 1389, 1445**
0 246: **1387**
0 250: **1145**
0 260: **1532**
0 261: **1387, 1532**
0 262: **1584**
0 263: **1385**
0 264: **1532, 1590**
0 268: **1532**
0 273: **1659, 1685**
0 275: **1368**
0 281: **1812**
0 283: **1545, 1799, 2451**
0 284: **1021**
0 285: **1815**
0 287: **1827**
0 289: **1892**
0 291: **1052**
0 297: **1640, 1903**
0 300: **1933**
0 302: **1917**
0 304: **1162**
0 306: **1689**
0 309: **1596**
0 310: **1387**
0 312: **2451**
0 313: **1368**
0 314: **2034**
0 316: **1528**
0 319: **1638**

0 330: **1543, 1545, 1677, 2451**
0 333: **1015, 1543, 1544, 1545, 1546, 1548, 1611, 2418, 2451**
0 334: **1773**
0 335: **1636**
0 337: **1419**
0 340: **1048, 1422, 1423, 1424, 1425, 2039, 2040**
0 347: **1354**
0 349: **1528, 2460**
0 352: **1890**
0 370: **1721, 1722**
0 373: **1385, 2148**
0 378: **2419**
0 385: **1869**
0 393: **1623**
0 395: **1431**
0 397: **2034**
0 406: **1146**
0 407: **1145**
0 408: **1145, 2208, 2435**
0 409: **1145, 2016, 2208**
0 411: **1387**
0 412: **1184**
0 413: **1572, 2208**
0 414: **1364, 1844**
0 415: **1747**
0 416: **1573**
0 419: **1184, 1821**
0 420: **1844**
0 421: **1844**
0 426: **1890**
0 431: **1405**
0 433: **2208**
0 434: **1145, 1404, 1407, 2208**
0 435: **1405, 1406, 2208**
0 436: **1660, 1784, 2208**
0 440: **1869**
0 443: **1194, 1659**
0 450: **1423, 2040**
0 451: **2068, 2460**
0 452: **2068, 2460**

0 453: **2068**
0 455: **2050**
0 460: **1243, 1640**
0 470: **1915, 2236**
0 471: **1915, 2046, 2236**
0 477: **2449**
0 485: **1058**
0 486: **1211**
0 500: **1855**
0 510: **1089**
0 521: **1149**
0 522: **2058**
0 525: **2068**
0 540: **1089, 1670, 2208**
0 550: **1506**
0 551: **1387, 1388**
0 552: **1869**
0 553: **1869**
0 563: **1075, 1076**
0 564: **1125**
0 565: **1606**
0 566: **1354**
0 567: **1197**
0 571: **1297, 2460**
0 572: **1321**
0 573: **1330**
0 575: **1349**
0 582: **2054, 2450, 2530**
0 583: **1387**
0 586: **1387**
0 590: **1770**
0 592: **1145**
0 593: **1869**
0 600: **1382, 1383, 2208**
0 602: **1345**
0 603: **1383, 2208**
0 624: **2514**
0 627: **2516**
0 631: **1093, 1529**
0 632: **1094**
0 636: **2507**
0 642: **1855, 2010**
0 642 106: **2063**
0 642 130: **2061**
0 643: **2020**
0 644: **2010**

0 660: **2109, 2112, 2180**
0 662: **2109**
0 669: **2149**
0 670: **1661, 2068, 2460**
0 671: **1803, 2451**
0 673: **2034**
0 674: **1390**
0 679: **1722**
0 684: **1803**
0 7005: **1619**
0 7007: **1229**
0 7008: **1283**
0 7011: **1188, 1722**
0 7012: **1188, 1722**
0 7015: **2054**
0 7016: **2046**
0 7018: **2049**
0 7020: **1067, 1384, 1763**
0 7021: **2501**
0 7022: **2073**
0 7028: **1386**
0 7043: **1711, 1924**
0 7045: **1354**
0 7054: **1864**
0 7055: **2454**
0 7062: **1898**
0 7063: **1897**
0 7064: **1382**
0 7070: **2388**
0 7073: **1753, 1776**
0 7078: **1604**
0 7083: **1895**
0 7089: **1862**
0 7090: **1379**
0 7091: **1379**
0 7095: **1134**
0 7097: **1135**
0 7103: **1488**
0 7105: **1378**
0 7106: **1479**
0 7108: **1700**
0 7110: **1022**
0 7111: **1540**
0 7112: **1525**
0 7117: **1481**
0 7119: **1630**
0 7121: **1685**

0 7123: **1127, 1128, 1130, 1131**
0 7126: **1071, 1722**
0 7130: **1161**
0 7131: **1048, 1422, 2039, 2040**
0 7136: **1015, 1072, 1089**
0 7137: **1096**
0 7141: **1132, 1855**
0 7145: **1114, 1148**
0 7146: **1161**
0 7148: **1668**
0 7151: **1193**
0 7152: **1756**
0 7153: **1237**
0 7155: **1493**
0 7156: **1255**
0 7158: **1089**
0 7160: **1272**
0 7161: **1354**
0 7162: **1282**
0 7163: **1298**
0 7165: **2396**
0 7167: **1329**
0 7169: **1344**
0 7171: **2394**
0 7175: **1861**
0 7181: **1485, 1661, 2068, 2460**
0 7185: **1516**
0 7188: **1538**
0 7190: **1553**
0 7195: **1594**
0 7197: **1597**
0 7198: **1379**
0 7199: **1609, 1671**
0 7201: **1556**
0 7202: **1621**
0 7206: **1644**
0 7207: **1485, 2068**
0 7214: **1504, 2068**
0 7216: **1384, 1763**
0 7217: **1769**
0 7219: **1792**
0 7220: **1793**
0 7223: **1831**
0 7225: **1387**
0 7226: **2460**
0 7229: **1858**
0 7230: **1386, 1387**

0 7232: **1661, 1899, 2068, 2460**	0 7725: **2160**	0 85124: **1820**	0 85486: **1907**	0 86071: **1588**	0 86417: **2048**
	0 7726: **2213**	0 85131: **1023**	0 85487: **1910**	0 86072: **1711**	0 86431: **2009**
0 7235: **1929**	0 7730: **2122**	0 85142: **1055**	0 85491: **1499**	0 86078: **1052**	0 86433: **2057**
0 7239: **1495**	0 7735: **2171**	0 85143: **1056**	0 85496: **1083**	0 86082: **1598**	0 86438: **2074**
0 7241: **2062, 2077**	0 7744: **2189**	0 85151: **1069**	0 85498: **1467**	0 86084: **1284**	0 86439: **2015**
0 7242: **2071**	0 7748: **2213, 2230**	0 85152: **1387**	0 85503: **1563**	0 86091: **1885**	0 86440: **2046**
0 7243: **2027**	0 7766: **2191**	0 85157: **1524**	0 85527: **1700**	0 86093: **1632**	0 86442: **2053**
0 7253: **2041**	0 7770: **2204**	0 85165: **1780**	0 85532: **1783**	0 86101: **1758**	0 86445: **2002**
0 7254: **2049**	0 7780: **2188**	0 85169: **1171**	0 85533: **1585, 2208**	0 86104: **1691**	0 86450: **2074**
0 7255: **2041**	0 7817: **2034**	0 85170: **1085**	0 85543: **1387**	0 86112: **1124**	0 86462: **2076**
0 7270: **2049**	0 7900: **2208**	0 85174: **1136**	0 85546: **1738**	0 86121: **2380, 2391**	0 86469: **2440**
0 7277: **1853**	0 7923: **1501**	0 85177: **1015, 1089**	0 85567: **2018**	0 86125: **1760**	0 86473: **2468**
0 7278: **1790**	0 7974: **2532**	0 85183: **1166**	0 85572: **2038**	0 86131: **1760**	0 86492: **2142**
0 7279: **1100**	0 7981: **2500**	0 85186: **1750**	0 85574: **2025**	0 86132: **1760**	0 86505: **1220**
0 7286: **1771**	0 7986: **2502**	0 85202: **1908**	0 85575: **2001**	0 86140: **1811**	0 86531: **1905**
0 7293: **1361**	0 7994: **2517**	0 85205: **1218**	0 85597: **1409**	0 86145: **1001**	0 86542: **1094**
0 7294: **1894**	0 8020: **1867**	0 85206: **1231**	0 85598: **1646**	0 86146: **1168**	0 86569: **1368**
0 7295: **2033**	0 8037: **2068**	0 85207: **1233**	0 85614: **1320**	0 86153: **1756**	0 86571: **2182**
0 7301: **2075**	0 8039: **1754**	0 85213: **1597**	0 85628: **1273**	0 86155: **1605**	0 86715: **1714**
0 7305: **2080**	0 8053: **2054**	0 85224: **1264**	0 85633: **1619**	0 86158: **1861**	0 86720: **1483**
0 7306: **2077**	0 8065: **1158**	0 85229: **1278**	0 85635: **1155**	0 86163: **1063**	0 86760: **2003**
0 7308: **2027**	0 8089: **1384**	0 85231: **1728**	0 85640: **1091**	0 86175: **1466**	0 86788: **2030**
0 7310: **2080**	0 8094: **1864**	0 85234: **1289**	0 85646: **1040**	0 86186: **1106**	0 86793: **1094, 2014**
0 7312: **2076**	0 8133: **1905**	0 85236: **1303**	0 85648: **1527**	0 86187: **1681**	0 86799: **2028**
0 7324: **2003**	0 8153: **1337, 2034**	0 85238: **1094**	0 85650: **1198**	0 86188: **1676**	0 86806: **2032**
0 7327: **2059**	0 8160: **1300**	0 85241: **1322**	0 85654: **1285**	0 86190: **1587**	0 86817: **2517**
0 7444: **1538**	0 8168: **2056**	0 85242: **1618**	0 85660: **1872**	0 86196: **1522**	0 86819: **2021**
0 7445: **1896**	0 8184: **1158**	0 85243: **1325**	0 85661: **1005**	0 86201: **1781**	0 86840: **2065**
0 7449: **1012**	0 8212: **1528**	0 85244: **1356**	0 85667: **1917**	0 86202: **1258**	0 86852: **2495, 2497**
0 7450: **1698, 1700**	0 8216: **1158**	0 85245: **1710**	0 85668: **1046**	0 86210: **1032**	0 86896: **2079**
0 7451: **1190**	0 8240: **2034**	0 85249: **1826**	0 85670: **1006**	0 86211: **1716**	0 86914: **2068**
0 7453: **1691**	0 8289: **2460**	0 85255: **1228**	0 85683: **1796**	0 86217: **2404**	0 86917: **2029**
0 7456: **1093, 1693**	0 8306: **2056**	0 85258: **1705**	0 85684: **1461**	0 86220: **1190**	0 86922: **2531**
0 7459: **1086, 1527, 1812**	0 8352: **1112**	0 85259: **1343**	0 85692: **1262**	0 86232: **1936**	0 86925: **2529**
	0 8356: **1858**	0 85263: **1798**	0 85694: **1868**	0 86238: **1187**	0 86975: **2512**
0 7460: **1881**	0 8371: **1368**	0 85269: **1387**	0 85696: **1398**	0 86239: **1499**	0 86981: **2515**
0 7463: **1622**	0 8379: **1112**	0 85274: **1467**	0 85819: **2047**	0 86241: **1153**	0 86991: **2503**
0 7470: **1089**	0 8385: **1698**	0 85278: **1417**	0 85825: **2026**	0 86242: **1009**	0 86997: **2505**
0 7472: **1401**	0 8386: **1348**	0 85288: **1447**	0 85828: **3054**	0 86243: **1932**	0 87055: **1701**
0 7475: **1098**	0 8387: **1348**	0 85290: **1119, 1449**	0 85847: **2008**	0 86248: **1539**	0 87070: **1855**
0 7478: **1798**	0 8389: **1029**	0 85291: **1008**	0 85910: **2066**	0 86250: **2042**	0 87140: **1623**
0 7486: **1264, 1694**	0 8419: **1017, 1428**	0 85292: **1457**	0 85924: **1387, 2035, 2036**	0 86251: **2028**	0 87196: **1300**
0 7487: **1861**	0 8442: **1886**	0 85295: **1458**		0 86259: **1489**	0 87217: **1112**
0 7490: **1025**	0 8453: **1348**	0 85296: **1459**	0 85934: **1065**	0 86264: **1033**	0 87322: **1434**
0 7492: **1634, 1635**	0 8487: **1528**	0 85298: **1560**	0 85935: **1112**	0 86272: **1506**	0 87348: **1654**
0 7493: **1554, 1582, 2208**	0 85003: **1643**	0 85299: **1186**	0 85937: **1559**	0 86278: **2400**	0 87413: **1348**
	0 85009: **1926**	0 85303: **1161**	0 85938: **1484**	0 86281: **1042**	0 87436: **1003**
0 7494: **1502**	0 85012: **1093**	0 85305: **1478**	0 85941: **1698, 1701**	0 86291: **1112**	0 87630: **2034**
0 7495: **1001**	0 85021: **1909**	0 85306: **1481**	0 85946: **1454**	0 86292: **1857**	0 87879: **1037**
0 7497: **1551, 2208**	0 85025: **1213**	0 85308: **1484**	0 85950: **1861**	0 86299: **1843**	0 87893: **1329**
0 7498: **1929**	0 85030: **1387**	0 85315: **1511**	0 85952: **3057**	0 86303: **1568**	0 87901: **1329, 2034**
0 7499: **1676**	0 85031: **1025**	0 85320: **1526**	0 85953: **1189**	0 86311: **1760**	0 87975: **1707**
0 7500: **1541**	0 85032: **1233**	0 85323: **1530**	0 85956: **1224**	0 86315: **1312**	0 87982: **1348**
0 7502: **1541, 1901**	0 85033: **1671**	0 85331: **1537**	0 85964: **1177**	0 86316: **1930**	0 88010: **1828**
0 7503: **1467**	0 85036: **1569**	0 85340: **1901**	0 85965: **1690**	0 86318: **1248**	0 88011: **1434**
0 7506: **1145, 2208**	0 85038: **1502**	0 85342: **2399**	0 85967: **1052, 1774**	0 86319: **1616**	0 88029: **1886**
0 7507: **1301**	0 85039: **1340**	0 85364: **1653**	0 85969: **1795, 1812**	0 86322: **2381**	0 88048: **1030**
0 7508: **1320**	0 85045: **1642**	0 85365: **1524**	0 85973: **1861**	0 86325: **1172**	0 88088: **1920**
0 7509: **1843**	0 85046: **1190**	0 85368: **1047**	0 85976: **1246**	0 86327: **2405**	0 88167: **2034**
0 7510: **1418**	0 85052: **1660**	0 85369: **1669**	0 85978: **1233**	0 86332: **1103**	0 88168: **1026**
0 7513: **1248**	0 85059: **1829**	0 85370: **1672**	0 85979: **1019**	0 86338: **1287**	0 88173: **1698**
0 7514: **1184**	0 85066: **1851**	0 85372: **1684**	0 85985: **1189**	0 86339: **1655**	0 88188: **1466**
0 7515: **1528**	0 85070: **1210**	0 85389: **1807**	0 85989: **1294**	0 86341: **1459**	0 88192: **1863**
0 7517: **1116**	0 85078: **1901**	0 85390: **2404**	0 85991: **1115**	0 86343: **1323**	0 88509: **2158**
0 7520: **1332, 1659**	0 85083: **1281**	0 85398: **1342**	0 85997: **1190**	0 86347: **1259**	0 88625: **2132**
0 7521: **1403**	0 85084: **1748**	0 85403: **1749**	0 86009: **1549**	0 86356: **1761**	0 88629: **2114**
0 7522: **1113**	0 85086: **1682**	0 85404: **1750**	0 86012: **1141**	0 86358: **1387**	0 88646: **2132**
0 7523: **1506**	0 85088: **1350**	0 85412: **1759**	0 86020: **1881**	0 86359: **1466**	0 88677: **2068**
0 7524: **1178**	0 85091: **2055**	0 85421: **1781**	0 86021: **1420**	0 86368: **1216**	0 88734: **1688**
0 7531: **1468**	0 85105: **1811**	0 85429: **1320**	0 86022: **1140**	0 86369: **1890**	0 88736: **1561**
0 7623: **1475**	0 85110: **1461**	0 85435: **1233**	0 86023: **1715**	0 86372: **1472**	0 88750: **2188**
0 7701: **2128**	0 85111: **1461**	0 85439: **1757**	0 86025: **1410**	0 86377: **1709**	0 88751: **2196**
0 7705: **2139, 2173**	0 85112: **1376**	0 85440: **1828**	0 86031: **1620**	0 86380: **1734**	0 88754: **2197**
0 7710: **2169**	0 85115: **1115**	0 85442: **1830**	0 86037: **1470**	0 86382: **1581**	0 88755: **2174**
0 7715: **2139, 2173**	0 85119: **1190**	0 85449: **1347**	0 86051: **1743**	0 86383: **1350**	0 88760: **2104**
0 7718: **2213**	0 85120: **1332**	0 85473: **1453**	0 86065: **1499**	0 86388: **1921**	0 88776: **2228**
0 7720: **2160**	0 85121: **1332**	0 85476: **1499**	0 86068: **1889**	0 86411: **2060**	0 88784: **2156**

0 88796: **2115**	0 901269: **1371**	0 905114: **1513**	0 907349: **1818**	0 919203: **2220**	0 921332: **2226**
0 88801: **2229**	0 901291: **1595**	0 905118: **1288**	0 907383: **1476, 1477**	0 919349: **2144**	0 921411: **2107**
0 88833: **2129**	0 901366: **1490**	0 905138: **1400**	0 907462: **1039**	0 919380: **2185**	0 921556: **2145**
0 88839: **2146**	0 901462: **1456**	0 905140: **2400**	0 907476: **1692**	0 919441: **2224**	0 921573: **2201**
0 88844: **2199**	0 901495: **1588**	0 905203: **1580**	0 907486: **1382**	0 919462: **2220**	0 921586: **2183**
0 88850: **2207**	0 901595: **3053**	0 905209: **1887**	0 907496: **1316**	0 919473: **2130**	0 921627: **2113**
0 88854: **1867, 2214**	0 901665: **1494**	0 905249: **1307**	0 907547: **1439**	0 919493: **2163**	0 921689: **2099**
0 88864: **2092**	0 901714: **2403**	0 905263: **1441**	0 907566: **1873**	0 919519: **2104**	0 921692: **2162**
0 88878: **2097**	0 901716: **1456**	0 905273: **1851**	0 907579: **1019**	0 919566: **2193**	0 921788: **2165**
0 88882: **2155**	0 901759: **1700**	0 905291: **1667**	0 907590: **1816**	0 919573: **2183**	0 921827: **2195**
0 88884: **2179**	0 901762: **1317**	0 905366: **1082**	0 907610: **1865**	0 919591: **2198**	0 921842: **2233**
0 88887: **2102**	0 901764: **1225**	0 905392: **1216**	0 907621: **1713**	0 919599: **2238**	0 921881: **2145**
0 88894: **2129**	0 901771: **1335**	0 905450: **1112**	0 907628: **1380**	0 919618: **2099**	0 921912: **2170**
0 88899: **2129, 2143**	0 901783: **1007**	0 905451: **1208**	0 907638: **1882**	0 919619: **2099**	0 929005: **2215**
0 88910: **2120**	0 901787: **1936**	0 905459: **1727**	0 907679: **1142**	0 919626: **2105**	0 929032: **2238**
0 88920: **2237**	0 901791: **1600**	0 905478: **1033**	0 907683: **1200**	0 919627: **2203**	0 929087: **1473**
0 88922: **2222**	0 901805: **1772**	0 905483: **1911**	0 907758: **1768**	0 919654: **2146**	0 929262: **2093**
0 88924: **2131, 2216**	0 901819: **1193**	0 905492: **1036**	0 907768: **1217**	0 919670: **2131**	0 930454: **3061**
0 88954: **2152**	0 901824: **1565**	0 905703: **1180**	0 907849: **1054**	0 919769: **2111**	0 931146: **1863**
0 88962: **2177**	0 901877: **1771**	0 905715: **1811**	0 907850: **1245**	0 919783: **2103**	0 931250: **1434**
0 88968: **2117**	0 901905: **1878**	0 905762: **1936**	0 907938: **1886**	0 919797: **2165**	0 931340: **1863**
0 88971: **2147**	0 901976: **1880**	0 905838: **1436**	0 907969: **1120**	0 919813: **2108**	0 931421: **1037**
0 88975: **2137**	0 902028: **1039**	0 905895: **1252**	0 908031: **2086**	0 919822: **2103**	0 931477: **1739**
0 88978: **2096**	0 902088: **1499**	0 905998: **1105**	0 908081: **1320**	0 919834: **2197**	0 933516: **1026**
0 88982: **2190**	0 902129: **1249**	0 906008: **1690**	0 908086: **2053**	0 919888: **2183**	0 934223: **1348**
0 88984: **2200**	0 902145: **1155**	0 906031: **1087**	0 908090: **2043**	0 919890: **2232**	0 934977: **1920**
0 89006: **1051**	0 902197: **1443**	0 906048: **1459**	0 908094: **2032**	0 919913: **2095**	0 935702: **1329**
0 89042: **1030**	0 902363: **1195**	0 906053: **1061**	0 908112: **2002**	0 919926: **2124**	0 937091: **1654**
0 89158: **1905**	0 902561: **2385**	0 906070: **1567**	0 908237: **2065**	0 919946: **2098**	0 939481: **1490**
0 89232: **1475**	0 902726: **1886**	0 906127: **2392**	0 908300: **2534**	0 919948: **2104**	0 939643: **2401**
0 89433: **2056**	0 902992: **1451**	0 906156: **1508**	0 908307: **2533**	0 919957: **2153**	0 940866: **1348**
0 89454: **1329**	0 902996: **2393**	0 906212: **1848**	0 908308: **2530**	0 919964: **2164**	0 941664: **1348**
0 89471: **1752**	0 903001: **1311**	0 906214: **1844**	0 908310: **2530**	0 920057: **2099**	0 943231: **1838**
0 89746: **1158**	0 903031: **1463**	0 906224: **1105**	0 908311: **2528**	0 920059: **2140**	0 944190: **1348**
0 89766: **1617**	0 903102: **1232**	0 906247: **1041**	0 908387: **2495**	0 920063: **2239**	0 944256: **1339**
0 89789: **1368**	0 903317: **1341**	0 906273: **1860**	0 908540: **2028**	0 920066: **2225**	0 945636: **1348**
0 89862: **1375**	0 903354: **1452**	0 906285: **1041**	0 908567: **2457**	0 920079: **2136**	0 946003: **1935**
0 89930: **1368**	0 903393: **1226**	0 906294: **1875**	0 908569: **2458**	0 920080: **2147**	0 946015: **1599**
0 900068: **2378**	0 903450: **1003**	0 906348: **1257**	0 908608: **2434**	0 920110: **2142**	0 946097: **1347**
0 900075: **1920**	0 903461: **1474**	0 906362: **1353**	0 908610: **2433**	0 920121: **2212**	0 946137: **1320**
0 900087: **1173**	0 903466: **1176**	0 906369: **1250**	0 908629: **2438**	0 920236: **2094**	0 946139: **1274**
0 900090: **1054**	0 903534: **1126**	0 906391: **1550**	0 908630: **2462**	0 920277: **2231**	0 946183: **1167**
0 900125: **1066**	0 903540: **1312**	0 906393: **1020**	0 908652: **2456**	0 920303: **2094**	0 946211: **2379**
0 900162: **1065**	0 903715: **1452**	0 906397: **2104**	0 908704: **2466**	0 920304: **2145**	0 946242: **1662**
0 900178: **1235**	0 903729: **1472**	0 906399: **1028**	0 908756: **2441**	0 920316: **2184**	0 946270: **1665**
0 900246: **1170**	0 903804: **1681**	0 906427: **1097**	0 908757: **2462**	0 920417: **2206**	0 946284: **1227**
0 900274: **1439**	0 903843: **1628, 1653**	0 906506: **3018**	0 908783: **2453**	0 920474: **2181**	0 946313: **1147**
0 900312: **1215**	0 903895: **1743**	0 906517: **1808**	0 908790: **2447**	0 920490: **2127**	0 946323: **1614**
0 900319: **1226**	0 903909: **1507**	0 906520: **1577**	0 908812: **2436**	0 920502: **2162**	0 946328: **1163**
0 900332: **1564**	0 903983: **1436**	0 906527: **1649**	0 908864: **2465**	0 920534: **2157**	0 946395: **1275**
0 900379: **1314**	0 904011: **2393**	0 906540: **1269**	0 908876: **2448**	0 920541: **2193**	0 946439: **1487**
0 900382: **1705**	0 904017: **1603**	0 906554: **1199**	0 908877: **2443**	0 920544: **2175**	0 946451: **1374**
0 900384: **1328**	0 904110: **1163**	0 906579: **1687**	0 908884: **2467**	0 920633: **2225**	0 946462: **1289, 1355**
0 900458: **1414**	0 904357: **1456**	0 906584: **1078**	0 908906: **2441**	0 920663: **2154**	0 946487: **1536**
0 900470: **1614**	0 904387: **1843**	0 906619: **1775**	0 908912: **2469**	0 920717: **2144**	0 946495: **1837**
0 900549: **1589**	0 904498: **1697**	0 906710: **1725**	0 908916: **2457**	0 920722: **2135**	0 946510: **1739**
0 900550: **1398**	0 904503: **1043**	0 906717: **1505**	0 908990: **2439**	0 920763: **2133**	0 946550: **1571**
0 900559: **1601**	0 904568: **1612**	0 906731: **1191**	0 909144: **2031**	0 920802: **2133**	0 946551: **1339**
0 900568: **1387**	0 904597: **1578**	0 906754: **1305**	0 909268: **2028**	0 920813: **2217**	0 946559: **1705**
0 900592: **1671**	0 904631: **3010**	0 906780: **1215**	0 909532: **1112, 2084**	0 920814: **2201**	0 946590: **1849**
0 900625: **1256**	0 904651: **1042**	0 906782: **1363**	0 910230: **1029**	0 920847: **2202**	0 946616: **1415**
0 900630: **1737**	0 904705: **1275**	0 906791: **1583**	0 911285: **1882**	0 920852: **2185**	0 946621: **1471**
0 900652: **1072**	0 904722: **1416**	0 906798: **1053**	0 911797: **2401**	0 920862: **2110**	0 946626: **1240**
0 900675: **1811**	0 904724: **1901**	0 906896: **1652**	0 912138: **1319**	0 920897: **2184**	0 946640: **2397**
0 900680: **1813**	0 904725: **1491**	0 906969: **1412**	0 912704: **1031**	0 920911: **2104**	0 946653: **1288**
0 900751: **1315**	0 904727: **1704**	0 906980: **2395**	0 913460: **1654**	0 920953: **2123**	0 946688: **1463**
0 900768: **1895**	0 904748: **1430**	0 907018: **1845**	0 914294: **1752**	0 921051: **2219**	0 946699: **1835**
0 900771: **1294**	0 904766: **1918**	0 907033: **1438**	0 916422: **1738**	0 921054: **2185**	0 946707: **1462**
0 900778: **1891**	0 904836: **1213**	0 907061: **1704**	0 917072: **1698**	0 921102: **2211**	0 946724: **1160**
0 900886: **1923**	0 904864: **1932**	0 907070: **1789**	0 917304: **1863**	0 921103: **2164**	0 946771: **1817**
0 900898: **1290**	0 904910: **1377**	0 907115: **1237**	0 918016: **1348**	0 921128: **2185**	0 946796: **1034**
0 900967: **1427**	0 904919: **1694**	0 907188: **1466**	0 918438: **1434**	0 921149: **2106**	0 946819: **1373**
0 900976: **1455**	0 905005: **1849**	0 907206: **1455**	0 919091: **2209**	0 921215: **2134**	0 946826: **1678**
0 900977: **1040**	0 905028: **1591**	0 907264: **1934**	0 919100: **2116**	0 921217: **2194**	0 946857: **1241**
0 901072: **1811**	0 905099: **1515**	0 907271: **2387**	0 919143: **2195**	0 921282: **2186**	0 946889: **1445**
0 901116: **1777**	0 905104: **1800**	0 907304: **1286**		0 921284: **2098**	0 946890: **1735**
0 901223: **1459**		0 907345: **1518**		0 921299: **2215**	

0 946897: **1645**	0 948905: **1099**	1 55138: **2194**	1 85184: **1450**	1 85429: **1935**	1 85715: **1151**
0 946960: **1327**	0 948911: **1310**	1 55141: **2115**	1 85196: **1679**	1 85431: **1092**	1 85717: **1497**
0 946962: **1377**	0 948955: **1740**	1 55144: **2141**	1 85200: **1880**	1 85433: **1133**	1 85723: **1528**
0 946983: **1117**	0 948965: **1299**	1 55145: **2187, 2238**	1 85210: **1901**	1 85435: **3041**	1 85725: **1081**
0 947062: **2043**	0 949138: **2070**	1 55152: **2096**	1 85213: **1637**	1 85437: **1849**	1 85727: **1767**
0 947087: **2067**	0 949206: **2031**	1 55164: **2099**	1 85223: **1227**	1 85444: **1054**	1 85728: **1876**
0 947138: **2024**	0 949225: **2534**	1 55166: **1385, 2148**	1 85224: **1097**	1 85448: **1403**	1 85732: **1585, 2208**
0 947351: **2090**	0 949284: **2088**	1 55180: **2159**	1 85225: **1869**	1 85450: **1274**	1 85733: **1503**
0 947464: **2495**	0 949414: **2087**	1 55192: **2206**	1 85227: **1890**	1 85452: **1226**	1 85739: **1112**
0 947533: **1121**	0 949659: **2045**	1 55193: **2140**	1 85228: **1813**	1 85455: **1216**	1 85741: **1814**
0 947553: **1080**	0 949714: **2037**	1 55197: **2121**	1 85230: **1269**	1 85458: **1882**	1 85742: **1052**
0 947554: **1222**	0 949773: **2052**	1 55199: **2170**	1 85234: **1861**	1 85459: **1413**	1 85743: **1288**
0 947568: **1852**	0 949795: **2002**	1 55587: **1739**	1 85235: **2393**	1 85461: **1622**	1 85744: **1147**
0 947645: **1600**	0 949924: **2048**	1 55598: **1739**	1 85238: **1614**	1 85470: **1207**	1 85750: **1331**
0 947655: **1824**	0 949937: **2495, 2497**	1 55729: **1229**	1 85239: **1371**	1 85479: **1629**	1 85753: **1118, 1834**
0 947672: **3029**	0 9500508: **1416**	1 55786: **1093**	1 85242: **1787**	1 85485: **1901**	1 85754: **1155**
0 947697: **1192**	0 9500528: **1176**	1 55853: **1886**	1 85249: **1152, 1886**	1 85486: **1618**	1 85756: **1480**
0 947754: **1147**	0 9501351: **1914**	1 55938: **1475**	1 85251: **1552**	1 85489: **1741**	1 85758: **1251**
0 947795: **1324**	0 9501735: **1168**	1 55972: **1158**	1 85252: **1552**	1 85490: **1006**	1 85759: **1917**
0 947850: **1204**	0 9502686: **1290**	1 56000: **2054**	1 85260: **1829**	1 85497: **1077**	1 85770: **1766**
0 947877: **1737**	0 9504543: **1020**	1 56138: **1752**	1 85264: **1072**	1 85503: **1513**	1 85775: **1717**
0 947898: **1366**	0 9504797: **2387**	1 56593: **1805**	1 85270: **1407**	1 85506: **1859**	1 85776: **1103**
0 947962: **2378**	0 9505828: **1274**	1 56779: **1592**	1 85271: **1440**	1 85510: **1382**	1 85778: **1708, 1839**
0 947971: **1802**	0 9506431: **1873**	1 57098: **2401**	1 85273: **1232**	1 85513: **1736**	1 85780: **1579**
0 947981: **1589**	0 9506882: **1380**	1 57106: **2153**	1 85276: **1313**	1 85514: **1603**	1 85781: **1230**
0 947988: **1914**	0 9507735: **1871**	1 57230: **1375**	1 85278: **1052, 1271**	1 85521: **1052, 1235**	1 85782: **1095**
0 947992: **1531**	0 9507892: **1660**	1 57392: **1707**	1 85284: **1195**	1 85524: **1226**	1 85788: **1119**
0 947993: **1444**	0 9508050: **1535**	1 57488: **1118**	1 85285: **1380**	1 85532: **1642**	1 85791: **2377**
0 948003: **1176**	0 9508285: **1122**	1 77901: **2534**	1 85286: **1865**	1 85538: **1387**	1 85792: **1191**
0 948006: **1856**	0 9508725: **2402**	1 77903: **2530**	1 85291: **1712, 3036**	1 85549: **1219**	1 85793: **1656**
0 948058: **1267**	0 9509182: **1745**	1 77990: **2529**	1 85292: **1150**	1 85554: **1093**	1 85794: **1802**
0 948061: **1647**	0 9509432: **1641**	1 81058: **1676**	1 85296: **1506**	1 85557: **1097**	1 85797: **1639, 1640**
0 948075: **1566**	0 9509487: **1318**	1 85000: **1301, 1851**	1 85297: **1044**	1 85561: **1080, 2208**	1 85798: **1639, 1640**
0 948080: **1871**	0 9509792: **1068**	1 85008: **1326**	1 85302: **1498**	1 85567: **1681**	1 85799: **1639, 1640**
0 948107: **1887**	0 9511508: **1744**	1 85010: **1398**	1 85304: **1725**	1 85568: **1231**	1 85800: **2402**
0 948135: **1512**	0 9513240: **1144**	1 85015: **1295**	1 85306: **1216**	1 85573: **1925**	1 85802: **1683**
0 948149: **1061**	0 9513492: **1024**	1 85022: **1873**	1 85310: **1020**	1 85575: **1487**	1 85810: **1813**
0 948158: **1111**	0 9513759: **1879**	1 85028: **1252**	1 85311: **1439**	1 85576: **1870**	1 85811: **1203**
0 948183: **2384**	0 9514490: **1832**	1 85029: **1209, 2208**	1 85312: **1208**	1 85578: **1697**	1 85820: **1708**
0 948205: **3065**	0 9515151: **1064**	1 85038: **1426**	1 85314: **1308**	1 85584: **1828**	1 85821: **1665**
0 948230: **1004**	0 9516129: **1217**	1 85043: **1718, 1850**	1 85315: **1751**	1 85585: **1207**	1 85823: **1113, 1528**
0 948240: **3045**	0 9516295: **1212**	1 85044: **1533**	1 85317: **1257**	1 85591: **1407, 2208**	1 85825: **1810**
0 948248: **1393**	0 9516402: **1214**	1 85049: **1290**	1 85321: **1192**	1 85592: **1185, 1639, 1640**	1 85835: **1449**
0 948251: **1680**	0 9516844: **3049**	1 85051: **1382, 2208**	1 85324: **1420**	1 85594: **2379**	1 85836: **1418**
0 948253: **1822**	0 9517700: **3003**	1 85052: **1382, 2208**	1 85326: **1928**	1 85596: **1377**	1 85852: **1571**
0 948259: **1318**	0 9519489: **1846**	1 85054: **1411**	1 85327: **1704**	1 85597: **1409**	1 85856: **1871**
0 948265: **1727**	0 9521414: **1562**	1 85055: **1306**	1 85328: **1510**	1 85600: **1758**	1 85860: **1339**
0 948268: **2386**	0 9521964: **1797**	1 85057: **1549**	1 85333: **1501**	1 85602: **1238**	1 85862: **1007**
0 948269: **1257**	0 9523571: **1319**	1 85058: **1800**	1 85339: **1463**	1 85604: **1524**	1 85864: **1452**
0 948275: **1694**	0 9527302: **1365**	1 85065: **1436**	1 85340: **1678**	1 85607: **2384**	1 85866: **1174**
0 948285: **1044**	0 9592597: **2007**	1 85070: **1651**	1 85341: **1649**	1 85608: **1435**	1 85868: **1157**
0 948353: **1627**	0 9597884: **2462**	1 85072: **1788**	1 85343: **1327**	1 85610: **1318**	1 85876: **1432**
0 948358: **1589**	0 9690438: **2212**	1 85074: **1279**	1 85346: **1333**	1 85617: **1275**	1 85879: **1507**
0 948397: **1629**	0 9690454: **2216**	1 85075: **1794**	1 85352: **1418**	1 85619: **1804, 2208**	1 85881: **1639, 1640**
0 948456: **1725**	1 55002: **2131**	1 85078: **1628, 1653**	1 85355: **1008**	1 85628: **1052**	1 85882: **1886**
0 948462: **1726**	1 55013: **1886, 2163**	1 85079: **1615**	1 85356: **1598**	1 85629: **1260**	1 85886: **1357**
0 948509: **1391**	1 55017: **2147**	1 85089: **1468**	1 85359: **1591**	1 85635: **2399**	1 85894: **1570**
0 948513: **1840**	1 55022: **2133**	1 85091: **1502**	1 85361: **1732**	1 85640: **1369**	1 85895: **1802**
0 948535: **1519**	1 55037: **2094**	1 85097: **1714**	1 85368: **1614**	1 85648: **1708**	1 85898: **1052, 1271**
0 948549: **1206**	1 55039: **2220**	1 85103: **1586, 2129**	1 85372: **1018, 1469**	1 85649: **1936**	1 85902: **1350**
0 948555: **1164**	1 55046: **2103**	1 85109: **1003**	1 85375: **3050**	1 85656: **1721**	1 85903: **1549**
0 948564: **2382**	1 55050: **2124**	1 85116: **1179, 1791**	1 85381: **1889**	1 85669: **1496, 1855**	1 85918: **2385**
0 948577: **1275**	1 55054: **2129**	1 85127: **1106**	1 85383: **1261**	1 85675: **1334**	1 85922: **1724**
0 948578: **1292**	1 55059: **2127**	1 85128: **1359**	1 85389: **1549**	1 85681: **1722**	1 85931: **1773**
0 948636: **1602**	1 55065: **2232**	1 85145: **1656**	1 85390: **2404**	1 85685: **1809**	1 85941: **1169**
0 948661: **1073**	1 55068: **2231**	1 85149: **1039**	1 85391: **1566**	1 85688: **1824**	1 85946: **1737**
0 948690: **1649**	1 55071: **2144**	1 85150: **1753**	1 85396: **1183**	1 85691: **1840**	1 85960: **1398**
0 948691: **1923**	1 55074: **2164**	1 85152: **1382, 2208**	1 85398: **1053**	1 85695: **1468**	1 85962: **1079**
0 948699: **1249**	1 55077: **2226**	1 85153: **1738**	1 85399: **1255**	1 85697: **1506**	1 85964: **1338**
0 948724: **1106**	1 55081: **2104**	1 85158: **1550**	1 85404: **1269**	1 85703: **1432**	1 85967: **1038**
0 948725: **1106**	1 55082: **2203**	1 85168: **1631**	1 85406: **1002**	1 85704: **1002**	1 85968: **1153**
0 948817: **1372**	1 55092: **2182**	1 85170: **1837**	1 85409: **1047**	1 85707: **1847, 3055**	1 85972: **1052**
0 948848: **1523**	1 55109: **2185**	1 85172: **1691**	1 85410: **1061**	1 85710: **1746**	1 85973: **1083**
0 948867: **3049**	1 55111: **2106**	1 85175: **1439**	1 85411: **1692**	1 85711: **1011**	1 85983: **1120**
0 948875: **1564**	1 55125: **2231**	1 85177: **1887**	1 85418: **1395**	1 85713: **1099**	1 85984: **1885**
0 948877: **1779**	1 55130: **2113**	1 85182: **2392**	1 85422: **1391**	1 85714: **1719**	1 85986: **1408**
0 948894: **1300**		1 85183: **1801**	1 85425: **1569**		1 85993: **1592, 3068**

1 86003: **1777**
1 86007: **1013**
1 86024: **1926**
1 86033: **1062**
1 86034: **1346**
1 86035: **1038**
1 86039: **1637**
1 86046: **1392**
1 86049: **1889**
1 86058: **1560**
1 86064: **1718, 1850**
1 86094: **1446**
1 86099: **1358**
1 86105: **1743**
1 86108: **1373**
1 86110: **1549**
1 86126: **1227**
1 86134: **1857**
1 86165: **1657**
1 86171: **1223**
1 86176: **1255**
1 86197: **1263, 1706**
1 86199: **3004**
1 86204: **1269**
1 86205: **1656**
1 86207: **1362**
1 86291: **2079**
1 86302: **2049**
1 86307: **2007**
1 86315: **2052**
1 86330: **2208**
1 86340: **2012**
1 86343: **1566**
1 86351: **2078**
1 86366: **2022**
1 86368: **2031**
1 86371: **2035, 2036**
1 86378: **2060**
1 86399: **2051**
1 86400: **1702**
1 86403: **2070**
1 86407: **2047**
1 86429: **2025**
1 86812: **2513**
1 86813: **2499**
1 86814: **2518**
1 86826: **2514**
1 86839: **2504**
1 86842: **2495**
1 86934: **2444**
1 86940: **2432**
1 86941: **2461**
1 86943: **2464**
1 86946: **2455**
1 86950: **2446**
1 86953: **2433**
1 86955: **2454**
1 86956: **2442**
1 86962: **2443**
1 869833: **1916**
1 869839: **1138**
1 869844: **1736**
1 869860: **1059, 1920**
1 869868: **1724**
1 869888: **1421**
1 869890: **1396**
1 869922: **1567**
1 869928: **1555**
1 870003: **1729**
1 870045: **1934**
1 870071: **1810**
1 870080: **1226**
1 870098: **1365**
1 870109: **1808**
1 870127: **1893**
1 870196: **1471**

1 870248: **1917**
1 870259: **1626**
1 870322: **1764**
1 870325: **1912**
1 870332: **1913**
1 870441: **1293**
1 870451: **1613**
1 870458: **1270**
1 870532: **1500**
1 870562: **1625**
1 870586: **1696**
1 870655: **1755**
1 870668: **1503**
1 870673: **1039**
1 870708: **1766**
1 870727: **1646**
1 870732: **3048**
1 870758: **1762**
1 870775: **1658**
1 870817: **1719**
1 870889: **1854**
1 870890: **1043**
1 870905: **1717**
1 870946: **1482**
1 870948: **1713**
1 870956: **3058**
1 870979: **1074**
1 870989: **1066**
1 871044: **1397**
1 871048: **1816**
1 871080: **1657**
1 871201: **1217**
1 871349: **1492**
1 871381: **1913**
1 871402: **1861**
1 871438: **1806**
1 871440: **1230**
1 871471: **1667**
1 871489: **1917**
1 871512: **1027**
1 871516: **1460**
1 871552: **2387**
1 871569: **1089, 1412**
1 871585: **1842**
1 871612: **1108**
1 871647: **1660**
1 871676: **1191**
1 871814: **1742**
1 871824: **1116**
1 871846: **1223**
1 871869: **3004**
1 871871: **1633**
1 871876: **1817**
1 871901: **1335**
1 871980: **1686**
1 871993: **1057**
1 872002: **2395**
1 872004: **1919**
1 872082: **1490**
1 872148: **1874**
1 872167: **1438**
1 872180: **1324**
1 872362: **1201**
1 872414: **1215**
1 872424: **1122**
1 872457: **1827**
1 872489: **1765**
1 872501: **1580**
1 872524: **1687**
1 872557: **1068**
1 872571: **1262**
1 872576: **3022**
1 872610: **1474**
1 872670: **1549**
1 872699: **1486**
1 872727: **1612**

1 872747: **1825**
1 872803: **1745**
1 872815: **1507**
1 872868: **1028**
1 872876: **1789**
1 872885: **1695**
1 872921: **1922**
1 872941: **1601**
1 872971: **1727**
1 872988: **1090**
1 873012: **1835**
1 873041: **1402**
1 873045: **1473**
1 873047: **1448**
1 873150: **1591**
1 873190: **1753**
1 873245: **1217**
1 873308: **1137**
1 873357: **1451**
1 873376: **1817**
1 873385: **1514**
1 873394: **1247**
1 873410: **1229**
1 873429: **1650**
1 873432: **1559**
1 873454: **1019**
1 873475: **1838**
1 873575: **1857**
1 873580: **1911**
1 873600: **1832**
1 873626: **1120**
1 873631: **1064**
1 873644: **1565**
1 873656: **1846, 1886**
1 873730: **2034**
1 873784: **1624**
1 873790: **2386**
1 873793: **1577**
1 873824: **1781**
1 873829: **3016**
1 873836: **1112**
1 873868: **1126**
1 873884: **1877, 1888**
1 873929: **1167**
1 873936: **1477**
1 873938: **1338**
1 873968: **1110**
1 873982: **1240**
1 873994: **1833**
1 874016: **1176**
1 874041: **2413**
1 874044: **1050**
1 874045: **2403**
1 874052: **1205**
1 874061: **1627**
1 874105: **1884**
1 874164: **1016**
1 874241: **1169**
1 874250: **1225**
1 874371: **1399**
1 874422: **1351**
1 874430: **1664**
1 874488: **3069**
1 874504: **1886**
1 874529: **1010, 1367**
1 874545: **1557**
1 874557: **1400**
1 874567: **1566**
1 874634: **3027**
1 874640: **1045**
1 874644: **1277**
1 874675: **2397**
1 874687: **1445, 1886**

1 874700: **2383**
1 874735: **1886, 3006**
1 874744: **1088**
1 874754: **1316**
1 874774: **1161, 1529**
1 874783: **1019**
1 874785: **3056**
1 874790: **1394**
1 875145: **2006**
1 875327: **2023**
1 875498: **2044**
1 875589: **2084**
1 875606: **2013**
1 875627: **2024**
1 875656: **2005**
1 875657: **2043**
1 875695: **2069**
1 875739: **2089**
1 875840: **2082**
1 875857: **2090**
1 877133: **2458**
1 877161: **2447**
1 879105: **1805**
1 879373: **2401**
1 881616: **1855**
1 882013: **1030**
1 882092: **2401**
1 882100: **1030**
1 882807: **1592**
1 885108: **1475**
1 885582: **1592**
1 886106: **2332**
1 889080: **2159**
1 895070: **2212**
1 895073: **2209**
1 895198: **2118**
1 895246: **2169**
1 895340: **2157**
1 895411: **2193**
1 895431: **2099**
1 895449: **2225**
1 895555: **2168**
1 895562: **2238**
1 895569: **2223**
1 895571: **2110**
1 895579: **2227**
1 895618: **2136**
1 895629: **2234**
1 895700: **2153**
1 895714: **2206**
1 895854: **2126**
1 895897: **2219**
1 896081: **2095**
1 896095: **2198**
1 896133: **2102**
1 896151: **2116**
1 896210: **2202**
1 896300: **2184**
1 896329: **2121**
1 896357: **2098**
1 896647: **2107**
1 897580: **1639, 1640**
1 897675: **1123**
1 897766: **1159**
1 897767: **1242**
1 897784: **1610**
1 897799: **1341**
1 897817: **1444**
1 897853: **1531**
1 897884: **3015**
1 897913: **1415**
1 897959: **1785**
1 898000: **1070**
1 898001: **1517**

1 898128: **1175**
1 898217: **1509**
1 898218: **1778**
1 898283: **1223**
1 898298: **1462**
1 898307: **1154**
1 898323: **1117**
1 898351: **1927**
1 898507: **1421**
1 898591: **1144**
1 898601: **1173**
1 898617: **1212**
1 898660: **1305**
1 898697: **1372**
1 898716: **1666**
1 898718: **1104**
1 898769: **1143**
1 898785: **1662**
1 898839: **1444, 1720**
1 898883: **1239**
1 898885: **1370**
1 898931: **1709**
1 898994: **3052**
1 899025: **1156**
1 899047: **2390**
1 899120: **1764**
1 899163: **1713**
1 899247: **1060**
1 899296: **3003**
1 899324: **1535**
1 899365: **1508**
1 899396: **1505**
1 899399: **1464**
1 899524: **1866**
1 899527: **1317**
1 899573: **3038**
1 899579: **1918**
1 899606: **1272**
1 899607: **1520, 1521**
1 899618: **1848**
1 899760: **1063**
1 899827: **1778**
1 899863: **1534**
1 899870: **1589**
1 900018: **1370**
1 900019: **1370**
1 900104: **1286**
1 900127: **1723**
1 900152: **1835**
1 900188: **1645**
1 900207: **1819**
1 900300: **1441**
1 900322: **1365**
1 900455: **1073**
1 900506: **1037**
1 900512: **1574**
1 900541: **1348**
1 900600: **1657**
1 900652: **1593**
1 900693: **2383**
1 900834: **1036**
1 900887: **1558**
1 900949: **1315**
1 916567: **2401**
1 947450: **2508**
1 985537: **2130**
2 034: **1506**
2 06: **1575**
2 7600: **2091**
2 7603: **2191**
2 7605: **2204**
2 7606: **2176**
2 7613: **2210**
2 7619: **2218**
2 7625: **2151**

2 7637: **2166**
2 8315: **1084**
2 89019: **2126**
2 89021: **2125**
2 89029: **2218**
2 89043: **2218**
2 89044: **2218**
2 89052: **2101**
2 89105: **2138**
2 89109: **2158**
2 89117: **2218**
2 89135: **2144**
2 89310: **2119**
2 89423: **2201**
2 89461: **2119**
2 89462: **2126**
2 920073: **2204**
2 921310: **2167**
3 540: **1823**
3 598: **1112**
3 7913: **1855**
3 85604: **1738**
3 92107: **1575**
4 385: **1882**
4 87417: **1714**
81 07233: **2360**
81 202: **2258**
81 204: **2332**
81 205: **2332**
81 206: **2265**
81 207: **2366**
81 208: **2321**
81 209: **2340**
81 211: **2275**
81 212: **2297**
81 215: **2322**
81 216: **2300**
81 222: **2331**
81 246: **2285**
81 250: **2330**
81 7003: **2362**
81 7005: **2323**
81 7008: **2315**
81 7010: **2298**
81 7011: **2277**
81 7012: **2290**
81 7013: **2327**
81 7014: **2367**
81 7017: **2256**
81 7018: **2288**
81 7019: **2371**
81 7020: **2283**
81 7021: **2310**
81 7022: **2282**
81 7024: **2264**
81 7026: **2299**
81 7030: **2304, 2356**
81 7033: **2349**
81 7034: **2272**
81 7035: **2286**
81 7036: **2354**
81 7045: **2267**
81 7058: **2270**
81 7059: **2370**
81 7066: **2262**
81 7069: **2322**
81 7074: **2271**
81 7087: **2332, 2334**
81 7094: **2375**
81 7100: **2287**
81 7103: **2337**
81 7111: **2314**
81 7116: **2326**
81 7117: **2329**
81 7122: **2276**
81 7130: **2284**
81 7132: **2341**

81 7133: **2348**	81 7533: **2317**	81 85319: **2363**	91 44: **1187**	969 441: **2472**	9964 87: **2241**
81 7154: **2342**	81 7551: **2345**	81 85357: **2357**	92 826: **2389**	969 461: **2477**	9964 959: **2243**
81 7167: **2353**	81 85015: **2324**	81 85386: **2255**	939 35: **2478**	969 466: **2476**	9964 978: **2247**
81 7172: **2358**	81 85017: **2309**	81 85401: **2318**	955 24: **2519**	976 605: **2410**	9964 979: **2244**
81 7180: **2369**	81 85028: **2303**	81 85402: **2361**	955 552: **2521**	976 6410: **2019**	9966 21: **2421**
81 7181: **2316**	81 85046: **2360**	81 85428: **2357**	955 9098: **2520**	976 8010: **2406**	9966 46: **2414**
81 7214: **2306**	81 85047: **2350**	81 85457: **2336**	962 07: **2250**	976 8097: **2019**	9966 47: **2422**
81 7215: **2262**	81 85069: **2259**	81 85517: **2335**	962 08: **2254**	976 8100: **2409**	9966 49: **2417**
81 7289: **2260**	81 85076: **2280**	81 85559: **2302**	962 201: **2249**	978 163: **2470**	9966 836: **2412**
81 7307: **2344**	81 85116: **2292**	81 85604: **2342**	962 209: **2252**	981 00: **2485**	9966 847: **2416**
81 7314: **2351**	81 85120: **2281**	81 85613: **2280**	962 255: **2250**	981 208: **2491**	9966 848: **2414**
81 7315: **2343**	81 85135: **2325**	81 85711: **2348**	962 290: **2250**	981 215: **2488, 2491**	9966 884: **2415**
81 7317: **2266, 2328**	81 85173: **2289**	81 85860: **2308**	962 302: **2251**	981 218: **2484**	9966 885: **2418**
81 7318: **2266, 2328**	81 85195: **2319**	81 85880: **2317**	962 329: **2250**	981 3018: **2489**	9971 0: **2486**
81 7319: **2324**	81 85198: **2324**	81 85972: **2350**	962 7160: **2248**	981 3029: **2483**	9971 69: **2492**
81 7359: **2365**	81 85200: **2372**	81 86224: **2347**	967 91: **2426**	981 3045: **2481**	9971 83: **2485**
81 7368: **2279**	81 85212: **2263**	81 86378: **2274**	967 917: **2428**	981 3068: **2483**	9971 84: **2485**
81 7371: **2373**	81 85218: **2345**	81 86765: **2374**	967 919: **2429**	983 9629: **2427**	9971 985: **2483**
81 7387: **2307**	81 85250: **2352**	81 86766: **2374**	967 966: **2424**	983 9808: **2425**	9976 63: **2525**
81 7473: **2255**	81 85276: **2368**	83 86208: **1107**	969 29: **2479**	9964 3: **2246**	9976 66: **2524**
81 7494: **2372**	81 85288: **2295,**	90 411: **1501**	969 402: **2480**	9964 70: **2240**	9976 956: **2523**
81 7505: **2257**	**2296**	90 5703: **2019, 2029**	969 412: **2473**	9964 72: **2245**	9982 00: **2527**
81 7510: **2350**	81 85301: **2257**	90 6544: **1501**	969 436: **2474**	9964 78: **2242**	9982 01: **2527**

7.7 INDEX OF PERSONAL NAMES

Ms Annette Aaronson 6300
Afraz Abbasi 2477
Sally Abbey 1889
S. A. Abbott 3010
Stan Abbott 1512, 6035
F. H. Abdullah 2523
Brenda V. Abercrombie 1326
Nicholas Abercrombie 1326
Sheila Ableman 1075
Mark Abonyo 2414
D. Abraham 1564
Mrs Hildegard Abraham 4032
Rowland Abram 6242
Miss Bathsheba Abse 5085
Dannie Abse 5017
Billy Adair 1295
Imogen Adam 1739
Max Adam 1485, 1661
Patricia Adam 2068
Richard Adam 1401
Audrey Adams 1033
Bill Adams 5018
Colin Adams 1098
Firgal Adams 2056
Geoffrey Adams 5039
Imogen Adams 1368
John Adams 1248
Karen Adams 5150
Mrs Kathleen Adams 5071
Lynn Adams 1754
M. Adams 1320, 1632, 1829
Michael Adams 2392, 2402
Will Adams 1802
H. Adamson 1066
Priya B. Adarkar 2330
Ray Addicott 6025
Jeremy Addis 6333
David Addison 6142
Karen Addison 4021
Michael Addison 1009
Dotun Adebayo 1931
Chief (Mrs) C. O. Ademuyiwa
  2470
Rukun Advani 2333
David Affleck 1280, 6222, 6236
Ahmad Afzaal 2478
S. Ager 1439
Jaideep Aggarwal 2260, 2340
Manish Aggarwal 2260, 2274,
  2340
Dr V. B. Aggarwal 2340

D. J. Aggersberg 1343
Ronald Agius 2431
Dharamvir Agrawal 2343
Parasnath Agrawal 2343
Pawan Agrawal 2343
Piyush Agrawal 2343
Raghuvir Agrawal 2343
Helen Agutter 6039
Shabbir Ahmad 2475
Jameel Ahmed 2472
Noor Ahmed 2472
M. M. Ahsan 1470
John Airlie 6270
Gillon Aitken 4003
Alhaji S. A. S. Ajala 2470
Donald H. Akenson 2171
Jenny Akester 5097
Mrs Agatha Akonor-Mills 2247
Ams Alawdeen 2427
Jean-Pierre Albert 2210
Michael Alcock 1113
Jan Alcoe 1657
David Alcorn 1167
Patricia Aldana 2143
Patsy Aldana 2129
Brian Alderson 5052
Clare Alexander 1381, 1661
David Alexander 1269, 1527
Julian Alexander 4004
Nick Alexander 2020
Pat Alexander 1527
Susanne Alexander 2142
Precy Alfonso 2476
Ino Algranti 2210
Akbar Ali 2427
Steve Allam 6029
David Allan 1022
Gordon Allan 1027
H. Allan 2461
Katrena Allan 1027
Kevin Allard 6243
Bruce Allardice 2058
Barbara Allen 1512, 6035
Chris Allen 1419
Diane Allen 1549
Jean Allen 1794
Jenny Allen 1733
Joseph A. Allen 1023
Judith Allen 6252
K. Allen 1705
Liz Allen 1401

Mary Allen 5019
Piers R. Allen 1475
Robert Allen 1506
Rosemary Allen 1257
Stephanie Allen 1594
K. Allen Jones 1157
Keith Allen-Jones 3020
Katharine Allenby 1193
John Allgrove 1237
Mark Allin 1685
Jim Allpass 6033
Peter Allsop 1909
Mike Allsopp 6303
Marisa Alps 2147
Judith Alsop 6067
Robert Alton 2197
John Altus 2066
M. K. J. A. Alwis 5178
Upali Amarasiri 5179
Christine Amer 1236
Mohamed Amin 2413
Ashish Amos 2306
Lyn Amy 2068
K. Anand 2376
K. N. Anantharaman 2370
Habel Andati 2416
E. Anders 2054
Barbara Anderson 3042
Barry Anderson 1750
Bob Anderson 6167
D. Anderson 1823
Darley Anderson 4005
M. Anderson 2038
R. Anderson 6199
Trevor Anderson 2085
Willie Anderson 5036
David Ando 1010
L. K. Andreasen 5119
Hugh Andrew 1088, 1153, 1534
J. Andrew 1014
Jeff Andrew 5068
W. R. Andrewes 1648
Adrian Andrews 1211
Dr Malcolm Andrews 5064
Robert Andrews 1750
Prof A. H. Angelo 2468
Brian Angle 6277, 6283
Gordon Angus 1246
Juliet Annan 1049, 1722
Paul Anness 1038
Guisseppie Annoscia 1278

Paul Anonen 2236
Aleem Ansari 2480
Zamir Ansari 2339
Roger Antrobus 6173
Pedr ap Llwyd 5124, 6258
H. John Appleby 1355
Aileen Apps 1816, 6124
Steven Apps 1816, 6124
Brian April 2137
Mrs Sarah Apronti 2242
Jeff Archer 1327
Jeffrey Archer 1101
J. G. Archibald 1340
Joe Arcuri 6266
Sophie Arditti 1885
Anthony Aridegbe 2470
Anthony Aris 1786
Elizabeth A. Aris 1046
Evelyn A. Aris 1046
Doreen Armbruster 2237
Clare Armstrong 1423, 1425
David Armstrong 6055
H. R. Armstrong 1600
Jodi Armstrong 2197
Paul Armstrong 2086
Ronald Armstrong 1138
T. Armstrong 1915
Tom Armstrong 1387
William Armstrong 1799
Simon Arnison 6053
E. R. Arnold 2517
John Arnold 5044
Phyllis Arnold 2095
James Arnold-Baker 1648
Ms Jyoti Arora 2308
M. G. Arora 2372
Manish Arora 2372
Pradeep Arora 2372
Sanjeev Arora 2372
Sushil Arora 2308
A. B. Arshad 1469
Mrs Inger Arthur 1141, 1783
P. Arthur 1355
Roger Arthur 6020
Kim Arthurton 6243
Virender Kumar Arya 2255
Wilfrid Asciak 2431
Michael Ash 6224
Stephen Ash 6224
John Ashby 1682

B. V. Ashcroft-Hawley 2054, 2450
Charles Ashford 6181
J. Ashling 1459
Steve Ashman 2406
Toby Ashmore 1656
Dolores Ashton 1403
Norma Ashton 1553
Mary Asirifi 5153
William G. Askew 1734
Muhammad Aslam 2472
Jane Aspden 1585
J. Aspinall 6267
Jenny Aspinall 1089
Ivon Asquith 1648
Pascal Assathiany 2101
Ray Astbury 6375
Neil Astley 1097
M. Aston 1016
Richard Astor 1833
Angela Atcheson 1510
Jill Athey 1057
Lionel Athey 1057
Maria Atkin 3053
Julie Atkins 1834
Michelle Atkins 2064
J. Atkinson 1281
John Atkinson 1085
Nigel Atkinson 1149
Mrs R. Atkinson 1536
T. W. Atkinson 1536
Philip Attenborough 5040
Ray Attwood 5091
Tony Attwood 1309
David Attwooll 1408
Amit Atwal 2258
Sneh Atwal 2258
Au Bak Ling 1898, 3011
Stephen Aucutt 6015
Timothy Auger 1072, 2489
Derek Auld 1756
J. Austin 1398
Mrs Jane Austin 1748
Stephen Averiss 6242
Karen Avery 2446
Phyllis Avery 1238
John Axon 5095
Nahlah Ayed 2114
J. Ayre 1014
Sean Ayres 1689
Pete Ayrton 1787
Fatima Azzam 1471

Brian D. Babani 1360
Michael H. Babani 1065
Peter L. Babani 1360
Mrs S. Babani 1065
Veronica Babington Smith 1468
Maral Bablanian 2094
S. Baboneau 1545
Michael Bach 2212
Debbie Backhouse 3057
Phil Bacon 1499
K. K. Bagchi 2271
P. K. Bagchi 2271
Mike Baggallay 1261, 1502
Iradj Bagherzade 1850
Ujjal Singh Bahri 2272
Andrew Bailey 1870, 6141
Antonia Bailey 1799
Bill Bailey 6071
Dana Bailey 2122
David Bailey 1277, 1870
J. R. Bailey 6197
John Bailey 6135
Rhonda Bailey 2190
Roberta Bailey 1541

Sue Bailey 1296
Warwick Bailey 6250
Yvonne Baillie 1651
George Bain 1093
Gordon Bain 5146
Robin Baird-Smith 1255
Barry Baker 3042
Christine Baker 1586
David Baker 2146
F. Baker 1014
G. Baker 1140
Joan Baker 2464
K. Baker 1439
M. Baker 1664
Michael R. Baker 1007
Nick Baker 1275
Simon Baker 1294
Balakrishnan 2369
Kailash Balani 5156
L. A. Balarin 2522
Karen Balasaglou 2435
David Balatti 5149
Robert Baldock 1933
David Baldwin 1179, 1791
Mrs Gillian Baldwin 1179,
Richard Balkwill 5100, 6005
J. Ball 2498
J. A. B. Ball 2497
Jonathan Ball 2495
K. M. Ball 1881
Karen Ball 6144
Pamela Ball 2027
T. Ball 2522
Sara Ballard 3015
May Ballerio 1342
Joyce Ballinger 1396
Sister Rosemary Ballini 2421
S. Balwant 2258
Laura Bamford 1382
Ian Banbery 1067, 1763
Miss Mangalika Bandupala 2521
Joe Banel 2139
Arunjeet Banerjee 2376
K. Banerji 1338, 1472
Frances Banfield 3027
D. J. Banister 1851
Nigel Banister 1093
Peter Banki 5130
Bodunde Bankole 5171
Mary Banks 1100
W. B. R. Banks 2007
David Bann 1574
Linda Banner 1637, 1900
Ian Bannerman 1094
Vijay Bansal 2295, 2296
Antonia Banyard 2097
Jean-Luc Barbanneau 1445, 1902
C. Barber 1354
E. Barber 1623
H. R. Barber 1115
R. W. Barber 1115
Robert Barber 2026
Sharron Barber 2464
Anthony Baring 4076
Michelle Baring 1839
Christine R. Barker 1438
Keith Barker 6375
R. Barker 1547
Lloyd Barkham 1434
Howard Barkway 6159
Derek Barley 1245
Anne Barlow 6060
Geoff Barlow 1061
Steve Barlow 1659
R. N. Barman 2353
M. Barnard 1016
M. J. Barnard 1547

Nicholas Barnard 1398
Anne Barnes 1595
Dr J. D. Barnes 1010
Jan Barnes 1212
Julia Barnes 1740
Bill Barnett 1782
D. Barnett 2054
Marie L. Barnett 6080
Paul Barnett 3007
Roger Barnett 6080
U. A. Barnett 4047
W. M. Barnett 1067, 1384, 1429,
1763
Glyn Barnicoat 6242
Jonathan Barnicoat 6242
Paul Barnicoat 6242
Victoria Barnsley 1324
Richard Baron 1116
John Barr 5163
Stephen Barr 1754
Helen Barrett 1293
George Barrington 1240
B. A. Barron 6200
Fergus Barrowman 2468
E. W. Barry 1648
Jean Barry 2393
Birgit Bartels 6171
Mervyn T. Barter 1069
Alick Bartholomew 1339
Mari Bartholomew 1339
Richard Bartlett 2039, 2040
Sue Bartlett 6242
Mrs Vivian Bartlett 1066
Ms Deborah Bartley 6170
Ian Bartley 1855
Joan Barton 2108
Mark Barty-King 1869
Joachim Bartz 6270
Wadad Bashour 2207
John Bassett 1230
Rachael Bastian 6242
D. N. Basu 2262
Veena Baswani 2331
Robin Batchelor-Smith 1433
Bob Bateman 2079
David Bateman 2433
Graham Bateman 3004
Paul Bateman 2433
Lucy Bater 1409
Chris Bates 1538
Eric Bates 1855
Joan Bates 1733
Linda Batham 1502
Julian R. Batson 1190
Nigel Batt 1528
Nicholas Battle 1216
Suzanne Battle 1216
Libby Baulch 5130
H. Baum 1851
L. Baum 5119
Louis Baum 6334
R. F. Baum 1909, 5119
G. P. S. Bawa 2309
Andrew Bax 1717
Colin Baxter 1073
Keith Baxter 1839
Nick Baxter 5118
Paul Baxter 1131
Mrs N. Baye 2496
J. B. Bayne 1906
Sarah Beal 1098
Jeremy Beale 1711
John Beale 6106
Simon Beale 1685
Robert Beard 1147
Ronald Beard 1049
Janice Bearg 2129

John Beaton 1550
Alaina Beattie 5163
Irene Beattie 2024
Joe H. Beauduin 2207
John Beaufoy 1614
Ms Lesley Beaumont 2090
Gordon Becker 1759
Debbie Beckerman 1869
John Bedding 1330
Dianne Bedford 2060
Anne Beech 1691
Diana Beech 1800
Graham Beech 1800
Donald Beecher 2130
Sophie Beecher 2130
Kathryn Beecroft 1524, 6382
Robin Beecroft 1460
Mark Beedell 1527
Lorraine Beele 1717
John Beer 1635
Allan Beesley 6141
Michael W. Beevers 1622, 6191
Miss Yolanda Beh 5174
Sabine Behle 5011
Gwenda Beishon 6351
Jessica Beishon 6351
John Beishon 6351
Marc Beishon 6351
Jana Bek 1329
Tønnes Bekker-Nielsen 5009
Christian Bélair 6156
Noreen Belanger 6310
Barry Belasco 1321
Jane Belford 1203
Eddie Bell 1387
Mrs Hazel Bell 5025
Hilary Bell 1091
John Bell 5043
Joyce Bell 5102
Andrea de Belleroche 1121
Ib Bellew 1081
Martine Benard 2125
Lionel Bender 3009
Michelle Benjamin 2198
Laurence Benkhabeb 1166
C. G. Benn 1231
Pansy Benn 2408
Timothy Benn 1231
Avie Bennett 2169
David Bennett 1238
Francis Bennett 1102
J. Bennett 2220
Mrs L. Bennett 6262
Michelle Bennett 2219
Paul Bennett 1391
Regena Bennett 2153
Rosemary Bennett 1849
Sarah Bennison 1032
Judy Benson 2077
Dominic Bentham 1751
Guy Bentham 1463
Georgina Bentliff 1048
Helen Benton 2467
Stephen Benz 1766
Anil Beri 2301
Krishna Chand Beri 2301
Rajendra Prasad Beri 2301
Vijay Prakash Beri 2301
Vivek Beri 2301
Jenny Berich 2072
Jean Bernier 2101
James Berry 1149
Linda Berry 2127
Edowan Bersma 2248
Alison Bertram 6243
Mrs Elsie Bertram 6243
Kip Bertram 6243

Nigel Bertram 6243
Katherine Besomi 1138
Chris Besse 2139
Ronald Besse 2139
Richard Beswick 1528
Tina Betts 4060
Marga Beuth 1703, 6039
Linda Bevan Smith 5166
Frank Bevis 6056
M. S. Beyers 1014
Tony Bezzina 2430
M. S. Bhalla 5156
Prabir Bhambal 2333
Seema Bharti 2259
Shri V. K. Bharti 2305
Mrs Durgesh Bhatia 2350
G. S. Bhatia 2287
Miss Geeta Bhatia 2339, 2350
H. S. Bhatia 2287
K. D. S. Bhatia 2287
Manish K. Bhatia 2350
Dr S. K. Bhatia 2350, 5156
Harsha Bhatkal 2342
Ramdas Bhatkal 2342
T. Bhaumik 2333
C. H. Bhote 3051
Anand Bhushan 2340
Kul Bhushan 2419
Sushil Bhushan 2340
Ved Bhushan 2260, 2340
Tony Bianchi 5020
K. Bickmore 1845
Mark Bicknell 1151
Caroline Bidwell 1150, 1678
Katharina Bielenberg 1392
Freddy Bienstock 1825
A. A. C. Bierrum 1621
Fiona Biggs 2404
Carol Bignell 1350
Stuart Biles 1075
John Billingham 1403
Stewart Binne 1162
Ruth Binney 1837
Adrian Binsted 1314
Howard Binsted 1314
Clive Birch 1715
Mike Birch 1754
Nicola Birch 6067
Sarah Birdsey 6158
Zev Birger 6300
Victoria Birkett 1770
Anthony Birks-Hay 3003
Leslie Birks-Hay 3003
Caroline Birrell 6383
D. Bishop 2016
C. Biss 1103
Anna Bisztyga 1184, 1821
Emma Bittleston 1165
Caroline Black 1724
Charles Black 1015, 1089, 1412
Jim Black 2161
Rhonda Black 2032
Simon Blackall 2088
Diane Blackbourn 1936
Gina Blackham 1442
Lyn Blackman 1248
Jane Blackstock 1162, 1349
Julian Blackwell 1093
Nigel Blackwell 1093, 1094
Susan Blackwell 5133, 6285
Joe Blades 2107
Sarah Blair 5021
Alison Blake 6279
C. Blake 1844
Carole Blake 4007
Deborah Blake 1255
John Blake 1095, 1869

Tony Blake 6044
Ian Blakemore 1653
G. Blanc 6255
David Blanch 6339
Jenny Blanch 6339
Jean-François Blanchette 2112
Glenice Bland 2076
Peter B. Blaney 2171
Mark Blaug 1271
David Bleasdale 1770, 6282
Clare Blick 1553
P. R. Bligh 5074
Ian Bloodworth 1770, 6282
A. L. Bloom 6213
Adam Bloom 6294
Andy Bloom 1041
M. I. Bloom 6213
Roy Bloom 6213
Suzie Bloom 1685
David G. T. Bloomer 1651
Paula F. Bloomer 1651
Judith Bloor 1317
Charles Blount 1593
Nicholas Bloxam 6301
Robin Bloxsidge 1530
Brian W. Blunden 6051
Margaret Blunden 1613
Dr Margot H. Blunden-Willms
  6051
John Blunsden 1589
David Blunt 1490
Deirdre Blunt 1490
Dorothy Blythe 2185
Victor K. Boadu 2246
Wendy Boase 1896
Dr Andreas Bode 5015
Swami Bodhasarananda 2257
Bhikkhu Bodhi 2519
Jackie Bodley 1413
John Bodley 1297
Arden Boehm 2163
Paul Bogart 2152
Karin Bogliolo 1307
Thierry Bogliolo 1307
Francine Bois 6310
Nicholas Boisseau 6247
A. Bokalamulla 2519
Anna Bolger 2053
James de Gaspé Bonar 2218
Frances Bond 4114
John Bond 1890
Phillip Bond 1181
Vivian Bone 1264
Richard L. Bong 1171
R. Boning 1648
Roger Bonnett 1935
Heather Bonning 1695
Luigi Bonomi 1485
A. W. Boon 1385
John T. Boon 1385
Laurel Boone 2142
Anne Boore 1377
Gwilym Boore 1377
Roger Boore 1377
Barbara Boote 1528
Kathryn S. A. Booth 1308
Stuart Booth 1308
Edward Booth-Clibborn 1110
James Booth-Clibborn 1110
Judy Boothroyd 6009, 6063
Tracey Borgfeldt 2433
Emma Borghesi 2030
Jose Borghino 5136
Marie-Claire Borgo 2176, 2191
Rev Emmanuel Borlabi Bortey
  2242
L. Born 2448

Sebastian Born 4002
Sara Borthwick 1525
Rosanna Bortoli 1089
T. G. Borton 6139
Sharmila Bose 2333
Penny Boshoff 1781
J. K. Bosomtwe 2246
Suzanne Bossé 2191
Suzy Boston 1334
Rajni Boswell 5125
Michael Boswood 1276
Prof E. Botha 2516
Andrea Bottella 1006
Philippe Boucheron 5054
Marie-Victoire Boudillet 6308
Rachel Boulding 1812
Michael Bounds 6257
Niàmh Bourke 1440
Adrian Bourne 1387
Derek Bourne-Jones 1250
David Bousfield 1275
Angela Bovell 6279
Miss Jean K. Bowden 5083
Rev Dr John Bowden 1773
Nicky Bowden 1525
Sarah Bowden 2447
Tim Bowdler 6269
William Bowe 1278
Mike Bowen 1190
P. D. Bowen 1635
B. L. Bowen-Davies 6037
C. M. Bowen-Davies 6037
W. Bowen-Davies 6037
Delian Bower 3013
Elanor Bower 1364
Susie Bower 3013
Roger Bowes 5021
Neal Bowhay 1535
Ms J. Bowler 1652
Vivien Bowler 1528
D. S. Bowman 6136
Mrs K. J. Bowman 6136
Marg Bowman 2045
Mrs B. M. Bowsher 1281
Marion Boyars 1114
Simon Boyd 1403
Sharon Boyle 2108
Ann Braben 2046
David Bradbury 1127
Emma Bradford 3002
Neil Bradford 1437
Ian Bradie 1149
John Brading 5107
Clive Bradley 5056, 5099
Derek Bradley 6019
Graham Bradley 2065
Irene Bradley 6019
J. Bradley 2388
Philip Bradley 1922
Michael Bradstock 2436
Mrs Hilary Bradt 1117, 6147
Suzy Brain England 6267
Peter F. Braithwaite 6353
Barbara Bramall 1906
Betty Brammer 1458
E. Bramwell 1705
Carl Brand 2131
Tim Brandt 2217
Trudy Brannan 1606
Cheryl Brant 2518
Daphne Brasell 5162
Stephen Bray 1387
George Braye 2240
Jan Brazier 1245
Nicholas Brealey 1119
Prof. C. A. Brebbia 1208
Josephine Breese 5163

Martin R. Breese 1121
Brian M. Brennan 2033
Des Brennan 1005, 1067, 1384,
  1429, 1763
Paula Brennan 1824, 6198
Joe Breslawski 6046
Paula Breslich 3014
D. S. Brewer 1115
C. T. Breytenbach 2500
Nadine Brianceau 6308
J. Brierley 1769
Dr Peter Brierley 1192
G. Briffin 2099
Dr Peter Briggs 5024
Tim Briggs 6242
Lord Briggs of Lewes 5046
Katherine Bright-Holmes 1741
Jannie Brightman 6024
The Baroness Brigstocke 5004
Chris Brilz 2121
Mrs P. Brine 2528
Adrian Brink 1199, 1538
Katharine Brisbane 2021
Jean-Francois Brisson 2176, 2191
Kevin Bristow 6220
Rod Bristow 1685
Anna Britten 1607
Catherine Britton 1303
J. Broadfoot 2016
Allen Brobyn 5037, 5080
Dr M. Brock 5086
Mike Broderick 1049, 1722
Charles F. Brook 1438
Davina C. Brook 1438
Mrs P. M. Brook 1322
Phillip Brook 6192
Alan Brooke 1401
Michael Z. Brooke 6004
Netie Brooke 1248
M. Brookes 6260
Rosalie Brookhouse 1225
Alessina R. Brooks 2044
Ali Brooks 3045
Judith Brooks 1884
Phillip Brooks 1419
Frank Broomhead 5016
Stephen Brough 1263, 1706
Daniel Broughton 1859
Jean Brouillet 2207
A. Brown 6225
Mrs A. R. Brown 5034
Ailsa Brown 3016
Andrew Brown 1149, 1894, 5044
Ann Rosina Brown 5034
Beverley Brown 1484
Bob Brown 6064
Brian Brown 1140
Cameron Brown 1080, 1207
Campbell Brown 1064
Chris Brown 1846
Christine Brown 1113
D. C. Brown 1575
David Brown 1645, 6073, 6145
George Brown 1916
Graham Brown 3016
J. Trevor Brown 1867, 6148
P. Brown 6261
Patty Brown 2082
Robert Brown 2073
Sarah Brown 1376
Sheridan Brown 6102
T. Nigel Brown 1136
Terence Brown 2397
Trevor E. Brown 1327
Diane Browne 2410
Greg Browne 2064, 2454
Lionel Browne 5114

Joanne Browning Wroe 1513
K. Brownlie 1533
Deborah Brownrigg 2112
Hamish Bruce 1193
Beth Bruder 2236
Jacqui Bruff 1716
Clark Brundin 1094
Charlotte Bruton 4012
Catherine Bruzzone 3006
Felicity Bryan 4009
Michael Bryan 2121
Richard Bryant 1843
Tony Bryars 6146
D. Bryce 1531
Elizabeth Buchan 5102
Karen Buchan 1097
Edwin Buckhalter 1790
Alan Buckingham 1248
John Buckingham 1184
Marlene Buckland 1814
Nadine Buckland 2408
Annie Buckley 1305
Patrick Buckley 2403
Nina Bueno Del Carpio 1504
Anne-Marie Bulat 1248
Tom Bulgarelli 1803
Jeffery Bull 2435
Michael Bullard 6327
Lord Bullock 1623
P. Bulos 1385
Dr Alan Bundy 2006
Judith Bundy 2006
Anne Burbage 1774
Rodney Burbeck 6373
Paul Burby 6283
H. K. I. Burchell 6260
Lynn Burden 2122
Neil Burden 1520, 1521
Pierre Burdon 2218
Judy Burdsall 1896
Charles Burfitt 2052
Donal Burke 1933
T. Burke 5075
Thomas Burke 6193
Brie Burkeman 4017
Lindy Burleigh 1161
L. Burnand 6225
J. F. Burnett 6103
Piers Burnett 1061
Jonathan Burnham 1188
Les Burnham 1592
Boaden Burns 5139
Caroline Burns 1803
David Burns 1346
Gerard Burns 2460
Kate Burns 1520, 1521
Paul Burns 1141
Adrienne Burrows 1168
Cari Burrows 2173
Diane Burston 4011
Leighton Burston 6149
Caroline Burt 1023
Revd Gerald Burt 1282, 1571
Miss Juliet Burton 4078
Lesley Burton 1887
N. E. Burton 1463
Robbie Burton 2437
E. Busangabanye 2529
Paul Busby 6277
Edward Buscombe 1085, 5042
Julie Bushell 1420
Eugene Bustamante 1613
Peggy Butcher 1297
Stephen Butcher 1162, 1182, 1556, 1590
A. C. Butler 6208
Dr Eamonn Butler 1808

G. A. Butler 6151
Marian Butler 6338
Mary Butler 1887
Mike Butler 6243
Steve Butler 6079
M. D. Buttler 1001
Dennis Butts 5052
David Buxton 1178
Fred Buxton 1376
Nicholas Byam Shaw 1547, 1677
Jamie Byng 1153
Kathryn Byrd 5073
Kevin Byrne 1534
Dr Tony Byrne 1204
D. A. Byrom 2532
Michael Byron Davis 2160

Stephanie Cabot 4066
Louis Cabral 5141
Mary Cadogan 5052
Elizabeth Caffin 2432
Ramsey Caffull 1759
Gilles Cahn 1522
J. W. S. Cairns 6268
R. Caithness 2068
Dr M. Calcraft-Rennie 5047
Jenni Calder 1602
John Calder 1148
Liz Calder 1098
Rachel Calder 4085
Jill Caldwell 2086
Gerard Callaghan 1142
Kate Callaghan 1676
Paul Callaghan 1142
Trevor Callaghan 1466
Michael Callahan 4097
Dr Anthea Callen 5022
Heather Cam 2032
Ian Cameron 6008
Ian A. Cameron 3018
J. D. Cameron 1560
Linda D. Cameron 2408
R. A. Cameron 1623
Robin Cameron 6010
B. Camichel 1725
Peter Camilleri 6059
A. Campbell 2174
Bill Campbell 1550
C. I. Campbell 2484
D. G. Campbell 2484
David Campbell 1151
Eileen Campbell 1387, 1388
Mrs F. G. Campbell 1652
K. C. Campbell 2484
Maggie Campbell 6035
Malcolm G. Campbell 1229
Martina B. Campbell 1229
Ramsey Campbell 5041
Robert Campbell 1094
Robin Campbell 1053, 6140
Rod Campbell 1150
S. J. Campbell 2148
Sally-Ann Campbell 1721
Simon Campbell 1535
Suzie Campbell 2061
Edmund Campion 5136
Beryll Camplin 1457
Jamie Camplin 1855
Gordon Camsey 1759
V. Canning 4118
Jeffrey Canton 5148
Simon Capelin 1149
Keith Carabine 5057
Dana Carciumaru 2212
Danny Carey 6141
Martine Cariou-Keen 1094

Mrs Helen Carley 1524, 5087, 6382
A. E. Carlile 1713
I. Carlile 1478
Richard Carlisle 3058
Dr Diane Carlyle 2013
L. W. Carp 1262
Fiona Carpenter 1545, 1677
Jon Carpenter 1159
Philip Carpenter 1093
Thomas F. Carpenter 5083
Alyson Carr 1921
D. Carr 2174
Jane Carr 1128, 1130
Nigel Carr 6088
Richard Carr 1251
Tim Carr 1125
Robert Carr-Archer 1603
Roch Carrier 5144
Michael Carroll 2206
Patricia Carroll 2385
Peter Carson 1381, 1661
William Carson 1166
Ann Carter 5027
Prof. Ian Carter 2432
Margaret Carter 1789
Philip Carter 1594
Charlotte Cartwright 6024
Denis Cartwright 1616
B. D. Carvell 1861
Giorgio R. Casarotto 4013
Jenne Casarotto 4013, 4014
Shelagh Casebourne 6277
Shawn Casey 2046
Seamus Cashman 2405
Lorna Casimir 1644
Sybil Caslin 1356
Frank Cass 1161
Stewart Cass 1161
Linda Cassells 2459
P. A. Cassidy 1180
Vincent Cassidy 1005
Dr Stephen Castell 6045
Ian Castello-Cortes 1376
Eduardo Castillo 6311
Bunny Castle 2499
Kevin Castle 6247
Jenny Cattell 2078
Dr J. A. Catterall 1456
W. M. Catto 2148
Achilles F. Cauchi 2430
R. Cauthery 1014
P. Cauwood 2016
Claire Cavanaugh 2074
Joan Cave 1168
Paul Cave 1168
Sandy Caven 1614
Patrick Cavendish 1260
Keith Cavers 5030
Marsha Cawthorne 6315
Philip Cercone 2171
Yolanda Cerdá 1379
Giovanna Ceroni 1497
Sam Chacko 2365
A. J. Chadwick 6271
David Chadwick 6134
J. A. Chadwick 6271
P. G. Chadwick 6271
Peter Chadwick 1502
Timothy Chadwick 1002
Lady A. M. Chadwyck-Healey 1177
Sir C. E. Chadwyck-Healey 1177
Henry Chakava 2414
Narisa Chakra 1612
S. Chakraborti 2291
Debashis Chakraborty 2338

Goutam Chakraborty 2338
Shri A. K. Chakravarty 2305
Manish Chakravorty 2320
Tapan Chakravorty 2320
Miss Heather Chalcroft 4078
Martina Challis 1721
Ginette Chalmers 4076
Mark Chaloner 1477
Graham Chamberlain 6166
Aidan Chambers 1874
David Chambers 5016
Dawn Chambers 2407
Frank Chambers 1334
Harry Chambers 1667
Jeff Chambers 6167
Lynn Chambers 1667
C. C. Chan 2254
Raymond Chan 2428
Dr Chan Man Hung 2250
Ms Chan Yun King 2250
Shri Prakash Chand 2367
Prem Chand 2340
Kishor Chandarana 6270
Jennifer Chandler 5007
Mrs J. Chant 2528
David Chaplin 1484
D. A. Chapman 6034
Geoffrey Chapman 1025
Ian S. Chapman 1545, 1677
Ian Chapman 1376, 1799
Jennifer Chapman 1025
Keith Chapman 1568
Kevin Chapman 2141
Lucy Chapman 1033
Martyn Chapman 1047, 1096, 1162, 1182, 1556, 1590, 1615, 1892, 1897
Mary Chapman 1236
Melissa Chapman 1201, 1483
Paul Chapman 1183
Philip Chapman 1658
Ruth Chapman 1226
J. N. Chapple 1635
Kate Charles 5060
Chris Charlesworth 1630
R. I. H. Charlton 1054
Geoffrey Charters 1047, 1096, 1162, 1615, 1892, 1897
Ms Chumki Chatterjee 2338
S. Chatterjee 2376
Winnie Y. W. Chau 2252
Nirmalya Roy Chaudhuri 2339
Nabab Singh Chauhan 2343
Lesley Chaundy 1468
B. R. Chawla 2299
Himanshu Chawla 2299
Ann Checchia 2192
Joan Checkley 1034
Philip Checkley 1034
Prof Chan Heng Chee 2487
Gillian Chee 2494
Anthony Cheetham 1640
Hal Cheetham 4012
Ron Cheetham 6241
Rosie Cheetham 1639
Michel de la Chenelière 2119
Douglas Cheng 2251
Grace Cheng 5155
Christoph Chesher 1648
Geoffrey Chesler 3035
K. A. Chesson 2007
Dennis W. C. Cheung 2252
Jean-Marc Chevrier 2158
Robin Chew Hee Leong 2252
M. L. A. Chiappelli 6269
Christine Chick 1758
Fine Chilomo 2527

Mark Chilver 6152
Audrey Chin 2014
Wan Mun Ching 2428, 2429
Mike Chinn 5041
Emilia Chiocca 2144
Henry Chipewo 2527
B. C. Chitsike 5182
Chris Chittenden 2452
Greg Chiykowski 2192
Kelvyn Chong 2490
Mohinder Kumar Chowdhry 2323, 2337
Naresh Kumar Chowdhry 2323, 2337
A. K. Rai Chowdhury 2333
A. Roy Chowdhury 2333
Sheila Christie 6391
Philippa Christmas 5167
Karen Christopherson 6171
Chua Hong Koon 2488
Rajiv Chugh 2280
Ramesh Chugh 2280
Ritu Chugh 2280
Anthony Chung 2483
Mrs P. Church 1283
Peter Churcher 1580
D. W. Churchill 1340
G. J. Churchill 5088
Jane Churchill 6259
John Churchill 1078
G. B. Churchman 2448
Massimo Ciavolella 2130
L. Claerhout 1501
Thérèse Claffey 1735
Marcus Clapham 1928
Hilary Clare 1250
Deirdre Clark 1787
Mrs Fiona Clark 5103
Lynne Clark 1295
Margaret Clark 5052
P. M. Clark 1306
Paul Clark 1125
Philip Clark 3019
Stephen Clark 1466
T. J. Clark 1357
Anthony Clarke 1198
Barbara Clarke 2252
Barry Clarke 1636, 2482
David Clarke 1447
Denis Clarke 1198
Elaine Clarke 1198
Fiona Clarke 1648
Miss Gloria Clarke 5160
J. A. Clarke 1635
James Clarke 2435
Jaqui Clarke 1487
Lisa Clarke 1787
Malcolm Clarke 6082
Margaret Clarke 1651
Michèle Clarke 5114
Pauline Clarke 6188
Prof. Richard Clarke 1878
Roger Clarke 1485, 1661
Serafina Clarke 4015
Anna Clarkson 1301
Malcolm Clarkson 1301
Bev Clasohm 2076
Barbara Classen 6394
Eric W. Classey 1202
Peter D. Classey 1202
Miss Marie Clayton 1399
Peter Cleal 2079
Celia Clear 1849
David Cleary 2187, 2238
John Cleary 1244
Patrick Cleary 5111
R. J. Dick Cleary 2018

John Clement 1389, 1506
Mary Clemmey 4016
Normand Cléroux 2210
G. Cleveland 2496
Glenn Clever 2102
Ann Clifford 2442, 5165
P. C. Clifford 2532
Peter Clifford 1843
Hilary Clifford Brown 1671
Hugh W. P. Clift 1856
Susan Cline 2122
Prof. David J. A. Clines 1794
Liam Clooney 2399
Jonathan Clowes 4017
Frances Coady 1362
Dudley Coates 1571
Katharine Coates 1389
Ken Coates 1820
Bob Cobbing 5026
Elspeth Cochrane 4018
Carol Cockaday 1671
David Cocking 2040
L. Cocking 1014
A. B. Cocks 1115
Lyn Codrai 1293
M. Coetzee 2500
Ray Coffey 2031
Jeannie Cohen 1633
L. Cohen 2517
Michael Cohen 1890
Stephen Coke 1050, 6138
Dr A. J. Colborne 1522, 1823
Melvyn Colby 1134
Alan Cole 1419
Colin Cole 1249, 6282
Denis Cole 1527
Linda Cole 1248
Peter Coleborn 5041
Peter Colebrook 1221
Stephen Colebrooke 6248
Bill Colegrave 1407
Ms C. G. Coleman 1144
Jill Coleman 1089, 1412
Gill Coleridge 4083
Adrian Coles 1138
Mrs B. Coles 1478
B. R. Coles 1851
John Coles 5052
Peter Coles 1020
Thomas Coles 1509
Sue Coll 1338, 1472
L. H. R. Collard 1144
Robert Collie 6235, 6294
Felicity Collier 1126
Mahara Collier 6110
Suzanne Collier 5118
P. H. Collin 1206
S. M. H. Collin 1206
Mark Collingbourne 4024
Allison Collins 1717
David Collins 1445, 1886, 3006, 6128
Joyce Collins 1133
Mark Collins 1080, 1207
Mike Collins 1341
Penny Collins 1886, 6128
Richard Collins 1758
Nicholas Combrinck 5177
Jon Conibear 1094, 2014
Robert B. Conklin 1863
D. Conniffe 2388
Claudia Connolly 2194
G. Connolly 6261
Jay Connolly 2190
S. Connolly 2507
Jane Connor 2443
Barbara Conolly 2106

Philip Conrad 5057
Róisín Conroy 2379
Peter Constable 1189
Christophe Conte 6308
Jane Conway-Gordon 4020
Tim Conyers 6013
Michael Coogan 1138
Andrew Cook 1462
Deborah Cook 1077
G. Cook 1398
Graham Cook 1521
John Cook 6039
Alistair B. Cooke 1210
Isabel Cooke 4117
R. J. Cooke 2501
Richard Cooke 5177
Douglas Cooksey 1077
Vikki Cookson 1689
N. Cooles 2522
Dulcie Coombs 2162
Jack Cooper 6219
Janet Cooper 1758
Jenny Cooper 2458
Naomi Cooper 1541
P. Cooper 1289
Sara Cooper 1434
Wendy Cooper 1768
David Cope 6152
Ivan Corbett 1213, 1873
Sue Corbett 1093
Anne Cordwent 1457
David Corkill 4006
Ania Corless 4041
Gill Cormode 1676
Ron Cornelius 2149
C. W. Cornell 6263
Robert Cornford 1646
Tim Corrie 4076
Ian Corsie 1684
R. Cortie 6233
Christine Corton 1113
Bill Cosans 1403
Bryony Cosgrove 2068
Pamela Costain 6353
David Costello 1143
Seán Costello 1565
E. Costigan 2050
Philip Cotterell 1676
Brian Cotton 1039
Peter Cotton 1528
Simon Couchman 1409
Pam Coulas 2112
Joanne Cournoyer 5141
K. R. Courtney 1851
Yvonne Courtney 6134
Ann Cowan 6392
Jane Cowan 6392
Helen Coward 1631
Peter Cowell 1083
Athol E. Cowen 1663
Geoff Cowen 6131
Lesley Cowen 1278
J. Cowhig 1467
Raymond Cowie 1550
Stewart Cowley 3063
Mrs Doreen Cowling 6214
Peter Cowling 5105
Barry Cox 1231
Colin Cox 2460
Deidre Cox 2057
Sara Jane Coxon 1047, 1096, 1892
Gabrielle Coyne 2068
Alan Crabb 6142
John Crabb 1480
Richard A. B. Crabbe 2241, 5153
Ludo Craddock 1529

Alan Craig 1333
Ian Craig 1387
M. Craig 1014
Susie Craigie-Halkett 1711
J. Cramp 1533
Leslie Cramphorn 1252
Carole Crampton 6148
B. Crane 2050
Paul Crane 1517
Philip Cranfield 6073, 6145
Mike Cranidge 1638
Lesley Craven 1278
Cameron Crawford 2212
Mrs H. C. Crawford 1344
James Crawford 1258
N. J. Crawford 1344
Chris Crawshaw 5120
Patrick Crean 2219
Barbara Creary 2125
Elizabeth Cree 4041
Sara Creech 1581, 6325, 6365, 6367, 6369
Stephanie Creed 4111
Robert Creffield 1006
John Cressey 1549
R. Cressey 1705
Ruth Cresswell 6044
F. Rupert Crew 4022
Kathleen Crew 4022
Peter Cribb 2035
Simon Crine 1298
Bob Cripps 1927, 6121
Max Crisfield 1103
S. Critchlow 1385
Robert Crocker 1743
Howard Croft 1751
Jon Croft 1004
Henrietta Crompton 1225
Melissa Crompton 1225
Paul Crompton 1225
Lester Crook 1718
Cathie Crooks 2209
Steven Cross 1853
William K. Cross 2117
Anthony Crouch 4041
Alan Crowden 1149
Rev Colville Crowe 2047
Harriet Cruickshank 4023
Dennis Crutcher 1297
Edward Crutchley 1094
David Crystal 6152
Alan Cubitt 1750
Lord Cuckney 1640
Dr Fintan Cullen 5022
Tony Cullis 6141
Andrew Cullua 1419
Barbara Cumming 2114
S.L. Cummings 1385
Blair Cummock 1371
Jan Cundy 6133
Alan Cunningham 1409
Arthur Cunningham 1129
Barry Cunningham 1098
David Cunningham 2042
Helen Cunningham 2005
Jean Cunningham 2042
S. Curnow 1600
Tim Curnow 4024, 4102
Patrick Curran 1297
Clare Currey 1228
James Currey 1228
Tina Currie 1339
Jane Curry 2049
Richard Curry 6154
Eleanor Curtain 2023
Craig Curtis 6325
Jenny Curtis 2057

Nina Curtis 1834
Dr Simon Curtis 5077
Tony Curtis 1539, 1837
Martin Cuss 1648
Chris Custance 6155
Neville Cusworth 1146
Tom Cutler 1166
Gillian Cutress 1299
A. Cutting 1087
Laura Czerniewicz 2499, 5177

Antonio D'Alfonso 2144
Trevor D'Cruz 1008
Radomir Dabanovic 6170
David Dackson M. Patawah 2240
F. Dada 2507
Gillean Daffern 2211
Tony Daffern 2211
Deena Daher 3008
C. Dahlstrom 2174
Mrs P. Dahn 2496
Shelley Daigh 2401
Dr John Daintith 3040
Ms Meva Daka 2526
Jean Dale 2117
Mike Dale 6060
T. A. Dale 1470
Nicholas Dale-Harris 1552
Joan Dale-Lace 1161
Sheena Daley 1795, 1812
John Dalton 1783
M. J. Daly 1771
Tom Danby 2053
Bill Dancer 3020
Dr Louise Dandurand 5151
Marc-André Dandurand 2218
Cliff Dane 1562
Margaret Dane 1562
Mrs Elma Dangerfield 5048
Dr J. S. Daniel 1635
Jane Daniel 1100
Penny Daniels 1072
Sandra Daniels 1845
Victor G. Daniels 1234
Sarah Dann 1076
Miss G. A. Danson-Smith 6179
Rev Dr T. C. Danson-Smith 6179
M. B. Dar 2411
Noreen Dar 2411
S. M. Dar 2411
Simon Dardick 2232
Margaret Dardis 2378
Rena Dardis 2378
Sharon Dare 1233
Tim Dare 1611
K. G. Darke 1793
Loren Darroch 2161
P. W. Dart 2068
Peter Darvill-Evans 1890
Brajmohan Das Gupta 2278
Vanessa Daubney 5060
Beverley Daurio 2175
Donald Daurio 2175
A. Davenport 1467
Marjorie Davenport 6079, 6331
Genevieve Davey 1294
John Davey 1093
Teresa Davey 1257
A. David 2521
Jack David 2133
David Davidar 2339
Andy Davidson 1450
Bob Davidson 3069
Ian Davidson 1264
Jim Davidson 2034
John Davidson 6162
Merric Davidson 6084

Paul Davidson 5139
Mrs R. Davidson 1357
S. G. Davidson 1109
Hugh Davie 1023
Mrs S. J. Davie 1738, 6195
A. L. Davies 2017
Alun Davies 1869
Bill Davies 1149
Brian Davies 1499, 1830
C. Davies 1320, 1632, 1829
C. M. G. Davies 1284
Colleen Davies 2159
D. Philip Davies 5124, 6258
Don Davies 1638
Elgan Davies 5124
Gerallt Wyn Davies 1290
Gill Davies 1327, 3047
Gwen Davies 5020
H. Davies 1014
Heather Davies 2094
John Davies 1372
John R. M. Davies 5059, 5068
Mike Davies 6221
Paul Davies 1799, 2133
Dr Philip R. Davies 1794
Ray Davies 1255
Rebecca Davies 6134
Robert Davies 2126
Sheila Davies 5125
Simone Davies 1395
Stephen Davies 1515
Sue Davies 1350
Sydney Davies 6344
Tim Davies 1297
Alan Davis 1184, 1821
Alison Davis 1097
Christopher Davis 1248
Janet Davis 1046
Jeremy Davis 2065
John Davis 6096, 6123
Lenelle Davis 5107
Linda Davis 1248
Meg Davis 4063
Michael Byron Davis 2156
Nicola Davis 1173
P. Davis 2522
Penny Davis 3033
Veronica Davis 3067
Kimberly Davison 2234
Peter Davison 1149
S. Davison 1511
Tim Davison 1305
T. C. Davy 1014
Brian Dawes 1923
Caroline Dawnay 4076, 5023
Abigail Dawson 1386
Imogen Z. Dawson 3069
James Dawson 1315
Liz Dawson 1510
Patrick Dawson 1315
Ro Dawson 1315
D. Day 2016
Ed Day 3042
Jackie Day 1301
Jon Day 1154
Julia Day 1154
Peter Day 1025
Shirley Day 1697
Asok De 2291
Robin De Beaumont 5016
Theo de Boer 6236
Crispin de Boos 1044
Dr H. de Brouwer 1744
Jean-Marc de Chauvigny 6308
Denis de Freitas 5039
Caroline de Fries 2019
Dr H. de Glanville 6014

Countess de la Bedoyère 1141, 1783
Giles de la Mare 1297
Mrs M. de Lange 1156
C. Baile de Laperriere 1416
S. Baile de Laperriere 1416
Christine De Poortere 1506
Taya de Reyniès 6308
Denzil de Silva 4078
Joe De Souza 1265, 3039
Louis de Sybaris 6001
Tiny de Vries 3057
Frans de Wit 5088
Felix de Wolfe 4025
A. Dean 6137
C. J. Dean 1532
Christopher Dean 5107
S. Dean 6137
John F. Deane 2386
Miss S. Deane 1281
Dominic Deeson 6007
Jane Deeson 6007
Dr Tony Deeson 6007
A. Dei-Awuku 2241
W. A. Dekutsey 2247
Hilary Delamere 4002
Gino Della-Ragione 6232
Xavier Delmas 6308, 6309
Vicki Demmsico 2202
Philip Denby 1477
Andrew Denham 1625
John Denison 2103
Geoffrey Denner 1737
John Dennis 1227
Nicki Dennis 1048
R. A. Denniston 1623
Adam Dent 6119
G. R. H. Dent 1910
Mary Denton 1665
George Depotex 6074
Jenny Dereham 1485
Ken Derham 1689
Helene Derome 2125
Dr Robin Derricourt 2029
J. P. Desmond 1288
A. A. DeSouza 1760
Grace Deutsch 2227
Michael Devenish 1248
R. Dever 1819
Anne Deveson 5134
Diana Devin 1683
Anne Dewe 4060
Lilian Dhahabu 2414
Dr R. K. Dhawan 2345
Sumesh Dhawan 2345
D. Diamond 2522
Manuela Dias 2229
Jill Dick 1778, 6346
Mollie Dickenson 1484
E. Dickinson 2016
Nigel Dickinson 1256
Philippa Dickinson 1869
R. A. Dickinson 6263
C. J. Dicks 1915
Brian Dickson 1075
David Dickson 2397
Susanne Dickson 5109
Keith Diggle 1735
John Dilger 1166
John Dill 2172
Andrew Dilnot 1451
Jenny Diment 1408
Dave Dimmell 2161
Alastair Dingwall 1448
Denis Dion 2166
Edmund Dixon 1635
Isobel Dixon 4007

John Dixon 2377
Louise Dixon 1743
Dr M. Dixon 1915
Mary Dixon 2193
Dr Michael Dixon 1184, 1724
Ryan Dixon 2193
Patience Dizon 1798
N. Dlodlo 2530
Richard Dlucik 1125
R. Dobbing 1823
Angela Dobler 2231
Charlene Dobmeier 2136
Elizabeth Dobson 1349
Gerry Dobson 6312
Philip Dodd 1890
Richard Dodman 1211
Broo Doherty 1869
Joan Donald 1733
Anne Dondertman 5142
Nathalie Donikian 6309
John Donlan 2105
Hilary Donlon 1630
Patricia Donlon 6359
Clare Donnelly 1116
Walter Donohue 1297
Peter Donoughue 2046, 5133
Prof B. T. Donovan 5025
Paul Donovan 2004
Peter Donovan 1149
Sue Donovan 2059
Rosemary Dooley 6068
Novin Doostdar 1631
Esther Dordoe 2241
Fleure Dorrell 1236
Nelson Doucet 2141
Mike Dougdale 1033
Carolyn Dougherty 1093
Bronwen Douglas 1004
D. Douglas 5075
Deron Douglas 2186
Diana Douglas 2159
Jackie Douglas 1248
Josie Douglas 2045
Michael Dover 1903
Francesca Dow 1637, 1900
Shirley Dow 1741
Mrs Lesley Down 6091
Allan Downend 5030
Stephanie Dowrick 1924
Andrea Dowsett 1418
Cathy Doyle 1457
Ashley Drake 6085
Helen Drake 1058
Joy Drake 6085
Norman Drake 6085
R. G. Drake 1156
R. Geoffrey Drake 1253
R. Jonathan Drake 1253
I. Drane 1844
P. Dray 6126
Dana Dreibelbis 1184
Ms Suzanne Drew 1208
Rob van Driesum 2053
John Driscoll 1759
Paul Driver 1149
Sheila Drummond 2032
Nevill Drury 2019, 2029
Paul Drury 6167
Adrian Du Plessis 1149
Nann du Sautoy 1528
S. F. du Toit 2502
Eoin Duane 1442
A. D. Dubbins 5075
J. P. Dubois 1901
Andrew Duff 1304
Gilly Duff 1119, 1691
Mrs Patricia Duff 5160

Rachel Duffield 5063
Maureen Duffy 5039, 5058
Patric Duffy 1324
S. Duggan 1384
Sean Duggan 1067, 1763, 1782
Peter Duke 1125
Christine Dulat 2229
Geneviève Dumas 2167
Ian Dumbleton 6073, 6145
Gerard Dummett 1112, 6318, 6341, 6354, 6357, 6386
Jeannine Dumont 2167
Wendy Dunbar 1091
Andrew Duncan 3022
Caroline Duncan 1101
Jo Duncan 5163
John E. Duncan 1369
Moira Duncan 1055
Martin Dunford 3054
Martin Dunitz 1257
Vivienne Dunlop 1754
Ian Dunnet 1756
Nick Dunton 1184
Ellen Dupont 3041
Diane Dupuis 2114
Nicholas Durbridge 4021
Stephen Durbridge 4002
B. M. Dureja 2268
Mary Durkin 1605
Andrew B. Durnell 6086
Michael Durnin 1297
P. W. Durrance 1033
John Durrant 1468
Shiv Dutt 2279
Stella Dutton 1100
Evelyne Duval 6077
Anthony Dwyer 2025
Michael Dwyer 1436
Richard Dwyer 2003
Raymond Dyer 6242
Kathy Dyke 1388
Nadia Dyman 2212
Pamela Dymock 1326
Roderick Dymott 1047, 1096, 1162
Dinah Dysart 2029
A. Dyson 1687
I. Dyson 1705
Pippa Dyson 4037
Nichola Dyson Walker 2019
Francis K. Dzokoto 2243
Moses K. Dzokoto 2243

Bert Eadon 2035
Toby Eady 4027
Brian Eagle 1457
Brian G. Eagle 6191
Graham Eames 1890
Jonathan Earl 1255
Kathryn Earle 1083
Michael Earley 1572
Graeme East 3058
Jilly Easterby 1677
Ian Eastment 1754
Mark Eastment 1849
David Easton 1780
Mrs Fiona Easton 5076
Robert Easton 1161
Stephen Easton 1044
Annie Eastwood 1800
R. Eastwood 1358
Annie Eaton 1869
Michael Eaton 1419
Pamela Ebdon 1326
Jacob Ecclestone 5092
A. O. Echebiri 5171
Nick Eddison 3025

John Eddowes 6036
Mike Edgar 1888
Jacqui Edge 6174
Wendy Edge 6174
HRH The Duke of Edinburgh 5004, 5031
Dr J. J. Edley 2509
John Edmondson 1448
E. A. Edwards 1568
Jan Edwards 5041
Malcolm Edwards 1387, 2039, 2040
Margot Edwards 1678
Nicholas Edwards 1431
Penny Edwards 1098
Phil Edwards 6250
Ros Edwards 1297
Benita Edzard 4086
John Eggleston 1871
Madeleine Ehm 1080
Peter Eichhorn 2004
Max Eilenberg 1784
Z. El-Rayyes 1736
Nick el Rio 1008
Alex Elder 1386
J. Elder 1246
Peter Elek 4028
John Elford 1365
Edward Elgar 1052, 1271
Sandy Elgar 1271
B. Eliot 1560
Valerie Eliot 1297
D. Elis-Gruffydd 1350
J. Elkin 2068
Gordon Ell 2434
Mark Ellingham 3054
A. Clive Elliot 1272
Malcolm G. Elliot 1272
D. Elliott 1385
Judith Elliott 1639
Marion Elliott 2122
Aidan Ellis 1273
C. R. Ellis 1915
Glen Ellis 2214
Helen Ellis 1387
Jennifer Ellis 1773
Lucinda Ellis 1273
Martin Ellis 1492
R. W. Ellis 4001
Wayne Ellis 1094, 6181
Valerie Elliston 5114
Peter Ellway 6343
Richard Elman 3041
Caroline Elmslie 5100
John Elrtul 1598
Suzi Elsden 1207
Barbara Else 4113
Chris Else 4113
Graham Elton 1659
Mary Elverson 1301
David Elworthy 2466
Luke Elworthy 2466
Jan Pieter Emans 6013
Jean Emmerson 1217
John Emmerson 1217
C. Emmett 1564, 1665
John A. Emmett 2047
Harry Endrulat 2234
Dilshad Engineer 2188
Mick England 1473
Ricky Englander 2164
Cecily Engle 1485, 1661
N. Entract 5086
J. Entwiste-Baker 1560
Frank R. Entwistle 1461
Tony Entwistle 2445
Paul Eprile 2098

Hugh Epstein 5057
Tom Erhardt 4013, 4014
Anne Erickson 2192
Jane Erskine 6328
Jenny Ertle 1723
Robert Ertle 1723
Judith Escreet 1525
Mike Esplen 1406
Angela Espley 1719, 6194
Nicholas Esson 1876
Stephen Esson 1049, 1722
Jamie Etherington 1717
A. Evans 1195
Ann Evans 4017
Bethan Evans 4002
David Evans 1685, 2034
Gareth Evans 6282
Jacinta Evans 1636
John Evans 6242
Martin F. Marix Evans 3012
Matthew Evans 1297
P. Evans 6395
P. M. Evans 1352
R. B. Evans 1195
Richard Evans 1349
Steve Evans 1409
Timothy Evans 1855
Yvette Evans-Foster 1211
Martin Eve 1569
Lisa Eveleigh 4099
Bryony Evens 4055
Richard Evenst 2053
Joanna Everard 1239
Sara Everett 1083
Elona Ewing 2206
Kenneth Ewing 4076
Michael Ewins 1005, 1067, 1384, 1763
Helen M. Exley 1295
Lincoln Exley 1295
Richard A. Exley 1295
Cristina Externest 3063
K. Eyston 1600

T. E. Faber 1297
Gaye Facer 4028
Chief Bayo Fadoju 2470
Christopher Fagg 1892
Jan Fairley 6295
Bertil Falck 6286
Bonnie Falconer 6353
Peter Fallon 2393
Lorraine Fannin 5109
Martin Fanning 2392
Diane Farewick 2234
Terry Farley 2073
Anna Farmar 2390
Tony Farmar 2390
T. M. Farmiloe 1546
I. Farnell 6199
Ian Farr 1441
Acrelda Farrell 1877
Antony Farrell 2397
Giovanna Farrell-Vinay 4052
P. M. Farrer 1281
T. C. Farries 6262
Imogen Farrow 1498
Nigel A. E. Farrow 1052, 1235, 1271, 1354, 1774, 6171
Akin Fasemore 5171
S. Fathers 1705
R. T. Fawcett 6249
J. A. Fawibe 5171
Pat Fawley 6166
Simon Fearnehough 1519
Barry Featherstone 1188
A. S. Feldman 6052

Michael Feldman 1376
Tony Feldman 4045, 6098
R. A. Fell 1109
Dr Robert Fellham 1619
Mick Felton 1692
Franz Fenke 6299
Patrick Fenouil 1462
Pierre Fenouil 1462
Mike Fenton 1093
Trevor Fenwick 1287, 5066
Enid Ferdinand 2207
Christopher Ferguson 1855
E. Ferguson 1851
James Ferguson 1508
Mrs L. Fernandez 1558
Trish Fernandez 3063
M. J. B. Fernando 5178
David Fernbach 1347
Grahame Fernback 6172
Roger Ferneyhough 1432
Karen Ferns 2460
Francesco Ferri 2151
Edwina Ferris 2049
P. W. Ferris 1915
Stewart Ferris 1838
T. G. Ferris 1579
David Fickling 1770, 6282
D. Fidler 1560
Elizabeth Fidlon 1741
Lisa Field 1094
P. J. Field 2054, 2068
Gordon Fielden 5121
David Fielder 1847, 3055
John Fielder 6076
Rachel Fielding 1147
Jennifer Fifield 3063
Barry Finch 1685
Chris Finch 1697
Peter Finch 5026
Sarah Finch 1331
T. Finch 6233
Trevor Finch 1066
Ian Findlay 1929
John J. Finlay 5147
Larry Finlay 1869
Matthew Finlay 1561
J. M. Finn 6087
P. Finneran 2050
O. C. Finnie 6267
Gilberto Fiocco 1391
Leonz Fischer 2531
Cyril Fish 6182
Rodney Fishbien 2113
Chester Fisher 1506
Francesca Fisher 3035
Jeremy Fisher 2056
John Fisher 3054
Larry Fisher 1487
Paula Fisher 2219
R. Fisher 1086
R. W. Fisher 2054, 2068
Richard Fisher 1149
Robert Fisher 2450
Sara Fisher 4040
Michael Fishwick 1387
Tony Fisk 2446
J. D. Fitz Gerald 2388
M. FitzGerald 1654
Mary Anne Fitzgerald 1317
Gaynor Fitzpatrick 2149
Robert Flanagan 1231
Ken Fleet 1820
Louise Fleming 2145
Nancy B. Fleming 5143
Andrew Fletcher 1275
Clare Fletcher 1336
Martin Fletcher 1803

Mrs S. Fletcher 1439
Sue Fletcher 1423
Terry Fletcher 1231
Ivy Flett 2186
Suzanne Flett 2195
Nellie Flexner 1485
John Flint 1172
John Flood 2114
Timothy Flood 1855
I. Florance 1619
Mrs Karen Flower 6014
Carol Floyd 2025
Sally Floyer 1661, 1899, 3062
J. Flugge 1033
Klaus Flugge 1033
A. Flynn 2148
Rob Flynn 2053
Siobhan Flynn 1865
Dirk Folens 1313
Ian Folkes 1332
Brenda Follett 1908
A. M. Fondo 2420
Angel Fong 2251
Lionel Foot 1837
Rt Hon Michael Foot 5048
Peter Forbes 5096
Anthony Forbes Watson 1661
Arden Ford 2171
B. Ford 1823
R. E. Ford 2068
Adrian Forman 1319
Allan Forrie 2225
Bill Forster 1414
K. T. Forster 1837
Markus Forster 2525
Michael Forster 1375, 1709, 6157
Francois Fortin 2205
Jacques Fortin 2205
John Foster 5092
Maria Foster 2065
Tim Foster 1239
David Fothergill 1611
A. Fouché 2504
John Fowler 2248
Miss Karen Fox 6091
Ken Fox 1837, 6217
Michael Alan Fox 1863
P. Fox 1687
Simon Fox 1386
T. Fox 1546
Graham Foxcroft 2056
Anthony M. Foye 1709, 1851
R. A. J. Francis 1014
Miss Sydney Francis 3030
Teresa Francis 1132
Yvonne Francis 1504
Joanna Frank 1803
J. P. Frankel 1340
Annie Frankland 1248
Andrew Franklin 1263, 1706
Ian Franklin 1921
Paul Franklin 1638
Theresa Franklin 1269
Jane Franks 1726
Carlos Franz 6311
Anne Fraser 1051
Anthea Fraser 5060
Lady Antonia Fraser 5028
Ian C. Fraser 2009
Lindsey Fraser 5035, 6315
Sarah Fraser 1068
D. Fratsanos 2517
Sue Freathy 4024
Derek Free 6327
Andrew Freeman 1855
Ms D. Freeman 1016
Oliver Freeman 2065, 2072

Robin Freeman 2035
Sue Freestone 1437
Sibyl Frei 2145
Anna French 1498
Christopher French 1138
John French 4030
Colin Fricker 5065
Julian Friedmann 4007
Bridget Frost 1679
Matthew Frost 1553
Nick Frost 6353
Susan Froud 2192
C. Fry 1669
Ms M. Fry 1545
Minna Fry 1799
Ron Fry 1466
C. Fryer 2514
Eileen Fryer 6247
M. Fryer 2500
M. A. Fuller 6263
K. C. Fullman 1398
David Fulton 1333
Pamela Fulton 1333
Y. K. Fung 2249
Michael Funga 2527
David Furse-Roberts 1574
Blossom Furtado 2352
Rock Furtado 2352
Vernon E. Futerman 4031
Charlotte Fyfe 1053, 6140
Alexander Fyjis-Walker 1650

Michael Gabb 1504
Juri Gabriel 1240
Waruingi Gacheche 2422
David Gadsby 1089
O. Gadsby 1861
Hakeem Gaffar 2470
Gajendra Singh Gahlot 2275
Janet Gainham 6244
Justin Gainham 6244
Leslie Gainham 6244
Lian Gainham 6244
John Gaisford 1670
Kathy Gale 1924
Neeraj Galgotia 2293
Suneel Galgotia 2294
Naomi Galinski 1827
James Gallacher 1072
Brian Gallagher 1245
Margaret Gallagher 1913
Patrick Gallagher 2004
Ronan Gallagher 2392
N. Gallehawk 1501
Sue Galley 2053
Peter Galliner 4032
D. A. Galloway 2148
Kelly Galusha 6306
Angela Galvin 1609
Berni Galway 2236
Anthony C. Gamble 1735
Carl Gamble 6057
John Gamble 1898, 3011
Mrs S. Gamble 1807
Sally Gaminara 1869
M. Gandy 1087
Edward Gannan 2064
Ms Julie Ganner 2034
Ted Gannon 2454
K. M. Ganu 2246
Steven Gardiner 1542
Brenda Gardner 1678
D. Gardner 6223
Philip Gardner 3065, 6002
W. H. Gardner 6223
Amit Garg 2297
B. P. Garg 2297

Deborah D. Garman 1863
Luc Garneau 2210
Diane Garnell 1008
Barry Garner 2065
D. Garner 1702
G. N. S. Garner 1266
Graham Garner 1710
Frank Garofalo 6146
Pat Garrett 5052
Charlotte Gascoigne 3051
André Gaspard 1761
Lucy Gasson 1812
Murray Gatenby 2440
Bertrand Gauthier 2125
Julie Gauthier 5141
R. E. Gauvin 1611
John Gavin 1754
Kate Gavron 1155
Richard Gay 1075
Jo Gearing 1301
Karen Geary 1423
Jan Geddes 2123
K. Gee 1087
Peter Gee 1643
Jeremy Geelan 1012
Michael Geelan 1029, 1030,
   1031, 1368, 6161
Friedel Gehring 2057
Adam Gelbtuch 1682
Howard Gelman 2085
Tricia Genat 2009
Alastair George 1872
Jamie George 1353
Anton Gerits 5012
Paul Gerrish 1189
Frances Gertler 1239
Joanna Gertler 2192
Gaurav Ghai 2316, 2365, 2366
S. K. Ghai 2366
Vikas Ghai 2316, 2365, 2366
S. N. Ghosal 2265
Sunanda Ghosh 2354
Mai Ghoussoub 1761
Nóirín Ní Ghrádaigh 2383
A. Gibb 1218
R. Gibb 1545
John Gibbins 6241
Prof Michael Gibbons 1056
Julie Gibbs 2068
Simon Gibbs 1190
Susie Gibbs 1543
C. Gibson 1545
Caroline Gibson 1248
Chris Gibson 1677
Douglas Gibson 2169
Gilbert Gibson 4006
Jane Gibson 2181
Lee Gibson 6057
R. G. C. Gibson 1344
Roma Gibson 1085
Anthony Giddens 1693
Michael Gifkins 4110
Luigi Gigliotti 6001, 6347, 6348
David Gilbert 6242
Mike Gilbert 6049
D. Gilbertson 1533
John Gilder 2059
Dan Giles 1917
T. E. Giles 2127
Terence H. E. Giles 6177
Andrew Gilfillan 1149
D. Gilhooly 1777
M. H. Gill 2394
Steve Gill 2413
Joanne Gillam 1716
Col Gillespie 2076
Joyce Gillespie 5135

Patricia Gillette 1124
B. Gillham 1664
Michael Gilliat 1226
Emily Gillingham 1035
C. Gillitt 2507
Eileen Gillow 1265, 3039
Mike Gilmore 1922
R. M. Gilmour 2083
Harry Gilonis 1726
Susan Girvan 2173
Gitau Githenji 5161
Morwenna Given 6092
Janet Glass 4033
Justin Glass 5048
Jenny Glayzer 5091
Benjamin Glazebrook 1211
Ken Glen 1279
T. Glover 1109
Trevor Glover 5099
Barry Glynn 6174
Stasz Gnych 3015
Bill Godber 6201
David Goddard 1710
Anne Godden 2043
Susie Godden 2043
Tim Godfray 5036, 6289, 6335,
   6344
David Godfrey 1233
Nicky Godfrey 6250
Joanne Godziuk 2211
Alison Goff 1162, 1892, 1897
Anthony Goff 4041
Martyn Goff 5070, 6292, 6315
Michael Goff 1047, 1096, 1162,
   1349, 1892, 1897
Bernard Goggin 2381
Brenda Goh 2488
Claire Goh 2490
Edwin Goh 5174
Jerry Goh 2488, 2491
Steven Goh 2481
R. N. Gokarn 2342
Ian Golding 1124
Richard Gollner 4082
Suneel Gomber 2308
Ms Sweety Gomber 2308
Dr I. R. Gomersall 1139
Lindi Gonzalez 1105
Mrs Rosemary Good 1359
Stephen Goodchild 1094
David Goodere 6167
Josephine Gooderham 1052
Andrew Goodfellow 3050
Lennie Goodings 1889
Paul Goodland 6162
Ken Goodlet 2003
J. Goodman 1157
George Goodwin 2169
Pauline Goodwin 1502
Alan Goodworth 1300, 1746
Stan Googe 6090
L. C. Gooneratne 2521
Michelle Goossen 2186
Adam Gordon 1351
Giles Gordon 4024
Martin Gordon 2019
Sanjeev Goswami 2333
Prof. Dr D. Götze 1823
Nicholas Gould 1270
M. Goulding 1486
Pat Gouldstone 1598
Alastair Gourlay 3015
A. Gouws 2517
D. K. Govindaraj 2370
Colin Gower 1758
Lesley Gowers 1490
Lord Gowrie 5019

Ashwani Goyal 2295, 2296
Kaushal Goyal 2295, 2296
Malcolm Grabham 1630
A. M. W. Graham 1358
Arlene Graham 6188
Betty Graham 6362
Chris Graham 1359
Gordon Graham 6362
John Graham 1258
Ronnie Graham 1359
Tim Graham 1359
Vanessa Graham 1553
Helen Graham-Cameron 3029,
    6030
Mike Graham-Cameron 3029,
    6030
Rod Grainger 1884
Peter Grala 1278
Katie Gramich 6332
B. Grandage 1844
Dr Douglas Grant 1776
Gary Grant 1837
Sandy Grant 1730
Louise Grantham 2513
Tudor Grashoff 6050
Pat Graves 6135
Alison Gray 5127
Cat Gray 1353
D. Gray 6260
Prof D. J. Pereira Gray 1748
David Gray 1167
J. C. F. Gray 1616
Jenny Gray 1401
Mrs Jill Pereira Gray 1748
Randal Gray 1161
Robert Gray 3026
Sue Gray 1363, 6024
John Grayston 1781
Barry Graystone 1848
Brian Green 5032, 5056
Carole A. Green 1801
Christine Green 4034
David R. Green 1326
Duncan Green 1508
Geoff Green 1801
Dr Geoffrey F. Green 1197
J. Green 1600
Julie Green 2444
Lynn Green 1583
Maureen Green 1745
Paul Green 5026
Peter Green 1236
Ray Green 1161
Rod Green 1890
Stuart Green 1087
T. S. Green 1745
Vivien Green 4086
Avis Greenaway 1511
Alan Greene 1919
Bee Greene 1077
Graham Greene 4095
George Greenfield 1869
Adrian Greenwood 6148
J. J. Greenwood 1713
Ros Greenwood 2008
Lawrence Greer 1091
David Gregor 6129
C. Gregory 2504
Jane Gregory 4036, 4037
Paul Gregory 6219
Tim Gregson-Williams 1422
Elspeth Greig 1525
John Grenier 1418
Anthony Gresford 1724
Wendy Gresser 4002
Oonagh Gretton 1541, 1901
Diana Gribble 2082

Liz Grieve 2184
Andrew Griffin 1203
Kate Griffin 1362
Tom Griffin 2404
Dave Griffiths 5080
Ian Griffiths 1269
Naomi Griffiths 2114
Terence Griffiths 1418
Clare Grist 1443, 1698, 1699,
    1700, 1701
Alexandra Groom 4031
Debby de Groot 2513
Peter Grose 1370
Roslyn Grose 1370
Tamara Grose 1370
Beth Grossman 6135
Jane Grounsell 1197
Marjukka Grover 1591
Mike Grover 1591
Peter Groves 1567
Garmon Gruffudd 1932
Robat Gruffudd 1932
Alain Gründ 5013
Elio Guarnuccio 2076
David Gudgin 1287
Mrs Martine Gueguen 5001
Ginette Guetat 2151
Conrad Guettler 1149
Joy Gugeler 2097
D. K. Guha 6093
David Guild 1904
Vivienne Guinness 2397
Sevak Gulbekian 1828
Fred Gullette 6328
Helen Gummer 1803
L. Gunn 1352
Ms L. Gunn 6395
Jane Gunton 1671
Alok Gupta 2347
Amit Gupta 2346
Anil Gupta 2304, 2356
Anjani Gupta 2347
Anurag Gupta 2347
Dr Ashok Kumar Gupta 2346
K. R. Gupta 2269
Manoj Das Gupta 2270
Mira Gupta 2270
Naresh Gupta 2304, 2356
Nikunj Gupta 2295, 2296
Om Parkash Gupta 2347
R. K. Gupta 2315
Ramesh Kumar Gupta 2346
Shri R. S. Gupta 2305
Sunil Gupta 2304, 2356
Vikas Gupta 2346
Vinod Gupta 2346
Virender Gupta 2304, 2356
Prabhu Guptara 6117
Mrs Josephine Gurira 5183
Alan Gurney 6209
R. F. Gurnham 2122
Graham Gurr 2445
Prof William Gutteridge 1733
Robert Guy 1391
R. Guzner 1385
Philip Gwyn Jones 1387
Robert Gwyn Palmer 3035

Mrs Yim Ng Seen Ha 2254
Barend ter Haar 1184, 1821
Madeleine Hacking 1227
Mrs Lesley Hadcroft 4078
Maureen Hadden 2079
Sue Hadden 1636
David Haddock 1378
Jemima Haddock 6169
Peter Haddock 1378

Colin P. Hadley 5058
Michael Hagen 1645
Mary Hagger 1504
Iqbal Haidari 2471
Saleem Haidari 2471
Andrew T. Haigh 6259
Louise Haines 1485
Peter Hains 2511
Prof P. E. H. Hair 5076
Mrs A. Haistor 1023
Mary Halbmeyer 2075
Hilary Hale 1528
John Hale 1379
Sylvia Hale 2032
Graham Hales 1120
Chris Hall 1247
D. Hall 1014
Derek Hall 3004
Diane Hall 2088
Gary Hall 1636
Geoffrey Hall 1101
Mrs Hazel Hall 3061
Ken Hall 1591
Lorraine Hall 1379
Nigel Hall 1345
Penny Hall 1200
Rod Hall 4099
S. Hall 1177
Prof S. Hall 1635
Stephen Hall 1661, 1899
Tony Hall 5032
Sue Halliday 1921
Meryl Halls 6289
Charles Halpin 1112, 6318, 6341,
    6354, 6357, 6358, 6377, 6379,
    6385, 6386, 6388
Joseph Halpin 6259
Christine Halsey 1255
Margaret Halton 1387
Ingrid Hamer 1167
Captain P. Hames 5126
David Hamill 6073, 6145, 6260
Harry Hamill 6254
Tony Hamill 2197
Alaine Hamilton 1737
Florence Hamilton 1679
Maggie Hamilton 2085
Mark Hamilton 4040
Matthew Hamilton 1098
Susan Hamilton 6007
Ted Hamilton 2020
William Hamilton 4040
Catherine Hammond 2025
Jill Hammond 2447
Margaret Hanbury 4038
David Hancock 2146
Mike Hancock 1683
Ralph Hancox 6392
Peter Bernard Hands 1241
David Hanley 2137
William B. Hanna 2156
Priscilla Hannaford 1123
Judith Hannam 1548
D. Hannan 2388
Carol Hannawin 1256
Lisa Hanrahan 2078
Richard Hansen 6150
Victoria Hansen 6150
James Hanson 2111
Sir John Hanson 5040
Rukhsana Haq 2413
Michael Haralambos 1167
Pauline Haralambos 1167
Joan Harcourt 2171
Claire Harcup 1902
Ian Harding 1819
Rudy Harding 6170

Anne Hardy 2188
Rod Hare 1248
Susanne Hargrave 2081
Mrs M. Hargraves 5176
Tony Harkins 2460
Mrs E. Harkness 1807
Jennifer Harland 6079, 6331
Peter Harland 6079, 6331
Prof. W. Harlen 1777
Richard Harman 3042
A. E. Harold 1444
Tony Harold 1720
John Harper 6169
Judy Harper 2453
R. D. Harper 2054
John Harper-Nelson 2002
Wendy Harrex 2456, 2458, 5162
Anthony Harris 1741
Bonnie Harris 2163
David Harris 2079, 6193
Gillian Harris 6279
Jonathan Harris 1251
Kate Harris 1387
Kim W. Harris 2017
Michael Harris 2232
Nick Harris 2219
Philip Harris 1671
Sue Harris 6079
C. Harrison 1014
Christopher Harrison 1544
Clare Harrison 6075
John Harrison 5043
Joy Harrison 1485
Michael Harrison 2106
Miranda Harrison 1887
P. S. Harrison 1115
Patricia Harrison 1313
Philippa Harrison 1528
Mrs Sara Harrity 5031
Tessa Harrow 1815
Dennis R. Hart 1928
Jim Hart 2053
D. Harte 1881
Kathleen Harte 2395
Richard H. Hartgill 1544, 1546
Andre Harthill 1444, 1720
Tony Hartley 6162
Desmond Harty 2135
K. E. Harvey 1391
Roland Harvey 2037
Vance Harvey 1391, 6226
Viv Harvey 1094
Antony Harwood 4003
Lyn Harwood 2067
R. K. Haselden 5126
Prof. A. Alamghir Hashmi 2477
Harriet Hastings 6116
Ken Hathaway 1227
N. Hattle 2528
Richard Hatton 4039
Kathy Hatzi 2076
R. Hauman 2500
Therese Haussener 2085
Anne Haward 5120
Tony Hawke 2155
Chris Hawkes 1712, 3036
Jean Hawkes 5117
Pauline Hawkes 2109
P. Hawkey 1393
Bob Hawkins 1737
Clive Hawkins 6358, 6379
Gillian Hawkins 1248
Dr R. Hawkins 1394
Stephen Hawthorne 1091
Mrs Julie Hay 1797
Andrew Hayes 1593
Colin Hayes 1149

Patrick J. Hayes 2132
Richard Hayes 6033
Stephanie Haygarth 2001
William Hayhurst 1869
J. H. Haynes 1320, 1398, 1632, 1829
Ven. Derek Hayward 1773
J. C. Hayward 1910
Mark Hayward 1877, 1888
Philip Hayward 6164
Stephen Hayward 1785
Mrs Y. G. Hayward 1910
Brian Haywood 6166
Peter Haywood 1313
Philip Haywood 1313
Anthony Head 6159
Gwyn Headley 6095
Mrs Stephanie Heald 1461
J. Heals 1014
Linda Healy 1097
Martin Healy 2392
Bill Heaney 6157
David Heap 2455
Roger Hearn 6026
Louisa Hearnden 1603
E. Heasman 1861
David Heatherwick 1896
Carol Heaton 4035, 5023
Margaret Heaton 5052, 5097
Caroline Hebblethwaite 2139
Ernest Hecht 1815
John K. Hedgecock 5010
N. Hedges 1858
Malcolm Hedley 6163
Jean Heffernan 1390
Clare Hegarty 1640
Mary Hegarty 2401
Oscar Heini 1089
David Held 1693
C. Hellawell 1223
Lucy Heller 1885
Martin Heller 3044
Michael Hellyar 1751
Tim Hely-Hutchinson 1401, 1425
Mary Hemming 1924
Jo Hemmings 1614
T. Hemmingway 2115
Barry Hempstead 1869
Felicia Hen 2428, 2429
Ms S. Henbrey 6151
Allan Henderson 1411
Barrie Henderson 1409
Cris Henderson 1170
F. Henderson 1843
Fiona Henderson 2085
Philip Henderson 1527
Stuart Henderson 1207
Eric Hendry 1419
Chiam Heng Him 2493
E. W. Henry 2388
Katherine Henry 1452
L. Michael Henry 2407
Olivine Henry 3041
Robin Henry 6356, 6380
Ros Henry 2466
Donald Henson 1215
Jacki Heppard 2085
Peter Hepple 5061
Sev Hepton 1087
Richard Hepworth 1647
David Herbert 1412
Lorna Herbert 6332
Susan Herbert 1148
Richard Herkes 1499
Nick Hern 1413
Tracy Heron 1102
B. C. T. Herridge 1074

L. C. Herridge 1074
Mike Herridge 1929
Dr M. Herriger 6274
Dennis Heslop 1922
Paul Hetherington 2063, 5137
Teresa van den Heuvel 2135
Leon Heward-Mills 1853
Andrew Hewetson 3033, 3063
Sarah Hewetson 3046
M. Hewinson 1546
Sir Nicholas Hewitt 1660, 1906
T. G. Hewitt 1660, 1906
Andrew Hewson 4049
Margaret Hewson 4049
Peter Hey 1929
Michael Heyward 2082
Michael Heyworth 1215
Steve Hibbard 2053
Roger Hibbert 3033, 3063
Ms Shirley Hibbert 1338, 1472
B. E. Hickey 2148
David Hicks 5034
Simon Hicks 1692
Sophie Hicks 4095
Jane Hickson 1189
Lynn Hieatt 1149
Keith Higgins 6275
Veronica Higgs 1556
Lisa Highton 2040
Bob Hilderley 2203
Herb Hilderley 2161
David Hill 1754
Derek Hill 1125
Diane Hill 1676
Greg Hill 1399
Jimmie Hill 1505
Matthew Hill 1139
Melissa Hill 1480
Richard Hill 6329
Rose Hill 1898
Sally Hill 6279
Vivienne Hill 1309
Paul Hillcrup 2234
Susanne Hillen 3054
Bruce Hilliard 2055
Caroline Hillier 1525
Janet Hillman 2059
Trevor Hills 2149
P. Hilsdon 6185
R. Hilsdon 6185
Beverley Hilton 1260
Chris Hilton-Childs 1226
A. Hinder 1016
C. Hindle 6178
John Hindley 1052
Jean Hindmarch 6391
Kai Jörg Hinz 5123
Paul Hippsley 1374
Alex Hippsley Cox 1437
Carolyn Hird 1542
Gemma Hirst 4071
Tony Histed 1194
Sue Hitchen 1635
Ute Hitchin 1176
Barrie Hitchon 2034, 2036
Ms Clara Ho 2252
Hari Ho 2029
Penny Hoare 1804
Tony Hobbs 1781
Matthew Hoben 6242
Georgina Hobhouse 1534
Anthony R. A. Hobson 5002
Henry Hochland 1421
Katherine Hockley 1244
Jamie Hodder-Williams 1423
David Hodge 1843
H. Hodgkins 2504

Barrie B. Hodgson 6132
Josanne Hodgson 6132
Adrian Hodnett 1356
Anna Hodson 1772
Philip J. Hodson 6313
S. Hoedt 1501
Fr S. Hofbeck 2525
Jean Hoff 2199
Antonia Hoffman 4103
John Hoffman 2435
Larry Hoffman 4103
James Hogan 1626
David Hogg 1843
Richard Hoggart 5128
Sarah Hoggett 1207
Paul Holberton 1570
Franca Holden 1363, 1608
J. K. Holden 6265
Leandra Holder 6188
Michael Holdsworth 1149
Jill Hole 1291
Douglas Holford 1132
Chris Holifield 6283
Jonathan W. Holland 1426, 6227
Mark Holland 1703, 6039
Mike Holland 1744
R. Holland 1109
R. E. Holland 1463
Richard Holland 1232
Sheila M. Holland 6227
William C. Holland 1426, 6227
Frances Hollingdale 1787
Paula Hollings 6163
Richard Hollingsworth 6171
Jill Hollis 3018, 6008
Michael Holloway 1818
Richard Holloway 1009
Barry Holmes 1892, 5005
Chris Holmes 6238
Colm Holmes 1313, 2380, 2391
David Holmes 1248
Miriam Holmes 1017, 1428
P. Holmes 1915
Peter Holmes 1020
Michael Holroyd 5028
Charlotte J. Holt 1592
J. Holt 2054
Melanie Holt 1217
Vanessa Holt 4042
Tim Holton 1849
Michael Holyoak 1035
Ken Hone 2106
W. D. Honeybone 2462
P. Honohan 2388
T. Hook 1501
Pat Than Sow Hoon 2429
Deborah Hooper 3062
Cherry Hope 1695
Peter Hopkins 1488
Andy Hopkinson 1605
David Horgan 2030
Ian Hornby 1616
John Hornby 1378
P. Hornby 1001
Pat Hornby 1378
Eileen Horne 1194
Timothy Horne 1194
Neil Hornick 4082
Brad Horning 2113
Pat Hornsey 4048
Marlyn Horsdal 2154
Val Horsler 1279
Dr David Horton 2001
Roger Horton 1301, 1851
Eve Horwitz 2501, 5177
Irene Horwood 2024
T. Hoskins 6011

Richard Houdmont 1895
C. Hougaard 2517
Susan Houlden 2405
Mark Houlton 1093
David Houston 1387
Rob Hoverman 1105
J. Kirk Howard 2131, 2216
J. V. Howard 1001
Kirk Howard 2155
Sue Howard 2072
Frances Howard-Gordon 1353
Will Howarth 1504
David Howe 5041
G. Howe 1385
Mary Howell 2040
Robert Howells 6106
R. J. Howitt 2462
John Howkins 6242
Jean Howlett 1848
Mrs S. M. Howlett 1662
Barbara Howson 2164
Judy Hubbard 1008
Alannah Hubbart 5102
David C. Hubber 1792
Alison Hubert 1544
Ruth Huddleston 3058
Christopher Hudson 5009
Ian Hudson 1721
John Hudson 1419, 6356, 6380
Marilyn Hudson 2165
Richard Hudson 1484
Roger Huggins 1072
C. Hughes 1223
James Hughes 1021
Mrs M. Hughes 6137
Medwyn Hughes 6094
Peter Hughes 6259
Phil Hughes 1541
R. M. Hughes 1288
Paula Huhtala 2106
Bob Hulks 1625
Brian Hulme 1622
P. Hulme 1066
Karl Humberstone 1280, 6222, 6236
Daniel Hume 5118
John Hume 6189
Christopher Humphrys 6097
Erica Hunnigher 1525
Anne Hunt 1882
Candida Hunt 3008
Fenella Hunt 1248
Greg Hunt 4013
J. Hunt 1478, 5018
John Hunt 1435, 6146
L. Hunt 1881
Liz Hunt 6171
Bruce Hunter 4041
David Oliver Hunter 6032
Jenny Hunter 6032
Simon Huntley 1855
Anne Hurley 2179
Mary Hurley 6359
Paula Hurley 2068
Vincent Hurley 2397
Christopher A. R. Hurst 1436
Jacqueline Hushion 5146
William Hushion 2169
A. Hussain 1893
F. Hussain 1893
Richard Hussey 1640
Valerie Hussey 2164
Jackie Hutchings 2442
Kim Hutchins 6323
C. Hutchinson 1371
Christine Hutchinson 1199, 1538
Mike Hutchinson 1707

R. Hutchinson 1479
Douglas Hutchison 1411
Hazel Hutchison 1933
James V. Hutchison 2229
Pippa Hutchison 1411
Victoria Huxley 1920
Charles Hyde 1077
Jane Hyden 2061
David Hyland 1473
Robin Hyman 1496, 3017

Allan Ibarra 2163
Janet Ibbotson 5063
Ahmad Ijaz 2478
Michael Illingworth 1295
Graham Imeson 2053
Michael Imison 4044
Tamsyn Imison 4044
Malcolm Imrie 1885
Vicki Ingle 1147
B. C. Ingleby 6261
Fiona Inglis 4102
Karen Ingram 1434
Verna Ingram 1286
L. Ingram-Brown 1136
Elke Inkster 2200
Tim Inkster 2200
David Inman 1113
Glen Innes 1553
Keith Ireland 1614
Paula Ireland 6230
Rita Ireland 1637, 1900
Dotti Irving 6083
Niamh Irving 1435
Chris Irwin 1376
J. L. Irwin 1052
John Irwin 1235
Robert Irwin 1240
Sarah Isaac 6294
Dr Alan Isaacs 3040
Mark Isherwood 5088
Nazrul Islam 2338
K. Abdulla Ismaily 2420
Ron Ive 6229
N. Ivel 6269
Karen Iversen 2095
N. V. Iyer 2333
Bruce Izard 6242

C. van Jaarsveld 2517
M. A. C. Jacklin 2504
R. Jackman 6014
Stuart Jackman 1248
Anne Jackson 1589, 1917
Bob Jackson 6250
Carol Jackson 4083
Emma Jackson 1301
Ian Jackson 3025
M. Jackson 1456, 1619
Matt Jackson 1754
Peter Jackson 1288
R. Jackson 1320, 1398, 1632,
  1829
Terry Jackson 1528
Shaji Jacob 4107
R. Jacobson 2461
Selwyn Jacobson 2463
Sir Martin Jacomb 5040
Stephen Jaeger 1162
Helen Jager 2113
O. P. Jaggi 2331
Philip Jago 2062
Anurag Jain 2321
Ashok Jain 2310, 2322
Devendera Jain 2322
J. P. Jain 2321
K. L. Jain 2259

Kuldeep Jain 2310
M. K. Jain 2361
N. P. Jain 2321
Dr P. N. Jain 2310
Pankaj Jain 2322
Shri R. K. Jain 2371
R. P. Jain 2321
Rajiv P. Jain 2321
Ravi P. Jain 2321
Shri S. K. Jain 2371
S. K. Jain 5156
Shashi Jain 2341
Vipin Jain 2341
Suneel Jaitly 1708, 1839
Dr Alhaji L. K. Jakande 2470
Lukeman K. Jakande 2470
Clifford Jakes 1162
Charles James 1882, 3025
Graham James 1853
Helen James 1080
J. A. James 1728
Pat James 1528
Vivien James 1099, 1656
Philippa Jamieson 2458
Martin Jane 1901
Patrick Janson-Smith 1869
David Japp 1825
Cherry Jaquet 6033
Sarah Jardine-Willoughby 5052
Angela Jarman 1576
Linda Jarret 1375
Antony Jarrold 1481
Caroline Jarrold 1481
John Jarrold 1049
E. A. Jarvis 1672
Dr J. Jarvis 1915
John Jarvis 5059
Shri Sunil K. Jashi 2305
Susan Jasper 2208
Peter Jawardena 1917
Mary Jay 6069
Peter Jay 1040
Gamini Jayawickrema 2521
Kevin Jeans 2020
Micheline Jebb 6181
H. Jefferies 1343
Mark Jefferson 1677
Mark Jeffrey 1295
Julian Jeffs 5054
Cathy Jenkins 2036
Emyr Jenkins 5020
Gerald Jenkins 1848
Rhonda Jenkins 1595
Susan Jenkins 1895
Rt Hon Lord Jenkins of Hillhead
  5104
Andrea Jenn 1491
Cathy Jennings 1161
Lawrence Jennings 6180
Patricia Jennings 3046
Susan Jerdan-Taylor 1194
Ms S. Jespersen 5087
Grant Jessé 3038
Vinod Jethra 2339
Gaurav Jetley 2265
Gautam Jetley 2265
Jagdish Jetley 2265
Mrs Saroj Jetley 2265
Henri Jobbé-Duval 6308
David Joel 2452
Siv Johansson-Falk 6286
Derek Johns 4099
Alan Johnson 1189
Dale E. Johnson 1863
Miss E. M. Johnson 5077
Frances Johnson 1668
Herbert M. Johnson 1475

Hilary Johnson 5102
I. M. Johnson 1352
Ken Johnson 1199, 1538
Linda Johnson 1010, 1367
M. A. Johnson 6199
M. B. Johnson 1792
Marlene Johnson 1637, 1900
Stephen Johnson 2511
Tracy Johnson 6287, 6288, 6307
W. R. Johnson 5170
Alison Johnston 1214
Andrew Johnston 1020
Brian Johnston 6169
Catherine Johnston 1516, 1556,
  1681
David Johnston 1172, 1226
F. P. M. Johnston 6269
Ian Johnston 1821
Janet Johnston 1346
Madeleine V. Johnston 1475
Pamela Johnston 1043
Steve Johnston 6029
T. V. W. Johnston 6101
Timothy S. Johnston 1214
Drummond Johnstone 1814
Tom Johnstone 1565
Denise Johnstone-Burt 1033
Tim Jollands 1614
Christopher Jolly 1482
Ken Jolly 2079
Allison Jones 2058
Anthony Jones 4076
April Jones 1379
Barbara Jones 4007
Brian Jones 1291
Chris Jones 5026
Dafydd Charles Jones 5124, 6258
Diana Jones 1855
Eiry Jones 1932
Glyn Jones 1697
Gwerfyl Pierce Jones 5124, 6258
J. Jones 1014
J. L. Jones 1014
Jane Jones 1138
Julia Jones 5127
Julie Jones 6085
Lindy Jones 2187, 2238
Liz Jones 1645
Morfydd Jones 1872
N. Jones 1611
P. A. Jones 6265
R. Gerallt Jones 6332
Robert Jones 1881
Roger Jones 1292, 1876
Ruth Jones 1721
B. Joseph 1358
K. L. Joseph 2279
Ms Mary Joseph 2316
Richard Joseph 1486, 6376
Janet Joyce 1516, 1556, 1681
K. Joyson 2376
Jane C. Judd 4050
S. Judd 2054
Katherine Judge 1525
Tim Julien 2116
Jean-Pascal Jullien 6309
Michael Juma 2416
Luc Jutras 5138

J. W. Kabugi 2422
Barry Kadoch 2196
Helen R. Kahn 5012
Paula Kahn 1668
Constance Kaine 1855
Anjul Kalra 2354
M. K. Kalsi 6203
Bob Kalyan 6170

Alex Kaminsky 1041
Sammy Kamota 2526
Grace Kan 2490
Mrs Sarah Dorothy Kanda 5152
Stella Kane 1711
Anand Kanekar 2303
Pramod Kapoor 2344
Mrs Rani Kapoor 2283
Subodh Kapoor 2283
Sunil Kapoor 2283
Ms Vandana Kapoor 2344
Vinod Kapoor 2344
Joanna Kaptein 1083
Sebastian Karamuelil 1757
Muthoni Karega 2422
Tamar Karet 3043
Professor Enamul Karim 5086
Bo A. Karlsson 6286
Vytas Karpavicius 1904
M. W. Karunaratne 2520
R. W. Karunaratne 2520
Mr Garesan Kasee 2484
Kiran Kataria 4079
Ms Davinder Kaur 2276
Pat Kavanagh 4076
R. A. Kay 1564
S. Kay 1479
Liz Kaydos 2078
Martin Kaye 6175
Jean Kazan 1223
Antony Kearns 1826
Linda Keeble 1859
D. Keel 1320, 1398, 1632, 1829
Robin Keeley 1812
Brian Keen 1795, 1812
Chris Keen 2169
Ms Diane Keen 6170
Linda Keene 1933
Joachim Kehl 6299
Russell Keirnan 2015
Michael Keith 2465
Stanley Kekwick 1050, 6138
Tom Kelleher 1297
Dr Peter Kelley 5047
David Kellock 2076
Bob Kelly 1803, 1865
Eileen Kelly 2395
Frances Kelly 4051
Judith Kelly 2080
Kenneth Kelly 2382
Les Kelly 1581, 6367
Shirley Kelly 6333
A. Kemball 2220
Richard Kemoli 2414
Helen Kemp 1602
Kenneth Kemp 1822
Kirstie Kemp 6152
Simon Kemp 1313
T. Kemp 1320, 1632, 1829
Martin Kendall 1379
Robert Kendrew 3063
R. Kendrick 6151
Steve Kenis 4066
A. Kennedy 1491
Mrs C. Kennedy 1491
Hilary Kennedy 5158
J. Kennedy 1491
Prof K. A. Kennedy 2388
Mrs Rosalind Kennedy 5086
S. Kennedy 1546
W. M. Kennedy 6260
Nick Kenney 1297
Fiona Kenshole 1425
David Kent 1528
Debbie Kent 1566
Nick Kent 1104, 1740
Mel Kenyon 4013

Chenile Keogh 2400
K. W. Keohane 1851
Victoria Keown-Boyd 1623
John Keppler 2506
Ann Kerr 5163
Gordon J. Kerr 1066
John Kerr 6060
Martin Kerr 6038
Rachael Kerr 1392
Liza Kershaw 1737
Peter Kershaw Taylor 1494
David M. R. Kewley 1770, 6282
Samir Saad Khalil 6290
Abdul Waheed Khan 2475
Manzar Khan 2333
Masood Husain Khan 2476
Rana Allah Dad Khan 2475
R. C. Khanna 2312
Vineet Khanna 2312
Thomas Khng 5174
Ms H. Khoosal 2509
H. R. Khurana 2277
J. J. Kiambu 2523
John Kiarie 2420
Peter Kibby 1854
David Kidger 1504
Sean Kidney 2070
Anne Kidson 1161
Robert Kiernan 1747
N. R. Killip 1648
Jan Kimber 6159
Anthony Kinahan 1364
Peter Kindersley 1248
Andrew King 1630
C. King 1016
Caradoc King 4099
David King 1267, 1504
Diana King 1704
John King 2108
Jonathan King 1640
Julia King 1076
Julian King 1704
Kathryn King 1591
Laurence King 1496, 3017
Richard King 2436
Robin King 1865
Simon King 1049, 1437, 1722
Ann King-Hall 4052
Jessica Kingsley 1498
Richard Kingsley 5037
John Kingsmill 6243
Simon Kingston 1795, 1812
James Kinnear 1843
Dr Ben Kipkoir 2414
Emma Kirby 1098
Joan Kirby 2457
Robert Kirby 4086
Philip Kirk 2435
Robert Kirk 1089
Sue Kirkland 1056
Nicole Kirkman 1190
George Kirkpatrick 2106
Roger Kirkpatrick 1084
J. Kirkup 1385
Colin Kirkwood 1073
David Kirkwood 2149
Karen Kirtley 1863
P. Kisray 1915
Graham Kitchen 1321
Penny Kitchenham 1898, 3011
Rose Kitching 2043
Peter Kitley 1542
Ric Kitowski 2192
Michael Kitson 1230
Guy Kitteringham 1275
Alan Kittridge 1875
Gillian Klein 1871

Lydia Klimovitch 5169
Chris Kloet 1349
Dr B. J. Knapp 1059, 3024
Al Knight 2043
Andrew Knight 4052
D. J. G. Knight 1546
John Knight 1685
Peter Knight 4052
G. A. Knights 1439
Liz Knights 1162, 1349
Robin Knights 1638
Roger Knights 1519
Margaret Ko 1647
Konrad Kochanski 6373
Susan Kodicek 1015, 1089
Marion Koenig 6103
Philip Kogan 1502
Khrystyna Kohut 2110
Peter Kokoi 5153
Mrs Anita Kolb-Goyal 2295,
   2296
Lorinne Kon 2428
Chang Chee Kong 2428, 2429
Chua Hong Koon 2491
Lai Nam Koong 2429
Ben Kooter 2231
Jacqueline Korn 4041
Ipuseng Kotsokoane 2512
H. Kotze 2517
Jeremy Kourdi 1454
J. Alexis Koutchoumow 5013
Phang Yow Kow 2429
Berit Kraus 2230
Emmanuelle Kreh 1593
Julia Kreitman 4002
Anna Kress 2139
Michelle de Kretzer 2053
Gary Krikler 2172
G. Krishnamurti 5070
K. Kroeger 2499
Jennifer Kroezen 2094
Ranjit Kuar 2428, 2429
Mike Kudar 1409
A. Kühn 2500
Ms Aarti Kumar 2363
Amrendra Kumar 2279
Ms Anita Kumar 2363
Ashok Kumar 6093
Krishan Kumar 2363
Manish Kumar 2269
Pawan Kumar 2360
Sanchit Kumar 2363
Satish Kumar 2329
Vijaya Kumar 2366
Vinod Kumar 2362
Asha Kumaran 2490
Driden Kunaka 5183
Joshua Kuperard 1503, 6175
Hans Küpfer 1141
G. C. Kurup 2277
Pieter Kwant 1628, 1653
Blaine Kyllo 2096
Iris Kynaston 1379
Robert Kynaston 1379

Colette Laberge 6156
Marc Laberge 6156
Christine LaBlanc 2114
Marise Labresque 2176
J. J. Labuschagne 2514
Tony Lacey 1661
Gilles Lachance 2204
Dani Lacusta 2147
Liz Laczynska 1869
Jeanette Laffan 2012
Gilberte Lafolie 1462
Marianne Lagrange 1183

Adrian Laing 1387
Alison Lake 1486
Jane Lake 1023
P. Lake 1705
Simon Lake 1685
B. P. Lakhani 6216
M. G. Lalji 2523
Louise Lallier 5141
Brian Lam 2096
Louisa Lam 5155
David Lamb 1248
James Lamb 1515
Mrs M. Lamb 1725
Murray Lamb 2172
Susan Lamb 1639
Tony Lamberton 6142
Brad J. Lambertus 2113
Robert Lambolle 6016
D. S. Lamm 1623
Athena Lamnisos 1331
Sylvain Lamoureux 2218
Julie Lancashire 1051
N. Lancaster 6269
Rupert Lancaster 1423
Shaun Lancaster 1723
Sonia Land 1837, 4086
D. W. N. Landale 6262
P. D. R. Landale 6262
Nick Landau 1865
C. Lander 1014
William-Alan Landes 1688
Roger Lane 1269
Gavin Lang 1770, 6282
Muoneen Lang 2506
S. C. Lang'at 5161
D. J. Langford 6012
Dr Chris Langley 6013
Matthew Langman 2072
Paul Langridge 1015, 1089
Peter Langworth 1149
Íde Ní Laoghaire 2400
Céline Laprise 2138
Angela Larcombe 1111
Naomi Laredo 6018
Judy Large 1396
Martin Large 1396
Colin Larkin 1825
Mark Larsen 2111
Roger Lascelles 1507
C. P. de Laszlo 1474
A. Lategan 2500
Paul A. Latham 2044
Rodney Latham 6270
J. Lau 2253
Mrs Fiona Lauder 2253
Beverly Laughlin 1618
Huguette Laurent 2218
Hilary Laurie 1243
Rebecca Laurier 2099
Anne de Lautour 2464
Claire Lavedan 6094
Kim Lavely 1908
John Lavender 1184
Robert Lavender 1583
Peter D. Laverack 1037
P. Lavery 1545
Adrian Lavis 1220, 6185
Fay W. Lavis 1220, 6104
James H. Lavis 1220, 6104
A. J. Law 6087
A. M. Law 6087
Alan Law 2010, 5131
J.L. Law 1197
Kathy Law 1528
Mary Law 1194
N. S. Law 1564, 1665
O. M. Lawal-Solarin 5171

John Lawes 1082
Christine Lawless 1149
Joanna Lawrence 1689
Ruth Lawrence 1510
S. R. Lawrence 1623
Mrs Fianach Lawry 6393
Jill Lawson 4048
Linden Lawson 1933
Mark Le Fanu 5028, 5112, 5113,
   5122
Nigel Le Page 1576
Robert Leach 1598
Michael R. Leaman 1726
Mrs M. Leamon 1343
Mrs Lam Yuk Lean 2428
Pippa Leask 1643
Sarah Leask 1409
Timothy Leates 1795, 1812
M. Lebi 6040
Matthew Lebus 1260
Robert Lecker 2133
Jacques Leclerc 2218
Catherine Ledger 4053
Trudy Ledsham 2128
Alan Lee 1721
Anne Lee 2385
Candy Lee 2148
Chris Lee 1508
Donna Kay Lee 4115
Ms Evelyn Lee 2484
Ms Gael Lee 2484
Laura Lee 2212
Myra Lee 2079
Ronald Lee 6169
Stewart Lee 2251
Susan D. M. Lee 1164
Terry Lee 5155
Robert Leech 6110
Barbara Leedham 3031
Nicola Leedham 2117
Janice Leeming 6013
Duncan Leeper 1925
Roger LeGarrec 2176
Roger Legarrel 2191
Joanna Legg 1161
Rodney Legg 1249
Jon Leibowitz 6284
Janet Leibster 6382
David Leigh-Hunt 5085
Hon B. Leith 1066
Erica Leith 1342
Prue Leith 5105
Sheila Lemon 4002
Gerard Lemos 1517
Helen Leng 1753
David Leonard 1232
Miss Kath Leonard 1204
Mark Leonard 1665
Sonny Leong 1169
Don LePan 2106
Nicholas Lerwill 1022
Humphrey Lesley 6319
Pierre Lespérance 2218
Julie Lessels 1212
Colin Lester 1199, 1538
Malcolm Lester 2168
Marie Lester 6360
Joseph Arap Leting 2414
Edmond Leung 2251
Lionel Leventhal 1366, 1537
Dan Levey 1017, 1428, 6076
George Levin 1121
Michael Levine 4106
Joanna Levinson 1520
Jonathan Levy 1418
Avis Lewallen 1767
R. M. Lewell 1532

Brian Lewis 1824, 6198
Christopher Lewis 1423
Dinah Lewis 2037
Elaine Lewis 1917
Emma Lewis 2410
J. Lewis 1575
J. H. Lewis 1350
John Lewis 1653, 1901
Jonathan Lewis 1350
Kitty Lewis 2105
Martyn Lewis 3057
Michael Lewis 1505
N. P. Lewis 1578, 1579
R. G. Lewis 1500
Dy Leyland 1527
S. Li 2253
Tsze Sun Li 2251
Gan Bee Lian 2490
John Libbey 1522
Ian Liddiard 1276
Denise Lie 1038
Janet Liebster 1524, 5087
Canon James Lifa 2524
Geoffrey Lill 1678
Keith Lilley 1901
Clarence Lim 2490
Jeffrey Lim 2482
Richard Lim 1446
Lim Kim Wah 2425
Lim Li Kok 2483
Foong Chui Lin 2429
Brian Lincoln 1125
Frances Lincoln 1525
Andrew Lindesay 1348
Ms Tamar Lindesay 1348
Ken Lindsay 1258
I. Lindsay-Smith 1533
David Lines 6230
Eleanor Lines 1334
Lydia Linford 1161
David Ling 2439
Kuek Tang Ling 2429
Margaret Ling 1936
P. Ling 2253
Chris Lingard 1376
Ruth Linka 2124, 2206
J. H. Linsky 4003
Julia Lippiatt 6086
Mrs Marian Lisk 5172
Graham Lister 6176
Avril Litchmore 1525
Alan Little 6250
Amanda Little 4098
Andrew Little 6250
Carol Little 6250
Christopher John Little 4055
Greg Little 2085
Jean Little 6250
Jonathan Little 6250
Miss S. Little 6260
Tony Littlechild 1363, 6024
Simon Littlewood 1401
Colette Littman 1529
Robert Littman 1529
Linda Liu 5139
Francesca Liversidge 1869
Tony Llewellyn 5003
Christopher Lloyd 1279, 1308,
6105
Colin Lloyd 5065
David Lloyd 1896
Davina Lloyd 1181
Jonathan Lloyd 4024, 4102
Linda Lloyd 1631
Menna Lloyd Williams 5124
Don Loader 1468
Judith Loades 1674

Judith Ann Loades 1402
Peter G. Lock 1433
D. W. Locke 1371
Elizabeth B. Locke 1371
Mrs P. Locke 6245
Lynn Lockett 3001
Paul Lockwood 2196
D. Lodge 1533
Clare Loeffler 4083
Ruth Logan 1098
Ms C. Y. Loh 1806
Mrs Homa Lohrasb 6065
Johnny Loke 2428
Shri R. R. Lokeshwar 2305
R. Lomax 1014
Cécile Lomer 6022, 6316, 6371
Talat Lone 2411
Elizabeth Long 2139
Lisa Long 6106
R. Long 1915
David Longfoot 6055
The Countess of Longford 5070
Tom Longford 1356
Martyn Longley 1248
Judith Longman 1424
Gene Longson 2187, 2238
Allison Longstaff 1666
Hugh E. Look 6349
Julian Loose 1297
Joanna Lorenz 1038
Rowland Lorimer 6392
Samuel Loring Asiedu 2242
Kathy Lorringer 2228
Peter Lothian 2055
Norman Lott 6237
Lina Lotto 1535
A. Lourie 1844
Jonathan Lovat Dickson 2196
Jane Lovell 1645
M. Lovell 1806
Peter Lovering 1400
Chris Loveys 6062
Ian A. B. Low 2131
D. M. Lowe 1881
P. S. Lowe 1285
Stephen Lowe 6241
Kathy Lowinger 2168
Andrew Lownie 4057
R. M. Loydell 1835
F. Luard 1600
Mrs Talabi A. Lucan 5172
Bill Lucas 1022
David Lucas 6039
Mark Lucas 4076
G. Luciano 1623
Ms Lui Siu Ping 2250
Jennifer Luithlen 4058
Dr Steven K. Luk 2250
Lydia Lum 2483
Dorothy Lumley 4026
Elizabeth Lumley 6338
Aidan Lunn 1004, 6127
Nicola Lutte 5143
Sarah Lutyens 4059
John Lycett 1909
Miss Margaret Lydamore 1773
Leah-Ann Lymer 2209
Catherine Lyn-Jones 1360
Brian Lynch 2404
Rachel Lynch 1774
Jean Lyne 6219
Simon Lyne 1513
Mike Lynn 1419

Kingsley K. H. Ma 2249
L. Mabandla 2502

Juliet Mabey 1631
Robert Mabro 1647
Barra Mac Aoilha Bhuí 2377
Susanne McAdam 2171
Andrew McAllister 1097
Catherine McAllister 1921
Gerri McAndrew 1599
Jane Macandrew 3059
Shane McAteer 1878
Alec McAulay 1052
Alex McAulay 1774
Prof Donald MacAulay 5055
Paul McAvoy 1042
Colin MacCabe 5042
Kristin McCahon 2137
James McCall 6393
Colleen McCallum 2510
Dean McCallum 2212
Kate McCallum 2510, 5177
Mark McCallum 1437
Moira McCann 3020
D. McCarthy 1054
Daniel C. McCarthy 2398
Pat McCarthy 1661
Liz McCarty 1857
Mary Macchiusi 2194
Tim McCleary 2149
Margaret McClintock 2120
Peg McColl 2068
Janet McConkey 1514
Stephen McConkey 1514
Anthony McConnell 1188, 1722
Bill McConnell 2076
John McConnell 2189
W. J. McCormack 2397
D. McCrae 1177
D. L. R. McCrae 1059, 3024
W. J. McCreadie 1061
M. McCreanor 6199
Patrick McCreeth 3027
Robert McCrum 1297
G. McCullough 2528
David McCune 1754
Sara Miller McCune 1754
Van McCune 2048
Steve McCurdy 3008
Ruth McCurry 1182, 1516, 1556,
1590, 1681
Julia McCutcheon 1269
Susanne McDadd 1574
John McDavitt 4111
Ms E. McDonald 2055
Fiona MacDonald 1160, 1896
Fiona McDonald 2076
Gavin McDonald 1184, 1821
Ian MacDonald 5055
John Macdonald 5005
Keith McDonald 2073
Michael McDonald 1135, 1495
Tim McDonald 2139
Jonathan McDonnell 1850
Terri McDonnell 2402
Steve MacDonogh 2381
Alison MacDougall 1659
Allan MacDougall 2206
Beth McDougall 1574
Jennifer MacDougall 2160
John McDougall 1387
Rosalie MacFarlane 1528
Yvonne McFarlane 1614
W. D. McFeely 1623
Brian McGahon 1849
Colin McGee 2511
Hamish MacGibbon 1476
Joan McGilvray 2171
Hugh McGinlay 2047
P. A. McGinley 1288

Hilary McGlynn 1408
Jason McGovern 1291
Dr Ian McGowan 6393
Neil MacGowan 6162
S. F. McGowan 1831
Karen McGrath 1638
Nicola McGrath 1455
A. McGregor 3010
Christine Macgregor 1496, 3017
David McGregor 6174
J. McGrillis 6262
S. McGuinness 1702
Eilish McGuire 2402
Dennis McGuirk 1504
Kris Machala 1107
Franscois McHardy 2518
Tom Machin 5044
Hamish McIlwrick 1149
Catherine McInerney 1779
Susan McIntosh 2129, 2143
Grant McIntyre 1594
Ian G. McIntyre 6107
Mrs K. A. McIntyre 6107
Dr Douglas Mack 6393
Diana Mackay 4024, 4102
Don McKay 2105
John Mackay 1504
Peter McKay 1067, 1384, 1429,
1724, 1763
Barbara Mackay Miller 6252
Hamish Mackay Miller 6252
J. D. McKell 1728
Mark McKell 1656
D. R. Mackenzie 2530
Heather Mckenzie 1440
Joan Mackenzie 2451
Peter MacKenzie 1550
Ursula Mackenzie 1869
William MacKenzie 1191
E. M. Mackenzie-Wood 1621
Clare McKeon 2163
Margaret McKeown 1717
Andy McKillop 1049
Pauline McKillop 2114
Bernadette McKinlay 2076
Jenny McKinley 1128
Joanna Mackle 1297
Michael Macklem 2188
Nicholas Macklem 2188
Linda McKnight 4106
Susanna McKnight 6279
Helen McLachlan 6303
Sylvia McLauchlan 1836
Guillaume McLaughlin 1304
John McLaughlin 4012
Patrick McLaughlin 1161
Christian Maclean 1312, 5109
Kathleen McLean 2184
Malcolm Maclean 1191
Mark Maclean 2045
Sue MacLean 2195
Christopher Maclehose 1392
R. J. McLennan 6143
Alasdair MacLeod 1132
Brigid Macleod 1408
Kerrie McLeod 2032
Margaret MacLeod 1335
Murdo MacLeod 1069
Max McMaster 5135
Andrew McMillan 1047, 1096
Andrew McMillan 1162
Andrew McMillan 1349, 1892
Andrew Macmillan 1897
The Hon. D. M. B. Macmillan
1547
David Macmillan 1677
Karen McMullin 2127

Simon McMurtrie 1239
Julie McNair 1261, 1502
Caroline McNamara 1194
Tony McNamara 2395
S. McNaughton 1052
Gil McNeil 1885
Susan McNish 2111
Wendy McPeake 2180
Christina Macphail 1528
Kate MacPhee 1080, 1207
Noel McPherson 1805
Alistair MacQueen 1092
Anna McQuinn 1239
William McRobert 1150
Richard McRoberts 2089
Valerie McRoberts 2089
Michael McWhinne 1541
Bruce MacWillson 6041
Sunil Madan 2313
Miss O. E. Madden 5106
George Maddison 2230
Mazvita Patricia Madondo 2529
J. N. Magan 2372
Adrian Magson 1172
Adrienne Maguire 1096, 1162,
    1349, 1892
Sheridan Maguire 1449
Vicky Mahadeva 2072
Sarah Mahaffy 1113
Dinker Mahajan 2318
Pratibha Mahajan 2318
Sudha Mahapatra 2339
Danny Maher 1029, 1031, 1617,
    6161
Dawn Mahon 1135
Murray Mahon 6169
Mary Mahoney-Robson 2092
Hubert J. Mahony 2394, 5159
Jane Mahony 1679
Andrew Mailey 1277
Mrs Maureen Main 6182
R. S. Mair 1915
Leena Maissen 5008
Therese Maitland 1035
Chandralekha Maitra 2303
Jimmi Makotsi 2414
Yoel Makov 6300
A. H. Male 1173
J. F. Malherbe 2516
C. Shekhar Malhotra 2300
D. N. Malhotra 2281, 2300
Kapil Malhotra 2331, 2375
Miss Madhvi Malhotra 2300
Ms Poonam Malhotra 2300
Shekhar Malhotra 2281
Sudhir Malhotra 2331, 2375
Abhinav Malik 2256
Ateev Malik 2256
C. L. Malik 2290
Kamal Malik 2290
P. L. Malik 2290
Shakti Kumar Malik 2256
Sumain Malik 2290
Surendra Malik 2290
Vijay Malik 2290
Louise Mallard 6073, 6145
Jacqueline Mallet 2138
Diana Mallett 1682
Michael J. Mallett 1794
Hasir Mallick 2338
Ann Mallinson 2453
Lorraine Mallon 1006
Gillian Malpass 1933
Henry Malt 6273
Liz Mammat 1528
Virman Man 1601
Jeanne Manchee 1815

Evie Mandel 2230
Dallas Manderson 1640
Ruth Mandrake 1555
Emmanuel Manful 2240
John Manger 1648
Polly Manguel 2129
Ian Manhire 1869
James Manis 2209
Jonathan Manley 1161
Deborah Mann 1859
Doreen Mann 1017, 1428, 6076
Michael Mann 1269
Morris Mann 6254
Moyra Mann 6254
T. Mann 1014
Clare Manning 2391
Garry Manning 3033, 3063
Pat Manning 1097
Elena Mannion 1614
Maire Mannion 1356
N. E. Manohar 2369
A. Mansell 1014
David Mansfield 6073, 6145
Michael Manson 1557
Monica Manwaring 1356
Sabelo Mapasure 5183
Sister Teresa Marcazzan 2421
Joseph J. Marcelle 1443, 1698,
    1699, 1700, 1701
Joe March 2208
Vicki Marcok 2232
Tony Margolis 1041
Anne Marimuthu 1900
Andy Marino 4082
Sue Mariscal 1414
Kevin Mark 2035
Ms I. Markan 1177
Frank Markham 1489
Sarah Markham 1052
J. Marks 1546
Anne Marley 5051
Dawn Marley 1449
Clemency Marlowe 1449
Chris Marsden 1473
Edmund Marsden 1463
John Marsh 1563
P. Marsh 1635
Paul Marsh 4061
Robert Marsh 2510
Adam Marshall 1697
Amanda Marshall 1252
Bill Marshall 1666
Bruce Marshall 3042
Douglas Marshall 1042
Eileen Marshall 6197
John Marshall 2185
Lewis Marshall 1683
Lynn Marshall 1625
Peter Marshall 1685
S. Marshall 5021
Marie Marsolais 6156
Belinda Marston 3053
Nick Marston 4099
Alan Martin 1720
Barbara Martin 1636
C. H. Martin 1288
Dr Connie Martin 1036
David M. Martin 2534
Miss Elizabeth Martin 3040
Fergal Martin 1166
Gaby Martin 4052
Jane Martin 1834
Nick Martin 6106
P. K. Martin 6199
Penny Martin 2056
Richard Martin 1499
Ross Martin 2028

Mrs S. I. Martin 6260
Stephanie Martin 2217
Toy Martin 2028
Trevor Martin 6154
Laurie Martinelli 2020
Leigh Martins 5044
Blanche Marvin 4062
Mrs A. H. Marwah 2325
Erroll Marx 2513
Andrew Maslen 1287
A. Mason 1559
B. H. Mason 2504
Julie Mason 1245
K. Mason 1559
M. Mason 1559
P. Mason 1559
R. J. Mason 6246
André Massicotte 2218
Simon Master 1722, 5099
John Masters 1865, 6070
Donald L. Matheson 2132
Edward C. Matheson 2093
Samuel Matsangaise 2533
Belinda Matthews 1297
Gary J. Matthews 2055
Juliet Matthews 4061
Kevin Matthews 6224
Lee Matthews 1239
Peter Matthews 2506
Roger Matthews 1252
Victoria Matthews 6322
Darryl Mattocks 6099
Scott Mauck 1398
Rachel Maund 1354
Rolf Maurer 2183
Simon Maurice 1400
Langton Mavhudzi 5183
S. M. Mawani 1114
Bob Mawhinney 2140
David Maxwell 2219
John Maxwell 6219
Robert J. Maxwell 1497
Sarah Maxwell 2442
Barry May 1391
Ann Mayer 1396
P. M. Mayer 2068
Peter Mayer 1661
Chris Maynard 1272
J. Maynard 1157
A. J. Mayne 1813
Alain Mayotte 2201
Trish Mbanga 6314
Jane Mbaya 2414
Basil Mbewe 5180
Miss Mary Mbuthia 2418
Robert Mead 2121
Rod Mead 2057
Anne Meade 2457, 5168
Chris Meade 5096
Alice Meadows 1596, 1905, 6111
Kirsty Meadows 1309
Mrs Janet Mears 1117, 6147
Mrs M. Mears 1439
John Meckan 2058
Ka Meechan 1102
David Meggs 1468
John Mehan 2064
C. K. Mehra 2353
D. Mehra 2353
N. K. Mehra 2324
R. K. Mehra 2353
S. Mehra 2324
S. K. Mehra 2353
Anil Mehta 2266, 2328
Miss Anita Mehta 2350
Hemant Mehta 2302
Ravinder Kumar Mehta 2328

S. N. Mehta 2309
Salil Mehta 2266, 2328
Shri S. S. Mehta 2255
L. Meiller 1014
Terry Melia 6108
H. Melkman 1744
David Mellin 1549
Adrian Mellor 1685
R. Mellors-Bourne 1459
David Membrey 5031
Valerie Mendes 6021
Sara Menguc 4079
Nana Yaa Mensah 1785
A. Meredith 1385
Luis Merola 6257
Hugh Merrell 1570
Robert Merrell 6313
John N. Merrill 1316
Roger Merritt 1598
Annabel Merullo 3026
Charles Merullo 3026
S. J. Mesquita 1001
Michael Messenger 1875
Yvonne Messenger 5078
Jo Messham 1708
Joanne Messham 1839
John Metcalf 2200
Sheron Metcalf 2173
Prof. Edwin Metcalfe 1010
I. J. Metcalfe 1545
Daphne Metland 1608
Pierre Meunier 5141
Chand Mian 2472
Roger Michael 1581
HRH Princess Michael of Kent
    5070
C. Michaletz 1823
Miss Gilly Michie 1364
Ian Middleton 1855
Jane Middleton 5125
Kathy Middleton 1220
John Miell 1638
Nancy Miles 1425
Richard Miles 1094
Edward Milford 1477
Julie Millard 1569
R. Millbank 1456
Cathy Miller 1327, 4064
Elly Miller 1580
G. Miller 6199
Gavin Miller 6133
Genevieve Miller 1233
Graham Miller 6167
Harvey Miller 1580
Ian Miller 1233
Jane Miller 1233
Jeff Miller 2122
Louise Miller 1520
Mike Miller 5109
Nancy Miller 2146
P. Miller 1533
Sue Miller 1596, 1905, 6111
Didier Millet 2489
Lynn Millhouse 1606
Corrine Millroy 2121
Chris Mills 1606
Ion Mills 1627, 6100
J. Mills 1014
John Mills 1615, 1892, 1897
Nicholas Mills 1843
S. J. Mills 2122
William R. Mills 6004
Kate Millward 1175
Anne W. Millyard 2094
Chris Milne 1149
Flair Milne 1403
Sally Milner 2078

Terèsine Milner 1199
Teresine Milnes 1538
Philippa Milnes-Smith 1661
R. Peter Milroy 2230
F. Milton 1819
M. R. Milton 1288
Steve Mimmack 5005
Brian Minett 1419
Pamela Minett 1832
Roberto Minio 6051
Matthew Minter 1398
Deepak Mirchandani 2303
Padmini G. Mirchandani 2303
May Misfeldt 2127
Alan Mitchell 1193
Catherine Mitchell 2228
Catriona Mitchell 1563
David Mitchell 1768
J. C. V. Mitchell 1577
Lawrence Mitchell 1542
Paul Mitchell 5005
Valerie Mitchell 5004
John Mitchinson 1392
Anne Mithamo 2414
Swapan Mitra 2359
Anil Mittal 2286
Arvind Kumar Mittal 2282
Ashok Kumar Mittal 2282
Lata Mittal 2285
Parmil Mittal 2288
Pradeep Mittal 2288
Praveen Mittal 2288
Susheel Kumar Mittal 2285
Alan E. Mitton 6004
Simon Mitton 1149
Carmel Mizzi 2430
Ms M. P. Moberly 2509
Barbara Moeller 1048
David Moeller 1540
Paul Mogford 1499
H. A. Mohamed 2420
Peer Mohamed 2427
Shireen Mohammad Ali 2471
Bob Moheebob 6152
Ms Maimanat Mohsin 2480
Iain Moir 1367
Dawn Mokhobo 2511
John Mole 1323
A. Mollison 5119
Ken Molloy 2121
Sarah Molloy 4040
Tim Molloy 1440
D. Moloantoa 2522
Robert Molteno 1936
Eileen Molver 4114
Susan Molyneux 1773
Dr Wendi Momen 1066, 1342
Girish S. Mondkar 2330
Nigel Money 1360
George Monger 5007
Philippa Monks 6144
Mary Monteith 5177
Caroline Montgomery 4022
Doreen Montgomery 4022
Nigel Montgomery 6177
Saric Moolman 2515
A. F. Moon 1276
Bridget Moon 1594
Andrew Moore 6123
Billie Moore 3053
Chris Moore 1386
Christopher Moore 1312
Diane Moore 3052
Gillian Moore 1420
Isabel Moore 1260
John Moore 3052
Leslie Moore 2108

Tony Moore 1446
John R. Moorley 1588
Peter Moran 1301
Paul Moreton 1637
Paulene Morey 2084
Bernard Morgan 1597
Kris Morgan 1555
Leon Morgan 4095
M. Morgan 1420
Pip Morgan 1334
Joanna Moriarty 1795, 1812
Gaëtan Morin 2138
Emiko Morita 2198
Ms G. Morley 1545
Georgina Morley 1548
Mary Morley 5091
Neil Morley 6089
R. J. Morley 3051
Sally Morley 6089
Jane Morpeth 1401
Ros Morpeth 1598
Kirsten Morphet 1043
D. J. Morrell 6271
Liz Morrell 1508
Alison Morris 1521
Deirdre Morris 2084, 6363, 6383
Marshall Morris 2172
Michael J. Morris 3033, 3063
Richard Morris 1215
Mrs S. Morris 1915
Steven Morris 2049
Dewi Morris Jones 5124
Alex Morrison 2111
Dawn Morrison 2122
Donald Morrison 1246
Marg Anne Morrison 2098
Patricia Morrison 1925
Darryl E. Morriss 2220
David Morrow 2161
Michael Morrow 2248
John Mortimer 5104
Julia Mortimer 1857
Sheila Mortimer 3068
Robin Mortimore 6142
Anthea Morton-Saner 4024
Anthea Morton Saner 4102
Elena Morus 1932
Monica Moseley 1655
Ms A. Moss 1177
Margarethe Mostert 2499
P. Mothersole 1648
Michael Motley 4067
Anthony Mott 1869
Sir Nevill Mott 1851
Marion Motts 1465
Mrs Myra Mouland 1208
Ferdinand Mount 6378
M. J. Mousley 3051
Gregory Moxon 1717
Tim Moyler 1424
M. Moynahan 2461
N. Mthenge 2417
P. Mtinshilana 2517
A. Muchaziwepi 2528
Philip Mudd 1502
Jeremy Mudditt 1628
Ray Mudie 1890
Ben Mugabe 2529
Elliot Mugamu 6314
Caroline Muir 1896
Robert Muir 2027
David N. Muita 2418
Sushil Mukherjea 2319
T. K. Mukherjee 2319
Klaasje Mul 4069
Gerard Mullen 2036
Gervase Muller 6202

Laurie Muller 2073
Geoff Mulligan 1582
Tony Mulliken 6109
Martin Mulloy 1077
Benito Mulota 2527
Barrack O. Muluka 2414
Jennifer Mulvanny 1291
J. Mumford 1014
Mark Mumford 1466
Mary Mumford 2030
Ray Munamwimbu 2527, 5180
Stephen Muncaster 1386
C. Oduor Munjal 2414
Alison Munro 1264
Dr Craig Munro 2073
Ron Munro 2172
Gad N. Munyaka 2418
J. K. Muraya 5161
P. Murby 2522
Donal P. Murphy 2382
Janet Murphy 1015, 1089
John Murphy 1042
John T. Murphy 1143
K. D. Murphy 2382
Nick Murphy 1178
P. Murphy 1358
Patrick Murphy 6066
Peter Murphy 4024
Sheila Murphy 1061
Allison Murray 1666
Anne Murray 1770
Gail Murray 1683
Iain H. Murray 1069
Janet Murray 2115
John Murray 1138
John R. Murray 1594
Judith Murray 4035
Louise Murray 1936
Phil Murray 1666
P. Murray Hill 1157
Ann-Janine Murtagh 1506
Fabian Murugu 2414
Barry Musto 5060
Obrien Mutero 2531
Enoch Mwale 2527
Ms Unity Mwanza 2526
John Mwika Githae 2412
Lucy Myers 1537
R. G. Myers 6271
Alan Myles 6173
Jeremy Mynott 1149

C. J. Nagle 1325
Jagdish Nair 2313
N. T. Nair 5175
V. R. Radhakrishnan Nair 2284
Christine Nalder 1339
Vesna Nall 1102
Angela Namoi 2004
Shashi Bhushan Nangia 2264
David Napier 1759
Ronald Napier 2511
David Nash 1837
Paul Nash 6367
J. Nataf 2099
Ranga Nathan 6113
Carol Natsis 2074
E. Naudé 2500
Bharat Nayee 5180
Mrs F. Naylor 1915
Kevin Naylor 6123
Trevor Naylor 1855
E. Ndwandwe 2522
Stephen B. Neal 1709, 1851
Andrew Neale 1686
John Neale 5146
Rachel Neaman 1834

Christine Needham 1326
Ruth Needham 4063
J. E. Needleman 6225, 6228, 6233
Angie Needs 1522
Alexander Negri 2099
G. Negus 1014
Helen Negus 6073, 6145
Martin Neild 1423
Andy Neilson 2053
Ann Nelles 2173
Julie Nellthorp 4021
Elizabeth Nelson 2450
Graham Nelson 6251
M. E. Nelson 3051
Magnus Nelson 5063
Han Moh Neoh 2428
Laurence Nérée 6308
J. S. Nesbitt 1769
Charles Nettleton 1424
Thomas Neurath 1855
Robert Neville 1003
Bernard Nevin 1901
James New 1343
Claire Newbery 1303
Julia Newbluard 2410
Gary Newbrook 6099
Catherine Newman 1401
Clive Newman 2031
Fred Newman 6373
Mark Newman 2060
Peter Newsom 1401
Brian Newson 1542
Michelle Newton 2451
Nigel Newton 1098
Ms Rebecca Ng 2253
Tom Ng 2251
David Nganga 2418
Jeremy Nganga 2414
Cletus Ngwaru 2529
Aaron Ngwenya 5183
Déirdre Ní Thuathail 2383
Ahmad Niaz 2478
Charles Nicholas 3001
John Nicholas 1254
P. J. Nicholas 1831
Alison Nicholls 1615
Andrea Nicholls 1834
J. Nicholls 6006
Bob Nichols 6241
Ann Nicholson 2189
P. Nicholson 1632
Susanna Nicklin 4061
Patricia Nicol 2393
Helen Nicoll 1219
John Nicoll 1933
Sarah Niel 1491
M. Nieuwenhuis 1501
Najiye Nihat 2043
Ms Jyoti Nijhawan 2361
Terry Nikkel 2160
Gillian Nineham 1717
Ms Hila Nir 6300
J. Nissen 1103
G. M. Nissen, CBE 1103
Julie Nix 6167
Deborah Nixon 2049
M. Nixon 1501
Janet Njoroge 2417
Victor Nmakwe 2470
Maggie Noach 4068
Debra Noakes 1150
Charly Nobbs 1149
Chantal Noel 1113
Dorothy Noel 2406
Brid Nolan 2388, 2389
Peter van Noorden 2046

Andrew Nopper 2128, 5146
Paul Norbury 1346
Greg Nordal 2115
John Norman 6224
Cresta Norris 1387
Robert Norris 5092
William Norris 6152
David North 1543, 1545, 1548, 1677, 1799
Norman North 4076
Rosemary North 1781
Anne-Lucie Norton 1408
C. Notarmarco 1823
Felicity Nottingham 2012
Jonathan Nowell 1909, 6334
Claire Nozières 1525
Caroline Ntoshya 2526
Isidore Gerd Ntoshya 2526
Patrick Nugent 1334
Sarah Nundy 4069
Leslie Nunn 1793
Andrew Nurnberg 4069, 5023
Colin Nutt 1527
Hesbon Nyongesa 2412
Bridgid C. Nzekwu 6047
R. Mutua Nzioki 2414
Benedict Nzomo 2419

Priscilla Oakeshott 6115
E. Oakley 1398
Séan O Boyle 2384
Carol O'Brien 1211
Ivan O'Brien 2400
Leacy O'Brien 5150
M. D. O'Brien 2394
Michael O'Brien 2400
Orna O'Brien 6391
Mrs Irene O'Brien-Coker 5172
Emma O'Bryen 1678
Eileen O'Carroll 2385
Micheal Ó Conghaile 2383
Janine O'Connor 2506
John O'Connor 1313, 2380, 2391
Kaori O'Connor 1488
Pamela O'Connor 1694
Mrs Asenath Bole Odaga 2416
James C. Odaga 2416
Sarah Odedina 1637, 1900
Ian Odgers 5135
Peter N. Odhiambo 2416
Anne O'Donnell 6333
Brian O'Donnell 2160, 5146
Jim O'Donnell 2395
Jo O'Donoghue 5158
Anna O'Donovan 2380
Jo O'Driscoll 1261
M. D. O'Dwyer 2394
Martin Oestreicher 1614
Eric Ofei 2240
Dr Colin Ogbourne 5003
Nick Ogden 1841
James Ogola 2414
Onyango Ogutu 2414
Suzanne O'Hare 6171
Suzanne Ohlson 6286
N. N. Ojha 2279
Moses Okech 2416
M. O'Keeffe 2394
Richard Olafson 2134
Wale Olaniawo 5171
Alan Oldfield 4096
Cora-Louise Oldfield 4096
J. Oldham 1385
Peter Oldham 6146
Jim Oldroyd 6230
David O'Leary 4070
A. G. Oliver 1288

Chris Oliver 1933
Mark Oliver 6181
Rhonda Oliver 1697
Rene Olivieri 1093
Kari Olsen 6303
Dr Lai Olurode 2470
Peter Olver 1215
Lesley O'Mara 1629
Michael O'Mara 1629
Caoimhín Ó Marcaigh 2377
Philip O. Omondi 2420
David Omuruli 2417
Brown Onduso 2415
H. O'Neil 1385
A. M. O'Neill 2050
P. A. O'Neill 6267
S. O'Neill 1546
I. K. Ong 1806
Jocelyn Ong 2196
Triena Ong 2487
Shirley A. Onn 2108
Greta Ooro 2414
Mark Opzoomer 6146
L. F. Orbach 3051
Susan Orchard 6171
Karen O'Reilly 2173
Seamus O'Reilly 2385
Sheila O'Reilly 1005, 1067, 1384, 1429, 1763
Patrick O'Rourke 2225
Charles Orwin 2489
Peter Osborn 1080
Bob Osborne 1405
Eva Osborne 1380
Mary Osborne 1917
Noel H. Osborne 1671
Arlene O. Osen 2157
Hayley Osen 1161
Jim Osgerby 1714
Catherine O'Shea 4013
Martine O'Shea 2458
Kirsten Osland 2121
Chris Ostrom 1909
Matthew O'Sullivan 1640
Janetta Otter-Barry 1525
Marcel Ouellette 2091
Kenn Oultram 5018, 5049, 5050
Francesca Ovington 1334
Carol Owen 1124
Chris Owen 1403
David Owen 1094, 3025, 6108
Deborah Owen 4071
L. Owen 1014
Peter Owen 1644
William Owen 1499
John Owens 1333
Mrs P. Owens 1813
Sian Owens 1434
Vincent Owusu-Ansah 2244

Mary Pachnos 1803
John Pacione 1477
Susan Pacitti 1133
Michael Packard 1649
John Paculabo 1499
David Padbury 5044
Nigel Padbury 1541
Donald Page 1125
Gillian Page 6112
Neil Page 1237, 6280
Stephen Page 1324
Miranda Page Wood 6114
Clare Painter 1408
Martin Paisner 5070
Kua Hong Pak 2493
Sarah Pakenham 1033
Dr S. Palanichamy 2335

Dr I. Palin 1066
Irene Palko 1254
Michael Pallis 1936
Mireille de Palma 2210
Alison Palmer 1079
Gary Palmer 1172
Hon H. W. Palmer 6081
Judith E. Palmer 6015
K. A. Palmer 1340
Martin Palmer 1387
Nigel Palmer 1094
Roger Palmer 6015
Steven Palmer 1400
Tony Palmer 1079
Jim Palmieri 2128
Judith Pamplin 1623
Y. P. Pandey 2362
A. J. Pandit 1343
Gopinder Panesar 1070
Monica Pang 5155
Brian Pannhausen 1378
Shri Manohar Pant 2367
Sarah Pape 1003
Vonai B. Paradza 2531
J. Pares 1014
Maggie Parham 5104
Chris Parish 6163
Grahame Parish 6237
Sue Parish 6237
Adrian Parker 1158, 1752, 6207
Chris Parker 1657
Derek Parker 6324
Gill Parker 1462
Jim Parker 5098
John Richard Parker 4063
Jonathan Parker 1642
Richard Parkes 3031
Kate Parkin 1049
P. E. Parkin 6215
Bunty Parkinson 5107
Dic Parkinson 2161
Dinah Parkinson 1096, 1897
Paul C. Parkinson 2433
Robert Parkinson 5041
Madeleine Parkyn 1764
W. M. Parmar 2318
Rosemary Parravani 1925
Dr J. Parris 1066
C. Parrish 1600
David Parrish 1033, 1049, 6188
Charlotte Parry-Crooke 1614
Catherine Parson 6094
Prof. John Parsonage 1367
Matt Parsons 6071
Nicholas Parsons 2021
Elaine Partington 3025
Bruce Pascoe 2067
Marie-Hélène Pasdeloup 6308
Ted Pashley 6174
Harikant Patel 2270
Ms Manisha Patel 6170
R. B. Patel 2333
Rramukhbhai Patel 2318
Shruti Patel 1603
Michael A. Pateman 6253
Christopher J. Paterson 1544, 1547, 1548
Claire Paterson 1362
Gill Paterson 1182, 1590
Laura Paterson 2085
Mark Paterson 4072
C. J. Pateson 2522
Jean Paton 2216
Julie Patten 6166
Shirley Patton 1566
Ashok Paul 2267
B. C. Paul 2255

Gill Paul 6023
R. K. Paul 2267
Mrs Sharda Paul 2267
Tony Paulaskas 6190
Dr K. Paulus 1467
Pedja Pavlicic 6170
Stephen Pawley 1291
John Pawsey 4073
Dave Paxton 6167
Jacques Payette 2151
Luc Payette 2151
Anthony Payne 5076
Margaret Payne 5052
J. W. Peacock 1546
John Peacock 1544
M. Peacock 2507
Peter Peacock 1526
David Peagram 2464
Rodney Peake 6174
Sebastian Peake 5090
Jill Pearce 1247
Jonathan Pearce 1515
Karen Pearce 3049
Liz Pearce 6242
Sarah Pearce 5166
Maggie Pearlstine 4074
Phyllis Pearsall 1340
Anne Pearson 6234
David Pearson 1334
Diane Pearson 1869
J. E. Pearson 1564
Joss Pearson 1334
Anne Peel 1770
Annie Peel 6282
John Pelan 1753
Line Pellerin 2158
Paul Pels 2035
John Pemberthy 1163
D. Pemberton 6199
David Pemberton 6167
E. B. Pemberton 6218
M. J. Pemberton 6218
Mike Pembry 2186
Rebecca Pembry 2186
Barry Penhale 2181
Fiona Penn 1619
Jane Pennells 2076
Tracey Pennington 1013
Lynn Penrod 5151
J. Penrose 1014
Jane Penrose 1691
Gail Penston 1387
Pentagram 1297
Laura Pentecost 2003
George Pentney 6239
Edward Peppitt 1251
Alison Percival 1708, 1839
Mike Percival 5120
Jules Perel 1072
Charles Perkins 3067
Fred Perkins 1542
Brian Perman 5035, 5128, 6292, 6315
Nicholas Perren 1594
John Perrett 6174
K. Perrett 1320, 1632, 1829
David G. Perry 1464
Kathryn Perry 1936
Louisa Perry 1035
Rohays Perry 1709
Ann Peters 6191
Jean Peters 2163
Malcolm Peters 5032
Elisabeth Petersdorff 1633
Mel Petersen 3022
A. Peterson 2054
P. Petker 1394

Inga Petri 2145
L. Petriw 2122
David Pettifor 6157
Rosemary Pettit 5033, 5066
Stephen Pettitt 5061
Pamela Petty 2057
Paul Petzold 1060
J. M. Pewtress 6265
Sister Maria Pezzini 2421
Chris Pfeiffer 2066
Mrs Maria Phantis 1748
Roger Phay 2490
Don Phelan 2121
Neil Philip 3002
Tony Philip 2074
HRH the Prince Philip, Duke of
    Edinburgh 5128, 6292, 6315
Alan Philipp 1041
Gail Philipp 1041
Roland Philipps 1423
A. A. Phillips 1046
Alan Phillips 1373
Andrew Phillips 1542
Brian Phillips 2443
J. A. Phillips 1665
Katrina Phillips 1599
Kevin Phillips 1708, 1839
L. M. Phillips 1046
Margaret Phillips 4095
Sue Phillips 6082
Penny Phipps 6114
Roger Phua 2486
D. S. Phull 2276
Judy Piatkus 1676
David Pickin 1743
Mrs A. V. Picton-Phillips 1680
D. B. Picton-Phillips 1680
William Pidduck 1011
Hanri Pieterse 2510
Christine Pietrowski 1215
Mrs J. Piggott 1316
Lois Pike 2215
Terence Pilchick 1918
Miss C. Pillath 6260
Laurence Pine 6313
Nicholas J. Pine 1775
J. Pineo 2115
N. Pinfield 1823
Terry Pink 1869
B. Pinker 1311
Mrs M. M. Pinkerton 1344
Maggie Pinkney 2030
Frances Pinter 1174
M. Piper 2016
Dr Madsen Pirie 1808
Bret Pitchfork 1781
Norma Pitman 1053, 6140
Nicholas Pitt 2234
Teresa Pitt 2058
Melissa Pitts 2097, 2217
J. Pixton 1014
Alan Plank 1843
Christopher Plant 2182
Judith Plant 2182
J. S. Platts 1769
David Playne 3047
F. du Plessis 2503, 2505
Chris Plews 1172
Kate Pocock 1933
Bernard Poirier 2207
Dr Douglas C. Pollard 2152
Lois Pollard 2152
Sarah Pollard 1094
Stephen Pollard 1298
Gerald J. Pollinger 4078
Gina Pollinger 4079
Murray Pollinger 4079

Celia Pollock 5129
Bella Pomer 4104
A. Pomroy 1467
Dr Mark Ponnampalam 1879
A. P. Pool 1109
Kate Pool 5069, 6324
Mrs J. Poole 1439
John D. Poole 6197
Linda Pooley 4021
Jim Pope 3050
Steve Pope 1931
Neil Poppmacher 1100
Erik Pordes 6033
Henry Pordes 6231
Rita Pordes 6231
Sharon Port 2160
David Porteous 1696
Anna Porter 2163
C. L. M. Porter 1587
Chantal Porter 1103
Helen Porter 1236
R. Porter 1157
Terence Porter 1690
Richard Portes 1175
Mrs M. Portsmouth 6194
Julia Posen 1291
Carl Posluns 2172
N. W. Posnett 1452
A. Potgieter 2500
J. C. Potgieter 2501
Andrew Potter 5095
Catherine Potter 1506
Christopher Potter 1324
Roger Potter 1566
Dr Tony Potter 3068
Craig Potton 2437
Ray Potts 1388
Serge Poulin 6156
Poul Jan Poulsen 5012
P. F. Poulter 6040
Richard Poulter 1400
Robert Poulton 1468
Paul Pounsford 1909
Clive Powell 2172
David J. Powell 6028, 6047,
    6052, 6349
Dawn Powell 1870
Graham Powell 6078
James Powell 1679
Judy Powell 2108
Ms Liz Powell 1895
Richard Powell 1277, 1870
Tony Powell 1440
Shelley Power 4080
Chris Powling 6329
M. E. Powter 1544, 1548
Frances Pra-Lopez 3034
Pedro Pra-Lopez 3034
Peter Prado 6169
G. Pratt 1306
Jeremy M. Pratt 1019
Keith Pratt 6173
Chris Prebble 2046
Patricia Preece 4093
Frank Preiss 6160
S. Prendiville 1467
Alison Press 1562
Edward G. Preston 5064
Frank Priatel 2035, 2036
Alec Price 6146
Andrew Price 1668
Humphrey Price 1113, 1790
Mathew Price 3049
Paul Price 1904
Terry Price 6219
Trevor Price 1236
Kenneth Prichard-Jones 5085

Roger Priddy 1248
Andrew Prideaux 1203
Bo Priestley 1764
Dr A. M. Primlani 2334
Gulab Primlani 2261, 2332, 2334
Mohan Primlani 2332
Raju Primlani 2332
Vijay Primlani 2332
Georgia Prince 1689
Robert Prince 6058
Roger Pring 6026
Alexandra Pringle 4027
Garry Prior 1869
Joanna Prior 1324
Adrian Pritchard 6099
J. D. Pritchard 5072
M. E. Pritchard 6213
Sara Pritchard 4013
Sir Victor Pritchett 5112
Andrew Proctor 1452
Joanne Proctor 6176
Ken Proctor 2161
Stuart Proffitt 1387
Lorraine Prosser 2081
D. H. Provan 1136
W. D. B. Prowse 1180
Pierre Prud'Homme 2210
Mairwen Prys Jones 1350
Dawn Louise Pudney 1857
Sonia Pugh 1207
Heddwen Pugh-Evans 1932
Ashok Puliani 2273
D. C. Puliani 2273
Mahesh Puliani 2273
Ravi Puliani 2273
Gary Pulsifer 1644
Penny Pumphrey 3022
Jaffe K. Punnoose 4107, 6387
K. P. Punnoose 4107, 6387
Marja-Liisa Puolakka 1689
Lucy Purkis 1412
Christopher Pursehouse 1571
Sir Neville Purvis 5045
Walter Puszczynski 1824, 6198
Penelope Putnikovich 3048
Radomir Putnikovich 3048
Roger Pygram 1773
J. Pym 2517
Carol Pyrah 1215
Roger Pytel 1278

Diane Quick 2065
Anne Quigley 6211, 6275
J. Quilter 1533
Sue Quincey 1309
Darran Quinn 6142
Hilary Quinn 1271
J. Quinney 1288
Prof. Sarfraz K. Qureshi 2477
Jerry Quy 1161

Andrew H. Rabin 1360
Agatha Raboli 2412
Eva Radford 2184
Dr Lisanne Radice 4037
Bridget Radnedge 6162
Karen Rafferty 1305
Mohamed Rafique 2427
E. Raghavan 2330
Dinesh Raghu 2303
Thomas C. Railton 1426, 6227
Chris Raine 2085
Laurence Raine 1221
Michael Raine 1002
Julie Rainford 1530
Danielle Raitzes 2212
Shri Hans Raj 2305

P. T. Rajasekharan 2336
K. Rakhudu 2522
Philip Ralli 1415
Simon Rallison 1094
Pauline Ralston 2028
Labhaya Ram 2372
Rohier Ramachandran 6382
Rohini Ramachandran 1524
Kevin Ramage 6335
Christine Ramos 1300
Ramesh Ranade 2358
S. K. Ranade 2358
Y. P. Ranade 2358, 5157
Graham Rand 6256
Ms S. Randall 6126
Carlene Randle 2409
Ian Randle 2409
The Countess of Ranfurly 5031
Ranganath 2270
Stephen Rangecroft 1685
Pippa Rann 6117
A. Ransom 1014
J. Krishnadev Rao 2330
J. Rameshwar Rao 2330
Judy Rasmussen 1496, 3017
H. K. Rastogi 2348
R. K. Rastogi 2348
Jo Ratcliffe 1356
Philip Rathkey 1635
Michel Ratthé 2158
H. G. Raubenheimer 2516
Jean Ravine 1418
Kailash Rawat 2349
Pranit Rawat 2349
Sachin Rawat 2349
Elizabeth Rawlings 2452
Jill Rawnsley 2451
Mrs J. Rawson 1813
Jo Anne Ray 6392
Tarapada Ray 2338
Wayne Ray 2153
Mrs Shashi Razdan 2305
Fiona Razvi 1515
D. Reach 1829
D. J. Reach 1320, 1398, 1632
Phillip Read 1184, 1821
Reg Readings 6039
D. Reaney 1467
Angela Rebeiro 2197
Gail Rebuck 1071, 1722
G. Rechner 2496
Nicholas Reckert 1149
Shane Redding 6106
D. Yoga Reddy 2355
Jagan Mohan Reddy 2330
Jo Reddy 1169
Madhu Reddy 2330, 2373
R. Sunandan Reddy 2330
A. Moira Redfern 1793
Martin Redfern 1793
Janice Redlin 2211
C. Redman 1444
Kevin Redpath 1339
Andrea Reece 1425
Henry Reece 1659
Philippa Reece 6278
Ed Reed 5150
Glyn Reed 6327
Mrs Lyn Reed 6072
S. L. Reed 1398
Paul W. Reekie 2020
Lord Rees-Mogg 1679
Morag Reeve 1236
Christine Regan 3050
S. Rehman 2279
Tarique Rehman 2472
Chris Reid 1297

Girsha Reid 4002
Patrick Reid 2209
Sarelle Reid 1914
Tony Reid 1286
Mrs Valerie Reid 5160
Judith Reinhold 1594
John Reiss 1825
Matthew Reisz 1457
Ms M. Rejt 1545
David Rendel 2453
Patricia Rennie 1933
Susan Renouf 2163
Amanda Renshaw 1668
Ms D. Renu 2345
H. J. M. Retief 2504
David Rex-Taylor 1087
Clive Reynard 1928
Alan Reynolds 2030
David Reynolds 1098
Ian Rhind 2221
Louise Rice 2076
Barbara Richards 4112
Cindy Richards 1207
Ian Richards 6251
John Richards 1506
Phil Richards 6133
Ray Richards 4112
S. A. Richards 1109
Stephen Richards 6242
Carol Richardson 2106
Helen Richardson 2139
John Richardson 1194
Kim Richardson 3009
Mike Richardson 2173
Paul Richardson 6402
Peter Richardson 1194
Rob Richardson 6188
Mrs A. K. Ricketts 1323
H. M. Ricketts 1323
Peter J. Ridder 2457, 5168
P. W. Riddle 1844
Jonathan Ridge 6259
Diane Ridley 1492
Amanda Ridout 1423
Rosie Ries 1095
Jennifer Rigby 1860
Frances Riley 1295
J. Riley 1545
Janet Riley 1504
Sally Riley 4003
Rick Rinehart 2401
Marcia H. Rioux 2212
Lee Ripley Greenfield 1496,
  3017
Eric Rippington 1447
Anton Rippon 1120
Trudy L. Rising 2227
Colin Risk 6033
Mrs M. Risseeuw 5014
Denyse Ritchie 2051
Ian Ritchie 2051
Mark Ritchie 3004
Sheila Ritchie 1274
Anna Rivers 1094
Barney Rivers 2069
Julian Rivers 6243
Stuart Rivett 6099
Tim Rix 5031, 6075
Mandy Roads 1482
Luc Roberge 2205
Mr Robert 6266
Alison Roberts 1936
Andrew Roberts 5057
Caroline Roberts 1721
David Roberts 1625, 1629
Mrs G. Roberts 6136
J. Roberts 6274

K. Roberts 1014
Dr M. Roberts 6136
M. P. Roberts 1728
P. Roberts 1823
Paul Roberts 1116
Peter Roberts 1503, 6175
Phil Roberts 1842
Sarah Roberts 1525
Terry Roberts 6097
Valerie Roberts 1685
Sally Roberts Jones 5017
Bruce Robertson 3021
Isobel Robertson 1239
Liz Robertson 1602
Mark Ian Robertson 2014
Miranda Robertson 1337
Barbara Robins 2207
Dorothy Robins 6141
Richard Robins 1491
Andrew Robinson 1094
Barry Robinson 6243
Colin Robinson 1885
Dawn Robinson 6209
Hal Robinson 6023
Ian Robinson 1296, 5026
J. E. Robinson 1014
Jeremy Robinson 1223
Jim Robinson 2033
Karen Robinson 1434
Kim Robinson 2407
Pamela Robinson 2120
Peter Robinson 4024
S. C. Robinson 6054
Sandra Robinson 1530
David Robottom 5065
Annabel Robson 1424
Carole Robson 1743
Jeremy Robson 1743
Peter Robson 2147
Chris Roby 5030
Peter Roche 1113, 1640, 6177
Nora Rock 2135
Arwyn Roderick 5124
Anne Rodford 1936
Derek Rodger 1045
David Rodgers 1553
Sally Rodoham 1041
Neil Rodol 1360
Christopher Roering 2024
Dawn Roering 2024
Bruce Roff 2026
Alan Rogers 2081
Dafydd Rogers 5017
Deborah Rogers 4083
J. Rogers 2461
Stephen Rogers 1773
John Rolfe 1661, 1899
A. Rolington 1479
Glenn Rollans 2092
Jean Rollason 6017
Robert Rollason 6017
Suzanne Rollinson 1491
Kirstan Romano 4004
Mrs Joyce Ronald 1714
Eoin Ronayne 5092
Frank Roney 1047, 1096, 1162,
  1182, 1349, 1556, 1590, 1892,
  1897
Emma Rookledge 1762
Gordon Rookledge 1762
Jennie Rookledge 1762
Sarah Rookledge 1762
Kathy Rooney 1098
Andy Roper 1747
Isobel Rorison 1362
Clyde Rose 2104
Guy Rose 4031

John Rose 6242
Michael Rose 1278
David Rosenberg 2048
Jeannine Rosenberg 2123
John Rosenberg 2128
Scilla Rosenberg 2048
T. G. Rosenthal 1244
Lance Rosolowich 2239
Bob Ross 2467
D. Ross 1103
David Ross 1042
Jamie Ross 1509
Neill Ross 1395
Pat Ross 1504
Robbie Ross 2149
Sue Ross 1798
Susan Ross 1076
R. Ross Stanton 1480
David Rosser 1781
Paul Rossiter 1365
Julian Rothenstein 1729
Gina Rotherford 1935
Jacqueline P. Rotheroe 1798
John W. Rotheroe 1798
Pam Roud 1102
Terry Rouelett 1089
Malik Abdul Rouf 2479
John Roughan 2388
Carina Rourke 1091
Mark Rouse 1139
D. Andrew Rousseau 2410
J. Roux 2099
Doc Rowe 5007
John Rowe 2056
Tricia Rowland 6024
Matthew Rowlands 1491
John Rowlanes 1759
Diane Rowley 1401
Gill Rowley 1908
Kenneth Roy 1160
Ms J. M. Royle 1352, 6395
Diana Ruault 1635
J. H. Rubens 1289
Stephen Rubin 1869
Felicity Rubinstein 4059
Hilary Rubinstein 4084
Pippa Rubinstein 1252
David J. Rudiger 1171
Ann Rudkin 6119
Anthony Rudkin 6119
Yvonne Rue 1751
Oriana Ruffini 2084, 6323, 6363,
  6383
Margaret Ruhfus 2001
Patrick Rukodzi 2531
John Rule 6196
Geoffrey Rumpf 1869, 2085
Mrs Rupa 6266
John Rush 4086
Marie Rushton 1683
Anna Russell 1598
Byron Russell 1084
J. C. Russell 1177
Lucy Russell 2046
Nora Russell 2136
Andrea Russo 1656
Peter Russum 1891
S. Rutt 1546
Carol Ryan 4095
Dr W. F. Ryan 5076
Susan Ryan-Sheridan 2389
David Rye 1386
David Rylands 2235

Mrs Margaret Saah 2241
Alan Sabatini 1918
K. L. Sabharwal 5156

Hassan Sabri 1342
Cesare D. S. Sacerdoti 1487
Mrs J. F. Sacerdoti 1487
Christopher Sackett 1843
Robert Sackville-West 3059
John Saddler 1869
Hashim M. Saeed 1018
Sheri Safran 1847, 3055
S. Sagar 2314
V. Sagar 2314
Colin Sage 6280
Angela Sainsbury 1755
George Sainsbury 1755
Mrs Suberleena Sajid 2474
Mrs Muhammad Sajid Saeed
  2474
Gordon M. Saks 1026
Batul Salazar 1471
Judith Sale 1020
Michael Salinger 1795, 1812
Sue Salisbury 1293
E. K. Sallah 2245
Glynis Salmon 2408
Helen Salmon 1936
C. J. Salter 1578, 1579
Debra Salvoni 1510
Michael Salzman 6389
Oliver Salzmann 2208
Kweku E. Sam-Woode 2244
Kwesi Sam-Woode 2244
Henry Samaranayake 2521
Keith Sambrook 1228
Alan Samson 1528
Alison Samuel 1188
Ron Samuels 3030
Amelia la Fuente Sanchez 1885
Michael Sanders 1802
Rob Sanders 2129
Charles Sanderson 1504
John Sanderson 6234
Sylvia Sanderson 1794
Ms Sandhya 6093
Sandi 1930
Gunilla Sandin 6286
Susan Sandon 1049, 1722
John Sands 6318
Ruth Sandys 1248
Pierre Sané 1032
John V. Sankey 6042
Angela Sansom 1727
John Sansom 1727
Marisol Santos 2207
Barbara Sapergia 2124
Peter Sapsed 3040
D. Sar 1276
Alan Sargent 2248
Rosemary Sarginson 1427
Mrs P. Sarojini 2335
Robert Sarsfield 2074
Jeff Satterley 1504
Peter Saugman 1094
Paula Saunders 1525
Peter Saunders 2140
Ruth B. Saunders 1141, 1783
Sarah Saunders 5038
Tony Saunders 1022
Philip Saunderson 1048
Lyne Sauvé 2116
John Saville 1419
R. Savolainen 2115
Heather Saward 1092
Eleanor Sawyer 2116
Nick Sayers 1387
Mark Sayes 2441
Christopher Scarles 1149
Peter Scarlett 1853
Todd Scarth 2100

Hubert Schaafsma 1252
Arlene Schale 2165
Veronica Schami 5138
Dr Barbara Scharioth 5015
Ms R. Scheepers 2514
Paul Scheinberg 1360
Sue Schenk 2105
Warren Schirmer 2066
Richard Schlagman 1668
Kirsten Schlesinger 1566
V. Schmalzer 1623
Leah Schmidt 4002
Michael Schmidt 1155
Cathy Schofield 1803
P. S. Scholtz 2502
B. Schouwstra 2517
D. Schroeder 2517
Michael Schubart 2154
Vivienne Schuster 4024
Lysa Schwartz 6055
Mike Schwartzentruber 2187, 2238
Volker Schwarz 5006
John Scotney 5127
A. F. D. Scott 2253
Allan Scott 6002
Ashley Scott 1125
Donna M. Scott 5144
Jeanie Scott 1694
Judith Scott 1028
Leslie-Ann Scott 2109
P. Scott 1384
Pat Scott 1005
Peter Scott 6209
Roz Scott 6220
Bill Scott-Kerr 1869
Michael Scott Rohan 6002
Julie Scriver 2142
Susan Scull-Carvalho 2415
James Scullion 2484
Mrs Jan Scutt 2047
Matthew Seal 2512
Emma Sealey 1424
Derek Searle 6121
June Searle 6121
John Seccombe 1840
Julia Sedger 2230
Michael Sedgwick 6167
Monica Seeber 2512
Yvonne Seeley 6095
Fraser Seely 2136
Richard Seet 2490
C. K. Segbawu 2245
Mrs F. G. Segbawu 2245
F. K. Segbawu 2245
H. J. Seghal 2366
Daljit Sehbai 1620
Mrs Anju Sehgal 2350
Jamie Sehmer 1067, 1384, 1429, 1763
Lauri Seidlitz 2235
M. S. Sejwal 2324
John F. Selby 4054
John Sellers 1740
Anthony R. Selvey 1709, 1851
Aidan Selwyn 6182
Roy Selwyn 6182
Barb Semple 2108
J. K. Sen 2333
Chong Huai Seng 2491
Robert Senior 1287
S. P. Sephton 2501
Jean-Pierre Servant 2205
S. Seshadari 2333
R. P. Sessions 2068
W. K. Sessions 1788
W. Mark Sessions 1788

Bali Sethi 6266
Harsh Sethi 2354
David Settle 1789
J. Seward 2016
Robin Sewell 6044
Thom Sewell 1173
Ann Sexsmith 1390, 1584
J. J. Sexton 2388
John Sexton 6162
Elena Seymenliyska 1091
Rebecca Seymour 1182, 1516, 1556, 1590, 1681
Andrew Shackleton 6002
Arvimd A. Shah 2423
Ashok A. Shah 2423
C. D. Shah 2423
Hillen Shah 1888
S. V. Shah 2423
Mrs Shahida Shah 2418
Shaila Shah 1126
Mohan Shahani 2303
S. L. Shaily 2300
Andrea Shallcross 1525
M. D. Shams 1018, 1469
Furqan Ahmad Shamsi 2473
Ravi Shankar 2277
Gareth Shannon 5053
Anil Sharma 2263
Gopal Sharma 2264
I. J. Sharma 2358
Miss Meenu Sharma 2350
Nalin Sharma 2263
S. K. Sharma 2297
S. R. Sharma 2263
Shri Kuldip Sharma 2305
George Sharp 1162
Sylvia Sharp 1801
Jill Sharpe 1900
Martha Sharpe 2156
Peter Sharpe 2065
K. N. Sharples 4065
R. M. Sharples 4065
O. P. Shastri 5157
Linda Shaughnessy 4099
Terry Shaughnessy 1656
Sandra Shaul 2214
Alison Shaw 1857
Dave Shaw 2445
Jenny Shaw 1118
Kiel Shaw 6201
Margaret Shaw 6166
Michael Shaw 4024
Paul Shaw 1147
Philip Shaw 1145
Liz Shearn 6173
Angela Sheehan 3005
Qaseemuddin Sheikh 2472
Anthony Sheil 4086
Caroline Sheldon 4087
David Sheldrake 1929
Chris Shelley 1612
Gavin Shepherd 2079
Peter Shepherd 1194
William Shepherd 1731
Martin Sheppard 1236, 1380, 1880
Paul Sherer 5034
Linda Sheridan 1837
Timothy Sherwen 1526
Alan Shields 6141
Hugh Shiels 2403
John Shillingford 6212
Martin Shillingford 6212
Patricia Anne Shillingford 6212
R. Shimmon 5087
R. W. Shingleton 6256
Mrs Charles Shirley 1719, 6194

Jamie Shmer 1005
P. M. Shnji 2523
Rev N. O. Sholesi 2470
Jo-ann Shore 1008
Don Short 4090
S. Short 1705
Tony Short 1747
Wendy Short 4090
Rob Shreeve 1890
Julian Shuckburgh 1071
Myron Shutty 2146
Winnie Sibeko 2518
Judy Sibley 1260
Liz Sich 6083
Zi Siddique 1877, 1888
Naved Islam Siddiqui 2475
Paul Sidey 1437
Nick Sidle 1024
Ira Siegal 1112
Jan Siegler 6003
Karl H. Siegler 2222
Ruth Siems 2069
Alfred Sikajanga 2527
David Silk 6174
Bernard Silver 6067
Mark Silver 1659
Makeda Silvera 2217
Marian Silvester 1207
Pierre Simard 2151
Jasmine Simeone 5107
John Simkin 5135
Allan Simmons 5057
C. Simmons 2050
Ruth Simmons 6259
A. D. R. Simpson 1020
Bethan Simpson 6039
C. J. Simpson 1354
Jacqueline Simpson 5007
Lisa Simpson 3041
M. C. T. Simpson 5067
Peter Simpson 1297
Tony Simpson 1820
A. Simpson-Muellner 1867
Thomas Sims 6306
Mrs W. Sin 2253
Marion Sinclair 1694
Jonathan Sinclair-Wilson 1261
Sing Wong 5154
Mrs Nirmal Singal 2327
Mrs Nisha Singal 2327
Sushil Singal 2327
David Singer 1387
Arvinder Singh 2298
Deepinder Singh 2298
G. P. Singh 2298
Paramjit Singh 2326
Pritam Singh 2276
Rajendra Singh 2343
Tejeshwar Singh 2354
A. Singleton 1467
Rita Singleton 2404
Adrian Sington 1113
Atish Sinha 2359
J. Sinha 2359
Mrs Prakriti Sinha 2359
Mrs Rajashi Sinha 2359
S. Sinha 2359
Satin Sinha 2359
Snehamay Sinha 2359
N. D. Sinker 1463
Rosemary Anne Sisson 5127
Michael Sissons 4076
R. J. Sissons 1788
Ric Sissons 2070
Sitakumari 1024
Mrs Vasantha Kumaree Siva 5173

K. P. Sivam 5175
Bob Siwecki 6224
E. Siyangapi 2532
Bernard Skalli 5002
Beryl Skellern 2034
Eva Skelley 6351
John Skelton 1636
David Skinner 1445
Eric Skinner 6048
Jane Skinner 1048
Simon Skinner 1909, 6345, 6360, 6364, 6374, 6384
Peter Skipper 6044
Don Skirving 6135
Sue Slater 6279
Rachel Slattery 2076
John Slaytor 1257
Graham Sleight 1487
Janet Slingsby 3060
Jeff Sloan 2114
Jeremy Sloan 1856
Tony Slogget 1003
Michael Sloly 2115
Petra Sluka 1423
Helena Smalman-Smith 1193
Tim Smartt 6171
John Smedley 1052
Erica Smishek 2124
Alan Smith 1162, 1615
Amanda Smith 1330
Barbara Smith 1594
Betty Smith 1468
Bruce Smith 1137, 1927
Mrs C. Smith 1439
Carol Smith 4089
Colin W. Smith 2438
Colleen Smith 1473
Miss D. Smith 6260
D. A. Smith 1014
D. J. Smith 1861
Dag Smith 6391
David Smith 1929, 6180
Deborah Smith 1790
Donald Smith 1506
Fiona Smith 1050, 6138
Geoffrey Smith 1920
Mrs J. Smith 1156
Jennifer Smith 2208
John Smith 1419
Kenneth Smith 1810
Malcolm Smith 1487
Mark Smith 2060
Michele Smith 3004
Mike Smith 6212
N. H. Smith 1635
Paul Smith 1466
Rt Rev Peter Smith 1166
Quentin Smith 2046
R. D. Smith 6151
R. G. Smith 1303
R. H. Smith 1792
Robert Smith 1809
Roger Smith 1188, 1515
Ron Smith 2190
Mrs Rosemary Smith 5048
Rosemary Smith 6106
Sue Smith 1801
Tracey Smith 4013
Victoria Smith 5118
William Smith 1775
Paul Smitz 2053
Ms B. Smoker 5110
John Smoker 1085, 5042
Mike Smuts 2499
Sarah Smye 1039
Sarah Smyth 6291
Colin Smythe 1811

Donna Snelgrove 2162
Diana Snell 6210
Graham Snell 6210
Catharine Snow 1637
Robert Snuggs 1389, 1506
W. A. Snyder 6122
Piet Snyman 1721, 1722
Ms P. T. So 2252
Nicolas Soames 1607
A. Soar 1543, 1544, 1545, 1546,
   1547, 1548
C. Sobro 1600
The Society of Authors 5062
Rupinder Sohal 1102
Farouk Sohawon 1936
Carol Ann Solcoloff 2134
B. Somekh 1777
James Somerville 1278
Jane Somerville 2219
Elaine Soni 1581, 6367
Rajesh Sood 2295, 2296
Savitrie Sookdeo 6266
Stephen Lim Kee Soon 2426
Glen Sorestad 2225
Sonia Sorestad 2225
Mark Sorrell 4075, 5094
Simon Sossion 2417
Dan Soucoup 2185
Brian Southam 1058
Doris Southam 1058
Rob Southam 2464
Mrs D. Southern 1915
Phillipa Southern 1112
Peter Sowden 1747
Angela Spall 1395
Clive Sparling 3004
M. Spears 2054
Miss J. Speed 1439
David Spence 1758
Piers Spence 1237
K. M. Spencer 6265
Mick Spencer 1419
Nikki Spencer 1275
Lynne Spender 5134
A. Sperring 1398
George Spicer 1637, 1900
Stephen Spick 6167
Amanda Spiers 1614
Stephan Spies 2503, 2505
John F. Spillane 2399
Diane Spivey 1897
A. Spooner 1664
Deborah Spring 1453
Robert Springall 1613
Truda Spruyt 1726
Jean Spurr 1443, 1698, 1699,
   1700, 1701
Steven Spurrier 5054
Richard Squibb 6205
Sarah Squibb 6205
G. Sreekumar 2284
Arvind Srivastava 2333
Sajal Srivastava 2339
Hans Staal 1172, 1226
Vikki Stace 6116
Jack Stacey 6187
Mark A. Stacey 6177
John Stachiewicz 1387
R. Stagg 2054
Rosemary Stagg 2450
T. Stagg 2496
Juliet Standing 1644
Mark Stanley 1260
J. Stanton 1014
Julie Stanton 2085
Mark Stanton 2206
Heather Staples 6224

Peter G. Stark 5164
Harold K. Starke 1827
Mary Starkey 1584
Naomi Starkey 1812
Pat Starkey 2449
Bernhard Starkmann 6270
Jim Starr 1589
M. Staton 1479
Mrs I. Staunton 2528
Marie Staunton 1332
G. Steddy 1501
Paul Steedman 2513
Alan J. Steel 1118
Diana Steel 1039
Hunter Steele 1090
Abner Stein 4091
Jeremy Stein 1092
John Stengelhofen 1875
Heather Stephens 1254
Adrian Stephenson 1712, 3036
Rosemary Stephenson 3036
M. Stern 1354
Mai Kim Stern 6279
Julie Sternberg 2113
Brian Steven 1422
Aletta Stevens 1310
C. J. Stevens 1385
Elizabeth Stevens 4024
Ian Stevens 1419, 6356, 6380
Irene Stevens 5136
Kevin Stevens 6057
Matthew Stevens 1310
P. J. Stevens 1340
Pam Stevens 1568
G. Stevens-Cox 1868
Andrew Stevenson 1194
B. A. Stevenson 2148
Peter Stevenson 1593
Richard Stevenson 5024
Tony Stevenson 1885
Wilf Stevenson 5042
J. Steward 6218
Sally Steward 2053
Anne Stewart 2444
Carolyn Stewart 2183
Catherine Stewart 3007
David Stewart 1648, 2069
Graham C. Stewart 2444
Joan Stewart 2076
Philippa Stewart 1900
Alastair Steyn 2498
J. Steyn 2514
Jonathan Steyn 1922
Ms L. Steyn 2514
Chris Stibbs 1332
Henrietta Stickland 1719, 6194
J. Stidolph 3010
Richard Stileman 1048
Mrs Madeline Stiles 1417
R. Stock 6040
Peter Stockham 6125
Celia Stocks 1017, 1428, 6076
Barbara M. Stockwell 1568
Derek Stockwell 1568
R. J. G. Stockwell 1831
Andrew Stoddart 6264
John Stoddart 1006
Susan Stoddart 2128
K. Stoecker 1385
C. Stoffberg 2500
Sally Stokes 2049
R. Stoltenkamp 5176
S. Stonard 1087
Brian Stone 4003, 5023
Katie Stone 1497
Nicky Stonehill 1890
Dr Miriam Stoppard 6114

Miss L. Storey 1858
Louise Storry 6061
B. F. Stott 6126
Carl Stott 1640
Suzanne Stott 2114
John Strange 1094
Peter Straus 1545, 1677
Polly Strauss 1375
Mark Streatfeild 1640
Patricia Streotin 1491
Mike Stribbling 1737
Rolf Stricker 1299
Jennie Strickland 2114
Tessa Strickland 1070
J. C. Strike 2068
Roy Strode 1466
Denise Strong 2114
John Stroud 1659
Stephen Stuart-Smith 1644
Philip Sturrock 1047, 1096, 1162,
   1182, 1349, 1556, 1590, 1615,
   1892, 1897
L. Sucharov 1208
Claire Suckling 5181
Robert Sulley 2499
T. Sully 1880
D. Summers 1014
Linda Summers 1721
Lorna Summers 6202
John W. Sumsion 1523
Fran Supple 1661
Suresh 2345
W. J. Suresh 2265
Debra Surette 2217
Frank Surry 5090
W. Sutcliffe 1626
A. J. Sutherland 1547
D. Sutherland 5110
D. D. Sutherland 2462
D. F. Sutherland 2532
M. Sutherland 4118
Ed Suthon 1685
Alan Sutton 1178
Clare Sutton 1029, 1031
M. Sutton 6260
R. Sutton 1705
Adrian Swallow 1124
Su Swallow 1291
Dr Alma Swan 6102
Anna Swan 4082
Maureen Swanage 2008
A. Swanepoel 2514
A. H. Swann 1907
Bridget Swann 1512, 6035
Christopher K. Swann 1907
Rachel Swann 4013
Nellie Swart 2515
Leonie Sweeney 2079
Sean Sweeney 6113
Christopher Sweeten 5032
Tom Sweetman 1909
Mary Sweny 1288
B. Swidecki 6087
Christine L. Swift 1360
Ms E. Swift 1813
Peter Swift 1295
Mary Swinney 4072
A. Symonds 1001
John Symonds 2162
Anna Synenko 2100
J. N. Syrett 1340
John Szabo 2065

Judith Tabern 1457
Jon Tacey 1672
Mohammad Abid Taimuri 2473
Angie Tainsh 1119

Brenda Tait 2087
Nicasio M. Takawira 2531
Atsuko Takenaka 6064
John Talbot 6250
T. B. Talwatte 2519
Yvonne Tam 2249
Anna Tamar Thame 1524
Albert Tan 5139
Constance Tan 2490
Margaret Tan 2488
Siew Lan Tan 2494
Wu Cheng Tan 2485
Tan Poay Lim 2486
Tan Wu Cheng 5175
Shelley Tanaka 2143
Dr H. L. S. Tandon 2292
R. Taneja 2376
Anne Tannahill 1091
Bob Tanner 4048
Mary Tapissier 1424, 1425
Geoffrey Tapper 5077
Jean Tardif 2210
Maxim Tarnawsky 2110
Susan Tarsky 1002
Peter Tauber 4092
Robert Tauber 4092
L. M. Taunyane 2516
Bessie Tay 2482
Patricia Tay 2492
Alan Taylor 6256
Ann Taylor 3032
Cora Taylor 5145
Daphne Taylor 2407
David Taylor 1360, 1466
E. Taylor 1087
Elizabeth Taylor 1494
G. S. Taylor 1014
George Taylor 1648
Imogen Taylor 1528
John Taylor 1537, 1634, 1749,
   3032
Jonathan Taylor 1035
Judy Taylor 5097
Lesley Taylor 5109
Lesley A. Taylor 1756
Dr Michael Taylor 5052
Michael Taylor 6240
Milan Taylor 1683
Neil Taylor 6186
Paul Taylor 1330
Peter J. Taylor 1852
Peter Kershaw Taylor 6168
R. J. E. Taylor 1284
R. V. Taylor 2514
Stuart Taylor 1094
Susan K. V. Taylor 1494, 6168
Keith Taylorson 1686
David Teale 6281
Warwick Teale 2085
David Tebbutt 1747
Charlotte Teeple 5148
Clive Tempest 1535
Mrs Nicola S. Temple 6182
Terry Temple 4116
Bill Templeman 2075
Ray Templeton 5087
Diane Tennant 6241
Steven Teo 2488
Peter Terrell 3037
J. Terry 2005
Brian Tetley 2413
Brian Thackray 1055, 5021
Anna Tamar Thame 6382
Lyn Thane 2022
Christina Theile 2130
Sonja Thein 1149
Serge Thériault 2179

P. A. Thew 2394
Nansi Thirsk 1097
Simon Thirsk 1097
Rudi Thoemmes 1859
Amanda Thomas 1925
Caroline Thomas 6118
Christina Thomas 5101
Karen Thomas 2124
Kevin Thomas 5017
Michael Thomas 4040
Ned Thomas 1895
Neil Thomas 1395
Richard Thomas 1735
Russ Thomas 2162
Siân Thomas 1401
B. G. Thompson 1262
Claire Thompson 6201
David Thompson 6036
Glenn Thompson 1930
Ian Thompson 1191
John Thompson 1693
Keith Thompson 2226
Lois Thompson 2449
Margaret Thompson 2068
Merril Thompson 2011
Mike Thompson 1673
Nicolas Thompson 5058, 5100
Peter Thompson 1758
Tony Thompson 1481
Prof A. W. J. Thomson 1635
Derick S. Thomson 1335
Janice Thomson 1297
Ken Thomson 2169
Ron B. Thomson 2199
Sarah Thomson 1401
Jeremy Thor 2424
Eunice A. Thorne 2093
Brenda Thornley 2045
Brian Thornton 1571
Juliet Thorp 1503
Paul Thorp 1230
Amelia Thorpe 1071, 1722
D. F. Thorpe 1862
David Thorpe 1549
F. A. Thorpe 1862
Jill Thorpe 1900
Simon Thraves 1178
James Throssell 2086
Jon Thurley 4093
Anthony Thwaite 1244
Lesley Thwaites 2035
Frank Tierney 2102
Anita Tiessen 1032
Catherine Tilley 1251
Suzanne Timbers 1625
John Timmis 6154
Chris Timms 6166
J. Timothy 1564
H. L. Timpe 1672
Andrew Tindall 1391, 6226
Stuart Tipping 1505
T. Tippler 1014
Alan Titley 6333
K. P. Tiwari 2314
Chris Tixerant 1866
to be appointed 1866
To be appointed 1094
Julian Tobin 1244
Richard Tobin 1878
Janet Tod 5063
G. R. U. Todd 1547
M. W. Todd 1014
Neil Todd 2333
Lesley Toll 1095, 1574, 1809
Anthony Tomei 5093
Richard Tomkins 1211
Liz Toms 6010

William B. Toohey 2074
S. Toop 1467
Sandra Tooze 2117
Joseph Tortell 2431
Sue Toseland 6242
Pat Touchie 2159
Amber Toullelan 2121
Frances Townsend 1802
Peter Townsend 1802
Maggie Toy 1006
David Tranah 1149
Catherine Trarelle 2113
Erica Travers 2005
Nancy Traversy 1070
Michael C. W. Trayler 1928
Mark Tredinnick 2034
Angèle Tremblay 2204
Carmen Tremblay 5138
David Trenaman 1597
Ronnie Trenter 2028
Tracey Trenter 2028
Jeremy Trevathan 1545
Lavinia Trevor 4094
Stan Trevor 5026
Ion Trewin 1903
Simon Trewin 4086
Elisabeth Tribe 1422
B. Trigg 1467
Richard Trillo 3054
Jane Trinder 1077
Annabel Trodd 1732
B. H. Trodd 1732
Miss N. Trodd 1732
Andy Fiennes Trotman 1872
P. S. Trotman 1547
Mark Trotter 6166
Mrs H. C. Troughton 5115
Denise Truax 2201
Michael Trup 6172
Gerry Truscott 2213
F. Tse 2253
Linda Tsevi 2246
Alex Tucker 6031
Darryl Tucker 6242
Del Tucker 3060
Pat Tucker 2518
Peter Tucker 6027, 6031
Richard Tucker 1423
C. Tullo 1844
His Honour Judge Stephen Tumim 5103
David J. Tuppa 2524
Dr A. Turnbull 6393
Andrew Turnbull 1781
Charles Turner 6153
Clare Turner 1783
David Turner 6153
Gaye Turner 1194
Graham Turner 1491
Greg Turner 2063, 5137
Helen Turner 3053
J. M. S. Turner 6271
Judy Turner 1869
Steve Turner 1418
Geraldine Turpie 1112
David Turton 1874
Dr Marvis Tutiah 2157, 2223
John Tuttle 1611
Alan Twiddle 1906
John Twiggs 1013
Michael Twinn 1189
Ann Twiselton 1584
Mrs Sarah Tyacke 5076
David Tyler 1011
Diana Tyler 4063
J. Tyler 1881
Jeremy Tyndall 6291

W. Uiterwijk 2522
Michael E. Ulyatt 1438
Mohammed Umar 1936
Christopher Underwood 5084
Pat Underwood 1840
Sue Unstead 1248
D. Unsworth 1195
W. Unsworth 1195
Fred Unwalla 2199
Lyndsey Unwin 1497
Vanessa Unwin 1025
Carl Upsall 1510
Michael Upshall 1408
Mary Ellen Upton 1026
Laurence Urdang 3061, 6381
Geoffrey Ursell 2124
T. P. Usborne 1881
P. Uttley 1014
R. Uttley 1501

Ahmad Vahdat 6065
Christine Vale 2076
Peter Vallee 2008
Catherine Vallet 2138
C. Vamvadelis 2507
Dirk van Corter 2515
Theo van de Bilt 1689
Dirk van der Toorn 2498
Phoebe van der Walt 2515
Charles Van Nostrand 1330
Basil Van Rooyen 2513
Basil van Rooyen 5177
P. van Schuik 2503
Roger Van Zwanenberg 1691
Willem VanZon 2132
Peter Varey 1458
G. Varghese 2530
Amarnath Varma 2364
Anil Varma 2364
Sanjay Varma 2364
Sunil Varma 2364
B. V. Varney 6011
Lata Vasvani 2303
Denis Vaugeois 2166
Paul Vaughan 4081
Veeraraghavan 2261
Marianne Velmans 1869
J. J. M. Velterop 1005, 1384
Ariadne van de Ven 1623
Mrs Debbie Venables 1168
Mrs H. Venter 2503, 2505
Lisa Ventura 4081
Pasquale Verdicchio 2144
Sara-Jane Vere Nicoll 1165
F. Verhagen 1276
Francine Vernac 2167
J. Vernay 1546
Delphine Verroest 1403
Sarah Vicary 1913
Ed Victor 4095
S. Vidyarthi 1106
Mrs S. Vidyarthi 1106
Nikki Viinikka 1553
L. Viljoen 2500
Gerald de Villiers 2512
Jane Villiers 4085
Francis Vincent 2218
Maureen Vincent 4076
Tom Vincent 5142
Charles Viney 1528
Leslie Viney 6184
P. Vinson 1861
Michael Virtue 1891
A. Visser 1501
Alberto Vitale 1722
Penny Vogler 1181
Agnes Vogt 3063

Dr Roopa Vohra 2259
Norman Vokey 6053
Mrs E. M. Volschenk 2503, 2505
Mechthild von Alemann 5006
Malko von Osten 2158
T. Vosloo 2516
Doreen Vostinar 2076
Christiane Vuidar 5010

Amy Wack 1692
Karl Waddicor 1434
Mrs Caroline Wade 1066
Susanna Wadeson 1113
Victor Waese 2137
Anthony Wagstaff 6073, 6145
Allison Wainman 1765
Susannah Wainman 1765
M. K. Wait 6263
Mrs R. Wake 1777
Richard Wake 5091
Sandra Wake 1690
Carol Wakefield 1826
Keith Wakefield 1826
E. A. Wakley 6246
V. L. C. Walatara 2521
Susan Walby 1334
Guido Waldman 1392
Tony Wales 1527
Alan Gordon Walker 1897
Brenda Walker 1318
Caroline Walker 2136
Derek Walker 6129
Dwight Walker 5135
E. K. Walker 4096
Geoff Walker 2460
Henrietta Walker 1449
Dr M. A. Walker 2137
Nicholas S. Walker 2013
Penny Walker 1869
Peter Walker 5060
Sophie Walker 6331
Steve Walker 2160
Anthony Wall 1744
A. Wallace 2528
Ian Wallace 1904
John Wallace 1209
Penelope Wallace 5123
Veronica Wallace 1734
B. Waller 1533
Ann Wallin 2187, 2238
Charles Wallis 1527
Diane Wallis 2088
Mrs E. Wallis 5115
Helen Wallis 3038
Morwenna Wallis 1604
Michael Walmer 1114
Dr Hartmut Walravens 5011
Andrew Walsh 6209
Christine Walsh 6183
Colin Walsh 1363, 1608, 6024
Diana Walsh 6183
John Walsh 6144
Liz Walsh 6118
Neil Walsh 2014
Patrick Walsh 4055
Philip Walsh 6312
Sarah Walsh 6009, 6063
Virginia Walsh 5132
Rebecca Walshe 2012
Aubrey Walter 1347
Jan Walter 2170
Philip Walters 1422
Stuart Walters 1489
Michael Walton 1178
Prof. Shem Wandiga 2414
Cathrine Wanezycki 2112
Cissy Wang 6266

William Wang 5174
Christopher Ward 6257
Jacquie Ward 6036
Jane Ward 1541
Peter Ward 6113
Richard Ward 6113
Roy Ward 2171
A. Ware 1014
M. Ware 1467
P. Wareing 6215
R. D. Warman 1558
Elizabeth Warner 1329
G. Warner 1546
Richard Warner 1201, 1483
Brian C. J. Warnes 1641
Ann Warnford-Davies 4083
Darcel Warren 1863
Jane Warren 1528
Peter Warwick 1659, 2122
Ken R. Wasley 6191
John Waterhouse 2003
Jane Waterman 1278
K. Waterman 1861
C. P. Watkins 6269
Anthony Watkinson 1724
Andrew Watson 2058
Anna Watson 1338
Anne Watson 1472
Christine Watson 1659
J. R. Watson 1823
John Watson 1544
Malcolm G. Watson 1313
Sheila Watson 4098
Ian Watt 2446
Kelly Watt 2217
Susan Watt 1485, 1661
Linda Watters 1520
Gordon Watts 1502
Judith Watts 1336
Julie Watts 2068
Nick Watts 1331
Tony Watts 1455
Simonne Waud 1248
Juliet Waugh 1076
David Wavre 1259
David Way 1128, 1130
Emma Way 1132
Debbie Wayment 6024
Deborah Wayment 1608
Ian Wayne 2113
Jack Wayne 2113
Janice Weaver 2168
Colin Webb 1656
G. H. Webb 5086
J. Webb 2522
Ken Webb 6217
Kenneth R. L. Webb 1837
Mark Webb 1137, 1152
Mary Webb 2400
Nic Webb 1613
Nick Webb 1803
Pamela Webb 1656
Richard Webb 3064
Timothy Webb 4035, 4063
Ronald Weber 6299
Adrian Webster 1902
Michael Webster 2084, 6322,
  6323, 6363
Mike Webster 1869
Rick Webster 5080
Susannah Webster 1902
Geoff Weedon 6239
Cathryn Weekes 1866
Gerd Weidemann 5011
Peter Weidhaas 6299
Brian Weight 1751
Linda A. Weigl 2235

M. van de Weijer 1861
Ms J. Weir 1669
Louise Weir 1401
Daphne Weiss 1161
Carole Welch 1423
John Welch 4100
Fay Weldon 4109
Tom Weldon 1404, 1554
Stella Welford 1093
Andrew Welham 1661
Robert Welham 1750, 6202
Chris Weller 1075
Helen Weller 2002
P. J. Weller 1669
Louise Wellington 2045
Alan Wells 1332
Nick Wells 3027
Penny Wells 1150
Pat Wemyss 1161
John Wendon 1518
Robert Wendover 1527
Anthony R. A. Werner 1796
Mrs M. M. Werner 1796
Marian Werner 5097
Henryk Wesolowski 1896
Ros Wesson 1248
Ann J. West 2220
Cecilia West 2384
Christopher West 1544
Colin West 1222
Janet West 1492
Julian West 1492
Justin West 1116
Martin West 1484
Tim Westbrook 1747
Sarah Westcott 1392
Paul Westlake 1785
Adrian Weston 6116
Betty Weston 1379
Trevor Weston 1598
Bruce Westwood 4106
Guy Westwood 1003
Jeremy Westwood 1386
Malcolm Wetherill 6238
Andrew Wheatcroft 6393
Suzanne Wheatley 1003
Christopher Wheeler 1048
Maureen Wheeler 2053
Rupert Wheeler 1147
Tony Wheeler 2053
B. J. Whelan 2388
C. T. Whelan 2388
Deirdre Whelan 2380
Elizabeth Whelan 1094
Alan Wherry 1098
Sarah Wherry 1656
Carolyn Whitaker 4056
David Whitaker 1909, 5119
Martin Whitaker 1909, 5119
Sally Whitaker 1909, 5119
John Whitby 6133
Judy Whitby 6133
Amanda White 4015
Antony White 1917
Ben White 3009
Brenda White 4042
Caroline White 1845
Chris White 1047, 1892, 1897
Christine White 1883
Christopher White 1096
Denise White 1245
Derek White 5016
Diane White 6141
G. N. White 1532
Heather White 1614
Howard White 2147
Jim White 1042

Maria White 3025
Mary White 2147
Murray White 1388
Nick White 1611
Nicky White 1263, 1706
Pat White 4083
Paul White 1103, 1213, 6213
S. White 1844
Sarah White 1889
Stephen White-Thomson 1541,
  1901
Helen Whitehorn 1048
P. J. B. Whiteing 1662
H. C. H. Whiteside 1358
Tim Whitfield 1485
Janice Whitford 4106
C. L. Whiting 1444
Catherine Whiting 1720
Andrew Whittaker 6251
Sue Whittaker 1084
Noel Whittall 3065
Annabel Whittet 1911
Lizzy Whittingham 1723
Dr Keith Whittles 1912
Tony Whittome 1437
A. Whitton 1157
Paul Whitton 1527
Colin Whurr 1913, 6362
Florence Whyte 1098
Conrad Wiberg 6074
Pauline Wickham 1174
Mrs N. M. Wickremesinghe 2521
B. M. Wiener 4101
D. P. Wiener 4101
Dinah Wiener 4101
F. J. Wiese 2516
Pamela Wiggin 5151
Barbara Wiggins 1871
Steven Wiggins 1064
A. B. T. Wijeratne 2521
D. N. Wijewardene 2521
R. S. Wijewardene 2521
Sara Wilbourne 2385
Clair Wilcox 1298
Katy Wild 1865
Brian Wilder 2058
Glen Wilders 1853
Don Wildey 1267
Jannie Wilken 2499
Ian Wilkes 1410, 1688
Andrew Wilkins 2043
Mary-Jane Wilkins 1080
Stephen Wilkins 1186
Martin Wilkinson 1094
Ronald Wilkinson 1063
Rosemary Wilkinson 3066
Rick Wilks 2094
B. Willan 1014
S. Willcox 1501
Margaret Willes 1604
Duncan Willetts 2413
Alastair Williams 1838
Anthony Williams 6240
Bridget Williams 2432, 2469
C. H. Williams 5079
Caerwyn Williams 5017
Christine Williams 1494
Clive Williams 1222
Conrad Williams 4007
Crispin Williams 1792
David Williams 1047, 1096,
  1615, 1892, 1897
Emyr Williams 5020
Graham Williams 1926
James Williams 3049
Jana Williams 2217
Jonathan Williams 4108

Kevin Williams 2206
Lawrence Williams 6257
Michael Williams 1111, 1759
Monica Constantinou Williams
  6264
P. A. Williams 1560
Patricia Williams 1600
Peter Williams 1138
Phil Williams 5041
Roz Williams 1363, 6024
Ruth Williams 1678
S. Williams 1511, 1672
Mrs S. E. Williams 3028
Miss Samantha Williams 3028
Mrs Saundrea Williams 6165
Sonia Williams 1111
Steven Williams 6109
Susan A. Williams 1122
T. Williams 1014
Tony Williams 1916
W. Alister Williams 1122
Iain Williamson 2202
Dr J. J. Williamson 1813
James Williamson 1221, 2234
Jane Williamson 1859
Gareth Willis 3030
Nicola Willmot 1671
Iris Willsher 1256
Connie Wilsack 1529
Adam Wilson 1806
Anne Wilson 2060
Annie Wilson 1269
Brian Wilson 1461
Bruce Wilson 2022
David Wilson 1244, 2046
David F. Wilson 1108
E. N. Wilson 1447
Elisabeth Wilson 1917
Georg Wilson 2146
Ian Wilson 1359
J. Wilson 1669
Jacqueline Wilson 1458
Jamie Wilson 1817
Jean Wilson 2230
John Wilson 1119, 1904
John S. Wilson 6130
Joyce M. Wilson 6337
Kate Wilson 1543
Neil Wilson 1610
Nigel Wilson 1316
Pat Wilson 6130
Philip Wilson 1917
Phyllis Wilson 2192
Quentin Wilson 2447
S. R. M. Wilson 1115
Sarah Wilson 1921
Sue Wilson 1174
Susan Wilson 4111
Tony Wilson 1149
William Wilson 1447
J. R. Winckler 1546
Helen Windrath 1924
Martin Windrow 1919
Rebecca Winfield 1869
Barry Winkleman 3050
John Winkley 1139
D. Winter 1533
Mary Kay Winter 2227
Rebecca Winter 1527
Jane Winterbotham 1383, 1407,
  1551, 1573
Susan Winton 3062
Julia Wisdom 1387
Derek Wise 5048
Robert Wise 1630
Tim Wise 6062
Mrs M. Wiseman 1478

Trevor Witcher 6166
Alan Witherby 1923
Mary Witts 2076
E. Wolfaard 2500
L. J. Wolfe 6269
Margie Wolfe 2215
Sally Wolfe 5091
Mrs A. M. Wolfenden 1624
M. H. Wolfenden 1624
Angelina L. F. Wong 2249
Paul S. L. Wong 2249
Tony Wong 2056
Vincent Wong 2251
Wong Chin Teng 2425
Wong To 2250
Wong Wai-Man 2253
Alison Wood 1049
Amanda Wood 3058
Anita Wood 2178
Barrie Wood 2513
Boo Wood 1090
D. Wood 3056
Diane Wood 2236
Jane Wood 1639
Jenny Wood 3045
Julie Wood 1141, 1783
Dr Juliette Wood 5007
Kate Wood 2239
Nicola Wood 1843
Norman Wood 2389
Robin Wood 1387
Roger Wood 1466
Rosalie Wood 6353

S. L. Wood 3056
Tim Wood 3045
Janson Woodall 1332
Ms Pamela Woode 2244
Laura Woodford 2104
Roger Woodham 6180
Alison Woodhead 1301
Kate Woodhead 5022
Martin Woodhead 1925
Amanda Woodrow 2235
Allan Woods 1264
Jeanette Woods 6140
Julia Woods 2172
R. N. Woodward 1014
Ron Woodward 6392
David Woodworth 1882
Gill Woolcott 1890
Sandra Woolfrey 2237
Gillian B. Woolven 1056
Sam Wootten 1163
Ian Wordsworth 6191
David R. Worlock 4045, 6028,
   6047, 6052, 6098, 6349
Kim Worts 1060
Miss Heather Wraight 1192
Simon Wratten 1648
Warwick Wratten 5181
Mark Wray 1366, 1537
J. Wrench 1103
Alex Wright 1812
Deborah Wright 1485, 6220
E. Wright 1881

Geoff Wright 2090
Giles Wright 1298
Miss J. Wright 1439
James Wright 6170
Jean Wright 1651
Jennifer Wright 2087
Judith Wright 5168
Mrs Karen Wright 1204
M. Wright 5087
Malcolm Wright 1742
Patrick M. M. Wright 1132
Timothy Wright 1194
Steve Wuerz 2239
Ian Wylie 1497
Nesta Wyn Jones 5017
David Wynn 1648
Jonathan Wynne 6171
Anna Wypych 2118
George Wypych 2118

R. P. Yadav 2297
Colin Yam 2493
Elaine Yap 2490
Constance Yates 1934
Roy Yates 1934, 6272
Jeremy Yates-Round 1388
Lau Chor Yau 5174
M. Yazdani 1460
Rosalind Yeow 2490
Jonathan Yglesias 1661
Richard York 1788
Sarah York 1238

Stephen York 1860
Philip Yorke 1187
Andrew Young 1261
Anne Young 1128
Barbara Young 2403
David Young 6160
Gwen Young 1581, 6367
Julie Young 1132
Nigel R. Young 1052, 1235,
   1271, 1354
Greg Young-Ing 2224
Laura Yuen 2057

Gary Zabel 1427
Marc Zagar 1506
Syed Hasan Zaidi 2475
M. P. Zaidner 1161
Sugra Zaman 4098
Debbie Zampieri 2049
Jack Van Zandt 2401
Stephanie Zarach 1363
Leo Zeglovskis 1625
Hans M. Zell 6022, 6316, 6317,
   6371
Christopher Zielinski 5029
M. Zifcak 2038
Catie Ziller 2060
Daniela Zimmermann 6394
Henriette Zoughebi 6309
Suzanna Zsohar 1075
Sabelo Zulu 2499
Jan Zwicky 2105

7.8 INDEX OF COMPANIES & IMPRINTS

Bold figures indicate a principal entry in the Directory; other figures refer to citations within principal entries.

Uitgeverij 010 6139
10/18 6160
100 Best Books **6315**
21st Century **6243**
3 & 5 Promotion **6068**
3-D City Guides 3022
3-D Revelations 6166

AA Publishing **1001**, 6162, 6243
AAB Editorial Research Centre – Oxford **6001**
Aarti Books 2363
Aavishkar Publishers' Distributors 2341
AB Books **6208**
A & B Personal Management Ltd **4001**
Abacus 1528, 2460, 2506
ABAGE Publications 1416
Abbeville Press Inc 1594, 6167, 6243
Abbey Press 1198
ABC Books 6154
ABC-Clio International 6182
ABC-Clio Ltd **1003**, 1444, 6191
ABC-Clio (UK) 1003
ABC Verlag 1050, 6138
ABC – The All Children's Co Ltd **1002**
Abdo & Daughters Publishing 6166
Abercastle Publications 6258
Abhinav Publications 1106, **2256**
Abingdon Press 6181
Abington Publishing 1925, 6202
Ablex Publishing Corporation 6157
Aboriginal Studies Press **2001**
Harry N. Abrams Inc 6243
Editora Abril 1385
Absolute Classics **1004**
Absolute Press **1004**, 6152, 6243
Acacia 2517
Yr Academi Gymreig / The Welsh Academy **5017**, 6258
Academic Books 2528
Academic Press Inc **1005**, 1384
Academic Press Ltd **1005**, 1384, 2033, 6182
Academic Publishers 1760
Academic Therapy Publications 1037
Academic & University Publishers Group (AUPG) 6145
Academy Chicago Publishers Ltd 6166
Academy Editions 1006

Academy Group Ltd **1006**, 1883, 6174
Academy Manuscript 1466
Academy Science Publishers 6069
Les Éditions d'Acadie **2091**
Acadiensis Press 2142
Editions Acatos 1416
ACBLF **5141**
ACC Publications **1007**
Accent Educational Publishers Ltd 6160
Access Press **2002**
Accountancy Books **1008**
Contemporary Issues in Accounting Series 2341
Ace Books **1009**
Acid Jazz 6243
Acol-Biotol **1010**
Acorn Editions 1199
Acorn Publications Ltd 1395
ACR 1050, 6138
Acrobat Books Publishers 6166
Acropolis South LC 6166
ACS Publications 6135
Acta Kurdica 1229
Actinic Press 1224
Active Press 6146
Adam Editions 6152
Adam Matthew Publications **1011**
Adam Software 1659, 6182
Adamantine Press Ltd **1012**
Bob Adams 6146
Addax Retail Publishing Ltd **1013**, 6243
Addison-Wesley 1014, 2054, 2068
Editions Addison-Wesley France SA 1014
Addison-Wesley Interactive 1014
Addison-Wesley Italia Editoriale SpA 1014
Addison Wesley Longman Australia Pty Ltd 1014
Addison Wesley Longman Inc 1014
Addison Wesley Longman Ltd **1014**, 2068, 2450, 2530
Addison Wesley Longman Nederland BV 1014
Addison Wesley Longman New Zealand Ltd 1014
Addison Wesley Longman Publishers BV 1014
Addison Wesley Longman Verlag 1014
Henri Addor & Associates 1416
ADEC 1416
Adelphi Papers (Monograph Series) 1834
Adlard Coles 1015, 1089, 6243

Adlard Coles Nautical **1015**, 1089
Adlib 1770
Advaita Ashrama **2257**
Advance Publications Inc 1722
Advanced Marketing (UK) Ltd 6162
Advances in Fluid Mechanics 1208
Adventures Unlimited 6166
Advertising Press Ltd 1625
Advisory Unit: Computers in Education **1016**
Aedes Gallery 6139
Aerofax 1579
Aerospace Publishing 1020
Aesthetic Holdings Pty Ltd 2007
AFNIL **5001**
Afram Publications (GH) Ltd **2240**, 6069
Africa Book Services (EA) Ltd **2411**
Africa Christian Press **2241**
Africa Community Publishing & Development Trust 6069
The African Book Publishing Record **6316**
The African Book World & Press: A Directory / Répertoire du Livre et de la Presse en Afrique **6317**
African Books Collective **6069**
African Books in Print **6318**
African Occasional Papers 2108
African Publishers' Network **6319**
Africana Publishing Co **1017**
Afrisoft Grahamstown 1016
Afritech 2517
Afro Publishers (Eastern Cape) 2517
Age Concern 1009, 6145, 6243
Agence Francophone pour la Numérotation Internationale du Livre (AFNIL) **5001**
The Agency (London) Ltd **4002**
Ages Publications 6136
The Agricultural Development, Commercial Credit & Industrial Investment Co Ltd 2373
AGS 1619
Ahmadiyya Muslim Publications **1018**
Aids Readers 2522
AIM Productions 6172
Aircraft Monographs 1107
Aird Books Pty Ltd 6166
Airdata Publications **1019**
Airlife Publishing Ltd **1020**, 6243
Airlift Book Company 6071, **6135**, 6243
Airplan Flight Equipment Ltd 1019
A.I.T.B.S. Publishers & Distributors **2255**
Aitken & Stone Ltd **4003**
A J-Press 1107

Ajanta Books International **2258**
Ajanta Publications 1106, 2258
AK Press 1328
Akademie Verlag 1883
AKME Publications 6152
Akshat Publications **2259**
Aktok 6152
Al-Ghazali Series 1471
University of Alabama Press 6161
Aladdin Books Ltd 1900, **3001**
Aladdin/Watts 1900
Alaw 6258
Alba House 1757
Alban Books 6181
Albany Book Co Ltd **6259**
Albatross Books Pty Ltd 1527, **2003**
University of Alberta Press **2092**, 6104
Albion Press Ltd **3002**
Albion Publishing 6191
Albright-Knox Gallery 6139
Albums 1725
Albyn Press **1021**
ALCS **5029**
Alderney Books 6205
A Level Questions & Answers 1251
A Level Study Guides 1251
Jacintha Alexander Associates **4004**
Alexandria Press 1838
Alfaguara 6160
Alhambra Longman SA 1014
Alianza 6160
All about food series 3069
All Books for Children 1002, 6191
All India Traveller Book Seller 2255
Ian Allan Group Ltd 1022
Ian Allan Ltd **1022**, 6243
Ian Allan Publishing 6177
Philip Allan 1443
Allegretto Publications 6152
Allen Lane 6243
J. A. Allen & Co Ltd **1023**, 1793
Allen & Unwin 1876, 6181, 6194
Allen & Unwin Pty Ltd **2004**
Aller Leaser Service 1385
Alliance Music 1653
Alliance of Literary Societies **5018**
Allied Dunbar Board 1685
Allied Information Technologies Ltd 1625
Allied Mouse Ltd **1024**
Allied Newspapers Ltd 2431
Allison & Busby **1025**, 6162, 6243
Allworth Press 6131
Allyn & Bacon 1698
Alma House 6153
The Almanac Software Publishing Co 1016
Almo Music Inc 1466
Aloray Inc 1458
ALP Snc 2493
Alpha Press 6085, 6105, 6142
Alpha Sigma Pte Ltd **2424**
Alphabet & Image Ltd **3003**
Alphabooks 1089
Alpine Fine Art Books Ltd **1026**, 6205
Alpine Fine Arts Collection 1026
ALPSP 6202
Altamira Press Inc 1754
Altman Publications 6174
Alun Books 6258
Alvina Publishing House 2358
Alyson Publications 6152
Amacom 1542
Amadeus Press 1863
The Amaising Publishing House Ltd 1444, **1027**
Amalgam Publishing Co 6166
Amalgamated Book Services Ltd **6070**, 6146, 6243

Amanda Publications 6152
Edition de l'Amateur 1416
Amateur Winemaker Publications 6105
Frank Amato Publications Inc 1325
Ambar Parkashan **2260**, 2274, 2340
Ambe Books 2258
Amber Lane Press Ltd **1028**
Amecea Gaba Publications **2412**
University Press of America 6161
America West Distributors 6166
American Academy of Ophthalmology 1100
American Academy of Orthopaedic Surgeons 6161
American Association for Artificial Intelligence Press 1584
American Association of Cereal Chemists 1314
American Association of Orthopedic Surgery 6191
American Bible Society 1125
American Book Trade Directory **6320**
American Booksellers Association Convention & Trade Exhibit **6284**
American Chemical Society 1750, 6202
American College of Physicians 1100
American Conference of Governmental Industrial Hygienists 6182
American Contract Bridge League 1087
American Early Medieval Studies 1645
American Enterprise Institute 6161
American Federation of Astrologers 1325
American Guidance Services 1253
American Institute of Baking 1314
American Institute of Chemical Engineers (AIChE) 1458
American Institute of Physics 1648
American Library Association **1029**, 6161
American Library Directory **6321**
American Management Association 1705
American Map Corporation 1507, 1746
American Mathematical Society 1648
American Nostalgia Library 1393
American Psychiatric Press **1030**, 6161, 6191
American Psychological Association **1031**, 6161
American Public Health Association 1184, 6174
American Quilters Society 6176
American Society of Mechanical Engineers 1560
American Society of Microbiology 6181
American Society of Neurological Surgeons 6181
American Technical Publishers Inc 6166
American Trust Publications 6137
The American Welding Society 1925
Amerind Publishing Co Pvt Ltd **2261**, 2334
Amethyst Books 1339
AMG Publishers 6179
Amgueddfa Genedlaethol Cymru / National Museum of Wales 6258
Amnesty International International Secretariat **1032**, 6152
Ampersand Communications Inc **2093**
Galerie Amrad African Art 1050
Amrita Editions 1325
Amrita Prakashan 2338
AMS 6161
Amsterdam University Press 6104
An Gúm **2377**
Anako Editions 1922
The Analytic Press 1487
Analytical Chemistry by Open Learning/ Biotechnology by Open Learning (ACOL/ BIOTOL) 1010
Anand Paperbacks 2331, 2375
Ananda Publishers Pvt Ltd **2262**

Anarchist Classics Series 1328
Anatomical Chart Co 6166
Anaya Publishers Ltd 1207, 6145, 6160, 6243
Anchor Press 1053, 6140
Anchorage Press Inc 1224, 1493
Ancient History & Medieval Book Club **6274**
Ancient Indian Tradition & Mythology 2321
Andersen Artists (greetings cards) 1033
Andersen Press Ltd **1033**, 6199, 6243
Andersen Young Readers' Library 1033
Darley Anderson Literary, TV & Film Agency **4005**
Peter Andrew Publishing Co Ltd **1034**
Andromeda Interactive Ltd **1035**, 3004, 6180, 6182, 6243
Andromeda Oxford Ltd **3004**, 6180
Angel Books 6135
Angel City Press 6166
Angell Editions 6191
Anglia Multimedia 6243
Anglia Young Books 1583
Anglican Book Centre 1439
The Anglo-American Book Co Ltd **6136**
Anglo-Catalan Society 1794
The Anglo-Chinese Textbook Publishers Organization Ltd **5154**
Anglo-German Foundation for the Study of Industrial Society **1036**
Anglo-Pic Music Co Ltd 1466
Angus & Robertson Publishers 6166
Animals & their Ecosystems Series 1220
Ann Arbor Publishers Ltd **1037**
Ann Arbor Science 1145
Annals of Experimental and Clinical Medicine 1357
Anness Publishing Ltd **1038**
Anness Publishing Pty 1038
Annick Press Ltd 1719, **2094**, 6194
Annual Reviews Inc 6166
Annuals Publishing Ltd 6146, 6243
Annwn 6258
Anodyne Publishing Services 1325
Anthroposophic Press 1828
Antiquarian Publication & Reprographic Services Pvt Ltd 2265
Antique Collectors' Club Ltd **1039**
Antique Publications 6176
Anvil Books/Children's Press **2378**
Anvil Editions 1040
Anvil Press Poetry **1040**
ANWB 1447
ANY 1043
AP Information Services **1041**
APA Australian Book Fair **6285**
APA Insight Guides 6243
APAC Publishers Services **2481**
APB **6241**
Aperture Foundation 1379
Apex Book Distributors 2308
Apex Books Concern **6137**
Apex Press 1159
Apex Publishing 6095
Apollo Books 1416
Apollos 1461
APP (Academic Press Professional) 1005
Appa 1658
Apparitions Press 1835
Applause Books 1089, 6153
Apple Press 3051, 6167, 6243
Appleton-Century-Crofts 1698
Appleton & Lange 1698
Appletree Press Ltd **1042**, 6146, 6243
Applications 2449
APS 6153
Apsen 2034
Aquafitness 6243
Aquarian 1387, 6243

Aquarius Literary Agency & Picture Library **4006**
Aran Book Publishers 6152
ARC Edition 1416
Arcadia 1050, 6138, 6139
Arcania Press 6140
Arcania Publications 1053
Archaeological Yearbook 1215
Archaeology of Lincoln 1215
Archaeology of York 1215
Archibel SA 6191
Archipelago Press 2489
Architectural Association Publications **1043**
Architectural Book Publishers Co Inc 6166
Architectural Design 1006
Architectural Monographs 1006
Architecture Design & Technology Press (ADT) 1668
Archival Facsimiles Ltd **1044**
The Archive Photographs Series 1178
Archway 6243
Arco 1698
Arco Editorial 1050, 6138
Arctic World Series 1220
Ardmore & Beechwood Ltd 1466
ARE Press 6155
Areen Projects (Jersey) 1399
Arena 1052
Argus Books 6243
Argyll Publishing **1045**, 1444, 6243
Ariadne Press 6152
Aris & Phillips Ltd **1046**
University of Arizona Press 6181
Arkana 1661
Arkitektens Forlag 6071
Arlekin Wydawnictwo 1385
Arlington Books 6073, 6145, 6243
Armada 1387
Armour in Detail 1107
Arms & Armour Press **1047**, 1096, 1162, 1615, 6243
Armstrong Publishing Corp 1475
Arnette Blackwell 1094
Arnold **1048**, 1401, 1422, 1425, 6202
E. J. Arnold 6174
Edward Arnold Ltd 1424, 2040, 6146, 6243
Arnold Publishing Ltd **2095**
Arnolfini Gallery 6139
Jason Aronson 1503, 6161, 6175
Arrow Books Ltd **1049**, 1188, 1722, 6199, 6243
Ars Edition 6194
Ars Obscura 1813
Arsenal Pulp Press **2096**
Arsenale Editrice 1039
Art Address Verlag 1416
Art Books International **1050, 6138**
Art Data **6139**
Art & Design 1006
Art Direction Book Co 6122
Art Gallery of New South Wales 6139
Art Gallery of Nova Scotia 2142
Art Institute of Chicago 6139
Art Metropole 6139
Art of Painting on Silk 1783
Art Random 6139
Art Review 6152
Art Unlimited 1050, 6138
Artech House **1051**
Artemis Publishing **2005**
Article 19 6152
Artis 1050, 6138
Artists Associated Pty Ltd 2015
Artists Bookwork 6139
Artists' Choice Ltd **6273**
Arts Council of England 1871, **5019**
Arts Council of Wales **5020**

Arts Guild **6274**
Artulen 6243
Artus Books 1640
Arun Publishing House Pvt Ltd **2263**
AS 2079
AS Publishing **3005**
ASA Editions 6104
Ascherberg, Hopwood & Crew Ltd 1466
Asempa Publishers Christian Council of Ghana **2242**
Asgard Publishing Services **6002**
Ashgate-Gower Asia Pacific Pte Ltd 2482
Ashgate Publishing Asia Pacific Pte Ltd **2482**
Ashgate Publishing Group 1052, 2482
Ashgate Publishing Ltd **1052**, 1774
Ashgrove Distribution 1053
Ashgrove Press Ltd **1053, 6140**, 6243
Ashish Publishing House **2264**
Ashley Courtenay 6145
Ashmolean Museum Publications **1054**, 6166
Sh Muhammad Ashraf 6137
Ashton Scholastic 2079
Ashwood Medical 2024
ASI (Research) Ltd 1808
Asia 2000 Ltd **2248**
The Asia Collection 2490
Asia Pacific Press 2493
Asia Publishing House 1106
Asian Arts & Archaeology Series Office 2356
Asian Educational Press 1106
Asian Educational Services **2265**
Asian Health Press 1106
Asian Humanities Press 1922
Asian Publishers **2266**, 2328
Asiapac Books Pte Ltd **2483**, 6183
Aslan Publishing 1527, 1920
Aslib Directories 1055
Aslib Guide to Copyright 1055
ASLIB (The Association for Information Management) **1055, 5021**, 6182
ASP 1328
Aspen Gold Books 6166
Aspen Publishers 6191
Assess Your Child's Progress at Key Stage 2 1251
Assimil 6160
Associated Booksellers of Southern Africa **5176**
Associated Publishing House **2267**
Associated University Presses Inc 1348
Association Canadienne des Bibliothecaires de Langue Française **5141**
Association des Presses Universitaires Canadiennes **5140**
Association for Bahá'í Studies 1066
Association for Computing Machinery 6182
The Association for Information Management **5021**
Association for the Export of Canadian Books **5138**
Association Internationale de Bibliophilie **5002**
Association Management Press 6122
Association of American Petroleum Geologists 1341
Association of Art Historians **5022**
Association of Authors' Agents **5023**
Association of British Science Writers **5024**
Association of Canadian Publishers **5139**
Association of Canadian University Presses / Association des Presses Universitaires Canadiennes **5140**
Association of Christian Teachers of Wales 1290
Association of Commonwealth Universities (ACU) **1056**
Association of County Councils 1007

Association of Indian Universities **2268**
Association of Learned & Professional Society Publishers **5025**
Association of Little Presses **5026**
Association pour l'Avancement des Sciences et des Techniques de la Documentation **5141**
Editions Assouline 1050, 6138
ASTED Inc **5141**
At A Glance Self-folding Maps 1503, 6175
At Cost Travel Guides 2052
Athey Educational **1057**
The Athlone Press Ltd **1058**
Atlantic Disk Publishers 2153
Atlantic Europe Publishing Co Ltd **1059**, 1920, 3024
Atlantic Publishers & Distributors **2269**
Atlantic Transport Publishing 1022
Atlantis 6205
Atlanto Publishing 1491
Atlas Press 6135
Atlas Publishers (North West Province) 2517
Atrium Publishers Group 1920
Attainment Inc 1657
Attic Press Ltd **2379**
Attica Cybernetics 6243
Attwood & Binsted Ltd 1314
ATV Music 1466
Éditions Aubrey Walter 1347
Auburn House Publishing Co 1368, 6161
Auckland University Press 1648, **2432**
Auckland University Press/Bridget Williams Books 2432
Audio 1549
Audio Press 2401
Augener 1826
Augsburg 6181
Aukana 1922
Aura Books Plc **6141**
Aurelian Information Ltd **1060**
Aureus Editions (Editions Saint Michel) 1325
Sri Aurobindo Ashram Publication Department **2270**
Aurora Enterprises Ltd **6209**
Aurora Metro Publications 6152
Aurora Press 6135
Aurum Press **1061**, 6162, 6243
Auslib Press **2006**
Austed Publishing Co **2007**
Austen Cornish Publishers Ltd 1547
Austin & Winfield 6161
Austral 6160
Australian Academy of Science **2008**
Australian Books in Print 6322
Australian Bookseller & Publisher **6323**
Australian Booksellers Association **5129**
Australian Business Network 2072
The Australian Centre for Egyptology 1046
Australian Copyright Council **5130**
Australian Council for Educational Research (ACER) 1619, 1777, **2009**
Australian Doll Digest 6166
Australian Government Publishing Service 2010, **5131**
Australian Institute of Aboriginal and Torres Strait Islanders Studies 2001
Australian Institute of Criminology **2011**
Australian Large Print Audio & Video Pty Ltd **2012**
Australian Library & Information Association **5132**
Australian National Gallery 2061
Australian Publishers Association Ltd **5133**
Australian Scholarly Publishing **2013**
Australian Society of Authors Ltd **5134**
Australian Society of Indexers **5135**
The Author **6324**
Authors' Advisory Service **6003**

Authors' Club **5027**
Authors' Foundation **5028**
Authors' Licensing & Collecting Society
  (ALCS) **5029**
Authors' Marketing Services Ltd **4103**
Autobridge 1087
Automobile Association 1001, 1139
Autonomedia 6152
Ave Maria Press 1728
Avebury Aviation 1052
Avery Publishing Group 6207
Aviation Publications Inc 1019
Avo Books 1920
Avon Books **1062**
A Vos Marques Cassettes 1719, 6194
Award Publications Ltd **1063**
Axle Music Ltd 1466
M/S Ayaz Bookbinding Works 2479
La Azotea 1050, 6138

Babani Press 1065
Bernard Babani (Publishing) Ltd **1065**
Babbage Press (Local History) 1402
Babelcom 6166
Babhali Besiswati 2522
Audrey Babington's Workbox 6166
Babylon 1466
Back Roads (One Word) Guides 3022
Back to Basics 1251
Backpacking Guide Series 1117
Baen 1803
K. P. Bagchi & Co **2271**
Bahá'í Publications Canada 1066
Bahá'í Publishing Trust **1066**
Bahá'í Publishing Trust of Japan 1066
Bahá'í Verlag GmbH 1066
Bahri Publications **2272**
BAIE **5037**
Bailey Distribution Ltd **6142**
Bill Bailey Publishers' Representatives **6071**
Baillière Tindall **1067**, 1384, 2033, 6243
Bain & Cox, Publishers 2100
Duncan Baird Publishers 6180
W. G. Baird 1091
Baker Book House 1289, 1653
Balch Institute Press 1348
Balintore Holdings 1191
Jonathan Ball Publishers **2495**, 2497, 2514
Ballena Press 6085
Balloon Books 6145
Balnain Books **1068**
Baltimore Museum of Art 6139
The Banff Centre for Management 2108
The University Press Bangladesh 6085
Banking Technology Ltd 1440
Banmar Inc 6166
The Banner of Truth Trust **1069**
Bantam Australia 2085
Bantam Books (Canada) Inc / Doubleday
  Canada Ltd 1869
Bantam Doubleday Dell Publishing Group Inc
  1869, 2085
Bantam Press 1869, 6243
Baobab Books (Pvt) Ltd **2528**, 6069
BAPLA **5038**
Barbican Art Gallery 1050, 6138
Bard Graduate Centre 1039
Virginia Barder **6043**
Barebones Books 1680
Barefoot Beginners 1070
Barefoot Books **1070**, 6243
Barefoot Collections 1070
Bargain Book Sales **6210**
I Libri del Bargello 6166
Barnes & Noble Inc 6128
Paul Barnett Editorial **3007**
J. Barnicoat Ltd **6242**

Barnsley Chronicle Holdings Ltd 1660, 1906
Baron 1715
Barricade Books 1746
Barrie & Jenkins Ltd **1071**, 1188, 1722, 6243
Barrons 6154, 6243
Barrytown Ltd 6135
Bartholomew 1386, 1387, 6243
Barton House 6135, 6243
Basic Books 1503, 6175
Bastet Books 2216
Barnabe Riche Society in Early English Prose
  Fiction 2130
Bateleur Books (Northern Province) 2517
David Bateman Ltd 1050, **2433**, 6138
Bath University Press 6085
B. T. Batsford Ltd **1072**, 3035, 6243
Bauhaus Archive 6139
Colin Baxter Photography Ltd **1073**, 6243
Bay Books 2060
Bay View Books Ltd **1074**, 6105, 6142, 6243
Bayeux Publishers 6085
BBC Books **1075**, 1077, 6154, 6162, 6243
BBC Educational Publishing **1076**
BBC English **1077**, 6144
BBC Enterprises Ltd 1076
BBC for Business Videos 1449
BBC Music Guides 1630
BBC Publications 6095
BBC Radio Collection 1075
BBC Worldwide Ltd 1075
BBL Distribution Services Ltd **6143**
BCA **6274**
BCS Publishing Ltd **3008**
Be-Ma Editrice 1050, 6138
Beach Holme Publishers **2097**
Beacon Press 6135
Beaconsfield Publishers Ltd **1078**
Glenys Bean Literary Agency **4109**
Bear & Co 6135
Beaver Publishing Ltd **1079**, 6190
Beaverbrook Art Gallery 2142
BEBC Distribution **6144**
Peter Bedrick Books 1719, 6194
Beech Tree 6202
Beercan Books 1846
Beginners' Nature Guides 2434
Frederic Beil Publisher Inc 6166
Bekking & Blitz Uitgevers bv 6166
Belair Publications 1313, 2506
George Beldam Collection 6205
Belgrove Publishing 1022
Belitha Press Ltd **1080**, 1207, 6142
Bell Tower 1356
Bellevue Books 6166
Bellew Publishing **1081**, 6191
The Belmont Press **1082**
Belser 1668
Edition Belvedere 6145
Belvedere Fine Publishing Co 6166
Belwin Mills Publishing Corporation 1466
R. J. Bender Publishing 1319
Bender Richardson White **3009**
Benedictine Publications 2525
Benedikt Taschen 6153
Benefactum Publishing Ltd 6152
Benjamin/Cummings 1014, 2054
Ernest Benn 1089
David Bennett Books 1719, 6194
Benn's Media **6325**
E. F. Benson Society **5030**
Benteli Verlag 6139
Bera Dialogues 1591
Berg Publishers Ltd **1083**, 6145
Bergh Publishing Inc 6166
Berghahn Books 6191
Berghaus Oberauer Offset 6073
Bergin & Garvey 1368, 6161

Bergli Books AG 6166
Berkley Publishing Group 6108
Berkshire House Publishers 6166
Berkswell Illustrated Guides 3010
Berkswell Publishing Co Ltd **3010**
Irving Berlin (London) 1466
Berlinn Ltd 1444
Berlitz Publishing Co Inc 1084
Berlitz Publishing Co Ltd **1084**, 1614, 2506,
  6177, 6243
Bernan Press 1419
Bernards (Publishers) Ltd 1065
Berndtson & Berndtson (Maps) 1503
Berol Ltd 6146
Berrett-Koehler 1542
Bertram Books Ltd **6243**
Bespoke Audio Ltd 6146, 6243
Best Books for Public Libraries **6326**
Best Mailing Services Ltd **6072**
Best of New Zealand 2434
Better Homes & Gardens 2060
Better Yourself Books 1757
Betty Crocker 1803
Between the Lines **2098**
Beuth (The German Standards Institute) 1925
Beyond Words Publishing Inc 6155
BFI Publishing **1085**
BFP Books 1072
Bhaktivedanta Book Trust 6143
Bharat Law House Pvt Ltd **2273**
Bharat Publishing House 2260, 2273, **2274**,
  2340
Bhatkal Books International 2342
Bhatkal & Sen 2342
BHS Bridleways Publications 1023
Bible Reading Fellowship **1086**
Bible Society 1125, 6243
Bible Society in Northern Ireland 1125
Bibliagora 1087
Bibliographical Society 1648
Bibliographical Society of Canada **5142**
Bibliographisches Institut Mannheim 6160
Bibliography of British Newspapers 1128
Bibliolog **6327**
Bibliophile Books **6211**, **6275**
Bibliopolis 6104
Biblios Marketing Services **6073**
Biblios Publishers Distribution Services Ltd
  6145
Bibliotheque De L'image 1050
Bibliotheca Indo-Buddhica Series Office
  2304, 2356
Bibliothèque de l'Image 6138
Bibliotheque des Arts 1416
Bicycle Books Inc 6105, 6142, 6243
Big Books 1370
Big Database Publishing Pvt Ltd 2331, 2375
Big Pig Music Ltd 1466
Big Time 1378
Bilal Muslim Mission of Tanzania **2523**
Bild Publications 6191
Bilingual Education & Bilingualism 1591
Billboard Books 6131
Clive Bingley Ltd 1524
Binsted Frères SA 1314
Biochemical Society 1697
BioCommerce Data 6182
Biodiversity 2000 1723
Biography Press 6191
Biography & Self Development 1396
Birch Lane Press 1158
Birlinn Ltd **1088**
Edition Galerie Bruno Bischofberger 1050,
  6138
Biscuit Music 6145
Bishen Singh Mahendra Pal Singh **2275**
BLA Publishing Ltd 1898, **3011**

Black Ace Books **1090**
Black Ace Enterprises 1090
Black Butterfly Children's Books 1930
Black Cat Press Ltd 6152
Black Dagger Crime 1190
A. & C. Black (Publishers) Ltd 1015, **1089**, 1412, 6243
Black Pudding Press 6152
Black Rose Books Ltd 1159, **2099**, 6152
Black Sparrow Press 6135
Black Spring Press 6135
Black Swan 1869
Blackberry Books 6152
Blackie 1611, 1661, 6243
Blackie Academic & Professional 1184
Blackie Educational 6174
Blackie Scientific 6174
Blacklace 1890
Blackstaff Press Ltd **1091**
Blackstone Press Ltd **1092**, 1116, 1251
Blackwater Press **2380**
Blackwell Business 6181
Blackwell Journals 1093
Blackwell Polity 1093
Blackwell Publishers Inc 1093
Blackwell Publishers Ltd 1093, 6181, 6243
Blackwell Science (Australia) Pty Ltd 1094
Blackwell Science Inc 1094
Blackwell Science Japan 1094
Blackwell Science Ltd 1094, 2014, 6181, 6243
Blackwell Science Pty Ltd 1094, **2014**
Blackwell Wissenschafts-Verlag 1094
Blake Friedmann Literary Agency Ltd **4007**
Blake Publishing Ltd **1095**, 6145, 6166, 6243
Blaketon Hall Ltd **6212**
Blandford Press 1047, **1096**, 1162, 1615, 1892, 6243
Editions Blay 1507
The Blew Blanket Library 1536
BLH Publishers' Distributors Pvt Ltd 2273
Blizzard Publishing **2100**, 6166
Bloodaxe Books Ltd **1097**, 6243
Roy Bloom Ltd **6213**
Bloomsbury Publishing Ltd 6162, 6243
Bloomsbury Publishing Plc **1098**
Bloomsbury/Warne 6243
Blue Dolphin Publishing Inc 1325
Blue Guides 1089
Blue Moon Books 6207
Blue Poppy Press 6155
Blueprint **1099**, 6152, 6174
Blueprint Monographs 1324
Bluffers Guides 1725
BMJ Publishing Group **1100**
BMMR 6174
BMP **1101**
BNA International 6182
Boardwalk 6104
Boatswain Press Ltd 1559
Bobcat Books 1630
The Bodley Head Ltd 1188, 1721, 1722, 6243
Bogle-L'Ouverture Press Ltd 6152
Bok & Bibliotek **6286**
Bolinda Audio 2012
Bolinda Press 2012
David Bolt Associates **4008**
Bonacci Editore 6160
Frances Bond Literary Services **4114**
Sandra Bondhus 6176
Bonfini Art Books 6131
Bonnie Gaunt 1218
Bonnington Books 1474
Bonus Books Inc 6166
Book Aid International (Ranfurly Library Service) **5031**
Book and Periodical Council **5143**
Book Club of Ireland **6274**

Book Connections 1363
Book Creation Services Ltd **6023**
Book Data Ltd **1102**, 6151, 6182
The Book Depot **6074**
Book Express 2206
Book Guild 1103
The Book Guild Ltd **1103**, 6205
Book House Training Centre **6391**
Book Industry Communication **5032**
Book Makers 2346
Book Marketing Ltd **6075**
Book News Inc **6328**
Book of the Breed 1740
Book of the Month Club **6274**
Book Packagers Association **5033**
Book Packaging and Marketing **3012**
Book Print (London) **6287**
Book Production Consultants Plc 1363, 1608, **6024**
Book Publishers' Association of New Zealand Inc **5162**
Book Publishing Co 6135
Book Rat **2107**
Book Representation and Distribution Ltd (BRAD) **6076**
The Book Shop Ltd (Retailers) 2410
Book Trade Benevolent Society **5034**
Book Trade Services Remainder & Promotional Books (Frankfurt) **6288**
Book Traders (Caribbean) Ltd (Distributors) 2410
Book Trust **5035**
Bookcraft Ltd **6069**
Bookking International 1050, 6138
Booklink **6077**
Bookman Projects Ltd **1104**, 6145
Bookmark International **6214**
Bookmarks **1105**
Bookmarks Chicago 1105
Bookmarks Club **6276**
Bookmarks Melbourne 1105
Bookmart Ltd **6215**, 6243
Bookpoint Ltd **6146**
Bookprint Consultants Ltd 2444
Books Americana Inc 6166
Books Continental Ltd **6078**
Books Direct **6274**
Books Exports **6216**
Books for All 2288
Books for Children **6277**
Books for Keeps **6329**
Books from India (UK) Ltd **1106**
Books in English (*microfiche*) 1129
Books in Print **6330**
Books in the Media **6331**
Books in Wales / Llais Llyfrau **6332**
Books International **1107**
Books International (Poland) 1107
Books Ireland **6333**
Books on Disk 2153
Books UK Ltd **1108**
The Bookseller **6334**
Booksellers and Publishers Association of Zambia (BPAZ) **5180**
Booksellers Association Annual Conference **6289**
Booksellers Association Directory of Members **6335**
Booksellers Association of Great Britain and Ireland **5036**
Booksellers New Zealand **5163**
Books & Toys Ltd **6224**
BookTrack Ltd 1909
Bookwatch Ltd **6079**
Bookworld Services Inc 6166
Bookworld Wholesale **6244**
Bookworm Book Club **6278**

Boolarong Press **2015**
Boosey & Hawkes Inc 1109
Boosey & Hawkes Music Publishers Ltd **1109**, 6145
Boosey & Hawkes Musikverlag 1109
Boosey & Hawkes Plc 1109
Booth-Clibborn Editions **1110**
Bootstrap Press 1159
Bootstrap & Apex Press 6152
Pierre Bordas & fils 6160
Editions du Boréal **2101**
Boréal Compact 2101
Boréal Express 2101
Boréal Inter 2101
Boréal Junior 2101
Borealis Press Ltd **2102**
Bossiney Books **1111**
The Boston Mills Press **2103**
Bote & Bock 1109
Boulevard 6152
Boundary Books 6205
Bounty 2208
Bounty Books 1730, 6243
Bourne Music Ltd 1466
Bow Wow Books 1360
Delian Bower Publishing **3013**
Bowerdean Publishing 6152
R. R. Bowker 1112
The Bowker Annual Library and Book Trade Almanac **6336**
Bowker-Saur **1112**, 6151, 6182
Bowker/Whitaker Global Books in Print Plus **6352**
Bowmar Publications 1466
Boxtree **1113**, 6071, 6177, 6243
Marion Boyars Publishers Inc 1114
Marion Boyars Publishers Ltd **1114**, 6142
Boydell & Brewer Inc 1115
Boydell & Brewer Ltd **1115**, 6095, 6243
boyd & fraser 6174
BPIF **5044**
BPL 6167
BPL Remainders Ltd **6217**
BPP Holdings Plc 1116, 1251
BPP (Letts Educational) Ltd 1116
BPP Publishing Ltd **1116**, 1251, 6243
B R Publishing Corporation 2288
A. C. Braby **2496**
Braby's Business Directories **2496**
Bracken Books 1837, 6167
Bracken Publishing 1216, 6205
Bradbury Wood 1466
Bradford Books 1584
Bradford Technology Ltd 1139
Henry Bradshaw Society 1115
Bradt Publications **1117**, 1824, **6147**, 6243
Brady 1698
Bramble Books US 6136
Bramcote Press 6085
Brampton Publications 1766
Branden Publishing Co 6166
Brandon Book Publishers Ltd **2381**, 6201
Graham Brash Pte Ltd **2484**, 6166
Brassey Sports 6243
Brassey (UK & US) Ltd 1118
Brassey's Inc (Washington) 1118
Brassey's (UK) Ltd **1118**, 6181, 6202
Braus **6139**
George Braziller 1039
Breakwater Books Ltd **2104**
Nicholas Brealey Publishing Ltd **1119**, 6199, 6243
Nicholas Bredey Publishing 1449
Breedon Books Publishing Co Ltd **1120**
Breese Books Collector's Series 1121
Breese Books Ltd **1121**
Brefi Press 6258

Breslich & Foss Ltd **3014**
Breton Books 2142
D. S. Brewer 1115
Brick Books **2105**
Bridge Book Club 1087
The Bridge Book Co Ltd **6218**
Bridge Books **1122**, 6258
Bridge Publications 1613
Bridge World 1087
Briefings 1114
Brigantia Monographs 1843
Bright Careers Institute **2276**
Bright Careers Ltd 2276
Bright Distributing Co 2276
Bright Media Impex (P) Ltd 2276
Bright Music Ltd 1466
E. J. Brill 6137
Brilliant Publications **1123**
Brimax Books **1124**, 1730, 6243
Bristol Classical Press 1255
Bristol Publishing Enterprises Inc 6166
University of Bristol Press 1857
Britain Books 6166
Britannia Crest 6146
Britannia Press 1262, 6243
Britannica Book of the Year 1278
Britannica Software Inc 6182
British Academic Press 1850
British Academy 1648
British Agencies for Adoption & Fostering
    1126
British Association for Local History 1671
British Association of Communicators in
    Business **5037**
The British Association of Picture Libraries and
    Agencies (BAPLA) **5038**
British Bus Publishing 1687
British Consultants Bureau (BCB) 1419
British & Continental Music Agencies Ltd
    1466
British Copyright Council **5039**
British Council **5040**
British Deaf Association 6166
British Fantasy Society **5041**
British Film Institute 1085, **5042**, 6191
British & Foreign Bible Society **1125**
British Geotechnical Society 1853
The British Guild of Travel Writers **5043**
The British Institute of Archaeology at Ankara
    1645
British Institute of Radiology 6205
British Library 1127, 1128, 6151, 6182, 6202
British Library, Document Supply Centre
    1127
British Library, Humanities & Social Sciences
    1128
British Library, National Bibliographic Service
    1129
British Library Occasional Papers 1128
The British Library, Public Services Publishing
    1130
The British Library, Science Reference &
    Information Service **1131**
The British Library Studies in the History of the
    Book 1128
British Medical Association 1100
British Medical Journal 1100
British Mountaineering Council 6243
British Museum Press **1132**, 1855, 6243
British Museum Publications Ltd 1132
British National Bibliography 1129
British National Film & Video Guide 1129
British Nuclear Energy Society 1853
British Printing Industries Federation (BPIF)
    5044
British Psychological Society (BPS Books)
    1133, 6191, 6202

British Railways Series 1241
The British School at Rome 1645
The British School of Archaeology in Egypt
    1046
British School of Archaeology in Iraq 1645
British Small Animal Veterinary Association
    (BSAVA) 1557
British Standards Institution **5045**
British Tourist Authority 1001, **1134**
Broadcast Book Services 6145
Broadcast Books 1269, 1444
Broadview Press Ltd **2106**
Brockhampton Press Ltd **6219**, 6243
Brockhaus 6160
Andrew Brodie Publications 6243
Broken Jaw Press/M. A. Productions **2107**
The Brontë Society **5046**
Brooke Publications Ltd **6004**
Brookers 2050
Paul H. Brookes 1498, 1502
Brookline Books 1253
Brooklyn Museum of Art 6139
Brooks Cole 6174, 6243
Brooks Waterloo 2046
Broomtail Publications 1154
Brotherhood of Life 1233
de Brouwer & Melkman Publishing 1744
Trevor Brown Associates **6148**
Brown Books 3015, 6145
Karen Brown Guides 1824
Brown Packaging (Books) Ltd **3015**
John Brown Publishing 6199, 6243
Brown Watson Ltd **1135**
Brown Wells & Jacobs Ltd **3016**
The Browning Society **5047**
Brown, Son & Ferguson, Ltd **1136**
D. Brown & Sons 6258
Bruce Smith Books Ltd **1137**
Bruguera 6160
Brunner/Mazel Publishers **6157**
The Bruschettini Foundation 1648
Felicity Bryan **4009**
BSA/CML Bookshop **1138**
b small publishing 1886, **3006**, 6128
BTEC 1685
BTL Publishing **1139**, 6243
Buchu Books 6069
Bill Buckley Music 1466
Rosemarie Buckman **4010**
Bucknell University Press 1348
Bucks Music 1466
Buddhadhamma Foundation 1922
Buddhist Publication Society 1922, 2520,
    6104
Buddhist Publication Society Inc **2519**
Buddhist Publishing Group 1922
The Buddhist Society 1922
Buddhist Tradition Series 2321
Budo-Store 1225
The Building Services Research & Information
    Association **1140**, 6182
Building & Construction Books 6174
Buildings of England, Ireland, Scotland and
    Wales 1661
Bulfinch 1528, 2506
Bull Publishing 6166
Bulletin 1452
Burall Ltd 1311
Burchell & Martin Ltd **6260**
Bureau Development Inc 6182
Bureau of Business Practice 1698
Bureau van Dijk 6182
Burke's Peerage 6146
Burlington Music Co Ltd 1466
Burns & Oates Ltd **1141**, 1783
Diane Burston **4011**

Burston Distribution Services **6149**
Bus Enthusiast Publishing Co 1687
Bush Films 2434
Bush Pictorials 2434
The Bush Press **2434**
Bush Press Communications Ltd 2434
Bush Press Production 2434
Bushwood Books **6150**
Business Books Direct 6144
Business Education Publishers **1142**
Business English Video Magazine 1464
Business Information Books 2427
Business & Professional Publishers Pty Ltd
    6166
Business Ratio Plus 1442
Business Terms (Pocket Books) 1464
Butcherbest Ltd 1221
Butterfingers **1144**, 6243
Butterworth-Heinemann **1145**, 2208, 2499,
    6182, 6243
Butterworth-Heinemann Business 2208
Butterworth Medical 1145
Butterworth Overseas Subsidiary Companies
    1145
Butterworth Scientific 1145
Butterworths **2016**, 2208
Butterworths Ltd **1146**
Butterworths of New Zealand Ltd **2435**
Buying a Home in... Guides 6175
Buzz Books 1407, 1730, 2208, 6243
B & W Publishing Ltd **1064**
Byron Douglas Publications 1466
The Byron Society **5048**

CA 2011
CAB INTERNATIONAL **5003**
Caddo Gap Press 6085
Cadogan Books Plc **1147**, 6167
Cadogan Bridge Books 1147
Cadogan Chess Books 1072, 1147
Cadogan Guides 1147, 6243
Cadogan Pergamon Chess 1147
Caduceus Press 1023
Cadw 6258
Cairo International Book Fair **6290**
Calabria Press 1328
Randolph Caldecott Society **5049**
The Calder Educational Trust 1148
John Calder Ltd 6153
Calder Publications Ltd **1148**
Calderbooks Paperbacks 1148
Calendar Makers Corp 2309
University of Calgary Press **2108**
California University Press 1915
The University Presses of California, Columbia
    & Princeton Ltd **6204**
Calmann & King Ltd 1496, **3017**
Cambax Publishing 6197
Cambridge Academic 6243
Cambridge CD-ROM Ltd **6151**
University of Cambridge – Dept of Land
    Economy 1363
Cambridge International Publishers 1633
Cambridge Multimedia Systems Plc **6044**
Cambridge Publishing Group 6243
Cambridge University Press 1125, **1149**, 2017,
    6151, 6243
Cambridge University Press Australian Branch
    2017
Cambridgeshire Records Society 1843
Cambrix Publishing Ltd 1592
Camden House 1115
Camerapix **2413**, 6167
Cameron Books **3018**
Cameron & Hollis 3018
Camouflage and Markings 1107
Campaign for Real Ale Ltd 1152

Campbell Books **1150**, 1543, 6243
David Campbell Publishers 1147, **1151**
Campbell Thomson & McLaughlin Ltd **4012**
Campden Food Preservation Research Association 1314
Campion Press 2034
Camra Books **1152**, 1886, 6128, 6243
CAMRA (Campaign for Real Ale) 1886
Canada Communication Group — Publishing **2109**, 6182
The Canada Council **5144**
Canada & International Relations 2230
Canada Law Book 2135
Canada Publishing Corporation 2139, 2173
Canadian Almanac & Directory Publishing Co 6122
Canadian Archival Inventory Series 2108
Canadian Authors Association **5145**
Canadian Book Publishers Council **5146**
Canadian Book Review Annual **6337**
Canadian Booksellers Association **5147**
Canadian Centre for Occupational Health & Safety 6182
Canadian Centre for Studies in Publishing **6392**
The Canadian Children's Book Centre **5148**
Canadian Children's Classics 2203
Canadian Energy Research Institute 2108
Canadian Golf Press Inc 2234
Canadian Healthcare Association 2116
Canadian Institute of Resources Law Series 2108
The Canadian Institute of Strategic Studies (CISS) **2111**
Canadian Institute of Ukrainian Studies Press **2110**
Canadian ISBN Agency **5149**
Canadian Library Association 1524, **5150**
Canadian Museum of Civilization 1746, **2112**
Canadian Poetry Association: Bookclub 2153
Canadian Radio Drama Series 2203
Canadian Scholars' Press **2113**
Canadian Social History 2169
Canal & Stamperia 1039
Candle Books 1653
Candlewick Press Inc 1896
J. S. Canner 1689
Cannon International **2485**
Canoe Press UWI 2408
Canolfan Adnoddau CPC Aberystwyth / UCW Aberystwyth Resources Centre 6258
Canolfan Astudiaethau Iaith / Language Studies Centre 6258
Canolfan Genedlaethol Addysg Grefyddol / Welsh National Centre for Religious Education 6258
Canongate Audio 1153
Canongate Books **1153**, 6243
Canongate Classics 1153
Canongate Kelpies 1153
Canplay 2216
Canterbury Press Norwich 1439
Canterbury University Press **2436**
Canterbury & York Society 1115
Edition Cantz 6139
Capall Bann Publishing **1154**
Cape Distribution 2067
Jonathan Cape Ltd 1188, 1722, 6243
Capital Transport Publishing 1687
Capscan 6182
The Carbery Press 1323
Carcanet Press Ltd **1155**, 6177, 6243
Cardiff Academic Press **1156**
Cardoza Publications 1627
Care Concern Handbook Series 1394
Better Care Guides 1394

Carey Publications 1289
The Caribbean Law Publishing Co Ltd 2409
Carleton Contemporary Series 2114
Carleton Library Series 2114
Carleton Renaissance Plays — in Translation Series 2130
Carleton University Press **2114**
Carlin Music Corporation 1466, 1825
Carlong Assessment Tests Series 2406
Carlong Practice Papers for Common Entrance Series 2406
Carlong Primary Social Studies Series 2406
Carlong Publishers (Caribbean) Ltd **2406**
Carlsen 6160
Carlton Books Ltd 1098, **1157**, 6243
Carlton Communications Plc 1157
Carol Publishing Group **1158**, 6071, 6145, 6207
Carolina Biological Supply Co Inc 1649
Carousel — the Guide to Children's Books **6339**
Jon Carpenter Publishing **1159**, 6152
Carrick Media **1160**
Carroll & Graf 6207
Daresbury Lewis Carroll Society **5050**
Carswell Co of Canada 6174
Cartermill 1659, 6151, 6170, 6182
Cartwight Omni Corporation 2135
Cary & Co 1466
Casarotto Co Ltd **4013**, 4067
Casarotto Marsh Ltd 4013
Casarotto Ramsay Ltd 4013, **4014**
Case Studies for Practice 1498
Cassandra Press 6135
Frank Cass & Co Ltd **1161**, 6145
Cassell 1047, 1096, 1162, 1615, 1673, 1892, 6243
Cassell Educational 1162
Cassell Plc 1047, 1096, **1162**, 1182, 1349, 1431, 1516, 1556, 1590, 1615, 1681, 1892, 1897
Cassell Publishers 1162
Castalia 6160
Castell Computer & Systems Telecommunications Ltd **6045**
Casterman 6160
Castle Communications 1661, 6243
Castle Kent Associates 6166
Castle Publications 6258
Castlemain Books **1163**
Castlemead Publications **1164**
Catedra 6160
Catesby Press (Historical Novels) 1402
Kyle Cathie Ltd **1165**, 6177
Catholic Communications Institute of Ireland 2404
Catholic Institute for International Relations 6152
The Catholic Truth Society **1166**
Catholic University of America Press 6161
John Catt Educational Ltd 1433
Causeway Press Ltd **1167**
Cavalcade Story Cassettes 1190
Godfrey Cave Associates **6220**, 6243
Godfrey Cave Holdings Ltd 1661
Paul Cave Publications Ltd **1168**
Cavendish Publishing (Australia) Pty Ltd 1169
Cavendish Publishing Ltd **1169**
Caversham Printing & Publishing 2496
CBA Research Reports 1215
CBD Research 1170
CBD Research Ltd **1170**
CCBI Publications **1171**
CCH Canadian Ltd **2115**
CCH Editions Ltd **1172**
CCH/FM Ltée 2115
CCH Inc 1172

CD Pubco Inc **6046**
CD-ROM Directory 95 **6340**
CD Specialties 6166
CEC Information Market Observatory (IMO) reports 1055
Cedar 1730
Cedar Tree House **6080**
Cedco Calendars 6073
Cedco Publishing 6145
Celestial Arts 6135
Centaur 2499
Centaur Communications Ltd 1526
Centenary Series 1328
Center for Creative Photography 6139
Center Press 6136
Central African Correspondence College (Pvt) Ltd 2532
Central Asian Studies 1046
Central Books **6152**, 6243
The Central Bureau **1173**, 1503, 6243
Central European University Press **1174**
Central Tanganyika Press **2524**
Central TV 1871
Centre d'Arts Plastiques Contemporains 6139
Centre for Alternative Technology 1444
Centre for Applied Research in Education 1698
Centre for Economic Policy Research **1175**
Centre for Information on Language Teaching & Research **1176**
The Centre for Interfirm Comparison **6081**
Centre for Policy on Ageing 6142
Centre for Professional Development (Australia) Pty Ltd 2050
The Centre for Publishing Studies **6393**
Centre for Social Research 6069
Centre Georges Pompidou 6139
Centro Di 1050, 6138
Century 22 1886, 6128
Century Publishing Co Ltd 1188, 1722, 6243
CENWOR (Centre for Women's Research) 2520
Cerved International 6182
CESA 5 1619
CHA Press **2116**
Chadwyck-Healey Ltd **1177**, 6151, 6170, 6182
Chalcott Marketing 6152
The Chalford Publishing Co Ltd **1178**
Chalksoft Ltd **1179**, 1791
Chambers 1506, 6243
Chambers-Macmillan Dictionaries 2522
Chambers & Partners 6145
Chancellor 1382
Chancellor Publications Ltd 1793
Chancerel International Publishers Ltd **1180**
Chancery House Press 1170
Chancery Law Publishing Ltd 1915
Channel 4 Learning **1181**
Channel Tunnel at a Glance 6175
Channel View Publication 1591
Chansitor Publications Ltd 1439
Geoffrey Chapman 1162, **1182**
Paul Chapman Publishing Ltd **1183**, 6191, 6243
Chapman & Hall Ltd 1099, **1184**, 1724, 1821, 6174, 6182
Chapmans **1185**, 1639, 1640, 6177, 6243
Chappell-Aznavour Ltd 1466
Chappell-Morris Ltd 1466
Chappell Music Ltd 1466
Chappell Plays Ltd 1466
Character Colour/Activity 1929
Character Publishing 6153
Charities Address Book–UK 1060
Charities on Disk 1060
The Charlton Press **2117**
Charming Small Hotel Guides 3022

Charnwood Hardback Series 1862
Chart Books 6162
Charta 1050, 6138, 6139
Chartered Institute of Bankers 1685
The Chartered Institute of Public Finance &
    Accountancy 1186
Chartered Insurance Institute 1363
Chartered Society of Designers 1737
Chartwell-Bratt (Publishing & Training) Ltd
    1187
Chase Production Services 6025
Chatham House Publishers 1746, 6153
Chatham Publishing 1255
Chatto & Windus Ltd 1188, 1722, 6243
Zelda Cheatle Press 6138
Cheerman Ltd 6152
Chelsea Football Club 6095
Chelsea Green Publishing Co 1365, 6152
Cheltenham Festival of Literature 6291
Chemical Abstracts Service 6182
Chemical Publishing Co Inc 1314
ChemTec Publishing 2118
Les Editions de la Chenelière 2119
Chenelière/McGraw-Hill 2119
Cherokee Literacy Agency 4115
Cherry Lane Music Inc 1466
Cherrytree Press Ltd 1190
Cheshire Publishing 2054
Chetana (Bombay) 1106
University of Chicago Press 1915, 6243
Chick Publications 6179
Child Poverty Action Group 6152
Children in Charge 1498
Children's Book Circle 5051
Children's Book of the Month Club 6274
Children's Book Trust 2277
Children's Book Week 6292
Children's Books History Society 5052
Children's Books in Print 6341
Children's Britannica 1278
Children's Britannica Yearbook 1278
The Children's Guides to New Zealand Nature
    2434
Children's Large Print Galaxy 1190
Children's Picture Books 1033
Children's Society 6152
Children's Writers & Illustrators Group 5053
Child's Play (International) Ltd 1189, 6243,
    6258
Chilton Book Co 1072
China Library 1229
The Chinese University Press 2249
Chiriotti Editori Srl 1314
Chiron Publications 1487, 6135
Chivers Press Ltd 1190, 6243
Chocolate World 1491
Choices 2449
Choose Your Own Adventure 1869
Chopsticks Publications Ltd 6166
Chowkhamba Sanskrit Series Office 2278
Christian Booksellers' Association (NZ
    Chapter) 5164
Christian Booksellers Convention 6293
Christian Classics Inc 1793
Christian Focus Publications 1191
Christian Medical Fellowship 1461
Christian Research Association 1192
Chronicle Books 2279, 6243
Chronicle Group of Publications 2279
Chronicle Publications (P) Ltd 2279
Chronosports 6205
Chugh Publications 2280
Chuoshuppan-Sha 1757
Church House Publications 1439
Church House Publishing 1193
Church of Scotland Stationery 1756

Church of Scotland's Board of Communication
    1756
Churchill Livingstone 1194, 1659, 2068, 6182,
    6243
Churchill Livingstone Inc 1194
Ciana Ltd 6294
Cicerone Press 1195
Cimino Publishing Group Inc 6166
Cimtech 1414
Cin-Dav Inc 6166
Circle of Wine Writers 5054
Circustuff 1144
Cirone Publications 1466
CIS 6170
Citadel Press 1158
CITIS Ltd 2382, 6170
City Lights 6135
Civil Liberties Trust 6152
Claiborne Publications 1196
Clarabella Music Ltd 1466
Claremont 1661
Clarendon Press 1648
Clarion 1272
Clarion Books 2281, 2300
Clarity English Software 6144
Philip Clark Ltd 3019
Robin Clark 1711, 6191
T. & T. Clark 1197
Clark Boardman Callaghan 6174
Clark, Lawrence Publishers 6197
James Clarke 1199
Serafina Clarke 4015
Clarke Associates – Europe Ltd 6082
Anthony Clarke Books 1198
James Clarke & Co 1199, 1538
I. E. Clarke Inc 1224
Nigel J. Clarke Publications 1200
Class Publishing 1201, 6191
E. W. Classey Ltd 1202
Classic Collection 1323
Classical Association 1648
Classical Music Direct 6274
Classical Press of Wales 1255
Classical Texts 1046
CLB Publishing Ltd 3020
CLE International 6160
Clear Light Publishers 6166
Clear Point Press 1922
R. J. Cleary 2018
Clematis Press 1236
Clemis Group Ltd 1267
Mary Clemmey Literary Agent 4016
Clever Clogs 1409
Cliff College Publishing 1588
Cliffs Notes Inc 6166
Clinical Neuroscience 6174
Clinical Press 6166
Clio Press 6191
Cló Iar-Chonnachta 2383
Clothes and Crafts series 3069
Cloverleaf 1291
Jonathan Clowes Ltd 4017
William Clowes (Publishers) Ltd 1439
CLT Professional Publishing 1203
Clunie Press 1487
CMC Publishing 6166
CMC ReSearch Inc 6182
CNA Gallo 2499
C/- Network Distributors 1385
CNS Publications 1724
C.O.N.DOMS Series 1725
Coach House Press Inc 2120
Coachwise Ltd 1204
Cobble & Mickle Books 6166
Elspeth Cochrane Agency 4018
Coco Creations 2298
Richard Cohen 6162, 6243

Lloyd Cole 1205
Cole Group 6243
Colegio de España 6160
Cole & Whurr Ltd 1913
Colgems-EMI Music Ltd 1466
Armand Colin 6160
Rosica Colin Ltd 4019
Colleagues Press 1115
Collected Papers on South Asia 1229
Collector Books 6176
Collector Grade Publications 1816
College Press Publishers (Pvt) Ltd 1547, 2529
Peter Collin Publishing Ltd 1206, 6181
Collins 1387, 6151
Collins Bibles 1387
Collins & Brown 1080, 1207, 6145, 6243,
Collins Cartographic 1386, 1387
Collins Classics 1387
Collins COBUILD 1387
Collins Crime 1387
Collins Dove, Australia 1387
Collins English Dictionaries 1387
Collins Harvill 1392
Collins Liturgical 1387
Collins Longman 1386, 1387
Collins Natural History 1387
Collins New Naturalist Library 1387
CollinsEducational 1387
CollinsGems 1387
CollinsWillow 1387
Colman Getty Ltd 6083
Colonial Williamsburg 1039
Colorado University Press 6166
Colour Library Books Ltd 3020
Colporteur 6152
Colt Books 6243
Columba 2384
The Columba Press 2384
Columbia Books Inc 6122
Columbia Pictures Publications 1466
Columbia University Press 1915
Franco Columbo 1466
Combined Book Services 1366, 6153
Comedia Publications 6152
Comerford, Miller & Associates 6152
CoMet Verlag 1016
Comhairle nan Leabhraichean / The Gaelic
    Books Council 5055
The Comic Book Price Guide (Price Guide
    Productions) 1308
Commentary 1451
Commerce Clearing House Inc 2115
The Commercial Press (Hong Kong) Ltd 2250
The Commercial Press International Co Ltd
    2250
The Commercial Press (Singapore) Ltd 2250
Commission of the European Communities
    2389
Common Knowledge Press 1159
Commonwealth Publications Inc 2121
Community Health Foundation 6152
Companion Press 6166
Compass Press 2012
Compass Star Publications 6243
The Complete Directory of Large Print Books
    and Serials 6342
Comprehensive 2186
Compton's Interactive Encyclopaedia 1278
Computational Engineering Services 1208
Computational Mechanics International Ltd
    1208
Computational Mechanics Publications 1208
Computer Library 6170, 6182
Computer Science Press 1329
Computer Technology Research Corp 6159
Computerized Interactive Tutorials (CITs)
    2186

Conari Press 6135
Concept Publishing Co **2282**
Concord Publications Co 1366
Concorde 6146
Condor Books 1815
The Confederation of Information
    Communication Industries **5056**
Conference of European Churches 1171
Conflict 1396
Conflict Studies 1733
Congressional Information Service 6182
Connections 6108
The Joseph Conrad Society (UK) **5057**
Conran Octopus **1209**, 1730, 2208, 6243
Conservative Central Office 1210
Conservative Political Centre **1210**
The Consortium 6152
Constable & Co Ltd **1211**, 2506, 6199, 6243
Consultants Bureau 1689
Consumers Association 1661
Consumers Association Penang 6152
Contact Illustration Agents 1270
Contact Illustrators 1270
Contact Photographers 1270
Contemporary Books Inc 6166
The Content Co Inc **4028**
Context 6151, 6170, 6182
Continental Publications 1613
Continuing Education Press 6085, 6142
Continuum Publishing Co 1773
Continuum Publishing Group 1746
Controversies and Dilemmas Series 1751
Jane Conway-Gordon **4020**
Conway Maritime Press 1118, 6181, 6243
Conway Printers Pvt Ltd 2302
David C. Cook 1499
Thomas Cook Rail Maps 1507
Leo Cooper 1660, 6243
Cooper Dale **6026**
Copp Clark Ltd **2122**
Copper Beech Publishing Ltd **1212**
The Copyright Licensing Agency Ltd **5058**
Copyrights America Inc 4021
Copyrights Australasia (Pty) Ltd 4021
The Copyrights Co (Europe) Ltd 4021
The Copyrights Co (UK) Ltd **4021**
The Copyrights Group Ltd 4021
Copyrights Japan Ltd 4021
Copytrain **6005**
Cora Verlag AG 2148
Cora Verlag GmbH & Co 1385
Coral Cay Conservation 1723
Ivan Corbett Publishing **1213**, 6258
Cordee 6243
Corel Systems Corp. 6182
Corgi 1869
Cork University Press **2385**, 6152
Cormorant Books Inc **2123**
Cornelius Books 1507
Cornell University Press 6191
Cornelsen-Velhagen & Klasing 6160
Cornerhouse (Trade Counter) 6071
Cornerstone Press 1835
Cornish Connection 1053, 6140
Cornwall Books 1348
Coronet 1423, 6243
Corpus Information Services 2221
Corpus of British Medieval Library Catalogues
    1128
Corpus of Spanish Drawings 1580
Corpus Rubenianum Ludwig Burchard 1580
Cortina Learning International Inc 6166
Corwin Press Inc 1754
Cosmo Dictionaries 2283
Cosmo Key Facts 2283
Cosmo Publications **2283**
Cosmopolitan Book House 2283

Costa Rica Books 6166
Coteau Books **2124**
Cottage Publications **1214**
Michael E. Coughlin 1328
Council for British Archaeology **1215**
Council for the Development of Science and
    Technology (CODESRIA) 6069
Council Oak Books 1365
Council of Academic and Professional
    Publishers **5059**
Council of Churches for Britain & Ireland
    1171
Council of Europe 1419
Country Diary of an Edwardian Lady Ltd 3064
Country Roads Press 6166
Country Sports Book Society **6280**
Countryman Press Inc 6166
Countryside Books **1216**
Countyvise Ltd **1217**
Courage Books 1752
Course Technology Inc 6174
La Courte Echelle **2125**
Covenant Media Production 1218
Covenant Publishing Co Ltd **1218**
Cover to Cover Cassettes Ltd **1219**, 1525,
    6146, 6243
Cowgirlsinkilts 2107
Cowley Publications 1812
T. Cox & Son (Cash & Carry) Ltd **6245**
CPC Publishing 6139
Crabapples Series 1220
Crabtree Environment Series 1220
Crabtree Publishing Co **1220**, 6104
CRAC 1420
The Craft Library Series 1783
Craftsman Book Society **6280**
Craftsman House **2019**, 2029
Craig Potton Publishing Ltd **2437**
Craig Printing Co Ltd **2438**
Cramer 1109
C. R. Competition Refresher (P) Ltd 2276
CRCS 1325, 6135
Patrick Crean Books 2219
Creation Books **1221**
Creative Books Plus **6280**
Creative Bound Inc 6166
Creative Career Publishers 2289
Creative Editions 6108
Creative Living **6280**
Creative Monochrome 6205
Creatures at Large Press 6166
Creciendo con matemáticas 2059
Crécy Books Ltd **1222**
Creed 1661
Creel Publishing 6105
Creole Music Ltd 1466
Crescent Moon Publishing **1223**
Cressrelles Publishing Co Ltd **1224**, 1493
Rupert Crew Ltd **4022**
Crime Prevention Readers 2522
Artemis Crime Series 2005
Crime Writers' Association **5060**
Critical Guides to French Texts 1361
Critical Guides to German Texts 1361
Critical Guides to Spanish Texts 1361
Critics' Circle **5061**
Crompton Bequest Fund **5062**
Paul H. Crompton Ltd **1225**, 6135
Cromwell Editions 1026
Croner Publications 1226
Croner Publications Ltd **1226**
Croom Helm 6174
Crossing Press 6135
Crossroads 6181
Crossroads of Prague 6205
Crossway Books 1461
Crown Outlet 6166

The Crowood Press Ltd **1227**, 6146, 6243
CRS Records 6073
Cruelty-Free London 6152
Cruickshank Cazenove Ltd **4023**
Crystal Clarity Publishers 6155
CSA Press 1325
CSA Telltapes 6073, 6145
CSIRO Australia 2020
CSIRO Publishing **2020**
C & T Publishing 6091, 6131
CTI Publications Inc 1314
CTS Publications 1166
Cube Publications Ltd **1216**
Cuisenaire 1014
Cuisenaire Co of America 1513
Culinary Arts 1920
Culture Shock! Guides 1503, 6175
Cumbria Social Services 1657
Curator 6161
Currency Press **2021**, 4111, 6166
Current Biology 1337
Current Clinical Strategies Publishing 6166
Current Legal Publications 2290
Current Science Group 6191, 6202
Current Technology Index **6343**
Current Topics in Drug Researh 1357
James Currey Publishers **1228**, 6191
Curriculum Corporation **2022**
Eleanor Curtain Publishing 1253, **2023**
Curtis Brown **4024**
Curtis Brown (Australia) Pty Ltd 4024, **4102**
Curtis Brown Group Ltd 4102
Curtis Brown Ltd 4102
Curzon Press Ltd **1229**, 6181
Cwmni Cyhoeddi Gwynn 6258
Cy Decosse 1864
C.Y.P. Audio 2506
Cyd-Bwyllgor Addysg Cymru / Welsh Joint
    Education Committee 6258
Cygnet Press 1050, 6138
Cygnus Arts 1348
Cyhoeddiadau Barddas 6258
Cyhoeddiadau Curiad 6258
Cyhoeddiadau Modern Cymreig / Modern
    Welsh Publications 6258
Cyhoeddiadau'r Gair 6258
Cymdeithas Lyfrau Ceredigion 6258
Cyngor Llyfrau Cymraeg **5124**
Cyngor Llyfrau Cymraeg: Canolfan
    Ddosbarthu **6258**
CYP Ltd — Children's Audio **1230**, 6146
Czech Publishers & Booksellers Association
    6095

D Services **6154**
Da Capo Press 6161
Daily Mail & General Trust Group 1420
Daily Telegraph Maps 1507
Dake Bible Sales 6179
Dale Seymour 1014
Dalebank Books 6073, 6145
Dalesman Publishing Co Ltd **1231**
Daltons Weekly 6146
Dance Books Ltd **1232**, 6205
Dance Horizons 1232, 6205
The C. W. Daniel Company Ltd **1233**, 1325,
    6243
Daniels Medica **1234**
Dar Al Jaqi Sarl 1761
Dar es Salaam University Press 6069
Darby Publications 1588
Herman Darewski 1466
Dartmouth Publishing Co Ltd 1052, **1235**
Darton, Longman & Todd Ltd **1236**
Darwen County History 1671
Darwen Finlayson Ltd 1671
Data News Press 1325

Data Service & Information 6182
DataMedia 6182
David Bennett Books Ltd **1238**
David Ling Publishing Ltd **2439**
David & Charles Publishers **1237**, 6162, 6243
Merric Davidson, Marketing Consultancy
   6084
Christopher Davies 6258
Mike Davies Books **6221**
Robert Davies Publishing **2126**, 6085
Davis Publications Inc 6166
Davo Publications 1343
DAW 2068
Dawn Publications 6155
Dawson UK Ltd **6261**
Daya Publishing House **2286**
Francis Day & Hunter Ltd 1466
DBI Books Inc 1047, 1162
D. C. Books and Current Books **2284**
DC Publishing 6105, 6142
DCM Publications 6205
DD Editorial Services **6006**
Y Ddraig Fach 6258
De Agostini Children's Books 1239
De Agostini Editions 1001, **1239**, 6162, 6243
De Vorss & Co 1325
Felix de Wolfe **4025**
De Wolfe Ltd 1466
Dead Sea Physh Products 2107
Dean 1383, 1730, 2208
Debrett's Peerage 6146, 6243
Debut Books 6153
Decent Books 2285
Dedalus European Classics 1240
Dedalus Ltd **1240**, 6152
The Dedalus Press **2386**
Dee Books **6246**
Ivan R. Dee Inc 6166
Deep Books Ltd 6071, **6155**
Deep & Deep Publications **2287**
Deerfield Publications Inc 2393
Deerhurst Publications 6205
Deeson Editorial Services **6007**
Defiant Publications **1241**
Degremont 1462
Delacorte 1869
University of Delaware Press 1348
Delectus Books **1242**
Delectus Classics of Erotic Literature 1242
Delectus Vampire Classics 1242
Delft University Press 6139
Delhi State Booksellers' & Publishers'
   Association **5156**
Dell Yearling 1869
Dellasta **2024**
Delmar 6174
Delos/Tafelberg 2514
Delphi Press 1920
Delta Books (Pty) Ltd 2495, 2497
Delta Editions Sdn Bhd 2425, 6166
Delta Ltd **6247**
Delta Publishing Group of Companies
   (Malaysia) 2425
Delta Publishing Sdn Bhd **2425**
Democratic Left 6152
Demos 6152
Demos Vermande 6166
Deneway Guides 6146
J M Dent **1243**, 1640, 6177, 6243
Department of Administrative Services (DAS)
   2010
Department of Adult & Higher Education,
   University of Manchester 1421
Department of Education 2377
DermaPet Inc 6166
Derry's Walls 1374
Derwent Scientific & Patent Information 6182

Deshon Music Inc 1466
Design and Artists Copyright Society Ltd **5063**
Design and Technology Association 1871
Design Handbooks 1412
Design Systems **6027**
Destino 6160
Destiny Publishers 1218
Detselig Enterprises Ltd **2127**
André Deutsch Children's Books 1770, 6243
André Deutsch Ltd **1244**, 6177, 6243
Deutscher Taschenbuch Verlag 6160
Development Bibliographies 1452
Devyn Press Inc 6166
Dhaka University Press 6137
Dharma Cloud 1920
Dharma Communications 1922
Dharma Drum 1922
Dharma Publishing 1918
Dharmachakra Tapes 1918
Dharmafarer 1922
DHP Books 2132
Diadem Books 6243
Diagram Visual Information Ltd **3021**
Dial Electrical/Electronics 1996 1245
Dial Engineering 1996 1245
Dial House 1022
Dial Publications **1245**, 2068
Diamond Publishing 1886, 6128, 6153
Dick Leahy Music Ltd 1466
Dickens Fellowship **5064**
Didier 6160
Didier-Millet 6183
Dido Press 6205
Verlag Moritz Diesterweg 6160
Diffulivre Inc 2139, 2173, **6156**
Diffusion du Livre Mirabel 2210
Difusión 6160
Digirule Inc 6166
Digital Media Resources 6182
Dimension Books 1728
Diogenes 6160
Dioscorides Press 1863
Dipalo 2522
Direct Distribution **6157**, 6243
Direct English Srl 1014
Direct Marketing Association (UK) Ltd **5065**
Direction Book Sales 6145
Director Books 1701
Directory of Book Publishers, Distributors and
   Wholesalers **6344**
Directory of Irish Family History Research
   1878
Directory of Publishers 1996 **6345**
Directory of Writers' Circles **6346**
Directory Publishers Association **5066**
Directory Publishers of Zambia Ltd **5181**
Disability Alliance 6152
Disability and Rehabilitation Series 1498
Discover 1084
Discover New Zealand 2434
Discoverers 1586
Discovering Series 3069
Discovery House 6179
Discussion Papers 1452
Disha Books 2330
Disha Publications 2299
Disney 1466
Disney Studio Albums 1725
Distican Inc **2128**
Divya Jyoti 2360
Dix Ltd 1466
DK Agencies (P) Ltd 2285
DK Printworld (P) Ltd **2285**
DK Publishers Distributors (Pvt) Ltd **2288**
DLM Teaching Resources 1619
Do Not Press 6162
Doaba House **2289**

Eric Dobby Publishing 1886, 6128
Doctor Who 1890
Document Management Yearbook (for
   Cimtech) – Series 1414
Documentation Française 6160
Anthony d'Offay Gallery 6139
Dog Publishing Inc 6152
Dolmen Press 1811
Dolphin 6177
Dominican Publications **2387**
The Dominie Group 2028
Dominique 2101
Les Editions Domino 2218
Domino Books 6258
John Donald Publishers Ltd 1216, **1246**
Donhead Publishing Ltd **1247**
Ad Donker (Pty) Ltd 2495, **2497**
Tom Donovan Publishing Ltd 1816
Donna Music Ltd 1466
Doral Publishing Inc 6166
Dorian Literary Agency **4026**
Dorling Kindersley Inc 1248
Dorling Kindersley Ltd **1248**, 1409, 6151,
   6173, 6243
Dorling Kindersley Marketing Services 6145
Dorset House Publishing Co Inc 1915
Dorset Press/Barnes & Noble Books 1886
Dorset Publishing Co **1249**
Doubleday 1728, 1869, **6158**, 6243
Doubleday Australia 2085
Douglas & McIntyre Ltd 1719, 1746, **2129**
The Dovecote Press 1216
Dovehouse Editions Canada **2130**
Dovehouse Editions Inc 1530
Dover Books 6199
Dover Publications Inc 1211
Dover Thrift Editions 6243
Downlander Publishing **1250**
DP Publications Ltd 1116, 6243
DP Publications & Letts Educational **1251**
Dragon Books Publishing Corp 6255
Dragon Door Publications 1225
Dragon's World Ltd **1252**, 6162, 6243
Drake Educational Associates Ltd **1253**
Drake Group Ltd 1253
Drake International Services **6085**, 6142
Drama Book Publishers 1413
Drama Series 2144
Dramaline Publications 6166
Dramatic Lines **1254**
Draw Books 1089
Dreamer's Guide Series 1121
The Dryad Press Ltd 1072
The Dryden Press 2033
DS4 A 1328
dtv 6160
Brian Dubé Inc 1144
Duckworth 2506, 6071
Gerald Duckworth & Co Ltd **1255**, 6243
Duden 6160
Dulwich Picture Gallery 1050, 6138
Dulwich Press 6142
The Dun & Bradstreet Corporation 1256
Dun & Bradstreet Ltd **1256**, 6182
Duncan Petersen Publishing Ltd **3022**
University of Dundee 1657
The Dundurn Group **2131**
Dundurn Press 2155, 2216, 6104
Martin Dunitz Ltd **1257**, 6181
Dunmore Press Ltd **2440**
Sara Dunn **3023**
Dunod 6160
Dunrod Press **1258**
Duns Tew 2506
Duquesne University Press 6085
Durham Indological Series 1229
Durkin Hayes Audio/Paperback Audio 2132

Durkin Hayes Publishing Ltd **2132**
Andrew Durnell — Publishers European
  Marketing Agency **6086**
Durrant's Press Cuttings Ltd **6087**
Verlag Dürr & Kessler 6160
Dutton 1661, 2068, 6243
E. J. Dwyer (Australia) Pty Ltd **2025**
E. J. Dwyer (Holdings) Pty Ltd 2025
Dye & Durham 2135
Dyllansow Truran 1213
Dynotech Ltd 6166

EA Books (Engineers Australia Pty Ltd) **2026**
Toby Eady Associates Ltd **4027**
Eagle **1259**, 1653, 6153
Eaglemoss International GmbH 1260
Eaglemoss International Ltd 1260
Eaglemoss Publications Ltd **1260**
Early Childhood Learning 2506
Early English Church Music 1826
Early English Text Society 1115, 1648
Early Settler Life Series 1220
Earlybird Books 2493
Earth Heart 1920
Earth Magic Productions Inc 6166
Earthscan Publications Ltd **1261**, 1502
Earthscape Editions 1059, **3024**
Earthspirit Inc 6155
East African Educational Publishers Ltd **2414**,
  6069
East West Express 6166
East West Nigel Carr Publishers Consultants
  6088
East-West Publications (UK) Ltd 1053, **1262**,
  6140
Eastern Book Company **2290**
Eastern Dragon Series 2427
Eastern Law House Pvt Ltd **2291**
Eastern University Press 2493
Eastview Publications Sdn Bhd 2488, 2491
EBC Publishing Pvt Ltd 2290
Ebony Holdings Pty Ltd 2051
EBSCO 6151, 6182
Ebury Press 1722, 6243
Ecco Press 1623
ECCTIS 2000 Ltd 6182
Echoes 1761
Eclipse 1387
Ecole des loisirs 6160
Economic Forecasting Service 2471
Economic & Industrial Publications **2471**
Economic Review 2471
Economic & Social Research Institute **2388**
The Economist Books **1263**
Editions Ecosociété 2099
ECRA Publishing Ltd 6152
ECS Publishing Co 1826
ECW Press **2133**
Eddington Hook 6153
Eddison Press Ltd 1564
Eddison Sadd Editions Ltd **3025**
EDELSA (Ediseis) 6160
Eden Grove Editions 6135, 6243
Eden Toys Inc 1661
Edgemore Enterprises 6104
Edicinco 1016
Ediciones SM 6160
Edinburgh Bibliographical Society **5067**
Edinburgh Book Festival **6295**
Edinburgh University Press **1264**, 1694, 6181
Edinburgh University, Dept of Archaeology
  1645
Editions Edisud 1507
Edition **6008**
Les Editions françaises 2218
Editora Index 6138
Editorial Moll 6205

Department for Education and Children's
  Services, South Australia **2027**
Educational Bookshelf 6145
Educational Broadcasting Trust 1657
Educational Heretics Press 6085, 6142
Educational Low-Priced Books Scheme
  (ELBS) **1265**
Educational Planning Books **1266**
Educational Productions Ltd 1253
Educational Publications Department **5178**
Educational Publishers Council **5068**
Educational Publishing 1770
Educational Sciences Series co-published with
  UNESCO 1498
Educational Series 1878
Educational Software for Microcomputers
  (ESM) 1513
Educational Supplies Lty Ltd **2028**
Educational Titles 2527
Educational Writers Group **5069**
Eel Pie 1690
Wm B. Eerdmans 1197, 6181
Efstathiadis Group 6166
Egmont 1929
The Egyptian International Publishing Co —
  Longman 1014
EHSSB 1657
Eiffel Editions 1050, 6138
The Eighteen Nineties Society **5070**
Eilers & Schunemann 6160
Einaudi 1050, 6138
EIP Investors' Service 2471
Ekstasis Editions **2134**
El-Sayed Publications 6166
élan press 2141
Eland Books 1211
ELC International **1267**
Electa 1050, 6138
Electa España 1050, 6138
Electric Paper 1719
Electronic Bibliography of Out-of-Print Books
  6347
Electronic Books **6296**
Electronic Meeting Services 6205
Electronic Publishing 96 **6297**
Electronic Publishing Services Ltd **1268**,
  4045, **6028**, **6047**
Electronic Publishing Services (Publications)
  Ltd 4045
Electronic Register of Wanted Publications
  6348
Electronica Books Ltd **6159**
Elefanten Press 6139
Peter Elek Associates/Elek International Rights
  Agent USA **4028**
Elektor Electronics 6166
Element Books Ltd **1269**, 1661, 6243
Element Communications Ltd 1269
Element Inc 1269
Elementary, Readers, Junior Readers,
  Secondary Readers Series 2414
Elephant Editions 1328
Elfande Art Publishing 6104
Elfande Ltd **1270**
Edward Elgar Publishing Ltd 1052, **1271**
Elias Publishing 6137
The George Eliot Fellowship **5071**
Elite International Publications Ltd 1469
Elliot Right Way Books **1272**, 6243
Andrew Elliot & Sons Ltd 1272
Elliott & Clark 1920
Ellipsis London Ltd 6177
Thomas Ellis Memorial Fund **5072**
Aidan Ellis Publishing **1273**, 6182, 6243
Ellison Educational 1842
Elm Publications **1274**
Elm Training 1274

Carlos H. Elmer Publishing 6166
Elms Hunt International 6145
Elsevier Advanced Technology **1275**, 1276
Elsevier Applied Science 1276
Elsevier Science BV 1276
Elsevier Science Inc 1276
Elsevier Science Ltd 1275, **1276**, 6174
Elsevier Trends Journals 1276
Elstead Maps **6248**
Elstree Music Ltd 1466
ELT Press 1811
Elysium Growth Press 6166
EMAP Business Publications 6243
EMB 1109
EMC Publishing 6160
Guide Emer 1416
EMFEC 1657
EMI Distribution Centre 6243
EMI Film Music Ltd 1466
EMI Music Publishing Ltd 1466
EMI Songs Ltd 1466
EMI-Virgin Music Ltd 1466
Emma Books Ltd **1277**, 1870
Emond Montgomery Publications Ltd 1169,
  2135
Emperors Press 1366
Empire of the Senses 1240
Encore Series 1845
Encyclopaedia Britannica Inc 1278
Encyclopaedia Britannica International Ltd
  1278, 6151, 6182
Encyclopaedia Universalis 1278
Encyclopedia of Indian Philosophies 2321
Encyclopedia of Popular Music 1825
Endangered Animals Series 1220
Endeavour Group UK **3026**
Enerdata 6182
Engineering Index 6170
Engineering Software 1208
Engineering Training Authority 1281
English Book Clubs **6274**
English Heritage **1279**, 6105, 6142
English House Publishing Services **6089**
English-Speaking Union of the Commonwealth
  5004
English Theosophical Trust 1858
English Tourist Board 1001
Ennsthaler GmbH & Co KG 6166
ENO Opera Guides 1148
Enterprise Transport Books Ltd **1280**
Enterprises Publishers 6166
EnTra Publications Ltd **1281**
Envirobook Pty 1159
Environmental Development Action in the
  Third World (ENDA) 6069
Verlag Enzyklopädie 6160
EP Publishing 1089
EPB Publishers Pte Ltd **2486**, 6166
EPB Retail Pte Ltd 2486
EPJournal **6349**
Eponymists in Medicine Series 1751
ePublishing **6029**
Epworth Press **1282**, 1571, 1773
Equestrian Book Society **6280**
Era Publications 1719, 6194
ERA Technology Ltd **1283**
Ercomer 6104
Lawrence Erlbaum Associates 6157
Erlbaum UK 6243
Ermor Enterprises 6166
The Ernest Press 6258
Ernst & Sohn Verlag 1883
Eros Plus 1865
Erskine Press 1044
ESA Publications (NZ) Ltd **2441**
ESC Publishing 1844, 6174
Escreet Publications 6152

The Esoteric Story Trilogy 1666
Espasa-Calpe 6160
Essay Series 2144
Essential Poets Series 2144
Essential Series 1559
Estamp 6152
Estate Publications **1284**, 6243
ETCH (Essays & Texts in Cultural History) 2397
Ethical Consumer 6152
Ethics & Public Policy Centre 6161
L'Etincelle Editeur 2126
ETS/Warner Publications (GMAT & MBA) 1652
Eurobook Ltd **1285**
Eurofi Guide to European Community Grants and Loans 1286
Eurofi Ltd **1286**
Euromoney Books 1701, 6191
Euromonitor International Inc 1287
Euromonitor Plc **1287**, 6182
Europa Militaria Series 1919
Europa Pages 1838
Europa Publications Ltd **1288**
Europe 1992–95 1240
The European Book World **6350**
European Bookseller Magazine **6351**
European Business Books Ltd 6152
European Christian Booksellers Association **5005**
European Communities (EC) 1419
European Contact 1270
European Economic Perspectives (bi-monthly) 1175
European Foundation for the Improvement of Living and Working Conditions **2389**
European Institute of Education & Social Policy 1871
European Labor Forum (Elf Books) 1820
European Language Institute 6160
European Law Centre 6174
European Library Publishers 6145
European Patent Office 6182
European Photography 6152
European Schoolbooks Hatier Ltd 6160
European Schoolbooks Ltd **6160**
European Schoolbooks Publishing Ltd 6160
Europresse SARL 1289
The Eurospan Group **6161**
Eusidic **6298**
Evangelical Library (London) 1290
Evangelical Library of Wales 1290
Evangelical Movement of Wales 1290
Evangelical Press of Wales **1290**
Evangelical Press & Services Ltd **1289**
Faith Evans Associates **4029**
Evans Brothers (Kenya) Ltd 1291
Evans Brothers Ltd **1291**, 6146, 6243
Evans Brothers (Nigeria Publishers) Ltd 1291
Evening Standard 6073, 6243
Everest 6160
Everyday Phrase Books 1503, 6175
Everyday Science Series 1220
Everyman Guides 1151
Everyman Paperbacks 1243, 1640, 6177, 6199, 6243
Everyman's Library 1151, 6243
Everyone's Guide To (Art) Series 1725
Everywoman 6152
Ex Libris Press **1292**
Excalibur Press 1744, 6166
Excel Books 2321
Excellent Press 6243
Executive Grapevine International Ltd **1293**
Executive World **6274**
Exel Logistics Media Services **6162**
Exeter Multimedia 1483

University of Exeter Press **1294**, 1843, 6191
Exhibitions International 1050, 6138
Exley Giftbooks 1295
Exley Publications Ltd **1295**, 6095, 6243
Exley SA 1295
Exoterica Corporation, Publishing Software **6048**
Expansion Publishing Co 1325
Expert 6243
Expert Gardening Books 1869
Export Success 6191
Express Newspapers Plc **1296**
Extraordinary Classics 1787
E–Z Legal Forms Inc 1509

Fabbri-Bompiani 6160
Faber 2460
Geoffrey Faber Holdings Ltd 1297
Faber Music Ltd 1297
Faber & Faber 6095, 6243
Faber & Faber Inc 1297
Faber & Faber Ltd **1297**
Fabian Pamphlet 1298
Fabian Society **1298**
FACE Distribution **6163**
Facticity Trainings 6136
The Factory Shop Guide **1299**
Facts on File **1300**, 1746, 6146
Facts On File Inc 1300, 1746
Factwell Ltd **6153**
J. B. Fairfax International 1566
J. B. Fairfax Press Ltd 1566
J. B. Fairfax Pty Ltd 1566
Fairleigh Dickinson University Press 1348
Fairmont Press 1698
Fairview Press 6166
Falcon Books 2283
Falk 1824
Editions du Fallois 6160
Falmer Press Ltd **1301**, 1851, 6243
Familia 1878
Family Books Pvt Ltd 2346
Family Circle 2060
Family Law 1484
Family Publications 1356
Family Walks Series 1768
Fantail Books **1302**, 2068
Fantasy & SF Book Club **6274**
Far East Publications Ltd 2493
Far East Trade Press Business Publications Ltd 2493
A. & A. Farmar **2390**
Farming Press **1303**, 6243
Farrand Press 1697
Farrar, Straus & Giroux 6177
T. C. Farries & Co Ltd **6262**
Fast Forward 1444, 6145
Faulkner Information Services 6182
Ian Faulkner Publishing 1843
R. T. & A. Fawcett **6249**
Fazleesons (Pvt) Ltd **2472**
Fearless Publications 1687
Federal Publications Ltd **2251**, 2493
Federal Publications Pte Ltd 2426
Federal Publications (S) Pte Ltd 2251, 2493
Federal Publications Sdn Bhd **2426**, 2493
Federal Trust **1304**
Fédération des Éditeurs Européens (FEE) **5006**
Féderation Internationale de la Précontrainte (Slough, UK) 1853
The Federation of Educational Publishers in India **5157**
Federation of K.S.I. Jarnaats of Africa 2523
The Federation Press 1092
J. J. Fedorowicz 6150
Feedback Theatrebooks 6166

Feldman & Co Ltd 1466
Fellowship Press 6137
Feltrinelli 6160
The Feminist Press 6166
Editions 'des femmes' 6160
Fernhurst Books **1305**, 6243
Fernwood Press 6183
Ferozsons Ltd 6137
Ferry Publications 6258
Fertiliser Development and Consultation Organisation **2292**
Festerman 1050, 6138
FETP Business Publications Pte Ltd 2493
FHG Publications Ltd **1306**, 6243
Fiddlehead Poetry Books 2142
FIEC 1289
Field Studies Council 1738, 6195
Fifth House Publishers **2136**
Fig Tree Press 1810
Filmtrax Plc 1466
Financial Surveys 1442
Financial Times 1685
The Financial Training Co 1861
Findex 1287
Findhorn Press 1053, **1307**, 6140
Fine Arts Press 2019, **2029**
Finesse Press 1144
Firebird Books Ltd **1308**, 6105, 6142, 6243
Firebox Audiovisual Productions 3027
Firebrand Books 6135
Fireside 1803
Firestone Hispania SA 1507
First Aid in English 1344
First Discovery 1586
First Edition Translations Ltd **6009, 6063**
A First Guide to.....Series 3069
First Nations Languages Series 2230
First sports science series 3069
First Steps in Science Series 2406
First & Best Business Press 1309
First & Best in Education Ltd **1309**
Fischer 6160
Carl Fischer 1109
Fisher Books 1323
J. Fisher & Bros 1466
Fishing News Books 1094, 6181
Fitzhenry & Whiteside 1746
The Fitzjames Press 1589
Fitzroy Dearborn Publishers 6181
Five Leaves Publications 6152
The Five Mile Press Pty Ltd **2030**, 6105, 6142, 6243
Fivedit 1824
Flag Communications **6010**
Flame Tree Publishing 3027
Flamingo 1387
Flammarion SA 1855, 6160
Fleetfoot Books 6166
Fletel Business Services **6090**
Flicks Books **1310**
Flint River Press Ltd 1917
Flohic 1050, 6138
Floodlight 6152
Burall Floraprint Ltd **1311**, 6073, 6145
University Press of Florida 6161
Florilegium 6205
Floris Books **1312**, 6243
Flowers East Gallery 1050, 6138
Flugzeug Publikations 1019
Focal Press 1145, 2208
Focus Books 2342, 6139
Focus on the Bible 1191
Fodor 1722, 6199, 6243
Folens Distribution **6164**
Folens Investment Co 2391
Folens Ltd **1313**, 2391
Folens Publishing Co 2380, **2391**

Charles Foley Inc 1466
Folger Shakespeare Library 1348
Folio 6160
Folio Holdings 1155
The Folklore Society **5007**
Folly Fellowship 6095
Fontana Press 1387
Food & Agriculture Organisation (FAO) 1419
Food & Nutrition Press Inc 1314
Food Processors Institute 1314
Food Trade Press Ltd **1314**
Footprint Handbooks **1315**
Footprint Press Ltd **1316**
Footprint/Trade & Travel Handbooks 1315
For Beginners 1930
Forbes Publications Ltd **1317**, 6191
Forbidden Planet Ltd, UK 1865
Mary Ford Publications 6162, 6243
Fordham University Press 6161
Forensic Focus 1498
Forest Books **1318**
Formac 6104
Adrian Forman Books **1319**
Fortress Press 6181
Foucher 6160
G. T. Foulis & Co **1320**, 1398, 1632, 1829
W. Foulsham & Co Ltd **1321**, 6095, 6180, 6243
Foundation for Education with Production 6069
The Foundational Book Company **1322**
The Foundery Press 1571
The Foundry Creative Media Co Ltd **3027**
Fount 1387, 1388
Fountain Press Ltd **1323**, 6069, 6243
Four Courts Press **2392**
Four Walls Eight Windows 6201
Fourth Dimension Publishing Co Ltd 6069
Fourth Estate 6199, 6243
Fourth Estate Ltd **1324**
L. N. Fowler & Co Ltd **1325**
Fowler Wright Books 1356
Sam Fox Publishing Co 1466
W. G. Foyle Ltd 6146
FPA 1657
Fragment 6139
Framework Press Educational Publishers Ltd **1326**
Frameworks 1461
Franey & Co 1705
Frank Publishing Ltd **2243**
Frankfurt Book Fair **6299**
Franklin Watts 1900
Franklin Watts Australia 1637
The Fraser Institute **2137**
Fraser Stewart Book Wholesale Ltd **6222**
Robert Frederick 6073, 6145
Free Association Books **1327**, 1793
Free Lance Press 6205
Free Presbyterian Publishing 1289
Free Press 1803
Freedom House 6161
Freedom Ministries 1588
Freedom Press **1328**, 6069
Freelance Press Services **3028**, **6165**
W. H. Freeman **1329**, 1466, 1546, 6180, 6243
Freestone Collective 1920
Freeway 1869
Fremantle Arts Centre Press 1530, **2031**
French Company Handbook 6122
Samuel French Inc 1330
Samuel French Ltd **1330**
Samuel French Trade 6166
French Sociolinguistics 1591
French Surrealism 1148
French's **4030**
Sigmund Freud Copyrights 4072

Freytag & Berndt 1824
Barry Friedman 6139
Michael Friedman Publishing Group 1566
Friends General Conference 1710
Friends of the Earth **1331**
Friends United Press 1710
Frommer 1803
Frontier Publishing 6243
Frontline 6152
FT Law & Tax **1332**, 1659, 6182
David Fulton Publishers Ltd **1333**, 6181
Fun Files 1409
Fun to Learn 1929
Fun with Phonics Series 2406
Fundacion Caja de Pensiones 6139
Funfax 1409
Fuse Press 6152
Vernon Futerman Associates **4031**
Futura Publishing 1094, 6181
Future Publishing 1566
Futurepace Inc 6136
Fyfield Books 1155

Gadabout Guides 1503
Gaelic Books Council **5055**
Gaëtan Morin Publisher 2138
Gage Distribution 2139
Gage Educational Publishing Co **2139**, 2173
Gaia Books Ltd **1334**, 6243
Gairm Publications **1335**
Galde Press Inc 6166
Gale Centre Publications 6135
Gale Research Inc 1336
Gale Research International Ltd **1336**, 6174, 6182
Galerie Amrad African Art 6138
Galerie Claude Bernard 6139
Galerie Isy Brachot 6139
Galerie Lelong 6139
Galerie Thaddeus Ropac 6139
Galgotia Booksource Pvt Ltd **2293**
Galgotia Publications (Pvt) Ltd **2294**
E. D. Galgotia & Sons 2294
Gallaudet University Press 6166
Galleria Editrice 1050, 6138
Gallery Children's Books 1262, 1719, 6194, 6243
The Gallery Press **2393**
Galliard Ltd 1826
Gallimard 6160
Peter Galliner Associates **4032**
Gambling Times 1158
Gamsberg Macmillan Publishers 2522
Garamond Press **2140**
Garden Art Press 1039
Gardeners Book Society **6280**
Walter H. Gardner Ltd **6223**
Gardner Press 6161
Gardners Books Ltd **6250**
Garfield 1725
Sri Garib Dass Oriental Series Office 2304, 2356
Garland Publishing Inc **1337**, 2034, 6181, 6243
La Librairie Garneau 2218
Garnet Publishing Ltd **1338**, 1472, 6131
Garnier 6160
Garnier Flammarion 6160
Garrett Publishing Inc 1509
Garzanti 6160
Gateway Books **1339**, 6243
Gateway Books & Tapes 6166
Gateways Books 6166
Gault Millau 6160
Gautier-Langereau 6160
Gautier-Villars 6160
Gävle 1016

Gay Authors Workshop **5073**
The Gay Men's Press 1347
Gaza Books 6154
Gazelle Book Services Ltd **6166**
GBS Distribution & Marketing Ltd **6091**
GCSE Passcards 1251
GCSE Questions & Answers 1251
GCSE Study Guides 1251
GCSE Textbooks 1251
Gedung Ilmu Sdn Bhd 2425
Gee & Co 1705
Geeta Graphics 2350
General 2141
General Book Depot **2295**, 2296
General Publishing Co Ltd **2141**, 2160, 2170
General Synod of the Church of England 1193
Genesis Publishing Pvt Ltd 2283
Genius Publishing Co 2250
Geocart 1824
Geocenter 6071
Geocentre International UK Ltd 6167, 6243
Geographers' A–Z Map Co Ltd **1340**, 6243
Geography Detective Series 3069
Geological Society of America 1341
Geological Society Publishing House **1341**
George Padmore Research Library on African Affairs **5152**
George Ronald Publisher Ltd **1342**
Georgetown University Press 6191
University of Georgia Press 6161
Geoscience 6108
German Expressionism 1148
German Historical Institute, London 1648
German Tuition – Barbara Classen **6394**
Germany's Top 500 6122
Gestalt Journal Press 6136
Die Gestalten Verlag 1050, 6138
Getting to Grips 1251
Getty Trust Publications 6131
De Geus 6152
Ghana Book Publishers Association **5153**
Ghana Publishing Corporation 6069
Ghana Universities Press **2246**, 6069
Ghost Gum Press 2012
Gibb Memorial Trust 1046, **5074**
Stanley Gibbons Publications **1343**
Douglas Gibson Books 2169
Robert Gibson & Sons (Glasgow) Ltd **1344**
The Gieves Group Plc 1190
Michael Gifkins & Associates **4110**
Mike Gilbert Productions **6049**
Gilde Buchhandlung 6160
Gustavo Gili 6071, 6139
Gill & Macmillan Ltd 1547, **2394**, 6100, 6243
Etienne Gilson Series 2199
K. S. Giniger Co Inc 6206
Ginn & Co **1345**, 1731, 2499
Gita Enterprises 2350
Given & Partners **6092**
The Glamorgan County History Trust 1895
Mary Glasgow Publications 1861
Glasgow Royal Concert Hall 6243
Glasgow University, Department of Archaeology 1843
Eric Glass Ltd **4033**
Global Books Ltd **1346**
Global Business Press 2300
Global Oriental 1346
Global Press 2139, 2173
Globe Pequot 1824
Globe Publishing Ltd 1547
Gloucester Reprints 1843
Sean Glyn 6166
GMC Publications 6105, 6142
GMP Publishers Ltd **1347**, 6152, 6201
Go Teach Publications 1289
Goanna Crime 2012

Godfrey Book Sales Ltd **6220**
David R. Godine **6135**
Godsfield Press Ltd 1435, 6146, 6243
Godwit Publishing Ltd **2443**
Gold Eagle 2148
Golden Aura Publishing 6166
Golden Cockerel Press Ltd, Associated
    University Presses **1348**, 6145
Golden Dawn 1555
The Golden Dog 6085
Golden Gates Press 1053, 6140
Golden Memories 6162
Golden Palm Books 1471
The Golden Sufi Centre 1325
Goldmann 6160
Golfermania 1725
Golfer's Dictionary 1725
Golgonooza 6152
Gollancz Children's Paperbacks 1349
Victor Gollancz Ltd 1047, 1162, **1349**, 1615,
    6243
Gollancz Paperbacks 1349
Gomer Press **1350**
The Good Book Guide **6353**
Good Books 6139, 6153, 6166
Good Company for Children Co 6142
Good Food Retailing Publications 6205
Goodall Publications 1019
Goodlife Publications 1466
Goodnight, Sleeptight Books 1360
Goose Lane Editions **2142**
Adam Gordon **1351**
The Gordon Press Ltd 1792
The Robert Gordon University **1352**, **6395**
Gordon & Breach 6181
Gordon & Breach Arts International 2019
Gorham House Publishing 6166
Gospel Standard Publications 1289
Gothic Image Publications 1053, **1353**, 6140
Goulden Reports Ltd 1267
H. M. Gousha Co 1503, 1507
Gousha Road Atlases 6175
Govardhan Hill 6143
Government of Canada 2109
Government Printing Office 6182
James Gowans (Trade Bookbinders) Ltd 1136
Gower Asia-Pacific Pte Ltd 1052, 1354
Gower Publishing Co Inc 1354
Gower Publishing Ltd 1052, **1354**, 1657, 6182
Goyl SaaB Publishers & Distributors 2295,
    2296
Gozo Press **2430**
GP Publications Ltd **2442**, **5165**
GPC Books 1895
Grabert Verlag 1050, 6138
Grace Publications Trust 1289, **1355**
Gracewing/Fowler Wright Books Ltd **1356**,
    6243
Publications of the Graduate Institute of
    International Studies, Geneva 1488
Graffham Press Ltd **1357**
Graficor 2138
Grafisk Forlag 6160
Grafocarte 1447
Graham-Cameron Illustration 3029, **6030**
Graham-Cameron Publishing & Illustration
    3029
Francis Graham-Dixon Gallery 1050, 6138
W. F. Graham (Northampton) Ltd **1359**
Graham & Whiteside Ltd **1358**
Grail Publications 1356, 6153
Gramophone 1630
Grandreams Ltd **1360**
Grange Books Plc **6224**, 6243
Grant Books 6166
Grant & Cutler Ltd **1361**
Grant Jessé Associates 3038

Granta 1098, **1362**, 6243
Granta Editions **1363**, 6205
Granta Publications Ltd 1362
Granta USA Ltd 1362
Granth Akademi 2343
Grantham Book Services Ltd **6167**
Grantham House Publishing **2444**
Graphic Arts Center 6205
Graphical, Paper & Media Union **5075**
Graphis 1110
Grashoff Consulting Group **6050**
Grassfield Press 6139
Gravestone Inscription Series 1878
H. W. Gray Co Inc 1466
Great 20th Century Expeditions 3069
Great African American Series 1220
Great Battles & Sieges 3069
Great Books of the Western World 1278
Great Ocean Publishing 6136
Greek Index Project Series 2199
Christine Green Authors' Agent **4034**
Green Books **1365**, 6152
J. Green Books 1813
Green Books & Resurgence Books 1365
Green Croc Pty Ltd 2037
Green Earth Books 1365
Warren H. Green Inc 6166
Green Print 1569
The Green Street Book Shop Mail Order 1471
Green Submarine 1230
W. Green The Scottish Law Publisher **1364**,
    1844, 6174
Stephen Greene 2460
Greene & Heaton Ltd **4035**
Greenhill Books / Lionel Leventhal Ltd **1366**,
    6146
Greenprint 6152
Greenwich Editions **6225**
Greenwich Exchange 6152
Greenwich University Press 1010, **1367**
Greenwood Press 1368, 6161
Greenwood Publishing Group **1368**
Gregg Publishing Co Ltd 1052
The Jane Gregory Agency **4036**, 4037
Gregory & Radice Authors' Agents 4036,
    4037
Gregory's 1824
Gremese International 1746, 6146
Gresham Books 1925
Grey House Publishing 6122
Grey Seal Books **1369**, 6152
The Greyhound Press 6166
Greystone Books 1746, 2129
Griffin Publishing 6166
The Griffith Institute of the University of
    Oxford 1046
Grijalbo 6160
Grinder Delozier and Associates 6136
Grolier Electronic Publishing 6182
Grolier Inc 1900
Grondahl Dreyers Forlag AS 6166
Groningen Museum 6139
Peter Grose Ltd **1370**, 6145, 6146, 6243
Grosvenor Books **1371**
Grosvenor Productions Ltd 1371
Groundwood Books 2129, **2143**
Groupe de la Cité 1506
Grove's Dictionaries Inc 1547
Grove's Dictionaries of Music Ltd 1547
Growing Series 2048
Grub Street **1372**, 6142, 6243
GRUND 1416
Gründ 6160
Grune & Stratton Inc 1384
Grune & Stratton Ltd 1384, 2033
Guardian Books 1324, 6152
Guernica Editions **2144**, 6166

Guernsey Museums and Galleries 1843
The Guernsey Press Co 1843
Guerra 6160
Guggenheim Museum 1849, 6139
Dipak Kumar Guha **6093**
Guide des Prêts et Subventions de la
    Communauté Européenne 1286
Guide to Microforms in Print (GMIP) **6354**
Guide to New Australian Books **6355**
Guide to Series 1117
Guides to the West of Scotland 1536
Guild of Master Craftsman Publications Ltd
    1373, 6105, 6243
Guildford Reading Services **6011**
Guildhall Press **1374**
Guildhall School of Music 1109
Guilford Press **1375**, 6157
Guilford Press Inc 1375
Guinness Publishing Ltd **1376**, 6180, 6243
Guinness World of Records Inc 1376
Gulf Publishing Co 6191
Gunsmoke Westerns 1190
Gursharan Sahota 6166
Gwasg Addysgol Drake Cyf 1253, 6258
Gwasg Cambria 6258
Gwasg Carreg Gwalch 6258
Gwasg Dwyfor 6258
Gwasg Efengylaidd Cymru / Evangelical Press
    of Wales 6258
Gwasg Ffrancon 6258
Gwasg Gee 6258
Gwasg Gomer / Gomer Press 6258
Gwasg Gwalia 6258
Gwasg Gwynedd 6258
Gwasg Pantycelyn 6258
Gwasg Prifysgol Cymru 1895
Gwasg Prifysgol Cymru / University of Wales
    Press 6258
Gwasg Taf 6258
Gwasg y Dref Wen **1377**, 6258
Gyan Books (P) Ltd **2297**
Gyan Ganga 2343
Gyan Publishing House 2297
gynergy books 2145

Haags Gemeentemuseum 6139
Habib & Co 6137
Hachette 6160
Hackett Publishing Co Inc 6166
Peter Haddock Ltd **1378**, 6167
Hadeda Books 2509
The Hakluyt Society 1115, **5076**
Peter Halban Publishers 1640, 6177
Halcyon Publishing Ltd **2445**
Haldane Mason Ltd **3030**
Robert Hale Ltd **1379**, 6243
Hale & Iremonger **2032**
Half Halt Press Inc 1490
G. K. Hall & Co 1190
Hallwag 1386
The Hambledon Press **1380**
Hamdard Foundation Press **2473**, 6137
Hamish Hamilton Children's Books Ltd 1381,
    1661
Hamish Hamilton Ltd **1381**, 1661, 2068, 2460,
    6095, 6243
Hamlyn **1382**, 1383, 1730, 2208, 6243
Hamlyn Children's Reference **1383**, 1730
Hampshire Field Club 1843
Hampton Press 6161
Margaret Hanbury **4038**
Hancock House Publishers Ltd **2146**, 6166
Handbag Books 1559
Handsaw 1050, 6138
Hanen Programme 1921
Hanover Gallery 6139
Hans-Nietsch-Verlag 6152

Carl Hanser Verlag 1883
Edition Hansjorg Mayer 6139
Happy Cat Books 1719, 6194
Harbinger International 6145
Harbord Publishing 6152
Harbour Publishing Co Ltd 2049, **2147**
Harcourt Brace & Co Inc 1384
Harcourt Brace & Co Ltd 1067, **1384**, 1429,
  1763, 2033
Harcourt Brace & Co, Australia Pty Ltd 1384,
  2033
Harcourt General Inc 2033
Hardens Guides 6145
Patrick Hardy 1538
The Thomas Hardy Society **5077**
Harenberg Kommunikation 6160
Harlan Davidson Inc 6166
Forlaget Harlekin AB 1385
Harlem River Press 1930
Harlen Books 2462
Harlenic Hellas AE 2148
Harlenic Hellas SA 1385
Harlequin Books SA 2148
Harlequin Bulgaria EOOD 1385
Harlequin Enterprises (Australia) Pty Ltd 2148
Harlequin Enterprises BV 1385
Harlequin Enterprises Ltd 1385, **2148**
Harlequin Finland 1385
Harlequin Iberica SA 1385, 2148
Harlequin KFT 1385, 2148
Harlequin KK 1385
Harlequin Mills & Boon Ltd **1385**, 6162, 6243
Harlequin Mills & Boon Pty Ltd 1385
Harlequin Mondadori SPA 1385, 2148
Harlequin Poland 2148
Harlequin Publishers (NZ) Ltd 1385
Harlequin Publishers SR 1385
Harlequin Retail Ltd 2148
Harlequin SA 1385, 2148
Harlequin Taiwan Ltd 1385
Harlequin Yayincilik Ltd Sti 1385
Harmex 1385
Harmony Guides 1540
Harmsworth Publishing Ltd 1420, 6243
Harp Publications 6243
Harper Educational (Australia) **2034**
HarperCollins 1125, 1386, 1387, 2034, 6182
HarperCollins Audio 1387
HarperCollins Audiobooks 1387
HarperCollins Cartographic **1386**
HarperCollins Electronic 6243
HarperCollins ELT 6174
HarperCollins India 1106
HarperCollins Medical 6174
HarperCollins Paperbacks 1387, 6243
HarperCollins Publishers Inc 2034, 2446
HarperCollins Publishers Ltd **1387**, 2034,
  6243
HarperCollins Publishers (Melbourne) **2035**,
  2036
HarperCollins Publishers (New Zealand) Ltd
  2446
HarperCollins Publishers Pty Ltd 2034
HarperCollins Publishers (SA) (Pty) Ltd **2498**
HarperCollins Religious 1387, **1388**, 1653,
  2036
HarperCollins San Francisco 1197, 1387, 1388
HarperCollins Science Fiction & Fantasy 1387
Harrap **1389**, 1506, 6182, 6243
Harrap Educational 6174
O. Harrassowitz 6137
Harrods Publishing 6162, 6243
John Hart Publicity Ltd 1439
Adam Hart Publishers 6085
Hartley & Marks 1537
Hart & Sole (Publishers) Ltd 6197
Harvard Associates Inc 1016

Harvard Business School Press 1542
Harvard Common Press 6166
Harvard University Press **1390**, 1915, 6243
Roland Harvey Books 2037
Harvest (Harcourt Brace – San Diego) 6071
Harvester Wheatsheaf 1443, 1698, 6173
Roland Harvey Studios **2037**
Harveys Books **1391**
Harveys Books (Magna Books) **6226**
The Harvill Press **1392**, 6162, 6243
Harwood Academic Publishers 6181
Hastings House 6166
Hatier 6160
Hatje 6139
Richard Hatton Ltd **4039**
Editions Haug 1233
Karl F. Haug Verlag 1233
La Haule Books Ltd 1046
University of Hawaii Press 1447, 6148Hawk
  Books **1393**, 6243
Hawk Comics 1393
Hawker Consumer Publishing 1394
Hawker Publications **1394**, 6191
Hawksmere Group Ltd **1395**, 6146
Hawthorn Press **1396**
Hawthorns Publications Ltd **1397**
Hay House 6135, 6243
Hayden 1698
Hayit Publishing GB Ltd 6146
Haymarket Specialist Motoring Publications
  6205
Haynes North America Inc 1398
Haynes Publishing Group Plc 1320, 1398,
  1632, 1829, 6243
Editions Haynes SA 1398
J. H. Haynes & Co Ltd 1320, **1398**, 1632, 1829
Hazan Editions 6139
Hazar Graphics 1399
Hazar Publishing Ltd **1399**, 6180
Hazard Poets Series 2447
Hazard Press Ltd **2447**
Hazard Short Fiction Series 2447
Hazelden 6135
Hazleton Publishing Ltd **1400**, 6145, 6243
He Purapura 2449
Headline Book Publishing Ltd 1048, **1401**,
  1422, 1423, 1424, 1425, 6146, 6243
Headline Delta 1401
Headline Feature 1401
Headline Liaison 1401
Headline Review 1401
Headstart History **1402**, 1674, 1746, 6258
Headstart History Papers 1402
Headstart Lecture Series 1402
Headstock Publications 1687
Healing Tao Books 6135
Health Communications 6135
Health Education Authority **1403**, 6181, 6243
Health Press 1746
Health Professions Press 1498
Health Resource Series 2427
Health Science Press 1233
The Health Series 1666
Hearst Books International 1110
Heart of America 6176
Hearthstone Publications 6085
A. M. Heath & Co Ltd **4040**
D. C. Heath Canada Ltd **2149**, 6181
Heathcoat Publishing 6166
Heathcote Books **6251**
Hebreware 1744
Hedera Press 1202
Heffers Booksellers & Library Suppliers **6263**
Heibonsha 6139
William Heinemann **1404**, 1730, 1731, 2076,
  2208, 2499, 6095, 6151, 6243
Heinemann-Centaur 2499

Heinemann Drama 6152
Heinemann Drama US 2208
Heinemann Educational **1405**, 1731
Heinemann Educational Books (Nigeria) 6069
Heinemann Educational Botswana Pty Ltd
  1731
Heinemann English Language Teaching **1406**,
  1731
Heinemann Higher & Further Education 2499
Heinemann Iberia SA 1731
Heinemann Inc 1162
Heinemann International Education 1405
Heinemann (Latin America) 1731
Heinemann Le Monnier (50%) 1731
Heinemann Library 1405, 1731, 6243
Heinemann Professional Publishing 1145
Heinemann Publishers 1731
Heinemann Publishers (Pty) Ltd **2499**
Heinemann Publishing Oxford 6243
Heinemann USA 1731
Heinemann Young Books **1407**, 1730, 2208
Heinle & Heinle 6174
Helicon **1408**, 1722, 6199, 6243
Helix Editions Ltd 6166
Hellenic Bookservice (The Greek Bookshop)
  6264
Christopher Helm 1072, 1089, 6243
Helm Information 6205
Helsinki School of Economics & Business
  6182
Hemkunt Press Publishers **2298**
Henderson Publishing Plc **1409**, 6243
Henderson Study System 1409
Hendricksen Publishers 1289
Thomas Heneage 1050, 6138
Ian Henry Publications Ltd **1410**
Henston Ltd **1411**
Herald Press **2150**
The Herbert History of Art & Architecture
  1412
The Herbert Press 1089, **1412**, 6243
Heretic Books Ltd 1347
Heritage House 1507
Heritage Impex Worldwide 2299
Editions Heritage Inc **2151**
Heritage Publishers **2299**
Hermetician Press 1920
Nick Hern Books **1413**, 6199, 6243
Heroes & Warriors Series 1308
Hertfordshire Archaeological Trust 1843
University of Hertfordshire 1414
University of Hertfordshire Press **1414**
Heyne 6160
Heythrop Monographs 1793
Hi Marketing Ltd 6071, **6094**, 6146, 6199
Hidden Worlds 3069
High Noon Books 1037
High Risk Books 1787
High View Publications 1225
David Higham Associates Ltd **4041**
Higher Education Policy Series 1498
Highgate/Price Milburn Ltd 2454
Highland Books **1415**, 1653
Highsmith 1253
HighText Publications Inc 6166
Highway Book Shop **2152**
Hikoki Publications 1107
Adam Hilger 1467
Hilit Publishing Co Ltd 6166
Hill of Content Publishing Co Pty Ltd **2038**
Hillside Publications 1213
Hillside Publishing 1597
Hilmarton Manor Press **1416**
Hind Pocket Books Pvt Ltd 2281, **2300**
Hind Pustak Bhandar 2346
Hindi Book Centre 2364
Hindi Pracharak Publications Pvt Ltd 2301

Hindi Pracharak Sansthan **2301**
Hippo 1770, 6243
Hippocrene Books Inc 1240, 6166
Hiralal Printing Works Ltd **2302**
Hirmer Verlag 1050, 6138
Ron Hirshberg Publishing 6166
Hisarlik Press 6085
Hispanic Classics 1046
Histoires & Collections 6105, 6142
Historic Community Series 1220
The Historical Association **1417**
Historical Perspectives 1148
Historical Publications Ltd 1671
Historical Series 1878
History Detectives 3069
History from the Sources 1671
History of Christian Doctrine Series 1744
History Guild
History Starters Series 3069
The HLT Group Ltd 1418
HLT Publications **1418**
HM Stationery Office 6182
HMS Press: Books on Disk **2153**
HMSO Books **1419**, 1447, 1608, 6071, 6151,
6170, 6243
HNH International 1607
Hobby House Press 6166
Hobsons Publishing Plc **1420**, 6073, 6145,
6243
Hochland & Hochland Ltd **1421**
Hodder Children's Books **1425**
Hodder Education 2039, 6243
Hodder Headline (Australia) Pty Ltd 2039,
2040
Hodder Headline Plc 1048, 1401, 1422, 1423,
1424, 1425, 2040, 6151
Hodder & Stoughton 1048, 1125, 1422, 1423,
1424, 2040, 6146, 6243
Hodder & Stoughton Educational **1422**, 2512
Hodder & Stoughton General **1423**
Hodder & Stoughton Religious **1424**
Hoepli 6160
The Hogarth Press 1188, 1722
Hohm Press 6091
Holbrook Design Oxford Ltd **6031**
Holidays & Festivals Series 1220
The Holistic Centre 1325
Holland Enterprises Ltd **1426, 6227**
Holland Press 1614
Hollanden Publishing 6145, 6243
Hollis Arts Funding Handbook 1427
Hollis Business Entertainment (the annual
guide to corporate hospitality) 1427
Hollis Directories Ltd **1427**
Hollis Europe 1427
Hollis Press & Public Relations Annual 1427
Hollis Sponsorship & Donations Yearbook
1427
Holloway House 2506
Martin Holmes Rallying 6205
Holmes & Meier Publishing 1017, **1428**
Henry Holt 6180
Vanessa Holt Ltd **4042**
The Holt Jackson Book Co Ltd **6265**
Holt, Rinehart & Winston 1384, **1429**, 2033
Holtzbrinck Publishers Holdings Ltd 1544,
1545, 1548
Verlagsgruppe Georg von Holtzbrink GmbH
2452
Home Computer Club **6274**
Home Health Education Service **1430**
Home Planners Inc 6091
Home Time 1409
Les Editions de l'Homme 2218
Homoeopathic Book Service 1106
Honey Press 1325
Honeyglen Publishing 6145

Hong Kong Educational Publishing Co 2250
Hong Kong Library Association **5155**
Hong Kong Tai Ping Book Co 2250
The Hong Kong University Press **2252**, 6085
Honno 6258
Hope Publishing Co 1826
Hopeful Monster 1050, 6138
Hoppenstedt Bonnier Information GmbH
1442
Horizon House Inc 1051
Horizon Publishers & Distributors Inc 6166
Jonathan Horne Publications 1039
Horsdal & Schubart Publishers Ltd **2154**
Horwitz Publications Pty Ltd **2041**
Ellis Horwood 1698, 6173
Hospitality Press Pty Ltd **2042**
Hospitality Publications Ltd 1314
Hospital & Social Service Publications Ltd
1547
Hostaction Ltd 1393, 6146
Hostelling International 1824
Hotlicks 1466
Houghton Mifflin Co Inc 6181
Houghton Mifflin Co International **1431**
Hounslow Press 2131, **2155**, 6104
House of Anansi Press Ltd **2156**
Houston Fine Art Press 6139
Hove Books 1323
Hove Collectors Books 1323
Hove Foto Books 1323
How To Books Ltd **1432**, 6191, 6243
Tanja Howarth Literary Agency **4043**
Howell Book House 1740
Howell Press 1022, 1838
Howells House 6166
HPR 6095
HPS Publications Pvt Ltd 2301
HRD Human Resource Development Press
6166
HT (Book Distribution) Ltd **6168**
HTV 6258
Norman Hudson 6073, 6145, 6243
Hudson Centre 6136
Hudson Hills Press 1050, 6138
Max Hueber Verlag 6160
Hughes a'i Fab 6258
Hugo's Language Books Ltd **1433**, 6243
Hulton Deutsch 6182
Hulton Educational Publications Ltd 1861
Human Horizons 1815
Human Kinetics (Europe) Ltd **1434**
Human Kinetics Inc 1434
Human Sciences Press 1689, 6161
Humana Press 1184, 6174
Humanics New Age 6135
Humanities Press 6152
Human & Rousseau Pty Ltd **2500**, 2514
Humberside Industrial Publications **6096**
Humphrey Series (for Children) 1845
Humphrys Roberts Associates **6097**
Hunkydory Designs Ltd **6169**
Hunt and Thorpe **1435**, 1653, 6146, 6243
D. & J. Hunter **4042**
Hunter House Inc 6166
Hunter Publishing 1824
C. Hurst & Co (Publishers) Ltd **1436**, 6181
Hussami Book Depot 6137
Hutchinson 1188, **1437**, 1721, 1722, 6243
Hutton Press Ltd **1438**
Hydrographic Department 1447
Hydrographic Office 1447
The Hyland House/Monash Asia Institute
Series 2043
Hyland House Publishing Pty Ltd **2043**, 6166
Hymns Ancient & Modern Ltd & **1439**
Hyperion Press Ltd **2157**, 2506
Hyphen Press 6152

I Can Learn 1929
IAL Consultants Ltd 1267
Ibadan University Press 6069
IBBY — International Board on Books for
Young People **5008**
IBC Business Publishing **1440**
IBC Group Plc 1440
Iberia Press 1507
IBIS 6106
Ibis Books Ltd 2441
ICA (Institute of Contemporary Arts) **1441**
ICA Video 1441
ICC Information Group Ltd **1442**
Ice Publishing 6180
ICL 6182
ICN 6064
Icon Books 1661, 6152, 6243
ICS Books Inc 6166
ICS Publications 1728
ICSA Publishing Ltd **1443**, 1701, 6173
Idea Books Edizioni 6139
Idea Group Publishing 6161
The Ideas Factory 3027
Ideas in Progress 1114
IDG Computer Books 1869, 6243
IDS Commisioned Studies 1452
IEAS 1229
IEEE 6159
IEEE Computer Society 6159
IEPRC — International Electronic Publishing
Research Centre **6051**
IES Report Series 1450
IFI Plenum Data Corporation 1689
Ikeda & Lokker 1050, 6138
ILI 6170
Iliffe Books Ltd 1145
University of Illinois Press 6148
Illustrated Biographies 1412
Illustrated Musical Biographies 1148
Dar el Ilm 6137
IM Guides 1685
Images 1050, 1444, 6138
Images Australia P/c 2044
Images of Asia 2490
Images Publishing 6145
The Images Publishing Group Pty Ltd **2044**
Images Publishing (Malvern) Ltd **1444**
Imago Publishing Ltd **6033**
Michael Imison Playwrights Ltd **4044**
Immediate Publishing 1709, 6157
Immel Publishing 6145
IMP 6146
Impact Books / Olive Press **1445**, 1886, 6128,
6135, 6166
Impala Books 6166
Imperial College Press **1446**
Impilo Enhle 2522
Imprimerie Richard Vézma Inc 2167
IMP & Warner Chappell 1466
Imray Laurie Norie & Wilson Ltd **1447**
IMS World Publications Ltd 6182
In Camera 1715
In Focus Country guides series 1508
In My World Series 1220
In Print Publishing Ltd **1448**, 6142, 6202
In-Tune Books 1053, 6140
Edições Inapa 1050, 6138
Inbal Travel Information Ltd 1503, 6175
Independent Magazines 6145
Independent Music Press 1630
Independent Publishers' Association **5139**
Independent Publishers Guild **5078**
Independent UK Sports Publications 6243
Editora Index 1050
Index Translationum **6356**
India Book House Pvt Ltd **2303**
Indian Books Centre **2304**, 2356

Indian Council of Agricultural Research **2305**
Indian Defence Review 2313
Indian Society for Commonwealth Studies 2345
The Indian Society for Promoting Christian Knowledge **2306**
Indiana University Press 1636, 1915
Indigo 1349, 6243
Indus Publishing Co **2307**
Indus Publishing House 1760
Industrial Press Inc 6166
Industrial Research Service 2471
The Industrial Society 1119, **1449**, 6146
Industry Forecasts Ltd 1625
Infinity Press 6243
Info Technology Supply Ltd (ITS) **6170**
Infobase 6095, 6243
Informania 6182
Informatics 1055
Information Access Co 6182
Information Agents Ltd **4045, 6052, 6098**
Information Publications International **6171**
InfoSource Inc 1093
InfoSource International 1093, 6181
Jennie Ingham Associates Ltd 1934
Ingham Yates 1934
Ink Inc Ltd **3031**
Inner Circle 1676
Inner City Books 6135
Inner Light Publications 6166
Inner Traditions International 6155
Innotech Inc 6182
Innotech Multimedia Corporation **6053**
Insect Publications 6166
Insel 6160
Insight Books 1922
Insoft Ltd **6054**
Institute for Aboriginal Development (IAD) Press **2045**, 6166
Institute for African Alternatives 6152
Institute for Employment Studies **1450**
Institute for Fiscal Studies **1451**
Institute for Palestine Studies 1850, 6145
Institute for Public Policy Research 6152
Institute Manpower Studies 6144
The Institute of Chartered Accountants in England & Wales 1008
Institute of Contemporary Art 6139
Institute of Development Studies **1452**
Institute of Education **1453**
Institute of Fiscal Studies 1701
Institute of Historical Research, University of London 1648
Institute of Islamic Culture 6137
Institute of Islamic Thought **1470**
The Institute of Management **1454**
The Institute of Marine Engineers **1455**
The Institute of Materials **1456**
Institute of Personnel & Development **1457**, 6191
Institute of Petroleum 1915
Institute of Physics 1467
Institute of Policy Studies 1470
Institute of Printing **5079**
Institute of Psycho-Analysis, London 1487
Institute of Psychological Research Inc **2158**
Institute of Public Administration **2395**
Institute of Public Policy Research titles — Series 1741
Institute of Risk Management 1923
Institute of Scientific and Technical Communicators (ISTC) **5080**
Institute of Southeast Asian Studies **2487**
Institute of Southern African Studies 6069
Institute of Translation & Interpreting **5081**
Institution of Chemical Engineers **1458**
Institution of Civil Engineers 1853

Institution of Electrical Engineers **1459**
Institution of Engineers 2026
Instituto Geografico de Agostini 1239
Intellect Ltd **1460**, 6104
Inter Publishing Service (IPS) Ltd 1259
Inter-Varsity Press **1461**
Interactive Ideas Ltd **6172**
Interactive Media Publications Ltd 4045, 6182
Interart sarl 1855
Interbook Business Co 6166
Interbook International 1416
Intercept Ltd **1462**
Intercommunication 1591
Intercontinental Literary Agency **4046**
Intercultural Networking Ltd (ICN) **6064**
The Interface Collection Series 1414
Interfisc Publishing 1793
Interlink Books 1153
Intermediate Technology Development Group Ltd **1463**
Intermediate Technology Publications Ltd **1463**, 6191
International Academy at Santa Barbara 6182
International African Institute 1648
International Agency for Research on Cancer 1648
International Association of Scholarly Publishers **5009**
International Atomic Energy Agency (IAEA) 1419
International Authors Series 2203
International Bible Reading Association 1597
International Biographical Centre 1564
International Book Development Ltd **3039**
International Book Distributing Co **2308**
International Book Distributors Ltd 1830, **6173**
International Books in Print 1994 **6357**
International Booksellers Federation (IBF) **5010**
International Broadcasting Services Ltd 6166
International Business Images Ltd **1464**
The International Business Library Ltd **1143**, 6205
International Centre for Public Enterprises 6104
International Chamber of Shipping 1923
International Chess Enterprises Inc 6166
International Computer Programs 6182
International Congress and Symposium Series 1751
International Development Research Centre (IDRC) 1463
International Imaging **6034**
International ISBN Agency **5011**
International Jewelry Publications 6166
International Labour Office **1465**
International Labour Organization 6182
International League of Antiquarian Booksellers (ILAB) **5012**
International Library of African Studies 1850
International Library of Historical Studies 1850
International Literary Market Place **6358**
International Marine 1020
International Monetary Fund (IMF) 1419
International Monographs in Prehistory 1645
International Music Publications Ltd **1466**
The International Press Agency **4047, 4116**
The International Press Agency (Pty) Ltd 4047
International Press Publications Inc **6266**
International Publishers Association (IPA) **5013**
International Publishers Distributor 6181
International Publishers NY 6152
International Scholars Publications 6161
International Scripts Ltd **4048**

International Self-Counsel Press Ltd **2159**
International Society for General Semantics 6136
International Standard Book Numbering Agency **5166**
International Studies in Mathematics 1494
International Tanker Owners' Pollution Federation 1923
International Theatre Bookshop 6166
International Thomson Corporation 1479
International Thomson Publishing Services Ltd **6174**
International Translations Centre **5014**
International Travel Maps & Books (ITMB) 1284
International Venture Handbooks 1432
The International Youth Library **5015**
The Internet Bookshop **6099**
Internos Books 1110, 6199
Interprint **2309**
Intersong Music Ltd 1466
Interworld Publications 6166
Intrac 6152
Intratex 2496
Investor's Chronicle 1685
Inwardpath Publishers 1325
IOJ **5084**
Ion Press 6146
The Iona Community 1914
IOP Publishing **1467**
IOS Press 6104
Iowa State University Press 6161
Ipalele 2522
Ipanema Music Ltd 1466
IPAT 1619
IPL Books **2448**
IPL Publishing Group Ltd 2448
IPL Video 2448
IPL Wordprint 2448
Iqbal Academy 6137
IR—Multiclient Studies 2471
Irish Academic Press 1161, **2396, 2402**
Irish Book Publishers Association (CLÉ) **5158**
Irish Book Sales **6100**
Irish Cruising Club 1447
Irish Educational Publishers Association **5159**
Irish Publishing Record **6359**
Irish University Press 2396
IRL Press 1648
Irvington Publishers Inc 6166
Irwin Publishing **2160**
Isando Books 2499
ISBN Listing—on Microfiche 1996 **6360**
ISEAS 2487
ISER 6104
Ishiyaku EuroAmerica Inc 6166
ISI 6170
ISIS Publishing Ltd **1468**, 6243
Islam International Publications Ltd 1018, **1469**
Islamic Art Foundation, New York 1648
Islamic Book Centre **2474**
Islamic Book Publishers 1470
The Islamic Foundation **1470**
Islamic Publications (Pte) Ltd **2475**
Islamic Research Institute 6137
The Islamic Texts Society **1471**, 6152
Al-Shirkatul Islamiyyah 1018, 1469
Island Press 1261, 1502
Isle of Avalon Press 1154
Isma'ili Heritage Series 1850
ISSN UK Centre **5082**
ISTC **5080**
Italica Press 1920
Ithaca Press 1338, **1472**
ITI Conference Proceedings 1055
ITP Nelson Canada **2161**

IVP 1653
IW Books **1473**

Jacaranda Buku Sdn Bhd 2491
Jacaranda Designs Ltd **2415**
The Jacaranda Press 2046
Jacaranda Wiley Ltd **2046**, 2236
Bernard Jacobson Gallery 1050, 6138
Jade Publishers **1474**, 6146
Jaeger & Waldmann 6182
Jaffe International Education Service 4107
Jaffe Publishing Management Service **4107**
Jaffe Punnoose & Co 4107
Fred Jahn Galerie 6139
J'ai lu 6160
JAI Press Inc 1475
JAI Press Ltd **1475**, 6181
JAI Software Publishing 1475
B. Jain Publishers (P) Ltd **2310**
Jain Brothers **2311**
Jain Publishing 1922
Jamaica Library Association **5160**
Arthur James Ltd **1478**
James & James (Publishers) Ltd **1476**
James & James (Science Publishers) Ltd **1477**
Jane Austen Memorial Trust **5083**
Jane's Information Group Ltd **1479**, 6170, 6174, 6182
Peter Janson-Smith Ltd 4012
Janus Poetry Series 1480
Janus Publishing Co Ltd **1480**, 6142
Japan Information Center of Science & Technology 6182
Japan Library 1229, 6181
Japan Publication Trading Co (JPT) 6145
Japanese Studies Series 1488
Japanska 6255
Jarrold Publishing **1481**, 6243
Jayatinta Sdn Bhd 2425
Jerusalem International Book Fair **6300**
Jesperson Press Ltd **2162**
Grant Jessé 3038
Jets 1387
Jeux Nathan 6160
Jewel Music Publishing Co Ltd 1466
Jewel Publishing House 1922
Jewish Lights Publishing 6155
Jewish Publication Society 1503, 6175
Jinaver Associates 1546
JMC Press Ltd 2158
JMLS Ltd **6267**
Jobete Music (UK) Ltd 1466
Joe's Press 1223
Johansens/CRAC 6145
Johansens Publications Ltd 1420, 6073, 6243
John Taylor Book Ventures **3032**
Johns Hopkins University Press 6191
Johnson Associates Inc 1475
John Johnson Ltd **4049**
Johnson Reprint Co Ltd 1384
The Johnston Educational Service **6101**
Johor State Economic Development Corp 2424
The Joint Board of Christian Education 1597, **2047**
La Jolla Museum of Contemporary Art 6139
Jolly Learning **1482**, 6243
John Jones Publishing 6085, 6258
Bob Jones University Press 6179
Jones & Bartlett Inc 1201, 1483
Jones & Bartlett International **1483**, 6182, 6191
Die Jonglerie 1144
Jordan Publishing Ltd **1484**
Michael Joseph Ltd & Pelham Books **1485**, 1661, 2068, 2460, 6095, 6243
Richard Joseph Publishers Ltd **1486**

Joshua Morris **3033**, 3063
Joshua Morris Publishing Inc 3033, 3063
Le Jour Editeur 2218
Journal of Reproduction & Fertility Ltd 1697
Chartered Institute of Journalists **5084**
Journeyman Press 1691, 6181
Joy Books 6137
JPL Fine Art 6139
JPM Publications SA 6180
Editions JR 6205
J&S Publishing Co Inc 6166
JSOT Press 1794
J. S. R. Junior Science Refresher (P) Ltd 2276
Jane Judd Literary Agency **4050**
Edward E. Judge & Sons 1314
Jumpahead Ltd 1559
Jumping Bean 2254
Junior Funfax 1409
Junior Secondary Social Studies 2522
Juta & Co Ltd **2501**
Juta Holdings (Pty) Ltd 2501
Juta Zimbabwe (Pvt) Ltd 2501
Jutastat (Pty) Ltd 2501
Juventud 6160

Kabushiki Kaisha Union Enterprises 2493
Kagiso Publishers **2502**
Kagiso Readers 2522
Kahn & Averill 6142
Kala Mula Shastra 2321
Kala Press 1050, 6138, 6152
Kala Tattva Kosha 2321
Kalimát Press 1066
Edwin F. Kalmus Music Publications 1466
Kami-Case 2101
Kangaroo Press Pty Ltd **2048**
University Press of Kansas 6161
Kapco Library Products 6142
Karavadra : Multimedia 3038
Kar-Ben Copies Inc 1503, 6175
H. Karnac (Books) Ltd **1487**
Karto & Graphic 1824
Karunaratne & Sons Ltd **2520**
Kaye & Ward 6243
Kazi Publications, Chicago 6137
Keats 1053, 6140
Keats-Shelley Memorial Association **5085**
Kedros Publishing 6152
Keep Busy Series of Books 2302
Kegan Paul International Ltd **1488**, 1915
The Frances Kelly Agency **4051**
Kelly's Directories 1245
Kempen Pers BV 1050, 6138
Kemps Publishing Ltd **1489**
Kendall/Hunt 6136
The Kenilworth Press Ltd **1490**, 6243
Kenlyn Publishing 1680
Kennedy's Publications Ltd **1491**
Kensington West Productions **1492**, 6243
Kent Archaeological Society 1843
Evelyn Kent Associates 6166
Kent County Council 1216
Kent State University Press 6161
University Press of Kentucky 6148
Kenway Publications 2414
Kenya Factbook 2419
Kenya Literature Bureau **5161**
Kenyon-Deane Ltd 1224, **1493**
N. G. Kerk-Uitgewers **2503**, 2505
Kershaw Publishing Co Ltd **1494**
Michael Kesend Publishing Ltd 6166
Kettle's Yard 6139
Key British Enterprises 1256
Key Issues in the Information Business Series 1414
Key Paper Conferences Series 1751
Key Perspectives **6102**

Key Porter Books Ltd 1886, **2163**, 2168, 6128
Key Stage 2 National Tests 1251
Key Stage 3 National Tests 1251
Key Stage 3 Study Guides 1251
Key to Art Series 1783
Keyboard 6181
Keyfacts GCSE Passbooks 1251
Keynote Reports 1442
Keytone Publications 6205
KGP Publishing 6243
Khaniqahi Nimatullahi Publications (KNP) 6155
Khanna Publishers **2312**
Khula Educational Investments (50%) 2507
Kibworth Books **1495**
Kids 1708
Kids Can Press **2164**
Kiepenheuer & Witsch 6160
Killie Campbell Africana Library 2509
Kindred Productions **2165**
Laurence King Publishing **1496**, 1855, 3017, 6243
Kingfisher 1506, 6243
Kingfisher Design Services **3034**
King's Fund **1497**, 6144
Kingscourt Publishing 2059
Jessica Kingsley Publishers **1498**, 1502
Kingston Publishers Ltd **2407**, 6166
Kingsway Communications Ltd 1499
Kingsway Music 1499, 1653
Kingsway Publications Ltd **1499**, 1653
Kingsway Publishers 2485
Kinnell Publications Ltd **1500**, 6205
The Kipling Society **5086**
Kirin Publishing Pty Ltd 2049
Kiscadale 6104
Kistler Graphics 1507
KIT Press 1463
Kitab Bhavan 6137
K. L. Commercial Book Co (M) Sdn Bhd 2250
Klutz 6243
Kluwer Algemene Uitgeverijen 6166
Kluwer Law International **1501**
Kluwer Publishing 1226
Knaur 6160
Knight Features **4052**
Knight Ridder 6151, 6170
Knight-Ridder Information OnDisc 6182
Knights Templar of Aquarius 1325
Know Alls 1409
Know How Series 1055
Know the Game 1089
Knowledge Systems (GB) 6152
Knowledge Unlimited (Pty) Ltd **2504**
Knox Press 1289
Kodak Publications 1323
Kodansha 1922
Kodansha Europe 6145
Kodansha/Tuttle (Biblios) 6071
Kogan Page Ltd 1261, **1502**, 6202, 6243
Kohler 2496
Kompass Publishers 1245
Kompass (Reed Information Services) 6182
Konark Publishers 1760
Konecky & Konecky 1026, 6205
Walther Konig 6139
Konsep Lagendia 6183
Kosei 1922
Kozmik Press 6205
KPI Paperbacks 1488
KPM Music Group 1466
H. J. Kramer 6135, 6243
Krause Publications 6166
Krieger Publishing Co 6161, 6191
KSB Publishers' Services **6103**
Kunsthaus Zürich 6139

Kuperard (London) Ltd **1503**, 6142, **6175**, 6243
Kwela Books 2514
Kyle Cathie 6243
Kyoto Shoin 6139
Kyoto Zen Centre 1922

La Trobe University Press 1697
Labor Publications 1473
Labour Research Department 6152
Labyrinth Group Plc 1072, 3035
Labyrinth Publishing (UK) Ltd **3035**
Ladybird Books Ltd **1504**, 1661, 2068, 6243
R. Laffont 6137
University of Lagos Press 6069
Lake House Investments Ltd **2521**
Lake Publishers & Enterprises Ltd **2416**
Lala Sunderlal Jain Series 2321
Lame Turtle Press 1922
Lancaster House Pub. 6152
Lancer International 2313
Lancer Paperbacks 2313
Lancer Publishers & Distributors **2313**
Land Rover 6205
Lands Peoples & Cultures Series 1220
Landscape Institute 1737
Landscapes Series 1840
Langenscheidt Dictionaries 6160, 6243
Langenscheidt/Longman GmbH 1014
Langsyne Publishers 6243
Language & Education Library 1591
Language Forum Monograph Series (LSMF) 2272
Language Teaching Publications **1505**
Lannoo 6073, 6145
Lansdowne Press 2049
Lansdowne Publishing **2049**
Lapis Press 6139
Large Print 1549
Large Print Chivers 1190
Largest Companies Series 1267
Lark Publishing 1162
Larousse Plc 1389, **1506**, 6160, 6243
Larson 1053, 6140
Roger Lascelles **1507**
Latin America Bureau **1508**, 6152
Laughing Stock Productions 6243
Laurel House Publishing Co Inc 6166
Wilfrid Laurier University Press 6148
Les Presses de l'Université Laval **2166**
Lavis Marketing **6104**
Lavoisier Publishing 1462
Lavoisier Tec et Doc 1462
Law Book Co 1747
Law Book Co of Australia 6174
Law Pack Publishing Ltd **1509**
Law Publishers **2314**
Law Society Publications & Multimedia **1510**
Law Times Press 2290
Lawrence & Wishart Ltd **1511**, 6152
Lawson-Price 6095
Lawyers Co-operative 6174
Laxmi Publications **2315**
LBC Information Services **2050**
LDA 1513
Leading Edge Press & Publishing **1512**, **6035**
Learned Enterprises International 6166
Learners Press **2316**, 2365
Learning Development Aids (LDA) **1513**, 6105, 6142, 6243
Learning Media Ltd **2449**
Learning Resources 1513
Learning Rewards 1929
Learning Solutions **2051**
Learning Strategies Corporation 6136
Learning Through Landscapes Trust 1814
Learning Together **1514**, 6073, 6145

Leatherhead Food Research Association 1314, 6182
Cat Ledger Literary Agency **4053**
Left Bank Books 1328
Legal Action Group **1515**
Legastat Copying & Scanning **6036**
Legend 1722
Lehigh University Press 1348
Leicester University Press 1162, **1516**, 1681
Leipzig Book Fair **6301**
Leisure Art Series 1783
Leisure Books 6145, 6207
Lemma 1498
Uitgeverij Lemman BV 1502
Lemon Unna & Durbridge Ltd 4002
Lemos & Crane **1517**
Lennard Associates Ltd 1712, **3036**
Lennard Publishing 3036, 6243
Christopher Lennox-Boyd 1050, 6138
Leo Books 2514
Hal Leonard 1466
Leopard Books 6167
Leosong Copyright Services Ltd 1466
Lesome Press **6183**
Lester & Orpen Dennys 2163
Lester Publishing Ltd 2163, **2168**
Let's Learn to Write Series 2406
Letterbox Library **6279**
Letterland Direct Ltd 6243
Letterland International Ltd **1518**
Lettermen Publishing Ltd **1519**, 6145, 6243
Letts 1614
Letts/Channel 4 Exam Kit 1251
Letts Educational 1251, 6243
Letts Explore Literature Guides 1251
Letts (General Publishing Division) 6243
Lionel Leventhal Ltd 1366
Hugh Lauter Levin Associates 6166
Levinson Books Ltd **1520**, 1521, 6243
Levinson Children's Books Ltd **1521**, 1719, 6194
Barbara Levy Literary Agency **4054**
H. K. Lewis 6174
J. D. Lewis & Sons Ltd 1350
Lexicon 2499
Lexus Ltd **3037**
L.I.R. (Legal Information Resources) 1844
John Libbey CIC srl 1522
John Libbey Eurotext Ltd 1522
John Libbey & Co Pty Ltd 1522
John Libbey & Company Ltd **1522**
Liberation & Theology 1141
Libertarian Education 6152
Liberty Fund 6202
Librairie du Liban 1649
Librapharm 6191
Libraries Unlimited 6161
Library Association **5087**, 6146
Library Association Publishing **1524**
Library Challenges Series 2006
Library Council of NSW 2080
Library of Analytical Psychology 1487
Library of Arabic Linguistics 1488
Library of Congress 6182
Library & Information Statistics Unit (LISU) **1523**
Library of International Relations 1850
Library of Modern Middle East Studies 1850
Library of Tibetan Works and Archives 1922
Library Research Agency **6012**
Libris Ltd 6085
LIBRIS (Thailand) Co Ltd 1648
Libro Port 6139
Libtech – International Library Technology Fair **6302**
Lidel Edições Técnicas 6160
Lifestar 6136

Lifetime Books Inc 6166
Lifeways 1396
Light Technology 1920
Liguori 1728
The Lilliput Press Ltd **2397**, 6100, 6152
Lily Publications 6258
Limelight Editions 6166
Limetree Calendars 6145
Frances Lincoln Ltd **1525**, 6146, 6243
Lincoln Records Society 1115
Lindisfarne Press 1312
Lineage Research Unit 1087
Linford Soft Cover Series 1862
Ling Kee (UK) Ltd 1898, 3011
Linguapac Distributors Pte Ltd 1526
Linguaphone Institute Ltd **1526**
Linguaphone Institute (Hong Kong) Ltd 1526
Linguaphone Japan KK 1526
Linguasia 1106
Link House 6243
Link House Media Ltd 1306
Links Publications 6160
Lion Library 1527
Lion Manuals 1527
Lion Publishing Corp 1527
Lion Publishing Plc **1527**, 6243
Lionheart Music 1466
Lions 1387
Lion's Den Publications Inc 6166
Lip Smackers Inc 6166
J. B. Lippincott 2034, 6182
Lippincott-Raven Publishers 6191
Listen for Pleasure 2418
Lister Art Books (of Southport) **6176**
LISU Reports 1523
Literacy Links/2000 2059
Literary Dynamics **4117**
The Literary Guild **6274**
Literary Market Place 1994 **6361**
The Literary Review 1711
The Literature Bureau **5182**
Literature Fund of the Australia Council **5136**
Litografia Artistica Cartografica Srl 1507
Little Ark Books (Allen & Unwin Pty) 1719, 2004
Little Barefoot Books 1070
Little, Brown & Co Inc 1528
Little, Brown & Co (UK) 1169, **1528**, 1889, 2506, 6166, 6182, 6199, 6243
Little, Brown Medical 1194, 1659
Little, Brown USA 2506
Little Hills Press Pty Ltd 1587, **2052**
Little Lions 1527
Christopher Little Literary Agency **4055**
Little Mammoth 1551
Little People Books **3038**
Little Wizard Ltd 1819, 6180Littlehampton Book Services Ltd 1640, **6177**
The Littman Library of Jewish Civilization 1161, **1529**
Liver Press 1217
Liveright 1623
Liverpool University Press **1530**, 6202
Living Books 6243
Living & Learning (Cambridge) Ltd 1513
Living & Learning Inc 1513
Living Media India Ltd 1620
Living Quest 6166
Living Stories Inc 6179
Living & Working in... Guides 6175
Livres de poche 6160
Livres de poche classique 6160
Llais Llyfrau **6332**
Llanerch Enterprises 6258
Llanerch Publishers **1531**
Llewellyn 6135

Chris Lloyd Sales & Marketing Services 6105, 6142, 6243
Lloyd's Register of Shipping 1532
LLP (Asia) Ltd 1533
LLP Inc 1533
LLP Ltd 1533
Llyfrau'r Faner 6258
Llyfrgell Genedlaethol Cymru / National Library of Wales 6258
Local Heritage Books UK 1216
House of Lochar 1534
Locker Verlag 6139
Loeb Classical Library 1390, 1915
Login Publishers Consortium 6166
Logis of Great Britain 1824
Logos 6362
Logotron 1014
Loizeaux Brothers Inc 6179
London College of Printing and Distributive Trades 6396
London Independent Books 4056
The London Institute 6397
London International Book Fair 6303
The London Mosque Publications 1469
London Papers (now European Research in Regional Science) (Series) 1682
London Review of Books 6152
London School of Publishing 6398
London Studies on South Asia 1229
Lone Eagle Publishing Co 6166
Lonely Planet Publications 2053, 6167, 6178, 6243
Lonely Planet Publications Inc 2053
Lonely Planet Publications Pty Ltd 2053
Barry Long Books 1535
The Barry Long Foundation 1535
Longhorn Kenya Ltd 2417
Longhorn Publishers (Uganda) Ltd 2417
Longman Asia Ltd 1014
Longman Australia Pty Ltd 2054
Longman Botswana (Pty) Ltd 1014
Longman de Mexico SA de CV 1014
Longman France SA 1014
Longman Group Ltd 2068, 2507, 6243
Longman Hellas Publishing SA 1014
Longman Italia Srl 1014
Longman Japan KK 1014
Longman Lesotho (Pty) Ltd 1014
Longman Malaysia Sdn Bhd 1014
Longman Namibia (Pty) Ltd 1014, 2507
Longman Nigeria Plc 1014
Longman Paul Ltd 2450, 2460
Longman Singapore Publishers Ltd 1014
Longman Zambia Ltd 1014
Longman Zimbabwe (Pvt) Ltd 1014, 2530
Loony Balloonies 1409
Lorenz Books 1038, 1061, 6243
James Lorimer & Co 6104
Lothian Books 2055, 6166
Thomas C. Lothian Pty Ltd 2055
Lotsawa 1922
Loughborough University 1523, 6399
Le Loup de Gouttière Inc 2167
L. A. Louver Gallery 1050, 6138
Love Child Publishing 6166
Love Line Books 6135
Love Publishing 1498
Low Priced British Books (LPBB) 2288, 3039
Peter Lowe 1285, 6243
Margaret Lowenfeld Trust 6085
Lower Saint John River Association 2142
Lowery-Chappell 1466
Andrew Lownie Literary Agency 4057
Loyola University Press 1198
Luath Press Ltd 1536
Luchterhand 6160
Jennifer Luithlen Agency 4058

Lund Humphries Publishers 6146
Lund Humphries Publishers Ltd 1537
Lund University Press 1187
Lunwerg Editores 1050, 6138
The Lutterworth Press 1538, 1199
Lutyens & Rubinstein 4059
Lux Verbi 2503
Lux Verbi Ltd 2505
Luzac Storytellers 1934
LW Book Sales 6176
Lyle Publications Ltd 1539, 6243
Lyle Stuart 1158
Lynx Communication 1812
Lyons & Burford 1824
Lyric Books Ltd 1540, 6145, 6243

M.33 Ltd 3004
McAfee Music Corporation 1466
B. McCall Barbour 6179
McClelland & Stewart Inc 2169, 2228, 6108
Deirdre McDonald Books 6108
McDonald Publishing Ltd 1135, 1495
Macdonald Purnell (Pty) Ltd 2506
Macdonald Young Books 1541, 6142, 6243
McFarland & Co Inc 6197
MacFarlane Walter & Ross 2170
McGill-Queen's University Press 1876, 2171, 6181
McGraw-Hill Book Co Australia Pty Ltd 1542, 2056
McGraw-Hill Book Co New Zealand Ltd 2056
Libros McGraw-Hill de Mexico SA de CV 1542
McGraw Hill Healthcare & Medical 6181
McGraw-Hill Inc 1542, 2056, 2172
McGraw-Hill/Interamericana (Colombia) SA 1542
McGraw-Hill/Interamericana de España SA 1542
McGraw-Hill/Interamericana de Portugal Ltda 1542
McGraw-Hill/Interamericana (Venezuela) SA 1542
McGraw-Hill International Book Co 1542
McGraw-Hill Libri Italia srl 1542
McGraw-Hill Publishing Co 1094, 1542, 2172, 6151, 6182, 6243
McGraw-Hill Ryerson Ltd 1542, 2172
Mackwin & Co 2476
Maclean Press 1088
MacLennan & Petty Pty Ltd 1498, 1502, 2057
Macmillan 1545, 1803, 2451, 6095, 6151, 6243
Macmillan Accounts and Administration Ltd 1547
Macmillan Atlases 2522
Macmillan Boleswa (Lesotho) Publishing Co 2522
Macmillan Boleswa Publishers Pty Ltd 1547, 2522
Macmillan Book Publishing Group 6180
Macmillan Botswana Publishing Co (Pty) Ltd 1547, 2522
Macmillan Canada 2139, 2173
Macmillan Children's Books 1543, 1545, 1547
Macmillan Computer Publishing 1698
Editorial Macmillan de Mexico SA de CV 1547
The Macmillan Dictionary of Art Ltd 1547
Macmillan Direct Ltd 1547
Macmillan Distribution Ltd 1547, 6180
Macmillan do Brasil 1547
Macmillan Education Ltd 1544, 1547, 2418, 6174, 6243
Macmillan General Books Ltd 1544, 1545, 1546, 1547, 1548

Macmillan India Ltd 1547
Macmillan Information Systems Ltd 1547
Macmillan Interactive 6243
Macmillan Journals Ltd 1547
Macmillan Journals Subscriptions Ltd 1547
Macmillan Kenya Publishers 1547, 2418
Macmillan Language House Ltd 1547
Macmillan Library Series 2522
Macmillan London Ltd 1545, 1547
Macmillan Ltd 1543, 1546, 1547, 1677
Macmillan Magazines Ltd 1547
Macmillan Multimedia Ltd 1547
Macmillan Nigeria Publishers Ltd 1547
Macmillan Press Ltd 1544, 1545, 1546, 1547, 1548
Macmillan Press UK Ltd 1547
Macmillan Primary English Project (MAPEP) 2522
Macmillan Primary English Readers 2522
Macmillan Primary Maths 2522
Macmillan Production Ltd 1547
Macmillan Publishers 2451, 2522
Macmillan Publishers Australia Pty Ltd 1547
Macmillan Publishers (China) Ltd 1547
Macmillan Publishers (Hong Kong) Ltd 1547
Macmillan Publishers Ltd 1544, 1545, 1546, 1547, 1548, 2452
Macmillan Publishers New Zealand Ltd 1547, 2452
Macmillan Publishers (Zambia) Ltd 1547
Macmillan Reference Books 1547, 1548
Macmillan Reference Publications Ltd 1547
Macmillan Schoolbooks 1611
Macmillan Shuppan KK 1547
Macmillan South Africa (Pty) Ltd 2522
Macmillan Subscriptions Ltd 1547
Macmillan Swaziland National Publishing Co (Pty) Ltd 1547, 2522
Macmillan Uganda Ltd 1547
Macmillan US Subscriptions Ltd 1547
McPhee Gribble 2068
McPherson & Co 6139
Macquarrie University Ancient History Documentary Research Centre 1530
Julia MacRae 1722, 6243
Mad Jack 1409
Mad River Press 1738, 6195
Madeleine 2101
Louis E. Madison 6166
Madison Publishing 6205
Madoc Books 6166
Maeght Editeur 1050, 6138
Maelor Interactive Publishing 1122
Magazine Design & Publishing Ltd 6180
Magi Publications 1089
Magic Image Filmbooks 6166
Magination Press 6136
Magna Books 1391, 6226
Magna Books Inc 1391
Magna Large Print Books 1549
Magwood Press 1835
Mahajan Publishers Pvt Ltd 2318
Mahayana Publications 1922
Mahayana Sutra & Tantra Press 1922
Mainstream Baptists for Life & Growth 1588
Mainstream (Bookpoint) 6071
Mainstream Publishing Co (Edinburgh) Ltd 1550, 6243
S. Abdul Majeed & Co 2427
Make-A-Model Books 1409
Malayan Law Journal Pte Ltd 1112
Malice Aforethought Press 6152
Mallinson Rendel Publishers Ltd 2453
Malone Society 1648
Malthouse Press Ltd 6069, 6104
The Malvern Publishing Co Ltd 1444
Mambo Press 2531

Mammoth **1551**, 1730, 2208
Mamre Press 1920
Management Books 2000 Ltd **1552**, 6145
Management Guides 1725
Management Publications 1314
Manav Law House 2290
Manchester City Art Galleries 1050, 6138
Manchester University Press **1553**
Mandarin **1554**, 1730, 2208, 6243
Mandarin Educational Publishers Pte Ltd 2491
Manderino Books 6166
Mandrake of Oxford **1555**
Manhattan Press (HK) Ltd 2488, 2491
Manhattan Press (S) Pte Ltd **2488**, 2491
University of Manitoba Press **2174**, 6104
Andrew Mann Ltd **4060**
Leah Manning Trust 1825
Mansell Publishing 1162, **1556**
Manson Publishing Ltd **1557**
Manticore Europe Ltd **1558**
Manticore Publishers Inc 1558
Manufacture Française des Pneumatiques
    Michelin 1575
Mapeasy 1746
Mapin Publishing Pvt Ltd 6166
Maplehouse Press 1503
MARC International 1192
Marco Polo Guides 6243
Mardev Ltd **6106**
Maresfield Library 1487
Marian Communications 1356
Marian Series 1198
Dairat al Marif 6137
Market House Books Ltd **3040**
Market Street Press 6166
Markt & Technik 1698
Markus Wiener 1183
Marlborough Fine Art 6139
Marlin Books 1803
Marling Menu Masters 1323
Marlowe & Co 6166
Marquis Who's Who 1112
The Marsh Agency **4061**
Marshall Cavendish (Australia) Pty Ltd 2493
Marshall Cavendish Books 2493, **3041**
Marshall Cavendish Corporation 2493
Marshall Cavendish International Ltd 2493
Marshall Cavendish Ltd 2251
Marshall Cavendish Partworks Ltd 2493
Marshall Cavendish, US 1746
Marshall Editions Developments Ltd 3042
Marshall Information Ltd **3042**
H. H. Marshall Ltd 2185
Marshall Media Ltd 3042
Marshall Pickering 1387, 1388
Marston Book Services Ltd 1093, **6181**
Marston House 3003, 6105, 6142
John Martin & Artists Ltd **6037**
Martin Books 6173
Martin-Coulter Music Ltd 1466
Martin Education 2041
Martindale-Hubbell 1112
Martins Printing Group UK Ltd 1288
Marval 1050, 6138
Blanche Marvin **4062**
Marwain Publishing 1824
Edition Marzona 6139
Mask Noir 1787
Maskew Miller Longman (Pty) Ltd 1014, **2507**
Kenneth Mason Publications Ltd **1559**, 6073,
    6145, 6243
Masquerade Books 6207
Masquerade Publications 6205
University of Massachusetts Press 6161
Editions Charles Massin 1507
Master Bridge Series 1349
Master Class 1409

Masters 1225
Masters Press 6166
Material History Review 2180
Harold Matson Co Inc 4046
Peter Maurice Music Co Ltd 1466
Mautoglade Music Ltd 1466
Maxi Books 1846
Maxwell Aley Associates 4008
Mayer Edition 1416
Mayfield Publishing Co 1431, 6181
Maypop Books 1920
Mazzota Editore 6139
MBA Literary Agents **4063**
MCA Music Inc 1466
MCI (Music College International) 6243
M D Publications Pvt Ltd **2317**
M & E 1685
Meadowbrook Press 6105, 6142
P. D. Meany Co Inc 1811
Mechanical-Copyright Protection Society Ltd
    5088
Mechanical Engineering Publications **1560**
Institution of Mechanical Engineers 1560
Mecklermedia Ltd **1561**
Medallion Publishing Ltd **3043**
Médecins sans Frontières 6152
Media Masters Pty Ltd 6146, 6243
Media Research Publishing Ltd **1562**
Media Resource Service **6013**
Mediaeval Sources in Translation 2199
Mediakey Plc 3042
Medialine Holdings Ltd 2462
Median Books Ltd **6107**
Medias Paul 1757
Medical Economics 6181, 6182
Medical & Health Annual 1278
Medical Writers Group **5089**
The Medici Society Ltd **1563**
Mediterraneans 6152
Meditext **6014**
Meher Baba Books 3049
Melbourne University Press 2058, 6166
Melia Publishing Services **6108**, 6167, 6243
Robert Mellin Ltd 1466
Melrose Press Ltd **1564**
Melstamps 6205
MELTS Readers 2522
Memorabilia Pack Co 6146
Memory Lane Music Ltd 1466
Menard Press 6152
Editions Menges 1050, 6138
Mennonite Brethren Church of North America
    2165
Mentor 1191, 2068
Mentor Publications **2398**
Mercantila Publishing AS 1314
Mercat Press **1565**
Mercator Fonds 1050, 6138
Mercier Press Ltd **2399**, 6100
Mercury Arts Publications 1828
Mercury Business Books 1552
Mercury House 6166
The Mercury Press **2175**
Mercury Press (Pvt) Ltd **2532**
Meredith Books 1072
Merehurst Books 1566, 6146, 6243
Merehurst Fairfax 1566
Meresborough Books Ltd **6252**
Meridian Books 1216, **1567**
Meridian Classic 2068
Meriwether Publishing Ltd 6166
Merlin 6152
Merlin Books Ltd **1568**
Merlin Press Ltd **1569**
Merlin Unwin 6243
Mermaid 1661, 2460
Merrell Holberton Publishers Ltd **1570**, 6145

Merry Walk Antiques 6176
Merseyside Port Folios 1217
The Mervyn Peake Society **5090**
Messidor Books 6205
Meta Publications 6136
Metaphysical Research Group 1813
Metasystems 6136
Methodist Publishing House **1571**, **2508**
Methuen **1572**, 1730, 2208, 6243
Methuen Children's Books **1573**, 1730, 2208
Methuen Drama 2208
Metro Books **1574**, 6162, 6243
Metropolis Promotions Ltd 1444
Mews Music Ltd 1466
MH Editions 1050, 6138
Michaelmas Books 6205
Michael's Guides 1503, 6175
Michelin Tourist Guides (Red & Green) 1575
Michelin Tyre Plc **1575**, 6243
University of Michigan Press 6148, 6191
The Michigan State University Press 6166
Microform Academic Publishers **1576**
Microinfo Ltd **6182**
Micromedex 6170, 6182
Micropatent 6170
Microsoft 1248, 6151, 6182, 6243
Midas Public Relations Ltd **6109**
Middle East Cultures Series 1472
Middle School Maths 2522
Middlesex University **6400**
Middlesex University Press 6152
Middleton Press **1577**
Midland Counties Publications (Aerophile) Ltd
    1578, 1579
Midland Publishing Ltd 1578, **1579**, 6243
Midnight Classics 1787
Midsummer Books 1801
Miegunyah Press 2058
Mighty Minds Corporation Ltd 6091
Milady Publications 6174
Milepost Publications 1687
Milestone Publications 1775
Milex Data Corporation **6055**
Milia – International Illustrated Book & New
    Media Publishing Fair **6304**
Editrice Militare 1050, 6138
Military & Aviation Book Society **6274**
The Military Balance (Annual) 1834
Millbank Books Ltd 6153, **6183**
Millennium 1639, 1640, 2025, 6155, 6177,
    6243
J. Garnet Miller Ltd 1224
The Cathy Miller Foreign Rights Agency **4064**
Miller Freeman Inc 6166
Miller Freeman Information Services **1581**
Miller Freeman Plc 1581
Robert Miller Gallery 6139
Harvey Miller Publishers **1580**
Millers 1730
Editions Didier Millet **2489**
Mills & Boon 1385, 1549, 2148
Mills Music Inc 1466
Millstream Books 1022
Milne Books Pty Ltd 6155
Richard Milne Ltd **4065**
Milner 2078, 6243
Milner Craft Series 2078
Sally Milner Publishing 1162, 6166
Mimosa Publishing Ltd 1731, **2059**
Mind and Miracles 6166
Mind Matters 6136
Minder Music Ltd 1466
Mindscape 6243
The Minerals Metals and Materials Society
    (TMS) 6159
Minerva **1582**, 1730, 2208

Minerva Associates (Publications) Pvt Ltd **2319**
Minimax Books Ltd **1583**
Ministero de Cultura (Spain) 6139
Minneapolis Institute of Art 6139
University of Minnesota Press 1876, 6181
Minority Rights Group 6152
Minuit 6160
Minus 6152
Mira 1385, 2148
Mirchandani & Co Ltd 2303
Mirror Books 6243
Mirror Group 1104
MIS Press (M & T Books) 1685
Mispol 1591
Mission Earth 1613
University Press of Mississippi 1746, 6071
Mississippi Museum of Art 6139
University of Missouri Press 6161
The MIT Press Ltd **1584**, 1915
Mitchell Beazley **1585**, 1730, 2208, 6243
Mitchell-Filby 1323
Mitra & Ghosh Publishers Pvt Ltd **2320**
M&J Publications 6105, 6142
MJS Books 1050, 6138
Mkuki na Nyota Publishers 6069
MLBD Books International 2321
MLBD Series in Linguistics 2321
M & M Publishing 6154, 6243
Mmaletsatsi 2522
Mobile Communications International Ltd 1440
Modello 6154
Modern African Library 2422
Modern African Writers Library 2414
The Modern Book Depot 2363
Modern Book Service **6268**
Modern Egyptology 1046
Modern English Fiction 1240
Modern Languages in Practice 1591
The Modern Library 1503
The Modern Library (Random House) 6175
Modern Welsh Publications 6085
Moeller Foundation 1325
M/S Siraj Mohammadi Press 2479
Molino 6160
Momenta Publishing Ltd **6110**
Monacelli 1661
Monate Wa Setswana 2522
Mondadori España 6160
Mondadori UK Ltd 6160, **6184**
Monitoring European Integration (annual) 1175
Montagud Editores SA 1314
Montfort Publications 1356
Monthly Review Foundation 6152
Montignac Publishing 6073, 6145
Les Presses de l'Université de Montréal 2138, **2176**
Monumenta Indica Series 2304, 2356
Moon Travel Handbooks 6243
Moonlight First Encyclopaedia 1586
Moonlight Publishing Ltd **1586**, 1719, 6194
Moorland Publishing Co Ltd **1587**, 6167, 6243
Moorley's Bible & Bookshop Ltd 1588
Moorley's Print & Publishing **1588**
Moral Re-Armament (The Oxford Group) 1371
Morehouse Publishing 1356
Morgan Interactive 1139
Morgan Kaufmann Publishers 6157
Morgan & Morgan Inc 6166
Morgen Publishing 6136
Morley Books **6269**
Morpheus International 6153
Joshua Morris 6243
William Morris Agency Inc 4066

William Morris Agency (UK) Ltd **4066**
Morrison Leahy Ltd 1466
Morriss Publishing 2220
Mosaic Educational Publications 1814
Mosaic Press 1148, **2177**, 6085
Moscovitch & Co 6152
Mosupatsela 2522
Motilal Banarsidass Publishers 1050, 1922, **2321**, 6138
Motilal Books (UK) 6104, **6185**
Motivation Cassettes 1552
Michael Motley Ltd **4067**
Moto Magazine (Pvt) Ltd 2531
Motor Racing Publications Ltd **1589**, 6145
Motorbooks International Inc 1398
Motta 1050, 6138
Mount 1356
Mount Series 2052
Moving into Math 2059
Moving Publications Ltd **2178**
Mowbray 1162, **1590**, 6243
Moyer Bell Ltd 6166
MPW Lasec Software Ltd **6056**
Mr Humpty Cassettes 1719
Mr Little 3062
Mr Men Library 1929
M & S Paperback 2169
M/S Prints India 2317
MTD Rigg 1810
De Muiderkring 1658
John Muir 6154
Frederick Muller 6243
Muller GmbH & Co KG 1416
Lars Muller Publishers 1110
Multi Media Investments Ltd 1841
Multi-Sensory Learning 1309
Multicom Publishing Inc 6166
Multilingual Matters Ltd 1591, 6191, 6243
Multimedia Library Ltd **1592**
Multimedia Revision Guides for GCSE 1251
Multimedia Solutions 6243
Multimedia Zambia 6069
James Munro & Co 1136
Munshiram Manoharlal Publishers Pvt Ltd **2322**
Mike Murach & Associates Inc 6166
Murchison's Pantheon Ltd **1593**
Murdoch Books **2060**
Murdoch Magazines Pty Ltd 2060
John Murray Publishers Ltd **1594**, 6167, 6243
Murray Remainders **6228**
The Phil Murray Success Programme 1666
Ugo Mursia 6160
Musée de la Mode et du Costume 6139
Musée de Marseille 6139
Museum of Fine Arts, Boston 1039
Museum of London 1050, 6138
Museum of Modern Art, New York 1855
Museum of Modern Art (Oxford) 6139
Museum of New Mexico Press 6139
Museum Quilts Publications 1113, 6145, 6243
Museum Tusculanum Press 6166
Mushroom Bookshop 6152
Music Book Distributors Ltd **6186**
Music Collection International 6146
Music Direct **6274**
Music for London Entertainment 1826
Music Master 1630
Music Sales Corp 1630
Music Sales Ltd 1630
Music Sales (Pty) Ltd 1630
Musica Britannica 1826
Musicord Publications 1466
Muslim Publications Ltd 1469
Mustang Publishing 6166
Mustaqim 6085
Mute Records 6152

My Little Funfax 1409
Mykologia Lucerne 1738, 6195
Mystery & Thriller Guild **6274**

Nadder Books 1269
NAG Press Ltd 1379
Peter Nahum 1050, 6138
Naiad Press 6135
Nairobi University Press 6069
NAL 2068, 2460
Namara Group 1711
Name Authority List 1129
Napier University **6401**
John Napir 6162
Napoleonic Library 1366
Naresh Publishers **2323**, 2337
Narosa Book Distributors Pvt Ltd 2324
Narosa Publishing House **2324**, 6161
Nasionale Boekhandel Beperk 2500, 2516
Nasionale Pers 2514
Nasjonal Læremiddelscenter 1016
Nasou 2514
Nat West 1685
University of Natal Press **2509**
Nataraj Publishing 6135
NATE (National Association for the Teaching of English) **1595**
Nathan 1513, 6160
National Academy Press **1596**, 6191
National Acquisitions Group **5091**
National Aviation Museum 2180
National Bible Societies 1125
National Book Development Council of Singapore **5173**
National Book Distributors 1614
National Book Foundation 6137
National Book Network 6166
National Book Organisation **2325**
National Book Shop **2326**
National Building Specification (NBS) 1737
National Center for Non-Profit Boards 1609
National Childbirth Trust 1608
National Christian Education Council **1597**
The National Coaching Foundation 1204
National Council for Civil Liberties 6152
National Council for Voluntary Organisations 1609
National Educational Group 2517
National Extension College Trust Ltd **1598**
National Foreman's Institute 1698
National Foster Care Association (NFCA) **1599**
National Gallery of Australia 1855, **2061**
National Gallery of Canada **2179**
National Gallery of Victoria **2062**
National Gallery Publications Ltd **1600**
The National Gallery Trust 1600
National Gardens Scheme 6243
National Geographic 6191
National Information Services Corp 6182
National Institute of Adult Continuing Education **1601**
National Joint Consultative Committee for Building 1737
National League for Nursing 6166
National Library of Australia **2063**, **5137**
National Library of Medicine 1127
National Museum of Science & Technology Corporation **2180**
National Museum of Wales 1843, 1895
National Museums of Scotland **1602**, 6166
National Oceanographic & Atmospheric Administration 6182
National Portrait Gallery Publications **1603**, 6145
National Press 2495, 2497, 2498, 6166
National Radiological Protection Board 1419

National Register Publishing 1112
National Society / Church House Publishing 1193
National Sound Archive 1128
National Spiritual Assembly of Bahá'ís of the United Kingdom 1066
National Technical Information Service, US Dept of Commerce 6182
National Textbook Co 6071, 6160
The National Trust 1604, 6146, 6243
National Union of Journalists 5092
National Youth Agency 1605
NATO – Publications Office 6182
Natural Heritage/Natural History Inc 1746, 2181
The Natural History Museum – Publications Section 1462, 1606
Nature America Inc 1547
Nature Detectives 2434
Nature Japan KK 1547
Naturist Society 6166
The Naur Foundation 1648
Nautical Books 1015, 1089
Nautical Publishing Co Ltd 1089
Nav Din Prakashan Kendra 2306
Naval Institute Press 1020
Navigator series of maps 1082
Navrang, Booksellers & Publishers 2327
Naxos Audiobooks 1607
NC Press 6104
NCC Blackwell 1093, 6181
NCLC Publishers Ltd 1298
NCT Publishing Ltd 1363, 1608
NCVO Management Guides 1609
NCVO Publications 1609
Ndanda Mission Press 2525
N E Publications 1613
Neal-Schuman Publishers 6161
University of Nebraska Press 6071
Nebula Encounters Series 1744
Needlecrafts with Cross Stitch Book Society 6280
Neha Mini Katha 2363
Neil Wilson Publishing Ltd 1610
NEL 2040
Thomas Nelson 1125, 1611, 2460, 6174
Thomas Nelson Australia 2064, 6174
Thomas Nelson Inc 1926
Thomas Nelson & Sons Ltd 1611, 2506, 6179Nelson-Hall Inc 6166
Nelson Price Milburn Ltd 2064, 2454
Nene Valley Publishing 1179, 1791
Nepal Sahitya Kendra 2374
Neptune Press 6166
Net.works 1846
Neugebauer Press 1719
University of Nevada Press 6161
Neville Spearman Publishers 1233
New Age Publications 6085
New Amsterdam Books 6166
New Asian Publishers 2266, 2328
New Brunswick Geographic Information Corporation 2142
New Canadian Library 2169
New Canadian Poets Series 2203
New Cavendish Books 1612, 6153, 6243
New Chapter Press 6166
New Cherwell Press 6085
New City 1356
New Clarion Press 6152
New Consumer Publications 1159
New Dimensions in Maths 2522
New Directions Publishing Corporation 1623
New Earth Press 1835
University of New England Press 6166, 6191
New English Library 1423
New Era Book Agency 2263

New Era Publications UK Ltd 1613
New Falcon Publications 6135
New Harbinger 6135
New Holland (Publishers) Ltd 1614, 6177, 6243
New Home & Garden Guild 6274
New Horizons 2522, 6152
New Horn Press Ltd 6069
New House Publishers Ltd 2455
New Humanity Books 6155
New Internationalist Books 6152
New Island Books 6100, 6152
New Knowledge Books 1828
New Leaf Publishers 1113, 6176
New Lifestyle Publishing 1444
New Media Investments Ltd 1547
New Mermaids 1089
University of New Mexico Press 6071
New Millennium Publishing 1325
New Muse Award (annual) 2107
New Namibia Books (Pty) Ltd 6069
New Orchard Editions 1047, 1096, 1162, 1615
New Paris Editions 1148
New Playwrights' Network 1616
The New Press 1850, 6145
New Society Publishers 1159, 2182, 6152
University of New South Wales Press 1878, 2065
New Star Books Ltd 2183
New Testament Commentaries 1089
New Ventures in History 2522
New Women's Press Ltd 2456
New World Library 6135, 6243
The New York Academy of Sciences 1617, 6161
State University of New York Press 6191
New York University Press 6191
New York Zoetrope Inc 6166
New Zealand Book Council 5167
New Zealand Books in Print 6363
New Zealand Council for Educational Research 1619, 1777, 2457, 5168
New Zealand Library and Information Association – Te Rau Herenga o Aotearoa 5169
New Zealand Past and Present 2434
Newcastle Publishing 6135
NeWest Publishers Ltd 2184, 6104
Newmarket Press 6207
Newnham College, Cambridge 1843
The News Corp Ltd 1387
News International 1388
News Multimedia 6151, 6182
Newsletter Information Services Pty Ltd 2050
Newsplan 1128
Newspread International 2419
Newstech Publishing Inc 2419
Nexus Special Interests 1618, 1890, 6105, 6142, 6243
NFER (National Foundation for Educational Research) & The Thomson Corporation 1619
NFER-Nelson Publishing Co Ltd 1619
NFER Routledge 6174
Ngwao Boswa 2522
NIACE (National Institute for Adult Continuing Education) 6152
Nicholson 1386
Nico Editions 1859
Nierwand Verlag GmbH 6139, 6166
University of Nigeria Press 6069
Nigerian Institute of International Affairs 6069
Nigerian Publishers Association 5171
Nightingale Books 1066
Nightingale Press 6190
Nile & Mackenzie Ltd 1620
Nimbus Publishing Ltd 1588, 2185, 6166

The Nine Club 2002
Nine Gates Press 1922
Nippan Educational Books 6145
Nippan Visual Art Books 6145
N. Ireland Tourist Board 1001
James Nisbet & Co Ltd 1621
NLP Comprehensive 6136
No Exit Press 1627, 2506, 6243
The Maggie Noach Literary Agency 4068
Noble Porter Press 6166
The Noble Rider 6152
Nolo Press Inc 1169
Nolwazi Educational Publishers Pty Ltd 2522
Non-Parliamentary Publications 1419
Noon Music Ltd 1466
Norbry Publishing Ltd 2186
Norden Publishing House 6142
Nordic Council of Ministers 1419
A. E. Norris Ltd 1559
North American Wildlife Series 1220
North Atlantic Books 6135
University of North Carolina Press 6148
North-South Books 1719, 6194
North Star Publications 1746
Northcliffe Books 1185, 1640
Northcote House Publishers Ltd 1622, 6191
Northern Bee Books 1824
Northern Ireland Publications 1419
Northern Nigerian Publishing Co Ltd 1547
Northstone Publishing Inc 2187
Northwestern University Press 1876, 6181
W. W. Norton & Co Ltd 1447, 1623, 1915
Norwegian University Press 1648
Norwood Publishers 1624
University of Notre Dame Press 6161
Nott Organisation 6205
Notting Hill Publishers 6162, 6243
Nova Science Publishers Inc 1499, 6166
Novalis 1356
New Canadian Novelists Series 2203
Novelsound 1064
NRP 1698
NSPCC 1657
NTC Publications Ltd 1625, 6243
NTC Publishing Group 1886, 6128
NTC Research Ltd 1625
Nuffield Foundation 5093
Nuffield Provincial Hospitals Trust 1648
Nuova Alfa 1050
Andrew Nurnberg Associates Ltd 4069
Andrew Nurnberg Associates, Bucharest 4069
Andrew Nurnberg Associates, Budapest 4069
Andrew Nurnberg Associates, Prague 4069
Andrew Nurnberg Associates, Sofia 4069
Andrew Nurnberg Associates, Warsaw 4069
Andrew Nurnberg Literary Agency (Moscow) 4069
Nutshell Press 1680

Oak Tree Press 6152
Oakwood Publishers 1198
Obafemi Awolowo University Press 6069
Oberon Books Ltd 1626, 6243
Oberon Classics 1626
Oberon/Lamda (London Academy of Music & Dramatic Art) 1626
Oberon Modern Playwrights 1626
Oberon Press 2188
O'Brien Educational 2400
The O'Brien Press 2400, 6100, 6243
Editions de l'Ocean Indien 6069
Ocean Press 6152
OCLC 6170
Octagon Books (Wholesale) Ltd 6229
Octopus 1382
Octopus Distribution 6153
Oddball Publishing 6243

Odyssey Illustrated Guides 6243
Off The Shelf Publishing 6105
Office for Official Publications 2389
Office of Public Works 1419
Ohio State University Press 6161
Oil Companies International Marine Forum 1923
Oise Press **2189**
Oishin Publishing 6152
University of Oklahoma Press 6161
Okonomisk Litteratur 1267
Old Bailey Press 1418
Old Colony 1658
Oldcastle Books Gambling Books 1627
Oldcastle Books Ltd **1627**, 2506, 6146
Jim Oldroyd Books **6230**
David O'Leary Literary Agents **4070**
Olive Press 1445
Oliver & Boyd 2068
Oliver Freeman Pty Ltd 2072
The Olivia & Hill Press 6160
OM Publishing **1628**, 1653
Michael O'Mara Books Ltd 1545, **1629**, 6180, 6243
Omnibus Press **1630**, 2079, 6243
Omnigraphics 6122
Omsons Publications **2329**
On the Road **6274**
Oneworld Publications 1269, **1631**
Online Guides 1055
Online Inc 1854
Online — European Congress & Fair for Technical Communications **6305**
Onlywomen Press 6135
ONT 6205
Ontario Institute for Studies in Education 1777, 2189
Onyx 2068
Oolichan Books **2190**
OP Title Listing — On Microfiche **6364**
OPA Overseas Publishing 6145
OPC (Oxford Publishing Company) 1398, **1632**
Open Book 1356
Open Court Publishing Co 6161
Open Gate Press **1633**
Open Horizons Publishing Co 6166
Open Road Publishing 6166
The Open University **1634**, 1635, 6243
Open University Educational Enterprises Ltd 1634, **1635**
Open University Press **1636**
Openbook Publishers **2066**
Opera Library 1148
Optima 1722
Optonica Ltd **6057**
Opus Publishing Ltd **3044**
Oral Traditions 6155
Orbis Books 6181
Orbit 1528, 2506
Orca Publishing Services Ltd 2447
Orchard Books **1637**, 1900, 6243
Orda-B 6182
Order of Battle Series 3052
Ordnance Survey 1284, **1638**, 6243, 6258
Ordnance Survey of Northern Ireland 1284
O'Reilly Associates 6174
Orfeus Software Publishing 1016
Organic Handbooks Series 1783
Organisation for Economic Cooperation & Development (OECD) 1419, 6182
Orient Book Club 2331
Orient Longman Ltd 1014, 1760, **2330**, 2373
Orient Paperbacks 1106, **2331**, 2375
Oriental Books Reprint Corporation 2322
Oriental Institute, Oxford 1648
Orion Books Ltd **1639**, 1640, 6177, 6243

Orion Children's 1639, 1640, 6177
Orion Paperbacks 1639, 1640, 6243
The Orion Publishing Group Ltd 1185, 1243, 1639, **1640**, 1903
Orpheus Publications 1658
The Oryx Press 6161
Osborne 2056, 6243
Osborne TAB 1542
Oscar 6160
OSDATA (Orient Software Development & Training Co Ltd) 2330
Osmosis Publications **1641**
Osprey **1642**, 1730, 6243
Osservatore Romano 1166
University of Otago Press **2458**
Ottawa Hispanic Studies 2130
University of Ottawa Press **2191**
OUP Singapore 2490
Our Generation 2099
Our Sunday Visitor 1356
Outcomes Incorporated 6136
Outline Press Ltd (Balafon) 1323
Oval Publishing 6205
Overseas Book Service **6306**
Overseas Development Institute **1643**
OVP — Editions du Vidal 6182
Deborah Owen Ltd **4071**
Peter Owen Ltd **1644**, 6177, 6243
Owl Man 1719, 6194
Oxbow Books **1645**
Oxbow Monographs in Archaeology 1645
Oxenwood Press (Gardening Books) 1219
Oxfam Audio-Visual 1646
Oxfam Education 1646
Oxfam Information 1646
Oxfam Publishing **1646**, 6152
University of Oxford 1894
Oxford Book & Stationery Co 2334
Oxford Centre for Publishing Studies **6402**
Oxford Childrens 6243
Oxford Electronic 6243
Oxford Illustrated Press 1320, 1398, 1632, 1829
Oxford in Asia Hardback Reprints 2490
Oxford in Asia Students Editions 2490
Oxford in Asia Studies in Ceramics 2490
Oxford Institute for Energy Studies **1647**, 1648
Oxford Jardine Electronic Publications Ltd 2253
Oxford Literary Review 6152
Oxford Paperbacks 2490
Oxford Publicity Partnership **6111**
Oxford Publishing Co (OPC) 1320, 1398, 1829, 6243
Oxford School of Learning Ltd 6166
Oxford University Committee for Archaeology 1645
Oxford University Press 1125, **1648**, 2192, 2253, 2333, 2420, 2459, 2490, 2510, 6095, 6151, 6182, 6243
Oxford University Press (Canada) **2192**
Oxford University Press (China) Ltd **2253**
Oxford University Press Eastern Africa **2420**
Oxford University Press (Indian Branch) **2333**
Oxford University Press (New Zealand Branch) **2459**
Oxford University Press Pte Ltd **2490**
Oxford University Press (Southern Africa) **2510**
Oxford & IBH Publishing Co Pvt Ltd 1106, **2332**, 2334
Oxmoor House 6108
Oxonian Press Pvt Ltd **2334**
Oyster Books Ltd **3045**

Pace Communications 1171
Pace Gallery 6139
Pacific Basin Books 1488
Pacific View Press 1846
Pacific Writers Series 2208
Les Editions du Pacifique 2489, 2493
Packard (Arabic titles) 1649
Packard Publishing Ltd 1039, **1649**, 6166
Paddleless Press 6243
Padma Publishing 1922
Paganiniana Books (THF Publications Ltd) 1466
Pageant Publishing **6112**
Pakistan Institute of Development Economics **2477**
Paladour Books 6258
Palani Paramount Publications **2335**
Pali Text Society 1922, 6104
The Pall Mall Publishing Co 1444
Pallas Athene 1115, **1650**, 6243
Pallas Guides 1650
G. D. Palmer & Sons Ltd 1439
Roger Palmer Ltd Media Contracts & Copyright **6015**
Pamphleteer's Press 6152
PAMS Promotions **6307**
Pan 1545, 2451
Pan Books (Holdings) Ltd 1547
Pan Books Ltd 1545, 1547, 1677, 1799, 2451, 6243
Pan Bookshops Ltd 1547
Pan Macmillan Australia Pty Ltd 1547, 2451
Pan Macmillan Ltd 1799
Pan Pacific Public Co Ltd 2488
Pan Pacific Publications (S) Pte Ltd 2488, **2491**
Panaf Books 1936
Pandemic Ltd **6187**
Pandon Press Ltd 1097
Pandora 1387
The Panizzi Lectures 1128
Panopus Manuscript 1466
Panorama Information Group 6085
Panos Institute 6152
Panther Publishers Pvt Ltd **2336**
Panurge 6152
Paper European Data Book **6365**
Paper Tiger Books 1252
Paperbound Books in Print **6366**
Paperfronts 1272
PaperJacks 2128
Papermac 1545
Papers in Mediaeval Studies 2199
Papiers collés 2101
PAR 1619
Paragon House 1746
Paragon Softcover Large Print 1190
Parallax Press 6166
Paramount Sales (India) Pvt Ltd 2323, **2337**
Paraninfo 6160
Parapress Ltd **6153**
Parasol 6166
Parco View 6139
Parent & Child 1407, 1730
The Parents' Guide to Children's Holidays 6175
Parent's Guides to the National Curriculum 1251
Parent's Monthly 2254
Paris Audiovisuel 6139
Paris Musées 1050, 6138
Paris Publishing 6166
Park Publications 1507
Parker Associates 6145
Parkett Verlag 6152
Parkstone Press 6166
Parliamentary Publications 1419

Parliamentary Research Services 1235
Parragon 6154, 6243
The Parthenon Publishing Group Inc 1651
Parthenon Publishing Group Ltd **1651**
Parthian Books 6258
Partridge Press 1869, 6243
PASA **5177**
Pascoe Publishing Pty Ltd **2067**
Pasold Research Fund 1648
Passport Publications 1444
Password (Books) Ltd 1116, **6188**
Password Training **6403**
Past & Present Publishing Ltd 1802
PasTest **1652**
Pastime Publications 1001, 6243
Patemans Wholesale Book Service **6253**
Paternoster Periodicals 1653
The Paternoster Press 1653
Paternoster Publishing **1653**
Mark Paterson & Associates **4072**
Pathfinder Distribution Ltd **6191**
Pathfinder Press **1654**
Pathway Productions 1756, 1869
Patra Bharati **2338**
Patricia Music Ltd 1466
Stanley Paul 6243
Paulines Publications **2421**
Paulist Press 1356
Peter Pauper Press 1920
PAVIC Publications **1655**
Pavilion Books Ltd **1656**, 6146, 6243
Pavilion Publishing (Brighton) Ltd **1657**
Pavilions of Splendour 6095
John Pawsey **4073**
Payback Press 1153
PC Publishing **1658**
Peabody Museum 1039
Peachpit Press 1014, 2054
Peachtree Publishers 6122
F. E. Peacock Publishers Inc 6166
Maggie Pearlstine Associates Ltd **4074**
Pearson Peacekeeping Centre – The
  Peacekeeping Press 2111
Pearson Professional Ltd 1014, 1194, 1332,
  1659, 1685, 2054, 2122
Pearson Professional Pty Ltd **2068**
J. M. Pearson & Sons 1447
Pebbleshore Ltd **6189**
Pedigree Books 6146, 6243
Peerage 1382
Pegasus Distribution Ltd **6190**
Peguis Publishers Ltd **2193**, 6085
Pelanduk Publications **6183**
Pelham 1485, 1661, 2068, 6243
Pelican 1661, 2068, 2460
Pembroke Publishers Ltd 1253, **2194**
Pemmican Publications **2195**
Pendle Hill Publications 1710
Pendragon Partnership 1022
Pendulum Gallery Press 6073, 6145
Pendulum Plus Inc 6166
Penguin Audiobooks 1661
Penguin Books Australia Ltd 1661, **2068**
Penguin Books Canada Ltd 1661, 2068
Penguin Books India Pvt Ltd **2339**
Penguin Books Ltd 1302, 1381, 1485, **1661**,
  1899, 2068, 2339, 2460, 6151, 6182, 6243
Penguin Books (NZ) Ltd 1661, 2068, **2460**
Penguin Books USA Inc 1661, 2068
Penguin Electronic 1661, 6243
Penguin Group 1504, 3062
Penguin Popular Classics 6243
Penguin Publishing Co Ltd 1661, 2068
Peninsula Production & Distribution Ltd 1547
The Penman Club **5094**
The Penman Literary Service (Agency
  Department) **4075**

Penn State Press 6161
Pennant Professional Books 1657
Penrose Press 6152
The Pensions Management Institute **1662**
Pen & Sword Books Ltd **1660**, 1906, 6243
Pentathol Publishing **1663**
Pentaxion Ltd **1664**
Pentech Press 1915
Penthe Publishing Co 1325
Pentland Press Inc 1665
The Pentland Press Ltd 1564, **1665**
Penton Overseas Inc 6166
Penton Press 1498, 1502
Pepet letso 2522
Pepin Press 6167
Peppercanister Series 2386
Peter Peregrinus Ltd 1459
Perfect Words and Music Ltd **1666**
Performing Art Series 2321
Performing Right Society Ltd **5095**
Pergamon 1276, 6170
Pergamon Chess 1147
Peridot Press 6152
Pet Owners' Guide 1740
Peter Ward Book Exports **6113**
Peterloo Poets **1667**
A. K. Peters 1755, 6191
The Peters Fraser & Dunlop Group Ltd 4046,
  4076
Duncan Petersen 1001, 6243
John Peterson Music 6179
Peterson's Guides 1882
Petheric Press 2185
Pevensey Press 1237
Phaidon Press Ltd **1668**, 6243
Phanes Press 6135
The Pharmaceutical Press **1669**
Philadelphia Art Alliance 1348
Philadelphia Museum of Art 6139
George Philip **1670**, 1730, 2208, 6243
Philip & Tacey Ltd 1672
Philippine Book Distributors Inc 1385
Philips School 2000 CD-i educational software
  6151
Phillimore & Co Ltd **1671**
Phoebe Phillips **4077**
Phillips International Paper Directory **6367**
Philograph Publications Ltd **1672**
Philosophical Research Society (PRS) 6155
Phipps Public Relations Ltd **6114**
Phoenix 1639, 1640, 1673, 6177, 6243
Phoenix Education Pty Ltd **2069**
Phoenix ELT **1673**
Phoenix House 1639, 1640, 6177, 6243
Phoenix Paperbacks 6243
Phoenix Press (Oxford) 1328, 1402, **1674**
Phoenix Publications **1675**
Phoenix Publishers Ltd **2422**
Phoenix Publishing Inc 6155
Phoenix Young Readers Library 2422
Photographers Gallery 6139
Photographic Book Society **6280**
Photovision 6139
Pi34 Publishing 6152
Piatkus Books **1676**, 2506, 6167, 6243
PIC 6243
Pica Pica Press 2092
Pica Press 6205, 6243
Picador 1545, **1677**, 2451
Picas Series 2144
Piccadilly Press 1113, **1678**, 6199, 6243
Piccin Editore 6166
Piccolo 2451
Pickering & Chatto (Publishers) Ltd **1679**,
  6202
Picton Press (Liverpool) 1217
Picton Publishing (Chippenham) Ltd **1680**

Pictorial Presentations Ltd 1815
Pictorial Publications 1507
Picture Corgi 1869
Picture Lions 1387
Picture Press 6152
Picture Roo Books 2048
Pictures from the Past 2434, 3069
Pilgrim Book Services 1325
Pilgrim Publications 1289
Pilkington Brothers 6095
Pimlico 1722, 6243
Pine Forge Press Inc 1754
Pineloft Publications 1323
The Pinpoint Design Co **6038**
Pinter Publishers Ltd 1162, **1681**
Pinwheel Publishing Ltd **3046**
Pion Ltd **1682**, 6202
The Pioneers of British Columbia Series 2230
Pipeline Books 1711
Piper 2451
Pippin Publishing Ltd **2196**, 6085
Pira International **1683**
Pirate Press 1328
Pisces Publications 1433
Pitambar Publishing Co Pvt Ltd 2260, 2274,
  2340
Pitjantjatjava Bible Translation Project 2081
Pitkin Guides **1684**, 1730
Pitman Publishing 1659, **1685**, 6243
University of Pittsburgh Press 6161
Piyush Printers Publishers Pvt Ltd 2260
Erin Pizzy 6243
PJB Publications 6182
Planet 6258
Planet Dexter 1014
Planeta 6160
The RHS Plant Finder 1587
Plateway Press **1686**
Platform 5 Publishing Ltd **1687**
Platform Books 1148
Plato Publishing **6115**
Players Press Inc 1688
Players Press (UK) 1410, **1688**
Playmarket **4111**
Playne Books Ltd **3047**
Playne Plays **3047**
Playscripts 1148
Playwrights Canada Press **2197**
Playwrights Union of Canada 2197
Plaza & Janes 6160
Plenum Insight 1689
Plenum Medical Book Co 1689
Plenum Press 1689
Plenum Publishing Co Ltd **1689**
Plenum Publishing Corporation 1689
Plenum Publishing Corporation, Moscow
  1689
Plexus Publishing Ltd **1690**, 6146, 6243
Editions Plume 1050, 2068, 6138
Pluto Press Australia 1691, **2070**, 6181, 6243
Pluto Publishing Ltd **1691**
Plymbridge Distributors Ltd **6191**
University of Plymouth **6404**
Plymouth Music Inc 1466
PMA Publishing 6161
The PMI Tuition Service 1662
PMP Guitar Publications 1466
Pocket 1803, 6173, 6243
Pocket Bears 1586
Pocket Classics Series 1843
Pocket Worlds 1586
Pocketbond Ltd **6192**
Poddington Publishing 6180
Poetica 1040
Poetry Canada Review 2203
Poetry Review 6152
The Poetry Society **5096**

Poetry Wales Press Ltd **1692**
Point 1770
Point Loma Publications Inc 6166
Pointer Books Ltd **2526**
Pointer Publishers **2341**
Polebridge Press 1773
Polestar Book Publishers **2198**
Police Review Publishing Co Ltd 1705
Policy Studies Institute 6144
Polin Series 1529
Giancarlo Politi Editore 6152
Political Risk Services 6182
Polity Press 1093, **1693**, 6181
Laurence Pollinger Ltd **4078**
Murray Pollinger **4079**
Pollock's Toy Theatres 1816
Polo Publishing 6166
Polygon 1264, **1694**, 6181
Polygram 6243
Pomegranate Europe Ltd **6193**
Pomegranate Press 1766
Bella Pomer Agency Inc **4104**
Pond View 1397
Pont Books 1350, 6258
Pontifical Institute of Mediaeval Studies **2199**
The Pony Club 1023, 1793, 6243
Pookie Productions Ltd **1695**
Poolbeg Group Services 6162, 6243
Robert Pooley Ltd 1020
Poorna Publications 2369
Pop Universal Ltd 1815
Popular Book Depot 2342
Popular Culture, Inc 6161
Popular Prakashan (Pte) Ltd 1760, **2342**
Porcepic 2097
Porcupine Press 6152
The Porcupine's Quill **2200**
H. Pordes Ltd **6231**
Henry Pordes Books Ltd **6232**
University of Port Harcourt Press 6069
Portage & Main Press 2193
David Porteous Editions **1696**, 6146, 6243
David Porteous Editions (Bookpoint) 6071
Porthill Publishers **3048**
Portikus 6139
Portland Press Ltd **1697**
Porto Editora 6160
A Portrait in Old Picture Postcards (series) 1766
Positive Changes 6136
Post Graduate Institute of Pali & Buddhist Studies 2520
Post Music Ltd 1466
Postcards from......Series 3069
The Beatrix Potter Society **5097**
Pour en finir 2101
Shelley Power Literary Agency Ltd **4080**
Power Publications 1216
Powerhouse (PR) Ltd **6116**
T. & A. D. Poyser 1005, 1384
PR Planner UK **6368**
Prabhat Prakashan **2343**
Practical Handbooks in Archaeology 1215
Practice Tests In Series 1514
Praeger Publishers 1368, 6161
Pragati Publications **2344**
Pratibha Pratishthan 2343
Prayer & Practice 1793
PRC (Promotional Reprint Co) 1708
Precept Press Inc 6166
Prehistory Press 1645
Premier Book Co 2367
Premier Book Marketing 6145
Premier Books 6105, 6142
Prentice Hall Europe 1443, 1673, **1698**, 1701, 6182
Prentice Hall/Ellis Horwood **1699**

Prentice Hall/Harvester Wheatsheaf **1700**
Prentice Hall Hispanoamericana 1698
Prentice Hall International 6173, 6243
Prentice Hall Macmillan 1698
Prentice Hall of Canada Ltd 1698
Prentice Hall of India Pte Ltd 1698
Prentice Hall of Japan Inc 1698
Prentice Hall Press 1803
Prentice Hall Regents 1673, 1698
Prentice Hall/Woodhead Faulkner **1701**
Prepare to Pass 1344
Presbyterian & Reformed 1289
Presidio Press 1366
The Press University of the West Indies **2408**
Les Editions la Presse 2218
Presses de la cité 6160
Presses de l'Université d'Ottawa (University of Ottawa Press) 2138
Presses de l'Université du Québec 2204
Presses Interuniv. Européennes 6166
Les Presses Libre 2218
Presses Pocket 6160
Presses Universitaires de France 6160
Presses Universitaires de Grenoble 6160
Presswork 6152
Prestel Verlag, Munich 1855
Prestige Books **2345**
Preston Corporation (Pte) Ltd 2428, 2429
Preston Corporation Sdn Bhd **2428**, 2429
Preston Publications 6182
Preston-Times Printing & Publishing Co Sdn Bhd 2428, 2429
Mathew Price Ltd **3049**
Pride of Place Publishing 6243
Prim-Ed Publishing **1702**
Prima Publishing 6146
Primary Ecology Series 1220
Department of Primary Industries **2071**
Primary Maths (Botswana) **2522**
Primary Science **2522**
Primary Shona 2534
Primary Social Studies **2522**
Primary Source Media **1703**, **6039**, 6182
Robert Prince – Publishing Solutions **6058**
Prince's Trust Events Ltd 6152
Princeton Architectural Press 6145
Princeton Book Co 1232, 6205
Princeton University Press 1915, 6243 Printing Industries New Zealand (Inc) **5170**
Printing Trades Directory **6369**
Prion Books Ltd **3050**, 6162, 6243
Priory Press Ltd 1901
Priory Publications 1321
Éditions Prise de Parole **2201**
Prism Press Book Publishers Ltd **1704**, 6105, 6142, 6243
Private Eye Books 1869
Private Libraries Association **5016**
Pro Art Publications 1466
Pro-Ed 1619
Productive Publications **2202**
Professional Publishing Ltd **1705**
Professional & Scientific Publications 1100
Profile Books Ltd **1706**
Profiles in Aeronautical History 2180
Progress in Engineering 1208
Progress Press Co Ltd **2431**
Progress Press Publications 2431
Project in Secondary Mathematics (PRISM) 2522
Project Renaissance 6136
Prolog 1503
Prometheus Books UK **1707**, 6104
Promotional Reprint Co Ltd **1708**, 1839
Proper Pictures 6152
Prose Series 2144
Prospect Media Pty Ltd **2072**

Prospect Publishing 2072
Protection Publications 1838
Prous Science Publishers 6182
Keith Prowse Music Publishing Co Ltd 1466
Pruett Publishing Co 6166
The Psychological Corporation 1384, 2033
Psychological & Educational Publications 1037
Psychology Press of Erlbaum (UK) Taylor & Francis **1709**
Psygnosis 6243
PT (Playtime) 1230
PTB 6153
Public Lending Right **5098**
Public Policy Series 2114
Publications de l'Institut d'Études Médiévales 2199
Publications of the Dictionary of Old English 2199
Publications Sci. Nat. 1202
Publisher Marketing Ltd **2485**
The Publishers Association **5099**
Publishers' Association of South Africa (PASA) **5177**
Publishers Distribution Services 6166
Publishers' International ISBN Directory **6370**
Publishers Licensing Society Ltd **5100**
Publishers Publicity Circle **5101**
Publishing and Book Development in Sub-Saharan Africa **6371**
Publishing and Development in the Third World **6372**
Publishing Copyrights Ltd 3004
The Publishing Corporation 6243
Publishing News **6373**
Puffin 1661, 2068, 2460
Pulp Faction 6152
Punches Productions 6166
Purdy Hicks Gallery 1050, 6138
Purelight Publishing 6136
Pustak Mahal **2346**
Pustaka Baiduri Sdn Bhd 2330
Pustaka Delta Pelajaran Sdn Bhd 2425
Putnam Aeronautical Books 1118, 6181
Putnam Publishing Group 6108
PVA Management Limited **4081**
PWS 6174
Pyramid 1382

QED Publishing Ltd 3051
Q-Multimedia (UK) Ltd **6040**
QPD (Quality Paperbacks Direct) **6274**
Quadrille Publishing Ltd 6180, 6243
Quadrillion Publishing Ltd 3068
Quail Map Co 1687
Quaker Home Service **1710**
Qualitex 6258
Quarry B. M. S. (Body, Mind, Spirit) 2203
Quarry Magazine 2203
Quarry Press Inc **2203**
Quarry Rocks! 2203
Quartet Books **1711**, 6191, 6243
Quartet Encounters 1711
Quarto Children's Books Ltd 3051
The Quarto Group Inc 3051
Quarto Publishing Plc **3051**
Que 1698
Presses de l'Université du Québec **2204**
Les Editions Québec/Amérique Inc **2205**
Québec Science Editeur 2204
Queen Anne Press **1712**, 6243
Queen Music Ltd 1466
The University of Queensland Press **2073**
Quentin Books Ltd 4072
Quest Books 6135, 6205
Questron 1189
Quill Publishing Ltd 3051

Quiller Press Ltd **1713**, 6153, 6243
Quilliam 6152
Quinta Essentia 1471, 6152
Quintessence Publishing Co Inc 1714
Quintessence Publishing Co Ltd **1714**, 1793
Quintessenz Verlags GmbH 1714
Quintet Publishing Ltd 3051
Quorum Books 1368, 6161
Quotes Ltd **1715**

Raab Gallery 1050, 6138
Raben & Sjogren Bokforlag 6194
RAC Callbooks 6131
RAC Motoring Services 1716, 6146
RAC Publishing **1716**, 6154, 6243
Radala & Associates **4082**
Radcliffe Medical Press Ltd **1717**
The Radcliffe Press **1718**, 6145
Radiant Publishers 1760
RAF Benevolent Fund 6105, 6142
Ragged Bears Ltd 1586, **1719**, **6194**, 6243
Ragweed Press/ gynergy books **2145**
Rail Photoprints 1687
RailTrail 1512
Railway and Canal Historical Society 1843
Railway Book Club 6280
The Rainbow Co (Retail) 1499
Raincoast Book Distribution Ltd **2206**
Rajpal & Sons 2331, 2375
RAK Publishing Ltd 1466
Ramblers Association 1321
Ramblers & Climbers Book Society **6280**
Ramboro Books **6233**
Ramesh Publishing House **2347**
Rampant Horse Ltd 1444, **1720**
Rand McNally & Co 1824, 6243
Ian Randle Publishers Ltd **2409**
Random House Audio Books 1722, 6243
Random House Australia Pty Ltd 1722, 2461
Random House Children's Books **1721**
Random House Group Ltd 2461, 2511, 6166
Random House Inc 1503, 1722, 2461
Random House New Media 1721
Random House New Zealand Ltd 1722, **2461**
Random House South Africa (Pty) Ltd 1722, 2461, **2511**
Random House UK Ltd 1033, 1049, 1071, 1188, 1437, 1721, **1722**, 6151, 6199
Random New Media 6243
Ranjung Yeshe 1922
Pippa Rann Books **6117**
Ransom Publishing **1723**, 6181
Rapid Communications of Oxford 6174
Rapid Science Publishers **1724**
Rapport Learning Ltd 1317
RAPRA 6182
Raqeen Press 1469
Rastar Pty Ltd 6152
Rastogi Publications **2348**
Rathdowne Publishing 2004
Rato Publicatins 1922
Ravan Press (Pty) Ltd **2512**
Ravelin Ltd **3052**
Raven 2034
Ravenstein Verlag 1503, 1507, 6175
Ravette Publishing Ltd **1725**, 2506, 6190, 6243
Ravindra Printing Press 2331, 2375
Rawat Publications **2349**
The Ray Society 1462
Raytheon International Inc 2149
RCC Pilotage Foundation 1447
Editions RD 2126
RD Press 2074
Readers Choice **6274**
The Reader's Digest Association (Canada) Ltd **2207**

The Reader's Digest Association Inc 2074, 2207, 3033, 3063
Reader's Digest (Australia) Pty Ltd **2074**
Reader's Digest Books 1237, 2074, 6162, 6243
Reader's Digest Young Families 3033, 3063
Readers International 6191
Readers' Union **6280**
Readers' Union Group of Book Clubs 1237
Reading Readiness Series 2406
Reading & Righting (Robert Lambolle Services) **6016**
Reading Science 2449
Read & Wonder 1896
Ready-Ed 1814
Ready to Read 2449
Reaktion Books Ltd **1726**, 6177
Real People Press 6135
Rebel Inc 1153
Reclam 6160
Red Fox Books 1721, 6243
Red House Children's Book Club **6281**
Red Sea Press 6201
Redback (Audio) 6243
Redcliffe Press Ltd **1727**
Redemptorist Publications **1728**
Redstone Press **1729**, 6152
Redwood Music Ltd 1466
Reed Audio 6243
Reed Books **1730**, **2075**
Reed Books Australia 2075, 2076, 2208
Reed Books Canada **2208**
Reed Books Pty Ltd 2493
William Reed Directories **3053**
Reed Educational Publishing **1731**
Reed Educational Publishing USA 1731
Reed Elsevier Australia Pty Ltd 2016
Reed Elsevier Plc 1382, 1383, 1404, 1407, 1551, 1554, 1572, 1573, 1582, 1585, 1642, 1670, 1730, 1784, 1804, 2084, 2208, 2435, 2499
Reed Elsevier UK 1146
Reed Information Services 1245, 6085, 6151, 6170, 6182, 6243
Reed Interactive 6243
Reed International Books Ltd 1124, 1145, 1209, 1345, 1405, 1406, 1684, 1731
Reed New Zealand 2208
William Reed Publishing Ltd 3053
Reed Reference Publishing 1112
Reed Technology & Information Services **6059**
Reeve Books 2002
Reeve Pty Ltd 2002
The Reference Press 6122
Reflected Images Publishing 6176
Reflex Publishers 6139
Regency House Publishing Ltd **1732**
Regies Actions Publicitaires 1314
Regina Press 1728
Regional Policy and Development Series 1498
Regional Sales Leads 1442
Regional Tourist Boards 1001
Regnum 1653
REH Music 1466
Reidmore Books Inc **2209**
Max Reinhardt 6243
Dar Al Reisha 1399
Reliance Publishing House **2350**
Religious Books in Print 1996 **6374**
Religious & Moral Education Press 1439
Religious Society of Friends (Quakers) 1710
Remedia 1592
Renaissance House Publishers 6166
Editions du Renouveau Pédagogique Inc **2210**
Editions Rényi 6160

Repertoire du Livre et de la Presse en Afrique **6317**
Report 1451
ReSearch 6135
Research Bibliographies & Checklists 1361
Research & Education Association 6191
Research Highlights in Social Work 1498
Research Information Systems 6182
Research Institute for the Study of Conflict & Terrorism (RISCT) **1733**
Research Press **2351**
Research Publications International 1703, 6137
Research Reports 1452, 1454
Research Series 2388
Research Studies Press Ltd **1734**, 1915
Resolutions Ltd **6118**
Resource Center (Country Guide Series) 1508
Resources in Education 1622
Retail Entertainment Data 6182
Retrograph Archive Ltd 1121
Reward Music Ltd 1466
Reynolds Music 1466
Rhinegold Publishing Ltd **1735**
Rhode Island School of Design 6139
R.I.C. 1702
R.I.C. (Australia) 1702
Riad El-Rayyes Books Ltd **1736**
RIBA Companies Ltd **1737**
RIBA Information Services 1737
RIBA Publications **1737**
Francisco Ribeiro 1840
The Richard III and Yorkist History Trust 1843
The Richard III Society 1843
Richards Literary Agency **4112**
The Richmond Publishing Co Ltd **1738**, 6144, **6195**
Ricordi 1109
Rider 1922, 6243
Ridge Books 2492
Lynne Rienner Publishers **1739**, 6161
Gerrit Rietveld Academie 6139
Rigby Education USA 1731
Rigby Heinemann 1731, **2076**
Rigby Publishers 2049
Right Way 1272
RightAngle Books 1462
RIGPA Publications 1922
Rinchen Editions 1922
Roberts Rinehart Publishers **2401**
Leonard Ring Associates Ltd 6166
Ringpress Books Ltd **1740**, 6145, 6243
Ringpull Press 6243
Rinsen 1922
Ripping Publishing 6180
Ritana Books **2352**
Ritter Verlag 6139
River Books 1612
Riverrun Press Inc 1148
Rivers Oram **1741**
Riverside Bibles 6179
Riverswift 6243
Rizzoli/Biblios Marketing 6071
Rizzoli International Publications Inc 6073, 6145, 6160
RJX Publications Inc 1466
RMIT Publishing **2077**
Road Books 6152
Roadmaster Publishing **1742**
Robbins Music Corp Ltd 1466
Roberts Rinehart Publishers 6135
Robertson Scientific Publications 1477
Robinson Publishing 6243
Robson Books Ltd **1743**, 6145, 6243
Roc 1661, 2068
University of Rochester Press 1115
Rock Accounts 1995 1562

Rocket Publishing 1466
Rockport 1110
Rocky Mountain Books 2211
The Roeher Institute 2212
Alan Rogers Good 6243
Rogers, Coleridge & White Ltd 4083
Robert Rollason Associates 6017
Rollo Publishing Co 6166
Romantic Novelists Association 5102
Romer Publications 1744
George Ronald, Publisher 1066
Rondor Music 1466
Roof Publications 6152
Rookledge International Publications 1762
Rosendale Press Ltd 1113, 1745, 6177, 6243
Rosetree Publishing Inc 6166
Roth Publishing 6182
Rotovision SA 6131
Rough Guides Ltd 1661, 3054, 6243
The Round Hall Press 2402
Round Table Series 1751
Roundhouse Publishing Ltd 1746, 6146
Roundhouse Reference Books 1746
Les Routiers Guides 1503, 6175
Routledge 1724, 1747, 6174, 6243
Routledge, Chapman & Hall Inc 1747
Routledge Kegan Paul 6174
Rowman & Littlefield Publishers 6161
Rowohlt 6160
Roximillion Publications Co 1325
Royal Anthropological Institute 6202
Royal Asiatic Society 6104
Royal British Columbia Museum 2213
Royal College of General Practitioners 1748
Royal College of Nursing, Baillière Tindall,
    Harcourt Brace 1782, 6166
Royal College of Physicians 6166
Royal Commission on Ancient & Historical
    Monuments in Wales 1843
Royal Incorporation of Architects in Scotland
    1753
Royal Institute of International Affairs 6191
Royal Irish Academy 2403
Royal Literary Fund 5103
The Royal Marsden Hospital, Patient
    Information Group 1421
Royal Melbourne Institute of Technology
    6182
Royal Ontario Museum 1867, 2214
The Royal Pharmaceutical Society of Great
    Britain 1669
Royal Priest Publishing 1920
Angela Royal Publishing 6152
The Royal Society 1749
The Royal Society for the encouragement of the
    Arts, Manufactures and Commerce 5105
The Royal Society of Chemistry 1750
Royal Society of Chemistry 6202
Royal Society of Literature 1115, 5104
Royal Society of Medicine Press Ltd 1751
R&R Enterprises 6182
R&S Books 1719
R. S. Holdings Ltd 1118
RSPB 1089
Hilary Rubinstein Books 4084
Anthony Rudkin Associates 6119
Rugby Press 2462
Rugby Publishing Ltd 2462
John Rule, Publishers Sales Agent 6196
John Rule Sales & Marketing 6120, 6145
Running Press Book Publishers 1752, 6145
Running Press Mini Editions 6243
Running Press Miniature Editions™ 1752
Runpast Publishing 1022
Rupa & Co 1106, 2353
Rushmere Wynne Ltd 6146
The Ruskin Society of London 5106

Diana E. H. Russell 6152
Michael Russell 6145
Bertrand Russell Peace Foundation Ltd 1820
Russell Sage Foundation 6191
Russian Federation Chamber of Commerce &
    Industry 6182
E. Russum & Sons Ltd 1891
Rutgers University Press 6071
Rutherford House 1191, 1653
The Rutland Press 1064, 1753
Rutledge Hill Press 1886, 6128
Rux 6160
Ryland Peters & Small 6180

S1 Editrice Srl 6166
Sached Books (Pty) Ltd 2507
Sacred Books of the East 2321
Sadie Fields Management Inc 3055
Sadie Fields Productions Ltd 1847, 3055
SAF Publishing 6135
Saga 1715
Sagamore Publishing Inc 6166
Sage Publications Inc 1754, 2354
Sage Publications India Pvt Ltd 2354
Sage Publications Ltd 1754, 2354, 6243
Sage Publications Pvt Ltd 1754
Sage Publications Software 1754
Sagebrush 2012
Sagep 1050, 6138
Sahitya Bharati Publications Pvt Ltd 2301
Sain 6258
Sainsbury Publishing Ltd 1755
Saint Andrew Press 1756, 6243
University of St Andrews 1657
St Anne's Music Society 6145
St Anthony Messenger Press 1728
St Antonys Middle East Series 1472
St Bede's Publications 1356
St George & Dragon Press 1087
St James Press 1336, 6174
St Louis Press 6152
St Lucie Press 1261, 1502
St Martin's Enterprises Inc 1547
St Martins Press 1545, 2451
St Martin's Press Inc 1547
St Matthew's Ngukurr—Kriol 2081
St Pauls 1757
St Pauls Publications 1757
St Petersberg Shipbuilding Institute 1016
Saint Publishing Ltd 2463
St Vladimir's Seminary Press 1162, 1590
Salamander Books 1758, 6146, 6243
Salamander Holdings NV 1758
Sally Milner Publishing Pty Ltd 2078
J. Salmon Ltd 6243
Salon du Livre 6308
Salon du Livre de Jeunesse 6309
Salon du Livre de Montreal 6310
Salvationist Publishing & Supplies Ltd 1759
University of Salzburg Studies in English
    Literature 6085
Sam Language Series 2427
Sam-Woode Ltd 2244
Sammelwerk Redaktions Service GmbH 2493
Sams 1698
Sams.Net 1698
San Francisco Museum of Art 6139
Ediciones San Pablo 1757
Edições San Pablo 1757
Edizioni San Paolo 1757
Sand Sedge Publishers 1122
Sandcastle Books 2031
Sanderson Books Ltd 6234
Sandpiper Books Ltd 6235
Sandton Literary Agency 4118
Sang-E-Meel Publications 2478
Sangam Books (I) Ltd 1760, 2330, 2355, 2373

Sangam Books Ltd 1760, 2330
Sankofa Educational Publishers 6069
Sankore Publishers 6069
Sansom & Co 1727
Santiago International Book Fair (Cámara
    Chilena del Libro) 6311
Santillana 6160
Sanya 2342
Sapling 1113
Sapphire Publishing Corporation 6166
Saqi Books 1761, 6085
Sarema Press (Publishers) Ltd 1762
Saros International Publishers 6069
Sarpedon Publishers 1817
Sri Satguru Publications 2356
Satprakashan Sanchar Kendra 2357
Satrap Publishing & Translation 6065, 6152
Satsahitya Prakashan 2343
Satwant Book Agency 2326
Saudi Education '97 6312
W. B. Saunders Co Ltd 1384, 1763, 2033
The Saunders Group 1323
W. B. Saunders Inc 1763
K. G. Saur 1112
K. G. Saur Verlag 1112
A. Saurabh & Co Pvt Ltd 2315
SAUS Publications 1857
Savas Woodbury 1366
Save the Children 1764
Sawd Books 1765
Alastair Sawday Publishing 6243
The Dorothy L. Sayers Society 5107
Sayes Corporation Ltd 2441
Tessa Sayle Agency 4085
Saztec Europe Ltd 6060
S. B. Publications 1766, 6145
SBP Consultants & Engineers Pvt Ltd 2346
Scala Books 1039
Scala Publications Ltd 1917
Scallywag 1409
Scalo, Zurich 1855
Scandinavian Institute of Asian Studies
    Monograph Series 1229
Scandinavian Institute of Asian Studies
    Occasional Papers 1229
Scandinavian University Press 1648, 6148
Scanvik Books 6071
Scarecrow Press Inc 6197
Scarlet Press 1767, 6191
Scarthin Books 1768
Sceptre 1423
Schaltauer 1100
Schellman Edition 6139
Schemeco Enterprises 2358
Schiffer Collectibles Arts & Crafts 6150
Schiffer Publishing Ltd 6150, 6183
Schirmer-Mosel 6139
Schirn Kunsthalle (Frankfurt) 6139
F. X. Schmid 1189
Schmitt Publications 1466
Schocken Books 1503, 6175
Schoettle Publishing House 6179
Schofield & Sims Ltd 1769
Scholar Publishing House (P) Ltd 2358
Scholarly Resources Inc 6161
Scholarstown Educational Publishers 1313
Scholastic Australia Pty Ltd 1770, 2464
Scholastic Canada 1770, 2079, 2464
Scholastic Inc 1770, 2079, 2464
Scholastic Ltd 1770, 6282
Scholastic New Zealand Ltd 1770, 2464
Scholastic Pty Ltd 2079
Scholastic UK 2079
School Book Fairs Ltd 6313
School & College Press (Zambia) Ltd 2501
School Garden Co 1179
School Journal 2449

The School Librarian **6375**
School Library Association **5108**
School of Oriental and African Studies
    (University of London) 1648, **1771**
School Zone Publishing Co 6091
Schubi 1513
Michael Schwinn 6152
Science Alive 2059
Science and Behavior Books 6136
Science for All 2522
Science Museum Publications **1772**
Science Press NY 6122
Science Publishers Inc 2261, 2332
Science & Technology Book Store **6254**
Scientific American Books Inc 1329
Scientific American Inc 1329
Scientific American Medicine Books 1329,
    6182
Scientific Book Agency **2359**
Scientific Press 6174
Scientific Publishers **2360**
SCM Press Ltd **1773**
Scolar Press 1052, **1774**
Scolari 1754
Scope International Ltd **1775**
Scope Special Reports 1775
Scott Foresman/Addison Wesley 1014
Scottish Academic Press **1776**
Scottish Children's Press **1778**
Scottish Council for Research in Education
    1777
Scottish Cultural Press **1778**, 6243
Scottish Gaelic Texts Society 1776
Scottish Library 1148
Association for Scottish Literary Studies **1779**
Scottish Publications 1419
Scottish Publishers Association **5109**
Scottish Text Society 1778
Scottish Tourist Board 1001
The Scout Association **1780**
University of Scranton Press 1348
Screen Gems EMI Music Ltd 1466
Scribners 1197, 1803
Scriptmate Editions 6205
Scripture Union Publishing **1781**
Scutari Press 1384, **1782**
SDK Verlags GmbH 1248
SDU Publishers 6139
Seaby Books 1072
Seafarer 1569, 6152
Seafile 1559
Seaflower Books 1292
Seagull Books 1103
Seal Press 6135
Seameo Regional Language Centre **5174**
Search Press Ltd 1141, **1783**, 6243
Searchlight 6152, 6166
Derek Searle Associates Ltd **6121**, 6146
Martin Secker & Warburg 1730, **1784**, 2208,
    6243
Second Story Press **2215**, 6135
Secondary Selection Portfolio Series 1057
Secondary Shona 2534
Sedco Publishing Ltd **2245**
Seeing is Believing? – Murals in Derry 1374
Seibu Museum 6139
Seix Barral 6160
Self-Counsel Press Inc 1746, 2159
Self-Realization Fellowship 1053, 6140
Sellquick Co Ltd **6236**
Seloc 1305
Seminery Publishers 2358
Semiotext 6152
Sempringham Publishing 6152
Senate 6167
Senate Paperbacks 1837
Send The Light Ltd 1628, 1653, 6243

Sensor Verlag 1513
SEPM 1341
Seren 6152, 6258
Series in Indian Languages and Linguistics
    (SILL) 2272
Series in Indian Studies in Theoretical and
    Applied Linguistics (SISTAL) 2272
Series in Semiotics and Linguistics 2272
Series in Semiotics and Literature 2272
Serif **1785**, 6152
Serindia/Kiscadale (Wisdom) 6071
Serindia Publications **1786**, 1922
Serpentine Gallerie 6139
Serpent's Tail Ltd **1787**, 6191, 6243
Servant Publications 1728
Servedit-Acatos 1416
Services for Export and Language (SEL) **6066**
William Sessions Holdings Ltd 1788
Sessions of York **1788**
Settle Press **1789**, 6145
Editions du Seuil 6160
Seven Seas 6137
Sevenstar Communications 6155
Severn House Publishers Inc 1790
Severn House Publishers Ltd **1790**, 6199
SGC Books 1179, **1791**
SGEL 6160
Shade Tree Press 6166
Shadows Music Ltd 1466
Frank Shaffer Publications 1313
Shakespeare Series 1725
Shambhala 1922, 6135
Shambhala/Redstone 1729
Shanghai AWL Education Software Ltd 1014
The Sharland Organisation 4098
See Sharp Press 1328
M. E. Sharpe Publishing 6161
Kate Sharpley Library 1328
Harold Shaw 1653
The Shaw Society **5110**
Shaway 1792
Shaw & Sons Ltd **1792**, 6146
Shearwater Associates Ltd **2465**
Sheed & Ward Ltd 1356, **1793**
Sheffield Academic Press **1794**
Sheil Land Associates Ltd **4086**
Caroline Sheldon Literary Agency **4087**
Sheldon Press **1795**, 1812, 6243
Sheldrake Press 1061
Shelwing Ltd **6197**
Shepheard-Walwyn (Publishers) Ltd **1796**,
    6085, 6243
Sheppard 1486
Sheppard's Book Dealers **6376**
Sher Music 1466
Sheriar Press Ltd 3049
Sheridan House Inc 1015
Sherwood Press 1796
Sherwood Publishing **1797**
Shikosha 6139
Shiksha Bharati 2331, 2375
Shipra Publications **2361**
Shire Publications Ltd **1798**, 6243
Shishuswapna Prakashan 2338
Shoal Bay Press Ltd 2451, **2466**
The Shoe String Press Inc 6166
Shoestring Publications 6166
Shogun International Ltd **6255**
Shola 6152
The Short Publishing Co Ltd 6180
Shri Jaintendra Press 2321
Shufonotomo 6255
Sidan Press 6146
Siddhi Books 2283
Sidgwick & Jackson Ltd 1545, 1547, **1799**,
    2451, 6243
Siemens 1883

Sierra Leone Library Board **5172**
Sierra Press 1920
Sigma Forlag 1498
Sigma Leisure 1800
Sigma Press **1800**
Sigma Science 1800
Signature 2169
Signature Series 1148
Signet 1661, 2068, 6243
Signpost Books Ltd 1920, **3056**
Sigo Press 6135
Silent Books Ltd **1801**
Silhouette 1385, 2148
Silhouette Folktales for Children 2203
Silicon Press 1698
Silkworm Books 6104
Silman James Press 6166
Silver Link Publishing Ltd **1802**, 6146
Silver Moon Books 6135
Silver Pixel Press 1323
SilverPlatter 6170, 6182
Simba Information Inc 1854
Jeffrey Simmons **4088**
Simon & Pierre Publishing Co Ltd 2131, **2216**,
    6104
Simon & Schuster 1503, **1803**, 2451, 6175,
    6243
Simon & Schuster (Asia) Pte Ltd 1698
Simon & Schuster Audio 1803
Simon & Schuster (Australia) Pty Ltd 1698
Simon & Schuster Inc 1803
Simon & Schuster International Group
    (Academic Division) 1803
Simon & Schuster Trade 6173
Simon & Schuster Young Books 6243
Simple Guides 1346
Simply Classics 6205
Sinauer Associates 1329
Sinclair-Stevenson 1730, **1804**, 2208, 6243
Singapore Book Publishers Association **5175**
Singapore University Press Pte Ltd 2492, 6085
Singspiration Inc 6179
Singular Publishing Group Inc **1805**, 6174,
    6191
Sino Group Enterprises Ltd 2253
Sino United Publishing (Holdings) Ltd 2250
Malik Sirajuddin & Sons **2479**
Sister Vision Press **2217**
S & J 1545
Skellig Press Ltd 1811
Charles Skilton Ltd 1021
Skoob Books Ltd **1806**, 6166
Skoob Esoterica 1806
Skoob Pacifica 1806
Skoob Seriph 1806
Skotaville Publishers 6069
Skratch Music Publishing & Productions 1466
Sky Books 6166
Sky Writing (Publishing) Ltd 1466
Skyblue Publishing 6146
Sleeping Bear 6243
Beverley Slopen Literary Agency **4105**
SLS Legal Publications (NI) **1807**
Small Print **6018**
Gibbs M. Smith 6135
Monica Smith 1050, 6138
Adam Smith Institute **1808**
Carol Smith Literary Agency **4089**
Smith Gryphon Publishers 1113, **1809**, 6199,
    6243
Smith & Kraus Inc 1004, 6152
Smith Settle Ltd **1810**
Smithsonian (History of Aviation Series) 1020
Smithsonian Institution Press 6191
Colin Smythe Ltd **1811**
Snow Lion Graphics 1922
Snow Lion Publications USA 1922

SNP Corporation Ltd 2486
SNP Publishers Pte Ltd 2486
William Snyder Publishing Associates **6122**
Soccer Book Publishing 6243
Social Change Media 2070
Social Ecology 1396
Social Sciences and Humanities Research
  Council **5151**
Social Scientists Association 2520
Socialist Health Association 6152
Socialist Workers Party 1105
Societe Jersaise 1843
Society and Culture in the Modern Middle East
  1850
Society for Endocrinology 6202
Society for Experimental Biology 1697
Society for Industrial and Applied Mathematics
  (SIAM) **6159**
The Society for Promoting Christian
  Knowledge 1795, **1812**, 2306
Society for Research into Higher Education
  Series 1636
Society of Antiquaries of Scotland 1645
Society of Archivists **5111**
Society of Authors **5112**
Society of Authors Pension Fund **5113**
Society of Chemical Industry 6202
The Society of Consulting Marine Engineers
  and Ship Surveyors 1923
Society of Dairy Technologists 1314
Society of Freelance Editors & Proofreaders
  5114
Society of Indexers **5115**
Society of International Gas Tanker & Terminal
  Operators 1923
The Society of Metaphysicians Ltd **1813**
Society of Metaphysicians (Nigeria) Ltd 1813
Society of Picture Researchers and Editors
  (SPREd) **5116**
The Society of Women Writers and Journalists
  5117
Society of Young Publishers **5118**
SoftbABCks 1002
The Softback Review **6283**
Softcover Large Print Camden 1190
Softmill Oy 1016
Software Toolworks 6182
Softwaves Educational Software Inc 2104
Sogides Ltée **2218**
Soho Book Co Ltd 6166
Solipaz Publishing Co 1144
Solo Books Ltd 4090, 6162
Solo Literary Agency Ltd **4090**
Solo Syndication Ltd 4090
Solo Vision Ltd 4090
Solos Press 1053, 6140
Solum Forlag AS 6104
Solutions Software 6182
Solway 1653
Somerville House Books Ltd **2219**
Editions Somogy 1050, 6138
Songs of the World Church 1914
Sono Nis Press **2220**
Sony Music 6243
Sopena 6160
Sophia Books 1828
Sotheby's Publications 1917
Sound View Press 1416
Sound & Vision 1323
Soundings Audio Books 1862
Source Books 1198
Source Books California 1198
South Asia Books 2282
South Asian Publishers Pvt Ltd **2362**
Government of South Australia 2027
South Coast Transport Publishing 1687

South East Asian Social Science Monographs
  2490
South Wales Record Society 1843
South Western 6174
South Western Publishing Co (School
  Division) 1611
Southam Magazine & Information Group
  2221
Southampton City Museums 1843
Southern African Printing and Publishing
  House / SAPES Trust 6069
Southern African Research and Documentation
  Centre (SARDC) 6069
Southern Book Publishers (Pty) Ltd **2513**,
  6183
Southern Directories 2513
Southern Printing 2506
University of Southern Queensland 2087
Southgate Publishers **1814**, 6145
Soutron Ltd **6061**
Souvenir Press Ltd **1815**, 6146, 6243
Sovereign Books Ltd 1901
Sovereign Publications 1289
Sovereign Systems **6123**
SPA 6122
Spa Books Ltd 1236, **1816**, **6124**
Spantech & Lancer 2313
Spare Time Editions 2107
Spare Tyre Publications 6152
Sparrow Hawk Press 6155
Sparrowhawk 1393
SPC Software Publishing 6182
SPCK 1812
Spear Books 2414
Spearhead Monograph Series 2412
Spectrum 1546
Spectrum Books Ltd 6069
Spectrum Publications **2363**
Spektrum Academic Publishers UK 1329
Spellmount Ltd 1211, **1817**, 6153, 6243
Spinal Publications (NZ) Ltd 6243
Spindlewood 1719, **1818**, 6194
Spindrift Music Ltd 1466
Spinsters Ink 6135
Spiritual Masters 1793
SPLASH! Animation Ltd 1819
SPLASH! Holdings Ltd 1819
SPLASH! Publishing Ltd **1819**, 6180
Spokesman **1820**
E. & F. N. Spon 1184, **1821**, 6174
Sport in Word 6167
The Sporting Press 1444, 2462
Sporting & Leisure Press 1715
Sports Support Syndicate Inc 6166
Sportsbooks 6205
The Sportsman's Press **1822**, 6145, 6243
Sportsprint 1246
Spot Books 3062
SPREd **5116**
Spredden Press 1810
Spring Publications 6135
Springer Books (India) Pvt Ltd 2324
Springer International Student Edition 2324
Springer Publishing 1659
Springer Verlag GmbH & Co KG 1823
Springer-Verlag London Ltd **1823**, 6182
Springfield Books Ltd **1824**, **6198**, 6243
Springfield Music 1466
Springs of Wisdom 1141, 1783
Sprinters 1896
Square One Books Ltd **1825**
Sri Lanka National Library Services Board
  5179
Sri Satguru Publications 2304
Stable 6145
Stabur Corp 6166
Stacey International 6145

Stackpole Books 1366
Stagbooks 1793
Stahleisen (The German Iron & Steel Institute)
  1925
Stainer & Bell Ltd **1826**
Stam Press Ltd 1861
Stamps Baxter Music 6179
Stanborough Press Ltd 1430
Standard Book Numbering Agency Ltd 1909,
  5119
Standard Catalogue Publishers 6243
Stanford Maritime 1015, 1089
Stanford University Press 1149
Stanley Paul & Co Ltd 1188, 1722
Stanley Thornes 6243
Staple First Editions 6085
Star Bright Books 1719, 6194
Star Publications (P) Ltd **2364**
Harold Starke Medical 1827
Harold Starke Publishers Ltd **1827**
Starkmann Ltd **6270**
Start Exploring™ 1752
Starting Out.... 1622
State Library of NSW Press **2080**, 6085
Station Hill Press 6135
Station Press 1050, 6138
Statistical Office of the European Communities
  6182
Statistics Canada 6161, 6182
Abner Stein **4091**
Rudolf Steiner Press 1396, **1828**, 6145
Stemmer House Publishers Inc 6166
Edition Stemmle 1050, 6138
Stenhouse Publishers 1183, 6191
Step-by-Step 2186
Patrick Stephens Ltd 1320, 1398, 1632, **1829**,
  6243
Stepping Stones 1866
Sterling 2365, 6243
Sterling Information Technologies **2365**
Sterling Languages 2365
Sterling Management 2365
Sterling Publishers Inc 1162
Sterling Publishers Pvt Ltd 2316, 2365, **2366**
Sterling Publishing Co 1096
Stevens & Sons 1844, 6174
Stevenson Publications 6243
Stewart House 2169
Stewart Tabori & Chang 6167
Sticky History Books 1409
Stillpoint Publishing 6135
Stills Gallery 6139
Stilwell Publishing 6105, 6142, 6243
Stipes Publishing Co 1649
Stobart Davies Ltd **1830**
Stobart Publishing Ltd 1830
Peter Stockham Associates **6125**
Stockholm International Peace Research
  Institute 1648
Stockton Press Inc 1544, 1546, 1547, 1548
Stockton Press Ltd 1547
Arthur H. Stockwell Ltd **1831**
Stoddart (Anansi) 6104
Stoddart Publishing 1022, 2103, 2156, 6128
Stoeger Publishing Co 1020
Stokesby House Publications **1832**
Stonebridge Music 1466
Stonewall Press 6152
Storey/Garden Way Publishing 1072
Story Library 2449
Straightforward Press Ltd **1833**
Strand Editorial Services **6019**
International Institute for Strategic Studies
  1834
Strategic Survey (Annual) 1834
Stratford Music Ltd 1466
Straw Hat 6153

Streamline 1507
Stree 2342
Streetwise Maps Inc 1004
Stride Publications **1835**
The Stroke Association **1836**
The Strong Oak Press Ltd 1816
Struik Publishers 1614
Studentlitteratur AB 1187
Studies in Egyptology 1488
Studies in Society & Space (Series) 1682
Studies on Asian Topics 1229
Studies on Sri Lanka Series Office 2304, 2356
Studies & Texts 2199
Studio Designs 1837
Studio Editions Ltd 1722, **1837**, 2506, 6243
Studio PR 1466
Studio Vista 1096, 1162, 1615, 6243
Study Skills 1251
H. S. Stuttman Inc 2493
Subject Guide to Australian Children's Books in Print **6377**
Subsidia Mediaevalia 2199
Success Strategies 6136
Success Study Books 1594
Suffolk Record Society 1115
Suhrkamp 6160
Sultan Chand & Sons **2367**
Summer Institute of Linguistics (Australian Aborigines & Islanders Branch) **2081**
Summer Institute of Linguistics International 2081
Summersdale Publishers **1838**, 6177, 6243
Summit 1803
Summit Beacon International 6166
Summit Books 1503, 6175
Summit Publications 1466
Summit Publishing Promotion Services **6020**
Summy Birchard 1466
Sun Books 1813
Sun Books Pty Ltd 1547
Sun-Pacific Music (London) Ltd 4006
Sun Ya Publications (HK) Ltd **2254**
Sunburst Books 1708, **1839**, 6180, 6243
Suncrest Ventures Ltd 1316
Sunday Books 1370
Sunflower Books 1089, **1840**
Sunk Island Publishing 6152
Sunna Books 1471
Sunny Classics 2363
Sunset 1528
Sunset Books 6166
Supernet **1841**
Supplements to Zambezia Series 2533
Supportive Learning Publications (SLP) **1842**
Surrealism 1240
Surrey Beatty 1649
Surrey Books 6166
Survey of Manuscripts Illuminated in the British Isles 1580
Survival Books 1503
Surya International Publications **2368**
Susquehanna University Press 1348
University of Sussex 1657
Sussex Academic Press 6085
Sussex Videos 6145
Sustainability & The Environment 2230
Alan Sutton Publishing Ltd **1843**, 6177, 6243
Editions Alan Sutton 1178
SVS Press (Icons) 1356
Swallow Press 1824
Swan Hill Press 1020
Swan Publishing 2496
Swan Raven & Co 1920
Swansea Institute of Higher Education **6405**
Swapmeet Ltd 6243
Sweet Dreams 1869
Sweet & Maxwell Ltd **1844**, 6174, 6243

Sweet Valley High 1869
Sweet Valley Kids 1869
Sweet Valley Twins 1869
Sword of the Lord Publishers 6179
Sybex 1659, 1685
Sybylla Co-operative Press 6152
Synergy Books International 2427
Syntony Publishing 6136
Syracuse University Press 6161
Syrens 1661
Systemic Thinking Theory & Practice Series 1487

Tab/Aero Books Inc 1020
Tab Books 2056
Casa Editrice Tabacco 1507
Tabb House **1845**
Tabor Publishing 1728
Tafe Educational Books 2065
TAFE Publications 2077
Tafelberg Publishers **2514**
Taffeta Publications 6166
Tafol 6258
TAFT 1336
Taft 6174
Taj Co 6137
Take One Publications 6205
Take That Ltd **1846**, 1886
Takshica Hardbounds 2258
Tales of Heaven & Earth 1586
Tallents Press 6085
Tallis Press 1021
Talon Books Ltd **2222**
Talos Books 3052
Taltrade Sales Pty Ltd 2055
Tamarind 1781
Tamesis 1115
Tamos Books Inc **2223**
Tanam Press 6139
Tandem Press **2467**
Tango Books **1847**, 3055, 6146
Tanker Structure Co-operative Forum 1923
Tanzania Commission for Science and Technology 6069
Tanzania Publishing House 6069
Tardy 1416
Tarmac 6095
Tarquin Publications **1848**
Tarragon Press 6104
Taschen (Benedikt) UK Ltd 6243, 6167
Tasende Gallery 1050, 6138
Tasman Studio 6180
Tata-McGraw-Hill Publishing Co Ltd 1542
Cath Tate 6152
Tate Gallery Publishing Ltd **1849**
Peter Tauber Press Agency **4092**
The Taunton Press 1072
Tauris Academic Studies 1850
Tauris Parke Books 1850, 6145
I. B. Tauris & Co Ltd **1850**, 6145
Tavistock Institute of Marital Studies (TIMS) 1487
Tavistock Publications 6174
Taxus Press 1835
David Taylor 1303
John Taylor Book Ventures 1816
Taylor Graham Publishing **1852**
Taylor Nelson 6182
Taylor Publishing Co 6166
Taylor & Francis Group 1301
Taylor & Francis Inc 1301, 1851
Taylor & Francis Ltd 1709, **1851**
TBS Publishers' Distributors **2369**
TDS Inform 6182
Te Neues Publishing 6153
Tea Rooms of Britain 6175
Teacher Created Materials 1313

Teacher Ideas Press 6161
Teachers' College Press 6161
TeakWood Press Inc 6166
Tear Fund 1653
Technical & Educational Services 6191
Technical Indexes 6182
The Tecumseh Press Ltd 2102
Teeney Books Ltd **3057**
Teens 1551
Teitan Press Inc 6166
TELDAN Information Systems 6182
Teledynamics **6126**
Telegraph Books 1502
TeleOrdering Ltd 1909
Thomas Telford Services Ltd **1853**
Tellastory 1721
The Templar Co Plc **3058**
Templar Publishing 1719, 3058, 6194
Temple Gallery 1050, 6138
Temple House Books 1103, 6205
Temple University Press 1895, 6161
Templegate 1356
Tempo Publishing Sdn Bhd 2425
Ten 8 6152
Ten Speed Press 6135, 6243
Pierre Terrail Editions 6071, 6145
Tessloff 6160
Tetra Publications Ltd 1447
Tetradon Publications 1567
Texas A & M University Press 6148
University of Texas Press 6137, 6148
Text Book Centre Ltd 2423
The Text Publishing Co Pty Ltd **2082**
Textile Museum 6139
TFH Publications 6243
TFPL Inc 1854
TFPL Ltd 1854
TFPL Multimedia Ltd 1547
TFPL Publishing **1854**, 6170
TFS Literary Agency 4113
TFS Total Fiction Services **4113**
T & H Holdings Ltd 1855
Thames Head 3011
Thames Publishing 6142
Thames Valley University **6406**
Thames & Hudson (Australia) Pty Ltd 1855, **2083**
Thames & Hudson (Distributors) Ltd 1855
Thames & Hudson Inc 1855
Thames & Hudson Ltd **1855**, 2083, 6243
Thames & Hudson (S) Pte Ltd 1855
Editions Thames & Hudson sarl 1855
Thankyou Music 1499
Tharpa Publications **1856**, 1922
The Policy Press **1857**
Theatre Communications Group 1413
Themis Books 1365
Theosophical Books Ltd **1858**, 2370
The Theosophical Publishing House 1858, 2370
Theytus Books Ltd **2224**
James Thin Ltd 1565
Thistledown Press Ltd **2225**
Thoemmes Antiquarian Books Ltd 1859
Thoemmes Press **1859**, 6145
Thomas Cook Publishing 1001, **1860**
Thomas International Publishing Co 6161
Thomas Marketing & Distribution 6182
Thompson Educational Publishing Inc **2226**
D. C. Thomsen & Co Ltd 1378
Thomson Australia Holdings Ltd 2454
The Thomson Corporation 1184, 1336, 1364, 1611, 1705, 1724, 1747, 1844, 2050, 2064, 2161
Thomson Directories 6174
Thomson Professional Publishing 6174
Stanley Thornes (Publishers) Ltd **1861**

Thornton Cox Publishers 1886
Thornton Cox Travel Guides 6128
Thorogood Ltd 1395
D. W. Thorpe 1112, **2084**
F. A. Thorpe (Publishing) Ltd **1862**
Thorsons 1387, 6243
Thoth Publishing 6145
Thoth Uitgeverij 6139
Three Rivers Books 1028
Threshold Books/The Kenilworth Press Ltd
    1490, 6155
Threshold Publishing Ltd 1785
Thubten Dhargye Ling 1922
Thunder Bay Publishing Co 6166
Thunders Mouth 6135
J. M. Thurley Management **4093**
Tiger Books International Plc 2506, **6237**
Tigers—Read Alone Fiction 1033
Timber Press 1801, **1863**
Timber Press Inc 1863
Time-Life Books **1864**, 6131, 6146
Time Warner Publisher Services International
    6108
Time Warner Publishing BV 2504
Timeless Books 6155
Times Academic Press 2493
Times Books 1386, 1387, 6243
Times Books International 2493
Times Editions 1503, 2493, 6183
Times Editions Pte Ltd 2493
Times Educational Co Ltd 2429
Times Educational Co Sdn Bhd 2428, **2429**
The Times Literary Supplement **6378**
Times Mirror International 6151, 6162, 6182,
    6243
Times Publishing Ltd 2251, 2426, **2493**, 3041
Times Trade Directories Pte Ltd 2493
Times Warner International 6243
Tip-Top Guides Series 1838
Tiptree Book Services Ltd **6199**
Tir Eolas 1811
Titan Books Ltd **1865**, 6162, 6243
Nga Rerenga o te Titi Tuhiwai 2465
Tixerant Dean Publications/Stepping Stones
    1866
Toccata Press 1323
Today & Tomorrow's Printers & Publishers
    2371
Todd Publications 6166
Tolkien 1387
The Tolkien Society **5120**
Tolley Publishing 6243
Tomart Publications 6176
Topaz 2068
Topics in Engineering 1208
Topics in Translation 1591
Tor Mark Press 1213
Torchlight Publishing 6143
Toronto Medieval Latin Texts 2199
University of Toronto Italian Studies 2130
University of Toronto Press **1867**, 1878, 6148,
    6181
Torstar Corporation 2148
Total Book Distribution (TBD) **6256**
Toucan Books Ltd **3059**
Toucan Press **1868**
Touchstone 1803, 6135, 6243
Tough Dove Books 6155
Touring Australia Road Atlases 6175
TR Publications 6085
T & R United 1507
Tracks 1387
The Trade Counter Ltd **6200**
Trade & Technical Press 1275
Trade & Travel 6243
Tradewind Books 6243
Trafton 1824

Trailblazer Publications 1507
Training Matters **6407**
Training Media Group (Videos) 1449
Training Publications 6166
Trait Design **6041**
Trans-SABD (Pty) Ltd 1869
Transformation Series 2180
Translating and the Computer Series 1055
Translators Association **5121**
Translegal 6105, 6142
Transnational Juris Publications 6122
Transparent Language 6172
Transport for Leisure 1512
Transworld Publishers (Aust) Pty Ltd 1869,
    2085
Transworld Publishers Ltd **1869**, 2085, 6243
Transworld Publishers (NZ) Ltd 1869, 2085
Travellers 1084
Traveller's Histories 1920
Traveller's Literary Companion Series 1448
Traveller's Phrase Book & Dictionary Series
    1725
The Traveller's Wine Guides 3019
Travelling Scholarship Fund **5122**
Travelus Publishing 6166
Tre Graig Press 6258
Treasure 1382
Tree of Life Publications 1920
Treehouse Children's Books Ltd 1277, **1870**,
    6180, 6243
Trends & Issues in Crime & Criminal Justice
    2011
Trentham Books **1871**
Trentham Print Design Ltd 1871
Trescher Verlag GmbH 6166
Treville 6139
Lavinia Trevor **4094**
Tri Star Publishing 6182
Triad Publishers Pty Ltd 6166
Triangle Books 1812
Tricolour Books 1106
Trifolium Books Inc **2227**, 6085
Trimarket Co 6166
Trinity Estates 6095
Trinity Press International 1773
Triple Gem Press 1922
Trisea Publications 2374
Tristan Music Ltd 1466
Troddy Books 1732
Troika **6127**
Trojan Horse 1050, 6138
Troll Bookclubs 2231
Trombone Press 1835
Trotman & Co Ltd **1872**
Trotman Africa Pte Ltd 1872
Trotman Australia Pty Ltd 1872
Truedata Computer Services 1588
Dyllansow Truran **1873**
Trust Study for Adolescence 1657
TSAR Publications 6085
Tshedimoso 2522
TSR 6199, 6243
Tucker Slingsby **3060**
Tui, Tui Junior and Tui Turbo young fiction
    2446
Tundra Books Inc 1719, **2228**, 6194
Tundra Books of Northern New York 2228
Tupu 2449
Turnaround Publisher Services Ltd **6201**, 6243
Turner Publishing Inc 6190
Turning Point 6136
Turnstone Press Ltd **2229**
Turpin Distribution Services Ltd **6202**
Turpion 1682, 6202
Turton & Armstrong Pty Ltd **2086**
Turton & Chambers **1874**
Tuttle 1922

TVRT Studios (Sound) 3038
Twelve Trees Press 6139
Twelveheads Press **1875**
Twenty-Third Publications 2384
TWI (The Welding Institute) 6182
Twin Palms Publishing 6139
Two-can/Watts 1900
Two Heads Publishing 6105, 6142, 6243
Tŷ John Penry 6258
Tynron Press Ltd 2484, 6166

UBC Press **2230**, 6181
UBS Publishers' Distributors Ltd **6203**
UCL Press Ltd **1876**, 6181, 6243
UFO Music Ltd **1877**
UGMT Ltd 1010, 1367
UK Atomic Energy Authority 1419
UK Record Industry Annual Survey 1995
    1562
UK Standard Address Numbering Agency Ltd
    1909
UK Standard Book Numbering Agency Ltd
    1909
UKHM 1507
Ullstein 6160
Ulrich's International Periodicals Directory
    6379
Ulster Historical Foundation **1878**
Ultimate Editions 1038
The Ulverscroft Group 1549
Ulverscroft Hard Cover Series 1862
Ulverscroft Large Print Books Ltd 1862
Umberleigh Press 1402
UMI 6170
UN Food & Agriculture Organization 6182
Yr Undeb Cristnogol 1290
Undercurrents 2385
Understand How to Draw Series 1783
Understanding Global Issues 6160
P. A. Underwood Ltd 1840
Unemployment Unit 6152
UNESCO 1419, 6182
UNESCO Institute for Educational Planning
    1871
UNESCO Statistical Yearbook 1995 **6380**
Uitgeverij Uniepers bv 6152
Unisa Press **2515**
United Book Traders 2360
United Kingdom Council for Human Rights
    (UKCHR) **1879**
United Nations (UN) 1419, 6182
United Nations University (UNU) 1419
United News & Media Plc 1581
United Newspapers Ltd 1296, 1303
United Publishers Services (HK) Ltd 2493
United Publishers Services Ltd 2493
United Publishers Services Pte Ltd 2493
United States Institute of Peace 6191
United Writers Publications Ltd **1880**
Uniting Church Press 2047
Universal Book Traders **2372**
Universal Reference Publishing 6122
Universe Publishing 6073, 6131, 6145
Universities & Colleges Christian Fellowship
    1461
Universities Press (I) Ltd 1760, 2330, **2373**
University Art Museum (Santa Barbara) 6139
University Book Marketing 6145
University Bookshop 2485
University Central Admissions System
    (University & College Entrance) 1793
University College of Cape Breton Press 2142
University Microfilms Inc 6182
University Press Ltd 1648
University Press Plc 6069
University Publishing Inc 6166
University Science Books 1329, 1546

Harvey Unna & Stephen Durbridge Ltd 4002
Unwin Hyman 6174
UPM Agencies 6191
The Upper Room Nashville 1571
UPS Translations 6067
Urban Institute Press 6161
Urbanization in Asia 2230
Laurence Urdang Inc 3061
Urdd Gobaith Cymru 6258
Ure Smith Press 2049
Ursus Press 1039
US Patent & Trademark Office 6182
Usborne Books at Home 6146
Usborne Publishing Ltd 1770, 1881, 6154,
   6243
Usha Publications 6108
USQ Press 2087
University of Utah Press 6137
Utilis 2218
Utryck 1914

Vac Job 1882
Vacation Work 1507, 1882, 6243
Vagabond Publishing Inc 6166
Editions Vagnon 1447
Valhalla Publishing 6166
Vallardi e Associati 6205
Vallentine Mitchell 1161
Valley Books Trust Ltd 6257
Valley of the Sun 1920
Valor Foundation 1325
Van + Van Publiciteit 6205
Van Abbe Museum 6139
Van Duren 1811
Van Nostrand Reinhold 6174
J. L. van Schaik Publishers 2514, 2516
John Van Weenen 6073, 6145
Editions Van Wilder 1416
Vanderbilt University Press 6148
Vanguard Books Pvt Ltd 2480
Vanguard Publications 6137
Vans Information & Investor Services Ltd
   2342
Vantage Press 6137
Vanwell Publishing Ltd 2231
Variorum 1052
VCH Publishers Inc 1006, 1883
VCH Publishers (UK) Ltd 1006, 1883
VCH Verlag AG 1006, 1883
VCH Verlagsgesellschaft 1006, 1883
VDI (The Association of German Engineers)
   1925
Véhicule Press 2232
Veloce Publishing Plc 1884, 6073, 6145
Cynthia Venn 6166
Ventura Publishing Ltd 1661, 3062
Verbaid Ltd 1886
Verbatim Books 3061
Verbatim, the Language Quarterly 6381
Verenigde Boekhandelaars van Suidelike
   Afrika 5176
Javier Vergara 6160
Veritas Book & Video Distribution Ltd 2404
Veritas Publications 2404
Verlag am Goetheanum 1828
Verlag für Deutsch 6160
Vermilion 1722
Verrocchio Arts 6152
Versatile Guides 3022
Verso 1885, 6181, 6243
Verulam (IBD) 6071
Verulam Publishing Ltd 1050, 1886, 6128,
   6138, 6243
Vestal Press Ltd 6166
Veterinary Business Development Ltd 1411,
   6166
The Veterinary Press Ltd 1557

VG Crime 1349
VG Horror 1349
VGSF 1349
Via Afrika 2514, 2517
Viacom Inc 1673, 1698, 1699, 1700, 1701
Ed Victor Ltd 4095
Victoria & Albert Museum Publications 1887,
   6177
Victoria House Publishing Ltd 3063, 6177
Victoria University Press 2468
Video Direct 6274
Vidya Vihar 2343
Vidyarthi Prakashan (Pvt) Ltd 2374
Vikas Publishing House Pvt Ltd 1760
Viking 1661, 2068, 2460, 6243
Viking Children's Books 1661
Viking Kestrel 2460
Le Groupe Ville-Marie Littérature 2218
Villiers Publications Ltd 6042
Vine House Distribution 6205, 6243
Vineyard Books 3004
Vineyard Press (London) 6197
Vintage 1722, 6243
Vintage Aviation Library 1366
Vinyl Experience Ltd 1888, 6146, 6243
Vippassana Dhura 1922
Virago Press 1889, 2506, 6199, 6243
Virgin Books 6243
Virgin Group Ltd 1890
Virgin Publishing 1890, 6162
The University Press of Virginia 6161
Virtue Books Ltd 1891
Virtuosity : Animations 3038
Visible Ink Press 1336
Vision Books Pvt Ltd 2331, 2375
Visiria 1016
Vista 1349, 6243
Studio Vista 1892
Vista Iberica 1503
Vista Point Verlag GmbH 6166
Vista Productions Ltd 2428, 2429
Vita Books 1148
Vitra Design Museum 1050, 6138
Vivation Publishing 6135
VNR 1491
VNU Business Publications 6182
Vocational Technologies 6182
Voix (Collection) 2144
Volcano Press Ltd 1893
Volkwein Bros 1466
Voltaire Foundation Ltd 1894
Voluntary Sector Press 6205
Voyageur Press 1020
Voyageur Publishing 2233
VU University Press 6085
VUB University Press 6166

Wadsworth Publishing 6174
Wag Books 1919
Waite Group 1659
Wakefield Press 6152
University of Wales Press 1895, 6095
Walford's Guide to Reference Material 6382
Walker Books Ltd 1297, 1896, 6243
S. Walker Literary Agency 4096
Derek Walker Partnership 6129
Edgar Wallace Society 5123
H. R. Wallingford 1853
Walters Lexikon 6182
Wandishi wa Kiafrika (African Writers in
   Kiswahili) 2414
Ward Lock Educational Co Ltd 1898, 3011,
   6146
Ward Lock Ltd 1047, 1096, 1162, 1615, 1892,
   1897, 6243
Ward's Publishing Services 1164

Frederick Warne & Co Ltd 1661, 1899, 2068,
   2460, 6243
Warner Books 1528, 6243
Warner Bros. Publications Inc 1466
Warner Chappell Music Ltd 1466, 4097
Warner Chappell Plays Ltd 1466, 4097
Warner-Futura 1528
Warner Music Group 1466
Warner UK 2506
Warplanes (Interactive CD-ROM Series) 3052
Warwick Interactive Inc 2234
Warwick Publishing Inc 2234
University of Washington Press 6148
Wat Tyler Books 6197
Watchword Videos & Cassettes 1719, 6194
The Water Press 1050, 6138
Water Research Centre 6182
Waterkant Publishers 2503, 2505
Waterline 1020
William Waterman Publications 1816
The Watermark Press 1920, 2088
Watershed Arts Trust Ltd 6152
Watershed Productions Ltd 6146, 6243
Waterside Productions Inc 4082
Watson, Little Ltd 4098
A. P. Watt Ltd 4099
The Watts Publishing Group 1637, 1900,
   6199, 6243
Waverley 1770 3020
Waverly Europe Ltd 6181, 6182
Wayland Paperbacks 6243
Wayland Publishers Ltd 1541, 1901, 6142
Wayne State University Press 6161
Wayzata Technology 6182
W. E. Associates (Swindon) Ltd 6238
WeatherDisc Associates Inc 6182
Weatherhill Inc 1614, 6243
Weatherlight Press 1918
Richard Webb Ltd 3064
Webb & Bower (Publishers) Ltd 3064, 6095
Adrian Webster Ltd 1902
Webster Publishing 1723
Websters International Publishers Ltd 1902
Websters Multimedia Ltd 1902
Webster's New World Dictionaries 1803
Webster's Unified Inc 2493
Geoff Weedon Books Ltd 6239
Weekes 1826
Weekly Book Newsletter 6383
WEF 1653
Wei-Chuan Publishing Inc 6166
Weidenfeld & Nicolson 1640, 1903, 6177,
   6243
Weigl Educational Publishers 2235
Weingarten GmbH, Kunstverlag 6166
Weirknightsbridge & Associates 1325
Samuel Weiser Inc 6135
John Welch 4100
Weldon International 2059
Wellesley College Museum 6139
Wellspring Publications 6135
Welsh Academic Press 6085
Welsh Books Council / Cyngor Llyfrau Cymru
   5124
Welsh Books Council: Distribution Centre /
   Cyngor Llyfrau Cymru: Canolfan
   Ddosbarthu 6258
Welsh Rugby Union 6095
Wer liefert was? 6182
Wesleyan University Press 6191
West 2034
West Herts College 6408
University of the West Indies 2408
West Indies Publishing Ltd 2410
West Meadow Books 1801
West of England Trust 1484
John West Publications Ltd 2470

West Publishing Co 6173
Westermann 6160
Western Archaeological Trust 1843
University Western Australia 6243
Western Book Depot 2329
Western Buddhist Review 1918
Western Publishing Co Inc **1904**, 6243
Western World Publishers 6176
Westgate Press 6166
University of Westminster **6409**
Westminster/John Knox Press 1197, 1773
Westport Publishers Inc 6166
Westview Press **1905**, 6191
Westwood Creative Artists Ltd **4106**
Westwood Publishing 6136
Wexas International 1315
Wharncliffe Publishing Ltd 1660, **1906**
What's That Over There? 3065
A. H. Wheeler & Co Ltd **2376**
Wheldon & Wesley Ltd **1907**
Whereabouts Press 6166
Which? Books **1908**, 6243
Which? Consumer Guides 1908
Which? Ltd 1908
Which? Travel Guides 1908
Whitaker's Books in Print 1996 **6384**
J. Whitaker & Sons Ltd **1909**, 6145, 6151,
    6170, 6182, 6243
Whitcoulls Group 2442
White Dove International 6135
White Eagle Publishing Trust 1325, **1910**
White Line Press 6166
White Line Publishing Services **3065**
White Orchid Press 6104
White Wolf 6145
Whitechapel 6139
Whitetree Books 1727
Whitford Press 6135
Whitter Nohedes 6166
Whittet Books Ltd **1911**, 6145, 6243
Whittles Publishing **1912**
Paul Whittome 6243
Who Owns Whom Series 1256
Who's Who in British History series 1796
Who's Who in Italy 6161
Who's Who in the Voluntary Sector 1060
Who's Who of Australian Writers **6385**
Whurr Publishers Ltd **1913**, 6202
Wide World Publishing/Tetra 6166
Dinah Wiener Ltd **4101**
Michael Wiese Production 6166
Wild Flower Press 1920
Wild Goose Prints (Drama) 1914
Wild Goose Publications 1756, **1914**
Wild Goose Song Books 1914
Wildwood House 1354
Wiley Eastern Ltd 2046
Wiley Europe Ltd 1915
Wiley Heyden Ltd 1915
John Wiley & Sons Canada Ltd 2046, **2236**
John Wiley & Sons Inc 2046, 2236
John Wiley & Sons Ltd **1915**, 2046, 2236,
    6095, 6182, 6243
John Wiley & Sons (SEA) Pte Ltd 2046, 2236
Wilfrid Laurier University Press **2237**
Rosemary Wilkinson Publishing **3066**
Joseph Williams 1826
Bridget Williams Books Ltd **2469**
Jonathan Williams Literary Agency **4108**
Tony Williams Publications **1916**
Williamson Music Ltd 1466
Williamson Publishing Co 6166
W. J. Williams & Son (Books) Ltd **6240**
Willis Music Co 1466
Willow Park Press 1159
Wilmette Publications Sdn Bhd 6166
Philip Wilson 1917

John Wilson Booksales **6130**, 6146
H. W. Wilson Co. 6170
Neil Wilson Publishers Ltd 6162, 6243
Philip Wilson Publishers Ltd **1917**
Wilson & Day Ltd 1025
Wincanton Press 1249
Windbell 1922
Windhorse Publications **1918**
Windmill Publishing 6176
Windrow & Greene 1022, **1919**, 6177, 6243
Windrush Island Guides 1920
Windrush Press Ltd **1920**, 6191, 6243
Windsor Books International **6131**
Windsor Large Print 1190
Wing Forward — Publishers Regional Service
    6132
Wingham Press 1019
Winnicott Studies (Series) 1487
Winning International 6166
Winslow Press Ltd 1657, **1921**, 6105, 6142
Winterthur 1039
The Wire 1711
University of Wisconsin Press 6161
Wisden 1661, 6243
Wisdom Books **1922**
Wisdom Publications (Boston) 1922
Wisdome Press 1325
Wise Owl Books 1418
Wise Owl Quiz Promotions 1308
Wise (University of the Witwatersrand
    Initiative in Science Education) 2522
Wise & Loveys Ltd **6062**
Wishing Well 3033
Wishwa Prakashan 6085
Wisley Handbooks (Royal Horticultural
    Society) 1162, 6243
H. F. & G. Witherby 1349, 6243
Witherby Monument 1923
Witherby & Co Ltd **1923**
Witwatersrand University Press **2518**
Wizard Books Pty Ltd **2089**
Wizard Classroom Kits 2089
Wizard English Teaching Modules 2089
Wizard Fiction 2089
Wizard Study Modules 2089
Woburn Press 1161
Woeli Publishing Services **2247**, 6069
Mrs Mariella Wolf **6206**
Wolfhound Press **2405**, 6100
Wolters Kluwer NV 1172, 1226, 1501, 1541
Wolters Kluwer UK Plc 1861, 1901
Women in Publishing **5125**
Women's Experience Series 2114
The Women's Press 1711, **1924**, 6191, 6243
The Women's Press Book Club 1924
Women's Studies Series 2005
Women's Voices, Women's Lives Series 2005
Wonders of the World Series 1220
Wood Lake Books Inc **2238**
Woodbine House 6166
Woodbridge Press Publishing Co 6166
Woodfield & Stanley Ltd **6271**
Woodhead Faulkner (Publishers) Ltd 1443,
    1698, 1701, 6173
Woodhead Publishing Ltd **1925**, 6153, 6202
Woodpond Press 6152
Word Inc 1926
Word Publishing **1926**
Words on Cassette 1994 **6386**
Words on Sport Ltd **1927**, 6146, 6243
Wordsearch 6152
Wordsmith Publishing Co 6243
Wordsworth Editions Ltd **1928**, 6243
Wordware Publishing Inc 6166
Wordwise **6021**
Wordwright **3067**
Working Books Ltd 1886, 6128

Working Holidays Abroad 6175
Working Press 6152
Workman Publishing 6108, 6167
World Bank Publications 1648, 6182
World Book — Childcraft International 6182
World Book Industry **6387**
World Books **6274**
World Council of Churches 1171
World Customs Organisation 1419
World Guide to Libraries **6388**
World Health Organisation (WHO) 1419
World in Crisis Series 1148
World Intellectual Property Organisation 6182
World International Publishing Ltd **1929**,
    2506, 6162, 6243
World Leisure Corporation 1507
World Leisure Marketing 6071, **6133**, 6167,
    6243
World Library Inc 6182
World Library Ltd 1592
World Music Press 1746
The World of Learning **6389**
World of Transport 1022
World One Day Novel Cup 6095
World Resources Institute 1261
World Scientific Publishing Co 2494
World Scientific Publishing Co Inc 2494
World Scientific Publishing Co Pte Ltd **2494**,
    6166
World Scientific Publishing (HK) Co Ltd 2494
World Tourism Organization (WTO) 1419
World Trade Organisation 1419, 6182
World Trade Press 1542
World Wide Adventures 1344
Worldlife Library 1073
The World's Best Loved Hotels 6166
World's Toughest Tongue Twisters 1725
Worldsmith 1106
WorldView Publications 6152
Worldwide Government Directories Inc 6122
Worldwide Media / Adrian Parker Associates /
    Running Press (Biblios) 6071
Worldwide Media Service Inc 6145, **6207**
Worshipful Company of Stationers and
    Newspaper Makers **5126**
Worth 1329, 1546, 2034
WPS 1619
Wright Publishing 6166
Wrightbooks Pty Ltd **2090**
Wrightson Biomedical 6202
Write Stuff Syndicate Inc 6166
Writer Inc 3028, 6165
Writers and Their Work 1622
Writer's Digest 3028, 6165
Writers' Guild of Great Britain **5127**
Writers House 4008
Writer's House Inc **4082**
Writers' & Artists' Yearbook **6390**
Writers & Readers Ltd **1930**, 6243
Writers & Readers Publishing Inc 1930, 6135
Writings of Mary Baker Eddy 1746
Wuerz Publishing Ltd 1793, **2239**
WWF United Kingdom 1738, 6195
Wyrick & Co 6166

The X Press **1931**, 6201, 6243
Xenophobe's Guides 1725
Xpress Reprints 1773

Yale Representation Ltd 1933
Yale University Press 1600, 1915, 1933
Yale University Press London **1933**
Yapaka — Warlpiri 2081
Roy Yates Books **1934**, **6272**
Yearbook of Science & the Future 1278
Yes International 1920
Y Lolfa Cyf **1932**, 6085, 6258

YMAA 1225
Yoga Publications Society 1325
York University, Dept of Archaeology 1645
Yorkshire Art Circus Ltd 6243
Yorkshire International Thomson Multimedia 6151
Yorkshire TV Enterprises 6243
T. Young 1588
Young Book Trust **5128**
Young Corgi 1869
Young Generation Series 2486
Young Hylanders (children's paperback reprint) 2043
Young Library Ltd **1935**
Young Lions 1387, 1527
Nat Young Surfing Books 1305
Yourdon Press 1698
Youth Hostel Association 6243

Youth Work Press 1605
Youthaid 6152
Yuam Focus on the Family 1926
Yurisha Press 6136
Yvonne Courtney PR **6134**

Zambia Educational Publishing House **2527**
Zanichelli 6160
Zardos Books 6166
Dale Zdenek Publications 1466
Zebra Books 6243
Zed Books Ltd **1936**, 6191
Zelda Cheatle Press 1050
Hans Zell Publishing Consultants 1112, **6022**
Zen Centre (London) 1922
Zena Publications 1895

Zephyr Press 6135, 6136
Zigzag Books 3068
Zigzag Publishing 1592, 3020, **3068**, 6243
Zimbabwe Book Publishers Association 6069
Zimbabwe International Book Fair **6314**
Zimbabwe Library Association **5183**
University of Zimbabwe Publications **2533**, 6069
Zimbabwe Publishing House **2534**, 6069
Zimbabwe Women Writers 6069
Zoë Books Ltd **3069**, 6142
Zoilus Press 6152
Zon International 6183
Zondervan Corporation 1387, 1388, 6179
Zone Books (Urzone Publishing Ltd) 1584
Zwemmer 1917

7.9 UK PUBLISHERS BY POSTCODE

London & South-East England

Brighton
BN1 4GB   **1657**
BN1 9RE   **1452**
BN1 9RF   **1450**
BN2 2SU   **1448**
BN2 2TG   **1686**
BN3 1JD   **1541, 1901**
BN3 2BE   **1505**
BN3 2FA   **1375, 1709**
BN6 9EL   **3068**
BN7 1XU   **1373**
BN7 2LU   **1103**
BN18 9AJ   **1305**
BN22 0RS   **1250**
BN23 6NT   **1499**
BN25 1TP   **1766**
Bromley
BR1 2NE   **1187**
BR3 2JS   **1170**
BR6 7SQ   **1355**
Canterbury
CT20 3LZ   **1346**
Croydon
CR0 3RY   **1589**
CR2 6XW   **1716**
CR5 2NH   **1479**
Dartford
DA1 1JG   **1010, 1367**
DA1 4BZ   **1792**
Enfield
EN2 6DJ   **1376**
Guildford
GU2 5HN   **1259**
GU5 6YD   **1740**
GU7 2EP   **1415**
GU7 3DJ   **1823**
GU9 8HT   **1486**
GU10 2AQ   **1018, 1469**
GU11 3HR   **1052, 1235, 1354, 1774**
GU14 6EY   **1107**
GU27 1AF   **1474**
GU29 9AZ   **1577**
GU33 7HY   **1910**
GU34 3HQ   **1728**
Harrow
HA3 8RU   **1082**
HA9 9EA   **3048**

Hemel Hempstead
HP2 7EZ   **1443, 1673, 1698, 1699, 1700, 1701**
HP2 7ST   **1618**
HP5 2SH   **1101**
HP7 0NB   **1866**
HP9 1PL   **1078**
HP12 4UL   **1256**
HP17 9AA   **1798**
HP20 1TN   **3040**
HP20 2HY   **3061**
HP20 2QZ   **1345**
Ilford
IG2 7HH   **1161**
IG7 8DL   **1482**
IG8 8HD   **1426**
IG8 8HN   **1466**
IG10 4PZ   **1707**
Kingston-upon-Thames
KT1 2EW   **3031**
KT1 3HD   **1323**
KT2 6SR   **1226**
KT2 7JT   **3006**
KT3 4AD   **1714**
KT12 5PL   **1611**
KT15 1HY   **1022**
KT20 6TD   **1272**
KT22 7RU   **1683**
KT22 7SA   **1283**
KT23 3EU   **1270**
London
E1 1LU   **1689**
E1 6EP   **1760**
E1 6LQ   **1744**
E1 7LS   **1662**
E1 7QX   **1328**
E3 5DA   **1785**
E4 7AY   **1318**
E8 2HN   **1767**
E8 4PH   **1931**
E9 5LN   **1511**
E10 6RG   **1500**
E14 4JD   **1853**
E14 5AP   **1104**
E14 9FT   **1844**
E17 9AA   **1922**
EC1A 7HE   **1150**
EC1A 9JR   **1593**
EC1M 5NA   **1287**
EC1M 5NQ   **1854**
EC1N 8BS   **3059**

EC1N 8RT   **1881**
EC1R 0ET   **1923**
EC1R 0HT   **1379**
EC1R 1UL   **1508**
EC1R 4SX   **1268**
EC1R 5AR   **1221**
EC1V 0DX   **1924**
EC1V 8BB   **1737**
EC1V 9AP   **1055**
EC1Y 8JJ   **1836**
EC2A 4PU   **1754**
EC2A 4RH   **1637, 1900**
EC3M 4BS   **1532**
EC3R 7JN   **1455**
EC4A 3DE   **1301**
EC4P 4EE   **1336, 1747**
N1 0NX   **1773**
N1 1BE   **1228**
N1 1DE   **1741**
N1 1EN   **1066**
N1 1LA   **1183**
N1 1LX   **3015**
N1 1RD   **1392**
N1 2UN   **1913**
N1 6PB   **1255**
N1 7JQ   **1331**
N1 8BE   **1362**
N1 9BN   **1809**
N1 9DZ   **1262**
N1 9HG   **1563**
N1 9JB   **1498**
N1 9JF   **1930, 1936**
N1 9JN   **1261, 1502**
N1 9PA   **1668**
N1 9RL   **1609**
N1 9UN   **1515**
N2 9NR   **3034**
N3 1DZ   **1826**
N4 1AD   **1369**
N4 2BT   **1491, 1787**
N4 2DE   **1105**
N5 1UP   **1070**
N6 5AA   **1691**
N6 6BA   **1517**
N7 9LG   **1758**
N7 9RH   **1626**
N12 0AF   **1607**
N16 0NA   **3023**
NW10 AE   **1257**
NW10 AG   **1520, 1521**
NW1 2BJ   **1710**

NW1 3BH   **1048, 1401, 1422, 1423, 1424, 1425**
NW1 3DZ   **1063**
NW1 4DF   **1908**
NW1 4DU   **1795, 1812**
NW1 4NS   **1643**
NW1 7DX   **1005, 1067, 1384, 1429, 1763, 1782**
NW1 8BD   **1825**
NW1 8HX   **1380**
NW1 8NZ   **1477**
NW1 8PR   **1678**
NW1 9XA   **3044**
NW2 5JN   **1682**
NW3 2PN   **1933**
NW3 3PG   **1705**
NW3 4DU   **1174**
NW5 1AJ   **3067**
NW5 1LP   **3050**
NW5 1LX   **1476**
NW5 2JU   **1360**
NW5 2QE   **3035**
NW5 2RZ   **1525**
NW5 3HR   **1569**
NW5 8SY   **3021**
NW6 1DZ   **1633**
NW6 2HL   **1503**
NW10 3PS   **1060**
NW11 7DL   **1557**
NW11 7SG   **1058**
NW11 9DU   **3005**
NW11 9NN   **1366, 1537**
NW11 9PZ   **1041**
SE1 0LX   **1126**
SE1 0UP   **1865**
SE1 1EP   **1599**
SE1 1YT   **1445, 1570, 1902**
SE1 3AG   **1732**
SE1 4YH   **1509**
SE1 7JN   **1669**
SE1 7RL   **1171**
SE1 8HN   **1099, 1184, 1724, 1821**
SE1 8LL   **1654**
SE1 9PD   **1656**
SE1 9PL   **1113**
SE1 9UX   **1296**
SE5 8RD   **1764**
SE9 2TZ   **1192**
SE10 8PX   **1040**
SE11 4JH   **1417**

SE11 5HJ 1896	SW19 5DT 1358	W10 5BN 1393	WC2R 0BB 1047, 1096,
SE19 3RY 3016	SW19 6JA 1822	W10 5SU 1729	1162, 1182, 1349, 1516, 1556,
SE21 7DF 3019	W1H 0AH 1072	W11 2ER 1121	1590, 1615, 1681, 1892, 1897
SE28 0AX 1641	W1H 3HJ 1858	W11 2SJ 1612	Medway
SW1A 2BN 1173	W1H 6DQ 1614	W11 3LR 1789	ME5 9AQ 1742
SW1E 5JF 1371	W1H 7LN 1449	W12 0TT 1075, 1077	ME9 8BA 1765
SW1E 5XA 1051	W1M 0AN 1497	W12 7TS 1076	Portsmouth
SW1H 9AS 1604	W1M 1FH 1733	W12 8AW 1092, 1116, 1251	PO9 6EE 1775
SW1H 9BN 1298	W1M 1LE 1291	W14 0BY 1911	PO10 7DQ 1559
SW1P 1EP 1757	W1M 5PE 1026	W14 0YP 3022	PO19 1RP 1838
SW1P 1RT 1561	W1M 7HF 1833	W14 9PB 1095	PO19 1UD 1915
SW1P 1SB 1745	W1M 8AE 1751	W10 5AH 1890	PO19 2EN 1649
SW1P 2NB 1465	W1M 9HB 1620	WC1A 1DF 1909	PO20 6BG 1671
SW1P 3BL 1808	W1M 9LA 1263, 1706	WC1A 1LD 1002	Reading
SW1P 3HH 1210	W1N 3AJ 1697	WC1A 1LR 1106	RG1 4QS 1338, 1472
SW1P 3NZ 1193	W1N 5FB 1917	WC1A 1PU 1623	RG1 8HF 1703
SW1P 3QB 1304	W1N 7AP 1837	WC1A 2AH 1348	RG9 1EJ 1625
SW1P 4RG 1849	W1N 7RE 1480	WC1A 2LP 1036	RG9 4PG 1059, 3024
SW1V 1DE 1501	W1N 7RJ 1440	WC1A 2QH 1806	RG9 5RT 1273
SW1V 1PD 1166	W1P 0BY 1867	WC1A 2TH 1119, 1679	RG12 7AH 1140
SW1V 2SA 1033, 1049,	W1P 1DE 1726	WC1B 3AT 1061	RG14 5DS 1216
1071, 1165, 1188, 1437, 1721,	W1P 1HF 1676	WC1B 3BN 1496, 3017	RG20 8TF 1154
1722	W1P 1LR 1334	WC1B 3DG 1128, 1130	RG21 2EA 1001
SW1W 0DH 1395	W1P 2LD 1711	WC1B 3ES 1043	RG21 6XS 1329, 1543, 1544,
SW1W 0EL 1023	W1P 2LN 1085	WC1B 3JN 1288	1546
SW1W 9BH 1007	W1P 3FJ 3014	WC1B 3LJ 1244	RG24 8PR 1851
SW1W 9NF 1545, 1547,	W1P 5FB 1337	WC1B 3PA 1815	Redhill
1548, 1677, 1799	W1P 5PA 1327	WC1B 3QP 1855	RH4 1JE 3058
SW1X 7NJ 1736	W1P 6JR 1330	WC1B 3QQ 1132	RH8 0AE 1158, 1752
SW1Y 5AG 1749	W1P 7AA 1181	WC1B 3SW 1488	RH8 0DY 1252
SW1Y 5AH 1441	W1P 7AD 1506	WC1B 4DZ 1718, 1850	RH11 9RT 3053
SW1Y 5BA 1600	W1P 8LE 1743	WC1B 4HH 1463	RH12 3DE 1934
SW1Y 5DB 1456	W1P 9DD 1877, 1888	WC1E 6BT 1876	RH13 8RA 1725
SW2 4DQ 1299	W1P 9FB 1110	WC1E 7AE 1451, 1524	RH19 1HU 1112
SW3 1HW 1887	W1P 9FF 3001	WC1E 7ET 1390, 1584	RH19 1XA 1245
SW3 4AH 1021	W1P 9LL 1659	WC1H 0AL 1453	RH19 2PE 1666
SW3 6RB 1382, 1383, 1404,	W1R 2HD 1279	WC1H 0PF 1056	RH19 3BT 1898, 3011
1407, 1551, 1554, 1572, 1573,	W1R 5FA 1852	WC1H 0XG 1771	RH19 4FS 1212
1582, 1585, 1642, 1670, 1730,	W1R 8JH 1109	WC1H 9JR 1100	RH19 4JY 1613
1784, 1804	W1V 2AY 1361	WC1H 9NN 1759	Romford
SW3 6SJ 1322	W1V 3AW 1157	WC1H 9SU 1904	RM1 4LH 1410, 1688
SW4 6HR 3026	W1V 3HR 1885	WC1H 9TX 1403	RM6 4DH 1325
SW4 6PS 1143	W1V 3PF 1151	WC1N 1LD 1008	Slough
SW4 7NQ 1629	W1V 3TD 3041	WC1N 2AT 1118	SL1 5AP 1321
SW4 9BX 1690	W1V 4AX 1526	WC1N 3AU 1297	SL2 3RS 1738
SW5 0RE 1644	W1V 5TZ 1630	WC1N 3JX 1333	SL4 1DF 1619
SW6 1TN 1713	W1V 6HB 1098	WC1N 3NJ 1332	SL6 2QL 1542
SW6 4NZ 1708, 1839	W1V 7LA 1574	WC1N 3XX 1242	SL6 6AZ 1205
SW6 4TJ 3046	W1V 7LS 1919	WC1R 4JH 1015, 1089, 1412	SL9 0LA 1117
SW7 1PU 1748	W1V 9DD 3042	WC1X 8DJ 1032	SL9 8XA 1811
SW7 1RB 1580	W1X 1AF 1138	WC1X 9BZ 1025, 1148	Southall
SW7 2AZ 1446	W1X 1LB 1175	WC1X 9DH 3025	UB7 0DA 1661
SW7 2DD 1772	W1X 4BD 1594	WC1X 9PX 1169	UB9 5NX 3009
SW7 2HR 1260	W1Y 1HB 3043	WC2A 1AW 1131	UB11 1DP 1864
SW7 3HG 1840	W1Y 7DS 1239	WC2A 1EL 1146	Southampton
SW7 4QY 1487	W2 2AQ 1803	WC2A 1SX 1510	SO9 4DH 1638
SW7 5BD 1606	W2 3AN 1006	WC2E 7EN 1528, 1889	SO15 2DF 1168
SW7 5JS 1780	W2 4HJ 1650	WC2E 7NQ 1834	SO23 7AB 3069
SW8 4UD 1050	W2 5BP 3030	WC2E 7PB 1475	SO24 9JH 1435
SW11 1HT 1372	W2 5RH 1761	WC2E 8JZ 1436	SO40 7AA 1208
SW11 4LR 1062	W3 0RG 1847, 3055	WC2E 8LU 1012, 1029,	Southend
SW11 4NB 1394	W3 7ST 1413	1030, 1031, 1368, 1494, 1617,	SS7 2DE 1017, 1428
SW11 4NQ 1080, 1147, 1207	W4 1RX 1265, 3039	1739	St Albans
SW12 9EA 1081	W4 2DT 1399	WC2E 8PS 1248	AL1 4LW 1152
SW14 8SN 1519	W4 5HY 3027	WC2E 9AN 1685	AL1 5EB 1238
SW15 1DQ 1225	W5 3RA 1540	WC2E 9ED 1317	AL2 2AU 1886
SW15 1JX 1856	W5 5SA 1869	WC2E 9PA 1180	AL2 3JD 1137, 1927
SW15 1NL 1114	W5 5TL 1267	WC2H 0DH 1796	AL4 8RF 1198
SW15 1PR 1566	W6 7NF 1065	WC2H 0HE 1603	AL5 1EQ 1627
SW15 2NU 1218	W6 7PA 1201, 1483	WC2H 8EH 1735	AL5 1ST 1879
SW15 2RP 3060	W6 8JB 1386, 1387, 1388	WC2H 9EA 1185, 1243,	AL5 2MA 1293
SW15 6NH 1786	W6 9EL 1134	1639, 1640, 1903	AL5 5DR 1712, 3036
SW16 4ER 1009	W6 9ER 1211	WC2H 9HN 1209	AL7 1EW 1164
SW16 6DA 1675	W6 9QL 1828	WC2H 9QL 3054	AL9 5JZ 1016
SW18 4HR 1522	W8 5TZ 1302, 1381, 1485,	WC2N 4EZ 1232	AL10 8AW 3032
SW18 4JJ 1236	1899, 3062	WC2N 4LB 1176	AL10 9AD 1414
SW19 4UW 1457	W8 6QA 1586	WC2N 6BH 1186	

Sutton (Surrey)
SM1 1DF 1790
SM5 4JS 1762
SM6 0DA 1278
Tonbridge
TN2 3DR 1141, 1783
TN9 1SE 1581
TN9 2PJ 1658
TN11 0DD 1013
TN12 0AZ 1817
TN12 8EA 1418
TN14 5PQ 1397
TN15 8PP 1340
TN16 1BZ 1314
TN30 6EP 1284
TN35 4PG 1813
Twickenham
TW1 3RZ 1102
TW2 5RN 1254
TW8 0QP 1507
TW9 1SR 1385
TW9 2QA 1229
TW10 6RE 1400
TW10 6UA 1872
TW11 8DT 1206
TW11 8EY 1427
TW12 2HQ 1442
TW14 8JF 1087
Watford
WD1 1SX 1575
WD1 4BN 1295
WD1 4QF 1797
WD1 7EN 1281
WD3 5DN 1558
WD4 9PW 1280

South-West England

Bath
BA1 1LF 3033, 3063
BA1 2BT 1004
BA1 3DZ 1053
BA1 3JN 1341
BA2 3AX 1190
BA2 3DZ 1315
BA2 8QJ 1339
BA3 6SN 1277
BA5 2PJ 1870
BA6 9DP 1353
BA9 9AT 1249
BA12 8PQ 1046
BA12 9XB 3010
BA14 8HD 3057
BA14 9AN 1310
BA15 1JS 1292
BA22 7JJ 1320, 1398, 1632, 1829
BA22 8DH 3003
Bournemouth
BH14 0AX 1308
BH24 3SH 1343
Bristol
BS1 5RR 1859
BS1 6JS 1484
BS1 6NX 1467
BS4 4AX 1222
BS8 3LA 1727
BS8 4EA 1857
BS18 2ED 1144
BS21 7SJ 1591
BS23 2UX 1562
BS26 2QH 3045
Dorchester
DT2 7AE 1884
DT9 4HP 3049
DT10 2DP 1704

Exeter
EX1 2HL 3007
EX2 6AS 1460
EX4 4QR 1294
EX4 6EW 1835
EX4 6JA 3013
EX8 2QE 1814
EX31 2HY 1818
EX33 2LD 1568
EX34 8BA 1831
EX39 2PZ 1074
Jersey
JE2 4TD 1841
Plymouth
PL6 7PY 1622
PL6 7PZ 1432
PL18 9SA 1667
PL28 8BG 1845
PL30 3JH 1111
Salisbury
SP7 8BP 1269
SP7 9LY 1247
SP10 1YG 1462
SP10 2AA 1684
SP10 5BA 1672
SP11 9HX 1719
Swindon
SN5 7DG 1125
SN5 7YD 1189
SN7 7JP 1202
SN8 1AP 1011
SN8 2HR 1227
SN8 3UG 1219
SN11 8SB 1416
SN13 9BX 1935
SN15 2NS 1680
Taunton
TA1 1HD 1734
TA3 6DU 1916
TA4 2UJ 1535
TA24 8YX 1319
Torquay
TQ6 9PY 3064
TQ9 6EB 1365
TQ12 4PU 1237
TQ13 0YZ 1696
Truro
TR4 8EE 1873
TR4 8SN 1875
TR10 8AT 1213
TR20 8BG 1880

Midlands

Birmingham
B9 4AA 1918
B26 1BU 1489
B29 6LB 1597
B29 7EU 3038
B68 9LA 1567
B72 1SX 1203
B90 3RN 1241
Coventry
CV11 6RY 1702
CV21 3HQ 1458
CV31 1EB 1123
CV32 5PR 1770
Derby
DE1 1DA 1120
DE4 3QF 1768
DE5 3DA 1316
DE6 1HD 1587
DE7 5DA 1588
Dudley
DY10 3AD 1223
Gloucester
GL5 1BJ 1396

GL5 2BU 1843
GL5 5EQ 1874
GL6 8HP 1552
GL6 8NX 1178
GL15 6JD 1163
GL50 1YW 1861
GL50 2HU 1271
GL56 0LL 1920
Hereford
HR3 8QU 1624
HR6 0QF 1356
Leicester
LE1 6GD 1605
LE1 7DR 1133
LE1 7GE 1601
LE1 7GP 1461
LE2 2YH 1893
LE7 7FU 1862
LE8 0HR 1495
LE8 0HG 1135
LE9 7NA 1578, 1579
LE11 2NQ 1504
LE11 3TU 1523
LE15 6HU 1066
LE18 4ZH 1391
LE67 9RN 1470
Milton Keynes
MK1 1QU 1926
MK2 2EB 1781
MK7 6AA 1634
MK11 1BY 1635
MK18 1XW 1636
MK18 2JR 1490
MK18 4LB 1351
Northampton
NN3 6RT 1359
NN12 8UT 3012
NN12 8XS 1715
NN17 1TT 1454
Nottingham
NG7 4ET 1820
NG14 7GH 1755
NG31 9SL 1430
Oxford
OX1 1AP 1555
OX1 1HJ 1882
OX1 1HN 1645
OX1 2EP 1408
OX1 2PH 1054
OX2 0EL 1094
OX2 0ES 1468
OX2 6AS 1529
OX2 6AT 1003
OX2 6DP 1648
OX2 6FA 1647
OX2 6JX 1894
OX2 7AR 1631
OX2 7DZ 1646
OX2 7FF 1300, 1746
OX2 8DP 1145
OX2 8EJ 1405, 1406, 1731
OX2 9JJ 1596, 1905
OX3 0AB 3056
OX3 7AD 1220
OX4 1JF 1093
OX4 1JJ 1083
OX4 2TX 1084
OX4 5HG 1086, 1527
OX5 1AS 1275
OX5 1GB 1276
OX5 2DN 1342
OX6 0TS 1921
OX6 0XD 1172
OX6 8TD 3008
OX7 3PQ 1159
OX7 3PR 1028
OX7 6RU 3002

OX8 6DY 1592
OX9 5PS 1723
OX10 0XU 1285
OX14 1AA 1717
OX14 3PX 1035, 3004
OX14 4YN 1431
Shrewsbury
SY3 9EB 1020
Stoke-on-Trent
ST4 5NP 1871
Worcester
WR9 7RP 1034
WR11 6BH 1478
WR13 6RN 1224, 1493
WR14 4LH 1444, 1720

East Anglia

Cambridge
CB1 1HZ 1883
CB1 2NT 1199, 1538
CB1 6AH 1925
CB1 6PX 1471
CB2 1LZ 1420
CB2 1NS 1234
CB2 1UR 1693
CB2 2HN 1598
CB2 2RU 1149
CB3 7AY 1518
CB4 1ND 1363, 1608
CB4 4WF 1750
CB4 5QG 1801, 1863
CB5 8SW 1177
CB7 5BA 1564
CB8 7AU 1124
CB10 1JP 1233
Chelmsford
CM8 3YP 1464
CM18 6LY 1230
CM20 2JE 1014
Colchester
CO3 3LP 1533
CO7 0SX 1196
Ipswich
IP1 4LG 1303
IP12 1BY 1409
IP12 1DS 1039
IP12 3DF 1115
IP13 0AG 1433
IP21 5JP 1848
IP21 5NG 1827
IP32 6BW 1560
Norwich
NR3 1PD 1419
NR3 1TR 1481
NR3 3BH 1439
NR16 2HW 1044
NR26 8NB 3029
NR29 3ET 1832
Peterborough
PE3 7PG 1282, 1571
PE3 8BQ 1860
PE4 6NA 1411
PE6 8HD 1583
PE8 4HJ 1309
PE8 5TE 1802
PE9 4NT 3052
PE11 1NZ 1179, 1791
PE13 2AE 1513
PE13 2TH 1311
PE17 2NJ 1274
PE17 4BT 1447
PE17 5XE 1240
PE37 8PA 1347
Stevenage
SG1 2AY 1459
SG2 8UH 1816

SG4 8TE   **1907**
SG5 2DY   **1621**
SG12 9ET   **1928**
SG14 1RN   **1830**

North-East England

Bradford
  BD7 1BX   **1139**
  BD23 3AE   **1231**
  BD23 4ND   **1549**
Darlington
  DL1 1RQ   **1289**
  DL8 3PB   **1512**
  DL14 6XB   **1665**
Harrogate
  HG1 4XB   **1846**
Huddersfield
  HD8 0NQ   **1769**
  HD8 8TH   **1824**
Hull
  HU17 7SB   **1438**
Leeds
  LS6 3BJ   **1204**
  LS15 8EQ   **1819**
  LS16 6EB   **1434**
  LS19 6DP   **3065**
  LS21 3JP   **1810**
  LS23 7BQ   **1127, 1129**
Newcastle-upon-Tyne
  NE1 2TE   **1664**
  NE28 6UZ   **1108**
  NE46 1NJ   **1492**
  NE70 7JX   **1037**
  NE99 1SN   **1097**
Sheffield
  S2 4HG   **1687**
  S8 0XJ   **1595**
  S10 2BP   **1655**
  S11 9AS   **1794**
  S30 1DJ   **1266**
  S60 1LB   **1891**
  S60 1SU   **1473**

S70 2AS   **1660, 1906**
Sunderland
  SR2 7BN   **1142**
Wakefield
  WF3 2AT   **1576**
York
  YO1 2UA   **1215**
  YO3 9HS   **1788**
  YO16 5BT   **1378**
  YO25 9LA   **1057**

North-West England

Carlisle
  CA3 0QS   **1628, 1653**
Lancaster
  LA1 4TZ   **1326**
  LA6 2LA   **1651**
  LA7 7PY   **1195**
Liverpool
  L39 5HP   **1167**
  L42 3XS   **1217**
  L69 3BX   **1530**
Manchester
  M4 3BY   **1155**
  M6 6GG   **3028**
  M13 9NR   **1553**
Stockport
  SK9 3FB   **1929**
  SK9 4LL   **1019**
  SK9 6AR   **1800**
  SK9 7DT   **1079**
  SK17 6BJ   **1024**
Warrington
  WA15 6EF   **1616**
  WA15 9SF   **1421**
  WA16 8DX   **1652**

Wales

Cardiff
  CF2 4YD   **1895**
  CF4 2EA   **1377**

CF5 3AE   **1156, 1253**
CF31 1FT   **1692**
CF31 4DX   **1290**
Llandudno
  LL12 7AW   **1122**
  LL13 7NS   **1663**
  LL14 5HL   **1842**
  LL57 1SB   **1402, 1674**
Mid-Wales
  SY24 5HE   **1932**
Newport (Gwent)
  NP5 4BL   **1370**
Swansea
  SA44 4BQ   **1350**
  SA48 8PJ   **1531**
  SA62 5AU   **3047**

Scotland

Aberdeen
  AB9 2TQ   **1352**
  AB11 7ZE   **1778**
Borders
  TD1 3NR   **1539**
  TD11 3SG   **1090**
Dumfries
  DG10 9SU   **3018**
Edinburgh
  EH1 1JF   **1602**
  EH1 1NQ   **1064**
  EH1 1TE   **1088, 1153**
  EH1 1YS   **1565**
  EH1 2BE   **1753**
  EH1 3AF   **1194**
  EH1 3EP   **1357**
  EH1 3UG   **1550**
  EH2 2DX   **1776**
  EH2 2LQ   **1197**
  EH2 4PS   **1364**
  EH2 4YN   **1756**
  EH3 5AA   **1246**
  EH3 7HF   **1286**
  EH3 7HF   **1286**
  EH7 4AZ   **1389**

EH8 8JR   **1777**
EH8 9LF   **1264, 1694**
EH10 5LN   **1695**
EH11 1SH   **1312**
EH12 6EL   **1069**
EH52 6PG   **1027**
Glasgow
  G2 4HZ   **3037**
  G2 6BZ   **1335**
  G3 7SF   **1344**
  G3 8AZ   **1610**
  G12 8QH   **1779**
  G41 2SD   **1136**
  G51 3UU   **1914**
Inverness
  IV12 5LF   **1068**
  IV20 1TW   **1191**
  IV36 0TZ   **1307**
Kilmarnock
  KA12 0LL   **1160**
  KA26 9TN   **1536**
Orkney
  KW5 6DW   **1912**
Paisley & Isles
  PA1 1TJ   **1306**
  PA22 3AE   **1045**
  PA61 7YR   **1534**
Perth
  PH26 3NA   **1073**

Northern Ireland

Belfast
  BT1 6DD   **1878**
  BT2 8DL   **1042**
  BT5 6NW   **1514**
  BT7 1NN   **1807**
  BT16 0AN   **1091**
  BT21 0NG   **1214**
  BT36 8RN   **1258**
  BT48 7DF   **1374**